The
Grey House
Performing Arts
Directory

2011/12

The Grey House Performing Arts Directory

Seventh Edition

- Dance
- Instrumental Music
- Vocal Music
- Theatre
- Series & Festivals
- Facilities
- Information Resources
- Six Indexes

Grey House Publishing

4919 Route 22
Amenia, NY 12501

PUBLISHER: Leslie Mackenzie
EDITOR: Richard Gottlieb
EDITORIAL DIRECTOR: Laura Mars

PRODUCTION MANAGER: Kristen Thatcher
PRODUCTION ASSISTANTS: Diana Delgado, Erica Schneider, Donna Vanicky

MARKETING DIRECTOR: Jessica Moody

Grey House Publishing, Inc.
4919 Route 22
Amenia, NY 12501
518.789.8700
FAX 845.373.6390
www.greyhouse.com
e-mail: books@greyhouse.com

First edition published 2000
Seventh edition published 2011
Printed in the USA
The Grey House performing arts directory – 7th ed.
1018v.; 4.03 cm.
Bi-Annual
ISSN: 1540-8655

1. performing arts – United States – Directories. I. Grey House Publishing, Inc., II. Title: Performing arts directory

PN1561.G74
792
ISBN 13: 1-59237-551-6 softcover

Table of Contents

Introduction

This is the seventh edition of *The Grey House Performing Arts Directory* – a premier resource of performing arts organizations. It offers unequaled coverage of major performance categories, as well as resources for performers and artist managers alike.

Praise for previous edition:

> *"A no-frills, straight-forward fund of information . . . [a] methodically detailed resource. . . . Clear-cut, easy-to-use, uncomplicated but comprehensive, the* Directory *is a great resource for public and academic libraries alike, as well as any performing arts-related entity."*
>
> ARBA, 2010

Arrangement

The Grey House Performing Arts Directory provides access to 9,013 performing organizations and resources – hundreds more than the previous edition – and 22,417 key contact names, both Artistic Management and Business titles. The listings are arranged first by performance category ***Dance *Instrumental Music *Vocal Music *Theatre *Series & Festivals**, then by state, then by city, making it easy to research listings by both category and location. Following these five performing arts chapters are **Facilities** by state, and **Information Resources** by type of resource – Associations, Newsletters, Magazines & Journals, Trade Shows, Directories & Databases, and Industry Web Sites.

Performing Arts Chapters

Each of these five chapters includes a vast range of listings in size, budget, and recognition. From *Alaska Dance Theatre* to the *New York City Ballet*, from *Gooseberry Park Players* to the *National Shakespeare Company*, from the *Tahoe Arts Project* to *Tanglewood Music Festival*, the scope of listings is unequalled in this format. In addition to the range of listings, the number of listings in each chapter are impressive: 558 Dance; 1,088 Instrumental Music; 454 Vocal Music; 1,568 Theatre; and 1,878 Series & Festivals.

Each listing begins with important contact information – name, address, phone, fax, email and web site. You will find long lists of key staff – both Artistic Management and Business titles – and dozens of valuable details, such as: *Specialized Arts Fields; Number of Paid/Volunteer Staff; Income Sources; Budget; Year Founded; Affiliations; Annual Attendance;* and *Seating Capacity.* **NEW** to this edition is a list of entities utilized by the organization – *Guest Writers/Directors; Local Talent; Instructors; Artists-in-Residence; Singers, Multimedia; Student Interns; Special Technical Talent,* etc.

Performance Facilities

This chapter includes 2,752 listings of venues for the performing arts, and is organized first by state, then by city. Many facilities are multi-purpose, such as arenas, stadiums and college and university spaces. Some are devoted stages for dance or theater. All facilities listed include important contact information, most with key staff and important details, such as *Stage Dimensions, Seating Capacity*, and *Rental Contact.*

Information Resources

Taken from our popular *Directory of Business Information Resources*, this section includes 715 resources for the performing arts industry. Whether the need is educational or professional, users will find detailed listings for Associations, Newsletters, Magazines, Journals, Trade Shows, Directories, Databases, and Web Sites, with the contact information and key executive names needed for in depth research into the dynamic performing arts industry.

Six Indexes

The Grey House Performing Arts Directory has six indexes to make it easy for researchers to locate the exact data they are looking for using a variety of criteria.

Entry Name Index: An alphabetical listing of all performance organizations.

Executive Name Index: An alphabetical listing of 22,417 key executives in the performing arts industry.

Facilities Index: An Alphabetical listing of 2,752 performance facilities.

Specialized Field Index: An alphabetical listing of more than 250 performing arts categories within major categories of Dance, Vocal Music, Instrumental Music, Theatre, and Series & Festivals.

Geographic Index: 9,013 performing arts listings and facilities listed by state

Information Resources Index: An alphabetical listing of performing arts Associations, Newsletters, Magazines, Journals, Trade Shows, Directories, Databases, and Web Sites.

For even easier access to data, *The Grey House Performing Arts Directory* is available for subscription on G.O.L.D. – Grey House OnLine Database. Subscribers to G.O.L.D. have immediate access to 9,013 performing arts resources and 22,417 key industry contacts, and can search by dozens of criteria, including performance area, key staff, budget, keyword and so much more. Plus, subscribers can download contact sheets to create their own mailing list.

Alabama

1
ALABAMA BALLET
2726 1st Avenue S
Birmingham, AL 35233
Phone: 205-322-4300
Fax: 205-322-4444
e-mail: information@alabamaballet.org
Web Site: www.alabamaballet.org
Management:
  Artistic Director: Tracey Alvey
  Executive Director: Gia Rabito
Mission: To promote and foster the development of classical and contemporary ballet through high-quality performances, dance education, and community outreach.
Utilizes: Choreographers; Dance Companies; Dancers; Educators; Guest Artists; Local Artists & Directors; Soloists; Theatre Companies
Founded: 1981
Specialized Field: Classical Ballet; Contemporary Ballet
Status: Non-Profit, Professional
Paid Staff: 10
Volunteer Staff: 4
Paid Artists: 22
Non-paid Artists: 13
Budget: $1.5 million
Income Sources: Ticket sales; donations; grants
Performs At: Samford Wright Center; Alabama Theatre; Ayls Stephens Center
Organization Type: Performing; Touring

2
SOUTHEAST ALABAMA DANCE COMPANY
909 S Saint Andrews Street
PO Box 125
Dothan, AL 36301
Phone: 334-702-7139
Fax: 334-702-7139
e-mail: seadac@graceba.net
Mission: To provide performance opportunities and formal training to serious dance students, primarily in classical ballet.
Utilizes: Choreographers; Dance Companies; Dancers; Guest Accompanists; Guest Artists; Guest Ensembles; Guest Musicians; Original Music Scores; Resident Professionals; Scenic Designers; Singers; Soloists; Student Interns; Theatre Companies; Touring Companies; Volunteer Artists
Founded: 1978
Specialized Field: Jazz; Modern
Status: Non-Profit:Professional
Performs At: Dothan Civic Center

3
HUNTSVILLE BALLET COMPANY
800 Regal Drive
PO Box 373
Huntsville, AL 35804
Phone: 256-539-0961
Fax: 256-539-1837
e-mail: info@huntsvilleballet.org
Web Site: www.huntsvilleballet.org
Officers:
  President: Dannye Drake
  First VP: Sherry Polk
  Second VP: Marion Merrell
  Treasurer: Lynn Kerkhof
Management:
  Artistic Director: Keren Gibb
  School Administor: Keren Gibb
  Office Manager: Lori Lindstrom
Founded: 1964
Specialized Field: Ballet; Modern; Jazz; Tap; Pointe; Creative Movement
Status: Semi-professional; Nonprofit
Paid Staff: 20
Volunteer Staff: 100
Paid Artists: 20
Non-paid Artists: 100
Income Sources: Fundraising; Corporate Sponsorship; Individual Giving
Performs At: Ron Vaughn Center Concert Hall
Seating Capacity: 2,153
Year Built: 1975
Organization Type: Touring; Resident

4
MOBILE BALLET INC
4351 Downtowner Loop N
Mobile, AL 36608
Phone: 251-342-2241
e-mail: info@mobileballet.org
Web Site: www.mobileballet.org
Management:
  Artistic Director: Winthrop Corey
  Ballet Mistress: Lori Bilbrey-Vaghefi
Mission: To provide superior dance education, to present quality performances, and to promote the ballet to the community as an expression of the human spirit.
Founded: 1987
Specialized Field: Ballet

5
ALABAMA DANCE THEATRE
Armory Learning Arts Center
1018 Madison Avenue
Montgomery, AL 36104
Mailing Address: PO Box 11327 Montgomery, AL 36111
Phone: 334-241-2590
Fax: 334-241-2504
e-mail: ADTDance1@aol.com
Web Site: www.alabamadancetheatre.com
Management:
  Artistic Director: Kitty Seale
  Ballet Master: Foye DuBose
  Director of Development: Brenda Robertson Dennis
  Public Relations/Dancer: Casey Vaughan
  Choreographer: Sara Sanford
  Choreographer: Jenny Plunkett Letner
  Choreographer: Janie Allen Atford
Mission: To train and educate students in the disciplined art of dance and to educate and develop the future audience for dance in central Alabama. ADT hosts a number of educational activities in the community which serve to build our audience and enhance the cultural life of our city.
Utilizes: Choreographers; Dance Companies; Dancers; Guest Accompanists; Guest Artists; Guest Ensembles; Soloists; Theatre Companies
Founded: 1986
Specialized Field: Classical Ballet; Modern Ballet; Jazz; Hip Hop; Tap
Performs At: Davis Theater
Seating Capacity: 1,200
Year Built: 1930

6
MONTGOMERY BALLET
2102 Eastern Boulevard
Suite 223
Montgomery, AL 36117
Mailing Address: PO Box 230097 Montgomery, AL 36123
Phone: 334-409-0522
e-mail: info@montgomeryballet.orgm
Web Site: www.montgomeryballet.org
Officers:
  President: Jan Hodgson
  VP/Special Events: Dottye Hannan
  VP/Marketing: Catherine Woodson
  Secretary: Lucie McLemore
  Treasurer: Renee Smith
Management:
  Artistic Director: Elie Lazar
  Artistic Advisor: Galina Panova
  Ballet Master: Haynes Owens
  Executive Artistic Director: Priscilla Crommelin-Ball
  Administrator/Finance Manager: Jan Alexander
  Marketing Director: Katy Olsen
Mission: To provide unparalleled excellence in training and annual performance opportunities.
Founded: 1958
Specialized Field: Ballet
Status: Professional; Nonprofit
Paid Staff: 4
Volunteer Staff: 10
Paid Artists: 55
Income Sources: Southeast Regional Ballet Association
Performs At: Alabama Shakesphere Festival
Seating Capacity: 700
Organization Type: Performing; Educational

Alaska

7
ALASKA DANCE THEATRE
550 E 33rd Avenue
Anchorage, AK 99503
Phone: 907-277-9591
Fax: 907-274-3078
e-mail: info@alaskadancetheatre.org
Web Site: www.alaskadancetheatre.org
Officers:
  President: Heather Grahame
  Treasurer: Michael Burke
  Secretary: Maryann Frazier
  Vice President: Barbara Simpson Kraft
Management:
  Artistic/School Director: Alice Bassler Sullivan
  Associate/Director: Coutland Weaver
  Interim Executive Director: Michelle Guisinger
Mission: To promote dance through performance, professional education and avocacy in Alaska and to provide a place within the dance comunity for local and visiting artists to expand their creative talent while nurturing discipline, confidence, fitness and the experience of movement. Alaska Dance Theatre strives to keeps its program affordable to a wide range of the population.
Utilizes: Choreographers; Collaborations; Dancers; Guest Accompanists; Guest Artists; High School Drama; Instructors; Local Artists; Multimedia; Music; Resident Artists; Soloists
Founded: 1981
Specialized Field: Ballet
Status: Nonprofit Organization
Paid Staff: 23
Volunteer Staff: 150
Paid Artists: 5
Non-paid Artists: 30
Budget: $50,000
Income Sources: Grants; Donations; Tuition

Performs At: Atwood Concert Hall
Type of Stage: Proscenium
Stage Dimensions: 120' wide by 52'deep
Seating Capacity: 2,000
Year Built: 1988
Organization Type: Performing

Arizona

8

CROSSROADS PERFORMANCE GROUP
1870 W 5th Place
Mesa, AZ 85201
Phone: 480-969-6683
Fax: 480-692-1887
e-mail: lrchow@cox.net
Management:
   Dance Instructor: Step Rapist
   Dance Instructor: Lisa R Chow
Mission: The duo explore the merging of movement, sound, and drama to create new forms of performance art in its purest form. They strive to capture the imagination and intrigue the senses.
Specialized Field: Interdisciplinary; Collaborative Dance
Status: Non-Profit
Volunteer Staff: 5
Income Sources: Educational Programs; Performances

9

BALLET ARIZONA
3645 E Indian School Road
Phoenix, AZ 85018
Phone: 602-381-0184
Fax: 602-381-0189
e-mail: info@balletaz.org
Web Site: www.balletaz.org
Officers:
   Chairman: Harold Dorenbecher
   Vice Chairman: Steve Johnson
   Treasurer: Melinda Poppe
Management:
   Artistic Director: Ib Andersen
   Interim Executive Director: Jo Leong
   Director of Finance: Pat Diekan
Mission: To creat, perform and teach classical and contemporary ballet.
Utilizes: Commissioned Composers; Commissioned Music; Dancers; Designers; Five Seasonal Concerts; Guest Accompanists; Guest Artists; Guest Conductors; Guest Instructors; Multimedia; Original Music Scores; Resident Professionals; Student Interns; Theatre Companies
Founded: 1986
Specialized Field: Dance
Status: Professional; Nonprofit
Paid Staff: 14
Volunteer Staff: 5
Paid Artists: 21
Budget: $5 Million
Income Sources: Ticket Sales; Donations; Ballet School Tuition
Performs At: Orpheum Theatre
Facility Category: Performing Arts
Seating Capacity: 2,800
Year Built: 1927
Organization Type: Performing; Touring; Resident; Educational

10

DESERT DANCE THEATRE
PO Box 25332
Tempe, AZ 85285-5332
Phone: 480-962-4584
Fax: 480-962-1887
e-mail: info@desertDanceTheatre.org
Web Site: www.desertdancetheatre.com
Officers:
   Vice President: Lisa R Chow
   Secretary: Pualani Blackmon
   Treasurer: Thomas Bass
   Continuing Director: Marion K Jones
   Continuing Director: Margie Romero Wolf
Management:
   Artistic Director/Choreographer: Lisa R Chow
   Associate Artistic Director: Renee Davis
   Music Director: Step Raptis
Mission: Performers, choreographers and educators who strive to bring the openness, spontaneity and diversity of dance to the public.
Utilizes: Actors; Choreographers; Collaborating Artists; Collaborations; Commissioned Music; Dance Companies; Dancers; Educators; Fine Artists; Five Seasonal Concerts; Guest Artists; Guest Choreographers; Guest Companies; Guest Ensembles; Guest Lecturers; Guest Musical Directors; High School Drama; Instructors; Multi Collaborations; Multimedia; Music; Organization Contracts; Original Music Scores; Sign Language Translators; Soloists; Student Interns
Founded: 1979
Specialized Field: Modern; Jazz; Ballet; Creative Movement
Status: Non-Profit
Volunteer Staff: 15
Paid Artists: 15
Budget: 50,000
Income Sources: Corporate Support; Private Sponsors
Performs At: Scottsdale Center For The Performing Arts
Seating Capacity: 838
Organization Type: Performing; Educational

11

YUMA BALLET THEATRE & PERFORMING ARTS COMPANY
3140 S 4th Avenue
Suite D-7
Yuma, AZ 85364
Phone: 928-341-1925
Fax: 928-341-1925
e-mail: ybt_dance@yahoo.com
Web Site: www.yumaballet.org
Officers:
   President: Lou Miller
   Vice President: Carolyn Miller
   Secretary: Lorry Podolsky
   Treasurer: Liz Laster
Management:
   Artistic Director: Erika Farrar-Romanyuk
   Executive Director: Lisa Mendez
   Instructor: Zabie Nields
   Instructor: Berbara Miller
   Instructor: Taylor Podolsky
   Instructor: Jared Mesa
Mission: To encourage and promote the excellence of dance in Yuma and Arizona by nurturing the highest artistic and moral values in our dancers, to showcase and support the work of emerging and established choreography, bring dance and its education to residents of Yuma and the surrounding areas, and

fortify the artistic community of Yuma County through partnerships and resource sharing with art groups in the area.
Utilizes: Five Seasonal Concerts; Singers
Founded: 1979
Specialized Field: Ballet
Status: Non-Professional; Nonprofit; Part-Time Special Dancers
Paid Staff: 06
Volunteer Staff: 20
Income Sources: Regional Dance America; Honor Company; Ticket Sales; Friends Of Ballet
Performs At: Snider Auditorium
Seating Capacity: 700
Organization Type: Performing; Educational

Arkansas

12

FOUNDATION OF ARTS
115 E Monroe Avenue
Jonesboro, AR 72403
Mailing Address: PO Box 310
Phone: 870-935-2726
Web Site: www.jonesborofoa.com
Officers:
   Board Of Director, Chair: Josie Welsh
Management:
   Executive Director: Sherri Beatty
   Education Director: Heather Intres
   Director; Development: Kristi Pulliam
   Instructor: Amber Bond
   Instructor: Michelle Edwards
   Instructor: Stephanie Gurley Hardy
   Instructor: Heather Intres
   Instructor: Elena Johns
   Instructor: Naomi Lawrence
Mission: The Foundation of Arts for Northeast Arkansas is a regional non-profit organization that passionately strives to enhance the community's quality of life by providing and fostering arts programming that includes education, outreach and entertainment.
Utilizes: Actors; Choreographers; Educators; Guest Artists; Guest Designers; High School Drama; Instructors; Local Artists; Lyricists; Multimedia; Organization Contracts; Sign Language Translators; Soloists; Student Interns; Touring Companies
Founded: 1978
Specialized Field: Ballet, Hip-Hop, Tap Dance and Art and Painting Classes
Status: Non-Profit
Paid Staff: 15
Budget: $35,000-$100,000
Income Sources: Box Office; Grants; Private Donation; Class Tuition
Annual Attendance: 25,000
Facility Category: Theatre
Type of Stage: Proscenium
Seating Capacity: 670
Year Built: 1940
Year Remodeled: 2000
Rental Contact: Executive Director Sherri Beatty
Resident Groups: NEA Symphony; Theatre on the Ridge; Act Experience; Jonesboro City Ballet

13

BALLET ARKANSAS
PO Box 26203
Little Rock, AR 72221-6203
Phone: 501-223-5150
Fax: 501-227-0662
Web Site: balletarkansas.org
Officers:

President: Holly Whitcombe
Vice President: P Delanna Padilla
Treasurer: Mike Heald
Secretary: Cami Love
Guild President: Jammie Ziller
Management:
   Executive Director: Tammye Hall
Mission: Ballet Arkansas is committed to enriching the community through development of its young performers and providing high caliber performances.
Utilizes: Guest Artists; Guest Companies; Singers
Founded: 1978
Specialized Field: Ballet
Status: Semi-Professional; Nonprofit
Paid Staff: 13
Income Sources: Southwest Regional Ballet Association; National Association for Regional Ballet
Performs At: Robinson Center Music Hall
Seating Capacity: 2,600
Organization Type: Performing; Touring; Educational; Sponsoring

California

14
CENTRAL CALIFORNIA BALLET

Lively Arts Foundation
1379 Crown Drive
Alameda, CA 94501
Phone: 877-608-5883
e-mail: livelyarts2@aol.com
Web Site: www.livelyarts.org
Management:
   Artistic Director: Diane K Mosier
Mission: To help establish the Fresno metropolitan area as a major cultural force in California by providing a variety of world class music, dance and dramatic entertainment and by fostering a challenging and enriched environment for talented local students in the performing arts.
Founded: 1989
Specialized Field: Ballet
Paid Staff: 1
Volunteer Staff: 6
Performs At: Historic Tower Theatre
Seating Capacity: 900
Year Built: 1939
Organization Type: Performing; Touring

15
SUHAILA DANCE COMPANY & SUHAILA SALIMPOUR SCHOOL OF DANCE

425 San Pablo Avenue
Albany, CA 94706
Phone: 510-527-2400
e-mail: suhaila@therealsuhaila.com
Web Site: www.therealsuhaila.com
Officers:
   Founder: Suhaila Salimpour
Mission: To create instructional and performance videos for all dance levels, as well as fully orchestrated middle eastern dance musicals and cd recordings of the latest percussion artists
Utilizes: Five Seasonal Concerts
Founded: 1996
Specialized Field: Belly Dance; Middle Eastern Dance
Status: Professional
Performs At: Zellerbach Hall; Berkeley Community Theater
Seating Capacity: 1,600
Organization Type: Performing; Educational

16
CLARITA & THE ARTE FLAMENCO DANCE THEATRE

Arte Flamenco Dance Theatre, Inc.
230 W Main Street
Alhambra, CA 91801
Phone: 626-458-1234
Fax: 626-458-0113
e-mail: info@clarita-arteflamenco.com
Web Site: www.clarita-arteflamenco.com
Officers:
   Founder/President/Artistic Director: Clarita
   VP/CFO/Managing Director: Art Jauregui
Management:
   Artistic Director: Clarita
   Administrative Assisstant: Renee Tabizon
   Managing Director: Art Jauregui
   Instructor - Spanish Dance: Ana-Lupe Morado
   Instructor - Belly Dance - Pilates: Aubre Hill
   Instructor - Belly Dance: Kamala
   Instructor - Folklorico: Cindy Eligio
   Instructor - Folklorico - Zumba: Andrea Ramirez
   Instructor - Hawaiian/Tahitian: Keaki
Mission: Arte Flamenco is dedicated to promoting the value of dance in contemporary society by enthusiastically introducing the public to Spanish dance and its relevance as a positive way to develop appreciation of artistic and cultural diversity.
Utilizes: Artists-in-Residence; Choreographers; Dance Companies; Dancers; Educators; Grant Writers; Guest Artists; Guest Choreographers; Guest Ensembles; Guest Musical Directors; Guest Musicians; Guest Speakers; Original Music Scores; Paid Performers; Sign Language Translators; Soloists; Students
Founded: 1989
Specialized Field: Spanish; Flamenco
Status: Professional, Non-Profit
Paid Staff: 3
Volunteer Staff: 3
Paid Artists: 15
Organization Type: Performing

17
ANAHEIM BALLET

280 E Lincoln Avenue
Anaheim, CA 92805-3226
Phone: 714-520-0904
Fax: 714-520-0914
e-mail: info@anaheimballet.org
Web Site: www.anaheimballet.org
Management:
   Executive Director: Lawrence Rosenberg
   Administrator: Ashley Duree
Mission: To enlighten and entertain audiences with classically rooted programming and contemporary presentation. Provides quality performances to audiences of balletomanes as well as novice ballet-goers and acts as a haven to talented Southern California artists and as a magnet to international talents.
Utilizes: Community Talent; Dance Companies; Dancers; High School Drama; Instructors; Original Music Scores; Resident Artists; Soloists
Founded: 1985
Specialized Field: Ballet; Jazz; Tap; Hip Hop
Status: Non-Profit
Budget: $326,000
Income Sources: Arts of Orange County; Discount Dance Supply; Anaheim Community Foundation; Pacific Life Foundation; Samueli Foundation; Target; Orange County Community Foundation
Affiliations: Anaheim Chamber of Commerce; Downtown Anaheim Association; Anaheim Arts Council

Organization Type: Performing

18
CRASH, BURN AND DIE DANCE COMPANY

Moving and Storage Performance Company
259 Rio Del Mar Boulevard
Aptos, CA 95003-4658
Phone: 831-688-3371
Web Site: www.ferrucci.com/crash
Officers:
   President: Darryl Ferrucci
Management:
   Artistic Director: Leslie Swaha
Mission: To enlighten the audience's point of view on the dancers' perspective of adventure, physical pleasure, and a sublime consciousness of the world.
Specialized Field: Contemporary
Status: Non-Profit
Budget: $280,000
Income Sources: Arts of Orange County; Discount Dance Supply; Anaheim Community Foundation; Pacific Life Foundation; Samueli Foundation; Target; Orange County Community Foundation
Affiliations: Anaheim Chamber of Commerce; Downtown Anaheim Association; Anaheim Arts Council
Organization Type: Performing

19
YOUNG ARTISTS BALLET THEATRE

425 Harbor Boulevard #3
Belmont, CA 94002
Phone: 650-598-0796
Web Site: www.yabt.org
Management:
   Co-Director: Zoltan Peter
   Co-Director: Carmela Peter
Mission: To serve as a stepping stone for young committed people towards a professional career, along with providing enriching performance experiences to those young dancers who may not meet professional physical criteria or who are simply dancing for pleasure.
Founded: 1993
Specialized Field: Ballet
Status: Non-Profit; Semi-Professional
Affiliations: Joffrey Ballet; San Francisco Ballet; Boston Ballet; Pennsylvania Ballet; Kirov Ballet Institute

20
BERKELEY BALLET THEATER

2640 College Avenue
Berkeley, CA 94704
Phone: 510-843-4687
Fax: 510-843-2606
e-mail: idance@berkeleyballet.org
Web Site: ww.berkleyballet.org
Management:
   Director Emerita: Sally Streets
   Artistic Director: Sarah Marcus
   Artistic Director: Susan Weber
Mission: Berkeley Ballet Theater believes that the joy of dance with all its physical, mental and aesthetic benefits should be available to everyone. Whatever a student's goal, we believe it is best achieved in a well-disciplined but positive and loving environment.
Founded: 1908
Specialized Field: Ballet
Status: Non-Profit
Paid Staff: 22
Volunteer Staff: 150
Performs At: Julia Morgan Theatre
Seating Capacity: 385
Year Built: 1908

21
SHA SHA HIGBY
PO Box 152
Bolinas, CA 94924
Phone: 415-868-2409
Fax: 415-868-2409
e-mail: shasha@shashahigby.com
Web Site: www.shashahigby.com
Officers:
> **Founder:** Sha Sha Higby

Mission: To approach dance through the medium of sculpture
Utilizes: Dance Companies; Dancers; Fine Artists; Guest Artists; Lyricists; Paid Performers; Resident Professionals; Touring Companies; Visual Arts
Founded: 1984
Specialized Field: Interpretive Dance
Paid Staff: 2
Paid Artists: 1
Performs At: Zellerbach Hall; Berkeley Community Theater
Seating Capacity: 500
Organization Type: Performing; Educational

22
LA DANSERIE
9759 Mason Avenue
Chatsworth, CA 91311
Phone: 818-341-0530
e-mail: jpgladanserie@yahoo.com
Web Site: www.ladanserie.com
Officers:
> **President/CEO:** Patricia Davis

Management:
> **Artistic Director/Choreographer:** Patrick Frantz
> **Choreographer/Administrative Dir:** Judy Pisarro-Grant

Mission: To support and advance the art of dance. The company is guided by the belief that dance can act as a universal language to facilitate understanding among people of diverse cultures and backgrounds, and that dance has a tremendous potential to positively impact through an embodiment of positive values, including self respect, team work and persistence.
Utilizes: Collaborations; Dance Companies; Dancers; Designers; Five Seasonal Concerts; Guest Accompanists; Guest Artists; Organization Contracts; Resident Professionals
Founded: 1997
Specialized Field: Ballet
Paid Staff: 4
Volunteer Staff: 8
Paid Artists: 10
Non-paid Artists: 6

23
CAROLINA LUGO'S BRISAS DE ESPANA FLAMENCO DANCE COMPANY
1301 Franquette Avenue
Concord, CA 94520
Phone: 925-939-7850
Fax: 925-939-9773
e-mail: carolinalugo1@msn.com
Web Site: www.carolinalugo.com
Management:
> **Artistic Director:** Carolina Lugo
> **Manager:** Richard Tonkin

Mission: The company represents a diversity of cultures from around the globe, appearing in a broad spectrum of creative mediums, including television, dinner theater, cabaret venues, opera and symphonic formats.
Founded: 1997

Specialized Field: Flamenco Dance
Status: Non-Profit

24
SAMAHAN FILIPINO AMERICAN PERFORMING ARTS
1442 Hillsmont Drive
El Cajon, CA 92020
Phone: 619-444-7528
Fax: 619-444-3695
e-mail: samahaphildance@gmail.com
Web Site: www.samahaphilippinedance.com
Management:
> **Executive Director:** Lolita D Carter, PhD
> **Artistic Director:** Ruby Pearl B Chiong
> **Music Coordinator:** Juanita Caccam

Mission: To provide Filipino youth opportunity to gain knowledge and appreciation of their cultural heritage.
Utilizes: Dancers; Five Seasonal Concerts; Guest Accompanists; Guest Artists; Music; Soloists
Founded: 1974
Specialized Field: Flilipino Dance
Status: Semi-Professional; Nonprofit
Volunteer Staff: 20
Paid Artists: 18
Budget: 50,000
Income Sources: Grants; Admissions; Individual Contributions; Fundraisers; Classes
Affiliations: Saville Theatre
Facility Category: Theaters, informal spaces
Seating Capacity: 500
Year Built: 1960
Organization Type: Performing; Touring; Educational; Sponsoring

25
REDWOOD CONCERT BALLET
426 F Street
Eureka, CA 95501
Mailing Address: PO Box 680 Eureka, CA 95501
Phone: 707-442-7779
Officers:
> **President:** Sally Biggin
> **VP:** Mary Glavich
> **Secretary:** Marie Boylan
> **Treasurer:** Kathy Ehnebuske

Management:
> **Artistic Director:** Virginia Niekrasz-Laurent

Mission: RCB's performances touch a wide rnage of styles, and give opportunity to experience the dedication ands skill required to successfully dance professionally.
Specialized Field: Ballet; Modern; Jazz
Volunteer Staff: 30
Non-paid Artists: 1
Income Sources: Trition

26
JOHN CHOOKASIAN ARMENIAN CONCERT ENSEMBLE
2511 W Browning Avenue
Fresno, CA 93711
Phone: 559-449-1777
Fax: 559-432-6666
e-mail: chook3@qnis.net
Web Site: www.chookasian.com
Management:
> **Artistic Director/Founder:** John Chookasian, chook3@qnis.net

Mission: To present, preserve and perpetuate traditional Armenian music, folkdance, and culture through tours, concerts, festivals, special events

venues, and the sale and distribution of multi award-winning live concert and festival CD's for the general public at large.
Utilizes: Dance Companies; Dancers; Filmmakers; Grant Writers; Guest Accompanists; Guest Musical Directors; Guest Musicians; Multimedia; New Productions; Organization Contracts; Original Music Scores; Paid Performers; Sign Language Translators; Theatre Companies
Founded: 1994
Specialized Field: Armenian Folk Dance
Status: Professional, Nonprofit
Paid Artists: 12
Income Sources: Grants; Fundraisers; Concerts; Concert Halls; Museums; Arts Centers; Churches; Cultural Organizations; Festivals; Colleges & Universities; Corporations; Individuals; Touring
Annual Attendance: 4,000 - 10,000
Organization Type: Performing; Touring; Educational

27
ANTELOPE VALLEY BALLET
2763 W Avenue L
Lancaster, CA 93536
Phone: 661-722-9702
e-mail: kimburnett@verizon.net
Web Site: www.avballet.com
Officers:
> **President:** Bradford Boyd
> **Secretary:** Gina Rossall
> **Treasurer:** Kimberly Brouwer

Management:
> **Artistic Director:** Kathleen Burnett

Mission: To provide dancers from across the Antelope Valley region with professional quality performance opportunities in a company setting. To provide high quality performances locally and regionally, stimulating interest in and appreciation for dance as a performing art. To be a positive force in the cultural climate of Antelope Valley and the State of California.
Founded: 1998
Specialized Field: Ballet
Status: Nonprofit
Performs At: Lancaster Performing Arts Center
Seating Capacity: 720
Year Built: 1992

28
REGINA KLENJOSKI DANCE COMPANY
PO Box 7732
Long Beach, CA 90807
Phone: 310-292-7024
e-mail: info@rkdc.org
Web Site: www.rkdc.org
Officers:
> **President:** Hirofumi Kawano
> **Treasurer/Marketing Director:** Stephen Schmidt
> **Secretary:** Albertossy Espinoza

Management:
> **Artistic Director:** Regina Klenjoski
> **Managing Director:** Cory Nakasue

Mission: To promote the understanding of and to create a passion for the art of contemporary dance, making it accessible to both seasoned and new audiences.
Founded: 1999
Specialized Field: Modern; Ballet
Income Sources: Los Angeles County Arts Commision And The Cultural Services Division Of The City Of Torrance
Performs At: Torrance Cultural Arts Center
Seating Capacity: 120
Year Built: 1938

All listings are in alphabetical order by state, then city, then organization within the city.

29
RHAPSODY IN TAPS
4812 Matney Avenue
Long Beach, CA 90807
Phone: 562-428-6411
e-mail: linda@rhapsodyintaps.com
Web Site: rhapsodyintaps.com
Management:
Artistic Director/Choreographer: Linda
Sohl-Ellison
Rehearsal Dircetor: Pauline Hagino
Marketing Director: Carolyn Clarke
Mission: To promote and perform the act of rhythm tap
dance while exploring new choreographic directions.
Utilizes: Singers
Founded: 1981
Specialized Field: Tap Dance
Status: Nonprofit
Budget: $50,000-$100,000
Organization Type: Performing; Touring

30
AEOLIAN BALLET THEATRE
914 Westwood Boulevard
Suite 250
Los Angeles, CA 90024
Phone: 310-838-0849
e-mail: info@aeolianballet.org
Web Site: www.aeolianballet.org
Officers:
Executive Director: Maria Serafica-Stermer
Management:
Artistic Advisor: Marat Daukayev
Artistic Advisor: Stefan Wenta
Mission: The company is dedicated to enriching the
human experience through live dance performance, to
the creation of new works and the revival of historical
pieces.
Founded: 1998
Specialized Field: Ballet
Status: Nonprofit, Professional
Volunteer Staff: 10
Paid Artists: 20
Budget: $500,000
Performs At: Ucla
Seating Capacity: 650
Year Built: 1919

31
AISHA ALI DANCE COMPANY
3270 Kelton Avenue
Los Angeles, CA 90034
Phone: 310-474-4867
e-mail: info@aisha-ali.com
Web Site: www.aisha-ali.com
Management:
Artistic Director: Aisha Ali
Mission: To introduce the arts of Middle Eastern and
North African dance to audiences around the globe.
Founded: 1973
Specialized Field: Belly Dance; Middle-Eastern; North
African Dance
Status: Professional

32
COLLAGE DANCE THEATRE
2934-1/2 Beverly Glen Circle
Suite 25
Los Angeles, CA 90077
Phone: 818-784-8669
Fax: 818-981-4116
e-mail: info@collagedancetheatre.org
Web Site: www.collagedancetheatre.org

Officers:
President: Liliane Corzo
Secretary: Terry Wolverton
Treasurer: Lanie Graham
Management:
Artistic Director: Heidi Duckler
Mission: We actively seek collaborations with artists,
arts organizations and community groups in order to
forge a link between professional performance, public
space and audience. We seek non-traditional venues
and methods for creating contemporary dance theatre
works that seek new forms of relationship between
audience and performer.
Utilizes: Actors; Collaborating Artists; Collaborations;
Dancers; Designers; Filmmakers; Five Seasonal
Concerts; Instructors; Multi Collaborations; Multimedia;
Organization Contracts; Original Music Scores;
Playwrights; Resident Artists; Resident Professionals;
Selected Students; Soloists; Touring Companies; Visual
Arts
Founded: 1987
Specialized Field: Contemporary Dance
Status: Non-Profit
Paid Staff: 3
Volunteer Staff: 20
Budget: $100,000
Income Sources: Grants; Fundraising; Ticket Sales
Performs At: California Science Center
Annual Attendance: 5,000
Seating Capacity: 435
Year Built: 1989
Organization Type: Performing; Touring

33
DIAVOLO
616 Moulton Avenue
Los Angeles, CA 90031
Phone: 714-979-4700
Fax: 714-979-4740
e-mail: marah.diavolo@gmail.com
Web Site: www.diavolo.org
Officers:
Chairman: Patrick Bolek
Vice President: Peter Lesnik
Management:
Artistic Director: Jacques Heim
Mission: Redefine dance through dynamic movement,
enlightening communities through trust, teamwork and
individual expression.
Founded: 1992
Specialized Field: Interdisciplinary Dance
Status: Profit
Paid Staff: 7
Volunteer Staff: 15
Non-paid Artists: 3
Income Sources: Friends Of Diavolo; California Arts
Commission; City Of Los Angeles, Cultural Affairs
Department; The James Irvine Foundation
Performs At: The Carpenter Center
Seating Capacity: 2,041
Year Built: 1928
Organization Type: Performing; Touring; Educational

34
JAPANESE AMERICAN CULTURAL AND
COMMUNITY CENTER
244 S San Pedro Street
Suite 505
Los Angeles, CA 90012
Phone: 213-628-2725
Fax: 213-617-8576
Web Site: www.jaccc.org
Officers:
Chairman: Sandra Sakamoto

Vice Chair: Gary Kawaguchi
Vice Chair: Nancy Matsui
Secretary: Rinban Noriaki Ito
Treasurer: Gary Kawaguchi
Management:
Artistic Director: Hirokazu Kosaka
Executive Director: Chrisazu Aihara
Mission: To present, perpetuate, transmit and promote
Japanese and Japanese American arts and culture to
diverse audiences and to provide a center to enhance
community programs.
Founded: 1971
Specialized Field: Japanese Dance; Japanese Arts
Paid Staff: 25
Volunteer Staff: 15
Performs At: Sakaye Aratant Japan American Theatre
Seating Capacity: 840

35
JAZZ TAP ENSEMBLE
1416 Westwood Boulevard
Suite 207
Los Angeles, CA 90024
Phone: 310-475-4412
e-mail: jtensemble@aol.com
Web Site: www.jazztapensemble.org
Management:
Artistic Director: Lynn Dally
Managing Director: Gayle Hooks
Music Director: Jerry Kalaf
Mission: The Ensemble brings together the virtuosic
talents of itss several dancers and musicians in a
spirited display of creativity and spontaneity to express
its dedication to tap dancing and jazz music.
Utilizes: Dancers; Guest Accompanists; Guest Musical
Directors; Instructors
Founded: 1979
Specialized Field: Tap; Jazz
Status: Nonprofit
Paid Staff: 2
Paid Artists: 15
Budget: $200,000-$500,000
Income Sources: Grants; Ticket Sales
Performs At: John F. Kennedy Center For The
Performing Arts
Seating Capacity: 2,100
Year Built: 1968

36
LOS ANGELES BALLET
11755 Exposition Boulevard
Los Angeles, CA 90064
Phone: 310-477-7411
Fax: 310-477-7414
e-mail: contact@losangelesballet.org
Web Site: www.losangelesballet.org
Management:
Artistic Director: Thordal Christensen
Artistic Director: Colleen Neary
Company Manager: Dan Rib,
rib@losangelesballet.org
Director Of Sales: Laurel Long
Mission: To passionately pursue innovation and
creativity in performances. To preserve the best
choreographic work of the past and become the
impetus for the best choreography yet to come.
Founded: 2006
Specialized Field: Ballet
Status: Professional

37
LULA WASHINGTON DANCE THEATRE
3773 S Crenshaw Boulevard
Los Angeles, CA 90016

Phone: 323-292-5852
Fax: 323-292-5851
e-mail: luladance@aol.com
Web Site: lulawashington.com
Officers:
President: Todd Reznik
Chair: Lula Washington
Publicist: Emma Pullen
Bookkeeper: Brenda Walker
Development Associate: Gail Christian
Management:
Artistic Director: Lula Washington
Executive Director: Erwin Washington
Associate Director/Choreographer: Tamica Washington-Miller
Choreographer: Donald McKayle
Mission: To provide a creative outlet for minority artists in South Los Angeles. To build a world class, professional, contemporary modern dance company that reflects many aspects of African American culture and history.
Utilizes: Choreographers; Dance Companies; Dancers; Designers; Five Seasonal Concerts; Guest Artists; Resident Professionals
Founded: 1980
Specialized Field: African American Dance
Status: Professional, Nonprofit
Income Sources: Black Dance Companies Association
Performs At: John F. Kennedy Center For The Performing Arts
Seating Capacity: 2,100
Year Built: 1968
Organization Type: Performing; Touring; Educational; Sponsoring

38
GROUNDING POINT DANCE COMPANY

PO Box 123
Manhattan Beach, CA 90267
Phone: 942-302-1208
e-mail: gpdance@att.net
Web Site: www.gpdance.com
Officers:
President: Carrie A Smaczny
Management:
Artistic Director: Carrie A Smaczny
Mission: To showcase artistic and entertaining dance forms through outreach residencies, dance for the camera projects and multimedia stage performances.camera projects, and multimedia stage performances.
Founded: 1998
Specialized Field: Multidisciplinary Dance
Status: Non-Profit, Semi-Professional
Paid Staff: 1
Volunteer Staff: 10
Income Sources: Tuition; Performances
Performs At: Scottsdale Center For Performing Arts
Seating Capacity: 838
Organization Type: Performing

39
CENTRAL WEST BALLET

3125 McHenry Avenue
Suite D
Modesto, CA 95350
Phone: 209-576-8957
Fax: 209-576-1308
e-mail: info@centralwestballet.com
Web Site: www.centralwestballet.com
Officers:
President: Ann Endsley
Vice President: Sandra Cash
Treasurer: Hugh Rose III

Secretary: Linda West
Management:
Artistic Director: Rene Daveluy
Ballet Mistress: Leslie Ann Larson
Executive Director: Cynthia Coughlin
Mission: The company has a dedication to inspiring excellence in dance and infusing passion that fosters a high quality, financially supported, professional dance company.
Utilizes: Choreographers; Collaborating Artists; Collaborations; Dance Companies; Dancers; Five Seasonal Concerts; Guest Artists; Guest Composers; Guest Designers; Guest Ensembles; Instructors; Local Artists; Organization Contracts; Resident Professionals; Soloists; Student Interns; Touring Companies
Founded: 1987
Specialized Field: Ballet
Status: Non-Profit, Pre-Professional
Paid Staff: 3
Volunteer Staff: 100
Paid Artists: 2
Non-paid Artists: 40
Budget: $250,000
Income Sources: Ads; Ticket Sales; Fund-Raising; Grants; Donations
Performs At: High school auditorium
Affiliations: Regional Dance America/Pacific
Annual Attendance: 10,000-14,000

40
INLAND PACIFIC BALLET

5050 Arrow Highway
Montclair, CA 91763
Phone: 909-482-1590
Fax: 909-482-1589
e-mail: info@ipballet.org
Web Site: www.ipballet.org
Officers:
President: Neal Archer
Treasurer: C A Sheppard
Management:
Artistic Director: Victoria Koenig
Ballet Mistress: Sarah Spradlin
Mission: To build and sustain a professional ballet company of national stature in the Inland Empire of Southern California. Inland Pacific Ballet strives to introduce new audiences to the magic of ballet, and to make the experience more available and accessible to all.
Founded: 1993
Specialized Field: Ballet
Paid Staff: 7
Volunteer Staff: 20
Paid Artists: 3
Non-paid Artists: 11
Income Sources: Tickets Sales; Merchandise Contributed Income; Foundation; Corporate; Individual
Performs At: Bridges Auditorium
Annual Attendance: 20,000
Facility Category: Opera House
Type of Stage: Proscenium
Seating Capacity: 2,500
Year Built: 1931
Year Remodeled: 1975
Cost: $600,000

41
INLAND PACIFIC BALLET

5050 Arrow Highway
Montclair, CA 91763
Phone: 909-482-1590
Fax: 904-482-1589
e-mail: info@ipballet.org
Web Site: www.ipballet.org

Officers:
Founder: Victoria Koenig
Founder: Kevin Myers
President: Neal Archer
Treasurer: C A Sheppard
Management:
Artistic Director: Victoria Koenig
Co-Artistic Director: Kevin Myers
Ballet Mistress: Sarah Spradlin-Bonomo
Ballet Mistress: Jill Voznick
Mission: Inland Pacific Ballet's mission is to build and sustain a professional ballet company of national stature in the Inland Empire of Southern California.
Specialized Field: Ballet
Status: Professional, Nonprofit

42
WESTERN BALLET

The Mountain View Ballet Company and School
914 N Rengstorff Avenue
Unit A
Mountain View, CA 94043
Phone: 650-968-4455
Fax: 650-968-4465
e-mail: info@westernballet.org
Web Site: www.westernballet.org
Officers:
President: Robin Ching
Secretary: Sara Lake
Treasurer: Julia Liu
Management:
Artistic Director: Alexi Zubiria
Mission: We strive to create an environment that grooms young artists for professional careers, providing the best possible training and performance experience, bringing out each dancer's personal best.
Founded: 1976
Specialized Field: Ballet

43
AXIS DANCE COMPANY

1428 Alice Street
Suite 200
Oakland, CA 94612
Phone: 510-625-0110
Fax: 510-625-0321
e-mail: judy@axisdance.org
Web Site: www.axisdance.org
Officers:
President: Deborah Kaplan
Vice President: Mishana Hosseinioun
Secretary/Treasurer: Girish Satya
Management:
Development Manager: Mollie McFarland, mollie@axisdance.org
Education Director: Annika Nonhebel
Artistic Director: Judith Smith
Mission: To create and perform contemporary dance that is developed through the collaboration of dancers with and without disabilities. AXIS teaches dance and educates about collaboration and disability through community education and outreach programs. AXIS is committed to promoting and supporting this form of dance locally and abroad.
Founded: 1987
Specialized Field: Contemporary Physically Integrated Dance
Status: Non-Profit
Paid Staff: 4
Paid Artists: 7
Budget: $489,900
Income Sources: Touring; Performances; Commissions; Education/Outreach Work; Government; Foundation; Corporate & Individual Donations

Performs At: The Malonga Casquelourd Center for Performing Arts
Seating Capacity: 350
Year Built: 1927
Organization Type: Educational; Performing

44
DIMENSIONS DANCE THEATER
Malonga Casquelourd Center for the Arts
1428 Alice Street
Suite 308
Oakland, CA 94612-4004
Phone: 510-465-3363
Fax: 510-465-3364
e-mail: dimensionsdance@prodigy.net
Web Site: www.dimensionsdance.org
Management:
  Artistic Director: Deborah B Vaughan
  Administrative Coordinator: Latanya D Tigner
Mission: To create, perform, and teach dance that reflects the historical experiences and contemporary lives of African Americans.
Founded: 1972
Specialized Field: Modern; African Dance; Jazz
Performs At: Calvin Simmons Theatre
Seating Capacity: 1,924
Year Built: 1914
Organization Type: Performing

45
OAKLAND BALLET
The Ronn Guidi Foundation
2626 Harrison Street
Oakland, CA 94612
Phone: 510-452-9288
e-mail: info@rgfpa.org
Web Site: www.rgfpa.org
Officers:
  Chair/Executive Director: Richard Cowan
  Secretary: Michelle Migdal Gee
  Treasurer: Marcia Olsen Joseph
Management:
  Artistic Director: Ronn Guidi
  Dance Mistress: JoAnn Hall Jung
Mission: To administer the operation of the Oakland Ballet Company, and to offer ballet training for young dancers while preserving and presenting historically significant ballet, including works from the Diaghilev Ballet Russers era.
Utilizes: Choreographers; Commissioned Music; Dancers; Five Seasonal Concerts; Grant Writers; Guest Accompanists; Guest Artists; Guest Conductors; Guest Musical Directors; Guest Musicians; Instructors; Local Artists; Original Music Scores; Resident Professionals; Visual Arts
Founded: 1968
Specialized Field: Ballet
Status: Professional, Nonprofit
Paid Staff: 3
Volunteer Staff: 50
Paid Artists: 33
Budget: $1,000,000-$2,500,000
Income Sources: Fundraising; Donations
Annual Attendance: 42,000
Type of Stage: Proscenium
Seating Capacity: 3,000
Organization Type: Performing; Touring

46
WING IT! PERFORMANCE ENSEMBLE
2273 Telegraph Avenue
Oakland, CA 94612
Phone: 510-814-9584
Fax: 510-836-3312
e-mail: bodywiz@aol.com
Web Site: www.interplay.org
Founded: 1989
Specialized Field: Modern; Improvisation; Theatrical Dance
Status: Professional; Non-Profit
Paid Staff: 3
Volunteer Staff: 100
Budget: 500,000
Annual Attendance: 3,000

47
WEST COAST CONSERVATORY BALLET
1014 W Collins Avenue
Orange, CA 92867
Phone: 714-639-8525
e-mail: info@wccballet.com
Web Site: www.wccballet.com
Management:
  Instructor: Jeng Halili
  Instructor: Li-Ann Lim
  Instructor: Julie Parker
  Instructor: Angela Talmadge
  Instructor: Tara Tillman
Mission: We feel that careful training given with individual attention on technique, expression, musicality and approach gives each student the greatest opportunity to fulfill his or her potential.
Specialized Field: Ballet
Status: Non-Profit
Performs At: Fullerton College Campus Theatre
Seating Capacity: 536
Year Built: 1913

48
DANZA FLORICANTO/USA
2758 East Orange Boulevard
Pasadena, CA 91107-2735
Phone: 626-796-2403
Fax: 626-796-2403
e-mail: floricanto@att.net
Web Site: www.danzafloricantousa.com
Management:
  Founder: Gema Sandoval
Mission: Their purpose is to preserve Mexican culture, validate it as a cultural and artistic expression of the Latino people in the American Southwest, and create awareness and appreciation or it through live performance.
Utilizes: Choreographers; Dancers; Original Music Scores
Founded: 1975
Specialized Field: Mexican Folk Dance/Chicano Dance
Status: Professional; Non-Profit
Paid Staff: 20
Volunteer Staff: 6
Paid Artists: 20
Budget: $75,000
Income Sources: Foundations; Government; Corporate; Individual; Ticket Sales
Performs At: John Anson Ford Theatre; Luckman Fine Arts Complex
Annual Attendance: 10,000

49
PASADENA CIVIC BALLET
253 North Vinedo Avenue
Pasadena, CA 91107
Phone: 626-792-0873
e-mail: inforequest@pcballet.com
Web Site: www.pcballet.com
Management:
  Artistic Director: Diane De Franco Browne
  Artistic Director: Tania Grafos
  School Director: Zoe Vidalakis
Mission: Provides quality instruction in the art and technique of dance, with an emphasis on ballet as the foundation for discipline and vocabulary; to create performance opportunities to allow the dancers to grow as artists as well as develop self confidence, poise and presentation skills; to provide a nuturing, supportive environment the emphasizes dance as an avenue to growth as an individual.
Utilizes: Choreographers; Collaborations; Dance Companies; Dancers; Five Seasonal Concerts; Guest Accompanists; Guest Artists; Guest Teachers; High School Drama; Lyricists; Original Music Scores
Founded: 1980
Specialized Field: Modern; Ballet; Jazz; Tap; Musical Theater; Character Dance; Hip Hop
Status: Pre-Professional; Nonprofit
Paid Staff: 11
Income Sources: Pasadena Arts Council
Performs At: San Gabriel Civic Auditorium
Seating Capacity: 1,500
Year Built: 1927
Rental Contact: Diane Browne
Organization Type: Performing; Educational

50
PASADENA DANCE THEATRE
1985 E Locust Street
Pasadena, CA 91107
Phone: 626-683-3459
Fax: 626-683-3559
Web Site: www.pasadenadance.org
Officers:
  President: James Watterson
  Vice President: Gwen Whitson
Management:
  Artistic Director: Cynthia Young
  Associate Director: Laurence Blake
Mission: To provide classical and innovative contemporary choeography through professional dance performance and to offer a high caliber of dacne training through its conservatory.
Founded: 1958
Specialized Field: Ballet
Status: Semi-Professional, Nonprofit
Paid Staff: 12
Volunteer Staff: 4
Paid Artists: 2
Non-paid Artists: 20
Income Sources: National Association for Regional Ballet; California Arts Council; Los Angeles County Arts Commission
Performs At: San Gabriel Civic Auditorium
Seating Capacity: 1,500
Year Built: 1927
Organization Type: Performing; Touring; Resident

51
PETALUMA CITY BALLET
110 Howard Street
Petaluma, CA 94952
Phone: 707-765-2660
e-mail: petballet@aol.com
Web Site: www.petalumacityballet.org
Officers:
  President: Katherine Reiff
  Vice President: Barbara Fields
  Treasurer: Heather Strand
  Secretary: Rebecca Patrascu
Management:
  Artistic Director: Ann Derby

Co-Artistic Director: Zoura O'Neill
Mission: To be a part of Petaluma's growing cultural community, offering quality productions of classical and comtemporary works by local and guest choreographers.
Founded: 1981
Specialized Field: Ballet
Status: Non-Profit, Pre-Professional
Paid Staff: 2
Volunteer Staff: 10
Non-paid Artists: 20
Budget: $50,000
Income Sources: Fund Raising; Grants
Performs At: SSU Everet B. Person Theatre; Spreckel's Performing Arts Center
Affiliations: Reginal Dance Of America
Annual Attendance: 2,500
Type of Stage: Full
Stage Dimensions: 40' X 35'
Seating Capacity: 475-511

52
CALIFORNIA RIVERSIDE BALLET
3840 Lemon Street
Riverside, CA 92501
Phone: 909-787-7850
Fax: 951-787-0879
Web Site: www.crballet.com
Officers:
President: Lisa Vinsingardisly
Secretary: Richerd Brent Reed
CFO: Marilyn Luckett
Management:
Artistic Director: Glenda Carhart
Artistic Advisor/Choreographer: David Allan
Choreographer: Michael Gervais
Ballet Mistress: Kathleen Riker
Ballet Master: Damien Diaz
Mission: Promoting excellence and enriching life through its presentation of the finest in classical and contemporary ballet. California Riverside Ballet accomplishes this through community outreach and performances, which educate and provide artistic experience to dancers and patrons alike. The ballet cultivates awareness of this traditional art expression to benefit the community and the arts.
Utilizes: Singers
Founded: 1969
Specialized Field: Modern; Ballet
Status: Professional, Nonprofit
Paid Staff: 75
Performs At: Landis Auditorium
Organization Type: Performing; Educational; Sponsoring

53
MAGIC CIRCLE THEATER
241 Vernon Street
Roseville, CA 95678
Phone: 916-782-1777
Fax: 916-782-1766
e-mail: stagemanager@mcircle.org
Web Site: www.mcircle.org
Officers:
President: Brent Null
Vice President: Paul March
Treasurer: Russ Sproull
Secretary: Dave Wooldridge
Management:
Artistic Director: Rosemarie Gerould
Executive Producer: Robert Gerould
Mission: To educate and entertain people of all ages, thereby enriching the cultural life of our community at large.

Founded: 1987
Specialized Field: Theatrical Dance
Budget: $800,000
Income Sources: Ads in the Program; Grants; Donations; Ticket Sales; Concessions; Sponsorships; Workshop Fees; Acting Class Fees
Performs At: Community Theatre
Affiliations: Roseville Theatre
Type of Stage: Proscenium
Seating Capacity: 500
Year Built: 1929
Year Remodeled: 2001
Rental Contact: Executive Director Robert Gerould

54
SACRAMENTO BALLET
1631 K Street
Sacramento, CA 95814-4019
Phone: 916-552-5800
Fax: 916-552-5815
e-mail: info@sacballet.org
Web Site: www.sacballet.org
Officers:
President: Jillrt Kaiser Newcom
First VP: Wahida Sharman
Second VP: Jay Radke
Secretary: Lydia Cohen
Management:
Artistic Director: Carrine Binda
Artistic Director: Ron Cunningham
Mission: The Sacramento Ballet entertains, educates, inspires and engages people through the powerful vehicle of dance.
Utilizes: Artists-in-Residence; Choreographers; Collaborating Artists; Collaborations; Dance Companies; Dancers; Designers; Educators; Grant Writers; Guest Accompanists; Guest Artists; Guest Composers; Guest Conductors; Guest Ensembles; Guest Musical Directors; High School Drama; Lyricists; Multimedia; Original Music Scores; Resident Artists; Student Interns; Visual Arts
Founded: 1954
Specialized Field: Ballet
Status: Professional, Nonprofit
Paid Staff: 11
Volunteer Staff: 2
Paid Artists: 28
Non-paid Artists: 5
Budget: 2.1 million
Income Sources: Ticket Sales; Program Ads; Grants; Contributions
Performs At: Monclavi Center
Affiliations: Dance USA; NSFRE; Regional Dance Pacific America
Annual Attendance: 80,000
Facility Category: Community Center Theatre
Type of Stage: Proscenium
Seating Capacity: 2,426
Organization Type: Performing; Touring; Resident

55
SAN DIEGO BALLET COMPANY
Dance Place San Diego
2650 Truxtun Road
San Deigo, CA 92106
Phone: 619-294-7378
Fax: 619-294-7315
e-mail: info@sandiegoballet.org
Web Site: www.sandiegoballet.org
Officers:
President: Greg Cartwright
Management:
Co-Artistic/Executive Director: Robin Sherertz Morgan

Co-Artistic Director/Choreographer: Javier Velasco
Ballet Mistress: Ahita Ardalan
Mission: To excite, enrich and entertain our diverse audience.
Founded: 1991
Specialized Field: Ballet
Status: Professional, Nonprofit

56
CALIFORNIA BALLET COMPANY
4819 Ronson Court
San Diego, CA 92111
Phone: 858-560-5676
Fax: 858-560-0072
e-mail: info@califoniaballet.org
Web Site: www.californiaballet.org
Management:
Director: Maxine Mahon
Program Director: Clarissa Palhegyi
Mission: To perform, educate and create new ballets.
Utilizes: Choreographers; Collaborations; Dance Companies; Dancers; Five Seasonal Concerts; Local Artists; Resident Artists
Founded: 1968
Specialized Field: Ballet
Status: Semi-Professional, Nonprofit
Budget: $950,000
Income Sources: Membership; Tickets; CAC; San Diego City Commission for Arts and Culture; Sponsors
Performs At: San Diego Civic Theatre
Seating Capacity: 3,000
Year Built: 1965
Organization Type: Performing; Touring; Resident

57
CITY BALLET SAN DIEGO
941 Garnet Avenue
PO Box 99072
San Diego, CA 92169
Phone: 858-274-6058
Fax: 858-272-8375
e-mail: artistic.director@cityballet.org
Web Site: www.cityballet.org
Management:
Artistic Director: Steven Wistrich
Choreographer: Elizabeth Wistrich
Mission: City Ballet is a non-profit organization committed to furthering the ballet art form.
Specialized Field: Ballet
Status: Nonprofit
Paid Staff: 2
Paid Artists: 10
Non-paid Artists: 9
Budget: $450,000
Income Sources: Ticket Sales; Donations
Performs At: Spreckels Theatre
Annual Attendance: 16,000
Type of Stage: Fly Theatre; Proscenium Stage
Seating Capacity: 120-150
Year Built: 1928

58
CIVIC DANCE COMPANY
2125 Park Boulevard
San Diego, CA 92101
Phone: 619-702-3408
Web Site: www.citydancearts.org
Management:
Instructor: Ava Towne Bishop
Instructor: Rachel Mitchell
Instructor: Katie McMahon
Instructor: Leslie Hayse Padilla

Mission: To support and promote a premier dance arts program and an appreciation of the arts, in cooperation with the San Diego Park and Recreation Department Dance Arts Program.
Founded: 1983
Specialized Field: Ballet; Jazz; Tap
Status: Non-Profit
Paid Staff: 18
Volunteer Staff: 120
Paid Artists: 4
Non-paid Artists: 40
Income Sources: Scholarships; Box Office Sponsor; Patron of the Arts; Management Sponsor; Parnership Sponsor Board of Directors Sponsors; Corporate Sponsor; Private Sponsor

59

MALASHOCK DANCE & THE MALASHOCK DANCE SCHOOL

2650 Truxton Road
Suite 202
San Diego, CA 92106
Phone: 619-260-1622
Fax: 619-523-0603
e-mail: info@malashockdance.org
Web Site: www.malashockdance.org
Officers:
    President: Russell King
Management:
    Artistic Director: John Malashock
    Associate Artistic Director: Michael Mizerany
    Education Director: Molly Puryear
Mission: To create, educate, collaborate and put emotion in motion.
Utilizes: Artists-in-Residence; Choreographers; Collaborations; Commissioned Composers; Community Members; Dance Companies; Dancers; Educators; Filmmakers; Guest Artists; Guest Ensembles; Guest Speakers; High School Drama; Instructors; Multi Collaborations; Soloists; Theatre Companies
Founded: 1988
Specialized Field: Theatrical Dance
Status: Professional
Paid Staff: 5
Volunteer Staff: 65
Paid Artists: 7-12
Budget: $500,000-$600,000
Income Sources: Government; Foundation; Corporate; Individuals
Affiliations: Dance/USA; SD Performing Arts League; TCG; CA Arts Council Touring Artists
Annual Attendance: 2000
Organization Type: Performing; Touring

60

SAN DIEGO DANCE THEATER

Dance Place San Diego
2650 Truxton Road
Suite 108
San Diego, CA 92106
Phone: 619-255-1803
Fax: 619-255-1803
e-mail: jean@sandiegodancetheater.org
Web Site: www.sandiegodancetheater.org
Management:
    Artistic Director: Jean Isaacs
    Music Director: Steve Baker
Mission: Create and perform intelligent dances that breathe life into the people of our region and beyond. Provide acces to viewing, training in and dancing of Isaacs' dances by people of many ages, nationalities, body types, sexual preferences and physical abilities.
Founded: 1972
Specialized Field: Ballet; Modern; Theatre Dance

Status: Professional, Non-Profit
Paid Staff: 2
Volunteer Staff: 10
Paid Artists: 9
Budget: $250,000-$300,000
Income Sources: Public Grants; Foundations; Individual Donors; Ticket Sales; The City of San Diego/Commission for Arts and Culture; County of San Diego; California Arts Council.
Annual Attendance: 5,000
Organization Type: Touring; Performing

61

SUSHI PERFORMANCE & VISUAL ART

390 Eleventh Avenue
San Diego, CA 92101
Mailing Address: PO Box 152761, San Diego CA 92115
Phone: 619-235-8466
Fax: 619-235-8552
e-mail: info@sushiart.org
Web Site: sushiart.org
Officers:
    President: Stephen Silverman
    Treasurer: Ed Koijane
    Secretary: Barbara Measelle
Management:
    Executive Director: Lynn Schuette
Mission: Sushi is commited to providing its artists and audiences with a laboratory where creative exploration, community engagement and new ideas flourish.
Founded: 1980
Specialized Field: Contemporary Dance
Status: Professional, Nonprofit
Paid Staff: 1
Budget: $200,000
Income Sources: Grants; Individual Donations; Membership; Admissions
Annual Attendance: 4,000 - 6,000
Facility Category: Alternative Loft Space
Organization Type: Performing; Touring; Educational

62

ALONZO KING LINES BALLET

26 Seventh Street
San Francisco, CA 94103
Phone: 415-863-3040
Fax: 415-863-1180
e-mail: info@linesballet.org
Web Site: www.linesballet.org
Officers:
    Executive Director/CEO: Ann Marie Nemanich
    Associate Artistic Director: Robert Rosenwasser
    Ballet Master: Arturo Fernandez
    Chair: Jocelyn Lamm Startz
    Treasurer: Merredith Treaster
Management:
    Artistic Director: Alonzo King
    Marketing: Tom Dill, tdill@linesballet.org
Mission: LINES Ballet nurtures dynamic artistry and the development of auhtentic, creative expression through dance. The company is dedicated to exploring the possibilities of movement from a global perspective.
Utilizes: Choreographers; Collaborating Artists; Collaborations; Commissioned Composers; Commissioned Music; Dancers; Designers; Filmmakers; Five Seasonal Concerts; Guest Accompanists; Guest Artists; Guest Companies; Guest Conductors; Guest Ensembles; Guest Musical Directors; Guest Musicians; High School Drama; Multimedia; Original Music Scores; Resident Artists; Resident Professionals; Soloists; Theatre Companies; Visual Arts
Founded: 1982

Specialized Field: Ballet; Modern Ballet
Paid Staff: 20
Volunteer Staff: 50
Paid Artists: 14
Budget: $2,000,000-$3,500,000

63

CHITRESH DAS DANCE COMPANY

32 Saint Charles Avenue
San Francisco, CA 94132
Phone: 415-333-9000
Web Site: www.kathak.org
Management:
    Artistic Director: Pandit Chitresh Das
Mission: Produce exemplary traditional, innovative, and collaborative works of North Indian classical Kathak dance, increase awareness of Kathak dance, to train future generations and build local, national and international community support for the Kathak tradition.
Founded: 1980
Specialized Field: Kathak Dance
Status: Professional
Paid Staff: 6
Volunteer Staff: 25
Paid Artists: 09
Budget: $285,000-300,000
Income Sources: Touring; Performances; Tuition

64

DANCE BRIGADE

3316 24th Street
San Francisco, CA 94110
Phone: 415-826-4401
Fax: 415-826-4401
Web Site: www.dancebrigade.org
Management:
    Artistic Director: Krissy Keefer
Mission: To create and perform dance theater that addresses the complex problems of contemporary American women. The company has created, performed, presented and produced issue-oriented dance theater exploring socio-political issues such as voilence against women, class injustice, war, racism, breast cancer, sexual abuse and homophobia.
Utilizes: Five Seasonal Concerts; Guest Artists; Singers
Founded: 1984
Specialized Field: Contemporary Dance
Status: Professional, Non-Profit
Paid Staff: 3
Volunteer Staff: 18
Paid Artists: 8
Performs At: Mission Theatre
Organization Type: Performing; Touring; Resident; Sponsoring

65

DANCERS' GROUP

1360 Mission Street
Suite 200
San Francisco, CA 94103
Phone: 415-920-9181
Fax: 415-920-9173
Web Site: www.dancersgroup.org
Officers:
    President: Mary Armentrout
    Vice President: Ken James
    Secretary: Dana Lawton
    Treasurer: Denise Pate
Management:
    Executive Director: Wayne Hazzard
Mission: We strive to bring a variety of artists and organizations together that create engaging partnerships and civic collaborations and we work to

build the quality and accessibility of dance in the San Fransisco Bay Area. Our presenting and co-presenting programs increase visibility for dance artists that engage in a diverse community in an effort to bring new audiences to dance.
Founded: 1982
Specialized Field: Contemporary Dance
Paid Staff: 2
Volunteer Staff: 5
Income Sources: Dance Bay Area; Donations; Sponsors
Performs At: ODC Theater
Organization Type: Performing; Educational; Sponsoring

66

JOE GOODE PERFORMANCE GROUP

1007 General Kennedy Avenue
Suite 209
San Francisco, CA 94129
Phone: 415-561-6565
Fax: 415-561-6562
e-mail: info@joegoode.org
Web Site: www.joegoode.org
Officers:
  President: Lynne Blair
Management:
  Artistic Director: Joe Goode
  Managing Director: Maia Rosal
Mission: To promote understanding, compassion and tolerance among people through the innovative use of dance and theater, as interpreted by the artistic vision and work of Joe Goode.
Founded: 1986
Specialized Field: Theatrical Dance
Budget: $200,000-$500,000
Income Sources: Donations; Fundraising

67

KULARTS

Bayanihan Center
1010 Mission Street
San Francisco, CA 94112
Phone: 415-239-0249
e-mail: info@kularts.org
Web Site: www.kularts.org
Officers:
  President: Francis Wong
Management:
  Artistic/Executive Director: Alleluia Panis
Mission: To inform and expand the understanding of American Philippino culture and preserve the spirit and integrity of ancient Pilipino art forms.
Founded: 1985
Specialized Field: Presenter of Contemporary And Tribal Pilipino Dance
Paid Staff: 2
Volunteer Staff: 100
Paid Artists: 10
Non-paid Artists: 5
Budget: $130,000
Income Sources: California Arts Council; California Council for the Humanities , San Francisco Grants for the Arts; San Francisco Arts Commission-Cultural Equity,Zellerbach Foundation;LIA Fnd
Annual Attendance: 5,000
Seating Capacity: 80
Year Built: 2008

68

LILY CAI CHINESE DANCE COMPANY

Chinese Cultural Productions
Fort Mason Center
Landmark Building C-353
San Francisco, CA 94123
Phone: 415-474-4829
Fax: 415-651-9589
e-mail: info@ccpsf.org
Web Site: www.ccpsf.org
Management:
  Artistic Director: Lily Cai
  Executive Director/Music Director: Gang Situ
Mission: To promote greater public awareness of Chinese dance and music, to produce original contemporary work that is firmly rooted in Chinese cultural traditions, to challenge American conceptions of traditional Chinese and Chinese American culture and to encourage our community artists to explore new avenues of self expression.
Utilizes: Dance Companies
Founded: 1989
Specialized Field: Chinese Dance
Status: Nonprofit Organization
Paid Staff: 4
Volunteer Staff: 10
Paid Artists: 7
Income Sources: Funders; Corporate Sponsors; Donations
Performs At: Extensively throughout California and the United States; Major Performing Arts Venues; Festivals; University Theatres
Organization Type: Performing; Touring

69

MARGARET JENKINS DANCE COMPANY

149-9th Street
Suite 300
San Francisco, CA 94103
Phone: 415-861-3940
Fax: 415-861-3872
e-mail: info@mjdc.org
Web Site: www.mjdc.org
Management:
  Artistic Director: Margaret Jenkins
  Development & Operations Manager: Todd Eckert
  Administrative Assistant/Tour Mngr: Jackie Bendzinski
Mission: To perform the work of choreographer Margaret Jenkins.
Founded: 1972
Specialized Field: Modern Dance
Status: Professional; Nonprofit
Paid Staff: 3
Paid Artists: 9
Affiliations: Margaret Jenkins Dance Laboratory
Annual Attendance: 2,000
Organization Type: Performing; Touring; Resident; Educational

70

MARK FOEHRINGER DANCE PROJECT

798 Ashbry Street
San Francisco, CA 94117
Phone: 415-640-2784
Fax: 415-665-8485
e-mail: gary@mfdpsf.org
Web Site: www.mfdpsf.org
Officers:
  Founder: Mark Foehringer
  President: Allen Habel
  Treasurer: Gary Lindsay
  Secretary: Susanna Douthit

Management:
  Artistic Director/Choreographer: Mark Foehringer
  Managing Director: Susanna Douthit
  Production Manager/Technical Dir: Frederic O Boulay
  Business Manager: Gary Lindsay
Mission: It is made of a repertoire of contemporary ballet works created by founder and choreographer Mark Foehringer and professional dancers.
Founded: 1996
Specialized Field: Contemporary
Status: Professional

71

NANCY KARP & DANCERS

The New Arts Foundation
60 Guy Place
San Francisco, CA 94105
Phone: 510-653-1195
Fax: 510-652-0898
e-mail: info@nancykarp.org
Web Site: www.nancykarp.org
Management:
  Artistic Director/Choreographer: Nancy Karp
Mission: The New Arts Foundation is dedicated to the creation and presentation of new work that reflects the artistic vision of director/choreographer Nancy Karp and her dance company, Nancy Karp & Dancers.
Utilizes: Choreographers; Collaborating Artists; Collaborations; Commissioned Composers; Dancers; Designers; Fine Artists; Guest Companies; Guest Conductors; Guest Musical Directors; Instructors; Local Artists; Lyricists; Organization Contracts; Original Music Scores; Poets; Resident Artists; Resident Professionals; Singers; Student Interns; Visual Arts
Founded: 1981
Specialized Field: Interdisciplinary; Collaborative Dance
Status: Professional, Nonprofit
Performs At: Cowell Theater; Theater Artaud
Type of Stage: Proscenium
Organization Type: Performing; Touring

72

ODC THEATER

ODC Theater at Project Artaud Theater
351 Shotwell Street
San Francisco, CA 94110
Phone: 415-863-6606
Fax: 415-863-9833
e-mail: info@odctheater.org
Web Site: www.odctheater.org
Management:
  Theater Director: Rob Bailis
  Artistic Director: Brenda Way
Mission: To inspire audiences, cultivate artists, engage community and foster diversity and inclusion through dance.
Founded: 1971
Specialized Field: Modern Dance
Paid Staff: 6
Volunteer Staff: 2
Budget: $300,000
Performs At: The Kennedy Center; Jacob's Pillow; The Joyce Theater, NYC; The Olympic Arts Festival;, The Spoletto Festival
Annual Attendance: 18,000
Facility Category: Studio Theater
Type of Stage: Sprung Wood
Stage Dimensions: 48'x40'
Seating Capacity: 187
Year Built: 1920
Year Remodeled: 1980
Rental Contact: Director Andrew Wood

Organization Type: Performing; Touring; Resident; Educational

73
PURPLE MOON DANCE PROJECT

26 7th Street
6th Floor
San Francisco, CA 94103
Phone: 415-552-1105
e-mail: project@purplemoondance.org
Web Site: purplemoondance.org
Management:
 Executive/Artistic Director: Jill Togawa
 Administrative Manager: Frances Gay Teves Sedayao
Mission: To increase the visability of lesbians and women of color and to encourage social change, peace and healing in our society through the medium of dance. Purple Moon's work is diversity made physical.
Founded: 1992
Specialized Field: Western; Non-Western; Multidisciplinary Collaboration Dance
Paid Staff: 5
Volunteer Staff: 32
Non-paid Artists: 2
Performs At: The Gay Games Cultural Festival in New York; Santa Monica, California; Oregon
Annual Attendance: 4,500

74
ROBERT FRIEDMAN PRESENTS

451 30th Avenue
San Francisco, CA 94121
Phone: 415-759-1992
Fax: 415-752-0576
e-mail: rf@rfpresents.com
Web Site: www.rfpresents.com
Officers:
 President: Robert Friedman
Management:
 Director: Robert Friedman
Mission: To bring variant forms of theatrical art to the San Francisco area.
Founded: 1973
Specialized Field: Theatrical Performance

75
SAN FRANCISCO BALLET

455 Franklin Street
San Francisco, CA 94102
Phone: 415-861-5600
e-mail: sfbmail@sfballet.info
Web Site: www.sfballet.org
Officers:
 Chair: Richard Barker
Management:
 Artistic Director/Choreographer: Helgi Tomasson
Mission: The San Francisco Ballet Company is dedicated to sharing our love of dance with the broadest possible audience.
Founded: 1933
Specialized Field: Ballet
Status: Professional, Non-Profit
Paid Staff: 70
Volunteer Staff: 300
Paid Artists: 69
Performs At: The War Memorial Opera House
Annual Attendance: 100,000
Facility Category: War Memorial Opera House
Type of Stage: Dance; Opera
Seating Capacity: 3,200
Year Remodeled: 1996
Organization Type: Performing; Touring

76
SAN FRANCISCO ETHNIC DANCE FESTIVAL

World Arts West
Fort Mason Center
Landmark Building D
San Francisco, CA 94123-1382
Phone: 415-474-3914
Fax: 415-474-3922
e-mail: info@worldartswest.org
Web Site: www.worldartswest.org
Management:
 Executive Director: Julie Mushet
 Artistic Director: Carlos Carvajal
 Artistic Director: CK Ladzekpo
Mission: To honor and celebrate culturally diverse dance forms through presentation, education and support of artists and their tradititons.
Specialized Field: Munticultural Dance
Status: Professional, Non-Profit
Paid Staff: 4
Volunteer Staff: 15
Budget: $60,000-$150,000
Income Sources: Sponsors; Donations
Season: June
Affiliations: Palace of Fine Arts
Annual Attendance: 7,600
Seating Capacity: 1,000

77
SMUIN BALLET

44 Gough Street #103
San Francisco, CA 94103
Phone: 415-556-5000
Fax: 415-556-5200
e-mail: info@smuinballet.org
Web Site: www.smuinballet.org
Officers:
 President: Pattie Hume
 Vice President: Thomas Aden
 Company Manager: Jo Ellen Arntz
Management:
 Director: Celia Fushille
 Ballet Master: Amy London
Mission: To bring enjoyment of dance to new as well as to existing audiences through works of uncompromising originality and quality.
Founded: 1994
Specialized Field: Ballet
Status: Non-Profit, Professional
Paid Staff: 12
Volunteer Staff: 36
Paid Artists: 18
Budget: $2.3 million
Income Sources: Ticket Sales; Donations
Performs At: Palace of Fine Arts; Mountain View Center for Performing Arts; Yerba Buena Novellus Theatre; Lesher Center-Walnut Creek
Annual Attendance: 50,000

78
THE LIVELY FOUNDATION

2565 Washington Street
Suite 4
San Francisco, CA 94115-1828
Phone: 415-346-8959
Fax: 415-474-3058
e-mail: livelyhedgehog@mac.com
Web Site: livelyfoundation.org
Management:
 Artistic Director: Leslie Friedman

Mission: The foundation is devoted to the ptoduction of artistic and educational programs in dance, music and related arts.
Founded: 1983
Specialized Field: Contemporary Dance
Performs At: Herbst Theater; Vetrans' Building Green Room
Organization Type: Performing; Touring; Educational

79
THEATER ARTAUD

499 Alabama Street
San Francisco, CA 94110
Phone: 415-621-4240
Fax: 415-621-3824
e-mail: info@artaud.org
Web Site: www.artaud.org
Officers:
 President: Susan Sullivan
 VP: Mari Eliza
 Secretary: Angelica Bogner
 Treasurer: Judy West
Mission: To provide support for artists and arts activities and a model of how artist communities can be shelters for artisans and resources for a city.
Utilizes: Five Seasonal Concerts; Guest Artists; Guest Companies; Singers
Founded: 1971
Specialized Field: Performing Arts
Status: Professional
Income Sources: National Performance Network; California Presenters
Organization Type: Performing

80
WORLD ARTS WEST

Fort Mason Center
Landmark Building D
San Francisco, CA 94123-1382
Phone: 415-474-3914
Fax: 415-474-3922
e-mail: info@worldartswest.org
Web Site: www.worldartswest.org
Management:
 Executive Director: Julie Mushet
 Artistic Director: Carlos Carvajal
 Artistic Director: CK Ladzekpo
Mission: To honor and celebrate culturally diverse dance forms through presentation, education and support of artists and their traditions.
Utilizes: Dance Companies; Dancers
Specialized Field: Multicultural Performing Arts
Status: Nonprofit, Professional
Paid Staff: 4
Volunteer Staff: 15
Income Sources: Sponsors; Donations
Performs At: Palace of Fine Arts; Cowell Theater; Other Venues
Annual Attendance: 7,600
Organization Type: Performing; Resident; Educational; Sponsoring

81
YAELISA AND CAMINOS FLAMENCOS

26th Seventh Street
5th Floor
San Francisco, CA 94103
Phone: 510-531-9986
e-mail: info@caminosflamencos.com
Web Site: www.caminosflamencos.com
Management:
 Artist Director: Yaelisa

Mission: To create and present contemporary, traditional and theatrical dance programs showcasing artists from Spain and the US which reflect the changing face of Flamenco in the 21st century.
Founded: 1993
Specialized Field: Spanish; Flamenco
Performs At: ODC Theater

82
ZACCHO DANCE THEATRE

1777 Yosemite Avenue
Studio 330
San Francisco, CA 94124
Phone: 415-822-6744
Fax: 415-822-6745
e-mail: office@zaccho.org
Web Site: www.zaccho.org
Officers:
President: Sean Cullen
Treasurer: Jose Maria Francos
Management:
Artistic Director: Joanna Haigood
Executive Director: Jennifer Ross
Mission: Zaccho dance theater creates and presents performance work that investigates dance as it relates to place.
Founded: 1979
Specialized Field: Contemporary Performing Arts
Paid Staff: 4
Non-paid Artists: 1
Income Sources: Ticket Sales; Performances; Fundraising; Class Fees
Performs At: Walker Art Center; Theatre Artaud

83
ABHINAYA DANCE COMPANY OF SAN JOSE

52 Harold Avenue
San Jose, CA 95117
Phone: 408-983-0491
Fax: 408-983-0492
e-mail: Abhinaya_sj@yahoo.com
Web Site: www.abhinaya.org
Management:
Artistic Director/Choreographer: Mythili Kumar
Mission: The company is dedicated to promoting the classical dance forms of South India through instructional classes and professional performances.
Founded: 1980
Specialized Field: South Indian Dance
Status: Non-Profit, Professional
Paid Staff: 2
Volunteer Staff: 50
Income Sources: Corporate Sponsors; Grants
Performs At: Mexican Heritage Theater; Louis B Meyer Theater; Center For Performing Arts
Organization Type: Performing

84
BALLET SAN JOSE

40 N First Street
San Jose, CA 95113-1200
Phone: 408-288-2820
Fax: 408-993-9570
e-mail: ikopp@balletsj.org
Web Site: www.balletsj.org
Management:
Artistic Director: Dennis Nahat
Marketing Director: Lee Kopp
Mission: To provide the South Bay with theatrically produced ballet and professional dance education in a manner that is in vision of the artists, meets the highest

technical and artistic standards, contributes to the fulfillment of the cultural needs of the community, and is accessible to as wide an audience as possible.
Utilizes: Collaborating Artists; Contract Orchestras; Dancers; Guest Accompanists; Guest Artists; Guest Conductors; Guest Speakers; Original Music Scores; Resident Artists; Resident Professionals
Founded: 1983
Specialized Field: Ballet
Paid Staff: 23
Paid Artists: 44
Income Sources: Corporate Sponsors
Performs At: Performing Arts Center With Continental Seating
Affiliations: AGMA; Musicians Union
Annual Attendance: 50,000
Type of Stage: Proscenium
Stage Dimensions: 48'x35'
Seating Capacity: 2,600
Year Built: 1972

85
PENINSULA BALLET THEATRE

1880 S Grant Street
San Mateo, CA 94402
Phone: 650-342-3262
Fax: 650-342-3265
e-mail: marketing@penisulaballet.org
Web Site: www.penisulaballet.org
Officers:
President/CEO: Christine Leslie
Chairman: Michael Berube
Treasurer: Katherine Jones
Secretary: Lance Huntley
Management:
Artistic Director/Conservatory Dir.: Bruce I Steivel
Music Director: Chris Christenson
Company Manager: Sharon Torrano
Marketing Director: Lance Huntley
Mission: To support and foster a vital arts community in the greater Bay area through educational outreach and by engaging local art talent in the production and presentation of professional, live dance performances at prices affordable to all segments of the population.
Utilizes: Artists-in-Residence; Choreographers; Commissioned Composers; Community Members; Community Talent; Composers-in-Residence; Contract Orchestras; Dancers; Guest Artists; High School Drama; Local Artists; Original Music Scores; Singers; Soloists
Founded: 1967
Specialized Field: Ballet
Status: Professional, Nonprofit
Paid Staff: 4
Volunteer Staff: 25
Paid Artists: 52
Income Sources: Corporate; Foundation; Individual; Merchant Donors
Performs At: San Mateo Performing Arts Center
Organization Type: Performing; Resident

86
PERSPECTIVE DANCE THEATRE/RENO BALLET

Peninsula Ballet Theatre School
333 S B Street
PO Box 1804
San Mateo, CA 94401
Phone: 650-340-9444
Fax: 650-340-9495
e-mail: marketing@peninsulaballet.org
Web Site: peninsulaballet.org
Officers:
President: Christine Leslie

Chairman: Judy David
Secretary: William U Savage
Treasurer: Keith Kaiser
Management:
Artistic Director: Carlo Carvajal
Music Director: Chris Christenson
Mission: To support and foster a vital arts community in the greater Bay Area through educational outreach and by engaging local art talent in the production and presentation of professional, live dance performances at prices affordable to all segments of the population.
Founded: 1967
Specialized Field: Modern
Income Sources: Corporate; Foundation; Individual; Merchant Donors

87
SAN PEDRO CITY BALLET

1231 S Pacific Avenue
San Pedro, CA 90731
Phone: 310-732-1861
Fax: 310-732-1543
e-mail: info@sanpedrocityballet.org
Web Site: www.sanpedrocityballet.org
Management:
Artist Director: Cynthia Bradley
Artistic Director: Patrick Bradley
Mission: To identify, train and promote a world class pre-professional dance company from the diverse population of the Los Angeles Harbor area that is founded in the base of classical works and traditions, and goes beyond to explore new contemporary and original modern works and to provide training to schools throughout Los Angeles for arts education and after school programs.
Founded: 1994
Specialized Field: Ballet

88
MARIN BALLET/CENTER FOR DANCE

100 Elm Street
San Rafael, CA 94901
Phone: 415-453-6705
Fax: 415-453-5894
e-mail: info@marinballet.org
Web Site: www.marinballet.org
Management:
Artistic Director: Cynthia Lucas
Executive Director: Lawrence Ewing
Mission: To provide excellent dance training and education and to promote the art of dance.
Founded: 1963
Specialized Field: Ballet
Status: Nonprofit; Non-Professional
Paid Staff: 17
Volunteer Staff: 20
Paid Artists: 5
Budget: $500,000-$1,000,000
Performs At: The Marin Center Veteran Memorial Auditorium; Phyllis Thelen Studio Theatre
Annual Attendance: 300-350

89
STATE STREET BALLET

322 State Street
Santa Barbara, CA 93101
Phone: 805-965-6066
Fax: 805-965-3590
e-mail: ssbdance@aol.com
Web Site: www.statestreetballet.com
Management:
Artistic Director: Rodney Gustafson

Mission: The compant is dedicated to presenting excellence in dance through public performances and educational outreach programs. By combining classical tradition with diversity and sophisticated style we are committed to exploring new avenues in dance while preserving the classics.
Founded: 1994
Specialized Field: Ballet
Paid Staff: 2
Volunteer Staff: 20
Budget: $1,000,000
Income Sources: Donations; Grants; Ticket Sales
Performs At: Palmdale Playhouse

90

SANTA CLARA BALLET

3123 Millar Avenue
Santa Clara, CA 95051
Phone: 408-247-9178
e-mail: scballet@bigfoot.com
Web Site: www.santaclaraballet.org
Officers:
　　President: Dennis Mullen
Management:
　　Artistic Director: Josefa Villanueva
Mission: To stimulate and promote interest in ballet, primarily as an art form, by providing high-quality ballet performances at a reasonable cost to the general public. To provide performing opportunities to local dancers by helping them develop their talents and achieve their goals. To enhance the quality of life in the South Bay/Silicon Valley community through cultural awareness and diversity.
Utilizes: Actors; AEA Actors; Arrangers; Artists-in-Residence; Choreographers; Collaborating Artists; Collaborations; Commissioned Composers; Commissioned Music; Community Members; Community Talent; Composers; Composers-in-Residence; Contract Actors; Contract Orchestras; Curators; Dance Companies; Dancers; Designers; Educators; Equity Actors; Fine Artists; Guest Accompanists; Guest Musicians; Guest Speakers; High School Drama; Local Artists; Original Music Scores; Paid Performers; Singers; Soloists
Founded: 1973
Specialized Field: Ballet
Paid Staff: 3
Volunteer Staff: 8
Paid Artists: 8
Non-paid Artists: 15
Income Sources: Partially funded by the City of Santa Clara; memberships; donations; fund-raising
Performs At: Santa Clara Convention Center Theatre
Type of Stage: Wood
Seating Capacity: 607
Organization Type: Performing; Touring; Resident

91

DANCING CAT PRODUCTIONS

PO Box 4287
Santa Cruz, CA 95063
Phone: 831-429-5085
Fax: 831-423-7057
e-mail: ml@dancingcat.com
Web Site: www.dancingcat.com
Management:
　　Marketing: Jennifer Gallacher
Specialized Field: Contemporary Dance
Status: Professional
Paid Staff: 5

92

DR. SCHAFFER AND MR. STERN DANCE ENSEMBLE

PO Box 8055
Santa Cruz, CA 95061-8055
Phone: 831-335-1861
Fax: 831-335-1876
e-mail: schafferkarl@fhda.edu
Web Site: www.schafferstern.org
Management:
　　Co-Artistic Director: Karl Schaffer
　　Co-Artistic Director: Erik Stern
　　Creative Collaborator: Gregg Lizenbery
Mission: Presents the artistic and educational work of Karl Schaffer and Erik Stern.
Utilizes: Collaborating Artists; Collaborations; Commissioned Music; Dancers; Educators; Lyricists; Original Music Scores; Resident Professionals; Scenic Designers; Sign Language Translators; Singers; Student Interns; Visual Arts; Visual Designers; Volunteer Artists; Volunteer Directors & Actors; Writers
Founded: 1987
Specialized Field: Modern
Status: Professional; Non-Profit
Paid Staff: 2
Paid Artists: 5
Budget: 20,000-60,000
Income Sources: Grants; Fee for Service; Touring; Donations
Performs At: Center for the Arts; Henry J. Mello Center;The Mondavi Center; The John F. Kennedy Center for the Performing Arts
Annual Attendance: 5,000-25,000

93

ALLAN HANCOCK COLLEGE DANCE PROGRAM

800 S College Drive
Santa Maria, CA 93454
Phone: 805-922-6966
Fax: 805-928-7905
Toll-free: 866-354-5242
e-mail: dmcmahon@hancockcollege.edu
Web Site:
www.hancockcollege.edu/default.asp?page=478
Management:
　　Dance Program Coordinator: Diane McMahon
　　Dance Spectrum Director: Larissa Nazarenko
Mission: Students and faculty are given the opportunity to choreograph as well as perform.
Utilizes: Actors; Arrangers; Choreographers; Commissioned Music; Composers-in-Residence; Dance Companies; Dancers; Educators; Equity Actors; Guest Artists; Guest Choreographers; Guest Companies; Guest Directors; Guest Ensembles; Guest Instructors; Guest Lecturers; Guest Musical Directors; Guest Musicians; Guest Soloists; Guest Speakers; Guest Teachers; Guest Writers; Guild Activities; High School Drama; Organization Contracts; Original Music Scores; Soloists
Specialized Field: Ballet; Jazz
Paid Staff: 50
Volunteer Staff: 200
Paid Artists: 10
Budget: $100,000
Income Sources: Community College Budget; Box Office Receipts
Performs At: Marian Theatre; Severson Theatre
Facility Category: Theater
Type of Stage: Thrust stage
Stage Dimensions: 40' x 40'
Year Built: 1967

94

DONNA STERNBERG & DANCERS

911 9th Street
#206
Santa Monica, CA 90403
Phone: 310-260-1198
Fax: 310-260-1198
e-mail: dsdancers@earthlink.net
Web Site: www.dsdancers.com
Management:
　　Artistic Director: Donna Sternberg,
　　dsdancers@earthlink.net
Mission: An interdisciplinary dance company whose mission is to build bridges and make connections between dance, science, philosophy and other art forms so that people and ideas come together in ways that expand human awareness leading audiences to envision the world as theirs to create in a unique way.
Utilizes: Choreographers; Collaborating Artists; Collaborations; Dance Companies; Dancers; Designers; Educators; Guest Accompanists; Guest Instructors; Guest Musical Directors; Guest Soloists; Instructors; Lyricists; Multi Collaborations; Organization Contracts; Original Music Scores; Theatre Companies
Founded: 1985
Specialized Field: Contemporary Dance
Status: Non-Profit; Professional
Paid Staff: 1
Volunteer Staff: 2
Paid Artists: 6
Budget: 38,000
Income Sources: Government Grants; Foundations; Business; Individuals; Ticket Sales; Contracted Performances and Teaching Programs; Touring
Annual Attendance: 3,000

95

BANAFSHEH SAYYAD AND NAMAH

1537 Berkeley Street
Suite 2
Santa Monica, CA 90404
Phone: 310-499-7100
Fax: 818-888-3484
e-mail: namah@namah.net
Web Site: www.namah.net
Management:
　　Artistic Director: Banafsheh Sayyad
Mission: To promote and educate the broadest possible public appreciation and interest in Iranian and world performing arts, including dance, music and theater, through public performances, educational outreach programs, workshops, lectures and studio instruction.
Founded: 1994
Specialized Field: Contemporary Persian Dance; Sufi Whirling; Flamenco
Paid Staff: 1
Volunteer Staff: 1
Paid Artists: 6

96

KESHET CHAIM DANCE ENSEMBLE

4155 Dixie Canyon Avenue
Sherman Oaks, CA 91423
Phone: 818-784-0344
Fax: 818-896-1496
e-mail: general_info@kcdancers.org
Web Site: www.kcdancers.org
Management:
　　Executive Director: Genie Benson
　　Artistic Director: Eytan Avisar

Mission: A non-profit American-Israeli contemporary dance troupe, mission is to express the global spirit of Judaism and Israeli culture throughout the world, and to combat prejudice through education and the arts.
Founded: 1983
Specialized Field: Israeli Contemporary Folk Dance
Status: Non-Profit; Professional
Paid Staff: 3
Volunteer Staff: 5
Non-paid Artists: 20
Budget: $1,170,000
Income Sources: Government; Foundations; Corporate; Private Donors
Performs At: Various; Concert; Festival; School
Annual Attendance: 10,000

97
SANTA CRUZ BALLET THEATRE

2800 S Rodeo Gulch Road
Soquel, CA 95073
Phone: 831-477-1600
Fax: 831-464-1219
e-mail: info@scbt.org
Web Site: http://scbt.org
Management:
　Artistic Director: Diane Cypher
　Artistic Director: Robert Kelley
Mission: To inspire the community and create opportunities for young artists through the advamcement of the art of ballet.
Founded: 1978
Specialized Field: Ballet
Status: Non-Profit, Pre-Professional

98
LAURIDSEN BALLET CENTRE

1261 Sartori Avenue
Torrance, CA 90501
Phone: 310-533-1247
e-mail: southbayballet@yahoo.com
Web Site: www.southbayballet.org
Management:
　Artistic Director: Diane Lauridsen
Mission: To provide quality artistic performances to the community as well as outstanding training to young and pre-professional dancers.
Founded: 1987
Specialized Field: Ballet

99
MENDOCINO BALLET

205 S State Street
Ukiah, CA 95482
Phone: 707-463-2290
e-mail: balletoffice@sbcglobal.net
Web Site: www.mendocinoballet.org
Management:
　Artistic/Executive Director: Trudy McCreanor
Mission: To provide the highest professional dance instruction and performance opportunities in Mendocino County and the surrounding areas.
Founded: 1984
Specialized Field: Ballet

100
FRANCISCO MARTINEZ DANCE THEATRE

6723 Matilija Avenue
Valley Glen, CA 91405
Phone: 818-988-2192
e-mail: info@fmdt.org
Web Site: www.fmdt.org
Management:
　Artistic Director: Francisco Martinez

Mission: Francisco Martinez's dances are as varied as his far ranging interests, yet all reflect his deep affection for movement, music and the intriguing possibilities for combining the two.
Founded: 1971
Specialized Field: Ballet
Status: Non-Profit, Professional
Paid Staff: 8
Volunteer Staff: 2
Budget: $40,000-$400,0000
Performs At: Government; Corporate; Individual; Foundations
Annual Attendance: 25,000
Organization Type: Performing; Touring

101
VENTURA COUNTY BALLET COMPANY

2750 East Main Street
Ventura, CA 93003
Phone: 805-648-2080
Fax: 805-643-6771
e-mail: info@venturacountyballet.com
Web Site: www.venturacountyballet.com
Management:
　Executive Director: Kathleen Noblin
　Artistic Director: Colleen O'Callaghan
Mission: To provide the community with a prestigious professional/pre-professional ballet company to reach audiences countywide. Our goal is also to offer the county's underserved population quality ballet performances without charge.
Founded: 1998
Specialized Field: Ballet
Paid Staff: 4
Volunteer Staff: 100

102
DIABLO BALLET

PO Box 4700
Walnut Creek, CA 94596
Phone: 925-943-1775
Fax: 925-943-1115
e-mail: diablo@diabloballet.org
Web Site: www.diabloballet.org
Management:
　Artistic Director: Lauren Jonas
　Artistic Advisor: Sally Streets
Mission: To train and provide professional performance opportunities to dancers who have outstanding potential through Diablo Ballet's Apprentice and Professional Intermediate Programs.
Founded: 1993
Specialized Field: Theatrical Dance
Income Sources: Corporate; Merchant; Individual Donors
Performs At: Zellerbach Hall, University of California at Berkeley; Yerba Buena Center for the Arts
Organization Type: Performing; Touring; Educational

Colorado

103
HELANDER DANCE THEATER

Dairy Center For the Arts
2590 Walnut Street
Boulder, CO 80302-5700
Phone: 303-473-9438
Fax: 303-449-4614
e-mail: danelle@peakpeak.com
Web Site: www.helanderdance.org
Management:
　Artistic Director: Danelle Helander

Mission: To make a vital contribution to the community through dance as a vehicle for greater understanding, sharing and healing.
Founded: 1980
Specialized Field: Ballet
Status: Non-Profit; Professional
Paid Staff: 2
Volunteer Staff: 15
Paid Artists: 10
Non-paid Artists: 3
Budget: 30,000
Income Sources: Grants; Foundations; Classes
Performs At: Dairy Center For The Arts
Annual Attendance: 10,500-2,000

104
LE CENTRE DU SILENCE MIME SCHOOL

PO Box 1015
Boulder, CO 80306-1015
Phone: 303-661-9271
e-mail: savital@bodyspeak.com
Web Site: www.bodyspeak.com
Management:
　Director: Samuel Avital
Mission: To surpass the normal means of communication offered by the entertainment industry and society's abuse of the spoken word.
Founded: 1971
Specialized Field: Mime
Status: Professional, Profit
Volunteer Staff: 2
Performs At: International
Annual Attendance: 15-20

105
CLEO PARKER ROBINSON DANCE

119 Park Avenue W
Denver, CO 80205
Phone: 303-295-1759
Fax: 303-295-1328
e-mail: cleodance@aol.com
Web Site: www.cleoparkerdance.org
Management:
　Executive Artistic Director: Cleo Parker Robinson
　Company Manager: Malik Robinson
Mission: Cleo Parker Robinson Dance is an international, cross-cultural, dance arts and educational institution rooted in African American traditions and dedicated to excellence in providing instruction, performances and community programs for intergenerational students, artists and audiences.
Utilizes: Five Seasonal Concerts
Founded: 1970
Specialized Field: African Dance; Ballet; Jazz; Break Dancing; Hip Hop
Paid Staff: 7
Volunteer Staff: 30
Paid Artists: 18
Budget: $1,500,000,000
Income Sources: Ensemble Performances; School; Government; Grants
Performs At: Theatre; 3 Studios
Affiliations: Denver Center for the Performing Arts
Facility Category: Concert Hall; Performance Center
Type of Stage: Proscenium
Seating Capacity: 300 plus 6 for special needs
Year Built: 1886
Rental Contact: Operations Director Mary Hart
Organization Type: Performing; Touring; Resident; Educational
Resident Groups: Cleo Parker Robinson Dance Ensemble

106
COLORADO BALLET
1278 Lincoln Street
Denver, CO 80203
Phone: 303-837-8888
Web Site: www.coloradoballet.org
Management:
   Artistic Director: Gil Boggs
   Ballet Mistress: Lorita Travaglia
   Ballet Mistress: Sandra Brown
Mission: To provide enriching, inspiring opportunities to people of all ages and backgrounds, fostering and appreciation of the artistry and athleticism of ballet, and making dance accsssible as a culturally important means of creativity and expression.
Utilizes: Dancers; Guest Companies; Singers
Founded: 1951
Opened: 1961
Specialized Field: Ballet
Status: Professional; Nonprofit
Paid Staff: 35
Volunteer Staff: 20
Budget: 5,000,000
Income Sources: Corporate; Individual; Auxiliary
Performs At: Denver Auditorium Theatre; Temple Hoyne Buell Theatre
Annual Attendance: 50,000
Organization Type: Performing; Touring; Resident; Sponsoring

107
HANNAH KAHN DANCE COMPANY
75 S Cherokee Street
Denver, CO 80223
Phone: 303-789-4181
e-mail: hannahkahndance@gmail.com
Web Site: www.hannahkahndance.org
Management:
   Artistic Director: Hannah Kahn,
   hannahkahndance@gmail.com
Mission: The Hannah Kahn Dance Company has been dedicated to making quality, innovative art and sharing it with the community.
Utilizes: Choreographers; Collaborating Artists; Collaborations; Dance Companies; Dancers; High School Drama; Instructors; Soloists; Visual Arts
Founded: 1992
Specialized Field: Modern Dance
Status: Professional; Non-Profit
Paid Staff: 12
Volunteer Staff: 1
Non-paid Artists: 1
Budget: $70,000
Income Sources: Grants; Contributions; Box Office; Performance & Teaching Fees; Classes
Annual Attendance: 11,000
Organization Type: Performing; Touring

108
KIM ROBARDS DANCE
The KRD Dance Loft
1379 S Inca Street
Denver, CO 80223
Phone: 303-825-4847
Fax: 303-825-4846
e-mail: info@kimrobardsdance.org
Web Site: www.kimrobardsdance.org
Management:
   Artistic Director: Kim Robards
Mission: To expand awareness of modern dance as a unique art form that inspires and transforms lives through creating, performing and educating.
Founded: 1987

Specialized Field: Modern
Paid Staff: 4
Volunteer Staff: 30
Paid Artists: 15
Budget: $100,000-$200,000
Income Sources: Foundation; Grants; Ticket Sales
Performs At: Newman Performing Arts Center
Annual Attendance: 4,000

109
PDAC/ARTS FOR ALL
216 S Grant Street
Denver, CO 80209
Phone: 303-722-2624
e-mail: info@artsforallcolorado.org
Web Site: http://artsforallcolorado.org
Officers:
   President: Linda Weiler
Management:
   Artistic Director: Gwen Bowen
Mission: To protect and promote the arts in the face of the threats that jeopardize arts programming in our schools and comunities today.
Founded: 1963
Specialized Field: Ballet; Tap; Modern; Jazz; Hip Hop; Flamenco
Income Sources: Fundraising; Performances; Ticket Sales
Performs At: The Metro Area

110
DAVID TAYLOR DANCE THEATRE
PO Box 140750
Edgewater, CO 80214
Phone: 303-789-2030
Fax: 303-789-2165
e-mail: dtdt@dtdt.org
Web Site: www.dtdt.org
Management:
   Artistic Director: David Taylor
   Artistic Director: James Wallace
Mission: To provide and present the highest standards in contemporary ballet performance, technical instruction and educational programs to the State of Colorado and throughout the Rocky Mountain Region.
Utilizes: Choreographers; Collaborating Artists; Collaborations; Commissioned Composers; Commissioned Music; Dance Companies; Dancers; Designers; Fine Artists; Grant Writers; Guest Accompanists; Guest Artists; Guest Choreographers; Guest Conductors; Guest Directors; Guest Ensembles; High School Drama; Instructors; Lyricists; Multi Collaborations; Multimedia; New Productions; Organization Contracts; Original Music Scores; Resident Professionals; Theatre Companies; Touring Companies; Visual Arts
Founded: 1979
Specialized Field: Contemporary Ballet
Status: Professional, Nonprofit
Paid Staff: 12
Volunteer Staff: 6
Paid Artists: 11
Non-paid Artists: 8
Budget: $500,000
Income Sources: Box Office; Grants; Individual Contributions
Performs At: Lakewood Cultural Center; Town Hall Arts Center; Auditorium Theatre
Annual Attendance: 70,000
Facility Category: Performance
Type of Stage: Proscenium
Stage Dimensions: 44' x 32'
Organization Type: Performing; Educational

Comments: Artist Management: Gary Lindsey Artist Services

111
CANYON CONCERT BALLET
1031 Conifer Street
Suite 3
Fort Collins, CO 80524-5313
Phone: 970-472-4156
Fax: 970-472-4158
e-mail: info@ccballet.org
Web Site: www.ccballet.org
Officers:
   President: Hilton Campbell
Management:
   Artistic Director: Kim Carter
Mission: To create and share the passion of dance through artistically enriching performances and dance education. Our vision is to provide a sustainable community forum for dance performance and education.
Founded: 1978
Specialized Field: Ballet
Paid Staff: 20
Volunteer Staff: 2
Income Sources: Friends of Canyon Concert Ballet Dance Fund; Ticket Sales
Performs At: Lincoln Center Performance Hall
Annual Attendance: 7,000

Connecticut

112
ADAM MILLER DANCE PROJECT
94 Huntington Street
Hartford, CT 06105
Phone: 860-249-7748
e-mail: adamballet@aol.com
Web Site: www.adammillerdanceproject.com
Officers:
   President: Ken Warner Esq
   Chief Financial Officer: Michael J Giglio
Management:
   Artistic Director: Adam Miller
Mission: The mission of the Adam Miller Dance Project is to provide the greater Hartford area with a first rate professional dance organization which focuses on the creation and production of leading edge and ballet-based work.
Founded: 2001
Specialized Field: Ballet
Income Sources: Grants

113
CONNECTICUT BALLET
20 Acosta Street
Stamford, CT 06902
Phone: 203-964-1211
e-mail: ctballet@ix.netcom.com
Web Site: www.connecticutballet.com
Officers:
   President: Brett Raphael
   Vice President: Marie Seymour
Management:
   Artistic Director: Brett Raphael
Mission: To be Connecticut's premier classical and contemporary ballet company, performing a diverse repertoire of new works, masterworks and great story ballets.
Utilizes: Five Seasonal Concerts
Founded: 1981
Specialized Field: Modern; Ballet
Status: Professional; Non-Profit

Paid Staff: 3
Volunteer Staff: 3
Budget: 500,000-1,000,000
Performs At: Stamford Center For The Arts
Annual Attendance: 25,000
Organization Type: Performing; Touring; Educational

114
ZIG ZAG BALLET
20 Acosta Street
Stamford, CT 06902
Phone: 203-964-1211
Fax: 203-961-1928
e-mail: zigzagballet@hotmail.com
Web Site: www.connecticutballet.com
Officers:
    President: Marie Seymour
Management:
    Director: Brett Raphael
Mission: To be Connecticut's premier classical and comtemporary ballet company, performing a diverse repertoire of new works, masterworks and great story ballets.
Specialized Field: Contemporary Dance
Status: Non-Profit; Professional
Paid Staff: 2
Paid Artists: 10
Budget: $250,000
Annual Attendance: 25,000

115
NUTMEG BALLET
Nutmeg Conservatory for the Arts
58 Main Street
Torrington, CT 06790
Phone: 860-482-4413
Fax: 860-482-7614
Web Site: www.nutmegconservatory.org
Officers:
    President: Susan Patterson
    Vice President: Marc Trivella
Management:
    Artistic Director: Sharon Dante
    Senior Ballet Mistress: Denise Warner Limoli
Mission: To provide professional level ballet training to aspiring young dance artists.
Utilizes: Artists-in-Residence; Dance Companies; Dancers; Grant Writers; Guest Accompanists; Guest Artists; Guest Companies; High School Drama; Multimedia; Original Music Scores; Resident Artists; Singers; Soloists
Founded: 1969
Specialized Field: Ballet
Paid Staff: 40
Paid Artists: 20
Budget: $500,000-$1,000,000
Facility Category: Dance/Music Instruction
Year Built: 2001
Organization Type: Performing; Touring; Resident; Educational; Sponsoring

116
HARTT SCHOOL
University of Hartford
200 Bloomfield Avenue
West Hartford, CT 06117-1599
Phone: 860-768-4465
e-mail: harttadm@hartford.edu du
Web Site: http://harttweb.hartford.edu
Management:
    Public Relations: Sheri Ziccardi
Mission: The Hartt School seeks to enhance the practice and appreciation of all aspects of the performaing arts through professial training in a conservatory environment, avocational programs & service and advocacy in its immediate and extended community.
Utilizes: Actors; Arrangers; Artists-in-Residence; Choreographers; Collaborating Artists; Collaborations; Composers; Composers-in-Residence; Dance Companies; Dancers; Designers; Educators; Fine Artists; Grant Writers; Guest Accompanists; Guest Artists; Guest Choreographers; Guest Companies; Guest Composers; Guest Conductors; Guest Designers; Guest Directors; Guest Ensembles; Guest Instructors; Guest Lecturers; Guest Musical Directors; Guest Musicians; Guest Soloists; Guest Speakers; High School Drama; Instructors; Local Artists; Local Unknown Artists; Lyricists; Multi Collaborations; Multimedia; Music; Organization Contracts; Paid Performers; Poets; Resident Companies; Resident Professionals; Sign Language Translators; Singers; Soloists; Students; Student Interns; Special Technical Talent; Visual Arts
Founded: 1920
Specialized Field: Theatrical Dance
Performs At: Millard Theatre; Lincoln Theatre
Annual Attendance: 689

Delaware

117
DELAWARE DANCE COMPANY
168 Elkton Road
Suite 101 Madeline Crossing
Newark, DE 19711
Phone: 302-738-2023
Fax: 302-738-1820
e-mail: ddcoffice@verizon.net
Web Site: www.delawaredance.org
Management:
    Artistic Director: Sunshine Webster Latshaw
Mission: To advance the nowledge and appreciation of dance in the community and region through instruction, performances and outreach programs. To provide the highest quality educational opportunities possible in all aspects of dance to anyone desiring such education. To be viewed as a community and regional leader in preparing vocational students for a professional career in dance.
Utilizes: Five Seasonal Concerts; Singers
Founded: 1978
Specialized Field: Modern; Ballet; Tap; Theatre Dance
Paid Staff: 30
Income Sources: Fundraising; Private; Donations
Performs At: Dickinson Theatre; Delaware Theatre Company
Annual Attendance: 3,000
Organization Type: Performing; Touring; Educational

118
MID-ATLANTIC BALLET
108A E Main Street
PO Box 161
Newark, DE 19715-0161
Phone: 302-266-6362
Fax: 302-266-6372
Web Site: www.midatlanticballet.org
Officers:
    President: Dolores Ballintyn
Management:
    Artistic Director: Patrick Korstange
Mission: Mid-Atlantic Ballet is dedicated to developing the minds and bodies of its students as well as promoting dance as an art form.
Founded: 1997
Specialized Field: Ballet

119
FIRST STATE BALLET THEATRE
818 N Market Street
Wilmington, DE 19801
Phone: 302-658-7897
Toll-free: 800-374-7263
e-mail: fsbt@grandopera.org
Web Site: www.firststateballet.com
Management:
    Artistic Director: Pavel Kambalov
    Assistant Artistic Director: Lev Assouliak
Mission: To present professional quality ballet performances to audiences throughout Delaware, to provide performing opportunities to aspiring dancers and to educate the Delaware dance audience of the future.
Founded: 1999
Specialized Field: Ballet
Paid Staff: 3
Volunteer Staff: 36
Paid Artists: 10
Income Sources: Donations; Sponsors; Private; Fundraising
Performs At: The Grand Opera House
Annual Attendance: 4,000

District of Columbia

120
DANA TAI SOON BURGESS & COMPANY
2745 Arizona Avenue NW
Washington, DC 20016
Phone: 202-297-2436
Fax: 202-232-2786
e-mail: dtsbco@cs.com
Web Site: www.dtsbco.com
Management:
    Director/Founder: Dana Tai Soon Burgess
    Manager: Alyson Brokenshire
Founded: 1990
Specialized Field: Modern
Status: Non-Profit; Professional
Paid Staff: 3
Volunteer Staff: 25
Performs At: The Lincoln Center

121
DANCE PLACE
3225 Eighth Street NE
Washington, DC 20017
Phone: 202-269-1600
Fax: 202-269-4103
Web Site: www.danceplace.org
Officers:
    Chairman: Rich Bernardi
    President: Carla Perlo
Management:
    Artistic Director: Carla Perlo
Mission: To transform lives through performing arts and creative education programs that inspire personal growth, professional success, physical wellness and community enegagement.
Utilizes: Dance Companies; Dancers; Five Seasonal Concerts; Guest Artists; Guest Choreographers; Guest Ensembles; Guest Musical Directors; Instructors; Local Artists; Sign Language Translators
Founded: 1980
Specialized Field: Modern; Ethnic Dance; Theatrical Dance
Paid Staff: 14
Volunteer Staff: 25
Budget: $900,000

Income Sources: Theater; Studio
Annual Attendance: 9,000
Facility Category: Studio/Theatre/Community Center
Type of Stage: Black Box
Seating Capacity: 165
Year Built: 1936
Year Remodeled: 2000
Organization Type: Performing; Touring; Resident; Educational; Sponsoring

122
DEBORAH RILEY DANCE PROJECTS
Dance Place
3255 8th Street NE
Washington, DC 20017-3502
Phone: 202-269-1600
Fax: 202-269-4103
Web Site: www.danceplace.org
Officers:
   Chairman: Richard Bernardi
Management:
   Artistic Director: Deborah Riley
Mission: To transform lives through performing arts and creative education programs that inspire personal growth, professional success, physical wellness and community engagement.
Founded: 1987
Specialized Field: Modern
Performs At: The Dance Place

123
GALLAUDET DANCE COMPANY
Gallaudet University
800 Florida Avenue NE
Washington, DC 20002
Phone: 202-651-5493
Web Site: dance.gallaudet.edu
Management:
   Director: Diane Hottendorf
Mission: Gallaudet University is a bilingual, diverse. multicultural institution of higher education that ensures the intellectual and professional advancement of deaf and hard of hearing individuals through American Sign Language and English.
Founded: 1955
Specialized Field: Modern; Jazz; Tap; American Sign Language
Income Sources: Gallaudet University
Annual Attendance: 15-20
Organization Type: Educational; Performing

124
MAIDA WITHERS DANCE CONSTRUCTION COMPANY
800 21st Street NW
Washington, DC 20052
Phone: 202-994-0739
Fax: 202-994-9403
e-mail: m.withers@verizon.net
Web Site: www.maidadance.com
Officers:
   Board of Directors: Greg Hunter
   Board of Directors: Alison Beesley
   Board of Directors: Nancy Tartt
   Board of Directors: Aimee Fullman
Management:
   Founder/Artistic Director: Maida Withers
Mission: Project based company that creates/presents fresh and inspiring one of a kind dance works and films, conceived and choreographed by Maida Withers, that have social/political relevance in today's global society. Withers also creates site-specific works: recent projects include street performances in Washington, DC, the Lenin Museum in Krasnoyarsk, Siberia, Russia.

Founded: 1974
Specialized Field: Post-Modern Dance; New Media; Multi-Media Dance
Status: Non-Profit; Professional
Paid Staff: 2
Volunteer Staff: 15
Paid Artists: 10
Non-paid Artists: 10
Budget: $89,000
Income Sources: Box Office; US Department of State; Foundation/Corporation Support; Individual
Performs At: Betts Marvin Theatre
Affiliations: DC International Improvisation Plus Festival
Annual Attendance: 2000
Facility Category: Theatres; Sites; Festivals;
Type of Stage: Proscenium & Galleries/Museums

125
ST. MARK'S DANCE STUDIO
The Arts At St Mark's
St. Mark's Episcopal Church
301 A Street SE
Washington, DC 20003
Phone: 202-543-0054
Web Site: www.stmarks.net/arts/dance.html
Management:
   Artistic Director: Rosetta Brooks
   Ballet Mistress: Dorothy Rogers-Walker
Mission: To support the arts in the St. Mark's community by providing opportunities for each parishioner to develop and expand his or her creativity as an expression of spiritual life.
Founded: 1991
Specialized Field: Ballet; Jazz
Paid Staff: 4
Volunteer Staff: 3
Budget: $40,000-$100,000
Income Sources: Tuition
Performs At: St. Mark's Church

126
WASHINGTON BALLET
3515 Wisconsin Avenue NW
Washington, DC 20016
Phone: 202-362-3606
Fax: 202-362-1311
Web Site: www.washingtonballet.org
Management:
   Artistic Director: Septime Webre
   Associate Artistic Director: David Palmer
   Ballet Master: John Goding
Mission: The company is dedicated to presenting the best in classical and contemporary ballet and is devoted to bringing ballet to broad communities throughout Washington DC.
Utilizes: Artists-in-Residence; Choreographers; Collaborating Artists; Commissioned Music; Dancers; Five Seasonal Concerts; Guest Artists; Guest Companies; Guest Conductors; High School Drama; Resident Professionals; Sign Language Translators; Soloists; Student Interns
Founded: 1976
Specialized Field: Ballet
Paid Staff: 25
Volunteer Staff: 15
Budget: $6 million
Income Sources: Earned; Donations
Performs At: John F Kennedy Center for the Performing Arts; Warner Theatre
Organization Type: Performing; Touring

127
BOCA BALLET THEATRE
7630 NW 6th Avenue
Boca Raton, FL 33487
Phone: 561-955-0709
Fax: 561-995-8356
e-mail: mail@bocaballet.org
Web Site: www.bocaballet.org
Management:
   Artistic/Executive Director: Dan Guin
   Co Artistic Director: Jane Tyree
Mission: To enrich the cultural landscape of our community and educate our youth in classical ballet and concert dance through focused training, interaction with professional dancers and participation in full-length ballets and contemporary choreography.
Founded: 1990
Specialized Field: Modern; Jazz; Ballet; Pilates
Status: Non-Profit; Non-Professional
Paid Staff: 6
Volunteer Staff: 50
Budget: $875,000
Performs At: FAU University Theatre
Annual Attendance: 5,000
Seating Capacity: 498

128
MOMENTUM DANCE COMPANY
PO Box 331973
Coconut Grove, FL 33233-1973
Phone: 305-858-7002
e-mail: mdanceco@bellsouth.net
Web Site: www.mometumdance.com
Management:
   Artistic Director: Delma Iles
Mission: To develop and educate the audience for dance in South Florida, with emphasis on non-traditional and modern dance forms; and to educate and train students for the purposes of professional careers as well as personal appreciation and enjoyment of dance.
Utilizes: Five Seasonal Concerts; Singers
Founded: 1982
Specialized Field: Modern; Ballet; Jazz
Status: Professional; Non-Profit
Paid Staff: 2
Paid Artists: 10
Budget: $100,000-$200,000
Income Sources: Government; Earned; Foundations; Contributions
Annual Attendance: 5,000-7,000
Organization Type: Performing; Touring; Resident; Educational

129
NORTHWEST FLORIDA BALLET
310 Terry Avenue SE
Fort Walton Beach, FL 32548
Phone: 850-664-7787
Fax: 850-664-0130
Web Site: www.nfballet.org
Management:
   Artistic Director: Todd Eric Allen
   Assistant Artistic Director: Sharon Allen
   Ballet Mistress: Dorothytte Daniels Lister
Mission: To provide quality dance performances and instruction for Northwest Florida, to identify and develop talented dancers and increase appreciation of the arts through public education and outreach.
Utilizes: Five Seasonal Concerts
Founded: 1969

Specialized Field: Ballet
Paid Staff: 12
Budget: $200,000-$500,000
Income Sources: Florida Dance Association
Performs At: The Sanger Theatre
Annual Attendance: 7,000-10,000
Organization Type: Performing; Touring; Resident; Educational; Sponsoring

130
DANCE ALIVE NATIONAL BALLET
1325 NW Second Street
Gainesville, FL 32601
Phone: 352-371-2986
Fax: 352-371-2986
e-mail: dalive@bellsouth.net
Web Site: www.dancealive.org
Officers:
President: Tim Cannon
Treasurer/Fundraising Chair: Elaine Connolly
Secretary: Courtney Holmes
Management:
Artistic Director: Kim Tuttle
Residence Choreographer: Judy Skinner
Mission: Dance Alive National Ballet, State Touring Company of Florida is based in Gainesville. With a cast of superb international dancers, the Company presents ravishing classical and the most provocative of contemporary dance. From sensuality and athleticism to the neoclassical beauty of Balanchine with humor, passion and jazzy playfulness, this company does it all.
Specialized Field: Classical Ballet; Contemporary Dance
Season: October-December
Performs At: Curtis M Phillips Center
Type of Stage: Proscenium Hall, Black Box Theatre
Seating Capacity: 1,700, 200

131
FLORIDA BALLET AT JACKSONVILLE
300 E State Street
Suite E
Jacksonville, FL 32222
Phone: 904-353-7518
Fax: 904-353-7709
e-mail: floridaballet@floridaballet.org
Web Site: www.floridaballwe.org
Officers:
President: Leslie H Krieger PhD
VP: Laurie Picinich-Byrd
Treasurer: Micheal Kenney
Secretary: Susan H Adams
Mission: To take a contemporary approach to performance of classical guest choreographers' ballet.
Utilizes: Five Seasonal Concerts
Founded: 1978
Specialized Field: Ballet
Status: Professional; Nonprofit
Budget: $40,000-$100,000
Organization Type: Performing; Touring; Resident

132
JACKSONVILLE BALLET THEATRE
10131 Atlantic Boulevard
Jacksonville, FL 32225
Phone: 904-727-7515
e-mail: info@jacksonvilleballettheatre.com
Web Site: http://jacksonvilleballettheatre.com
Officers:
President: David R Sutton Jr MD
Management:
Artistic Director: Duce Anaya

Mission: To Bgive Jacksonville dancers the opportunity to participate in original choreographies of full-length classical and modern works, present high quality ballet performances for the benefit of the community and to encourage appreciation for and enjoyment of the art of dance.
Founded: 1970
Specialized Field: Ballet
Performs At: Civic Auditorium
Organization Type: Performing; Educational

133
DEMETRIUS KLEIN DANCE COMPANY
811 Lake Avenue
Lake Worth, FL 33460
Phone: 561-586-1889
e-mail: info@kleindancecompany.com
Web Site: www.kleindancecompany.com
Management:
Artistic Director: Kathleen Klein
Mission: Klein Dance has served South Florida by making the art of dance accessible for all who wish to be a part of it.
Utilizes: Actors; Artists-in-Residence; Choreographers; Collaborating Artists; Collaborations; Dance Companies; Dancers; Five Seasonal Concerts; Grant Writers; Guest Artists; Guest Choreographers; Guest Conductors; Guest Ensembles; Guild Activities; Instructors; Local Artists; Lyricists; Organization Contracts; Original Music Scores; Resident Professionals; Soloists
Founded: 1987
Paid Staff: 4
Volunteer Staff: 10
Paid Artists: 10
Budget: $200,000-$500,000
Income Sources: Grants; Earned Income; Donations
Affiliations: Dans USA; Florida Dance Association
Annual Attendance: 10,000
Type of Stage: Sprung
Stage Dimensions: 30'x 40'
Seating Capacity: 500-700

134
FLORIDA DANCE ASSOCIATION
111 SW 5th Avenue
Miami, FL 33130
Phone: 305-547-1117
Fax: 305-547-1118
Web Site: www.floridadanceassociation.org
Officers:
President: Ric Rose
Vice President: Anjali Austin
Management:
Director of Operations: Bill Doolan
Mission: To encourage excellence, support artistic and cultural diversity in dance, and increase opportunities for all people to experience dance and the arts.
Founded: 1972
Specialized Field: Ethnic Dance
Status: Professional, Nonprofit
Paid Staff: 2
Volunteer Staff: 10
Paid Artists: 40
Budget: $400,000
Income Sources: Sponsors; Foundations; Corporate; Community Partners
Affiliations: Dance/USA; National Performance Network; Florida Cultural Alliance; Association of Performing Arts Presenters
Organization Type: Educational; Sponsoring; Service

135
VLADIMIR ISSAEV'S SCHOOL OF CLASSICAL BALLET
2646 NE 189th Terrace
Miami, FL 33180
Phone: 305-935-3232
Web Site: www.clasicalballetschool.com
Management:
Artistic Director/Ballet Master: Vladimir Issaev
Mission: To enhance the lives of all who learn with us and while we shall demand from each student, whether or not a dance career is planned, the best effort of which he or she is capable, we shall give in return the care and attention that each student deserves.
Specialized Field: Ballet; Pointe; Jazz; Tap
Status: Professional
Affiliations: Arts Ballet Theatre of Florida
Facility Category: 2,200 Square Feet/2 Studios/Marley Covered Spring Floors

136
MIAMI CITY BALLET
2200 Liberty Avenue
Miami Beach, FL 33139
Phone: 305-929-7010
Web Site: www.miamicityballet.org
Officers:
CEO: Edward Villella
Management:
Founding Artistic Director: Edward Villella
Executive Director: Pamela Gardiner
Principal Ballet Mistress: Roma Sosenko
Mission: From Edward Villella, the creative inspiration and artistic soul of the company, to the dancers whose artistry and talent have awed a nation, Miami City Ballet brings a gold standard of excellence to the cultural landscape of our community.
Utilizes: Five Seasonal Concerts; Guest Artists; Singers
Founded: 1986
Specialized Field: Ballet
Status: Professional, Nonprofit
Budget: $10.7 million
Performs At: The Naples Philharmonic Center
Organization Type: Performing; Touring; Resident

137
ORLANDO BALLET
1111 N Orange Avenue
Orlando, FL 32804
Phone: 407-426-1739
Fax: 407-999-9098
e-mail: jleon@orlandoballet.org
Web Site: www.orlandoballet.org
Management:
Artistic Director: Bruce Marks
Mission: Orlando Ballet has grown to become Central Florida's only professional resident ballet company and is one of the few ballet companies of its sixe and budget that is performing the full length classical ballets.
Utilizes: Artists-in-Residence; Choreographers; Collaborations; Commissioned Composers; Commissioned Music; Dance Companies; Dancers; Educators; Five Seasonal Concerts; Grant Writers; Guest Accompanists; Guest Artists; Guest Companies; Guest Composers; Guest Conductors; Guest Ensembles; Guest Instructors; Guest Musical Directors; Guest Musicians; Guest Soloists; High School Drama; Instructors; Local Artists; Lyricists; Multimedia; Organization Contracts; Original Music Scores; Resident Artists; Resident Professionals; Soloists; Visual Arts
Founded: 1973

Specialized Field: Ballet
Status: Professional, Nonprofit
Paid Staff: 53
Volunteer Staff: 2
Paid Artists: 28
Budget: $4.5 Million
Income Sources: State Dance Association of Florida
Annual Attendance: 100,000
Organization Type: Performing; Touring; Sponsoring

138
RUSSIAN BALLET OF ORLANDO
421 N Bumby Avenue
Orlando, FL 32803
Phone: 407-443-5045
Fax: 407-275-2405
Web Site: www.orlandocityballet.com
Officers:
President: Michele Paymer
Management:
Artistic Director: Irina Depler
Mission: To sponsor students of the Russian Academy of Ballet of all ages and levels, and to give them opportunity to perform in profesional quality performances.
Founded: 1989
Specialized Field: Russian Ballet

139
BALLET PENSACOLA
400 S Jefferson Street
Pensacola, FL 32502
Phone: 850-432-9546
Fax: 850-432-3297
e-mail: board@balletpensacola.com
Web Site: www.balletpensacola.com
Officers:
President of the Board: Hilda Jones
Management:
Artistic Director: Richard Steinert
Director of Development & Marketing: Courtney Dell
Mission: To enhance the cultural life of the community by developing an appreciation and knowledge of the art of dance through excellent dance training and quality performances.
Utilizes: Singers
Founded: 1978
Specialized Field: Dance
Status: Professional, Nonprofit
Income Sources: Private; Corporate; Fundraising; Grants; Foundations
Performs At: The Sanger Theatre
Annual Attendance: 8,000
Organization Type: Performing; Resident; Educational

140
FREDDICK BRATCHER & COMPANY
525 Jeffrey Drive
Saint Augustine, FL 32086
Phone: 305-302-8947
e-mail: fbcompany@att.net
Web Site: www.freddickbratchercompany.com
Management:
Founding Artistic Director: Freddick Bratcher
Mission: To provide local audiences with superior quality jazz, modern, classical and narrative choreographic works and to offer local talent a challenging and rewarding opportunity to mature artistically in a creative environment.
Utilizes: Five Seasonal Concerts; Singers
Founded: 1980
Specialized Field: Contemporary Dance
Status: Professional, Nonprofit

Performs At: Gusman Center for the Performing Arts
Organization Type: Performing; Touring; Educational

141
SARASOTA BALLET OF FLORIDA
5555 N Tamiami Trail
Sarasota, FL 34243
Phone: 941-359-0099
Fax: 941-358-1504
Toll-free: 866-722-5538
Web Site: www.sarasotaballet.org
Management:
Artistic Director: Iain Webb
Mission: To be committed to artistic excellence through the presentation of the highest quality of classical and contemporary dance, through the encouragement of choreographic talent, through the ongoing expansion of education programs and opportunities for community outreach and service.
Utilizes: Choreographers; Dancers; Lyricists; Organization Contracts
Founded: 1990
Specialized Field: Ballet
Paid Staff: 24
Volunteer Staff: 10
Paid Artists: 28
Budget: $2,500,000
Income Sources: Ticket Sales; Foundation and Corporate Grants; Individual Donations
Performs At: Van Wezel Performing Arts Hall; FSU Center for the Performing Arts
Affiliations: Sarasota Ballet Association
Annual Attendance: 35,000
Seating Capacity: 1700 and 500

142
THOMAS ARMOUR YOUTH BALLET
5818 SW 73rd Street
South Miami, FL 33143
Phone: 305-667-5543
Fax: 305-667-1024
e-mail: info@thomasarmouryouthballet.org
Web Site: www.thomasarmouryouthballet.org
Management:
Program Administrator: Geannina Burgos
Artistic Director: Ruth Wiesen
Mission: The Thomas Armour Youth Ballet puts an emphasis on community outreach, ballet education and making the world of ballet accessible to under privileged youth both as audience members and as performers.
Utilizes: Dancers; Educators; Five Seasonal Concerts; Guest Artists; Instructors; Local Talent; Students; Visual Designers
Founded: 1951
Specialized Field: Ballet; Tap
Status: Non-Professional, Non-Profit
Paid Staff: 30
Budget: $119,000
Income Sources: Private; Foundations; Corporate and Government
Performs At: Dade County Auditorium and Public Schools
Annual Attendance: 9,000
Organization Type: Performing; Resident

143
THE ACADEMY OF BALLET ARTS
2914 First Avenue N
St Petersburg, FL 33713
Phone: 727-327-4401
Web Site: www.academyofballetarts.org
Management:
Artistic Director: Suzanne Pomerantzeff

Mission: To develop each student's creative potential by allowing them to express their individual ideas and emotions through the beauty of movement.
Founded: 1969
Specialized Field: Ballet
Status: Professional, Non-Profit
Paid Staff: 7
Volunteer Staff: 6
Non-paid Artists: 15
Income Sources: Tuition; Fundraising; Donations
Annual Attendance: 1,000

144
THE TALLAHASSEE BALLET
218 E Third Avenue
Tallahassee, FL 32302
Phone: 850-224-6917
Fax: 850-224-7681
e-mail: info@tallaballet.com
Web Site: www.tallaballet.com
Management:
Executive Director: Janet Pichard
Mission: The Tallahassee Ballet is a non-profit dance company which provides an outstanding training ground for emerging professionals while stimulating appreciation of the dance arts through quality productions of classical and contemporary works.
Utilizes: Five Seasonal Concerts; Guest Companies; Singers
Founded: 1972
Specialized Field: Ballet
Status: Non-profit, Semi-Professional
Paid Staff: 4
Volunteer Staff: 3
Non-paid Artists: 55
Budget: $200,000-$500,000
Income Sources: Ticket Revenue; Advertising Sales; Memberships; Annual Fundraisers
Performs At: Ruby Diamond Auditorium; Opperman Music Hall
Affiliations: Florida Dance Association
Annual Attendance: 7,000-10,000
Organization Type: Performing; Resident; Educational

145
FIRETHORN DANCE ACADEMY
10630 N 56th Street
Suite 3
Temple Terrace, FL 33617
Phone: 813-985-2555
e-mail: info@firethorn-dance.com
Web Site: www.firethorn-dance.com
Management:
Director/Instructor: Carine Puckett
Instructor: Cheryl Coombs-Farfan
Mission: Firethorn has provided quality dance training for dancers of all levels in a friendly and enjoyable environment.
Founded: 1979
Specialized Field: Modern; Ballet; Jazz; Tap; Hip Hop
Paid Staff: 2

146
BALLET FLORIDA
500 Fern Street
West Palm Beach, FL 33401
Phone: 561-659-1212
Fax: 561-659-2222
Web Site: WWW.balletflorida.com
Management:
Founding Artistic Director: Marie Hale
Ballet Mistress: Claudia Cravey
Ballet Master: Steven Hoff

Mission: To produce and present ballets danced by professional dancers; create an eclectic repertoire choreographed by contemporary choreographers of note or of historical importance; maintain the highest levels of design and production; reach, expose and educate the widest audience possible with its programs.
Utilizes: Five Seasonal Concerts
Founded: 1986
Specialized Field: Ballet; Contemporary Ballet
Status: Professional, Nonprofit
Paid Staff: 60
Volunteer Staff: 8
Budget: $4,500,000
Income Sources: Grants; Foundations; Corporate; Private Sponsors
Performs At: Eissey Theatre; Kravis Center for the Performing Arts
Organization Type: Performing; Touring; Resident; Educational

Georgia

147
UGA BALLET ENSEMBLE
University of Georgia
263 Dance Building
Athens, GA 30602-3653
Phone: 706-542-4415
Fax: 706-542-4084
e-mail: ugadance@uga.edu
Management:
　Director: Joan Buttram
Mission: The UGA Department of Dance provides a variety of performance company options focused towards pre-professional training, student choreography and student performance. These companies provide performances to local, community, state, national and international audiences.
Founded: 1993
Specialized Field: Ballet
Status: Non-Profit, Pre-Professional
Paid Staff: 3
Volunteer Staff: 3
Income Sources: UGA Foundation; Student Activities; Grant Support

148
UGA CORE CONCERT DANCE COMPANY
University of Georgia
1030 Sanford Drive
Athens, GA 30602
Phone: 706-542-4415
Fax: 706-542-4084
e-mail: ugadance@uga.edu
Web Site: www.franklin.uga.edu/dance
Management:
　Artistic Director: Bala Sarasvati
Mission: The UGA Department of Dance provides a variety of performance company options focused towards pre-professional training, student choreography and student performance. These companies provide performances to local, community, state, national, and international audiences.
Founded: 1991
Specialized Field: Modern; Ballet
Status: Non-Profit, Pre-Professional
Paid Staff: 3
Volunteer Staff: 3
Annual Attendance: 1,200

149
ATLANTA BALLET
1695 Marietta Boulevard NE
Atlanta, GA 30318
Phone: 404-873-5811
Fax: 404-874-7905
e-mail: tekholm@atlantaballet.com
Web Site: www.atlantaballet.com
Officers:
　President: Karen Vereb
　Chairman: Allen Nelson
Management:
　Artistic Director: John McFall
　Executive Director: Arthur Jacobs
Mission: To provide professional ballet performances for the people of metropolitan Atlanta and the surrounding area.
Utilizes: Choreographers; Dancers; Guest Artists; Guest Companies; Guest Conductors; Resident Artists; Singers
Founded: 1929
Specialized Field: Ballet
Status: Professional, Nonprofit
Paid Staff: 27
Paid Artists: 45
Budget: $6,659,609
Income Sources: National Association for Regional Ballet; Corporate; Tuition
Performs At: Fabulous Fox Theatre; Cobb Energy Performing Arts Centre
Annual Attendance: 60,000
Facility Category: Theatre
Seating Capacity: 4,500; 2,750
Rental Contact: Gene Conroy
Organization Type: Performing; Touring; Resident

150
BALLETHNIC DANCE COMPANY
2587 Cheney Street
PO Box 7749
Atlanta, GA 30344-3118
Phone: 404-762-1416
Fax: 404-762-6319
e-mail: cynthiab@ballethnic.org
Web Site: www.ballethnic.org
Officers:
　Company Manager: Cynthia Benefield
Management:
　Artistic Director: Nena Gilreath
　Artistic Director: Waverly Lucas
　Company Manager: Amy Hazzlewood
　Musical Director: L Gerard Reid
　Make-Up Artist: Cheryl Barney
　Company Photographer: Keiko Guest
Mission: Ballethnic Dance Company is a classically trained, culturally diverse professional performing company producing innovative performances of artistic excellence and is committed to providing opportunities to those who are overlooked because of race and ethnicity.
Founded: 1990
Specialized Field: Ballet
Status: Professional, Non-Profit
Paid Staff: 4
Volunteer Staff: 8
Paid Artists: 9
Non-paid Artists: 5
Income Sources: Foundations; Corporate
Performs At: Robert Far Center

151
FULL RADIUS DANCE
PO Box 54453
Atlanta, GA 30308
Phone: 404-724-9663
Fax: 404-724-9663
e-mail: fullradiusdance@aol.com
Web Site: www.fullradiusdance.org
Officers:
　Chairman: Marcelo Roman
　Vice Chairman: David Cable
Management:
　Artistic/Executive Director: Douglas Scott
Mission: To promote, advance and enhance the modern dance form for persons with disabilities, for dance artists and the general community.
Utilizes: Dancers; Original Music Scores
Founded: 1991
Specialized Field: Modern
Status: Non-Profit, Professional
Paid Staff: 1
Volunteer Staff: 8
Budget: $70,000
Income Sources: Private; Government; Corporations; Business; Earned
Annual Attendance: 9,000

152
MYSTICAL ARTS OF TIBET
1781 Dresden Drive
Atlanta, GA 30319
Phone: 404-982-6437
Fax: 404-982-6435
e-mail: mystical@drepung.org
Web Site: www.mysticalartsoftibet.org
Management:
　Director: Lobsang Tenzin
　Assistant Director: Irene S Lee
Mission: The Mystical Arts of Tibet is a world tour to promote peace and healing by sharing Tibet's rich and authentic sacred performing and visual arts with modern audiences. The two most requested programs are the Sacred Music Sacred Dance performance and Mandala Sand Painting exhibition.
Founded: 1991
Specialized Field: World Music
Status: Non-Profit; Professional
Paid Staff: 6
Income Sources: Performances
Organization Type: Performing; Touring

153
BEACON DANCE COMPANY
PO Box 1553
Decatur, GA 30031-1553
Phone: 404-377-2929
Fax: 404-377-2929
e-mail: patton@beacondance.org
Web Site: www.beacondance.org
Management:
　Artistic Director: D Patton White, patton@beacondance.org
Mission: To develop peoples's understanding of the art of movement as a means of communication.
Utilizes: Actors; Artists-in-Residence; Choreographers; Collaborating Artists; Collaborations; Community Members; Dance Companies; Dancers; Educators; Filmmakers; Five Seasonal Concerts; Guest Accompanists; Guest Artists; Guest Companies; Guest Designers; Guest Soloists; Guest Speakers; Guest Teachers; Instructors; Lyricists; Multi Collaborations; Original Music Scores; Paid Performers; Sign Language Translators; Student Interns; Theatre Companies

Founded: 1952
Specialized Field: Modern; Ballet; Jazz
Status: Professional, Nonprofit
Volunteer Staff: 12
Non-paid Artists: 1
Budget: $20,000
Income Sources: Earned Income; Grants; Contributions
Performs At: Beacon Hill Arts Center Studio Theatre
Annual Attendance: 4,000
Organization Type: Performing; Educational

154
SEVERAL DANCERS CORE

PO Box 2045
Decatur, GA 30031-2045
Phone: 404-373-4154
Fax: 404-377-1815
e-mail: sdcinfo@mindspring.com
Web Site: www.severaldancerscore.org
Officers:
    Founder: Sue Schroeder
Management:
    Artistic Director: Sue Schroeder
    Company/Production Manager: D Patton White
    Tour Coordinator: Elizabeth Geiger
Mission: To create, present and produce contemporary dance.
Founded: 1980
Specialized Field: Contemporary Dance
Status: Non-Profit, Professional
Paid Staff: 3
Volunteer Staff: 2
Paid Artists: 6
Budget: $270,000
Income Sources: Foundations; Corporate; Individual
Affiliations: The Field
Annual Attendance: 80,000
Facility Category: Studio Theater

155
NORTHEAST ATLANTIC BALLET ENSEMBLE

4047 Darling Court
Lilburn, GA 30047
Phone: 770-921-7277
e-mail: balletensemble@yahoo.com
Web Site: www.northeastatlantaballet.org
Management:
    Artistic Director: Jennifer Byokawski-Gordon
Mission: Mission and purpose is to provide performing opportunities to talented young dancers and to provide quality arts programming at prices affordable to families of all socioeconomic groups.
Founded: 1996
Specialized Field: Ballet; Jazz; Tap
Status: Non-Profit

156
GEORGIA BALLET

1255 Field Parkway
Marietta, GA 30066
Phone: 770-528-0881
Fax: 770-528-0891
e-mail: info@georgiaballet.org
Web Site: www.georgiaballet.com
    School Director:
Management:
    Artistic Director: Gina Hyatt-Mazon
    Executive Director/School Director: Michele Ziemann-Devos
    Ballet Mistress: Gina Hyatt Mazon

Mission: Dedicated to promoting excellence in ballet performance and training, fostering an increased public awareness and appreciation for dance, and providing dedicated and talented dancers with the opportunity for advanced training and professional preforming venues.
Founded: 1960
Specialized Field: Ballet
Status: Non-profit
Paid Staff: 5
Volunteer Staff: 15
Performs At: The Anderson Theatre
Annual Attendance: 19,500

157
RUTH MITCHELL DANCE COMPANY

49 West Park Square
Marietta, GA 30060
Phone: 770-426-0007
e-mail: info@georgiadance.com
Web Site: www.georgiadance.com
Officers:
    President: Sandra Ratchford
    Vice President: Courtney Kennedy
    Treasurer: Carmen Dillard
    President of the Guild: Judy Freeman
Management:
    Artistic Director: Ruth Mitchell
    Production Manager: Courtney Kennedy
Mission: To provide the community with a small, eclectic company to perform in places not suited for large ballet companies.
Utilizes: Five Seasonal Concerts
Founded: 1956
Specialized Field: Modern; Ballet; Jazz
Status: Professional, Nonprofit
Income Sources: National Association for Regional Ballet; Dance Coalition of Atlanta; Young Audiences of Atlanta
Organization Type: Performing; Touring

158
ATLANTA FESTIVAL BALLET COMPANY

416 Eagle's Landing Parkway
Stockbridge, GA 30281
Phone: 770-507-2775
Fax: 770-507-9182
e-mail: fbcatl@aol.com
Web Site: www.atlantafestivalballet.com
Management:
    Artistic Director: Gregory Aaron
    Artistic Director: Nicolas Pacana
    Company Manager: Gesielle DiBlasi
Mission: To thrill and move our audience, dancers, choreographers, students, supporters and staff with art and discipline to enrich and inspire lives.
Founded: 1989
Specialized Field: Ballet
Status: Non-Profit, Professional
Paid Staff: 12
Volunteer Staff: 12
Paid Artists: 19
Non-paid Artists: 12
Budget: $300,000
Income Sources: Partners in Education; Grants; Donations; Ticket Sales
Affiliations: Clayton County Schools; Henry County Schools
Annual Attendance: 20,000

Hawaii

159
WEST HAWAII DANCE THEATRE AND DANCE ACADEMY

74-5626 Alapa Street
Kailua-Kona, HI 96740
Phone: 808-329-8876
Fax: 808-329-1033
e-mail: vh2dns4@ilhawaii.net
Web Site: www.whdt.org
Management:
    Artistic Director: Virginia Holte, vh2dns4@ilhawaii.net
    Teacher/Choreographer/Designer: Megan Hoyt Chapman
Mission: The dance company sponsors educational outreach programs, public performances, guest artists and workshops while the academy provides professional dance training from preschool through advanced.
Founded: 1989
Specialized Field: Classical Ballet, Contemporary Dance, Modern, Jazz, Hip Hop, Hula, Yoga, Pilates Mat, Gyrotonic Expansion System

Idaho

160
BALLET IDAHO

Esther Simplot Performing Arts Academy
501 S 8th Street
Boise, ID 83702
Phone: 208-343-0556
Fax: 208-424-3129
e-mail: info@balletidaho.org
Web Site: www.balletidaho.org
Officers:
    Chairman: AJ Balukof
    Secretary: Kerrie Quinn
    Vice Chairman: Jane Cliff
    Treasurer: Jason Sneed
Management:
    Artistic Director: Peter Anastos
    Executive Director: Julie Numbers Smith
Mission: To promote the value of classical and contemporary dance in Idaho through excellence in performance and education.
Utilizes: Artists-in-Residence; Choreographers; Dancers; Designers; Five Seasonal Concerts; Guest Accompanists; Guest Artists; Guest Ensembles; Lyricists; Multimedia; Original Music Scores; Resident Artists; Resident Professionals; Student Interns
Founded: 1972
Specialized Field: Modern; Ballet
Status: Professional, Non-Profit
Paid Staff: 6
Paid Artists: 23
Budget: 1,150,000
Income Sources: Corporate; Foundations; Individual; Business Alliance
Season: September-May
Performs At: Morrison Center for the Performing Arts
Affiliations: Eugene Ballet Company
Annual Attendance: 14000
Seating Capacity: 2090
Organization Type: Performing; Touring; Resident; Educational; Sponsoring

161
OINKARI BASQUE DANCERS
1224 Rose Park Circle
Boise, ID 83702
Phone: 208-336-8219
e-mail: yanci@msn.com
Web Site: www.oinkari.org
Officers:
Board Director: Tyler Smith
Board Director: Nick Bicandi
Board Director: Emily Martin
Business Manager: John Kirtland
Management:
Girls Dance Director: Toni Ansotegui
Boys Dance Director: Dan Ansotegui
Mission: The promotion and enhancement of our culture through dance, song, language and education.
Utilizes: Guest Companies; Singers
Specialized Field: Ethnic Dance; Folk Dance
Status: Nonprofit
Paid Staff: 70
Income Sources: Euskaldunak
Performs At: Boise Basque Center
Organization Type: Performing; Touring; Educational

Illinois

162
BALLET CHICAGO
218 S Wabash Avenue
3rd Floor
Chicago, IL 60604
Phone: 312-251-8838
Fax: 312-251-8840
e-mail: info@balletchicago.org
Web Site: www.balletchicago.org
Management:
Artistic Director: Daniel Duell
School Director: Patricia Blair
Operations Director: Robert Bondlow
Co-Artistic Director: Sara Ford
Mission: To develop future career classical dancers for Chicago and the dance world at large through the study and performance of the aesthetic and repertory of George Balanchine, this century's most influential and widely performed choreographer.
Utilizes: Guest Accompanists
Founded: 1987
Specialized Field: Ballet
Status: Pre-Professional, Nonprofit
Paid Staff: 20
Volunteer Staff: 5
Income Sources: Tuition; Performances; Donations; Corporate; Individual; Foundations
Performs At: Athenaeum Theatre
Annual Attendance: 20,000
Organization Type: Performing;Educational

163
CHICAGO MOVING COMPANY
3035 N Hoyne Street
Chicago, IL 60618
Phone: 773-880-5402
Fax: 773-384-4292
Web Site: www.chicagomovingcompany.org
Officers:
Board Director: Jeff Abell
Board Director: Larry Blust
Board Director: Chris Gent
Board Director: William Gilmore
Board Director: Lois Grossman
Board Director: Nana Shineflug

Management:
Artistic Co-Director: Nana Shineflug
Director Of Business/Development: Kay Wendt Lasota
Mission: To perform art that speaks to life to touch the spirit of the audience, and engage them in feeling and reflections.
Utilizes: Singers
Founded: 1972
Specialized Field: Modern
Status: Professional, Nonprofit
Income Sources: Performances; Touring; Workshops; Grants
Performs At: Columbia Dance Center
Annual Attendance: 30,000
Organization Type: Performing; Touring; Educational

164
DANCE CENTER OF COLUMBIA COLLEGE
1306 S Michigan Avenue
Chicago, IL 60605
Phone: 312-344-8300
Fax: 312-344-8036
e-mail: info@dum.edu
Web Site: www.dancecenter.org
Officers:
Chair: Bonnie Brooks
Associate Chair: Margi Cole
Management:
Executive Director: Phil Reynolds
Operations Manager: Shannon Epplett
Marketing Director: Heather Hartley
Music Director: Richard Woodbury
Visiting Artist: Mariah Maloney
Mission: To provide dance instruction to a variety of people from culturally diverse backgrounds.
Utilizes: Artists-in-Residence; Choreographers; Collaborating Artists; Collaborations; Commissioned Music; Dance Companies; Dancers; Educators; Guest Accompanists; Guest Artists; Guest Choreographers; Guest Ensembles; Guest Instructors; Guest Soloists; High School Drama; Local Artists; Multi Collaborations; Original Music Scores; Selected Students; Theatre Companies
Founded: 1969
Specialized Field: Modern; Ballet; Jazz; Ethnic Dance; Improvisation
Status: Professional, Nonprofit
Paid Staff: 7
Paid Artists: 35
Budget: $2,100,000
Income Sources: Earned and Contributed Income
Performs At: The Harris Theatre
Affiliations: APAP; IPN; MADTC
Annual Attendance: 10,000
Facility Category: Black Box
Type of Stage: Dance
Seating Capacity: 272
Year Built: 2000
Cost: $3,500,000
Rental Contact: Shannon Epplett
Organization Type: Performing; Educational

165
JOEL HALL DANCERS & CENTER
1511 W Berwyn Street
Chicago, IL 60640
Phone: 773-293-0900
Fax: 773-293-1130
e-mail: joelhalldance@hotmail.com
Web Site: www.joelhall.org
Management:
Artistic Director: Joel Hall

Managing Director: Susan Dickson
Associate Director: Vanessa Truvillion
Associate Artistic Director: Nancy Teinowitz
Mission: To build and serve a constituency that is racially, ethnically, culturally and socially diverse, to promote a philosophy of inclusiveness, and to enrich the lives of community members through dance education and performance.
Utilizes: Five Seasonal Concerts
Founded: 1974
Specialized Field: Jazz; Ballet; Modern; Hip Hop; Tap; Egyptian Dance; Educational Dance
Status: Professional, Nonprofit
Annual Attendance: 10,000
Facility Category: Dance Studio
Organization Type: Performing; Touring; Resident; Educational

166
JOFFREY BALLET
70 E Lake Street
Suite 1300
Chicago, IL 60601
Phone: 312-739-0120
Fax: 312-739-0119
e-mail: information@joffrey.com
Web Site: www.joffrey.com
Officers:
Chairman: Pamela Stroebel
Vice Chairman: Miles B. White
Vice Chairman: Gary Holdren
Vice Chairman: Fred Eychaner
Secretary: Connie Lindsay
Management:
Artistic Director: Gerald Arpino
Executive Director: Jon H Teeuwissen
Marketing/Public Relations: Amanda Golucki
Mission: To preserve, recreate and present historical masterpieces of the twentieth century and to nurture, commission and present works of young artists, particularly Americans, to audiences worldwide.
Founded: 1956
Specialized Field: Ballet
Status: Non-Profit, Professional
Budget: $2,500,000+
Income Sources: Tickets Sales; Touting; Contributions
Performs At: Auditorium Theatre of Roosevelt University

167
LIRA DANCERS OF THE LIRA ENSEMBLE
6525 N Sheridan Road
Chicago, IL 60626
Phone: 773-508-7040
Fax: 773-508-7043
e-mail: lira@liraensemble.org
Officers:
Co-Conductor: Philip Seward
Choreographer: Iowna Puc
President: Lucyna Migala
Secretary: Frances Weit
Treasurer: Bernard Tresnowski
Management:
Artistic Director/General Manager: Lucyna Migala
Co-Conductor: Paul Dijkstra
Mission: To help acquaint Polish Americans with the richness of their thousand year old heritage of music and dance and to help other Americans learn about and appreciate Polish culture and traditions.
Founded: 1975
Specialized Field: Polish Folk Dance
Status: Non-Profit, Professional
Non-paid Artists: 30
Budget: $200,000-$500,000

Organization Type: Performing

168
MORDINE AND COMPANY DANCE THEATRE

1016 N Dearborn Parkway
Chicago, IL 60610-2804
Phone: 312-654-9540
Fax: 847-864-9730
e-mail: info@morfine.org
Web Site: morfine.org
Officers:
   President: Allen Doderlein
   Secretary/Treasurer: Philip Martini
   Vice President: Shirley Mordine
Management:
   Artistic Director: Shirley Mordine
Mission: To create innovative dance works and to collaborate with outstanding artists as well as conduct educational programs for high school students and young choreographers.
Utilizes: Community Members; Five Seasonal Concerts; Singers; Special Technical Talent
Founded: 1969
Specialized Field: Modern
Status: Professional, Nonprofit
Paid Staff: 3
Non-paid Artists: 2
Income Sources: Association for Performing Arts Presenters; Dance USA; Chicago Dance Coalition
Performs At: The Dance Center of Columbia College
Annual Attendance: 4,000
Organization Type: Performing; Resident; Educational

169
MUNTU DANCE THEATRE

7127 S Ellis Avenue
Suite 2
Chicago, IL 60619
Phone: 773-241-6080
Fax: 773-241-6089
e-mail: info@muntu.comcom
Web Site: www.muntu.com
Officers:
   President: Joan Gray
Management:
   Company Manager: Lynn Stevenson
   Artistic Director: Amanda Payne
   Operations Director: Barbara Maxon
   Program Director: Vaune Blalock
Mission: The performance of traditional and contemporary African and African American dance, music and folklore.
Founded: 1972
Specialized Field: Ethnic Dance
Status: Professional, Nonprofit
Budget: $500,000-$1,000,000
Organization Type: Performing; Touring; Resident

170
NAJWA DANCE CORPS

1900 W Van Buren Street
Chicago, IL 60612
Phone: 312-850-7224
e-mail: najwadancecorps@sbcglobal.net
Web Site: www.najwadance.org
Officers:
   Executive Director: Sheila Walker-Wilkens
Management:
   Artistic Director: Najwa I,
   najwadancecorps@sbcglobal.net

Mission: To perserve dance styles and techniques of different era's as it relates to the African American dance experience. Najwa Dance Corps is dedicated to being a live historical dance archive.
Utilizes: Artists-in-Residence; Choreographers; Collaborating Artists; Collaborations; Dance Companies; Dancers; Educators; Guest Accompanists; Guest Ensembles; Guest Speakers; High School Drama; Instructors; Local Talent; Multimedia; Original Music Scores; Playwrights; Poets; Scenic Designers; Students; Theatre Companies
Founded: 1978
Opened: 1979
Specialized Field: African; Carribean; Tap; Jazz; Modern Dance
Status: Professional, Nonprofit
Paid Staff: 4
Volunteer Staff: 4
Paid Artists: 12
Budget: $40,000-$100,000
Income Sources: Chicago Dance Art Coalition; African-American Arts Alliance
Organization Type: Performing; Touring; Educational

171
NATYAKALALAYAM DANCE COMPANY

410 South Michigan Avenue
Suite 725
Chicago, IL 60605-1387
Phone: 312-212-1240
Fax: 312-212-1250
e-mail: info@natya.com
Web Site: www.natya.com
Management:
   Artistic Director: Hema Rajagopalan
   Assistant Artistic Director: Krithika Rajagopalan
Mission: To promote the classical dance of India in today's contemporary world.
Founded: 1975
Specialized Field: Indian Dance
Status: Non-Profit, Professional
Paid Staff: 3
Volunteer Staff: 8
Paid Artists: 15
Non-paid Artists: 25
Income Sources: Foundations; Corporations; Earned Income; Ticket Revenue
Annual Attendance: 40,000

172
RIVER NORTH CHICAGO DANCE COMPANY

1016 N Dearborn Parkway
Chicago, IL 60610
Phone: 312-944-2888
Fax: 312-944-2581
e-mail: info@rivernorthchicago.com
Web Site: www.rivernorthchicago.com
Officers:
   Executive Director: Angela Combact
Management:
   Artistic Director: Frank Chaves
Mission: Established for the purpose of cultivating and promoting Chicago's wealth of jazz dance talent.
Founded: 1989
Specialized Field: Jazz; Contemporary Dance
Status: Professional, Non-Profit
Paid Staff: 3
Paid Artists: 24
Budget: $1,100,000
Income Sources: Performance Fees; Corporate, Foundation, and Government Contributions; Individual Contributions
Annual Attendance: 30,000

173
T DANIEL PRODUCTIONS

6619 N Campbell Street
Chicago, IL 60645
Phone: 773-743-0277
Fax: 773-743-0276
e-mail: tdaniel@tdanielcreations.com
Web Site: www.tdanielcreations.com
Officers:
   Co-Founder: T Daniel
   Co-Founder: Laurie Willets
Management:
   Artistic Co-Director: T Daniel
   Artistic Co-Director: Laurie Willets
Mission: To create, educate and tour theatrical productions, shows and concert programs dynamically based upon the Art of Mime for audiences of all ages.
Utilizes: Collaborations; Multi Collaborations
Founded: 1971
Specialized Field: Theatrical Dance
Status: Professional, Non-Profit
Paid Staff: 2
Paid Artists: 2

174
TRINITY IRISH DANCE COMPANY

2936 N Southport
3rd Floor
Chicago, IL 60657
Phone: 773-549-6135
Fax: 773-549-6325
e-mail: info@trinityirishdancecompnay.org
Web Site: www.trinity-dancers.com
Officers:
   Founder: Mark Howard
Management:
   Artistic Director: Mark Howard
   Company Manager: Michael Carr
   Instructor: Anne McCarthy
Mission: Trinity Academy of Irish Dance is the most widely recognized dance program in the world. The program gives everyone the opportunity to embark on a unique journey of Irish dance.
Founded: 1990
Specialized Field: Irish Dance
Status: Professional, Non-Profit
Budget: $980,000
Income Sources: Touring Revenue; Individual Grants; Corporation Grants
Annual Attendance: 57,000

175
ZEPHYR DANCE

1627 N Oakley Avenue
Chicago, IL 60647-5318
Phone: 773-489-5069
Fax: 773-489-9930
e-mail: michelle@zephyrdance.com
Management:
   Artistic Director: Michelle Kranicke
   Associate Artistic Director: Emily Stein
Mission: To bring experiences in self-expression and creative development to diverse communities through its educational outreach programming.
Founded: 1989
Specialized Field: Ballet; Modern; Creative Movement
Status: Non-Profit; Professional
Paid Staff: 1
Volunteer Staff: 10
Annual Attendance: 500-1,000

176
JUDITH SVALANDER DANCE THEATRE
83 E Woodstock Street
Crystal Lake, IL 60014-4363
Phone: 815-455-2055
Fax: 815-477-0313
e-mail: jsschoolofballet@hotmail.com
Web Site: www.jsvalander.com
Officers:
Business Administrator: Nora Kay Belt
Founder: Judith Svalander
Management:
Artistic Director: Judith Svalander
Creative Dance Director: Laura Bobkowski
Resident Guest Artist: Greg Begley
Mission: Dedication to the development of dance and the combination of skills and the joy of music.
Specialized Field: Ballet

177
GUS GIORDANO JAZZ DANCE CHICAGO
614 Davis Street
Evanston, IL 60201
Phone: 847-866-6779
Fax: 847-866-9228
e-mail: ggjdc@giordnojazzdance.com
Web Site: www.giordanojazzdance.com
Officers:
President: John Seeback
Vice President: Beth Stephens
Treasurer: A Steven Crown
Secretary: Stephanie Weidenborner
Founder: Gus Giordano
Management:
Artistic Director: Nan Giordano
Executive Director: Ben Hodge
Director: Gus Giordano
Mission: To excite audiences about dance in general, specifically jazz dance.
Utilizes: Choreographers; Collaborations; Dancers; Designers; Guest Artists; Guest Conductors; High School Drama; Original Music Scores; Student Interns
Founded: 1962
Specialized Field: Jazz; Contemporary Dance
Status: Professional, Non-Profit
Paid Staff: 4
Paid Artists: 16
Budget: $200,000-$500,000
Income Sources: Illinois Arts Council; Foundations; Ticket Sales; Performing Fees; Government; Corporations; Individual Donations
Affiliations: Jazz Dance World Congress
Annual Attendance: 56,000
Organization Type: Performing; Touring; Educational

178
VON HEIDECKE'S CHICAGO FESTIVAL BALLET
1239 S Naper Boulevard
Naperville, IL 60540
Phone: 630-527-1052
Fax: 630-527-8427
e-mail: general@chicagofestivalballet.org
Web Site: www.chicagofestivalballet.com
Officers:
Chairman: Christopher Rosean
Secretary: Sue Doser
Tresurer: Ron Pavlacka
Founder: Kenneth Von Heidecke
Management:
Director: Kenneth Von Heidecke
Artistic Honorary Advisor: Maria Tallchief
Artistic Advisor: Nathalie Krassovska

Studio Manager: Timothy Cremeens
Mission: To maintain the highest artistic standards and uncompromising quality of spirted performances through the traditions of classical ballet.
Specialized Field: Ballet
Status: Nonprofit

179
MOMENTA
Academy of Movement and Music
605 Lake Street
Oak Park, IL 60302
Phone: 708-848-2329
Fax: 708-848-2391
e-mail: stephanieclemens@hotmail.com
Web Site: www.momenta-dance.org
Management:
Press Represetative/Artistic Dir: Stephanie Clemens
Artistic Co-Director: Larry Ippel
Artistic Co-Director: Stephanie Clemens
Mission: To produce and present dance concerts.
Founded: 1983
Specialized Field: Historical Dance; Modern; Contemporary Dance
Paid Staff: 2
Volunteer Staff: 3
Paid Artists: 15
Non-paid Artists: 50
Budget: $175,000
Income Sources: Tickets; Memberships; Fundraising
Performs At: Doris Humphrey Memorial Theatre
Annual Attendance: 2500
Facility Category: Black Box Theatre
Type of Stage: Proscenium
Stage Dimensions: 45'x 30'x 125'
Seating Capacity: 150
Year Built: 1924
Year Remodeled: 1983
Cost: negotiable
Rental Contact: Stephanie Clemens

180
PEORIA BALLET
8800 N Industrial Road
Peoria, IL 61615
Phone: 309-690-7990
Fax: 309-690-7991
e-mail: info@peoriaballet.com
Web Site: www.peoriaballet.com
Officers:
President: Scot Fairfield
Vice President: Laurie Pearl Cane
Treasurer: Stephanie Rickets
Secretary: Linda Hallman
Management:
Artistic Director: Erich Yetter
General Manager: Paula Sapinski
Marketing/Advertising Director: Rachael Hamilton
Office Manager: Laura Kessler
Development Director: Amy Bearce
Mission: To further the participation, education and appreciation of all disciplines of dance as a cultural art form with a particular emphasis in ballet.
Founded: 1965
Specialized Field: Ballet
Status: Professional, Nonprofit
Paid Staff: 11
Paid Artists: 6
Budget: $400,000
Income Sources: Corporate and Private Donations; Grants; Fundraising Events; Tuition; Illionis Arts Counsil
Performs At: Peoria Civic Center
Annual Attendance: 6,000

Organization Type: Performing; Touring; Resident

181
BALLET QUAD CITIES
613 17th Street
Rock Island, IL 61201
Phone: 309-786-3779
e-mail: jcookdalletqc@sbglobal.net
Web Site: www.balletquadcities.com
Officers:
President: Paul Van Duyne
Vice President: Linda Bowers
Secretary: Ruth Lee
Treasurer: Dennis Miller
Management:
Artistic Advisor: Dominic Walsh
Artistic Affiliate: Stuart Loungway
Associate Director: Courtney Lyon
Ballet Mistress: Erica Wood
Resident Choreographer: Deanna Carter
Resident Artist/Choreographer: Domingo Rubio
Guest Choreographer: Cleo Mack
Mission: Ballet Quad Cities provides classical and contemporary dance to the entire bi-state region through oustanding performances, entertainig lecture-demonstrations and innovative educational outreach programs for people of all ages.
Founded: 1996
Specialized Field: Ballet

182
ROCKFORD DANCE COMPANY
711 N Main Street
Rockford, IL 61103
Phone: 815-963-3341
Fax: 815-963-3541
Web Site: www.rockforddancecompany.com
Officers:
President: Doug Mark
Vice President: Carole Newcomer
Treasurer: Ron Foran
Secretary: Cheryl Balsam
Management:
Executive Director: Cindy Lance
Artistic Director: Margaret Faust
Mission: Committed to serving as an arts resource in dance through its presentations, performances and education.
Utilizes: Five Seasonal Concerts
Founded: 1972
Specialized Field: Modern; Ballet; Jazz
Status: Semi-Professional, Nonprofit
Paid Staff: 15
Volunteer Staff: 10
Income Sources: Corporate; Foundations; Tuition; Ticket Sales
Performs At: The Cornado Theatre
Organization Type: Performing; Resident; Educational; Sponsoring

183
SPRINGFIELD BALLET COMPANY
420 S Sixth Street
Springfield, IL 62704
Phone: 217-544-1967
Fax: 217-544-1968
e-mail: info@springfieldballetco.org
Web Site: springfieldballetco.org
Officers:
Business Manager: Sally Hamilton
Management:
Artistic Director: Julie Dunn
Ballet Mistress: Gina DeCroix

All listings are in alphabetical order by state, then city, then organization within the city.

Mission: To use beauty, energy, and diversity of dance to speak to the community; to foster dance as the common language that encourages freedom of expression, bridges generations and cultures, and adds to the richness of life in Central Illinois.
Utilizes: Guest Companies; Singers
Founded: 1975
Specialized Field: Modern; Ballet; Jazz; Folk Dance
Status: Non-Professional, Nonprofit
Paid Staff: 03
Volunteer Staff: 150
Budget: $30,000
Income Sources: Corporate; Individual; Grants;
Performs At: The Sangamon Auditorium
Affiliations: Illionis Arts Counsil; Springfield Arts Counsil
Annual Attendance: 25,000
Organization Type: Performing; Touring; Educational; Sponsoring

184
SALT CREEK BALLET
98 E Naperville Road
Westmont, IL 60559-1559
Phone: 630-769-1199
Fax: 630-769-0052
e-mail: saltcreekballet@aol.com
Web Site: www.saltcreekballet.org
Management:
  Co-Director: Sergey Kozadayev
  Co-Director: Zhanna Dubrovskaya
  Artistic Director: Jan Templeton
Mission: to bring professional quality dance programming to area audiences
Utilizes: Choreographers; Collaborations; Dance Companies; Dancers; Educators; Guest Accompanists; Guest Artists; Guest Composers; Guest Conductors; Guest Musical Directors; Original Music Scores; Resident Professionals; Soloists; Student Interns
Founded: 1985
Specialized Field: Ballet
Status: Non-Profit; Non-Professional
Paid Staff: 15
Budget: $750,000
Income Sources: Grants; Contributions; Ticket Sales
Annual Attendance: 10,000
Organization Type: Touring Company

Indiana

185
ANDERSON YOUNG BALLET THEATRE
29 Dillon Street
PO Box 631
Anderson, IN 46016-1805
Phone: 765-643-2184
Web Site: www.andersonyoungballet.org
Officers:
  President: Tracy Skiles
  Founder: Lou Ann Young
  Vice President: Amy Sizemore
  Treasurer: Terra Skinner
Management:
  Artistic Director: LouAnn Young
  Assistant Artistic Director: Kory Browder
  Instructor/Choreographer: Audra Sokol
Specialized Field: Ballet

186
CARMEL DANCE ARTS-INDY LATIN DANCE
575 W Carmel Drive
Carmel, IN 46032
Phone: 317-844-9131
e-mail: carmeldancearts@indylatindance.com
Web Site: www.indylatidance.com
Mission: Our dance group offers typical folkloric dancing, salsa and latin dance performances.
Specialized Field: Folkloric Dance; Salsa; Latin

187
EVANSVILLE DANCE THEATRE
333 Plaza East Boulevard
Suite E
Evansville, IN 47715
Phone: 812-473-8937
Fax: 812-473-0392
e-mail: evvdance@cigecom.net
Web Site: www.edtdance.org
Officers:
  President: Mary Mably
  VP: Martha Alle
  Secretary: Kelly Gates
  Treasurer: Klara Stone
Management:
  Artistic Director: Keith J Martin
  Ballet Mistress: BJ Martin
  Guest Artist: Jason Keith Martin
Mission: Increase public awareness and appreciation of dance as a performing art as well as producing and presenting excellent dance performances, invrntive choreography and showcasing unique talents.
Utilizes: Collaborations; Dance Companies; Dancers; Five Seasonal Concerts; Guest Writers
Founded: 1981
Specialized Field: Ballet; Theatrical Dance
Status: Professional,Nonprofit
Paid Staff: 12
Paid Artists: 7
Income Sources: Corporate; Foundations; Grants
Performs At: Victory and Shankein Theatre
Organization Type: Performing; Touring; Educational

188
FORT WAYNE BALLET
324 Penn Avenue
Fort Wayne, IN 46805
Phone: 260-484-9646
Fax: 260-484-9647
e-mail: acadamy@fortwayne.org
Web Site: www.info@fortwayneballet.org
Officers:
  President: James F Coughlin
  Vice President: Tim Manges
  Treasurer: Jessica Thompson
  Secretary: Catherine Christoff
Management:
  Artistic/Executive Director: Karen Gibbons Brown
  Managing Director: Anna Ross
  Business Director: Christine Thompson
Mission: The mission of the Fort Wayne Ballet, Inc., is to inspire and nurture an appreciation for the art of dance through educational excellence, artistic achievement, performance experiences and outreach activities in the community and beyond.
Utilizes: Guest Companies; Singers
Founded: 1956
Specialized Field: Ballet; Jazz; Contemporary Dance; Character Dance
Status: Semi-Professional, Nonprofit
Paid Staff: 17
Volunteer Staff: 250
Budget: $897,000
Performs At: Performing Arts Center
Affiliations: Arts United of Greater Ft. Wayne
Annual Attendance: 28,000
Organization Type: Performing; Educational

189
FORT WAYNE DANCE COLLECTIVE
437 E Berry Street
Suite 203
Fort Wayne, IN 46802
Phone: 260-424-6574
Fax: 260-424-2789
e-mail: info@fwdc.org
Web Site: www.fwdc.org
Officers:
  President: Mark Angelos
  VP: Jill Barkenstein
  Secretary: Robert Grayless
  Treasurer: Gregg Smith
Management:
  Artistic Director: Liz Monnier
  Managing Director: Cat Moors
Mission: To promote and expand the development of human creativity and expression through movement, as well as to sustain and develop the Fort Wayne Dance Collective's traditions by presenting dance, inter- and multi-disciplinary arts, and educational programs of the highest quality to diverse audiences and student populations.
Utilizes: Artists-in-Residence; Choreographers; Collaborating Artists; Collaborations; Commissioned Music; Community Talent; Composers; Dance Companies; Dancers; Educators; Five Seasonal Concerts; Guest Accompanists; Guest Artists; Guest Choreographers; High School Drama; Instructors; Lyricists; Multi Collaborations; Original Music Scores; Soloists; Theatre Companies
Founded: 1979
Specialized Field: Modern; Jazz; Belly Dance; Yoga
Status: Professional; Nonprofit
Paid Staff: 3
Paid Artists: 16
Budget: $300,000
Income Sources: Earned Income; Local Foundations; State and National Grants
Affiliations: Arts United
Annual Attendance: 24,000
Organization Type: Performing; Educational; Sponsoring; Video Producer for Public Access

190
BALLET INTERNATIONALE
502 N Capitol Avenue
Suite B
Indianapolis, IN 46204
Phone: 317-637-8979
Fax: 317-637-1637
e-mail: info@balletinternational.org
Web Site: www.balletinternational.org
Officers:
  President: Clare D Coxey
  Treasurer: Patrick J Burley
Management:
  Artistic Director: Eldar Aliev
  Executive Director: Bill Wilson
  Company/Booking Manager: Carolyn Treebee
  Marketing/Public Relations Director: Kevin O'Donohue
Mission: To stimulate the evolution of our community in those ways only possible with world-class ballet.
Founded: 1973
Specialized Field: Classical Ballet
Status: Professional; Non-Profit
Paid Staff: 20
Volunteer Staff: 25
Paid Artists: 27
Budget: $2.5 million

Income Sources: Ticket Sales; Contributed Income; Touring; Residencies; Merchandise Sales; Production Rental
Performs At: Murat Centre
Affiliations: Association of Performing Arts Presenters; Arts Midwest; Western Arts Alliance
Annual Attendance: 40,000
Facility Category: Multi-use
Type of Stage: Proscenium
Seating Capacity: 2,500
Rental Contact: General Manager Terry Hennessey
Organization Type: Performing; Touring; Resident; Educational; Sponsoring

191
DANCE KALEIDOSCOPE
4603 Claredon Road
Room 32
Indianapolis, IN 46208-3485
Phone: 317-940-6555
Fax: 317-940-6557
e-mail: dk@dancekal.org
Web Site: www.dancekal.org
Officers:
   President: Harry Kurkowski
   Treasurer: Bernadette Fletcher
Management:
   Artistic Director: David Hochoy
   Resident Lighting Designer: Laura Glover
   Executive Director: Janice Virgin
   Marketing Director: Karen Knotts
   Office Manager: Janie Snyder
Mission: To inspire, educate and entertain through the experience of outstanding professional contemporary dance.
Founded: 1972
Specialized Field: Modern; Contemporary Dance
Status: Professional, Nonprofit
Paid Staff: 7
Paid Artists: 11
Budget: $1,032,000
Income Sources: Earned; Developed; Special Events
Performs At: Pike Performing Arts Center; Indiana Repertory Theatre
Affiliations: Indian Repretory
Annual Attendance: 10,000
Facility Category: Professional Theatre
Type of Stage: Proscenium
Seating Capacity: 600
Organization Type: Performing; Touring; Resident

192
INTO SALSA DANCE STUDIO
1833 Expo Lane
Indianapolis, IN 46204
Phone: 317-496-4196
Web Site: www.intosalsa.com
Management:
   Dance Instructor: Yang Xiao
   Dance Instructor: Erin Lamb
Mission: Yang Xiao and Erin Lamb have performed and captivated thousands of audiences in Central America. In the spring of 2005 they opened IntoSalsa Latin Dance Studio.
Opened: 2005
Specialized Field: Ethnic Dance; Salsa

193
INDIANA BALLET THEATRE NORTHWEST
8888 Louisiana
Merrillville, IN 46410

Phone: 219-755-4444
Fax: 219-226-0920
e-mail: info@ibtnw.org
Web Site: www.ibtnw.org
Officers:
   Founder: Gloria Tuohy
   President: Jane Leslie
   VP: Blossom Mabon
   Treasurer: Cynthia Davis
Management:
   Artistic/Executive Director: Gloria Tuohy
Mission: Indiana Ballet Theatre Northwest is dedicated to the art of dance and to enriching the cultural life of our community.
Founded: 1980
Specialized Field: Ballet
Status: Professional, Nonprofit

194
MUNCIE BALLET STUDIO
520 W Main Street
Muncie, IN 47305
Phone: 765-282-1480
Web Site: www.muncieballet.org
Management:
   Director: Lisa Love
Mission: Muncie ballet studio is creating audiences for today, tomorrow and memories to last a lifetime.
Specialized Field: Ballet

Iowa

195
CO' MOTION DANCE THEATER
129 E Seventh Street
Ames, IA 50010
Phone: 515-232-7374
Fax: 515-233-9290
e-mail: dance@comotion.org
Web Site: www.comotion.org
Officers:
   President: Ronald Jackson
   VP: Beth Clarke
   Secretary: Brenda Witherspoon
   Treasurer: Larry Gleason
Management:
   Director: Valerie Williams
   General Manager: Susan Jackson
Mission: To bring high-caliber and professional dance to Midwestern sponsors at affordable prices and to offer the highest quality in dance education to its students.
Utilizes: Choreographers; Collaborating Artists; Dance Companies; Dancers; Guest Musical Directors; High School Drama; Instructors; Local Artists & Directors; Lyricists; Original Music Scores; Paid Performers; Poets; Student Interns
Founded: 1978
Specialized Field: Modern
Status: Professional, Nonprofit
Paid Staff: 1
Volunteer Staff: 6
Paid Artists: 3
Non-paid Artists: 3
Performs At: The Ames City Auditorium
Organization Type: Performing; Touring; Resident; Educational

196
IOWA DANCE THEATRE
Po Box 65755
Des Moines, IA 50265-0755

Phone: 515-979-6622
Fax: 515-276-2694
Web Site: www.iowadancetheatre.com
Management:
   Executive Director: Mary Joyce Lind
   Project Director: Janice Baker-Haines
   Co-Director: Lisa Hamilton
   Co-Director: Cathy Bergman
   Co-Director: Lana Lyddon-Hattan
   Head Chamber Dances: Kathleen Hurley
Mission: Dedicated to supporting a company of dancers who will perform and promote the art form of dance.
Founded: 1983
Specialized Field: Modern; Ballet; Jazz
Status: Semi-Professional; Nonprofit
Volunteer Staff: 15
Paid Artists: 12
Non-paid Artists: 15
Income Sources: Grants; Fundraisers
Performs At: Civic Center of Greater Des Moines
Annual Attendance: 5,000
Seating Capacity: 2,750
Year Built: 1979
Year Remodeled: 2000
Organization Type: Performing; Touring; Educational

Kansas

197
COHAN/SUZEAU DANCE COMPANY
University of Kansas Dept. of Dance
Robinson Center
Room 251
Lawrence, KS 66045
Mailing Address: 1002 Avalon Road, Lawrence, KS 66044
Phone: 785-841-6394
Fax: 785-864-5089
e-mail: suzeau@ku.edu
Web Site: www.cohansuzeau.org
Management:
   Co-Artistic Director: Patrick Suzeau
   Co-Artistic Director: Muriel Cohan
   Manager: Suan Whitfield
Founded: 1973
Specialized Field: Contemporary Dance; East Indian Classical Dance; Contemporary/Indian Fusion
Status: Professional; Non-Profit
Paid Staff: 2
Income Sources: Touring; Performing
Performs At: The Lied Center
Affiliations: University Of Kansas
Type of Stage: Proscenium

198
KANSAS REGIONAL BALLET
11728 Quivira Road
Overland Park, KS 66210
Phone: 913-451-9292
Fax: 913-498-2222
e-mail: krbdance@mindsping.com
Web Site: krb.homestead.com
Officers:
   President: Dennis Landsman
   Vice President: Kathy Landsman
   Secretary: Linda Smith
   Treasurer: Dennis Landsman
Management:
   Artistic Co-Director: Kathy Landsman
   Artistic Co-Director: Dennis Landsman
Mission: To introduce and educate all ages to the art form of dance.

Utilizes: Choreographers; Dancers; Guest Accompanists; Guest Artists; Multimedia; Soloists
Founded: 1979
Specialized Field: Ballet
Status: Pre-Professional; Nonprofit
Paid Staff: 2
Volunteer Staff: 27
Non-paid Artists: 27
Budget: $100,000
Income Sources: Fund Raisers; Grants; Ticket Sales
Performs At: Johnson Community College/The Carlson Center
Affiliations: Midstates Regional Dance America
Annual Attendance: 5,000
Facility Category: Community College
Type of Stage: Proscenium
Stage Dimensions: 55'x 45'
Seating Capacity: 1,300
Year Built: 1988
Rental Contact: Johnson County Community College
Organization Type: Performing; Touring; Educational

199
WICHITA CONTEMPORARY DANCE THEATRE

Witchita State University
1845 N Fairmount
Box 101
Wichita, KS 67260-0101
Phone: 316-978-3530
Fax: 316-978-3071
e-mail: renea.goforth@wichita.edu
Management:
    Director Dance: C Nicholas Johnson
    Instructor: Sabrina Vasquez
    Choreographer: Denise A Celestin
Mission: To provide high quality entertaining dance performances and to foster understanding and appreciation for dance through educational programs as well as provide a venue for artists to live and work.
Founded: 1924
Specialized Field: Modern; Ballet; Jazz; Tap
Status: Non-Professional, Non-Profit
Paid Staff: 3
Budget: $20,000
Income Sources: Performances; Tuition; Foundations; Corporate; Individual
Annual Attendance: 2,500

Kentucky

200
KENTUCKY BALLET THEATRE

736 National Avenue
Lexington, KY 40502
Phone: 859-252-5245
Fax: 859-252-7925
e-mail: info@kyballet.com
Web Site: www.kyballet.com
Management:
    Artistic Director: Norbe Risco
    Public Relations: Sandy Robinson
Mission: To establish through performance and education a professional company and academy committed to the art of dance.
Utilizes: Artists-in-Residence; Choreographers; Dance Companies; Dancers; Guest Artists; Guest Musical Directors; Guest Writers; High School Drama; Multimedia; Original Music Scores; Soloists
Founded: 1998
Specialized Field: Ballet; Theatrical Dance
Status: Non-Profit, Professional
Performs At: The Lexington Opera House

201
LEXINGTON BALLET

161 N Mill Street
4th Floor
Lexington, KY 40507
Phone: 859-233-3925
Fax: 859-252-0505
e-mail: info@lexingtonballet.org
Web Site: www.lexingtonballet.org
Officers:
    President: Amber Renee Jones
    VP: Michael Potapov
    Treasurer: Allen Porter
    Assistant Treasurer: Mark Weimer
    Secretary: Scott Benton
    Assistant Secretary: Felipe Drucker
Management:
    School Director/Artistic Director: Luis Dominguez
Mission: Committed to offering a variety of performances in contemporary and classical dance.
Utilizes: Five Seasonal Concerts
Founded: 1974
Specialized Field: Ballet
Status: Professional, Nonprofit
Paid Staff: 05
Volunteer Staff: 20
Budget: $200,000-$500,000
Income Sources: Donations; Tuition; Ticket Revenue
Annual Attendance: 9,500
Organization Type: Performing; Resident

202
LOUISVILLE BALLET

315 E Main Street
Louisville, KY 40202-1215
Phone: 502-583-3150
Fax: 502-583-0006
e-mail: info@louisvilleballet.org
Web Site: www.louisvilleballet.org
Management:
    Artistic Director: Bruce Simpson
    Associate Artistic Director: Helen Starr
    School Director: Elizabeth Hartwell
    Director Operations: Michael Harris
Mission: To bring to the broadest audience high-quality professional dance.
Utilizes: Guest Artists; Guest Companies; Singers
Founded: 1952
Specialized Field: Ballet
Status: Professional; Nonprofit
Paid Staff: 120
Budget: $3,000,000
Income Sources: Dance USA; Southeast Regional Ballet Association; Individual; Corporate; Foundations
Affiliations: Dance USA; Southeast Regional Ballet Association
Organization Type: Performing; Touring; Resident; Educational; Sponsoring

Louisiana

203
BATON ROUGE BALLET THEATER

10745 Linkwood Court
PO Box 82288
Baton Rouge, LA 70884
Phone: 225-766-8379
Fax: 225-766-8230
e-mail: admin@batonrougeballet.org
Web Site: www.batonrougeballet.org
Management:
    Artistic Co-Director: Sharon Mathews

Artistic Co-Director: Molly Buchmann
    Director Development/Communications: Mary Boyle
Mission: To promote, aid and assist, in any manner whatsoever, the development, improvement and advancement of ballet by maintaining a performing dance company.
Utilizes: Choreographers; Dance Companies; Dancers; Guest Accompanists; Guest Artists; Guest Choreographers; Multimedia; Original Music Scores
Founded: 1963
Specialized Field: Dance
Status: Professional; Nonprofit
Paid Staff: 5
Budget: $200,000-$500,000
Income Sources: Ticket Sales; Grants; Donations
Performs At: Baton Rouge River Center; Performing Arts Theatre
Organization Type: Performing; Touring; Resident

204
DELTA FESTIVAL BALLET OF NEW ORLEANS

P.O. Box 7425
Metairie, LA 70010
Phone: 504-888-0931
Fax: 504-888-0941
e-mail: deltafestballet@aol.com
Web Site: deltafestivalballet.org
Management:
    Artistic Director: Joseph Giacobbe
    Artistic Diector: Maria Giacobbe
Mission: Advancing the art of dance through professional performance, education, cultural outreach and community involvement. Delta Festival Ballet is committed to arts-in-education.
Utilizes: Dancers
Founded: 1967
Specialized Field: Ballet
Status: Professional; Nonprofit
Paid Staff: 15
Budget: 300,000
Income Sources: National Association for Regional Ballet; Arts Counsil of New Orleans
Annual Attendance: 12,000
Organization Type: Performing; Touring; Resident; Educational

205
NEW ORLEANS BALLET ASSOCIATION

226 Carondelet Street
3rd Floor
New Orleans, LA 70130
Phone: 504-522-0996
Fax: 504-595-8454
e-mail: noba@nobadance.com
Web Site: www.nobadance.com
Officers:
    Chair: Michael Allday
    Secretary: Charlotte Bollinger
Management:
    Executive Director: Jenny R Hamilton
Mission: To cultivate understanding, appreciation, and enjoyment of dance through performance, education, and community service.
Utilizes: Artists-in-Residence; Choreographers; Collaborating Artists; Collaborations; Dance Companies; Dancers; Educators; Grant Writers; Guest Accompanists; Guest Artists; Guest Choreographers; Guest Instructors; Guest Soloists; High School Drama; Instructors; Local Artists; Lyricists; Original Music Scores; Theatre Companies
Founded: 1969
Specialized Field: Dance

Status: Nonprofit, Professional
Paid Staff: 6
Volunteer Staff: 37
Paid Artists: 125
Non-paid Artists: 1
Budget: $1,500,000
Income Sources: Ticket Sales; Contributions
Performs At: Mahalia Jackson Theater for the Performing Arts
Affiliations: Dance/USA; National Guild of Community Schools of the Arts; National Dance Education Organization
Annual Attendance: 25,000
Facility Category: Concert Hall
Type of Stage: Proscenium
Seating Capacity: 2,317
Organization Type: Sponsoring; Presenting; Educational

206
TULANE UNIVERSITY NEWCOMB DEPARTMENT OF MUSIC

102 Dixon Hall
New Orleans, LA 70118
Phone: 504-865-5267
Fax: 504-865-5270
e-mail: music@tulane.edu
Web Site: www.tulane.edu/~music
Officers:
   Chair: B Michael Howard
Management:
   Artistic Director: B Michael Howard
   Office Manager: Kathleen S Crago
Paid Staff: 8
Volunteer Staff: 5
Income Sources: University Budget; Donations; Ticket Sales
Performs At: Dixon Hall
Annual Attendance: 1,000
Type of Stage: Black Box; Proscenium
Seating Capacity: Proscenium theatre seats 1,000

207
SHREVEPORT METROPOLITAN BALLET

6654 St Vincent Avenue
Shreveport, LA 71106
Phone: 318-866-9916
Fax: 318-866-9927
e-mail: info@shreveportmetroballet.org
Web Site: www.shreveportmetroballet.org
Management:
   Artistic Director: Kendra Feazel Meiki
   Executive Director: Kate Pedrotty
Mission: To promote the art of classical ballet in Shreveport-Bossier City.
Utilizes: Five Seasonal Concerts
Founded: 1973
Specialized Field: Classical Ballet
Status: Semi-Professional, Nonprofit
Paid Staff: 2
Income Sources: Memberships; Grants; Fundraising; Corporate; Foundations; Ticket Sales
Performs At: The Shreveport Civic Theatre
Annual Attendance: 5,000-12,000
Organization Type: Performing; Resident; Educational

Maine

208
MAINE STATE BALLET

348 US Route One
Falmouth, ME 04105
Phone: 207-781-7672
Fax: 207-781-3663
e-mail: msballet@maine.rr.com
Web Site: www.mainestateballet.org
Officers:
   President: William McKinley
   Treasurer: Peter Hall
   Secretary: Julia Finn
Management:
   Artistic Director: Linda MacArthur Miele
   Associate Director: Gail Csoboth
   Conductor: Karla Kelley
Mission: Maine State Ballet's mission is to enrich the Maine community through education, outreach and expanded enjoyment of dance and the performing arts.
Founded: 1986
Specialized Field: Ballet
Status: Professional, Nonprofit
Paid Artists: 25

209
BATES DANCE FESTIVAL

Bates College
163 Wood Street
Lewiston, ME 04240-6016
Phone: 207-786-6381
Fax: 207-786-8282
e-mail: dancefest@bates.edu
Web Site: www.batesdancefestival.org
Management:
   Director: Laura Faure
   Associate Director/Registrar: Nancy Salmon
Mission: The Bates Dance Festival brings an artistically and ethnically diverse group of the best contemporary dance artists to Maine during the summer season to teach, perform, and create new work; encourages and inspires established and emerging artists by providing them with a creative, supportive environment in which to work; and actively engages people from the community and region in a full range of dance activities.
Founded: 1982
Specialized Field: Dance; Music
Status: Professional, Non-Profit
Paid Staff: 8
Volunteer Staff: 14
Paid Artists: 40
Budget: over $600,000
Income Sources: Public; Private; and Earned Income
Performs At: Schaeffer Theatre
Affiliations: Bates College
Annual Attendance: 4,000
Type of Stage: Proscenium
Stage Dimensions: 28'x35'
Seating Capacity: 300
Year Built: 1952
Organization Type: Resident; Educational; Sponsoring

210
BAY CHAMBER CONCERTS

18 Central Street
PO Box 599
Rockport, ME 04856
Phone: 207-236-2823
Fax: 207-230-0454
Toll-free: 888-707-2770
e-mail: info@baychamberconcerts.org
Web Site: www.baychamberconcerts.org
Officers:
   President: Carole Brand
   Treasurer: Laurence Novotney
   Secretary: Jacob Gerritsen
Management:
   Executive Director: Monica Kelly

Mission: To present a variety of music styles and educational programs to reach a diverse audience along the coast of Maine.
Utilizes: Commissioned Music; Dancers; Fine Artists; Grant Writers; Guest Accompanists; Guest Choreographers; Guest Directors; Guest Musical Directors; Guest Musicians; Lyricists; Multimedia; Original Music Scores; Resident Artists; Sign Language Translators; Singers; Special Technical Talent
Founded: 1960
Specialized Field: Music
Status: Non-Profit, Professional
Paid Staff: 9
Budget: $500,000
Performs At: Rockport Opera House
Facility Category: Opera House; Strom Auditorium
Type of Stage: Proscenium; Auditorium
Seating Capacity: 400; 800
Organization Type: Performing

Maryland

211
BALLET THEATRE OF MARYLAND

801 Chase Street
Annapolis, MD 21401
Phone: 410-263-2909
Fax: 410-626-1835
e-mail: info@balletmaryland.org
Web Site: www.balletmaryland.org
Officers:
   Chairman: Larry Earle
   First Vice Chairman: Debbie Mayer
   Second VP: Andy Moser
   Secretary: Mary Ann Kingsley
Management:
   Artistic Director: Dianna Cuatto
   Office Manager/Admin Assistant: Charlotte McNutt
Mission: To provide Maryland with a fully profesional ballet company and training academy that meets the aesthetic and recreational needs of Maryland through expressive movement. To promote interest in and enjoyment of the dance arts in the state of Maryland by providing dancers an opportunity to study, perform and grow artistically.
Utilizes: Actors; Collaborating Artists; Dancers; Five Seasonal Concerts; Resident Professionals
Founded: 1978
Specialized Field: Ballet
Status: Professional; Nonprofit
Paid Staff: 03
Volunteer Staff: 100
Paid Artists: 16
Non-paid Artists: 15
Budget: $200,000-$500,000
Annual Attendance: 10,000
Organization Type: Touring; Resident

212
DOUG HAMBY DANCE

University of Maryland
Department of Dance UMBC
1000 Hilltop Circle
Baltimore, MD 21250
Phone: 410-455-2950
e-mail: hamby@umbc.edu
Web Site: www.umbc.edu
Management:
   Artistic Director: Doug Hamby
Specialized Field: Ballet; Modern
Status: Non-Profit, Professional
Budget: $10,000-$25,000

Income Sources: Grants; Ticket Sales; Private Donations
Annual Attendance: 1,000

213
MARYLAND BALLET THEATRE
PO Box 4783
Crofton, MD 21114
Phone: 410-428-8099
e-mail: arleene@marylandballettheatre.org
Web Site: marylandballettheatre.org
Officers:
   Founder: Arleene Monahan
Management:
   Artistic Director: Arleene Monahan
Mission: To train and inspire students to further develop their performing capabilities through professionally oriented training.
Founded: 1989
Specialized Field: Ballet; Russian Classical

214
FROSTBURG STATE UNIVERSITY DANCE COMPANY
Frostburg State University
Department of Theatre and Dance
101 Braddock Road
Frostburg, MD 21532-2303
Phone: 301-687-4145
Fax: 301-687-7961
e-mail: myost@frostburg.edu
Web Site: www.frostburg.edu
Officers:
   Chair, Dept. of Theatre and Dance: Mairzy Yost-Rushton
Mission: To prepare students for the theatre profession through pre-professional training and production experience.
Utilizes: Actors; AEA Actors; Artists-in-Residence; Choreographers; Dancers; Designers; Educators; Equity Actors; Five Seasonal Concerts; Grant Writers; Guest Artists; Guest Conductors; Guest Ensembles; Guest Lecturers; Guest Musical Directors; Guest Soloists; Guest Speakers; Guest Teachers; Instructors; Multi Collaborations; Music; Paid Performers; Performance Artists; Sign Language Translators
Specialized Field: Modern; Ballet; Jazz; Tap; Designing; Directing; Playwriting; Singing; Musical Theatre; Improv; Shakespeare; Stage Combat; Movement & Speech;Pilates
Paid Staff: 20
Performs At: Performing Arts Center
Affiliations: SAFD; AEA; SAG
Facility Category: Recital Hall, Studio Theatre, Large Drama Theatre

215
NATIONAL TAP ENSEMBLE
PO Box 4102
Hagerstown, MD 21741-2439
Phone: 301-790-1180
Fax: 270-964-1476
Toll-free: 800-683-8277
e-mail: pr1@usatap.org
Web Site: www.usatap.org
Management:
   Public Relations Director: Miles Johnson
Mission: Over 2,000 programs performed worldwide.
Founded: 1989
Specialized Field: Tap; Jazz; American Vernacular Dance
Paid Staff: 3
Paid Artists: 12
Budget: $200,000-$500,000

Annual Attendance: 250,000

216
METROPOLITAN BALLET THEATRE AND ACADEMY
10076 Darnestown Road
Suite 202
Rockville, MD 20850
Phone: 301-762-1757
Fax: 301-762-1757
e-mail: contact@metropolitanballettheatre.com
Web Site: www.metropolitanballettheatre.com
Officers:
   President: Paul Hlavinka
   Vice President: Brenda Lipowsky
Management:
   Director: Suzanne Erlon
   Administrator: Gail Minning
   Director Of Development: Anita Anderson
   Artistic Advisor: Dennis Price
Mission: Teaching dancers to be the best they can be.
Founded: 1989
Specialized Field: Ballet; Jazz
Status: Nonprofit; Professional
Paid Staff: 3
Volunteer Staff: 150
Budget: 350,000
Income Sources: Donation; Grants; Tuition; Ticket Revenue; Fundraisers
Performs At: Robert E. Parilla Performing Arts Center
Annual Attendance: 5,500

217
SACRED DANCE GUILD
550M Ritchie Highway
#271
Severna Park, MD 21146
Phone: 877-422-8678
e-mail: info@sacreddanceguild.org
Web Site: www.sacreddanceguild.org
Officers:
   President: Karen Josephson
   Vice President: P Merle Wade
   Recording Secretary: Carolynn Hine-Johnson
Management:
   Executive Director: Karen Josephson
   Public Relations: Linda Telesco
Founded: 1958
Specialized Field: Ballet; Jazz; Tap; Hip Hop; Modern; Indigenous
Status: Non-Profit; Professional
Affiliations: American Dance Guild; IACD; ILDA/NPM; National Dance Association; American Alliance for Health
Annual Attendance: 150-300

218
ARKA BALLET
309 Philadelphia Avenue
Takoma Park, MD 20912
Phone: 301-587-6225
Fax: 301-587-6225
Web Site: www.arkaballet.org
Officers:
   President: Roudolf Kharatian
Management:
   Artistic Director: Roudolf Kharatian
   Executive Director: Tania J Chichmanian
Mission: ARKA Ballet's mission is to bring high level dance to diverse audiences and to nurture, develop and showcase international level dance talent through inspiring and challenging choreography.
Founded: 1999
Specialized Field: Ballet

Status: Non-Profit, Professional
Volunteer Staff: 5
Income Sources: Donations; Ticket Sales;
Performs At: The Kennedy Center

219
LIZ LERMAN DANCE EXCHANGE
7117 Maple Avenue
Takoma Park, MD 20912
Phone: 301-270-6700
Fax: 301-270-2626
e-mail: mail@danceexchange.org
Web Site: www.danceexchange.org
Officers:
   Chair: Ellen Bogage
   Chair Emeritus: Elliot Rosen
Management:
   Founding Artistic Director: Liz Lerman
   Managing Director: Jane Hirshberg
Mission: A professional company of dance artists that creates, performs, teaches and engages people in making art. They provide groundbreaking new dance works performed by a cross-generational company on major stages both in the U.S and internationally.
Utilizes: Five Seasonal Concerts; Singers
Founded: 1976
Specialized Field: Contemporary Dance
Status: Professional, Nonprofit
Paid Staff: 8
Volunteer Staff: 4
Paid Artists: 7
Non-paid Artists: 6
Budget: $1.3 Million
Income Sources: Corporate; Foundations; Grants; Private
Organization Type: Performing; Touring; Resident; Educational

220
NATIONAL BALLET COMPANY
PO Box 620
Tracy's Landing, MD 20779
Phone: 301-218-9822
Fax: 240-334-4894
e-mail: balletnbcoffice@aol.com
Web Site: www.nationalballet.com
Officers:
   Founder: Helen Moore
Management:
   Director: Pamela Moore
   Assistant Director: Bat Erdene Udval
Mission: Performing a wide range of ballets from the full length classics to contemporary works. There is always something that appeals to the individual audience member that brings artistic satisfaction.
Founded: 1948
Specialized Field: Ballet

Massachusetts

221
COMMONWEALTH BALLET COMPANY
PO Box 892
Acton, MA 01720-0892
Phone: 978-263-6533
e-mail: chip.morris@commonwealthballet.org
Web Site: www.commonwealthballet.org
Officers:
   Founder: Chip Morris
   Founder: Kathryn Anderson
   Chair/President: Susan Moncrieff
Management:
   Artistic Director: Chip Morris

Stage Manager: Tom Sikina
Mission: The purpose of the Commonwealth Ballet Company (CBC) is to develop, foster, and promote the performance and appreciation of classical and contemporary ballet among the citizens of Massachusetts. Specifically, the company's main objectives are to: maintain strong ties with the communities it serves, provide a substantial educational opportunity for young dancers and demonstrate the highest level of artistic quality.
Founded: 1992
Specialized Field: Classical Ballet; Contemporary Ballet
Status: Nonprofit
Income Sources: Acton-Boxborough Local Cultural Council; Corporate; Individual
Season: September-May

222
AMHERST BALLET THEATRE COMPANY
29 Strong Street
Amherst, MA 01002
Phone: 413-549-1555
e-mail: info@amherstballet.org
Web Site: www.amherstballet.org
Officers:
Founder: Therese Brady Donohue
President: Tom Dumm
Vice President: Robin Diamond
Treasurer: Delcie Bean
Secretary: Mitch G Aslin
Management:
Artistic Director: Catherine Fair
Mission: A non-profit organization run by a volunteer Board of Directors and is dedicated to dance education and professional training. Through nurturing and inspiring local young dancers, we help them strive toward an understanding of artistic excellence, discipline, leadership and a lifelong appreciation of dance.
Utilizes: Five Seasonal Concerts
Founded: 1971
Specialized Field: Ballet; Creative Movement; Jazz; Modern
Status: Nonprofit
Income Sources: Tuition; Grants; Donations

223
BOSTON BALLET
19 Clarendon Street
Boston, MA 02116-6100
Phone: 617-695-6950
Fax: 617-695-6995
Toll-free: 800-447-7400
e-mail: pr@bostonballet.com
Web Site: www.bostonballet.org
Officers:
Chief Executive Officer: Bruce Bernier
Management:
Artistic Director: Mikko Nissien
Music Director/Principal Conductor: Jonathan McPhee
Resident Choreographer: Jorma Elo
Production Stage Manager: Craig Margolis
Mission: Boston Ballet's mission is to bring new levels of excellence to ballet both on and offstage. We will accomplish this through a process that is inclusive in scope, educational and creative.
Founded: 1963
Specialized Field: Ballet
Status: Professional, Nonprofit
Income Sources: Corporate; Foundations; Grants; Donations
Season: October-May

Performs At: Boston Opera House; Wang Theatre

224
JEANNETTE NEILL DANCE STUDIO
261 Friend Street
5th Floor
Boston, MA 02114
Phone: 617-523-1355
Fax: 617-557-4404
e-mail: info@jndance.com
Web Site: www.jndance.com
Officers:
Founder: Jeannette Neill
Management:
Artistic Director: Jeannette Neill
Mission: The Jeannette Neill Dance Studio has provided personalized and comprehensive dance training to both the professional and recreational adult dancer.
Founded: 1979
Specialized Field: Hip Hop; Jazz; Theatre Dance
Paid Staff: 3
Volunteer Staff: 10
Performs At: Tsai Performance Center
Type of Stage: Proscenium
Stage Dimensions: 41 « W x 17 9« H

225
INCA SON: MUSIC AND DANCE OF THE ANDES
Cambridge, MA 02238-1899
Mailing Address: PO Box 381899
Phone: 781-284-4622
Fax: 781-284-9365
e-mail: CIncaSonV@aol.com
Web Site: www.incason.com
Management:
Founder/Creative Director: Cesar Villalobos
Manager: Marianne Ruggiero
Mission: To introduce and educate peoples to the riches of Andean Culture.
Founded: 1988
Specialized Field: Andean Music and Dance
Status: Professional
Performs At: Festivals; Museums; University; Private Parties; Theatre; Schools
Annual Attendance: 1,000,000

226
JOSE MATEO BALLET THEATRE
400 Harvard Street
Cambridge, MA 02138
Phone: 617-354-7467
Fax: 617-354-7856
Web Site: www.ballettheatre.org
Officers:
Founder: Jose Mateo
Chair: Richard P Shea
Management:
Artistic Director/Choreographer: Jose Mateo
Managing Director: Scott Fraser
Mission: Our mission is to create new ballets of excellence that are stimulating and culturally relevant to diverse audiences and reposition the role of dance in our culture and expand its purpose in the education of youth and enrichment of community locally and beyond.
Founded: 1986
Specialized Field: Ballet
Status: Professional, Nonprofit
Income Sources: Corporate; Foundations, Gifts; Grants; Individuals
Season: October-December
Performs At: The Sanctuary Theatre
Annual Attendance: 10,000

227
SNAPPY DANCE THEATER
PO Box 400075
Cambridge, MA 02140
Phone: 617-718-2497
Fax: 775-248-4980
e-mail: info@snappydance.com
Web Site: www.snappydance.com
Officers:
President: Ellen Grossman
Treasurer: Jerry Boos
Management:
Artistic Director: Martha Mason
General Manager: Philippe Naulot
Mission: The group is dedicated to creating compelling performances which work the edge of oxymoron-emotions and images which contradict themselves in art, as in real life.
Founded: 1997
Specialized Field: Contemporary; Modern
Status: Nonprofit

228
DANCE PRISM
33 Bradford Street
Concord, MA 01742
Mailing Address: 23 Hastings Road, Boston, MA 02421-6806
Phone: 978-371-1038
e-mail: dance_prism@verizon.net
Web Site: www.danceprism.com
Management:
Artistic Director: Mary Demaso
Mission: A Boston area ballet company dedicated to making affordable professional ballet available to the secondary communities of New England.
Founded: 1982
Specialized Field: Ballet
Season: November-December
Performs At: Bristol Community College; Performing Arts Center; Mechanics Hall; The Collins Center

229
ALBANY BERKSHIRE BALLET
116 Fenn Street
Pittsfield, MA 01201
Phone: 413-442-1307
Toll-free: 866-476-6964
e-mail: abballet@rnetworx.com
Web Site: www.berkshireballet.org
Officers:
Founder: Madeline Cantarella Culpo
President: Victile Donahue
Treasurer: Janine Maschino
Secretary: Claire Dalton
Management:
Artistic Director: Madeline Cantarella Culpo
Stage Manager: Laura Claus
Mission: The Albany Berkshire Ballet is nationally recognized for its versatility in performing both classical and contemporary dance works with excellence.
Founded: 1960
Specialized Field: Classical; Contemporary

230
ART OF BLACK DANCE AND MUSIC
32 Cameron Avenue
Somerville, MA 02144
Phone: 617-666-1859
Fax: 617-666-1859
e-mail: Deamabattle@abdm.net
Web Site: www.abdm.net
Officers:

Founder: DeAma Battle
Management:
 Artistic/Executive Director: DeAma Battle
Mission: Our mission is to bridge cultural gaps by teaching the common history of humankind through African-rooted dance, music and folklore, and to entertain audiences of all ages with culturally diverse expressions of African-American heritage.
Utilizes: Five Seasonal Concerts; Singers
Founded: 1975
Specialized Field: Folk Dance
Paid Staff: 1
Volunteer Staff: 2
Paid Artists: 7
Non-paid Artists: 3
Performs At: Veterans War Memorial Auditorium
Annual Attendance: 30,000 - 50,000

Michigan

231
ANN ARBOR DANCE WORKS
University of Michigan Dance Department
3501 Dance Building
Ann Arbor, MI 48109-2217
Phone: 734-763-5460
e-mail: cmicklez@umich.edu
Web Site: www.music.umich.edu
Officers:
 Chair: Angela Kane
Management:
 Dance Administrator: Carla Mickler-Konz
Mission: Our mission is to bridge dance practice and scholarship and to foster interdisciplinary inquiry. As an internationally renowned faculty, we bring a challenging range of perspectives to our teaching and research and we continually reexamine our curriculum in order to prepare both young and mature dancers for careers in an ever-evolving field.
Utilizes: Choreographers; Collaborating Artists; Collaborations; Commissioned Music; Dance Companies; Dancers; Designers; Filmmakers; Five Seasonal Concerts; Grant Writers; Guest Accompanists; Guest Artists; Guest Choreographers; Guest Companies; Guest Conductors; Guest Directors; Guest Musical Directors; Guest Musicians; Instructors; Lyricists; Multi Collaborations; Multimedia; Organization Contracts; Touring Companies
Founded: 1984
Specialized Field: Modern
Status: Professional, Nonprofit
Paid Artists: 9
Non-paid Artists: 10
Budget: $20,000
Income Sources: Corporate; Endowments; Individal; Matching Gifts, Planned Giving
Performs At: Power Center for the Performing Arts
Affiliations: University of Michigan
Annual Attendance: 800
Type of Stage: Proscenium
Stage Dimensions: 55'3-3/4 x 28'
Orchestra Pit: y
Seating Capacity: 1368
Resident Groups: Dance Company of the University of Michigan.

232
GRAND RAPIDS BALLET COMPANY
Meijer-Royce Center for Dance
341 Ellsworth
Grand Rapids, MI 49503

Phone: 616-454-4771
Fax: 616-454-0672
e-mail: school@grballet.com
Web Site: www.grballet.com
Management:
 Artistic Director/Choreographer: Gordon Peirce Schmidt
 Associate Artistic Director: Laura Schwenk-Berman
Mission: Original programming, innovative choreography, and a commitment to excellence are hallmarks of the Grand Rapids Ballet Company. With artists invested in the community and a community that supports the arts, the Grand Rapids Ballet Company has created a flourishing arts center for all of Michigan and continues to provide the highest level of excellence in dance theatre and education for all individuals.
Utilizes: Choreographers; Collaborations; Commissioned Music; Dancers; Educators; Grant Writers; Guest Accompanists; Guest Artists; Guest Composers; Guest Conductors; Guest Musical Directors; Guest Musicians; High School Drama; Local Unknown Artists; Lyricists; Multimedia; Resident Professionals; Sign Language Translators
Founded: 1971
Specialized Field: Ballet
Status: Professional, Nonprofit
Paid Artists: 16
Budget: $1-2.5 million
Income Sources: Corporate; Endowment; Individual
Season: October-May
Performs At: DeVos Performance Hall; Peter Martin Wege Theatre
Seating Capacity: 300

233
INTERLOCHEN CENTER FOR THE ARTS
PO Box 199
Interlochen, MI 49643-0199
Phone: 231-276-7200
Fax: 231-276-7464
Toll-free: 800-681-5912
e-mail: admission@interlochen.org
Web Site: www.intelochen.org
Officers:
 Chair: Steve Hayden
 President: Jeffrey Kimpton
Management:
 Dance Director: Mark Borchelt
Mission: Interlochen Center for the Arts engages and inspires people worldwide through excellence in educational, artistic and cultural programs, enhancing the quality of life through the universal language of the arts.
Founded: 1928
Specialized Field: Ballet; Modern
Status: Nonprofit
Income Sources: Corporate; Employer Match; Individual
Season: September-May
Performs At: Corson Auditorium; Dendrinos Chapel; Harvey Theatre; Kresge Auditorium
Annual Attendance: 5,000+
Type of Stage: Proscenium, Amphitheater
Seating Capacity: 952, 200, 4,000, 200

234
KALAMAZOO BALLET COMPANY
431 E South Street
Kalamazoo, MI 49007
Phone: 269-343-3027
Fax: 269-342-8788
Web Site: www.kalamazoomi.com
Officers:

Founder: Therese Bullard
Management:
 Artistic Director: Therese Bullard
Mission: The company's artistic philosophy focuses on excellence in professional performance together with fine arts education, coupled with a commitment to developing and maintaining a varied repertoire consisting of traditional (including Highland), classical and innovative dance works.
Utilizes: Five Seasonal Concerts; Guest Artists; Singers
Founded: 1969
Specialized Field: Ballet; Classical; Traditional Ballet
Income Sources: Corporate; Fundraisers; Grants; Individuals
Performs At: Kalamazoo Civic Theatre; Miller Auditorium
Affiliations: Mid-States Regional Dance America Association
Organization Type: Performing; Touring; Educational

235
WELLSPRING/CORI TERRY & DANCERS
359 S Kalamazoo Mall
Suite 204
Kalamazoo, MI 49007
Phone: 269-342-4354
Fax: 269-342-4245
e-mail: wellspring@wellspringdance.org
Web Site: www.wellspringdance.org
Officers:
 President: Judah Gesmundo
 Treasurer: Sarah Mallo-Hoff
 Secretary: Barbara Harkins
 VP: Matthew Downey
Management:
 Artistic Director: Cori Terry
 Executive Director: Maria Suszynski
Mission: Exists to offer a unique and authentic voice in modern dance, which serves to move, challenge and inspire the community.
Utilizes: Actors; Arrangers; Collaborating Artists; Collaborations; Dance Companies; Dancers; Guest Accompanists; Guest Artists; Guest Lecturers; Guest Musical Directors; Guest Musicians; Instructors; Lyricists; Resident Professionals; Soloists; Touring Companies; Visual Arts
Founded: 1981
Specialized Field: Modern Dance
Status: Professional
Paid Staff: 9
Volunteer Staff: 13
Income Sources: Grants, Donations, Tickets Sales, Rentals
Performs At: Dance/Music
Annual Attendance: 6,000
Facility Category: Stadium Seating
Type of Stage: Sprung Wood
Stage Dimensions: 36' x 26'
Seating Capacity: 140
Year Built: 2000

236
EISENHOWER DANCE ENSEMBLE
1541 W Hamlin Road
Rochester Hills, MI 48309
Phone: 248-852-5850
Web Site: www.ededance.org
Officers:
 Founder: Laurie Eisenhower
Management:
 Artistic Director: Laurie Eisenhower
 Associate Artistic Director: Stephanie Pizzo
 Executive Director: Maury Okun

Mission: To educate and inform the public about the art of dance through concert performances, educational residencies and workshops.
Founded: 1991
Specialized Field: Contemporary Dance
Paid Staff: 5
Volunteer Staff: 15
Paid Artists: 9
Non-paid Artists: 2

Minnesota

237
MINNESOTA BALLET

301 W First Street
Suite 800
Duluth, MN 55802-1613
Phone: 218-529-3742
Fax: 218-529-3744
e-mail: info@minnesotaballet.org
Web Site: www.minnesotaballet.org
Management:
   Artistic Director: Robert Gardner
   Production/Tour Manager: Kenneth Pogin
Mission: To maintain a high-quality school of ballet and a company of professional dancers; to present a regular series of performances.
Utilizes: Choreographers; Dance Companies; Dancers; Designers; Five Seasonal Concerts; Guest Accompanists; Guest Artists; Guest Ensembles; Guest Musical Directors; High School Drama; Instructors; Local Artists; Multimedia; Original Music Scores; Resident Artists; Resident Professionals; Soloists; Theatre Companies
Founded: 1965
Specialized Field: Ballet; Jazz; Tap; Modern
Status: Professional, Nonprofit
Paid Staff: 4
Volunteer Staff: 30
Paid Artists: 12
Budget: $500,000-$600,000
Income Sources: Foundations; Corporate; Individual
Performs At: Duluth Entertainment & Convention Center
Type of Stage: Proscenium
Stage Dimensions: 60'x45'
Seating Capacity: 2,400
Organization Type: Performing; Touring; Resident; Educational; Sponsoring

238
HAUSER DANCE COMPANY

1940 Hennepin Avenue
Minneapolis, MN 55403
Phone: 612-871-9077
Fax: 612-871-9077
e-mail: nhdc@tcinternet.net
Web Site: www.mnartists.org/hauser_dance2
Management:
   Artistic Director/Choreographer: Heidi Hauser
   Jasmin, nhdc@tcinternet.net
Mission: The mission of Houser Dance is to promote and sustain the living language of music and dance. Our mission is accomplished by performing and teaching the constantly evolving Houser aesthetics and to provide opportunities for people of all ages and abilities to participate in and appreciate the art form. We are commited to presenting the highest quality of music dance performance and educational programming for the broadest possible audience
Utilizes: Choreographers; Collaborating Artists; Commissioned Composers; Composers; Dance Companies; Dancers; Designers; Educators; Grant

Writers; Guest Ensembles; Guest Speakers; High School Drama; Original Music Scores; Resident Artists; Selected Students
Founded: 1961
Specialized Field: Modern
Status: Professional, Nonprofit
Paid Staff: 2
Volunteer Staff: 20
Paid Artists: 6
Non-paid Artists: 15
Budget: $55,000
Income Sources: Foundations; Corporations; Individuals
Performs At: Small Theatre
Annual Attendance: 1,000
Facility Category: Dance studio; Small black box theater
Stage Dimensions: 28'x40'
Seating Capacity: 100
Year Built: 1925
Year Remodeled: 1989
Organization Type: Performing; Touring; Educational; Sponsoring

239
JAMES SEWELL BALLET

528 Hennepin Avenue
Suite 215
Minneapolis, MN 55403-1810
Phone: 612-672-0480
e-mail: info@jsballet.org
Web Site: www.jsballet.org
Officers:
   Co-Founder: James Sewell
   Co-Founder: Sally Rousse
Management:
   Artistic Director/Choreographer: James Sewell
   Artistic Associate: Penelope Freeh
   Lighting Designer/Production Mgr: Kevin A Jones
   Executive Director: George Sutton
Mission: James Sewell Ballet's mission is to create and perform works that connect artists with audiences and to advance contemporary ballet.
Founded: 1990
Specialized Field: Ballet

240
MINNESOTA DANCE THEATRE & DANCE INSTITUTE

528 Hennepin Avenue
6th Floor
Minneapolis, MN 55403
Phone: 612-338-0627
Fax: 612-338-5160
e-mail: info@mndance.org
Web Site: www.mndance.org
Officers:
   Executive Director: Francis McGovern
Management:
   Artistic Director: Lise Houlton
   School Director: Jeffrey Hawkinson
   Artistic Associate: Abdo Sayegh
   Executive Director: Morrie Hartman
Mission: Minnesota Dance Theatre & the Dance Institute is renowned as one of Minnesota's cultural treasures with an eclectic international voice performing dance.
Utilizes: Singers
Founded: 1962
Specialized Field: Theatrical Dance; Traditional Dance; Contemporary Dance
Status: Professional, Nonprofit
Paid Staff: 140
Volunteer Staff: 150

Paid Artists: 35
Budget: $1,000,000
Income Sources: Ticket Revenue; Donations; State Funding; Grants
Performs At: State Theatre; Illusion Theater; Fitzgerald Theater
Annual Attendance: 23,000
Organization Type: Performing; Touring; Resident; Educational

241
NORTHROP DANCE SEASON

Department of Concerts and Lectures
84 Church Street SE
Minneapolis, MN 55455
Phone: 612-625-6600
Fax: 612-626-1750
Web Site: www.1.umn.edu
Management:
   Artistic Director: Ben Johnson
   Event Manager: Eileen May
   Stage Manager: Mike Damman
   Stage Manager: Justin Burke
Mission: To offer an annual season featuring six to eight of the finest national and international dance companies.
Utilizes: Students
Founded: 1928
Specialized Field: Jazz
Status: Professional, Nonprofit
Paid Staff: 13
Volunteer Staff: 20
Budget: $4,000,000
Income Sources: Association of Performing Arts Presenters; International Society of Performing Arts Administrators
Performs At: Northrop Memorial Auditorium
Annual Attendance: 235,560
Organization Type: Sponsoring

242
STUART PIMSLER DANCE & THEATER

1937 Glenwood Parkway
Minneapolis, MN 55422
Phone: 763-521-7738
e-mail: spdanth@aol.com
Web Site: www.stuartpimsler.com
Management:
   Co-Artistic Director: Stuart Pimsler
   Co-Artistic Director: Suzanne Costello
Mission: Stuart Pimsler Dance and Theater's work stands apart in the field of contemporary performance for its vast emotional range, intellectual provocations and stunning visual environments.
Utilizes: Guest Companies; Singers
Founded: 1978
Specialized Field: Modern
Status: Professional
Budget: $200,000-$500,000
Income Sources: Ohio Dance; Association for Performing Arts Presenters; Alliance for Dance & Movement Arts
Organization Type: Performing

243
ZENON DANCE COMPANY AND SCHOOL

528 Hennepin Avenue
Suite 400
Minneapolis, MN 55403
Phone: 612-338-1101
Fax: 612-338-2479
e-mail: info@zenondance.org
Web Site: www.zenondance.org
Management:

Artistic Director: Linda Andrews
Managing Director: Katherine Dunbar
Mission: Our mission is to sustain an artistically excellent, professional dance company in the Twin Cities by commissioning the works of emerging and locally, nationally and internationally recognized modern and jazz choreographers and to present this work to diverse communities, including those with disabilities.
Utilizes: Commissioned Composers; Commissioned Music; Dance Companies; Dancers; Five Seasonal Concerts; Guest Artists; Guest Companies; High School Drama; Local Artists; Multimedia; Original Music Scores; Resident Artists; Selected Students
Founded: 1983
Specialized Field: Modern; Jazz
Status: Professional, Nonprofit
Paid Staff: 5
Volunteer Staff: 30
Paid Artists: 8
Facility Category: 2 Dance Studios
Stage Dimensions: 54'x46'; 56'x27'
Rental Contact: Managing Director Ann Willemssen
Organization Type: Performing; Touring; Resident; Educational

244
ETHNIC DANCE THEATRE
4000 Winnetka Avenue N
New Hope, MN 55427
Phone: 763-545-1333
e-mail: info@ethnicdancetheatre.com
Web Site: www.ethnicdancetheatre.com
Officers:
Founder: Donald LaCourse
Chair: Leila Poullada
Chief Financial Officer: Lynn Petros-Winn
Secretary: Jeanne Schultz
Management:
Artistic Director: Donald LaCourse
Mission: Our mission is to foster understanding and awareness of world cultures through the re-creation and presentation of traditional ethnic dance and music.
Founded: 1974
Specialized Field: Ethnic Dance
Status: Professional, Nonprofit
Budget: 154,000
Income Sources: Grants; Federal; Government; Corporation; Individual; Ticket Sales
Performs At: Concordia University
Annual Attendance: 40,000
Organization Type: Performing; Touring; Resident; Educational

Mississippi

245
BALLET MISSISSIPPI
PO Box 1787
Jackson, MS 39215-1787
Phone: 601-960-1560
Fax: 601-960-2135
e-mail: keary@balletms.com
Web Site: www.balletms.com
Management:
Artistic Director: David Keary
Mission: Ballet Mississipi has continued the tradition begun by the founders, by reestablishing the Ballet Mississippi School which focuses on classical technique, discipline and performance opportunities.
Utilizes: Five Seasonal Concerts; Singers
Founded: 1983
Specialized Field: Classical
Status: Professional, Nonprofit

Budget: $100,000-$200,000
Organization Type: Performing; Touring; Resident; Educational

Missouri

246
ALEXANDRA BALLET
68 E Four Seasons Center
Chesterfield, MO 63017
Phone: 314-469-6222
Fax: 314-469-6222
e-mail: alexandraballet@msn.com
Web Site: www.alexandraballet.com
Officers:
President: Peter Karutz
Vice President: Donnagail Carr
Secretary: Sally Duncan
Treasurer: Juliet Chayat
Management:
Artistic Director: Alexandra Zaharias
Company Administrator: CiCi Houston
Marketing/Communications: Lisa Howe
Mission: Repertoire ranges from classic to contemporary. Performance showcases original works through the restaging of classics by locally and internationally known choreographers and the collaboration of professional guest artists.
Utilizes: Choreographers; Collaborations; Dancers; Educators; Guest Artists
Founded: 1984
Specialized Field: Ballet
Status: Non-Profit; Semi-Professional
Paid Staff: 3
Volunteer Staff: 56
Income Sources: Foundations; Fundraising; Corporate; Missouri Arts Council; Regional Arts Commission-St. Louis; Arts & Education Council of Greater St. Louis
Performs At: Touhill Performing Arts Center; Purser Center; Sheldon Concert Hall, Edison Theatre
Affiliations: Regional Dance America
Annual Attendance: 8,000
Resident Groups: Dance

247
SAINT LOUIS BALLET
218 THF Boulevard
Chesterfield, MO 63005
Phone: 636-537-1998
e-mail: info@stlouisballet.org
Web Site: www.stlouisballet.org
Officers:
Co-Chairperson: Ann Cortinovis
Co-Chairperson: David Weller PhD
Treasurer: William J Florent
Secretary: Linda Crist
Management:
Artistic/Executive Director: Gen Horiuchi
Ballet Mistress: Heather Iler
Mission: Dedicated to bringing audiences quality performances through a diverse repertoire that is both classical and contemporary.
Specialized Field: Classical; Contemporary
Status: Professional, Nonprofit

248
BALLET NORTH
6308 N Prospect Avenue
Gladstone, MO 64119-1825
Phone: 816-454-4859
Web Site: www.balletnorth.com
Officers:

Co-Founder: Laura Luzicka Reinschmidt
Co-Founder: Matthew Reinschmidt
Management:
Artistic Director: Laura Luzicka Reinschmidt
Mission: Perform rarely seen full-length classical ballets and modern works in theatre.
Founded: 1986
Specialized Field: Classical
Status: Nonprofit
Paid Staff: 4
Volunteer Staff: 12
Paid Artists: 8
Non-paid Artists: 20
Budget: $55,000
Income Sources: Performance revenue; Fund raisers; Grants
Affiliations: Independent
Facility Category: Professional theater

249
KANSAS CITY BALLET
1616 Broadway Street
Kansas City, MO 64108-1208
Phone: 816-931-2232
Fax: 816-931-1172
Toll-free: 888-968-2538
e-mail: info@kcballet.org
Web Site: www.kcballet.org
Management:
Artistic Director: William Whitener
Ballet Master: James Jordan
Ballet Mistress: Karen Brown
Production Manager: Amy Taylor
Stage Manager: Heather O'Mara
Executive Director: Jeffrey J Bentley
Mission: To establish Kansas City Ballet as an indispensable asset of the Kansas City community through exceptional performances, excellence in dance training and community education for all ages.
Utilizes: Sign Language Translators; Students
Founded: 1957
Specialized Field: Ballet
Status: Professional
Paid Artists: 25
Budget: $5,000,000
Performs At: Lyric and Midland Theatre
Affiliations: MAC, National Endowment for the Arts
Annual Attendance: 48,000

250
DANCE SAINT LOUIS
3547 Olive Street
Suite 301
Saint Louis, MO 63103
Phone: 314-534-5000
Fax: 314-534-5001
e-mail: bmacrobie@dancestlouis.org
Web Site: www.dancestlouis.org
Officers:
Founder: Annelise Mertz
Chairman: Richard Kluesner
President: Tom Voss
Management:
Artistic/Executive Director: Michael Uthoff
Mission: Dance Saint Louis' mission is to provide the Saint Louis region with the world's best dance and to develop an appreciation of dance as an art form. Dance Saint Louis fulfills this mission through dance presentation, creation and education outreach.
Utilizes: Singers
Founded: 1966
Specialized Field: Classical Ballet; Contemporary Ballet; Modern; Ethnic Dance; Ballroom; Tap; Jazz; Hip Hop

Status: Nonprofit
Income Sources: Dance USA; Individual; Corporate
Performs At: Kiel Opera House; Edison Theatre; Washington University
Organization Type: Resident; Educational; Sponsoring

251
SPRINGFIELD BALLET
420 S Sixth Street
Springfield, MO 62701
Phone: 217-544-1967
Fax: 217-544-1968
e-mail: info@springfieldballetco.org
Web Site: www.springfieldballetco.org
Management:
  Artistic Director: Julie Dunn
  Ballet Mistress: Gina DeCroix
Mission: Dance is the language of movement that gives voice to the human spirit. The Springfield Ballet Company uses the beauty, energy and diversity of dance to speak to the community. It is this common language that encourages freedom of expression, bridges generations and cultures and adds to the richness of life in central Illinois.
Utilizes: Choreographers; Collaborations; Dance Companies; Dancers; Designers; Guest Artists; Guest Choreographers; Guest Companies; Guest Conductors; Guest Writers; High School Drama; Local Artists; Resident Professionals; Soloists
Founded: 1975
Specialized Field: Classical; Contemporary; Jazz; Modern; Tap; Theatre Dance
Status: Nonprofit
Paid Staff: 3
Paid Artists: 30

Montana

252
MONTANA BALLET COMPANY
1195 Stoneridge Drive
Suite 4
Bozeman, MT 59718
Phone: 406-582-8702
Fax: 406-586-9659
e-mail: mbcmanager@mindspring.com
Web Site: www.montanaballet.com
Officers:
  Founder: Ann Bates
Management:
  Artistic Director: Ann Bates
  Choreographer: Amy Lynn Stoddart
Mission: The mission of Montana Ballet Company has been to produce top quality dance performances from a variety of cultural and ethnic traditions and to provide outstanding education outreach opportunities to the underserved populations.
Utilizes: Collaborating Artists; Composers; Dance Companies; Dancers; Five Seasonal Concerts; Guest Accompanists; Guest Choreographers; Guest Musical Directors; Guest Musicians; Guest Speakers; Guest Writers; Organization Contracts; Theatre Companies
Founded: 1984
Specialized Field: Ballet
Status: Pre-Professional, Nonprofit
Paid Staff: 3
Volunteer Staff: 75
Budget: $210,000
Income Sources: Grants; Donations; Ticket Sales
Performs At: Willson Auditorium
Annual Attendance: 7,000-10,000
Facility Category: School
Stage Dimensions: 32'x 26'

Seating Capacity: 1,100
Organization Type: Performing; Touring; Educational; Sponsoring

Nebraska

253
NEBRASKA THEATRE CARAVAN
Omaha Community Playhouse
6915 Cass Street
Omaha, NE 68132-2696
Phone: 402-553-4890
Fax: 402-553-6288
e-mail: info@omahaplayhouse.com
Web Site: www.nebraskatheatrecaravan.com
Management:
  Artistic Director: Carl Beck
  Executive Director: Tim Schmad
  Technical Director: Don Hook
  House Manager: Matt Bross
Mission: To provide quality theatrical experiences and educational opportunities to communities in which they would not otherwise be available. The Nebraska Theatre Caravan is the professional touring wing of the Omaha Community Playhouse.
Founded: 1975
Specialized Field: Theatrical Dance; Educational Dance

Nevada

254
NEVADA BALLET THEATRE
1651 Inner Circle
Las Vegas, NV 89134
Phone: 702-243-2623
Fax: 702-804-0365
e-mail: info@nevadaballet.com
Web Site: www.nevadaballet.com
Officers:
  CFO: Lorin Wolfe
Management:
  Artistic Director: James Canfield
  Artistic Associate: Clarice Rathers
  Executive Director/CEO: Beth Barbre
Mission: Our mission is to educate and inspire regional, statewide and national audiences and vitally impact community life through professional company productions, dance training, education and outreach.
Founded: 1972
Specialized Field: Ballet
Status: Nonprofit
Budget: $1,000,000-$2,500,000

New Hampshire

255
ST. PAUL'S SCHOOL BALLET COMPANY
325 Pleasant Street
Concord, NH 033012591
Phone: 603-229-4600
e-mail: srandolph@sps.edu
Web Site: www.sps.edu
Management:
  Dance Director: Sharon Randolph
Mission: The dance program is designed to accommodate the needs of a variety of students, including beginners seeking a new experience, athletes working on agility and coordination, students with developed interest and a love of the study of dance, and those with professional aspirations.

Specialized Field: Ballet
Income Sources: Corporate; Gifts; Individual; Planned Giving
Annual Attendance: 50

256
NORTHERN BALLET THEATRE
Northern Ballet Theatre Dance Centre
36 Arlington Street
Nashua, NH 03060
Phone: 603-889-8406
Web Site: www.nbti.org
Officers:
  Founder: Doreen Cafarella
  President: Andrew Piela
  VP: Rhonda Rendina
  Treasurer: Patricia Lavoie
  Secretary: Janice Bauer
Management:
  Artistic Director: Doreen Cafarella
Mission: Northern Ballet Theatre is dedicated to providing world class dancers, exciting sets and breathtaking choreography.
Founded: 1986
Specialized Field: Ballet
Status: Professional, Nonprofit

257
BALLET NEW ENGLAND
135 Daniel Street
Portsmouth, NH 03802-4501
Phone: 603-430-9309
Fax: 603-436-5396
e-mail: martha.balletnewengland@verizon.net
Web Site: www.balletnewengland.org
Management:
  Artistic Director: Barbara Pontecorvo
  Executive Director: Martha Lemire
Mission: Dedicated to producing the highest standard in excellence in professional dance performance, educating dancers of all ages and levels and providing outreach programming throughout the New England area.
Specialized Field: Ballet
Status: Pre-Professional, Nonprofit
Budget: $200,000-$500,000

New Jersey

258
NEW JERSEY TAP ENSEMBLE
340 Franklin Street
1st Floor
Bloomfield, NJ 07003
Phone: 973-743-0600
Fax: 973-743-3899
e-mail: njtapinfo@njtap.org
Web Site: www.njte.org
Officers:
  Treasurer: Sonia Vance
  Chairman: Donald Kalfus
  Vice Chairman: Barbara Hoffman
Management:
  Artisitc Director: Deborah Mitchell
Mission: This touring dance company's mission is to preserve and celebrate the american art form of rythym tap dancing through public performances.
Founded: 1994
Specialized Field: Rythym Tap
Status: Non-Profit

259
ATLANTIC CONTEMPORARY BALLET
713 W Moss Mill Road
Egg Harbor City, NJ 08215
Phone: 609-804-1995
e-mail: acbt@acbt.org
Web Site: www.acbt.org
Officers:
    Founder: Phyllis Papa
Management:
    Artistic Director: Phyllis Papa
Mission: The Atlantic City Ballet is a unique chamber ballet company with an exciting repertoire which cherishes the great tradition of classical ballet and explores the contemporary. The Atlantic City Ballet is in residence at the Atlantic Contemporary Ballet.
Utilizes: Actors; Dancers; Five Seasonal Concerts; Guest Ensembles; Guest Musical Directors; Guest Musicians; High School Drama; Original Music Scores; Sign Language Translators; Soloists
Founded: 1982
Specialized Field: Chamber Ballet
Paid Artists: 9
Budget: $40,000-$100,000

260
NAI-NI CHEN DANCE COMPANY
PO Box 1121
Fort Lee, NJ 07024
Fax: 201-242-9807
Toll-free: 800-650-0246
e-mail: info@nainichen.org
Web Site: www.nainichen.org
Officers:
    Chair: Nai-Ni Chen
    President: Arlene Yang
    Treasurer: Shu Lan Tong
    Secretary: Ellen B Simon
Management:
    Artistic Director/Choreographer: Nai-Ni Chen
Mission: Nai-Ni Chen's distinctive style blends the discipline of Chinese classical movement with the freedom of American modern dance. Her work finds inspiration in everything from the flowing lines of calligraphy to the thunderous motion of martial arts to the grace and beauty of nature itself.
Founded: 1988
Specialized Field: Contemporary; Traditional Ballet
Status: Professional, Nonprofit
Paid Staff: 3
Paid Artists: 09
Budget: $10,100,000
Income Sources: New Jersey State Council of the Arts; Corporate; Foundations; Grants
Annual Attendance: 100,000

261
MOSAIC DANCE THEATER COMPANY
Glen Ridge, NJ
Phone: 973-783-2395
e-mail: mosaicdtc@att.net
Web Site: www.mosaicdancetheaterco.org
Officers:
    President: Celeste Varricchio
    Secretary: Robert Greenwald
    Treasurer: Karen Lindsay
Management:
    Artistic Director: Morgiana Celeste
    Artisitc Director/Choreographer: Samara
Mission: This performing and touring dance company presents original dance, theater, and educational programs celebratinbg the rich diversity of cultures and folkloric traditions of the Mediterranean, including the Middle East, North Africa, Turkey, Greece, Italy and spain.
Founded: 2003
Specialized Field: Middle Eastern; Mediterranean Dance
Status: Non-Profit

262
RANDY JAMES DANCE WORKS
PO Box 4452
Highland Park, NJ 08904
Phone: 732-247-2653
Fax: 732-247-5353
e-mail: rjdw4452@yahoo.com
Web Site: www.rjdw.org
Officers:
    President: Dr Philip Levy
    Vice President: Dorothy Bitetto
    Treasurer: Marvin Auerbach
Management:
    Artistic Director/Choreographer: Randy James
    Executive Director: Ruth Lanza
Mission: The company is deeply committed to dance education and providing a forum for nurturing creative thoughts and ideas and exposing the public to physical, emotional, mental and spiritual benefits of dance through the production of dance performances and workshops.
Founded: 1993
Specialized Field: Modern
Paid Staff: 8
Volunteer Staff: 20
Paid Artists: 12
Budget: $100,000-$200,000
Income Sources: State Government; Foundations; Individual Supporters; Earned Income
Affiliations: Member of Dance USA, Dance NJ, DTW

263
KENNEDY DANCERS
79 Central Avenue
Jersey City, NJ 07306
Phone: 201-659-2190
e-mail: kennedydancers@aol.com
Web Site: www.kennedydancers.org
Officers:
    President: Diane Dragone
    Chairman: Guy Catrillo
Management:
    Artistic Director: Diane Dragone
Mission: This contemporary performing and touring dance company offers outreach programs, lectures, demonstrations and a cable tv series with a mission of bringing high quality dance to the New york/New Jersey metro area.
Founded: 1976
Specialized Field: Contemporary Dance
Status: Non-Profit; Professional

264
ROXEY BALLET
243 N Union Street
Lambertville, NJ 08530
Phone: 609-397-7616
Fax: 609-397-6889
e-mail: info@roxeyballet.org
Web Site: www.roxeyballet.com
Officers:
    President: Judith Leviton
    Vice President: Kelly Griffiths
    Founder/Executive Director: Mark Roxey
    Founder: Melissa Roxey
Management:
    Artistic Director: Mark Roxey
Mission: Through touring and performing, Roxey Ballet delivers artistic and cultural excellence through professional dance.
Founded: 1995
Specialized Field: Ballet
Status: Non-Profit

265
NEW JERSEY BALLET COMPANY
15 Microlab Road
Livingston, NJ 07039
Phone: 973-597-9600
e-mail: info@njballet.org
Web Site: www.njballet.org
Officers:
    Chairman: Donald A Robinson Esq
    President: Peter Maloff Esq
    Executive Vice President: Carolyn Clark
    Treasurer: Scott T Tross Esq
    Secretary: Gale Difabio Raffield
Management:
    Artistic Director: Carolyn Clark
    Assistant Artistic Director: Paul Hilliard McRae
    Ballet Mistress: Marina Bogdanova
    Ballet Mistress: Luba Gulyaeva
    Production Manager: Brian Coakley
Mission: The Company brings the magic of dance theatre to thousands every year in every part of the state. It makes ballet accessible to New Jersey seniors and families with children through subsidized low-cost tickets.
Utilizes: Five Seasonal Concerts; Guest Artists; Guest Companies
Founded: 1958
Specialized Field: Ballet
Status: Professional, Nonprofit
Budget: $1,000,000-$2,500,000
Organization Type: Performing; Touring; Educational

266
NEW JERSEY DANCE CENTER
202 Maplewood Avenue
Maplewood, NJ 07040
Phone: 973-762-3033
e-mail: info@njerseydancecenter.com
Web Site: www.njerseydancecenter.com
Management:
    Artistic Director: Anne Krohley
Mission: Dedicated to giving students the highest quality dance training with a curriculum based program from ages 3 to 18 at all levels of experience in a friendly, nurturing environment.
Founded: 1982
Specialized Field: Ballet
Status: Semi-Professional, Commercial
Performs At: New Jersey Dance Theatre
Organization Type: Resident

267
RENATE BOOE DANCE COMPANY
239 Midland Avenue
Montclair, NJ 07042
Phone: 973-783-9845
Fax: 973-783-0001
e-mail: yass@bellatlantic.net
Officers:
    Chairperson: Barbara Francett
Management:
    Assistant Director: Muriel Daino
    Artistic Director: Renate Boue
Utilizes: Student Interns
Founded: 1972
Specialized Field: Modern

Status: Professional
Paid Staff: 4
Volunteer Staff: 15
Budget: 50,000
Income Sources: Performance; Classes; Tuition
Annual Attendance: 4,000
Organization Type: Performing; Educational

268
AMERICAN REPERTORY BALLET
New Brunswick Studio
80 Albany Street 2nd Floor
New Brunswick, NJ 08901
Phone: 732-249-1254
Fax: 732-249-8475
e-mail: info@arballet.org
Web Site: www.arballet.org
Officers:
Chairman: Charles Metcalf
Treasurer: Nancy MacMillan
Secretary: Barbara J Bergen
Management:
Artistic Director: Graham Lustig
Executive Director: Marvin Preston
Ballet Master: Bat Abbitt
Ballet Mistress: Kathleen Moore
Stage Manager: Matthew Keefe
Mission: American Repertory Ballet is committed to helping ensure the survival and accountability of dance as an art form through educational initiatives.
Utilizes: Actors; AEA Actors; Arrangers; Artists-in-Residence; Choreographers; Collaborating Artists; Collaborations; Commissioned Composers; Commissioned Music; Community Members; Community Talent; Composers; Composers-in-Residence; Contract Actors; Contract Orchestras; Dance Companies; Dancers; Designers; Educators; Five Seasonal Concerts; Grant Writers; Guest Accompanists; Guest Artists; Guest Conductors; Guest Ensembles; Guest Musical Directors; Instructors; Local Artists; Lyricists; Multi Collaborations; Multimedia; Resident Professionals; Selected Students; Soloists; Student Interns; Visual Arts
Founded: 1987
Specialized Field: Ballet
Status: Professional, Nonprofit
Budget: $2,500,000+
Organization Type: Performing; Resident; Touring; Educational

269
LKB DANCE
9 Livingston Avenue
New Brunswick, NJ 08901
Phone: 732-742-1523
e-mail: info@lkbdance.org
Web Site: www.lkbdance.org
Management:
Artistic Director: Leah Kreutzer Barber
Assistant Artistic Director: Emily Edwards
Mission: Dedicated to the creation and performance of new modern dance works by Leah Kreutzer Barber with an emphasis on collaborations with living composers and other artists.
Founded: 1999
Specialized Field: Modern
Status: Professional, Nonprofit
Volunteer Staff: 3
Paid Artists: 8
Budget: $30,000
Income Sources: Foundations; Corporations; Individual; Government
Performs At: George Street Playhouse
Affiliations: Dance USA; Dance Theatre Workshop

Annual Attendance: 2,000
Seating Capacity: 350

270
IRINE FOKINE BALLET COMPANY
33 Chestnut Street
Ridgewood, NJ 07450
Phone: 201-652-9653
Fax: 201-652-9286
Web Site: www.fokineballet.com
Management:
Artistic Director: Irine Fokine
Mission: To provide training for young dancers and bring ballet to young people in suburban communities.
Utilizes: Singers
Founded: 1957
Specialized Field: Classical; Jazz; Character Dance
Status: Semi-Professional
Budget: $100,000-$200,000
Organization Type: Performing; Touring; Educational

271
CAROLYN DORFMAN DANCE COMPANY
2780 Morris Avenue
Suite 1-A
Union, NJ 07083
Phone: 908-687-8855
Fax: 908-686-5245
Toll-free: 800-887-9322
e-mail: info.cddc@verizon.net
Web Site: www.carolyndorfmandanceco.org
Management:
Artistic Director/Choreographer: Carolyn Dorfman
Stage Manager: Jennifer Mesce
Production Manager: Sean Perry
Mission: With cohesive artistic and educational programming, the Carolyn Dofrman Dance Company works on and off the stage to bring contemporary dance to its audiences.
Utilizes: Choreographers; Commissioned Composers; Commissioned Music; Dancers; Designers; Five Seasonal Concerts; Guest Accompanists; Guest Artists; Guest Conductors; Guest Musical Directors; Lyricists; Multi Collaborations; Organization Contracts; Original Music Scores; Resident Artists; Resident Professionals; Sign Language Translators
Founded: 1982
Specialized Field: Modern
Status: Professional, Nonprofit
Budget: $500,000
Income Sources: New Jersey State Council on the Arts; Foundation; Corporate; Individual

New Mexico

272
KESHET DANCE COMPANY
214 Coal Avenue SW
Albuquerque, NM 87102
Phone: 505-224-9808
e-mail: info@keshetdance.org
Web Site: www.keshetdance.org
Officers:
Founder: Shira Greenberg
President: Mark Hartman
Vice President: Hilary Noskin
Treasurer: Kris Haanes
Secretary: Karen Wright
Management:
Artistic Director: Shira Greenberg

Mission: Keshet Dance Company is a professional company of dance artists committed to inspiring passion and opening unlimited possibilities through the experience of dance. Keshet dancers use movement, music and spoken word to connect people with art and to build a stronger community.
Founded: 1996
Specialized Field: Modern
Status: Professional, Non-Profit
Paid Staff: 3
Volunteer Staff: 200
Paid Artists: 10
Non-paid Artists: 20
Budget: 250,000
Income Sources: Tickets; Foundations; Government; Private
Annual Attendance: 6,000

273
NEW MEXICO BALLET COMPANY
4200 Wyoming Boulevard NE
PO Box 21518
Albuquerque, NM 87154-1518
Phone: 505-292-4245
Web Site: www.nmballet.org
Management:
Artistic Director: Patricia Dickinson
Mission: Our mission is to create and produce unique, innovative ballet and classical ballet performances for the people of New Mexico through dance education, ticket sales, major contributors, grants and a strong volunteer Board and Guild.
Founded: 1972
Specialized Field: Classical
Status: Nonprofit
Budget: $100,000-$200,000
Income Sources: Ticket Sales; Major Contributors; Grants
Organization Type: Performing; Touring

274
ASPEN SANTA FE BALLET
550B Saint Michael's Drive
Suite 1
Santa Fe, NM 87505
Phone: 505-983-5591
e-mail: Cherie@aspensantafeballet.com
Officers:
Founder: Bebe Schweppe
President: Laurie Farber-Conlon
President-Elect: Keith Gorges
Vice President: Leigh Moiola
Management:
Artistic Director: Tom Mossbrucker
Executive Director: Jean-Philippe Malaty
Mission: A company of eleven classically trained dancers who perform an eclectic repertoire by some of the world's foremost choreographers. Performs year-round at home in Aspen and Santa Fe and on tour throughout the United States.
Founded: 1990
Specialized Field: Ballet
Status: Professional, Non-Profit
Budget: $2,500,000
Income Sources: Ticket Revenue; Earned Income; Foundations
Annual Attendance: 45,000

New York

275
MAUDE BAUM & COMPANY DANCE THEATRE
EBA Inc
351 Hudson Avenue
Albany, NY 12210
Phone: 518-465-9916
Fax: 518-465-9916
e-mail: ebadance@eba-arts.org
Web Site: www.eba-arts.org
Officers:
   Chief Executive Officer: Maude Baum
Management:
   Artistic Director: Maude Baum
   Stage Manager/Technical Director: Richard Chafin
Mission: With a mission to bring the best of American Modern Dance Theatre choreography and performance to audiences and to inspire creativity, Maude Baum & Company Dance Theatre creates, performs and tours acclaimed American Modern Dance works and offers a superb repertoire of dance theatre works.
Founded: 1972
Specialized Field: Modern
Status: Professional, Nonprofit
Budget: $200,000-$500,000
Income Sources: Grants; Contributions; Tuition; Foundations
Annual Attendance: 40,000

276
LES GUIRIVOIRES DANCE COMPANY
Guiraud-McDonald Cultural Exchange Inc
2195 Grand Concourse
Suite 6B
Bronx, NY 10453
Phone: 718-562-8656
Fax: 347-879-6766
e-mail: info@guiraudmredec.org
Web Site: www.guiraudmredec.org
Officers:
   Founder: Rose Marie Guiraud
   Treasurer/Secretary: Emmett O McDonald
Management:
   Artistic/Executive Director: Rose Marie Guiraud
   Choreographer: Christal Brown
Mission: Les Guirivoires Dance Theatre Company is the New York based professional performance organ of Guiraud-McDonald Cultural Exchange whose mission is to provide inter-cultural performances which include African traditional and contemporary dance, modern and jazz dance, music concerts and theater.
Founded: 1973
Specialized Field: African Traditional; Contemporary; Modern; Jazz
Status: Profesisonal, Nonprofit
Performs At: Throughout New York

277
MERIAN SOTO DANCE & PERFORMANCE
1001 Grand Concourse #10F
Bronx, NY 10452
Phone: 718-588-1936
Fax: 718-537-3973
e-mail: pepatian@aol.com
Management:
   Artistic Director: Merian Soto
   Associate Director: Jane Gabriels
Founded: 1983
Specialized Field: Traditional Dance; Ethnic Dance

Paid Staff: 2
Paid Artists: 10

278
BRIGHTON BALLET THEATRE COMPANY
The School Of Russian American Ballet
Kingsborough Community College
2001 Oriental Boulevard Building T7
Brooklyn, NY 11235
Phone: 718-769-9161
Fax: 866-812-7646
Toll-free: 866-812-7646
e-mail: brightonballet@gmail.com
Web Site: www.brightonballet.org
Officers:
   Founder: Irina Roizin
Management:
   Artistic Director/Choreographer: Edouard Kouchnarev
   Executive Director: Irina Roizin
Mission: Brighton Ballet Theater was created to preserve and further the tradition of Russian classical and folk dance in New York City.
Utilizes: Artists-in-Residence; Choreographers; Collaborating Artists; Collaborations; Community Members; Community Talent; Dance Companies; Dancers; Educators; Five Seasonal Concerts; Grant Writers; Guest Accompanists; Guest Artists; Guest Musicians; High School Drama; Instructors; Local Artists & Directors; Original Music Scores; Paid Performers; Resident Artists; Resident Companies; Soloists; Students; Visual Designers; Volunteer Artists
Founded: 1987
Specialized Field: Classical Ballet; Folk Dance
Status: Nonprofit

279
BROOKLYN ARTS EXCHANGE
421 Fifth Avenue
3rd Floor
Brooklyn, NY 11215
Phone: 718-832-0018
Fax: 718-832-9189
e-mail: info@bax.org
Web Site: www.bax.org
Officers:
   Founder: Marya Warshaw
   Chair: Oliver Fein
   Treasurer: Steven Flax
Management:
   Artistic Director/Executive Dir: Marya Warshaw
   Technical Director: Emma Rivera
Mission: Our mission is to provide a nurturing, year-round performance, rehearsal and educational venue in Brooklyn that encourages artistic risk-taking and stimulates dialogue among diverse constituencies.
Utilizes: Artists-in-Residence; Curators; Dance Companies; Guest Artists
Founded: 1991
Specialized Field: Theatrical Dance; Educational Dance
Status: Nonprofit
Paid Staff: 5
Budget: $200,000-$500,000
Income Sources: Individual; Foundation; Corporate
Facility Category: Theatre and rehearsal studios
Stage Dimensions: 25'X 30'
Seating Capacity: 75

280
CHARLES MOORE DANCE THEATRE
Dances & Drums of Africa
397 Bridge Street
2nd Floor
Brooklyn, NY 11201
Phone: 718-254-0670
Officers:
   Co-Founder: Ella Thompson-Moore
   Co-Founder: Charles Moore
Management:
   Artistic Director/Choreographer: Ella Thompson-Moore
Mission: To demonstrate the beauty and great variety of African, Caribbean and African-American culture, the company also proves that multiculturalism and traditional black American arts are inseparable.
Utilizes: Singers
Founded: 1974
Specialized Field: African Dance; Caribbean
Status: Professional, Nonprofit
Paid Staff: 2
Volunteer Staff: 15
Paid Artists: 12
Income Sources: New York State Council Dance Arts; Department of Cultural Affairs; New York Division of the Humanities Education Department
Performs At: Charles Moore Center for Ethnic Studies
Organization Type: Performing; Touring; Educational

281
DANCEWAVE
45 4th Avenue
Brooklyn, NY 11217
Phone: 718-522-4696
Fax: 718-522-4769
e-mail: info@dancewave.com
Web Site: www.dancewave.org
Management:
   Executive/Artistic Director: Diane Jacobowitz
   Education/Marketing Manager: Veronica Carnero
Mission: A unique dance troupe in which boys and girls perform works by world choreographers such as Mark Morris, Twyla Tharp, David Dorfman and others.
Utilizes: Choreographers; Commissioned Composers; Dance Companies; Grant Writers; Guest Accompanists; Guest Choreographers; Guest Companies; Guest Ensembles; Singers
Founded: 1979
Specialized Field: Modern
Status: Semi-Professional, Non-Profit
Paid Staff: 3
Paid Artists: 25
Budget: $150,000
Performs At: NYC theaters
Annual Attendance: 5,000
Organization Type: Performing; Touring; Resident; Educational; Sponsoring

282
ERICA ESSNER PERFORMANCE CO-OP
26 Berkeley Place
Suite #1
Brooklyn, NY 11217
Phone: 646-335-5264
e-mail: essner@eecop.org
Web Site: www.eecop.org
Management:
   Director/Choreographer: Erica Essner
   Composer: Erik Walker

Mission: Striving for the essence of individuality, the cooperative process is revealed in the merging of unique and idiosyncratic movement styles based on each member of the company.
Founded: 1990
Specialized Field: Modern
Paid Staff: 3
Volunteer Staff: 10
Paid Artists: 6

283
MARK MORRIS DANCE GROUP

3 Lafayette Avenue
Brooklyn, NY 11217-1415
Phone: 718-624-8400
Fax: 718-624-8900
e-mail: info@mmdg.org
Web Site: www.markmorrisdancegroup.org
Officers:
Vice President: Mark Selinger
Executive Director: Nancy Umanoff
Management:
Artistic Director: Mark Morris
Production/Facilities Manager: Mathew Eggelton
Studio Manager: Karyn w Treadneu
Mission: Mark Morris Dance Group's mission is to develop, promote and sustain dance, music and opera productions by Mark Morris and serve as a cultural resource to engage and enrich the community.
Utilizes: Singers
Founded: 1980
Specialized Field: Dance
Status: Professional, Nonprofit
Budget: $4,000,000
Organization Type: Performing; Touring

284
MARTHA BOWERS DANCE THEATRE ETCETERA

480 Van Brunt Street
Room 3
Brooklyn, NY 11231
Phone: 718-643-6790
Fax: 718-643-6733
Web Site: www.dancetheatreetcetera.org
Management:
Executive Director: Martha Bowers
Mission: Premised on the belief that the arts are an effective vehicle for social transformation, Dance Theatre Etcetera unites artists and community members as co-creators in dynamic cultural activities. Through site-specific performances, festivals, parades, and performing arts and media education programs, Dance Theatre Etcetera stimulates the social imagination through acts of informed expression.
Founded: 1981
Specialized Field: Theatrical Dance; Street Theatre
Status: Professional, Nonprofit
Budget: $40,000-$100,000
Income Sources: Foundations; Corporations; Individual
Performs At: Throughout Brooklyn
Annual Attendance: 5,000

285
POLISH AMERICAN FOLK DANCE COMPANY

261 Driggs Avenue
Brooklyn, NY 11222
Phone: 718-907-6199
Web Site: www.pafdc.org
Officers:
Vice President: Andrzej Buczek
Vice President: Richard Mazur
Treasurer: Margaret Pasanowic
Executive Director: Mariusz Bernatowicz
Secretary: Magdalena Kras
Management:
Artistic Director: Ryszard Sudol
Mission: Our mission is to stimulate public interest in Polish culture primarily through presentation of authentic Polish songs and dances.
Founded: 1938
Specialized Field: Polish American Folk Dance
Status: Nonprofessional, Nonprofit
Budget: $75,000
Performs At: The Lincoln Center
Annual Attendance: 300,000
Organization Type: Performing; Touring

286
URBAN BUSH WOMEN

138 S Oxford Street
Suite 4B
Brooklyn, NY 11217
Phone: 718-398-4537
Fax: 718-398-4783
e-mail: info@urbanbushwomen.org
Web Site: www.urbanbushwomen.org
Officers:
Executive Director: Jana La Sorte
Chair: Tammy Bormann
Management:
Program Manager: Pia Murray
Mission: Urban Bush Women seeks to bring the untold and under-told histories and stories of disenfranchised people to light through dance. We do this from a woman-centered perspective, as members of the African Diaspora community, in order to create a more equitable balance of power in the dance world and beyond.
Founded: 1984
Specialized Field: African Dance
Status: Professional, Nonprofit
Paid Staff: 12
Volunteer Staff: 24
Budget: $600,000-$700,000
Income Sources: Earned; Government; Individual; Foundations
Organization Type: Performing; Touring

287
YOUNG DANCERS IN REPERTORY

Sunset Station
PO Box 205037
Brooklyn, NY
Phone: 718-567-9620
Fax: 347-702-7157
e-mail: ydr@youngdancersinrep.org
Web Site: www.youngdancersinrep.org
Officers:
CEO/Artistic Director: Maude Baum
Administrator: JuliAnn Goronkin
Management:
Technical Director: Richard Chafin
Mission: Classical modern dance
Specialized Field: Modern; Ballet; Ethnic Dance

288
AFRICAN-AMERICAN CULTURAL CENTER

350 Masten Avenue
Buffalo, NY 14209
Phone: 716-884-2013
Fax: 716-885-2590
e-mail: aacc@wzrd.com
Web Site: www.africancultural.org
Officers:
Executive Director: Agnes Bain
Treasurer: Paulette S. Counts
Board Of Directors, Chairperson: Harry Stokes
Board Of Director, Vice Chairperson: Emma Bassett
Management:
Artistic Director: Paulette D Harris
Dance Director: Linda Barr
Assistant Director: Alicia Banner
Mission: Committed to promoting a positive sense of self among the community it was founded to serve. Its programs and services are still structured to motivate personal growth, stimulate untapped potential and facilitate a better understanding of cultural diversity among all people.
Founded: 1958
Specialized Field: African Dance; Ethnic Dance
Status: Semi-Professional, Nonprofit

289
MID-HUDSON BALLET COMPANY

Estelle & Alfonso, Inc.
4 Old Route 9 W
Fishkill, NY 12524
Phone: 845-897-2667
Fax: 845-897-7052
e-mail: director@estelleandalfonso.com
Web Site: www.estelleandalfonso.com
Management:
Artistic Director: Alfonso Weinlein
Artistic Director: Estelle Weinlein
Mission: To promote interest in the art of dance including but not limited to ballet and to foster, promote all activities and movements for the social and educational benefits of its members and public.
Utilizes: Dance Companies; Dancers; Educators; Fine Artists; Guest Artists
Founded: 1959
Specialized Field: Ballet
Status: Nonprofit
Income Sources: Northeast Regional Ballet; Dutchess County Arts Council
Performs At: Mid-Hudson Civic Center
Affiliations: Eisenhower Hall Theatre
Organization Type: Performing; Educational

290
BILL EVANS DANCE COMPANY

6908 Benedict Beach
Hamlin, NY 14464
Phone: 585-964-9196
Fax: 585-385-5134
e-mail: billevansdance@hotmail.com
Web Site: www.billevansdance.org
Officers:
Founder: Bill Evans
Management:
Artistic Director/Choreographer: Bill Evans
Mission: To support the creation and performance of contemporary dance and rhythm tap dance work.
Utilizes: Soloists
Founded: 1975
Specialized Field: Contemporary Dance; Jazz
Status: Professional, Nonprofit
Paid Staff: 2
Volunteer Staff: 2
Budget: $100,000
Income Sources: Ticket sales; grants
Annual Attendance: 7,000
Facility Category: Theatre
Type of Stage: Proscenium
Stage Dimensions: 40'x 35'
Seating Capacity: 420

Year Built: 1969
Year Remodeled: 1996
Resident Groups: Bill Evans Dance Company

291
ITHACA BALLET
PO Box 4341
Ithaca, NY 14464
Phone: 607-277-1967
Web Site: www.ithacaballet.org
Officers:
    President: Elmer Fairbank
Management:
    Artistic Director: Alice Reid
    Associate Director: Cindy Ried
    Technical Director: Craig Eagleson
    Stage Manager: Jeff Franzese
Mission: The ballet is a professional ensemble corps, having a varied repertoire of classical and contemporary works. The Ithaca Ballet is Upstate New York's only repertory company and is the resident ballet company at State Theatre.
Utilizes: Singers
Founded: 1961
Specialized Field: Classical; Contemporary
Status: Professional
Budget: $40,000-$100,000
Organization Type: Performing; Touring

292
DINIZULU AFRICAN DANCERS, DRUMMERS AND SINGERS
Dinizula Ctr for African Culture & Research
11562 Sutphin Boulevard
Jamaica, NY 11434
Phone: 718-843-6213
Fax: 718-528-3065
e-mail: dancecompany@dinizulu.org
Web Site: www.dinizulu.org
Management:
    Executive Director: Alice Dinizulu
    Artistic Director: Kiamati Dinizulu
Mission: Dedicated to presenting the beauty and majesty of African culture through dance.
Founded: 1950
Specialized Field: Ethnic Dance; African Dance
Status: Professional; Nonprofit
Organization Type: Performing; Touring; Resident; Educational; Sponsoring

293
AMERICAN BOLERO DANCE COMPANY
42-24 9th Street
Long Island City, NY 11101
Phone: 718-392-8888
Fax: 718-392-3840
e-mail: info@ambolero.com
Web Site: www.ambolero.com
Officers:
    Founder: Gabriela Granados
Management:
    Artistic Director/Choreographer: Gabriela Granados
Mission: American Bolero Dance Company's primary goal is to bring the music, history and tradition of Spanish Dance to the United States.
Founded: 1996
Specialized Field: Flamenco; Spanish; Bolero

294
EGLEVSKY BALLET
999 Herricks Road
New Hyde Park, NY 11040

Phone: 516-746-1115
Fax: 516-746-1117
e-mail: info@eglevskyballet.com
Web Site: www.eglevskyballet.com
Management:
    Artistic Director/Choreographer: Ali Pourfarrokh
    Ballet Mistress: Kristen McGrew
    Production/Stage Manager: Kelly Brown
Mission: The Eglevsky Ballet endeavors to develop a distinct artistic identity through performance and outreach programs furthering the appreciation of the art form. The company aspires to develop a unique and innovative repertoire of classical and contemporary works to enrich the Long Island community and to strive for national and international recognition.
Founded: 1961
Specialized Field: Contemporary; Classical
Status: Professional

295
VANAVER CARAVAN
10 Main Street
Suite 322
New Paltz, NY 12561
Phone: 845-256-9300
Fax: 845-256-9400
e-mail: vcoffice@vanavercaravan.org
Web Site: www.vanavercaravan.org
Officers:
    Co-Founder: Bill Vanaver
    Co-Founder: Livia Vanaver
Management:
    Artistic Director: Bill Vanaver
    Artistic Director: Livia Drapkin Vanaver
Mission: To mision of The Vanaver Caravan is to enlighten, educated and inspire diverse audiences through performances of traditional dance and music at concerts, festivals, workshops and school presentations. Our work is based on concepts of ancestry, ethnic/cultural & spiritual origins. We create and perform work that celebrates and promotes international (multi-cultural) understandiing and appreciation of the global family tree.
Utilizes: Selected Students; Sign Language Translators; Soloists; Theatre Companies
Founded: 1972
Specialized Field: Modern; Ethnic Dance; Folk Dance
Status: Professional, Nonprofit
Paid Staff: 5
Volunteer Staff: 10
Paid Artists: 25
Budget: $50,000-$100,000
Income Sources: New York State Counsil for the Arts; Grants
Organization Type: Performing; Touring; Educational

296
AILEY II
Alvin Ailey Dance Foundation
Joan Weill Center for Dance
405 W 55th Street
New York, NY 10019
Phone: 212-405-9000
Fax: 212-405-9001
e-mail: info@alvinailey.org
Web Site: www.alvinailey.org
Officers:
    Executive Director: Sharon Gersten Luckman
    Senior Director: Calvin Hunt
    Chief Financial Officer: Pamela Robinson
Management:
    Artistic Director: Sylvia Waters
    Associate Artistic Director: Troy Powell
    Stage Manager: Brian Emens

Mission: Ailey II couples the energy of young dance talent with emerging choreography, thus bringing exciting dance and innovative outreach programs to diverse communities throughout the country.
Founded: 1974
Specialized Field: Modern

297
AJKUN BALLET THEATRE
193 Cross Street
New York, NY 10464-1225
Phone: 914-235-2265
e-mail: AJKUN@aol.com
Web Site: www.ajkunbt.org
Management:
    Artistic Director: Leonard Ajkun
    Artistic Director: Chiara Ajkun
    Company Scheduler: Ichiko Nakajama, artisticstaff@arkunbt.org
    Office Manager: Aimira Bubesi
Mission: Professional company with a repertoire of traditional ballets and contemporary creations performed during its 48 week season. Part of the company mission is the goal to open the avenues of opportunities to youngest artists thru funding, summer intensives in New York and Italy, and arts in education programs.
Utilizes: Artists-in-Residence; Choreographers; Community Members; Community Talent; Contract Orchestras; Dance Companies; Dancers; Educators; Filmmakers; Five Seasonal Concerts; Guest Accompanists; Guest Artists; Guest Musicians; Instructors; Original Music Scores; Resident Companies; Students
Founded: 2000
Opened: 2001
Specialized Field: Ballet
Status: Non-Profit
Paid Staff: 15
Paid Artists: 35
Income Sources: Public & Private Funding
Affiliations: The Field; LUDT

298
ALLNATIONS DANCE COMPANY
Performing Arts Foundation
500 Riverside Drive
New York, NY 10027
Phone: 212-316-8431
Management:
    Artistic Director: Sophia Pachecano
    Executive Director: Herman Rottenberg
Mission: The troupe is composed of dynamic ethnic dancers, who present their own cultures through music and dance and unite with each other to perform dances from around the world.
Utilizes: Singers; Student Interns
Founded: 1967
Specialized Field: Ethnic Dance
Status: Professional, Nonprofit
Budget: $100,000
Performs At: International House
Organization Type: Performing; Touring; Educational

299
ALPHA OMEGA THEATRICAL DANCE COMPANY
711 Amsterdam Avenue
Suite 4E
New York, NY 10025
Phone: 212-749-0095
Fax: 212-749-0095
e-mail: info@alphaomegadance.org
Web Site: www.alphaomegadance.org

Management:
Artistic Director: Enrique Cruz De Jesus
Executive Director: Dolores Vanison-Blakely
Associate Director: Donna Clark
Mission: The company was founded with the purpose of expanding opportunities for minority choreographers and dancers and to work with a variety of art forms. It is committed to promoting knowledge and appreciation of artistic activities related to dance through schools, repertory ensembles and a professional company.
Utilizes: Artists-in-Residence; Choreographers; Commissioned Music; Dance Companies; Dancers; Designers; Educators; Five Seasonal Concerts; Guest Artists; Original Music Scores; Singers
Founded: 1972
Specialized Field: Modern; Jazz; Ballet
Status: Professional, Nonprofit
Paid Staff: 3
Volunteer Staff: 5
Paid Artists: 12
Budget: $69,000
Income Sources: Individual, NYSCA
Organization Type: Performing

300
ALVIN AILEY AMERICAN DANCE THEATER

Alvin Ailey Dance Foundation
Joan Weill Center for Dance
405 W 55th Street
New York, NY 10019
Phone: 212-405-9000
Fax: 212-405-9001
e-mail: info@alvinailey.org
Web Site: www.alvinailey.org
Management:
Artistic Director: Judith Jamison
Associate Artistic Director: Masazumi Chaya
Rehearsal Director: Ronni Favors
Mission: Alvin Ailey American Dance Theater is dedicated to the preservation of unique Black cultural expression and the enrichment of the American modern dance heritage.
Utilizes: Choreographers; Dancers; Grant Writers; Guest Artists; Guest Companies; Guest Conductors; Singers; Soloists
Founded: 1958
Specialized Field: Modern; Ballet; Jazz; Ethnic Dance
Status: Professional, Nonprofit
Budget: $18,000,000
Income Sources: Earned Revenue; Contributed
Performs At: City Center
Annual Attendance: 450,000
Organization Type: Performing; Touring; Educational

301
AMERICAN BALLET THEATRE

890 Broadway
New York, NY 10003
Phone: 212-477-3030
Fax: 212-254-5938
Web Site: www.abt.org
Officers:
Executive Director: Rachael Moore
Management:
Artistic Director: Kevin McKenzie
Production/Operations Manager: David Lansky
Mission: To develop a repertoire of the best ballets from the past and to encourage the creation of new works by gifted young choreographers, wherever they might be found.
Founded: 1940
Specialized Field: Ballet
Status: Professional, Non-Profit

Budget: $2,500,000
Performs At: Metropolitan Opera House
Affiliations: Dance/Usa; The Arts and Business Council
Organization Type: Performing; Touring

302
AMERICAN TAP DANCE FOUNDATION

Christopher Street #2B
New York, NY 10001
Phone: 646-230-9564
Fax: 646-230-7777
e-mail: info@atdf.org
Web Site: www.atdf.org
Officers:
Board Chair: Deb Beard
Board Member, Artistic Mentor: Brenda Bufalino
Board C-Chair, Producer: Hoagy B Carmichael
Director Of Marketing/Sales: Lisa Scotto
Management:
Artistic/Executive Director: Tony Waag
Choreographer/Director: Mercedes Ellington
Technical Director: Tony Mayes
Operations Director: Hjordis Linn
Mission: A nonprofit tap dance company dedicated to celebrating, preserving and perpetuating one of America's few indigenous art forms and tap dance.
Utilizes: Singers
Founded: 1986
Specialized Field: Jazz; Tap
Status: Professional, Nonprofit
Performs At: American Tap Dance Center
Organization Type: Performing; Touring; Educational

303
ANNABELLA GONZALEZ DANCE THEATER

4 E 89th Street
Suite #P-C
New York, NY 10128-0645
Phone: 212-722-4128
Fax: 718-701-1777
e-mail: agdt@mindspring.com
Web Site: www.agdt.org
Management:
Artistic Director/Choreographer: Annabella Gonzalez, agdt@mindspring.com
Board Chair: Richard Grimm, richard.grimm@mindspring.com
Mission: To create excellent and original dances; to educate individuals of all ages and circumstances on modern dance, Mexican dance, jazz and creative improvisations.
Utilizes: Choreographers; Collaborations; Commissioned Composers; Dancers; Designers; Five Seasonal Concerts; Guest Accompanists; Guest Artists; Guest Companies; Guest Conductors; Guest Musical Directors; Multimedia; Original Music Scores
Founded: 1976
Opened: 1976
Specialized Field: Modern; Ethnic Dance
Status: Professional, Nonprofit
Paid Staff: 1
Volunteer Staff: 2
Paid Artists: 6
Budget: $80,000-$100,000
Income Sources: Government Foundations, Corporate Support; Individual Contributions; Fall Galas
Affiliations: Dance Theater Worshop; ART/New York; The Association of Hispanic Arts
Annual Attendance: 8,500
Facility Category: Rental theatres, school theatres, libraries, etc.
Organization Type: Performing; Touring; Educational

304
APOLLO'S BANQUET

Grand Central Station
PO Box 523
New York, NY 10163
Phone: 203-838-1904
Fax: 203-838-1904
e-mail: louixiv203@aol.com
Web Site: www.apollosbanquet.com
Officers:
Founder: Thomas Baird
Co-Founder: Hugh Murphy
Management:
Artistic Director/Choreographer: Thomas Baird
Music Director: Hugh Murphy
Mission: To present baroque dance and music of the highest quality possible in concert venues.
Founded: 1995
Specialized Field: Eighteenth-Century Dance

305
AVODAH DANCE ENSEMBLE

C/O HUC-JIR
1 West 4th Street
New York, NY 10012
Phone: 917-822-9665
e-mail: avodahdance@gmail.com
Web Site: www.avodahdance.org
Officers:
Founding Director: JoAnne Tucker
Management:
Artistic Director: Julie Gayer
Mission: Avodah is a modern dance company that uses ancient sacred texts to connect and reconnect our spiritual selves to god and community, reaching deep within the jewish tradition, using dance, music and movement.
Utilizes: Artists-in-Residence; Choreographers; Collaborating Artists; Dancers; Five Seasonal Concerts; Guest Accompanists; Guest Artists; Local Artists; Lyricists; Original Music Scores; Singers
Founded: 1973
Specialized Field: Modern
Status: Professional, Nonprofit
Paid Staff: 2
Paid Artists: 6
Budget: $75,000
Income Sources: Bookings; Grants; Individual Contributions; Foundations
Annual Attendance: 2,000-10,000
Organization Type: Performing; Touring; Resident; Educational

306
BALLET HISPANICO OF NEW YORK

167 W 89th Street
New York, NY 10024
Phone: 212-362-6710
Fax: 212-362-7809
Web Site: www.ballethispanico.org
Officers:
Executive Director: Marie-Louise Silva Stegall
Executive Director: Anthony Patton
Management:
Artistic Director: Eduardo Vilaro
General Manager: Derek R Munson
Mission: Providing performances and training in traditional and contemporary Hispanic-American dance.
Utilizes: Artists-in-Residence; Dance Companies; Educators; Five Seasonal Concerts; Guest Artists; Touring Companies; Visual Arts
Founded: 1970

Specialized Field: Latin; Contemporary; Classical; Concert
Status: Professional, Nonprofit
Paid Artists: 39
Budget: $3,000,000
Income Sources: Earned Revenue; Public and Private Sector Contributions
Affiliations: Dance/USA; Association of Performing Arts Presenters
Organization Type: Performing

307
BALLET TECH
890 Broadway
New York, NY 10003
Phone: 212-777-7710
Fax: 212-353-0936
e-mail: questions@ballettech.org
Web Site: www.ballettech.org
Officers:
   President/Artistic Director: Eliot Feld
   Vice President: Carol Zerbe Hurford
   Treasurer: Robert Freedman
   Secretary: Yvette Neier
Management:
   Operations Director: Maggie Christ
   Facilities Manager: Patrick Crowson
Mission: Ballet Tech is dedicated to seeking out talented New York City public school students and provides a continuum of training from introductory through professional level training.
Utilizes: Dancers; Designers; Guest Artists; Guest Conductors; Multimedia; Original Music Scores; Resident Professionals; Visual Arts
Founded: 1974
Specialized Field: Ballet
Status: Nonprofit
Budget: $3,000,000
Income Sources: Individual; Corporate; Foundation
Performs At: Joyce Theater
Affiliations: The Ballet Tech School

308
BATTERY DANCE COMPANY
380 Broadway
5th Floor
New York, NY 10013-3518
Phone: 212-219-3910
Fax: 212-219-3918
e-mail: peggy@batterydance.org
Web Site: www.batterydanceco.com
Management:
   Artistic/Executive Director: Jonathan Hollander
   Managing Director: Peggy Coleman
   Program Manager: Sarah Dell'Orto
Mission: Battery Dance Company performs on the world's stages, teaches, presents and advocates for the field of dance.
Founded: 1976
Specialized Field: Modern; Contemporary Dance
Status: Professional, Non-Profit
Budget: $200,000-$500,000
Income Sources: Pace University
Performs At: Tribeca Performing Arts Center
Annual Attendance: 100,000
Organization Type: Performing; Touring; Resident; Educational; Sponsoring

309
BEBE MILLER COMPANY
140 Second Avenue
Suite 404
New York, NY 10033
Phone: 212-777-1340
Web Site: www.bebemillercompany.org
Officers:
   President: Michael Mazzola
   Treasurer: Dana Whitco
Management:
   Artistic Director: Bebe Miller
   Company Director: Caterina Bartha
Mission: The mission of Bebe Miller Company is to support the artistic vision of choreographer Bebe Miller in creative, cross-disciplinary explorations and in creating and performing new works.
Founded: 1985
Specialized Field: Modern
Status: Professional, Nonprofit
Paid Staff: 2
Paid Artists: 6
Budget: $200,000-$500,000
Organization Type: Performing; Touring; Resident

310
BILL T JONES/ARNIE ZANE DANCE COMPANY
27 W 120th Street
Suite 1
New York, NY 10027
Phone: 212-426-6655
Fax: 212-426-5883
Web Site: www.billtjones.org
Officers:
   Executive Director: Jean Davidson
Management:
   Artistic Director: Bill T Jones
   Associate Artistic Director: Janet Wong
   Creative Director: Bjorn G Amelan
   Resident Costume Designer: Liz Prince
   Resident Lighting Designer: Robert Wierzel
   Band Leader: Christopher Lancaster
   Artistic Consultant: Bill Katz
   Program Director: David Archuletta
Mission: The 10 member company has performed worldwide in over 200 cities and 30 countries. The Harlem based company is recognized as one of the most innovative and powerful forces in the modern dance world.
Specialized Field: Modern

311
BILL YOUNG/COLLEEN THOMAS AND DANCERS
100 Grand Street
2nd Floor
New York, NY 10013
Phone: 212-426-6655
Web Site: www.nyc-arts.org
Management:
   Artistic Director: Bill Young
Mission: Abstract and extremely physical dance performed by a group of international dancers.
Specialized Field: Modern

312
BLANCO PERFORMING ARTS FOUNDATION
Old Chelsea Station
PO Box 985
New York, NY 10011
Phone: 212-362-6061
Fax: 212-877-0814
e-mail: blancoarts@aol.com
Web Site: www.blancoarts.org
Management:
   Co-Artistic Director: Carol Blanco
   Co-Artistic Director: R Michael Blanco
Mission: Produces innovative cross-media performances in dance, theater, music and visual design.
Founded: 1993
Specialized Field: Theatre Dance; Dramatic Dance
Status: Professional, Nonprofit
Income Sources: Donations; Grants; Earned Income

313
CELEBRATION TEAM
National Dance Institute
594 Broadway
Room 805
New York, NY 10012
Phone: 212-226-0083
Fax: 212-226-0761
e-mail: cgriffin@nationaldance.org
Web Site: www.nationaldance.org
Officers:
   Founder: Jacques D'Amboise
Management:
   Artistic Director: Ellen Weinstein
   Associate Artistic Director: Tracy Straus
   Music Director: Jerry Korman
   Program Director: Aileen Barry
Mission: National Dance Institute was founded in the belief that the arts have a unique power to engage children and motivate them toward excellence.
Founded: 1976
Specialized Field: Ballet; Modern; Jazz
Status: Semi-Professional

314
CHINESE FOLK DANCE COMPANY
NY Chinese Cultural Center
390 Broadway 2nd Floor
New York, NY 10013
Phone: 212-334-3764
Fax: 212-334-3768
e-mail: info@chinesedance.org
Web Site: www.chinesedance.org
Management:
   Artistic Director: Jiang Qi
   Executive Director: Helen H Wu
   Managing Director: Belle Lam
Mission: To inspire and educate through Chinese cultural arts.
Founded: 1973
Specialized Field: Chinese Dance
Status: Professional, Nonprofit
Paid Staff: 5
Volunteer Staff: 2
Paid Artists: 20
Budget: $500,000
Annual Attendance: 150,000
Facility Category: Dance Studio
Rental Contact: Belle Lam
Organization Type: Performing; Touring; Educational

315
DANCE COLLECTIVE NEW YORK
463 West Street #953H
New York, NY 10014
Phone: 212-627-4275
Fax: 212-627-4275
e-mail: cnolte2344@aol.com
Web Site: www.nydancecollective.org
Management:
   Artistic Director/Choreographer: Carol Nolte
Mission: Comprised of dancers from a variety of ethnic and cultural backgrounds, creative artists in their own right, the company is committed to both community involvement and the expansion of creative potential.

Founded: 1974
Specialized Field: Modern
Status: Professional, Nonprofit
Paid Staff: 1
Volunteer Staff: 4
Paid Artists: 6
Affiliations: Dance Theatre Workshop; The Field
Organization Type: Performing; Touring

316
DANCE JUNE LEWIS AND COMPANY
PO Box 2025
New York, NY 10159
Phone: 212-741-3044
Fax: 718-996-1433
Management:
    Publicity Manager: Mel Leifer
    Artistic Director: June Lewis
    Associate Artistic Director: Claudio Assante
Founded: 1968
Specialized Field: Modern; Contemporary Dance
Status: Professional
Organization Type: Performing; Touring; Resident; Educational

317
DANCE NEW AMSTERDAM
280 Broadway
New York, NY 10007
Phone: 212-625-8369
Fax: 212-625-8313
e-mail: info@dnadance.org
Web Site: www.dnadance.org
Officers:
    Board Director: Martha Chapman
    Board Director: Cookie Harlin
    Board Director: Thomas Flagg
    Founder: Laurie DeVito
    Founder: Michael Geiger
    Founder: Danny Pepitone
    Founder: Lynn Simonson
    Founder: Charles Wright
    Founder: Danny Pepitone
Mission: To present and promote artistic excellence in dance performance, education and the creation process through ballet, jazz, hip hop and modern dance with over 40 performances annually.
Founded: 1984
Specialized Field: Ballet; Jazz; Hip Hop; Modern

318
DANCE THEATRE OF HARLEM
466 W 152nd Street
New York, NY 10031-1814
Phone: 212-690-2800
Fax: 212-690-8736
e-mail: info@dancetheatreofharlem.org
Web Site: www.dancetheatreofharlem.org
Management:
    Artistic Director: Virginia Johnson
    Executive Director: Laveen Naidu
    Marketing Associate: Brittany Liburd
Mission: A leading dance institution as unparalleled global acclaim, encompassing a Classically American dance company, a leading arts education center and Dancing Through Barriers an International outreach program.
Founded: 1969
Specialized Field: Dance
Status: Professional, Nonprofit
Organization Type: Touring; Performing; Educational

319
DANCES PATRELLE
139 Fulton Street
Suite 310
New York, NY 10038
Phone: 212-722-7933
Fax: 212-966-2978
e-mail: info@dancespatrelle.org
Web Site: www.dancespatrelle.org
Management:
    Artistic Director: Francis Patrelle
    Rehearsal Director: Leda Meredith
    Co-Managing Director: Lisa Iannacito
    Co-Managing Director: Hana Ginsburg
Mission: Dances Patrelle's mission has been to bring dramatic ballet, with an emphasis on societal and historical concerns, to the stage. We strive to address all elements of the human condition and by so doing, make ballet accessible to a wider audience.
Founded: 1998
Specialized Field: Ballet

320
DANCING IN THE STREETS
545 Eighth Avenue
Suite 1830
New York, NY 10018
Phone: 212-625-3505
Fax: 212-625-3510
e-mail: info@dancinginthestreets.org
Web Site: www.dancinginthestreets.org
Officers:
    Founder: Elise Bernhardt
Management:
    Artistic/Executive Director: Aviva Davidson
    Marketing/Media Manager: Mathew Heggem
Mission: Dancing in the Streets strives to illuminate the urban experience with free public performances and site-specific installations that examine the kinetic life and history of natural and architectural public spaces.
Founded: 1984
Specialized Field: Street Theatre
Status: Professional, Nonprofit
Organization Type: Producing

321
DANSPACE PROJECT
131 E 10th Street
New York, NY 10003
Phone: 212-674-8112
Fax: 212-529-2318
e-mail: info@danspaceproject.org
Web Site: www.danspaceproject.org
Officers:
    President: Christina Adair Smith
    First Vice President: Frances Milberg
    Second Vice President: Ann Tuomey-DePiro
    Treasurer: David Fanger
    Executive Director: Judy Hussie-Taylor
Management:
    Program Manager: Abby Harris Holmes
    Technical Director: Leo Janks
Mission: The mission of the Danspace Project is to stimulate, promote and present challenging new work in dance from a broad range of artistic voices within a distinguished and nurturing environment.
Utilizes: Curators; Dance Companies; Theatre Companies
Founded: 1974
Specialized Field: Modern; Experimental Dance; Post-Modern Dance
Status: Professional, Nonprofit
Paid Staff: 5

Volunteer Staff: 15
Paid Artists: 30
Budget: $1,000,000
Performs At: Sanctuary Performace Space at St. Mark's Church
Annual Attendance: 15,000
Stage Dimensions: 36'x48'
Seating Capacity: 200
Year Built: 1799
Year Remodeled: 1980
Organization Type: Performing; Artists Services

322
DOUG VARONE AND DANCERS
Doug Varone and Dancers/DOVA, Inc.
260 W Broadway
Suite 4
New York, NY 10013
Phone: 212-279-3344
Fax: 212-279-6397
e-mail: info@dougvaroneanddancers.org
Web Site: www.dougvaroneanddancers.org
Officers:
    Executive Director: Thomas Ward
Management:
    Artistic Director: Doug Varone
    Program Director: Sarah Bodley
    Company Manager: Alex Springs
Mission: A dance performance company headed by Doug Varone, performs at such venues as London's Queen Elizabeth Hall and at the Jacob's Pillow Dance festival in western Massachusettes. It also performs an annual season in New York City at the Joyce theatre and other venues.
Specialized Field: Dance

323
DOUGLAS DUNN AND DANCERS
Rio Grande Union, Inc.
541 Broadway
3rd Floor
New York, NY 10012
Phone: 212-966-6999
Fax: 212-274-1804
e-mail: info@douglasdunndance.com
Web Site: www.douglasdunndance.com
Management:
    Artistic Director: Douglas Dunn
Mission: Dedicated to producing and promoting the works of contemporary choreographer Douglas Dunn.
Utilizes: Singers
Founded: 1976
Specialized Field: Modern
Status: Professional; Nonprofit
Organization Type: Performing; Touring; Educational

324
EIKO AND KOMA
246 W 38th Street
8th Floor
New York, NY 10018-5805
Phone: 212-278-8111
Fax: 212-278-8555
e-mail: info@eikoandkoma.org
Web Site: www.eikoandkoma.org
Management:
    Artistic Director/Choreographer: Eiko Otake
    Artistic Director/Choreographer: Koma Otake
Mission: Established to perform the theater choreography of Eiko and Koma.
Specialized Field: Contemporary Dance
Status: Professional, Nonprofit
Organization Type: Performing; Touring; Resident; Educational

325

ELISA MONTE DANCE

481 8th Avenue
Suite 543
New York, NY 10001
Phone: 212-868-4488
Fax: 212-868-4494
e-mail: info@elisamontedance.org
Web Site: www.elisamontedance.org
Officers:
Executive Director: Gary De Mattei
Management:
Artistic Director: Elisa Monte
Stage Manager: Sarissa Michaud
Mission: In order to advance and enrich the art of dance, Elisa Monte Dance will present the choreography of Elisa Monte to an American and international audience to create a bridge between cultures.
Founded: 1981
Specialized Field: Modern
Status: Professional, Nonprofit
Income Sources: Dance USA
Performs At: The Joyce Theater
Organization Type: Performing; Touring; Educational

326

ERNESTA CORVINO'S DANCE CIRCLE COMPANY

451 W 50th Street
New York, NY 10019
Phone: 212-247-2564
e-mail: ecdoesit3@att.net
Web Site: www.corvinoballet.org
Management:
Director: Ernesta Corvino
Ballet Mistress: Andra Corvino
Mission: To provide the public with high quality and affordable dance performances, as well as workshops and lecture demonstrations.
Founded: 1981
Specialized Field: Ballet
Status: Professional, Nonprofit
Performs At: Marymount Manhattan Theatre
Organization Type: Performing

327

EUGENE JAMES DANCE COMPANY

PO Box 2504
New York, NY 10116
Phone: 212-564-1026
Fax: 212-564-1026
Management:
Manager: Richard Williams
Artistic Director: Eugene James
Mission: Dedicated to extending the contributions of Afro-American rhythms to dance.
Founded: 1967
Specialized Field: Modern; Ethnic Dance
Status: Professional; Nonprofit
Volunteer Staff: 3
Organization Type: Performing; Touring; Resident

328

FELICE LESSER DANCE THEATER

484 W 43rd Street
#9T
New York, NY 10036
Phone: 212-594-3388
Fax: 215-594-3388
e-mail: fldtny@aol.com
Web Site: www.fldt.org
Management:

Artistic/Executive Director: Felice Lesser
Mission: Creates and performs multi-disciplinary works-mixing dance with video, computer animation, contemporary music, drama and art. Committed to education as well as performance, it has developed an extensive program of lecture-demonstrations, classes, residencies and workshops to develop audiences and bring the general public and students into the creative process.
Utilizes: Singers
Founded: 1975
Specialized Field: Modern; Ballet
Status: Professional, Nonprofit
Affiliations: Dance USA
Organization Type: Performing; Touring; Resident; Educational

329

H.T. CHEN AND DANCERS

Chen Dance Center
70 Mulberry Street 2nd Floor
New York, NY 10013
Phone: 212-349-0126
Fax: 212-349-0494
e-mail: info@chendancecenter.org
Web Site: www.chendancecenter.org
Officers:
Founder: H.T. Chen
Chairperson: Rita Gail Johnson
Management:
Artistic Director: HT Chen
Associate Director: Dian Dong
Mission: Chen Dance Center (CDC) is a not-for-profit organization that provides for the cultural vitality of the performing arts community through its company, theater and school. All of CDC's programs and activities reflect its ongoing mission to provide moving experiences in Asian-American and contemporary dance through artistic creation, arts education, and presentation.
Utilizes: Artists-in-Residence; Choreographers; Collaborations; Community Members; Dance Companies; Dancers; Five Seasonal Concerts; High School Drama; Paid Performers; Soloists; Students; Theatre Companies
Founded: 1978
Specialized Field: Modern; Asian American Dance
Status: Professional, Nonprofit
Paid Staff: 5
Volunteer Staff: 3
Paid Artists: 25
Non-paid Artists: 2
Budget: $600,000
Income Sources: Association for Performing Arts Presenters
Performs At: Black box theater for Modern Dance only
Affiliations: Dance/USA, Dance Theater Workshop, Asian American Arts Alliance
Annual Attendance: 20,000
Facility Category: Marley flooring over wood
Type of Stage: Marley floor for Modern Dance
Stage Dimensions: 24 x 22
Seating Capacity: 70
Year Built: 1892
Year Remodeled: 2010
Cost: $1800
Rental Contact: Artistic Director H.T. Chen

330

ICE THEATRE OF NEW YORK

59 Chelsea Piers
Room 5911
New York, NY 10011

Phone: 212-929-5811
Fax: 212-929-0105
e-mail: itny@icetheatre.org
Web Site: www.icetheatre.org
Management:
Founder/Artistic Director: Moira North
Executive Director: Jirina Ribbens
Mission: Committed to developing figure skating as a performing art. They build an artistic repertory of ice skating performance pieces; to allow professional skaters from various backgrounds to collaborate with choreographers, musicians and visual artists.
Utilizes: Choreographers; Collaborations; Commissioned Composers; Commissioned Music; Dancers; Guest Artists; Guest Companies; High School Drama; Lyricists; Original Music Scores
Founded: 1984
Specialized Field: Modern
Status: Professional; Nonprofit
Budget: $450,000
Income Sources: Performances; Ticket Sales
Performs At: The Rink at Rockefeller Plaza
Annual Attendance: 20,000
Organization Type: Performing; Touring; Educational

331

ISADORA DUNCAN DANCE FOUNDATION

141 W 26th Street
3rd Floor
New York, NY 10001-6800
Phone: 212-691-5040
Fax: 212-627-0774
e-mail: info@isadoraduncan.org
Web Site: www.isadoraduncan.org
Officers:
Founder: Lori Belilove
Management:
Artistic Director: Lori Belilove
Associate Artistic Director: Cherlyn Smith
Music Director: John Link
Mission: The Isadora Duncan Dance Foundation's mission is to preserve, present and teach the work of Isadora Duncan through the performance and educational programs.
Founded: 1979
Specialized Field: Traditional Dance; Educational Dance
Status: Professional, Non-Profit
Paid Staff: 6
Volunteer Staff: 20
Paid Artists: 12
Non-paid Artists: 5
Budget: $200,000
Income Sources: Grants; Individual & Corporate Contributions

332

JANIS BRENNER AND DANCERS

123 W 93rd Street
Suite #3E
New York, NY 10025-7554
Phone: 212-864-3874
Fax: 212-864-3874
e-mail: janis@janisbrenner.com
Web Site: www.janisbrenner.com
Management:
Artistic Director/Choreographer: Janis Brenner
Mission: Established to perform the work of Janis Brenner and to conduct teaching workshops in technique, improvisation, composition, repertory and sounding.
Utilizes: Collaborations; Commissioned Composers; Dancers; Educators; Soloists; Students

Founded: 1985
Specialized Field: Modern; Contemporary
Status: Professional, Nonprofit
Paid Staff: 1
Volunteer Staff: 1
Paid Artists: 7
Organization Type: Performing; Touring; Educational

333
JENNIFER MULLER: THE WORKS
131 W 24th Street
4th Floor
New York, NY 10011
Phone: 212-691-3803
Fax: 212-206-6630
e-mail: twinfo@jmtw.org
Web Site: www.jmtw.org
Officers:
  Chairman: Barbara Massey
Management:
  Artistic Director/Choreographer: Jennifer Muller
  Associate Artistic Director: John Brooks
  Production Stage Manager: Jason C Kaiser
Mission: Jennifer Muller: The Works' mission is to create work through a multi-discipline approach combining technical virtuosity with dance and theater, to subject matter that is accessible and communicates directly to audiences about issues that touch their lives.
Utilizes: Actors; Collaborating Artists; Collaborations; Dancers; Designers; Educators; Filmmakers; Fine Artists; Five Seasonal Concerts; Guest Companies; Guest Conductors; Guest Directors; Guild Activities; Lyricists; Multi Collaborations; Multimedia; New Productions; Organization Contracts; Original Music Scores; Resident Professionals
Founded: 1974
Specialized Field: Contemporary Dance
Status: Professional, Nonprofit
Paid Staff: 4
Volunteer Staff: 2
Paid Artists: 12
Budget: $200,000-$700,000
Income Sources: Individual; Corporate; Foundations; Government
Performs At: The Joyce Theatre
Annual Attendance: 10,000
Organization Type: Performing; Touring; Resident

334
JOAN MILLER DANCE PLAYERS
1380 Riverside Drive
Suite 10B
New York, NY 10033
Phone: 212-568-8854
Fax: 212-795-5212
Management:
  Artistic Director/Choreographer: Joan Miller
Mission: A unique, multi-ethnic, street smart, mixed media company with a zany sense of humor, a slightly off-beat point of view and an eclectic sense of dance theater.
Utilizes: Singers
Founded: 1970
Specialized Field: Modern; Ballet; Jazz; Ethnic Dance
Status: Professional; Non-Profit
Paid Staff: 5
Budget: $60,000-$100,000
Income Sources: Grants; Foundations; Bronx Counsil For The Arts
Annual Attendance: 5,000-6,000
Organization Type: Performing; Touring

335
JODY OBERFELDER DANCE PROJECTS
234 E 4th Street
Suite 16
New York, NY 10009
Phone: 212-777-6227
e-mail: jody@jodyoberfelder.com
Web Site: www.jodyoberfelder.com
Management:
  Artistic Director: Jody Oberfelder
  Co-Director: David Lachman
  Company Manager: Clair Cook
Mission: Jody Oberfelder Dance Projects endeavors to bring boldly physical dance to both a traditional and a non-traditional dance audience.
Founded: 1989
Specialized Field: Contemporary Dance
Status: Professional, Nonprofit
Budget: $45,000
Annual Attendance: 6,000

336
JOSE LIMON DANCE FOUNDATION
307 W 38th Street
Suite 1105
New York, NY 10018
Phone: 212-777-3353
Fax: 212-777-4764
e-mail: info@limon.org
Web Site: www.limon.org
Officers:
  Executive Director: Gabriela Poler-Buzali
Management:
  Artistic Director: Carla Maxwell
  Associate Artistic Director: Roxane D'Orleans Juste
Mission: Presents modern classics, jazz works and other contemporary works through performances and residencies throughout the United States and abroad. The foundation also offers a variety of educational programs.
Founded: 1946
Specialized Field: Modern
Status: Nonprofit, Professional
Budget: $1.5 Million
Income Sources: Corporate; Foundation; Government Grants; Individual Donations; Performance Fees; Liscensing Fees

337
JUILLIARD SCHOOL
Dance Division
60 Lincoln Center Plaza
New York, NY 10023-6588
Phone: 212-799-5000
Fax: 212-724-0263
e-mail: admissions@juilliard.edu
Web Site: www.juilliard.edu
Management:
  Dance Director: Lawrence Rhodes
Mission: Juilliard's central mission is to educate talented performing musicians, dancers and actors so that they may achieve the highest artistic standards, as well as become leaders in their professions.
Founded: 1951
Specialized Field: Contemporary Dance
Status: Pre-professional, Nonprofit
Paid Staff: 30
Budget: $500,000-$1,000,000
Organization Type: Performing; Resident

338
KATHAK ENSEMBLE & FRIENDS/CARAVAN
141 E 3rd Street
12H
New York, NY 10009
Phone: 212-673-1282
Fax: 212-673-1282
e-mail: info@kathakensemble.com
Web Site: www.kathakensemble.com
Management:
  Artistic/Administrative Director: Janaki Patrik
Mission: To teach and perform classical Northern Indian Kathak dance with live musical accompaniment, to create new repertoire inspired by classical and modern Indian music and dance.
Founded: 1978
Specialized Field: North Indian Dance
Status: Professional, Nonprofit

339
KEI TAKEI'S MOVING EARTH
28 Vesey Street
#2200
New York, NY 10007
Phone: 212-459-4383
Fax: 212-732-3926
e-mail: keitakei@aol.com
Web Site: www2.gol.com/users/keitakei
Officers:
  Chairperson: Kei Takei
  President: Louise Roberts
  VP: Maldwyn Pate
  Secretary/Treasurer: Lawrence Brezer
Management:
  Executive Director: Laz Brezer
Mission: To perform the internationally acclaimed, award-winning choreography of Kei Takei.
Founded: 1968
Specialized Field: Modern
Status: Professional
Paid Staff: 8
Organization Type: Performing; Touring

340
LABAN/BARTENIEFF INSTITUTE OF MOVEMENT STUDIES
520 8th Avenue
Suite 304
New York, NY 10018
Phone: 212-643-8888
Fax: 212-643-8388
e-mail: info@limsonline.org
Web Site: www.limsonline.org
Officers:
  President: Virginia Reed
  Executive Director: Karen Bradley
  Financial Manager: Lorraine Benjamin
Mission: To teach Laban movement analysis, Bartenieff fundamentals on the introductory and professional level. Devoted to the study, exploration and teaching of movement as a human fundamental experience.
Founded: 1978
Specialized Field: Laban Movement Analyis; Bartenieff Fundamentals; Anatomy & Kinesiology; Bartenieff X-Class for Fitness
Status: Professional; Nonprofit
Paid Staff: 6
Paid Artists: 12
Budget: $350,000

Income Sources: National Association of Schools of Dance; Emergency Fund for Student Dancers; Dance Theatre Workshop: American Dinner Theatre Association; International Movement Therapists
Organization Type: Performing; Educational; Sponsoring

341
LAR LUBOVITCH DANCE COMPANY
229 W 42nd Street
8th Floor
New York, NY 10036-7201
Phone: 212-221-7909
Fax: 212-221-7938
e-mail: lubovitch@aol.com
Web Site: www.lubovitch.org
Officers:
  President: Virginia Kinzey
Management:
  Executive Director: Richard J Caples
  Artistic Director: Lar Lubovitch
  Company Manager: Leticia D Baratta
Mission: To create, perform and teach modern dance throughout the United States and the world.
Founded: 1968
Specialized Field: Modern
Status: Professional; Nonprofit
Paid Staff: 4
Volunteer Staff: 20
Paid Artists: 20
Budget: $1,000,000-$2,500,000
Affiliations: Dance USA; Association of Performing Arts Presenters
Annual Attendance: 85,000
Type of Stage: Sprung Floor
Stage Dimensions: 40'x42'

342
LES BALLETS TROCKADERO DE MONTE CARLO
Cathedral Station
Box 46
New York, NY 10025
Phone: 212-865-7925
Fax: 212-865-7925
e-mail: mail@trockadero.org
Web Site: www.trockadero.org
Management:
  General Director: Eugene McDougle
  Artistic Director: Tory Dobrin
  Technical Director: Isabel Martinez Rivera
  Ballet Master: Paul Gheslin
Mission: The original concept of Les Ballets Trockadero De Monte Carlo has not changed. It is a company of professional male dancers performing the full range of the ballet and modern dance repertoire, including classical and original works in faithful renditions of the manners and conceits of those dance styles.
Founded: 1974
Specialized Field: Ballet
Status: Professional, Nonprofit
Budget: $500,000-$1,000,000
Organization Type: Performing; Touring

343
LES GRANDS BALLETS DE LOONY
484 W 43rd Street
#32H
New York, NY 10036
Phone: 212-279-5169
Fax: 212-279-5169
e-mail: nephties@earthlink.net
Management:

Artistic Director/Choreographer: Marco Galante
Mission: Marco Galantes goal is to present a show in which the work is solid, clever and very funny, a show which is diverse in its programming and is audience friendly.
Founded: 1992
Specialized Field: Ballet

344
LOTUS MUSIC & DANCE
109 W 27th Street
8th Floor
New York, NY 10001
Phone: 212-627-1076
Fax: 212-675-7191
e-mail: info@lotusmusicanddance.org
Web Site: www.lotusmusicanddance.org
Management:
  Artistic Director: Kamala Cesar
  Development Director: Simmi Malhotra Degenemark
  Studio Manager: Angelina Hines-Jones
Mission: Our mission is to protect, promote and celebrate the music and dance traditions of all world cultures.
Founded: 1989
Specialized Field: Ethnic Dance
Status: Nonprofit
Performs At: Throughout New York City

345
MARJORIE LIEBERT
New York, NY 10025
Mailing Address: PO Box 20456, Parkwest Station
Phone: 212-724-3238
Fax: 212-724-3238
Mission: To nurture and develop artistry and help healthy artists develop proper alignment. Rehabilitates injuries. Prevents future injuries. Reduces stress and develops muscles without stress.
Founded: 1980
Specialized Field: Ballet; Educational Dance
Status: Professional
Paid Staff: 1

346
MARK DEGARMO AND DANCERS
Dynamic Forms Inc
107 Suffolk Street
Suite 310
New York, NY 10002
Phone: 212-375-9214
Fax: 212-375-9216
e-mail: info@markdegarmoarts.org
Web Site: www.markdegarmoarts.org
Officers:
  President: Marybeth Nelson
  Treasurer: Mario Baez
  Executive Director: Mark DeGarmo, Phd
Mission: Established to develop and perform the original choreography of Mark DeGarmo.
Founded: 1982
Specialized Field: Modern
Status: Professional, Nonprofit
Income Sources: Dance USA
Organization Type: Performing; Touring; Resident; Educational

347
MARK KAPPEL
252 W 76th Street
Suite 6E
New York, NY 10023

Phone: 212-724-3889
Fax: 212-874-5039
e-mail: markkapl1@aol.com
Web Site: eee.markkappeldance.com
Mission: Presents an international array of dancers and choreographers.
Specialized Field: Ballet

348
MARTHA GRAHAM DANCE COMPANY
316 E 63rd Street
New York, NY 10065
Phone: 212-838-5886
Fax: 212-838-0339
e-mail: info@marthagraham.org
Web Site: www.marthagraham.org
Management:
  Executive Director: LaRue Allen
  Artistic Director: Janet Eilber
  Senior Artistic Associate: Denise Vale
  General Manager: Faye Rosenbaum
  Director: Virginie Mecene
Mission: Established to perform the original works of Martha Graham.
Founded: 1926
Specialized Field: Contemporary Dance
Status: Professional, Nonprofit
Performs At: Citi Centre
Organization Type: Performing; Touring; Educational

349
MERCE CUNNINGHAM DANCE COMPANY
55 Bethune Street
New York, NY 10014
Phone: 212-255-8240
Fax: 212-633-2453
e-mail: info@merce.org
Web Site: www.merce.org
Officers:
  Chair: Molly Davies
  Co-Chair: Loyd Lewis
  Vice Chairman: Alvin Chereskin
Management:
  Artistic Director: Merce Cunningham
  Executive Director: Jeffrey James
  General Manager: Trevor Carlson
Mission: Committed to developing, understanding and public interest in dance through performances, dance instruction and videotapes.
Utilizes: Singers; Special Technical Talent
Founded: 1964
Specialized Field: Modern
Status: Professional; Nonprofit
Budget: $5,000,000
Income Sources: American Guild of Musical Artists; National Association of Schools of Dance; Dance USA
Performs At: Merce Cunningham Studio
Organization Type: Performing; Touring; Educational

350
MICHAEL MAO DANCE
1841 Broadway
Suite 1008
New York, NY 10023
Phone: 212-757-9669
Fax: 212-757-4198
e-mail: admin@michaelmaodance.org
Management:
  Marketing Director: Vadim Ghin
Mission: Dance Performance; Touring; Community Outreach; Arts-in-Education; WSL Dance

Utilizes: Choreographers; Collaborations; Commissioned Composers; Commissioned Music; Dancers; Designers; Educators; Five Seasonal Concerts; Grant Writers; Multimedia; Music; Original Music Scores; Performance Artists; Resident Professionals; Selected Students; Student Interns; Touring Companies; Visual Arts
Specialized Field: Modern
Status: 501c3
Paid Staff: 3
Paid Artists: 15
Budget: $200,000-$500,000
Income Sources: NEA; NYSCA; DCA; Foundations; Corporations; Fees; Tickets
Affiliations: ISPA; DTN; APAP

351
MIMI GARRARD DANCE COMPANY
Two Penn Plaza
Suite 1500
New York, NY 10121
Phone: 212-674-6868
Fax: 845-386-4883
e-mail: mimimgdc@aol.com
Web Site: www.mimigarrarddance.com
Management:
   Director/Choreographer: Mimi Garrard
Mission: Established to present original, professional dance theatre productions to the public and offer classes and workshops for individuals of all ages.
Founded: 1965
Specialized Field: Modern
Status: Professional, Nonprofit
Budget: $40,000-$100,000
Income Sources: Dance Theatre Workshop
Performs At: Mimi Garrard Dance Company
Organization Type: Performing; Touring; Resident

352
MOLISSA FENLEY AND DANCERS
Momenta Foundation
260 Broadway
Suite 1
New York, NY 10013
Phone: 212-941-8911
Fax: 212-334-5149
e-mail: artservicesinc@mindspring.com
Web Site: www.molissafenley.com
Management:
   Artistic Director/Choreographer: Molissa Fenley
   Administration: Mimi Johnson
Mission: Molissa Fenley is noted for incorporating quotes from classical and traditional dance worldwide into her choreography and for using unmediated physicality to convey emotional and psychic intensity.
Founded: 1977
Specialized Field: Ballet; Modern
Budget: $100,000-$200,000

353
MUNA TSENG DANCE PROJECTS
115 Christopher Street
4th Floor
New York, NY 10014
Phone: 212-627-5638
Fax: 212-645-5319
e-mail: info@munatseng.org
Web Site: www.muntatseng.org
Officers:
   Chairman: Christopher Gray
   President: Muna Tseng
   Secretary: Ray Tseng
Management:
   Artistic Director/Choreographer: Muna Tseng

Administrative Assistant: Cindy Lee
Mission: Muna Tseng Dance Projects was founded to produce art in a culture of creative ideas, with collaborators bringing a gesture, a text, a melody, a picture or a story. We work through live performances, books, visual art installations, exhibitions and media projects such as video, film and DVD.
Utilizes: Actors; Choreographers; Collaborating Artists; Collaborations; Commissioned Composers; Composers; Curators; Dancers; Designers; Educators; Fine Artists; Guest Artists; Lyricists; Multi Collaborations; Multimedia; Organization Contracts; Original Music Scores; Paid Performers; Performance Artists; Playwrights; Resident Professionals; Scenic Designers; Students; Theatre Companies; Touring Companies; Visual Arts; Volunteer Directors & Actors; Writers
Founded: 1988
Specialized Field: Dance; Visual Art; Contemporary Photography
Status: Professional, Non-Profit
Paid Staff: 2
Paid Artists: 6
Budget: $100,000
Annual Attendance: 5,000

354
NATIONAL DANCE INSTITUTE
594 Broadway
Room 805
New York, NY 10012
Phone: 212-226-0083
Fax: 212-226-0761
e-mail: cgriffin@nationaldance.org
Web Site: www.nationaldance.org
Officers:
   Founder: Jacques D'Amboise
   Chair: John Fullerton
   Treasurer: Robert D Krinsky
   Secretary: Richard DeScherer
Management:
   Artistic Director: Ellen Weinstein
   Associate Artistic Director: Tracy Straus
   Technical Director/Producer: Kit Westerman
   Program Director: Aileen Barry
Mission: To make the arts a foundation of children's education through the medium of dance to reach children who would otherwise not have the opportunity to become involved in the arts.
Utilizes: Singers
Founded: 1976
Specialized Field: Modern; Jazz; Tap
Status: Professional, Nonprofit
Paid Staff: 20
Volunteer Staff: 100
Income Sources: Grants; Foundations; Government
Performs At: LaGuardia High School
Annual Attendance: 17,000
Seating Capacity: 1,000
Organization Type: Performing; Educational

355
NETA DANCE COMPANY
Our Children's Foundation
449 W 125th Street
Apartment 5D
New York, NY 10027
Phone: 212-866-4626
e-mail: neta@ufl.edu
Web Site: www.netacompany.org
Management:
   Artistic Director/Choreographer: Neta Pulvermacher
   Rehearsal Director: Lanileigh Ting

Administrative Director: Kristen Schifferdecker
Mission: To present contemporary performance arts to the public.
Founded: 1986
Specialized Field: Modern; Ballet; Contemporary
Status: Professional
Paid Staff: 2
Budget: $40,0000-$200,000
Income Sources: Dance Theatre Workshop; Circum Arts
Organization Type: Performing; Touring; Resident; Educational; Sponsoring

356
NEUER TANZ
Bernard Schmidt Productions
461 W 49th Street, E Office
New York, NY 10019
Phone: 212-307-5046
Fax: 212-397-2459
e-mail: bschmidtpd@aol.com
Web Site: www.bernardschmidtproductions.com
Management:
   Artists Representative: Bernard Schmidt
Mission: Performers from around the world at the crossroads of innovation and tradition.
Founded: 1986
Specialized Field: Modern; German Dance
Paid Staff: 3
Paid Artists: 10

357
NEW YORK CITY BALLET
David H Koch Theatre
20 Lincoln Center
New York, NY 10023
Phone: 212-870-5656
e-mail: webmaster@nycballet.com
Web Site: www.nycballet.com
Officers:
   Founder: George Balanchine
   Founder: Lincoln Kirstein
   Chairman: John L Vogelstein
   President: David W Heleniak
   Treasurer: Gordon B Pattee
   Secretary: Marlene Hess
Management:
   Chief Ballet Master: Peter Martins
   Ballet Mistress: Rosemary Dunleavy
   Founding Choreographer: George Balanchine
   Founding Choreographer: Lincoln Kirstein
   Music Director: Faycal Karoui
Mission: The goal of producing and performing a new ballet repertory that would reimagine the principles of classical dance.
Utilizes: Singers
Founded: 1948
Specialized Field: Ballet
Status: Professional, Nonprofit
Volunteer Staff: 350
Paid Artists: 350
Budget: $2,500,000
Performs At: New York State Theater
Facility Category: Proscenium
Seating Capacity: 2,779
Organization Type: Performing; Touring; Resident; Educational

358
NEW YORK THEATRE BALLET/BALLET SCHOOL OF NY
30 E 31st Street
5th Floor
New York, NY 10016

Phone: 212-679-0401
Fax: 212-679-8171
e-mail: admin@nytb.org
Web Site: www.nytb.org
Officers:
   President & Artistic Director: Diana Byer
   Executive Director: Christina Paolucci
   Administrative Assistant: Eve Karlin
Mission: New York Theatre Ballet provides an intimate environment for the performance, study and appreciation of classical and contemporary dance, with a commitment to cultural enrichment and enjoyment for all.
Utilizes: Choreographers; Dancers; Guest Artists; Original Music Scores
Founded: 1978
Specialized Field: Ballet; Theatrical Dance
Status: Professional, Nonprofit
Paid Staff: 12
Paid Artists: 14
Budget: $500,000-$1,000,000
Annual Attendance: 40,000

359
PARSONS DANCE COMPANY

229 W 42nd Street
8th Floor
New York, NY 10036
Phone: 212-869-9275
e-mail: info@parsonsdance.org
Web Site: www.parsonsdance.org
Officers:
   President: Steven Morris
   VP: Barbara Rohdie
   VP Finance, Development, Treasurer: Chris Yegen
Management:
   Company & Stage Manager: Rebecca Josue
   Program, Marketing & Development: Colleen Cashman
   Executive Director: David Harrison
Mission: Parsons Dance is an internationally renowned contemporary dance company under the artistic direction of choreographer David Parsons. Parsons Dance creates and performs contemporary American dance of extraordinary artistry that is entertaining and enriching to diverse audiences.
Founded: 1985
Specialized Field: Modern; Contemporary Dance
Status: Professional, Non-Profit
Budget: $1,000,000-$2,500,000
Income Sources: Individual; Foundations; Corporate
Performs At: Nationally; Internationally
Organization Type: Performing; Touring; Resident; Educational

360
PAUL TAYLOR DANCE COMPANY

551 Grand Street
New York, NY 10012-3947
Phone: 212-431-5562
Fax: 212-966-5673
e-mail: jt@ptdc.org
Web Site: www.paultaylor.org
Officers:
   Chairman: Paul Taylor
   President: Robert E Aberlin
   Treasurer: Joseph A Smith
   Secretary: Joan C Bowman
   Vice President: Elise Jaffe
   Vice President: Carol Strickland
   Vice President: C F Stone, III
Management:
   Executive Director: Martin Kagan

General Manager: John Tomlinson
Mission: The Paul Taylor Dance Foundation generates the resources Mr. Taylor needs to create new works; maintains the Paul Taylor Dance Company as one of the finest ensembles in the world; ensures that Mr. Taylor's work is seen by the largest possible audience; promotes the Taylor style through education initiatives; and preserves Mr. Taylor's dances for future generations.
Utilizes: Dancers; Singers
Founded: 1954
Specialized Field: Modern Dance
Status: Professional; Nonprofit
Paid Staff: 15
Volunteer Staff: 8
Paid Artists: 25
Budget: $6,200,000
Income Sources: Grants; Individual Donations; Ticket Sales; Matching Gifts; In Kind Donations; Touring Fees
Facility Category: Dance Studio/Dance School/Offices
Organization Type: Performing; Touring; Resident

361
PHYLLIS ROSE DANCE COMPANY

Dance Vectors, Inc.
102-00 Shore Front Parkway
Suite 10P
New York, NY 11694
Mailing Address: Rockaway Park
Phone: 718-474-1672
Fax: 718-634-0348
e-mail: dvi7@verizon.net
Web Site: www.phyllisrosedance.com
Officers:
   President: Phyllis Rose
   Secretary: Miriam Bird
   Treasurer: Richard Lambert
Management:
   Company Director: Phyllis Rose
   Engagement Coordinator: Morgayne West
Mission: To provide arts-in-education experiences in the areas of dance, music, and folklore to young audiences, via performances, workshops and residency programs special focus on young audiences.
Utilizes: Singers
Founded: 1969
Specialized Field: Modern; Jazz; Ethnic Dance; Folk Dance; Novelty Dance; Theatrical Dance
Status: Professional; Nonprofit
Paid Staff: 3
Volunteer Staff: 1
Paid Artists: 15
Budget: $100,000-200,000
Income Sources: Earned; Donations
Performs At: Touring
Organization Type: Performing; Resident; Educational; Sponsoring

362
PICK UP PERFORMANCE COMPANY

520 8th Street
3rd Floor, Room 303
New York, NY 10018
Phone: 212-244-7622
Web Site: www.pickupperformance.org
Officers:
   Founder: David Gordon
Management:
   Director: David Gordon
   Co-Director: Ain Gordon
   Producer: Alyce Dissette
Mission: Dedicated to producing and promoting the work of David Gordon and Ain Gordon.
Founded: 1971

Specialized Field: Modern; Theatrical Dance
Status: Professional, Nonprofit
Income Sources: Dance USA; Association for Performing Arts Presenters; Western Alliance of Arts Administrators
Organization Type: Performing; Touring; Resident

363
POPPO & THE GOGO BOYS

165 W 26th Street
6th Floor
New York, NY 10001
Phone: 212-989-4819
Fax: 212-989-4819
e-mail: mikopop@gis.net
Management:
   Artistic Director: Poppo Shiraishi
   Manager: Miko Otake
Specialized Field: Modern

364
REBECCA KELLY BALLET

579 Broadway
Suite 4B
New York, NY 10012
Phone: 212-431-8489
e-mail: rkballet1@verizon.net
Web Site: www.rebeccakellyballet.com
Officers:
   Founder: Rebecca Kelly
   Executive Director: Craig D. Brashear
   Secretary: Eve S Wolfsohn
Management:
   Artistic Director/Choreographer: Rebecca Kelly
Mission: Rebecca Kelly creates abstract and narrative ballets which convey her humanistic outlook. The works features Kelly's vibrant expression, fusing classical dance with modern forms resulting in an arresting lyrical yet earthy quality.
Founded: 1979
Specialized Field: Contemporary Ballet
Status: Professional, Nonprofit
Paid Artists: 8
Budget: $180,000-$220,000
Income Sources: Grants; Contributions; Foundations; Classes; Performances
Performs At: The Duke Theater; Kaye Playhouse; Tribeca Performing Arts Center
Annual Attendance: 1,000-2,000

365
RIOULT

246 W 38th Street
8th Floor
New York, NY 10018
Phone: 212-398-5901
Fax: 212-398-5902
e-mail: info@rioult.org
Web Site: www.rioult.org
Officers:
   Founder: Pascal Rioult
   Company Manager: Holly Evans
Management:
   Executive Director: Joyce Herring
   Lead Teaching Artist: Anastasia Soroczynski
   Artistic Director: Pascal Rioult
Mission: Educating and expanding audiences for modern dance at home and throuh touring nationally and internationally.
Specialized Field: Modern Dance

DANCE / New York

366
RISA JAROSLOW AND DANCERS
139 Fulton Street
Suite 310
New York, NY 10038
Phone: 212-233-0330
e-mail: rjdinfo@verizon.net
Web Site: www.hightidedance.com
Officers:
President: Mark Elliott
Management:
Artistic Director/Choreographer: Risa Jaroslow
Managing Director: Chantel Bell
Mission: Dedicated to merging performance and community work and to including diverse communities as participants and audience.
Founded: 1985
Specialized Field: Modern
Status: Professional, Nonprofit
Paid Staff: 3
Volunteer Staff: 1
Paid Artists: 6
Budget: $170,000-180,000
Income Sources: Foundations; Government; Private Donors; Earned Income
Affiliations: Dance Theater Workshop
Annual Attendance: 2,000-3,000
Organization Type: Performing; Touring; Resident; Educational

367
ROD RODGERS DANCE COMPANY & STUDIOS
62 E 4th Street
New York, NY 10003
Phone: 212-674-9066
Fax: 212-674-9068
e-mail: rodrodgers.dance@verizon.net
Web Site: www.rodrodgersdance.org
Officers:
Founder: Rod Rodgers
Management:
Artistic Director: Kim Grier
Mission: Rod Rodgers Dance Company considers use of dance as a vehicle for human development, including helping people realize their positive potential and inner beauty, to provide information and stimulate dialogues about our and about historic contributions of landmark figures, are considered central to the Rod Rodgers Dance Company mission.
Utilizes: Guest Artists
Founded: 1960
Specialized Field: Modern; Theatrical Dance
Budget: $100,000-$200,000

368
SAEKO ICHINOHE DANCE COMPANY
159 W 53rd Street
New York, NY 10019
Phone: 212-757-2531
e-mail: ichinohedance@earthlink.net
Web Site: www.ichinohedance.org
Officers:
Founder: Saeko Ichinohe
Management:
Artistic Director/Choreographer: Saeko Ichinohe
Technical Director: Chenault Spence
Mission: Saeko Ichinohe has been creating dance by merging traditional Japanese movement, music and costumes with modern Western movement continuously since 1970.
Founded: 1970
Specialized Field: Contemporary Western Dance

Volunteer Staff: 3
Paid Artists: 10
Budget: $40,000-$100,000
Income Sources: Grants; Contributions; Foundations; Corporate; Individual
Performs At: The Kaye Playhouse

369
SALIA NI SEYDOU
Bernard Schmidt Productions
461 W 49th Street, E Office
New York, NY 10019
Phone: 212-307-5046
Fax: 212-397-2459
e-mail: bschmidtpd@aol.com
Web Site: www.bernardschmidtproductions.com
Management:
Executive Director: John Hassle
Mission: Performers from around the world at the crossroads of innovation and tradition.
Specialized Field: African Dance; West African Dance
Paid Staff: 3
Volunteer Staff: 5

370
SENSEDANCE
1425 3rd Avenue
Suite 3C
New York, NY 10028
Phone: 212-717-6869
Fax: 212-717-6869
e-mail: sensedance@sensedance.org
Web Site: www.sensedance.org
Management:
Artistic Director/Choreographer: Henning Rubsam
Mission: Sensedance has been created in the hope that through the senses for a moment we can still all meet.
Founded: 1991
Specialized Field: Modern
Status: Nonprofit
Paid Staff: 2
Volunteer Staff: 2
Paid Artists: 9
Budget: $40,000-$100,000

371
SOLARIS DANCE THEATRE & VIDEO
264 W 19th Street
Room 53
New York, NY 10011
Phone: 215-563-8108
Fax: 212-242-2201
e-mail: solaris@libertynet.org
Web Site: www.lakotasolarisdancetheatre.org
Management:
Artistic Director: Henry Smith
Mission: To create experimental dance theatre through the workshop process and through cross-cultural performance; to create bonds with people otherwise unrecognized in our society.
Utilizes: AEA Actors; Artists-in-Residence; Choreographers; Collaborating Artists; Collaborations; Commissioned Composers; Commissioned Music; Composers-in-Residence; Dancers; Designers; Educators; Filmmakers; Five Seasonal Concerts; Guest Accompanists; Guest Artists; Guest Ensembles; Guest Lecturers; Guest Musical Directors; Guest Musicians; Guest Soloists; Instructors; Lyricists; Multi Collaborations; Multimedia; Organization Contracts; Original Music Scores; Poets; Resident Professionals; Touring Companies
Founded: 1976

Specialized Field: Modern; Ethnic Dance; Folk Dance; Martial Arts
Status: Professional; Nonprofit
Paid Staff: 4
Volunteer Staff: 6
Paid Artists: 12
Budget: $165,000
Income Sources: Grants; Performances
Performs At: Studio
Affiliations: Arts; Business Council
Organization Type: Performing; Touring; Resident; Educational

372
STEPHEN PETRONIO DANCE COMPANY
140 2nd Avenue
Suite 504
New York, NY 10003
Phone: 212-473-1660
Fax: 212-477-3471
e-mail: info@stephenpetronio.com
Web Site: www.stephenpetronio.com
Management:
Artistic Director/Choreographer: Stephen Petronio
Managing Director: June Poster
Production Stage Manager: Lynda Erbs
Mission: Stephen Petronio Dance Company creates an expansive body of work marked by an unmistakable movement language and groundbreaking choreography in collaboration with contemporary innovators in the fields of music, visual arts and fashion.
Founded: 1984
Specialized Field: Modern
Status: Professional; Nonprofit
Performs At: The Joyce Theatre
Organization Type: Performing; Touring

373
SUSAN MARSHALL AND COMPANY
63 Greene Street
Suite 506
New York, NY 10012
Phone: 212-219-0005
Fax: 212-966-2978
e-mail: dance@sumacdance.org
Web Site: www.susanandmarshallandcompany.org
Management:
Artistic Director/Choreographer: Susan Marshall
Managing Director: Robert Dorf
Mission: Susan Marshall's choreography illuminates the contemporary condition by interweaving movement, structure, imagery and drama.
Founded: 1982
Specialized Field: Modern
Status: Professional, Nonprofit
Paid Staff: 4
Volunteer Staff: 1
Paid Artists: 21
Budget: $450,000
Income Sources: Dance USA
Annual Attendance: 30,000
Organization Type: Performing; Touring

374
TRISHA BROWN DANCE COMPANY
625 W 55th Street
2nd Floor
New York, NY 10019
Phone: 212-582-0040
Web Site: www.trishabrowncompany.org
Officers:
Founder: Tricia Brown
Chairman: Robert Rauschenberg

All listings are in alphabetical order by state, then city, then organization within the city.

President: Kirk Radke
VP: Jeanne Linnes
Treasurer: Michael Hecht
Secretary: David Blasband
Management:
    Artistic Director/Choreographer: Trisha Brown
    Executive Director: Michele Thompson
    Assistant Artistic Director: Rebecca Davis
    Rehearsal Director: Irene Hultman
    General Manager: Nicole Taney
    Production Stage Manager: Tricia Toliver
Mission: The Trisha Brown Dance Company has initiated the Legacy and Preservation Program, to ensure that future generations have access to the artistry of Trisha Brown.
Founded: 1970
Specialized Field: Modern
Status: Professional, Nonprofit
Paid Staff: 6
Paid Artists: 17
Budget: $1,000,000-$2,500,000
Income Sources: Foundation; Corporate; Grants; Performance Fees; Individual Contribution
Organization Type: Performing; Touring; Resident; Educational

375
WOFA! PERCUSSION AND DANCE FROM GUINEA, WEST AFRICA
Bernard Schmidt Productions
461 W 49th Street, E Office
New York, NY 10019
Phone: 212-307-5046
Fax: 212-397-2459
e-mail: bschmidtpd@aol.com
Web Site: www.bernardschmidtproductions.com
Management:
    Artists Representative: Bernard Schmidt
Mission: Performers from around the world at the crossroads of innovation and tradition.
Specialized Field: African Dance; Contemporary Dance
Paid Staff: 2
Paid Artists: 10

376
WORLD MUSIC INSTITUTE
49 W 27th Street
Suite 930
New York, NY 10001-6936
Phone: 212-545-7536
Fax: 212-889-2771
e-mail: chris@worldmusicinstitute.org
Web Site: www.heartheworld.org
Officers:
    Chair: Zeyba Rahman
    Secretary: Zette Emmons
Management:
    Executive/Artistic Director: Robert H Browning
    Promotion Director: Helene Browning
    Finance/Administration Director: Elias El-Hage
    Development Director: Chris Tokar
    Produciton Coordinator: Song Lee
Mission: Dedicated to the research and presentation of the finest in traditional and contemporary music and dance from around the world. World Music Institute supports and encourages musicians from immigrant communities and collaborates with universities, cultural organizations and other presenting organizations that have similar goals.
Founded: 1985
Specialized Field: Ethnic Dance; Folk Dance; World Music
Status: Nonprofit

Paid Staff: 10
Volunteer Staff: 20
Income Sources: Ticket Sales; Grants
Performs At: Symphony Space; Town Hall; Merkin Hall; Zankel Hall
Annual Attendance: 35,000
Organization Type: Touring

377
YOSHIKO CHUMA AND THE SCHOOL OF HARD KNOCKS
201 E 4th Street
New York, NY 10009
Phone: 212-533-9473
Fax: 915-773-3891
Web Site: www.yoshikochuma.org
Management:
    Artistic Director/Choreographer: Yoshiko Chuma
Mission: Yoshiko Chuma has been building unique structures in the liminal area between her native Japanese culture and her adopted American one. Using trained and pedestrian movers, virtuoso instrumentalists (whose playing she often conducts), film, video and sculptural forms by collaborating artists, she develops unusual time based art works that blend the live and the recorded, the flat and the three-dimensional, people and things.
Founded: 1984
Specialized Field: Post-Modern Dance
Status: Professional, Nonprofit
Income Sources: Grants; Foundations; Corporations
Organization Type: Performing; Touring

378
POSEY DANCE COMPANY
PO Box 254
Northport, NY 11768
Phone: 631-757-2700
e-mail: msposey@optonline.net
Web Site: www.poseyschool.com
Management:
    Founder/Director: Elsa Posey
Mission: Education.
Founded: 1953
Specialized Field: Modern; Ballet; Jazz
Status: Professional; Nonprofit
Income Sources: American Dance Guild
Organization Type: Performing; Touring; Educational

379
DEBRA WEISS DANCE COMPANY
51 Summit Street
Nyack, NY 10960
Phone: 845-353-3860
Fax: 845-353-3860
e-mail: dnweiss@aol.com
Web Site: www.debraweissdance.org
Officers:
    President: Debra Weiss
Management:
    Artistic Director: Debra Weiss
Mission: We use dance as a medium for storytelling and living history programs for children, teens and adults. Much of our work is in schools and museums, where we supplement and enrich existing cirricula and exhibits with our programming.
Utilizes: Actors; Artists-in-Residence; Choreographers; Collaborations; Commissioned Music; Dancers; Grant Writers; Guest Lecturers; Guest Musical Directors; Guild Activities; High School Drama; Instructors; Local Artists; Lyricists; Original Music Scores; Singers; Students
Founded: 1983
Specialized Field: Storytelling; Educational Dance

Status: Professional, Nonprofit
Paid Artists: 3
Organization Type: Performing; Touring; Resident; Educational

380
WESTCHESTER BALLET COMPANY
PO Box 694
Ossining, NY 10562
Phone: 914-941-4532
Fax: 941-923-7693
e-mail: westchesterballet@gmail.com
Web Site: www.westchesterballet.org
Officers:
    President: Denise Rempe
    VP: Terri Richards
    VP: Jeanne Carroll
    Treasurer: Antonia Newbury
    Secretary: Maria Weyrauch
Management:
    Artistic Director: Beth Fritz-Logrea
    Co-Artistic Director: Jean Logrea
Mission: To promote the awareness and appreciation of dance through all the communitites of Westchester County. Westchester Ballet Company has become known for excellence in performance and dance education.
Utilizes: Singers
Founded: 1950
Specialized Field: Ballet
Status: Professional, Nonprofit
Paid Staff: 70
Performs At: Westchester County Center For The Arts
Organization Type: Performing; Educational

381
BALLET NY
4445 Post Road
Suite 3H
Riverdale, NY 10471
Phone: 718-543-2760
Fax: 718-543-2760
e-mail: balletny.directors@gmail.com
Web Site: www.balletny.org
Officers:
    Chair: Lauren B Cramer
Management:
    Artistic Director: Judith Fugate
    Co-Artistic Director: Medhi Bahiri
Mission: Foremost in Ballet New York's mission is to offer emerging choreographers the opportunity to create new works on accomplished dancers. The company is also committed to keeping ticket prices affordable in an effort to attract, cultivate and educate new audiences for dance.
Founded: 1997
Specialized Field: Ballet

382
GARTH FAGAN DANCE
50 Chestnut Street
Rochester, NY 14604
Phone: 585-454-3260
Fax: 585-454-6191
e-mail: johanna@garthfagandance.org
Web Site: www.garthfagandance.org
Officers:
    Founder/President: Garth Fagan
    Chairman: Kenneth D Bell
    Treasurer: Jesse Dudley
    Secretary: Louise H Klinke
Management:
    Artistic Director/Choreographer: Garth Fagan
    Executive Director: Ruby P Lockhart

Rehearsal Director: Norwood Pennewell
Controller: Susanna Kreilick
Company Manager: Bit Knighton
Marketing Coordinator: Johanna M Lester
Production Stage Manager: Bets Quackenbush
Mission: To perform modern dance and compete on a national level with original choreography by Garth Fagan.
Founded: 1970
Specialized Field: Modern; Ethnic Dance
Status: Professional, Nonprofit
Budget: $1,000,000-$2,500,000
Income Sources: Grants; Performances; Foundations
Performs At: Nazareth College Arts Center
Organization Type: Performing; Touring; Resident; Educational

383
ROCHESTER CITY BALLET

1326 University Avenue
Rochester, NY 14607
Phone: 585-461-5850
Fax: 585-473-8847
e-mail: info@rochestercityballet.com
Web Site: www.rochestercity ballet.org
Management:
Artistic Director: Jamey Leverett
Executive Director: Kathy Ertsgaard
Mission: Rochester City Ballet will nurture, promote and demonstrate the art of dance through education and performances of the highest technical exellence.
Specialized Field: Ballet

384
BALLET LONG ISLAND

1863 Pond Road
Ronkonkoma, NY 11779
Phone: 631-737-1964
e-mail: dance@balletlongisland.com
Web Site: www.balletlongisland.com
Management:
Artistic Director: Debra Punzi
Mission: Our mission is to make dance available and affordable to everyone.
Utilizes: Artists-in-Residence; Choreographers; Collaborating Artists; Commissioned Music; Dancers; Guest Artists; High School Drama; Local Artists; Original Music Scores; Poets
Founded: 1985
Specialized Field: Ballet
Status: Professional, Nonprofit
Budget: $200,000-$500,000
Performs At: Islip Town Hall West; Long Island Ballet Center Performance Space
Affiliations: Ballet Center
Annual Attendance: 40,000
Seating Capacity: 500

385
PICK OF THE CROP DANCE

2344 Lake Road
Silver Creek, NY 14136
Phone: 716-934-0515
e-mail: info@poc.org
Web Site: www.poc.org
Management:
Artistic Director: Elaine Gardner
Music Director/Executive Director: Curt Steinzor
Mission: Pick of the Crop Dance's mission is to produce and promote excellence in contemporary dance through community performances, educational programs and the training of young dancers.
Founded: 1979
Specialized Field: Contemporary Dance

Budget: $100,000-$200,000

386
PAT CANNON'S FOOT & FIDDLE DANCE COMPANY

115 Johnsontown Road
Sloatsburg, NY 10974
Phone: 845-753-6950
Fax: 845-753-6949
e-mail: info@footandfiddle.org
Web Site: www.footandfiddle.org
Officers:
Founder/President: Pat Cannon
Management:
Artistic Director: Pat Cannon
Mission: Pat Cannon's Foot & Fiddle Dance Company is a versatile ensemble of dancers and musicians who present American dance and music in creative new ways.
Utilizes: AEA Actors; Choreographers; Dancers; Original Music Scores
Founded: 1981
Specialized Field: Tap; Square Dance; Appalachian Clogging; Swing Dance; Irish Dance
Status: Professional, Nonprofit
Paid Staff: 2
Budget: $125,000
Income Sources: Concert venues, Arts In Education, Square Dancers
Performs At: throughout the Northeast
Organization Type: Performing; Touring; Resident; Educational

387
MOWHAWK VALLEY BALLET

Mohawk Valley Performing Arts Inc
270 Geneseee Street
Utica, NY 13502-4617
Phone: 315-738-7646
e-mail: info@mvperformingarts.org
Web Site: www.mvperformingarts.org
Officers:
Founder: Delia Foley
Management:
Artistic Director: Delia Foley
Mission: The Mohawk Valley Ballet offers a subscription series including The Nutcracker and an Education through Experience Series for students and teachers.
Founded: 1973
Specialized Field: Ballet
Year Built: 1920

388
MANHATTAN TAP

PO Box 571
Valley Cottage, NY 10989
Phone: 845-480-1396
e-mail: hcornell@manhattantap.org
Web Site: www.manhattantap.org
Officers:
Founder: Heather Cornell
Management:
Artistic Director/Choreographer: Heather Cornell, hcornell@manhattantap.org
Mission: Manhattan Tap continues to create a new style of concert tap that has never lost the art of improvisation or the individual strengths of its members.
Utilizes: Singers
Founded: 1986
Specialized Field: Tap
Status: Professional, Non-Profit
Paid Staff: 2
Paid Artists: 09

Budget: $100,000 - $250,000
Facility Category: Theater
Seating Capacity: 5,000

North Carolina

389
TERPSICORPS THEATRE OF DANCE

Pack Place
2 S Pack Square
Asheville, NC 28801
Phone: 828-252-6342
e-mail: info@terpsicorps.org
Web Site: www.terpsicorps.org
Officers:
Chair: Karen Ramshaw
President: Stephanie Biziewski
Treasurer: Elizabeth Bright
Secretary: Alison Watson
Management:
Artistic Director: Heather Maloy
Managing Director: Lucia Del Vecchio
Ballet Master: Timothy Rinehart Yeager
Mission: A summer season from June to mid-August gives Terpsicorps the chance to introduce it's innovative style of dance to the citizens of Asheville through two concert performances at Pack Place.
Founded: 2003
Specialized Field: Contemporary Ballet
Status: Professional, Nonprofit

390
NORTH CAROLINA DANCE THEATRE

622 E 28th Street
Charlotte, NC 28205
Phone: 704-372-0101
Fax: 704-375-0260
e-mail: awright@ncdance.org
Web Site: www.ncdance.org
Officers:
President: Jean-Pierre Bonnefoux
Chair: Thomas Brydon
Treasurer: Stephen Hasty Jr
Secretary: Stuart Goldstein
Management:
Artistic Director: Jean-Pierre Bonnefoux
Associate Artistic Director: Patricia McBride
Executive Director: Doug Singleton
Program Director NC Dance Theatre 2: Mark Diamond
Rehearsal Director: Sasha Janes
Musical Associate/Facilities Mgr: Gene Gledsoe
Resident Choreographer: Dwight Rhoden
Development Director: Anthony M Wright
Marketing Manager: Marketing Ralon
Mission: The North Carolina Dance Theatre's mission is to provide artistically excellent programming to diverse audiences in its home city of Charlotte, the Southeast region and to the varied communities it serves while on tour across the nation.
Utilizes: Choreographers; Commissioned Composers; Dancers; Designers; Educators; Five Seasonal Concerts; Guest Accompanists; Guest Artists; Guest Composers; Guest Conductors; Guest Ensembles; Guest Instructors; Guest Musical Directors; Guest Musicians; Instructors; Resident Artists; Resident Professionals; Sign Language Translators; Soloists; Visual Arts
Founded: 1970
Specialized Field: Modern; Ballet
Status: Professional, Nonprofit
Budget: 4,200,000

Income Sources: Arts and Science Council of Charlotte; Corporate; Individual
Performs At: North Carolina Blumenthal Performing Arts Center
Type of Stage: Proscenium
Stage Dimensions: 44'x34'
Seating Capacity: 1920
Year Built: 1992
Organization Type: Performing; Touring

391
AFRICAN AMERICAN DANCE ENSEMBLE
120 Morris Street
Durham, NC 27701
Phone: 919-560-2729
Fax: 919-560-2743
Web Site: www.africanamericandanceensemble.org
Officers:
  Founder: Chuch Davis
  President: Donald Baker
Management:
  Artistic Director: Chuck Davis
  Associate Artistic Director: Stafford C Berry Jr
  Interim Executive Director: Beverly A Cureton
  Musical Director: Kwabena Osei Appiagyei
  Program Director/Tour Manager: Normadien Gibson-Woolbright
  Technical Director: Elizabeth Droessler
Mission: The African American Dance Ensemble seeks to preserve and share the finest traditions of African and African American dance and music through research, education and entertainment.
Utilizes: Choreographers; Collaborating Artists; Collaborations; Dance Companies; Dancers; Guest Accompanists; Guest Musical Directors; Instructors; Lyricists; Original Music Scores; Sign Language Translators; Student Interns; Theatre Companies
Founded: 1984
Specialized Field: African Dance; African American Dance
Status: Professional, Non-Profit
Paid Staff: 12
Volunteer Staff: 10
Paid Artists: 9
Budget: $500,000
Income Sources: Federal, State and Private Funding; Earned Income from Performances
Performs At: Nationally; Internationally
Annual Attendance: 150,000

392
GREENSBORO BALLET
200 N Davie Street
Box 12
Greensboro, NC 27401
Phone: 336-333-7480
Fax: 336-333-7482
e-mail: greensboroballet@yahoo.com
Web Site: www.greensboroballet.org
Officers:
  CEO: Maryhelen Mayfield
Management:
  Artistic Director: Maryhelen Mayfield
  School Director: John Dennis
  Ballet Mistress: Elissa Fuchs
  Director of Children's Dance: Becky Turner
Mission: The Greensboro Ballet provides professional ballet performances and training to the people of Greensboro and surrounding communities.
Utilizes: Choreographers; Dance Companies; Dancers; Educators; Five Seasonal Concerts; Guest Artists; Guest Choreographers; Guest Musicians; Guest

Speakers; High School Drama; Original Music Scores; Paid Performers; Resident Companies; Singers; Soloists; Volunteer Artists
Founded: 1980
Specialized Field: Classical Ballet
Status: Professional, Nonprofit
Paid Staff: 10
Volunteer Staff: 22
Paid Artists: 4
Non-paid Artists: 2
Budget: $325,000
Income Sources: Performances; Tuition; Foundations
Performs At: throughout Greensboro
Annual Attendance: 8,000-10,000

393
JAN VAN DYKE DANCE GROUP
NC Dance Project Inc
306 Aberdeen Terrace
Greensboro, NC 27403-1817
Phone: 336-370-4819
Fax: 336-334-3238
e-mail: vandykedance@hotmail.com
Web Site: www.janvandykedance.org
Officers:
  President: Tracie Foster
  Treasurer: Peggy Markham
  Secretary: Julia Mulyihill
Management:
  Artistic Director/Choreographer: Jan Van Dyke
Mission: To present the work of Jan Van Dyke through a variety of professional performances and educational programs to all ages.
Utilizes: Artists-in-Residence; Choreographers; Collaborations; Commissioned Composers; Commissioned Music; Community Talent; Composers; Dance Companies; Dancers; Designers; Filmmakers; Guest Companies; Guest Musical Directors; Instructors; Multi Collaborations; Multimedia; Organization Contracts; Original Music Scores; Playwrights; Resident Artists
Founded: 1989
Specialized Field: Modern
Status: Professional, Nonprofit
Paid Staff: 2
Paid Artists: 5
Budget: $20,000
Income Sources: Grants; Fundraising; Donations; Ticket Sales
Affiliations: North Carolina Dance Project; UNC Greensboro Department of Dance; United Arts Council of Greensboro
Organization Type: Performing; Touring
Resident Groups: University of North Carolina at Greensboro

Ohio

394
OHIO BALLET
354 E Market Street
Akron, OH 44325
Phone: 330-972-7900
Fax: 330-972-7902
Web Site: www.ohioballet.org
Management:
  General Manager: Stephan Newenhisen
  Artistic Director: Jeffrey Graham Hughes
Mission: Delivering the magic of dance. To be a driving force creating a passion for dance.
Utilizes: Five Seasonal Concerts
Founded: 1968
Specialized Field: Ballet

Status: Professional; Nonprofit
Budget: $1,500,000
Performs At: Akron; Cleveland; Youngstown
Organization Type: Performing; Touring

395
CANTON BALLET
1001 N Market Avenue
Canton, OH 44702
Phone: 330-455-7220
Fax: 330-455-6977
e-mail: cantonballet@cantonballet.com
Web Site: www.cantonballet.com
Management:
  Artistic Director/Executice Dir: Cassandra Crowley
  Manager: Deby Barath
Mission: Committed to offering progressive levels of dance training of the highest quality and providing performance opportunities for dancers.
Utilizes: Singers
Founded: 1965
Specialized Field: Ballet
Status: Pre-professional; Nonprofit
Paid Staff: 15
Volunteer Staff: 100
Paid Artists: 10
Non-paid Artists: 150
Budget: $600,000
Income Sources: Tuition; Performance Admissions; Memberships; Foundations; Arts In Starks; Ohio Arts Council
Performs At: Palace Theatre
Affiliations: Regional Dance America; Ohio Citizens for the Arts; Ohio Dance
Annual Attendance: 7,000
Type of Stage: Proscenium
Seating Capacity: 1500
Year Built: 1929
Organization Type: Performing; Touring; Resident; Educational

396
BI-OKOTO CULTURAL INSTITUTE
7030 Reading Road
Suite 662 & 654
Cincinnati, OH 45237
Phone: 513-221-6112
Fax: 330-238-0023
e-mail: bi-okoto@bi-okoto.com
Web Site: www.bi-okoto.com
Management:
  Artistic/Executive Director: Adebola T Olowe Sr
Mission: Our mission is to preserve, promote and share the rich cultural heritage of Africa and Africans using drums, music, dance, food, languages and other arts.
Founded: 1996
Specialized Field: Edo Dance; Apepe; Koroso; Jameba; Apeja Dance
Status: Nonprofit
Paid Staff: 5
Volunteer Staff: 7
Paid Artists: 20
Income Sources: Corporate; Grants; Individuals
Rental Contact: Courtney Smith

397
CINCINNATI BALLET
1555 Central Parkway
Cincinnati, OH 45214
Phone: 513-621-5219
Fax: 513-621-4844
Web Site: www.cincinnatiballet.com

Officers:
CEO: Victoria Morgan
Chair: Otto M Budig Jr
President: Kathy Selker
VP: Rhonda Sheakley
VP: Russ Shelton
Treasurer: Michael J Sewell
Secretary: Judy Dalambakis
Management:
Artistic Director: Victoria Morgan
Associate Artistic Director: Devon Carney
Music Director: Carmon DeLeone
Principal Ballet Mistress: Johanna Bernstein Wilt
Finance/Operations Director: Craig Lattarulo
Development Director: Stephanie Harris
Interim Marketing Director: Melissa Santomo
Mission: Cincinnati Ballet continues to thrill audiences with unparalleled performances. From excellence on stage to outreach in local schools and community Cincinnati Ballet takes pride in the fact that it is an integral part of the culture of the city.
Utilizes: Five Seasonal Concerts; Guest Companies
Founded: 1958
Specialized Field: Ballet
Status: Professional, Nonprofit
Budget: $5,000,000
Income Sources: Foundations; Earned; Government
Performs At: Music Hall
Annual Attendance: 9,000
Organization Type: Performing; Touring; Resident; Educational

398
CONTEMPORARY DANCE THEATER

College Hill Town Hall
1805 Larch Avenue
Cincinnati, OH 45224
Phone: 513-591-1122
Fax: 513-591-1222
e-mail: info@cdt-dance.org
Web Site: www.cdt-dance.org
Officers:
Founder: Jefferson James
Management:
Artistic/Executive Director: Jefferson James
Assistant Director: Laura Stewart
Mission: Our mission is moving bodies moving souls, the essence of contemporary dance. Connecting the community with diverse and socially relevant dance and performance art.
Utilizes: Actors; Choreographers; Collaborating Artists; Collaborations; Commissioned Composers; Community Members; Community Talent; Dance Companies; Dancers; Guest Accompanists; Guest Artists; Guest Choreographers; Guest Ensembles; Guest Musical Directors; Guest Speakers; Instructors; Local Artists; Local Artists & Directors; Original Music Scores; Paid Performers; Scenic Designers; Soloists; Visual Designers
Founded: 1972
Specialized Field: Modern; Jazz; Ballet; Tap; Improvisation; Hip Hop
Status: Professional, Nonprofit
Paid Staff: 2
Paid Artists: 7
Non-paid Artists: 12
Income Sources: Ohio Dance; Cincinnati Commission of the Arts; Dance Action
Performs At: The Dance Hall
Organization Type: Performing; Touring; Resident; Educational; Sponsoring

399
CLEVELAND STATE UNIVERSITY DANCE COMPANY

Dance Program
2121 Euclid Avenue PE 214
Cleveland, OH 44115-2214
Phone: 216-687-4883
Fax: 216-687-5410
e-mail: dance@csuohio.edu
Web Site: www.csuohio.edu
Officers:
President: Michael Schwartz
Management:
Director: Lynn H Deering
Mission: Cleveland State University Dance Company offers students the opportunity to rehearse and perform their own work, as well as works by nationally renowned artists in the Greater Cleveland Area.
Founded: 1979
Specialized Field: Contemporary Dance
Status: Pre-Professional, Nonprofit

400
DANCECLEVELAND

13110 Shaker Square
Suite 106
Cleveland, OH 44120
Phone: 216-991-9000
Fax: 216-991-9001
e-mail: dex@dancecleveland.org
Web Site: www.dancecleivland.org
Management:
Executive Director: Pam Young
Marketing Director: Heather Greer-Sikora
Development Manager: Barbara Badalamenti
Administrative Coordinator: Rachael Sauber
Projects Coordinator: Kitty McWilliams
Mission: Our mission is to bring the passion and verve of modern and contemporary dance to Northeast Ohio.
Founded: 1956
Specialized Field: Dance
Status: Nonprofit
Income Sources: National Endowment for the Arts; Association for Performing Arts Presenters; International Society of Performing Arts Administrators; Arts Midwest; Dance USA; Arts Presenters
Performs At: Ohio Theatre; Playhouse Square Center
Organization Type: Educational; Sponsoring

401
INLET DANCE THEATRE

11125 Magnolia Drive
Cleveland, OH 44106
Phone: 216-721-8580
Fax: 216-721-8580
e-mail: info@inletdance.org
Web Site: www.inletdance.org
Officers:
Founder: Bill Wade
Chairperson: Steve Citerin
Management:
Artistic Director: Bill Wade
Mission: Inlet Dance Theatre is one of the region's most exciting professional contemporary dance companies dedicated to performing with a high level of quality, skill, innovation and purpose. Inlet utilizes the art form of dance to bring about personal development in the lives of individuals through training and mentoring, and to speak creatively about life and the issues we face.
Utilizes: Artists-in-Residence; Choreographers; Composers; Dancers; Educators; Filmmakers; Guest Artists; Local Talent; Theatre Companies

Founded: 2001
Specialized Field: Contemporary Dance
Season: November-December

402
MORRISONDANCE

4201 Lorain Avenue
Cleveland, OH 44113
Phone: 216-281-9558
e-mail: sarah@morrisondance.com
Web Site: www.morrisondance.com
Officers:
Founder: Sarah Morrison
Treasurer: Jennifer Bennett
Secretary: Kimi Nose
Management:
Artistic Director/Choreographer: Sarah Morrison
Artist/Visual Designer: Scott Radke
Mission: To inspire and cultivate public awareness of the art of dance through performances, crossdisciplinary collaborations, in combination with various other art forms and disciplines. To provide, promote and participate in educational and outreach programs that increase the awareness of dance and that assist and encourage community cultural and artistic endeavors.
Founded: 1997
Specialized Field: Modern
Status: Professional, Nonprofit

403
VERB BALLETS

2140 Lee Road
Suite 216
Cleveland, OH 44118
Phone: 216-397-3757
Fax: 216-397-7872
e-mail: info@verbballets.org
Web Site: www.verbballets.org
Officers:
President: Jeri Chaikin
Treasurer: Robert M Shwab
Secretary: Jill Cotterman
VP: Richard Rinehart
Management:
Director: Margaret Carlson
Outreach Coordinator: Katie Gnagy
Mission: The mission of Verb Ballets is to promote and develop interest in and appreciation for contemporary dance nationally, regionally and locally through performance, programs that promote learning and nurture wellness, audience and community dialogue and advocacy efforts to support the art form.
Founded: 1987
Specialized Field: Dance
Status: Professional, Non-Profit
Paid Staff: 5
Volunteer Staff: 3
Paid Artists: 15
Budget: $400,000
Income Sources: Ticket Sales; Grants; Foundations; Coroprate

404
BALLETMET DANCE CENTRE

322 Mount Vernon Avenue
Columbus, OH 43215
Phone: 614-229-4860
Fax: 614-229-4858
e-mail: shunt@balletmet.org
Web Site: www.balletmet.org
Officers:
Chair: Susan Porter
Chair-Elect: Randall Walters

Treasurer: Thomas H Brinker
Secretary: Trish Cadwallader
Management:
Artistic Director: Gerard Charles
Executive Director: Cheri Mitchell
Resident Music Director: Mikhail Popov
Ballet Mistress: Rebecca Rodriguez-Hodory
Ballet Master: Hisham Omardien
Development Director: Pam Bishop
Marketing/Communications Director: Sheila Hunt
Production Manager: Jaime Gross
Mission: BalletMet will celebrate dance by engaging the community through quality performances, instruction, education programs and creation of new work.
Utilizes: Singers
Founded: 1978
Specialized Field: Ballet
Status: Professional, Nonprofit
Income Sources: National Association for Regional Ballet; Dance USA
Performs At: Ohio Theatre
Organization Type: Performing; Touring; Resident; Educational; Sponsoring

405
OHIO STATE UNIVERSITY OF DANCE
1813 N High Street
Columbus, OH 43210
Phone: 614-292-7977
Fax: 614-292-0939
e-mail: dance@osu.edu
Web Site: www.dance.ohio-state.edu
Officers:
Chair: Susan Van Pelt Petry
Management:
Music Director: Susan Chess
Production Manager: David Covey
Mission: The department of dance at the Ohio State University is a community of diverse individuals trained on a common nexus of inquiry, the rich and complex phenomenon of dance.
Specialized Field: Traditional Dance; Educational Dance

406
CUYAHOGA VALLEY YOUTH BALLET
PO Box 3131
Cuyahoga Falls, OH 44223
Phone: 330-996-1100
e-mail: lakulwicki@yahoo.com
Web Site: www.cvyb.org
Officers:
Founder: Mia Klinger
President: Laura Kulwicki
Marketing: Rick Davidson
Management:
Artistic Director: Mia Klinger Welch
Artistic Consultant: Lori Klinger
Mission: To provide performing experience for talented young dancers, educating them in the realities of professional ballet to educate area children and families in the appreciation of ballet as an art form at affordable prices.
Utilizes: Five Seasonal Concerts
Founded: 1975
Specialized Field: Modern; Ballet
Status: Pre-Professional, Nonprofit
Paid Staff: 33
Income Sources: Ohio Arts Council; Foundations; Corporate; Individual
Performs At: Akron Civic Theatre; EJ Thomas Hall
Organization Type: Performing; Resident; Educational

407
CONTEMPORARY DANCE OF SINCLAIR
444 W 3rd Street
Sinclair Community College
Dayton, OH 45402
Phone: 937-512-2751
Fax: 937-512-2054
e-mail: patricia.fox@sinclair.edu
Web Site: www.sinclair.edu
Management:
Artisitc Advisor: Patricia Fox
Artistic Director: Rodney Veal
Artistic Director: Denise Miller
Mission: Contmeporary Dance of Sinclair is a modern dance company for the performing aspiring adult trained dancers of the community college environment.
Founded: 1978
Specialized Field: Contemporary Dance

408
DAYTON BALLET
Dayton Ballet Association
140 N Main Street
Dayton, OH 45402
Phone: 937-223-1542
Fax: 934-461-8353
e-mail: info@daytonballet.org
Web Site: www.daytonballet.org
Officers:
Chairman: Douglas Franklin
President: Craig Brown
Management:
Artistic/Executive Director: Dermot Burke
Ballet Mistress: Karen Russo
Ballet Mistress: Sharon Lancaster
Resident Designer/Costumer: Lowell A Mathwich
Marketing Director: Diane Schoeffler-Warren
Production Manager: Stacie R Bigl
Mission: Dayton Ballet's mission is to educate, enlighten and entertain the widest audience possible with the very best in performance, outreach and community service.
Utilizes: Artists-in-Residence; Choreographers; Collaborating Artists; Collaborations; Commissioned Music; Dance Companies; Dancers; Fine Artists; Guest Artists; Guest Choreographers; Guest Conductors; Local Artists; Organization Contracts; Original Music Scores; Resident Artists; Resident Professionals; Soloists; Theatre Companies
Founded: 1927
Specialized Field: Ballet; Contemporary Dance
Status: Professional, Nonprofit
Paid Staff: 32
Budget: $2,000,000
Income Sources: Ticket Revenue; Community Support; State and Local Government
Performs At: The Victoria Theatre; Schuster Performing Arts Center
Annual Attendance: 30,000
Seating Capacity: 1,100
Year Built: 1866
Year Remodeled: 1989
Organization Type: Performing

409
DAYTON CONTEMPORARY DANCE COMPANY
126 N Main Street
Suite 240
Dayton, OH 45402-1710

Phone: 937-228-3232
Fax: 937-223-6156
e-mail: office@dcdc.org
Web Site: www.dcdc.org
Officers:
Chair: Richard Lapedes
Management:
Artistic Director: Debbie Blunden-Diggs
Executive Director: Ro Nita Hawes-Saunders
Touring/Production Manager: Teri Fritze
Mission: Dayton Contemporary Dance Company's mission is to deliver contemporary dance of the highest quality to the broadest possible audience. Dayton Contemporary Dance Company reaches this audience with local performances, through national and international touring and through the company's educational programs in the Miami Valley and on tour.
Utilizes: Actors; AEA Actors; Artists-in-Residence; Choreographers; Collaborating Artists; Collaborations; Community Members; Dance Companies; Dancers; Educators; Five Seasonal Concerts; Guest Artists; Guest Composers; Guest Writers; High School Drama; Multi Collaborations; Multimedia; Original Music Scores; Resident Professionals; Singers
Founded: 1968
Specialized Field: Contemporary Dance; Jazz; Modern
Status: Professional, Nonprofit
Paid Staff: 12
Paid Artists: 11
Non-paid Artists: 15
Budget: $1,300,000
Income Sources: Government; Corporate; Foundations; Individuals
Performs At: The Victoria Theatre
Annual Attendance: 4,500
Type of Stage: Proscenium
Organization Type: Performing; Touring; Resident

410
RHYTHM IN SHOES
126 N Main Street
Suite 420
Dayton, OH 45402
Phone: 937-226-7463
Fax: 937-910-1048
Web Site: www.rhythminshoes.org
Management:
Artistic Director/Choreographer: Sharon Leahy
Artistic Director/Composer: Rick Good
Executive Director: Noreen Willhelm
General Manager: Maggie Cooper
Mission: Rooted in traditional forms of american music and dance swing tunes, tap, hoedowns and clogging the varied repertoire of Rhythm in Shoes directed by choreographer Sharon Leahy and composer Rick Good is at once original and recognizable.
Utilizes: Actors; AEA Actors; Choreographers; Composers-in-Residence; Dancers
Founded: 1987
Specialized Field: Swing Dance; Tap; Clogging
Paid Staff: 2
Paid Artists: 15
Budget: $200,000-$500,000

411
SINCLAIR DANCE
Sinclair Community College
444 West Third Street
Dayton, OH 45402-1460
Phone: 937-512-2751
Fax: 937-512-2054
Toll-free: 800-315-3000
e-mail: pfox@sinclair.edu
Management:

Artistic Director: Patricia Fox
Artistic Director: Dawn Quigley
Specialized Field: Ballet; Modern; Tap

412
ZIVILI DANCE COMPANY
1753 Loudon Street
Granville, OH 43023
Phone: 740-587-7715
Toll-free: 877-906-8314
e-mail: mobenauf@alltel.net
Web Site: www.home.columbus.rr.com
Officers:
Founder/President: Melissa Pintar Obenauf
Co-Founder/VP: Pamela Lacko Kelley
Management:
Artistic Director: Pamela Lacko Kelley
Dance/Executive Director: Melissa Pintar Obenauf
Mission: Zivili Dance Company was created to help preserve a strong cultural legacy of primarily Croatian dance and music.
Utilizes: Five Seasonal Concerts; Singers
Founded: 1973
Specialized Field: Croatian Dance
Status: Professional, Nonprofit
Budget: $250,000
Income Sources: Performances; Arts Counsil Grants; Individual Contributions
Performs At: Southern Theatre
Annual Attendance: 50,000
Organization Type: Performing; Touring; Educational

413
OHIO DANCE THEATRE
New Union Center for the Arts
39 S Main Street Suite 241
Oberlin, OH 44074
Phone: 440-774-6077
Fax: 440-774-6160
e-mail: odt@oberlin.net
Web Site: www.ohiodancetheatre.org
Officers:
Founder: Denise Gula
Management:
Artistic Director: Denise Gula
Faculty Coordinator/Dir Summer Prog: Nancy Brenstuhl
Mission: Ohio Dance Theatre will encourage the growth and support of serious dance through the presentation of exceptional performances, instruction and educational programs that enhance the community's quality of life.
Specialized Field: Classical; Contemporary Dance; Theatre Dance
Income Sources: Community Foundation; Corporate; Fundraising; Individual; Matching Gifts; Nord Family Foundation; Ohio Arts Council; Stocker Foundation
Season: October-May

414
THEATER AND DANCE PROGRAM
Oberlin College
30 N Professor Street
Oberlin, OH 44074
Phone: 440-775-8152
Fax: 440-775-8340
e-mail: janice.sanborn@oberlin.edu
Web Site: www.oberlin.edu
Officers:
Associate Chair: Nusha Martynuk
Management:
Dance Professor: Ann Cooper Albright
Assistant Technical Director: David Bugher

Mission: The Theater and Dance Program offers students an interrelated series of courses and performance activities designed to provide a sound liberal arts grounding in the theory and practice of the arts of theater and dance.
Specialized Field: Modern
Performs At: Finney Chapel; Hall Auditorium; Warner Center

415
MIAMI UNIVERSITY DANCE THEATRE
106 E Phillips Hall
Oxford, OH 45056
Phone: 513-529-2730
Fax: 513-529-5006
e-mail: rosenblk@muohio.edu
Web Site: www.muohio.edu/dancetheatre
Management:
Artistic Director/General Manager: Lana Kay Rosenberg, rosenblk@umohio.edu
Founded: 1933
Specialized Field: Contemporary/Modern; Ballet; Jazz; Tap
Status: Semi-Professional; Non-Profit
Income Sources: Ticket Sales; Miami University
Performs At: Hall Auditorium
Affiliations: Ohio Dance; ACDFA
Annual Attendance: 1,100
Type of Stage: Proscenium
Seating Capacity: 730

416
BALLET THEATRE OF OHIO
PO Box 2255
Stow, OH 44262
Phone: 330-688-6065
Fax: 330-688-7781
e-mail: info@ballettheatreohio.org
Web Site: www.ballettheatreohio.org
Officers:
Founder: Christine Meneer
Management:
Artistic Director: Christine Meneer
Mission: Ballet Theatre of Ohio will present repertory performances and extensive educational outreach programs for the youth and the Akron area community.
Utilizes: Five Seasonal Concerts; Singers
Founded: 1993
Specialized Field: Ballet
Status: Professional, Nonprofit
Income Sources: Corporate; Foundation; Individual
Performs At: Akron Civic Theatre
Organization Type: Performing; Touring; Resident

417
LEAVEN DANCE COMPANY
2292 Lynnwood Drive
Stow, OH 44224
Phone: 330-688-8806
Fax: 330-686-6103
e-mail: kmleaven@neo.rr.com
Web Site: www.leavendance.org
Officers:
Founder: Kathryn Mihelick
President: Thomas J Froehlich PhD
VP/Secretary: Robert Stadulis PhD
Treasurer: C Branton Shearer PhD
Management:
Artistic Director/Choreographer: Kathryn Mihelick
Associate Artistic Director: Andrea Tecza Shearer

Mission: Leaven Dance Company is a professional dance ensemble whose work addresses spiritual, ethical, social and wholeness issues through performance and worship venues and educational, motivational workshops.
Founded: 1992
Specialized Field: Liturgical Dance; Experimental Dance
Status: Professional, Nonprofit
Paid Staff: 1
Volunteer Staff: 8
Paid Artists: 6
Budget: 10,000
Annual Attendance: 8,000

418
TOLEDO BALLET ASSOCIATION
5001 Monroe Street
Toledo, OH 43623
Phone: 419-471-0049
Fax: 419-471-9005
e-mail: info@toledoballet.net
Web Site: www.toledoballet.net
Officers:
Founder: Marie Bollinger Vogt
President: Robert Koenig
VP: Gayle Parseghian
Treasurer: Jodi Busack
Secretary: Traci Coleman
Management:
Executive Director: Mari Davies
Artistic Director Emerita: Marie Bollinger Vogt
School Director: Lisa Mayer
Marketing/Outreach Coordinator: Michael Lang
Business Coordinator: Elizabeth White
Mission: The Toledo Ballet is dedicated to providing the highest quality of training, from the earliest stages and progressing through the pre-professional level, by blending the discipline of classical ballet with the respect for the entire spectrum of dance.
Utilizes: Collaborations; Dance Companies; Dancers; Educators; Five Seasonal Concerts; Guest Accompanists; Guest Artists; Guest Composers; Guest Writers; Theatre Companies
Founded: 1958
Specialized Field: Ballet
Status: Professional, Nonprofit
Paid Staff: 10
Volunteer Staff: 2
Budget: $633,000
Income Sources: Various
Performs At: Stranahan Theater; Franciscan Center
Annual Attendance: 15,000
Organization Type: Performing; Touring; Resident; Educational; Sponsoring

419
BALLET WESTERN RESERVE
218 W Boardman Street
Youngstown, OH 44501-1684
Phone: 330-744-1934
Fax: 330-744-2631
e-mail: info@balletwesternreserve.org
Web Site: www.balletwesternreserve.org
Officers:
President: Don Foley
VP: Aundrea Cika Heschmeyer
Treasurer: Robert Smith
Secretary: Amy Gelfand
Management:
Artistic Director: Richard Dickinson
Director Emeritus: Anita S Lin
Business Manager: James McClellan

Mission: Ballet Western Reserve students are offered the opportunity to develop the skills, experience and discipline that provide the necessary foundation for a professional career in dance.
Utilizes: Five Seasonal Concerts; Singers
Founded: 1962
Specialized Field: Modern; Ballet; Jazz
Status: Nonprofessional, Nonprofit
Income Sources: Tuition; Fundraising
Performs At: Youngstown State University; Powers Auditorium
Annual Attendance: 5,000-6,000
Organization Type: Performing; Educational

Oklahoma

420
WESTERN OKLAHOMA BALLET THEATRE

711 Frisco Avenue
Clinton, OK 73601
Phone: 580-323-7400
e-mail: debbie.brown@swosu.edu
Web Site: www.western-oklahoma-ballet.org
Officers:
Founder: Candance Jones Smalley
Management:
Artistic/Executive Director: Penny Askew
Mission: Western Oklahoma Ballet Theatre is dedicated to bringing quality dance performances and instruction to Western Oklahoma, focusing on the fine art of classical ballet.
Utilizes: Five Seasonal Concerts
Founded: 1977
Specialized Field: Classical Ballet
Status: Nonprofessional, Nonprofit
Paid Staff: 9
Income Sources: Regional Dance America; Southwestern Regional Ballet Association
Performs At: Southwestern Oklahoma State University Fine Arts
Organization Type: Performing; Educational

421
DUNCAN LAWTON CITY BALLET

1006 SW E Avenue
Lawton, OK 73501
Mailing Address: PO Box 3714 Lawton OK, 73502
Phone: 580-357-2700
Fax: 580-353-3527
e-mail: dlcballet@hotmail.com
Officers:
Chair: Dr. Lloyd A Dawe
Management:
Artistic Director/Founder: Margaret Gray
Managing Director: Roger Gray
Mission: Dedicated to the presentation of ballet.
Founded: 1994
Specialized Field: Ballet
Status: Nonprofit
Volunteer Staff: 3
Non-paid Artists: 16
Income Sources: Local Foundations
Performs At: Simon Center Theatre
Annual Attendance: 7,200

422
CONTEMPORARY DANCE OKLAHOMA

University of Oklahoma School of Dance
560 Parrington Oval
Room 1000
Norman, OK 73019-0319

Phone: 405-325-4051
Fax: 405-325-7024
e-mail: dance@ou.edu
Web Site: www.ou.edu/finearts/dance
Officers:
Chair: Mary Margaret Holt
Management:
School Dance Director: Mary Margaret Holt
Artistic Director: Austin Hartel
Assistant to the Director: Rhonda Hill
Mission: To present an eclectic repertoire of modern and contemporary dance works presented by a company of young, talented dancers.
Founded: 1961
Specialized Field: Modern
Status: Semi Professional, Non-Profit
Paid Staff: 6
Non-paid Artists: 24
Budget: Less than $40,000
Income Sources: University Of Oklahoma; Tours
Performs At: The Rupel Jones Theatre; Donald W Reynolds Performing Arts Center Theatre (Holmberg Hall)
Annual Attendance: 5,500
Type of Stage: Proscenium Arch Stage (Both)
Stage Dimensions: 4,935sq ft(Jones); 5,000sq ft (Hall
Seating Capacity: 700;677
Year Built: 1965
Year Remodeled: 2002

423
OKLAHOMA FESTIVAL BALLET

560 Parrington Oval
Room 1000
Norman, OK 73019-0319
Phone: 405-325-4051
Fax: 405-325-7024
e-mail: dance@ou.edu
Web Site: www.ou.edu
Officers:
Chair: Mary Margaret Holt
Management:
School of Dance Director: Mary Margaret Holt
Assistant to the Director: Rhonda Moore
Mission: To present an eclectic repertoire through a classical ballet company of young dancers.
Utilizes: Choreographers; Collaborations; Dancers; Designers; Grant Writers; Guest Accompanists; Guest Artists; Original Music Scores; Soloists
Founded: 1961
Specialized Field: Ballet
Status: Semi-Professional, Non-Profit
Paid Staff: 6
Non-paid Artists: 30
Budget: $200,000-$500,000
Income Sources: University of Oklahoma; Tours
Performs At: The Rupel Jones Theatre; Donald W Reynolds Performing Arts Center Theatre(Holmberg Hall)
Annual Attendance: 5,500
Type of Stage: Proscenium arch stage (Both)
Stage Dimensions: 4,935sq ft(Jones);5,000sq ft(Hall)
Seating Capacity: 700;677
Year Built: 1965
Year Remodeled: 2002
Organization Type: Performing; Touring; Resident; Educational

424
ANN LACEY SCHOOL OF AMERICAN DANCE AND ARTS MANAGEMENT

Oklahoma City University
2501 N Blackwelder Avenue
Oklahoma City, OK 73106

Phone: 405-521-5322
Fax: 405-521-5313
e-mail: dance@okcu.edu
Web Site: www.okcu.edu
Officers:
Chairman: Jo Rowan
Dean: John Bedford
Associate Dean: Melanie Shelley
Management:
External Affairs/Special Projects: Jennifer Polvado
Mission: A single place within a respected university where American dance art forms and arts management can be nurtured and developed to their highest level and properly recognized for their contributions to art and culture throughout the world.
Founded: 1981
Specialized Field: Jazz; Tap; Musical Theater Dance; Rhythm Tap and Ballet

425
OKLAHOMA CITY BALLET

7421 N Classen
Oklahoma City, OK 73116
Phone: 405-843-9898
Fax: 405-843-9894
e-mail: balleto@sbcglobal.net
Web Site: www.balletoklahoma.com
Officers:
President: Phil Clayton
Treasurer: Randy Foraker
Secretary: Desiree LaVigne-Roan
Management:
Artistic Director: Robert Mills
Executive Director: Judith Hankins
Ballet Master: Jacob Sparso
Company Teacher/Coach: Alexa Fioroni
Technical/Lighting Director: Dale Hall
Stage Manager: David Pape
Mission: Continues to provide superb training for students interested in becoming professional ballet dancers as well as for others who want recreational ballet classes.
Utilizes: Five Seasonal Concerts; Singers
Founded: 1972
Specialized Field: Ballet; Jazz
Status: Professional, Non-Profit
Paid Staff: 7
Volunteer Staff: 5
Paid Artists: 18
Budget: $1,000,000-$2,500,000
Income Sources: Ticket Sales; Grants
Performs At: Oklahoma City Civic Center
Annual Attendance: 20,000
Organization Type: Performing; Touring; Resident; Educational; Sponsoring

426
PRAIRIE DANCE THEATRE

2100 NE 52nd
Kirkpatrick Center
Oklahoma City, OK 73111
Phone: 405-424-2249
Fax: 405-475-9366
e-mail: comgr@prairiedance.org
Web Site: www.prairiedance.org
Management:
Executive Director: Beth Shumway
Mission: Prairie Dance Theatre offers full concerts of contemporary dance and is known for original works based on Southwestern and Native American themes.
Utilizes: Five Seasonal Concerts; Guest Companies; Singers
Founded: 1978

Specialized Field: Modern; Ethnic Dance; Folk Dance
Status: Professional; Nonprofit
Budget: $100,000-$200,000
Income Sources: Kirpatrick Center Museum;
MidAmerica Dance Network
Organization Type: Performing; Touring; Resident;
Educational

427
TULSA BALLET
1212 E 45th Place
Tulsa, OK 74105
Phone: 918-749-6030
Fax: 918-749-0532
e-mail: admin@tulsaballet.org
Web Site: www.tulsaballet.org
Officers:
   President: Georgia Snoke
Management:
   Artistic Director: Marcello Angelini
   Music Director: Nathan Fifield
   Ballet Mistress: Daniela Busonm
   Ballet Mistress: Susan Frei
   Resident Choreographer: Val Caniparoli
   Production/Stage Manager: Jessica Flores
Mission: The artistic mission of the Tulsa Ballet has
remained constant throughout the years to combine the
beauty and joy expressed by dance with the drama and
entertainment of the theatre.
Utilizes: Collaborations; Dancers; Five Seasonal
Concerts; Guest Accompanists; Guest Artists; Guest
Conductors; Guest Ensembles; Guest Writers;
Multimedia; Music; Resident Professionals; Sign
Language Translators
Founded: 1956
Specialized Field: Ballet
Status: Professional, Nonprofit
Paid Staff: 15
Paid Artists: 30
Budget: $2,700,000
Income Sources: Contributions; Ticket Sales
Performs At: Tulsa Performing Arts Center
Annual Attendance: 60,000
Organization Type: Performing; Touring

Oregon

428
DANCE THEATRE OF OREGON
815 Dorris Street
Eugene, OR 97404
Phone: 541-689-5189
Fax: 541-688-9235
e-mail: dto@efn.org
Web Site: www.dtodance.org
Officers:
   Founder: Marc Siegel
   Co-Founder: Pamela Lehan Siegel
Management:
   Co-Artistic/Managing Director: Marc Siegel
   Co-Artistic Director: Pamela Lehan-Siegel
Mission: Dance Theatre of Oregon is known for its
daring, exuberant, entertaining and intriguing brand of
dance theater, packed with emotion and humor for
audience of all ages.
Founded: 1991
Specialized Field: Modern
Status: Professional, Nonprofit
Performs At: Hult Center For The Arts

429
EUGENE BALLET COMPANY
PO Box 11200
Eugene, OR 97440
Phone: 541-485-3992
Fax: 541-485-3992
Web Site: www.eugeneballet.org
Officers:
   President: David Ramos
   VP: Marty Moran
   Secretary: Hannah Swan
Management:
   Artistic Director/Choreographer: Toni Pimble
   Assoc Artistic Dir/Ballet Master: Peter
Pawlyshynor
   Managing Director: Riley Grannan
   Development/Education Director: Jaclyn LaRue
   Marketing Director: Rob Bean
   Production Manager: Josh Neckles
Mission: To provide quality professional dance
productions and innovative educational services to a
broad based audience throughout the United States.
Utilizes: Choreographers; Collaborations; Dance
Companies; Dancers; Designers; Guest Accompanists;
Guest Artists; Guest Companies; Guest Composers;
Guest Conductors; Resident Professionals
Founded: 1978
Specialized Field: Classical; Contemporary
Status: Professional, Nonprofit
Paid Artists: 21
Budget: $1,500,000
Income Sources: Individuals; Corporations;
Foundations
Performs At: Hult Center for the Performing Arts
Annual Attendance: 25,000
Facility Category: Performing Arts Center
Type of Stage: Proscenium
Stage Dimensions: 52'x48'
Seating Capacity: 2,460
Year Built: 1982
Cost: $23 million
Organization Type: Performing; Touring; Resident;
Sponsoring

430
UNIVERSITY OF OREGON DEPARTMENT
OF DANCE
161 Gerlinger Annex
1214 Unversity of Oregon
Eugene, OR 97403-1214
Phone: 541-346-3386
Fax: 541-346-3380
e-mail: rhonka@uoregon.edu
Web Site: www.dance.uoregon.edu
Officers:
   President: Dave Frohnmayer
Management:
   Director: Rita Honka
Mission: The primary aim of the department of dance is
to enrich the lives of majors, non majors and the
Oregon community with diverse dance experiences.
Founded: 1993
Specialized Field: African Dance
Status: Pre-Professional, Non-Profit
Budget: $3,000
Income Sources: Donations; Performances
Annual Attendance: 500

431
BODYVOX
1300 NW Northrup Street
Portland, OR 97209

Phone: 503-229-0627
Fax: 503-224-8227
e-mail: info@bodyvox.com
Web Site: www.bodyvox.com
Management:
   Artistic Director: Jamey Hampton
   Artistic Director: Ashley Roland
   Artistic Associate: Eric Skinner
Mission: BodyVox contemporary dance company
performs and creates innovative multidisciplinary dance
works.
Utilizes: Collaborating Artists; Dancers; Guest
Accompanists; Guest Artists; Lyricists; Multimedia
Founded: 1997
Specialized Field: Contemporary Dance
Status: Professional, Non-Profit
Paid Staff: 4
Volunteer Staff: 20
Paid Artists: 13
Budget: $400,000
Income Sources: Artistic Fees; Private & Foundation
Support
Annual Attendance: 10,000-15,000

432
METRO DANCERS
Portland Metro Arts
9003 SE Stark Street
Portland, OR 97216
Phone: 503-408-0604
e-mail: info@pdxmetroarts.org
Web Site: www.pdxmetroarts.org
Officers:
   Chair: Dan Hess
   Treasurer: Tamara Larison
Management:
   Artistic/Executive Director: Nancy Yeamans
Mission: To create an avenue for gifted advanced
dancers to perform traditional full length ballets, as well
as modern, jazz, character and contemporary ballet
pieces.
Founded: 1978
Specialized Field: Classical; Ballet; Modern; Jazz;
Character Dance; Contemporary Ballet
Status: Pre-Professional, Nonprofit
Paid Staff: 10
Volunteer Staff: 30
Income Sources: Grants; Performances
Type of Stage: Sprung Floor
Stage Dimensions: 50'x50'
Seating Capacity: 165
Year Built: 2000
Year Remodeled: 2010
Rental Contact: Artistic/Executive Director Nancy
Yeamans
Organization Type: Performing

433
OBO ADDY MASTER DRUMMER
7725 N Fowler Avenue
Portland, OR 97211
Phone: 503-288-3025
e-mail: susan@homowo.org
Web Site: www.oboaddy.com
Management:
   Artistic Director/Master Drummer: Obo Addy
   Booking Manager: Susan Addy
Mission: To bring traditional and popular Ghana music
to Europe and America.
Founded: 1980
Specialized Field: Ghana Dance; Ghana Music

434
OREGON BALLET THEATRE
818 SE Sixth Avenue
Portland, OR 97214
Phone: 503-227-0977
Fax: 503-227-4186
e-mail: info@obt.org
Web Site: www.obt.org
Officers:
   Chairman: Thomas E Cody
   Treasurer: Richard A Pierce
   Secretary: Brent Barton
Management:
   Artistic Director: Christopher Stowell
   Music Direcetor/Conductor: Niel DePonte
   Ballet Master: Lisa Kipp
   Lighting Director: Michael Mazzola
Mission: To entertain and educate audiences and to encourage the creative talents of dancers, choreographers, composers and musicians.
Utilizes: Choreographers; Dancers; Guest Artists
Founded: 1989
Specialized Field: Modern; Ballet; Jazz
Status: Professional, Nonprofit
Paid Artists: 18
Budget: $4.5 Million
Income Sources: Public and Private Funding Organizations; Individual Donations; Ticket Sales; Gift Boutique
Season: October - June
Performs At: Keller Auditorium, Newmark Theatre, Portland Center
Organization Type: Performing; Touring; Resident; Educational; Sponsoring

Pennsylvania

435
ALLEGHENY BALLET COMPANY
PO Box 369
Altoona, PA 16603
Phone: 814-941-9944
Fax: 814-943-6081
e-mail: info@alleghenyballet.com
Web Site: www.alleghenyballet.com
Management:
   Artistic Director: Cristin Burwellor
Mission: Provides audiences the opportunity to experience a professional ballet in their own community.
Founded: 1981
Specialized Field: Ballet
Status: Pre-Professional, Nonprofit
Income Sources: Business Community, Individuals Patrons, Foundations, And Grants
Performs At: Mishler Theatre
Organization Type: Performing; Resident

436
PENNSYLVANIA YOUTH BALLET
Ballet Guild of the Lehigh Valley Inc
556 Main Street
Bethlehem, PA 18018
Phone: 610-865-0353
Fax: 610-865-2698
e-mail: pyb@rcn.com
Web Site: www.bglv.org
Officers:
   President: Barry Pell
   VP: Jennifer L Altemose Esq
   Treasurer: Stephen E Prange
   Secretary: Donna-Marie Daday Esq
Management:

Artistic Director: Karen Kroninger Knerr
Mission: Dedicated to fostering the art of theatre dance, primarily classical ballet, through education and performances.
Utilizes: Dancers; Guest Accompanists; High School Drama; Original Music Scores
Founded: 1958
Specialized Field: Classical Ballet; Theatre Dance
Status: Semi-Professional, Nonprofit
Paid Staff: 6
Budget: $200,000 - $250,000
Performs At: Zoellner Arts Center, Lehigh University
Organization Type: Performing; Educational

437
CENTRAL PENNSYLVANIA YOUTH BALLET
5 N Orange Street
Suite 3
Carlisle, PA 17013
Phone: 717-245-1190
Fax: 717-245-1189
e-mail: info@cpyb.org
Web Site: www.cpyb.org
Officers:
   President: David Hukill
   VP: Teresa N Slocomb
   Treasurer: Reinhard W Beel
   Secretary: Craig Jurgensen MD
Management:
   Artistic Director: Marca Dale Weary
   Associate Artistic Director: Darla Hoover
   Executive Director: Maurinda C Wingard
   Resident Choreographer: Alan Hineline
   Public Relations Director: Sarah Kopac
   Production Manager: David Nash
Mission: Central Pennsylvania Youth Ballet continues to provide exceptional dance training for beginning to pre-professional dancers, with many alumni going on to perform with top companies throughout the world.
Founded: 1956
Specialized Field: Ballet; Jazz; Hip Hop; Tap
Status: Pre-Professional, Nonprofit
Income Sources: The Allied Arts Fund; The Pennsylvania Council Of The Arts; The Greater Harrisburg Foundation; Generous Support From Many Individuals; Corporations; Foundations.
Performs At: The Whitaker Center; The Hershey Theatre
Affiliations: Resident Ballet Company

438
VOLOSHKY UKRAINIAN DANCE ENSEMBLES
700 Cedar Avenue
Jenkintown, PA 19046
Phone: 215-663-0294
Fax: 215-763-8503
e-mail: info@voloshky.com
Web Site: www.voloshky.com
Management:
   Artistic Director: Taras Lewckyj
   Assistant Artistic Director: Oleg Goudimiak
Mission: The Voloshky Ukrainian Dance Ensemble is committed to sharing the wealth of Ukrainian dance and folklore.
Founded: 1973
Specialized Field: Classical Ballet; Ukrainian Dance
Income Sources: Federal; State; Local Organizations; Pennsylvania Arts Counsil

439
PITTSBURGH YOUTH BALLET COMPANY & SCHOOL
St Petersburg Center
210 Valley Brook Road
McMurray, PA 15317
Phone: 724-969-6000
Fax: 724-969-6900
e-mail: info@pybco.com
Web Site: www.pybco.com
Officers:
   Founder: Jean Gedeon
   President: Mary Roman
   VP: Leslie Borandi
   VP: Cara Strock
   Treasurer: Mohylyn Yocca
Management:
   Artistic Director: Jean Gedeon
   Ballet Mistress: Tamar Rachelle
   Ballet Master: Steven Annegarn
   Choreographer: Andrew Blight
Mission: The Pittsburgh Youth Ballet Company's mission is to train, inspire and nurture young dancers towards artistic excellence, perform works by choreographic masters and to bring the art of dance, through outreach efforts, to new multi-generational audiences.
Founded: 1983
Specialized Field: Contemporary Ballet
Status: Professional, Nonprofit

440
PENNSYLVANIA ACADEMY OF BALLET
Pennsylvania Academy of Ballet Society
29 N Narberth Avenue
Narberth, PA 19072
Phone: 610-664-3455
Fax: 610-664-6733
e-mail: info@paacademyofballet.com
Web Site: www.paacademyofballet.com
Officers:
   Founder: John White
   Founder: Margarita De Saa
Management:
   Co-Aristic Director: John White
   Co-Artistic Director: Margarita De Saa
   Assistant Director: Melinda Pendleton
   Ballet Master: Bryan Koulman
Mission: To provide essential training for talented students with professional aptitudes and interest in pursuing careers in classical ballet.
Founded: 1974
Specialized Field: Classical Ballet

441
NEW CASTLE REGIONAL BALLET
210 W Washington Street
New Castle, PA 16105
Phone: 724-652-1822
Officers:
   Founder: Debbie Menichino Parou
Management:
   Artistic Director: Debbie Menichino Parou
Mission: A professional program using dance as the vehicle to teach children respect, commitment, honesty, teamwork and discipline. To educate a child's mind, body and to develop character on a professional level that will be useful in aspects of their life whether or not they choose dance as a profession.
Founded: 1987
Specialized Field: Ballet; Jazz; Tap
Status: Nonprofit
Income Sources: Pennsylvania Counsil Of The Arts

442
DANCE AFFILIATES
4701 Bath Street
Building 46B
Philadelphia, PA 19137
Phone: 215-636-9000
Fax: 267-672-2912
e-mail: jane@danceaffiliates.org
Web Site: www.dancecelebration.org
Officers:
    President: Ira S Lefton Esq
    VP: Nancy Purcell
    VP: Nicole D Galli Esq
    Treasurer: Christine M Lussier
    Secretary: Michael C Lillys
Management:
    Artistic Director: F Randolph Swartz
    Development Director: Jane Bensignor
Mission: The mission of Dance Affiliates is to advance the growth, development and well being of the art of dance.
Utilizes: AEA Actors; Artists-in-Residence; Choreographers; Collaborating Artists; Commissioned Composers; Commissioned Music; Composers-in-Residence; Curators; Dance Companies; Dancers; Designers; Educators; Filmmakers; Five Seasonal Concerts; Grant Writers; Guest Accompanists; Guest Artists; Guest Choreographers; Guest Companies; Guest Conductors; Guest Ensembles; Guest Lecturers; Guest Soloists; High School Drama; Instructors; Lyricists; New Productions; Original Music Scores; Poets; Resident Professionals; Sign Language Translators; Soloists; Theatre Companies
Founded: 1979
Specialized Field: Modern; Ballet; Jazz; Ethnic Dance; Folk Dance
Status: Professional, Nonprofit
Paid Staff: 4
Volunteer Staff: 20
Budget: $1,000,000
Income Sources: Ticket Sales; Public & Private Funding
Performs At: Annenberg Center for the Performing Arts; Univ. of the Arts
Annual Attendance: 30,000
Facility Category: Theatre
Stage Dimensions: 48'x31'
Seating Capacity: 911
Year Built: 1972
Organization Type: Sponsoring

443
KORESH DANCE COMPANY
2020 Chestnut Street
Philadelphia, PA 19103
Phone: 215-751-0959
Fax: 215-665-0805
e-mail: info@koreshdance.org
Web Site: www.koreshdance.org
Officers:
    President: Steve Lazin
    VP: David Cooper
    Treasurer: Cary Borish
Management:
    Artistic Director: Ronen Koresh
    Executive Director: Alon Koresh
    Assistant Artistic Director: Melissa Rector
    Development Director: Deborah Crocker
Mission: Dedicated to the enrichment of the cultural landscape and artistic reputation of Philadelphia.
Founded: 1991
Specialized Field: Traditional Dance

Paid Staff: 5
Volunteer Staff: 15
Paid Artists: 31

444
PENNSYLVANIA BALLET
1819 JFK Boulevaard
Suite 210
Philadelphia, PA 19103
Phone: 215-551-7000
Fax: 215-551-7224
e-mail: info@paballet.org
Web Site: www.paballet.org
Officers:
    Chairman: Janis Goodman
    Vice Chair: Barbara A. Austell
    Chair: Penny Fox
    Esq.: Cary Levinson
Management:
    Artistic Director: Roy Kaiser
    Executive Director: Michael Scolamiero
    Assistant Artistic Director: Michael Sheridan
    Development Director: Hilary Alger
    Marketing/Communications Director: Shawn D Stone
    Production Director: John Hoey
Mission: Our mission is to maintain and nurture a financially sound, Philadelphia-based ballet company that presents the finest in artistry and performance to the widest possible audience. To expand & diversify its classical and contemporary repertoire, and provide the highest caliber of instruction for aspiring professional dancers. The ballet strives to enrich and expand the cultural lives of children and adults through the art of ballet.
Founded: 1963
Specialized Field: Ballet
Status: Professional, Nonprofit
Paid Staff: 30
Paid Artists: 44
Budget: $8,000,000
Income Sources: Earned; Unearned; Corporate; Foundation
Performs At: The Merriam Theatre
Organization Type: Performing; Touring; Resident

445
PHILADELPHIA DANCE COMPANY
Philadanco
9 N Preston Street
Philadanco Way
Philadelphia, PA 19104-2210
Phone: 215-387-8200
Fax: 215-387-8203
e-mail: shaughton@philadanco.org
Web Site: www.philadanco.org
Officers:
    Founder: Joan Myers Brown
    Chairman: Spencer Wertheimer Esq
    President: Beverly A Harper
Management:
    Artistic/Executive Director: Joan Myers Brown
    Assistant Artistic Director: Kim Bears-Bailey
    General Manager: Vanessa Thomas-Smith
    Development Director: Sandra N Haughton
    Marketing Director: Gail Bennett
Mission: To perform, instruct and train offering tuition-free instruction and performing opportunities to young dancers.
Utilizes: Actors; Choreographers; Collaborations; Commissioned Composers; Commissioned Music; Community Members; Dancers; Designers; Five Seasonal Concerts; Guest Accompanists; Guest Artists; Guest Companies; Guest Conductors; Guest

Ensembles; Guest Writers; High School Drama; Instructors; Organization Contracts; Original Music Scores; Selected Students
Founded: 1970
Specialized Field: Modern; Contemporary Dance
Status: Professional, Nonprofit
Paid Staff: 6
Volunteer Staff: 4
Paid Artists: 19
Budget: $1,000,000-$2,500,000
Income Sources: Dance USA; International Association for Blacks in Dance; American Dance Guild; Greater Philadelphia Cultural Alliance; PDA; Philadelphia C.C.
Affiliations: IABD; GRCA; Dance/USA; PDA; American Dance Guild
Annual Attendance: 60,000
Facility Category: Performing Arts Center
Type of Stage: Proscenium
Seating Capacity: 990
Organization Type: Performing; Touring; Resident; Educational

446
DANCE ALLOY THEATER
5530 Penn Avenue
Pittsburgh, PA 15206
Phone: 412-363-4321
Fax: 412-363-4320
e-mail: info@dancealloy.org
Web Site: www.dancealloy.org
Officers:
    President: Thomas K Whitford
    VP: J Nicole Wilson
Management:
    Artistic Director: Beth Corning
    Managing Director: Susan Sparks
Mission: We are a performing professsional company, a studio open for dance and movement classes as well as a provider of dance education in the Pittsburgh Public Schools.
Utilizes: Choreographers; Commissioned Music; Curators; Dance Companies; Dancers; Educators; Five Seasonal Concerts; Grant Writers; Guest Artists; Guest Companies; Guest Conductors; High School Drama; Original Music Scores; Poets; Soloists
Founded: 1976
Specialized Field: Modern
Status: Professional, Nonprofit
Paid Staff: 6
Paid Artists: 5
Budget: $700,000
Income Sources: Foundations; Corporations; Government
Performs At: Kelly Strayhorn Theatre
Annual Attendance: 4,500
Organization Type: Performing; Touring; Educational

447
LABCO DANCE
1113 E Carson Street
3rd Floor
Pittsburgh, PA 15203
Toll-free: 800-607-0857
e-mail: labcodance@penn.com
Web Site: www.labcodance.net
Officers:
    President: Eric A Stroud
    VP: Michael J Forlenza PhD
    Treasurer: Timothy W Garland
    Secretary: Marla N Stayduhar
Management:
    Artistic Director/Choreographer: Gwen Hunter Ritchie

Mission: A company committed to its mission of passionately advancing the daring art of movement while nurturing unity within the dance community.
Founded: 1996
Specialized Field: Contemporary Dance
Status: Professional, Nonprofit
Paid Staff: 1
Volunteer Staff: 50
Paid Artists: 6
Non-paid Artists: 20
Performs At: Kelly Strayhorn Performing Arts Center

448
MARY MILLER DANCE COMPANY
601 Wood Street
Pittsburgh, PA 15222-2503
Phone: 412-434-1169
e-mail: marymillerdanceco@netzero.net
Web Site: www.maymillerdanceco.org
Officers:
President: William Lafe
Treasurer: Debora Brenner Brown
Secretary: Sheila Collins
Management:
Artistic Director/Choreographer: Mary Miller
Mission: Our mission is to create, develop and present modern dance works that reflect on our daily life and today's social, psychological and political issues.
Founded: 1985
Specialized Field: Modern
Status: Professional, Non-Profit

449
PITTSBURGH BALLET THEATRE
2900 Liberty Avenue
Pittsburgh, PA 15201-1500
Phone: 412-281-0360
Fax: 412-281-9901
Web Site: www.pbt.org
Officers:
Chairperson: Carolyn M Byham
Treasurer: James E Crockard III
Secretary: Shelley Taylor
Management:
Artistic Director: Terrence S Orr
Executive Director: Harris N Ferris
Assistant Artistic Director: Robert Vickrey
Ballet Mistress: Marianna Tcherkassky
Ballet Master: Steven Annegarn
Marketing/Communications Director: Bear Brandegee
Mission: Pittsburgh Ballet Theatre, the professional and classical ballet company of Western Pennsylvania.
Utilizes: Five Seasonal Concerts; Guest Artists
Founded: 1969
Specialized Field: Ballet
Status: Professional, Nonprofit
Budget: $2,500,000
Income Sources: National Endowment for the Arts; Dance USA
Organization Type: Performing; Touring; Resident; Educational

450
PITTSBURGH DANCE COUNCIL
Pittsburgh Cultural Trust
803 Liberty Avenue
Pittsburgh, PA 15222
Phone: 412-471-1916
Web Site: www.pgharts.org
Officers:
President: J Kevin McMahon
Management:
Executive Director: Paul Organisak

Mission: Committed to expanding the visibility, appreciation and presentation of dance as an art form in the Pittsburgh area while nurturing the field of dance on national and international levels.
Utilizes: Singers
Founded: 1969
Specialized Field: Modern; Ballet
Status: Professional, Nonprofit
Income Sources: Ticket Sales; Grants; Sponsorships
Performs At: Benedum Center; Byham Theater
Organization Type: Sponsoring; Presenting

451
PENNSYLVANIA DANCE THEATRE
PO Box 792
State College, PA 16801
Phone: 814-883-6907
Fax: 814-865-3039
e-mail: info@pdtdance.org
Web Site: www.pdtdance.org
Management:
Artistic Director/Choreographer: Andre Koslowski
Mission: Pennsylvania Dance Theatre provides dance enrichment through performance and educational outreach.
Utilizes: Five Seasonal Concerts; Singers
Founded: 1979
Specialized Field: Modern; Contemporary Dance
Status: Professional, Nonprofit
Paid Staff: 1
Budget: $100,000-$200,000
Organization Type: Performing; Touring; Educational

452
NOTARA DANCE THEATRE
700 Phillips Street
Stroudsburg, PA 18360
Phone: 570-421-1718
e-mail: notara@verizon.net
Management:
Co-Artistic Director: Sally Notara
Co-Artistic Director: Darrell Notara
Specialized Field: Ballet; Modern; Jazz; Tap
Status: Nonprofit

453
GREATER YORK YOUTH BALLET
Greater York Center for Dance Education
3524 E Market Street
York, PA 17402
Phone: 717-755-6683
Fax: 717-755-6688
e-mail: dance@gycde.com
Web Site: www.gycde.org
Officers:
Founding Director: Shana Garling
President: Verna Stilwell
VP: Jill Snell
Management:
Artistic Director: Lori Pergament
Executive Director: Melinda Fritz
Mission: The Greater York Youth Ballet provides intensive training, individual coaching, performance opportunities and the discipline of a pre-professional dance environment to aspiring dancers.
Founded: 1971
Specialized Field: Ballet
Status: Pre-Professional, Nonprofit
Performs At: Strand Capital Performing Arts Center

454
KELLI WICKE DAVIS/SHODA MOVING THEATRE
110 Highland Avenue
Barrington, RI 02806
Phone: 401-245-6956
e-mail: kwickedavis@earthlink.net
Management:
Director/Choreographer: Kelli Wicke Davis, kwickedavis@earthlink.net
Mission: Ms. Davis ' choreography and direction of performanes, original or existing, are an imaginative incorporation of dance, mime, voice, masks and gesture which create a movement/theatre style which is innovative and unusual in its presentation
Utilizes: Actors; AEA Actors; Choreographers; Composers; Dancers; Educators; Equity Actors; Organization Contracts; Original Music Scores; Paid Performers
Founded: 1974
Specialized Field: Movement; Theatrical Dance
Paid Artists: 3
Affiliations: Director/Choreographer; Stage Directors And Choreographers Society

455
FUSIONWORKS DANCE COMPANY
PO Box 402
Lincoln, RI 02865-0402
Phone: 401-946-0607
e-mail: fusionwk@cox.net
Web Site: www.fusionworksdance.org
Officers:
President: Mathew Montgomery
Vice President: Tree Callanan
Management:
Artistic Director: Deb Meunier
Mission: Fusionworks Dance Company provides access to and an understanding of contemporary dance through the presentation of high quality professional dance with an emphasis on direct audience experience. This is accomplished in an educational framework of concerts, public performances and school-based programming intended to introduce audiences to both the beauty that inspires and the processes behind the dances performed.
Founded: 1987
Specialized Field: Contemporary Dance
Status: Nonprofit
Income Sources: Individual; Corporate
Season: November-April

456
STATE BALLET OF RHODE ISLAND
52 Sherman Avenue
Lincoln, RI 02865
Phone: 401-334-2560
Fax: 401-334-0412
e-mail: info@stateballet.com
Web Site: www.stateballet.com
Officers:
Chairperson: Herci Marsden
Treasurer: Ana Mardsen Fox
Recording Secretary: Barbara Ann Marsden
VP of The State Ballet of RI: Mark Marsden
Management:
Artistic Director: Herci Marsden
Executive Director: Ana Marsden Fox
Email Correspondant: Mia Nocera Godbout
VP/Coordinator: Shana Fox Marceau

Mission: To create, present, preserve and extend the great repertoire of classical dancing through exciting performances and educational programming of the highest quality, presented to the widest possible audience
Utilizes: Guest Artists
Founded: 1959
Specialized Field: Classical Ballet
Status: Semi-Professional; Nonprofit; Civic; Regional Ballet Comp
Paid Staff: 2
Volunteer Staff: 35
Paid Artists: 13
Non-paid Artists: 60
Budget: $110,000
Income Sources: Admission; Benefactors; Members Contributor; Fund Raisers
Performs At: Roberts Auditorium; Rhode Island College
Affiliations: Brae Crest School of Ballet
Annual Attendance: 10,000
Facility Category: College Theatreium
Stage Dimensions: 45x60
Seating Capacity: 1,100
Rental Contact: Michael Dusharme
Organization Type: Performing; Touring; Resident; Educational

457
RHODE ISLAND'S BALLET THEATRE

20 Loring Street
Middletown, RI 02842
Phone: 401-847-5301
e-mail: ribt-nm@cox.net
Web Site: www.riballet.org
Officers:
   President: Robert Newbert
   VP/Secretary: Barbara Jean Medeiros
Management:
   Artistic Director: Nancy McAuliffe
   Executive Director: Warren McAuliffe
Specialized Field: Ballet

458
ISLAND MOVING COMPANY

PO Box 746
Newport, RI 02840-4192
Phone: 401-847-4470
e-mail: info@islandmovingco.org
Web Site: www.islandmovingco.org
Officers:
   Chairman: Ellen Barnes
   Treasurer: David Silvia
   Secretary: Joan Martin
Management:
   Artistic Director: Miki Ohlsen
   Executive Director: Dominique Alfandre
   Technical Director: Roy K Omori
Mission: Island Moving Company is a classically trained contemporary ballet company founded on the belief that collaboration and a supportive environment enhance the creative process, producing great works of art representing profound expressions of the human spirit and experience.
Utilizes: Choreographers; Collaborating Artists; Commissioned Music; Dance Companies; Dancers; Guest Artists; Guest Choreographers; Instructors; Local Artists; Original Music Scores; Playwrights; Resident Artists
Founded: 1982
Specialized Field: Contemporary Ballet
Status: Professional, Nonprofit
Paid Staff: 6
Paid Artists: 15

Budget: $250,000
Income Sources: Admissions; Foundations; Grants; Membership
Affiliations: Newport Academy of Ballet
Annual Attendance: 4,000
Organization Type: Performing; Touring; Resident; Educational

459
EVERETT DANCE THEATRE

9 Duncan Avenue
Providence, RI 02906
Phone: 401-831-9479
Fax: 401-455-0581
e-mail: info@everettdancetheatre.org
Web Site: www.everettdancetheatre.org
Officers:
   Co-Founder: Dorothy Jungels
   Co-Founder: Aaron Jungels
Management:
   Artistic Director: Dorothy Jungels
Founded: 1986
Specialized Field: Theatrical Dance
Status: Professional, Non-Profit
Paid Staff: 3
Paid Artists: 15
Income Sources: Performances, Foundations; Government; Individual
Annual Attendance: 20,000

460
FESTIVAL BALLET PROVIDENCE

Center for Dance Educaiton
825 Hope Street
Providence, RI 02906
Phone: 401-353-1129
Fax: 401-353-8853
e-mail: info@festivalballet.com
Web Site: www.festivalballet.com
Officers:
   President: Don Wineburg
   VP: Laura Love Rose
   Treasurer: David Von Hemat
   Secretary: Stacy Nakasians
Management:
   Artistic Director: Milhailo Djuric
   Ballet Mistress: Milica Bijelic
   Managing Director: Lisa LaDew
   Marketing/Public Relations Manager: Mark Morin
Mission: Festival Ballet Providence enriches the community by expanding dance awareness through education and performance.
Utilizes: Collaborations; Dancers; Guest Accompanists; Guest Artists; Guest Ensembles; High School Drama
Founded: 1977
Specialized Field: Ballet
Status: Professional, Nonprofit
Paid Staff: 20
Paid Artists: 12
Non-paid Artists: 3
Budget: $1,500,000
Income Sources: Ticket Sales; School Tuition; Donations; Grants
Performs At: Providence Performing Arts Center; Veterans Memorial Aud.
Affiliations: The Festival Ballet Center for Dance Education
Annual Attendance: 35,000
Facility Category: Dance School; Performing Company
Type of Stage: Rent Providence Area Stages
Organization Type: Performing; Touring; Resident

461
DANCE STATION

1632 Chapin Road
Chapin, SC
Phone: 803-932-9999
e-mail: tjdancestation@aol.com
Web Site: www.dancestationfeaturingcarolinafreetyle.com
Management:
   Artistic Director: Tammy Johns
Specialized Field: Dance

462
ROBERT IVEY BALLET

College of Charleston School of the Arts
1910 Savannah Highway
Charleston, SC 29407-9679
Phone: 843-556-1343
Fax: 843-757-0960
e-mail: ribart@mindspring.com
Web Site: www.home.mindspring.com
Management:
   Artistic Director: Robert Ivey
Mission: To promote and educate in the art of dance.
Utilizes: Five Seasonal Concerts
Founded: 1977
Specialized Field: Modern; Ballet; Jazz
Paid Staff: 50
Volunteer Staff: 3
Paid Artists: 3
Non-paid Artists: 30
Income Sources: Grants; Fundraiser; Donations; Addmission Sales
Performs At: Sottioe Theatre
Annual Attendance: 7,000
Facility Category: Rental Theatre
Type of Stage: Proscenium
Stage Dimensions: 48' x 32'
Seating Capacity: 785
Organization Type: Resident

463
SPOLETO FESTIVAL USA

14 George Street
Charleston, SC 29401-1524
Phone: 843-722-2764
Fax: 843-723-6383
e-mail: info@spoletousa.org
Web Site: www.spoletousa.org
Officers:
   Chairman: Martha Rivers Ingram
   President: Carlos E. Evans
Management:
   Artistic Director-Choral Activities: Joseph Flummerfelt
   Director, Chamber Music: Geoff Nuttall
   General Director: Nigel Redden
   Producer: Nunally Kersh
   Director Of Development: Julia Forster
   Director Marketing/Public Relations: Paula Edwards
Mission: To present opera, dance, theater, symphonic, choral and chamber music, jazz and visual arts exhibits of the highest quality; to serve as an educational environment for young artists and audiences alike.
Utilizes: Singers
Founded: 1977
Specialized Field: Jazz; Theatrical Dance
Status: Professional; Semi-Professional; Non-Profit
Paid Staff: 18
Budget: $7,000,000

Income Sources: Ticket Revenues; Contributions
Performs At: Gaillard Municipal Auditorium; Dock Street Theater
Annual Attendance: 70,000-80,000
Organization Type: Performing; Educational; Sponsoring

464
COLUMBIA CITY BALLET
1545 Main Street
Columbia, SC 29201
Phone: 803-799-7605
Fax: 803-799-7928
e-mail: marketing@columbiacityballet.com
Web Site: www.columbiacityballet.com
Officers:
    President: Fred Sheheen
    Vice President: Coralee Harris
    Treasurer: Chris Ray
Management:
    Artistic/Executive Director: William Starrett
    Ballet Mistress: Patricia Miller
    Ballet Mistress: Mariclare Miranda
    Technical Director/Lighting: Barry Sparks
    Marketing/Public Relations Manager: Skot Garrick
Mission: Columbia City Ballet's mission is to offer South Carolina and Southeastern audiences the highest quality ballet and to provide dancers with only the best professional dance training.
Utilizes: Artists-in-Residence; Dance Companies; Dancers; Five Seasonal Concerts; Guest Artists; Guest Conductors; High School Drama; Lyricists; Organization Contracts; Resident Professionals; Student Interns
Founded: 1961
Specialized Field: Ballet
Status: Professional, Nonprofit
Paid Staff: 9
Paid Artists: 34
Non-paid Artists: 7
Budget: $1,000,000
Income Sources: Box Office; Grants; Corporate Support
Performs At: Koger Center for the Arts
Annual Attendance: 125,000
Facility Category: Opera
Type of Stage: Proscenium
Seating Capacity: 2,100
Year Built: 1989
Rental Contact: Michael Taylor
Organization Type: Performing; Touring; Resident; Educational

465
COLUMBIA CITY JAZZ DANCE COMPANY & SCHOOL
550 River Drive
Columbia, SC 29210
Phone: 803-252-0252
Fax: 803-779-6291
Web Site: www.columbiacityjazz.com
Management:
    Choreographer/Artistic Director: Dale Lam
Mission: Internationally known not-for-profit pre-professional jazz dance troupe.
Specialized Field: Dance
Status: Nonprofit

466
COLUMBIA COMMUNITY ARTS CENTRE
1001 Piney Woods Road
Columbia, SC 29210

Phone: 803-772-1462
Fax: 803-772-1462
e-mail: lyben1@bellsouth.net
Web Site: www.lybenchristiandance.com
Management:
    Founder/Director: Gail Faust
Mission: To encourage and develope the worship of god through dance.
Founded: 2010
Specialized Field: Dance; Music; Drama
Income Sources: Donations; Grants; Fundraisers

467
COLUMBIA'S BALLROOM COMPANY
1333 Omarest Drive
Columbia, SC 29210
Phone: 803-750-0181
Fax: 803-750-0181
Mission: Beginner to advance ballroom dancing.
Specialized Field: Dance

468
SC CHRISTIAN DANCE THEATER
736 St Andrews Road
Columbia, SC 29210
Phone: 803-609-4777
e-mail: cynthia@scchristiandance.com
Management:
    Director: Cynthia Dewar
Mission: Offers dancers more opportunities for performance workshops and understanding what it means to worship through dance.
Specialized Field: Dance

469
SOUTHEASTERN SCHOOL OF BALLET
1120 Sparkleberry Lane Extension
Suite C-2
Columbia, SC
Phone: 803-419-5512
Toll-free: 866-411-5512
e-mail: ssb@southeasternschoolofballet.com
Web Site: www.southeasternschoolofballet.com
Management:
    Director: Hillary Krieger
    Director: Gabor Toth
Mission: Offer the highest quality of instruction in the various disciplines of ballet.
Specialized Field: Dance

470
STEPPING OUT DANCE STUDIO
1019 Assembly Street
Columbia, SC 29072
Phone: 803-808-7766
e-mail: steppingout@windstream.net
Web Site: www.steppingoutdancestudio.com
Management:
    Owner: Fred Kelly
    Owner: Ann Kelly
Mission: Dance workshop programs taught by guest artists and staff.
Specialized Field: Dance

471
VISTA BALLROOM
1019 Assembly Street
Columbia, SC 29201
Phone: 803-546-3705
e-mail: vistaballroom@gmail.com
Web Site: www.vistaballroom.net
Management:
    Director: Erin Bolshakov

Mission: Offering instruction in argentine tango, salsa, ballroom, latin, shag and swing dancing.
Specialized Field: Dance

472
GILBERT STUDIO OF DANCE ARTS
311 Broad Street
PO Box 191
Gilbert, SC 29054
Phone: 803-892-5374
e-mail: dancewithnelle@yahoo.com
Web Site: gilbertstudioofdance.wordpress.com
Management:
    Owner/Director/Instructor: Linelle Yates
Mission: Ballet, tap, jazz, clogging, pom pon and praise dance.
Specialized Field: Dance

473
CAROLINA BALLET THEATRE
PO Box 135
Greenville, SC 29602
Phone: 864-421-0940
Fax: 864-297-1635
Web Site: www.carolinaballet.org
Management:
    Artistic Director: Hernan Justo
    Executive Director: Kelly Baird
    Ballet Mistress/Principal Dancer: Anita Sun Pacylowski Justo
Mission: Carolina Ballet Threatre strives to offer quality performances that will educate and entertain a wide variety of audiences in the art of ballet.
Founded: 1972
Specialized Field: Classical Ballet; Contemporary
Status: Professional, Nonprofit
Paid Staff: 8
Volunteer Staff: 40
Budget: $250,000
Income Sources: Private; Grants; Ticket Sales; Community Outreach
Performs At: The Peace Center For The Performing Arts

474
GREENVILLE BALLET SCHOOL AND COMPANY
105 Woodruff Industrial Lane
Greenville, SC 29607-4101
Phone: 864-234-5677
Fax: 864-268-5653
e-mail: info@greenvilleballet.com
Web Site: www.greenvilleballet.com
Management:
    Director: Andrew Kuharsky
    Director: Merry Kuharsky
Mission: To provide the finest quality dance instruction in a fun and loving environment in order to promote life-long learning, fitness, and appreciation of the arts.
Specialized Field: Ballet
Status: Semi-Professional, Nonprofit
Budget: $20,000
Income Sources: Individual; Foundations; Ticket Sales
Performs At: Furman University
Annual Attendance: 3,000
Stage Dimensions: 35x45
Seating Capacity: 1900

475
THE SOUTHERN STRUTT STUDIO
90 Ashbourne Road
Irmo, SC 29063
Phone: 803-781-3980
Web Site: www.southernstruttdance.com

Management:
Owner/Director: Nancy Giles
Mission: To build individuals self confidence and to help them learn discipline and team work
Specialized Field: Dance

476
CAROLINA BALLET
3401-131 Atlantic Avenue
Raleigh, SC 27604
Phone: 919-719-0800
Fax: 919-719-0910
Web Site: www.carolinaballet.com
Officers:
Chairman: Daniel Risku
Treasurer: Ed Thomas
Secretary: Peggy Wilks
Management:
Artistic Director: Robert Weiss
Music Director: Alfred E Sturgis
Executive Director: Lisa Jones
Assistant Artistic Director: Elizabeth R Parker
Resident Guest Choreographer: Lynne Taylor-Corbett
Development Director: Steve Bishop
Production Manager: Robert Auchter
Mission: Carolina Ballet's mission is to perform world-class professional ballet, entertaining and enlightening audiences in Raleigh and beyond.
Founded: 1984
Specialized Field: Ballet
Status: Pre-Profesisonal, Nonprofit
Paid Staff: 6
Volunteer Staff: 22
Paid Artists: 8
Non-paid Artists: 45
Budget: $180,000
Income Sources: Grants; Memberships; Earned; Unearned
Performs At: The Township Auditorium; Cmfa Black Box Theatre
Annual Attendance: 15,000

Tennessee

477
BALLET TENNESSEE
John A Patten Center
3202 Kelly's Ferry Road
Chattanooga, TN 37419
Phone: 423-821-2055
Fax: 423-821-2156
e-mail: anna@ballettennessee.org
Web Site: www.ballettennessee.org
Officers:
President: Rosemarie Bryan
VP: Stacy Goodwin-Lightfoot
Treasurer: Julia Sanford
Secretary: Shonda Caines
Management:
Artistic Director: Anna Baker-VanCura
Executive Director: Barry VanCura
Associate Director: Laurel Shastri
Mission: Strives to make a positive impact on people of all ages, races, abilities and economic levels through the art of ballet by providing professional quality performance and instruction.
Founded: 1987
Specialized Field: Classical Ballet; Contemporary Ballet
Status: Professional, Nonprofit
Budget: $200,000-$500,000

Income Sources: Allied Arts Of Greater Chattanooga, Tennessee Arts Commission, National Endowment For The Arts, Corporate Grants, Individual Contributions.
Performs At: The Tivoli Theatre
Annual Attendance: 20,000

478
CHATTANOOGA BALLET
PO Box 6175
Chattanooga, TN 37401
Phone: 423-265-0617
e-mail: info@chattanoogaballet.net
Web Site: www.chattanoogaballet.net
Management:
Executive Director: Bob Willie
Assistant Director: Laurne Abney
Ballet Master: Frank Hay
Mission: The mission of the Chattanooga Ballet is to stimulate artistic growth and to increase public awareness and participation in the art of dance in our community and region.
Utilizes: Guest Companies; Singers
Founded: 1980
Specialized Field: Classical Ballet
Status: Professional, Nonprofit
Paid Staff: 11
Volunteer Staff: 100
Paid Artists: 11
Non-paid Artists: 110
Budget: $450,000
Income Sources: Corporations; Individual; Foundations; Government
Performs At: Fine Arts Center; University of Tennessee-Chattanooga; Tivoli Theatre
Affiliations: Tennessee Association of Dance; University of Tennessee
Annual Attendance: 36,000
Organization Type: Performing; Touring; Resident; Educational; Sponsoring

479
TENNESSEE ASSOCIATION OF DANCE
PO Box 4368
Chattanooga, TN 37405
Phone: 423-855-7890
e-mail: info@tennesseedance.org
Web Site: www.tennesseedance.org
Officers:
President: Bonny Copenhaver
VP: Heidi Lambert
Treasurer: Janet Clough
Secretary: Marcus Hayes
Management:
Executive Director: Karen Wilson
Mission: Tennessee Association of Dance is a statewide network of organizations and individuals dedicated to artistic excellence and committed to ensuring that dance is a vital and respected part of life for all Tennesseans.
Founded: 1971
Specialized Field: Modern; Ballet; Jazz; Tap
Status: Professional, Nonprofit
Performs At: Middle Tennessee State University
Organization Type: Educational

480
CITY BALLET
PO Box 1664
Knoxville, TN 37901
Phone: 865-544-0495
Fax: 865-522-3043
e-mail: cityballet@nxs.net
Officers:
President: John King

Management:
Executive Director: John King
Mission: To raise the calibre of dance in this area through public performances; to build technically proficient dancers through the use of professional teachers, choreographers, and performers brought in by the company.
Utilizes: Five Seasonal Concerts; Guest Artists
Founded: 1988
Specialized Field: Modern; Ballet; Jazz
Status: Semi-Professional; Nonprofit
Paid Staff: 2
Budget: $550,000
Income Sources: Grants; Donations
Performs At: The Tennessee Theatre; Civic Coliseum
Organization Type: Educational; Sponsoring

481
TENNESSEE CHILDREN'S DANCE ENSEMBLE
4216 Sutherland Avenue
Knoxville, TN 37919
Phone: 865-588-2770
Web Site: www.discoveret.org
Officers:
Founder: Dorothy Floyd
Management:
Artistic Director: Irena Linn
Managing Director: Judy Robinson
Ballet Master/Choreographer: Lenette Perra
Utilizes: Five Seasonal Concerts; Singers
Founded: 1981
Specialized Field: Modern
Status: Professional, Nonprofit
Paid Staff: 5
Paid Artists: 22
Budget: $200,000-$500,000
Income Sources: Corporations; Foundations; Grants; Individuals
Annual Attendance: 10,000-15,000
Type of Stage: 7
Organization Type: Performing; Touring; Resident; Educational

482
APPALACHIAN BALLET COMPANY
215 W Broadway
Maryville, TN 37801
Phone: 865-982-8463
Fax: 865-982-8463
Web Site: www.appalachianballet.com
Management:
Artistic Director: Amy Moore Morton
Mission: To promote and foster a love and appreciation of the arts through performances and lecture demonstrations within the community.
Utilizes: Singers
Founded: 1972
Specialized Field: Classical Ballet
Status: Semi-Professional, Nonprofit
Paid Staff: 1
Volunteer Staff: 60
Performs At: Knoxville Civic Auditorium; Tennessee Theater
Affiliations: Southeast Regional Ballet Association
Organization Type: Performing; Touring; Resident; Educational

483
BALLET MEMPHIS
Ballet Memphis Studios
7950 Trinity Road
Memphis, TN 38018

Phone: 901-737-7322
Fax: 901-737-7037
e-mail: callen@balletmemphis.org
Web Site: www.balletmemphis.org
Officers:
  Founder: Dorothy Gunther Pugh
Management:
  Artistic Director: Dorothy Gunther Pugh
  Associate Artistic Director: Karl Condon
  Managing Director: Philip West
  Ballet Mistress: Tamara Hoffmann
  Development Director: Roger Johnson
  Production Manager: Allan Kerr
Mission: Ballet Memphis is a creative resource to the nation as a maker and interpreter of the South's cultural legacy through dance, production and training.
Founded: 1986
Specialized Field: Ballet
Status: Professional, Non-Profit
Paid Artists: 19
Budget: $3,100,000
Performs At: Orpheum Theatre
Organization Type: Performing; Resident; Touring; Educational

484
NASHVILLE BALLET

3630 Redman Street
Nashville, TN 37209-4827
Phone: 615-297-2966
Fax: 615-297-9972
e-mail: jjohnson@nashvilleballet.com
Web Site: www.nashvilleballet.com
Officers:
  President: Dan Slipkovich
  VP: Patricia Eastwood
  Treasurer: Bill Haralson
Management:
  Artistic Director/CEO: Paul Vasterling
  Executive Director: Angie Adams
Mission: Create, perform, teach and promote dance as an essential and inspiring element of our community.
Utilizes: Community Members; Curators; Dancers; Five Seasonal Concerts; Guest Artists; Singers
Founded: 1986
Specialized Field: Ballet
Status: Professional, Nonprofit
Paid Staff: 15
Paid Artists: 15
Budget: $1,000,000-$2,500,000
Organization Type: Performing; Touring; Educational

Texas

485
BALLET AUSTIN

Ballet Austin Academy
501 W Third Street
Austin, TX 78701
Phone: 512-476-9151
Fax: 512-476-3973
Web Site: www.balletaustin.org
Officers:
  Chairperson: Sarah Butler
  President: Dan Byrne
Management:
  Artistic Director: Stephen Mills
  Executive Director: Cookie Gregory Ruiz
  Associate Artistic Director: Michelle Martin
  Production Director: Bill Sheffield
  Marketing Director: Lance Johnson

Mission: As distinctive and dynamic as the city calls home, welcomes people near and far to participate in it's Classically Innovative vision of dance.
Utilizes: Artists-in-Residence; Collaborating Artists; Collaborations; Commissioned Composers; Commissioned Music; Dancers; Designers; Five Seasonal Concerts; Grant Writers; Guest Accompanists; Guest Artists; Guest Companies; Guest Conductors; Guest Directors; Guest Instructors; Guest Lecturers; Local Artists; Resident Artists; Touring Companies
Founded: 1956
Specialized Field: Ballet
Status: Professional, Nonprofit
Paid Staff: 16
Paid Artists: 47
Income Sources: Corporate; Foundation
Performs At: Performing Arts Center; University of Texas at Austin
Organization Type: Performing; Touring; Educational

486
JOHNSON/LONG DANCE COMPANY

PO Box 516
Austin, TX 78767
Phone: 512-467-0704
Fax: 512-475-3908
e-mail: along@bga.com
Management:
  Co-Artistic Director: Darla Johnson
  Co-Artistic Director: Andrew Long
Specialized Field: Ballet; Modern

487
TAPESTRY DANCE COMPANY

2302 Western Trails
Austin, TX 78745
Phone: 512-474-9846
Fax: 512-474-9212
e-mail: dance@tapestry.org
Web Site: www.tapestry.org
Officers:
  Co-Founder: Acia Gray
  Co-Founder: Deirdre Strand
  President: Judy Witkin
Management:
  Artistic/Executive Director: Acia Gray
Mission: Created with the goal of cross discipline choreography and training, the company supports the artistic development in the mixture of tap, modern and jazz creating new works.
Founded: 1989
Specialized Field: Ballet; Tap; Jazz; Modern
Status: Pre-Professional, Nonprofit
Paid Artists: 7

488
CORPUS CHRISTI BALLET

1621 N Mesquite Street
Corpus Christi, TX 78401
Phone: 361-882-4588
Fax: 361-881-9291
e-mail: ccballet@sbcglobal.net
Web Site: www.corpuschristiballet.com
Officers:
  President: Kimberly Kemp
  VP: Dominga Ramos
  Treasurer: Shay Raymond
  Secretary: Amanda Urban
Management:
  Artistic Director: Cristina Stirling Munro
Mission: Dedicated to providing professional ballet productions for the South Texas community.
Utilizes: Five Seasonal Concerts; Guest Artists

Founded: 1974
Specialized Field: Ballet
Status: Non-Professional, Nonprofit
Income Sources: Grants
Performs At: Bayfront Plaza Auditorium
Organization Type: Performing; Touring; Resident; Educational; Sponsoring

489
DALLAS BLACK DANCE THEATRE

2700 Flora Street
Dallas, TX 75201
Phone: 214-871-2376
Fax: 214-871-2842
e-mail: e.flood@dbdt.com
Web Site: www.dbdt.com
Officers:
  Founder: Ann M Williams
  President: Georgia Scaife
  Treasurer: Terry Sanders
  Secretary: Paulette Turner
Management:
  Artistic Director: Ann M Williams
  Executive Director: Zenetta S Drew
  Associate Artistic Director: Melissa M Young
  Sr Marketing/Public Relations Dir: Errika Flood
Mission: The mission of Dallas Black Dance Theatre is to create and produce contemporary modern dance at its highest level of artistic excellence.
Founded: 1976
Specialized Field: Modern; Jazz; Ethnic Dance
Status: Professional, Nonprofit
Paid Staff: 12
Paid Artists: 12
Budget: $1.7 Million
Income Sources: Corporate Sponsorship; City of Dallas; Individuals Donations; Ticket Sales/Touring
Performs At: Majestic Theater
Affiliations: City of Dallas OCA; TCA; National Endowment for the Arts; IABA
Annual Attendance: 125,000
Facility Category: Dee and Charles Wyly Theater
Seating Capacity: 556
Year Built: 2009
Organization Type: Performing; Touring; Educational

490
DALLAS METROPOLITAN BALLET

6815 Hillcrest Avenue
Dallas, TX 75205
Phone: 214-361-0278
e-mail: dallasballet@msn.com
Web Site: www.dallasmetroballet.com
Officers:
  Founder: Ann Etgen
  Founder: Bill Atkinson
Management:
  Artistic Director: Ann Etgen
  Artistic Director: Bill Atkinson
Mission: The aims and focus of the company have remained consistent, to encourage and support ambitious, talented young dancers pursuing professional careers in ballet and to provide an opportunity for the serious student to continue quality dancing as an avocation.
Utilizes: Choreographers; Dancers; Guest Accompanists; Guest Artists; Original Music Scores
Founded: 1964
Specialized Field: Ballet
Status: Semi-Professional, Nonprofit
Paid Staff: 48
Volunteer Staff: 10
Paid Artists: 8
Non-paid Artists: 14

Income Sources: Ticket Sales; Donations; Grants; Fund Raisers
Performs At: McFarlin Auditorium; Southern Methodist University
Affiliations: Regional Dance America/Southwest
Organization Type: Performing; Touring; Resident; Educational

491
BALLET CONCERTO
3803 Camp Bowie Boulevard
Fort Worth, TX 76107-3355
Phone: 817-738-7915
e-mail: balletconcerto@hotmail.com
Web Site: www.balletconcerto.com
Officers:
Founder: Margo Dean
Management:
Artistic Director: Margo Dean
Mission: Ballet Concerto is dedicated to continuing this tradition with a focus on providing lecture, demonstrations and other dance programs to school-aged children.
Utilizes: Guest Artists; Guest Companies; Singers
Founded: 1969
Specialized Field: Ballet
Status: Semi-Professional, Nonprofit
Paid Staff: 2
Volunteer Staff: 5
Paid Artists: 10
Non-paid Artists: 10
Organization Type: Performing

492
CONTEMPORARY DANCE/FORT WORTH
PO Box 11652
Fort Worth, TX 76110
Phone: 817-922-0944
e-mail: cdfw@cdfw.org
Web Site: www.cdfw.org
Officers:
Founder: Susan Douglas Roberts
Management:
Co-Artistic Director: Susan Douglas Roberts
Co-Artistic/Executive Director: Kerry Kreiman
Mission: Contemporary Dance/Fort Worth was formed with the mission of promoting and producing modern dance in the Fort Worth and Tarrant County area.
Specialized Field: Modern
Status: Professional
Affiliations: Dance USA

493
TEXAS BALLET THEATER
1600 Green Oaks Road
Fort Worth, TX 76116
Phone: 817-763-0207
Fax: 817-763-0624
e-mail: margo@texasballettheater.org
Web Site: www.texasballet.org
Officers:
Chairman: Suzanne Charriere
Chairman Elect: Courtney Marcus
Secretary: Laila Minder Gleason
Management:
Artistic Director: Ben Stevenson, O.B.E.
Associate Artistic Director: Tim O'Keefe
Managing Director: Margo McCann
Assistant Artistic Director: Li Anlin
Principal Ballet Master: Anna Donovan
Mission: To bring a world class ballet to North Texas in order to engage in the community, contribute to cultural knowledge and inspire an appreciation for the art of dance; to educate and train the next generation of world

class dancers; to encourage creativity; collaboration and expression by creating a nationally recognized environment for dancers and choreographers to develop and showcase their talent.
Founded: 1961
Specialized Field: Ballet; Modern
Status: Professional, Nonprofit
Budget: $5,000,000+

494
ALLEGRO BALLET OF HOUSTON
Allegro Academy
12680 Goar Road
Houston, TX 77077
Phone: 281-496-4670
Fax: 281-496-1007
Web Site: www.allegroballetofhouston.com
Management:
Artistic Director: Glenda Brown
Artistic Director: Vanessa Brown
Mission: Dedicated to offering a performing outlet for gifted dancers by presenting them in performances both at home and abroad in both classical and contemporary repertoire.
Utilizes: Dance Companies; Dancers; Guest Artists; Singers
Founded: 1951
Specialized Field: Classical; Contemporary
Status: Semi-Professional, Nonprofit
Paid Staff: 2
Volunteer Staff: 6
Non-paid Artists: 15
Income Sources: Private Donations
Performs At: Wortham Center
Affiliations: Regional Dance America
Annual Attendance: 10,000
Organization Type: Performing; Resident; Educational

495
BAY AREA HOUSTON BALLET & THEATRE
PO Box 580466
Houston, TX 77258
Phone: 281-480-1466
e-mail: office@babt.org
Web Site: www.bahbt.org
Officers:
Founder: Lynette Mason Gregg
Management:
Artistic/Executive Director: Lynette Mason Gregg
Associate Artistic Director: Heather Steele
Mission: Bay Area Houston Ballet & Theatre strives to enhance cultural awareness through performing arts and develop aspiring performers with diversified performing skills as well as stimulate public participation and regional involvement.
Utilizes: AEA Actors; Artists-in-Residence; Choreographers; Dancers; Designers; Guest Accompanists; Guest Artists; Guest Choreographers; Guest Ensembles; Guest Musicians; High School Drama; Original Music Scores; Resident Professionals
Founded: 1976
Specialized Field: Theatrical Dance
Status: Semi-Professional, Nonprofit
Paid Staff: 10
Volunteer Staff: 200
Paid Artists: 20
Non-paid Artists: 75
Budget: $800,000
Income Sources: Grants; Patrons; Government; Cities; Foundations
Performs At: University of Houston at Clear Lake
Annual Attendance: 11,000
Facility Category: University

Type of Stage: Proscenium
Stage Dimensions: 50'x60'
Seating Capacity: 500
Year Built: 1975
Rental Contact: Tyler Gavin
Organization Type: Performing

496
CHRYSALIS REPERTORY DANCE COMPANY
PO Box 980398
Houston, TX 77098-0398
Phone: 713-661-9855
Fax: 713-664-0643
e-mail: drjsbak@gateway.net
Web Site: www.chrysalisdance.org
Officers:
President: Harold Eisenmann
VP: Elin Grossman, Esquire
Secretary: Kay Warhol
Treasurer: Christine Lindall
Management:
Artistic Associate: Christine Lidvall
Director: Linda Phenix
Mission: To present innovative, quality dance to enhance Houston and other communities.
Utilizes: Five Seasonal Concerts; Singers
Founded: 1883
Specialized Field: Modern; Post-Modern Dance
Status: Professional; Nonprofit
Paid Staff: 3
Paid Artists: 7+
Budget: $100,000
Income Sources: Individuals; Foundations; Corporations; Performances; Government; Private
Performs At: Heinen Theatre; Houston Community College
Facility Category: Proscenium and Black Box Theaters
Organization Type: Performing; Touring; Resident; Educational; Sponsoring

497
CITY BALLET OF HOUSTON
9902 Long Point Road
Houston, TX 77055
Phone: 713-468-3670
Fax: 713-468-8708
e-mail: mmarshall9902@houston.rr.com
Web Site: www.cityballethouston.com
Management:
Artistic Director: Margo Marshall
Artistic Advisor: Dennis Marshall
Associate Artistic Director: Mary Elizabeth Arrington
Mission: City Ballet of Houston is recognized as a company that brings quality performances to the community and prepares young dancers for professional careers.
Utilizes: Five Seasonal Concerts
Founded: 1958
Specialized Field: Ballet
Status: Semi-Professional, Nonprofit
Volunteer Staff: 10
Paid Artists: 4
Non-paid Artists: 20
Income Sources: Fundraising; Grants; Donations
Performs At: Galveston Grand Opera House; Music Hall
Organization Type: Performing

498
HOUSTON BALLET
PO Box 130487
Houston, TX 77219-0487
Phone: 713-523-6300
Fax: 713-523-4038
Toll-free: 800-828-2787
e-mail: nutcrackermarket@houstonballet.org
Web Site: www.houstonballet.org
Officers:
President: Karl S. Stern
Chairman: Joseph A. Hafner, Jr.
Secretary: Margaret Alkek Williams
Management:
Artistic Director: Stanton Welch
Managing Director: Cecil C Conner Jr
Music Director: Ermanno Florio
Artistic Coordinator: Kelly Ann Vitacca
Associate Choreographer: Christopher Bruce
Production Director: Thomas Boyd
Mission: To inspire a lasting love and appreciation for dance through artistic excellence, exhilarating performances, innovative choreography and superb educational programs.
Founded: 1969
Specialized Field: Ballet
Status: Professional, Nonprofit
Budget: $13,000,000
Income Sources: Corporate; Foundation; Individual Contributions
Performs At: Wortham Center for the Performing Arts
Annual Attendance: 250,000
Organization Type: Performing; Touring; Resident; Educational

499
HOUSTON METROPOLITAN DANCE COMPANY AND CENTER
1202 Calumet
PO Box 980457
Houston, TX 77098
Phone: 713-522-6375
Fax: 713-849-2766
e-mail: houstonmet@aol.com
Web Site: www.houstonmetdance.com
Management:
Executive Director: Michelle Smith
Managing Director: Marlana Doyle
Mission: To enhance the quality of life for individuals and society through instruction in, and the performance of dance. Committed to the development of dance using movement as a learning tool.
Utilizes: Artists-in-Residence; Choreographers; Collaborations; Dancers; Guest Artists; Guest Choreographers; Guest Ensembles; Guest Speakers; High School Drama; Original Music Scores; Resident Artists; Soloists
Founded: 1995
Specialized Field: Contemporary Dance
Status: Professional; Nonprofit
Paid Staff: 25
Volunteer Staff: 50
Paid Artists: 15
Non-paid Artists: 15
Income Sources: Grants; Foundation; Corporations
Performs At: The Wortham Center
Annual Attendance: 10,000
Organization Type: Performing; Touring; Resident; Educational

500
SANDRA ORGAN DANCE COMPANY
PO Box 130936
Houston, TX 77219-0936
Phone: 713-225-0677
Fax: 713-222-1426
e-mail: sorgansodc@aol.com
Web Site: www.organdance.org
Officers:
Founder: Sandra Organ Solis
VP: Nicole Montgomery
Management:
Artistic Director: Sandra Organ Solis
Mission: To promote contemporary dance, educate the public and attract a diverse audience.
Founded: 1997
Specialized Field: Contemporary Dance

501
IRVING BALLET COMPANY
3333 N McArthur Boulevard
Irving, TX 75062
Phone: 972-717-3926
Fax: 972-254-0802
Management:
Artistic Director: Dale Riley
Mission: Dedicated to expanding ballet audiences in the Irving area and establishing a permanent base for future dance audiences.
Utilizes: Five Seasonal Concerts; Guest Companies
Founded: 1982
Specialized Field: Ballet; Jazz
Status: Semi-Professional; Professional
Paid Staff: 25
Income Sources: Irving Symphony; Cultural Affairs Council
Performs At: Irving Arts Center
Organization Type: Performing

502
MOMENTUM DANCE COMPANY
4121 Village Green Drive
Irving, TX 75038
Phone: 972-255-2338
e-mail: jaforcher@momentumdancecompany.org
Web Site: www.momentumdancecompany.org
Officers:
President: Barbara Munday
VP: Dixie Yu
Treasurer: Jerry Forcher
Secretary: Sandy Del Rio
Management:
Artistic Director: Jacquelyn Ralls Forcher
Mission: The Momentum Dance Company's goal is to bring the highest quality dance to the North Texas area.
Founded: 2005
Specialized Field: Ballet
Status: Nonprofit
Paid Staff: 3
Volunteer Staff: 12
Non-paid Artists: 15
Budget: $47,000
Income Sources: Grants; Donations; Ticket Sales
Performs At: Dance
Affiliations: Irving Arts Center

503
KERRVILLE PERFORMING ARTS SOCIETY
PO Box 291884
Kerrville, TX 78029-1884
Phone: 830-896-5727
e-mail: info@kpas.org
Web Site: www.kpas.org
Officers:
President: Tom Murray
Treasurer: Bettye Warnock
Secretary: Jeanie Smith
Mission: To promote and present professional level performing artists, to provide outreach workshops to community schools and organizations, and to offer scholarship aid to area students pursuing higher education in the performing arts.
Utilizes: Singers
Founded: 1983
Status: Non-Profit
Income Sources: Tickets; Donations; Sponsorships; Grants
Performs At: Auditorium
Annual Attendance: 10,000
Facility Category: Municipal Auditorium
Seating Capacity: 8000
Organization Type: Performing

504
RIO GRANDE VALLEY BALLET
5240 N Tenth Street
McAllen, TX 78504
Phone: 956-682-2721
Fax: 956-686-7672
e-mail: deborah@dcda.com
Web Site: www.dcda.com
Management:
Artistic Director: Deborah Case
Mission: Dedicated to promoting the enjoyment and art of dance in all its forms in the Rio Grande Valley and all across the State of Texas.
Utilizes: Five Seasonal Concerts; Singers
Founded: 1972
Specialized Field: Ballet; Jazz; Ethnic Dance; Folk Dance
Status: Semi-Professional, Nonprofit
Paid Staff: 10
Volunteer Staff: 30
Paid Artists: 15
Non-paid Artists: 50
Budget: $40,000-$100,000
Organization Type: Performing; Touring; Resident; Educational; Sponsoring

505
PAMPA CIVIC BALLET
315 N Nelson Street
Pampa, TX 79065
Phone: 806-669-6361
Management:
Artistic Director: Jeanne M Willingham
Assistant Director: Glennette Goode
Mission: To provide encouragement and performance opportunities to the more gifted and dedicated dancers in the area.
Utilizes: Choreographers; Community Talent; Dance Companies; Dancers; Five Seasonal Concerts; Guest Accompanists; Guest Artists; Guest Companies; Guest Musicians; Guest Speakers; High School Drama; Instructors; Local Artists; Multimedia; Resident Artists; Singers
Founded: 1972
Specialized Field: Ballet
Status: Non-Professional, Nonprofit
Income Sources: Contributions; Ticket Sales
Performs At: M.K. Brown Auditorium
Annual Attendance: 300
Facility Category: Civic Auditorium
Type of Stage: Proscenium

Stage Dimensions: 51x22
Seating Capacity: 1,200
Organization Type: Performing; Resident; Educational; Sponsoring

506
GUADALUPE DANCE ACADEMY
Guadalupe Cultural Arts Center
1300 Guadalupe Street
San Antonio, TX 78207
Phone: 210-271-3151
Fax: 210-271-3480
e-mail: info@guadalupeculturalarts.org
Web Site: www.guadalupeculturalarts.org
Officers:
   Chairman: Sammy Nieto
   Treasurer: Fernando Garcia
Management:
   Interim Executive Director: Dan Gonzalez
   Dance Program Director: Belinda Menchaca
Mission: The mission of the Guadalupe Dance Academy is to preseve, present and promote cultural heritage through traditional and contemporary styles of music and dance.
Founded: 1992
Specialized Field: Folkloric Dance; Flamenco
Status: Professional, Nonprofit
Paid Staff: 23
Budget: $1,700,000
Income Sources: Federal; State; Local; Private
Performs At: Guadalupe Theater
Annual Attendance: 190,000
Type of Stage: Proscenium; Thrust
Seating Capacity: 379
Year Built: 1940
Year Remodeled: 1984
Cost: $1,000,000
Organization Type: Resident

507
TYLER CIVIC BALLET
PO Box 9494
Tyler, TX 75711-9494
Phone: 903-596-0224
e-mail: kym@ballettyler.com
Web Site: www.ballettyler.org
Officers:
   President: Beth Price
   VP: Mary Wright
   Treasurer: Monique Dominguez
   Secretary: LeAnn Murphy
Management:
   Artistic Director: Kym Lanier
   Assistant Artistic Director: Jennifer Bailey
Mission: Our mission is to promote education in the art of dance and to provide performing experience and scholarships for promising young dancers in East Texas.
Founded: 1988
Specialized Field: Ballet
Status: Professional, Nonprofit

508
WICHITA FALLS BALLET THEATRE
3412 Buchanan Avenue
Wichita Falls, TX 76308
Phone: 940-322-2552
Web Site: www.wf.net
Officers:
   President: Cynthia Brock
   Treasurer: Joey Wilson
   Secretary: Lisa Williams
Management:
   Artistic Director: Gari Boehm

Artistic Director: Patricia Thornton
   Development: Chris Marvel Loskot
Mission: Dedicated to the creation of dance repertory and the advancement of the arts for the community.
Utilizes: Singers
Founded: 1963
Specialized Field: Modern; Ballet
Status: Semi-Professional, Nonprofit
Paid Staff: 18
Budget: $120,000
Income Sources: Southwest Regional Ballet Association
Performs At: Memorial Auditorium
Annual Attendance: 80,000
Seating Capacity: 2,717
Organization Type: Performing; Touring; Resident

Utah

509
ODYSSEY DANCE THEATRE
11537 S Berryknoll Circle
Draper, UT 84020
Phone: 801-495-3262
Fax: 801-998-3445
e-mail: avanalstyne@odysseydance.com
Web Site: www.odysseydance.com
Officers:
   Treasurer/Secretary: Tori Lima
Management:
   Artistic Director: Derryl Yeager
Mission: To provide quality entertainment and artistic excellence in theatrical dance as a professional dance company as well as creating and recreating classical and full length works that are exciting to young and old alike.
Founded: 1994
Specialized Field: Theatrical Dance; Ballet; Jazz
Status: Professional, Nonprofit
Income Sources: Ticket Sales

510
UTAH REGIONAL BALLET
Utah Valley State College
493 N 1030 W
Lindon, UT 84042
Phone: 801-796-7323
e-mail: shauna@jacquelinesballet.com
Web Site: www.utahregionalballet.org
Management:
   Founder/Artistic Director: Jacqueline P Colledge
Mission: One of the goals of Utah Regional Ballet is to bring world class ballet to Utah audiences as well as those nationally and even abroad.
Founded: 1980
Specialized Field: Ballet
Status: Professional, Nonprofit
Volunteer Staff: 50
Paid Artists: 11
Non-paid Artists: 20
Performs At: Covey Center for the Arts
Annual Attendance: Over 8,000 children
Year Built: 2005
Organization Type: Performing; Touring

511
BALLET WEST
50 W 200 S
Salt Lake City, UT 84101
Phone: 801-323-6900
Fax: 801-359-3504
e-mail: info@balletwest.org
Web Site: www.balletwest.org

Officers:
   Chairman: David Leta
   Treasurer: Harold L Rosenthal
   Secretary: Barbara Clark
Management:
   Artistic Director: Adam Sklute
   Executive Director: JoHann Jacobs
   Assistant Artistic Director: Nick Mullikin
   Principal Ballet Mistress: Pamela Robinson-Harris
   Ballet Master: Mark Goldweber
   Ballet Master: Bruce Caldwell
   Development Director: Denise Begue
Mission: Dedicated to presenting high quality ballet performances.
Utilizes: Five Seasonal Concerts; Guest Artists; Singers
Founded: 1963
Specialized Field: Ballet
Status: Professional, Non-Profit
Paid Staff: 30
Budget: $6,500,000
Income Sources: Contributions; Ticket Sales
Organization Type: Performing; Touring; Resident; Educational

512
INTERNATIONAL DANCE THEATER
Eastern Arts
PO Box 526362
Salt Lake City, UT 84152
Phone: 801-485-5824
e-mail: kstjohn@burgoyne.com
Web Site: www.easternartists.com
Management:
   Artistic Director/Choreographer: Katherine St John
Mission: Presenting traditional dance from many nations and ethnicities.
Founded: 1960
Specialized Field: Ethnic Dance
Status: Professional, Nonprofit
Paid Staff: 10
Income Sources: Western Alliance of Arts Administrators; Society for Ethno-Musicology; Middle East Studies Association; Society for Dance Ethnology
Organization Type: Performing; Educational; Sponsoring

513
REPERTORY DANCE THEATRE
PO Box 510427
Salt Lake City, UT 84151-0427
Phone: 801-534-1000
Fax: 801-534-1110
e-mail: rdt@rdtutah.org
Web Site: www.rdtutah.org
Officers:
   President: John Bogard
   Treasurer: Scott Schwendiman
Management:
   Artistic/Executive Director: Linda C Smith
   Development Director: Susan Sandack
Mission: Repertory Dance Theatre is dedicated to the creation, performance, perpetuation and appreciation of modern dance.
Founded: 1966
Specialized Field: Modern
Status: Professional, Non-Profit
Paid Staff: 4
Paid Artists: 9
Budget: $500,000-$1,000,000
Income Sources: Grants; Foundations; Ticket Sales
Organization Type: Performing; Touring; Resident; Educational; Sponsoring

514

RIRIE WOODBURY DANCE COMPANY

138 W Broadway
Salt Lake City, UT 84101
Phone: 801-297-4241
Fax: 801-297-4235
e-mail: info@ririewoodbury.com
Web Site: www.ririewoodbury.com
Officers:
 Chairman: Joan Woodbury
 Vice Chairman: Rhees Ririe
 Secretary: Shirley Ririe
Management:
 Marketing/Public Relations: Jessica Ballard
 Associate Managing Director: Jena Woodbury
 Development: David Pace
 Artistic Director: Charlotte Boye Christensen
Mission: Furthers contemporary dance as an
accessible and valued art form though performance and
dance education that raises the standards, deepens the
understanding and promotes personal connections with
contemporary dance.
Utilizes: Choreographers; Collaborating Artists;
Dancers; Educators; Five Seasonal Concerts; Guest
Artists; Guest Companies; Singers; Soloists
Founded: 1964
Specialized Field: Modern
Status: Professional; Nonprofit
Budget: $900,000
Income Sources: Government; Foundations;
Corporations
Performs At: The Rose Wagner Performing Arts
Center; Capital Theatre
Annual Attendance: 50,000
Organization Type: Performing; Touring; Resident;
Educational; Sponsoring

515

CLOG AMERICA

Worldwide Association of Performing Artists
6645 Castleview Drive
West Valley City, UT 84128
Phone: 801-968-2411
Fax: 801-981-8222
e-mail: iae123@comcast.net
Web Site: www.wwapa.org
Officers:
 Founder: Shawnda Bishop
 President: Duane Bishop
Management:
 Artistic/Executive Director: Shawnda Bishop
 Assistant Director: Bonnie Romney
Mission: The promotion of clogging workshops,
festivals, tours and performances throughout the USA
and abroad.
Founded: 1990
Specialized Field: Folk Dance
Status: Semi-Professional, Commercial
Income Sources: Utah Arts Council; National Clogging
Leaders Organization
Performs At: Scera Shell Amphitheatre
Organization Type: Performing; Touring; Educational

Vermont

516

BURKLYN BALLET THEATRE

Johnson State College
337 College Hill
Johnson, VT 05656

Phone: 802-635-0438
Fax: 973-586-3556
Toll-free: 877-287-5596
e-mail: info@burklynballet.com
Web Site: www.burklynballet.com
Officers:
 President: James Whitehall
Management:
 Artistic Director: Joanne Whitehill
Mission: Burklyn Ballet Theatre's goal is to bring to the
world of dance a program of the highest artistic caliber
and give performance opportunities to all participating
dancers in a beautiful and safe environment.
Utilizes: Artists-in-Residence; Choreographers;
Dancers; Educators; Guest Artists; Guest Ensembles;
Guest Musical Directors; Guest Soloists; Guest
Speakers; High School Drama; Resident Companies;
Scenic Designers; Soloists; Students; Student Interns;
Theatre Companies
Founded: 1976
Opened: 1976
Specialized Field: Ballet; Dance
Status: Pre-Professional
Paid Staff: 12
Paid Artists: 20
Non-paid Artists: 55
Budget: $500,000
Income Sources: Box Office; Tuition
Performs At: Dibden Center for the Arts
Affiliations: Burklyn Youth Ballet
Annual Attendance: 2-5000
Type of Stage: Proscenium
Stage Dimensions: 42'x 39'
Seating Capacity: 600
Year Built: 1968
Year Remodeled: 1992
Organization Type: Performing; Touring; Educational

Virginia

517

ARLINGTON DANCE THEATRE

PO Box 3091
Arlington, VA 22205
Phone: 703-524-4750
e-mail: adt@arlingtondance.org
Web Site: www.arlingtondance.org
Officers:
 President: Andrew Rylyk
 VP: Susan Tyson
 Secretary/Treasurer: Cheryl Scannell
Management:
 Youth Ballet Company Director: Martha Rutter
 Administrative Director: Amanda Smith
 School Director: Ann Kelly
Mission: To promote excellence in the performance
and teaching of dance.
Utilizes: Singers
Founded: 1956
Specialized Field: Ballet; Jazz; Tap
Status: Semi-Professional, Nonprofit
Paid Staff: 16
Income Sources: Arlington County Cultural Affairs
Office
Performs At: Thomas Jefferson Community Theatre
Organization Type: Performing; Educational

518

JANE FRANKLIN DANCE

3700 S Four Mile Run Drive
Arlington, VA 22206

Phone: 703-933-1111
e-mail: info@janefranklin.com
Web Site: www.janefranklin.com
Officers:
 President: Charlotte Hollister
 Treasurer: Cheryl Stevens
 Secretary: Christina Friedl
Management:
 Artistic Director: Jane Franklin
Mission: Jane Franklin Dance celebrates movement
and makes dance accessible to a wide range of
audiences through public performances, community
engagement, dance education and collaborations with
artists from other disciplines.
Founded: 1997
Specialized Field: Movement; Educational Dance;
Traditional Dance
Status: Professional, Nonprofit
Paid Staff: 3
Volunteer Staff: 15
Budget: $65,000
Income Sources: Government; Foundations; Individual
Performs At: The Gunston Theatre
Annual Attendance: 9,000
Organization Type: Performing; Touring; Educational

519

DANCEVERT

3017 James Street
Fairfax, VA 22031
Phone: 301-529-7750
Fax: 301-529-7684
e-mail: dancevert@aol.com
Web Site: www.dancevert.org
Management:
 Artistic Director/Choreographer: Susana
 Weingarten
 Co-Artistic Director: Tom Evert
Mission: To share the innate vitality of movement as a
form of expression and the body as an instrument
connected with the mind and spirit.
Utilizes: Musical Directors; Singers
Founded: 1986
Specialized Field: Modern
Status: Professional, Nonprofit
Budget: $150,000
Income Sources: Association for Performing Arts
Presenters; Arts Midwest; Arts Presenters Network;
Ohio Dance; Ohio Citizens Committee for the Arts
Performs At: Cleveland Play House
Annual Attendance: 20,000
Organization Type: Performing; Touring; Resident;
Educational; Special Events

520

HAMPTON ROADS CIVIC BALLET

Academy of Ballet
4218 Victoria Boulevard
Hampton, VA 23669
Phone: 757-722-8216
e-mail: info@hrcivicballet.org
Web Site: www.hrcivicballet.org
Officers:
 Founder: Muriel Shelley Evans
 President: Karen Page
 VP: Paula Hogg
 Treasurer: Debbie Scott
 Secretary: Frances Brown
Management:
 Artistic Director: Muriel Shelley Evans
Mission: Provides students with differing goals the
opportunity to grow artistically and technically in a
supportive, dynamic environment.
Founded: 1959

Specialized Field: Ballet
Status: Professional, Nonprofit
Organization Type: Performing; Resident; Educational

521
LOUDOUN BALLET COMPANY
PO Box 916
Leesburg, VA 20178
Phone: 703-771-1522
e-mail: info@loudounballet.org
Web Site: www.loudounballet.org
Officers:
  Founder: Sheila Hoffmann-Robertson
  Chairman: Steve Spaseff
  Treasurer: Cherilynne Piper
  Secretary: Patricia Potts
Management:
  Artistic Director: Maureen Miller
  Ballet Mistress: Lisa Startsman
Mission: The Loudoun Ballet Company's purpose is to support a professional dance company and offer a performing season for the Loudoun community.
Founded: 1978
Specialized Field: Ballet
Status: Professional, Nonprofit

522
MALINI'S DANCES OF INDIA TROUPE
1510 Bordeaux Place
Norfolk, VA 23509
Phone: 757-533-5594
Fax: 757-533-4616
e-mail: maindance@dancesofindia.org
Web Site: www.danceofindia.org
Management:
  Artistic Director: Malini Srirama
Mission: The programs have been crafted to offer western audiences an understanding of the historical background and cultural development of India's art forms.
Utilizes: Singers
Specialized Field: Ethnic Dance
Status: Professional, Nonprofit
Volunteer Staff: 7
Organization Type: Performing; Touring; Resident; Educational; Sponsoring

523
THEATRE ARTS DANCE PROGRAM
Old Dominion University
4810 Elkhorn Avenue
Diehn Room 147
Norfolk, VA 23529
Phone: 757-683-4354
Fax: 757-683-6098
e-mail: mmarloff@odu.edu
Web Site: www.odu.edu
Officers:
  President: John R Broderick
Management:
  Artistic Director: Marilyn Marloff
Mission: Focuses on intellectual understanding of the systems of motion, performance opportunities for creative expression and collaborative efforts that create synergy.
Specialized Field: Ballet; Jazz; Modern
Status: Nonprofit

524
VIRGINIA BALLET THEATRE
Virginia Ballet Academy
134 W Olney Road
Norfolk, VA 23510

Phone: 757-622-4822
Fax: 757-622-7904
e-mail: virginiaballettheatre@gmail.com
Web Site: www.virginiaballettheatre.com
Officers:
  President: Angela Martin Blackwell
  Treasurer: Gregory French
  Secretary: Michael Morisi
Management:
  Artistic Director: Jurijs Safonovs
  Executive Director: Thom Prevette
Mission: Professional ballet dance theatre bringing dance and dance education to Virginia and beyond.
Founded: 1961
Specialized Field: Ballet
Status: Non-Professional, Nonprofit
Paid Staff: 04
Volunteer Staff: 20
Paid Artists: 20
Organization Type: Performing; Resident

525
CONCERT BALLET OF VIRGINIA
Box 25501
Richmond, VA 23260
Phone: 804-798-0945
e-mail: concertballetofvirginia@yahoo.com
Web Site: www.concertballet.com
Officers:
  President: Susan McCoy
  VP: Annie Tibbett
  Treasurer: Amy Christopher
Management:
  Artistic Director: Robert Watkins
  Associate Director: Scott Boyer
  Executive Director: Eleanor Rennie
  Production Manager: Tim Ryder
Mission: To foster an appreciation of classical and contemporary dance by staging affordable productions at convenient locations throughout the state, while providing excellent training and challenging creative opportunities within a professional dance company.
Utilizes: Five Seasonal Concerts; Guest Artists
Founded: 1976
Specialized Field: Classical; Contemporary Dance
Status: Professional, Nonprofit
Paid Staff: 15
Income Sources: Fundraising; Foundations; Individual
Performs At: The Woman's Club Auditorium; Blackwell Auditorium
Organization Type: Performing; Touring; Educational

526
RICHMOND BALLET
407 E Canal Street
Richmond, VA 23219
Phone: 804-344-0906
Fax: 804-344-0903
e-mail: smckinney@richmondballet.com
Web Site: www.richmondballet.com
Officers:
  President: Libby Robertson
  Chairman: Mary Anne Hooker
  President: Carroll Hurst
  Treasurer: David Beran
  Secretary: Cyane B Crump
Management:
  Artistic Director: Stoner Winslett
  Operations Director: Sue McKinney
  Artistic Associate/Ballet Master: Malcolm Burn
  Ballet Master: Jerri Kumery
  Resident Artist: Igor Antonov
  Development Director: Susan Coogan

  Marketing/Communications Director: Aaron Sutten
Mission: Dedicated to the promotion, preservation and continuing evolution of the art form of ballet according to specific aesthetic and institutional values established by the vision of the artistic director.
Utilizes: Choreographers; Commissioned Music; Dance Companies; Dancers; Five Seasonal Concerts; Grant Writers; Guest Artists; Guest Companies; Guest Conductors; Original Music Scores
Founded: 1957
Specialized Field: Ballet
Status: Professional, Nonprofit
Paid Artists: 19
Budget: $2,500,000+
Organization Type: Performing; Touring; Resident; Educational

527
SCHOOL OF THE ARTS
Virginia University
1315 Floyd Avenue
PO Box 843007
Richmond, VA 23284
Phone: 804-828-1711
Fax: 804-828-7356
e-mail: dance@vcu.edu
Web Site: www.vcu.edu
Officers:
  Chair: Richard E Toscan
Management:
  Assistant Professor: Lea Marshall
Mission: Offers a vibrant, stimulating atmosphere where students are prepared for careers in the field of dance.
Founded: 1981
Specialized Field: Educational Dance; Theatrical Dance
Paid Staff: 6
Paid Artists: 24
Affiliations: NASD; CODA
Annual Attendance: 9,167
Facility Category: Theater
Seating Capacity: 225
Year Built: 1934
Year Remodeled: 1996
Rental Contact: Grace Street Theater House Manager Cynthia Theakston

528
MUSIC IN MOTION®ACADEMY OF DANCE
629 N Lynnhaven Road
Virginia Beach, VA 23452
Phone: 757-340-1534
e-mail: darlene@musicinmotionva.com
Web Site: www.musicinmotionva.com
Management:
  Artistic Director: Darlene Stephens
Mission: Music in Motion® has an ongoing program of performances with public school systems and young audiences in Virginia.
Founded: 1987
Specialized Field: Ballet; Modern; Jazz
Status: Pre-Professional
Annual Attendance: 750

529
WILLIAMSBURG BALLET THEATRE
Institute for Dance
3356 Ironbound Road
Suite 501
Williamsburg, VA 23188

Phone: 757-229-1717
Fax: 757-229-4953
e-mail: info@institutefordance.org
Web Site: www.institutefordance.org
Officers:
Founder: Heidi Robitshek
President: Putul Rogowski
VP: John Burton
Treasurer: Laura Colvin
Secretary: Laura Ekstrom
Management:
Artistic Director: Kristine Antis
Studio Director/Instructor: Kathy Martin-Palmo
Mission: Our mission is to bring cultural enrichment to Williamsburg and surrounding areas by presenting to our audiences professional quality performances.
Founded: 1968
Specialized Field: Ballet
Status: Nonprofit

Washington

530
PENINSULA DANCE THEATRE

515 Chester Avenue
Bremerton, WA 98377
Phone: 360-377-6214
e-mail: joandscott@comcast.net
Web Site: www.peninsuladancetheatre.org
Officers:
President: Scott Dempski
Management:
Artistic Director: Lawan Morrison
Junior Company Assistant Director: Diana Lau
Music Director: Alan Futterman
Mission: Peninsula Dance Theatre is dedicated to furthering classical and contemporary forms of dance in the Kitsap county region.
Founded: 1973
Specialized Field: Classical; Contemporary Dance
Status: Professional, Nonprofit
Performs At: Win Graulund Performing Arts Center
Organization Type: Performing; Resident

531
OLYMPIC BALLET THEATRE

Olympic Ballet School
700 Main Street
Edmonds, WA 98020
Phone: 425-774-7570
Fax: 425-672-2827
e-mail: dance@olympicballet.com
Web Site: www.olympicballet.com
Officers:
Founder: Helen Wilkins
Founder: John Wilkins
Management:
Artistic Director: Helen Wilkins
Associate Artistic Director: John Wilkins
Mission: Olympic Ballet Theatre seeks to develop and sustain professional dance, promote dance as a creative performing art and engage the widest possible audience with a stimulating repertoire of classical contemporary and dramatic ballets.
Utilizes: Singers
Founded: 1981
Specialized Field: Ballet
Status: Semi-Professional, Nonprofit
Paid Staff: 21
Budget: $200,000-$500,000
Performs At: The Moore Theatre; Everett Performing Arts Center
Organization Type: Resident

532
ARIA DANCE COMPANY

9th Avenue Performing Arts Center
33639 Ninth Avenue S
Federal Way, WA 98003
Phone: 253-924-0621
e-mail: aria@intodance.com
Web Site: www.intodance.com
Officers:
President: Martha Lawson
VP: Carol Karalus
Treasurer: Guy Pittman
Secretary: Susan Rao
Management:
Artistic/Executive Director: Christina Vandenberg-Suju
Mission: Aria is dedicated to helping dancers achieve self-discipline and artistic expression through dance.
Founded: 1996
Specialized Field: Ballet; Modern; Jazz, Folk; Character Dance
Status: Nonprofit

533
CHAMBER DANCE COMPANY

University of Washington
Box 351150
Seattle, WA 98195-1150
Phone: 206-543-1150
Fax: 206-543-8610
e-mail: uwdance@u.washington.edu
Web Site: www.meany.org
Officers:
Founder: Hannah C Wiley
Management:
Artistic Director: Hannah C Wiley
Mission: The Chamber Dance Company's mission is to present and record works of historical and artistic significance.
Founded: 1990
Specialized Field: Educational Dance; Theatrical Dance
Status: Professional
Paid Artists: 6

534
DANCE PROGRAM

University of Washington
Box 351150
Seattle, WA 98195-1150
Phone: 206-543-9843
Fax: 206-543-8610
e-mail: uwdance@u.washington.edu
Web Site: www.depts.washington.edu/uwdance
Management:
Associate Professor: Elizabeth Cooper
Music Director: Paul Moore
Production Manager: Peter Bracilano
Mission: The mission of the University of Washington Dance Program is to educate performers, educators, arts advocates and cultural leaders.
Specialized Field: Ballet; Modern
Status: Professional, Nonprofit
Paid Staff: 10
Paid Artists: 30
Income Sources: University of Washington; Private; Corporations; Foundations
Performs At: Meany Hall
Organization Type: Sponsoring; Presenting

535
OCHEAMI AFRICAN DANCE COMPANY

PO Box 31635
Seattle, WA 98103
Phone: 206-329-8876
e-mail: ocheami@earthlink.net
Web Site: www.home.earthlink.net
Officers:
Founder: Amma Anang
Founder: Kofi Anang
Management:
Artistic Director: Kofi Anang
Manager: Amma Anang
Mission: Ocheami's purpose is to share West African culture by providing authentic, quality instruction and performances in African Arts and to have these experiences accessible to all.
Utilizes: Five Seasonal Concerts
Founded: 1978
Specialized Field: Historical Dance; African Dance
Status: Professional, Nonprofit
Organization Type: Performing; Touring; Educational

536
PACIFIC NORTHWEST BALLET

Pacific Northwest Ballet School
301 Mercer Street
Seattle, WA 98109
Phone: 206-441-9411
Fax: 206-441-2440
e-mail: marketing@pnb.org
Web Site: www.pnb.org
Officers:
Chairman: Carl Behnke
President: Aya Hamilton
Treasurer: Hallock W Beals
Secretary: W Daniel Heidt
Management:
Artistic Director: Peter Boal
Executive Director: David Brown
Music Director: Stewart Kershaw
Mission: Dedicated to maintaining a professional ballet company and school.
Utilizes: Choreographers; Collaborations; Commissioned Composers; Commissioned Music; Dancers; Designers; Educators; Fine Artists; Five Seasonal Concerts; Grant Writers; Guest Accompanists; Guest Artists; Guest Companies; Guest Conductors; Guest Ensembles; Guest Musical Directors; Guest Musicians; Guest Writers; High School Drama; Instructors; Lyricists; Multimedia; New Productions; Organization Contracts; Original Music Scores; Poets; Resident Professionals; Singers; Soloists; Student Interns
Founded: 1974
Specialized Field: Ballet
Status: Professional, Nonprofit
Paid Artists: 51
Budget: $12,000,000
Performs At: The McCaw Hall
Organization Type: Performing; Touring; Resident

537
PAT GRANEY COMPANY

1419 S Jackson Street
Studio 11
Seattle, WA 98144
Phone: 206-329-3705
Fax: 206-329-3730
e-mail: staff@patgraney.org
Web Site: www.patgraney.org
Officers:
Founder: Pat Graney

Management:
Artistic/Executive Director: Pat Graney
Mission: The mission of the Pat Graney Company is to create and perform new dance and performance works and to conduct arts education programming.
Utilizes: Collaborating Artists; Dancers; Designers; Educators; Guest Companies; Instructors; Local Artists; Multimedia; Original Music Scores; Student Interns
Founded: 1990
Specialized Field: Contemporary Dance
Status: Professional, Nonprofit
Volunteer Staff: 10
Paid Artists: 05
Budget: $200,000
Income Sources: Individual Donors; Foundations; Corporate Grants

538
RADOST FOLK ENSEMBLE

PO Box 31295
Seattle, WA 98103
Phone: 206-860-5251
e-mail: admin@radost.org
Web Site: www.radost.org
Management:
Co-Director: Sidney Deering
Mission: Radost Folk Ensemble is an ethnic dance company dedicated to teaching, preserving and presenting the dance traditions of Eastern Europe.
Utilizes: Scenic Designers; Sign Language Translators; Singers; Students; Theatre Companies
Founded: 1976
Specialized Field: Ethnic Dance; Eastern Europe Dance
Status: Semi-Professional, Nonprofit
Paid Staff: 1
Volunteer Staff: 4
Paid Artists: 8
Non-paid Artists: 12
Budget: $20,000
Income Sources: Touring Concerts; Teaching; Grants; Private Donations
Organization Type: Performing; Touring; Educational; Sponsoring

539
PIONEER DANCE ARTS

172 Bell Meadow Lane
PO Box 238
Sequim, WA 98382
Phone: 360-683-3693
e-mail: mpirouette@earthlink.net
Web Site: www.pioneerdancearts.com
Officers:
Secretary: Stacey Forshaw
Treasurer: Kathy Clark
Management:
Academy Director: Kathleen Moore
Mission: The mission of the company is to raise the dance art awareness on the North Olympic Penninsula.
Utilizes: Five Seasonal Concerts
Founded: 1974
Specialized Field: Classical Ballet; Modern; Contemporary Jazz; Tap
Status: Non-Professional, Nonprofit
Volunteer Staff: 100
Performs At: Port Angeles High School Auditorium
Organization Type: Performing; Resident; Educational; Sponsoring

540
FILIPINIANA DANCE COMPANY

569 N 166th Street
Shoreline, WA 98133

Phone: 206-542-7245
e-mail: rogervidal2005@yahoo.com
Officers:
Founder/President: Roger Del Rosario
Management:
Director: Roger Del Rosario
Mission: Traditional Filipino dance group that combines rich pageantry, elegant costumes, music and dance to create an exciting intermingling of very different cultures.
Utilizes: Five Seasonal Concerts; Singers
Founded: 1969
Specialized Field: Philippino Dance
Status: Semi-Professional, Nonprofit
Volunteer Staff: 30
Non-paid Artists: 50
Budget: $25,000
Income Sources: Festivals
Performs At: Shoreline Arts Center
Annual Attendance: 10,000
Organization Type: Performing; Touring; Resident; Educational; Sponsoring

541
TACOMA CITY BALLET

508 6th Avenue
Tacoma, WA 98402
Phone: 253-272-4219
Fax: 253-272-4219
e-mail: tacomacityballet@gmail.com
Web Site: www.tacomacityballet.com
Officers:
Chairman: John Hodder
Management:
Artistic Director: Erin M Ceragioli
Executive Director: Nikki Smith
Mission: To provide quality, fully-staged classical ballets for the Southern Puget Sound area.
Founded: 1955
Specialized Field: Ballet
Status: Semi-Professional
Paid Staff: 20
Income Sources: National Association for Regional Ballet; Pacific Regional Ballet Association
Performs At: Pantages Theater
Organization Type: Performing

542
TACOMA PERFORMING DANCE COMPANY

Jo Emery Ballet School
5212 D S Washington Street
Tacoma, WA 98409
Phone: 253-627-8272
e-mail: info@tacomaperformingdance.org
Web Site: www.tacomaperformingdance.org
Officers:
Founder: Jo Emery
President: Bernie Plancich
VP: Sarah Heckman
Treasurer: Helene Cox
Secretary: Tom Kimpel
Management:
Artistic Director: Jo Emery
Mission: The mission of Tacoma Performing Dance Company is to provide outstanding, versatile dance presentations to the greater south Puget Sound region at an affordable price for the enjoyment of all.
Utilizes: Guest Companies
Founded: 1967
Specialized Field: Modern; Ballet; Jazz
Status: Semi-Professional, Nonprofit
Performs At: Pantages Centre
Organization Type: Performing; Touring; Resident

543
CHARLESTON BALLET

822 Virginia Street E
Charleston, WV 25301
Phone: 304-342-6541
e-mail: info@thecharlestonballet.com
Web Site: www.thecharlestonballet.com
Management:
Artistic Director/CEO: Kim R Pauley
Office Manager: Elaine Baldwin
Production: Becky Turley
Mission: To present ballet concerts for professional and talented young dancers.
Utilizes: Artists-in-Residence; Collaborating Artists; Collaborations; Composers; Contract Orchestras; Dancers; Educators; Filmmakers; Grant Writers; Guest Accompanists; Guest Artists; Guest Choreographers; Guest Ensembles; Guest Speakers; Instructors; Local Talent; Organization Contracts; Original Music Scores; Students
Founded: 1956
Specialized Field: Modern; Ballet; Folk Dance
Status: Semi-Professional, Nonprofit
Paid Staff: 3
Volunteer Staff: 20
Paid Artists: 20
Non-paid Artists: 30
Season: October-March
Performs At: Charleston Civic Center Theater; Maier Performance Hall at Clay Center; Walker Theater at Clay Center
Organization Type: Performing; Touring

544
MID OHIO VALLEY BALLET COMPANY

Nash School
1311 Ann Street
PO Box 4204
Parkersburg, WV 26101
Phone: 304-422-5538
Fax: 304-422-6730
Toll-free: 800-882-1148
e-mail: movdance@wirefire.com
Web Site: www.movballet.com
Management:
Artistic Director: Suzy Gunter
Executive Director: Norma J Gunter
Music Director: Joy Held
Educational Director: Terry Donne Gunter
Artistic Advisor: Mark Jelks
Artistic Advisor: Brian Palmer
Mission: Mid Ohio Valley Ballet is dedicated to quality performances, training and education and the preservation of classical ballet.
Founded: 1994
Specialized Field: Ballet; Modern
Status: Professional, Nonprofit
Paid Staff: 6
Budget: $1,000,000-$2,500,000
Income Sources: Artsbridge
Season: October-May

545
APPALACHIAN YOUTH JAZZ-BALLET COMPANY

605 D Street
South Charleston, WV 25303
Phone: 304-343-1076
Toll-free: 800-409-4646
Officers:
President: Ricklin Brown

VP: John Breed
Secretary: Catherine Halloran
Treasurer: Carol Velasquez
Management:
    Artistic Director: Nina Denton
Mission: To provide talented aspiring dancers liaisons between the classroom and the professional stage; to enrich the community through concerts and lecture demonstrations; to provide inspiration to youngsters in the audience.
Founded: 1982
Specialized Field: Ballet; Jazz
Status: Nonprofit
Paid Staff: 2
Income Sources: Washington Community Education
Performs At: Charleston Civic Center; Municipal Auditorium
Organization Type: Performing; Touring; Educational

Wisconsin

546
DANCE PROGRAM

University of Wisconsin
1050 University Avenue
Lathrop Hall
Madison, WI 53706
Phone: 608-262-1641
Fax: 608-265-3841
e-mail: uwdance@education.wisc.edu
Web Site: www.dance.wisc.edu
Officers:
    Dean: Julie K Underwood
Management:
    Professor: Jin-Wen Yu
    Professor: Li Chiao-Ping
    Professor/Music Director: Joseph N Koykkar
Mission: To create and maintain high standards for dance in the Midwest and to bring quality modern dance to the largest public eye possible.
Utilizes: Singers
Founded: 1985
Specialized Field: Modern
Status: Professional, Nonprofit
Paid Staff: 1
Income Sources: University of Wisconsin-Madison
Organization Type: Performing; Touring

547
KANOPY DANCE COMPANY

341 State Street
Madison, WI 53703
Phone: 608-255-2211
Web Site: www.kanopydance.org
Officers:
    President: Suzanne Voeltz
    VP: Richard Zillman
    Treasurer: Sue Gardner
    Secretary: Chuck Hahn
Management:
    Artistic Director/Choreographer: Lisa Andrea Thurrell
    Artistic Director/Choreographer: Robert E Cleary
Mission: To promote, encourage and increase the public's knowledge of and appreciation for the arts including the art of dance.
Utilizes: Singers
Founded: 1976
Specialized Field: Modern; Jazz
Status: Professional
Income Sources: Wisconsin Dance Council
Season: November-May
Performs At: Kanopy Studio; Wisconsin Union Theatre

Organization Type: Performing; Touring; Resident; Educational; Sponsoring

548
MADISON SCOTTISH COUNTRY DANCERS

4805 Regent Street
Madison, WI 53705
Phone: 608-232-0512
e-mail: Madison_Scottish_Country_Dancers@yahoogroups.com
Web Site: www.sprott.physics.wisc.edu
Officers:
    Chair: Nancy McClements
    Treasurer: Dyan Steenport
    Secretary: Kate Deck
Management:
    Teacher: Norma Briggs
    Teacher: Chuck Snowdon
Mission: Madison Scottish Country Dancers is a social group that enjoys learning and dancing the traditional reels, jigs and strathspeys of Scotland.
Founded: 1977
Specialized Field: Ethnic Dance
Status: Non-Professional, Nonprofit
Paid Staff: 60
Income Sources: Royal Scottish Country Dance Society (Scotland)
Performs At: University of Wisconsin; Memorial Union
Organization Type: Performing; Educational

549
MM COLBERT

1321 E Johnson Street
Madison, WI 53703
Phone: 608-257-9807
Officers:
    Chairperson: Nancy Idaka Sheran
Management:
    Director/Choreographer: MM Colbert
Mission: To present original modern ballets in collaboration with other living artists.
Utilizes: Singers
Founded: 1980
Specialized Field: Modern; Ballet; Jazz
Status: Nonprofit
Organization Type: Performing

550
TAPIT/NEW WORKS ENSEMBLE THEATER

1957 Winnebago Street
Madison, WI 53704
Phone: 608-244-2938
Fax: 608-244-9114
e-mail: info@tapitnewworks.org
Web Site: www.tapitnewworks.com
Officers:
    President: Steve Holtzman
    Treasurer: Larry Lundy
Management:
    Producing Artistic Director: Danielle Dresden
    Producing Artistic Director: Donna Peckett
    Secretary: Carolyn Hegeler
    Treasurer: Larry Lundy
Mission: Creates, produces and performs original works, collaborating with artists working in the disciplines of theater, tap dance, visual arts and music; brings the arts to audiences of all ages and backgrounds; encourages participation in the arts through outreach; and enriches the lives of individuals and communities.

Utilizes: Actors; Artists-in-Residence; Collaborating Artists; Collaborations; Commissioned Composers; Educators; Equity Actors; Grant Writers; Guest Companies; Guest Conductors; Guest Designers; Guest Ensembles; Guest Instructors; Guest Musical Directors; Guest Speakers; Guild Activities; High School Drama; Instructors; Local Artists; Local Talent; Original Music Scores; Playwrights; Selected Students; Students; Touring Companies; Visual Arts
Founded: 1985
Specialized Field: Theatre Dance; Multi-Disciplinary Work; Tap; Residencies; Workshops
Paid Staff: 3
Volunteer Staff: 3
Paid Artists: 15
Budget: $50,000-$120,000
Income Sources: Public; private; fees; tickets
Performs At: Perform in their storefront venue and tour throughout the US and abroad.
Annual Attendance: 12,000
Seating Capacity: 50
Year Remodeled: 1994
Rental Contact: Producing Artistic Director Donna Peckett

551
WILLOW: A DANCE CONCERN

122 State Street
Lower Level
Madison, WI 53703
Phone: 608-280-9601
Management:
    Director: Phyllis Sanfilippo
Mission: To promote dance as a performing art and form of personal expression.
Utilizes: Singers
Founded: 1975
Specialized Field: Modern
Status: Nonprofit
Paid Staff: 5
Organization Type: Performing

552
MESOGHIOS DANCE TROUPE

3813 S Meadow Drive
Middleton, WI 53562
Phone: 608-831-4485
Officers:
    Founder/President: Vicky Knoedler
Management:
    Artistic Director: Vicky Knoedler
Mission: To perform Greek, Turkish, Russian and Azerbayjan ethnic and folk dances.
Founded: 1978
Specialized Field: Ethnic Dance; Folk Dance
Status: Semi-Professional, Nonprofit
Paid Staff: 15
Organization Type: Performing; Educational

553
DANCECIRCUS

527 N 27th Street
Milwaukee, WI 53208
Phone: 414-277-8151
e-mail: dance@dancecircus.org
Web Site: www.dancecircus.org
Officers:
    VP: Jean Dean
    Treasurer: Robert Lamb
Management:
    Artistic Director: Betty Salamun

Mission: With concern for the people and the land we bring affordable accessible programs to the entire community creating original works in music, dance and theatre true to our midwestern heritage.
Utilizes: Actors; Artists-in-Residence; Collaborating Artists; Collaborations; Commissioned Composers; Commissioned Music; Dance Companies; Dancers; Educators; Filmmakers; Guest Accompanists; Guest Artists; Guest Companies; Guest Musical Directors; Guest Musicians; Guest Teachers; Guild Activities; Instructors; Local Artists; Lyricists; Multimedia; Organization Contracts; Original Music Scores; Poets; Selected Students; Soloists; Touring Companies; Visual Arts
Founded: 1975
Specialized Field: Modern Dance
Status: Professional, Nonprofit
Paid Staff: 1
Volunteer Staff: 2
Paid Artists: 14
Budget: $62,000
Income Sources: Grants; Earned; Donations
Affiliations: Dance USA
Annual Attendance: 45,000-50,000
Organization Type: Performing; Touring; Educational

554
KO-THI DANCE COMPANY
PO Box 1093
Milwaukee, WI 53201
Phone: 414-273-0676
Fax: 414-273-0727
Toll-free: 800-442-8422
e-mail: kkothi@aol.com
Web Site: www.ko-thi.org
Officers:
Chair-Board: Mark Ernest
Treasurer: Vincent Ciccolini
Secretary: Sharon Williams
Management:
Artistic Director: Ferne Yangyeitie Caulker
Associate Artistic Director: Valencia Turner
Managing Director: Una Van Duvall
Mission: To promulgate and preserve the African, African American and Caribbean art forms.
Utilizes: Choreographers; Collaborating Artists; Collaborations; Dance Companies; Dancers; Five Seasonal Concerts; Guest Artists; Guest Musical Directors; Guest Musicians; Local Artists; Lyricists; Multimedia; New Productions; Organization Contracts; Original Music Scores; Playwrights; Student Interns; Special Technical Talent; Touring Companies
Founded: 1969
Specialized Field: African Dance
Paid Staff: 6
Volunteer Staff: 10
Paid Artists: 28
Budget: $294,000
Income Sources: Instruction; Tickets
Performs At: UWM Deck School Of The Arts

555
MILWAUKEE BALLET COMPANY
504 W National Avenue
Milwaukee, WI 53204
Phone: 414-643-7677
Fax: 414-649-4066
e-mail: 2thepointe@milwaukeeballet.org
Web Site: www.milwaukeeballet.org
Officers:
Chair: Mary Leahy
Treasurer: Dorinda Floyd
Management:
Artistic Director: Michael Pink

Executive Director: Dennis Buehler
Ballet Mistress: Nadia Thompson
Ballet Master: Denis Malinkine
Production Director: Steve Vallee
Mission: Representing traditional and contemporary ballet performances expressing the highest aspirations and deepest emotions of the human spirit.
Utilizes: Dancers; Guest Artists; Guest Conductors; Singers
Founded: 1970
Specialized Field: Traditional Ballet; Contemporary Ballet
Status: Professional, Nonprofit
Budget: $4,800,000
Income Sources: Corporate; Individual; Donation
Performs At: Uihlein Hall; Milwaukee Performing Arts Center
Annual Attendance: 70,000
Organization Type: Performing; Touring; Resident; Educational

556
WILD SPACE DANCE COMPANY
Lincoln Center Middle School of the Arts
820 E Knapp Street
PO Box 511665
Milwaukee, WI 53202
Phone: 414-271-0307
Fax: 414-271-6087
e-mail: info@wildspacedance.org
Web Site: www.wildspacedance.org
Management:
Founder/Artistic Director: Debra Loewen, DebLoewen@wildspacedance.org
Managing Director: Richard T Clark, rick@wildspacedance.org
Business Manager: Sheri Urban
Mission: Its mission is to expand the audience for contemporary dance through inventive performances and innovative outreach programs throughout southeastern Wisconsin.
Utilizes: Actors; Artists-in-Residence; Choreographers; Collaborating Artists; Collaborations; Community Members; Composers; Dance Companies; Dancers; Educators; Five Seasonal Concerts; Grant Writers; Guest Accompanists; Guest Artists; Guest Designers; Guest Directors; Guest Lecturers; Guest Musical Directors; Guest Musicians; Guest Soloists; High School Drama; Instructors; Local Artists; Local Artists & Directors; Lyricists; Multi Collaborations; Multimedia; Music; Organization Contracts; Original Music Scores; Paid Performers; Poets; Resident Artists; Resident Companies; Scenic Designers; Sign Language Translators; Singers; Soloists; Students; Student Interns; Touring Companies; Visual Arts; Volunteer Artists
Founded: 1986
Specialized Field: Contemporary/Modern Dance
Status: Nonprofit
Paid Staff: 3
Volunteer Staff: 40
Paid Artists: 12
Non-paid Artists: 2
Budget: $175,000
Income Sources: Donations; Foundations; Ticket Sales; Partnerships; Contracted Residencies
Annual Attendance: 15,000+
Type of Stage: Warehouse
Seating Capacity: 175-400

557
DANCE WISCONSIN
6332 Monona Drive
Monona, WI 53716

Phone: 608-221-4535
Fax: 608-221-9632
e-mail: jojeanr@sbcglobal.net
Web Site: www.dancewisconsin.com
Officers:
President: Roger White
VP: Jean Adams
Secretary: Vicki Hearing
Management:
Artistic Director: JoJean Retrum
Mission: To promote and foster dance in Wisconsin and develop appreciation of the arts including dance, music and theatre by creating productions of the highest caliber geared towards entertaining, educating and enriching our diversified audience.
Utilizes: Sign Language Translators
Founded: 1999
Specialized Field: Ballet
Status: Pre-Professional, Nonprofit
Volunteer Staff: 6
Paid Artists: 4
Non-paid Artists: 20
Budget: $100,000
Income Sources: Regional Dance America
Performs At: Madison Civic Center; Wisconsin Union Theatre; Milby Theatre
Seating Capacity: 2,000
Organization Type: Performing; Resident; Educational

558
LI CHIAO-PING DANCE
5973 Purcell Road
Oregon, WI 53575
Phone: 608-835-6590
Fax: 608-835-6592
e-mail: mgr@lichiaopingdance.org
Web Site: www.lichiaopingdance.org
Officers:
Founder/President: Li Chiao-Ping
VP: Blair Mathews
Treasurer: David Johnsen
Management:
Artistic Director/Choreographer: Li Chiao-Ping
Visual Artisti: Douglas Rosenberg
Communications Manager: Demetrios Lallas
Mission: Dedicated to offering programs of emotionally charged and athletic works with striking visual design and the music of contemporary composers.
Utilizes: Choreographers; Collaborating Artists; Collaborations; Commissioned Composers; Dancers; Guest Accompanists; Guest Artists; Guest Companies; Guest Conductors; Multi Collaborations; Original Music Scores; Soloists
Founded: 1990
Specialized Field: Modern
Paid Staff: 1
Volunteer Staff: 9
Paid Artists: 10
Budget: $80 k
Income Sources: Grants; Fees; Ticket Revenue

Alabama

559
ALABAMA SYMPHONY ORCHESTRA
3621 6th Avenue S
Birmingham, AL 35222
Phone: 205-251-6929
Fax: 205-251-6840
e-mail: orchestra@alabamasymphony.com
Web Site: www.alabamasymphony.org
Officers:
President: Charles Perry
Chairman: H Corbin Day
Vice Chairman: Gloria N Moody
VP: Ruffner Page
Treasurer: Allen W Ritchie
Secretary: K Wood Herren
Management:
Executive Director: Curtis Long
Development Director: Kathy Yarbrough
Music Director/Principal Conductor: Justin Brown
Artistic Administration Director: Emma Kapley
Mission: To provide high quality, professional musical performances and educational opportunities for the Central Arkansas community.
Utilizes: Fine Artists; Grant Writers; Guest Composers; Guest Lecturers; Guest Musical Directors; Guest Musicians; Instructors; Multimedia; Original Music Scores; Sign Language Translators; Singers
Founded: 1933
Specialized Field: Symphony; Orchestra
Status: Nonprofit
Paid Staff: 25
Volunteer Staff: 300
Paid Artists: 54
Budget: $7 million
Income Sources: Box Office; Grants; Corporate; Private Donations; Sponsorships
Performs At: Alys Stephens Center; Performing Arts Center; Indian Springs School Concert Hall; BJCC Concert Hall; Alabama Theatre
Affiliations: American Symphony Orchestra League; American Federation of Musicians
Annual Attendance: 100,000+
Type of Stage: Proscenium
Stage Dimensions: 28x88
Seating Capacity: 3,000
Year Built: 1996
Organization Type: Performing

560
RED MOUNTAIN CHAMBER ORCHESTRA
868 6th Street W
Birmingham, AL 35204
e-mail: sbeaudry@asfa.k12.al.us
Web Site: www.rmco.org
Officers:
Founder: Robert Markush
President: Suzanne Beaudry
Secretary: Gwen Knowlton
Treasurer: Nancy Watson
Management:
General Manager: Oliver Roosevelt
Mission: To educate and give pleasure to the public by performing music not otherwise heard in Birmingham.
Utilizes: Guest Lecturers; Guest Musical Directors; Guest Musicians; High School Drama; Local Artists; Multimedia; Sign Language Translators; Singers
Founded: 1980
Specialized Field: Classical Orchestra
Budget: $35,000

Income Sources: State and Local Grants; Private Donors
Performs At: Colleges; Churches; Birmingham Museum of Art
Affiliations: Birmingham Southern College
Annual Attendance: 1,200
Facility Category: Concert Hall
Type of Stage: Small Performance Space
Seating Capacity: 300

561
GADSDEN SYMPHONY ORCHESTRA
2828 Scenic Highway
PO Box 13
Gadsden, AL 35902
Phone: 256-543-9187
e-mail: mdupont@bellsouth.net
Officers:
President: Mitch DuPont
Founded: 1991
Specialized Field: Symphony
Volunteer Staff: 20
Budget: $20,000-$30,000
Income Sources: Local Contributions; Grants
Affiliations: American Symphony Orchestra League
Annual Attendance: 1,100
Facility Category: Concert Hall; Outdoor Ampitheatre
Seating Capacity: 800
Year Built: 1960
Year Remodeled: 1999

562
HUNTSVILLE CHAMBER MUSIC GUILD
301 Sparkman Drive NW
Huntsville, AL 35899
Phone: 256-824-6540
Fax: 256-824-6083
e-mail: hcmg@uah.edu
Web Site: www.hcmg.uah.edu
Officers:
President: Dr David B Williams
Chair: Don Bowyer
Mission: To provide the community of Huntsville and the region of Northern Alabama with a season of performances of the highest quality musicianship.
Specialized Field: Classical Music
Income Sources: Jane K Lowe Foundation; Marilyn Horne Foundation; Alabama State Council on the Arts; National Endowment for the Arts
Season: October-April
Performs At: Trinity United Methodist Church; Roberts Recital Hall-University of Alabama

563
HUNTSVILLE SYMPHONY ORCHESTRA
Von Braun Center
700 Monroe Street SW
Huntsville, AL 35801
Mailing Address: PO Box 2400, Huntsville, AL 35804
Phone: 256-539-4818
Fax: 256-539-4819
e-mail: hso@hiwaay.net
Web Site: www.hso.org
Officers:
President/CEO: Daniel Halcomb
Management:
Music Director: Carlos Miguel Prieto
Symphony School Director: Joe Lee
Mission: To serve the community as an aid to industrial development. Huntsville Symphony strives to perform high quality performances to satisfy the community's high standards for leisure time activities.
Utilizes: Guest Artists; Sign Language Translators
Founded: 1954

Specialized Field: Symphony
Status: Non-Professional, Nonprofit, Commercial
Paid Staff: 75
Budget: $1,050,000-$3,600,000
Income Sources: American Symphony Orchestra League; Sponships and Gifts from local corporations; Ticket Sales
Performs At: Von Braun Civic Center - Concert Hall
Organization Type: Performing; Educational; Sponsoring

564
HUNTSVILLE YOUTH ORCHESTRA
PO Box 2532
Huntsville, AL 35804
Phone: 256-880-0622
e-mail: hyo@hiwaay.net
Web Site: www.huntsvilleyouthorchestra.org
Officers:
President: Ellie Lienau
Secretary: Kelly Manley
Treasurer: Jim Chafin
Management:
Director: Joseph Lee
Mission: To provide a rewarding and challenging experience for its members by means of active participation in the performance of good music
Utilizes: Guest Artists
Specialized Field: Youth Orchestra; Classical Music
Paid Staff: 270
Income Sources: American Symphony Orchestra League (Youth Orchestra Division); Alabama Federation of Music; Alabama Arts Council
Performs At: Von Braun Civic Center
Organization Type: Performing; Touring; Educational; Sponsoring

565
MOBILE CHAMBER MUSIC SOCIETY
University of Alabama Music Department
1913 Timberly Road W
Mobile, AL 36609
Phone: 251-476-8794
Fax: 334-460-7328
e-mail: music@mobilechambermusic.org
Web Site: www.mobilechambermusic.org
Officers:
President: Gordon Moulton
Management:
Director: Dr Greg Turner
Mission: to present the best in Chamber Music to the Southern Alabama region
Specialized Field: Chamber Music
Volunteer Staff: 4
Income Sources: Mobile Arts Council; Alabama State Council on the Arts
Season: October-April
Performs At: Alabama School of Mathematics and Science Auditorium; Laidlaw Performing Arts Center Recital Hall

566
MOBILE SYMPHONY
257 Dauphin Street
Mobile, AL 36652-3127
Mailing Address: PO Box 3127 Mobile AL 36652-3127
Phone: 251-432-2010
Fax: 251-432-6618
Web Site: www.mobilesymphony.org
Officers:
Chair: Celia Mann Baehr
Secretary: Dr Richard Wilson
Treasurer: Linda Steele
Management:

Director: Scott Speck
General Manager: Greg Gordon
Development Director: Mary Hadley
Marketing Director: Heather Pace
Mission: To enhance the lives of every member of the community by achieving the highest standards in live symphonic music and music education
Specialized Field: Classical Music
Paid Staff: 10
Paid Artists: 65
Budget: $900,000-1,050,000
Income Sources: Ticket Sales; Corporate Sponsors; Grants; Individual Donations
Performs At: Mobile Civic Center Theatre; Larkins Music Center
Annual Attendance: 3,000
Stage Dimensions: 90x60
Seating Capacity: 2,000

567
MONTGOMERY SYMPHONY ORCHESTRA
301 N Hull Street
Montgomery, AL 36104
Phone: 334-240-4004
Fax: 334-240-4034
e-mail: mysymphony@bellsouth.net
Web Site: www.montgomerysymphony.org
Officers:
  President: James E Klinger
  First VP: Arthur Mazyck
  Second VP: Lisa B Capell
  Secretary: Edith J Crook
  Treasurer: George A Kent
Management:
  Orchestra Manager: Helen Steineker
Mission: To perform great orchestral works by invested volunteers in the community.
Founded: 1976
Specialized Field: Symphony; Orchestra; Pops; Classical
Status: Semi-Professional, Volunteer
Non-paid Artists: 75
Budget: $70,000
Income Sources: American Symphony Orchestra League; Corporate and Patrol Sponsorships; Program Advertising
Performs At: Davis Theater for the Performing Arts
Type of Stage: Flexible Backbox Studio Theatre
Seating Capacity: 1250
Year Built: 1938
Organization Type: Performing; Educational

568
TUSCALOOSA SYMPHONY ORCHESTRA
PO Box 20001
Tuscaloosa, AL 35402
Phone: 205-752-5515
Fax: 205-345-2787
e-mail: tso@tsoonline.org
Web Site: www.tsoonline.org
Officers:
  President: Alistair Harding-Smith
  Secretary: Jo Ann Cook
  Treasurer: John Cade
  President Elect: Ed Shotts
Management:
  Executive Director: Elizabeth McGuire
Mission: To enrich the livelihood of the community through high quality musical performances
Founded: 1979
Specialized Field: Instrumental Music
Paid Staff: 5
Volunteer Staff: 75

Paid Artists: 70
Budget: $260,000-1,050,000
Income Sources: Sponsorships; Donations; Gloria Moody Narramore Foundation; City of Tuscaloosa; Corporate Gifts
Performs At: Moody Concert Hall
Seating Capacity: 1,000
Year Built: 1926
Organization Type: Performing; Educational

Alaska

569
ANCHORAGE SYMPHONY ORCHESTRA
400 D Street
Suite 230
Anchorage, AK 99501
Phone: 907-274-8668
Fax: 907-272-7916
e-mail: aso@youraso.org
Web Site: www.anchoragesymphony.org
Officers:
  President: Aron Wolf
  Secretary: Bill Bernier
  Treasurer: Brian Hoefler
  President-Elect: Walter Featherly
Management:
  Music Director: Randall Craig Fleischer
  Executive Director: Sherri Burkhart Reddick
  Marketing Director: Kristin Cosgrove
  Associate Director: Darleen Fernandez
Mission: To inspire, engage and educate our community through the live performance of great music
Utilizes: Collaborations; Guest Accompanists; Guest Artists; Guest Companies; Guest Composers; Guest Musical Directors; Guest Musicians; Instructors; Multimedia; Original Music Scores; Poets; Selected Students; Singers; Student Interns
Founded: 1948
Specialized Field: Classical Music; Ballet
Paid Staff: 4
Paid Artists: 90
Budget: $1.2 Million
Income Sources: ASL
Performs At: Evangeline Atwood Concert Hall
Annual Attendance: 240,000
Type of Stage: Proscenium
Stage Dimensions: 120x52
Seating Capacity: 2,000
Year Built: 1988
Organization Type: Performing; Educational

570
ANCHORAGE YOUTH SYMPHONY
PO Box 240541
Anchorage, AK 99524
Phone: 907-566-7297
Fax: 907-333-0576
e-mail: ancys@juno.com
Web Site: www.anchorageyouthsymphony.org
Officers:
  President: Robert Harris
  Secretary: Celia Rozen
  Treasurer: Dennis Berry
Management:
  Music Director/Conductor: Linn Weeda
  General Manager: Ron Flugum
Mission: To train young musicians through concert experience, tours and community involvement which produces high quality orchestra performances.
Founded: 1965
Specialized Field: Symphony; Orchestra
Status: Non-Professional, Non-Profit

Paid Staff: 2
Income Sources: American Symphony Orchestra League (Youth Orchestra Division)
Performs At: Discovery Theatre/ACPA West High Auditorium; Atwood Concert Hall; Alaska Center for the Performing Arts (three theatres)
Facility Category: Theatre
Seating Capacity: 750; 2,000; 300
Year Built: 1988
Cost: $87,000,000
Organization Type: Performing; Touring; Educational

571
FAIRBANKS RED HACKLE PIPE BAND
PO Box 82782
Fairbanks, AK 99708-2782
Phone: 907-479-0807
e-mail: luckydog451@yahoo.com
Web Site: www.fairbanksredhacklepipeband.org
Officers:
  President: Ed Debevec
  Treasurer: Rocky Janiroc
  Secretary: John Moriarty
  Vice President: Dennis Stephens
Mission: Promoting the Scottish arts and traditions in the North
Utilizes: Community Members; Dance Companies; Dancers; Guest Ensembles; Guest Musical Directors; High School Drama; Soloists
Founded: 1974
Specialized Field: Scottish Music; Bag Pipes and Drums; Highland Dance
Performs At: Weddings; Parades; Picnics; Civic Events; Funerals
Organization Type: Performing; Educational

572
FAIRBANKS SYMPHONY ASSOCIATION
234 Fine Arts Complex
312 Tanana Loop
Fairbanks, AK 99775
Phone: 907-474-5733
Fax: 907-474-5147
e-mail: symphony@fairbankssymphony.org
Web Site: www.fairbankssymphony.org
Officers:
  President: Chuck Lemke
  Treasurer: Ted Fathauer
  Secretary: Sue Evans
Management:
  Executive Director: Laura Bergh
  Director: Eduard Zilberkant
  Marketing Director: George Rydlinski
Mission: To provide a significant positive cultural and educational influence to its region by fostering, promoting, and developing the musical knowledge and appreciation of the public for symphonic music and the arts
Utilizes: Artists-in-Residence; Commissioned Music; Guest Accompanists; Guest Artists; Guest Musical Directors; Guest Musicians; Multimedia; Singers
Specialized Field: Symphony; Orchestra; Chamber; Classical
Paid Staff: 4
Volunteer Staff: 70
Income Sources: American Symphony Orchestra League; Alaska Alliance on the Arts; Individual Patrons; Foundations; Corporations; Fairbanks Symphony Endowment Fund
Performs At: Concert Hall
Affiliations: University of Alaska, Fairbanks
Annual Attendance: 7,000-10,000
Type of Stage: Concert
Seating Capacity: 910

Year Built: 1974
Organization Type: Performing; Touring; Resident; Educational; Sponsoring
Resident Groups: Fairbanks Symphony Orchestra; Arctic Chamber Orchestra

573
JOCELYN CLARK
1109 C Street
Juneau, AK 99801
Phone: 907-586-9601
e-mail: jocelyn@jocelynclark.com
Web Site: www.jocelynclark.com
Officers:
President: Jocelyn Clark
Mission: Solo performances and collaboration with non-Western musical ensembles
Specialized Field: Non-Western Music; Korean Music
Performs At: Meyerson Hall; Renee Weiler Concert Hall; Springstep Center

574
JUNEAU JAZZ AND CLASSICS
Juneau Arts & Culture Center
350 Whittier Street, Suite 105
Juneau, AK 99802
Mailing Address: PO Box 22152 Juneau AK 99801
Phone: 907-463-3378
Fax: 907-463-3385
e-mail: info@jazzandclassics.org
Web Site: www.jazzandclassics.org
Officers:
Chair: Kathy Kolkhurst Ruddy
Treasurer: Galen Tromble
Secretary: Ren DeCherney
Management:
Artistic Director: Linda Rosenthal
Executive Director: Sandy Fortier
Mission: To provide a rich musical experience to music lovers in Juneau, the remote towns of Southeast Alaska and the entire state
Specialized Field: Classical; Jazz; Blues
Volunteer Staff: 100
Budget: $250,000
Income Sources: Private Donations
Season: May
Performs At: Alaska Native Brotherhood Hall
Seating Capacity: 1,000; 250; 250
Organization Type: Educational; Sponsoring

575
JUNEAU SYMPHONY
PO Box 21236
Juneau, AK 99802
Phone: 907-586-4676
Fax: 907-463-2555
e-mail: info@juneausymphony.org
Web Site: www.juneausymphony.org
Officers:
President: Colleen Torrence
VP: Lucy Merell
Secretary: John DeCherney
Treasurer: Judy G Knight
Management:
Music Director: Kyle Wiley Pickett
Concertmaster: Steve Tada
Executive Director: Valerie Snyder
Mission: Dedicated to give local musicians a platform to perform and develop musically, to provide live symphonic music for the community, and to offer musical opportunities and support for youth.
Founded: 1962
Specialized Field: Symphony
Status: Semi-professional; Volunteer

Paid Staff: 2
Paid Artists: 1
Non-paid Artists: 55
Budget: $185,000
Performs At: Juneau Douglas High School, Juneau Arts And Humanities Council
Seating Capacity: 900

Arizona

576
FLAGSTAFF SYMPHONY ORCHESTRA
113 E Aspen Avenue
Suite A
Flagstaff, AZ 86001
Mailing Address: PO Box 122 flagstaff AZ 86002-0122
Phone: 928-774-5107
Fax: 928-774-5109
e-mail: info@flagstaffsymphony.org
Web Site: www.flagstaffsymphony.org
Officers:
President: Jeff Hall
Treasurer: Paul Bjorklund
Executive Director: Laura Kelly
Management:
Director: Elizabeth Schulze
Mission: To enrich the cultural life of northern Arizona and expand the understanding, appreciation and love of music in people of all ages
Utilizes: Educators
Specialized Field: Symphony; Orchestra
Status: Nonprofit
Paid Staff: 3
Volunteer Staff: 65
Paid Artists: 65
Budget: $260,000-1,050,000
Income Sources: Individual; Private Donations
Season: September-May
Performs At: Ardrey Auditorium
Annual Attendance: 1,500
Type of Stage: proscenium
Stage Dimensions: 26x54
Seating Capacity: 1,941
Organization Type: Educational; Performing

577
SYMPHONY OF THE SOUTHWEST
56 S Center Street
Mesa, AZ 85210
Phone: 480-827-2143
Fax: 480-827-2070
e-mail: symphonyofthesouthwest@gmail.com
Web Site: www.symphonyofthesouthwest.org
Officers:
President: Virginia Ikeda
Treasurer: Dawn Cain
Management:
Executive Director: Alycia De Mesa
Director: Cal Stewart Kellogg
Marketing Director: Paul Dlouhy
Mission: To present the highest quality live, professional, orchestral and chamber concerts that compete in impact and significance with commerical productions
Utilizes: Collaborations; Guest Accompanists; Guest Companies; Guest Composers; Guest Directors; Guest Lecturers; Guest Musical Directors; Guest Musicians; Lyricists; Multimedia; Organization Contracts; Original Music Scores; Sign Language Translators; Soloists
Specialized Field: Symphony
Paid Staff: 3
Volunteer Staff: 20
Paid Artists: 70

Budget: $150,000-260,000
Income Sources: American Symphony Orchestra League
Performs At: Chandler Central Arts
Annual Attendance: 60,000
Facility Category: 2 Halls, 1 Amphitheatre
Type of Stage: Proscenium
Stage Dimensions: 82x69
Seating Capacity: 1,550
Organization Type: Performing; Educational

578
PHOENIX CHAMBER MUSIC SOCIETY
Scottsdale Center for the Arts
5517 N Thrid Street
Phoenix, AZ 85012
Phone: 602-252-0095
Web Site: www.phoenixchambermusicsociety.org
Officers:
President: Janet Green
Mission: To bring the finest chamber music in the world to the valley
Founded: 1961
Specialized Field: Chamber
Status: Nonprofit
Income Sources: Private Donations; Ticket Sales; American Symphony Orchestra League
Performs At: Scottsdale Center for the Arts - Virginia Piper Theatre
Affiliations: Culture Finder.Com; Northwest Valley Chamber of Commerce; Chamber Music America
Type of Stage: Flexible
Seating Capacity: 838
Organization Type: Sponsoring; Performing; Educational

579
PHOENIX SYMPHONY
One N. 1st Street
Phoenix, AZ 85004
Phone: 602-495-1117
Fax: 602-253-1772
e-mail: info@phoenixsymphony.org
Web Site: www.phoenixsymphony.org
Officers:
President/CEO: Maryellen H Gleason
Chairman: C A Howlett
Treasurer: Michael F Casey
Management:
Music Director: Michael Christie
General Manager: Jay Good
Operations Manager: Kimberly Koniecki
Marketing Director: Laura Schairer
Development Director: Frank Bourget
Assistant Conductor: Joseph Young
Mission: Evoking a passion for orchestral music within the entire community
Utilizes: Commissioned Composers; Commissioned Music; Dancers; Educators; Guest Accompanists; Guest Composers; Guest Directors; Guest Lecturers; Guest Musical Directors; Guest Musicians; Local Artists; Original Music Scores; Sign Language Translators; Singers; Theatre Companies
Founded: 1947
Specialized Field: Symphony
Paid Artists: 75
Budget: $8,600,000
Income Sources: Private Donations; Institutional Supporters
Season: September-May
Performs At: Phoenix Symphony Hall; Orpheum Theatre; Sedona Cultural Park
Annual Attendance: 140,000
Facility Category: Symphony Hall

Stage Dimensions: 60x100
Seating Capacity: 2,587
Year Built: 1972
Organization Type: Performing; Touring; Educational

580
YAVAPAI SYMPHONY ASSOCIATION
228 N Alarcon Street
PO Box 2333
Prescott, AZ 86301
Mailing Address: PO Box 2333, Prescott, MA 86302
Phone: 928-776-4255
Fax: 928-778-5286
e-mail: ysa1@cableone.net
Web Site: www.yavapaisymphony.org
Officers:
        President: Jayne Nordstrom
Management:
        Office Manager: Sue Wilkes, ysa1@cableone.net
Mission: To provide high quality classical music performances and to develop, promote and enhance classical music appreciation in Yavapai county.
Utilizes: Contract Orchestras
Founded: 1966
Specialized Field: Classical; Symphony
Status: Nonprofit, Professional
Paid Staff: 1
Volunteer Staff: 19
Income Sources: Private Donations
Season: November-June
Performs At: Yavapai College Performance Hall
Annual Attendance: 1,100
Stage Dimensions: 60x100
Seating Capacity: 1,200
Year Built: 1972
Organization Type: Sponsoring, Performing

581
SCOTTSDALE SYMPHONY ORCHESTRA
8524 E Thomas Road
Scottsdale, AZ 85251
Phone: 480-945-8071
Fax: 480-946-8770
e-mail: sso@scotsymph.org
Web Site: www.scotsymph.org
Management:
        Music Director: Irving A Fleming
Mission: Provide the community with cultural entertainment and education through music.
Founded: 1975
Specialized Field: Classical; Symphony; Pops
Status: Nonprofit
Budget: $150,000-260,000
Season: November-June
Performs At: Grace Chapel Auditorium
Seating Capacity: 700

582
CHAMBER MUSIC SEDONA
1487 W Highway 89A
Suite 9
Sedona, AZ 86336
Phone: 928-204-2415
Fax: 928-282-0893
e-mail: info@chambermusicsedona.org
Web Site: www.chambermusicsedona.org
Officers:
        President: Edward Ingraham
        Treasurer: John Steinbrunner
        Secretary: Mary Lee Warner
Management:
        Executive Director: Albert P Harclerode III
        General Manager: Anna Cates
        Operations Director: Susan Saxton

Mission: To enrich the lives of Northern Arizona residents and visitors by presenting the finest international, national, and regional performing artists and to promote a love of the performing arts through arts education programs.
Utilizes: Artists-in-Residence; Collaborating Artists; Commissioned Music; Five Seasonal Concerts; Grant Writers; Guest Companies; Guest Directors; Guest Lecturers; Guest Musical Directors; Local Artists; Multimedia
Specialized Field: Chamber Music, Bluegrass, The Met: Live In HD
Paid Staff: 3
Volunteer Staff: 65
Paid Artists: 52
Budget: $300,000
Income Sources: Contributions, Grants, Ticket Sales, Advertising Sales
Performs At: St. John Vianney Church; Sedona Performing Arts
Affiliations: CMA, ACA, SWAP
Annual Attendance: 4000
Facility Category: Catholic Church
Seating Capacity: 250; 750
Organization Type: Performing; Educational; Presenters

583
SEDONA JAZZ ON THE ROCKS
15 Cultural Park Place
Suite 2B
Sedona, AZ 86336
Phone: 928-282-1985
Fax: 928-282-0590
e-mail: office@sedonajazz.com
Web Site: www.sedonajazz.com
Officers:
        President, Board of Directors: Bettye Wilson
Management:
        President: Bettye Wilson, president@sedonajazz.com
Mission: To celebrate jazz as a living art form through education and performance programs
Utilizes: Guest Accompanists; Instructors; Original Music Scores; Sign Language Translators; Soloists
Specialized Field: Jazz
Status: Non-Profit, Non-Professional
Volunteer Staff: 200
Budget: $400,000
Income Sources: Box Office; Corporate Sponsors; Grants
Season: September
Performs At: Poco Diablo Resort (Festival Site)
Affiliations: Sedona Arts & Culture Commission; Greater Sedona Community Foundation; Arizona Commission on the Arts; National Endowment for the Arts
Annual Attendance: 2,000
Facility Category: Various Venues
Seating Capacity: 200-4,000
Organization Type: Performing; Sponsoring

584
CHAMBER MUSIC WEST
10451 W Palmeras Drive
Suite 122E
Sun City, AZ 85373-2608
Phone: 623-972-0478
Fax: 623-972-8815
e-mail: SCChmbrMusSoc@aol.com
Web Site: www.chambermusicwest.com
Management:
        Executive Director: Mona Myhre

Mission: To present internationally acclaimed chamber music to the greater Phoenix area providing a balance of established and emerging performers who are culturally diverse and through school concerts and residencies, to foster lifelong appreciation of fine music.
Utilizes: Fine Artists; Grant Writers; Guest Instructors; Original Music Scores
Founded: 1978
Specialized Field: Chamber Music
Status: Nonprofit
Paid Staff: 1
Volunteer Staff: 30
Paid Artists: 20
Budget: $175,000
Income Sources: NEA; Arizona Commission on the Arts; WAA; Donors
Season: November-April
Affiliations: Chamber Music America; Culture Finder.com; Northwest Valley
Annual Attendance: 3,000
Facility Category: Church
Type of Stage: Chancel
Stage Dimensions: 35 x 10
Seating Capacity: 600
Organization Type: Sponsoring, Performing

585
WEST VALLEY SYMPHONY
PO Box 1417
Sun City, AZ 85372
Phone: 623-236-6781
e-mail: westvalleysymphony@yahoo.com
Web Site: www.westvalleysymphony.org
Management:
        Music Conductor/Director: Cal Stewart Kellogg
Mission: To continue our presentations of the finest classical music to our many valuable patrons
Founded: 1968
Specialized Field: Symphony; Classical
Paid Staff: 4
Budget: $260,000-$1,050,000
Income Sources: Individual Contributions; Corporate Contributions; Grants
Season: November-March
Performs At: Various locations in the Northwest Valley of Phoenix Metro Area
Annual Attendance: 7,169
Organization Type: Performing

586
UNIVERSITY CHAMBER ORCHESTRA
Arizona State University
Herberger College of the Arts
PO Box 870405
Tempe, AZ 85287-0405
Phone: 480-965-3371
Web Site: music.asu.edu
Officers:
        President: Michael M Crow
        Secretary: Yvonne Delgado
Management:
        Director: Timothy Russell
Mission: To provide the highest level of instruction and research fo music professionals in the fields of performance, conducting, pedagogy, music education, music therapy, music history, music theory and composition.
Utilizes: Guest Musicians; Singers
Specialized Field: Orchestra; Ensemble; Classical
Volunteer Staff: 100
Budget: $100,000-150,000
Performs At: Grady Gammage Auditorium
Annual Attendance: 15,000
Facility Category: Auditorium

Seating Capacity: 3000
Year Built: 1963

587

UNIVERSITY SYMPHONY ORCHESTRA

Arizona State University
Herberger College of the Arts
PO Box 870405
Tempe, AZ 85287-0405
Phone: 480-965-3371
Web Site: music.asu.edu
Officers:
President: Michael M Crow
Secretary: Yvonne Delgado
Management:
Director: Timothy Russell
Mission: To provide the highest level of instruction and research for music professionals in the fields of performance, conducting, pedagogy, music education, music therapy, music history, music theory and composition.
Utilizes: Guest Musicians; Singers
Specialized Field: Orchestra; Ensemble; Classical
Volunteer Staff: 100
Budget: $100,000-150,000
Performs At: Grady Gammage Auditorium
Annual Attendance: 15,000
Facility Category: Auditorium
Seating Capacity: 3000
Year Built: 1963

588

EASTERN ARIZONA COLLEGE-COMMUNITY ORCHESTRA

615 N Stadium Avenue
Thatcher, AZ 85552
Phone: 928-428-8266
Toll-free: 800-678-3808
e-mail: franklin.alvarez@eac.edu
Web Site: www.eac.edu
Officers:
President: Mark Bryce
Chair: Patricia Jordahl
Management:
Director: Franklin Alvarez
Marketing Director: Todd Haynie
Mission: To display a passion for music that manifests into a lively and entertaining performance
Specialized Field: Symphony; Chamber
Budget: $35,000
Income Sources: Private Donations
Performs At: Fine Arts Auditorium
Seating Capacity: 960
Organization Type: Performing; Educational

589

ARIZONA EARLY MUSIC SOCIETY

4440 N Campbell Avenue
Tucson, AZ 85737
Mailing Address: PO Box 68512 tucson AZ 85737-8512
Phone: 520-297-3448
Fax: 520-297-3448
e-mail: aems@azearlymusic.org
Web Site: www.azearlymusic.org
Officers:
President: Lois Anne Nagy
Treasurer: Kathleen Krause
Secretary: Gary Kern
Mission: Dedicated to the enrichment of contemporary life with the music of the past
Founded: 1982
Specialized Field: Medieval; Renaissance; Baroque
Status: Nonprofit

Budget: $10,000-20,000
Income Sources: Ticket Sales; Grants; National Endowment for the Arts; Western States Arts Federation; Arizona Commission on the Arts; Tucson/Pima Arts Council; Private Donations
Season: October-April
Performs At: St. Philip's in the Hills Episcopal Church
Seating Capacity: 500

590

ARIZONA FRIENDS OF CHAMBER MUSIC

PO Box 40845
Tucson, AZ 85717
Phone: 520-577-3769
Fax: 520-881-2009
e-mail: friends@arizonachambermusic.org
Web Site: www.arizonachambermusic.org
Officers:
President: Dr Jean-Paul Bierny
Management:
Office Manager: Cathy Anderson
Mission: Presenters of chamber music concerts.
Founded: 1951
Specialized Field: Chamber
Status: Nonprofit
Paid Staff: 1/2
Volunteer Staff: 15
Paid Artists: 50
Budget: $200,000
Income Sources: Audience; AZ Commission on the Arts
Performs At: Leo Rich
Annual Attendance: 8,400
Facility Category: Concert Hall
Type of Stage: Proscenium
Stage Dimensions: 130x40
Seating Capacity: 511
Year Built: 1970
Organization Type: Performing; Sponsoring

591

CHAMBER MUSIC PLUS SOUTHWEST

8322 E Snyder Road
Tucson, AZ 85745
Phone: 520-400-5439
Web Site: www.chambermusicplus.org
Officers:
President: Eric Abrams
Management:
Artistic Director: Harry Clark
Executive Director: Sanda Schuldmann
Utilizes: Actors; Artists-in-Residence; Collaborating Artists; Commissioned Music; Composers-in-Residence; Guest Companies; Guest Directors; Guest Instructors; Guest Musical Directors; Guest Soloists; Multimedia; Original Music Scores
Budget: $400,000
Income Sources: Private and Corporate Donations, Ticket Sales
Season: October-April
Annual Attendance: 200 per performance

592

CIVIC ORCHESTRA OF TUCSON

PO Box 42764
Tucson, AZ 85733-2764
Phone: 520-798-0062
Fax: 520-818-6584
e-mail: civicorchestra@att.net
Web Site: www.cotmusic.com
Officers:
President: Audra Koereert
General Manager: Terry Sullivan
Management:

Artistic Director: Dr. Hersel Kreloff
Mission: Dedicated to continue the tradition of presenting free symphonic concerts.
Founded: 1975
Specialized Field: Symphony; Pops
Volunteer Staff: 60
Budget: $10,000-$15,000
Season: August-May
Performs At: UA Crowder Hall
Annual Attendance: 800
Seating Capacity: 544
Year Built: 1957
Year Remodeled: 1991

593

SOUTHERN ARIZONA SYMPHONY ORCHESTRA

PO Box 43131
Tucson, AZ 85733
Phone: 520-323-7166
e-mail: info@sasomusic.org
Web Site: www.sasomusic.org
Officers:
President: Debbie Bouchard
Treasurer: Dee Schroer
Secretary: Sherry Jameson
Management:
Director: Linus Lerner
Mission: Dedicated to exploring the classical repertoire and introducing new works to the community
Specialized Field: Classical
Status: Nonprofit
Budget: $35,000
Income Sources: Private Donations; Art Groups; Advertisers
Season: October-May
Seating Capacity: 60
Organization Type: Performing; Educational

594

TUCSON CHAMBER ORCHESTRA

PO Box 13925
Tucson, AZ 85732
Phone: 520-401-4369
e-mail: patrickgibbons@cox.net
Web Site: www.tucsonchamberorchestra.org
Officers:
President: Patrick Gibbons
Management:
Director: Enrique Lasansky
Mission: To provide high quality, live performances of orchestral music in Tucson as well as throughout southern Arizona and northern New Mexico
Specialized Field: Chamber
Volunteer Staff: 60
Budget: $35,000-$100,000
Season: October-May
Performs At: Catalina High Magnet School Auditorium
Affiliations: Tucson Pima Arts Council; Arizona Commission on the Arts

595

THE TUCSON JAZZ SOCEITY

6061 E Broadway
Suite 121
Tucson, AZ 85711
Phone: 520-903-1265
Fax: 520-903-1266
e-mail: office@tucsonjazz.org
Web Site: www.tucsonjazz.org
Officers:
President: Rick Gregson
Vice President: Jeff Lewis
Treasurer: John Dennis

Secretary: Sally West
Management:
Office Manager: Pat Young,
development@tucsonjazz.org
Mission: Dedicated to promoting and preserving America's original music-jazz.
Founded: 1977
Specialized Field: Jazz
Status: Nonprofit
Volunteer Staff: 65
Income Sources: National Jazz Service Organization; International Association of Jazz Educators
Performs At: Berger Perfoming Arts Center
Type of Stage: Proscenium
Stage Dimensions: 48x28
Seating Capacity: 500
Year Built: 1990
Organization Type: Sponsoring

596
TUCSON PHILHARMONIA YOUTH ORCHESTRA
166 W Alameda Street
Tucson, AZ 85701
Phone: 520-623-1500
e-mail: info@tpyo.org
Web Site: www.tpyo.org
Management:
Director: Suzette Battan
Mission: To provide the finest quality symphonic training and performance opportunities for young musicians in a professional environment that promotes advanced musical education, performance competition and responsibility
Founded: 1953
Specialized Field: Classical
Season: November-March
Performs At: Tucson Convention Center Music Hall; Armory Park Center
Type of Stage: Proscenium
Stage Dimensions: 128Wx49.5D
Seating Capacity: 2,289
Organization Type: Performing; Educational

597
TUCSON SYMPHONY ORCHESTRA
2175 N Sixth Avenue
Tucson, AZ 85705
Phone: 520-792-9155
Web Site: www.tucsonsymphony.org
Officers:
President: Nancy J March
Secretary: John E Wahl
Treasurer: Robert A Jennens
Management:
Executive Director: Susan Franano
Development Director: Wanda L Kay
Marketing Director: Sue DeBenedette
General Manager: Norman Ross
Mission: To present live symphonic performances and music education at the highest level of artistic excellence, enriching and entertaining the people of Southern Arizona
Utilizes: Guest Composers; Guest Musicians
Specialized Field: Symphony
Paid Staff: 30
Paid Artists: 85
Budget: $4,098,500
Performs At: Tucson Convention Center Music Hall
Affiliations: ASOL, BMI, ASCAP
Facility Category: Music hall

598
TUCSON WINTER CHAMBER MUSIC FESTIVAL
PO Box 40845
Tucson, AZ 85717
Phone: 520-577-3769
e-mail: office@arizonachambermusic.org
Web Site: www.arizonachambermusic.org
Management:
Artistic Director: Peter Rejto
Mission: To be one of the country's most active commissioning programs
Specialized Field: Chamber
Volunteer Staff: 15
Paid Artists: 20
Budget: $60,000-$150,000
Income Sources: Arizona Chamber Association
Season: February - March
Performs At: Leo Rich Theatre - Tucson Convention Center
Type of Stage: Proscenium
Seating Capacity: 560
Organization Type: Performing; Sponsoring

Arkansas

599
ARKANSAS STATE MUSIC PROGRAMS
Arkansas State University- Beebe
Howell Music Center
1000 Iowa Street
Beebe, AR 72012-1000
Mailing Address: PO Box 1000 Beebe AR 72012-1000
Phone: 870-972-2094
Web Site: www.asub.edu
Officers:
President: Dr Les Wyatt III
Chair: Mike Gibson
Secretary: Florine Tousant Milligan
Chair: Tom O'Connor
Management:
Director: Neale Bartee
Mission: To provide students the opportunity to seek success in many different areas of the music profession through varied degree offerings
Specialized Field: Orchestra
Status: Nonprofit
Income Sources: Ticket Sales; Donations
Organization Type: Performing; Educational

600
CONWAY SYMPHONY ORCHESTRA
PO Box 1307
Conway, AR 72033
Phone: 501-269-1066
e-mail: symphony@conwaycorp.net
Web Site: www.conwaysymphony.org
Officers:
Board President: Allison Vetter
Management:
Conductor/Music Director: Israel Getzof
Manager: Vicki Crockett
Mission: To create meaningful experiences through performances and education.
Founded: 1984
Specialized Field: Orchestra
Status: Pre-Professional, Professional
Paid Staff: 1
Affiliations: League Of American Orchestras
Seating Capacity: 1,000
Year Built: 2000

601
SOUTH ARKANSAS SYMPHONY
315 E Oak Street
Suite 206
El Dorado, AR 71730
Toll-free: 800-792-0521
e-mail: sasomail@sbcglobal.net
Web Site: www.southarkansassymphony.com
Management:
Director: Kermit Poling
Executive Director: Scott Watkins
Operations Director: Virginia Matthews
Mission: To promote symphonic music to the area and to introduce this music to children.
Founded: 1956
Specialized Field: Orchestra
Status: Professional
Paid Staff: 2
Volunteer Staff: 23
Paid Artists: 100
Budget: $100,000-$150,000
Income Sources: Corporate; Private Donations
Season: September-May
Performs At: Municipal Auditorium; Harton Theatre
Annual Attendance: 2,500
Type of Stage: Proscenium
Seating Capacity: 500
Year Built: 1924
Organization Type: Performing; Educational

602
NORTH ARKANSAS SYMPHONY SOCIETY
605 W Dickson Street
Fayetteville, AR 72702
Mailing Address: PO Box 1243 Fayetteville AR 72702
Phone: 479-521-4166
Web Site: www.nasymphony.org
Officers:
Chairman: Bob Gaddy
Secretary: Joan Campbell
Treasurer: Tom Garrison
Management:
Director: Jeannine Wagar
General Manager: Aldee Marquis
Mission: To provide north Arkansas with a fully professional regional orchestra presenting quality music, education and programs to enrich the communities
Utilizes: Guest Artists
Founded: 1954
Specialized Field: Symphony
Status: Semi-Professional; Nonprofit
Paid Staff: 6
Income Sources: University of Arkansas
Season: October-April
Performs At: Walton Arts Center
Seating Capacity: 1,200
Year Built: 1992
Organization Type: Performing; Educational

603
FORT SMITH SYMPHONY
PO Box 3151
Fort Smith, AR 72913
Phone: 479-452-7575
Fax: 479-452-8985
e-mail: fssymphony@aol.com
Web Site: www.fortsmithsymphony.org
Officers:
Chair: Marilyn Patterson
Management:
Director: John Jeter

Development Director: Allison B Walden
Marketing Director: Becky Yates
Mission: Bringing wonderful music to the youth in our community- Kids first.
Utilizes: Artists-in-Residence; Commissioned Music; Composers-in-Residence; Educators; Fine Artists; Guest Accompanists; Guest Composers; Guest Lecturers; Guest Musicians; Local Artists; Multimedia; Original Music Scores; Singers
Specialized Field: Classical; Symphony
Paid Staff: 4
Volunteer Staff: 60
Budget: $260,000-$1,050,000
Income Sources: Arkansas Arts Council; National Endowment for the Arts
Performs At: Arkansas Best Corporation Performing Arts Center - Fort Smith Civic Center
Facility Category: Performing Arts Center
Seating Capacity: 1,400
Year Remodeled: 2000
Organization Type: Performing; Educational

604
ARKANSAS SYMPHONY ORCHESTRA

2417 N Tyler
PO Box 7328
Little Rock, AR 72207
Phone: 501-666-1761
Fax: 501-666-3193
e-mail: gwixson@arkansassymphony.org
Web Site: www.arkansassymphony.org
Officers:
   Chair: Michael Shelley
Management:
   Music Director: David Itkin
   Assistant Conductor: Geoffrey Robson
   Executive Director: Galen Wixson
   Public Relations: Tamara Clement
Mission: To create a positive environment for the musical education of youth throughout Arkansas.
Founded: 1966
Specialized Field: Classical; Pops; Symphony
Status: Nonprofit
Paid Staff: 14
Volunteer Staff: 2000
Paid Artists: 60
Budget: $1,050,000-$3,600,000
Income Sources: Individual; Corporate; Foundation Donations
Season: September-May
Performs At: Robinson Center Music Hall
Affiliations: Arkansas Symphony Orchestra Society Guild, ASO Ovation
Annual Attendance: 250,000
Type of Stage: Proscenium
Stage Dimensions: 60Wx42Dx35H
Seating Capacity: 2,609
Organization Type: Performing; Educational

605
PINE BLUFF SYMPHONY ORCHESTRA

211 W 3rd Avenue
Pine Bluff, AR 71601
Phone: 870-536-7666
Web Site: arkansasarts.com
Officers:
   President: William H Fox
Management:
   Director: Dr Charles Evans
Mission: To enlarge the symphony's demographic audience, supporting the health and wellness of the region's community and enbedding the educational value of classical music within every aspect of the new and emerging cultural infrastructure

Founded: 1987
Specialized Field: Orchestra; Symphony
Paid Staff: 3
Paid Artists: 70
Budget: $225,000
Income Sources: Private and Corporate Donations
Season: October-April
Annual Attendance: 25,000
Seating Capacity: 1,900
Organization Type: Performing; Educational

California

606
BACHMAN'S MUSIC STUDIO

7555 San Gabriel Road
Atascadero, CA 93422
Phone: 805-466-8383
e-mail: kbachman466@charter.net
Web Site: www.bachmansmusicstudio.com
Mission: Our specialty is Music Education and Performance. We offer private lessons, in most instruments including voice. We offer classes in beginning and intermediate guitar. Our lessons are structured to the student's individual wants and needs. We do in home as well as studio lessons. We also offer instrumental performances in Classical, Jazz guitar and other instruments.
Founded: 1990
Specialized Field: Classical; Folk Music; Jazz

607
BAKERSFIELD SYMPHONY ORCHESTRA

1328 34th Street
Suite A
Bakersfield, CA 93301
Phone: 661-323-7928
Fax: 661-323-7331
e-mail: music@bakersfieldsymphony.org
Web Site: www.bakersfieldsymphony.org
Officers:
   President: Marci Maynard
   Chairman: Hon Jon Stuebbe
   Secretary: Candace Davies
   Treasurer: Nile Kinney Esq
Management:
   Director: John Farrer
   Operations Director: Mary Moore
   Marketing Director: Alice Oden
Mission: To provide the best possible performances of great music for the widest possible audience and provide musical education for the young people of Kern County
Founded: 1932
Specialized Field: Classical; Symphony
Paid Staff: 7
Volunteer Staff: 25
Paid Artists: 60
Budget: $260,000-$1,050,000
Income Sources: Individual and Corporate Donations, Foundations, Symphony Associates, Bakersfield Symphony Orchestra Endowment Foundation
Season: October-May
Performs At: Rabobank Theater
Affiliations: Bakersfield Masterworks Chorale, Bakersfield Youth Symphony, Bakersfield Summer Band
Annual Attendance: 5,000
Facility Category: Convention Center & Theater
Type of Stage: Full with Pit
Seating Capacity: 2,800
Year Built: 1965
Rental Contact: Ed Dorsey

608
BERKELEY SYMPHONY ORCHESTRA

1942 University Avenue
Suite 207
Berkeley, CA 94704
Phone: 510-841-2800
Fax: 510-841-5422
e-mail: info@berkeleysymphony.org
Web Site: www.berkeleysymphony.org
Officers:
   President: Kathleen G Henschel
   Treasurer: Buzz Hines
   Secretary: Ronald Choy
Management:
   Director: Kent Nagano
   Executive Director: James A Kleinmann
   Operations Director: Theresa Gabel
   Development Director: Urray E Nelson
   General Manager: Rene Mandel
Mission: Ensuring that our programming continues to touch the lives of many, inside and outside the concert hall
Utilizes: Guest Artists; Singers
Founded: 1969
Specialized Field: Symphony; Contemporary
Status: Semi-Professional
Paid Staff: 37
Volunteer Staff: 20
Budget: 1 million
Income Sources: Private and Corporate Donations
Season: September-April
Performs At: Zellerbach Hall; University of California at Berkeley, Roda Theatre, St John's Presbyterian Church
Affiliations: Ameican Symphony Orchestra League
Annual Attendance: 20,000
Seating Capacity: 2,089
Year Built: 1968
Organization Type: Performing

609
SAN FRANCISCO EARLY MUSIC SOCIETY

PO Box 10151
Berkeley, CA 94709
Phone: 510-528-1725
e-mail: sfems@sfems.org
Web Site: www.sfems.org
Officers:
   Chair, Board Of Directors: Meryl Sacks
Management:
   Executive Director: Harvey Malloy, hmalloy@sfems.org
   Administrative Assistant: Dorothy Manly, dorothy@sfems.org
Mission: Seeks to create an appreciative and supportive environment for the study and performance of medieval, renaissance, and baroque music by both amateurs and professionals in Northern California
Utilizes: Contract Orchestras; Educators; Guest Directors; Multimedia; Original Music Scores
Founded: 1975
Specialized Field: Chamber; Ensemble
Status: Professional; Nonprofit
Paid Staff: 2
Budget: 1/4 million
Income Sources: Private and Corporate Donations, Grants
Season: October-May
Performs At: First Lutheran Church, St. John's Presbyterian Church; First Congregational Church; St. Mark's Lutheran Church
Affiliations: Early Music America; Chamber Music America

Year Built: 1920
Year Remodeled: 1991
Organization Type: Performing; Touring, Presenters

610
SAN FRANCISCO CHAMBER ORCHESTRA

PO Box 591566
Berkeley, CA 94159
Phone: 415-248-1640
Fax: 510-524-3683
e-mail: info@sfchamberorchestra.org
Web Site: www.sfchamberorchestra.org
Officers:
Executive Director: Richard Aldag
Management:
Music Director: Benjamin Simon
Personnel Manager: Robin May
Mission: Dedicated to bringing immediacy and intimacy of music for small orchestra and chamber ensemble to audiences of all ages by presenting classical, contemporary, and commissioned works as well as to educate and enlighten the next generation of music lovers through outreach programs.
Utilizes: Theatre Companies
Founded: 1952
Specialized Field: Classical
Status: Professional
Budget: $260,000-$1,050,000
Income Sources: Private Donations
Season: December-May
Performs At: Louise M Davies Symphony Hall, Florence Gould Theatre, Various Venues
Seating Capacity: 2,741, 316
Year Built: 1980
Organization Type: Performing; Educational

611
YOUNG PEOPLE'S SYMPHONY ORCHESTRA

PO Box 5593
Berkeley, CA 94705
Phone: 510-849-9776
Fax: 510-654-0274
e-mail: ypsomusic@yahoo.com
Web Site: www.ypsomusic.net
Officers:
President: Janice Stewart
Treasurer: Mark Leverette
Secretary: Lynn Mackay
Management:
Executive Director: Wendy Howe
Director: David Ramadanoff
Mission: To provide orchestra education to young adults ranging from 13 to 21 living in the Bay Area
Utilizes: Soloists
Founded: 1935
Specialized Field: Symphony; Chamber
Paid Staff: 2
Paid Artists: 10
Budget: $100,000
Income Sources: Private and Corporate Donations, Grants
Performs At: Dean Lesher Regional Center for the Arts
Seating Capacity: 580
Rental Contact: Operations Manager David Davis
Organization Type: Performing; Educational

612
LOREN L ZACHARY SOCIETY FOR THE PERFORMING ARTS

2250 Gloaming Way
Beverly Hills, CA 90210
Phone: 310-276-2731
Fax: 310-275-8245
Web Site: www.zacharysociety.org
Officers:
President: Nedra Zachary
Management:
Conductor: Frank Fetta
Competition Director: Nedra Zachary
Mission: Dedicated to producing the National Vocal Competition for Young Singers and Grand Finals Concert.
Utilizes: Guest Composers; Multimedia; Original Music Scores; Sign Language Translators
Founded: 1972
Specialized Field: Opera Singing
Status: Non-profit
Volunteer Staff: 100
Paid Artists: 35
Non-paid Artists: 1
Income Sources: Private Donations
Performs At: Wilshire Ebell Theatre
Annual Attendance: 1,260
Facility Category: Theatre
Type of Stage: Proscenium
Stage Dimensions: 28Dx48Wx60H
Seating Capacity: 1,270
Year Built: 1927
Year Remodeled: 1989

613
YOUNG MUSICIANS FOUNDATION DEBUT ORCHESTRA

195 S Beverly Drive
Suite 414
Beverly Hills, CA 90212
Phone: 310-859-7668
Fax: 310-859-1365
e-mail: info@ymf.org
Web Site: www.ymf.org
Officers:
Chairman: Paul Marshall
Secretary: Louise Danelian
Treasurer: Arnold Seidel
Management:
Executive Director: Edye Rugolo
Director: Case Scaglione
Artistic Director: Delores Stevens
Mission: To preserve the classical music heritage by providing performance opportunities, financial assistance and community outreach programming that contributes to the personal, academic and artistic development of youth from all socio-economic and ethnic backgrounds
Founded: 1955
Specialized Field: Chamber; Classical
Status: Professional
Budget: $260,000-$1,050,000
Income Sources: Private and Corporate Donations, Grants, Ticket Sales
Season: November-August
Performs At: Wilshire Ebell Theatre
Annual Attendance: 17,000
Stage Dimensions: 28Dx48Wx60H
Seating Capacity: 1,270
Organization Type: Performing; Educational

614
SOUTHEAST SYMPHONY

1985 Rolling Vista Drive
Suite 55
Burbank, CA 91508
Phone: 323-293-7372
e-mail: cedickersoniii@sbcglobal.net
Web Site: www.southeastsymphony.org

Officers:
President: Sandra Wheeler
VP: Frank Harris
Treasurer: Rosemarie Cook Glover
Secretary: Allison Cook
Management:
Music Director/Conductor: Charles Dickerson
Mission: To perform concerts for the diverse community and to foster musical training for aspiring musicians, most of whom are African American.
Founded: 1948
Specialized Field: Symphony
Status: Nonprofit
Paid Staff: 14
Volunteer Staff: 30
Paid Artists: 60
Budget: $100,000-$150,000
Income Sources: Grants; Memberships; Donations
Affiliations: Association of California Symphony Orchestras
Seating Capacity: 1,100

615
SJG SCHOOL OF MUSIC

1 W Campbell Avenue
Suite K-59
Campbell, CA 95008
Phone: 408-370-6590
e-mail: lessons@sanjoseguitar.com
Web Site: www.sjgschoolofmusic.com
Officers:
Owner/Founder: Chris Shahin
Mission: The music school has expanded to include other instruments and relocated to Campbell, California. Chris has gathered an accomplished group of music teachers who are also professional performers to bring SJG School of Music to the forefront of music education. With this team of professionals, SJG's instructors have created a dynamic and collaborative program that helps students move their learning from the private classroom to the public arena.
Specialized Field: Instrumental

616
CARMEL BACH FESTIVAL

PO Box 575
Carmel, CA 93921
Phone: 831-624-1521
Fax: 831-624-2788
e-mail: info@bachfestival.org
Web Site: www.bachfestival.org
Officers:
Board President: Cyril Yansouni
First Vice President: Fran Lozano
Director Finance/Administration: Elizabeth Pasquinelli
Treasurer/CFO: Mary Kay Crockett
Recording Secretary: Susan Watts DuCoeur
Management:
Music Director/Conductor: Bruno Weil
Associate Conductor: William Jon Gray
Artistic Director: Nana Fardiany
Managing Director: Jesse Read
Concertmaster: Elizabeth Wallfisch
Vocal Coordinator Education Dir: David Gordon
Ticket Manager: Karma Simons
Mission: We celebrate the genius of Johann Sebastian Bach, as well as his contemporaries and musical heirs, through performances and educational activities of the highest caliber.
Founded: 1935
Specialized Field: Bach; Ensemble; Educational
Status: Professional; Nonprofit
Paid Staff: 35

Paid Artists: 100
Non-paid Artists: 30
Budget: 1.5 million
Income Sources: Private and Corporate Donations, Sponsors
Season: July-August
Performs At: All Saints Church, Sunset Theatre, Historic Carmel Mission Basilica, Church in the Forest in Pebble Beach
Affiliations: Various Sites in the vicinity of Carmel-by-the-Sea
Annual Attendance: 17,000
Facility Category: Community Auditorium
Type of Stage: Proscenium
Seating Capacity: 259
Year Built: 1928
Organization Type: Performing; Educational

617

CHAMBER MUSIC MONTEREY BAY

3785 Via Nona Marie
Suite 307
Carmel, CA 93923
Mailing Address: PO Box 221458 Carmel CA 93922
Phone: 831-625-2212
Fax: 831-625-3555
e-mail: info@chambermusicmontereybay.org
Web Site: www.chambermusicmontereybay.org
Officers:
 President: Amy Anderson
Management:
 Director: John Newkirk
Mission: Enrich the cultural life of the community by producing an annual concert series of world renowned chamber ensembles, developing and delivering a variety of outreach and educational programs
Utilizes: Guest Directors; Guest Musical Directors; Multimedia
Founded: 1966
Specialized Field: Chamber
Status: Nonprofit
Paid Staff: 2
Volunteer Staff: 14
Paid Artists: 5
Budget: $105,000
Income Sources: Donations; Ticket Sales; Grants
Season: September-April
Performs At: Sunset Theatre
Annual Attendance: 3,000
Facility Category: Theatre and Community Center
Type of Stage: Proscenium
Seating Capacity: 700
Year Built: 1940
Year Remodeled: 2002
Organization Type: Sponsoring

618

MONTEREY BAY SYMPHONY

PO Box 146
Carmel, CA 93921
Phone: 831-373-8450
e-mail: ronweitzman@redshift.com
Web Site: www.montereybaysymphony.org
Officers:
 President: Ron A Weitzman
 Secretary: Dr John Castagna
 Treasurer: Sharyn Evers
Management:
 Director: Dr Carl Christensen
Mission: To bring pops and patriotic orchestral music performed by professional musicians to the residents and visitors of Monterey County free of charge, while providing musical support to local arts organizations
Founded: 1985

Specialized Field: Pops; Patriotic Orchestral Music
Status: Nonprofit
Volunteer Staff: 20
Paid Artists: 56
Budget: $35,000-$100,000
Performs At: Naval Postgraduate School

619

MONTEREY SYMPHONY

Room 17 Sunset Center
Mission and 10th Avenue
Carmel, CA 93921
Mailing Address: PO Box 3965 Carmel CA 93921
Phone: 831-624-8511
Fax: 831-624-3837
Toll-free: 800-698-1138
e-mail: info@montereysymphony.org
Web Site: www.montereysymphony.org
Officers:
 President: Janet McDaniel
 Secretary: Joanne Taylor Johnson
 Treasurer: Stephen Mangelsen
Management:
 Executive Director: Joseph Truskot
 Director: Max Bragado=Darman
 Development Director: Michelle Lange
Mission: To bring music of high quality to the people of Monterey and San Benito Counties and to foster and encourage the appreciation of it by people of all ages.
Utilizes: Guest Accompanists; Guest Companies; Guest Composers; Guest Musical Directors; Guest Musicians; Guest Writers; Organization Contracts; Original Music Scores
Founded: 1947
Specialized Field: Symphony; Orchestra;
Status: Professional; Nonprofit
Paid Staff: 6
Volunteer Staff: 7
Paid Artists: 80
Budget: $1,500,000
Income Sources: Association of California Symphony Orchestras, American Symphony Orchestra League, Cultural Council, Grants
Season: October-May
Performs At: Sunset Theatre; Sherwood Hall; Pacific Grove Middle School
Affiliations: ACSO; American Symphony Orchestra League
Annual Attendance: 20,000
Seating Capacity: 733; 1511
Year Remodeled: 2002
Organization Type: Performing

620

CARMEL ACADEMY OF PERFORMING ARTS

Mission & 8th
PO Box 1586
Carmel-by-the-Sea, CA 93921-1586
Phone: 831-624-3729
e-mail: info@carmelacademyofperformingarts.com
Web Site: www.carmelacademyofperformingarts.com
Officers:
 Owner: Carol Benton Richmond
Management:
 Director: Carol Benton Richmond
 Studio Manager: Sarah Felsinger
Mission: Students of all levels enjoy year-round instruction in a friendly, caring, loving and creative environment. From the toddler to the beginner to the pre-professional, each student feels the excitement and energy in the air at the Carmel Academy of Performing Arts! We have a program to fit each student's goals and

aspirations and we look forward to finding the perfect schedule for your family. Welcome to the Carmel Academy of Performing Arts!
Utilizes: Dance Companies; Dancers; Educators; Guest Artists; Guest Ensembles; Guest Speakers; Guild Activities; High School Drama; Multimedia; Sign Language Translators; Soloists
Specialized Field: Instrumental

621

SACRAMENTO SYMPHONIC WINDS

PO Box 1503
Carmichael, CA 95608
Phone: 916-489-2576
Fax: 916-489-2576
e-mail: michr@sbcglobal.net
Web Site: www.sacwinds.org
Management:
 Conductor: Lester E Lehr
Utilizes: Collaborations; Educators; Five Seasonal Concerts; Guest Accompanists; Guest Companies; Guest Musicians; Local Artists; Lyricists; Multimedia; Organization Contracts; Sign Language Translators; Singers
Volunteer Staff: 65
Non-paid Artists: 4
Annual Attendance: 1,500
Seating Capacity: 500

622

CARSON-DOMINGUEZ HILLS SYMPHONY

California State University at Dominguez Hills
1000 E Victoria Street
Carson, CA 90747
Phone: 310-243-3543
Web Site: cah.csudh.edu
Officers:
 President: Mildred Garcia
 Chair: Richard Kravchak PhD
Management:
 Director: David Bradfield MM
Mission: To provide music students with career-oriented skills for use in the music industry
Founded: 1976
Specialized Field: Orchestra
Status: Nonprofit; Professional
Budget: 148,000
Income Sources: Fundraising, Donations, National Endowment for the Arts
Season: December-May
Performs At: University Theatre; California State University of Los Angeles

623

CALIFORNIA E.A.R. UNIT

29654 Driver Avenue
Castaic, CA 91384
Phone: 661-775-9975
Fax: 661-775-3855
Web Site: www.earunit.org
Officers:
 Founder: Dorothy Stone
 Founder/Executive Director: Amy Knoles
Management:
 Artistic Director: Vicki Ray
Mission: Dedicated to the performance, promotion, and creation of some of the most exciting music of our time
Founded: 1981
Specialized Field: Contemporary
Status: Professional; Nonprofit
Paid Staff: 2
Volunteer Staff: 2
Paid Artists: 6

Performs At: Los Angeles County Museum of Art
Organization Type: Performing; Touring; Resident; Educational
Resident Groups: New Chamber Music

624
CLAREMONT SYMPHONY ORCHESTRA
PO Box 698
Claremont, CA 91711
Phone: 909-593-5620
Web Site: www.claremontso.org
Officers:
President: Barbara Bonzo
Management:
Director: Dr James Fahringer
Mission: To provide free concerts for the community that features an exciting variety of musical experiences
Founded: 1953
Specialized Field: Symphony
Status: Nonprofit
Budget: $18,000
Income Sources: Private Donations
Season: October-July
Performs At: Bridges Hall of Music
Affiliations: Association of California Symphony Orchestras
Seating Capacity: 600
Year Built: 1915
Year Remodeled: 1972
Organization Type: Performing; Educational

625
POMONA COLLEGE ORCHESTRA
Pomona College Department of Music
340 N College Avenue
Claremont, CA 91711-6324
Phone: 909-621-8155
Fax: 909-621-8645
e-mail: elindholm@pomona.edu
Web Site: music.pomona.edu
Officers:
Chair: Genevieve Lee
Management:
Director: Eric Lindholm
Mission: To meet the needs of both students who choose one of the concentration programs and students who wish to explore music one course at a time
Specialized Field: Orchestra
Status: Nonprofit
Paid Staff: 2
Volunteer Staff: 5
Budget: $15,000
Income Sources: Private and Corporate Donations
Season: October-April
Performs At: Bridges Hall of Music
Affiliations: Association of California Symphony Orchestras, Los Angeles County Arts Commission
Annual Attendance: 2,500-3,000
Seating Capacity: 600
Year Built: 1915
Year Remodeled: 2001
Organization Type: Performing

626
DIABLO SYMPHONY ASSOCIATION
PO Box 2222
Concord, CA 94595
Phone: 925-676-5888
Web Site: www.diablosymphony.org
Officers:
President: Patrick Campbell
Secretary: Ed Ragalia
Treasurer: Ron Cassano
Management:

Director: Joyce Johnson-Hamilton
Marketing Director: Bob Rezak
Mission: Provide great concerts in the Diablo/Walnut Creek area
Founded: 1962
Specialized Field: Orchestra
Status: Professional; Nonprofit
Paid Staff: 7
Volunteer Staff: 15
Paid Artists: 12
Budget: 125,000
Income Sources: Tickets; Sponsors; Members; American Symphony Orchestra League; Association of California Symphony Orchestras
Performs At: Dean Lesher Center for the Performing Arts
Annual Attendance: 7,000
Facility Category: Art Center Music Hall
Type of Stage: 3 Stage Music Hall
Stage Dimensions: 40x50
Seating Capacity: 297
Year Built: 1989
Organization Type: Performing; Sponsoring

627
MOZART CLASSICAL ORCHESTRA
Renee and Henry Segerstrom Concert Hall
600 Town Center Drive
Costa Mesa, CA 92626
Phone: 949-387-9197
Fax: 714-556-8984
e-mail: info@mozartorchestra.org
Web Site: www.mozartorchestra.org
Officers:
President: Jack Teberg
Management:
Director: Ami Porat
Founded: 1985
Status: Non-Profit; Professional
Budget: 328,000
Income Sources: Individual and Corporate Donations
Performs At: Zipper Hall; Colburn School for the Performing Arts
Seating Capacity: 415
Year Built: 1998
Organization Type: Performing

628
CULVER CITY SYMPHONY ORCHESTRA
Westchester Symphony Society
PO Box 4846
Culver City, CA 90231
Phone: 310-717-5500
e-mail: info@culvercitysymphony.org
Web Site: www.culvercitysymphony.org
Officers:
President: Matthew Hetz
Manager: Helene Mirich-Spear
Management:
Director: Frank Fetta
Mission: Dedicated to providing the highest artistic standards in presenting music to our loyal audience
Utilizes: Educators; Multimedia
Founded: 1963
Specialized Field: Symphony; Orchestra
Status: Nonprofit; Professional
Budget: $35,000-$100,000
Income Sources: Membership in Symphony Society, Donations, and Grants
Performs At: Veterans Memorial Auditorium
Annual Attendance: 1,800-2,400
Seating Capacity: 1,000
Year Built: 1950
Organization Type: Performing; Educational

629
CYPRESS POPS ORCHESTRA
PO Box 434
Cypress, CA 90630
Phone: 714-527-4276
e-mail: cjm1@cypresspops.org
Web Site: www.cypresspops.org
Officers:
President: Paula English
Treasurer: Allyson Davis
Secretary: Liz Royce
Management:
Music Director: John E Hall III
Mission: Dedicated to providing quality performances at no cost to the public
Founded: 1988
Specialized Field: Pops
Status: Nonprofit
Budget: $75,000-$125,000
Income Sources: Audiences; Patrons; Corporate Sponsors; City of Cypress; Orchestra's Guild
Season: June-November
Performs At: Cypress Civic Center Green
Seating Capacity: 1,000
Year Built: 1967
Organization Type: Educational; Performing

630
CAPISTRANO VALLEY SYMPHONY
24681 La Plaza
Suite 360
Dana Point, CA 92629
Phone: 949-240-8540
Fax: 949-847-6828
e-mail: info@capovalleysymphony.com
Web Site: www.capovalleysymphony.com
Officers:
President: Patti Short
Management:
Director: David Matthies
Mission: To provide concerts and educational programs of the highest quality symphonic music for the residents of South Orange County and to make this music affordable and accessible to the broadest possible audience.
Utilizes: Five Seasonal Concerts; Guest Accompanists; Guest Companies; Singers
Founded: 1984
Specialized Field: Symphony
Status: Nonprofit
Paid Staff: 1
Budget: $260,000
Income Sources: Grants from local goverments and corporations; Individual Sponsors
Season: May-September
Performs At: Mission San Juan Capistrano
Annual Attendance: 100,000
Year Built: 1776
Organization Type: Educational; Performing

631
TASSAJARA SYMPHONY ORCHESTRA
696 San Ramon Valley Boulevard
Suite 104
Danville, CA 94526
Phone: 925-820-2494
e-mail: greatmusic@tassajarasymphony.org
Web Site: www.tassajarasymphony.org
Officers:
President: Cheryl Williamson
Management:
Founding Musical Director/Conductor: Sara Jobin

Artistic Director: Dawn Wade
Mission: Aims to provide an exciting and enjoyable playing environment that encourages camradery and emphasizes fine ensemble playing.
Utilizes: Collaborations; Commissioned Composers; Commissioned Music; Dance Companies; Educators; Fine Artists; Five Seasonal Concerts; Guest Instructors; Guest Lecturers; Guest Musicians; Guest Writers; Multimedia; Original Music Scores; Sign Language Translators; Singers; Soloists
Founded: 1998
Specialized Field: Orchestra; Symphony
Paid Staff: 2
Volunteer Staff: 10
Paid Artists: 45
Budget: $140,000
Income Sources: Donors; Grants
Performs At: Community Church and Regional Center for the Arts
Annual Attendance: 1500

632
DOWNEY SYMPHONY ORCHESTRA

Downey Symphonic Society
PO Box 763
Downey, CA 90241-0763
Phone: 562-403-2944
Fax: 562-861-9499
Web Site: www.downeysymphony.org
Officers:
 President: Larry Lewis
 VP: Nick Frankart
 Secretary: Ruth Hillecke
 Treasurer: William Hare
Management:
 Music Director: Sharon Lavery
Mission: Provides leadership in bringing symphonic music to the community, encouraging and supporting the orchestra's artistic, organizational and fiscal development. The Society fosters accessibility, diversity, and excellence in its programs and promotes, to the public, the value and importance of symphonic music.
Founded: 1962
Specialized Field: Symphony
Status: Professional, Nonprofit
Paid Staff: 3
Volunteer Staff: 16
Paid Artists: 60
Budget: $150,000
Income Sources: Donations; Ticket Sales; Grants
Performs At: Downey Civic Center
Affiliations: ASCO
Annual Attendance: 3,000
Seating Capacity: 740
Organization Type: Performing

633
IMPERIAL VALLEY SYMPHONY

1904 Johnson Lane
PO Box 713
El Centro, CA 92243-9547
Phone: 760-355-6287
Fax: 760-355-6398
e-mail: joel@imperial.cc.ca.us
Web Site: http://faculty.imperial.cc.ca.us
Management:
 Music Director/Conductor: Joel Jacklich
Founded: 1974
Specialized Field: Symphony; Orchestra
Status: Nonprofit
Paid Staff: 1
Volunteer Staff: 4
Paid Artists: 25

Non-paid Artists: 35
Budget: $20,000
Affiliations: American Symphony Orchestra League
Annual Attendance: 1950
Seating Capacity: 1050
Year Built: 1996

634
FREMONT SYMPHONY ORCHESTRA

PO Box 104
Fremont, CA 94537
Phone: 510-371-4860
Fax: 510-794-1658
e-mail: info@fremontsymphony.org
Web Site: www.fremontsymphony.org
Officers:
 General Manager: Susan L Rose
 Development Director: Ann Millican
Management:
 Music Director: David Sloss
 Orchestra Personnel Manager: Carole Klein
Mission: To provide and develop, for the greater Fremont area, a professional symphony orchestra. The orchestra will fulfill the community's needs and wants by offering a balanced program of established symphonic repertoire.
Utilizes: Collaborations; Commissioned Composers; Dance Companies; Five Seasonal Concerts; Guest Composers; Guest Musicians; Guest Writers; Instructors; Local Artists & Directors; Organization Contracts; Original Music Scores; Paid Performers; Scenic Designers; Singers
Founded: 1964
Specialized Field: Symphony; Orchestra; Ensemble; Educational
Status: Professional
Paid Staff: 5
Volunteer Staff: 45
Paid Artists: 70
Budget: $270,000
Income Sources: Ticket Sales; Government; Corporate & Foundation Grants; Individual Contributions; Fundraising Events
Season: September-May
Performs At: Smith Center; Ohlone College
Affiliations: American Symphony Orchestra League; ACSO; Fremont Chamber; American Society of Composers, Authors and Publishers
Annual Attendance: 2,500-6,000
Facility Category: Theatre
Type of Stage: Proscenium
Stage Dimensions: 30x50
Seating Capacity: 405
Year Built: 1998
Rental Contact: Christopher Boorasa
Organization Type: Performing; Educational

635
CHOOKASIAN ARMENIAN CONCERT ENSEMBLE

2511 W Browning Avenue
Fresno, CA 93711-2508
Phone: 559-449-1777
Fax: 559-432-6666
e-mail: chook3@qnis.net
Web Site: www.chookasian.com
Management:
 Armenian Ensemble Director: John Chookasian
Mission: To preserve, present, and promote the traditional Armenian music, dance and culture through our concert and festival presentations around the world and our live concert/festival cD albums. Secondly, we have presented numerous educational programs that

has broadened the understanding and appreciation of traditional Armenian music and culture to the students and general public at large.
Utilizes: Dancers; Filmmakers; Grant Writers; Guest Musical Directors; Organization Contracts; Paid Performers; Theatre Companies
Founded: 1994
Specialized Field: Armenia Music
Status: Professional
Paid Staff: 15
Paid Artists: 15
Income Sources: Grants; Concert Halls; University/College Concert Halls, Museums, Institutions, Art Center, Corporations, Churches, Festivals, Films, Individuals
Performs At: California State University Performing Arts Center
Seating Capacity: 600
Year Built: 1987

636
FRESNO PHILHARMONIC

2377 West Shaw Lane
Suite 101
Fresno, CA 93711
Phone: 559-261-0600
Fax: 559-261-0700
e-mail: info@fresnophil.org
Web Site: www.fresnophil.org
Officers:
 President: Judith Peracchi
 VP: Sasan Rahmatian
 Treasurer: Tim Buchanan
 Secretary: Beanie Irola
Management:
 Music Director: Theodore Kuchar
 Orchestra Manager: Boris Nixon
 Executive Director: Don Reinhold
Mission: To present high quality, live orchestral music to audiences throughout the San Joaquin Valley.
Utilizes: Collaborations; Guest Accompanists; Guest Artists; Guest Composers; Guest Lecturers; Guest Musical Directors; Guest Musicians; Multimedia; Singers
Founded: 1954
Specialized Field: Symphony; Orchestra
Status: Nonprofit
Paid Artists: 80
Budget: 1.8 million
Income Sources: Association of California Symphony Orchestras
Season: September-May
Performs At: William Saroyan Theatre; Fresno Convention Center
Seating Capacity: 2,353
Year Built: 1966
Organization Type: Performing; Touring; Resident

637
JOHN CHOOKASIAN INTERNATIONAL FOLK ENSEMBLE

2511 W Browning Avenue
Fresno, CA 93711-2508
Phone: 559-449-1777
Fax: 559-449-1777
e-mail: chook3@qnis.net
Web Site: www.chookasian.com
Management:
 Performing Director: John Chookasian, chook3@qnis.net
Mission: To promote the folk music, folk dance, and folk instruments of the Near & Middle East, including: Armenian, Arabic, and Greek culture & traditions.

Available for tours, concerts, festivals, conventions, corporate events, concert halls, colleges & universities, weddings, dances, private parties, night clubs and films.
Utilizes: Collaborating Artists; Dance Companies; Dancers; Grant Writers; Guest Accompanists; Guest Artists; Guest Musical Directors; Guest Musicians; Lyricists; Multimedia; Original Music Scores; Paid Performers; Poets; Sign Language Translators; Theatre Companies
Founded: 1964
Specialized Field: Near-East Music; Middle-Eastern Music
Status: Professional; Nonprofit
Paid Artists: 12
Income Sources: Grants; Concerts; Festivals; Arts Councils; Corporations; Cultural Institutions; Organizations; Individuals; Art Centers; Colleges & Universities; Churches
Annual Attendance: 4,000 - 6,000
Organization Type: Performing; Touring; Educational

638
PHILIP LORENZ MEMORIAL KEYBOARD CONCERTS
PO Box 14162
Fresno, CA 93650
Phone: 559-278-2337
Fax: 559-278-6800
e-mail: andreasw@csufresno.edu
Web Site: www.keyboardconcerts.com
Management:
 Artistic Director: Andreas Werz
Mission: Memorial Keyboard Concerts presents eight to ten pianists/organists from around the world.
Founded: 1971
Opened: 1971
Specialized Field: Piano
Status: Nonprofit
Paid Staff: 5
Volunteer Staff: 5
Paid Artists: 10
Budget: $60,000
Income Sources: Private and Corporate Donations, Ticket Sales
Performs At: Concert Hall; California State University, Fresno
Seating Capacity: 400

639
SOUTH VALLEY SYMPHONY
PO Box 1347
Gilroy, CA 95021-1347
Phone: 408-842-3934
Fax: 408-842-9776
e-mail: bbottini@verizon.net
Web Site: www.southvalleysymphony.org
Officers:
 President: Barbara Bottini
 VP: John Graham
 Secretary: Jean Lance
Management:
 Music Director/Conductor: Anthony Quartuccio
Mission: To provide music from Verdi, Vivaldi, Mandel, Copeland, Donizetti, and much more. South Valley Symphony performs a series of 6 concerts.
Founded: 1974
Specialized Field: Symphony
Status: Nonprofit
Volunteer Staff: 10
Non-paid Artists: 40
Budget: $30,000-$35,000
Income Sources: Fundraisers, Advertising
Season: October-May
Performs At: Gavilian College Theatre

Annual Attendance: 275-425

640
GLENDALE SYMPHONY ORCHESTRA ASSOCIATION
PO Box 1986
Glendale, CA 91209-1986
Phone: 818-500-8720
Fax: 818-500-8721
e-mail: info@glendalesymphony.org
Web Site: www.glendalesymphony.org
Officers:
 President: Patrick Shahijanian
 VP: Jack Kabateck
 VP: Edna Karinski
 VP: Mary Ann Plumley
 Recording Secretary: Sheila Farrell Murray
 Corresponding Secretary: Jane Garcin
 Treasurer: Rita Burns
Management:
 Music Director: Olivia Tsui
 COO: Jack Kabateck
Mission: To contribute to the diversity of the community and to encourage an appreciation of music for future generations.
Utilizes: Guest Companies
Founded: 1924
Specialized Field: Symphony; Orchestra
Status: Professional, Nonprofit
Paid Staff: 1
Income Sources: American Symphony Orchestra League, Grants
Performs At: Alex Theater
Organization Type: Performing; Educational

641
GLENDALE YOUTH ORCHESTRA
PO Box 4401
Glendale, CA 91222-0401
Phone: 818-321-3083
Fax: 818-552-2043
e-mail: gyo@mindspring.com
Web Site: www.glendale-online.com/gyo
Officers:
 President: Elinor Lloyd
 VP Operations: Manisha Rea
 Treasurer: Stephen Staudenmeir
 Assistant Treasurer: Jennifer Babcock
 VP Fundraising/Solicitations: Eitan Sadeg
 VP Fundraising Events: Sue Kelly
 VP Publicity: Tom Metzler
 VP Recruiting: Helen Crosby
 Corresponding Secretary: Tim Kelley
Management:
 Music Director: Brad Keimach
Mission: To provide qualified young musicians an environment in which to explore, comprehend, appreciate and develop a lasting interest in music in a quality orchestral setting. As orchestra members, to perform concerts of standard symphonic music; to learn the value of achievement, teamwork, and discipline; to work with top teaching professionals as coaches.
Founded: 1989
Specialized Field: Youth Symphony
Status: Nonprofit
Budget: $35,000-$100,000
Income Sources: Individual and Corporate Donations, Fundraisers
Season: December-June
Performs At: Alex Theatre

642
RUSSIAN RIVER BLUES FESTIVAL
Omega Events
26429 Rancho Parkway S
Suite 135
Guerneville, CA 92630
Phone: 707-869-1595
Fax: 949-362-5366
e-mail: info@omegaevents.com
Web Site: www.omegaevents.com
Officers:
 President/CEO: Rich Sherman
Management:
 Operations: Ryan Hardin
 Manager: Pamela Forney
Utilizes: Singers
Status: For-Profit
Income Sources: Fundraisers, Private and Corporate Donations, Ticket Sales
Season: September
Performs At: Johnson's Beach; Guerneville
Organization Type: Performing

643
RUSSIAN RIVER CHAMBER MUSIC
1803 Vine Street
Suite 136
Healdsburg, CA 95448
Phone: 707-524-8700
Fax: 707-431-7622
e-mail: info@russianrivermusic.org
Web Site: www.russianrivermusic.org
Officers:
 President: Scott Daley
 Treasurer: Jane Oriel
Management:
 Artistic Director: Gary McLaughlin
Mission: To promote the appreciation of chamber music in Sonoma County
Founded: 1992
Specialized Field: Chamber
Status: Nonprofit
Paid Staff: 1
Income Sources: Private and Corporate Donations, Ticket Sales, Grants
Season: October-May
Performs At: Healdsburg Community Church
Facility Category: Church
Seating Capacity: 300

644
HOLLYWOOD BOWL ORCHESTRA
The Hollywood Bowl
2301 N Highland Avenue
PO Box 1951
Hollywood, CA 90078-1951
Phone: 323-850-2000
Fax: 323-850-2155
Web Site: www.hollywoodbowl.com
Officers:
 Chairman: David C Bohnett
 President: Deborah Borda
 Secretary: Alan Wayte
Management:
 Artistic Director: Chad Smith
 Director: Laura Connelly
 Manager: Johanna Rees
Founded: 1922
Status: Professional
Income Sources: Private and Corporate Donations
Performs At: Hollywood Bowl
Affiliations: Los Angeles Philharmonic
Annual Attendance: 18,000

Seating Capacity: 17,680

645

MOZART CLASSICAL ORCHESTRA
PO Box 54404
Irvine, CA 92619
Phone: 949-387-9197
e-mail: info@mozartorchestra.org
Web Site: www.mozartorchestra.org
Officers:
Founder: Ami Porat
Management:
Music Director/Conductor: Ami Porat
Mission: To encourage greater audience appreciation of the music from the great masters of chamber orchestra music.
Founded: 1980
Specialized Field: Chamber; Orchestra
Budget: $150,000-$260,000
Income Sources: Ticket Sales; Private and Corporate Donations
Performs At: St. Andrews Presbyterian Church; Irvine Barclay Theatre
Year Built: 1990

646

PHILHARMONIC SOCIETY OF ORANGE COUNTY
2082 Business Center Drive
Suite 100
Irvine, CA 92612
Phone: 949-553-2422
Fax: 949-553-2421
e-mail: contactus@philharmonicsociety.org
Web Site: www.philharmonicsociety.org
Officers:
Chairman/CEO: Sabra Bordas r
Secretary/Treasurer: Noel Hamilton
Management:
Artistic Director: Dean Corey
Marketing: Chantel Chen
Operations: Jeffrey Mistri
Founded: 1954
Status: Non-Profit
Budget: $3.7 million
Income Sources: Fundraising; Gifts from Individuals; Ticket Sales
Season: September-June
Performs At: Orange County Performing Arts Center
Seating Capacity: 2900
Year Built: 1969
Organization Type: Presenters

647

COLLEGE OF MARIN
Department of Performing Arts
835 College Avenue
Kentfield, CA 94904
Phone: 415-485-9460
Fax: 415-485-0135
e-mail: commusic@marin.edu
Web Site: www.marin.edu
Officers:
Superintendent/President: David Wain Coon Ed.D
Management:
Co-Chair, Performing Arts: Tara Flandreau, tara.flandreau@marin.edu
Administrative Assistant: Joanna Pinckney, joanna.pinckney@marin.edu
Utilizes: Actors; Collaborations; Community Members; Community Talent; Dance Companies; Dancers; Educators; Guest Instructors; Guest Musical Directors; Guest Musicians; Guest Soloists; High School Drama; Local Artists; Multimedia; Music; Resident Professionals; Sign Language Translators; Singers; Soloists; Student Interns; Special Technical Talent
Specialized Field: Music, Drama & Dance
Status: Non-Profit
Performs At: Fine Arts Theatre
Affiliations: Association of California Symphony Orchestras, American Symphony Orchestra League, Theatre Bay Area
Seating Capacity: 600
Rental Contact: Cheryl Carlson
Organization Type: Performing; Educational

648

LA JOLLA MUSIC SOCIETY
7946 Ivanhoe Street
Suite 309
La Jolla, CA 92037
Phone: 858-459-3724
Fax: 858-459-3727
e-mail: lrosenthal@ljms.org
Web Site: www.ljms.org
Officers:
Board Chairman: Leigh Ryan
President: Christopher Beach
Management:
Artistic Administrator: Leah Z Rpsenthal
Productions Manager: Hannes Kling
Mission: To enhance the vitality and deepen the cultural life of San Diego by presenting and producing a dynamic range of performing arts for our increasingly diverse community.
Founded: 1941
Specialized Field: Symphony; Chamber; Ensemble; Piano; Jazz; Family Programming
Status: Professional, Nonprofit
Paid Staff: 25
Budget: $3.6 Million
Income Sources: Ticket Sales; Contributions
Performs At: Sherwood Auditorium; Civic Theatre; Copley Symphony Hall; Qualcomm Hall; Birch North Park Theatre; Neuroscience Institute
Annual Attendance: 35,000
Organization Type: Performing, Presenting

649

LA JOLLA SYMPHONY & CHORUS
9500 Gilman Drive
La Jolla, CA 92093-0361
Phone: 858-534-4637
Fax: 858-534-9947
e-mail: boxoffice@lajollasymphony.com
Web Site: www.lajollasymphony.com
Officers:
President: Amee Wood
Treasurer: Jennifer Smerud
Secretary: George Anderson
Management:
Executive Director: Diane Salisbury
Manager: Ted Bietz
Utilizes: Educators; Multimedia
Status: Non-Profit
Budget: $150,000-$260,000
Season: October-January
Performs At: Mandeville Center for the Performing Arts, Neurosciences Institute Auditorium
Affiliations: University of California; San Diego, City of San Diego Commission for Arts and Culture; County of San Diego; California Arts Council
Seating Capacity: 788, 350
Organization Type: Educational; Performing

650

LIVERMORE AMADOR SYMPHONY
Livermore Valley Performing Arts Center
2222 Second Street
Suite 18
Livermore, CA 94550
Phone: 925-373-6100
Fax: 925-373-6099
e-mail: receptionist@livermoreperformingarts.org
Web Site: www.livermoreperformingarts.org
Officers:
Chairman: Philip R Wente
President: Joan K Seppala
Secretary: Tom Reitter
Treasurer: Michael Bocchicchio
Management:
Executive Director: David Dial
Development Director: Kimberly Moore
Status: Nonprofit
Budget: $35,000-$100,000
Income Sources: Fundraisers, Grants, Corporate Donations, Estate Sales
Season: September-May
Performs At: First Presbyterian Church, Amador Theatre
Seating Capacity: 450

651

LONG BEACH SYMPHONY ORCHESTRA
110 W Ocean Boulevard
Suite 22
Long Beach, CA 90802
Phone: 562-436-3203
Fax: 562-491-3599
e-mail: lbso@lbso.org
Web Site: www.lbso.org
Management:
Music Director: Enrique Diemecke
Executive Director: Robert Jones
General Manager: Janet Nyquist
Production/Stage Manager: Ryan Lee
Special Events Manager: Kari Regan
Mission: To provide high quality symphonic music for the entertainment and education of the community.
Founded: 1935
Specialized Field: Symphony; Orchestra
Status: Nonprofit, Professional
Paid Staff: 13
Volunteer Staff: 300
Paid Artists: 83
Income Sources: Ticket Sales, Individual and Corporate Donations, Conductor's Circle, Corporate Circle, Sponsorships, Fundraisers
Season: October-May
Performs At: Terrace Theater, Long Beach Arena; Long Beach Performing Arts Center
Annual Attendance: 40,000
Seating Capacity: 3,000, 7,000
Organization Type: Performing

652

PENINSULA SYMPHONY ORCHESTRA
146 Main Street
Suite 102
Los Altos, CA 94002
Phone: 650-941-5291
Fax: 650-941-5292
e-mail: info@peninsulasymphony.org
Web Site: www.peninsulasymphony.org
Officers:
Chair: Dick Bennett
Vice Chair: Frank Rahn
Treasurer: Roy Bukstein

Management:
Executive Director: Steve Carlton
Marketing/Outreach Coordinator: Katie Bartholomew
Development Associate: Angela Ragni
Mission: To enrich the lives of our community with the highest quality musical presentations at modest prices, inspire greater appreciation for music and promote music education.
Utilizes: Educators; Music
Founded: 1949
Status: Non-Profit, Professional
Paid Staff: 6
Paid Artists: 2
Budget: 600,000
Income Sources: Private and Corporate Donations, Sponships
Season: October-May
Performs At: Flint Center, Fox Theatre; Redwood City, San Mateo Performing Arts Center
Type of Stage: Proscenium
Stage Dimensions: 89.9Wx39.2Dx40H
Seating Capacity: 2,500, 1,460

653
ADAMS MUSIC
10612 W Pico Boulevard
Los Angeles, CA 90064
Phone: 310-839-3575
e-mail: saxshop@gmail.com
Web Site: www.adamsmusic.com
Officers:
Owner: Adam Lerman
Mission: Adam's music offers private music lessons for children and adults. Whether you play the trombone, guitar or clarinet.
Specialized Field: Instrumental

654
AMERICAN YOUTH SYMPHONY
2365 Westwood Boulevard
Suite 23
Los Angeles, CA 90064
Phone: 310-470-2332
Fax: 310-470-2772
e-mail: info@aysymphony.org
Web Site: www.aysymphony.org
Officers:
Chairman: Herbert Gelfand
President: David Newman
Treasurer: Sonia J Luna
Secretary: Krystyna Newman
Management:
Executive Director: Janneke Straub
Manager: Mason Dille
Utilizes: Educators; Five Seasonal Concerts; Guest Composers; Guest Lecturers; Guest Musical Directors; High School Drama; Multimedia; New Productions; Organization Contracts; Singers; Soloists
Founded: 1959
Status: Non-Professional, Non-Profit
Budget: $700,000
Income Sources: American Symphony Orchestra League; Youth Orchestra Division, Private and Corporate Donations, Foundation and Government Support
Season: October-June
Performs At: Royce Hall; UCLA
Annual Attendance: 12,000
Type of Stage: Proscenium
Seating Capacity: 1,818
Year Built: 1929
Year Remodeled: 1994
Organization Type: Performing; Educational

655
LOS ANGELES BACH FESTIVAL
First Congregational Church
540 S Commonwealth Avenue
Los Angeles, CA 90020-1298
Phone: 213-385-1341
Fax: 213-487-0461
e-mail: jtalberg@fccla.org
Web Site: www.fccla.org
Management:
Director: Jonathan Talberg
Budget: $20,000-$35,000
Affiliations: First Congregational Church of Los Angeles
Seating Capacity: 150
Year Built: 1867

656
LOS ANGELES CHAMBER ORCHESTRA
707 Wilshire Boulevard
Suite 1850
Los Angeles, CA 90017
Phone: 213-622-7001
Fax: 213-955-2071
e-mail: info@laco.org
Web Site: www.laco.org
Officers:
Chairman: Gregory J Soukup
President: Michael Rosen
Treasurer: Titus Brenninkmeijer
Secretary: Debra Gastler
Management:
Executive Director: Andrea Laguni
Marketing: Nicolette Atkins
Operations: Devin Thomas
Utilizes: Collaborations; Commissioned Composers; Commissioned Music; Composers-in-Residence; Guest Composers; Guest Designers; Guest Lecturers; Guest Musical Directors; Guest Musicians; Guest Soloists; Local Artists; Music; Selected Students; Singers
Founded: 1968
Status: Professional; Non-Profit
Budget: $2.2 million
Income Sources: Ticket Sales; Contributed Income from Foundations; Corporations; Government Agencies; Individual Donations
Season: October-May
Performs At: Alex Theatre; Glendale, Royce Hall; UCLA
Affiliations: American Symphony Orchestra League; Association of California Symphony Orchestras; Western Arts Alliance; International Society of Performing Art
Annual Attendance: 1,500
Organization Type: Performing; Touring; Resident

657
LOS ANGELES DOCTORS SYMPHONY ORCHESTRA
PO Box 642949
Los Angeles, CA 90064
Phone: 323-662-1045
e-mail: info@ladso.org
Web Site: www.ladso.org
Officers:
President/Orchestra Council: Richard Chen
Vice President: Louis Fantasia
Treasurer: Ken Alexander
Management:
Music Director/Conductor: Ivan Shulman

Mission: To provide for the comradeship of music for its musicians, to contribute culturally to the community, to help raise funds for medical and other charities and provide concerts at low cost to the public.
Utilizes: Commissioned Music; Guest Musical Directors; Guest Musicians; Multimedia; Singers; Soloists
Founded: 1953
Specialized Field: Orchestra
Status: Nonprofit
Volunteer Staff: 10
Non-paid Artists: 3
Budget: $25,000
Income Sources: Dues; Grants; Donations
Season: October-July
Performs At: No Official Base
Annual Attendance: 2,500

658
LOS ANGELES PHILHARMONIC ASSOCIATION
135 N Grand Avenue
Los Angeles, CA 90012
Phone: 323-850-2000
Fax: 323-850-2155
Web Site: www.laphil.org
Officers:
Chairman: David C Bohnett
President: Deborah Borda
Secretary: Alan Wayte
Management:
Director: Esa-Pekka Salonen
Artistic Director: Chad Smith
Manager: Johanna Rees
Founded: 1919
Status: Nonprofit
Income Sources: Private and Corporate Donations, Ticket Sales, Grants
Season: October-June
Performs At: Walt Disney Concert Hall; Hollywood Bowl (summer)
Seating Capacity: 3,189, 20,000
Year Built: 1999
Organization Type: Educational; Performing; Touring

659
SANTA CECILIA ORCHESTRA
2759 W Broadway
Los Angeles, CA 90041
Phone: 323-259-3011
Fax: 323-257-0889
e-mail: info@scorchestra.org
Web Site: www.scorchestra.org
Management:
Artistic Director: Sonia Marie De Leon De Vega
Founded: 1993
Status: Non-Profit
Budget: 7,000
Income Sources: Private and Corporate Donations, Foundations
Performs At: Greystone Mansion

660
THORNTON SYMPHONY
University of Southern California
Bovard Auditorium
3551 Trousdale Parkway
Los Angeles, CA 90089 1
Phone: 213-740-6935
Fax: 213-740-3217
e-mail: bovprod@usc.edu
Web Site: www.usc.edu
Officers:
Chair: Michael Gorfaine

Chair: Ian White Thomson
Management:
Operations: Pamela Hopson
Manager: Michelle Maestas
Status: Non-Profit
Budget: $35,000
Season: September-December
Performs At: Bovard Auditorium
Seating Capacity: 1,544

661
PEPPERDINE UNIVERSITY ORCHESTRA
Pepperdine University
Fine Arts Division
24225 Pacific Coast Highway
Malibu, CA 90263-4966
Phone: 310-506-4462
Fax: 310-506-4077
e-mail: tony.cason@pepperdine.edu
Web Site: seaver.pepperdine.edu
Officers:
Chair: Dr. Gary Cobb
Management:
Director: Tony Cason
Status: Semi-Professional
Organization Type: Performing

662
MILL VALLEY CHAMBER MUSIC SOCIETY
38 Miller Avenue
Suite 521
Mill Valley, CA 94941
Phone: 415-381-4453
Fax: 415-381-2039
e-mail: mychambermusicsociety@yahoo.com
Web Site: www.chambermusicmillvalley.org
Officers:
President: Larry Snyder
VP: Fred W Taylor
Treasurer: Robert Glasson
Secretary: John Cutler
Chair: William Home
Management:
Artist Relations Coordinator: Sylvia Gang
Programs Coordinator: Tina Kun
Mission: To promote an appreciation of classical music for the next generation to enjoy.
Founded: 1974
Specialized Field: Chamber; Ensemble
Status: Nonprofit
Season: September-April
Performs At: Mt Tamalpais United Methodist Church
Organization Type: Educational; Sponsoring

663
MODESTO SYMPHONY ORCHESTRA
911 Thirteenth Street
Modesto, CA 95354
Phone: 209-523-4156
Fax: 209-523-0201
e-mail: info@modestosymphony.org
Web Site: www.modestosymphony.org
Officers:
Chair: Brian McCaffrey MD
President: Paul Jan Zdunek
Treasurer: Lisa Finer
Secretary: Robert Saunders
Management:
Director: David Lockington
Marketing: Caroline Nickel
Development Director: Cathy Mendoza

Utilizes: Guest Directors; Guest Instructors; Guest Musicians; Guest Writers; Instructors; Multimedia; Music; Original Music Scores; Singers
Founded: 1931
Status: Professional, Non-Profit
Budget: $1.7 Million
Income Sources: Association of California Symphony Orchestras; American Symphony Orchestra League; Fundraising; Private and Corporate Donations; Ticket Sales
Season: September-December
Performs At: Modesto Junior College Auditorium
Seating Capacity: 940
Organization Type: Performing; Educational

664
MUSIC IN THE VINEYARDS
Napa Valley Chamber Music Festival
PO Box 6297
Napa, CA 94581
Phone: 707-258-5559
Fax: 707-258-5566
e-mail: mitv@sonic.net
Web Site: www.musicinthevineyards.org
Officers:
President: Greg Evans
Secretary: Rosemary Richardson
Treasurer: Peter McCrea
Management:
Artistic Directors: Michael & Daria Adams
Executive Director: Evie Ayers
Marketing: Christy Bors
Mission: Music in the vineyards is dedicated to bringing together outstanding artists to perform in the unique vineyard settings of the Napa Valley so that both the performers and the audience can experience the intimacy of chamber music as it was intended to be performed.
Utilizes: Multimedia; Original Music Scores; Poets
Founded: 1995
Specialized Field: Chamber Music Festival
Status: Non-Profit
Paid Staff: 3
Volunteer Staff: 120
Paid Artists: 45
Budget: $140,000
Season: August
Performs At: Napa Valley; Festival Site, San Gabriel Civic Auditorium
Affiliations: Various vineyards and related venues
Seating Capacity: 150 - 250

665
PACIFIC CHAMBER SYMPHONY
Napa Valley Opera House
1030 Main Street
Napa Valley, CA 94559
Phone: 707-226-7372
Fax: 707-226-5392
Web Site: www.pacificchambersymphony.org
Management:
Director: Lawrence Kohl
Founded: 1989
Status: Non=Profit
Budget: $260,000-1,050,000
Performs At: Kanbar Hall; Jewish Community Ctr; Hofman Theatre; Dean Lesher Regional Ctr; Neighborhood Theater; Valley Community Theater

666
SAN FERNANDO VALLEY SYMPHONY ORCHESTRA
20210 Haynes Street
Ninnetka, CA 91306

Phone: 818-347-4807
Web Site: www.sfvsymphony.com
Officers:
President: Gloria Pollack
VP: Gary Thomas
Founder: James Elza Domine
Management:
Music Director/Conductor: James Elza Domine
Mission: To present classical concerts.
Utilizes: Guest Artists; Poets; Singers; Theatre Companies
Founded: 1980
Specialized Field: Symphony
Status: Professional, Nonprofit
Income Sources: Individual and Corporate Donations
Season: September-June
Performs At: Pierce College Performing Arts Theatre
Affiliations: Valley Cultural Center, American Symphony Orchestra League, Association Of California Symphony Orchestras
Seating Capacity: 400
Year Built: 1981
Organization Type: Performing; Touring; Resident; Educational; Sponsoring

667
CSUN YOUTH ORCHESTRAS
California State University Northridge
18111 Nordhoff Street
Northridge, CA 91330-8314
Phone: 818-677-3074
e-mail: yhorch@csun.edu
Web Site: www.csunyouthorchestra.org
Budget: $100,000
Income Sources: Private and Corporate Donations, Fundraisers, Ticket Sales
Season: August-May
Performs At: Performing Arts Community Center
Annual Attendance: 5,000-6,000
Type of Stage: Proscenium
Year Built: 1994

668
BERKELEY YOUTH ORCHESTRA
1587 Franklin Street
Oakland, CA 94612
Mailing Address: PO Box 1294 Berkeley CA 94701
Phone: 510-663-3296
e-mail: president@byoweb.org
Web Site: www.berkeley-youth-orchestra.org
Officers:
President: Julie Arca
Treasurer: Maya Rath
Secretary: Lynn Mackay
Management:
Executive Director: Al Maitland
Mission: BYO is an exceptional full symphonic orchestra fostering a musical community for dedicated young musicians grades 5-10+ from the greater Bay Area
Utilizes: Community Members; Music; Paid Performers
Founded: 1969
Specialized Field: Symphony; Orchestra
Status: Nonprofit
Volunteer Staff: 70
Budget: 55,000
Income Sources: Member Tuition Fees, Ticket Sales, Donations, Fundraising
Season: September-May
Performs At: Laney College Theatre
Affiliations: American Symphony Orchestra League
Annual Attendance: 1,500
Seating Capacity: 350
Organization Type: Performing; Educational

INSTRUMENTAL MUSIC / California

669
OAKLAND EAST BAY SYMPHONY
400-29th Street
Suite 501
Oakland, CA 94609
Phone: 510-444-0801
Fax: 510-444-0863
e-mail: admin@oebs.org
Web Site: www.oebs.org
Officers:
President: Paul E Garrison Esq
Management:
Music Director/Conductor: Michael Morgan
Assistant Conductor: Bryan Nies
Executive Director: Jennifer Duston
Development Director: Ken Ingraham
Mission: Oakland East Bay Symphony aims to make classical music accessible, particulary to those individuals in the community who might otherwise never hear live symphonic music.
Founded: 1988
Specialized Field: Classical; Folk Music
Paid Staff: 7
Volunteer Staff: 40
Paid Artists: 64
Budget: $2,000,000
Income Sources: Donations
Season: November-May
Performs At: Paramount Theatre
Annual Attendance: 75,000
Year Built: 1931
Year Remodeled: 1973

670
OAKLAND YOUTH ORCHESTRA
Malonga Casquelourd Center for Performing Arts
1428 Alice Street
Room 202M
Oakland, CA 94612
Phone: 510-832-7710
Fax: 510-832-2571
e-mail: manager@oyo.org
Web Site: www.oyo.org
Officers:
President: Debbra Wood Schwartz
Chairman: Conway B Jones Jr
Treasurer: Kathleen Pickard
Secretary: Janett Edrington
Management:
Artistic Director: Michael Morgan
General Manager: Gail Edwards
Executive Assistant: Zahra Mahloudji
Librarian: Kelly Jenkins
Utilizes: Instructors
Founded: 1964
Status: Non-Profit
Paid Staff: 3
Volunteer Staff: 20
Paid Artists: 2
Budget: $250,000
Income Sources: Private and Corporate Donations, Tuition, Foundation and Government Grants
Season: September-June

671
OJAI COMMUNITY CHORUS
304 N Foothill Road
PO Box 755
Ojai, CA 93023-2455
Phone: 805-208-6368
e-mail: info@ojaicommunitychorus.com
Web Site: www.ojaicommunitychorus.com
Management:

Artistic Director: Phil Harvey
Director: Connie Woodson
Status: Non-Profit
Budget: $35,000
Income Sources: Private and Corporate Donations, Ticket Sales, Grants, Foundations
Performs At: Ventura City Hall; Los Angeles County Museum of Art, Ojai Presbyterian Church

672
CHAPMAN UNIVERSITY SYMPHONY ORCHESTRA & CHAMBER ORCHESTRA
Chapman University Conservatory of Music
One University Drive
Orange, CA 92866
Phone: 714-997-6914
Fax: 714-744-7671
e-mail: wachs@chapman.edu
Web Site: www.chapman.edu
Officers:
Chair: Amy Graziano PhD
Management:
Director: Daniel Alfred Wachs
Utilizes: Theatre Companies
Budget: $100,000-150,000
Income Sources: Private and Corporate Donations, Fundraisers, Grants
Season: January-May
Performs At: Chapman Auditorium
Facility Category: Concert Hall
Seating Capacity: 1,100
Organization Type: Performing; Educational; Touring

673
ORANGE COUNTY YOUTH SYMPHONY ORCHESTRA
Chapman University Conservatory of Music
One University Drive
Orange, CA 92866
Phone: 714-744-7927
Fax: 714-744-7671
e-mail: info@ocyso.org
Web Site: www.ocyso.org
Management:
Executive Director: Heather Ter-Jung
Director: Daniel Alfred Wachs
Operations: John Acosta
Utilizes: Educators; Theatre Companies
Status: Non-profit, Pre-Professional
Budget: $35,000-100,000
Income Sources: Private and Corporate Donations, Fundraisers, Grants, Ticket Sales
Season: December-March
Performs At: Chapman Auditorium
Seating Capacity: 1,100
Organization Type: Performing; Educational; Touring

674
DESERT SYMPHONY
72925 Fred Waring
Suite 101
Palm Desert, CA 92260
Phone: 760-773-5988
Fax: 760-773-5652
e-mail: admin@desertsymphony.org
Web Site: www.desertsymphony.org
Officers:
President: Nancy Tapick
Secretary: Rhona S Kauffman
Management:
Manager: Shane A Bitner
Business Manager: Mariyn Benachowski
Conductor: Gary Berkson

Founded: 1989
Status: Nonprofit, Professional
Seating Capacity: 1,127
Year Built: 1988

675
CALIFORNIA YOUTH SYMPHONY
441 California Avenue
Suite 5
Palo Alto, CA 94306
Phone: 650-325-6666
Fax: 650-325-1243
e-mail: californiayouthsymphony@gmail.com
Web Site: www.cys.org
Officers:
President: Dave Morley
Secretary: Ken Chu
Treasurer: Bob Srinivas
Management:
Executive Director: Jim Hogan
Director: Leo Eylar
Marketing: Elizabeth Frazier
Founded: 1952
Status: Non-Professional, Non-Profit
Season: November-May
Performs At: Flint Center for Performing Arts, San Mateo Performing Arts, Spangenber Theater; Gunn High School, Smithwick Theater
Affiliations: American Symphony Orchestra League, Youth Orchestra Division; Association of California Symphony Orchestras
Annual Attendance: 8,000
Organization Type: Performing; Educational; Touring

676
EL CAMINO YOUTH SYMPHONY
4055 Fabian Way
Palo Alto, CA 94303
Phone: 650-213-7111
Fax: 650-493-1525
e-mail: ecys@earthlink.net
Web Site: www.ecys.org
Officers:
President: Peter Farmer
Vice President: Li-Wha Chen
Secretary: Darel Chapman
Treasurer: Helen Zhang
Management:
Executive Director: Cathy Spieth
Development Director: Matthew Taylor
Administrative Assistant: Lori Bingham
Artistic Operations Manager: Sara Hancock
Mission: To nurture, train and develop young musicians from culturally diverse backgrounds, encouraging their appreciation of music.
Utilizes: Theatre Companies
Founded: 1963
Specialized Field: Orchestra; Chamber
Status: Non-Profit
Budget: $900,000
Income Sources: Private and Corporate Donations, Grants
Season: November-May
Performs At: Flint Center
Type of Stage: Proscenium
Seating Capacity: 2300
Organization Type: Performing; Educational; Touring

677
COLEMAN CHAMBER CONCERTS
225 S Lake Avenue
Suite 300
Pasadena, CA 91101

Phone: 626-793-4191
e-mail: info@colemanchambermusic.org
Web Site: www.coleman.caltech.edu
Officers:
President: Susan Grether
VP: Robert Winter
Secretary: Donna Swayze
Treasurer: Jerome Hamburger
Management:
Executive Director: Kathy Freedland
Mission: To present international chamber ensembles and to reach local children with demonstration performances.
Utilizes: Guest Directors
Founded: 1904
Specialized Field: Chamber
Status: Nonprofit
Paid Staff: 1
Volunteer Staff: 50
Income Sources: Western Alliance of Arts Administrators; Chamber Music America; California Presenters; Ticket Sales, Membership Dues, Endowment Income and Gifts from Organizations
Season: October-April
Performs At: Caltech Beckman Auditorium
Stage Dimensions: 24x43x16
Seating Capacity: 1,150
Year Built: 1964
Organization Type: Sponsoring

678
PASADENA CONSERVATORY OF MUSIC

100 N Hill Avenue
Pasadena, CA 91106
Phone: 626-683-3355
e-mail: music@pasadenaconservatory.org
Web Site: www.pasadenaconservatory.org
Officers:
Chairman: Linda Dickason
Executive Director: Stephen McCurry
Development Director: Gina DiMassa
Marketing Director: Beverly Lafontaine
Director Finance/Administration: Charles Ro
Management:
Program Coordinator/Facilities Mgr: Jeannie Robbins
Mission: We provide an independent nonprofit community music school that is proud to provide a comprehensive curriculum of music study to students in and around Pasadena, California.
Founded: 1983
Specialized Field: Instrumental
Status: Nonprofit

679
PASADENA POPS ORCHESTRA

117 E Colorado Boulevard
Suite 200
Pasadena, CA 91105
Phone: 626-793-7172
Fax: 626-793-7180
e-mail: dbailey@theorchestras.org
Web Site: www.theorchestras.org
Officers:
President: Diane Rankin
CEO: Paul Jan Zdunek
Management:
Director: Rachael Worby
General Manager: Darice Bailey
Status: Non-Profit
Income Sources: Private and Corporate Donations, Grants
Season: June-September
Annual Attendance: 16,000

680
PASADENA SYMPHONY

117 E Colorado Boulevard
Suite 200
Pasadena, CA 91105
Phone: 626-793-7172
Fax: 626-793-7180
e-mail: dbailey@theorchestras.org
Web Site: www.theorchestras.org
Officers:
President: Diane Rankin
CEO: Paul Jan Zdunek
Management:
Director: Jorge Mester
General Manager: Darice Bailey
Utilizes: Guest Accompanists; Guest Musicians
Status: Professional
Budget: 2.3 million
Income Sources: Private and Corporate Donations, Ticket Sales, Foundations
Season: October-June
Performs At: Pasadena Civic Auditorium
Annual Attendance: 100,000
Seating Capacity: 3,000
Year Built: 1931
Organization Type: Performing

681
SOUTHWEST CHAMBER MUSIC

2500 E Colorado Boulevard
Pasadena, CA 91107
Phone: 626-685-4455
Fax: 626-685-4458
Toll-free: 800-726-7147
e-mail: mail@swmusic.org
Web Site: www.swmusic.org
Officers:
President: Kenneth Blaydow
VP: Betsy Tyler
Secretary: Natalie Poole
Treasurer: Samuel Jang
Founder: Fritzie Culick
Management:
Artistic Director: Jeff von der Schmidt
Executive Director: Jan Karlin
Mission: To provide multiculutral music through concert, recording and educational programming.
Founded: 1987
Specialized Field: Chamber
Status: Nonprofit
Season: September-May
Performs At: Norton Simon Museum; Colburn School of Performing Arts, Huntington Library
Annual Attendance: 100,000
Seating Capacity: 300; 400; 250

682
VILLAGE MUSIC SCHOOL

1200 Contra Costa Boulevard
Pleasant Hill, CA 94523
Phone: 925-676-8400
e-mail: villagemusicschool@gmail.com
Web Site: www.phmusicstudios.com
Management:
Director: Robert Konkle
General Manager: Katie Wills
Mission: We believe that when music is fun and presented in a supportive environment using materials that inspire practice and commitment students develop a love and understanding for music that will last a lifetime.
Specialized Field: Music

683
SHASTA SYMPHONY ORCHESTRA

11555 N Old Oregon Trail
PO Box 496006
Redding, CA 96049
Phone: 530-242-2365
Fax: 530-225-4763
e-mail: rfiske@shastacollege.edu
Web Site: www.shastacollege.edu
Management:
Music Director: Dr. Richard Allen Fiske
General Manager: Ralph Perrin
Mission: To provide a symphony orchestra for the college and the community.
Utilizes: Guest Artists; Guest Companies
Founded: 1950
Specialized Field: Symphony
Status: Nonprofit
Budget: $10,000
Income Sources: Private and Corporate Donations, Tuition, Grants
Performs At: Shasta College Theater
Affiliations: ASOL; ACSO
Annual Attendance: 1,600-2,000
Seating Capacity: 474
Year Remodeled: 2008

684
REDLANDS SYMPHONY ASSOCIATION

1200 E Colton
PO Box 3080
Redlands, CA 92373-0999
Phone: 909-748-8018
Fax: 909-335-5213
e-mail: symphony@redlands.edu
Web Site: www.RedlandsSymphony.com
Officers:
Board President: Zack Tucker
Board VP: Bruce Satzger
Board Secretary: Nancy Spencer
Board Treasurer: Phillip Doolittle
Management:
Music Director/Conductor: Jon Robertson
Operations Manager: Rachel Wade
Development Manager: Julie Nichols
Executive Director: Karen Idmes
Mission: Developing and maintaining an excellent symphony orchestra which offers an annual series of concerts and coordinating outreach programs.
Founded: 1950
Specialized Field: Symphony
Status: Professional, Nonprofit
Paid Staff: 6
Paid Artists: 60
Budget: $800,000
Income Sources: Grants; Ticket Sales; Annual Fund Raising Gala
Season: September-April
Performs At: Memorial Chapel; University of Redlands
Affiliations: American Symphony Orchestra League, Association of California Symphony Orchestras
Seating Capacity: 1,486
Organization Type: Performing, Educational

685
BEACH CITIES SYMPHONY ASSOCIATION

PO Box 248
Redondo Beach, CA 90277-0248
Phone: 310-379-9725
Fax: 310-798-2834
e-mail: info@beachcitiessymphony.org
Web Site: www.beachcitiessymphony.org

Officers:
Chairman: Ruth McFarlane
President: Robert L Peterson
Treasurer: Yong Reuter
Secretary: Bill Malcolm
Management:
Music Director/Conductor: Barry Brisk
Concertmaster: Rebecca Rutkowski
Assistant Concertmaster: Joanne Satterburg
Mission: The Beach Cities Symphony Association believes that music enriches individuals whether performers or members of the audience and community at large.
Founded: 1949
Specialized Field: Symphony; Classical
Status: Semi-Professional, Nonprofit
Income Sources: American Symphony Orchestra League; Symphony League of Los Angeles County; Private and Corporate Donations
Season: October-May
Performs At: Marsee Auditorium; El Camino College
Annual Attendance: 4,000
Organization Type: Performing

686
REDWOOD SYMPHONY

1031 16th Avenue
Redwood City, CA 94063
Phone: 650-366-6872
e-mail: info@redwoodsymphony.org
Web Site: www.redwoodsymphony.org
Officers:
Chair: Stephen Ruppenthal
Treasurer: Richard Steinberg
Management:
Director: Eric Kujawsky
Status: Non-Profit
Budget: $35,000
Income Sources: Private and Corporate Donations
Season: October-May
Performs At: Bayside Performing Arts Center, Notre Dame de Namur University Theatre, San Mateo Performing Arts Center & Theatre

687
RIVERSIDE COUNTY PHILHARMONIC

Riverside Municipal Auditorium
3485 Mission Inn Avenue
PO Box 1601
Riverside, CA 92502
Phone: 909-787-0251
Toll-free: 877-744-5849
e-mail: info@thephilharmonic.org
Web Site: www.thephilharmonic.org
Officers:
President: James Henderson
Treasurer: Paul Sundeen
Secretary: Geraldine Bowden
Management:
Director: Patrick Flynn
Executive Director: Wayne Hinton
General Manager: Katherine Wilson
Founded: 1958
Status: Professional, Non-Profit
Budget: $260,000-1,050,000
Income Sources: Ticket Sales; Contributions; Grants
Season: October-May
Performs At: Riverside Municipal Auditorium; Gardiner W Spring Auditorium
Annual Attendance: 1,500
Seating Capacity: 1,776
Organization Type: Performing

688
ASIA AMERICA SYMPHONY ORCHESTRA

608 Silver Spur Road
Suite 320
Rolling Hills Estates, CA 90274
Phone: 310-377-8977
Fax: 310-377-8949
e-mail: aasa@asiaamericasymphony.org
Web Site: www.asiaamericasymphony.org
Officers:
President: Donald M Okada MD
Secretary: Cynthia Kawaguchi Dunn
Treasurer: Valena Noguchi
Management:
Director: David Benoit
Utilizes: Community Talent; Multimedia
Founded: 1961
Budget: $150,000-$260,000
Performs At: Norrise Center for the Performing Arts, Japanese American Cultural Center
Affiliations: Norris Center for the Performing Arts
Seating Capacity: 450
Organization Type: Performing; Educational

689
CHAMBER ORCHESTRA OF THE SOUTH BAY

Norris Theatre for the Performing Arts
27570 Crossfield Drive
Rolling Hills Estates, CA 90274
Phone: 310-544-0403
Fax: 310-544-0403
e-mail: joanmoe@cox.net
Web Site: www.norristheatre.org
Officers:
President: Robert Miller
Management:
Director: Frances Steiner
Artistic Director: Joan Moe
Operations: Gilbert Cheng
Utilizes: Guest Musicians; Original Music Scores; Resident Artists; Singers
Status: Professional
Budget: $170,000
Income Sources: National Endowment for the Arts, Los Angeles County Arts Comission, Norris Foundation Cooperatives, Ticket Sales And Industrial Contributions
Season: October-April
Performs At: Norris Center for the Performing Arts
Affiliations: American Symphony Orchestra League; Association of California Symphony Orchestra
Annual Attendance: 2,200
Facility Category: Theatre
Type of Stage: Proscenium
Seating Capacity: 450
Year Built: 1983

690
CAMELLIA SYMPHONY ORCHESTRA

PO Box 19786
Sacramento, CA 95819
Phone: 916-929-6655
Fax: 916-929-4292
e-mail: camelliaorch@aol.com
Web Site: camelliasymphony.org
Officers:
President: Gus Guichard
VP: Barbara Monroe
Treasurer: Krista Dunzweiler
Management:
Conductor: Allan Pollack
Executive Director: Roberta McCellan
Mission: To expand the growth of music in the Sacramento area by presenting unique repertoire at reasonable prices, as well as provide opportunities for area musicians and composers.
Utilizes: Multimedia; Singers
Founded: 1962
Specialized Field: Orchestra
Status: Volunteer, Nonprofit
Paid Staff: 2
Budget: $175,000
Income Sources: Private and Corporate Donations; Ticket Sales; Grants
Performs At: Memorial Auditorium, Sacramento
Affiliations: Numerous Community Affiliations
Annual Attendance: 6,000
Facility Category: Community Center Theater
Seating Capacity: 2400
Year Built: 1925
Year Remodeled: 2008
Organization Type: Performing

691
SACRAMENTO PHILHARMONIC ORCHESTRA

2617 K Street
Suite 200
Sacramento, CA 95816
Phone: 916-732-9045
Fax: 916-732-9049
e-mail: office@sacphil.org
Web Site: www.sacphil.org
Officers:
President: David K. Nystrom
Chief Financial Officer: Marta Quinn
Treasurer: David Motes
Secretary: Nancy Pearl
Management:
Music Director: Michael Morgan
Executive Director: Marc Feldman
Status: Non-Profit
Budget: $1.4 Million
Income Sources: Sacramento Philharmonic Orchestra Foundation; Sacramento Metropolitan Arts Commission; Private and Corporate Donations; Ticket Sales
Season: October-April
Performs At: Sacramento Convention Center, Community Center Theater
Annual Attendance: 9,540

692
SACRAMENTO YOUTH SYMPHONY & ACADEMY OF MUSIC

3443 Ramona Avenue
Suite 22
Sacramento, CA 95826
Phone: 916-731-5777
Fax: 916-736-3874
e-mail: cathytaylor@sacramentoyouthsymphony.org
Web Site: www.sacramentoyouthsymphony.org
Officers:
President: Jack Holmes
Secretary: Steffen Brown
Treasurer: Henry Kim
Management:
Artistic Director: Michael Neumann
Executive Director: Cathy Taylor
Mission: To educate and advance the musical skills of youth in our communities in ways that engage, challenge and inspire them to reach their highest potential.
Founded: 1956
Status: Non-Profit

Budget: 400,000
Season: September-May
Performs At: CSUS Music Recital Hall, Memorial Auditorium; Various Venues
Annual Attendance: 7,500
Organization Type: Performing; Educational; Touring

693
CHAMBER MUSIC IN NAPA VALLEY

4375 Atlas Peak Road
Saint Helens, CA 94558
Phone: 707-226-2190
Fax: 707-226-2936
e-mail: cmnv@napanet.net
Web Site: www.chambermusicnapa.org
Management:
Director: John Kongsgaard
Director: Maggy Kongsgaard
Status: Non-Profit
Income Sources: Private and Corporate Donations, Ticket Sales, Grants
Season: October-May
Performs At: United Methodist Church, Napa Valley Opera House
Seating Capacity: 320

694
SAN BERNARDINO SYMPHONY ORCHESTRA

415 W 2nd Street
San Bernardino, CA 92401
Phone: 909-381-5388
Fax: 909-883-6428
e-mail: sbsymphon1y@aol.com
Web Site: sanbernardinosymphony.org
Officers:
President: Mary Schnepp
Treasurer: Lisa Doherty
Secretary: Grace Baldwin
Management:
Director: Carlo Pointi Jr
Utilizes: Actors; Grant Writers; Guest Lecturers; Guest Musicians; Guest Soloists; Guest Writers; Instructors; Music; New Productions; Original Music Scores; Singers; Soloists
Founded: 1929
Status: Non-Profit
Budget: 500,000
Income Sources: Box Office; Donations; Special Events; Fundraising
Season: October-May
Performs At: California Theatre for the Arts
Affiliations: American Symphony Council Orchestra; Broadcast Music, Inc.
Annual Attendance: 10,000
Facility Category: Theatre
Type of Stage: Wood
Stage Dimensions: 28'x56'
Seating Capacity: 1,728
Year Built: 1928

695
MAINLY MOZART

2802 Juan Street
Suite 29
San Diego, CA 92110
Phone: 619-239-0100
Fax: 619-233-4292
e-mail: admin@mainlymozart.org
Web Site: www.mainlymozart.org
Officers:
President: Christopher Weil
Chairman: Alexander Pearson
Treasurer: Jerrold Weller

Secretary: Linda Satz
Management:
Artistic Director: David Atherton
Executive Director: Nancy Laturno Bojanic
Utilizes: Educators; Guest Accompanists; Guest Musical Directors; Guest Musicians; Multimedia
Founded: 1988
Status: Non-Profit
Budget: $1.4 million
Income Sources: Box Office; Grants; Donations; Ticket Sales; Fundraisers
Season: January-May
Performs At: Neurosciences Institute; Copley Symphony Hall
Annual Attendance: 19,000
Seating Capacity: 352;2247

696
SAN DIEGO CHAMBER ORCHESTRA

11772 Sorrento Valley Road
Suite 212
San Diego, CA 92121
Phone: 858-350-0290
Fax: 858-350-0297
Toll-free: 888-848-7326
e-mail: info@sdco.org
Web Site: www.sdco.org
Officers:
President: Gay Hugo Martinez
Management:
Executive Director: Tyler Hewes
Customer Relations Manager: Erin Oleno
Mission: To provide a resident orchestra of the highest professional caliber for the greater San Diego area.
Utilizes: Guest Artists
Founded: 1984
Specialized Field: Symphony; Orchestra; Chamber
Status: Professional, Nonprofit
Paid Staff: 5
Volunteer Staff: 1
Paid Artists: 60
Budget: $1.3 million
Income Sources: Ticket Sales; Donations; Sponsors
Season: October-May
Performs At: Sherwood Auditorium, St Paul's Cathedral; La Jolla, Rancho Santa Fe; Fairbanks Ranch Country Club
Affiliations: American Symphony Orchestra League; Association of California Symphony Orchestras
Annual Attendance: 15,000
Seating Capacity: 100-3,000
Organization Type: Performing
Resident Groups: Chamber Orchestra

697
SAN DIEGO EARLY MUSIC SOCIETY

PO Box 82008
San Diego, CA 92138
Phone: 619-226-4266
Fax: 619-688-1684
e-mail: sdems@sdems.org
Web Site: www.sdems.org
Officers:
President: Penelope Hawkins
Secretary: Angela Quinn
Treasurer: Peter Cramer
Management:
Director: Diemet Rose
Utilizes: Guest Musical Directors; Instructors; Multimedia; Original Music Scores; Sign Language Translators
Founded: 1981
Status: Non-Profit
Budget: $65,000

Income Sources: Box Office; Members; Ads; Grants
Season: October-April
Performs At: St. James-by-the-Sea; Sherwood Auditorium At S.D. Museum of Contemporary Art, La Jolla; S.D. Museum of Art
Affiliations: Early Music America; San Diego Performing Arts League
Annual Attendance: 2,500
Seating Capacity: 400; 500; 100

698
SAN DIEGO SYMPHONY ORCHESTRA

1245 7th Avenue
San Diego, CA 92101
Phone: 619-235-0800
Fax: 619-235-0005
e-mail: marketing@sandiegosymphony.org
Web Site: www.sandiegosymphony.com
Officers:
Chairman: Theresa J Drew
Vice Chairman: Dennis W Arriola
Vice Chairman: Joyce Grosvenor
Vice Chairman: Paul Hering
Treasurer: John Zygowicz
Secretary: Evelyn Olson Lamden
Management:
Music Director: Jahja Ling
Concertmaster: Jeff Thayer
Assistant Concertmaster: Nick Grant
Artistic Administrator: Tommy Phillips
Production Manager: Jennifer Ringle
Executive Director: Edward B Gill
Mission: To present the highest quality performances of classical music to the San Diego community.
Utilizes: Guest Artists
Founded: 1910
Specialized Field: Symphony; Orchestra
Status: Professional; Nonprofit
Income Sources: American Symphony Orchestra League; Association of California Symphony Orchestras; Private and Corporate Donations; Ticket Sales; Foundations
Season: October-May
Performs At: Copley Symphony Hall
Seating Capacity: 2,245
Year Built: 1929
Organization Type: Performing; Educational; Sponsoring

699
SAN DIEGO YOUTH SYMPHONY

1650 El Prado
Suite 207A
San Diego, CA 92101
Phone: 619-233-3232
Fax: 619-233-3236
e-mail: sdys@sdys.org
Web Site: www.sdys.org
Officers:
Chair: Jim Whitesell
President/CEO: Dalouge Smith
Treasurer: Robert Gaan
Secretary: Nai Hwang
Management:
Artistic Director: Jeff Edmons
Operations: Alexis Alfaro
Marketing: Molly Clark
Founded: 1945
Status: Semi-professional
Budget: $150,000-260,000
Income Sources: Private and Corporate Donations, Ticket Sales, Grants, Foundations
Season: November-June
Performs At: Copley Symphony Hall

Annual Attendance: 600-4,000
Seating Capacity: 2,400

700
TIFERETH ISRAEL COMMUNITY ORCHESTRA
6660 Cowles Mountain Boulevard
San Diego, CA 92119
Phone: 619-697-6001
Fax: 619-697-1102
e-mail: tifereth@tiferethisrael.com
Web Site: www.tiferethisrael.com
Officers:
President: Marla Lobenstein
Secretary: Randy Philipp
Management:
Director: David Amos
Utilizes: Commissioned Composers;
Composers-in-Residence; Guest Accompanists; Guest
Companies; Guest Lecturers; Guest Musical Directors;
Guest Musicians; Singers; Touring Companies
Founded: 1974
Budget: 15,000
Income Sources: Tickets, donations
Season: Novemebr-July
Performs At: Tifereth Israel Synagogue
Affiliations: Tifereth Israel Synagogue
Annual Attendance: 4000
Facility Category: Social Hall
Seating Capacity: 400-1500

701
KRONOS QUARTET
PO Box 225340
San Francisco, CA 94122
Phone: 415-731-3533
Fax: 415-664-7590
e-mail: talk@kronosquartet.org
Web Site: www.kronosquartet.org
Management:
Director: Janet Cowperthwaite
Artistic Administrator: Sidney Chen
Development: Laird Rodet
Utilizes: Choreographers; Collaborating Artists;
Collaborations; Commissioned Composers;
Commissioned Music; Composers; Filmmakers; Guest
Accompanists; Guest Choreographers; Guest
Companies; Guest Musical Directors; Guest Musicians;
Multimedia; Organization Contracts; Original Music
Scores; Paid Performers; Sign Language Translators;
Singers; Visual Arts
Founded: 1973
Status: Professional, Non-Profit
Budget: $1.5 Million
Income Sources: Earned; Contributions; Individual;
Foundations; Government Sources
Season: July-May
Performs At: Various Venues
Affiliations: Association of Performing Arts Presenters;
Western Arts Alliance; Chamber Music America;
National Academy of Recording Arts Sciences
Annual Attendance: 1,000,000
Organization Type: Performing; Touring; Sponsoring

702
MIDSUMMER MOZART FESTIVAL
760 Market Street
Suite 749
San Francisco, CA 94102
Phone: 415-627-9141
Fax: 415-627-9142
e-mail: amadeus@midsummermozart.org
Web Site: www.midsummermozart.org
Officers:

Chair: Behzad Khosrovi
Management:
Executive Director: Marcy Straw
Music Director: George Cleve
Mission: To present the music of Wolfgang Amadeus
Mozart to expanding Bay Area audiences through
performances of unparalleled excellence.
Founded: 1974
Specialized Field: Mozart; Ensemble
Status: Professional; Nonprofit
Budget: $10,000
Income Sources: American Symphony Orchestra
League; California Confederation of the Arts;
Association of California Symphony Orchestras; Private
and Corporate Donations; Ticket Sales
Season: July-August
Performs At: Berkeley's First Congregational Church;
San Farncisco's Palace of the Legion of Honor; Various
Venues
Annual Attendance: 800
Organization Type: Performing

703
NEW CENTURY CHAMBER ORCHESTRA
665 Third Street
Suite 200
San Francisco, CA 94107
Phone: 415-357-1111
Fax: 415-357-1101
e-mail: info@ncco.org
Web Site: www.ncco.org
Officers:
Chairman: Gordon P Getty
President: Paula Gambs
Treasurer: Richard Lonegran
Management:
Music Director: Nadja Salemo Sonnenberg
Executive Director: Parker E Monroe
Operations Director: Everett L Doner
Mission: To communicate vibrant orchestral music to
the audience, blending each instrument harmoniously
together without the guidance of a conductor.
Founded: 1992
Specialized Field: Chamber
Paid Staff: 7
Paid Artists: 19
Budget: $1.4 million
Income Sources: Private and Corporate Donations;
Foundations; Goverment Agencies
Season: September-June
Performs At: Herbst Theatre; First Congregational
Church; First United Methodist Church; Osher Marin
JCC
Annual Attendance: 4,000
Seating Capacity: 926
Year Built: 1991

704
PAUL DRESHER ENSEMBLE
Musical Traditions Inc
333 Valencia Street
Suite 301
San Francisco, CA 94103-3552
Phone: 415-558-9540
Fax: 510-834-4102
e-mail: info@dresherensemble.org
Web Site: www.dresherensemble.org
Management:
Artistic Director: Paul Dresher
Operations: Sarah Lockhart
Development: Michele Fromson
Utilizes: Commissioned Music; Theatre Companies
Status: Professional, Non-Profit
Budget: 150,000

Income Sources: Private and Corporate Donations,
Donations of Stock or other Appreciated Items
Season: October-May
Performs At: Various Venues
Organization Type: Performing; Touring; Educational

705
PHILHARMONIA BAROQUE ORCHESTRA
180 Redwood Street
Suite 200
San Francisco, CA 94102-3281
Phone: 415-252-1288
Fax: 415-252-1488
e-mail: info@philharmonia.org
Web Site: www.philharmonia.org
Officers:
President: Paul Sugarman
Treasurer: E Paul Swatek
Secretary: Douglas Tanner
Management:
Executive Director: Cindi Hubbard
Artistic Director: Jeff Phillips
Development: Courtney Beck
Utilizes: Guest Artists
Founded: 1981
Status: Professional, Non-Profit
Budget: 2.8 million
Income Sources: Ticket Sales, Private and Corporate
Donations
Season: August-June
Performs At: Performs throughout the Bay area, US
and in Europe
Annual Attendance: 30,000
Organization Type: Performing; Touring

706
ROVA SAXAPHONE QUARTET
333 12th Street
San Francisco, CA 94103
Phone: 415-487-1701
Fax: 415-487-1501
e-mail: rova@rova.org
Web Site: www.rova.org
Management:
Manager: Julia Melancon
Utilizes: Collaborating Artists; Collaborations;
Commissioned Composers; Commissioned Music;
Dance Companies; Dancers; Educators; Five Seasonal
Concerts; Grant Writers; Guest Companies; Guest
Directors; Guest Instructors; Guest Musical Directors;
Instructors; Lyricists; Multimedia; Organization
Contracts; Sign Language Translators
Status: Professional, Non-Profit
Income Sources: Ticket Sales, Members of Rova Arts,
Private and Corporate Donations, William and Flora
Hewlett Foundation
Season: September-October
Annual Attendance: 5,000
Organization Type: Performing; Touring

707
SAN FRANCISCO COMMUNITY MUSIC CENTER
544 Capp Street
San Francisco, CA 94110
Phone: 415-647-6015
Fax: 415-647-3890
e-mail: mission@sfcmc.org
Web Site: www.sfcmc.or
Officers:
President: Patricia Taylor Lee
VP: Catharine L Kalin
Secretary/Treasurer: Paul Sussman
Secretary: David J Neuman

Management:
Executive Director: Stephen R Shapiro PhD
Development: Fran Hildebrand
Marketing: Sonia Caltvedt
Mission: To make high quality music accessible to all people, regardless of their financial status.
Founded: 1921
Opened: 1921
Specialized Field: Music Education
Status: Non-Profit
Paid Staff: 11
Budget: $2 million
Income Sources: Endowment; Planned Giving Program; Private and Corporate Donations; Tuition
Performs At: Music Center Recital Hall
Affiliations: National Guild of Community of the Arts, California Arts Council
Annual Attendance: 18,000
Seating Capacity: 250
Rental Contact: Linda Hitchcock
Organization Type: Performing; Educational

708
SAN FRANCISCO CONTEMPORARY MUSIC PLAYERS

55 New Montgomery
Suite 708
San Francisco, CA 94105
Phone: 415-278-9566
Fax: 415-778-6402
e-mail: info@sfcmp.org
Web Site: www.sfcmp.org
Officers:
President: Susan Hartzell
Executive Director: Adam L Frey
Management:
Music Director/Conductor: David Milnes
Operations Director: Carrie Blanding
Mission: To professionally perform contemporary chamber music using a mixed ensemble.
Utilizes: Collaborations; Commissioned Composers; Five Seasonal Concerts; Guest Composers; Guest Musicians; Multimedia; Original Music Scores
Founded: 1971
Specialized Field: Chamber; Ensemble
Status: Professional; Nonprofit
Paid Staff: 3
Paid Artists: 45
Budget: 400,000
Income Sources: Government and Foundation Grants; Individual Donations; Ticket Sales; Stock Gift, Corporate Match, Planned Giving
Season: September-April
Performs At: Yerba Buena Center for the Arts
Annual Attendance: 2,000
Facility Category: Arts Center
Seating Capacity: 335
Organization Type: Performing; Touring

709
SAN FRANCISCO CONSERVATORY OF MUSIC

50 Oak Street
San Francisco, CA 94102-6011
Phone: 415-864-7326
Fax: 415-503-6299
e-mail: admit@sfcm.edu
Web Site: www.sfcm.edu
Officers:
President: Colin Murdoch
Dean: Mary Ellen Poole
Management:
Concert Operations Manager: Seth Ducey

Assist Concert Operations Manager: Lauren Brown
Mission: The training of classical musicians for professional careers in performing, composing, conducting and teaching.
Utilizes: Singers
Founded: 1917
Specialized Field: Orchestra; Chamber; Ensemble; Electronic; Live Electronic
Status: Nonprofit
Season: September-March
Performs At: Three performance spaces
Affiliations: Western Association of Colleges and Schools, National Association of Schools of Music
Annual Attendance: 22,000
Seating Capacity: 350
Organization Type: Performing; Educational

710
SAN FRANCISCO JAZZ ORGANIZATION

3 Embarcadero Center
Lobby Level
San Francisco, CA 94111
Phone: 415-398-5655
Fax: 415-398-5569
Toll-free: 800-850-7353
e-mail: sfjazz@sfjazz.org
Web Site: www.sfjazz.org
Officers:
Founder/President: Randall Kline
Chair: Srinija Srinivason
Vice Chair: Michael Lazarus
Secretary: Roberta Katz
Management:
Artistic Director: Randall Kline
Artist Administrator: Laura Evans
Marketing Director: Mike Charlasch
Mission: To feature the jazz performers from the local Bay Area as well as performers from around the country in San Francisco venues.
Utilizes: Poets
Founded: 1983
Specialized Field: Ensemble; Jazz; World Music
Status: Professional, Nonprofit
Paid Staff: 25
Volunteer Staff: 300
Paid Artists: 40
Non-paid Artists: 25
Budget: $6 million
Income Sources: Private and Corporate Donations, Organizations
Season: June-March
Performs At: Various Venues
Annual Attendance: 100,000
Organization Type: Performing; Resident; Educational; Presenter

711
SAN FRANCISCO SYMPHONY

Davies Symphony Hall
201 Van Ness Avenue
San Francisco, CA 94102
Phone: 415-552-8000
Fax: 415-431-6857
e-mail: tickets@sfsymhpony.org
Web Site: www.sfsymphony.org
Officers:
President: John D Goldman
Secretary: Robert R Tufts
Management:
Executive Director: Brent Assink
Artistic Director: Gregg Gleasner
Development: Robert W Lasher
Utilizes: Guest Artists

Founded: 1911
Status: Professional, Non-Profit
Budget: $150,000-400,000
Income Sources: Private and Corporate Donations, Ticket Sales, Advertising
Performs At: Louise M Davies Symphony Hall, Flint Center
Affiliations: American Symphony Orchestra League; Association of California Symphony Orchestras
Annual Attendance: 600,000
Seating Capacity: 2,700, 2,500
Organization Type: Performing; Touring; Resident; Educational

712
SAN FRANCISCO SYMPHONY YOUTH ORCHESTRA

Davies Symphony Hall
201 Van Ness Avenue
San Francisco, CA 94102
Phone: 415-503-5350
Fax: 415-431-6857
e-mail: yo@sfsymphony.org
Web Site: www.sfsymphony.org
Officers:
Chair: Claire N Barnes
Management:
Director: Benjamin Shwartz
Manager: Jefferson Packer
Utilizes: Guest Artists
Founded: 1981
Status: Non-Professional, Non-Profit
Income Sources: American Symphony Orchestra League; Youth Orchestra Division, Private and Corporate Donations
Performs At: Louise M Davies Symphony Hall
Annual Attendance: 25,000
Seating Capacity: 2,700
Organization Type: Performing; Touring; Resident; Educational; Sponsoring

713
EAST WEST MUSIC AND DANCE

7283 Coronado Drive
San Jose, CA 95129
Phone: 408-865-0654
Web Site: www.eastwestmusicanddance.com
Mission: All we do is teach. We do not sell or rent instruments of music. This leaves us free to specialize in one thing - providing the highest quality of music instruction.
Specialized Field: Instrumental

714
SAN JOSE CHAMBER MUSIC SOCIETY

PO Box 108
San Jose, CA 95103-0108
Phone: 408-286-5111
Fax: 510-651-0389
e-mail: sjcm@sjchambermusic.org
Web Site: www.sjchambermusic.org
Management:
Artistic Director: Ted Lorraine
Founded: 1986
Status: Non-Profit
Budget: 100,000
Income Sources: Private and Corporate Donations, Ticket Sales
Season: October-April
Performs At: Le Petit Trianon Theatre
Annual Attendance: 2,600
Seating Capacity: 348
Year Built: 1920
Organization Type: Performing

715
SAN JOSE JAZZ SOCIETY
145 W San Carlos
San Jose, CA 95113
Phone: 408-288-7557
Fax: 408-288-7598
e-mail: info@sanjosejazz.org
Web Site: www.sanjosejazz.org
Officers:
Chairman: Arturo Riera
Secretary: David Kennedy
Treasurer: Henry Wang
Management:
Executive Director: Geoff Roach
Marketing: Lucie Paye
Development: Madelyn Crawford
Founded: 1986
Status: Non-Profit
Income Sources: Grants; Donations; Sponsors; Members
Season: January-March
Performs At: Main Stage; Plaza de Cesar Chavez
Annual Attendance: 165,000
Seating Capacity: 200

716
SAN JOSE TAIKO GROUP
565 N 5th Street
PO Box 26895
San Jose, CA 95159
Phone: 408-293-9344
Fax: 408-293-9366
e-mail: taiko@taiko.org
Web Site: www.taiko.org
Officers:
Executive Director: Roy Hirabayashi
Management:
General Manager: Wisa Uemura
Artistic Director: PJ Hirabayashi
Associate Artistic Director: Franco Imperial
Mission: San Jose Taiko, with a deep respect of cultural traditions and a commitment to artistic excellence, is dedicated to the advancement of the taiko art form through the development of its world-class Performing Ensemble and the San Jose Taiko Conservatory.
Utilizes: Artists-in-Residence; Choreographers; Collaborating Artists; Collaborations; Commissioned Music; Five Seasonal Concerts; Guest Artists; Guest Companies; Guest Directors; Guest Musical Directors; Local Artists; Multimedia; Original Music Scores; Poets; Singers; Soloists; Student Interns
Founded: 1973
Specialized Field: Traditional Folk Arts/Music
Status: Professional, Nonprofit
Paid Staff: 1
Volunteer Staff: 20
Paid Artists: 5
Non-paid Artists: 4
Income Sources: Private and Corporate Donations, CD's, Ticket Sales, Performance Fees
Season: May-October
Performs At: Various Venues
Organization Type: Performing; Touring; Educational

717
SOUTH BAY GUITAR SOCIETY
72 North Fifth Street
Suite 18
San Jose, CA 95112
Phone: 408-292-0704
Fax: 408-280-0407
e-mail: sbgs@sbgs.org
Web Site: www.sbgs.org
Officers:
President: Jerry Snyder
VP: Tom Ingalz
Treasurer: Suzanne Patrick
Secretary: Bob Orr
Management:
Artistic Director: Jerry Snyder
Managing Director: Tom Ingalz
Mission: To make classical guitar music accessible to people of diverse cultures, ages, abilities and economic means by offering performance opportunities to professional and amateur muscians, providing classical guitar music education, and by presenting the music of many cultures to the public.
Founded: 1986
Specialized Field: Classical Guitar
Status: Nonprofit
Income Sources: Local Government Arts Grants, Ticket Sales, Member Dues, Concert Subscriptions
Season: September-April
Performs At: Le Petit Trianon Theatre, Espresso Garden & Cafe
Seating Capacity: 348
Organization Type: Presenters

718
SAN LUIS OBISPO MOZART FESTIVAL
3165 Broad Street
Suite 110
San Luis Obispo, CA 93401
Mailing Address: PO Box 311, San Luis Obispo, CA 93406
Phone: 805-781-3008
Fax: 805-781-3011
e-mail: info@mozartfestival.com
Web Site: www.mozartfestival.com
Officers:
President: Dwyne Willis
VP: Charles Myers
Secretary: Peter Zaleski
Treasurer: Rodger Mastako
Management:
Music Director: Scott Yoo
Executive Director: Curtis Pendleton
Project Manager: Cary Woll
Mission: To present a classical music festival highlighting Mozart and other classical and contemporary composers.
Utilizes: Commissioned Composers; Commissioned Music; Guest Composers; Guest Lecturers; Guest Musical Directors; Multimedia; Original Music Scores; Singers
Founded: 1971
Specialized Field: Mozart; Ensemble; Jazz; Children's Concerts; Educational
Status: Professional, Nonprofit
Volunteer Staff: 200
Budget: $150,000-$400,000
Income Sources: Private and Corporate Donations, Ticket Sales
Season: July-August
Performs At: Throughout San Luis Obispo County (Festival Sites)
Affiliations: San Luis Performing Arts Center; Wineries; Chapels
Seating Capacity: 1,300
Organization Type: Performing; Educational

719
SAN LUIS OBISPO SYMPHONY
PO Box 658
San Luis Obispo, CA 93406
Phone: 805-543-3533
Fax: 805-781-3534
e-mail: staff@slosymphony.com
Web Site: www.slosymphony.com
Officers:
President: Dr. Michael Zigelman
Treasurer: Cle Van Beurden
Management:
Music Director/Conductor: Michael Nowak
Co-Concertmaster: Pam Dassenko
Co-Concertmaster: Paul Severtson
Music Education Director: Andrea Stoner
Executive Director: Brian Hermanson
Mission: To support an outstanding community orchestra, to foster symphonic and chamber music education and to contribute to the cultural and economic vitality of the central coast community.
Utilizes: Collaborations; Commissioned Composers; Community Members; Five Seasonal Concerts; Singers; Soloists; Students
Founded: 1961
Specialized Field: Orchestra
Paid Staff: 7
Paid Artists: 83
Budget: $260,000-1,300,000
Income Sources: Ticket Sales; Donations; Grants; Fundraisers; Tuition
Season: October-June
Performs At: Performing Arts Center, Clark Center for the Performing Arts, United Methodist Church of Los Osos, Avila Beach Resort
Annual Attendance: 10,000
Seating Capacity: 1100 (Center) 3000 (Avila) 300-600 (sm. venu)
Organization Type: Performing, Touring

720
CALIFORNIA PHILHARMONIC ORCHESTRA
1120 Huntington Drive
San Marino, CA 91108
Phone: 626-300-8200
Fax: 626-300-8010
e-mail: info@calphil.org
Web Site: www.calphil.org
Officers:
President/CEO: Victor Vener
Chairman Emeritus: Robert W Miller
Chairman: Roger Ward
Controller: Curtis Morris
Management:
Music Director: Victor Vener
Artistic Administrator: Roger Allen Ward
Mission: To bring excellent professional performances of great music to the widest possible audience.
Founded: 1997
Specialized Field: Classical
Paid Staff: 10
Volunteer Staff: 500
Paid Artists: 70
Income Sources: Ticket Sales; Gifts from Corporate Sponsors; Community Foundations and Private Donations
Season: January-May
Performs At: Los Angeles County Arboretum and Botanic Garden
Annual Attendance: 170,000
Facility Category: Outdoor Amphitheatre

721
MARIN SYMPHONY ORCHESTRA
4340 Redwood Highway
Suite 409C
San Rafael, CA 94903
Phone: 415-479-8100
Fax: 415-479-8110
e-mail: greatmusic@marinsymphony.org
Web Site: www.marinsymphony.org
Management:
Artistic Director: Alasdair Neale
Executive Director: Noralee Monestere
Marketing: Suzanne Crawford
Utilizes: Commissioned Composers;
Composers-in-Residence; Grant Writers; Guest
Accompanists; Guest Companies; Guest Designers;
Guest Lecturers; Instructors; Multimedia; Music;
Organization Contracts; Original Music Scores; Poets;
Sign Language Translators; Singers
Budget: 1.2 million
Season: October-May
Performs At: Marin Veterans' Memorial Auditorium in
San Rafael
Affiliations: Association of California Symphony
Orchestra, Americany Symphony Orchestra League
Annual Attendance: 24,000
Seating Capacity: 2,000
Architect: Frank Lloyd Wright

722
MARIN SYMPHONY YOUTH ORCHESTRA
4340 Redwood Highway
Suite 409C
San Rafael, CA 94903
Phone: 415-479-8100
Fax: 415-479-8110
e-mail: greatmusic@marinsymphony.org
Web Site: www.marinsymphony.org
Management:
Artistic Director: George Thompson
Executive Director: Noralee Monestere
Marketing: Suzanne Crawford
Income Sources: American Symphony Orchestra
League, Youth Orchestra Division; Private and
Corporate Donations; Ticket Sales; Tuition
Season: September-June
Performs At: San Rafael High School Auditorium
Annual Attendance: 3,000
Organization Type: Performing; Touring; Educational;
Sponsoring

723
PACIFIC SYMPHONY
3631 S Harbor Blvd
Suite 100
Santa Ana, CA 92704
Phone: 714-755-5788
Fax: 714-755-5789
e-mail: info@pacificsymphony.org
Web Site: www.pacificsymphony.org
Officers:
Chairman: John W Daniels
President: John E Forsyte
Treasurer: Sarah J Anderson
Secretary: Susan Anderrson
Management:
Music Director: Carl St Clair
Principal Pops Conductor: Richard Kaufman
Assistant Conductor: Maxim Eshkenazy
Concertmaster: Raymond Kobler

Mission: Offers moving musical experiences with
repertoire ranging from the great orchestral
masterworks to music from today's most prominent
composers, highlighted by the annual American
Composers Festival.
Founded: 1978
Specialized Field: Orchestra
Volunteer Staff: 400
Budget: 3,600,000-10,000,000
Income Sources: Private and Corporate Donations,
Ticket Sales, Foundations, Luncheons, Fundraisers
Season: All Year
Performs At: Orange County Performing Arts Center,
Summer Concerts in the park in Santa Ana and
Anaheim
Annual Attendance: 18,000

724
MUSIC ACADEMY OF THE WEST
1070 Fairway Road
Santa Barbara, CA 93108-2899
Phone: 805-969-4726
Fax: 805-969-0686
e-mail: admissions@musicacademy.org
Web Site: www.musicacademy.org
Officers:
President: Scott Reed
VP Finance: Barbara Robertson
VP Marketing/Communications: Susan Gwynne
Management:
VP Artistic Programs: Richard Feit
Dean of Students: Tiffany Schoemaker
Special Events Manager: Brooke E Jacobs
Director Operations: Leslie Kelleher
Mission: The Music Academy of the West is dedicated
to advancing the development of gifted young classical
musicians and classical music professionals through a
unique combination of intensive personal instruction,
educational programs and performance opportunities,
all of the highest quality.
Utilizes: Artists-in-Residence; Collaborating Artists;
Grant Writers; Guest Artists; Guest Companies; Guest
Composers; Guest Musical Directors; Guest Musicians;
Multimedia
Founded: 1947
Specialized Field: Chamber; Classical; Opera;
Orchestra
Paid Staff: 25
Budget: $5,000,000-6,000,000
Income Sources: Individual Contributions;
Foundations; Corporations; Stock Gifts; Planned Giving
Season: June-August
Performs At: Campus and City Venues
Affiliations: Association of California Symphony
Orchestra, League of American Orchestras
Annual Attendance: 36,000
Facility Category: Recital Hall
Rental Contact: Leslie Kelleher

725
SANTA BARBARA CHAMBER ORCHESTRA
PO Box 90903
Santa Barbara, CA 93101
Phone: 805-966-2441
Fax: 805-966-2448
e-mail: info@sbco.org
Web Site: www.sbco.org
Officers:
President: Donald Lafler
Chairman: Pamela Taylor
Management:
Music Director/Conductor: Heiichiro Ohyama
Concertmaster: Amy Hershberger

General Manager: Daniel Kepl
Artistic Operations Manager: Rachel Galvin
Development Director: Leslie Bisno
Mission: To present the Santa Barbara community with
high quality music by skilled musicians and soloists.
Founded: 1978
Specialized Field: Chamber; Orchestra
Paid Staff: 4
Paid Artists: 30
Budget: 450,000-500,000
Income Sources: Private and Corporate Donations,
Matching Gifts, Donations of Stock, Planned Giving
Season: October-March
Performs At: Lobero Theatre, Natural History Museum
Annual Attendance: 11,000
Seating Capacity: 680

726
SANTA BARBARA SYMPHONY ASSOCIATION
1330 State Street
Suite 102
Santa Barbara, CA 93101
Phone: 805-898-9386
Fax: 805-898-9326
e-mail: info@thesymphony.org
Web Site: www.thesymphony.org
Officers:
President: Stefan Riesenfeld
VP: Paksy Plackis-Cheng
Treasurer: Howard Simon
Secretary: John Matuszeski
Management:
Music & Artistic Director: Nir Kabaretti
Conductor Laureate: Gisele Ben-Dor
Principal Concertmaster: Caroline Campbell
Executive Director: John Robinson
Mission: To be a highly respected symphony orchestra
performing great works with passion and excellence.
Founded: 1953
Specialized Field: Orchestra
Paid Staff: 11
Volunteer Staff: 3
Budget: $1,050,000-3,600,000
Income Sources: Sustaining Funds; Endowment Fund;
Private and Corporate Donations ;Planned Giving;
Foundations
Season: October-May
Performs At: Arlington Theatre
Annual Attendance: 40,000
Seating Capacity: 1,550

727
WEST COAST CHAMBER ORCHESTRA
1812 La Coronilla Drive
Santa Barbara, CA 93109
Phone: 805-962-6609
Fax: 805-962-6609
e-mail: info@westcoastsymphony.com
Web Site: www.westcoastsymphony.com
Officers:
President: Christopher Story IV
VP: Jacqueline Sarrgeri
Secretary: Lawrence Hilton
Treasurer: Gary Gray
Management:
Music Director/Conductor: Christopher Story VI
Mission: To present the finest music from local
musicians.
Utilizes: Guest Artists
Founded: 1987
Specialized Field: Symphony; Orchestra; Chamber
Status: Professional, Nonprofit
Volunteer Staff: 1

All listings are in alphabetical order by state, then city, then organization within the city.

Paid Artists: 20
Non-paid Artists: 2
Budget: 40,000
Income Sources: Private and Corporate Donations, Ticket Sales
Performs At: Trinity Episcopal Church
Annual Attendance: 800
Facility Category: Church
Organization Type: Performing

728
YELLOW BIRD MUSIC STUDIO

2726 De La Vina
Santa Barbara, CA 93105
Phone: 805-898-9070
e-mail: deebird6@yahoo.com
Web Site: www.yellowbirdmusic.com
Officers:
    Owner: Alexandra Adams
Management:
    Maestro: Alexandra Adams
Mission: Yellow Bird Music incorporates Kindermusik® based curriculum along with brand new ways to explore the world musically. Some new and exciting additions to the program include special performances by local musicians giving children an up-close and personal opportunity to view musical expression by professionals. Yellow Bird Music also features special events and offers birthday and tea parties. Yellow Bird Music is an unique place to explore.
Specialized Field: Instrumental

729
SANTA CRUZ BAROQUE FESTIVAL

PO Box 482
Santa Cruz, CA 95061
Phone: 831-457-9693
e-mail: info@scbaroque.org
Web Site: www.scbaroque.org
Officers:
    Founder: Linda Burman-Hall
    President: Kathryn Tobish
    VP: Patti Julin
    Treasurer: Donald Wilson
    Secretary: Sophy Chou
Management:
    Artistic Director: Linda Burman-Hall
    General Manager: Alissa Roedig
Mission: The Santa Cruz Baroque Festival has brought to life a broad spectrum of music written by composers of centuries past.
Founded: 1974
Specialized Field: Ensemble; Baroque
Status: Professional, Nonprofit
Budget: 40,000
Income Sources: Private and Corporate Donations, Government Agencies, Advertisers, Media, Grants
Season: February-May
Performs At: Various Auditoriums
Annual Attendance: 1,500
Facility Category: Various auditoriums
Organization Type: Performing; Sponsoring

730
SANTA CRUZ COUNTY SYMPHONY

307 Church Street
Santa Cruz, CA 95060
Phone: 831-462-0553
Fax: 831-426-1193
e-mail: sccs@santacruzsymphony.org
Web Site: www.santacruzsymphony.com
Officers:
    President: Beth Bates
    Executive Director: Virginia Wright

Management:
    Music Director: John Larry Granger
    Executive Director: Mark Huber
    Production Manager: Rick Larsen
    Stage Manager: Eileen Flynn
Utilizes: Collaborations; Guest Artists; Guest Musical Directors; Guest Musicians; Guest Writers; Instructors; Resident Artists
Founded: 1957
Specialized Field: Classical
Status: Professional
Paid Staff: 4
Paid Artists: 80
Budget: $260,000-1,050,000
Income Sources: Private and Corporate Donations, Ticket Sales, Sponsoring a Concert
Season: September-February
Performs At: Santa Cruz Civic Auditorium, Henry J Mello Center
Annual Attendance: 15,000
Facility Category: Civic Auditorium
Seating Capacity: 1,300
Year Built: 1930

731
BRENTWOOD-WESTWOOD SYMPHONY ORCHESTRA

1010 19th Street
Suite 8
Santa Monica, CA 90403
Phone: 310-829-3149
e-mail: alvin@brentwoodwestwoodsymphony.org
Web Site: www.brentwoodwestwoodsymphony.org
Officers:
    Founder: Alvin Mills
    Chairwoman: Erin Prouty
    President: Bob Engelman
    Treasurer: George Beck
    Secretary: Grusha Paterson-Mills
Management:
    Music Director/Conductor: Alvin Mills
    General Manager: Grusha Paterson-Mills
Mission: In these times of turmoil and unrest music is still the universal language that enriches our lives. Let us share this treasure with each other.
Founded: 1952
Specialized Field: Symphony
Status: Nonprofit
Budget: 100,000-150,000
Income Sources: Grants, Foundations, Private and Corporate Donations
Season: October-May
Performs At: Paul Revere Middle School Auditorium
Annual Attendance: 12,000

732
LOS ANGELES BAROQUE ORCHESTRA

1007 Montant Avenue
Suite 304
Santa Monica, CA 90403
Phone: 323-664-2535
Fax: 310-393-6423
e-mail: music@labaroque.org
Web Site: www.labaroque.org
Management:
    Music Director: Gregory Maldonado
    Managing Director: Annette Simons
Founded: 1985
Specialized Field: Baroque
Status: Professional
Budget: $260,000-1,050,000
Income Sources: Grant Awards from National Endowment for the Arts, James Irvine Foundation, Andrew Mellon Foundation, California Arts Council

Performs At: Water Garden; Zipper Concert Hall; Miles Memorial Playhouse

733
SANTA MONICA MUSIC CENTER (SMMC)

1901 Santa Monica Boulevard
Santa Monica, CA 90404
Phone: 310-453-1928
Fax: 310-453-0619
e-mail: pfernandez@santamonicamusic.com
Web Site: www.santamonicamusic.com
Officers:
    President/Director: Paul Fernandez
    VP/General Manager: Victor Fernandez
    Sales Manager: Craig Spendlove
Mission: Our goal to provide the best in products and service and educational excellence is foremost in our planning and direction.
Founded: 1972
Specialized Field: Instrumental
Facility Category: Music School

734
SANTA MONICA SYMPHONY ORCHESTRA

PO Box 3101
Santa Monica, CA 90408-3101
Phone: 310-395-6330
e-mail: office@smsymphony.org
Web Site: www.smsymphony.org
Officers:
    Chair/President: Nathaniel Trives
    Treasurer: Richard Lawrencfe
    Secretary: Ian McIlraith
Management:
    Music Director/Conductor: Allen Gross
    Concertmaster: David Stenske
    Operations Manager: Ryan Bullard
    Stage Manager: Robert Godfrey
Mission: To provide high-quality admission-free concerts from the classical and contemporary symphony repertoire to Santa Monica and West Lost Angeles.
Founded: 1945
Specialized Field: Orchestra
Status: Nonprofit
Budget: $35,000-100,000
Income Sources: Private and Corporate Donations, Grants from City of Santa Monica, County of Los Angeles, Friends of the Santa Monica Symphony
Season: October-May
Performs At: Santa Monica Civic Auditorium
Affiliations: Association of California Symphony Orchestra, American Symphony Orchestra League, Santa Monica Chamber of Comemrce
Annual Attendance: 5,600
Seating Capacity: 3,000
Year Built: 1958

735
SANTA ROSA JUNIOR COLLEGE CHAMBER CONCERT SERIES

1501 Mendocino Avenue
Music Department
Santa Rosa, CA 95401
Phone: 707-427-4249
Fax: 707-521-7988
e-mail: ljohns@santarosa.edu
Web Site: www.santarosa.edu/music/chamber
Officers:
    Department Chair: Bennett Friedman
Management:
    Administrative Assistant: Linda Johns

Mission: Santa Rosa Junior College's Chamber Concert Series has been delighting audiences with wonderful music performed by superb musicians in an intimate environment.
Specialized Field: Classical; Chamber
Income Sources: Private and Corporate Donations, Ticket Sales
Season: October-December
Performs At: Burbank Auditorium, Randolph Newman Auditorium
Annual Attendance: 1,200
Seating Capacity: 700, 350

736
SANTA ROSA SYMPHONY

50 Santa Rosa Avenue
Suite 410
Santa Rosa, CA 95404
Phone: 707-546-7097
Fax: 707-546-0460
e-mail: info@santarosasymphony.com
Web Site: www.santarosasymphony.com
Officers:
   President: Eric Rossin
   VP: Charlie Schlangen
   Treasurer: Jim Hinton
   Secretary: Peggy Elliott
Management:
   Music Director: Bruno Ferrandis
   Executive Director: Alan Silow
   Conductor Laureate: Jeffrey Kahane
   Choral Director: Robert Worth
   Concertmaster: Joseph Edelberg
   Artistic Operations Director: Tim Beswick
   Marketing Director: Sara Obuchowski
Mission: To inspire and engage people with the highest quality musical performances and educational programs.
Utilizes: Collaborations; Commissioned Composers; Composers-in-Residence; Guest Artists; Guest Directors; Guest Musicians; Original Music Scores; Resident Artists; Sign Language Translators; Singers
Founded: 1928
Specialized Field: Symphony; Orchestra; Chamber; Ensemble
Status: Nonprofit
Paid Staff: 13
Volunteer Staff: 100
Paid Artists: 225
Budget: $20 Million
Income Sources: Underwriters, Grants, Donations, Endowments, Ticket Sales
Season: October-May
Performs At: Wells Fargo Center for the Arts
Affiliations: Association of California Symphony Orchestras, American Symphony Orchestra League
Annual Attendance: 50,000
Seating Capacity: 1,500
Organization Type: Performing; Resident; Educational

737
STANFORD SYMPHONY ORCHESTRA

Department of Music Stanford University
Braun Music Center
541 Lasuen Mall
Stanford, CA 94305-3076
Phone: 650-724-6738
Fax: 650-725-2686
e-mail: marioch@stanford.edu
Web Site: music.stanford.edu/deptinfo/index.hmtl
Officers:
   Chairman: Stephen M Sano
   Financial Officer: Velda Williams
Management:

Administrative Director: Mario Champagne
Facilities/Production Manager: Scott Kepley
Publicist: Delane Haro
Academic Administrator: Debbie Barney
Mission: The Stanford Symphony Orchestra is an on campus student organization supported by the Music Department and the Associated Students of Stanford University.
Utilizes: Theatre Companies
Founded: 1891
Paid Staff: 2
Volunteer Staff: 5
Budget: $35,000-100,000
Income Sources: Friends of Music at Stanford, Private and Corporate Donations, Ticket Sales
Season: October-June
Performs At: Dinkelspiel Auditorium, Campbell Recital Hall
Facility Category: Recital Hall (Campbell)
Seating Capacity: 221
Year Built: 1985
Organization Type: Performing, Educational, Touring

738
CONSERVATORY OF MUSIC

University of the Pacific
3601 Pacific Avenue
Stockton, CA 95211
Phone: 209-946-2285
Web Site: www.pacific.edu
Officers:
   Interim Dean: William Hipp
Management:
   Development Director: Renna Beninoris
   Stage/Technical Direcgtor: James Gonzales
   Operations Manager: Stephen Perdicaris
Mission: We are dedicated to the education and training of musicians for the highest levels of artistic performance, creative endeavor and intellectual inquiry.
Specialized Field: Symphony
Budget: $35,000
Income Sources: Ticket Sales, Private and Corporate Donations, Grants
Season: October-April
Performs At: Faye Spanos Concert Hall
Annual Attendance: 12,000
Seating Capacity: 1,000

739
FRIENDS OF CHAMBER MUSIC

University of the Pacific
PO Box 4874
Stockton, CA 95204
Phone: 209-946-0540
e-mail: info@chambermusicfriends.org
Web Site: www.chambermusicfriends.org
Officers:
   President: Carole Gilbertson
   VP: Dwane Milnes
   Treasurer: Sara milnes Milnes
   Secretary: Madeleine Lynch
Mission: The mission of the Friends of Chamber Music of Stockton is to develop, sustain and advance an interest in professional quality chamber music for the citizens of Stockton and surrounding communities.
Founded: 1955
Specialized Field: Chamber
Status: Nonprofit
Volunteer Staff: 8
Paid Artists: 19
Income Sources: Ticket Sales, Private and Corporate Donations
Season: September-March

Performs At: Faye Spanos Concert Hall in the Conservatory of Music, University of the Pacific
Seating Capacity: 1,000

740
STOCKTON SYMPHONY ASSOCIATION

1024 Robinhood Drive
Stockton, CA 95207
Phone: 209-951-0196
Fax: 209-951-1050
e-mail: jkenworthy@stocktonsymphony.org
Web Site: www.stocktonsymphony.org
Officers:
   President: Mike Whelan
   Treasurer: Daniel Terry
   Secretary: Maury Marengo
Management:
   Music Director/Conductor: Peter Jaffe
   Executive Director: Jane E Kenworthy
   Orchestra Personnel Manager: Joanna Pinckney
Mission: The mission of the Stockton Symphony is to engage, educate and inspire the community through a commitment to excellence in its performances and programs.
Utilizes: Commissioned Composers; Guest Artists; Guest Musical Directors; Guest Musicians; Instructors; Multimedia; Music; Original Music Scores; Sign Language Translators; Soloists
Founded: 1926
Specialized Field: Symphonic Music
Status: Professional, Nonprofit
Paid Staff: 90
Paid Artists: 6
Budget: $1.3 Million
Income Sources: Ticket Sales, Contributions, Grants
Season: September-April
Performs At: Atherton Auditorium, San Joaquin Delta College, Stockton Memorial Civic Auditorium, Stockton's Weber Point Event Center
Affiliations: American Symphony Orchestra League, Association of California Symphony Orchestras
Annual Attendance: 35,000
Type of Stage: Proceisum
Seating Capacity: 1,456
Year Built: 1976
Organization Type: Performing; Educational

741
CONEJO POPS ORCHESTRA

3648 Mountclef Boulevard
Thousand Oaks, CA 91358
Phone: 805-492-2764
Fax: 805-498-7092
Management:
   Music Director/Conductor: Elmer Ramsey
Mission: Dedicated to maintaining a nonprofit corporation for the education and enhancement of the musical, cultural and social interests of the community, through the medium of a symphony orchestra.
Utilizes: Guest Artists; Singers
Founded: 1961
Specialized Field: Symphony; Chamber
Status: Semi-Professional; Nonprofit
Paid Staff: 37
Income Sources: American Symphony Orchestra League, Private and Corporate Donations, Ticket Sales
Performs At: Preus-Brandt Forum; California Lutheran University
Seating Capacity: 246
Organization Type: Performing

742
NEW WEST SYMPHONY ASSOCIATION
2100 E Thousand Oaks Boulevard
Suite D
Thousand Oaks, CA 91362
Phone: 805-497-5800
Fax: 805-497-5839
e-mail: symphony@newwestsymphony.org
Web Site: www.newwestsymphony.org
Officers:
    President: Leonard Linton
    Interim VP: Judith Linton
    Treasurer: Neil Sunkin Esq
    Secretary: Miriam Wille
Management:
    Music Director/Conductor: Boris Brott
    Executive Director: Nelson Dodge
    Concertmaster: Charles Stegeman
    Concertmaster: Elizabeth Pitcairn
Mission: To present concerts of classical music for the community and to promote an increased public knowledge and appreciation of concert music.
Utilizes: Commissioned Composers; Commissioned Music; Composers-in-Residence; Educators; Guest Accompanists; Guest Artists; Guest Companies; Guest Composers; Guest Conductors; Guest Lecturers; Guest Musical Directors; Guest Musicians; Instructors; Local Artists; Multimedia; Music; Original Music Scores; Sign Language Translators; Singers
Founded: 1995
Specialized Field: Symphony; Chamber; Ensemble
Status: Professional, Nonprofit
Paid Staff: 9
Budget: 2 million
Season: October-May
Performs At: Oxnard Performing Arts Center
Annual Attendance: 37,000
Facility Category: Multi-Purpose Theatre
Type of Stage: Proscenium
Seating Capacity: 528
Organization Type: Performing

743
SYMPHONY ORCHESTRA
El Camino College
Center for the Arts
16007 Crenshaw Boulevard
Torrance, CA 90506
Phone: 310-532-3670
Fax: 310-660-3734
Toll-free: 800-832-2787
e-mail: dteter@elcamino.edu
Web Site: www.elcamino.edu
Officers:
    President: Mary E Combs
    VP: Nathaniel Jackson
    Secretary: Maureen O'Donnell
Management:
    Music Director: Dane Teter
    Executive Director: Bruce Spain
    Production Manager: Nancy Adler
    Stage Manager: Jerry Root
Mission: The mission of the El Camino College Center for the Arts is to present high quality performing arts in a positive environment for the education and entertainment of the student, faculty, staff and communities.
Utilizes: Poets
Founded: 1949
Specialized Field: Orchestra
Status: Non-Professional, Nonprofit
Paid Staff: 1

Income Sources: Ticket Sales, Private and Corporate Donations, Grants
Season: September-June
Performs At: Marsee Auditorium
Annual Attendance: 700
Seating Capacity: 2,000
Organization Type: Performing; Educational

744
HERB ALPERT SCHOOL OF MUSIC
California Institute of the Arts
24700 McBean Parkway
Valencia, CA 91355
Phone: 661-253-7817
Fax: 661-255-0938
Toll-free: 800-545-2787
e-mail: info@music.calarts.edu
Web Site: www.music.calarts.edu
Officers:
    Dean/Chair: Dean Rosenboom
    President: Steven D Lavine
Management:
    Artistic Director: David Rosenboom
Mission: Committed to providing the resources and support necessary for our intimate community of students and faculty to stretch and reach beyond themselves and their disciplines to new heights of art making and thinking.
Founded: 1970
Specialized Field: Symphony; Orchestra; Chamber; Classical; Jazz
Status: Professional, Nonprofit
Income Sources: Private and Corporate Donations, Ticket Sales, Tuition
Season: September-January
Performs At: Roy O. Disney Music Hall
Seating Capacity: 266
Year Built: 1970
Year Remodeled: 1994
Organization Type: Resident

745
VALLEJO SYMPHONY ASSOCIATION
PO Box 568
Vallejo, CA 94590
Phone: 707-643-4441
Fax: 707-643-5746
e-mail: info@vallejosymphony.org
Web Site: www.vallejosymphony.org
Officers:
    President: Bonnie Bernhardt
    VP: Rosemary Thurston
Management:
    Music Director/Conductor: David Ramadanoff
    Concertmaster: Kathleen Comalli Dillon
    Personnel Manager: Holly Nichols
Mission: To enjoy year round entertainment from this symphony that performs everything from classical to pops.
Utilizes: Guest Accompanists; Guest Musical Directors
Founded: 1931
Specialized Field: Symphony; Orchestra
Paid Staff: 6
Volunteer Staff: 25
Paid Artists: 85
Budget: $150,000-200,000
Income Sources: Donors, Subscribers, Vallejo Symphony League, Fundraisers
Season: September-April
Performs At: Hogan Auditorium
Annual Attendance: 800

746
TULARE COUNTY SYMPHONY
208 W Main Street
Suite 5A
Visalia, CA 93291
Phone: 559-732-8600
Fax: 559-732-8617
e-mail: tcsymph@abcglobal.net
Web Site: www.tcsymphony.org
Officers:
    President: Phil Bourdette
    Executive Director: Francie Levy
    Vice President: Ellen Gorelick
    Secretary: Roger Hall
Mission: To educate the community and introduce people to symphonic music.
Utilizes: Guest Artists; Guest Companies
Founded: 1960
Specialized Field: Symphony; Orchestra
Status: Professional, Nonprofit
Paid Staff: 2
Volunteer Staff: 20
Paid Artists: 75
Budget: $350,000
Income Sources: Ticket Sales; Sponsorships; Grants; Donations
Season: September-April
Performs At: Visalia Fox Theatre
Annual Attendance: 8,000
Facility Category: Fox Theatre
Seating Capacity: 1,200
Year Built: 1929
Year Remodeled: 1999
Rental Contact: Paul Fry
Organization Type: Performing; Resident; Educational

747
CALIFORNIA SYMPHONY
877 Ygnacio Valley Road
Suite 200
Walnut Creek, CA 94596
Phone: 925-280-2490
Fax: 925-280-2494
e-mail: info@californiasymphony.org
Web Site: www.californiasymphony.org
Officers:
    Founder: Barry Jekowsky
    Chairman: Gordon Getty
    President: William M Eames
    Treasurer: Lewis W Teel
    Secretary: Carlotta Dathe
Management:
    Music Director: Barry Jekowsky
    Executive Director: Stacey Street
    Concertmaster: Roy Malan
    Development Director: Jenna Ervice
Mission: The California Symphony is passionately committed to providing music education programs to children and adults in the San Francisco East Bay.
Founded: 1986
Specialized Field: Symphony
Status: Professional
Paid Staff: 6
Volunteer Staff: 62
Paid Artists: 5
Budget: $1,050,000-3,600,000
Income Sources: Private and Corporate Donations
Season: September-April
Performs At: Concord Pavilio; Dean Lesher Regional Center for the Arts, Hofmann Theatre; Todos Santos Plaza
Annual Attendance: 33,000
Seating Capacity: 12,000

Year Built: 1970

748
SACRAMENTO JAZZ JUBILEE
2787 Del Monte Street
West Sacramento, CA 95691
Phone: 916-372-5277
e-mail: info@sacjazz.com
Web Site: www.sacjazz.com
Officers:
President: Jim Roberson
VP: Molly Greene
Treasurer: Lisa Negri
Secretary: Alicia Fullbright
Management:
Executive Director: Jill Harper
Mission: The mission of the Sacramento Jazz Jubilee is to preserve and promote traditional jazz, Dixieland and classic jazz music.
Founded: 1974
Specialized Field: Jazz
Status: Nonprofit
Paid Staff: 4
Volunteer Staff: 2500
Budget: $1.8 million
Income Sources: Admissions, Sponsorships, Grants, Food Concession Sales, Souvenir Sales, Private and Corporate Donations, Memberships, Ticket Sales
Season: September-June
Performs At: Old Sacramento and Midtown
Affiliations: 30 Sacramento Area Venues (Indoor & Outdoor)
Annual Attendance: 65,000 +/-
Seating Capacity: 250-1,800

749
RIO HONDO SYMPHONY ASSOCIATION
PO Box 495
Whittier, CA 90608
Phone: 562-698-8626
e-mail: rhsymphony@verizonmail.com
Web Site: www.riohondosymphony.org
Officers:
President: Bonnie Price
VP: Laurie Baccus
Secretary: Carolyn McFarland
Treasurer: Charles Barth
Management:
General Manager: Sue Walker
Orchestra Manager: Lue Ann Barth
Orchestra Manager: Kathleen Egbert
Mission: To provide free concerts of symphonic music for the residents in the Rio Hondo Area and to encourage young talented artists with musical pursuits.
Founded: 1933
Specialized Field: Symphony; Orchestra
Status: Nonprofit
Paid Staff: 5
Income Sources: Rio Hondo Symphony Guild, Private and Corporate Donatins, Grants, Endowment, Tuition
Season: October-April
Performs At: Victor Lopez Auditorium, Whittier Union High School
Annual Attendance: 5,000
Organization Type: Performing; Resident

750
WHITTIER COLLEGE BACH FESTIVAL
Whittier College
13406 E Philadelphia Street
PO Box 634
Whittier, CA 90608
Phone: 562-907-4237
Fax: 562-907-4592
e-mail: dlozano@whittier.edu
Web Site: www.whittier.edu/academic/musicdepartment
Management:
Director: Danilo Lozano
Mission: To present diverse, high quality music in appropriate venues throughout the San Gabriel Valley.
Specialized Field: Bach; Ensemble
Budget: $10,000
Season: October-June
Performs At: Whittier College Campus; Skyrose Chapel, Various Venues
Annual Attendance: 900
Facility Category: Whittier College Memorial Chapel & other venues
Seating Capacity: 300

751
HARMONIA BAROQUE PLAYERS
19795 Villager Circle
Yorba Linda, CA 92886-4452
Phone: 714-970-8545
e-mail: harmoniabaroque@sbcglobal.net
Web Site: www.harmoniabaroque.org
Management:
Director: Marika Frankl
Mission: Harmonia Baroque has been established to perform rich and plentiful repertoire written for small ensembles in the Renaissance and Baroque period. The ensemble is committed to perform not only the popular works, but also the lesser known masterpieces of these times. The groups is also deeply committed to providing affordable and high quality performances.
Utilizes: Guest Musical Directors; Multimedia
Founded: 1981
Specialized Field: Baroque
Volunteer Staff: 15
Non-paid Artists: 6
Income Sources: Box Office; Private Donations
Season: October-May
Performs At: Oneonta Congregational Church; Concordia University; Peninsula Community Church; Norton Simon Museum; San Diego Art Museum
Affiliations: Arts Orange County
Annual Attendance: 700

752
NAPA VALLEY SYMPHONY
100 California Drive
Yountville, CA 94599
Mailing Address: 3379 Solano Ave., Suite 1000, Napa CA 94558
Phone: 707-944-9910
Fax: 707-944-9912
e-mail: info@napavalleysymphony.org
Web Site: www.napavalleysymphony.org
Officers:
President: Kent Kuhlmann
VP: Cookie Deckter
Secretary: Marissa Schleicher
Management:
Production Manager: James Collins
Executive Director: Richard Aldag
Operations Manager: Karen Frost
Development Director: Andrea Lyons
Mission: To provide the Napa Valley with Symphonic music performances and education programs.
Founded: 1933
Specialized Field: Symphony
Status: Non-Profit
Paid Staff: 10
Paid Artists: 55
Budget: $1 Million

Income Sources: Fundraisers, Private and Corporate Donations, Grants, Foundations
Performs At: Lincoln Theatre; Yountville
Annual Attendance: 15,000
Seating Capacity: 1,200
Organization Type: Performing; Educational

Colorado

753
AURORA SYMPHONY ORCHESTRA
PO Box 4441481
Aurora, CO 80044
Phone: 303-873-6622
e-mail: info@aurorasymphony.org
Web Site: www.aurorasymphony.org
Officers:
Chairman: E Dwight Taylor Esq
Treasurer: Claire Junker-Counts
Secretary: Lori Hanson
Management:
Music Director/Conductor: Richard Niezen
Executive Director: Rich Duston
Concertmaster: Samuel Baker
Assistant Concertmaster: Magdalena Lesniak
Mission: The Aurora Symphony Orchestra have a strong commitment to educating the young musicians in the community to develop a lifelong love of music.
Specialized Field: Orchestra

754
BOULDER BACH FESTIVAL
PO Box 1896
Boulder, CO 80306
Phone: 303-776-9666
Fax: 303-682-9888
e-mail: BolderBach@aol.com
Web Site: www.boulderbachfest.org
Officers:
Co-President: Eileen O'Neill
Co-President: Frederick Denny
Executive Director: Carol Bartel
Treasurer: Thurston Manning
Production Manager: Jeff Rusnak
Secretary: Albert Lundell
Management:
Music Director: Robert Spillman
Concertmaster: William Terwilliger
Assistant Concertmaster: Annamaria Karacson
Chorus Manager: Caroline Van Pelt
Board Member/Volunteer Coordinator: Judy Barkley
Mission: To present the music of Johann Sebastian Bach and to encourage knowledge and appreciation of the Baroque master. Provides a three day festival each year, featuring an orchestra, chorus, and soloists drawn from the pool of area musicians, with a few nationally-known artists from other parts of the country.
Founded: 1981
Specialized Field: Bach; Ensemble
Status: Professional, Nonprofit
Paid Staff: 1
Volunteer Staff: 200
Paid Artists: 40+
Budget: $100,000
Income Sources: Admissions, Grants, Private and Corporate Donations, Foundations
Season: October-May
Performs At: University Lutheran Church, Mountain View Methodist Church, St John's Episcopal Church, Boulder High School
Affiliations: First Prebyterian Church
Annual Attendance: 2,500

Seating Capacity: 800

755
BOULDER PHILHARMONIC ORCHESTRA
2995 Wilderness Place
Suite 100
Boulder, CO 80301
Phone: 303-449-1343
Fax: 303-443-9203
e-mail: info@boulderphil.org
Web Site: www.boulderphil.org
Management:
    Executive Director: Sue Levine
    Director: Michael Butterman
    Operations: Glenn Ross
    Marketing: Jillian Crandall
    Development: Maegan Ball
Status: Non-Professional, Non-Profit
Budget: 1 million
Income Sources: American Symphony Orchestra League; Western Alliance of Arts Administrators, Endowment
Season: September-October
Performs At: Macky Auditorium Concert Hall
Organization Type: Performing; Sponsoring

756
BRECKENRIDGE MUSIC INSTITUTE ORCHESTRA
PO Box 1254
217 S Ridge Street
Breckenridge, CO 80424
Phone: 970-453-9142
Fax: 970-453-9143
e-mail: bmi@breckenridgemusicfestival.net
Web Site: www.nationalrepertoryorchestra.com
Officers:
    President: Sandy Mortensen
    Vice President: Samantha Morris
    Executive Director: Jeff D Braum
    Treasurer: John Krakauer
    Secretary: Suzy Witzler
Management:
    Music Director/Principal Conductor: Gerhardt Zimmermenn
    Co-Concertmaster: Nicholas DiEugenio
    Co-Concertmaster: Elbert Tsai
    Assistant Concertmaster: Helen Liu
    Assistant Concertmaster: Brent Price
Mission: Provide musicians the experience necessary to enhance their skills through an intense repertory performance experience.
Founded: 1960
Specialized Field: Jazz; Folk Music; Educational
Status: Nonprofit
Paid Staff: 16
Volunteer Staff: 35
Budget: $260,000-1,050,000
Income Sources: Grants, Private and Corporate Donations
Season: June-August
Performs At: Riverwalk Center
Facility Category: Amphitheater
Seating Capacity: 750
Year Built: 1993

757
BRECKENRIDGE MUSIC FESTIVAL ORCHESTRA
PO Box 1254
Breckenridge, CO 80424
Phone: 303-453-9142
Fax: 303-453-1423
e-mail: bmi@breckenridgemusicfestival.com
Web Site: www.breckenridgemusicfestival.com
Officers:
    President: Wally Ducayet
    Treasurer: Linda Hague
    Secretary: Rick Oshlo
Management:
    Music Director/Conductor: Gerhardt Zimmermann
    Executive Director: Jeff D Baum
    Concertmaster: Nathan Olson
    Production Manager: Vito Ciccone
Mission: The Breckenridge Music Festival's mission is to provide performing arts programs and arts education to the communities of Summit, Park and Lake Counties.
Utilizes: Guest Artists
Founded: 1980
Specialized Field: Jazz, Folk Music; Educational
Status: Professional, Nonprofit
Performs At: Breckenridge Event Tent
Organization Type: Performing; Educational

758
COLORADO SPRINGS PHILHARMONIC
PO Box 60730
Colorado Springs, CO 80960
Mailing Address: PO Box 60730
Phone: 719-884-2110
Fax: 719-884-2111
e-mail: constance@csphilharmonic.org
Web Site: www.csphilharmonic.org
Officers:
    President: Doug Adams
Management:
    Music Director: Lawrence Leighton Smith
    Associate Conductor: Thomas Wilson
    Executive Directror: Nathan Newbrough
    Concertmaster: Michael Hanson
    Associate Concertmaster: Lydia Svyatlovskaya
    Development Director: Constance Gelvin
Mission: To spread the joy of classical music beyond its traditional boundaries.
Utilizes: Guest Artists
Founded: 2003
Specialized Field: Symphony; Orchestra; Chamber
Status: Professional, Nonprofit
Budget: 1.12 million
Income Sources: Private and Corporate Donations, Foundations, Ticket Sales
Performs At: Pikes Peak Center
Annual Attendance: 45,000
Organization Type: Performing; Educational; Sponsoring

759
CRESTED BUTTE MUSIC FESTIVAL
308 3rd Street
PO Box 2117
Crested Butte, CO 81224
Phone: 970-349-0619
e-mail: swan@rmii.com
Web Site: www.cbmountaintheatre.org
Officers:
    Director Development/Marketing: Emily Bond
    COO: Barbara Chistian
Management:
    Co-Artistic Director/CEO: Debra Ayers
    Co-Artistic Director: Alexander Scheirle
    Principal Guest Conductor: Roland Kluttig
    Opera Director: David Malis
Mission: We are proud to have carried on the tradition of presenting a broad spectrum of performing arts here in Crested Butte. Our goal is to create a unique festival for a unique town.
Founded: 1997
Specialized Field: Ensemble; Folk Music; Ethnic Music
Status: Nonprofit
Budget: $20,000-$35,000
Income Sources: Funding from Colorado Council on the Arts, Colordo General Assembly, National Endowment for the Arts
Season: July
Performs At: Crested Butte, CO (Festival Site)
Facility Category: Crested Butte Chamber Music Festival
Seating Capacity: 250

760
COLORADO SYMPHONY ASSOCIATION
Boettcher Concert Hall
1000 14thn Street Suite 15
Denver, CO 80202
Phone: 303-292-5566
Fax: 303-293-2649
e-mail: admin@coloradosymphony.org
Web Site: www.coloradosymphony.org
Officers:
    Interim President: Kevin Duncan
    Treasurer: Tensie Homan
    Secretary: Abby Raymond
Management:
    Music Director: Jeffrey Kahane
    Conductor Laureate: Marin Alsop
    Associate Conductor: Scott O'Neil
    Concertmaster: Yumi Hwang-Williams
    Associate Concertmaster: Claudia Sim
Mission: The Colorado Symphony Orchestra embraces a tradition of musical excellence by presenting a wide variety of symphonic performances from classical repertoire to innovative new forms in Boettcher Concert Hall.
Utilizes: Guest Artists
Founded: 1990
Specialized Field: Symphony; Orchestra
Status: Professional, Nonprofit
Paid Staff: 30
Volunteer Staff: 1
Paid Artists: 804
Non-paid Artists: 250
Budget: $11 Million
Income Sources: Ticket Revenue, Donations From Individuals, Foundations; Businesses, Public Agencies, Grants
Performs At: Denver Performing Arts Complex; Boettcher Concert Hall
Annual Attendance: 202,000
Facility Category: Concert hall, performance center
Type of Stage: In the round
Stage Dimensions: 35 x 80
Orchestra Pit: 1
Seating Capacity: 2,650
Year Built: 1974
Organization Type: Performing; Touring; Resident; Educational; Sponsoring
Resident Groups: Colorado Symphony Orchestra

761
DENVER MUNICIPAL BAND
2253 Bellaire Street
Denver, CO 80207
Phone: 303-322-8608
Fax: 303-322-8608
e-mail: gendsley@ecentral.com
Web Site: www.dmamusic.org

Management:
Music Director/Conductor: Gerald Endsley
Mission: Presenting free summer concerts in Denver parks.
Founded: 1891
Specialized Field: Band; Folk Music
Status: Professional
Income Sources: Association of Concert Bands, Individuals, Foundations, Businesses
Season: May-December
Performs At: Various Venues, Parks
Organization Type: Performing

762
DENVER YOUNG ARTISTS ORCHESTRA

1245 E Colfax Avenue
Suite 302
Denver, CO 80218
Phone: 303-433-2420
Fax: 720-836-3335
e-mail: info@dyao.org
Web Site: www.dyao.org
Officers:
President: Paul Keebler
VP: Eileen Griffin
Treasurer: Lisa Mitchell
Secretary: Donna Bloomer
Management:
Music Director/Conductor: Scott O'Neil
Assistant Conductor: Devin Hughes
Executive Director: Chris Silberman
Assistant Director: Deborah De La Torre
Orchestra Manager: Peter Hellyer
Mission: Its mission is to provide the finest possible youth orchestra programs inspiring and educating young musicians through the performance of great works of music and offering valuable cultural opportunities to the community.
Utilizes: Commissioned Composers; Five Seasonal Concerts; Guest Accompanists; Guest Composers; Instructors; Multimedia; Organization Contracts; Soloists
Founded: 1980
Specialized Field: Symphony
Status: Nonprofit
Paid Staff: 2
Volunteer Staff: 10
Paid Artists: 2
Non-paid Artists: 85
Budget: $150,000
Income Sources: Grants, Ticket Sales, Member Fees, Individuals, Foundations and Corporations, Fundraisers
Season: October-May
Performs At: Boettcher Concert Hall
Affiliations: Colorado Chamber Players
Annual Attendance: 5,000

763
SAN JUAN SYMPHONY

PO Box 1073
Durango, CO 81302
Phone: 970-382-9753
Web Site: www.sanjuansymphony.com
Officers:
President: Polly Morgenstern
Management:
Music Director: Arthur Post
Executive Director: Kathy Myrick
Mission: The San Juan Symphony is a regional orchestra uniting the Four Corners area by nurturing the art of music through education and high quality performances that touch the soul.
Founded: 1973
Specialized Field: Symphony; Orchestra

Status: Nonprofit
Budget: $35,000- $100,000
Income Sources: Grants from Regional and National Foundations, Private and Corporate Donations
Season: September-April
Performs At: Farmington Civic Center, Community Concert Hall; Fort Lewis College
Affiliations: American Symphony Orchestra League
Annual Attendance: 4000
Seating Capacity: 900, 600

764
COLORADO STATE UNIVERSITY ORCHESTRA

Music Department
1778 Campus Delivery
Fort Collins, CO 80523-1778
Phone: 970-491-5529
Web Site: www.music.colostate.edu
Officers:
Chair: Michael H Thaut
Management:
Music Director/Conductor: Wes Kenney
Co-Executive Director: Michaelh Thaut
Mission: To prepare students to become highly skilled music educators, music therapists, performers, composers and conductors.
Specialized Field: Symphony
Status: Nonprofit
Income Sources: Private and Corporate Donations, Grants, Ticket Sales
Performs At: Edna Rizley Griffin Concert Hall
Annual Attendance: 2,000
Seating Capacity: 567

765
FORT COLLINS SYMPHONY ORCHESTRA

PO Box 1963
Fort Collins, CO 80522
Phone: 970-482-4823
Fax: 970-482-4858
e-mail: note@fcsymphony.org
Web Site: www.fcsymphony.org
Officers:
President: Jan Jorgensen
Treasurer: Maryann Ruck
Secretary: Jody Johnson
Management:
Music Director/Conductor: Wes Kenney
Executive Director: Terese Kaptur
Orchestra Manager: Cille Lutsch
Concertmaster: Stacy Lesartre
Assistant Concertmaster: Hee-Jung Kim
Mission: To provide orchestral music of the highest artistic standard for the purposes of entertainment, education and enhancement of the cultural environment.
Utilizes: Guest Accompanists; Guest Composers; Guest Lecturers; Guest Writers; Lyricists
Founded: 1949
Specialized Field: Symphony
Status: Professional
Paid Staff: 4
Volunteer Staff: 100
Paid Artists: 100
Budget: $391,000
Income Sources: Individual and Corporate Donations, Foundations, Ticket Sales, Matching Gifts, Planned Giving, Endowment
Performs At: Edna Rizley Griffin Concert Hall; Lincoln Center Auditorium
Affiliations: American Symphony Orchestra League

Annual Attendance: 10,000
Facility Category: City Auditorium Concert Hall
Type of Stage: Proscenium
Seating Capacity: 567
Year Remodeled: 1979

766
JEFFERSON SYMPHONY ORCHESTRA

PO Box 546
Golden, CO 80402-0546
Phone: 303-278-4237
e-mail: info@jeffersonsymphony.org
Web Site: www.jeffersonsymphony.org
Officers:
Chairman: Dennis Orr
Treasurer: Katherine Moeller
Secretary: Carol Irwin
Management:
Music Director/Conductor: William Morse
Associate Conductor: David Ackerman
Assistant Conductor: J Stephen Mallinson
Mission: To achieve our vision we enrich the greater Jefferson County community through quality musical experiences and educational programs.
Utilizes: Collaborations; Guest Artists; Guest Musical Directors; Guest Musicians; Guest Writers; Multimedia; Organization Contracts; Original Music Scores; Sign Language Translators; Singers; Touring Companies
Founded: 1953
Specialized Field: Symphony; Orchestra; Ensemble
Status: Semi-Professional, Nonprofit
Paid Staff: 2
Volunteer Staff: 150
Budget: $275,000
Income Sources: Chamber of Commerces, Supported by Scientific and Cultural Facilities District, Fundraisers, Private and Corporate Donations
Season: October-May
Performs At: Green Centre; Colorado School of Mines
Annual Attendance: 10,000
Facility Category: auditorium
Seating Capacity: 1,100
Year Built: 1973
Organization Type: Performing

767
GRAND JUNCTION MUSICAL ARTS ASSOCIATION

225 N 5th
Suite 120
Grand Junction, CO 81501
Mailing Address: PO Box 3039
Phone: 970-243-6787
Fax: 970-243-6792
e-mail: info@gjsymphony.org
Web Site: www.gjsymphony.org
Management:
Music Director: Kirk Gustafson
Concertmaster: Carlos Elias
Executive Director: Michael Schwerin
Technical Director: Gordon Rhoades
Mission: To provide symphonic music for the enjoyment and enrichment of the Grand Junction area community.
Founded: 1978
Specialized Field: Symphony; Orchestra; Band
Status: Nonprofit
Paid Staff: 6
Volunteer Staff: 10
Paid Artists: 60
Budget: 400,000
Season: May-August
Performs At: Grand Junction High School Auditorium
Annual Attendance: 20,000

Facility Category: High School
Type of Stage: Proscenium
Stage Dimensions: 45x55
Seating Capacity: 1,500
Year Built: 1951
Organization Type: Performing; Touring; Educational; Sponsoring

768
GREELEY PHILHARMONIC ORCHESTRA

PO Box 1535
Greeley, CO 80632-1535
Phone: 970-356-6406
Fax: 970-352-8761
e-mail: jk@greeleyphilharmonic.com
Web Site: www.greeleyphilharmonic.com
Officers:
   President: Robert Waldo
   Treasurer: Joy Waters
   Secretary: Patricia Streeter
Management:
   Music Director/Conductor: Glen Cortese
   Executive Director: Jeannette Kolokoff
   Concertmaster: Lynelle Harding
   Associate Concertmaster: Aaron Lande
   Production Manager: Benjamin Whitley
Mission: To develop, foster and promote a professional orchestra that satisfies the various musical needs of Greeley and the surrounding area.
Utilizes: Commissioned Music; Guest Composers; Guest Lecturers; Guest Musicians; Multimedia; Original Music Scores; Soloists
Founded: 1911
Specialized Field: Symphony; Orchestra
Status: Professional
Paid Staff: 4
Paid Artists: 80
Budget: $260,000-1,050,000
Income Sources: Tickets; Grants; Fund Drives; Sponsors
Season: September-April
Performs At: Union Colony Civic Auditorium
Annual Attendance: 12,000
Facility Category: Performance Hall
Seating Capacity: 1,665
Year Built: 1984

769
SYMPHONY ORCHESTRA

University of Northern Colorado
College of Performing and Visual Arts
Fraiser 18 Campus Box 28
Greeley, CO 80639
Phone: 970-351-2993
Fax: 970-351-1923
e-mail: info@arts.unco.edu
Web Site: www.arts.unco.edu
Officers:
   Dean: Andrew Jay Svedlow
Management:
   Music Drirector: Russell Guyver
   Administrative Assistant: Jennifer Beck
Mission: Provides rich and well founded tradition of excellence and has developed into a program that has received national and international recognition.
Utilizes: Educators; Guest Composers; Guest Musical Directors; Guest Musicians; High School Drama; Multimedia; Singers
Specialized Field: Orchestra
Budget: $35,000
Performs At: Union Colony Civic Center; Foundation Hall

770
ARAPAHOE PHILHARMONIC

2100 W Littleton Boulevard
Suite 250
Littleton, CO 80120
Phone: 303-781-1892
Fax: 303-781-4918
e-mail: ame@arapahoe.phil.org
Web Site: www.arapahoe.phil.org
Officers:
   Chair: Bert Glandon
   Treasurer: George Burnside
Management:
   Music Director/Conductor: Vincent C LaGuardia Jr
   Associate Conductor: Steve Asheim
   Symphonic Strings/Symphony Director: Tracy LaGuardia
   Assistant Concertmaster: Giga Romero
   Administrator: Ame Leonard
   Administrative Director/APYO: John Leiniger
Mission: Dedicated to providing quality live orchestra performances for the community's enjoyment, appreciation and education.
Founded: 1953
Specialized Field: Symphony
Status: Nonprofit
Paid Staff: 1
Volunteer Staff: 75
Paid Artists: 15
Non-paid Artists: 60
Budget: $245,000
Income Sources: Box Office; Donations; Grants
Season: September-May
Performs At: South Suburban Christian Church
Annual Attendance: 5,000
Facility Category: Church

771
LONGMONT SYMPHONY ORCHESTRA

519 Main Street
PO Box 74
Longmont, CO 80502
Phone: 303-772-5796
Web Site: www.longmontsymphony.org
Management:
   Music Director/Conductor: Robert Olson
   Associate Conductor: Brian St John
Mission: Dedicated to providing the highest possible classical music.
Utilizes: Educators; Fine Artists; Guest Companies; Guest Composers; Guest Designers; Guest Lecturers; Guest Musical Directors; Guest Musicians; Guest Writers; Instructors; Local Artists; Multimedia; Music; Original Music Scores; Singers; Soloists
Founded: 1966
Specialized Field: Classical
Status: Nonprofit
Budget: $150,000-260,000
Season: October-May
Performs At: Vance Brand Civic Auditorium
Annual Attendance: 15,000

772
PUEBLO SYMPHONY

301 N Main Street
Suite 106
Pueblo, CO 81003
Phone: 719-545-7967
Web Site: www.pueblosymphony.com
Officers:
   President: Donna Seilheimer
Management:

Music Director/Conductor: Jacob Chi
Mission: The purpose of the Pueblo Symphony is to provide a quality musical experience for the people of the City and County of Pueblo by recognizing that music is a vital feature of the artistic, cultural and educational life of a community.
Founded: 1928
Specialized Field: Orchestra
Status: Nonprofit
Budget: $300,000
Income Sources: American Symphony Orchestra League, Private and Corporate Donations, Fundraisers
Season: October-February
Performs At: Hoag Recital Hall; CSU Pueblo Campus
Annual Attendance: 7,000
Organization Type: Performing

773
STRINGS IN THE MOUNTAINS

Po Box 774627
Steamboat Springs, CO 80477
Phone: 970-879-5056
Fax: 970-879-7460
Web Site: www.stringsinthemountains.com
Officers:
   Chair: Mary Brown
   Treasurer: Ron Whaley
Management:
   Music Director: Andres Cardenes
   Music Director: Monique Mead
   Music Director/Chamber: Katherine Collier
   Music Director/Chamber: Yizhak Schotten
   Executive Director: Kay Clagett
Mission: Presents innovative programs of distinctive classical and popular contemporary music in an intimate and friendly setting to audiences of all ages, enhancing the cultural, educational and entertainment experiences of the community of Northwest Colorado and its visitors.
Utilizes: Artists-in-Residence; Guest Musical Directors; Guest Musicians; Multimedia; Music; Original Music Scores
Founded: 1988
Specialized Field: String Ensemble; Jazz; Children's Chamber Music
Status: Professional, Nonprofit
Paid Staff: 5
Volunteer Staff: 125
Paid Artists: 170
Budget: $1,000,000
Income Sources: American Symphony Orchestra League, Chamber Music America, Western Arts Alliance, Private and Corporate Donations, Grants, Ticket Sales, Festival Program Advertising
Season: July - August
Performs At: Tensile Fabric Structure
Facility Category: Strings Music Tent
Stage Dimensions: 13'x30'
Seating Capacity: 540
Year Built: 1982
Rental Contact: Facility Manager Jessie Burns
Organization Type: Performing

774
TELLURIDE CHAMBER MUSIC FESTIVAL

PO Box 115
Telluride, CO 81435
Phone: 970-728-8686
Toll-free: 800-525-3455
e-mail: info@telluridechambermusic.org
Web Site: www.telluridechambermusic.org
Officers:
   Founder: Roy Malan
Management:

Artistic Director: Roy Malan
Mission: Our festival creates a spontaneous connection between audience and musicians which lifts the human spirit.
Founded: 1973
Specialized Field: Chamber
Status: Professional
Budget: $10,000
Income Sources: Individual Donations, Grants, Telluride Foundation
Season: August
Performs At: Telluride; Festival Site
Facility Category: Sheridan Opera House
Seating Capacity: 240

Connecticut

775
HARTFORD JAZZ SOCIETY
116 Cottage Grove Road
Room 202
Bloomfield, CT 06002-3200
Phone: 860-242-6688
Fax: 860-243-3130
e-mail: hartjazzsocinc@aol.com
Web Site: www.hartfordjazzsociety.com
Officers:
  President: Daniel Feingold
  Treasurer: Robert Pernell
  Secretary: Leslie Manselle
Mission: To foster interest, understanding, and appreciation of jazz by presenting a variety of live jazz events and by nurturing new generations of jazz performers and audiences.
Founded: 1960
Specialized Field: Jazz
Status: Professional
Paid Staff: 2
Income Sources: Ticket Sales; Fund Raisers; Grants; Private and Corporate Donations
Performs At: Wadsworth Atheneum Museum of Art
Facility Category: Theater
Seating Capacity: 284
Year Built: 1842
Organization Type: Sponsoring

776
GREATER BRIDGEPORT SYMPHONY ORCHESTRA
446 University Avenue
Bridgeport, CT 06604
Phone: 203-576-0263
Fax: 203-367-0064
Web Site: www.bridgeportsymphony.org
Officers:
  Chairman: Robert S Tellalian
  President: Marianne Laska
  VP: H Michael Keden
  Treasurer: Peter Guenther
  Secretary: Preston Tisdale
Management:
  Music Director/Conductor: Gustav Meier
  Executive Director: Jena Maric
  Concertmaster: Deborarh Wong
  Assistant Concertmaster: Nina Crothers
Mission: Dedicated to enriching the lives of young people within a musical community.
Utilizes: Guest Accompanists; Guest Composers; Guest Musicians; Original Music Scores; Singers
Founded: 1945
Specialized Field: Symphony
Status: Professional, Nonprofit
Budget: $260,000-1,050,000

Income Sources: Private and Corporate Donations, Foundations, Grants, Ticket Sales
Season: October-April
Performs At: Klein Memorial Auditorium
Annual Attendance: 7,500
Facility Category: Auditorium
Seating Capacity: 1,468

777
ASTON MAGNA FOUNDATION
PO Box 3167
Danbury, CT 06813-3167
Phone: 203-792-4662
Fax: 203-744-7244
Toll-free: 800-875-7156
e-mail: info@astonmagna.org
Web Site: www.astonnmagna.org
Officers:
  Chairman: Robert B Strassler
Management:
  Artistic Director: Daniel Stepner
  Acadmey Director: Raymond Erickson
  Executive Director: Ronnie Boriskin
Mission: The mission of the Aston Magna Foundation is to enrich the appreciation of music of the past and the understanding of the cultural, political and social contexts in which it was composed and experienced.
Utilizes: Educators
Founded: 1972
Specialized Field: Chamber; Early Music
Status: Professional, Nonprofit
Paid Staff: 4
Volunteer Staff: 6
Income Sources: Massachusetts Cultural Council, Grants
Season: July-August
Performs At: St James Church Festival in Great Barrington, Daniel Arts Center at Simon's Rock College
Organization Type: Performing; Touring; Educational; Sponsoring

778
GREATER BRIDGEPORT SYMPHONY YOUTH ORCHESTRA
PO Box 645
Fairfield, CT 06824-0645
Phone: 203-459-4249
Fax: 203-459-4249
e-mail: gbyo@gbyo.org
Web Site: www.gbyo.org
Officers:
  President: Mark Halstead
Management:
  Music Director: Christopher Hisey
  Symphony Orchestra Conductor: Leo Ficks
  Concert Orchestra Conductor: Jeff Albright
  String Orchestra Conductor: Erica Messian
  Wind Ensemble Conductor: Aaron Barkon
  Executive Director: Barb Upton
Mission: To offer young musicians in the Greater Bridgeport area a quality orchestral experience.
Founded: 1961
Specialized Field: Symphony; Orchestra
Status: Non-Professional
Income Sources: Private and Corporate Donations, Foundations, Grants, Ticket Sales, Membership fees
Season: November-May
Performs At: Klein Auditorium
Organization Type: Performing; Educational

779
AMERICAN CLASSICAL ORCHESTRA
PO Box 441
Greenwich, CT 06836

Phone: 212-362-2727
Fax: 212-362-2729
e-mail: admin@aconyc.org
Web Site: www.americanclassicalorchestra.org
Officers:
  President: Reba Beeson
  Treasurer: Victor Germack
  Secretary: William Lee
  Founder: Thomas Crawford
Management:
  Music Director: Thomas Crawford
  Development Associate: Glen Askin
Mission: To recreate classical music in its original form to revive and preserve period instrumentation.
Founded: 1985
Specialized Field: Classical
Paid Staff: 2
Volunteer Staff: 29
Paid Artists: 45
Budget: $260,000-700,000
Income Sources: Private and Corporate Donations, Ticket Sales, American Classical Orchestra Guild, Advertising
Season: October-April
Performs At: Halls; Museums; Private Residences
Annual Attendance: 3,000
Seating Capacity: 1,062

780
GREENWICH SYMPHONY ORCHESTRA
299 Greenwich Avenue
PO Box 35
Greenwich, CT 06836
Phone: 203-869-2664
Fax: 203-869-2664
e-mail: gsorch@verizon.net
Web Site: www.greenwichsym.org
Officers:
  President: Mary J Radcliffe
  VP: Richard J Slagle
  Treasurer: Richard Chase
Mission: To offer a subscription series, youth concert series and chamber players series.
Founded: 1958
Specialized Field: Classical
Status: Professional
Budget: $260,000-1,050,000
Income Sources: Ticket Sales; Private and Corporate Donations; Greenwich Symphony Guild; Endowment Fund
Performs At: Dickerman Hollister Auditorium; Greenwich High School
Annual Attendance: 11,000
Facility Category: Greenwich High School Auditorium
Seating Capacity: 850

781
SYMPHONY ON THE SOUND
RD 1, 18 Zygmont Lane
Greenwich, CT 06830
Phone: 203-661-7413
Fax: 203-661-7413
Officers:
  Executive Director: P Steinborn
  General Manager: P M Lewis
Management:
  Music Director/Conductor: Joseph Leniado-Chira
Specialized Field: Symphony
Status: Professional, Nonprofit
Annual Attendance: 20,000

782
CONNECTICUT CLASSICAL GUITAR SOCIETY
PO Box 1528
Hartford, CT 06114-1528
Phone: 860-249-7041
e-mail: info@ctguitar.org
Web Site: www.ctguitar.org
Officers:
President: H Vivero
Management:
Artistic Director: Daniel Salazar
Executive Director: Joyce Magee
Status: Non=Profit
Budget: 150,000
Income Sources: Funded in part by the Connecticut Commission of the Arts; The Greater Hartford Arts Council; Takamine Guitar; The Roberts Foundation: The D'Addario Foundation
Season: September-May
Performs At: Carol Autorino Center; St Joseph College, Autorino Great Hall, Belding Theater; Bushnell
Annual Attendance: 6,500

783
HARTFORD SYMPHONY ORCHESTRA
99 Pratt StreetAvenue
Suite 500
Hartford, CT 06103-1629
Phone: 860-244-2999
Fax: 860-249-5430
e-mail: info@hartfordsymphony.com
Web Site: www.hartfordsymphony.org
Officers:
President: Kenneth A Jacobson
VP: James S Remis
VP: Pierre H Guertin
Chairman: David M Roth
Management:
Music Director/Conductor: Edward Cumming
Executive Director: Kristin M Phillips
Assistant Director: Karen L Degrace
Mission: To bring music and educational programs of the highest artistic standards to the widest possible audience.
Utilizes: Actors; Collaborating Artists; Collaborations; Commissioned Composers; Commissioned Music; Dancers; Five Seasonal Concerts; Grant Writers; Guest Accompanists; Guest Companies; Guest Composers; Guest Lecturers; Guest Musical Directors; Guest Musicians; Instructors; Lyricists; Multi Collaborations; Multimedia; Original Music Scores; Sign Language Translators; Singers; Theatre Companies
Founded: 1934
Specialized Field: Orchestra
Budget: 6.1 million
Income Sources: Subscribers, Donors, Ticket Sales
Season: October-May
Performs At: Bushnell Center for the Performing Arts
Annual Attendance: 173,000
Seating Capacity: 2,805

784
MANCHESTER SYMPHONY ORCHESTRA/CHORALE
PO Box 861
Manchester, CT 06045-0861
Phone: 860-228-2921
e-mail: musicsix@cox.net
Web Site: www.msoc.org
Officers:
President: Linda Cromwell
Treasurer: John Belbruno
VP Orchestra: Sean McDonald
VP Chorale: Lydia Messerschmidt
Management:
Orchestra Director: Lewis J Buckley
Chorale Director: Kevin L Mack
Mission: To enhance the enjoyment and enrichment of members while furthering performing arts in the community.
Utilizes: Artists-in-Residence; Guest Artists
Founded: 1960
Specialized Field: Symphony; Orchestra; Chorus
Status: Non-Professional, Nonprofit, Volunteer, Community
Paid Staff: 4
Volunteer Staff: 100
Income Sources: Private and Corporate Donations, Ticket Sale, Endowment
Season: Octber-May
Performs At: Manchester Community College
Affiliations: Greater Manchester Chamber of Commerce, Association of Connecticut Choruses
Organization Type: Performing; Resident

785
NEW BRITAIN SYMPHONY ORCHESTRA
PO Box 1253
New Britain, CT 06050
Phone: 860-826-6344
Fax: 860-826-6344
Web Site: www.newbritainsymphony.org
Officers:
President: Barbara Kirejczyk
Secretary: Mel Ellis
Treasurer: Norman Holland
Management:
Director: Jesse Levine
Founded: 1950
Status: Non-Profit
Income Sources: Private and Corporate Donations, Endowment Fund
Season: October-September
Performs At: Darius Miller Shell; Walnut Hill Park
Seating Capacity: 3,000
Organization Type: Performing

786
SILVERMINE GUILD SUMMER MUSIC SERIES
1037 Silvermine Road
New Canaan, CT 06840
Phone: 203-966-9700
Fax: 203-996-2763
e-mail: sgac@silvermineart.org
Web Site: www.silvermineart.org
Officers:
Chair: Fran Henry Meehan
Secretary: Roger Williams
Treasurer: Richard Cohen
Management:
Executive Director: Pamela Davis
Marketing: Robin Axness
Status: Non-Profit
Income Sources: Ticket Sales, Fundraisers
Performs At: Gillford Hall
Annual Attendance: 800

787
NEW HAVEN SYMPHONY ORCHESTRA
PO Box 9718
New Haven, CT 06536
Phone: 203-865-0831
Fax: 203-931-2999
Toll-free: 800-292-6476
e-mail: nforbes@newhavensymphony.org
Web Site: www.newhavensymphony.com
Officers:
President: Christopher H Getman
Executive Committee Chair: David W Benfer
VP: William S Gedge
VP: Alice Hummel
VP: Tracey Scheer
Treasurer: Stehphen P August
Recording Secretary: Carol von Pressentin Wright
Management:
Executive Director: Natalie Forbes
Principal Conductor/Music Director: William Boughton
Associate Conductor: Gerald Steichen
Mission: Our mission is to reach a diverse audience and promote excellence in the performing arts. Our orchestra consists of 70 professionals.
Founded: 1894
Specialized Field: Orchestra
Status: Professional, Nonprofit
Paid Staff: 6
Paid Artists: 70
Budget: $1.8-2 million
Income Sources: Box Office, Sponsorship, Private and Corporate Donations, Commemorative Gifts, Foundations, Grants
Season: September-April
Performs At: Woolsey Hall

788
ORCHESTRA NEW ENGLAND
PO Box 200123
New Haven, CT 06520-0123
Phone: 203-777-4690
Fax: 203-772-0578
e-mail: info@orchestranewengland.org
Web Site: www.orchestranewengland.org
Management:
Director: James Sinclair
Founded: 1974
Budget: $35,000-100,000

789
YALE SYMPHONY ORCHESTRA
PO Box 201945
New Haven, CT 06520
Phone: 203-432-4140
Fax: 203-432-7642
e-mail: brian.s.robinson@yale.edu
Web Site: www.yale.edu
Officers:
Dean: Robert L Blocker
President: Larua Britton
VP: Matthew Smith
Management:
Music Director/Conductor: Toshiyuki Shimada
Concertmaster: Kensho Watanabe
Manager: Brian Robinson
Mission: To present diverse and high quality music.
Specialized Field: Orchestra; Symphony
Paid Staff: 1
Non-paid Artists: 200
Income Sources: Private and Corporate Donations, Endowment, Grants, Foundations, Ticket Sales
Season: October-February
Performs At: Woolsey Hall, Morse Recital Hall; Sprague Memorial Hall
Affiliations: ASOL
Annual Attendance: 8,000-10,000
Seating Capacity: 2,695

Year Built: 1901

790
EASTERN CONNECTICUT SYMPHONY

289 State Street
New London, CT 06320
Phone: 860-443-2876
Fax: 860-444-7601
e-mail: ectsymphony@snet.net
Web Site: www.ectsymphony.com
Officers:
President: Tom Castle
VP: Barbara Richards
Treasurer: Robert Salmonsen
Secretary: Lois Andrews
Management:
Executive Director: Isabelle G Singer
Music Director: Toshiyuki Shimada
Mission: The mission of the Eastern Connecticut Symphony is to enrich the cultural life of the region by performing high quality music and by conducting educational outreach programs.
Founded: 1946
Specialized Field: Symphony; Orchestra; Ensemble
Status: Professional, Nonprofit
Paid Staff: 7
Paid Artists: 75
Budget: $795,000
Income Sources: Ticket Sales; Grants; Corporate Sponsorships; Individual Donations; Fundraising Events
Season: October-May
Performs At: Garde Arts Center
Annual Attendance: 8,400
Facility Category: Restored theater at Garde Arts Center
Seating Capacity: 1440
Year Built: 1926
Year Remodeled: 1998
Organization Type: Performing; Educational

791
NORWALK SYMPHONY ORCHESTRA

1 Park Street
Norwalk, CT 06851
Phone: 203-847-8844
Fax: 203-847-2455
e-mail: info@norwalksymphony.org
Web Site: www.norwalksymphony.org
Management:
Director: Diane Wittry
Founded: 1939
Status: Professional
Budget: $260,000-1,050,000
Income Sources: Ticket Sales, Private and Corporate Donations, Grants
Season: October-May
Performs At: Norwalk Concert Hall
Annual Attendance: 5,000
Seating Capacity: 1,062

792
NORWALK YOUTH SYMPHONY

71 E Avenue
Norwalk, CT 06851
Mailing Address: PO Box 73
Phone: 203-866-4100
Fax: 203-866-0012
e-mail: info@norwalkyouthsymphony.org
Web Site: www.norwalkyouthsymphony.org
Management:
Executive Director: Sara Watkins
Utilizes: Artists-in-Residence; Commissioned Composers; Educators; Fine Artists; Guest Companies; High School Drama; Multimedia; Theatre Companies

Founded: 1956
Status: Non-Profit
Budget: $800,000
Income Sources: Tuition; Box Office; Donations; Grants
Season: November-May
Performs At: Norwalk Concert Hall
Affiliations: ASOL; MCNC; ASCAP: BMI
Annual Attendance: 5,500
Seating Capacity: 1,062
Organization Type: Performing; Educational

793
RIDGEFIELD SYMPHONY ORCHESTRA

90 East Ridge Avenue
Ridgefield, CT 06877
Phone: 203-438-3889
Fax: 203-438-0222
Web Site: www.ridgefieldsymphony.org
Officers:
President: Donna Case
Treasurer: Suzanne Escola
Secretary: Mary Kaletta
Management:
Executive Director: Sarah Miller
Music Director: Gerald Steichen
Operations Manager: Catherine da Cruz
Mission: To present high quality classical music programs in the communities surrounding Ridgefield.
Utilizes: Fine Artists; Guest Accompanists; Guest Musicians; Multimedia; Original Music Scores; Sign Language Translators; Singers
Founded: 1964
Specialized Field: Symphony
Status: Professional, Nonprofit
Paid Staff: 1
Volunteer Staff: 34
Paid Artists: 70+
Budget: $500,000
Income Sources: American Symphony Orchestra League; Broadcast Music Incorporated; American Society of Composers, Authors and Publishers, Private and Corporate Donations, Ticket Sales
Season: September-April
Performs At: Ann S Richardson Auditorium; Ridgefield High School, Ridgefield Playhouse
Annual Attendance: 6,000
Organization Type: Performing

794
STAMFORD SYMPHONY ORCHESTRA

263 Tresser Boulevard
Stamford, CT 06901
Phone: 203-325-1407
Fax: 203-325-8762
e-mail: office@stamfordsymphony.org
Web Site: www.stamfordsymphony.org
Officers:
Chair: James Marpe
President/CEO: Barbara J Soroca
Management:
General Manager: Elaine C Carroll
Operations Manager: Susan Oetgen
Mission: To develop an appreciation for classical music through diverse programming on a professional level.
Utilizes: Collaborations; Guest Accompanists; Guest Musical Directors; Guest Musicians; Multimedia; Resident Artists
Founded: 1968
Specialized Field: Symphony; Orchestra; Ensemble
Status: Professional, Nonprofit
Paid Staff: 7
Paid Artists: 70
Budget: $1.3 million

Income Sources: Ticket Sales, Contributions, Grants, Friends of SSO
Performs At: Palace Theatre
Annual Attendance: 15,000
Seating Capacity: 1,586
Organization Type: Performing; Resident; Educational

795
STAMFORD YOUNG ARTISTS PHILHARMONIC

Ridgeway Station
PO Box 3301
Stamford, CT 06905
Phone: 203-532-1278
e-mail: executivedirector@syap.org
Web Site: www.syap.org
Officers:
President: Michael Marotto
Secretary: Leah Rumbough
Co-Treasurer: William Webster
Co-Treasurer: Susanne Webster
Management:
Executive Director: Joyce DiCamillo
Mission: To create an outlet for young musicians to perform, developing their skills and abilities, while exposing the community to this cultural art.
Founded: 1960
Specialized Field: Orchestra; Ensemble; Jazz
Status: Non-Professional, Nonprofit
Paid Staff: 150
Season: September-May
Performs At: Stamford High School
Organization Type: Performing; Educational

796
WALLINGFORD SYMPHONY ORCHESTRA

Choate Rosemary Hall- Paul Mellon Arts Center
333 Christian Street
Wallingford, CT 06492
Phone: 203-697-2671
e-mail: annwhitman@snet.net
Web Site: www.wallingfordsymphony.org
Officers:
President: Ann Whitman
Treasurer: Donald Kirschbaum
Secretary: Karen Grava
Management:
Music Director: Philip T Ventre
Mission: To provide professional quality orchestral performances to reach and inspire the greater Wallingford community.
Founded: 1974
Specialized Field: Symphony; Orchestra
Status: Nonprofit
Paid Artists: 65
Budget: $35,000-100,000
Income Sources: Subscription, Individual and Corporate Donations, Grants, Fundraisers
Facility Category: Theater
Seating Capacity: 780
Year Built: 1972

797
WATERBURY SYMPHONY ORCHESTRA

110 Bank Street
PO Box 1762
Waterbury, CT 06702
Phone: 203-574-4283
Fax: 203-755-6948
e-mail: waterbury.symphony@snet.net
Web Site: www.waterburysymphony.org
Officers:

President: David Sfara
Treasurer: Malcolm H Forbes
Recording Secretary: Rosemary Renda
Corresponding Secretary: Kris Jacobi
Management:
Executive Director: Fran Goldman
Marketing Director: Kathryn Dennen
Mission: To bring a diverse audience together through live symphonic music.
Utilizes: Artists-in-Residence; Choreographers; Collaborating Artists; Collaborations; Commissioned Composers; Commissioned Music; Dance Companies; Dancers; Educators; Five Seasonal Concerts; Grant Writers; Guest Accompanists; Guest Artists; Guest Choreographers; Guest Companies; Guest Composers; Guest Designers; Guest Directors; Guest Lecturers; Guest Musical Directors; Guest Musicians; Guest Soloists; High School Drama; Instructors; Local Artists; Lyricists; Multi Collaborations; Multimedia; Music; Organization Contracts; Original Music Scores; Resident Artists; Sign Language Translators; Singers; Soloists
Specialized Field: Classical; Pops
Status: Professional, Nonprofit
Paid Staff: 2
Volunteer Staff: 50
Paid Artists: 70
Budget: $260,000-1,050,000
Income Sources: Annual Fund, Corporate Sponsors, Memberships, Grants
Performs At: Main Stage; Naugatuck Valley Community College
Annual Attendance: 15,000
Facility Category: Community College
Type of Stage: Proscenium
Stage Dimensions: 38x34
Seating Capacity: 800

798
CONNECTICUT YOUTH SYMPHONY
Hartt School Community Division
200 Bloomfield Avenue
West Hartford, CT 06117
Phone: 860-768-4451
Fax: 860-768-4777
e-mail: harttcomm@hartford.edu
Web Site: www.hartford.edu
Management:
Music Director: Dan D'Addio
Mission: To provide programs for talented young musicians.
Founded: 1930
Specialized Field: Youth Symphony
Budget: $35,000
Income Sources: Tuition; Fundraising
Performs At: Lincoln Theater
Affiliations: Hartt School
Annual Attendance: 2,000
Seating Capacity: 700

799
ORCHESTRA NEW ENGLAND
University of New Haven
300 Orange Avenue
West Haven, CT 06516
Phone: 203-934-8863
Fax: 203-934-8379
Web Site: www.orchestranewengland.org
Management:
Music Director: James Sinclair
Mission: To present exciting and versatile performances to enhance music appreciation in the community.
Founded: 1974

Specialized Field: Orchestra
Status: Professional, Nonprofit
Paid Staff: 3
Non-paid Artists: 25
Budget: $200,000
Income Sources: Fundraising, Ticket Sales, Private and Corporate Donations
Season: November-May
Performs At: Battell Chapel; Yale University, Dodds Hall Auditorium; University of New Haven Campus
Annual Attendance: 3,000
Seating Capacity: 850

Delaware

800
NEWARK SYMPHONY ORCHESTRA
PO Box 7775
Newark, DE 19714-7775
Phone: 302-369-3466
e-mail: info@newarksymphony.org
Web Site: www.newarksymphony.org
Officers:
President: Carl Luft
VP: J. Kevin Chapmond
Management:
Music Director: Simeone Tartaglione
Personnel Manager: Jennifer Hugh
Business Manager: Denice Grawe
Mission: To give volunteer musicians the opportunity to play symphonic literature and to provide live performances for the community.
Utilizes: Community Talent; Five Seasonal Concerts; Guest Directors; Guest Musicians
Founded: 1966
Specialized Field: Symphony
Status: Non-Professional, Nonprofit
Paid Staff: 3
Volunteer Staff: 80
Budget: $55,000
Income Sources: University of Delaware, Grants, National Endowment for the Arts, Delaware Division of the Arts
Season: October-April
Performs At: Newark United Methodist Church; The Independence School
Annual Attendance: 2,000-2,500
Organization Type: Performing

801
BRANDYWINE BAROQUE
PO Box 730
Wilmington, DE 19899
Phone: 302-594-4544
Web Site: www.brandywinebaroque.org
Management:
Artistic Director: Karen Flint
Director: Robert Munsell
Mission: To provide lively Baroque music on period instruments to make the chamber music accessible to the modern audience.
Specialized Field: Chamber
Budget: $100,000-150,000
Income Sources: Ticket Sales, Private and Corporate Donations
Performs At: Christ Church Christiana Hundred; Wilmington, St Peter's Church; Lewes

802
DELAWARE SYMPHONY ORCHESTRA
PO Box 1870
Wilmington, DE 19899

Phone: 302-656-7442
Fax: 302-656-7754
e-mail: lucindaw@delawaresymphony.org
Web Site: www.delawaresymphony.org
Officers:
Chairman: Jerome Grossman
Secretary: Mary Jo Anderson
Management:
Executive Director: Lucinda Williams
Development Director: Christopher Van Bergen
Mission: Seeks to enrich the quality of life through live orchestral music by pursuing artistic excellence in symphonic and chamber music performances and cultivating a life-long love of orchestral music through education and community engagement programs.
Utilizes: Guest Artists
Founded: 1929
Specialized Field: Symphony; Orchestra; Classical; Pops; Chamber
Status: Professional, Nonprofit
Paid Staff: 10
Volunteer Staff: 100
Paid Artists: 86
Budget: $2.5 Million
Income Sources: American Symphony Orchestra League, Ticket Sales, Private and Corporate Donations, Advertising, Grants
Season: October-May
Performs At: Grand Opera House, Gold Ballroom; Hotel duPont
Organization Type: Performing; Educational

803
DICKINSON THEATRE ORGAN SOCIETY
1801 Milltown Road
PO Box 7263
Wilmington, DE 19803-0296
Phone: 302-995-2603
e-mail: president@dtoskimball.org
Web Site: www.dtoskimball.org
Officers:
President: Robert E Dilworth
Mission: To present theatre pipe organ concerts on the pipe organ located in the Dickinson High School Auditorium.
Utilizes: Guest Accompanists; Guest Directors; Guest Musical Directors; Instructors; Local Talent; Original Music Scores
Founded: 1973
Opened: 1969
Specialized Field: Organ Music
Status: Professional, Semi-Professional, Nonprofit
Volunteer Staff: 60
Paid Artists: 6
Budget: $75,000
Income Sources: Tickets; Donations
Season: September-July
Performs At: Dickinson High School Auditorium
Affiliations: American Theatre Organ Society
Annual Attendance: 5,000
Type of Stage: Proscenium
Stage Dimensions: 48'x35'
Organization Type: Sponsoring

District of Columbia

804
UNITED STATES AIR FORCE BAND
201 McChord Street
Bolling AFB, DC 20332-0202
Phone: 202-767-4225
Fax: 202-767-0686
Web Site: www.usaband.af.mil

Officers:
Commander: Col Dennis M Layendecker
Deputy Commander: Lt Col Alan C Sierichs
Management:
Manager: CM Sgt Jerry Thomas
Operations Director: CM Sgt Richard Pearson
Marketing Director: CM Sgt Elizabeth Campeau
Mission: To provide music support for American troops, to encourage service in the Air Force and to increase the public awareness and reputation of the armed forces.
Utilizes: Singers
Founded: 1941
Specialized Field: Symphony; Orchestra; Chamber; Ensemble; Chorus; Band
Status: Professional, Nonprofit
Paid Staff: 230
Volunteer Staff: 2
Budget: $1,800,000
Income Sources: Department of Defense Funds
Season: October-December
Performs At: DAR Constitution Hall
Organization Type: Performing; Touring

805
CAPITAL CITY SYMPHONY

1333 H Street NE
Washington, DC 20002
Phone: 202-399-7993
Web Site: www.capitalcitysymphony.org
Officers:
Chair: Virginia Elgin
Vice Chair: Meredith Maslich
Treasurer: Judit Nagy Eichenberger
Recording Secretary: Howard Spendelow
Management:
Music Director: Victoria Gau
Associate Conductor: David Grandis
General Manager: Debbie Grossman
Mission: To present affordable programs with a relaxed atmosphere to make orchestral music approachable to the metropolitan DC community.
Founded: 1967
Specialized Field: Orchestra

806
CONTEMPORARY MUSIC FORUM

500 17th Street NW
Washington, DC 20006
Phone: 877-263-8431
e-mail: info@cmf-verge.org
Web Site: www.contemporarymusic.org
Officers:
Chair: David Curry
Vice Chair: Steve Soderberg
Treasurer: Fred Weck
Secretary: Michael Stover
Management:
Executive Director: Lina Bahn
Artistic Advisor: Steve Antosca
Mission: To provide the Greater Washington area with quality contemporary music performances.
Founded: 1973
Specialized Field: Chamber
Status: Nonprofit
Income Sources: Private and Corporate Donations, Ticket Sales
Season: May-November
Performs At: Armand Hammer Auditorium; Corcoran Gallery of Art; Millennium Stage; CMF at the Kennedy Center
Organization Type: Performing; Resident

807
DC YOUTH ORCHESTRA PROGRAM

Brightwood Station
PO Box 56198
Washington, DC 20011
Phone: 202-723-1612
Fax: 202-723-6040
e-mail: info@dcyop.org
Web Site: www.dcyop.org
Officers:
President: Gary Carleton
Secretary: Maya Weil
Treasurer: Tina Kelly
Management:
Executive Director: Ava Spece
Mission: To facilitate a creative outlet for young people, regardless of experience level, to practice and perform music.
Founded: 1960
Specialized Field: Symphony; Orchestra; Chamber
Status: Nonprofit
Budget: 642,000
Income Sources: American Symphony Orchestra League Youth Orchestra Division, Private and Corporate Donations, Ticket Sales, Matching Gifts, Planned Gifts
Performs At: Various Venues
Organization Type: Performing; Touring; Educational

808
GEORGE WASHINGTON UNIVERSITY SYMPHONY ORCHESTRA

George Washington University Music Department
801 22nd Street NW
Washington, DC 20052
Phone: 202-994-6245
e-mail: gwumusdir@mac.com
Web Site: www.gwu.edu
Officers:
Chair: Karen Ahlquist
Management:
Director: Nancia D'Alimonte
Mission: To rehearse and perform diverse orchestral music ranging from contemporary music to traditional.
Founded: 1961
Specialized Field: Orchestra
Budget: $35,000
Income Sources: Private and Corporate Donations, Ticket Sales
Performs At: Lisner Auditorium

809
KENNEDY CENTER OPERA HOUSE ORCHESTRA

John F Kennedy Center
2700 F Street NW
Washington, DC 20566
Phone: 202-467-4600
Toll-free: 800-444-1324
Web Site: www.kennedy-center.org
Officers:
President: Michael Kaiser
Founding Chair: Roger L Stevens
Chair: Stephen A Schwarzman
Secretary: Jean Kennedy Smith
Treasurer: Roland Betts
Management:
Artistic Director: Heinz Fricke
Manager: Kristy Dolbeare
Mission: To accompany opera performances with orchestral music.
Founded: 1978
Specialized Field: Orchestra

Volunteer Staff: 500
Budget: $1,050,000-3,600,000
Income Sources: Private and Corporate Donations, Charitable Estate Planning
Season: September-May
Performs At: John F Kennedy Center for the Performing Arts

810
NATIONAL GALLERY ORCHESTRA

National Gallery Of Art
4th and Constitution Avenue NW
Washington, DC 20565
Phone: 202-842-6941
e-mail: G-Manos@nga.gov
Web Site: www.nga.gov
Officers:
Chair: John C Fontaine
President: Victoria P Sant
Management:
Music Director: George Manos
Mission: To provide the public with free concerts at the National Gallery of Art.
Utilizes: Commissioned Composers; Curators; Educators; Fine Artists; Guest Accompanists; Guest Directors; Guest Musical Directors; Multimedia; Original Music Scores
Founded: 1941
Specialized Field: Symphony; Orchestra; Chamber; Ensemble
Status: Nonprofit
Paid Staff: 8
Season: October-June
Performs At: Museum Garden Courts; National Gallery
Annual Attendance: 500
Seating Capacity: 500
Organization Type: Performing

811
NATIONAL SYMPHONY ORCHESTRA ASSOCIATION

Kennedy Center for the Performin Arts
2700 F Street NW
Washington, DC 20566
Phone: 202-467-4600
Toll-free: 800-444-1324
Web Site: www.kennedy-center.org
Officers:
Founding Chairman: Robert L Stevens
Chair: Stephen A Schwarzman
President: Michael M Kaiser
Secretary: Jean Kennedy Smith
Treasurer: Roland Betts
Management:
Artistic Director: Nigel Boon
Manager: Cynthia Pickett Steele
Mission: To fulfill President Kennedy's vision to produce and present a diverse selection of performing arts for all ages.
Utilizes: Guest Artists
Founded: 1930
Specialized Field: Symphony; Orchestra; Chamber
Status: Nonprofit
Income Sources: American Symphony Orchestra League; John F. Kennedy Center for the Performing Arts
Performs At: John F. Kennedy Center for the Performing Arts
Organization Type: Performing; Touring

812
WASHINGTON BACH CONSORT
1010 Vermont Avenue NW
Suite 202
Washington, DC 20005
Phone: 202-429-2121
Fax: 202-429-2269
e-mail: creifel@bachconsort.org
Web Site: www.bachconsort.org
Officers:
  President: Shannon Davis
  VP: Jill Kent
  Secretary: John Wohlstetter
Management:
  Executive Director: Charles Reifel
  Music Director: J Reilly Lewis
  Assistant Conductor: Scott Dettra
  Concertmaster: Jeanne Johnson
Mission: To perform the music of Johan Sebastian Bach and his contemporaries to the highest standards to expand the appreciation of Bach in the community.
Founded: 1977
Specialized Field: Chorus; Classical
Status: Professional
Paid Staff: 6
Budget: $260,000-1,050,000
Income Sources: Private and Corporate Donations, Ticket Sales, Appreciated Stock, Membership
Season: September-June
Performs At: National Presbyterian Church, Basilica of the Shrine of the Immaculate Conception, Clarice Smith Performing Arts Center
Organization Type: Performing, Touring

813
COMMODORES
United States Navy Band
617 Warrington Avenue SE
Washington Navy Yard, DC 20374-5054
Phone: 202-433-2525
e-mail: navyband.comments@navy.mil
Web Site: www.navyband.navy.mil
Officers:
  Executive Officer: LCDR Richard H Bailey
  Commanding Officer: CAPT George N Thompson
Management:
  Senior Chief Musician: Philip M Burlin
Mission: To provide musical support to the President, Navy and government officials to inspire patriotism and increase troop morale.
Founded: 1969
Specialized Field: Jazz
Income Sources: Private Donations
Performs At: Official Military Ceremonies, Special Events
Annual Attendance: 1,300
Organization Type: Performing; Touring; Educational

814
COUNTRY CURRENT/US NAVY BAND
United States Navy Band
617 Warrington Ave SE
Washington Navy Yard, DC 20374-5054
Phone: 202-433-3676
Fax: 202-433-4108
e-mail: NavyBand.Public.Affairs@navy.mil
Web Site: www.navyband.navy.mil
Officers:
  Commanding Officer/Leader: CAPT Geogre M Thompson
  Executive Officer/Assistant Leader: LCDR Richard H Bailey
Management:

  Associate Conductor: LT Michael S Grant
  Operations Chief: MUCM Mark C Cochran
Mission: Provides musical support to the President of the United States, the Department of the Navy and other senior military and government officials.
Founded: 1973
Performs At: Official Military Ceremonies, Special Events
Annual Attendance: 1,300
Organization Type: Performing; Touring

815
CRUISERS
617 Warrington Avenue SE
Washington Navy Yard, DC 20374-5054
Phone: 202-433-3676
Fax: 202-433-4108
e-mail: public.affairs@navyband.navy.mil
Web Site: www.navyband.navy.mil
Management:
  Senior Chief Musician: John L Fisher
Mission: To provide music for such ceremonies, functions and other occasions as may be directed by proper authority in order to best represent the Navy in a musical capacity at the seat of government and elsewhere as directed.
Founded: 1973
Specialized Field: Contemporary; Rock; Rythym; Blues
Performs At: Official Military Ceremonies, Special Events
Annual Attendance: 1,300
Organization Type: Performing; Touring

816
UNITED STATES NAVY BAND
617 Warrington Avenue SE
Washington Navy Yard, DC 20374-5054
Phone: 202-433-3676
Fax: 202-433-4108
e-mail: public.affairs@navyband.navy.mil
Web Site: www.navyband.navy.mil
Officers:
  Lieutenant/Assistant Leader: Melvin P Kessler
  Lieutenant/Third Officer: Issac Daniel, Jr
Management:
  Commander/Directr/Officer in Charge: Ralph Gambone
  Master Chief Musician: Jeffrey C Myers
  Chief Musician: John L Fisher
  Chief Musician: Earl E Powers
Mission: To provide music for such ceremonies, functions and other occasions as may be directed by proper authority in order to best represent the Navy in a musical capacity at the seat of government and elsewhere as directed.
Founded: 1925
Specialized Field: Ceremonial Music; Classical Rock; Jazz; Country
Status: Professional
Performs At: Official Military Ceremonies, Special Events
Annual Attendance: 1,500,000
Organization Type: Performing; Touring; Educational

Florida

817
MIAMI INTERNATIONAL PIANO FESTIVAL
20191 E Country Club Drive
Suite 709
Aventura, FL 33180

Phone: 305-935-5115
Fax: 305-935-9087
e-mail: info@miamipianofest.com
Web Site: www.miamipianofest.com
Officers:
  Founder: Giselle Brodsky
Management:
  Artistic Director: Giselle Brodsky
  Executive Director: Barbara Muze
Mission: To discover, promote and support the great masters of the keyboard while providing audiences with a unique musical experience.
Founded: 1998
Specialized Field: Classical
Status: Nonprofit
Paid Staff: 2
Volunteer Staff: 10
Paid Artists: 15
Budget: $360,000
Income Sources: Private Donations; Grants; Ticket Sales; Merchandise
Season: February
Performs At: Lincoln Theatre
Annual Attendance: 5,000
Facility Category: Lincoln Theatre
Seating Capacity: 700

818
TAMPA BAY SYMPHONY
PO Box 4653
Clearwater, FL 33758
Phone: 727-442-3696
e-mail: info@tampabaysymphony.com
Web Site: www.tampabaysymphony.com
Officers:
  President: James R Parady
  VP: Kurt M Klotz
  Treasurer: Victoria G Patterson
  Secretary: Carol M Skey
Management:
  Musica Director/Conductor: Jack Heller
Mission: To promote interest in classical music in the Tampa Bay area and to encourage and educate youth throughout Florida with a Young Artist Competition.
Specialized Field: Orchestra

819
MIAMI BACH SOCIETY/TROPICAL BAROQUE MUSIC FESTIVAL
PO Box 4034
Coral Gables, FL 33114
Phone: 305-669-1376
e-mail: info@miamibachsociety.org
Web Site: miamibachsociety.org
Officers:
  Chairman: Gordon Fales
  Treasurer: Kingsley Bewley
  Secretary: Claire Veater
Management:
  Artistic Director: Donald Oglesby
  Executive Director: Kathryn B Gaubatz
Mission: To perform and present the music of Johann Sebastian Bach.
Utilizes: Guest Directors; Guest Musical Directors; Guest Musicians; Multimedia; Original Music Scores
Founded: 1984
Specialized Field: Baroque
Status: Nonprofit
Paid Staff: 4
Budget: $300,000
Income Sources: Corporations; Government; Indivdual Donations; Ticket Sales
Season: October-January

Performs At: Plymouth Congregational Church; First United Methodista Church of Coral Gables
Annual Attendance: 5,000
Organization Type: Performing, Touring and Presenting Musical Organization
Resident Groups: MBS Chorus and Orchestra

820
DAYTONA BEACH SYMPHONY SOCIETY
PO Box 2
Daytona Beach, FL 32115
Phone: 386-253-2901
Fax: 386-253-5774
e-mail: info@dbss.org
Web Site: www.dbss.org
Officers:
 President: Carol Lively Platig
 VP: Harvey Morse
 Secretary: Yolanda Reilly
 Treasurer: Carolyn S Brewer
 Chair: Dallas Weekley
Management:
 Executive Director: Carol Anderson McLean
Mission: To present diverse musical and cultural programs to stimulate the community with an appreciation for music.
Utilizes: Composers; Five Seasonal Concerts; Guest Soloists; Multimedia
Founded: 1952
Specialized Field: Symphony; Orchestra; Chamber
Status: Nonprofit
Paid Staff: 2
Budget: 35,259
Income Sources: Grants; Donations; Ticket Sales
Season: November-March
Performs At: Peabody Auditorium
Affiliations: None
Annual Attendance: 20,000
Organization Type: Sponsoring, Presenters

821
FLORIDA INTERNATIONAL FESTIVAL
210-212 S Beach Street
Daytona Beach, FL 32114
Phone: 386-872-2323
Fax: 386-238-1663
e-mail: fifcfce@fif-lso.org
Web Site: www.fif-lso.org
Officers:
 General Manager: Eric Lariviere
 Operations Manager: Robert Cox
 Marketing Coordinator: Christine Preston
Mission: Through a variety of performances ranging from music, dance and comedy are presented through both free and paid programs. It takes place over a 17 day period with 80 or more performances.
Utilizes: Artists-in-Residence; Dance Companies; Guest Choreographers; Guest Composers; Guest Instructors; Guest Musicians; Multimedia; Original Music Scores; Singers; Theatre Companies
Founded: 1974
Specialized Field: Classical; Pops
Paid Staff: 6
Volunteer Staff: 100
Paid Artists: 200
Budget: $400,000 - 1,000,000
Income Sources: Ticket Sales; Contributions; Grants
Season: July, Biennial
Performs At: Our Lady of Lourdes Church, Mary McLeod Bethune Performing Arts Center, Ormond Beach Performing Arts Center
Annual Attendance: 2,000-40,000
Facility Category: Peabody Aud; Ocean Cntr; Ormond Beach Cntr; etc.

822
SYMPHONY OF THE AMERICAS
2425 East Commercial Blvd
Suite 405
Fort Lauderdale, FL 33308
Phone: 954-335-7002
Fax: 945-335-7008
e-mail: sympamer@aol.com
Web Site: www.symphonyoftheamericas.org
Officers:
 President: Beth Hollandi
 Secretary: Sherill Capi
 Treasurer: Stanley Marks
Management:
 Artistic Director: James Brooks-Bruzzese
 Executive Director: Renee LaBonte
Mission: To present diverse orchestral music to enrich the cultural environment of South Florida and the Americas.
Utilizes: Contract Orchestras; Guest Soloists
Founded: 1988
Specialized Field: Classical
Status: Nonprofit
Paid Staff: 4
Volunteer Staff: 2
Paid Artists: 60
Budget: $260,000-1,050,000
Income Sources: Sponsers; Grants; Donations; Program Ads
Performs At: Broward Performing Arts Center-Lmetoro Theater
Annual Attendance: 2.700
Seating Capacity: 2,700

823
SOUTHWEST FLORIDA SYMPHONY ORCHESTRA & CHORUS ASSOCIATION
12651 McGregor Blvd. #4-403
Fort Myers, FL 33919
Phone: 239-418-0996
Fax: 239-418-0725
e-mail: info@swflso.org
Web Site: www.swflso.org
Officers:
 President: Christine Lacroix
 Vice President: J Thomas Uhler
 Secretary: Toni Mather
 Treasurer: John Hudson
Management:
 Development Director: Tiffany Doer
 Marketing: Andrew Bassila
 Operations: Heidi Kelley
Mission: Sharing the gift of classical music to more people in the communities through the Sanibel Series and the Around Town concerts.
Utilizes: Collaborations; Commissioned Composers; Composers; Contract Orchestras; Educators; Grant Writers; Guest Accompanists; Guest Companies; Guest Composers; Guest Directors; Guest Lecturers; Guest Musical Directors; Guest Musicians; Local Unknown Artists; Lyricists; Multimedia; Music; Resident Companies; Sign Language Translators; Soloists; Students
Founded: 1962
Specialized Field: Classical
Status: Professional
Volunteer Staff: 450
Budget: $1.3 Million
Income Sources: Ticket Sales, Private and Corporate Donations, Fundraising, Symphony Society
Season: November-April
Performs At: Barbara B. Mann Performing Arts Hall
Annual Attendance: 22,000

Organization Type: Performing

824
GAINESVILLE CHAMBER ORCHESTRA
PO Box 357011
Gainesville, FL 32635-7011
Phone: 352-336-5448
Web Site: www.gcomusic.org
Officers:
 President: Lynn Noffsinger
 VP: Rebecca Micha
 VP: Greg Johnson
 Treasurer: Tim Hoskinson
 Secretary: Lispbeth Gets
Management:
 Music Director/Conductor: Evans Haile
 Orchestra Representative: Terence Muir
 Orchestra Representative: Grace Kang
 Personnel Director: Virginia Lamboley
Mission: To provide to Alachua County and surrounding areas quality programs of traditional and contemporary repertoire, which will entertain, enrich and educate a diverse and broad-based audience.
Founded: 1983
Specialized Field: Classical
Status: Professional
Budget: $200,000
Income Sources: Private and Corporate Donations, Ticket Sales
Performs At: Center for the Performing Arts; University of Florida and Santa Fe Community College
Annual Attendance: 15,000

825
MELBOURNE CHAMBER MUSIC SOCIETY
PO Box 033403
Indialantic, FL 32903
Phone: 321-956-8775
Fax: 321-956-8775
e-mail: mcms@cfl.rr.com
Web Site: www.melbournechambermusicsociety.com
Officers:
 President: Diane Taylor
 Secretary: Peggy Snead
 Treasurer: Irene Quilleux
Mission: To showcase international chamber artists for the Brevard community.
Founded: 1997
Specialized Field: Chamber
Income Sources: Private and Corporate Donations, Ticket Sales
Season: October-March
Performs At: St Mark's United Methodist Church
Organization Type: Presenters, Sponsors

826
JACKSONVILLE SYMPHONY ORCHESTRA
300 W Water Street
Suite 200
Jacksonville, FL 32202
Phone: 904-354-5479
Fax: 904-354-9238
Toll-free: 877-662-6731
e-mail: frontdesk@jaxsymphony.org
Web Site: www.jaxsymphony.org
Officers:
 Chair: Jim Van Vleck
 Treasurer: James A Heinz
 Secretary: Halcyon E Skinner
Management:
 Exeucutive Director: Stacy Ridenour

Operations: Kevin Roberts
Development: Kaye Glover
Mission: To contribute to the artistic culture of the community by performing high quality music to Florida audiences.
Utilizes: Commissioned Composers; Composers; Guest Artists; Guest Musical Directors; Poets; Singers
Founded: 1949
Specialized Field: Symphony; Orchestra
Status: Professional, Nonprofit
Paid Staff: 25
Volunteer Staff: 1700
Paid Artists: 52
Budget: 6.2 million
Income Sources: Ticket sales, Private donations, Grants, Fundraisers, Jacksonville Symphony Guild
Season: October-May
Performs At: Robert E Jacoby Symphony Hall; Times Union Center For The Performing Arts
Annual Attendance: 220,000
Type of Stage: Platform
Seating Capacity: 1800
Year Built: 1997
Year Remodeled: 1999
Rental Contact: Director Adina Alford
Organization Type: Performing; Touring; Educational

827
KEY WEST SYMPHONY

PO Box 744
Key West, FL 33041
Phone: 305-292-1774
Fax: 305-292-5623
e-mail: info@keywestsymphony.com
Web Site: www.keywestsymphony.com
Officers:
Founder: Sebrina Alfonso
Management:
General Manager: Susan Collins
Marketing: Rebecca Tomlinson
Mission: To reach, entertain and educate the community with live symphonic music.
Founded: 1997
Specialized Field: Symphony
Status: Professional, Nonprofit
Paid Staff: 3
Paid Artists: 80
Budget: 700,000
Income Sources: Private and Corporate Donations, Ticket Sales, Grants
Season: December-April
Performs At: Tennessee Williams Fine Arts Center
Annual Attendance: 2,000

828
IMPERIAL SYMPHONY ORCHESTRA

1037 S Florida Avenue
Suite 125
Lakeland, FL 33806
Phone: 863-688-3743
Fax: 863-686-2881
e-mail: info@imperialsymphony.org
Web Site: www.imperialsymphony.org
Officers:
President: Curt Wheeler
Secretary: Lu Fitzwater
Treasurer: Tom Mack
Chair: Brock Self
Management:
Music Director/Conductor: Mark Thielen
Mission: To serve the community by providing touching musical performances.
Founded: 1965
Specialized Field: Symphony; Orchestra

Status: Professional, Nonprofit
Budget: $260,000-1,050,000
Income Sources: Private and Corporate Donations, Ticket Sales, Grant from National Endowment for the Arts
Season: September-May
Performs At: Youkey Theater; Lakeland Center

829
BREVARD SYMPHONY ORCHESTRA

1500 Highland Avenue
PO Box 361965
Melbourne, FL 32935
Phone: 321-242-2024
Fax: 321-259-4716
e-mail: info@brevardsymphony.com
Web Site: www.brevardsymphony.com
Officers:
Chairman: Harry Brandon
Treasurer: Brian Nemeroff
Secretary: Leasha Flammio-Watson
Management:
Music Director/Principal Conductor: Christopher Confessore
Executive Director: Fran Detsie
Mission: The Brevard Symphony Orchestra shall inspire and enhance the quality of life within our community by providing exceptional orchestral music.
Utilizes: Resident Artists
Founded: 1954
Specialized Field: Musical
Status: Professional
Paid Staff: 6
Volunteer Staff: 250
Paid Artists: 50
Budget: $620,020
Income Sources: Private and Corporate Donations, Memorial Gift Contributions, Endowment Fund
Season: October-April
Performs At: King Center for the Performing Arts
Annual Attendance: 40,000+
Facility Category: In Residence

830
FRIENDS OF CHAMBER MUSIC OF MIAMI

2665 S Bayshore Drive
Miami, FL 33133
Phone: 305-372-2975
Fax: 305-381-8734
e-mail: info@miamichambermusic.org
Web Site: www.miamichambermusic.org
Officers:
President: Julian H Kreeger
Mission: To present exemplary chamber musicians to preserve and develop appreciation for chamber music.
Founded: 1955
Specialized Field: Chamber
Status: Nonprofit
Income Sources: Private and Corporate Donations, Ticket Sales
Season: December-May
Performs At: Gusman Concert Hall, University of Miami
Organization Type: Presenters, Performing

831
MIAMI CLASSICAL GUITAR SOCIETY

PO Box 0725
Miami, FL 33265-0725
Phone: 305-412-2494
e-mail: info@miamiguitar.org
Web Site: www.miamiguitar.org
Officers:
Founder/President: Carlos Molina

Mission: To promote appreciation for classical guitar music performed by local, national and international artists.
Utilizes: Composers; Guest Accompanists; Guest Musical Directors; Multimedia; Singers
Founded: 1987
Specialized Field: Classical Guitar
Volunteer Staff: 4
Paid Artists: 6
Budget: $45,000
Income Sources: Grants; Sponsors; Members; Ticket Sales
Performs At: Theaters; Churches
Annual Attendance: 2,000
Seating Capacity: 300

832
SOUTH FLORIDA YOUTH SYMPHONY

12645 SW 114 Avenue
Miami, FL 33176
Phone: 305-238-2729
e-mail: foertter@gmail.com
Web Site: www.sfys.net
Mission: To foster the musical growth of young people.
Utilizes: Actors; Artists-in-Residence; Collaborating Artists; Collaborations; Commissioned Music; Dancers; Educators; Guest Accompanists; Guest Companies; Guest Composers; Guest Designers; Guest Directors; Guest Ensembles; Guest Musical Directors; High School Drama; Instructors; Lyricists; Multi Collaborations; Multimedia; Organization Contracts; Selected Students; Soloists; Special Technical Talent; Theatre Companies
Founded: 1964
Specialized Field: Orchestra; Ensemble
Status: Nonprofit
Paid Staff: 1
Volunteer Staff: 6
Budget: 160,000
Income Sources: Grants, Private and Corporate Donations, Tuition, Fundraisers, Grant National Endowment for the Arts
Season: December-May
Performs At: Local Halls; Parks; Schools
Annual Attendance: 3,500
Organization Type: Performing; Educational
Resident Groups: All

833
NEW WORLD SYMPHONY

541 Lincoln Road
Miami Beach, FL 33139
Phone: 305-673-3330
Fax: 305-673-6749
Toll-free: 800-597-3331
e-mail: email@nws.edu
Web Site: www.nws.edu
Officers:
Founder: Michael Tilson Thomas
President/CEO: Howard Herring
Management:
Artistic Director: Michael Tilson-Thomas
Marketing Director: Sabrina Anico
Development: Paul Woehrle
Mission: To prepare young music graduates for orchestral leadership with an advanced, three year training program.
Utilizes: Collaborations; Five Seasonal Concerts; Guest Accompanists; Guest Artists; Guest Companies; Guest Composers; Guest Ensembles; Guest Instructors; Guest Musical Directors; Guest Musicians; Guest Soloists; High School Drama; Instructors; Local

Artists; Multimedia; Organization Contracts; Original Music Scores; Sign Language Translators; Singers; Soloists; Visual Arts
Founded: 1987
Specialized Field: Symphony; Orchestra; Chamber; Educational; Ensemble
Status: Professional, Nonprofit
Paid Staff: 48
Budget: $7.5 Million
Income Sources: Endowment, Ticket Sales, Private and Corporate Donations
Season: August-May
Annual Attendance: 22,000
Facility Category: Theatre
Type of Stage: Sprung Beech
Stage Dimensions: 49'32 x 42'4 x 25
Seating Capacity: 705
Year Built: 1936
Year Remodeled: 1988
Organization Type: Performing; Touring

834
PHILHARMONIC CENTER FOR THE ARTS

5833 Pelican Bay Boulevard
Naples, FL 34108
Phone: 239-597-1900
Fax: 239-597-7856
Toll-free: 800-597-1900
e-mail: info@thephil.org
Web Site: www.thephil.org
Officers:
   Founder/CEO: Myra Janco Daniels
Mission: To enlighten, educate and entertain people of all ages and backgrounds in Southwest Florida by presenting the very best of the visual and performing arts.
Founded: 1989
Opened: 1989
Specialized Field: Orchestra; Show Tunes
Status: Professional
Paid Staff: 412
Annual Attendance: 500,000
Seating Capacity: 1,425

835
OCALA SYMPHONY ORCHESTRA

416 SE Fort King Street
Ocala, FL 34471
Phone: 352-351-1606
e-mail: toni.james@embarqmail.com
Web Site: www.cfsymphony.com
Officers:
   President: Toni James
   Treasurer: Bill Nassal
Management:
   Music Director: James Plondke
   General Manager: Dorothy Pitone
Mission: To present orchestral music performances for the community.
Founded: 1975
Specialized Field: Orchestra
Budget: 200,000
Performs At: CFCC Fine Arts Auditorium; Lecanto Auditorium
Annual Attendance: 5,000

836
FLORIDA SYMPHONY YOUTH ORCHESTRA

812 E Rollins Street
Suite 300
Orlando, FL 32803
Phone: 407-999-7800
Fax: 407-898-5250
e-mail: kerry@fsyo.org
Web Site: www.fsyo.org
Officers:
   President: Norberto Katz
   Treasurer: Brett Hendley
   Secretary: Susan Jones
Management:
   Executive Director: Kerry McGlone
   Operations Manager: Carl Rendek
Mission: To educate young musicians, strengthening their skills and appreciation of music.
Founded: 1957
Specialized Field: Symphony
Status: Nonprofit
Paid Staff: 3
Volunteer Staff: 50
Paid Artists: 3
Budget: $150,000-260,000
Income Sources: Private and Corporate Donations, Box Office, Grants, United Arts and Florida Arts
Season: October-May
Performs At: Performing Arts Centre
Annual Attendance: 5,000
Seating Capacity: 2,359
Organization Type: Performing Arts Center

837
ORLANDO PHILHARMONIC ORCHESTRA

812 E Rollins Street
Suite 300
Orlando, FL 32803
Phone: 407-896-6700
Fax: 407-896-5512
e-mail: mfischer@orlandophil.org
Web Site: www.orlandophil.org
Officers:
   President: Carol Conner
   Secretary: Susan M Curran
   Treasurer: Marc L Hagle
Management:
   Executive Director: David Schillhammer
   General Manager: Mark Fischer
   Operations: Sally Carter
   Marketing Director: Sandy Rendek
Mission: To share symphonic music with the community through performance, education and cultrual leadership.
Founded: 1993
Specialized Field: Orchestra; Classical; Pops
Budget: $1,050,000-3,600,000
Income Sources: Private and Corporate Donations, State of Florida, Philharmonic's Endowment, Foundations, Grants
Season: October-April
Performs At: Margeson Theater; Lowndes Shakespeare Center, Community Presbyterian Church
Seating Capacity: 2,500

838
UNIVERSITY OF CENTRAL FLORIDA ORCHESTRA

UCF Music Department
4000 Central Florida Boulevard
Orlando, FL 32816-1354
Phone: 407-823-2869
Fax: 407-823-3378
e-mail: ucfmusic@mail.ucf.edu
Web Site: www.music.ucf.edu.
Officers:
   Chair: Johnny Pherigo
Mission: To give students an artistic outlet to perform for the public in an orchestral setting.
Founded: 1929
Specialized Field: Ensemble; Chamber
Status: Nonprofit
Income Sources: University Of Central Florida
Performs At: Music Rehearsal Hall; University of Central Florida
Annual Attendance: 3,200
Seating Capacity: 500

839
PALM BEACH SYMPHONY

Palm Beach Towers
44 Cocoanut Row
Suite M207B
Palm Beach, FL 33480
Phone: 561-655-2657
Web Site: www.palmbeachsymphony.com
Management:
   Music Director/General Manager: Ray Robinson
Mission: To bring quality music programs to the Palm Beach community.
Utilizes: Guest Artists
Founded: 1963
Specialized Field: Symphony
Status: Nonprofit
Volunteer Staff: 2
Paid Artists: 60
Budget: $200,000
Income Sources: Private and Corporate Donations, Ticket Sales
Season: November-April
Performs At: Flagler Museum, Society of the Four Arts, Bethesda by the Sea Church, Colony Pavilion
Annual Attendance: 2,500-3,000
Facility Category: multi-venues
Seating Capacity: 1,000

840
JAZZ SOCIETY OF PENSACOLA

PO Box 18337
Pensacola, FL 32523-8337
Phone: 850-433-8382
Fax: 850-433-8790
e-mail: jsop1@juno.com
Web Site: www.jazzpensacola.com
Officers:
   President: Crystal Joy Albert
Management:
   Administrator: Kathy Lyon
Mission: The Jazz Society of Pensacola aspires to be the premier Jazz Society on the Central Gulf Coast dedicated to promoting all forms of jazz-America's Music. We endeavor to provide a social forum for jazz performance, education and enjoyment for listeners and musicians.
Founded: 1983
Specialized Field: Jazz
Status: Non-Profit
Paid Staff: 1
Volunteer Staff: 50
Budget: 40,000
Income Sources: Individual Donors, Corporate Sponsors, NWFL, Florida Arts Councils, Volunteers
Season: April
Performs At: Annual Pensacola JazzFest held in outdoor park; Seville Square; Monthly Concerts/Jam sessions In Local Venues
Affiliations: Charter Member; Jazz Education Network
Annual Attendance: 14,000
Facility Category: City Park
Type of Stage: Gazebo, Tented Stage

841
PENSACOLA SYMPHONY ORCHESTRA
205 E Zarragossa Street
PO Box 1752
Pensacola, FL 32502
Phone: 850-435-2533
e-mail: info@pensacolasymphony.com
Web Site: www.pensacolasymphony.com
Officers:
    President: William B Dollarhide
    Treasurer: Milton Usry
    Secretary: Margaret J Couch
Management:
    Executive Director: Christina Littlejohn
    Development: Bret Barrow
    Marketing Director: Crystal Lohman
Mission: To educate and enrich the Pensacola community through music.
Utilizes: Guest Artists
Founded: 1926
Specialized Field: Symphony
Status: Nonprofit
Budget: $260,000-1,050,000
Income Sources: Grants, Private and Corporate Supporters, Ticket Sales, Endowment Fund
Season: October-May
Performs At: Saenger Theatre
Annual Attendance: 43,000

842
SARASOTA YOUTH ORCHESTRAS
709 N Tamiami Trail
Sarasota, FL 34236
Phone: 941-953-4252
Fax: 941-953-3059
e-mail: rmccabe@sarasotaorchestra.org
Web Site: www.sarasotaorchestra.org
Officers:
    President/CEO: Joseph McKenna
    CFO: Douglas Shanley
    CMO: Gordon Greenfield
    Education Director: Rose Ann McCabe
Mission: The Sarasota Youth Orchestras consist of five orchestras, affording students the opportunity to participate in an orchestra comparable to their skill level.
Utilizes: Composers-in-Residence; Educators; Fine Artists; Guest Composers; Multimedia; Poets; Resident Artists; Resident Companies; Soloists
Founded: 1959
Specialized Field: Youth Philharmonic; Youth Symphony; String Ensemble
Status: Non-Professional, Nonprofit
Income Sources: Ticket Sales; Sponsorships; Special Gifts; Scholarships; Endowment Gifts; Planned Giving; Fundraisers
Performs At: Sarasota Opera House; Van Wezel Performing Arts Hall; Holley Hall
Facility Category: Performing; Resident; Touring
Organization Type: Performing; Educational

843
JAZZ CLUB OF SARASOTA
330 S Pineapple Avenue
Suite 111
Sarasota, FL 34236
Phone: 941-366-1552
Fax: 941-366-1553
e-mail: admin@jazzclubsarasota.com
Officers:
    VP: Wes Bearden
Management:
    Volunteer Artistic Director: Gordon Garrett
Mission: To promote, preserve, perform and educate people about jazz the original American art form.
Utilizes: Original Music Scores; Sign Language Translators
Founded: 1980
Specialized Field: Jazz
Paid Staff: 1
Volunteer Staff: 60
Paid Artists: 100
Non-paid Artists: 10
Income Sources: Membership Dues, Grants
Season: October-April
Performs At: Van Wezel Performing Arts Hall, Holley Hall, Bayfront Community Center
Annual Attendance: 8,000

844
SARASOTA ORCHESTRA STRING QUARTET
709 N Tamiami Trail
Sarasota, FL 34236
Phone: 941-953-4252
Fax: 941-953-3059
Toll-free: 866-508-0611
e-mail: rmmcabe@sarasotaorchestra.org
Web Site: www.sarasotaorchestra.org
Officers:
    President/CEO: Joseph McKenna
    CFO: Douglas Shanley
    CMO: Gordon Greenfield
    Chairman: Virginia Toulmin
    Secretary: Marie Monsky
    Treasurer: George Allison
Management:
    Artistic Director: Leif Bjaland
    Operations Director: Patricia Joslyn
Mission: To provide a showcase for new, young string players in the Sarasota Orchestra.
Utilizes: Multimedia; Original Music Scores
Founded: 1967
Specialized Field: Ensemble
Status: Professional, Nonprofit
Paid Artists: 4
Income Sources: Ticket Sales, Sponsorships, Special Gifts, Scholarships, Endowment Gifts, Planned Giving, Fundraisers, Florida West Coast Symphony Association
Season: October-May
Performs At: Holley Hall
Organization Type: Performing; Touring; Resident

845
SARASOTA ORCHESTRA
709 N Tamiami Trail
Sarasota, FL 34236
Phone: 941-953-4252
Fax: 941-953-3059
e-mail: rmccabe@sarasotaorchestra.org
Web Site: www.sarasotaorchestra.org
Officers:
    President/CEO: Joseph McKenna
    CFO: Douglas Shanley
    CMO: Gordon Greenfield
Management:
    Artistic Director: Leif Bjaland
    Operations Director: Patricia Joslyn
Mission: To build an orchestra of resident musicians with talented musical skills, to present diverse music programming in Florida and to attract visiting soloists of international accclaim. The orchestra also strives to involve as many people as possible in classical and symphonic music, providing lifelong learning opportunities for the community.

Utilizes: Collaborations; Fine Artists; Five Seasonal Concerts; Grant Writers; Guest Companies; Guest Musical Directors; Guest Musicians; Guest Writers; Local Artists; Multimedia; Organization Contracts; Original Music Scores; Singers; Student Interns
Founded: 1956
Specialized Field: Symphony
Status: Nonprofit, Professional
Budget: $4 million
Season: September-May
Seating Capacity: 1,736
Year Built: 1968
Organization Type: Performing; Resident

846
SARASOTA ORCHESTRA NEW ARTISTS PIANO QUARTET
709 N Tamiami Trail
Sarasota, FL 34236
Phone: 941-953-4252
Fax: 941-953-3059
Toll-free: 866-508-0611
e-mail: rmmcabe@sarasotaorchestra.org
Web Site: www.sarasotaorchestra.org
Officers:
    President/CEO: Joseph McKenna
    CFO: Douglas Shanley
    CMO: Gordon Greenfield
    Chairman: Virginia Toulmin
    Secretary: Marie Monsky
    Treasurer: George Allison
Management:
    Artistic Director: Leif Bjaland
    Operations Director: Patricia Joslyn
Mission: To promote classical music locally, statewide and nationally by presenting high quality music programs.
Utilizes: Artists-in-Residence; Multimedia; Poets; Resident Artists; Resident Companies
Founded: 1991
Specialized Field: String Ensemble
Status: Professional, Nonprofit
Paid Artists: 4
Income Sources: Ticket Sales, Sponsorships, Special Gifts, Scholarships, Endowment Gifts, Planned Giving, Fundraising, Florida West Coast Symphony Association
Season: October-May
Performs At: Holley Hall
Organization Type: Performing; Resident; Touring

847
SARASOTA ORCHESTRA WIND QUINTET
709 N Tamiami Trail
Sarasota, FL 34236
Phone: 941-953-4252
Fax: 941-953-3059
Toll-free: 866-508-0611
e-mail: rmmcabe@sarasotaorchestra.org
Web Site: www.sarasotaorchestra.org
Officers:
    President/CEO: Joseph McKenna
    CFO: Douglas Shanley
    CMO: Gordon Greenfield
    Chairman: Virginia Toulmin
    Secretary: Marie Monsky
    Treasurer: George Allison
Management:
    Artistic Director: Leif Bjaland
    Operations Director: Patricia Joslyn
Mission: To promote classical music locally, statewide and nationally by presenting high quality music programs.
Utilizes: Artists-in-Residence; Poets; Resident Artists; Resident Companies

Founded: 1984
Specialized Field: Wind Ensemble
Status: Professional, Nonprofit
Income Sources: Ticket Sales, Sponsorships, Special Gifts. Scholarships, Endowment Gifts, Planned Giving, Fundraising, Florida West Coast Symphony Association
Season: October-May
Performs At: Holley Hall
Facility Category: Performing; Resident; Touring

848
SARASOTA ORCHESTRA BRASS QUINTET
709 N Tamiami Trail
Sarasota, FL 34236
Phone: 941-953-4252
Fax: 941-953-3059
Toll-free: 866-508-0611
e-mail: rmmcabe@sarasotaorchestra.org
Web Site: www.sarasotaorchestra.org
Officers:
President/CEO: Joseph McKenna
CFO: Douglas Shanley
CMO: Gordon Greenfield
Chairman: Virginia Toulmin
Secretary: Marie Monsky
Treasurer: George Allison
Management:
Artistic Director: Leif Bjaland
Operations Director: Patricia Joslyn
Mission: To promote classical music locally, statewide and nationally by presenting high quality music programs.
Utilizes: Multimedia; Original Music Scores
Founded: 1967
Specialized Field: Ensemble
Status: Professional, Nonprofit
Paid Artists: 4
Income Sources: Ticket Sales, Sponsorships, Special Gifts, Scholarships, Endowment Gifts, Planned Giving, Fundraisers, Florida West Coast Symphony Association
Season: October-May
Performs At: Holley Hall
Organization Type: Performing; Touring; Resident

849
PINELLAS YOUTH SYMPHONY
PO Box 4106
Seminole, FL 33775
Phone: 727-438-3149
e-mail: pysdirector@yahoo.com
Web Site: www.pysmusic.org
Officers:
President: Leo Meirose
Secretary: John Creveling
Treasurer: Wayne Raymond
Management:
Executive Director: Jane T Hine
Conductor: Dr Susan Robinson
Serenade String Orchestra: Lei Liu
Operations Director: Wayne Raymond
Mission: To enhance the music education of the youth in Pinellas County.
Founded: 1958
Specialized Field: Orchestra; Ensemble
Status: Professional
Income Sources: Tuition, Grants, Contributions
Performs At: Murray Studio; Ruth Eckerd Hall
Organization Type: Performing

850
FLORIDA ORCHESTRA
244 Second Avenue N
Suite 420
St Petersburg, FL 33701
Phone: 727-892-3331
Fax: 727-892-3338
e-mail: admin@floridaorchestra.org
Web Site: www.floridaorchestra.org
Officers:
Chairman: Thomas Farquhar
President: Michael Pastreich
Secretary: Susan B. Betzer, MD
Management:
Music Director: Stefan Sanderling
Coffee Concert Conductor: Allistair Willis
Artistic Administrator: David Rogers
Development Director: Emily McClain
Mission: To enrich the life of the Tampa Bay area as it inspires, entertains and educates a wide and diverse audience with the unique experience of live symphonic music ensuring that future generations will continue to enjoy this legacy that so magnificently celebrates the human spirit.
Founded: 1968
Specialized Field: Symphony; Orchestra
Status: Professional, Nonprofit
Paid Staff: 21
Paid Artists: 72
Budget: 8 Million
Income Sources: Ticket Sales; Private & Corporate Donations; Fundraising Events
Performs At: Progress Energy Center For The Arts; Mahaffey Theatre; Stroz Center For The Performing Arts; Ruth Eckerd Hall
Annual Attendance: 150,000
Organization Type: Performing; Touring; Resident; Educational

851
BIG BEND COMMUNITY ORCHESTRA
The Artist Series
1897 Capital Circle NE
Suite 204
Tallahassee, FL 32308
Phone: 850-224-9934
Fax: 850-224-1730
e-mail: ginnyden@comcast.net
Web Site: www.bbcorch.org
Officers:
Board Chair: Richard Hopkins
Management:
Conductor: Shleby Chipman
Associate Conductor: Ed Kawakami
Assistant Director: Jame Mick
Mission: All volunteer community orchestra provides area with The Artist Series.
Utilizes: Community Members; Community Talent; Educators; Guest Composers; Guest Designers; Guest Musical Directors; Guest Musicians; Instructors; Local Artists & Directors; Multimedia; Scenic Designers; Singers; Soloists
Founded: 1994
Specialized Field: Orchestra
Status: Nonprofit
Budget: $6,000
Income Sources: Funded by members of the Orchestra, City of Tallahassee, Leon County, Private and Corporate Donations
Season: October-April
Performs At: Lee Hall Auditorium
Affiliations: American Symphony Orchestra League
Annual Attendance: 600

Facility Category: FAMU Lee Hall Auditorium/TCC Turner Aud
Seating Capacity: 1,200

852
TALLAHASSEE SYMPHONY ORCHESTRA
1345 Thomasville Road
Tallahassee, FL 32303
Phone: 850-224-0461
Fax: 850-222-9092
e-mail: operations@tallahasseesymphony.org
Web Site: www.tallahasseesymphoony.org
Officers:
President: Mary Bedford
Treasurer: Sean Singleton
Secretary: Chris Sloan
Management:
Music Director: Miriam Burns
Executive Director: Lois D Griffin
VP Artistic Affairs: Don Gibson
Assistant Concertmaster: Rang Hee Kim
Operations Director: Laura Figo
Mission: To maintain and further develop a resident, professional symphony orchestra to produce musical performances of the highest artistic quality and to provide cultural and educational opportunities in the Tallahassee, North Florida and South Georgia communities.
Founded: 1979
Specialized Field: Symphony
Status: Professional; Nonprofit
Paid Staff: 3
Income Sources: American Symphony Orchestra League, Private and Corporate Donations, Grants, Ticket Sales
Season: September-April
Performs At: Ruby Diamond Auditorium; Florida State University
Organization Type: Performing; Resident; Presenters

853
VENICE SYMPHONY
PO Box 1561
Venice, FL 34284
Phone: 941-488-1010
Fax: 941-488-7074
e-mail: venicesymphony@aol.com
Web Site: www.thevenicesymphony.org
Management:
Artistic Director/Conductor: Kenneth Bowermeister
Personnel Manager: Michael Fiore
Executive Director: Jean Peters
Mission: To cultivate, promote and sponsor an appreciation of musical arts in the community, secure patrons of these arts, and perform concerts
Utilizes: Guest Accompanists; Guest Companies; Guest Musicians; Guest Writers; Local Unknown Artists; Multimedia; Original Music Scores; Sign Language Translators; Singers; Soloists
Founded: 1974
Specialized Field: Classical
Status: Professional
Paid Staff: 5
Paid Artists: 75
Budget: $450,000
Income Sources: Tickets; Contributions; Grants
Performs At: Church of the Nazarene
Annual Attendance: 11,875
Facility Category: Church
Seating Capacity: 625
Organization Type: Performing

854
PALM BEACH POPS

Palm Beach Pops, Inc.
500 S Australian Avenue
Suite 100
West Palm Beach, FL 33401
Phone: 561-832-7677
Fax: 561-832-9686
Toll-free: 800-448-2472
e-mail: info@palmbeachpops.org
Web Site: www.palmbeachpops.org
Officers:
   President/Chairman/Founder: Robert Lappin
Management:
   Executive Director: David Quilleon,
   dquilleon@palmbeachpops.org
   Music Director/Conductor: Robert Lappin
Mission: To provide artistic excellence and education
with each performance.
Utilizes: Guest Accompanists; Guest Musicians;
Multimedia; Original Music Scores; Paid Performers;
Singers; Students
Founded: 1991
Specialized Field: Symphony; Pops; Orchestra
Status: Nonprofit
Paid Staff: 12
Season: November-April
Performs At: Kravis Center for the Performing Arts;
Florida Atlantic University Center Auditorium; Palm
Beach Gardens Eissey Campus
Annual Attendance: 65,000
Organization Type: Presenters, Performing

Georgia

855
ALBANY SYMPHONY ORCHESTRA

PO Box 70065
Albany, GA 31708-0065
Phone: 229-430-6799
Fax: 229-430-6798
e-mail: albanysymphony@yahoo.com
Web Site: www.albanysymphony.org
Officers:
   President: Diane Cunningham
   General Manager: Marie Galamba-Pierce
   Publicity/Marketing: Robert M Drake
   Assistant Publicity Director: Richard H Waller
   Operations Manager: Edward J Trammell
Management:
   Music Director/Conductor: Claire Fox Hillard
   Concertmaster: Matson Topper
   Assistant Concertmaster: Alicija Vsarek
Mission: Dedicated to providing and promoting quality
symphonic music for Southwest Georgia through the
maintenance of a symphony orchestra and related
educational activities.
Utilizes: Artists-in-Residence; Collaborations;
Composers-in-Residence; Guest Accompanists; Guest
Companies; Guest Musicians; Instructors; Organization
Contracts; Original Music Scores; Singers; Soloists
Founded: 1965
Specialized Field: Symphony; Orchestra
Status: Nonprofit
Paid Staff: 4
Volunteer Staff: 10
Budget: $275,000
Income Sources: American Symphony Orchestra
League, Albany Arts Council, Private and Corporate
Donations, Ticket Sales, Grants
Season: August-May

Performs At: Albany Municipal Auditorium, Albany
Civic Center, Parks at Chehaw, Mount Zion Baptist
Church, Veterans Park Amphitheater
Facility Category: Municipal Auditorium
Seating Capacity: 980
Year Built: 1915
Year Remodeled: 1993
Organization Type: Performing; Educational

856
GEORGIA SOUTHWESTERN STATE UNIVERSITY CHAMBER CONCERT SERIES

Georgia Southwest State University
800 Wheatley Street
Americus, GA 31709-4693
Phone: 229-931-2204
Fax: 229-931-2927
e-mail: jem@canes.gsw.edu
Management:
   Director: Dr Julie Megginson
   Conductor: Dr Herschel Beazley
Mission: The series features a variety of chamber
ensembles including string quartets and trios. Six
classical performances are held each year.
Specialized Field: Chamber
Status: Nonprofit
Income Sources: Private and Corporate Donations,
Ticket Sales, Grants
Season: October-April
Performs At: Jackson Performance Hall
Seating Capacity: 250

857
ATLANTA CHAMBER PLAYERS

PO Box 5438
Atlanta, GA 30343
Phone: 404-872-4952
Fax: 404-872-4952
e-mail: paulapeace@bellsouth.net
Web Site: www.atlantachamberplayers.com
Officers:
   President, Board Of Advisors: James
   Throckmorton
Management:
   Founder/Artistic Managing Director: Paula Peace
Mission: Atlanta Chamber Players is a professional
ensemble of musicians committed to offering audiences
world class traditional and contemporary masterpieces
as well as commissioned new works.
Founded: 1976
Specialized Field: Chamber
Status: Professional; Nonprofit
Paid Staff: 3
Paid Artists: 11
Season: September-March
Performs At: Walter Hill Auditorium; High Museum Of
Art
Organization Type: Performing; Touring; Resident;
Educational

858
ATLANTA JAZZ FESTIVAL

Atlantic Bureau of Cultural Affairs
675 Ponce De Leon
Atlanta, GA 30308
Phone: 404-817-6851
Fax: 404-658-6945
Web Site: www.atlantafestivals.com
Officers:
   Manager: Alonzo Craig
   Supervisor: Lisa Baker
Management:

   Festivals Manager: Jackie Davis
   Coordinator: Nnena U Nchege
Mission: To offer a showcase for talented local and
national performers; to provide Atlanta citizens with jazz
music.
Founded: 1978
Specialized Field: Jazz
Status: Professional; Nonprofit
Income Sources: Private and Corporate Donations,
Grants, Ticket Sales
Performs At: Piedmont Park, Centennial Olympic Park,
Woodruff Park, Chastain Park Amphitheatre, Sambuca
Jazz Cafe, Churchill Grounds
Organization Type: Performing; Educational

859
ATLANTA SYMPHONY ORCHESTRA

1280 Peachtree Street NE
Atlanta, GA 30309-3552
Phone: 404-733-4900
Fax: 404-733-4901
e-mail: aso-info@woodruffcenter.org
Web Site: www.atlantasymphony.org
Officers:
   President/CEO: Allison Vulgamore
   Chair: Ben F Johnson III
   Vice Chair: Clayton F Jackson
   Treasurer: John D Rogers
   Secretary: Joni Winston
Management:
   Music Director: Robert Spano
   Orchestral Manager: Julie Fish
   Artistic Planning Director: Evans Mirageas
   Project Director: Tom Tomlinson
Mission: To serve audiences with performances and
educational opportunities, while striving for excellence.
Utilizes: Actors; Artists-in-Residence; Choreographers;
Collaborating Artists; Collaborations; Commissioned
Composers; Commissioned Music;
Composers-in-Residence; Dancers; Designers;
Educators; Five Seasonal Concerts; Guest
Accompanists; Guest Artists; Guest Choreographers;
Guest Companies; Guest Composers; Guest
Designers; Guest Directors; Guest Instructors; Guest
Musical Directors; Guest Musicians; Guest Soloists;
Guest Writers; High School Drama; Instructors; Local
Artists; Lyricists; Multi Collaborations; Multimedia;
Music; New Productions; Organization Contracts;
Original Music Scores; Resident Artists; Resident
Professionals; Sign Language Translators; Singers;
Soloists; Student Interns; Theatre Companies; Touring
Companies; Visual Arts
Founded: 1945
Specialized Field: Symphony; Orchestra; Chamber
Status: Professional, Nonprofit
Paid Staff: 50
Paid Artists: 99
Income Sources: American Symphony Orchestra
League, Private and Corporate Donations, Grants,
Ticket Sales
Performs At: Symphony Hall; Chastain Park
Amphitheatre
Annual Attendance: 500,000 +
Facility Category: Concert Hall
Type of Stage: Full Theater Facilities
Seating Capacity: 1749 / 82
Year Built: 1968
Rental Contact: Operations Manager Sandra Schaffer
Organization Type: Performing

860
ATLANTA SYMPHONY YOUTH ORCHESTRA
1293 Peachtree Street NE
Suite 300
Atlanta, GA 30309
Phone: 404-733-4870
Fax: 404-733-4901
e-mail: melanie.darby@woodruffcenter.org
Web Site: www.atlantasymphony.org
Officers:
    Parents Association President: Bill Cecil
    Treasurer: Wayne Musselwhite
    Secretary: Nancy Musselwhite
Management:
    Music Director/Conductor: Jere Flint
Mission: Atlanta Symphony Youth Orchestra plays a larger role in promoting the arts and arts education.
Utilizes: Guest Artists
Founded: 1974
Specialized Field: Youth Orchestra; Educational
Status: Nonprofit
Paid Staff: 60
Volunteer Staff: 22
Paid Artists: 100
Non-paid Artists: 120
Budget: $35,000-100,000
Income Sources: Lanie and Ethel Foundation, Halle Foundation, Private and Corporate Donations, Grants, Ticket Sales
Season: November-February
Performs At: Robert W Woodruff Arts Center
Annual Attendance: 9,600
Seating Capacity: 1748
Rental Contact: Sandi Schaffer

861
CHASTIAN PARK AMPHITHEATRE ATLANTA SYMPHONY ORCHESTRA FESTIVAL POPS
1293 Peachtree Street NE
Suite 300
Atlanta, GA 30309
Phone: 404-733-4900
Fax: 404-733-4901
e-mail: aso-info@woodruffcenter.org
Web Site: www.classicchastian.org
Officers:
    Executive Director: Allison Vulgamore
    Director Public Relations: Minde Herbert
    Staff Accountant: April Satterfield
Management:
    Music Director: Robert Spano
    Conductor: Jere Flint
    Conductor: Michael Krajewski
    Principal Guest Conductor: Donald Runnicles
Mission: Provides young instrumentalists an opportunity to perform orchestral masterworks under the city's finest conductors.
Founded: 1945
Specialized Field: Orchestra
Status: Nonprofit
Paid Staff: 40
Volunteer Staff: 200
Budget: $6 million
Income Sources: Donations and Sponsors.
Season: June - August
Performs At: Atlanta Symphony Hall; Woodruff Arts Center
Affiliations: Atlanta Symphony Orchestra
Annual Attendance: 160,000
Facility Category: Chastian Park Amphitheatre
Type of Stage: Plywood/ Shell

Seating Capacity: 6,291
Year Built: 1933
Year Remodeled: 1989
Resident Groups: Atlanta Symphony Orchestra

862
EMORY SYMPHONY ORCHESTRA
Emory University
Dept Of Music., Donna & Marvin Schwartz Cntr.
1700 N Decatur, Suite 314
Atlanta, GA 30322
Phone: 404-727-6445
Fax: 404-727-0074
e-mail: music@emory.edu
Web Site: www.music.emory.edu
Management:
    Conductor: Richard Prior
    Managing Director: Robert McKay
    Assoc. Director For Programming: Tracy Clark
    Stage Manager: Mark Teague
    Production Manager: Lewis Fuller
    Department Of Music Chair: Kevin Karnes
Mission: Provides works selected from the rich heritage of symphonic literature and symphonic choral literature. Each spring their concert features a guest soloist the winner of the Music Department's Student Concerto Competition.
Utilizes: Artists-in-Residence; Educators; Guest Accompanists; Guest Composers; Guest Designers; Guest Directors; Guest Ensembles; Guest Instructors; Guest Musical Directors; Local Artists; Multimedia; Sign Language Translators; Soloists
Founded: 1836
Specialized Field: Symphony; Chamber
Status: Nonprofit
Budget: $5,104,801
Income Sources: Grants, Tuition, Ticket Sales, Private and Corporate Donations
Season: October
Performs At: Performing Arts Studio
Seating Capacity: 220

863
SYMPHONY ORCHESTRA OF AUGUSTA
Augusta Symphony, Inc.
1301 Greene Street, Suite 200
PO Box 579
Augusta, GA 30903-0579
Phone: 706-826-4705
Fax: 706-826-4735
e-mail: sandraesoaugusta.org
Web Site: www.soaugusta.org
Officers:
    President: Joseph H. Huff
    Vice President: W.L. Fletcher
    Executive Director: Sandra Self
    Treasurer: Alicia Markyna
    Finance Manager: Martha Robinson
Management:
    Music Director/Conductor: Shizuo Kuwahara
    Production Manager: Arthur Ross III
Mission: To share the joy of great performance with our audience. Together we are music.
Utilizes: Artists-in-Residence; Collaborating Artists; Collaborations; Commissioned Composers; Commissioned Music; Dance Companies; Fine Artists; Guest Accompanists; Guest Composers; Guest Musical Directors; Guest Musicians; Guest Writers; Instructors; Lyricists; Multimedia; New Productions; Original Music Scores; Sign Language Translators; Singers
Founded: 1954
Specialized Field: Music; Orchestra
Status: Nonprofit
Paid Staff: 14

Volunteer Staff: 3
Paid Artists: 250
Budget: $1,200,000
Income Sources: Tickets; Contributions
Season: September-May
Performs At: First Baptis Of Augusta Bell Auditorium
Annual Attendance: 50,000
Facility Category: Symphony; Pops;Chamber;Outdoor & Educational Concerts
Seating Capacity: 800; 2,000; 300; 686
Year Built: 1950
Year Remodeled: 2000
Organization Type: Performing, Touring,
Resident Groups: Augusta Symphony String Quartet; Augusta Symphony Woodwind Trio

864
COLUMBUS SYMPHONY ORCHESTRA
101 13th Street
PO Box 1499
Columbus, GA 31902
Phone: 706-323-5059
Fax: 706-323-7051
e-mail: customerservice@columbussymphony.com
Web Site: www.csoga.org
Officers:
    Executive Director: Bill Faust
    Marketing Director: Becky Young
    Development Director: Timothy R Watkins
Management:
    Music Director/Conductor: George Del Gobbo
    Personnel Manager/Operations: Jeanette Ross
Mission: To provide quality music to area residents.
Utilizes: Commissioned Music; Grant Writers; Guest Accompanists; Guest Companies; Guest Musical Directors; Multimedia
Founded: 1855
Specialized Field: Symphony
Status: Semi-Professional
Paid Staff: 8
Volunteer Staff: 3
Budget: $715,000
Income Sources: American Symphony Orchestra League, Private and Corporate Donations, Ticket Sales
Performs At: River Center Bill Heard Theatre
Annual Attendance: 25,000
Facility Category: Theatre
Seating Capacity: 2,000
Organization Type: Performing; Touring; Resident; Educational; Sponsoring

865
GAINESVILLE SYMPHONY ORCHESTRA
Brenau University
422 Brenau Avenue
PO Box 162
Gainesville, GA 30503
Phone: 770-532-5727
Fax: 770-535-0554
e-mail: gso-pam@mindspring.com
Web Site: www.gsomusic.com
Officers:
    Executive Director: Pam Slaton
Management:
    Music Director/Conductor: Larry Sims
Mission: Dedicated to the promotion and appreciation of music throughout Alachua County and the State of Florida through performance and education.
Utilizes: Collaborations; Fine Artists; Grant Writers; Guest Companies; Local Artists; Lyricists; Original Music Scores; Touring Companies
Founded: 1981
Specialized Field: Symphony
Status: Professional, Nonprofit

Paid Staff: 2
Volunteer Staff: 30
Non-paid Artists: 80
Budget: 35,000-100,000
Income Sources: Grants, National Endowment for the Arts, Private and Corporate Donations, Ticket Sales
Season: October-July
Performs At: Pearce Auditorium; Brenau University
Annual Attendance: 10,000

866
MACON SYMPHONY ORCHESTRA

400 Poplar Street
Macon, GA 31201
Phone: 478-301-5300
Fax: 478-301-5505
e-mail: mso@maconsymphony.com
Web Site: www.maconsymphony.com
Officers:
President: Katherine B Vitale
Direcgtor Development/Marketing: Tanya Edge
VP Audience Development: Susan T McDuffie
General Manager: Doris Wood
Management:
Music Director/Conductor: Adrian Gnam
Personnel Manager: Melissa Klein
Mission: To offer live quality classical music performances for the enjoyment of the community; to foster the appreciation of music through educational programs.
Utilizes: Artists-in-Residence; Collaborating Artists; Collaborations; Commissioned Music; Composers-in-Residence; Educators; Fine Artists; Five Seasonal Concerts; Guest Accompanists; Guest Companies; Guest Composers; Guest Lecturers; Guest Musical Directors; Guest Musicians; Guest Writers; Instructors; Local Artists; Lyricists; Multimedia; Organization Contracts; Original Music Scores; Sign Language Translators; Singers; Soloists
Founded: 1976
Specialized Field: Orchestra
Status: Professional; Nonprofit
Paid Staff: 6
Volunteer Staff: 1
Paid Artists: 75
Budget: $650,000
Income Sources: Ticket Sales, Donations, Grants
Performs At: Grand Opera House
Annual Attendance: 12,000+
Seating Capacity: 1,025
Year Built: 1887
Year Remodeled: 2000
Organization Type: Performing; Resident; Educational

867
COBB SYMPHONY ORCHESTRA

PO Box 680993
Marietta, GA 30068-0017
Phone: 770-426-1509
Fax: 770-424-5541
e-mail: executivedirector@cobbsymphony.com
Web Site: www.cobbsymphony.com
Officers:
Executive Director: Sherry M Roedl
Management:
Music Director/Conductor: Michael Alexander
Head Music Education Program: Nate Casey
Mission: To enrich the cultural life of Cobb County and surrounding communities by performing and promoting music of the highest quality and to provide an opportunity for local musicians to perform in a professional symphony orchestra that serves a culturally diverse population and aids in the music education of the community.

Founded: 1951
Specialized Field: Classical
Status: Nonprofit
Budget: $150,000-260,000
Income Sources: Fundraising, Ticket Sales, Private and Corporate Donations
Season: August-May
Performs At: Stillwell Theatre

868
ROME SYMPHONY ORCHESTRA

540 Broad Street
PO Box 553
Rome, GA 30161
Phone: 706-291-7967
Fax: 706-291-3840
e-mail: symphony@romesymphony.org
Web Site: www.romesymphony.org
Officers:
President: Barbara L Beninato
VP: Katie Dempsey
Executive Director: MaryAnn Kelly Bray
Treasurer: Ira Levy
Secretary: Suzanne Smith
Management:
Music Director/Conductor: Philip O Rice
Mission: Promoting and providing quality musical programs.
Founded: 1921
Specialized Field: Symphony
Paid Staff: 2
Volunteer Staff: 5
Paid Artists: 65
Budget: $35,000-100,000
Income Sources: Donations, Ticket Sales, Program Sales, Fund Raisers, Rome Symphony Women's Association
Season: October-September
Performs At: Rome City Auditorium
Seating Capacity: 1,094

869
ORCHESTRA ATLANTA

1000 Holcomb Woods Parkway
Suite 112
Roswell, GA 30076
Phone: 770-992-2559
Fax: 770-998-6877
e-mail: orchatl@aol.com
Web Site: www.orchestraatlanta.com
Management:
Orchestra Manager: Charles Little
Mission: Provides quality classical orchestral music to Atlanta audiences, while providing a venue for top-drawer volunteer and semi-professional musicians to present their talents to the community.
Founded: 1984
Specialized Field: Classical
Status: Nonprofit
Paid Staff: 1
Volunteer Staff: 10
Paid Artists: 15
Non-paid Artists: 8
Budget: $100,000-150,000
Income Sources: Private and Corporate Donations, Ticket Sales, Grants
Season: November-May
Performs At: Roswell Cultural Arts Center

870
DEKALB SYMPHONY ORCHESTRA

PO Box 1313
Tucker, GA 30085

Phone: 678-891-3565
Fax: 678-891-3575
e-mail: dso@dekalbsymphony.com
Web Site: www.dekalbsymphony.com
Officers:
Orchestra Manager: Richard Rogers
Management:
Music Director & Conductor: Fyodor Cherniavsky
Mission: Provides outstanding soloists and polished orchestral playing.
Founded: 1964
Specialized Field: Orchestra
Paid Staff: 2
Volunteer Staff: 4
Paid Artists: 12
Budget: $140,000
Income Sources: Private and Corporate Donations, Ticket Sales, Grants, Fundraisers
Season: November-July
Performs At: Marvin Cole Auditorium
Annual Attendance: 8,000
Facility Category: College Auditorium
Seating Capacity: 500

871
VALDOSTA SYMPHONY ORCHESTRA

Valdosta State University
Valdosta, GA 31698
Phone: 229-333-5804
Fax: 229-259-5578
e-mail: jploendue@valdosta.edu
Web Site: www.valdosta.edu/music
Officers:
Executive Director: Taylor Harding
Management:
Artistic Director: Dr J Plondke
Concertmaster: Nina Lutz
Stage Manager: Andy Baxter
Mission: Provides both the cultural life of the community and the regional academic mission of Valdosta State University.
Founded: 1990
Specialized Field: Symphony
Status: Nonprofit, Professional
Income Sources: Fundraisers, Ticket Sales, Private and Corporate Donations, Valdosta Symphony Guild, Valdosta State University
Season: September-April
Performs At: Whitehead Auditorium
Type of Stage: Proscenium
Seating Capacity: 774

Hawaii

872
CHAMBER MUSIC HAWAII

1466 Akeakamaie Street
Honolulu, HI 96816
Phone: 808-738-0202
Fax: 808-738-0202
Web Site: www.chambermusichawaii.com
Officers:
President: James Moffitt
Vice President: Robert Berssenbrugge
Executive Director: David S Wallerstein
Treasurer: Paul Lemcke
Secretary: Norma Nichols
Mission: To provide the people of Hawaii with chamber music through support of resident chamber music ensembles.
Founded: 1982
Specialized Field: Chamber; Ensemble
Status: Professional; Nonprofit

Income Sources: Grants, State Foundation on Culture and the Arts, Hawaii Community Foundation, Cooke, Atherton & McInerny Foundations, National Endowment for the Arts, Michael Paul Foundation
Season: September-May
Performs At: Paliku Theatre; Windward Community College, Doris Duke Theatre; Honolulu Academy of Arts
Organization Type: Presenting

873
HAWAII CHAMBER ORCHESTRA SOCIETY
3810 Maunaloa Avenue
Honolulu, HI 96816
Phone: 808-734-0397
Fax: 808-926-8004
Officers:
General Manager: Jacqueline Ward
Mission: To increase interest in and appreciation of classical music.
Founded: 1967
Specialized Field: Chamber; Ensemble
Status: Professional; Nonprofit
Income Sources: Ticket Sales, Grants
Performs At: Unity Church
Annual Attendance: 1,000+
Organization Type: Performing; Educational

874
HAWAII YOUTH SYMPHONY ASSOCIATION
1110 University Avenue
Suite 201
Honolulu, HI 96826-1508
Phone: 808-941-9706
Fax: 808-941-4995
e-mail: admin@hiyouthsymphony.org
Web Site: www.hiyouthsymphony.org
Officers:
President: Roy E King, Jr
Executive Director: Selena Ching
Treasurer: Michael Onofrietti
VP Resource Development: Tina Lau
VP Operations: Les Murata
Operations Manager: Judy Vierck
Secretary: David Matsumoto
Management:
Music Director/Conductor: Henry Miyamura
Conductor Youth Symphony II: Michael Nakasone
Conductor Concert Orchestra: Derrick Yamane
Conductor Concert String Orchestra: Joan Doike
Conductor Preparatory Strings: Helen Nguyen
Co-Conductor Beginning Strings: Sandy Ching
Co-Conductor Beginning Strings: Winnie Ching
Mission: Dedicated to nurturing the educational and artistic development of student musicians.
Utilizes: Commissioned Composers; Commissioned Music; Educators; Five Seasonal Concerts; Guest Companies; Guest Composers; Guest Musical Directors; Guest Musicians; High School Drama; Instructors; Multimedia; Music; Original Music Scores; Soloists
Founded: 1964
Specialized Field: Youth Symphony; Youth Orchestra
Status: Nonprofit
Paid Staff: 13
Volunteer Staff: 50
Paid Artists: 6
Budget: $600,000
Income Sources: Registration; Grants; Donations; Sponsorships; Tickets

Performs At: Venues range from shopping malls to the professional concert hall
Affiliations: American Symphony Orchestra League, HAAE
Annual Attendance: 15,000
Organization Type: Performing; Educational

875
HONOLULU CHAMBER MUSIC SERIES
University of Hawaii
Box 2233
Honolulu, HI 96804
Phone: 808-528-8226
Fax: 808-956-9422
e-mail: panpac@lava.net
Officers:
President: Richard Lachmann
Board Director: Andrew Bunn
Mission: Dedicated to providing chamber music.
Founded: 1954
Specialized Field: Chamber
Status: Professional, Nonprofit
Performs At: Orvis Auditorium

876
HONOLULU SYMPHONY ORCHESTRA
650 Iwilei Road
Suite 202
Honolulu, HI 96817
Phone: 808-524-0815
Fax: 808-524-1507
e-mail: jmancuso@honolulusymphony.com
Web Site: www.honolulusymphony.com
Officers:
Chair: Carolyn A Berry
President: Steve Bloom
Interim Executive Director: John Graham
VP Finance/Administration: Suzanne Ruiz
Marketing Manager: Ryan Lum
Public Relations Manager: Suzanne Lee
VP Development: Angela Smith
Personnel Manager: Jennifer Lovejoy
Management:
Music Director: Samuel Wong
Pops Conductor: Matt Catingub
Assistant Conductor: Joan Landry
Chorus Director: Karen Kennedy
Artistic Advisor: Maestro JoAnn Falletta
Concertmaster: Ignace Jang
Associate Concertmaster: Claire Sakai Hazzard
Assistant Concertmaster: Judy Barrett
Orchestra Operations Manager: Jim Mancuso
Mission: To enhance the quality of life of the people of Hawaii by sustaining a symphony orchestra of the highest artistic quality.
Founded: 1900
Specialized Field: Symphony
Status: Nonprofit
Budget: $3,600,000-10,000,000
Income Sources: Private and Corporate Donations, Ticket Sales, Grants
Performs At: Neal Blaisdell Concert Hall

877
MUSIC AT MANOA/UNIVERSITY OF HAWAII AT MANOA OUTREACH COLLEGE
2530 Dole Street
Honolulu, HI 96822
Phone: 808-956-2042
Fax: 808-956-9657
e-mail: tslaughter@outreach.hawaii.edu
Web Site: www.hawaii.edu/uhmmusic

Management:
Director: Tim Slaughter
Mission: Dedicated to presenting quality musical, dance, theater and special attractions to Hawaii audiences, including the Honolulu Chamber Music Series.
Founded: 1907
Specialized Field: Chamber; Ensemble; Ethnic Music; Soloists
Status: Professional
Income Sources: Western Alliance of Arts Administrators, Association for Performing Arts Presenters, Private and Corporate Donations, Ticket Sales
Season: January-December
Performs At: Blaisdell Concert Hall; Orvis Auditorium
Organization Type: Sponsoring

Idaho

878
BOISE CHAMBER MUSIC SERIES
Boise State University
1910 University Drive
Boise, ID 83725-1560
Phone: 208-426-1216
Fax: 208-426-1771
e-mail: jbelfy@boisestate.edu
Officers:
Media Contact: Pat Pyke
Management:
Artistic Director: Dr Jeanne Belfy
Mission: To provide quality chamber music.
Specialized Field: Chamber
Season: September-February
Performs At: Morrison Center Recital Hall

879
BOISE PHILHARMONIC ASSOCIATION
Esther Simplot Performing Arts Academy
516 S 9th Street
Boise, ID 83702
Phone: 208-344-7849
Fax: 208-336-9078
Toll-free: 888-300-7849
e-mail: info@boisephilharmonic.org
Web Site: www.boisephilharmonic.org
Officers:
President: Don Hendrickson
Vice President: Jeanie Smith
Treasurer: Louis Henry
Director Finance: Gordon Swenson
Education Coordinator: Jamey Lamar
Secretary: Alan Katseanes
Management:
Music Director/Conductor: James Ogle
Concertmaster: Geoffrey Trabichoff
Associate Concertmaster: Jill Rowley
Orchestra Personnel Manager: Marilyn Goerrich
Stage Manager: Forrest Hartvigsen
Mission: Provide an opportunity to share the passion and talent of the members of teh Boise Philharmonic as they celebrate the great music of all ages.
Utilizes: Guest Artists
Founded: 1887
Specialized Field: Orchestra
Status: Nonprofit
Paid Staff: 10
Volunteer Staff: 50
Paid Artists: 72
Budget: $1.3 million
Income Sources: Private and Corporate Donations, Ticket Sales

Season: October-May
Performs At: Morrison Center for the Performing Arts
Annual Attendance: 58,000

880
BOISE STATE UNIVERSITY CLASSICAL GUITAR SOCIETY
Boise State University
1910 University Drive
Boise, ID 83725-1560
Phone: 208-426-1507
Fax: 208-426-1771
Web Site: www.boisestate.edu/music
Management:
Director: Dr Joseph Baldassarre
Specialized Field: Classical Guitar
Status: Nonprofit
Performs At: Morrison Center for the Performing Arts
Seating Capacity: 2,000

881
IDAHO FALLS SYMPHONY
498 A Street
Suite A
Idaho Falls, ID 83402
Phone: 208-529-1080
Fax: 208-529-1097
Web Site: www.srv.net/~ifsymph
Officers:
President: Kevin O'Brien
Vice President: Bruce Turner
Treasurer: DeAnn Maart
Marketing: Karen Cornwell
Development: Mary Lynn Hartwell
Education: Renie Clements
Secretary: Anne Voilleque
Management:
Music Director/Conductor: George Adams
Concertmaster: Rick Hansen
Associate Concertmaster: Myrna South
Orchestra Representative: Linda Neeley
Mission: Instrumental music.
Founded: 1950
Specialized Field: Symphony; Orchestra
Status: Semi-Professional; Nonprofit
Paid Staff: 3
Volunteer Staff: 50
Budget: 250,000
Income Sources: American Symphony Orchestra League, Private and Corporate Donations, Ticket Sales, Endowment Fund
Season: October-May
Performs At: Colonial Theater, Civic Auditorium
Annual Attendance: 10,000+
Seating Capacity: 948
Organization Type: Performing; Resident; Educational

882
AUDITORIUM CHAMBER MUSIC SERIES
University of Idaho
PO Box 444015
Moscow, ID 83844-4015
Phone: 208-885-7557
Fax: 208-885-7254
e-mail: mdupree@uidaho.edu
Management:
Director: Mary DuPree
Administrative Assistant: Matthew Pilcher
Mission: Offers a yearly concert series and we also sponsor activities throughout the Palouse bringing visiting artists into direct contact with school children, university students and community members.
Specialized Field: Chamber
Status: Nonprofit

Paid Staff: 2
Paid Artists: 20
Income Sources: National Endowment for the Arts, Idaho Commission on the Arts
Season: September-April
Performs At: University of Idaho Auditorium

883
IDAHO STATE CIVIC SYMPHONY
Campus Box 8099
5 Dillon
Pocatello, ID 83201
Phone: 208-234-1587
Fax: 208-236-4884
e-mail: hurlangi@isu.edu
Web Site: www.thesymphony.us
Officers:
President: Allan Jackson
Vice President: Jedd Thomas
Executive Director: Sue Parker
Treasurer: Faye Booth
Secretary: Roger Wheeler
Management:
Music Director/Conductor: Dr. Thom Ritter George
Mission: To build and maintain a symphony orchestra which performs musical programs of high artistic quality.
Founded: 1954
Specialized Field: Symphony
Status: Nonprofit
Budget: $100,000-150,000
Income Sources: Friends of Symphony, Fundraising, Ticket Sales, Private and Corporate Donations
Season: September-April
Performs At: Goranson Hall, Pocatello High School Auditorium
Annual Attendance: 12,000
Seating Capacity: 450
Year Built: 1965

884
MAGIC VALLEY SYMPHONY
PO Box 1805
315 Falls Avenue
Twin Falls, ID 83303-1805
Phone: 208-734-6549
Fax: 208-733-6161
Officers:
President: George Halsell
Symphony League President: Elaine Bowen
Business Manager: H Richard Cook
Management:
Music Director/Conductor: Theodore H Hadley
Mission: Committed to enhancing the cultural life of the community and providing an outlet for performers.
Utilizes: Guest Composers; Guest Musicians
Founded: 1959
Specialized Field: Symphony; Orchestra
Status: Non-Professional; Nonprofit
Paid Staff: 3
Budget: $25,500
Income Sources: Ticket Sales; Donations
Performs At: College of Southern Idaho Fine Arts Auditorium
Affiliations: American Society of Composers, Authors and Publishers
Annual Attendance: 2,000
Facility Category: Junior College
Seating Capacity: 900
Year Built: 1970
Organization Type: Performing

Illinois

885
BELLEVILLE PHILHARMONIC ORCHESTRA
116 N Jackson Street
Belleville, IL 62220
Phone: 618-235-5600
Fax: 618-235-4975
Web Site: www.bellphil.com
Officers:
Executive Director: Kathleen J AuBuchon
Management:
Conductor: Robert Charles Howard
Assistant Conductor: Dr Leon Burke
Mission: Committed to serving the interests of music and musicians in the Greater Belleville area.
Founded: 1867
Specialized Field: Symphony; Orchestra
Status: Non-Professional; Nonprofit
Paid Staff: 100
Budget: 61,600
Income Sources: Advertising, Sponsor a Concert, Private and Corporate Donations, Ticket Sales
Season: October-May
Performs At: St Henry's Catholic Church, Scottish Rite Cathedral, Our Lady of the Snows, Union United Methodist Church, St Teresa Church
Annual Attendance: 1,500-1,800
Organization Type: Performing; Educational

886
CENTRALIA PHILHARMONIC ORCHESTRA
Centralia Cultural Society
1250 E Rexford Street
Centralia, IL 62801
Phone: 618-532-2951
Fax: 618-532-2964
e-mail: artcntr@msn.com
Web Site: www.centraliaarts.org
Officers:
Administrative Coordinator: Jane Pacey
Mission: To connect arts with the community and the community with the arts.
Utilizes: Artists-in-Residence; Touring Companies
Founded: 1961
Specialized Field: Orchestra; Show Tunes
Status: Nonprofit
Paid Staff: 1
Budget: $120,000
Income Sources: Ticket Sales, Patrons, Trust Funds, Illinois Arts Council, Private and Corporate Donations
Season: October-August
Annual Attendance: 25,000
Seating Capacity: 300
Year Built: 1971
Year Remodeled: 1981

887
CHAMPAIGN-URBANA SYMPHONY ORCHESTRA
701 Devonshire Drive, C-24
Champaign, IL 61820-7337
Phone: 217-351-9139
Fax: 217-351-1698
e-mail: music@cusymphony.org
Web Site: www.cusymphony.org
Officers:
President: Sam Krug
Vice President: Elaine Peppers
Treasurer: Peggy Schneider
General Manager: Megan Holland

Development Director: Wayne Nagy
Operations Director: Kevin McGuire
Management:
　Music Director/Conductor: Steven Larsen
　Orchestra Representative: Marina Antoline
Mission: To provide live, symphonic music performances of the highest quality and music education for our community's children.
Founded: 1960
Specialized Field: Symphony
Status: Nonprofit, Professional
Budget: $150,000-260,000
Income Sources: Private and Corporate Donations, Ticket Sales, Champaign-Urbana Symphony Guild
Season: September-April
Performs At: Krannert Center for the Performing Arts
Annual Attendance: 7,000

888
EASTERN SYMPHONY ORCHESTRA

Eastern Illinois University
Department of Music
Charleston, IL 61920
Phone: 217-581-3111
Fax: 217-581-7137
e-mail: music@io.eiu.edu
Web Site: www.eiu.edu/~music
Management:
　Music Director: Richard Robert Rossi
Mission: To provide the finest symphony music.
Utilizes: Collaborations; Commissioned Composers; Commissioned Music; Educators; Fine Artists; Five Seasonal Concerts; Guest Accompanists; Guest Companies; Guest Composers; Guest Designers; Guest Directors; Guest Ensembles; Guest Instructors; Guest Lecturers; Guest Musical Directors; Guest Musicians; Guest Soloists; High School Drama; Instructors; Local Artists; Local Unknown Artists; Lyricists; Multi Collaborations; Multimedia; New Productions; Organization Contracts; Original Music Scores; Playwrights; Sign Language Translators; Singers; Soloists; Touring Companies
Specialized Field: Symphony
Status: Nonprofit
Volunteer Staff: 20
Paid Artists: 15
Non-paid Artists: 60
Budget: $50,000
Income Sources: Private and Corporate Donations, Ticket Sales
Performs At: Dvorak Hall

889
ANNUAL CHICAGO JAZZ FESTIVAL

Mayor's Office of Special Events
121 N LaSalle Street
Chicago, IL 60602
Phone: 312-744-3315
Fax: 312-744-0613
e-mail: specialevents@cityofchicago.org
Web Site: www.cityofchicago.org/specialevents
Management:
　Coordinator: Jennifer J Washington
Mission: To present a festival, free to the public featuring jazz in all of its forms.
Founded: 1979
Specialized Field: Jazz Ensemble
Status: Professional
Season: September
Performs At: Symphony Music Shell; Petrillo Music Shell
Organization Type: Performing

890
CHICAGO CHAMBER ORCHESTRA

65 W Jackson Blvd. #133
Chicago, IL 60604
Phone: 312-357-1551
e-mail: koberdieter@aol.com
Web Site: www.chicagochamberorchestra.org
Management:
　Founder/Music Director/Conductor: Dieter Kober
　Assoc Conductor/Music Dir Designate: Edward Benyas
　Concertmaster: Charles Pikler
　Assistant Concertmaster: Steven Boe
Mission: Dedicated to bringing great music directly to the community, to people from many different backgrounds, and to all ages. All concerts are presented admission free.
Founded: 1952
Specialized Field: Chamber Orchestra; Classic Repertory; New Music
Income Sources: Private and Corporate Donations, Governmental Subsidies, Grants
Season: September-May
Performs At: Chicago Cultural Center, First United Methodist Church; Oak Park, Second Presbyterian Church, Fourth Presbyterian Church

891
CHICAGO SINFONIETTA

70 East Lake Street
Suite 700
Chicago, IL 60601
Phone: 312-236-3681
Fax: 312-235-5429
Web Site: www.chicagosinfonietta.org
Officers:
　Chairperson: Michelle Collins
　President: Roger G Wilson
　VP: Weldon Rougeau
　Secretary: Robert Wootton
Management:
　Music Director: Paul Freeman
　General Manager: Thomas De Walle
　Development Administrator: Maria Mowbray
　Director Marketing: Ferris O'Shaughnessy
Mission: Offering classical music in original orchestration and promoting ethnic diversity in the concert hall.
Utilizes: Guest Artists
Founded: 1986
Specialized Field: Classical; Jazz; World Music
Status: Nonprofit
Paid Staff: 16
Volunteer Staff: 120
Paid Artists: 65
Non-paid Artists: 1
Income Sources: Chicago Music Alliance
Performs At: Lund Auditorium; Rosary College
Organization Type: Performing; Touring; Educational

892
CHICAGO SYMPHONY ORCHESTRA

Symphony Center
220 S. Michigan Ave.
Chicago, IL 60604
Phone: 312-294-3000
Fax: 312-294-3329
Toll-free: 800-223-7114
Web Site: http://www.cso.org/
Officers:
　Chairman: William A. Osborn
　Vice Chairman: Paul C. Gignilliat
　President: Deborah R. Card

Management:
　Principal Conductor: Bernard Haitink
Utilizes: Composers; Composers-in-Residence; Guest Artists; Guest Companies; Student Interns
Founded: 1890
Specialized Field: Symphony; Orchestra
Status: Nonprofit
Income Sources: American Symphony Orchestra League
Organization Type: Performing

893
CHICAGO YOUTH SYMPHONY ORCHESTRA

410 S Michigan Avenue
Suite 833
Chicago, IL 60605
Phone: 312-939-2207
Fax: 312-939-2015
e-mail: sdodson@cyso.org
Web Site: www.cyso.org
Officers:
　Chairman: John Schladweiler
　Executive Director: Holly H. Hudak
　Director Development: R. Scott Dodson
Management:
　Music Director: Allen Tinkham
　Associate Director: Terrance Oliver-Gray
　Director Chamber Music: Kathie Johnson
Mission: To provide the finest quality orchestral training and performance opportunities for Chicagoland musicians 8 - 18
Utilizes: Commissioned Composers; Educators; Fine Artists; Guest Artists; Guest Companies; Guest Composers; Guest Directors; Guest Instructors; Guest Musical Directors; Instructors; Multimedia; Original Music Scores; Singers; Soloists
Founded: 1946
Specialized Field: Orchestra
Status: Nonprofit
Paid Staff: 12
Budget: $848,450
Income Sources: Government; Foundations/Corporations; Benefit; Individuals
Performs At: Orchestra Hall
Facility Category: Large Rehearsal/Performance Hall
Organization Type: Performing; Touring; Sponsoring

894
CLASSICAL SYMPHONY ORCHESTRA & THE PROTEGE PHILHARMONIC

218 South Wabash Avenue
Siute 260
Chicago, IL 60604
Phone: 312-341-1521
Fax: 312-341-1835
e-mail: theorchestras@classicalsymphonyorchestra.org
Management:
　Music Director: Joseph Glymph
Specialized Field: Orchestra
Budget: $150,000-260,000
Performs At: Preston Bradley Hall

895
CSO PRESENTS

220 S Michigan Avenue
Chicago, IL 60604
Phone: 312-294-3000
Fax: 312-294-3329
Officers:
　President: Henery Fogel
Management:

Conductor Emeritus: Pierre Boulez
Principal Conductor: Bernard Haiitink
Specialized Field: Orchestra
Budget: $400,000-$1,000,000
Performs At: Orchestra Hall at Symphony Center

896
LIRA DANCERS OF THE LIRA ENSEMBLE

6525 N Sheridan Road
Chicago, IL 60626
Phone: 773-508-7040
Fax: 773-508-7043
e-mail: lira@liraensemble.org
Officers:
Co-Conductor: Philip Seward
Choreographer: Iowna Puc
President: Lucyna Migala
Secretary: Frances Weit
Treasurer: Bernard Tresnowski
Management:
Artistic Director/General Manager: Lucyna Migala
Co-Conductor: Paul Dijkstra
Mission: To help acquaint Polish Americans with the richness of their thousand-year-old heritage of music and dance, and to help other Americans learn about and appreciate Polish culture and traditions.
Founded: 1975
Specialized Field: Polish Music
Status: Non-Profit; Professional
Non-paid Artists: 30
Budget: $200,000-$500,000
Organization Type: Performing

897
NEW BLACK MUSIC REPERTORY ENSEMBLE

Center for Black Music Research
Columbia College, 600 S Michigan
Chicago, IL 60605
Phone: 312-344-7559
Fax: 312-344-8029
Web Site: www.cbmr.org
Officers:
Director: Resita M Sands, Jr
Management:
Coordinator of Perf. Activities: Coleridge Parkinson
Mission: To perform works by black composers from 1700 to the present.
Founded: 1988
Specialized Field: Chamber; Ensemble; Ethnic Music
Status: Professional; Nonprofit
Paid Staff: 13
Paid Artists: 40
Income Sources: Columbia College, Federal and State Grants, Foundation and Corporate Grants
Organization Type: Performing; Touring

898
PERFORMING ARTS CHICAGO

410 S Michigan Avenue
#911
Chicago, IL 60605
Phone: 312-663-1628
Fax: 312-663-1043
Web Site: www.pachicago.org
Officers:
Chair: Helyn Goldenberg
President Director: Maya Polsky
President: Judy Neisser
Treasurer: David Ellis
Management:
Executive Director: Susan Lipman
Programs Manager: CJ Mitchell

Director: Christy Uchida
Operations Manager: Laurell Zahrobsky
Development Assistant: Brigid Flynn
Mission: Performing Arts Chicago is dedicated to the presentation of new work by local, national, and international artists from a wide cultural spectrum, and in doing so, reaching out in collaboration with the Chicago arts and education communities to challenge our diverse urban audience.
Utilizes: Actors; Artists-in-Residence; Choreographers; Collaborating Artists; Dance Companies; Dancers; Local Artists; Multimedia; Original Music Scores; Special Technical Talent
Founded: 1959
Specialized Field: Chamber
Status: Professional; Nonprofit
Paid Staff: 6
Budget: $1,000,000
Performs At: The Civic Theater
Organization Type: Performing; Resident; Educational; Sponsoring

899
ROOSEVELT UNIVERSITY ORCHESTRA: CHICAGO COLLEGE OF PERFORMING ARTS

430 S Michigan Avenue
Chicago, IL 60605
Phone: 312-341-3780
Fax: 312-341-6358
Web Site: www.roosevelt.edu
Management:
Chief Resident Conductor: Steven Squires
Utilizes: Artists-in-Residence; Guest Directors; High School Drama; Soloists
Specialized Field: Orchestra
Performs At: Rudolph Ganz Memorial Hall

900
UNIVERSITY OF CHICAGO SYMPHONY ORCHESTRA

1010 E 59th Street
Chicago, IL 60637
Phone: 773-702-8484
Fax: 773-753-0558
e-mail: musicdept@uchicago.edu
Officers:
President: Gilberto Zaldivar
VP: Rene Buch
Secretary/Treasurer: Robert Weber Federico
Management:
Music Director/Conductor: Barbara Schubert
Director Public Relations: Kristine Kohler-Hall
Specialized Field: Orchestra
Budget: $100,000
Performs At: Leon Mandel Hall
Affiliations: University of Chicago

901
DANVILLE SYMPHONY ORCHESTRA

2917 N Vermillion Street
Danville, IL 61832
Phone: 217-443-5300
Fax: 217-443-5313
e-mail: info@danvillesymphony.com
Web Site: www.danvillesymphony.org
Officers:
President: Dr. Alice Marie Jacobs
Vice President: Dr. Shawn Mallady
Executive Director: Meda Bateman
Management:
Music Director: Jeremy Swerling
Orchestra Manager: Stuart A. de Haro

Mission: To serve our community and to inspire it to achievement and excellence by presenting music at the highest possible levels of artistic excellence.
Utilizes: Dancers; Grant Writers; Guest Accompanists; Guest Choreographers; Guest Musical Directors; Guest Musicians; Guest Writers; Instructors; Multimedia; Sign Language Translators; Singers; Soloists
Founded: 1967
Specialized Field: Symphony; Orchestra; Chamber
Status: Semi-Professional; Nonprofit
Paid Staff: 2
Paid Artists: 80
Budget: $190,000
Income Sources: Illinois Council of Orchestras; Illinois Presenters Network
Performs At: High School Auditorium; David Palmer Civic Center
Seating Capacity: 1,700
Organization Type: Performing; Educational

902
MILLIKIN-DECATUR SYMPHONY ORCHESTRA

Millikin University
1184 W Main
Decatur, IL 62522
Phone: 217-424-6300
Fax: 217-420-6652
Toll-free: 800-373-7733
e-mail: mluxner@mail.millikin.edu
Management:
Music Director/Conductor: Michael Luxner
Artistic Administrator: Nancy Freeman
Specialized Field: Orchestra
Budget: $150,000-260,000
Performs At: Kirkland Center Theatre

903
ELGIN SYMPHONY ORCHESTRA

20 DuPage Court
Elgin, IL 60120-6424
Phone: 847-888-4000
Fax: 847-888-0400
e-mail: boxoffice@elginsymphony.org
Web Site: www.elginsymphony.org
Officers:
President: Dr Jerry Cain
Management:
Music Director: Robert Hanson
Associate Conductor: Stephen Squires, ssquires@roosevelt.edu
Education Coordinator: Randal Swiggum, rswiggum@wisc.edu
Founded: 1950
Specialized Field: Symphony; Orchestra

904
ELMHURST SYMPHONY ORCHESTRA

PO Box 345
Elmhurst, IL 60126
Phone: 630-941-0202
Fax: 630-941-0627
e-mail: boxoffice@elmhurstsymphony.org
Management:
Music Director: Stephen Alltop
Symphony Manager: Jennifer Thompson
Executive Director: Cynthia Kraine
Founded: 1959
Specialized Field: Symphony; Orchestra
Paid Staff: 3
Volunteer Staff: 35
Paid Artists: 27
Non-paid Artists: 53
Budget: $250,000

Performs At: Hammerschmidt Memorial Chapel at Elmhurst College
Annual Attendance: 4,500
Facility Category: Chapel
Type of Stage: Closed Proscenium
Seating Capacity: 853

905
CHICAGO PHILHARMONIC

1123 Emerson Street
Suite 207
Evanston, IL 60201
Phone: 847-866-6888
Fax: 847-866-6896
e-mail: info@chicagophilharmonic.org
Officers:
   President: Dr. James Berkenstock
Management:
   Music Director: Larry Rachleff
   Artistic Administrator: Barbara Haffner
Mission: The ensemble is dedicated to building new audiences for serious music by offering moderately priced concerts, at the highest professional level, in convenient venues. Its presentations of the full range symphonic works embody the excitement of live performances and exemplify a special relationship between performers and audiences.
Specialized Field: Orchestra
Budget: $260,000-1,050,000
Performs At: Pick - Staiger Concert Hall

906
DUPAGE SYMPHONY

PO Box 488
Glen Ellyn, IL 60137
Phone: 630-690-8644
Fax: 630-690-8644
Web Site: www.dupagesymphony.org
Management:
   Music Director/Conductor: Barbara Schubert
   Business Manager: Doris Purdie
Mission: To provide area citizens an opportunity to hear live music; to offer a performance outlet for musicians.
Utilizes: Guest Artists
Founded: 1954
Specialized Field: Symphony; Orchestra; Chamber; Ensemble
Status: Non-Professional; Nonprofit
Paid Staff: 65
Income Sources: Illinois Council of Orchestras
Performs At: Dupage County Auditorium
Organization Type: Performing; Touring

907
NEW PHILHARMONIC

College of DuPage
Fawell and Park Boulevards
Glen Ellyn, IL 60137
Phone: 630-942-4000
Fax: 630- 79—980
e-mail: raffel@cdnet.cod.edu
Management:
   Music Director: Kirk Muspratt
   Marketing Coordinator: Roland Raffel
Specialized Field: Orchestra
Budget: $150,000-260,000
Seating Capacity: 800

908
WHEATON SYMPHONY ORCHESTRA

344 Spring Avenue
Glen Ellyn, IL 60137
Phone: 630-790-1430
Fax: 630-790-9703
Management:
   General Manager: Donald C Mattison
   Music Director: Kevin McMahon
Mission: Dedicated to performing the music of 19th and 20th-century composers which was composed for large orchestras.
Utilizes: Guest Musicians; Organization Contracts
Founded: 1959
Specialized Field: Symphony
Status: Non-Professional
Volunteer Staff: 2
Income Sources: American Symphony Orchestra League
Performs At: Auditorium
Type of Stage: Large In An Auditorium
Stage Dimensions: Large Holds Chorus & Orchestra
Seating Capacity: 700
Year Built: 1995
Organization Type: Performing

909
CHAMBER MUSIC SOCIETY OF THE NORTH SHORE

PO Box 470
Glencoe, IL 60022
Phone: 847-835-5084
e-mail: iris@interaccess.com
Web Site: www.cmsns.org
Officers:
   President: Iris Cosnow
   Administrator: Sandra Weiss
Founded: 1984
Specialized Field: Chamber
Performs At: Pick-Staiger Concert Hall
Seating Capacity: 900

910
ALTON SYMPHONY ORCHESTRA

5800 Godfrey Road
PO Box 1205
Godfrey, IL 62035
Phone: 618-467-2326
Fax: 618-465-7435
e-mail: info@altonsymphony.org
Web Site: www.altonsymphony.org
Officers:
   President: Mark Landon
   Vice President: Gayle Hill
   Treasurer: Anne Cacciottoli
   President Public Relations: Lynden Schuyler
   Secretary: Tom Johnson
Management:
   Music Director/Conductor: Edward Dolbashian
   Pops Concert Director: William Shane Williams
   Concertmaster: Deberah Haferkamp
   Concert Manager: Mark Landon
   Orchestra Manager: Elizabeth Zenk
   Stage Manager: Brian McKinney
Mission: To provide a training ground for the development of instrumental abilities of area musicians; to increase interest in orchestral music; to present concerts to the public.
Founded: 1946
Specialized Field: Symphony
Status: Non-Professional; Nonprofit
Budget: 32,000
Income Sources: Illinois Council of Orchestras, Private and Corporate Donations, Ticket Sales
Season: October-April
Performs At: Hatheway Hall; Lewis & Clark Community College
Organization Type: Performing

911
MIDWEST YOUNG ARTISTS

878 Lyster Road
Highwood, IL 60040
Phone: 847-926-9898
Fax: 847-926-4787
e-mail: mya@mya.org
Officers:
   President: Richard Sugar
   VP: John Chipman
   Secretary: Tom Sharp
   Treasurer: Tom Drake
Management:
   Director: Dr. Allan Dennis
   Director Administration: Karen Dennis
   Director Development: Richard Gage
Founded: 1993
Specialized Field: Orchestra; Ensemble; Chamber; Jazz
Paid Staff: 6
Paid Artists: 18
Budget: $260,000-1,050,000
Income Sources: Tuition; Ticket Sales; Program Ad Revenues
Performs At: Pick - Staiger Concert Hall
Affiliations: Illinois Council of Orchestras

912
WEST SUBURBAN SYMPHONY

PO Box 565
Hinsdale, IL 60522
Phone: 630-887-7464
e-mail: info@westsubsymphony.org
Management:
   Music Director: Peter Lipari
Mission: Offers Chicago-area audiences both intimate chamber music and grand works for symphony orchestra. Has inspires thousands of young people annually with the power of live music through special educational concerts and free concert admission for preteens. Provides a stage for outstanding local soloists and gives rewarding performance opportunities to volunteer players and singers annually.
Founded: 1947
Specialized Field: Orchestra

913
LAKE FOREST SYMPHONY

50 E Old Mill Road
Lake Forest, IL 60045-3844
Phone: 847-295-2135
Fax: 847-295-2747
e-mail: info@lakeforestsymphony.org
Web Site: www.lakeforestsymphony.com
Officers:
   Treasurer: G Christopher Coffin
Management:
   Music Director: Alan Heatherington
   Interim Executive Director: Joanne Bernstein
   Controller: Gayle Heatherington
   Director Marketing: Pat Nissen
Mission: Present five classical concerts during the regular season.
Utilizes: Guest Accompanists; Guest Musicians; Multimedia; Original Music Scores; Sign Language Translators; Singers
Founded: 1956
Specialized Field: Symphony; Orchestra
Paid Staff: 5
Volunteer Staff: 1
Budget: $1.3 million
Income Sources: Donations; Ticket Sales

Performs At: James Lumber Center For The Performing Arts
Annual Attendance: 4,000-5,000
Type of Stage: Thrust
Seating Capacity: 600

914

CEDARHURST CHAMBER MUSIC

PO Box 923
Mount Vernon, IL 62864
Phone: 618-242-1236
Fax: 618-242-9530
e-mail: Shar@midwest.net
Web Site: www.cedarhurst.org
Management:
    Executive Director: Sharon Bradham
Mission: To generate enthusiastic participation in and support for the performing arts in Southern Illinois and surrounding region.
Utilizes: Artists-in-Residence; Collaborating Artists; Collaborations; Commissioned Composers; Commissioned Music; Curators; Educators; Five Seasonal Concerts; Guest Writers; Multimedia; Organization Contracts; Original Music Scores; Sign Language Translators; Special Technical Talent; Theatre Companies; Touring Companies
Founded: 1979
Specialized Field: Orchestra; Chamber; Ensemble; Ethnic Music
Status: Professional; Nonprofit
Paid Staff: 4
Volunteer Staff: 12
Income Sources: Chamber Music America; Illinois Presenters Network
Performs At: Main Gallery; Mitchell Art Museum
Annual Attendance: 1,000
Facility Category: Museum
Type of Stage: Permanent
Stage Dimensions: 16' x 24'
Seating Capacity: 350
Year Remodeled: 2008
Rental Contact: Brett Gibbs
Organization Type: Sponsoring

915

NORTHBROOK SYMPHONY ORCHESTRA

899 Skokie Boulevard
#LL12
Northbrook, IL 60062
Phone: 847-272-0755
Fax: 847-272-0787
e-mail: nso@theramp.net
Web Site: www.northbrooksymphony.org
Officers:
    President: Susan Laing
    Treasurer: Joseph Kitzes
    VP Administration: John Amrein
    VP Marketing: James Kahan
    Secretary: Linda Wachtel
Management:
    Music Director: Lawrence Rapchak
    General Manager: JC Wacholz
    VP Development: Judith Gelleerd
Mission: To offer classical music concerts at an affordable price as well as outreach programs.
Utilizes: Collaborations; Educators; Guest Accompanists; Guest Composers; Guest Instructors; Guest Writers; Instructors; Multimedia; Original Music Scores; Sign Language Translators; Singers; Soloists
Founded: 1980
Specialized Field: Classical; Symphony; Orchestra; Educational
Paid Staff: 2

Volunteer Staff: 30
Paid Artists: 75
Non-paid Artists: 25
Budget: $260,000-1,050,000
Income Sources: Ticket Sales; Foundations; Corporate & Individual Donations; Special Events
Performs At: Sheely Center for the Performing Arts
Affiliations: CHG Music Alliance; Illinois Council of Orchestra; American Symphony Orchestra League
Annual Attendance: 10,000
Seating Capacity: 1,484

916

SYMPHONY OF OAK PARK & RIVER FOREST

PO Box 3564
Oak Park, IL 60303
Phone: 708-218-2648
Fax: 708-524-9892
e-mail: KCM908@aol.com
Officers:
    General Manager: Beth Gavriel
Management:
    Music Director: Jay Friedman
    Board President: David Leehey
Specialized Field: Orchestra
Budget: $35,000-100,000

917

ILLINOIS PHILHARMONIC ORCHESTRA

377 Artists Walk
Park Forest, IL 60466
Phone: 708-481-7774
Fax: 708-481-7998
e-mail: ED@ipomusic.org
Management:
    Music Director: Carmon DeLeone
    Executive Director: Edmund Feingold
Specialized Field: Orchestra; Jazz
Budget: $260,000-1,050,000

918

PEORIA SYMPHONY ORCHESTRA

203 Harrison
Peoria, IL 61602
Phone: 309-637-2787
Fax: 309-637-7388
e-mail: execdir@peoriasymphony.org
Officers:
    President: Sidney Banwart
    VP: Walter Kuppman
    Treasurer: Bill O'Malley
    Secretary: Winsley Durand, Jr
Management:
    Music Director: David Commanday
    Executive Director: Judy Furniss
Mission: We provide excellent performances of fine music to a large and diverse audience in a variety of settings. Through a team effort of musicians, volunteers, staff and boards, we develop aggressive programs of education, marketing, and development. Cooperative efforts with local organizations enable us to enrich the mind, life, and culture which is the soul of our community.
Utilizes: Guest Musicians; Guest Writers; Multimedia
Specialized Field: Orchestra
Budget: $950,000
Performs At: Peoria Civic Center

919

QUINCY SYMPHONY ORCHESTRA

428 Main Street
Suite 270
Quincy, IL 62301

Phone: 217-222-2856
Fax: 217-222-2869
e-mail: qsoa@adams.net
Web Site: www.adams.net/~qsoa
Officers:
    President: Anda Zirnitis
Management:
    General Manager: Stacy Taylor
    Managerial Assistant: Pam Snider
Mission: To provide the area with fine orchestral music; to offer local musicians the opportunity to perform; to provide educational programs.
Utilizes: Fine Artists; Guest Composers; Guest Musical Directors; Guest Musicians; Guest Writers; Instructors; Lyricists; Multimedia; Sign Language Translators; Singers
Founded: 1947
Specialized Field: Symphony; Orchestra; Chamber
Status: Non-Professional; Nonprofit
Paid Staff: 45
Volunteer Staff: 40
Budget: $130,000
Income Sources: Grants; Donations; Tickets
Performs At: Quincy Junior High School Auditorium
Organization Type: Performing; Resident; Educational

920

AUGUSTANA SYMPHONY ORCHESTRA

Augustana College Music Department
639 38 Street
Rock Island, IL 61201
Phone: 309-794-7233
Fax: 309-794-7678
e-mail: jon-hurty@augustana.edu
Management:
    Music Director: Daniel Culver
    Department Chair: Jon Hurty
Specialized Field: Orchestra; Chamber; Band; Ensemble
Budget: $35,000
Performs At: Centennial Hall

921

MENDELSSOHN CLUB

415 N Church Street
Rockford, IL 61103-6881
Phone: 815-964-9713
Fax: 815-964-9929
e-mail: info@mendelsohnclub.org
Web Site: www.mendelssohnclub.org
Management:
    Executive Director: Lynn Andreini
Mission: To promote, support and present quality music for all.
Founded: 1884
Specialized Field: Classical
Paid Staff: 5
Volunteer Staff: 45
Paid Artists: 41
Non-paid Artists: 406
Affiliations: Rockford Area Arts Council; Illinois Arts Council
Facility Category: Auditorium with Stage
Stage Dimensions: 18'x 40'
Seating Capacity: 220
Year Built: 1952
Year Remodeled: 2002

922

ROCKFORD AREA YOUTH SYMPHONY ORCHESTRA

Riverfront Museum Park
711 N Main Street
Rockford, IL 61103-6903

Phone: 815-965-0049
Fax: 815-965-0642
e-mail: info@rockfordsymphony.com
Web Site: www.rockfordsymphony.com
Officers:
Board President: E. Gerald Gale
Management:
RSO Musical Director/Conductor: Steven Larsen
RSO Executive Director: Scott Provancher
Utilizes: Soloists
Founded: 1965
Specialized Field: Youth Symphony; Educational
Paid Staff: 1
Paid Artists: 6
Non-paid Artists: 65
Budget: $260,000-1,050,000
Income Sources: Grants; Ticket sales; Individual gifts; Sponsorshipos
Performs At: Coronado Theatre

923
ROCKFORD SMYPHONY ORCHESTRA
711 North Main Street
Rockford, IL 61103
Phone: 815-965-0049
e-mail: info@rockfordsymphony.com
Officers:
Education and Community Relations: Lorie Langan
Management:
Executive Director: Brian Ritter
Marketing and Development Director: Julie Schaper
Education Director: Lorie Langan
Patron Services Coordinator: Athea Halsey
Music Director: Steven Larsen
Personnel Manager: Paul Semanic
Music Librarian: Becky Asher
Mission: Committed more than ever to fulfilling its mission to educate and to entertain the people of northern Illinois through symphonic music performances of the highest artistic excellence.
Founded: 1943
Specialized Field: Orchestra

924
SKOKIE VALLEY SYMPHONY ORCHESTRA
9501 Skokie Boulevard
Skokie, IL 60077
Phone: 847-679-9501
Fax: 847-679-1879
e-mail: info@svso.org
Web Site: www.skokievalleysymphony.org
Officers:
President Board Of Directors: Kathryn Canny
Artistic Vice President: Karen Frost
Administrative Vice President: Sara Diaguardi
Management:
Music Director: Francesco Miliato
General Manager: Leslie Brodie
Mission: Our community symphony, the Skokie Valley Symphony Orchestra, was founded in 1962 by musicians who wanted to enrich the lives of others through music.
Founded: 1962
Specialized Field: Symphony Music
Budget: $35,000-100,000
Income Sources: Ticket sales; Donations; Grants
Affiliations: Illinois Council of Orchestra's
Facility Category: Concert Hall
Type of Stage: Proscenium
Seating Capacity: 839
Year Built: 1996

925
ILLINOIS SYMPHONY ORCHESTRA
PO Box 5191
Springfield, IL 62705-5191
Phone: 217-522-2838
Fax: 217-522-7374
e-mail: info@ilsymphony.org
Web Site: www.ilsymphony.org
Management:
Executive Director: Trevor Orthmann
Music Director: Karen Lynne Deal
Utilizes: Collaborations; Commissioned Composers; Grant Writers; Guest Accompanists; Guest Companies; Guest Musicians; Guest Writers; Instructors; Original Music Scores; Singers
Specialized Field: Orchestra
Budget: $260,000-1,050,000

926
ILLINOIS CHAMBER SYMPHONY
12 S 1st Avenue
St Charles, IL 60174
Phone: 630-377-6423
Fax: 630-377-3105
Officers:
President: Charles Brown
VP: Jeffrey Hunt
Secretary/Treasurer: William Simmons
Management:
Music Director: Stephen Squires
Marketing Director: Robert Murphy
Executive Director: Catherine Squires
Librarian: Tim Juergensen
Personnel Manager: Amy Scarlato
Mission: Promoting live classical music of the highest artistic caliber and furthering cultural growth in the state of Illinois.
Founded: 1983
Specialized Field: Orchestra; Chamber
Status: Professional; Nonprofit
Income Sources: Indiana Orchestra Consortium; Kane County Tourism Association; American Symphony Orchestra League; Fox Valley Arts Council
Performs At: Norris Cultural Arts Center; Baker Methodist Church
Organization Type: Performing

927
SINFONIA DA CAMERA
909 W Oregon
Urbana, IL 61801
Phone: 217-244-4350
Fax: 217-244-4350
e-mail: sinfonia@uiuc.edu
Web Site: www.sinfonia.illinois.edu
Management:
Music Director: Ian Hobson
General Manager: Rebecca Hill Riley
Specialized Field: Orchestra
Budget: $150,000-260,000
Performs At: Foellinger Great Hall

928
WAUKEGAN SYMPHONY ORCHESTRA & CONCERT CHORUS
39 Jack Benny Drive
Waukegan, IL 60085
Phone: 847-360-4740
Fax: 847-662-0592
Web Site: www.waukeganparks.org/jbc
Management:
Music Director: Stephen Blackweldor
Specialized Field: Symphony

Paid Staff: 2
Paid Artists: 6
Non-paid Artists: 60
Budget: $100,000-150,000
Income Sources: Waukegan Park District; Corporation; Grants
Performs At: Orlin D. Trapp Auditorium
Affiliations: Waukegan Park District
Annual Attendance: 1500
Facility Category: Auditorium
Type of Stage: Proscenium
Seating Capacity: 1800

929
CHINESE CLASSICAL ORCHESTRA AND EDUCATIONAL PROGRAM
PO Box 5275
Woodridge, IL 60517-0275
Phone: 630-910-1551
Fax: 630-910-1561
Web Site: www.chinesemusic.net
Officers:
President: Dr. Sin-yan Shen
VP: Kok-Koon Ng
Management:
Director Concert Lecture Department: Dr. Yuan-Yuan Lee
Mission: The music society is the largest Chinese music educational service institution in North America; publishes the Chinese Music Monograph Series, the international journal of Chinese Music, and educational material on music and acoustics.
Utilizes: Guest Artists; Guest Companies; Singers
Founded: 1976
Specialized Field: Symphony; Orchestra; Chamber; Ensemble; Ethnic Music; Folk Music; Electronic; Live Electronic
Status: Professional; Nonprofit
Budget: $260,000 - $1,050,000
Organization Type: Performing; Touring; Resident; Educational; Sponsoring

930
SILK AND BAMBOO ENSEMBLE
Chinese Music Society of North America
PO Box 5275
Woodridge, IL 60517-0275
Phone: 630-910-1551
Fax: 630-910-1561
Web Site: www.chinesemusic.net
Management:
Music Director/Conductor: Dr. Sin-yan Shen
Manager: Johson Hsu
Mission: To create chamber music of the 21st century; to perform works utilizing silk and bamboo instrumentation and just intervals; to tour internationally and in the US year round.
Utilizes: Guest Artists; Guest Companies; Singers
Founded: 1981
Specialized Field: Chamber; Ensemble; Ethnic Music
Status: Professional; Nonprofit
Budget: $260,000 - 1,050,000
Organization Type: Performing; Touring; Educational

931
WOODSTOCK MOZART FESTIVAL
PO Box 734
Woodstock, IL 60098
Phone: 630-983-7072
Fax: 630-717-7782
e-mail: mozartfest@aol.com
Web Site: www.mozartfest.org
Officers:
Interim President: Edward L. Streit

Management:
General Director: Anita Whalen
Artistic Advisor: Mark Peskanov
Utilizes: Guest Accompanists; Guest Composers; Guest Musicians; Multimedia; Original Music Scores
Founded: 1987
Specialized Field: Mozart
Paid Staff: 1
Budget: $185,000
Income Sources: Individuals, Corporations, Foundations
Facility Category: Woodstock Opera House (121 Van Buren Street)
Seating Capacity: 412
Year Built: 1889
Year Remodeled: 1977

Indiana

932
ANDERSON SYMPHONY ORCHESTRA ASSOCIATION

PO Box 741
Anderson, IN 46015-0741
Phone: 765-644-2111
Fax: 317-642-1477
Toll-free: 888-644-9490
e-mail: aso@andersonsymphony.org
Officers:
Adminisrative Assistant: RuthAnn Ginder
Management:
Music Director: Richard Sowers
Executive Director: Dana Stone, dana@andersonsymphony.org
Founded: 1978
Specialized Field: Orchestra
Paid Staff: 74
Budget: $150,000-260,000
Performs At: Paramount Theatre Centre

933
BLOOMINGTON SYMPHONY ORCHESTRA

PO Box 1823
Bloomington, IN 47402
Phone: 812-331-2320
Fax: 812-331-2320
e-mail: bso@bloomingtonsymphony.com
Officers:
President: Joseph R. Carr
Management:
Music Director: Charles Latshaw
Office Manager: Kathy Barton
Mission: Strives to provide serious music to the community; to encourage interest in hearing and participating in serious music; and to offer a professional environment for performing that music for both amateurs and professionals.
Utilizes: Arrangers; Collaborations; Community Members; Composers; Grant Writers; Guest Composers; Guest Musical Directors; Guest Musicians; Instructors; Local Artists & Directors; Local Talent; Multimedia; Music; Organization Contracts; Sign Language Translators; Soloists; Students; Student Interns; Visual Designers
Specialized Field: Orchestra
Paid Staff: 2
Non-paid Artists: 70

934
CARMEL SYMPHONY ORCHESTRA

PO Box 761
11 First Avenue NE
Carmel, IN 46082
Phone: 317-844-9717
Fax: 317-844-9916
e-mail: info@carmelsymphony.com
Web Site: www.carmelsymphony.org
Management:
Executive Director: Alan Davis
Office Manager: Denise Ryan
Mission: Committed to enhancing our community's quality of life in a fically responsible manner through creative, artistically excellent performances and educational experiences for diverse audiences of all ages.
Founded: 1975
Specialized Field: Symphony
Status: Nonprofit
Paid Staff: 3
Volunteer Staff: 14
Paid Artists: 13
Non-paid Artists: 60
Budget: $150,000-175,000
Income Sources: Box Office; Grants; Donations
Affiliations: American Symphony Orchestra League
Annual Attendance: 31,000
Organization Type: Performing; Educational

935
COLUMBUS INDIANA PHILHARMONIC

393 Commons Mall
Columbus, IN 47201
Phone: 812-376-2638
Fax: 812-376-2567
e-mail: info@columbus-in-phil.org
Web Site: www.columbus-in-phil.org
Officers:
President: Kaye Ellen Conner
VP: Ronald F Sewell
Treasurer: Robert Williamson
Secretary: Bruce Pollert
Immediate Past President: Jane B. Hoffmeister
Management:
Manager: Alice O. Curry
Administrative Assistant: Elizabeth Mullich
Music Director: David Bowden
Mission: To enhance the quality of life in our community so that all citizens have the opportunity to be touched by live, classical music in a manner and style meaningful to them.
Founded: 1986
Specialized Field: Symphony
Status: Semi-Professional; Nonprofit
Budget: $260,000-$1,050,000
Income Sources: American Symphony Orchestra League; Indiana Orchestra Consort; Indiana Arts Commission; Columbus Area Arts Council
Performs At: Columbus North Erne Auditorium
Facility Category: Orchestra Professional
Organization Type: Performing; Educational; Sponsoring

936
EVANSVILLE PHILHARMONIC ORCHESTRA

530 Main Street
PO Box 84
Evansville, IN 47708
Phone: 812-425-5050
Fax: 812-426-7008
e-mail: euphil@evansvillephilharmonic.org
Web Site: www.evansvillephilharmonic.org
Officers:
President: Philip Fisher
VP: James Dodd
Secretary: Thomas F Clayton
Treasurer: Ken Robinson
Board of Director: Danny Bateman
Management:
Executive Director: Ken Krantz
Administrative Assistant: Sandy Oldham
Director Marketing: Lynette McClusky
Mission: To provide the Tri-State Area of Southern Indiana, Illinois and Kentucky with symphonic music of the highest quality; to present programs for adult audiences and students in the school systems.
Founded: 1934
Specialized Field: Symphony; Orchestra; Chamber; Ensemble
Status: Professional
Paid Staff: 18
Budget: $2,000,000
Income Sources: American Symphony Orchestra League; Indiana Orchestra Consortium; Evansville Arts & Education Council
Performs At: Victory Theatre
Seating Capacity: 1,800
Year Remodeled: 1998
Organization Type: Performing; Educational

937
FORT WAYNE PHILHARMONIC ORCHESTRA

2340 Fairfield Avenue
Fort Wayne, IN 46807
Phone: 219-744-1700
Fax: 219-456-8555
Web Site: www.FortWaynePhilharmonic.com
Officers:
Chairman: Michael McCollum
Secretary: Nancy Stewart
Treasurer: John Shoaff
Management:
Music Director: Edvard Tchivzhel
Assistant Conductor: David Borsnold
Director Concert Operations: Laura Bordner
President: Christopher Guerin
Founded: 1946
Specialized Field: Orchestra; Educational
Paid Staff: 22
Paid Artists: 88
Budget: $4,100,000
Income Sources: Box office, grants, private donations
Performs At: Embassy Theatre
Affiliations: America Symphony Orchestra League, Indiana Orchestra Consortium
Annual Attendance: 220,000
Type of Stage: Proscenium
Seating Capacity: 2434
Year Built: 1928

938
DEPAUW UNIVERSITY CHAMBER SYMPHONY

DePauw University
PO Box 37
Greencastle, IN 46135-0037
Phone: 765-658-4380
Fax: 765-658-4401
Toll-free: 800-447-2495
e-mail: music@depauw.edu

Management:
Conductor: Orcenith Smith
Specialized Field: Orchestra; Band; Jazz
Budget: $6,000
Performs At: Kresge Auditorium
Type of Stage: Concert Stage
Stage Dimensions: 60'x 40'
Year Built: 1976
Rental Contact: 765-658-4828 Byron Craft

939

AMERICAN CONSERVATORY OF MUSIC

252 Wildwood Road
Hammond, IN 46324
Phone: 219-931-6000
Fax: 219-931-6089
e-mail: registrar@americanconservatory.edu
Officers:
Registrar: Dr. Mary Ellen Newson
Dean: Dr. Marvin Zaporyn
Chairman Emeritus: Dr. Richard Schulze
Chairman: Dr. Otto Schulze
Management:
President: Theodora Schulze
Dean: Reverend Daniel Gorham
Utilizes: Artists-in-Residence;
Composers-in-Residence; Educators; Fine Artists;
Guest Companies; Guest Composers; Guest Directors;
Guest Lecturers; Guest Musical Directors; Guest
Musicians; High School Drama; Lyricists; Multi
Collaborations; Multimedia; Music; Original Music
Scores; Playwrights; Singers; Soloists; Touring
Companies
Founded: 1886
Specialized Field: Orchestra; Jazz; Sacred Music

940

BUTLER UNIVERSITY SYMPHONY ORCHESTRA

Jordan College of Fine Arts
4603 Clarendon Road
Indianapolis, IN 46208
Phone: 317-940-9246
Fax: 317-940-9258
Toll-free: 800-368-6852
e-mail: info@butler.edu
Officers:
Admissions Representative: Kathy Lang
Management:
Conductor and Orchestra Director: Richard
Auldon Clark
Music Chair: Andrea Gullickson
Specialized Field: Orchestra; Jazz; Ensemble
Performs At: Clowes Memorial Hall

941

INDIANAPOLIS CHAMBER ORCHESTRA

32 East Washington Street
Suite 600
Indianapolis, IN 46204-2919
Phone: 317-262-1100
Fax: 317- 26—115
e-mail: iso@indianapolis Symphony.org
Officers:
Vice President /General Manager: Thomas
Ramsey
Management:
Music Director: Jack Everly
President and CEO: Simon Crookall
Specialized Field: Orchestra
Budget: $260,000-1,050,000
Seating Capacity: 2,200

942

INDIANAPOLIS SYMPHONY ORCHESTRA

45 Monument Circle
Indianapolis, IN 46204
Phone: 317-262-1100
Fax: 317-262-1159
e-mail: iso@indyorch.org
Web Site: www.indyorch.org
Officers:
President/CEO: Richard R Hoffert
Chairman: James B Steichen, MD
Management:
VP/General Manager: Thomas R Ramsey
VP Finance/Administration: Susan L Prenatt
VP Marketing: Ellen Schantz
VP Development: Kevin Garvey
Director Public Relations: Thomas N Akins
Mission: To perform live symphonic music at the
highest artistic level; to promote, support and sustain
interest in symphonic music in Indiana; to present
programs that enrich, entertain and challenge all
audiences.
Utilizes: Guest Artists; Singers
Founded: 1930
Specialized Field: Symphony; Orchestra; Chamber;
Ensemble
Status: Professional; Nonprofit
Paid Staff: 60
Paid Artists: 90
Budget: $23 Million
Income Sources: Ticket Sales; Contributions;
Endowment
Performs At: Hilbert Circle Theatre
Affiliations: ASOL
Annual Attendance: 500,000+
Type of Stage: Proscenium
Stage Dimensions: 50x40
Seating Capacity: 1786
Year Built: 1916
Year Remodeled: 2002
Organization Type: Performing; Touring; Resident;
Educational

943

INTERNATIONAL VIOLIN COMPETITION OF INDIANAPOLIS

32 E Washington Street
Suite 1320
Indianapolis, IN 46204
Phone: 317-637-4574
Fax: 317-637-1302
e-mail: kwok@violin.org
Web Site: www.violin.org
Management:
Executive Director: Glen Kwok
Operations Director: Mindy Miller
Development Director: Mary Jane Sobera
Mission: Recognizes, rewards and promote's the
world's finest young classical violinists and encourages
understanding, appreciation and support of the violin
repertoire by a large and diverse audience. Utilizes its
world prominence to bring international attention to
Indianapolis, and maintains its efforts to be a visible and
collaborative member of the arts communities in
Indianapolis and Indiana.
Founded: 1979
Specialized Field: Chamber; International
Paid Staff: 4

944

NEW WORLD YOUTH SYMPHONY ORCHESTRA

32 East Washington Street
Suite 950
Indianapolis, IN 46204
Phone: 317-229-2365
Fax: 317- 23—490
Officers:
General Manager: Ruth Wollf
Management:
Founder & Artistic Director: Susan Kitterman
Music Director: Nanna G Vaughn
Specialized Field: Orchestra; Chamber; Ensemble
Budget: $100,000-150,000
Performs At: Circle Theater

945

PHILHARMONIC ORCHESTRA OF INDIANAPOLIS

17 W Market
Suite 910
Indianapolis, IN 46204
Phone: 317-916-0178
Fax: 317-656-8754
Web Site: www.philharmonicindy.org
Officers:
President: Deana Slater
VP: Craig Parmerlee
Treasurer: Joyce Boxman
Secretary: Rolanda Haycox
Management:
General Manager: Jeff Maess
Artistic Director: Orcenith Smith
Mission: We provide educational opportunities to the
community and enhance the musical growth of
volunteer membership.
Utilizes: Guest Artists
Founded: 1940
Specialized Field: Symphony; Orchestra; Chamber
Status: Non-Professional; Nonprofit
Paid Staff: 3
Paid Artists: 7
Non-paid Artists: 80
Budget: $100,000-150,000
Performs At: Caleb Mills Hall
Organization Type: Performing; Resident; Educational

946

KOKOMO SYMPHONY

2601 S Webster Street
PO Box 6115
Kokomo, IN 46904-1659
Phone: 765-455-1659
Fax: 765-453-0048
e-mail: ksoexec@kokomosymphony.org
Web Site: www.kokomosymphony.org
Management:
Executive Director: Paul L Wood
Mission: To maintain a local orchestra, chorus and
youth orchestra; to provide the highest quality of music
under the direction of a capable conductor; to provide
musical education programs in underserved areas.
Utilizes: Collaborations; Commissioned Music; Dance
Companies; Guest Accompanists; Guest Directors;
Guest Musicians; Instructors; Lyricists; Multimedia; Sign
Language Translators; Singers
Founded: 1971
Specialized Field: Symphony; Orchestra; Chamber
Status: Nonprofit
Paid Staff: 2
Volunteer Staff: 460
Paid Artists: 65

Budget: $239,000
Income Sources: American Symphony Orchestra League; Indiana Orchestra Consortium; Indiana Advocates for the Arts
Performs At: Havens Auditorium
Affiliations: ASOL
Annual Attendance: 5400
Facility Category: Auditorium
Seating Capacity: 905
Organization Type: Performing; Touring; Resident; Educational; Sponsoring

947
LAFAYETTE SYMPHONY

111 N 6th Street
Lafayette, IN 47902-0052
Mailing Address: PO Box 52, Lafayette, IN 47902-0052
Phone: 765-742-6463
Fax: 765-742-2375
e-mail: executivedirector@lafayettesymphony.org
Web Site: www.lafayettesymphony.org
Officers:
   President: Doug Gutridge
   VP: Sandy Bollenbacher
   Treasurer: Chuck Wolpat
   Secretary: Mary Beth Buescher
Management:
   Executive Director: Kitty Campbell
   Conductor: Nick Palmer
   Operations Manager: Erica Pence
   Business Manager/Ticket Sales: Rockie Allee
   Development Director: Ken Bootsma
   Education Director: Allison Edberg
   Personnel Manager: Kara Stolle
   Librarian: Amanda Baer
Mission: The mission of the Lafatette Symphony Orchestra is to enrich the community by engaging audiences and inspiring a love of music through exciting live symphony performances, innovative programming, and educational outreach.
Utilizes: Guest Artists; Multimedia
Founded: 1951
Specialized Field: Symphony; Orchestra
Status: Semi-Professional; Nonprofit
Budget: $260,000-$1,050,000
Income Sources: American Symphony Orchestra League; Indiana Orchestra Consortium
Performs At: Long Center for the Performing Arts
Organization Type: Performing; Educational

948
TIPPECANOE CHAMBER MUSIC SOCIETY

638 N Street
Lafayette, IN 47901
Phone: 765-497-6440
Fax: 765-583-2386
Management:
   Artistic Director: Verna Aloe
Mission: Fosters and promotes the appreciation of chamber music. Promotes the pursuit of musical excellence in the area's youth through diverse educational programs, including master classes, coaching and special school programs.
Founded: 1997
Specialized Field: Chamber
Status: Nonprofit

949
MARION PHILHARMONIC ORCHESTRA

PO Box 272
Marion, IN 46952
Phone: 765-662-0012
Fax: 765- 66—266
e-mail: mpo@marionphil.org
Officers:
   President: Robert Stone
   First VP: Donna Carroll
   Secretary: Susan Munn
   Treasurer: Bob Hogan
Management:
   Music Director: Alexander Platt
   Executive Director: Mary Kirby
Utilizes: Guest Artists
Founded: 1969
Specialized Field: Orchestra
Paid Staff: 80
Budget: $150,000-260,000
Performs At: Marion High School Auditorium

950
MUNCIE SYMPHONY ORCHESTRA

2000 University Avenue
Bail State University
Muncie, IN 47306
Phone: 765-285-5531
Fax: 765-285-9128
e-mail: manager@munciesymphony.com
Web Site: www.munciesymphony.com
Officers:
   President: Jerome J Gassen
   VP: Don Whitaker
   Past President: Paul C Powers
   Secretary: Charles Hetrick
Management:
   Executive Director: Judy A Kirkwood
Mission: To stimulate, educate, and entertain audiences in East Central Indiana, and to provide meaningful musical experience for professional, community, and student musicians, through the performance of fine music and other activities.
Utilizes: Guest Artists
Founded: 1948
Specialized Field: Symphony
Status: Semi-Professional; Nonprofit
Paid Staff: 11
Paid Artists: 80
Income Sources: American Symphony Orchestra League; American Society of Composers, Authors and Publishers; Broadcast Music Incorporated; Indiana Orchestra Consortium
Performs At: Emens Auditorium
Affiliations: Ball State University
Organization Type: Performing; Educational

951
NORTHWEST INDIANA SYMPHONY ORCHESTRA AND SOCIETY

1040 Ridge Road
Munster, IN 46321
Phone: 219-836-0525
Fax: 219-836-0690
e-mail: info@NISOrchestra.org
Web Site: NISOrchestra.org
Officers:
   President: Christopher Morrow
   Treasurer/Secretary: Rick Suetanoff
Management:
   Music Director/Conductor: Kirk Muspratt
   Executive Director: John M Cain
   Marketing Director: Tricia Hernandez
   Orchestra Manager: Phil Bauman
Mission: Dedicated to presenting subscription, special, and children's concerts and maintaining the Youth Orchestra and Chorus.
Utilizes: Guest Musicians

Founded: 1941
Specialized Field: Symphony; Orchestra; Chamber; Ensemble
Status: Professional; Nonprofit
Paid Staff: 14
Paid Artists: 75
Non-paid Artists: 120
Budget: $1.2 Million
Income Sources: Grants; Donations; Ticket Sales
Performs At: Star Plaza Theatre; Merrillville
Organization Type: Performing; Resident; Educational

952
CHANTICLEER STRING QUARTET

944 Woods Road
Richmond, IN 47374
Phone: 765-966-6214
Fax: 765-973-4570
Management:
   Founder/Violinist/Agent: Caroline Klempe Green
Mission: Sharing in creative ways with people in all walks of life and of all ages the beauty of chamber music.
Founded: 1977
Specialized Field: Chamber
Status: Professional; Nonprofit
Organization Type: Performing; Touring; Educational

953
RICHMOND SYMPHONY ORCHESTRA

380 Hub Etchison Parkway
PO Box 982
Richmond, IN 47374
Phone: 765-966-5181
Fax: 765-973-3346
e-mail: rso@richmondsymphony.org
Officers:
   First VP: Karen Roeper
   Second VP: Sue Miller
   VP: Diana Pappin
   Secretary: Bobbi Whitlock
   Treasurer: Carol Smyth
Management:
   Music Director/Conductor: Guy Victor Bordo
   President: Diiana Pappin
Utilizes: Dance Companies; Guest Accompanists; Guest Companies; Guest Directors; Guest Musical Directors; Guest Musicians; Multimedia; Original Music Scores; Sign Language Translators; Singers; Theatre Companies
Founded: 1957
Specialized Field: Orchestra
Budget: $260,000-1,050,000
Performs At: Civic Hall Performing Arts Center

954
SOUTH BEND SYMPHONY ORCHESTRA

120 W LaSalle
Suite 404
South Bend, IN 46601-1305
Phone: 219-232-6343
Fax: 219-232-6627
e-mail: managingdirector@sbsymphony.com
Web Site: sbsymphony.org
Management:
   Music Director/Conductor: Tsung Yeh
   Managing Director/Executive VP: W Mack Richardson
Mission: To perform classical, pops, chamber orchestra, and educational programs.
Utilizes: Actors; Artists-in-Residence; Choreographers; Collaborating Artists; Collaborations; Commissioned Composers; Commissioned Music; Composers-in-Residence; Dance Companies; Dancers;

Educators; Fine Artists; Grant Writers; Guest Accompanists; Guest Artists; Guest Choreographers; Guest Composers; Guest Directors; Guest Musical Directors; Guest Musicians; Guest Soloists; Instructors; Local Artists; Lyricists; Multimedia; Original Music Scores; Poets; Resident Professionals; Sign Language Translators; Singers; Soloists; Student Interns; Special Technical Talent
Founded: 1932
Specialized Field: Symphony; Orchestra
Paid Staff: 11
Paid Artists: 95
Budget: $1,050,000-3,600,000
Income Sources: Sales; Contributions; Investments
Performs At: Morris Performing Arts Center
Affiliations: ASOL
Annual Attendance: 150,000
Type of Stage: Proscenium
Seating Capacity: 2,500
Year Built: 1920
Year Remodeled: 2000
Cost: 16,000,000
Rental Contact: Dennis Andres

955
TERRE HAUTE SYMPHONY ORCHESTRA

25 N 6th Street
Terre Haute, IN 47807
Phone: 812-242-8476
Fax: 812-232-2781
Toll-free: 800-878-8476
e-mail: thso@juno.com
Web Site: www.terrehautesymphony.org
Officers:
    President: Dr. Wieke Van der Weiden Bejamin
    Secretary: Richard Layton
    Treasurer: Lowell Bourne
Management:
    Executive Director: Jean Elliott Williams
    Music Director: David Bowden
    Librarian/Resident Composer: Daniel Powers
    Personnel Manager: Laura Q Savage
    Personnel Manager: Chad Roseland
    Bloomington Contractor: Gesa Kordes
    Stage Manager: Alice Yuritic
    House Manager: Emily L Fisher
    Box Office Assitant: Julliane Brandt
Mission: To increase the enjoyment and cultural enrichment of audiences in the Wabash Valley area by maintaining an orchestra dedicated to excellent performances of symphonic literature.
Utilizes: Collaborations; Dance Companies; Five Seasonal Concerts; Guest Accompanists; Guest Companies; Guest Musical Directors; Guest Musicians; Instructors; Lyricists; Multimedia; Organization Contracts; Original Music Scores; Sign Language Translators; Singers; Soloists; Special Technical Talent
Founded: 1926
Specialized Field: Symphony
Status: Professional
Paid Staff: 8
Paid Artists: 80
Budget: $345,000
Income Sources: Private; Corporate; State
Performs At: Tilson Auditorium; Indiana State University
Annual Attendance: 7,500
Facility Category: Music hall
Seating Capacity: 1478
Year Remodeled: 2002
Rental Contact: 812-237-3737 Hulman Center
Organization Type: Performing; Educational; Run-Outs

956
VALPARAISO UNIVERSITY SYMPHONY ORCHESTRA

VU Center for the Arts
Valparaiso, IN 46383
Phone: 219-464-5455
Fax: 219-464-5244
e-mail: joseph.bognar@valpo.edu
Web Site: www.valpo.edu
Officers:
    Department Chair: Joseph Bognar
Management:
    Conductor: Dennis Friesen-Carper
Specialized Field: Orchestra
Budget: $35,000

Iowa

957
AMES TOWN AND GOWN CHAMBER MUSIC ASSOCIATION

3222 Oakland Street
Ames, IA 50014-3518
Phone: 515-292-3891
e-mail: ForrestPS@aol.com
Web Site: www.amestownandgown.org
Officers:
    President: Karl Gwiasda
    VP: Linda Hagge
    Secretary: Sherry Dragula
Management:
    Artistic Director: Paula Forrest Helmuth
Mission: The presentation of four to six chamber music concerts annually.
Founded: 1950
Specialized Field: Chamber; Ensemble
Status: Nonprofit
Income Sources: Iowa State University Music Department
Performs At: Iowa State University Music Hall Recital Hall
Organization Type: Sponsoring

958
CENTRAL IOWA SYMPHONY

PO Box 1080
Ames, IA 50014-1080
Phone: 515-250-1121
Fax: 515-292-4115
e-mail: jamienieman@mschsi.com
Officers:
    Vice President: Donita McCoy
    General Manager: Jamie Nieman
    Treasurer: Tom Jackson
Management:
    Music Director/Conductor: James Hannon
    Board President: Wendi Nutini
Mission: To foster quality performance of orchestral music for the people of the Central Iowa communities; to offer satisfying musical experience for its musicians; and to provide leadership in the arts community.
Specialized Field: Orchestra
Budget: $35,000-100,000
Performs At: Ames City Hall Auditorium

959
WATERLOO-CEDAR FALLS SYMPHONY ORCHESTRA

Gallagher-Bluedorn Center
Cedar Falls, IA 50614-0803

Phone: 319-273-3373
Fax: 319-273-3363
e-mail: information@wcfsymphony.org
Web Site: www.wcfsymphony.org
Officers:
    President: Kathleen Wernimont
    President-Elect/VP: Richard Congdon
    Secretary: Charles Wheeland
    Treasurer: Louis Fettkether
Management:
    Executive Director: Rachel Ford
Mission: To educate, entertain, and enrich listeners by presenting performances of the highest quality.
Utilizes: Collaborations; Guest Accompanists; Guest Artists; Guest Composers; Guest Musical Directors; Guest Musicians; Instructors; Multimedia; Original Music Scores; Sign Language Translators; Soloists
Founded: 1929
Specialized Field: Symphony; Orchestra; Chamber; Ensemble
Status: Nonprofit
Paid Staff: 7
Income Sources: American Symphony Orchestra League; American Society of Composers, Authors and Publishers; Broadcast Music Incorporated
Performs At: Kersenbrock Auditorium
Annual Attendance: 15,000
Facility Category: Performing Arts Center
Seating Capacity: 1,500
Year Built: 2000
Organization Type: Performing

960
CEDAR RAPIDS SYMPHONY ORCHESTRA

205 2nd Avenue SE
Cedar Rapids, IA 52401
Phone: 319-366-8206
Fax: 319-366-5206
Web Site: www.crsymphony.org
Management:
    Executive Director: Marc D Levy
    Music Director/Conductor: Christian Tiemeyer
Founded: 1922
Specialized Field: Symphony; Orchestra; Chamber; Ensemble
Status: Professional; Nonprofit
Budget: $1,050,000-$3,600,000
Income Sources: American Symphony Orchestra League
Performs At: Paramount Theatre
Organization Type: Performing; Educational

961
CLINTON SYMPHONY ORCHESTRA

PO Box 116
Clinton, IA 52733-0116
Phone: 319-243-2049
e-mail: execdirector@clinsonsymphony.org
Officers:
    President: Richard J Phelan
Management:
    Executive Director: Robert Whipple
    Concertmaster: Jerry Henry
Specialized Field: Orchestra; Chamber
Budget: $35,000-100,000

962
QUAD CITY SYMPHONY ORCHESTRA ASSOCIATION

327 Brady Street
PO Box 1144
Davenport, IA 52805-1144

Phone: 563-322-0931
Fax: 563-322-6864
e-mail: info@qcsymphony.com
Web Site: www.qcsymphony.com
Officers:
President: Patricia E Duffy
Executive VP: Dan Churchill
Secretary: Beth Dietz
Treasurer: Sue Hansey
Honorary Chairman: Elsie von Maur
Management:
Executive Director: Lance O Willett
Orchestra Manager: Dennis Loftin
Music Director/Conductor: Donald Schleicher
Marketing Director: Karen Brooke
Mission: Dedicated to supporting symphonic performances; committed to fostering, stimulating and encouraging orchestral ensemble and other music through developmental programs and scholarships.
Utilizes: Guest Companies; Guest Musicians; Multimedia; Original Music Scores; Singers
Founded: 1915
Specialized Field: Symphony; Orchestra
Status: Professional; Nonprofit
Paid Staff: 6
Volunteer Staff: 375
Paid Artists: 90
Budget: $1,600,000
Income Sources: Ticket Sales; Contributions; Fund-raising
Performs At: Centennial Hall; Rock Island; Adler Theater; Davenport
Affiliations: American Symphony Orchestra League; Illinois Council of Orchestra
Annual Attendance: 40,000
Facility Category: Theatres
Type of Stage: Proscenium
Seating Capacity: 2,350; 1,620
Year Built: 1931
Year Remodeled: 1984
Organization Type: Performing; Educational

963
QUAD CITY YOUTH STRING ENSEMBLE

327 Brady Street
Davenport, IA 52801
Mailing Address: PO Box 1144, Davenport, IA. 52805
Phone: 563-322-0931
Fax: 563-322-6864
e-mail: LWillett@qcsymphony.com
Officers:
Orchestra Manager: Dennis Loftin
Management:
Music Director /Conductor: Donald Schleicher
Executive Director: Lance Willett
Utilizes: Multimedia
Specialized Field: Youth Orchestra; Ensemble; Chamber
Paid Staff: 1
Budget: $5,000
Performs At: Adler Theatre; Centennial Hall
Annual Attendance: 500
Facility Category: Recital Hall

964
LUTHER COLLEGE SYMPHONY ORCHESTRA

Luther College
700 College Drive
Decorah, IA 52101-1045
Phone: 563-387-1209
Fax: 563- 38—107
Toll-free: 800-369-8863
e-mail: selfje01@luther.edu

Management:
Director/Choral: Arnold Craig
Director/Orchestra: Daniel Baldwin
Specialized Field: Orchestra; Ensemble; Jazz
Budget: $35,000
Performs At: Center for Faith & Life

965
DES MOINES SYMPHONY

221 Walnut Street
Des Moines, IA 50309
Phone: 515-280-4000
Fax: 515-280-4005
e-mail: info@dmsymphony.org
Web Site: www.dmsymphony.org
Management:
Music Director/Conductor: Joseph Giunta
Executive Director: Richard L Early
Artistic Administrator: John Roloff
Managing Director, Symphony Academy: Joshua Barlage
Mission: To create and engage our community in extraordinary musical experiences and outstanding educational opportunities.
Utilizes: Guest Artists
Founded: 1937
Specialized Field: Symphony; Orchestra; Chamber; Ensemble
Status: Professional; Nonprofit
Paid Staff: 9
Budget: $1,700,000
Income Sources: Ticket Sales; Grants; Private Donations
Performs At: Civic Center of Greater Des Moines
Affiliations: American Symphony Orchestra League
Annual Attendance: 80,000
Facility Category: Civic Center
Type of Stage: Proscenium
Stage Dimensions: 61'x30'
Seating Capacity: 2,653
Year Built: 1979
Organization Type: Performing; Educational

966
DRAKE SYMPHONY ORCHESTRA

Drake University Music Department
2507 University Avenue
Des Moines, IA 50311
Phone: 515-271-2011
Fax: 515-271-2558
Toll-free: 800-44 -RAKE
e-mail: Clarence.Padilla@drake.edu
Management:
Orchestral Studies Director: John Canarina
Muisc Chair: Clarence Padilla
Specialized Field: Orchestra; Ensemble; Jazz
Budget: $35,000
Performs At: Sheslow Auditorium

967
DUBUQUE SYMPHONY ORCHESTRA

2728 Asbury Road
Suite 900
Dubuque, IA 52004
Phone: 563-557-1677
Fax: 563-557-9841
Toll-free: 866-803-9280
e-mail: info@dubuquesymphony.org
Web Site: www.dubuquesymphony.org
Officers:
President: Keith Bibelhausen
Preseident-Elect: Alan Avery
Executive Director: Jeff Goldsmith
Director Development: Jean Tucker

Management:
Music Director: William Intriligator
Mission: To provide quality performances; to offer educational programs in the field of classical music.
Founded: 1959
Specialized Field: Symphony; Orchestra; Chamber; Ensemble
Status: Semi-Professional; Nonprofit
Income Sources: Symphony League
Performs At: Five Flags Center Theatre
Organization Type: Performing; Resident; Educational; Sponsoring

968
DES MOINES COMMUNITY ORCHESTRA

PO Box 1796
Johnston, IA 50306
Phone: 515-964-4562
e-mail: webmaster@desmoinescommunityorchestra.org
Officers:
President: Steve Urion
VP: Josh Whitver
Treasurer: Laura Valle
Secretary: Kendall Childs
Social: Deb Gordley
Music Acquisition: Rich Gordley
Fund Raising: George Mosley
Management:
Music Director/Conductor: Carl Johnson
Specialized Field: Orchestra
Budget: $35,000
Performs At: Hoyt Sherman Place

969
SOUTHEAST IOWA SYMPHONY ORCHESTRA

601 N Main
Mount Pleasant, IA 52641
Phone: 319-385-8021
Fax: 319-385-6352
Web Site: www.geocities.com/Broadway/Orchestra/1844
Management:
Conductor/Music Director: Robert McConnell
Manager: Joy Rayman Anderson
Mission: Dedicated to educating, encouraging and performing orchestral music in Southeast Iowa.
Founded: 1950
Specialized Field: Symphony; Orchestra
Status: Non-Professional; Nonprofit
Paid Staff: 40
Income Sources: American Symphony Orchestra League; Broadcast Music Incorporated; American Society of Composers, Authors and Publishers
Performs At: James Madison Auditorium; Iowa Wesleyan Chapel Auditorium
Organization Type: Performing

970
OTTUMWA SYMPHONY ORCHESTRA

PO Box 173
Ottumwa, IA 52501
Phone: 641-682-4812
Fax: 515-682-8255
e-mail: lynnd@lisco.com
Officers:
President: John Cobler
Management:
Manager: Lynn Dew
Specialized Field: Orchestra
Budget: $35,000-100,000
Performs At: St. John Auditorium

971
CENTRAL COLLEGE COMMUNITY ORCHESTRA
Central College, Music Department
812 University
Pella, IA 50219
Phone: 877-462-3687
Fax: 641-628-5316
e-mail: lawsone@central.edu
Management:
    Director of Music Connection: Rita Burghart
Specialized Field: Orchestra; Ensemble
Budget: $1000
Performs At: Douwstra Performing Arts Center
Facility Category: Auditorium
Seating Capacity: 650
Rental Contact: Lowell Olivier

972
NORTHWEST IOWA SYMPHONY ORCHESTRA
498 4th Avenue NE
Sioux Center, IA 51250
Phone: 712-722-6230
Fax: 712- 72—637
e-mail: ngaines@dordt.edu
Officers:
    Development Director: James Koldenhoven
Management:
    Music Director: Henry Duitman
    General Manager: Norman Gaines
Specialized Field: Orchestra
Budget: $35,000
Seating Capacity: 1,200

973
SIOUX CITY SYMPHONY ORCHESTRA
520 Pierce Street
Suite 375
Sioux City, IA 51102
Mailing Address: PO Box 754, Sioux City, IA 51102
Phone: 712-277-2111
Fax: 712-252-0224
e-mail: info@siouxcitysymphony.org
Web Site: www.siouxcitysymphony.org/
Officers:
    Board President: Peter Thoreen
    Board Vice President: Eunice Acker
    Board Secretary: Marilyn Hagberg
    Board Treasurer: Rusty Clark
Management:
    Music Director/Conductor: Ryan Haskin, ryan@scsym.org
    Executive Director: David G. Krogh, dkrogh@scsym.org
Mission: To enhance the quality of life in Siouxland through symphonic music
Founded: 1915
Specialized Field: Symphony; Orchestra; Ensemble
Status: Professional; Nonprofit
Paid Staff: 5
Paid Artists: 100
Budget: $800,000
Income Sources: Sponsors; Grants; Individual Giving; Ticket Sales
Performs At: Orpheum Theatre
Seating Capacity: 2,500
Year Built: 1927
Year Remodeled: 2001
Cost: $9,200,000
Rental Contact: Orpheum Theatre Jennifer Canny
Organization Type: Performing; Resident; Educational

974
SIOUXLAND YOUTH SYMPHONY ORCHESTRA
PO Box 754
Sioux City, IA 51102
Phone: 712-277-2111
Fax: 712-252-0224
e-mail: info@scsym.org
Web Site: www.siouxcitysymphony.org
Management:
    Executive Director: David G Krogh
    Music Director: Joe Shufro
Founded: 1955
Specialized Field: Youth Orchestra
Facility Category: College Auditorium

975
WARTBURG COMMUNITY SYMPHONY ORCHESTRA
Wartburg College
222 9th Street NW
Waverly, IA 50677
Phone: 319-352-8370
Fax: 319-352-8501
Web Site: www.wartburg.edu/symphony
Management:
    Music Director/Conductor: Dr. Janice E Wade
Founded: 1952
Specialized Field: Symphony; Orchestra
Volunteer Staff: 20
Paid Artists: 5

Kansas

976
EMPORIA SYMPHONY ORCHESTRA
Emporia State University
105 Beach Hall Campus Box 4029
Emporia, KS 66801
Phone: 620-341-5431
Fax: 620- 34—560
Management:
    Music Director: Allan Comstock
    Chairman: Marie Miller
Specialized Field: Orchestra

977
HAYS SYMPHONY ORCHESTRA
Fort Hays State University
Hays, KS 67601
Phone: 913-628-5360
Fax: 913-628-4096
Web Site: www.ellisco.org/symphony.htm
Management:
    Conductor/Music Director: Christine Webber
Mission: Offering Western Kansas musical and cultural activities and providing music students with artistic and educational opportunities.
Utilizes: Singers
Founded: 1920
Specialized Field: Symphony; Orchestra
Status: Nonprofit
Paid Staff: 2
Income Sources: American Society of Composers, Authors and Publishers; American Symphony Orchestra League
Performs At: Beach/Schmidt Performing Arts Center
Organization Type: Performing; Educational

978
HUTCHINSON SYMPHONY ASSOCIATION
PO Box 1241
Hutchinson, KS 67504-1241
Phone: 620-728-0246
Fax: 620-728-8157
e-mail: keithtematt@sbcglobal.net
Management:
    Conductor: Richard Koshgarian
Specialized Field: Orchestra
Budget: 100,000

979
NEWTON MID-KANSAS SYMPHONY ORCHESTRA
Bethel College
300 East 27th Street
North Newton, KS 67117-0531
Phone: 316-283-0814
Fax: 316-284-5286
Officers:
    Manager: Jill Gatz
Management:
    Principal Conductor: Diego Sanchez Haase
Founded: 1956
Specialized Field: Orchestra
Paid Staff: 1
Volunteer Staff: 20
Paid Artists: 2

980
YOUTH SYMPHONY ASSOCIATION OF KANSAS
7301 Mission Road
Suite 333
Prairie Village, KS 66208
Phone: 913-722-6810
Fax: 913-722-6806
e-mail: ysymph@crn.org
Officers:
    Program Manager: Ingrid Stolzel
    President: Stephen Kort
Management:
    Music Director/Conductor: Dr. Glenn Block
    Executive Director: Mary Corneil
Mission: To provide educational opportunities for young musicians by performing before community-wide audiences and by inspiring excellence in performance.
Specialized Field: Youth Orchestra; Ensemble; Chamber
Budget: $260,000-1,050,000

981
TOPEKA SYMPHONY
PO Box 2206
Topeka, KS 66601-2206
Phone: 785-232-2032
Fax: 785-232-6204
e-mail: tso@TopekaSymphony.org
Web Site: www.topkeasymphony.org
Officers:
    President: Michael Lennen
    Treasurer: Neil Dobler
Management:
    Music Director/Conductor: John Strickler
    General Manager: Kathy Maag
Mission: To encourage and cultivate appreciation and support for fine music in northeast Kansas by presenting performances of high quality and by providing educational and performance opportunities for youth.
Founded: 1946
Specialized Field: Orchestra

Paid Staff: 3
Paid Artists: 88

982
WICHITA SYMPHONY
Century II Concert Hall
225 W Douglas
Wichita, KS 67202
Phone: 316-267-5259
Fax: 316-267-1937
e-mail: symphony@wso.org
Web Site: www.wso.org
Management:
    General Manager: Mitchell Berman
    Music Director/Conductor: Andrew Sewell
Mission: To rpovide Southcentral Kansas with the
highest quality of cultural, educational and
entertainment presentations through the maintencance
of a symphony orchestra and related activities.
Utilizes: Guest Accompanists; Guest Lecturers; Guest
Musicians; Multimedia; Singers
Founded: 1944
Specialized Field: Symphony; Orchestra; Chamber
Status: Professional; Nonprofit
Paid Staff: 6
Volunteer Staff: 350
Paid Artists: 95
Budget: $2.15 million
Income Sources: Ticket Sales; Donations; Program
Advertising; Performance Fees; Investment Income
Performs At: Century II Concert Hall
Facility Category: Convention Center
Stage Dimensions: 49'x60'x29'
Seating Capacity: 2,250
Year Built: 1969
Organization Type: Performing; Touring; Educational;
Sponsoring

Kentucky

983
BOWLING GREEN-WESTERN SYMPHONY ORCHESTRA
416 E Main Street
Bowling Green, KY 42101
Phone: 270-782-2787
Fax: 270-782-2894
Web Site: www.wku.edu/Dept/Academic/AHSS/Music/
Management:
    Music Director/Conductor: Jooyong Ahn
Mission: Offering the people of Southern Kentucky
classical music.
Founded: 1982
Specialized Field: Symphony; Orchestra; Chamber
Status: Semi-Professional; Nonprofit
Paid Staff: 35
Income Sources: American Symphony Orchestra
League
Performs At: Van Meter Auditorium
Organization Type: Performing; Resident; Educational

984
CENTRAL KENTUCKY YOUTH ORCHESTRAS
161 N Mill Street
Lexington, KY 40507-1125
Phone: 859-254-0796
Fax: 859-254-9644
e-mail: ckyo@ckyo.org
Officers:
    Santa Fe Office Manager: Robert Stadelman
    Seceretery: Fred Bachmeyer

    Tresurer: Jeff Garstka
Management:
    Music Director: William Briggs
    Office Manager: Penny Mazur
Mission: Dedicated to the musical education and
growth of its student members. Provides performance
opportunities, motivational workshops, small group
instruction, travel, mentoring and social interaction.
Specialized Field: Youth Orchestra

985
CHAMBER MUSIC SOCIETY OF CENTRAL KENTUCKY
Box 12032
Lexington, KY 40579
Phone: 859-246-6396
e-mail: Mlfreyoo@uky.edu
Officers:
    Past President/Information Services: Marcia
    Freyman
Management:
    President: Charles Thompson
    VP: Benjamin Karp
Mission: The purpose of this society is to foster and
promote chamber music in Central Kentucky and the
organization remains the only one in the area devoted
exclusively to the presentation of music written for small
ensembles.
Founded: 1950
Specialized Field: Chamber
Status: Nonprofit

986
LEXINGTON PHILHARMONIC SOCIETY
161 N Mill Street
Lexington, KY 40507
Phone: 859-233-4226
Fax: 859-233-7896
Web Site: www.lexingtonphilharmonic.org
Officers:
    President: Dr. Michael J Morrill
    President Elect: Larry Deener
    Foundation Chairman: John Burrus
    Secretary: Sharon C. Reed
    Guild President: Doris King Shepherd
    Guild President Elect: Cindy Leveridge
    Chamber of Commerce: Barbara Wagner
Management:
    Music Director/Conductor: George Zack
    Executive Director: Peter Kucirko
    Orchestra Representative: Elaine Cook
Mission: To offer entertainment and enjoyment to the
local community.
Utilizes: Guest Accompanists
Founded: 1961
Specialized Field: Symphony; Chamber; Ensemble
Status: Nonprofit
Income Sources: Lexington Arts & Cultural Council;
Kentucky Arts Council
Performs At: Singletary Center for the Arts
Organization Type: Performing; Educational
Comments: Special Seating and Facilities; Program in
Large Type: Assistive Listening Devices

987
LOUISVILLE BACH
4607 Hanford Lane
Louisville, KY 40207
Phone: 502-585-2224
Fax: 502-893-7954
Web Site: www.louisvillebachsociety.org
Management:
    Music Director: Melvin Dickinson

Mission: To perform the choral and orchestral music of
Bach, as well as other baroque, modern, classical and
romantic composers.
Founded: 1964
Specialized Field: Orchestra
Status: Nonprofit
Paid Staff: 80
Income Sources: Kentucky Arts Council; Greater
Louisville Fund for the Arts; American Federation of
Musicians
Performs At: University of Louisville
Organization Type: Performing; Touring; Resident;
Educational

988
LOUISVILLE CHAMBER MUSIC SOCIETY
University of Louisville
School of Music
Louisville, KY 40292
Phone: 502-852-6907
Fax: 502-852-0520
Toll-free: 800-334-UOFL
e-mail: gomusic@louisville.edu
Officers:
    Artist/Program Committee Chairman: Dr. Acton
    Ostling, Jr
Specialized Field: Chamber
Performs At: Recital Hall

989
LOUISVILLE ORCHESTRA
300 W Main Street
Suite 100
Louisville, KY 40202
Phone: 502-587-8681
Fax: 502-589-7870
e-mail: info@louisvilleorchestra.org
Web Site: www.louisvilleorchestra.org
Officers:
    Chairman of the Board: Joe Pusateri
Management:
    Operations Director: Toni M Robinson, Esq
    Music Director: Jorge Mester
    Principal Pops Coordinator: Robert Bernhardt
Mission: To educate, enlighten, entertain, excite and
enrich listeners of all ages by presenting live orchestral
performances of the highest possible quality to
audiences in Louisville, throughout the Commonwealth
of Kentucky, and in the surrounding states.
Founded: 1937
Specialized Field: Symphony; Orchestra; Chamber
Status: Professional; Nonprofit
Paid Artists: 70
Budget: $7,000,000
Performs At: Whitney Hall; Brown Theatre; Olge
Center; Louisville Palace
Organization Type: Performing; Touring; Educational;
Sponsoring

990
LOUISVILLE YOUTH ORCHESTRA
623 W Main
Louisville, KY 40208
Phone: 502-582-0135
Fax: 502-582-0149
Management:
    Music Director: Daniel Spurlock
    Executive Director: Melody Welsh
Mission: To provide high quality musical experiences
and the opportunity of performing for the benefit of the
community and its young musicians regardless of race,
creed, or economic circumstances.
Utilizes: Guest Artists
Founded: 1958

Specialized Field: Youth Orchestra
Status: Nonprofit
Income Sources: Greater Louisville Fund for the Arts; Youth Performing Arts Council
Performs At: Youth Performing Arts Center
Organization Type: Performing; Educational

991
KENTUCKY SYMPHONY ORCHESTRA

540 Linden Avenue
PO Box 72810
Newport, KY 41072
Phone: 859-431-6216
Fax: 859-431-3097
e-mail: info@kyso.org
Web Site: www.kyso.org
Management:
  Music/Executive Director: James R Cassidy
  General Manager: Angela Williamson
Mission: To culturally enrich, educate and entertain the residents of Northern Kentucky and Greater Cincinnati through unique and innovative presentations designed to make symphonic music and the concert experience, accessible and affordable.
Utilizes: Guest Accompanists; Multimedia
Founded: 1992
Specialized Field: Orchestra
Paid Staff: 5
Volunteer Staff: 79
Paid Artists: 96
Non-paid Artists: 10
Budget: $600,000
Income Sources: Sponsorship; Grant; Ticket Sales; Gala Proceeds
Performs At: Performing Arts Center And Amphitheatre
Annual Attendance: 35,000
Seating Capacity: 405-6,000

992
OWENSBORO SYMPHONY ORCHESTRA

122 E 18th Street
Owensboro, KY 42303-3751
Phone: 270-684-0661
Fax: 270-683-0740
e-mail: info@owensborosymphony.org
Web Site: www.owensborosymphony.org
Officers:
  President: Robert G Reed
  President Elect: Leslie Hines
  Secretary: Sandy Wood
  Treasurer: Joe Hancock
Management:
  Executive Director: M Wade Kelly
  Music Director/Conductor: Nicholas Palmer
  General Manager: Paula Knott
Mission: To enhance the cultural environment of Western Kentucky through performances of symphonic music.
Utilizes: Artists-in-Residence; Collaborations; Commissioned Composers; Commissioned Music; Dance Companies; Fine Artists; Guest Accompanists; Guest Artists; Guest Choreographers; Guest Companies; Guest Composers; Guest Directors; Guest Instructors; Guest Lecturers; Guest Musical Directors; Guest Musicians; Guest Writers; Instructors; Local Artists; Lyricists; Multimedia; Organization Contracts; Original Music Scores; Sign Language Translators; Singers; Soloists; Touring Companies
Founded: 1966
Specialized Field: Symphony; Orchestra
Status: Professional; Nonprofit
Paid Staff: 5
Volunteer Staff: 3

Paid Artists: 75
Budget: $759,000
Income Sources: American Symphony Orchestra League
Performs At: River Park Center
Annual Attendance: 7,400
Facility Category: Performing Arts Center
Seating Capacity: 1,482
Year Built: 1991
Rental Contact: Assistant Director Roxi Witt
Organization Type: Performing; Touring; Resident; Educational; Recording

993
PADUCAH SYMPHONY ORCHESTRA

2101 Broadway
Box 1763
Paducah, KY 42002-1763
Mailing Address: PO Box 1763
Phone: 270-444-0065
Fax: 270- 44—045
Toll-free: 800-738-3727
e-mail: symphony@apex.net
Officers:
  Secretaty: Dick Holland
Management:
  Music Director & Conductor: Jordan Tang
  President: Tom Miller
Utilizes: Guest Musical Directors; Guest Musicians; High School Drama; Local Artists; Multimedia; Original Music Scores
Specialized Field: Orchestra
Paid Staff: 12
Volunteer Staff: 75
Paid Artists: 100
Budget: $400,000+

Louisiana

994
RAPIDES SYMPHONY ORCHESTRA

PO Box 12093
Alexandria, LA 71315-2093
Phone: 318-442-9709
Fax: 318-442-9755
Management:
  Conductor: William Kushner
Founded: 1967
Specialized Field: Orchestra
Paid Staff: 1
Volunteer Staff: 30
Non-paid Artists: 50

995
BATON ROUGE SYMPHONY ORCHESTRA

7300 Highland Road
2nd Floor
Baton Rouge, LA 70898
Mailing Address: PO Box 14209
Phone: 225-383-0500
Fax: 225-767-4609
e-mail: info@brso.org
Web Site: www.brso.org
Officers:
  President: Johnny Tate
  President Elect: Anthony Kurlas
  Director Marketing: Allen Wagner
Management:
  Executive Director: Alan T. Hopper, ahopper@brso.org
  Director Operations/Education: Derrien Tolden, dtolden@brso.org

Marketing & Development: Miriam Overton, moverton@brso.org
Mission: The mission of the Baton Rouge Symphony Orchestra is to develop and maintain a financially sound, first-class symphony orchestra with a regional and national profile which will provide education and cultural enrichment for the people of the Baton Rouge region and neighboring communities.
Founded: 1947
Specialized Field: Symphony; Orchestra; Chamber; Ensemble
Status: Nonprofit
Paid Staff: 6
Paid Artists: 84
Budget: $1.5 Million
Income Sources: Individual And Corporate Gifts; Ticket Sales
Performs At: Riverside/Centroplex Theatre for Performing Arts
Affiliations: Louisiana Youth Orchestra; Baton Rouge Symphony League
Annual Attendance: 36,000
Seating Capacity: 1,905
Organization Type: Performing

996
ACADIANA SYMPHONY ORCHESTRA

PO Box 53632
412 Travis Street
Lafayette, LA 70505
Phone: 337-232-4277
Fax: 337-237-4712
e-mail: info@acadianasymphony.org
Officers:
  Conservatory Director: Denise Melancon
Management:
  Music Director: Mariusz Smolij
  Executive Director: Timothy J Bergman
Mission: To promote music and music education with focus on the youth throughout the entire region of Acadiana.
Founded: 1984
Specialized Field: Orchestra
Paid Staff: 5
Paid Artists: 9

997
LAKE CHARLES SYMPHONY

PO Box 3102
Lake Charles, LA 70602
Phone: 337-433-1611
Fax: 337-433-1615
e-mail: lclasym@aol.com
Web Site: www.lcsymphony.org
Officers:
  President: Lucie Earhart
Management:
  Executive Director: Debbie Reed
Founded: 1958
Specialized Field: Symphony; Orchestra
Status: Nonprofit
Paid Staff: 2
Volunteer Staff: 50
Paid Artists: 70
Affiliations: Southwest Regional Ballet Association

998
MONROE SYMPHONY ORCHESTRA

PO Box 4353
Monroe, LA 71211-4353
Phone: 318-435-0029
Fax: 318-435-6761
e-mail: symphony@bayou.com
Web Site: www.bayou.com/symphony

Management:
Music Director: Dr. Roger Jones
Executive Director: Naomi Cordill
Mission: To provide the region with live symphonic music of quality and to educate the public about its music.
Founded: 1971
Specialized Field: Symphony; Orchestra

999
LOUISIANA PHILHARMONIC ORCHESTRA

1010 Common Street
Suite 2120
New Orleans, LA 70112
Phone: 504-523-6530
Fax: 504-595-8468
e-mail: info@lpomusic.com
Web Site: www.lpomusic.com
Mission: Strives to continue its artistic growth, continue its financial success, provide cultural enrichment to the community, as the only player-owned ochestra in the country.
Utilizes: Actors; Artists-in-Residence; Collaborating Artists; Collaborations; Educators; Five Seasonal Concerts; Grant Writers; Guest Accompanists; Guest Choreographers; Guest Companies; Guest Composers; Guest Directors; Guest Lecturers; Guest Musical Directors; Guest Musicians; Instructors; Lyricists; Multi Collaborations; Multimedia; Music; Organization Contracts; Original Music Scores; Resident Artists; Sign Language Translators; Singers; Soloists; Student Interns; Special Technical Talent; Theatre Companies; Touring Companies; Visual Arts
Founded: 1991
Specialized Field: Symphony; Orchestra
Paid Staff: 15
Volunteer Staff: 100
Paid Artists: 70
Budget: $4 Million
Income Sources: Ticket Sales, Contributions, Grants
Season: September-May
Performs At: Orpheum Theater
Annual Attendance: 50,000
Facility Category: Theatre
Type of Stage: Orchestra
Seating Capacity: 1800
Year Built: 1921
Rental Contact: Jeff Montalbaro

1000
NEW ORLEANS CONCERT BAND

UNO Box 522
New Orleans, LA 70148-0522
Phone: 504-455-9380
e-mail: nocb@email.com
Web Site: www.gnofn.org/~nocb
Officers:
President: John Risey
VP: Norman Robinson
Secretary: Jackie Gillane
Treasurer: Donna Thompson
Board Member: Keith Buccola
Board Member: Steve Carter
Board Member: Henry Lowentritt
Board Member: Ed Mulderick
Board Member: Charlene Strain
Management:
Conductor: Dr. Richard Dugser
Mission: An adult community band providing quality music at free concerts.
Founded: 1915
Specialized Field: Band; Wind Ensemble
Status: Professional; Non-Professional

Paid Artists: 80
Budget: $5,000
Income Sources: Dues, grants
Performs At: University of New Orleans Recital Hall
Affiliations: Association of Concert Bands
Annual Attendance: 10,000
Facility Category: University owned
Seating Capacity: 85
Year Built: 1965
Organization Type: Resident

1001
NEW ORLEANS JAZZ AND HERITAGE FOUNDATION

1205 N Rampart Street
New Orleans, LA 70116
Phone: 504-522-4786
Fax: 504-522-5456
Toll-free: 800-854-4714
Web Site: www.nojhf.org
Officers:
Executive Director: Wali Abdel-Ra'oof
Management:
Program Director: Sharon Martin
Mission: The presentation and preservation of Louisiana's culture and music.
Founded: 1970
Specialized Field: Band; Jazz; Historical Music
Status: Nonprofit
Paid Staff: 12
Organization Type: Performing

1002
SHREVEPORT SYMPHONY ORCHESTRA

619 Louisiana Avenue
Suite 400
Shreveport, LA 71101
Mailing Address: PO Box 205
Phone: 318-222-7496
Fax: 318-222-7490
e-mail: office@shreveportsymphony.com
Web Site: www.shreveportsymphony.com
Officers:
President: Dr. David Lilien
Treasurer: Sidney E Kent
Secretary: Anna Epling
Chairman: Virginia Shehee
President Board Development: Gene Eddy
VP Education/Outreach: Janie Samuels
VP Development: Donald A Webb
Member-At-Large: Debbie Rathburn
Management:
Music Director/Conductor: Dennis Simons
Marketing Director: Melissa Baldwin
Mission: Dedicated to providing the three-state area with the highest possible quality musical performances.
Utilizes: Choreographers; Collaborations; Commissioned Music; Dance Companies; Dancers; Educators; Guest Accompanists; Guest Artists; Guest Composers; Guest Musical Directors; Guest Writers; Instructors; Local Artists; Lyricists; Multimedia; Organization Contracts; Sign Language Translators; Singers; Student Interns
Founded: 1947
Specialized Field: Symphony; Orchestra; Chamber; Ensemble
Status: Professional; Nonprofit
Paid Staff: 12
Budget: 1.2 million
Income Sources: American Symphony Orchestra League, Annual Fund, Ticket Sales
Performs At: Civic Theatre
Affiliations: American Symphony Orchestra League; Chamber of Commerce

Type of Stage: Proscenium
Seating Capacity: 1,737
Year Built: 1963
Organization Type: Performing; Touring; Educational

Maine

1003
BANGOR SYMPHONY ORCHESTRA

PO Box 1441
Bangor, ME 04402-1441
Phone: 207-942-5555
Fax: 207-990-1272
Toll-free: 800-639-3221
e-mail: symphony@bangorsymphony.com
Web Site: www.bangorsymphony.com
Officers:
Executive Director: Susan Jonason
Mission: The Bangor Symphony Orchestra performs locally as well as on tour.
Utilizes: Collaborations; Commissioned Composers; Guest Artists; Guest Companies; Guest Composers; Guest Musical Directors; Instructors; Multimedia; Original Music Scores; Sign Language Translators; Soloists
Founded: 1896
Specialized Field: Symphony; Orchestra; Chamber; Ensemble
Status: Professional; Nonprofit
Paid Staff: 7
Paid Artists: 90
Income Sources: American Symphony Orchestra League; Greater Bangor Arts Council
Performs At: Bangor Opera House
Annual Attendance: 12,000
Organization Type: Performing; Touring; Resident; Sponsoring

1004
ARCADY MUSIC SOCIETY

PO Box 780
Bar Harbor, ME 04609
Phone: 207-288-3151
Fax: 207-288-3151
e-mail: arcady@arcady.org
Web Site: www.arcady.org
Management:
Artistic Director: Masanobu Ikemiya
Mission: To offer the finest contemporary and classical music to Maine residents, particularly chamber music and presentations for youth.
Utilizes: Guest Artists
Founded: 1981
Specialized Field: Ensemble; Classical Music
Status: Professional; Nonprofit
Paid Staff: 2
Volunteer Staff: 30
Paid Artists: 70
Budget: $307,000
Income Sources: Chamber Music America
Organization Type: Performing; Educational; Sponsoring

1005
BOWDOIN INTERNATIONAL MUSIC FESTIVAL

6300 College Station
Bowdoin College
Brunswick, ME 04011
Phone: 207-373-1400
Fax: 207-373-1441
e-mail: info@bowdoinfestival.org
Web Site: www.bowdoinfestival.org

Officers:
Chairman of the Board: James Morgan
Management:
Artistic Director: Lewis Kaplan
Executive Director: Peter Simmons
Admissions Director: Jen Means
Business Manager: Chris Grosser
Mission: To provide the most promising music students from around the world with opportunities to further their musical development, and to present chamber music performed to the highest standards by distinguished professional musicians.
Utilizes: Composers; Composers-in-Residence; Guest Ensembles; High School Drama; Scenic Designers
Founded: 1964
Specialized Field: Chamber
Status: Nonprofit
Budget: $1,100,000
Income Sources: Contributions; Ticket Sales; Tution
Performs At: Crooker Theater, Brunswick High School, Studzinski Recital Hall, Bowdoin College
Affiliations: Chamber Music America; Major Conservatories; Maine Performing Arts Network
Annual Attendance: 10,000
Seating Capacity: 600;200
Year Built: 1995
Organization Type: Educational; Presenting

1006
PIERRE MONTEUX SCHOOL
PO Box 157
Hancock, ME 04640
Phone: 207-422-3931
Fax: 207-422-9122
e-mail: www.monteuxschool.org
Web Site: pmonteux@aol.com
Officers:
Chamber Music Instructor: Claude Monteux
Management:
Administrative President: Nancie Monteux-Barendse
Music Director: Michael Jinbo
Mission: To acquaint young conductors and future orchestra musicians with the full symphonic repertoire.
Founded: 1943
Specialized Field: Symphony
Status: Professional; Nonprofit
Organization Type: Performing; Educational

1007
MAINE MUSIC SOCIETY
215 Lisbon Street
Lewiston
Lewiston, ME 04240
Phone: 207-782-1403
Fax: 207-783-1851
e-mail: info@mainemusicsociety.org
Web Site: www.mainemusicsociety.org
Officers:
President: Judith W Andrucki
VP: David M Blocher
Treasurer: Anne M Jarvis
Management:
Interim Director: John Corrie
Mission: To support the artistic and educational activities of the professional Maine Chamber Ensemble and the auditioned, mixed-voice Androscoggin Chorale.
Founded: 1991
Specialized Field: Chamber; Ensemble
Status: Professional
Income Sources: Maine Community Foundation; Davis Family Foundation; Helen & George Ladd Charitable Foundation; Maine Arts Commision; Maine Humanities Commission

Performs At: Orchestral; Chamber and Coral Music; Educational Programs
Affiliations: American Symphony Orchestra League; Maine Arts Sponsors Association; Androscoggin County Chamber of Commerce; Maine Association Of Non-Profits

1008
LARK SOCIETY FOR CHAMBER MUSIC
PO Box 11
Portland, ME 04112
Phone: 207-761-1522
Fax: 207-780-6554
e-mail: lark1@prexar.com
Web Site: http://www.portlandstringquartet.org/lark
Management:
Executive Director: Giselle A/ Auger
Mission: Committed to supporting and presenting a Portland concert series and educational presentations by the Portland String Quartet. Presenters of the Portland Concert Series, and supporters of the PSQ's outreach activities, we promote chamber music and music education in the state of Maine.
Specialized Field: Chamber; Ensemble
Status: Professional
Income Sources: Chamber Music America
Organization Type: Performing; Touring; Resident; Educational

1009
PORTLAND STRING QUARTET
CONCERT SERIES/WORKSHOP
The Lark Society
PO Box 11
Portland, ME 04112-4866
Phone: 207-774-5144
Fax: 207-780-6554
e-mail: lark1@prexar.com
Management:
LARK Society Executive Director: Giselle A Auger
Founded: 1969
Specialized Field: Chamber; String Ensemble

1010
PORTLAND SYMPHONY ORCHESTRA
50 Monument Square, 2nd Floor
PO Box 3573
Portland, ME 04104
Phone: 207-773-6128
Fax: 207-773-6089
e-mail: psobox@portlandsymphony.org
Web Site: www.portlandsymphony.org
Officers:
President: Peter Haynes
Management:
Executive Director: Lisa Dickson
Director Marketing & Communications: Alice Kornhouser
Director Of Finance: Ellie Chotto
Music Director/Conductor: Robert Moody
Director Artistic Operations: Carolyn Nishon
Education/Community Engagement Mngr: Heather Kienow
Associate Director, Development: Leah Robertson
Mission: The PSO is a professional orchestra aspiring to the highest artistic quality; serving its city, state, and Northern New England. Its mission is to engage diverse audiences in the enjoyment of live orchestral music.
Founded: 1924
Specialized Field: Symphony; Orchestra
Status: Nonprofit
Paid Staff: 12
Volunteer Staff: 150

Budget: $2.5 Million
Performs At: Merrill Auditorium
Organization Type: Performing

1011
BAY CHAMBER CONCERTS
18 Central Street
PO Box 599
Rockport, ME 04856
Phone: 207-236-2823
Fax: 207-230-0454
Toll-free: 888-707-2770
e-mail: info@baychamberconcerts.org
Web Site: www.baychamberconcerts.org
Officers:
President: Carole Brand
Treasurer: Laurence Novotney
Secretary: Jacob Gerritsen
Management:
Executive Director: Monica Kelly
Mission: To present a variety of music styles and educational programs to reach a diverse audience along the coast of Maine.
Utilizes: Commissioned Music; Dancers; Fine Artists; Grant Writers; Guest Accompanists; Guest Choreographers; Guest Directors; Guest Musical Directors; Guest Musicians; Lyricists; Multimedia; Original Music Scores; Resident Artists; Sign Language Translators; Singers; Special Technical Talent
Founded: 1960
Specialized Field: Music
Status: Non-Profit, Professional
Paid Staff: 9
Budget: $500,000
Performs At: Rockport Opera House
Facility Category: Opera House; Strom Auditorium
Type of Stage: Proscenium; Auditorium
Seating Capacity: 400; 800
Organization Type: Performing

Maryland

1012
ANNAPOLIS CHAMBER ORCHESTRA
Maryland Hall for the Creative Arts
801 Chase Street
Annapolis, MD 21401
Phone: 410-263-1906
Fax: 410-263-5989
e-mail: annapolischorale@erols.com
Officers:
President: John Vickerman
VP: Jim Harle
Treasurer: Marilyn Rhodovi
Secretary: Katherine Hilton
Management:
Music Director: J Ernest Green
General Manager: Pamela Godfrey
Founded: 1973
Specialized Field: Chamber; Orchestra
Annual Attendance: 12,000

1013
BALTIMORE CHAMBER ORCHESTRA
5807 Hartford Road
Baltimore
Baltimore, MD 21214
Phone: 410-426-0157
Fax: 410- 42—016
e-mail: info@baltchamberorch.org
Officers:
Executive Director: Lockwood Hoehl
Management:

Music Director: Markand Rhakar
Concertmaster: Jonathan Carney
Utilizes: Actors; Guest Companies; Guest Composers; Guest Lecturers; Guest Musicians; Multimedia; Singers
Founded: 1984
Specialized Field: Orchestra
Income Sources: Legg Mason; Lockheed Martin; The Rouse Company
Annual Attendance: 8,000

1014
BALTIMORE CLASSICAL GUITAR SOCIETY

4607 Maple Avenue
Baltimore, MD 21227
Phone: 410-247-5320
Officers:
  President: David Hepple
Mission: To promote awareness of the classical guitar as an art form.
Specialized Field: Classical Guitar

1015
BALTIMORE SYMPHONY ORCHESTRA

Joseph Meyerhoff Symphony Hall
1212 Cathedral Street
Baltimore, MD 21201-5545
Phone: 410-783-8000
Fax: 410-783-8077
e-mail: tweber@baltimoresymphony.org
Web Site: www.baltimoresymphony.org
Management:
  President: John Gidwitz
  VP Artistic/Education Programming: Lucinda Williamsch
  Music Director: Yuri Temirkanov
Utilizes: Commissioned Composers; Commissioned Music; Dance Companies; Grant Writers; Guest Accompanists; Guest Artists; Guest Companies; Guest Composers; Guest Musical Directors; Guest Musicians; Multimedia; Original Music Scores
Founded: 1916
Specialized Field: Symphony
Status: Professional
Income Sources: American Symphony Orchestra League; American Arts Alliance
Performs At: Joseph Meyerhoff Symphony Hall
Organization Type: Performing

1016
CONCERT ARTISTS OF BALTIMORE

1114 St. Paul Street
Baltimore, MD 21202-2615
Phone: 410-625-3525
Fax: 410-625-9343
e-mail: cab@cabalto.org
Web Site: www.cabalto.org
Officers:
  Managing Director: Felice Homann
Management:
  Artistic Director: Edward Polochick
  General Manager: Cheryl Kauffman, cheryl@cabalto.org
  President Of The Board: Barry Williams, bfw53@aol.com
Mission: To present varied classical music programs, featuring an all professional orchestra and vocal ensemble.
Founded: 1987
Specialized Field: Chamber; Orchestra; Vocal Ensemble
Paid Staff: 4
Volunteer Staff: 10
Paid Artists: 70

Budget: $ 300,000
Income Sources: Grants; Ticket Sales; Corporate Foundations; Individual Giving
Annual Attendance: 7,500-10,000

1017
PEABODY CONSERVATORY OF MUSIC

1 E Mount Vernon Place
Baltimore, MD 21202-2397
Phone: 410-659-8140
Fax: 410-659-8140
e-mail: lpollack@peabody.jhu.edu
Officers:
  Dean of the Conservatory: Wolfgang Justin
Management:
  Concert Manager: Elizabeth Pollack
  Director: Jeffrey Sharkey
Specialized Field: Orchestra
Performs At: Miriam A. Friedberg Concert Hall

1018
UNIVERSITY OF MARYLAND BALTIMORE COUNTY SYMPHONY

1000 Hilltop Circle
Baltimore, MD 21250
Phone: 410-455-6872
Fax: 410-455-1181
e-mail: benton@umbc.edu
Management:
  Music Department Chair: Linda Dusman
  Associate Chair: Joseph Morin
Specialized Field: Orchestra; Electronic
Performs At: Fine Arts Building

1019
MONTGOMERY COUNTY YOUTH ORCHESTRA

5301 Tuckerman Lane
Bethesda, MD 20852-3385
Phone: 301-654-2018
e-mail: info@mcyo.org
  Tresurer: Ginny Jacoby
  Secretary: Georganne Larsen
Management:
  Artistic Director: Olivia W Gutoff
  Operations Manager: Cheryl Jukes
Mission: Mission of the orchestras is to nurture, develop, and advance young, talented musicians in a quality orchestral program.
Founded: 1946
Specialized Field: Youth Orchestra; Chamber

1020
MARYLAND PRESENTS

Clarice Smith Performing Arts Center
University of Maryland Suite 3800
College Park, MD 20742-1625
Phone: 301-405-2787
Fax: 301- 40—597
e-mail: cscaccess@umd.edu
Officers:
  Director of Finance and Administrat: Bob Miller
Management:
  Executive Director: Susie Farr
  Executive Administrative Assistant: Kim Thorne
  Director of Cultural Participation: Ruth Waalkes
Founded: 2001
Specialized Field: Orchestra; Chamber; Ensemble
Paid Staff: 50
Performs At: The Inn and Conference Center
Annual Attendance: 250,000
Facility Category: Performing Arts Center with 6 stages

Year Built: 2001
Rental Contact: Claudia Telliho

1021
NATIONAL ORCHESTRAL INSTITUTE

2110 Clarice Smith Performing Arts Center
University of Maryland
College Park, MD 20742-1620
Phone: 301-405-2317
Fax: 301-314-9504
e-mail: noi@accmail.umd.edu
Web Site: www.nationalaorchestralinstitute.com
Management:
  Assistant Manager: Phil Kancianic
  Manager: Richard Scerbo
  Aristic Director: James Ross
  Artistic Director: Christopher Kendall
Mission: The NOI offers an intensive three-week training experience in orchestral musicianship and professional development for musicians on the threshold of their careers.
Founded: 1987
Specialized Field: Orchestra
Paid Staff: 2
Paid Artists: 41
Budget: $380,000
Income Sources: University Funds, Ticket Revenue
Performs At: University Performing Arts Facility
Annual Attendance: 3500
Facility Category: Concert Hall
Type of Stage: Open
Seating Capacity: 1100
Year Remodeled: 2001

1022
UNIVERSITY OF MARYLAND: INTERNATIONAL WILLIAM KAPELL PIANO COMPETITION & FESTIVAL

Clarice Smith Performing Arts Center
University of Maryland
College Park, MD 20742
Phone: 301-405-8174
Fax: 301-405-5977
Web Site: www.claricesmithcenter.umd.edu
Founded: 1971
Specialized Field: Piano
Status: Nonprofit
Income Sources: University of Maryland
Season: 2003
Performs At: Clarice Smith Performing Arts Center
Organization Type: Educational; Sponsoring

1023
CANDLELIGHT CONCERT SOCIETY

8970-A Route 108
Columbia, MD 21045
Phone: 410-715-0034
Fax: 410-715-0034
Management:
  Executive Director: Bonita J Bush
Mission: To offer Central Maryland audiences professional chamber music.
Founded: 1974
Specialized Field: Ensemble; Chamber; Children's Concerts
Status: Professional; Nonprofit
Paid Staff: 1
Volunteer Staff: 75
Budget: $178,000
Income Sources: Columbia Foundations; MSAC; HCAC; Chamber Music America; Contributions
Season: October - May

Performs At: Smith Theatre; Howard Community College
Annual Attendance: 16,000
Type of Stage: Proscenium
Seating Capacity: 417
Organization Type: Performing; Sponsoring

1024
COLUMBIA ORCHESTRA
8510 High Ridge Road
Ellicott City
Ellicott City, MD 21043
Phone: 410-465-8777
Fax: 461-465-8778
e-mail: execdir@columbiaorchestra.org
Officers:
President: Bruce Kuehne
Executive Director: Tedd Griepentrog
Management:
Conductor: Jason Love
Concertmaster: Brenda Anna
Personnel/Strings: Annette Szawan
Personnel/Winds: Ann Ward
Mission: The Columbia Orchestra is dedicated to serving local audiences, musicians, and students. This is accomplished by: providing the community with high-quality musical performances , providing area students, teachers and educational institutions witha classical music resource and providing local classical musicians with an opportunity to explore and perform orchestral literature and chamber music.
Founded: 1977
Specialized Field: Orchestra

1025
SUSQUEHANNA SYMPHONY ORCHESTRA
PO Box 485
Forest Hill, MD 21050-0485
Mailing Address: PO Box 485
Phone: 410-838-6465
Fax: 410- 83—082
e-mail: susan73@yahoo.com
Officers:
Orchestra Manager: Susan Burdette
Marketing and Publicity: Tonya Woody
Management:
Music Director: Sheldon Bair
President: Susan Zollers
Mission: The Susquehanna Symphony Orchestra is a nonprofit community orchestra, providing education and entertainment for Harford County, Maryland.
Specialized Field: Orchestra

1026
MARYLAND YOUTH SYMPHONY ORCHESTRA
PO Box 27
Glenwood, MD 21738
Phone: 410-442-5645
Fax: 410-489-7268
e-mail: mgattomyso@aol.com
Web Site: www.myso.info
Management:
Music Director: Angelo Gatto
General Manager: Margaret Gatto
Mission: The symphony provides the opportunity for talented young musicians to learn and perform major symphonic repertoire at a high professional level, thus providing cultural enrichment for both performer and audience
Founded: 1964
Specialized Field: Youth Symphony

Paid Staff: 3
Paid Artists: 6

1027
MUSIC AT PENN ALPS
PO Box 668
Grantsville, MD 21536
Phone: 240-382-0903
Fax: 301-895-4603
e-mail: musicatpennalps@gmail.com
Web Site: www.musicatpennalps.org
Officers:
President: Fred C Bolton
VP: Bernice Friedland
Management:
Program Director: Nancy Salmon
Administrator: Julyen Norman
Mission: To present high-quality classical chamber music to the communities of rural Western Maryland.
Founded: 1992
Specialized Field: Chamber Music
Paid Staff: 1
Volunteer Staff: 8
Budget: $40,000
Income Sources: Corporate Sponsors; Individual Contributions; Ticket Sales
Performs At: Informal Small Halls, Good Accoustics

1028
MARYLAND SYMPHONY ORCHESTRA
13 South Potomac Street
Hagerstown, MD 21740
Phone: 301-797-4000
Fax: 301-797-2314
e-mail: mellifritz@marylandsymphony.org
Web Site: http://www.marylandsymphony.org/
Officers:
Executive Director: Andrew Kipe
Director Marketing/PR: Mary Anne Ellifritz
Management:
Music Director: Elizabeth Schulze
Orchestra Manager: Sharon Buck-Ahrens
Box Office Manager: Beth Ann Deodorff
Administrative Assistant: Carolyn Reed
Utilizes: Commissioned Composers; Commissioned Music; Fine Artists; Five Seasonal Concerts; Guest Accompanists; Guest Musicians; Local Artists; Multimedia; Music; New Productions; Organization Contracts; Original Music Scores; Sign Language Translators; Singers
Founded: 1982
Specialized Field: Symphony
Status: Professional
Paid Staff: 5
Budget: $1,000,000
Income Sources: Donors; Grants
Performs At: Maryland Theatre
Annual Attendance: 20,000
Seating Capacity: 1377
Organization Type: Performing

1029
NATIONAL MUSICAL ARTS
9506 Culver Street
PO Box 39162
Kensington, MD 20895-3628
Phone: 301-946-0355
Fax: 336-855-8494
e-mail: pgraypiano@msn.com
Officers:
Chairman: Jane Siena
Executive Director: Anne Taylor
General Manager: Joe Ragan
Secretary: Christopher Griner

Management:
Artistic Director: Patricia Gray
Orchestra Manager: Kate Gorecki
Mission: To revolutionize the way audiences experience musically innovative live performances and outreach projects, and by exploring music's role throughout the biosphere via transdisciplinary projects.
Utilizes: Collaborations; Commissioned Composers; Commissioned Music; Composers; Composers-in-Residence; Educators; Five Seasonal Concerts; Guest Accompanists; Guest Artists; Guest Companies; Guest Composers; Guest Instructors; Guest Musical Directors; Guest Musicians; Guest Soloists; Lyricists; Multi Collaborations; Multimedia; Organization Contracts; Original Music Scores; Resident Artists; Singers; Student Interns
Founded: 1980
Specialized Field: Chamber; Ensemble
Status: Professional; Nonprofit
Paid Staff: 2
Paid Artists: 20
Budget: $150,000
Income Sources: Grants, Ticket Sales, Private and Corporate Donations
Annual Attendance: 3,000
Facility Category: Auditorium
Type of Stage: Speaker Stage
Seating Capacity: 650
Year Built: 1970
Organization Type: Performing; Touring; Resident
Resident Groups: National Music Arts

1030
NATIONAL CHAMBER ORCHESTRA SOCIETY
Music Center at Strathmore
5301 Tuckerman Lane
North Bethesda, MD 20852-3385
Phone: 301-493-9283
Fax: 301-493-9284
e-mail: office@nationalphilharmonic.org
Web Site: http://www.nationalphilharmonic.org/
Officers:
President: Kenneth Oldham, Jr.
Management:
Music Director/Conductor: Piotr Gajewski
Chorale Artistic Director: Stan Engebretson
Mission: To provide concerts and programs that foster an appreciation for great classical music.
Utilizes: Commissioned Composers; Commissioned Music; Composers-in-Residence; Educators; Five Seasonal Concerts; Guest Companies; Guest Composers; Guest Lecturers; Guest Musical Directors; Guest Musicians; Multimedia; Music; Organization Contracts; Original Music Scores; Sign Language Translators; Singers; Soloists
Specialized Field: Orchestra; Chamber
Status: Professional; Nonprofit
Paid Staff: 3
Volunteer Staff: 5
Paid Artists: 32
Budget: $350,000
Performs At: Duke Ellington School of the Arts; F. Scott Theatre
Annual Attendance: 8,000
Facility Category: Theatre
Organization Type: Resident

1031
PRINCE GEORGE'S PHILHARMONIC
6611 Kenilworth Avenue
PO Box 1111
Riverdale, MD 20738

Mailing Address: PO Box 1111
Phone: 301-454-1462
Fax: 301-454-1454
Officers:
Vice President: Blake Lorenz
Management:
Music Director: Charles Ellis
President: Mary Ann White
Mission: The Philharmonic's partnership with Prince George's County schools helps cultivate a new generation of musicians and audiences. With a focus on helping children develop to their fullest potential, the schools and orchestra together clarify the best role for each to play.
Specialized Field: Orchestra
Organization Type: Performing; Educational

1032
JEWISH COMMUNITY CENTER SYMPHONY

6125 Montrose Road
Rockville, MD 20852
Phone: 301-881-0100
Fax: 301-881-5512
e-mail: info@jccso.org
Management:
Music Director: Joel Lazar
Director of Music JCCGW: Sarah N Schallern
Specialized Field: Orchestra

1033
WASHINGTON JEWISH THEATRE

6125 Montrose Road
Rockville, MD 20852
Phone: 301-230-3775
Fax: 301-881-5512
Officers:
President: Eric Slipp
Vice President: Dr. Jean Owener
Secretary: Jameser Pannabecker
Treasurer: Cynthis A. Thomas
Management:
Executive Director: Missy Shives
Founded: 1969
Specialized Field: Orchestra
Status: Nonprofit

Massachusetts

1034
BOSTON BAROQUE

68 Leonard Street
Belmont, MA 02478
Phone: 617-484-9200
Fax: 617-484-9200
e-mail: info@bostonbaroque.org
Web Site: www.bostonbaroque.org
Officers:
Founder/Music Director: Martin Pearlman
Executive Director: David Gaylin
Management:
Operations Manager: Laurie Szablewski
Marketing Associate: Christopher Jones
Mission: To present performances of Baroque and classical music on period instruments with a chorus.
Utilizes: Collaborations; Contract Orchestras; Guest Accompanists; Guest Soloists; Multimedia; Paid Performers
Founded: 1973
Specialized Field: Orchestra; Baroque
Status: Professional; Nonprofit
Income Sources: Memberships
Performs At: Jordan Hall; Sanders Theatre

Organization Type: Performing; Touring; Resident

1035
NORTH SHORE PHILHARMONIC ORCHESTRA

PO Box 95
Beverly, MA 01915-0095
Phone: 617-631-6513
Fax: 617-247-3087
e-mail: nsphil@hotmail.com
Web Site: www.nspo.org
Officers:
President: Robert A Marra, Jr
VP: Mary Miller
Treasurer: William Justin Shahan
Secretary: Thad Coverdale
Management:
Manager: Herbert A Cohen
Music Director: Max Hobart
Mission: Committed to providing access to quality music at an affordable price to communities on Boston's North shore; to developing, training and providing opportunities for young muscians; and to providing a large range of programs.
Founded: 1948
Specialized Field: Symphony; Orchestra
Status: Semi-Professional; Nonprofit
Paid Staff: 35
Organization Type: Performing; Resident

1036
ALEA III

855 Commonwealth Avenue
Boston, MA 02215
Phone: 617-353-3340
Fax: 781-793-8903
e-mail: aleaiii@bu.edu
Web Site: www.aleaiii.com
Officers:
Chairman: Andra de Quadros
President: George Demeter
Co-President: Ellen Demeter
Treasurer: Samuel Headrick
Management:
Executive Administrator: Alexandros Kalogeras
Music Director: Theodore Antoniou
Mission: Dedicated to performing and promoting twentieth and twenty first century classical music and supporting the work of contemporary composers.
Utilizes: Guest Artists; Guest Companies; Guest Lecturers
Founded: 1979
Specialized Field: Chamber; Ensemble; Electronic; Live Electronic
Status: Professional; Nonprofit
Income Sources: Boston University
Performs At: Tsai Performance Center
Organization Type: Performing; Resident

1037
BOSTON POPS ORCHESTRA

Symphony Hall
301 Massachusetts Avenue
Boston, MA 02115
Phone: 617-266-1492
Fax: 617-638-9493
Web Site: www.bso.org
Management:
Conductor: Keith Lockhart
Manager: Tony Beadle
Artistic Administrator: Dennis Alves
Sales & Marketing Director: Kim Noltemy
Director Finance: Thomas D May
Operations Manager: Christopher W Ruigomez

Chorus Manager: Felicia A Burrey
Production Coordinator: Jana Gimenez
Opened: 1885
Specialized Field: Orchestra; Pops
Status: Professional; Nonprofit
Income Sources: Memberships
Performs At: Symphony Hall
Organization Type: Performing; Touring

1038
BOSTON SYMPHONY CHAMBER PLAYERS

Symphony Hall
301 Massachusetts Avenue
Boston, MA 02115
Phone: 617-266-1492
Fax: 617-638-9367
Web Site: www.bso.org
Management:
Orchestra Manager: Ray F Wellbaum
Artistic Administrator: Anthony Fogg
Mission: The Chamber Players comprise the 12 first-chair players of the Boston Symphony Orchestra. They present programs of standard and contemporary literature not only in Boston and at Tanglewood, but on tour throughout this country and abroad, especially to audiences in locations which would not ordinarily be able to hear the Boston Symphony Orchestra in person.
Founded: 1964
Specialized Field: Chamber; Ensemble
Status: Professional; Commercial
Income Sources: Boston Symphony Orchestra
Performs At: Jordan Hall; Tanglewood
Organization Type: Performing; Touring

1039
BOSTON SYMPHONY ORCHESTRA

Symphony Hall
301 Massachusetts Avenue
Boston, MA 02115
Phone: 617-266-1492
Toll-free: 888-266-1200
Web Site: www.bso.org
Officers:
Managing Director: Mark Volpe
Director Development: Peter Minichiello
Director Media Relations: Bernadette Horgan
Management:
Music Director: James Levine
Music Director Laureate: Seiji Ozawa
Artistic Administrator: Anthony Fogg
Mission: To bring great music to the widest possible audience; the Boston Symphony Orchestra, Inc. is the parent organization of the Boston Symphony Orchestra, the Boston Pops, the Boston Symphony Chamber Players, Tanglewood and the Tanglewood Music Center. To foster and maintain an organization dedicated to the making of music consonant with the highest aspirations of musical art.
Utilizes: Guest Artists; Singers
Founded: 1881
Specialized Field: Symphony; Orchestra; Chamber; Ensemble
Status: Professional; Nonprofit
Performs At: Symphony Hall Tanglewood
Organization Type: Performing; Touring; Resident; Educational

1040
DINOSAUR ANNEX MUSIC ENSEMBLE

PO Box 5824
Boston, MA 02114

Phone: 617-482-3852
Fax: 617-482-4972
e-mail: manager@dinosaurannex.org
Web Site: www.dinosaurannex.org
Management:
   Artistic Director: Scott Wheeler
   Manager: Michael J Veloso
Mission: Presenting the best in contemporary music for chamber ensemble.
Founded: 1975
Specialized Field: Orchestra; Chamber; Ensemble; Electronic; Live Electronic
Status: Professional; Nonprofit
Paid Staff: 1
Paid Artists: 22
Performs At: First and Second Church; Boston
Organization Type: Performing

1041
GREATER BOSTON YOUTH SYMPHONY ORCHESTRAS

855 Commonwealth Avenue
Boston, MA 02215
Phone: 617-353-3348
Fax: 617-353-5205
Web Site: www.gbyso.org
Officers:
   President: David M Welch
   VP: Pamela Petri Humphrey
   Secretary: Anne Cademenos
   Treasurer: Doris Fritz Welch
Management:
   Executive Director: Catherine Weiskel
   Music Director: Federico Cortese
   Orchestra Manager: Ed Feingold
   Director Public Relations/Marketing: Jessica Tanner
   Director of Development: Ryan Losey
Mission: To organize and promote a youth orchestra program that provides the highest quality musical education, training and performance opportunities for young people.
Founded: 1958
Specialized Field: Youth Symphony; Chamber
Status: Non-Professional; Nonprofit
Paid Staff: 5
Volunteer Staff: 25
Budget: $800,000
Income Sources: Boston University; Public/Private Grants; Tuition
Affiliations: Boston University
Organization Type: Performing; Touring; Resident; Educational

1042
HANDEL AND HAYDN SOCIETY

300 Massachusetts Avenue
Boston, MA 02115
Phone: 617-262-1815
Fax: 617-266-4217
e-mail: info@handelandhaydn.org
Web Site: www.handelandhaydn.org
Management:
   Music Director: Grant Llewellyn
   Conductor Laureate: Christopher Hogwood
   Executive Director: Mary Deissler
Mission: Dedicated to promoting the performance, study, composition and appreciation of music.
Utilizes: Commissioned Composers; Guest Composers; Guest Directors; Guest Musical Directors; Guest Musicians; Multimedia; Music; Original Music Scores; Sign Language Translators; Singers
Founded: 1815
Specialized Field: Chamber; Ensemble

Status: Professional; Nonprofit
Paid Staff: 16
Budget: $2,600,000
Performs At: Symphony Hall; Jordan Hall
Annual Attendance: 40,000
Organization Type: Performing; Touring; Educational; Sponsoring

1043
MASSACHUSETTS YOUTH WIND ENSEMBLE

290 Huntington Avenue
Boston, MA 02115
Phone: 617-585-1130
Fax: 617-585-1135
e-mail: prep@newenglandconservatory.edu
Management:
   Music Director/Conductor: Michael Mucci
   Extension Division Dean, NE: Mark Churchill
Mission: Providing exceptionally talented high school musicians with an opportunity to study and perform the quality literature written for wind, brass, and percussion instruments.
Utilizes: Guest Artists; Guest Companies; Singers
Founded: 1970
Specialized Field: Youth Orchestra; Chamber; Ensemble; Band
Status: Nonprofit
Income Sources: New England Conservatory
Performs At: Jordon Hall
Organization Type: Performing; Touring; Educational

1044
NEW ENGLAND PHILHARMONIC

6 Hemenway Street
Boston, MA 02140
Phone: 617-868-1222
Fax: 617-868-1222
Web Site: www.nephilharmonic.org
Officers:
   President: Kathleen Cragin Brittan
   VP: Jennifer Snodgrass
   Secretary/Director of Development: Jeff Bigler
   Treasurer: John Guthrie
Management:
   General Manager: Brian Ritter
   Music Director: Richard Pittman
   Personnel Manager: Elizabeth Dinwiddie
Mission: To nurture and encourage the enjoyment and appreciation of new and unusual orchestral music and perform standard orchestral literature in community locations.
Utilizes: Community Talent
Founded: 1976
Specialized Field: Orchestra
Status: Non-Professional
Paid Staff: 65
Income Sources: American Symphony Orchestra League
Performs At: Sanders Theatre; Cambridge; Dwight Hall
Organization Type: Performing; Resident

1045
BROCKTON SYMPHONY ORCHESTRA

156 West Elm Street
Brockton, MA 02301
Phone: 508-588-3841
Fax: 508- 58—381
e-mail: exec.dir@brocktonsymphony.org
Officers:
   Conductor: Jonathan Cohler
Management:
   Board of Directors Chair: Paul J Carchidi

   Executive Director: Andrea Bates
Founded: 1948
Specialized Field: Orchestra

1046
BOSTON CHAMBER MUSIC SOCIETY

60 Gore Street
Cambridge, MA 02141
Phone: 617-349-0086
Fax: 617-349-0080
e-mail: info@bostonchambermusic.org
Web Site: www.bostonchambermusic.org
Officers:
   President: Stephen Friedlaender
   Vice President: Jeffrey Berman, MD
   Clerk: Pamela Brownberg
   Treasurer: Susan M Ikeda
Management:
   Artistic Director: Ronald Thomas
   Executive Director: Alan Mann
   Operations Manager: Wen Huang
Mission: To provide Boston's concert-going public with exceptional performance of the great chamber music repertoire of the 18th, 19th, and 20th centuries while fostering understanding and appreciation of the artform.
Utilizes: Guest Accompanists; Guest Musical Directors; Multimedia
Founded: 1982
Specialized Field: Chamber
Paid Staff: 3
Budget: $520,000
Income Sources: Box Office; Grants; Contributions
Performs At: Concert Hall

1047
BOSTON MUSICA VIVA

114 Auburn Street
4th Floor
Cambridge, MA 02138
Phone: 617-354-6910
Fax: 617-354-8513
e-mail: bmv@pobox.com
Web Site: www.bmv.org
Officers:
   President: Micheline de Bievre
   Treasurer: Grant Anderson
   Clerk: Robert Soorian
Management:
   General Manager: Miguel A Rodriguez
   Music Director: Richard Pittman
Mission: To promote the work of living American composers as well as comtemporary classics.
Founded: 1969
Specialized Field: Chamber; New Music
Status: Professional
Paid Staff: 2
Volunteer Staff: 4
Paid Artists: 10
Budget: $450,000
Income Sources: Box Office; Grants; Donations
Performs At: Edward Pickman Hall; Blackman Auditorium; Tsai Performance Center
Affiliations: Chamber Music America
Organization Type: Performing; Touring; Educational

1048
BOSTON PHILHARMONIC ORCHESTRA

295 Huntington Avenue
Suite 210
Cambridge, MA 02115
Phone: 617-236-0999
Fax: 617-236-8613
e-mail: office@bostonphil.oeg
Web Site: www.bostonphil.org

Management:
 General Manager: Rod Birtles
Mission: Committed to reaching and educating a wide audience in fine arts.
Founded: 1979
Specialized Field: Symphony; Orchestra
Status: Professional; Semi-Professional; Nonprofit
Paid Staff: 4
Paid Artists: 60
Non-paid Artists: 25
Budget: $1,000,000
Income Sources: Arts Boston
Performs At: Jordan Hall; Sanders Theater; Symphony Hall
Annual Attendance: 7,000
Organization Type: Performing; Touring

1049
CAMBRIDGE SOCIETY FOR EARLY MUSIC: CHAMBER MUSIC SERIES

PO Box 380-336
Cambridge, MA 02238-0336
Phone: 617-489-2062
Fax: 617-489-0686
e-mail: info@csem.org
Mission: To entertain, enlighten, educate, and in general promote the rich musical culture of five centuries of Western music occuring up to the early nineteenth century.
Specialized Field: Chamber; Early Music
Performs At: Fogg Art Museum

1050
HARVARD-RADCLIFFE ORCHESTRA

Harvard University
Music Building
Cambridge, MA 02138
Phone: 617-496-6276
Fax: 617-496-8081
e-mail: hro@hcs.harvard.edu
Management:
 Music Director/Conductor: Dr. James Yannatos
 President: Chrix Finne
Specialized Field: Orchestra

1051
KLEZMER CONSERVATORY BAND

83 Inman Street
Cambridge, MA 02139
Phone: 617-354-2884
Fax: 617-776-0955
Web Site: www.klezmerconservatory.com
Management:
 Business Manager Aaron Concert Man: James Guttmann
Mission: To offer Yiddish instrumental and vocal music with many influences (Jazz, Dixieland, Ragtime, Latin and Broadway).
Founded: 1980
Specialized Field: Ethnic Music; Folk Music; Band
Status: Professional
Organization Type: Performing; Touring

1052
PRO ARTE CHAMBER ORCHESTRA

99 Bishop Allen Drive
Cambridge, MA 02139
Phone: 617-661-7067
Fax: 617-492-6596
Web Site: www.proarte.org
Management:
 Executive Director: Ryan Fleur
 Music Director: Isaiah Jackson
 Chair: W. Easley Hamner

President: Barbara Englesberg
Mission: Seeks to make classical music accessible to the entire community. Through our Access to the Best Music program, low income, at-risk, disabled, and elderly individuals experience fine music.
Utilizes: Guest Accompanists
Founded: 1978
Specialized Field: Orchestra; Chamber
Status: Professional; Nonprofit
Paid Staff: 9
Volunteer Staff: 510
Paid Artists: 40
Budget: $550,000
Income Sources: Ticket Sales; Contributed Sources
Performs At: Sanders Theater
Annual Attendance: 6,500
Seating Capacity: 1,200
Year Built: 1870
Year Remodeled: 1994
Organization Type: Performing

1053
CONCORD BAND

Box 302
Concord, MA 01742
Phone: 978-897-9969
Fax: 978-369-1367
Web Site: www.concordband.org
Officers:
 President: BP Troup
 Treasurer: J Grace
Management:
 Music Director: Dr. William G McManus
 Manager/Librarian: J Kemson
 Fundraising: L Matson
Utilizes: Guest Artists
Founded: 1959
Specialized Field: Band
Status: Non-Professional; Nonprofit
Paid Staff: 70
Income Sources: Association of Concert Bands
Organization Type: Performing

1054
CONCORD ORCHESTRA

PO Box 381
Concord, MA 01742
Phone: 978-369-4967
e-mail: jlbo@rcn.com
Management:
 Conductor: Richard Pittman
Mission: Dedicated to providing our amateur musicians the enjoyment of playing music and offering good music to the community.
Founded: 1952
Specialized Field: Symphony; Orchestra
Status: Non-Professional; Nonprofit
Paid Staff: 70
Income Sources: American Symphony Orchestra League
Organization Type: Performing

1055
INTERNATIONAL MUSIC NETWORK

278 Main Street
Gloucester, MA 01930
Phone: 978-283-2883
Fax: 978-283-2330
Web Site: www.imnworld.com
Management:
 Co-Director/Co-Owner: AnneMarie Southard
 Co-Director/Co-Owner: Scott Southard
 International Agent: Scott Southard
 European Agent: Katherine McVicker

International Coordinator: Kristen Teixeria
Accountant: Pat Lefebvre
Contract Administrator: Laurie Zylicz
Mission: Booking agency
Founded: 1989
Specialized Field: Jazz; World Music; International

1056
CAPE ANN SYMPHONY ORCHESTRA

PO Box 1343
Gloucester
Gloucster, MA 01930
Phone: 508-326-1111
Fax: 508-362-7916
e-mail: casadvbe@shore.net
Management:
 Music Director: Yoichi Udagawa
Specialized Field: Orchestra

1057
PIONEER VALLEY SYMPHONY

91 Main Street
Greenfield, MA 01301
Phone: 413-773-3664
Fax: 413-772-6800
Toll-free: 800-681-7870
e-mail: pvsoffice@pvso.org
Officers:
 Orchestra Manager: Cecilia R Berger
Management:
 Music Director: Paul Phillips
 Executive Director: Constance Clark
Mission: To serve the Pioneer Valley.
Specialized Field: Orchestra

1058
SYMPHONY PRO MUSICA

PO Box 332
Hudson, MA 01749-0332
Phone: 978-562-0939
Fax: 978-562-0939
e-mail: spm@symphonypromusica.org
Web Site: www.symphonypromusica.org
Officers:
 President: Dan Sweeney
 Vice President: Ruth Washington Mayhew
Management:
 Music Director: Mark Churchill
 General Manager: Alison Doherty
Mission: Symphony Pro Musica have enriched the cultural life of our communities with live performances of the best symphonic music from the eighteenth, nineteenth, and twentieth centuries.
Founded: 1983
Specialized Field: Classical
Paid Staff: 2
Volunteer Staff: 15
Paid Artists: 6
Non-paid Artists: 65

1059
THAYER SYMPHONY ORCHESTRA

14 Monument Square
Suite 406
Leominster, MA 01453
Phone: 978-466-1800
Fax: 978-466-1000
e-mail: info@thayersymphony.org
Web Site: www.thayersymphony.org
Management:
 General Manager: Francis Wada
 Conductor/ Artistic Director: Toshimasa Wada
 Executive Director: Kathleen Corcoran

Mission: To sustain and develop a symphony orchestra of the highest quality for the education, enrichment, and pleasure of the citizens and musicians of Central Massachusetts.
Founded: 1973
Specialized Field: Symphony
Status: Semi-Professional; Nonprofit
Paid Staff: 20
Income Sources: American Symphony Orchestra League; North Central Massachusetts Chamber of Commerce
Organization Type: Performing; Educational

1060
INDIAN HILL SYMPHONY

36 King Street
PO Box 1484
Littleton, MA 01460
Phone: 978-486-9524
Fax: 978-486-9844
Toll-free: 800-439-2370
e-mail: Info@indianhillmusic.org
Officers:
Director of Education: Jo-Ann Wangh
Director of Performance: Cheryl DaSilva
Management:
Music Director: Bruce Hangen
Executive Director: Susan Randazzo
Utilizes: Artists-in-Residence; Collaborations; Composers-in-Residence; Educators; Guest Companies; Guest Composers; Guest Directors; Guest Lecturers; Guest Musical Directors; Guest Musicians; Multimedia; Original Music Scores
Founded: 1974
Specialized Field: Orchestra
Paid Staff: 75
Annual Attendance: 7,000
Facility Category: various venues

1061
BOSTON MODERN ORCHESTRA PROJECT

376 Washington Street
Malden, MA 02148
Phone: 781-324-0396
Fax: 781-324-0397
e-mail: bmop@bmop.org
Web Site: www.bmop.org
Officers:
Orchestra Manager: Sissie Siu
Management:
Artistic Director: Gil Rose
Development Director: Margaret Lias
Label Manager: Hannah Field
Orcehstra Manager: Sissie Cohen
Mission: Boston Modern Orchestra project's mission is to illuminate the connections that exist naturally between contemporary music and contemporary society by reuniting composers and audiences in a shared concert experience.
Specialized Field: Orchestra

1062
TUFTS UNIVERSITY: MUSIC DEPARTMENT

48 Professor Row
Medford, MA 02155
Phone: 617-627-3564
Fax: 617-627-3712
e-mail: musicadmin@tufts.edu
Management:
Department Chair: Joseph Auner
Department Administrator: Lucille Jones

Specialized Field: Orchestra; Chamber; Ensemble

1063
MELROSE SYMPHONY ORCHESTRA

PO Box 175
Melrose, MA 02176
Phone: 781-662-0641
Fax: 781-662-0641
e-mail: millierich@aol.com
Web Site: melrosesymphony.org
Officers:
President: Millie Rich
First VP: Anne Fremont-Smith
Second VP: Katherine Radley
Secretary: Rita Moore
Treasurer: Albert J Traveis
Management:
Executive Director: Millie Rich
Mission: To give the citizens of Melrose and surrounding area an opportunity to participate in the joy of music.
Utilizes: Commissioned Composers; Commissioned Music; Composers; Educators; Guest Accompanists; Guest Companies; Guest Composers; Guest Directors; Guest Instructors; Guest Lecturers; Guest Musical Directors; Guest Musicians; Lyricists; Multi Collaborations; Multimedia; Music; Organization Contracts; Scenic Designers; Singers
Founded: 1918
Specialized Field: Symphony; Orchestra
Status: Nonprofit
Volunteer Staff: 17
Paid Artists: 1
Non-paid Artists: 72
Performs At: Memorial Building (590 Main Street, Melrose)
Annual Attendance: 5,000
Facility Category: Auditorium Performance Center
Type of Stage: Performance Stage
Stage Dimensions: 30x40
Seating Capacity: 900
Year Built: 1912
Rental Contact: 7189794185 Millie Rich
Organization Type: Performing

1064
BOSTON CLASSICAL ORCHESTRA

Box 152
Newton, MA 02468
Phone: 617-423-3883
Fax: 617-527-4764
Web Site: www.bostonclassicalorchestra.org
Officers:
President: Diana Bishop
VP: Richards L Edwards
Treasurer: Rand Folta
Management:
Executive Director: Carolyn Copp
Music Director: Steven Lipsitt
Mission: To offer outstanding performances of the chamber orchestra repertoire in an intimate setting, concentrating on music of the Classical period. Through imaginatively presented live concerts in a relaxed atmosphere, the BCO seeks to foster a sense of connection between audience and performers and to strengthen its appeal to a growing and varied public.
Founded: 1980
Specialized Field: Symphony; Orchestra; Chamber
Status: Professional; Nonprofit
Paid Staff: 3
Volunteer Staff: 25
Budget: $300,000
Performs At: Faneuil Hall
Organization Type: Performing

1065
NEWTON SYMPHONY ORCHESTRA

61 Washington Park
Newton, MA 02460
Phone: 617-965-2555
Fax: 617-965-0450
e-mail: newtonsymphony@compuserve.com
Web Site: www.newtonsymphony.org
Officers:
President: Walter F Carter
VP: Andris Vizolis
Secretary: Nancy O'Brien
Treasurer: Joel Corman
Management:
Administrative Coordinator: Arks Smith
Music Director/Conductor: Jeffrey Rink
Personnel Manager: Mark Perreovlt
Mission: To provide area volunteer musicians the opportunity to maintain and develop their skills, and to enhance music appreciation, promote cross-cultural understanding, and build community through outreach programs for students and seniors.
Founded: 1965
Specialized Field: Symphony; Orchestra
Status: Nonprofit; Volunteer
Paid Staff: 3
Volunteer Staff: 7
Paid Artists: 10
Non-paid Artists: 60
Budget: $100,000
Income Sources: Box office; grants; private donations
Performs At: Rashi Auditorium
Annual Attendance: 3,000 - 4,000
Seating Capacity: 852
Organization Type: Performing

1066
CAPE COD CHAMBER MUSIC FESTIVAL

216C Orleans Road
Nickerson Corners
North Chatham, MA 02650
Phone: 508-945-8060
Fax: 508-945-8059
Toll-free: 800-229-5739
e-mail: contact@capecodchambermusic.org
Web Site: www.capecodchambermusic.org
Officers:
President: Lawrence M Handley
Treasurer: Laura S Emmons
Secretary: George Dillion
Management:
Artistic Director: Nicholas Kitchen
Executive Directoror: Pamela Patrick
Director Development: Lynne Pleffner
Mission: To present the finest classical and contemporary chamber music by both world-class ensembles and exceptional young emerging artists to Cape Cod audiences; to develop new and younger audiences for chamber music; to commission new chamber works whenever possible; and to provide educational activities and programs which encourage, broaden and deepen appreciation of the chamber music art form.
Founded: 1979
Specialized Field: Chamber
Status: Professional; Nonprofit
Paid Staff: 3
Paid Artists: 30
Facility Category: Usually churches
Seating Capacity: 250 - 300
Organization Type: Performing; Educational

1067

SMITH COLLEGE ORCHESTRA

Smith College Musical Department
Sage Hall, Smith College
Northampton, MA 01063
Phone: 413-584-2700
Fax: 413-585-3180
e-mail: jhirsh@email.smith.edu
Management:
Conductor: Jonathan Hirsh
Utilizes: Original Music Scores; Soloists
Specialized Field: Orchestra
Performs At: Concert Halls

1068

STOCKBRIDGE CHAMBER CONCERTS AT SEARLES CASTLE

68 Kenilworth Street
Pittsfield, MA 01201
Phone: 413-442-7711
Fax: 413-442-7711
Toll-free: 888-528-7728
e-mail: elizabethhagenah@altavista.com
Officers:
President: Elizabeth A Hagenah
VP: Dr. David Anderegg
Treasurer: Dr. Norma Thompson
Management:
Artistic Director/Founder: Elizabeth A Hagenah
Clerk: Eunice Agar
Mission: To promote cultural activities and help outstanding young talents by giving them scholarship performances with mature artists.
Utilizes: Sign Language Translators; Students
Founded: 1975
Specialized Field: Ensemble; Chamber
Status: Professional; Nonprofit
Paid Artists: 15
Budget: $16,000 - $22,000
Income Sources: Ticket sales, contributions
Performs At: Searles Castle
Affiliations: Chamber Music America (member)
Annual Attendance: 175
Facility Category: Concert hall and reception atrium
Type of Stage: Small elevated
Seating Capacity: 175, 250 childrens programs
Year Built: 1886
Rental Contact: At John Dewey Academy Dr. Thomas Bratter
Organization Type: Performing; Touring; Resident; Educational; Sponsoring
Resident Groups: Stockbridge Chamber Concerts (summer)

1069

PLYMOUTH PHILHARMONIC ORCHESTRA

16 Court Street
Plymouth, MA 02361
Mailing Address: PO Box 3174, Plymouth, MA 12361
Phone: 508-746-8008
Fax: 508-746-0115
e-mail: thephil@adelphia.com
Web Site: www.plymouthphilharmonic.com
Officers:
President: Louise Woodruff
VP: Thomas Hurley
VP: Michael Coleman
Secretary/Clerk: Donna Frugoli
Treasurer: Paul Kiley
VP: N. Thompson Bosanquet
Management:
Executive Director: Roberta J Otto

Office Manager: Linda Hurley
Development Manager: Christine Wells
Marketing Specialist: Judith Ingram
Music Director/Conductor: Steven Karidoyanes
Mission: To present excellent, professional symphonic music to the broadest possible audience and to encourage a life-long love of music through a variety of educational programs.
Utilizes: Collaborations; Commissioned Music; Educators; Five Seasonal Concerts; Guest Musical Directors; Guest Musicians; Local Artists; Multi Collaborations; Multimedia; Music; Organization Contracts; Original Music Scores; Sign Language Translators; Singers; Volunteer Artists
Founded: 1913
Specialized Field: Symphony; Orchestra; Chamber; Ensemble
Status: Professional; Semi-Professional; Nonprofit
Paid Staff: 8
Paid Artists: 75
Budget: $519,468
Income Sources: Ticket Sales; Grants; Contributions
Performs At: Memorial Hall - Plymouth, Massachusetts
Affiliations: American Symphony Orchestra League; Plymouth County Development Council; Plymouth Area Chamber of Commerce
Annual Attendance: 15,500
Facility Category: Municipal Auditorium
Seating Capacity: 1285
Year Built: 1926
Year Remodeled: 2002
Organization Type: Performing; Educational; Sponsoring

1070

ROCKPORT CHAMBER MUSIC FESTIVAL

PO Box 312
Rockport, MA 01966
Phone: 978-546-7138
e-mail: rcmf@shore.net
Web Site: www.rcmf.org
Officers:
President: Phillip D Cutter MD
VP: Dianne Anderson
VP: Barbara Sparks
Treasurer: William Hausman
Clerk/Secretary: Mollie Byrnes
Management:
Artistic Director: David Deveau
Mission: The presentation of a 16-concert series in June, featuring chamber ensembles performing alone and in collaboration.
Specialized Field: Chamber
Status: Professional; Nonprofit
Performs At: Rockport Art Association
Organization Type: Presenting

1071

MUSICORDA FESTIVAL & SUMMER STRING PROGRAM

PO Box 557
South Hadley, MA 01075
Phone: 413-538-2590
Fax: 413-538-3021
e-mail: musicorda@aol.com
Web Site: www.musicorda.org
Management:
Artistic Director: Leopold Teraspulsky
Executive Director: Jacqueline Melnick
Mission: To forge an international community of artists and students dedicated to sharing their joy in making music and to enriching the lives of diverse audiences through excellence in performance and education.
Founded: 1987

Specialized Field: String Ensemble
Status: Professional; Nonprofit
Paid Staff: 4
Volunteer Staff: 4
Performs At: Chapin Auditorium; Mount Holyoke College
Facility Category: Concert Hall
Seating Capacity: 800
Organization Type: Performing; Touring; Resident; Educational

1072

SPRINGFIELD ORCHESTRA ASSOCIATION

75 Market Place
1ST Floor
Springfield, MA 01103
Phone: 413-733-0636
Fax: 413-781-4129
Management:
Music Director: Kevin Rhodes
Executive Director: Michael Jonnes
Mission: To provide symphonic music and other musical entertainment to the residents of Western Massachusetts; to nurture music appreciation.
Specialized Field: Symphony
Status: Professional; Nonprofit
Performs At: Springfield Symphony Hall
Organization Type: Performing; Touring; Educational

1073

SPRINGFIELD SYMPHONY ORCHESTRA

75 Market Street
Springfield, MA 01103
Phone: 413-733-2291
Fax: 413-781-4129
Web Site: www.springfieldsymphony.org
Management:
General Manager: Linda G Moore
Music Director/Conductor: Kenneth Kiesler
Orchestra Manager: Judith Lampert
Mission: To sponsor, promote and assist in the presentation of symphonic concerts; encourage and develop a desire for symphonic music; instruct, assist and develop musical abilities; assist in training and education; provide concerts, musical programs and other entertainment.
Founded: 1921
Specialized Field: Symphony; Orchestra; Chamber; Ensemble
Status: Professional; Nonprofit
Income Sources: American Symphony Orchestra League; Chamber Music America; Illinois Arts Alliance
Performs At: Braden Auditorium at Illinois State University
Organization Type: Performing; Touring; Resident; Educational

1074

MARTHA'S VINEYARD CHAMBER MUSIC SOCIETY

PO Box 4189
Vineyard Haven, MA 02568
Phone: 508-696-8055
Fax: 508-696-8055
e-mail: mvcms@vineyard.net
Web Site: mvcms.vineyard.net/
Officers:
President: Daniel J Culkin
VP: Dr. Sofia Anthony
Treasurer: Marilyn Hollinshea
Secretary: Susan Phelps
Management:

Executive Director: Nancy Rogers
Artistic Director: Delores Stevens
Mission: To produce chamber music concerts, promote and support classical music learning opportunities and create awareness of the value and significance of fine music on the island.
Utilizes: Collaborations; Commissioned Composers; Guest Musical Directors; Multimedia; Original Music Scores; Sign Language Translators
Founded: 1971
Specialized Field: Chamber
Status: Professional; Nonprofit
Paid Staff: 1
Paid Artists: 30
Budget: $100,000
Income Sources: Box Office; Grants; Private Donations
Performs At: Old Wharling Church; Chilmark Community Center
Annual Attendance: 2,800
Facility Category: Historic Church; Peformance & Community Center
Type of Stage: Proscenium
Seating Capacity: 500; 200

1075
NEW ENGLAND STRING ENSEMBLE
599 N Avenue, Suite 8
PO Box 2012
Wakefield, MA 01880
Phone: 781-224-1117
Fax: 781-224-3547
e-mail: info@nese.net
Web Site: www.nese.net
Officers:
 President: Gordon Conrad
 VPresident: James Wisdom
 Tresurer: Bob Sanferrare
 Clerk: John Wall
Management:
 Music Director: Susan Davenny Wyner
 Executive Director: Peter Stickel
 Orchestra Manager: John Bumstedd
Mission: The New England String Ensemble was founded to bring string music both to the concertgoing public and to those who might not overwise have the opportunity to hear a professional string orchestra.
Founded: 1994
Specialized Field: Classical; String Ensemble
Paid Staff: 3
Volunteer Staff: 2
Paid Artists: 30
Annual Attendance: 390,000
Facility Category: Concet Hall
Seating Capacity: 1,000

1076
BRANDEIS UNIVERSITY DEPARTMENT OF MUSIC
PO Box 5491110
South Street
Waltham, MA 02454-9110
Phone: 781-736-3310
Fax: 781-736-3320
e-mail: music@brandies.edu
Web Site: www.brandeis.edu/departments/music
Mission: Pesenting a university concert series including Professional Series, Concerts at Noon and student performances.
Utilizes: Guest Artists
Founded: 1940
Specialized Field: Orchestra; Chamber; Ensemble; Electronic; Live Electronic
Status: Professional; Non-Professional; Nonprofit

Performs At: Slosberg Recital Hall
Organization Type: Performing; Resident

1077
BOSTON CIVIC SYMPHONY ORCHESTRA OF BOSTON
PO Box 1082
Brookline
Westwood, MA 02446-0009
Phone: 617-923-6333
Fax: 781-329-7293
e-mail: info@csob.org
Officers:
 Orchestra Manager: Jane Zanichkowsky
 Personnel Manager: Mona Chang
Management:
 Music Director/Conductor: Max Hobart
 President: Richard Blacher
Specialized Field: Orchestra

1078
WILLIAMS CHAMBER PLAYERS
Williams College Department of Music
54 Chaplin Hall Drive
Williamstown, MA 01267
Phone: 413-597-2736
Fax: 413-597-3100
Management:
 Chair/Department Music: Douglas B Moore
 Concert Manager: Ernest Clark
Mission: To bring high-quality performance of chamber music repertoire to Williams students and the community-at-large.
Founded: 1999
Specialized Field: Chamber
Status: Professional; Nonprofit
Performs At: Brooks-Rogers Recital Hall; Bernhard Music Center
Organization Type: Performing; Touring; Resident

1079
QUINCY SYMPHONY ORCHESTRA
PO Box 2
Wollaston, MA 02170
Phone: 781-961-3790
Fax: 617-376-1297
Toll-free: 800-579-1618
e-mail: quincysymphony@netscape.net
Officers:
 President: Barbara Clement
 First VP: Lee Salerno
 Second VP: Roberta Kopelman
 Secretary: Eleanor Nelson
 Treasurer: David Levy
Management:
 Music Director: Yoichi Udagawa
 Concertmaster: Anne Hopper Webb
Founded: 1954
Specialized Field: Orchestra

1080
CAPE COD SYMPHONY ORCHESTRA
712A Main Street
Yarmouth Port, MA 02675-2000
Phone: 508-362-1111
Fax: 508-326-7916
e-mail: csoadmin@capesymphony.org
Web Site: www.capesymphony.org
Officers:
 Acting Executive Director: Jerome Karter
Management:
 Music Director/Conductor: Royston Nash
 Vice Chair: Jerome Karter

Mission: The program is designed to encourage appreciation and to futher develop the students understanding of classical music.
Specialized Field: Symphony

Michigan

1081
ADRIAN SYMPHONY ORCHESTRA
110 S Madison Street
Adrian, MI 49221
Phone: 517-264-3121
Fax: 517-264-3833
e-mail: aso@adrian.edu
Web Site: www.adriansymphony.org
Management:
 Executive Director: Elizabeth Watson
 Music Director: John Dodson
Mission: To remain Lenawee County's premiere musical ensemble and Adrian College's professional orchestra-in-residence; to perform classical, family, holiday, pops, chamber and young peoples' concerts.
Utilizes: Grant Writers; Guest Accompanists; Guest Artists; Guest Composers; Guest Musicians
Founded: 1981
Specialized Field: Symphony; Orchestra; Chamber; Ensemble
Status: Professional; Nonprofit
Paid Staff: 5
Budget: $350,000
Income Sources: American Symphony Orchestra League; Michigan Orchestra Association
Performs At: Dawson Auditorium
Affiliations: Adrian College
Organization Type: Performing; Touring; Resident; Educational

1082
ALMA SYMPHONY ORCHESTRA
614 W Superior Street
Alma, MI 48801
Phone: 989-463-7167
Fax: 517-463-7277
Toll-free: 800-321-2562
e-mail: masley@alma.edu
Management:
 Music Director: Murray Gross
 Director of Percussion Ensemble and: David Zerbe
Specialized Field: Orchestra; Ensemble; Band

1083
ANN ARBOR SYMPHONY ORCHESTRA
220 E Huron
Suite 470
Ann Arbor, MI 48104
Phone: 734-994-4801
Fax: 734-994-3949
e-mail: a2so@a2so.com
Web Site: www.a2so.com
Officers:
 President: Kim Eagle
 VP: William Maxbauer
 Secretary: Joan Singer
 Treasurer: Richard Hendricks
Management:
 Executive Director: Mary Steffek Blaske
 Personnel Manager: Gregg Emerson Powell
 Librarian: Kit Weber
Mission: Enrich musical culture of Ann Arbor and surrounding area, foster growing appreciation for orchestral music.

Utilizes: Collaborations; Commissioned Music; Guest Accompanists; Guest Musical Directors; Guest Musicians; Instructors; Multimedia; Organization Contracts; Original Music Scores; Sign Language Translators; Singers; Soloists
Founded: 1928
Specialized Field: Symphony; Orchestra
Status: Professional
Paid Staff: 8
Volunteer Staff: 3
Paid Artists: 220
Budget: $979,000
Income Sources: Tickets; Contributions; Grants
Performs At: Historic Theater
Annual Attendance: 18,000
Organization Type: Performing; Educational

1084
UNIVERSITY OF MICHIGAN SYMPHONY ORCHESTRAS

1100 Baits Drive
E V Moore Building
Ann Arbor, MI 48109-2085
Phone: 734-764-0583
Fax: 734-763-5097
e-mail: aderente@umich.edu
Officers:
   Dean: Christopher Kendall
Management:
   Music Director: Kenneth Kiesler
   Ensembles Manager: David R Aderente
Specialized Field: Orchestra
Budget: $35,000
Performs At: Hill Auditorium

1085
BATTLE CREEK SYMPHONY ORCHESTRA

PO Box 1613
Battle Creek, MI 49016
Phone: 269-963-1911
Fax: 269-966-2547
e-mail: bcso@musiccenterscmi.com
Officers:
   President: Penny DeGarmo
Management:
   Music Director/Conductor: Matthew Hazelwood
   General Manager: Glenn Klassen
Mission: The performance of classical and pops concerts.
Utilizes: Collaborations; Commissioned Music; Guest Accompanists; Guest Composers; High School Drama; Multimedia; Sign Language Translators; Singers
Founded: 1899
Specialized Field: Symphony; Orchestra; Chamber
Status: Professional; Nonprofit
Paid Staff: 6
Paid Artists: 80
Budget: $500,000
Income Sources: American Symphony Orchestra League; Michigan Council for Arts and Cultural Affairs; United Arts Council
Performs At: WK Kellogg Auditorium
Organization Type: Performing; Educational

1086
MUSIC CENTER OF SOUTH CENTRAL MICHIGAN

PO Box 1613
Battle Creek, MI 49016
Phone: 269-963-1911
Fax: 269-966-2547
Web Site: www.musiccenterscmi.com

Management:
   Symphony Music Director: Anne Harrigan
   General Manager: Kelly Redmond
   Box Office Manager: Kevin Cort
Mission: Your nonprofit resource for learning and performance in the Battle Creek region, featuring the symphony, music schools and choruses.
Specialized Field: Concert Band; Folk Music; Orchestra
Status: Nonprofit
Income Sources: Individual
Performs At: W K Kellogg Auditorium; Lakeview High School; First Presbyterian Church; First Congregational Church
Type of Stage: Black Box

1087
BIRMINGHAM-BLOOMFIELD SYMPHONY

1592 Buckingham
Birmingham, MI 48009
Phone: 248-645-2276
Fax: 248-645-2276
Web Site: www.bbso.org
Management:
   Executive Director: Carla Lamphere
   Personnel Manager: Jon Boyd
   Librarian: Eldonna May
   Administrative Assistant: Joe Labuta
Mission: To foster an appreciation of the musical arts.
Utilizes: Guest Artists
Founded: 1975
Specialized Field: Symphony; Orchestra; Ensemble
Status: Professional; Nonprofit
Income Sources: American Society of Composers, Authors and Publishers; Michigan Orchestra Association; Michigan Orchestra Volunteer Association
Performs At: Temple Beth El
Organization Type: Performing; Educational

1088
MACOMB SYMPHONY ORCHESTRA

PO Box 381062
4-4575 Garfield
Clinton Township, MI 48038
Phone: 586-286-2045
Fax: 248-643-0808
e-mail: thomusic@prodigy.net
Web Site: www.macombsymphony.org
Management:
   Music Director: Thomas Cook
Utilizes: Multimedia
Founded: 1974
Specialized Field: Orchestra
Paid Staff: 2
Volunteer Staff: 28
Paid Artists: 82
Non-paid Artists: 6
Budget: $35,000-100,000
Seating Capacity: 1,230
Year Built: 1981
Year Remodeled: 2002

1089
DEARBORN ORCHESTRAL SOCIETY / DEARBORN SYMPHONY

PO Box 2063
Dearborn, MI 48123
Phone: 313-565-2424
Fax: 313-565-2411
e-mail: info@dearbornsymphony.org
Officers:
   President: Sandra Butler
   VP: Stanley Nycek
   Treasurer: John Carr

Management:
   Music Director: Kypros Markou
   Office Manager: Debora Brazakis
Utilizes: Guest Companies; Guest Lecturers; Local Artists; Multimedia; Sign Language Translators; Singers
Specialized Field: Orchestra
Paid Staff: 3
Income Sources: Donations; Corporate Support
Annual Attendance: 5,000
Facility Category: Ford Community and Performing Arts Center
Seating Capacity: 1,201
Year Built: 2001

1090
DETROIT SYMPHONY ORCHESTRA

3711 Woodward Avenue
Detroit, MI 48201
Phone: 313-576-5111
Fax: 313-576-5109
Web Site: www.detroitsymphony.com
Officers:
   Chairman: James B Nicholson
Management:
   Director: Leonard Slatkin
   Executive Director: Anne Parsons
   Marketing: Ross Binnie
Utilizes: Guest Artists
Founded: 1914
Status: Non-Profit, Professional
Performs At: Orchestra Hall; Meadow Brook Music Festival
Organization Type: Performing; Touring; Resident; Educational; Sponsoring

1091
CHAMBER MUSIC SOCIETY OF DETROIT

31731 Northwestern Highway
Suite 259 W
Farmington Hills, MI 48334
Phone: 248-737-9980
Fax: 248-737-9981
e-mail: Administrator@ComeHearCMSD.org
Web Site: www.ComeHearCMSD.org
Officers:
   President: Lois R Bezuus
Management:
   Administrative Director: Willa R Walker
Utilizes: Collaborations; Commissioned Music; Guest Directors; Multimedia; Original Music Scores; Singers
Founded: 1944
Specialized Field: Chamber Music; Recitals
Performs At: Seligman Performing Arts Center; Orchestra Hall
Affiliations: Chamber Music America
Seating Capacity: 715; 2,035

1092
FLINT SCHOOL OF PERFORMING ARTS: YOUTH ENSEMBLES

1025 E Kearsley
Flint, MI 48503
Phone: 810-238-1350
Fax: 810-238-6385
e-mail: fim@thefim.com
Officers:
   Manager: Tom Glasscock
Management:
   Music Director: Davin Pierson Torre
   President: Paul Torre
Specialized Field: Orchestra; Youth Orchestra
Annual Attendance: 3500

1093
FLINT SYMPHONY ORCHESTRA
Flint Institute of Music
1025 E Kearsley Street
Flint, MI 48503
Phone: 810-238-1350
Fax: 810-238-6385
Web Site: www.thefim.com/fso
Management:
Manager: Tom Glasscock
Utilizes: Guest Artists
Founded: 1917
Specialized Field: Symphony; Orchestra
Status: Professional; Nonprofit
Budget: $260,000-1,50,000
Performs At: James H. Whiting Auditorium
Organization Type: Performing; Resident; Educational

1094
GRAND RAPIDS SYMPHONY
169 Louis Campau Promenade NW
Suite One
Grand Rapids, MI 49503
Phone: 616-454-9451
Fax: 616-454-7477
e-mail: grsinfo@grsymphony.org
Web Site: www.grsymphony.org
Officers:
Chairperson: Thomas Hilliker
Management:
President: William A Ryberg
VP Marketing/Public Relations: Karen Mueller
Public Relations Manager: Carol Tanis
VP Development: Jan McKinnon
Mission: The purpose of the Grand Rapids Symphony Society is to provide concerts of orchestral and chamber music and educational programs of the highest quality to the widest possible audience.
Utilizes: Guest Artists; Guest Companies
Founded: 1929
Specialized Field: Symphony; Orchestra; Chamber; Ensemble
Status: Nonprofit
Paid Staff: 25
Paid Artists: 75
Budget: $6.2 million
Income Sources: Concert and Event Income; Grants; Private Donations
Annual Attendance: 200,000
Organization Type: Performing; Touring; Resident; Educational

1095
GRAND RAPIDS YOUTH SYMPHONY
220 Lyon Street NW
Suite 415
Grand Rapids, MI 49503
Phone: 616-454-9451
Fax: 616-454-7477
Management:
Conductor: John Varineau
Outreach Director: Pam French
Mission: The Grand Rapids Youth Symphony affords the area's finest young musicians the opportunity to perform orchestral compositions ats a high standard.
Founded: 1959
Specialized Field: Youth Symphony; Orchestra
Status: Non-Professional; Nonprofit
Paid Staff: 80
Income Sources: American Symphony Orchestra League (Youth Orchestra Division); Grand Rapids Symphony

Performs At: Forest Hills Northern High School Auditorium
Organization Type: Performing; Educational

1096
ST. CECILIA MUSIC SOCIETY
24 Ransom Avenue NE
Grand Rapids, MI 49503
Phone: 616-459-2224
Fax: 616-459-2997
e-mail: scms_pwp@iserv.net
Web Site: www.scmsonline.org
Management:
Executive Director: Sharon Mack
Music Director: Philip Pletcher
Mission: To promote and support chamber music performance in Western Michigan, specifically Grand Rapids.
Utilizes: Actors; AEA Actors; Artists-in-Residence; Choreographers; Collaborating Artists; Collaborations; Dance Companies; Dancers; Educators; Fine Artists; Grant Writers; Guest Accompanists; Guest Choreographers; Guest Companies; Guest Directors; Guest Instructors; Guest Musical Directors; Guest Musicians; Guest Soloists; High School Drama; Instructors; Local Artists; Lyricists; Multi Collaborations; Multimedia; Organization Contracts; Original Music Scores; Selected Students; Sign Language Translators; Singers; Soloists; Student Interns; Theatre Companies
Specialized Field: Educational; Classical Music
Status: Nonprofit
Paid Staff: 20
Volunteer Staff: 300
Paid Artists: 50
Non-paid Artists: 100
Budget: $700,000
Income Sources: Membership, Grants, Corporate Funding
Performs At: Royce Auditorium
Annual Attendance: 35,000
Facility Category: Historic Landmark Building
Type of Stage: Proscenium
Seating Capacity: 650
Year Built: 1894
Year Remodeled: 1998
Organization Type: Sponsoring

1097
PRO MUSICA OF DETROIT
181 Beaupre Avenue
Grosse Pointe Farms, MI 48236-3448
Phone: 313-885-0793
Fax: 313-885-6685
e-mail: alex@suczek.com
Web Site: www.promusicadetroit.com
Officers:
First VP: Alice Haidostian
Second VP: Dr. Hershel Sandberg
Secretary: Ann Kondak
Treasurer: James Diamond
President: Alexander Suczek
Mission: To present world-class emerging performers in debut recitals; to offer performances of composers.
Utilizes: Guest Companies; Guest Directors; Guest Musical Directors; Guest Musicians; Multimedia; Original Music Scores; Sign Language Translators; Singers
Founded: 1927
Specialized Field: Ensemble; New Music; World Music; Classical Music
Status: Professional; Nonprofit
Volunteer Staff: 40
Paid Artists: 3-30
Budget: $60,000

Income Sources: Ticket Sales; Membership; Endowment; Corporate Sponsors
Performs At: Recital Hall of the Detroit Institute of the Arts
Annual Attendance: 3,000
Facility Category: Auditorium; Concert Hall
Seating Capacity: 1,100
Year Built: 1927
Organization Type: Performing

1098
HILLSDALE COLLEGE COMMUNITY ORCHESTRA
Hillsdale College
33 E College Street
Hillsdale, MI 49242
Phone: 517-437-7341
Fax: 517-437-3923
Management:
Music Director/Manager: James A Holleman
Specialized Field: Orchestra; Ensemble
Budget: $35,000
Performs At: Markel Auditorium; Sage Center for the Arts

1099
HOLLAND CHAMBER ORCHESTRA
583 Riley
Holland, MI 49424
Mailing Address: PO Box 8084, Holland, MI. 49422-8084
Phone: 616-786-3172
Fax: 616-393-7616
e-mail: hco@macatawa.org
Management:
Music Director: Mihai Craioveanu
Orchestra Director: Thomas Working
Mission: Belongs to the community and allows adult musicians to share their love of music and further develop their talents; provides enjoyable and informative programs to promote classical music and inspire our listeners.
Specialized Field: Chamber
Budget: $35,000

1100
HOLLAND SYMPHONY ORCHESTRA
294 W Lakewood
PO Box 8054
Holland, MI 49422-8084
Phone: 616-494-0256
Fax: 616-392-7871
e-mail: hso@hollandsymphony.org
Web Site: www.hollandsymphony.org
Management:
Executive Director: Kay Walvoord
Utilizes: Artists-in-Residence; Collaborating Artists; Collaborations; Commissioned Composers; Commissioned Music; Fine Artists; Guest Accompanists; Guest Composers; Guest Lecturers; Guest Musical Directors; Guest Musicians; Multimedia; Music; Original Music Scores; Singers
Founded: 1990
Specialized Field: Orchestra
Paid Staff: 4
Volunteer Staff: 30
Paid Artists: 1
Non-paid Artists: 80
Budget: $100,000
Income Sources: Donations; Ticket Sales; Grants; Corporate Sponsorships
Performs At: High School Performing Arts Centers
Annual Attendance: 4000
Facility Category: Performing Arts Center

Seating Capacity: 942

1101
HOPE COLLEGE ORCHESTRA
Hope College, Music Department
127 E 12th Street
Holland, MI 49423
Phone: 616-394-7652
Fax: 616-395-7182
e-mail: ritsema@hope.edu
Management:
    Conductor: Robert Ritsema
Mission: The presentation of concerts on campus as well as in other cities.
Utilizes: Guest Artists; Guest Companies
Founded: 1949
Specialized Field: Orchestra; Chamber
Status: Non-Professional; Nonprofit
Paid Staff: 60
Budget: $35,000
Income Sources: American Symphony Orchestra League; Michigan Orchestra Association
Performs At: Dimnent Chapel
Organization Type: Performing; Touring; Resident; Educational

1102
KEWEENAW SYMPHONY ORCHESTRA OF MICHIGAN TECHNOLOGICAL UNIVERSITY
Michigan Technological University
1400 Townsend Drive 209 Walker
Houghton, MI 49931-1295
Phone: 906-487-2067
Fax: 906- 48—184
Toll-free: 888-MTU-1885
e-mail: Fineart@mtu.edu
Management:
    Director of Orchestra and Chorus: Milton Olsson
    Administrator: Shane Crist
Utilizes: Commissioned Music; Guest Companies; Guest Composers; Guest Musical Directors; Guest Musicians; Instructors; Multimedia; Original Music Scores; Singers
Founded: 1971
Specialized Field: Orchestra
Budget: $35,000-100,000
Performs At: Rozsa Center for the Performing Arts
Affiliations: ASOL

1103
FONTANA CHAMBER ARTS
359 S. Kalamazoo Mall
Suite 200
Kalamazoo, MI 49007
Phone: 269-382-7774
Fax: 269-382-0812
e-mail: bwong@fontanachamberarts.org
Web Site: www.fontanachamberarts.org
Officers:
    Chairman: B. William Maxey
    Co-Vice Chairman: Bruce W. Martin
    Treasurer: Martha Ream
    Secretary: Lawrence Schlack
Management:
    Executive/Artistic Director: Anne Berquist
Mission: Offering diverse, high quality chamber music programs in a relaxed rural setting.
Founded: 1980
Specialized Field: Chamber; Ensemble
Status: Professional; Nonprofit
Performs At: The Art Emporium
Organization Type: Performing; Sponsoring

1104
KALAMAZOO SYMPHONY ORCHESTRA
359 South Kalamazoo Mall
Suite 100
Kalamazoo, MI 49007
Phone: 269-349-7759
Fax: 269-349-9229
e-mail: jbarlament@kalamazoosymphony.com
Web Site: www.kalamazoosymphony.com
Officers:
    President: Linda Depta
    President-Elect: Craig Lubben
    Executive Director: Jennifer Barlament
    Director Marketing/PR: Thom Andrews
Management:
    Music Director: Raymond Harvey
    Assistant Conductor: Barry Ross
Mission: To support a professional symphony orchestra and staff; to present concerts of symphonic music and related programs of the highest possible artistic level; to support effective regional music education; to serve and involve the people of the greater Kalamazoo area in the Symphony Society.
Utilizes: Artists-in-Residence; Collaborating Artists; Commissioned Composers; Commissioned Music; Educators; Five Seasonal Concerts; Guest Accompanists; Guest Artists; Guest Composers; Guest Directors; Guest Instructors; Guest Musical Directors; Guest Musicians; Local Artists; Multimedia; Original Music Scores
Founded: 1921
Specialized Field: Symphony; Orchestra; Chamber; Ensemble
Status: Professional; Nonprofit
Paid Staff: 12
Paid Artists: 85
Budget: $2,000,000
Income Sources: Individual & Corporate Sponsors; Local; State & National Grants
Performs At: Miller Auditorium
Annual Attendance: 25,000
Seating Capacity: 3,496
Organization Type: Performing; Educational

1105
LANSING SYMPHONY ORCHESTRA
5016 Capital Avenue
Suite 400
Lansing, MI 48933
Phone: 517-487-5001
Fax: 517-487-0210
e-mail: info@lansingsymphony.org
Web Site: www.lansingsymphony.org
Officers:
    Director Finance & Operations: Karen Dichoza
Management:
    Executive Director: Courtney Millbrook
    Dir Education/Community Engagement: Catherine Guarino
    Director, Marketing & Development: Kristin Petersen
    Music Director: Timothy Muffitt
Mission: Enriching lives through excellence in music and in educational outreach
Utilizes: Guest Musical Directors; Multimedia
Founded: 1929
Specialized Field: Symphony; Orchestra; Chamber; Ensemble
Status: Professional; Nonprofit
Performs At: Wharton Center for Performing Arts
Affiliations: League Of American Orchestras
Seating Capacity: 2,800
Organization Type: Performing; Educational

1106
LIVONIA SYMPHONY ORCHESTRA
37637 Rive Mile Road #398
Livonia, MI 48154
Phone: 734-421-1111
Fax: 734-464-8713
e-mail: promoman@kelseypromo.com
Officers:
    President: Tom Bjorklund
Management:
    Music Director/Conductor: Volodymyr Schesiuk
    Assistant Conductor: Carl Karoub
Specialized Field: Orchestra
Budget: $100,000-150,000

1107
MIDLAND SYMPHONY ORCHESTRA
Midland Center for the Arts
1801 W. St. Andrews Rd.
Midland, MI 48640-2695
Phone: 989-631-5390
Fax: 989-631-7890
e-mail: info@mcfta.org
Web Site: http://www.mcfta.org/A_Symphony
Officers:
    Interim President/CEO: Bill Henninger
    Vice President: Dick Jellum
Management:
    Artistic Director: Jim Hohmeyer
    Managing Director: Tami Ramaker
    Conductor: Carlton Woods
Mission: Encouraging and supporting the Midland Symphony Orchestra in its pursuit of artistic excellence.
Utilizes: Guest Artists
Founded: 1936
Specialized Field: Symphony; Orchestra; Chamber; Ensemble
Status: Professional; Semi-Professional; Non-Professional; Nonprofit
Income Sources: Michigan Orchestra Association; American Symphony Orchestra League
Performs At: Midland Center for the Arts
Organization Type: Performing; Touring; Educational; Sponsoring

1108
MUSIC SOCIETY: MIDLAND CENTER FOR THE ARTS
1801 W St. Andrews
Midland, MI 48640
Phone: 517-631-1072
Fax: 517-631-7890
Web Site: www.mcfta.org/main.html
Management:
    Artistic Director: Dr. Victor A Klimash
Mission: Committed to providing performing and educational opportunities that would not otherwise exist.
Utilizes: Guest Artists; Guest Companies; Singers
Founded: 1943
Specialized Field: Orchestra; Chamber; Ensemble; Folk Music; Band
Status: Nonprofit
Performs At: Midland Center for the Arts
Organization Type: Performing; Educational; Sponsoring

1109
WEST SHORE YOUTH SYMPHONY ORCHESTRA
425 W Western Avenue
Suite 409
Muskegon, MI 49440

Phone: 231-726-3231
Fax: 231-722-6913
e-mail: info@wsso.org
Web Site: www.wsso.org
Officers:
Executive Director: Gretchen Cheney Rhoades
President: A Sawyer
Mission: To bring fine live music to the West Michigan area.
Utilizes: Actors; AEA Actors; Artists-in-Residence; Choreographers; Dance Companies; Dancers; Guest Accompanists; Guest Companies; Guest Conductors; Guest Designers; Guest Directors; Instructors; Local Artists; Multimedia; Music; Original Music Scores; Performance Artists; Resident Professionals; Sign Language Translators; Singers; Soloists; Special Technical Talent; Theatre Companies
Founded: 1940
Specialized Field: Youth Symphony; Orchestra; Chamber
Status: Professional; Nonprofit
Paid Staff: 5
Budget: 12,500
Type of Stage: thrust
Stage Dimensions: 30' x 50'
Seating Capacity: 1,700
Year Remodeled: 1999
Organization Type: Performing

1110

PLYMOUTH SYMPHONY

470 Forest Place, Suite 18
PO Box 6349
Plymouth, MI 48170-0379
Phone: 734-451-2112
Fax: 734-451-3458
e-mail: plymouthsymphony@aol.com
Web Site: www.plymouthsymphony.com
Officers:
President: Linda Alvarado
VP: John Lewis
Secretary: Robert Pray
Treasurer: Michelle Burger
Management:
Executive Director: Darlene A Dreyer
Music Director/Conductor: Nan Washburn
Office Manager: Pat Derderian
Mission: To provide high quality orchestral and music education experiences for the surrounding community.
Utilizes: Choreographers; Collaborating Artists; Collaborations; Commissioned Music; Dance Companies; Educators; Fine Artists; Five Seasonal Concerts; Grant Writers; Guest Companies; Guest Directors; Guest Musicians; Guest Soloists; Guest Writers; Instructors; Local Artists; Lyricists; Multi Collaborations; Multimedia; Music; New Productions; Original Music Scores; Poets; Sign Language Translators; Soloists
Founded: 1945
Specialized Field: Orchestra
Paid Staff: 8
Volunteer Staff: 50
Paid Artists: 80
Budget: $271,000
Income Sources: Ticket Sales; Grants; Donations; Auction; Raffle
Performs At: Variety of Public Venues
Affiliations: ASOL
Facility Category: Churches, Auditoriums, Banquet Halls

1111

SAGINAW BAY SYMPHONY ORCHESTRA

901 S Washington Avenue
Saginaw, MI 48601
Phone: 989-755-6471
Fax: 989-755-1420
Toll-free: 877-755-7276
e-mail: info@saginawbayorchestra.com
Web Site: www.saginabayorchestra.com
Management:
Music Director/Conductor: Patrick Flynn
Executive Director: Michael G Dunkel
Office Manager: Kelly Belcher
Production Manager: Anna Leppert-Largent
Founded: 1935
Specialized Field: Orchestra
Paid Staff: 3

1112

SOUTHWEST MICHIGAN SYMPHONY ORCHESTRA

513 Ship Street
Saint Joseph, MI 49085
Phone: 269-982-4030
Fax: 269-982-4181
e-mail: info@smso.org
Web Site: www.smso.org
Management:
General Manager: Jeffrey G White
Music Director: Robert Vodnoy
Mission: To present concerts and sponsor an orchestra; to provide music educational activities.
Founded: 1950
Specialized Field: Symphony; Orchestra
Status: Professional
Performs At: Mendel Center; Lake Michigan College
Organization Type: Performing; Educational

1113

DETROIT CHAMBER WINDS & STRINGS

20300 Civinc Center Drive
Suite 100
Southfield, MI 48076-4166
Phone: 248-559-2095
Fax: 248-559-2098
e-mail: info@detroitchamberwinds.org
Web Site: www.detroitchamberwinds.org
Management:
Artistic Advisor: H. Robert Reynolds
Executive Director: Maury Okun
Mission: To offer performances of works featuring between 6 and 20 winds.
Utilizes: Collaborating Artists; Collaborations; Commissioned Music; Dance Companies; Guest Companies; Guest Musicians; Instructors; Multimedia; Organization Contracts; Original Music Scores; Singers
Founded: 1982
Specialized Field: Chamber; Wind Ensemble; String Ensemble
Status: Professional; Nonprofit
Organization Type: Performing

1114

METROPOLITAN YOUTH SYMPHONY

PO Box 244
Southfield, MI 48037-0244
Phone: 503-239-4566
Toll-free: 888-752-9697
Management:
Conductor: Kevin D Miller
President: Craig Cornwall
Conductor: Dr. John Richards
Conductor: Bill Hunt

Specialized Field: Youth Orchestra

1115

LAKE ST. CLAIR SYMPHONY ORCHESTRA

PO Box 806249
St. Clair Shores, MI 48080-6249
Phone: 586-777-8944
Fax: 810-776-1012
e-mail: tulrich@home.com
Web Site: www.lscso.com
Management:
Music Director: Zeljko Milicevic
Mission: To promote and provide a symphony orchestra for the residents of the communities adjacent to Lake St. Clair; to provide a continuing educational program in symphonic music for students of the various school districts in the communities served by the Orchestra; and to provide a community-based organization for the expression and enjoyment of the music.
Founded: 1962
Specialized Field: Symphony; Orchestra
Status: Semi-Professional; Nonprofit
Budget: $35,000-100,000
Income Sources: American Symphony Orchestra League; Michigan Orchestra Association
Performs At: Schaublin Auditorium
Organization Type: Performing

1116

TRAVERSE SYMPHONY ORCHESTRA

123 1/2 E Front Street
PO Box 1247
Traverse City, MI 49685
Phone: 231-947-7120
Fax: 231-947-8118
e-mail: vschneider@tso-online.org
Web Site: www.tso-online.org
Officers:
Administrative Manager: Victoria Schneider
Utilizes: Guest Musical Directors; Guest Musicians
Founded: 1951
Specialized Field: Symphony; Orchestra; Chamber
Status: Professional
Budget: $500,000
Income Sources: Ticket Sales; Grants; Donations; Sponserships
Annual Attendance: 7,000
Organization Type: Performing; Touring; Sponsoring

Minnesota

1117

BEMIDJI SYMPHONY ORCHESTRA

Bemidji State University
PO Box 3136
Bemidji, MN 56619
Phone: 218-751-0665
Fax: 218-755-4369
e-mail: Podium314@aol.com
Officers:
Co-Chair: Diane Wahl
Management:
Conductor: Dr Beverly Everett
Co-Chair: Mary Auger
Mission: Dedicated to communicating the richness of a variety of African cultures and customs through dance, rythym, and song in an exciting, energetic and colorful manner.
Specialized Field: Orchestra
Budget: $35,000

Performs At: Bangsberg Fine Arts Complex Theatre & Recital Hall

1118
DULUTH-SUPERIOR SYMPHONY ORCHESTRA
506 W Michigan Street
Duluth, MN 55802
Phone: 218-733-7575
Fax: 218-733-7537
Web Site: www.dsso.com
Management:
    Executive Director: Andrew Berryhill
    Music Director: Markand Thakar
Mission: To generate the required financial and artistic resources to maintain the finest possible symphony orchestra as well as related programs and services; to develop future musicians and audiences.
Utilizes: Collaborations; Commissioned Music; Composers-in-Residence; Fine Artists; Guest Accompanists; Guest Composers; Guest Directors; Guest Musical Directors; Guest Musicians; Instructors; Multimedia; Music; New Productions; Original Music Scores; Singers
Founded: 1932
Specialized Field: Symphony; Orchestra; Chamber; Ensemble
Status: Professional; Nonprofit
Budget: $1,000,000
Income Sources: American Symphony Orchestra League; Saint Louis County Heritage & Arts Center
Performs At: Duluth Auditorium
Annual Attendance: 40,000
Facility Category: DECC Auditorium
Type of Stage: Normal Stage
Seating Capacity: 2,400
Year Built: 1966
Organization Type: Performing; Educational

1119
DULUTH-SUPERIOR YOUTH ORCHESTRAS & SINFONIA
506 W Michigan Street
Duluth, MN 55802
Phone: 218-733-7575
Fax: 218-733-7537
Mission: To offer a learning and performing experience for students in the Youth Orchestra (high school) and Sinfonia (junior and senior high school).
Founded: 1940
Specialized Field: Youth Orchestra; Chamber; Ensemble
Status: Non-Professional; Nonprofit
Paid Staff: 100
Income Sources: American Symphony Orchestra League (Youth Orchestra Division); Duluth-Superior Symphony Orchestra
Organization Type: Performing; Educational

1120
HEARTLAND SYMPHONY ORCHESTRA
122 SE 1st Street
BOBox 241
Little Falls, MN 56345
Phone: 320-632-0960
Fax: 320-632-9025
Toll-free: 800-826-1997
Management:
    Music Director: Richard Haglund
    Business Manager: William Adkins

Mission: To bring orchestral music to concert-goers in our area, to aquaint young people with the beauty of classical music, and to provide an opportunity for trained musicians to play together.
Utilizes: Guest Musicians
Founded: 1977
Specialized Field: Orchestra
Status: Nonprofit
Budget: $35,000-100,000
Performs At: Tornstrom Auditorium; Charles Martin Auditorium

1121
MANKATO SYMPHONY ORCHESTRA
120 South Broad Street
Mankato, MN 56001
Mailing Address: PO Box 645 Mankato MN, 56002
Phone: 507-625-8880
Fax: 507-625-5792
e-mail: mso@mnic.net
Web Site: www.symphony.mankato.com
Officers:
    Executive Director: Jane Stetta
    President: Lisa Haman
    VP: Lorin Ruthenbeck
    Secretary: Sally Trask
    Treasurer: Ann Coleman
Mission: The orchestra plays five subscription concerts each year plus three Youth Concerts, and provides many educational and artistic opportunities to area students, including the Young artist and Young Composer contests. The orchestra also plays one free outdoor concert in June.
Utilizes: Collaborating Artists; Collaborations; Guest Accompanists; Guest Musical Directors; Guest Musicians; Guest Writers; Instructors; Multimedia; Organization Contracts; Original Music Scores; Singers; Soloists; Theatre Companies
Founded: 1952
Specialized Field: Symphony; Orchestra
Status: Non-Professional; Nonprofit
Paid Staff: 1
Volunteer Staff: 65
Paid Artists: 90
Budget: $190,000
Income Sources: Grants; Sponsors; Contributions
Performs At: Mankato West High School Auditorium
Facility Category: High school auditorium
Organization Type: Performing; Resident; Educational

1122
CIVIC ORCHESTRA OF MINNEAPOLIS
PO Box 50604
Minneapolis, MN 55405-0604
Phone: 612-332-4842
Fax: 612-649-1288
e-mail: manager@civicorchestrampls.org
Officers:
    President: Scott Sterling
    VP: Laurie McFaul
Management:
    Music Director: Cary John Franklin
    Orchestra Manager: Rachel Hest
Specialized Field: Orchestra
Budget: $35,000

1123
GREATER TWIN CITIES YOUTH SYMPHONIES
528 Hennepin Avenue
Suite 404
Minneapolis, MN 55403

Phone: 612-870-7611
Fax: 612-870-7613
e-mail: mail@gtcys.org
Web Site: www.gtcys.org
Officers:
    President: Loisd Hesselroth
    Treasurer: Kerry Spaven
    VP: Nancye Rystrom
    Secretary: Kristin Schoephoerster
Management:
    Interim Artistic Director: Marlene Pauley
    Operations Manager: Devin Thomas
    Office Manager: Denise Culshaw
    Executive Director: Christine Corcoran
Mission: In the conviction that music nourishes the mind, body, and spirit of the individual and enriches the community, the Greater Twin Cities Youth Symphonies provides a rigorous and inspiring orchestral experience for qualifying young muscians.
Utilizes: Educators; Multimedia; Soloists
Founded: 1972
Specialized Field: Youth Symphony; Chamber; Ensemble
Status: Non-Professional; Nonprofit
Paid Staff: 6
Paid Artists: 8
Non-paid Artists: 5
Budget: $645,000
Performs At: Orchestra Hall; Landmark Center
Organization Type: Performing; Touring; Educational

1124
METROPOLITAN SYMPHONY ORCHESTRA
PO Box 581213
Minneapolis, MN 55458-1213
Phone: 651-645-4283
e-mail: info@msoa.net
Officers:
    Personnel Manager: David Wall
    VP: Terry Wilson
    Treasurer: Scott Simmons
    Secretary: Scott Simmons
Management:
    Music Director: William Schrickel
    General Manager: Mark Warhol
Specialized Field: Orchestra
Budget: $35,000

1125
MINNESOTA SINFONIA
901 N Third Street
Suite 112
Minneapolis, MN 55401-1022
Phone: 612-871-1701
Fax: 612-871-1701
e-mail: mnsinfonia@aol.com
Officers:
    Chairperson: Mary Weber
    Treasurer: Laura Carlson
Management:
    Conductor: Jay Fishman
    Manager: Raphael Fishman
Specialized Field: Orchestra

1126
ORCHESTRA HALL
1111 Nicollet Mall
Minneapolis, MN 55403
Phone: 612-371-5600
Toll-free: 800-292-4141
e-mail: info@mnorch.org
Web Site: www.minnesotaorchestra.org
Officers:

President: Michael Henson
Management:
General Manager: Robert Neu
Mission: To enrich lives with great music.
Utilizes: Guest Artists; Guest Companies; Sign Language Translators; Singers
Founded: 1903
Status: Non-Profit; Professional
Paid Staff: 150
Paid Artists: 100
Budget: $28,000,000
Annual Attendance: 400,000
Type of Stage: Proscenium
Seating Capacity: 2,450
Year Built: 1974
Organization Type: Performing; Touring; Resident; Educational; Sponsoring

1127
FARGO-MOORHEAD SYMPHONY ORCHESTRA AND ASSOCIATION
810 Fourth Avenue S
Suite 250
Moorhead, MN 56560
Phone: 218-233-8397
Fax: 218-236-1845
e-mail: fmsymphony@i29.net
Management:
Executive Director: Bill Law
Mission: To provide our region with the opportunity to experience live orchestral music, including performances by local, regional, national, and international guest artists; to provide musicians in the community with the opportunity to perform.
Utilizes: Fine Artists; Guest Accompanists; Guest Companies; Guest Composers; Guest Lecturers; Guest Musicians; Multimedia; Music; Original Music Scores; Sign Language Translators; Singers
Founded: 1931
Specialized Field: Orchestra
Paid Staff: 8
Paid Artists: 75
Budget: $260,000-1,050,000
Income Sources: Individual; Corporate; Foundations
Performs At: Reineke Fine Arts Center
Annual Attendance: 15,000
Facility Category: Concert hall- University
Stage Dimensions: 987
Seating Capacity: 1,000
Year Built: 1990
Rental Contact: 7012817932 Division of Fine Arts

1128
SAINT OLAF COLLEGE ORCHESTRA
Saint Olaf College
1520 St. Olaf Avenue
Northfield, MN 55057
Phone: 507-786-3180
Fax: 507-786-3527
e-mail: music@stolaf.edu
Web Site: music@stolaf.edu
Officers:
Music Organizations Manager: BJ Johnson
Music Organizations Secretary: Denise Bundgaard
Management:
Conductor: Steven Amundson
Manager: Terra Widdifield
Music Organizations Admin. Asst.: Marinda Bryan
Utilizes: Arrangers; Artists-in-Residence; Choreographers; Collaborations; Composers; Dancers; Educators; Guest Composers; Guest Directors; Guest Musical Directors; Guest Speakers; High School

Drama; Multimedia; New Productions; Sign Language Translators; Singers; Soloists; Students; Theatre Companies
Specialized Field: Orchestra; Ensemble
Budget: $35,000-100,000
Performs At: Skoglund Center Auditorium
Seating Capacity: 4,000

1129
ST. CLOUD SYMPHONY ORCHESTRA
PO Box 234
Saint Cloud, MN 56302
Phone: 320-252-7276
e-mail: snadeau@stcloudsymphony.com
Web Site: www.stcloudsymphony.com
Officers:
Executive Director: Sandy Nadeau
Treasurer: Lori Johnson
Secretary: Sharon Cogdill
Board President: Deanna Boone
Management:
Executive Director: Sandy Nadeau
Artistic Dir/Principal Conductor: Andrew Altenbach
Assistant Conductor: Daniel O'Bryant
Stage Manager: Paul Bernard
Librarian/Personnel Manager: Andrew Altenbach
Mission: The mission is to present high quality performance of orchestral music and educational outreach activities to Central Minnesota, to encourage participation by local and area musicians, and to further the understanding and appreciation of this music.
Founded: 1975
Specialized Field: Orchestra
Paid Staff: 4
Paid Artists: 85

1130
451ST ARMY BAND
Fort Snelling
Building 506
Saint Paul, MN 55111
Phone: 612-713-3339
Fax: 612-713-3519
Management:
Commander/Band Master: CW4 Bruce J Hedblom
Assistant Conductor: SSG Robert A Lake
Mission: Representing the 88th United States Army Reserve Command to the military and to the general public as well as promoting and encouraging the performing arts.
Utilizes: Guest Artists; Guest Companies
Founded: 1923
Specialized Field: Ensemble; Ethnic Music; Folk Music; Band
Status: Professional; Nonprofit
Organization Type: Performing; Touring; Educational

1131
MINNESOTA STATE BAND
651 Mackubin Street N
Saint Paul, MN 55103-1624
Phone: 651-282-4077
Web Site: www.mnband.org
Management:
Music Director/Conductor: Joseph Komro
Public Relations: Neil Danielson
Stage Manager: Adam Torres
Concert Coordinator: Helmut Kahlert
Mission: Dedicated to furthering the musical development and appreciation of America's concert band and wind ensemble movement.
Utilizes: Guest Artists; Guest Companies; Singers
Founded: 1898

Specialized Field: Ensemble; Ethnic Music; Band
Status: Professional; Nonprofit
Paid Staff: 70
Income Sources: Association of Concert Bands
Organization Type: Performing; Touring; Educational

1132
SAINT PAUL CHAMBER ORCHESTRA
Hamm Building, 408 St. Peter Street
Suite 500
Saint Paul, MN 55102-1497
Phone: 651-292-3248
Fax: 651-292-3281
e-mail: info@spcomail.org
Web Site: www.thespco.org
Officers:
President/Managing Director: Bruce Coppock
Management:
Artistic Partner: Pierre-Laurent Aimardn
Artistic Partner: Dawn Upshaw
Artistic Partner: Nicholas McGegan
Artistic Partner: Douglas Boyd
Artistic Partner: Roberto Abbado
Mission: To present a world-class professional chamber orchestra in the Twin Cities, dedicated to superior performance and artistic innovation, for the enrichment of community life and world audiences.
Utilizes: Actors; Artists-in-Residence; Collaborations; Composers-in-Residence; Dance Companies; Educators; Fine Artists; Guest Accompanists; Guest Artists; Guest Choreographers; Guest Composers; Guest Composers; Guest Directors; Guest Instructors; Guest Musical Directors; Guest Musicians; Instructors; Multi Collaborations; Multimedia; Organization Contracts; Original Music Scores; Sign Language Translators; Singers; Soloists; Special Technical Talent; Touring Companies
Founded: 1959
Specialized Field: Orchestra; Chamber; Ensemble
Status: Professional; Nonprofit
Paid Artists: 33
Budget: $9,200,000
Income Sources: Government & Corporate Donors; Sales
Season: 38 weeks
Performs At: Ordway Center for the Performing Arts
Affiliations: American Symphony Orchestra League; Association of Performing Arts Presenters
Organization Type: Performing; Touring; Resident; Educational; Recording

Mississippi

1133
GULF COAST SYMPHONY
PO Box 542
Biloxi, MS 39533-0542
Phone: 228-435-9800
Fax: 228-435-9807
e-mail: gcso@worldnet.att.net
Web Site: www.gulfcoastsymphony.net
Officers:
President: Harold Roberts
VP: Jim Wooten
Secretary: Peggy Schloegel
Music Director/Conductor: John Wesley Strickler
Management:
Executive Director: Natalie Robohm
Development Director: Signe Cutrone
Mission: The presentation of symphonic music to Gulf Coast residents.

Utilizes: Artists-in-Residence; Collaborating Artists; Collaborations; Commissioned Composers; Commissioned Music; Composers-in-Residence; Guest Companies; Guest Composers; Guest Lecturers; Guest Musicians; Local Artists; Multimedia; Organization Contracts; Original Music Scores; Singers; Soloists; Student Interns; Special Technical Talent
Founded: 1963
Specialized Field: Symphony
Status: Professional; Nonprofit
Paid Staff: 3
Volunteer Staff: 150
Paid Artists: 4
Budget: $460,000
Performs At: Saenger Theatre; Biloxi
Annual Attendance: 20,000
Facility Category: Theater
Seating Capacity: 1,050
Rental Contact: Lee Hood
Organization Type: Performing; Touring; Educational

1134
UNIVERSITY OF SOUTHERN MISSISSIPPI SYMPHONY

College Of Arts And Letters
118 College Drive #5081
Hattiesburg, MS 39406-0001
Phone: 601-266-5418
Fax: 601-266-6541
e-mail: arts@usm.edu
Web Site: www.usm.edu/arts
Management:
   Dean: Dr. Denise von Herrmann
   Marketing & Event Manager: Dr. Mike Lopinto
   Public Relations/Recruiting Manager: Tearanny Street
Mission: Founded in 1910, The University of Southern Mississippi is a comprehensive doctoral and research-driven university with a proud history and an eye on the future. Our primary mission is to cultivate intellectual developmental creativity through the generation, dissemination, application and preservation of knowledge. The arts programs are internationally regarded as some of the finest ranking among only 31 fully accredited in all four discipline
Founded: 1910
Specialized Field: Art; Dance; Music; Theatre
Budget: $100,000-150,000
Performs At: Bennett Auditoirum
Seating Capacity: 1,000

1135
MISSISSIPPI SYMPHONY ORCHESTRA

201 E Pascagoula Street
PO Box 2052
Jackson, MS 39225-2052
Phone: 601-960-1565
Fax: 601-960-1564
Toll-free: 800-898-5050
e-mail: development@msorchestra.com
Web Site: www.msorchestra.com
Officers:
   Chairman: Alan Leach
Management:
   President/CEO: Robert A Reed
   Director Finance: Sarajean Babin
   Director Operations: Richard Hudson
   Director Education: Patrick Johnson
   Music Director & Conductor: Crafton Beck
Utilizes: Collaborations; Commissioned Composers; Commissioned Music; Dance Companies; Dancers; Educators; Filmmakers; Five Seasonal Concerts; Grant Writers; Guest Companies; Guest Composers; Guest Directors; Guest Lecturers; Guest Musical Directors;

Guest Musicians; High School Drama; Instructors; Lyricists; Multi Collaborations; Multimedia; Music; Organization Contracts; Original Music Scores; Sign Language Translators; Singers; Soloists; Touring Companies
Founded: 1944
Specialized Field: Symphony; Orchestra; Chamber; Pops
Paid Staff: 7
Volunteer Staff: 1
Budget: $1,300,000
Performs At: Brianwood Presbyterian; Thalia Mara Hall; Galloway United Methodist Church
Seating Capacity: 2430

1136
MISSISSIPPI YOUTH SYMPHONY ORCHESTRA

PO Box 2052
Jackson, MS 39225-2052
Phone: 601-960-1565
Fax: 601-960-1564
Toll-free: 800-898-5050
Web Site: www.msorchestra.com
Officers:
   Chairman: Phil Posey
   Chairman Elect: Hugh Parker
   President/Executive Director: Michael Beattie
   Director Marketing: Crystal Allen Skelton
   Director Development: Phoebe Smith-Porter
Management:
   Music Director/Conductor: Crafton Beck
Mission: To promote education and appreciation of classical music through participation in the junior or senior youth orchestras.
Specialized Field: Youth Symphony
Status: Non-Professional; Nonprofit
Income Sources: American Symphony Orchestra League(Youth Orchestra Division)
Performs At: Chastain Junior High School
Organization Type: Performing; Touring; Educational

1137
MERIDIAN SYMPHONY ORCHESTRA

PO Box 2171
Meridian, MS 39307
Phone: 601-693-2224
Fax: 601-482-8824
e-mail: mdnsymph@mississippi.net
Management:
   Music Director: Claire Fox Hillard
   General Manager: Carolyn Abdella
Specialized Field: Orchestra
Budget: $260,000-1,050,000
Performs At: Meridian Community College Auditorium
Seating Capacity: 600

1138
TUPELO SYMPHONY ORCHESTRA ASSOCIATION

PO Box 474
Tupelo, MS 38802
Phone: 662-842-8433
Fax: 662-842-9565
e-mail: tso@tupelosymphony.com
Web Site: www.tupelosymphony.com
Officers:
   Chairman: Dr Matthew Wesson
   Executive VP: Robert E Rice
   Secretary: Jo Miller Orr
   Executive Administrator: Nancy Diffee
Management:
   Music Director: Steven Byess

   President/Executive Director: Margaret Anne Murphy
Mission: To offer high quality performances of symphonic works.
Utilizes: Educators; Fine Artists; Five Seasonal Concerts; Guest Accompanists; Guest Composers; Guest Lecturers; Multimedia; Original Music Scores; Sign Language Translators; Singers
Founded: 1971
Specialized Field: Symphony; Orchestra
Status: Professional
Paid Staff: 1
Volunteer Staff: 3
Budget: $300,000
Income Sources: Ticket Sales; Contributors; Corporate Sponsors; Grants
Performs At: Tupedo Civic Auditorium
Affiliations: American Symphony Orchestra League
Facility Category: Concert Hall
Seating Capacity: 535
Year Built: 1965
Year Remodeled: 2000
Organization Type: Performing; Touring

Missouri

1139
MISSOURI SYMPHONY SOCIETY

203 S 9th Street
Columbia, MO 65201
Phone: 573-875-0600
Fax: 573-449-4214
e-mail: motheatre@socket.net
Web Site: www.missouritheatre.com
Mission: The enhancement of the cultural environment through fine music, education and the nurturing of young musicians.
Utilizes: Guest Composers; Guest Ensembles; Guest Musical Directors; Guest Musicians; Multimedia
Founded: 1971
Specialized Field: Symphony; Orchestra; Chamber
Status: Professional; Nonprofit
Paid Staff: 40
Budget: $375,000
Income Sources: Pops Orchestra; Chamber Orchestra Festival Symphony
Performs At: Missouri Theatre
Type of Stage: Proscenium
Seating Capacity: 1,220
Year Built: 1928
Rental Contact: Executive Director David A White
Organization Type: Performing; Touring; Educational; Sponsoring

1140
INDEPENDENCE SYMPHONY ORCHESTRA

PO Box 2276
Lee's Summit
Independence, MO 64063
Phone: 816-373-8151
Fax: 816-220-6511
e-mail: LynnP12@juno.com
Officers:
   VP: Cathy Lawrey
   House Manager: Dave Mayta
   Treasurer: Helen Newlin
   Secretary: Betty Liston
Management:
   Conductor/Music Director: James Murray
   President: Jeff Quibell
Specialized Field: Orchestra
Budget: $35,000

Seating Capacity: 1500-5000

1141
FRIENDS OF CHAMBER MUSIC
4635 Wyandotte Street
Suite 201
Kansas City, MO 64112-1542
Phone: 816-561-9999
Fax: 816-561-8810
Toll-free: 877-697-3287
e-mail: marketing@chambermusic.org
Officers:
    Chairman of the Board: Jerome Wolf
    Vice Chairman & Treasurer: David M Eisenberg
Management:
    President and Founder: Cynthia Siebert
    Marketing Director: Daniel Billingsley
Specialized Field: Chamber
Status: Not-for-profit

1142
KANSAS CITY CHAMBER ORCHESTRA
11 East 40th Street
Kansas City, MO 64111
Phone: 816-960-1324
Fax: 816-960-1325
e-mail: kcco@earthlink.net
Management:
    Music Director/Conductor: Bruce Sorrell
Utilizes: Guest Accompanists; Guest Musicians;
Instructors; Local Artists; Original Music Scores; Sign
Language Translators; Singers; Soloists
Founded: 1987
Specialized Field: Chamber; Ensemble
Budget: $150,000-200,000
Income Sources: Donations, Grants, Ticket sales

1143
KANSAS CITY SYMPHONY
1020 Central
Suite 300
Kansas City, MO 64105-1672
Phone: 816-471-1100
Fax: 816-471-0976
e-mail: tkutey@kcsymphony.org
Officers:
    President: Shirley Bush Helzberg
    VP: Robert A Kipp
    VP: Michael D Fields
    VP: Arthur B. Krause
    Secretary/Treasurer: William B. Taylor
Management:
    Music Director: Michael Stern
    Executive Director: Frank Byrne
    Assistant to the Executive Director: Mary Allen
    Director Marketing/Public Relations: Rose Sinn
Specialized Field: Orchestra

1144
NORTHLAND SYMPHONY ORCHESTRA
PO Box 12255
PO Box 12255
Kansas City, MO 64152-2255
Phone: 816-420-3137
Fax: 816-759-9084
e-mail: northlandsymphonyorchestra@yahoo.com
Officers:
    VP: David Rumsey
    Treasurer: Bev Roggenkamp
Management:
    Music Director/Conductor: James Murray III
    President: Amber Bourek

Mission: To offer professional, amateur and student
musicians an opportunity to preform fin orchestral music
and free public concerts fir diverse audiences.
Specialized Field: Orchestra
Budget: $35,000
Performs At: Park Hill South School Auditorium
Seating Capacity: 950

1145
LIBERTY SYMPHONY ORCHESTRA
WJC 1137
500 College Hill
Liberty, MO 64068
Phone: 816-781-7700
Fax: 816-415-5012
e-mail: cunninghaf@william.jewell.edu
Web Site: www.libertysymphony.org
Officers:
    President: Ann Reed
    Treasurer: Peggy Barr
Management:
    Conductor: Dr Tony Brandolino
    Managing Director: Florence Cunningham
Mission: Contributes to the cultural life of the Kansas
City community by performing four concerts a season in
the Liberty Performing Arts Theatre. In addition, two
educational concerts for school-aged children are
performed. More than 3,000 citizens in the area are
reached through these programs. The Orchestra is
transitioning through founder leadership and artistic
direction to more active, hands-on participation by the
Board of Directors.
Utilizes: Guest Musicians; Multimedia; Original Music
Scores; Singers; Soloists
Founded: 1970
Specialized Field: Orchestra
Paid Staff: 2
Volunteer Staff: 50
Non-paid Artists: 58
Budget: $50,000
Income Sources: Sponsors; Patrons; Donors; Grants;
Box Office
Performs At: Liberty Performing Arts Theatre; Liberty
Community Center
Affiliations: Missouri Citizens for the Arts; American
Symphony Orchestra League; Missouri Arts Council;
Liberty Chamber of Commerce
Annual Attendance: 4,200
Facility Category: Performing Arts Theatre
Seating Capacity: 700
Year Built: 1991
Organization Type: Performing; Educational

1146
SAINT JOSEPH SYMPHONY SOCIETY
120 S Eighth Street
Saint Joseph, MO 64501
Phone: 816-233-7701
Fax: 816-233-6704
e-mail: info@saintjosephsymphony.org
Web Site: www.saintjosephsymphony.org
Officers:
    President: Ray Sisson
    VP: Jan Mehl
    Treasurer: Charles Salanski
Management:
    Managing Director: Ann Brock
Mission: To present symphonic concerts and
educational activities for the citizens of Northwest
Missouri and Eastern Kansas.
Founded: 1959
Specialized Field: Symphony
Status: Professional; Nonprofit
Performs At: Missouri Theatre

Organization Type: Performing; Educational

1147
KIRKWOOD SYMPHONY ORCHESTRA
PO Box 410053
Saint Louis, MO 63141
Phone: 314-569-3220
Fax: 314-569-3220
e-mail: violinist@claytonsymphony.org
Officers:
    President: Rusell A Willis
Management:
    Artistic Direcor: Edward Dolbashian
Specialized Field: Orchestra
Budget: $35,000
Performs At: St. John's Lutheran Church
Seating Capacity: 500

1148
NEW MUSIC CIRCLE
142 Willow Brook Road
Saint Louis, MO 63146
Phone: 314-432-6073
Fax: 314-567-5384
e-mail: alumrod@aol.com
Management:
    Music Director: Rich O'Donnell
Mission: To advocate for new music; to commission
new works; to promote promising composers and
ensembles.
Specialized Field: Electronic; Live Electronic; New
Music; Avant Garde
Status: Professional; Nonprofit
Organization Type: Presenting

1149
SAINT LOUIS CLASSICAL GUITAR
SOCIETY
PO Box 11425
Saint Louis, MO 63105
Phone: 314-567-5566
e-mail: info@guitarstlouis.net
Web Site: www.guitarstlouis.net
Officers:
    President: William Ash
Mission: To promote and foster an understanding and
appreciation of the guitar, to encourage a high standard
in instruction and performance, to encourage the
creation and preservation of music for the guitar to
sponsor the society.
Specialized Field: Classical Guitar
Status: Nonprofit
Budget: $100,000
Performs At: The Ethical Society

1150
SAINT LOUIS PHILHARMONIC
ORCHESTRA
PO Box 220437
Saint Louis, MO 63122
Phone: 314-421-3600
Web Site: www.stlphilharmonic.org
Officers:
    President: Marilyn K Humiston
    VP: Stephen Larmore
    Secretary: Doug Kenner
    Treasurer: David Lyon
Mission: To offer musicians an opportunity to play good
music under the direction of an able conductor.
Utilizes: Guest Artists
Founded: 1860
Specialized Field: Symphony
Status: Non-Professional; Nonprofit

Performs At: Scottish Rite Cathedral
Organization Type: Performing

1151
SAINT LOUIS SYMPHONY ORCHESTRA

Powell Symphony Hall
718 N Grand Boulevard
Saint Louis, MO 63103
Phone: 314-533-2500
Fax: 314-286-4142
Toll-free: 800-232-1880
e-mail: orchestra@slso.org
Web Site: www.slso.org
Officers:
    Chairman: Cynthia Brinkley
    President: Randy Adams
    VP Operations: Robert McGrath
Management:
    Executive Director: Randy Adams
    Chorus Director: Amy Kaiser
    Artistic Administration Director: Jeremy Geffen
    Stage Manager: Mike Lynch
    Director Marketing: Stephen Duncan
    Concertmaster: David Halen
Utilizes: Guest Artists
Founded: 1879
Specialized Field: Symphony
Status: Professional; Nonprofit
Paid Staff: 150
Volunteer Staff: 200
Paid Artists: 97
Budget: $22,000,000
Income Sources: Ticket Sales, Sponsorships, Donations
Performs At: Powell Symphony Hall at Grand Center
Seating Capacity: 2,700
Year Built: 1925
Year Remodeled: 1966
Rental Contact: Melissa Lange
Organization Type: Performing; Touring; Educational

1152
SAINT LOUIS SYMPHONY YOUTH ORCHESTRA

Powell Symphony Hall
718 N Grand Boulevard
Saint Louis, MO 63103
Phone: 314-533-2500
Fax: 314-286-4142
Web Site: www.slso.org/performers/yo.htm
Management:
    Manager: Margaret Neilson
    Music Director: David Amado
    Founder: Leonard Slatkin
Mission: The Saint Louis Symphony Youth Orchestra was founded in 1970 by Leonard Slatkin to acquaint young instrumentalists with the atmosphere of a professional orchestra, to introduce them to the environment of the Saint Louis Symphony and to provide them with the opportunity of investigating and performing a wide spectrum of symphonic music.
Utilizes: Guest Artists
Founded: 1970
Specialized Field: Youth Orchestra; Chamber
Status: Non-Professional; Nonprofit
Paid Staff: 100
Income Sources: American Symphony Orchestra League (Youth Orchestra Division)
Performs At: Powell Symphony Hall at Grand Center
Organization Type: Performing; Touring; Educational; Sponsoring

1153
KANSAS CITY YOUTH SYMPHONY ASSOCIATION OF KANSAS

7301 Mission Road
Suite 143
Shawnee Mission, MO 66208
Phone: 913-722-6810
Fax: 913-722-6806
e-mail: ysymph@crn.org
Web Site: www.crn.org/kcys
Management:
    Music Director/Conductor: Glenn Block
Mission: To provide educational opportunities for young muscians by performing before community-wide audiences and by inspiring excellence in performance.
Specialized Field: Youth Symphony

1154
SPRINGFIELD SYMPHONY ASSOCIATION

1536 E Division
Springfield, MO 65803
Phone: 417-864-6683
Fax: 417-864-8967
Web Site: www.orion.org/~symphony/history.html
Officers:
    President: Randal L Saul
    VP: Jason Hemingway
    Treasurer: Lisa C Officer
    Secretary: Sheryl Wachter
    Guild President: Libby Falk
Management:
    Executive Director: Dana C Randall
    Conductor: Charles Bontrager
Mission: To provide the highest level of symphonic music and music education to all of Southwest Missouri, commensurate with sound fiscal policies.
Utilizes: Guest Artists; Guest Companies; Singers
Founded: 1934
Specialized Field: Symphony
Status: Semi-Professional
Income Sources: American Symphony Orchestra League; Missouri Arts Council
Performs At: Juanita K. Hammons Hall for the Performing Arts
Organization Type: Performing

1155
CENTRAL MISSOURI STATE UNIVERSITY SYMPHONY ORCHESTRA

Music Department
Utt 109
Warrensburg, MO 64093
Phone: 660-543-4330
Fax: 660-543-8271
e-mail: rutland@cmsu1.cmsu.edu
Web Site: www.cmsu.edu/music
Officers:
    Chairman Music Department: Charles McAdams
Management:
    Music Director/Conductor: John Rutland
Mission: To give university students and community members exposure to the standard orchestral repertoire and serve as a cultural force within the greater Warrensburg area.
Founded: 1871
Specialized Field: Symphony
Paid Staff: 2
Paid Artists: 1
Non-paid Artists: 55
Budget: $35,000
Performs At: Hart Recital Hall
Seating Capacity: 350

1156
BILLINGS SYMPHONY SOCIETY

201 N Broadway
Suite 350
Billings, MT 59103
Phone: 406-252-3610
Fax: 406-252-3353
e-mail: symphony@billingssymphon.org
Web Site: www.billingssymphony.org/
Management:
    Music Director: Dr. Uri Barnea
    Chorale Director: David Barnet
    General Manager: Maxine Pihlaja
Mission: To offer the community and the region live symphonic music.
Utilizes: Guest Artists
Founded: 1951
Specialized Field: Symphony; Orchestra
Status: Semi-Professional; Nonprofit
Budget: $260,000-1,050,000
Income Sources: American Symphony Orchestra League; Montana Association of Symphony Orchestras
Performs At: The Alberta Bair Theater for the Performing Arts
Seating Capacity: 1,200
Organization Type: Performing

1157
YELLOWSTONE CHAMBER PLAYERS

1204 Rimhaven Way
Billings, MT 59102
Phone: 406-248-2832
Fax: 406-248-2832
e-mail: mclamonaca@hotmail.com
Officers:
    Board Member: Mary LaMonaca
    VP: Delores Vigessa
    Secretary: Lisa Lombardy
    Treasurer: Ramona Turnbull
Management:
    President: Elizabeth Adcock
    Ticket Manager: Caron Schultz
Mission: The performance of a wide variety of chamber music, from string quartets and piano quintets, to small ensembles employing clarinet, flute and guitar.
Utilizes: Artists-in-Residence; Collaborating Artists; Educators; Guest Companies; Guest Musical Directors; Multimedia; Original Music Scores; Sign Language Translators
Founded: 1980
Specialized Field: Chamber; Ensemble
Status: Professional; Nonprofit
Volunteer Staff: 20
Paid Artists: 15
Income Sources: Friends of YCP; Donations; Business Sponsors
Performs At: Churches; Small Recital Halls
Annual Attendance: 1,000
Organization Type: Performing; Touring; Resident

1158
GREAT FALLS SYMPHONY ASSOCIATION

113 Street N
PO Box 1078
Great Falls, MT 59401
Phone: 406-453-4102
Fax: 406-453-9779
e-mail: info@gfsymphony.org
Web Site: www.gfsymphony.org
Management:

Executive Director: Carolyn Valacich
Music Director/Conductor: Gordon J Johnson
Choir Director: Paul Ritter
Mission: To produce and present symphonic, chamber and choral music and to serve as a s resource for education and outreach for the people of Montana.
Utilizes: Collaborations; Grant Writers; Guest Companies; Guest Directors; Multimedia; Organization Contracts; Original Music Scores; Theatre Companies
Founded: 1959
Specialized Field: Symphony; Orchestra; Chamber; Youth Orchestra
Status: Professional; Nonprofit
Paid Staff: 8
Paid Artists: 65
Non-paid Artists: 80
Budget: $450,000-$500,000
Income Sources: American Symphony Orchestra League; Montana Association of Symphony Orchestras; Tickets
Performs At: Great Falls Civic Center
Annual Attendance: 35,000
Seating Capacity: 1,776
Organization Type: Performing; Touring; Resident; Educational; Sponsoring

1159
HELENA SYMPHONY SOCIETY

15 N Ewing Street
PO Box 1073
Helena, MT 59624
Phone: 406-442-1860
Fax: 406-443-6620
e-mail: helenasymphony@hotmail.com
Web Site: www.helenasymphony.org
Officers:
    President: John Mundinger
    VP: Frank Graham
    Secretary: Ross Common
Management:
    Executive Director: Leslie Gilkey
    Music Director: Eric Funk
    Chorale Director: Gary Funk
Mission: The presentation of classical and popular symphony concerts, including choral and chamber concerts.
Utilizes: Composers-in-Residence; Guest Composers; Guest Musical Directors; Guest Musicians; Singers; Soloists
Founded: 1955
Specialized Field: Symphony; Orchestra; Chamber; Ethnic Music
Status: Nonprofit
Paid Staff: 4
Volunteer Staff: 20
Non-paid Artists: 140
Budget: $175,000
Income Sources: American Society of Composers; Authors and Publishers; Broadcast Music Incorporated; Donations; Tickets
Performs At: Helena Civic Center
Affiliations: American Symphony Orchestra League; Montana Association of Symphony Orchestra
Organization Type: Performing; Educational

1160
MISSOULA SYMPHONY ASSOCIATION

PO Box 8301
Missoula, MT 59807
Phone: 406-721-3194
Fax: 406-541-3194
e-mail: info@missoulasymphony.org
Web Site: http://www.missoulasymphony.org/
Officers:

President: Jim Valeo
Vice President: Lynda Frost
Executive Director: John Driscoll
Management:
    Music Director: John Henry
    Choral Director: Dean Peterson
Mission: To present artistic programs of excellence to Missoula and the surrounding areas, provide an opportunity for young persons and develop an interest in the arts through concerts and master classes.
Utilizes: Commissioned Composers; Commissioned Music; Composers-in-Residence; Educators; Guest Accompanists; Guest Directors; Guest Lecturers; Guest Writers; Instructors; Original Music Scores; Singers; Theatre Companies
Founded: 1954
Specialized Field: Symphony
Status: Nonprofit
Paid Staff: 4
Paid Artists: 10
Non-paid Artists: 60
Budget: $200,000
Income Sources: American Symphony Orchestra League
Performs At: University Theatre
Annual Attendance: 7,500
Facility Category: University Theatre
Stage Dimensions: 37'x 36'
Seating Capacity: 1,040
Year Built: 30's
Year Remodeled: 1997
Organization Type: Performing; Sponsoring

Nebraska

1161
HASTINGS SYMPHONY ORCHESTRA

Hastings College
Fuhr Hall - 710 N Turner Avenue
PO Box 597
Hastings, NE 68901
Phone: 402-461-7361
Fax: 402-469-9396
e-mail: hso@hastingssymphony.com
Web Site: http://www.hastingssymphony.com
Officers:
    President: Dale Duensing
    Executive Secretary: Jodi Mackin
Management:
    Conductor/Artistic Director: Bryon Jensen, PhD
Mission: To enrich the cultural environment for people of all ages by providing quality, live performances of music in a symphonic setting, music education, and performance opportunities for talented musicians.
Utilizes: Artists-in-Residence; Commissioned Music; Guest Companies; Guest Composers; Guest Musicians; Local Artists; Multimedia; Original Music Scores; Sign Language Translators; Soloists
Founded: 1926
Specialized Field: Symphony; Orchestra
Status: Non-Professional; Nonprofit
Paid Staff: 2
Volunteer Staff: 40
Paid Artists: 6
Non-paid Artists: 4
Budget: $90,000
Income Sources: Tickets; Contributions; Grants
Performs At: Auditorium at Masonic Center
Annual Attendance: 2,500-3,500
Facility Category: City Auditorium
Seating Capacity: 850
Year Built: 1920

Organization Type: Performing; Touring; Resident; Educational
Resident Groups: American Symphony Orchestra League

1162
KEARNEY AREA SYMPHONY ORCHESTRA

University of Nebraska at Kearney
Music Department, 2506 12th Avenue
Kearney, NE 68849
Phone: 308-865-8618
Fax: 308-865-8806
e-mail: crockerr@unk.edu
Officers:
    President: Vernon Plambeck
    VP: John Johnson
    Secretary: C J Sabah
    Treasurer: Steven J Lind
Management:
    Conductor: Dr. Ron Crocker
Mission: Provides quality symphonic concerts for University and community members in Central Nebraska
Founded: 1905
Specialized Field: Orchestra
Paid Staff: 1
Volunteer Staff: 16
Budget: $25,000
Income Sources: Donations; Ads
Performs At: Auditorium
Affiliations: University Of Nebraska @ Kearney
Annual Attendance: 2000
Seating Capacity: 500
Year Built: 1970
Year Remodeled: 2005

1163
LINCOLN CIVIC ORCHESTRA

Nebraska Wesleyan University
Department of Music
5000 St. Paul
Lincoln, NE 68504
Phone: 402-465-2267
e-mail: jjc@nebrwesleyan.edu
Web Site: http://music.nebrwesleyan.edu/lco
Management:
    Music Director: Dr. Pat Fortney
    Executive Director: Dean W Haist
Mission: Offering community members an opportunity to perform serious music.
Utilizes: Singers
Specialized Field: Orchestra
Status: Nonprofit
Paid Staff: 130
Budget: $35,000
Performs At: O'Donnell Aud.; Rogers Arts Center; Nebraska Wesleyan Univ.
Organization Type: Resident

1164
LINCOLN FRIENDS OF CHAMBER MUSIC

5211 W Chadderton Circle
Lincoln, NE 68521
Phone: 402-472-5121
Fax: 402-472-8962
e-mail: jkraus1@unl.edu
Web Site: www.lfcm.org
Officers:
    President: Joe Kraus
    Head Artists Subcommittee: Anne Chang-Barnea
Mission: Presenting chamber music; promoting community appreciation of chamber music; aiding talented local chamber music artists.

Utilizes: Guest Directors; Multimedia
Founded: 1965
Specialized Field: Chamber; Ensemble
Status: Nonprofit
Volunteer Staff: 15
Budget: $25,000
Income Sources: Ticket Sales; Donations; Grants
Performs At: Sheldon Art Gallery Auditorium
Annual Attendance: 1250
Facility Category: Art Gallery Auditorium
Stage Dimensions: 25'W x 10'D
Seating Capacity: 300
Year Built: 1963
Rental Contact: P.J. Jacobs
Organization Type: Sponsoring

1165
LINCOLN SYMPHONY ORCHESTRA

233 S 13th Street
Suite B102
Lincoln, NE 68508
Phone: 402-476-2211
Fax: 402-476-2236
e-mail: info@lincolnsymphony.com
Web Site: lincolnsymphony.com
Officers:
President: Roxann Brinnfoerder
Management:
Music Director: Edward Polochick
Executive Director: Barbara Bach
Office /Box Office Manager: Erin Hilsabeck
Operations/Personnel Manager: Travis Kulnicki
Development Director: Tari Hendrickson Svvzency
Mission: Will enrich, educate and entertain current and potential audiences through the performances and advancement of symphonic music.
Founded: 1927
Specialized Field: Symphony; Orchestra
Status: Professional; Nonprofit
Paid Staff: 7
Paid Artists: 60
Budget: $260,000- $ 1,050,000
Performs At: Lied Center for the Performing Arts; Kimball Recital Hall
Affiliations: American Symhpony Orchestra League
Seating Capacity: 2285/ 850
Organization Type: Performing; Sponsoring

1166
LINCOLN YOUTH SYMPHONY

7201 Woody Creek Lane
Lincoln, NE 68501
Phone: 402-423-5343
Fax: 435-797-3150
Officers:
President: Joyce Glaesemann
Secretary: Linda Maack
Treasurer: Carl Olson
Administrator: Richard Scott
Business Manager: Micheal Swartz
Management:
Music Director/Conductor: Dr Brain Moore
Mission: The Lincoln Youth Symphony Orchestra was organized to perform symphonic literature unable to be played within regular school instruction through participation in the Youth Orchestra or the Junior Youth Orchestra.
Founded: 1953
Specialized Field: Youth Symphony
Status: Non-Professional; Nonprofit
Paid Staff: 76
Income Sources: American Symphony Orchestra League (Youth Orchestra Division); Lincoln Public Schools

Performs At: Kimball Recital Hall; University of Nebraska
Organization Type: Performing; Touring; Educational; Sponsoring

1167
NEBRASKA JAZZ ORCHESTRA

216 N 11 Street
Suite 202
Lincoln, NE 68508-1401
Phone: 402-477-8446
Fax: 402-477-8222
e-mail: njo@artsincorporated.org
Officers:
President: David Shiffermiller
Vice President: Tom Grafton
Management:
Music Director: Ed Love
Executive Director: Dean Haist
Founded: 1975
Specialized Field: Jazz
Budget: $35,000- $100,000
Performs At: Embassy Suites;Joslyn Art Museum, Omaha
Seating Capacity: 450/ 1500
Organization Type: Performing

1168
OMAHA AREA YOUTH ORCHESTRAS

PO Box 34518
Omaha, NE 68134-0518
Phone: 402-238-2044
Fax: 402-238-2310
e-mail: oayo@radiks.net
Web Site: www.oayo.org
Officers:
President: Kathleen Vance
Secretary: Dara Spivack
Treasurer: Craig Vance
President-Elect: Ron Mimick
Management:
Music Director: Aviva Segall
General Manager: Jan Braden
Associate Conductor: Jennifer L Bloomgarden
Mission: To enhance the musical education of aspiring and talented young musicians through the medium of orchestral performance; to help them become appreciative listeners; and to build discipline, cooperation, and other skills necessary for a group accomplishment.
Founded: 1958
Specialized Field: Youth Orchestra; Chamber; Ensemble
Status: Non-Professional; Nonprofit
Paid Staff: 6
Volunteer Staff: 250
Budget: $200,000
Income Sources: American Symphony Orchestra League; Omaha Symphony Guild; ASTA; Music Educators National Conference; Nebraska Arts Council
Performs At: University Recital Hall
Annual Attendance: 7,000-8,000
Organization Type: Performing; Educational; Sponsoring

1169
OMAHA SYMPHONY

1605 Howard Street
Omaha, NE 68102-2705
Phone: 402-342-3560
Fax: 402-342-3819
e-mail: info@omahasymphony.org
Web Site: www.omahasymphony.org
Officers:

Chairman: William A. Fitzgerald
President/CEO: Robert J. Hallam
Management:
Music Director: Thomas Wilkins
Resident Conductor: Ernest Richardson
Utilizes: Collaborations; Commissioned Music; Five Seasonal Concerts; Guest Accompanists; Guest Artists; Guest Composers; Guest Musical Directors; Guest Musicians; Guest Writers; Lyricists; New Productions; Organization Contracts; Resident Professionals
Founded: 1921
Specialized Field: Symphony; Orchestra; Chamber; Ensemble
Status: Professional; Nonprofit
Paid Staff: 27
Paid Artists: 70
Budget: $4,500,000
Income Sources: American Symphony Orchestra League; National Endowment for the Arts; Nebraska Arts Council
Organization Type: Performing; Touring; Resident; Educational; Sponsoring

1170
OMAHA SYMPHONY CHAMBER ORCHESTRA

1605 Howard Street
Omaha, NE 68102-2705
Phone: 402-342-3560
Fax: 402-342-3819
e-mail: bravo@omahasymphony.org
Officers:
President and CEO: Robert J Hallam
Executive Assistant: Diane Coffin
Management:
Music Director: Thomas Wilkins
Resident Conductor: Ernest Richardson
General Manager: Jennifer Bareament
Operations Manager: Sherrie Goeden
Artistic Coordinator: Tara M Cowherd
Personnel Manager: Jay Wise
Stage Manager: Rick Jones
Box Office Manager: Howard Coffin
Public Relations Manager: Marjorie Maas
Specialized Field: Orchestra
Budget: $1,050,000- $3,600,000
Performs At: Orpheum Theatre; Joslyn Art Museum; Witherspoon Concert Hall
Seating Capacity: 2750/ 1174

Nevada

1171
CARSON CITY SYMPHONY

PO Box 2001
Carson City, NV 89702-2001
Phone: 775-883-4154
Fax: 775-883-4371
e-mail: ehbugli@aol.com
Web Site: CCSymphony.com
Officers:
President: Elinor Bugli
Vice President: Grant Mills
Treasurer: Charlotte Tucker
Secretary: Edith Isidoro-Mills
Management:
Music Director/Conductor: David Bugli
Director Chamber Singers: Judy Monson
Youth Orchestra Director: Sue Kritts
Mission: To provide amateur and volunteer professional musicians with opportunity to learn and perform various musical styles to entertain and educate the community.

Utilizes: Arrangers; Commissioned Composers; Community Members; Community Talent; Composers; Guest Choreographers; Guest Companies; Guest Directors; Guest Musical Directors; Guest Musicians; High School Drama; Instructors; Local Artists & Directors; Music; Soloists
Founded: 1984
Opened: 1984
Specialized Field: Educational; Symphony; Chorus; Youth Strings
Status: Nonprofit
Volunteer Staff: 10
Non-paid Artists: 55
Budget: $25,000
Income Sources: Memberships; Ticket sales; Grants; Donations
Performs At: Concert Hall at Carson City Community Center
Affiliations: Carson Chamber Singers, Strings In The School
Annual Attendance: 2,000
Facility Category: Concert hall in community center
Type of Stage: Proscenium
Seating Capacity: 800

1172
LAS VEGAS CIVIC SYMPHONY
821 Las Vegas Boulevard N
Las Vegas, NV 89101
Phone: 702-229-6211
Fax: 702-382-5199
Web Site: www.ci.las-vegas.nv.us
Management:
    Cultural Supervisor: Patricia L Harris
    Cultural Center Coordinator: Ellis Rice
    Cultural Publicist: Stephanie Fosse
Mission: Provide culturally enriched performances and classes to the Greater Las Vegas area.
Specialized Field: Symphony
Paid Staff: 20
Paid Artists: 50
Non-paid Artists: 200
Budget: $260,000- $1,050,000
Performs At: Reed Whipple Cultural Arts Center
Seating Capacity: 300

1173
LAS VEGAS PHILHARMONIC
1412 South Jones Blvd
Las Vegas, NV 89146
Phone: 702-258-5438
Fax: 702-893-7757
e-mail: jeri@lvphil.com
Web Site: www.lvphil.com
Officers:
    Executive Director: Jeri Crawford
    Finance Manager: Doug Van Gilder
    Treasurer: Kep Sweeney
    Secretary: Pat Fink
Management:
    Music Director/Conductor: David Itkin
Mission: To provide live symphony music at the highest artistic standards. Encourage and build appreciation of music to all through educaitonal programming and community initiatives.
Founded: 1998
Specialized Field: Orchestra
Paid Staff: 4
Volunteer Staff: 2
Paid Artists: 76

1174
NEVADA SYMPHONY ORCHESTRA
4505 Maryland Parkway
VNLV Department of Music
Las Vegas, NV 89154
Phone: 702-895-3332
Fax: 702-895-4239
Web Site: www.nevadasymphony.org
Officers:
    President: M Rex Baird
    VP: Bruce B Borgelt
    Secretary: Collen Schoeder
    Treasurer/ President Elect: B. Michl Lloyd
Management:
    Artistic Director: Virko Baley
    Executive Dorector: Judith Markham
    Director Operations: Timothy Bonenfant
    Chairman: Paul Kreider
Mission: To offer symphonic performances, services and educational opportunities to the Las Vegas community.
Founded: 1980
Specialized Field: Orchestra; Ensemble
Status: Professional; Nonprofit
Organization Type: Performing; Educational; Sponsoring

1175
RENO CHAMBER ORCHESTRA
PO Box 547
Reno, NV 89504
Phone: 775-348-9413
Fax: 775- 34—064
e-mail: info@renochamberorchestra.org
Officers:
    Operations Manager: Chris Morrison
    Board President: Jim M Winter
Management:
    Music Director/Conductor: Theodore Kuchar
    Executive Director: Scott Faulkner
    Operations Manager: Chris Morrison
    Music Director: Theordore Kirchar
Mission: To provide the highest quality performance of repertoire written for the smaller orchestra and educate and promote the appreciation of the music among diverse audiences.
Specialized Field: Chamber; Orchestra
Paid Staff: 4
Volunteer Staff: 45
Paid Artists: 40 +
Budget: $400,000 - $425,000
Income Sources: Individual contributions; Tickets sales; Foundations; Grants; Corparate soliciations
Performs At: Nightingale Concert Hall
Facility Category: Concert Hall
Seating Capacity: 615

1176
RENO PHILHARMONIC
925 Riverside Drive
Suite 3
Reno, NV 89503
Phone: 775-323-6393
Fax: 775-323-6711
e-mail: renophil@renophil.com
Officers:
    President/CEO: Tim Young
Management:
    Music Director/Conductor: Laura Jackson
    Personnel Manager: Mary Miller
    Marketing Director/Box Office: Francine Burge

Mission: To bring the best of symphonic music to the Truckee Meadows and surrounding communities; to ensure a high quality musical experience; to bring that musical experience to the youth of our community; to foster strong individual and corporate support for the Reno Philharmonic; to engage in sound business and fiscal planning and execution; to work in cooperation with the other local arts groups.
Founded: 1969
Specialized Field: Orchestra
Paid Staff: 7
Paid Artists: 150
Non-paid Artists: 300
Budget: $1.9 Million
Income Sources: Earned Revenue/Contributions
Annual Attendance: 60,000

New Hampshire

1177
NEVERS' 2ND REGIMENT BAND
110 South State Street
P O Box 2352
Concord, NH 03301
Phone: 603-642-6623
e-mail: info@neversband.org
Web Site: www.neversband.org
Officers:
    Treasurer: Doug Osborne
    Secretary: Deborah Lincoln
    Member-at-Large: Peter Clark
    Business Manager: George West
Management:
    Conductor/Treasurer: Douglas Osborne
Mission: To perpetuate its tradition of live, high quality performances of music for the benefit and enjoyment of all people; to promote and demonstrate the continuing relevance of modern and traditional concert band music and to preserve the history of the Band's regimental origins.
Utilizes: Community Talent; Guest Artists; Guest Musical Directors; Guest Musicians; Instructors; Lyricists; Multimedia; Scenic Designers; Singers; Students
Founded: 1861
Specialized Field: Band
Status: Semi-Professional; Nonprofit
Paid Staff: 6
Paid Artists: 30
Income Sources: City of Concord
Affiliations: American Federation of Musicians
Facility Category: Outdoors; Wagner Bandwagon
Seating Capacity: unlimited
Year Built: 1968
Organization Type: Performing

1178
APPLE HILL CENTER FOR CHAMBER MUSIC
Apple Hill Road
PO Box 217
East Sullivan, NH 03445
Phone: 603-847-3371
Fax: 603-847-9734
Toll-free: 800-472-6677
e-mail: info@applehill.org
Web Site: www.applehill.org
Officers:
    President: John Hoffman
    VP: Julian Bergeron
    Secretary: Samdra Phipps
    Board Treasurer: Drew Landry
Management:

Executive Director/Pianist: Eric Stumacher
Administrative Associate: April Weed
Fiscal Manager: Deborah Ford
Summer School Administrator: Vicky Pittmann
Mission: To further the performing and teaching of chamber music at the highest standard and in so doing to play for peace. It pursues these goals through the internationally celebrated performance and coaching of its Artists-in-Residence, the Apple Hill Chamber Players.
Founded: 1971
Specialized Field: Chamber; Ensemble
Status: Professional; Semi-Professional; Non-Professional; Nonprofit
Paid Staff: 6
Paid Artists: 5
Performs At: Louise Shonk Kelly Concert Barn
Organization Type: Performing; Resident; Educational; Sponsoring

1179
NEW HAMPSHIRE PHILHARMONIC ORCHESTRA

83 Hanover Street
4th Floor
Manchester, NH 03101
Phone: 603-647-6476
Fax: 603-647-4130
e-mail: info@nhpo.com
Officers:
 President: Walter Zanchuk
 VP: Adele Baker
 Secretary: George Jobel
 Treasurer: John Gunther
Management:
 Executive Director: Steven A Olans
Mission: To offer classical concerts; to enhance music education; to provide opportunities for nonprofessionals to work with music professionals.
Founded: 1905
Specialized Field: Symphony; Orchestra
Status: Professional; Non-Professional; Nonprofit
Paid Staff: 2
Volunteer Staff: 2
Paid Artists: 2
Non-paid Artists: 65
Budget: $100,000
Income Sources: Box office; donations; foundations
Performs At: Palace Theatre
Annual Attendance: 10,000
Facility Category: Concert Hall
Type of Stage: Proscenium
Seating Capacity: 850
Year Built: 1920
Year Remodeled: 1975
Organization Type: Performing; Resident; Educational

1180
NEW HAMPSHIRE SYMPHONY ORCHESTRA

1087 Elm Street #306
Manchester, NH 03105-1298
Phone: 603-669-3559
Fax: 603-623-1195
Toll-free: 800-639-9320
e-mail: info@nhso.org
Web Site: www.nhso.org
Management:
 Music Director: Kenneth Kiester
 Executive Director: Douglas Barry CAE
 Director Development: George Regan
Founded: 1974
Specialized Field: Symphony; Orchestra

Status: Professional; Nonprofit
Performs At: Palace Theatre and Music Hall in Portsmouth, NH/ Capitol Center For The Arts in Concord
Affiliations: American Symphony Orchestra League
Organization Type: Performing; Touring; Educational

New Jersey

1181
COLONIAL SYMPHONY

246 B Madisonville Road
Basking Ridge, NJ 07920
Phone: 908-766-7555
Fax: 908-953-9799
e-mail: colonialsy@verizon.net
Web Site: www.colonialsymphony.org
Officers:
 President: Mark C Rosenblum
 VP: Carol Wead
 VP: Daniel H Olmsted
 Vice-President: Ross Longfield
 Treasurer: Thomas P. Bintinger
 Secretary: Lawrence J. Hunt
Management:
 Music Director/Conductor: Yehuda Gilad
 Executive Director: Suzanne Samson
Mission: Dedicated to nurturing and sustaining a superior orchestra performing a balance of classical and contemporary music and enhancing the understanding of music through education.
Utilizes: Choreographers; Collaborations; Commissioned Composers; Composers-in-Residence; Dancers; Guest Composers; Guest Musical Directors; Guest Musicians; Instructors; Singers
Founded: 1950
Specialized Field: Symphony
Status: Professional; Nonprofit
Paid Staff: 2.5
Volunteer Staff: 12
Paid Artists: 50
Budget: $500,000
Income Sources: Corporate Donations; Individual Donations; Government Endowments; Foundations
Performs At: Community Theatre in Morristown, N.J.
Affiliations: American Symphony Orchestra League
Annual Attendance: 5,000
Facility Category: Community Theatre of Morristown
Organization Type: Performing; Educational

1182
ORCHESTRA OF ST. PETER BY THE SEA

2456 Hooper Avenue
PO Box 215
Bay Head, NJ 08742
Phone: 732-920-4444
Fax: 732-477-6277
e-mail: seasymphonyinc@aol.com
Management:
 Music Director/Manager: Father Alphonse Stephenson
Founded: 1986
Specialized Field: Orchestra; Ensemble
Performs At: Touring Orchestra
Annual Attendance: 2,500

1183
BLOOMFIELD MANDOLIN ORCHESTRA

Bloomfield Recreation Commission
PO Box 1776
Bloomfield, NJ 07003

Phone: 973-743-8828
Fax: 973-743-0343
e-mail: nj.mandolins@worldnet.att.net
Web Site: http://nj.mandolins.home.att.net
 Treasurer: Filomena Peloro
Management:
 Musical Director: Gabriel Nevola
 Manager: Russell Kelner
 Orchestra Librarian: Yugo Re
Mission: To promote the mandolin by way of entertainment as well as instruction.
Utilizes: Singers
Founded: 1941
Specialized Field: Mandolin Orchestra
Status: Nonprofit
Non-paid Artists: 35
Performs At: Presbyterian Church on the Green
Organization Type: Performing, Touring, Educational

1184
GARDEN STATE PHILHARMONIC SYMPHONY YOUTH ORCHESTRA

150 Brick Boulevard
Brick, NJ
Brick, NJ 08723
Phone: 732-451-0064
Fax: 732-451-0094
e-mail: gsmusic@earthlink.net
Officers:
 Business Manager: Sandra Campbell
Management:
 Artistic Director/Conductor: Anthony LaGruth
 Executive Director: Darlene A Dreyer
Specialized Field: Youth Orchestra
Budget: $250,000- $1,050,000
Performs At: Toms River H.S. Auditorium/ Ocean County College Arts Center
Seating Capacity: 1,266/ 604

1185
BAY-ATLANTIC SYMPHONY

59 East Commerce Street
Bridgeton, NJ 08302
Phone: 856-451-1169
Fax: 856-451-4380
e-mail: info@bayatlanticsymphony.org
Officers:
 Executive Director: Paul H Herron
 Development Director: Rhonda Jackson
Management:
 Music Director/Conductor: Jed Gaylin
 Concertmaster: Ruotao Mao
Founded: 1983
Specialized Field: Orchestra
Budget: $514,000
Income Sources: Geraldine R Dodge Foundation, New Jersey State Council Of Arts, Fleet Bank, Bergen Family Foundation, Silento Family Foundation, Basile Tesa, LLC
Performs At: Richard Stockton PAC in Atlanta, Performing Arts Center in Vinland, Cap May Music

1186
SOLID BRASS

5 Sunset Drive
Chatham, NJ 07928-1141
Phone: 201-768-6970
Fax: 201-768-7257
e-mail: haislip@solidbrass.com
Web Site: www.solidbrass.com
Management:
 Artistic Director: Douglas Haislip
 Management: Lois Scott, lsminc@aol.com

Mission: Preserving and perpetuating brass chamber music through performance, recording, composing and related activities.
Utilizes: Multimedia
Founded: 1982
Specialized Field: Chamber; Brass Ensemble
Status: Professional
Non-paid Artists: Yes
Annual Attendance: 1,500
Organization Type: Performing; Touring; Educational

1187
NEW JERSEY INTERGENERATIONAL ORCHESTRA

PO Box 432
Cranford, NJ 07016
Phone: 908-522-0100
Fax: 908-665-0929
e-mail: info@njio.org
Management:
    Founder: Lorraine Marks
    Conductor: Todd VanBeveren
Mission: To nurture the belief that senior citizens can share their wisdom and become vital resources for children by bringing youth and the elderly together to share experiences that promote mutual growth and understanding between generations.
Founded: 1994
Specialized Field: Orchestra
Status: Non-Professional
Paid Staff: 3
Volunteer Staff: 10
Paid Artists: 30
Non-paid Artists: 100

1188
ALL SEASONS CHAMBER PLAYERS

115 Orchard Road
Demarest, NJ 07627
Phone: 201-768-1331
e-mail: jeanstri@bellatlantic.net
Web Site: www.allseasonschamberplayers.org
Mission: A leading chamber music ensemble in New Jersey performing music from baroque to contemporary periods in mixed ensembles
Founded: 1981
Specialized Field: Baroque; Contemporary

1189
HADDONFIELD SYMPHONY

41 S Haddon Avenue
Suite 7
Haddonfield, NJ 08033
Phone: 856-429-1880
Fax: 856-428-5634
e-mail: symphony@haddonfield-symphony.org
Web Site: www.haddonfield-symphony.org
Officers:
    President: Trevor Orthmann
Management:
    Music Director/Conductor: Rossen Milanov
    Assistant Conductor: Benjamin Loeb
    Director Marketing/Public Relations: Michele Holcomb
    Director Development: Eileen K Myers CFRE
    Director Educational Artistic Oper.: Erin Bewsher
    Marketing /Development Assistant: Erica Heyer
Mission: Dedicated to enriching the musical lives of the residents of the state of New Jersey.
Utilizes: Guest Artists; Guest Companies; Singers
Founded: 1952
Specialized Field: Symphony; Orchestra
Status: Professional; Nonprofit
Paid Staff: 6

Organization Type: Performing; Educational

1190
NEW JERSEY CITY UNIVERSITY ORCHESTRA

2039 Kennedy Boulevard
New Jersey University/Music Department
Jersey City, NJ 07305-1597
Phone: 201-200-2017
Fax: 201-200-3130
e-mail: eraditz@njcu.edu
Management:
    Music Director: Edward Raditz
Utilizes: Guest Musical Directors; Guest Musicians; Multimedia; Soloists
Specialized Field: Orchestra; Ensemble
Paid Staff: 2
Volunteer Staff: 10
Paid Artists: 3
Budget: $35,000
Performs At: Margaret William Auditorium, New Jersey City University
Annual Attendance: 3000
Facility Category: Theatre\Auditorium
Seating Capacity: 1,000
Year Built: 1960
Year Remodeled: 1975

1191
NEW JERSEY MUSIC SOCIETY

311 Claremont Avenue
Montclair, NJ 07042
Phone: 973-746-6068
Fax: 973-746-0685
e-mail: njchambermusicsociety@att.net
Web Site: njcms.org
Management:
    Executive Director: Michael Lawson
    Assistant Executive Director: Marie Figueredo
    Artist in Residence: Paquito D'Rivera
Mission: To create, produce and maintain a repertoire of outstanding musical performances in classical, jazz and world music with core artists-in-residence and frequent nationally prominent guest artists. To provide new opportunities to a wider audience through innovative and stimulating children's programs, family concerts and workshops in area school system.
Founded: 1974
Specialized Field: Chamber
Status: Professional; Nonprofit
Performs At: Montclair Art Museum; Union Congregatinal Church
Organization Type: Performing; Touring; Resident; Educational

1192
PHILHARMONIC OF SOUTHERN NEW JERSEY

PO Box 768
Moorestown
Moorestown, NJ 08057
Phone: 856-779-2600
Fax: 609-654-8792
e-mail: raineyo@geocities.com
Officers:
    Concert & Production Manager: William Joyce
    President: Jack Paolin
    Secretary: Marcia Steinbock, Esq
    Treasurer: Madelyn Niessner
Management:
    Music Director/Conductor: Philip Travaline
    Personnel Manager: Barbara Travaline
    Concert/Production Manager: William Joyce

Mission: Provides quality classical music for the community; and offer rehearsal/performance opportunities for the talented musician.
Founded: 1991
Specialized Field: Orchestra
Budget: $35,000- $100,000
Income Sources: Grants and Contributions
Performs At: Forrest Rowland Auditorium
Affiliations: American Symphony Orchestra League; South Jersey Cultural Alliance
Seating Capacity: 1,300

1193
WEST JERSEY CHAMBER MUSIC SYMPHONY & SOCIETY

101 Bridgeboro Road
Moorestown, NJ 08057
Phone: 856-778-1899
Fax: 856-234-3666
Management:
    Music Director: Joel Krott
    Executive Assistant: Cindi Schneider
Utilizes: Guest Artists; Guest Companies
Founded: 1980
Specialized Field: Orchestra; Chamber
Status: Professional; Nonprofit
Paid Staff: 2
Volunteer Staff: 15
Paid Artists: 40
Budget: $35,000 - $100,000
Performs At: Various churches and schools
Organization Type: Performing; Touring

1194
NEW JERSEY YOUTH SYMPHONY

570 Central Avenue
Murray Hill, NJ 07974
Phone: 908-771-5544
Fax: 908-771-9839
e-mail: office@njys.org
Web Site: www.njys.org
Management:
    Executive Director: Linda Abrams
    Artistic Director: Barbara Barstow
    Executive Director: Susan Cauldwell
    Operations Manager: Robert Varner
Mission: To provide talented young musicians with orchestral and related music education experiences that will enable them to reach their highest potential as performers and listeners.
Founded: 1979
Specialized Field: Youth Symphony
Status: Non-Professional; Nonprofit
Non-paid Artists: 95
Budget: $500,000
Organization Type: Performing; Touring; Educational

1195
CATHEDRAL BASILICA OF THE SACRED HEART CONCERT SERIES

89 Ridge Street
Newark, NJ 07104
Phone: 973-484-2400
Fax: 973-497-9336
e-mail: jmiller@cathedralbasilica.org
Web Site: www.cathedralbasilica.org/concert/
Management:
    Director Music Ministry: John J Miller
Mission: Offering quality musical programs to Newark area residents.
Founded: 1983
Specialized Field: Symphony; Orchestra; Chamber; Ensemble

1196
NEW JERSEY SYMPHONY ORCHESTRA
2 Central Avenue
Newark, NJ 07102
Phone: 973-624-3713
Fax: 973-624-2115
e-mail: information@njsymphony.org
Web Site: www.njsymphony.org
Officers:
President: Lawrence J Tamburrit
General Operation: Susan Stucker
Chairman: Victor Parsonnet
Executive Vice Chairman/Treasurer: Victor Bauer
Management:
Music Director: Zdenek Macal
Mission: To engage the people of New Jersey by performing the full symphonic repertoire at the highest caliber in a variety of settings for diverse audiences.
Utilizes: Guest Artists
Founded: 1922
Specialized Field: Symphony; Orchestra; Chamber; Ensemble
Status: Professional; Nonprofit
Paid Staff: 43
Volunteer Staff: 76
Budget: $14.5 Million
Performs At: New Jersey Performing Arts Center; John Harms Center for the Arts/Englewood; Community Theatre/Morristown; State Theatre
Affiliations: War Memorail Trenton
Seating Capacity: 2,600/1,900
Organization Type: Performing

1197
NEW JERSEY SYMPHONY ORCHESTRA
2 Central Avenue
Newark, NJ 07102
Phone: 973-624-3713
Fax: 973-624-2115
e-mail: information@njsymphony.org
Web Site: www.njusymphony.org
Officers:
Chairman: Dr. Victor Parsonnet
Vice Chairman: Albert D. Angel
President/CEO: Stephen Sichak, Jr.
Management:
Music Director: Neeme Jarvi
Conductor: Henry Kao
Specialized Field: Orchestra
Budget: $35,000- $100,000
Performs At: New Jersey Performing Arts Center
Seating Capacity: 2,700

1198
OCEAN CITY POPS
901 Asbury Avenue
Ocean City, NJ 08226
Phone: 609-525-9291
Fax: 609-339-0374
e-mail: oceancitypops@aol.com
Officers:
Board Chair: John S Gabel
Vice Chair/Finances: Janey Perotti
Management:
Music Director: William Scheible
Executive Director: Michael Dattilo
Specialized Field: Orchestra; Pops
Budget: $250,000- $1,050,000
Performs At: auditorium
Seating Capacity: 930

1199
PLAINFIELD SYMPHONY
PO Box 5093
Plainfield, NJ 07061
Phone: 908-561-5140
e-mail: info@plainfieldsymphony.org
Web Site: www.plainfieldsymphony.org
Officers:
President: James Rowland
Vice President: Joseph Stuczynski
Treasurer: Lesley Rogers
Secretary: Pat Fox
Management:
Music Director: Charles Prince
Executive Director: James Rowland
Mission: To prepare and present musical programs of a symphonic type; to stimulate interest in symphonic music in the Central New Jersey area; to provide educational opportunities through youth and family concerts; and to provide a medium of performance for talented nonprofessional musicians.
Founded: 1919
Specialized Field: Symphony; Ensemble
Paid Staff: 2
Paid Artists: 40
Non-paid Artists: 40
Budget: $100,000-$125,000
Performs At: Crescent Avenue Presbyterian Church
Seating Capacity: 600

1200
GREATER PRINCETON YOUTH ORCHESTRA
PO Box 3037
Princeton, NJ 08543
Phone: 609-936-8700
Fax: 908- 87—017
e-mail: gpyo@patmedia.net
Officers:
Manager: Jan Fish Lewis
President: Richard Bilotti
Treasurer: Peter Cahill
Secretary: Noreen Coutin
Management:
Music Director/Conductor: Fernando Raucci
Executive Director: Margaret Plante Borah
Operations Manager: Melinda Strauss
Mission: To provide exciting and unique educational opportunites for many of our community's young people. Through their involvement in the Orchestra, gifted young musicians from across Central New Jersey and Pennsylvania hone their skills as performers in a large orchestra and in chamber music groups, and learn to work with others in pursuing common goals.
Founded: 1961
Specialized Field: Youth Orchestra
Budget: $35,000- $100,000
Performs At: Richard Auditorium, Princeton University
Seating Capacity: 868

1201
PRINCETON SYMPHONY ORCHESTRA
PO Box 250
Princeton, NJ 08542
Phone: 609-497-0020
Fax: 609-497-0904
e-mail: info@princetonsymphony.org
Web Site: www.princetonsymphony.org
Officers:
President: David Tierno
Vice President: Richard Levine
Management:
Music Director/Conductor: Rosen Milanov

Executive Director: Melanie Clarke
Mission: To present the finest classical compositions from the widest range, including unusual and seldom heard works; to enhance audience appreciation of the often unfamiliar works through lectures and presentations; to create an outstanding performance opportunity for the many excellent musicians in the New Jersey region; and to reach out to new audiences both geographically and demographically.
Founded: 1980
Specialized Field: Orchestra
Paid Artists: 55
Budget: $250,000-$1,050,000
Performs At: Richardson Auditorium
Seating Capacity: 850

1202
RIDGEWOOD SYMPHONY ORCHESTRA
PO Box 176
Ridgewood, NJ 07451-0176
Phone: 201-612-0118
Fax: 201-445-2762
Web Site: www.ridgewoodsymphony.org
Officers:
President: E Sosinsky
Treasurer: Richard A. Marri
Management:
General Manager: Karin A Todd
House Manager: Clermon Bachelor
Personnel Manager: Donna Dixon Olson
Personnel Manager: Louise Butler
Conductor/Music Director: Gary S Fagin
Secretary: Knarig Meyer
Founded: 1940
Specialized Field: Symphony; Orchestra
Paid Staff: 4
Volunteer Staff: 10
Non-paid Artists: 90
Budget: $90,000
Income Sources: Box Office; Grants; Private Donations; Fundraising
Performs At: Benjamin Franklin Middle School Auditorium
Annual Attendance: 3,700
Seating Capacity: 775

1203
SUMMIT SYMPHONY
100 Morris Avenue
Summit, NJ 07901
Phone: 908-277-2932
Fax: 908-277-2978
Management:
Music Director: James Sadewhite
Manager Orchestra Personnel: Barry Davidson
Mission: To offer orchestra music to Summit and surrounding communities and provide an opportunity for nonprofessionals to perform major works.
Founded: 1937
Specialized Field: Symphony
Status: Non-Professional; Nonprofit
Income Sources: Summit Board of Recreation; New Jersey Council on the Arts
Performs At: Summit Senior High School; Summit Middle School
Organization Type: Performing

1204
BERGEN PHILHARMONIC ORCHESTRA
PO Box 174
Teaneck, NJ 07666
Phone: 201-837-1980
Management:
Music Director: David Gilbert

Specialized Field: Orchestra

1205
GARDEN STATE PHILHARMONIC SYMPHONY ORCHESTRA
7 Hadley Avenue
Toms River, NJ 08753
Phone: 732-349-6277
Fax: 732-349-2401
e-mail: garden1idt.net
Web Site: www.islandhts.com/garden.htm
Management:
    Music Director/Conductor: Anthony LaGruth
Mission: Dedicated to maintaining a professional orchestra in Ocean County and surrounding NJ counties, that will give concerts of the highest cultural and educational value for the community and to providing both educational and training programs as well as fostering activities to encourage appreciation of music.
Utilizes: Multi Collaborations
Founded: 1956
Specialized Field: Symphony; Orchestra
Status: Professional; Nonprofit
Paid Staff: 30
Volunteer Staff: 2
Paid Artists: 70
Income Sources: Grants
Performs At: Toms River High School North; The Strand Theatre
Seating Capacity: 1200
Organization Type: Performing

1206
GREATER TRENTON SYMPHONY ORCHESTRA
28 W State Street
Suite 202
Trenton, NJ 08608
Phone: 609-394-1338
Fax: 609-394-1394
e-mail: info@trentonsymphony.org
Web Site: www.trentonsymphony.org
Management:
    Executive Director/Conductor: John Peter Holly
Mission: To offer residents of the greater Trenton area high-quality performances of classical music for orchestra.
Utilizes: Artists-in-Residence; Guest Writers; Local Artists; Multimedia; Original Music Scores
Founded: 1921
Specialized Field: Symphony; Orchestra
Status: Professional; Nonprofit
Performs At: War Memorial Theater
Organization Type: Performing; Educational

1207
MONMOUTH SYMPHONY ORCHESTRA
P O Box 1302
Wall, NJ 07719
Phone: 732-747-2063
Fax: 732-747-2063
e-mail: veep@monsym.org
Officers:
    Membership Chairperson: Karen Slobodin
Management:
    Conductor: Roy D Gussman
    President: Joan M Berzansky
Founded: 1948
Specialized Field: Orchestra
Performs At: Count Basie Theatre, Red Bank
Annual Attendance: 500
Seating Capacity: 1,700

1208
DISCOVERY ORCHESTRA
PO Box 4064
Warren, NJ 07059
Phone: 908-226-7300
Fax: 908-226-7337
e-mail: info@discoveryorchestra.org
Web Site: www.discoveryorchestra.org
Management:
    Artistic Director: George Marriner Maull
    Manager Director: Virgina Johnson
    Executive Director: Hewitt V Johnson
    Administrator: Diane Lester
Mission: In response to the cultural forces that regelate music to a background presence in people's lives, the mission of the Discovery Orchestra is to sensitize people to the difference between listening and hearing music through meaningful and compelling music educational experiences.
Founded: 1987
Specialized Field: Orchestra
Paid Staff: 95
Budget: $250,000- $1,050,000
Performs At: New Jersey Performing Arts Center
Seating Capacity: 2,800/785

1209
WILLIAM PATERSON UNIVERSITY PERFORMING ARTS
300 Pompton Road
Wayne, NJ 07470
Phone: 973-720-3178
Fax: 973-720-2408
e-mail: reedc7@wpunj.edu
Web Site: www.wpunj.edu/coac/UPA/htm
Management:
    Performing Arts Director: Christine L Reed
    Operations Director: Al Schaefer
Mission: To increase arts offerings and education within New Jersey's Tri-County area and present dynamic performances of great music, lectures and art.
Founded: 1986
Specialized Field: Orchestra
Status: Professional
Paid Staff: 10
Budget: over $100,000
Performs At: Shea Center for the Performing Arts
Seating Capacity: 960
Year Built: 1967
Rental Contact: Operations Director (973)720-2384 Al Schaefer
Organization Type: Performing

1210
ARBOR CHAMBER MUSIC SOCIETY
PO Box 2901
Westfield, NJ 07091
Phone: 908-232-1116
Fax: 908-232-2423
e-mail: arbormusic@comcast.net
Management:
    Director: Lenore Fishman Davis
Mission: To bring the highest artistic standards of chamber music performance to New Jersey's audiences, to educate audiences and to develop the next generation of listeners and musicians.
Founded: 1991
Specialized Field: Chamber
Status: Professional
Income Sources: Private Foundations; Business/Corporate Donations; Box Office; Individual Donations

Performs At: Union City Arts Center; St. Paul's Episcopal Church-Westfield
Organization Type: Performing; Touring; Educational

1211
NEW JERSEY WORKSHOP FOR THE ARTS
150-152 E Broad Street
Westfield, NJ 07090
Phone: 908-789-9696
Fax: 908-789-9101
e-mail: njwa2@aol.com
Web Site: www.njworkshopforthearts.com
Officers:
    Chairman: Josh Porter
    Founder/Executive Director: Dr Theodore K Schlosberg
    Vice Chairman: Walter Metzger
    Treasurer: Dennis Simon
    Secretary: Janet Elby
Management:
    NJWA Concert Band: Howard Toplansky
    Music Director Big Band: Jon Paterson
    Symphony Director: Janet Lyman
    International Alphorn Ensemble: Dr. Ted Schlosberg
Mission: Where talent develops and creativity thrives, to enrich lives by providing opportunities to develop creative talents and encourage a greater appreciation of the arts through both instruction and performance.
Founded: 1972
Specialized Field: Music; Dance; Arts; Crafts
Status: Nonprofit
Budget: $1,000,000
Income Sources: Tuition, Grants
Performs At: Recital Hall

1212
WESTFIELD SYMPHONY ORCHESTRA
224 E Broad Street
Suite 6
Westfield, NJ 07090
Phone: 908-232-9400
Fax: 908-232-2446
e-mail: wso@westfieldsymphony.org
Web Site: www.westfieldsymphony.org
Officers:
    President: Mark Fleder, Esq
    Treasurer: Alan Smith
    First VP: Norman Luka, MD
    Second VP: James T Dettre
Management:
    Executive Director: Elizabeth Ryan
    Music Director: David Wroe
Mission: Westfield Symphony Orchestra is one of New Jersey's premiere fully professional regional symphonies. It's mission is to promote the world's legacy of symphonic and operatic music to audiences involving them in the rich heritage through a diversity of professional musical experience, including performance education and mentoring.
Utilizes: Guest Musicians; Original Music Scores; Singers
Founded: 1983
Specialized Field: Symphony
Status: Professional; Nonprofit
Paid Staff: 5
Volunteer Staff: 5
Paid Artists: 106
Budget: $600,000
Income Sources: Government Grants; Box Office; Corporate Donations; Foundation Contributions; Individual Donations

Performs At: Union County Arts Center; The Presbyterian Church, Westfield; Westfield High School; Kean University; PNC Arts Center
Affiliations: American Symphony Orchestra League; Westfield Area Chamber of Commerce; Center for Nonprofits
Organization Type: Performing; Resident; Touring; Educational
Comments: For information concerning accessibility for special needs, call (908) 232-9400

New Mexico

1213
CHAMBER ORCHESTRA OF ALBUQUERQUE

PO Box 35081
Albuquerque, NM 87176-5081
Phone: 505-881-2078
Fax: 505-881-2634
e-mail: coaoch@aol.com
Web Site: coa.aosys.com
Management:
   Music Director/Conductor: David Oberg
   Operations Manager: Diane Bonnell
   Personnel Manager: Carol Swift-Matton
   Stage Manager: Karla Simmet
   Music Librarian: Oscar Mendelson
Mission: To provide a broad range of listening and participatory musical opportunities to the State of New Mexico; to maintain a professional orchestra whose work enriches the quality of community life.
Founded: 1976
Specialized Field: Orchestra; Chamber
Status: Professional; Nonprofit
Paid Staff: 3
Paid Artists: 1
Performs At: St. John's United Methodist Church
Organization Type: Performing

1214
NEW MEXICO SYMPHONY ORCHESTRA

4407 Menaul Boulevard North East
Suite 4
Albuquerque, NM 87107
Mailing Address: PO Box 30208, Albuquerque, NM. 87190-0208
Phone: 505-881-9590
Fax: 505-881-9456
e-mail: postmaster@nmso.org
Web Site: www.nmso.org/
Management:
   Principal Pops Conductor: Michael Krajewski
   Resident Conductor/Choral Director: Roger Melone
   Music Director: Guillermo Figueros
   Marketing/Public Relations: Colleen Harris-Kistner
   Development Director: Joan Allen
Mission: To present live concerts of music for small ensembles through full orchestra in both educational and concert settings.
Utilizes: Singers
Founded: 1932
Specialized Field: Symphony; Orchestra
Status: Professional; Nonprofit
Paid Staff: 22
Paid Artists: 80
Income Sources: American Symphony Orchestra League; American Arts Alliance
Performs At: Popejoy Hall; National Hispanic Cultural Center
Organization Type: Performing; Educational

1215
SOUTHWEST SYMPHONY

3307 N Grimes Street
PO Box 101
Hobbs, NM 88241
Phone: 505-738-1041
Fax: 505-392-5980
e-mail: swshobbs@hotmail.com
Management:
   Music Director: Dr. Mark Jelinek
Utilizes: Dancers; Guest Directors; Local Artists; Multimedia; Original Music Scores; Theatre Companies
Founded: 1983
Specialized Field: Orchestra
Paid Staff: 2
Volunteer Staff: 120
Budget: $100,000- $150,000
Income Sources: Fund Drives: Season Tickets, Grants, Donations
Performs At: Auditorium
Seating Capacity: 2,000

1216
LAS CRUCES SYMPHONY ORCHESTRA

PO Box 1622
Las Cruces, NM 88004
Phone: 505-646-3709
Fax: 505-646-1086
e-mail: info@lascrucessymphony.com
Officers:
   Educational Outreach: Kathleen Albers
   Board President: Carolyn M Stolberg
   Treasurer: Tom Tate
   Secretary: Nancy Carlson
   VP: Nita Swartz
Management:
   Music Director/Conductor: Dr. Lonnie Klein
   Executive Director: Cindy Robbins
Utilizes: Five Seasonal Concerts; Guest Accompanists; Guest Musicians; Guest Writers; Instructors; Multimedia; Original Music Scores; Singers; Soloists
Specialized Field: Orchestra
Paid Staff: 1
Volunteer Staff: 70
Paid Artists: 8
Non-paid Artists: 1
Budget: $100,000- $150,000
Income Sources: Box Office; Grants; Private Donations
Performs At: NMSU Performance Center
Affiliations: American Symphony Orchestra League
Annual Attendance: 8,000
Facility Category: Music Hall
Type of Stage: Thrust
Seating Capacity: 540
Year Built: 1985

1217
ROSWELL SYMPHONY ORCHESTRA

W Office Plaza
1717 W Second, Suite 205
Roswell, NM 88201
Phone: 505-623-5882
Fax: 505-623-5882
Toll-free: 800-300-9822
e-mail: rso@dfn.com
Web Site: www.roswellsymphony.org
Officers:
   President: Sam Pettit
Management:
   Director of Financial Operations: Melynda Roberson
   Director of Concert Operations: Rhonda Robinson
   Music Director: John Farrer
Mission: To provide Roswell and Southeast New Mexico with the best orchestral literature by providing an annual concert season, music education programs for children, and a multi cultural chamber concert series.
Utilizes: Guest Accompanists; Guest Musicians; Guest Writers; Multimedia; Music; Original Music Scores
Founded: 1960
Specialized Field: Symphony; Orchestra
Paid Staff: 2
Paid Artists: 84
Budget: $150,000- $260,000
Income Sources: Tickets; Grants; Gifts; Fund Raising
Performs At: Pearson Auditorium
Affiliations: American Symphony Orchestra League
Annual Attendance: 11,000
Facility Category: Auditoriums
Seating Capacity: 930

1218
MUSIC FROM ANGEL FIRE

130 Grant Avenue
#202
Santa Fe, NM 87501
Mailing Address: PO Box 502, Angel Fire, NM 87710
Phone: 575-377-3233
Fax: 505-820-2539
Toll-free: 888-377-3300
e-mail: info@musicfromangelfire.org
Web Site: www.musicfromangelfire.org
Management:
   General Director: Nancy Ondov
   Artistic Director: Ida Kavafian
   Associate Director: Lynne S Mazza
Mission: To bring world-class chamber music performed by international artists to the Northern New Mexico communities of Angel Fire, Taos, Raton and Las Vegas
Founded: 1984
Specialized Field: Chamber
Status: Professional; Nonprofit
Paid Staff: 2
Volunteer Staff: 40
Paid Artists: 40
Budget: $650,000
Affiliations: Chamber Music America; Classical Music Festivals Of The West; New Mexico Arts
Annual Attendance: 15,000
Facility Category: Concert Hall; Venues in Taos, Angel Fire, Raton, Las Vegas
Organization Type: Performing

1219
SANTA FE PRO MUSICA

1405 Luisa Street- Suite 2
PO Box 2091
Santa Fe, NM 87505
Phone: 505-988-4640
Fax: 505-984-2501
Toll-free: 800-960-6680
e-mail: info@santafepromusica.com
Web Site: www.santafepromusica.com
Officers:
   President: David Cost
Management:
   Executive Director: Linda Armer
   Artistic Director: Tom O'Connor
   Operations Manager: Toni Pittman
Mission: To provide the highest quality chamber music possible and make youth programs available to the public.

Utilizes: Guest Accompanists; Original Music Scores; Sign Language Translators
Founded: 1980
Specialized Field: Symphony; Orchestra; Chamber; Classical Music
Status: Professional; Nonprofit
Paid Staff: 5
Volunteer Staff: 35
Paid Artists: 80
Budget: $900,000
Performs At: Lensic Theatre
Annual Attendance: 14,000
Organization Type: Performing; Touring; Educational

1220
SANTA FE SYMPHONY
551 W Cordova Road, Suite D
PO Box 9692
Santa Fe, NM 87504
Phone: 505-983-3530
Fax: 505-982-3888
Toll-free: 800-480-1319
e-mail: symphony@rt66.com
Web Site: www.sf-symphony.org
Officers:
    President: Mick Ramsey
    VP: Gregory Heltman
    Secretary: Janet Zlatoff-Mirsky
    Treasurer: Michael Melody
Management:
    Founder/General Director: Gregory Heltman
    Operations Manager: Diane Stengle
    Music Director: Steven Smith
    Chorus Director: Linda Raney
Utilizes: Sign Language Translators
Founded: 1984
Specialized Field: Symphony; Orchestra; Chamber
Status: Professional; Nonprofit
Paid Staff: 5
Volunteer Staff: 40
Paid Artists: 100
Non-paid Artists: 80
Budget: $950,000
Income Sources: Ticket Sales; Grants; Contributions
Performs At: Lensic Performing Arts Center
Affiliations: American Symphony Orchestra League; Santa Fe Performing Arts Association
Annual Attendance: 11,000
Facility Category: Theatre
Type of Stage: Proscenium
Stage Dimensions: 40' x 50'
Seating Capacity: 791
Year Built: 1927
Year Remodeled: 2000
Organization Type: Performing; Resident; Educational; Sponsoring

New York

1221
ALBANY SYMPHONY ORCHESTRA
19 Clinton Avenue
Albany, NY 12207
Phone: 518-465-4755
Fax: 518-465-3711
e-mail: info@albanysymphony.com
Web Site: www.albanysymphony.com
Officers:
    Chairman: Alan P Goldberg
Management:
    Artistic Director: David Alan Miller

Mission: One of their major programs is Key's American Music Festival featuring new American Composers. The Albany Symphony Orchestra is committed to the live presentation and recording of top quality musical programming, with an emphasis on the creation and promotion of contemporary or overlooked American works and its dissemination to a broad-based regional audience from all cultural and economic backgrounds.
Utilizes: Artists-in-Residence; Commissioned Composers; Commissioned Music; Composers-in-Residence; Guest Accompanists; Guest Companies; Guest Musical Directors; Guest Musicians; Multi Collaborations; Multimedia; Organization Contracts; Original Music Scores; Sign Language Translators; Singers; Soloists
Founded: 1931
Specialized Field: Symphony; Ensemble
Status: Professional; Nonprofit
Paid Staff: 6
Volunteer Staff: 250
Paid Artists: 68
Budget: $1.4 million
Income Sources: American Symphony Orchestra League
Season: September-May
Performs At: Albany's Palace Theatre, Troy Savings Bank Music Hall, Canfield Casino, Saratoga Springs, NY
Annual Attendance: 18,000
Seating Capacity: 2,800; 1,200
Organization Type: Performing

1222
CAPITOL CHAMBER ARTISTS
263 Manning Boulevard
Albany, NY 12206
Phone: 518-458-9231
Fax: 518-458-9231
e-mail: info@capitolchamberartists.com
Web Site: www.capitolchamberartists.com
Management:
    Co-Founder/Director/Violinist: Mary Lou Saetta
    Co-Founder/Flutist: Irvin E Gilman
    Cellist: Helene Annas
    Pianist: Aniko Szokody
Mission: Performing the highest quality chamber music and educating a new audience.
Founded: 1969
Specialized Field: Chamber
Status: Professional; Nonprofit
Season: October-June
Performs At: First Congregational Church, Albany; Community Hall, Benson VT
Annual Attendance: 15,000
Organization Type: Performing; Touring; Resident; Educational

1223
GOLIARD CHAMBER SOLOISTS
Goliard Concerts
21-65 41st Street
Astoria, NY 11105
Phone: 718-728-8927
Fax: 718-728-8927
e-mail: info@goliardconcerts.com
Web Site: http://www.goliardconcerts.com
Officers:
    Executive Director: James Blanton
Management:
    Artistic Director: Arielle Levioff
    Development Associate: Gregg Lauterbach
Mission: Performing eclectic chamber music in various vocal and instrumental combinations.

Founded: 1983
Specialized Field: Chamber; Soloists
Status: Professional; Nonprofit
Paid Staff: 3
Volunteer Staff: 1
Paid Artists: 40
Performs At: Merkin Concert Hall at the Abrahman Goodman House
Organization Type: Performing; Touring; Presenting

1224
AUBURN CHAMBER ORCHESTRA
Willard Memorial Chapel 17 Nelson Street
PO Box 985
Auburn, NY 13021-0339
Phone: 315-252-0065
e-mail: info@willardchapel.org
Officers:
    President: Karen Deming
    Treasurer: Marion Fritz
Management:
    Conductor/Music Director: Ubaldo Valli
Founded: 1997
Specialized Field: Chamber
Budget: $4,000
Performs At: Willard Chapel
Seating Capacity: 300

1225
ONONDAGA CIVIC SYMPHONY ORCHESTRA
Ed Brennan
3667 Woodland Drive
Baldwinsville NY
Baldwinsville, NY 13027
Phone: 315-622-3933
e-mail: tmecox@yahoo.coM
Officers:
    President: Ryan Coburn
    Vice President: Charles Moore
Management:
    Music Director: Erik Kibelsbeck
    Personnel Manager: Tom Cox
Specialized Field: Orchestra

1226
GENESEE SYMPHONY ORCHESTRA
PO Box 391
Batavia, NY 14021
Phone: 845-343-9313
Toll-free: 800-774-7372
e-mail: gso@geneseesymphony.com
Officers:
    Co-President: Dave Funston
    Co-President: Marjorie Fulmer
    Vice President: Ann Reid
    Secretary: Marcia Gann
    Treasurer: Henry Emmans
Management:
    Conductor/Music Director: Raffaele Ponti
    Orchestra Manager: Jeanette Partis
Specialized Field: Orchestra
Season: October-April
Performs At: Stuart Steiner Theater, Genesee Community College

1227
BINGHAMTON PHILHARMONIC ORCHESTRA
31 Front Street
Binghamton, NY 13905

Phone: 607-722-6717
Fax: 607-722-6526
e-mail: info@binghamtonphilharmonic.org
Web Site: www.binghamtonphilharmonic.org
Officers:
President: Corinne Farrell
Vice President: Geralyn Yousuf
Treasurer: Susan Burtis
Secretary: Jane Cotnoir
Management:
Executive Director: Stephan Raube-Wilson
Music Director: Jose-Luis Novo
Marketing Director: Cynthia K Kelly
Stage Manager: Judith Mica
Development Director: Sandra J Griffiths
Accounts/Office Manager: June M Christensen
Mission: Presentation of classical and pops concerts.
Utilizes: Commissioned Composers; Commissioned Music; Guest Accompanists; Guest Directors; Guest Musical Directors; Guest Musicians; Multimedia; Music; Organization Contracts; Original Music Scores
Founded: 1996
Specialized Field: Orchestra; Pops
Status: Professional; Nonprofit
Paid Staff: 6
Paid Artists: 76
Budget: $260,000-1,050,000
Income Sources: Ticket sales, Grants, Donations
Season: October-April
Performs At: Forum Theatre; Anderson Center for Performing Arts at Binghamton University
Annual Attendance: 17,000
Seating Capacity: 1,188; 1,590
Organization Type: Performing

1228
BRONX ARTS ENSEMBLE
Golf House
100 Van Cortlandt Park
Bronx, NY 10471
Phone: 718-601-7399
Fax: 718-549-4008
e-mail: baeconcert@aol.com
Web Site: www.bronxartsensemble.org
Officers:
Chairperson: Gail McMillan
Counsel: Lorance Hockert
Secretary: John W Freeman
Treasurer: Karen Wasserman
Management:
Executive/Artistic Director: William Scribner
Assistant Director/Office Manager: Louise Scribner
Development Consultant: Constantine G Vasiliadis
Education Coordinator: Carmen Bu
Mission: Offering chamber music programs and chamber orchestras at a variety of locations in the Bronx at affordable prices.
Utilizes: Guest Musical Directors; Guest Musicians; Multimedia; Original Music Scores; Singers
Founded: 1972
Specialized Field: Symphony; Chamber
Status: Professional; Nonprofit
Paid Staff: 5
Volunteer Staff: 10
Budget: $260,000-1,050,000
Income Sources: Various
Season: Year-round
Performs At: Fordham University
Organization Type: Performing; Resident; Educational
Resident Groups: Fordham University

1229
BARGEMUSIC
Fulton Ferry Landing
Brooklyn, NY 11201
Phone: 718-624-2083
Fax: 718-624-1155
e-mail: info@bargemusic.org
Web Site: www.bargemusic.org
Officers:
President: Olga Bloom
Management:
Executive Director: Pat Scala
Business Manager: Angela Nahagian
Mission: Presenting year-round chamber music concerts on a permanently moored barge in New York Harbor.
Founded: 1977
Specialized Field: Chamber
Status: Nonprofit
Budget: $1.5 million
Income Sources: Ticket Sales; Individual; Foundations; Contributions
Seating Capacity: 125
Organization Type: Performing

1230
BROOKLYN FRIENDS OF CHAMBER MUSIC
140 Bond Street
Brooklyn, NY 11217-2242
Phone: 718-855-3053
Fax: 212-308-2442
e-mail: wflecknaf@aol.com
Web Site: www.brooklynfriendsofchambermusic.com
Management:
Manager: Wanda Fleck
Mission: Six chamber music concerts, commissioning of new work.
Founded: 1988
Specialized Field: Chamber
Volunteer Staff: 10
Paid Artists: 50
Season: September-April
Performs At: Lafayette Avenue Presbyterian Church at 85 S Oxford Street

1231
BROOKLYN PHILHARMONIC ORCHESTRA
55 Washington Street
Suite 656
Brooklyn, NY 11201
Phone: 718-488-5700
Fax: 718-488-5901
e-mail: info@brooklynphilharmonic.org
Web Site: www.brooklynphilharmonic.org
Management:
Operations Director: Sarah Stephens
Executive Director: Greg Pierson
Mission: To be a nationally recognized symphony orchestra, introducing the best new music of our time while shining light on the great repertoire of the past. The Brooklyn Philharmonic is committed to education and serving the needs of diverse communitites of New York's most popular borough.
Founded: 1954
Specialized Field: Symphony; Orchestra; Chamber; Ensemble; Ethnic Music
Status: Professional; Nonprofit
Paid Staff: 5
Paid Artists: 80
Budget: $1.5 Million
Annual Attendance: 24,000

Organization Type: Performing; Educational

1232
BROOKLYN SYMPHONY ORCHESTRA
PO Box 020-334
Brooklyn, NY 11202-0334
Phone: 718-852-0677
Fax: 718-951-5412
e-mail: info@brooklynsymphonyorchestra.org
Web Site: www.brooklynsymphonyorchestra.org
Officers:
President: Jaye Zuckerman
Management:
Music/Artistic Director: Nicholas Armstrong
Concert Mistress: Judy Spokes
Founded: 1973
Specialized Field: Orchestra; Chamber
Status: Professional; Semi-Professional
Budget: $35,000
Season: September-April
Performs At: Saint Ann's Church in Brooklyn Heightst; Park Slope
Seating Capacity: 500

1233
SEM ENSEMBLE
25 Columbia Place
Brooklyn, NY 11201
Phone: 718-488-7659
Fax: 718-243-0964
e-mail: info@semEnsemble.org
Web Site: www.semensemble.org
Officers:
President: Jerald Ordover
Secretary: Paula Cooper
Management:
Artistic director: Peter Kotik
Managing Director: Martina Perry
Mission: To offer performances of and education in new music.
Founded: 1970
Specialized Field: Orchestra; Chamber
Status: Professional
Performs At: Willow Place Auditorium
Organization Type: Performing; Touring; Resident; Educational

1234
ARS NOVA MUSICIANS CHAMBER ORCHESTRA
6820 E Quaker Road
Buffalo, NY 14127
Phone: 716-896-2515
e-mail: arsnovamusicians@aol.com
Management:
Music Director/Conductor: Marylouise Nanna
Manager Director: Susan Willet
Founded: 1974
Specialized Field: Chamber; Orchestra
Budget: $35,000- $100,000
Performs At: various locations

1235
BUFFALO CHAMBER MUSIC SOCIETY
PO Box 349
Buffalo, NY 14216
Mailing Address: PO Box 349, Buffalo, NY 14207
Phone: 716-462-4939
e-mail: bcms@bflochambermusic.org
Web Site: www.bflochambermusic.org
Management:
Executive Director: Clementina Fleshler, bcms@bflochambermusic.org

Mission: Present world renowned chamber ensembles in Western New York.
Utilizes: Guest Directors; Guest Ensembles
Founded: 1924
Specialized Field: Chamber
Budget: $60,000-150,000
Income Sources: Subscriptions
Performs At: Kleinhans Music Hall
Annual Attendance: 7,000
Seating Capacity: 700

1236
BUFFALO PHILHARMONIC ORCHESTRA
499 Franklin Street
Buffalo, NY 14202
Phone: 716-885-0331
Fax: 716-885-9372
e-mail: dianam@bpo.org
Officers:
 Music Director: JoAnn Falletta
Management:
 Executive Director: Daniel Hart
 Director Finance & Administration: Patrick McInerney
 Director Learning Resources: Carol Timmerman-Yorty
 Box Office Manager: Kevin Hahn
 Dir. Orchestra & Artistic Operation: Lisa J. Gallo
 Development Assistant: Megan Dean
Mission: Perhaps the Orchestra's greatest accomplishment is its contribution to the artistic life of Western New York, made possible by more than six decades of support from its dedicated patrons. The Orchestra has performed over a thousand Youth Concerts for more than two million students as well as many concerts at campuses across the United States.
Specialized Field: Orchestra

1237
PUTNAM SYMPHONY ORCHESTRA
P O Box 534
Carmel, NY 10512
Phone: 914-299-6646
Fax: 845-228-4415
e-mail: putnamsymphonyorchestra@yahoo.com
Web Site: www.putnamsymphony.homestead.com
Management:
 Conductor: Christine Smith
 Secretary: Kimberly Riesdorph
 Assistant To The Conductor: Kyle Kayler
Mission: To expand opportunities for cultural entertainment within the community and to provide an opportunity to perform for community musicians.
Founded: 1976
Specialized Field: Music; Entertainment
Volunteer Staff: 12
Non-paid Artists: 100

1238
CHAUTAUQUA SYMPHONY ORCHESTRA
Chautauqua Institution
PO Box 28
Chautauqua, NY 14722
Phone: 716-357-6217
Fax: 716-357-9014
Toll-free: 800-836-2787
e-mail: cso@ciweb.org
Web Site: www.symphony.ciweb.org
Management:
 VP/Program Director: Marty Merkley
 Business/Personnel Manager: Jason Weintraub
Mission: To provide orchestral music to summer residents and attendees of Chautauqua Institution
Founded: 1929

Specialized Field: Summer Festival Orchestra
Status: Professional; Nonprofit
Budget: $1.7 Million
Income Sources: Chautauqua Institution
Season: July-August
Affiliations: Chautauqua Institution
Annual Attendance: 100,000
Facility Category: Outdoor Roofed Ampitheater
Type of Stage: Thrust
Stage Dimensions: 50' x 40'
Seating Capacity: 5,000
Year Built: 1893
Year Remodeled: 1984
Organization Type: Performing; Resident; Educational

1239
MAMADOU DIABATE
On Queue Performing Artists
PO Box 145
Cooperstown, NY 13439
Phone: 607-547-9494
Fax: 607-547-9494
e-mail: concerts@OnQueueArtists.com
Web Site: http://www.onqueueartists.com/diabate
Management:
 Founder/Agent: Sandra Bernegger
Mission: To perform music from Mali, touring with balafon, ngoni, guitar, players and singer, Abdoulaye Diabate.
Founded: 1997
Specialized Field: World Music; Ethnic Music
Paid Staff: 4

1240
MATAPAT
PO Box 145
Cooperstown, NY 13326
Phone: 607-547-9494
Fax: 607-547-9494
e-mail: info@matapat.com
Web Site: www.onqueuartists.com
Management:
 Founder/Agent: Sandra Bernegger
 Administrative Assistant: Linda Van Slyke
 Administrative Assistant: Frances Breslin
Mission: To perform the traditional music, song and dance of Quebec with contempoary and world music influences.
Founded: 1997
Specialized Field: Ethnic Music
Paid Staff: 3
Paid Artists: 3

1241
QUINTET OF THE AMERICAS
15 Circle Road
Douglaston, NY 11363
Phone: 718-230-5189
Fax: 718-398-2737
e-mail: quintet@rcn.com
Web Site: www.quintet.org
Officers:
 Chair: Kenneth Thomas, Esq
Management:
 Director: Barbara Oldham
Mission: The presentation of chamber music and contemporary music, with an emphasis on North and South America.
Founded: 1976
Specialized Field: Chamber; Ethnic Music
Status: Professional; Nonprofit
Paid Staff: 3
Paid Artists: 5
Performs At: Center for Inter-American Relations

Organization Type: Performing; Touring; Resident; Educational

1242
ISLIP ARTS COUNCIL CHAMBER MUSIC SERIES
50 Irish Lane
East Islip, NY 11730
Phone: 631-224-5420
Fax: 631-224-5440
e-mail: iacouncil@aol.com
Web Site: www.islipartscouncil.org/chamber.html
Officers:
 President: Helene Katz
 VP: Nicholas Wartella
 Secretary: Jean Lipshie
 Treasurer: Edward E. Wankel
Management:
 Executive Director: Lillian Barbash
 Co-Director: Jodi Gianni
 Artist Administrator: Dorothy Kalson
 Clerk Typist: Angela Wallace
Mission: To present a variety of disciplines ranging from fine classical music to young persons' programs to avant garde performance art; to enable and emerging art organizations to gain information and assistance from the Arts Council library and staff in applying for not-for-profit status, funding, computer services, publicity, mailing lists, etc.
Utilizes: Singers
Founded: 1974
Specialized Field: Chamber; Ensemble
Status: Professional; Nonprofit
Budget: $250,000
Income Sources: Town of Islip; Suffolk County
Performs At: David Jones Concert Hall; Sayville Schools; Dowling College
Type of Stage: Semi-Thurst
Seating Capacity: 400
Organization Type: Performing

1243
FOREST HILLS SYMPHONY ORCHESTRA OF QUEENS
107-23 71 Road
Suite 240
Forest Hills, NY 11375
Phone: 718-374-1627
e-mail: Fhso44@aol.com
Management:
 Music Director: Franklin Verbsky, fhso44@aol.com
 Manaer: Marilyn Verbsky, fhs044@aol.com
Mission: The mission is to provide the local community with an orchestra to perform with and an audience to attend inexpensively without traveling to Manhattan
Founded: 1964
Specialized Field: Orchestra
Budget: $16,000
Income Sources: Donations
Performs At: Forest Hills Jewish Center
Annual Attendance: 900
Seating Capacity: 300

1244
WESTERN NEW YORK CHAMBER ORCHESTRA
Mason Hall
State University College
Fredonia, NY 14063
Phone: 716-673-3463
Fax: 716-673-3154
Web Site: www.fredonia.edu/rac/wnyco.html
Officers:

President: James Merrins
VP: Lydia Evans
Secretary: Ruth Mohoney
Treasurer: John Wrigley
Management:
    Executive Director: James East
    Artistic Director: Joel Revzen
    Business/Orchestra Manager: Signe Rominger
Mission: To present concerts throughout Western New York, Pennsylvania and on tour; to sponsor a chamber orchestra and chamber music series; to sponsor an ensemble-in-residence at the State University of New York, Fredonia School of Music.
Founded: 1981
Specialized Field: Orchestra; Chamber
Status: Professional; Nonprofit
Paid Staff: 3
Volunteer Staff: 1
Paid Artists: 55
Income Sources: Arts Council for Chautauqua County; Fund for the Arts in Chautauqua County
Performs At: King Concert Hall at State University of New York
Organization Type: Performing; Touring; Resident; Educational; Sponsoring

1245
FRIENDS OF MUSIC ORCHESTRA

Brodie Fine Arts Building
State University of New York - Geneseo
Geneseo, NY 14454
Phone: 716-243-2958
Fax: 716-245-5826
Management:
    Music Director: James Walker
Mission: To provide to the Geneseo Valley region a wide range of repertoire on a professional level, with emphasis on new music for chamber orchestra.
Founded: 1970
Specialized Field: Orchestra
Status: Professional; Profit
Volunteer Staff: 12
Paid Artists: 38
Non-paid Artists: 1
Performs At: Saint Michael's Church
Organization Type: Performing; Educational; Sponsoring

1246
GENESEO CHAMBER SYMPHONY

Brodie Fine Arts Building
State University of New York-Geneseo
Geneseo, NY 14454
Phone: 716-245-5824
Fax: 716-245-5826
e-mail: jwalker@geneseo.edu
Management:
    Music Director: James Walker
Mission: Committed to providing younger performers an opportunity to interact with respected, established artists in performance as well as educational environments.
Founded: 1970
Specialized Field: Chamber
Status: Semi-Professional; Nonprofit
Paid Staff: 39
Performs At: Wadsworth Auditorium
Organization Type: Performing; Educational; Sponsoring

1247
TREMONT STRING QUARTET

PO Box 396
Geneseo, NY 14454

Phone: 716-243-4429
Fax: 716-245-5005
Management:
    Artistic Director: Richard Balkin
    Executive Director: James Kirkwood
Mission: Performing the best contemporary and standard chamber music repertory in venues throughout the world.
Specialized Field: Chamber; String Ensemble
Status: Professional; Nonprofit
Organization Type: Performing; Touring; Resident; Educational; Sponsoring

1248
QUEENS SYMPHONY ORCHESTRA

70-31 84th Street
Building 38
Glendale, NY 11385
Phone: 718-326-4455
Fax: 718-326-4499
e-mail: qso@queenssymphony.org
Web Site: www.queenssymphony.org
Officers:
    President: Herb Chain
    Executive VP: Elsi Levy
    Secretary: Joseph Murphy
Management:
    Executive Director: Lynda Herndon
    Music Director: Constantine Kitsopoulos
    Marketing & Communications Manager: Kate Oberjat
Mission: To provide world-class music and education to the international community of Queens.
Founded: 1953
Specialized Field: Orchestral Music
Status: Professional; Nonprofit
Paid Staff: 5
Volunteer Staff: 45
Paid Artists: 65
Budget: $600,000
Income Sources: Government, Foundations, Corporate, Individuals
Performs At: Varies/Concert Halls
Facility Category: Queensborough Community College Performing Arts Center
Seating Capacity: 875
Organization Type: Performing

1249
GLENS FALLS SYMPHONY ORCHESTRA

7 Lapham Place
PO Box 2036
Glens Falls, NY 12801-2036
Phone: 518-793-1348
Fax: 518- 79—912
e-mail: Info@GlensFallsSymphony.org
Officers:
    President: Samuel Friedman
    First Vice President: K Bryan Kirk
Management:
    Music Director/Conductor: Charles Peltz
    Executive Director: Robert B Rosoff
Specialized Field: Orchestra

1250
GREAT NECK PHILHARMONIC

38 Hicks Lane
Great Neck, NY 11024
Phone: 516-482-4225
Management:
    Music Director: Mark Russell Amsterdam
    Executive Director: Susan Amsterdam
Specialized Field: Orchestra

1251
FOUNDATION FOR BAROQUE MUSIC

165 Wilton Road
Greenfield Center, NY 12833-1704
Phone: 518-893-7527
Fax: 518-893-2351
e-mail: impresario48@yahoo.com
Web Site: www.baroquefestival.org
Officers:
    President: Robert Conant
    VP: Nancy Conant
    Secretary/Treasurer: James P Ketterer
Management:
    Co-Artistic Director: Robert Conant
    Co-Artistic Director: Kenneth Slowik
    Artistic Advisor: Judson Griffin
Mission: Promoting 17th and 18th century music by performing with historically accurate techniques on period instruments.
Utilizes: Commissioned Music; Educators; Guest Accompanists; Guest Artists; Guest Composers; Guest Ensembles; Guest Musical Directors; Guest Musicians; Instructors; Multimedia; Original Music Scores; Sign Language Translators; Singers
Founded: 1959
Specialized Field: Baroque; Ensemble
Status: Professional; Nonprofit
Paid Staff: 1
Volunteer Staff: 2
Paid Artists: 28
Budget: $32,000
Income Sources: New York State Council on Arts; Private & Business Donations
Performs At: Baroque Festival Studio; Saratoga Springs City Center
Affiliations: ALA; SCAC; Early Music America; Chamber Music America; Greater Saratoga Chamber of Commerce
Annual Attendance: 800
Facility Category: Chamber music hall - all wood
Stage Dimensions: 25'x40'
Seating Capacity: 110
Year Built: 1973
Year Remodeled: 1996
Rental Contact: President Robert Conant
Organization Type: Performing; Resident; Educational

1252
WESTCHESTER PHILHARMONIC

123 Main Street
Lobby Level
Hartsdale, NY 10601
Phone: 914-682-3707
Fax: 914-682-3716
e-mail: info@Westchesterphil.org
Web Site: www.westchesterphil.org
Officers:
    Artistic Director: Itzhak Perlman
    President, Board of Directors: Neil D Aaron
Management:
    Executive Director: Joshua Worby
Mission: The New Orchestra of Westchester is committed to bringing the highest quality music to the Westchester area with a goal of featuring music by living American composers as part of annual programming.
Utilizes: Artists-in-Residence; Commissioned Composers; Commissioned Music; Guest Musicians; Guest Soloists; Multimedia; New Productions; Original Music Scores; Playwrights; Singers
Founded: 1983
Specialized Field: Classical Music
Status: Professional; Nonprofit

Paid Staff: 3
Volunteer Staff: 25
Paid Artists: 100
Budget: $1,450,000
Income Sources: Westchester Council for Arts; New York State Coucil on Arts; National Endowment for the Arts
Performs At: Performing Arts Center; State University of New York
Annual Attendance: 27,650
Organization Type: Performing; Educational

1253
CAYUGA CHAMBER ORCHESTRA

116 N Cayuga Street
Ford Hall, Ithaca College
Ithaca, NY 14850
Phone: 607-273-8981
Fax: 607-273-4816
e-mail: cco.orch@verizon.net
Officers:
President: Jim Johnston
Vice President: Craig Evans
Management:
Music Director: Kimbo Ishii-Eto
General Manager: Danielle Farnbaugh
Specialized Field: Orchestra; Chamber

1254
NEW DIRECTIONS CELLO FESTIVAL

501 Linn Street
Ithaca, NY 14850
Phone: 607-277-1686
Fax: 607-277-1686
Toll-free: 877-665-5815
e-mail: info@newdirectionscello.com
Web Site: www.newdirectionscello.com
Management:
Director: Chris White
Education Director: Sera Surslen
Mission: To bring together cellists and others interested in nonclassical uses of cello (jazz, blues, folk, rock, etc.). Workshops, jams, concerts.
Utilizes: Artists-in-Residence; Collaborations; Guest Accompanists; Guest Directors; Guest Musical Directors; Guest Musicians; Multimedia; Organization Contracts; Original Music Scores; Soloists
Founded: 1995
Specialized Field: Cello Ensemble
Paid Staff: 2
Volunteer Staff: 10
Paid Artists: 12
Budget: Under $10,000
Income Sources: Sponsors, Participants, Donations
Season: July 11 - 13, 1999
Performs At: University of Connecticut, Storrs [Festival Site]
Annual Attendance: 100
Facility Category: Mehden Auditorium/Recital Hall
Stage Dimensions: 50x25
Seating Capacity: 500
Year Built: 1985
Cost: $150 - 3 day

1255
JAMESTOWN CONCERT ASSOCIATION

315 N Main Street
Suite 200
Jamestown, NY 14701-5124
Phone: 716-487-1522
Fax: 716- 48—152
e-mail: icamusic@excite.com
Officers:
President: Corbin

VP: Sally Ulrich
Treasurer: F John Fuchs
Secretary: Mary Weeden
Management:
Programming: Sally Ulrich
Mission: Purpose of presenting live classical performances in the Jamestown area.
Founded: 1934
Specialized Field: Orchestra; Band; Ensemble
Volunteer Staff: 16
Income Sources: Arts Association Chautauqua County
Performs At: Civic Center
Organization Type: Educational; Sponsoring

1256
LAKE GEORGE JAZZ WEEKEND

Lake George Arts Project
1 Amherst Street
Lake George, NY 12845
Phone: 518-668-2616
Fax: 518-668-3050
e-mail: mail@lakegeorgearts.org
Web Site:
www.lakegeorgearts.org/lakegeorge-jazz.htm
Officers:
President: Ed Ostberg
Management:
Executive Director: John Strong
Music Director: Paul Pines
Mission: Sponsoring a two-day jazz festival every September featuring nationally acclaimed as well as emerging jazz artists.
Founded: 1984
Specialized Field: Ensemble; Jazz
Status: Professional; Nonprofit
Income Sources: Grants; Donations; Patrons
Performs At: Shepard Park Bandstand
Organization Type: Performing; Touring

1257
BEETHOVEN FESTIVAL

Friends of the Arts
Locust Valley, NY 11560-0702
Mailing Address: PO Box 702
Phone: 516-922-0061
Fax: 516-922-0770
e-mail: info@fotapresents.org
Web Site: www.FOTApresents.org
Officers:
President: Gary Andersen
Vice President: Mitchell Rechler
Treasurer: George M Simeone
Management:
Executive Director: Maryann K Beaumont
Director Marketing/Development: Debbie Honorof
Director Arts Education: Lois Kipris
Director Audience Services: Elisabeth Sinniger
Finance Manager: Mariann Fresiello
Conductor: Richard Owen Jr
Mission: Presenting Beethoven's lifetime body of work during one spectacular weekend.
Founded: 1981
Specialized Field: Ensemble; Classical Music
Status: Professional; Nonprofit
Income Sources: Sponsors
Performs At: Planting Fields Arboretum
Organization Type: Performing

1258
LONG ISLAND BAROQUE ENSEMBLE

PO Box 7
Locust Valley, NY 11560-0007

Phone: 631-724-7386
Fax: 631-864-4426
e-mail: gribzi@optonline.net
Web Site: www.longislandbaroqueensemble.com
Officers:
President: Vipin Barathan
Treasurer: Alfred Zoller
Secretary: Bernice Kudysch
VP: Alice Ross
Management:
Artistic Director: Sonia Gezairlian Grib
Administator: Patricia Berman
Mission: Performing early music on period instruments in conjunction with vocal specialists.
Founded: 1970
Specialized Field: Chamber; Ensemble; Baroque
Status: Professional; Nonprofit
Paid Staff: 2
Volunteer Staff: 10
Budget: $40,000
Income Sources: Government; Counties; Private; Ticket Sales
Season: October-April
Performs At: St. Andrews Lutheran Church, Smithtown; Christ Church, Oyster Bay
Annual Attendance: 2,000
Organization Type: Performing; Touring; Educational

1259
LONG ISLAND PHILHARMONIC

One Huntington Quadrangle
Suite 2C21
Melville, NY 11747-4401
Phone: 631-293-2223
Fax: 631-293-2655
e-mail: liphil@liphilharmonic.org
Web Site: www.liphilharmonic.com
Officers:
Chairman: Larry Austin
President: John T Russell
First Vice President: Robert F Kearns
Second Vice President: Jane Shalam
Treasurer: Joesph F Purcell
Management:
Executive Director: Neil Birnbaum
Music Director: David Wiley
Orchestra/Production Manager: Matthew E Flood
Concertmaster: Erica Kiesewetter
Personnel Manager: Jonathan Taylor
General Manager: Linda Morrisey
Director Education: Joanne Spencer
Utilizes: Sign Language Translators; Singers; Soloists; Special Technical Talent; Touring Companies
Founded: 1979
Specialized Field: Symphony; Orchestra; Chamber
Status: Professional
Budget: $1.7 million
Income Sources: Ticket Sales; Fundraisers; Private Contributions; Grants
Performs At: Tilles Center; Staller Center
Organization Type: Performing; Resident; Educational

1260
NOMADICS

PO Box 1073
Millbrook, NY 12545
Phone: 845-677-3319
Fax: 845-677-3319
e-mail: flautist107@yahoo.com
Web Site: www.thenomadics.com
Officers:
Public Relations: Lynnette Benner

Mission: To expose people, children in particular, to ethnic music from countries other than our own. We perform Ethnic Folk Music, discuss its history, performance practices and traditional instruments. Some of the countries we touch on are Sweden, Austria, The British Isles, Turkey, Argentina and many others. Our concerts are interactive and informative.
Founded: 2001
Specialized Field: World Music; Folk Music; Celtic; Classical Music; Colonial
Paid Staff: 2
Paid Artists: 2
Performs At: Various Venues
Affiliations: American Federation of Musicians

1261
DEL-SE-NANGO OLDE TYME FIDDLERS ASSOCIATION
RD #3
PO Box 233
New Berlin, NY 13411
Phone: 607-843-6745
Mission: Dedicated to the preservation, promotion and perpetuation of the art of olde tyme fiddling, its music and dances.
Founded: 1978
Specialized Field: Folk Music
Status: Nonprofit
Paid Staff: 40
Organization Type: Performing; Educational; Sponsoring

1262
TANNERY POND CONCERTS
PO Box 446
New Lebanon, NY 12125
Fax: 413-442-7813
Toll-free: 800-820-1696
Officers:
 President: Brenda Archer Adams
 VP: Lois E Dickson
 Treasurer: Brian Baker
 Secretary: Cindy Puccio
 President Emeritus: Christina Wirth
Management:
 Artistic Director: Christian Steiner
 Administrative Director: Linda McGinley Papas
Specialized Field: Chamber; Ensemble; Classical Music
Performs At: Tannery Pond
Seating Capacity: 300

1263
AEOLIAN CHAMBER PLAYERS
173 Riverside Drive
New York, NY 10024
Phone: 212-595-4688
Fax: 212-595-8431
e-mail: Lewiskap@aol.com
Web Site: www.lewiskaplan.net
Management:
 Director: Lewis Kaplan
Mission: Committed to performing a broad repertoire of music from the classical to the contemporary.
Founded: 1961
Specialized Field: Chamber
Status: Professional
Income Sources: National Endowment for the Arts; New York State Council on Arts; Bowdoin Summer Music Festival
Organization Type: Performing; Touring; Resident

1264
AMERICAN COMPOSERS ORCHESTRA
240 W 35th Street
Suite 405
New York, NY 10001-2506
Phone: 212-977-8495
Fax: 212-977-8995
e-mail: acoinfo@americancomposers.org
Web Site: www.americancomposers.org
Officers:
 President: Francis Thorne
 Executive VP/Executive Director: Michael Geller
 Treasurer: Bernadette Murphy
 Treasurer: Bernadette Murphy
 Secretary: Robert D. Taisey
Management:
 Executive Director: Michael Geller, michael@americancomposers.org
 Operations Manager: John Glover, john@americancomposers.org
 Operations Assistant: Jenny Kampmeier, jenny@americancomposers.org
 Artistic Director: Robert Beaser
Mission: The ACO's purpose is to discover, produce and present the widest possible spectrum of American repertoire, past and present, in performances of the highest quality, thereby focusing national awareness and support of American composers and their music.
Utilizes: Collaborations; Commissioned Composers; Commissioned Music; Educators; Guest Accompanists; Guest Choreographers; Guest Companies; Guest Directors; Guest Instructors; Guest Lecturers; Guest Musical Directors; Guest Musicians; Guild Activities; Instructors; Multi Collaborations; Multimedia; Organization Contracts; Original Music Scores; Singers
Founded: 1977
Specialized Field: Symphony; Orchestra
Status: Professional; Nonprofit
Paid Staff: 7
Paid Artists: 84
Budget: $1,900,000
Income Sources: American Symphony Orchestra League
Season: November-May
Performs At: Carnegie Hall
Annual Attendance: 20,000
Organization Type: Performing

1265
AMERICAN SYMPHONY ORCHESTRA
333 West 39th Street
Suite 1101
New York, NY 10018
Phone: 212-868-9276
Fax: 212-868-9277
e-mail: dconroy@americansymphong.org
Web Site: www.americansymphony.org
Officers:
 Chair: Jan Krukowski
 Vice-Chair: Eileen Rhulen
 Treasurer: Dimitri Papadimitriou
 Secretary: Mary Miller
 General Manager: Dennis Conroy
Management:
 Executive Director: Lynne Meloccaro
 Music Director: Leon Botstein
 Composer in Residence: Richard Wilson
 Assistant Executive Director: Andrew Elsesser
 Assistant Conductor: Teresa Cheung
 Director Operations: Alex Johnston
 Orchestra Librarian: Jack Parton
 Associate Director Marketing: Chris Schimpf
 Personnel Manager: Ronald Sell

Mission: American Symphony Orchestra is the only self-governing orchestra in the United States with a subscription series at Carnegie Hall. It is also a resource organization providing musical service to communities nurturing young artists.
Utilizes: Guest Musical Directors; Guest Musicians; Instructors; Multimedia; Singers
Founded: 1962
Specialized Field: Symphony; Orchestra; Ensemble
Status: Professional; Nonprofit
Paid Staff: 8
Season: October-April
Performs At: Carnegie Hall
Organization Type: Performing

1266
BACHANALIA CHAMBER ORCHESTRA
400 W 43rd Street
Suite 7D
New York, NY 10036
Phone: 212-239-5906
Fax: 212-239-5906
e-mail: info@bachanalia.org
Web Site: www.bachanalia.org
Officers:
 President: Harvey J. Stein
 Vice President and Treasurer: Philip A. Mousin
 Secretary: Elizabeth Pinkhasov, PhD
Management:
 Founder/Artistic Director: Nina Beilina
 Assistant To Artistic Director: John-Paul Norpoth
 Composer-in-Residence: Raphael Fusco
Mission: The consort of professional musicians dedicated to innovative programming, a high level of performance, and a collaborative philosophy that does away with a conductor.
Specialized Field: Chamber; Ensemble

1267
BLOOMINGDALE SCHOOL OF MUSIC
323 W 108th Street
New York, NY 10025
Phone: 212-663-6021
Fax: 212-932-9429
e-mail: info@bsmny.org
Web Site: www.bsmny.org
Officers:
 Executive Director: Lawrence Davis
Management:
 Project Manager: Margalit Cantor
 Assistant Director: Jeremy Conley
Mission: To promote, foster and develop the love of and interest for the musical arts.
Founded: 1964
Specialized Field: Orchestra; Chamber; Ensemble; Ethnic Music; Folk Music; Electronic; Live Electronic
Status: Professional; Nonprofit
Income Sources: National Guild of Community Schools of the Arts
Organization Type: Performing; Educational; Sponsoring

1268
CARNEGIE CHAMBER PLAYERS
514 W 110th Street
Suite 41
New York, NY 10025
Phone: 212-645-7424
Management:
 Artistic Director: Richard Goldsmith
 Artistic Director: Yari Bond

Mission: The promotion of chamber music in a mixed string and woodwind ensemble; the commissioning of new works; the performing of a traditional chamber music repertoire.
Specialized Field: Chamber; Ensemble
Status: Professional; Nonprofit
Performs At: Montshire Science Museum; Norwich VT
Organization Type: Performing; Touring; Resident; Educational

1269
CHAMBER MUSIC AMERICA
305 Seventh Avenue
New York, NY 10001
Phone: 212-242-2022
Fax: 212-242-7955
Web Site: www.chamber-music.org
Officers:
  CEO: Margaret Loi
Management:
  Program Director: Susan Dadian, sdadian@chamber-music.org
  Consulting Editor: Fred Cohn, fcohn@chamber-music.org
  Publications Director: Ellen Goldensohn, egoldensohn@chamber-music.org
Mission: To make chamber music a vital part of American cultural life through promoting professional chamber music.
Founded: 1977
Specialized Field: Chamber
Status: Professional; Nonprofit
Organization Type: Educational; Service Organization

1270
CHAMBER MUSIC SOCIETY OF LINCOLN CENTER
70 Lincoln Center Plaza
New York, NY 10023
Phone: 212-875-5775
Fax: 212-875-5799
e-mail: info@chambermusicsociety.org
Web Site: www.chambermusicsociety.org
Officers:
  Executive Director: Norma Hurlburt
Management:
  Artistic Director: David Finckel
  Artistic Director: Wu Han
  Production Manager: Lana Mione
  Marketing Manager: Trent Casey
Mission: To present chamber music concerts.
Founded: 1969
Specialized Field: Chamber; Ensemble; Classical Music
Status: Professional; Nonprofit
Performs At: Alice Tully Hall
Organization Type: Performing; Touring; Resident; Educational

1271
CHINESE MUSIC ENSEMBLE OF NEW YORK
PO Box 1062
New York, NY 10002
Phone: 212-925-6110
e-mail: info@chinesemusic.org
Web Site: www.chinesemusic.org
Officers:
  Director: Yu-chiung Teng
  Associate Director: Terence Yeh
  Associate Director: Oiman Chan
Management:
  Co-Director: Yu-chung Teng

  Co-Director: Terence Yeh
Mission: To introduce the music of China to Western audiences.
Founded: 1961
Specialized Field: Chinese Music; Ensemble; Ethnic Music; Folk Music
Status: Semi-Professional; Nonprofit
Organization Type: Performing; Touring; Educational

1272
CLASSICAL QUARTET
225 W 99th Street
New York, NY 10025
Phone: 212-222-2700
Web Site: saturdaybrass.org
Officers:
  President: Nancy Wilson
  Treasurer: David Miller
Management:
  Artist Representative: Beverly Simmons
Mission: The Classical Quartet was founded to present masterpieces of the Classic Era, string quartets of Hayden, Mozart, Beethoven and their contemporaries, on period instruments.
Founded: 1979
Specialized Field: Chamber; Brass Ensemble
Status: Professional
Performs At: Saint Michael's Church
Organization Type: Performing; Touring; Resident; Educational

1273
COLUMBIA UNIVERSITY ORCHESTRA
Music Department
806 Dodge Hall, Columbia University
New York, NY 10027
Phone: 212-854-5409
Fax: 212-854-8191
e-mail: cuo@columbia.edu
Web Site: www.columbia.edu
Officers:
  Board President: Alexandra Rice
Management:
  Assistant Conductor/Librarian: Mahir Cetiz, mc2765@columbia.edu
  Assistant Manager: Charlene Lee, cjl2144@columbia.edu
Mission: As a course in the department of music, students are given the opportunity to perform in a challenging ensemble.
Founded: 1896
Opened: 1899
Specialized Field: Orchestra

1274
EARLY MUSIC NEW YORK (EM/NY)
10 West 68 Street
New York, NY 10023
Phone: 212-749-6600
Fax: 212-749-2848
e-mail: info@EarlyMusicNY.org
Web Site: www.earlymusicny.org
Officers:
  President: Audrey Boughton
Management:
  Founder/Director: Frederick Renz, f.renz@EarlyMusicNY.org
  Operations Manager: Aaron Smith, admin@EarlyMusicNY.org
Mission: To foster historically informed performances
Founded: 1974
Specialized Field: Early Music; Dance & Music Drama; Medieval; Renaissance; Baroque;Classical
Status: Professional; Nonprofit

Paid Staff: 4
Paid Artists: 100
Budget: $300,000
Income Sources: Ticket Sales; CD Sales; Private Contributions & Grants; Government Awards
Performs At: Cathedral of Saint John the Divine
Affiliations: Early Music Foundation; New York Early Music Central (NYEMC)
Organization Type: Performing; Touring; Resident

1275
ENSEMBLE 21 ARTISTS
500 W 111th Street
Suite 3E
New York, NY 10025-1910
Web Site: www.ensemble21.com
Management:
  Artistic Director: Marilyn Nonken
  Executive Director: Jason Eckardt
Mission: Ensemble 21, the contemporary classical music performance group is recognized for its top caliber performances and has earned a reputation as a champion of innovative European composers rarely heard in America, specifically those associated with the new complexity and spectral movements.
Founded: 1993
Specialized Field: Instrumental Music

1276
INTERSCHOOL ORCHESTRAS OF NEW YORK
1556 Third Avenue
Suite 601
New York, NY 10128
Phone: 212-410-0370
Fax: 212-410-1606
e-mail: info@isorch.org
Web Site: www.isorch.org
Management:
  Executive Director: Nora Gibson, ngibson@isorch.org
  Program Associate: Gary Tigner, gtigner@isorch.org
  Operations Manager: Beverly Simon, bsimon@isorch.org
Mission: To provide a graded, systematic orchestral education program for children of all ages and abilities, bringing together students from all economic, cultural and racial backgrounds to play orchestral and chamber music.
Founded: 1972
Specialized Field: Chamber; Concert Band; Folk Music; Orchestra; Symphony
Income Sources: Individual; Corporate
Season: November-June
Performs At: Avery Fisher; Alice Tulley Halls; Symphony Space; New York Botanical Garden; Carnegie Hall

1277
JAZZ AT LINCOLN CENTER'S ESSENTIALLY ELLINGTON JAZZ FESTIVAL
33 W 60th Street
11th Floor
New York, NY 10023-7999
Phone: 212-258-9800
Fax: 212-258-9900
e-mail: jsarles@jalc.org
Web Site: www.jazzatlincolncenter.org
Officers:
  Vice Chair: Shahara Ahmad-Llewellyn
  Chairman: Robert H Burns

President: John Arnhold
Treasurer: Alan D Cohn
Managing Director: Christopher Dark
Management:
Artistic Director: Wynton Marsalis
Executive Director: Katherine E Brown
Chief Financial Officer: Freda Gimpel
Mission: To promoting the appreciation and understanding of jazz through performance, education and preservation.
Founded: 1991
Specialized Field: Jazz
Status: Not-for-Profit
Performs At: Lincoln Center of Performing Arts
Organization Type: Performing; Touring; Education; Residence

1278
LITTLE ORCHESTRA SOCIETY OF NEW YORK

330 W 42nd Street
12th Floor
New York, NY 10036-6902
Phone: 212-971-9500
Fax: 212-971-9501
e-mail: info@littleorchestra.org
Web Site: www.littleorchestra.org
Officers:
Co-Chair: William S Ohlemeyer Esq
Co-Chair: Carol D Schaefer
Management:
Music Director/Conductor: Dino Anagnost
Executive Directo: Joanne Bernstein-Cohen
Mission: Shares the vitality of live classical music and seeks to build future audiences by presenting innovative concerts that incorporate multiple art forms with a variety of artists to foster a deeper understanding and enjoyment of music.
Founded: 1947
Specialized Field: Music Performance
Paid Staff: 13
Volunteer Staff: 12
Paid Artists: 60

1279
LYRIC CHAMBER MUSIC SOCIETY OF NEW YORK

20 W 64th Street
Suite 27H
New York, NY 10023
Phone: 212-239-9190
Fax: 212-496-9927
e-mail: info@lyricny.org
Web Site: www.lyricny.org
Officers:
Board President: Dr. Joan Thompson Kretschmer
Treasurer: Taylor Hanex
Secretary: Ambrose Richardson
Board Member: Dr. Len Horovitz
Board Member: Julia C. Reinhart
Associate Board Member: Judith Binney
Management:
Artistic Director: Dr. Joan Thomson Kretschmer
Managing Director: Julia Reinhart
Mission: To provide exceptionally gifted musicians an opportunity to perform chamber music.
Utilizes: Artists-in-Residence; Composers-in-Residence; Educators; Five Seasonal Concerts; Guest Musical Directors; Instructors; Local Talent; Multimedia; Music; Organization Contracts; Original Music Scores; Sign Language Translators; Students; Volunteer Artists
Founded: 1997

Specialized Field: Chamber
Status: Non-Profit
Paid Staff: 2
Paid Artists: 15

1280
MARGOT ASTRACHAN MUSIC

1050 5th Avenue
New York, NY 10028
Phone: 212-722-6394
Fax: 212-828-9026
Officers:
Auction Chair: Vicki Downey
Management:
Owner: Margot Astrachan
Marketing Director: Sol Lieberman
Event Producer: Margot Astrachan
Director of Development: Nancy Barry
Founded: 1994
Specialized Field: Show Tunes; Traditional Classics

1281
MUSIC BEFORE 1800

Music Before 1800, Inc.
Corpus Christi Church
529 W 121st Street
New York, NY 10027
Phone: 212-666-9266
Fax: 212-666-9266
e-mail: mb1800@aol.com
Web Site: www.mb1800.org
Management:
Executive Director: Louise Basbas, mb1800@aol.com
Mission: Offering performances of vocal and instrumental chamber music from before 1800 on historic instruments
Founded: 1975
Opened: 1975
Specialized Field: Chamber; Early Music
Status: Professional
Paid Staff: 2
Volunteer Staff: 20
Paid Artists: 60
Budget: $150,000
Performs At: Corpus Christi Church
Affiliations: Chamber Music America; Early Music America
Annual Attendance: 2,600
Seating Capacity: 500
Year Built: 1935
Year Remodeled: 2007
Organization Type: Performing; Sponsoring

1282
NATIONAL ORCHESTRAL ASSOCIATION

New York, NY 10150-7016
Mailing Address: Po Box 7016
Phone: 212-208-4691
Fax: 212-208-4691
e-mail: info@nationalorchestral.org
Web Site: www.nationalorchestral.org
Officers:
Chairman: Matthew J Trachtenberg
Vice President/Secretary: David Levitman
Vice President/Treasurer: Reka Souwapawong
Executive Director: Eric Kuttner
Management:
Director of Public Affairs: Steven B Allnatt
Marketing/Special Events Consultant: Laurie Stokes Bott
Director: Bright M Judson
Executive Director: Teri Orr

Mission: Trains American musicans in orchestral technique and repertoire, providing them with necessary experience for professional orchestral careers.
Founded: 1930
Specialized Field: Orchestra; Chamber
Status: Nonprofit
Performs At: Carnegie Hall
Organization Type: Educational

1283
NEW YORK CITY SYMPHONY ORCHESTRA

481 Eight Avenue
New York, NY 10001
Phone: 212-967-7538
Fax: 212-465-2367
e-mail: nycsym@aol.com
Web Site: www.nycsymphony.org
Management:
Music Director: David Eaton
Mission: The presentation of young performers at the major concert halls in New York City; the presentation of performances and music by artists of different ethnic backgrounds.
Specialized Field: Symphony; Chamber
Status: Professional; Nonprofit
Performs At: Carnegie Hall; Alice Tully Hall
Organization Type: Performing

1284
NEW YORK CONSORT OF VIOLS

201 W 86th Street
Suite 905
New York, NY 10024
Phone: 212-580-9787
e-mail: info@nyconsortofviols.org
Web Site: www.nyconsortofviols.org
Management:
Artistic Director: Judith Davidoff
Mission: Performing the vast repertoire of music for violas from the Renaissance and Baroque periods; encouraging the composition of new works for the viola.
Founded: 1972
Specialized Field: Chamber
Status: Professional; Nonprofit
Paid Staff: 1
Paid Artists: 4
Organization Type: Performing; Touring; Educational

1285
NEW YORK HARP ENSEMBLE

140 W End Avenue
Suite 3K
New York, NY 10023
Phone: 212-799-5989
Fax: 212-799-5989
Management:
Music Director: Dr. Aristid von Wurtzler
Metropolitan Artists Management:
Mission: To perform concerts worldwide; to offer new contemporary compositions for four harps; to provide master classes; to produce recordings and appear in television performances.
Founded: 1970
Specialized Field: Harp Ensemble
Status: Professional; Nonprofit
Organization Type: Performing; Touring; Resident; Educational

1286
NEW YORK PHILHARMONIC
Avery Fisher Hall
10 Lincoln Center Plaza
New York, NY 10023-6990
Phone: 212-875-5900
Fax: 212-875-5717
Web Site: www.newyorkphilharmonic.org
Officers:
President: Zarin Mehta
Assistant to President: Susan O'Dell
Assistant to Chairman of the Board: Shelia Smith
Manager: Daniel Boico
Management:
Artistic Adiminstrator: Matias Tarnopolsky
Artistic Department Assistant: Courtenay Scholwalter
Director of Development: Melanie Forman
Reasearch Manager: Barbars Shear
Director of Projects: Steven Parkey
Director of Marketing: David Snead
Director of Operations: Miki Takebe
Founded: 1842
Specialized Field: Symphony; Orchestra; Chamber
Status: Professional
Income Sources: American Symphony Orchestra League
Performs At: Avery Fisher Hall
Organization Type: Performing; Touring; Resident; Educational

1287
NEW YORK PHILOMUSICA CHAMBER ENSEMBLE
105 W 73rd Street
Suite 4C
New York, NY 10023
Phone: 212-580-9933
Fax: 212-580-3902
e-mail: info@ntphilomusica.org
Web Site: www.nyphilomusia.org
Officers:
Chairman: Peter Smith
President: Robert Johnson
Vice President: Eugene L Scott
Secretary/Treasurer: John Masten
Management:
Artistic Director: Robert Johnson
Mission: Performing and recording the music written from 1750 to the present for wind, strings and piano, with guest soloists.
Founded: 1971
Specialized Field: Chamber; Ensemble
Status: Professional; Nonprofit
Performs At: American Concert Hall; Merkin Concert Hall
Organization Type: Performing; Recording

1288
NEW YORK POPS
881 7th Avenue
Suite 903
New York, NY 10019
Phone: 212-765-7677
Fax: 212-315-3199
e-mail: info@newyorkpops.org
Web Site: www.newyorkpops.org
Management:
Executive Director: James M Johnson
Director of Operations: Anne M Swanson
Education Director: Sherrie Maricle
Office Coordinator: Joanne Winograd
Development Assistant: Shannon L Robinson
Production Manager: Casey L McClellan
Stage Manager: Chan Chandler
Mission: Publicly-supported, not-for-profit corporation dedicated to broadening public awareness and enjoyment of America's rich popular music heritage through presentation of orchestral concerts of the highest quality in traditional and non-traditional settings.
Founded: 1983
Specialized Field: Symphony; Pops
Status: Professional; Nonprofit
Paid Staff: 5
Paid Artists: 79
Budget: 2.1 million
Income Sources: Concert Fees, Ticket Sales, and Institutional Support From Individuals, Corporations, Foundations, and Government Sources.
Performs At: Carnegie Hall
Affiliations: American Syphony Orchestra League, NYC & Company
Facility Category: Concert Hall
Organization Type: Performing; Touring

1289
NEW YORK YOUTH SYMPHONY
850 7th Avenue
Suite 505
New York, NY 10019-5230
Phone: 212-581-5933
Fax: 212-582-6927
e-mail: info@nyyouthsymphony.org
Web Site: www.nyyouthsymphony.org
Officers:
Chair: Leslie J Garfield
President: A. Slade Mills Jr
Vice Chairman: Robert L Poster
Treasurer: Cyrus Deboo
Senior Vice President: Barry Goldberg
Secretary: Susan S Rai
Management:
Executive Director: Barry Goldberg
Operations Manager: Larry Bomback
Adiminstrative Assistant: Jordan Stokes
Program Manager: Jabell Hamilton
Assistant Manager: Cassandra Olsen
Assistant Director: Brad Siebeking
Mission: New York Youth Symphony is established as the premier orchestra in metropolitan New York offering a unique learning experience and musical showcase for the gifted, young musician, conductor, soloist and composer.
Utilizes: Singers
Founded: 1963
Specialized Field: Youth Symphony; Chamber; Jazz Ensemble
Status: Non-Professional; Nonprofit
Paid Staff: 5
Volunteer Staff: 60
Budget: $1,000,000
Income Sources: Contributions; Ticket Sales
Performs At: Carnegie Hall
Affiliations: American Symphony Orchestra League; Chamber Music America
Annual Attendance: 14,000
Seating Capacity: 2,800
Organization Type: Performing; Educational; Sponsoring

1290
NOONDAY CONCERTS
74 Trinity Place
New York, NY 10006-2088
Phone: 212-602-0800
Fax: 212-602-9630
Web Site: www.trinitywallstreet.org

Management:
Director Trinity Concerts: Earl Tucker
Founded: 1933
Specialized Field: Ensemble; Jazz; Classical Music
Paid Staff: 2

1291
NORTH/SOUTH CONSONANCE
Cathedral Station
PO Box 698
New York, NY 10025-0698
Phone: 212-663-7566
e-mail: ns.concerts@att.net
Web Site: www.northsouthmusic.org
Management:
Director: Max Lifchitz, ns.concerts@att.net
Mission: Performing and furthering the music of living composers with particular emphasis on music from the Americas.
Founded: 1980
Specialized Field: Chamber; Ensemble; Electronic; Live Electronic; New Music
Status: Professional; Nonprofit
Volunteer Staff: 2
Budget: 35,000
Income Sources: Chamber Music America
Performs At: Christ & St. Stephen's Church; Merkin Hall; Weil Recital Hall
Annual Attendance: 1,750
Organization Type: Performing; Touring; Resident; Educational

1292
ORCHESTRA OF ST. LUKE'S
330 W 42nd Street
9th Floor
New York, NY 10036
Phone: 212-594-6100
Fax: 212-594-3291
e-mail: senelow@oslmusic.org
Web Site: http://www.oslmusic.org/home
Officers:
President/Executive Director: Marianne C. Lockwood
Vice President/General Manager: Edward P. Sweeney
Chairman: Norma S Benaquen
Management:
Co-Director Chamber Music: Daire Fitzgerald
Co-Director Chamber Music: Stephen Taylor
Artistic Associate: Maiko Kawabata
Director Marketing: Noel Hayashi
Director Education: Liz Norman
Marketing Consultant: Wende Persons
Director of Operations: Valerie Broderick
Mission: St. Lukes is a gathering of outstanding musicians whose purpose is to bring the beauty of music and the enlightened communication that is unique to music to as broad an audience as possible.
Founded: 1974
Specialized Field: Orchestra
Status: Professional; Nonprofit
Paid Staff: 15
Income Sources: St. Luke's Chamber Ensemble
Performs At: Merkin Concert Hall; Carnegie Hall
Organization Type: Performing

1293
ORPHEUS CHAMBER ORCHESTRA
490 Riverside Drive, 11th Floor
New York, NY 10027-5788
Phone: 212-896-1700
e-mail: info@orpheusnyc.org
Web Site: www.orpheusnyc.com

Officers:
Chairman: Richard S Lannamann
Vice Chairman: Spencer Stuart
Secretary: Martin D Jacobson
Treasurer: Ed Sermier
Management:
Executive Assistant: Ginelle Nicolas
Finance Manager: Kristine Rapp
Marketing Manager: Alan J Benson
Development/ Executive Associate: Adam Platka
Artistic Coordinator: Eric Wyrick
Personnel Coordinator: Stewart Rose
General Director: Graham Parker
Managing Director: Ronnie Bauch
Program Coordinator: Alan Kay
Mission: To provide members an opportunity to work in collaboration on the selection and interpretation of pieces.
Founded: 1972
Specialized Field: Orchestra; Chamber
Status: Professional; Nonprofit
Performs At: Carnegie Hall
Organization Type: Performing; Touring

1294
PEOPLES' SYMPHONY CONCERTS

201 W 54th Street
Suite 1 C
New York, NY 10019
Phone: 212-586-4680
Fax: 212-581-4029
e-mail: info@pscny.org
Web Site: www.pscny.org
Officers:
Chairperson: Susan Porter
President: Richard R Howe
Treasurer: Stefan H Cushman
Secretary: Frederick Wertheim
Manager: Frank Salomon
Management:
Production Manager: Christina Klapper
Mission: To bring the best music to students and workers at minimum prices.
Specialized Field: Chamber; Ensemble; Symphony

1295
RIVERSIDE SYMPHONY

225 W 99th Street
New York, NY 10025-5014
Phone: 212-864-4197
Fax: 212-864-9795
e-mail: riverside@riversidesymphony.org
Web Site: www.riversidesymphony.org
Management:
Artistic Director: Anthony Korf
Conductor/Music Director: George Rothman
Production Manager: Justin Stanley
Mission: To present new and less-familiar work; to present emerging artists; to produce American music.
Utilizes: Commissioned Composers; Commissioned Music; Guest Companies; Guest Musical Directors; Multimedia; Original Music Scores; Sign Language Translators; Singers; Soloists; Student Interns
Specialized Field: Symphony; Orchestra
Status: Professional; Nonprofit
Budget: $500,000
Performs At: Alice Tully Hall Lincoln Center
Organization Type: Performing; Resident; Educational

1296
ROULETTE INTERMEDIUM

228 W Broadway
New York, NY 10013

Phone: 212-219-8242
e-mail: info@roulette.org
Web Site: www.roulette.org
Officers:
President: Jim Staley
Management:
Producer: Jim Staley
Adiministrative Director: Elizabeth Halem
Publicity Director: Jessica Feldman
Development Director: Mary Griffin
Production Manager: Matthew Mehlan
Mission: To be a presenting organization and facility for innovative composers and musicians through its concert series, commissions and recording distribution services; to support a broad range of new music by young established artists.
Specialized Field: Chamber; Ensemble; Ethnic Music; Folk Music; Electronic; Live Electronic; Band
Status: Nonprofit
Performs At: Roul
Organization Type: Presenting

1297
SAINT LUKES CHAMBER ENSEMBLE

330 West 42nd Street, 9th Floor
New York, NY 10036
Phone: 212-594-6100
Fax: 212-594-3291
e-mail: senelow@oslmusic.org
Web Site: www.orchestraofstlukes.org
Officers:
Chairman: Norman S Benzaquen
President/Executive Director: Marianne C Lockwood
Vice President/ General Manager: Edward P Sweeney
Management:
Director of Artistic Planning: Elizabeth Ostrow
Co-Director: Daire Fitzgerald
Co-Director: Stephen Taylor
Artistic Associate: Maiko Kawabata
Director of Education: Liz Asuen
Business Manager: Irene Asuen
Marketing Director: Bill Rhoads
Director of Operations: Valerie Broderick
Artistic Personnel Manager: Julian Plyter
Mission: Encompasses St. Luke's Chamber Ensemble, Orchestra of St. Luke's, Children's Free Opera and Dance of New York.
Specialized Field: Orchestra; Chamber
Status: Nonprofit
Performs At: Avery Fisher Hall; Merkin Concert Hall; Brooklyn
Organization Type: Performing; Touring; Educational; Sponsoring

1298
SATURDAY BRASS QUINTET

St. Michael's Episcopal Church
225 W 99th Street
New York, NY 10025
Phone: 212-222-2700
Fax: 212-678-5916
Mission: Presenting classics of the brass chamber genre; soliciting and performing new selections for brass.
Specialized Field: Chamber; Brass Ensemble
Status: Professional; Nonprofit
Organization Type: Performing; Touring; Resident; Educational

1299
SHEILA-NA-GIG MUSIC

Hibernian Music
New York, NY 10009-2349
Mailing Address: Po Box 2349
Phone: 212-260-2302
Fax: 212-260-9645
e-mail: hibernian@earthlink.net
Web Site: www.house-of-music.com
Mission: To represent artists from Ireland, Scotland and the US in world and acoustic music.
Founded: 1998
Specialized Field: Ethnic Music

1300
ST. PATRICK'S CATHEDRAL CHAMBER MUSIC SERIES

St. Patrick's Cathedral
460 Madison Avenue
New York, NY 10022-6863
Phone: 212-753-2261
Fax: 212-753-3925
e-mail: RMESPC@aol.com
Management:
Music Adminstrator: Robert Evans
Specialized Field: Chamber; Ensemble
Budget: $10,000

1301
TAIPEI THEATER OF CHINESE INFORMATION & CULTURE

1230 Avenue of the Americas
New York, NY 10020
Phone: 212-373-1852
Fax: 212-373-1878
e-mail: utheatre@tpts8.seednet.net
Specialized Field: Chinese Music

1302
TISCH CENTER FOR THE ARTS

92nd Street Y
1395 Lexington Avenue
New York, NY 10128
Phone: 212-415-5740
Officers:
President: Fredic Mack
Chair of the Board: Michael Goldstein
Vice President: Len Blavatnik
Treasurer: Jeffery B Goldenberg
Secretary: Oliver Stanton
Co-Chair: Thomas S Kaplan
Co-Chair: Jonathan P May
Management:
Associate Executive Director: Helaine Geismar Katz
Associate Executive Director Financ: Greg J Brooks
Executive Officer: Eleanor Goldhar
Executive Director: Sol Adler
Mission: Promotes individual and family development and participation in civic life within the context of Jewish values and American pluralism.
Utilizes: Singers
Specialized Field: Orchestra; Chamber; Ensemble; Pops; Jazz
Status: Nonprofit
Performs At: Kaufmann Concert Hall
Organization Type: Performing; Educational

1303
PHILHARMONIA VIRTUOSI CORPORATION
PO Box 645
North Salem, NY 10560
Phone: 914-693-5595
Fax: 914-693-7040
Toll-free: 800-973-7729
e-mail: info@pvmusic.org
Web Site: www.pvmusic.org
Officers:
Chairman: Lucille Werlinich
President: Stuart Finkelstein
Vice President: Marion Swett Robinson
Secretary: Deborah Senft
Treasurer: Denny P Jacobson
Management:
Music Director: Richard Kapp
Executive Director: Barbara Kapp
Volunteer Coordinator: Barbara Babad
Concertmaster: Mela Tenenbaum
Orchestra Librarian: Alexandr Tenenbaum
Mission: To perform an exceptionally broad spectrum of music from the 1600s to the present; to remain a flexible ensemble that performs orchestra concerts with up to 45 players and chamber music programs with as few as three.
Founded: 1968
Specialized Field: Orchestra; Chamber
Status: Professional; Nonprofit
Paid Staff: 5
Volunteer Staff: 60
Paid Artists: 100
Budget: $650,000
Organization Type: Performing; Touring; Educational; Recording

1304
CATSKILL SYMPHONY ORCHESTRA
PO Box 14
Oneonta, NY 13820
Phone: 607-436-2670
Fax: 607-436-2718
Management:
General Manager: Deborah Wolfanger
Personnel Manager: Charles England
Mission: Bringing quality music to the immediate and outlying areas of Central New York State.
Founded: 1972
Specialized Field: Symphony; Orchestra
Status: Professional; Nonprofit
Paid Staff: 7
Performs At: Hunt Union; State University of New York-Oneonta
Organization Type: Performing; Educational

1305
WAVERLY CONSORT
Patterson, NY 12563
Mailing Address: PO Box 286
Phone: 845-878-3723
Fax: 845-878-3817
Management:
Artistic Director: Michael Jaffee
Mission: The presentation of early music to audiences in NY and across the country.
Founded: 1964
Specialized Field: Ensemble
Status: Professional; Nonprofit
Organization Type: Performing; Touring

1306
PENFIELD SMYPHONY ORCHESTRA
1587 Jackson Road
Penfield, NY 14526
Phone: 585-872-0774
e-mail: ps_info@penfieldsymphony.org
Management:
Music Director: David Harman
Mission: Penfield Symphony Orchestra's purpose is to bring enjoyment and appreciation of fine music to the residents of Penfield and the greater Rochester area. An artistic organization with high performance standards, providing an outlet for dedicated and talented musicians and has frequent collaborations with area educational institutions and community groups.
Founded: 1955
Specialized Field: Orchestra

1307
HUDSON VALLEY PHILHARMONIC
35 Market Street
Poughkeepsie, NY 12601
Phone: 845-473-5288
Fax: 845-473-2074
e-mail: SLAMARCA@bardavon.org
Web Site: WWW.BARDAVON.ORG
Management:
Music Director: Randall Craig Fleischer
Executive Director: Chris Silva
Managing Director: Stephen LaMarca
Mission: Dedicated to sponsoring and supporting a professional symphony orchestra which will present performances of the highest artistic quality and further the musical growth of the region.
Founded: 1959
Specialized Field: Symphony; Orchestra; Chamber
Status: Professional
Income Sources: American Symphony Orchestra League; American Society of Composers, Authors and Publishers; Broadcast Music Incorporated
Performs At: Ulster Performing Arts Center; Bardavon 1869 Opera House
Organization Type: Performing; Resident; Sponsoring

1308
CHAMBER MUSIC AT RODEF SHALOM WITH STEPHEN STARKMAN & FRIENDS
51 Ackerthook Road
Rhinebeck, NY 12572
Phone: 845-876-2742
Management:
Artistic Director: Stephen Starkman
Specialized Field: Chamber
Budget: $10,000-20,000
Seating Capacity: 500+

1309
RHINEBECK CHAMBER MUSIC SOCIETY
PO Box 465
Rhinebeck, NY 12572
Phone: 845-876-2870
Fax: 845- 87—198
e-mail: info@rhinebeckmusic.org
Management:
Artistic Director: Kurt Grishman
Specialized Field: Chamber
Budget: $10,000-20,000
Performs At: Church of Messiah

1310
EASTMAN PHILHARMONIA
26 Gibbs Street
Eastman School of Music
Rochester, NY 14604
Phone: 585-274-1000
Fax: 716-274-1110
e-mail: scharles@esm.rochester.edu
Officers:
Department Secretary: Sheryle Charles
Ensemble Coordinator: Katherine Zager
Management:
Conductor: Neil Varon
Department Chair: Mark David Scatterday
Specialized Field: Orchestra; Ensemble

1311
GREECE SYMPHONY ORCHESTRA
950 E Avenue
Rochester, NY 14607
Phone: 716-663-4693
Fax: 716-581-1015
Management:
Director: David Fetler
Mission: Committed to enhancing the cultural life of Greece and the surrounding area through free concerts and other performances and to sponsoring young artists competitions in local schools.
Founded: 1968
Specialized Field: Orchestra
Status: Semi-Professional; Nonprofit
Paid Staff: 65
Income Sources: Greece (NY) Performing Arts Society
Organization Type: Performing; Sponsoring

1312
CASTLEMAN QUARTET PROGRAMS
1163 E Avenue
#4
Rochester, NY 14607
Phone: 585-274-1592
Fax: 585-442-4282
e-mail: ccastleman@gmail.com
Web Site: www.quartetprogram.com
Officers:
Chairman: Joesph Cuningham
Management:
Director: Charles Castleman, ccastleman@gmail.com
Mission: Develop individual and ensemble skills and explore group dynamics for the finest preprofessional musicians.
Founded: 1970
Specialized Field: Ensemble
Status: Professional; Non-Profit
Paid Staff: 15
Paid Artists: 8
Non-paid Artists: 40
Performs At: Grusin Hall in Boulder, CO; Rosch Hall in Fredonia, NY
Seating Capacity: 150
Organization Type: Performing; Resident; Educational; Sponsoring

1313
ROCHESTER CHAMBER ORCHESTRA
950 E Avenue
Rochester, NY 14607
Phone: 716-473-6711
Fax: 716-271-8879
Web Site: www.rochester.edu/College/MUR/ursourco/
Management:
Director: David Fetler

Mission: Offering the Rochester community an outstanding chamber orchestra repertoire from the 17th century to the present; presenting newly commissioned works.
Founded: 1964
Specialized Field: Orchestra; Chamber
Status: Professional; Nonprofit
Performs At: Asbury First Methodist Church
Organization Type: Performing; Sponsoring

1314
SOCIETY FOR CHAMBER MUSIC IN ROCHESTER

PO Box 20715
Rochester, NY 14602
Phone: 585-586-5690
Fax: 716-359-1132
e-mail: info@chambermusicrochester.org
Officers:
   Chairman: Edna Claunchy
   Presidnet: Donald Hunsberger
Management:
   Co-Artistic Director: Stefan Reuss
   C0-Artistic Director: Joseph Werner
Specialized Field: Chamber
Budget: $35,000-60,000
Performs At: Memorial Art Gallery Auditorium; Roberts Wesleyan Auditorium

1315
SARATOGA PERFORMING ARTS CENTER

108 Avenue of the Pines
Saratoga Springs, NY 12866
Phone: 518-587-9330
e-mail: media@spac.org
Web Site: www.spac.org
Officers:
   President/Executive Director: Marcia J. White
   Director Development/Marketing: Vesna Gjaja
   Production Manager: Coleen Grignon
Management:
   Principal Conductor/Artistic Dir: Charles Dutoit
   Box Office Manager: Bonnie Jones
Mission: To host performing arts events.
Utilizes: Singers
Founded: 1966
Specialized Field: Ensemble; Show Tunes; Band; Classical Music; Pops
Status: Professional; Nonprofit
Budget: $11 Million
Income Sources: International Association of Auditorium Managers; New York Performing Arts Association; Membership ticket sales
Affiliations: Summer home of New York City Ballet, Philadelphia Orchestra and Saratoga Chamber Music Festival
Annual Attendance: 350,000
Facility Category: Ampitheatre
Type of Stage: Proscenium
Stage Dimensions: 80 W x 60 D
Seating Capacity: 5100
Year Built: 1966
Organization Type: Performing; Educational; Sponsoring

1316
STATEN ISLAND SYMPHONY

1 Campus Road
Staten Island, NY 10301
Phone: 718-390-3426
Fax: 718-420-4145
e-mail: sisymphony@aol.com

Officers:
   President: Sandra Sperry
Management:
   Office Manager: Marie Penza
   Executive Director: Elizabeth LaCause
Founded: 1980
Specialized Field: Classical; Symphony
Paid Staff: 3
Volunteer Staff: 20
Paid Artists: 10
Non-paid Artists: 40

1317
ROSEWOOD CHAMBER ENSEMBLE

43-31 39th Street
Sunnyside, NY 11104
Phone: 718-784-6160
Mission: Providing the community with quality classical music and offering musical education to young people.
Founded: 1980
Specialized Field: Chamber; Ensemble
Status: Professional; Nonprofit
Organization Type: Performing; Educational

1318
SYRACUSE FRIENDS OF CHAMBER MUSIC

35 Drumlins Terrace
Syracuse, NY 13224
Phone: 315-446-0994
Fax: 315-446-0994
Web Site: www.syr.edu/arts/chambermusic/
Management:
   Music Director: Henry Palocz
Mission: To provide high quality chamber music concerts to Central New York audiences.
Founded: 1950
Specialized Field: Chamber
Volunteer Staff: 10
Budget: $20,000-35,000
Performs At: High School Auditorium

1319
SYRACUSE SYMPHONY ORCHESTRA

411 Montgomery Street
Syracuse, NY 13202
Phone: 315-424-8222
Fax: 315-424-1131
Toll-free: 800-724-3810
e-mail: webmaster@syracusesymphony.org
Web Site: www.syracusesymphony.org
Management:
   Music Director: Daniel Hege
   Resident Conductor: Grant Cooper
   Conductor Emeritus: Kazuyoshi Akiyama
Mission: To maintain and further develop a resident, professional symphony orchestra; to produce musical performances of the highest artistic quality; to fulfill the cultural, educational and entertainment needs of the Central and Northern New York communities we serve.
Utilizes: Dance Companies; Dancers; Educators; Guest Accompanists; Guest Companies; Guest Directors; Guest Musical Directors; Guest Musicians; Instructors; Local Artists; Multimedia; Original Music Scores; Sign Language Translators; Singers; Soloists; Special Technical Talent
Founded: 1960
Specialized Field: Symphony; Orchestra; Chamber
Status: Professional; Nonprofit
Income Sources: American Symphony Orchestra League; Association of Performing Arts Presenters
Performs At: John H. Mulroy Civic Center
Organization Type: Performing; Touring; Resident; Educational

1320
SYRACUSE SYMPHONY YOUTH ORCHESTRA

411 Montgomery Street
Syracuse, NY 13202
Phone: 315-424-8222
Fax: 315-424-1131
Web Site: www.syracusesymphony.org
Officers:
   Chairman: Dr. Arthur Rosenbaum
Management:
   Conductor: Kenneth Andrews
   Orchestra Manager: Cornelia Brewster
   Education Manager: Cher Leszczewicz
   Youth String/Orchestra Conductor: Muriel Bodley
Founded: 1961
Specialized Field: Youth Orchestra
Status: Non-Professional; Nonprofit
Paid Staff: 80
Income Sources: American Symphony Orchestra League (Youth Orchestra Division); Syracuse Symphony Orchestra
Performs At: H.W. Smith Elementary School
Organization Type: Performing; Touring; Resident; Educational

1321
FRIENDS OF CHAMBER MUSIC OF TROY

45 Maple Avenue
Troy, NY 12180-5129
Phone: 518-266-0044
Fax: 518-276-2649
e-mail: herroi@rpi.edu
Web Site: www.friendsofchambermusic.org
Officers:
   President: Isom Herron
Management:
   Programming: Susan Blandy
Founded: 1949
Specialized Field: Classical; Chamber
Budget: $10,000-20,000
Performs At: Kiggins Hall; Emma Willard School

1322
TROY CHROMATICS CONCERTS

PO Box 1574
Troy, NY 12181
Phone: 518-273-0038
Fax: 518-273-1564
Web Site: www.troychromatics.org
Officers:
   Board President: Joseph Erkes
Mission: Providing world class artists and programs to New York State's capital region.
Founded: 1895
Specialized Field: Symphony; Chamber; Ensemble; Soloists
Status: Nonprofit
Performs At: Troy Savings Bank Music Hall
Organization Type: Sponsoring

1323
NASSAU SYMPHONY SOCIETY

185 California Avenue
Uniondale, NY 11553
Phone: 516-565-0646
Fax: 516-481-3382
Management:
   Executive Director: Sherry Smolev
Mission: The performance of the highest quality symphonic music for residents of all ages on Long Island.
Specialized Field: Symphony

Status: Professional; Nonprofit
Performs At: John Cranford Adams Playhouse; Hofstra University
Organization Type: Performing; Educational

1324
CHAMBER MUSIC SOCIETY OF UTICA
310 Genesee Street
Utica, NY 13502
Phone: 315-822-4392
e-mail: jimit@borg.com
Web Site: www.uticachambermusic.org
Management:
    Trustee: James Taylor
    Head Music Selection: Dr. Jon Magendanz
Mission: The presentation of an annual series of high-quality chamber music concerts.
Specialized Field: Chamber
Status: Nonprofit
Budget: $10,000-$20,000
Performs At: Munson-Williams-Proctor Museum of Art Auditorium
Annual Attendance: 1,200
Facility Category: Arts Museum
Type of Stage: Open
Stage Dimensions: 15x30
Seating Capacity: 271
Year Remodeled: 1992
Organization Type: Presenting

1325
AMHERST SYMPHONY ORCHESTRA
PO Box 1083
Williamsville, NY 14221-1083
Phone: 716-633-4606
Fax: 716-836-4972
e-mail: asorch46@aolcom
Officers:
    President: John Olson
    Personnel Director: Richard Sowinski
Management:
    Director: Mark Ahrens
    Director: Linda Arzola
Specialized Field: Orchestra
Budget: $35,000- $100,000
Performs At: Amherst Middle School
Seating Capacity: 1475

1326
CHAMBER PLAYERS INTERNATIONAL
45 Crossways Park Boulevard
Woodbury, NY 11797
Fax: 212-481-7690
Toll-free: 877-444-4488
e-mail: info@chamberplayersinternational.org
Officers:
    Executive Director: David Winkler
Management:
    President: Steven Leventhal
    Vice President: Joseph F Martorano
Specialized Field: Chamber; Ensemble
Performs At: Poway Center for the Performing Arts
Seating Capacity: 850

1327
MAVERICK CONCERTS
PO Box 102
Woodstock, NY 12498
Phone: 845-679-8217
Web Site: www.maverickconcerts.org
Mission: To provide Sunday afternoon chamber music concerts in summer.
Specialized Field: Chamber
Status: Professional; Nonprofit

Performs At: Maverick Concert Hall
Organization Type: Performing

North Carolina

1328
ASHEVILLE CHAMBER MUSIC SERIES
25 Brook Forest Drive
Arden, NC 28704
Mailing Address: PO Box 1003 Arden, NC 28802
Phone: 828-298-5085
e-mail: marybarth@aol.com
Web Site: http://www.main.nc.us
Officers:
    President: Dr. Harold Rotman
    VP: Philip Walker
    Secretary: Perien Gray
    Treasurer: JH Wynn
Management:
    Program Director: Bill van der Hoeven
Mission: To provide chamber music concerts.
Founded: 1952
Specialized Field: Chamber; Ensemble
Status: Non-Professional; Nonprofit
Budget: $10,000-20,000
Income Sources: Chamber Music America
Organization Type: Performing

1329
ASHEVILLE SYMPHONY ORCHESTRA
P O Box 2852
Asheville, NC 28802
Phone: 828-254-7046
Fax: 828-254-1716
e-mail: epvarner@ashevillesymphony.org
Officers:
    Artistic Administrator: Sally J Keeney
    Office Administrator: Elisabeth P Varner
Management:
    Executive Director: Steven R Hagerman
    Concertmaster: Mary Byrd Daniels
    Treasurer: .Edward Towson II
    Vice President/Programming: John R Anderson
    Vice President/Outreach: Barbara Chisolm
    Guild President: Janice Orson
    Vice President/Finance: Dr. Karl S Quisenberry
    Vice President/Human Resources: Herbert Smith, Jr.
Specialized Field: Orchestra

1330
HOWARD HANGER JAZZ FANTASY
31 Park Avenue N
Asheville, NC 28801
Phone: 828-254-1174
Fax: 828-254-1174
Toll-free: 800-345-1174
e-mail: info@howardhanger.com
Web Site: www.howardhanger.com
Management:
    Music Director: Howard Hanger
Mission: Performing new age as well as traditional jazz; introducing children aged 6-12 to jazz.
Founded: 1966
Specialized Field: Ensemble; Electronic; Live Electronic; Jazz
Status: Professional
Paid Artists: 4
Organization Type: Performing; Touring; Educational

1331
MOORE COMMUNITY BAND
Route 1
PO Box 98
Cameron, NC 28326
Phone: 919-245-7267
Management:
    Director: David Sieberling
Mission: Offering the opportunity to perform quality band literature; supporting community programs.
Utilizes: Guest Artists; Guest Companies
Founded: 1984
Specialized Field: Band
Status: Nonprofit
Paid Staff: 35
Income Sources: Sandhills Arts Council
Performs At: Performing Arts Center
Organization Type: Performing; Resident

1332
CAROLINA PRO MUSICA
PO Box 32022
Charlotte, NC 28232
Phone: 704-334-3468
Fax: 704-333-5239
e-mail: kjacob@vnet.net
Web Site: www.carolinapromusica.org
Officers:
    Executive Director: Karen Hite Jacob
    Education Director: Holly Wright Maurer
    Outreach: Rebecca Miller Saunders
Management:
    Artistic Director: Karen Hite Jacob
    Research: Edward Ferrell
Mission: The performance of music primarily written before 1800 in an historically-correct style, on period instruments.
Utilizes: Collaborations; Curators; Educators; Guest Accompanists; Guest Directors; Guest Musical Directors; Guest Musicians; Instructors; Lyricists; Multimedia; New Productions; Original Music Scores; Sign Language Translators; Singers; Soloists
Founded: 1977
Specialized Field: Early Music; Medieval; Baroque; Educational
Status: Professional; Nonprofit
Paid Artists: 4
Budget: $15,000- $20,000
Income Sources: Ticket sales; Education grants; Promoters
Performs At: St. Mary's; St. Martin's
Affiliations: Early Music America
Annual Attendance: 750
Facility Category: Churches. St. Mary's; St. Martin's
Seating Capacity: 125/175
Year Built: 1925
Year Remodeled: 1975
Organization Type: Performing; Touring; Educational; Sponsoring
Resident Groups: Belmont Abbey College, Belmont NC

1333
CHAMBER MUSIC OF CHARLOTTE
2114 Amboy Court
Charlotte, NC 28205
Phone: 704-535-3024
Mission: To foster the composition, performance and enjoyment of chamber music.
Founded: 1977
Specialized Field: Chamber
Status: Professional; Semi-Professional; Nonprofit
Paid Staff: 15

Organization Type: Performing; Educational

1334
CHARLOTTE PHILHARMONIC ORCHESTRA AND CHORUS
PO Box 470987
Charlotte, NC 28247-0987
Phone: 704-846-2788
Fax: 704-847-6043
e-mail: info@charlottephilharmonic.org
Web Site: www.charlottephilharmonic.org
Officers:
    Chairman: Dr. J Arlen Smith
    President: Albert E Moehring
    Treasurer: C Chandler
Management:
    Maestro: Albert E Moehring
    Orchestra Manager: Patricia Moehring
    Choral Director: Marc Setzer
    Administrative Assistant: Barbara Guenzi
Mission: Perform a variety of musical entertainment, classical/popular. Provide educational programming for all ages.
Utilizes: Choreographers; Collaborating Artists; Collaborations; Dance Companies; Dancers; Educators; Fine Artists; Five Seasonal Concerts; Guest Accompanists; Guest Artists; Guest Companies; Guest Composers; Guest Directors; Guest Lecturers; Guest Musical Directors; Guest Musicians; Guest Writers; Instructors; Lyricists; Multimedia; Original Music Scores; Resident Professionals; Sign Language Translators; Singers; Soloists
Founded: 1990
Specialized Field: Orchestra
Status: Not-for-profit; Professional Symphonic Orchestra; Amateur Volunteer Chorus
Paid Staff: 4
Volunteer Staff: 100
Paid Artists: 125
Budget: $705,000
Income Sources: Box Office, Private Donations, Grants/Gifts
Affiliations: American Symphony Orchestra League, Association of Symphony Orchestras of North Carolina, Chamber of Commerce, Charlotte Convention Center
Annual Attendance: 15-20,000
Facility Category: Performing Arts Center/Concert Hall
Type of Stage: Proscenium
Stage Dimensions: 60 x 30
Seating Capacity: 2,100
Year Built: 1993

1335
CHARLOTTE SYMPHONY
Two Wachovia Center
301 S Tryon Street
Suite 1700
Charlotte, NC 28202
Phone: 704-714-5113
Fax: 704-972-2012
e-mail: scottb@charlottesymphony.org
Web Site: www.charlottesymphony.org
Officers:
    Chairperson: Elizabeth J McLughlin
Management:
    Executive Director: Jonathan Martin
    Music Director: Christopher Warren-Green, 7
Utilizes: Collaborating Artists; Commissioned Composers; Commissioned Music; Dance Companies; Educators; Five Seasonal Concerts; Grant Writers; Guest Accompanists; Guest Companies; Guest Composers; Guest Directors; Guest Lecturers; Guest Musical Directors; Guest Musicians; Guest Writers; Instructors; Local Unknown Artists; Lyricists;

Multimedia; Music; Organization Contracts; Original Music Scores; Resident Artists; Sign Language Translators; Singers
Founded: 1932
Specialized Field: Symphony; Orchestra; Ensemble
Paid Staff: 25
Income Sources: American Symphony Orchestra League; Association of Symphony Orchestras of North Carolina; Arts Advocates of North Carolina
Performs At: North Carolina Blumenthal Performing Arts Center and Various Other Facilities
Facility Category: Multi-purpose performing arts center
Type of Stage: Proscenium
Stage Dimensions: 55 W x 50 D
Seating Capacity: 1970
Year Built: 1992
Cost: $65 Million
Rental Contact: Booking Manager NC Blumenthal

1336
QUEENS UNIVERSITY: QUEENS FRIENDS OF MUSIC CHAMBER SERIES
1900 Selwyn Avenue
Charlotte, NC 28274
Phone: 704-337-2204
Fax: 704-337-2356
e-mail: steelea@queens.edu
Web Site: www.queens.edu/friends-of-music
Management:
    Artistic Director: Paul Nitsch
Mission: To present Chamber music concerts and support music education and the Queens Music Department.
Utilizes: Artists-in-Residence; Educators; Guest Musical Directors; Multimedia; Original Music Scores
Founded: 1983
Specialized Field: Chamber
Paid Staff: 1
Volunteer Staff: 28
Paid Artists: 6
Budget: $10,000-$20,000
Income Sources: Gifts; Ticket Sales
Performs At: Dana Auditorium
Affiliations: Queens University Of Charlotte
Annual Attendance: 1,200
Seating Capacity: 1,000
Year Built: 1962
Year Remodeled: 1995

1337
CHAMBER ARTS SOCIETY
PO Box 90685
Duke University
Durham, NC 27708
Phone: 919-660-3356
Fax: 919-660-3381
e-mail: bryant@math.duke.edu
Web Site: www.chamberartssociety.org
Officers:
    Board Chair: Robert Bryant
Mission: Committed to providing five or six chamber music concerts of the highest possible quality annually, with an emphasis on string quartet.
Founded: 1945
Specialized Field: Chamber
Status: Nonprofit
Paid Staff: 2
Volunteer Staff: 6
Budget: $60,000
Income Sources: Tickets Sales; Contributions Duke Performances
Performs At: Bryan Center
Annual Attendance: 3,000
Seating Capacity: 600

Organization Type: Sponsoring

1338
DURHAM SYMPHONY ORCHESTRA
120 Morris Street
Durham, NC 27701
Mailing Address: PO Box 1993, Durham, NC 27702
Phone: 919-491-6576
e-mail: Office@durhamsymphony.org
Web Site: www.durhamsymphony.org
Management:
    General Manager: Kelly Kovalesky
    Music Director/Conductor: William Henry Curry
    Executive Director: Mary Sherk
Mission: Foster the appreciation of orchestral music through the production of high-quality music for and by the residents of Durham and the surrounding communities
Specialized Field: Orchestra

1339
MALLARME CHAMBER PLAYERS
Durham Arts Council
120 Morris Street
Durham, NC 27701
Phone: 919-560-2788
Fax: 919-560-2743
e-mail: mallarme@mindspring.com
Web Site: www.marllarmemusic.org
Officers:
    President: Jimmy Gibbs
    VP: Shelly Green
Management:
    Artistic Director: Anna Ludwig Wilson
    Office Manager: Robin Vail
Mission: To perform concerts that enhance that intamacy of communication that is the special province of chamber music, with professional artists featuring all of the orchestral instruments.
Founded: 1984
Specialized Field: Chamber
Paid Staff: 2
Paid Artists: 30
Budget: $150,000
Income Sources: Earned Revenue; Corporate; Foundations Grants; Individual Donors; Merchandise
Performs At: People Security Insurance Theatre
Affiliations: North Carolina Arts Council
Annual Attendance: 10,000

1340
CUMBERLAND COUNTY FRIENDS OF THE ORCHESTRA
1624 Ireland Drive
Fayetteville, NC 28304
Phone: 910-484-8121
Fax: 910-323-4127
Officers:
    President: David J Phleeger
    Secretary: Rita Warren
    Treasurer: Lynn Gloyeski
Management:
    Orchestra Coordinator: Janice Swoope
Mission: To maintain a community support group for the Cumberland County School Orchestra Program, lending volunteer hours and financial aid where needed to maintain excellence in the program.
Utilizes: Guest Companies
Founded: 1980
Specialized Field: Orchestra
Status: Nonprofit
Organization Type: Educational; Sponsoring

1341
HIGHLAND BRITISH BRASS BAND ASSOCIATION
2405 Morganton Road
Fayetteville, NC 28303
Phone: 910-484-0281
Officers:
Chairman: Robert Downing
Mission: To provide suitable outlet for musically talented adults who are interested in promoting good band music in the British Brass Band format for the instruction and edification of the general public.
Utilizes: Guest Artists
Founded: 1980
Specialized Field: Band; Brass Ensemble
Status: Semi-Professional; Nonprofit
Income Sources: Arts Council of Fayetteville & Cumberland County
Performs At: Methodist College
Organization Type: Performing

1342
GREENSBORO SYMPHONY ORCHESTRA/CAROLINA POPS
200 N Davie Street
Suite 328
Greensboro, NC 27401
Phone: 336-335-5456
Fax: 336-335-5580
e-mail: scordick@greensborosymphony.org
Web Site: www.greensborosymphony.org/home.html
Officers:
President/CEO: Lisa Crawford
Managing Director: Stephanie Cordick
Management:
Music Director/Conductor: Dmitry Sitkovetsky
Principal Pops Conductor: Michael Berkowitz
Mission: To strive seriously for the highest quality of performance, with the ultimate goal of attaining a truly professional sound, the love of playing orchestral literature remaining the prime factor for participation.
Utilizes: Guest Artists
Founded: 1977
Specialized Field: Orchestra; Pops
Status: Professional
Income Sources: City of Greensboro
Performs At: War Memorial Auditorium
Organization Type: Performing

1343
PHILHARMONIA OF GREENSBORO
200 N Davie Street, Box 2
The Music Center, City Arts
Greensboro, NC 27401
Phone: 336-373-2549
Fax: 336-373-2659
e-mail: britanygreen@hotmail.com
Management:
Music Director: Robert Gutter
Executive Director: Lynn H Donovan
Specialized Field: Orchestra

1344
SUMMER STRINGS ON THE MEHERRIN
303 S Elm Street
Greenville, NC 27858
Phone: 919-752-2542
Officers:
President: John R Kernodle, Jr
Secretary: Angela Seawell
Management:
Music Director: Paul Topper
Chowan College Officer: James Chamblee

Mission: Summer Strings on the Meherrin offers a three-week program for 12 to 18-year-old bowed string players to improve their musicianship and techniques and to present chamber music concerts.
Founded: 1972
Specialized Field: Chamber; String Ensemble
Status: Nonprofit
Income Sources: Chowan College
Performs At: Daniels Hall; Chowan College
Organization Type: Performing; Resident; Educational

1345
HENDERSONVILLE SYMPHONY ORCHESTRA
PO Box 1811
Hendersonville, NC 28793
Phone: 828-697-5884
Fax: 828-697-5765
e-mail: info@hendersonvillesymphony.net
Officers:
President: William Humleker
VP: Don Hupe
Management:
Music Director/Conductor: Dr. Thomas Joiner
General Manager: Katie Cilluffo
Orchestra: Candace Norton
Founded: 1971
Specialized Field: Orchestra
Paid Staff: 4
Paid Artists: 65
Budget: $211,000

1346
WESTERN PIEDMONT SYMPHONY
243 3rd Avenue NE
Suite 1-N
Hickory, NC 28601
Phone: 828-324-8603
Fax: 828-324-1301
e-mail: chrisbrown@wpsymphony.org
Officers:
Personnel Manager: Dr Philip Paul
Business Manager: Eileen Rogers
Secretary: Nancy Rockett
Management:
Music Director/Conductor: John G Ross
Executive Director: Chris Brown
Business Manager: Rochelle Hull
Utilizes: Educators
Founded: 1964
Specialized Field: Orchestra
Income Sources: Unifour; Fund-raisers
Performs At: P.E. Monroe Auditorium

1347
SMOKY MOUNTAIN BRITISH BRASS
PO Box 1467
Lake Juanaluska, NC 28745
Phone: 828-253-6842
e-mail: smbrass@asapgroup.com
Web Site: http://www.smbrass.com
Management:
General Manager: Bert Wiley
Artistic Director: Dr. William Bryant
Mission: Offering quality music for brass band covering all artists and eras.
Utilizes: Guest Artists
Founded: 1981
Specialized Field: Chamber; Band; Brass Ensemble
Status: Semi-Professional
Organization Type: Performing; Touring; Educational

1348
TRINKLE BRASS WORKS
803 W 24th Street
Lumberton, NC 28358
Phone: 919-671-4556
Officers:
President: Steven Trinkle
VP: Genie Burkett
Secretary: Dr. Alan Kalkor
Treasurer: Joel Gordon
Mission: Established in 1977 to provide art centers, universities and schools with concerts and lecture-recitals in brass and percussion chamber music. Concerts include performances on Renaissance, Baroque and modern instruments.
Utilizes: Singers
Founded: 1977
Specialized Field: Chamber; Brass Ensemble
Status: Professional; Nonprofit
Income Sources: Wisconsin Arts Board
Organization Type: Performing; Touring; Resident; Educational

1349
NORTH CAROLINA SYMPHONY
2 E South Street
Raleigh, NC 27601
Phone: 919-733-2750
Fax: 919-733-9920
e-mail: tickets@ncsymphony.org
Web Site: www.ncsymphony.org
Officers:
Chairman: William P Furr
Vice Chairman: Henry Mitchell
Secretary: Carolyn Turner
Treasurer: Wade Reece
Management:
Music Director/Conductor: Gerhardt Zimmermann
Artistic VP: Scott Freck
Assistant Conductor: Jeffrey. Pollock
Stage Manager: Granville H Spry, III
Assistant Stage Manager: Prentis Lambert
Mission: Presenting live orchestral music for residents of North Carolina; providing music education programs in the schools.
Utilizes: Commissioned Composers; Commissioned Music; Composers-in-Residence; Guest Artists; Guest Musicians; Multimedia; Original Music Scores
Founded: 1932
Specialized Field: Symphony; Orchestra; Chamber; Ensemble
Status: Professional; Nonprofit
Budget: $8.4 Million
Income Sources: American Symphony Orchestra League
Organization Type: Performing; Touring; Resident; Educational; Sponsoring

1350
RALEIGH RINGERS
8516 Sleepy Creek Drive
Raleigh, NC 27613
Phone: 919-847-7574
Fax: 919-847-7574
Toll-free: 866-637-7464
e-mail: rrmgdir@nc.rr.com
Management:
Director: David M Harris
Managing Director: Nancy Ritter
Artistic Consultant: Dr. William A Payn
Specialized Field: Handbell Ensemble
Status: Nonprofit

1351
RALEIGH SYMPHONY ORCHESTRA
119 S Pason Street
PO Box 25878
Raleigh, NC 27611-5878
Phone: 919-546-9755
Fax: 919-546-0251
e-mail: manager@raleighsymphony.org
Web Site: www.raleighsymphony.org
Management:
    Music Director: Jim Widdelow
    Executive Director: Irene Burke
Mission: The Raleigh Symphony Orchestra (RSO) is a non-profit organization whose mission is to promote and encourage the understanding and appreciation of music through high quality performances of orchestral and chamber music; to make programs available at a reasonable cost to an increasing and diverse audience from Raleigh and surrounding communities; and to feature and provide opportunities for outstanding musicians of the area.
Founded: 1979
Specialized Field: Symphony; Orchestra; Chamber Music
Status: Non-Profit
Paid Staff: 3
Paid Artists: 70
Non-paid Artists: 40

1352
TAR RIVER CHORAL & ORCHESTRAL SOCIETY
The Dunn Center 1200
PO Box 8255
Rocky Mount, NC 27804
Phone: 252-985-3055
e-mail: abouttroc@suddenlink.net
Management:
    Conductor: Alfred Sturgis
    General Manager: Beth Kupsco
Specialized Field: Orchestra; Band; Swing

1353
SALISBURY SYMPHONY ORCHESTRA
PO Box 4264
Salisbury, NC 28145
Phone: 704-637-4314
Fax: 704-637-4268
e-mail: mshives@catawba.edu
Web Site: www.ci.salisbury.nc.us/symphony
Officers:
    President: Martha West
    VP: Jean Owen
    Secretary: Judy Robinson
Management:
    Music Director/Conductor: David Hagyes
Mission: Performing symphonic music and increasing musical appreciation in the area; offering four full concerts annually, including one free concert for youth.
Utilizes: Collaborations; Guest Accompanists; Guest Musicians; Guest Writers; Multimedia; Singers
Founded: 1966
Specialized Field: Symphony; Orchestra
Status: Professional; Nonprofit
Paid Staff: 3
Paid Artists: 70
Budget: $241,900
Income Sources: Ticket Sales; Program Ads; Sponsorships; Contributions
Performs At: Varick Auditorium; Livingstone College
Seating Capacity: 1,500
Year Built: 1964
Organization Type: Performing; Educational

1354
PADDYWHACK
Route 2
PO Box 60
Tryon, NC 28782
Phone: 704-894-8091
Mission: Playing and promoting 16th-19th century popular music.
Founded: 1978
Specialized Field: Ensemble; Ethnic Music; Folk Music; Band
Status: Semi-Professional
Income Sources: Schiele Museum
Organization Type: Performing; Touring; Educational

1355
WILMINGTON SYMPHONY ORCHESTRA
4608 Cedar Avenue
Suite 105
Wilmington, NC 28403
Phone: 910-791-9262
Fax: 910-791-8970
Web Site: www.wilmingtonsymphony.org
Officers:
    President: John R Stike
    Treasurer: Ralph Godwin
Management:
    Executive Director: Reed M Wallace
Mission: To provide music of the highest integrity and performance quality to the community.
Founded: 1971
Specialized Field: Symphony
Status: Non-Professional; Nonprofit
Paid Staff: 3
Budget: $250,000
Income Sources: Box office; Private donations; Grants
Performs At: Kenan Auditorium
Annual Attendance: 6,000
Seating Capacity: 987
Organization Type: Performing; Educational

1356
NORTH CAROLINA SCHOOL OF THE ARTS SYMPHONY ORCHESTRA
North Carolina School of the Arts
School of Music, 1533 South Main Street
Winston-Salem, NC 27127-2188
Phone: 336-770-3399
Fax: 336-770-3248
e-mail: tclark@ncarts.edu
Management:
    Conductor: Serge Zehnacker
    Dean: Thomas Clark
Founded: 1963
Specialized Field: Orchestra

1357
WAKE FOREST UNIVERSITY SYMPHONY ORCHESTRA
Reynolda Station
Box 7345
Winston-Salem, NC 27109
Phone: 336-758-5364
Fax: 336-758-4935
e-mail: dhagy@wfu.edu
Management:
    Conductor: Dr. David Hagy
    Music Department Chair: Stewart Carter
Specialized Field: Orchestra

1358
WINSTON-SALEM SYMPHONY
201 N Broad Street
Suite 200
Winston-Salem, NC 27101
Phone: 336-725-1035
Fax: 336-725-3924
e-mail: mvale@wssymphony.org
Web Site: www.wssymphony.org
Officers:
    President: Ray McKinney
    President/CEO: Roger Bear
    Treasurer: Dick Deem
    Secretary: Jerry Silber
Management:
    Music Director: Robert Moody
    Ticket Sales/Donor Administration: Latonya Wright
Mission: To present high quality symphonic literature and to provide music education for Winston-Salem children.
Utilizes: Collaborations; Commissioned Composers; Commissioned Music; Educators; Five Seasonal Concerts; Guest Accompanists; Guest Artists; Guest Choreographers; Guest Companies; Guest Composers; Guest Directors; Guest Instructors; Guest Lecturers; Guest Musical Directors; Guest Musicians; Guest Soloists; High School Drama; Local Artists; Lyricists; Multimedia; New Productions; Singers; Visual Arts
Founded: 1947
Specialized Field: Symphony; Orchestra; Chamber; Ensemble
Status: Professional, Nonprofit
Paid Staff: 14
Volunteer Staff: 120
Paid Artists: 75
Non-paid Artists: 80
Budget: $1.4 million
Income Sources: The Arts Council of Winston-Salem/Forsyth County, Wachovia Wealth Management, RJ Reynolds, Partners Medicare Choice, Michael & Mardene Morykwas
Performs At: E. Stevens Center for the Performing Arts
Annual Attendance: 100,000
Seating Capacity: 1,380
Year Remodeled: 1985
Organization Type: Performing; Resident; Educational

North Dakota

1359
BISMARCK-MANDAN SYMPHONY ORCHESTRA
215 N 6th Street
PO Box 2031
Bismarck, ND 58502
Phone: 701-258-8345
Fax: 701-258-8345
e-mail: bmso@bisman.com
Web Site: www.bismarckmandansymphony.org
Officers:
    President: William Pearce
    Treasurer: Al Wolf
    Treasurer: Richard Weber
Management:
    Executive Director: Susan Lundberg
    Music Director: Thomas Wellin
Mission: To share orchestral music and educational programs of all kinds with the public in many venues.
Utilizes: Guest Musical Directors; Guest Musicians; Local Artists; Multimedia; Original Music Scores; Sign Language Translators

Founded: 1975
Specialized Field: Symphony; Orchestra; Ensemble
Status: Nonprofit
Paid Staff: 3
Volunteer Staff: 200
Paid Artists: 70
Budget: $300,000
Income Sources: Private; Corporate; Grants
Performs At: Belle Mehus City Auditorium
Annual Attendance: 4,000
Facility Category: Auditorium
Type of Stage: Conventional
Stage Dimensions: 40 x 60
Seating Capacity: 836
Year Built: 1914
Year Remodeled: 1997
Cost: 32.5 Million
Organization Type: Performing

1360
GREATER GRAND FORKS SYMPHONY ORCHESTRA

University of North Dakota
3350 Campus Road Stop 7125
Grand Forks, ND 58202
Phone: 701-777-2644
Fax: 701-777-3320
Toll-free: 800-225- 863
e-mail: tamara.mulske@und.nodak.edu
Management:
 Department Chair: Royce Blackburn
 Director of Strings/Orchestra: Eric Lawson
 Theatre Symphony Music Director: James Popejoy
Mission: The greater Grand Forks Symphony Association is a regional center for classical music performance and education.
Specialized Field: Orchestra; Ensemble; Chamber
Paid Staff: 3
Paid Artists: 50
Non-paid Artists: 10

1361
MINOT SYMPHONY ASSOCIATION

500 University Avenue W
Minot, ND 58707
Phone: 701-858-4228
Fax: 701-858-3823
Web Site: warp6.cs.misu.nodak.edu/music/mso/
Officers:
 President: Lou Whitmer
 Treasurer: David Herzig
 Conductor: Dr. Daniel Hornstein
Mission: To foster and perpetuate the Minot Symphony Orchestra, a college-community orchestra.
Founded: 1965
Specialized Field: Symphony; Orchestra
Status: Professional; Nonprofit
Paid Staff: 70
Income Sources: North Dakota Council of Arts; Minot Area Council of Arts; North Dakota Arts Alliance; American Symphony Orchestra League; National Endowment for the Arts
Performs At: McFarland Auditorium
Organization Type: Performing; Resident

Ohio

1362
AKRON SYMPHONY ORCHESTRA

17 N Broadway
Akron, OH 44308
Phone: 330-535-8131
Fax: 330-535-7302
e-mail: msnider@akronsymphony.org
Web Site: www.akronsymphony.org
Officers:
 President: George Rosin
Management:
 Interim Executive Director: Margo Snider
 Director Marketing/Public Relations: Wendy Turrell
Mission: Enhance the quality of life for the greater Akron community through exccellence in music performance and education.
Utilizes: Guest Artists
Founded: 1949
Specialized Field: Ensemble; Symphony
Status: Professional; Nonprofit
Paid Staff: 8
Budget: $1.6 million
Income Sources: American Symphony Orchestra League; Ohio Arts Council; Private/Corporate Donations; Grants; Funding
Performs At: E.J. Thomas Performing Arts Hall
Facility Category: University Performing Arts Hall
Seating Capacity: 3,000
Organization Type: Performing; Educational

1363
AKRON YOUTH SYMPHONY ORCHESTRA

17 N Broadway
Akron, OH 44308-1946
Phone: 330-535-8131
Fax: 330-535-7302
e-mail: WTurrell@akronsymphony.org
Web Site: www.akronsymphony.org
Management:
 Music Director/Conductor: Ya-Hui Wang
 Executive Director: Jeffrey K Sperry
 Director Marketing: Wendy A Turrell
Founded: 1949
Specialized Field: Youth Symphony
Status: Professional; Nonprofit
Paid Staff: 75
Income Sources: Akron Symphony Orchestra; American Symphony Orchestra League (Youth Orchestra Division)
Performs At: E.J. Thomas Performing Arts Hall
Organization Type: Performing; Educational; Sponsoring

1364
ASHLAND SYMPHONY ORCHESTRA

401 College Avenue
Ashland, OH 44805
Phone: 419-289-5115
Fax: 419-289-5329
e-mail: symphony@ashland.edu
Officers:
 President: Fred Lavender
 VP: Paula Watson
 Secretary: Elissa Huffman
 Treasurer: Mindy Reef
Management:
 Executive Director: Ann Mohr
 Music Director/Conductor: Arie Lipsky
 Office Manager: Candace Drake
 Personnel/Production Manager: Michele Gedrge
Mission: Offering symphonic orchestra programs to all residents of Ashland as well as the surrounding area.
Utilizes: Collaborations; Guest Accompanists; Guest Musicians; Original Music Scores; Sign Language Translators
Founded: 1970

Specialized Field: Symphony; Orchestra
Status: Semi-Professional; Nonprofit
Paid Staff: 5
Volunteer Staff: 10
Paid Artists: 7
Budget: $190,000
Income Sources: Box Office; Private Donations; Business Donations
Performs At: Hugo Young Theatre
Affiliations: American Symphony Orchestra League
Annual Attendance: 3,500-6,000
Organization Type: Performing; Educational

1365
ASHTABULA CHAMBER ORCHESTRA

3325 W 13th Street
Ashtabula, OH 44004
Mailing Address: PO Box 415 Ashtabula, OH 44005
Phone: 440-964-3322
e-mail: hdra!alltel.net
Web Site: www.ashtabulaareaorchestra.com
Officers:
 President: Joesph Petros
 VP: May Lou Jaskela
 Treasurer: Betty Heitikko
 Secretary: Dianne Lahti
Management:
 Music Director: Michael Gelfand
Mission: To educate the people of the area in all types of stringed music; to provide string ensemble music for public enjoyment; to encourage young people on strings.
Utilizes: Guest Artists; Guest Companies; Singers
Founded: 1982
Specialized Field: Orchestra; Chamber
Status: Non-Professional; Nonprofit
Paid Staff: 35
Income Sources: Kent State University; Ashtabula Campus
Performs At: Kent State University Auditorium; Ashtabula Campus
Organization Type: Performing; Resident

1366
CLERMONT PHILHARMONIC

1501 Cincinnati-Batavia Pike
Batavia
Batavia, OH 45103
Phone: 513-732-2561
Fax: 513- 73—293
e-mail: asantoro@clermontphilharmonic.com
Officers:
 Board President: Debbie Siegroth
 Treasurer: Ed Brady
Management:
 Music Director/Conductor: David Smarelli
 General Manager: Angelo Santoro
Specialized Field: Orchestra

1367
CLEVELAND POPS ORCHESTRA

24000 Mercantile Road
Unit 11
Beachwood, OH 44122
Phone: 216-765-7677
Fax: 216-765-7677
e-mail: shirleymorgenstern@clevelandpops.com
Web Site: www.clevelandpops.com
Officers:
 Chairman of the Board: Thomas J Scanlon
 Vice Chairman: Randall Solomon
 Vice Chairman: Sondra Boyd
Management:
 President & CEO: Shirley Morgenstern

Artistic Director & Conductor: Carl Topilow
Marketing Director: Gordon Petitt
Mission: The Cleveland POPS Orchestra is committed to presenting pops music of the highest artistic quality that is entertaining and exciting to a wide and diverse audience.
Founded: 1994
Specialized Field: Orchestra; Broadway; Jazz; Movie Themes; Patriotic
Paid Staff: 5
Paid Artists: 65
Budget: $800,000
Income Sources: Ticket Sales; Private Contributions; Foundation Grants; Corporate Sponsorships
Performs At: Severance Hall, Playhouse Square Center

1368
OHIO CHAMBER ORCHESTRA

3659 Green Road #118
Beachwood, OH 44122
Phone: 216-464-1755
Fax: 216-464-8628
e-mail: oco@ix.netcom.com
Officers:
    President: Paul R Bunker
    Chairman Executive Committee: William Steffee MD
    Executive Vice Chairman: Robert H Jackson
    Treasurer: James E. Wilcosky
    Secretary: Martha Vail
    President Ohio Chamber Orchestra: Norma Glazer
Management:
    Executive Director: Eugenia L Epperson
Mission: To perform at the highest artistic level possible programs specializing in works written specifically for chamber orchestra in appropriate (intimate) settings, featuring soloists of local and international standing.
Utilizes: Guest Artists
Founded: 1972
Specialized Field: Symphony; Orchestra; Chamber; Ensemble
Status: Professional
Performs At: The Cleveland Play House
Organization Type: Performing; Touring; Resident

1369
SUBURBAN SYMPHONY ORCHESTRA

PO Box 22653
Beachwood, OH 44122
Phone: 216-449-2389
Management:
    Music Director: Martin Kessler
    General Manager: Paul Pride
Mission: To offer accomplished professionals and nonprofessionals an opportunity to be part of a symphony orchestra; to present five free concerts each season.
Utilizes: Guest Artists
Founded: 1954
Specialized Field: Symphony; Orchestra
Status: Professional; Semi-Professional; Non-Professional; Nonprofit
Paid Staff: 70
Performs At: Beachwood High School Auditorium
Organization Type: Performing

1370
BALDWIN-WALLACE COLLEGE SYMPHONY ORCHESTRA

275 Eastland Road
Fanny Nast Gamble Auditorium 650
Berea, OH 44017
Phone: 440-826-2362
Fax: 440-826-3239
Web Site: www.bw.edu
Management:
    Conductor: Dwight Ottman
    Conservatory of Music Director: Peter Landgren
Specialized Field: Orchestra

1371
VENTI DA CAMERA

Bowling Green State University
Bowling Green, OH 43403
Phone: 419-372-2955
Fax: 419-372-2938
Management:
    Oboe/College Musical Arts: John Bentley
    Flute/College Musical Arts: Christina Jennings
    Clarinet; College of Musical Arts: Kevin Schempf
    Bassoon College of Musical Arts: Winston Collier
    Horn; College of Musical Arts: Rosemary Williams
Mission: Presenting works composed for wind quintet as well as other ensembles and offering a wide-ranging repertoire to a broad audience.
Utilizes: Guest Musical Directors; Guest Musicians; Sign Language Translators; Soloists
Founded: 1965
Specialized Field: Chamber; Wind Ensemble
Status: Professional
Income Sources: Bowling Green State University College of Music
Performs At: Bryan Recital Hall
Annual Attendance: 800
Facility Category: Recital Hall
Stage Dimensions: 50'x30'
Seating Capacity: 250
Year Built: 1976
Organization Type: Performing; Touring; Resident; Educational

1372
CANTON SYMPHONY ORCHESTRA

1001 Market Avenue N
Canton, OH 44702-1024
Phone: 330-452-3434
Fax: 330-452-3429
e-mail: lmoorhouse@cantonsymphony.org
Web Site: www.cantonsymphony.org
Officers:
    President/CEO: Stephen Wogaman
    Chair: Jeffrey Halm
Management:
    Music Director: Gerhard Zimmermann
Mission: To maintain an orchestra of the highest quality as a cultural and educational resource and to bring the enjoyment and enrichment of great music to increasing numbers of citizens in Northeastern Ohio.
Utilizes: Guest Artists
Founded: 1937
Specialized Field: Symphony; Orchestra; Chamber; Ensemble
Status: Professional; Nonprofit
Paid Staff: 5
Paid Artists: 17
Income Sources: American Symphony Orchestra League
Performs At: William E. Umstattd Performing Arts Hall
Seating Capacity: 1490

Year Built: 1976
Organization Type: Performing

1373
CANTON YOUTH SYMPHONY

1001 North Market Avenue
Canton, OH 44702
Phone: 330-452-3434
Fax: 330-452-4429
Officers:
    President: Stephen Wogaman
    Education Programs Manager: Irene Barker
Founded: 1962
Specialized Field: Youth Symphony
Status: Non-Professional; Nonprofit
Income Sources: American Symphony Orchestra League (Youth Orchestra Division); Canton Symphony Orchestra
Performs At: Fine and Professional Arts Building
Organization Type: Performing; Educational; Sponsoring

1374
DAYTON CLASSICAL GUITAR SOCIETY

8530 Cherrycreek Drive
Centerville, OH 45458-3215
Phone: 937-435-1858
e-mail: Dcgs@mccutcheon.com
Officers:
    President: Jim McCutcheon
Management:
    President: Jim McCutcheon
    Vice President: David Ferrara
Founded: 1975
Specialized Field: Classical Guitar
Budget: $1,000
Annual Attendance: 500-700
Seating Capacity: 175

1375
CCM PHILHARMONIA & CONCERT ORCHESTRA

College-Conservatory of Music
PO Box 210003
Cincinnati, OH 45221-0003
Phone: 513-556-6638
Fax: 513-556-2698
e-mail: PJ.Woolston@us.edu
Officers:
    Conductor: Xian Zhang
    Assistant to the Dean: Carol Brown
Management:
    Dean: Douglas Lowry
    Assistant Dean Performance Manageme: Katherine Mohylsky
Specialized Field: Orchestra; Chamber

1376
CINCINNATI CHAMBER ORCHESTRA

105 W Fourth Street
Suite 810
Cincinnati, OH 45202
Phone: 513-723-1182
Fax: 513-723-1057
e-mail: info@ccocinnati.com
Web Site: www.ccocinnati.com
Officers:
    President: Rosemary Schlachter
    VP: Robert Chavezr
    Secretary: Brian Hickey
    Treasurer: Michael Comer
Management:
    Executive Director: Jennifer Nagel
    Operations Manager: Daren Fuster

Music Director: Mischa Santora
PR/Communications Manager: Ann Stewart
Mission: To provide high quality classical music in an engaging, innovative, accessible and affordable manner
Utilizes: Guest Composers; Guest Lecturers; Guest Musicians
Founded: 1974
Specialized Field: Chamber; Orchestra
Paid Staff: 5
Volunteer Staff: 40
Paid Artists: 32
Budget: $485,000
Affiliations: American Symphony Orchestra League
Organization Type: Performing; Touring; Educational

1377
CINCINNATI ORCHESTRA
23 South Front Street Hamilton
Cincinnati, OH 45011
Phone: 513-895-5151
Fax: 513-474-1584
e-mail: info@hfso.org
Management:
Music Director: Paul Stanbery
Mission: Presentation of symphonic concerts, educational activities and pops.
Specialized Field: Orchestra; Ensemble
Paid Staff: 4
Volunteer Staff: 16
Paid Artists: 75

1378
CINCINNATI SYMPHONY YOUTH ORCHESTRA
1241 Elm Street
Music Hall
Cincinnati, OH 45202
Phone: 513-621-1919
Fax: 513- 74—353
Management:
Conductor: Eric Dudley
Music Director: Paavo Jarvi
Specialized Field: Youth Orchestra

1379
LINTON CHAMBER MUSIC SERIES/ENCORE! LINTON
Music Hall
1241 Elm Street
Cincinnati, OH 45202
Phone: 513-381-6868
e-mail: linton_info@lintonmusic.org
Web Site: www.lintonmusic.org
Officers:
Anne Black: Anne Black
Management:
Artistic Director: Richard Waller
Specialized Field: Chamber
Budget: $20,000-35,000
Performs At: First Unitarian Church; Cinicinnati City Council Chambers

1380
CLEVELAND CHAMBER SYMPHONY
2647 Eaton Road
University Heights
Cleveland, OH 44118
Phone: 216-687-9243
Fax: 216-687-9279
Personnel Manager: James Taylor
Management:
Conductor: Steven Smith
Program Annotator: Robert Finn

Mission: Works to commission, perform, record and promote the dissemination of musical works exclusively by composters of our time.
Utilizes: Guest Composers; Guest Musical Directors; Guest Musicians
Founded: 1980
Specialized Field: Chamber; Symphony
Paid Staff: 3
Paid Artists: 37
Budget: $400,000 - 500,000
Income Sources: Individuals; Government & Distinguished Private Foundations; Ohio Arts Council
Performs At: Drinko Recital Hall
Affiliations: National Endowment for the Arts; The Ohio Arts Council; The Ohio Board of Regents; The Cleveland Foundation; The George Gund Foundation
Annual Attendance: 2,700 - 3,300
Facility Category: Recital Hall
Type of Stage: Proscenium
Seating Capacity: 300
Year Built: 1990
Rental Contact: Facilities Coordinator Toni Lovejoy

1381
CLEVELAND INSTITUTE OF MUSIC
11021 E Boulevard
Cleveland, OH 44106
Phone: 216-791-5000
Fax: 216-791-3063
e-mail: cimmktg@po.cwro.edu
Web Site: www.cim.edu
Officers:
President: David Cerone
Management:
Director Marketing/Communications: Susan M Schwartz
Mission: To provide talented students with a professional, world-class education in the art of music.
Utilizes: Artists-in-Residence; Collaborations; Guest Accompanists; Guest Composers
Founded: 1920
Specialized Field: Educational; Classical Music; World Music
Paid Staff: 65
Paid Artists: 180
Budget: $13,175,000
Affiliations: Cleveland International Piano Competition; Art Song Festival; Western Reserve University
Annual Attendance: 47,000
Facility Category: Music
Seating Capacity: 550
Year Built: 1961
Rental Contact: Lori Wright
Resident Groups: Faculty and Student Performers

1382
CLEVELAND JAZZ ORCHESTRA
PO Box 31666
Cleveland, OH 44131
Phone: 216-524-2263
Fax: 216-524-8349
Web Site: www.clevelandjazz.org
Officers:
President: Jill Brotman
VP: Jim Remond
Management:
Managing Director: Larry Patch Paciorek
Music Director: Jack Schantz
Mission: To establish Cleveland Jazz Orchestra in Northeast Ohio; to enhance availability and quality of jazz; to assist in educating young musicians; to encourage involvement and training of minority musicians.
Founded: 1985

Specialized Field: Jazz Ensemble; Band
Status: Professional; Nonprofit
Paid Staff: 2
Volunteer Staff: 6
Paid Artists: 80
Income Sources: Cuyahoga Community College; Northeast Ohio Jazz Society; Cleveland Playhouse
Annual Attendance: 5,000
Organization Type: Performing; Resident; Educational; Sponsoring

1383
CLEVELAND OCTET
1510 Crest Road
Cleveland, OH 44121
Phone: 216-381-9031
Fax: 216-291-0502
Officers:
Founder/Director: Erich Eichhorn
Management:
Columbia Artist Management, NY:
Mission: To present and perform rarely performed masterpieces for ensembles of six to eight players.
Founded: 1977
Specialized Field: Chamber; Ensemble
Status: Professional; Nonprofit
Income Sources: Cleveland Museum of Art; Cleveland Orchestra
Performs At: Cleveland Museum of Art
Organization Type: Performing; Touring

1384
CLEVELAND ORCHESTRA
11001 Euclid Avenue
Severance Hall
Cleveland, OH 44106
Phone: 216-231-7372
Fax: 216-231-0202
e-mail: info@clevelandorchestra.com
Web Site: www.clevelandorch.org
Officers:
Chairman: Larry Milder
Management:
Executive Director: Reobert Porco
Music Director: Christoph Von Dohnanyi
Manager: Nancy Bell Cue
Director Choruses: Robert Porco
Concert Master: William Preucil
Utilizes: Guest Artists
Founded: 1918
Specialized Field: Symphony; Orchestra; Ensemble
Status: Professional; Nonprofit; Semi-Volunteer
Paid Staff: 6
Volunteer Staff: 168
Income Sources: American Symphony Orchestra League
Performs At: Severence Hall; Blossom Music Center
Organization Type: Performing; Touring; Resident; Educational; Sponsoring

1385
CLEVELAND ORCHESTRA YOUTH ORCHESTRA
11001 Euclid Avenue
Severance Hall
Cleveland, OH 44106-1796
Phone: 216-231-7352
Fax: 216-231-4077
e-mail: coyo@clevelandorchestra.com
Web Site: www.clevelandorchestrayouthorchestra.com
Management:
Music Director: James Feddeck
Manager: Ashley Smith
Founded: 1986

Specialized Field: Youth Orchestra
Paid Staff: 2
Paid Artists: 18
Budget: $170,000
Income Sources: Musical Arts Association
Performs At: Concert Hall
Affiliations: The Cleveland Orchestra
Facility Category: Concert Hall
Seating Capacity: 2,000
Year Remodeled: 2000

1386
CLEVELAND PHILHARMONIC ORCHESTRA

8702 Bessemer Avenue
PO Box 16251
Cleveland, OH 44116
Phone: 216-556-1800
Management:
General Manager: Martha Hamilton
Music Director/Conductor: William B Slocum
Mission: Providing performances of quality at reasonable ticket prices; to train aspiring musicians; to offer musicians a technical education.
Utilizes: Guest Artists
Founded: 1938
Specialized Field: Symphony; Orchestra
Status: Semi-Professional; Nonprofit
Paid Staff: 60
Income Sources: American Symphony Orchestra League; Saint Vincent Quadrangle Association
Performs At: Cuyahoga Community College
Organization Type: Performing; Resident; Sponsoring

1387
NORTHEAST OHIO JAZZ SOCIETY

4614 Prospect Avenue
#533
Cleveland, OH 44103
Phone: 216-426-9900
Fax: 216-426-9906
Specialized Field: Jazz Ensemble
Budget: $60,000-150,000

1388
SHAKER SYMPHONY ORCHESTRA

Cleveland Institute of Music
11021 East Boulevard
Cleveland, OH 44106
Phone: 216-464-6170
Fax: 216- 79—303
e-mail: hinkleal@adelphia.net
Management:
Conductor: Allan Hinkle
Director: David Cerone
Specialized Field: Orchestra

1389
UNIVERSITY CIRCLE CHAMBER ORCHESTRA

Music Department
Case Western Reserve University
Cleveland, OH 44106
Phone: 216-368-2400
Fax: 216-368-6557
Web Site:
www.cwru.edu/artsci/musc/ensembles/orchestra.
Mission: Offering an opportunity to university students as well as interested amateurs, to perform stimulating repertoire in a pleasant but serious atmosphere.
Specialized Field: Symphony; Orchestra; Chamber; Ensemble
Status: Non-Professional; Nonprofit

Paid Staff: 18
Income Sources: Case Western Reserve University
Performs At: Harkness Chapel
Organization Type: Performing; Resident; Educational

1390
CLEVELAND CHAMBER MUSIC SOCIETY

2532 Lafayette Drive
University Heights
Cleveland Heights, OH 44118
Phone: 216-291-2777
Fax: 216- 29—913
e-mail: information@clevelandchambermusic.org
Management:
Executive Secretary: Sharon Muskin
President: Mary Von Herrmann
Founded: 1949
Specialized Field: Chamber
Paid Staff: 1
Budget: $60,000-150,000
Income Sources: Ticket Sales; Endowment
Performs At: Fairmount Temple Auditorium; Church of the Convenant
Annual Attendance: 2,800
Facility Category: Rent
Seating Capacity: 736

1391
HEIGHTS CHAMBER ORCHESTRA

PO Box 18413
Cleveland Heights, OH 44118
Phone: 216-921-4339
Fax: 440-775-8886
e-mail: susanblackwell@hotmail.com
Web Site: http://129.22.153.16/hco/
Officers:
President: Susan Blackwell
Vice President: Sue Schieman
Treasurer: Marlene Englander
Secretary: Carol Boyd
Management:
Music Director: Kelly Corcoran
Resident Conductor: Anthony Addison
Concertmaster: Gino Raffaelli
Mission: To provide the community with an orchestra and the schools with music education.
Founded: 1983
Specialized Field: Symphony; Orchestra
Status: Nonprofit
Paid Staff: 52
Income Sources: Cleveland Heights Board of Education; Cleveland Heights Parks & Recreation Department
Performs At: Performing Arts Center; Cleveland Heights High School
Organization Type: Performing

1392
CHAMBER MUSIC COLUMBUS

PO Box 14445
Columbus, OH 43214
Phone: 614-267-2267
e-mail: info@CMColumbus.org
Management:
President: Charles Warner, president@CMColumbus.org
Vice President: Daniel Jensen, vice_president@CMColumbus.org
Treasurer: Saul Blumenthal, treasurer@CMColumbus.org
Secretary: Sally Griffiths
Specialized Field: Chamber
Status: Non Profit
Budget: $150,000

Seating Capacity: 950

1393
COLUMBUS SYMPHONY ORCHESTRA

55 East State Street
Columbus, OH 43215
Phone: 614-228-8600
Fax: 614-224-7273
Web Site: www.columbussymphony.com
Officers:
Chairman: Linda Kass
Management:
Executive Director/President: Daniel Hart
General Manager: Susan L Rosenstock
Music Director: Alessandro Siciliani
Public Relations Manager: Linda Brill
Mission: To nurture and further the public's musical knowledge through educational activities and musical performances.
Utilizes: Actors; Dancers; Educators; Grant Writers; Guest Accompanists; Guest Companies; Guest Composers; Guest Designers; Guest Instructors; Guest Lecturers; Guest Musical Directors; Guest Musicians; Instructors; Local Artists; Multimedia; Music; Original Music Scores; Sign Language Translators; Singers; Soloists
Founded: 1950
Specialized Field: Symphony; Orchestra; Chamber; Ensemble
Status: Professional
Budget: $10.8 million
Income Sources: American Symphony Orchestra League
Performs At: Ohio Theatre; Mershon Auditorium
Annual Attendance: 205,000
Organization Type: Performing; Educational; Sponsoring

1394
COLUMBUS SYMPHONY YOUTH ORCHESTRAS

55 East State Street
Columbus, OH 43215
Phone: 614-228-9600
Fax: 614-224-7273
e-mail: eberman@columbysymphony.org
Web Site: csyoa.org
Management:
Music Director/Conductor: Peter Stafford Wilson
Education Director: Jane Hahn
Youth Orchestra Manager: Erica C Berman
Mission: To provide the highest quality educational and performance experiences for Central Ohio's most gifted instrumentalists.
Utilizes: Collaborations; Commissioned Composers; Composers-in-Residence; Educators; Fine Artists; Five Seasonal Concerts; Guest Accompanists; Guest Companies; Guest Composers; Guest Designers; Guest Lecturers; Guest Musical Directors; Multimedia; Music; Organization Contracts; Singers; Soloists
Founded: 1955
Specialized Field: Youth Orchestra; Chamber
Status: Non-Professional; Nonprofit
Paid Staff: 7
Income Sources: American Symphony Orchestra League (Youth Orchestra Division); Columbus Symphony Orchestra; donations; tuiton
Performs At: Mess Hall, Capital University; Capitol Theatre; Verne Ritte Center; Hughes Auditorium; Ohio State University
Organization Type: Performing; Touring; Educational

1395
JAZZ ARTS GROUP OF COLUMBUS
930 N High Street
Columbus, OH 43201
Phone: 614-294-5200
Fax: 614-298-6149
e-mail: info@jazzartsgroup.org
Web Site: www.jazzartsgroup.org
Officers:
Director Of Donor Stewardship: Elizabeth Jewell
Grants Manager: Kerri Mollard
Finance Manager: Yvette Boyer
Executive Director: Robert Breithaupt
Management:
Orchestra Manager: Karen Atria aupt
Artistic Director: Bryon Stripling
Artistic Director Emeritus: Ray Eubanks
Managing Director/Operations Dir.: Carol Argiro
Director Of Jazz In Schools: Judy Shafer
Director Of Affiliate Musicians: Louis Tsamous
Business Operations Assistant: Jennifer
Pettibone
Librarian: Jay Miglia
Director Marketing/Communications: Scott
Vezdos
Mission: To advance the art of jazz through
performance and education.
Founded: 1973
Specialized Field: Performing Arts
Status: Professional; Nonprofit
Paid Staff: 12
Volunteer Staff: 15
Budget: $1.4 million
Income Sources: Ohio Arts Council; Greater
Columbus Arts Council; Columbus Foundation;
Subscriptions; Sponsorships; Individual Donations;
Corporate Donations
Performs At: Southern Theatre, Lincoln Theatre
Affiliations: Experience Columbus; Columbus
Chamber; CAMA; OAPN; APAP; Jazz Education
Network
Organization Type: Performing; Touring; Resident;
Educational

1396
PRO MUSICA CHAMBER ORCHESTRA OF COLUMBUS
243 N 5th Street
Columbus, OH 43215
Phone: 614-464-0066
Fax: 614-464-4141
Web Site: www.promusicacolumbus.org
Management:
Executive Director: Alan Silon
Music Director/Conductor: Dr. Timothy Russell
Mission: To establish a partnership with the audience
in order to understand and fulfill audience needs for a
variety of entertaining and enlightening musical
performances as well as educational experiences.
Utilizes: Collaborations; Guest Accompanists; Guest
Artists; Guest Composers; Guest Instructors; Guest
Musical Directors; Guest Musicians; Instructors;
Lyricists; Multi Collaborations; Multimedia; Organization
Contracts; Original Music Scores; Selected Students;
Sign Language Translators
Founded: 1978
Specialized Field: Symphony; Orchestra; Chamber
Status: Professional; Nonprofit
Paid Staff: 7
Budget: $800,000
Performs At: Southern Theatre
Seating Capacity: 939
Year Built: 1896

Year Remodeled: 1999
Organization Type: Performing; Touring

1397
DAYTON PHILHARMONIC ORCHESTRA ASSOCIATION
109 North Main Street
Suite 200
Dayton, OH 45402
Phone: 937-224-3521
Fax: 937-223-9189
e-mail: info@daytonphilharmonic.com
Web Site: www.daytonphilharmonic.com
Officers:
President: Paul Helfrich
Dir. Marketing & Public Relations: David Bukvic
Management:
Music Director: Neal Gittleman
Mission: Maintaining and nurturing the highest quality
professional symphonic orchestra; offering live concerts
that promote cultural enhancement.
Utilizes: Guest Artists
Founded: 1933
Specialized Field: Symphony; Orchestra; Chamber
Status: Professional; Nonprofit
Paid Staff: 16
Volunteer Staff: 6
Paid Artists: 88
Non-paid Artists: 120
Income Sources: American Symphony Orchestra
League; American Arts Alliance; American Council for
the Arts
Performs At: Montgomery County's Memorial Hall;
Dayton Convention Center
Organization Type: Performing; Resident; Educational;
Sponsoring

1398
DAYTON PHILHARMONIC YOUTH ORCHESTRA
Performance Place
109 N Main Street, Suite 200
Dayton, OH 45402
Phone: 937-224-3521
Fax: 937-223-9189
e-mail: info@daytonphilharmonic.com
Web Site: www.daytonphilharmonic.com
Management:
Conductor: Patrick Reynolds
Director Education: Gloria Pugh
Mission: To give aspiring young musicians of the
Dayton area an opportunity to work together studying
challenging orchestral music; to attempt to strengthen
and expand the musical skills, knowledge, talent and
experience through the study of the symphonic
orchestral literature.
Founded: 1982
Specialized Field: Youth Orchestra
Status: Professional; Nonprofit
Paid Staff: 15
Volunteer Staff: 3
Non-paid Artists: 90
Income Sources: American Symphony Orchestra
League (Youth Orchestra Division); Ohio Music Club;
Dayton Philharmonic Orchestra
Performs At: Concert Hall; Wright State University
Organization Type: Performing; Educational

1399
SOIREES MUSICALES PIANO SERIES
834 Riverview Terrace
Dayton, OH 45407-2433

Phone: 937-228-5802
Fax: 937-228-2380
e-mail: hagpia@interaxs.net
Web Site: www.soireesmusicales.com
Management:
Series Director: Donald C Hageman
Founded: 1969
Specialized Field: Soloists; Piano
Volunteer Staff: 7
Budget: $10,000-20,000
Performs At: Shiloh Church

1400
CENTRAL OHIO SYMPHONY ORCHESTRA
PO Box 619
Delaware, OH 43015
Phone: 740-362-1799
Fax: 740-362-1733
Toll-free: 888-999-2676
e-mail: mail@coso-orchestra.org
Web Site: www.COSO-Orchestra.oeg
Management:
Executive Director: Warren W Hyer
Interim Conductor: Jamie Morales Matos
Founded: 1978
Specialized Field: Orchestra
Paid Staff: 4
Paid Artists: 65
Non-paid Artists: 10
Budget: $120,000
Annual Attendance: 20,000
Facility Category: Concert Hall
Seating Capacity: 1,079
Year Built: 1893
Year Remodeled: 1980

1401
HAMILTON-FAIRFIELD SYMPHONY & CHORALE
22 South Front Street
Hamilton, OH 45011
Phone: 513-895-5151
Fax: 513-474-1584
e-mail: info@hfso.org
Management:
Music Director/Conductor: Paul Stanbery
Specialized Field: Orchestra

1402
MUSIC FROM THE WESTERN RESERVE
Western Reserve Academy
116 College Street
Hudson, OH 44236
Phone: 330-650-9714
Fax: 330-688-4839
Officers:
President: Bruce F Rothmann, MD
VP: Walter Watson
Treasurer: Robert L Henke
Secretary: David Hunter, Esquire
Recording Secretary: Diana Truyell
Management:
Concert Manager: Lola Rothmann
Mission: Showcasing the abundant musical talent of
Northeast Ohio.
Utilizes: Instructors; Multimedia; Original Music Scores;
Sign Language Translators; Singers
Founded: 1982
Specialized Field: Chamber
Status: Nonprofit
Volunteer Staff: 6
Budget: $10,000

Performs At: The Chapel, Western Reserve Academy
Annual Attendance: 600-700
Seating Capacity: 450
Year Built: 1836
Organization Type: Sponsoring

1403
LAKELAND CIVIC ORCHESTRA

Lakeland Community College
Lakeland Performing Arts Center 430
Kirtland, OH 44094-5198
Phone: 440-473-9929
Fax: 440-975-4738
Toll-free: 800-589-8520
e-mail: kharsha@lakelandcc.edu
Management:
    Orchestra Director: Kathryn Harsha
    Senior Secretary: Theresa Myllykoski
Specialized Field: Orchestra

1404
LAKESIDE SYMPHONY

236 Walnut Avenue
Lakeside, OH 43440
Phone: 419-798-4461
Fax: 419-798-5033
e-mail: schedule@lakesideohio.com
Web Site: www.lakesideohio.com
Management:
    Executive Director: Bud Cox
    Music Director: Robert L Conquist
    Program Director: G Keith Addy
Mission: To maintain a professional resident orchestra for part of the summer season at Lakeside.
Founded: 1925
Specialized Field: Symphony; Orchestra; Chamber
Status: Professional; Nonprofit
Paid Staff: 75
Volunteer Staff: 60
Paid Artists: 10
Performs At: Hoover Auditorium
Organization Type: Performing; Resident; Educational

1405
LIMA SYMPHONY ORCHESTRA

PO Box 1651
67 Town Square
Lima, OH 45802
Phone: 419-222-5701
Fax: 419-222-6587
e-mail: staff@limasymphony.org
Web Site: www.limasymphony.com
Officers:
    Symphony Board President: Linda Burkhalter
    VP: Tom Leininger
    Secretary: Scott Shafer
    Friends of the Symphony, President: Kim Shanahan
Management:
    Music Director/Conductor: Crafton Beck
    Executive Director: Paul Assenheimer
    Personnel Manager: Anita Sims Skinner
Mission: Promoting the public's musical appreciation and knowledge through live musical performances, including chamber, opera and symphonic.
Utilizes: Guest Artists; Guest Companies
Founded: 1953
Specialized Field: Symphony; Orchestra; Chamber
Status: Semi-Professional; Nonprofit
Paid Staff: 8
Volunteer Staff: 1
Paid Artists: 85
Budget: $350,000- $400,000

Income Sources: American Symphony Orchestra League
Performs At: Veterans Memorial Civic and Convention Center
Seating Capacity: 1,670
Organization Type: Performing; Educational; Sponsoring

1406
MANSFIELD SYMPHONY ORCHESTRA

PO Box 789
Mansfield, OH 44901-0789
Phone: 419-522-2726
Fax: 419-524-7005
e-mail: tomc@rparts.org
Officers:
    Choral Director: Richard L Wink
    Director of Finance: Alison Crabb
Management:
    President/CEO: Dr. Thomas J Carto
    Music Director: Robert Franz
Specialized Field: Orchestra
Facility Category: Theater
Type of Stage: Proscenium
Seating Capacity: 1406
Year Built: 1928
Year Remodeled: 1982

1407
RICHLAND PERFORMING ARTS

138 Park Avenue W
Mansfield, OH 44902
Phone: 419-524-5927
Fax: 419-524-7098
Officers:
    President: William McIntyre
    VP: Jeanne Alexander
    Secretary: J Brad Preston
    Treasurer: Dan Scurci
Management:
    General Manager: Dr. Thomas J Carto
    Music Director/Conductor: Jeff Holland Cook
    Development Director: Janet E Keeler
Mission: To present symphony concerts mainly from symphony repertoire including educational and pops programming.
Utilizes: Guest Artists
Founded: 1930
Specialized Field: Symphony; Orchestra; Ensemble
Status: Professional; Nonprofit
Income Sources: American Symphony Orchestra League; ORACLE; OCCA
Performs At: Renaissance Theatre
Organization Type: Performing; Touring; Educational

1408
MIDDLETOWN SYMPHONY ORCHESTRA

130 N Verity Parkway
PO Box 411
Middletown, OH 45042
Phone: 513-424-2426
e-mail: mso@middletownsymphony.com
Management:
    Music Director: Carmon DeLeone
Founded: 1941
Specialized Field: Orchestra

1409
SOUTHEASTERN OHIO SYMPHONY ORCHESTRA

PO Box 42
Muskingum College
New Concord, OH 43762

Phone: 740-826-8197
Fax: 740-826-8404
e-mail: maestra1@roadrummer.com
Officers:
    Symphony Manager: John Kunkel
Management:
    Music Director: Laura E Schumann
    Executive Director: Elizabeth E Broschart
Specialized Field: Orchestra

1410
TUSCARAWAS PHILHARMONIC

PO Box 406
New Philadelphia, OH 44663
Phone: 330-364-1843
Fax: 330-364-1843
Officers:
    President: Steve Jenkins
    VP: Sheila Snead
    Secretary: Patricia Karnosh
    Treasurer: Patricia Tolloti
Management:
    Music Director/Conductor: Eric Benjamin
    General Manager: Melanie Winn
    Finance Manager: Robert L Henke
Mission: To offer musical enjoyment to all ages and enhance the cultural development of the community.
Utilizes: Commissioned Music; Guest Accompanists; Guest Musical Directors; Guest Musicians; Instructors; Local Artists; Original Music Scores; Sign Language Translators; Singers; Soloists
Founded: 1935
Specialized Field: Symphony; Orchestra
Status: Semi-Professional; Nonprofit
Paid Staff: 35
Performs At: Dover High School
Annual Attendance: 4,000 - 6,000
Facility Category: Auditorium
Type of Stage: Proscenium
Seating Capacity: 1,084
Organization Type: Performing

1411
NORTHERN OHIO YOUTH ORCHESTRAS

39 S Main
Suite 244
Oberlin, OH 44074
Phone: 440-775-3059
Fax: 440-774-6160
e-mail: noyo@noyo.org
Management:
    Artistic Director/Conductor: Dr. Joanne Erwin
    General Manager: Patty Rush
Specialized Field: Youth Orchestra

1412
OBERLIN BAROQUE ENSEMBLE

Conservatory of Music
Oberlin College
Oberlin, OH 44074
Phone: 440-775-8121
Fax: 440-775-8886
Mission: The ensemble performs 17th and 18th-century compositions on period instruments.
Founded: 1973
Specialized Field: Chamber; Ensemble; Baroque
Status: Professional
Income Sources: Oberlin College Conservatory of Music
Performs At: Oberlin Conservatory
Organization Type: Performing; Touring; Resident; Educational

1413
MIAMI UNIVERSITY SYMPHONY ORCHESTRA
209 A Presser
Hall Auditorium 730
Oxford, OH 45056
Phone: 513-529-3086
Fax: 513-529-3027
e-mail: muso@muohio.edu
Management:
Music Director: Jose-Luis Novo
Orchestra Manager: Kristin Pyles
Specialized Field: Orchestra

1414
MIAMI WIND QUINTET
Department of Music
Miami University
Oxford, OH 45056
Phone: 513-529-1809
Fax: 513-529-3841
Management:
Director Audience Development: Jeanne Conners
Mission: Offering chamber music composed for winds; assisting young wind players.
Founded: 1985
Specialized Field: Chamber; Wind Ensemble
Status: Professional
Income Sources: Miami University
Performs At: Souers Recital Hall; Miami University
Organization Type: Performing; Touring; Resident; Educational

1415
SPRINGFIELD SYMPHONY ORCHESTRA
300 S Fountain Avenue
PO Box 1374
Springfield, OH 45501
Phone: 937-325-8100
Fax: 937-325-2299
e-mail: info@springfieldsym.org
Web Site: www.springfieldsym.org
Officers:
President: Margaret Roark
VP: Marlies Hemmann
Management:
Executive Director: David Dietrick
Music Director/Conductor: Peter Stafford Wilson
Mission: Providing the best symphonic music for the community; offering music education to youth.
Utilizes: Educators; Guest Accompanists; Guest Artists; Guest Composers; Multimedia
Founded: 1944
Specialized Field: Symphony; Chamber
Status: Professional; Nonprofit
Paid Staff: 60
Paid Artists: 80
Budget: $850,000
Income Sources: American Symphony Orchestra League
Performs At: Kuss Auditorium; Clark State Performing Arts Center
Affiliations: Clark State College
Annual Attendance: 1,200
Seating Capacity: 1,200
Organization Type: Performing; Sponsoring

1416
WITTENBERG UNIVERSITY DEPARTMENT OF MUSIC
Ward Street at Woodlawn Avenue
Box 720
Springfield, OH 45501-0720
Phone: 937-327-7354
Fax: 937-327-7347
Toll-free: 800-677-7558
e-mail: dkazez@wittenberg.edu
Web Site: www4.wittenberg.edu
Management:
Professor of Music: Daniel Kazez
Mission: For over 100 years, Wittenberg has excelled in preparing students for careers in music education, performance, church music, composition, arts administration, and other music fields. Wittenberg's music department has been a member of the National Association of Schools of Music (NASM) for over 75 years.
Specialized Field: Chamber; Folk Music; Jazz; Symphony
Performs At: Krieg Hall; Weaver Chapel
Affiliations: National Association of Schools of Music
Seating Capacity: 135

1417
TOLEDO JAZZ SOCIETY
151 Michigan Street
Suite 307
Toledo, OH 43604
Phone: 419-241-5299
Fax: 419-241-4777
Web Site: www.toledojazzsociety.org
Officers:
President: Jon Richardson
VP: Jeff Jaffe
Secretary: Joanne Treuhaft
Management:
Executive Director: Kim Buehler
Membership/Marketing Coordinator: Anne Biel
Mission: Promoting the performance of jazz and its preservation as an art form; providing concerts, educational programs and lectures.
Founded: 1980
Specialized Field: Orchestra; Jazz Ensemble; Band
Status: Professional; Nonprofit
Paid Staff: 12
Paid Artists: 100
Income Sources: Association of Performing Arts Presenters; Arts Midwest
Performs At: The Franciscan Theatre And Conference Center In Toledo, Ohio
Organization Type: Performing; Resident; Educational; Sponsoring

1418
TOLEDO SYMPHONY
1838 Parkwood Avenue
Suite 310
Toledo, OH 43624
Phone: 419-246-8000
Fax: 419-321-6890
Toll-free: 800-348-1253
e-mail: music@toledosymphony.com
Web Site: www.toledosymphony.com
Officers:
President/CEO: Robert Bell
Management:
Principal Conductor: Stefan Sanderling
Resident Conductor: Chelsea Tipton, II
Mission: To furnish performances of the highest artistic caliber to the widest possible audience; to conduct public service and education functions.
Utilizes: Commissioned Music; Guest Accompanists; Guest Artists; Guest Composers; Guest Lecturers; Original Music Scores; Sign Language Translators; Singers
Founded: 1943
Specialized Field: Symphony; Orchestra; Chamber; Ensemble
Status: Professional; Nonprofit
Performs At: Toledo Museum of Art Peristyle
Organization Type: Performing; Touring; Educational

1419
WESTERVILLE SYMPHONY
28 S State Street
PO Box 478
Westerville, OH 43081
Phone: 614-890-5523
Fax: 614-882-2085
e-mail: wsymphony@otterbein.edu
Web Site: www.westervillesymphony.org
Officers:
President: Donna Kerr
VP: John Gale
Secretary: Lyle Barkhymer
Treasurer: Michael Howard
Executive Director: Jeanne Browne
Management:
Music Director: Peter Stafford Wilson
Mission: A nonprofit, charitable corporation functioning as an aesthetic, educational and cultural resource, presenting performances primarily of symphonic music; an artistic outlet for amateur and semi-professional musicians.
Founded: 1982
Specialized Field: Symphony; Orchestra; Ensemble
Status: Non-Professional; Nonprofit
Paid Staff: 50
Performs At: Cowan Hall; Otterbein College
Organization Type: Performing; Educational

1420
WOOSTER SYMPHONY ORCHESTRA
College of Wooster
217 Scheide Music Center
Wooster, OH 44691
Phone: 330-263-2047
Fax: 330-263-2051
e-mail: jlindberg@acs.wooster.edu
Management:
Director: Jeffrey Lindberg
Mission: Bringing the community live orchestral repertoire.
Utilizes: Artists-in-Residence; Collaborating Artists; Commissioned Music; Curators; Five Seasonal Concerts; Guest Accompanists; Guest Companies; Guest Composers; Guest Directors; Guest Ensembles; Guest Instructors; Guest Musicians; Guest Soloists; Guest Speakers; Instructors; Local Artists; Multimedia; Music; Organization Contracts; Original Music Scores; Sign Language Translators; Singers; Soloists; Student Interns
Founded: 1915
Specialized Field: Symphony; Orchestra
Status: Non-Professional
Paid Staff: 1
Volunteer Staff: 5
Paid Artists: 18
Non-paid Artists: 55
Budget: $20,000
Income Sources: Women's Committee; ticket sales
Performs At: McGaw Chapel
Affiliations: Colllege of Wooster
Annual Attendance: 6,000 per concert
Organization Type: Performing; Resident

1421
CHAMBER MUSIC YELLOW SPRINGS
Box 448
Yellow Springs, OH 45387

Phone: 937-767-2912
Fax: 937-767-9350
e-mail: mary.t.white@wright.edu
Officers:
  President: Mary T White
Mission: Performing professional chamber music of high quality.
Founded: 1983
Specialized Field: Chamber
Status: Professional; Nonprofit
Budget: 25-30,000
Income Sources: Donations: Grants; Tickets
Performs At: First Presbyterian Church
Seating Capacity: 240
Organization Type: Sponsoring

1422
YOUNGSTOWN SYMPHONY ORCHESTRA

260 W Federal Street
Youngstown, OH 44503
Phone: 330-744-4269
Fax: 330-744-1441
e-mail: symphony@youngstownsymphony.com
Web Site: www.youngstownsymphony.com
Officers:
  Chairman of the Board: Gary Balog
  President/CEO: Patricia A Syak
  Vice Chairman: Lewis Kasper
  Secretary: Gloria Detesco
  Treasurer: James Baker
Management:
  Facility Booking Agent: Jane Beckner
  Theater/Facility Manager: Joe Woronka
Utilizes: Guest Composers; Guest Musicians; Singers; Special Technical Talent
Founded: 1931
Specialized Field: Orchestra; Educational
Status: Professional; Nonprofit
Paid Staff: 7
Paid Artists: 500
Budget: $200,000
Income Sources: American Symphony Orchestra League
Performs At: Youngstown Symphony Center; Edward W. Powers Auditorium
Annual Attendance: 131,347
Facility Category: Auditorium
Type of Stage: Proscenium
Stage Dimensions: 60 x 40
Seating Capacity: 2310
Year Built: 1931
Year Remodeled: 1968
Cost: 1.5 Million
Rental Contact: Theatre Coordinator Leslie A. Brown
Organization Type: Performing; Resident; Educational
Resident Groups: Youngstown Symphony Orchestra

Oklahoma

1423
BARTLESVILLE SYMPHONY ORCHESTRA

Bartlesville Community Center
300 E Adams Boulevard
Bartlesville, OK 74005
Phone: 918-333-7989
Fax: 918-333-7989
e-mail: lauren@bartlesvillesymphony.org
Web Site: www.bartlesvillesymphony.org
Management:

Music Director/Conductor/Manager: Lauren Green
Mission: Offering community musicians and audiences an opportunity to experience symphonic professional quality symphonic musical expirences and world-class quest soloists.
Utilizes: Guest Artists; Singers
Founded: 1957
Specialized Field: Symphony; Orchestra
Status: Non-Professional; Nonprofit
Paid Staff: 1
Volunteer Staff: 2
Paid Artists: 20
Non-paid Artists: 45
Budget: $200,000
Income Sources: Tickets; Donations; Fundraising Products
Performs At: Bartlesville Community Center
Annual Attendance: 4,000
Facility Category: Auditoriuam
Type of Stage: Proscenium
Seating Capacity: 1700
Year Built: 1982
Cost: $ 13 Million
Organization Type: Resident

1424
OKLAHOMA MOZART INTERNATIONAL FESTIVAL

500 SE Dewey, Suite A
PO Box 2344
Bartlesville, OK 74005
Phone: 918-336-9900
Fax: 918-336-9525
e-mail: boxoffice@okmozart.com
Web Site: www.okmozart.com
Management:
  Executive Director: Dr Manuel Prestamo
  Development Director: Linda Keller
Utilizes: Actors; Artists-in-Residence; Collaborations; Commissioned Music; Dance Companies; Fine Artists; Grant Writers; Guest Accompanists; Guest Companies; Guest Composers; Guest Conductors; Guest Directors; Guest Instructors; Guest Musicians; Multi Collaborations; Multimedia; Original Music Scores; Sign Language Translators; Singers; Touring Companies
Founded: 1985
Specialized Field: Ensemble; Mozart; Chamber; Orchestra
Status: Professional; Nonprofit
Paid Staff: 8
Volunteer Staff: 800
Paid Artists: 150
Non-paid Artists: 300
Budget: $995,000
Income Sources: Oklahoma State Arts Council; National Endowment for the Arts; Individuals; Businesses
Performs At: Bartlesville Community Center
Annual Attendance: 30,000
Facility Category: Concert Hall, Community Center
Seating Capacity: 1700
Year Built: 1982
Organization Type: Sponsoring
Resident Groups: New York Orchestra

1425
ENID-PHILLIPS SYMPHONY ORCHESTRA

300 W Cherokee
Suite 109
Enid, OK 73701
Phone: 405-237-9646
Fax: 405-237-7646
Management:

Artistic Director: Douglas Newell
Administrative Associate: Eleanor Hornbaker
Utilizes: Guest Artists
Founded: 1906
Specialized Field: Symphony; Orchestra
Status: Professional; Nonprofit
Income Sources: American Symphony Orchestra League
Performs At: Eugene S. Briggs Auditorium
Organization Type: Performing; Educational

1426
LAWTON PHILHARMONIC ORCHESTRA

6425 NW Cache Road
Suite 115
Lawton, OK 73502
Mailing Address: PO Box 1473
Phone: 580-531-5043
Web Site: www.lawtonphil.org
Management:
  Music Director: Jon Kalbfleisch
Mission: To provide high quality cultural experiences to Southwest Oklahoma.
Utilizes: Guest Artists
Founded: 1962
Specialized Field: Symphony; Orchestra
Status: Professional
Paid Staff: 3
Volunteer Staff: 40
Paid Artists: 62
Budget: $260,000
Income Sources: Box office; Grants; Private donations
Performs At: McMahon Memorial Auditorium
Affiliations: American Symphony Orchestra League
Annual Attendance: 10,000
Facility Category: Concert Hall
Seating Capacity: 1,560
Year Built: 1962
Year Remodeled: 2000
Organization Type: Performing; Touring; Resident; Educational; Sponsoring

1427
JAZZ IN JUNE

PO Box 2405
Norman, OK 73070
Phone: 405-325-3388
e-mail: postmaster@jazzinjune.org
Web Site: www.jazzinjune.org
Management:
  Executive Director: Phoebe Morales
Mission: To offer Oklahoma residents a jazz festival.
Utilizes: Singers
Founded: 1985
Specialized Field: Jazz; Ensemble
Status: Professional; Semi-Professional
Income Sources: American Federation of Musicians
Organization Type: Performing

1428
UNIVERSITY OF OKLAHOMA SYMPHONY ORCHESTRA

University of Oklahoma School of Music
500 West Boyd Room 138
Norman, OK 73019-2071
Phone: 405-325-2081
Fax: 405-325-7574
e-mail: ousymphonyt@ou.edu
Officers:
  Assistant Director: Brian Britt
Management:
  Director of Orchestra and Opera St: Jonathan Shames
  Music School Director: Dr Steven Curtis

Personnel Director: Shara Long
Operations Director: Timothy Verville
Founded: 1920
Specialized Field: Orchestra; Ensemble
Paid Staff: 6
Performs At: Catlett Music Center

1429
CHAMBER MUSIC IN OKLAHOMA
PO Box 54624
Oklahoma City, OK 73154-1624
Phone: 405-974-3333
Fax: 405-974-3844
Web Site: www.cmok.org
Officers:
Vice President & Treasurer: Brad Ferguson
Vice President & Special Projects: Mary J Rutherford
Secretary: Martha Blaine
Management:
Artists & Bookings: Dr Mark A Everett
Publicity & Webmaster: Dr. H Dean Everett
Founded: 1960
Specialized Field: Chamber
Status: Nonprofit
Budget: $20,000-35,000
Performs At: Christ the King Church

1430
GO FOR BAROQUE
PO Box 20178
Oklahoma City, OK 73120
Phone: 405-840-0278
Mission: To offer formal baroque concerts and young people's concerts.
Founded: 1982
Specialized Field: Chamber; Ensemble; Baroque
Status: Professional
Organization Type: Performing; Touring; Educational

1431
OKLAHOMA CITY PHILHARMONIC ORCHESTRA
428 W California
Suite 210
Oklahoma City, OK 73102
Phone: 405-232-7575
Fax: 405-232-4353
e-mail: info@okcphilharmonic.org
Web Site: www.okcphilharmonic.org
Officers:
President: John P McMillin
President Elect: Michael Joseph
VP: Grace Ryan
Treasurer: Doug Stussi
Management:
Music Director/Conductor: Joel Levine
Executive Director: Edward Walker
General Manager: Joe Ragan
Finance Director: Vanessa Etheridge
Mission: Performing classical, orchestral, and popular music; entertaining and educating; enhancing the cultural environment of Oklahoma City as well as the state.
Utilizes: Guest Artists; Singers
Founded: 1988
Specialized Field: Symphony; Orchestra
Status: Professional; Nonprofit
Performs At: Rose State Performing Arts Theatre
Affiliations: American Symphony Orchestra League; Allied Arts of Oklahoma City
Organization Type: Performing; Resident

1432
CHAMBER MUSIC TULSA
2210 South Main
Tulsa, OK 74128-2006
Phone: 918-587-3802
Fax: 918-587-0698
e-mail: executivedirector@chambermusictulsa.org
Web Site: www.chambermusictulsa.org
Management:
Executive Director: Rose McCracken
Mission: To continue cultivating audiences to enjoy chamber music.
Founded: 1954
Specialized Field: Chamber
Status: Professional; Nonprofit
Income Sources: Chamber Music America
Performs At: John H. Williams Theater; Tulsa Performing Arts Center
Organization Type: Performing; Educational

1433
TULSA PHILHARMONIC
2901 S Harvard Avenue
Suite A
Tulsa, OK 74114
Phone: 918-747-7473
Fax: 918-747-7496
Web Site: www.tulsaphilharmonic.org
Officers:
President: Dr. Gordon D Lantz
VP: Larry E Lee
VP: Richard B Williamson
Secretary: Robert K. Gardnine
Treasurer: Ronald R. Glass
Management:
CEO: Thomas Greedom
Director Operations: Wendy Jones
Stage Manager: Tomnt Cortwright
Librarian: Marc Facci
Personnel Manager: Phillip Wachowski
Mission: To offer live performances of symphony music.
Utilizes: Guest Artists
Founded: 1947
Specialized Field: Symphony; Orchestra; Chamber; Ensemble
Status: Professional; Nonprofit
Performs At: Tulsa Performing Arts Center; Brady Theater
Affiliations: Walter Arts Center at Holland Hall School
Organization Type: Performing; Touring; Resident; Educational; Sponsoring

1434
TULSA YOUTH SYMPHONY
1409 S Elwood Avenue
Tulsa, OK 74119
Phone: 918-592-7725
e-mail: ron.wheeler@tyso.org
Web Site: www.tyso.org
Management:
Conductor/Administrator: Ronald Wheeler
Administrative Assistant: Sue Loomis
Mission: Tulsa Youth Symphony Orchestra aims to encourage and develop students' musical abilities through rehearsal, concert performance and regular contact with professional musicians, offering training and performance opportunities.
Utilizes: Guest Artists
Founded: 1963
Specialized Field: Youth Symphony; Chamber
Status: Non-Professional; Nonprofit
Paid Staff: 85

Income Sources: American Symphony Orchestra League (Youth Orchestra Division); Tulsa Philharmonic
Performs At: Union High School Performing Arts Center
Seating Capacity: 1,900
Organization Type: Performing; Touring; Educational
Resident Groups: Philharmonic Society; Tulsa Area Youth Association

Oregon

1435
CHAMBER MUSIC CONCERTS
SOSC
1250 Siskiyou Boulevard
Ashland, OR 97520
Phone: 541-552-6419
Fax: 541-552-6380
e-mail: chamber-music@sou.edu
Web Site: www.sou.edu/cmc
Management:
Founder/Director: Dr Gregory Fowler
Assistant: Lesley Pohl
Mission: To offer Southern Oregon residents the highest possible quality of chamber music.
Founded: 1984
Specialized Field: Chamber
Status: Professional; Nonprofit
Performs At: SOSC Music Building Recital Hall
Organization Type: Performing

1436
ROGUE VALLEY SYMPHONY
SOU Music Hall
1250 Siskiyou Boulevard
Ashland, OR 97520
Phone: 541-552-6354
Fax: 541-552-6353
e-mail: office@rvsymphony.org
Web Site: www.rvsymphony.org
Officers:
President: Margaret Scarborough
President Elect: Glenn Cunningham
Secretary: Lynn Thompson
Management:
Executive Director: Cybele Abbett
Music Director/Conductor: Martin Majkut
Utilizes: Choreographers; Commissioned Composers; Dancers; Guest Musicians; Instructors; Sign Language Translators; Singers
Founded: 1966
Specialized Field: Symphony
Paid Staff: 6
Paid Artists: 73
Budget: $500,000
Performs At: SOU Music Recital Hall
Annual Attendance: 20,000
Facility Category: 3 Facilities

1437
CHAMBER MUSIC CORVALLIS
5576 SW Windflower Drive
Corvallis, OR 97333
Phone: 541-752-7222
e-mail: millmari@comcast.net
Web Site: www.violins.org
Officers:
Chairman: Marilyn Miller
Management:
Artistic Director: Chris Rochester, mc_rochester@gmail.com
Program Editor: Carol Fischler, fischler@teleport.com

Mission: Present chamber music concerts; outreach to k-12 students
Founded: 1958
Specialized Field: Chamber Music
Status: Non-Profit
Volunteer Staff: 25
Non-paid Artists: 7
Budget: $35,000-70,000
Income Sources: Ticket Sales; Donations; Grants
Performs At: LaSells Stewart Center; Oregon State University

1438
OSU-CORVALLIS SYMPHONY ORCHESTRA

Corvallis-OSU Symphony
Corvallis, OR
Phone: 541-758-3052
Fax: 541-737-4268
e-mail: syminfo@peak.org
Management:
　　Music Director/Conductor: Marian Carlson
Specialized Field: Orchestra

1439
EMERALD CHAMBER PLAYERS

3080 Potter
Eugene, OR 97405
Phone: 541-344-0483
e-mail: ORVALETTER@netscape.net
Management:
　　Convener: Orval Etter
Mission: To provide amateurs with opportunities to play and perform chamber music.
Founded: 1962
Specialized Field: Orchestra; Chamber; Ensemble
Status: Non-Professional; Nonprofit
Organization Type: Performing

1440
EUGENE SYMPHONY ASSOCIATION

115 W 8th Avenue
Suite 115
Eugene, OR 97401
Phone: 541-687-9487
Fax: 541-687-0527
e-mail: paul.winberg@eugenesymphony.org
Web Site: www.eugenesymphony.org
Officers:
　　President: Mary Ann Hanson g
　　Vice President: Dunny Sorensen
　　Treasurer: Warren Barnes
　　Secretary: Carolyn Chambers
Management:
　　Operations Director: Christopher Collins
　　Music Director/Conductor: Daniel Racheu in
Mission: Enriching lives through the power of music.
Utilizes: Commissioned Composers; Composers-in-Residence; Fine Artists; Guest Accompanists; Guest Artists; Guest Directors; Guest Musicians; Guest Writers; Instructors; Original Music Scores; Resident Artists; Sign Language Translators; Singers
Founded: 1966
Specialized Field: Symphony; Orchestra
Status: Professional; Nonprofit
Paid Staff: 9
Volunteer Staff: 160
Paid Artists: 82
Budget: $2.2 million
Income Sources: Ticket Revenues; Contributions
Performs At: Hult Center for the Performing Arts
Facility Category: Hult Center for the Performing Arts
Seating Capacity: 2400

Year Built: 1982
Organization Type: Performing; Resident

1441
OREGON BACH FESTIVAL

1257 University of Oregon
Eugene, OR 97403
Phone: 541-346-5666
Fax: 541-346-5669
Toll-free: 800-457-1486
e-mail: bachfest@uoregon.edu
Web Site: www.oregonbachfestival.com
Management:
　　Artistic Administrator: Michael Anderson
　　Executive Director: John Evans
　　Marketing Director: George Evano
Mission: Further the work, spirit and influence of J.S. Bach.
Utilizes: Singers
Founded: 1970
Specialized Field: Choral-Orchestral, Chamber Music
Paid Staff: 8
Volunteer Staff: 200
Paid Artists: 250
Budget: $2.5 Million
Income Sources: Ticket Sales; Sponsorships; Donations
Performs At: Concert Halls
Affiliations: University of Oregon; Chorus America; League of Amer Orchs
Annual Attendance: 42,000
Facility Category: Concert Hall
Type of Stage: Proscenium
Seating Capacity: 2500/550
Organization Type: Performing; Resident; Educational

1442
OREGON MOZART PLAYERS

1590 Williamette Street
Eugene, OR 97440
Mailing Address: PO Box 11474
Phone: 541-345-6648
Fax: 541-345-7849
e-mail: omp@oregonmozartplayers.org
Web Site: www.oregonmozartplayers.org
Management:
　　Executive Director: Jeffrey Eaton
　　President: Charles Wright
Mission: To offer chamber orchestra music; to provide talented, local musicians with opportunities to perform as orchestra members and soloists as well as in chamber ensembles.
Utilizes: Guest Artists; Singers
Founded: 1982
Specialized Field: Orchestra; Chamber; Mozart
Status: Professional; Nonprofit
Performs At: Hult Center For The Performing Arts; Beall Concert
Organization Type: Performing; Touring; Resident; Educational

1443
PACIFIC UNIVERSITY COMMUNITY WIND ENSEMBLE

Pacific University
Music Department
Forest Grove, OR 97116
Phone: 503-357-6151
Fax: 503-359-2910
Management:
　　Conductor: Michael Burch-Pesses
Mission: To provide music students with educational training; to offer community members a performing outlet.

Founded: 1849
Specialized Field: Orchestra; Chamber; Wind Ensemble
Status: Non-Professional; Nonprofit
Performs At: University Center
Organization Type: Performing; Resident; Educational

1444
MT HOOD JAZZ FESTIVAL

PO Box 226
Gresham, OR 97030
Phone: 503-669-1937
Fax: 503-667-2848
Web Site: www.mthoodjazz.com
Officers:
　　President: Susie Jones
　　Public Relations: Amy Maxwell
Mission: To provide for the performance of contemporary and classical music and to help promote the fine arts in the Eastern part of Multnoman, Clackamps and Clark counties.
Specialized Field: Pops; Orchestra
Paid Artists: 65
Performs At: Auditorium

1445
GRANDE RONDE SYMPHONY ORCHESTRA

Eastern Oregon University
One University Boulevard
La Grande, OR 97850-2899
Phone: 541-963-9066
Fax: 541-962-3596
e-mail: music@eou.edu
Management:
　　Orchestra Director: Leandro Espinosa
Specialized Field: Orchestra
Performs At: Loso Hall

1446
BRITT FESTIVALS

PO Box 1124
Medford, OR 97501
Phone: 541-779-0847
Fax: 541-776-3712
Toll-free: 800-882-7488
e-mail: info@brittfest.org
Web Site: www.brittfest.org
Officers:
　　Board President: Ken Wells
Management:
　　Executive Director: Jim Fredericks
　　Music Director: Peter Bay
　　Marketing: Sara King Cole
Mission: To present and sponsor, in Southern Oregon, performing arts of the highest quality for the education, enrichment and enjoyment of all.
Utilizes: Commissioned Music; Dance Companies; Dancers; Guest Musical Directors; Guest Musicians; Multi Collaborations; Multimedia; Original Music Scores; Singers; Special Technical Talent; Theatre Companies
Founded: 1963
Specialized Field: Classical; Jazz; Pops; Country; Folk Music; Bluegrass; World Music; Show Tunes
Paid Staff: 12
Volunteer Staff: 600
Performs At: Outdoor Auditorium
Annual Attendance: 70,000
Facility Category: Outdoor Amphitheatre
Seating Capacity: 2200
Year Built: 1963
Year Remodeled: 1992

1447
OREGON EAST SYMPHONY
424 S Main
Pendleton, OR 97801
Phone: 541-276-0320
Fax: 541-278-6114
e-mail: info@oregoneastsymphony.org
Management:
Executive Director: Cheryl Marier
Utilizes: Dancers; Five Seasonal Concerts; Grant
Writers; Guest Accompanists; Guest Composers; Guest
Directors; Guest Musical Directors; Guest Musicians;
Guest Writers; Local Artists; Music; Original Music
Scores; Sign Language Translators; Singers; Soloists
Founded: 1976
Specialized Field: Symphony
Paid Staff: 2
Volunteer Staff: 10
Paid Artists: 70
Non-paid Artists: 30
Budget: $125,000
Income Sources: Sales; Grants; Sponsorship
Performs At: Vert Auditorium
Annual Attendance: 4,000
Facility Category: Hall
Type of Stage: Wooden
Stage Dimensions: 40 x 30
Seating Capacity: 750
Year Built: 1925
Year Remodeled: 1995

1448
CHAMBER MUSIC NORTHWEST
522 SW Fifth Avenue
Suite 725
Portland, OR 97204
Phone: 503-223-3202
Fax: 503-294-1690
e-mail: info@cmnw.org
Web Site: www.cmnw.org
Officers:
Educations & Communications Manager:
Adrienne Leverette
Management:
Executive Director: Linda Magee
Artistic Director: David Shifrin
Operations Director: Franck Avril
Finance Director: Katherine King
Marketing Manager: Garen Horgend
Mission: To present an annual summer music festival
(five weeks/25 concerts) with world renowned
performers in residence; to present concerts and
educational activities on a year-round basis.
Founded: 1971
Specialized Field: Chamber; Ensemble; Classical
Music
Status: Professional; Nonprofit
Paid Staff: 6
Volunteer Staff: 50
Paid Artists: 75
Budget: One Million
Affiliations: Kaul Auditorium at Reed College; Cabell
Theatre at Catlin Gabel School
Annual Attendance: 19,000
Facility Category: Small Concert Hall (private college)
Seating Capacity: 550
Year Built: 1998
Organization Type: Performing

1449
CHAMBER MUSIC SOCIETY OF OREGON
1935 NE 59th Avenue
Portland, OR 97213-4117

Phone: 503-287-2175
e-mail: delorenzoh@earthlink.net
Web Site: www.oregonchambermusic.org
Officers:
President: Patricia Ann Haim
VP: Dr. Floyd Grant Jackson
Secretary: Beatrice Matin
Treasurer: John B. Gould
Executive Director: Hazel M. DeLorenzo
Mission: To promote music in our schools for its value
in teaching children how to learn.
Utilizes: Singers
Founded: 1973
Specialized Field: Orchestra; Chamber; Ensemble
Status: Non-Professional; Nonprofit
Performs At: St. Philip Neri Church; Hood River Middle
School
Organization Type: Performing; Resident; Educational

1450
FRIENDS OF CHAMBER MUSIC
PO Box 397
Portland, OR 97207
Phone: 503-224-9842
Fax: 503-725-8215
Mission: To present a season of five chamber-music
concerts annually; to sponsor outreach activities,
including workshops and master classes.
Specialized Field: Chamber
Status: Nonprofit
Organization Type: Presenting

1451
FRIENDS OF CHAMBER MUSIC
222 NW Davis Street
Suite 405
Portland, OR 97209
Phone: 503-224-9842
Fax: 503-228-1407
e-mail: info@focm.org
Management:
Executive Director: Pat Zagelow
Operations Manager: Lori Fitch
Utilizes: Guest Directors; Multimedia; Original Music
Scores
Specialized Field: Chamber
Budget: $400,000
Income Sources: Tickets; Contributors
Performs At: Lincoln Performance Hall; Kaul
Auditorium
Annual Attendance: 7,000
Type of Stage: Proscenium
Seating Capacity: 476
Year Remodeled: 2010

1452
METROPOLITAN YOUTH SYMPHONY
PO Box 5254
Portland, OR 97208
Phone: 503-239-4566
Toll-free: 888-752-9697
Web Site: www.metroyouthsymphony.org
Management:
Music Director/Conductor: Lajos Balogh
Conductor Symphonic Band: Dr. John K Richards
Conductor Concert Orchestra: Bill Hunt
Associate Conductor: Mike Ott
Associate Conductor: Nita Van Pelt
Conductor Preparatory Band: Larry Wells
Conductor Overture Orchestra: Kathie Reed
Specialized Field: Youth Symphony; Educational
Performs At: Arlene Schnitzer Concert Hall;
Intermediate Theater

1453
OREGON SYMPHONY
921 SW Washington
Suite 200
Portland, OR 97205
Phone: 503-228-4294
Fax: 503-228-4150
e-mail: ecalder@orsymphony.org
Web Site: www.orsymphony.org
Officers:
President: Elaine Calder
Management:
VP/General Manager: Mary Crist
Founded: 1896
Specialized Field: Symphony Orchestra
Paid Staff: 34
Paid Artists: 79
Budget: $15 Million
Income Sources: Ticket Sales; Contributions; Grants

1454
PORTLAND BAROQUE ORCHESTRA
1020 SW Taylor Street
Suite 275
Portland, OR 97205
Phone: 503-222-6000
Fax: 503-226-6635
e-mail: admin@pbo.org
Web Site: www.pbo.org
Officers:
Executive Director: Thomas Cirillo
Chairman: Aron Faegre
Management:
Artistic Director: Monica Huggett
Utilizes: Guest Accompanists; Guest Musical Directors;
Guest Musicians; Local Artists; Multimedia; Original
Music Scores
Founded: 1984
Specialized Field: Baroque; Orchestra; Classical on
Period Instruments
Status: Tax-exempt

1455
PORTLAND CHAMBER ORCHESTRA
ASSOCIATION
PO Box 9024
Portland, OR 97205
Phone: 503-227-7902
Fax: 503-227-7066
Officers:
President: Ellwood Miller
VP: Mildred Berthelsdorf
Treasurer: Margaret Sutherland
Recording Secretary: Jane Perkins
Management:
Director: Mildred Berthelsdorf, MD
Conductor: Anthony Armore
Mission: To present free and/or low fee concerts of fine
chamber music by outstanding local talent.
Founded: 1946
Specialized Field: Classical; Chamber
Paid Artists: 30
Budget: $44,948
Income Sources: Private; Foundations; Grants;
Endowments; Business/corporate donations; Individual
donations
Performs At: Scottish Rite Center
Annual Attendance: 255/concert
Facility Category: Performing Arts Center
Type of Stage: Raised
Seating Capacity: 400

1456

PORTLAND COLUMBIA SYMPHONY

PO Box 6559
Portland, OR 97228
Phone: 503-234-4077
Fax: 503-234-4017
e-mail: cso@pacifier.com
Web Site: www.columbiasymphony.org
Management:
   Executive Director: Betsy Hatton,
   cso@pacifier.com
   Music Director/Conductor: Huw Edwards,
   cso@pacifier.com
   Operations Manager: Shelly Williams
Utilizes: Community Members; Community Talent; Fine
Artists; Guest Accompanists; Guest Companies; Guest
Composers; Guest Designers; Guest Musical Directors;
Guest Musicians; Local Artists; Local Artists &
Directors; Organization Contracts; Original Music
Scores; Paid Performers; Singers; Soloists; Visual
Designers
Founded: 1982
Specialized Field: Orchestra
Paid Staff: 2
Volunteer Staff: 40
Paid Artists: 65
Non-paid Artists: 3
Performs At: Auditorium
Facility Category: Church
Seating Capacity: 600

1457

PORTLAND YOUTH PHILHARMONIC ASSOCIATION

1119 SW Park Avenue
Portland, OR 97205
Phone: 503-223-5939
Fax: 503-223-5003
e-mail: information@portlandyouthphil.org
Web Site: www.portlandyouthphil.org
Officers:
   President: Bruce Samson
   VP: George C Reinmiller
   Corporate Secretary: Wayne Landeverk
   Treasurer: Robert M. Nibley
Management:
   Music Director/Conductor: Mei-Ann Chen
   Executive Director: Paul Barthelemy
Mission: It is the purpose of the Portland Youth
Philharmonic to maintain the finest possible resident
youth orchestra in order to inspire, train and educate
young people in the performance and appreciation of
symphonic music and to provide a cultural asset to the
community.
Founded: 1924
Specialized Field: Youth Philharmonic; Ensemble
Status: Non-Professional; Nonprofit
Paid Staff: 7
Non-paid Artists: 206
Budget: $500,000
Income Sources: American Symphony Orchestra
League (Youth Orchestra Division)
Performs At: Arlene Schnitzer Concert Hall; Civic
Auditorium
Organization Type: Performing; Touring; Resident;
Educational

1458

ROSE CITY CHAMBER ORCHESTRA

PO Box 6652
Portland, OR 97228-6652
Phone: 503-921-2785
e-mail: info@rosecity.org
Web Site: www.rosecity.org
Mission: The Rose City Chamber Orchestra was
formed in Portland, Oregon by a group of dedicated
musicians with the goal to achieve the highest quality
musical experience, enjoyed by both performers and
the community.
Founded: 1998
Specialized Field: Chamber; Orchestra

1459

SINFONIA CONCERTANTE ORCHESTRA

1640 SE Holly Street
Portland, OR 97214
Phone: 503-231-1421
Fax: 503-236-1655
e-mail: sueminde@aol.com
Management:
   Artistic Director & Conductor: Stefan Minde
Mission: To provide the community of the greater
metropolitan area with outstanding performances that
preserve the classical music tradition. To support
mentoring and educational programs for students.
Founded: 1990
Specialized Field: Chamber; Orchestra
Volunteer Staff: 20
Performs At: Lewis & Clark College; Evans Hall; St.
Mary's Cathedral

1460

UMPQUA SYMPHONY ASSOCIATION

PO Box 241
Roseburg, OR 97470
Phone: 503-672-4320
Web Site: members.nbci.com/UmpquaSymphony/
Management:
   Production Director: Bob Robbins
   President: Loren Hinkle
   VP: Virginia Roth
   Secretary: Barbara Dugas
   Treasurer: Deborah Dixon
Mission: To offer the local community classical music.
Founded: 1955
Specialized Field: Symphony; Orchestra; Chamber;
Ensemble
Status: Nonprofit
Performs At: Umpqua Community College Auditorium
Organization Type: Sponsoring

1461

CAMERATA MUSICA

PO Box 2782
Salem, OR 97302
Phone: 503-364-8263
Fax: 503-362-3290
e-mail: gstubble@williamette.edu
Web Site: www.open.org
Officers:
   President: George Struble
Mission: To present free chamber music concerts by
local professional musicians. Concerts presented on
Sunday afternoons, seven Sundays a year.
Utilizes: Commissioned Composers; Community
Talent; Guest Accompanists; Guest Directors; Guest
Instructors; Guest Musical Directors; Instructors;
Multimedia; Original Music Scores; Singers
Founded: 1976
Specialized Field: Chamber
Status: Professional; Non-Professional; Nonprofit
Volunteer Staff: 3
Paid Artists: 30
Budget: $5,000

Income Sources: Patrons; Grants; Memorial Gifts;
Donations at concerts
Performs At: Salem Public Library Lecture Hall
Affiliations: Mid-Valley Arts Council, Salem
Annual Attendance: 1,600
Seating Capacity: 300
Year Built: 1990
Rental Contact: Camerata Musica (free)
Organization Type: Performing; Sponsoring

1462

SALEM CHAMBER ORCHESTRA

PO Box 768
Salem, OR 97308
Phone: 503-378-5483
e-mail: kkenaston@willamette.edu
Web Site: www.open.org/~scomusic/
Management:
   Executive Director: Kimberly Kenaston
Mission: The Salem Chamber Orchestra, through a
partnership between Willamette University and the
Salem-Keizer community, enriches the Willamette
Valley by promoting classical music that entertains,
educates, and provides performance opportunities for
Willamette students and area musicians.
Founded: 1984
Specialized Field: Classical; Chamber
Paid Staff: 2
Volunteer Staff: 4
Paid Artists: 15
Non-paid Artists: 35
Performs At: Smith Auditorium Willamette university

1463

SUNRIVER MUSIC FESTIVAL

PO Box 4308
Sunriver, OR 97707
Phone: 541-593-1084
Fax: 541-593-6959
e-mail: tickets@sunrivermusic.org
Web Site: www.sunrivermusic.org
Officers:
   President: Jim Putney
Management:
   Executive Director: Pamela Beezley
   Office Manager: Vicki Udlock
   Ticket Office Manager: Robin Burford
Mission: To present quality performances of classical
music and support music education programs for the
youth of Central Oregon.
Utilizes: Fine Artists; Guest Lecturers; Multimedia;
Original Music Scores
Founded: 1971
Specialized Field: Chamber; Orchestra
Paid Staff: 3
Volunteer Staff: 4
Budget: $250,000
Income Sources: Private; Business; Grants
Performs At: Great Hall
Annual Attendance: 3,500

Pennsylvania

1464

ALLENTOWN SYMPHONY ASSOCIATION

Symphony Hall
23 N 6th Street
Allentown, PA 18101
Phone: 610-432-6715
Fax: 610-871-0142
e-mail: info@allentownsymphony.org
Web Site: www.allentownsymphony.org
Officers:

President: John Berseth
Management:
Music Director/Conductor: Diane M Whittry
Executive Director: Robert Ditmars
Mission: To promote cultural values by providing high quality symphonic music and performing arts events, with broad community appeal, and education concerning them, in Allentown's historic Symphony Hall.
Utilizes: Singers
Founded: 1950
Specialized Field: Symphony; Orchestra
Status: Nonprofit
Income Sources: American Symphony Orchestra League; Association of Pennsylvania Orchestras; Lehigh Valley Arts Council; American Society of Composers, Authors and Publishers
Performs At: Symphony Hall
Annual Attendance: 20,000
Seating Capacity: 1246
Year Built: 1899
Year Remodeled: 1998
Rental Contact: John Ebert
Organization Type: Performing; Educational

1465
ALTOONA SYMPHONY ORCHESTRA

1331 12th Avenue, Suite 107
PO Box 483
Altoona, PA 16603
Phone: 814-943-2500
Fax: 814-943-7115
Web Site: www.altoona.net/symphony/home
Officers:
President: Al Massod
VP: Karen Shauf
Second VP: Phil Sukenik
Secretary: Edith Isacke
Assistant Secretary: Judy Halbritter
Treasurer: Heidi Rexford
Assistant Treasurer: Robert Lamort
Management:
Music Director: Nicolas Palmer
Executive Director: A Diane Schoeffler
Accounts Manager: Bruce Brower
Personnel Manager/Librarian: Sandy Woodward
Office Manager: Nancy Bickel
Mission: To provide the highest quality fine arts performances to everyone in our community.
Specialized Field: Orchestra

1466
NORTHEASTERN PENNSYLVANIA PHILHARMONIC

957 Broadcast Center
Avoca, PA 18641-1654
Phone: 570-457-8301
Fax: 570-457-5901
e-mail: info@nepaphil.org
Web Site: www.nepaphil.org
Officers:
President: Susan S Belin
VP Administration: Nicholas H Niles
VP Development: Anna Cervenak
VP Marketing/Public Relations: Mark Thomas
Treasurer: Thomas Robinson
Assistant Treasurer: Richard I. Rosenthal
Management:
Executive Director: Glenn T Roberts
Music Director/Conductor: Clyde Mitchell
Operations Manager: Jamie Kurtz
Director Development: Karen Kelly Mears
Marketing/Public Relations: Lisa Philips
Executive Assistant: Jean Spindler
Education Manager: Laura Craig

Mission: To produce the highest quality symphony orchestra and chamber ensemble performances possible; to provide musical services; to maintain an organizational environment in which local and national talent serve as a cultural resource.
Utilizes: Collaborations; Dance Companies; Educators; Grant Writers; Guest Accompanists; Guest Choreographers; Guest Companies; Guest Composers; Guest Designers; Guest Directors; Guest Instructors; Guest Lecturers; Guest Musical Directors; Guest Musicians; Guest Writers; Instructors; Multimedia; Music; Resident Professionals; Sign Language Translators; Singers; Soloists; Students
Founded: 1972
Specialized Field: Symphony; Orchestra
Status: Professional; Nonprofit
Paid Staff: 11
Paid Artists: 64
Income Sources: American Symphony Orchestra League; Citizens for the Arts in Pennsylvania
Performs At: Masonic Temple; Kirby Center for the Performing Arts
Organization Type: Performing; Touring; Educational

1467
CHAMBER MUSIC SOCIETY OF BETHLEHEM

PO Box 4336
Bethlehem, PA 18018-0336
Phone: 610-435-7611
Fax: 610-967-6569
e-mail: chambermusic@cmsob.org
Web Site: www.cmsob.org
Officers:
President: Ursla Levy
VP: Jennifer Scavuzzo
Treasurer: Christine Roysdan
Secretary: William McGlinn
Mission: To further appreciation of chamber music by presenting concerts to the Lehigh Valley community featuring the highest quality ensembles.
Founded: 1951
Specialized Field: Chamber
Status: Nonprofit
Volunteer Staff: 15
Budget: $50,000
Income Sources: Donations; Subscriptions; Tickets Sales
Annual Attendance: 1,500
Seating Capacity: 425
Organization Type: Performing; Sponsoring

1468
ERIE PHILHARMONIC

1006 State Street
Erie, PA 16501
Phone: 814-455-1375
Fax: 814-455-1377
e-mail: eriephil@ncinter.net
Web Site: www.eriephil.org
Management:
Music Director: Hugh Keelan
Executive Director: William F Faust
Mission: To offer symphonic, youth orchestra and pops concerts; to provide quality music educational experiences; to exhibit leadership in cultural affairs of the tri-state area.
Utilizes: Collaborations; Commissioned Composers; Composers-in-Residence; Dance Companies; Educators; Grant Writers; Guest Accompanists; Guest Artists; Guest Composers; Guest Lecturers; Guest Musical Directors; Guest Musicians; Guest Writers; Instructors; Local Artists; Multimedia; Music; Original Music Scores; Singers

Founded: 1913
Specialized Field: Symphony; Orchestra
Status: Nonprofit; Professional
Paid Staff: 12
Volunteer Staff: 120
Income Sources: Individual; Foundation; Grants
Performs At: Warner Theatre
Seating Capacity: 2500
Organization Type: Performing

1469
WESTMORELAND SYMPHONY ORCHESTRA

105 N Pennsylvania Avenue
Greensburg, PA 15601
Phone: 724-837-1850
Fax: 724-837-1342
e-mail: info@westmorelandsymphony.org
Web Site: www.westmorelandsymphony.org
Officers:
President: JoAnn R Lightcap
Treasurer: William Friedlander
Management:
Music Director: Kypros Markov
Executive Director: Morris A Brand
Mission: Expanding accessibility to the cultural enrichment provided by music; offering enjoyment, inspiration and motivation.
Utilizes: Guest Musicians; Music; Original Music Scores
Founded: 1969
Specialized Field: Symphony; Orchestra; Ensemble
Status: Semi-Professional; Nonprofit
Paid Staff: 4
Budget: $450,000
Performs At: Palace Theatre
Seating Capacity: 1,300
Organization Type: Performing; Educational

1470
GREENVILLE SYMPHONY SOCIETY

PO Box 364
Greenville, PA 16125
Phone: 724-588-2911
Web Site: www.geocites.com/Vienna/Strasse/2224
Management:
Manager: John H Evans
Personnel Director: Vicki Poe
Personnel Director: Jamie Scott
Librarian: Jean Sankey
Music Director/Conductor: Paul Chenevey
Mission: To provide music education through performances.
Founded: 1927
Specialized Field: Symphony; Orchestra
Status: Nonprofit
Income Sources: Pennsylvania Council on the Arts
Performs At: Passavant Memorial Center; Thiel College
Organization Type: Performing

1471
CENTRAL PENNSYLVANIA FRIENDS OF JAZZ

5721 Jonestown Road
Harrisburg, PA 17112
Phone: 717-540-1010
Fax: 717-540-7735
e-mail: dave@pajazz.org
Web Site: www.pajazz.org
Officers:
President: Ray Bogardus
First VP: Frank Paul

Second VP: Keith Thomas
Third VP: Karen Sheaffer
Treasurer: Fred Guion
Secretary: Bunny Hottenstein
Management:
Executive Director: Dave Lazorcik
Mission: To present, promote and preserve America's unique art form, jazz.
Utilizes: Soloists
Founded: 1980
Specialized Field: Jazz Ensemble
Status: Nonprofit
Paid Staff: 30
Budget: $76,000
Income Sources: Allied Arts Fund; Metro Arts of Central Pennsylvania; Mellon Bank; PA Council on the Arts
Facility Category: Hotel Ballroom
Organization Type: Performing; Educational; Sponsoring

1472
HARRISBURG SYMPHONY ASSOCIATION

800 Corporate Circle
Suite 101
Harrisburg, PA 17110
Phone: 717-545-5527
Fax: 717-545-6501
Web Site: www.harrisburgsymphony.org/
Management:
Music Director: Stuart Malina
Mission: To offer Central Pennsylvania quality symphonic music.
Utilizes: Actors; Collaborations; Dance Companies; Dancers; Grant Writers; Guest Accompanists; Guest Artists; Guest Companies; Guest Directors; Guest Lecturers; Guest Musical Directors; Guest Musicians; Multi Collaborations; Multimedia; Organization Contracts; Original Music Scores; Selected Students; Sign Language Translators; Singers; Touring Companies
Founded: 1930
Specialized Field: Symphony; Orchestra
Status: Professional; Nonprofit
Paid Staff: 15
Volunteer Staff: 300
Income Sources: Grants; Ticket Sales; Fundraising; Corporate and Individual Donations
Performs At: The Forum
Annual Attendance: 140,000
Facility Category: The Forum, State-owned Hall
Seating Capacity: 1,763
Year Built: 1931
Organization Type: Performing

1473
HARRISBURG YOUTH SYMPHONY ORCHESTRA

128 Locust Street
Harrisburg, PA 17101
Phone: 717-545-5527
Fax: 717-545-6501
Web Site: www.angelfire.com/pa3/hyso/
Management:
Music Director/Conductor: Dr. Ronald E Schafer
Mission: To provide young people with an opportunity to participate in an orchestra.
Specialized Field: Youth Symphony
Status: Non-Professional; Nonprofit
Paid Staff: 70
Income Sources: American Symphony Orchestra League (Youth Orchestra Division)

Performs At: Susquehanna Township Middle School
Organization Type: Performing; Touring; Educational; Sponsoring

1474
HERSHEY SYMPHONY ORCHESTRA

PO Box 93
Hershey, PA 17033
Phone: 717-533-8449
Fax: 717-520-9227
e-mail: info@hersheysymphny.org
Officers:
General Manager: Sharon Fuller
Assistant General Manager: Marsha Roscoe
Management:
Music Director: Dr. Sandra Dackow
Assistant Conductor: Robert Sproul
Concertmistress: MaryLee Yerger
General Manager: Diane Cook
Personnel Manager: KellyLee Yerger
Librarian: Kim Elicker
Archivist: Annette Kilpatrick
Founded: 1969
Specialized Field: Orchestra
Paid Staff: 7
Non-paid Artists: 15

1475
BALTIMORE CONSORT

93 Old York Road
222 Jenkintown Plaza
Jenkintown, PA 19046
Phone: 215-885-6400
Fax: 215-885-9929
e-mail: artists@rilearts.com
Web Site: www.file.com
Management:
Artist Management: Joanne Rile
Mission: To perform popular music of the fifteen and sixteen hundreds from England, France and Scotland.
Founded: 1980
Specialized Field: Chamber; Ensemble; Folk Music
Status: Professional; Nonprofit
Income Sources: Walters Art Gallery
Organization Type: Performing; Touring; Resident; Educational

1476
JOHNSTOWN SYMPHONY ORCHESTRA

227 Franklin Street
Suite 302
Johnstown, PA 15901
Phone: 814-535-6738
Fax: 814-535-6739
e-mail: info@johnstownsymphony.org
Web Site: www.johnstownsymphony.org
Officers:
President: James Beener
VP: Karen Azer
Treasurer: William Locher
Management:
Executive Director: Patricia Hofscher
Business Manager: Lawrence R Samay
Administrative Assistant: Doris Lapinski
Music Director: Istvan Jaray
Mission: To provide classical music for greater Johnstown area residents.
Utilizes: Actors; Collaborations; Educators; Fine Artists; Grant Writers; Guest Accompanists; Guest Composers; Guest Lecturers; Guest Musical Directors; Guest Musicians; Guest Writers; Instructors; Local Artists; Multimedia; Original Music Scores; Sign Language Translators; Singers; Soloists
Founded: 1929

Specialized Field: Symphony; Orchestra; Chamber
Status: Professional
Paid Staff: 7
Volunteer Staff: 150
Paid Artists: 80
Non-paid Artists: 80
Budget: $638,000
Income Sources: Individuals; Corporations; Grants; Sponsors
Affiliations: Pasquerilla Performing Arts Center On Campus or University Of Pittsburgh At Johnstown
Annual Attendance: 16,680
Facility Category: Auditorium
Type of Stage: Proscenium with Pit
Stage Dimensions: 40x50
Seating Capacity: 1,000
Year Built: 1990
Cost: $9.6 million
Rental Contact: Bev Walery
Organization Type: Performing

1477
KENNETT SYMPHONY

206 E State Street
Kennett Square, PA 19438
Phone: 610-444-6363
Fax: 610-925-1599
e-mail: info@kennettsymphony.org
Officers:
Board President: Bill Simeral
Board VP: Paul Merluzzi
Management:
Music Director/Conductor: Mary W Green
Executive Director: Barb Bullock
Office Manager: Barbara Belt
Personnel Manager: Ardath Belzer
Mission: To support professional symphonic music, to encourage young musicians and to educate young audiences.
Founded: 1940
Specialized Field: Orchestra
Volunteer Staff: 3
Budget: $400,000

1478
RIVERSIDE SYMPHONIA

PO Box 650
Lambertville, New Jersey
Lambertville, PA 8530
Phone: 609-397-7300
e-mail: info@riversidesymphonia.org
Officers:
Chair: Kathy Hausman
Young Artists Competition: Candace Phillips
Management:
Music Director: Mariusz Simolij
Executive Director: Benita Ryan
Founded: 1990
Specialized Field: Orchestra
Budget: $150,000- $260,000
Performs At: auditorium
Seating Capacity: 450

1479
LEHIGH VALLEY CHAMBER ORCHESTRA

PO Box 20641
Lehigh Valley, PA 18002
Phone: 610-266-8555
Fax: 610-266-8525
e-mail: lvco@fast.net
Web Site: www.lvco.org
Management:
Executive Director: Llyena Boylan

Music Director: Donald Spieth
Office Manager: Holly Stackhouse
Mission: To support and appreciate classical music through performances of the highest standard of excellence; to enhance the quality of life in our community by fostering musical heritage and promoting contemporary American music, providing educational programming and presenting virtuoso performers of international stature; to create and seek opportunities to enhance our reputation.
Founded: 1979
Specialized Field: Orchestra; Chamber
Status: Professional; Nonprofit
Paid Staff: 3
Volunteer Staff: 100
Paid Artists: 100
Income Sources: Individual; Government; Business
Performs At: Dorothy & Dexter Baker Center for the Arts
Annual Attendance: 8,000-10,000
Seating Capacity: 500
Organization Type: Performing; Touring; Educational; Recording

1480
MCKEESPORT SYMPHONY ORCHESTRA
PO Box 354
McKeesport, PA 15134-0354
Phone: 412-664-2854
Fax: 412-460-1415
e-mail: mail@mckeesportsymphony.org
Officers:
Composer-in-residence: Todd Goodman
Personnel Manager: John Hall
Management:
Conductor: Bruce Lauffer
Concert master: Jason Posnock
Mission: To present orchestra concerts and other musical events of professional quality for the benefit of the public.
Specialized Field: Orchestra

1481
ALLEGHENY CIVIC SYMPHONY
Music Department
Allegheny College
Meadville, PA 16335
Phone: 814-332-3356
e-mail: rbond@allegro.edu
Management:
Conductor: Robert Bond
Mission: To provide student artists with an opportunity to perform with experienced musicians; to offer high quality performances.
Founded: 1957
Specialized Field: Symphony
Status: Semi-Professional; Nonprofit
Paid Staff: 60
Income Sources: Allegheny College
Performs At: Raymond P. Shafer Auditorium
Organization Type: Performing; Educational

1482
PHILADELPHIA CLASSICAL SYMPHONY
71 Merbrook Lane
Merion
Merion, PA 19066
Phone: 610-664-8481
Fax: 610-664-6667
e-mail: info@classicalsymphony.org
Management:
Artistic Director: Karl Middleman

Mission: Believing that music can be a healing, ennobling force in modern life, we present intriguing concerts that aim to make classical music accessible to audiences of all ages. Symphony events are organized around thematic programs and historical practices and frequently offer audience participation.
Founded: 1993
Specialized Field: Orchestra

1483
BACH FESTIVAL OF PHILADELPHIA
8806 Germantown Avenue
Philadelphia, PA 19118
Phone: 215-247-BACH
e-mail: office@bach-fest.org
Web Site: www.Bach-Fest.org
Officers:
President: John L. Fowler, Esq
Management:
Executive Director: Dr Guido Houden
Artistic Director: Jonathan Sternberg
Mission: The Bach Festival of Philadelphia is dedicated to enriching the community through concerts and educational programs presented by some of the best Baroque interpreters in the world.
Utilizes: Collaborations; Guest Composers; Guest Directors; Guest Musical Directors; Guest Musicians; Guest Soloists; Multimedia; Original Music Scores; Sign Language Translators; Singers
Founded: 1976
Specialized Field: Bach; Ensemble; Chamber
Status: Professional; Nonprofit
Paid Staff: 2
Volunteer Staff: 8
Income Sources: Government; Corporate and private foundations; Donations; Ticketsales; Advertising books
Performs At: Churches, Performance halls
Annual Attendance: 2,000-3,000
Organization Type: Educational; Presenting

1484
CHESTNUT BRASS COMPANY
PO Box 30165
Philadelphia, PA 19103
Phone: 215-204-6792
Fax: 215-204-9792
Web Site: www.chestnutbrass.com/
Mission: Offering a historical perspective on brass instruments to the public.
Founded: 1977
Specialized Field: Chamber; Brass Ensemble; Jazz
Status: Professional; Nonprofit
Income Sources: Greater Philadelphia Cultural Alliance; Temple University; Esther Boyle School
Organization Type: Performing; Touring; Resident; Educational

1485
CONCERTO SOLOISTS
Walnut Street Theatre Building
9th and Walnut Streets
Philadelphia, PA 19107
Phone: 215-574-3550
Fax: 215-574-3598
Web Site: www.wstonline.org
Management:
Artistic/Music Director: Marc Mostovoy
General Manager: Ken Wesler
Artistic Administrator: Kelli Marshall
Mission: To belong to the Philadelphia community as one of its cultural institutions.
Utilizes: Guest Artists
Founded: 1964

Specialized Field: Orchestra; Chamber; Ensemble; Soloists
Status: Nonprofit
Income Sources: Greater Philadelphia Arts Council; Performing Arts League of Philadelphia; American Symphony Orchestra League
Performs At: Walnut Street Theatre; Church of the Holy Trinity
Organization Type: Performing; Touring; Resident; Educational; Sponsor Produced

1486
MARLBORO SCHOOL OF MUSIC
1616 Walnut Street
Suite 1600
Philadelphia, PA 19103
Phone: 215-569-4690
Fax: 215-569-9497
e-mail: info@marlboromusic.org
Web Site: www.marlboromusic.org
Management:
Administrator: Anthony P Checchia
Manager: Philip Maneval
Director Of Admissions: Carol Faris
Mission: Professional school providing advanced training for chamber musicians.
Founded: 1951
Specialized Field: Chamber; Educational
Status: Professional; Nonprofit
Income Sources: Grants; Ticket Sales; Endowments; Patron Gifts
Performs At: Marlboro College Concert Hall
Annual Attendance: 8,000+
Seating Capacity: 670
Organization Type: Performing; Educational

1487
PETER NERO AND THE PHILLY POPS
260 South Broad Street
16th Floor
Philadelphia, PA 19102
Phone: 215-893-1900
Fax: 215-875-7649
e-mail: ThePOPS@philadelphiaorchestra.org
Officers:
Management Assistant: Cynthia Heininger
Vice President of Marketing: J Edward Cambron
Management:
Artistic Director/C onductor: Peter Nero
President and CEO: James Undercofler
Public Relations Director: Maria Venuti Forrest
Artistic Administrator: Laura Bordner Adams
Patron Services Manager: Michelle Messa
Patron Services: Matthew Baehr
Mission: POPS concerts run the gamut, from classics to big band, Broadway to rock n' roll. Audiences want an eclectic mix, thats the success of our concerts for we provide quality, variety and a great orchestra that can play anything.
Specialized Field: Orchestra; Pops

1488
PHILADELPHIA CHAMBER MUSIC SOCIETY
1616 Walnut Street
Suite 1600
Philadelphia, PA 19103
Phone: 215-569-8587
Fax: 215-569-9497
e-mail: mail@pcmsconcerts.org
Officers:
Manager: Miles Cohen
Development Director: Derek Delaney
President: Elizabeth P Glendinning

INSTRUMENTAL MUSIC / Pennsylvania

VP: Horace W Schwarz
Treasurer: Park B Dilks
Secretary: Sandor S Shapiro MD
Management:
Artistic Director: Anthony Checchia
Executive Director: Philip Maneval
Administrator/Concert Manager: Miles Cohen
Development Director: Derek Delaney
Marketing Director: Susan Grody
Mission: The Philadelphia Chamber Music Society (PCMS) is one of the largest, most accessible music presenting forums in the United States.
Founded: 1986
Specialized Field: Chamber
Performs At: Perelman Theater; Pennsylvania Convention Center

1489
PHILADELPHIA CLASSICAL GUITAR SOCIETY

2038 Sansom Street
Philadelphia, PA 19103
Phone: 215-567-2972
Fax: 215-963-9950
Web Site: www.phillyguitar.com
Officers:
Acting President: Joseph Mayes
Secretary: Arnold Gessel
Treasurer: George Thomas
Management:
Artistic Director: Joseph Mayes
Marketing Director: Michael Simmons
Mission: To present and foster classical guitar-related activities throughout the Greater Philadelphia area; to provide a forum for informal performance, lectures, outreach, and communication between fellow classical guitar enthusiasts.
Specialized Field: Chamber; Classical Guitar
Status: Professional; Nonprofit
Paid Staff: 40
Budget: $10,000-20,000
Income Sources: Ticket Sales; Patron Gifts; Grants
Performs At: Pennsylvania Convention Auditorium
Seating Capacity: 610

1490
PHILADELPHIA ORCHESTRA

260 S Broad Street
16th Floor
Philadelphia, PA 19102
Phone: 215-893-1900
Fax: 215-875-7649
e-mail: philadelphia_orchestra@philorch.org
Web Site: www.philorch.org
Officers:
Vice Chairman (Rpac Oversight): Robert J Butera
Vice Chairman (Artistic): John G Christy
Vice Chairman (Planning): Peter G Ernster
Vice Chairman (Education): Carole Haas Gravagno
Vice Chairman Marketing: Beverly A Harper
Vice Chairman (Human Resources): Martin A Heckscher
Vice Chairman (Development): John N Park, Jr
(Nominating & Governance): Robert H Rock
Vice Chairman (Investments): Ellen C Wolf
Management:
President/CEO: Joseph H Kluger
Music Director/Conductor: Wolfgang Sawallisch
Director Finance: Ben Hayllar
Executive VP: Shel Thompson
Chairman: Richard L Smoot
Vice Chairman/Audit: Roland K Bullard II
Director Public Relations: Judith Kurnick

Director Development: Maria T Giliotto
Director Ecucation: Gary Alan Wood
Mission: Maintaining the Philadelphia Orchestra's preeminence as one of the city's outstanding cultural assets.
Utilizes: Guest Artists
Founded: 1900
Specialized Field: Symphony; Orchestra
Status: Professional; Nonprofit
Income Sources: American Symphony Orchestra League
Performs At: Academy of Music
Seating Capacity: 2,897
Organization Type: Performing

1491
PHILADELPHIA YOUTH ORCHESTRA

PO Box 41810
Philadelphia, PA 19101-1810
Phone: 215-545-0502
Fax: 215-545-7399
e-mail: info@pyos.org
Web Site: www.pyos.org
Officers:
President: Louis Scaglione
Chairman: Trude Haecker, M.A.
Mission: To promote, encourage and foster the study and practice of music by making available to deserving and talented youth opportunities for orchestra instruction and supervision of their work and to provide concerts for promoting musical art and its appreciation.
Founded: 1939
Specialized Field: Youth Orchestra; Chamber; Ensemble
Status: Non-Professional; Nonprofit
Paid Staff: 2
Volunteer Staff: 200
Non-paid Artists: 190
Income Sources: American Symphony Orchestra League (Youth Orchestra Division); Greater Philadelphia Cultural Alliance
Performs At: Academy of Music
Facility Category: Theatres; Schools
Organization Type: Performing; Touring; Educational

1492
PIFFARO: THE RENAISSANCE BAND

2258 Fairmount Ave
Philadelphia, PA 19130
Phone: 215-235-8469
Fax: 215-235-8469
e-mail: info@piffaro.com
Web Site: www.piffaro.com
Officers:
Chairman: William Gross
Management:
Director: Robert Wiemken
Director: Joan Kimball
Mission: Performing early Baroque and Renaissance music using period instruments.
Utilizes: Actors; Collaborations; Dance Companies; Dancers; Guest Musical Directors; Guest Musicians; Multimedia; Original Music Scores; Sign Language Translators; Singers
Founded: 1980
Specialized Field: Chamber; Ensemble; Early Music; Renaissance
Status: Professional; Nonprofit
Paid Staff: 3
Volunteer Staff: 10
Paid Artists: 7
Budget: $170,000
Income Sources: Government; Pennsylvania Council Art Foundation; Ticket sales; Concert fees

Organization Type: Performing; Touring; Educational

1493
PRESIDENTIAL JAZZ WEEKEND

African-American History Museum
701 Arch Street
Philadelphia, PA 19106
Phone: 215-574-0380
Fax: 215-574-3110
Management:
Jazz Live Director: Rhoda Blount
Museum Director: Dr. Rowena Stewart
Mission: To celebrate the classical music of African-Americans.
Utilizes: Singers
Founded: 1989
Specialized Field: Jazz Ensemble; Ethnic Music
Status: Professional; Semi-Professional; Nonprofit
Income Sources: Greater Philadelphia Cultural Alliance; American Association of Museums; Coalition of Afro-American Organizations
Organization Type: Performing; Educational; Sponsoring

1494
RELACHE ENSEMBLE

715 S Third Street
Philadelphia, PA 19147
Phone: 215-574-8246
Fax: 215-574-0253
e-mail: relache@att.net
Web Site: www.relache.org/indexWin.htm
Management:
Executive Artistic Director: Joseph Franklin
Director Planning/Development: Arthur Stidfole
Director Educational Projects: Laurel Wyckoff
Mission: Developing, producing and presenting the works of living composers.
Specialized Field: Chamber; Ensemble; Electronic; Live Electronic; Contemporary
Status: Professional; Nonprofit
Performs At: Mandell Theater
Organization Type: Performing; Touring; Resident; Educational; Sponsoring

1495
PITTSBURGH CHAMBER MUSIC SOCIETY

315 S. Bellefield Avenue #305
Pittsburgh, PA 15213
Phone: 412-624-4129
Fax: 412-624-6461
e-mail: info@pittsburghchambermusic.org
Web Site: www.pittsburghchambermusic.org
Officers:
Executive Director: Kelli Clevenger
Mission: To present chamber music of the highest quality performed by internationally and nationally recognized ensembles to tri-state residents; to support and extend the full range of chamber music repertoire through performances and commissions; to support educational activities that encourage more adults and students to appreciate the art form; and to nurture exceptional emerging chamber music ensembles.
Founded: 1961
Specialized Field: Chamber Music
Status: Professional; Nonprofit
Paid Staff: 2
Income Sources: Chamber Music America; PA Presenters
Performs At: Carnegie Music Hall, Oakland
Affiliations: Chamber Music America
Organization Type: Sponsoring

1496
PITTSBURGH NEW MUSIC ENSEMBLE
Duquesne University School of Music
Pittsburgh, PA 15282
Mailing Address: PO Box 99476
Phone: 412-682-2955
Fax: 412-682-2955
Officers:
President: Bruce Wilder
VP: Liza Weis
Secretary: Roger Dannenberg
Treasurer: Bonnie Hellman
Management:
Executive Director: Michelle Greenlaw
Artistic Director: Kevin Noe
Mission: To encourage the creation, performance, dissemination and appreciation of contemporary music, with special emphasis on American Music and living composers.
Utilizes: Guest Artists
Founded: 1976
Specialized Field: Chamber; Ensemble; Contemporary
Status: Professional; Nonprofit
Paid Staff: 2
Paid Artists: 50
Income Sources: Chamber Music America
Performs At: Levy Hall at The Fulton Theatres
Organization Type: Performing; Touring; Resident; Educational; Sponsoring

1497
PITTSBURGH SYMPHONY ORCHESTRA
Pittsburgh Symphony Heinz Hall
600 Penn Avenue
Pittsburgh, PA 15222-3259
Phone: 412-392-4900
Fax: 412-392-4909
e-mail: customerservice@pittsburghsymphony.org
Web Site: www.pittsburghsymphony.org
Officers:
President: Tom Todd
Executive VP: Gideon Toeplitz
Management:
Resident Conductor: Daniel Meyer
Mission: Striving for and attaining excellence in artistic achievement.
Utilizes: Guest Artists
Founded: 1895
Specialized Field: Symphony; Orchestra; Chamber
Status: Nonprofit
Income Sources: Pittsburgh Symphony Society
Performs At: Heinz Hall for the Performing Arts
Seating Capacity: 2,661
Organization Type: Performing; Touring; Educational; Presenting

1498
PITTSBURGH YOUTH SYMPHONY ORCHESTRA ASSOCIATION
Heinz Hall
600 Penn Avenue
Pittsburgh, PA 15222-3259
Phone: 412-392-4872
e-mail: info@pyso.us
Web Site: www.pittsburghsymphony.org
Officers:
President: Jerry Gindrele
VP: Suzanne Cafferty Ross
Secretary: Bethne Cheberenchic
Treasurer: Roberts Milspaw
Management:
Music Director: Lawrence Loh
Executive Director: Craig Johnson

Program Coord/Music Lib/Pers Mngr.: Eve Goodman
Mission: To provide the best possible musical training to members of the orchestra and to develop new audiences for symphonic music among youth.
Founded: 1946
Status: Non-Professional; Nonprofit
Income Sources: Grants; Foundations; Corporate/Individual Contribution
Performs At: Pittsburgh Symphony Heinz Hall
Annual Attendance: 5,000
Seating Capacity: 2663
Organization Type: Performing; Touring; Resident; Educational; Sponsoring

1499
RENAISSANCE AND BAROQUE SOCIETY OF PITTSBURGH
303 S Craig Street
PO Box 10156
Pittsburgh, PA 15213
Phone: 412-682-7262
Fax: 412-682-5253
e-mail: director@rbsp.org
Web Site: www.rbsp.org
Management:
Executive Director: Ann F Mason
President: Rosemary Hogan
VP: Laura Haibeck
Secretary: Susan Godfrey
Treasurer: Margaret M Barth
Mission: Sponsoring national and international touring ensembles who use period instruments to perform early music.
Founded: 1969
Specialized Field: Orchestra; Chamber; Early Music; Baroque
Status: Professional
Performs At: Synod Hall; Sacred Heart Cathedral
Organization Type: Sponsoring
Comments: Special parking/entry for handicap access; Large print programs

1500
RIVER CITY BRASS BAND
PO Box 6436
Pittsburgh, PA 15212
Phone: 412-322-7222
Fax: 412-322-6821
Toll-free: 800-292-7222
e-mail: kshaffer@rcbb.com
Web Site: www.rcbb.com
Officers:
Chairman: Michael C Barbarita
Management:
Conductor: Denis Colwell
Executive Director: Marilyn Thomas
Contracted Performances Rep.: Milton Orkin
General Manager: Joseph Zuback
Mission: The mision of the River City Brass Band is to propagate and perpetuate musical culture, primarily American musical culture, across a broad spectrum of the public through the presentation of brass band performances, educational programs and the production of recordings. The River City Brass Band has as its central obligation service to the people of Western Pennsylvania.
Utilizes: Commissioned Composers; Dance Companies; Educators; Guest Accompanists; Guest Companies; Guest Musical Directors; Guest Musicians; Local Artists; Organization Contracts; Singers
Founded: 1981
Specialized Field: Band; Brass Ensemble
Status: Professional; Nonprofit

Paid Staff: 8
Paid Artists: 28
Budget: $2 million
Income Sources: Association of Performing Arts Presenters; American Concert Band; National Endowment for the Arts
Performs At: Carnegie Music Hall
Annual Attendance: 140,000
Organization Type: Performing; Touring; Resident; Educational; Recording

1501
TAMBURITZANS FOLK ENSEMBLE
1801 Boulevard of the Allies
Pittsburgh, PA 15219
Phone: 412-396-5185
Fax: 412-396-5583
e-mail: stafura@duq2.cc.duq.edu
Web Site: www.duq.edu/Tamburitzans
Management:
Managing Director: Paul G Stafura
Mission: The Duquesne University Tamburitzans is dedicated to preserving and perpetuating the cultural heritages of Eastern Europe and its neighbors through performance, while awarding scholarships to talented and deserving student performers.
Utilizes: Singers
Founded: 1937
Specialized Field: Ensemble; Ethnic Music; Folk Music
Status: Non-Professional; Nonprofit
Paid Staff: 40
Income Sources: Duquesne University
Organization Type: Performing; Touring

1502
READING SYMPHONY ORCHESTRA
147 N 5th Street
Reading, PA 19601-3502
Phone: 610-373-7557
Fax: 610-373-5446
e-mail: readingsym@aol.com
Web Site: www.readingsymphony.com
Management:
Executive Director: Joseph Tackett
Music Director: Andrew Constantine
Mission: Providing the city of Reading and Berks County with high quality orchestral concerts.
Utilizes: Guest Artists
Founded: 1912
Specialized Field: Symphony
Status: Professional; Nonprofit
Paid Staff: 10
Non-paid Artists: 80
Income Sources: Grants; Ticket Sales; Fundraisers
Performs At: Rajah Theatre
Annual Attendance: 10,000+
Seating Capacity: 2,150
Organization Type: Performing; Educational; Sponsoring

1503
NITTANY VALLEY SYMPHONY
PO Box 1375
State College, PA 16804-1375
Phone: 814-231-8224
Fax: 814-231-0140
e-mail: info@nvs.org
Web Site: www.nvs.org
Management:
Music Director: Michael Jinbo
Mission: Pledging to program the best in orchestral music, it presents six concerts a year, including one specially designed for families.
Founded: 1967

Specialized Field: Orchestra
Status: Nonprofit
Income Sources: Ticket Revenue; Grants; Foundation Earnings; Donor Contributions

1504
VILLANOVA UNIVERSITY CHAMBER SERIES

Office of Musical Activities
Villanova University
Villanova, PA 19085-1603
Phone: 610-519-7214
Fax: 610-519-7596
e-mail: john.dunphy@villanova.edu
Management:
   Manager: Peter Marino
Specialized Field: Chamber
Budget: $20,000-35,000
Performs At: St. Mary's Hall

1505
WILLIAMSPORT SYMPHONY ORCHESTRA

220 W 4th Street
Williamsport, PA 17701
Phone: 570-322-0227
Fax: 570-327-7662
e-mail: info@williamsportsymphony.com
Management:
   Music Director: Robin Fountain
Mission: To be a cultural asset to the community by providing quality orchestral music, education and performance opportunities for regional talent to an ever-expanding audience.
Specialized Field: Orchestra

Rhode Island

1506
KINGSTON CHAMBER MUSIC FESTIVAL AT URI

PO Box 1733
Kingston, RI 02881
Phone: 401-874-2060
Fax: 401-874-2380
e-mail: sadd@egr.uri.edu
Web Site: www.mce.uri.edu
Management:
   Artistic Director/Violin: David Kim
Mission: To provide outstanding classical music programs in New England. Offers both summer and winter concerts, and also outreach programs at local area schools.
Utilizes: Guest Musical Directors; Multimedia; Original Music Scores
Founded: 1989
Specialized Field: Classical; Chamber
Volunteer Staff: 15
Paid Artists: 1045
Budget: $60,000
Income Sources: Donations; Ticket sales
Affiliations: University of Rhode Island
Annual Attendance: 2800

1507
UNIVERSITY OF RHODE ISLAND SYMPHONY ORCHESTRA

Music Department
105 Upper College Road Suite 2
Kingston, RI 02881

Phone: 401-)74—243
Fax: 401-874-2772
e-mail: music@etal.uri.edu
Officers:
   Secretary: Jeannette Ruhle
Management:
   Music Department Chair: Ronald Lee
   Administrative Assistant: Lucienne Andrew
Specialized Field: Orchestra
Performs At: Recital Hall, Fine Arts Center

1508
BROWN UNIVERSITY ORCHESTRA

Brown University
One Young Orchard Avenue
Providence, RI 02912
Mailing Address: PO Box 1924
Phone: 401-863-1472
Fax: 401-863-1256
e-mail: orchestra@brown.edu
Web Site: www.brown.edu/Orchestra
Management:
   Music Director/Conductor: Paul Phillips
Utilizes: Collaborating Artists; Collaborations; Commissioned Composers; Community Members; Composers; Educators; Guest Companies; Guest Composers; Guest Lecturers; Guest Musical Directors; Guest Musicians; Multi Collaborations; Multimedia; Music; Original Music Scores; Singers; Soloists
Founded: 1918
Specialized Field: Orchestra
Performs At: Sayles Hall
Seating Capacity: 400

1509
RHODE ISLAND CHAMBER MUSIC CONCERTS

PO Box 41356
Providence, RI 02940
Phone: 401-863-2416
e-mail: info@ricmc.org
Officers:
   President: Joan Lusk
Specialized Field: Chamber
Budget: $10,000-20,000
Income Sources: Tickets; Grants; Donations
Facility Category: Church
Type of Stage: Raised Platform
Stage Dimensions: small
Seating Capacity: 400

1510
RHODE ISLAND CIVIC CHORALE & ORCHESTRA

33 Chestnut Street
Providence, RI 02903
Phone: 401-521-5670
Fax: 401-521-5276
e-mail: info@ricco.org
Web Site: www.ricco.org
Management:
   Music Director: Edward Markward
Mission: To enrich the public and performers through artistic concert presentations.
Specialized Field: Orchestra
Status: Non-Profit
Performs At: Veterans Memorial Auditorium

1511
RHODE ISLAND COLLEGE SYMPHONY ORCHESTRA

600 Mount Pleasant Avenue
Rhode Island College
Providence, RI 02908
Phone: 401-456-9883
Fax: 401-874-2772
Management:
   Music Director: Dr. Edward Markward
Specialized Field: Orchestra
Performs At: Roberts Auditorium

1512
RHODE ISLAND PHILHARMONIC ORCHESTRA AND MUSIC SCHOOL

222 Richmond Street
Providence, RI 02903
Phone: 401-831-3123
Fax: 401-831-4577
e-mail: information@ri-philharmonic.org
Web Site: www.ri-philharmonic.org
Officers:
   Executive Director: David M Wax
   Operations Director: David W Gasper
Utilizes: Actors; Choreographers; Collaborating Artists; Composers-in-Residence; Dance Companies; Dancers; Educators; Fine Artists; Five Seasonal Concerts; Grant Writers; Guest Accompanists; Guest Artists; Guest Choreographers; Guest Companies; Guest Composers; Guest Designers; Guest Directors; Guest Lecturers; Guest Musical Directors; Guest Musicians; Instructors; Local Artists; Multimedia; Music; Original Music Scores; Resident Artists; Sign Language Translators; Singers; Student Interns; Special Technical Talent; Theatre Companies
Founded: 1945
Specialized Field: Symphony; Educational
Status: Professional; Nonprofit
Paid Staff: 10
Paid Artists: 72
Income Sources: Individual; Corporate; Foundation Grants
Performs At: VMA Arts and Cultural Center
Seating Capacity: 2,100
Organization Type: Performing; Resident; Educational

South Carolina

1513
ANDERSON SYMPHONY ORCHESTRA

126 Foxcroft Way
Anderson, SC 29621
Phone: 864-224-5508
Officers:
   President: Marion Hovermale
   Treasurer: John Kane
Management:
   Music Director: Richard Sowers
   Exeuctive Director: Pamela Coletti
Utilizes: Guest Artists
Founded: 1978
Specialized Field: Orchestra
Paid Staff: 74
Budget: $150,000-260,000
Performs At: Paramount Theatre Centre

1514
CHARLESTON SYMPHONY ORCHESTRA

77 Calhoun Street
Charleston, SC 29403

Phone: 843-723-7528
Fax: 843-722-3463
e-mail: darrell@charlestonsymphony.com
Web Site: www.charlestonsymphony.com
Officers:
President: Bronwyn Lester
Management:
Executive Director: Darrell G Edwards
Music Director/Conductor: David Stahl
Associate Conductor: Bundit Ungrangsee
Assistant Manager: Cynthia Branch
Mission: Offering South Carolina residents quality musical performances; educating children through the use of smaller orchestras and ensembles.
Utilizes: Collaborations; Commissioned Composers; Commissioned Music; Fine Artists; Guest Accompanists; Guest Artists; Guest Companies; Guest Directors; Guest Lecturers; Guest Musical Directors; Guest Musicians; Guest Writers; Multimedia; Original Music Scores; Sign Language Translators; Singers
Founded: 1936
Specialized Field: Symphony; Orchestra; Chamber; Ensemble
Status: Professional; Nonprofit
Paid Staff: 11
Volunteer Staff: 1
Budget: $2.5 Million
Income Sources: Ticket Sales; Business; Individual Contributions; Grants
Performs At: Gaillard Municipal Auditorium
Facility Category: Multipurpose
Seating Capacity: 2730
Organization Type: Performing; Touring; Resident; Educational

1515
SPOLETO FESTIVAL USA
14 George Street
Charleston, SC 29401-1524
Phone: 843-722-2764
Fax: 843-723-6383
e-mail: info@spoletousa.org
Web Site: www.spoletousa.org
Officers:
Chairman: Martha Rivers Ingram
President: Carlos E. Evans
Management:
Artistic Director-Choral Activities: Joseph Flummerfelt
Director, Chamber Music: Geoff Nuttall
General Director: Nigel Redden
Producer: Nunally Kersh
Director Of Development: Julia Forster
Director Marketing/Public Relations: Paula Edwards
Mission: To present opera, dance, theater, symphonic, choral and chamber music, jazz and visual arts exhibits of the highest quality; to serve as an educational environment for young artists and audiences alike.
Utilizes: Singers
Founded: 1977
Specialized Field: Jazz; Theatrical Dance
Status: Professional; Semi-Professional; Non-Profit
Paid Staff: 18
Budget: $7,000,000
Income Sources: Ticket Revenues; Contributions
Performs At: Gaillard Municipal Auditorium; Dock Street Theater
Annual Attendance: 70,000-80,000
Organization Type: Performing; Educational; Sponsoring

1516
CAROLINA YOUTH SYMPHONY
PO Box 534
Greenville, SC 29602
Phone: 864-232-3963
e-mail: gordon@carolinayouthsymphony.org
Officers:
Conductor Repertory Orchestra: James Kilgus
Management:
Executive Director: Lee Elmore
Director of Bands: Leslie W Hicken
Director: Leslie W Hicken
Specialized Field: Youth Orchestra

1517
GREENVILLE SYMPHONY ORCHESTRA
The Symphony Center
S Main Street
Greenville, SC 29601
Phone: 803-232-0344
Fax: 803-240-3113
Web Site: www.greenvillesymphony.org
Management:
Office Manager: Patricia G Quarles
Operations Manager: Julie Greer
Music Director/Conductor: Edvard Tchivzhel
General Manager: Joel E Keller
Ticket Manager: Edith K Diver
Librarian: Susan Bocook
Mission: Providing our community with the highest quality musical entertainment and education.
Founded: 1948
Specialized Field: Symphony; Chamber; Ensemble; Pops
Status: Professional
Income Sources: American Symphony Orchestra League; American Society of Composers, Authors and Publishers; Broadcast Music Incorporated
Performs At: Peace Center for the Performing Arts
Organization Type: Performing; Resident; Educational

1518
CONVERSE SYMPHONY ORCHESTRA
Converse College
580 E Main Street
Spartanburg, SC 29302
Phone: 864-596-9021
Fax: 864-596-9167
Toll-free: 800-766-1125
e-mail: music@converse.edu
Web Site: www.converse.edu
Management:
Conductor: Paul Davis
Department Chair: Dr Douglas Weeks
Mission: College student orchestra.
Founded: 1899
Specialized Field: Orchestra
Paid Staff: 2

South Dakota

1519
BROOKINGS CHAMBER MUSIC SOCIETY
Music Department
S Dakota State University, Brookings
Brookings, SD 57007
Phone: 605-688-5187
Fax: 605-688-4307
Web Site: web.sdstate.edu/sites/bcms
Officers:
President: David Reynolds
Management:

Program Coordinator: John Walker
Mission: Offering the South Dakota State University community and the Brookings area the highest quality artists and ensembles.
Utilizes: Collaborations; Fine Artists; Grant Writers; Guest Companies; Guest Directors; Guest Musical Directors; Guest Musicians; Multimedia; Organization Contracts; Original Music Scores; Sign Language Translators; Singers
Founded: 1982
Specialized Field: Orchestra; Chamber; Ensemble
Status: Nonprofit
Volunteer Staff: 16
Paid Artists: 20
Budget: $18,000
Income Sources: Season tickets; Gate; Donations; Endowments; Grants
Performs At: Peterson Recital Hall
Affiliations: SDSU
Annual Attendance: 1,800
Facility Category: Recital Hall
Type of Stage: Open
Stage Dimensions: 40' x 25'
Seating Capacity: 350
Year Built: 1980
Year Remodeled: 1995
Organization Type: Performing; Educational; Sponsoring

1520
SOUTH DAKOTA STATE UNIVERSITY CIVIC SYMPHONY
Music Department
S Dakota State University
Brookings, SD 57007
Phone: 605-688-5187
Fax: 605-688-4307
e-mail: john_brawand@sdstate.edu
Management:
Music Director/Conductor: John Browand
Mission: Performing symphonic literature from Baroque through contemporary and highlighting outstanding soloists.
Utilizes: Collaborations; Five Seasonal Concerts; Guest Accompanists; Guest Musical Directors; Guest Musicians; Instructors; Local Artists; Multimedia; Original Music Scores; Singers; Soloists; Visual Arts
Founded: 1966
Specialized Field: Symphony; Orchestra
Status: Non-Professional; Nonprofit
Paid Staff: 3
Paid Artists: 10
Non-paid Artists: 40
Budget: $13,000
Income Sources: South Dakota State University; South Dakota Arts Council; Corporate Sponsors; Local Businesses
Performs At: Peterson Recital Hall
Facility Category: Performing Arts Center
Type of Stage: Concert Hall
Stage Dimensions: 96'x63'
Seating Capacity: 1000
Year Built: 2001
Cost: $6.4 million
Organization Type: Performing; Educational

1521
BLACK HILLS SYMPHONY ORCHESTRA
Rapid City, SD
Mailing Address: PO Box 2246, Rapid City SD 57709
Phone: 605-348-4676
Web Site: www.rapidnet.com/~ecorwin/symphony
Management:
Conductor: Jack Knowles

Concertmaster: Coral White
Mission: To promote music appreciation and knowledge in the area; to offer opportunities for local musicians to grow through performance and education.
Founded: 1931
Specialized Field: Symphony; Orchestra
Status: Nonprofit
Paid Staff: 10
Performs At: Rushmore Plaza Civic Center Theater
Organization Type: Performing; Resident; Educational

1522

SOUTH DAKOTA SYMPHONY

300 N Dakota
Suite 116
Sioux Falls, SD 57104
Phone: 605-335-7933
Fax: 605-335-1958
e-mail: sdsymphony@sdsymphony.org
Web Site: www.sdsymphony.org
Officers:
Executive Director: Tom Bennett
Administrative Assistant: Linda Clement
Marketing Coordinator: Heidi Sehr
President: Fene Uher
Management:
Music Director: Susan Haig
Mission: Providing the highest quality orchestral music to the people of the Northern Plains, the South Dakota Symphony takes leadership in enhancing the cultural environment of the region, developing an understanding and interest in the people of the state for fine artistic expression.
Utilizes: Commissioned Music; Guest Companies; Guest Composers; Guest Designers; Guest Directors; Guest Lecturers; Guest Musical Directors; Guest Musicians; Local Artists; Multimedia; Original Music Scores; Sign Language Translators; Singers
Founded: 1922
Specialized Field: Symphony; Orchestra; Chamber; Ensemble
Status: Professional; Nonprofit
Paid Staff: 8
Paid Artists: 10
Budget: $1,500,000
Income Sources: Ticket Sales, Donations, grants, fundraising events
Performs At: Washington Pavilion of Arts and Science
Facility Category: Performing arts center
Type of Stage: Multi-purpose
Stage Dimensions: 50'x60'
Seating Capacity: 1,850
Year Remodeled: 1998
Rental Contact: Jeff Venekamp
Organization Type: Performing; Touring; Resident; Educational

Tennessee

1523

CHATTANOOGA SYMPHONY AND OPERA

630 Chestnut Street
Chattanooga, TN 37402
Phone: 423-267-8583
Fax: 423-265-6520
Web Site: www.chattanoogasymphony.org
Management:
Executive Director: John Wehrle
Music Director: Robert Bernhardt
Utilizes: Commissioned Composers; Commissioned Music; Educators; Five Seasonal Concerts; Grant Writers; Guest Accompanists; Guest Companies; Guest

Composers; Guest Designers; Guest Lecturers; Guest Musical Directors; Guest Musicians; Guest Writers; Instructors; Multimedia; Organization Contracts; Original Music Scores; Playwrights; Sign Language Translators; Singers
Specialized Field: Symphony
Status: Professional; Nonprofit
Paid Staff: 40
Budget: $1.2 Million
Income Sources: Tennesseans for the Arts; Opera America; American Symphony Orchestra League
Performs At: Tivoli Theatre
Annual Attendance: 50,000 - 75,000
Facility Category: Theatre and Outdoor
Seating Capacity: 1700
Organization Type: Performing; Touring; Educational

1524

JACKSON SYMPHONY ASSOCIATION

1903 N Highland, Suite 6
PO Box 3429
Jackson, TN 38303
Phone: 901-427-6440
Fax: 901-427-6417
Toll-free: 800-951-6440
e-mail: jso@aeneas.net
Web Site: www.jso.tn.org
Officers:
Board President: Nancy Oberg
Board President Elect: Brenda Whalley
Executive Director: Matthew Stover
Management:
Music Director: Dr. Jordan Tang
Mission: To support a performing orchestra of increasing quality for Jackson and its surrounding area; to promote the preservation of our musical heritage and audience exposure to the finer aspects of that heritage by providing programs that are attractive and entertaining.
Utilizes: Educators; Grant Writers; Guest Accompanists; Guest Directors; Guest Instructors; Guest Musical Directors; Guest Musicians; Multimedia; Original Music Scores; Sign Language Translators; Singers
Founded: 1961
Specialized Field: Symphony; Orchestra
Status: Semi-Professional
Paid Staff: 6
Volunteer Staff: 1
Budget: $600,000
Performs At: The Jackson Civic Center
Affiliations: American Symphony Orchestra League
Annual Attendance: 30,000
Organization Type: Performing; Touring; Resident; Educational

1525

JOHNSON CITY SYMPHONY ORCHESTRA

3201 Bristol Highway
Suite 2, PO Box 533
Johnson City, TN 37605
Phone: 423-926-8742
Fax: 423-926-8979
e-mail: jcsymphony@earthlink.net
Web Site: www.jcsymphony.com
Officers:
Chairman: Lynn Brown
Management:
Conductor: Tom Stites
General Manager: Lewis Senger
Mission: To be a vital regional force providing orchestral music for all ages through education, entertainment, and cultural enrichment.

Founded: 1969
Specialized Field: Orchestra
Paid Staff: 2
Budget: $ 191,900
Income Sources: Tennessee Arts Commission Grant; Johnson City Area Arts Council Grant; Corporate and Individual Sponsorships and Contributions; Foundation Grants
Performs At: College Chapel; City Auditorium
Affiliations: ASOL; BMI
Annual Attendance: 20,000
Seating Capacity: 1194

1526

KINGSPORT SYMPHONY ORCHESTRA

1200 E Center Street
Kingsport, TN 37660
Phone: 423-392-8423
Fax: 423-392-8428
e-mail: ksorch@aol.com
Web Site: www.kso.bigstep.com
Management:
Music Director: Cyrus Ginwala
Executive Director: Ann Meyers
Personnel Mgr./Education Director: Elaine Barker
Office Manager: Judy Branfield
Mission: To offer the public orchestral concerts as well as educational programs.
Utilizes: Collaborations; Guest Artists; Guest Musical Directors; Guest Musicians; Multimedia; Music; Singers
Founded: 1947
Specialized Field: Symphony; Orchestra; Chamber; Ensemble
Status: Semi-Professional; Non-Professional; Nonprofit
Paid Staff: 4
Volunteer Staff: 1
Paid Artists: 75
Budget: $285,000
Income Sources: Tickets sales, TN Arts, Commission grants, private contribution, corp. contributions
Performs At: Tom F Reid Employee Center
Affiliations: ASOL
Facility Category: Auditorium
Seating Capacity: 1,700 +
Organization Type: Performing; Resident; Educational; Sponsoring

1527

KNOXVILLE SYMPHONY ORCHESTRA

708 Gay Street
Knoxville, TN 37902
Phone: 865-523-1178
Fax: 865-546-3766
Web Site: www.ksoknox.org/
Management:
Executive Director: Constance Harrison
Director Development: Martha Weaver
Mission: To offer the region of East Tennessee a symphony orchestra for its enjoyment and education.
Utilizes: Guest Artists
Founded: 1935
Specialized Field: Symphony; Orchestra
Status: Professional; Nonprofit
Performs At: Tennessee Theater
Organization Type: Performing; Touring; Educational

1528

MEMPHIS SYMPHONY ORCHESTRA AND YOUTH SYMPHONY ORCHESTRA

585 S Mendenhall Road
Suite 501
Memphis, TN 38117

Phone: 901-537-2500
Fax: 901-537-2550
e-mail: information@memphissymphony.org
Web Site: www.memphissymphony.org
Officers:
  Chairman: David Ferraro
  Chairman Elect: George E Cates
  President/Executive Director: Martha Ellen
  Maxwell
Management:
  Music Director/Conductor: David Loebel
  Resident Conductor: Vincent L Danner
  Director Operations: Amylou Porter
  Personnel Manager: Doug Mayes
Utilizes: Guest Artists
Founded: 1952
Specialized Field: Youth Orchestra; Chamber
Status: Professional; Nonprofit
Paid Artists: 75
Performs At: Eudora Auditorium
Affiliations: American Symphony Orchestra League;
Memphis Arts Council
Organization Type: Performing; Educational;
Sponsoring

1529
NASHVILLE SYMPHONY
2000 Glen Echo Road
Suite 204
Nashville, TN 37215
Phone: 615-783-1200
Fax: 615-783-1575
Web Site: www.nashvillesymphony.org
Officers:
  Chairman: Martha R Ingram
  Secretary: Pamela K Pfeffer
  Treasurer: David Williams II
  Vice-Chairman: Joseph K Presley
  Vice-Chairman: Lou Todd
  Vice-Chairman: Anne Russell
Management:
  Music Director: Kenneth Schermerhorn
  Associate Conductor: Byung-Hyun Rhee
  Executive Director: Alan D Valentine
  Executive Assistant: Laura Faust
Mission: Dedicated to enhancing the quality of life in
Nashville and the surrounding communities by
providing opportunities for all citizens to enjoy live
performances of symphonic music in its various forms.
Utilizes: Guest Artists; Singers
Founded: 1946
Specialized Field: Symphony; Orchestra; Chamber
Status: Professional
Income Sources: American Symphony Orchestra
League; American Arts Alliance; American Society of
Composers, Authors and Publishers; Broadcast Music
Incorporated
Performs At: Tennessee Performing Arts Center; War
Memorial Auditorium
Organization Type: Performing; Resident; Touring;
Educational

1530
OAK RIDGE CIVIC MUSIC ASSOCIATION
205 Badger Road
PO Box 4271
Oak Ridge, TN 37831-4271
Phone: 865-483-5569
e-mail: office@orcma.org
Web Site: www.orcma.org
Management:
  President: Charles Coutant
  Vice President: David Gurd

  Music Director/Conductor: Cornelia Kodkami
  Laemmli
Mission: Offering the community quality music;
providing gifted performers with an outlet.
Utilizes: Guest Artists; Singers
Founded: 1942
Specialized Field: Symphony; Orchestra
Status: Semi-Professional; Nonprofit
Paid Staff: 35
Income Sources: American Symphony Orchestra
League; Tennesseans for the Arts
Performs At: Oak Ridge High School Auditorium
Organization Type: Performing; Educational

Texas

1531
ABILENE PHILHARMONIC ASSOCIATION
402 Cypress
Suite 130
Abilene, TX 79601
Phone: 915-677-6710
Fax: 915-676-6343
Web Site: www.abilene.com/philharmonic/home.html
Management:
  Music Director/Conductor: George Yaeger
  Manager/Librarian: Ed Allcorn
  Executive Secretary: Susan Saver
Mission: Offering the finest in symphonic literature to
Abilene area residents.
Utilizes: Guest Artists
Founded: 1950
Specialized Field: Symphony; Orchestra
Status: Professional; Nonprofit
Income Sources: American Symphony Orchestra
League
Performs At: Abilene Civic Center
Organization Type: Performing; Educational

1532
AMARILLO SYMPHONY
1000 South Polk Street
PO Box 2586
Amarillo, TX 79105-2586
Phone: 806-376-8782
Fax: 806-376-7127
e-mail: info@amarillosymphony.org
Web Site: www.amarillosymphony.org
Management:
  Executive Director: Nathan Newbrough
  Music Director/Conductor: James Setapen
Mission: Providing symphonic music to residents of the
Texas Panhandle; expanding musical appreciation and
knowledge in the area.
Utilizes: Artists-in-Residence; Commissioned
Composers; Commissioned Music; Fine Artists; Guest
Accompanists; Guest Companies; Guest Composers;
Guest Directors; Guest Lecturers; Guest Musical
Directors; Guest Musicians; Guest Writers; Instructors;
Multimedia
Founded: 1924
Specialized Field: Symphony; Orchestra; Chamber;
Ensemble
Status: Professional; Nonprofit
Paid Staff: 6
Budget: $1,300,000
Income Sources: Tickets; Donations
Performs At: Amarillo Civic Center
Affiliations: American Symphony Orchestra League
Annual Attendance: 80,000
Facility Category: Auditorium; Outdoor
Seating Capacity: 2,300
Year Built: 1960

Organization Type: Performing; Educational

1533
AUSTIN CHAMBER MUSIC CENTER
3814 Medical Parkway
Austin, TX 78756
Phone: 512-454-7562
Fax: 512-454-0029
e-mail: info@austinchambermusic.org
Web Site: www.austinchambermusic.org
Management:
  Director: Michelle Schumann
  Business Manager: Ora Shay
  Assistant Director Education: Joel Bright
  Assistant Director Operations: Valerie Kremer
Mission: To improve the quality of community life by
nurturing and expanding the knowledge, understanding,
and appreciation of chamber music through education
and performance.
Utilizes: Artists-in-Residence; Collaborations;
Commissioned Composers; Commissioned Music;
Composers-in-Residence; Fine Artists; Guest
Accompanists; Guest Directors; Guest Ensembles;
Guest Musical Directors; Instructors; Local Artists;
Multimedia; Original Music Scores
Founded: 1981
Specialized Field: Chamber
Status: Professional; Nonprofit
Paid Staff: 4
Budget: $350,000
Income Sources: Grants from government;
Foundations and corporations; Underwriting; Individuals
and corporations; Ticket sales
Annual Attendance: 13,000
Facility Category: Various locations
Organization Type: Performing; Educational;
Sponsoring

1534
AUSTIN CLASSICAL GUITAR SOCIETY
PO Box 4072
Austin, TX 78765
Phone: 512-300-2247
e-mail: M@MatthewHinsley.com
Officers:
  President: Mike Harris
Management:
  Executive Director: Matthew Hinsley
Specialized Field: Classical Guitar
Budget: $10,000

1535
AUSTIN SYMPHONY ORCHESTRA SOCIETY
1101 Red River
Austin, TX 78701
Phone: 512-476-6064
Fax: 512-476-6242
e-mail: tickets@austinsymphony.org
Web Site: www.austinsymphony.org
Officers:
  President: Joe Long
Management:
  Executive Director: Jim Reagan
  Music Director: Peter Bay
  Director Educational Programs: Diana Eblen
  Assistant to Executive Director: Barbara
  Uhlaender
Mission: To enhance the cultural quality of life for the
adults and young people of Austin and Central Texas by
providing excellence in music performance and
educational programs.
Utilizes: Guest Artists
Founded: 1911

Specialized Field: Symphony; Orchestra; Chamber; Ensemble; Ethnic Music; Folk Music; Band
Status: Professional
Paid Staff: 15
Budget: $3.8 million
Season: September-April
Performs At: University of Texas Theater for the Performing Arts
Affiliations: ASOL
Annual Attendance: 400,000
Organization Type: Performing; Touring; Resident; Educational; Sponsoring

1536
SYMPHONY OF SOUTHEAST TEXAS

4345 Phelan Boulevard
Suite 105
Beaumont, TX 77707
Phone: 409-892-2257
Fax: 409-892-0117
e-mail: sost@sost.org
Web Site: www.sost.org
Management:
    Executive Director: Galen Wixson
    Communications Director: Craig Escamilla
    Administrative Assistant: Laura Lightfoot
Mission: Offering residents of Southeast Texas high quality musical performances of all types.
Founded: 1953
Specialized Field: Symphony; Orchestra
Status: Semi-Professional; Nonprofit
Paid Staff: 5
Income Sources: American Symphony Orchestra League; American Society of Composers, Authors and Publishers; Broadcast Music Incorporated
Performs At: Julie Rogers Theatre
Organization Type: Performing; Resident

1537
BRAZOS VALLEY SYMPHONY ORCHESTRA

800 S Coulter
PO Box 3524
Bryan, TX 77802
Phone: 979-779-6100
e-mail: office@bvso.org
Web Site: www.bvso.org
Officers:
    President: Keith Brooks
    First VP: Douglas Menarchik
    Second VP: Jim Singleton
    Secretary: Jennifer de Jong
    Treasurer: Kay Dobbins
Management:
    Music Director/Conductor: Marcelo Bussiki
    Concermaster: Javier Chaparro
Mission: To bring fine orchestral music to the Brazos Valley, home of Bryan/College Station and Texas A&M University. Each year, with generous support from our patrons, the BVSO puts on a full season of performances that delight young and old alike.
Founded: 1981
Specialized Field: Symphony; Orchestra; Chamber
Status: Non-Professional
Organization Type: Performing

1538
CORPUS CHRISTI CHAMBER MUSIC SOCIETY

4709 Curtis Clark
Corpus Christi, TX 78411
Mailing Address: PO Box 60124 Corpus Christi, TX 78466-0124
Phone: 361-855-0264
e-mail: jallison@the-1.net
Management:
    Program Director: Joan Allison
    President: David Parker
Mission: To promote the appreciation and enjoyment of chamber music by bringing the world's finest ensembles together.
Founded: 1982
Specialized Field: Chamber
Volunteer Staff: 25
Paid Artists: 22
Budget: $30,000-$45,000
Income Sources: Private Donors; foundations; ticket sales
Performs At: Wolfe Recital Hall; Art Museum of South Texas
Affiliations: Chamber Music America
Annual Attendance: 2,000
Facility Category: Recital Hall; Auditorium
Seating Capacity: 300; 400

1539
TEXAS JAZZ FESTIVAL SOCIETY

403 N Shoreline Boulevard
Corpus Christi, TX 78403
Phone: 361-808-9515
Fax: 361-883-4500
e-mail: ricksanchez@grandecom.net
Web Site: www.texasjazz-fest.org/
Management:
    Festival Originator: Al Beto Garcia
    President: Rick Sanchez
Mission: Producing the Texas Jazz Festival to the public annually, free of charge; promoting and preserving American jazz.
Utilizes: Singers
Founded: 1969
Specialized Field: Jazz Ensemble
Status: Professional; Nonprofit
Performs At: Bayfront Plaza Convention Center
Organization Type: Performing

1540
CHAMBER MUSIC INTERNATIONAL

PO Box 140092
Dallas, TX 75214
Phone: 972-385-7267
Fax: 214-324-1868
e-mail: admin@chambermusicinternational.org
Officers:
    Board President: Paul Theiss
    Executive Director: Maggie Bauer
    Treasurer: David Witherspoon
Management:
    Artistic Director: Phillip Lewis
    Board President: Ann Jeter
Utilizes: Fine Artists; Guest Accompanists; Guest Musical Directors; Guest Musicians; Instructors; Multimedia; Original Music Scores; Soloists
Founded: 1986
Specialized Field: Chamber
Paid Staff: 1
Paid Artists: 26
Budget: $100,000
Performs At: St. Barnabas Presbyterian Church

1541
DALLAS BACH SOCIETY

PO Box 140201
Dallas, TX 75214-0201
Phone: 214-320-8700
e-mail: DBachSoc@cs.com
Web Site: www.dallasbach.org
Management:
    Artistic Director: James Richman
    General Manager: Angeline Churchill
Mission: Uniting the finest vocalist and instrumentalists specializing in Baroque and Classical period music, brings lively and informed performances of Handel, Bach, Vivaldi, Mozart and friends to the Dallas-Fort Worth area, featuring outstanding performers from around the Metroplex, New York, the United States and abroad, to assure the highest professional standards of performance practice and technical virtuosity.
Founded: 1982
Specialized Field: Orchestra; Chamber
Status: Professional; Semi-Professional; Nonprofit
Paid Staff: 20
Income Sources: Chorus America; International Bach Society
Performs At: Dallas Museum of Art; Saint Thomas Aquinas Church
Organization Type: Performing; Sponsoring

1542
DALLAS CHAMBER MUSIC SOCIETY

4808 Drexel Drive
Dallas, TX 75205
Phone: 214-526-7301
e-mail: dcms@netscape.net
Web Site: dcms.us
Officers:
    President: George Lee, Jr
    VP Development/Financial: Bill Barstow
    VP Membership/Accommodations: Arend-Julius Koch
    Secretary: Pat Baldwin
Management:
    Manager: Don Ort
    Artistic Director: Dorothea Kelley
Mission: To offer Dallas audiences low cost chamber music concerts of the highest professional quality.
Founded: 1954
Specialized Field: Chamber
Status: Professional; Nonprofit
Performs At: Caruth Auditorium; Southern Methodist University
Organization Type: Performing; Sponsoring

1543
DALLAS WIND SYMPHONY

1465 First Avenue
Dallas, TX 75210
Phone: 214-565-9463
Fax: 214-421-2263
Officers:
    Operations Manager: Courtney Dodson
    1465: Lee Papert
Management:
    Artistic Director: Jerry Junkin
    Executive Director/Founder: Kim J Campbell
    Box Office Manager: Sharron Morgan
    Accountant: Janet Massey
    Artistic Director: Jerry F Junkin
    Principal Guest Conductor: Frederick Fennell
    Associate Conductor: David Kehler
    Composer-In-Residence: John Gibson
Mission: The Dallas Wind Symphony is the leading professional civilian wind bandin the United States today. Comprised of 50 woodwind, brass and percussion players, the band performs an eclectic blend of musical styles ranging from Bach to Bernstein and

Sousa to Strauss. They combine the tradition of the British brass band with the musical heritage of the American town band.
Specialized Field: Wind Ensemble; Orchestra

1544
GREATER DALLAS YOUTH ORCHESTRA ASSOCIATION

Sammons Center for the Arts
3630 Harry Hines Boulevard
Dallas, TX 75219
Phone: 214-528-7747
Fax: 214-528-7749
e-mail: info@gdyo.org
Web Site: www.gdyo.org
Management:
    Executive Director: Charles R Moore
    Artistic Director: Richard Giangiulio
Mission: To provide music education and performance opportunities to musically talented youth.
Utilizes: Guest Artists; Guest Companies
Founded: 1972
Specialized Field: Youth Orchestra; Ensemble
Status: Non-Professional; Nonprofit
Budget: $470,000
Income Sources: Tuition; Diversified Grants
Performs At: Morton H Meyerson Symphony Center
Affiliations: League Of American Ochestras
Annual Attendance: 15,000
Organization Type: Performing; Resident; Educational

1545
VOICES OF CHANGE

11300 N Central Expressway
Suite 316
Dallas, TX 75243
Phone: 214-378-8670
Fax: 214-378-5043
e-mail: info@voicesofchange.org
Web Site: www.voicesofchange.org
Officers:
    President: Jack Waldenmaier
    Secretary: Francis Ostentowski
    Treasurer: William F Barstow
Management:
    Artistic Director: Maria Schleuning
Mission: To present the works of living composers and classics of the 20th & 21st centuries; to offer a seasonal series, tours, monthly radio broadcasts, recordings, special-event concerts and commissions.
Utilizes: Artists-in-Residence; Collaborations; Commissioned Composers; Commissioned Music; Guest Accompanists; Guest Artists; Guest Companies; Guest Composers; Guest Musical Directors; Guest Musicians; Lyricists; Multimedia; Original Music Scores; Playwrights; Singers
Founded: 1975
Specialized Field: Chamber; Ensemble
Status: Professional; Nonprofit
Paid Staff: 2
Budget: $115,000
Income Sources: Tickets, Gifts, Grants
Performs At: Caruth Auditorium; Southern Methodist University
Affiliations: Chamber Music America; Southern Methodist University; American Music Center; Meet the Composers; Texas Commission on the Arts
Annual Attendance: 5,000
Organization Type: Performing; Touring; Resident; Educational

1546
WALDEN PIANO QUARTET/WALDEN CHAMBER MUSIC SOCIETY

PMB 729
PO Box 29081
Dallas, TX 75372
Phone: 214-750-1561
Fax: 214-369-4711
e-mail: laucl@excite.com
Management:
    Management Consultant: Clara Lau
Founded: 1981
Specialized Field: Chamber
Status: Professional
Paid Staff: 1
Volunteer Staff: 1
Paid Artists: 5
Budget: $20,000-35,000
Income Sources: Private; City; Foundations
Performs At: Sanctuary, First Unitarian Church
Annual Attendance: 1,200
Stage Dimensions: 15 x 20
Year Built: 1965

1547
SOUTH TEXAS SYMPHONY ASSOCIATION

1201 W University
Edinburg, TX 78539
Mailing Address: PO Box 2832 McAllen, TX 78501
Phone: 956-393-2293
Fax: 956-393-2290
e-mail: southtexassymphony@prodigy.net
Web Site: www.southtexassymphony.com
Officers:
    President: Suzie McDonald
    VP: Bill Buerns
    Secretary: Matt Weber
    Treasurer: Cecilio Rodriguez
Management:
    Administrator: Glynda Boykin
    Administrative Secretary: Velma Ranirez
    Clerk: Rolando Gonzalez
Mission: Promoting, nurturing and supporting symphonic music performances in South Texas.
Utilizes: Singers
Founded: 1976
Specialized Field: Symphony; Chamber
Status: Semi-Professional; Nonprofit
Paid Staff: 78
Volunteer Staff: 40
Budget: $529,000
Income Sources: American Symphony Orchestra League; Pan American University
Performs At: Pan American University Fine Arts Auditorium
Annual Attendance: 6,500
Facility Category: Fine Arts Center
Seating Capacity: 1,055
Organization Type: Performing; Resident; Educational

1548
EL PASO PRO-MUSICA

3557 N Mesa
PO Box 13328
El Paso, TX 79913-3328
Phone: 915-833-9400
Fax: 915-833-9425
e-mail: info@elpasopromusica.org
Web Site: www.elpasopromusic.org
Officers:
    Chairman/President: Ellen Lacy
    President Elect: Jaime Lowensberg

Management:
    Executive Director: Karen Paul
    Office Manager: Nancy Ellis
Mission: Promoting musical and cultural growth in the El Paso area; presenting chamber music and a chamber music festival.
Utilizes: Guest Artists; Guest Companies
Founded: 1977
Specialized Field: Chamber; Classical Music
Status: Professional; Nonprofit
Organization Type: Performing; Educational; Presenter

1549
EL PASO SYMPHONY ORCHESTRA

PO Box 180
El Paso, TX 79942
Phone: 915-532-3776
Fax: 915-533-8162
e-mail: epsoorg@htp.net
Web Site: www.epso.org
Officers:
    Chairman: William V Ballew, III
Management:
    Executive Manager: Ruth Ellen Jacobson
    Music Director/Conductor: Gurer Aykal
Mission: Fostering appreciation of symphonic music in the El Paso area.
Utilizes: Collaborations; Commissioned Composers; Commissioned Music; Educators; Grant Writers; Guest Accompanists; Guest Artists; Guest Companies; Guest Composers; Guest Instructors; Guest Lecturers; Guest Musicians; Guest Writers; Guild Activities; Local Artists; Lyricists; Multimedia; Original Music Scores; Singers; Theatre Companies; Touring Companies
Founded: 1930
Specialized Field: Symphony; Orchestra
Status: Professional; Nonprofit
Paid Staff: 100
Budget: $1,000,000
Income Sources: Ticket sales, contributions
Performs At: El Paso Civic Center Theatre
Annual Attendance: 35,000
Facility Category: Theatre
Seating Capacity: 2,400
Organization Type: Performing; Educational; Sponsoring

1550
CLIBURN CONCERTS

Van Cliburn Foundation
2525 Ridgmar Boulevard, Suite 307
Fort Worth, TX 76116
Phone: 817-738-6536
Fax: 817-738-6534
e-mail: clistaff@cliburn.org
Web Site: www.cliburn.org
Officers:
    President & CEO: David Chambless Worters
Management:
    Artist Liaison: Sandra Doan, sdoan@cliburn.org
    President & CEO: David Chambless Worters, dcworters@cliburn.org
Mission: To produce the Cilburn Piano Series.
Founded: 1962
Specialized Field: Series & Festivals; Instrumental Music; Vocal Music
Status: Non-Profit; Professional
Paid Staff: 13
Paid Artists: 15
Budget: $150,000-400,000
Performs At: Nancy Lee & Perry R. Bass Performance Hall

1551
FORT WORTH SYMPHONY ORCHESTRA
330 E 4th Street
Suite 200
Fort Worth, TX 76102
Phone: 817-665-6500
Fax: 817-665-6600
e-mail: admin@fwsymphony.org
Web Site: www.fwsymphony.org
Officers:
    Executive Director: Ann Koonsman
Management:
    Music Director: Miguel Harth-Bedoya
    General Manager: John Toohey
    Production Manager: Jim Brady
    Marketing Manager: Stacey Newman
Mission: To provide the leadership and financial support required to maintain a symphony orchestra of first rank and to build an internationally-recognized chamber orchestra, dedicated to artistic development and performances of superior quality.
Utilizes: Guest Composers; Guest Instructors; Guest Musical Directors; Guest Musicians
Founded: 1925
Specialized Field: Symphony; Orchestra; Chamber
Status: Professional; Nonprofit
Paid Staff: 25
Volunteer Staff: 400
Paid Artists: 80
Budget: $9,900,000
Income Sources: Ticket Sales; Grants; Individual & Corporate Donors
Performs At: Tarrant County Convention Center; Ed Landreth Auditorium
Affiliations: American Symphony Orchestra League
Annual Attendance: 290,000
Rental Contact: Rental Contact Carl Davis
Organization Type: Performing; Touring

1552
YOUTH ORCHESTRA OF GREATER FORT WORTH
4401 Trail Lake Drive
Fort Worth, TX 76109
Phone: 817-923-3121
Fax: 817-924-0007
Web Site: www.yofw.org
Management:
    Executive Director: William Jordan
    Orchestra Manager: Lindsey E Stortz
    Operations Manager: Sylvia Stoddard
Mission: Educating young musicians from the ages of 3 to 22.
Founded: 1965
Specialized Field: Youth Orchestra
Status: Nonprofit
Paid Staff: 1
Volunteer Staff: 100
Paid Artists: 6
Budget: $200,000
Income Sources: Grants; tuitions; concerts
Performs At: Orchestra Hall
Annual Attendance: 4,000
Type of Stage: Proscenium
Stage Dimensions: 70x40
Seating Capacity: 384
Year Built: 1940
Year Remodeled: 1980
Rental Contact: 817-921-6222 Mike Haley
Organization Type: Performing; Touring; Educational

1553
DALLAS BRASS
4321 Clemson Drive
Garland, TX 75042
Phone: 972-276-7114
Web Site: www.dallasbrass.com/
Management:
    Director: Michael Levin
    Booking Coordinator: Wiss Rudd
Mission: Striving to bridge musical gaps from classical to pop.
Founded: 1982
Specialized Field: Brass Ensemble
Status: Professional; Commercial
Organization Type: Performing; Touring; Resident; Educational

1554
GARLAND SYMPHONY ORCHESTRA
1721 Reserve
Garland, TX 75042
Phone: 972-926-0611
Fax: 972-926-0811
Web Site: www.garlandsymphony.org/
Officers:
    President: Dick Sutton
    VP: Mike Lancaster
    Secretary: Celia Swiger
    Treasurer: Rick Trimble
Management:
    Music Director: Robert Carter Austin
    Assistant General Manager: Richard Stieber
Mission: Presenting the finest possible concerts.
Utilizes: Guest Artists
Founded: 1978
Specialized Field: Symphony; Orchestra
Status: Professional; Nonprofit
Performs At: Garland Performing Arts Center
Organization Type: Performing; Educational

1555
CLEAR LAKE SYMPHONY
PO Box 890582
Houston, TX 77289-0582
Phone: 713-639-0702
e-mail: arthurs@blkbox.com
Web Site: www.serve.com/Violin
Management:
    General Manager: Betty Wall
    Music Director: Charles Johnson
Mission: To present classical music for the residents of the Bay area and to provide opportunities to qualified musicians both to perform with a classical orchestra and to participate in the music education of the area.
Founded: 1976
Specialized Field: Symphony; Orchestra
Status: Non-Professional; Nonprofit
Paid Staff: 34
Income Sources: National Symphony Orchestra League
Performs At: Clear Lake Theatre; Gloria Dei Lutheran Church Auditorium
Organization Type: Performing

1556
HOUSTON CIVIC SYMPHONY ORCHESTRA
4378 Harrest Lane
Houston, TX 77004-6606
Phone: 713-747-0018
e-mail: harris@bcm.tmc.edu
Web Site: www.civicsymphony.org
Officers:
    President: Mark Andrews
    VP: John Snyder
    Secretary: Susan Weaver
    Treasurer: Betty Thompson
Management:
    Music Director: Clifton Evans
    Assistant Conductor: Richard Spitz
Mission: To provide a playing and performance opportunity for professional and nonprofessional musicians who earn the major portion of their livelihood outside full-time, professional music performances.
Utilizes: Guest Companies
Founded: 1967
Specialized Field: Symphony; Orchestra; Chamber
Status: Semi-Professional; Nonprofit
Paid Staff: 65
Income Sources: University of Houston
Performs At: Cullen Hall; University of Houston
Organization Type: Performing

1557
HOUSTON EARLY MUSIC
PO Box 271193
Houston, TX 77277
Phone: 713-432-1744
e-mail: info@HoustonEarlyMusci.org
Web Site: www.HoustonEarlyMusic.org
Officers:
    President: Rodney Koenig
    Secretary: Bettie Anderson
    Treasurer: Terece McGovern
Management:
    Executive Director: Helga Aurisch
    Artistic Director: Nancy Ellis
Mission: Houston Early Music is a chartered, nonprofit, organization whose purpose is to present historically-informed performances of early music from the European traditions and other world cultures in concerts featuring internationally renowned vocal, instrumental and chamber musicians. In addition, we reach out to new and diverse audiences through a cross-disciplinary educational program.
Founded: 1968
Specialized Field: Chamber; Ensemble; Ethnic Music; Folk Music
Status: Professional; Nonprofit
Paid Staff: 8
Organization Type: Educational; Sponsoring

1558
HOUSTON FRIENDS OF CHAMBER MUSIC
Rice University, MS 532
6100 Main Street
Houston, TX 77005
Phone: 713-348-5400
Fax: 713-348-5405
e-mail: friends@rice.edu
Web Site: www.houstonfriendsofchamber.org
Officers:
    President: Dr Ann Fairbanks
Mission: Presenting chamber ensembles of national and international reputation; developing new audiences.
Founded: 1960
Specialized Field: Chamber; Ensemble
Status: Professional; Nonprofit
Paid Staff: 1
Income Sources: Shepherd School of Music
Performs At: Seude Concert Hall
Organization Type: Performing; Sponsoring

1559
HOUSTON SYMPHONY
615 Louisiana Street
Suite 102
Houston, TX 77002
Phone: 713-224-4240
Officers:
Music Director: Hans Graf
Management:
Executive Director/CEO: Matthew VanBesien
General Manager: Steven Brosvik
Director Human Resources: Suzanne McArdle
Malock
Manager Projects/Communication: Amy
Thompson
General Manager: Matthew Vanbesien
Director Operations: Donald Hightower
Orchestra Personnel Manager: Janni Toomes
Senior Director Finance/Planning: Michael D
Pawson
Mission: The mission of the Houston Symphony is to
foster excellence and innovation in the performance
and presentation of great music. To enrich the lives of
our diverse citizens, to educate current and future
audiences and to bring distinciton to our community
through the orchestra's international presence and
standing.
Specialized Field: Orchestra

1560
SYMPHONY NORTH OF HOUSTON
PO Box 73591
Houston, TX 77273
Phone: 713-867-3465
Officers:
Vice President: Rubena Buerger
Secretary: Marie Rogoff
Management:
Conductor: Dr Reynaldo Ochoa
President: Bob Henricksen
Publicity: Lynn Coalmer
Treasurer: Karla Marchell
Secretary: Marie Rogoff
Librarian: Stanley Lewis
Personnel Manager: Connie Yancey
Mission: A community based orchestra composed of a
very special group of classical musicians, which include
teachers, homemakers, engineers, lawyers, bankers
and many other professionals that enjoy playing
classical music.
Founded: 1974
Specialized Field: Orchestra

1561
IRVING SYMPHONY ORCHESTRA ASSOCIATION
225 E John Carpenter Freeway
Suite 120
Irving, TX 75062
Phone: 972-831-8818
Fax: 972-831-8817
e-mail: irvingsymphony@irvingsymphony.com
Web Site: www.irvingsymphony.com
Officers:
President: Rene Castilla
President Elect: Beverly Adams
Secretary: Nancie Rissing
Treasurer: Carol Little
Management:
Music Director/Conductor: Hector Guzman
Executive Director: Marguerite Korkmas
Mission: Offering Irving and its surrounding
communities outstanding music.

Founded: 1962
Specialized Field: Symphony; Orchestra
Status: Nonprofit
Paid Staff: 1
Volunteer Staff: 220
Paid Artists: 85
Performs At: Carpenter Performance Hall
Affiliations: ASOL; TASO
Organization Type: Performing

1562
LAREDO PHILHARMONIC ORCHESTRA
PO Box 1399
Laredo, TX 78042
Phone: 956-727-8886
e-mail: lpo@laredophilharmonic.org
Web Site: www.laredophilharmonic.org
Management:
Music Director/Conductor: Terence Frazor
Co-President: Consuelo Lopez
Co-President: Elmo Lopez
Executive VP: Teresa Nimcham
Mission: Contributing to the cultural enrichment of
Laredo and the surrounding area.
Founded: 1980
Specialized Field: Symphony; Orchestra; Chamber
Status: Professional; Nonprofit
Performs At: Laredo Civic Center
Organization Type: Performing; Touring; Resident;
Educational

1563
LONGVIEW SYMPHONY ORCHESTRA
PO Box 1825
Longview, TX 75606
Phone: 903-236-9739
Web Site: www.longviewtx.com
Management:
Music Director/Conductor: Tonu Kalam
Business Manager: Gary Bruns
Mission: Presenting the highest calibre orchestral
music to Texas citizens.
Utilizes: Guest Artists
Founded: 1968
Specialized Field: Symphony; Orchestra
Status: Semi-Professional; Nonprofit
Volunteer Staff: 36
Paid Artists: 75
Budget: $260,000
Income Sources: Ticket sales; Grants; Contributions
Performs At: T.G. Field Auditorium
Annual Attendance: 5,000
Organization Type: Performing; Resident; Educational

1564
LUBBOCK SYMPHONY ORCHESTRA
1313 Broadway
Suite 2
Lubbock, TX 79401
Phone: 806-762-1688
Fax: 806-762-1824
Web Site: www.lubbocksymphony.org
Management:
Executive Director: Pam Parkman
Music Director/Conductor: Andrews Sill
Chairman: Ray Fargason
Mission: Offering the Lubbock Area symphonic music
and an enhanced quality of life.
Utilizes: Artists-in-Residence; Collaborating Artists;
Collaborations; Commissioned Music; Dance
Companies; Dancers; Educators; Fine Artists; Grant
Writers; Guest Accompanists; Guest Companies; Guest

Instructors; Guest Musical Directors; Guest Musicians;
Guest Writers; Instructors; Multimedia; Original Music
Scores
Founded: 1942
Specialized Field: Symphony; Orchestra; Chamber;
Ensemble
Status: Professional; Nonprofit
Paid Staff: 8
Volunteer Staff: 450
Paid Artists: 84
Budget: $900k
Income Sources: American Symphony Orchestra
League; American Society of Composers, Authors and
Publishers
Performs At: Lubbock Memorial Civic Center
Annual Attendance: 12,000
Seating Capacity: 1,400
Organization Type: Performing; Educational

1565
MARSHALL SYMPHONY ORCHESTRA
Marshall, TX 75671
Mailing Address: PO Box 421
Phone: 903-935-5266
Fax: 903-938-3531
Management:
Artistic Director/Conductor: Leonard Kacenjar
Management Consultant: Fran Hurley
Mission: To provide local musicians with an opportunity
to perform along with professional musicians; to provide
symphonic music for area audiences.
Utilizes: Guest Artists; Singers
Founded: 1952
Specialized Field: Symphony; Orchestra
Status: Semi-Professional; Nonprofit
Paid Staff: 45
Income Sources: Marshall Regional Arts Council;
Texas Association of Symphony Orchestras
Performs At: Marshall Civic Center Theatre
Organization Type: Performing

1566
MIDLAND-ODESSA SYMPHONY AND CHORALE
3100 LaForce Boulevard
PO Box 60658
Midland, TX 79711
Phone: 915-563-0921
Fax: 915-498-9251
e-mail: symphony@mosc.org
Web Site: www.mosc.org
Management:
Office Manager: Crys Crichfield,
symphony@mosc.org
Mission: To offer residents of the Permian Basin
symphonic, chamber and choral music.
Utilizes: Collaborations; Commissioned Music;
Educators; Grant Writers; Guest Artists; Guest
Companies; Guest Directors; Guest Lecturers; Guest
Writers; High School Drama; Local Artists; Lyricists;
Multi Collaborations; Multimedia; Organization
Contracts; Original Music Scores; Singers; Theatre
Companies
Founded: 1962
Specialized Field: Symphony; Orchestra; Chamber;
Ensemble
Status: Nonprofit
Paid Staff: 6
Volunteer Staff: 100
Paid Artists: 65
Budget: $750,000
Income Sources: Tickets; Grants; Donations
Affiliations: ASOL
Annual Attendance: 10,000

Organization Type: Performing; Educational

1567
SAN ANGELO SYMPHONY ORCHESTRA AND CHORALE
PO Box 5922
San Angelo, TX 76902
Phone: 915-658-5877
Fax: 915-653-1045
Web Site: www.sanangelosyphony.org
Officers:
President: Fred Key
VP: Doris Rousselot
Secretary: Johnell Vincent
Treasurer: Bill McKinney
Past President: Teady George
Management:
Music Director/Conductor: Hector Guzman
Executive Director: Mercyla Sheiburne
Mission: To further cultural advancement and enjoyment of symphonic music in the San Angelo area.
Utilizes: Singers
Founded: 1948
Specialized Field: Symphony
Status: Professional; Non-Professional; Nonprofit
Paid Staff: 140
Income Sources: Broadcast Music Incorporated; American Society of Composers, Authors and Publishers; American Symphony Orchestra League
Performs At: City Auditorium
Annual Attendance: 50,000
Seating Capacity: 1,590
Organization Type: Performing

1568
SAN ANTONIO CHAMBER MUSIC SOCIETY
PO Box 12702
San Antonio, TX 78212
Phone: 210-408-1558
Fax: 210-408-1558
e-mail: bat@ccsi.com
Web Site: www.ccsi.comg
Officers:
President: Dale Bennett
VP Administration: Diane Stevens
VP Membership: Daavid Shapiro
Financial Secretary: Mary K Vaughan
Treasurer: William Montville
Secretary: George M Vaughan
Management:
Artist Committee: Ruth J Guriuitz
Artist Committee: Marilyn Cockburn
Mission: Chamber music series featuring world chamber music artists.
Founded: 1943
Specialized Field: Chamber; Ensemble
Volunteer Staff: 25
Paid Artists: 5
Budget: $35,000-60,000
Performs At: Incarnate Word College Auditorium

1569
SAN ANTONIO SYMPHONY
222 E Houston Street
Suite 200
San Antonio, TX 78205
Phone: 210-554-1000
Fax: 210-554-1008
Web Site: www.sasymphony.org
Management:
Music Advisor: Christopher Wilkins
Executive Director: Steven R Brosvik

Gen. Manager/Artistic Administrator: Lawrence J Fried
Public Relations: Nancy Diehl
Mission: Providing an outstanding professional symphony; meeting cultural, entertainment and educational needs of the community.
Utilizes: Choreographers; Dance Companies; Dancers; Educators; Guest Accompanists; Guest Artists; Guest Composers; Guest Conductors; Instructors; Music; Sign Language Translators; Soloists; Student Interns
Founded: 1939
Specialized Field: Symphony; Orchestra
Status: Professional; Nonprofit
Paid Staff: 21
Paid Artists: 77
Budget: $7,500,000
Income Sources: American Symphony Orchestra League
Performs At: Majestic Theatre
Seating Capacity: 2400
Organization Type: Performing; Educational

1570
YOUTH ORCHESTRAS OF SAN ANTONIO
106 Auditorium Circle
Suite 130
San Antonio, TX 78205
Phone: 210-737-0097
Fax: 210-732-7233
e-mail: info@yosa.org
Management:
Executive Director: Steven Payne
Marketing & Community Relations: Nicte Hayes
Specialized Field: Youth Orchestra

1571
MID-TEXAS SYMPHONY ORCHESTRA
Texas Lutheran University
PO Box 3216 TLU
Seguin, TX 78155
Phone: 830-372-8089
Fax: 830-372-8112
e-mail: mts@tlu.edu
Web Site: www.mtsymphony.org
Officers:
President: Kathy Nossaman
Secretary: Martha Rinn
Treasurer: Heidi Franzen
Management:
Musical Director: David Mairs
Orchestra Manager: Cheryl Fisher
Development Director: Courtney Lyons-Garcia
Stage Manager: Tau Beta Sigma
Mission: The MTS provides a broad array of music from the classics to more modern selections.
Founded: 1978
Specialized Field: Orchestra
Paid Staff: 1
Income Sources: Grants

1572
SHERMAN SYMPHONY ORCHESTRA
900 N Grand Avenue
Suite 61567
Sherman, TX 75090
Phone: 903-813-2251
Fax: 903-813-2273
e-mail: ddominick@austincollege.edu
Web Site: shermansymphony.com
Management:
Conductor: Daniel Dominick

Mission: To offer concert performances featuring standard orchestral repertoire to area audiences; to provide guest appearances by nationally-known soloists.
Utilizes: Commissioned Music; Guest Musicians; Multimedia; Original Music Scores; Singers; Soloists
Founded: 1966
Specialized Field: Symphony; Orchestra
Status: Non-Professional; Nonprofit
Paid Staff: 2
Volunteer Staff: 40
Paid Artists: 30
Budget: $50,000
Performs At: Wynne Chapel
Annual Attendance: 3,200
Facility Category: College Chapel; City Concert Hall
Seating Capacity: 300; 1,300
Year Built: 1930
Year Remodeled: 2000
Organization Type: Performing; Educational; Sponsoring

1573
FORT BEND SYMPHONY ORCHESTRA
PO Box 16861
Sugar Land, TX 77496
Phone: 281-276-9642
Officers:
Vice President: David Flores
Treasurer: Marilyn Conger
Management:
Music Director: Dr John Antonio Ricarte
President: Amy Floyd
Secretary: Susan Watts
Treasurer: Marilynn Conger
Director Auditions: Heather Carty
Director Performance: Barry Ward
Director Publicity: Charity James
FBSO Musical Director & Conductor: Dr John Antonio Ricarte
Mission: This full-size orchestra, complete with brass, woodwind, percussion, and strings section, consists of approximately 60 talented and dedicated musicians primarily from the Fort Bend area.
Founded: 1992
Specialized Field: Orchestra

1574
EAST TEXAS SYMPHONY ORCHESTRA
305 S Broadway
Suite 603
Tyler, TX 75702
Phone: 903-592-1427
Fax: 903-592-7649
Web Site: www.etso.org/
Officers:
VP Operations: Jean Davoust
President/CEO: Les Talbert
President Elect: LaVerne Gollop
VP Administration: Nancy Wrenn
Mission: To bring excellent orchestral music to East Texas.
Utilizes: Collaborations; Educators; Fine Artists; Guest Accompanists; Guest Artists; Guest Composers; Guest Writers; Lyricists; Multimedia; Original Music Scores; Singers; Student Interns
Founded: 1936
Specialized Field: Symphony; Orchestra
Status: Professional; Semi-Professional
Paid Staff: 7
Paid Artists: 70
Performs At: Cowan Performing Arts Center; UT-Tyler
Affiliations: American Symphony Orchestra League
Seating Capacity: 2,073

Organization Type: Performing

1575

WACO SYMPHONY ORCHESTRA

600 Austin Avenue
Suite 10
Waco, TX 76701
Mailing Address: PO Box 1201 Waco, TX 76703
Phone: 254-754-0851
Fax: 254-752-8611
e-mail: exdir@wacosymphony.com
Web Site: www.wacosymphony.com
Officers:
  Board President: Linda Hatchel
Management:
  Executive Director: Susan Taylor
  Music Director/Conductor: Stephen Heyde
  Development Director: Ann Owen
Mission: To present live classical music that will enrich the cultural life of the community.
Founded: 1962
Specialized Field: Symphonic Orchestral Music
Paid Staff: 7
Paid Artists: 80
Budget: $750,000
Income Sources: Sponsors; Program Ad Sales; Ticket Sales; Donations
Performs At: Waco Hall, Baylor University
Seating Capacity: 2,200

1576

WICHITA FALLS SYMPHONY ORCHESTRA

30005 Garnett
Parker Square
Wichita Falls, TX 76308
Phone: 940-723-6202
Fax: 817-322-4480
Web Site: members.aol.com/WFSO/WFSO.htm
Management:
  Manager: Alex Rouggieri
  Music Director/Conductor: Theodore Plute
Mission: Offering the community the highest quality of symphonic music; educating area youth.
Founded: 1946
Specialized Field: Symphony; Orchestra
Status: Nonprofit
Performs At: Memorial Auditorium
Organization Type: Performing

Utah

1577

UTAH CLASSICAL GUITAR SOCIETY

1466 E 920 S
Provo, UT 84606

Management:
  President: James Mahood
  Program Director: David Norton
  Secretary: Stephen Hanka
Mission: Furthering performance and study of classical guitar repertoire in Utah.
Founded: 1984
Specialized Field: Classical Guitar
Status: Nonprofit
Paid Staff: 5
Performs At: First Presbyterian Church; Salt Lake City
Organization Type: Performing

1578

CHAMBER MUSIC SOCIETY OF SALT LAKE CITY

807 N Juniperpoint Drive
Salt Lake City, UT 84103
Phone: 801-364-1322
Fax: 801-581-4148
e-mail: wwallcomp@aol.com
Officers:
  President: Gene Scoggins
  VP: Henriette Mohebbizadeh
  Treasurer: Paul Griffin
Management:
  Artist Transportation: Bill Wallace
  Artist Transportation: David George
Mission: To entertain and enlighten.
Utilizes: Guest Accompanists; Guest Musical Directors
Founded: 1966
Specialized Field: Chamber
Budget: $40,000-45,000
Income Sources: Ticket Sales; Contributions
Performs At: Libby Gardner Auditorium - David Gardner Hall
Facility Category: Auditorium
Seating Capacity: 650
Year Remodeled: 1999

1579

EASTERN ARTS INTERNATIONAL DANCE THEATER

PO Box 526362
Salt Lake City, UT 84152
Phone: 801-485-5824
e-mail: kstjohn@burgoyne.com
Web Site: www.easternartists.com
Officers:
  Dance Director: Katherine St. John
  Music Director: Lloyd Miller
Management:
  Director: Katherine St. John
Mission: To promote time-honored traditions by offering concerts, lectures, and workshops of cultures from Asia and Eastern Europe.
Founded: 1960
Specialized Field: Ethnic Music
Status: Professional; Nonprofit
Paid Staff: 10
Income Sources: Western Alliance of Arts Administrators; Society for Ethno-Musicology; Middle East Studies Association; Society for Dance Ethnology
Organization Type: Performing; Educational; Sponsoring

1580

GINA BACHAUER INTERNATIONAL PIANO FOUNDATION

138 W Broadway
Suite 220
Salt Lake City, UT 84101
Phone: 801-297-4250
Fax: 801-521-9202
Web Site: www.bachauer.com
Officers:
  Chairman: Linda M Babcock
  Vice Chairman: Jeffrey T Simmons
  Secretary/Treasurer: Taylor Vriens
Management:
  Artistic Director/Founder: Dr. Paul C Pollei
  Manager: Kimi Kawashima
  Accountant: Jared Christensen

Mission: To further the pianistic art by holding international piano competitions, solo recitals and educational sessions; to enrich the community and build an artistic and educational environment for musicians and nonmusicians alike.
Founded: 1976
Specialized Field: Piano
Status: Nonprofit
Paid Staff: 8
Performs At: Symphony Hall; Salt Lake City Assembly Hall
Organization Type: Performing; Educational; Sponsoring

1581

GRANITE YOUTH SYMPHONY

340 E 3545 S
Salt Lake City, UT 84115
Phone: 801-268-8542
Fax: 801-263-6128
Management:
  PhD Staff Assoc., Music Education: Ellis C Worthen
Mission: Dedicated to studying and performing standard symphonic literature.
Utilizes: Guest Artists
Founded: 1957
Specialized Field: Youth Symphony
Status: Nonprofit
Income Sources: Granite School District
Organization Type: Performing; Touring; Educational

1582

ORCHESTRA AT TEMPLE SQUARE

50 E North Temple Street
20th Floor
Salt Lake City, UT 84150
Phone: 801-240-4150
Fax: 801-240-4886
e-mail: Bradfordbd@ldschurch.org
Officers:
  President: Mac Christensen
  Manager: Brent R Peterson
Management:
  Church President: Gordon B Hinckley
  Conductor: Igor Gruppman
Founded: 1999
Specialized Field: Orchestra
Paid Staff: 2
Volunteer Staff: 6
Non-paid Artists: 110
Performs At: Tabernacle on Temple Square
Affiliations: The Church of Jesus Christ of Latter-day Saints
Annual Attendance: 10,000
Facility Category: Church

1583

SALT LAKE SYMPHONY

220 Morris Avenue
Suite 200
Salt Lake City, UT 84115
Phone: 801-463-2440
e-mail: contact@saltlakesymphony.com
Officers:
  Managing Director: Joyce Mahoney
  Secretary/Treasurer: Louise Mathews
Management:
  Music Director/Conductor: Robert Baldwin
  Chair: Joe Dickinson
Founded: 1976
Specialized Field: Orchestra
Income Sources: Individuals; Corporations

Performs At: Abravanel Hall; Jeanne Wagner Concert Hall; Temple Square

1584
UNIVERSITY OF UTAH: SCHOOL OF MUSIC

1375 E Presidents Circle
Room 204
Salt Lake City, UT 84112-0030
Phone: 801-581-6762
Fax: 801-581-5683
e-mail: robert.baldwin@music.utah.edu
Web Site: www.music.utah.edu
Management:
    Interim Director: Robert Baldwin
Specialized Field: Educational
Performs At: David P. Gardner Hall; Libby Gardner Concert Hall; Thompson Chamber Music Hall; Dumke Recital Hall; Mckay Music Library

1585
UTAH SYMPHONY

123 W S Temple
Salt Lake City, UT 84101
Phone: 801-533-5626
Fax: 801-869-9026
e-mail: info@utahsymphonyopera.org
Web Site: www.utahsymphony.org
Officers:
    President & CEO: Melia Tourangeau
    Senior Vice President: David S Green
    Chairman: Patricia A Richards
Management:
    VP Symphony Artistic Planning: Anthony Tolokan
    Music Director: Thierry Fischer
Mission: To maintain a symphony orchestra capable of providing performances of the highest possible quality; to provide performance opportunities for skilled professional musicians; to foster musical education for persons of all ages.
Utilizes: Artists-in-Residence; Collaborating Artists; Commissioned Music; Educators; Fine Artists; Guest Accompanists; Guest Companies; Guest Composers; Guest Directors; Guest Lecturers; Guest Musical Directors; Instructors; Multimedia; Sign Language Translators; Singers; Student Interns; Visual Arts
Founded: 1940
Specialized Field: Symphony
Status: Professional; Nonprofit
Budget: $12,000,000
Income Sources: American Symphony Orchestra League; American Arts Alliance
Performs At: Symphony Hall
Annual Attendance: 200,000
Facility Category: Concert Hall
Seating Capacity: 2,800
Year Built: 1979
Architect: $12,000,000
Organization Type: Performing; Educational

Vermont

1586
BURLINGTON DISCOVER JAZZ FESTIVAL

156 College Street
Suite 202
Burlington, VT 05401
Phone: 802-863-7992
Fax: 802-864-3927
e-mail: info@discoverjazz.com
Web Site: www.discoverjazz.com

Officers:
    Director, Flynn Center: Andrea Rogers
Management:
    Managing Director: Brian Mital
    Chief Programming Officer: Arnie Malina
    Associate Director: Geeda Searfoorce
Mission: Offering the widest possible range of jazz and music educational programs; ticketed and free events.
Utilizes: Community Members; Community Talent; Composers; Educators; Guest Directors; Guest Musical Directors; Instructors; Local Artists & Directors; Lyricists; Multimedia; Music; Scenic Designers; Sign Language Translators
Founded: 1984
Specialized Field: Jazz
Status: Non-Profit, Professional
Paid Staff: 2
Volunteer Staff: 350
Budget: $600,000
Income Sources: Burlington City Arts; Flynn Center
Performs At: Multi-disciplinary
Annual Attendance: 45,000
Facility Category: City-wide (Burlington)
Organization Type: Performing; Educational; Sponsoring

1587
VERMONT MOZART FESTIVAL

3 Main Street
Suite 217
Burlington, VT 05401
Phone: 802-862-7352
Fax: 802-862-2201
Web Site: www.vtmozart.org
Management:
    Executive Director: Timothy Riddle
    Operations Assistant: Christina Brooker
    PR & Development Coordinator: Rachel Mulis
Mission: Enriching people's lives through beautiful music in special Vermont places.
Utilizes: Singers
Founded: 1973
Specialized Field: Northwestern Vermont
Status: Professional; Nonprofit
Paid Staff: 7
Volunteer Staff: 30
Paid Artists: 80
Income Sources: Ticket sales, sponsorship, membership
Organization Type: Performing

1588
VERMONT SYMPHONY ORCHESTRA

2 Church Street
Suite 19
Burlington, VT 05401-4457
Phone: 802-864-5741
Fax: 802-864-5109
Toll-free: 800-876-9293
e-mail: info@vso.org
Web Site: www.vso.org
Officers:
    Chairman: John Dinse
    Vice Chairman: Ken Singer
    Treasure: Jesse F Sammis, III
    Secretary: Patricia Mandeville
Management:
    Executive Director: Alan Jordan
    Orchestra Manager: Eleanor Long
    Music Director: Jaime Laredo
Founded: 1934
Specialized Field: Symphony; Ensemble
Status: Professional; Nonprofit
Paid Staff: 14

Paid Artists: 54
Budget: $1,400,000
Performs At: Flynn Theatre
Affiliations: American Symphony Orchestra League
Annual Attendance: 65,100
Organization Type: Performing; Touring; Educational

1589
VERMONT YOUTH ORCHESTRA ASSOCIATION

Elley-Long Music Center at St Michael's College
223 Ethan Allen Avenue
Colchester, VT 05446
Phone: 802-655-5030
Fax: 802-655-5034
e-mail: info@vyo.org
Web Site: www.vyo.org
Officers:
    Executive Director: Caroline Whidden
Management:
    Director Of Operations: Art DeQuasie
    Director Marketing: Lisamarie Charlesworth
    Development Manager: Liza Reed
Mission: To provide young musicians and singers with superior orchestral and choral performance and educational experiences.
Utilizes: Collaborations; Guest Accompanists; Guest Artists; Guest Companies; Guest Musicians; Instructors; Multimedia; Organization Contracts; Singers; Soloists
Founded: 1964
Specialized Field: Youth Orchestra
Status: Non-Professional; Nonprofit
Paid Staff: 7
Budget: $400,000
Income Sources: American Symphony Orchestra League (Youth Orchestra Division)
Performs At: Private Performance Hall; Rental Available
Seating Capacity: 350
Year Built: 1888
Year Remodeled: 2001
Rental Contact: Kate Graham
Organization Type: Performing; Educational

1590
BANJO DAN AND THE MID-NITE PLOWBOYS

49 School Street
Vergennes, VT 05491
Phone: 802-877-2077
e-mail: banjodan@pshift.com
Management:
    Band Leader/Booking Agent: Dan Lindner
Mission: A professional 5 piece band available to play bluegrass music at concerts, schools and festivals.
Founded: 1972
Specialized Field: Folk Music
Status: Professional
Organization Type: Performing

1591
SKY BLUE BOYS

49 School Street
Vergennes, VT 05491
Phone: 802-877-2077
e-mail: banjodan@pshift.com
Management:
    Band Leader/Booking Agent: Dan Lindner
Mission: A professional band available to play acoustic duo at concerts, schools and festivals.
Founded: 1972
Specialized Field: Folk Music
Status: Professional

Organization Type: Performing

Virginia

1592
ALEXANDRIA SYMPHONY ORCHESTRA
2121 Eisenhower Avenue
#608
Alexandria, VA 22314
Phone: 703-548-0885
Fax: 703-548-0985
e-mail: alex@alexsym.org
Web Site: www.alexsym.org
Officers:
President: Mark O Wilkoff
Secretary: Ronal Butler
Management:
Executive Director: Molly Danforth
Mission: The Alexandria Symphony Orchestra, through its highly respected, innovative, professional programming, is an integral force in the bulding of community in the greater Alexandria area, bringing affordable and accessible music to it families.
Specialized Field: Orchestra

1593
FAIRFAX SYMPHONY ORCHESTRA
4024 Hummer Road
Annandale, VA 22003
Phone: 703-642-7200
Fax: 703-642-7205
e-mail: info@fairfaxsymphony.org
Web Site: www.fairfaxsymphony.org
Officers:
President: R Dennis McArver
Management:
Executive Director: Rachel Garrity
Mission: To provide high quality orchestra performances as well as music appreciation and education programs to enhance the quality of life in the metropolitan Washington area.
Utilizes: Guest Musicians; Local Artists
Founded: 1957
Specialized Field: Symphony; Orchestra; Chamber; Ensemble
Status: Professional; Nonprofit
Budget: $1,200,000
Performs At: George Masson University
Affiliations: American Symphony Orchestra League; SOI
Organization Type: Performing; Touring; Resident; Educational

1594
AMERICAN BALALAIKA SYMPHONY
3811 North 14th Street
Arlington, VA 22201
Phone: 703-351-1331
e-mail: Peter@balalaika.biz
Management:
Founder/Artistic Director/Conductor: Peter Trofimenko
Specialized Field: Orchestra; Ethnic Music

1595
HESPERUS
3706 N 17th Street
Arlington, VA 22207
Phone: 703-525-7550
Fax: 703-908-9207
Management:
Artistic Director: Scott Reiss
Producing Director: Tina Chancey

Mission: To trace, through music, the cultural parallels existing between the Old and New Worlds.
Specialized Field: Chamber; Folk Music; Early Music; Classical Music
Status: Professional; Nonprofit
Performs At: Smithsonian Institute; National Museum of America
Organization Type: Touring; Resident

1596
CHARLOTTESVILLE CLASSICAL GUITAR SOCIETY
1074 Simmons Gap Road
Dyke, VA 22935
Phone: 434-973-0115
Fax: 434-975-3935
e-mail: dave@rediscov.com
Web Site: www.rediscov.com/ccgs
Officers:
President: David Edwards
VP: Keith Stevens
Mission: Develop interest in the Classical Guitar, educate and perform community service.
Founded: 1993
Specialized Field: Classical Guitar
Volunteer Staff: 4
Paid Artists: 2
Budget: $2,000
Income Sources: Donations; Ticket Sales
Annual Attendance: 400
Facility Category: Dinner Theater or Church
Type of Stage: Elevated
Seating Capacity: 250
Year Built: 1900

1597
WASHINGTON AND LEE UNIVERSITY CONCERT GUILD
Washington and Lee University
201 DuPont Hall, Department of Music
Lexington, VA 24450
Phone: 703-463-8855
Fax: 540-463-8104
e-mail: gaylardt@wlu.edu
Web Site: http://music.wlu.edu/guild.htm
Management:
Music Department: Timothy Gaylard
Mission: To bring nationally and internationally recognized classical artists to the campus.
Specialized Field: Chamber; Soloists
Status: Professional; Nonprofit
Paid Artists: 4
Performs At: Lenfest Centre
Organization Type: Educational; Sponsoring

1598
TIDEWATER CLASSICAL GUITAR SOCIETY
PO Box 777
Norfolk, VA 23501
Phone: 757-627-6229
e-mail: tcgs@mac.com
Officers:
Treasurer: C Jordan Ball
Grant Applications: W Mead Stith
Management:
President: Sam Dorsey
Vice President: Christopher Basford
Specialized Field: Classical Guitar

1599
VIRGINIA SYMPHONY
861 Glenrock Road
Suite 200
Norfolk, VA 23502
Phone: 757-466-3060
Fax: 757-466-3046
e-mail: ejohnson@virginiasymphony.org
Officers:
Music Director/Conductor: JoAnn Falletta
Associate Conductor: Shizuo Kuwahara
Management:
Executive Director: Carla Johnson
General Manager: Jim Bredeson
Vice Chairman: Withrop Allen Short, Jr.
Secretary: Susan Goode
Treasurer: R Bruce Bradley
Mission: To present classical, pops, family and educational performances each season and time and time again being recognized for its national caliber of execllence. This acclaimed orchestra includes over seventy professional musicians.
Founded: 1920
Specialized Field: Orchestra

1600
RICHMOND SYMPHONY ORCHESTRA
300 West Franklin Street
Richmond, VA 23220
Phone: 804-788-4717
Fax: 804-788-1541
Web Site: www.richmondsymphony.com/
Management:
Music Director: Mark Russell Smith
Executive Director: Michele Walter
Assistant Executive Director: Felicia Pompa
Office Manager: Nancy Wyatt
Accounting Manager: Celia Powell
Associate Conductor: Gerard Edeistein
Orchestra Manager: Patricia Vorhis
Operations Assistant: Jennifer Green
Manager Chorous: Barbie Baker
Mission: To perpetuate the orchestral tradition, develop audience enthusiasm, educate future generations of concert goers, and contribute to the enjoyment of the art of symphonic music. We invite you and encourage you to join with us in carrying out the Richmond Symphony's mission.
Utilizes: Singers
Founded: 1908
Specialized Field: Symphony; Orchestra; Chamber; Ensemble
Status: Professional; Nonprofit
Income Sources: American Symphony Orchestra League; Indiana Orchestra Consortium
Performs At: Civic Auditorium
Organization Type: Performing; Resident; Educational

1601
ROANOKE SYMPHONY ORCHESTRA
541 Luck Avenue
Suite 200
Roanoke, VA 24016
Phone: 540-343-9127
Fax: 540-343-6221
Toll-free: 866-277-9127
e-mail: music@rso.com
Officers:
Director of Operations: Grant Ellis
Executive Director: Brian Black
VP: Melissa Giles
VP: R Jay Irons
Management:

Music Director/Conductor: David Wiley
Chorus Master: John Hugo
Director/Public Relations: Joe Cobb
Mission: To enrich lives, educate, and entertain audiences in Western Virginia with the highest quality instrumental and choral concerts, and to enhance traditional performances with innovative programming in a welcoming acoustical environment.
Founded: 1953
Specialized Field: Orchestra
Status: Nonprofit; Education
Paid Staff: 10
Paid Artists: 1
Budget: $1.7 million
Income Sources: Gifts and ticket sales
Facility Category: Civic Center/Auditorium
Seating Capacity: 2,400/848

1602
VIRGINIA BEACH SYMPHONY ORCHESTRA

PO Box 2544
Virginia Beach, VA 23450
Phone: 757-671-8611
Fax: 757-671-8704
e-mail: VBSOED@aol.com
Web Site: www.vbso.org
Officers:
President: L Jean Stewart
VP: Harvey Stokes
Secretary: Anna Stewart
Treasurer: Lee Edmondson
Management:
Music Director/Conductor: David S Kunkel
Executive Director: Wendy T Young
Concertmaster: Dora M Mullins
Mission: The Virginia Beach Symphony provides a high quality music for everyone, affords an opportunity for players, and young musicians. We perform over 18 concerts a year for the citizens of Virginia Beach and the Hampton Roads area.
Founded: 1981
Specialized Field: Orchestra
Paid Staff: 8
Volunteer Staff: 150
Paid Artists: 2
Non-paid Artists: 100
Performs At: Pavilion Theater, Virginia Beach
Affiliations: ASCAP; BMI; American Symphony Orchestra; Virginians for the Arts; Central Business District; Cultural Alliance of Greater Hampton Roads Chamber
Annual Attendance: 55,000
Facility Category: Theater; Convention
Type of Stage: Proscenium
Seating Capacity: 1000
Year Built: 1981
Rental Contact: Mary Collins

Washington

1603
BELLEVUE PHILHARMONIC ORCHESTRA

PO Box 1582
Bellevue, WA 98009-1582
Phone: 425-455-4171
Fax: 425-455-9170
e-mail: info@bellevuephil.org
Officers:
Marketing and Special Events Coordi: Cam Williams

Director of Education , Grants: Emily R Morgan
Management:
Music Director/Conductor: Fusao Kajima
Executive Director: Lawrence Fried
Specialized Field: Orchestra

1604
BREMERTON SYMPHONY ORCHESTRA

PO Box 996
535B 6th Street
Bremerton, WA 98337
Phone: 206-373-1722
Fax: 360-405-1158
e-mail: symphony@symphonic.org
Web Site: www.symphonic.org
Officers:
President: Anita Williams
First VP: Caron Cromwell
Second VP: Mahlon Christensen
Secretary: Nancyen Reid
Management:
Music Director/Conductor: John Welsh
Executive Director: Laurie Strange
General Manager: Laurie Strange
Mission: To bring high quality classical instrumental and vocal music to our diverse communities; to serve the skilled amateur musicians of the region by providing performance opportunities; and develop enthusiasm and love of music for the enrichment of the cultural environment of the West Sound.
Utilizes: Singers
Founded: 1942
Specialized Field: Symphony; Orchestra; Ensemble
Status: Non-Professional; Nonprofit
Paid Staff: 60
Paid Artists: 10
Budget: $200,000
Income Sources: American Symphony Orchestra League
Performs At: Bremerston High School; Admiral Theatre
Organization Type: Performing; Resident; Educational

1605
CASCADE SYMPHONY ORCHESTRA

PO Box 550
Edmonds, WA 98026
Phone: 425-778-4688
Fax: 425-672-3951
Management:
Conductor: Ropen Shakarian
Executive Director: Ruby Fusaro
Mission: Performing symphonic literature which ranges from the baroque to the contemporary.
Utilizes: Guest Artists
Founded: 1962
Specialized Field: Symphony; Orchestra; Chamber; Ensemble
Status: Semi-Professional; Non-Professional
Income Sources: American Symphony Orchestra League; Broadcast Music Incorporated; American Society of Composers, Authors and Publishers; American Federation of Musicians
Performs At: Puget Sound Christian College
Organization Type: Performing; Resident; Sponsoring

1606
FEDERAL WAY SYMPHONY

PO Box 4513
Federal Way, WA 98063-4513
Phone: 253-529-9857
e-mail: admin@federalwaysymphony.org
Officers:
Office Administrator: Lisa Ernst

Board President: Kathy Franklin
Management:
Conductor: A Brian Davenport
Executive Director: Mary Gates
Mission: The Federal Way symphony Orchestra remains committed to bringing the finest classical music to residents of the South Puget Sound region.
Specialized Field: Orchestra

1607
OLYMPIA SYMPHONY ORCHESTRA

3400 Capitol Boulevard S
Suite 203
Olympia, WA 98501-3351
Phone: 360-753-0074
Fax: 360-753-4735
e-mail: ecavin@olympiasymphony.com
Web Site: www.olympiasymphony.com
Officers:
President: Philip Hall
First Vice President: Dick Blinn
Second Vice President: Larry Goodman
Management:
Administrative Manager: Erin Cavin
Music Director: Haw Edwards
Development Director: Kathleen Thornton
Mission: To encourage the growth and development of the symphony orchestra and maintain the orchestra; to promote musical and cultural entertainment in diverse forms; to provide the musicians of Thurston County and its surrounding areas with the opportunity to play in a symphony.
Founded: 1970
Specialized Field: Symphony; Orchestra
Status: Professional; Nonprofit
Paid Staff: 4
Income Sources: American Symphony Orchestra League
Performs At: Washington Center for the Performing Arts
Organization Type: Performing; Educational

1608
WASHINGTON IDAHO SYMPHONY

PO Box 9185
Pullman, WA 99163
Phone: 509-332-3408
Fax: 509-335-2220
e-mail: symphony@pullman.com
Web Site: www.c-5.com/symphony/
Officers:
Board President: Cicely Wingate
Management:
Music Director/Conductor: L Keating
Mission: To offer the enjoyment of music to people of all ages and provide area musicians an opportunity to participate in an orchestra or chorus.
Founded: 1972
Specialized Field: Symphony; Ensemble
Status: Non-Professional; Nonprofit
Paid Staff: 40
Income Sources: American Symphony Orchestra League, Chair Sponsorship Program, Private and Corporate Donations, Ticket Sales
Season: September-April
Performs At: Lewiston High School Auditorium, Clarkston High School Auditorium, Gladish Auditorium
Organization Type: Performing; Resident; Educational

1609
MID-COLUMBIA SYMPHONY

716 Jadwin
PO Box 65
Richland, WA 99352

Phone: 509-943-6602
Fax: 509-946-7917
e-mail: email@midcolumbiasymphony.org
Web Site: www.midcolumbiasymphony.org
Officers:
    Executive Director: Ken Pointer
Management:
    Concert Manager: Carma Kimball
    Music Director/Conductor: Dr Robert Bode
Mission: The Mid-Columbia Symphony is committed to implementing an inclusive strategy that embraces everyone in the region, creating a cultural entity that is a source of regional pride, creating and implementing a strong educational program.
Founded: 1945
Specialized Field: Symphony; Orchestra
Status: Non-Professional; Nonprofit
Income Sources: American Symphony Orchestra League
Performs At: Richland High School Auditorium
Organization Type: Performing; Resident; Educational

1610
EARLY MUSIC GUILD OF SEATTLE

2366 Eastlake Avenue E
Suite 335
Seattle, WA 98102
Phone: 206-325-7066
Fax: 206-860-9151
e-mail: emg@earlymusicguild.org
Web Site: www.earlymusicguild.org
Officers:
    Executive Director: August Denhard
Mission: Presenting an annual international six concert series featuring touring ensembles.
Utilizes: Collaborations; Guest Directors; Guest Instructors; Guest Musical Directors; Guest Musicians; High School Drama; Instructors
Founded: 1977
Specialized Field: Chamber; Early Music
Status: Professional; Nonprofit
Budget: $250,000
Organization Type: Educational; Sponsoring

1611
LAKE UNION CIVIC ORCHESTRA

Northgate Station PO Box 75387
Seattle, WA 98175
Phone: 206-343-5826
e-mail: info@luco.org
Officers:
    Vice President: Pam McDonald
Management:
    Music Director/Conductor: Christophe Chagnard
    President: Janet Young
    Secretary: Susan Lubetkin
    Treasurer: Jennifer Whitaker
    Orchestra Manager: Steven Noffsinger
    Orchestra Representative: Nicola Shangrow
    Production Manager: Brant Allen
    Fund Raising: John Dunne
    Music Director: Christopher Chagnard
Mission: The Lake Union Civic Orchestra is dedicated to the exploration and performance of symphonic and chamber music with energy and passion, and to sharing that experience with individuals throughout the community.
Founded: 1995
Specialized Field: Orchestra

1612
NORTHWEST CHAMBER ORCHESTRA

1305 4th Avenue
#522
Seattle, WA 98101
Phone: 206-343-0445
Fax: 206-343-3955
Web Site: www.nwco.org
Officers:
    President: Mark Charles Paben
    VP: James Simpkins
    VP: Bruce King
    Secretary: Katie Matison
    Treasurer: Maureen Swanson
Management:
    Executive Director: Deborah K Daoust
    Artistic Director: Marjorie Kransberg-Talvi
    Music Director/Principal Conductor: Ralf Gothoni
Mission: To present pre-baroque through contemporary repertoire for chamber orchestra and ensembles. NWCO accomplishes this through concerts, tours, educational outreach programs, broadcasts, free public concerts and recordings. Includes a core of twenty string players with adjunct musicians added based on the repertoire.
Utilizes: Guest Accompanists; Guest Artists; Guest Composers; Guest Musicians
Founded: 1973
Specialized Field: Orchestra; Chamber
Status: Professional; Nonprofit
Paid Staff: 3
Volunteer Staff: 2
Paid Artists: 25
Budget: $600,000
Income Sources: American Federation of Musicians
Performs At: Nordstrom Recital Hall; Benarova Hall
Annual Attendance: 11,000
Facility Category: Concert Hall
Seating Capacity: 532
Year Built: 1999
Organization Type: Performing; Touring; Resident; Educational

1613
NORTHWEST SYMPHONY ORCHESTRA

PO Box 16231
Seattle, WA 16231
Phone: 206-292-2787
e-mail:
anthonyspain@northwestsymphonyorchestra.org
Officers:
    President: Diane Macewicz
Management:
    Music Director: Anthony Spain
Founded: 1987
Specialized Field: Orchestra
Budget: $35,000
Performs At: Highline Performing Arts Center
Seating Capacity: 900

1614
PHILADELPHIA STRING QUARTET

PO Box 45776
Seattle, WA 98145
Phone: 206-527-8839
Fax: 206-526-8621
Web Site: www.musicfest.net/
Management:
    Executive Director: Alan Iglitzin
Mission: Performing string quartets; producing the Olympic Music Festival.
Founded: 1960
Specialized Field: Chamber; String Ensemble

Status: Professional; Nonprofit
Organization Type: Performing; Touring; Educational; Sponsoring

1615
PUGET SOUND CHAMBER MUSIC SOCIETY

93 Pike Street
#315
Seattle, WA 98101
Phone: 253-383-2674
Fax: 253-383-1709
Web Site: www.mcnw.org/pscw
Officers:
    President: Stuart Rolfe
Management:
    Executive Director: Kyle Siebrecht
Mission: To offer the highest quality chamber music festival.
Specialized Field: Chamber
Status: Nonprofit
Organization Type: Presenting

1616
SEATTLE BAROQUE

2366 Eastlake Avenue E
Suite 428
Seattle, WA 98102
Phone: 206-322-3118
Fax: 206-322-3119
e-mail: info@seattlebaroque.org
Web Site: www.seattlebaroque.org/
Management:
    Music Director: Ingrid Matthews
    Artistic Director: Bryon Schenkman
    Executive Director: Joann Mendelsohn
    Marketing/Development Coordinator: Karen Nestvold
Mission: To awaken contemporary audiences to the vitality of 17th and 18th century music through historically informed performance of both familiar and unknown works.
Founded: 1993
Specialized Field: Classical; Baroque
Paid Staff: 6
Volunteer Staff: 6
Paid Artists: 35

1617
SEATTLE PHILHARMONIC ORCHESTRA

PO Box 177
Seattle, WA 98111
Phone: 206-528-6878
e-mail: questions@seattlephil.com
Officers:
    Vice President: Martha J Weiss
    Treasurer: Walter Moore
Management:
    Music Director: Adam Stern
    Board President: Carol Wollenberg
    Treasurer: Carol Wollenberg
    Secretary: Meg Holmes
Founded: 1944
Specialized Field: Orchestra

1618
SEATTLE SYMPHONY ORCHESTRA

200 University Street
PO Box 21906
Seattle, WA 98111-3906
Phone: 206-215-4700
Fax: 206-215-4701
e-mail: info@seattlesymphony.org
Web Site: www.seattlesymphony.org

Officers:
Co-Chairman: Alexandra A Brookshire
Co-Chairman: Cyrus R Vance, Jr
Vice Chair: Alexander W Clouts
Vice Chair: Robert L Collett
Vice Chair: David Friedenberg
Management:
Executive Director: Deborah R Card
Mission: To present symphonic music of the highest quality in a distinctive way for the enjoyment, enrichment and education of the people of the Pacific Northwest.
Utilizes: Commissioned Composers; Commissioned Music; Composers-in-Residence; Curators; Educators; Five Seasonal Concerts; Guest Accompanists; Guest Artists; Guest Companies; Guest Lecturers; Guest Musicians; Guest Soloists; Multimedia; Original Music Scores; Sign Language Translators; Singers; Soloists; Theatre Companies
Founded: 1903
Specialized Field: Symphony; Orchestra; Chamber; Ensemble
Status: Professional; Nonprofit
Paid Staff: 63
Volunteer Staff: 270
Paid Artists: 90
Budget: $20,000,000
Income Sources: Ticket Sales; Donations
Performs At: Benaroya Hall, Seattle
Annual Attendance: 338,000
Facility Category: Symphony Hall
Seating Capacity: 2500; 540
Year Built: 1998
Cost: $11.8 Million
Rental Contact: Troy Skubitz
Organization Type: Performing; Resident; Educational

1619
SEATTLE YOUTH SYMPHONY ORCHESTRA

11065 5th NE
Suite A
Seattle, WA 98125
Phone: 206-362-2300
Fax: 206-361-9254
e-mail: info@syso.org
Web Site: www.syso.org/
Management:
Executive Director: Daniel Petersen
Box Office Manager: John Empey
Community Relations Director: Stuart Wolferman
Mission: To offer performances that promote music appreciation.
Founded: 1942
Specialized Field: Youth Orchestra
Status: Nonprofit
Paid Staff: 7
Volunteer Staff: 100
Paid Artists: 100
Non-paid Artists: 999
Income Sources: American Society of Composers, Authors and Publishers; Broadcast Music Incorporated
Performs At: Seattle Center Opera House
Organization Type: Performing; Educational

1620
SPOKANE SYMPHONY ORCHESTRA

929 W Sprage
Spokane, WA 99201
Phone: 509-326-3136
Fax: 509-326-3921
e-mail: info@spokanesymphony.org
Web Site: www.spokanesymphony.org/
Officers:

President: Elizabeth Cowles
Management:
Executive Director: John Hancock
Music Director: Fabio Mechetti
Director Marketing: Annie Matton
Director Marketing: Amanda Livingston
Mission: The Spokane Symphony Society believes that orchestral music nurtures the human spirit and is integral to the presentation and development of our American culture. We are committed to providing performances of the symphonic and chamber orchestra repertoire and to promoting educational and cultural activities which will enhance the knowledge and appreciation of that music for people of all ages.
Utilizes: Guest Artists; Guest Companies; Singers
Founded: 1945
Specialized Field: Symphony; Orchestra; Chamber
Status: Professional; Nonprofit
Paid Staff: 17
Volunteer Staff: 20
Paid Artists: 65
Budget: $3.4 million
Income Sources: Ticket Sales; Contributions; Endorsement
Performs At: Spokane Opera House
Affiliations: ASOL
Annual Attendance: 150,000
Organization Type: Performing; Touring; Resident; Educational; Sponsoring

1621
TACOMA PHILHARMONIC

901 Broadway
Tacoma, WA 98402
Phone: 253-272-0809
Fax: 253-591-0537
e-mail: info@TacomaPhilharmonic.org
Web Site: www.tacomaphilharmonic.org
Management:
Executive Director: Andrew Wood
Founded: 1936
Specialized Field: Classical
Paid Staff: 2
Volunteer Staff: 24
Budget: $150,000-400,000
Income Sources: Grants; Donations; Ticket Sales
Performs At: Pantages Theater
Annual Attendance: 7,600+
Seating Capacity: 1,186

1622
TACOMA SYMPHONY ORCHESTRA

738 Broadway, Suite 301
PO Box 19
Tacoma, WA 98401
Phone: 253-272-7264
Fax: 253-274-8187
e-mail: tacomasymphonyorchstra@hotmail.com
Management:
Executive Director: Mitchell Owens
Music Director: Harvey Felder
Administrative Assistant: Karen Pickett
Mission: To offer the community affordable classical music.
Utilizes: Guest Artists
Founded: 1959
Specialized Field: Symphony; Orchestra
Status: Professional; Nonprofit
Paid Staff: 10
Performs At: Pantages Theatre
Organization Type: Performing

1623
TACOMA YOUTH SYMPHONY

901 Broadway Plaza
Suite 500
Tacoma, WA 98402
Phone: 253-627-2792
Fax: 253-627-1682
e-mail: info@tysamusic.org
Web Site: www.tysamusic.org
Management:
Executive Director: Dr. Loma L Cobbs
Artistic Director: Dr. Paul-Elliot Cobbs
Mission: Committed to the development of the Tacoma Youth Symphony Association as a quality music education organization that attracts and sustains the highest level of musical excellence for training and performance in the Puget Sound area. The TYSA challenges young musicians to pursue musical excellence, to seek intellectual stimulation, and to experience the love and joy of music making.
Founded: 1963
Specialized Field: Youth Symphony; Chamber; Ensemble
Status: Non-Professional; Nonprofit
Paid Staff: 9
Volunteer Staff: 120
Paid Artists: 8
Non-paid Artists: 15
Income Sources: Tuition/Fees; Ticket Sales; Public & Private Support
Performs At: Rialto Theatre
Organization Type: Performing; Educational

1624
WALLA WALLA SYMPHONY

PO Box 92
Walla Walla, WA 99362
Phone: 509-529-8020
Fax: 509-529-1353
e-mail: wwsorch@wwics.com
Web Site: www.symphony.com
Officers:
President: Martin Thorson
VP: Barbara Stubblefield
Secretary: Gretchen de Grasse
Treasurer: Dudley Joyce
Management:
Executive Director: Russ Martin
Production Assistant: Trudy Ostby
Mission: Continuing the tradition of outstanding symphonic music; bringing high-quality performances to the entire community, including children.
Utilizes: Artists-in-Residence; Collaborations; Commissioned Composers; Commissioned Music; Composers-in-Residence; Dancers; Fine Artists; Five Seasonal Concerts; Guest Accompanists; Guest Companies; Guest Composers; Guest Directors; Guest Lecturers; Guest Musical Directors; Guest Musicians; Guest Writers; Multimedia; Organization Contracts; Original Music Scores; Sign Language Translators; Soloists
Founded: 1906
Specialized Field: Symphony; Orchestra
Status: Non-Professional; Nonprofit
Paid Staff: 7
Paid Artists: 80
Budget: $300,000
Performs At: Cordinet Hall
Annual Attendance: 10,000
Seating Capacity: 1,384
Organization Type: Performing

All listings are in alphabetical order by state, then city, then organization within the city.

1625
YAKIMA SYMPHONY ORCHESTRA
32 N 3rd Street
Suite 333
Yakima, WA 98901
Phone: 509-248-1414
Fax: 509-457-0980
e-mail: noel@yakimasymphony.org
Web Site: yakimasymphony.org
Management:
Executive Director: Noel Moxley
Director Development: Lawrence Golan
Mission: Performing and promoting symphonic music.
Utilizes: Guest Artists
Founded: 1971
Specialized Field: Symphony; Orchestra
Status: Professional; Nonprofit
Paid Staff: 6
Paid Artists: 65
Income Sources: American Symphony Orchestra League
Performs At: Capitol Theatre
Seating Capacity: 1,500
Year Built: 1971
Organization Type: Performing; Educational

1626
YAKIMA YOUTH ORCHESTRA
PO Box 307
Yakima, WA 98907
Phone: 509-966-3394
Fax: 509-457-0980
Management:
Conductor: Dennis Clauss
Specialized Field: Youth Orchestra; Chamber
Status: Non-Professional; Nonprofit
Paid Staff: 20
Income Sources: Yakima Symphony Orchestra
Organization Type: Performing; Educational

West Virginia

1627
CHARLESTON CHAMBER MUSIC SOCIETY
PO Box 641
Charleston, WV 25323
Phone: 304-344-5389
Fax: 304-344-5389
e-mail: ndavids@aol.com
Management:
Executive Director: N David Stem
Mission: To bring outstanding chamber-music ensembles to Charleston.
Utilizes: Guest Directors; Multimedia; Original Music Scores
Founded: 1941
Specialized Field: Chamber; Ensemble
Status: Nonprofit
Paid Staff: 1
Volunteer Staff: 7
Budget: $40,000
Income Sources: Association of Performing Arts Presenters; Chamber Music America
Performs At: Christ Church United Methodist
Affiliations: Association od Performing Arts Presenters; Chamber Music America
Annual Attendance: 1500
Facility Category: Church Sanctuary
Type of Stage: 3/4 Round
Seating Capacity: 400+
Organization Type: Performing; Sponsoring

1628
MONTCLAIRE STRING QUARTET
1205 Oakmont Road
Charleston, WV 25314
Phone: 304-345-5743
Fax: 304-342-0152
Web Site: www.wvsymphony.org/montclaire_string_quartet.
Officers:
President: John L McClaugherty
Management:
Executive Director: Paul Helfrich
Mission: To present the highest quality string quartet repertoire throughout the state of West Virginia; to provide leadership in the West Virginia Symphony Orchestra; to present educational programs in West Virginia schools.
Founded: 1982
Specialized Field: Symphony; Chamber; Ensemble
Status: Professional
Paid Artists: 4
Performs At: Kanawha United Presbyterian Church
Organization Type: Performing; Touring; Resident; Educational; Sponsoring

1629
HUNTINGTON SYMPHONY ORCHESTRA
PO Box 2434
Huntington, WV 25725
Phone: 304-781-8343
Fax: 304-781-0670
e-mail: levans@huntingtonsymphony.org
Web Site: www.huntingtonsymphony.org
Officers:
President: Brandi Jacob-Jones
Vice President: Dr. Maurice Mufson
Secretary: Pat Bertoia
Management:
Music Director: Kimo Furumoto
Executive Director/CEO: T. Hogan Haasmoto
Mission: To perform the finest music written for chamber orchestras.
Utilizes: Community Members; Composers; Contract Orchestras; Educators; Five Seasonal Concerts; Guest Composers; Guest Lecturers; Instructors; Local Artists; Multimedia; Organization Contracts; Original Music Scores
Founded: 1970
Specialized Field: Orchestra; Chamber
Status: Professional; Nonprofit
Paid Staff: 3
Income Sources: American Symphony Orchestra League
Performs At: Keith Albee Performing Arts Center
Annual Attendance: 20,000
Organization Type: Performing; Resident

1630
WHEELING SYMPHONY
1025 Main Street
Suite 307
Wheeling, WV 26003
Phone: 304-232-6191
Fax: 304-232-6192
e-mail: wso@wheelingsymphony.com
Web Site: www.wheelingsymphony.org
Officers:
President Board of Directors: Betty H Mullen
Management:
Executive Director: Susan C Hogan
Mission: To provide balanced and diversified musical programs which broaden audience appreciation and improve the quality of life in our area.
Founded: 1926
Specialized Field: Symphony; Orchestra
Status: Professional; Nonprofit
Paid Staff: 10
Income Sources: Grants; Donations; Ticket Sales
Performs At: Capitol Music Hall
Organization Type: Performing; Touring; Resident; Educational

Wisconsin

1631
BELOIT JANESVILLE SYMPHONY ORCHESTRA
PO Box 185
Beloit, WI 53512
Phone: 608-363-2554
Fax: 608-363-2718
e-mail: bjso@beloit.edu
Web Site: www.beloit.edu/~bjso
Officers:
President: Leslie Brunsell
VP: Bonnie Welter
Management:
Music Director: Robert Tomaro
Executive Director: Nancy Sonntag
Founded: 1953
Specialized Field: Orchestra
Paid Staff: 5
Volunteer Staff: 130
Paid Artists: 80

1632
FOND DU LAC SYMPHONIC BAND
PO Box 1483
Fond du Lac, WI 54936-1483
Phone: 920-907-7678
e-mail: marthur@fdlsymphonicband.org
Officers:
Business Manager: Mary A. Arthur
Mission: To provide quality musical entertainment for our area and beyond; to enhance the image of the concert band as a performing medium; to provide a sophisticated performing opportunity for adult instrumentalists.
Founded: 1898
Specialized Field: Band
Status: Semi-Professional; Nonprofit
Paid Staff: 20
Income Sources: Association of Concert Bands; American Federation of Musicians
Organization Type: Performing; Touring

1633
GREEN BAY SYMPHONY ORCHESTRA
115 S Jefferson Street
PO Box 222
Green Bay, WI 54305
Phone: 920-435-3465
Fax: 920-435-1427
Web Site: www.gbsymphony.org/
Officers:
President: Kent Ciak
VP: Jim Bowley
Treasurer: Jean Vande Hey
Management:
Executive Director: John Kelley
Business Manager: Pete Schmeling
Education Drirector: Jill Quigley
Administrative Assistant: Dana Blodgett

Mission: To promote orchestras and performances of the highest quality for the enjoyment of ever-widening audiences and pursue educational experiences for youth and adults through musical collaborations.
Founded: 1914
Specialized Field: Symphony; Orchestra; Chamber
Status: Nonprofit
Paid Staff: 7
Volunteer Staff: 135
Paid Artists: 71
Income Sources: American Symphony Orchestra League; Association of Wisconsin Symphony Orchestra
Performs At: Weidner Center for The Performing Arts
Organization Type: Performing; Educational

1634
CARTHAGE CHAMBER MUSIC SERIES

2001 Alford Drive
Carthage College
Kenosha, WI 53140-1994
Phone: 262-551-8554
Fax: 262-551-6208
e-mail: jripley@carthage.edu
Officers:
    Chairman Music Department: Dr. RD Sjoerdsma
Management:
    Music Department Chair: James Ripley
Specialized Field: Chamber; Ensemble
Budget: $20,000-35,000
Performs At: Siebert Chapel

1635
KENOSHA SYMPHONY ASSOCIATION

6501 Third Avenue
Kenosha, WI 53143
Phone: 262-654-9080
Fax: 262-654-8809
e-mail: kso@acronet.net
Web Site: www.kenoshasymphony.org
Officers:
    President: Joseph Mayne
    First VP: Donnalee Bain
    Second VP: Dr. Greg Lyne
    Secretary: Ksthleen Braun
    Treasurer: Donald Michie
Management:
    President: Richard Fields
    Vice President: Edward Block
Mission: To provide a symphony orchestra in a community setting.
Founded: 1941
Specialized Field: Symphony; Orchestra; Chamber
Status: Professional; Semi-Professional; Non-Professional; Nonprofit
Paid Staff: 1
Volunteer Staff: 50
Paid Artists: 70
Income Sources: Kenosha Unified Schools
Performs At: Reuther Auditorium
Organization Type: Performing; Educational

1636
MADISON SYMPHONY ORCHESTRA

6314 Odana Road
Madison, WI 53719
Phone: 608-257-3734
Fax: 608-280-6192
e-mail: info@madisonsymphony.org
Web Site: www.madisonsymphony.org
Officers:
    President: Doug Reuhl
Management:
    Executive Director: Richard Mackie
Utilizes: Sign Language Translators

Founded: 1926
Specialized Field: Symphony
Status: Professional
Paid Staff: 9
Paid Artists: 90
Budget: $2,000,000
Performs At: Oscar Meyer Theatre
Affiliations: Civic Center Box Office
Annual Attendance: 40,000+
Facility Category: Multi Purpose Performance Hall
Seating Capacity: 2,110
Organization Type: Performing; Educational

1637
WISCONSIN CHAMBER ORCHESTRA

22 N Carroll Street
Suite 104
Madison, WI 53701-0171
Mailing Address: PO Box 171
Phone: 608-257-0638
Fax: 608-257-0611
e-mail: wco@wcoconcerts.org
Web Site: www.wcoconcerts.com
Officers:
    President: Richard Leeping
    VP: Jill Sommers
    Treasurer: Don Rahn
    Secretary: Chris Berry
Management:
    Executive Director: Robert Sorge
    Music Director: Andrew Sewell
Mission: To perform musical works.
Utilizes: Singers
Founded: 1962
Specialized Field: Orchestra; Chamber
Status: Professional; Nonprofit
Performs At: Capitol Square; First Congregational Church; Wisconsin Union Theater
Seating Capacity: 1,200
Organization Type: Performing

1638
WISCONSIN YOUTH SYMPHONY ORCHESTRAS

1625 Humanities Building
455 N Park Street
Madison, WI 53706
Phone: 608-263-3320
Fax: 608-265-3751
Web Site: www.wyso.music.wisc.edu/
Officers:
    President: Randall Diamond
    Treasurer: Christopher Rich
    Secretary: Coe Williams
Management:
    Music Director: James R Smith
    Executive Director: Bridget Fraser
    Manager: Joe Bernstein
    Development Director: Sarah Seres
    Administrative Assistant: Elizabeth Allman
    Associate Music Director: Tom Buchhauser
Mission: To meet the symphonic needs of the musically-talented youth of Southern Wisconsin.
Utilizes: Artists-in-Residence; Collaborating Artists; Commissioned Music; Five Seasonal Concerts; Guest Accompanists; Guest Companies; Guest Directors; Organization Contracts; Singers; Soloists
Founded: 1966
Specialized Field: Youth Orchestra
Status: Nonprofit
Paid Staff: 25
Volunteer Staff: 50
Performs At: Mills Concert Hall; University of Wisconsin

Annual Attendance: 2,500
Facility Category: music hall
Stage Dimensions: 40x40
Seating Capacity: 750
Organization Type: Performing; Touring; Educational

1639
MARSHFIELD-WOOD COMMUNITY SYMPHONY

2000 W 5th Street
Marshfield, WI 54449
Phone: 715-387-1147
Fax: 715-389-6517
Officers:
    President: Sarah Hanson
Management:
    Conductor: Timothy McCollum
Mission: To present the best music possible for the least possible cost.
Founded: 1965
Specialized Field: Symphony; Orchestra
Status: Nonprofit
Income Sources: American Symphony Orchestra League
Performs At: Fine Arts Building Theatre
Organization Type: Performing; Educational

1640
FOX VALLEY SYMPHONY

1477 Kenwood Center
Menasha, WI 54952
Phone: 920-729-5000
Fax: 920-729-5468
e-mail: info@foxvalleysymphony.com
Web Site: www.foxvalleysymphony.com/
Officers:
    President, Fox Valley Symphony: Tom Gottsacker
    President Symphony League: Priscilla Daniels
Management:
    Executive Director: Carley Miller
    Music Director: Brian Goner
Mission: To provide symphonic music for all; to sponsor youth orchestras and to introduce school children to orchestra music.
Utilizes: Commissioned Music; Guest Musical Directors; Guest Musicians; Multimedia; Singers
Founded: 1966
Specialized Field: Symphony
Status: Nonprofit
Paid Staff: 7
Volunteer Staff: 125
Paid Artists: 65
Budget: $424,000
Performs At: Pickard Auditorium; Lawrence University Chapel
Annual Attendance: 6000
Organization Type: Performing; Resident; Educational; Sponsoring

1641
MILWAUKEE SYMPHONY ORCHESTRA

700 N Water Street
Suite 700
Milwaukee, WI 53202
Phone: 414-291-6010
Fax: 414-291-7610
Toll-free: 800-291-7605
e-mail: info@mso.org
Web Site: www.mso.org
Officers:
    VP Marketing & Communications: Susan Loris
    Chairman Of The Board: Chris Abele
    Director Public Relations: Erin Kogler
    Human Resources Manager: Mary Novak

Management:
Orchestra Personnel Manager: Linda Unkefer
Founded: 1959
Specialized Field: Symphony; Orchestra
Status: Professional; Nonprofit
Paid Staff: 5
Budget: $16M
Income Sources: Ticket Sales; Fees for Services; United Performing Arts Fund; Wisconsin Arts Board; Milwaukee County CAMPAC; Corporate And Individual Giving
Performs At: Marcus Center for the Performing Arts; Uihlein Hall
Annual Attendance: 270,000
Organization Type: Performing; Touring; Educational; Recording

1642
MILWAUKEE YOUTH SYMPHONY ORCHESTRA

325 W Walnut Street
Milwaukee, WI 53212
Phone: 414-267-2950
Fax: 414-267-2960
e-mail: general@myso.org
Web Site: www.myso.org
Officers:
President: Susan Wernecke
Management:
Executive Director: Frances S Richman
Artistic Edu/Resident Conductor: Carter Simmons
Music Director/Senior Symphony: Margery Deutsch
Mission: Provides training in the finest techniques of orchestral and ensemble musicianship to students ages 8-18 in the greater Milwaukee area, through an extensive schedule of rehearsals, performances and enrichment activities.
Utilizes: Collaborating Artists; Collaborations; Commissioned Composers; Community Members; Composers; Composers-in-Residence; Educators; Grant Writers; Guest Companies; Guest Composers; Guest Musical Directors; Guest Musicians; Guest Soloists; Guest Teachers; High School Drama; Instructors; Lyricists; Multimedia; Music; Original Music Scores; Scenic Designers; Sign Language Translators; Singers; Soloists; Students
Founded: 1956
Specialized Field: Youth Orchestra; Chamber; Ensemble
Status: Non-Professional; Nonprofit; Youth Orchestra
Paid Staff: 40
Budget: $1.5 Million
Performs At: Uihlein Hall
Affiliations: LAO; AWSO; YOD
Annual Attendance: 10,000
Seating Capacity: 2,300

1643
PRESENT MUSIC

158 N Broadway
Milwaukee, WI 53202
Phone: 414-271-0711
Fax: 414-271-7998
e-mail: newmusic@presentmusic.org
Web Site: www.presentmusic.org
Management:
Artistic Director: Kevin Stalheim
Managing Director: Eric Lind
Mission: Present music engages artists and audiences in imaginative experiences with new music through ensemble performace education and commissioning.

Utilizes: Artists-in-Residence; Collaborations; Commissioned Music; Guest Companies; Guest Directors; Multimedia; Organization Contracts
Founded: 1982
Specialized Field: Chamber; Ensemble
Status: Professional; Nonprofit
Paid Staff: 35
Paid Artists: 25
Budget: $400,000
Income Sources: Ticket Sales; Philanthropic Support
Annual Attendance: 5,000
Facility Category: Art Museum
Seating Capacity: 750
Year Built: 2001
Organization Type: Performing; Touring; Resident; Educational; Recording

1644
OSHKOSH SYMPHONY ORCHESTRA

290 City Center
PO Box 522
Oshkosh, WI 54902
Phone: 920-233-7510
Fax: 620-233-5091
Officers:
President: John Bermingham
Executive VP: Sam Adams
Secretary: Victoria Beltran
Treasure: Stuart N. Tribbey
Executive Director: Susan Traska
Marketing Director: Mary Whitlock
Management:
Business Manager: Rebecca Spurlock
Founded: 1940
Specialized Field: Symphony; Orchestra
Status: Semi-Professional
Income Sources: Association of Wisconsin Symphony Orchestra; American Symphony Orchestra League
Performs At: Osh Kosh Civic Auditorium
Organization Type: Performing

Wyoming

1645
WYOMING SYMPHONY ORCHESTRA

111 Westsecond Street
Suite 103
Casper, WY 82601
Mailing Address: PO Box 667 Casper, WY 82602
Phone: 307-266-1478
Fax: 307-266-4522
e-mail: wso@coffey.com
Web Site: www.wyomingsymphony.com
Officers:
President: Bobbie Brown
Management:
Executive Director: Jennifer Thompson
Music Director: Jonathan Shames
Librarian: Roger Hedlund
Mission: To enhance cultural life; to expand childrens' musical horizons; to offer area musicians a performance outlet.
Founded: 1950
Specialized Field: Symphony; Orchestra
Status: Professional; Nonprofit
Paid Staff: 4
Paid Artists: 75
Budget: $300,000
Income Sources: City of Casper; Wyoming Council on the Arts; National Endowment for the Arts; American Symphony Orchestra League; Private Foundations
Performs At: John F. Welsh Auditorium; Natrona County High School

Affiliations: American Symphony Orchestra League
Annual Attendance: 6,400
Facility Category: High School
Organization Type: Performing; Touring; Educational

1646
CHEYENNE SYMPHONY ORCHESTRA

PO Box 851
Cheyenne, WY 82003
Phone: 307-778-8561
Fax: 307-634-7512
e-mail: email@cheyennesymphony.org
Web Site: www.cheyennesymphony.org
Management:
Executive Director: Christine De Poorter
Music Director: William Intriligator
Mission: Presenting excellent professionally performed symphonic music to as wide as possible an audience, emphasizing educational outreach.
Utilizes: Guest Artists
Founded: 1954
Specialized Field: Symphony; Orchestra; Chamber
Status: Professional; Nonprofit
Income Sources: American Symphony Orchestra League; Symphony & Choral Society of Cheyenne
Performs At: Cheyenne Civic Center
Organization Type: Performing; Educational

Alabama

1647
BIRMINGHAM MUSIC CLUB
PO Box 10486
Birmingham, AL 35202
Phone: 205-252-7548
Fax: 205-322-6206
e-mail: info@bhammusicclub.org
Web Site: www.bhammusicclub.org
Officers:
President: Wyatt R Haskell
VP: Eloise Williams
Treasurer: Malcolm K Miller Jr
Secretary: Judy H Wiggins
Management:
Executive Director: Cynthia Harper
Mission: To present talented artists from around the world to the community of Birmingham.
Specialized Field: Ethnic Music; Classical; Contemporary
Status: Non-Profit, Professional
Paid Staff: 4

1648
OPERA BIRMINGHAM
1807 3rd Avenue N
Birmingham, AL 35203
Phone: 205-322-6737
Fax: 205-322-6206
e-mail: john@bhammusiccoop.org
Web Site: www.bhammusiccoop.org
Officers:
President: John T Natter
Guild President: Summer Currier
Management:
President: Philippe Rathrop
Executive Director: John Jones
Principal Conductor: Steven White
Education and Outreach Manager: Mary K Jackson
Mission: Opera Birmingham is committed to creating the finest opera productions, developing local and regional talent through competition and exposure to major artists, and preserving the operatic art form through community-wide education.
Founded: 1955
Specialized Field: Grand Opera; Lyric Opera; Youth Chorus; Classical; Contemporary
Status: Non-Profit, Professional
Paid Staff: 4
Performs At: Alabama Theater

1649
HUNTSVILLE OPERA THEATER
8802 Willow Hills Drive
Huntsville, AL 36660-1633
Phone: 334-476-7377
Fax: 334-476-7373
e-mail: mbeutjer@hiwaay.net
Web Site: www.huntsvilleopera.com/hot.html
Officers:
President: Steve Russell
Guild President: Sonja Bruek
Management:
General Director/Princ Conductor: Jerome Shannoni
Administrative Director: Merv White-Spunner
Financial Secretary: Nancy Thomas
Education Director: Charles Smoke
Publications Manager: Sarah Wright
Marketing Director: Larry Wooley
Development Director: Paul Klotz

Mission: Nurturing the growth of young dancers, singers and technicians.
Founded: 1981
Specialized Field: Grand Opera
Status: Nonprofit
Performs At: Von Braun Civic Center - Playhouse
Organization Type: Performing

1650
MOBILE OPERA
257 Dauthin Street
Mobile, AL 36602
Phone: 251-432-6772
Fax: 251-431-7613
e-mail: info@mobileopera.org
Web Site: www.mobileopera.org
Officers:
President: Sheryl Bates
Executive Vice President: Cesar Roca
Treasurer: Ann Broughton
Management:
President: Sheryl Bates
General Director: Scott Wright
Artistic Director: Andy Anderson
Mission: Present professional productions of opera and musical theatre and programs dedicated to in school arts education and community outreach while providing performance opportunities for national and regional artists.
Utilizes: Actors; Artists-in-Residence; Dance Companies; Grant Writers; Guest Accompanists; Guest Artists; Guest Companies; Guest Composers; Guest Conductors; Guest Designers; Guest Writers; Original Music Scores
Founded: 1946
Specialized Field: Grand Opera; Operetta
Status: Non-Profit, Professional
Paid Staff: 4
Volunteer Staff: 10
Paid Artists: 150
Budget: $700,000
Performs At: Mobile Saenger Theatre
Affiliations: Opera America
Annual Attendance: 9,120
Type of Stage: Proscenium
Seating Capacity: 1,900
Year Built: 1927
Year Remodeled: 2004

Alaska

1651
ALASKA LIGHT OPERA THEATRE
639 W International Airport Road
#34
Anchorage, AK 99502
Fax: 907-345-2568
Officers:
President: James Feeney
VP: Duane Heyman
Treasurer: Frank Danner
Secretary: Jacquie Turpin
Management:
General Director: Gloria Marinacc Allen
Administrative Assistant: Judy O'Neal
Mission: To produce professional-quality musical theatre; to produce musical-theatre education programs for Alaska school children; to provide professional development to Alaskan musical-theatre performers through the Resident Artists Program.
Utilizes: Guest Artists; Guest Companies; Singers
Founded: 1984
Specialized Field: Light Opera

Status: Professional; Nonprofit
Performs At: Fourth Avenue Theatre
Organization Type: Performing; Resident; Educational

1652
ANCHORAGE CONCERT CHORUS
PO Box 100364
Anchorage, AK 99510
Phone: 907-274-7464
Fax: 907-563-5980
e-mail: concertchorus@gci.net
Web Site: www.anchorageconcertchorus.org
Officers:
President: Shaun Baines
Management:
Artistic Director/Conductor: Dr. Grant Cochran, concertchorus@gci.net
Executive Director: Sandra Adams, concertchorus@gci.net
Mission: To serve Anchorage and surrounding communities by fostering excellence in choral music through world-class vocal performance, community events, and music education.
Utilizes: Guest Artists
Founded: 1947
Specialized Field: Choral
Status: Non-Profit, Non-Professional
Paid Staff: 2
Non-paid Artists: 160
Budget: $240,000
Income Sources: Municipality of Anchorage; Alaska State Council on the Arts, Donations, Dues, Performances
Performs At: Alaska Center for the Performing Arts
Affiliations: Chorus America
Annual Attendance: 12,000-16,000
Organization Type: Performing
Resident Groups: Alaska Center for the Performing Arts

1653
ANCHORAGE OPERA COMPANY
1507 Spar Avenue
Anchorage, AK 99501-1812
Phone: 907-279-2557
Fax: 907-279-7798
e-mail: info@anchorageopera.org
Web Site: www.anchorageopera.org
Officers:
President: Robert Bracco
Treasurer: Alan Clark
Secretary: Amy Kropp
VP: Donald Endres
Management:
General Director: Torrie Allen
Production Manager/Technical Dir: Lauren Miller
Director of Individual Giving: Eva Aigner
Grants & Education Manager: Lauren Green
Mission: Provides the finest operatic experiences to residents and visitors while also serving as a professional resource for American artist's, admistrators and technical staff helping them to refine their talent and perfect craft.
Utilizes: Actors; Artists-in-Residence; Collaborations; Community Members; Community Talent; Contract Orchestras; Dancers; Designers; Educators; Five Seasonal Concerts; Grant Writers; Guest Artists; Guest Composers; Guest Lecturers; Guest Musicians; Guest Writers; Instructors; Local Artists & Directors; Lyricists; Multi Collaborations; Multimedia; Music; Original Music Scores; Poets; Resident Artists; Resident Professionals; Scenic Designers; Sign Language Translators; Singers; Students; Student Interns; Visual Arts

Founded: 1962
Specialized Field: Grand Opera; Light Opera; Lyric Opera; Classical
Status: Non-Profit, Professional
Paid Staff: 6
Volunteer Staff: 90
Paid Artists: 100
Performs At: Alaska Center for the Performing Arts

1654
FAIRBANKS CHORAL SOCIETY
1815 Carr Avenue
Fairbanks, AK 99709-4208
Phone: 907-456-1144
e-mail: sing@mosquitonet.com
Web Site: www.fairbankschoralsociety.org
Management:
 Executive Director: Suzanne Summerville, ssummerville@gmail.com
Mission: Sponsoring the Fairbanks Sing-It-Yourself-Messiah, and concerts for the animals
Utilizes: Guest Artists; Guest Companies; Singers
Founded: 1984
Specialized Field: Classical; Contemporary; Religious
Status: Non-Profit, Non-Professional
Paid Artists: 3
Income Sources: Fairbanks City Bed-Tax And Private Donations
Performs At: University of Alaska; Fairbanks Concert Hall
Organization Type: Performing; Educational; Sponsoring

1655
FAIRBANKS LIGHT OPERA THEATRE
PO Box 72787
Fairbanks, AK 99707
Phone: 907-456-3568
Fax: 907-456-3662
e-mail: flot@flot.org
Web Site: www.flot.org
Officers:
 President: Theresa Reed
 VP: Tami Holland
 Treasurer: Phyllis Church
 Secretary: Dorothea Moravec
Management:
 President: Diane Coughlan
Mission: To offer our community musical theatre and light opera.
Founded: 1969
Specialized Field: Light Opera
Status: Non-Professional; Nonprofit
Performs At: Hering Auditorium; Alaskaland Civic Center
Organization Type: Performing; Touring

1656
JUNEAU LYRIC OPERA
PO Box 21456
Juneau, AK 99802-1456
Phone: 907-789-4604
e-mail: opera@juneau.com
Officers:
 President: Susan Auer
 Vice President: Alan Davis
 Treasurer: Jim Kennedy
 Secretary: Karen Allen
Mission: To present high quality vocal performances and workshops to encourage the growth and education of our musical community. To provide singing, choral and theatrical opportunities for community members.
Founded: 1975
Specialized Field: Opera

1657
JUNEAU ORATORIO CHOIR
PO Box 32760
Juneau, AK 99803-2760
Phone: 907-789-0320
Fax: 907-586-6261
e-mail: jallanmackinnon@gmail.com
Officers:
 President: J Allan MacKinnon
Management:
 Artistic Director: J Allan MacKinnon
Specialized Field: Choral
Status: Non-Profit, Non-Professional

Arizona

1658
ARIZONA OPERA
4600 N 12th Street
Phoenix, AZ 85014
Phone: 602-266-7464
Fax: 602-266-5806
e-mail: phoenixdev@azopera.com
Web Site: www.azopera.com
Management:
 Artistic Director: Joel Rezeven
 General Director: Scott Altman
 Box Office Manager-Phoenix: Michael Tomaszek
 Box Office Associate: Terri Staats
 Box Office Associate: Paloma Routh
 Administrative Associate: Melanie Booth
 Artistic Administrative Assistant: Shannon Whidden
 Chorus Director: John Massaro
Mission: To offer grand opera to Arizona, in both the Tucson and Phoenix areas.
Utilizes: Guest Artists; Guest Designers; Sign Language Translators
Founded: 1971
Specialized Field: Grand Opera
Status: Professional; Nonprofit
Budget: $5,400,000
Income Sources: Contributed Income; Corporate; Government; Foundations; Individual Donations
Performs At: Tucson Community Center Music Hall; Phoenix Symphony Hall
Annual Attendance: 80,000
Organization Type: Performing

1659
ORPHEUS MALE CHORUS OF PHOENIX
PO Box 217
Phoenix, AZ 85001
Phone: 602-271-9396
e-mail: info@orpheus.org
Web Site: www.orpheus.org
Officers:
 Chorus President: Tom Eccles
 Treasurer: Robert L Merer
Management:
 Accompanist: Rou Rhode
 Artistic Director: Robb Butler
Mission: To employ music as a tool to further goodwill as well as to offer an outlet for men who love singing.
Utilizes: Collaborating Artists; Original Music Scores; Singers
Founded: 1929
Specialized Field: Choral; Men's Chorus
Status: Non-Professional, Nonprofit
Paid Artists: 2
Non-paid Artists: 40+

Income Sources: Dues; CD Sales; Contract Concerts; Patron Contributions
Performs At: Trinity Cathedral, Camelback Bible Church, Dupherm Theatre
Organization Type: Performing; Touring

1660
PHOENIX BACH CHOIR
PO Box 16956
Phoenix, AZ 85011-6956
Phone: 602-253-2224
Fax: 602-253-5772
Web Site: www.bachchoir.org
Management:
 Managing Director: Joel M Rinsema
 Artistic Director: Charles Bruffy
Founded: 1958
Specialized Field: Classical
Status: Non-Profit, Professional
Paid Staff: 5
Paid Artists: 30

1661
PHOENIX BOYS CHOIR
1131 E Missouri Avenue
Phoenix, AZ 85014
Phone: 602-264-5328
Fax: 602-264-6778
e-mail: pat@boyschoir.org
Web Site: www.boyschoir.org
Management:
 President: Sal Rivera
 Executive Director: Jeth Mill
 Artistic Director: George Stangelberger
Mission: To educate boys in the art of singing.
Founded: 1948
Specialized Field: Youth Chorus
Status: Non-Profit, Non-Professional
Paid Staff: 7
Volunteer Staff: 100
Paid Artists: 8

1662
ARIZONA OPERA
3501 N Mountain Avenue
Tucson, AZ 85719
Phone: 520-293-4336
Fax: 520-293-5097
e-mail: info@azopera.com
Web Site: www.azopera.com
Management:
 Artistic Director: Joel Revzen
Mission: To offer grand opera to Arizona, in both the Tucson and Phoenix areas.
Utilizes: Guest Composers; Guest Designers; Sign Language Translators
Founded: 1972
Specialized Field: Grand Opera; Light Opera; Lyric Opera; Choral
Status: Non-Profit, Professional
Paid Staff: 30
Budget: $5,400,000
Income Sources: Contributed Income; Corporate; Government; Foundations; Individual Donations
Performs At: Tucson Community Center Music Hall; Phoenix Symphony Hall
Annual Attendance: 80,000
Organization Type: Performing

1663
DESERT VOICES
PO Box 270
Tucson, AZ 85702-0270

Phone: 520-791-9662
Fax: 520-791-3360
e-mail: office@desertvoices.org
Web Site: www.desertvoices.org
Officers:
President: Carolyn Schurulst
VP: Sylvia Yeager
Secretary: Shar Loper Bloch
Treasurer: Dick Rehse
Office Manager: Becky Cohen
General Manager: Jeffrey Scotland
Management:
Artistic Director: Chris Tackett
Mission: Arizona premiere GLBTS chorus organization is committed to developing talent, fostering artistic integrity, enteraining our audiences and encouraging cooperation across differences supporting diversity.
Founded: 1988
Specialized Field: Alternative
Status: Non-Profit, Non-Professional
Paid Staff: 3
Budget: $60,000
Income Sources: Arizona Commission on the Arts; National Endowment for the Arts; Tucson Pima Arts Council; Amazon Foundation; Southern Arizona Community Foundation
Performs At: Performing Arts Auditorium; Church Sanctuaries
Annual Attendance: 1,000

1664
TUCSON ARIZONA BOYS CHORUS
5770 E Pima Street
Tucson, AZ 85712
Phone: 520-296-6277
Fax: 520-296-6751
e-mail: tabc@boyschorus.org
Web Site: www.boyschorus.org
Officers:
President: Michael B Smith
VP: David Roher
Treasurer: Art Flagg
Secretary: Kelly Bequette
Management:
Director: Dr Julian Ackerley
Director of Development: Jennifer Ackerley
Office Manager: Lisa Slechta
Mission: Presents a varied program including traditional boy choir repertoire, songs of the southwest with trick rodeo roping, a choreographed medley of populartunes and stirring patriotic selections.
Founded: 1939
Specialized Field: Youth Chorus
Paid Staff: 4
Paid Artists: 5
Budget: $680,000
Income Sources: Performance Fees; Ticket Sales; Fundraising Programs; Corporate Partners; Foundation Support; Governmental Grants
Affiliations: International SocietyO Children's Choral and Performing Arts; Alliance For Arts and Understanding; American Choral Directors Association

Arkansas

1665
OPERA IN THE OZARKS AT INSPIRATION POINT
16311 Highway 62 W
Holiday Island, AR 72632

Phone: 479-253-8595
Fax: 501-253-8595
e-mail: operaintheozarks@ipa.net
Web Site: www.opera.org
Management:
Artistic Director: Vern Sutton
Underworld Conductor: Kostis Protopap
Specialized Field: Opera; Youth Chorus; Classical for Young Audiences; Educational
Budget: $60,000-$150,000
Season: May - July
Affiliations: South Central of National Federated Music Clubs
Facility Category: Amphitheater
Seating Capacity: 300

California

1666
BERKELEY OPERA
1700 Shattuck Avenue
Suite 312
Berkeley, CA 94709
Phone: 510-841-1903
Web Site: www.berkeleyopera.org
Management:
Artistic Director: Jonathan Khuner
Audition Secretary: Jane Rateaver
Orchestra Manager: Bonnie Lockett
Artistic Director: Jonathan Khuner
Mission: The presentation of opera.
Utilizes: High School Drama
Founded: 1979
Specialized Field: Lyric Opera
Status: Semi-Professional
Paid Staff: 20
Income Sources: Theater Bay Area
Performs At: Julia Morgan Theater; Hillside Club Theater
Organization Type: Performing

1667
CALIFORNIA CHAMBER ORCHESTRA & CHAMBER OPERA
53 Osage Avenue
Los Altos
Berkeley, CA 94022
Phone: 510-524-3682
Fax: 510-524-3683
e-mail: info@californiachamberopera.com
Officers:
Musical Director: Roy Firestone
Management:
Co-Artistic Director: Diane Squires
Co-Artistic Director: Gretchen McNeil
Specialized Field: Opera
Budget: $260,000-$1,050,000

1668
LOS ANGELES CONCERT OPERA ASSOCIATION
2250 Gloaming Way
Beverly Hills, CA 90210
Phone: 310-276-2731
Fax: 310-275-8245
Management:
Acting Director: Nedra Zachary
Mission: To provide young opera singers with performance opportunities of lesser known opera and Viennese operetta.
Founded: 1987
Specialized Field: Operetta; Vocal Music

Status: Nonprofit
Paid Artists: 30
Performs At: Wilshire Ebell Theatre
Organization Type: Performing

1669
CASA ITALIANA OPERA COMPANY
902 N Screenland Drive
Burbank, CA 91505
Phone: 818-559-8696
Fax: 310-411-9349
Web Site: www.casaitaliana.org
Officers:
Founder: Mario Leonetti
Management:
General Director: Mario E Leonetti
Mission: To reach a growing audience with appreciation for opera, in the classical Italian form as well as expanding the repertoire with lesser known productions.
Founded: 1971
Specialized Field: Opera
Performs At: Casa Italiana Hall and Theater; Wilshire Ebell Theater

1670
HIDDEN VALLEY MUSIC SEMINAR
PO Box 116
Carmel Valley, CA 93924
Phone: 831-659-3115
Fax: 831-659-7442
e-mail: hvms@aol.com
Web Site: www.hiddenvalleymusic.org
Management:
General Director: Peter Meckel
Mission: Arts training for pre-professional and early professional artists
Founded: 1963
Specialized Field: Choral; Educational
Status: Non-Profit, Professional
Paid Staff: 25
Volunteer Staff: 50
Paid Artists: 30
Non-paid Artists: 30

1671
ALL AMERICAN BOYS YOUTH CHORUS
PO Box 1527
Costa Mesa, CA 92628
Phone: 714-708-1670
Fax: 714-557-5447
e-mail: taabc@aol.com
Web Site: www.allamericanboyschorus.org
Management:
President: Anthony S Manrique
Music Director: Wesley Martin
Production Manager: Jason Gannon
Marketing Director: Juan Ayala
Mission: To provide each member with the training, motivation, and opportunity to develop and exercise qualities of leadership within an exceptional program of choral music conducted in an environment of high moral standards.
Founded: 1970
Specialized Field: Youth Chorus; Entertainment Chorus
Status: Non-Profit, Non-Professional
Paid Staff: 12

1672
MASTER CHORALE OF ORANGE COUNTY
660 W Baker
Suite 273
Costa Mesa, CA 92626
Mailing Address: PO Box 2156, Costa Mesa, CA. 92628
Phone: 714-997-6504
Fax: 714-556-6341
e-mail: info@whmc.org
Management:
Music Director: Dr. William D Hall
Associate Music Director: Dr. Thomas Sheets
Administrative Director: Sheri Sheperd
Administrative Assistant: Jean Updegraff
Founded: 1956
Specialized Field: Choral
Status: Nonprofit
Paid Staff: 140
Budget: $10,000
Performs At: Orange County Performing Arts Center
Organization Type: Performing

1673
CAPITOL OPERA SACRAMENTO
1907 Donner Ave
Unit 3
Davis, CA 95616
Phone: 707-450-8850
e-mail: capitolopera2004@yahoo.com
Web Site: www.capopera.com
Management:
General Director: Kathleen Torchia
Acting Artistic Director: Corey Wilkins
Scene Artist: Roger Smith
Mission: To keep opera alive and provide performing opportunities for developing artists.
Utilizes: Actors; Artists-in-Residence; Choreographers; Dance Companies; Dancers; Designers; Fine Artists; Five Seasonal Concerts; Guest Accompanists; Guest Composers; Guest Writers; Instructors; Local Artists; Multimedia; Music; Resident Professionals; Sign Language Translators; Singers; Soloists; Student Interns
Founded: 1990
Specialized Field: Opera
Volunteer Staff: 10
Income Sources: Tickets; Donations; Seasonal Subscriptions
Affiliations: AACT; Opera America
Annual Attendance: 5,000
Facility Category: Small Theater
Type of Stage: Black Box
Seating Capacity: 50
Year Remodeled: 1993

1674
SACRAMENTO CHORAL SOCIETY AND ORCHESTRA
4025 A Bridge Street
Fair Oaks, CA 95628
Phone: 916-536-9065
Fax: 916-962-0352
e-mail: scso2005@yahoo.com
Web Site: www.sacramentochoral.com
Officers:
President: James McCormick
Vice President: Lee Blachowicz
Second VP/Conductor: Donald Kendrick
Secretary: Marya Kasch
Treasurer: Truman Rishard
Management:

Conductor/Artistic Dirctor: Donald Kendrick
Mission: To continue the tradition of performing important choral orchestral masterworks for the community; to develop an appreciation of choral music in the community; to encourage choral music education and creativity through workshops, clinics and mentoring; to achieve professional standards of performance; to secure a lasting foundation as a symphonic music organization.
Utilizes: Collaborations; Educators; Five Seasonal Concerts; Guest Accompanists; Guest Composers; Guest Directors; Guest Instructors; Guest Lecturers; Guest Musical Directors; Guest Musicians; Multimedia; Sign Language Translators; Singers; Soloists
Founded: 1996
Specialized Field: Choral
Status: Nonprofit
Paid Staff: 1
Volunteer Staff: 10
Paid Artists: 60
Non-paid Artists: 180
Budget: $500,000
Income Sources: Annual Fund; Program Ads; Fundraising; Corporate Grants; Ticket Sales; CD Sales; Contract Fees
Performs At: Cathedral of the Blessed Sacrament; Sacramento and the Mondavi Center; UC Davis
Type of Stage: Concert Hall
Year Remodeled: 2003
Cost: $34.5 Million

1675
FULLERTON CIVIC LIGHT OPERA
218 W Commonwealth Avenue
Fullerton, CA 92832
Phone: 714-526-3832
Fax: 714-992-1193
e-mail: marilyn@fclo.com
Web Site: www.fclo.com
Officers:
President: Gordon Haag
Management:
President: Norma Jones
Executive Director: Griff Duncan
Artistic Director: Jan Duncan
Mission: To present live stage musicals and nationwide costume and scenery rentals.
Utilizes: Actors; AEA Actors; Choreographers; Collaborations; Community Talent; Contract Orchestras; Dancers; Designers; Guest Artists; Guest Companies; Guest Conductors; Guest Designers; Guest Lecturers; Guest Writers; Guild Activities; Instructors; Local Artists; Lyricists; Multi Collaborations; Multimedia; Music; Original Music Scores; Resident Professionals; Singers; Students; Special Technical Talent
Founded: 1971
Specialized Field: Light Opera
Status: Non-Profit, Professional
Paid Staff: 34
Volunteer Staff: 40
Paid Artists: 90
Non-paid Artists: 40
Budget: $1.6 million
Income Sources: Ticket Sales; Costume/Scenery Rentals; Contributions
Performs At: Plummer Auditorium
Affiliations: National Alliance of Musical Theatre Producers
Annual Attendance: 50,000
Facility Category: Stage Auditorium
Type of Stage: Proscenium
Stage Dimensions: 36x31
Seating Capacity: 1,314
Year Built: 1934

Year Remodeled: 1993
Cost: $2,700,000
Rental Contact: Fullerton Union High School District
Organization Type: Performing; Resident

1676
ALBERT MCNEIL JUBILEE SINGERS OF LOS ANGELES
Aya World Productions
Management
Hermosa Beach, CA
Phone: 323-459-3007
Fax: 323-375-1783
e-mail: aaron@ayaworld.com
Management:
Director: Albert McNeil
Management: Aaron Nigel Smith
Utilizes: Multimedia; Singers
Founded: 1968
Specialized Field: Gospel Chorus
Paid Staff: 1

1677
MASTERWORKS CHORALE
PO Box 323
Lexington, CA 02420
Phone: 781-235-6210
e-mail: info@masterworkschoral.org
Web Site: www.masterworkschoral.org
Management:
Music Director: Bryan Baker
Music Director Emeritus: Galen Marshall
Mission: Mission is the performance of manjor choral works
Founded: 1964
Specialized Field: Choral
Status: Non-Profit, Semi-Professional
Paid Staff: 1
Paid Artists: 1
Performs At: Sanders Theatre; Harvard University

1678
LONG BEACH CIVIC LIGHT OPERA
PO Box 20280
Long Beach, CA 90801
Phone: 562-435-7605
Fax: 310-372-8685
Management:
Managing Director: Pegge Logefeil
Producer: Martin Wiviott
Mission: Maintaining artistic excellence in professional musical theatre; training young people and preprofessionals in musical theatre.
Utilizes: Guest Artists; Guest Companies; Singers
Founded: 1950
Specialized Field: Light Opera; Operetta
Status: Professional; Nonprofit
Performs At: Terrace Theater
Organization Type: Performing

1679
LONG BEACH OPERA
PO Box 14895
Long Beach, CA 90803
Phone: 562-439-2580
Web Site: www.lbopera.com/
Management:
General Director: Michael Milenski
Mission: To offer professional opera to the community of Southern California and to nurture the love for opera and performing arts.
Utilizes: Guest Artists; Guest Companies; Singers
Founded: 1978
Specialized Field: Grand Opera; Lyric Opera

Status: Professional, Nonprofit
Paid Staff: 25
Performs At: Center Theater; Terrace Theater
Organization Type: Performing; Educational

1680
LOS ANGELES CHAMBER SINGERS ACAPPELLA

PO Box 64888
Los Angeles, CA 90064-0888
Phone: 310-575-9790
Fax: 310-575-3405
Toll-free: 866-296-9414
e-mail: voices@lacs.org
Web Site: www.lacs.org
Management:
   Music Director: Peter Rutenberg
Mission: Los Angeles Chamber Singers excels in the art and performance of choralchamber music; preserves and promotes the art form; presents concert programs for the general public and educational programs for elementary, high school and college students; appears on records and radio
Founded: 1990
Specialized Field: Choral
Paid Staff: 1
Volunteer Staff: 5
Paid Artists: 25
Affiliations: Chorus America; Early Music America; RCM Records

1681
LOS ANGELES MASTER CHORALE

The Music Center
135 N Grand Avenue
Los Angeles, CA 90012
Phone: 213-972-7282
Fax: 213-687-8238
e-mail: lamc@lamc.org
Web Site: www.lamc.org
Officers:
   Executive Director: Terry Knowles
   Chairman: Mark Foster
   Treasurer: Cheryl Petersen
Management:
   Music Director: Grant Gershon
Mission: To educate the public in the art of choral singing and to foster an appreciation of the art form.
Founded: 1963
Specialized Field: Choral
Status: Professional
Paid Staff: 12
Budget: $4 Million
Income Sources: Ticket Sales; Individual Contributions; Business and Foundation Contributions
Performs At: Walt Disney Concert Hall
Organization Type: Performing; Resident; Educational

1682
LOS ANGELES OPERA

135 N Grand Avenue
Suite 327
Los Angeles, CA 90012
Phone: 213-972-7219
Fax: 213-687-3490
e-mail: wehelpyou@laopera.com
Web Site: www.losangelesopera.org
Officers:
   Chairman Emeritus: Richard Seaver
   Chairman/CEO: Marc I Stern
   President: Frank E Baxter
   Chairman Executive Committee: Bernard A Greenberg
   Secretary/Treasurer: Eugene P Stein

CFO: Seth I Weintraub
   Administration Director: Elizabeth Kennedy
Management:
   Executive Director: Elizabeth Kennedy
   Artistic Director: Placido Domingo
   Principal Conductor: Kent Nagano
   Artistic Administrator: Edgar Baitzel
   Costume Director: Jennifer Green
Mission: To present opera at its highest professional standard with international guest artists and a resident company.
Utilizes: Artists-in-Residence; Collaborations; Dancers; Designers; Educators; Grant Writers; Guest Artists; Guest Companies; Guest Conductors; Guest Ensembles; Guest Instructors; Guest Musicians; Guest Soloists; Guest Writers; High School Drama; Instructors; Local Artists; Lyricists; Multimedia; Organization Contracts; Original Music Scores; Poets; Resident Professionals
Founded: 1986
Specialized Field: Opera
Status: Non-Profit, Professional
Income Sources: Ticket Revenue, Contributed Income
Season: July-May
Performs At: Dorothy Chandler Pavilion
Annual Attendance: 160,000
Facility Category: Performing Arts Center
Type of Stage: Proscenium
Seating Capacity: 3,086
Year Built: 1964
Organization Type: Performing; Resident; Educational

1683
OPERA A LA CARTE

PO Box 39606
Los Angeles, CA 90039
Phone: 626-791-0844
Fax: 626-791-4806
e-mail: info@operaalacarte.org
Web Site: www.operaalacarte.org
Management:
   President: Richard Sheldon
Founded: 1970
Specialized Field: Musical Theatre; Opera; Gilbert and Sullivan
Status: Non-Profit, Professional
Paid Staff: 1
Paid Artists: 55

1684
UNIVERSITY OF SOUTHERN CALIFORNIA THORNTON OPERA

Booth Hall of Music, Room 112
University Park Campus, 820 W 34th Street
Los Angeles, CA 90089-0851
Phone: 213-740-6451
Fax: 213-821-1603
e-mail: opera@thornton.usc.edu
Web Site: www.usc.edu/music/uscopera
Management:
   Dean: Robert Cutietta
   Conductor/Music Director: Brent McMunn
   Resident Staqe Director: Ken Cazan
   Opera Manager: Damien Elwood
Mission: Providing a performance outlet and training for talented young singers in all aspects of performance; presenting two full operas as well as various single scenes.
Founded: 1940
Specialized Field: Grand Opera; Lyric Opera; Light Opera; Operetta
Status: Non-Profit, Non-Professional
Paid Staff: 25
Income Sources: University of Southern California

Performs At: Bing Theater
Organization Type: Performing; Touring; Educational

1685
TOWNSEND OPERA PLAYERS

605 H Street
Modesto, CA 95354
Mailing Address: PO Box 4519, Modesto, CA. 95352
Phone: 209-523-6426
Fax: 209-579-0532
e-mail: top@ainet.com
Web Site: www.townsendoperaplayers.com
Officers:
   President: Robert Fisk
   Secretary: Judy Schmidt
   Treasurer: Dale McKinney
Management:
   President: Steve Collins
   Executive Director: Erik Buck Townsend
   Operations Manager: Erika Townsend
   Production Coordinator: Barbara Wesley
   Education Director: Charles Sheaffer
   Public Relations/Marketing: Martha Martin
Mission: Performing great opera as well as classics of American Musical Theatre for the enjoyment of San Joaquin Valley and surrounding area residents.
Utilizes: Actors; Choreographers; Collaborations; Dance Companies; Dancers; Designers; Educators; Five Seasonal Concerts; Grant Writers; Guest Accompanists; Guest Artists; Guest Composers; Guest Designers; Guest Directors; Guest Instructors; Guest Musicians; Guest Writers; Guild Activities; Instructors; Local Artists; Lyricists; Multimedia; Music; Resident Professionals; Selected Students; Sign Language Translators; Singers; Soloists; Student Interns; Visual Arts
Founded: 1982
Specialized Field: Grand Opera; Light Opera; Choral; Youth Chorus; Classical
Status: Non-Profit, Professional
Paid Staff: 4
Paid Artists: 100
Non-paid Artists: 150
Budget: $400,000
Income Sources: Membership, Grants, Donation and Ticket Sales
Annual Attendance: 10,000
Facility Category: High School Auditorium
Stage Dimensions: 44'x38'x16'
Seating Capacity: 1,100
Year Built: 1900
Organization Type: Performing; Touring; Educational

1686
CANTABILE YOUTH SINGERS

953 Industrial Avenue #122
Mountain View, CA 94303
Phone: 650-424-1410
Fax: 650-424-1430
e-mail: info@cantabile.org
Web Site: www.cantabile.org
Officers:
   Chairman Of The Board: Lori Mirek
Management:
   Executive Director: Sonja Wohlgemuth
   Artistic Director: Eman Isadiar
   Managing Director: Denise Lewis
Founded: 1979
Specialized Field: Vocal Choral
Status: Non-Profit, Non-Professional
Paid Staff: 2
Paid Artists: 4

1687
SCHOLA CANTORUM
1605 W El Camino Real
Suite 200
Mountain View, CA 94040-2452
Phone: 650-254-1700
Fax: 650-254-1701
e-mail: info@scholacantorum.org
Web Site: www.scholacantorum.org
Officers:
Chairman: Henry Lesser
Management:
Music Director: Gregory Wait
Executive Director: Nicola Rees
Mission: To celebrate the joy of singing with our community: by performing choral music of all styles, including masterpieces and commissioned works; by educating and inspiring our singers and our audiences.
Utilizes: Collaborations; Commissioned Composers; Grant Writers; Guest Directors; Guest Ensembles; Guest Instructors; Guest Musical Directors; Guest Musicians; Guest Soloists; Instructors; Local Artists; Multimedia; New Productions; Original Music Scores; Sign Language Translators; Singers; Soloists
Founded: 1964
Specialized Field: Choral
Status: Non-professional; Nonprofit
Paid Staff: 4
Volunteer Staff: 3
Paid Artists: 2
Budget: $218,000
Income Sources: Ticket Sales; Grants; Donations; Sponsorships;
Annual Attendance: 5,000

1688
MUSICAL AMERICA
North Hollywood High School
5231 Colfax Avenue
North Hollywood, CA 91607
Phone: 818-980-3095
Management:
Director: Cornelia Korney
Mission: Educating through the presentation of fine choral music; providing the community with entertainment.
Utilizes: Guest Artists; Singers
Founded: 1969
Specialized Field: Choral
Status: Semi-Professional; Non-Professional
Income Sources: Los Angeles Unified School District
Performs At: North Hollywood High School
Organization Type: Performing; Touring; Educational

1689
KITKA WOMEN'S VOCAL ENSEMBLE
1201 Martin Luther King Jr Way
Suite 103
Oakland, CA 94612
Phone: 510-444-0323
Fax: 510-444-1013
e-mail: info@kitka.org
Web Site: www.kitka.org
Officers:
President: Rodney Pasion
Treasurer: Chitra Arunasalam
VP: Norman Gelbart
Management:
Executive Director: Shira Cion, shira@kitka.org
Interim Music Director: Elizabeth Setzer, elizabeth@kitka.org
Ensemble Manager: Briget Boyle
Mission: An American women's vocal arts ensemble inspired by traditional songs and vocal techniques from Eastern Europe. Dedicated to developing new audiences for music rooted in Balkan, Slavic, and Caucasian women's vocal traditions, Kitka also strives to expand the boundaries of folk song as a living and evolving expressive art form.
Founded: 1979
Specialized Field: Choral; Ethnic Music; Classical; Contemporary
Status: Non-Profit, Professional
Paid Staff: 9
Volunteer Staff: 26
Paid Artists: 10
Budget: $330,000
Income Sources: National Endowment for the Arts; California Arts Council ARRA Program; City of Oakland Cultural Funding Program; Creative Capital's MAP Fund; William & Flora Hewlett Found
Affiliations: Knudsen Productions; Folk Alliance; Chorus America; Western Arts Alliance; Arts Presenters
Annual Attendance: 12,000-24,000
Facility Category: Concert Halls, Festivals

1690
OAKLAND OPERA THEATER
1734 Campbell Street
Oakland, CA 94607
Phone: 510-763-1146
e-mail: info@oaklandopera.org
Officers:
President: Jo Vincent Parks
Treasurer: Steve Snider
Management:
Artistic Director: Tom Dean
Director: Brian C Mulhern
Music Director: Brian C Mulhern
Executive Director: Lori Zook
Mission: Produce fully staged productions featuring artists and performers of color, geared to the pace of the 21st century and addressing issues of modern day urban life.
Specialized Field: Opera
Performs At: Oakland Metro

1691
OAKLAND YOUTH CHORUS
2501 Harrison Street
Oakland, CA 94612
Phone: 510-287-9700
Fax: 510-832-2211
e-mail: mail@oaklandyouthchorus.org
Web Site: www.oaklandyouthchorus.org
Management:
Executive Director: Sharon Dolan
Director: Rachelle Rogers Ard
Interim Managing Director: Jessica Manta Meyer
Mission: Providing multicultural youth from ages 14-21 with quality professionally-directed training; to advance the choral art form.
Utilizes: Artists-in-Residence; Collaborating Artists; Grant Writers; Guest Accompanists; Guest Artists; Guest Companies; Multimedia; Original Music Scores; Sign Language Translators; Soloists
Founded: 1974
Specialized Field: Opera; Choral; Youth Chorus; Ethnic Music; Classical; Contemporary
Status: Non-Profit, Professional
Paid Staff: 12
Non-paid Artists: 80
Budget: $6,000
Performs At: First Presbyterian Church; Calvin Simmons Theater
Organization Type: Performing; Touring; Sponsoring

1692
WILLIAM HALL CHORALE
1 University Drive
Orange, CA 92866
Phone: 714-997-6891
Fax: 714-997-6504
e-mail: whall@chapman.edu
Officers:
Founder: Dr. William D Hall
Management:
President: Robert Guyett
VP: David Masone
Artistic Director: William Hall
Founded: 1956
Specialized Field: Choral Orchestral Literature
Status: Non-Profit, Professional
Paid Staff: 3
Paid Artists: 24

1693
WEST BAY OPERA
221 Lambert Street
Palo Alto, CA 94306
Phone: 650-424-9999
Fax: 650-843-3904
Web Site: www.wbopera.org
Officers:
President: Yvonne Holcomb
VP: Riva Bacon
Secretary: Nan McKenna
Treasurer: Richard Bogart
Management:
General Director: Jose Luis Moscovich
Mission: To provide quality opera for the San Francisco Bay Area community and to nurture emerging and established artists.
Utilizes: Guest Artists; Guest Companies
Founded: 1955
Specialized Field: Musical Theatre; Opera; Classical
Status: Non-Profit, Professional
Paid Staff: 3
Performs At: Lucie Stern Theatre
Organization Type: Performing; Educational

1694
LIGHT OPERA THEATRE OF SACRAMENTO
PO Box 188641
Sacramento, CA 95818-8641
Phone: 916-978-5800
e-mail: info@lightoperasac.org
Officers:
Business Manager: Bill Bourne
Management:
Artistic Director: Mike Baad
Artistic Director: Debbie Baad
Founded: 1982
Specialized Field: Opera

1695
SACRAMENTO MASTER SINGERS
PO Box 417997
Sacramento, CA 95841
Phone: 916-788-7464
Fax: 916-784-1248
e-mail: rehchoir@aol.com
Web Site: www.mastersingers.org
Officers:
President: Kathy Ossmann
Management:
Director: Ralph Hughes
Managing Director: Julie Jenness
Founded: 1983

Specialized Field: Choral
Status: Non-Profit, Professional
Paid Staff: 4

1696
SACRAMENTO MEN'S CHORUS

PO Box 188726
Sacramento, CA 95818
Phone: 916-484-5789
e-mail: info@sacmenschorus.org
Web Site: www.sacmenschorus.org
Management:
President: Mark Ebenhoch
VP: Darryl Strohl
Chairman Of Board: Daniel Kiermaier
Artistic Director: Carl Naluai Jr
Founded: 1984
Specialized Field: Men's Chorus
Status: Non-Professional; Nonprofit
Paid Staff: 30
Performs At: First United Methodist
Organization Type: Performing; Touring

1697
SACRAMENTO OPERA COMPANY

PO Box 161027
Sacramento, CA 95816
Mailing Address: PO Box 161027, Sacramento, CA. 95816
Phone: 916-737-1000
Fax: 916-737-1032
e-mail: info@sacopera.org
Web Site: www.sacopera.org
Officers:
President: Michael E Chase
Vice President: Joe Hartzog
Secretary: Sue Miller
Treasurer: Sue Huscroft
Management:
Artistic Director: Timm Rolek
Executive Director: Rod Gideons
Managing Director: Rod Gideons
Managing Director: Rod Gideons
Mission: To produce outstanding regional opera, to develop & cultivate public interst in opera & its allied arts and to further music education.
Utilizes: Guest Artists; Guest Companies; Singers
Founded: 1947
Specialized Field: Opera
Status: Non-Profit, Professional
Paid Staff: 7
Paid Artists: 150
Budget: 1.6 M
Income Sources: Earned Revenue Donations
Performs At: Theater
Affiliations: Opera America
Annual Attendance: 18,000
Type of Stage: Proscenum
Seating Capacity: 2,380
Organization Type: Performing; Educational

1698
SAN DIEGO CHILDREN'S CHOIR

6635 Flanders Drive
Suite H
San Diego, CA 92121
Phone: 858-587-1087
Fax: 858-587-0071
e-mail: info@sdcchoir.org
Web Site: www.sdcchoir.org
Management:
Director: Ken Herman
President: Maureen Lochtefeld
Chairman: Steve Schroeter

Utilizes: Collaborations; Composers-in-Residence; Educators; Guest Musical Directors; High School Drama; Instructors; Multimedia; Music; Organization Contracts; Resident Artists; Sign Language Translators; Soloists
Founded: 1990
Specialized Field: Youth Chorus; Choral; Educational
Status: Non-Profit
Budget: $250,000
Affiliations: Chorus America; ACDA;
Annual Attendance: 10,000
Facility Category: Different Venues
Type of Stage: Traditional at all venues
Stage Dimensions: varies
Seating Capacity: 200-2100

1699
SAN DIEGO COMIC OPERA/LYRIC OPERA SAN DIEGO

2891 University Avenue
Suite 1
San Diego, CA 92104
Phone: 619-231-5714
Fax: 619-231-0662
Web Site: www.lyricoperasandiego.com
Officers:
President: Roberto Cueva
VP: Richard Brown
Secretary: Kristin Schuler Hint
Treasurer: William Mayleas
Management:
General Director: Leon Natker
Artistic Director: J Sherwood Montgomery
Mission: To offer quality musical theater and to provide creative employment for area professional artists.
Utilizes: Actors; AEA Actors; Choreographers; Collaborations; Commissioned Composers; Commissioned Music; Dancers; Designers; Grant Writers; Guest Accompanists; Guest Artists; Guest Companies; Guest Composers; Guest Conductors; Guest Writers; Guild Activities; Instructors; Local Artists; Lyricists; Multimedia; Music; Original Music Scores; Resident Professionals; Sign Language Translators; Singers; Soloists; Student Interns; Theatre Companies; Touring Companies
Founded: 1979
Specialized Field: Opera; English Operetta
Status: Non-Profit, Professional
Paid Staff: 6
Paid Artists: 75
Budget: $500,000
Income Sources: Ticket Sales; Membership Dues; Foundations; Grants
Performs At: Indoor Casa del Prado Theater
Affiliations: San Diego Performing Arts League; Opera America; San Diego Arts & Culture Coalition; Downtown Partnership
Annual Attendance: 15,000
Facility Category: Rental
Seating Capacity: 550
Organization Type: Performing; Touring; Resident; Educational

1700
SAN DIEGO MEN'S CHORUS

3749 Park Boulevard
PO Box 33825
San Diego, CA 92163
Phone: 619-296-7664
Fax: 619-296-3471
e-mail: webmaster@sdmc.org
Web Site: www.sdmc.org
Officers:
President: Jonathon N Myatttt

VP: Todd D Ebert
Treasurer: Jamie Royak
Secretary: Tony Hammond
Management:
President: Todd D Ebert
VP: Anthony Hammond
Artistic Director: Christopher Allen
Mission: To foster unity and a love of music through our performances.
Utilizes: Choreographers; Collaborating Artists; Commissioned Composers; Commissioned Music; Composers; Contract Orchestras; Guest Accompanists; Guest Artists; Guest Choreographers; Guest Musical Directors; Guest Musicians; Instructors; Multi Collaborations; Paid Performers; Selected Students; Singers
Founded: 1985
Specialized Field: Men's Chorus
Status: Non-Professional; Nonprofit
Paid Staff: 2
Volunteer Staff: 130
Budget: $150,000
Income Sources: Membership Dues; Ticket Sales; Individual & Business Donations
Performs At: First Unitarian Universalist Church
Affiliations: GALA Choruses
Annual Attendance: 5,000
Seating Capacity: 541
Organization Type: Performing; Touring
Comments: Donates $4,000 annually to local HIV/AIDS organizations

1701
SAN DIEGO OPERA

1200 3rd Avenue
18th Floor, Civic Center Plaza
San Diego, CA 92101-4112
Phone: 619-232-7636
Fax: 619-231-6915
e-mail: sdostaff@sdopera.com
Web Site: www.sdopera.com
Officers:
President: William R Stensrud
Executive VP: Robert B Horsman
VP Finance: L Renee Comeau
VP Special Projects: James L. Fitzpatrick
VP Marketing/Membership: Lisa Briggs
VP Individual Gifts: Iris Lynn Strauss
Secretary: James H. Amos Jr.
Management:
General Director: Ian D Campbell
Director Strategic Planning: Ann S Campbell
Resident Conductor: Karen Keltner
Resident Conductor: Karen Keltner
Director Education/Outreach: Nicolas M Reveles
Director Marketing/Public Relations: Todd Schultz
Director Production: Ronald G Allen
Director Finance: John Sleeper
Founded: 1965
Specialized Field: Opera
Status: For-Profit, Non-Professional
Paid Staff: 35
Performs At: Civic Theatre

1702
STARLIGHT MUSICAL THEATRE

1549 El Padro - Balboa Park
PO Box 3519
San Diego, CA 92101
Phone: 619-544-7800
Fax: 619-544-0496
Management:
Executive Director: CE Bud Farnks

Producing Artistic Director: Don Ward
Producing Artistic Director: Bonnie Ward
Mission: The preservation and promotion of the art form of musical theatre.
Utilizes: Guest Artists; Guest Companies; Singers
Founded: 1946
Specialized Field: Light Opera; Musical Theatre
Status: Professional; Nonprofit
Performs At: Starlight Bowl; Civic Theatre; Spreckles Theatre
Organization Type: Performing; Educational

1703
MEROLA OPERA PROGRAM
301 Van Ness Avenue
San Francisco, CA 94102
Phone: 415-565-6427
Fax: 415-255-6774
e-mail: mop@sfopera.com
Web Site: www.sfopera.com/merola
Officers:
President: Karl O. Mills
Vice President/Treasurer: Doreen Woo Ho
President: Rusty Rolland
Mission: Discovering and developing professional opera singers; sponsoring the Merola Opera Program at the San Francisco Opera and the San Francisco Opera Center auditions.
Utilizes: Guest Artists; Guest Companies; Singers
Founded: 1923
Specialized Field: Grand Opera; Lyric Opera
Status: Nonprofit
Income Sources: Central Opera Service
Performs At: War Memorial Opera House
Rental Contact: Bill Bowles
Organization Type: Educational; Sponsoring

1704
POCKET OPERA
469 Bryant Street
San Francisco, CA 94107
Phone: 415-972-8930
Fax: 415-348-0931
e-mail: info@pocketopera.org
Web Site: www.pocketopera.org
Officers:
President: Jim Erhort
Management:
Artistic Director: Donald Pippin
Executive Director: Dianna Shuster
Mission: To present and promote opera in an accessible, affordable and engaging way by using English settings, minimal props and orchestrations
Utilizes: Choreographers; Guest Designers; Instructors; Organization Contracts; Original Music Scores; Sign Language Translators
Founded: 1978
Specialized Field: Grand Opera; Lyric Opera; Light Opera; Operetta
Status: Professional, Nonprofit
Paid Staff: 5
Volunteer Staff: 2
Paid Artists: 60
Budget: $350,000
Income Sources: Central Opera Service
Performs At: Marines Memorial Theatre In San Francisco; Hillside Club In Berkeley
Organization Type: Performing; Touring; Resident

1705
SAN FRANCISCO BACH CHOIR
3145 Geary Boulevard
PMB 210
San Francisco, CA 94118-3300
Phone: 415-441-4942
Fax: 415-922-2819
e-mail: singet@flash.net
Officers:
Assistant Conductor and Librarian: Joseph Gregorio
Management:
Concert Master: Cynthia Roberts
Orchestra Manager: John Thiessen
Specialized Field: Choral

1706
SAN FRANCISCO CHORAL ARTISTS
PMB 344, 601 Van Ness Avenue
Suite E
San Francisco, CA 94102
Phone: 415-979-5779
e-mail: info@sfca.org
Web Site: www.sfca.org
Officers:
President: John A. Kelley
Management:
Artistic Director: Magen Solomon, info@sfca.org
Assistant Conductor: Tina Harrington, info@sfca.org
Executive Director: Natalie Churchill, info@sfca.org
Publicity: Wieneke Gorter
Mission: Specializing in the music of living compoisers, present both contemporary compositions and finest choral works of the last 600 years, delighting audiences, composers, and singers alike.
Utilizes: Arrangers; Collaborating Artists; Collaborations; Commissioned Composers; Commissioned Music; Community Talent; Composers-in-Residence; Guest Accompanists; Guest Companies; Guest Directors; Guest Instructors; Guest Musical Directors; Instructors; Local Artists; Local Artists & Directors; Multimedia; Music; Original Music Scores; Sign Language Translators; Singers; Students
Founded: 1984
Specialized Field: Choral
Status: Professional; Nonprofit
Budget: $2,300,000
Income Sources: Earned and donated revenue sources
Performs At: Primarily acoustically-satisfying church venues such as St. Mark's Lutheran, SF; St. Mark's Episcopal;Marin, CA
Affiliations: Composer's Inc.; Chorus America, American Chorus Director's Association; Various high schools and universities In the San Francisco Bay Area
Organization Type: Performing; Touring; Resident; Educational

1707
SAN FRANCISCO CHORAL ARTISTS
601 Van Ness Avenue
Suite E 3344
San Francisco, CA 94102
Phone: 415-979-5779
e-mail: info@sfca.org
Web Site: www.sfca.org
Officers:
President: Maureen Stone
Management:
Music Director: Claire Giovannetti
Associate Conductor: Doug Wyatt
Development Manager: Teresa Byrne
Publicity: Audrey Wong
Mission: To develop and maintain an outstanding performing choral ensemble dedicated to the art of modern classical music.
Specialized Field: Choral

Status: Professional; Nonprofit
Performs At: Calvary Presbyterian Church; St. Mark's Episcopal
Organization Type: Performing

1708
SAN FRANCISCO GIRLS CHORUS
44 Paige Street
Suite 200
San Francisco, CA 94102
Phone: 415-863-1752
Fax: 415-934-0302
e-mail: info@sfgirlschorus.org
Web Site: www.sfgirlschorus.org
Officers:
Board President: Douglas M Ireland
Management:
Artistic Director: Susan McMane
Executive Director: Melanie Smith
Communications Manager: Naho Yoshida
Mission: To create outstanding performances featuring the unique and compelling sound of young women's voices through an exemplary music education program.
Founded: 1978
Specialized Field: Choral; Youth Chorus
Status: Non-Profit, Non-Professional
Budget: $2,000,000
Income Sources: Earned Income, Institutional Giving And Individual Giving.

1709
SAN FRANCISCO GIRLS CHORUS AND ASSOCIATION
44 Page Street
Suite 200
San Francisco, CA 94102-5986
Phone: 415-863-1752
Fax: 415-934-0302
e-mail: info@sfgirlschorus.org
Web Site: www.sfgirlschorus.org
Management:
Artistic Director: Susan McMane
Executive Director: Melanie Smith
Director Marketing/Communication: Jay Krohnengold
Utilizes: Collaborating Artists; Commissioned Music; Educators; Five Seasonal Concerts; Grant Writers; Guest Artists; Guest Companies; Guest Instructors; Guest Lecturers; Multimedia; Music; Original Music Scores; Sign Language Translators; Soloists
Specialized Field: Youth Chorus

1710
SAN FRANCISCO OPERA CENTER
San Francisco Opera
301 Van Ness Avenue
San Francisco, CA 94102
Phone: 415-861-4008
Fax: 415-626-1729
e-mail: mop@sfopera.com
Web Site: www.sfopera.com
Officers:
Chairman: Franklin P Johnson, Jr
President of the Association: William W Godward
VP: Francis W Chen
VP: Howard H. Leach
VP: Leslie P. Hume
VP/Treasurer: Doreen Woo Ho
Secretary: Robert E. Sullivan
Chairman Emeritus: Reid W. Dennis
Management:
General Director: Pamela Rosenberg
Music Director: Donald Runnicle
Executive Director: Keithy Cerny

Production Director: Patrick Markle
Mission: To enhance cultural life; to present masterworks of opera with the San Fransico Opera Orchestra and outstanding casts; to offer training and outreach; to nurture new audiences and talent.
Utilizes: Actors; Artists-in-Residence; Choreographers; Collaborating Artists; Collaborations; Commissioned Composers; Commissioned Music; Composers-in-Residence; Curators; Dance Companies; Dancers; Designers; Educators; Fine Artists; Five Seasonal Concerts; Grant Writers; Guest Accompanists; Guest Artists; Guest Companies; Guest Composers; Guest Conductors; Guest Designers; Guest Ensembles; Guest Instructors; Guest Lecturers; Guest Musical Directors; Guest Musicians; Guest Soloists; Guild Activities; High School Drama; Instructors; Local Artists; Local Unknown Artists; Lyricists; Multi Collaborations; Multimedia; Music; New Productions; Organization Contracts; Original Music Scores; Performance Artists; Poets; Resident Professionals; Selected Students; Sign Language Translators; Singers; Soloists; Student Interns; Theatre Companies; Touring Companies; Visual Arts
Founded: 1932
Specialized Field: Grand Opera; Lyric Opera; Light Opera; Operetta
Status: Professional; Nonprofit
Budget: 51 Million
Income Sources: Private and Corporate Donations; Instituional Gifts; Ticket Sales; Government Assistance
Performs At: War Memorial Opera House

1711
SAN FRANCISCO OPERA CENTER

War Memorial Opera House
301 Van Ness Avenue
San Francisco, CA 94102
Phone: 415-861-4008
Fax: 415-255-6774
e-mail: chancock@sfopera.com
Web Site: www.sfopera.com
Management:
    Director: Sheri Greenwald
    Administrative Director: Curt Hancock
Mission: To utilize the various affiliate components of the San Francisco Opera Association in a comprehensive and unique professional training program for artists.
Utilizes: Five Seasonal Concerts; Guest Artists; Guest Companies; Singers
Founded: 1982
Specialized Field: Grand Opera; Lyric Opera; Light Opera; Operetta
Status: Professional; Nonprofit
Performs At: Cowell Theater; Herbst Thater; Old First Chruch; Yerba Buena Theater; Stern Grove
Rental Contact: Bill Bowles
Organization Type: Performing; Touring; Resident; Educational; Sponsoring

1712
SAN FRANCISCO SYMPHONY CHORUS

San Francisco Symphony
Pouise M. Davies Symphony Hall
San Francisco, CA 94102
Phone: 415-552-8000
Fax: 415-431-6857
Web Site: www.sfsymphony.org
Officers:
    President: Nancy H Bechtle
    VP: John D Goldman
    VP: Robert D Glynn, Jr
    VP: Eff W. Martin
    Secretary: Robert R. Tufts

Management:
    Chorus Director: Vance George
    Chorus Administrator: Gregory Boals
Mission: Recognition as a world-class chorus; performance of a wide repertoire of fine music under leading conductors.
Founded: 1973
Specialized Field: Choral
Status: Professional; Nonprofit
Performs At: Louise M. Davies Symphony Hall
Organization Type: Performing

1713
SAN FRANCISCO OPERA

301 Van Ness Avenue
San Francisco, CA 94102
Phone: 415-861-4008
Fax: 415-626-1729
e-mail: webmaster@sfopera.com
Officers:
    Executive Director: Keith Cerny
    Director of Artistic and Music Admi: Shane Gasbarra
Management:
    General Director: David Gockley
    Music Director/Principal Conductor: Donald Runnicles
    Production Director: Patrick Markle
    Artistic Administrator: Brad Trexell
Founded: 1923
Specialized Field: Opera
Rental Contact: Bill Bowles

1714
WESTERN OPERA THEATER

San Francisco Opera
301 Van Ness Avenue
San Francisco, CA 94102-4509
Phone: 415-861-4008
Fax: 415-255-6774
e-mail: webmaster@sfopera.com
Management:
    Director: Richard Harrell
    Tour Manager: William Bowles
Utilizes: Artists-in-Residence; Grant Writers; Guest Composers; Guest Designers; Guest Ensembles; Guest Lecturers; Guest Musical Directors; Guest Musicians; Guest Soloists; High School Drama; Instructors; Multimedia; Music; Original Music Scores; Poets; Resident Professionals; Sign Language Translators; Singers; Soloists; Theatre Companies
Specialized Field: Opera; Musical Theatre
Rental Contact: Bill Bowles

1715
AMERICAN MUSICAL THEATRE OF SAN JOSE

1717 Technology Drive
San Jose, CA 95110
Phone: 408-453-7100
Fax: 408-453-7123
Toll-free: 888-455-7469
e-mail: amtsj@amtsj.org
Web Site: www.amtsj.org
Officers:
    President: Michael Miller
    Chairman: Jim Louch
    Vice Chairman: John Michael Sobrato
Management:
    Executive Producer: Michael Miller
    CFO: Robert Nazarenus
    Production Director: Bob Bones
Mission: To create the highest quality musical theatre that inspires the spirit of the community.

Utilizes: Actors; AEA Actors; Choreographers; Commissioned Music; Dancers; Designers; Five Seasonal Concerts; Guest Artists; Guest Companies; Guest Conductors; Guild Activities; Local Artists; Local Unknown Artists; Multimedia; Music; Performance Artists; Resident Professionals; Selected Students; Sign Language Translators; Soloists; Student Interns; Theatre Companies
Founded: 1934
Specialized Field: Musical Theatre
Status: Non-Profit, Professional
Paid Staff: 55
Volunteer Staff: 80
Paid Artists: 40
Non-paid Artists: 10
Season: August - September
Performs At: San Jose Center for the Performing Arts
Annual Attendance: 200,000
Seating Capacity: 2,600

1716
OPERA SAN JOSE

2149 Paragon Drive
San Jose, CA 95131
Phone: 408-437-4450
Fax: 408-437-4455
e-mail: info@operasj.org
Web Site: www.operasj.org
Officers:
    President: Frank Veloz
    VP/Chair of Finance: Sharon McCorkle
    Secretary: Jack Schneider
Management:
    Executive Director: Irene Dalis
    Artistic Director: Matt Siek
    Managing Director: Lynda Osborne
    Music Director: David Rohrbaugh
    Director/Marketing: Larry Hancock
    Director Communications: Christine Spielberger
    Corporate Relations Manager: Glen Won
Mission: To maintain and enhance a professional opera company of artistic excellence; to provide principally in opera of all periods and secondarily in operetta; to provide opera singers with professional development and performance opportunities; to develop, educate and entertain.
Utilizes: Artists-in-Residence; Commissioned Composers; Commissioned Music; Grant Writers; Guest Artists; Guest Companies; Guest Conductors; Guest Musical Directors; High School Drama; Local Artists; Original Music Scores; Resident Professionals; Sign Language Translators; Singers; Student Interns
Founded: 1984
Specialized Field: Grand Opera; Musical Theatre; Classical
Status: Non-Profit, Professional
Paid Staff: 18
Volunteer Staff: 155
Paid Artists: 224
Budget: $2,765,000
Performs At: Montgomery Theater
Seating Capacity: 519
Organization Type: Performing; Touring; Educational; Sponsoring

1717
OPERA PACIFIC

600 W Warner Avenue
Santa Ana, CA 92707
Phone: 714-546-6000
Fax: 714-546-6077
Toll-free: 800-346-7372
e-mail: flitteral@operapacific.org
Web Site: www.operapacific.org

Officers:
Chairman: Patrick Seaver
Management:
Executive Director: Martin G Hubbard
Artistic Director: John Demain
Producing Director/Artistic Advisor: Mitchell Krieger
Marketing/Development Director: Adrian Stevens
Music Administrator/Chorusmaster: Henri Venanzi
Director Finance: Bree Noble
Mission: To present a broad repertoire of opera and American musicals with the highest artistic standards; to provide opportunities for emerging opera talent; to reach out to area communities with educational and performance opportunities.
Utilizes: Guest Artists; Guest Companies; Singers
Founded: 1986
Specialized Field: Grand Opera; Light Opera; Lyric Opera; Musical Theatre; Choral; Youth Chorus; Classical
Status: Non-Profit, Professional
Performs At: Orange County Performing Arts Center
Affiliations: Opera America
Organization Type: Performing; Touring; Resident; Educational

1718
PACIFIC CHORALE

3621 S Harbor Boulevard
Suite 220
Santa Ana, CA 92704
Phone: 714-662-2345
Fax: 714-662-2395
e-mail: contactus@pacificchorale.org
Web Site: www.pacificchorale.org
Officers:
President/CEO: Kelly Ruggirello
Management:
Artistic Director: John Alexander
Operations Director: Brian Sullivan
Marketing Director: Ryan McSweeney
General Manager: Dana Ramos
Mission: Committed to the highest quality performance and recording of existing choral masterworks and to the creation, performance and recording of future masterworks. We will enrich and educate our current audience as well as singers and audiences of the future.
Utilizes: Collaborations; Commissioned Composers; Composers-in-Residence; Fine Artists; Guest Accompanists; Guest Choreographers; Guest Musical Directors; Guest Musicians; Guest Writers; Multimedia; Original Music Scores; Sign Language Translators
Founded: 1968
Specialized Field: Choral
Status: Non-Profit, Professional
Paid Staff: 7
Paid Artists: 40
Non-paid Artists: 130
Budget: $1.2 million
Income Sources: Ticket revenue, Contributions
Performs At: Orange County Performing Arts Center
Affiliations: Chorus America, ACDA
Annual Attendance: 10,000+
Organization Type: Performing; Touring; Educational

1719
OPERA SANTA BARBARA

1330 State Street
Suite 209
Santa Barbara, CA 93101
Phone: 805-898-3890
Fax: 805-898-3892
e-mail: info@operasb.com
Web Site: www.operasb.com
Officers:
President: Duncan Mellichamp
VP: Sarah Chrisman
Secretary: Ida Rickborn
Treasurer: Dan Reicker
Management:
Company Manager: Brian Hotchkin, brian@operasb.com
Artistic Director: Jose Maria Condemi
General Director: Steven Sharpe
Mission: Opera Santa Barbara contributes to the cultural enrichment of our audiences by presenting exciting high-quality productions and community programs that celebrate the breadth and beauty of opera. Opera Santa Barbara aspires to be a destination opera company, producing a diverse repertoire of traditional and contemporary operas that engage and excite a broad audience.
Utilizes: Dancers; Grant Writers; Guest Artists; Guest Companies; Guest Composers; Guest Conductors; Guest Designers; Guest Musical Directors; Guest Musicians; High School Drama; Local Artists & Directors; Multimedia; Music; Sign Language Translators; Visual Designers
Founded: 1994
Specialized Field: Opera
Status: Non-Profit, Professional
Paid Staff: 6
Volunteer Staff: 75
Paid Artists: 500
Performs At: Granada; Lobero Theater

1720
GOLDEN GATE OPERA

3030 Bridgeway
(Sausalito)
Sausalito, CA 94965
Phone: 415-339-9546
Fax: 415-339-9547
e-mail: rw-b@sbcglobal.net
Officers:
Technical Director: Rod Mortensen
Development Director: Rachel Ward
Community Outreach: Maria Chang-Calderon
Management:
Artistic Director/General Manager: Roberta Becker
Music Director/Conductor: Geoggrey Gallegos
Mission: A cooperative of professional musicians, singers and technicians dedicated to producing professional, high-quality and affordable opera.
Founded: 1996
Specialized Field: Opera
Season: September-May
Performs At: Marin Civic Center Showcase Theatre; Marin Center Veteran's Memorail Auditorium; Legion of Honor Florence Gould Theatre

1721
ROGER WAGNER CHORALE

25744 Hood Way
Stevenson Ranch
Stevenson Ranch, CA 91381
Phone: 661-287-3864
Fax: 661-287-3865
e-mail: info@rogerwagnerchorale.com
Management:
Director of Music: Jeannine Wagner
Specialized Field: Choral

1722
LA MARCA AMERICAN VARIETY CHORUS SINGERS

2655 W 230th Place
Torrance, CA 90505
Phone: 310-325-8708
Fax: 310-325-8708
e-mail: lamarcamusic@earthlink.com
Web Site: www.getlessonsnow.lamarcamusic
Management:
President: Priscilla Lamarca-Kandel
Mission: To educate and entertain
Utilizes: Musical Directors; Singers
Founded: 1974
Specialized Field: Southern California
Status: Non-Profit, Professional
Paid Staff: 2
Income Sources: International Federation of Festival Organizations
Organization Type: Performing; Touring; Resident; Educational

1723
DIABLO LIGHT OPERA COMPANY

PO Box 5034
Walnut Creek, CA 94596
Phone: 925-944-1565
Fax: 925-944-1510
e-mail: dloc@dloc.org
Web Site: www.dloc.org
Officers:
President: Bobbi Bach
Management:
Artistic Advisor: Rhoda Klitsner
Producer: Grete Egan
Mission: Dedicated to enriching our community by producing quality musicals and light opera and by providing educational opportunities in the arts.
Utilizes: Five Seasonal Concerts; Guest Artists; Guest Companies; Singers
Founded: 1960
Specialized Field: Light Opera; Operetta; Musical Theatre
Status: Non-Professional; Nonprofit
Paid Staff: 50
Performs At: Regional Center for the Arts
Organization Type: Performing; Educational

1724
FESTIVAL OPERA

675 Ygnacio Valley
#B125
Walnut Creek, CA 94596
Phone: 925-944-9610
Fax: 925-944-1078
e-mail: hsheaff@festivalopera.com
Web Site: www.festivalopera.com
Officers:
Board Chair: Roberta Emerson
Executive Director: Helen Sheaff
Management:
Artistic Director: Michael Morgan
Founded: 1991
Specialized Field: Grand Opera
Status: Non-Profit, Professional
Paid Staff: 2
Performs At: Hofmann Theater; Regional Center for the Arts

1725
THE FESTIVAL OPERA ASSOCIATION INC
675 Ygnacio Valley Road
Suite B215
Walnut Creek, CA 94596
Phone: 925-944-9610
Fax: 925-944-1078
e-mail: info@festivalopera.com
Web Site: www.festivalopera.com
Management:
Executive Director: Helen C Sheaff
Artistic/Music Director: Michael Morgan
Production Director: Frederic O Boulay
Founded: 1991
Specialized Field: Opera
Status: Non-Profit, Professional
Paid Staff: 3
Paid Artists: 150
Performs At: Redlands Bowl

1726
ANGELES CHORALE
20929 Ventura Boulevard
Suite 47-120
Woodland Hills, CA 91364
Phone: 818-591-1735
Fax: 818-701-7703
Web Site: www.angeleschorale.org
Officers:
Chair: Werner Keller
President: Mary Whittemore
Management:
Executive Director: Rae MacDonald
Mission: To reach the community of Los Angeles with high quality choral concerts while developing the talent of the performing musicians.
Utilizes: Collaborations; Guest Musical Directors; Guest Musicians; Instructors; Sign Language Translators
Founded: 1975
Specialized Field: Choral
Status: Non-Profit, Professional
Paid Staff: 1
Paid Artists: 20
Non-paid Artists: 125
Budget: $180,000
Income Sources: Tickets; Donations; Grants
Performs At: Concert hall
Annual Attendance: 7,000
Facility Category: Royce Hall, UCLA + First United Methodist Church-Pasadena
Seating Capacity: 1,800
Year Built: 1924
Cost: $3,000

Colorado

1727
ASPEN OPERA THEATER CENTER
2 Music School Road
Aspen, CO 81611
Phone: 970-925-3254
Fax: 970-925-3802
e-mail: festival@aspenmusic.org
Web Site: www.aspenmusicfestival.com
Officers:
President/CEO: Alan Fletcher
Management:
Managing Director: James Berdahl
Music Director: David Zinman
Founded: 1949

Specialized Field: Grand Opera; Light Opera; Lyric Opera; Musical Theatre; Choral; Ethnic Music; Classical; Contemporary
Status: Non-Profit, Professional
Paid Staff: 35
Performs At: Wheeler Opera House
Annual Attendance: 5000
Facility Category: Opera House
Type of Stage: Proscenium
Stage Dimensions: 27 x 24
Seating Capacity: 490
Year Built: 1889
Year Remodeled: 1984

1728
WHEELER OPERA HOUSE
320 E Hyman Avenue
Aspen, CO 81611
Phone: 970-920-5770
Fax: 970-920-5780
e-mail: heather.larson@ci.aspen.co.us
Web Site: www.wheeleroperahouse.com
Management:
Executive Director: Gram Slaton
Operations Manager: Heather Larson
Utilizes: Singers
Founded: 1889
Specialized Field: Opera; Folk Music
Status: Non-Profit; Professional
Performs At: Proc Theatre
Facility Category: Theatre
Type of Stage: Procenium
Stage Dimensions: 28'x28'
Seating Capacity: 503
Year Built: 1984
Year Remodeled: 2006
Rental Contact: Operations Manager Heather Larson
Organization Type: Sponsoring

1729
CHAMBER SINGERS OF THE COLORADO SPRINGS CHORALE
P.O. Box 2304
Colorado Springs, CO 80901
Phone: 719-634-3737
Fax: 719-473-0077
e-mail: csc@cschorale.org
Web Site: www.cschorale.org
Management:
Executive Director: Mark Dempsey, mark@cschorale.org
Conductor: Kimberly Schultz
Administrative Assistant: Jackie Foorman
Mission: A representative ensemble of the Colorado Springs Chorale, performing a repertoire of diverse musical styles, performing in schools, service clubs, retirement homes and businesses, and private and public functions.
Founded: 2010
Specialized Field: Lyric Opera; Musical Theatre; Choral; Ethnic Music; Classical; Contemporary; Religious
Status: Non-Profit, Non-Professional
Paid Staff: 2
Volunteer Staff: 14
Paid Artists: 1
Organization Type: Performing; Resident; Educational

1730
COLORADO SPRINGS CHORALE
16 E Platte, Ste. 204A
PO Box 2304
Colorado Springs, CO 80901

Phone: 719-634-3737
Fax: 719-473-0077
e-mail: csc@cschorale.org
Web Site: www.cschorale.org
Officers:
Chairman: Judith Kramer
Vice Chairman: Kenneth Myers
Secretary: Linda Cummings
Treasurer: Diane Olvieri
Management:
Executive Director: Mark Dempsey, mark@cschorale.org
Artistic Director/Conductor: Donald P Jenkins, don@cschorale.org
Accompanist & Assistant Conductor: Daniel S. Brink, dbrink@coloradocollege.edu
Administrative Assistant: Jackie Foorman
Mission: To serve the Pikes Peak region by celebrating the human voice in song and its power to rejoice, console, educate, enrich, unite and inspire
Founded: 1956
Specialized Field: Choral
Status: Non-Profit, Non-Professional
Paid Staff: 4
Non-paid Artists: 150
Budget: $216,000
Income Sources: Grants; Donations; Ticket Sales
Performs At: Pikes Peak Center
Seating Capacity: 1885
Organization Type: Performing; Resident

1731
CENTRAL CITY OPERA HOUSE ASSOCIATION
400 S Colorado Boulevard
Suite 530
Denver, CO 80246
Phone: 303-292-6500
Fax: 303-292-4958
Toll-free: 800-851-8175
e-mail: admin@centralcityopera.org
Web Site: www.centralcityopera.org
Management:
General/Artistic Director: Pelham G Pearce
Music Director: John Baril
Artistic Director Emeritus: John Moriarty
Mission: Central City Opera is the nations fifth oldest opera company. The national summer opera festival draws patrons from 48 states, presenting works of artistic excellence from standard and contemporary repertoire.
Utilizes: Sign Language Translators
Founded: 1932
Specialized Field: Opera
Status: Non-Profit, Professional
Paid Staff: 17
Paid Artists: 100
Budget: $4.2 million
Income Sources: Scientifrand Cultural Facilities District
Season: July - August
Performs At: Central City (Festival Site)
Affiliations: Opera America League of Historic-America Theatres
Annual Attendance: 27,000
Facility Category: Opera House
Type of Stage: Proscenium
Stage Dimensions: 25x34x171/2
Seating Capacity: 552
Year Built: 1878
Cost: $23,000 (built)

1732
COLORADO CHILDREN'S CHORALE
2420 W 26th Avenue
Suite 350 D
Denver, CO 80211
Phone: 303-892-5600
Fax: 303-892-0828
e-mail: mail@childrenschorale.org
Web Site: www.childrenschorale.org
Officers:
    President: Fritz Trask
    Vice President: Jim Thomas
Management:
    Artistic Director: Deborah DeSantis
Mission: Providing the nation with a performing-arts group that features children and strives for excellence.
Utilizes: Guest Artists
Founded: 1974
Specialized Field: Youth Chorus; Choral; Classical; Folk Music; Ethnic Music; Musical Theatre
Status: Non-Profit, Non-Professional
Paid Staff: 14
Organization Type: Performing; Touring; Educational

1733
OPERA COLORADO
695 S Colorado Boulevard
Suite 20
Denver, CO 80246
Phone: 303-778-1500
Fax: 303-778-6533
e-mail: info@operacolorado.org
Web Site: www.operacolorado.org
Officers:
    Chairman: Jack Finlaw
Management:
    Artistic Director: James Robinson
    General Director: Peter Russell
    Director Marketing: Rex Fuller
    Development Director: Susan Evans
Mission: To develope a better appreciation and understanding of opera throughout the community; to produce the highest quality performances of grand operas in their original languages with projected English supertitles translation.
Utilizes: Actors; Artists-in-Residence; Choreographers; Collaborations; Dancers; Designers; Five Seasonal Concerts; Grant Writers; Guest Accompanists; Guest Artists; Guest Composers; Guest Conductors; Guest Designers; Guest Ensembles; Guest Lecturers; Guest Musical Directors; Guest Musicians; Guest Writers; High School Drama; Instructors; Lyricists; Multimedia; Original Music Scores; Resident Professionals; Selected Students; Sign Language Translators; Student Interns; Visual Arts
Founded: 1981
Specialized Field: Grand Opera
Status: Professional; Nonprofit
Paid Staff: 75
Budget: $2,000,000-5,000,000
Income Sources: Opera America
Rental Contact: Gordon Robertson
Organization Type: Performing; Resident; Educational

1734
DURANGO CHORAL SOCIETY
PO Box 1043
Durango, CO 81302
Mailing Address: PO Box Durango, CO 81302
Phone: 970-247-7251
Fax: 970-382-6910
e-mail: mack_1@fortlewis.edu
Web Site: www.durangochoralsociety.com

Officers:
    President: Gene M Bradley
    Executive Vice-President: Bob Westerwick
    VP Development: Wynn Berven
    Treasurer: Bob Dolphin
    Assistant Treasurer: Sarah Jones
    Secretary: Trisha Burbach
Management:
    President: Wendy Gilliis
    Executive VP: Jacque Hendrick
    Artistic Director: Linda Mack
    Director: Richard Cumming
Mission: To provide fine choral and orchestral performances for the four-corners area.
Utilizes: Singers
Founded: 1961
Specialized Field: Choral
Status: Non-Profit
Paid Staff: 45
Income Sources: American Choral Directors Association
Organization Type: Performing; Touring; Resident; Educational; Sponsoring

1735
LARIMER CHORALE
PO Box 884
Fort Collins, CO 80522
Phone: 970-416-9348
Fax: 970-491-4142
e-mail: lc@fortnet.org
Officers:
    Executive Director: Vicki Fogel Mykles
    Board President: David Lindstron
    Treasurer: Andrew Hinds
Management:
    Artistic Director: Dr Michael T Krueger
    Assistant Conductor: Jean Johnson
Mission: To bring classical choral music to Northern Colorado by singing choral music of the masters.
Utilizes: Actors; Artists-in-Residence; Collaborating Artists; Collaborations; Dance Companies; Dancers; Designers; Educators; Grant Writers; Guest Companies; Guest Composers; Guest Directors; Guest Instructors; Guest Lecturers; Guest Musical Directors; Guest Musicians; Instructors; Local Artists; Lyricists; Multi Collaborations; Multimedia; Organization Contracts; Original Music Scores; Playwrights; Sign Language Translators
Founded: 1977
Specialized Field: Choral
Status: Non-Profit
Paid Staff: 5
Volunteer Staff: 30
Paid Artists: 8
Non-paid Artists: 105
Budget: $80,000+
Income Sources: Audiences, grants, fundraising
Performs At: Lincoln Center
Annual Attendance: 4,000+
Facility Category: Large community auditorium building, 2 stages
Type of Stage: Large for 200 singers/50 symphony
Seating Capacity: 1180, smaller stage 350
Year Built: 1978

1736
OPERA FORT COLLINS
PO Box 503
Fort Collins, CO 80522
Phone: 970-482-0220
e-mail: opera@msn.com
Officers:
    Executive Director: Kelin Queen

    President: Steven Lovaas
Management:
    Artistic Director: Todd Queen
    Music Director: Wes Kenny
Founded: 1991
Specialized Field: Opera
Status: Non-Profit

1737
AURORA SINGERS
Palo Alto Universalist Church
505 E Charleston Road
Palo Alto, CO 94306
Phone: 650-323-6912
e-mail: mchethik@sbcglobal.net
Web Site: www.aurorasingers.net
Officers:
    President: Millie Chethik
Management:
    Director: Dawn Reyen
Mission: To bring quality music to listeners in convalescent homes or senior centers who might otherwise not be able to attend traditional live music concerts.
Utilizes: Guest Companies
Founded: 1988
Specialized Field: Choral
Status: Non-Profit
Paid Staff: 50
Income Sources: City of Aurora
Performs At: Aurora Fox Arts Center
Organization Type: Performing; Resident

Connecticut

1738
NEW ENGLAND LYRIC OPERETTA
PO Box 1007
Darien, CT 06820
Phone: 203-655-0566
Fax: 203-655-8066
Officers:
    Chairman: Stephen Pierson
Management:
    President: William H Edgerton
Mission: Performing the entire range of American and European operetta.
Utilizes: Designers; Guest Musicians; Multimedia; Original Music Scores; Resident Artists; Resident Professionals; Sign Language Translators
Founded: 1986
Specialized Field: Light Opera; Musical Theatre
Status: Non-Profit, Professional
Performs At: Rich Forum; Stauford Center for the Arts
Organization Type: Performing; Resident

1739
FAIRFIELD COUNTY CHORALE
61 Unguowa Road
Fairfield, CT 06824
Phone: 203-254-1333
Fax: 203-319-8273
e-mail: fairfieldcountyc@aol.com
Web Site: www.fairfieldcountychorale.org
Officers:
    President: Lucinda Kuuth
Management:
    President: Mary Filipelli
    Executive Director: John Parkinson
    Artistic Director: Johannes Somary

Mission: To perform classical choral music with professional orchestra and soloists, in the manner in which the composer intended it. To present this to people living in Fairfield County, with the hope of enriching their musical lives.
Utilizes: Collaborations; Guest Accompanists; Guest Musicians; Multimedia; Music; Original Music Scores; Sign Language Translators; Singers
Founded: 1965
Specialized Field: Choral; Classical; Contemporary; Religious
Status: Non-Profit, Non-Professional
Paid Staff: 3
Paid Artists: 120
Budget: $80,000
Income Sources: Tickets; Advertisement Sales; Donations; Fund Raising
Performs At: Norwalk Concert Hall
Annual Attendance: 2,000
Facility Category: Concert Hall
Seating Capacity: 1,064
Rental Contact: City of Norwalk

1740
GREENWICH CHORAL SOCIETY
PO Box 5
Greenwich, CT 06836
Phone: 203-622-5136
Fax: 203-325-8762
Management:
    Music Director/Conductor: Paul F Mueller
    Executive Director: Greg Wold
Mission: To offer audiences a wide variety of choral music for their enjoyment and education.
Founded: 1925
Specialized Field: Choral
Status: Nonprofit
Performs At: State University of New York at Purchase
Organization Type: Performing

1741
CONNECTICUT OPERA
226 Farmington Avenue
Hartford, CT 06105
Phone: 860-527-0713
Fax: 860-293-1715
e-mail: info@ctopera.org
Web Site: www.ctopera.org
Officers:
    Chairman: John G Ewen
    Vice Chairman: Thomas K Standish
    President: Calvin S Price
Management:
    President: John Kreitler
    Managing Director: Linda Jackson
    Artistic Director: Willie Waters
Mission: To preserve and advance the operatic art form; to make opera accessible to a diverse population; to educate, enlighten and entertain through the medium of opera; to assist young artists, directors, designers and technicians.
Utilizes: Guest Artists; Guest Companies; Singers
Founded: 1942
Specialized Field: Grand Opera; Light Opera
Status: Non-Profit, Professional
Paid Staff: 8
Income Sources: Opera America
Performs At: Horace Bushnell Memorial Hall
Organization Type: Performing; Touring; Resident; Educational; Sponsoring

1742
CONNECTICUT CHORAL ARTISTS
52 Main Street
New Britain, CT 06051
Phone: 860-224-7500
Fax: 860-827-8890
e-mail: contact@concora.org
Web Site: www.concora.org
Officers:
    President: Matthew Schreck
    Vice President: Harold Rives
    Marketing Director: Stacy Grimaldi
Management:
    Managing Director: Christine Laird
    Development Director: Cynthia Mellon
    Artistic Director: Richard Coffey
Mission: To perpetuate and perform with excellence, choral music of the highest quality for the broadest possible audience.
Utilizes: Guest Artists
Founded: 1974
Specialized Field: Choral; Classical; Contemporary; Religious
Status: Non-Profit, Professional
Paid Staff: 4
Paid Artists: 53
Budget: $300,000
Income Sources: Government; Foundations; Individuals
Affiliations: Chorus America
Organization Type: Performing; Touring; Resident; Educational

1743
GREATER NEW BRITAIN OPERA ASSOCIATION
662 E Street
New Britain, CT 06051
Phone: 860-224-2466
Fax: 860-584-9687
Management:
    General Manager: Kenneth A Larson
Mission: To offer a showcase for young artists cast in principal roles; to expose Connecticut youth to opera through work-study programs and classes.
Utilizes: Guest Artists; Guest Companies; Singers
Founded: 1976
Specialized Field: Grand Opera
Status: Professional; Nonprofit
Organization Type: Performing; Resident

1744
YALE RUSSIAN CHORUS
Yale Station
PO Box 202032
New Haven, CT 06520-2032
Phone: 203-432-4776
e-mail: ilyana.sawka@yale.edu
Officers:
    Business Manager: Stephen Bruce
Management:
    President: Ilyana Sawka
    Concert Manager: Helen Deng
    Business Manager: Andrew Schram
    Artistic Director: Mark Bailey
Founded: 1953
Specialized Field: Choral

1745
YALE SCHOLA CANTORUM
Yale Institute Of Sacred Music
409 Prospect Street
New Haven, CT 06511

Phone: 203-432-3222
Fax: 203-432-5296
e-mail: melissa.maier@yale.edu
Web Site: www.ylle.edu/schola
Management:
    External Relations Manager: Melissa Maier
    Founder and Conductor: Simon Carrington
Mission: The Yale Schola Cantorum, founded in 2003, is a 24-voice chamber choir, specializing in music from before 1750 and from the last 100 years, supported by the Yale Institute of Sacred Music with the School of Music and open by audition to all Yale students. Simon Carrington is the group's founder and conductor. In addition to performing regularly in New Haven, New York and Boston, Schola Cantorum records and tours nationally and internationally.
Utilizes: Sign Language Translators
Founded: 2003
Specialized Field: Vocal Music
Non-paid Artists: 200

1746
CONNECTICUT GRAND OPERA AND ORCHESTRA
307 Atlantic Street
Stamford, CT 06901
Phone: 203-327-2867
Fax: 203-327-1417
e-mail: mail@ctgrandopera.org
Web Site: www.ctgrandopera.org
Officers:
    Chairman: Robert A Wilson
    Secretary: Robert Scrofani
    Treasurer: Philip Giordano
Management:
    General Director: Laurence Gilgore
    Assistant General Manager: Ronald Land
Mission: Dedicated to presenting to area residents and visitors world-class operatic and orchestral performances featuring international music talent and innovative productions.
Utilizes: Guest Artists; Guest Companies; Singers
Founded: 1993
Specialized Field: Grand Opera
Status: Non-Profit, Professional
Paid Staff: 6
Volunteer Staff: 40
Income Sources: American Guild of Musical Artists; International Association of Theatrical Stage Employees
Performs At: Palace Theatre of the Arts; Klein Auditorium
Organization Type: Performing; Resident

1747
PRO ARTE CHAMBER SINGERS OF CONNECTICUT
PO Box 4251
Stamford, CT 06905
Phone: 203-322-5970
Management:
    Managing Director: Cynthia King
Mission: Presenting the full depth of choral repertoire, ranging from medieval times to the contemporary.
Utilizes: Singers
Founded: 1974
Specialized Field: Choral
Status: Professional
Performs At: First Presbyterian Church
Organization Type: Performing; Touring

1748
CONNECTICUT CONCERT OPERA
PO Box 370341
West Hartford, CT 06137-0341
Phone: 860-722-2300
Fax: 860-726-1839
e-mail: ctconcert@aol.com
Management:
Artistic Director: Wayne Rivera
President: John Wadhams
VP: Robert Merritt
Mission: To present less frequently heard operas in original language with supertitles in concert format and to expand opera opportunites in Connecticut and Western Massachusetts.
Founded: 1991
Specialized Field: Opera
Volunteer Staff: 25
Paid Artists: 30

Delaware

1749
DIAMOND STATE CHORUS OF SWEET ADELINES
42 Craig Road
Bear, DE 19701
Phone: 609-358-8995
Fax: 302-378-0935
Web Site: www.diamondstatechorus.org
Officers:
President: Emily Pinder
VP: Louisa Leipold
Secretary: Sylvia Taggart
Treasurer: Celia Renal
Management:
Chores Manager: Becky Diamond
Mission: Entertaining and educating the public in barber shop harmony as an American art form.
Utilizes: Singers
Founded: 1978
Specialized Field: Women's Chorus
Status: Semi-Professional; Nonprofit
Paid Staff: 50
Organization Type: Performing; Educational

1750
BELLE VOIX
PO Box 7065
Wilmington, DE 19803
Phone: 302-792-9498
Fax: 215-358-5789
Web Site: www.madrigal-singers.org
Officers:
President: Carol Lind
Treasurer: Dave Vallee
Management:
Artistic Director: Jeffrey Anderson
Accompanist: Kevin Freaney
Mission: To bring audiences great chamber choral music of all periods and genres.
Founded: 1959
Specialized Field: Choral
Status: Non-Profit
Paid Staff: 20
Organization Type: Performing; Touring; Educational

1751
GRAND YOUTH CHORUS
818 Market Street Mall
Wilmington, DE 19801
Phone: 302-658-7897
Fax: 302-652-5346
Toll-free: 800-37 -rand
e-mail: grandopera@grandopera.org
Web Site: www.grandopera.org
Management:
Marketing Direstor: Cindy Frankey
Executive Director: Kenneth A Wesler
Controller: Barbara Kelly
Director Of Development: Beth Press
Director Development: Jennifer Mackey
Controller: Barbara Kelly
Director Operations: Jamie Bowman
Media Manager: Paige Wolf
Utilizes: Singers
Founded: 1871
Specialized Field: Classical; Opera; Classical for Young Audiences; Entertainment Chorus
Status: Professional; Nonprofit
Performs At: Grand Opera House
Affiliations: Association of Performing Arts Presenters; League of Historic American Theatres
Seating Capacity: 1190; 300
Year Built: 1871
Year Remodeled: 1973
Rental Contact: Jennifer Uro
Organization Type: Performing; Educational; Sponsoring

1752
OPERA DELAWARE
OperaDelaware
4 South Poplar Street
Wilmington, DE 19801
Phone: 302-658-8063
Fax: 302-659-4991
e-mail: opinfo@operade.org
Web Site: www.operade.org
Officers:
President: John W Rollins III
Treasurer: John Rollins
VP: Charles Platznzie
VP: Linda O'Conner
Management:
General & Artistic Director: Leland P Kimball III, jkimball@operade.org
Director Of Development: Carin Brastow
Mission: Mission is to enrich the cultural life of people in the Deleware Valley by producing opera, educational and outreach programs.
Utilizes: Choreographers; Collaborations; Commissioned Composers; Commissioned Music; Composers-in-Residence; Designers; Educators; Grant Writers; Guest Accompanists; Guest Artists; Guest Companies; Guest Composers; Guest Conductors; Guest Designers; Guest Lecturers; Guest Musical Directors; Guest Soloists; Instructors; Local Artists; Lyricists; Multimedia; Music; New Productions; Organization Contracts; Original Music Scores; Resident Professionals; Selected Students; Sign Language Translators; Singers; Student Interns; Theatre Companies; Visual Arts
Founded: 1948
Specialized Field: Grand Opera
Status: Non-Profit, Professional
Paid Staff: 3
Volunteer Staff: 30
Paid Artists: 100
Budget: $800,000
Income Sources: Delaware Division Of The Arts
Performs At: Grand Opera House
Annual Attendance: 27,000
Type of Stage: Proscenium
Stage Dimensions: 38x30
Seating Capacity: 1,100
Year Built: 1876
Year Remodeled: 1976
Organization Type: Performing; Educational

District of Columbia

1753
UNITED STATES AIR FORCE SINGING SERGEANTS
The United States Air Force Base
201 McChord Street
Bolling AFB, DC 20032-0202
Phone: 202-767-5665
Fax: 202-767-0686
e-mail: bandpublicaffairs@bolling.af.mil
Web Site: www.usafband.com
Management:
Conductor: Moore Urrutia
Manager: Patricia Wolfe
Commander/Music Director: Col Dennis M Layendecker
Utilizes: Fine Artists; Guest Composers; Guest Lecturers; Guest Musical Directors; Organization Contracts; Singers
Founded: 1945
Specialized Field: Choral
Status: Non-Profit, Professional
Paid Staff: 26
Paid Artists: 25
Affiliations: Chorus America; American Choral Directors Association

1754
CATHEDRAL CHORAL SOCIETY
Washington National Cathedral
Massachusetts & Wisconsin Avenues NW
Washington, DC 20016-5098
Phone: 202-537-8980
Fax: 202-537-5648
e-mail: choralsociety@cathedral.org
Web Site: www.cathedralchoralsociety.org
Officers:
President: Roberta J Duffy
VP: Steven W Smith
Secretary: Neal Jackson
Treasurer: Gerald Padwe
Management:
President: Janice Hall
Executive Director: Mark W Ohnmacht
Artistic Director: J Reilly Lewis
Utilizes: Commissioned Composers; Commissioned Music; Educators; Guest Composers; Guest Directors; Guest Instructors; Guest Musical Directors; Guest Musicians; Local Artists; Multimedia; Original Music Scores; Sign Language Translators; Singers
Founded: 1942
Specialized Field: Classical; Contemporary; Religious; Choral
Status: Non-Profit, Professional
Paid Staff: 7
Paid Artists: 3
Non-paid Artists: 220
Budget: $1,044,400
Performs At: Washington National Cathedral
Affiliations: Chorus America; Cultural Alliance of Greater Washington
Annual Attendance: 23,626
Facility Category: Cathedral
Seating Capacity: 1618
Year Built: 1907

1755
CHORAL ARTS SOCIETY OF WASHINGTON
5225 Wisconsin Avenue NW
2nd Floor, Suite 603
Washington, DC 20015
Phone: 202-244-3669
Fax: 202-244-4244
e-mail: choralarts@choralarts.org
Web Site: www.choralarts.org
Officers:
Chairman: Eric Frauntelle
Treasurer: Charles E Hoyt
Vice Chairman: Patrica B Sagon
Vice Chair: Elizabeth Holleman
Secretary: Lorraine Wallace
Immediate Past Chair: Anne Keiser
General Counsel: David Brown
Vice Chair: Cinnie Fehr
Management:
President: Elizabeth Hollman
Executive Director: Debra Kraft
Artistic Director: Norman Scribner
Director Public Relations: Jonathan Kerr
General Counsel: David N Brown
Chorus President: Jim McHugh
Associate Conductor: Joseph Holt
Director Comm./Education Programs: Alicia Mills
Mission: Committed to the highest standards of excellence in its programming and performance.
Utilizes: Collaborations; Commissioned Music; Guest Artists; Guest Companies; Guest Composers; Guest Directors; Guest Instructors; Guest Lecturers; Guest Musicians; Multi Collaborations; Organization Contracts; Selected Students; Sign Language Translators; Singers; Soloists
Founded: 1965
Specialized Field: Choral
Status: Non-Profit, Professional
Paid Staff: 10
Non-paid Artists: 190
Budget: $2,000,000
Income Sources: Individual Donors; Corporate; Government and Foundation Grants; Gifts
Performs At: John F. Kennedy Center for the Performing Arts
Affiliations: Kennedy Center; Chorus America
Annual Attendance: 17,500
Type of Stage: Concert Hall
Organization Type: Performing; Resident

1756
CHORUS AMERICA
1156 15th Street NW
Suite 310
Washington, DC 20005
Phone: 202-331-7577
Fax: 202-331-7599
e-mail: service@chorusamerica.org
Web Site: www.chorusamerica.org
Officers:
President: John Alexander
Management:
President: Ann Meier Baker
Office Manager: Adam Hall
Mission: To promote the high quality and artistic growth of vocal ensembles; to stimulate further development of remuneration for singers; to encourage greater understanding, appreciation and enjoyment of choral music by all segments of society.

Utilizes: Artists-in-Residence; Collaborating Artists; Collaborations; Commissioned Composers; Commissioned Music; Composers-in-Residence; Educators; Guest Companies; Guest Soloists; Sign Language Translators
Founded: 1977
Specialized Field: Choral
Status: Non-Profit, Non-Professional
Paid Staff: 8
Volunteer Staff: 2

1757
MASTER CHORALE CHAMBER SINGERS
1200 29th Street NW
LL 2
Washington, DC 20007
Phone: 202-471-4050
Fax: 202-471-4051
Web Site: www.masterchorale.org
Officers:
Chair of the Board: Kae Dakin
Management:
Music Director: Donald McCullough
Assitant Conductor/Artistic Admin: Danny Ozment
Mission: To present choral music concerts.
Utilizes: Collaborating Artists; Collaborations; Commissioned Composers; Commissioned Music; Educators; Grant Writers; Guest Companies; Guest Composers; Guest Designers; Guest Directors; Guest Ensembles; Guest Instructors; Guest Lecturers; Guest Musical Directors; Guest Musicians; Local Artists; Lyricists; Multimedia; Music; Organization Contracts; Original Music Scores; Sign Language Translators; Singers; Soloists; Theatre Companies
Founded: 1967
Specialized Field: Choral
Status: Non-Profit, Professional
Paid Staff: 5
Volunteer Staff: 4
Paid Artists: 20
Non-paid Artists: 100
Budget: $1,100,000
Performs At: John F. Kennedy Center for the Performing Arts
Organization Type: Performing

1758
MASTER CHORALE CHAMBER SINGERS
1200 29th Street NW
LL 2
Washington, DC 20007
Phone: 202-471-4050
Fax: 202-471-4051
Web Site: www.masterchorale.org
Management:
Music Director: Donald McCullough
Concert Operations Director: Dennis Martin
Executive Director: Lea Joergenson
Specialized Field: Choral

1759
OPERA CAMERATA OF WASHINGTON
1819 Shepherd Street NW
Suite 100
Washington, DC 20011
Phone: 202-722-5335
Fax: 202-291-0877
e-mail: OCW@operacamerata.org
Management:
Artistic Director/Conductor: Gregory Buchalter
Chairman/Executive Director: Michael J Reilly
Mission: Production of Opera/Operetta rarities, infrequently produced great works.

Founded: 1990
Specialized Field: Opera; Operetta
Volunteer Staff: 25
Budget: $70,000

1760
OPERA MUSIC THEATER INTERNATIONAL
1201 Pennsylvania Avenue NW
Suite 300
Washington, DC 20004
Phone: 202-683-7874
Fax: 202-661-4699
e-mail: info@omti.org
Web Site: www.omti.org
Officers:
President: James K McCully
Management:
General Director: James K McCully
Mission: To showcase multi-cultural opera and music theater performances to draw the diverse DC region together through music.
Specialized Field: Opera; Musical Theatre

1761
SUMMER OPERA THEATRE COMPANY
Music School- CUA
620 Michigan Avenue NE
Washington, DC 20064
Phone: 202-526-1669
Fax: 202-319-5433
Web Site: www.summeropera.org
Officers:
Chairman: Leilane G Mehler
Vice Chairman and Dev. Chairman: Elizabeth C Sara
Secretary: Jaqueline Havener
Treasurer: Helen Toomey
Membership Chairman: Mary Frances Lombard
Board/Staff Liaison: F. Victoria Tresansky
Management:
General Manager: Deanne Giarraputo
Artistic Director: Elaine R Walter
Mission: To seek, promote and present young artists ready for work with major opera and musical theatre companies; to offer more established artists the opportunity to prepare and perform new roles.
Utilizes: Guest Artists; Singers
Founded: 1978
Specialized Field: Opera; Musical Theatre
Status: Non-Profit, Professional
Paid Staff: 4
Volunteer Staff: 4
Paid Artists: 200
Budget: $750,000
Income Sources: Private Donations/ Grants/ Box Office
Performs At: The Hartke Theatre
Annual Attendance: 5,900
Facility Category: Theatre
Organization Type: Performing; Resident; Educational

1762
VOCAL ARTS SOCIETY
1818 24th Street NW
Washington, DC 20008
Phone: 202-265-8177
Fax: 202-265-7164
e-mail: gperman@aol.com
Web Site: www.vocalartssociety.org
Officers:
President: Gerald Perman
Chair Board of Director: Martha Ellison
Treasurer: Ernest Hamel

Secretary: Mary Lynne McElroy
Management:
  President: Gerald Perman
  Executive Director: William O Wears
Mission: To promote the classical recital and bring to the Greater Washington area the finest vocals artists in programs of the great and largely underpreformed song literature.
Founded: 1990
Specialized Field: Choral; Classical
Status: Non-Profit, Professional
Paid Staff: 1
Paid Artists: 22
Budget: $170,000
Income Sources: Board/Audience Contributions; Foundation Grants
Performs At: Terrace Theater of the Kennedy Center; French Embassy
Annual Attendance: 3,600
Facility Category: Recital Hall
Seating Capacity: 475; 800

1763
WASHINGTON BACH CONSORT
1220 19th Street
Suite 300
Washington, DC 20036
Phone: 202-429-2121
Fax: 202-429-2269
e-mail: info@bachconsort.org
Web Site: www.bachconsort.org
Officers:
  President: Ann Meier
  Treasurer: Robert Inglis
  Secretary: Craig Hosmer
Management:
  President: Frank Dillow
  Executive Director: Stephen Borko
  Music Director: J Reilly Lewis
Mission: Perform to the highest artistic standards the music of JS Bach and his Baroque contemporaries. Expand our audience through concerts, collaborations with other performing ensembles, media appearances, marketable recordings, and tours. Promote current and future appreciation of Bach in our community through compelling music education programs presented by members of the Consort.
Founded: 1977
Specialized Field: Choral; Classical
Status: Non-Profit, Professional
Paid Staff: 6
Paid Artists: 40
Organization Type: Performing; Touring; Educational

1764
WASHINGTON CHORUS
1010 Wisconsin Avenue NW
Suite 310
Washington, DC 20007
Phone: 202-342-6221
Fax: 202-342-8208
e-mail: staff@thewashingtonchorus.org
Officers:
  Chorus/Outreach Administrator: Deborah Paez
  Chair Board of Trustees: Catherine French
  Vice Chair Board of Trustees: August Schumach
  Secretary: Katherine Roberts
Management:
  Music Director/Conductor: Robert Shafer
  Executive Director: Dianne Peterson
  Executive Director: Dianne Peterson
  Music Director: Robert Shafer

Mission: The Washington Chorus shares, preserves and advances the art of choral singing to help expirence the transforming power od choral music.
Utilizes: Commissioned Music; Guest Accompanists; Guest Musical Directors; Guest Musicians; Multimedia; Original Music Scores; Selected Students; Sign Language Translators; Singers
Founded: 1961
Specialized Field: Choral
Paid Staff: 8
Non-paid Artists: 200
Budget: $807,000
Income Sources: Individual; Foundation; Corporate & Government Support; Ticket Sales
Performs At: Kennedy Center Concert Hall
Annual Attendance: 25,000
Facility Category: Concert Hall

1765
WASHINGTON CONCERT OPERA
1808Connecticut Avenue NW
Suite 101
Washington, DC 20009
Phone: 202-364-5826
Fax: 202-364-5836
e-mail: info@concertopera.org
Management:
  Artistic Director/ Conductor: Anthony Walker
Specialized Field: Opera
Performs At: Kennedy Center Concert Hall

1766
WASHINGTON NATIONAL OPERA
2600 Virginia Avenue NW
Suite 104
Washington, DC 20037
Phone: 202-295-2420
Fax: 202-295-2479
Toll-free: 800-876-7372
e-mail: info@dc-opera.org
Web Site: www.dc-opera.org
Officers:
  President: Michael R Sonmenreich
  Board of Trustees, Life Chairperson: Mrs. Eugene B Casey
  Chairperson: James V Kimsey
  Chair of the Executive Committee: Mrs. Cristine F Hunter
Management:
  President: Micheal Sonnenreich
  Executive Director: Blair Caple
  Artistic Director: Placido Domingo
Mission: To provide highest quality opera; to broaden public awareness and understanding of opera through education and community programming; to support development of young American singers; to encourage work of new composers to maintain opera as a living art form.
Utilizes: Guest Artists; Guest Companies; Singers
Founded: 1956
Specialized Field: Opera
Status: For-Profit, Professional
Paid Staff: 60
Volunteer Staff: 150
Budget: $30,000,000
Income Sources: Box Office; Grants; Private Donations
Performs At: John F. Kennedy Center for the Performing Arts
Affiliations: OPERA America; Washington Opera Guild/Edcuational
Annual Attendance: 135,500
Type of Stage: Open Stage; Proscenium
Seating Capacity: 2,200

Organization Type: Performing; Resident; Educational

1767
CRUISERS
617 Warrington Avenue SE
Washington Navy Yard, DC 20374-5054
Phone: 202-433-6090
Fax: 202-433-4108
e-mail: navyband.public.affairs@navy.mil
Web Site: www.navyband.navy.mil
Management:
  Musician First Class: Kenneth H Carr
  Chief Musician: John L Fisher
  Musician First Class: Benjamin L Grant
  Musician First Class: Benjamin L Grant
  Musician First Class: John T Parsons
Mission: To provide music for such ceremonies, functions and other occasions as may be directed by proper authority in order to best represent the Navy in a musical capacity at the seat of government and elsewhere as directed.
Founded: 1999
Specialized Field: Contemporary
Organization Type: Performing; Touring

1768
SEA CHANTERS
617 Warrington Avenue SE
Washington Navy Yard, DC 20374-5054
Phone: 202-433-3676
Fax: 202-433-4108
e-mail: navyband.public.affairs@navy.mil
Web Site: www.navyband.navy.mil
Management:
  Master Chief Musician: John R Bury
  Chief Musician and Musical Director: Keith D Hinton
Mission: To provide music for such ceremonies, functions and other occasions as may be directed by proper authority in order to best represent the Navy in a musical capacity at the seat of government and elsewhere as directed.
Founded: 1925
Specialized Field: Traditional Choral Music; Sea Chanteys; Broadway Musicals
Organization Type: Performing; Touring

1769
US NAVY BAND
617 Warrington Avenue SE
Washington Navy Yard, DC 20374-5054
Phone: 202-433-3366
Fax: 202-433-4108
e-mail: public.affairs@navyband.navy.mil
Web Site: www.navyband.navy.mil
Management:
  Senior Chief Musician: Wayne C Taylor
Mission: To provide music for such ceremonies, functions and other occasions as may be directed by proper authority in order to best represent the Navy in a musical capacity at the seat of government and elsewhere as directed.
Founded: 1925
Specialized Field: Choral
Status: For-Profit, Professional
Paid Staff: 172
Paid Artists: 172
Organization Type: Performing; Touring

Florida

1770
PICCOLO OPERA COMPANY
24 Del Rio Boulevard
Boca Raton, FL 33432-4734
Fax: 561-394-0520
Toll-free: 800-282-3161
e-mail: leejon51@msn.com
Officers:
    Board: Harold Pinales
    Board: Barbara Goldstein
    Secretary: Merry Silber
    Treasurer: M Gordon
Management:
    Executive Director: Marjorie Gordon
Mission: To present opera in English to adults and youngsters with local orchestras, chorus, dancers, or with piano.
Utilizes: Commissioned Music; Music
Founded: 1963
Specialized Field: Opera
Status: Nonprofit, Professional
Budget: Varies
Income Sources: Performances; Grants to Sponsors
Performs At: Varied
Affiliations: Touring Company
Organization Type: Travelling troupe

1771
GOLD COAST OPERA
1420 North Swinton Avenue
Delray Beach, FL 33444
Phone: 561-276-8085
Fax: 561-276-8740
e-mail: sunsetet@aol.com
Web Site: www.goldcoastopera.com
Officers:
    President-Gold Coast Opera, Inc: Joan Readding
    Secretary-Gold Coast Opera, Inc: Salvatore Cordini
Management:
    Operations Director: Dr Joseph Ferrer
    Artistic Director/Conductor: Dr Thomas Cavendish
Mission: To offer the South Florida residents from Ft. Pierce to Ft. Lauderdale fully staged operatic masterpieces using the finest talent from Europe and North America.
Utilizes: Guest Companies; Singers
Founded: 1979
Specialized Field: Opera
Status: Professional; Nonprofit
Paid Staff: 10
Budget: 458,000,000
Income Sources: Tickets Sales, Grants and Contributions
Performs At: theaters in Ft. Pierce, Palm Beach Gardens, Boca Raton, Coral Springs, and Ft. Lauderdale
Organization Type: Performing; Touring; Educational

1772
OPERA GUILD
221 SW 3rd Avenue
Fort Lauderdale, FL 33312
Phone: 954-728-9700
Fax: 954-728-9702
Toll-free: 800-741-1010
e-mail: info@fgo.org
Web Site: www.fgo.org
Management:
    President: Robert Heuer

Executive Director: Patrick Flynn
Artistic Director: Stewart Robinson
Mission: Promoting opera and the newer performing arts.
Utilizes: Guest Artists; Guest Companies
Founded: 1944
Specialized Field: Opera
Status: Non-Profit, Professional
Income Sources: Junior Opera Guild/Children's
Performs At: Broward Center for the Performing Arts
Organization Type: Touring

1773
FLORIDA GRAND OPERA
1200 Coral Way
Miami, FL 33145-2980
Phone: 305-854-1643
Fax: 305-856-1042
Toll-free: 800-741-1010
e-mail: info@fgo.org
Officers:
    Director of Young Artist Studio: Cecelia Schieve
    Principal Coach: Scott Gilmore
Management:
    General Director: Robert Heuer
    Conductor: Stewart Robertson
    Artistic Administation Director: Karl Hesser
    Music Director: Stewart Robertson
Utilizes: Commissioned Music; Educators; Grant Writers; Guest Artists; Guest Composers; Guest Conductors; Guest Designers; Guest Instructors; Guest Soloists; Guest Writers; Original Music Scores; Sign Language Translators
Specialized Field: Opera
Budget: 10,000,000

1774
ORLANDO OPERA
1111 N Orange Avenue
Orlando, FL 32804
Phone: 407-426-1717
Fax: 407-426-1705
Toll-free: 800-336-7372
Web Site: www.orlandoopera.org
Officers:
    President/CEO: James D. Ireland, Jr.
    Director Public Relations: Celeste Hart
Management:
    General Director: Robert Swedberg
    Music Director: Robin Stamper
    Production Director: Elizabeth Sutton
Utilizes: Guest Artists; Guest Companies; Sign Language Translators; Singers; Student Interns; Visual Arts
Founded: 1958
Specialized Field: Grand Opera; Light Opera; Youth Chorus; Classical
Status: Non-Profit, Professional
Paid Staff: 18
Paid Artists: 30
Income Sources: Opera America
Performs At: Bob Carr Performing Arts Center
Organization Type: Performing

1775
CHORAL SOCIETY OF PENSACOLA
1000 College Boulevard
Room 803
Pensacola, FL 32504
Phone: 850-484-1806
Fax: 850-484-1835
e-mail: csop1@juno.com
Web Site: www.choralsocietyofpensacola.org
Management:

President: Pamela Brown
Executive Director: Andrew R Metzger
Artistic Director: Xiaolun Chen
Orchestra Personnel Manager: Rosemary R Pearce
Mission: The performance of choral literature.
Founded: 1935
Specialized Field: Choral
Status: Non-Profit, Non-Professional
Paid Staff: 4
Paid Artists: 25
Income Sources: Arts Council of North West Florida; Chorus America; Florida Cultural Action Alliance
Performs At: Saenger Theatre; Cokesbury United Methodist Church
Organization Type: Performing; Resident

1776
PENSACOLA OPERA
PO Box 1790
Pensacola, FL 32598-1790
Phone: 850-433-6737
Fax: 850-433-1082
e-mail: morgan@pensacolaopera.com
Web Site: www.pensacolaopera.com
Officers:
    Chairman: Ruth Orth
    Vice-Chairman: Fred Carmody
Management:
    Artistic Director: Kyle Marrero
    Business Manager/Dir Of Development: Erin Sammis
Mission: The mission of Pensacola Opera is to enrich the culture of Northwest Florida by producing professional opera performances, educational programs and other opera related community events for people of all ages, interests and backgrounds.
Utilizes: Artists-in-Residence; Choreographers; Commissioned Composers; Commissioned Music; Dance Companies; Dancers; Designers; Educators; Grant Writers; Guest Accompanists; Guest Artists; Guest Composers; Guest Conductors; Guest Designers; Guest Ensembles; Guest Instructors; Guest Lecturers; Guest Musical Directors; Guest Musicians; Guest Soloists; Guest Writers; High School Drama; Instructors; Multimedia; Music; New Productions; Original Music Scores; Resident Professionals; Sign Language Translators; Singers; Student Interns; Visual Arts
Founded: 1983
Specialized Field: Opera
Status: Non-Profit, Professional
Paid Staff: 5
Volunteer Staff: 15
Paid Artists: 75
Non-paid Artists: 40
Budget: $1,130,000
Income Sources: Ticket Sales; Public and Private Contributions; Other Income
Performs At: Vaudeville Era Theater
Affiliations: OPERA America
Annual Attendance: 12,000
Facility Category: Performing
Type of Stage: Proscenium
Stage Dimensions: 71' X 38'
Seating Capacity: 1,650
Year Built: 1925
Year Remodeled: 2009
Cost: $15 Million

1777
SARASOTA OPERA ASSOCIATION
61 N Pineapple Avenue
Sarasota, FL 34236

Phone: 941-366-8450
Fax: 941-955-5571
Toll-free: 888-673-7212
e-mail: info@sarasotaopera.org
Web Site: www.sarasotaopera.org
Officers:
  Chairman: Joan H. Wood
  Vice Chairman: Ulysses Brualdi
  Treasurer: Julian L. Clarkson
  Secretary: Richard Hull
Management:
  Artistic Administrator: Greg Trupiano
  Youth Opera Music Director: Lance Inouye
  Technical Director: Jeff Ellis
  House Manager: Chris Burtless
Mission: To continue to bring quality opera to our community and to showcase it in our own opera house; to educate the general community in an appreciation of opera and send our outreach programs into the schools of both Manatee and Sarasota counties; to offer statewide touring programs.
Utilizes: Guest Artists; Guest Companies; Singers
Founded: 1959
Specialized Field: Grand Opera; Light Opera; Lyric Opera; Musical Theatre; Choral; Youth Chorus; Classical
Status: Non-Profit, Professional
Paid Staff: 25
Paid Artists: 100
Income Sources: Opera America; Central Opera Service; American Guild of Musical Artists
Performs At: Sarasota Opera House
Organization Type: Performing; Educational; Sponsoring

1778
FLORIDA STATE OPERA AT FLORIDA STATE UNIVERSITY
School Of Music
002 Hmu
Tallahassee, FL 32306-1180
Phone: 850-645-4903
Fax: 850-644-2566
e-mail: opera@cmr.fsu.edu
Officers:
  President, Florida State University: Eric Barron
  Dean, College of Music: Don Gibson
Management:
  Director Opera Activities: Douglas Fisher
  Production Manager: June Dollar
  Technical Director: James Meade
  Stage Director/Professor Opera: Matthew Lata
Mission: Providing training for students at Florida State University; serving as a quality cultural resource.
Utilizes: Choreographers; Composers-in-Residence; Designers; Educators; Guest Artists; Guest Companies; Guest Conductors; Guest Designers; Local Artists; Resident Professionals; Singers
Founded: 1963
Specialized Field: Grand Opera; Lyric Opera; Operetta; Musical Theatre
Status: Semi-Professional; Nonprofit
Paid Staff: 10
Volunteer Staff: 200
Performs At: Ruby Diamond Auditorium; Opperman Music Hall
Affiliations: National Opera Association; Central Opera Service; TOG
Organization Type: Performing

1779
MASTER CHORALE OF TAMPA BAY
PO Box 20591
Tampa, FL 33622-0591

Phone: 813-258-9468
Fax: 813-258-0988
e-mail: mchorale@tampabay.rr.com
Web Site: www.masterchorale.com
Officers:
  Chairman: Robert B Hicks
  Operations Manager: Sandy Ray
Management:
  Executive Director: Bill Faucett
  Operations Manager: Sandy Ray
  Music and Artistic Director: Richard Zielinski
Mission: To enrich the community by performing and sustaining high quality choral music.
Utilizes: Guest Musical Directors; Organization Contracts
Founded: 1979
Specialized Field: Choral
Status: Non-Profit, Non-Professional
Paid Staff: 4
Paid Artists: 125

1780
SPANISH LYRIC THEATER
2819 Safe Harbor Drive
Tampa, FL 33548
Phone: 813-936-0217
Fax: 813-936-0217
e-mail: jcgonzalez@spanishlyrictheatre.com
Web Site: www.spanishlyrictheatre.com
Officers:
  President/CEO: Thomas P. Keating
Management:
  Founder/Artistic Director: Rene Gonzalez
  Touring Production Manager: Juan Carlos Gonzalez
Founded: 1959
Specialized Field: Light Opera; Lyric Opera; Musical Theatre; Ethnic Music; Classical; Contemporary
Status: Non-Profit, Professional
Paid Staff: 1
Paid Artists: 200
Performs At: Tampa Bay Performing Arts Center

1781
PALM BEACH OPERA
415 S Olive Avenue
West Palm Beach, FL 33401
Phone: 561-833-3709
Fax: 561-833-8294
e-mail: pbopera@pbopera.org
Web Site: www.pbopera.org
Management:
  General Director: William A Ryberg
  Artistic Operations Director: Daniel Biaggi
  Marketing/Sales Manager: Alexandra Wasil
Mission: Dedicated to producing world-class opera and diverse educational programs which play an integral role ni the artistiv and overall enrichment of the communities it serves.
Founded: 1961
Specialized Field: Opera
Status: Non-Profit, Professional
Paid Staff: 25
Volunteer Staff: 5
Paid Artists: 120
Performs At: Kravis Center for the Performing Arts
Organization Type: Performing; Touring; Resident; Educational

Georgia

1782
ATLANTA BOY CHOIR
1215 S Ponce De Leon Avenue
Atlanta, GA 30306
Phone: 404-378-0064
Fax: 404-378-4722
e-mail: mail@atlantaboychoir.org
Web Site: www.atlantaboychoir.org
Officers:
  Administrative/Business Manager: Roberta Kahne
Management:
  President: David White
  Administrative/Business Manager: Roberta Kahne
Founded: 1957
Specialized Field: Choral
Status: Non-Profit, Non-Professional
Paid Staff: 3
Paid Artists: 2

1783
ATLANTA OPERA
1575 Northside Drive NW
Atlanta, GA 30318
Phone: 404-881-8801
Fax: 404-881-1711
Toll-free: 800-356-7372
e-mail: info@atlantaopera.org
Web Site: www.atlantaopera.org
Officers:
  Chairman: Gregory F Johnson
  President: Charles R Yates Jr
  Treasurer: Denis J Duncan
  Secretary: Robert G Woodward
Management:
  General Director: Dennis Hanthorn
  Artistic Administration Director: Eric Mitchko
  Company Manager: Elecia Crowley
  Production Manager: Michael Benedict
  Orchestra Manager: Mark McConnell
Mission: To present opera productions of the highest standards possible, while fostering education about the art form and encouraging growth with services and programs designed to fill the needs of the community
Utilizes: Actors; Choreographers; Collaborating Artists; Collaborations; Dancers; Designers; Educators; Five Seasonal Concerts; Grant Writers; Guest Accompanists; Guest Artists; Guest Composers; Guest Conductors; Guest Designers; Guest Ensembles; Guest Instructors; Guest Musical Directors; Guest Musicians; Guest Soloists; Guest Writers; High School Drama; Instructors; Local Artists; Lyricists; Multi Collaborations; Multimedia; New Productions; Original Music Scores; Selected Students; Sign Language Translators; Singers; Soloists; Student Interns; Visual Arts
Founded: 1979
Specialized Field: Grand Opera
Status: Non-Profit, Professional
Paid Staff: 25
Volunteer Staff: 40
Non-paid Artists: 10
Budget: $5.4 Million
Income Sources: Ticketing, Foundations, Individuals, Coporate, Government
Performs At: Alliance Theatre; Symphony Hall
Annual Attendance: 50,000+
Seating Capacity: 4514
Year Built: 1920
Organization Type: Performing; Educational

1784
ATLANTA SYMPHONY ORCHESTRA CHORUS
Robert W. Woodruff Arts Center
1293 Peachtree Street
Suite 300
Atlanta, GA 30309-3552
Phone: 404-733-4900
Fax: 404-733-4901
e-mail: aso-info@woodruffcenter.org
Web Site: www.atlantasymphony.org
Management:
President: Allison Vulgamore
Chief Financial Officer: Donald Fox
VP: John Sparrow
Choral Administrator: Jeff Baxter
Founded: 1945
Specialized Field: Grand Opera; Operetta; Arias
Status: Non-Professional; Nonprofit; Volunteer
Performs At: Robert W. Woodruff Arts Center
Symphony Hall
Organization Type: Performing; Touring

1785
ATLANTA YOUNG SINGERS OF CALLANWOLDE
980 Briarcliff Road NE
Atlanta, GA 30306
Phone: 404-873-3365
Fax: 404-873-0756
e-mail: info@aysc.org
Web Site: www.aysc.org
Officers:
President: David Hughes
VP: Rita Brett
Secretary: Amanda Freer
Treasurer: Virginia Ling
Management:
Executive Director: Virginia M Thompson
Music Director: Paige Mathis
Mission: To provide a program of exceptionally fine training in choral singing for boys and girls, which will develop their appreciation of and talents in choral and musical artistry; to encourage the personal growth of each singer through individual responsibility and group cooperation; to advance the choral art form by presenting traditional and innovative music through the voices of children in live performances to local, national and international com
Utilizes: Guest Accompanists; Guest Musical Directors; Multimedia; Original Music Scores
Founded: 1975
Specialized Field: Youth Chorus
Paid Staff: 4
Volunteer Staff: 400
Paid Artists: 15
Non-paid Artists: 10
Budget: $630,000
Income Sources: Grants; Donations; Performances; Tuition
Annual Attendance: 60,000-90,000

1786
CAPITOL CITY OPERA
1266 West Paces Ferry Road
#451
Atlanta, GA 30327
Phone: 404-454-6213
e-mail: info@ccityopera.com
Officers:
Administrative Assistant: Heather Dittus
Management:
Artistic Director/Founder: Donna Angel

Stage Director: Michael Nutter
Stage Director: Michael Nutter
Director Production: Steven Cernek
Director Marketing: Nichol Julia Jacobs
New Projects Coordinator: Kathleen Szalay
Mission: To provide Atlanta area classically trained singers the opportunity to learn and perform complete opera roles and continue to develop their vocal and acting skills on a professional level.
Utilizes: Community Talent; Instructors; Local Talent
Founded: 1983
Specialized Field: Opera
Season: October-January;July
Performs At: Falany Performing Arts Center at Reinhardt College; 14th Street Playhouse

1787
CHORAL GUILD OF ATLANTA
PO Box 550772
Atlanta, GA 30355
Phone: 404-223-6362
Fax: 770-641-1385
e-mail: info@cgatl.org
Web Site: www.cgatl.org
Management:
Chairman: Pat Snider
Vice Chairman: George Taylor
Music Director and Conductor: Jim Bohart
Mission: Recognition as the foremost large civic chorus in the metro Atlanta area; performance of major works of nonstandard repertoire; increasing financial solvency.
Founded: 1939
Specialized Field: Choral
Status: Semi-Professional; Nonprofit
Organization Type: Performing; Touring

1788
TROIKA BALALAIKES WORLD ARTISTS
World Artists
3126 Bolero Drive
Atlanta, GA 30341
Phone: 770-939-4343
Fax: 770-908-1231
Web Site: www.lynnmcconnell.com
Management:
Director: Lynn Connell
Specialized Field: Russian Folk Music
Affiliations: Cucanandy (Irish), Cowboy Envy, Deluxe Vaudeville Orchestra, Atlanta Brassworks, Hotlanta (Dixieland), Mariachi Vasqukez, Else Witt

1789
AUGUSTA OPERA ASSOCIATION
1301 Greene Street
Suite 100
Augusta, GA 30903
Phone: 706-826-4710
Fax: 706-826-4732
e-mail: kbopera@aol.com
Web Site: www.augustaopera.org
Officers:
President: Sandra Blackwood
Treasurer: Davenport Bruker
Secretary: Doris Begley
Executive VP: Gerald Chamber S
Management:
President: Liz Hopkins
Artistic Director: Mark Flint
Managing Director: Katherine Deloach
Marketing Associate: Mary Ann Woodworth
Mission: Strives to present opera music theater productions of the highest standards while encouraging growth of the art form through its programs and outreach services.

Utilizes: Collaborations; Fine Artists; Grant Writers; Guest Artists; Guest Choreographers; Guest Composers; Guest Conductors; Guest Lecturers; Guest Writers; Local Artists; Lyricists; Multi Collaborations; Multimedia; Original Music Scores; Singers; Special Technical Talent
Founded: 1967
Specialized Field: Grand Opera; Light Opera; Lyric Opera; Musical Theatre; Choral
Status: Non-Profit, Professional
Paid Staff: 3
Volunteer Staff: 35
Paid Artists: 3
Non-paid Artists: 128
Budget: $500,000
Income Sources: Subscriptions; Single Ticket Sales; Iundividual Donations; Foundations; Corporations; Government Grants
Performs At: Imperial Theatre
Affiliations: Opera America
Annual Attendance: 9,000
Seating Capacity: 850
Organization Type: Performing; Resident; Educational

1790
GRAND OPERA HOUSE SEASON AT THE GRAND
651 Mulberry Street
Macon, GA 31201
Phone: 478-301-5470
Fax: 912-301-5469
e-mail: goss_km@mercer.edu
Management:
Managing Director: Karen Lambert
Artistic Administration Director: Karen Goss
Specialized Field: Musical Theatre; Opera
Performs At: Grand Opera House

Hawaii

1791
HAWAII ECUMENICAL CHORALE
3752 Old Pali Road
Honolulu, HI 96817
Phone: 808-595-3447
Fax: 808-521-4595
Management:
Artistic Director: Eileen Lum
Mission: To provide an opportunity for local singers to participate in more challenging music than average choirs offer; to sponsor a local choral composition contest to encourage indigenous choral work.
Utilizes: Guest Artists; Guest Companies; Singers
Founded: 1979
Specialized Field: Grand Opera; Choral; Ethnic Music; Folk Music
Status: Semi-Professional; Nonprofit
Volunteer Staff: 4
Affiliations: State Foundation on Culture and the Arts
Organization Type: Performing; Resident; Educational

1792
HAWAII OPERA THEATRE
987 Waimanu Street
Honolulu, HI 96814
Phone: 808-596-7858
Fax: 808-596-0379
Toll-free: 800-836-7372
e-mail: hotopero@hawaii.rr.com
Web Site: www.hawaiiopera.org
Management:
President: Henry G Akina
Executive Director: Karen Tiller

Mission: To offer opera in Hawaii.
Utilizes: Guest Artists; Guest Companies
Founded: 1962
Specialized Field: Grand Opera
Status: Non-Profit, Professional
Paid Staff: 13
Income Sources: Opera America; Central Opera Service
Performs At: Neal S. Blaisdell Center-Concert Hall
Orchestra Pit: 1
Organization Type: Performing; Touring; Resident; Educational

1793
HONOLULU CHILDREN'S OPERA CHORUS

PO Box 22304
Honolulu, HI 96822
Phone: 808-521-2982
Fax: 808-521-4595
Officers:
  Business Manager: Malla Ka'ai
Management:
  Music Director: Nola A Nahulu
  Accompanist: Wendy Chang
Mission: Developing and nurturing the performing arts by means of choral music; providing educational and artistic resources for Hawaii.
Founded: 1961
Specialized Field: Grand Opera; Light Opera; Choral; Ethnic Music
Status: Nonprofit
Organization Type: Performing; Educational

1794
OAHU CHORAL SOCIETY

650 Iwilei Road
Suite 202
Honolulu, HI 96817
Phone: 808-524-0815
Fax: 808-524-1507
e-mail: Oahuchoral@aol.com
Officers:
  Artistic Director: Nola A Nahulu
  Chorus Manager and Executive Direct: Joseph McAlister
Management:
  President: Valerie Ossipoff
  VP: Christine Philben
  Artistic Director: Karen Kennedy
  Executive Director: Joseph McAlister
Founded: 1995
Specialized Field: Choral
Status: Nonprofit

Idaho

1795
BIOTZETIK BASQUE CHOIR

PO Box 1011
Boise, ID 83701
Phone: 208-336-8219
Management:
  Business Manager: John Kirtland
  Business Manager: Miren Artiach
  Communicator: Ricardo Yanci
Mission: The promotion and enhancement of our culture through dance, song, language and education.
Utilizes: Guest Companies; Singers
Specialized Field: Ethnic Music; Folk Music
Status: Nonprofit
Paid Staff: 70
Income Sources: Euskaldunak

Performs At: Boise Basque Center
Organization Type: Performing; Touring; Educational

1796
BOISE MASTER CHORALE

PO Box 2244
Boise, ID 83701
Phone: 208-344-7901
e-mail: info@boisemasterchorale.org
Web Site: www.boisemasterchorale.org
Officers:
  President: Alana Seacord
  Secretary: Cindy Geile
  Treasurer: Bob Ball
  Membership: Diane Campbell
  Program Director: Leon Collins
  Advertising: Barbara Myhre
Management:
  President: Joanne C Anderson
  Artistic Director: Dr James Jirak
Mission: Offering the community fine choral music; enabling community members to participate in a high quality choral group.
Founded: 1975
Specialized Field: Choral
Status: Professional; Semi-Professional; Nonprofit
Paid Staff: 125
Performs At: Saint John's Cathedral; Morrison Center for the Arts
Organization Type: Performing

1797
OPERA IDAHO

513 S 8th Street
Boise, ID 83702
Phone: 208-345-3531
Fax: 208-342-7566
e-mail: officemgr@operaidaho.org
Web Site: www.operaidaho.org
Mission: Opera Idaho's mission for it's professional resident company is to promote opera in general by providing traing and performance opportunities for many talented singers in the Boise area.
Specialized Field: Opera
Performs At: Morrison Center; Esther Simplot Performing Arts Annex

Illinois

1798
BELLA VOCE

Department of Performing Arts
UIC 1040 W Harrison Street
Room L018 MSC 255
Chicago, IL 60607
Phone: 312-479-1096
e-mail: mail@bellavoce.org
Web Site: www.bellavoce.org
Management:
  Artistic Director: Andrew Lewis
  Artistic Director Emeritus: Anne Heider
Mission: To entertain, inspire and educate through the performance of choral chamber music.
Utilizes: Commissioned Composers; Community Talent; Educators; Five Seasonal Concerts; Guest Musicians; Instructors; Local Artists; Local Artists & Directors; Local Talent; Lyricists; Multimedia; Music; Resident Companies; Sign Language Translators; Singers; Soloists
Founded: 1982
Specialized Field: Choral; Classical; Contemporary; Religious
Status: Non-Profit, Professional

Paid Staff: 2
Volunteer Staff: 30
Paid Artists: 21
Budget: $125,000
Income Sources: Grants; Donations; Concert tickets; CD's
Annual Attendance: 2,500
Organization Type: Performing

1799
CHICAGO A CAPPELLA

2936 N Southport Avenue
2nd Floor
Chicago, IL 60657
Phone: 773-281-7820
Fax: 773-296-0968
Toll-free: 800-746-4969
e-mail: info@chicagoacappella.org
Web Site: www.chicagoacappella.org
Management:
  Executive Director: Matthew Greenberg
  Artistic Director: Jonathan Miller
Mission: Nine professional vocal soloists committed to furthering the art of singing together without instruments. Chicago a cappella aims to speak directly to the human spirit, through repertoire from the ninth to the twenty-first centuries.
Founded: 1933
Specialized Field: Traditional Choral Music; A Cappella
Status: Professional
Performs At: Civic Center Music Hall

1800
CHICAGO CHILDREN'S CHOIR

78 E Washington
Chicago, IL 60602
Phone: 312-849-8300
Fax: 312-849-8309
e-mail: info@ccchoir.org
Web Site: www.ccchoir.org
Management:
  President: Christina Deaton
  Artistic Director: Josephine Lee
  Development Director: Eileen Epstein
  Marketing Director: Pat Washington
Utilizes: Artists-in-Residence; Collaborations; Commissioned Music; Educators; Grant Writers; Guest Companies; Guest Composers; Guest Designers; Guest Lecturers; Guest Musical Directors; Guest Musicians; Lyricists; Multimedia; New Productions; Organization Contracts; Sign Language Translators; Singers; Soloists; Special Technical Talent; Theatre Companies; Touring Companies
Founded: 1956
Specialized Field: Grand Opera; Light Opera; Lyric Opera; Musical Theatre; Choral; Youth Chorus; Ethnic Music; Classical; Contemporary; Religious
Status: Non-Profit, Non-Professional
Paid Staff: 31
Volunteer Staff: 100
Budget: $2,500,000
Income Sources: Performance Fees; Corporate; Civic and Private Sponsorships
Performs At: Concert halls, Churches, etc.
Annual Attendance: 1500
Organization Type: Performing; Touring; Educational

1801
CHICAGO OPERA THEATER

70-E Lake Street
Suite 815
Chicago, IL 60601-5907

Phone: 312-704-8420
Fax: 312-704-8421
e-mail: info@chicagooperatheater.org
Web Site: www.chicagooperatheater.org
Management:
   President: Gregory O'Leary
   General Manager: Roger Weitz
   General Director: Brian Dickie
   Marketing & Public Relations Dir.: Colleen
   Flanigan
Mission: To present Classical, Baroque, and 20th
century operas with a strong empasis on education for
people young and old.
Founded: 1974
Specialized Field: Classical; Baroque; 20th Century
Operas
Status: Professional
Performs At: Harris Theatre
Type of Stage: Athenaeum

1802
CHICAGO SYMPHONY CHORUS

Symphony Center
220 S Michigan Avenue
Chicago, IL 60604
Phone: 312-294-3430
Fax: 312-294-3450
e-mail: chorus@cso.org
Web Site: www.cso.org
Management:
   President: Deborah Card
   Manager: Mark Rulison
   Artistic Director: Duane Wolfe
Mission: Performance with a leading symphony
orchestra.
Founded: 1957
Specialized Field: Choral
Status: Non-Profit, Professional
Paid Artists: 105
Non-paid Artists: 80
Budget: $1,000,000
Performs At: Orchestra Hall; Ravinia Festival
Organization Type: Performing; Touring; Educational

1803
L'OPERA PICCOLA

5239 N. LaCrosse Ave
Chicago, IL 60630
Phone: 312-560-1072
Fax: 847-823-3165
e-mail: sasha@loperapiccola.org
Web Site: www.loperapiccola.org
Officers:
   President: Jerry Lee Brown
   VP: Mark D Holihan
   Treasurer: John Sasser
   Secretary: Lawrence Zimmerman
Management:
   General Manager/Executive Director: Shasha
   Gerritson
   Music Director: David Richards
   Artistic Director: Shifra Werch
   Executive Producer: Madeline Nelson
   Events Coordinator: Aggie Zarkadas
Mission: To provide a creative outlet for Chicago's
aspiring musicians and to reach members of the
community with Italian opera production.
Founded: 1996
Specialized Field: Italian Opera
Status: Non-Profit, Professional
Paid Staff: 4
Volunteer Staff: 250
Paid Artists: 200
Budget: $250,000

Income Sources: Grants; Individual Donations; Ticket
Sales
Performs At: Athenaeum Theatre
Annual Attendance: 6,000
Seating Capacity: 985

1804
LIRA CHAMBER CHORUS

6525 N Sheridan Road
#CH-LL
Chicago, IL 60626
Phone: 773-508-7040
Fax: 773-508-7043
e-mail: lira@liraensemble.org
Management:
   Artistic Director/General Manager: Lucyna Migala
Mission: To bring back Polish Culture into American
life.
Specialized Field: Choral; Youth Chorus
Paid Staff: 5
Paid Artists: 50

1805
LIRA DANCERS OF THE LIRA ENSEMBLE

6525 N Sheridan Road
Chicago, IL 60626
Phone: 773-508-7040
Fax: 773-508-7043
e-mail: lira@liraensemble.org
Officers:
   Co-Conductor: Philip Seward
   Choreographer: Iowna Puc
   President: Lucyna Migala
   Secretary: Frances Weit
   Treasurer: Bernard Tresnowski
Management:
   Artistic Director/General Manager: Lucyna Migala
   Co-Conductor: Paul Dijkstra
Mission: To help acquaint Polish Americans with the
richness of their thousand-year-old heritage of music
and dance, and to help other Americans learn about
and appreciate Polish culture and traditions.
Founded: 1975
Specialized Field: Polish Music
Status: Non-Profit; Professional
Non-paid Artists: 30
Budget: $200,000-$500,000
Organization Type: Performing

1806
LIRA SINGERS

6525 N Sheridan Road
#CH-LL
Chicago, IL 60626
Phone: 773-508-7040
Fax: 773-508-7043
e-mail: lira@liraensemble.org
Management:
   Artistic Director/General Manager: Lucyna Migala
   Assistant Manager: Susan Smentek
Mission: The Lira Ensemble is the nation's only
professional performing arts company specializing in
Polish music, song, and dance.
Specialized Field: Choral
Organization Type: Performing

1807
LYRIC OPERA OF CHICAGO

20 N Wacker Drive
Suite 840
Chicago, IL 60606
Phone: 312-332-2244
Fax: 312-419-8345
Web Site: www.lyricopera.org

Management:
   General Director: William A Mason
   Music Director: Andrew Davis
   Aristic Director Emeritus: Bruno Bartoletti
Mission: Offering quality opera to Chicago area
residents.
Utilizes: Educators; Guest Artists; Guest Companies;
Singers
Founded: 1954
Specialized Field: Grand Opera
Status: Professional, Nonprofit
Income Sources: Lyric Opera Center for American
Artists
Performs At: Civic Opera House
Seating Capacity: 3,563
Organization Type: Performing, Sponsoring

1808
MUSIC OF THE BAROQUE CHORUS & ORCHESTRA

111 North Wabash Ave
Suite 810
Chicago, IL 60602
Phone: 312-551-1414
Fax: 312-551-1444
e-mail: baroque@baroque.org
Web Site: www.baroque.org
Officers:
   Chairman: Leland E Hutchinson
   Vice Chairman: Stanley L Ferguson
   Vice Chairman: Thomas O Kuhns
   Secretary: Pamela Baker
   Treasurer: Lawrence E Strickling
Management:
   Music Director: Jane Glover
   Chorus Director: Edward Zelnis
   Executive Director: Karen Fishman
   House Manager: Andrew Baldeschwiler
   Artistic Operations Manager: Vincent Carbone
Mission: To perform and increase audience
appreciation for choral and orchestral music of the 17th
and 18th centuries.
Founded: 1972
Specialized Field: Baroque; Choral
Status: Professional
Paid Staff: 6
Paid Artists: 60
Budget: $1,500,000
Performs At: Church Venues
Annual Attendance: 13,000
Facility Category: Church venues
Type of Stage: Varies
Seating Capacity: 600-2,521

1809
PATRICK G AND SHIRLEY W RYAN OPERA CENTER

20 N Wacker Drive
Suite 700
Chicago, IL 60606
Mailing Address: 20 N Wacker Drive Suite #860
Phone: 312-332-2244
Fax: 312-345-8425
e-mail: atakushi@lyricopera.org
Web Site: www.lyricopera.org/about/ryanoperacenter
Officers:
   Director: Gianna Rolandi
   Administrative/Auditions Coord.: Alicia Takushi
Management:
   Manager: Dan Novak

Mission: To administer an apprentice artist program in conjunction with and under the overall direction of the Lyric Opera of Chicago to bridge the gap between a singer's preparation in school and performance on a professional stage.
Utilizes: Guest Companies; Singers
Founded: 1974
Specialized Field: Opera
Status: Vocal Music; Professional Development Program
Paid Staff: 3
Volunteer Staff: 2
Paid Artists: 13
Income Sources: Sponsors; Audition Fees; Lyric Opera of Chicago
Affiliations: Lyric Opera of Chicago
Organization Type: Performing; Educational

1810
WILLIAM FERRIS CHORALE
Loyola University
1032 W. Sheridan Road
Chicago, IL 60660
Phone: 773-508-2940
e-mail: requests@williamferrischorale.org
Web Site: www.williamferrischorale.org
Management:
Music Director: Paul French
Artistic and Executive Director: John Vorrasi
Utilizes: Collaborating Artists; Composers; Contract Orchestras; Guest Accompanists; Guest Companies; Guest Directors; Guest Musical Directors; Guest Musicians; Guest Soloists; Instructors; Multimedia; Music; Organization Contracts; Original Music Scores; Sign Language Translators; Singers; Students
Founded: 1972
Specialized Field: Choral
Paid Staff: 3
Volunteer Staff: 3
Paid Artists: 35
Budget: $195,000
Annual Attendance: 2,000
Seating Capacity: 400

1811
WINDY CITY PERFORMING ARTS
3023 N Clark Street
Suite 329
Chicago, IL 60657
Phone: 773-404-9242
Fax: 773-404-6815
e-mail: info@windycitysings.org
Web Site: www.windycitysings.org
Officers:
Chair: Trung T. Tieu
Vice Chair: Ray Lesniewski
Management:
Interim Music Director: Alan Wellman
Utilizes: Actors; Artists-in-Residence; Commissioned Composers; Dancers; Guest Companies; Guest Composers; Guest Lecturers; Guest Musical Directors; Guest Musicians; Instructors; Local Artists; Multimedia; Music; Resident Professionals; Sign Language Translators; Singers; Student Interns
Founded: 1979
Specialized Field: Musical Theatre; Choral
Paid Staff: 2
Volunteer Staff: 20
Paid Artists: 6
Non-paid Artists: 100
Budget: $400,000
Annual Attendance: 5,000

1812
MILLIKIN UNIVERSITY OPERA THEATRE
Millikin University
School of Music
1184 West Main
Decatur, IL 62522
Phone: 217-424-6300
Fax: 217-420-6652
Toll-free: 800-373-7733
e-mail: tstone@mail.millikin.edu
Web Site: www.millikin.edu
Officers:
President: Douglas E. Zemke
VP University Development: Peggy S. Luy
Management:
Director: Terry Stone
Mission: To provide professional training and numerous performance opportunities for undergraduates in productions including scenes, chamber operas, fully produced operas and musical theatre.
Utilizes: Artists-in-Residence; Dancers; Designers; Grant Writers; Guest Artists; Guest Composers; Guest Conductors; Guest Designers; Guest Instructors; Guest Lecturers; Guest Musical Directors; Resident Professionals; Soloists; Student Interns
Founded: 1955
Specialized Field: Grand Opera; Light Opera; Lyric Opera; Musical Theatre; Choral; Ethnic Music; Classical; Operetta
Status: Non-Profit, Professional
Paid Staff: 3
Paid Artists: 67
Budget: $15,000
Income Sources: Annual budget; ticket sales
Performs At: Kirkland Fine Arts Center, Albert Taylor Hall, Kaeuper Hall
Affiliations: Opera America, Musical America
Annual Attendance: 2,000
Type of Stage: Proscenium w/hydraulic pit
Organization Type: Educational

1813
DOWNERS GROVE CHORAL SOCIETY
PO Box 655
Downers Grove, IL 60515
Phone: 630-515-0030
Fax: 630-910-8254
e-mail: President@dgcs.org
Management:
Music Director/Conductor: Robert Holst
Orchestra Manager: Patricia Smith
Specialized Field: Choral

1814
LIGHT OPERA WORKS
927 Noyes Street
Suite 225
Evanston, IL 60201
Phone: 847-869-6300
Fax: 847-869-6388
Web Site: www.light-opera-works.org
Officers:
President: Dr. Robert Greendale
Management:
Artistic Director: Rudy Hogenmiller
General Manager: Briget McDonough
Business Manager: Mike Kotze
Production Manager: Paige Keedy
Mission: To produce and present music theater from a variety of world traditions
Utilizes: Guest Artists; Guest Companies
Founded: 1980

Specialized Field: Musical Theatre
Status: Non-Profit, Professional
Paid Staff: 7
Volunteer Staff: 20
Budget: $1.5 Million
Income Sources: Tickets, Donations
Performs At: University Theater
Affiliations: National Alliance for Musical Theater, Leagues of Chicago Theaters
Annual Attendance: 25,000
Type of Stage: Proscenium
Stage Dimensions: 45 x 35
Seating Capacity: 1,000
Year Built: 1940
Year Remodeled: 1994
Organization Type: Performing

1815
DUPAGE OPERA THEATER
Arts Center; College of Dupage
Glen Ellyn, IL 60137
Phone: 630-942-3005
Fax: 630-790-9806
e-mail: cebula@cod.edu
Web Site: www.cod.edu
Management:
Executive Director: Stephen Cummins
Artistic Director: Kirk Muspratt
Managing Director: Paula Cebula
Founded: 1977
Specialized Field: Light Opera; Lyric Opera
Status: Non-Profit, Professional
Paid Staff: 5
Paid Artists: 15
Income Sources: Ticket Sales; Individual Donor
Performs At: Arts Center; Mainstage
Seating Capacity: 793
Year Built: 1985

1816
GLEN ELLYN CHILDREN'S CHORUS
799 Roosevelt Road
Building 6, Suite 100
Glen Ellyn, IL 60137
Phone: 630-858-2471
Fax: 630-858-2476
e-mail: info@gechildrenschorus.org
Web Site: www.gechildrenschorus.org
Officers:
President: David Fox
Management:
Executive Director: Priscilla Smith
Artistic Director: Emily Ellsworth
Mission: To provide any interested child, regardless of previous musical experience, with an outstanding performance-based music education program offered in a positive and nurturing environment which fosters self-esteem and personal growth.
Utilizes: Guest Companies; Guest Musical Directors; Guest Musicians; Multimedia; Sign Language Translators; Soloists
Founded: 1964
Specialized Field: Youth Chorus; Choral
Status: Non-Profit, Non-Professional
Paid Staff: 12
Organization Type: Performing; Touring; Educational

1817
MOLINE BOYS CHOIR
3426 Avenue of City
Moline, IL 61265
Phone: 309-764-3109
e-mail: mobocho@mchsi.com
Management:

President: John Mickiewicz
Director: Kermit Wells
Managing Director: Margaret Mangelsdorf
Mission: To perform choral literature of a variety of styles; to provide vocal/choral training to boys of talent, interest and ability.
Founded: 1948
Specialized Field: Light Opera; Musical Theatre; Choral; Youth Chorus; Ethnic Music; Classical; Contemporary; Religious
Status: Non-Profit, Non-Professional
Paid Staff: 2
Volunteer Staff: 1
Organization Type: Performing; Touring; Educational

1818
OPERA ILLINOIS
416 Hamilton Boulevard
Suite 309
Peoria, IL 61602
Phone: 309-673-7253
Fax: 309-673-7211
Web Site: www.operaillinois.com
Officers:
President: Karl Kuppler
Vice-President: Camille Gibson
Treasurer: Mildred Arends
Management:
President: Joan Janssen
Executive Director: Margaret Swain
Artistic Director: Fiora Contino
General Manager: William Swain
Mission: The mission is to enhance the cultural, educational and economic life of Downstate Illinois by the promotion of opera and the production of professional opera performances.
Utilizes: Actors; Choreographers; Dance Companies; Designers; Educators; Grant Writers; Guest Accompanists; Guest Artists; Guest Composers; Guest Conductors; Guest Designers; Guest Musical Directors; Guest Musicians; Instructors; Local Artists; Multimedia; Music; Original Music Scores; Resident Professionals; Sign Language Translators; Student Interns
Founded: 1972
Specialized Field: Opera; Classical; Musical Theatre
Paid Staff: 5
Volunteer Staff: 25
Budget: $565,000
Income Sources: Ticket Revenue; Contributed Revenue
Performs At: Peoria Civic Center Theater
Affiliations: Opera America
Annual Attendance: 10,000+
Facility Category: Peorkia, Civic Center, Theatre
Type of Stage: Proscenium
Stage Dimensions: 45'x35'x45'
Seating Capacity: 2131
Year Built: 1981

1819
MUDDY RIVER OPERA COMPANY
428 Maine Street
Suite 270
Quincy, IL 62301-3930
Phone: 217-222-2856
Fax: 217-222-2869
e-mail: abernzen12@gmail.com
Web Site: www.muddyriveropera.org
Officers:
President: Jason Stone
Management:
President/Artistic Director: Avril Marie Bernzen

Mission: To create an opportunity for local performers to work in collaboration with professionals, creating a professional opera experience for the pleasure and education of the local community. To introduce children to the art of Opera.
Utilizes: Actors; Dancers; Designers; Fine Artists; Grant Writers; Guest Accompanists; Guest Artists; Guest Conductors; Guest Designers; Guest Musical Directors; Guest Musicians; Instructors; Local Artists; Lyricists; Multimedia; Music; Original Music Scores; Resident Professionals; Sign Language Translators; Singers; Student Interns; Touring Companies
Founded: 1989
Opened: 1990
Specialized Field: Opera
Status: Non-Profit, Professional
Volunteer Staff: 16
Budget: $49,500
Income Sources: Grants; Memberships; Donations; Ticket Fees
Annual Attendance: 2000
Facility Category: Several theatres
Seating Capacity: 500650
Year Built: 1994

1820
AUGUSTANA CHOIR
Augustana College
Department of Music
639 38th Street
Rock Island, IL 61201
Phone: 309-794-7233
Fax: 309-794-7678
Toll-free: 800-798-8100
e-mail: jonhurty@augustana.edu
Web Site: www.augustana.edu/academics/music
Officers:
President: Steven Bahls
Management:
Director Choral Activities: Jon Hurty
Manager Performance/Outreach: Christiana Conner
Mission: Augustana Choir brings sacred choral music of the highest caliber to people around the region, nation and the world.
Founded: 1860
Specialized Field: A Cappella; Choral
Status: Non-Profit, Non-Professional
Paid Staff: 6
Paid Artists: 1

1821
ARCH-OPERA HOUSE OF SANDWICH
140 E Railroad Street
Sandwich, IL 60548
Phone: 815-786-2555
Fax: 815-786-7855
e-mail: sandwichoperahouse@hotmail.com
Web Site: www.sandwichoperahouse@hotmail.com
Officers:
President: Rich Bryan
Vice President: Tom Merkel
Secretary: Ellen Faulk
Mission: To present a variety of high cultural programs to people of all ages in Sandwich and througout our region.
Utilizes: Actors; Dance Companies; Dancers; Educators; Fine Artists; Grant Writers; Guest Accompanists; Guest Directors; Guest Musical Directors; Guest Musicians; Instructors; Multimedia; Original Music Scores; Sign Language Translators; Singers; Soloists; Special Technical Talent; Theatre Companies; Touring Companies
Founded: 1878

Specialized Field: Light Opera; Lyric Opera; Musical Theatre; Choral; Ethnic Music; Classical; Contemporary; Religious
Status: Non-Profit, Non-Professional
Paid Staff: 1
Volunteer Staff: 50
Budget: 110,000
Income Sources: Ticket Sales; Memberships; Donations
Performs At: ARCH-Opera House of Sandwich
Annual Attendance: 20,000
Facility Category: Restored 1878 Opera House
Type of Stage: Proscenium
Stage Dimensions: 20 x 20
Seating Capacity: 310
Year Built: 1878
Year Remodeled: 1986
Cost: $1.75 Million
Rental Contact: Executive Director Sandra Black

1822
WAUKEGAN CONCERT CHORUS
First Presbyterian Church
122 N Martin Luther King Jr Avenue
Waukegan, IL 60085
Phone: 847-360-4740
Fax: 847-622-6621
Management:
President: Janet Kilkelly
VP: Joe Favero
Treasurer: Wayne Motley
Commissioner: Terry Duffy
Utilizes: Guest Lecturers; Guest Writers; Multimedia; Music; Original Music Scores
Founded: 1917
Specialized Field: Choral
Non-paid Artists: 30

1823
WAUKEGAN SYMPHONY ORCHESTRA & CONCERT CHORUS
Jack Benny Center for the Arts
39 Jack Benny Drive
Waukegan, IL 60085
Phone: 847-360-4740
Fax: 847-662-0592
Management:
Music Director: Stephen Blackweldor
Performance Supervisor: Rik Covalinski
Specialized Field: Choral
Paid Staff: 2
Paid Artists: 6
Non-paid Artists: 60
Budget: $100,000-150,000
Income Sources: Waukegan Park District Corporation, grants
Performs At: Orlin D. Trapp Auditorium
Annual Attendance: 1500
Facility Category: Auditorium
Type of Stage: Proscenium
Seating Capacity: 1500

1824
WOODSTOCK OPERA HOUSE
121 Van Buren Street
Woodstock, IL 60098
Phone: 815-338-4212
Fax: 815-334-2287
e-mail: operahouse@woodstock-il.com
Web Site: www.woodstockoperahouse.com
Management:
Executive Director: John Scharres

Mission: Providing McHenry County, Illinois with a cultural center; showcasing Illinois artists as well as American and international performers; working closely with the local Woodstock community.
Utilizes: Dance Companies; Dancers; Fine Artists; Guild Activities; Local Artists; Multi Collaborations; Multimedia; Original Music Scores; Resident Professionals; Sign Language Translators; Student Interns; Special Technical Talent; Theatre Companies
Founded: 1890
Specialized Field: Opera; Musical Theatre
Status: Non-Profit, Professional
Paid Staff: 15
Volunteer Staff: 20
Income Sources: International Society of Performing Arts Administrators; Association of Performing Arts Presenters
Performs At: Woodstock Opera House
Annual Attendance: 55,000
Facility Category: Theatre
Type of Stage: Proscenium
Stage Dimensions: 24'x26'
Seating Capacity: 420
Year Built: 1890
Year Remodeled: 1974
Organization Type: Performing; Resident; Educational; Sponsoring

Indiana

1825
INDIANAPOLIS OPERA

250 E 38th Street
Indianapolis, IN 46205
Phone: 317-283-3531
Fax: 317-923-5611
e-mail: ticket@indyopera.org
Web Site: www.indyopera.org
Officers:
 President: Norman Oman
Management:
 Executive Director: John Pickett
 Artistic Director: James Caraher
 Marketing and Customer Relations: Mathew Tippel
 Marketing and Customer Relations: Matthew Tippel
Mission: To produce and present opera in performances of the highest quality and to develop audiences for opera.
Utilizes: Artists-in-Residence; Choreographers; Collaborating Artists; Collaborations; Dance Companies; Dancers; Designers; Educators; Grant Writers; Guest Accompanists; Guest Artists; Guest Composers; Guest Conductors; Guest Designers; Guest Instructors; Guest Musical Directors; Guest Musicians; Guest Soloists; Guest Writers; Instructors; Local Artists; Lyricists; Multimedia; Music; New Productions; Original Music Scores; Resident Professionals; Sign Language Translators; Singers; Soloists; Student Interns
Founded: 1975
Specialized Field: Grand Opera; Light Opera; Lyric Opera; Musical Theatre; Choral; Ethnic Music; Classical; Contemporary; Operetta
Status: Non-Profit, Professional
Paid Staff: 10
Paid Artists: 130
Budget: $2,312,000
Performs At: Clowes Memorial Hall; Butler University
Affiliations: Opera America
Annual Attendance: 16,800

Facility Category: Multiple Use, Concert, Performance Hall
Type of Stage: Proscenium
Stage Dimensions: 52'x 60'
Year Built: 1965
Organization Type: Performing; Touring; Resident; Educational; Sponsoring
Resident Groups: Indianapolis Opera Ensemble

1826
INDIANAPOLIS SYMPHONIC CHOIR

4600 Sunset Avenue
Indianapolis, IN 46208
Phone: 317-940-9057
Fax: 317-940-9058
e-mail: information@indychoir.org
Officers:
 Assistant Conductor: Michael Davis
Management:
 Artistic Director: Eric Stark
 Managing Director: Michael Pettry
Specialized Field: Choral

1827
MACALLISTER

PO Box 1941
Indianapolis, IN 46206
Phone: 317-546-6387
Fax: 317-546-6399
e-mail: opera@iquest.net
Officers:
 President: PE MacAllister
 VP: Melvin Carroway
 Secreatary: Dede Commons
 Treasurer: Alan Thompson
Management:
 General Director: Elaine Bookwalter
 President/Board of Directors: P E MacAllister
Mission: To provide opera opportunities for young artists through opera productions and sponsorship of the MacAllister Awards, the largest sponsored, nonrestricted opera competition on the continent; to provide, through productions, training for young artists, both artistic and technical.
Utilizes: Guest Artists; Guest Companies; Singers
Founded: 1980
Specialized Field: Grand Opera; Lyric Opera; Light Opera; Operetta
Status: Professional; Nonprofit
Paid Staff: 2
Income Sources: Central Opera Service; Butler University Romantic Festival
Performs At: Frederic M. Ayers Auditorium
Organization Type: Performing; Touring; Sponsoring

1828
PELLA OPERA HOUSE

611 Franklin Street
PO Box 326
Pella, IN 50219
Phone: 641-628-8625
Fax: 641-628-8628
Toll-free: 800-720-6327
e-mail: boxoffice@pellaoperahouse.com
Web Site: www.pellaoperahouse.com
Management:
 General Manager: Barbara Filer
 Assistant Manager: Emily Riley
 Volunteer Coordinator: Vicki Meyers
Mission: Present a variety of performing arts throughout the year for entertainment and educational purposes. To enhance and support the arts community.
Founded: 1900
Specialized Field: Opera; Musical Theatre

Paid Staff: 2
Volunteer Staff: 30
Budget: $260,000
Income Sources: Ticket Sales; Donations; Tours
Annual Attendance: 32,000
Type of Stage: Proscenium
Stage Dimensions: 22x22
Seating Capacity: 324
Year Built: 1900
Year Remodeled: 1990
Cost: $2,000,000
Rental Contact: Emily Riley

1829
VALPARAISO UNIVERSITY CHORALE

Valparaiso University Music Department
1709 Chapel Drive
Valparaiso, IN 46383
Phone: 219-464-5453
Fax: 219-464-5244
Web Site: www.valpo.edu
Management:
 Managing Director: Jeff Hazewinkel
 Choral Director: Christopher M Cock
Mission: To perform works that represent the university's Lutheran heritage and multi-cultural perspectives.
Specialized Field: Choral; Classical; Religious
Status: Non-Profit, Non-Professional
Paid Staff: 30
Non-paid Artists: 50

Iowa

1830
CEDAR RAPIDS OPERA THEATRE

1120 Second Avenue SE
Cedar Rapids, IA 52401
Phone: 319-365-7401
e-mail: cropera@webtv.net
Officers:
 President: Mark Zimmerman
 Vice President: Sarah Antin
 Treasurer: John Botkin
 Secretary: Kim Blankenship
Management:
 Executive Director/Conductor: Daniel Kleinknecht
 Development Director: Virginia Michalicek
Mission: To present two to three operas featuring international and American artists each season, as well as opera outreach performances.
Founded: 1988
Specialized Field: Opera
Status: Nonprofit
Season: January-June

1831
DORIAN MUSIC FESTIVALS

Luther College 700 Drive
Decorah, IA 52101
Phone: 563-387-1389
Fax: 563-387-1076
e-mail: buzzja01@luther.edu
Web Site: www.luther.edu
Officers:
 President: Robert Lillie
 VP: Justine Lionberger
 Secretary/Treasurer: Lynette Wilson
 Director Marketing: Vicki Bjerke
Management:
 Artistic Director: Weston Noble
 Managing Director: Jim Buzza
 Chairman of Music Department: John Strauss

Mission: Offering performance experience to young professionals as well as student artists.
Utilizes: Singers
Founded: 1949
Specialized Field: Multi-Disciplinary; Musical Theatre
Status: Non-Profit, Non-Professional
Paid Staff: 25
Performs At: Luther College Center for Faith and Life
Organization Type: Touring; Resident; Educational

1832
DES MOINES CHORAL SOCIETY
PO Box 93852
Des Moines, IA 50393
e-mail: dmcs@dmchoral.org
Web Site: www.dmchoral.org
Officers:
President: Wayne Bauman
VP/Community Relations: LuAnn White
Treasurer: Carolyn Knittle
Secretary: Lois O'Donnell
Management:
Artistic Director/Conductor: Dr James Rodde
Mission: To inform, educate and stimulate the public toward a better appreciation of choral music.
Specialized Field: Choral; Educational
Paid Staff: 1
Paid Artists: 6
Budget: $85,000
Income Sources: Tickets; Grants; Private Donations
Affiliations: Chorus America; Metro Alliance of Greater Des Moines
Annual Attendance: 2,000

1833
DES MOINES METRO OPERA
106 W Boston Avenue
Indianola, IA 50125-8175
Phone: 515-961-6221
Fax: 515-961-8175
e-mail: dmmo@dmmo.org
Web Site: www.dmmo.org
Officers:
President: Wendy Carlson
CEO: Thomas S Smith
Management:
Artistic Director: Robert L Larsen
Executive Director: Thomas S Smith
Artistic Administrator: Michael Egel
Development Director: Robert Montana
Mission: To provide a stage for young american artists, produce high quality performances and educate audiences to opera in the Midwest.
Utilizes: Artists-in-Residence; Choreographers; Dance Companies; Dancers; Designers; Educators; Fine Artists; Guest Writers; High School Drama; Instructors; Local Artists; Multimedia; Organization Contracts; Original Music Scores; Resident Professionals; Sign Language Translators; Soloists; Student Interns
Founded: 1973
Specialized Field: Opera
Status: Non-Profit, Professional
Paid Staff: 9
Paid Artists: 175
Budget: 2.1 Million
Income Sources: Revenue and Contributions
Season: June - July
Performs At: Indianola (Festival Site)
Affiliations: Opera America
Annual Attendance: 8,000
Facility Category: Blank Performing Arts Center
Type of Stage: Proscenium with thrust stage
Seating Capacity: 488
Year Built: 1972

Rental Contact: Jim Lile
Organization Type: Performing; Touring; Resident; Educational
Resident Groups: OPERA Iowa - 13 week tour

Kansas

1834
TOPEKA SYMPHONY CHORUS
PO Box 2206
Topeka, KS 66601-2206
Phone: 785-232-2032
Fax: 785-232-6204
e-mail: tso@topekasymphony.org
Web Site: www.topekasymphony.org
Management:
Music Director: John Strickler
General Manager: Kathy Mahe
Founded: 1945
Specialized Field: Choral
Status: Non-Profit, Professional
Paid Artists: 80

Kentucky

1835
KENTUCKY OPERA
Kentucky Opera Building
101 S 8th Street
Louisville, KY 40202
Phone: 502-584-4500
Fax: 502-584-7484
Toll-free: 800-690-9236
e-mail: info@kyopera.org
Web Site: www.kyopera.org
Management:
General Director: Deborah Sandler
Finance Director: Brett Landow
Development Director: Jeff Sodowsky
Development Director: Jeff Sodowsky
Marketing Director: Steve Kelley
Mission: To entertain and educate a broad, diverse audience by producing opera of the highest quality.
Utilizes: Collaborations; Designers; Educators; Grant Writers; Guest Companies; Guest Composers; Guest Conductors; Guest Designers; Guest Writers; Instructors; Lyricists; Multimedia; Original Music Scores; Resident Professionals; Sign Language Translators
Founded: 1952
Specialized Field: Grand Opera; Light Opera; Lyric Opera; Musical Theatre; Choral; Youth Chorus; Ethnic Music; Classical; Contemporary; Religious
Status: Non-Profit, Professional
Paid Staff: 20
Volunteer Staff: 200
Paid Artists: 80
Budget: $2,200,000
Income Sources: Fund for the Arts; Mainstage Performances; Education Programs; Public/Private Philanthropy
Performs At: Kentucky Center for the Arts; Whitney Hall
Annual Attendance: 14,000/25,000 edu
Type of Stage: Proscenium
Stage Dimensions: 59'9"x52'6"x32'
Seating Capacity: 2,406
Year Built: 1983
Year Remodeled: 2002
Organization Type: Performing; Touring; Educational

1836
LOUISVILLE BACH SOCIETY
4607 Hanford Lane
Louisville, KY 40207
Phone: 502-585-2224
Fax: 502-893-7954
e-mail: bach@louisvillebachsociety.org
Web Site: www.louisvillebachsociety.org
Management:
Founder/Director: Melvin Dickinson
Founder/Director: Margaret Dickinson
Mission: To perform the choral and orchestral music of Bach, as well as other baroque, modern, classical and romantic composers.
Founded: 1964
Specialized Field: Classical
Status: Non-Profit, Professional
Paid Staff: 4
Income Sources: Kentucky Arts Council; Greater Louisville Fund for the Arts; American Federation of Musicians
Performs At: University of Louisville
Organization Type: Performing; Touring; Resident; Educational

1837
LOUISVILLE CHORUS
6303 Fern Valley Pass
Louisville, KY 40228
Phone: 502-968-6300
Fax: cal-l f-irst
e-mail: louisvillechorus@louisvillechorus.org
Web Site: www.louisvillechorus.org
Officers:
President: Jordan Engler
VP: Paul Patterson
Secretary: Sue Juett
Management:
Executive Director: Therese Davis
Artistic Director: Dr S Timothy Glasscock
Mission: To foster the art of choral music for singers, audiences, students and special constituents by presenting the widest variety of performances and outreach programs.
Utilizes: Guest Artists
Founded: 1939
Specialized Field: Choral
Status: Non-Profit, Professional
Paid Staff: 4
Paid Artists: 45
Income Sources: Individual, Corporate, State Arts Council, Local Metro Government
Performs At: Concert Halls; Churches
Affiliations: Chorus America
Organization Type: Performing; Touring; Educational; Entertaining; Sponsoring

Louisiana

1838
JPAS CHILDREN'S CHORUS/YOUTH CHORALE
Jefferson Performing Arts Society
1118 Clearview Parkway
Metairie, LA 70001
Phone: 504-885-2000
Fax: 504-885-3437
e-mail: jpasinfo@jpas.org
Web Site: www.jpas.org
Officers:
Chairman: Hannah Cunningham
President: Wayne Keating

Past President: Dr. Bud Willis
Secretary: Subhash Kulkarni
Management:
President: Andrea Babin
Executive Director: Dennis Assaf
Conductor: Louise Labruyere
Conductor: Dr. Louise LaBruyere
Mission: To provide a complete music education experience for young people.
Founded: 1984
Specialized Field: Youth Chorus; Opera; Musical Theatre
Status: Non-Profit, Professional
Paid Staff: 4
Volunteer Staff: 20
Paid Artists: 300
Non-paid Artists: 130
Budget: $150,000
Income Sources: JPAS; Tuitions

1839
NEW ORLEANS OPERA ASSOCIATION
305 Baronne
Suite 500
New Orleans, LA 70112-1618
Phone: 504-529-2278
Fax: 504-529-7668
Toll-free: 800-881-4459
Web Site: www.neworleansopera.org
Officers:
President: Lois Hawkins
Executive VP: Robert Monroe
Treasurer: Ronald Dyer
Secretary: Charles Dupin
Management:
President: Lovell Jr John
Executive Director: Robert Lyall
Scenic Studios Manager: G Alan Rusnak
Administration Director: Rebecca Hildabrant
Mission: Providing the highest quality grand opera for Louisiana and its surrounding area.
Utilizes: Choreographers; Dancers; Designers; Five Seasonal Concerts; Grant Writers; Guest Accompanists; Guest Composers; Guest Designers; Guest Lecturers; Guest Musicians; Local Artists; Multimedia; Original Music Scores; Resident Professionals; Sign Language Translators
Founded: 1943
Specialized Field: Grand Opera
Status: Non-Profit, Professional
Paid Staff: 8
Paid Artists: 50
Budget: $2.5 Million
Income Sources: Individual; Corporate; Foundation; Ticket Sales
Season: October- April
Performs At: Mahalia Jackson Theater of the Performing Arts
Annual Attendance: 18,500
Facility Category: Theater
Year Built: 1975
Organization Type: Performing; Resident; Educational

1840
SYMPHONY CHORUS OF NEW ORLEANS
PO Box 50542
New Orleans, LA 70150
Phone: 504-737-0647
e-mail: resoj@cox.net
Web Site: www.symphonychorus.org
Management:
Director: Steven Edwards
Accompanist: Carmen Leerstang
President: Enrico J Sterlling

Founded: 1981
Specialized Field: Choral; Classical; Religious
Status: Non-Profit, Professional
Paid Staff: 3
Paid Artists: 40

1841
SHREVEPORT OPERA
212 Texas Street
Suite 101
Shreveport, LA 71101
Phone: 318-227-9503
Fax: 318-227-9518
e-mail: edillner@shreveopera.org
Web Site: www.shreveopera.org
Officers:
President: Joe Kane
VP: Bob Robinson
Treasurer: Mikey Carlisle
Management:
General/Artistic Director: Eric Dillner
VP Fund Development: Sybil Patten
Mission: To foster and promote the production of quality performances of opera and music drama; to aid in furthering the development of opera; and to further educational efforts which support the growth, development, and appreciation of opera as a viable art form within the tri-state region.
Utilizes: Collaborations; Dance Companies; Educators; Fine Artists; Guest Composers; Guest Designers; Guest Writers; Original Music Scores; Resident Professionals; Sign Language Translators; Soloists
Founded: 1949
Specialized Field: Opera/Musical Theatre
Status: Non-Profit, Professional
Paid Staff: 7
Volunteer Staff: 450
Paid Artists: 450
Non-paid Artists: 30
Budget: $800,000
Income Sources: Individual; Corporate; Facility; State; Grants
Performs At: Theater
Annual Attendance: 5,500
Facility Category: Civic Theater
Type of Stage: Proscenium
Stage Dimensions: 50' x 40'
Seating Capacity: 2,000
Organization Type: Performing; Touring; Resident; Educational

Maine

1842
MAINE MUSIC SOCIETY
PO Box 711
Auburn, ME 4212
Phone: 207-782-1403
Fax: 207-783-1851
e-mail: info@mainemusicsociety.org
Web Site: www.mainemusicsociety.org
Officers:
President: Judith W Andrucki
VP: Charles W Scheib
Treasurer: Jeffrey R Gosselin
Management:
President: Robert Grieshaber
Artistic Director: Peter Frewen
Mission: The Maine Music Society supports the artistic and educational activities of the professional Maine Chamber Ensemble and the auditioned, mixed-voice Androscoggin Chorale.
Founded: 1991

Specialized Field: Choral; Classical; Religious
Status: Non-Profit, Professional
Paid Staff: 3
Income Sources: Maine Community Foundation; Davis Family Foundation; Helen & George Ladd Charitable Foundation; Maine Arts Commision; Maine Humanities Commission
Performs At: Orchestral; Chamber and Coral Music; Educational Programs
Affiliations: American Symphony Orchestra League; Maine Arts Sponsors Association; Androscoggin County Chamber of Commerce; Maine Association of Non-Profits

1843
PORTLAND SYMPHONIC CHOIR
PO Box 1517
Portland, ME 97207
Phone: 503-223-1217
Fax: 503-223-4840
e-mail: info@pschoir.org
Officers:
Development Director: Kathy Pape
Management:
Artistic Director/Conductor: Dr Steven Zopfi
General Manager: Mark Petersen
Founded: 1946
Specialized Field: Choral

1844
PORTOPERA
PO Box 7733
Portland, ME 04112
Phone: 207-879-7678
Fax: 207-879-7681
e-mail: portopera@aol.com
Web Site: www.portopera.org
Officers:
Immediate Past President: Dona D Vaughn
Management:
President: Donald Head
Office Manager: Julia Underwood
Mission: PORTopera is dedicated to equally high standards of artisitc excellence and personal effectiveness. Its mission is to present to the people of Maine great operatic masterpieces in productions that are lively, beautiful and important locally, regionally and nationally. Its objective is to do so within a principled and empowered environment.
Utilizes: Choreographers; Collaborating Artists; Collaborations; Dance Companies; Dancers; Educators; Five Seasonal Concerts; Grant Writers; Guest Accompanists; Guest Artists; Guest Composers; Guest Conductors; Guest Designers; Guest Instructors; Guest Writers; Local Artists; Lyricists; Multimedia; Original Music Scores; Resident Artists; Resident Professionals; Sign Language Translators; Soloists; Student Interns
Founded: 1995
Specialized Field: Grand Opera
Status: Non-Profit, Professional
Paid Staff: 1
Volunteer Staff: 2
Paid Artists: 179
Budget: $500,000
Income Sources: Corporate; Individual Support
Annual Attendance: 6,000
Facility Category: Municipal Theatre
Type of Stage: Proscenium
Stage Dimensions: 52'x40'x35'
Seating Capacity: 1830
Year Built: 1912
Year Remodeled: 1997

1845
BAY CHAMBER CONCERTS
18 Central Street
PO Box 599
Rockport, ME 04856
Phone: 207-236-2823
Fax: 207-230-0454
Toll-free: 888-707-2770
e-mail: info@baychamberconcerts.org
Web Site: www.baychamberconcerts.org
Officers:
    President: Carole Brand
    Treasurer: Laurence Novotney
    Secretary: Jacob Gerritsen
Management:
    Executive Director: Monica Kelly
Mission: To present a variety of music styles and educational programs to reach a diverse audience along the coast of Maine.
Utilizes: Commissioned Music; Dancers; Fine Artists; Grant Writers; Guest Accompanists; Guest Choreographers; Guest Directors; Guest Musical Directors; Guest Musicians; Lyricists; Multimedia; Original Music Scores; Resident Artists; Sign Language Translators; Singers; Special Technical Talent
Founded: 1960
Specialized Field: Music
Status: Non-Profit, Professional
Paid Staff: 9
Budget: $500,000
Performs At: Rockport Opera House
Facility Category: Opera House; Strom Auditorium
Type of Stage: Proscenium; Auditorium
Seating Capacity: 400; 800
Organization Type: Performing

Maryland

1846
BALTIMORE CHORAL ARTS SOCIETY
1316 Park Avenue
Baltimore, MD 21217
Phone: 410-523-7070
Fax: 410-523-7097
Toll-free: 800-750-0875
e-mail: info@baltimorechoralarts.org
Web Site: www.baltimorechoralarts.org
Officers:
    President: Arnold Paskoff
    VP: Linda C Goldberg
    Treasurer: Jeffrey Austin
    Secretary: Andrea Bowman-Moore
Management:
    Music Dir: Tom Hall
    Chorus Manager: Ellen Clayton
    Administrative Director: Laura Byrne
    Chorus Manager: Ellen Clayton
Utilizes: Collaborating Artists; Collaborations; Commissioned Composers; Dance Companies; Dancers; Grant Writers; Guest Accompanists; Guest Choreographers; Guest Directors; Guest Instructors; Guest Musical Directors; Guest Musicians; Instructors; Multimedia; Original Music Scores; Sign Language Translators; Singers
Founded: 1966
Specialized Field: Choral
Paid Staff: 4
Volunteer Staff: 1
Paid Artists: 65
Non-paid Artists: 75
Budget: $500,000

Income Sources: Ticket Sales; Contributions; Maryland State Arts Council; Baltimore County Commission on Arts & Science; Mayor's Advisory Committee on Art & Culture; Local Contributors
Performs At: Joseph Meyerhoff Symphony Hall; Krausbaar Auditorium
Affiliations: Member of Chorus America
Annual Attendance: 15,000

1847
BALTIMORE OPERA COMPANY
110 W Mount Royal Avenue
Suite 306
Baltimore, MD 21201
Phone: 410-625-1600
Fax: 410-625-6474
e-mail: jharp@baltimoreopera.com
Web Site: www.baltimoreopera.com
Management:
    President: Micheal Harrison
    Music Director: James Harp
Utilizes: Dancers; Designers; Grant Writers; Guest Accompanists; Guest Composers; Guest Conductors; Guest Designers; Guest Instructors; Guest Writers; Resident Professionals; Sign Language Translators
Founded: 1950
Specialized Field: Grand Opera; Light Opera; Lyric Opera; Musical Theatre; Choral; Youth Chorus; Ethnic Music; Classical; Contemporary; Religious
Status: Non-Profit, Professional
Paid Staff: 100
Volunteer Staff: 50
Paid Artists: 20
Budget: $7 million
Annual Attendance: 60,000
Facility Category: Opera House
Type of Stage: Proscenium
Seating Capacity: 2460
Year Built: 1894
Year Remodeled: 1981

1848
BALTIMORE SYMPHONY CHORUS
1212 Cathedral Street
Baltimore, MD 21201-5545
Phone: 410-783-8100
Fax: 410-783-8077
e-mail: jglicker@baltimoresymphony.org
Web Site: www.baltimoresymphony.org
Management:
    President: James Glicker
    VP: Karen Swanson
    Director Of Operations: Susan Anderson
    Artistic Coordinato: Carol Oppelaar
Mission: The choir is the choral arm of the Baltimore Symphony and performs when the Symphony needs singers.
Founded: 1916
Specialized Field: Choral
Status: Nonprofit
Performs At: Joseph Meyerhoff Symphony Hall
Organization Type: Performing

1849
HANDEL CHOIR OF BALTIMORE
3600 Clipper Mill Road
Suite 240
Baltimore, MD 21211
Phone: 410-366-6544
Fax: 410-366-6554
e-mail: music@handelchoir.org
Web Site: www.handelchoir.org
Officers:

    President: Audrey Theis
    VP: Howard Kymptom
    Treasurer: John Keenan
Management:
    President: Daryl Sidle
    Artistic Director: Melinda O'Neal
    Managing Director: Linda Talley
Founded: 1934
Specialized Field: Choral; Youth Chorus; Classical
Status: Non-Profit, Non-Professional
Paid Staff: 2
Paid Artists: 3
Income Sources: Southwest Airlines; David Ashton & Associates

1850
OPERA VIVENTE
811 Cathedral Street
Baltimore, MD 21201
Phone: 410-547-7997
Fax: 847-557-2175
e-mail: paul@chemicalgraphics.com
Management:
    General Director: John Bowen
    Music Director: Aaron Sherber
Utilizes: Collaborations; Grant Writers; Guest Writers; Instructors; Local Artists; Multimedia; Music; Original Music Scores; Resident Professionals; Sign Language Translators
Specialized Field: Opera

1851
WASHINGTON SAVOYARDS
916 G Street NW
Bethesda, MD 20001
Phone: 202-315-1323
Fax: 202-315-1303
Web Site: www.savoyards.org
Officers:
    President: Kathleen Mitchell
    VP: Tom Npedersen
    Treasurer: Christine McEvroy
Management:
    Executive Director: Katheleen Mitchell
Mission: Provide professional performances of musicals & Gilbert & Sulivans Operettas
Founded: 1973
Specialized Field: Gilbert and Sullivan; Operetta; Light Opera
Status: Non-Profit, Professional
Income Sources: Ticket Sales; Grants
Performs At: Atlas Performing Arts Center

1852
CHILDREN'S OPERA THEATER
3203 Pickwick Lane
Chevy Chase, MD 20815
Phone: 301-656-2442
Fax: 301-656-2442
Management:
    Artistic Director: Michael Kaye
Mission: Introducing and involving youth in opera; providing employment for artists as they make the transition to a professional career.
Founded: 1976
Specialized Field: Light Opera; Choral
Status: Professional; Nonprofit
Organization Type: Touring; Educational

1853
COLUMBIA PRO CANTARE
5404 Iron Pen Place
Columbia, MD 21044

Phone: 410-730-8549
Fax: 410-730-8634
e-mail: chorus@procantare.org
Web Site: www.procantare.org
Officers:
President: Judith Weintraub
VP: Gregory Stanford
Secretary: Joyce Halasz
Treasurer: Kevin T Howard
Management:
Executive Director: Elladean Brigham
Director: Frances Dawson
Accompanist: Alison Matuskey
Assistant Director: Laura Lee Fischer
Mission: A nationally recognized mixed chorus of 130 auditioned volunteer singers based in Howard County which seeks to present the finest choral literature in concerts of high artistic quality to a growing regional audience. It aspires to provide enriching musical experiences for both singers and audience. Its mission is to nourish the human need we all have to participate in something greater than ourselves through the performance of great choral music.
Founded: 1977
Specialized Field: Vocal Music
Status: Non-Profit, Professional
Paid Staff: 5
Volunteer Staff: 1
Paid Artists: 3
Non-paid Artists: 130
Budget: $180,000
Income Sources: Public and Private Grants; Corporations; Individuals
Performs At: Public Theater for performing arts; Also use 2 large churches for smaller concerts.
Affiliations: Maryland State Arts Council; Howard County Arts Council; Chorus America
Annual Attendance: 2,500
Stage Dimensions: 60' x 30'
Seating Capacity: 740
Year Built: 1997

1854
INSTITUTE OF MUSICAL TRADITIONS

PO Box 5930
Takoma Park, MD 20913
Phone: 301-754-3611
Fax: 301-754-3612
e-mail: office@imtfolk.org
Web Site: www.imtfolk.org
Officers:
President: David Richardson
Vice-President: Kent Murray
Treasurer: Arthur Shaw
Secretary: James Byrne
Founder, President Emeritus: David Eisner
Management:
Executive Director: Siobhan Quinn
Mission: To present concerts, workshops and educational programs that preserve traditional folk music from around the world and nurtures new styles evolving from these cultural roots.
Utilizes: Arrangers; Collaborating Artists; Collaborations; Community Members; Dance Companies; Educators; Five Seasonal Concerts; Guest Accompanists; Guest Choreographers; Guest Companies; Guest Directors; Guest Ensembles; Guest Musical Directors; Guest Musicians; Guest Speakers; Instructors; Local Talent; Local Unknown Artists; Lyricists; Multi Collaborations; Multimedia; Original Music Scores; Paid Performers; Resident Companies; Sign Language Translators; Student Interns; Theatre Companies; Visual Designers
Founded: 1981

Opened: 1981
Specialized Field: Traditional Folk
Status: Non-Profit
Paid Staff: 3
Volunteer Staff: 20
Paid Artists: 135
Budget: $131,000
Income Sources: Tickets; Public & Private Foundation Grants; Private Donations
Affiliations: Folklore Society Of Greater Washington; International Folk & Dance Alliance; Washington Arts & Music Association
Annual Attendance: 3,500
Facility Category: Church Hall
Type of Stage: Elevated
Stage Dimensions: 16x6
Seating Capacity: 150; 230; 500

1855
CHILDREN'S CHORUS OF MARYLAND & SCHOOL OF MUSIC

100 E Pennsylvania Avenue
Suite 202
Towson, MD 21286
Phone: 410-494-1480
Fax: 410-494-4673
e-mail: ccm@ccmsings.org
Officers:
Education Director & Associate Cond: Dr Betty Bertaux
Concert Manager: Andrea Burgoyne
Management:
General Director: Ramona Galey
Artistic Director: Mairee Pantzer
Assistant Artistic Director: Mairee Pantzer
Concert Manager: Andrea Burgoyne
Mission: Children's Chorus of Maryland empowers musical children and promotes the fine art of music. This mission is achieved by providing children with the tool of self-expression, through choral music education and professional performance opportunities, in a program dedicated tio excellence, aesthetic sensitivity, play-based learning, respect, and diversity.
Founded: 1976
Specialized Field: Youth Chorus

Massachusetts

1856
VALLEY LIGHT OPERA

PO Box 2143
Amherst, MA 01004-2143
Phone: 413-549-1098
e-mail: wcvenman@comcast.net
Web Site: www.vlo.org
Management:
President: Glen Gordon
Managing Director: Jacqueline Kidwell
Artistic Director: Joseph Donohue
General Manager: Bill Venman
Mission: Promotes broad participation and produces fine entertainment.
Founded: 1975
Specialized Field: Light Opera
Status: Non-Profit, Non-Professional
Performs At: Amherst Regional High School Auditorium
Organization Type: Performing

1857
BOSTON CAMERATA

45 Ash Street
Auburndale, MA 02466

Phone: 617-262-2092
Fax: 617-262-2091
Toll-free: 866-427-2092
e-mail: manager@bostoncamerata.com
Web Site: www.bostoncamerata.org
Management:
Artistic Director: Anne Azema
Mission: To reach large audience through teaching, recording and performance by touring.
Founded: 1954
Specialized Field: Lyric Opera; Musical Theatre; Choral; Ethnic Music; Classical
Status: Non-Profit, Professional
Paid Staff: 2
Paid Artists: 30

1858
CANTATA SINGERS

161 First Street
Boston, MA 02142
Phone: 617-868-5885
Fax: 617-868-3772
e-mail: bach@cantatasingers.org
Web Site: www.cantatasingers.org
Management:
Executive Director: Jeffrey George
Artistic Director: David Hoose
General Manager: Jessica Goodyear
Mission: Through vital performances of works old and new, familiar and unfamiliar, Cantata Singers engages and shared with the community the power of music to enrich the human spirit.
Utilizes: Commissioned Composers; Commissioned Music; Educators; Fine Artists; Five Seasonal Concerts; Grant Writers; Guest Directors; Guest Instructors; Guest Musicians; Local Artists; Multimedia; Organization Contracts; Original Music Scores; Sign Language Translators; Singers; Soloists
Founded: 1964
Specialized Field: Choral
Status: Non-Profit, Professional
Paid Staff: 3
Volunteer Staff: 5
Paid Artists: 1
Non-paid Artists: 44
Budget: $400,000
Income Sources: Ticket sales; Contributions; Government Endowments
Performs At: Rented Hall
Affiliations: Chorus America
Annual Attendance: 7,000
Facility Category: Rented Concert Hall at New England Conservatory
Rental Contact: Jon Wulp

1859
HANDEL AND HAYDN SOCIETY

300 Massachusetts Avenue
Boston, MA 2115
Phone: 617-262-1815
Fax: 617-266-4217
e-mail: info@handelandhaydn.org
Web Site: www.handelandhaydn.org
Management:
Executive Director: Mary Deissler
Music Director: Grant Llewellyn
Executive Director: Mary Deissler
Mission: Dedicated to promoting the performance, study, composition and appreciation of music.
Utilizes: Commissioned Composers; Guest Composers; Guest Directors; Guest Musical Directors; Guest Musicians; Multimedia; Music; Original Music Scores; Sign Language Translators; Singers
Founded: 1815

Specialized Field: Choral; Classical
Status: Non-Profit, Professional
Paid Staff: 16
Paid Artists: 100
Budget: $2,600,000
Performs At: Symphony Hall; Jordan Hall
Annual Attendance: 40,000
Organization Type: Performing; Touring; Educational; Sponsoring

1860
OPERA BOSTON

25 Kingston Street
3R
Boston, MA 02111-2200
Phone: 617-451-3388
Fax: 617-451-6633
e-mail: info@operaboston.org
Officers:
 Chairman: Winifred Perkin Gray
 President: Randolph Fuller
 Treasurer: Campbell Steward
 Office Administrator: Gillian Morrison
 Secretary: Timothy Gillette
Management:
 General Director: Carole Charnow
 Music Director: Gil Rose
 Director Operations: William Chapman
 Production Manager: Emma Donoghue
 Patron Services Associate: Chloe Quail
 Production Photographer: Clive Grainger
Mission: The company produces staged opera and special events in Boston, as well as presents new productions of rarely-heard works, innovative repertoire, groundbreaking opera education and outreach programs.
Specialized Field: Opera
Status: Professional
Income Sources: Donations
Season: October-April
Performs At: Cutler Majestic Theatre
Year Built: 1903

1861
OPERA NEW ENGLAND

45 Franklin Street
4th Floor
Boston, MA 02110-1300
Phone: 617-542-4912
Fax: 617-542-4913
Web Site: www.blo.org
Officers:
 Chair: Steven P Atkin
 Vice Chair: Thomas D Gill Jr
 Treasurer: J Stephanie Giacalone
 Clerk: Catherine E Grein
Management:
 Marketing Director: Judith McMichael
 General/Artistic Diretor: Esther Nelson
 Production Director: Dan Duro
Mission: To present diverse productions by emerging opera musicians to entertain, educate and inspire audiences.
Founded: 1973
Specialized Field: Lyric Opera; Light Opera
Status: Professional, Nonprofit
Income Sources: Opera Company of Boston
Organization Type: Educational; Sponsoring

1862
BRAINTREE CHORAL SOCIETY

346 Washington Street
PMB #154
Braintree, MA 02184
Phone: 508-583-5662
e-mail: braintreechoral@bigfoot.com
Web Site: www.braintreesings.com
Management:
 President: Kathleen Mullen
 Artistic Director: Justin Smith
Mission: Promoting interest in choral music.
Utilizes: Singers
Founded: 1923
Specialized Field: Classical; Choral
Status: Non-Profit, Non-Professional
Paid Staff: 2
Paid Artists: 2
Organization Type: Performing

1863
KLEZMER CONSERVATORY BAND

83 Inman Street
Cambridge, MA 02139
Phone: 617-354-2884
Fax: 617-776-0955
Web Site: www.klezmerconservatory.com
Management:
 Business Manager Aaron Concert Man: James Guttmann
Mission: To offer Yiddish instrumental and vocal music with many influences (Jazz, Dixieland, Ragtime, Latin and Broadway).
Founded: 1980
Specialized Field: Ethnic Music; Folk Music; Band
Status: Professional
Organization Type: Performing; Touring

1864
RADCLIFFE CHORAL SOCIETY

Harvard University
Holden Chapel
Cambridge, MA 02138
Phone: 617-495-5730
Fax: 617-496-5166
e-mail: rcs@hcs.harvard.edu
Web Site: www.radcliffechoralsociety.org
Officers:
 President: Molly O'Laughlin
Management:
 Conductor: Andrew Clark
 Manager: Molly Storer
Founded: 1899
Specialized Field: Choral; Youth Chorus; Ethnic Music; Classical; Contemporary; Religious
Status: Non-Profit, Non-Professional
Paid Artists: 3

1865
SAVOYARD LIGHT OPERA COMPANY

PO Box 333
Carlisle, MA 01741
Phone: 978-371-7562
Officers:
 Secretary: Laura Gouillart
Management:
 President: Larry Millner
 Vice President: Liana Pacilli
 Secretary: Susan Schmidt
 Treasurer: Tedford Armistead
 Archivist: Patti Lopoulos
Mission: To associate ourselves for the purpose of encouraging and making generally available performances of the works of W.S. Gilbert and A.S. Sullivan, and other works of similar operatic, musical or theatrical nature in Carlisle and nearby areas.
Founded: 1971
Specialized Field: Light Opera

1866
COLLEGE LIGHT OPERA COMPANY

162 S Cedar Street
Falmouth, MA 02541
Phone: 440-774-8485
Fax: 440-775-8642
e-mail: cloc@oberlin.net
Web Site: www.collegelightopera.com
Officers:
 President: DeWitt C Jones III
 Treasurer: Robert A Haslun
 Secretary: Ursula R Haslun
Management:
 Producer/General Manager: Robert A Haslun
 Producer/Business Manager: Ursula R Haslun
Mission: Musical theatre training ground for undergraduates, singers, musicians, tech & costume staff, business office and production staff.
Utilizes: Actors; Choreographers; Contract Orchestras; Designers; Guest Artists; Guest Companies; Guest Conductors; Guest Designers; Guest Lecturers; Music; Resident Artists; Resident Professionals; Sign Language Translators; Students
Founded: 1969
Specialized Field: Light Opera; Operetta; Musical Theatre
Status: Non-Professional, Nonprofit
Paid Staff: 25
Paid Artists: 18
Non-paid Artists: 32
Budget: $300,000
Income Sources: Box Office; Annual Fund
Performs At: Highfield Theatre
Annual Attendance: 15,200
Type of Stage: Proscenium
Seating Capacity: 300
Year Built: 1947
Year Remodeled: 2007
Cost: $450,000
Organization Type: Performing, Resident, Educational

1867
COMMONWEALTH OPERA

140 Pine Street #12
Florence, MA 01062
Phone: 413-586-5026
Fax: 413-587-0380
Toll-free: 866-733-6737
Web Site: www.commonwealthopera.org
Officers:
 President: Gerry Katz
 VP: Richard Strongren
 Treasurer: Anita Regish
 Guild President: Katherine Willey
Management:
 President: Richard L Stromgren
 Artistic Director: Ron Luchsinger
 Executive Director: Janet Sadler
Mission: Enhancing professional opportunities in and appreciation of grand opera and broadway musicals in the region.
Utilizes: Choreographers; Collaborations; Dance Companies; Dancers; Five Seasonal Concerts; Grant Writers; Guest Accompanists; Guest Companies; Guest Composers; Guest Instructors; Guest Lecturers; Guest Musicians; Guest Writers; Instructors; Multimedia; Original Music Scores; Resident Professionals; Sign Language Translators; Singers
Founded: 1972
Specialized Field: Grand Opera; Lyric Opera
Status: Semi-Professional
Paid Staff: 3
Volunteer Staff: 40

Budget: 250,000
Income Sources: Tickets; Sponsors; Donations
Performs At: Calvin Theatre; Smith College
Organization Type: Performing; Touring

1868

BERKSHIRE OPERA COMPANY

297 N Street
Great Barrington, MA 01201
Phone: 413-442-9955
Fax: 413-442-5995
Web Site: www.berkshireopera.org
Officers:
  Chairman/Treasurer: Norman M Michaels
Management:
  General Director: Ryaniam Taylor
  Artistic Director: Kathleen Kelly
Mission: To produce and present the very finest in
professional opera. To provide and enhance
educational programming and community activities to
people of all ages in Berkshire County.
Utilizes: Guest Companies; Singers
Founded: 1985
Specialized Field: Opera
Status: Non-Profit, Professional
Budget: $1.3 million
Income Sources: Berkshire Hills Visitors Bureau
Performs At: Mahaiwe Theater
Annual Attendance: 3,000
Seating Capacity: 700
Year Built: 1905
Rental Contact: Al Shwartz
Organization Type: Performing; Touring; Resident;
Educational

1869

PRISM OPERA

5 Linebrook Road
Ipswich, MA 01938
Phone: 978-356-1787
Toll-free: 888-236-8181
e-mail: prism@prismopera.org
Management:
  Executive Director: Arthur Rishi
  Artistic Director: Thomas Stumpf
Mission: Prism Opera is committed to producing
effective and moving productions of operatic
masterpieces, with a special emphasis on neglected
works and on twentieth century repertoire.
Founded: 1995
Specialized Field: Opera

1870

MASTER SINGERS

PO Box 172
Lexington, MA 02173
Phone: 781-862-6459
e-mail: msingers@themastersingers.org
Web Site: www.themastersingers.org
Officers:
  President: Sarah Getty
  Treasurer: Shaylor Lindsay
  Secretary: Virginia Fitzgerald
Management:
  President: Haris Papamichael
  Accompanist: Eric Mazonson
  Music Director: Adam Grossman
Mission: To present the chamber chorus repertoire of
all eras in an intimate setting aimed at maximum
enjoyment for both singers and listeners.
Founded: 1967
Specialized Field: Classical; Contemporary; Grand
Opera; Choral; Religious
Status: Non-Profit, Professional

Paid Staff: 30
Income Sources: Massachusetts Cultural Alliance
Performs At: First Parish Church in Lexington
Organization Type: Performing; Touring

1871

LONGWOOD OPERA

42 Hawthorne Avenue
Needham, MA 02192-3806
Phone: 781-455-0960
Fax: 781-455-0960
e-mail: Encore@LongwoodOpera.org
Officers:
  Musical Director: Wayne Ward
  Director of Marketing Communication: Harding
  Ounanian
Management:
  General Director: Scott Brumit
  Musical Director: Jeffrey Brody
Specialized Field: Opera

1872

ZAMIR CHORALE OF BOSTON

PO Box 590126
Newton Center, MA 02459
Phone: 617-916-2008
Toll-free: 866-926-4720
e-mail: manager@zamir.org
Web Site: www.zamir.org
Officers:
  Chairman: Joyce Bohnen
  Co-Treasurer: Marvin Mandelbaum
  Clerk: Andrew M Greene
Management:
  Executive Director: Dianne Simmons
  Artistic Director: Joshua Jacobson
  Accompanist: Edwin Swanborn
Mission: To promote, develop and encourage the
growth of Jewish choral music through scholarship,
performances, recordings and educational programs.
Founded: 1969
Specialized Field: Choral; Ethnic Music
Status: Non-Professional; Nonprofit
Paid Staff: 5
Organization Type: Performing; Touring; Resident;
Educational

1873

SMITH COLLEGE GLEE CLUB & CHOIRS

Smith College, Music Department
Northampton, MA 01063
Phone: 413-585-3150
Fax: 413-585-3180
e-mail: gleeclub@smith.edu
Web Site: www.smith.edu/music
Management:
  President: Anna Monas
  Artistic Executive Director: Jonathan Hirsh
Founded: 1885
Specialized Field: Grand Opera; Light Opera; Lyric
Opera; Musical Theatre; Choral; Youth Chorus; Ethnic
Music; Classical; Contemporary; Religious
Status: Non-Profit, Non-Professional
Paid Staff: 2

1874

GLORIAE DEI ARTES FOUNDATION

PO Box 2831
Orleans, MA 02653
Phone: 508-255-3999
Fax: 508-240-1989
e-mail: gda@gdaf.org
Web Site: www.gdaf.org
Officers:

President: Sarah R Kanaga
Management:
  Choir Director: Elizabeth C Patterson
  Concert Manager: Gail Gibson
Mission: The pursuit of excellence in the performing
and visual arts and to the inspiration and education of
others. The foundation encompasses twelve arts
groups and soloist, including the world renowned choir
Gloriae Dei Cantores, Spirit of America band, Stages
Theatre Company, Tapestry Dance Company,
Archangelus Brass Ensemble, Gloria Dei Ringers, Vox
Caeli Sinfonia, Gloriae Dei Chamber Ensemble, Master
Schola educational series.
Utilizes: Artists-in-Residence; Choreographers;
Collaborating Artists; Composers; Dancers; Designers;
Fine Artists; Guest Writers; High School Drama; Multi
Collaborations; Multimedia; Music; Paid Performers;
Poets; Resident Professionals; Sign Language
Translators; Singers; Theatre Companies; Visual Arts;
Volunteer Directors & Actors; Writers
Founded: 1995
Specialized Field: Classical; Contemporary; Religious;
Choral; Musical Theatre
Status: Non-Profit, Professional

1875

BERKSHIRE LYRIC THEATRE

PO Box 347
Pittsfield, MA 01202
Phone: 413-499-0258
Web Site: www.berkshirelyrictheatre.org
Officers:
  President: Laurel Caluori
Management:
  Artistic Director: Jack Brown
Mission: To nurture the art of choral singing through
diverse concert performances and to educate young
musicians.
Utilizes: Singers
Founded: 1963
Specialized Field: Light Opera; Choral
Status: Non-profit
Paid Staff: 40
Organization Type: Performing

1876

PAUL MADORE CHORALE

PO Box 992
Salem, MA 01970-6092
Phone: 781-639-8062
Fax: 781-639-8065
e-mail: djmurph@mediaone.net
Officers:
  President: Kathleen Snarry
  Vice President: Chris Lemoine
  Treasurer: Marcia Hunkins
  Recording Secretary: Eileen Mackey
  Corresponding Secretary: Elaine Shindle
  Librarian: Judy Pierce
Management:
  Director: Paul Madore
  Orchestra Manager: Alan Hawery
  Chorus Manager: Donna Murphy
Mission: Offering choral masterpieces for the
enjoyment and cultural advancement of the North
Shore/Boston areas.
Utilizes: Guest Musical Directors; Guest Soloists;
Multimedia; New Productions; Original Music Scores;
Sign Language Translators; Singers
Founded: 1966
Specialized Field: Opera; Choral
Status: Semi-Professional; Nonprofit
Volunteer Staff: 1
Paid Artists: 1

Budget: $50,000
Income Sources: Box Office; Private Donations
Performs At: Churches; Municipal Buildings
Affiliations: Salem Chamber of Commerce; Greater Boston Choral Consortium
Organization Type: Performing

1877
FINE ARTS CHORALE

779 Main Street
South Weymouth, MA 02190
Phone: 617-337-3023
Toll-free: 800-230-7555
Officers:
    President: Deborah Kohl
    VP: Kate Lacatell
    Secretary: Eleanor MacDonald
    Treasurer: Louise Bacon
Management:
    Music Director/Founder: Peter L Edwards
Mission: The presentation of sacred choral masterworks accompanied by a professional orchestra and soloists. There are no dues required.
Founded: 1966
Specialized Field: Choral
Status: Non-Professional; Nonprofit
Paid Staff: 130
Organization Type: Performing

1878
REVELS

80 Mount Auburn Street
Watertown, MA 02472
Phone: 617-972-8300
Fax: 617-972-8400
e-mail: infor@revels.org
Web Site: www.revels.org
Officers:
    President: Carl Corey
    VP: Richard Goettle
    Treasurer: Christopher Hughes
Management:
    Executive Director: Gayle Rich
    Artistic Director: Patrick Swanson
    Music Director: George Emlen
Mission: To cultivate authentic cultural traditions and celebrate the cycles of the seasons through staged performances of song, dance and drama, education programs, and opportunities for participation by all.
Founded: 1971
Specialized Field: Music; Dance; Theatre
Status: Non-Profit, Professional
Paid Staff: 7
Paid Artists: 20
Performs At: Sanders Theatre; Harvard University
Organization Type: Performing; Educational

1879
SALISBURY SINGERS

370 Main Street
Suite 1200
Worcester, MA 01608
Phone: 508-799-3848
Fax: 508-792-3067
e-mail: info@salisburysingers.org
Web Site: www.salisburysingers.org
Officers:
    Treasuer: James Monroe
Management:
    Music Director: Dr Michelle Graveline
    Chorus Manager: Joyce Messinger
Mission: To perform classical works for the community of central Massachusetts.
Founded: 1973

Specialized Field: Choral
Status: Non-Profit
Paid Staff: 1
Non-paid Artists: 80
Performs At: Church; Concert Halls

Michigan

1880
ADRIAN SYMPHONY ORCHESTRA

110 S Madison Street
Rush Hall
Adrian, MI 49221
Phone: 517-264-3121
Fax: 517-264-3121
Web Site: www.aso.org
Officers:
    Co-Chair: Robert Bell
    Co-Chair: Muriel Bell
Management:
    Music Director: John Dodson
    Executive Director: Susan Hoffman
    Producer: Jimmy Hilburger
Mission: To create grand opera performances for the citizens of Lenawee County, Michigan; to sponsor the Friedrich Schorr Memorial Performance Prize in Voice; to collaborate between the Adrian Symphony and the Croswell Opera House.
Utilizes: Singers
Founded: 1989
Specialized Field: Grand Opera; Lyric Opera; Operetta
Status: Professional; Nonprofit
Income Sources: National Opera Association; Opera America
Performs At: Croswell Opera House
Organization Type: Performing; Resident; Educational

1881
BOYCHOIR OF ANN ARBOR

1100 N Main Street
Ann Arbor, MI 48104
Phone: 734-663-5377
e-mail: office@aaboychoir.org
Web Site: www.aaboychoir.org
Management:
    Founder & Music Director: Thomas Strode, office@aaboychoir.org
Mission: Through excellence in vocal training and choral performance, the Boychoir of Ann Arbor enriches the life of the community and enhances the social, emotional, and musical development of boys who love to sing.
Utilizes: Community Members; Community Talent; Educators; Grant Writers; Guest Composers; Guest Designers; Guest Directors; Guest Musical Directors; High School Drama; Local Artists & Directors; Lyricists; Multimedia; Music; Original Music Scores; Scenic Designers; Sign Language Translators; Singers; Soloists; Volunteer Artists
Founded: 1986
Specialized Field: Choral; Youth Chorus; Classical
Status: Non-Profit
Paid Staff: 3
Volunteer Staff: 40
Paid Artists: 2
Non-paid Artists: 2
Budget: $55,000
Income Sources: Performances; Tuition; Donations; Grants
Affiliations: Royal School of Church Music

1882
COMIC OPERA GUILD

PO Box 1922
Ann Arbor, MI 48106
Phone: 734-973-3264
Fax: 734-973-6281
e-mail: constu@comcast.net
Web Site: www.comicoperaguild.org
Officers:
    President: Patrick Johnson
    Secretary: Patricia Petiet
    Treasurer: George Valenta
Management:
    Managing Director: Thomas Petiet
Mission: To revive popularity and interest in the medium of comic opera and operetta through performance and recording.
Utilizes: Guest Artists; Guest Companies; Singers
Founded: 1973
Specialized Field: Light Opera; Musical Theatre; Classical
Status: Non-Profit, Non-Professional
Paid Staff: 6
Volunteer Staff: 40
Paid Artists: 25
Non-paid Artists: 50
Performs At: Village Theater
Organization Type: Performing; Touring; Resident

1883
UNIVERSITY MUSICAL SOCIETY CHORAL UNION

University Musical Society
Burton Memorial Tower, 881 N University Avenu
Ann Arbor, MI 48109-1011
Phone: 734-764-2538
Fax: 734-647-1171
Toll-free: 800-221-1229
e-mail: umstix@umich.edu
Web Site: www.ums.org
Officers:
    President: Ken Fisher
    Director Administration: John Kennard
    Director Of Development: Susan McClanahan
    Interim Director Education: Claire Rice
    Chairperson: Dr. James Stanley
    Vice Chair: David Herzig
    Secretary: Martha Darling
    Treasurer: Robert C. Macek
Management:
    Director Of Programming: Michael Kondziolka
    Director oOf Marketing/Communicatio: Sara Billmann
Mission: To provide professional theatre, dance and music for Southeastern Michigan students and residents.
Utilizes: Guest Artists
Founded: 1879
Specialized Field: Series & Festivals; Musical Performance
Status: Non-Profit; Professional
Paid Staff: 30
Budget: $8,000,000
Income Sources: Ticket Sales; Fundraising
Performs At: Hill Auditorium; University of Michigan
Affiliations: Association of Performing Arts Presenters; International Society of Performing Arts Administrators
Annual Attendance: 150,000
Organization Type: Performing; Touring; Resident; Educational

1884
UNIVERSITY OF MICHIGAN GILBERT AND SULLIVAN

The Michigan League Building
911 N University
Ann Arbor, MI 48109
Phone: 734-647-8436
e-mail: umgassexec@umich.edu
Web Site: www.umgass.org
Officers:
   President: Daniel Florip
   VP: Julia Head
   Secretary: Andriana Pachella
   Treasurer: Elizabeth Crabtree
Management:
   Company Promoter: Matthew D Grace
   Ticket Manager: Barbara Fleming
   Programmer: James Allen
Founded: 1947
Specialized Field: Operetta
Status: Non-Professional; Nonprofit
Paid Artists: 30
Performs At: Mendelssohn Theatre; University of Michigan
Organization Type: Performing; Resident; Educational

1885
CHEBOYGAN AREA ARTS COUNCIL/OPERA HOUSE

403 N Huron Street
PO Box 95
Cheboygan, MI 49721
Phone: 231-627-5432
Fax: 231-627-2643
e-mail: pamtheoperahouse.org
Web Site: www.theoperahouse.org
Management:
   Assistant Director: Vicky Pyrzynski
   Executive Director: Pamela Westover
Mission: To promote and encourage cultural and educational activities within the Straits Area of Northern Michigan and to provide services that stimulate and encourage participation in and appreciation of the arts.
Utilizes: Actors; AEA Actors; Artists-in-Residence; Collaborations; Dance Companies; Dancers; Grant Writers; Guest Accompanists; Guest Choreographers; Guest Lecturers; Guest Musical Directors; Guest Musicians; Guild Activities; Local Artists; Multi Collaborations; Multimedia; Original Music Scores; Resident Artists; Sign Language Translators; Singers; Soloists; Special Technical Talent; Theatre Companies
Founded: 1972
Specialized Field: Multi-Disciplinary
Status: Non-Profit, Professional
Budget: $250,000
Income Sources: Membership; Ticket Sales; Fundraisers; Grants; Other Earned Income
Performs At: Opera House
Affiliations: Association of Performing Arts Presenters; MACAA; LHAT
Annual Attendance: 30,000
Facility Category: Historic Theatre
Type of Stage: Proscenium
Stage Dimensions: 34x20
Seating Capacity: 582
Year Built: 1877
Year Remodeled: 1984
Rental Contact: Pamela Westover
Organization Type: Educational; Sponsoring

1886
TIBBITS OPERA FOUNDATION AND ARTS COUNCIL

14 S Hanchett Street
Coldwater, MI 49036
Phone: 517-278-6029
Fax: 517-279-7594
e-mail: boxoffice@tibbits.org
Web Site: www.tibbits.org
Officers:
   President: Randall Hazelbaker
   Treasurer: Brian Hodson
Management:
   Executive Director: Christine Delaney
   Artisic Director: Charles Burr
Mission: Improve the quality of life by preserving the Tibbits Opera House and promoting arts culture and education.
Founded: 1964
Specialized Field: Live Performance
Status: Non-Profit, Professional
Paid Staff: 8
Volunteer Staff: 300
Budget: $500,000
Income Sources: Membership; Ticket Sales; Annual Auction; Grants - Michigan Council for Arts and Cultural Affairs; Michigan Humanities Council; Branch County Community Foundation; Corporate
Performs At: Tibbits Opera House
Affiliations: League Of Historic American Theatres
Annual Attendance: 30,000
Facility Category: Historic Theatre/Opera House
Type of Stage: Proscenium
Stage Dimensions: 25'x35'
Seating Capacity: 500
Year Built: 1882
Year Remodeled: 1965
Rental Contact: Christine Delaney
Organization Type: Performing; Touring; Resident; Educational; Sponsoring
Resident Groups: Tibbits Summer Theatre - Professional Repertory Company

1887
MICHIGAN OPERA THEATRE

1526 Broadway
Detroit, MI 48226
Phone: 313-961-3500
Fax: 313-237-3412
e-mail: webadministrator@motopera.org
Web Site: www.michiganopera.org
Management:
   General Director: David Dichiera
   Productioin Director: David Osborne
   Director Of Artistic Administration: Roberto Mauro
   Facilities Director: Karen Tjaden
   Administration Director: John Eckstrom
   Marketing Director: Steve Haviaras
   Assistant Marketing Director: Susan Fazzini
Mission: To be one of the outstanding opera companies in the United States, serving as a major cultural resource.
Utilizes: Artists-in-Residence; Collaborations; Dance Companies; Educators; Five Seasonal Concerts; Grant Writers; Guest Accompanists; Guest Choreographers; Guest Composers; Guest Conductors; Guest Designers; Guest Instructors; Guest Musical Directors; Guest Musicians; Guest Soloists; Guild Activities; Instructors; Local Artists; Lyricists; Multimedia; Original Music Scores; Playwrights; Resident Artists; Resident

Professionals; Selected Students; Sign Language Translators; Singers; Soloists; Student Interns; Theatre Companies
Founded: 1971
Specialized Field: Grand Opera; Operetta; Musical Theatre
Status: Professional; Nonprofit
Paid Staff: 54
Volunteer Staff: 800
Paid Artists: 74
Budget: 12,000,000
Income Sources: Earned and Unearned
Performs At: Stage; Rehearsal Room
Affiliations: International Association of Auditorium Managers
Annual Attendance: 194,608
Facility Category: Performing Arts
Type of Stage: Proscenium
Stage Dimensions: 65x110
Seating Capacity: 2,800
Year Built: 1922
Year Remodeled: 1996
Rental Contact: Facilities Director Karen Tjaden
Organization Type: Performing; Touring

1888
RACKHAM SYMPHONY CHOIR

555 Brush Street
Number 2311
Detroit, MI 48226
Phone: 313-272-0333
Fax: 313-272-5111
Web Site: www.rackhamchoir.org
Management:
   Music Director: Suzanne Mallare Acton
   Assistant Director And Accompanist: Donald Kukier
   Managing Director: Anne Bak
Mission: To provide choral symphonic performances featuring the works of the classical masters to the Detroit metropolitan area.
Founded: 1949
Specialized Field: Choral
Status: Nonprofit
Paid Staff: 60
Organization Type: Performing; Educational

1889
OPERA LITE

27284 Winterset Circle
Farmington Hills, MI 48334
Phone: 248-888-7640
Fax: 248-888-7641
e-mail: dsp96@aol.com
Management:
   President: David Pulice
   Assistant Director: Don Daniels
Founded: 1986
Specialized Field: Grand Opera; Light Opera; Lyric Opera; Musical Theatre; Choral; Youth Chorus; Classical; Religious
Status: Non-Profit, Professional
Paid Staff: 3
Paid Artists: 47
Organization Type: Performing; Touring; Resident

1890
OPERA GRAND RAPIDS

161 Ottawa NW
Suite 204
Grand Rapids, MI 49503
Phone: 616-451-2741
Fax: 616-451-4587
Web Site: www.operagr.com

Management:
President: Earle Irwin
Executive Director: John Peter Jeffries
Artistic Director: Robert Lyall
Mission: To enhance the quality of life in the Grand Rapids area and Western Michigan by providing professional-quality operatic/musical theater productions; to raise the level of appreciation and understanding of opera in all residents.
Utilizes: Actors; Dancers; Designers; Five Seasonal Concerts; Grant Writers; Guest Accompanists; Guest Artists; Guest Composers; Guest Conductors; Guest Designers; Guest Instructors; Guest Lecturers; Guest Musical Directors; Guest Musicians; Guest Soloists; Guest Writers; Instructors; Local Artists; Lyricists; Multimedia; Music; Original Music Scores; Resident Professionals; Sign Language Translators; Singers; Soloists; Student Interns
Founded: 1967
Specialized Field: Opera
Status: Non-Profit, Professional
Paid Staff: 5
Budget: $1.2 million
Performs At: DeVos Hall; Van Andel Arena
Annual Attendance: 17,000
Seating Capacity: 2,340
Year Built: 1979
Organization Type: Performing; Educational; Sponsoring

1891
HOLLAND CHORALE

150 East 8th Street
Holland, MI 49423-3504
Phone: 616-494-0256
Fax: 616-396-6298
e-mail: julia@hollandchorale.org
Web Site: www.hollandchorale.org
Officers:
President: Ronald J Toering
Management:
Operations Manager: Julia Johnson
Artistic Director: Ryan M Kelly
Founded: 1959
Specialized Field: Choral; Ethnic Music; Classical; Contemporary; Religious
Status: Non-Profit, Non-Professional
Paid Staff: 2
Volunteer Staff: 85

1892
SAGINAW CHORAL SOCIETY

326 S Jefferson Avenue
Saginaw, MI 48647
Phone: 989-753-1812
Fax: 989-753-1043
Web Site: www.saginawchoralsociety.com
Officers:
President: Joan McGlaughlin
Management:
President: William Millar
Business Manager: Tamara Grafe
Mission: To provide an opportunity for quality singers to join together in singing and performing fine choral music so as to contribute to the enjoyment, musical growth and education of the residents of Saginaw Valley. Regularly performs master works from the classical choral music literature, as a priority in maintaining the firm artistic integrity of the organization.
Founded: 1935
Specialized Field: Choral
Status: Non-Profit, Non-Professional
Paid Staff: 2

Minnesota

1893
AUGSBURG CHOIR

Augsburg College
2211 Riverside Avenue South
Minneapolis, MN 55454
Phone: 612-330-1000
Fax: 612-330-1264
e-mail: hendricp@augsburg.edu
Management:
Choral Activities Director: Dr Peter Hendrickson
Specialized Field: Choral

1894
MINNESOTA CHORALE

528 Hennepin Avenue
Suite 407
Minneapolis, MN 55408
Phone: 612-333-4866
Fax: 612-344-1503
e-mail: we_sing@mnchorale.org
Web Site: www.mnchorale.org
Management:
General Manager: Bob Peskin
Operations Director: Melissa Morey
Mission: The Minnesota Chorale is a nationally acclaimed symphonic chorus with a signature flexibility to perform masterfully in ensembles ranging from 20 to 200 voices. Celebrates the human voice in its ability to educate, enrich, and inspire.
Founded: 1972
Specialized Field: Choral; Ethnic Music; Classical
Status: Non-Profit, Professional
Paid Staff: 8
Paid Artists: 40
Non-paid Artists: 230
Income Sources: Chorus America
Performs At: Orchestra Hall; Ordway Music Theatre
Affiliations: Minnesota Orchestra's Principal Chorus
Organization Type: Performing

1895
MINNESOTA OPERA

620 N First Street
Minneapolis, MN 55401
Phone: 612-333-2700
Fax: 612-333-0869
Toll-free: 800-676-6737
e-mail: staff@mnopera.org
Web Site: www.mnopera.org
Officers:
President/CEO: Kevin Smith
Artistic Director: Dale Johnson
Management:
President: Kevin Smith
Artistic Director: Dale Johnson
Mission: To produce opera and opera education programs at the highest artisic level that inspire and entertain our audiences and enrich the cultural life of our community.
Utilizes: Choreographers; Dance Companies; Designers; Educators; Guest Accompanists; Guest Artists; Guest Composers; Guest Conductors; Instructors; Local Artists; Original Music Scores; Resident Professionals; Sign Language Translators
Founded: 1963
Specialized Field: Opera
Status: Non-Profit, Professional
Income Sources: Opera America
Performs At: Ordway Music Theatre
Annual Attendance: 55,000

Facility Category: Rent Ordway Center for the Performing Arts
Seating Capacity: 1764
Year Built: 1985
Organization Type: Performing; Touring; Resident; Educational; Recording

1896
NATIONAL LUTHERAN CHOIR

528 Hennepin Avenue
Suite 302
Minneapolis, MN 55403
Phone: 612-722-2301
Fax: 612-216-4777
Toll-free: 888-747-4589
e-mail: info@nlca.com
Web Site: www.nlca.com
Management:
General Manager: Debby Harrer
Music Director: David Cherwien
Administrative Assistant: Kellie Gabrick
Mission: The National Lutheran Choir seeks to strengthen, renew, and preserve the heritage of sacred choral music through the highest standards of performance and literature.
Founded: 1986
Specialized Field: Choral; Religious
Status: Professional
Paid Staff: 3
Paid Artists: 4
Non-paid Artists: 55
Budget: $250,000
Income Sources: Ticket Sales; General Donations; Corporate Donations
Affiliations: American Council for the Arts; American Lutheran Church Musicians; Chorus America
Annual Attendance: 25,000
Organization Type: Performing

1897
TWIN CITIES GAY MEN'S CHORUS

528 Hennepin Avenue
Suite 307
Minneapolis, MN 55403
Phone: 612-339-7664
Fax: 612-332-8141
e-mail: chorus@tcgmc.org
Web Site: www.tcgmc.org
Management:
Executive Director: Jeff Heirr
Artistic Director: Stan Hill
Marketing/Development Manager: Christopher Taykalo
Office Manager: Stephanie Gaw
Mission: Gay men building community through music.
Utilizes: Choreographers; Commissioned Composers; Commissioned Music; Grant Writers; Guest Accompanists; Guest Artists; Guest Musicians; Selected Students; Sign Language Translators; Singers; Visual Arts
Founded: 1981
Specialized Field: Choral
Status: Non-Profit, Non-Professional
Paid Staff: 5
Volunteer Staff: 20
Non-paid Artists: 150
Budget: $625,000
Income Sources: Ticket Sales; Merchandise; Contributions
Performs At: Ted Menn Concert Hall
Annual Attendance: 9,000
Facility Category: Concert hall
Seating Capacity: 1,100
Organization Type: Performing, Touring, Recording

1898
VOCALESSENCE
1900 Nicollet Avenue
Minneapolis, MN 55403
Phone: 612-547-1451
Fax: 612-547-1484
e-mail: info@vocalessence.org
Web Site: www.vocalessence.org
Management:
   President: Janice Marturano
   Executive Director: Mary Ann Pulk
   Artistic Director: Philip Brunelle
Mission: Founded as The Plymouth Music Series,
explores the interaction of voices and instruments
through innovative programming of music, both
newly-commissioned and rarely heard.
Founded: 1969
Specialized Field: Musical Theatre; Choral; Classical;
Contemporary; Religious
Status: Non-Profit, Professional
Paid Staff: 10
Paid Artists: 32
Non-paid Artists: 80

1899
MINNETONKA CHAMBER CHOIR
Music Association of Minnetonka
18285 Highway 7
Minnetonka, MN 55345
Phone: 952-401-5954
Fax: 952-401-5959
e-mail: mamoffice@musicassociation.org
Web Site: www.musicassociation.org
Officers:
   Office Administrative: Joyce Barnes
Management:
   Artistic Director/Conductor: Roger S Hoel
Mission: Provides enriching classical musical
experiences for people of all ages and abilities.
Approximately 70 concerts are performed each year.
Founded: 1974
Specialized Field: Choral; Youth Chorus; Ethnic Music;
Classical; Contemporary; Religious
Status: Non-Profit, Non-Professional
Paid Staff: 3
Paid Artists: 300

1900
MINNETONKA SYMPHONY CHORUS
Music Association of Minnetonka
18285 Highway 7
Minnetonka, MN 55345
Phone: 952-401-5954
Fax: 952-401-5959
e-mail: mamoffice@musicassociation.org
Web Site: www.musicassociation.org
Officers:
   Office Administrator: Joyce Barnes
Management:
   Music Director/Conductor: Roger Satrang Hoel
Mission: Provides enriching classical musical
experiences for people of all ages and abilities.
Approximately 70 concerts are performed each year.
Founded: 1974
Specialized Field: Community Chorus
Status: Non-Profit; Non-Professional
Paid Staff: 3

1901
CONCORD SINGERS OF NEW ULM
PO Box 492
New Ulm, MN 56073
Phone: 507-354-8850
Fax: 507-354-1504
e-mail: concord31@newulmtel.net
Web Site: www.concordsingers.com
Officers:
   President: Joseph Meyer
   VP: Lenny Donahue
Management:
   Manager: John Konz
   Music Director: Robert Beussman
   Secretary: Dick Wilbrecht
Mission: To promote the German language through
singing.
Founded: 1931
Specialized Field: Festive German Music
Status: Non-Profit, Non-Professional
Paid Staff: 2
Volunteer Staff: 4
Non-paid Artists: 36
Income Sources: Stipend From The City Plus
Performances In Our 5 State Area
Organization Type: Performing; Sponsoring

1902
ST OLAF CHOIR
St Olaf College
1520 St Olaf Avenue
Northfield, MN 55057-1098
Phone: 507-786-3179
Fax: 507-786-3521
Toll-free: 800-363-5487
e-mail: music@stolaf.edu
Web Site: www.stolaf.edu/music
Management:
   Artistic Director: Anton Armstrong
   Managing Director: B J Johnson
Founded: 1912
Specialized Field: Choral; Ethnic Music; Classical;
Contemporary; Religious
Status: Non-Profit, Non-Professional
Paid Staff: 6

1903
ROCHESTER SYMPHONY ORCHESTRA & CHORALE
400 S Broadway
Suite 302
Rochester, MN 55904
Phone: 507-286-8742
Fax: 507-280-4136
e-mail: info@rochestersymphony.org
Web Site: www.rochestersymphony.org
Officers:
   President: Lester Horntvedt
Management:
   Interim Executive Director: Laurie Mond
   Artistic Director: Jere Lantz
   Business Administrator: Amy Lindstrom
   Education Coordinator: Nancy Eastman
Mission: Rochester Symphony Orchestra and Chorale
seeks to serve our community and region by
preserving, nurturing and advancing the art of music
through education and high quality performances that
seek to touch the soul.
Utilizes: Collaborating Artists; Collaborations; Dancers;
Five Seasonal Concerts; Guest Artists; Guest Musical
Directors; Guest Musicians; Multimedia; Music; New
Productions; Original Music Scores; Sign Language
Translators; Singers
Founded: 1919
Specialized Field: Choral; Orchestra
Status: Non-Profit, Professional
Paid Staff: 4
Volunteer Staff: 80

Paid Artists: 75
Non-paid Artists: 80
Budget: $550,000
Income Sources: Ticket Sales; Contributions; Grants
Performs At: Mayo Civic Center
Affiliations: ASOL
Annual Attendance: 5,000
Facility Category: Mayo Civic Center

1904
NORTH STAR OPERA
75 W 5th Street
Suite 414
Saint Paul, MN 55102
Phone: 651-224-1640
e-mail: steve@northstaropera.org
Web Site: www.northstaropera.com
Management:
   Planning Director: Craig Fields
   Artistic Director: Steve Stucki
   Operations Director: Alison Albrecht
   President: Mariellen Jacob
Mission: Developing and showcasing highly-talented,
well-qualified professional musicians, singers and
related personnel of the local area and upper Midwest;
sponsoring college internship programs.
Utilizes: Guest Artists; Guest Companies; Singers
Founded: 1980
Specialized Field: Lyric Opera; Light Opera; Operetta
Status: Professional; Nonprofit
Performs At: O'Shaughnessy Auditorium; Drew Fine
Aris Theatre
Organization Type: Performing; Touring; Resident;
Educational

1905
MINNESOTA CENTER CHORALE
PO Box 471
St Cloud, MN 56302
Phone: 320-257-0603
e-mail: pwelter@csbsju.edu
Web Site: minnesotacenterchorale.org
Officers:
   President: Charles J Welter
   Secretary: Tom Ramsey
   Treasurer: Chris Morgan
Management:
   Music Director/Conductor: J Michele Edwards
Mission: The MCC performs a mixture of classical and
contemporary music, often with orchesrtal
accompaniment.
Utilizes: Guest Companies; Guest Composers; Guest
Lecturers; Guest Musical Directors; Guest Musicians;
Local Artists; Singers
Specialized Field: Choral
Paid Staff: 1
Budget: $60,000
Annual Attendance: 3,000
Facility Category: Auditorium
Year Built: 1965

Mississippi

1906
GULF COAST OPERA THEATRE
PO Box 118
Biloxi, MS 39533
Phone: 228-436-6514
Fax: 228-374-0152
Web Site: www.datasync.com/~micksch/gco.htm
Management:
   President: Lisa Michell
   General Director: David Daniels

Artistic Director: Jane Hardin
Mission: Educating Mississippi Gulf Coast residents regarding musical theatre and opera.
Founded: 1973
Specialized Field: Grand Opera; Light Opera; Lyric Opera; Musical Theatre; Choral; Youth Chorus; Classical; Religious
Status: Non-Profit, Professional
Paid Staff: 40
Performs At: Saenger Theatre for the Performing Arts
Organization Type: Performing; Resident

1907
MISSISSIPPI OPERA
PO Box 1551
Jackson, MS 39215
Phone: 601-960-2300
Fax: 601-960-1526
Toll-free: 877-676-7372
e-mail: info@msoperaa.org
Web Site: www.msopera.org
Management:
    Executive Director: Elizabeth Buyan
    Artistic Director: Jay Dean
    Marketing Director: Sherry Harfst
Mission: To enhance Mississippi's cultural and economic development by presenting high quality opera performances in an accessible manner; to identify and develop regional operatic artists; and to promote the understanding and appreciation of Opera through education, outreach, and audience development.
Utilizes: Guest Artists; Guest Companies; Singers
Founded: 1945
Specialized Field: Grand Opera; Lyric Opera; Light Opera; Operetta; Musical Theatre
Status: Non-Profit, Professional
Paid Staff: 2
Volunteer Staff: 3
Paid Artists: 1
Non-paid Artists: 1
Budget: $300,000
Performs At: Jackson Municipal Auditorium
Organization Type: Performing; Touring; Educational

Missouri

1908
SAINT LOUIS CHAMBER CHORUS
PO Box 11558
Clayton, MO 63105
Phone: 636-458-4343
Fax: 314-993-6458
e-mail: stchamberchorus@gmail.org
Web Site: www.chamberchorus.org
Officers:
    President: Barbara Uhlemann
    Treasurer: Deane Thompson
Management:
    Executive Director: Linda Ryder
    Artistic Director: Philip Barnes
    Assistant Conductor: Mary Chapman
    Assistant Conductor: Orin Johnson
Mission: Presenting unaccompanied classical choral music, not merely to entertain, but to educate and inspire.
Utilizes: Commissioned Music
Founded: 1956
Specialized Field: A Cappella Choral Music
Status: Not-For-Profit
Paid Staff: 2
Volunteer Staff: 2
Paid Artists: 46
Income Sources: Ticket Sales; Donations; Grants

Affiliations: American Choral Directorss' Association
Annual Attendance: 1,000
Facility Category: Houses of Worship & Concert Halls
Organization Type: Performing; Educational

1909
HEARTLAND MEN'S CHORUS
PO Box 32374
Kansas City, MO 64171-5374
Phone: 816-931-3338
Fax: 816-531-1367
e-mail: hmc@hmckc.org
Web Site: www.hmckc.org
Officers:
    Chairman: Matthew Stretz
Management:
    Artistic Director: Joseph Nadeau
    Executive Director: Rick Fisher
Mission: A not-for-profit, volunteer chorus of gay and gay-sensitive people joining together to make a positive cultural contribution to the entire community; advancing men's choral music through excellence in performance.
Founded: 1986
Specialized Field: Choral
Status: Non-Profit, Non-Professional
Paid Staff: 3
Paid Artists: 20
Non-paid Artists: 135
Budget: $695,000
Income Sources: Program Revenues; Donations
Performs At: The Folly Theater
Affiliations: Gay and Lesbian Association Choruses; Chorus America
Annual Attendance: 7,000
Seating Capacity: 1,078
Year Built: 1900
Year Remodeled: 2000
Organization Type: Performing

1910
LYRIC OPERA OF KANSAS CITY
Lyric Theatre
1029 Central
Kansas City, MO 64105-1677
Phone: 877-673-7252
Fax: 816-471-0602
Web Site: www.kc-opera.org
Management:
    Artistic Director: Ward Holmquist
    General Director: Evan R Luskin
Mission: The Lyric Opera of Kansas engages people of diverse backgrounds and ages through the region in a broad range of professional operatic experiences to enrich their lives.
Utilizes: Guest Artists; Guest Companies; Singers
Founded: 1958
Specialized Field: Grand Opera; Light Opera; Lyric Opera; Musical Theatre; Choral; Classical; Operetta
Status: Non-Profit, Professional
Paid Staff: 21
Paid Artists: 120
Budget: $5.1 Million
Income Sources: Ticket Sales; Contributions
Performs At: Lyric Theatre
Affiliations: Opera America
Annual Attendance: 20,000
Facility Category: Theatre
Type of Stage: Proscenium
Stage Dimensions: 50'x36'
Seating Capacity: 1640
Year Built: 1926
Year Remodeled: 1974
Organization Type: Performing; Touring; Resident

1911
KANSAS CITY SYMPHONY CHORUS
William Jewell College
Music Department
Liberty, MO 64068
Mailing Address: 800 West 47 Street, Kansas City, MO. 64112
Phone: 816-781-7700
Fax: 816-415-5027
e-mail: epleya@william.jewell.edu
Management:
    Music Department Chair: Ian Coleman
Specialized Field: Choral

1912
BACH SOCIETY OF SAINT LOUIS
634 N Grand Boulevard
12th Floor
Saint Louis, MO 63103-1002
Phone: 314-652-2224
Fax: 314-652-0450
Officers:
    Chairman: Dan Lesicko
    Vice Chairman: Sally M Williams
    Treasurer: Susan Thomson
    Secretary: Ellen Walters
Management:
    Executive Director: Alayne D Smith
    Music Director and Conductor: Dr A Dennis Sparger
Mission: To educate, enrich and entertain the people of the St. Louis region by performing the choral works of Johann Sebastian Bach and other composers.
Founded: 1939
Specialized Field: Choral
Paid Staff: 1
Paid Artists: 25
Non-paid Artists: 35
Budget: $250,000
Income Sources: Individual & Corporate Contributions; Local; Regional & State Grants
Annual Attendance: 5,000

1913
OPERA THEATRE OF SAINT LOUIS
210 Hazel Avenue
PO Box 191910
Saint Louis, MO 63119
Phone: 314-961-0171
Fax: 314-961-7463
e-mail: info@opera-stl.org
Web Site: www.opera-stl.org
Officers:
    Chairman: Donna Wilkinson
    Vice Chair: Arnold W Donald
    Vice Chair: Jo Ann Harmon
Management:
    Artistic Director: Colin Graham
    General Director: Charles R Mackay
    Music Director: Stephen Lord
    Director Finance: Heather Kemp
Mission: To offer opera in English; to provide career advancement for young American singers; to offer the direction of renowned conductors and directors.
Utilizes: Guest Companies; Guest Composers; Guest Conductors; Multimedia; Original Music Scores; Sign Language Translators; Singers
Founded: 1976
Specialized Field: Grand Opera; Light Opera; Lyric Opera; Musical Theatre; Choral; Youth Chorus; Ethnic Music; Classical; Contemporary
Status: Non-Profit, Professional
Paid Staff: 25

Budget: $6,500,000
Income Sources: 75% Contributions
Performs At: Loretto-Hilton Center for the Performing Arts
Affiliations: Missouri Arts Council; Regional Arts Commission; National Endowment for the Arts; Arts & Education Council of Greater Saint Louis
Annual Attendance: 29,000
Facility Category: Theater
Type of Stage: Thrust
Seating Capacity: 987
Rental Contact: Stephen Ryan
Organization Type: Performing; Touring; Educational

1914

SAINT LOUIS SYMPHONY CHILDREN'S CHOIRS
2842 N Ballas
Saint Louis, MO 63131
Phone: 314-993-9626
Fax: 314-993-0264
Web Site: www.slccsing.org
Management:
    President: Charlotte Dohlmann
    Artistic Director: Barbara Berner
    Program Director: Pheeby Telschow
Mission: Performing orchestral works with a chorus.
Utilizes: Guest Artists
Founded: 1978
Specialized Field: Choral; Youth Chorus; Ethnic Music; Classical; Religious
Status: Non-Profit, Non-Professional
Paid Staff: 32
Non-paid Artists: 114
Income Sources: Chorus America
Performs At: Powell Symphony Hall
Organization Type: Performing; Touring; Educational

1915

SAINT LOUIS CHILDREN'S CHOIRS
2842 N Ballas Road
Saint Louis, MO 63131-2311
Phone: 314-993-9626
Fax: 314-993-0264
e-mail: info@slccsing.org
Management:
    Development Director: Sheryl Bennett
    Program Director: Phebe Telschow
    Artistic Director: Barbara Berner
Mission: To provide young artits the opportunity to experience musical excellence and character development.
Specialized Field: Youth Chorus; Classical; Ethnic Music; Choral
Paid Staff: 32
Budget: $600,000
Income Sources: Concert Fees; Tuition; Donations; Grants
Performs At: Symphony Halls
Affiliations: Chorus America
Annual Attendance: 38,000

1916

SRO - A LYRIC THEATRE COMPANY
411 N Sherman Parkway
Springfield, MO 65802
Phone: 417-863-1960
Fax: 417-862-7877
e-mail: info@srolyrictheatre.org
Web Site: www.srolyrictheatre.org
Officers:
    President: Les Brown
    Vice President: Jeff Carney
    Secretary: Mary Christiano

    Treasurer: Sara Hitesman
    Treasurer: Irma Leidig
Management:
    Managing Director: Derek Munson
    Artistic Director/Conductor: Amy Muchnick
Mission: Create lasting memories by presenting, promoting, and developing the art of opera, music, and theatre.
Utilizes: Guest Accompanists; Guest Designers; Local Artists; Multimedia
Founded: 1979
Specialized Field: Grand Opera; Lyric Opera; Light Opera; Operetta
Status: Professional, Nonprofit
Paid Staff: 2
Volunteer Staff: 13
Budget: $189,000
Income Sources: Box Office, Grants, Private Donations
Performs At: Landers Theatre; Hammons Hall
Affiliations: Opera America
Facility Category: Theatre
Type of Stage: Proscenium
Seating Capacity: 600
Year Built: 1920
Year Remodeled: 2005
Organization Type: Performing

Montana

1917

BILLINGS SYMPHONY ORCHESTRA & CHORALE
201 N Broadway
Suite 350
Billings, MT 59101
Phone: 406-252-3610
Fax: 406-252-3353
e-mail: symphony@billingssymphony.org
Web Site: www.billingssymphony.org
Officers:
    President: Robert Griffin
    VP: Jon Phillips
    Secretary: John Green
    Treasurer: Nicki Larson
Management:
    Music Director/Conductor: Uri Barnea
    Executive Director: Rina Reynolds
Mission: To encourage artistic excellence and offer symphonic performances and educational programs to the region.
Utilizes: Artists-in-Residence; Collaborations; Composers-in-Residence; Dance Companies; Guest Accompanists; Guest Companies; Guest Composers; Guest Musical Directors; Guest Musicians; Local Artists; Multimedia; Original Music Scores; Sign Language Translators; Touring Companies
Founded: 1950
Specialized Field: Choral
Status: Non-Profit, Professional
Paid Staff: 4
Paid Artists: 85
Budget: $260,000-1,050,000
Income Sources: Individual; Businesses; Foundations; Government; Ticket Revenue
Performs At: Alberta Bair Theater for the Performing Arts
Annual Attendance: 30,000

1918

MONTANA CHORALE
214 24th Street SW
Great Falls, MT 59406

Phone: 406-453-0248
Fax: 406-453-7248
Web Site: www.montana-chorale.org
Officers:
    President: Ann Cogswell
    VP: Lorrin Darby
    Treasurer: Sharon Knowles
Management:
    Artistic Director: Kenyard Smith
Mission: To inspire and develop the choral arts in Montana, provide continuing education and employment for professional singers in Montana and develop an artistic climate with international reputation in Montana.
Utilizes: Guest Artists
Founded: 1976
Specialized Field: Choral
Status: Professional; Nonprofit
Income Sources: Chorus America
Performs At: Great Falls Civic Center
Organization Type: Performing; Touring; Sponsoring

Nebraska

1919

OPERA OMAHA
1625 Farnam
Omaha, NE 68102
Phone: 402-346-4398
Fax: 402-346-7323
Toll-free: 877-846-7872
Web Site: www.operaomaha.org
Management:
    President: David Gardels
    Executive Director: Joan Desens
    Artistic Director: Hal France
Utilizes: Singers
Founded: 1958
Specialized Field: Grand Opera; Light Opera; Lyric Opera; Musical Theatre; Choral; Youth Chorus; Classical; Contemporary
Status: Non-Profit, Professional
Paid Staff: 13
Budget: $2.4 million
Income Sources: Individuals; Foundations; Corporations; NEA; Nebraska Arts Council; Douglas County; NE Ticket Income
Performs At: Orpheum Theatre; Witherspoon Concert Hall
Annual Attendance: 9,000
Facility Category: Theater
Type of Stage: Proscenium
Stage Dimensions: 54'w x 30'h x 44'd
Seating Capacity: 2,500
Year Built: 1927
Year Remodeled: 2002
Organization Type: Performing; Touring; Resident; Educational; Sponsoring

Nevada

1920

NEVADA OPERA
925 Riverside Drive
PO Box 3256
Reno, NV 89505
Mailing Address: PO Box 3256
Phone: 775-786-4046
Fax: 775-786-4063
e-mail: info@nevadaopera.org
Web Site: www.nevadaopera.org
Management:

Artistic Director: Michael Borowitz
Artistic Director: Robin Stamper
Marketing Director: Zoe Rose
Mission: To produce quality professional opera for the broadest possible audience.
Utilizes: Singers
Founded: 1968
Specialized Field: Grand Opera; Light Opera; Lyric Opera; Choral; Classical
Status: Non-Profit, Professional
Paid Staff: 6
Volunteer Staff: 10
Income Sources: Corporate & Donors
Performs At: Pioneer Center for the Performing Arts
Organization Type: Performing; Resident

New Hampshire

1921
CLAREMONT OPERA HOUSE
City Hall on Opera House Square
PO Box 664
Claremont, NH 03743
Phone: 603-542-0064
Fax: 603-542-7014
Web Site: www.claremontoperahouse.com
Management:
    President: John Bennett
Mission: Multi-use performing arts center.
Utilizes: Guest Accompanists; Guest Musical Directors; Local Artists; Multimedia; Original Music Scores; Soloists; Special Technical Talent; Theatre Companies
Opened: 1977
Specialized Field: Opera; Contemporary
Status: Non-Profit, Professional
Paid Staff: 1
Budget: $150,000
Income Sources: Tickets; Membership; Sponsors
Affiliations: APAP; APNNE
Annual Attendance: 15,000
Facility Category: Theatre
Type of Stage: Proscenium
Seating Capacity: 780
Year Built: 1897
Year Remodeled: 1975

1922
OPERA NORTH
20 W Park Street
Hanover, NH 03766
Phone: 603-448-4141
Fax: 603-448-0999
e-mail: info@operanorth.org
Web Site: www.operanorth.org
Officers:
    President: Virginia Rolett
    President Elect: Caroline Vaillant
    Treasurer: Timothy Wager
    Secretary: Carl Brandon
Management:
    Artistic Director: Louis Burkot
    Executive Director: Patricia Compton
    Executive Producer: Florence Klausner
    Director Productions: Ron Luchsinger
Mission: To produce opera for Northern New England with the highest musical and dramatic standards; to recognize that opera is both entertaining and spiritually enriching, we seek diversified audience through educational and performance programs. Opera North is also committed to the development of young artists through performance opportunities and production experience.

Utilizes: Actors; Artists-in-Residence; Dancers; Designers; Educators; Fine Artists; Five Seasonal Concerts; Grant Writers; Guest Accompanists; Guest Artists; Guest Conductors; Guest Instructors; Guest Musicians; Guest Soloists; Guest Writers; Guild Activities; Local Artists; Multimedia; Original Music Scores; Resident Professionals; Singers; Student Interns
Founded: 1981
Specialized Field: Opera
Paid Staff: 3
Volunteer Staff: 350
Paid Artists: 150
Budget: $540,000
Income Sources: Ticket Sales, Grants, Contributions
Performs At: Lebanon Opera House
Affiliations: Opera America
Annual Attendance: 11,000
Facility Category: Auditorium
Type of Stage: Proscenium
Stage Dimensions: 30 x 30 x 27
Seating Capacity: 800
Year Built: 1920
Year Remodeled: 2001

New Jersey

1923
METRO LYRIC OPERA
PO Box 35
Allenhurst, NJ 07711
Phone: 732-531-2378
Fax: 732-531-2752
e-mail: metrolyricopera@yahoo.com
Web Site: www.metrolyricopera.org
Officers:
    President: John Mullins
    VP: John Plunkett
    Secretary: Joan Benoist
Management:
    Founder And Artistic Director: Era Tognoli
    Assistant Artistic Director: Luccio Zachary
    Conductor: Anton Coppola
Mission: To bring opera of a high standard to all people at popular prices; to create a professional outlet for deserving young artists as well as experienced professionals; to bring opera in English to public schools.
Utilizes: Guest Artists; Singers
Founded: 1959
Specialized Field: Grand Opera; Operetta
Status: Professional
Income Sources: Monmouth Opera Guild
Performs At: Paramount Theatre; Strand Theatre
Organization Type: Performing; Educational; Community Service

1924
PHILOMUSICA CHOIR
PO Box 6032
East Brunswick, NJ 08816-6032
Phone: 732-545-8434
Toll-free: 888-744-5668
e-mail: info@philomusica.org
Web Site: www.philomusica.org
Officers:
    President: Faith Knabe
    VP: Julie Ann Glaz
    Treasurer: Louise Hyland
    Secretary: Ann Chicchi
    Member at Large: Miguel Cruz
    Member at Large: Jean Meyers
Management:

Director: Dennis Boyle
Mission: Excellence in choral sound, performance and musicianship.
Utilizes: Collaborations; Community Members; Community Talent; Composers; Contract Orchestras; Five Seasonal Concerts; Guest Directors; Guest Musical Directors; Guest Musicians; Multimedia; Visual Designers
Founded: 1969
Specialized Field: Grand Opera; Light Opera; Lyric Opera; Musical Theatre; Choral; Ethnic Music; Classical; Contemporary; Religious
Status: Non-Profit, Non-Professional
Non-paid Artists: 40+
Affiliations: Middlesex County Cultural/Heritage Commission
Organization Type: Performing; Touring

1925
NEW JERSEY ASSOCIATION OF VERISMO OPERA
PO Box 3024
Fort Lee, NJ 07024-9024
Phone: 201-342-1970
Fax: 201-224-6911
e-mail: comments@njavo.org
Management:
    Artistic Director: Lucine Amara
    Music Director/Principal Conductor: Anthony Morss
Mission: NJAVO is able to offer scholarship aid and performance opportunities through its Annual International Vocal Competition. It plays a leading role in the arts education in Bergen County.
Founded: 1989
Specialized Field: Opera; Choral
Performs At: Orrie de Nooyer Auditorium

1926
VERISMO OPERA/NEW JERSEY ASSOCIATION OF VERISMO OPERA
PO Box 3024
Fort Lee, NJ 07024-9024
Phone: 201-342-1970
Fax: 201-224-6911
Web Site: www.njavo.org
Officers:
    President: Giovanni Simone
    VP: Lucine Amara
    VP: Evelyn Quaife
    VP: Stan Staniloff
    Secretary: Fran Staniloff
    Treasurer: Adora Crager
Management:
    President: Gianni Simone
    Artistic Director: Lucine Amara
    Managing Director: Evelyn La Quaife
    Music Director: Anthony Morss
Mission: The New Jersey Association of Verismo Opera has been a part of the New Jersey music scene since 1989. It began by sponsoring a vocal competition and an opera workshop.
Founded: 1989
Specialized Field: Grand Opera; Light Opera; Lyric Opera; Musical Theatre; Choral; Youth Chorus; Ethnic Music; Classical; Contemporary; Religious
Status: Non-Profit, Professional

1927
RARITAN VALLEY CHORUS
PO Box 6044
Hillsborough, NJ 08844
Phone: 908-281-8509

Officers:
President: Diane Wisenski
Recording Secretary: Bobbi Agins
Management:
Artistic Director/Conductor: Rodney Briscoe
Accompnaist: Christopher Nittoli
Mission: A community based ensemble of varying ages, backgrounds and careers. The choir is open to all residents of the region and offers a range of musical experiences unparalleled in Central New Jersey.
Founded: 1990
Specialized Field: Choral

1928
NEW JERSEY STATE OPERA
50 Park Place
9th Floor
Newark, NJ 07102
Phone: 973-623-5757
Fax: 973-623-5761
e-mail: info@njstateopera.org
Web Site: www.njstateopera.org
Officers:
Chairman: Bernard J. D'Avella, Jr.
Board President: Kenneth B. Kashkin, MD
Secretary: Laura Barrett
Treasurer: Margareth De Jesus
Management:
Music Director Young Artists Prog: David Maiulloni
Acting Managing Director: Donna Nichols-Lawrence
Utilizes: Guest Companies; Singers
Founded: 1966
Specialized Field: Opera
Status: Non-Profit, Professional
Paid Staff: 50
Income Sources: Essex County Arts Council; New Jersey State Arts Council
Performs At: New Jersey Performing Arts Center; Prudential Hall
Seating Capacity: 2,750
Organization Type: Performing

1929
ARS MUSICAL CHORALE & ORCHESTRA
PO Box 525
Paramus, NJ 07653
Phone: 973-628-8793
Fax: 201-358-6405
e-mail: arsmusica@hotmail.com
Web Site: www.arsmusica.org
Management:
President: Mark Kantrowitz
Administrative Director: Alexandra Cramer
Music Director: Robert Long
Founded: 1965
Specialized Field: Choral
Status: Non-Profit, Non-Professional
Paid Staff: 2

1930
PRO ARTE CHORALE
400 Paramus Road, Scoskie Hall
Suite 2
Paramus, NJ 07652
Phone: 201-445-9052
Fax: 201-445-1421
e-mail: info@proartechorale.org
Web Site: www.proartechorale.org
Officers:
President: Howard Hanes
Management:
President: Enid Hayflick

Music Director: David Crone
Managing Director: Sharon Sauer
Founded: 1964
Specialized Field: Choral
Status: Non-Profit, Professional
Paid Staff: 3
Paid Artists: 4
Budget: $130,000
Income Sources: State Grant, Corporation Foundation, Private Donations, Ticket Sales, Fund raisers, Membership Dues
Performs At: Concert Hall, Church/Temple
Affiliations: Chorus America

1931
AMERICAN BOYCHOIR
19 Lambert Drive
Princeton, NJ 08540
Phone: 609-924-5858
Fax: 609-924-5812
Web Site: www.americanboychoir.org
Officers:
Chairman: Chester W Douglass
President: John Ellis
Management:
Music Director: Fernando Malvar-Ruiz
General Manager: Janet Kaltenbach
Mission: The Boychoir includes choristers from throughout North America, who are students at the internationally-renowned boarding and day choir school (which offers a full academic program).
Utilizes: Commissioned Composers; Commissioned Music; Guest Artists; Theatre Companies
Founded: 1937
Specialized Field: Choral; Youth Chorus
Status: Professional; Nonprofit
Paid Staff: 42
Budget: $3,000,000
Organization Type: Performing; Touring; Educational

1932
PRINCETON PRO MUSICA CHORUS & ORCHESTRA
PO Box 1313
Princeton, NJ 08542
Phone: 609-683-5122
Web Site: www.princetopromusic.org
Officers:
President: John V Phelan
Treasurer: Martin Wheelwright
Management:
Executive Director: Janet Pfeiffer
Music Director: Frances Fowler Slade
Mission: To perform masterpieces of the choral repertoire with a professional orchestra and soloists.
Utilizes: Guest Artists
Founded: 1979
Specialized Field: Choral; Classical
Status: Nonprofit
Paid Staff: 4
Volunteer Staff: 25
Income Sources: NJSCA; Individuals
Performs At: Richardson Auditorium; Princeton University
Affiliations: Chorus America; Art Pride
Organization Type: Performing

1933
WESTMINSTER CHOIR COLLEGE
101 Walnut Lane
Princeton, NJ 08540-3899

Phone: 609-921-7100
Fax: 609-921-3012
e-mail: wccinfo@rider.edu
Web Site: www.rider.edu/westminster
Management:
President: Mordechai Roznski
Managing Director: Robert Annis
Director of External Affairs: Anne Sears
Utilizes: Actors; Arrangers; Artists-in-Residence; Collaborations; Commissioned Composers; Community Members; Composers; Guest Accompanists; Guest Designers; Guest Lecturers; Guest Musical Directors; Guest Soloists; High School Drama; Instructors; Multimedia; Music; Original Music Scores; Resident Artists; Resident Companies; Scenic Designers; Sign Language Translators; Singers; Soloists; Students; Special Technical Talent
Founded: 1926
Specialized Field: Grand Opera; Light Opera; Lyric Opera; Musical Theatre; Choral; Youth Chorus; Ethnic Music; Classical; Contemporary; Religious
Status: Non-Profit, Non-Professional
Paid Staff: 25
Paid Artists: 75

1934
RIDGEWOOD GILBERT AND SULLIVAN OPERA COMPANY
975 E Ridgewood Avenue
Ridgewood, NJ 07450
Phone: 973-423-0300
Officers:
President: William Ramey
Treasurer: Philip Sternenberg
Secretary: Thomas Basile
Management:
Business Manager: Mike Wiley
Mission: To present and encourage an appreciation of Gilbert and Sullivan operas.
Founded: 1937
Specialized Field: Light Opera
Status: Non-Professional, Non-profit
Paid Staff: 50
Income Sources: Ticket Sales; Program Ads; Sponsored Performances
Performs At: Local Middle School; Outside Facilities
Affiliations: NJ Council on the Arts
Seating Capacity: 700
Year Built: 1954
Organization Type: Performing; Touring

1935
BROADWAY CENTER STAGE
Po Box 68
South Orange, NJ 07079
Phone: 973-378-3244
Fax: 973-378-3242
e-mail: squaredusa@comcast.net
Web Site: www.broadwaycenterstage.com
Management:
Producer: Suzanne Ishee
Business Manager: Lucy Bowers
Marketing Director: Jean Kerley
Mission: Presenting the finest, most affordable Broadway programming available, the duo of Broadway stars captures the most memoriable moments of Broadway.
Founded: 1995
Specialized Field: Theatrical Dance; Educational
Paid Staff: 2
Volunteer Staff: 1
Paid Artists: 6

1936
COMMUNITY OPERA
417 Morris Avenue
22
Summit, NJ 07901
Phone: 908-277-1934
Management:
President: Edward Q Watts
Mission: Showcasing opera singers as well as modern composers.
Utilizes: Singers
Founded: 1981
Specialized Field: Light Opera; Lyric Opera; Classical; Contemporary; Musical Theatre
Status: Non-Profit, Professional
Income Sources: Orpheus Society
Performs At: Hudson Guild; South Street Seaport-Fulton Center

1937
SUMMIT CHORALE
PO Box 265
Summit, NJ 07902-0265
Phone: 973-762-8486
Fax: 908-464-0959
e-mail: info@summitchorale.org
Officers:
President: Terry Perkins
Membership Chair: Ellie Winslow
Management:
Music Director: Richard Garrin
Accompanist: Douglas Keilitz
Conductor: Richard Garrin
Music Director: Richard Garrin
Mission: To promote and cultivate choral music by providing an opportunity for those who enjoy ensemble singing to explore the rich heritage of choral music while studying and singing under the best professional leadership obtainable; to foster public appreciation and enjoyment of choral music through performance as well as educational and community outreach endeavors.
Founded: 1909
Specialized Field: Choral
Status: Non-professional
Volunteer Staff: 12
Budget: $70,000
Income Sources: Private; Public; Box Office; Grants; Fundraising
Performs At: University; Churches; Schools
Organization Type: Performing; Education

1938
CHORAL ARTS SOCIETY OF NEW JERSEY
PO Box 2036
Westfield, NJ 07091
Phone: 908-756-5154
Officers:
President: James Zgoda
VP: Ted Schirm
Treasurer: Linda Jacobey
Secretary: Suzanne Beeny
Management:
Music Director: Evelyn Bleeke
Mission: To study, perform and promote choral works.
Founded: 1962
Specialized Field: Choral
Status: Non-Professional
Organization Type: Performing

New Mexico

1939
OPERA SOUTHWEST
515 15th Street NW
PO Box 27671
Albuquerque, NM 87125
Phone: 505-243-0591
e-mail: info@operasouthwest.org
Web Site: www.operasouthwest.org
Management:
President: Karen K Lynch
Vice President: George Richmond
Artistic Director: David Bartholomew
Founded: 1972
Specialized Field: Grand Opera
Status: Non-Profit, Professional
Paid Staff: 30

1940
OPERA SOUTHWEST
515 15th Street NW
Albuquerque, NM 87104
Phone: 505-243-0591
e-mail: operaSW@aol.com
Web Site:
www.unm.edu/~shapiro/MUSIC/opera_southwest.ht
Officers:
President: Sheila Johnson
Management:
Production Manager/General Director: Justine Tate-Opel
Artistic Director: Kyle Marrero
Music Director: Michael Butterman
Mission: To present fully staged, costumed operas with accomplished musicians at the highest artistic level.
Utilizes: Singers
Founded: 1972
Specialized Field: Grand Opera; Lyric Opera; Light Opera; Operetta
Status: Professional; Nonprofit
Paid Staff: 30
Income Sources: Central Opera Service
Performs At: KiMo Theatre
Organization Type: Performing; Educational

1941
SANGRE DE CRISTO CHORALE
PO Box 4462
Santa Fe, NM 87502-4462
Phone: 505-455-3707
Fax: 505-665-4433
Officers:
Treasurer: Don Raish
Publicity: Andrea Fechter
Development Chair: Gary Bell
Performance Chair: Joan Ellis
Management:
Director: Doyle Preheim
Board Presidnet: Jerry Nelson
Business Manager: Ed Van Eeckhout
Chorale President: Gary Buff
Mission: Performance of choral music and educational outreach.
Utilizes: Commissioned Composers; Commissioned Music; Guest Composers; Guest Lecturers; Multimedia; Music; Original Music Scores; Sign Language Translators; Soloists
Founded: 1978
Specialized Field: Choral
Volunteer Staff: 10
Paid Artists: 35
Budget: $52,000

Income Sources: Admissions; Contributions; Advertising; Grants
Performs At: Churches, Hotels
Annual Attendance: 1,800
Facility Category: Various venues: churches, hotels
Type of Stage: Choral Risers off Floor

1942
SANTA FE DESERT CHORALE
811 St Michels Drive
Suite 208
Santa Fe, NM 87505
Phone: 505-988-2282
Fax: 505-988-7522
Toll-free: 800-244-4011
e-mail: info@desertchorale.org
Web Site: www.desertchorale.org
Officers:
President: Mary Ann Nelson
Management:
President: Margaret Wright
Executive Director: Erich Covollmer
Artistic Director: Linda Mack
Mission: To perform music from the choral repertoire within the last five centuries, especially Baroque and Modern.
Founded: 1982
Specialized Field: Choral; Youth Chorus; Classical; Religious
Status: Non-Profit, Professional
Paid Staff: 5
Paid Artists: 20
Income Sources: Chorus America
Performs At: Santuario de Guadalupe; Loretto Chapel
Organization Type: Performing; Educational

1943
SANTA FE SYMPHONY ORCHESTRA AND CHORUS
PO Box 9692
Santa Fe, NM 87504
Phone: 505-983-3530
Fax: 505-982-3888
Toll-free: 800-480-1319
e-mail: symphony@rt66.com
Web Site: www.sf-symphony.org
Management:
President: Jenny Auger-Maw
Founder/General Director: Gregory Heltman
Artistic Director: Steven Smith
Development Director: Jennifer Schiffmacher
Founded: 1984
Specialized Field: Choral; Classical
Status: Non-Profit, Professional
Paid Staff: 4
Paid Artists: 80

1944
SANTA FE SYMPHONY ORCHESTRA AND CHORUS
551 West Cordova Road
Suite D
Santa Fe, NM 87504
Phone: 505-983-3530
Fax: 505-982-3888
Toll-free: 800-480-1319
e-mail: symphony@santafesymphony.org
Officers:
Choral Director: Linda Raney
Personnel Manager: Nicolle Maniaci
Management:
Founder/General Director: Gregory Heltman
Operations Manager: Diane Stengle

Development Director: Jennifer Schiffmacher
Music Director: Steven Smith
Utilizes: Guest Lecturers; Guest Musicians; Lyricists; Multimedia; Sign Language Translators
Specialized Field: Choral
Budget: $550,000
Income Sources: Contributions; Ticket Sales; Grants
Performs At: Lensic Performing Arts Center
Seating Capacity: 800

New York

1945
ALBANY PRO MUSICA
PO Box 3850
Albany, NY 12203-0850
Phone: 518-438-6548
Fax: 518-442-4197
e-mail: info@albanypromusica.org
Officers:
  Administrative Director: William Tuthill
  Artistic Administrator: Kate Pruzek
Management:
  Artistic Director/Conductor: David Griggs-Janower
  Assistant Conductor: Joseph Farrell
  Artistic Director and Conductor: David Griggs-Janower
Mission: To be a mixed chorus of selected volunteers who are dedicated to the enhancement of the cultural life in upstate New York and their own musical growth. Albany Pro Musica achieves these objectives through professional quality a cappella performance and accompanies choral repertoire drawn from diverse traditions and styles.
Founded: 1981
Specialized Field: Choral
Performs At: Civic and Community Musical Events
Affiliations: Albany Symphony Orchestra

1946
TRI-CITIES OPERA COMPANY
315 Clinton Street
Binghamton, NY 13905
Phone: 607-729-3444
Fax: 607-797-6344
e-mail: info@tricitiesopera.com
Web Site: www.tricitiesopera.com
Officers:
  President: Grant Best
  First VP: Dr. Fran Goldman
  Second First President: Juames Thomas
  Treasurer: Dirk Olds
Management:
  President: Grant Best
  Executive Director: Reed Smith
  Artistic Director: Duane Skrabalak
  Associate Artistic Director: Peter Sicilian
Mission: To produce opera
Utilizes: Artists-in-Residence; Choreographers; Designers; Five Seasonal Concerts; Guest Accompanists; Guest Conductors; Guest Writers; Multimedia; Original Music Scores; Poets; Resident Professionals; Sign Language Translators; Soloists; Student Interns
Founded: 1949
Specialized Field: Grand Opera
Status: Non-Profit, Professional
Paid Staff: 50
Paid Artists: 123
Budget: $1,000,000

Income Sources: American Guild of Musical Artists; American Federation of Musicians; International Association of Theatrical Stage Employees
Performs At: Broome County Forum
Affiliations: Binghamton University
Annual Attendance: 15,000
Seating Capacity: 1500
Year Built: 1920
Year Remodeled: 1975
Organization Type: Performing; Resident; Educational

1947
BERKSHIRE-HUDSON VALLEY FESTIVAL OF OPERA
1400 Benson Street
Suite 5A
Bronx, NY 10461
Phone: 718-877-4211
e-mail: lgalagarza@ramonalsina.org
Web Site: www.ramonalsina.org
Mission: Create and market concerts, recitals and operas to showcase.
Utilizes: Actors; Artists-in-Residence; Choreographers; Collaborating Artists; Collaborations; Commissioned Composers; Commissioned Music; Dance Companies; Dancers; Designers; Educators; Fine Artists; Grant Writers; Guest Accompanists; Guest Artists; Guest Choreographers; Guest Conductors; Guest Designers; Guest Directors; Guest Ensembles; Guest Lecturers; Guest Musical Directors; Guest Musicians; Guest Teachers; High School Drama; Instructors; Local Artists; Lyricists; Multimedia; Music; Organization Contracts; Original Music Scores; Poets; Resident Artists; Resident Professionals; Selected Students; Sign Language Translators; Singers; Soloists; Special Technical Talent; Theatre Companies
Founded: 1971
Specialized Field: Grand Opera; Lyric Opera; Youth Chorus; Classical; Contemporary
Status: Non-Profit, Professional
Volunteer Staff: 5
Paid Artists: 15
Budget: Varies
Income Sources: Tickets; Sponsors; Donations; Grants
Affiliations: Touring Concert Opera Company
Annual Attendance: 5,000 - 10,000
Organization Type: Performing; Touring

1948
BRONX OPERA COMPANY
5 Minerva Place
Bronx, NY 10468
Phone: 718-365-4209
Fax: 718-563-8379
e-mail: michael@bronxopera.org
Web Site: www.bronxopera.org
Officers:
  President: Eva Schulz
  Treasurer: Manny Nadelman
Management:
  President: Peter Heiman
  Artistic Director: Michael Spierman
  Assistant Artistic Director: Ben Spierman
  Production Manager: Gayle Jeffries
Mission: Bronx Opera has established a record of continuous growth, excellence and community involvement.
Founded: 1967
Specialized Field: Opera
Status: Non-Profit, Professional
Paid Staff: 3
Paid Artists: 120

1949
AMERICAN OPERA PROJECTS INC
138 S Oxford Street
Brooklyn, NY 11217
Phone: 718-398-4024
Fax: 718-398-3489
e-mail: info@operaprojects.org
Web Site: www.operaprojects.org
Management:
  Artistic Director: Steven Osgood
  Executive Director: Charles Jarden
  Project Manager: Matthew Gray
Specialized Field: Opera

1950
REGINA OPERA COMPANY
1251 Tabor Court
Brooklyn, NY 11219
Phone: 718-232-3555
Fax: 718-232-3555
e-mail: reginaopera@yahoo.com
Web Site: www.reginaopera.org
Officers:
  President: Marie Cantoni
  Executive VP: Francine Garber-Cohen
  VP/Legal Advisor: Linda Cantoni
Management:
  Artistic Director: Alex Alejandro Guzman
  Executive Director: Francine Garber Cohen
  Stage Director: Linda Lehr
  Conductor: Scott Jackson Wiley
Mission: Training young professionals and showcasing experienced directors and performers.
Utilizes: Grant Writers; Guest Musicians; Instructors; Local Artists; Sign Language Translators; Singers
Founded: 1970
Specialized Field: Choral; Opera; Musical Theatre
Status: Non-Profit, Non-Professional
Volunteer Staff: 15
Non-paid Artists: 50
Budget: Under $100,000
Income Sources: Public & Private Funding; Ticket Sales
Performs At: Regina Hall
Annual Attendance: 5,000
Facility Category: School Auditorium
Type of Stage: Proscenium
Stage Dimensions: 30'x18'
Seating Capacity: 325
Year Built: 1950
Organization Type: Performing

1951
BUFFALO PHILHARMONIC CHORUS & CHAMBER SINGERS
PO Box 176
Buffalo, NY 14207-0176
Phone: 716-)33—664
Fax: 716-874-0486
e-mail: katysings@yahoo.com
Officers:
  Accompanist: Bettyalice Riehle
Management:
  President: Steven Bench
  Music Director: L Brett Scott
Founded: 1936
Specialized Field: Choral
Paid Staff: 3
Volunteer Staff: 15
Paid Artists: 10
Non-paid Artists: 100

1952
CHAUTAUQUA SUMMER SCHOOLS OF FINE AND PERFORMING ARTS
PO Box 1098
Schools Office
Chautauqua, NY 14722
Phone: 716-357-6233
Fax: 716-357-9014
e-mail: smalinoski@ciweb.org
Web Site: www.ciweb.org
Management:
   Student Services Coordinator: Sarah Malinoski
Mission: To be a center for the arts, education, religion and recreation.
Utilizes: Singers
Founded: 1989
Specialized Field: Theatrical Dance
Status: Pre-Professional
Paid Staff: 120
Paid Artists: 1500
Budget: $15,000,000
Income Sources: Box Office; Grants; Private Donations
Performs At: Amphitheater; Lenna Hall
Affiliations: Opera America; Chamber Music America
Annual Attendance: 150,000
Organization Type: Performing; Religious; Educational; Recreational

1953
GLIMMERGLASS OPERA
PO Box 191
Cooperstown, NY 13326
Phone: 607-547-0700
Fax: 607-547-6030
e-mail: info@glimmerglass.org
Web Site: www.glimmerglass.org
Management:
   Artistic/General Director: Francesca Zambello
   Managing Director: Linda Jackson
   Music Director: David Angus
   Administratio/Operations Director: Andrea Lyons
   Director of Production: Abby Rodd
   Marketing/Public Relations Director: June Dziolo
   Artistic Events/Music Manager: Eric Schnobrick
Mission: A professional non-profit summer opera company dedicated to producing new productions each season. Mission is to produce new, little-known and familiar operas and works of music theater in innovative productions which capitalize on the intimacy and natural setting of the Alice Busch Opera Theater; to promote an artistically-challenging work environment for young Americans; and to engage important directors, designers and conductors
Founded: 1975
Specialized Field: Performing Arts
Status: Non-Profit, Professional
Paid Staff: 25

1954
GLIMMERGLASS OPERA
PO Box 191
Cooperstown, NY 13326
Phone: 607-547-5704
Fax: 607-547-6030
Web Site: www.glimmerglass.org/
Management:
   General Director: Esther Nelson
   Music Director: Stewart Robertson
Mission: To produce new, little known, and familiar operas and works of music theater in innovative productions which capitalize on the intimacy and natural setting of The Alice Busch Opera Theater; to promote

an artistically challenging work environment for young American performers, and to engage important directors, designers and conductors who provide high standards of achievement.
Utilizes: Artists-in-Residence; Choreographers; Collaborations; Commissioned Composers; Designers; Educators; Guest Accompanists; Guest Writers; Guild Activities; Multimedia; Organization Contracts; Resident Professionals; Student Interns
Founded: 1975
Specialized Field: Lyric Opera; Grand Opera
Status: Professional; Nonprofit
Paid Staff: 25
Income Sources: Opera America
Season: July - August
Performs At: Alice Busch Opera Theater
Facility Category: Theater
Seating Capacity: 900
Year Built: 1987
Organization Type: Performing

1955
1891 FREDONIA OPERA HOUSE
9 Church Street
PO Box 384
Fredonia, NY 14063
Phone: 716-679-0891
Fax: 716-679-0899
e-mail: operahouse@fredopera.org
Web Site: www.fredopera.org
Officers:
   Business Manager: Marsha Finley
Management:
   Executive Director: Rick Davis
   Technical Director: Daniel Allen
Mission: Year round performing arts center offering the best in music, theatre and films.
Founded: 1994
Specialized Field: Multidisciplinary
Paid Staff: 3
Volunteer Staff: 60
Performs At: Theatre
Type of Stage: Proscenium
Seating Capacity: 444
Year Built: 1891
Rental Contact: Technical Director Daniel Allen

1956
NEW ROCHELLE OPERA
PO Box 55
New Rochelle, NY 10804
Phone: 914-576-0365
e-mail: newrochelleopera@aol.com
Web Site: www.nropera.org
Officers:
   Co-Founder/Artistic Director: Camille Coppola
   Co-Founder/Board President: Billie Tucker
   Vice President: Paulette Soffin
   Secretary: Louise Shepherd
   Treasurer: Edward C Flanagan
   Corresponding Secretary: John Fraioli
Management:
   Executive Director: Camille Coppola, camillecoppola@aol.com
   Company Coordinator: Billie Tucker, purepurplelady@yahoo.com
   Conductor: Gregory Ortega
Utilizes: Collaborations; Community Members; Community Talent; Dancers; Designers; Grant Writers; Guest Artists; Guest Composers; Guest Musical Directors; Original Music Scores; Paid Performers; Resident Professionals; Sign Language Translators; Soloists
Founded: 1985

Specialized Field: Grand Opera; Light Opera; Lyric Opera; Musical Theatre; Choral; Youth Chorus; Classical; Religious
Status: Non-Profit, Professional
Volunteer Staff: 15+
Budget: $100,000
Income Sources: Box Office; Grants; Contributions
Performs At: Mainstage: Ursuline Performing Arts Center, New Rochelle, NY; Concerts at Various Locations
Annual Attendance: 3000
Type of Stage: Proscenium
Stage Dimensions: 18 x 30
Seating Capacity: 318

1957
AMATO OPERA THEATRE
319 Bowery
New York, NY 10003
Phone: 212-228-8200
Fax: 212-228-8201
e-mail: info@amato.org
Web Site: www.amato.org
Officers:
   President: Anthony Amato
Management:
   Artistic Director: Anthony Amato
Mission: The Amato Opera Theater, has survived on a collective artistic desire to present grand opera that is good theater and, at the same time, has created a platform for aspiring young artists.
Utilizes: Sign Language Translators; Singers
Founded: 1948
Specialized Field: Grand Opera; Light Opera
Status: Non-Profit
Volunteer Staff: 25
Non-paid Artists: 200
Budget: $160,000
Income Sources: Tickets; Donations
Seating Capacity: 103
Organization Type: Performing

1958
AMERICAN INTERNATIONAL LYRIC THEATRE
322 Duke Ellington Boulevard
New York, NY 10025
Phone: 212-662-3468
Fax: 212-678-0571
Web Site: hometown.aol.com/ppress322/music1/index.htm
Management:
   Managing Director: Paulette Singer
   Artistic Director: Russel Miller
Mission: A traveling company that presents Operettas, Broadway shows, European Operas and dance shows of all kinds using native performers from many different countries.
Utilizes: Theatre Companies
Founded: 1984
Specialized Field: World Music; Theatrical Dance
Status: Non-Profit; Professional
Budget: $500,000
Performs At: Throughout The United States

1959
AMERICAN OPERA MUSIC THEATER
400 W 43rd Street
Suite 19-D
New York, NY 10036
Phone: 212-594-1839
Fax: 212-695-4350
Web Site: www.americanoperacompany.com
Officers:

Administrator: Christian Miles
Management:
President: Diana Cortot
Stage Director: Theodore Mann
Mission: Promote emerging artists with major talent, present new famililar music, with costumed and staged quality productions.
Utilizes: Choreographers; Designers; Fine Artists; Grant Writers; Guest Artists; Guest Composers; Guest Conductors; Guest Designers; Guest Directors; Guest Lecturers; Guest Musical Directors; Guest Musicians; Lyricists; Music; New Productions; Original Music Scores; Sign Language Translators; Singers; Theatre Companies
Founded: 1995
Specialized Field: Lyric Opera; Musical Theatre; Choral; Youth Chorus; Ethnic Music; Classical; Contemporary
Status: Non-Profit, Professional
Paid Staff: 3
Volunteer Staff: 3
Paid Artists: 50
Budget: $350,000-$450,000
Income Sources: Corporate; Donations; Service Revenues
Performs At: Theaters, Concert Halls
Annual Attendance: 30,000
Facility Category: Theaters
Type of Stage: Proscenium, round
Stage Dimensions: 26 x 35 minimum
Seating Capacity: 500 - 3,000

1960
AMERICAN-INTERNATIONAL LYRIC THEATRE
322 Duke Ellington Boulevard
New York, NY 10025-3471
Phone: 212-662-3468
Fax: 212-678-0517
e-mail: ppress322@aol.com
Management:
Artistic Director: Russell Miller
Managing Director: Paulette Singer
Founded: 1985
Specialized Field: Lyric Opera; Musical Theatre
Status: Non-Profit, Professional
Paid Staff: 3
Paid Artists: 50
Budget: $500,000
Season: Year round

1961
BACH VESPERS AT HOLY TRINITY
3 W 65th Street
New York, NY 10023
Phone: 212-877-6815
e-mail: office@bachvespersnyc.org
Web Site: www.bachvespersnyc.org
Officers:
President: Kelly Hall
Secretary: Robert Crump
Treasurer: Stephen Hucko
Office Manager: Tobin Schmuck
Office Assistant: Bonnie Minger
Management:
Cantor: Rick Erickson
Mission: To bring the cantatas of Bach, and other early music, to the community in context of worship, as was done in 18th century Leipzig.
Utilizes: Guest Soloists; Sign Language Translators; Singers
Founded: 1968
Specialized Field: Baroque; Period Instruments; Choral

Paid Staff: 4
Volunteer Staff: 10
Paid Artists: 24
Income Sources: Donations; Offerings; Endowment
Affiliations: Lutheran (ELCA)
Annual Attendance: 7,500
Facility Category: Church
Seating Capacity: 500
Year Built: 1904
Resident Groups: Bach Choir; Period In

1962
BOYS CHOIR OF HARLEM
2005 Madison Avenue
New York, NY 10035-1298
Phone: 212-289-1815
Fax: 212-289-4195
e-mail: info@boyschoirofharlem.org
Web Site: www.boyschoirofharlem.org
Officers:
President: Tim Battle
Vice President: Willam Byrd
Secretary: Gilbert Robinson
Management:
Parliamentarian: Terrance Wright
Mission: The Boys Choir of Harlem program evolves directly from our mission and a vision of consistent, compassionate, communal strength in raising children.
Specialized Field: Choral; Youth Chorus; Educational
Paid Staff: 60
Paid Artists: 32
Non-paid Artists: 28
Season: One or two tours a year
Comments: Boys Choir age are 9 to 18 years.

1963
CANTERBURY CHORAL SOCIETY
2 E 90th Street
Church of the Heavenly Rest
New York, NY 10128
Phone: 212-222-9458
Fax: 212-222-9458
e-mail: dodsley@aol.com
Web Site: www.canterburychoral.org
Management:
Conductor: Charles D Walker
Utilizes: Guest Musicians; Original Music Scores; Sign Language Translators; Singers
Founded: 1952
Specialized Field: Religious; Choral
Status: Non-Profit, Professional
Paid Staff: 1
Paid Artists: 12
Non-paid Artists: 100
Performs At: Church
Annual Attendance: 2,000
Facility Category: Church
Seating Capacity: 900
Year Built: 1929

1964
CHILDREN'S AID SOCIETY CHORUS
219 Sullivan Street
New York, NY 10012
Phone: 212-533-1675
Fax: 212-420-9153
Web Site: www.childrensaidsociety.org
Management:
Director of Music: Peter Frost
Assistant Director: Yi-Ching Lin
Assistant Program Director: Kelly Campbell
Associate Conductor: Phyllis Clark

Mission: Strives to provide every child, regardless of socioeconomic situation, the opportunity to study and perform quality choral music with other children from New York City.
Founded: 1997
Specialized Field: Choral; Youth Chorus; Ethnic Music; Classical; Contemporary
Status: Non-Profit, Professional
Paid Staff: 15
Paid Artists: 12
Budget: $142,000

1965
COLLEGIATE CHORALE
115 E 57th Street
11th Floor
New York, NY 10022
Phone: 646-202-9623
e-mail: info@collegiatechorale.org
Web Site: www.collegiatechorale.org
Officers:
Co-Chairman: Susan L Baker
Co-Chairman: George J Grumbach Jr
Secretary: Christie C Salomon
Treasurer: Lois Conway
Management:
Music Director: James Bagwell
Executive Director: Jennifer Collins
General Manager: Julie Morgan
Mission: To enrich the audience through innovative programming and exceptional performances of a broad range of vocal music featuring a premier choral ensemble.
Founded: 1941
Specialized Field: Choral
Status: Non-Profit, Professional

1966
DICAPO OPERA THEATRE
184 E 76th Street
New York, NY 10021
Phone: 212-288-9438
e-mail: dotproduction@aol.com
Web Site: www.dicapo.com
Management:
Artistic Director: Diane Martindale
General Director: Michael Capasso
Mission: After the Metropolitan Opera and New York City Opera, Dicapo Opera Theatre is the only opera company in New York to present an entire season of opera productions, musical theatre, concerts, family fare, and other events, and it does so in a gem of a facility tucked away on the Upper East Side.
Founded: 1982
Specialized Field: Grand Opera
Status: Non-Profit, Professional
Season: September - June
Performs At: Dicapo Theatre
Facility Category: Theatre
Type of Stage: Proscenium
Stage Dimensions: 40'x 40'
Seating Capacity: 200
Rental Contact: General Director Michael Capasso

1967
EARLY MUSIC NEW YORK (EM/NY)
10 West 68 Street
New York, NY 10023
Phone: 212-749-6600
Fax: 212-749-2848
e-mail: info@EarlyMusicNY.org
Web Site: www.EarlyMusicNY.org
Officers:
President: Audrey Boughton

Management:
Founder/Director: Fredrick Renz,
f.renz@EarlyMusicNY.org
Operations Manager: Aaron Smith,
admin@EarlyMusicNY.org
Founded: 1975
Specialized Field: Early Music; Drama & Dance;
Medieval; Renassiance; Baroque; Classical
Status: Non-Profit, Professional
Paid Staff: 4
Paid Artists: 100
Budget: $300,000
Income Sources: Ticket Sales; CD Sales; Private
Contributions & Grants; Government Awards
Affiliations: Early Music Foundation; New York Early
Music Central (NYEMC)

1968
GRACE CHURCH CHORAL SOCIETY
802 Broadway
New York, NY 10003
Phone: 212-254-2000
Fax: 212-673-4938
Web Site: www.thechoralesociety.org
Management:
Music Director: John Maclay
Associate Conductor: Tony Bellomy
Mission: A 150-voice ensemble of experienced
professional and avocational singers who volunteer
their time and talents inthe service of the choral at form.
Utilizes: Artists-in-Residence; Commissioned
Composers; Commissioned Music;
Composers-in-Residence; Guest Companies; Local
Artists; Organization Contracts; Original Music Scores;
Sign Language Translators; Singers; Soloists
Founded: 1961
Specialized Field: Choral
Paid Staff: 2
Volunteer Staff: 6
Paid Artists: 12
Non-paid Artists: 100
Performs At: Church
Affiliations: Grace Church in New York
Annual Attendance: 2,400

1969
HIBERN IAN MUSIC
513 E 13th Street
Apartment 3
New York, NY 10009
Mailing Address: PO Box 2349
Phone: 212-260-2302
Fax: 212-260-9645
e-mail: sngmusic@earthlink.net
Web Site: www.hibernianmusic.com
Management:
Director: Brandan Jamieson
President: Susan McKeown
Founded: 1998
Specialized Field: Ethnic Music; Contemporary
Status: For-Profit, Professional
Paid Staff: 1
Paid Artists: 10

1970
I CANTORI DI NEW YORK
PO Box 1376
New York, NY 10185
Phone: 212-439-4758
e-mail: info@cantorinewyork.com
Web Site: www.cantorinewyork.com
Officers:
President: Gerald Metz
VP: Sarah Graham

Treasurer: Mary Jo Mace
Secretary: Alex Guerrero
Management:
Artistic Director: Mark Shapiro
Assistant Conductor: Jason Wirth
General Manager: Erol Gurol
Founded: 1984
Specialized Field: Choral
Status: Semi-Professional
Affiliations: Chorus America; Vocal Area Network;
Classical Domain
Organization Type: Performing

1971
L'OPERA FRANCAIS DE NEW YORK
PO Box 33
New York, NY 10185
Phone: 212-933-1793
e-mail: yabel@ofny.org
Web Site: www.ofny.org
Management:
Co-Artistic/Stage Directors: Jean-Philippe Clarac
Co-Artistic/Stage Director: Olivier Deloeuil
Manager: Susan Oetgen
Music Director/Founder: Yves Abel
Mission: The only professional opera company in
America devoted exclusively to French operas, a
repertory which has been unjustly neglected and
under-served by American companies in recent time.
Utilizes: Original Music Scores; Resident
Professionals; Sign Language Translators; Singers
Founded: 1988
Specialized Field: Lyric Opera
Status: Professional
Income Sources: French Institute; Alliance Francaise
Performs At: Alice Tull Hall; Kaye Playhouse
Organization Type: Performing

1972
LA GRAN SCENA OPERA COMPANY
211 E 11th Street
Suite 9
New York, NY 10003
Phone: 212-460-9124
Fax: 212-460-9124
e-mail: irasiff@aol.com
Web Site: www.granscena.org
Management:
President: Ira Siff
Managing Director: Antonio Tessitore
Utilizes: Five Seasonal Concerts; Grant Writers; Guest
Lecturers; Guest Musicians; Sign Language
Translators; Singers; Student Interns
Founded: 1981
Specialized Field: Opera
Status: Non-Profit, Professional
Paid Staff: 2
Volunteer Staff: 6
Paid Artists: 15
Budget: $150,000
Income Sources: Funding and Performances
Performs At: Various Auditoriums
Annual Attendance: varies
Facility Category: varies

1973
METROPOLITAN OPERA
Lincoln Center
New York, NY 10023
Phone: 212-362-6000
Web Site: www.metopera.org
Officers:
Co-Chairman: Christine F Hunter
Co-Chairman: Ann Ziff

President/CEO: William C Morris
Secretary: Betsy Cohen
Management:
General Manager: Peter Gelb
Music Director: James Levine
Mission: A vibrant home for the mose creative and
talented artists, including singers, conductors,
composers, orchestra musicians, stage directors,
designers, visual artists, choreographers, and dancers
from around the world.
Founded: 1883
Specialized Field: Grand Opera
Status: Non-Profit, Professional
Season: January-December

1974
MUSIC-THEATRE GROUP
10 Jay Street
Suite 900
New York, NY 11201
Phone: 718-797-1145
Fax: 718-408-9575
e-mail: info@musictheatregroup.org
Web Site: www.musictheatregroup.org
Officers:
Chair: Bill Clark
President: Diane Wondisford
Treasurer: Steven L Krueger
Management:
Producing Director: Diane Wondisford
Managing Director: Lisa Phillips
Mission: Occupies the unique space between music
theatre and opera. Generates original work by telling
stories driven by music, in experimental forms and
interdisciplinary combinations, offering artists the
opportunity to carefully and throughfully create new
work in a safe, collaborative environment.
Utilizes: Singers
Founded: 1971
Specialized Field: Musical Theatre
Status: Non-Profit, Professional
Paid Staff: 5
Paid Artists: 50
Income Sources: Opera America
Organization Type: Performing; Touring

1975
NEW AMSTERDAM SINGERS
PO Box 373
Cathedral Station
New York, NY 10025
Phone: 212-568-5948
e-mail: info@nasingers.org
Web Site: www.nasingers.org
Management:
Music Director: Clara Longstreth
Mission: A mid-sized, mixed-voice, avocational chorus
dedicated to sharing the love of choral music with each
other and with audiences in New York City and abroad.
Mission is to educate the listeners and ourselves by
performing a diverse and extended repertoire
combining traditional choral gems with new and
lesser-knows works, many of them a cappella.
Founded: 1972
Specialized Field: Choral

1976
NEW YORK CHORAL SOCIETY
119 W 57th Street
Suite 1215
New York, NY 10019

Phone: 212-247-3878
Fax: 973-948-4878
e-mail: info@nychoral.org
Web Site: www.nychoral.org
Officers:
  Chair: Michael Colosi
  President: Rosanne Zoccoli
  Executive VP: Joanne W Lawson
Management:
  Executive Director: John Lawson
  Music Director: John Daly Goodwin
  Assistant Conductor: Malcolm Merriweather
  Accompanist: David Ralph
Mission: To share a variety of choral music to enrich the culture of the community, foster community outreach to children and provide challenging experiences for the choir members.
Founded: 1958
Specialized Field: Choral
Status: Non-Professional, Nonprofit
Paid Staff: 280
Volunteer Staff: 50
Paid Artists: 2
Performs At: Carnegie Hall; Lincoln Center
Organization Type: Performing; Touring

1977
NEW YORK CITY OPERA
David H Koch Theater
20 Lincoln Center
New York, NY 10023
Phone: 212-870-5570
Web Site: www.nycopera.com
Management:
  General Manager/Artistic Director: George Steel
  Music Director: George Manahan
  Marketing Director: Tom Trayer
Mission: Producing grand opera; developing and presenting young American artists; presenting opera as theater.
Utilizes: Singers
Founded: 1943
Specialized Field: Grand Opera
Status: Non-Profit, Professional
Budget: $ 34 Million
Income Sources: Opera America
Performs At: New York State Theatre; Lincoln Center
Annual Attendance: 275,000+
Seating Capacity: 2,763
Organization Type: Performing; Touring; Resident; Educational

1978
NEW YORK GILBERT AND SULLIVAN PLAYERS
302 W 91st Street
New York, NY 10024
Phone: 212-769-1000
Fax: 212-769-1002
e-mail: info@nygasp.org
Web Site: www.nygasp.org
Officers:
  President: Albert Bergeret
  Treasurer: Alan Hill
  Secretary: John Behonek
  Board Chair: Michael Strone
Management:
  Artistic Director/General Manager: Albert Bergeret
  Managing Director: David Wannen
Mission: Producing and promoting Gilbert and Sullivan's works, along with related works employing orchestras as well as small ensembles.

Utilizes: Sign Language Translators; Singers; Theatre Companies
Founded: 1974
Specialized Field: Operetta; Musical Theatre; Gilbert and Sullivan
Status: Non-Profit, Professional
Paid Staff: 2
Paid Artists: 85
Budget: $1,500,000
Income Sources: Sales; Individual Contributions; Fees for Performance; Government Endowments
Performs At: Symphony Space; City Center; Tour
Affiliations: Actors' Equity Association; American Federation of Musicians of the United States and Canada
Annual Attendance: 20,000
Facility Category: Multiple Locations
Type of Stage: Proscenium
Stage Dimensions: 48 x 30
Seating Capacity: 2500
Year Remodeled: 2001
Cost: $35,000
Rental Contact: Eugene Lowery
Organization Type: Performing; Touring; Resident; Educational

1979
NEW YORK GRAND OPERA COMPANY
250 W 54th Street
Suite 807
New York, NY 10019
Phone: 212-245-8837
Fax: 212-245-8840
e-mail: info@newyorkgrandopera.org
Web Site: www.newyorkgrandopera.org
Management:
  Conductor/Artistic Director: Vincent La Selva
Mission: Unique in the world for presenting professional fully-staged grand opera productions free of charge to the public, giving all people access to opera, regardless of their financial means.
Founded: 1973
Specialized Field: Grand Opera
Season: Summer
Performs At: New York Central Park

1980
NEW YORK OPERA PROJECT
PO Box 0677
New York, NY 10025
Phone: 212-749-6603
Fax: 212-749-6603
e-mail: info@nyop.org
Web Site: www.nyop.org
Officers:
  Board Chairperson: Dorothy Heyl, Esq
  Secretary/Treasurer: Daniel O'Connell Esq
Management:
  Artistic/Executive Director: Fredrick Martell
Mission: To produce the highest possible professional presentation of operatic, concert and chamber vocal music works, to provide educational, performace and professional development opportunities for emerging artists and to provide a high caliber and affordable performing company to the community.
Founded: 1992
Specialized Field: Opera
Paid Staff: 2
Volunteer Staff: 3

1981
NEW YORK TREBLE SINGERS
210 W 89th Street
Suite 4L
New York, NY 10024-1811
Phone: 212-496-0094
Fax: 212-496-0094
e-mail: vsdavidson@nytreblesingers.org
Web Site: www.nytreblesingers.org
Officers:
  President: Virginia Davidson
Mission: A professional ensemble of twelve women who specialize in original music, particularly American 20th century, written for treble voices.
Founded: 1985
Specialized Field: Women's Chorus
Status: Non-Profit, Professional
Paid Staff: 1
Volunteer Staff: 3
Paid Artists: 12

1982
OPERA EBONY
2109 Broadway
Suite 1418
New York, NY 10023
Phone: 212-877-2110
Fax: 212-877-2110
e-mail: info@operaebony.org
Web Site: www.operaebony.org
Management:
  Artistic Director: Benjamin Matthews
  Musical Director: Wayne Sanders
Mission: Discovering and promoting singers, composers, directors, choreographers and technicians.
Utilizes: Singers
Founded: 1973
Specialized Field: Grand Opera; Light Opera; Lyric Opera; Musical Theatre; Choral; Ethnic Music; Classical; Contemporary; Religious
Status: Non-Profit, Professional
Paid Staff: 3
Paid Artists: 26
Income Sources: The American Music Center; Opera America
Performs At: Aaron Davis Hall
Organization Type: Performing; Touring; Educational

1983
OPERA NORTHEAST/CHILDREN'S OPERA THEATRE
PO Box 6700
New York, NY 10128
Phone: 212-472-2168
Fax: 212-472-6910
e-mail: donwestwood@earthlink.net
Web Site: www.operamgt.com
Management:
  Artistic Director: Donald Westwood
  Administrative Director: Tracy Throne
Mission: Build a first-class touring organization to produce and present authentic classical lyric theatre.
Utilizes: Collaborations; Grant Writers; Guest Artists; Guest Conductors; Guest Lecturers; Singers
Founded: 1972
Specialized Field: Youth Chorus; Classical for Young Audiences; Opera
Status: Non-Profit, Professional
Paid Staff: 6
Volunteer Staff: 10
Paid Artists: 10
Budget: $250,000
Organization Type: Performing; Touring; Educational

1984
OPERA ORCHESTRA OF NEW YORK
344 3 63rd Street
Suite B-1
New York, NY 10065
Phone: 212-906-9137
Fax: 212-906-9021
e-mail: oony@tiac.net
Web Site: www.oony.org
Officers:
President: Norman Raben
VP: Sandra Wagenfeld
Treasurer: Eearle W Kazis
Secretary: Francine Goldstein
Management:
Founder/Music Director: Eve Queler
Executive Director: Deborah Surdi
Office Manager: Evan Croen
Mission: Enriching the musical and cultural vitality of New York City. Gives new life to rarely-heard operas, providing the public with an opportunity to hear these operatic rarities in major concert performances at Carnegie Hall.
Utilizes: Guest Writers; Multimedia; Original Music Scores; Singers
Founded: 1972
Specialized Field: Opera
Status: Non-Profit, Professional
Paid Staff: 4
Volunteer Staff: 6
Paid Artists: 100
Budget: $1.5 million
Income Sources: Ticket sales and donations
Performs At: Carnegie Hall
Organization Type: Performing; Sponsoring

1985
ORATORIO SOCIETY OF NEW YORK
1440 Broadway
23rd Floor
New York, NY 10018
Phone: 212-400-7255
e-mail: webmaster@oratoriosocietyofny.org
Web Site: www.oratoriosocietyofny.org
Officers:
Chairwoman: Ellen L Blair
President: Richard A Pace
VP: Mary-Jo P Knight
VP: Janet Plucknett
Treasurer: Marie Gangemi
Secretary: Jay Jacobson
Management:
Music Director: Kent Tritle
Associate Conductor: David Rosenmayer
Mission: Brings together a diverse community of avocational singers who share a passion for choral music. Mission is to contribute to the cultural fabric of New York City through public performance of both classic and contemporary choral works at the highest musical standards. Committed to the musical development of members, audience and artists.
Founded: 1873
Specialized Field: Choral
Status: Non-Profit, Non-Professional
Paid Staff: 2
Paid Artists: 60
Budget: $475,000
Income Sources: Concert Tickets; Contributions; Chorus Dues
Performs At: Carnegie Hall
Seating Capacity: 2,700
Organization Type: Performing; Touring; Resident; Educational

1986
PALA OPERA ASSOCIATION
200 Riverside Boulevard
PH2A
New York, NY 10069-0917
Phone: 212-874-7866
Fax: 212-769-0563
e-mail: elizabethfalk@usa.net
Officers:
President: Elizabeth Falk
VP: Martin Piecuch
VP: Richard Woitach
Management:
Producer/Artistic Director: Elizabeth Falk
Music Director: Martin Piecuch
Chief Music Consultant: Richard Woitach
Mission: To present high-calibre, ascendant artists with professionalism and elegance, accompanied by a chorus and full orchestra; providing them the opportunity to be heard by discerning, paying audiences as well as critics.
Utilizes: Actors; Collaborating Artists; Dancers; Grant Writers; Guest Artists; Guest Directors; Guest Musical Directors; Guest Musicians; Lyricists; Singers; Student Interns
Founded: 1989
Specialized Field: Grand Opera; Musical Theatre
Status: Professional
Paid Staff: 2
Budget: 75,000-100,000
Income Sources: Contibutors
Performs At: Town Hall; Players
Organization Type: Performing

1987
CHAUTAUQUA OPERA
412 West 42nd Street Suite
Suite 4E4
New York City, NY 10036
Mailing Address: PO Box Q Chautauqua NY 14722
Phone: 212-779-3177
Fax: 212-779-3293
e-mail: admin@chautopera.org
Web Site: opera.ciweb.org
Management:
Artistic/General Director: Jay Lesenger
Music Administrator/Chorus Master: Carol Rausch
Administrative Director: Elizabeth Cheslock
Company Manager: Sallyann Turnbull
Director of Production: Michael Baumgarten
Mission: To produce music of the highest quality in order to extend the appreciation of opera for artists and audiences.
Utilizes: Singers
Founded: 1929
Specialized Field: Grand Opera; Light Opera; Lyric Opera; Musical Theatre; Classical; Contemporary
Status: Non-Profit, Professional
Paid Staff: 3
Income Sources: Opera America
Performs At: Norton Hall
Organization Type: Performing; Resident; Educational

1988
MATAPAT
517 County Highway 27
Richfield Springs, NY 13439
Phone: 315-858-1434
Fax: 315-858-1434
Web Site: www.onqueuartists.com
Management:
Founder/Agent: Sandra Bernegger

Administrative Assistant: Linda Van Slyke
Administrative Assistant: Frances Breslin
Mission: To perform the traditional music, song and dance of Quebec with contempoary and world music influences.
Founded: 1997
Specialized Field: Folk Music; Ethnic Music
Paid Staff: 3
Paid Artists: 3

1989
LAKE GEORGE OPERA AT SARATOGA
480 Broadway
Suite 336
Saratoga Springs, NY 12866
Phone: 518-584-6018
Fax: 518-584-6775
e-mail: info@lakegeorgeopera.org
Web Site: www.lakegeorgeopera.org
Officers:
Chairman: Robert C Miller
President: Theodore F Newlin III
Management:
General Director: Curtis Tucker
Education Director: Deborah Rocco
Development Director: Elizabeth Giblin
Mission: To produce high quality professional opera and develop the next generation of artists through our Apprentice and school programs.
Utilizes: Artists-in-Residence; Designers; Guest Accompanists; Guest Composers; Guest Designers; Guest Ensembles; Guest Lecturers; Guest Writers; Original Music Scores
Founded: 1962
Specialized Field: Opera
Status: Non-Profit; Professional
Paid Staff: 5
Paid Artists: 95
Budget: $950,000
Income Sources: Endowment; Individual Contributions; Tickets; Private/Public Grants
Performs At: Spac Little Theater; Saratoga Springs State Park
Affiliations: Opera America Professional Company Member
Annual Attendance: 16,000
Type of Stage: Modified Proscenium
Seating Capacity: 500

1990
SCHENECTADY LIGHT OPERA COMPANY
PO Box 1006
Schenectady, NY 12301-1006
Phone: 518-393-5732
Web Site: www.sloctheater.com
Officers:
President: Mellissa Jacijan
Secretary: Melinda Zarnoch
Treasurer: Mary Zarnoch
Management:
Business Manager: Joseph Concra
Mission: To present Broadway Musicals.
Founded: 1926
Specialized Field: Broadway Musicals; Light Opera
Status: Non-Profit
Affiliations: NYSTA
Organization Type: Performing

1991
CANTICUM NOVUM SINGERS
2 Cove Road
South Salem, NY 10590-1023

Phone: 914-763-3453
Fax: 914-763-3453
e-mail: haroldrosenbaum@gmail.com
Web Site: www.canticumnovum.org
Officers:
 Chairman: Linda Fusco
Management:
 Artistic Director/Conductor: Harold Rosenbuam
Founded: 1973
Specialized Field: Choral; Traditional Choral Music
Paid Staff: 1
Non-paid Artists: 24
Budget: $21,000
Income Sources: Individuals; Tickets; Merchandise; Contracted Services; Contributions; Fund Raisers
Performs At: Churches and Concert Halls
Affiliations: In Residence at St. Ignatius of Antioch Episcopal Church, NYC
Annual Attendance: 1,500

1992
THE NEW YORK VIRTUOSO SINGERS
2 Cove Road
South Salem, NY 10590
Phone: 914-763-3453
Fax: 914-763-3453
e-mail: haroldrosenbaum@gmail.com
Web Site: www.nyvirtuoso.org
Officers:
 Chairman: Linda Fusco
Management:
 President: Harold Rosenbaum
Mission: To perform chamber choral works from all periods with a special emphasis on 20th century repertoire; to commission, perform and record premieres.
Utilizes: Commissioned Composers; Grant Writers; Guest Companies; Guest Composers; Guest Musical Directors; Guest Musicians; Multimedia; Original Music Scores; Sign Language Translators; Singers
Founded: 1988
Specialized Field: Choral; Classical; Contemporary; Religious
Status: Non-Profit, Professional
Paid Staff: 1
Paid Artists: 16
Budget: $55,000
Income Sources: Foundations; Corporation; Individuals; Tickets; Merchandise; Contracted Services
Performs At: Churches and Concert Halls
Annual Attendance: 3,000
Organization Type: Performing

1993
WESTCHESTER ORATORIO SOCIETY
Box 6
South Salem, NY 10590
Phone: 914-763-3453
Fax: 914-763-8284
e-mail: bobmcdon@optonline.net
Web Site: www.westchesteroratorio.org
Management:
 President: Elizabeth McDonald
 Artistic Director: Harold Rosenbaum
Founded: 1997
Specialized Field: Choral; Traditional Choral Music
Status: Non-Profit, Non-Professional
Paid Staff: 2
Paid Artists: 60

1994
SYRACUSE OPERA
PO Box 1223
Syracuse, NY 13201-1223

Phone: 315-475-5915
Fax: 315-475-6319
e-mail: info@syracuseopera.com
Web Site: www.syracuseopera.com
Management:
 Artistic Director: Catherine Wolff
Mission: To produce for the community professional opera performances of the highest quality promoting young talent from across the country and cultivate a further appreciation of opera within the region, specifically Syracuse and the surrounding six county area by means of outreach and educational programs.
Utilizes: Sign Language Translators; Singers; Student Interns; Theatre Companies
Founded: 1963
Specialized Field: Grand Opera; Lyric Opera; Light Opera; Operetta
Status: Professional; Nonprofit
Paid Staff: 10
Budget: $1 Million
Income Sources: New York State Coucil on Arts; County of Onandaga; Natural Heritage Trust; Corporations; Foundations; Individuals
Performs At: Crouse-Hinds Concert Theater
Seating Capacity: 2,042
Organization Type: Performing; Touring; Resident; Educational

1995
TAGHKANIC CHORALE
PO Box 144
Yorktown Heights, NY 10598-0144
Phone: 914-737-6707
e-mail: maryc63533@aol.com
Web Site: taghkanicchorale.ontimeonline.com/
Officers:
 President: Peter Hauge
 VP: Pat Miller
 Secretary: Sandra Strubbe
 Treasurer: Dale Sharp
Management:
 President: David Jones
 VP: Pat Miller
 Music Director: Martin Rutishauser
Mission: Preparation and performance of choral works with emphasis on quality and authenticity.
Utilizes: Singers
Founded: 1967
Specialized Field: Choral
Status: Semi-Professional; Nonprofit
Paid Staff: 100
Income Sources: Chorus America
Organization Type: Performing; Educational

North Carolina

1996
ASHEVILLE LYRIC OPERA
2 South Pack Square
Asheville, NC 28801
Phone: 828-236-0670
e-mail: info@ashevillelyric.org
Web Site: www.ashevillelyric.org
Officers:
 President: Dr Barry Pate Jr
 Vice President: Dr Mario Dicesare
 Treasurer: Dr Perry Sprawls
 Secretary: Janis Bryant
Management:
 General/Artistic Director: David Craig Starkey
 Conductor: Delta David Gier
 Principal Guest Conductor: Dr Robert Hart Baker
 Principal Guest Director: Scott Parry

Mission: To build a professional opera company in Asheville and present an educational outreach in the area schools and universities, thereby becoming a part of and enhancing the life of the family of arts and culture in Western North Carolina.
Opened: 1999
Specialized Field: Opera
Income Sources: Sponsors
Season: October-April
Performs At: Diana Wortham Theatre

1997
CAROLINA VOICES
1900 Queens Road
Charlotte, NC 28207
Phone: 704-374-1564
Fax: 704-372-8733
Web Site: www.carolinavoices.org
Management:
 Chairman: Dennis Crowley
 Executive Director: Sue Wheldom
 Music Director: Donna Hill
 Music Director: Scott McKenzie
 Director: Jacqueline Robinson
Mission: To enrich and educate our community by sharing our passion for quality choral music and uniting the voices of all people in celebration of music, the international language of the soul.
Utilizes: Guest Artists; Guest Companies; Selected Students; Sign Language Translators; Visual Arts
Founded: 1953
Specialized Field: Choral; Ethnic Music; Classical; Contemporary; Religious
Status: Non-Profit, Non-Professional
Paid Staff: 7
Volunteer Staff: 1
Non-paid Artists: 175
Annual Attendance: 30,000

1998
CHARLOTTE PHILHARMONIC CHORUS
PO Box 470987
Charlotte, NC 28247-0987
Phone: 704-543-5551
Fax: 704-543-5542
e-mail: info@charlottephilharmonic.org
Officers:
 President: Deborah L Gould
Management:
 President: Albert E Moehring
 Choral Director: Marc S Setzer
Founded: 1994
Specialized Field: Choral
Performs At: The Carriage Club of Charlotte

1999
OPERA CAROLINA
Two Wachovia Center
301 S Tryon Street Suite 1550
Charlotte, NC 28282
Phone: 704-332-7177
Fax: 704-332-6448
Web Site: www.operacarolina.org
Officers:
 Chair: C. Wells Hall
 Chair Elect: Kay Allison Norris
 Vice Chair: Thomas Hughes
 Vice Chair: Catherine M Connor
 Secretary: Georgette Dixon
 Treasurer: Steven Hershfield
Management:
 General Director/Conductor: James Meena
 Director Production: Michael Baumgarten

Mission: To inspire the region's diverse population through the presentation of excellent professional opera, operetta, music, theatre and education and outreach programs that elevate the quality of life in the Carolinas.
Utilizes: Artists-in-Residence; Collaborating Artists; Community Talent; Contract Orchestras; Dancers; Educators; Guest Accompanists; Guest Artists; Guest Companies; Guest Composers; Guest Conductors; Guest Designers; Guest Lecturers; Guest Musical Directors; Guest Musicians; Guest Soloists; Guest Speakers; Guest Teachers; Guest Writers; Instructors; Local Artists; Music; Original Music Scores; Resident Artists; Resident Professionals; Scenic Designers; Sign Language Translators; Singers; Students
Founded: 1948
Specialized Field: Grand Opera
Status: Non-Profit, Professional
Paid Staff: 13
Paid Artists: 150
Budget: $2,500,000
Income Sources: Private Foundations/Grants/Endowments; Business/Coporate Donation; Government Grants; Individual Donations
Performs At: North Carolina Performing Arts Center
Affiliations: Opera America
Annual Attendance: 12,000
Facility Category: Performing Arts Center
Type of Stage: Proscenium
Stage Dimensions: 60'x43'
Year Built: 1970
Year Remodeled: 1992
Rental Contact: NC Performing Arts Center
Organization Type: Performing; Touring; Resident; Educational

2000
DURHAM CIVIC CHORAL SOCIETY
120 Morris Street
Durham, NC 27701
Phone: 919-560-2733
Web Site: www.choral-society.org
Officers:
    President: Dan Gunselman
    VP: Florence Nash
    Secretary: Celia Grasty Lata
    Treasurer: Lynn Wilson
Management:
    President: Dan Gunselman
    Director Of Upper School: Michael L Meye
    Artistic Director: Rodney Wynkoop
    Organist And Choir Director: Jane Lynch
Mission: Our mission is to bring together persons who share a common interest in high-quality performance of significant choral literature, both sacred and secular.
Founded: 1949
Specialized Field: Choral
Status: Non-Professional; Nonprofit
Paid Staff: 154
Performs At: Duke University Chapel; Baldwin Auditorium
Organization Type: Performing

2001
CHORAL SOCIETY OF GREENSBORO
200 N Davie Street
Box 2
Greensboro, NC 27401
Phone: 336-373-2549
Fax: 336-373-2659
Web Site: www.greensboro.com/choral
Management:
    President: Tom Wright
    Managing Director: Lynn H Donovan

Artistic Director: Welborn Young
Mission: Sharing musical understanding, appreciation, accomplishment and musicianship with the public.
Utilizes: Guest Artists
Founded: 1984
Specialized Field: Choral; Ethnic Music; Classical; Contemporary; Religious
Status: Non-Profit, Non-Professional
Paid Staff: 150
Income Sources: City of Greensboro; The Music Center
Performs At: Dana Auditorium
Organization Type: Performing

2002
GREENSBORO OPERA COMPANY
200 North Davie Street
Box 17
Greensboro, NC 27401
Phone: 336-273-9472
Fax: 336-273-9481
e-mail: opera2@bellsouth.net
Web Site: http://www.greensboroopera.org/index
Officers:
    President: George W. Aycock, III
    Treasurer/President-Elect: Frederick J. Smith
    Executive Director: David Barnwell
Management:
    Artistic Director: Valery Ryvkin
    Company Manager: Elena Deangelis
Mission: Enhancing cultural life in the Greensboro area through developing and promoting a quality program of operas and education.
Utilizes: Singers
Founded: 1981
Specialized Field: Grand Opera; Musical Theatre; Choral; Youth Chorus
Status: Non-Profit, Professional
Income Sources: Opera America; Central Opera Service
Performs At: War Memorial Auditorium; Carolina Theatre
Organization Type: Performing; Educational; Sponsoring

2003
RALEIGH BOYCHOIR
1329 Ridge Road
Raleigh, NC 27607
Mailing Address: PO Box 12481, Raleigh, NC. 27605
Phone: 919-881-9259
Fax: 919-881-0971
e-mail: rbc@ipass.net
Web Site: www.raleighboychoir.org
Management:
    Founder/Director: Thomas E Sibley
Mission: To educate and train boys in the art of singing; to perform the finest music in the boychoir tradition; to contribute to musical life in the greater Raleigh area; and to enhance North Carolina's cultural reputation. The Raleigh Boychoir experience develops character, discipline, leadership, and a strong commitment to excellence.
Founded: 1968
Specialized Field: Youth Chorus
Status: Non-Profit, Professional
Paid Staff: 3
Volunteer Staff: 5
Paid Artists: 2

2004
TAR RIVER CHORAL & ORCHESTRAL SOCIETY
The Dunn Center 1200
PO Box 8255
Rocky Mount, NC 27804
Phone: 252-985-3055
Fax: 252-985-3055
Web Site: www.abouttroc.org
Management:
    President: Daniel L Crocker
    Executive Director: Beth Kupsco
    Music Director: Alfred E Sturgis
Founded: 1986
Specialized Field: Choral; Youth Chorus; Classical
Status: Non-Profit, Professional
Paid Staff: 8

2005
PIEDMONT CHAMBER SINGERS
PO Box 20573
Winston-Salem, NC 27120
Phone: 336-722-4022
Fax: 336-722-4022
Web Site: www.piedmontchambersingers.org
Officers:
    President: Ed Carlson
    VP: Martha Claire Henzler
    Secretary: Joe Crocker
    Treasurer: Ken Carpenter
Management:
    President: Keith Kooken
    Executive Director: Marianne Levigne
    Artistic Director: William Osborne
Mission: Over the past two decades, PCS has gained a loyal following of supporters and patrons.
Founded: 1977
Specialized Field: Choral; Classical; Contemporary
Status: Non-Profit, Non-Professional
Paid Staff: 2

2006
PIEDMONT OPERA THEATRE
235 N Cherry Street
Suite 100
Winston-Salem, NC 27101-3929
Phone: 336-725-7101
Fax: 336-725-7131
Web Site: www.piedmontopera.org/
Officers:
    President: Guy Rudsill
    Treasurer: Gerard R Gunzenhauser
    Secretary: Clyde Fitzgerald
    VP Education: Margaret Kolb
Management:
    Board President: E Gail Phillips
    Artistic Director: James Allbritten
    Executive Director: John W Fichtel
Mission: To create and support consistently superior opera theatre productions and programs that ensure recognition of the company as an important community asset for entertainment and education, a force in city development, and a magnet attraction for regional and national audiences.
Utilizes: Guest Companies; Singers
Founded: 1978
Specialized Field: Grand Opera; Lyric Opera; Light Opera; Operetta
Status: Professional; Nonprofit
Income Sources: Opera America; Central Opera Service; National Opera Association; Arts Council; Winston-Salem

Performs At: Roger L. Stevens Center for the
Performing Arts
Organization Type: Performing; Resident; Educational

2007
WINSTON-SALEM PIEDMONT TRIAD SYMPHONY ASSOCIATION

610 Coliseum Drive
Winston-Salem, NC 27106
Phone: 336-725-1035
Fax: 336-725-3924
e-mail: mvale@wssymphony.org
Web Site: www.wssymphony.org
Officers:
    Operations/Stage Manager: Beverley Naiditch
    Financial Manager: Selina Carter
Management:
    Executive Director: E Merritt Vale
    Music Director: Peter Perret
    Director Marketing Development: William Cole
    Box Office Manager: Tinay Jeffers
Mission: Presenting the finest symphonic as well as choral literature; providing high quality music education for Winston-Salem and Forsythe County children.
Utilizes: Collaborations; Commissioned Composers; Commissioned Music; Educators; Five Seasonal Concerts; Guest Accompanists; Guest Artists; Guest Choreographers; Guest Companies; Guest Composers; Guest Directors; Guest Instructors; Guest Lecturers; Guest Musical Directors; Guest Musicians; Guest Soloists; High School Drama; Local Artists; Lyricists; Multimedia; New Productions; Singers; Visual Arts
Founded: 1947
Specialized Field: Choral
Status: Professional; Nonprofit
Paid Staff: 9
Paid Artists: 80
Budget: $1.4 million
Income Sources: American Symphony Orchestra League; Broadcast Music Incorporated; American Society of Composers, Authors and Publishers; Association of Symphony Orchestras of North Carolina
Performs At: E. Stevens Center for the Performing Arts
Annual Attendance: 100,000
Seating Capacity: 1,380
Year Remodeled: 1985
Organization Type: Performing; Resident; Educational

2008
WINSTON-SALEM SYMPHONY

201 N Broad Street
Suite 200
Winston-Salem, NC 27106
Phone: 336-725-1035
Fax: 336-725-3924
e-mail: mvale@wssymphony.org
Web Site: www.wssymphony.org
Officers:
    President/CEO: Merrit Vale
    President: Roger Bear
    Treasurer: Dick Deem
    Secretary: Jerry Silber
Management:
    Music Director: Robert Moody
    Ticket Sales/Donor Administration: Latonya Wright
Founded: 1947
Specialized Field: Choral
Status: Professional; Nonprofit
Paid Staff: 14
Volunteer Staff: 120
Paid Artists: 75
Non-paid Artists: 80

North Dakota

2009
FARGO-MOORHEAD OPERA COMPANY

114 Broadway
Suite S1
Fargo, ND 58102
Phone: 701-239-4558
Fax: 701-476-1991
Toll-free: 877-687-7469
e-mail: director@fmopera.org
Web Site: www.fmopera.org
Officers:
    President: Dennis Staton
    VP: Thomas Ortmeier
    Treasurer: David Duval
    Secretary: Beth Postema
Management:
    Office Manager: Iris Fogderud
    Artistic Director: David Hamilton
    Box Office Manager: Beau Brander
Mission: To produce professional opera and introduce people to one of the world's oldest art forms.
Utilizes: Selected Students; Singers; Soloists
Founded: 1968
Specialized Field: Opera
Status: Non-Profit, Professional
Paid Staff: 3
Budget: $356,900
Income Sources: National Endowment for the Arts; Alex Stern Family Foundation; Cities of Fargo and Moorhead; Bush Foundation; McKnight Foundation; Minnesota Council on the Arts
Performs At: NDSU Fine Arts Building
Annual Attendance: 3,600
Facility Category: Concert Hall
Organization Type: Performing; Touring; Educational
Resident Groups: Minnesota Association of Community Theatres, Lake Agassiz Arts Council, US Assoc. Community Theatre

2010
INTERNATIONAL MUSIC CAMP

1930 23rd Avenue SE
Minot, ND 58701
Phone: 701-838-8472
Fax: 701-838-8472
e-mail: info@internationalmusiccamp.com
Web Site: www.internationalmusiccamp.com
Officers:
    President: Vern Gerig
    VP: Clifford Grubb
    Secretary: Roy Johnson
    Treasurer: Randy Hall
Management:
    President: Donald Timmerman
    Executive Director: Joseph T Alme
Mission: To develop a greater appreciation among students of all nations through their mutual interest in the arts.
Utilizes: Singers
Founded: 1956
Specialized Field: Light Opera; Choral; Youth Chorus; Ethnic Music; Classical; Contemporary; Religious; Jazz; International
Status: Non-Profit, Professional
Paid Staff: 250
Volunteer Staff: 25
Paid Artists: 150
Budget: $600,000
Income Sources: Camp Fees
Performs At: International Music Camp
Annual Attendance: 3,000

Facility Category: Open Auditorium; Performing Arts Center
Stage Dimensions: 60' x 100'
Seating Capacity: 2000; 500
Year Built: 1982
Year Remodeled: 1999
Cost: $1,500,000
Rental Contact: Joseph T Alme
Organization Type: Performing; Resident; Educational

Ohio

2011
CINCINNATI BOYCHOIR

1926 Mills Avenue
Cincinnati, OH 45212
Phone: 513-396-7664
Fax: 513-396-7664
Web Site: www.cincinnatiboychoir.org
Management:
    Music Director: Randall Wolfe
    Business Manager: Patty Corfman
Mission: To provide high quality music, education, and performance opportunities to boys with unchanged voices and choral music to greater Cincinnati and other regions.
Utilizes: Collaborating Artists; Collaborations; Educators; Guest Artists; Guest Companies; Guest Directors; Guest Musical Directors; Multimedia; Music; Original Music Scores; Sign Language Translators; Soloists
Founded: 1965
Specialized Field: Choral; Youth Chorus; Ethnic Music; Classical; Religious
Status: Non-Profit, Non-Professional
Paid Staff: 2
Volunteer Staff: 10
Paid Artists: 5
Non-paid Artists: 110
Facility Category: Rehearsal Hall
Year Built: 1896
Organization Type: Performing; Touring; Resident; Educational

2012
CINCINNATI OPERA

1243 Elm Street
Cincinnati, OH 45202
Phone: 513-768-5500
Fax: 513-768-5552
Web Site: www.cincinnatiopera.com
Management:
    Artistic Consultant: Evans Mirageas
    General Director/CEO: Patricia K Beggs
Mission: To provide opera to the Cincinnati and Tri-State Area.
Utilizes: Guest Artists; Guest Companies; Singers
Founded: 1920
Specialized Field: Grand Opera; Lyric Opera; Operetta
Status: Professional; Nonprofit
Paid Staff: 28
Income Sources: Opera America
Performs At: Music Hall
Organization Type: Performing

2013
CLEVELAND OPERA

1422 Euclid Avenue
Suite 1052
Cleveland, OH 44115
Phone: 216-575-0903
Fax: 216-575-1918
e-mail: info@operacleveland.org

Officers:
Principal Conductor: Richard Buckley
Director of Finance and Administrat: Shari Lash
Management:
President Board of Trustees: Peter L Rubin
Artistic Advisor: Leon Major
Production Manager: William S Collister Jr
Director Production: Christopher Flinchum
Director Marketing: Catherine Guin
Director Development: William Cole
Manager Finance/Administration: Colleen G Sherman
Director Education/Outreach: Judith Ryder
Mission: Professional singers are allowed to gain experience in about 400 educational and entertainment events.
Founded: 1976
Specialized Field: Opera
Season: October-April

2014
CLEVELAND ORCHESTRA CHORUS
11001 Euclid Avenue
Cleveland, OH 44106
Phone: 216-231-1111
Fax: 216-231-0202
Toll-free: 800-686-1141
e-mail: info@clevelandorchestra.com
Web Site: www.clevelandorchestra.com
Officers:
Chairperson: Margaret B Robinson
The Cleveland Orchestra Chorus Oper:
Management:
President: Gary Hansen
Artistic Director: Franz Mose
Librarian: Eleanor Kushnick
Accompanist/Soloist: Joela Jones
Assitant Accompanist: Betty Meyers
Assitant Accompanist: Donald Shelhorn
Mission: To assist the Cleveland Orchestra in performing choral-orchestral works.
Utilizes: Guest Artists
Founded: 1952
Opened: cont
Specialized Field: Choral; Opera; Contemporary
Status: Non-Profit, Professional
Paid Staff: 170
Performs At: Severence Hall; Blossom Music Center
Organization Type: Performing; Touring; Resident

2015
LYRIC OPERA OF CLEVELAND
1422 Euclid Avenue
Suite 1052
Cleveland, OH 44115
Phone: 216-575-0903
Web Site: www.clevelandopera.org
Officers:
President: Don Scippione
President Guild: Becky Elliot
Management:
Director Of Production: Maidie O Rosenberg
Director Of Development: William Cole
Director Of Marketing/Communication: Catherine Guin
Direcotr Of Finance/Administration: Colleen G Sherman
President: Peter Rubin
Artistic Advisor: Leon Major
Mission: To utilize talented artists from the North in music theatre productions; to uncover new ideas, fresh concepts and illuminating perspectives in every work it produces; to emphasize training opportunities for professional development.

Utilizes: Actors; AEA Actors; Choreographers; Collaborations; Fine Artists; Grant Writers; Guest Artists; Guest Companies; Guest Composers; Guest Conductors; Guest Designers; Guest Soloists; Guest Writers; High School Drama; Local Artists; Lyricists; Multi Collaborations; New Productions; Resident Professionals; Sign Language Translators; Singers; Student Interns
Founded: 1974
Specialized Field: Opera; Musical Theatre
Status: Non-Profit, Professional
Paid Staff: 4
Paid Artists: 3
Non-paid Artists: 2
Budget: $500,000
Income Sources: Tickets, Cleveland Foundation, Gund & Kyles
Performs At: Cleveland Institute of Music
Annual Attendance: 4,800
Facility Category: Professional Theatre
Type of Stage: Proscenium
Stage Dimensions: 30 X 40
Seating Capacity: 500
Organization Type: Performing; Resident; Educational; Sponsoring

2016
SAINT SAVA FREE SERBIAN ORTHODOX CHURCH
2151 W Wallings
Cleveland, OH 44147
Phone: 216-741-3002
Management:
Director: Dragica Zamiska
Mission: To encourage and perpetuate Serbian music, dance, language, culture and heritage.
Founded: 1982
Specialized Field: Ethnic Music; Folk Music; Religious
Status: Non-Professional; Nonprofit
Income Sources: Saint Sava Free Serbian Orthodox Church; School Congregation; Cleveland Area Arts Council
Organization Type: Performing; Touring; Resident; Educational

2017
COLUMBUS SYMPHONY CHORUS
55 E State Street
Columbus, OH 43215
Phone: 614-228-9600
Fax: 614-224-7273
Web Site: www.columbussymphony.com
Management:
President: Rosen Stock
Conductor: Ronald J Jenkins
Mission: To expose the public to great music.
Utilizes: Commissioned Composers; Commissioned Music; Composers-in-Residence; Dance Companies; Grant Writers; Guest Accompanists; Guest Composers; Guest Lecturers; Guest Musicians; Instructors; Multimedia; Organization Contracts; Original Music Scores; Sign Language Translators; Singers
Founded: 1960
Specialized Field: Light Opera; Lyric Opera; Musical Theatre; Choral; Youth Chorus; Ethnic Music; Classical
Status: Non-Profit, Professional
Paid Staff: 100
Paid Artists: 70
Income Sources: Columbus Symphony Orchestra
Performs At: Ohio Theatre
Organization Type: Performing; Resident; Educational

2018
DAYTON OPERA ASSOCIATION
138 N Main Street
Dayton, OH 45402
Phone: 937-228-0662
Fax: 937-228-9612
Toll-free: 800-228-3630
e-mail: info@daytonopera.org
Web Site: www.daytonopera.org
Management:
General/Artistic Director: Thomas Bankston
Marketing/PR Director: Shannon McClure
Mission: To increase appreciation for opera through education; to present and promote opera of high quality to the Dayton region in balanced programs; to utilize international artists; to encourage local and regional artistic development.
Founded: 1960
Specialized Field: Grand Opera; Light Opera; Lyric Opera; Musical Theatre; Classical; Contemporary
Status: Non-Profit, Professional
Paid Staff: 30
Budget: 1.3 million
Income Sources: Box Office; Grants; Private Donations
Performs At: Memorial Hall
Affiliations: Opera America; American Arts Alliance; Dayton Performing Arts Fund
Facility Category: War Memorial Theater
Type of Stage: Proscenium
Stage Dimensions: 58 x 36 x 26
Seating Capacity: 2,501
Year Built: 1902
Year Remodeled: 1953
Organization Type: Performing; Resident; Educational

2019
HAMILTON-FAIRFIELD SYMPHONY & CHORALE
23 S Front Street
Hamilton, OH 45011
Phone: 513-895-5151
Fax: 513-844-1584
Web Site: www.hfso.org
Management:
President: Paul Stanbery
General Manager: Rita Line
Founded: 1994
Specialized Field: Choral
Status: Non-Profit, Professional
Paid Staff: 5
Paid Artists: 100

2020
LANCASTER CHORALE
109 N Broad Street
PO Box 2450
Lancaster, OH 43130
Phone: 740-687-5855
Fax: 740-653-7074
e-mail: officemanager@lancasterchorale.com
Web Site: www.lancasterchorale.com/
Officers:
President: Cathy Tolbert
Management:
Artistic Director: Robert Trocchia
Mission: To perform the finest choral literature, encompassing a wide range of styles, idioms and periods. The Chorale is characterized by its unique versatility, control, precision and blend.
Founded: 1985
Specialized Field: Choral
Status: Non-Profit

Income Sources: Chorus America
Organization Type: Performing; Touring

2021
SORG OPERA COMPANY
2 N Main Street
Suite 402
Middletown, OH 45042
Phone: 513-425-0180
Fax: 513-425-0181
Officers:
   President: Howard Johnson
   VP: William Hilsmier
   Secretary: Charles Robertson
Mission: To develop cultural awareness through opera education and to encourage community pride in the Miami Opera Valley through the presentation of high quality opera.
Utilizes: Actors; Artists-in-Residence; Choreographers; Collaborating Artists; Dance Companies; Dancers; Designers; Educators; Fine Artists; Five Seasonal Concerts; Grant Writers; Guest Accompanists; Guest Composers; Guest Designers; Guest Lecturers; Guest Writers; Instructors; Local Artists; Multimedia; Music; Original Music Scores; Sign Language Translators; Singers; Soloists; Visual Arts
Founded: 1990
Specialized Field: Opera
Status: Non-Profit, Professional
Volunteer Staff: 2
Seating Capacity: 700

2022
COLLEGE LIGHT OPERA COMPANY
1625 S Cedar Street
Oberlin, OH 44074
Phone: 440-724-8485
Fax: 440-775-8642
e-mail: bob.haslun@oberlin.edu
Web Site: www.collegelightopera.com
Officers:
   President: DeWitt C Jones III
   Treasurer: Robert A Haslun
   Secretary: Ursula R Haslun
Management:
   Producer/General Manager: Robert A Haslun
   Producer/Business Manager: Ursula R Haslun
Mission: Musical theatre training groud for undergraduates, singers, musicians, tech & costume staff, business office and production staff.
Founded: 1969
Specialized Field: Light Opera; Operetta; Musical Theatre
Status: Non-Professional; Nonprofit
Paid Staff: 25
Paid Artists: 19
Non-paid Artists: 32
Budget: $300,000
Income Sources: Box Office; Annual Fund
Performs At: Highfield Theatre
Annual Attendance: 15,200
Type of Stage: Proscenium
Seating Capacity: 300
Year Built: 1947
Year Remodeled: 1999
Cost: $450,000

2023
OHIO LIGHT OPERA
College of Wooster
329 E University Street
Wooster, OH 44691
Phone: 330-263-2345
Fax: 330-263-2272
e-mail: ohiolightopera@wooster.edu
Web Site: www.ohiolightopera.org
Officers:
   President: Grant Cornwell
Management:
   Executive Director: Laura Neill
   Artistic Director: Steven Daigle
   Music Director: Michael Borowitz
Mission: To promote, produce, and preserve the best operettas ever written, and to do them in traditional settings.
Utilizes: Choreographers; Commissioned Composers; Dancers; Designers; Guest Musical Directors; Multimedia; Original Music Scores; Resident Artists; Resident Professionals; Sign Language Translators; Student Interns
Founded: 1979
Specialized Field: Light Opera; Lyric Opera; Musical Theatre; Classical
Status: Non-Profit, Professional
Paid Staff: 120
Paid Artists: 75
Budget: $1,250,000
Income Sources: Private Donations, Ticket Sales
Performs At: Freedlander Theatre
Annual Attendance: 20,000
Seating Capacity: 394

Oklahoma

2024
CIMARRON CIRCUIT OPERA COMPANY
555 S University Boulevard
First Presbyterian Church
Norman, OK 73070
Mailing Address: PO Box 1085
Phone: 405-364-8962
Fax: 405-321-5842
e-mail: info@ccocopera.org
Web Site: www.ccocopera.org
Management:
   Director: Erica C Thomas
   Music Director: Kevin W Smith
   Development Manager: Carla Smitherman
   Technical Director: Mark Pooler
Mission: Offering training and experience to young Oklahoma singers; bringing opera to areas in Oklahoma where residents normally wouldn't have access to performances.
Utilizes: Guest Companies
Founded: 1975
Specialized Field: Grand Opera; Light Opera; Lyric Opera; Choral; Youth Chorus; Ethnic Music; Classical; Religious
Status: Non-Profit, Professional
Paid Staff: 5
Income Sources: Central Opera Service; Mid-America Arts Alliance
Performs At: Sooner Theatre; Holmberg Hall
Organization Type: Performing; Touring; Sponsoring

2025
CANTERBURY CHORAL SOCIETY
428 W California
#100
Oklahoma City, OK 73102-2454
Phone: 405-232-7464
Fax: 405-232-7465
e-mail: enquiries@canterburychoral.co.uk
Web Site: www.canterburychoral.co.uk
Management:

President: James W Bruce Jr
Executive Director: Kay E Holp
Artistic Director: Randi Von Ells
Founded: 1969
Specialized Field: Choral
Status: Non-Profit, Non-Professional
Paid Staff: 12
Non-paid Artists: 475

2026
OKLAHOMA OPERA AND MUSIC THEATER COMPANY
Oklahoma City University
2501 N Blackwelder
Oklahoma City, OK 73106-1493
Phone: 405-208-5700
Fax: 405-208-5316
Toll-free: 800-633-7242
e-mail: mparker@okcu.edu
Web Site: www.okcu.edu/music
Officers:
   President: Tom J. McDaniel
Mission: Offering the public high quality performances; providing students with a professional arena in which to develop their talents.
Utilizes: Guest Companies; Singers
Founded: 1904
Specialized Field: Grand Opera; Lyric Opera; Light Opera; Operetta; Choral
Status: Non-Profit, Non-Professional
Paid Staff: 40
Income Sources: Oklahoma City University
Performs At: Kirkpatrick Theater
Organization Type: Performing; Educational

2027
LIGHT OPERA OKLAHOMA - LOOK
Harwelden
2210 S Main
Tulsa, OK 74114
Phone: 918-583-4267
Fax: 918-583-1780
e-mail: eric@lightoperaok.org
Web Site: www.lightoperaok.org
Management:
   President: Leslie Shelton
   Artistic Director: Eric Gibson, frontoffice@lightoperaok.org
   Founder: John Everitt
Mission: To preserve and create awareness of the musical comedy/operetta art form by producing a festival of such every summer in Tulsa, OK.
Founded: 1984
Specialized Field: Light Opera; Musical Theatre
Status: Non-Profit, Professional
Paid Staff: 3
Volunteer Staff: 10
Paid Artists: 100
Non-paid Artists: 10
Budget: $750,000
Income Sources: Foundations; Corporations
Performs At: Tulsa Performing Arts Center - Williams Theatre
Annual Attendance: 6000-7500
Seating Capacity: 425

2028
TULSA OPERA
1610 S Boulder
Tulsa, OK 74119
Phone: 918-582-4035
Fax: 918-592-0380
Toll-free: 866-298-2530
Web Site: www.tulsaopera.com

Officers:
President: Scott Filstrup
Chairman: Jonathan Helmerich
Management:
General Director: Carol I Crawford
Director Finance and Planning: Elena Jackson-Forsyth
Director Operations: Amanda Foust
Mission: To produce opera of artistic integrity and enrich the regional community through innovative education and outreach programs.
Utilizes: Guest Artists; Guest Companies; Singers
Founded: 1948
Specialized Field: Youth Chorus; Grand Opera
Status: Non-Profit, Professional
Paid Staff: 15
Volunteer Staff: 100
Income Sources: Opera America; American Arts Alliance; Arts & Humanities Council of Tulsa
Performs At: Chapman Music Hall
Organization Type: Performing; Sponsoring

Oregon

2029
EUGENE OPERA
1590 Williamette Street
Eugene, OR 97401
Mailing Address: PO Box 11200, Eugene, OR 97400
Phone: 541-485-3985
Fax: 541-683-3783
Web Site: www.eugeneopera.com
Officers:
President: John Tilson
President-Elect: Richard Frye
VP: Philip Piele
Treasurer: Mark Reynolds
Secretary: Reggie Tonry
Management:
General Director: Mark Beudert
Production Manager: Josh Neckels
Chorus Master: John Jantzi
Mission: To contribute to the future of opera by increasing the audience, educating the community and utilizing the talents of emerging musicians.
Utilizes: Collaborations; Dancers; Designers; Guest Accompanists; Guest Composers; Guest Designers; Instructors; Multimedia; Original Music Scores; Resident Artists; Resident Professionals; Student Interns
Founded: 1976
Specialized Field: Grand Opera; Lyric Opera; Light Opera; Operetta
Status: Professional, Nonprofit
Paid Staff: 6
Volunteer Staff: 20
Budget: $800,000
Income Sources: Ticket Sales, Grants, Fund Raising
Performs At: Hugh Center for the Performing Arts
Seating Capacity: 2,400
Year Built: 1982
Organization Type: Performing; Educational

2030
PORTLAND OPERA
211 SE Caruther
Portland, OR 97215
Phone: 503-241-1407
Fax: 503-241-4212
Toll-free: 866-739-6737
e-mail: admin@portlandopera.org
Web Site: www.portlandopera.org
Management:

Executive Director: Christopher Matpaliano
Utilizes: Collaborations; Grant Writers; Guest Accompanists; Guest Artists; Guest Choreographers; Guest Companies; Guest Composers; Guest Conductors; Guest Designers; Guest Musical Directors; Guest Musicians; Guild Activities; Instructors; Organization Contracts; Original Music Scores; Resident Artists; Resident Professionals; Selected Students; Student Interns; Theatre Companies
Founded: 1964
Specialized Field: Grand Opera; Classical; Contemporary
Status: Non-Profit, Professional
Paid Staff: 50
Budget: $6.7 Million
Performs At: Portland Keller Auditorium
Affiliations: Opera America
Annual Attendance: 48,000
Facility Category: Auditorium
Type of Stage: Proscenium
Stage Dimensions: 30 x 60 x 43
Seating Capacity: 3,000
Year Built: 1917
Year Remodeled: 1967
Rental Contact: Lori Leyba Kramer
Organization Type: Performing; Touring; Resident

Pennsylvania

2031
MARY GREEN SINGERS
990 Old Huntingdon Pike
Huntingdon Valley, PA 19006
Phone: 215-572-5063
Fax: 215-884-5432
Officers:
Music Director/Conductor: Mary Woodmansee Green
Management:
President: Mary Green
Mission: Tax-exempt, non-profit cultural and educational institution.
Founded: 1986
Specialized Field: Choral
Status: Non-Profit, Non-Professional
Paid Staff: 1
Volunteer Staff: 6
Non-paid Artists: 150
Organization Type: Performing; Touring; Educational

2032
FULTON OPERA HOUSE
12 N Prince Street
PO Box 1865
Lancaster, PA 17608
Phone: 717-394-7133
Fax: 717-397-3780
Web Site: www.thefulton.org
Officers:
President: Harvey Owen
VP: J Bradley Scovill
Secretary: Karyn E Regite
Treasurer: Elizabeth H Habecker
Management:
Interim Artistic Director: Marc Robin
Managing Director: Aaron Young
Director Development: Richard Owen
Mission: To produce professional regional theatre of a quality that honors, affirms and extends the Fulton's role in the history of American theatre as a national historic landmark and to provide educational, artistic and cultural benefits that engender community ownership.

Utilizes: Actors; AEA Actors; Artists-in-Residence; Choreographers; Collaborations; Commissioned Music; Dance Companies; Dancers; Designers; Educators; Grant Writers; Guest Accompanists; Guest Artists; Guest Companies; Guest Conductors; Guest Designers; Guest Lecturers; Guest Teachers; Guest Writers; Guild Activities; Instructors; Local Artists; Lyricists; Multimedia; Music; Organization Contracts; Original Music Scores; Performance Artists; Poets; Resident Artists; Resident Professionals; Selected Students; Singers; Soloists; Student Interns
Founded: 1852
Specialized Field: Opera; Musical Theatre
Status: Non-Profit, Professional
Paid Staff: 30
Paid Artists: 300
Budget: $2,100,000
Income Sources: Earned, Contributed
Performs At: Fulton Opera House
Annual Attendance: 100,000+
Facility Category: Theatre
Type of Stage: Proscenium
Seating Capacity: 684
Year Built: 1852
Year Remodeled: 1995
Architect: $9,500,000
Rental Contact: Managing Director Rod McCullough
Organization Type: Performing, Touring, Educational

2033
LANCASTER OPERA COMPANY
PO Box 8382
Lancaster, PA 17604
Phone: 717-392-0885
Fax: 717-392-5650
e-mail: info@lancasteropera.com
Web Site: www.lancasteropera.com
Management:
President: Paul Fulmer
Executive Director: Cheryl Crider
Artistic Director: Scott Drackley
Marketing Manager: Dianne Fussaro
Founded: 1952
Specialized Field: Opera
Status: Non-Profit
Paid Staff: 1
Volunteer Staff: 25
Non-paid Artists: 120
Budget: $130,000
Income Sources: Tickets; Grants; Annual Appeal; Corporate Funding
Performs At: Fulton Opera House
Annual Attendance: 5,000+
Facility Category: 150 year-old theater
Type of Stage: Proscenium
Seating Capacity: 684
Year Built: 1852

2034
ACADEMY OF VOCAL ARTS OPERA THEATRE
1920 Spruce Street
Philadelphia, PA 19103
Phone: 215-735-1685
Fax: 215-732-2189
e-mail: info@avaopera.org
Web Site: www.avaopera.org
Officers:
President: Albert W Mandia
VP: John A Nyheim
VP: Laren Pitcairn
VP: James McKee Ridgway
VP: Conant Scott Rogers
Secretary: Martha R Hurt

Management:
 Public Relations Officer: Maryann Devine
 Executive Director: K James McDowell
 Music Director: Christofer Macatsoris
Mission: To train young singers for international careers in opera, and present in operas and recitals.
Utilizes: Artists-in-Residence; Guest Conductors; Guest Designers
Founded: 1934
Specialized Field: Lyric Opera; Classical
Status: Non-Profit, Non-Professional
Paid Staff: 33
Non-paid Artists: 25
Performs At: Helen Corning Warden Theater; Academy of Music
Affiliations: N.A.S.M.
Seating Capacity: 180

2035
CHORAL ARTS SOCIETY OF PHILADELPHIA

PO Box 22445
Philadelphia, PA 19110
Phone: 215-240-6417
e-mail: info@choralarts.com
Web Site: www.choralarts.com
Management:
 Artistic Director: Matthew Glandorf
Mission: To present a diverse selection of choral music spanning all musical periods.
Utilizes: Guest Companies; Guest Musical Directors; Guest Musicians; Instructors; Local Artists; Lyricists; Multimedia; Organization Contracts; Original Music Scores; Sign Language Translators; Singers; Theatre Companies
Founded: 1982
Specialized Field: Choral
Status: Professional, Nonprofit
Performs At: Mann Music Center; Academy of Music; Kimmel Center; Churches; Cathedrals
Organization Type: Performing; Touring; Educational

2036
DELAWARE VALLEY OPERA COMPANY

1731 Chandler Street
Philadelphia, PA 19111
Phone: 215-725-4171
e-mail: info@dvopera.org
Web Site: www.dvopera.org
Officers:
 President: Sandra Day
 Secretary: Carol Denenberg
 Treasurer: Alan Edelstein
Mission: To aid aspiring opera musicians with experience, training, education of opera through production and performance.
Utilizes: Singers
Founded: 1988
Specialized Field: Opera
Status: Non-Profit, Professional
Paid Staff: 41
Performs At: Tusten Theatre; Sullivan County Community College
Organization Type: Performing; Educational

2037
LYRIC OPERA THEATRE STREET

1608 S Broad
Philadelphia, PA 19145-1509
Phone: 215-755-1288
Fax: 215-551-1444
e-mail: llotop@aol.com
Web Site: www.surf.2/llotop.com
Officers:

President: AC Pugliese
VP/Secretary: Margaret Kastle
Management:
 President: Margaret Kastla
Mission: To provide repertoire experience for deserving amateur, professional and semi-professional singers.
Founded: 1987
Specialized Field: Musical Theatre; Educational
Status: For-Profit, Professional
Paid Staff: 2
Volunteer Staff: 10
Paid Artists: 10
Non-paid Artists: 50
Budget: $35,000-$60,000
Organization Type: Performing; Educational

2038
MENDELSSOHN CLUB OF PHILADELPHIA

1218 Locust Street
Philadelphia, PA 19107
Phone: 215-735-9922
Fax: 215-573-3786
Web Site: www.libertynet.org
Officers:
 President: James B Straw
 Chairman: C Christopher Cannon
 Vice Chairman: Dennis Alter
 Vice Chairman: Sara A Cerato
 Vice Chairman: Laurie Wagman
 VP: Benjamin Alexander
 VP: Jack R Bershad
 VP: Richard A Doran
 VP/Treasurer: Albert E Piscopo
Management:
 Executive Director: Jack Mulroney
 Producing Artistic Director: Robert B Driver
 Marketing/Communications: Gary Gansky
 Production: Susan Ashbaker
Mission: Mendelssohn's Club's mission has been to challenge, enrich, serve and fulfill its singing members, patrons and audiences through the excellence of its performances.
Utilizes: Collaborating Artists; Collaborations; Commissioned Composers; Guest Companies; Guest Composers; Guest Musicians; Sign Language Translators; Singers
Founded: 1874
Specialized Field: Choral; Classical
Paid Staff: 1
Volunteer Staff: 5
Paid Artists: 12
Non-paid Artists: 160
Budget: $222,000
Income Sources: Ticket Sales; Government and Foundation Grants; Individual Contributions
Performs At: Various: Symphony Halls to Churches

2039
OPERA COMPANY OF PHILADELPHIA

1420 Locust Street
Suite 210
Philadelphia, PA 19102
Phone: 215-893-3600
Fax: 215-893-7801
e-mail: marketing@operaphila.org
Web Site: www.operaphila.org
Officers:
 Chairman: Stephen A Madva
Management:
 Artisitc Director: Robert B Driver
 Executive Director: David B Devan
 CFO: Gary H Gansky

Mission: The city's professional opera company, committed to delivering outstanding productions of traditional repertoire, often presenting these operas in innovative and technologically creative ways, and underwriting and producing new and exciting operatic works that appeal to a socially and culturally diverse audience.
Utilizes: Guest Artists; Guest Companies; Singers
Founded: 1975
Specialized Field: Opera
Status: Professional; Nonprofit
Income Sources: Opera America; Greater Philadelphia Cultural Alliance
Performs At: Academy of Music
Organization Type: Performing

2040
PHILADELPHIA GAY MEN'S CHORUS

1315 Spruce Street
Philadelphia, PA 19107-5601
Phone: 215-731-9230
Toll-free: 877-462-7464
e-mail: info@pgmc.org
Web Site: www.pgmc.org
Officers:
 President: Gil Pereira
 VP Membership: Scott "Skip" Concilla
 VP Fundraising: Edward Stash
 VP Marketing: Sandy Smith
 VP Development: Mark Vernon
 VP Production: Patrick Hagerty
 Secretary: Paul Ackerman
 Treasurer: Chad Leonard
Management:
 Artistic Director: Joseph J Buches
 Collaborative Pianist: Bonnie Wagner
Mission: The Philadelphia Gay Men's Chorus is a diverse group of gay men presenting a variety of challenging musical experiences, seeking to improve the skills of the members and to reach out to the community.
Founded: 1981
Specialized Field: Alternative; Men's Chorus
Status: Non-profit

2041
PHILADELPHIA SINGERS

1211 Chestnut Street
Suite 610
Philadelphia, PA 19107
Phone: 215-751-9494
Fax: 215-751-9490
e-mail: info@philadelphiasingers.org
Web Site: www.philadelphiasingers.org
Officers:
 President: Doralene Davis
 VP: Robert E Mortensen
 VP: Chef Fritz Blank
 Secretary: Michael M. Mills
 Treasurer: James K. Abel
Management:
 President: Robert E Mortensen
 VP: Chef Fritz Blank
 Music Director: David Hayes
 Office Administration: Matthew Seneca
Mission: To produce high quality choral music and offer opportunities for professional singers.
Utilizes: Commissioned Music; Multimedia; Organization Contracts; Original Music Scores; Sign Language Translators; Singers
Founded: 1972
Specialized Field: Choral
Status: Professional
Paid Staff: 8

Volunteer Staff: 2
Paid Artists: 60
Non-paid Artists: 60
Performs At: Academy of Music; Church of the Holy Trinity
Affiliations: Resident Chorus of the Philadelphia Orchestra
Organization Type: Performing

2042
SINGING CITY
123 S 17th Street
Philadelphia, PA 19103
Phone: 215-569-9067
Fax: 215-569-9088
Web Site: www.singingcity.org
Officers:
   President: Robert H Holmes, MD
Management:
   Music Director: Jeffrey Brillhart
   Executive Director: Angela Scully
Mission: Present choral music concerts, educational and community outreach programs.
Founded: 1948
Specialized Field: Choral
Paid Staff: 4
Volunteer Staff: 3
Budget: $235,000
Income Sources: Charitable Donations; Contracted Musical Engagements

2043
BACH CHOIR OF PITTSBURGH
1108 S Braddock Avenue
Suite A
Pittsburgh, PA 15218
Phone: 412-241-4044
Fax: 412-241-4043
e-mail: info@bachchoirpittsburgh.org
Web Site: www.bachchoirpittsburgh.org
Officers:
   Chair: Paul Tellers
   Vice Chair: Penelope Morel
   Secretary: Marguerite Link
   Treasurer: Elizabeth Santillo
Management:
   Artistic Director: Thomas W Douglas
   Managing Director: Wrenn White
   Operations Manager: David A Kotler
   Choir President: Amy Richards
Mission: To perform highly artistic choral music from various musical traditions for the enjoyment of the community and as a discipline to enhance the training of the musicians.
Founded: 1934
Specialized Field: Choral; Classical

2044
MENDELSSOHN CHOIR OF PITTSBURGH
617 Audubon Avenue
PO Box 9350
Pittsburgh, PA 15228-2520
Phone: 412-561-3353
Fax: 412-561-5105
e-mail: mcp1908@verizon.net
Web Site: www.themendelssohn.org
Officers:
   President: George B Seeley
   Vice President: Mary Jane Jacques
   Secretary: Susan Beresik
   Treasurer: Joseph Schewe Jr
Management:
   Music Director/Conductor: Betsy Burleigh
   Jr Mendelssohn Conductor: Christine Frattare

Assistant Conductor: Susan Medley
   Managing Director: Elizabeth Andrews
   Choir Manager: Barry Miller
Mission: To perform a versatile repertoire of the highest musical standards to contribute to the choral art and to make an impact on the community.
Founded: 1908
Specialized Field: Choral; Classical

2045
OPERA THEATER OF PITTSBURGH
286 Main Street Third Floor
Pittsburgh, PA 15201
Phone: 412-621-1499
Fax: 412-621-2643
e-mail: eatonotp@netscape.net
Web Site: www.operatheaterpittsburgh.org
Management:
   Founder: Mildred Posvar
   Artistic Director: Jonathan Eaton
   General Manager: Raymond Very
Mission: To offer professional opera to people outside of metropolitan centers; to introduce opera to children; to nurture emerging professionals.
Founded: 1978
Specialized Field: Grand Opera; Youth Chorus; Chamber Opera; Musical Theatre
Status: Professional; Nonprofit
Budget: $35,000-$60,000
Performs At: Byham Theatre; Hazlett Theatre
Affiliations: Carnegie Mellon University
Seating Capacity: 1,200
Organization Type: Performing; Touring; Educational

2046
PITTSBURGH CAMERATA
PO Box 81546
Pittsburgh, PA 15217
Phone: 412-421-5884
e-mail: gmluley@pittsburghcamerata.org
Management:
   Artistic Director: Rebecca Rollett
   Business Manager: Gail Luley
Specialized Field: Choral

2047
PITTSBURGH CIVIC LIGHT OPERA
719 Liberty Avenue
Benedum Center
Pittsburgh, PA 15222
Phone: 412-281-3973
Fax: 412-281-5339
e-mail: mail@pittsburghclo.org
Web Site: www.pittsburghclo.org
Management:
   Executive Director: Van Kaplin
   Artistic Director Outreach: Buddy Thompson
Mission: To perpetuate, preserve and create musical, light opera and drama productions for the cultural and educational enrichment of our audiences, primarily in Western Pennsylvania and, secondarily, the United States.
Utilizes: Guest Companies; Singers
Founded: 1946
Specialized Field: Light Opera; Musical Theatre
Status: Non-Profit, Professional
Paid Staff: 25
Income Sources: Musical Theater Works; National Musical Theater Network
Season: June - August
Performs At: Benedum Center for the Performing Arts
Seating Capacity: 2,837
Organization Type: Performing; Educational

2048
PITTSBURGH OPERA
801 Penn Avenue
Pittsburgh, PA 15222-3681
Phone: 412-281-0912
Fax: 412-261-1123
e-mail: info@pittsburghopera.org
Web Site: www.pittsburghopera.org
Officers:
   President: H Woodruff Turner
   Secretary: Gracia Sheptak
   Treasurer: Kenneth Brand
Management:
   General Director: Mark J Weinstein
   Artistic Director: Christopher Hahn
   Music Director: Jhon Mauceri
   General Director and VP: Mark Weinstein
Mission: To culturally enrich Pittsburgh and the tri-state area and to draw national and international attention to the region.
Utilizes: Choreographers; Dancers; Educators; Grant Writers; Guest Artists; Guest Companies; Guest Conductors; Guest Lecturers; Guest Writers; Local Artists; Lyricists; Multimedia; Original Music Scores; Singers; Student Interns
Founded: 1939
Specialized Field: Grand Opera
Status: Professional; Nonprofit
Paid Staff: 30
Volunteer Staff: 300
Paid Artists: 300
Budget: $7.5 Million
Income Sources: Ticket Sales; Contributions; Grants
Performs At: Benedum Center for the Performing Arts
Affiliations: Opera America
Annual Attendance: 39,000
Facility Category: Opera House/Multi-purpose Theatre
Type of Stage: Proscenium
Seating Capacity: 2,770
Organization Type: Performing

2049
PITTSBURGH CONCERT CHORALE
PO Box 252
Warrendale, PA 15086
Phone: 412-635-7654
Fax: 412-635-0583
e-mail: pccsing@nauticom.net
Web Site: www.pghconcertchorale.org/about.html
Officers:
   President: Donald Maragon
   VP: Susan Mancuso
   VP: Charles Morrissey
   VP: Steve Radr
Management:
   Founder: Dr. Clark Bedford
   Executive Director: Betty Snyder
Mission: To share the joy of fine choral music with exceptional volunteer singers of the community.
Utilizes: Collaborations; Commissioned Composers; Commissioned Music; Grant Writers; Guest Companies; Guest Musicians; Multimedia; Sign Language Translators; Singers
Founded: 1985
Specialized Field: Choral
Status: Volunteer; Not-for-Profit; Tax-Exempt
Paid Staff: 1
Paid Artists: 2
Non-paid Artists: 85
Budget: $18,500
Income Sources: Ticket Sales, Grants, Government, Individuals

Performs At: Orchard Hill Church; Ingomar Methodist Church; Jewish Commuknity Center
Affiliations: Chorus America, Greater Pittsburgh Arts Alliance, Northern Allegheny County Chamber of Commerce
Annual Attendance: 3200

Rhode Island

2050
RHODE ISLAND CIVIC CHORALE AND ORCHESTRA

33 Chestnut Street
Providence, RI 02903
Phone: 401-521-5670
e-mail: info@ricco.org
Web Site: www.ricco.org
Officers:
President: Chester S Labedz, Jr
First VP: Roberta Padula
Second VP: Margaret Gidley
Third VP: Herman Eschentacher
Secretary: David T. Riedel
Treasurer: Walter Hope, Jr
Assistant Treasurer: Joseph A. Goldkamp
Management:
Director and Conductor: Edward Markward
Mission: To provide artistic enrichment to the public and the singers through presentation of at least three concerts of major choral works per year. These concerts feature the singers of the chorale, along with professional orchestra and soloists.
Utilizes: Guest Artists; Guest Companies
Founded: 1957
Specialized Field: Choral
Status: Nonprofit
Paid Staff: 70
Performs At: Veterans Memorial Auditorium; Grace Church
Organization Type: Performing

2051
CHORUS OF WESTERLY

119 High Street
Westerly, RI 02891
Phone: 401-596-8663
Fax: 401-596-1370
e-mail: notes@chorusofwesterly.org
Web Site: www.chorusofwesterly.org
Officers:
President: Deborah Dunham
VP: Ryan Saunders
Treasurer: Sharon Davis
Recording Secretary: Aimee Blanchette
Management:
Music Director: George Kent
Executive Director: Emma Palzere Rae
Operations/Marketing Mannager: Lee Eastbourne
Development Associate: Jodie Drapal Kluver
Mission: To perform, with artistic intergrity, both the major classic works of the choral literature and new or lesser known pieces of merit. To educate children and adults of diverse backgrounds in the appreciation, understanding and performance of great music. To grow and develop steadily as an organization important to the cultural experiences of the region.
Utilizes: Guest Artists; Guest Designers; Guest Musicians; Sign Language Translators
Founded: 1959
Specialized Field: Choral
Paid Staff: 6
Volunteer Staff: 200
Paid Artists: 16

Non-paid Artists: 200
Budget: $800,000
Income Sources: Tickets; Rental Fees; Gifts; Grants
Performs At: The Chorus of Westerly Performance Hall
Affiliations: Chorus America
Annual Attendance: 30,000
Facility Category: Historic Former Church Building
Seating Capacity: 440
Year Built: 1886
Year Remodeled: 2003
Cost: varies
Rental Contact: Emma Palzere Rae

Tennessee

2052
CHATTANOOGA BOYS CHOIR

4315-B Brainerd Road
Chattanooga, TN 37411
Phone: 423-622-3033
Fax: 423-622-1182
e-mail: info@cbchoir.org
Web Site: www.chattanoogaboyschoir.org
Management:
President: Micheal Brunson
Executive Director: Winston Oakes
Managing Director: Kelly Lusk
Mission: To offer comprehensive training that inspires boys to love and appreciate good music.
Founded: 1954
Specialized Field: Youth Chorus
Status: Non-Profit, Professional
Paid Staff: 7
Organization Type: Performing; Touring

2053
CHATTANOOGA SYMPHONY AND OPERA ASSOCIATION

630 Chestnut Street
Chattanooga, TN 37402
Phone: 423-267-8583
Fax: 423-265-6520
Web Site: www.chattanoogasymphony.org
Management:
Music Director/Conductor: Robert Bernhardt
Executive Director: John Wehrle
Administrative/Production Director: Charlotte Adkins
Director Of Cso Choruses: Darrin Hassevoort
Utilizes: Guest Artists; Guest Companies; Singers
Specialized Field: Grand Opera; Lyric Opera; Light Opera; Operetta
Status: Professional; Nonprofit
Paid Staff: 40
Budget: $60,000-$150,000
Income Sources: Tennesseans for the Arts; Opera America; American Symphony Orchestra League
Performs At: Tivoli Theatre
Seating Capacity: 1,680
Organization Type: Performing; Touring; Educational

2054
KNOXVILLE OPERA COMPANY

612 E Depot Avenue
Knoxville, TN 37917-0016
Phone: 865-524-0795
Fax: 865-524-7384
e-mail: info@knoxvilleopera.com
Web Site: www.knoxvilleopera.com
Management:
Executive Director/Conductor: Brian Salesky, bsalesky@knoxvilleopera.com

Production Manager: Don Townsend, dtownsend@knoxvilleopera.com
Director, Marketing & Public Rel.: Michael Torano, mtorano@knoxvilleopera.com
Mission: To provide the residents of East Tennessee with high quality locally produced operas
Utilizes: Dancers; Guest Writers; High School Drama; Instructors; Local Artists; Lyricists; Multi Collaborations; Music; Paid Performers; Scenic Designers; Sign Language Translators; Singers; Soloists; Touring Companies; Visual Designers
Founded: 1976
Specialized Field: Grand Opera; Light Opera; Lyric Opera; Musical Theatre; Choral; Classical
Status: Non-Profit, Professional
Paid Staff: 8
Paid Artists: 152
Budget: $1.1 Million
Income Sources: Opera America
Performs At: Historic Theatre
Annual Attendance: 9,000
Seating Capacity: 1,600
Year Built: 1928
Year Remodeled: 2005
Cost: $25.5 Million
Organization Type: Performing; Sponsoring

2055
LINDENWOOD CONCERTS

2400 Union Avenue
Memphis, TN 38112
Phone: 901-458-1652
Fax: 901-458-0145
e-mail: chris.nemec@lindenwood.net
Web Site: www.lindenwoodcc.com
Officers:
President: Gary Beard
Management:
Executive Director: Chris Nemec
Mission: To present the musical arts in a setting of a church, as in 17th and 18th century Europe.
Utilizes: Artists-in-Residence; Guest Accompanists; Guest Composers; Guest Musical Directors; Multimedia; Original Music Scores; Sign Language Translators; Singers
Founded: 1979
Specialized Field: Choral; Youth Chorus; Classical; Religious
Status: Non-Profit, Professional
Paid Staff: 2
Volunteer Staff: 25
Non-paid Artists: 85
Income Sources: Box Office and Benefactors
Affiliations: AGO; ACDA; Choristers Guild; Disciples of Christ
Annual Attendance: 1,000
Facility Category: Church Sanctuary
Seating Capacity: 1,000
Year Built: 1966
Year Remodeled: 2010
Rental Contact: Chris Nemec
Resident Groups: Gary Beard Chorale; Lindenwood Chancel Choir

2056
NASHVILLE OPERA ASSOCIATION

3622 Redmon Street
Nashville, TN 37209
Phone: 615-832-5242
Fax: 615-297-6337
e-mail: nashopera@nashvilleopera.org
Web Site: www.nashvilleopera.org
Officers:
President: Elizabeth Papel

Management:
Executive Director: Carol Penterman
Artistic Director: John Hoomes
Artistic Admin Director: Karen Haas
Mission: To present operatic productions to middle Tennesseeans.
Utilizes: AEA Actors; Choreographers; Collaborations; Commissioned Composers; Dancers; Designers; Educators; Five Seasonal Concerts; Grant Writers; Guest Accompanists; Guest Artists; Guest Composers; Guest Conductors; Guest Designers; Guest Directors; Guest Musical Directors; Guest Musicians; Instructors; Multimedia; Original Music Scores; Resident Professionals; Sign Language Translators
Founded: 1981
Specialized Field: Grand Opera; Light Opera; Lyric Opera; Classical; Contemporary
Status: Non-Profit, Non-Professional
Paid Staff: 14
Paid Artists: 60
Budget: $2.4 million
Income Sources: Contributed and Earned Income
Season: September - April
Performs At: Andrew Jackson Hall; Polk Theatre
Affiliations: Opera America
Annual Attendance: 13,000
Organization Type: Performing; Educational

2057
NASHVILLE SYMPHONY CHORUS
One Symphony Place
Nashville, TN 37201-2031
Phone: 615-687-6500
Fax: 615-783-1575
e-mail: info@nashvillesymphony.org
Management:
Choral Director: George Mabry
Music Director: Kenneth Schermerhorn
Specialized Field: Choral

Texas

2058
AUSTIN LYRIC OPERA
901 Barton Springs Road
PO Box 984
Austin, TX 78767
Phone: 512-472-5927
Fax: 512-472-4143
Toll-free: 800-316-7372
Web Site: www.austinlyricopera.org
Officers:
Chairman: Paul Burns
President: Betty King
Management:
Chairman: Steve Davis
President: Susan Lubin
Artistic Director: Richard Buckley
Managing Director: Tamara Hale
Mission: To promote and support opera; to foster public awareness of opera as a fine art.
Utilizes: Artists-in-Residence; Choreographers; Collaborations; Designers; Educators; Fine Artists; Five Seasonal Concerts; Guest Accompanists; Guest Composers; Guest Conductors; Guest Designers; Guest Soloists; Guest Writers; High School Drama; Instructors; Lyricists; Multi Collaborations; Multimedia; Original Music Scores; Resident Professionals; Selected Students; Sign Language Translators; Singers; Soloists; Student Interns; Theatre Companies; Visual Arts
Founded: 1985

Specialized Field: Grand Opera; Light Opera; Lyric Opera; Musical Theatre; Choral; Youth Chorus; Classical
Status: Non-Profit, Professional
Paid Staff: 30
Budget: $5,000,000
Income Sources: Central Opera Service
Season: November, January, March
Performs At: University of Texas Performing Arts Center
Annual Attendance: 48,000
Facility Category: Concert Hall
Type of Stage: Proscenium
Seating Capacity: 2,872
Organization Type: Performing; Educational

2059
CHORUS AUSTIN
PO Box 204361
Austin, TX 78720
Phone: 512-719-3300
Fax: 512-451-3110
Toll-free: 877-640-8836
Officers:
Chair: Catherine Huyck
Chairman: David Marks
Management:
Artistic Director: Dr Kenneth Sheppard
Executive Director: Christopher Roepke
Utilizes: Collaborations; Five Seasonal Concerts; Guest Accompanists; Guest Directors; Guest Musical Directors; Guest Musicians; Local Artists; Multimedia; Sign Language Translators; Singers
Specialized Field: Choral

2060
BEAUMONT CIVIC OPERA
4350 Thomas Glen
Beaumont, TX 77706
Phone: 409-892-5408
Management:
Conductor: L Randolph Babin
Business Manager: Delores Black
Mission: Presenting fine musical productions in Southwest Texas and giving young performers opportunities.
Utilizes: Guest Companies; Singers
Founded: 1962
Specialized Field: Grand Opera; Light Opera; Operetta
Status: Nonprofit
Budget: $35,000-$60,000
Income Sources: Opera America
Performs At: Julie Rogers Theatre for the Performing Arts
Seating Capacity: 1,775
Organization Type: Resident

2061
TEXAS A&M UNIVERSITY OPERA & PERFORMING ARTS
PO Box J-1
College Station, TX 77844-9081
Phone: 979-845-1661
Fax: 979-845-8043
Toll-free: 877-672-6727
e-mail: anne-black@tamu.edu
Web Site: www.mscopas.org
Management:
President: Mary Hatcher
Executive Director: Anne Black
Founded: 1972
Specialized Field: Grand Opera; Light Opera; Musical Theatre; Choral; Youth Chorus; Ethnic Music; Classical; Contemporary

Status: Non-Profit, Professional
Paid Staff: 4
Budget: $400,000-1,000,000

2062
DALLAS OPERA
Winspear Opera House
2403 Flora Street
Suite 500
Dallas, TX 75201
Phone: 214-443-1043
Fax: 214-443-1060
e-mail: suzanne.calvin@dallasopera.org
Web Site: www.dallasopera.org
Officers:
Chairman: Dr. Kern Wildenthal
General Director/CEO: Keith Cerny
Management:
Artistic Director: Jonathan Pell
Development Director: Cynthia Young
Mission: The Dallas Opera is an opera company committed to the presentation of opera at the international level. It enriches the community through performances of grand and chamber opera, operatic concerts, recitals and attendant education and community service programs.
Founded: 1957
Specialized Field: Grand Opera; Light Opera; Lyric Opera; Musical Theatre; Choral; Youth Chorus; Ethnic Music; Classical
Status: Non-Profit, Professional
Paid Staff: 35
Paid Artists: 60
Budget: $12,000,000
Performs At: Winspear Opera House Of The AT&T Performing Arts Center
Affiliations: Opera America; American Arts Alliance; Texas Arts Alliance
Annual Attendance: 79,754
Seating Capacity: 2,200
Year Built: 2009
Rental Contact: Director of Production John Gage
Organization Type: Performing; Educational; Sponsoring

2063
DALLAS SYMPHONY CHORUS
Dallas Symphony Association
2301 Flora Street
Dallas, TX 75201
Phone: 214-692-0203
Fax: 214-953-1218
e-mail: customerservice@dalsym.com
Web Site: www.dallassymphony.com
Officers:
Administrator: Donna Krauss
Management:
President: Fred Bronstein
Mission: Supporting the Dallas Symphony Association; performing major choral works in conjunction with the symphony.
Founded: 1900
Specialized Field: Lyric Opera; Light Opera; Operetta; Choral; Ethnic Music; Folk Music
Status: Nonprofit
Paid Staff: 3
Volunteer Staff: 1
Non-paid Artists: 240
Performs At: Meyerson Symphony Center
Organization Type: Performing; Touring; Resident

2064
TURTLE CREEK CHORALE
3630 Harry Hines Boulevard
PO Box 190137
Dallas, TX 75219
Phone: 214-526-3214
Fax: 214-528-0673
Toll-free: 800-746-4412
e-mail: info@turtlecreek.org
Web Site: www.turtlecreek.org
Officers:
    Chorus President: Craig Robinson
    Chair: Peter Anderson
Management:
    Executive Director: Craig Gregory
    Artistic Director: Jonathan Palant
Mission: To perform, unite and educate the audience through the presentation of male choral music and other musical activities.
Utilizes: Singers
Founded: 1980
Specialized Field: Choral
Status: Non-Professional, Nonprofit
Paid Staff: 8
Non-paid Artists: 200
Performs At: Meyerson Symphony Center
Annual Attendance: 30,000
Facility Category: Concert hall
Seating Capacity: 1875
Year Built: 1990
Organization Type: Performing

2065
FORT WORTH OPERA ASSOCIATION
1300 Gendy Street
Fort Worth, TX 76107
Phone: 817-731-0833
Fax: 817-731-0835
Toll-free: 866-396-7372
e-mail: admin@fwopera.org
Web Site: www.fwopera.org
Officers:
    President: Whit Smith
    President, Opera Guild of Ft. Worth: Petra Grimes
Management:
    President: Pollard Rogers
    Executive Director: Darren Woods
    Managing Director: Keith Wolfe
Mission: Cultivating and promoting the love and understanding of opera.
Utilizes: Actors; Dance Companies; Educators; Grant Writers; Guest Artists; Guest Composers; Guest Designers; Guest Writers; Local Artists; Multimedia; Resident Professionals; Sign Language Translators
Founded: 1946
Specialized Field: Opera
Status: Non-Profit, Professional
Paid Staff: 10
Paid Artists: 55
Budget: $2,700,000
Income Sources: Opera America; Arts Council of Fort Worth & Tarrant County; Private Foundations and Businesses.
Performs At: Bass Performance Hall
Affiliations: Opera America; Arts Council of Forth Worth and Tarrant County
Facility Category: Opera Performance Hall
Stage Dimensions: 57x65
Seating Capacity: 2,000
Year Built: 1999
Rental Contact: Paul Beard
Organization Type: Performing; Resident; Educational

2066
SCHOLA CANTORUM OF TEXAS
2463A Forest Park Boulevard
Fort Worth, TX 76110
Phone: 817-927-2114
Fax: 817-927-2443
e-mail: info@scholatexas.com
Web Site: www.scholatexas.com
Officers:
    President: Susan Seiter
    VP: George Muckleroy
Management:
    Choir Director: Jerry McCoy
Mission: To provide a performance outlet for talented singers, whereby providving outstanding choral music at the Metroplex.
Utilizes: Singers
Founded: 1962
Specialized Field: Choral
Status: Semi-Professional, Nonprofit
Paid Staff: 60
Performs At: Kimbell Art Museum; Irons Recital Hall
Organization Type: Performing

2067
TEXAS GIRLS' CHOIR
4449 Camp Bowie Boulevard
Fort Worth, TX 76107-3834
Phone: 817-732-8161
Fax: 817-732-4774
e-mail: tgc@texasgirlschoir.org
Web Site: www.texasgirlschoir.org
Management:
    Executive Director: Debi Weir
    Artistic Director: Layne Trent
Mission: To develop little girls' lives through excellence of music.
Utilizes: Commissioned Music; Community Talent; Grant Writers; Guest Accompanists; Guest Companies; Guest Designers; Guest Directors; Guest Lecturers; Guest Musical Directors; Guest Musicians; Guest Soloists; Instructors; Multimedia; Music; Original Music Scores; Sign Language Translators; Singers; Soloists
Founded: 1962
Specialized Field: Choral; Youth Chorus; Classical; Contemporary; Religious
Status: Non-Profit, Non-Professional
Paid Staff: 13
Volunteer Staff: 50
Budget: $622,370
Income Sources: Semester Fees; Donations; Concerts; Performances; Fundraisers
Performs At: Concert Hall; Auditorium
Facility Category: Former Church
Type of Stage: Full Width Of Auditorium
Seating Capacity: 600
Year Built: 1949
Rental Contact: Debi Weir
Organization Type: Performing; Touring; Educational

2068
HOUSTON CHAMBER CHOIR
PO Box 53388
Houston, TX 77052-3388
Phone: 713-224-5566
Fax: 713-222-2412
e-mail: becky.tobin@houstonchamberchoir.org
Web Site: www.houstonchamberchoir.org
Officers:
    President: Frank Hood
    Vice President: Harry C Webb
Management:
    Artistic Director: Robert Simpson
    Executive Director: Becky Tobin
Mission: A professional ensemble dedicated to increasing the awareness, appreciation and esteem of choral music and musicians through performance, outreach and education.
Utilizes: Commissioned Composers; Community Members; Guest Accompanists; Guest Companies; Guest Lecturers; Guest Musical Directors; Instructors; Multimedia; Organization Contracts; Original Music Scores; Playwrights; Sign Language Translators; Singers
Founded: 1995
Specialized Field: Choral; Chamber Opera
Status: Non-Profit, Professional
Paid Staff: 4
Volunteer Staff: 15
Paid Artists: 30
Budget: $350,000
Affiliations: Chorus America

2069
HOUSTON GRAND OPERA
510 Preston Street
Suite 500
Houston, TX 77002
Phone: 713-546-0200
Fax: 713-247-0906
Web Site: www.houstongrandopera.org
Officers:
    General Director/CEO: Anthony Freud
    Chief Advancement Officer: Greg Robertson
    Chairman Of The Board: Glen Rosenbaum
    Vice Chairman Of The Board: Lynn Wyatt
Management:
    Music Director: Patrick Summers
Mission: To produce opera of consistent excellence offering nontraditional and innovative works; to develop new forms, new artists and new audiences.
Utilizes: Composers; Guest Artists; Guest Companies; Guest Designers; Guest Musicians; Sign Language Translators; Singers
Founded: 1955
Specialized Field: Grand Opera; Lyric Opera; Light Opera; Operetta
Status: Professional; Nonprofit
Volunteer Staff: y
Budget: $20,000,000
Income Sources: Donations
Organization Type: Performing; Touring; Resident; Educational

2070
HOUSTON MASTERWORKS CHORUS
4119 Montrose Boulevard
Suite 260
Houston, TX 77006-2031
Phone: 713-529-8900
e-mail: houstonmasterworks@yahoo.com
Web Site: www.houstonmasterworks.org
Officers:
    President: Rita La Rue
    Secretary: Diane Hackem
    Treasurer: Tom Plapp
Management:
    Interim Managing Director: Martha Knotts
    Interim Conductor: Paula Acord Blackman
Mission: Dedicated to the presentation of great choral music, and to the continuation of the choral society tradition.
Utilizes: Five Seasonal Concerts; Guest Composers; Guest Musicians
Founded: 1986
Specialized Field: Choral; Classical
Status: Non-Profit, Non-Professional

Paid Staff: 4
Volunteer Staff: 150
Paid Artists: 25
Non-paid Artists: 129
Budget: 344,000
Income Sources: Endowment; Foundations; Individual Contributions

2071
HOUSTON SYMPHONY CHORUS
615 Louisiana Street
Houston, TX 77002-2798
Phone: 713-743-3160
Fax: 713-807-7824
e-mail: chorus@sbcglobal.net
Web Site: www.choral.org/grou/hsc/
Management:
   Director: Dr Charles Hausmann
   Chorus Manager: Susan Scarrow
Utilizes: Guest Artists
Founded: 1946
Specialized Field: Choral
Status: Non-Professional; Nonprofit
Paid Staff: 170
Income Sources: Chorus America
Performs At: Jesse H. Jones Hall for the Performing Arts
Organization Type: Performing; Resident

2072
IRVING CHORALE
3333 N MacArthur Blvd
Suite 300
Irving, TX 75062
Phone: 972-252-2787
Fax: 972-257-1417
Management:
   Artistic Director: Harry Wooten
   President: Phil Armstrong
Specialized Field: Choral

2073
MIDLAND-ODESSA SYMPHONY AND CHORALE
3100 LaForce Boulevard
PO Box 60658
Midland, TX 79711
Phone: 432-563-0921
Fax: 432-617-0087
e-mail: symphony@mosc.org
Web Site: www.mosc.org
Management:
   CEO: Wade Kelley
   General Manager: Ted Hale
Mission: To offer residents of the Permian Basin symphonic, chamber and choral music.
Utilizes: Collaborations; Commissioned Music; Educators; Grant Writers; Guest Artists; Guest Companies; Guest Directors; Guest Lecturers; Guest Writers; High School Drama; Local Artists; Lyricists; Multi Collaborations; Multimedia; Organization Contracts; Original Music Scores; Singers; Theatre Companies
Founded: 1962
Specialized Field: Choral
Status: Non-Profit, Professional
Paid Staff: 5
Volunteer Staff: 100
Budget: $670,000
Income Sources: Tickets; Grants; Donations
Affiliations: ASOL
Annual Attendance: 10,000
Organization Type: Performing; Educational

2074
SAN ANGELO SYMPHONY ORCHESTRA AND CHORALE
PO Box 5922
San Angelo, TX 76902
Phone: 915-658-5877
Fax: 915-653-1045
Web Site: www.sanangelosymphony.org
Officers:
   President: Fred Key
   VP: Doris Rousselot
   Secretary: Johnell Vincent
   Treasurer: Bill McKinney
   Past President: Teady George
Management:
   Music Director/Conductor: Hector Guzman
   Executive Director: Mercyla Sheiburne
Mission: To further cultural advancement and enjoyment of symphonic music in the San Angelo area.
Utilizes: Singers
Founded: 1948
Specialized Field: Choral
Status: Professional; Non-Professional; Nonprofit
Paid Staff: 140
Income Sources: Broadcast Music Incorporated; American Society of Composers, Authors and Publishers; American Symphony Orchestra League
Performs At: City Auditorium
Annual Attendance: 50,000
Seating Capacity: 1,590
Organization Type: Performing

2075
TWIN MOUNTAIN TONESMEN
PO Box 2711
San Angelo, TX 76902
Phone: 915-949-0608
Web Site: www.geocites.com/Broadway/Stage/3010/
Management:
   Director: Mark E Clark
Mission: To present Barbershop Singing in our area and compete in contests.
Founded: 1979
Specialized Field: Barbershop Quartet
Status: Non-Professional; Nonprofit; Charitable
Volunteer Staff: 38
Performs At: City Auditorium
Affiliations: Cultural Affairs Council; SOEBSQSA
Organization Type: Performing; Resident

2076
TEXAS BACH CHOIR
11 St Lukes Lane
San Antonio, TX 78209
Phone: 210-828-6425
Web Site: www.texasbachchoir.org
Officers:
   President: Mary Beth Garay
   VP: Katya Thompson-Cantu
   President Elect: Steve Matteson
   Secretary: Don Peterson
   Treasurer: Jim Harnish
Management:
   Music Director: Daniel Long
   Accompanist: Daniel Long
   Administrator: Samantha A Beer
Mission: The performance of classical sacred choral works of all periods, with emphasis on Baroque.
Utilizes: Singers
Founded: 1976
Specialized Field: Choral; Classical; Traditional Choral Music
Status: Non-Profit, Non-Professional

Paid Staff: 36
Paid Artists: 2
Income Sources: Chorus America
Organization Type: Performing; Touring; Resident

Utah

2077
UTAH FESTIVAL OPERA COMPANY
59 S 100 W
Logan, UT 84321
Phone: 435-750-0300
Fax: 435-753-5856
Toll-free: 800-262-0074
e-mail: opera@ufoc.org
Web Site: www.ufoc.org
Officers:
   Chairperson: Melanie Raymond
   Vice-Chair: Ralph Binns
   Treasurer: Brent Nyman
Management:
   General Director: Michael Ballam
   Development Director: Lila Geddes
   Marketing: Darla Seamons
Mission: Bringing people together to share ennobling artistic experiences.
Utilizes: AEA Actors; Choreographers; Collaborations; Commissioned Composers; Composers-in-Residence; Dancers; Designers; Grant Writers; Guest Artists; Guest Composers; Guest Conductors; Guest Designers; Guest Directors; Guest Instructors; Guest Lecturers; Guest Musical Directors; Guest Musicians; Guest Soloists; Instructors; Local Artists; Local Unknown Artists; Multimedia; Music; Original Music Scores; Resident Professionals; Sign Language Translators; Singers; Soloists
Founded: 1992
Specialized Field: Grand Opera; Light Opera; Musical Theatre; Operetta
Status: Non-Profit, Professional
Paid Staff: 12
Volunteer Staff: 1
Paid Artists: 200
Budget: $2 million
Income Sources: Box Office; Foundations; Endowment; Government Grants; Private Contributors
Performs At: Ellen Eccles Theatre
Affiliations: Opera America
Annual Attendance: 23,000
Facility Category: Theater
Type of Stage: Proscenium
Stage Dimensions: 36'x 35'x 25'
Seating Capacity: 1,110
Year Built: 1923
Year Remodeled: 1993
Organization Type: Performing; Educational

2078
MORMON TABERNACLE CHOIR
50 N West Temple Street
Salt Lake City, UT 84150
Phone: 801-240-3221
Fax: 801-240-4886
e-mail: scott.barrick@mormontabernaclechoir.org
Web Site: www.mormontabernaclechoir.org
Officers:
   President: Mac Christensen
Management:
   Music Director: Mark Wilberg
   General Manager: Scott Barrick
   Organist: Richard Elliott
Founded: 1847
Specialized Field: Choral; Religious

Status: Non-Profit, Non-Professional
Paid Staff: 14

2079
ORATORIO SOCIETY OF UTAH
PO Box 11714
Salt Lake City, UT 84147
Phone: 801-572-7464
Fax: 801-572-9398
Web Site: reality.sgi.com/csp/osutah/
Mission: Performing oratorio music and engaging in cultural exchanges with other countries.
Utilizes: Guest Artists
Founded: 1915
Specialized Field: Choral
Status: Semi-Professional; Nonprofit
Paid Staff: 250
Organization Type: Performing; Touring

2080
SALT LAKE SYMPHONIC CHOIR
3790 S 3145 E
Salt Lake City, UT 84109
Phone: 801-201-5451
Fax: 801-281-0563
e-mail: gbettinson@excite.com
Web Site: www.saltlakesymphonicchoir.com
Officers:
President: Greg Bettinson
VP: Ron Houston
Management:
Director: Erin Pike Tall nson
VP Public Relations: Vicki I Armitage
VP: Dennis Gunn
Mission: Presenting choral concerts world-wide.
Founded: 1949
Specialized Field: Choral
Status: Professional; Nonprofit
Non-paid Artists: 100
Organization Type: Performing; Touring

2081
UTAH OPERA
336 N 400 W
Salt Lake City, UT 84101
Phone: 801-736-4605
Fax: 801-581-5683
Toll-free: 888-901-7464
Web Site: www.utahsymphony.org
Officers:
President/CEO: Melia P Tourangeau
Management:
Artistic Director: Christopher McBeth
Operations Director: Lindsey Wood
Marketing Director: Kevin Bentz
Mission: To give performances which engage, educate and enrich the community.
Utilizes: Guest Composers; Guest Lecturers; Guest Musicians; Multimedia; Sign Language Translators
Founded: 1978
Specialized Field: Choral
Status: Professional
Paid Staff: 5
Volunteer Staff: 10
Budget: 55,000
Income Sources: Performances fees; Fundrasiers
Affiliations: Utah Symphony Orchestra

2082
UTAH OPERA COMPANY
Abravanel Hall
123 W South Temple
Salt Lake City, UT 84101

Phone: 801-533-5626
Fax: 801-869-9026
e-mail: info@utahsymphonyopera.org
Web Site: www.utahopera.org
Officers:
Chairman: William C Bailey
Management:
C E O: Anne Ewers
Office Manager: Rhea Bouman
Artistic Director: Christopher McBeth
General Director: Anne Ewers
Mission: To offer quality productions featuring standard opera repertoire; to educate the community.
Utilizes: Artists-in-Residence; Choreographers; Guest Composers; Guest Designers; Guest Ensembles; Instructors; Original Music Scores; Resident Professionals; Sign Language Translators
Founded: 1978
Specialized Field: Grand Opera; Light Opera
Status: Professional; Nonprofit
Paid Staff: 30
Budget: $4,500,000
Income Sources: Opera America; American Arts Alliance; Utah Arts Council; Salt Lake City Arts Council
Performs At: Capitol Theatre
Annual Attendance: 9,000
Facility Category: Capitol Theatre
Type of Stage: Proscenium
Seating Capacity: 1,835
Year Built: 1913
Year Remodeled: 1976
Organization Type: Performing; Resident; Educational

Vermont

2083
BRATTLEBORO MUSIC CENTER
38 Walnut Street
Brattleboro, VT 05301
Phone: 802-257-4523
e-mail: info@bmcvt.org
Web Site: www.bmcvt.org
Management:
Operations Director: Sabine Rhyne
Mission: Enriching lives through music. To promote the love and understanding of good music through performance and education, and to make music a vital part of the community.
Founded: 1952
Specialized Field: Classical; Contemporary; Choral
Status: Non-Profit, Professional
Paid Staff: 36
Paid Artists: 30
Performs At: Persons Auditorium; Marlboro College
Organization Type: Performing; Touring; Resident

2084
NORTH COUNTRY CHORUS
PO Box 184
Wells River, VT 05081
Phone: 802-429-2334
Web Site: www.northcountrychorus.org
Officers:
President: Marilyn Dempsey
Management:
Music Director: Alan Rowe
Mission: To enrich the musical lives of North Country Area residents; to offer participation to anyone who loves singing.
Utilizes: Guest Companies; Singers
Founded: 1948
Specialized Field: Choral
Status: Semi-Professional; Nonprofit

Season: June - August
Organization Type: Performing; Touring; Resident

Virginia

2085
OPERA THEATRE OF NO VIRGINIA
1916 Wilson Boulevard
Suite 301
Arlington, VA 22201
Mailing Address: PO Box 7027 Arlington, VA 22207
Phone: 703-528-1433
Fax: 703-812-5039
Web Site: www.novaopera.org
Officers:
President: Jean Shirhall
Management:
Artistic Director/Conductor: John Edward Niles
Mission: To provide affordable opera in English to the Northern Virginia and Greater Metropolitan Washington Area; to sponsor educational programs and performances geared to young audiences; to provide stage experience.
Utilizes: Guest Companies; Singers
Founded: 1961
Specialized Field: Grand Opera; Light Opera
Status: Professional; Nonprofit
Volunteer Staff: 25
Paid Artists: 50
Budget: $140,000
Income Sources: Ticket Sales; Individuals; Grants; Corporations
Performs At: Thomas Jefferson Community Theatre
Affiliations: Opera America; Cultural Alliance of Greater Washington; ASCAP
Organization Type: Performing; Resident

2086
VIRGINIA CHORAL SOCIETY
PO Box 1742
Newport News, VA 23601
Phone: 757-851-9114
e-mail: marketing@vachoralsociety.org
Web Site: www.vachoralsociety.org
Officers:
Secretary: Sarah Kressaty
Treasurer: Al Schweizer II
Management:
Artistic Director: James Powers
Managing Director: Charles Bump
Director Of Programming: Lou DeGrace
Director Of Personnel: James Branstetter
VCS Chorus President: Mark Sink
Artistic Director: James Powers
Mission: The goal of the Virginia Choral Society is to foster a broader awareness of vocal music in the community; cooperate with other groups in support of the arts; and continue our long tradition of presenting only the finest compositions from our rich choral heritage.
Founded: 1931
Specialized Field: Choral
Status: Nonprofit
Paid Staff: 2
Income Sources: Ticket Sales; Grants; Various Fund-Raising Activities
Organization Type: Performing

2087
VIRGINIA OPERA
160 E Virginia Beach Boulevard
Norfolk, VA 23510

Mailing Address: PO Box 2580, Norfolk, VA 23501
Phone: 757-627-9545
Fax: 757-622-0058
Toll-free: 866-673-7282
e-mail: info@vaopera.org
Web Site: www.vaopera.org
Officers:
   CEO: Paul A Stuhlreyer
Management:
   Artistic Director: Peter Mark
   Associate Artistic Director: Joseph Walsh
   General Director: Paul A Stuhlreyer
Mission: The mission of Virginia Opera is to attract, educate, develop and engage a diverse base of audiences, volunteers and professionals through the promotion and production of quality opera performances in the commonwealth of Virginia.
Utilizes: Guest Artists; Guest Companies; Singers
Founded: 1974
Specialized Field: Grand Opera; Light Opera; Lyric Opera; Choral; Classical
Status: Non-Profit, Professional
Paid Staff: 120
Budget: $4.8 million
Income Sources: Cultural Arts Alliance of Greater Hampton Roads; Opera America; American Arts Alliance; Patrons; Donors; Corporations; Grants
Performs At: Harrison Opera House; Carpenter Center; GMU
Organization Type: Performing; Touring; Educational

2088
VIRGINIA SYMPHONY CHORUS
861 Glenrock Road
Suite 200
Norfolk, VA 23502
Phone: 757-466-3060
Fax: 757-466-3046
Web Site: www.virginiasymphony.org
Management:
   President: Carla A Johnso
   Education Director: Ernestine Dole
   Education Assistant: Glenda Roberts
   Director Of Finance: Brad Kirkpatric
Mission: To perform symphonic choral repertoire.
Founded: 1920
Specialized Field: Choral

2089
OPERA ROANOKE
541 Luck Avenue
Suite 209
Roanoke, VA 24065
Phone: 540-982-2742
Fax: 540-982-3601
e-mail: mail@operaroanoke.org
Web Site: www.operaroanoke.org
Officers:
   President: Dana Maritn
   VP: Joseph Logan III
   Treasurer: Charles Troland
   Secretary: Mary Evelyn Tielking
Management:
   President: Joseph Logan III
   Executive Director: G Ronald Kastner
   Artistic Director: Craig Fields
Mission: Providing Southwestern Virginia with professional opera.
Utilizes: Guest Companies
Founded: 1977
Specialized Field: Opera
Status: Non-Profit, Professional
Paid Staff: 4
Paid Artists: 250

Budget: $500,000
Income Sources: Box Office; Grants; Individual Donations
Performs At: Shaftman Performance Hall
Facility Category: Performance Hall
Type of Stage: Proscenium
Seating Capacity: 950
Year Remodeled: 2000
Cost: $9.5 Million
Organization Type: Performing; Resident

2090
WOLF TRAP OPERA COMPANY
1645 Trap Road
Vienna, VA 22182-2063
Phone: 703-255-1935
Fax: 703-255-1896
e-mail: wtoc@wolftrap.org
Web Site: www.wolftrap.org
Management:
   Director: Kim Pensinger Witman
   Program Coordinator: Lee Anne Myslewski
Utilizes: Guest Composers; Guest Designers; Multimedia; Resident Artists; Resident Professionals; Sign Language Translators
Founded: 1971
Specialized Field: Grand Opera; Opera
Status: Non-Profit, Professional
Performs At: Barns of Wolf Trap; Filene Center
Seating Capacity: 350; 7,000

Washington

2091
ESOTERICS
4523A 40th Avenue SW
Seattle, WA 98116
Phone: 206-935-7779
Fax: 206-344-3327
e-mail: info@TheEsoterics.org
Management:
   Founding Director: Eric Banks
   Composer in Residence: Don Skirvin
Mission: Contemporary a cappella art music.
Founded: 1992
Specialized Field: Choral
Status: Nonprofit
Paid Staff: 1
Volunteer Staff: 1
Paid Artists: 4

2092
ORCHESTRA SEATTLE & SEATTLE CHAMBER SINGERS
PO Box 15825
Seattle, WA 98115
Phone: 206-682-5208
e-mail: osscs@osscs.org
Web Site: www.osscs.org
Management:
   Music Director: George Shangrow
Mission: To perform as a collaborative effort between the orchestra and singers to bring skilled artistry to the Seattle community.
Founded: 1969
Specialized Field: Classical; Choral
Status: Semi-Professional
Paid Staff: 10

2093
SEATTLE OPERA
1020 John Street
PO Box 9248
Seattle, WA 98109
Phone: 206-389-7600
Fax: 206-389-7651
e-mail: mary.brazeau@seattleopera.org
Officers:
   President: Steven C Phelps
   Treasurer: Jeffrey Hanna
Management:
   General Director: Speight Jenkins
   Chairman: John F Nesholm
   President: John F Nesholm
   Executive Vice President: Gerald L Hanauer
   Treasurer: Jeffrey Hanna
   Secretary: Rosemarie Anderson
Mission: Recognized internationally for its theatrically compelling and musically accomplished performances.
Specialized Field: Opera

2094
TACOMA OPERA ASSOCIATION
917 Pacific Avenue
Suite 407
Tacoma, WA 98402
Phone: 235-627-7789
Fax: 253-627-1620
e-mail: info@tacomaopera.com
Web Site: www.tacomaopera.com
Officers:
   President: Sue Stibbe
   VP: Wendy Phillips
   VP: Heidi Madson
   Treasurer: Catherine Adams
   Secretary: Mickey Kramer
Management:
   President: Wendy Phillips
   Executive Director: Kathryn Smith
   Artistic Director: Hans Wolf
   Business Manager: Marian Scheele
Mission: To offer residents of the South Puget Sound area light opera performed in English.
Utilizes: Grant Writers; Guest Artists; Guest Conductors; Resident Professionals; Sign Language Translators
Founded: 1968
Specialized Field: Opera
Status: Professional
Paid Staff: 4
Volunteer Staff: 4
Paid Artists: 100
Budget: $500,000
Performs At: Pantages Theater; Railto Theater
Affiliations: Opera America
Annual Attendance: 7,200
Facility Category: Renovated Vaudeville House
Type of Stage: Proscenium
Seating Capacity: 1,166
Year Built: 1920
Year Remodeled: 1983
Organization Type: Performing

West Virginia

2095
CHARLESTON CIVIC CHORUS
PO Box 2014
Charleston, WV 25327

Phone: 304-744-5078
e-mail: thedaltons@yahoo.com
Web Site: www.charleston-civic-chorus.com
Officers:
    President: C Conrad Haskell
    Vice President: Jim Merrill
    Treasurer: Evan Buck
Management:
    Artistic Director: J Truman Dalton
Mission: To perform high-quality choral classics as well as some lighter fare.
Founded: 1952
Specialized Field: Choral; Classical; Contemporary
Status: Non-Profit, Non-Professional
Paid Staff: 2
Paid Artists: 2
Performs At: The Baptist Temple
Organization Type: Performing; Resident

2096
WEST VIRGINIA SYMPHONY CHORUS

PO Box 2292
Charleston, WV 25328
Phone: 304-561-3552
Fax: 304-357-4715
Web Site: www.wvsymphony.org
Officers:
    President: Judy Wellington
Management:
    Director: Joseph Janisch
Mission: To assist the West Virginia Symphony Orchestra in performing major choral and orchestral works of high quality artistry.
Specialized Field: Choral
Status: Non-Profit

Wisconsin

2097
MADISON OPERA

333 Glenway Street
Madison, WI 53711
Phone: 608-238-8085
Fax: 608-233-3431
e-mail: stanke@madisonopera.org
Web Site: www.madisonopera.org
Officers:
    President: Karen Walsh
    VP: Paul Shain
    Secretary: Jo Greenhalgh
    Treasurer: J Marshall Osborn
Management:
    Director Development: Susan Buzby
    Executive Director: Ann Stanke
Mission: To bring quality opera, locally produced, to the city of Madison.
Utilizes: Actors; Commissioned Music; Guest Composers; Guest Designers; Guest Lecturers; Guest Musicians; Guest Writers; Original Music Scores; Singers
Founded: 1962
Specialized Field: Grand Opera
Status: Non-Profit, Professional
Paid Staff: 10
Paid Artists: 175
Budget: $900,000
Income Sources: Opera America
Performs At: Oscar Meyer Theatre
Organization Type: Performing; Educational

2098
OPERA FOR THE YOUNG

6441 Enterprise Lane
Suite 207
Madison, WI 53719
Phone: 608-277-9560
Fax: 608-277-9570
Web Site: www.operafortheyoung.org
Management:
    Artistic Director: Diane Garton Edie
    Managing Director: Dan Plummer
Mission: To engage and educate children about opera with school based performances, to involve students in performance, to provide professional opportunities for emerging artists and to foster the creativity for new opera targeting young audiences.
Utilizes: Sign Language Translators
Founded: 1970
Specialized Field: Classical
Status: Non-Profit, Professional
Paid Staff: 4
Paid Artists: 20
Budget: $235,000
Income Sources: School Fees; Grants
Performs At: Tour To Elementary Schools
Annual Attendance: 80,000
Organization Type: Performing; Touring; Educational

2099
BEL CANTO CHORUS

158 N Broadway
Milwaukee, WI 53202
Phone: 414-481-8801
Fax: 414-481-8807
e-mail: info@belcanto.org
Web Site: www.belcanto.org
Officers:
    President: Sally Hoyt
    Treasurer: Tom Thiele
    Secretary: Jim Hyland
Management:
    Managing Director: Marla Hahn
    Artistic Director: Richard Hynson
Mission: To enrich the lives of its audiences and its singing members through the outstanding live presentation of the finest choral music and to reach out to the community in order to share the benefits and joy of the singing arts.
Utilizes: Sign Language Translators
Founded: 1931
Specialized Field: Choral; Classical; Religious
Status: Non-Profit, Professional
Paid Staff: 3
Volunteer Staff: 10
Paid Artists: 10
Non-paid Artists: 800
Budget: $400,000
Performs At: Churches; Performing Arts Centers
Affiliations: Chorus America, UPAF
Facility Category: Various

2100
FLORENTINE OPERA COMPANY

700 N Water Street
Suite 950
Milwaukee, WI 53202
Phone: 414-291-5700
Fax: 414-291-5706
Toll-free: 800-326-7372
e-mail: info@florentineopera.org
Web Site: www.florentineopera.org
Officers:
    President: Clay Nesler

    Director Of Finance: Catherine Krekhofer
Management:
    General Director: William Florescu
    Marketing Director: Cindy Hosale
Mission: Producing Grand Opera for Wisconsin.
Utilizes: Artists-in-Residence; Collaborations; Dance Companies; Dancers; Designers; Educators; Fine Artists; Grant Writers; Guest Artists; Guest Companies; Guest Composers; Guest Conductors; Guest Instructors; Guest Musical Directors; Guest Musicians; Instructors; Local Artists; Lyricists; Multimedia; New Productions; Organization Contracts; Original Music Scores; Sign Language Translators; Soloists; Students; Touring Companies; Visual Arts
Founded: 1933
Specialized Field: Grand Opera
Status: Professional; Nonprofit
Paid Staff: 15
Paid Artists: 175
Budget: $3.2 million
Income Sources: Private Foundations; Grants; Endowments; Business/Corporate Donations; Government Grants; Individual Donations
Performs At: Marcus Center for the Performing Arts
Affiliations: Opera America; Downtown Theatre District; UPAF
Annual Attendance: 23,000 - 24,000
Seating Capacity: 2,219
Organization Type: Performing; Touring; Educational

Alabama

2101

AUBURN UNIVERSITY THEATRE

Auburn University
School of Fine Arts, Auburn University
Auburn, AL 36849
Phone: 334-844-4000
Fax: 334-844-4939
e-mail: webmaster@auburn.edu
Officers:
   Department Chair: Ralph E Miller
Management:
   Chair: John Varner
Founded: 1856
Specialized Field: Educational; Musical; Comedy;
Drama
Budget: $3,000-5,000
Affiliations: NAST; ATHE
Seating Capacity: 370
Year Built: 1973

2102

BIRMINGHAM CHILDREN'S THEATRE

2130 Richard Arrington Jr Boulevard N
Birmingham, AL 35203
Mailing Address: PO Box 1362
Phone: 205-458-8181
Fax: 205-458-8895
e-mail: spierce@bct123.org
Web Site: www.bct123.org
Officers:
   President: Clark Gillespy
   First VP: Robert M Lee
   Second VP: Betty McMahon
   Third VP: W. Wheeler Smith, Esquire
   Secretary: Larry Contri
   Treasurer: Jean P. Pierce
Management:
   Managing Director: Bert Brosowsky
   Administrator: Vivian S Lyle
   School Groups Coordinator: Teresa Shepperd
   Tour Coordinator: Darrell Revel
Mission: The Birmingham Children's Theatre is a
professional company providing quality theatre for
young people which incorporates literature, art, music
and drama into a medium that is both entertaining and
educational.
Utilizes: Actors; Artists-in-Residence; Choreographers;
Collaborating Artists; Collaborations; Commissioned
Composers; Commissioned Music;
Composers-in-Residence; Dancers; Designers;
Educators; Five Seasonal Concerts; Guest
Accompanists; Guest Artists; Guest Choreographers;
Guest Companies; Guest Conductors; Guest
Designers; Guest Directors; Guest Ensembles; Guest
Instructors; Guest Lecturers; Guest Teachers;
Instructors; Local Artists; Local Unknown Artists;
Lyricists; Multimedia; Music; Organization Contracts;
Original Music Scores; Performance Artists; Poets;
Resident Professionals; Selected Students; Sign
Language Translators; Singers; Student Interns;
Special Technical Talent; Theatre Companies
Founded: 1947
Specialized Field: Children's Theater
Status: Non-Profit
Paid Staff: 25
Paid Artists: 50
Budget: $1,425,000
Income Sources: City, County, State, Grants,
Corporate, Individuals, Ticket Sales, Tour Revenue
Performs At: Civic Center Theatre; Black Box; Studio
Theatre

Annual Attendance: 450,000
Facility Category: Civic Convention Center
Type of Stage: Flex Trust
Stage Dimensions: 140'w x 60'd
Seating Capacity: 250 - 1,100
Year Built: 1974
Year Remodeled: 1997
Organization Type: Performing; Touring; Resident;
Educational; Sponsoring

2103

GARDEN VARIETY SHAKESPEARE

Birmingham Botanical Gardens
2126 Lane Park Road
Birmingham, AL 35226
Mailing Address: PO Box 531034, Birnigham, AL.
35253
Phone: 205-879-1227
Specialized Field: Shakespeare; Outdoor Theater

2104

UNIVERSITY OF ALABAMA, BIRMINGHAM: DEPARTMENT OF THEATRE

ASC 255 1200 10th Avenue S
Birmingham, AL 35294-1263
Phone: 205-934-3236
Fax: 205-934-8076
Web Site: www.theatre.hum.uab.edu
Officers:
   Chair: Will York
Founded: 1969
Specialized Field: Educational; Theater Workshops
Status: Non-Profit, Non-Professional
Paid Staff: 23
Seating Capacity: 350
Year Built: 1999

2105

SOUTHEAST ALABAMA COMMUNITY THEATRE

PO Box 6065
Dothan, AL 36302
Phone: 334-794-0400
Fax: 334-794-0400
Web Site: www.seact.com
Officers:
   President: Doug Mann
Management:
   General Manager: Jane Long
Mission: To provide Southeast Alabama with
performing theatre.
Founded: 1974
Specialized Field: Musical; Comedy; Community
Theater; Contemporary
Status: Non-Profit, Non-Professional
Paid Staff: 2
Performs At: Dothan Opera House
Organization Type: Performing

2106

LOONEY'S TAVERN PRODUCTIONS

22400 Highway 278 E
Double Springs, AL 35553
Phone: 205-489-5000
Fax: 205-489-3500
Toll-free: 800-566-6397
e-mail: info@looneystavern.com
Web Site: www.looneystavern.com
Officers:
   President/CEO: Dwain Moody
Mission: To produce live performances of stage plays
to include drama, comedy, musical.

Founded: 1989
Specialized Field: Drama; Comedy; Musical
Status: Non-Equity
Paid Staff: 8
Volunteer Staff: 10
Paid Artists: 50
Budget: $500,000
Income Sources: Sales
Season: Year-round
Performs At: Amphitheater; Indoor Theatre
Annual Attendance: 25,000
Type of Stage: Amphitheatre; Theatre
Stage Dimensions: 90'x 40'
Seating Capacity: 1500; 275
Rental Contact: President/CEO Dwain Moody

2107

UNIVERSITY OF NORTH ALABAMA: DEPARTMENT OF COMMUNICATIONS & THEATRE

UNA Box 5011
Florence, AL 35632-0001
Mailing Address: PO Box 5007, University of North
Alabama, Florence, AL 35632
Phone: 256-765-4516
Fax: 256-765-4839
Toll-free: 800-825-5862
e-mail: dmmccullough@una.edu
Web Site: http://www.una.edu/m
Management:
   Chair: David McCullough
Mission: As an accredited institutional member of the
National Association of Schools of Music, the UNA
Department of Music and Theatre has much to
offer—outstanding faculty, exceptional performing
ensembles and quality degree programs, including
professional degree programs in music education and
liberal arts degree programs in music performance and
commercial music.
Specialized Field: Educational; Theater Workshops
Budget: $2,500-12,000
Seating Capacity: 1700
Year Built: 1969

2108

BROADWAY THEATRE

700 Monroe Street
Huntsville, AL 35801
Phone: 256-518-6155
Fax: 256-551-2990
Management:
   Director: Jean S Warren
   Executive Director: Andrew Willmon
   Membership Director: Debbie McCutcheon
   Group Director: Midori Maloney
Founded: 1959
Specialized Field: Musical; Comedy; Drama
Status: For-Profit, Professional

2109

SAENGER THEATRE

6 Joachim Street S
Mobile, AL 36602
Phone: 334-438-5686
Fax: 334-433-2087
Management:
   General Manager: Mihael D Maxwell
Specialized Field: Drama; Musical

2110

UNIVERSITY OF SOUTH ALABAMA

307 University Boulevard N
Mobile, AL 36688-0002

Phone: 251-460-6101
Fax: 334-461-1511
e-mail: webmaster@usouthal.edu
Officers:
    Department Chair: Dr. Eugene R Jackson
Management:
    President: Gordon Moulton
    Assoc VP: David Stearns
Founded: 1963
Specialized Field: Educational; Theater Workshops
Budget: $17,000-23,000
Affiliations: ATHE; Alabama Lyric Theatre
Seating Capacity: 180; 800
Year Built: 1999

2111
UNIVERSITY OF MONTEVALLO: DIVISION OF THEATRE

University of Montevallo
Station 6210
Montevallo, AL 35115
Mailing Address: Box 6210, Univ. of Montevallo, Montevallo, AL 35115
Phone: 205-665-6210
Fax: 205-665-6211
Web Site: www.montevallo.edu/thea
Management:
    Chairman of the Department: Randy Schott
    Director of Theatre: David Callaghan
Specialized Field: Educational; Theater Workshops
Status: Non-Profit, Non-Professional
Paid Staff: 6
Paid Artists: 6
Budget: $4,000-19,000
Seating Capacity: 1200
Year Built: 1931
Year Remodeled: 1978

2112
AUVURN UNIVERSITY MONTGOMERY THEATRE

Department Communication, Dramatic Arts
Montgomery, AL 36124
Mailing Address: PO Box 244023
Phone: 334-244-3379
Fax: 334-244-3740
e-mail: askaum@mail.aum.edu
Web Site: www.aum.edu
Management:
    Head of Theatre: Bob Gaines
    Department Head: Robert A Gaines
Founded: 1967
Specialized Field: Comedy; Classic; Contemporary
Status: Non-Profit, Non-Professional
Paid Staff: 600
Budget: $2,000
Affiliations: Alabama Shakespeare Festival
Seating Capacity: 180
Year Built: 1979

Alaska

2113
ANCHORAGE COMMUNITY THEATRE

1133 E 70th Avenue
Anchorage, AK 99518-2353
Phone: 907-344-4713
Fax: 907-344-6002
e-mail: acthome@gci.net
Web Site: www.act.alaska.org
Officers:
    President: Brian Saylor

Management:
    Executive Director: Bill Cotton
Mission: Building community through theatre since 1953.
Founded: 1953
Specialized Field: Community Theater
Status: Non-Profit, Non-Professional
Paid Staff: 1
Performs At: Live Theatre
Annual Attendance: 6,000

2114
CYRANO'S THEATRE COMPANY

413 D Street
Anchorage, AK 99501
Phone: 907-274-2599
Fax: 907-277-4698
e-mail: cyrano@ak.net
Web Site: www.cyranos.org
Management:
    Producer: Sandy Harper
Founded: 1992
Specialized Field: Drama; Comedy; Musical
Performs At: Cyrano's Off Center Playhouse
Type of Stage: Black Box
Seating Capacity: 86

2115
OUT NORTH - VSA ALASKA

3800 De Barr Road
Anchorage, AK 99508-2011
Phone: 907-279-8099
Fax: 907-279-8100
e-mail: art@outnorth.org
Web Site: www.outnorth.org
Management:
    Executive Artistic Director: Scott Schofield
    Director Of Operations: Eyvette Flynn
Mission: Out North exists to develop and present bold new work that challenges and changes the art, the artist, and the audience. We encourage artistic risk-taking and collaboration, examining today's world through diverse culturel perspectives, and creative community through the arts.
Founded: 1985
Specialized Field: Youth Theater; Ethnic Theater; Community Theater; Contemporary
Status: Non-Profit, Professional
Paid Staff: 5
Volunteer Staff: 50
Paid Artists: 12
Budget: $300,000
Income Sources: Ticket Sales; Government Grants; Private Foundations; Individual Donations
Performs At: Theatre; Film; Fine Arts
Affiliations: National Alliance for Media Arts & Culture; National Performance Network; National Association of Artists Organizations
Annual Attendance: 8,000
Facility Category: Multidisciplinary
Type of Stage: Flexible black box
Seating Capacity: 99
Year Built: 1958
Year Remodeled: 1994
Organization Type: Performing; Educational

2116
UNIVERSITY OF ALASKA, ANCHORAGE: DEPARTMENT OF THEATRE AND DANCE

3211 Providence Drive
Anchorage, AK 99508
Phone: 907-786-1792
Fax: 907-786-1799
Web Site: http://theatre.uaa.alaska.edu/index.html

Officers:
    Department Chair: Fran Lautenberger
Mission: The UAA Theatre program offers a well-rounded liberal arts approach in its curriculum, with courses covering all the basic areas of theatrical endeavor, including acting, directing, stagecraft, scene design, lighting, costuming, makeup, dramatic literature, theatre history, dramatic theory and criticism, and playwriting.
Specialized Field: Educational; Theater Workshops
Budget: $11,000-26,000
Affiliations: ATHE
Seating Capacity: 171; 99
Year Built: 1986

2117
PERSEVERANCE THEATRE

914 Third Street
Douglas, AK 99824
Phone: 907-364-2421
Fax: 907-364-2603
e-mail: info@perseverancetheatre.org
Web Site: www.perseverancetheatre.org
Officers:
    President: Glenda Carino
Management:
    President: Susan Koester
    Executive Director: P J Papareloi
    Director: Jeffrey Hermann
Founded: 1979
Specialized Field: Drama; Comedy; Musical
Status: Non-Profit, Professional
Paid Staff: 10
Paid Artists: 19

2118
UNIVERSITY OF ALASKA, FAIRBANKS: THEATRE DEPARTMENT

PO Box 755700
Fairbanks, AK 99775-5700
Mailing Address: PO Box 775700, Fairbanks, AK 99775
Phone: 907-474-6590
Fax: 907-474-7048
e-mail: fythtr@uaf.edu
Web Site: www.uaf.edu/theatre
Officers:
    Theatre Department Chair: Tara Maginnis
Management:
    President: Kade Mendelowitz
    Managing Director: Maya Salganek
    Stage Director: Anatoly Antohin
Founded: 1965
Specialized Field: Educational; Theater Workshops
Status: Non-Profit, Non-Professional
Paid Staff: 7
Paid Artists: 5
Budget: $3,700-11,000
Affiliations: Fairbanks Drama Associates & Children's Theatre; Fairbanks Shakespeare Theatre; Fairbanks Light Opera Theatre Summer Fine Arts Camp
Seating Capacity: 480; 110;
Year Built: 1968

2119
LYNN CANAL COMMUNITY PLAYERS

PO Box 1030
Haines, AK 99827
Phone: 907-766-2708
Fax: 907-766-2425
Officers:
    Treasurer: Annette Smith
    Secretary: Jane Sebena
    President: Kathy Pashigan

VP: Tod Sebens
Management:
President: Mark Sebens
Managing Director: Annette Smith
Mission: Performing in and sponsoring all forms of theatre; hosting the biennial presentation of the Alaska Community Theatre Festival.
Utilizes: Guest Companies; Singers
Founded: 1957
Specialized Field: Musical; Comedy; Youth Theater; Dinner Theater; Community Theater; Contemporary
Status: Non-Profit, Non-Professional
Paid Staff: 1
Volunteer Staff: 1
Income Sources: Arts Southeast
Performs At: Chilkat Center for the Arts
Organization Type: Performing

Arizona

2120
NORTHERN ARIZONA UNIVERSITY: THEATRE DIVISION, SCHOOL OF PERFORMING ARTS
PO Box 6040 Building 37
Room 120
Flagstaff, AZ 86011
Phone: 928-523-3781
Fax: 928-523-5111
e-mail: Theatre@nau.edu
Web Site: http://www.cal.nau.edu/theatre/
Officers:
Dean: Michael Vincent
Associate Dean: Jean Boreen
Marketing/Coordinator: Elizabeth Hellstern
Director of Development: Marjorie Kamine
Mission: Offers students the broadest possible understanding of the art and craft of theatre through creative, critical, and applied practice
Specialized Field: Educational; Theater Workshops
Budget: $5,000-9,650
Affiliations: ATHE
Seating Capacity: 300; 120
Year Built: 1968
Year Remodeled: 1999

2121
THEATER WORKS
10484 W Thunderbird Boulevard
Peoria, AZ 85351
Phone: 623-815-7930
Fax: 623-815-9043
Officers:
CEO: Michael Foulds
President: Robert T Root
VP: David Lunch
Treasurer: Vicky Holly
Secretary: Linda Kidwell
Management:
Executive Director: Michael Foulds
Artistic Director: Scott Campbell
Mission: To provide a diversified, strikingly creative performing arts program of the highest quality, accessible to all in the community.
Utilizes: Actors; Dancers; Resident Professionals; Sign Language Translators; Soloists
Founded: 1986
Specialized Field: Community Theater; Drama; Comedy
Status: Non professional; Nonprofit
Paid Staff: 8
Volunteer Staff: 100

Non-paid Artists: 70
Income Sources: Local Corporations; Arts Commissions; Patrons; Donations
Annual Attendance: 30,000
Seating Capacity: 150

2122
ACTORS THEATRE OF PHOENIX
Herberger Theater Center
222 E Monroe
Phoenix, AZ 85004
Mailing Address: PO Box 1924, Phoenix, AZ. 85001-1924
Phone: 602-253-6701
Fax: 602-252-8497
e-mail: info@actorstheatrephx.org
Web Site: www.actorstheatrephx.org
Officers:
Director Marketing: Janice Sweeter
Management:
Producing Artistic Director: Matthew Wiener
Mission: Actors Theater of Phoenix is unique in its presentation of contemporary professional theatre that amplifies the cultural conversation of our communities with powerful and innovative programming
Utilizes: Actors; AEA Actors; Choreographers; Guest Companies; Guest Conductors; Guest Designers; Local Artists; Local Artists & Directors; Music; Original Music Scores; Playwrights; Resident Professionals; Selected Students; Student Interns
Founded: 1985
Opened: 1985
Specialized Field: Political Comedy; Thenic Theater; Contemporary
Status: Non-Profit, Professional
Paid Staff: 8
Paid Artists: 40
Budget: $1.1 Million
Income Sources: Ticket Sales; Donations; Grants
Performs At: Herberger Theater Center; Stage West
Affiliations: Theatre Communications Group
Type of Stage: Proscenium
Stage Dimensions: 34'x40'
Seating Capacity: 300
Year Built: 1989
Year Remodeled: 2010
Rental Contact: Herberger Theatre Center Shannon O'Hara
Organization Type: Performing

2123
ARIZONA STATE UNIVERSITY THEATRE
Arizona State University
Tempe, AZ 85287
Mailing Address: PO Box 872002, Tempe, AZ 85287
Phone: 480-965-9011
Fax: 480-965-5351
e-mail: askasu@asu.edu
Officers:
Interim Chair: John Saldana
Specialized Field: Educational; Theater Workshops
Budget: $5,500-10,000
Affiliations: U/RTA; ATHE; Arizona Theatre Company
Seating Capacity: 525; 166; 70
Year Built: 1989

2124
CHILDSPLAY
PO Box 517
Tempe, AZ 85280
Phone: 480-350-8101
Fax: 480-350-8584
e-mail: info@childsplayaz.org
Web Site: www.childsplayaz.org

Management:
President: Dana Niell
Artistic Director: David Saar
Managing Director: Steve Martin
Mission: To create theatre so strikingly original in form, content, or both, that it instills in young people an enduring awe, love and respect for the medium, thus preserving imagination and wonder, the hallmarks of childhood, which are the keys to the future.
Founded: 1977
Specialized Field: Youth Theater; Puppet; Contemporary
Status: Non-Profit, Professional
Paid Staff: 15
Paid Artists: 10
Performs At: Herberger Theater, Scottsdale Center for the Arts, Stage West, Tempe Performing Arts Center
Type of Stage: Proscenium, Black Box
Seating Capacity: 800, 800, 350, 175

2125
ARIZONA THEATRE COMPANY
343 S. Scott Ave.
Tucson, AZ 85701
Mailing Address: Tuscon, AZ
Phone: 520-884-8210
Fax: 520-628-9129
e-mail: dgoldstein@arizonatheatre.org
Web Site: www.arizonatheatre.org
Officers:
President: Aubra Spaulding-Gaston
Board Chairman: Jack Davis
Management:
General Manager: Andrew Holtz
Artistic Director: David Ira Goldstein
Managing Director: Jessica Andrews
Marketing Director: Jennifer Spencer
Mission: Creating outstanding professional theatre for Arizona; having an impact locally and nationally.
Utilizes: Actors; AEA Actors; Artists-in-Residence; Collaborating Artists; Commissioned Composers; Commissioned Music; Curators; Dance Companies; Dancers; Designers; Educators; Fine Artists; Five Seasonal Concerts; Grant Writers; Guest Accompanists; Guest Artists; Guest Companies; Guest Composers; Guest Conductors; Guest Designers; Guest Directors; Guest Instructors; Guest Lecturers; Guest Musical Directors; Guest Soloists; Guest Teachers; Instructors; Local Artists; Multimedia; Music; Original Music Scores; Performance Artists; Poets; Resident Artists; Resident Professionals; Selected Students; Sign Language Translators; Singers; Soloists; Student Interns; Special Technical Talent; Visual Arts
Founded: 1967
Specialized Field: Musical; Comedy; Youth Theater; Ethnic Theater; Community Theater; Classic; Contemporary
Status: Non-Profit, Professional
Paid Staff: 50
Paid Artists: 80
Budget: $6.9 million
Income Sources: Ticket Sales; Donations; Grants; Government
Annual Attendance: 150,000
Facility Category: Temple of Music and Art; Herberger Theatre Center
Type of Stage: Proscenium
Seating Capacity: 622; 800
Year Built: 1927
Year Remodeled: 1990
Organization Type: Resident

2126
SCHOOL OF THEATRE ARTS
University of Arizona
Drama Building, Room 239
Tucson, AZ 85721-0003
Mailing Address: PO Box 210003
Phone: 520-621-7008
Fax: 520-621-2412
e-mail: theatre@email.arizona.edu
Web Site: www.arts.arizona.edu/theatre
Officers:
   President: Robert Shelton
Management:
   Director: Al Tucci
   Artistic Director: Brent Gibbs
Mission: Provides professional training and education leading to careers in acting, musical theatre, theatre design and technology, theatre education and outreach, and theatre history and dramaturgy. The School is dedicated to educating students through a highly visible production program enriching the university and Tucson communities.
Founded: 1936
Specialized Field: Educational; Theater Workshops
Status: Non-Profit, Professional
Performs At: Theatre
Affiliations: NAST; U/RTA; Arizona Theatre Company
Annual Attendance: 26,000
Facility Category: Theatre
Type of Stage: Proscenium; Black Box
Seating Capacity: 332; 300
Year Built: 1957
Year Remodeled: 1992

Arkansas

2127
LYON COLLEGE THEATRE DEPARTMENT
2300 Highland Road
Batesville, AR 72503
Mailing Address: PO Box 2317, Batesville, AR 72503
Phone: 870-793-1750
Fax: 870-698-4622
Toll-free: 800-423-2542
e-mail: mcounts@lyon.edu
Web Site: www.theatre.lyon.edu
Management:
   President: Walter Roettger
   Executive Director: John Peek
   Director of Theatre: Michael L Counts
Founded: 1925
Specialized Field: Educational; Theater Workshops; Drama
Status: Non-Profit, Non-Professional
Paid Staff: 2
Budget: $9,800 - 12,000
Affiliations: ATHE; KCACTF
Annual Attendance: 600-700
Type of Stage: Black Box
Seating Capacity: 150
Year Built: 1991
Year Remodeled: 1999

2128
UNIVERSITY OF CENTRAL ARKANSAS THEATRE PROGRAM
Ucato Box 4942
Conway, AR 7205
Mailing Address: PO Box 4942, University of Central AR, Conway, AR 72035
Phone: 501-450-5608

Fax: 501-450-3102
e-mail: gregb@uca.edu
Web Site: www.uca.edu/theatre
Officers:
   President: Alan Meadors
Management:
   Director of Theatre: Gregory Blakey
   Production Manager: Liz Parker
Founded: 1907
Specialized Field: BA/BS in Theatre
Status: Non-Profit, Non-Professional
Paid Staff: 4
Budget: $3,100-17,500
Affiliations: Home to Arkansas Shakespeare Theatre
Type of Stage: Proscenium/Black Box
Year Built: 1968
Year Remodeled: 1996

2129
UNIVERSITY OF ARKANSAS AT FAYETTEVILLE: DEPARTMENT OF DRAMA
619 Kimpel Hall
Fayetteville, AR 72701
Phone: 479-575-2953
Fax: 479-575-7602
e-mail: drama@cavern.uark.edu
Web Site: www.uark.edu/~drama
Officers:
   Chair: Dr. Andrew Gibbs
Management:
   President: John White
   Executive Director: Allan Sugg
   Artistic Director: D Andrew Gibbs
Founded: 1871
Specialized Field: Musical; Comedy; Ethnic Theater; Classic; Contemporary
Status: For-Profit, Non-Professional
Seating Capacity: 331; 1205; 75
Year Built: 1950

2130
FORT SMITH LITTLE THEATRE
401 N Sixth Street
PO Box 3752
Fort Smith, AR 72913
Phone: 479-783-2966
Web Site: www.fslt.org
Officers:
   President: Michael Richardson
   VP: Clara Jane Rubarth
   Treasurer: Mike Tickler
   Secretary: Wendy Quick
Management:
   President: Carole Rogers
   VP: Dennis Brown
   Secretary: Rosemary Johnson
   Treasurer: Paula Sharum
Founded: 1948
Specialized Field: Drama; Musical; Comedy
Status: Nonprofit
Income Sources: Ticket Sales
Performs At: Fort Smith Little Theatre
Organization Type: Performing

2131
FOUNDATION OF ARTS
115 W Monroe
PO Box 310
Jonesboro, AR 72403-0310
Phone: 870-935-2726
Fax: 870-933-9505
Officers:

Executive Director: Sherri Greuel
Marketing Director/Box Office: Danita Martin
Education Director: Lara Shelton
Technical Director: Brett Kellett
Management:
   Music Director: Dr. Neale King Bartee
   Executive Director: Margaret Peacock
   Education Director: Lara Shelton
   Marketing/Box Office: Danita Martin-Wilkins
Mission: Education, Community Theatre Workshops, Guest Directors, etc. to conduct workshops. Emphasis on youth, but offered to all ages.
Utilizes: Actors; Choreographers; Educators; Guest Artists; Guest Designers; High School Drama; Instructors; Local Artists; Lyricists; Multimedia; Organization Contracts; Sign Language Translators; Soloists; Student Interns; Touring Companies
Founded: 1978
Specialized Field: Community Theater; Musical; Drama; Comedy
Paid Staff: 5
Budget: $35,000-$100,000
Income Sources: Box Office, Grants, Private Donation, Class Tuition
Annual Attendance: 25,000
Facility Category: Theatre
Type of Stage: Proscenium
Seating Capacity: 670
Year Built: 1940
Year Remodeled: 2000
Rental Contact: Executive Director Sherri Greuel
Resident Groups: Nea Symphony, Theatre on the Ridge, Act Experience, Jonesboro City Ballet

2132
ARKANSAS ARTS CENTER CHILDREN'S THEATER
MacArthur Park, 9th Commerce Street
PO Box 2137
Little Rock, AR 72203
Phone: 501-372-4000
Fax: 501-375-8053
Toll-free: 800-264-2787
e-mail: mpreble@arkarts.com
Web Site: www.arkarts.com
Officers:
   President: Terri Erwin
Management:
   President: Ellen Thummel
   Artistic Director: Bradley D Anderson
Mission: Family theater.
Utilizes: Guest Companies; Singers
Founded: 1979
Specialized Field: Musical; Comedy; Youth Theater; Dinner Theater
Status: Non-Profit, Professional
Performs At: Arkansas Art Center Theater
Annual Attendance: 50,000
Facility Category: Auditorium
Type of Stage: Proscenium
Seating Capacity: 381
Year Built: 1930
Organization Type: Performing; Touring
Resident Groups: Resident Theatre Company

2133
ARKANSAS REPERATORY THEATRE
601 Main Street
PO Box 110
Little Rock, AR 72203

Phone: 501-378-0445
Fax: 501-378-0012
Toll-free: 866-6 T-EREP
e-mail: tickets@therep.org
Web Site: www.therep.org
Officers:
   Chairman: Wyck Nisbet
   Treasurer: Steve Strickland
   Secretary: Ann Bradford
Management:
   Executive Director: Robert Hupp
   Business Manager: Lynn Frazier
   Development Associate: Wanda Hoover
   General Manager: Michael McCurdy
   Marketing Director: Kelly Ford
Mission: To be a professional theatre of excellence that entertains and challenges local, regional, and national audiences. Through educational outreach, and as a creative forum for artists, The Rep strives to provide valuable services to the community and make significant contributions to the national theatre agenda.
Utilizes: Actors; AEA Actors; Choreographers; Collaborations; Dancers; Designers; Grant Writers; Guest Artists; Guest Choreographers; Guest Companies; Guest Composers; Guest Conductors; Guest Designers; Guest Ensembles; Guest Lecturers; Guest Musical Directors; Guild Activities; Instructors; Local Artists; Multimedia; Music; Organization Contracts; Original Music Scores; Resident Professionals; Selected Students; Singers; Theatre Companies; Touring Companies; Visual Arts
Founded: 1976
Specialized Field: Musical; Comedy; Youth Theater; Dinner Theater; Community Theater; Classic; Contemporary
Status: Non-Profit, Professional
Paid Staff: 35
Volunteer Staff: 200
Paid Artists: 160
Non-paid Artists: 10
Income Sources: Corporations; Private; Government; Ticket Sales
Performs At: Arkansas Repertory Theatre
Affiliations: Actors Equity Association and Theatre Communication Group
Annual Attendance: 60,000
Type of Stage: Modified Proscenium
Stage Dimensions: 40' x 30'
Seating Capacity: 350
Year Remodeled: 1988
Rental Contact: Michael McCurdy
Organization Type: Performing; Touring; Resident; Educational; Sponsoring

2134
UNIVERSITY OF ARKANSAS AT LITTLE ROCK: DEPARTMENT OF THEATRE AND DANCE

2801 South University
Little Rock, AR 72204
Phone: 501-569-3291
Fax: 501-569-8355
Management:
   Executive Director: Debra Baldwan
   Artistic Chair Person: Robert Hupp
Specialized Field: Musical; Comedy; Ethnic Theater; Classic; Contemporary
Status: Non-Profit, Non-Professional
Paid Staff: 17
Budget: $3,750-7,800
Affiliations: NAST; ATHE; Arkansas Repertory Theatre; Arkansas Arts Center Children's Theatre; Murray's Dinner Theatre

Seating Capacity: 680; 150

2135
SOUTHERN ARKANSAS UNIVERSITY THEATRE & MASS COMMUNICATIONS DEPARTMENT

100 E University
Magnolia, AR 71753
Mailing Address: Box 9203, Magnolia, AR 71754
Phone: 870-235-4257
e-mail: ddmurphy@saumag.edu
Web Site: www.saumag.edu
Officers:
   Chair: David Murphy
Management:
   President: David Rankin
   Artistic Director: David Murphy
Specialized Field: Comedy; Youth Theater; Ethnic Theater; Community Theater; Classic; Contemporary
Status: Non-Profit, Non-Professional
Paid Staff: 3
Paid Artists: 3
Budget: $550-2,100
Affiliations: ATHE
Seating Capacity: 475
Year Built: 1975

2136
TWIN LAKES PLAYHOUSE

600 W. 6th Street
Mountain Home, AR 72654
Mailing Address: PO Box 482 Mountain Home, AK
Phone: 870-481-5811
Toll-free: 870-240-44
Web Site: http://www.twinlakesplayhouse.org/
Officers:
   Chairman: Cindi Young
   Vice Chairman: Mike Baker
   Secretary: Chrissy Carney
   Treasurer: Chris Dyson
Mission: Providing live theater for the area.
Founded: 1971
Specialized Field: Community Theater
Status: Semi-Professional; Non-Professional; Nonprofit
Paid Staff: 40
Organization Type: Performing

California

2137
HUMBOLT STATE UNIVERSITY: DEPARTMENT OF THEATRE, FILM AND DANCE

1 Harpst Street
Arcata, CA 95521
Mailing Address: Arcata, CA
Phone: 707-826-3566
Fax: 707-826-5494
Web Site: http://www.humboldt.edu/theatrefilmanddance/index.shtml
Officers:
   Chair: Michael Goodman
Founded: 1913
Specialized Field: Musical; Comedy; Youth Theater; Ethnic Theater; Contemporary
Status: Non-Profit, Professional
Paid Staff: 12
Budget: $6,000-12,000
Affiliations: NAST; ATHE
Seating Capacity: 810; 140; 125
Year Built: 1959

2138
CALIFORNIA STATE UNIVERSITY, BAKERSFIELD: THEATRE PROGRAM

9001 Stockdale Highway
Bakersfield, CA 93311
Mailing Address: Bakersfield, CA
Phone: 661-664-3093
Fax: 661-665-6901
Web Site: http://www.csub.edu/theatre/
Officers:
   Chair: Annie DuPratt
Specialized Field: Educational; Theater Workshops
Budget: $6,500
Affiliations: ATHE
Seating Capacity: 500; 100
Year Built: 1980

2139
AURORA THEATRE COMPANY

2081 Addison Street
Berkeley, CA 94704
Mailing Address: PO Box 559, Berkeley, CA. 94701
Phone: 510-843-4042
Fax: 510-843-4826
e-mail: general@auroratheatre.org
Web Site: auroratheatre.org
Management:
   Artistic Director: Tom Ross
   Managing Director: Sandra Wright
   Secretary: Gail Oakley
   Treasurer: Hilary Perkins
Mission: Produce five professional plays per season.
Founded: 1991
Specialized Field: Drama; Musical; Comedy
Paid Staff: 8
Paid Artists: 50
Performs At: Airpra Theatre
Affiliations: Actor's Equity Theatre Company; Theatre Communications Group; Theatre Bay Area
Type of Stage: Arena
Seating Capacity: 67

2140
BERKELEY COMMUNITY THEATRE

1980 Allstom Way
Berkeley, CA 94703
Phone: 510-644-6863
Fax: 510-845-9674
Management:
   Theatre Manager: Judson H Owens
   Assistant Manager: Lance C James
   Facility Reservations: Yvonne Adams
Mission: To offer the community professional theatre.
Utilizes: Guest Artists; Guest Companies; Singers
Founded: 1950
Specialized Field: Community Theater
Status: Non-Profit, Non-Professional
Paid Staff: 4
Volunteer Staff: 60
Income Sources: Berkeley Unified School District
Performs At: Berkeley Community Theatre
Affiliations: Berkeley Unified School District
Seating Capacity: 3,500
Organization Type: Performing; Touring; Educational

2141
BERKELEY REPERTORY THEATRE

2025 Addison Street
Berkeley, CA 94704

Phone: 510-647-2900
Fax: 510-647-2976
Toll-free: 888-427-8849
e-mail: info@berkeleyrep.org
Web Site: www.berkeleyrep.org
Officers:
President: Nicholas M Graves
VP: Phillip R Trapp
Treasurerident: Kenneth P Avery
Secretary: Jean Strunsky
Management:
Executive Director: Susan Medak
Artistic Director: Tony Taccone
General Manager: Karen Racanelli
Mission: To set a national standard for ambitious programming, engagement with our audiences, and leadership within the community in which we reside. We endeavor to create a diverse body of work that expresses a rigorous, embracing aesthetic and relects the highest artistic standards, and seek to maintain an environment in which talented artists can do their best work.
Utilizes: Actors; AEA Actors; Choreographers; Collaborations; Designers; Educators; Five Seasonal Concerts; Guest Accompanists; Guest Artists; Guest Designers; Guest Instructors; Guild Activities; High School Drama; Instructors; Local Artists; Lyricists; Multimedia; Original Music Scores; Performance Artists; Resident Professionals; Student Interns; Visual Arts
Founded: 1968
Specialized Field: Drama; Comedy; Musical; Educational
Status: Non-Profit, Professional
Paid Staff: 75
Paid Artists: 50
Budget: $8.9 Million
Income Sources: Tickets; Grants; Donations; Subscriptions
Performs At: Berkeley Repertory Theatre
Affiliations: San Francisco Convention and Visitor Bureau; Berkeley Convention and Visitor Bureau
Annual Attendance: 150,000
Type of Stage: Thrust Stage and Proscenium Stage
Seating Capacity: 400 and 600
Year Built: 1980
Cost: $20 Million
Rental Contact: Alisha Tonsic
Organization Type: Performing; Touring; Resident; Educational

2142
BLACK REPERTORY GROUP

3201 Adeline Street
Berkeley, CA 94703
Phone: 510-652-2120
Fax: 510-652-8030
e-mail: keepersoftheculture@yahoo.com
Web Site: www.blackrepertorygroup.com
Officers:
President: Ella Wiley
VP: Pastor Earl Bill
Secretary: Doreen Zayas
Management:
President: Sean Vaughn Scott
Executive Director: Mona Vaughn Scott
Managing Director: Pamela Spikes
Mission: Building discipline and self-esteem in youth through drama. Showcasing the plays of black playwrights. Providing a folk arts venue for the community.
Utilizes: Guest Companies; Singers
Founded: 1964

Specialized Field: Musical; Comedy; Youth Theater; Dinner Theater; Ethnic Theater; Community Theater; Classic; Contemporary
Status: Non-Profit, Professional
Paid Staff: 4
Paid Artists: 250
Organization Type: Resident

2143
DELL'ARTE INTERNATIONAL SCHOOL OF PHYSICAL THEATRE

131 H Street
PO Box 816
Blue Lake, CA 95525
Phone: 707-668-5663
Fax: 707-668-5665
e-mail: info@dellarte.com
Web Site: www.dellarte.com.
Officers:
President: Bonnie Neely
Secretary/Treasurer: Bobbi Ricca
Management:
President: Bonnie Neely
Executive Director: Michael Fields
Co-Artistic Director: Joan Schirle
Mission: International in scope, grounded in the natural living world, inspired by the non-urban setting, explores theatre making, theatre practice and theatre training for ourselved, the world and the future.
Utilizes: Actors; AEA Actors; Choreographers; Collaborating Artists; Collaborations; Dancers; Designers; Educators; Five Seasonal Concerts; Guest Accompanists; Guest Choreographers; Guest Companies; Guest Designers; Guest Ensembles; High School Drama; Local Artists; Original Music Scores; Resident Professionals; Sign Language Translators; Soloists; Theatre Companies
Founded: 1971
Specialized Field: Theatre
Status: Non-Profit, Professional
Paid Staff: 22
Paid Artists: 15
Budget: $1 Million
Income Sources: Humboldt Arts Council; Theatre Communications Group, Theatre Bay Area
Performs At: Dell' Arte Theatre
Affiliations: NAST; ATHE
Facility Category: Black Box/Amphitheatre
Type of Stage: Sprung Floor
Seating Capacity: 113; 300
Year Remodeled: 1995
Organization Type: Performing; Touring
Resident Groups: Dell' Arte Company

2144
COLONY THEATRE COMPANY

555 N Third Street
Burbank, CA 91502-1103
Phone: 818-558-7000
Fax: 818-558-7110
e-mail: colonytheatre@colonytheatre.org
Web Site: www.colonytheatre.org
Officers:
President/Producing Director: Barbara Beckley
VP: Michael Wadler
Secretary: Priscilla Davis
Treasurer: Nonie Lann
Chairman: Keith Bardellini
Management:
President: Barbara Beckley
Managing Director: Sean Cutler
Mission: To produce full productions of plays for the public recognized to be of significant artistic, social, and/or historical value.

Utilizes: Actors; AEA Actors; Designers; Guest Conductors; Guest Lecturers; Guest Musical Directors; Instructors; Music; Resident Artists; Resident Professionals; Student Interns
Founded: 1975
Specialized Field: Drama; Comedy; Musical
Status: Non-Profit, Professional
Paid Staff: 7
Volunteer Staff: 10
Budget: $800,000
Income Sources: Subscription & Single Ticket Sales; Individual Donations
Performs At: Burbank Center Stage
Affiliations: Actors Equity Association
Annual Attendance: 20,500
Facility Category: Theater
Type of Stage: Thrust
Stage Dimensions: 37.5 x 22.5
Seating Capacity: 276
Year Built: 2000
Cost: $1,500,000 (built)
Rental Contact: Managing Director Amanda Diamond
Organization Type: Performing; Resident
Resident Groups: Colony Theatre Company

2145
CALIFORNIA STATE UNIVERSITY, DOMINGUEZ HILLS: DEPARTMENT OF THEATRE

California State University
Carson, CA 90747
Mailing Address: 1000 East Victoria St. LCH E303
Phone: 310-243-3588
Web Site: http://cah.csudh.edu/theatre/
Officers:
Chairman: Sydell Weiner
Specialized Field: Educational; Theater Workshops
Budget: $8,550-12,100
Affiliations: NAST
Seating Capacity: 475; 80

2146
CALIFORNIA STATE UNIVERSITY, CHICO

CSU Chico - Department Of Theatre
1205 West 7th Street
Chico, CA 95929-0810
Phone: 530-898-6161
Fax: 530-868-5263
e-mail: jprogers@csuchico.edu
Web Site: www.csuchico.edu/thea
Officers:
Chair: Joel P Rogers
Management:
Administrative Support Coordinator: Cindy Davidson
Paid Staff: 5
Affiliations: NAST; ATHE
Facility Category: Performing Arts Center
Type of Stage: Proscenium, Black Box
Seating Capacity: 450/150
Year Built: 1968
Organization Type: Educational

2147
CHICO PERFORMANCES

California State University Chico
400 W First Street
Chico, CA 95929-0116
Phone: 530-898-5917
Fax: 530-898-4797
e-mail: upe@csuchico.edu
Web Site: www.chicoperformances.com
Management:

President: Paul Zingg
Executive Director: Richard Jackson
Artistic Director: Dan Dewayne
Specialized Field: Multi-Media
Status: Non-Profit, Professional
Paid Staff: 9

2148
POMONA COLLEGE DEPARTMENT OF THEATRE AND DANCE

Pomona College
Claremont, CA 91711
Mailing Address: 300 E. Bonita Ave.
Phone: 909-621-8186
Fax: 909-621-8780
e-mail: mtr04747@pomona.edu
Web Site: http://theatre.pomona.edu/
Officers:
    Chair: Sherry Linnell
Management:
    President: David Oxtoby
    Managing Director: James Taylor
Specialized Field: Musical; Comedy; Ethnic Theater; Classic; Contemporary
Status: For-Profit, Non-Professional
Paid Staff: 15
Paid Artists: 2
Budget: $9,000-14,000
Affiliations: ATHE
Seating Capacity: 330; 150
Year Built: 1992
Year Remodeled: 1998

2149
LAMB'S PLAYERS THEATRE

1142 Orange Avenue
PO Box 18229
Coronado, CA 92178
Mailing Address: Lamb's Players Theatre P.O. Box 182229
Phone: 619-437-6050
Fax: 619-437-6053
e-mail: ed.hofmeister@lambsplayers.org
Web Site: http://www.lambsplayers.org/index.html
Officers:
    Chairman: Lisa Ledri-Aguilar
Management:
    Producing Artistic Director: W Robert Smyth
    Associate Director: Kerry Meads
    Associate Director: Deborah Smyth
    Art Director: Christian Turner
    Director of Operations: Brian Andrews
    Director of Marketing: Ed Hofmeister
    Production Manager: Paul Eggington
Mission: To be a theatre that probes and questions the values and choices of contemporary culture. Celebrates the joys, strengths and diverse traditions of family and community. Explores the spiritual dimension of life.
Utilizes: Guest Companies; Singers
Founded: 1973
Specialized Field: Drama; Comedy
Status: Professional; Nonprofit
Income Sources: Theatre Communications Group; California Theatre Council
Performs At: Harder Stage; Hahn; Lyceum
Type of Stage: Thrust/Proscenium, Flexible
Seating Capacity: 350, 250, 200
Organization Type: Performing; Touring; Resident; Educational

2150
SOUTH COAST REPERTORY

Professional Resident Theatre
655 Town Center Drive
Costa Mesa, CA 92626
Mailing Address: PO Box 2197 Costa Mesa, CA 92628
Phone: 714-708-5500
Fax: 714-708-5522
e-mail: boxoffice@scr.org
Web Site: www.scr.org
Management:
    Producing Artistic Director: David Emmes
    Artistic Director: Martin Benson
    Managing Director: Paula Tomei
    Public Relations Director: Soyia Ellison
    Director Development: Susan Reeder
    Director Marketing/Communications: Bil Schroeder
Mission: Founded in the belief that theatre is an artform with a unique power to illuminate the human experience. Commit ourselves to exploring the most urgent human and social issues of time, and to merging literature, design and performance in ways that test the bounds of theatre's artistic possibilities.
Utilizes: Actors; AEA Actors; Artists-in-Residence; Choreographers; Collaborating Artists; Commissioned Composers; Commissioned Music; Designers; Five Seasonal Concerts; Grant Writers; Guest Accompanists; Guest Artists; Guest Companies; Guest Conductors; Guest Designers; Guest Lecturers; Guest Musicians; High School Drama; Multimedia; Music; Original Music Scores; Performance Artists; Poets; Resident Artists; Resident Professionals; Selected Students; Soloists; Student Interns; Special Technical Talent; Visual Arts
Founded: 1964
Specialized Field: Classical; Contemporary; Multicultural; New York; Student/Youth Programs; Theatre for Young Audiences
Status: Non-Profit, Professional
Paid Staff: 70
Paid Artists: 150
Budget: $9 Million
Income Sources: Ticket Sales; Annual Fund Campaign
Affiliations: American Arts Alliance, the League of Resident Theatres (IORT), Theatre Communications Group (TCG), and Arts Orange County
Annual Attendance: 14,000; 50,000
Facility Category: Folino Theatre Center
Type of Stage: Flexible; Proscenium; End Stage
Seating Capacity: 507; 336; 95
Year Built: 1978
Year Remodeled: 2002
Cost: $29 million
Rental Contact: Nelson Denniston
Organization Type: Performing; Touring; Resident; Educational

2151
THE ACTORS' GANG THEATER

9070 Venice Boulevard
The Ivy Substation
Culver City, CA 90232
Phone: 323-465-0566
Fax: 323-978-0011
e-mail: production@theactorsgang.com
Web Site: www.theactorsgang.com
Management:
    Artistic Director: Tim Robbins
    Managing Director: Gregg Reiner
Founded: 1981

Specialized Field: Drama; Comedy
Status: Non-Profit, Professional
Paid Staff: 4
Paid Artists: 85
Performs At: Actors' Gang Theater, Actors' Gang El Centro
Type of Stage: Flexible Stage
Seating Capacity: 99, 40

2152
KIRK DOUGLAS THEATRE

Center Theatre Group
9820 Washington Boulevard
Culver City, CA 90232
Mailing Address: 601 W Temple St Los Angeles, CA 90012
Phone: 213-628-2772
Fax: 213-972-0746
e-mail: tickets@ctgla.com
Web Site: www.centretheatregroup.org
Officers:
    Chairman: Martin Massman
    President: William H Ahmanson
    VP: Ava Fries
    Secretary: Martin C Washton
    Treasurer: Dr Steven Nagelberg
Management:
    Artistic Director: Michael Ritchie
    Managing Director: Charles Dillingham
Mission: To serve the diverse audiences of Los Angeles by producing and presenting theatre of the highest caliber, by nurturing new artists, by attracting new audiences, and by developing youth outreach and arts education programs. This mission is based on a belief that the art of theatre is a cultural force with the capacity to transform the lives of individuals and society at large.
Utilizes: Actors; AEA Actors; Arrangers; Artists-in-Residence; Choreographers; Collaborating Artists; Collaborations; Community Members; Contract Actors; Dancers; Designers; Educators; Equity Actors; Five Seasonal Concerts; Guest Accompanists; Guest Artists; Guest Companies; Guest Composers; Guest Conductors; Guest Designers; Guest Lecturers; Guest Musical Directors; Guest Teachers; Instructors; Local Artists; Local Artists & Directors; Local Unknown Artists; Lyricists; Multi Collaborations; Multimedia; Music; Organization Contracts; Original Music Scores; Paid Performers; Performance Artists; Poets; Resident Artists; Resident Companies; Resident Professionals; Scenic Designers; Selected Students; Sign Language Translators; Singers; Soloists; Students; Student Interns; Special Technical Talent; Theatre Companies; Touring Companies; Visual Arts; Visual Designers; Volunteer Directors & Actors; Writers
Opened: 2004
Specialized Field: Musical; Comedy; Drama
Status: Non-Profit; Professional
Paid Staff: 350
Performs At: Performing Arts Center of Los Angeles
Affiliations: Ahmanson Theatre; Mark Taper Forum
Annual Attendance: 250,000
Facility Category: Music Center of Los Angeles
Type of Stage: Proscenium
Stage Dimensions: 40Wx28H
Seating Capacity: 317
Year Built: 2004

2153
UNIVERSITY OF CALIFORNIA, DAVIS: DEPARTMENT OF DRAMATIC ART

University of California - Davis
222 Wright Hall, One Shields Avenue
Davis, CA 95616

Mailing Address: 222 Wright Hall, One Shields Avenue
Phone: 530-752-0888
Fax: 530-752-8818
Web Site: http://theatredance.ucdavis.edu/
Officers:
   Chair: Barbara Sellers
Management:
   Chair: Barbara Sellers Young
Specialized Field: Educational; Theater Workshops
Budget: $3,600-11,000
Affiliations: ATHE; Sacramento Theatre Company;
Tahoe Shakespeare Festival; Magic Theatre; B Street
Theatre
Seating Capacity: 470; 250; 220; 150
Year Built: 1967

2154
CHRISTIAN COMMUNITY THEATER

1545 Pioneer Way
El Cajon, CA 92020
Phone: 619-588-0206
Fax: 619-588-4384
Toll-free: 800-696-1929
e-mail: info@cctcyt.org
Web Site: www.cctcyt.org
Management:
   President: Sheryl Russell
   Artistic Director: Paul Russell
   Managing Director: Diane Moses
   Marketing Director: Charles W Patmon, Jr
   Managing Director: Diane Mosce
   Operations Director: Mary Mwanger
   Development Director: Sharon Milligan
   Expansion Director: Justin Parks
   Graphic Designer: Lynette Fisk
Mission: To produce quality wholesome family
entertainment and reflect Judeo-Christian values
through training in the arts; to provide a children's
theatre training program.
Utilizes: Actors
Founded: 1980
Specialized Field: Musical; Youth Theater; Community
Theater
Status: Non-Profit, Non-Professional
Paid Staff: 25
Volunteer Staff: 50
Paid Artists: 5
Non-paid Artists: 200
Budget: $2,000,000
Income Sources: Box Office; Tuition; Grants; Private
Donations
Performs At: Rented- Outdoor amphitheater and public
performance center
Affiliations: American Alliance for Theatre and
Education; Christians in Theater Arts
Annual Attendance: 50,000+

2155
WELK RESORT SAN DIEGO THEATRE

8860 Lawrence Walk Drive
Escondido, CA 92026
Phone: 760-749-3448
Fax: 760-749-9592
Toll-free: 888-802-7469
e-mail: box.office@welktheatre.com
Web Site: www.welktheatre.com
Management:
   General Manager: Sean Coogan
   Producer/Theatre Manager: Joshua Carr
Utilizes: AEA Actors
Founded: 1981
Specialized Field: Musical
Status: For-Profit, Professional
Paid Staff: 40

Paid Artists: 20
Income Sources: Actors' Equity Association
Performs At: The Welk Resort; San Diego Theatre
Facility Category: Broadway Style Dinner Theatre
Seating Capacity: 339
Organization Type: Performing

2156
FERNDALE REPERTORY THEATRE

447 Main Street
PO Box 892
Ferndale, CA 95536-0096
Phone: 707-786-5483
Fax: 707-786-5480
e-mail: info@ferndale-rep.org
Web Site: www.ferndale-rep.org
Management:
   Director: Marilyn McCormick
   Technical Director: Daniel L Lawrence
Mission: To provide North Coast residents and visitors
theatrical performances of the highest quality.
Utilizes: Actors; Designers; Five Seasonal Concerts;
Guest Accompanists; Guest Artists; Guest Companies;
Guest Conductors; Guest Designers; Guest
Ensembles; Guest Instructors; Guest Lecturers; Guest
Soloists; High School Drama; Instructors; Local Artists;
Multimedia; Resident Professionals; Singers; Soloists;
Student Interns
Founded: 1972
Specialized Field: Community Theater
Status: Non-Profit, Non-Professional
Paid Staff: 3
Budget: $160,000
Income Sources: Grants; Ticket sales; Membership
Performs At: Ferndale Repertory Theatre
Facility Category: Live Stage Productions
Type of Stage: Thrust Percenium
Seating Capacity: 265
Year Built: 1922
Year Remodeled: 1972
Organization Type: Performing

2157
CALIFORNIA STATE UNIVERSITY, FRESNO: THEATRE ARTS DEPARTMENT

5201 North Maple
Fresno, CA 93740
Phone: 559-278-3987
Fax: 559-278-7512
Web Site: www.csufresno.edu/theatre
Officers:
   Chair: Kathleen McKinley
Management:
   President: John Wealthy
   Executive Director: Kathleen McKinley
Founded: 1911
Specialized Field: Musical; Comedy; Youth Theater;
Ethnic Theater; Community Theater; Classic;
Contemporary
Status: For-Profit, Non-Professional
Budget: $2,900-4,900
Affiliations: NAST; ATHE
Seating Capacity: 360; 200; 100
Year Remodeled: 1991

2158
CALIFORNIA STATE UNIVERSITY, FULLERTON: DEPARTMENT OF THEATRE AND DANCE

800 N State College
Fullerton, CA 92834

Phone: 714-278-3628
Fax: 714-278-7041
Web Site: www.arts.fullerton.edu/events
Officers:
   Chair: Susan Hallman
Management:
   Chairperson: Susan Hallman
Founded: 1957
Specialized Field: Musical; Comedy; Youth Theater;
Classic; Contemporary
Status: Non-Profit, Non-Professional
Paid Staff: 47
Budget: $9000-23,650
Affiliations: NASD; NAST; ATHE; South Coast
Repertory; A Noise Within
Seating Capacity: 500; 200; 100
Year Remodeled: 2000

2159
VANGUARD THEATRE ENSEMBLE

120 A W Wilshire Avenue
Fullerton, CA 92832
Phone: 714-526-8007
Fax: 714-451-1372
Web Site: www.vte.org
Management:
   Artistic Director: Wade Williamson
   Managing Director: Paulette Kendall
   Ensemble Director: Jill Cary Martin
Founded: 1992
Specialized Field: Comedy; Youth Theater; Ethnic
Theater; Community Theater; Classic; Contemporary
Status: Non-Profit, Professional

2160
GROVE THEATRE CENTER

12852 Main Street
Garden Grove, CA 92840-5207
Phone: 714-741-9555
Fax: 714-741-9560
Management:
   Artistic Director: Kevin Cochran
   Executive Director: Charles Johanson
   Company Manager: Gigi Horowitz
   Casting Coordinator: Hunter Stevenson
   Production Manager: Gabin PanGriff
   Production Stage Manager: Zac Prostein
Utilizes: Actors; AEA Actors; Choreographers;
Commissioned Music; Dance Companies; Dancers;
Designers; Grant Writers; Guest Accompanists; Guest
Artists; Guest Companies; Guest Conductors; Guest
Designers; Guest Lecturers; Guest Teachers; Guild
Activities; Instructors; Local Artists; Music; Original
Music Scores; Performance Artists; Resident
Professionals; Selected Students; Student Interns;
Theatre Companies
Specialized Field: Musical; Comedy; Drama; Theater
Workshops
Status: Nonprofit
Budget: $350,000
Season: Year Round
Annual Attendance: 15,000
Stage Dimensions: 35'x45',60'x45',40'x35',30'x60'
Seating Capacity: 172, 548, 246, 98

2161
AMERICAN ACADEMY OF DRAMATIC ARTS/HOLLYWOOD

1336 N LaBrea Avenue
Hollywood, CA 90028

Phone: 323-464-2777
Fax: 323-464-1250
Toll-free: 800-222-2867
e-mail: officeassistant@ca.aada.org
Web Site: www.aada.org
Management:
    Managing Director, Los Angeles: Barbara Hodgen
    Director of Instruction: Theresa Hayes
Mission: To provide students with the tools needed to make acting their profession.
Founded: 1884
Specialized Field: Educational; Acting Course of Study
Status: Non-Profit, Private, Professional
Paid Staff: 23
Paid Artists: 40
Income Sources: Tuition; Donations
Affiliations: NAST; Middle State Commission on Higher Education
Facility Category: Black Box Theater
Type of Stage: Proscenium
Seating Capacity: 150
Year Built: 2000
Year Remodeled: 2006

2162
BLANK THEATRE COMPANY

6500 Santa Monica Boulevard
Hollywood, CA 90038
Mailing Address: 1301 Lucile Avenue, Los Angeles, CA. 90026
Phone: 323-662-7734
Fax: 323-661-3903
e-mail: info@theblank.com
Web Site: www.theblank.com
Management:
    President: Daniel Henning
    Artistic Producer: Noah Wyle
    Producer: Stacy Reed
Founded: 1990
Specialized Field: Musical; Comedy; Youth Theater; Classic; Contemporary
Status: Non-Profit, Professional
Paid Staff: 3
Paid Artists: 60

2163
HUDSON THEATRE

6539 Santa Monica Boulevard
Hollywood, CA 90038
Phone: 323-856-7012
Fax: 323-856-4829
e-mail: leigh@hudsontheatre.com
Management:
    Managing Director: Trevor Ysaguirr
    Theatre Manager: Sandra Kuker
    Technical Director: Christian Smith
    Artistic Director: Leigh McLeod Fortier
    Managing Director: Trevor Ysaguiree
Utilizes: Guest Companies; Singers
Founded: 1991
Specialized Field: Avant-garde; Drama
Status: Professional; Nonprofit
Performs At: Hudson Theatre (Mainstage, Avenue Theatre, Guild Theatre)
Type of Stage: Modified Thrust; Proscenium
Seating Capacity: 99; 99; 43
Organization Type: Producing in House

2164
OPEN FIST THEATRE COMPANY

1625 N La Brea Avenue
Hollywood, CA 90028
Mailing Address: 6209 Santa Monica Boulevard, Los Angeles 90038
Phone: 323-882-6912
e-mail: mdemson@openfist.org
Web Site: www.openfist.org
Management:
    Director of Development: Samantha Bennett
    Artistic Director: Martha Demson
    Managing Director: David Castellani
    Literary Manager: Laura Flanagan
Mission: The Open Fist Theatre Company is a community of actors, playwrights, designers and directors.
Founded: 1989
Specialized Field: Comedy; Ensembles; Drama
Status: Non-Profit, Professional

2165
STAGES THEATRE CENTER

1540 N McCadden Place
210 S Westgate Avenue
Hollywood, CA 90028
Phone: 323-465-1010
Fax: 323-462-2176
e-mail: e-mail@stagestheatre.org
Officers:
    Chairperson: Pompea Smith
    Treasurer: Sonia Lloveras
Management:
    Artistic Director: Paul Verdier
    Managing Director: Sonia Lloveras
Mission: To expose new or unfamiliar works or styles of theater to Los Angeles audiences; to host unique artists-in-residence who utilize distinctive theatrical styles, such as Theater of the Absurd and Commedia del' Arte.
Utilizes: Guest Companies
Founded: 1981
Specialized Field: Experimental
Status: Professional; Nonprofit
Paid Staff: 3
Income Sources: Theatre Communications Group
Performs At: Stages Theatre
Stage Dimensions: 14'x14'
Organization Type: Performing

2166
HUNTINGTON BEACH PLAYHOUSE

7111 Talbert Avenue
Huntington Beach, CA 92648
Phone: 714-375-0696
Fax: 714-375-0698
Web Site: www.hbph.com
Officers:
    President: Dawn Conant
    Treasurer: Don Stanton
    Secretary: BJ O'Rourke-Smith
Mission: As a non-profit organization dedicated to community educational and cultural enrichment in dramatic arts, Huntington Beach Playhouse presents dramatic productions, sponsors student scholarships and offers stagecraft workshops.
Utilizes: Guest Companies; Singers
Founded: 1963
Specialized Field: Drama; Comedy; Musical
Status: Non-Profit, Non-Professional
Paid Staff: 4
Volunteer Staff: 100
Non-paid Artists: 75
Income Sources: Ticket Sales
Performs At: Central Library Theatre
Annual Attendance: 27,000
Type of Stage: Proscenium
Seating Capacity: 319

Year Built: 1994
Organization Type: Performing

2167
UNIVERSITY OF CALIFORNIA-IRVINE: DEPARTMENT OF DRAMA

249 Drama
Irvine, CA 92697-2775
Phone: 949-824-6614
Fax: 949-824-3475
e-mail: drama@uci.edu
Web Site: drama.arts.uci.edu
Officers:
    Chair: Eli Simon
Management:
    Information Coordinator: Marcus Beeman
Utilizes: Actors; Arrangers; Choreographers; Collaborating Artists; Composers; Dancers; Designers; Educators; Grant Writers; Guest Accompanists; Guest Artists; Guest Companies; Guest Conductors; Guest Designers; Guest Directors; Guest Instructors; Guest Musical Directors; Guest Soloists; Guest Speakers; Guest Teachers; Guest Writers; High School Drama; Instructors; Local Artists & Directors; Lyricists; Multi Collaborations; Multimedia; Music; Organization Contracts; Original Music Scores; Performance Artists; Resident Professionals; Scenic Designers; Soloists; Student Interns; Touring Companies; Visual Arts; Volunteer Directors & Actors; Writers
Founded: 1965
Specialized Field: Drama; Music Theater; Acting; Design (Costume, Lighting, Scene, Sound), Directing, Stage Management, Doctoral (PhD) Studies
Paid Staff: 30
Paid Artists: 20
Budget: $10,050-49,050
Affiliations: U/RTA;ATHE; South Coast Repertory
Facility Category: 6 Theaters, 2 Studios
Seating Capacity: Variable
Year Built: 1970
Rental Contact: Toby Wwiner

2168
PINE HILLS LODGE AND DINNER THEATRE

2960 La Posada Way
Julian, CA 92036
Phone: 760-765-1100
Fax: 760-765-1121
e-mail: events@pinehillslodge.com
Web Site: www.pinehillslodge.com
Founded: 2003
Specialized Field: Dinner Theater
Status: For-Profit, Professional

2169
KIDS 4 BROADWAY

PO Box 122
Kelseyville, CA 95451
Phone: 707-277-7550
Fax: 707-277-7557
e-mail: kidsplay@pacific.net
Mission: Offers a unique opportunity for a school or community to create love, laughter and magic in their childrens lives.
Specialized Field: Children's Theater; Educational

2170
LA JOLLA PLAYHOUSE

2910 La Jolla Villiage Drive
PO Box 12039
La Jolla, CA 92039

Phone: 858-550-1070
Fax: 858-550-1075
Web Site: www.lajollaplayhouse.com
Management:
   Executive Director: Terry Dwyer
   Artistic Director: Des McAnuff
   Literary Manager: Alison Horsley
Mission: Producing bold, innovative, adventurous theater; offering a summer home to America's leading theater artists.
Utilizes: Guest Companies; Singers
Founded: 1947
Specialized Field: Drama; Comedy; Musical
Status: Non-Profit, Professional
Paid Staff: 70
Paid Artists: 100
Income Sources: Actors' Equity Association; League of Resident Theatres; Theatre Communications Group
Season: April - December
Performs At: La Jolla Playhouse; Mandell Weiss Performing Arts
Type of Stage: Proscenium/Thrust
Seating Capacity: 500, 400
Organization Type: Touring; Resident; Educational

2171
UNIVERSITY OF CALIFORNIA-SAN DIEGO: DEPARTMENT OF THEATRE AND DANCE

9500 Gilman Drive
La Jolla, CA 92093
Phone: 858-534-3791
Fax: 858-534-1080
e-mail: theatrefrontdesk@ucsd.edu
Web Site: www.theatre.ucsd.edu
Officers:
   Department Chair: Allison Greene
   MSO: Mark Maltby
Founded: 1973
Specialized Field: Comedy; Youth Theater; Ethnic Theater; Community Theater; Classic; Contemporary
Status: Non-Profit, Non-Professional
Paid Staff: 33
Budget: $3,600-24,000
Performs At: Mandell Weiss Theater
Affiliations: ATHE; The La Jolla Playhouse
Seating Capacity: 500; 400; 100
Year Built: 1982

2172
UNIVERSITY OF LAVERNE

1950 Third Street
LaVerne, CA 91750
Phone: 909-593-3511
Fax: 909-392-2787
e-mail: tcisneros@ulv.edu
Web Site: www.ulv.edu
Officers:
   Chair: Elizabeth Pietrzak
Management:
   President: Steve Morgan
   VP: Thil Hawkey
Founded: 1891
Specialized Field: Educational; Theater Workshops
Status: Non-Profit, Non-Professional
Budget: $550-14,000
Affiliations: U/RTA; ATHE; The Guilford School of Acting (England); The Split International Theatre Festival (Croatia)
Seating Capacity: 175-250; 60; 475
Year Built: 1972

2173
LAGUNA PLAYHOUSE

606 Laguna Canyon Road
PO Box 1747
Laguna Beach, CA 92652-1747
Phone: 949-497-2787
Fax: 949-376-8185
Web Site: www.LagunaPlayhouse.com
Management:
   Executive Director: Richard Stein
   Artistic Director: Andrew Barnicle
   Managing Director: Kate Hicklin
   Youth Theatre Director: Joe Lauderdale
   Production Manager: Jim Ryan
   Business Manager: Kat Hiclklin
   Corporate Development Manager: Elaine Smith
   Systems Administrator: Deborah Purnell
   Telephone Sales Manager: June Rodgers
Mission: Committed to excellence in professional theatre.
Founded: 1920
Specialized Field: Musical; Comedy; Youth Theater; Ethnic Theater; Contemporary; Children's Theater
Status: Non-Profit, Professional
Paid Staff: 150
Paid Artists: 20
Income Sources: Inter-theatre Institute; American Association of Theatre Educators
Performs At: Moulton Theater
Organization Type: Performing; Educational

2174
CALIFORNIA REPERTORY COMPANY

1250 Bellflower Boulevard
Long Beach, CA 90840-2701
Phone: 562-985-1953
Fax: 562-985-2263
e-mail: publicrelations@calrep.org
Web Site: http://www.calrep.org/
Management:
   Managing Director: Eric Imley
   Artistic Producing Director: Joanne Gordon
   Founder: Howard Burman
   Technical Director: Jeff Hickman
Founded: 1989
Specialized Field: Educational; Theater Workshops
Performs At: UT Theatre, Studio Theatre, Edison Theatre, Players Theatre
Type of Stage: Proscenium, Flexible
Seating Capacity: 400, 225, 99, 90

2175
CALIFORNIA STATE UNIVERSITY, LONG BEACH: DEPARTMENT OF THEATRE

1250 Bellflower Boulevard
Long Beach, CA 90840
Phone: 562-985-5357
Fax: 562-985-2263
Web Site: www.csulb.edu
Officers:
   Chairman: Howard Burman
Management:
   Department Chairman: Joanne Gordon
   Managing Director: Eric Imley
Specialized Field: Educational; Theater Workshops
Status: Non-Profit, Non-Professional
Affiliations: NAST; California Repertory Company
Seating Capacity: 378; 250; 90; 99
Year Built: 1952
Year Remodeled: 1989

2176
FOUND THEATRE

599 Long Beach Blvd. at 6th St.
Long Beach, CA 90813
Phone: 562-433-3363
e-mail: info@foundtheatre.org
Web Site: http://www.foundtheatre.org/
Management:
   Artistic Managing Director: Cynthia Galles
   Literary Director: Virginia DeMoss
   Music Director: Alice Secrist
Mission: To provide professional-quality alternative theatre to the community as inexpensively as possible; to provide a place for actors, directors, and technicians to experiment, refine their craft, and grow as artists.
Founded: 1974
Specialized Field: Drama; Comedy; Musical
Status: Professional; Nonprofit
Performs At: The Found Theatre
Organization Type: Performing

2177
MYART

6285 East Spring Street
Long Beach, CA 90808
Toll-free: 800-400-2985
Web Site: http://www.myart.org/
Management:
   Artistic Director: Dana Hanstein-Hanlan
Mission: Providing instruction and performance experience in acting, singing, dancing, and stage movement. The program is endorsed as an excellent venue for training in the fine arts by a host of primary and secondary educators and by numerous entertainment professionals and by the Theatre Department at California State University.
Founded: 1989
Specialized Field: Youth Theater; Musical; Educational

2178
BUS BARN STAGE COMPANY

97 Hillview Avenue
PO Box 151
Los Altos, CA 94023-0151
Phone: 650-941-0551
Fax: 650-941-0884
e-mail: busbarn@busbarn.org
Web Site: www.busbarn.org
Officers:
   President: Vicki Reeder
   Secretary: Roy Lave
   Treasure: Chet Frankenfield
Management:
   President: Vicki Reeder
   Box Office Manager: Debbie Wells
   Artistic Director: Barbara Canon
   Production Manager and Publicist: Nichole Hamilton
Mission: To engage the community and the artists in a shared experience of intimate, professional-quality theatre. Bus Barn is a professionally managed, community based theatre company serving Los Altos, and the greater South Bay community.
Utilizes: Actors; Guest Artists; Guest Conductors; Guest Lecturers; Original Music Scores; Resident Professionals
Founded: 1995
Specialized Field: Drama; Musical
Status: Nonprofit
Paid Staff: 5
Budget: $260,000
Income Sources: Box Office; Grants; Individual donations

Performs At: Bus Barn Theatre
Affiliations: Theatre Bay Area
Annual Attendance: 7,000
Type of Stage: Proscenium
Seating Capacity: 100
Year Built: 1965
Year Remodeled: 1980

2179
A NOISE WITHIN
234 South Brand Boulevard
Los Angeles, CA 91204
Phone: 818-240-0910
Fax: 818-240-0826
e-mail: pr@anoisewithin.org
Web Site: www.anoisewithin.org
Management:
 Artistic Director/ Founder: Geoff Elliott
 Production Manager: Rebecca Baillie
 Artistic Director/ Founder: Julia Rodriquez
 General Manager: Todd Delliger
 Public Relations: Laura Stegman
 Public Relations: Libby Heubner
Mission: To present the classics of world literature in rotating repertory performed by a classically trained ensemble.
Founded: 1991
Specialized Field: Comedy; Youth Theater
Status: Non-Profit, Professional
Paid Staff: 11
Paid Artists: 35
Type of Stage: Thrust
Seating Capacity: 200 - 300

2180
ACTORS ART THEATRE
6128 Wilshire Boulevard
Los Angeles, CA 90048
Phone: 323-969-4953
Fax: 323-857-5891
e-mail: info@actorsart.com
Web Site: http://www.actorsart.com
Management:
 Artistic Director: Jolene Adams
 Managing Director: Douglas Coler
 Facility Manager: Grady Lee Richmond
Specialized Field: Theater Workshops; Ensembles

2181
ACTORS FOR THEMSELVES
Matrix Theatre
7657 Melrose Avenue
Los Angeles, CA 90048
Phone: 213-852-1445
Management:
 Artistic Director: Joe Stern
Mission: Giving actors a chance to hone their craft and affording them more opportunity to control the production process.
Utilizes: Guest Companies; Singers
Founded: 1974
Specialized Field: Theater Workshops; Drama; Movement Theater
Status: Professional; Nonprofit
Performs At: Matrix Theatre
Organization Type: Performing; Resident; Educational

2182
AHMANSON THEATRE
Center Theatre Group
135 N Grand Avenue
Los Angeles, CA 90012
Mailing Address: 601 W Temple St Los Angeles CA 90012
Phone: 213-628-2772
Fax: 213-972-7431
Web Site: www.centertheatregroup.com
Officers:
 Chairperson: Martin Massman
 President: William A Ahmanson
 VP: Ava Fries
 Secretary: Martin C Washton
Management:
 Artistic Director: Michael Ritchie
 Managing Director: Charles Dillingham
Mission: To serve the diverse audiences of Los Angeles by producing and presenting theatre of the highest caliber, by nurturing new artists, by attracting new audiences, and by developing youth outreach and arts education programs. This mission is based on a belief that the art of theatre is a cultural force with the capacity to transform the lives of individuals and society at large.
Utilizes: Actors; AEA Actors; Arrangers; Artists-in-Residence; Choreographers; Collaborating Artists; Collaborations; Community Members; Dancers; Designers; Educators; Equity Actors; Five Seasonal Concerts; Guest Accompanists; Guest Artists; Guest Companies; Guest Composers; Guest Conductors; Guest Designers; Guest Lecturers; Guest Musical Directors; Guest Teachers; Instructors; Local Artists; Local Artists & Directors; Local Unknown Artists; Lyricists; Multi Collaborations; Multimedia; Music; Organization Contracts; Original Music Scores; Paid Performers; Performance Artists; Poets; Resident Artists; Resident Companies; Resident Professionals; Scenic Designers; Selected Students; Sign Language Translators; Singers; Soloists; Students; Student Interns; Special Technical Talent; Theatre Companies; Touring Companies; Visual Arts; Visual Designers; Volunteer Directors & Actors; Writers
Founded: 1967
Opened: 1967
Specialized Field: Musical; Drama; Comedy
Status: Non-Profit; Professional
Performs At: Music Center of Los Angeles
Affiliations: Mark Taper Forum. Kirk Douglas Theatre
Facility Category: Music Center of Los Angeles
Type of Stage: Proscenium
Stage Dimensions: 190Wx47Dx67H; 40Wx28H
Seating Capacity: 1,600-2,000
Year Built: 1967
Year Remodeled: 1995
Rental Contact: Gordon Davidson

2183
ATTIC THEATRE CENTRE
5429 W Washington Boulevard
Los Angeles, CA 90016-1112
Phone: 323-525-0600
e-mail: info@attictheatre.org
Web Site: www.attictheatre.org
Management:
 Executive Producer: James Carey
 Artistic Director: August Vivirito
 Managing Producer: T L Kolman
 VP: John Szura
Mission: To provide a small theatre with its own resident company which is also available for rental to outside productions.
Utilizes: Singers
Founded: 1995
Specialized Field: Theater Workshops; Ensembles; Experimental
Status: Professional; Semi-Professional; Commercial
Income Sources: Theatre Los Angeles

Organization Type: Performing; Resident; Sponsoring

2184
BILINGUAL FOUNDATION OF THE ARTS
421 N Avenue 19
Los Angeles, CA 90031
Phone: 323-225-4044
Fax: 323-225-1250
Web Site: www.bfatheatre.org
Officers:
 Chairman: John Echeveste
Management:
 Artistic Director: Margarita Galban
 Managing Director: Luisa Cariaga
 Associate Professor: Estela Scarlata
Mission: Celebrating the richness and diversity of Hispanic Theater by offering theatre produced and directed in English and Spanish.
Utilizes: Guest Companies
Founded: 1973
Specialized Field: Classic; Ensembles; Spanish Language Company
Status: Non-Profit, Professional
Paid Staff: 6
Performs At: The Bilingual Foundation of the Arts Theatre
Affiliations: American Arts Alliance; Theatre Communications Group; California Confederation of the Arts
Annual Attendance: 125,000
Type of Stage: Thrust
Seating Capacity: 99 & 299
Organization Type: Performing; Touring; Educational

2185
BOB BAKER MARIONETTE THEATRE
1345 W First Street
Los Angeles, CA 90026
Phone: 215-250-9995
Fax: 213-250-1120
e-mail: bob@bobbakermarionettes.com
Web Site: http://www.bobbakermarionettes.com/
Mission: Marionette productions available for birthday parties and shop tours.
Utilizes: Soloists; Student Interns
Founded: 1963
Specialized Field: Puppet
Status: Professional
Income Sources: Admissions
Performs At: Marionette Theatre
Type of Stage: Proscenium; 3/4 Arena
Seating Capacity: 200
Year Built: 1950
Year Remodeled: 1963
Organization Type: Resident

2186
CALIFORNIA STATE UNIVERSITY-LOS ANGELES - PLAYERS
5151 State University Drive
Los Angeles, CA 90032
Phone: 323-343-4110
e-mail: srothma@exchange.calstatela.edu
Web Site: www.calstatela.edu
Management:
 Chair/Professor Of Theatre Arts: Stephen Rothman
 Assistant Professor Of Theatre Arts: Meredith Greenburg
Founded: 1947
Specialized Field: Educational; Theater Workshops

2187

CORNERSTONE THEATER COMPANY

708 Traction Avenue
Los Angeles, CA 90013
Phone: 213-613-1700
Fax: 213-613-1714
Management:
Founding Director: Alison Carey
Program Associate: Teeko Parran
Founded: 1986
Specialized Field: Multi-Cultural; Ensembles;
Contemporary; Drama
Status: Nonprofit
Season: Year Round

2188

EAST WEST PLAYERS

120 N Judge John Aiso Street
Los Angeles, CA 90012
Phone: 213-625-7000
Fax: 213-625-7111
e-mail: info@eastwestplayers.org
Web Site: www.eastwestplayers.org
Officers:
Chairperson: Lynn Fukuhara Arthurs
President: Wendy Fujihara Anderson
Vice President: Chirag Shah
Chief Financial Officer: David Solin Lee
Management:
PR/Marketing Manager: Jay Africa
Mission: To be a leader in creating engaging, and
empowering theatre that gives voice to the Asian Pacific
Islander community.
Utilizes: Actors; AEA Actors; Artists-in-Residence;
Choreographers; Collaborating Artists; Collaborations;
Commissioned Composers; Dancers; Designers;
Educators; Five Seasonal Concerts; Grant Writers;
Guest Accompanists; Guest Artists; Guest
Choreographers; Guest Companies; Guest Composers;
Guest Conductors; Guest Designers; Guest
Ensembles; Guest Instructors; Guest Lecturers; Guest
Musical Directors; Guest Musicians; Guest Soloists;
Guest Teachers; High School Drama; Instructors; Local
Artists; Local Unknown Artists; Lyricists; Multimedia;
Music; Organization Contracts; Original Music Scores;
Performance Artists; Playwrights; Poets; Selected
Students; Sign Language Translators; Singers; Soloists;
Student Interns; Special Technical Talent; Theatre
Companies; Visual Arts
Founded: 1965
Specialized Field: Drama; Musical
Status: Professional; Nonprofit
Paid Staff: 10
Volunteer Staff: 300
Paid Artists: 50
Non-paid Artists: 50
Budget: $1,000,000
Annual Attendance: 30,000
Facility Category: Theater
Type of Stage: Open/Modified Proscenium
Seating Capacity: 240
Year Built: 1922
Year Remodeled: 1997
Rental Contact: Meg Imamoto
Organization Type: Performing; Touring; Resident;
Educational

2189

EBONY SHOWCASE THEATRE

1285 S La Brea Avenue
Los Angeles, CA 90019
Mailing Address: Suite 203
Phone: 323-965-8837
Fax: 323-965-0420
Web Site: www.ebonyshowcase.org
Management:
Founder/Managing Director: Nick Stewart
Founder/Managing Director: Edna Stewart
Mission: To promote cultural enrichment and education
through entertainment.
Utilizes: Guest Companies
Founded: 1950
Specialized Field: Drama; Musical; Multi-Cultural
Status: Semi-Professional; Nonprofit
Performs At: Ebony Showcase Theatre
Organization Type: Performing; Resident

2190

FOUNTAIN THEATRE

5060 Fountain Avenue
Los Angeles, CA 90029
Phone: 323-663-2235
Fax: 323-663-1629
e-mail: info@fountaintheatre.com
Web Site: www.fountaintheatre.com
Management:
Producing Director/Dramaturg: Simon Levy
Producing Artistic Director: Deborah Lawlor
Managing Artistic Director: Stephen Sachs
Mission: A full season of theatre and flamenco.
Founded: 1990
Specialized Field: Theatre; Dance
Status: Non-Profit, Professional
Paid Staff: 5
Paid Artists: 45
Budget: 450,000
Performs At: Fountain Theatre
Affiliations: TCG; Theatre
Type of Stage: Thrust
Seating Capacity: 78

2191

GEFFEN PLAYHOUSE

11693 San Vicente Boulevard
#816
Los Angeles, CA 90049-5105
Phone: 310-208-6500
Fax: 310-208-0341
e-mail: boxoffice@geffenplayhouse.com
Web Site: www.geffenplayhouse.com
Officers:
General Manager: Paul Morer
Management:
President: Gilbert Cates
Artistic Director: Randall Arney
Managing Director: Stephen Eich
General Manager: Behnaz Ataee
Mission: To produce quality theatre in a broad range of
presentations of many moods and characters; to
present comedy, drama, musicals, new plays, revivals,
classics, experimental children's theatre, special
events, multimedia.
Utilizes: Guest Companies; Singers
Founded: 1995
Specialized Field: Drama; Comedy; Musical; Youth
Theater; New Plays
Status: Non-Profit
Performs At: Geffen Playhouse
Type of Stage: Proscenium
Seating Capacity: 498
Organization Type: Performing; Resident

2192

GREEK THEATRE

2700 N Vermont Avenue
Los Angeles, CA 90027
Phone: 323-665-1927
e-mail: yourcontact@greektheatrela.com
Web Site: www.greektheatrela.com
Management:
President: James N Landrella
General Manager: Susan Rosenbluth
Mission: Presenting a variety of Broadway plays,
concerts and comedy.
Utilizes: Singers
Founded: 1930
Specialized Field: Musical; Ethnic Theater
Status: Commercial
Performs At: Greek Theatre
Organization Type: Performing

2193

GROUNDLING THEATRE

7307 Melrose Avenue
Los Angeles, CA 90046
Phone: 323-934-4747
Fax: 323-934-8143
e-mail: staff@groundlings.com
Web Site: www.groundlings.com
Officers:
Business Director: Anesta Almonor
Management:
Executive Director: Eric Vennerbeck
Mission: To create new comedy talent and new
comedy productions.
Founded: 1974
Specialized Field: Comedy; Improvisation
Status: Nonprofit
Paid Staff: 5
Volunteer Staff: 15
Non-paid Artists: 30
Income Sources: Shows; Donations; School of
Improvitional Comedy
Performs At: The Groundling Theatre
Annual Attendance: 20,000
Seating Capacity: 99
Organization Type: Performing; Resident

2194

HOLLYWOOD COMPLEX THEATRE

6476 Santa Monica Boulevard
Los Angeles, CA 90038
Phone: 323-465-0383
Fax: 323-469-5408
Web Site: www.complexhollywood.com
Management:
Owner: Matt Chait
Assistant: Ryan Callahan
Utilizes: Actors; AEA Actors; Guest Instructors; High
School Drama; Resident Artists; Resident
Professionals; Student Interns; Special Technical Talent
Founded: 1990
Specialized Field: Drama; Comedy
Status: For-Profit, Non-Professional
Paid Staff: 2
Facility Category: 5 Theaters
Type of Stage: 4 Proscenium, 1 Black Box
Seating Capacity: 42-55
Cost: $150-225 per night
Rental Contact: Matt Ryan
Organization Type: Performing

2195

LOS ANGELES THEATRE CENTER: MOVING ARTS

514 S Spring Street
Los Angeles, CA 90013-2304
Phone: 213-622-8906
Fax: 213-622-8946
e-mail: info@movingarts.org
Web Site: www.movingarts.org
Management:
Director: J Hobart
Artistic Director: Kimberly Glann
Literary Director: Trey Nichols
Administrative Director: David Davidson
Mission: Providing professional training to students in theatre arts and supporting this training through professional-level productions.
Utilizes: Singers
Founded: 1992
Specialized Field: Drama; Movement Theater
Paid Staff: 1
Budget: 1,600-8,500
Income Sources: Equity-Waiver; Los Angeles Theatre Alliance; SCETA; American College Theatre Festival
Seating Capacity: 312; 99
Year Built: 1965
Organization Type: Performing; Educational

2196

LOS ANGELES THEATRE CENTER: MOVING ARTS

514 S Spring Street
Los Angeles, CA 90013-2304
Phone: 213-622-8906
Fax: 213-622-8946
e-mail: info@movingarts.org
Web Site: www.movingarts.org
Management:
Artistic Director: Lee Wochner
Artistic Director: Julie Briggs
Literary Director: Trey Nichols
Administrative Director: David Davidson
Mission: We produce new plays that challenge, illuminate, and reveal truths about the human condition in a fresh and startling way.
Utilizes: Actors
Founded: 1992
Specialized Field: Drama; Movement Theater
Paid Staff: 1
Volunteer Staff: 3
Non-paid Artists: 28

2197

LOYOLA MARYMOUNT UNIVERSITY THEATRE ARTS DEPARTMENT

Los Angeles, CA 90045
Phone: 310-338-2837
Web Site: http://cfa.lmu.edu/programs/theatre.htm
Management:
Chair/Theatre Arts Program: Diane Benedict
Specialized Field: Educational; Theater Workshops
Affiliations: NAST; ATHE
Seating Capacity: 174; 100
Year Built: 1961

2198

MARK TAPER FORUM

Center Theatre Group
601 W Temple Street
Los Angeles, CA 90012

Phone: 213-628-2772
Fax: 213-628-2796
e-mail: tickets@ctgla.com
Web Site: www.centretheatregroup.org
Officers:
Chairman: Martin Massman
President: William H Ahmanson
VP: Ava Fries
Secretary: Martin C Washton
Treasurer: Dr Steven Nagelberg
Management:
Artistic Director: Michael Ritchie
Managing Director: Charles Dillingham
Mission: To serve the diverse audiences of Los Angeles by producing and presenting theatre of the highest caliber, by nurturing new artists, by attracting new audiences, and by developing youth outreach and arts education programs. This mission is based on a belief that the art of theatre is a cultural force with the capacity to transform the lives of individuals and society at large.
Utilizes: Actors; AEA Actors; Arrangers; Artists-in-Residence; Choreographers; Collaborating Artists; Collaborations; Community Members; Contract Actors; Dancers; Designers; Educators; Equity Actors; Five Seasonal Concerts; Guest Accompanists; Guest Artists; Guest Companies; Guest Composers; Guest Conductors; Guest Designers; Guest Lecturers; Guest Musical Directors; Guest Teachers; Instructors; Local Artists; Local Artists & Directors; Local Unknown Artists; Lyricists; Multi Collaborations; Multimedia; Music; Organization Contracts; Original Music Scores; Paid Performers; Performance Artists; Poets; Resident Artists; Resident Companies; Resident Professionals; Scenic Designers; Selected Students; Sign Language Translators; Singers; Soloists; Students; Student Interns; Special Technical Talent; Theatre Companies; Touring Companies; Visual Arts; Visual Designers; Volunteer Directors & Actors; Writers
Founded: 1967
Opened: 1967
Specialized Field: Musical; Comedy; Drama
Status: Non-Profit; Professional
Paid Staff: 350
Performs At: Performing Arts Center of Los Angeles
Affiliations: Ahmanson Theatre; Kirk Douglas Theatre
Annual Attendance: 250,000
Facility Category: Music Center of Los Angeles
Type of Stage: Thrust
Stage Dimensions: 190Wx47Dx67H; 40Wx28H
Seating Capacity: 739
Year Built: 1967
Year Remodeled: 2008

2199

MOVING ARTS AT THE LOS ANGELES THEATRE CENTER

514 S Spring Street
Los Angeles, CA 90013-2304
Phone: 925-938-3300
Fax: 925-938-3300
e-mail: info@movingarts.org
Web Site: www.movingarts.org
Officers:
VP: Connie Leonard
Secretary: Darrell Kunitomi
Management:
Artistic Director: Kimberley Glann
Literary Director: Terry Nichols
Mission: Moving Arts is committed to producing high quality presentations of orginal dramas and comedies that are bold, challenging, edgy and relevant to the community
Founded: 1992

Specialized Field: Drama; Movement Theater
Paid Staff: 1
Volunteer Staff: 6
Budget: $79,000
Income Sources: Ticket Sales; Individual Donars; Government Grants
Annual Attendance: 1200
Type of Stage: Black Box
Seating Capacity: 51

2200

NINE O'CLOCK PLAYERS

1367 N St. Andrews Place
Los Angeles, CA 90028
Phone: 323-469-1970
Fax: 323-469-1443
Web Site: www.nineoclockplayers.com
Officers:
Chairman: Sue Leisner
Chairman/Production: Tricia Schaetzle
Mission: To provide free musical theater for culturally and physically disadvantaged children as well as paid performances for all children of Southern California; to donate proceeds to the services of the Assistance League of Southern California.
Utilizes: Commissioned Composers; Designers; Guest Companies; Music; Organization Contracts; Resident Professionals; Student Interns; Visual Arts
Founded: 1929
Specialized Field: Musical; Ensembles; Children's Theater; Classic Fairy Tales
Status: Semi-Professional; Nonprofit
Paid Staff: 4
Volunteer Staff: 145
Budget: $100,000
Income Sources: Donations; Tickets
Performs At: ALSC Playhouse
Affiliations: Assistance League of Southern California
Annual Attendance: 17,000
Facility Category: Theatre
Seating Capacity: 329
Year Built: 1938
Rental Contact: 323-469-1973 Janet Harrison
Organization Type: Performing; Touring

2201

OCCIDENTAL COLLEGE DEPARTMENT OF THEATRE

1600 Campus Road
1600 Campus Road
Los Angeles, CA 90041
Phone: 213-259-2771
Fax: 213-341-4987
e-mail: beatrice@oxy.edu
Officers:
Chair: Susan Gratch
Specialized Field: Educational; Theater Workshops
Budget: $4,400-6,800
Seating Capacity: 400
Year Built: 1988

2202

ODYSSEY THEATRE ENSEMBLE

2055 S Sepulveda Boulevard
Los Angeles, CA 90025
Phone: 310-477-2055
Fax: 310-444-0455
Web Site: www.odysseytheatre.com
Officers:
President: Sol Rabin
Secretary: Ben Olan
VP: David Simon
Treasurer: Fred Mantner
Management:

Artistic Director: Ron Sossi
Associate Artistic Director: Beth Hogan
Production Manager: Christina Burck
Associate Artistic Director: Beth Hogan
Mission: The creation of a theatre centre which is experimental and alternative and houses an ensemble company; the development of an international theatre center.
Utilizes: Guest Companies; Singers
Founded: 1969
Specialized Field: Ensembles; Ethnic Theater
Status: Non-Profit, Professional
Paid Staff: 14
Volunteer Staff: 86
Paid Artists: 126
Budget: $700,000
Income Sources: Theatre Consortium (Los Angeles Theatre Pass); League of Producers; Theatres of Los Angeles; Los Angeles Theatre Alliance; Theatre Communications Group
Performs At: Odyssey Theatre
Annual Attendance: 2000
Seating Capacity: 99
Rental Contact: Stephanie Meyer
Organization Type: Performing; Resident; Sponsoring

2203
PLAYWRIGHTS' ARENA

514 S Spring Street
Los Angeles, CA 90013
Phone: 213-473-0650
Fax: 213-473-0620
e-mail: jrivera923@juno.com
Management:
Artistic Director: Jon Lawrence Rivera
Mission: Dedicated to discovering, nurturing and producing bold new works for the stage written exclusively by Los Angeles playwrights. Develops new materials through several series of readings, workshops and round table discussions. Local playwrights are encouraged to create original, adventurous, daring materials with the intent of challenging the mind, touching the heart and provoking the spirit.
Founded: 1992
Specialized Field: New Plays
Status: Nonprofit
Season: January - December
Type of Stage: Proscenium
Seating Capacity: 35

2204
ROBEY THEATRE COMPANY

514 S Spring Street
(Los Angeles)
Los Angeles, CA 90013
Phone: 213-489-7402
Fax: 213-489-4520
e-mail: robeytc@sbcglobal.net
Web Site:
http://www.robeytheatrecompany.com/home.php
Management:
Artistic Director/ Co-Founder/ Boar: Bennet Guillory
Co-Founder: Danny Glover
Development Director: Judith Bowman
Board Secretary: Diana Smith
Treasurer: Sarisa Middleton
Founded: 1994
Specialized Field: African American; Multi-Cultural

2205
THEATRE WEST

3333 Cahuenga Boulevard W
Los Angeles, CA 90068
Phone: 323-851-4839
Fax: 323-851-5286
e-mail: theatrewest@theatrewest.org
Web Site: www.theatrewest.org
Management:
President: Jill Jones
Executive Director: John Gallogly
Artistic Moderator: Don Moore
Mission: Conducting weekly theater workshops; producing several plays annually; enhancing the cultural life of the community.
Utilizes: Actors; AEA Actors; Collaborations; Five Seasonal Concerts; Guest Companies; Multimedia; Organization Contracts; Original Music Scores; Performance Artists; Resident Professionals; Sign Language Translators; Visual Arts
Founded: 1962
Specialized Field: Musical; Comedy; Youth Theater; Community Theater; Classic; Contemporary
Status: Non-Profit, Professional
Paid Staff: 3
Volunteer Staff: 100
Paid Artists: 20
Income Sources: Dues; fund-raisers; grants; donations, ticket sales
Performs At: Theatre West
Annual Attendance: 19,000
Facility Category: Non-profit
Seating Capacity: 168
Organization Type: Performing; Resident; Educational

2206
UNIVERSITY OF CALIFORNIA-LOS ANGELES: DEPARTMENT OF THEATER

102 E Melnitz
Box 951622
Los Angeles, CA 90095
Phone: 310-825-7008
Fax: 310-825-3383
e-mail: info@tft.ucla.edu
Web Site: www.tft.ucla.edu
Management:
Chancellor: Albert Carnesale
Chairman of Theatre Department: William Ward
Founded: 1919
Specialized Field: Educational; Theater Workshops
Status: Non-Profit, Non-Professional
Paid Staff: 3
Paid Artists: 50
Budget: $7,100-22,500
Affiliations: Geffen Playhouse
Seating Capacity: 589; 200; 100
Year Built: 1963

2207
UNIVERSITY OF SOUTHERN CALIFORNIA: SCHOOL OF THEATRE

1029 Childs Way
Los Angeles, CA 90089-0791
Phone: 213-821-2744
Fax: 213-740-8888
e-mail: thtrinfo@usc.edu
Management:
Dean: Madeline Puzo
Founded: 1945
Specialized Field: Educational; Theater Workshops
Affiliations: 24th Street Theatre
Seating Capacity: 575; 99; 60
Year Built: 1965

2208
WEST COAST ENSEMBLE

PO Box 868
Los Angeles, CA 91408
Phone: 818-786-1900
Fax: 818-786-1905
e-mail: wcemgmt@aol.com
Web Site: www.wcensemble.org
Management:
Artistic Director and Founder: Les Hanson
Literary Associate: Don Cummings
Founded: 1981
Specialized Field: Musical; Comedy; Drama

2209
WILTERN THEATRE

3790 Wilshire Boulevard
Los Angeles, CA 90010
Phone: 213-388-4005
Fax: 213-388-1400
Management:
General Manager: Rena Wasserman
Specialized Field: Contemporary; Specialty Acts

2210
ZEPHYR THEATRE

7456 Melrose Avenue
Los Angeles, CA 90046
Phone: 323-653-4667
Fax: 323-852-0031
e-mail: thezephyr@aol.com
Management:
Managing Director: Linda Toliver
Technical Director: Gary Guidinger
Mission: Providing a rental venue for independent producers to mount shows.
Utilizes: Guest Companies
Founded: 1977
Specialized Field: Light Theater
Status: For-Profit, Professional
Paid Staff: 2
Income Sources: Los Angeles League of Theaters & Producers
Performs At: Zephyr Theatre
Organization Type: Performing

2211
MENDOCINO THEATRE COMPANY

45200 Little Lake Street
PO Box 800
Mendocino, CA 95460
Phone: 707-937-4477
Fax: 707-937-3625
e-mail: mtc@mcn.org
Web Site: www.1mtc.org
Officers:
President: Raven Deerwater
VP: Dorothy Wandruff
Treasurer: Ferren Taylor
Secretary: Lindsey Morin
Management:
President: Douglas Warner
Business Manager: Dick Ahrens
Program and Signage: Mervin Gibert
Mission: The mission of the Mendocino Theatre Company is to produce plays of substance and excitement ranging from classics to cutting edge; nurture local talent; and provide meaningful theatrical experiences for both local and visiting audiences.
Founded: 1977
Specialized Field: Comedy; Youth Theater; Community Theater; Contemporary
Status: Non-Profit, Non-Professional

Paid Staff: 12

2212
MENLO PLAYERS GUILD
601 Laurel Street
Menlo Park, CA 90028
Mailing Address: PO Box 301, Menlo Park, CA. 94026
Phone: 213-463-5336
Fax: 213-463-5356
Specialized Field: Community Theater; Drama;
Comedy

2213
THEATREWORKS
PO Box 50458
Menlo Park, CA 94303-0458
Phone: 650-463-1950
Fax: 650-463-1963
Management:
    Casting Director: Leslie Martinson
    Company Manager: Jennifer Brasher
    Artistic Director: Robert Kelley
    Managing Director: Randy Adams
Founded: 1970
Specialized Field: Educational; Theater Workshops;
Experimental

2214
MARIN THEATRE COMPANY
397 Miller Avenue
Mill Valley, CA 94941
Phone: 415-388-5208
Fax: 415-388-0768
e-mail: info@marintheatre.org
Web Site: www.marintheatre.org
Officers:
    President: Brian Houghton
    VP: Carl Berry
    Treasurer: Michael Pescatello
    Secretary: Kipp Delbyck
Management:
    Artistic Director: Jasson Minadakis
    Producing Director: Ryan Rilettech
    Development Director: Helen Rigby
    General Manager: Vivienne Dipeolu
    Production Manager: Jennifer Gadda
Mission: Presenting a season of performances;
developing and producing new plays; providing
educational programs to over 6,000 students each year.
Utilizes: Actors; AEA Actors; Artists-in-Residence;
Choreographers; Collaborations; Community Members;
Composers; Educators; Equity Actors; Five Seasonal
Concerts; High School Drama; Multimedia;
Performance Artists; Resident Professionals; Students
Founded: 1966
Specialized Field: Live Theatre (Contemporary;
Classic; Musicals)
Status: Non-Profit, Professional
Paid Staff: 12
Budget: $2.3 Million
Income Sources: Ticket Sales; Grants (Foundation
and Government); Individual Donations; Corporate
Sponsorship; Special Events
Performs At: Marin Theatre Company
Annual Attendance: 40,000
Seating Capacity: 264
Rental Contact: Production Manager Jennifer Gadda
Organization Type: Performing; Resident; Educational;
Sponsoring

2215
SADDLEBACK COLLEGE
28000 Marguerite Parkway
Mission Viejo, CA 92692-3635
Phone: 949-582-4763
Fax: 949-347-8653
e-mail: info@saddleback.cc.ca.us
Web Site: www.saddleback.edu
Management:
    President: Richard McCullough
    Director Performing Arts: Geof English
Specialized Field: Musical; Comedy; Youth Theater;
Community Theater; Classic; Contemporary
Status: Non-Profit, Professional
Paid Staff: 10
Performs At: McKinney Theatre; Cabaret Theatre

2216
TEATRO SHALOM
1811 Monarch Drive
Napa, CA 94558
Phone: 707-226-9918
Fax: 707-224-8065
Management:
    Artistic Director: David Gassner
    Managing Director: David Acevedo
Specialized Field: Ethnic Theater; Multi-Cultural;
Drama

2217
FOOTHILL THEATRE COMPANY
401 Broad Street
PO Box 1812
Nevada City, CA 95959
Phone: 530-265-9320
Fax: 530-265-9325
Toll-free: 888-730-8587
Web Site: www.foothilltheatre.org
Management:
    President: Alison Jones'Pomatto
    Executive Director: Cheri Slanigan
    Artistic Director: Philip Charles Sneed
Founded: 1977
Specialized Field: Musical; Comedy; Youth Theater;
Dinner Theater; Ethnic Theater; Community Theater;
Classic; Contemporary
Status: Non-Profit, Professional
Paid Staff: 12
Paid Artists: 100
Performs At: Nevada Theatre
Affiliations: AEA; CAC; TCG
Annual Attendance: 56,000
Facility Category: Historic Structure
Type of Stage: Proscenium
Seating Capacity: 246

2218
ACTORS FORUM THEATRE
10655 Magnolia Boulevard
North Hollywood, CA 91601
Phone: 818-506-0600
Fax: 818-506-0686
Management:
    Co-Artistic Director: Audrey Marlyn Singer
    Co-Artistic Director: Shawn Michael
Utilizes: Actors; AEA Actors; Artists-in-Residence;
Choreographers; Collaborating Artists; Collaborations;
Commissioned Composers; Commissioned Music;
Composers; Composers-in-Residence; Contract Actors;
Contract Orchestras; Curators; Dance Companies;
Dancers; Designers; Educators; Filmmakers; Fine
Artists; Five Seasonal Concerts; Grant Writers; Guest
Accompanists; Guest Artists; Guest Choreographers;
Guest Companies; Guest Composers; Guest
Conductors; Guest Designers; Guest Directors; Guest
Ensembles; Guest Instructors; Guest Lecturers; Guest
Musical Directors; Guest Musicians; Guest Soloists;
Guest Teachers; High School Drama; Instructors; Local

Artists & Directors; Multimedia; Music; Original Music
Scores; Paid Performers; Performance Artists; Sign
Language Translators; Singers; Soloists
Founded: 1975
Specialized Field: Musical; Comedy; Drama; Theater
Workshops
Status: Nonprofit
Income Sources: Patrons; Classes; Rentals; Shows
Facility Category: Theatre
Type of Stage: Floor with curtain
Stage Dimensions: 24' x 20'
Seating Capacity: 49
Year Remodeled: 1994

2219
GROUP REPERTORY THEATRE
10900 Burbank Boulevard
North Hollywood, CA 91601
Phone: 818-763-5990
e-mail: info@thegrouprep.com
Web Site: http://thegrouprep.com/index.php/1
Management:
    President: Richard Woody
    Secretary: Melissa Soso
    Treasurer: Lloyd Pedersen
Mission: To stage five to six productions each year
emphasizing new works by playwrights and young
actors; to work with the Los Angeles Unified School
District to produce theatrical presentations for those
learning English as a second language.
Founded: 1973
Specialized Field: Ensembles; Theater Workshops;
Drama
Status: Professional; Nonprofit
Income Sources: Valley Arts Council
Performs At: Group Repertory Theatre
Organization Type: Performing

2220
SYNTHAXIS THEATRE COMPANY
6310 Whitsett Avenue
North Hollywood, CA 91607
Phone: 213-877-4726
Management:
    Executive Director: Estelle Bush
Mission: Presenting new works as well as
lesser-known works of renowned authors; emphasizing
works by women; presenting benefit performances and
shows for children.
Founded: 1972
Specialized Field: Drama; Experimental; Theater
Workshops
Status: Professional; Nonprofit
Income Sources: Los Angeles Theatre Alliance; San
Fernando Valley Arts Council
Organization Type: Performing; Touring; Resident;
Educational

2221
CALIFORNIA STATE UNIVERSITY, NORTHRIDGE: DEPARTMENT OF THEATRE
18111 Nordhoff Street
Northridge, CA 91330
Phone: 818-677-3086
e-mail: theatre@csun.edu
Web Site: http://www.csun.edu/theatre/
Officers:
    Dept. Chair: Peter Grego
Specialized Field: Educational; Theater Workshops
Affiliations: NAST; ATHE; Mark Taper Forum
Seating Capacity: 400; 205; 100
Year Built: 1960

2222
MILLS COLLEGE DEPARTMENT OF DRAMATIC ARTS & COMMUNICATIONS
5000 MacArthur Boulevard
Oakland, CA 94613
Phone: 510-430-2327
Fax: 510-430-3314
Officers:
    Chair: Ken Burke
Specialized Field: Educational; Theater Workshops
Budget: $1,050-3,200
Seating Capacity: 196; 63
Year Built: 1901
Year Remodeled: 1972

2223
GREAT AMERICAN MELODRAMA AND VAUDEVILLE
1863 Pacific Boulevard, Highway 1
PO Box 1026
Oceano, CA 93475
Phone: 805-489-2499
Fax: 805-489-5539
e-mail: info@americanmelodrama.com
Web Site: www.americanmelodrama.com
Officers:
    President: John Schlenker
Management:
    Artistic Director: Eric Hoit
    Managing Director: Suzanne King
Mission: Produce 7 shows per year.
Founded: 1975
Specialized Field: Musical; Comedy; Drama
Status: For-Profit, Professional
Paid Staff: 8
Paid Artists: 9
Season: Year round
Type of Stage: Proscenium
Stage Dimensions: 20'x 25'
Seating Capacity: 260

2224
SHAKESPEARE ORANGE COUNTY
301 E Palm Street
www.chapman.edu
Orange, CA 92866
Mailing Address: PO Box 923, Orange, CA. 92856
Phone: 714-744-7016
Fax: 714-744-7015
Web Site: http://www.shakespeareoc.org/index.php
Management:
    Artistic Director: Thomas F Bradac
Founded: 1990
Specialized Field: Educational; Theater Workshops
Paid Staff: 5

2225
PALO ALTO CHILDREN'S THEATRE
1305 Middlefield Road
Palo Alto, CA 94301
Phone: 650-463-4930
Fax: 650-324-0291
Web Site: http://www.cityofpaloalto.org/default.asp
Management:
    Director: Patricia Briggs
    Assistant Director: Micheal Litfin
    Technical Director: Henry Loughman
    Costume Supervisor: Alison Williams
    Program Assistant: Sandy Rankin

Mission: To educate young people in all theatre arts including acting, dance, set design and construction, costuming and makeup, the design and use of sound and light systems, and performance direction and production.
Utilizes: Guest Companies; Guest Teachers; Singers
Founded: 1932
Specialized Field: Musical; Youth Theater; Children's Theater
Status: Non-Professional; Nonprofit
Performs At: Palo Alto Children's Theatre
Organization Type: Performing; Educational

2226
THEATREWORKS
PO Box 50458
Palo Alto, CA 94301
Mailing Address: 1100 Hamilton Court, Menlo Park, CA 94025
Phone: 650-463-1950
Fax: 650-463-1963
e-mail: boxoffice@theatreworks.org
Web Site: www.theatreworks.org
Officers:
    Chair: Mark Vershel
    Founder: Nancy Meyer
Management:
    Artistic Director: Robert Kelley
    Managing Director: Phil Santora
    Associate Artist: Leslie Martinson
Utilizes: Guest Companies; Singers
Founded: 1970
Specialized Field: Musical; Ensembles
Status: Professional; Semi-Professional; Nonprofit
Income Sources: Theatre Communications Group
Performs At: The Lucy Stern Theatre; The Mountain View Center
Organization Type: Performing

2227
PASADENA PLAYHOUSE
39 S El Molino Avenue
80 S Lake Avenue, Suite 500
Pasadena, CA 91101
Phone: 626-792-8672
Fax: 626-792-6142
Management:
    Executive Director: Lyla L White
    Artistic Director: Sheldon Epps
    Producing Director: Tom Ware
    General Manager: Tom Ware
Founded: 1917
Specialized Field: New Plays; Classic; Musical

2228
CINNABAR THEATER
3333 Petaluma Boulevard N
Petaluma, CA 94952
Phone: 707-763-8920
Fax: 707-763-8929
e-mail: info@cinnabartheater.org
Web Site: www.cinnabartheater.org
Management:
    President: Dick Kapask
    Executive Director: Elly Lichenstein
Founded: 1974
Specialized Field: Musical; Comedy; Youth Theater; Classic; Contemporary
Status: Non-Profit, Professional
Paid Staff: 11
Paid Artists: 40

2229
THEATRE EL DORADO
El Dorado County Fairgrounds
100 Placerville Drive
Placerville, CA 95667
Phone: 530-626-5193
Specialized Field: Community Theater; Educational

2230
CALIFORNIA STATE POLYTECHNIC UNIVERSITY: DEPARTMENT OF THEATRE
3801 W Temple Avenue
Pomona, CA 91768
Phone: 909-869-3900
Fax: 909-869-3184
Web Site: www.csupomona.edu
Officers:
    Chair: C. Julian White
Founded: 1963
Specialized Field: Educational; Theater Workshops; Tech Theater
Status: Non-Profit, Non-Professional
Paid Staff: 10
Budget: $5,375-20,650
Affiliations: Mark Taper Forum; South Coast Repertory
Seating Capacity: 543; 300-500
Year Built: 1965
Year Remodeled: 1998

2231
GARBEAU'S DINNER THEATER
12401 Folsom Boulevard
Rancho Cordova, CA 95742-6413
Phone: 916-985-6361
Fax: 916-985-7375
Web Site: www.garbeaus.com
Management:
    President: David Czarnecki
    Producer: Kitty Czarnecki
    Artistic Director: Allen Schmeltz
Founded: 1981
Specialized Field: Dinner Theater
Status: For-Profit, Professional

2232
PERFORMANCE RIVERSIDE
4800 Magnolia Avenue
Riverside, CA 92506
Phone: 951-222-8399
Fax: 951-222-8940
Web Site: http://www.performanceriverside.org/
Management:
    Executive Director: Steven A Glaudini
    Producing Artistic Director: Rey O'Day
    Production Coordinator: Raymond Couture
Founded: 1983
Specialized Field: Musical; Comedy; Community Theater; Puppet; Ensembles

2233
UNIVERSITY OF CALIFORNIA-RIVERSIDE: DEPARTMENT OF THEATRE
900 University Avenue
Riverside, CA 92521
Phone: 951-827-3343
Fax: 951-827-4651
e-mail: cindy.roulette@ucr.edu
Web Site: www.performingarts.ucr.edu
Management:
    Chairman: Eric Barr

Managing Director: Mark Longlois
Founded: 1955
Specialized Field: Comedy; Ethnic Theater; Classic; Contemporary
Status: Non-Profit, Professional
Paid Staff: 4
Paid Artists: 2
Budget: $20,500-22,500
Affiliations: ATHE; U/RTA
Seating Capacity: 500; 150; 120; 50

2234
SONOMA STATE UNIVERSITY THEATER DEPARTMENT
1801 E Cotati Avenue
Rohnert Park, CA 94928
Phone: 707-664-2474
Fax: 707-664-4332
Web Site: www.sonoma.edu/depts/performingartstheatre
Officers:
Chair: Jeff Langley
Management:
President: Ruben Arminana
Founded: 1968
Specialized Field: Educational; Theater Workshops
Status: Non-Profit, Non-Professional
Paid Staff: 50
Budget: $14,250-62,000
Affiliations: ATHE
Seating Capacity: 500; 300; 99
Year Built: 1990

2235
MAGIC CIRCLE THEATER
241 Vernon Street
Roseville, CA 95678
Phone: 916-782-1777
Fax: 916-782-1766
Web Site: www.mcircle.org
Officers:
President: Brian Null
Management:
Artistic Director: Rosemarie Gerould
Founded: 1987
Specialized Field: Musical; Comedy; Youth Theater; Dinner Theater; Community Theater; Contemporary
Status: Non-Profit, Non-Professional
Paid Staff: 7

2236
MAGIC CIRCLE THEATER
241 Vernon Street
Roseville, CA 95678
Phone: 916-782-1777
Fax: 916-782-1766
Officers:
President: Brian Null
Management:
Artistic Director: Rosemarie Gerould
Mission: To offer a high quality, full performing arts center for production and performance in the fields of dance, acting, and music. Additionally, we offer superior education and training of new talent in the areas of acting, dancing, technical support, production, and theatre management skills for all age groups. We will continue to invest in the future of our craft, to grow with the communities surrounding us, and to listen to our patrons.
Founded: 1987
Specialized Field: Theater in the Round; Drama
Budget: $500,000

Income Sources: Ads in the Program; Grants; Donations; Ticket Sales; Concessions; Sponsorships; Workshop Fees; Acting Class Fees
Performs At: Community Theatre
Affiliations: Roseville Theatre
Facility Category: Community Theatre
Type of Stage: Proscenium
Seating Capacity: 500
Year Built: 1929
Year Remodeled: 2001
Rental Contact: Executive Director Robert Gerould

2237
B STREET THEATER
2711 B Street
Sacramento, CA 95816
Phone: 916-443-5391
Fax: 916-443-0874
Web Site: www.bstreettheatre.org
Officers:
Treasurer: John Barrett
Secretary: Lisa Rossie
Management:
Producing Artistic Director/CEO: Buck Busfield
Founder/Owner: Randy Paragary
Executive Director: Allan Zaremberg
Utilizes: Actors; Five Seasonal Concerts; Guest Designers; Instructors; Local Artists; Multimedia; Original Music Scores; Resident Professionals
Founded: 1991
Specialized Field: New American Works
Status: Non-Profit, Professional
Paid Staff: 15
Income Sources: Ticket Sales; Donations; Grants
Performs At: 3/4 Thrust Stage
Facility Category: Small Theatre
Year Built: 1991

2238
BEST OF BROADWAY
4010 El Camino Avenue
Sacramento, CA 95821
Phone: 916-974-6280
Fax: 916-974-6281
Web Site: www.bestofbroadway.org
Management:
President: George Royston
Executive Director: Nina Johnson
Artistic Director: David L MacDonald
Mission: Dedicated to bringing a live theatrical experience to the community of Sacramento. Through music, song and dance its goals are to educate, entertain and inspire local children, youth and adults.
Utilizes: Selected Students; Sign Language Translators; Soloists; Student Interns
Founded: 1973
Specialized Field: Musical
Status: Non-Profit, Non-Professional
Paid Staff: 2
Volunteer Staff: 100
Paid Artists: 1
Non-paid Artists: 250
Budget: $250,000
Income Sources: Grants; Ticket sales; Concessions
Annual Attendance: 12,000
Facility Category: High School Auditorium
Type of Stage: Proscenium
Seating Capacity: 1,400 per performance
Year Built: 1950
Year Remodeled: 1990

2239
BEYOND THE PROSCENIUM PRODUCTIONS
1713 25th Street
Sacramento, CA 95816
Phone: 916-456-1600
Fax: 916-456-1600
e-mail: beyondpro@sbcglobal.net
Web Site: www.beyondtheproscenium.org
Management:
Artisistic Director: Nick Avdienko
Artistic Director Emeritus: Ann Tracy
Founded: 1994
Specialized Field: Ensembles; Contemporary
Status: Non-Profit, Professional
Paid Staff: 2

2240
CALIFORNIA MUSICAL THEATRE
1510 J Street
Suite 200
Sacramento, CA 95814
Phone: 916-446-5880
Fax: 916-446-1370
e-mail: subscribers@calmt.com
Web Site: www.californiamusicaltheatre.com
Officers:
President: Rick Frey
Market President: David Galasso
President: Cecilia Delury
Management:
CEO: Richard Lewis
Artistic Director: Scott Eckern
Executive Producer: Richard Lewis
Founded: 1951
Specialized Field: Musical
Status: Non-Profit, Professional
Paid Staff: 25
Season: June-August
Type of Stage: Arena
Seating Capacity: 2500

2241
CALIFORNIA STATE UNIVERSITY, SACRAMENTO: DEPARTMENT OF THEATRE OF DANCE
6000 J Street
Sacramento, CA 95819
Phone: 916-278-6368
Fax: 916-278-5681
Web Site: www.csus.edu/dram
Officers:
President: Alexander Gonzales
Chairman of the Department: Linda Goodrich
Management:
Administrative Coordinator: Andrea Cool
Administrative Secretary: Jill Armstrong
Founded: 1948
Specialized Field: Musical; Comedy; Youth Theater; Dinner Theater; Ethnic Theater; Community Theater; Puppet; Classic; Contemporary
Status: Non-Profit, Non-Professional
Paid Staff: 24
Performs At: Theatre (2); Small Outdoor/Indoor Stage; Dance Space (2)
Affiliations: NAST
Seating Capacity: 438;150;70
Year Built: 1957
Year Remodeled: 1970

2242
CAPITAL STAGE COMPANY
1000 Front Street
Sacramento, CA 95814
Phone: 916-995-5464
Fax: 916-444-5314
e-mail: info@capstage.org
Web Site: www.capstage.org
Management:
    Artistic Director: Stephanie Gularte
    General Manager: Keith Riedell
    Producing Dirctor: Jonathan Williams
    Marketing Director: Peter Mohrmann
Mission: To provide audiences with quality dinning/live theatre experience with contemporary plays performed by Sacramento top talent.
Founded: 2000
Specialized Field: Dinner Theater
Paid Staff: 3

2243
LAMBDA PLAYERS
1927 L Street
Sacramento, CA 95814
Phone: 916-442-0185
Officers:
    President: West Ramsey
    Secretary: Maureen Gaynor
    VP: Tom Swanner
    Business Manager: Charles Peer
Management:
    Production Manager: Stephen Abate
    Secretary: Gregg Peterson
    Business Manager: Charles Peer
    Fund Development: West Ramesy
    President: Marsha Swayze
    VP: Greg Brooks
Specialized Field: Alternative; Contemporary
Affiliations: Sacramento Area Regional Theater Alliance and The League of Sacramento Theaters.

2244
SACRAMENTO THEATRE COMPANY
1419 H Street
Sacramento, CA 95814
Phone: 916-443-6722
Fax: 916-446-4066
Toll-free: 888-782-49
e-mail: info@sactheatre.org
Web Site: www.sactheatre.org
Officers:
    President: Linda Clifford
    Vice President: Marq Truscott
    Secretary: Jack Mitchell
Management:
    Producing Director: Michael Laun
    Business Development Director: Martha Lake
    Artistic Director: Matt Miller
    Finance Manager: Natalie Lucas
Mission: To professionally produce contemporary and traditional theatrical works that are engaging to the hearts and minds of a diverse regional audience.
Founded: 1942
Specialized Field: Theater Workshops; Educational
Status: Non-Profit, Professional
Performs At: Mainstage Theatre; Stage 2
Facility Category: Theatre; Conservatory
Seating Capacity: 300/80

2245
WESTERN STAGE
156 Homestead Avenue
Salinas, CA 93901
Phone: 831-755-6987
Fax: 831-755-6954
e-mail: education@westernstage.org
Web Site: www.westernstage.org
Officers:
    President: Raul Chavez
Management:
    Artistic Program Director: Melissa J Chin Parker
    Artistic Director: Jon Selover
    Managing/Development Director: John Light
Mission: To provide theatre programs that educate and enrich the lives of the people of the Central Coast of California by utilizing professional artists, teachers, students and the community.
Utilizes: Actors; AEA Actors; Choreographers; Collaborations; Dancers; Designers; Educators; Fine Artists; Five Seasonal Concerts; Grant Writers; Guest Accompanists; Guest Artists; Guest Composers; Guest Conductors; Guest Designers; Guest Lecturers; Guest Musical Directors; Guest Teachers; Instructors; Local Artists; Multimedia; Music; Original Music Scores; Performance Artists; Resident Professionals; Sign Language Translators; Soloists; Student Interns; Visual Arts
Founded: 1973
Specialized Field: Drama; Musical
Status: Non-Equity; Nonprofit
Paid Staff: 16
Volunteer Staff: 18
Paid Artists: 41
Non-paid Artists: 11
Budget: $1,100,000
Income Sources: Ticket Sales; Donations; Contract Services
Season: June - August
Performs At: Main Theater; Black Box Studio
Affiliations: NAMT; TCG
Annual Attendance: 35,000
Type of Stage: Proscenium; Black Box
Seating Capacity: 501; 99
Year Built: 1973

2246
HORTON GRAND THEATRE
444 Fourth Avenue
San Diego, CA 92101
Phone: 619-234-3588
Fax: 619-234-3587
Management:
    General Manager: Matt Boden
Utilizes: Guest Companies
Founded: 1985
Specialized Field: Comedy
Paid Staff: 20
Paid Artists: 20
Income Sources: Ticket Sales
Affiliations: San Diego Arts Leauge; San Diego Regional Chamber of Commerce; San Diego Convention & Visitors Bureau
Annual Attendance: 50,000
Facility Category: Rental House
Type of Stage: Proscenium
Stage Dimensions: 29'9x18'x2s'6"
Organization Type: Performing; Educational; Sponsoring

2247
MARIE HITCHCOCK PUPPET THEATRE IN BALBOA
Balboa Park Management Office
2130 Pan American Plaza
San Diego, CA 92101
Mailing Address: 2130 Pan American Place
Phone: 619-685-5045
Fax: 619-235-1100
Web Site:
http://www.balboaparkpuppets.com/index.html
Officers:
    President: Joe Fitzpatrick
    Vice President: Gastin Morineau
    Treasurer: Millie Patterson
    Secretary: Terri Crook
Specialized Field: Puppet
Affiliations: San Diego Guild of Puppetry
Facility Category: Puppet Theatre
Type of Stage: Proscenium

2248
OLD GLOBE
1363 Old Globe Way
San Diego, CA 92101-1696
Mailing Address: PO Box 122171, San Diego, CA. 92112-2171
Phone: 619-231-1941
Fax: 619-231-5879
e-mail: tickets@TheOldGlobe.org
Web Site: www.theoldglobe.org
Officers:
    Chair: Donald Cohn
    Vice Chair Finance and Treasurer: Anthony Thornley
Management:
    Executive Director/ CEO: Louis G Spisto
    Artistic Director: Jack O'Brien
    Founding Director: Craig Noel
    General Manager: Michael Murphy
Mission: The mission of The Old Globe is to preserve, strengthen and advance American theatre by: creating theatrical experiences of the highest professional standards; producing and presenting works of exceptional merit, designed to reach current and future audiences; ensuring diversity and balance in programming; providing an environment for the growth and education of theatre professsionals, audiences and the community at large.
Utilizes: Actors; AEA Actors; Choreographers; Commissioned Composers; Commissioned Music; Dancers; Designers; Educators; Five Seasonal Concerts; Guest Accompanists; Guest Artists; Guest Companies; Guest Conductors; Guest Designers; Guest Lecturers; Guest Writers; Guild Activities; High School Drama; Instructors; Local Artists; Multimedia; Music; Original Music Scores; Performance Artists; Poets; Resident Professionals; Selected Students; Singers; Soloists; Special Technical Talent; Visual Arts
Founded: 1935
Opened: 1982
Specialized Field: Drama; Musical; Contemporary
Status: Non-Profit
Paid Staff: 200+
Volunteer Staff: 1555
Non-paid Artists: 150
Budget: $8.5 million
Income Sources: Theatre Communications Group; League of Resident Theatres; American Arts Alliance
Season: January - November
Performs At: Old Globe Theatre; Cassius Carter Centre Stage; Lowell Daives Festival Theatre
Affiliations: Actor's Equity Association; the Society Of Stage Directors and Choreographets; United Scenic Artists Local and International Alliance of Theatric
Annual Attendance: 300,000+
Type of Stage: Proscenium, black box, 3/4 thrust
Seating Capacity: OG Theatre 582; Stage 225; Lowell Theatre 612

Organization Type: Performing; Educational; Sponsoring

2249
PLAYWRIGHTS PROJECT
2590 Truxton Road
Suite 202
San Diego, CA 92106-6145
Phone: 619-239-8222
Fax: 619-239-8225
e-mail: write@playwrightsproject.org
Web Site: www.playwrightsproject.org
Officers:
Board President: Lisa Kirazian
Treasurer: David Carr
Secretary: Judy Leff
VP: Pat Jacoby
Management:
Executive Director: Cecelia Kouma
Mission: To advance literacy, creativity and communication by empowering individuals to voice their stories through playwriting programs and theatre productions.
Utilizes: Artists-in-Residence; Community Talent; Contract Actors; Educators; Five Seasonal Concerts; Guest Accompanists; Guest Conductors; Guest Designers; Guest Speakers; Guest Teachers; High School Drama; Instructors; Local Artists; Local Artists & Directors; Local Talent; Original Music Scores; Paid Performers; Performance Artists; Soloists; Visual Arts; Volunteer Directors & Actors; Writers
Founded: 1985
Specialized Field: Young Playwrights; New Plays
Status: Non-Profit, Professional
Paid Staff: 4

2250
SAN DIEGO JUNIOR THEATRE
1650 El Prado, Balboa Park
#208
San Diego, CA 92101
Phone: 619-239-1311
Fax: 619-239-5048
e-mail: info@juniortheatre.com
Web Site: www.juniortheatre.com
Officers:
President/Board of Trustees: David Braun
Management:
Executive Director: Will Neblett
Community Relations Director: Theresa Wers
Mission: To offer instruction in theatre arts to youth, aged 8-18.
Utilizes: Guest Companies
Founded: 1948
Specialized Field: Youth Theater; Theater Workshops
Status: Non-Profit, Professional
Paid Staff: 30
Income Sources: SCETA; San Diego Theatre League
Performs At: Casa del Prado Theatre
Organization Type: Performing; Educational

2251
SAN DIEGO REPERTORY THEATRE
79 Horton Plaza
San Diego, CA 92101-6144
Phone: 619-231-3586
Fax: 619-235-0939
e-mail: artistic@sandiegorep.com
Web Site: www.sandiegorep.com/
Management:
Artistic Director and Co-Founder: Sam Woodhouse
Public Relations Manager: Susan Enicoine
Mission: Adventurous theatre.

Founded: 1976
Specialized Field: Educational; Theater Workshops; Contemporary
Paid Staff: 43

2252
SAN DIEGO STATE UNIVERSITY: DEPARTMENT OF THEATRE
5500 Campanile Drive
San Diego, CA 92182
Phone: 619-594-5091
Fax: 619-594-7431
Web Site: www.sdsu.edu
Officers:
Chair: Alicia Annas
Management:
President: Stephen Weber
Executive Director: W Nick Reid
Marketing & Publicity Director: Paula Pearson
Founded: 1935
Specialized Field: Educational; Theater Workshops
Status: For-Profit, Non-Professional
Paid Staff: 25
Budget: $11,347-12,747
Affiliations: NAST; ATHE
Seating Capacity: 500; 175
Year Built: 1969
Year Remodeled: 1989

2253
SOUTHEAST COMMUNITY THEATRE
5140 Solola Avenue
San Diego, CA 92114
Phone: 619-262-2817
Management:
Artistic Director: Floyd Gaffney
Production Manager: Bonnie J Ward
Business Manager: Rufus DeWitt
Mission: Promoting African-American playwrights by showcasing non-professional, semi-professional and professional artists.
Utilizes: Guest Companies
Founded: 1976
Specialized Field: Community Theater
Status: Semi-Professional; Nonprofit
Income Sources: American Association of Community Theatres
Performs At: Educational Cultural Complex Performing Arts Theatre
Organization Type: Performing; Resident; Sponsoring

2254
STARLIGHT MUSICAL THEATRE
SAN DIEGO CIVIC LIGHT OPERA ASSOCIATION
1549 El Prado - Balboa Park
San Diego, CA 92101
Mailing Address: P.O Box 3519, San Diego, CA 92163
Phone: 619-232-7827
Fax: 619-232-1882
e-mail: info@starlighttheatre.org
Web Site: http://www.starlighttheatre.org/
Management:
Executive Director: CE Bud Farnks
Producing Artistic Director: Don Ward
Producing Artistic Director: Bonnie Ward
Mission: The preservation and promotion of the art form of musical theatre.
Utilizes: Guest Artists; Guest Companies; Singers
Founded: 1945
Specialized Field: Musical; Classic
Status: Professional; Nonprofit
Performs At: Starlight Bowl; Civic Theatre; Spreckles Theatre
Organization Type: Performing; Educational

2255
AFRICAN AMERICAN DRAMA COMPANY
394 5th Avenue
San Francisco, CA 94118
Phone: 415-378-0064
Fax: 877-376-0224
e-mail: DRAMART@comcast.net
Web Site: http://www.africanamericandramacompany.org/
Management:
Executive Director: Phillip E Walker
Executive Director: Ethel Pitts Walker
Mission: To offer American audiences Black history and African plays.
Utilizes: Guest Companies
Founded: 1977
Specialized Field: Drama; African American
Status: Professional
Organization Type: Touring

2256
AMERICAN CONSERVATORY THEATRE
30 Grant Avenue
6th Floor
San Francisco, CA 94108-5800
Mailing Address: 30 Grant Ave, Sixth Floor, San Francisco, CA 94108
Phone: 415-439-2350
Fax: 415-834-3300
e-mail: tickets@act-sf.org
Web Site: www.act-sf.org
Officers:
Chair: Jack Cortis
Vice Chair: Nancy Livingston
Vice Chair: Rusty Rueff
Vice Chair: Cheryl Sorokin
Volunteer Coordinator: Barbara Gerber
Finance Director: Jeffrey P. Malloy
Marketing Director: Andrew Smith
Management:
Executive Director: Ellen Richard
Artistic Director: Carey Perloff
Conservatory Director: Melissa Smith
Producing Director: James Haire
Director of External Affairs: Tim M. Whalen
Producing Director: James Haire
Mission: Performing contemporary and classical plays in conjunction with theatre training.
Utilizes: Guest Companies; Singers
Founded: 1965
Specialized Field: Youth Theater; Classic; Contemporary
Status: Non-Profit, Professional
Paid Artists: 400
Income Sources: League of Resident Theatres; Theatre Communications Group; American Arts Alliance; California Confederation of the Arts; National Corporation Theatre Fund
Performs At: Geary Theatre
Affiliations: American Conservatory Theatre
Type of Stage: Proscenium
Seating Capacity: 1014
Year Built: 1910
Year Remodeled: 1996
Rental Contact: Bob MacDonald (439-2392)
Organization Type: Performing; Resident; Educational

2257
ASIAN AMERICAN THEATER COMPANY
1840 Sutter Street
Suite 207
San Francisco, CA 94115

Phone: 415-440-5545
Fax: 415-440-5597
Management:
   Producing Director: Pamela Wu
Specialized Field: New Plays; Asian American; Asian Pacific Islander; Ethnic Theater

2258
BRAVA! FOR WOMEN IN THE ARTS
2781 24th Street
San Francisco, CA 94110
Phone: 415-641-7657
Fax: 415-641-7684
Management:
   Artistic and Executive Director: Ellen Gavin
   Co-Chair: David Mauroff
   Facilities Manager: Darren Hochstedler
   Interim Production Manager: Ari Poppers
Founded: 1986
Specialized Field: Community Theater; New Plays; Alternative; Ethnic Theater
Performs At: Brava Theatre Center, Barbie Stein Youth Theater
Type of Stage: Thrust, Black Box
Seating Capacity: 375, 100

2259
EL TEATRO DE LA ESPERANZA
PO Box 40578
San Francisco, CA 94140
Phone: 415-255-2320
Management:
   Artistic Director: Rodrigo Durte Clark
   General Manager: Eve Donovan
Mission: To present bi-cultural, bilingual plays that further theatre in the Chicano community.
Specialized Field: Spanish Language Company
Status: Professional; Nonprofit
Performs At: Mission Culture Center
Organization Type: Touring; Resident

2260
EUREKA THEATRE COMPANY
215 Jackson Street
San Francisco, CA 94111
Mailing Address: 555 Howard Street, Suite 201A, San Francisco, CA. 94105
Phone: 415-243-9899
Fax: 415-243-0789
Web Site: www.eurekatheatre.org
Officers:
   Chairman: Frederick Allardyce
   Treasurer: Anne Peskoe
Management:
   Co-Artistic Director: Andrea Gordon
   Co-Artistic Director: Benny Sato Ambush
   General Manager: Victoria Randall
   Executive Director: Torri Randall
Mission: Producing contemporary plays focusing on social and political issues.
Utilizes: Guest Companies; Singers
Founded: 1972
Specialized Field: Drama; Musical
Status: For-Profit, Professional
Income Sources: Actors' Equity Association; Coalition of Bay Area Theatres
Performs At: Eureka Theatre
Type of Stage: Proscenium
Stage Dimensions: 22' x 40'
Seating Capacity: 200
Organization Type: Performing; Resident; Educational

2261
GEORGE COATES PERFORMANCE WORKS
110 McAllister Street
San Francisco, CA 94102
Phone: 415-863-8520
Fax: 415-863-8520
Web Site: www.georgecoates.org
Officers:
   President: Craig Martin
   VP: Richard Cole
   Secretary: Cathy Elienberger-Ubell
   Treasurer: Michael McDonell
Management:
   Artistic Director: George Coates
   Managing Director: Friday Savathphoun
   Production Manager: Chris Read
Mission: To broaden the boundaries of contemporary performances and the creative experience itself; to explore new relationships between performer and audience; to develop new alliances between arts ensembles, individuals and emerging technology industries; emphasis on contemporary vocal expression and multimedia.
Utilizes: Local Talent; Singers
Founded: 1977
Specialized Field: New Plays; Musical
Status: Non-Profit, Professional
Paid Staff: 4
Performs At: Performance Works
Organization Type: Performing; Touring; Resident

2262
ILLUSTRATED STAGE COMPANY
PO Box 640063
San Francisco, CA 94164
Phone: 415-861-6655
Management:
   General Manager: Barbara Malinowski
Utilizes: Guest Companies
Founded: 1979
Specialized Field: Drama; Musical; Contemporary
Status: Professional; Nonprofit
Paid Staff: 1
Performs At: Alcazar Theatre
Organization Type: Performing; Resident

2263
JULIAN THEATRE
777 Valencia
San Francisco, CA 94110
Fax: 415-626-8986
Officers:
   Chairman: George Crowe
Management:
   Artistic/General Director: Richard Reineccius
   Library Manager: Veronica Masterson
   Development Director: Jackie Hayes
   Production Manager: Michael Dingle
Mission: To maintain interest in works that have a social or political sense of the times to serve as a multi-cultural theater working with new plays.
Utilizes: Guest Companies; Singers
Founded: 1965
Specialized Field: Ensembles; Drama
Status: Professional; Nonprofit
Income Sources: Actors' Equity Association
Organization Type: Performing; Touring; Resident; Educational; Sponsoring

2264
LORRAINE HANSBERRY THEATRE
620 Sutter Street
Suite 305
San Francisco, CA 94102
Phone: 415-474-8800
Fax: 415-288-0353
e-mail: stanley@LHTSF.org
Web Site: www.lorrainehansberrytheatre.com
Management:
   Executive Director: Quentin Easter
   Artistic Director: Stanley Williams
   Adminstrative Assistant: Albert Silva
   Administrative Director: Tod Green
   Production Associate: Marianella Macchiarini
Mission: To produce plays by America's and the world's leading Black writers; to foster the development of new Black writers through the ongoing activities of the playwrights workshop.
Utilizes: Actors; AEA Actors; Artists-in-Residence; Choreographers; Commissioned Music; Dance Companies; Dancers; Designers; Educators; Five Seasonal Concerts; Guest Designers; Guild Activities; High School Drama; Local Artists; Multimedia; Original Music Scores; Resident Professionals; Sign Language Translators; Soloists; Student Interns; Special Technical Talent
Founded: 1981
Specialized Field: Youth Theater; Ethnic Theater; Ensembles; Contemporary
Status: Non-Profit, Professional
Paid Staff: 5
Volunteer Staff: 30
Paid Artists: 5
Performs At: Lorraine Hansberry Theater
Type of Stage: Modified, Proscenium Thrust
Seating Capacity: 300
Organization Type: Performing; Educational

2265
MAGIC THEATRE
Fort Mason Center
Building D
San Francisco, CA 94123
Phone: 415-441-8001
Fax: 415-771-5505
Web Site: www.magictheatre.org
Management:
   President: Joe Matichak
   Artistic Director: Chris Smith
   Managing Director: David Gluck
Mission: Focused exclusively on developing new plays and playwrights and operating two professional theaters.
Founded: 1967
Specialized Field: Musical; Comedy; Youth Theater; Ethnic Theater; Contemporary; Ensembles
Status: Non-Profit, Professional
Paid Staff: 20
Paid Artists: 30
Budget: 1.1 million
Income Sources: Actors' Equity Association
Season: June - August
Performs At: Northside Theatre; Southside Theatre
Annual Attendance: 20,000
Type of Stage: Proscenium
Stage Dimensions: 18'x 24'
Seating Capacity: 160
Rental Contact: General Manager John Warren
Organization Type: Performing; Resident; Sponsoring

2266

MAKE A CIRCUS: ARCO SPORTS

639 Frederick Street
San Francisco, CA 94117
Phone: 415-665-2276
Fax: 415-566-0102
e-mail: info@acrosports.org
Web Site: www.acrosports.org
Management:
Executive Director: Dorri Huntington
Artistic Director: Stephanie Abrams
Mission: To provide opportunities for individuals, families and communities to experience self-empowerment through the magic of particapitory circus theatre.
Utilizes: Actors; Artists-in-Residence; Collaborations; Five Seasonal Concerts; Guest Artists; Guest Companies; Guest Designers; Guild Activities; High School Drama; Local Artists; Original Music Scores; Resident Professionals; Soloists
Founded: 1993
Specialized Field: Youth Theater; Community Theater; Contemporary
Status: Non-Profit, Non-Professional
Paid Staff: 45
Paid Artists: 5
Performs At: Any outdoor 100 x 100 flat, grassy area free of distractions
Annual Attendance: 40,000
Facility Category: Parks
Type of Stage: Outdoor
Stage Dimensions: 100' x 100'
Seating Capacity: 1,000
Organization Type: Performing; Touring; Educational; Participatory

2267

MUSICAL THEATRE WORKS

2340 Jackson Street
San Francisco, CA 94115-1323
Phone: 415-641-5988
e-mail: mtwmzmusic@aol.com
Web Site: www.musicaltheatreworks.org
Management:
General Director: Carolyn Miller
Stage Director: Christina Lazo
Production Manager: Matthew Royce
Mission: Developing and producing new works for American musical theatre.
Utilizes: Singers
Specialized Field: Musical; Ensembles
Status: Professional; Nonprofit
Income Sources: Actors' Equity Association; Theatre Communications Group; Alliance of Resident Theatres/New York
Organization Type: Performing; Resident

2268

NEW CONSERVATORY CENTER THEATRE

25 Van Ness Avenue
Lower Lobby
San Francisco, CA 94102
Phone: 415-861-4914
Fax: 415-861-6988
e-mail: email@nctcsf.org
Web Site: www.nctcsf.org
Officers:
Chairman: Thomas Burke
Chair Emeritus: George Vanberg Wolff
Treasurer: Paul R Brody
Secretary: Rich Kowalewski
Management:

Artistic/Executive Director: Ed Decker
Operations Manager: Jackie Jordan
Executive Assistant: Jesse Whittle-Utter
Mission: Through our work, we strive to make positive contributions to enrich the cultural and educational well-being of our world.
Utilizes: Actors; Choreographers; Dancers; Designers; Educators; Fine Artists; Five Seasonal Concerts; Grant Writers; Guest Accompanists; Guest Artists; Guest Conductors; Guest Ensembles; Guest Instructors; Guest Lecturers; Guild Activities; High School Drama; Local Artists; Multimedia; Music; Organization Contracts; Original Music Scores; Performance Artists; Resident Professionals; Sign Language Translators; Soloists; Student Interns; Special Technical Talent; Theatre Companies; Touring Companies
Founded: 1981
Specialized Field: Musical; Comedy; Youth Theater; Dinner Theater; Ethnic Theater; Community Theater; Puppet; Classic; Contemporary
Status: Non-Profit, Professional
Paid Staff: 14
Volunteer Staff: 5
Paid Artists: 20
Budget: $950,000
Income Sources: 60% Earned; 40% Contributed
Performs At: The New Conservatory Theatre Center
Annual Attendance: 75,000
Facility Category: Multi-theatre; Art Gallery
Type of Stage: 2 Black Box; 1 Proscenium
Seating Capacity: 50 - 140
Year Built: 1904
Year Remodeled: 1986
Organization Type: Performing; Touring; Educational

2269

PERSONA GRATA PRODUCTIONS

2 Alta Mar
San Francisco, CA 94121
Phone: 415-387-7898
e-mail: paulkwan@personagrataprod.org
Web Site: www.personagrataprod.org
Management:
Executive Director: Paul Kwan
Artistic Director: Arnold Iger
Mission: Educational and cross-cultural.
Utilizes: Singers
Founded: 1979
Specialized Field: Ensembles; Puppet
Status: Professional; Nonprofit
Paid Staff: 4
Organization Type: Performing; Educational

2270

PHOENIX ARTS ASSOCIATION THEATRE/WESTCOAST PLAYWRIGHTS ALLIANCE

Phoenix Theatre
414 Mason Street
San Francisco, CA 94117-3930
Mailing Address: 138 Carl Street
Phone: 415-336-1020
e-mail: lbaf23@aol.com
Web Site: www.phoenixtheatresf.org
Management:
Artistic Director/Managing Director: Linda B Ayres-Frederick
Technical Director: Ty McKenzie
Mission: To present new and often unperformed scripts and original adaptations of American, British, and European writers by Bay Area Artists as well as premiering the works of the West Coast Playwrights Alliance at their two intimate downtown San Francisco

theatres. In recent years to provide performance, rehearsal, and workshop space for the SF Bay area theatre community at reasonable rates.
Founded: 1985
Opened: 1985
Specialized Field: Contemporary & Original New Plays; Classics by the Phoenix & Other Nomadic Theatre Companies; Theatre Workshops in Acting; Scriptwriting; Movement
Paid Staff: 4
Volunteer Staff: 10
Paid Artists: 15
Non-paid Artists: 3
Income Sources: Performances; Contributions; Rentals
Affiliations: Theatre Bay Area
Facility Category: Theatre
Type of Stage: Thrust; Proscenium
Stage Dimensions: 30x20; 28'x20'
Seating Capacity: 49-65; 49
Year Built: 1985
Year Remodeled: 2001
Rental Contact: Artistic & Managing Director Linda Ayres-Frederick

2271

SAN FRANCISCO STATE UNIVERSITY: DEPARTMENT OF THEATRE ARTS

1600 Holloway Avenue
San Francisco, CA 94132
Phone: 415-338-1341
Fax: 415-338-0575
Web Site: www.sfu.edu/~tha/
Management:
President: Robert Corrigan
Executive Director: Roy Conboy
Specialized Field: Educational; Theater Workshops
Status: For-Profit, Non-Professional
Budget: $1,000-5,500
Affiliations: NAST
Seating Capacity: 250; 95

2272

SAN FRANCISCO MIME TROUPE

855 Treat Avenue
San Francisco, CA 94110
Phone: 415-285-1717
Fax: 415-285-1290
Web Site: www.sfmt.org
Management:
General Manager: Peggy Rose
Office Marketing Manager: Miche Hall
Production Manager: Natalie Saibel
Mission: Creating original, socially-relevant, musical theatre of high professional quality; performing for the broadest audience possible.
Utilizes: Actors; AEA Actors; Artists-in-Residence; Collaborations; Commissioned Composers; Dancers; Designers; Educators; Five Seasonal Concerts; Guest Accompanists; Guest Teachers; Guild Activities; High School Drama; Instructors; Local Artists; Local Unknown Artists; Multimedia; New Productions; Organization Contracts; Original Music Scores; Resident Artists; Resident Professionals; Sign Language Translators; Singers; Soloists; Visual Arts
Founded: 1959
Specialized Field: Musical; Comedy; Youth Theater; Ethnic Theater; Community Theater; Classic; Contemporary
Status: Non-Profit, Professional
Paid Staff: 5
Volunteer Staff: 25
Paid Artists: 10
Budget: $700,000

Income Sources: Free shows in Bay Area Parks; International Touring Engagements; Youth Project for At-risk Communities in San Francisco; Grants; Donations
Performs At: Varies (plays in parks for free in July)
Affiliations: Network of Ensemble Theaters, Theater Bay Area
Annual Attendance: 60,000
Type of Stage: Portable Raked Stage
Organization Type: Performing; Touring; Educational

2273
SHADOWLIGHT PRODUCTIONS
22 Chattanooga Street
San Francisco, CA 94114
Phone: 415-648-4461
Fax: 415-641-9734
e-mail: info@shadowlight.org
Web Site: http://www.shadowlight.org
Officers:
    President: Drew Takahashi
    Treasurer: Gail Silva
Management:
    Artistic/Executive Director: Larry Reed
    Managing Director: Sachiko Willis
    Director of Programs: Leslie Dreyer
Mission: To nurture indigenous shadow theater traditions and to explore and expand the possibilities of the shadow theatre medium by creating innovative interdisciplinary, multicultural works.
Specialized Field: Storytelling; Shadow Theater; Shadow Theater

2274
SOON 3 THEATER
951 Church Street
PO Box 460298
San Francisco, CA 94114-3028
Phone: 415-558-8575
e-mail: soon3@sirius.com
Web Site: www.soon3.com
Management:
    Executive Director: Edward Doherty
    Founder Artistic Director: Alan Finneran
Mission: Developing innovative forms of presentation for socially significant theatrical works.
Utilizes: Community Members; Educators; Guest Companies; Singers
Founded: 1972
Specialized Field: Ensembles; Multi-Media; Experimental
Status: Professional; Nonprofit
Income Sources: Theater Bay Area
Organization Type: Performing

2275
STEVE SILVER PRODUCTIONS
678 Green Street
San Francisco, CA 94133
Phone: 415-421-4222
Fax: 415-421-4817
e-mail: bbb@beachblanketbabylon.com
Web Site: www.beachblanketbabylon.com
Management:
    Producer: Jo Schuman Silver
Founded: 1974
Specialized Field: Musical; Comedy; Youth Theater
Status: Non-profit, Professional
Paid Staff: 100
Income Sources: San Francisco & California Chambers of Commerce; Theater Bay Area
Performs At: Club Fugazi
Annual Attendance: 150,000
Organization Type: Performing; Resident

2276
THEATER RHINOCEROS
2926 16th Street
San Francisco, CA 94103
Phone: 415-552-4100
Fax: 415-558-9044
e-mail: jfisher@therhino.org
Web Site: www.therhino.org
Management:
    Artistic Director: John Fisher
    Managing Director: John Simpson
    Development Director: Jim Boin
    Marketing Director: Jeffrey Hartgraves
Mission: The presentation of Lesbian and Gay theatre.
Utilizes: Actors; Collaborations; Guest Companies; Local Artists; Original Music Scores; Resident Professionals; Sign Language Translators; Student Interns
Founded: 1977
Specialized Field: Drama; Musical; Contemporary
Status: Professional; Nonprofit
Paid Staff: 4
Budget: $600,000
Income Sources: Non-profit
Performs At: Main Stage; Studio Theater
Annual Attendance: 20,000
Facility Category: Mainstage + Studio
Type of Stage: Proscenium
Seating Capacity: 112/54
Organization Type: Performing; Resident

2277
THEATRE ARTAUD
499 Alabama Street
Studio 445
San Francisco, CA 94110
Phone: 415-626-4370
Fax: 415-621-3824
e-mail: theater@artaud.org
Web Site: www.theatretaud.org
Management:
    General Manager: Donna Merlino
    President: John Sullivan
    Vice President: Allan Kessler
Founded: 1972
Specialized Field: Drama; Musical; Contemporary
Paid Staff: 7

2278
THICK DESCRIPTION
Thick House, 1695 18th Street
1695 18th Street
San Francisco, CA 94107
Mailing Address: P.O. Box 590603, San Francisco, CA 94159
Phone: 415-401-8081
e-mail: ÿinfo@thickhouse.org
Web Site: www.thickhouse.org
Management:
    Artistic Collective: Karen Amano
    Artistic Collective: Tony Kelly
    Artistic Collective: Rick Martin
Mission: Thick Description is run by a collective of three theater artists who share the duties and responsibilities of traditional artistic director.
Specialized Field: Drama; Classic; Contemporary

2279
TRAVELING JEWISH THEATRE
3130 20th Street
Suite 308
San Francisco, CA 94110
Phone: 415-285-8080
Fax: 415-399-1844
Web Site: www.atjt.com
Officers:
    Associate Artistic Director: Corey Fisher
Management:
    Director Of Marketing and Audience: Devra Aarons
    Company Manager: Jennifer Hoenigsberg
    Artistic Director: Aaron Davidman
    General Manager: Evan Specter
Mission: To create and perform original works of theatre, as an ensemble and in collaboration with theatre artists from a variety of cultural and ethnic backgrounds, that contribute to a generous vision of the human condition.
Utilizes: Guest Companies; Singers
Founded: 1978
Specialized Field: Touring Company; Ethnic Theater; Jewish
Status: Professional; Nonprofit
Income Sources: Theatre Communications Group
Organization Type: Performing; Touring; Educational

2280
CHILDREN'S MUSICAL THEATER-SAN JOSE
1401 Parkmoor Avenue
San Jose, CA 95128
Phone: 408-288-5437
Fax: 408-288-6241
Web Site: www.cmtsj.org
Officers:
    President: David J Stock
    VP: Rose Froehlich
    Treasurer: G Ron Lester
    Secretary: Kathy Custanza
Management:
    Executive Director: Jennifer Sandretto Hull
    Artistic Director: Kevin R Hauge
    Marketing/PR Director: Micki Sever
    Educational/Outreach Director: Drew Chappell
Mission: Committed to providing excellent, accessible musical theater training for youth, with high-quality performances for families and the entire community.
Founded: 1968
Specialized Field: Children's Theater; Musical
Status: Non-Profit, Non-Professional
Paid Staff: 9
Volunteer Staff: 35
Paid Artists: 86
Rental Contact: Facilities Manager/Rentals: Timme Reinhart

2281
CITY LIGHTS THEATRE COMPANY
529 S 2nd Street
San Jose, CA 95112
Phone: 408-295-4200
Fax: 408-295-8318
e-mail: citylights@cltc.org
Web Site: www.cltc.org
Management:
    Artistic Director: Lisa Mallette
    Production Manager: Kit Wilder
    Box Office Manager: Amy Haines
Mission: City Lights is a resident, non-profit company of theater artists dedicated to staging and hosting quality productions year round. This company prides itself on producing works you won't see at any other theater in the area.

Utilizes: Actors; Collaborations; Designers; Educators; Five Seasonal Concerts; Guest Designers; Instructors; Local Artists; Original Music Scores; Resident Professionals; Soloists; Student Interns; Special Technical Talent; Theatre Companies
Founded: 1982
Specialized Field: Musical; Comedy; Community Theater; Contemporary
Status: Non-Profit, Professional
Income Sources: Various
Annual Attendance: 10,000
Facility Category: Transformed Warehouse
Type of Stage: Flexible
Seating Capacity: 110
Rental Contact: Managing Director Lisa Mallette

2282
NORTHSIDE THEATRE COMPANY
848 E William Street
San Jose, CA 95116
Phone: 408-288-7820
e-mail: northside8@hotmail.com
Web Site: www.northsidetheatre.com
Officers:
   Chairperson: Dana Grover
   Vice Chairperson: Valerie Singer
   Treasurer: Matt Singer
   Secretary: Kathy Harwood
Management:
   Chairperson: Dana Grover
   Artistic Director: Richard T Orlando
   Assistant Director: Darcie Grover
   Communications Manager: Mertedith King
Mission: To provide high quality, theatrical opportunities for youth, regardless of economic, educational, cultural or physical limitations. Dedicated to the manifestation of the human spirit.
Utilizes: Singers
Founded: 1978
Specialized Field: Drama; Musical; Contemporary
Status: Non-Profit
Paid Staff: 6
Volunteer Staff: 12
Paid Artists: 25
Non-paid Artists: 50
Budget: $200,000
Income Sources: Community Foundation of Silicon Valley
Annual Attendance: 5,000
Type of Stage: Thurst
Stage Dimensions: 20x20
Year Built: 1965
Year Remodeled: 2000
Organization Type: Performing; Touring; Resident; Educational

2283
SAN JOSE CHILDREN'S MUSICAL THEATER
1401 Parkmoor Avenue
San Jose, CA 95126
Phone: 408-288-5437
Fax: 408-288-6241
e-mail: info@cmtsj.org
Management:
   Artistic Director: Kevin R Hauge
   Executive Director: Jennifer Sandretto Hull
   Development Director: Rebecca Purdin
   Director Marketing/Programs: Tegan McLane
Mission: Providing excellent, accessible musical theater training and youth theater performances for young audiences, families and the entire Silicon Valley region. Also providing a positive environment in which youth can learn teamwork and communication skills

and experience the pride of accomplishment. Recognizing diversity of racial, ethnic, social and economic backgrounds in our participants and audiences.
Founded: 1968
Specialized Field: Community Theater; Children's Theater; Musical; Puppet; Educational

2284
SAN JOSE REPERTORY THEATRE
101 Paseo De San Antonio
San Jose, CA 95113
Phone: 408-367-7255
Fax: 408-367-7237
e-mail: info@sjrep.com
Web Site: www.sjrep.com
Officers:
   President: John Michael Sobrato
Management:
   Artistic Director: Timothy Near
   Managing Director: Alexandra Urbanowski
Mission: The theatre exists to produce seasons of visually exciting, challenging, entertaining and evocative plays selected from classical and contemporary periods; provide a creative environment for theatre artists and offer opportunities for innovative approaches to existing work and the development of new work; to reflect and enhance the community.
Utilizes: Actors; AEA Actors; Artists-in-Residence; Collaborating Artists; Collaborations; Commissioned Composers; Designers; Five Seasonal Concerts; Grant Writers; Guest Accompanists; Guest Artists; Guest Choreographers; Guest Companies; Guest Conductors; Guest Designers; Guest Ensembles; Guest Lecturers; Guest Musical Directors; Guest Soloists; Guest Teachers; Instructors; Local Artists; Local Unknown Artists; Multimedia; Organization Contracts; Original Music Scores; Performance Artists; Poets; Resident Professionals; Student Interns; Visual Arts
Founded: 1980
Specialized Field: Comedy; Youth Theater; Ensembles; Classic; Contemporary
Status: Non-Profit, Professional
Paid Staff: 70
Volunteer Staff: 100
Budget: $5,900,000
Income Sources: League of Resident Theatres; Theatre Communications Group
Performs At: Performing Arts Complex
Annual Attendance: 110,000
Facility Category: Theater; Performing Arts
Seating Capacity: 533
Year Built: 1997
Cost: $24,000,000
Rental Contact: Drayton Foltz
Organization Type: Performing; Resident; Educational

2285
SAN JOSE STAGE COMPANY
490 S 1st Street
San Jose, CA 95113
Phone: 408-283-7142
Fax: 408-283-7146
e-mail: admin@sjstage.com
Web Site: www.sanjose-stage.com
Officers:
   President: Michael C Froncek
   VP: Faye Van Boxtel
   Secretary: Les Stevens
   Treasurer: Dr. Erik Cohen
Management:
   Executive Director: Cathleen King
   Artistic Director: Randall King
   Development Director: Mary Smith

Production Manager: Scott Tukloff
Technical Consultant: Scott Baker
Founded: 1984
Specialized Field: Classic; Contemporary
Status: Non-Profit, Professional
Income Sources: Private Contributions; Ticket/Subscription Revenues
Performs At: Professional Union Playhouse

2286
SAN JOSE STATE UNIVERSITY: DEPARTMENT OF THEATRE ARTS
One Washington Square
San Jose, CA 95192
Phone: 408-924-4530
Officers:
   Chair: Dr. Robert Jeenkins
Specialized Field: Educational; Theater Workshops
Budget: $8,100-17,000
Affiliations: NAST; ATHE; San Jose Repertory Theatre; Theatreworks; KQED; Paramount Great America; American Musical Theatre; The Barn Theatre
Seating Capacity: 400; 160; 60
Year Built: 1954

2287
TEATRO VISION
Mexican Heritage Plaza
1700 Alum Rock Avenue, Suite 265
San Jose, CA 95116
Phone: 408-272-9926
Fax: 408-928-5589
e-mail: teatrovision@teatrovision.org
Web Site: www.teatrovision.org
Management:
   President: Javier Augguire
   Executive Director: Raul Lozano
   Artistic Director: Elisa Marina Alvarado
   Production Manager: Dianne Vega
Mission: A Chicago theater company that celebrates culture, nurtures community, and inspires vision. Our art serves to move people to feel, think and act to create a better world.
Utilizes: Guest Companies
Founded: 1984
Specialized Field: Comedy; Youth Theater; Ethnic Theater; Community Theater; Contemporary
Status: Non-Profit, Professional
Paid Staff: 12
Paid Artists: 20
Income Sources: Movimiento de Arte y Cultura Latinoamericana; Theatre Bay Area
Organization Type: Performing; Touring

2288
EL TEATRO CAMPESINO
705 Fourth Street
San Juan Bautista, CA 95045
Mailing Address: PO Box 1240
Phone: 831-623-2444
Fax: 408-623-4127
Web Site: http://www.elteatrocampesino.com
Officers:
   Chairman: Luis Valdez
Management:
   Producing Artistic Director: Kinan Valdez
   Business Manager: Licha Munoz
   Artistic Director: Luis Valdez
Mission: To be recognized as one of the country's leading Latino/Chicano theaters.
Specialized Field: Ethnic Theater; Spanish Language Company
Status: Professional; Nonprofit
Performs At: El Teatro

Organization Type: Touring; Resident; Educational; Sponsoring

2289
SOUTH ORANGE COUNTY COMMUNITY THEATRE
Camino Real Playhouse
31776 El Camino Real
San Juan Capistrano, CA 92675
Phone: 949-489-8082
Fax: 949-489-8082
Specialized Field: Community Theater

2290
MARIN SHAKESPEARE COMPANY
PO Box 4053
San Rafael, CA 94913
Phone: 415-499-4485
Fax: 415-499-1492
e-mail: management@marinshakespeare.org
Web Site: www.marinshakespeare.org
Management:
   Executive Director: Lesley Schisgall Currier
   Artistic Director: Robert Currier
Mission: Our mission is to acheive excellence in the staging of Shakespearean plays; to celebrate Shakespeare; and to serve as a cultural and educational resource for Marin County, the San Francisco Bay Area and beyond.
Utilizes: Actors; AEA Actors; Choreographers; Collaborating Artists; Collaborations; Commissioned Composers; Commissioned Music; Community Members; Community Talent; Composers; Contract Actors; Designers; Educators; Equity Actors; Guest Accompanists; Guest Artists; Guest Conductors; Guest Designers; Guest Ensembles; Guest Instructors; Guest Musical Directors; Guest Soloists; Guest Speakers; Guest Writers; Guild Activities; High School Drama; Instructors; Local Artists; Local Artists & Directors; Local Talent; Multimedia; Organization Contracts; Original Music Scores; Performance Artists; Playwrights; Poets; Resident Companies; Resident Professionals; Sign Language Translators; Soloists; Students; Student Interns; Special Technical Talent; Theatre Companies; Visual Arts; Visual Designers; Volunteer Artists; Volunteer Directors & Actors; Writers
Founded: 1989
Specialized Field: Shakespeare
Status: Non-Profit, Professional
Paid Staff: 4
Paid Artists: 40
Season: July-September
Affiliations: Shakespeare Theatre Association of America; Theatre Bay Area Chamber of Commerce; Marin Arts Council; San Rafael Chamber of Commerce
Annual Attendance: 10,000
Facility Category: Outdoor Amphitheatre
Type of Stage: Thrust
Seating Capacity: 600
Year Built: 1967

2291
STOP-GAP
2900 Bristol Street
Suite D-105
Santa Ana, CA 92626
Phone: 714-979-7061
Fax: 714-979-7065
e-mail: get-info@stopgap.org
Web Site: www.stopgap.org
Officers:
   Executive Director/Founder: Don Laffoon
   Executive Director/Vice President: Kathleen Costello

Management:
   Artistic Director: Fionnuala Kenny
Mission: To use theatre as an educational and therapeutic tool to make a positive difference in individual lives.
Founded: 1978
Specialized Field: Ensembles; Contemporary
Status: Non-Profit, Professional
Paid Staff: 20
Organization Type: Performing; Touring; Educational

2292
ENSEMBLE THEATRE COMPANY OF SANTA BARBARA
914 Santa Barbara Street
Santa Barbara, CA 93101
Mailing Address: PO Box 2307, Santa Barbara, CA. 93120-9946
Phone: 805-963-0226
Fax: 805-568-3806
Management:
   President: Richard Banks
   Executive Director: Albert Ihde
   Artistic Director: Robert Grande-Weiss
Founded: 1978
Specialized Field: Comedy; Youth Theater; Classic; Contemporary
Status: Non-Profit, Professional

2293
SPEAKING OF STORIES
924 Anacapa Street
Suite B-1
Santa Barbara, CA 93101
Mailing Address: PO Box 21143, Santa Barbara, CA. 93121
Phone: 805-966-3875
Fax: 805-966-1107
Web Site: www.speakingofstories.org
Management:
   President: Carolyn Butcher
   Executive Director: Teri Ball
   Artistic Director: Maggie Mixsell
Mission: Mission is to promote the appreciation of literature through live theatrical readings and community educational programs.
Founded: 1994
Specialized Field: Storytelling; Drama; Ensembles
Status: Non-Profit, Professional
Paid Staff: 3
Volunteer Staff: 1
Paid Artists: 50
Budget: 250,000
Income Sources: Volunteers; Contributors; Supporters; Tickets
Facility Category: Theater

2294
UNIVERSITY OF CALIFORNIA-SANTA BARBARA: DEPARTMENT OF DRAMATIC ART
2217 Cheadle Hall
Santa Barbara, CA 93106
Phone: 805-893-4327
Fax: 805-893-2441
e-mail: nicole.klanfer@ia.ucsb.edu
Web Site: http://www.hfa.ucsb.edu/support_dramaticarts.html
Management:
   Professor: W. Davies King
   Dean: David Marshall
   Associate Dean: Carol Genetti
   Associate Dean: W.R. Garr

Specialized Field: Educational; Theater Workshops
Budget: $8,500-9,000
Affiliations: ATHE; Theatre Artists Group
Seating Capacity: 340; 110; 100
Year Built: 1964

2295
LYRIC THEATRE WAREHOUSE
430 Martin Avenue
Santa Clara, CA 95050-2911
Phone: 408-986-8631
Fax: 408-986-9090
e-mail: lyricmail@yahoo.com
Management:
   Managing Director: Angela Norlander
   Director: Jerald Enos
Mission: Lyric Theatre is a performing group of over 150 dedicated volunteers who have committed themselves to the art of stagecraft.
Founded: 1974
Specialized Field: Community Theater; Musical; Light Theater
Income Sources: Donations
Season: June 6th - August

2296
SANTA CLARA UNIVERSITY THEATRE AND DANCE DEPARTMENT
500 El Camino Real
Santa Clara, CA 95053
Phone: 408-554-4989
Fax: 408-554-5199
Web Site: http://www.scu.edu/theatre/
Management:
   Chair: Barbara Murray
   Office Manager: Robin Jiguor
Mission: Santa Clara University's Department of Theatre and Dance is a community of artist-scholars, faculty, staff, and students celebrating the creativity of the human spirit through a shared commitment to undergraduate liberal arts education in the Jesuit tradition.
Specialized Field: Educational; Theater Workshops
Budget: $4,650-10,200
Affiliations: NAST; ATHE; San Jose Repertory Theatre; TheatreWorks; SRI; AMT; PCPA
Seating Capacity: 388; 88-139
Year Built: 1975

2297
KIDS ON BROADWAY
PO Box 3461
Santa Cruz, CA 95063
Phone: 831-425-3455
Web Site: http://www.kidsonbroadway.org/
Officers:
   President: David Lundberg
   Vice President: Miguel Diaz
   Treasurer: John Chin
   Secretary: Nancy Main
Management:
   Executive Director: Mary Lundberg
Mission: To train students in all areas of theatrical production, including back stage aspects, thus providing through the arts, vital personal growth experiences to promote excellence and confidence.
Founded: 1995
Specialized Field: Children's Theater; Youth Theater

2298
SHAKESPEARE SANTA CRUZ
University of California
1156 High Street
Santa Cruz, CA 95064

Phone: 831-459-2121
Fax: 831-459-3316
e-mail: webmaster@shakespearesantacruz.org
Web Site: www.shakespearesantacruz.org
Officers:
  President: Nancy Austin
  Vice President: Don Rothman
  Vice President: Renee Winter
Management:
  Artistic Director: Marco Barricelli
  Managing Director: Marcus Cato
  Company Manager: Jennifah Chard
  Marketing/PR Director: Kyle Clausen
Mission: To produce Shakespeare and world drama in translation.
Founded: 1982
Specialized Field: Shakespeare
Paid Staff: 7
Paid Artists: 30
Non-paid Artists: 14
Budget: 1,800,000
Income Sources: Tickets; Grants; Donation
Season: July - August
Performs At: Outdoor, Stanley-Sinsheimer-Glen Theater; Indoor Mainstage
Affiliations: AEA; SSO & C; USA
Annual Attendance: 45,000
Type of Stage: Indoor-Thrust
Seating Capacity: Indoor, 540; Outdoor, 750+

2299
PCPA THEATERFEST
800 S College Drive
Santa Maria, CA 93454
Phone: 805-928-7731
Fax: 805-928-7506
Toll-free: 800-727-2123
e-mail: pcpa@pcpa.org
Web Site: www.pcpa.org
Management:
  Artistic Director: Mark Boher
  Managing Director: Michael Black
  Conservatory Direct./Actor Training: Roger DeLaurier
  Casting Director: Erik Stein
Mission: A professional conservatory theatre, committed to reflecting and transforming the diverse community with the art of live theatre. Believe that the theatre has a vital role and responsibility in the community to enrich cultural literacy and improve the quality of life. Committed to serving the current audience, cultivating the future audience and training the next generation of theatre professionals.
Utilizes: Actors; AEA Actors; Artists-in-Residence; Choreographers; Composers-in-Residence; Designers; Educators; Guest Accompanists; Guest Artists; Guest Companies; Guest Conductors; Guest Designers; Guest Lecturers; High School Drama; Instructors; Music; Poets; Resident Artists; Resident Professionals; Soloists; Student Interns
Founded: 1964
Specialized Field: Theatre
Status: Professional; Semi-Professional; Non-Professional; Nonprofit
Paid Staff: 35
Volunteer Staff: 2
Paid Artists: 18
Non-paid Artists: 5
Budget: $4.2 Million
Performs At: Performing Arts Center
Affiliations: U/RTA; AEA; TCG; USA
Annual Attendance: 80,000
Facility Category: Producing Theatre
Type of Stage: 3/4 Thrust

Seating Capacity: 448
Year Built: 1968
Year Remodeled: 2005

2300
ACTORS REPERTORY THEATRE AT SANTA MONICA PLAYHOUSE
1211 4th Street
Santa Monica, CA 90401
Phone: 310-394-9779
Fax: 310-393-5573
e-mail: theatre@santamonicaplayhouse.com
Web Site: www.santamonicaplayhouse.com
Management:
  Co-Artistic Director: Evelyn Rudie
  Co-Artistic Director: Chris DeCarlo
  Education Coordinator: Serena Dolinksy
Mission: To educate, enlighten, entertain and enrich the health and well-being of the local and global community through theatre arts, arts education and cultural exchange.
Utilizes: Singers
Founded: 1960
Specialized Field: Theatre and Theatre Arts Education
Status: Non-Profit
Paid Staff: 10
Volunteer Staff: 20
Paid Artists: 50
Income Sources: Theatre Communications Group; Actors' Equity Association; Theatre Los Angeles
Performs At: Santa Monica Playhouse
Facility Category: Theatre Arts Complex
Year Built: 1960
Year Remodeled: 1980
Rental Contact: Evelyn Rudie

2301
BROAD STAGE
Madison Project of Santa Monica College
1900 Pico Boulevard
Santa Monica, CA 90405
Phone: 310-434-3430
Fax: 310-434-3439
e-mail: franzen_dale@smc.edu
Web Site: www.thebroadstage.com
Officers:
  President: Dr. Chui Tsang
Management:
  Director: Dale Franzen
Founded: 1999
Specialized Field: Musical; Youth Theater; Ethnic Theater; Community Theater; Classic; Contemporary; Theater Workshops
Status: Non-Profit, Professional
Paid Staff: 4

2302
SUMMER REPERTORY THEATRE
1501 Mendocino Avenue
Santa Rosa, CA 95401
Phone: 707-527-4419
Fax: 707-524-1689
e-mail: jnewman@santarosa.edu
Web Site: www.summerrep.com
Officers:
  Business Manager: Shannon Stevens
Management:
  Artistic Director: James Newman
Utilizes: Actors; Choreographers; Collaborations; Community Members; Community Talent; Composers; Contract Orchestras; Dancers; Designers; Educators; Grant Writers; Guest Artists; Guest Composers; Guest Conductors; Guest Musical Directors; High School Drama; Local Artists; Local Unknown Artists;

Multimedia; Music; Resident Professionals; Scenic Designers; Sign Language Translators; Soloists; Students; Student Interns; Visual Arts
Founded: 1972
Specialized Field: Musical; Comedy; Youth Theater; Classic; Contemporary
Status: Non-Profit, Non-Professional
Paid Staff: 25
Season: May - August
Type of Stage: Proscenium
Stage Dimensions: 36'x 30'

2303
ANTENNA THEATER
Fort Cronkhite
Building 1057
Sausalito, CA 94965
Mailing Address: PO Box 939, Sausalito, CA. 94966
Phone: 415-332-8867
Fax: 415-332-8648
Web Site: www.antenna-theatre.org
Management:
  Artistic Director: Chris Hardman
  Managing Director: Sean Horton
  Assistant Director: Erica Wobensmith
Mission: Antenna seeks to invent, discover, and explore ways of involving a variety of artistic disciplines and new technologies in the theatre experience.
Utilizes: Actors; Choreographers; Commissioned Music; Dancers; Designers; Guest Conductors; Guild Activities; Local Artists; Lyricists; Multi Collaborations; Organization Contracts; Original Music Scores; Student Interns
Founded: 1980
Specialized Field: Musical; Comedy; Youth Theater; Dinner Theater; Ethnic Theater; Community Theater; Puppet; Classic; Contemporary
Status: Non-Profit, Professional
Paid Staff: 5
Paid Artists: 5
Budget: $500,000
Income Sources: Theatre Communications Group; California Confederaton of the Arts; Theatre Bay Area
Performs At: Site Specific
Organization Type: Performing; Touring

2304
INDEPENDENT EYE
502 Pleasant Hill
Sebastopol, CA 95472
Phone: 707-824-4307
Fax: 707-824-4307
Toll-free: 800-357-6016
Management:
  Artistic Director: Elizabeth Fuller
  Artistic Director: Conrad Fuller
Mission: The Independent Eye is a progressive theatre ensemble, now in its 30th year, devoted to creating new plays and new visions of classics. Based in Northern California, our work reaches a national audience.
Founded: 1974
Specialized Field: Drama; Specialty Acts; Radio Performances
Status: Nonprofit; Non-Equity
Season: Year Round

2305
LA CONNECTION COMEDY THEATRE
13442 Ventura Boulevard
Sherman Oaks, CA 91423
Phone: 818-710-1320
Fax: 818-710-8666
e-mail: madmovies@hotmail.com
Web Site: www.laconnectioncomedy.com

Management:
President: Kent Skov
Mission: To produce comedy productions for film, TV, industrial and theatrical shows. Live improvised comedy sketch, movie dubbing, year round. To become a member, performers may audition by appointment.
Founded: 1977
Specialized Field: Comedy; Specialty Acts
Status: For-Profit, Professional
Paid Staff: 6
Volunteer Staff: 1
Season: Year Round
Type of Stage: Thrust
Seating Capacity: 99

2306
NORTH COAST REPERTORY THEATRE

987D Lomas Santa Fe Drive
Solana Beach, CA 92075
Phone: 858-481-1055
Fax: 858-481-1527
Toll-free: 888-776-MCRT
e-mail: ncrt@northcoastrep.org
Web Site: www.northcoastrep.org
Officers:
President: Ira Epstein
VP: Lorraine Stamoulis
Treasurer: Michael Tedesco
Secretary: Marvin Read
Management:
President of the Board: Ira Epstein
Artistic Director: David Ellestein
Founder: Olive Blakistone
Managing Director: Paul Viera
Manager/Director: Veronica Baker
Mission: To produce artistically demanding plays of high quality, which include original works, neglected works of literary merit, both contemporary and classical and those which address social issues.
Utilizes: Actors; AEA Actors; Artists-in-Residence; Choreographers; Collaborating Artists; Collaborations; Commissioned Composers; Commissioned Music; Educators; Fine Artists; Grant Writers; Guest Accompanists; Guest Artists; Guest Choreographers; Guest Companies; Guest Conductors; Guest Designers; Guest Ensembles; Guest Instructors; Guest Lecturers; Guest Musical Directors; Guest Soloists; Guild Activities; High School Drama; Instructors; Local Artists; Multimedia; Music; Original Music Scores; Performance Artists; Soloists
Founded: 1982
Specialized Field: Musical; Comedy; Classic; Contemporary; Musical
Status: Non-Profit, Professional
Paid Staff: 10
Volunteer Staff: 300
Paid Artists: 40
Budget: $750,000 +
Income Sources: San Diego Theatre League; California Arts Council
Performs At: Thomas Santa Fe Plaza
Annual Attendance: 35,000 +
Facility Category: Indoor
Type of Stage: 3/4 Thrust
Seating Capacity: 194
Year Built: 1982
Year Remodeled: 1988
Rental Contact: Sue Schaffner
Organization Type: Performing

2307
SIERRA REPERTORY THEATRE AT EAST SONORA

13891 Highway 108
PO Box 3030
Sonora, CA 95370
Phone: 209-532-3133
Fax: 209-532-7270
e-mail: srt@mlode.com
Web Site: www.sierrarep.com
Management:
Producing Director: Dennis Jones
Managing Director: Sara Jones
Marketing Director: Jan Mangili
Utilizes: Actors; AEA Actors; Artists-in-Residence; Choreographers; Collaborating Artists; Collaborations; Dancers; Designers; Educators; Guest Accompanists; Guest Artists; Guest Companies; Guest Conductors; Guest Designers; Guest Lecturers; Guild Activities; Instructors; Local Artists; Multimedia; Music; Original Music Scores; Resident Artists; Resident Professionals; Sign Language Translators; Student Interns
Founded: 1980
Specialized Field: Educational; Theater Workshops; Drama; New Plays
Paid Staff: 30
Volunteer Staff: 2
Paid Artists: 140
Budget: $1,000,000
Income Sources: Ticket Sales; National Endowment for the Arts Grants; California Arts Council Grants; Fundraising & Sponsors
Season: Febuary - December
Performs At: Contemporary Live Theatre
Annual Attendance: 54,000
Facility Category: Live Theatre
Type of Stage: Proscenium
Stage Dimensions: 40x30
Seating Capacity: 202; 270
Year Built: 1980
Year Remodeled: 1992

2308
STAGE 3 THEATRE COMPANY

208 S Green Street
Sonora, CA 95370
Phone: 209-536-1778
Fax: 209-536-1778
e-mail: info@stage3.org
Web Site: www.stage3.org
Management:
President: Dan Quintom
Artistic Director: Don Bilotti
Managing Director: Neil Mill
Mission: Stage 3 Theatre Company is dedicated to the development and production of new plays by new playwrights, and contemporary works by established playwrights.
Utilizes: Actors; AEA Actors; Choreographers; Collaborating Artists; Collaborations; Community Talent; Designers; Educators; Guest Accompanists; Guest Artists; Guest Conductors; Guest Designers; Guest Lecturers; Guest Musical Directors; Guest Speakers; Instructors; Local Artists; Multimedia; Music; Original Music Scores; Paid Performers; Performance Artists; Resident Professionals; Scenic Designers; Sign Language Translators; Students; Visual Arts
Founded: 1993
Specialized Field: Comedy; Ensembles; Contemporary
Status: Non-Profit, Non-Professional
Paid Staff: 3
Paid Artists: 40
Budget: $100,000

Income Sources: Ticket Sales; Grants; Contributions; Rentals; Touring; Classes; Advertising Revenue
Annual Attendance: 6,000
Type of Stage: Black Box
Stage Dimensions: 20'x20'
Seating Capacity: 80-100
Year Built: 1996
Rental Contact: Artistic Director Barbara Segal-Mill
Resident Groups: Stage 3 Theatre Company

2309
STOCKTON CIVIC THEATRE

2312 Rose Marie Lane
Stockton, CA 95207
Phone: 209-473-2400
Fax: 209-473-1502
Web Site: www.sctlivetheatre.org
Management:
Producing Director: Jim Coleman
Development/Marketing Director: James Treganza
Mission: To provide the community with quality theatre.
Utilizes: Guest Companies
Founded: 1951
Specialized Field: Community Theater; Classic
Status: Non-Profit, Non-Professional
Paid Staff: 4
Volunteer Staff: 300
Non-paid Artists: 200
Income Sources: Patrons
Performs At: Civic Center
Annual Attendance: 25,000
Facility Category: Community Theatre
Type of Stage: Proscenium
Seating Capacity: 275
Year Built: 1980
Rental Contact: Producing Director Paul Bengston
Organization Type: Performing; Resident

2310
TILLIE LEWIS THEATER

Delta College
5151 Pacific Avenue
Stockton, CA 95207
Phone: 209-954-5266
Fax: 209-954-5755
e-mail: pfrancois@deltacollege.edu
Web Site: www.deltacollege.edu
Management:
President: Raul Rodriguez
Founded: 1977
Specialized Field: Drama
Status: Non-Profit, Non-Professional
Paid Staff: 4
Facility Category: Theatre
Type of Stage: Proscenium
Seating Capacity: 400
Year Built: 1973
Rental Contact: Dr. Charles Jennings

2311
UNIVERSITY OF THE PACIFIC: DEPARTMENT OF THEATRE ARTS

3601 Pacific Avenue
Stockton, CA 95211
Phone: 209-946-2116
Fax: 209-946-2118
e-mail: cmcclellan@pacific.edu
Web Site: http://web.pacific.edu/x13787.xml
Officers:
Department Chair: Cathie McClellan
Management:
Director: Gary Armagnac
Specialized Field: Educational; Theater Workshops

Budget: $2,550-8,600
Affiliations: U/RTA
Seating Capacity: 400; 80-120
Year Built: 1956
Year Remodeled: 1999

2312
ARK THEATRE COMPANY

PO Box 1188
Studio City, CA 91614
Phone: 323-969-1707
e-mail: info@arktheatre.org
Management:
Director: Richard Tatum
Artistic Director: Derek Medina
Associate Artistic Director: Richard Tatum
Mission: A new Los Angeles theatre company formed to produce and present a repertory season by an ongoing company of actors, writers, directors, and designers.
Specialized Field: Educational; Theater Workshops; Drama; Contemporary

2313
LOS ANGELES DESIGNERS' THEATRE

PO Box 1883
Studio City, CA 91614-0883
Phone: 323-650-9600
Fax: 323-654-3210
Management:
Artistic Director: Richard Niederberg
Founded: 1970
Specialized Field: Musical; Comedy; Ethnic Theater; Community Theater; Puppet; Classic; Contemporary
Status: Non-Profit, Professional

2314
THEATRE EAST

12655 Ventura Boulevard
Studio City, CA 91604
Phone: 818-760-4160
Web Site: www.angelfire.com/la/theatreeast
Officers:
President: Michael Harrity
VP: Linda DeMetrick
Treasurer: Susan O'Sullivan
Secretary: Jill Martin
Management:
President: Michael Harrity
VP: Linda Demetrick
Director: Gene Butler
Mission: Theatre East shall be an organization of dedicated professional artists in the theatrical and allied arts, banded together for the purpose of gaining artistic growth through performance and self-evaluation. We shall stimulate and encourage workshop activity that may be considered for public performance. We shall endeavor to make our influence felt as a creative force in the theatrical community.
Founded: 1960
Specialized Field: Drama; Musical
Status: Professional
Paid Staff: 125
Organization Type: Resident

2315
CALIFORNIA THEATRE CENTER

PO Box 2007
Sunnyvale, CA 94087
Phone: 408-245-2978
Fax: 408-245-0235
e-mail: ctc@ctcinc.org
Web Site: www.ctcinc.org
Management:

General Director: Gayle Cornelison
Resident Director: Will Huddleston
Box Office: Diana Burnell
Production Manager: Marley Morris
Administrative Director: Susan Earle
Tour Director: Lisa Mallette
Mission: Providing children and families with quality theatre.
Utilizes: Actors; AEA Actors; Artists-in-Residence; Choreographers; Commissioned Composers; Commissioned Music; Designers; Educators; Guest Accompanists; Guest Artists; Guest Companies; Guest Conductors; Guest Designers; Guest Lecturers; Guest Teachers; Instructors; Local Artists; Multimedia; Music; Original Music Scores; Performance Artists; Poets; Resident Artists; Resident Professionals; Singers; Theatre Companies
Founded: 1976
Specialized Field: Youth Theater
Status: Non-Profit, Professional
Paid Staff: 12
Paid Artists: 20
Budget: $1,750,000
Income Sources: Box Office; Touring; Education; Contributions
Performs At: The Performing Arts Center
Affiliations: Theatre Communications Group
Annual Attendance: 95,000; 150,000
Facility Category: Theatre
Type of Stage: Proscenium
Stage Dimensions: 34x25
Seating Capacity: 200
Year Built: 1974
Year Remodeled: 1991
Organization Type: Performing; Touring

2316
WILL GEER THEATRICUM BOTANICUM

1419 N Topanga Canyon Boulevard
Topanga Canyon, CA 90290
Phone: 310-455-2322
Fax: 310-455-3724
e-mail: theatricum@earthlink.net
Web Site: www.theatricum.com
Officers:
President: Mikko Sperber
Executive Director: Ellen Geer
Management:
Managing Director: Robert Camper
Mission: To elevate, educate, and entertain audiences of all ages by presenting thought-provoking classics, socially relevant plays, and educaiton programs in a beautiful, natural outdoor sanctuary for the arts. By passing on a sense of history to young people and adults alike, great works of art inform their present and inspire their future. A true renaissance theatre offering a diversity of programming from Shakespeare to poetry to folk music.
Utilizes: Actors; AEA Actors; Designers; Educators; Five Seasonal Concerts; Guild Activities
Founded: 1973
Specialized Field: Theatre
Status: Non-Profit, Professional
Paid Staff: 50
Paid Artists: 28
Budget: $500,000
Income Sources: Tuitions; Ticket Sales; Donations
Season: April - September
Performs At: Outdoor Amphitheatre
Type of Stage: Outdoor
Seating Capacity: 299
Organization Type: Performing; Resident; Educational

2317
CALIFORNIA STATE UNIVERSITY, STANISLAUS

801 W Monte Vista Avenue
Turlock, CA 95382
Phone: 209-667-3451
Fax: 209-667-3782
e-mail: cevett@csustan.edu
Web Site: www.csustan.edu
Officers:
Chair: Clay Everet
Management:
President: Hamid Shirvani
University President: Clay Everet
Mission: California State University Stanislaus offers the degree Bachelor of Arts, general acting and technical emphasis.
Founded: 1962
Specialized Field: Educational; Theater Workshops
Status: Non-Profit, Non-Professional
Paid Staff: 12
Budget: $20,000-25,000
Affiliations: NAST; ATHE
Facility Category: University Theatre
Seating Capacity: 300, 100
Year Built: 1970

2318
UKIAH PLAYERS THEATRE

1041 Low Gap Road
Ukiah, CA 95482
Phone: 707-462-1210
Fax: 707-462-1790
Web Site: www.wkohplayerstheatre.org
Management:
Executive Director: Kate Magruder
Artistic Director: Michael Ducharme
Production Manager: Jonathan Wipple
Publicity Manager: Dan Hibshman
Mission: Offering the general community a broad range of theatre experience; encouraging and educating theatre artists; providing a cultural venue.
Utilizes: Actors; Artists-in-Residence; Collaborations; Guild Activities; Instructors; Local Artists; Lyricists; Multi Collaborations; Multimedia; Performance Artists; Resident Professionals; Soloists; Touring Companies
Founded: 1977
Specialized Field: Musical; Comedy; Youth Theater; Ethnic Theater; Community Theater; Classic; Contemporary
Status: Non-Profit, Non-Professional
Paid Staff: 4
Volunteer Staff: 200
Paid Artists: 20
Non-paid Artists: 100
Budget: $175,000
Performs At: Community Theatre
Affiliations: AACT, TCS, TBA
Annual Attendance: 10,000
Facility Category: Playhouse
Type of Stage: Proscenium
Stage Dimensions: 24'x38'
Seating Capacity: 120
Year Built: 1981
Year Remodeled: 1985
Rental Contact: Michael Ducharme
Organization Type: Performing; Touring; Resident; Educational; Sponsoring

2319

CALIFORNIA INSTITUTE OF THE ARTS: SCHOOL OF THEATER

24700 McBean Parkway
Valencia, CA 91355
Phone: 661-255-7834
Fax: 661-255-0462
e-mail: theater@calarts.edu
Web Site: www.calarts.edu
Management:
Executive Director: John Gottlie
Founded: 1976
Specialized Field: Comedy; Youth Theater; Puppet; Classic; Contemporary
Status: For-Profit, Professional
Budget: $6,600-12,800
Affiliations: NAST; U/RTA
Seating Capacity: 300; 30-100; 30-80
Year Built: 1971
Year Remodeled: 1994

2320

SIX FLAGS MAGIC MOUNTAIN

26101 Magic Mountain Parkway
Valencia, CA 91355
Mailing Address: PO Box 5500, Valencia, CA. 91385
Phone: 661-255-4100
Fax: 661-255-4171
Web Site: www.sixflags.com
Management:
Entertainment Manager: Scott Sterner
Founded: 1971
Specialized Field: Youth Theater; Community Theater
Status: For-Profit, Professional
Type of Stage: Proscenium; Thrust; Flex
Seating Capacity: 200-3000

2321

LOS ANGELES THEATRE WORKS

681 Venice Boulevard
Venice, CA 90291
Phone: 310-827-0808
Fax: 310-827-4949
Toll-free: 800-708-8863
e-mail: latw@latw.org
Officers:
President: Doug Jaffe
Vice President: Aviva Covitz
Secretary: Doris Blaizely
Treasurer: Alan Finkel
Management:
President: Douglas Jeffe
Managing Director: Anne Gimbel
Producing Director: Susan Albert-Loewenberg
Mission: Los Angeles Theatre Works, a pioneering lab for playwrights, directors and other theatre artists, is committed to the exploration of contemporary work in theatre.
Utilizes: Actors; Artists-in-Residence; Collaborations; Educators; Fine Artists; Five Seasonal Concerts; Grant Writers; Guest Accompanists; Guest Designers; Guest Ensembles; Guest Lecturers; Guest Musical Directors; Guild Activities; High School Drama; Instructors; Local Artists; Multi Collaborations; Music; Original Music Scores; Performance Artists; Sign Language Translators
Founded: 1974
Specialized Field: Radio Performances; Children's Theater
Status: Professional; Nonprofit
Income Sources: California Arts Council
Performs At: Skirball Cultural Center
Facility Category: Auditorium

Seating Capacity: 350
Rental Contact: 310-440-4595 Skirball Cultural Center
Organization Type: Touring; Producing

2322

CELEBRATION THEATRE

7985 Santa Monica Boulevard
Suite 109-1
West Hollywood, CA 90046
Phone: 323-957-1884
Fax: 323-957-1826
Web Site: www.celebrationtheatre.com
Management:
Artistic Director: Michael Matthews
Managing Artistic Director: Derek Charles Livingston
Managing Director: David Tarlow
Mission: To illuminate all aspects of the gay and lesbian experience to the gay community and the community at large, while providing a safe and nurturing environment for gay and lesbian writers, directors, designers, and performers.
Utilizes: Guest Companies; Singers
Founded: 1982
Specialized Field: Drama; Contemporary; Classic
Status: Professional; Nonprofit
Paid Staff: 10
Income Sources: Grants; Ticket Sales; Indunderal Dancers
Performs At: Celebration Theatre
Annual Attendance: 4,000
Type of Stage: Three Quarter Stage
Seating Capacity: 64
Organization Type: Resident; Educational

2323

GROUP AT THE STRASBERG ACTING STUDIO

7936 Santa Monica Boulevard
West Hollywood, CA 90046
Phone: 323-650-7777
Fax: 323-650-7770
e-mail: admissionsla@strasberg.com
Web Site: www.strasberg.com
Management:
President: Victoria Krane
Executive Director: Anna Strasberg
Managing Director: David Strasberg
Founded: 1969
Specialized Field: Comedy; Youth Theater; Community Theater; Classic; Contemporary
Status: For-Profit, Professional
Paid Staff: 50
Paid Artists: 15
Performs At: Marilyn Monroe Theatre, Studio Stras, Stage Lee Strasberg
Type of Stage: Endstage
Seating Capacity: 99, 49, 49

2324

WHITTIER JUNIOR THEATRE

13230 Penn Street
Whittier, CA 90602
Phone: 562-945-8200
Fax: 562-464-3581
e-mail: admin@cityofwhittier.org
Web Site: www.whittierch.org
Management:
City Manager: Steve Helvey
Managing Supervisor: Dan Walker
Theatre Manager and Jt Director: Dan Walker
Mission: Offering performance opportunities to children 9 through 18 years old; presenting three productions per year.

Utilizes: Guest Companies
Founded: 1898
Specialized Field: Musical; Comedy; Youth Theater; Community Theater; Classic; Contemporary
Status: For-Profit, Non-Professional
Budget: $18,000
Income Sources: Box Office; Class Registration
Performs At: The Center Theatre
Type of Stage: Proscenium
Seating Capacity: 400
Year Built: 1961
Year Remodeled: 1987
Rental Contact: Michael Eiden
Organization Type: Performing; Touring; Educational

2325

YREKA COMMUNITY THEATRE

810 N Oregon Street
Yreka, CA 96097
Phone: 530-841-2332
Fax: 530-841-2339
Management:
Manager: Jeff Shinn
Mission: To provide a venue for community performances and productions both in-house and private.
Founded: 1976
Specialized Field: Community Theater
Status: Non-Profit, Non-Professional
Paid Staff: 3
Volunteer Staff: 4
Performs At: Yreka Community Theatre
Seating Capacity: 300
Year Built: 1976
Cost: $2 million
Rental Contact: Jeff Shirn

Colorado

2326

AURORA FOX CHILDREN'S THEATRE COMPANY

9900 E Colfax Avenue
Aurora, CO 80010
Mailing Address: PO Box 9 Aurora, CO 80040
Phone: 303-739-1970
Fax: 303-361-2909
Management:
Children's Theatre Coordinator: Thom Wise
Mission: To provide training and performance opportunities for young people.
Utilizes: Guest Companies; Singers
Founded: 1979
Specialized Field: Community Theater; Children's Theater
Status: Non-Professional
Paid Staff: 8
Non-paid Artists: 60
Budget: $550,000
Income Sources: City of Aurora; SCFO
Performs At: Aurora Fox Arts Center
Annual Attendance: 30,000
Facility Category: Theatre
Type of Stage: Proscenium
Stage Dimensions: 50'w x 40' d x 14'
Seating Capacity: 245
Year Built: 1946
Year Remodeled: 1985
Cost: $1 million
Organization Type: Performing; Resident; Educational

2327
LE CENTRE DU SILENCE MIME SCHOOL
PO Box 1015
Boulder, CO 80306-1015
Phone: 303-661-9271
Fax: 303-604-6046
e-mail: savital@bodyspeak.com
Web Site: www.bodyspeak.com
Management:
    Founder and Director: Samuel Avital
Mission: To surpass the normal means of communication offered by the entertainment industry, and society's abuse of the spoken word; to perpetuate and educate in the Art of Silence - MIME.
Founded: 1971
Specialized Field: Musical; Comedy; Youth Theater; Dinner Theater; Ethnic Theater; Community Theater; Puppet; Classic; Contemporary; Mime
Status: For-Profit, Professional
Paid Artists: 1

2328
UNIVERSITY OF COLORADO AT BOULDER: DEPARTMENT OF THEATRE AND DANCE
261 UCP
Boulder, CO 80309
Phone: 303-492-7355
Fax: 303-492-7722
e-mail: thrtdnce@colorado.edu
Web Site: www.colorado.edu/theatredance
Officers:
    Chair: Bud Coleman
    Associate Chair: Bruce Bergner
    Associate Chair: Onye Ozuzu
Management:
    President: Bruce Benson
    Graduate Theatre Studies Director: Dr Oliver Gerland
    Dance Graduate Studies Director: Michelle Ellsworth
Founded: 1872
Specialized Field: Musical; Youth Theater; Dinner Theater; Ethnic Theater; Community Theater; Classic; Contemporary
Status: Non-Profit, Non-Professional
Paid Staff: 9
Budget: $3,500-5,500
Affiliations: ATHE; Colorado Shakespeare Festival
Seating Capacity: 416; 140; 1004
Year Built: 1902
Year Remodeled: 1989

2329
UPSTART CROW THEATRE COMPANY
2131 Arapahoe
Boulder, CO 80302
Phone: 303-442-1415
e-mail: info@theupstartcrow.org
Web Site: www.theupstartcrow.org
Management:
    President: Richard Bell
Mission: A dedicated core group of actors not only supplies stage talent, but backstage support as well.
Founded: 1980
Specialized Field: Classic
Status: Non-Profit, Professional

2330
CASTLE ROCK PLAYERS
PO Box 1224
Castle Rock, CO 80104
Phone: 866-879-7373
e-mail: info@crplayers.org
Web Site: www.crplayers.org
Management:
    President: Sandy Haworth South
    Vice President: Anne McGhee Stinson
    Artistic Director: Michael A Parker
    Business Manager: Greg Bell
    Director Theatrical Instruction: Jacki Mangan
    Publicity Coordinator: Kimmy Brandon
Mission: Dedicated to providing quality theater experiences for the community.
Utilizes: Actors; Local Artists; Performance Artists
Founded: 1997
Opened: 1997
Specialized Field: Community Theater; Theater Workshops
Affiliations: Castle Rock Chamber of Commerce, Colorado Theatre Guild

2331
CREEDE REPERTORY THEATRE
124 N Main Street
PO Box 269
Creede, CO 81130
Phone: 719-658-2540
Fax: 719-658-2343
Toll-free: 866-658-2540
Web Site: www.creederep.org
Officers:
    Vice President: Arvin VanRy
    Secretary: Charlene Ameel
    Treasurer: Stan Lent
Management:
    President of Board: Robert Slater
    Executive Director: Maurice La Mee
    Managing Director: Tristan Wilson
    Development Director: Lynnaa Jackson
Mission: To produce a summer repertory season of eight plays; to promote knowledge of performing arts; to raise standards; to increase accessibility.
Utilizes: Guest Companies; Singers
Founded: 1966
Specialized Field: Musical; Comedy; Youth Theater; Puppet; Classic; Contemporary
Status: Non-Profit, Professional
Paid Staff: 5
Paid Artists: 50
Budget: $778,000
Income Sources: Donations; Grants; Box Office
Season: Late May - Early September
Performs At: Creede Repertory Theatre
Annual Attendance: 20,000
Facility Category: Performance Center
Type of Stage: Proscenium
Seating Capacity: 234
Year Remodeled: 1991
Organization Type: Performing; Touring; Educational; Sponsoring

2332
AVENUE THEATER
417 E 17th Avenue
Denver, CO 80203
Phone: 303-321-5925
e-mail: Avenuetheater@gmail.com
Web Site: http://www.avenuetheater.com/
Management:
    Artistic Director: Bob Wells
    Theatre Manager: Dave Johnson
    Administrative Coordinator: Heather Newman
Specialized Field: Comedy; Theater Workshops

2333
CHANGING SCENE THEATER
1527 1/2 Champa Street
Denver, CO 80202
Phone: 303-893-5775
Management:
    President: Alfred Brooks
    VP: Maxine Munt
Mission: To offer experience and performing space to young artists. Specializes in new works.
Utilizes: Guest Companies
Founded: 1968
Specialized Field: Drama; Contemporary; Experimental
Status: Nonprofit
Organization Type: Performing; Resident; Educational; Sponsoring

2334
DENVER CENTER THEATER COMPANY
1101 13th Street
Denver, CO 80204
Phone: 303-893-4000
Fax: 303-893-3206
Toll-free: 800-641-1222
e-mail: webmaster@dcpa.org
Web Site: www.denvercenter.org
Officers:
    President: Randy Weeks
Management:
    Artistic Director: Kent Thompson
    President: Randy Weeks
    Associate Artistic Director: Bruce K Sevy
    General Manager: Charles Varin
    Production Manager: Edward Lapine
    Education Director: Daniel Renner
    Vice President of Mktng & Comm.: Stacy Shaw
Mission: As the flagship theatre of the Rocky Mountain region, The Denver Center for the Performing Arts creates and presents exceptional theatre that engages, excits, provokes and inspires both artists and audience. We emrace the classics while striving to create new plays and musicals that advance the American theatre movement. We are committed to making The Denver Center a center for lifelong learning and civic engagement.
Utilizes: Guest Companies; Singers
Founded: 1979
Specialized Field: Theatre
Status: Non-Profit, Professional
Paid Staff: 78
Income Sources: The Denver Center; Theatre Communications Group; League of Resident Theatres
Performs At: Denver Center Theatre
Affiliations: League of Resident Theatres
Annual Attendance: 170,000
Facility Category: Four-Square Block, 12-Acre Denver Performing Arts Complex
Type of Stage: Thrust, Round, Proscenium, Thrust
Seating Capacity: 750, 650, 250, 200
Organization Type: Performing; Touring; Resident; Educational

2335
DENVER CIVIC THEATRE
721 Sante Fe Drive
Denver, CO 80204
Phone: 303-309-3773
Fax: 303-309-3774
Management:
    President: Richard Bernstein
    Executive Director: James Jay Cardwell
    General Manager: Gary Miller

Chairman: Mitchell Maxwell
Founded: 1985
Opened: 1991
Specialized Field: Musical; Comedy
Status: Non-Profit

2336
DENVER PUPPET THEATRE
3156 W 38th Avenue
Denver, CO 80211-2004
Phone: 303-458-6446
e-mail: annie@hypermall.net
Web Site: www.denverpuppettheater.com
Management:
   President: Annie Zock
Mission: Top quality puppet performance plus hands on puppet activities year round.
Utilizes: Scenic Designers
Founded: 1989
Specialized Field: Youth Theater; Puppet
Status: For-Profit, Professional
Paid Staff: 24
Paid Artists: 1
Budget: $90,000
Income Sources: Ticket Sales; Puppet Sales; Birthdays
Affiliations: Puppets of America; Theatre of Youth Coalition
Annual Attendance: 20,000
Stage Dimensions: 10'x20'
Seating Capacity: 100
Year Built: 1950
Year Remodeled: 1996
Resident Groups: Denver Puppet Theatre

2337
GERMINAL STAGE DENVER
2450 W 44th Avenue
Denver, CO 80211
Phone: 303-455-7108
e-mail: gsden@privatei.com
Web Site: www.germinalstage.com
Management:
   Director: Ed Baierlein
   Associate Producer: Sallie Diamond
Founded: 1974
Specialized Field: Drama; Contemporary
Status: Professional
Affiliations: Germinal Stage Denver
Stage Dimensions: 20'x15'
Orchestra Pit: 1
Architect: Ron Rinker

2338
IMPULSE THEATER
1634 18th Street
Lower Level
Denver, CO 80202
Phone: 303-297-2111
Fax: 303-297-1378
Toll-free: 877-467-8571
e-mail: info@impulsetheater.com
Web Site: www.impulsetheater.com
Management:
   Producer/Director: John Bauers
   Marketing: Noucha Noodele
Mission: Quick-witted cast of talented actors performing a funny mix of comedy, theater, and audience interaction.
Founded: 1987
Opened: 1987
Specialized Field: Musical; Comedy; Youth Theater; Dinner Theater; Ethnic Theater; Community Theater; Puppet; Classic; Contemporary

Status: For-Profit, Professional
Paid Staff: 20
Paid Artists: 15
Seating Capacity: 178

2339
JAFRIKA
3230 Clay Street
Denver, CO 80211
Phone: 303-433-7163
Fax: 303-433-7163
e-mail: tingzen@juno.com
Management:
   Dancer/Choreographer: Ricki Harada
   Musician/Composer: Chris Macor
Mission: Japanese dancer, black poet, white musician.
Utilizes: Soloists
Specialized Field: Drama; Contemporary; New Plays
Paid Artists: 3
Budget: $18,000
Income Sources: Paid by venue
Annual Attendance: 2,000
Facility Category: Schools, Libraries, Festivals

2340
METROPOLITAN STATE COLLEGE OF DENVER: DEPARTMENT OF THEATRE
Campus Box 34
Denver, CO 80217
Mailing Address: PO Box 173362
Phone: 303-556-3033
e-mail: hetzelm@mscd.edu
Web Site: http://www.mscd.edu/~cas/theatre/
Management:
   Director of Theatre: Dr. Marilyn Hetzel
Specialized Field: Educational; Theater Workshops
Budget: $4,000-7,000
Affiliations: Denver Civic Theatre; Denver Center for the Performing Arts
Seating Capacity: 99
Year Built: 1967

2341
NATIONAL THEATRE CONSERVATORY
1050 13th Street
Denver, CO 80204
Phone: 303-446-4855
Fax: 303-623-0693
Web Site: www.denvercenter.org
Management:
   Executive Director: Daniel Renner
Founded: 1984
Specialized Field: Educational; Theater Workshops
Status: Non-Profit, Non-Professional
Paid Staff: 28
Budget: $30,000-46,000
Affiliations: Denver Centre Theatre Company
Seating Capacity: 550; 420; 150
Year Built: 1979

2342
SU TEATRO
4725 High Street
Denver, CO 80216
Phone: 303-296-0219
Fax: 303-296-4614
e-mail: elcentro@suteatro.org
Web Site: www.suteatro.org
Officers:
   Board Member: Debra Gallegos
Management:
   Executive Director: Anthony J Garcia
   Development Director: Tonya Mote

Mission: Speaking to the struggles of the barrios of the Southwest; preserving and perpetuating Chicano culture and language.
Founded: 1971
Specialized Field: Musical; Comedy; Youth Theater; Ethnic Theater; Community Theater
Status: Non-Profit, Professional
Performs At: El Centro Su Teatro
Organization Type: Performing; Touring; Educational; Sponsoring

2343
UNIVERSITY OF COLORADO AT DENVER: DEPARTMENT OF PERFORMING ARTS
College Of Artsa, Campus Box 166
PO Box 173344
Denver, CO 80217-3364
Mailing Address: PO Box 173364, Denver, CO 80217
Phone: 303-556-4797
Fax: 303-556-2335
Web Site: www.cudenver.edu
Management:
   President: James Shore
   Executive Director: Laura Cuepara
   Managing Director: Nathan Thompson
Founded: 1995
Specialized Field: Classic; Contemporary
Status: Non-Profit, Non-Professional
Paid Staff: 15
Budget: $5,000-7,000
Affiliations: ATHE; Curious Productions; The Denver Center for the Performing Arts
Seating Capacity: 350; 120
Year Built: 2000

2344
UNIVERSITY OF DENVER DEPARTMENT OF THEATRE
MRH 104
Denver, CO 80208
Phone: 303-871-2518
Fax: 303-871-2505
Web Site: www.du.edu/thea
Management:
   Provost: John Seacoumb
   Chair of Dept: Fredrick Barbaur
   Assistant Professor: Paula Sperry
Founded: 1924
Specialized Field: Musical; Comedy; Youth Theater; Dinner Theater; Ethnic Theater; Community Theater; Puppet; Classic; Contemporary
Status: Non-Profit, Non-Professional
Paid Staff: 5
Paid Artists: 11
Budget: $2,700-4,900
Affiliations: ATHE; KC/ACTF
Seating Capacity: 200-450; 50
Year Built: 1938
Year Remodeled: 1991

2345
DIAMOND CIRCLE MELODRAMA
7th and Main
PO Box 3041
Durango, CO 81302
Phone: 970-247-3400
Fax: 970-375-7136
Web Site: www.diamondcirclemelodrama.com
Management:
   Musical Director: Helen Gregory
Mission: To present quality professional productions. We specialize in Melodrama and Vaudeville.

Founded: 1961
Specialized Field: Drama; Classic
Status: Non-Equity; Commercial
Paid Staff: 25
Paid Artists: 15
Season: June 2 - September 29
Type of Stage: Proscenium
Stage Dimensions: 30'x 20'
Seating Capacity: 250

2346
OPENSTAGE THEATRE AND COMPANY
PO Box 617
201 S College Avenue
Fort Collins, CO 80522
Phone: 970-484-5237
Fax: 970-221-6730
Web Site: www.openstage.com
Management:
Managing Director: Jeff Metzger
Mission: To develop and maintain a nationally recognized regional theatre company. Emphasis will be placed on providing the best in quality theatre for the public benefit, on providing educational outreach to the community, and on providing professional opportunities for company members.
Utilizes: Singers
Founded: 1973
Specialized Field: Drama; Contemporary; Experimental
Status: Semi-Professional; Nonprofit
Paid Staff: 25
Income Sources: American Association of Community Theatres; Colorado Theatre Producers Guild; Fort Collins Convention & Visitors Bureau; Fort Collins Chamber of Commerce.
Performs At: Lincoln Center Mini-Theatre
Organization Type: Performing

2347
MESA STATE COLLEGE THEATRE DEPARTMENT
Moss Performing Arts Center
1100 N Avenue
Grand Junction, CO 81501
Phone: 970-248-1795
Fax: 970-248-1159
e-mail: rcowden@mesastate.edu
Web Site: www.mesastate.edu
Management:
Department Head: Richard R Cowden
MSC President: Tim Foster
Specialized Field: Theatre and Dance
Status: Non-Profit, Non-Professional
Paid Staff: 7
Paid Artists: 7
Type of Stage: Proscenium
Stage Dimensions: 50' x 34'
Seating Capacity: 625

2348
LITTLE THEATRE OF THE ROCKIES
University of Northern Colorado
Frasier 115
Greeley, CO 80639
Phone: 970-351-2194
Fax: 970-351-1923
Management:
Theatre Arts Chairman: Dan Guyette
Utilizes: Actors; AEA Actors; Dancers; Educators; Guest Accompanists; Guest Conductors; Guest Musical Directors; Guild Activities; Instructors; Local Artists;

Multimedia; Music; Original Music Scores; Resident Artists; Resident Professionals; Sign Language Translators; Soloists; Student Interns
Founded: 1934
Specialized Field: Educational; Theater Workshops
Status: Nonprofit; Non-Equity
Season: Mid June - Early August
Type of Stage: Proscenium
Stage Dimensions: 34' x 32'
Seating Capacity: 600
Rental Contact: Diane Cays

2349
COUNTRY DINNER PLAYHOUSE
6875 S Clinton
Greenwood Village, CO 80112
Phone: 303-799-1410
Fax: 303-790-2615
Toll-free: 888-360-1026
Web Site: www.countrydinnerplayhouse.com
Officers:
President/Producer/CEO: David M Pritchard
Executive VP: David Lovinggood
VP/General Manager: Robert E Buffington
Management:
President: David Lovinggood
Artistic Director: Paul Dwyer
Assistant CEO/Producer/Casting: Patrick Alan Kearns
Utilizes: Singers
Founded: 1970
Specialized Field: Musical; Comedy; Dinner Theater; Contemporary
Status: Professional; AEA
Paid Staff: 85
Paid Artists: 25
Income Sources: Ticket Sales
Affiliations: NDTA; NTA; CTG; Tour Colorado
Annual Attendance: 170,000
Type of Stage: Theater-in-the-round
Seating Capacity: 470
Year Built: 1970
Year Remodeled: 2000
Rental Contact: Technical Director Jacob Weler
Organization Type: Performing

2350
PICKETWIRE PLAYERS
802 San Juan
La Junta, CO 81050
Mailing Address: PO Box 912 La Junta, CO
Phone: 719-384-8320
Web Site: www.ruralnet.net/~csn/business/picketwire
Mission: To provide a showcase for Southeastern Colorado's regional talent.
Utilizes: Guest Artists; Guest Companies
Founded: 1968
Specialized Field: Community Theater
Status: Non-Professional; Nonprofit
Income Sources: La Junta Chamber of Commerce; Colorado Community Theater Coalition
Performs At: Picketwire Center for the Performing and Visual Arts
Organization Type: Performing

2351
LONGMONT THEATRE COMPANY
513 Main Street
PO Box 573
Longmont, CO 80501
Phone: 303-772-5200
Fax: 303-651-0388
e-mail: manager@longmonttheatre.org
Web Site: www.longmonttheatre.org

Officers:
President: Chris Curtis
VP: Len Worland
Treasurer: Mick Finnegan
Secretary: Brain Curtiss
Management:
President: Kurt Keilbach
Executive Director: Cheri E Friedman
Mission: To provide high quality entertainment with a strong educational component for and by the citizens of the Greater Boulder County area and to successfully manage a self-sufficient performing arts center.
Utilizes: Scenic Designers; Soloists
Founded: 1957
Specialized Field: Community Theater
Status: Non-Profit, Non-Professional
Paid Staff: 1
Budget: $160,000
Income Sources: Ticket Sales; Advertising; Concessions; Grants; Donations; In Kind
Annual Attendance: 10,000
Type of Stage: Thurst
Seating Capacity: 294
Year Built: 1939
Year Remodeled: 1991

2352
BROADWAY THEATRE LEAGUE OF PUEBLO
PO Box 1394
Pueblo, CO 81002
Phone: 719-545-4721
Fax: 719-295-7230
e-mail: maggie@sdc-arts.org
Web Site: www.sdc-arts.org
Management:
President: Ron Dioeosio
Executive Director: Maggie Divelbiss
Box Office Manager: Cheryl Califano
Mission: To bring professional theatre to the community.
Utilizes: Original Music Scores; Theatre Companies
Founded: 1960
Specialized Field: Broadway Musical Revivals; Classic
Status: Non-Profit, Professional
Paid Staff: 1
Volunteer Staff: 20
Budget: $200,000
Income Sources: Ticket sales; Donations
Performs At: Pueblo Memorial Hall
Annual Attendance: 5,500
Type of Stage: Proscenium
Seating Capacity: 1,676
Year Built: 1920
Year Remodeled: 1960
Organization Type: Performing; Touring; Sponsoring

2353
IMPOSSIBLE PLAYERS
1201 N Main St
Pueblo, CO 81003
Mailing Address: PO Box 1005
Phone: 719-542-6969
e-mail: impossibleplayers@hotmail.com
Web Site: http://www.impossibleplayers.org/index.html
Officers:
President: Marlene Schmidt
Vice President: Bill Mattoon
Secretary: Carol Martin
Treasurer: Don Warren
Mission: To promote the enjoyment of the performing arts by the public; to further the education of both members and the public in the skills of those arts; to give people an opportunity to perform for the public.

Founded: 1966
Specialized Field: Community Theater
Status: Non-Professional; Nonprofit
Performs At: Public Community College; The Hoag Theater
Organization Type: Performing; Resident; Educational

Connecticut

2354
RENAISSANCE THEATER COMPANY/ACTOR'S ENSEMBLE
217 Greenwich Avenue
Branford, CT 06519
Mailing Address: 217 Greenwich Avenue New Haven, CT 06519
Phone: 203-772-2557
Web Site: www.actorsensemble.com
Management:
   President: Dana Sachs
   Managing Director: Joyce Tucker
Mission: For the purpose of providing quality theater for the general public and creative opportunities for local artists and technicians.
Founded: 1978
Specialized Field: Renaissance; Drama; Historical; Ensembles
Status: Non-Profit, Non-Professional
Income Sources: New England Foundation for the Arts
Organization Type: Performing; Touring; Educational

2355
CHESHIRE COMMUNITY THEATRE
PO Box 149
Cheshire, CT 06410
Phone: 203-272-2787
Web Site: www.cctonstage.org
Officers:
   President: John Grabar
   VP: Kristen Hinckley
   Secretary: Gayle Barrett
   Treasurer: Kim Wantroba
   Membership: Dawn Reiss
   Business Manager: Kurt Fusaris
   Publicity: Aleta Looker
   Play-Reading: Dorothy Brady
   Technical Director: Richard Conrad
Mission: To develop amateur dramatic talent, to produce plays in which members shall take part as actors, producers, and managers, to encourage the writing of plays by its members, and to encourage dramatic art.
Utilizes: Actors; Choreographers; Dancers; Local Artists; Music; Performance Artists; Sign Language Translators
Founded: 1953
Specialized Field: Musical; Community Theater
Status: Non-Professional; Nonprofit
Budget: $20,000
Income Sources: Ticket Sales; Program Ads; Membership Dues; Donations
Performs At: Cheshire High School
Annual Attendance: 1,800
Seating Capacity: 800
Rental Contact: Cheshire Board of Education
Organization Type: Performing; Resident

2356
EAST-WEST FUSION THEATRE
147 Kent Road
Cornwall Bridge, CT 06754
Phone: 860-672-3938
Fax: 860-672-3938

Management:
   Artistic Director: Teviot Fairservis
Mission: International and fusion theatre collaborations with artists and scholars from around the world, multicultural arts education.
Utilizes: Actors; Artists-in-Residence; Choreographers; Collaborating Artists; Collaborations; Community Talent; Composers; Contract Actors; Curators; Dancers; Educators; Fellows of Institute; Guest Accompanists; Guest Artists; Guest Choreographers; Guest Conductors; Guest Designers; Guest Speakers; Guest Teachers; High School Drama; Instructors; Local Artists; Lyricists; Multi Collaborations; Original Music Scores; Paid Performers; Performance Artists; Resident Companies; Scenic Designers; Students; Special Technical Talent; Theatre Companies; Visual Arts
Founded: 1975
Specialized Field: Multi-Cultural; International
Paid Staff: 6
Paid Artists: 6
Non-paid Artists: 25
Budget: $50,000
Income Sources: Tour Bookings; Grants; Corporate & Private Donors
Performs At: East-West Arts Retreat
Affiliations: AAP; UCTA
Annual Attendance: 500
Facility Category: Outdoor Spaces; Platforms; Grassy Areas
Stage Dimensions: 20x20 plus
Seating Capacity: 75-350
Year Built: 2001
Rental Contact: Teviot Fairservis

2357
WESTERN CONNECTICUT STATE UNIVERSITY: THEATRE ARTS DEPARTMENT
181 White Street
Danbury, CT 06810
Phone: 203-837-8258
Fax: 203-837-8611
e-mail: trapanis@wcsu.edu
Web Site: http://www.wcsu.edu/theatrearts/
Officers:
   Chairman: William Walton
Management:
   Chair: Sal Trapani
   Associate Chair: Pam McDanial
Specialized Field: Educational; Theater Workshops
Budget: $7,300-13,500
Affiliations: Circle Repertory; Barrow Group
Seating Capacity: 600; 200
Year Built: 1959
Year Remodeled: 1979

2358
AMERICAN MAGIC-LANTERN THEATER
Box 44
East Haddam, CT 06423
Phone: 860-345-2574
Fax: 860-345-7578
e-mail: tborton@magiclanternshows.com
   Artistic Director: Terry Borton
Founded: 1650
Specialized Field: Touring Company; Historical; Specialty Acts

2359
FAIRFIELD UNIVERSITY: DEPARTMENT OF VISUAL & PERFORMING ARTS
1073 North Benson Rd
Fairfield, CT 06824

Phone: 203-254-4000
Web Site: http://www.fairfield.edu/cas/vpa_index.html
Management:
   Director Theatre Program: Dr. Martha LoMonaco
Specialized Field: Educational; Theater Workshops
Budget: $10,250-20,500
Affiliations: ATHE
Type of Stage: Black Box
Seating Capacity: 150; 750
Year Built: 1989

2360
ARTISTS COLLECTIVE
1200 Albany Avenue
Hartford, CT 06112
Phone: 860-527-3205
e-mail: info@artistscollective.org
Web Site: http://artistscollective.org/
Management:
   Executive Director: Dollie Mclean
   Creative Consultant: Jackie McLean
Utilizes: Guest Companies; Singers
Founded: 1970
Specialized Field: Ensembles; Contemporary
Status: Non-Professional; Nonprofit
Organization Type: Resident

2361
HARTFORD STAGE COMPANY
50 Church Street
Hartford, CT 06103
Phone: 860-525-5601
Fax: 860-525-4420
Web Site: www.hartfordstage.org
Management:
   Board President: Jennifer Smith Turner
   Executive Director: Jim Ireland
   Artistic Director: Michael Wilson
   Director Marketing: Jacques Lamarre
Mission: Founded in 1963, the theatre is internationally known for entertaining audiences with a wide range of the best of world drama, from classics to provocative new works and neglected works from the past.
Founded: 1963
Specialized Field: Classic; Contemporary
Status: Non-Profit, Professional
Paid Staff: 50
Affiliations: Hartford Stage Company
Type of Stage: Thrust
Stage Dimensions: 40'x90'x90'
Orchestra Pit: 1
Seating Capacity: 489
Architect: Venturi & Rauch
Rental Contact: Production Manager Candice Chirgotis

2362
NATIONAL THEATRE OF THE DEAF
139 N Main Street
Hartford, CT 06107
Phone: 860-236-4193
Fax: 860-236-4163
Toll-free: 800-300-5179
e-mail: info@ntd.org
Web Site: www.ntd.org
Officers:
   Executive Director/President: Aaron M. Kuby
Management:
   Executive Director: Aaron M. Kuby
   Tour Director: Betty Beekman
   Maketing and Production Consultant: William C. Martin
   Development Director: Dr. Jonathan Spinner

Mission: To produce theatrically challenging work at a world class level, drawing from as wide a range of the world's literature as possible; to perform these original works in a style that links American Sign Language with the spoken work; to seek, train, and employ hearing impaired artists; to offer our work to as culturally diverse and inclusive an audience as possible; to provide community outreach activities.
Utilizes: Actors; Artists-in-Residence; Collaborations; Community Members; Community Talent; Educators; Filmmakers; Local Artists; Original Music Scores; Performance Artists; Resident Artists; Resident Companies
Founded: 1967
Specialized Field: Specialty Acts; Alternative
Status: Professional; Nonprofit
Facility Category: Touring Theatre
Organization Type: Performing; Touring; Educational

2363
THEATERWORKS
233 Pearl Street
Hartford, CT 06103
Phone: 860-727-4027
Fax: 860-525-0758
Web Site: http://www.theaterworkshartford.org/
Management:
    Executive Director: Steve Campo
    Production Manager: Michael Lenaghan
    General Manager: Nicole LaFlair Nieves
Mission: To provide unique works, especially recent American plays. We strive to address a diversified range of socially relevant works by important active authors.
Utilizes: Actors; AEA Actors; Original Music Scores; Resident Professionals; Student Interns
Founded: 1985
Specialized Field: Musical; Comedy; Youth Theater; Dinner Theater; Ethnic Theater; Community Theater; Puppet; Classic; Contemporary
Status: Non-Profit, Professional
Season: Year Round
Annual Attendance: 30,000+
Type of Stage: Modified Thrust
Seating Capacity: 197
Year Built: 1927
Year Remodeled: 1996

2364
TRINITY COLLEGE THEATRE AND DANCE DEPARTMENT
300 Summit Street
Hartford, CT 06106
Phone: 860-297-5122
Fax: 860-297-5380
e-mail: pkennedy@trincoll.edu
Web Site: http://www.trincoll.edu/depts/thdn/
Officers:
    Chair: Judy Dworin
    Dean: Katharine Power
Specialized Field: Educational; Theater Workshops
Budget: $12,550-17,600
Affiliations: La Mama (equity theatre company); National Theater Institute at the Eugene O'Neill Theater Center; Nikitsky-Gates Theater (Moscow)
Seating Capacity: 400; 100; 60
Year Built: 1967

2365
MANCHESTER MUSICAL PLAYERS
Cheney Hall
PO Box 626
Manchester, CT 06045

Phone: 860-649-9065
Web Site: www.geocities.com/broadway
Officers:
    President: David Gorman
    Vice President of Finance: Ann Azevedo
    VP Production: Marge Kelly
    Treasurer: Chris Stone
    Secretary: Dianne Burnham
Mission: 50-year-old community theater organization presenting one major Broadway musical each spring and a cabaret fundraiser in September. Other activities include holiday performances and annual scholarship.
Utilizes: Actors; Choreographers; Community Talent; Contract Orchestras; Dancers; Guest Artists; Guest Companies; Guest Conductors; Guest Designers; Guest Lecturers; Guest Musical Directors; Local Artists; Music; Resident Professionals; Sign Language Translators; Singers
Founded: 1947
Specialized Field: Musical
Status: Semi-Professional; Nonprofit
Non-paid Artists: 60+
Budget: $40,000
Income Sources: Tickets; Grants; Donations; Dues; Annual Fundraiser; Stock Rental; Fundraising Sales
Performs At: Cheney Hall
Annual Attendance: 2,000
Facility Category: Theater
Type of Stage: Theatrical
Seating Capacity: 325
Year Built: 1867
Organization Type: Performing

2366
ODDFELLOWS PLAYHOUSE
128 Washington Street
Middletown, CT 06457
Phone: 860-347-6143
e-mail: oddfellows@wesleyan.edu
Officers:
    Chair: Melissa Z Schilke
    Vice Chair: Alain Munkittrick
    Treasurer: Grady L Faulkner Jr
    Secretary: Robert Hoppenstedt
Management:
    Artistic Director: Dick Wheeler
    Managing Director: Mimi Rich
    Technical Director: Charlie McAfee
    Development Director and PR Coordin: Susan Brown
    Associate Artistic Director: Marcella Trowbridge
Mission: Oddfellows Playhouse is a non-profit youth theater and performing arts program that serves over 2,500 central CT young people, ages 6-20, each year through classes, workshops, mini-productions, mainstage shows, neighborhood-based troupes, and special events.
Founded: 1975
Specialized Field: Youth Theater; Theater Workshops
Status: Non-Profit

2367
WESLEYAN UNIVERSITY THEATER DEPARTMENT
70 Wyllys Avenue
Middletown, CT 06459
Mailing Address: Wesleyan Station
Phone: 860-685-2950
Fax: 860-685-2591
Web Site: http://www.wesleyan.edu/theater/
Officers:
    Chair: Claudia Nascimento
Management:
    President: Douglas J Benn

    Chair: Alan M Dachs
    Vice Chairs: Kofi Appenteng
Founded: 1831
Specialized Field: Educational; Theater Workshops
Budget: $1,500-9,000
Affiliations: ATHE
Seating Capacity: 400; 150
Year Built: 1973
Year Remodeled: 1994

2368
CENTRAL CONNECTICUT STATE UNIVERSITY: DEPARTMENT OF THEATRE
1615 Stanley Drive
New Britain, CT 06050
Phone: 860-832-3151
Fax: 860-832-3164
e-mail: siragusashm@ccsu.edu
Web Site: www.ccsu.edu
Officers:
    Chair: Lani Beck Johnson
Management:
    Executive Director: Lani Johnson
    Managing Director: Sheila Siragusaal, siragusashm@ccsu.edu
Mission: To provide a concentrated and varied experience in Dance, Performance, Educational Theatre, Directing, Technical Theatre and Costume Design. Students are provided with numerous opportunities to perform on and design for main stage productions, as well as learning about children's theatre and improvisation with touring experience.
Specialized Field: Musical; Comedy; Classic; Contemporary; Educational
Status: Non-Profit, Non-Professional
Paid Staff: 8
Paid Artists: 15
Budget: $38,000
Income Sources: Departmental Funding From State
Performs At: Black Box Theatre; Large and Small Proscenium Spaces
Affiliations: Hartford Stage Company; Goodspeed Opera; Hartford Children's Theatre; Newington Children's Theatre; Bushnell w/Internship Opportunities
Annual Attendance: varies
Type of Stage: Black Box and Proscenium
Seating Capacity: 150; 300; 80
Year Built: 1989

2369
HOLE IN THE WALL THEATRE
116-118 Main Street
New Britain, CT 06050-0942
Phone: 860-229-3049
e-mail: webmaster@hitw.org
Web Site: www.hitw.org
Mission: To allow anyone who walks through the door to enjoy theater at whatever level he or she desires.
Utilizes: Actors; Choreographers; Collaborating Artists; Collaborations; Community Talent; Designers; Guest Artists; Guest Conductors; Guest Lecturers; Local Artists; Music; Performance Artists; Resident Artists; Resident Professionals
Founded: 1972
Specialized Field: Musical; Community Theater; Staged Readings
Status: Professional; Nonprofit
Non-paid Artists: all
Budget: $40,000
Income Sources: Box Office; Grants; Individual Audience & Member Donations
Performs At: Black Box Studio Theatre

Affiliations: Greater New Britian Chamber of Commerce
Annual Attendance: 3,500
Facility Category: Thrust or 3/4 stage
Stage Dimensions: 42x30
Seating Capacity: 100
Year Remodeled: 1988
Rental Contact: Board of Directors
Organization Type: Performing; Resident

2370
ELM SHAKESPEARE COMPANY

PO Box 206029
New Haven, CT 06520-6029
Phone: 203-393-1436
Fax: 203-393-1405
e-mail: info@elmshakespeare.org
Web Site: www.elmshakespeare.org
Officers:
   President: Cheever Tyler
   Vice President: Andrew Boone
   Treasurer: John Conte
Management:
   Managing Director: Margaret Andreass
Mission: The Elm Shakespeare Company is a professional multicultural non-profit theater company committed to establishing a discourse with the New Haven community through the medium of Shakespeare's plays.
Utilizes: Actors; AEA Actors; Artists-in-Residence; Collaborations; Guest Conductors; High School Drama
Founded: 1995
Specialized Field: Summer Stock
Status: Nonprofit
Paid Staff: 3
Season: August 1 - September 1
Annual Attendance: 30,000
Facility Category: Outdoor
Seating Capacity: 3000

2371
LONG WHARF THEATRE

222 Sargent Drive
New Haven, CT 06511
Phone: 203-787-4284
Fax: 203-776-2287
Toll-free: 800-782-8497
e-mail: info@longwharf.org
Management:
   Associate Artistic Director: Kim Rubienstien
   Artistic Director: Gordan Eledlestein
   Managing Director: Michael Stotts
   General Manger: Deb Clapp
Mission: Offering full production plays.
Utilizes: Actors; Artists-in-Residence; Choreographers; Designers; Educators; Five Seasonal Concerts; Guest Companies; Instructors; Multimedia; Music; Organization Contracts; Performance Artists; Poets; Resident Professionals; Singers
Founded: 1965
Specialized Field: Musical; Drama; Comedy
Status: For-Profit, Professional
Budget: 120,000+
Income Sources: League of Resident Theatres; Theatre Communications Group; Connecticut Commission on the Arts; Actors' Equity Association
Performs At: Long Wharf Theatre
Facility Category: 2 stages
Seating Capacity: 487,199
Organization Type: Touring; Resident; Educational; Producing

2372
SOUTHERN CONNECTICUT STATE UNIVERSITY: DEPARTMENT OF THEATRE

501 Crescent Street
New Haven, CT 06515
Phone: 203-392-6100
Fax: 203-392-6105
e-mail: elwoodw1@southernct.edu
Web Site: www.scsu.ctstateu.edu
Officers:
   Chair: William R Ellwood
Management:
   President: Cheryl Norton
Specialized Field: Musical; Comedy; Ethnic Theater; Puppet; Classic; Contemporary
Status: Non-Profit, Non-Professional
Budget: $29,000-40,000
Affiliations: ATHE; USITT; NETC; Long Wharf Theatre; Hartford Stage; Shubert Performing Arts Center; Goodspeed Opera; Circle in the Square
Seating Capacity: 1,550; 150; 125
Year Built: 1969
Year Remodeled: 1973

2373
YALE REPERTORY THEATRE

222 York Street
PO Box 208244
New Haven, CT 06520
Phone: 203-432-1591
Fax: 203-432-8332
e-mail: yalerep@yale.edu
Web Site: www.yale.edu/yalerep
Management:
   Artistic Director: James Bundy
   Managing Director: Victoria Nolan
Mission: Producing new American plays, as well as little-known works and classics revisited through contemporary metaphors.
Utilizes: Guest Companies
Founded: 1966
Specialized Field: Comedy; Ethnic Theater; Community Theater; Puppet; Contemporary
Status: Non-Profit, Professional
Income Sources: Actors' Equity Association; Theatre Communications Group; American Arts Alliance; League of Resident Theatres; Connecticut Advocates for the Arts
Performs At: Yale Repertory Theatre; University Theatre
Organization Type: Performing; Resident; Educational

2374
YALE SCHOOL OF DRAMA

PO Box 208325
New Haven, CT 06520
Mailing Address: 149 York Street, New Haven, CT 06511
Phone: 203-432-1507
Fax: 203-432-9668
e-mail: yalerep@yale.edu
Web Site: http://drama.yale.edu/index.html
Management:
   President: Richard Charles Levin
   Dean: James Bundy
Founded: 1924
Specialized Field: Educational; Theater Workshops
Budget: 46,200-77,800
Affiliations: Yale Repertory Theatre
Seating Capacity: 487; 658; 200
Year Built: 1926
Year Remodeled: 2000

2375
CONNECTICUT COLLEGE DEPARTMENT OF THEATRE

270 Mohegan Avenue
New London, CT 06320
Mailing Address: Box 5512
Phone: 860-439-2605
Fax: 860-439-2595
e-mail: dthol@conncoll.edu
Web Site: http://www.conncoll.edu/departments/theater/index.htm
Management:
   Chairmam: Linda Nerr
   Department Chair: Leah Lowe
Specialized Field: Educational; Theater Workshops
Seating Capacity: 1300; 130; 75
Year Built: 1941
Year Remodeled: 2000

2376
CONNECTICUT CONSERVATORY OF THE PERFORMING ARTS

79 W Street
New Milford, CT 06776
Phone: 860-354-2978
Fax: 860-350-0221
Officers:
   President: Jim Wilder
   VP: Sarah Jane Chelminski
   Treasurer: Shirley Waters
   Secretary: Deborah Casey
Management:
   Executive Director: Kristin Marks
   Music Director: John Shackelford
   Dance Department Chair: Robert Maiorano
   Theatre Department Chair: Heather McNeil
Mission: Offers professional training in dance, music, theatre, and voice concurrently with an academic program for grades 7-12.
Utilizes: Artists-in-Residence; Choreographers; Composers; Educators; Guest Accompanists; Guest Artists; Guest Composers; Guest Designers; Guest Musical Directors; Guest Speakers; Guild Activities; High School Drama; Multimedia; Music; Scenic Designers; Students
Founded: 1980
Specialized Field: Educational; Theater Workshops
Paid Staff: 2
Paid Artists: 20
Performs At: Black Box
Facility Category: Small, informal
Seating Capacity: 75
Year Built: 1975
Resident Groups: Conservatory School

2377
GREENWOODS THEATRE AT NORFOLK

Route 44
Norfolk, CT 06058
Mailing Address: PO Box 490, Norfolk, CT. 06068-0569
Phone: 860-542-0026
Fax: 860-542-5205
Web Site: www.greenwoodstheatre.com
Management:
   Executive Director: Maura Cavanagh
   Artistic Director: Richard Smithies
Utilizes: Actors; AEA Actors; Artists-in-Residence; Guest Lecturers; Original Music Scores; Performance Artists; Poets; Resident Professionals; Student Interns
Founded: 1999
Specialized Field: Summer Stock; Historical; Classic
Status: Non-Profit, Professional

Paid Staff: 6
Paid Artists: 6
Income Sources: Ticket Sales, Donations
Performs At: Classic 1880's Opera House with Shops
Annual Attendance: 8000
Facility Category: Opera House
Type of Stage: Proscenium with Balcony
Seating Capacity: 280
Year Built: 1983
Year Remodeled: 1999
Cost: $650,000
Rental Contact: Maura Cavanaugh

2378
CLOCKWORK REPERTORY THEATRE
133 Main Street
Oakville, CT 06779
Phone: 860-274-7247
Fax: 860-274-7247
Web Site:
http://www.clockworkrep.com/Home_Page.php
Management:
    Executive Director: Harold J Pantely
    Artistic Director: Susan P Pantely
Mission: Producing plays, emphasizing new American
plays dealing with controversial events.
Utilizes: Guest Companies
Founded: 1977
Specialized Field: Comedy; Community Theater;
Contemporary
Status: Non-Profit, Professional
Paid Staff: 5
Paid Artists: 20
Income Sources: New England Theatre Conference
Organization Type: Performing; Resident

2379
TRIARTS SHARON PLAYHOUSE
49 Amenia Road
PO Box 1187
Sharon, CT 06069
Phone: 860-364-7469
Fax: 860-364-8043
e-mail: info@triarts.net
Web Site: www.triarts.net
Officers:
    President: David Sims
    VP: Mimi Estes
    Secretary: Emily Soell
    Treasurer: John Stimpson
Management:
    Executive Director: Alice Bemand
    Artistic Director: Michael Berkeley
    Artistic Director: John Simpkins
    Production Director: Erik Diaz
Mission: To create and administer a dynamic and
creative center for the arts, presenting live theatre and
other cultural events to the residents of the Tri-State
area (Connecticut, New York, and Massachusetts).
Utilizes: Actors; AEA Actors; Choreographers;
Community Talent; Educators; Guest Accompanists;
Guest Conductors; Guest Designers; Guest Lecturers;
Guest Musical Directors; Instructors; Music; Original
Music Scores; Resident Professionals; Sign Language
Translators; Students
Founded: 1989
Specialized Field: Summer Stock; Contemporary;
Drama
Budget: 250,000
Income Sources: Donations; Tickets
Performs At: Theater; Gallery
Annual Attendance: 13,000-15,000
Facility Category: Barn Style Summer Theater;
Year-Round Second Stage

Type of Stage: Proscenium
Seating Capacity: 370
Year Built: 1955
Year Remodeled: 1994
Resident Groups: Tri State Center for the Arts

2380
SHERMAN PLAYERS
PO Box 471
Sherman, CT 06784
Phone: 860-354-3622
Web Site: www.geocities.com/~shermanplayers
Officers:
    President: Elizabeth Scholze
    VP: Glenn Anderson
    Secretary: Jack Heidt
    Treasurer: Bobbie Tiebout
    Publicity: Jean Buoy
    Membership: Larry Buoy
    Board of Directors: Ellen Burnett
    Wardrobe: Alpha Castro
Mission: To provide good theater and related artistic
offerings to the CT area.
Utilizes: Actors; Collaborating Artists; Community
Talent; Dance Companies; Guest Accompanists; Guest
Artists; Guest Companies; Guest Designers; Guest
Lecturers; Guest Musical Directors; Guest Soloists;
Instructors; Local Artists; Performance Artists; Sign
Language Translators; Singers
Founded: 1929
Specialized Field: Musical; Community Theater;
Ensembles
Status: Non-Professional; Nonprofit
Paid Staff: n
Paid Artists: y
Budget: $16,000 - 32,000
Income Sources: Membership; Playbill Advertising;
Contributions; Occasional Fundraisers
Performs At: Sherman Playhouse
Annual Attendance: 3,200
Facility Category: Church, Converted to a Theater
Type of Stage: Proscenium
Stage Dimensions: 15x36
Seating Capacity: 126
Year Built: 1837
Year Remodeled: 1961
Rental Contact: Town of Sherman
Organization Type: Performing; Sponsoring

2381
PALACE THEATRE OF THE ARTS
61 Atlantic Street
307 Atlantic Street
Stamford, CT 06901
Phone: 203-358-2305
Fax: 203-358-2313
Management:
    Facilities Manager: John Hiddlestone
    Marketing Director: Nancy Koffin
    House Manager: Vicki Kieffer
    Managing Director: Mike Koffin
Founded: 1983
Specialized Field: Musical; Ensembles
Status: Professional; Commercial
Performs At: Palace Theatre
Affiliations: International Association of Theatrical
Stage Employees
Seating Capacity: 1580
Year Built: 1927
Year Remodeled: 1983
Architect: Thomas Lamb
Organization Type: Sponsoring

2382
STAMFORD THEATRE WORKS
95 Atlantic Street
Strawberry Hill Avenue
Stamford, CT 06901
Phone: 203-359-4414
Fax: 203-356-1846
e-mail: stwct@aol.com
Web Site: www.stamfordartstheatreworks.org
Officers:
    President: Steve Karp
    VP: Marietta Morrelli
    Secretary: Charry Boris
Management:
    Producing Director: Steve Karp
    General Manager: Patrick Shea
    Press/Marketing Director: Patricia Blaufuss
    Box Office Manager: Valarie Howard
    Administrative Assistant: Peter Young
Mission: To produce plays of cultural and social
significance for the benefit of the greater Stamford area;
to build a theatre of regional and national prominence,
acclaimed for its innovative productions of
contemporary and classical plays.
Utilizes: Actors; AEA Actors; Choreographers;
Designers; Guest Companies; Guest Designers;
Organization Contracts; Original Music Scores;
Resident Companies; Resident Professionals; Sign
Language Translators; Singers; Soloists; Student
Interns
Founded: 1988
Specialized Field: Drama; Musical; Contemporary
Status: Professional; Nonprofit
Paid Staff: 10
Volunteer Staff: 75
Paid Artists: 125
Budget: $800,000
Income Sources: Actors' Equity Association; Society
for Stage Directors and Choreographers
Annual Attendance: 16,000
Seating Capacity: 150
Organization Type: Performing

2383
PUPPET HOUSE THEATRE
128 Thimble Island Road
PO Box 3081
Stony Creek, CT 06405
Phone: 203-488-5752
Web Site: http://www.puppethouse.org/index.htm
Management:
    Manager: Christian Pacileo
Mission: Presenting theatrical programs of small
professional and community groups.
Utilizes: Guest Companies; Singers
Founded: 1972
Specialized Field: Summer Stock; Community
Theater; Ethnic Theater; Puppet
Status: Professional; Non-Professional; Nonprofit
Paid Staff: 75
Year Built: 1903
Organization Type: Performing; Touring; Sponsoring

2384
CONNECTICUT REPERTORY THEATRE
802 Bolton Road, Unit 1128
University of Connecticut
Storrs, CT 06269-1127
Phone: 860-486-3016
Fax: 860-486-3110
Web Site: www.sfa.uconn.edu
Management:
    Artistic Director: Gary M English

Managing Director: Frank Mack
Mission: Connecticut Repertory Theatre exists as the primary training mechanism for the Department of Dramatic Arts at the University of Connecticut, and as a nationally recognized professional theatre center for the University.
Founded: 1957
Specialized Field: Educational; Theater Workshops
Status: Nonprofit
Season: June - July
Type of Stage: Proscenium
Stage Dimensions: 30'x 25'
Seating Capacity: 492

2385
UNIVERSITY OF CONNECTICUT: DEPARTMENT OF DRAMATIC ARTS

U-1127, University of Connecticut
802 Bolton Road
Storrs, CT 06269-1127
Phone: 860-486-4025
Fax: 860-486-3110
e-mail: dramaoffice@uconn.edu
Web Site: www.drama.uconn.edu
Management:
   Artistic Director: Gary English
Specialized Field: Comedy; Youth Theater; Ethnic Theater; Puppet; Classic; Contemporary

2386
UNIVERSITY OF CONNECTICUT: DEPARTMENT OF DRAMATIC ARTS

U-127, University of Connecticut
802 Bolton Road
Storrs, CT 06269
Phone: 860-486-4025
Fax: 860-486-3110
Management:
   Professor: Gary English
Specialized Field: Educational; Theater Workshops
Budget: $8,500-18,800
Affiliations: NAST; U/RTA; Connecticut Repertory Theatre
Seating Capacity: 500; 100; 90
Year Built: 1960

2387
SEVEN ANGELS THEATRE

1 Plank Road, Historic Hamilton Park Pavilion
Waterbury, CT 06705
Mailing Address: PO Box 3358
Phone: 203-591-8223
Fax: 203-757-1807
e-mail: sterling@sevenangelstheatre.org
Web Site: http://sevenangelstheatre.org/page/6289-Home
Management:
   President of the Board: Allen Cipriano
   Executive Director: Teresa De Laurentis
   Artistic Director: Semina De Laurentis
   Development Director: Debra Bodnar
   Marketing Director: Paul Roth
Founded: 1991
Specialized Field: Musical; Comedy; Youth Theater; Community Theater; Contemporary
Status: Non-Profit, Professional
Paid Staff: 11
Paid Artists: 5

2388
EUGENE O'NEILL THEATER CENTER

305 Great Neck Road
Waterford, CT 06385

Phone: 860-443-5378
Fax: 860-443-9653
e-mail: theaterlives@theoneill.org
Web Site: www.theoneill.org
Officers:
   Chairman: Thomas Viertel
Management:
   Executive Director: Preston Whiteway
   Artistic Director: Wendy C Goldberg
Mission: Dedicated to the development of new works and new voices for the American theater. Home to more than 1,000 new works for the stage and to more than 2,500 emerging artists. Scores of projects developed at the O'Neill have gone on to full production at other theaters around the world, including Broadway, Off-Broadway, and major regional theaters.
Founded: 1964
Specialized Field: Theater/New Work Development
Status: Non-Profit, Professional
Season: July
Seating Capacity: 100-300

2389
NATIONAL THEATER INSTITUTE

EUGENE O'NEILL THEATER CENTER
305 Great Neck Road
Waterford, CT 06385
Phone: 860-443-5378
Fax: 860-443-9653
Web Site: www.oneilltheatre.org
Officers:
   Chairman: Thomas Viertel
   Vice Chair: Ruth Hendel
   Treasurer: Stephen Hendel
   Secretary: Linda Mariani
Management:
   Executive Director: Preston Whiteway
   Artistic Director: Jim Houghton
   Artistic Director: Paulette Hawpt
   Director: David B Jaffe
Mission: To support the development and education of theatrical artists, students and audiences.
Utilizes: Guest Companies
Founded: 1964
Specialized Field: Educational; Theater Workshops; Drama; Contemporary
Status: Professional; Nonprofit
Performs At: The Rose Barn; The Edith Oliver Theatre; The Amphitheatre
Affiliations: Theatre Communication Group; ATHE; Moscow Art Theater
Seating Capacity: 300; 50
Year Built: 1964
Organization Type: Performing; Educational; Sponsoring

2390
UNIVERSITY OF HARTFORD: DEPARTMENT OF ART HISTORY, CINEMA, DRAMA

200 Bloomfield Avenue
West Hartford, CT 06117
Phone: 860-768-4100
Fax: 860-768-4080
Toll-free: 800-947-4303
e-mail: calafiore@hartford.edu
Management:
   Dean: Power Boothe
   Associate Dean: Thomas Bradley
Founded: 1877
Specialized Field: Educational; Theater Workshops
Status: Non-Profit, Non-Professional
Budget: $6,000-9,000

Seating Capacity: 200
Year Built: 1960
Year Remodeled: 1996

2391
FAIRFIELD COUNTY STAGE COMPANY

25 Powers Court
Westport, CT 06880
Phone: 203-227-5137
Officers:
   Chairman: Rita Fredricks
   President: Marilyn Hersey
   Secretary: Christopher Cull
   Treasurer: Burry Fredrik
Management:
   Associate Artistic Director: Anne Ueefe
Mission: Professional regional theatre operating under the Letter of Agreement/LORT 'D' Contract with Actors' Equity Association.
Utilizes: Guest Companies
Founded: 1981
Specialized Field: Drama; Musical; Contemporary
Status: Professional
Paid Staff: 40
Paid Artists: 70
Income Sources: Actors' Equity Association; Theatre Communications Group
Organization Type: Performing; Resident

2392
WESTPORT COMMUNITY THEATRE

Town Hall
110 Myrtle Avenue
Westport, CT 06880
Mailing Address: 110 Myrtle Avenue
Phone: 203-226-1983
e-mail: info@westportcommunitytheatre.com
Web Site: http://www.westportcommunitytheatre.com/index.html
Management:
   Artistic Manager: H Edward Spires
Mission: Offering entertainment and instruction to the community regarding theatre; developing appreciation of theatre.
Utilizes: Guest Artists; Guest Companies
Founded: 1956
Specialized Field: Community Theater
Status: Non-Professional; Nonprofit
Paid Staff: 3
Season: June - September
Organization Type: Performing

2393
WESTPORT COUNTRY PLAYHOUSE

25 Powers Court
PO Box 629
Westport, CT 06880
Phone: 203-227-5137
Fax: 203-221-7482
Web Site: www.westportplayhouse.com
Management:
   Executive Director: Alison Harris
   Artistic Director: Joanne Woodward
Mission: Offering professional theatre to Connecticut.
Utilizes: Guest Companies
Founded: 1930
Specialized Field: Musical; Comedy; Youth Theater; Classic; Contemporary
Status: Non-Profit, Professional
Paid Staff: 16
Paid Artists: 50
Income Sources: Council of Stock Theatres
Season: June-September
Performs At: Westport Summer Country Playhouse

Facility Category: Summer Theatre
Type of Stage: Proscenium
Seating Capacity: 707
Year Built: 1930
Rental Contact: Julie Monahan
Organization Type: Performing; Resident

2394
WHITE BARN THEATRE
Newton Turnpike
Westport, CT 06880
Phone: 203-227-3768
Management:
General Manager: Vincent Curcio
Founder/Artistic Director: Lucille Lortel
Founded: 1947
Specialized Field: Summer Stock; Historical; Classic
Season: July - August
Type of Stage: Proscenium
Seating Capacity: 148

2395
WILTON PLAYSHOP
The Wilton Playshop
15 Lovers Lane
PO Box 36
Wilton, CT 06897
Phone: 203-762-7629
e-mail: webmaster@wiltonplayshop.org
Web Site: www.wiltonplayshop.org
Officers:
President: Skip Ploss
VP: Jon Murray
Chairman, Trustees: Karen Young
Management:
President: Zelie Pforzheimer,
president@wiltonplayshop.org
1st Vice President Production: Janice Dehn,
production@wiltonplayshop.org
2nd Vice President Production: Donna Savage,
fundraising@wiltonplayshop.org
3rd Vice President, House: Jane Alexander
4th Vice President, Special Project: Carin Freidag
Recording Secretary/Database Mngr.: Genia
Meinhold
Mission: The presentation of musicals and plays to the
general public at an affordable price under high quality
conditions.
Founded: 1937
Specialized Field: Ensembles; Drama; Contemporary
Status: Non-Professional
Volunteer Staff: 22
Paid Artists: 75
Non-paid Artists: 75
Budget: $50,000
Income Sources: Ticket Sales & Program Advertising
Performs At: Auditorium; Stage w/Loft;
Annual Attendance: 3,000 - 4,000
Facility Category: Live Theatre; Auditorium
Type of Stage: Proscenium
Stage Dimensions: 18x32
Seating Capacity: 125
Year Built: 1870
Year Remodeled: 2007
Cost: $75,000
Rental Contact: President Zelie Pforzheimer
Organization Type: Performing; Educational
Resident Groups: Community Theatre

2396
KENT COUNTY THEATRE GUILD
140 E Roosevelt Avenue
PO Box 783
Dover, DE 19903-0783
Phone: 302-674-3568
e-mail: kctg@kctg.org
Management:
Chairman: Mike Polo
Vice Chair: Pat Musto
Mission: Kent County has been providing quality
theatre to the central Delaware community since 1953.
Founded: 1953
Specialized Field: Community Theater; Drama;
Comedy

2397
POSSUM POINT PLAYERS
Old Laurel Highway
Po Box 96
Georgetown, DE 19947
Mailing Address: 441 Old Laurel Road
Phone: 302-856-3460
Fax: 302-856-4560
e-mail: mail@possumpointplayers.org
Web Site: www.possumpointplayers.org
Officers:
President: Louise Hartzell
Vice President: Cluadius Bowden
Secretary: Pat Erhardt
Treasurer: Kenny Workman
Management:
Executive Director: Andre Beaumont
Adminstrative Assistant: Mary Cahill
Mission: Offering quality theatrical productions to
Sussex County, Delaware.
Utilizes: Guest Companies
Founded: 1973
Specialized Field: Musical; Dinner Theater;
Community Theater
Status: Non-Professional; Nonprofit
Paid Staff: 50
Income Sources: Delaware Theater Association
Performs At: Possum Hall; Delaware Tech Theater
Organization Type: Performing; Educational

2398
RESIDENT ENSEMBLE PLAYERS
University of Delaware
Roselle Center for the Arts
110 Orchard Road
Newark, DE 19716
Phone: 302-831-2202
Fax: 302-831-8528
e-mail: ud-rep@udel.edu
Web Site: www.rep.udel.edu
Management:
Producing Artistic Director: Sanford Robbins
Coordinator of Marketing/PR: Nadine Howatt
Founded: 1743
Specialized Field: Theatre
Performs At: Thompson Theatre/Studio
Theatre/Hartshorn Theatre
Affiliations: ATHE, AEA, TCG, TAGP
Facility Category: Proscenium/Black Box/Black Box
Type of Stage: Proscenium; Black Box; Black Box
Seating Capacity: 400; 125; 185
Year Built: 1930
Year Remodeled: 1989

2399
ARTISTS THEATRE ASSOCIATION
PO Box 7258
Wilmington, DE 19803
Phone: 302-798-8775
Web Site: www.dca.net/ata
Officers:
President: L Jeffrey DiSabatino
Vice-President: Claire Ennis
Acting Treasurer: Claire Braun
Secretary: Tina M. Sheing
Past President: Tom Marshall
Mission: To further the dramatic arts; to encourage new
plays; to present workshops in high schools.
Utilizes: Guest Artists; Guest Companies
Founded: 1968
Specialized Field: Musical; Community Theater
Status: Non-Professional; Nonprofit
Paid Staff: 100
Income Sources: Delaware Theatre Association;
Delaware Alliance for Arts Education
Organization Type: Performing

2400
DELAWARE THEATRE COMPANY
200 Water Street
Wilmington, DE 19801-5048
Phone: 302-594-1104
Fax: 302-594-1107
Web Site: www.delawaretheatre.com
Officers:
Chairman: Gary Wilkinson
President: William Shea
Management:
Artistic Director: Fontaine Syer
General Manager: Rebecca Frederick
Marketing Director: Tom Kirkpatrick
Development Director: Gail O'Donnell
Mission: To create high quality professional theatre in
Delaware.
Utilizes: Actors; AEA Actors; Artists-in-Residence;
Designers; Educators; Five Seasonal Concerts; Grant
Writers; Guest Artists; Guest Companies; Guest
Conductors; Guest Designers; Guest Ensembles;
Guest Lecturers; Resident Professionals; Student
Interns
Founded: 1978
Specialized Field: Musical; Ensembles
Status: Professional; Nonprofit
Paid Staff: 35
Budget: $2.3 million
Performs At: The Delaware Theatre Company
Type of Stage: Semi-Thrust
Seating Capacity: 389
Year Built: 1985
Rental Contact: Tom Kirkpatrick
Organization Type: Performing; Educational

2401
SHOESTRING PRODUCTIONS LIMITED
214 W 18th Street
Wilmington, DE 19802
Phone: 302-655-0299
Management:
Artistic Director: Deborah Dehart
Mission: Creating, producing and touring original
musicals to entertain and educate young audiences.
Utilizes: Multimedia
Founded: 1978
Specialized Field: Musical; Ensembles
Status: Professional
Organization Type: Performing; Touring; Educational

2402
WILMINGTON DRAMA LEAGUE
10 W Lea Boulevard
Wilmington, DE 19802
Phone: 302-764-1172
Web Site: www.wdl.org
Management:
    President: Nick D'Argenio
    Treasurer: Dennis Williams
    VP Financial Development: Kate Monaghan
    VP Artistic Development: Alicia Chomo
Mission: To provide low-cost, quality theatre, theatrical activities, and education to the Greater Wilmington Region.
Utilizes: Singers
Founded: 1933
Specialized Field: Community Theater; Ensembles
Status: Non-Professional; Nonprofit
Paid Staff: 1
Volunteer Staff: 300
Budget: $195,000
Income Sources: Ticket Sales; Contribution; State Arts Council
Annual Attendance: 8,000
Facility Category: Theater
Seating Capacity: 256
Year Built: 1940
Year Remodeled: 1999
Organization Type: Performing; Educational

District of Columbia

2403
AFRICAN CONTINUUM THEATRE COMPANY (ACTCO)
3523 12th Street NE
2nd Floor
Washington, DC 20017-2545
Phone: 202-529-5763
Fax: 202-529-5764
e-mail: questions@africancontinuumtheare.com
Web Site: www.africancontinuumtheatre.com
Officers:
    President: Ivan Fitzgerald
    Secretary: Arden Phillips
Management:
    Executive Director: JoAnn Williams
    PR and Marketing Consultant: Renee Littleton
    Artisitic Associate: Jacqueline Lawton
Mission: To sustain and grow African-American theater by producing new and traditional art forms that contribute to the understanding and appreciation of the African-American culture.
Founded: 1989
Specialized Field: African American; Ethnic Theater
Paid Staff: 4
Volunteer Staff: 10

2404
AMERICAN UNIVERSITY THEATRE PROGRAM
4400 Massachusetts Avenue
Washington, DC 20016
Phone: 202-885-1092
e-mail: dpa@american.edu
Web Site:
http://www.american.edu/cas/performing-arts/theatre.cfm
Officers:
    Chair: Gail Humphries Breeskin
    Co-Chair: Daniel Abraham
Specialized Field: Educational; Theater Workshops

Affiliations: ATHE
Seating Capacity: 175-200; 175

2405
ARENA STAGE
1101 6th Street SW
Washington, DC 20024
Phone: 202-554-9066
Fax: 202-488-4056
e-mail: info@arenastage.org
Management:
    President: John M Derrick
    Artistic Director: Molly Smith
    Executive Director: Stephen Richard
    Chair: Wendy Farrow Raines
    Vp: Stephen Richard
    Vp: Riley K Temple
    Secretary: Helga Tarver
    Treasurer: David Shiffin
Mission: To offer huge plays that encompass all that is exuberant, passionate, deep, profound and dangerous in our American spirit. Arena Stage relentlessly pursues excellence and artistic process; flourishes by providing a dynamic and powerful artistic community; champions various diversities throughout our organization and in the community; is recognized as a leader throughout the world.
Utilizes: Guest Companies
Founded: 1950
Specialized Field: Drama; Comedy; Musical; Educational; Theater Workshops
Status: Professional; Nonprofit
Income Sources: Actors' Equity Association; Society for Stage Directors and Choreographers
Performs At: Arena Theatre (Fichandler & Kreeger)
Organization Type: Performing; Educational

2406
CATHOLIC UNIVERSITY OF AMERICA: DRAMA DEPARTMENT
105 Hartke
Washington, DC 20064
Phone: 202-319-5351
Fax: 202-319-5359
Web Site: www.cua.edu/as/drama
Officers:
    Chair: Dr. Greta Honegger PhD
Management:
    President: David M O'Conner
Founded: 1881
Specialized Field: Classic; Contemporary; Drama
Status: Non-Profit, Non-Professional
Paid Staff: 12
Budget: $10,100-15,500
Affiliations: Arena Stage
Seating Capacity: 590; 80; 40
Year Built: 1970
Year Remodeled: 1987

2407
DISCOVERY THEATER
Arts & Industries Building
900 Jefferson Drive SW
Washington, DC 20560
Phone: 202-357-1500
Fax: 202-357-2588
Web Site: www.discoverytheater.org
Management:
    Program Manager: Brigitte Blachere
    Artistic Director: Roberta Gasbarre
Mission: The Smithsonian's Discovery Theater, located in the Arts and Industries Building on the National Mall, is dedicated to offering the best in live performing arts for young people.

Founded: 1978
Specialized Field: Children's Theater
Status: Non-Profit, Professional
Paid Staff: 10
Season: September - August
Type of Stage: Thrust
Stage Dimensions: 25' x 10'
Seating Capacity: 175

2408
FLASHPOINT STUDIOS
916 G Street North West
Washington, DC 20001
Phone: 202-315-1324
e-mail: info@onestageproductions.com
Management:
    Founder/Artistic Director: Michael W McCorkle
    Chairperson: Monica S McCorkle
    Vice-Chairperson: Dana Trussell
    Treasurer: Nikisha Long
Mission: Purpose of providing individuals, who would not otherwise have the resources to benefit from the arts with the opportunity to develop and showcase their performing talents and capabilities within a professional environment. Through reading and writing dialogue, memorization, acting and peer mentoring, teens are provided with the academic and social enrichment needed to be successful in education.
Specialized Field: Theater Workshops; Youth Theater

2409
FOLGER SHAKESPEARE LIBRARY
201 E Capitol Street SE
Washington, DC 20003-1094
Phone: 202-544-4600
Fax: 202-544-4623
e-mail: webmaster@folger.edu
Web Site: www.folger.edu
Management:
    Director: Gail Kern Paste
    Executive Director: Janice Delaney
    Artistic Producer: Janet Alexander Griffin
    General Manager For Public Programs: Jane Pisano
Mission: Home of the world's largest Shakespeare collection, the Folger is a major international center for scholary research and a lively venue for exhibitions, literary programs, and the performing arts.
Utilizes: Actors; AEA Actors; Choreographers; Collaborations; Curators; Dancers; Educators; Five Seasonal Concerts; Guest Choreographers; Guest Conductors; Guest Designers; Guest Directors; Guest Instructors; Guest Musical Directors; Guest Musicians; Guild Activities; Instructors; Local Artists; Local Unknown Artists; Multimedia; Music; Original Music Scores; Performance Artists; Playwrights; Resident Professionals; Selected Students; Sign Language Translators; Singers; Soloists; Student Interns; Special Technical Talent; Theatre Companies
Founded: 1879
Specialized Field: Musical; Shakespeare; Historical; Specialty Acts
Status: Nonprofit
Paid Staff: 25
Volunteer Staff: 35
Paid Artists: 70
Budget: $9,000,000
Income Sources: Grants; Endowments
Performs At: Theater
Annual Attendance: 200,000
Type of Stage: Proscenium
Seating Capacity: 250
Year Built: 1932
Year Remodeled: 1992

2410
FORD'S THEATRE SOCIETY
511 10th Street NW
Washington, DC 20004
Phone: 202-638-2941
Fax: 202-347-6269
Toll-free: 800-899-2367
e-mail: onstage@fordstheatre.org
Web Site: www.fordstheatre.org
Officers:
Chairman: Hon. Joseph McDadeny
Vice Chairman: Gerald M Lowrie
Secretary: Mrs. Paul Laxalt
Treasurer: Richard L. Thompson
Management:
Managing Director: Paul Tetreault
Mission: Presenting live theatre productions to pay tribute to Abraham Lincoln's appreciation for the performing arts.
Founded: 1968
Specialized Field: Musical; Comedy; Youth Theater; Community Theater; Classic
Status: Non-Profit, Professional
Budget: $6,000,000
Performs At: Ford's Theatre
Annual Attendance: 150,000
Facility Category: Theatre House
Type of Stage: Proscenium/Thrust
Seating Capacity: 699
Year Built: 1860
Year Remodeled: 1968
Organization Type: Performing; Educational

2411
GALA HISPANIC THEATRE
PO Box 43209
Washington, DC 20010
Phone: 202-234-7174
Fax: 202-332-1247
e-mail: info@galatheatre.org
Web Site: www.galatheatre.org
Management:
Artistic Director: Hugo Medrono
Associate Producing Director: Abel Lopez
Mission: Expanding and promoting Hispanic culture.
Founded: 1976
Specialized Field: Spanish Language Company; Ethnic Theater
Status: Non-Profit, Professional
Paid Staff: 6
Performs At: GALA Hispanic Theatre
Type of Stage: Proscenium
Seating Capacity: 200
Organization Type: Resident; Educational

2412
GEORGE WASHINGTON UNIVERSITY: DEPARTMENT OF THEATRE AND DANCE
800 21st Street NW Suite 227
Washington, DC 20052
Phone: 202-994-8072
Fax: 202-994-9403
e-mail: onstage@gwu.edu
Web Site: http://theatredance.gwu.edu/
Officers:
Chair: Leslie B Jacobson
Management:
Chair: Dana Tai Soon Burgess
Executive Coordinator: Marjorie Coleman
Founded: 1875
Specialized Field: Educational; Theater Workshops
Status: For-Profit, Non-Professional
Budget: $2,900

Affiliations: ATHE
Seating Capacity: 484; 50
Year Built: 1968

2413
HOWARD UNIVERSITY DEPARTMENT OF THEATRE ARTS
Division of Fine Arts
2455 6th Street NW
Washington, DC 20059
Phone: 202-806-7050
Fax: 202-806-9193
e-mail: jljohnson@howard.edu
Web Site: www.howard.edu/collegefinearts/theatre
Officers:
Chair: Joe Selmon
Management:
President: Sidney A. Ribeau
Utilizes: Actors; Artists-in-Residence; Dancers; Educators; Guest Artists; Guest Soloists; High School Drama; Performance Artists; Resident Professionals; Sign Language Translators; Soloists; Theatre Companies
Founded: 1950
Specialized Field: Educational; Theater Workshops
Status: For-Profit, Non-Professional
Paid Staff: 20
Budget: $3,550-14,000
Affiliations: NAST; ATHE
Type of Stage: Black Box; Proscenium
Seating Capacity: 300; 75
Year Built: 1960
Year Remodeled: 1988
Rental Contact: Professor Denise Saunders Thompson

2414
KENNEDY CENTER AMERICAN COLLEGE THEATRE
John F Kennedy Center for the Performing Arts
Washington, DC 20566-0001
Mailing Address: 2700 F Street
Phone: 202-416-8864
Fax: 202-416-8860
Toll-free: 800-444-1324
Web Site: www.kennedy-center.org/education/actf
Management:
President: Michael Kaiser
Artistic Director: Ramon Terleckyi
Artistic Director: Gregg Henry
Co-Manager: Susan Shaffer
Utilizes: Actors; Artists-in-Residence; Collaborating Artists; Educators; Guest Accompanists; Guest Conductors; Guest Designers; Guest Soloists; High School Drama; Local Artists; Performance Artists; Resident Professionals; Soloists; Theatre Companies
Founded: 1971
Specialized Field: Educational; Theater Workshops; Classic
Status: Non-Profit, Professional
Paid Staff: 4
Volunteer Staff: 50
Non-paid Artists: 200
Season: April
Performs At: Kennedy Center [Festival Site]
Facility Category: Terrace Theatre; Theatre Lab
Seating Capacity: 513; 388

2415
LIVING STAGE
1101 6th Street SW
Washington, DC 20024

Phone: 202-234-5782
Fax: 202-797-1043
e-mail: info@arenastage.org
Web Site: www.arenastage.org
Management:
President: Molly Smith
Executive Director: Stephen Richards
Operations Manager: Jane Cassanajor
Managing Director: Guy Berquist
Mission: Change through creative empowerment.
Founded: 1966
Specialized Field: Community Theater
Status: Non-Profit, Professional
Paid Staff: 8
Volunteer Staff: 3
Paid Artists: 6
Non-paid Artists: 1
Performs At: Performance Workshops
Affiliations: A division of Community Engagement at Arena Stage
Type of Stage: Black Box
Stage Dimensions: 45'x 37'
Seating Capacity: varies
Year Built: 1985
Year Remodeled: 1990
Rental Contact: Anne Theisen
Organization Type: Resident

2416
NATIONAL CONSERVATORY OF DRAMATIC ARTS
1556 Wisconsin Avenue Northwest
Washington, DC 20007
Phone: 202-333-2202
Fax: 202-333-1753
e-mail: ncdadrama@aol.com
Web Site: www.theconservatory.org
Officers:
President: Raymond Ficca
Management:
Executive Director: Nan Fricca
Utilizes: Actors; AEA Actors; Collaborations; Designers; Educators; Equity Actors; Filmmakers; Grant Writers; Guest Designers; Guest Ensembles; Guest Instructors; Guest Musical Directors; Guest Soloists; Guest Teachers; High School Drama; Instructors; Local Artists; Multi Collaborations; Original Music Scores; Performance Artists; Scenic Designers; Soloists; Students; Student Interns; Special Technical Talent
Founded: 1975
Specialized Field: Educational; Theater Workshops
Status: Non-Profit, Non-Professional
Paid Staff: 4
Volunteer Staff: 10
Paid Artists: 22
Budget: $400,000
Income Sources: Tuition; Grants; Federal Funds
Performs At: Theatre; Film
Affiliations: TCG; CAGW; DC Arts & Humanities
Annual Attendance: 8,000
Type of Stage: Black Box
Stage Dimensions: 1,000 square feet
Seating Capacity: 60
Year Built: 1960
Year Remodeled: 2001

2417
NATIONAL THEATRE
1321 Pennsylvania Avenue NW
Washington, DC 20004
Phone: 202-628-6161
Toll-free: 800-447-7400
e-mail: dbm@nationaltheatre.org
Web Site: www.nationaltheatre.org

Officers:
   President: Donn B. Murphy
Management:
   General Manager: Harry Teter, Jr
   Theatre Manager: Guy Jordin Heard
Mission: The preservation of the historic playhouse; the presentation of top quality touring productions; the showcasing of professional and non-professional groups.
Utilizes: Singers
Founded: 1835
Specialized Field: Musical; Community Theater; Ethnic Theater; Puppet
Status: Professional; Nonprofit; Commercial
Paid Staff: 100
Paid Artists: 3
Income Sources: Actors' Equity Association; International Association of Theatrical Stage Employees; The Shubert Organization
Organization Type: Educational; Sponsoring

2418
SHAKESPEARE THEATRE COMPANY

516 8th Street SE
Washington, DC 20004
Phone: 202-547-3230
Fax: 202-547-0226
Web Site: www.shakespearetheatre.com
Management:
   Managing Director: Chris Jennings
   Artistic Director: Michael Kahn
   Director Marketing/Communications: Darby I Lunceford
   Managing Director: Nicholas Goldsborough
   Director Information Technology: Valerie Donegan
   Public Relations & Marketing: Barry M. Colfelt
Mission: The theatre's core mission is to present classic theatre in an accessible, skillful, imaginative, American style that honors playwrights' language and intentions while viewing their plays through a 21st-century lens.
Utilizes: Actors; AEA Actors; Artists-in-Residence; Choreographers; Collaborating Artists; Commissioned Composers; Guest Accompanists; Guest Artists; Guest Companies; Guest Conductors; Guest Designers; Guest Writers; Local Artists; Original Music Scores; Resident Artists; Resident Professionals; Selected Students; Soloists; Student Interns
Founded: 1986
Specialized Field: Shakespeare
Status: Non-Profit, Professional
Paid Staff: 90
Paid Artists: 75
Budget: $13 Million
Income Sources: League of Washington Theatres; Cultural Alliance of Greater Washington
Performs At: Shakespeare Theatre Company at the Lansburgh
Annual Attendance: 145,000
Facility Category: Theatre
Type of Stage: Proscenium
Seating Capacity: 451
Organization Type: Performing; Resident

2419
SOURCE THEATRE COMPANY

1835 14th Street NW
Washington, DC 20009
Phone: 202-204-7800
e-mail: info@sourcedc.org
Web Site: www.sourcetheatre.org
Management:
   Artistic Director: Joe Banno

   Literary Manager: Keith Parker
   Managing Director: Delia Taylor
   Contact: Heather Pagella
Mission: To present innovative and exciting productions of new works and contemporary plays that have relevance to our community; to offer reinterpretations of the classics.
Utilizes: Actors; AEA Actors; Artists-in-Residence; Collaborating Artists; Collaborations; Curators; Dance Companies; Designers; Educators; Fine Artists; Five Seasonal Concerts; Guest Accompanists; Guest Choreographers; Guest Companies; Guest Composers; Guest Designers; Guest Directors; Guest Ensembles; Guest Lecturers; Guest Musical Directors; Guest Musicians; Guest Teachers; Guild Activities; High School Drama; Instructors; Local Artists; Local Unknown Artists; Lyricists; Multi Collaborations; Multimedia; Music; New Productions; Organization Contracts; Original Music Scores; Performance Artists; Poets; Resident Professionals; Selected Students; Sign Language Translators; Singers; Soloists; Student Interns; Special Technical Talent; Theatre Companies; Touring Companies; Visual Arts
Founded: 1977
Specialized Field: Ensembles; Drama; Musical
Status: Professional; Nonprofit
Paid Staff: 4
Volunteer Staff: 40
Paid Artists: 20
Budget: $400,000
Income Sources: Ticket Sales, Grants
Performs At: Theatre
Affiliations: League of Washington Theatres; Theatre Communications Group; Actors' Equity Association
Annual Attendance: 15,000
Type of Stage: Black Box
Year Remodeled: 1998
Rental Contact: Heather Pagella
Organization Type: Performing; Touring; Resident

2420
STUDIO THEATRE

1333 P Street NW
Washington, DC 20005
Phone: 202-232-7267
Fax: 202-588-5262
e-mail: studio@studiotheatre.org
Web Site: www.studiotheatre.org
Officers:
   Chair of the Board of Trustees: Susan L Butler
   Vice Chair of the Board of Trustees: Janet L Dewar
   Chair Emeritus, Board of Trustees: Irene Harriet Blum
   Chair Emeritus, Board of Trustees: Jaylee M Mead
Management:
   Artistic Director: Joy Zinoman
   Managing Director: Keith Alan Baker
Mission: To produce the best in contemporary theatre and through its Secondstage and Acting Conservatory to provide opportunities for emerging artists and to offer rigorous theatre training. Our commitment to artistic excellence serves the diverse communities of the nation's capital.
Utilizes: Guest Companies
Founded: 1978
Specialized Field: Comedy; Youth Theater; Dinner Theater; Ethnic Theater; Community Theater; Classic; Contemporary
Status: Non-Profit, Professional
Paid Staff: 32
Budget: $3,000,000

Income Sources: Theatre Communications Group; Cultural Alliance of Greater Washington; League of Washington Theatres
Performs At: The Studio Theatre; The Secondstage
Facility Category: Theatre
Type of Stage: Proscenium
Seating Capacity: 182 Milton/218 Mead/50 Second Stage
Year Remodeled: 1997
Cost: 5.5 million
Rental Contact: Roma Rogers
Organization Type: Performing; Educational; Sponsoring

2421
VSA ARTS

1300 Connecticut Avenue
Suite 700
Washington, DC 20036
Phone: 202-628-2800
Fax: 202-737-0725
e-mail: info@vsarts.org
Web Site: www.vsarts.org
Officers:
   Director Nation Programs/Events: Dani Fox
   Information Specialist: Johanna Bontwood
Management:
   President: Soula Antonia
Utilizes: Actors; Artists-in-Residence; Fine Artists; Guest Accompanists; Guest Musical Directors; Guest Musicians; Guild Activities; Instructors; Multimedia; Playwrights; Singers; Touring Companies
Founded: 1974
Specialized Field: Musical; Youth Theater; Ethnic Theater; Community Theater; Puppet; Classic; Contemporary; Alternative; Educational
Status: Non-Profit, Professional
Affiliations: John F Kennedy Center for the Performing Arts

2422
WASHINGTON STAGE GUILD

4018 Argyle Terrace NW
#4
Washington, DC 20011
Phone: 240-582-0050
Web Site: http://www.stageguild.org/
Management:
   Producing Artistic Director: Bill Largess
   Executive Director: Ann Norton
Mission: To perform plays that are often overlooked, including lesser-known works of famous playwrights, classics, and new plays of merit.
Utilizes: Singers
Founded: 1986
Specialized Field: Drama; Musical
Status: Professional; Nonprofit
Income Sources: Actors' Equity Association; League of Washington Theatres; Cultural Arts Alliance of DC
Performs At: Carroll Hall
Organization Type: Performing; Resident; Educational

2423
WOOLLY MAMMOTH THEATRE COMPANY

641 D Street NW
Washington, DC 20004
Phone: 202-393-3939
Fax: 202-289-2446
e-mail: info@woollymammoth.net
Web Site: www.woollymammoth.net
Management:
   Artistic Director: Howard Shalwitz
   Managing Director: Jeffrey Herrmann

Mission: To ignite an explosive engagement between theatre artists and the community by developing, producing, and promoting new plays that explore the edges of theatrical style and human experience, and by implementing new ways to use the artistry of theatre to serve the people of Greater Washington, DC.
Utilizes: Guest Companies; Singers
Founded: 1980
Specialized Field: Theater
Status: Non-Profit, Professional
Paid Staff: 65
Budget: $4,085,814
Performs At: Woolly Mammoth Theatre
Type of Stage: Flex-Proscenium
Seating Capacity: 265
Year Built: 2005
Rental Contact: General Manager Brian Smith
Organization Type: Performing; Resident; Educational

Florida

2424
ISLAND PLAYERS

PO Box 20411, St. Simons Island
Anna Maria, FL 31522
Phone: 912-638-0338
e-mail: islandplayers@live.comÿ
Web Site: www.theislandplayers.com
Management:
President: Allan Ledingham
Vice President: Ronald Dempset
Secretary: Beverly Fetter
Treasurer: Joyce Ledingham
Mission: To present quality community theatre for the cultural enrichment of the area.
Utilizes: Guest Companies; Singers
Founded: 1948
Specialized Field: Community Theater
Status: Non-Professional; Nonprofit
Performs At: Island Players Theatre
Organization Type: Performing

2425
CALDWELL THEATRE COMPANY

7901 N Federal Highway
Levitz Plaza
Boca Raton, FL 33487
Phone: 561-241-7432
Fax: 561-997-6917
Toll-free: 877-245-7432
e-mail: clive@caldwelltheatre.com
Web Site: www.caldwelltheatre.com
Management:
Artistic And Marketing Director: Clive Cholerton
Company Manager: Patricia Burdett
Mission: To explore timeless and current human issues through the art of theater, and to provide a creative and caring artistic home for artists, staff, students and audiences of all ages. The Caldwell continues to provide an environment where imaginations soar-and professional theater thrives.
Utilizes: Designers; Guest Companies
Founded: 1975
Specialized Field: Drama; Musical
Status: Professional; Nonprofit
Income Sources: Theatre Communications Group; Florida Professional Theatre Association
Organization Type: Performing; Touring; Resident

2426
FLORIDA ATLANTIC UNIVERSITY: DEPARTMENT OF THEATRE

777 Glade Road
Boca Raton, FL 33431
Phone: 561-297-3810
Fax: 561-297-2180
e-mail: theatre@fau.edu
Web Site: www.fau.edu/theatre
Officers:
Chair: Gvozden Kopani
Founded: 1967
Specialized Field: Musical; Comedy; Youth Theater; Dinner Theater; Ethnic Theater; Community Theater; Puppet; Educational; Theater Workshops
Status: Non-Profit, Non-Professional
Paid Staff: 15
Paid Artists: 15
Budget: $40,750-51,000
Affiliations: ATHE
Seating Capacity: 540; 150; 100
Year Built: 1996

2427
MANATEE PLAYERS/RIVERFRONT THEATRE

102 12th Street W
Bradenton, FL 34205
Phone: 941-748-0111
Web Site: www.manateeplayers.com
Management:
Artistic Director: Rick Kerby
Production: Kristin Ribble
Marketing: Denny Miller
Mission: Improving the cultural and educational climate of our community through offering quality live theatre.
Utilizes: Guest Companies; Singers
Founded: 1948
Specialized Field: Community Theater
Status: Nonprofit
Paid Staff: 100
Income Sources: Festival of American Community Theatre; American Association of Community Theatres; Manatee County Cultural Alliance
Performs At: Riverfront Theatre
Organization Type: Performing; Educational

2428
ATLANTIC COAST THEATRE

8297 Champions Gate Boulevard #188
Champions Gate, FL 33896
Phone: 863-242-8656
Fax: 863-424-5130
Toll-free: 877-565-0828
Management:
Education Director: Noel Holland
Artistic Director: Don Gruel
Mission: Dedicated to bring the art of theatre to children and families. Believe in the amazing imaginations of children. Our mission is to create performances, workshops and educational programs that inspire and encourage discussion
Specialized Field: Children's Theater

2429
CITY PLAYERS

Clearwater Parks And Recreation
Po Box 4748
Clearwater, FL 34618
Phone: 813-462-6035
Management:
Cultural Arts Supervisor: Margo Walbolt
Technical Director: Phillip Terry

Music Director: B.J. Pucci
Mission: To offer the public quality theatre at nominal fees.
Founded: 1971
Specialized Field: Community Theater
Status: Non-Professional; Nonprofit
Paid Staff: 4
Performs At: Ruth Eckerd Hall; Saint Petersburg Junior College
Organization Type: Performing; Educational

2430
SHOWBOAT DINNER THEATRE

3405 Ulmerton Road
Clearwater, FL 34622
Phone: 727-571-1200
Fax: 813-573-2735
Management:
Owner/President/Producer: Virginia Sherwood
Utilizes: Guest Companies; Singers
Founded: 1967
Specialized Field: Dinner Theater
Status: Professional; Commercial
Organization Type: Performing

2431
SURFSIDE PLAYERS

PO Box 320053
Cocoa Beach, FL 32932
Phone: 321-783-3127
e-mail: box.office@surfsideplayers.com
Officers:
President: Dave McFarland
VP: Judy Bate
Secretary: Kay Grinter
Treasurer: Marilyn Rigerman
Mission: To produce high quality productions, and educate youth in the performing arts field.
Specialized Field: Children's Theater; Educational

2432
ACTORS' PLAYHOUSE AT THE MIRACLE THEATRE

280 Miracle Mile
Coral Gables, FL 33134
Phone: 305-444-9293
Fax: 305-444-4181
Web Site: www.actorsplayhouse.org
Officers:
Chairman: Lawrence Stein
Treasurer: Lawrence Kessler
Secretary: Leslie Gross
Management:
Chairman: Lawrence E Stein
Executive Producing Director: Barbara S Stein
Artistic Director: David Arisco
Assistant Technical Director: Chris Jahn
Mission: Actors' Playhouse at the Miracle Theatre is one of Florida's major, critically acclaimed, non-profit cultural institutions and is dedicated to entertaining and culturally enriching South Florida audiences by producing quality live theatre for adults and children at affordable prices.
Founded: 1988
Specialized Field: Musical
Status: Nonprofit
Season: October - June
Seating Capacity: 600

2433
GABLESTAGE

1200 Anastasia Avenue
Suite 230
Coral Gables, FL 33134

Phone: 305-446-1116
Fax: 305-445-8645
Web Site: www.gablestage.org
Management:
    Chair: Barbara Friedson Garrett
    General Manager: Maria Kronfeld
    Vice Chair: Denise K Ehrich
    Producing Artistic Director: Joseph Adler
Mission: To provide the South Florida community with classical contemporary theatrical productions of artistic excellence. FST hopes to challenge our multi-cultural audience with innovative productions that entertain as well as confront today's issues and ideas.
Utilizes: Singers
Founded: 1979
Specialized Field: Drama; Musical; Specialty Acts
Status: Professional; Nonprofit
Paid Staff: 10
Budget: $1 million
Income Sources: Foundations; Government; Corporations; Individuals; Box Office
Performs At: Biltmore Hotel
Affiliations: Theatre Leader of South Florida
Annual Attendance: 30,000
Type of Stage: Proscenium
Seating Capacity: 150
Year Built: 1995
Organization Type: Performing; Touring; Resident; Educational

2434
TEATRO AVANTE
744 S.W. 8th Street, 2nd Floor
Coral Gables, FL 33130
Phone: 305-445-8877
Fax: 305-445-1301
e-mail: TeAvante@aol.com
Web Site: www.teatroavante.com
Management:
    Producing Artistic Director: Mario Ernesto Sanchez
    Resident Director/Designer: Rolando Moreno
    Technical Coordinator: Manelo Mina
Mission: To further Hispanic theatre.
Utilizes: Guest Companies; Singers
Founded: 1979
Specialized Field: Summer Stock; Multi-Cultural
Status: Professional; Nonprofit
Performs At: El Carruse Theatre
Organization Type: Performing; Touring; Educational

2435
UNIVERSITY OF MIAMI: DEPARTMENT OF THEATRE ARTS
PO Box 248273
Coral Gables, FL 33124
Mailing Address: PO Box 248273, Coral Gables, FL 33124
Phone: 305-284-4474
Fax: 305-284-5702
e-mail: theatredepartment@miami.edu
Officers:
    Interim Chair: Bruce J Miller
Specialized Field: Educational; Theater Workshops
Budget: $20,000-30,000
Affiliations: City Theatre
Seating Capacity: 300-400;45
Year Built: 1951
Year Remodeled: 1996

2436
DAYTONA PLAYHOUSE
100 Jessamine Boulevard
Daytona Beach, FL 32118

Phone: 386-255-2431
Fax: 386-255-2432
e-mail: boxoffice@daytonaplayhouse.org
Web Site: www.daytonaplayhouse.org/
Management:
    Artistic Director: James F Sturgell
Mission: Since 1946, the Daytona Playhouse has entertained appreciative audiences with wonderful performances in the very best community theater tradition. The Playhouse, a nonprofit organization, is also a source of numerous and varied volunteer opportunities in theater management and production.
Utilizes: Commissioned Music
Specialized Field: Musical; Comedy; Community Theater; Classic; Contemporary
Status: Non-Profit, Non-Professional
Performs At: Daytona Playhouse
Organization Type: Performing; Resident

2437
SEASIDE MUSIC THEATER
901 6th Street
PO Box 2835
Daytona Beach, FL 32120
Phone: 386-252-3394
Fax: 386-252-8991
e-mail: lester.malizia@seasidemusictheater.org
Web Site: www.seasidemusictheater.org
Officers:
    President: William Gillespie
    Director Development: Monya Winzer
Management:
    Artistic Director: Lester Malizia
    Associate Producer/Executive Dir: Julia Truilo
    Production Manager: Bob Fetterman
    Company Manager: Jerry Lapidas
    Technical Director: Brian Kelley
Mission: To offer the finest examples of opera, operetta and musical theatre in repertory.
Utilizes: Actors; AEA Actors; Artists-in-Residence; Choreographers; Commissioned Composers; Dancers; Designers; Fine Artists; Five Seasonal Concerts; Grant Writers; Guest Accompanists; Guest Artists; Guest Companies; Guest Conductors; Guest Designers; Guest Lecturers; Guest Musical Directors; Music; Original Music Scores; Resident Professionals; Selected Students; Sign Language Translators; Singers; Soloists
Founded: 1977
Specialized Field: Musical
Status: Non-Profit, Professional
Paid Staff: 10
Paid Artists: 250
Budget: $2,800,000
Income Sources: Florida Professional Theatre Association; United States Institute for Theatre Technology; Southeastern Theatre Conference
Season: June - August
Annual Attendance: 40,000
Facility Category: Two Theaters
Type of Stage: Procenium
Stage Dimensions: 6'x30'; 47'x17'
Seating Capacity: 498; 576
Year Remodeled: 1999
Rental Contact: Director of Marketing Kelli Beasley
Organization Type: Performing; Touring; Educational

2438
DELRAY BEACH PLAYHOUSE
950 NW Ninth Street
Delray Beach, FL 33444

Phone: 561-272-1281
Fax: 561-272-5884
e-mail: delraybeachplayhouse@gmail.com
Web Site: www.delraybeachplayhouse.com
Officers:
    President: George Allenton
Management:
    Executive Director: Susan Easton
    Artistic Director: Randolph DelLago
    Box Office Manager: Sue Easton
Mission: To increase community involvement in the performing arts.
Founded: 1948
Specialized Field: Community Theater; Musical; Theater Workshops; Children's Theater
Status: Non-Profit, Non-Professional
Paid Staff: 4
Volunteer Staff: 150
Non-paid Artists: 100
Income Sources: Florida Theatre Conference
Performs At: Delray Beach Playhouse
Facility Category: Non-profit community theatre
Seating Capacity: 238
Organization Type: Performing; Educational

2439
BAY STREET PLAYERS
PO Box 1405
Eustis, FL 32727
Phone: 352-357-7777
e-mail: elmobsp@comcast.net
Web Site: www.baystreetplayers.org
Officers:
    President: Stephan Toth
    Executive Director: Elizabeth Scholl
Management:
    Director: Deborah Carpenter
    Managing Director: Michael Lake
Mission: To provide practical theater training through hands-on experience.
Utilizes: Guest Companies; Singers
Founded: 1975
Specialized Field: Community Theater
Status: Non-Profit, Non-Professional
Paid Staff: 3
Paid Artists: 6
Performs At: State Theatre
Organization Type: Performing; Touring; Educational

2440
FORT LAUDERDALE CHILDREN'S THEATRE
516 NE 13th Street
Fort Lauderdale, FL 33304
Phone: 954-763-6882
Fax: 954-523-0507
e-mail: info@FLCTStar.org
Web Site: www.flct.org
Officers:
    President: Janet Erlick
Management:
    Managing Director: Sean Cutler
    Education Director r: Patti Kimmel Meyers
    Business Manager: Rachal Solomon
Mission: To develop the full potential of students as members of our community; to celebrate the diversity of Broward County's population through the arts; to nurture communication among various performing groups; to advance the highest possible standards of the theatre; to encourage public appreciation of the art form; to develop future audiences and supporters of the cultural arts.

Utilizes: Actors; Collaborating Artists; Collaborations; Commissioned Music; Grant Writers; Guest Accompanists; Guest Artists; Guest Companies; Guest Conductors; Guest Designers; Guest Ensembles; Guest Instructors; Guest Lecturers; Guest Musical Directors; Guild Activities; High School Drama; Instructors; Local Artists; Lyricists; Multimedia; Music; Organization Contracts; Original Music Scores; Resident Professionals; Singers; Soloists
Founded: 1952
Specialized Field: Educational; Children's Theater; Theater Workshops
Status: Non-Profit, Non-Professional
Paid Staff: 12
Volunteer Staff: 50
Budget: $500,000
Income Sources: Classes; Plays; Outreach
Performs At: Dillard Center for the Arts; Hollywood Playhouse
Seating Capacity: 660; 262
Rental Contact: Business Manager Amy Rand
Organization Type: Performing; Touring; Educational

2441
ONE WAY PUPPETS

PO Box 5346
Fort Lauderdale, FL 33310
Phone: 954-491-4221
Management:
    Director: Bob Dolan
Mission: Entertainment and education through puppetry.
Founded: 1971
Specialized Field: Ensembles; Puppet
Status: Professional
Organization Type: Performing; Educational

2442
BROADWAY PALM DINNER THEATRE

1380 Colonial Boulevard
Fort Myers, FL 33907
Phone: 239-278-4422
Fax: 239-278-5664
Toll-free: 800-475-7256
e-mail: tickets@broadwaypalm.com
Web Site: www.broadwaypalm.com
Management:
    President and Owner: Will Prather
    Managing Director: Brian Enzmam
    General Manager: Susan Johnson
    Assistant General Manager: Maryi Lawton
Mission: Year-round professional dinner theatre presenting Broadway's brightest musicals and comedies.
Utilizes: Actors; Collaborations; Dancers; Designers; Fine Artists; Guest Artists; Guest Conductors; Guest Designers; Guest Lecturers; Guest Musical Directors; Instructors; Local Artists; Multimedia; Music; Original Music Scores; Resident Professionals; Sign Language Translators; Student Interns; Touring Companies
Founded: 1992
Specialized Field: Musical; Comedy; Youth Theater; Dinner Theater; Ethnic Theater; Community Theater; Contemporary
Status: Professional; Non-Equity
Paid Staff: 100
Paid Artists: 10
Income Sources: Ticket sales; Bar & gift shop revenue
Performs At: Broadway Palm Dinner Theatre
Affiliations: National Dinner Theatre Association
Annual Attendance: 150,000+
Facility Category: Dinner Theatre
Type of Stage: Proscenium
Seating Capacity: 450

Year Remodeled: 1993
Rental Contact: General Manager Susan Johnson

2443
FLORIDA REPERTORY THEATRE

2267 First Street
Fort Myers, FL 33901
Phone: 239-332-4665
Fax: 239-332-1808
Toll-free: 877-787-8053
e-mail: johnmartin@floridarep.org
Web Site: www.floridarep.org
Officers:
    Chairman: Dr Gerald Laboda
    Second Chair: Naomi Bloom
    Secretary: Sonya Lubner
    Treasurer: Arthur Zupko
Management:
    Producing Artistic Director/Pres: Robert Caciopto
    Managing Director/VP: John W Martin
    Associate Producer: Carrie Lund
Mission: Providing a first class regional theatre for Southwest Florida; creating, nurturing, and developing an ensemble of theatre professionals who will develop long term relationships working on a wide variety of plays; helping improve the quality of life in our community through all arts; and to making the arts-especially theatre-accessible to all.
Founded: 1998
Specialized Field: Educational; Drama; Theater Workshops
Status: Non-Profit, Professional
Paid Staff: 32
Volunteer Staff: 200
Paid Artists: 70
Budget: $1.8 Million
Income Sources: Ticket & Subscription Sales/Grants/Corporate & Individual Donations
Performs At: Professional Main Stage & Black Box Theatres; Children's Touring Theatre in the Region's Schools
Annual Attendance: 70,000
Type of Stage: Proscenium; 3/4 Thrust Black Box
Stage Dimensions: 40' x 30'; 15' x 10'
Seating Capacity: 393; 80
Year Built: 1908
Year Remodeled: 1994
Rental Contact: Production Manager Sean Griffin

2444
PENINSULA PLAYERS

1436 Rosada Way
Fort Myers, FL 33901
Phone: 941-476-7305
Officers:
    President: James Zgoda
    VP: Ted Schirm
    Treasurer: Linda Jacobey
    Secretary: Suzanne Beeny
Management:
    Director: Al Richter
    Director: Dan Perry
    Director/Producer: Martha Richter
    General Manager: Tom Birmingham
    Executive Producer: James B McKenzie
Mission: To study, perform and promote choral works.
Founded: 1935
Specialized Field: Dinner Theater; Community Theater
Status: Nonprofit
Income Sources: Lee County Alliance of Arts
Performs At: Peninsula Playhouse
Organization Type: Performing

2445
UNIVERSITY OF FLORIDA: SCHOOL, THEATER AND DANCE

Nadine McGuire Theater and Dance Pavilion
University of Florida
Gainesville, FL 32611
Phone: 352-273-0500
Fax: 352-392-5114
Web Site: www.arts.ufl.edu
Management:
    Chairperson: Kevin Marshall
Founded: 1853
Specialized Field: Musical; Comedy; Ethnic Theater; Classic; Contemporary
Status: Non-Profit, Non-Professional
Paid Staff: 30
Budget: $5,100-7,200
Affiliations: NAST; U/RTA; ATHE; Hippodrome State Theatre
Seating Capacity: 460; 100; 50
Year Built: 1967
Year Remodeled: 1996

2446
GOLDEN THESPIANS

900 Tyler Street
Hollywood, FL 33019
Phone: 305-920-5492
Officers:
    President: Ellen Bush
    VP: Gloria Williams
    Treasurer: Virginia Godfrey
    Secretary: Madeline Barauskas
Management:
    President/Director Shows: Ellen Bush
Mission: To bring together a senior group of men and women who were professional musicians, singers and dancers in their younger days to perform one-hour vaudeville shows in nursing homes, hospitals and at community affairs.
Founded: 1965
Specialized Field: Musical; Community Theater; Ethnic Theater; Classic
Status: Nonprofit
Paid Staff: 25
Income Sources: President's Council
Performs At: Recreation Center
Organization Type: Performing

2447
HOLLYWOOD PLAYHOUSE

2640 Washington Street
Hollywood, FL 33020
Phone: 954-922-0404
Fax: 954-922-0666
Web Site: http://playhousehollywood.com/
Officers:
    President: Bea Yianilos
    VP: Ivonne Morten
    Secretary/Treasurer: Kothi Glist
Management:
    Executive Artistic Director: Andy Rogow
    Technical Director: David Sherman
Mission: Bringing culture to our community through theatre.
Utilizes: Actors; AEA Actors; Choreographers; Collaborations; Five Seasonal Concerts; Guest Accompanists; Guest Artists; Local Artists; Performance Artists; Resident Professionals; Student Interns
Founded: 1948
Specialized Field: Drama; New Plays; Musical
Status: Professional Regional Theater
Paid Artists: 100

Budget: $750,000
Income Sources: Florida Theatre Conference
Affiliations: Theatre League of South Florida; Hollywood Chamber of Commerce
Facility Category: Proscenium Ttheatre with Ample Fly and Wing Space
Type of Stage: Proscenium
Seating Capacity: 262
Year Built: 1960
Organization Type: Performing

2448
ALHAMBRA DINNER THEATRE

12000 Beach Boulevard
Jacksonville, FL 32216
Phone: 904-641-1212
Fax: 904-642-3505
Toll-free: 800-688-7469
Web Site: www.alhambradinnertheatre.com
Officers:
    President: Tod Booth
Management:
    Executive Producer: Tod Booth
    Marketing Director: Jack Booth
Mission: Producing the finest professional theatrical productions.
Founded: 1880
Specialized Field: Dinner Theater
Status: Professional; Commercial
Paid Staff: 100
Income Sources: Actors' Equity Association; American Dinner Theatre Institute; Society for Stage Directors and Choreographers; American Federation of Musicians
Performs At: Alhambra Dinner Theatre
Annual Attendance: 120,000
Facility Category: Dinner Theatre
Type of Stage: Thrust
Seating Capacity: 400
Year Built: 1967
Rental Contact: Director of Marketing Jack Booth
Organization Type: Performing

2449
RITZ THEATRE AND LA VILLA MUSEUM

829 N Davis Street
Jacksonville, FL 32202
Phone: 904-632-5555
Fax: 904-632-5553
e-mail: ritztheatre@coj.net
Web Site: http://www.ritzjacksonville.com/
Management:
    Executive Director: Carol Alexander
    Production Manager: Teneese Williams
Founded: 1999
Specialized Field: Drama; Musical; Historical; Classic
Status: For-Profit, Professional
Paid Staff: 10

2450
KEY WEST PLAYERS

416 Eaton Street
Key West, FL 33040
Phone: 305-295-9493
Fax: 305-768-0465
e-mail: info@keywestfilm.org
Web Site: www.keywestfilm.org
Officers:
    President: Paul Hilson
    VP: Kelly Hedges-Peerman
    Treasurer: Florence Recher
Mission: Presenting live professional and amateur entertainment; providing a teaching experience; teaching all of the aspects of theater.

Utilizes: Actors; AEA Actors; Choreographers; Collaborating Artists; Collaborations; Composers; Dancers; Educators; Grant Writers; Guest Accompanists; Guest Artists; Guest Companies; Guest Designers; Guest Ensembles; Guest Instructors; Guest Lecturers; Guest Musical Directors; Guest Musicians; Guest Soloists; Guest Teachers; Guild Activities; High School Drama; Local Artists; Local Unknown Artists; Multimedia; Original Music Scores; Performance Artists; Poets; Resident Companies; Resident Professionals; Scenic Designers; Sign Language Translators; Singers; Soloists; Student Interns; Touring Companies
Founded: 1940
Specialized Field: Drama; Musical; Contemporary
Status: Nonprofit
Paid Staff: 5
Volunteer Staff: 12
Paid Artists: 150
Budget: $270,000
Income Sources: Box Office; Grants; Donations
Performs At: Waterfront Playhouse
Affiliations: FL. Professional Theater Association; League of South FL. Theaters; Theater Communications Group
Annual Attendance: 10,000
Facility Category: Live Performing Arts Theatre
Type of Stage: Proscenium
Stage Dimensions: 25'x35'
Seating Capacity: 180
Year Built: 1853
Year Remodeled: 1960
Rental Contact: George Gugleotti
Organization Type: Performing; Educational

2451
RED BARN THEATRE

319 Duval Street
PO Box 707
Key West, FL 33040
Phone: 305-293-3035
Fax: 305-293-3035
Web Site: www.redbarntheatre.com
Management:
    President: Steve Russ
    Managing Director: Mimi McDonald
Utilizes: Guest Companies
Founded: 1981
Specialized Field: Drama; Musical; Contemporary
Status: Professional; Nonprofit
Paid Staff: 7
Paid Artists: 90
Income Sources: Theatre Communications Group
Performs At: Red Barn Theatre
Organization Type: Performing; Resident; Educational

2452
FLORIDA SOUTHERN COLLEGE: DEPARTMENT OF THEATRE ARTS

111 Lake Hollingsworth Dr
111 Lake Hollingsworth Drive
Lakeland, FL 33801
Phone: 863-680-4226
Fax: 863-680-4457
Web Site: https://www.flsouthern.edu/academics/theatre/flash/program.html
Officers:
    Chairman: James F Beck
Management:
    Director of Theatre Dept: James Beck
Specialized Field: Educational; Theater Workshops
Budget: $600-5,000
Seating Capacity: 336; 75
Year Built: 1970

2453
KALEIDOSCOPE THEATRE

207 E 24th Street
Lynn Haven, FL 32444
Phone: 850-265-3226
e-mail: ktplays@kt-online.org
Web Site: http://www.kt-online.org/
Management:
    Board of Directors: Lois Carter
    Board of Directors: David Garcia
    Director/President: Sandy Wilson
Mission: To increase knowledge of theatre and provide cultural enrichment.
Utilizes: Guest Companies; Singers
Founded: 1972
Specialized Field: Musical; Dinner Theater; Community Theater
Status: Non-Professional; Nonprofit
Paid Staff: 300
Performs At: Kaleidoscope Theatre
Organization Type: Performing; Educational

2454
FLORIDA STAGE

262 S Ocean Boulevard
Manalapan, FL 33462
Phone: 561-585-3404
Fax: 561-588-4708
Toll-free: 800-514-3837
Web Site: www.floridastage.org
Officers:
    Chairman of the Board: Dennis Vlassis
    Immediate Past Chairman: Laurie Gildan
Management:
    Managing Director: Nancy Barnett
    President: Louis Tyrrell
    Director Communications: Larry Friedrich
Mission: Dedicated to the production of new American plays by our finest contemporary playwrights.
Founded: 1987
Specialized Field: Musical; Comedy; Drama
Status: Non-Profit, Professional
Paid Staff: 35
Budget: $2.5 Million
Season: October - August
Performs At: Florida Stage
Affiliations: AEA, SSDC, USA
Facility Category: Florida Stage
Type of Stage: Thrust
Seating Capacity: 258

2455
THEATRE CLUB OF THE PALM BEACHES

262 S Ocean Boulevard
Manalapan, FL 33462
Phone: 407-585-3404
Fax: 407-585-4708
Management:
    Producing Director: Louis Tyrrell
    Company Manager: Nancy Johnson
    Office Manager: Caroline Breder
    Marketing Director: Cheryl Dun
    Development Director: Alison Pruitt
Mission: To present the finest new works of young American playwrights.
Utilizes: Guest Companies
Specialized Field: Drama; Musical; Contemporary; Community Theater
Status: Professional
Paid Artists: Yes
Income Sources: Actors' Equity Association; Society for Stage Directors and Choreographers
Organization Type: Performing

2456

MARATHON COMMUNITY THEATRE

5101 Overseas Highway
Marathon, FL 33050
Mailing Address: PO Box 124
Phone: 305-743-0408
Fax: 305-743-0408
e-mail: http://www.marathontheater.org/
Web Site: http://www.marathontheater.org/
Management:
    Executive Director: Loretta Geotis
Mission: To offer quality theatre events to adults in our community; to give cultural programs in schools.
Utilizes: Guest Artists; Guest Companies; Singers
Founded: 1957
Specialized Field: Musical; Dinner Theater; Community Theater; Puppet
Status: Nonprofit
Paid Staff: 60
Organization Type: Performing; Sponsoring

2457

MELBOURNE CIVIC THEATRE

3030 W New Haven Avenue
Melbourne, FL 32904
Phone: 321-723-1668
Fax: 321-723-6935
Web Site: www.mymct.org
Officers:
    President: June Borowski
Management:
    President: Bob Sullivan
    Executive Director: Jew Morrow
Mission: Entertaining, educating and enriching the community through the theatre arts.
Utilizes: Guest Writers; Guild Activities; Lyricists; Touring Companies
Founded: 1952
Specialized Field: Community Theater
Status: Non-Profit, Non-Professional
Paid Staff: 1
Volunteer Staff: 60
Non-paid Artists: 30
Budget: 120,000
Income Sources: Ticket Sales, Advertisments, Donations
Annual Attendance: 5,100
Facility Category: Theatre
Type of Stage: variable
Stage Dimensions: variable
Seating Capacity: 97
Rental Contact: Anita Saczeciana
Organization Type: Performing; Educational

2458

COCONUT GROVE PLAYHOUSE

3500 Main Highway
Miami, FL 33133
Phone: 305-442-2662
Fax: 305-444-6437
Web Site: www.cgplayhouse.com
Officers:
    Chairperson: Vincent Post
    Vice Chairman: Judge Michael Chavies
    Secretary: Peggy Hollander
    Treasurer: Mitchell R. Less
Management:
    Producing Artistic Director: Arnold Mittelman
    Associate Producer: Earl Hughes
    Director Marketing: Debbie Eyerdan
    Director Finance and Operations: Bill Kerlin
Mission: Offering theater of quality to the community; expanding knowledge of theater.

Utilizes: Actors; AEA Actors; Choreographers; Commissioned Composers; Commissioned Music; Dancers; Designers; Guest Companies; Guest Soloists; High School Drama; Instructors; Local Artists; Local Unknown Artists; Multimedia; Music; Original Music Scores; Performance Artists; Resident Professionals; Sign Language Translators; Student Interns
Founded: 1956
Specialized Field: Drama; Musical; Contemporary
Status: Professional; Nonprofit
Budget: $5,000,000-$6,000,000
Income Sources: Theatre Communications Group
Performs At: Coconut Grove Playhouse
Affiliations: League of Resident Theatres, LORT B & D
Type of Stage: Proscenium/Black Box
Seating Capacity: 1000
Year Built: 1926
Organization Type: Performing; Touring; Educational

2459

FLORIDA INTERNATIONAL UNIVERSITY: DEPARTMENT OF THEATRE AND DANCE

Wertheim Performing Arts Center
SW 112 Avenue and 8th Street
Miami, FL 33199
Phone: 305-348-1684
Fax: 305-348-1803
Web Site: www.fiu.edu/~thedan
Officers:
    Chairman: Dr. Leroy Clark
Management:
    Executive Director: Leroy Clark
    Managing Director: Abel Cornejo
Founded: 1972
Specialized Field: Educational; Theater Workshops
Status: Non-Profit, Non-Professional
Paid Staff: 11
Budget: $7,100-11,900
Affiliations: NAST
Seating Capacity: 240; 150; 150
Year Built: 1996

2460

LAS MASCARAS THEATRE

2833 NW Seventh Street
Miami, FL 33125
Phone: 305-649-5301
Management:
    Artistic Director/Lead Actor: Alfonso Cremata
    Artistic Director/Lead Actor: Salvador Ugarte
Mission: To perform local and international plays in Spanish.
Founded: 1968
Specialized Field: Summer Stock; Musical
Status: Professional; Nonprofit
Performs At: Las Mascaras Theatre #1 & #2
Organization Type: Performing

2461

GOLD COAST THEATRE

PO Box 402964
Miami Beach, FL 33140-0964
Phone: 305-538-5500
Fax: 305-538-6315
e-mail: judeparry@aol.com
Web Site: www.goldcoasttheatre.org
Management:
    President: Warren Werner
    Executive Director: Jude Parry
Mission: To bring professional theatre to people from all walks of life with multi-media, original shows featuring the art of mime
Utilizes: Singers
Founded: 1982

Specialized Field: Musical; Comedy; Youth Theater; Ethnic Theater; Puppet; Contemporary; Mime
Status: Non-Profit, Professional
Paid Staff: 3
Volunteer Staff: 3
Paid Artists: 32
Budget: $100,000
Performs At: Touring Theatre Specializing in Mime
Annual Attendance: 100,000
Organization Type: Performing; Touring; Educational

2462

BERRY COLLEGE THEATRE COMPANY

Berry College
Mount Berry, FL 30149
Phone: 706-232-5374
Fax: 706-802-6739
e-mail: theatre@berry.edu
Web Site: www.berry.edu
Management:
    Technical Director: Christian Boy
    Costume and Make Up Director: Alice Bristow
    Director: John Countryman
Founded: 1952
Specialized Field: Musical; Comedy; Youth Theater; Community Theater; Classic; Contemporary
Status: Non-Profit, Non-Professional
Paid Staff: 30
Affiliations: ATHE; SETC
Seating Capacity: 240; 115
Year Built: 1984

2463

ICEHOUSE THEATRE

1100 North Unser Street 32757
Mount Dora, FL 32756-0759
Mailing Address: PO Box 759
Phone: 352-383-3133
Fax: 352-383-7897
e-mail: info@icehousetheatre.com
Web Site: http://www.icehousetheatre.com/
Officers:
    President: JC Bowling
    Vice President: Nanci Darst
    Treausrer: Carolyn Sonnentag
    Secretary: Brneda Aro
Management:
    Artistic Director: Darlin Barry
    Office Manager: Jean Robinson
Mission: Enhance the cultural life of Central Florida with first-quality theatrical productions and programs designed to inspire and educate patrons and their children. The theatre is also dedicated to providing talented area artists with numerous opportunities to refine their craft.
Utilizes: Actors; Artists-in-Residence; Collaborating Artists; Collaborations; Educators; Fine Artists; Five Seasonal Concerts; Grant Writers; Guest Artists; Guest Conductors; Guest Instructors; Guest Lecturers; Guest Soloists; Guest Writers; Guild Activities; High School Drama; Local Artists; Lyricists; Multimedia; Music; Performance Artists; Resident Professionals; Sign Language Translators; Soloists; Student Interns; Visual Arts
Specialized Field: Musical; Comedy; Drama
Status: Nonprofit
Paid Staff: 5
Paid Artists: 2
Income Sources: Memberships; Corporate Sponsorships
Affiliations: CFTA; AACT
Facility Category: Performing Arts Theatre
Type of Stage: Thrust/Proscenium Combination
Seating Capacity: 274

Year Built: 1947
Year Remodeled: 1953

2464
ORANGE PARK COMMUNITY THEATRE
2900 Moody Avenue
PO Box 391
Orange Park, FL 32067-0391
Phone: 904-276-2599
Fax: 941-472-0055
e-mail: opctweb@yahoo.com
Web Site: www.opct.org
Officers:
   President: Betty Detamore
Management:
   President: Barbara C Wells
   VP Of Production: Michael Ray
   Secretary: Regina Manning
Mission: Provides five stage productions annually, including at least one Broadway style musical, to the residents and visitors to the Jacksonville area and Northeast Florida.
Founded: 1969
Specialized Field: Musical; Community Theater
Status: Non-Professional; Nonprofit
Income Sources: Ticket Sales; Program Ads; Grants
Annual Attendance: 7,000
Facility Category: Community
Type of Stage: Proscenium
Stage Dimensions: 26x18
Seating Capacity: 101
Year Built: 1920
Year Remodeled: 1987
Organization Type: Performing; Educational

2465
ORLANDO BROADWAY DINNER THEATRE
3376 Edgewater Drive
Orlando, FL 32804
Phone: 407-843-6275
Fax: 407-398-0904
Web Site: www.orlandobroadway.com
Management:
   President/CEO: Dori Parker
   Director Of Operations: Scott Reeder
   Production Coordinator: Steve MacKinnon
Mission: Providing Orlando with full scale Broadway musicals and fine dining experience.
Founded: 1986
Specialized Field: Community Theater; Dinner Theater; Musical; Summer Stock; Puppet
Status: For-Profit, Professional
Paid Staff: 40
Paid Artists: 25
Income Sources: Actors' Equity Association; American Dinner Theatre Association
Performs At: Mark Two Dinner Theater
Organization Type: Performing

2466
SLEUTHS MYSTERY DINNER SHOWS
8267 International Drive
Orlando, FL 32819
Phone: 407-363-1985
Toll-free: 800-393-1958
e-mail: info@sleuths.com
Web Site: www.sleuths.com
Management:
   Show Director: Laurel Clark
Mission: Comedy mystery dinner shows.
Utilizes: Actors
Specialized Field: Comedy; Drama; Theatrical
Status: For Profit

Income Sources: Ticket Sales

2467
THEATRE-IN-THE-WORKS
PO Box 532016
Orlando, FL 32853
Phone: 407-365-7235
Management:
   Producing Director: Edward Dilks
Mission: Developing original musicals, operas and plays primarily written by Floridians.
Founded: 1984
Specialized Field: Drama; New Plays; Contemporary
Status: Professional; Nonprofit

2468
UCF CIVIC THEATRE
1001 E Princeton Street
Orlando, FL 32803
Phone: 407-896-7365
Fax: 407-897-3284
Management:
   Acting Executive Director: Kathryn Seidel
   Youth Program Coordinator: Jeff Revels
Mission: Providing entertainment, information, stimulation, education and an arena for artistic expression.
Utilizes: Guest Artists; Guest Companies; Singers
Founded: 1926
Specialized Field: Community Theater; Youth Theater
Status: Professional; Non-Professional; Nonprofit
Paid Staff: 2
Income Sources: American Association of Community Theatres; Florida Theatre Conference; United Arts
Performs At: Civic Theatre Complex
Organization Type: Performing; Touring; Educational

2469
UNIVERSITY OF CENTRAL FLORIDA: DEPARTMENT OF THEATRE
12501 Research Parkway
Suite 180
Orlando, FL 32816
Mailing Address: PO Box 162372, Orlando, FL 32816
Phone: 407-823-2862
Fax: 407-823-6446
Web Site: www.theatre.ucf.edu
Officers:
   Associate Chair: Joseph Rusnock
Management:
   Department Chairman: Christopher Niess
   Vice Department Chair: Kristina Tollefson
   Director of Production: Bert Scott
Mission: Educational theatre; BA; BFA; MA; MFA degrees
Specialized Field: Educational; Theater Workshops
Status: Non-Profit, Non-Professional
Paid Staff: 45
Paid Artists: 15
Budget: $800,000
Income Sources: State and revenue
Affiliations: ATHE; SEKC; USITT; FTC; TOC
Annual Attendance: 22,000
Type of Stage: Proscenium & Black Box
Seating Capacity: 300; 100
Year Built: 1982

2470
PENSACOLA LITTLE THEATRE
400 S Jefferson Street
Pensacola, FL 32502
Phone: 850-434-0257
Fax: 850-438-2787
Web Site: www.pensacolalittletheatre.com

Management:
   Technical Director: Jim Culton
   Executive Director: Donna Peoples
   Artistic Director: Ron Roston
   Managing Director: Heidi Schiller
Mission: To stimulate interest in performing arts; to provide community members a chance to participate in live theatre.
Founded: 1936
Specialized Field: Community Theater; Children's Theater
Status: Non-Professional; Nonprofit
Paid Staff: 100
Income Sources: Florida Theatre Conference; American Association of Community Theatres; Southeastern Theatre Conference
Performs At: Pensacola Little Theatre
Organization Type: Performing; Educational; Sponsoring

2471
UNIVERSITY OF WEST FLORIDA
Center for Fine and Performing Arts
11000 University Parkway
Pensacola, FL 32514
Phone: 850-474-2146
Fax: 850-474-2714
Toll-free: 800-263-1074
e-mail: admissions@uwf.edu
Web Site: www.uwf.edu
Management:
   President: John Cavanaugh
   Executive Director: Sandra Flake
   Artistic Director: Suzette Doyan
   Managing Director: Greg Lanier
Founded: 1968
Specialized Field: Educational; Theater Workshops
Status: Non-Profit, Professional
Budget: $13,000-33,000
Seating Capacity: 426; 120
Year Built: 1991

2472
PLANTATION THEATRE COMPANY
1829 N Pineland Road
Plantation, FL 33317
Phone: 954-424-9701
Fax: 954-424-0137
Mission: To afford community members an opportunity to participate in the arts.
Utilizes: Singers
Founded: 1975
Specialized Field: Musical; Community Theater
Status: Semi-Professional; Non-Professional; Nonprofit
Performs At: Diecke Auditorium
Organization Type: Performing; Educational

2473
POMPANO PLAYERS
PO Box 2045
Pompano Beach, FL 33061
Phone: 305-946-4646
Management:
   Box Office: Penny Manwell
   Technical: David Stockton
   Technical: Jerry Sullivan
Mission: To offer live theatre.
Utilizes: Guest Companies; Singers
Founded: 1956
Specialized Field: Musical; Community Theater
Status: Semi-Professional; Nonprofit
Income Sources: Florida Theatre Conference
Performs At: Pompano Players Theatre
Organization Type: Performing; Resident; Educational

2474
CHARLOTTE PLAYERS
PO Box 494088
Port Charlotte, FL 33949-4088
Phone: 941-255-1022
Fax: 941-743-7297
e-mail: charlotteplayers@nut-n-but.net
Web Site: www.charlotteplayers.org
Officers:
President: Gene Callan
Executive Director: Sherie M. Moody
Mission: To provide the highest quality theatre arts for our community's diverse culture through performance education and community involvement
Founded: 1960
Specialized Field: Community Theatre
Status: Non-Profit, Non-Professional
Paid Staff: 2
Performs At: Cultural Center Theater
Organization Type: Performing

2475
PIRATE PLAYHOUSE
975 Rabbit Road
Sanibel, FL 33957
Phone: 239-472-3511
Fax: 941-472-0055
Management:
Producing Artistic Director: Ralph Elias
General Manager: Kevin Mooney
Specialized Field: Drama; Comedy

2476
J HOWARD WOOD THEATRE
2200 Periwinkle Way
Sanibel Island, FL 33957
Phone: 941-472-0006
Fax: 941-472-0055
Web Site: www.thewoodtheatre.com
Officers:
President: Winnie Donoghue
Treasurer: Jim Lavelle
Secretary: Carla Benninga
Management:
Managing Director: Cindy Lee Overton
Artistic Producer: Robert Schelhammer
Marketing/Public Relations: Honey Larsen
Mission: To present live, professional theatre in Southwest Florida.
Utilizes: Actors; AEA Actors; Artists-in-Residence; Choreographers; Collaborations; Dancers; Designers; Fine Artists; Five Seasonal Concerts; Grant Writers; Guest Accompanists; Guest Artists; Guest Designers; Guest Ensembles; Guest Lecturers; Guest Musical Directors; Guest Teachers; Guild Activities; High School Drama; Instructors; Local Artists; Multimedia; Music; Original Music Scores; Performance Artists; Resident Professionals; Sign Language Translators; Soloists; Student Interns; Theatre Companies; Visual Arts
Founded: 1991
Specialized Field: Theater Workshops; Contemporary; Musical; New Plays; Young Playwrights; Children's Theater
Status: Not-for-Profit
Paid Staff: 10
Budget: 750k
Income Sources: Grants, Donations, Ticket Sales
Performs At: Theatre
Facility Category: Theater
Type of Stage: Thrust Stage
Seating Capacity: 180
Year Built: 1990

Organization Type: Performing; Touring; Resident; Educational; Sponsoring

2477
ASOLO REPERTORY THEATRE
5555 N. Tamiami Trail
Sarasota, FL 34243-2141
Phone: 941-351-9010
Fax: 941-351-5796
Toll-free: 800-361-8388
e-mail: asolorep@asolo.org
Web Site: www.asolorep.org
Management:
Managing Director: Linda DiGabriele
Producing Artistic Director: Michael Edwards
Assistant Managing Director: Corinne Deckard
Mission: Center for theatrical excellence, crafting the highest quality productions of classical, contemporary, and newly commissioned work all performed in the rarest form of rotating repertory. Featuring an accomplished resident company - complimented by distinguished guest artists - Asolo Rep offers audiences a unique and dynamic theatre experience.
Founded: 1960
Specialized Field: Educational; Theater Workshops
Status: Non-Profit
Performs At: Mertz Theatre, Cook Theatre
Affiliations: U/RTA; ATHE
Type of Stage: Proscenium
Seating Capacity: 499, 161

2478
FLORIDA STUDIO THEATRE
1241 N Palm Avenue
Sarasota, FL 34236
Phone: 941-366-9017
Fax: 941-955-4137
Web Site: www.fst2000.org
Management:
Associate Director: Kate Alexander
Artistic Director: Richard Hopkins
Managing Director: Rebecca Langford
Mission: To produce contemporary theatre with an emphasis on new plays and regional premieres.
Utilizes: Guest Companies; Singers
Founded: 1973
Specialized Field: Ensembles; Theater Workshops; Drama
Status: Professional; Nonprofit
Performs At: Florida Studio Theatre
Affiliations: Small Professional Theatre Assoication; Actors' Equity Association
Type of Stage: ThrustBox, Cabaret Space
Stage Dimensions: 30'x35'x25'
Seating Capacity: 173, 100
Rental Contact: John Jacobsen
Organization Type: Performing; Resident; Educational; Touring

2479
GOLDEN APPLE DINNER THEATRE
25 N Pineapple Avenue
Sarasota, FL 34236
Phone: 941-366-5454
Fax: 941-364-9100
Toll-free: 800-652-0920
Web Site: www.thegoldenapple.com
Management:
Managing Director: Ben Turoff
General Manager: Robert Turoff
Mission: To entertain, educate and enlighten.
Utilizes: Guest Artists; Singers
Founded: 1971
Specialized Field: Dinner Theater

Status: For-Profit, Professional
Paid Staff: 15
Paid Artists: 10
Income Sources: Actors' Equity Association
Performs At: Golden Apple Dinner Theatre
Organization Type: Sponsoring

2480
PLAYERS THEATRE
838 N Tamiami Trail
Sarasota, FL 34236
Phone: 941-365-2494
Fax: 941-954-0282
e-mail: info@theplayers.org
Web Site: www.theplayers.org
Officers:
President: Ken Shelin
Vice President: Barbara Johnson
Teasurer: Michael G Brown
Management:
Managing Director: Michelle Bianchi Pingel
Mission: To be the first and only community theatre in Sarasota offering live entertainment, full orchestra, professional direction and children's theatre.
Utilizes: Guest Artists; Guest Companies; Singers
Founded: 1930
Specialized Field: Musical
Status: Non-Profit, Non-Professional
Paid Staff: 7
Volunteer Staff: 700
Budget: $1.2 Million
Income Sources: Earned Income & Donations
Performs At: Community Theatre
Annual Attendance: 65,000
Seating Capacity: 497
Year Built: 1970
Organization Type: Performing; Touring; Educational

2481
ECKERD COLLEGE THEATRE DEPARTMENT
4200 54th Avenue South
St Petersburg, FL 33711
Phone: 813-864-8279
Fax: 813-864-7800
Toll-free: 800-569-09
Web Site: http://www.eckerd.edu/academics/theatre/
Officers:
Chair: Cynthia Totten
Specialized Field: Educational; Theater Workshops
Budget: $2,000-4,000
Affiliations: ATHE; SETC
Seating Capacity: 350; 60-80
Year Built: 1970

2482
VAUDEVILLE PALACE
7951 9th Street N
St Petersburg, FL 33702
Phone: 813-557-5515
Fax: 813-578-1024
Management:
Producer/Director: Buddy Graf
General Manager: Carol Graf
Box Office Manager: Skip Lewis
Mission: To offer amusing entertainment.
Founded: 1991
Specialized Field: Dinner Theater; Specialty Acts
Status: Professional; Commercial
Performs At: Vaudeville Palace
Organization Type: Performing; Resident

2483
LIMELIGHT THEATRE
11 Old Mission Avenue
PO Box 1196
St. Augustine, FL 32085-1196
Phone: 904-825-1164
Fax: 904-825-4662
e-mail: limeligt@bellsouth.net
Web Site: www.limelight-theatre.com
Officers:
   President: Paul McGuire
   VP: Wayne George
   Treasurer: Wayne Farrell
Management:
   President: Jeanne Krausz
   Artistic Director: Beth Lambert
   Director of Administration: Anne Kraft
   General Manager: Emma Lee Carpenter
Mission: To provide professional entertainment to visitors to the Saint Augustine area.
Utilizes: Actors; Choreographers; Collaborations; Dancers; Designers; Five Seasonal Concerts; Grant Writers; Guest Artists; Guest Conductors; Guest Ensembles; Guest Lecturers; Guest Musical Directors; Guest Musicians; Guest Teachers; Guest Writers; Guild Activities; High School Drama; Instructors; Local Artists; Lyricists; Music; Original Music Scores; Performance Artists; Resident Professionals; Selected Students; Sign Language Translators; Soloists; Student Interns; Theatre Companies; Touring Companies; Visual Arts
Founded: 1992
Specialized Field: Drama; Classic
Status: Non-Profit, Professional
Paid Staff: 4
Volunteer Staff: 80
Paid Artists: 60
Non-paid Artists: 10
Budget: 250,000
Income Sources: Admissions; Subsciptions; Individual and Corporate Donations and Grants
Performs At: Monson Resort
Affiliations: Flager College
Facility Category: Main Stage + Black Box
Type of Stage: Proscenium
Stage Dimensions: 36' x 20'
Seating Capacity: 99
Year Built: 1927
Year Remodeled: 2001
Rental Contact: General Manager Emma Lee Carpenter
Organization Type: Performing

2484
FLORIDA STATE UNIVERSITY: SCHOOL OF THEATRE
239 Fab
Florida State University
Tallahassee, FL 32306-1160
Phone: 850-644-6796
Fax: 850-644-7408
Web Site: www.fsu.edu/~theatre
Management:
   President: T K Wetherall
   Dean: Steven Wallace
Founded: 1973
Specialized Field: Musical; Educational; Theater Workshops
Status: Non-Profit, Non-Professional
Paid Staff: 40
Budget: $13,750-37,500
Affiliations: NAST; Asolo State Theatre
Seating Capacity: 500; 191; 200
Year Built: 1969

2485
YOUNG ACTORS THEATRE
609 Glenview Drive
Tallahassee, FL 32303
Phone: 850-386-6602
Fax: 850-422-2084
e-mail: info@youngactorstheatre.com
Web Site: www.youngactorstheatre.com
Officers:
   Executive Director: Cristina F. Williams
   Administrative Director: Valerie W. Smith
Management:
   Artistic Director: Robert A. Stuart
Mission: The education of youth in performance and theatre arts.
Utilizes: Actors; Guest Accompanists; Guest Artists; Guest Companies; Resident Professionals; Sign Language Translators
Founded: 1975
Specialized Field: Musical; Community Theater
Status: Non-Profit, Non-Professional
Paid Staff: 25
Volunteer Staff: 300
Paid Artists: 15
Non-paid Artists: 250
Budget: $550,000
Income Sources: Southeastern Theatre Conference; American Association of Theatre Educators, State of Florida, City of Tallahassee
Performs At: Young Actors Theatre
Affiliations: American Association of Theatre Educators, Southeastern Theatre Conference
Annual Attendance: 10,000
Facility Category: Theatre, Classrooms
Type of Stage: Proscenium
Seating Capacity: 215
Year Built: 1986
Year Remodeled: 1995
Cost: $150,000
Organization Type: Performing; Touring; Educational

2486
BITS 'N PIECES GIANT PUPPET THEATRE
12904 Tom Gallagher Road
Tampa, FL 33527
Phone: 813-659-0659
e-mail: info@PuppetWorld.com
Web Site: www.puppetworld.com
Management:
   President: Jerry Bickel
   Artistic Director: Holli Rubin
   Business Director: Jackie Hiendlmayr
Mission: To offer original, educational musicals featuring unique nine-foot puppets.
Utilizes: Singers
Founded: 1976
Specialized Field: Children's Theater
Status: Non-Profit, Professional
Paid Staff: 4
Paid Artists: 4
Organization Type: Performing; Touring; Resident; Educational

2487
CARROLLWOOD PLAYERS COMMUNITY THEATER
4333 Gunn Highway
Tampa, FL 33618-8729
Phone: 813-265-4000
e-mail: cwptampabay.rr.com
Web Site: carrollwoodplayers.com
Officers:

President: James Cass
Utilizes: Actors; Choreographers; Community Members; Community Talent; Dancers; Local Artists & Directors; Performance Artists; Sign Language Translators; Student Interns
Founded: 1981
Specialized Field: Community Theater; Classic; Contemporary
Status: Not-for-profit
Volunteer Staff: 30
Non-paid Artists: 100
Facility Category: Theater
Seating Capacity: 96

2488
FLORIDA SUNCOAST PUPPET GUILD
7107 N Howard Avenue
Tampa, FL 33604
Phone: 813-932-9252
Fax: 813-932-9252
e-mail: jodymcat@aol.com
Web Site: www.puppeteers.org/guilds/fla-sunc.htm
Officers:
   Guild President: Jody Wren
   Vice President: Katie Adams
   Secretary/Treasurer: Priscilla Lakus
   Historian: Frank Lakus
Mission: To promote the appreciation of the art of puppetry and all common interests of the membership. This is accomplished through a program of lectures, demonstrations, workshops, TV programs, exhibitions, newsletters, sponsored performances, conferences, etc.
Utilizes: Singers
Founded: 1973
Specialized Field: Puppet
Status: Non-Profit, Professional
Income Sources: Puppeteers of America
Organization Type: Educational; Sponsoring

2489
SPANISH LYRIC THEATRE
2819 Safe Harbor Drive
Tampa, FL 33618
Phone: 813-936-0217
Fax: 813-936-0217
Web Site: www.spanishlyrictheatre.com
Management:
   President: Dennis Diera
   Executive Director: Rene J Gonzalez
   Assistant Production Director: Marlyn Wadley
Mission: To promote Spanish musicals, or Zarzuelas; to offer lyric theatre in Spanish and English.
Utilizes: Singers
Founded: 1959
Specialized Field: Musical; Spanish Language Company
Status: Non-Profit, Professional
Paid Staff: 20
Paid Artists: 200
Performs At: Tampa Bay Performing Arts Center
Organization Type: Performing

2490
UNIVERSITY OF SOUTH FLORIDA: SCHOOL OF THEATRE
4202 E Fowler Avenue
TAR 230
Tampa, FL 33620-7450
Phone: 813-974-2701
Fax: 813-974-4122
e-mail: mpowers@arts.usf.edu
Web Site: www.arts.usf.edu/theatre
Officers:

Director Theatre/Dance: Marc Powers
Management:
President: Judy Genshaft
Dean Visual/Performing Arts: Ron Jones
Founded: 1956
Specialized Field: Educational; Theater Workshops
Status: Non-Profit, Non-Professional
Performs At: Proscenium Theatre, Black Box Theatre, Studio Theatres
Affiliations: NAST; ATHE
Seating Capacity: 552, 100-200, 80-125
Year Built: 1986
Year Remodeled: 95

2491
VENICE THEATRE
140 W Tampa Avenue
Venice, FL 34285
Phone: 941-488-1115
Fax: 941-484-9437
e-mail: info@venicestage.com
Web Site: www.venicestage.com
Management:
Executive/Artistic Director: Murray Chase
Mission: To present intellectual and instructive entertainment in the performing arts.
Founded: 1950
Specialized Field: Musical; Comedy; Youth Theater; Ethnic Theater; Community Theater; Classic; Contemporary
Status: Non-Profit, Non-Professional
Paid Staff: 12
Organization Type: Performing

2492
ACTING COMPANY OF RIVERSIDE THEATRE
3250 Riverside Park Drive
Vero Beach, FL 32963
Phone: 561-231-5860
Fax: 561-234-5298
Officers:
President: Marilyn Chenault
VP: Pat Trimble
Treasurer: Rebecca Allen
Board Secretary: Judy Balph
Management:
Artistic Director: Allen D Cornell
Production Manager: John Moses
Business Manager: Ida Spada
Development Director: Lynn Potter
Director Education: Linda Downey
Mission: To provide audiences of this region with productions that are relevant either by nature of their importance within a particular genre or as socially vital within the changing environment of our culture.
Utilizes: Guest Companies
Founded: 1995
Specialized Field: Theater Workshops; Drama; Contemporary; Classic
Status: Professional; Nonprofit
Paid Staff: 10
Income Sources: Actors' Equity Association; Theatre Communications Group; Florida Performing Theatre Association
Performs At: Riverside Theatre
Organization Type: Performing

2493
VERO BEACH THEATRE GUILD
2020 San Juan Avenue
Vero Beach, FL 32960

Phone: 772-562-8300
Fax: 772-562-8304
e-mail: verobeachtheatre@gmail.com
Web Site: www.verobeachtheatreguild.com
Officers:
President: Sara Dessureau
First VP: Larry Thompson
Secretary: Pat Kroger
Mission: To enhance appreciation of dramatic and musical pieces through community theater; to offer residents of Florida's Treasure Coast theatrical arts.
Utilizes: Singers
Founded: 1958
Specialized Field: Community Theater
Status: Non-Professional; Nonprofit
Paid Staff: 200
Performs At: Riverside Theatre
Facility Category: Production House
Organization Type: Performing; Educational

2494
PALM BEACH ATLANTIC COLLEGE: DEPARTMENT OF THEATRE
West Palm Beach, FL
Mailing Address: PO Box 24708, West Palm Beach, FL 33416
Phone: 561-803-2417
Fax: 561-803-2424
Officers:
Chair: Dr. Deborah McEniry
Specialized Field: Educational; Theater Workshops
Budget: $8,000-10,500
Affiliations: Florida Stage
Facility Category: Historical building
Seating Capacity: 220; 80

2495
THEATRE WINTER HAVEN
210 Cypress Gardens Boulevard
PO Drawer 1230
Winter Haven, FL 33882
Phone: 863-299-2672
Fax: 863-291-3299
e-mail: twh1970@aol.com
Web Site: www.theatrewinterhaven.com
Management:
Producing Director: Norman Small
Production Manager: Thom Altman
Mission: Fostering the community's cultural growth by offering quality live theatre.
Utilizes: Actors; AEA Actors; Choreographers; Grant Writers; Guest Artists; Guest Companies; Guest Conductors; Guest Designers; Guest Lecturers; Guest Musical Directors; Instructors; Music; Resident Professionals; Sign Language Translators; Singers
Founded: 1970
Specialized Field: Drama; Musical; Classic
Status: Non-Profit, Non-Professional
Paid Staff: 5
Volunteer Staff: 90
Paid Artists: 6
Non-paid Artists: 140
Budget: $618,000
Income Sources: Various
Affiliations: AACT, FTC
Type of Stage: Proscenium
Stage Dimensions: 30wx16hx28d
Seating Capacity: 332
Year Built: 1977
Rental Contact: Jane Waters
Organization Type: Performing; Educational

2496
ANNIE RUSSELL THEATRE
Rollins College
1000 Holt Avenue-2735
Winter Park, FL 32789
Phone: 407-646-2145
Fax: 407-646-2600
Web Site: www.rollins.edu/theatre
Officers:
VP/Treasurer: George Herbst
Management:
President: Thomas Ouellette
Managing Director: Scotty Campbell
Mission: Providing educational theatre; booking touring events for dance and theatre.
Utilizes: Guest Companies
Founded: 1931
Specialized Field: Musical; Educational; Theater Workshops
Status: Non-Profit, Non-Professional
Paid Staff: 9
Volunteer Staff: 12
Paid Artists: 3
Income Sources: Association of Performing Arts Presenters; Southeastern Theatre Conference; Florida Theatre Conference
Performs At: Annie Russell Theatre
Organization Type: Performing; Resident; Educational; Sponsoring

2497
ROLLINS COLLEGE: DEPARTMENT OF THEATRE AND DANCE
1000 Holt Avenue 2735
Winter Park, FL 32789
Phone: 407-646-2501
Fax: 407-646-2257
e-mail: bjohnson@rollins.edu
Web Site: www.rollins.edu/theater
Management:
Marketing Director: Olivia Horn, ohorn@rollins.edu
Department Chair: Dr. Jennifer Cavenaugh, jcavenaugh@rollins.edu
Founded: 1885
Specialized Field: Educational; Performance; Tech; Design; Dramaturgy
Status: Non-Profit, Non-Professional
Paid Staff: 4
Paid Artists: 7
Budget: $110,000
Performs At: Historic 377 Seat Broadway-Style Theatre
Annual Attendance: 300
Type of Stage: Proscenium
Seating Capacity: 400; 100
Year Built: 1931
Year Remodeled: 1978
Rental Contact: Kevin Griffin

Georgia

2498
THEATRE ALBANY
514 Pine Avenue
Albany, GA 31701
Mailing Address: PO Box 552 Albany GA 31702
Phone: 229-439-7193
Web Site: www.theatrealbany.com
Management:
Artistic Director: Mark Costello
Technical Director: Steve Felmet

Mission: To expose young people to the art of live performance.
Utilizes: Guest Companies
Founded: 1932
Specialized Field: Musical; Comedy; Youth Theater; Dinner Theater; Ethnic Theater; Community Theater; Puppet; Classic; Contemporary
Status: Non-Profit, Non-Professional
Paid Staff: 2
Income Sources: American Association of Community Theatres; Southeastern Theatre Conference; Georgia Theatre Conference
Performs At: Theatre Albany
Organization Type: Performing; Educational

2499
GABBIES PUPPETS

367 Lexington Heights
Athens, GA 30605
Phone: 706-353-2785
Management:
   Director: Carolyn S Gabb
Mission: Presenting and teaching language communication skills using puppets; storytelling; creative dramatics.
Utilizes: Singers
Founded: 1975
Specialized Field: Puppet
Status: Professional
Organization Type: Performing; Educational

2500
GEORGIA REPERTORY THEATRE

Dept Of Drama, Fine Arts Building
University Of Georgia
Athens, GA 30602-3154
Phone: 706-542-2836
Fax: 706-542-2080
Management:
   Producer: Stanley V Longman
   Dramaturg: Allen Partridge
Mission: The production of previously unproduced plays.
Founded: 1990
Specialized Field: Educational; Theater Workshops
Paid Staff: 6
Paid Artists: 5
Performs At: Fine Arts Theatre, Cellar Theatre, Seneyu Stovall Theatre
Type of Stage: Arena
Seating Capacity: 250
Year Built: 1941

2501
7 STAGES

1105 Euclid Avenue NE
Atlanta, GA 30307
Phone: 404-522-0911
Fax: 404-522-0913
Web Site: www.7stages.org
Officers:
   President: Del Hamilton
Management:
   Finance/Technical Director: Mack Headrick
   Producing Director: Faye Allen
Mission: A professional, non-profit theatre company devoted to engaging artists and audiences by focusing on the social, political, and spiritual values of contemporary culture. Give primary emphasis to international work and the support and development of new plays, new playrights and new methods of collaboration.
Founded: 1979

Specialized Field: Comedy; Youth Theater; Ethnic Theater; Contemporary
Status: Non-Profit, Professional
Paid Staff: 6
Volunteer Staff: 12
Paid Artists: 40
Non-paid Artists: 20
Budget: $650,000
Performs At: Renovated Cinema
Type of Stage: Flexible
Stage Dimensions: 45' x 30'
Seating Capacity: 200
Year Built: 1942
Rental Contact: Mark Headrick

2502
ACADEMY THEATRE

501 Means Street NW
Atlanta, GA 30318
Phone: 404-525-4111
Fax: 404-525-5659
Officers:
   Chairman: Jerry Dibble
   President: Frank Wittow
Management:
   Founder/Producing Artistic Director: Frank Wittow
   Managing Director: Lorenne Fey
   Development Director: Nick Rhoton
Mission: Creating and performing orginal plays about critical issues for children and young adults, training teachers in the use of innovative techniques to accelerate learning and retention of knowledge, introducing children to theatre as a measn of self-discovery and self-expression.
Utilizes: Guest Artists; Guest Companies; Singers
Founded: 1956
Specialized Field: Theater Workshops; Children's Theater
Status: Professional; Nonprofit
Paid Staff: 2
Volunteer Staff: 19
Paid Artists: 10
Budget: $370,000
Income Sources: NEA; Georgia Council for the Arts; Fulton County Arts Council; City of Atlanta and Foundations; Individuals
Affiliations: Theatre Communications Group; Atlanta Coalition of Performing Arts; Georgia Shares
Annual Attendance: 70,000
Organization Type: Performing; Touring; Resident; Educational; Sponsoring

2503
ACTOR'S EXPRESS THEATRE

887 W Marietta Street
Suite J-107
Atlanta, GA 30318
Phone: 404-875-1606
Fax: 404-875-2791
Web Site: www.actors-express.com
Officers:
   Board Chair: Donna Darroch
   Board Vice-Chair: David Robinson
   Board Secretary: Bruce Griffeth
Management:
   Producing Artistic Director: Bill Fennelly
   Marketing/New Media Director: Daniel Summers, Jr
   Development Director: Alexis Weiss
Mission: We produce a wildly eclectic mix of classic, contemporary, and cutting edge plays.

Utilizes: Actors; AEA Actors; Artists-in-Residence; Choreographers; Collaborations; Commissioned Composers; Commissioned Music; Five Seasonal Concerts; Guest Artists; Guest Companies; Guest Conductors; Guest Designers; Guest Lecturers; Guest Teachers; High School Drama; Instructors; Local Artists; Music; Original Music Scores; Performance Artists; Resident Professionals; Sign Language Translators; Student Interns
Founded: 1988
Specialized Field: Drama; Contemporary; Classic
Status: Non-Profit, Professional
Paid Staff: 714
Affiliations: AEA-GA
Facility Category: Flexible Black Box
Seating Capacity: 120-160
Year Built: 1994

2504
ALLIANCE THEATRE COMPANY

1280 Peachtree Street NE
Atlanta, GA 30309
Phone: 404-733-4650
Fax: 404-733-4625
e-mail: info@alliancetheatre.org
Web Site: www.alliancetheatre.org
Officers:
   Board Chair: Dan Reardon
   First Vice Chair: Vicki Palefsky
Management:
   Artistic Director: Susan V Booth
   Director of Finance/Administration: Brian Shively
   General Manager: Max Leventhal
Mission: Dedicated to celebrating diversity by building bridges that can connect us as human beings through the development and production of exciting, entertaining, and stimulating plays to nurture and enrich the art, the artists, and the audience.
Utilizes: Actors; AEA Actors; Artists-in-Residence; Choreographers; Commissioned Composers; Dancers; Designers; Educators; Guest Companies; High School Drama; Instructors; Local Artists; Multimedia; Music; Original Music Scores; Performance Artists; Resident Professionals; Selected Students; Sign Language Translators; Singers; Soloists
Founded: 1969
Specialized Field: Musical; Comedy; Youth Theater; Ethnic Theater; Classic; Contemporary
Status: Non-Profit, Professional
Paid Staff: 225
Paid Artists: 245
Budget: $10 Million
Performs At: Lort Regional Theater
Affiliations: Actors' Equity Association; Society for Stage Directors and Choreographers; League of Resident Theatres; USA
Annual Attendance: 225,000
Type of Stage: Proscenium; Flexible
Stage Dimensions: 40x96; 44x75
Seating Capacity: 800; 200
Year Built: 1968
Year Remodeled: 1996
Organization Type: Performing; Touring; Resident; Educational

2505
CENTER FOR PUPPETRY ARTS

1404 Spring Street
Atlanta, GA 30309
Phone: 404-873-3089
Fax: 404-873-9907
Web Site: www.puppet.org
Management:
   Executive Director: Vincent Anthony

Mission: To expand public awareness of puppetry.
Utilizes: Actors; Collaborating Artists; Commissioned Composers; Commissioned Music; Designers; Five Seasonal Concerts; Grant Writers; Guest Accompanists; Guest Choreographers; Guest Companies; Guest Conductors; Guest Designers; Guest Ensembles; Guest Instructors; Guest Soloists; High School Drama; Instructors; Local Artists; Multimedia; Original Music Scores; Performance Artists; Poets; Resident Professionals; Singers; Student Interns; Special Technical Talent; Theatre Companies; Visual Arts
Founded: 1978
Specialized Field: Puppet
Status: Non-Profit, Professional
Paid Staff: 59
Volunteer Staff: 30
Performs At: Mainstage Theater; Downstairs Theater
Annual Attendance: 900,000
Type of Stage: Mainstage
Seating Capacity: 345/Downstairs 170
Year Built: 1918
Year Remodeled: 96
Organization Type: Performing; Touring; Resident; Educational; Sponsoring

2506
DAD'S GARAGE THEATRE COMPANY
280 Elizabeth Street Suite C 101
Suite C-101
Atlanta, GA 30307
Phone: 404-523-3141
Fax: 404-688-6644
Web Site: http://www.dadsgarage.com/
Officers:
President: Andrew Chang
Vice President: Larry Wexler
Secretary: Melissa Honbach
Treasurer: Scott Bryan
Management:
Artistic Director: Kevin Gillese
Managing Director: Lena Carstens
Marketing Director: Linnea Frye
Founded: 1995
Specialized Field: Ensembles; Comedy; Improvisation

2507
ESSENTIAL THEATRE
887 W Marietta St. Suite J-107
#6
Atlanta, GA 30318
Phone: 404-212-0815
e-mail: pmhardy@aol.com
Web Site: http://www.essentialtheatre.com/
Management:
Producing Artistic Director: Peter Hardy
Founded: 1987
Specialized Field: Drama; Contemporary; Improvisation

2508
GATEWAY PERFORMANCE PRODUCTIONS
PO Box 8062
Atlanta, GA 31106
Phone: 404-982-9922
Fax: 404-982-9922
e-mail: info@masktheatre.org
Web Site: www.masktheatre.org
Officers:
President: Sandra Hughes
Chairperson: Chris Moser
Treasurer: Michael Hickey
Management:

Artistic Director: Sandra Hughes
Company Coordinator: Michael E Hickey
Mission: To create and produce high-quality outreach arts programming for touring theatres, festivals, museums, libraries, colleges, universities, schools, and other community sites. Gateway carries out this mission through touring the following programs and productions- Mask Theatre, Mime, Cultural Arts Programs, Workshops, Classes, Residencies, Demonstrations, and Exhibits.
Utilizes: Singers
Founded: 1974
Specialized Field: Mask Theater
Status: Non-Profit, Professional
Paid Staff: 2
Paid Artists: 2
Organization Type: Performing; Touring; Resident; Educational

2509
GEORGIA SHAKESPEARE
Conant Performing Arts Center
4484 Peachtree Road NE
Atlanta, GA 30319
Phone: 404-264-0020
Fax: 404-504-3414
e-mail: boxoffice@gashakespeare.org
Web Site: www.gashakespeare.org
Management:
Producing Artistic Director: Richard Garner
Marketing Director: Stacey Colosa Lucas
Mission: To produce professional plays written by Shakespeare and other enduring authors.
Founded: 1985
Specialized Field: Shakespeare; Classic
Status: Professional; Nonprofit
Paid Staff: 7
Income Sources: Southeastern Theatre Conference; Atlanta Theatre Coalition
Organization Type: Performing; Resident

2510
HORIZON THEATRE COMPANY
1083 Austin Avenue
Corner of Euclid & Austin Avenues
Atlanta, GA 30307
Mailing Address: PO Box 5376 Atlanta, GA 31107
Phone: 404-523-1477
Fax: 404-584-8815
Web Site: www.horizontheatre.com
Management:
President: Lisa Adler
Public Relationsmarketing Director: Andrea Minadakis
Coartistic Technical Director: Jeff Adler
Box Office Manager: Suehyla El-Attar
Managing Director: Alison Hayes
House Manager: Denny Zartman
Mission: To be a leader in the production and development of contemporary theatre in the Southeast. We present professional area premieres of new and recent plays and develop new artists and audiences for contemporary theatre through education and outreach programs.
Founded: 1983
Specialized Field: Musical; Comedy; Ethnic Theater; Contemporary
Status: Non-Profit, Professional
Paid Staff: 15
Paid Artists: 60
Income Sources: Grants
Performs At: Horizon Theatre
Type of Stage: Flexible
Seating Capacity: 170

2511
JUST US THEATER COMPANY
PO Box 42271
Atlanta, GA 30311
Phone: 404-753-2399
Fax: 404-758-9200
Officers:
President: Walter R Huntley
Treasurer: Pearle Cleage
Secretary: Zaron W Burnett, Jr
Management:
Artistic Director: Pearl Cleage
Producing Director: Zaron Burnett, Jr.
Mission: Just Us Theater Company is a Black professional company dedicated to the development of minority artists and the presentation of quality arts programs that reflect the diversity of our community; focus on sexism and racism.
Utilizes: Guest Companies; Singers
Founded: 1976
Specialized Field: Ensembles; Drama; Contemporary
Status: For-Profit,Non-Professional
Organization Type: Performing; Touring; Resident; Educational

2512
NEW AMERICAN SHAKESPEARE TAVERN
499 Peachtree Street NE
Atlanta, GA 30308
Phone: 404-874-5299
Fax: 404-874-9219
e-mail: becky@shakespearetavern.com
Web Site: www.shakespearetavern.com
Management:
Artistic Director: Jeffery Watkins
Managing Director: Kirstein Dunstan
Mission: The New American Shakespeare Tavern is unlike other theaters. It is a place out of time; a place of live music, hand-crafted period costumes, outrageous sword fights with the entire experience centered on the passion and poetry ofthe spoken word.
Founded: 1984
Specialized Field: Shakespeare
Status: Non-Profit, Professional
Paid Staff: 15
Paid Artists: 20

2513
NEW JOMANDI PRODUCTIONS
675 Ponce De Leon Avenue
City Hall East, 8th Floor
Atlanta, GA 30308
Phone: 404-876-6346
Fax: 404-872-5764
Toll-free: 877-217-4302
Web Site: www.jomandi.com
Officers:
Chairman/State Representative: Bob Holmes
Management:
General Manager: Jomal Vailes
Artistic Director: Carol Michell-Leon
Communicatons Director: Inda Royall
Production Manager: Lisa L Watson
Mission: Nurturing new works that reflect the African-American experience; providing theatre artists an opportunity for training and performance.
Utilizes: Guest Companies; Singers
Founded: 1978
Specialized Field: Musical; Comedy; Drama
Status: Non-Profit, Professional
Paid Staff: 10
Paid Artists: 3

Performs At: 14th Street Playhouse
Type of Stage: Proscenium/Thrust
Seating Capacity: 370
Organization Type: Performing; Touring; Resident

2514
OMILAMI PRODUCTIONS/PEOPLE'S SURVIVAL THEATRE
8 E Lake Drive NE
Atlanta, GA 30317
Phone: 404-377-6434
Fax: 404-584-9166
Management:
    Co-Artistic Director: Elizabeth Omilami
    Co-Artistic Director: Afemo Omilami
Mission: To produce, provide and encourage arts programming for impoverished areas that are not serviced by traditional groups; to stimulate and encourage new playwrights and directors to write and direct for the inner city and rural areas.
Utilizes: Guest Companies; Singers
Founded: 1977
Specialized Field: Community Theater
Status: Semi-Professional; Nonprofit
Paid Staff: 8
Organization Type: Performing; Touring; Educational

2515
SEVEN STAGES THEATRE
1105 Euclid Avenue
Atlanta, GA 30307
Phone: 404-523-7647
Web Site: www.7stages.org
Officers:
    Board Chair: Anne Yates
    Vice Chair: D'Asia Haley
    Secretary: Allison Walker
    Secretary: Gregory Pierce
Management:
    Artistic Director: Del Hamilton
    Producing Director: Faye Allen
    Director of Development: Catherine Pfitzer
Utilizes: Actors; Artists-in-Residence; Collaborating Artists; Dance Companies; Guest Companies; Local Artists; Multimedia; Original Music Scores; Playwrights
Paid Staff: 7
Volunteer Staff: 2
Paid Artists: 65
Budget: $850,000
Income Sources: Theatre Communications Group; National Endowment for the Arts; Georgia Council of the Arts; City of Atlanta Bureau of Cultural Affairs; Trust for Mutual Understanding; AT&T
Affiliations: Theatre Communications Group; Atlanta Coalition for the Performing Arts
Annual Attendance: 15,000
Facility Category: 2 Performing Arts Theatres
Type of Stage: Black Boxes
Seating Capacity: 90; 200
Year Built: 1928
Year Remodeled: 1994
Cost: $1.6 million
Organization Type: Performing; Resident
Resident Groups: Seven Stages

2516
SOUTHEASTERN SAVOYARDS
3270 Ivanhoe Drive
Atlanta, GA 30327
Phone: 404-233-7002
Officers:
    President: Jonn H Stevens
    VP: Robert B Langdon
    Treasurer: Fern M Stevens

    Secretary: Marcia Lane
Management:
    Executive Producer: John H Stevens
    Music Director/Artistic: J Lynn Thompson
Mission: Gilbert & Sullivan repertory company.
Utilizes: Guest Companies; Singers
Founded: 1980
Specialized Field: Musical
Status: Professional; Nonprofit
Performs At: Center Stage Theater Atlanta
Organization Type: Theatrical Group

2517
THEATER EMORY
Rich Building, Emory University
Room 230
Atlanta, GA 30322
Phone: 404-727-0524
Fax: 404-727-6253
e-mail: vmurphy@emory.edu
Web Site: www.emory.edu
Management:
    President: Vincent Murphy
    Managing Director: Rosalind Staiv
Founded: 1985
Specialized Field: Comedy; Ethnic Theater; Community Theater; Classic; Contemporary
Status: Non-Profit, Professional
Paid Artists: 50
Performs At: Mary Gray Munroe Theater at Emory University

2518
THEATER OF THE STARS
PO Box 11748
Atlanta, GA 30355
Phone: 404-252-8960
Fax: 404-252-1460
e-mail: theaterofstars@mindspring.com
Web Site: www.theaterofthestars.com
Management:
    President: Christopher B Manos
    Managing Director: Nicholas F Manos
    Artistic Director: Scott Bowker
Utilizes: Singers
Founded: 1953
Specialized Field: Musical
Status: Non-Profit, Professional
Paid Staff: 7
Organization Type: Performing; Touring; Sponsoring

2519
THEATRE GAEL
PO Box 77156
Atlanta, GA 30357
Phone: 404-876-1138
Fax: 404-876-1141
e-mail: theatregael@mindspring.com
Web Site: www.theatregael.com
Management:
    President: Thomas Brennan
    VP: Constance Callahan
    Artistic Director: John Stephens
    Managing Director: Sarah Dasher
Mission: The performance of plays from Scotland, Ireland and Wales.
Utilizes: Guest Companies; Singers
Founded: 1984
Specialized Field: Children's Theater
Status: Professional; Nonprofit
Paid Staff: 3
Volunteer Staff: 10
Paid Artists: 25

Income Sources: American Alliance for Theatre Arts; Alternate Rural Organization of Theaters South
Seating Capacity: 90
Organization Type: Performing

2520
THEATRICAL OUTFIT
Suite 36098
PO Box 1555
Atlanta, GA 30301
Phone: 404-577-5257
Fax: 404-577-5259
Web Site: www.theatricaloutfit.org
Officers:
    President: Bill Bolzer
Management:
    President: Bill Ballver
    Artistic Director: Tom Key
    Marketing/Development Director: Beth Haynes
Mission: Produces contemporary and classical scripts with an emphasis on Southern themes.
Utilizes: Guest Companies; Singers
Founded: 1976
Specialized Field: Drama; Musical; Contemporary
Status: Non-Profit, Professional
Paid Staff: 5
Paid Artists: 50
Budget: $700,000
Income Sources: Ticket Revenue; Private; Corporate; Foundations; Public
Performs At: Rialto Center for the Performing Arts
Organization Type: Performing; Educational

2521
AUGUSTA PLAYERS
PO Box 2352
Augusta, GA 30903-2352
Phone: 706-826-4707
Fax: 706-826-4709
e-mail: info@augustaplayers.org
Web Site: www.augustaplayers.org
Officers:
    President: Jenifer G. Hollett
Management:
    Executive Director: Debi Ballas
Utilizes: Actors; Community Members; Community Talent; Contract Orchestras; Five Seasonal Concerts; Guild Activities; Local Artists; Local Artists & Directors; Local Talent; Music; Paid Performers; Sign Language Translators; Visual Designers
Founded: 1945
Specialized Field: Musical Theatre
Status: Non-Professional; Nonprofit
Paid Staff: 2
Non-paid Artists: 150
Budget: $300,000
Income Sources: Donations; Grants; Ticket Sales
Affiliations: American Association Of Community Theatres
Organization Type: Performing; Educational

2522
WEST GEORGIA THEATRE COMPANY SUMMER CLASSIC
University Of West Georgia
Theatre Program
1601 Maple Street
Carrollton, GA 30117
Phone: 678-839-4708
Fax: 678-839-4708
e-mail: theatre@westgeorgia.edu
Management:
    Theatre Director: Shelly Elman
    Design Faculty/ Technical Director: Tommy Cox

Design Faculty/ Costumes: Alan Yoeng
Utilizes: Actors; Collaborating Artists; Collaborations; Designers; Educators; Grant Writers; Guest Accompanists; Guest Artists; Guest Designers; Guest Ensembles; Guest Lecturers; Guest Soloists; High School Drama; Resident Professionals; Sign Language Translators; Soloists; Student Interns; Special Technical Talent; Touring Companies; Volunteer Directors & Actors; Writers
Founded: 1991
Specialized Field: Educational; Theater Workshops
Status: Non-Equity; Nonprofit
Budget: $90,000
Season: June - August
Performs At: Multi-Stage
Affiliations: Georgia Theatre Conference; Southeastern Theatre Conference; Association for the Theatre in Higher Education; USITT
Facility Category: Performing Arts Center
Type of Stage: Proscenium; Balck Box
Seating Capacity: 450; 120

2523
SPRINGER OPERA HOUSE
THE STATE THEATER OF GEORGIA
103 Tenth Street
Columbus, GA 31901
Phone: 706-324-5714
Fax: 706-324-4681
Web Site: www.springeroperahouse.org
Management:
Executive Director: Porrin Trotter
Artistic Director: Paul R Pierce
Associate Artistic Director: Ron Anderson
Mission: Offering the Southeastern United States high quality productions; representing Georgia as its official State Theatre.
Utilizes: Actors; AEA Actors; Choreographers; Designers; Guest Accompanists; Guest Artists; Guest Companies; Guest Conductors; Guest Designers; Guest Instructors; Guest Soloists; High School Drama; Local Artists; Performance Artists; Resident Professionals; Sign Language Translators; Singers
Founded: 1871
Specialized Field: Musical; Light Theater; Classic
Status: Non-Profit, Professional
Paid Staff: 19
Volunteer Staff: 240
Paid Artists: 145
Non-paid Artists: 40
Budget: 1.6 Million
Income Sources: Private, Foundation, State, Municipal, Ticket Sales
Performs At: 130 year old National Historic Landmark Theatre
Annual Attendance: 125,000
Facility Category: Theatre
Type of Stage: Proscenium & Studio Theatre
Stage Dimensions: 32 W x 42 Deep
Year Built: 1871
Year Remodeled: 1998
Cost: 12 Million
Rental Contact: Allison Kent
Organization Type: Performing; Touring; Producing

2524
AGNES SCOTT COLLEGE: DEPARTMENT OF THEATRE AND DANCE
141 East College Ave
Decatur, GA 30030
Phone: 404-471-6251
Fax: 404-638-5369
e-mail: admission@agnesscott.edu

Web Site:
http://www.agnesscott.edu/academics/undergraduate/theatre
Officers:
Chair: Dudley Sanders
Management:
Associate Professor: Dudley W Sanders
Specialized Field: Educational; Theater Workshops
Budget: $2,800-4,000
Performs At: Winter Theatre
Affiliations: ATHE
Type of Stage: Semi-Thrust
Seating Capacity: 310
Year Built: 1965

2525
NEIGHBORHOOD PLAYHOUSE
430 W Trinity Place
Decatur, GA 30030
Phone: 404-373-3904
Fax: 404-373-4130
Web Site: www.nplayhouse.org
Management:
President: Gary Himes
Executive Director: Sonny Goff
Operations Manager: Micki Hibbs
Mission: Providing professional quality theatre that entertains, educates and challenges our community.
Utilizes: Actors; Choreographers; Collaborations; Dancers; Designers; Five Seasonal Concerts; Guest Companies; Guest Conductors; Guest Designers; Guest Lecturers; Guest Teachers; Instructors; Local Artists; Multimedia; Music; Organization Contracts; Original Music Scores; Performance Artists; Selected Students; Sign Language Translators; Singers
Founded: 1980
Specialized Field: Musical; Comedy; Youth Theater; Ethnic Theater; Community Theater; Classic; Contemporary
Status: Non-Profit, Professional
Paid Staff: 2
Paid Artists: 30
Income Sources: Box Office, Grants, Donations
Annual Attendance: 15,000
Stage Dimensions: 50x25 and 23x20
Seating Capacity: 170 and 70
Year Built: 1980
Year Remodeled: 1999
Rental Contact: Micki Hibbs
Organization Type: Performing

2526
PICCADILLY PUPPETS COMPANY
621 Densley Drive
Decatur, GA 30033
Phone: 404-636-0022
Fax: 404-636-0616
Web Site: www.piccadillypuppets.org
Officers:
President: Dr. Pat Penn
Secretary/Treasurer: Carol Daniel
Management:
President: Pat Temm
Executive Director: Carol Daniel
Mission: Perform puppet shows for children and families.
Founded: 1969
Specialized Field: Musical; Youth Theater; Community Theater; Puppet; Contemporary; Puppet; Touring Company
Status: Non-Profit, Professional
Paid Staff: 1
Paid Artists: 4
Budget: $75,000

Income Sources: Arts councils; Presenters; Foundation Support
Organization Type: Performing; Touring; Educational

2527
PARENTHESIS THEATRE CLUB
4336 Highborne Drive
Marietta, GA 30066
Phone: 404-977-8340
Management:
Artistic Director: Gregory Blum
Producing Director: Darrell Wofford
Mission: Producing ten minute plays that are socially relevant and original one acts.
Founded: 1991
Specialized Field: Dinner Theater
Status: Semi-Professional
Performs At: Cabaret Space
Organization Type: Performing; Resident

2528
THEATRE IN THE SQUARE
11 Whitlock Avenue
Marietta, GA 30064
Phone: 770-422-8369
Fax: 770-424-2637
Web Site: www.theatreinthesquare.com
Management:
Producing Director/CoFounder: Palmer Wells
Managing Director: Raye Varney
Assistant Artistic Director: Jessica Phelps West
Utilizes: Guest Companies; Singers
Paid Staff: 17
Performs At: Theatre in the Square
Organization Type: Performing; Touring

2529
PERRY PLAYERS
909 Main Street
Perry, GA 31069
Phone: 478-987-5354
e-mail: perryplayers@hotmail.com
Web Site: www.perryplayers.com
Officers:
President: Tom Saul
Treasurer: Marshall Hutten
Secretary: Bill Andrews
Management:
VP Of Production: Anita Williams
Mission: We offer high-quality entertainment and cultural activities to the citizens of middle Georgia. Individuals who enjoy acting, singing, dancing and producing cultural entertainment share and improve these skills in a welcoming environment of cooperation and enthusiasm.
Utilizes: Singers
Founded: 1982
Specialized Field: Musical; Community Theater
Status: Non-Profit
Paid Staff: 30
Income Sources: Houston County Arts Alliance; Macon Arts Alliance; Perry Chamber of Commerce

2530
GEORGIA ENSEMBLE THEATRE
950 Forrest Street
PO Box 607
Roswell, GA 30077-0607
Phone: 770-641-1260
Fax: 770-641-1360
e-mail: info@get.org
Web Site: www.get.org
Officers:
President: Andy Ross

Director Marketing: Tess Kincaias
Management:
Artistic Director: Robert J. Farley
Managing Director: Anita Allen-Farley
Founded: 1992
Specialized Field: Ensembles; Drama; Musical
Status: Non-Profit, Professional
Paid Staff: 8
Volunteer Staff: 200
Paid Artists: 25

2531
ART STATION THEATRE
ART Station Contemporary Art Center
5384 Manor Drive
Stone Mountain, GA 30083
Mailing Address: PO Box 1988 Stone Mountain GA
30086
Phone: 770-469-1105
Fax: 770-469-0355
e-mail: info@artstation.org
Web Site: www.artstation.org
Officers:
President: David Thomas
Chairman: Rusty McKeller
Vice Chairperson: Michele Henson
Secretary: Michael Hidalgo
Treasurer: Pam Culbersom
Management:
President and Artistic Director: David Thomas
Administrative Manager: Michael Hidalgo
Program Manager: Jon Goldstein
Mission: Celebration and presentation of southern arts
Founded: 1986
Opened: 1986
Specialized Field: Musical; Comedy; Classic;
Contemporary
Status: Non-Profit, Professional
Paid Staff: 5
Volunteer Staff: 2
Budget: $750,000
Income Sources: Government; Corporate;
Foundations; Private
Season: September - June
Affiliations: AEA
Annual Attendance: 10,000+
Facility Category: Small Theatre
Type of Stage: Proscenium
Stage Dimensions: 28' x 30'
Seating Capacity: 108
Year Built: 1900
Year Remodeled: 1990
Cost: $1.2 Million
Rental Contact: Jon Goldstein

2532
PEACH STATE SUMMER THEATRE
Department of Communication Arts
Valdosta, GA 31698
Phone: 229-333-5820
Fax: 229-249-2602
e-mail: dguthrie@valdosta.edu
Management:
Artistic Director: Jacque Wheeler
Managing Director: Duke Guthrie
Mission: Providing Georgia's Golden Isles residents
and visitors with quality musical theatre; offering college
interns professional training.
Utilizes: Guest Choreographers; Guest Companies;
Singers
Founded: 1990
Specialized Field: Summer Stock; Musical
Status: Professional; Nonprofit
Paid Artists: 65

Income Sources: Valdosta State University
Season: June - August
Performs At: Jekyll Island Amphitheater
Annual Attendance: 10,000
Facility Category: Professional Summer Stock Theatre
Type of Stage: Wooden, uncovered amphitheatre
Seating Capacity: 500
Year Built: 1970
Organization Type: Performing; Touring

2533
SOUTHERN APPALACHIAN STAGES
PO Box 499
Young Harris, GA 30582
Phone: 706-379-1711
Fax: 706-379-1542
Toll-free: 800-262-7664
Web Site: www.reachofsong.org
Management:
Executive Director: Philip Albert
Artistic Director: Sharon Albert
Mission: Preservation and presentation of the culture
and history of the Southern Appalachian Mountains
through the performing arts.
Founded: 1989
Specialized Field: Drama; Musical
Status: Non-Equity; Nonprofit
Paid Staff: 12
Volunteer Staff: 30
Paid Artists: 25
Season: June 20 - August 19
Type of Stage: Proscenium
Seating Capacity: 750

Hawaii

2534
ARMY ENTERTAINMENT PROGRAM
USASCH, DPCA, CRD, CSDAB
Entertainment Section
Fort Shafter, HI 96858
Phone: 808-438-1980
Fax: 808-438-1980
Management:
Chief Army Entertainment: Vanita Rae Smith
Technical Director: Tom Giza
Mission: The goals of the Army Entertainment Program
are to provide interested individuals with a constructive
outlet for talents, to maintain a high level of morals and
to promote good cultural relations with the local civilian
community.
Utilizes: Guest Artists; Guest Companies; Singers
Founded: 1949
Specialized Field: Musical; Community Theater
Status: Non-Professional; Nonprofit
Paid Staff: 30
Income Sources: American Association of Community
Theatres; Hawaii State Theatre Council
Performs At: Richardson Performing Arts Center
Organization Type: Performing; Resident; Educational

2535
HILO COMMUNITY PLAYERS
PO Box 46
Hilo, HI 96721
Phone: 808-935-9155
Web Site: www.hilocommunityplayers.org
Officers:
President: Gene Gold
Secretary: Angie Baker
Treasurer: Glen Swartwout
Management:
President: Laura Ward

Costume Manager: Judy Grogg
Equipment Manager: Amy Jackson
Mission: Organizing, promoting and conducting an
educational amateur drama program on the Island of
Hawaii.
Utilizes: Guest Companies
Founded: 1938
Specialized Field: Educational; Community Theater
Status: Non-Profit, Non-Professional
Paid Staff: 100
Paid Artists: 3
Organization Type: Performing; Educational

2536
DIAMOND HEAD THEATRE
520 Makapuu Avenue
Honolulu, HI 96816
Phone: 808-733-0277
Fax: 808-735-1250
e-mail: dht@diamondheadtheatre.com
Web Site: www.diamondheadtheatre.com
Officers:
Chairman: Chris Kanazawa
Management:
President: Dennis Francis
Artistic Director: John Rampage
Managing Director: Deena Dray
Mission: To present plays and musicals to the
community; to hold classes and workshops in acting for
all ages; to offer opportunities for all persons interested
to participate both on stage and backstage in theatre.
Utilizes: Actors; Choreographers; Dancers; Designers;
Guest Accompanists; Guest Artists; Guest Conductors;
Guest Designers; Guest Lecturers; Instructors; Local
Artists; Music; Resident Professionals; Sign Language
Translators; Soloists; Student Interns
Founded: 1915
Specialized Field: Musical; Comedy; Community
Theater; Educational
Status: Non-Profit, Non-Professional
Paid Staff: 12
Volunteer Staff: 400
Budget: $1,500,000
Income Sources: Tickets; Donations; State of Hawaii;
Foundations
Performs At: Diamond Head Theatre
Annual Attendance: 50,000
Facility Category: Community Theatre
Type of Stage: Proscenium
Seating Capacity: 500
Year Built: 1940
Year Remodeled: 1980
Rental Contact: Managing Director Deena Dray
Organization Type: Performing; Educational

2537
HAWAII THEATRE
1130 Bethel Street
Honolulu, HI 96813-2201
Phone: 808-528-5535
Fax: 808-529-8505
e-mail: burtonwhite@hawaii.rr.com
Web Site: www.hawiitheatre.com
Officers:
Chairman of the Board: Robert Midkiff
Treasurer: Paul Schraff
Vice Chairman: Mary Foster Weya
Management:
Theatre Manager: Burton White
Assistant Theatre Manager: Ryan Sueoka
Assistant Box Office Manager: Dawn Keeley
Stage Manager: Jude Lampitelli

Mission: Provide a professional venue for the celebration of cultures and the arts for the people of Hawaii and its visitors.
Founded: 1922
Specialized Field: Drama; Musical; Contemporary
Status: Nonprofit
Paid Staff: 13
Volunteer Staff: 300
Budget: $1,500,000
Annual Attendance: 5,000
Type of Stage: Proscenium
Stage Dimensions: 30x18
Seating Capacity: 325

2538
HONOLULU THEATRE FOR YOUTH
2846 Ualena Street
Honolulu, HI 96819-1910
Phone: 808-839-9885
Fax: 808-839-7018
e-mail: hty@htyweb.org
Management:
Artistic Director: Mark Lutwak
Managing Director: Louise Lanzilotti
Technical Director: Wade Kersey
Director Of Drama Education: Wade Kersey
Mission: To provide quality drama education and theatre to all children and their families in the state of Hawaii.
Founded: 1955
Specialized Field: Children's Theater; Educational
Status: Non-Profit
Paid Staff: 21
Volunteer Staff: 50
Paid Artists: 35
Budget: 1.4 million
Annual Attendance: 120,000

2539
KUMU KAHUA THEATRE
46 Merchant Street
Honolulu, HI 96813
Phone: 808-536-4222
Fax: 808-536-4226
e-mail: kumukahuatheatre@hawaiiantel.net
Web Site: www.kumukahua.org
Officers:
President: John Wat
Management:
Artistic Director: Harry Wong III
Managing Director: Scott Rogers
Mission: To produce plays by Hawai'i writers writing about Hawaii and plays of interest to Hawai'i's under served communites.
Utilizes: Actors; Collaborating Artists; Collaborations; Community Members; Community Talent; Designers; Educators; Five Seasonal Concerts; Guest Artists; Guest Choreographers; Guest Conductors; Guest Designers; Guest Ensembles; Guest Musical Directors; Guest Speakers; Guest Teachers; High School Drama; Instructors; Local Artists; Local Artists & Directors; Lyricists; Paid Performers; Performance Artists; Scenic Designers; Soloists; Students; Theatre Companies; Volunteer Directors & Actors; Writers
Founded: 1971
Specialized Field: Young Playwrights; Educational
Status: Non-Profit, Non-Professional
Paid Staff: 3
Income Sources: Patrons; Donations; Grants; Sponsors
Performs At: Live Theatre
Annual Attendance: 7,485
Type of Stage: Black Box(Flexible)
Seating Capacity: 1,871

Year Built: 1871
Year Remodeled: 1994
Rental Contact: Managing Director Scott Rogers

2540
WINDWARD THEATRE GUILD
PO Box 624
Kailua, HI 96734
Phone: 808-234-1751
Management:
Manager: Charles Brockman
Mission: Enhancing and promoting excellence in all aspects of theatrical production.
Utilizes: Guest Companies; Singers
Founded: 1956
Specialized Field: Musical; Dinner Theater; Community Theater
Status: Nonprofit
Paid Staff: 60
Income Sources: Hawaii State Theatre Council; State Foundation for Culture & the Arts; Alliance for Drama Education
Performs At: Boondocker Theatre; Kaneohe Marine Corps Air State
Organization Type: Performing; Educational

2541
WAIMEA COMMUNITY THEATRE
PO Box 1660
Kamuela, HI 96743
Phone: 808-885-5818
Web Site: www.waimeacommunitytheatre.org
Officers:
President: Jack Ross
VP: Julie Barreto
Secretary: Jennifer Hussong
Treasurer: Miguel Bray
Mission: Providing residents of North Hawaii with quality theatrical entertainment; offering community support and educational services in theatrical performance.
Utilizes: Guest Companies; Singers
Founded: 1964
Specialized Field: Musical; Dinner Theater; Community Theater
Status: Non-Profit
Paid Staff: 50
Income Sources: Hawaii State Theatre Council
Performs At: Parker School Auditorium
Organization Type: Performing; Educational

2542
KAUAI INTERNATIONAL THEATRE
Kauai Village
4-831 Kuhio Highway
Kapaa, Kauai, HI 96746
Phone: 808-821-1588
e-mail: thekit@GoKauai.org
Management:
Executive/Artistic Director: Gabriel Oberman
Specialized Field: New Plays; Dinner Theater
Status: Volunteer

2543
LEEWARD COMMUNITY COLLEGE THEATRE
University of Hawaii Colleges
96-045 Ala Ike
Pearl City, HI 96782
Phone: 808-455-0381
Fax: 808-455-0384
e-mail: lcctheatre@lcc.hawaii.edu
Web Site: www.lcctheatre.hawaii.edu
Management:

Theatre Manager: Joe Patti
Mission: Our primary goal of LCC Theatre is to promote cultural curiosity. We want our performances to make a connection to the mind, heart or spirit of our audiences; creating and stimulating a hunger for the experiences only achieved through the arts.
Founded: 1974
Opened: 1974
Specialized Field: Comedy; Musical; Educational
Status: Non-Profit, Professional
Paid Staff: 5
Type of Stage: Proscenium
Stage Dimensions: 50 ft x 41 ft
Orchestra Pit: y
Seating Capacity: 580
Year Built: 1974

2544
MAUI ACADEMY OF PERFORMING ARTS
81 N Church Street
Wailuku, HI 96732
Phone: 808-244-8760
Fax: 808-244-6530
Web Site: www.mauiacademy.org
Management:
President: Chris Hart
Executive Director: Donna C Breeden
Artistic Director: David C Johnston
Managing Director: Frances A Von Tempsky
Mission: Offering educational performing arts to youths and adults.
Utilizes: Actors; Artists-in-Residence; Choreographers; Collaborating Artists; Collaborations; Dance Companies; Dancers; Designers; Educators; Five Seasonal Concerts; Grant Writers; Guest Accompanists; Guest Artists; Guest Choreographers; Guest Conductors; Guest Designers; Guest Ensembles; Guest Lecturers; Guild Activities; Multi Collaborations; Music; Organization Contracts; Original Music Scores; Performance Artists; Resident Professionals; Special Technical Talent; Theatre Companies
Founded: 1974
Specialized Field: Comedy; Youth Theater; Ethnic Theater; Classic; Contemporary
Status: Non-Profit, Professional
Paid Staff: 35
Volunteer Staff: 200
Paid Artists: 3
Income Sources: Grants; Fundraising; Earned Revenue
Performs At: Maui Academy of Performing Arts
Annual Attendance: 10,000 +
Facility Category: Performing Arts Classrooms/ Theatre
Type of Stage: Multi-forum
Seating Capacity: 150 - 200
Year Built: 2000
Cost: $3.1 million
Rental Contact: David Johnson
Organization Type: Performing; Touring; Educational

Idaho

2545
IDAHO SHAKESPEARE FESTIVAL
PO Box 9365
Boise, ID 83707
Phone: 208-429-9908
Fax: 208-323-0700
Web Site: www.idahoshakespeare.org
Officers:
President: Cindy Bateman

Vice President: James Steele
Secretary: Brandy Stemmler
Treasurer: Henry Yun
Management:
Artistic Director: Charles Fee
Managing Director: Mark Hofflund
Director Of Development: Ann Dehner
Director Of Finance: Sherrill Livingstone
Mission: The Festival's mission is to produce great theater, entertain and educate.
Founded: 1975
Specialized Field: Shakespeare
Status: Non-Profit, Professional
Paid Staff: 12
Season: May - September
Organization Type: Performing; Touring; Educational

2546
COEUR D'ALENE SUMMER THEATRE/CAROUSEL PLAYERS

Hall Box Office Boswell Hall
W 1000 Garden Avenue, PO Box 1119
Coeur d'Alene, ID 83816-1119
Phone: 208-769-7780
Fax: 208-769-7856
Toll-free: 800-423-2849
Web Site: www.nic.edu/summertheatre
Management:
President: Ketty Martus
Artistic Director: Roger Welch
Managing Director: David Hollingshead
Development Director: Jim Speirs
Founded: 1968
Specialized Field: Summer Stock
Status: Non-Profit, Professional
Budget: $560,000
Income Sources: Patrons; Donors; Business Advertisers; Grants
Season: July 1 - August 29
Annual Attendance: 30,000
Facility Category: College Auditorium
Type of Stage: Proscenium
Stage Dimensions: 56'x 42'
Seating Capacity: 1100

2547
COMPANY OF FOOLS

PO Box 329
Hailey, ID 83333
Phone: 208-788-6520
Fax: 208-788-1053
Web Site: www.companyoffools.org
Management:
President: Benjamin Wood
Artistic Director: Rusty Wilson
Managing Director: R I Rowsey
Associate Artistic Director: Denise Simone
Founded: 1992
Specialized Field: Musical; Classic; Contemporary
Status: Non-Profit, Professional
Paid Staff: 6
Performs At: Liberty Theatre, Mint
Type of Stage: Proscenium, Flexible
Seating Capacity: 240, 30-90

2548
IDAHO FALLS ARTS COUNCIL COLONIAL THEATER

498 A Street
Idaho Falls, ID 83402

Phone: 208-522-0471
Fax: 208-522-0413
e-mail: ifac@idahofallsarts.org
Web Site: www.idahofallssarts.org
Management:
Executive Director: Carrie Getty
Artistic Director: Grey Gardner
Technical Director: Brad Higbee
Ticket and Front House Manager: Linda Evans
Mission: To promote and present visual and performing arts in Eastern Idaho.
Founded: 1990
Specialized Field: Drama; Movement Theater; Musical
Status: Non-Profit, Non-Professional
Paid Staff: 10
Paid Artists: 1
Type of Stage: Wood
Seating Capacity: 969
Year Built: 1919
Year Remodeled: 1999
Rental Contact: Linda Evans

2549
IDAHO REPERTORY THEATRE COMPANY

University of Idaho
PO Box 443074
Moscow, ID 83844-3074
Phone: 208-885-6465
Fax: 208-885-2558
e-mail: theatre@uidaho.edu
Web Site: www.uitheatre.com
Management:
President: Michael White
Artistic Director: Robert Caisley
Producing Director: David Lee Painter
Mission: Providing North Idaho with quality summer theatre.
Utilizes: Guest Companies; Singers
Founded: 1953
Specialized Field: Educational; Theater Workshops
Status: Non-Profit
Paid Staff: 8
Volunteer Staff: 10
Paid Artists: 50
Non-paid Artists: 5
Income Sources: Individual contribution; Business/Corporate Donations; Foundations
Season: May - August
Performs At: Hartung Theatre
Type of Stage: Semi-Thrust/Proscenium
Seating Capacity: 417
Year Built: 1973
Architect: $4,300,000
Organization Type: Performing; Educational

2550
PANIDA THEATRE

300 N 1st Avenue
Sandpoint, ID 83864
Phone: 208-263-9191
Fax: 208-263-1523
e-mail: panida@nidah.net
Web Site: www.panida.org
Management:
President: Debra McShane
Executive Director: Karen Bowers
Technical Director: Bill Lewis
Mission: Providing beautiful, versatile space for the presentation of quality performances; continuing to aid in the revitalization of downtown Sandpoint.
Utilizes: Singers
Founded: 1927
Specialized Field: Alternative

Status: Non-Profit, Professional
Paid Staff: 4
Income Sources: Fundraising; grants
Performs At: Panida Theatre
Annual Attendance: 25,000
Seating Capacity: 550
Year Built: 1927
Organization Type: Performing; Resident; Educational; Sponsoring

Illinois

2551
ABOUT FACE THEATRE

1222 W Wilson
Suite 2W
Chicago, IL 60640
Phone: 773-784-8565
Fax: 773-784-8557
e-mail: faceline1@aboutfacetheatre.com
Web Site: www.aboutfacetheatre.com
Management:
President: Christopher Sink
Artistic Director: Eric Rosen
Founded: 1995
Specialized Field: Musical; Comedy; Youth Theater; Community Theater; Contemporary
Status: Non-Profit, Professional
Paid Staff: 7
Type of Stage: Flexible Thrust Stage
Seating Capacity: 99

2552
AMERICAN THEATER COMPANY

1909 W Byron Street
Chicago, IL 60613
Phone: 773-409-4125
e-mail: info@atcweb.org
Web Site: www.atcweb.org
Officers:
President: Dino Biris
Vice President: Doug Diefanbach
Treasurer: Larry Levin
Management:
Artistic Director: P J Paparelli
Executive Director: Mary Ruth Coffey
Mission: American Theatre Company is an ensemble of artists committed to producing new and classic American stories that ask the question "What does it mean to be an American?". We provide a truly intimate home for the community to experience meaningful stories. We foster a nurturing environment for artists to take risks and create essential work.
Utilizes: AEA Actors; Artists-in-Residence; Choreographers; Collaborating Artists; Collaborations; Community Members; Community Talent; Contract Actors; Designers; Educators; Equity Actors; Five Seasonal Concerts; Grant Writers; Guest Accompanists; Guest Artists; Guest Choreographers; Guest Composers; Guest Conductors; Guest Designers; Guest Directors; Guest Ensembles; Guest Instructors; Guest Lecturers; Guest Musical Directors; Guest Speakers; Multimedia; Original Music Scores; Poets; Resident Companies; Resident Professionals; Students
Founded: 1985
Specialized Field: Musical; Comedy; Classic; Contemporary
Status: Non-Profit, Professional
Paid Staff: 6
Volunteer Staff: 12
Paid Artists: 85
Non-paid Artists: 20

Budget: $800,000
Income Sources: Private Foundations; Grants; Government Grants; Individual Donations
Performs At: American Theater Company
Affiliations: Actors' Equity Association
Annual Attendance: 10,000
Type of Stage: Modified Thrust
Seating Capacity: 107
Year Remodeled: 1993
Rental Contact: Production Manager Emily Ritger

2553
AMERICAN THEATRE

1225 W Belmont
Chicago, IL 60657
Phone: 773-327-5252
Management:
　　Co-Artistic Director: Jim Leaming
　　Co-Artistic Director: Kate Buddeke
Mission: Developing and producing new plays written by and for Midwesterners.
Founded: 1985
Specialized Field: New American Works; Classic; Historical
Status: Professional; Nonprofit
Paid Staff: 125
Income Sources: League of Chicago Theatres
Organization Type: Performing

2554
AUDITORIUM THEATRE OF ROOSEVELT UNIVERSITY

50 E Congress Parkway
Chicago, IL 60605
Phone: 312-922-2110
Fax: 312-431-2360
e-mail: info@auditoriumtheatre.org
Web Site: www.auditoriumtheatre.org
Officers:
　　Chief Marketing/Development Officer: Judie Green
Management:
　　Executive Director: Brett Batterson
Mission: Restoring the original architectural splendor of the Auditorium Theatre; presenting theatre, dance and music programs.
Utilizes: Singers
Founded: 1960
Specialized Field: Musical; Comedy; Educational
Status: Non-Profit, Professional
Paid Staff: 25
Paid Artists: 100
Performs At: Auditorium Theatre
Facility Category: Performing Arts Center
Type of Stage: Proecenium
Seating Capacity: 3,800
Year Built: 1884
Year Remodeled: 2003
Organization Type: Resident; Educational; Sponsoring

2555
BAILIWICK REPERTORY

Bailiwick Arts Center
1229 W Belmont
Chicago, IL 60657
Phone: 773-883-1090
Fax: 773-883-2017
Web Site: www.bailiwick.org
Officers:
　　President: Don Cortelyou
　　Treasurer: Elliot Ferdland
　　Secretary: Garth Person
　　Board of Directors: Gary Skala
Management:

Artistic Director: David Zak
Producer: Rusty Hernandez
Box Office Manager: Brannen Daugherty
General Manager: Jamie Axtell
Mission: To provide contemporary theater with a classical core; to produce vivid productions of the greatest dramatists of all times, alongside great works from our time; to serve as host or co-producer for other productions or attractions with similar artistic aims; to present festivals of one act plays; to showcase new directors and gay and lesbian plays.
Utilizes: Actors; AEA Actors; Artists-in-Residence; Choreographers; Dancers; Designers; Fine Artists; Five Seasonal Concerts; Guest Accompanists; Guest Artists; Guest Companies; Guest Conductors; Guest Designers; Guest Lecturers; Instructors; Local Artists; Local Unknown Artists; Multimedia; Music; Organization Contracts; Original Music Scores; Performance Artists; Playwrights; Poets; Resident Professionals; Selected Students; Sign Language Translators; Soloists; Students; Student Interns; Touring Companies; Visual Arts; Visual Designers
Founded: 1982
Specialized Field: Educational; Theater Workshops
Status: Non-Profit, Professional
Paid Staff: 5
Volunteer Staff: 200
Paid Artists: 195
Budget: $975,000
Income Sources: League of Chicago Theatres; Theatre Communications Group; Illinois Theater Association
Performs At: Bailwell Arts Center
Affiliations: League of Chicago Theatre; Theatre Communications Group
Annual Attendance: 95,000
Facility Category: Performing Arts Center
Year Built: 1995
Organization Type: Performing; Sponsoring

2556
BLACK ENSEMBLE THEATER

4520 N Beacon
Chicago, IL 60640
Phone: 773-769-4451
Fax: 773-769-4533
e-mail: blackensemble@aol.com
Web Site: www.blackensembletheater.org
Management:
　　Artistic Director/Producer: Jackie Taylor
　　Stage Manager: Jackie Taylor
Mission: Supplying continual employment for the Black artist; adhering to a philosophy of excellence.
Utilizes: Guest Companies
Founded: 1975
Specialized Field: Musical; Ensembles
Status: Non-Profit, Professional
Income Sources: Black Theater Alliance
Performs At: Leo Lerner Theater
Organization Type: Performing; Touring; Resident; Educational

2557
BLIND PARROT PRODUCTIONS

1446 W Berteau
Chicago, IL 60613
Phone: 312-549-3991
Officers:
　　President: Fred Hachmeister
　　Secretary: Sheri Jones
　　Treasurer: Frank Tourangeau
Management:
　　Executive Director: Jane Molnar
　　Co-Artistic Director: David Perkins

Mission: To produce innovative, intelligent, thought-provoking writing for the stage with a focus on scripts which test the limits of theatrical form; to introduce new concepts; to pursue new relationships between artists and the audience.
Utilizes: Guest Companies
Founded: 1983
Specialized Field: Drama; Musical; Contemporary
Status: Non-Professional
Paid Staff: 20
Income Sources: League of Chicago Theatres
Organization Type: Performing

2558
BODY POLITIC THEATRE

2261 N Lincoln Avenue
Chicago, IL 60614
Phone: 773-549-5788
Fax: 773-549-2777
Officers:
　　President: Richard Wier
Management:
　　Artistic Director: Albert Pertalion
　　Administrative Director: Kim Patrick Bitz
　　Business Director: Rick Sheingold
Mission: Provides an intimate forum for the best of classic and contemporary dramatic literature through thought-provoking and entertaining productions.
Utilizes: Guest Companies
Founded: 1966
Specialized Field: New Works of Social Importance; Experimental; Drama
Status: Professional; Nonprofit
Paid Staff: 10
Income Sources: Actors' Equity Association; United Scenic Arts; League of Chicago Theatres; Theatre Communications Group; Producers Association of Chicago Area Theatres
Organization Type: Performing; Touring; Resident; Educational

2559
CENTER THEATER AND THE TRAINING CENTER

1346 W Devon
Chicago, IL 60660
Phone: 773-508-0200
Fax: 773-508-9584
Management:
　　Artistic Director: Dan Lamorte
　　General Manager: RJ Coleman
Mission: Educating, inspiring and cultivating theatre audiences; offering actors an ongoing training program.
Utilizes: Guest Companies
Founded: 1985
Specialized Field: Educational; Theater Workshops
Status: Professional; Nonprofit
Paid Staff: 10
Income Sources: Theatre Communications Group; International Association of Theatre for Children and Youth
Performs At: Center Theater
Facility Category: Mainstage Theatre; Studio Theatre
Type of Stage: Thrust, Black Box
Seating Capacity: 60; 30
Organization Type: Performing; Touring; Resident; Educational

2560
CHICAGO ACTORS ENSEMBLE

941 W Lawrence Avenue
5Th Floor
Chicago, IL 60642
Phone: 312-275-4463

Management:
   Artistic Director: Richard Helweg
Utilizes: Guest Companies; Singers
Founded: 1984
Specialized Field: Ensemble
Status: Professional; Nonprofit
Income Sources: League of Chicago Theatres
Organization Type: Performing; Touring; Resident

2561
CHICAGO DRAMATISTS

1105 W Chicago Avenue
Chicago, IL 60622
Phone: 312-633-0630
Fax: 312-633-0840
e-mail: newplays@chicagodramatists.org
Web Site: www.chicagodramatists.org
Management:
   President of the Board: Ellen Krasnow
   Artistic Director: Russ Tutterow
   Managing Director: Brian Loevner
Mission: Chicago Dramatists is a professional, non-profit theatre, dedicated to the development and advancement of playwrights and new plays.
Utilizes: Actors; AEA Actors; Artists-in-Residence; Choreographers; Designers; Educators; Guest Companies; High School Drama; Instructors; Local Artists; Performance Artists; Poets; Resident Professionals; Student Interns; Special Technical Talent
Founded: 1979
Specialized Field: Young Playwrights; Educational
Status: Non-Profit, Professional
Paid Staff: 5
Volunteer Staff: 150
Paid Artists: 3
Budget: $250,000
Income Sources: Ticket Sales; Grant; Donations; Membership Fees; Class Fees
Performs At: Theatre
Affiliations: League of Chicago Theatre Actors' Equity Association; The Dramatists Guild; TCG
Annual Attendance: 8,000
Facility Category: Theatre
Type of Stage: Proscenium
Stage Dimensions: 24'x24'
Seating Capacity: 77
Year Built: 1884
Year Remodeled: 1998
Organization Type: Performing

2562
CHICAGO SHAKESPEARE THEATER ON NAVY PIER

800 E Grand Avenue
Navy Pier
Chicago, IL 60611
Phone: 312-595-5656
Fax: 312-595-5607
e-mail: customerservice@chicagoshakes.com
Web Site: www.chicagoshakes.com
Officers:
   Chairman: Raymond McCaskey
   Treasurer: Mark Ouweleen
Management:
   Executive Director: Criss Henderson
   Artistic Director: Barbara Gaines
Mission: Shakespeare offers countless paths of learning to students. Through one of the largest arts-in-education programs in the entire country, Team Shakespeare brings Shakespeare to life for middle school and secondary school students.
Founded: 1986
Specialized Field: Musical; Comedy; Classic; Contemporary

Status: Non-Profit, Professional
Paid Staff: 93
Volunteer Staff: 50
Paid Artists: 42
Performs At: Chicago Shakespeare Theater; Seven Story on Navy Pier
Annual Attendance: 200,000
Facility Category: Courtyard-style Theater
Type of Stage: Modified Thrust; Studio
Seating Capacity: 510; 175
Year Remodeled: 1999
Organization Type: Performing; Touring; Resident; Educational; Sponsoring

2563
CHILD'S PLAY TOURING THEATRE

2518 W Armitage Avenue
Chicago, IL 60647
Phone: 773-235-8911
Fax: 773-235-5478
Toll-free: 800-353-3402
e-mail: cptt@cptt.org
Web Site: www.cptt.org
Officers:
   President: Bernard Garbo
   VP: June Podagrosi
   Secretary: Eve Moran
   Treasurer: Mark Ackerman
Management:
   Executive Director and Producer: Nicole Rohr
   Founder and Executive Director: June Podagrosi
   Marketing: Karen Swatnik
Mission: Performing exclusively original literature authored by children; sharing, encouraging and validating children's creative writing; advancing children's literacy through theatre.
Utilizes: Actors; Collaborating Artists; Collaborations; Commissioned Composers; Educators; Multimedia; Music; Organization Contracts; Original Music Scores; Resident Professionals
Founded: 1978
Specialized Field: Touring Company
Status: Professional; Nonprofit
Paid Staff: 6
Volunteer Staff: 2
Paid Artists: 12
Budget: $800,000
Income Sources: Government; Foundations; Corporations; Individuals; Box Office
Performs At: Seasonal Run at the Goodman Theatre
Affiliations: Illinois Theater Association; Arts and Business Council; League of Chicago Theatres; NAPAMA; Donor's Forum of Chicago
Annual Attendance: 200,000
Facility Category: Off-site
Organization Type: Performing; Touring; Educational

2564
CITY LIT THEATER COMPANY

1020 W Bryn Mawr
Chicago, IL 60660
Phone: 773-293-3682
Fax: 773-293-3684
e-mail: info@citylit.org
Web Site: www.citylit.org
Officers:
   President: Gary Redeker
Management:
   Managing Director: Brian Pastor
   Artistic Director: Terry McCabe
   Casting Director: Shawna Tucker
Mission: City Lit Theater Company's presents both new adaptions of quality literature and extant with a literary bent.

Utilizes: Actors; Commissioned Music; Designers; Five Seasonal Concerts; Guest Accompanists; Guest Companies; Guest Conductors; Guest Designers; Guest Instructors; High School Drama; Instructors; Local Artists; Multimedia; Original Music Scores; Performance Artists; Resident Artists; Resident Professionals; Theatre Companies
Founded: 1979
Specialized Field: Drama; Musical; Historical; Educational
Status: Non-Profit, Professional
Paid Staff: 1
Volunteer Staff: 5
Paid Artists: 35
Budget: $176,000
Income Sources: Admissions; Grants
Annual Attendance: 5,526
Type of Stage: Thrust
Stage Dimensions: 16x25
Seating Capacity: 100
Year Remodeled: 2000
Organization Type: Performing; Touring; Resident; Educational

2565
CLASSICS ON STAGE!

PO Box 25365
Chicago, IL 60625
Phone: 773-989-0532
e-mail: classstage@aol.com
Web Site: www.classicsonstage.com
Management:
   Managing Director: Robert D Boburka
   Axtistic Director: Michele L Vacca
Mission: Developing future audiences for legitimate theatre through presentations of live professional theatre.
Utilizes: Singers
Founded: 1976
Specialized Field: Musical; Classic
Status: Professional; Commercial
Income Sources: Actors' Equity Association; Association of American Theatre for Youth; League of Chicago Theatres
Organization Type: Performing; Resident; Educational

2566
COURT THEATRE

5535 S Ellis Avenue
Chicago, IL 60637
Phone: 773-702-7005
Fax: 773-834-1897
e-mail: info@courttheatre.orgÿ
Web Site: www.courttheater.org
Officers:
   Chairman: Virginia Gerst
   Secretary: Mary Anton
   Treasurer: Margaret Zagel
Management:
   Executive Director: Stephen Albert
   Artistic Director: Charles Newell
Mission: To celebrate the immutable power and relevance of classic theatre.
Utilizes: Guest Companies; Singers
Founded: 1954
Specialized Field: Classic
Status: Non-Profit, Professional
Paid Staff: 18
Income Sources: Actors' Equity Association; League of Chicago Theatres; Theatre Communications Group; Producers Association of Chicago Area Theatres
Performs At: Court Theatre
Seating Capacity: 250
Organization Type: Performing; Educational

2567
DEPAUL UNIVERSITY MERLE RESKIN THEATRE
60 E Balbo Drive
Chicago, IL 60605
Phone: 312-922-1999
e-mail: jculbert@depaul.edu
Web Site:
http://theatreschool.depaul.edu/about_places.php
Management:
  Dean: John Culbert
Utilizes: Soloists
Specialized Field: Educational; Theater Workshops; Children's Theater
Status: Non-Profit, Non-Professional
Facility Category: Proscenium Theatre
Seating Capacity: 1325
Year Built: 1910
Rental Contact: Leslie Shook (773-325-7965)

2568
DREISKE PERFORMANCE COMPANY
1517 W Fullerton Avenue
Chicago, IL 60614
Phone: 312-281-9075
Officers:
  Chairman: David Edelberg
  Secretary: Emilye Hunterfields
Management:
  Artistic Director: Nicole Dreiske
  Managing Director: Milos Stehlik
  Literary Manager: Catherine Berkenstein
  General Manager: John Dreiske
Mission: Professional touring ensemble, many of whose productions were developed in historic and on-location projects; The Book of Lear in the Sahara Desert, Macondo in Columbia, South America; currently developing new theater works for performance for international TV and tours.
Utilizes: Guest Companies; Singers
Founded: 1975
Specialized Field: Ensembles; Drama
Status: Professional; Nonprofit
Income Sources: Association for Theatre in Higher Education; International Theatre Institute; League of Chicago Theatres
Performs At: International Performance Studio
Organization Type: Performing; Touring; Resident; Educational

2569
ENSEMBLE ESPANOL SPANISH DANCE THEATER
5500 N Saint Louis Avenue
Chicago, IL 60625
Phone: 773-583-4050
Fax: 773-794-5314
e-mail: ensemble-espanol@neiu.edu
Web Site: www.neiu.edu/~eespanol
Officers:
  President: Dr. Angelina Pedroso
  VP: Lou Altman
  Treasurer: Elba Maisonet
  Secretary: Lillian Heminover
Management:
  Director: Libby Komaiko
  Administrative Assistant: Jorge D Perez
  Accountant: Flor Dumblao
Mission: The Ensemble Espanol Spanish Dance Theater is chartered to share the rich traditions of Spanish dance, music, art and literature with all of our communities as the Spanish Dance Center in the United States.

Utilizes: Guest Companies
Founded: 1976
Specialized Field: Spanish Language Company; Musical; Educational; Ethnic Theater
Status: Professional; Nonprofit
Paid Staff: 4
Volunteer Staff: 2
Paid Artists: 30
Non-paid Artists: 31
Budget: $400,000
Income Sources: Foundations; Corporations; Government; Private Donations
Annual Attendance: 90,000
Facility Category: Auditorium; Dance Studios
Type of Stage: Proscenium
Stage Dimensions: 25x25
Seating Capacity: 650
Year Built: 1975
Year Remodeled: 2000
Organization Type: Performing; Touring; Resident; Educational; Sponsoring

2570
ETA CREATIVE ARTS FOUNDATION
7558 S Chicago Avenue
Chicago, IL 60619
Phone: 773-752-3955
Fax: 773-752-8727
e-mail: email@etacreativearts.org
Web Site: www.etacreativearts.org
Officers:
  Chairman: Milton Davis
  President: Abena Joan Brown
  Secretary/Treasurer: Velma Wilson
  Finance: Wiley Moore
Management:
  President: Abena Joan P Brown
  Artistic Director: Runako Jahi
  Business Manager: Teresa A White
  Building Manager: Kenneth Simmons
  Technical Director: Darryl Goodman
Mission: ETA provides training in the performing and technical aspects of the arts, encouraging the development and employment primarily of Black artists. ETA also works to encourage the development and propagation of the works of Black writers through its productions of original works.
Utilizes: Guest Companies
Founded: 1971
Specialized Field: Multi-Cultural
Status: Non-Profit, Professional
Paid Staff: 6
Volunteer Staff: 50
Paid Artists: 8
Budget: $1.6 million
Income Sources: Earned Funds; Corporate; Individuals
Performs At: ETA Square
Seating Capacity: 200
Organization Type: Performing; Touring; Resident; Educational

2571
FAMOUS DOOR THEATRE
Famous Door Theatre
Box 57029
Chicago, IL 60657
Phone: 773-404-8283
Fax: 773-404-8292
Web Site: www.famousdoortheatre.org
Officers:
  Chair: Dan Rivkin
  Vice-Chair: Don Copper
  Secretary: Leo Aubel

Treasurer: Jeff Anderle
Management:
  Co-Chairs: Ms Dara Altshu
  General Manager: Hanna Dworkin
  Artistic Director: Marc Grapey
  Managing Director: Dan Rivkin
Founded: 1987
Specialized Field: Drama; Musical; Classic; Contemporary
Paid Staff: 5
Volunteer Staff: 25
Paid Artists: 100
Non-paid Artists: 20
Budget: $500,000
Performs At: Victory Gardens Theatre
Affiliations: AEA; SSDC; TCG
Annual Attendance: 15,000
Type of Stage: Thrust
Seating Capacity: 200

2572
FREE STREET PROGRAMS
1419 W Blackhawk
Chicago, IL 60622
Phone: 773-772-7248
Fax: 773-772-7248
e-mail: gogogo@freestreet.org
Web Site: www.freestreet.org
Management:
  President: Deloris Axelrod
  Artistic Director: Ron Bieganski
  Managing Director: Rodney Terwilliger
  Creative Director: Anita Evans
Mission: Free Street Programs is an arts outreach organization that uses the performing arts to enhance the literacy, self-esteem, creativity and employability of populations consistently excluded from mainstream cultural programming.
Founded: 1969
Specialized Field: Youth Theater; Community Theater; Contemporary
Status: Non-Profit, Professional
Paid Staff: 12
Paid Artists: 90
Income Sources: Theatre Communications Group; Illinois Arts Alliance
Performs At: Free Street Teen Street Theater
Organization Type: Performing; Touring

2573
GOODMAN THEATRE
170 N Dearborn Street
Chicago, IL 60601
Phone: 312-443-3811
Fax: 312-443-3800
Web Site: www.goodman-theatre.org
Management:
  President: Roche Schuler
  Artistic Director: Robert Falls
  Associate Artistic Director: Steve Scott
Mission: To present the classics of our theatre heritage with freshness and new vision; to create an audience that reflects the diversity of the Chicago community; to showcase the finest local, national, and international artists; to provide its staff and artists with the best working conditions possible; to operate with fiscal responsibility.
Utilizes: Guest Companies; Singers
Founded: 1925
Specialized Field: Musical; Comedy; Youth Theater; Ethnic Theater; Puppet; Classic; Contemporary
Status: Non-Profit, Professional
Paid Staff: 100
Budget: $12 Million

Income Sources: Foundation; Corporate & Individual Contributions; Ticket Revenue
Performs At: Albert Iva Goodman, Owen Bruner Goodman Theater
Affiliations: TCG, Illinois Arts Alliance, League of Resident Theaters, American Arts Alliance, League of Chicago Theaters, Illinois Theater Association
Annual Attendance: 214,016
Type of Stage: Proscenium, Flexible Courtyard
Seating Capacity: 850 Albert, 345-467 Owen
Year Built: 2000
Organization Type: Performing; Educational; Sponsoring

2574
IMAGINATION THEATER

4802 N. Broadway
#201-B
Chicago, IL 60640
Phone: 773-303-0070
Fax: 773-303-0073
e-mail: info@imaginationtheater.org
Management:
   Artistic Director: Warren W Baumgart, Jr
Mission: Committed to the value of creative drama as a tool for learning through two basic programs: participatory theater for children, the elderly, and the disabled; and Child Sexual Abuse Prevention Program, a comprehensive program for teachers, parents and students.
Founded: 1966
Specialized Field: Touring Company; Improvisation
Status: Professional; Nonprofit
Organization Type: Performing; Touring; Educational

2575
LIFELINE THEATRE

6912 N Glenwood
Chicago, IL 60626
Phone: 773-761-4477
Fax: 773-761-4582
e-mail: info@lifelinetheatre.com
Web Site: www.lifelinetheatre.com
Management:
   Artistic Director: Dorothy Milne
   Managing Director: Melissa Bareford
Mission: Lifeline Theatre entertains, educates and empowers our community using an ensemble driven process to bring literature and new works to life.
Utilizes: Actors; Choreographers; Collaborating Artists; Commissioned Composers; Commissioned Music; Educators; Guest Companies; Guest Conductors; Guest Designers; Guest Lecturers; Local Artists; Music; Organization Contracts; Original Music Scores; Resident Professionals; Sign Language Translators; Soloists
Founded: 1982
Specialized Field: Drama; Classic
Status: Non-Profit, Professional
Paid Staff: 7
Volunteer Staff: 1
Budget: $500,000
Income Sources: League of Chicago Theatres, Contributes, Earned
Performs At: Lifeline Theatre
Affiliations: TGG, League of Chicago Theatres, AATE, PACT
Annual Attendance: 20,000
Facility Category: Theatre
Type of Stage: Flexible
Seating Capacity: 100
Year Built: 1930
Year Remodeled: 1992
Rental Contact: John Hildreth

Organization Type: Performing

2576
LIVE BAIT THEATRICAL COMPANY

3914 N Clark Street
Chicago, IL 60613
Phone: 773-871-1212
Fax: 773-871-3191
e-mail: sharon@livebaittheater.org
Web Site: www.livebaittheater.org
Management:
   President: Donna Benneth
   Executive Director: John Ragir
   Artistic Director: Sharon Evans
Mission: We produce all new, orginal works by Chicago area playwrights and solo performers.
Founded: 1987
Specialized Field: Musical; Comedy; Puppet; Contemporary; Drama
Status: Non-Profit, Professional
Paid Staff: 4
Performs At: Live Bait Theater
Type of Stage: Black Box
Seating Capacity: 70

2577
LOOKINGGLASS THEATRE COMPANY

875 North Michigan Ave Suite 2200
3rd Floor
Chicago, IL 60611
Phone: 773-477-9257
Fax: 773-477-6932
Web Site: www.lookingglasstheatre.org
Officers:
   Chairman: Lisa Green
   President: Alex Miller
   VP/Managing Director: Joseph Brady
   Secretary: Edward Filer
Management:
   Executive Director: Rachel Kraft
   Artistic Director: Andrew White
   General Manager: Michele Anderson
   Literary Manager: Marti Lyons
Founded: 1989
Specialized Field: Youth Theater; Classic; Contemporary
Status: Non-Profit, Professional
Paid Staff: 20
Paid Artists: 10

2578
LOYOLA UNIVERSITY DEPARTMENT OF THEATRE

6525 N Sheridan Road
Chicago, IL 60626
Phone: 773-508-3830
Fax: 773-508-8748
e-mail: theatre-info@luc.edu
Web Site: www.luc.edu/depts/theatre
Management:
   Chair Person: Sarah Gabel
   Managing Director: April Browning
Founded: 1960
Specialized Field: Educational; Theater Workshops
Status: Non-Profit, Non-Professional
Paid Staff: 3
Paid Artists: 8
Performs At: Kathleen Mullady Theatre

2579
MAYFAIR THEATRE/SHEAR MADNESS

636 S Michigan Avenue
Chicago, IL 60605
Phone: 312-786-9120

Management:
   Rompany Manager: 09252002 Gordon
   Producer: Marilyn Abrams
   Managing Director: Bruce Jordan
Mission: Mayfair Theatre presents 'Shear Madness,' the comedy whodunit that lets the audience play armchair detective. 'Shear Madness' is the longest running play in the history of Chicago theatre.
Founded: 1982
Specialized Field: Drama; Contemporary; Experimental
Status: Professional; Commercial
Income Sources: League of Chicago Theatres
Performs At: Mayfair Theatre
Organization Type: Performing

2580
PEGASUS PLAYERS

Truman College
1145 W Wilson
Chicago, IL 60640
Mailing Address: 1145 West Wilson Ave
Phone: 773-878-9761
Fax: 773-271-8057
e-mail: ÿinfo@pegasusplayers.org
Web Site: www.pegasusplayers.org
Management:
   Executive Director: Arlene Crewdson
   Production Manager: Marcus Petrella
Mission: To produce the highest quality artistic work and to provide exemplary theatre, entertainment, and arts education at no charge to people who have little or no access to the arts.
Utilizes: Guest Companies; Singers
Founded: 1979
Specialized Field: Classic; Drama
Status: Professional; Nonprofit
Income Sources: League of Chicago Theatres
Performs At: O'Rourke Center
Organization Type: Performing

2581
PERFORMING ARTS CHICAGO

410 S Michigan Avenue
#911
Chicago, IL 60605
Phone: 312-663-1628
Fax: 312-663-1043
Web Site: www.pachicago.org
Officers:
   President: Judys Neisser
   Executive Director: Susan Lipman
   Director: Christy Uchida
   Operations Manager: Laurell Zahrobsky
   Development Assistant: Brigid Flynn
   Treasurer: David Ellis
Management:
   Executive Director: Susan Lipman
   Director Marketing/Public Relations: Heidi Feldman
Mission: To present artists who explore the creative tension between tradition and innovation, to nurture an environment for and bring to performance new works and new performers, and to remain accountable to its community, furthering support for local artists, engagement and education, not only for its direct audience, but for society at large.
Utilizes: Special Technical Talent
Founded: 1960
Specialized Field: New Plays; Experimental; Improvisation; Drama; Musical
Status: Non-Profit, Professional
Paid Staff: 6
Budget: $1,000,000

Performs At: The Civic Theater
Organization Type: Performing; Resident; Educational; Sponsoring

2582
RAVEN THEATRE COMPANY
6157 N Clark
Chicago, IL 60660
Mailing Address: 2549 W Fargo Chicago, IL 60645
Phone: 773-338-2177
Fax: 773-508-9794
e-mail: info@raventheatre.com
Web Site: www.raventheatre.com
Officers:
  President: John Munson
  Vice President: Barbara King
  Secretary: Joni Gatz
  Treasurer: Ed Bray
Management:
  President: Michael Menendian
  Technical Director: John Munson
  Production Manager: Joni Gatz
Mission: To provide professional theatre affordable and accessible to the broadest cross-section of the people of Chicagoland and to provide the opportunity for local theatre artists to develop a showcase for their talents.
Utilizes: Guest Companies; Singers
Founded: 1983
Specialized Field: Youth Theater; Contemporary
Status: Non-Profit, Non-Professional
Paid Staff: 3
Paid Artists: 10
Income Sources: League of Chicago Theatres
Organization Type: Performing; Resident

2583
SAINT SEBASTIAN PLAYERS
St Bonaventure
1625 W Diversey Parkway
Chicago, IL 60614
Mailing Address: 1641 W Diversey Parkway, Chicago IL 60614
Phone: 773-404-7922
Fax: 312-728-0496
e-mail: info@saintsebastianplayers.org
Web Site: www.saintsebastianplayers.org
Officers:
  President: Jonathan Hagloch
  Secretary: Jill Chuckerman
  Treasurer: Jim Masini
Management:
  Public Relations Director: Jill Cluckerman
  Industry Liaison: Connie Anderko
Mission: To present comedies, dramas, musicals, mysteries and other theatrical events to the Chicago community.
Utilizes: Singers
Founded: 1981
Specialized Field: Classic; Ensembles
Status: Nonprofit
Paid Staff: 7
Income Sources: Ticket Revenue; Concessions Revenue; Playbill Ad Revenue; Donations
Performs At: Saint Bonaventure Parish
Annual Attendance: 1,200-1,500
Type of Stage: Flexible Proscenium
Seating Capacity: 70-100
Organization Type: Performing

2584
SEANACHAI THEATRE COMPANY
5108 N Ashland
#2
Chicago, IL 60640
Phone: 773-878-3727
Fax: 847-729-8274
e-mail: info@seanachai.org
Management:
  Artistic Director: Michael Grant
  Managing Director: John Dunleavy
  Literary Manager: Karen Tarjan
Specialized Field: Ensembles; Drama; Comedy

2585
SECOND CITY
1616 N Wells Street
Chicago, IL 60614
Phone: 312-664-4032
Fax: 312-664-9837
Toll-free: 877-778-4707
e-mail: aalexander@secondcity.com
Web Site: www.secondcity.com
Officers:
  Executive Producer/CEO: Andrew Alexander
Management:
  President: Andrew Alexander
  Managing Director: Jenna Aotoveoli
  Producer: Kelly Leonard
Mission: Satirical Revue.
Founded: 1959
Specialized Field: Comedy
Status: For-Profit, Professional
Paid Staff: 100
Paid Artists: 50
Performs At: Second City Mainstatge; Second City, Ect.
Type of Stage: Proscenium
Seating Capacity: 350; 180
Organization Type: Performing; Touring; Resident; Educational

2586
SHATTERED GLOBE THEATER
4001 N Ravenswood
Chicago, IL 60613
Phone: 773-404-1237
Fax: 773-404-1237
e-mail: shatteredglobetheater@gmail.com
Web Site: http://www.shatteredglobe.org/index.html
Officers:
  President: Brian Pudil
  VP: Joe Forbrich
  Secretary: Leigh Horsley
  Treasurer: Linda Reiter
Management:
  Artistic Director: Roger Smart
Mission: The foundation of the Shattered Globe is a core of actors, directors, playwrights, designers and teachers working together as the result of having received similar training in the Sanford Meisner technique.
Utilizes: Guest Companies; New Productions; Singers
Founded: 1990
Specialized Field: Contemporary
Status: Semi-Professional; Commercial
Paid Staff: 15
Income Sources: League of Chicago Theatres
Performs At: Chicago Actors Project
Organization Type: Performing; Resident; Educational

2587
STAGE LEFT THEATRE
3408 N Sheffield
Chicago, IL 60657
Phone: 773-883-8830
Fax: 773-472-1336
e-mail: sltchicago@aol.com
Web Site: www.stagelefttheatre.com

Officers:
  President: Jay Tarshis
  Treasurer: Wendy Istvanick
  Secretary: Dr Alice Martin
Management:
  Co-Artistic Director: Jessi D Hill
  Artistic Director: Kevin Heckman
  Development Director: Jacki Singleton
  Company Manager: Leigh Barrett
Mission: Producing plays that raise awareness of social and political issues.
Utilizes: Actors; Artists-in-Residence; Choreographers; Collaborating Artists; Collaborations; Designers; Five Seasonal Concerts; Guest Accompanists; Guest Choreographers; Guest Companies; Guest Conductors; Guest Designers; Guest Musical Directors; Guest Teachers; Instructors; Local Artists; Performance Artists; Poets; Resident Artists; Resident Professionals; Selected Students; Sign Language Translators; Student Interns; Special Technical Talent; Visual Arts
Founded: 1982
Specialized Field: Contemporary
Status: Non-Profit, Professional
Paid Staff: 2
Volunteer Staff: 19
Paid Artists: 20
Income Sources: League of Chicago Theatres
Facility Category: Storefront
Type of Stage: Black Box
Seating Capacity: 50
Organization Type: Performing; Touring; Educational

2588
STEPPENWOLF THEATRE COMPANY
1650 N Halsted Street
Chicago, IL 60614
Phone: 312-335-1650
Fax: 312-335-0808
e-mail: customerservice@steppenwolf.org
Web Site: www.steppenwolf.org
Management:
  Executive Director: David Hockinson
  Artistic Director: Martha Lavey
  Casting Director: Erica Daniels
  Internship Coordinator: Libby Ford
Mission: Committed to an ensemble approach.
Utilizes: Guest Companies; Scenic Designers; Singers; Students
Founded: 1976
Specialized Field: Ensemble
Status: Non-Profit, Professional
Paid Staff: 60
Income Sources: Theatre Communications Group; Actors' Equity Association; Producers Association of Chicago Theatres
Performs At: Steppenwolf Theater
Type of Stage: Removable Thrust
Seating Capacity: 510
Organization Type: Performing; Resident; Educational

2589
STRAWDOG THEATRE COMPANY
3829 N Broadway
Chicago, IL 60613
Phone: 773-528-9889
Fax: 773-528-7238
Web Site: www.strawdog.org
Management:
  Marketing Manager: Juile Stanton
  Press Public Relation: Shanon Hoag
  Artistic Director: Nic Diamond
  Managing Director: Tim Zingelman
Mission: To inspire and provoke through ensemble based theatrical works.

Founded: 1988
Specialized Field: Staged Readings; Drama
Status: Non-Profit, Professional
Volunteer Staff: 15
Paid Artists: 15
Non-paid Artists: 15

2590
THEATRE BUILDING CHICAGO
Performance Community
1225 W Belmont
Chicago, IL 60657
Phone: 773-929-7367
Fax: 312-327-1404
Web Site: www.theatrebuildingchicago.org
Management:
    Executive Director: Joan Mazzonelli
    Artistic Director: John Sparks
    Managing Director: Alan Chambers
Mission: To give exposure to new musicals; to support emerging artists in our Chicago area.
Founded: 1977
Specialized Field: Multi-Media; Musical
Status: Non-Profit, Professional
Paid Staff: 7
Income Sources: League of Chicago Theatres; Theatre Communications Group; National Alliance of Theatre Producers
Performs At: New Tuners Theatre Building
Organization Type: Performing; Resident

2591
THEATRE FIRST
6656 Sioux Avenue
Chicago, IL 60646
Phone: 773-792-2226
Management:
    Executive Producer: Joanne Notz
    Business Manager: William Mages
Utilizes: Guest Artists
Founded: 1952
Specialized Field: Contemporary
Status: Non-Professional
Income Sources: League of Chicago Theatres
Performs At: Athenaeum Theatre
Organization Type: Performing

2592
THEATRE II COMPANY
3700 W 103Rd Street
Chicago, IL 60655
Phone: 773-298-3000
Management:
    Artistic Director: Steve Micotto
    Managing Director: Joanne Fleming
Mission: Providing the Southwest Chicago community with quality live theater.
Utilizes: Singers
Founded: 1978
Specialized Field: Ensembles; Contemporary
Status: Professional; Nonprofit
Income Sources: League of Chicago Theatres; Saint Xavier University
Performs At: McGuire Hall
Organization Type: Performing

2593
TIMELINE THEATRE COMPANY
615 W Wellington Avenue
Chicago, IL 60657
Phone: 773-281-8463
Fax: 773-281-1134
e-mail: info@timelinetheatre.com
Web Site: www.timelinetheatre.com

Mission: To present plays inspired by history that connect with today's social and political issues.
Founded: 1997
Specialized Field: New Works of Social Importance

2594
VICTORY GARDENS THEATER AT THE BIOGRAPH
2243 N Lincoln Avenue
Chicago, IL 60614
Phone: 773-871-3000
e-mail: information,@victorygardens.org
Web Site: www.victorygardens.org
Management:
    Managing Director: Marcelle McVay
    Artistic Director: Dennis Zacek
Mission: Developing Chicago theatre artists, particularly playwrights.
Utilizes: Actors; AEA Actors; Designers; Educators; Five Seasonal Concerts; Guest Companies; Guest Conductors; Guest Designers; High School Drama; Instructors; Local Artists; Multimedia; Original Music Scores; Performance Artists; Poets; Resident Professionals; Selected Students; Singers; Soloists; Student Interns; Special Technical Talent
Founded: 1974
Specialized Field: Musical; Comedy; Ethnic Theater; Contemporary
Status: Non-Profit, Professional
Paid Staff: 14
Paid Artists: 3
Budget: $1.6M
Performs At: Block Box
Annual Attendance: 60,000+
Type of Stage: Black Box
Seating Capacity: 195
Rental Contact: Elizabeth Auman
Organization Type: Performing; Touring; Resident; Educational

2595
WOMEN'S THEATRE ALLIANCE
2936 N Southport
Suite 1775
Chicago, IL 60657
e-mail: wtachicago@gmail.com
Web Site: http://www.wtachicago.org/1401.html
Management:
    President: Brenda Kelly
    Vice President: Katie Carey
    Treasurer/Secretary: Scott Dray
Specialized Field: Ensembles; Theater Workshops; Specialty Acts

2596
DES PLAINES THEATRE GUILD
620 Lee Street
Des Plaines, IL 60016
Phone: 708-296-1211
Mission: Offering Northwest Suburban Chicago professional level community theatre for the education and entertainment of audiences.
Utilizes: Guest Companies
Founded: 1946
Specialized Field: Community Theater
Status: Non-Professional; Nonprofit
Performs At: Prairie Lake Community Center
Organization Type: Performing

2597
UNIVERSITY THEATRE: SUMMER SHOW BIZ
Southern Ilinois University
Campus Box 1777
Katherine Dunham Hall 1031
Edwardsville, IL 62026-1777
Phone: 618-650-2773
Fax: 618-650-3716
Toll-free: 888-328-5168
e-mail: dbrown@siue.edu
Web Site: www.siue.edu/theater
Management:
    Chairman: C Otis Sweezey
    Dance Director: C Otis Sweezey
    Director Design and Technical: James Dorethy
    Director Performance: Peter Cocuzza
Founded: 1975
Specialized Field: Musical; Comedy; Youth Theater; Dinner Theater; Ethnic Theater; Community Theater; Puppet; Classic; Contemporary
Status: Non-Profit, Professional
Paid Staff: 1
Paid Artists: 19
Season: June - July
Type of Stage: Proscenium
Stage Dimensions: 50' x 30'
Seating Capacity: 360

2598
NEXT THEATRE COMPANY
927 Noyes Street
Evanston, IL 60201
Phone: 847-475-1875
Fax: 847-475-6767
e-mail: info@nexttheatre.org
Web Site: www.nexttheatre.org
Officers:
    President: Judy Kemp
    Secretary: Ann Zastrow
    Treasurer: Jeff Enrich
Management:
    Artistic Director: Jennifer Avery
    Producing Director: Jim Davis
    Advance Services Manager: Amy Buckler
    Production Manager: Patrick Fries
Mission: We believe theatre promotes awarness and provokes change with more power than any other form of expression, and we are devoted to producing socially provocative artistically challenging entertainment.
Utilizes: Guest Companies; Singers
Founded: 1981
Specialized Field: Comedy; Puppet; Classic; Contemporary
Status: Non-Profit, Professional
Paid Staff: 5
Paid Artists: 50
Budget: $600,000
Income Sources: Actors' Equity Association; Theatre Communications Group; League of Chicago Theatres; Producers Association of Chicago Area Theatres
Performs At: Noyes Cultural Arts Center Theatre
Annual Attendance: 15,000
Type of Stage: Proscenium
Stage Dimensions: 24' x 33'
Seating Capacity: 167
Organization Type: Performing; Resident

2599
NORTHWESTERN UNIVERSITY THEATRE AND INTERPRETATION CENTER
1949 Campus Drive
Evanston, IL 60208

All listings are in alphabetical order by state, then city, then organization within the city.

Phone: 847-491-3170
Fax: 847-467-7135
Web Site: www.tic.northwestern.edu
Management:
 Managing Director: Claudia Kunin
Specialized Field: Musical; Comedy; Youth Theater;
Ethnic Theater; Community Theater; Puppet; Classic;
Contemporary
Status: Non-Profit, Non-Professional
Paid Staff: 20

2600
ORGANIC THEATER COMPANY
1125 W Loyola Avenue
Evanston, IL 60657
Phone: 847-675-5167
Fax: 847-675-2695
Officers:
 President: Holly I Myers
 VP/Secretary: Judith Thomson
 Treasurer: Mark Thomas
Management:
 Producing Artistic Director: Ina Marlowe
 Managing Director: Katie Klemme
Mission: To develop and produce new works of theatre
and to nurture the artists involved in that process;
interested in adventurous, challenging scripts that truly
explore the theatrical medium and its possibilities.
Utilizes: Actors; AEA Actors; Collaborations;
Designers; Educators; Five Seasonal Concerts; Guest
Companies; Guest Soloists; Guild Activities; High
School Drama; Instructors; Lyricists; New Productions;
Organization Contracts; Original Music Scores;
Performance Artists; Resident Professionals; Student
Interns
Founded: 1960
Specialized Field: Educational; Theater Workshops
Status: Professional; Nonprofit
Paid Staff: 5
Volunteer Staff: 15
Paid Artists: 40
Budget: $300,0000
Income Sources: League of Chicago Theatres;
Theatre Communications Group
Affiliations: AEA CAT, TYA
Annual Attendance: 15,000
Facility Category: House
Type of Stage: Proscenium
Seating Capacity: 260
Organization Type: Performing; Educational

2601
PIVEN THEATRE WORKSHOP
927 Noyes Street
Evanston, IL 60201
Phone: 847-866-6597
Fax: 847-866-6614
Web Site: www.piventheatreworkshop.org
Officers:
 President: Marcia Cahn
 Vice President: David Doyle
 Treasurer: Eric Rubenstein
 Secretary: Emily Neuberger
Management:
 Executive Director: Jen Green
 Artistic Director: Joyce Piven
 Managing Director: Jen Sultz
Mission: To provide professional theatre and an actors
training center for children and adults.
Utilizes: Actors; AEA Actors; Artists-in-Residence;
Choreographers; Collaborations; Commissioned
Composers; Commissioned Music; Dancers;
Designers; Five Seasonal Concerts; Grant Writers;
Guest Accompanists; Guest Artists; Guest Companies;

Guest Conductors; Guest Designers; Guest
Ensembles; Guest Musical Directors; Guest Teachers;
Guild Activities; High School Drama; Instructors; Local
Artists; Music; Original Music Scores; Performance
Artists; Poets; Resident Professionals; Sign Language
Translators; Soloists; Student Interns; Special Technical
Talent; Visual Arts
Founded: 1972
Specialized Field: Comedy; Youth Theater; Ethnic
Theater; Classic; Contemporary
Status: Non-Profit, Professional
Paid Staff: 20
Paid Artists: 10
Budget: $600,000
Income Sources: Illinois Arts Council; Evanston Arts
Council
Performs At: Noyes Cultural Arts Center
Annual Attendance: 7,500
Type of Stage: Black Box
Seating Capacity: 75
Organization Type: Performing; Educational

2602
ORPHEUM THEATRE
60 S Kellogg Street
Galesburg, IL 61401
Phone: 309-342-2299
Fax: 309-342-2515
Web Site: www.theorpheum.org
Management:
 Managing Director: Jennifer Rakestraw
Mission: To promote and preserve the Orpheum
Theatre as a premier presentation venue for the
community.
Utilizes: Actors; Dance Companies; Educators; Grant
Writers; Guest Accompanists; Guest Soloists;
Multimedia; Original Music Scores; Sign Language
Translators; Soloists; Special Technical Talent; Theatre
Companies
Founded: 1916
Specialized Field: Musical; Comedy; Youth Theater;
Dinner Theater; Ethnic Theater; Community Theater;
Puppet; Classic; Contemporary
Status: Non-Profit, Non-Professional
Paid Staff: 2
Volunteer Staff: 30
Budget: $252,000
Income Sources: City of Galesburg; Illinois
Affiliations: American Society of Composers, Authors
and Publishers
Facility Category: Performance Theatre
Type of Stage: Proscenium
Stage Dimensions: 59'x 40'
Seating Capacity: 952
Year Built: 1916
Year Remodeled: 1989
Rental Contact: Business Manager Danny Davis
Organization Type: Performing; Touring; Educational
Resident Groups: Prairie Players

2603
PRAIRIE PLAYERS CIVIC THEATRE
160 S Seminary S
Galesburg, IL 61402
Mailing Address: PO Box 831
Phone: 309-343-7728
e-mail: info@prairieplayers.com
Web Site: www.prairieplayers.com
Officers:
 President: Dennis Clark
 VP: Kenny Knox
 Secretary: Anita Reese
 Treasurer: Bob Gutermuth
Management:

President: Judy Diemer
VP: Jerry Hendel
Secretary: Don Blaheta
Treasurer: Vera Fornander
Mission: To sustain live theatre arts in a rural setting.
Utilizes: Guest Companies; Singers
Founded: 1915
Specialized Field: Dinner Theater; Community
Theater; Puppet
Status: Non-Profit
Income Sources: Association of Kansas Theatres
Organization Type: Performing; Resident

2604
WRITERS' THEATRE CHICAGO
Books on Vernon
664 Vernon Avenue
Glencoe, IL 60022
Phone: 847-835-7366
Fax: 847-835-5332
Management:
 Artistic Director: Michael Halberstam
 Executive Director: John W Adams
Mission: The Writers Theatre is a professional
company dedicated to a theatre of language and
passion.
Founded: 1992
Specialized Field: Drama; Young Playwrights
Paid Staff: 9
Performs At: Nichols Pennell Theatre

2605
CONKLIN'S BARN 2 DINNER THEATRE
Conklin Court
PO Box 310
Goodfield, IL 61742
Mailing Address: PO Box 310
Phone: 309-965-2545
Fax: 309-965-2735
Web Site: www.barn2.com
Management:
 President: Mary Simon
 Manager: Chaunce Conklin
Mission: To entertain, to educate and to promote live
performance.
Utilizes: Contract Orchestras; Resident Professionals
Founded: 1994
Specialized Field: Dinner Theater
Status: For-Profit, Professional
Organization Type: Performing; Resident

2606
APPLE TREE THEATRE
595 Elm Place
Suite 210
Highland Park, IL 60035
Phone: 847-432-8223
Fax: 847-432-5214
e-mail: appletreetheatre@yahoo.com
Web Site: www.appletreetheatre.com
Management:
 Executive/Artistic Director: Eileen Boevers
 Managing Director: Pim Statoer
 Producing Director: Cecilie Keenan
 Director Development: Mary Ellen Mason
 Production Manager: Tim Stadler
 Workshop/TYA Artistic Directors: Barbara Harris
Mission: Is committed to producing a diverse and
challenging selection of both dramas and musicals,
from new works to classics, all of which illuminate the
human condition.
Utilizes: Actors; AEA Actors; Choreographers;
Commissioned Composers; Dancers; Designers;
Educators; Five Seasonal Concerts; Grant Writers;

Guest Accompanists; Guest Artists; Guest Conductors; Guest Designers; Guest Ensembles; Guest Lecturers; Guest Musical Directors; High School Drama; Local Artists; Multimedia; Original Music Scores
Founded: 1983
Specialized Field: Musical; Comedy; Youth Theater; Dinner Theater; Ethnic Theater; Classic; Contemporary
Status: Non-Profit, Professional
Paid Staff: 8
Volunteer Staff: 15
Paid Artists: 40
Budget: $1,200,000
Income Sources: Grants; Donations; Ticket Sales
Annual Attendance: 30,000
Type of Stage: Thrust
Seating Capacity: 177+

2607
MARRIOTT'S THEATRE IN LINCOLNSHIRE
10 Marriott Drive
Lincolnshire, IL 60069
Phone: 847-634-0200
Fax: 847-634-7358
Web Site: www.marriotttheatre.com
Management:
    Executive Director: Terry E James
    Artistic Director: Aaron Thielen
    President of Marriott Corporation: J W Marriott
    Production Manager: Adam Ford
Mission: Presenting five productions annually, including classic musicals, rarely-seen musicals, and premieres of new works.
Utilizes: AEA Actors; Choreographers; Dancers; Designers; Local Artists; Music; Resident Professionals; Sign Language Translators
Founded: 1975
Specialized Field: Musical; Comedy; Youth Theater; Dinner Theater
Status: For-Profit, Professional
Income Sources: League of Chicago Theatres; American Dinner Theatre Institute
Performs At: Marriott's Lincolnshire Theatre
Affiliations: NAMT
Annual Attendance: 400,000
Type of Stage: In the Round
Seating Capacity: 882
Year Built: 1978
Organization Type: Performing; Resident

2608
ENCORE PLAYERS
222 E Sargent
Litchfield, IL 62056
Phone: 217-326-4414
Officers:
    President: Keith Purcell
    VP: Joel Schnur
    Treasurer: Dick Butler
    Secretary: Pauline Coughlan
Management:
    Director: Mae Morton
    Director: Dennis Plozizka
    Director: David Lewey
    Director: Tim Price
    Artistic Director: George Dawson
Mission: To promote art and the development of artistic ability as well as related theatrical skills; to encourage public appreciation of theatrical arts.
Utilizes: Guest Companies
Founded: 1968
Specialized Field: Musical; Dinner Theater; Community Theater
Status: Non-Professional; Nonprofit

Performs At: Community Center
Organization Type: Performing

2609
SUMMER MUSIC THEATRE
Western Illinois University Theatre/Dance Dep
Browne Hall 101
Macomb, IL 61455
Phone: 309-298-1543
Fax: 309-298-2695
e-mail: de-patrick@wiu.edu
Web Site: www.wiu.edu/theatre
Management:
    Managing Director: David Patrick
Mission: To offer professional musical theatre to the community; to provide training for students. Western Illinois University offers the BFA in musical theatre, BA and MFA degrees in acting, directing, and design.
Utilizes: Guest Companies; Singers
Founded: 1972
Specialized Field: Musical; Summer Stock
Status: Non-Profit, Non-Professional
Paid Staff: 10
Season: June - August
Performs At: Hainline Theatre and Horrabin Theatre
Type of Stage: Proscenium/Thrust
Seating Capacity: 387/150
Year Built: 1972
Organization Type: Performing; Resident; Educational

2610
COLEMAN PUPPET THEATRE
1516 S Second Avenue
Maywood, IL 60153
Phone: 708-344-2920
Management:
    Director: FR Coleman
    Director: Barbara Coleman
Mission: To preserve and perpetuate stories, both classic and modern through dramatization with puppets.
Founded: 1947
Specialized Field: Puppet
Status: Professional
Income Sources: Puppeteers of America; Chicagoland Puppetry Guild; Puppeteers of America
Organization Type: Performing; Touring

2611
TIMBER LAKE PLAYHOUSE
PO Box 29
Mt. Carroll, IL 61053
Phone: 815-244-2035
Fax: 815-244-2035
e-mail: info@timberlakeplayhouse.org
Web Site: www.timberlakeplayhouse.org
Officers:
    President: Diane Olds
Management:
    Artistic Director: Brad Lyons
Mission: Dedicated to providing a center for cultural opportunity for developing artists and a showcase of quality theatre for the residents of the Midwest, particularly in Northwestern Illinois and Eastern Iowa.
Founded: 1961
Specialized Field: Musical; Comedy; Youth Theater; Contemporary; Summer Stock
Status: Non-Profit, Professional
Paid Staff: 2
Season: June - September
Type of Stage: Semi-Thrust
Seating Capacity: 375

2612
ILLINOIS SHAKESPEARE FESTIVAL
Illinois State University
Box 5700
Normal, IL 61790-5700
Phone: 309-438-8974
Fax: 309-438-5806
Toll-free: 866-457-4253
e-mail: shake@ilstu.edu
Web Site: www.thefestival.org
Management:
    Managing Director: Dick Folse
    Artistic Director: Deb Alley
Utilizes: Actors; AEA Actors; Designers; Guest Conductors; Guest Designers; Guest Writers; Guild Activities; Original Music Scores; Resident Artists; Resident Professionals; Soloists; Student Interns
Founded: 1978
Specialized Field: Outdoor Theater; Classic; Shakespeare
Status: Non-Profit, Professional
Paid Staff: 80
Paid Artists: 40
Budget: $1.2 Million
Income Sources: Box Office, Fund Raising
Season: June - August
Performs At: Ewing Manor
Affiliations: U/RTA; Actors' Equity Association; SSDC
Annual Attendance: 14,000
Facility Category: Outdoor
Type of Stage: Thrust
Seating Capacity: 438
Year Built: 2000
Cost: $1.65 million
Organization Type: Performing; Educational

2613
OAK PARK FESTIVAL THEATRE
PO Box 4114
Oak Park, IL 60303
Phone: 708-445-4440
Fax: 708-524-4950
e-mail: ArtisticDirector@oakparkfestival.com
Web Site: http://oakparkfestival.com/
Officers:
    Co-President: Kevin Theis
    Co-President: Belinda Bremmer
    Treasurer: Robert Behr
    Secretary: Molly Surowitz
Management:
    Artistic Director: Jack Hickey
    Managing Director: Lisa Gordon
Utilizes: Actors; AEA Actors; Collaborations; Designers; Guest Companies; Guest Instructors; Instructors; Local Artists; Resident Professionals; Selected Students; Singers; Soloists; Student Interns
Founded: 1975
Specialized Field: Summer Stock
Status: Professional; Nonprofit
Paid Staff: 20
Volunteer Staff: 14
Budget: $160,000
Income Sources: Illinois Arts Council; Oak Park Area Arts Council; Foundations; Membership
Season: July - August
Performs At: Outside
Affiliations: Actors Equity Association; League of Chicago Theatres; Producers Association of Chicago
Facility Category: Outdoor
Type of Stage: Platform
Seating Capacity: 350
Organization Type: Performing

2614
VILLAGE PLAYERS THEATER
1010 W Madison Street
Oak Park, IL 60302
Phone: 708-921-0645
Fax: 708-383-9829
e-mail: tickets@village-players.org
Web Site: www.village-players.org
    Treasurer: Robby Robinson
Management:
    Artistic Director: Dan Taube
    Production Manager: Rick Julien
Mission: Promoting community involvement in cultural arts; developing theatrical ability through public performances and education.
Utilizes: Actors; AEA Actors; Choreographers; Dancers; Designers; Educators; Five Seasonal Concerts; Grant Writers; Guest Accompanists; Guest Artists; Guest Companies; Guest Conductors; Guest Directors; Guest Lecturers; Guest Musical Directors; High School Drama; Instructors; Local Artists; Multimedia; Music; New Productions; Original Music Scores; Performance Artists; Resident Professionals; Sign Language Translators; Soloists; Student Interns; Special Technical Talent
Founded: 1961
Specialized Field: Musical; Comedy; Youth Theater; Ethnic Theater; Community Theater; Classic; Contemporary
Status: Non-Profit, Professional
Paid Staff: 90
Paid Artists: 10
Budget: 280K
Income Sources: Tickets; Tuition; Grants
Performs At: Persidium
Affiliations: Village Players Theater School
Annual Attendance: 20,000
Facility Category: Mainstage/Blackbox
Type of Stage: Proscenium
Seating Capacity: 222
Organization Type: Performing Resident; Educational

2615
DRURY LANE OAKBROOK TERRACE
100 Drury Lane
Oakbrook Terrace, IL 60181
Phone: 708-530-8300
Fax: 630-530-0436
Web Site: www.drurylaneoakbrook.com
Management:
    Executive Director: Kyle DeSantis
    General Manager: John Tapia
    Artistic Director: Bill Osetek
    Production Manager: Juli Walker
Mission: To present large-scale musicals and comedies that feature leading theatre artists.
Utilizes: Actors; AEA Actors; Choreographers; Music; Resident Professionals
Founded: 1984
Specialized Field: Musical; Dinner Theater
Status: Professional; Non-Professional; Commercial
Income Sources: American Dinner Theatre Association
Performs At: Drury Lane Theater
Facility Category: Theatre/Conference House
Type of Stage: Proscenium
Seating Capacity: 959
Year Built: 1984
Organization Type: Performing; Touring

2616
ILLINOIS THEATRE CENTER
371 Artists' Walk
PO Box 397
Park Forest, IL 60466
Phone: 708-481-3510
Fax: 708-481-3693
e-mail: ilthetr@big planet.com
Web Site: www.ilthetr.org
Officers:
    President: Denyse Carreras
    Secretary: Candace Kleindorfer
Management:
    Producing Artistic Director: Etel Billig
    Music Director: Jonathan Roark Billing
    Administrative Assistant: Alexandra Murdoch
Mission: To bring professional, equity productions of new and award winning plays and musicals to residents of the Southland and surrounding communities; to provide a full season of seven productions, each running one month, and two summer specialized productions.
Utilizes: Actors; AEA Actors; Artists-in-Residence; Collaborating Artists; Dancers; Fine Artists; Five Seasonal Concerts; Guest Accompanists; Guest Artists; Guest Companies; Guest Conductors; Guest Designers; Guest Musical Directors; Instructors; Local Artists; Music; Organization Contracts; Original Music Scores; Performance Artists; Selected Students; Sign Language Translators; Singers; Soloists
Founded: 1976
Specialized Field: Drama; Musical
Status: Professional; Nonprofit
Paid Staff: 8
Volunteer Staff: 6
Paid Artists: 42
Performs At: Illinois Theatre Center
Affiliations: Actors' Equity Association; Theatre Communications Group; League of Chicago Theatres
Annual Attendance: 32,000
Facility Category: Theatre
Type of Stage: Proscenium
Seating Capacity: 179
Year Remodeled: 1999
Cost: $265,000
Organization Type: Performing; Touring; Resident; Educational

2617
PEORIA CIVIC CENTER
201 SW Jefferson Street
Peoria, IL 61602-1448
Phone: 309-673-8900
Fax: 309-673-9223
e-mail: info@peoriaciviccenter.com
Web Site: www.peoriaciviccenter.com
Management:
    Director Marketing: Marc Burnett
    General Manager: Debbie Ritschel
    Director Operations: Will Kenney
    Director Event Services: Jim Weatherington
Founded: 1982
Specialized Field: Musical; Comedy; Youth Theater; Dinner Theater; Ethnic Theater; Community Theater; Classic; Contemporary
Paid Staff: 450

2618
PEORIA PLAYERS THEATRE
4300 N University
Peoria, IL 61614
Fax: 309-688-4474
e-mail: players@mtco.com
Web Site: www.peoriaplayers.org
Officers:
    President: Stan Ellwood
    Business Administrator: Nicki Haschke
Mission: Enhances and promotes a tradition of excellence in community theatre by providing theatrical entertainment and by giving everyone an opportunity to participate in the theatre experience.
Founded: 1919
Specialized Field: Musical; Comedy; Youth Theater; Community Theater; Puppet; Classic; Contemporary
Status: Non-Profit, Non-Professional
Paid Staff: 2
Volunteer Staff: 50
Non-paid Artists: 100
Budget: $150,000
Income Sources: American Association of Community Theatres; Illinois Theatre Association
Performs At: Peoria Players Theatre
Annual Attendance: 13,000
Facility Category: Handicap-Accessible
Type of Stage: Proscenium
Stage Dimensions: 20x36
Seating Capacity: 350
Year Built: 1957
Year Remodeled: 2000
Rental Contact: Nicki Haschke
Organization Type: Performing; Resident; Educational

2619
CIRCA '21 DINNER PLAYHOUSE
1828 3rd Avenue
Rock Island, IL 61201
Phone: 309-786-7733
Fax: 309-786-4119
e-mail: dpjh@circa21.com
Web Site: www.circa21.com
Management:
    Producer: Dennis Hitchcock
Mission: To offer professional musicals and plays year-round along with the finest in dining.
Utilizes: Dancers; Grant Writers; Guest Artists; Guest Lecturers
Founded: 1921
Specialized Field: Dinner Theater
Status: Professional; Commercial
Paid Staff: 65
Affiliations: Vaudeville House Converted
Annual Attendance: 65,000
Type of Stage: Proscenium with Thrust
Seating Capacity: 336
Year Built: 1920
Year Remodeled: 1977
Cost: $500,000
Organization Type: Performing; Touring; Resident

2620
NEW AMERICAN THEATER
118 N Main Street
Rockford, IL 61101
Phone: 815-963-9454
Fax: 815-963-7215
Web Site: www.newamericantheater.com
Management:
    President: Stewart Cohn
    Artistic Director: Tony Vezner
Mission: Presenting classic and modern as well as new work.
Utilizes: Guest Companies; Singers
Founded: 1972

Specialized Field: Musical; Comedy; Youth Theater; Dinner Theater; Ethnic Theater; Community Theater; Puppet; Classic; Contemporary
Status: Non-Profit, Professional
Paid Staff: 10
Volunteer Staff: 400
Income Sources: Theatre Communications Group
Performs At: New American Theater
Type of Stage: Main; Second
Seating Capacity: 280; 90
Organization Type: Performing; Touring; Resident; Educational

2621
NORTHLIGHT THEATRE
9501 Skokie Boulevard
Skokie, IL 60077
Phone: 847-673-6300
Fax: 847-679-1879
e-mail: bjjones@northlight.org
Management:
    Artistic Director: BJ Jones
    Managing Director: Philip Santora
Mission: The theatre's objective is to challenge, as well as entertain its audiences with a focus to produce compelling new interpretations of contemporary plays drawn from an international repertoire and to create stage adaptions inspired by the full spectrum of artistic disciplines.
Founded: 1974
Specialized Field: Drama; Comedy; Educational
Status: Professional; Nonprofit
Income Sources: Theatre Communications Group; League of Resident Theatres; American Arts Alliance
Performs At: North Shore Center for the Performing Arts
Organization Type: Resident; Producing

2622
PHEASANT RUN THEATRE
4051 E Main
PO Box 64
St Charles, IL 60174
Phone: 708-584-6342
e-mail: info@pheasantrun.com
Web Site: http://www.pheasantrun.com/activities/theater.php
Management:
    Producer/Director: Diana Martinez
Utilizes: Guest Companies
Founded: 1964
Specialized Field: Dinner Theater
Status: Professional; Commercial
Organization Type: Performing

2623
LITTLE THEATRE ON THE SQUARE
16 E Harrison Street
PO Box 288
Sullivan, IL 61951-0288
Phone: 217-728-2065
Fax: 217-728-7525
Toll-free: 888-261-9675
Web Site: www.thelittletheatre.org
Management:
    President: Leonard A Anderson
    Artistic Director: M Seth Reines
Founded: 1957
Specialized Field: Musical; Comedy; Youth Theater; Community Theater; Contemporary
Status: Non-Profit, Professional
Paid Staff: 10
Paid Artists: 30
Season: June - August

Type of Stage: Proscenium
Stage Dimensions: 28' x 27'
Seating Capacity: 450
Year Built: 1928
Year Remodeled: 1958

2624
BOWEN PARK THEATRE & OPERA
39 Jack Benny Drive
Waukegan, IL 60087
Phone: 847-360-4740
Fax: 847-662-0592
Web Site: www.waukeganparks.org
Management:
    Executive Director: Claudia Patrauski
Founded: 1982
Specialized Field: Light Theater; Classic
Status: For-Profit, Professional
Paid Staff: 4
Paid Artists: 40

2625
THEATRE OF WESTERN SPRINGS
4384 Hampton Avenue
Western Springs, IL 60558
Phone: 708-246-3380
Fax: 708-246-4015
e-mail: ad@theatrewesternsprings.com
Web Site: www.theatrewesternsprings.com
Management:
    Business Manager: Allison Burkharht
    Artistic Director: Jack Phillips
    Children's Theatre Director: Scott Illingwarth
Mission: Promoting, developing and maintaining a community theatre that produces interesting, significant plays; providing a forum for artists.
Utilizes: Actors; Collaborations; Designers; Five Seasonal Concerts; Guest Artists; Guest Designers; Guest Lecturers; Guest Soloists; Guest Teachers; Guild Activities; High School Drama; Instructors; Local Artists; Multimedia; Music; Organization Contracts; Original Music Scores; Performance Artists; Resident Artists; Soloists; Student Interns; Special Technical Talent
Founded: 1928
Specialized Field: Community Theater; Children's Theater
Status: Non-Profit, Non-Professional
Paid Staff: 17
Volunteer Staff: 400
Paid Artists: 3
Budget: $750,000
Facility Category: Two theatres
Type of Stage: One open proscenium, one black box
Seating Capacity: 410; 120
Year Built: 1962
Rental Contact: Jeff Arena
Organization Type: Performing; Educational; Sponsoring

2626
INVENTIONS
1047 Gage Street
Winnetka, IL 60093
Phone: 847-446-0183
Fax: 847-446-0183
Web Site: http://home.earthlink.net/~inventions4
Management:
    Co-Founder: T Daniel
    Co-Founder: Laurie Willets
    Co-Founder: John Bruce Yeh
    Co-Founder: Teresa Reilly
Mission: An innovative foursome that strikes out in a new direction! A visual slant to cleverly interpret Classical Music and Mime for the new Century.

Founded: 2000
Specialized Field: Musical; Ensembles
Status: Professional
Paid Staff: 2
Volunteer Staff: 2
Organization Type: Performing; Touring

2627
T DANIEL PRODUCTIONS
6619 N Campbell Street
Winnetka, IL 60645
Phone: 773-743-0277
Fax: 773-743-0276
e-mail: tdaniel@tdanielcreations.com
Web Site: www.tdanielcreations.com
Management:
    Artistic Co-Director/Co-Founder: T Daniel
    Artistic Co-Director/Co-Founder: Laurie Willets
Mission: To create, educate and tour theatrical productions, shows and concert programs dynamically based upon the Art of Mime for audiences of all ages.
Utilizes: Collaborations; Multi Collaborations
Founded: 1971
Specialized Field: Movement Theater
Status: Non-Profit, Professional
Paid Staff: 2
Paid Artists: 2

2628
WOODSTOCK OPERA HOUSE
121 Van Buren Street
PO Box 190
Woodstock, IL 60098
Phone: 815-338-4212
Fax: 815-334-2287
e-mail: jscharres@woodstockil.gov
Web Site: www.woodstockoperahouse.com
Management:
    Managing Director: John H Scharres
Founded: 1890
Specialized Field: Musical; Comedy; Youth Theater; Ethnic Theater; Community Theater; Puppet; Classic; Contemporary
Status: Non-Profit, Non-Professional
Paid Staff: 11
Paid Artists: 4

2629
ZION PASSION PLAY
2500 Dowie Memorial Drive
Zion, IL 60099
Phone: 847-746-2221
Fax: 847-746-1452
e-mail: klangley@ccczion.org
Web Site: www.ccczion.org
Management:
    Artistic Director: Ron Arden
Mission: Biblical production about the life of Jesus Christ.
Utilizes: Singers
Founded: 1935
Specialized Field: Community Theater
Status: Non-Profit, Non-Professional
Paid Staff: 1
Paid Artists: 3
Income Sources: Christ Community Church
Performs At: Christian Arts Auditorium
Seating Capacity: 522
Organization Type: Performing; Resident; Educational

2630

LITTLE THEATRE OF BEDFORD

1704 Brian Lane Way
PO Box 142
Bedford, IN 47421
Phone: 812-279-3009
e-mail: boxoffice@ltb.org
Web Site: www.ltb.org
Officers:
   Treasurer: Denny Underwood
   VP: Tom Taylor
   Secretary: Rachel Fishback
   President: Roger Manning
Management:
   President: Todd Taylor
   VP: Nathan Walden
Mission: To offer an opportunity for amateur directors and performers to entertain our community.
Founded: 1960
Specialized Field: Musical; Community Theater
Status: Nonprofit
Paid Staff: 150
Performs At: Little Theatre
Organization Type: Performing

2631

SHAWNEE THEATRE OF GREENE COUNTY

PO Box 22
Bloomfield, IN 47424
Phone: 812-384-3559
Fax: 812-384-8773
e-mail: shawneetheatre@hotmail.com
Web Site: http://www.shawneetheatre.org/
Officers:
   President: Mary Aiken
Management:
   Producing Director: Matthew Graber
Founded: 1960
Specialized Field: Summer Stock
Status: Non-Equity; Nonprofit
Paid Staff: 6
Volunteer Staff: 26
Paid Artists: 20
Season: June - July
Annual Attendance: 4,900
Type of Stage: Proscenium
Stage Dimensions: 36' x 20'
Seating Capacity: 360
Year Built: 1979

2632

BLOOMINGTON COUNTY PLAYHOUSE

Indiana University
Bloomington, IN 47405
Phone: 812-855-0074
e-mail: hkibbey@indiana.edu
Specialized Field: Educational; Theater Workshops

2633

COMMUNITY THEATRE OF CLAY COUNTY

8 E National
Brazil, IN 47834
Phone: 812-442-1059
Fax: 973-455-1607
Officers:
   President: Susan M Bradbury
   VP: John Berry
   Secretary/Treasurer: Lois Myers

Mission: To provide opportunities for involvement in the arts in Clay County for all ages, by presenting dinner theatre, musicals, children's workshops, senior citizens programs, and sponsoring drama scholarships.
Utilizes: Guest Artists; Guest Companies; Singers
Founded: 1983
Specialized Field: Musical; Dinner Theater; Community Theater
Status: Non-Professional; Nonprofit
Paid Staff: 200
Income Sources: Arts Indiana; Indiana Theatre Association
Organization Type: Performing; Educational

2634

ELKHART CIVIC THEATRE

Bristol Opera House
210 E Vistula, PO Box 252
Bristol, IN 46507-0252
Phone: 574-848-5853
e-mail: webmaster@elkhartcivictheatre.org
Web Site: www.elkartcivictheatre.org
Officers:
   President: Cynthia Antonelli
   VP: Stephanie Yoder
   Treasurer: Timothy Yoder
   Secretary: Connie Deuschle
Management:
   Artistic Director: Leslie Torok
   Technical Director: John Shoup
Mission: To produce and present a high-quality and award-winning community theater.
Utilizes: Actors; Choreographers; Collaborations; Dancers; Grant Writers; Guest Artists; Guest Companies; Guest Conductors; Guest Lecturers; Guild Activities; High School Drama; Local Artists; Organization Contracts; Sign Language Translators; Soloists
Founded: 1946
Specialized Field: Community Theater
Status: Non-Professional; Nonprofit
Paid Staff: 2
Paid Artists: 2
Non-paid Artists: 200
Budget: $125,000
Income Sources: Indiana Arts Commission; Local & Regional Government & Foundation Sources; Business Community; Private & Individual Sources
Performs At: Bristol Opera House
Affiliations: American Association of Community Theatres; ICTL; Performing Arts & Cultural Entertainment of Elkhart County
Annual Attendance: 13,000
Facility Category: Intimate Vaudeville Style Wood Frame/Historic
Type of Stage: Proscenium/Thrust
Stage Dimensions: 17Wx25D
Seating Capacity: 192
Year Built: 1897
Year Remodeled: 1992
Organization Type: Performing; Resident; Educational

2635

JACKSON COUNTY COMMUNITY THEATRE

PO Box 65
Brownstown, IN 47220
Phone: 812-358-5228
e-mail: mail@jcct.org
Web Site: www.jcct.org
Management:
   President: Dot Goodwin
Mission: Producing live plays; bringing cultural programs to our community.

Utilizes: Guest Companies
Founded: 1971
Specialized Field: Dinner Theater; Community Theater
Status: Non-Professional; Nonprofit
Income Sources: Indiana Theatre Association
Performs At: Royal Office Square Theatre
Organization Type: Performing; Educational

2636

DERBY DINNER PLAYHOUSE

525 Marriott Drive
Clarksville, IN 47129
Phone: 812-288-8281
Fax: 812-288-2636
Toll-free: 877-898-8577
e-mail: tickets@derbydinner.com
Web Site: www.derbydinner.com
Management:
   Executive Director: Cindy Knopp
   Artistic Director: Lee Buckholz
   Owner: Bekki Jo Schneider
Mission: Professional dinner theatre.
Utilizes: Actors; Commissioned Composers; Commissioned Music; Designers; Educators; Guest Artists; Guest Companies; Guest Conductors; Guest Designers; Guild Activities; Organization Contracts; Original Music Scores; Performance Artists; Resident Artists; Singers; Soloists; Student Interns
Founded: 1974
Specialized Field: Musical; Comedy; Youth Theater; Dinner Theater
Status: For-Profit, Professional
Paid Staff: 80
Volunteer Staff: 10
Paid Artists: 30
Budget: $4 million
Income Sources: Ticket Sales; Gift Shop, Food, Drink
Performs At: Derby Dinner Playhouse
Affiliations: NAMT, NDTA, ABA, NTA
Annual Attendance: 200,000
Facility Category: Dinner Theatre
Type of Stage: Theatre-in-the-round
Stage Dimensions: 20'x20'
Seating Capacity: 520
Year Remodeled: 1998
Rental Contact: Group Sales Cindy Nevitt
Organization Type: Performing

2637

LINCOLN AMPHITHEATRE: MUSICAL OUTDOOR DRAMA

University of Southern Indiana
8600 University Boulevard
Evansville, IN 47712-3596
Phone: 812-465-1668
Fax: 812-464-0029
Toll-free: 800-264-4223
Web Site: www.lincoln-amphitheatre.com
Officers:
   Marketing Coordinator: Stacy A Brown
Management:
   Artistic Director: Elliot H Wasserman
   Managing Director: M Christopher Boyer
   Producer: Tom Wilhelmus
Founded: 1987
Specialized Field: Musical; Youth Theater; Community Theater; Classic; Contemporary; Outdoor Theater
Status: Non-Profit, Non-Professional
Paid Staff: 20
Volunteer Staff: 20
Paid Artists: 40
Non-paid Artists: 10
Season: June - August
Stage Dimensions: 150' x 80'

Seating Capacity: 150

2638
REPERTORY PEOPLE OF EVANSVILLE
Old Courthouse Building
Room 200
Evansville, IN 47708
Mailing Address: PO Box 3555, Evansville, IN 47734
Phone: 812-423-2060
Web Site: www.repertorypeople.net
Officers:
  Founder: Tom Angermeier
Management:
  Director: Jim Jackson
  Executive Producer: Tom Angermeier
Mission: To present serious American dramas and occasionally comedies.
Founded: 1973
Specialized Field: Community Theater; Educational
Status: Non-Professional; Nonprofit
Organization Type: Performing; Resident

2639
ARENA DINNER THEATRE
719 Rockhill Street
Fort Wayne, IN 46802
Mailing Address: PO Box 11992
Phone: 260-424-5622
Web Site: http://www.arenadinnertheatre.org/
Management:
  President: Dave Frey
  Vice President: Fred Karuskopf
  Secretary: David Siples
  Treasurer: Brian Schilb
Mission: To provide an additional option for actors and theatre-goers in the community.
Founded: 1974
Specialized Field: Dinner Theater; Community Theater
Status: Non-Professional
Paid Staff: 50
Income Sources: Fine Arts Foundation; Indiana Theatre Association
Organization Type: Performing

2640
FIRST PRESBYTERIAN THEATER
300 W Wayne Street
Fort Wayne, IN 46802
Phone: 260-422-6329
Fax: 260-422-5111
e-mail: thomhof@juno.com
Management:
  Artistic Director: Thom Hofrichter
Mission: To produce provocative contemporary and classical drama in a supportive atmosphere.
Utilizes: Guest Companies
Founded: 1968
Specialized Field: Community Theater
Status: Nonprofit
Paid Staff: 2
Volunteer Staff: 14
Non-paid Artists: 75
Income Sources: Fort Wayne Community Arts Council
Annual Attendance: 8000
Facility Category: 300 Seat Proscenium
Type of Stage: Proscenium
Stage Dimensions: 50 x 22
Seating Capacity: 300
Year Built: 1968
Year Remodeled: 2001
Organization Type: Performing; Educational

2641
FORT WAYNE CIVIC THEATRE
303 E Main Street
Fort Wayne, IN 46802
Phone: 260-422-8641
Fax: 260-422-6699
e-mail: pcolglazier@fwcivic.org
Web Site: www.fwcivic.org
Officers:
  President: Randall Steiner
  VP: John Burns
  Treasurer: Mark Rupp
  Secretary: Edward Kos
  VP: Ken Menefee
Management:
  President: Phillip Colglazier
  Business Manager: Mahlon Houlihan
  Marketing Director: Carolyn Hasty
Mission: Dedicated to strengthening itself as a significant cultural force in the Fort Wayne area through excellence in programming, theatre education and development of talent in the disciplines of theatre and the related performing arts.
Utilizes: Actors; Choreographers; Collaborating Artists; Collaborations; Commissioned Music; Dancers; Designers; Educators; Fine Artists; Five Seasonal Concerts; Grant Writers; Guest Accompanists; Guest Artists; Guest Designers; Guest Musical Directors; Guest Writers; Guild Activities; Instructors; Lyricists; Multimedia; Music; New Productions; Organization Contracts; Resident Professionals; Sign Language Translators; Soloists; Student Interns; Touring Companies; Visual Arts
Founded: 1928
Specialized Field: Musical; Comedy; Youth Theater; Community Theater
Status: Non-Profit, Non-Professional
Paid Staff: 11
Performs At: The Performing Arts Center
Annual Attendance: 50,000
Facility Category: Community Theatre
Type of Stage: Proscenium
Stage Dimensions: 60x30
Seating Capacity: 669
Year Built: 1973
Rental Contact: Shellie Englehart
Organization Type: Resident

2642
BRIDGEWORK THEATER
113 1/2 E Lincoln Avenue
Goshen, IN 46528-3228
Phone: 219-534-1085
Fax: 574-534-9493
Toll-free: 800-200-1602
e-mail: scripts@bridgework.org
Web Site: www.bridgework.org
Officers:
  President: Ruth Hollinger
  VP: Shirley Lint
  Treasurer: Cheryl Cooper
  Secretary: Lynn Miller
Management:
  Director: Donald C Yost
Mission: Goal is to help children through the art of theater. Plays address real life problems of young people, and model proven methods that empower youth to develop nonviolent solutions to those problems.
Utilizes: Actors; Five Seasonal Concerts; Guest Companies; Original Music Scores; Resident Professionals; Theatre Companies
Founded: 1979
Specialized Field: Drama; Contemporary

Status: Professional; Nonprofit
Organization Type: Performing; Touring

2643
BEEF AND BOARDS DINNER THEATRE
9301 N Michigan Road
Indianapolis, IN 46268
Phone: 317-872-9664
Fax: 317-876-0510
Web Site: www.beefandboards.com
Management:
  Managing Director: Robert Zehr
  Artistic Director: Douglas Stark
  Associate Producer: Eddie Curry
  Media Relations: JoEllen Miller
Utilizes: Actors; AEA Actors; Choreographers; Dancers
Founded: 1971
Specialized Field: Dinner Theater
Status: For-Profit, Professional
Paid Staff: 100
Income Sources: National Dinner Theatre Association; American Dinner Theatre Institute
Performs At: Beef and Boards Dinner Theatre
Facility Category: Dinner Theatre
Type of Stage: 3/4 Thrust
Seating Capacity: 480
Rental Contact: Pat Minneman
Organization Type: Performing

2644
CABARET AT THE COLUMBIA CLUB
The Cabaret at the Columbia Club
121 Monument Circle
Indianapolis, IN 46204
Phone: 317-275-1169
Fax: 317-686-5443
e-mail: info@thecabaret.org
Web Site: www.thecabaret.org
Management:
  Marketing & PR Manager: Ann Miller, anne@thecabaret.org
  Managing & Artistic Director: Shannon Forsell, shannon@thecabaret.org
Mission: To elevate the cabaret art form; attract, develop and retain high quality local performance talent; and to provide a unique and important contribution to the city's artistic and cultural life.
Utilizes: Actors; Choreographers; Dancers; Designers; Educators; Five Seasonal Concerts; Grant Writers; Guest Accompanists; Guest Artists; Guest Companies; Guest Conductors; Guest Soloists; Instructors; Multi Collaborations; Multimedia; Music; Organization Contracts; Original Music Scores; Performance Artists; Resident Professionals; Sign Language Translators; Student Interns
Founded: 1989
Specialized Field: Cabaret Theatre
Status: Non-Profit, Professional
Annual Attendance: 60,000
Facility Category: Theatre
Type of Stage: Proscenium
Seating Capacity: 125
Year Remodeled: 2010
Rental Contact: Shannon Forsell

2645
EDYVEAN REPERTORY THEATRE
University of Indianapolis
PO Box 47509
Indianapolis, IN 46227-7509
Phone: 317-788-2072
Fax: 317-788-2079
Toll-free: 800-807-7732
Web Site: www.edyvean.org

Management:
Artistic Director: Rose Kleiman
Managing Director: Bill Simmons
Administrative Director: Frederick Marshall
Market/Public Relations Director: Anne Penny
Sales/Box Office Manager: Brandon Truax
Tech Director/Production Manager: Michael Moffatt
Scenic Artist: Christian McKinney
Master Carpenter: Donald-Mac MacIntyre
Costumer: Chistopher Arthur
Mission: Illuminates the human journey by exploring its many dimensions and celebrating its possibilities.
Founded: 1967
Specialized Field: Educational; Theater Workshops
Status: Professional
Performs At: Ransburg Auditorium, University of Indianapolis
Annual Attendance: 12,000
Type of Stage: Proscenium
Seating Capacity: 750

2646
INDIANA REPERTORY THEATRE
140 W Washington Street
Indianapolis, IN 46204-3465
Phone: 317-635-5277
Fax: 317-236-0767
e-mail: info@irtlive.com
Web Site: www.indianarep.com
Officers:
President: William E Smith
Vice President: David Klapper
VP: Jane Schlegel
Secretary: Marjorie Herald
Treasurer: David L. Morgan
Management:
Artistic Director: Janet Allen
Managing Director: Daniel Baker
Marketing Director: Richard Ferguson
Development Director: Meg Gamage Tucker
Mission: Through innovative productions of classic and contemporary plays, the Indiana Repertory Theatre creates high quality, professional theatre of consistent artistic and cultural significance; the theatre also offers student programs.
Utilizes: Actors; AEA Actors; Artists-in-Residence; Choreographers; Collaborating Artists; Collaborations; Commissioned Composers; Commissioned Music; Designers; Educators; Fine Artists; Five Seasonal Concerts; Grant Writers; Guest Accompanists; Guest Artists; Guest Companies; Guest Composers; Guest Conductors; Guest Designers; Guest Ensembles; Guest Lecturers; Guest Musical Directors; Guest Musicians; Guest Soloists; Guest Teachers; High School Drama; Instructors; Local Artists; Lyricists; Multimedia; Music; Original Music Scores; Performance Artists; Playwrights; Poets; Resident Professionals; Selected Students; Sign Language Translators; Singers; Soloists; Visual Arts
Founded: 1972
Specialized Field: Musical; Comedy; Youth Theater; Classic; Contemporary
Status: Non-Profit, Professional
Paid Staff: 35
Paid Artists: 100
Budget: $4,900,000
Income Sources: League of Resident Theatres; Grants from the National Endowment for the Arts; Lila Wallace-Reader's Digest Fund; Schubert Foundation; Ticket Sales
Performs At: Indiana Theatre
Annual Attendance: 124,000
Facility Category: Historic Theatre; Ballroom

Type of Stage: Mainstage; Upperstage; Cabaret
Year Built: 1927
Year Remodeled: 2001
Rental Contact: Erika Keller
Organization Type: Performing; Resident; Educational

2647
PHOENIX THEATRE
749 N Park Avenue
Indianapolis, IN 46202
Phone: 317-635-2381
Fax: 317-635-0010
e-mail: info@phoenixtheatre.org
Management:
President: Frank M Basile
VP: John Fischer
Producing Director: Bryan Fonseca
Managing Director: Sharon Gamble
Founded: 1982
Specialized Field: Drama; Comedy; Theater Workshops
Status: Nonprofit
Budget: $400,000

2648
THEATRE ON THE SQUARE
627 Massachusetts Avenue
Indianapolis, IN 46204
Phone: 317-685-8687
Fax: 317-637-0302
Web Site: www.tots.org
Management:
Executive Artistic Director: Ron Spencer
Mission: To explore contemporary, classic plays and musicals in an intimate environment.
Founded: 1988
Specialized Field: Drama; Comedy

2649
STAR PLAZA THEATRE
I-65 & US 30
8001 Deleware Place
Merrillville, IN 46410
Phone: 219-769-6311
Fax: 219-756-0604
Web Site: www.starplazatheatre.com
Officers:
President: Charles Blum
Management:
President: Charles Blum
General Manager: Mark Bishop
Founded: 1979
Specialized Field: Musical
Status: For-Profit, Professional
Facility Category: Theatre
Seating Capacity: 3400
Year Built: 1979

2650
FOOTLIGHT PLAYERS, INC.
1705 Franklin Street
PO Box 46
Michigan City, IN 46360
Phone: 219-874-4035
e-mail: info@footlightplayers.org
Web Site: www.footlightplayers.org
Management:
General Manager: Kit Lyons
Designer and Technical Director: Richard Heffner
Artistic Director: Dorothy D'Anna
Director: Jacqueline Verdeyen
Treasure/Publicity/Chair: William Wild

Mission: To offer community members an opportunity for self-expression through amateur theatre; to provide education in drama and related subjects.
Utilizes: Guest Companies
Founded: 1950
Specialized Field: Community Theater; Drama
Status: Non-Professional; Nonprofit
Income Sources: Individual donors; business sponsors
Performs At: Footlight Players Theatre
Organization Type: Performing; Resident

2651
RIDGEWOOD ARTS FOUNDATION: THEATRE AT THE CENTER
1040 Ridge Road
Munster, IN 46321-1876
Phone: 219-836-3255
Fax: 219-836-0159
Toll-free: 800-511-1552
Management:
Artistic Director: Michael Weber
Utilizes: Actors; AEA Actors; Choreographers; Dancers; Designers; Five Seasonal Concerts; Grant Writers; Guest Artists; Guest Companies; Guest Composers; Guest Conductors; Guest Designers; Guest Lecturers; Guest Musical Directors; Local Unknown Artists; Multimedia; Music; Original Music Scores; Performance Artists; Resident Professionals; Sign Language Translators; Soloists
Founded: 1991
Specialized Field: Musical
Status: Nonprofit
Season: January - December
Type of Stage: Thrust; Flexible
Stage Dimensions: 12' x 8'
Seating Capacity: 454

2652
THE ROUND BARN THEATRE AT AMISH ACRES
Amish Acres, LLC
1600 W Market Street
Nappanee, IN 46550
Phone: 574-773-4188
Fax: 219-773-4180
Toll-free: 800-800-4942
e-mail: amishacres@amishacres.com
Web Site: www.amishacres.com
Management:
Artistic Director: Laurie Schotz
Producer: Richard Pletcher
Founded: 1986
Specialized Field: Musical; Comedy; Youth Theater; Dinner Theater; Ethnic Theater; Classic; Contemporary
Status: Professional
Income Sources: Ticket Sales
Season: April - December
Performs At: Relocated Historical Round Barn
Type of Stage: Proscenium
Stage Dimensions: 25' x 35'
Seating Capacity: 360
Year Built: 1911
Year Remodeled: 1999
Cost: $1,000,000

2653
BROWN COUNTY PLAYHOUSE
70 Buren Street S
Nashville, IN 47448

Mailing Address: PO Box 1187 Nashville, IN 47448
Phone: 812-988-2123
Fax: 812-856-0698
e-mail: jkinzer@indiana.edu
Web Site: www.indiana.edu/~thtr
Management:
   President: R Keith Michael
   Executive Director: Jonathan Michaelson
   Artistic Director: Dale McFadden
   Managing Director: Marilyn Norris
Mission: The Brown County Playhouse, a professional theatre operated in conjunction with the Indiana University Department of Theatre and Drama, is located in the center of scenic Nashville.
Founded: 1949
Specialized Field: Comedy; Contemporary
Status: Non-Profit, Professional
Paid Staff: 20
Paid Artists: 30

2654
UNIVERSITY OF NOTRE DAME DEPARTMENT OF FILM, TELEVISION & THEATRE

125 Washington Hall
Notre Dame, IN 46556
Phone: 219-631-5956
Fax: 219-631-3566
Management:
   Manager-Washington Hall: Tom Barkes
Specialized Field: Educational; Theater Workshops

2655
OLE OLSEN MEMORIAL THEATRE

154 S Broadway
PO Box 580
Peru, IN 46970
Phone: 765-472-3680
e-mail: postmaster@oleolsen.org
Web Site: www.oleolsen.org
Officers:
   President: Dick Schaffhausen
   Executive VP: Cheryl Jaquay
   Secretary: Michelle Boswell
   Treasurer: Sue Malloy
Management:
   Publicity: Kelly Voss
Mission: Purpose of this organization shall be to promote and encourage interest in the theatrical arts on a non-profit basis.
Founded: 1964
Specialized Field: Community Theater
Status: Non-Professional; Nonprofit
Income Sources: Indiana Community Theatre League; Division of Indiana Theaters
Performs At: High School Auditorium
Organization Type: Performing

2656
BROADWAY THEATRE LEAGUE OF SOUTH BEND

120 W Lasalle Avenue
Suite 101
South Bend, IN 46601
Phone: 574-234-4044
Fax: 219-288-0290
Toll-free: 877-315-1234
Web Site: www.broadwaytheatreleague.com
Management:
   President: Micheal Harding
   Executive Director: Andrew Hoffmann
Founded: 1959

Specialized Field: Youth Theater; Classic; Contemporary; Broadway Musical Revivals
Status: Non-Profit, Professional
Paid Staff: 4
Performs At: Morris Performing Arts Center

2657
INDIANA STATE UNIVERSITY SUMMER STAGE

Indiana State University
540 N 7th Street
Terre Haute, IN 47809
Phone: 812-237-3336
Fax: 812-237-3954
Management:
   Chairman/Artistic Director: Arthur Feinsod
   Production/Business Manager: David Del Colletti
Founded: 1965
Specialized Field: Educational; Theater Workshops
Status: Non-Equity; Nonprofit
Paid Staff: 20
Paid Artists: 20
Season: June 15 - July 28
Type of Stage: Thrust; Arena
Seating Capacity: 250

2658
VINCENNES UNIVERSITY SUMMER THEATRE

1002 N First
Vincennes, IN 47591
Phone: 812-885-4256
Fax: 812-885-5868
Management:
   Managing/Artistic Director: James J Spurrier, PhD
Mission: Offering quality theatrical entertainment to Vincennes and surrounding areas in the summer months.
Utilizes: Singers
Founded: 1968
Specialized Field: Summer Stock; Musical
Status: Semi-Professional; Nonprofit
Performs At: Shircliff Theatre
Organization Type: Performing; Resident; Educational

2659
WAGON WHEEL THEATRE

2517 E Center Street
PO Box 804
Warsaw, IN 46580
Phone: 219-267-8041
Fax: 219-269-7996
Toll-free: 866-823-2618
Web Site: http://www.wagonwheeltheatre.com/theatre
Officers:
   Business Maneger: Carol Craig
   Director Marketing: Carla Robinson
Management:
   Artistic Director: Roy Hine
   Director Marketing: Dan Rhodes
Utilizes: Actors; AEA Actors; Choreographers; Dancers; Designers; Guest Conductors
Founded: 1956
Specialized Field: Theater in the Round
Status: Non-Equity; Commercial
Season: June - September
Type of Stage: Arena
Stage Dimensions: 32' x 35'
Seating Capacity: 835

2660
PURDUE PROFESSIONAL SUMMER THEATRE

1376 Stewart Center
Room 85
West Lafayette, IN 47907
Phone: 317-494-3082
Fax: 317-494-3660
Management:
   Division Theater: Jim O'Connor
   Associate Professor of Theatre: Russ Jones
   Scenic Construction Supervisor: Ron Clark
   Secretary/Account Clerk: Darlene Flook
   Costume Shop Manager: Shauna Meador
   Operations Manager: Rosie Starks
   Marketing/Public Relations Director: Lori Sparger
Mission: To present more recent American plays both dramatic and comedic.
Utilizes: Guest Companies; Singers
Founded: 1958
Specialized Field: Educational; Theater Workshops
Status: Professional; Nonprofit
Income Sources: Purdue University
Performs At: Experimental Theater
Organization Type: Performing

Iowa

2661
OLD CREAMERY THEATRE COMPANY

39 38th Avenue
Suite 200
Amana, IA 52203
Phone: 319-622-6034
Fax: 319-622-6187
Toll-free: 800-352-6262
e-mail: octc@southslope.net
Web Site: www.oldcreamery.com
Officers:
   President: Bruce Eichacker
   VP: Richard Welch
   Treasurer: Vic Rathje
   Secretary: Ron Baldwin
Management:
   President: Tom P Johnson
   Associate Artistic Director: Meg Merckens
   Artistic Director: Sean McCall
   Managing Director: Pat Wagner
Mission: To bring live theater to as many people as possible in rural Iowa.
Utilizes: Actors; AEA Actors; Choreographers; Five Seasonal Concerts; Guest Accompanists; Guest Companies; Guest Conductors; Guest Designers; Multi Collaborations; Resident Professionals
Founded: 1971
Specialized Field: Musical; Comedy; Youth Theater; Community Theater; Contemporary
Status: Non-Profit, Professional
Paid Staff: 25
Paid Artists: 20
Season: March - December
Performs At: Main Stage; Courtyard Stage; The Old Creamery Theatre-Amana
Affiliations: Actors' Equity Association
Annual Attendance: 30,000
Type of Stage: Proscenium; Courtyard Stage
Seating Capacity: 300
Year Built: 1988
Organization Type: Performing; Touring; Resident; Educational

2662
CLINTON AREA SHOWBOAT THEATRE
PO Box 764
Clinton, IA 52733-0764
Phone: 563-242-6760
Fax: 563-242-9247
e-mail: boxoffice@clintonshowboat.org
Specialized Field: Summer Stock; Musical; Drama;
Comedy
Season: May - August

2663
BROADWAY THEATRE LEAGUE OF THE QUAD-CITIES
PO Box 130
Davenport, IA 52805
Phone: 319-326-1916
Mission: Supporting New York tours featuring
Broadway theatre productions.
Founded: 1960
Specialized Field: Broadway Musical Revivals
Status: Nonprofit
Performs At: Adler Theatre
Organization Type: Sponsoring

2664
JUNIOR THEATRE
2822 Eastern Avenue
Davenport, IA 52803
Phone: 563-326-7862
Fax: 563-888-2216
Web Site: http://www.davenportjuniortheatre.com/
Management:
    President: Rebecca Gulling
    Executive Director: Bonnie Guenther
    Artistic Director: Daniel Sheridan
Mission: To offer classes in dance play production and
creative drama to students in kindergarten through high
school; To present five major productions and twenty
eight touring productions.
Utilizes: Artists-in-Residence; Collaborations; Dancers;
Grant Writers; Guest Artists; Guest Lecturers; Guild
Activities; Instructors; Local Artists; Multimedia;
Soloists; Theatre Companies
Founded: 1951
Specialized Field: Musical; Youth Theater; Community
Theater; Children's Theater
Status: Non-Profit, Non-Professional
Paid Staff: 15
Volunteer Staff: 12
Paid Artists: 5
Income Sources: Local grants/class fees
Performs At: Mary Fluhrer Nighswander Junior
Theatre
Affiliations: AATE
Annual Attendance: Classrooms
Facility Category: Theatre, Dance Studio
Type of Stage: Proscenium
Stage Dimensions: 46 W x 30 D with thrust
Seating Capacity: 440
Year Remodeled: 1981
Organization Type: Performing; Touring; Educational
Resident Groups: Professional Modern Dance
Company

2665
GRAND OPERA HOUSE
135 8th Street
PO Box 632
Dubuque, IA 52001
Phone: 563-588-4356
Fax: 563-588-3497
e-mail: director@thegrandoperahouse.com
Web Site: www.thegrandoperahouse.com
Management:
    President: Peter Soraparu
    Executive Director: Paul Hemmer,
    director@thegrandoperahouse.co
    Box Office Manager: Jill Peterson
Mission: To offer quality entertainment and contribute
to the community's cultural growth.
Utilizes: Guest Companies
Founded: 1889
Specialized Field: Musical; Community Theater
Status: Non-Profit, Non-Professional
Paid Staff: 3
Volunteer Staff: 100
Paid Artists: 45
Budget: $450,000
Income Sources: Iowa Community Theatre
Association; Dubuque, Galena & Dyersville Area
Chambers of Commerce
Performs At: Community Theater
Annual Attendance: 10,000
Facility Category: Non union shop, utilizing volunteers
as operating personnel.
Type of Stage: Procenium arch 30' high x 35' wide
Stage Dimensions: 34' x 34', main curtain 4' back
Seating Capacity: 640
Year Built: 1989
Year Remodeled: 2010
Cost: $3.5 million
Rental Contact: Paul Hemmer
Organization Type: Performing; Educational

2666
IOWA SUMMER REPERTORY
University Theatre
N Riverside Drive
Iowa City, IA 52242
Phone: 319-335-2700
Fax: 319-335-3568
Toll-free: 800-426-2437
e-mail: eric-forsythe@uiowa.edu
Web Site: www.uiowa.edu/theatre
Management:
    President: Eric Forsythe
    Production Manager: Rick Loula
Mission: Retrospective of plays by a single
contemporary playwright each season and the
development of new scripts.
Utilizes: Actors; AEA Actors; Artists-in-Residence;
Commissioned Music; Composers-in-Residence;
Designers; Grant Writers; Guest Accompanists; Guest
Conductors; Guest Designers; Guest Lecturers;
Instructors; Local Artists; Multimedia; Music; Original
Music Scores; Performance Artists; Poets; Resident
Artists; Resident Professionals; Selected Students;
Student Interns; Visual Arts
Founded: 1920
Specialized Field: Comedy; Dinner Theater;
Contemporary
Status: Non-Profit, Professional
Paid Staff: 30
Paid Artists: 20
Budget: $170,000
Income Sources: Box Office, Grants
Season: May - July
Affiliations: AEA; URTA
Type of Stage: Proscenium; Flexible; Black Box
Seating Capacity: 477, 165, 135
Year Remodeled: 1986

2667
SIOUS CITY COMMUNITY THEATRE
1401 Riverside Boulevard
Sioux City, IA 51109
Mailing Address: PO Box 512
Phone: 712-233-2719
Fax: 712-233-1611
e-mail: scct@cableone.net
Web Site: www.scctheatre.org
Officers:
    President: Greg Gregerson
    Vice President: Mike Mattison
    Secretary: Jackie Kelly
    Treasurer: Heather Marreel
Management:
    Box Office Manager: Julie Ferris
    Education Director: Christine Wolf
    Concession Manager: Kent Martin
Mission: SCCT enhances quality of life by providing
opportunities for accessible and lifelong education,
volunteerism and entertainment in the performing arts
for people of all ages.
Founded: 1948
Specialized Field: Musical; Comedy; Drama
Status: Non-Profit, Non-Professional
Paid Staff: 3
Volunteer Staff: 500
Non-paid Artists: 100
Income Sources: Iowa Community Theatre
Association
Performs At: Shore Acres
Seating Capacity: 314
Organization Type: Performing

2668
RIVERSIDE THEATRE
3250 Riverside Park Drive
Vero Beach, IA 32963
Phone: 772-231-5860
Fax: 772-234-5298
Toll-free: 800-445-6745
e-mail: info@riversidetheatre.org
Web Site: www.riversidetheatre.org
Officers:
    President: E Bradley Jones
    VP: Marty Gibson
    Treasurer: Richard Stark
    Secretary: Thomas Slaughter
Management:
    Executive Director: Chuck Still
    Artistic Director: Allen D Cornell
    Education Director: Linda Downey
    Production Manager: Jon R Moses
Mission: To provide an artistic home for theatre
professionals from Iowa and beyond, and to entertain
audiences with intimate, engaging productions from the
classics to world premieres.
Utilizes: Actors; AEA Actors; Choreographers;
Commissioned Composers; Dancers; Designers;
Educators; Guest Conductors; Guest Designers; Guild
Activities; Instructors; Local Artists; Music; Performance
Artists; Resident Professionals; Soloists; Student
Interns
Founded: 1973
Specialized Field: Drama; Musical
Status: Nonprofit, Professional
Paid Staff: 35
Volunteer Staff: 150
Budget: $3 million
Income Sources: Ticket Sales; Annual Giving; Rentals;
Special Events
Affiliations: Actors' Equity Association; Florida
Professional Theatre Association; LORT

Annual Attendance: 110,000
Facility Category: Theatre
Type of Stage: Proscenium; Black Box
Stage Dimensions: 40x30
Seating Capacity: 610; 300
Year Built: 1973
Year Remodeled: 1990
Rental Contact: Jon Moses
Organization Type: Performing; Touring; Resident; Educational; Sponsoring

2669
WATERLOO COMMUNITY PLAYHOUSE & BLACK HAWK CHILDRENS THEATRE

225 Commercial Street
Waterloo, IA 50701
Phone: 319-235-0367
Fax: 319-235-7489
e-mail: info@wcpbhct.org
Web Site: www.wcpbhct.org
Management:
President of the Board: David Hildahl
Artistic Managing Director: Charles Stilwill
Marketing/Development Director: Danny Katz
Business Manager: Ethan Fischer
Designer/Production Manager: Katrina Sandvik
BHCT Director: Tyler Hayes Stilwill
Costume Director: Patricia Stilwill
Mission: Providing quality theatre productions; enhancing the cultural growth of Northeast Iowa.
Founded: 1916
Specialized Field: Musical; Comedy; Youth Theater; Community Theater; Classic; Contemporary
Status: Non-Profit, Non-Professional
Paid Staff: 9
Paid Artists: 6
Non-paid Artists: 400
Budget: $552,450
Income Sources: American Association of Community Theatres; Association of American Theatre for Youth; Waterloo, Cedar Falls & Waverly Chambers of Commerce; Iowa Community Theatre Association
Performs At: American Association of Community Theatres; Association of American Theatre for Youth; Waterloo/Cedar Falls/Waverly Chambers
Annual Attendance: 31,640
Facility Category: Arts Center
Type of Stage: Proscenium
Seating Capacity: 367
Year Built: 1965
Year Remodeled: 1977
Organization Type: Performing; Educational; Sponsoring

Kansas

2670
AUGUSTA ARTS COUNCIL/AUGUSTA HISTORIC THEATRE

PO Box 561
Augusta, KS 67010
Phone: 316-775-2900
Fax: 316-775-7475
e-mail: augustaarts@sbcglobal.net
Web Site: www.augustahistorictheatre.com
Officers:
President: William Morris
Executive Director: DeAnn Triboulet
Founded: 1975
Specialized Field: Musical; Comedy; Youth Theater; Dinner Theater; Ethnic Theater; Community Theater; Puppet; Historical; Classic

Status: Non-Profit, Professional
Paid Staff: 1
Performs At: Auditorium
Seating Capacity: 500
Year Built: 1935

2671
CHANUTE COMMUNITY THEATRE

PO Box 371
Chanute, KS 66720
Phone: 620-431-1628
e-mail: city@chanute.org
Web Site: www.chanute.org
Mission: To offer the community wide-ranging theatrical entertainment.
Founded: 1978
Specialized Field: Musical; Dinner Theater; Community Theater
Status: Non-Professional; Nonprofit
Income Sources: Association of Kansas Theatres
Performs At: Memorial Auditorium; Chanute Country Club
Organization Type: Performing; Resident; Educational

2672
COFFEYVILLE COMMUNITY THEATRE

400 West 11th
Coffeyville, KS 67337
Mailing Address: PO Box 317
Phone: 620-251-7700
e-mail: markf@coffeyville.edu
Web Site: http://www.coffeyville.edu/activities/theatre/index.htm
Management:
Director: Mark Frank
Mission: Providing live theatre for the community.
Founded: 1945
Specialized Field: Musical; Dinner Theater; Community Theater
Status: Non-Professional; Nonprofit
Paid Staff: 35
Income Sources: Association of Kansas Theatres; Kansas Arts Council
Performs At: Floral Hall
Organization Type: Performing

2673
BROWN GRAND THEATRE

310 W 6th Street
Concordia, KS 66901
Phone: 785-243-2553
e-mail: browngrand@nckcn.com
Web Site: www.browngrand.org
Officers:
President: Susan Sutton
VP: Luann Miller
Secretary/Treasurer: Wonda Brunkow
Management:
President: Susan Sutton
VP: Luann Miller
Vocal Music Director: Dr Everett Mill
Mission: Maintaining the historic Brown Grand Theatre; enhancing the cultural life of the area by providing quality theatre.
Utilizes: Guest Artists; Guest Companies; Singers
Founded: 1907
Specialized Field: Musical; Community Theater; Ethnic Theater; Puppet
Status: Professional; Nonprofit
Income Sources: Mid-America Arts Alliance
Organization Type: Performing; Educational; Sponsoring

2674
SALINA COMMUNITY THEATRE

303 E Iron
PO Box 2305
Salina, KS 67401
Phone: 785-827-6126
Fax: 785-827-6319
Toll-free: 877-414-2367
e-mail: sctstaff@salinatheatre.com
Web Site: www.salinatheatre.com
Management:
President: Shirley Braxton
Executive Director: Mike Spicer
VP Director: John Quinley
Technical Director: Tom Ward
Mission: To offer entertainment to the community; to provide recreation for those who would like to participate in theatrical productions.
Utilizes: Guest Companies
Founded: 1960
Specialized Field: Musical; Community Theater
Status: Non-Professional; Nonprofit
Paid Staff: 50
Organization Type: Performing; Sponsoring

2675
BARN PLAYERS THEATRE

6219 Martway
Shawnee Mission, KS 66202
Mailing Address: PO Box 12767
Phone: 913-432-9100
e-mail: admin@thebarnplayers.org.
Web Site: http://www.thebarnplayers.org/
Officers:
President: Margaret Godfrey
VP: Shirley Wagner
Secretary: Martha Coulter
Management:
Managing Director: Margaret Godfrey
Artistic Director: Max Beatty
Webmaster/Director: Richard Buswellk
Marketing Director/House Manager: Tricia Kyler
Webmaster/Developer/Technical Dir: Scott Bowling
Graphic Artist/Stage Manager: Bryan Colley
Co-Founder/Actor/Mistress Elec.: Diane Bulan
Mission: To promote artistic excellence through theatre; to produce community theatre productions; to encourage participation by interested persons; to promote theatre interest in the community.
Utilizes: Singers
Founded: 1956
Specialized Field: Community Theater
Status: Nonprofit
Income Sources: Association of Kansas Theatres; American Association of Community Theatres
Performs At: Overland Theatre
Organization Type: Performing

2676
TOPEKA CIVIC THEATRE & ACADEMY

3028 SW 8th Street
Topeka, KS 66606
Phone: 785-357-5211
Fax: 913-357-0719
Web Site: www.topekacivicteatre.com
Management:
Producing Artistic Director: Michael Wainstein
Business Manager: Brett Landow
Box Office Manager: Donna Jenks
Mission: Stimulating, entertaining, educating and serving our community; providing opportunities for performing and developing theatrical skills.

Utilizes: Guest Artists; Guest Companies
Founded: 1936
Specialized Field: Musical; Dinner Theater; Community Theater
Status: Non-Professional; Nonprofit
Paid Staff: 100
Income Sources: American Association of Community Theatres; Association of Kansas Theatres; Kansas Community Theatre Conference
Performs At: Topeka Civic Theatre
Type of Stage: Proscenium
Seating Capacity: 286
Organization Type: Performing

2677
COLUMBIAN THEATRE: MUSEUM & ART CENTER
521 Lincoln Avenue
PO Box 72
Wamego, KS 66547
Phone: 785-456-2029
Fax: 785-456-9498
Toll-free: 800-899-1893
e-mail: boxoffice@columbiantheatre.com
Web Site: www.columbiantheatre.com
Officers:
President: Lance White
Management:
Executive Director: Vivian Orndorff
Artistic Director: Ariane Chapman
Marketing/Events Director: Kayla Oney
Founded: 1989
Specialized Field: Specialty Acts; Historical; Drama
Status: Non-Profit, Non-Professional
Paid Staff: 4
Performs At: Peddicord Playhouse
Rental Contact: Marketing/Events Director Kayla Oney

2678
MUSIC THEATRE OF WICHITA
225 West Douglas
Suite 202
Wichita, KS 67202
Phone: 316-265-3253
Fax: 316-265-8708
e-mail: wayne@mtwichita.org
Web Site: www.mtwichita.org
Management:
Producing Artistic Director: Wayne Bryan, wayne@mtwichita.org
Producing Associate: Nancy Reeves, nancy@mtwichita.org
Mission: Dedicated to stimulating and nurturing interest in musical theatre by producing and or presenting Broadway quality productions, while entertaining and educating patrons, the community, and the theatrical artists.
Founded: 1972
Specialized Field: Musical
Status: Non-Profit, Professional
Paid Staff: 7
Volunteer Staff: 200
Paid Artists: 250
Budget: $3,000,000
Income Sources: Ticket Sales; Fundraisers; Set Rentals; State Funding; Grants
Season: June - August
Performs At: Century II Concert Hall
Affiliations: National Alliance for Musical Theatre
Annual Attendance: 60,000
Facility Category: Civic Arts Center
Type of Stage: Proscenium
Stage Dimensions: 44'Wx45'Dx22'H
Seating Capacity: 2,100

Year Built: 1969
Organization Type: Performing; Educational

2679
WICHITA COMMUNITY THEATRE
258 N Fountain
Wichita, KS 67208
Phone: 620-686-1282
e-mail: tdilport@cox.net
Web Site: www.wichitacommunitytheatre.com
Officers:
President: Dona Lancaster
VP: Terri Ingram
Secretary: Deanne Zogleman
Treasurer: Bob Lancaster
Management:
President: Mary Tush Green
VP: Diane Tinker
Mission: Providing the community with a wide range of theatrical entertainment; offering opportunities to amateur performers and technicians.
Founded: 1946
Specialized Field: Community Theater
Status: Non-Professional; Nonprofit
Income Sources: Association of Kansas Theatres
Performs At: Century II Civic Center; Workshop
Organization Type: Performing

2680
HORSEFEATHERS & APPLESAUCE SUMMER DINNER THEATRE
Southwestern College
100 College Street
Winfield, KS 67156-2499
Phone: 620-229-6328
Fax: 620-229-6335
e-mail: amoon@sckans.edu
Management:
Manager/Director: Nulson Moon
Founded: 1973
Specialized Field: Educational; Theater Workshops; Summer Stock
Status: Non-Equity; Nonprofit
Paid Staff: 35
Volunteer Staff: 10
Season: June 1 - July 31
Type of Stage: Proscenium
Seating Capacity: 240

Kentucky

2681
STEPHEN FOSTER-MUSICAL
411 East Stephen Foster Avenue
PO Box 546
Bardstown, KY 40004
Phone: 502-348-5971
Fax: 502-349-0574
e-mail: info@stephenfoster.com
Web Site: www.stephenfoster.com
Officers:
Chairman: Nicky Rapier
Vice Chairman: Louis Ballard
Management:
Artistic Director: Rick Dildine
General Manager: Betty Kelley
Mission: Fostering area cultural activities.
Utilizes: Actors; Choreographers; Commissioned Music; Educators; Fine Artists; Multimedia; Original Music Scores; Sign Language Translators; Singers
Founded: 1959
Specialized Field: Musical; Comedy; Youth Theater; Classic; Contemporary

Status: Non-Profit, Professional
Paid Staff: 70
Paid Artists: 50
Budget: $900,000
Performs At: J. Dan Talbott Amphitheatre
Annual Attendance: 60,000+
Facility Category: Outdoor Amphitheatre
Seating Capacity: 1,500
Year Built: 1958
Year Remodeled: 1997
Organization Type: Amphitheatre

2682
FOUNTAIN SQUARE PLAYERS
313 State Street
Bowling Green, KY 42101
Phone: 270-782-3119
e-mail: info@fountainsquareplayers.org fountainsquareplayers.org;
Web Site: http://www.fountainsquareplayers.org/
Officers:
President: Heather Bitterling
VP: Jeff Moore
Secretary: Miliska Knauft
Treasurer: Bill Russell
Mission: To promote appreciation and enjoyment of theatre.
Founded: 1978
Specialized Field: Community Theater
Status: Non-Professional; Nonprofit
Paid Staff: 150
Income Sources: American Arts Alliance
Performs At: Capitol Arts Center
Organization Type: Performing

2683
PIONEER PLAYHOUSE OF KENTUCKY
840 Stanford Road
Danville, KY 40422
Phone: 859-236-2747
Fax: 859-236-4321
e-mail: pioneer@mis.net
Web Site: www.pioneerplayhouse.com
Management:
Artistic Director: Holly Henson
Producer: Charlotte Henson
Mission: Maintaining an arts vocational training center with professionals as performers and teachers.
Founded: 1950
Specialized Field: Summer Stock; Musical; Dinner Theater
Status: Professional; Nonprofit
Paid Staff: 30
Income Sources: Southeastern Theatre Conference; Kentucky Theatre Association
Season: June - August
Performs At: Colonel Eben Henson Amphitheatre
Organization Type: Performing; Resident; Educational

2684
HARDIN COUNTY PLAYHOUSE
2382 S Dixie Avenue
Elizabethtown, KY 40160
Phone: 270-351-0577
e-mail: playhouse@hardincountyplayhouse.com
Web Site: www.hardincountyplayhouse.com
Management:
President: Danny Darnall
Managing Director: Dee Corkran
Mission: To provide performing arts for the community.
Utilizes: Guest Companies; Singers
Founded: 1969

Specialized Field: Musical; Comedy; Dinner Theater; Ethnic Theater; Community Theater; Contemporary
Status: Non-Profit, Non-Professional
Paid Staff: 1
Income Sources: Grants
Performs At: Hardin County Playhouse
Annual Attendance: varies
Organization Type: Performing

2685
KINCAID REGIONAL THEATRE
400 Main Street
Falmouth, KY 41040
Phone: 859-654-2117
Toll-free: 800-647-7469
e-mail: krtshows@fuse.net
Web Site:
http://www.krtshow.com/page/page/244016.htm
Officers:
Â Â Â Â President: Gene Kearns
Â Â Â Â VP: Myron Doan
Â Â Â Â Secretary: Barbara Browning
Management:
Â Â Â Â General Manager: Shirley Merrill
Mission: Employing talented actors and offering quality entertainment to the region.
Utilizes: Guest Artists; Guest Companies; Singers
Founded: 1983
Specialized Field: Musical; Ensembles
Status: Professional; Nonprofit
Income Sources: Southeastern Theatre Conference
Performs At: Falmouth Auditorium
Organization Type: Performing; Resident; Educational; Sponsoring

2686
FAR-OFF BROADWAY PLAYERS
115 East Main St
Glasgow, KY 42141
Phone: 270-651-8612
e-mail: president@faroffbroadwayplayers.org
Web Site: http://www.faroffbroadwayplayers.org/
Officers:
Â Â Â Â President: Peggy Goodman
Â Â Â Â VP: Denise Johnson
Â Â Â Â Secretary: Zona Cetera
Â Â Â Â Treasurer: Diane Beeckler
Mission: To study and perform amateur drama.
Founded: 1980
Specialized Field: Community Theater
Status: Non-Professional; Nonprofit
Paid Staff: 40
Organization Type: Performing; Resident

2687
MUHLENBERG COMMUNITY THEATRE
119 N Main Street
Greenville, KY 42345-7165
Phone: 270-338-7165
e-mail: mctipalacetheatre@live.com
Web Site: www.mctiky.com
Officers:
Â Â Â Â President: Jeff Dickinson
Â Â Â Â VP: Onalee Kidd
Â Â Â Â Recording Secretary: Karen Willis
Â Â Â Â Corresponding Secretary: David Eplett
Â Â Â Â Treasurer: Sherry Lorenzen
Â Â Â Â Assistant Treasurer: Daven Edmonds
Management:
Â Â Â Â President: Jeff Dicikinson
Mission: Promoting the theatrical arts.
Utilizes: Guest Artists; Guest Companies; Singers
Founded: 1980

Specialized Field: Musical; Dinner Theater; Community Theater
Status: Professional; Semi-Professional; Nonprofit
Paid Staff: 20
Income Sources: American Association of Community Theatres
Performs At: Palace Theatre
Year Remodeled: 1999
Organization Type: Performing; Touring; Resident; Educational

2688
LEGEND OF DANIEL BOONE/JAMES HARROD AMPHITHEATRE
Box 365
Harrodsburg, KY 40330
Phone: 606-734-3346
Fax: 602-734-3348
Management:
Â Â Â Â General Manager: Maureen Daly
Founded: 1963
Specialized Field: Summer Stock
Status: Non-Equity; Nonprofit
Season: Mid June - Late August
Type of Stage: Amphitheatre
Stage Dimensions: 60'x 40'
Seating Capacity: 600

2689
HORSE CAVE THEATRE
101 E Main Street
PO Box 215
Horse Cave, KY 42749
Phone: 270-786-1200
Fax: 270-786-5298
Toll-free: 800-342-2177
Web Site: www.horsecavetheatre.org
Officers:
Â Â Â Â President: Carla Wertzer
Management:
Â Â Â Â Artistic Director: Robert Brock
Â Â Â Â Education Associate: Lynn Gilcrease
Â Â Â Â Marketing Director: Melissa McGoire
Â Â Â Â Development Director: Kim Harrison
Mission: To be the only resident professional theater outside of metropolitan Louisville that provides a forum for Kentucky writers to produce their works; to present an annual Shakespeare production that assists in meeting the needs of students.
Utilizes: Actors; AEA Actors; Educators; Guest Artists; Guest Conductors; Guest Designers; Local Artists; Performance Artists; Poets; Resident Professionals; Soloists
Founded: 1977
Specialized Field: Comedy; Youth Theater; Classic; Contemporary
Status: Non-Profit, Professional
Paid Staff: 30
Paid Artists: 7
Budget: $625,000
Income Sources: Kentucky Arts Council; KY Tourism Cabinet; Corporations; Foundations; Businesses & Individuals
Season: June - December
Performs At: Horse Cave Theatre
Annual Attendance: 30,000
Facility Category: Theatre
Type of Stage: Thrust
Seating Capacity: 346
Year Built: 1977
Year Remodeled: 1993
Architect: Tate Jacobs
Cost: $1,500,000

Organization Type: Performing; Touring; Resident; Educational

2690
ACTORS' GUILD OF LEXINGTON
141 E Main Street
Lexington, KY 40507
Phone: 859-233-7330
Fax: 859-233-3773
e-mail: actorsguild@qx.net
Web Site: www.actorsguildoflexington.org
Management:
Â Â Â Â President: Richard Saintpeter
Â Â Â Â Managing Director: Steven Koehler
Mission: To produce compelling contemporary theatre for the region.
Founded: 1984
Specialized Field: Musical; Comedy; Ethnic Theater; Community Theater; Contemporary
Status: Non-Profit, Professional
Paid Staff: 4
Paid Artists: 40

2691
BROADWAY LIVE AT THE OPERA HOUSE
430 W Vine
Lexington, KY 40507
Phone: 859-233-4567
Fax: 859-253-2718
e-mail: mail@lexingtonoperahouse.com
Web Site: www.lexingtonoperahouse.com
Officers:
Â Â Â Â Chief Executive Officer: Bill Owen
Â Â Â Â Executive Officer: Luanne Franklin
Â Â Â Â Marketing Coordinator: Sheila Kenny
Management:
Â Â Â Â Managing Director: Tom Habermann
Utilizes: Actors; AEA Actors; Choreographers; Collaborations; Dance Companies; Dancers; Educators; Fine Artists; Guild Activities; Local Artists; Local Artists & Directors; Multimedia; Original Music Scores; Singers; Special Technical Talent; Theatre Companies
Founded: 1976
Specialized Field: Musical; Comedy; Youth Theater; Ethnic Theater; Classic; Light Theater
Status: Non-Profit, Non-Professional
Performs At: Broadway Live Series; Variety Series; Local Artist Groups
Affiliations: APAP; WTAT
Facility Category: Theatre
Type of Stage: Proscenium
Stage Dimensions: 37'3"x21'
Seating Capacity: 1,000
Year Built: 1886
Year Remodeled: 1976
Rental Contact: Program Director Luanne Franklin

2692
LEXINGTON CHILDREN'S THEATRE
418 W Short Street
Lexington, KY 40507
Phone: 859-254-4546
Fax: 859-254-9512
Toll-free: 800-928-4545
e-mail: info@lctonstage.org
Web Site: www.lctonstage.org
Management:
Â Â Â Â President: Wander Faircloth
Â Â Â Â Executive Director: Larry Snipes
Â Â Â Â Artistic Director: Vivian Snipes
Â Â Â Â Producing Director: Larry Snipes
Â Â Â Â Education Director: Jeremy Kisling
Â Â Â Â Production Stage Manager: Dawn Crabtree

Resident Designer: Eric Morris
Technical Director: Thomas Taylor
Founded: 1938
Specialized Field: Youth Theater; Children's Theater
Status: Non-Profit, Professional
Paid Staff: 10
Paid Artists: 30

2693
STUDIO PLAYERS
154 West Bell Court
Lexington, KY 40508
Mailing Address: PO Box 23252, Lexington, KY. 40523
Phone: 859-253-2512
e-mail: bsingleton@att.net
Web Site: http://www.studioplayers.org/index.htm
Officers:
President: Scott Turner
Past President: David Bratcher
President Elect: Debbie Sharp
Secretary: Ellen Hellard
Treasurer: Bob Kinstle
Mission: Studio Players has presented plays since 1953.
Founded: 1953
Specialized Field: Drama; Comedy
Status: Nonprofit

2694
ACTORS THEATRE OF LOUISVILLE
316-320 W Main Street
Louisville, KY 40202-4218
Phone: 502-584-1265
Fax: 502-561-3300
Toll-free: 800-422-5849
e-mail: mail@actorstheatre.org
Web Site: www.actorstheatre.org
Officers:
President: Bruce C Merrick
VP Finance: Frederic H Davis
Treasurer: Bruce K Dudley
Secretary: Sarah D. Fuller
Management:
Executive Director: Sandy Speer
Artistic Director: Marc Masterson
Managing Director: Fraizer Mash
Mission: To offer the finest in professional entertainment to a wide audience at reasonable prices; to maintain fiscal responsibility.
Utilizes: Actors; AEA Actors; Artists-in-Residence; Choreographers; Collaborations; Commissioned Composers; Commissioned Music; Dancers; Designers; Educators; Grant Writers; Guest Accompanists; Guest Artists; Guest Choreographers; Guest Companies; Guest Conductors; Guest Directors; Guest Ensembles; Guest Instructors; Guest Lecturers; Guest Musicians; Guest Teachers; Guest Writers; Guild Activities; Instructors; Local Artists; Multimedia; Music; Organization Contracts; Original Music Scores; Performance Artists; Playwrights; Poets; Resident Professionals; Selected Students; Sign Language Translators; Singers; Special Technical Talent; Touring Companies; Visual Arts
Founded: 1964
Specialized Field: Touring Company
Status: Non-Profit, Professional
Paid Staff: 152
Paid Artists: 150
Budget: $8 Million
Income Sources: Ticket sales; grants; contributions
Affiliations: League of Resident Theatres
Annual Attendance: 240,000
Facility Category: 3 theatre complex

Type of Stage: 2 thrust stages and an arena
Seating Capacity: 637; 318; 159
Year Built: 1972
Year Remodeled: 1994
Rental Contact: Mike Brooks
Organization Type: Performing; Resident

2695
KENTUCKY SHAKESPEARE FESTIVAL
1387 S 4th Street
Louisville, KY 40208
Phone: 502-583-8738
Fax: 502-583-8741
e-mail: tofter@aol.com
Web Site: www.kyshakes.org
Management:
President: Charles Keaton
Artistic Director: Curt Tofteland
Managing Director: Steven Renner
Mission: To provide accessible, professional, classical theatre and quality education touring programs.
Utilizes: Actors; Artists-in-Residence; Collaborating Artists; Collaborations; Designers; Educators; Five Seasonal Concerts; Guest Accompanists; Guest Conductors; Guest Ensembles; Guild Activities; High School Drama; Local Artists; Original Music Scores; Resident Artists; Resident Professionals; Selected Students; Soloists; Student Interns; Theatre Companies
Founded: 1960
Specialized Field: Shakespeare
Status: Non-Profit, Professional
Paid Staff: 7
Paid Artists: 20
Budget: $600,000
Income Sources: Corporate, Foundation, Individuals, Government, Fund, Earned
Season: May - August
Performs At: C. Douglas Ramey Amphitheater
Annual Attendance: 10,000
Facility Category: Outdoor Ampitheatre
Type of Stage: Thrust
Seating Capacity: 1000
Year Built: 1963
Year Remodeled: 1993
Organization Type: Performing; Resident; Touring; Educational

2696
MUSIC THEATRE LOUISVILLE
624 W Main Street
Suite 402
Louisville, KY 40202
Phone: 502-589-4060
Fax: 502-589-0741
e-mail: info@musictheatrelouisville.com
Web Site: www.musictheaterlouisville.com
Management:
President: Norma O'Berst
Artistic Director: Steven Jones
Director Marketing: Kara Brown
Director Education: Sharon Kinnison
Operations Supervisor: Bill Beauchamp
Box Office Manager: Michelle Kaelin
Administrative Coordinator: Greg Wood
Founded: 1981
Specialized Field: Musical; Comedy; Community Theater
Status: Non-Profit, Non-Professional
Paid Staff: 100
Paid Artists: 100
Season: May - August
Type of Stage: Proscenium
Stage Dimensions: 60' x 50'
Seating Capacity: 1600

2697
STAGE ONE: THE LOUISVILLE CHILDREN'S THEATRE
501 W Main Street
Louisville, KY 40202
Phone: 502-589-5946
Fax: 502-588-5910
Toll-free: 800-989-5946
e-mail: stageone@stageone.org
Web Site: www.stageone.org
Management:
Artistic Director: J Daniel Herring
Mission: To provide high-quality, professional, live theatre for young audiences that develops the whole child, supports the learning environment and builds strong family bonds.
Utilizes: Actors; AEA Actors; Collaborations; Designers; Educators; Guest Companies; Guest Conductors; Guest Lecturers; Multimedia; Original Music Scores; Performance Artists; Resident Artists; Resident Professionals; Singers
Founded: 1946
Specialized Field: Musical; Comedy; Youth Theater; Contemporary
Status: Non-Profit, Professional
Paid Staff: 25
Paid Artists: 15
Budget: 1.8 Million
Income Sources: Ticket sales; Grants; Donations
Performs At: Kentucky Center for the Arts; Brown Theatre
Affiliations: The Kentucky Center for the Arts
Annual Attendance: 150,000
Organization Type: Performing; Touring; Educational

2698
THEATRE WORKSHOP OF OWENSBORO
407 W 5th Street
PO Box 644
Owensboro, KY 42302
Phone: 270-683-5003
Fax: 270-683-5003
e-mail: twodrama@bellsouth.net
Web Site: www.theatreworkshop.org
Management:
President: Teresa Wills
Executive Director: Johnmike Filbin
Education Director: Sean Dysinger
House Manager: Tom Mudd
Mission: To offer quality amateur theatre to the Owensboro area; to provide area performers and technicians with opportunities to practice their crafts.
Utilizes: Actors
Founded: 1955
Specialized Field: Musical; Comedy; Youth Theater; Ethnic Theater; Theater Workshops
Status: Non-Profit, Non-Professional
Paid Staff: 4
Non-paid Artists: 350
Budget: 140,000
Income Sources: Corporate; Indivdual; Grants
Performs At: Old Trinity Centre; River Park Center
Annual Attendance: 4000
Facility Category: Church
Stage Dimensions: 20' x 22'
Seating Capacity: 100
Year Remodeled: 1999
Organization Type: Performing; Resident

2699
MARKET HOUSE THEATRE
141 Kentucky Avenue
Paducah, KY 42003

Phone: 270-444-6829
Fax: 270-575-9321
Toll-free: 888-648-7529
e-mail: info@mhtplay.com
Web Site: www.mhtplay.com
Management:
    Artistic/Executive Director: Michael Cochran
    Business Manager: Marsha Cash
Mission: To enrich the cultural and artistic life of the community through the presentation of a diverse season; touring; providing educational programs.
Utilizes: Guest Companies; Singers
Founded: 1963
Specialized Field: Community Theater
Status: Non-Professional; Nonprofit
Paid Staff: 7
Paid Artists: 10
Non-paid Artists: 200
Budget: $462,000
Income Sources: 70% Earned; 30% Contributed
Type of Stage: Proscenium
Stage Dimensions: 22' x 35'
Seating Capacity: 230
Year Remodeled: 1980
Organization Type: Performing; Touring; Educational

2700
JENNY WILEY THEATRE
121 Theatre Court
PO Box 22
Prestonburg, KY 41653
Mailing Address: PO Box 22
Phone: 606-886-9274
Fax: 606-886-8875
Toll-free: 877-225-5598
e-mail: marty@jwtheatre.com
Web Site: www.jwtheatre.com
Management:
    Executive Director: Martin Childers, marty@jwtheatre.com
Mission: Our mission is to enhance the quqality of life in eastern Kentucky by providing professional theatre and exceptional educational opportunities in the performing arts.
Utilizes: Actors; Choreographers; Collaborating Artists; Commissioned Composers; Community Talent; Contract Actors; Dancers; Designers; Educators; Filmmakers; Five Seasonal Concerts; Guest Artists; Guest Ensembles; Local Artists & Directors; Multimedia; Organization Contracts; Original Music Scores; Performance Artists; Resident Professionals; Selected Students; Sign Language Translators; Student Interns; Theatre Companies
Founded: 1965
Specialized Field: Musical
Status: Nonprofit; Non-Equity
Paid Staff: 4
Volunteer Staff: 30
Paid Artists: 30
Non-paid Artists: 20
Budget: $800,000
Income Sources: Grant; Ticket Sales; Donations; Corporate Support
Season: May 30 - August 24
Performs At: Amphitheatre; Convention Center; and Arts Center
Affiliations: Kentucky Theatre Association; TCG; IOD; SETC
Annual Attendance: 32,000
Type of Stage: Proscenium
Stage Dimensions: 44' x 28'
Seating Capacity: 580
Year Built: 1962
Year Remodeled: 1992

2701
RICHMOND CHILDREN'S THEATRE
114 West Broad St
Richmond, KY 23220
Phone: 804-783-1688
Fax: 859-254-9512
Web Site: http://www.theatreivrichmond.org/
Management:
    Artistic Director: Bruce Miller
    Managing Director: Phil Whiteway
Mission: To provide young people, ages 8-18, an opportunity to become involved in theatre arts through participation in performances, workhops, stagecraft and crew.
Utilizes: Guest Companies; Singers
Founded: 1978
Specialized Field: Musical; Community Theater
Status: Non-Professional; Nonprofit
Income Sources: Richmond Parks & Recreation Department
Performs At: Eastern Kentucky University Campus Theatre
Organization Type: Performing; Touring; Educational

Louisiana

2702
BATON ROUGE LITTLE THEATER
7155 Florida Boulevard
PO Box 64967
Baton Rouge, LA 70806
Phone: 225-924-6496
Fax: 225-924-9972
e-mail: boxoffice@brlt.org
Web Site: www.brlt.org
Officers:
    President: Sara Downing
    Vice President Administration: David Kiesel
    VP Publicity: Diane Mayer
    VP Production: Lynn Noland
    Treasurer: Louis LoBue
    Secretary: Gary Schaefer
Management:
    President: John Gum Jr
    Managing Director: Keith Dixon
    Theatre Manager: Jody Banta
Mission: Entertaining, educating and providing an artistic outlet.
Utilizes: Guest Artists; Guest Companies
Founded: 1946
Specialized Field: Community Theater
Status: Non-Profit, Non-Professional
Paid Staff: 7
Volunteer Staff: 100
Non-paid Artists: 200
Organization Type: Performing; Educational

2703
SWINE PALACE PRODUCTIONS
PO Box 18699
Baton Rouge, LA 70803
Phone: 504-388-3533
Fax: 504-388-4135
Management:
    Founding Artistic Director: Barry Kyle
    Executive Director: Marilyn Hersey
    Executive Producing Director: Michael Tick
Founded: 1992
Specialized Field: Educational; Theater Workshops; Touring Company
Status: Nonprofit
Performs At: Claude L. Shaver Theatre

Type of Stage: Traverse
Stage Dimensions: 111' x 47'
Seating Capacity: 488

2704
COLUMBIA THEATRE/FANFARE
220 E Thomas Street
SLU 10797
Hammond, LA 70402
Phone: 985-543-4366
Fax: 985-543-4369
e-mail: kcouret@selu.edu
Web Site: www.selu.edu
Management:
    Director: Donna Gay Anderson
    Associate Director/Marketing: Tonya Lowentritt
    Associate Director/Marketing: Pamela Mills
    Associate Director/Operations: Pete Pfeil
Mission: The mission and purpose of the Columbia Theatre for the Performing arts is to enhance and support Southeastern Louisiana University which serves the educational, economic and cultural needs of Southeastern Louisiana.
Founded: 1986
Specialized Field: Drama; Musical; Classic
Status: Non-Profit, Professional
Paid Staff: 8
Volunteer Staff: 55
Paid Artists: 25
Non-paid Artists: 10
Budget: $305,811
Income Sources: Ticket Renue; Rental Income; Sorporate Sponsorships; Business and Individual Donations; Poster Sales; Merchandise Commissions
Affiliations: Association of Performing Arts Presenters
Annual Attendance: 51,000
Stage Dimensions: 31'x6'x22'
Seating Capacity: 889
Year Built: 1928
Year Remodeled: 2001
Rental Contact: Pete Pfeil

2705
ARTISTS' CIVIC THEATRE AND STUDIO
One Reid Street
PO Box 278
Lake Charles, LA 70602
Phone: 337-433-2287
Fax: 337-436-5908
e-mail: marcpettaway@aol.com
Web Site: www.actstheatre.com
Management:
    President: Anita Fields-Gold
    Executive Director: Marc Pettaway
Mission: To give local talent a place to work under the direction of a trained professional director where production values are maintained at a high level; to offer formal classes in various aspects of theatre.
Utilizes: Singers
Founded: 1966
Specialized Field: Community Theater; Youth Theater
Status: Non-Profit, Non-Professional
Paid Staff: 1
Volunteer Staff: 70+
Non-paid Artists: 50-
Income Sources: Ticket sales; Grants
Performs At: ACTS' One Reid Street Theatre
Facility Category: Community Theatre
Seating Capacity: 125
Organization Type: Performing; Touring; Resident; Educational

2706

SOUTHERN REP THEATRE
333 Canal Street
PO Box 34
Lake Charles, LA 70130
Phone: 504-522-6545
Fax: 504-523-9859
e-mail: info@southernrep.com
Web Site: www.southernrep.com
Management:
    Managing Director: Marieke Gaboury
    Artistic Director: Aimee Hayes
Mission: Recognizing a need for professional theater in New Orleans, Dr. Rosary Hartel O'Neill, Dick O'Neill, Nancy Mendard and Clydia Davenport founded Southern Rep Theatre in 1986 with the goal of creating a leading center for Southern playwrights and plays.
Utilizes: Actors; AEA Actors; Collaborating Artists; Collaborations; Community Talent; Contract Actors; Designers; Educators; Equity Actors; Instructors; Local Artists; Local Artists & Directors; Original Music Scores; Performance Artists; Students
Founded: 1986
Specialized Field: Theatreys
Status: Non-Profit, Professional
Paid Staff: 8
Volunteer Staff: 40
Paid Artists: 100
Affiliations: NNPN; TCG
Facility Category: Indoor Theatre
Type of Stage: Modified Thrust
Seating Capacity: 144
Organization Type: Performing

2707

JUNEBUG PRODUCTIONS
PO Box 2331
New Orleans, LA 70176
Phone: 504-524-8257
Fax: ew -rle-n
Officers:
    Chairman: Wallace Young
    President: John O'Neal
    Treasurer: Theresa Holden
    Secretary: John T. Scott
Management:
    Artistic Director: John O'Neal
    Managing Director: Theresa Holden
Mission: To produce, present and support the development of high-quality theater, dance, music, storytelling and other artistic work that represents, supports and encourages African Americans in the Black Belt South.
Utilizes: Actors; AEA Actors; Artists-in-Residence; Choreographers; Collaborating Artists; Collaborations; Commissioned Composers; Commissioned Music; Composers-in-Residence; Dancers; Designers; Educators; Five Seasonal Concerts; Grant Writers; Guest Accompanists; Guest Choreographers; Guest Designers; Guest Ensembles; Guest Musical Directors; Guest Teachers; Guild Activities; High School Drama; Instructors; Local Artists; Lyricists; Multimedia; Organization Contracts; Original Music Scores; Performance Artists; Playwrights; Selected Students; Sign Language Translators; Singers; Soloists; Student Interns; Touring Companies
Founded: 1980
Specialized Field: Musical; Storytelling; African American
Status: Professional; Nonprofit
Budget: $300,000
Affiliations: Alternate ROOTs, National Performance Network

Facility Category: Touring theater
Organization Type: Performing; Touring; Educational; Sponsoring

2708

NEW ORLEANS RECREATION DEPARTMENT THEATRE
545 St. Charles Avenue, PO Box 791344
Lafayette Street Entrance
New Orleans, LA 70179
Phone: 504-565-7860
Fax: 504-565-6084
Mission: To present musical comedy productions three times yearly and to involve children, teenagers, and adults.
Utilizes: Sign Language Translators; Students
Founded: 1960
Specialized Field: Educational; Theater Workshops
Paid Staff: 4
Non-paid Artists: Var
Budget: Varies
Performs At: NORD Theatre
Annual Attendance: 5,000
Facility Category: Recreation Center
Type of Stage: Proscenium
Seating Capacity: 99

2709

SAENGER THEATRE
143 N Rampart Street
New Orleans, LA 70112
Phone: 504-524-2490
Fax: 504-569-1533
Web Site: www.saengertheatre.com
Management:
    General Manager: Cynthia Argo
    Booking and Special Sevents Manager: Patricia Baham
    Head of Production: Scott Stewart
    Marketing Director: Mason Wood
Founded: 1929
Specialized Field: Broadway Musical Revivals
Status: For-Profit, Professional
Paid Staff: 200

2710

SHAKESPEARE FESTIVAL AT TULANE
215 McWilliams Hall
Tulane University
New Orleans, LA 70118
Phone: 504-865-5105
Fax: 504-865-5205
e-mail: box@tulane.edu
Web Site: www.neworleansshakespeare.com
Management:
    Artistic Director: Ron Gural
    Managing Director: Clare Moncrief
    Operations Director: Brad Robbert
Mission: To provide professional Shakespeare productions to the Greater New Orleans and surrounding Gulf South area along with educational programs to the schools.
Utilizes: Actors; AEA Actors; Artists-in-Residence; Choreographers; Collaborating Artists; Collaborations; Commissioned Composers; Commissioned Music; Composers; Educators; Five Seasonal Concerts; Guest Artists; Guest Companies; Guest Instructors; Guest Musical Directors; Guest Soloists; Guest Teachers; High School Drama; Local Artists; Multimedia; Organization Contracts; Original Music Scores; Performance Artists; Resident Artists; Resident Professionals; Soloists; Students; Special Technical Talent
Founded: 1993

Specialized Field: Classic; Shakespeare; New Plays; Classic; Contemporary
Status: Professional; Nonprofit
Paid Staff: 6
Paid Artists: 60
Budget: $250,000
Income Sources: Public; Private; Corporate; Foundation; Box Office; Tuition
Facility Category: Equity Small Professional Theatre
Type of Stage: Black Box; Laboratory
Seating Capacity: 150; 60

2711

SOUTHERN REP
365 Canal Street
Box 34
New Orleans, LA 70130
Phone: 504-566-9212
Fax: 504-566-9214
e-mail: info@southernrep.com
Web Site: www.southernrep.com
Management:
    Managing Director: Marieke Gaboury
    Artistic Director: Aimee Hayes
Mission: Professional theatre created for the audience by paying the actors, stage manager, and designers for their art, as contrasted to community and educational theatres which create for educational and social experiences with volunteers. Selections for each season strive to include one masterpiece adapted to a Southern setting; a classic Southern play; and a play which addresses a Southern issue.
Utilizes: Actors; AEA Actors; Collaborating Artists; Collaborations; Community Talent; Contract Actors; Designers; Educators; Equity Actors; Instructors; Local Artists; Local Artists & Directors; Original Music Scores; Performance Artists; Students
Founded: 1986
Specialized Field: Theatre
Organization Type: Performing; Educational

2712

ST. JOHN THEATRE
115 W 4th Street
Reserve, LA 70084
Mailing Address: PO Box 188
Phone: 985-536-6630
e-mail: info@stjohntheatre.comÿ
Web Site: www.stjohntheatre.org
Management:
    President: Sterling Snowdy
    VP: Suzette Hullette
    Treasurer: Donna Conran
    Managing Director: Beverly Beard
    Secretary: Robert Beadle
Mission: Providing live theatre for the community, with particular emphasis on schools and students.
Utilizes: Guest Companies; Guest Speakers; Singers
Founded: 1981
Specialized Field: Musical; Community Theater
Status: Non-Professional; Nonprofit; Corporation
Paid Staff: 50
Performs At: St. John Theatre Stage
Organization Type: Performing; Educational

2713

SHREVEPORT LITTLE THEATRE
812 Margaret Place
Shreveport, LA 71101
Mailing Address: PO Box 4853
Phone: 318-424-4439
Fax: 318-424-4440
Web Site: www.shreveportlittletheatre.org
Officers:

President: Dr. David Pov
VP: Jan Pov
Treasurer: Janice Nelson
Secretary: Marcia Cassanova
Management:
President: Gene Bozeman
Artistic Director: Robert K Darrow
Mission: Committed to producing a variety of quality live theatre with predominantly volunteer participation from the community, with the guidance of trained artistic and managerial leadership, for entertainment, enlightenment and growth of audience awareness and pride.
Utilizes: Guest Companies
Founded: 1921
Specialized Field: Community Theater
Status: Non-Profit, Non-Professional
Paid Staff: 2
Budget: $165,000
Income Sources: Memberships; Ticket Sales; Contributions; Annual Fund; Grants
Affiliations: American Association of Community Theatres
Annual Attendance: 10,000+
Facility Category: Theater
Seating Capacity: 140
Year Built: 1925
Year Remodeled: 2002
Cost: $125,000
Organization Type: Performing; Touring

Maine

2714
ARUNDEL BARN PLAYHOUSE
53 Old Post Road
Arundel, ME 4046
Phone: 207-985-5552
Web Site: www.arundelbarnplayhouse.com
Management:
Executive Director: Adrienne Wilson Grant
Founded: 1998
Specialized Field: Drama; Musical
Status: For-Profit, Professional
Season: June - September
Type of Stage: Proscenium
Stage Dimensions: 25' x 22'
Seating Capacity: 225

2715
PENOBSCOT THEATRE COMPANY
183 Main Street
Bangor, ME 4401
Phone: 207-947-6618
Fax: 207-947-6678
e-mail: info@penobscottheatre.org
Management:
President: Daniel G McKay
Artistic Director: Mark Torres
Producing and Artistic Director: Mark Torres
Marketing Director: Mark Torres
Mission: To offer high quality, professional theatre experiences staged throughout the year; to provide educational outreach programs, and to develop and enrich new and existing audiences and artists.
Utilizes: Guest Companies; Singers
Founded: 1974
Specialized Field: Musical; Drama; Comedy; Youth Theater; Theater Workshops
Status: Professional; Nonprofit
Paid Staff: 8
Type of Stage: Proscenium
Seating Capacity: 132

Organization Type: Performing; Touring; Resident; Sponsoring

2716
HACKMATACK PLAYHOUSE
538 Route 9
Beaver Dam
Berwick, ME 03901
Phone: 207-698-1807
Fax: 207-698-1162
e-mail: HackPlayhouse@aol.com
Web Site: http://www.hackmatack.org/hackmatack/
Management:
Artistic/Production Director: Sharon Hilton
Founded: 1971
Specialized Field: Summer Stock; Drama; Theater Workshops
Status: Non-Equity; Nonprofit
Season: June 27 - September 2
Seating Capacity: 200

2717
CAROUSEL MUSIC THEATRE
196 Townsend Avenue
Boothbay Harbor, ME 04538
Mailing Address: PO Box 665
Phone: 207-633-5297
Fax: 207-663-5297
Toll-free: 800-757-5297
e-mail: info@carouselmusictheatre.com
Web Site: www.carouselmusictheatre.com
Management:
Owner/Producer: Theresa Falco
Director/Choreograper: Rosie North
Music Director: Rob Spring
Founded: 1978
Specialized Field: Cabaret; Musical
Status: For-Profit, Professional
Paid Staff: 10
Paid Artists: 6
Season: May - October
Type of Stage: Proscenium; Thrust

2718
MAINE STATE MUSIC THEATRE
22 Elm Street
Brunswick, ME 04011
Phone: 207-725-8760
Fax: 207-725-1199
Toll-free: 866-854-1200
e-mail: jobs@msmt.org
Web Site: www.msmt.org
Officers:
President: Kathy Greason
Vice President: Doug Niven
Secretary: Susan Sharpan
Treasurer: Thomas Pierle
Management:
Company Manager: Kathi Kacinski
Managing Director: Raymond M Dumontre
Marketing Director: Rob Jarrett
Mission: Live professional performances and outreach opportunities that entertain, educate, and enrich lives with power and passion.
Utilizes: Guest Companies; Selected Students; Sign Language Translators; Singers; Soloists; Student Interns
Founded: 1959
Specialized Field: Summer Stock; Musical
Status: Professional; Nonprofit
Paid Staff: 6
Volunteer Staff: 100
Budget: $4 Million

Income Sources: Ticket Sales; Sponsorships; Donations; Advertising
Season: May - August
Performs At: AEA summer musical theatre
Annual Attendance: 60,000+
Type of Stage: Proscenium
Stage Dimensions: 36 x 32, 5'5 R 5'5 L
Seating Capacity: 600
Organization Type: Performing; Resident; Educational

2719
FIGURES OF SPEECH THEATRE
77 Durham Road
Freeport, ME 4032
Phone: 207-865-6355
Fax: 207-865-6355
e-mail: figures@concentric.net
Web Site: www.figures.org
Management:
Managing Director: Carol Farrell
Artistic Director: John Farrell
Mission: Tours nationally and internationally. Award winning adult productions as well as family shows. Presenters include Kennedy Center, New Victory Theatre, Jim Henson festival.
Utilizes: Actors; Collaborating Artists; Collaborations; Commissioned Composers; Commissioned Music; Composers; Guest Companies; Guest Conductors; Guest Designers; Guest Lecturers; Guest Musical Directors; Local Artists; Original Music Scores; Resident Professionals; Sign Language Translators; Visual Arts
Founded: 1982
Specialized Field: Staged Readings; Contemporary
Status: Non-Profit, Professional
Paid Staff: 2
Volunteer Staff: 3
Paid Artists: 8
Non-paid Artists: 1
Income Sources: Earned & contributed
Annual Attendance: 25,000

2720
PUBLIC THEATRE
31 Maple Street
Lewiston, ME 04240
Phone: 207-782-3200
e-mail: info@thepublictheatre.org
Web Site: www.thepublictheatre.org
Officers:
President: Sheri Olstein
VP: Kathy Gleason
Treasurer: Thomas H Platz
Secretary: Andrea Quaid
Management:
Artistic Director: Christopher Schario
Office Manager: Carol Ham
Associate Artistic Director: Janet Mitchko
Mission: Founded to bring a high quality professional theatre to the people of Maine, at an affordable price. In choosing the season, we look for plays that speak from the ehart; that are life-affirming and uplifting even when the subject matter is dark or painful; that use our languageinpowerful and provocative ways; that invite the audience to see their worls in a new way.
Utilizes: Actors; AEA Actors; Collaborating Artists; Collaborations; Composers; Contract Actors; Designers; Equity Actors; Five Seasonal Concerts; Guest Accompanists; Guest Artists; Guest Designers; Guest Ensembles; Guest Speakers; Local Artists & Directors; Organization Contracts; Original Music Scores; Resident Professionals; Scenic Designers; Soloists; Students
Founded: 1991

Specialized Field: Mostly Contemporary Plays; Youth Theater
Status: Non-Profit, Professional
Paid Staff: 7
Volunteer Staff: 65
Budget: $500,000
Income Sources: Ticket Sales; Grants; Corporate Support; Donations
Affiliations: AEA
Annual Attendance: 17,000
Type of Stage: Proscenium
Stage Dimensions: 36' x 33'
Seating Capacity: 307

2721
DOWNRIVER THEATRE COMPANY
9 O'Brien Avenue
Machias, ME 04654-1397
Phone: 207-255-1200
Fax: 207-255-4864
Toll-free: 888-468-6866
e-mail: ummadmissions@maine.edu
Officers:
    President: Skip Cole
Management:
    President: Sue Huseman
    VP: Cynthia Huggins
Mission: The Downriver Theatre Company will present its 2003 bill of fare in the spacious and well-appointed Performing Arts Center at the University of Maine and Machias.
Founded: 1990
Specialized Field: Educational; Theater Workshops
Status: Non-Equity; Nonprofit
Season: June 15 - August 15

2722
THEATRE AT MONMOUTH
PO Box 385
Monmouth, ME 04259-0385
Phone: 207-933-9999
Fax: 207-933-2952
e-mail: tamoffice@theatreatmonmouth.org
Web Site: www.theatreatmonmouth.org
Management:
    Artistic Director: Sally Wood
    Producing Director: David Greenham
Founded: 1970
Specialized Field: Comedy; Youth Theater; Dinner Theater; Classic
Status: Non-Profit, Professional
Paid Staff: 50
Paid Artists: 20

2723
ACADIA REPERTORY THEATRE
PO Box 106
Mount Desert, ME 4660
Phone: 207-244-7260
Toll-free: 888-362-7480
e-mail: arep@acadia.net
Management:
    Artistic Director: Ken Stack
Mission: In our quaint performance space which seats 148, we have presented an impressive mix of comedies, dramas, mysteries, and children's theatre for over a quarter of a century.
Founded: 1973
Specialized Field: Summer Stock
Status: Non-Equity; Commercial
Season: July - September
Type of Stage: Flexible; Thrust
Stage Dimensions: 20'x 25'
Seating Capacity: 148

2724
MARITIME PRODUCTIONS
PO Box 2400
Ogunquit, ME 3907
Phone: 207-641-2313
Fax: 207-641-2314
Management:
    Artistic Director: Rene Risher
Founded: 1993
Specialized Field: Theater Cruise; Historical
Status: Non-Equity; Commercial
Season: June - October

2725
OGUNQUIT PLAYHOUSE
PO Box 915
Ogunquit, ME 3907
Phone: 207-646-2402
Fax: 207-646-4732
Web Site: www.ogunquitplayhouse.org
Officers:
    President: Larry Smith
Management:
    Producer: Roy Rogosin
    Marketing Director: Christina Williams
    Assistant Producer: Jean Benda
    Director Operations: Kimberly Starling
Founded: 1933
Specialized Field: Summer Stock
Status: Professional; Commercial
Paid Staff: 29
Volunteer Staff: 10
Paid Artists: 50
Season: June - September
Performs At: Ogunquit Playhouse
Annual Attendance: 40,000
Facility Category: Summer Theatre
Type of Stage: Proscenium
Seating Capacity: 750
Rental Contact: Kemberly Starling
Organization Type: Sponsoring

2726
PORTLAND STAGE COMPANY
25A Forest Avenue
Portland, ME 04101
Phone: 207-774-1043
Fax: 207-774-0576
e-mail: info@portlandstage.org
Web Site: www.portlandstage.org
Management:
    President: Valerie Gallin
    Artistic Director: Anita Stewart
    Managing Director: Camilla Barrantes
Mission: The leading professional theater in Northern New England, Portland Stage Company entertains, educates and engages its audiences by producing a wide range of artistic works and programs that explore basic human issues and concerns relevant to the communities served by the theater. The guiding principle is to promote creativity and dialogue among artists, staff, board and audience.
Utilizes: Actors; AEA Actors; Artists-in-Residence; Choreographers; Commissioned Composers; Dancers; Designers; Educators; Five Seasonal Concerts; Grant Writers; Guest Accompanists; Guest Artists; Guest Companies; Guest Conductors; Guest Designers; Guest Instructors; Guest Lecturers; Guest Musicians; Guest Soloists; Guild Activities; Local Artists; Local Unknown Artists; Multimedia; Music; Original Music Scores; Performance Artists; Selected Students; Soloists; Visual Arts
Founded: 1974

Specialized Field: Contemporary
Status: Non-Profit, Professional
Budget: $1,200,000
Income Sources: Ticket Sales; Donations
Performs At: Portland Performing Arts Center
Affiliations: LORT; SDC; USA; TCG
Annual Attendance: 50,000
Facility Category: Theater
Seating Capacity: 286
Year Built: 1920
Year Remodeled: 1979
Rental Contact: Camilla Barrantes
Organization Type: Performing; Resident; Educational

2727
LAKEWOOD THEATER
PO Box 331
Skowhegan, ME 4976
Phone: 207-474-7176
e-mail: generalinfo@lakewoodtheater.org
Web Site: http://www.lakewoodtheater.org/
Management:
    Treasurer: Jeffrey Quinn
Mission: Standing in a high grove of stately white birch, Lakewood Theater, the State Theater of Maine, presents high quality entertainment and stage education at a unique and beautiful site that is particularly Maine.
Founded: 1901
Specialized Field: Summer Stock; Drama; Comedy; Youth Theater
Status: Non-Equity; Nonprofit
Season: May - September
Type of Stage: Proscenium
Seating Capacity: 300

2728
SANFORD MAINE STAGE COMPANY
PO Box 486
Springvale, ME 4086
Phone: 207-324-9691
Officers:
    President: Leo Lunser
    Secretary: Melanie Emmons
Management:
    Buisness Manager: Mary Stair
Mission: We are a community theater located on Beaver Hill in Springvale, Maine. We offer quality, affordable entertainment for Southern Maine.
Founded: 1984
Specialized Field: Musical; Drama; Comedy
Status: Non-Equity; Nonprofit
Season: April - December
Type of Stage: Proscenium
Stage Dimensions: 30' x 30'
Seating Capacity: 160

Maryland

2729
ANNAPOLIS SUMMER GARDEN THEATRE
143 Compromise Street
Annapolis, MD 21401
Phone: 410-268-9212
Management:
    President: Jami Adkins
Founded: 1966
Specialized Field: Outdoor Theater; Musical; Theater Workshops; Youth Theater

2730
ARENA PLAYERS
801 McCulloh Street
Baltimore, MD 21201
Phone: 410-728-6500
Fax: 410-728-6503
Management:
   Artistic Director: Ed Terry
   Artistic Director: Donald Owen
   Managing Director: Rodney Orange Jr
   President: Edward Smith
Mission: Discovering, fostering and showcasing community talent.
Utilizes: Guest Companies
Founded: 1953
Specialized Field: Community Theater
Status: Non-Profit, Professional
Paid Staff: 1
Volunteer Staff: 20
Non-paid Artists: all
Income Sources: National Endowment for the Arts; Maryland State Arts Council; Mayor's Committee
Annual Attendance: 12,000
Facility Category: Community Theatre
Type of Stage: Thrust
Stage Dimensions: 22x14
Seating Capacity: 300
Year Remodeled: 1975
Organization Type: Performing; Touring; Educational

2731
BALTIMORE ACTORS' THEATRE
The Dumbarton House
300 Dumbarton Road
Baltimore, MD 21212
Phone: 410-337-8519
Fax: 410-337-8582
e-mail: batpro@baltimoreactorstheatre.org
Web Site: www.baltimoreactorstheatre.org
Officers:
   President: Helen M. Grigal
   Executive Director: Walter Anderson
Mission: Teaching and performing at a professional level.
Founded: 1959
Specialized Field: Musical; Educational
Status: Non-Profit, Professional
Paid Staff: 10
Paid Artists: 8
Performs At: Oregon Ridge Dinner Theatre
Organization Type: Performing; Touring; Educational

2732
CENTER STAGE
700 N Calvert Street
Baltimore, MD 21202-3686
Phone: 410-332-0033
Fax: 410-725-2522
e-mail: info@centerstage.org
Web Site: www.centerstage.org
Management:
   President: Lynn Deering
   Artistic Director: Irene Lewis
   Managing Director: Michael Ross
   Director of Audience Development: Barbara Watson
   Media Relations Director: Steve Lickteig
Mission: To serve as Maryland's official theatrical company.
Utilizes: Guest Companies
Founded: 1963
Specialized Field: Musical; Comedy; Youth Theater; Ethnic Theater; Classic; Contemporary
Status: Non-Profit, Professional
Paid Staff: 100
Volunteer Staff: 800
Paid Artists: 150
Performs At: Pearlstone Theater, Head Theater
Affiliations: BACVA; Baltimore Tourism Association; Baltimore Theatre Alliance; TCG; AEA
Annual Attendance: 106,462
Type of Stage: Thrust, Flexible
Stage Dimensions: 40' x 36'; 67' x 118'
Seating Capacity: 541, 100-400
Organization Type: Performing; Resident; Educational

2733
COCKPIT IN COURT SUMMER THEATRE
CCBC, Essex Campus
7201 Rossville Boulevard
Baltimore, MD 21237-3899
Phone: 443-840-2787
Fax: 443-840-1615
e-mail: cockpitincourt@ccbcmd.edu
Web Site: www.ccbc.edu
Officers:
   President: William Pheil
   VP: H Ray Lawson
   Recording Secretary: Ellen Moats
   Corresponding Secretary: Jennifer Otero
Management:
   Artistic Director: James Hunnicutt, jhunnicutt@ccbcmd.edu
   Administrative Manager: Lisa L Boeren, lboeren@ccbcmd.edu
Mission: Community-based performing arts organization dedicated to providing a variety of quality live theatre opportunities to our performers and audiences including musicals, Shakespeare, drama and children's theatre.
Founded: 1972
Specialized Field: Community Theater
Status: Non-Profit, Non-Professional
Paid Staff: 5
Volunteer Staff: 50
Paid Artists: 20
Non-paid Artists: 75
Season: June - August
Type of Stage: Proscenium

2734
DUNDALK COMMUNITY THEATRE
7200 Soillers Point Road
Baltimore, MD 21222
Phone: 443-840-2787
Fax: 443-840-1615
e-mail: lboeren@ccbcmd.edu
Officers:
   President: Kevin Ecker
   Vice President: John Amato
   Secretary: Cheryl Vourvoulas
Management:
   Artistic & Technical Director: Marc Smith
   Managing Director: Tom Colonna
Mission: Community-based performing arts organization of a professional quality at a reasonable ticket price and to be a resource for expanding the cultural experiences of the community
Utilizes: Actors; Choreographers; Community Talent; Educators; Instructors; Local Artists; Music; Resident Professionals
Founded: 1974
Specialized Field: Musical; Comedy; Community Theater; Contemporary
Status: Non-Profit, Non-Professional
Paid Staff: 3
Non-paid Artists: 104
Budget: $90,000
Income Sources: Ticket Sales; Subscription Sales; Private Donations; Grants
Performs At: Dundalk Community Theatre
Annual Attendance: 6,800
Seating Capacity: 388
Year Built: 1981
Rental Contact: Mary Huffman

2735
THEATRE HOPKINS
3400N Charles Street
The Johns Hopkins University
Baltimore, MD 21218
Phone: 410-516-7159
Fax: 410-261-1217
e-mail: thehop@jhu.edu
Web Site: www.jhu.edu/~theatre
Management:
   Artistic Director: Suzanne Straughn Pratt
   Managing Director: Graham Yearley
Mission: Theatre Hopkins presents a four-play season.
Founded: 1921
Specialized Field: Classic
Status: Non-Profit, Non-Professional
Paid Staff: 2

2736
THEATRE PROJECT
45 W Preston Street
Baltimore, MD 21201
Phone: 410-752-8558
e-mail: office@theatreproject.org
Web Site: www.theatreproject.org
Management:
   Producing Director: Anne C Fulwiler, anne@theatreproject.org
Mission: Through the presentation of a diverse array of original and experimental theatre, music, and dance, Theatre Project connects the artists and audiences of Baltimore with a global community of performers. We seek to nurture those artists who are actively experimenting with new forms of expression and support both performers of international reputation and emerging local companies creating new work.
Utilizes: Collaborating Artists; Collaborations; Community Members; Community Talent; Grant Writers; Guest Accompanists; Guest Artists; Guest Choreographers; Guest Companies; Guest Composers; Guest Conductors; Guest Designers; Guest Directors; Guest Ensembles; Guest Lecturers; Guest Musical Directors; Guest Musicians; Guest Speakers; Guest Teachers; Instructors; Local Artists & Directors; Local Talent; Lyricists; Multi Collaborations; Multimedia; Original Music Scores; Paid Performers; Soloists; Students
Founded: 1971
Opened: 1971
Specialized Field: Performing Arts; Theatre; Dance; Opera; Music
Status: Non-Profit, Professional; 501(3)k
Paid Staff: 3
Volunteer Staff: 10
Budget: $250,000
Income Sources: Ticket Sales; Individual & Corporate Donors; William G Baker Memorial Fund; Baltimore County; Baltimore City; Maryland State Arts Council
Performs At: Theatre Project
Affiliations: Theatre Communications Group
Annual Attendance: 11,000
Type of Stage: Modified Black Box
Stage Dimensions: 35' x 35'
Seating Capacity: 150
Year Built: 1887

Year Remodeled: 1985
Cost: $1,000/day; $3,000/week
Rental Contact: Anne Fulwiler
Organization Type: Sponsoring

2737
IMAGINATION STAGE
4908 Auburn Avenue
Bethesda, MD 20814
Phone: 301-961-6060
e-mail: boxoffice@imaginationstage.org
Management:
Founder/Executive Director: Janet Stanford
Artistic Director: Jerry Morenoff
Managing Director: Richard Bradbury
Coordinating Producer: Judi Canter
Director Instructional Advancement: Kathryn Chase Bryer
Associate Artistic Director: Patricia Kratzer
Director Financial Services: Laurie Levy-Page
Director Marketing/Public Relations: David Markey
Director Theatre Education: Charlotte Sommers
Mission: Nuture the creative spirit in all children and to cultivate skills that will serve them throughout their lives. In offering diverse and inclusive theatre education programs,aim to develop the whole child by encouraging self-expression, instilling respect for others and providing opportunities and accomplishment. Respect all talent, value all artistry and welcome all children.
Specialized Field: Children's Theater; Theater Workshops

2738
ROUND HOUSE THEATRE
PO Box 30688
Bethesda, MD 20902
Mailing Address: PO Box 30688 Bethesda, MD 20824-0688
Phone: 240-644-1099
Fax: 240-644-1090
e-mail: roundhouse@roundhousetheatre.org
Web Site: www.roundhousetheatre.org
Officers:
President: Peter A Jablow
VP: Judith H Zickler
Management:
President of Board of Trustees: Donald Boardman
Artistic Director: Jerry Whiddon
Managing Director: Ira Hillman
Director Production: Danshia Crosby
Mission: To vitalize an ever increasing circle of individuals and communities with a multitude of compelling theatre expirences through performance and education.
Utilizes: Guest Companies; Singers
Founded: 1978
Specialized Field: Musical; Comedy; Youth Theater; Contemporary
Status: Non-Profit, Professional
Paid Staff: 30
Income Sources: Actors' Equity Association
Performs At: Professional LORT-D Theatre
Organization Type: Performing; Touring; Resident Educational

2739
REP STAGE
10901 Little Patuxent Parkway
Columbia, MD 21044

Phone: 410-772-4484
Fax: 410-772-4040
e-mail: mstebbins@howardcc.edu
Web Site: www.repstage.org
Management:
Artistic Director: Michael Stebbins
Production Manager: Brett Ashley Crawford
Mission: Red Stage' mission is to provide Howard Country residents professional theatre, including classics, recently released plays from Broadway and off-Broadway plus new works.
Utilizes: Actors; AEA Actors; Choreographers; Designers; Guest Conductors; High School Drama; Instructors; Local Artists; Music; Performance Artists; Resident Professionals; Selected Students; Visual Arts
Founded: 1993
Specialized Field: Drama; Classic
Status: Non-Profit, Professional
Paid Staff: 5
Volunteer Staff: 100
Paid Artists: 75
Season: September - March
Affiliations: LOW7, BTA
Annual Attendance: 10,000
Facility Category: Two theatres
Type of Stage: Proscenium; Flexible
Stage Dimensions: 60' x 40'
Seating Capacity: 250; 200
Rental Contact: Janelle Broderick

2740
CUMBERLAND THEATRE
101 North Johnson Street
Cumberland, MD 21502
Phone: 301-759-4990
Fax: 301-777-7189
e-mail: boxoffice@cumberlandtheatre.com
Web Site: www.cumberlandtheatre.com
Management:
Artistic Director: Don Whisted
Utilizes: Community Members; Equity Actors
Founded: 1987
Specialized Field: Musical; Comedy; Youth Theater; Classic; Contemporary
Status: Non-Profit, Professional
Paid Staff: 30
Paid Artists: 30
Season: June - December
Type of Stage: Proscenium; Thrust
Stage Dimensions: 40' x 28'
Seating Capacity: 197

2741
ADVENTURE THEATRE: GLEN ECHO PARK
7300 MacArthur Boulevard
Glen Echo, MD 20812
Phone: 301-320-5331
Fax: 301-320-3108
e-mail: info@adventuretheatre.org
Web Site: www.adventuretheatre.org
Officers:
President: Carol Leahy
Management:
Marketing Manager: Tyler Whitmore
Founded: 1951
Specialized Field: Children's Theater
Status: Non-Profit, Professional
Paid Staff: 50
Paid Artists: 100

2742
PETRUCCI'S DINNER THEATRE
312 Main Street
Laurel, MD 20707
Phone: 301-490-1993
Management:
Producer: C David Petrucci
Producer: Angela Jo Leonard
Founded: 1977
Specialized Field: Dinner Theater
Status: Commercial
Income Sources: National Dinner Theatre Association
Organization Type: Performing

2743
YOUNG ARTISTS THEATRE
Route 29 & 216 Cherry Tree Center
Laurel, MD 20723
Mailing Address: 11200 Scaggsville Road #127, Laurel, MD 20723
Phone: 301-604-2844
Fax: 301-604-2845
e-mail: contactus@yatheatre.com
Web Site: www.yatheatre.com
Officers:
Chairman: William P Furr
Vice Chairman: Henry Mitchell
Secretary: Carolyn Turner
Treasurer: Wade Reece
Management:
Director: Kathryn MacDonald, contactus@yatheatre.com
Mission: Providing performing arts instruction, educational workshops, original musical comedies, field trips and artists in residence
Founded: 1994
Specialized Field: Children's Theater; Educational; Musical Theatre
Status: Non-Profit, Non-Professional
Affiliations: Howard County Arts Council; Girl Scouts of the Nation's Capital & Central Maryland
Facility Category: Theatre and Dance Studio
Type of Stage: Thrust
Stage Dimensions: 32'x15
Seating Capacity: 140
Year Built: 1996
Rental Contact: Director Kathy MacDonald

2744
SMALLBEER THEATRE COMPANY
4107 33rd Street
Mt. Rainier, MD 20712-1947
Phone: 301-277-8117
Fax: 703-993-2191
Management:
Artistic Director: Lynnie Raybuck
Founded: 1987
Specialized Field: Musical; Comedy; Ethnic Theater; Puppet; Contemporary
Status: Non-Profit, Professional
Paid Artists: 8
Season: September - June

2745
OLNEY THEATRE CENTER
NATIONAL PLAYERS
2001 Olney-Sandy Spring Road
Olney, MD 20832
Phone: 301-924-3400
Fax: 301-924-2654
e-mail: cbenjamin@olneytheatre.org
Web Site: www.olneytheatre.org
Management:

President: Harry Teter Jr
VP: Jim Petosa
Treasurer: Sandeep Saggar
Chairman: William H Graham Sr
Mission: Mission is to create professional theater productions and other programs to nurture the artist, student, technician, administrator and audience member; to develop each of these individual's potenial and skills using comprehensive possibilities of theater and the performing arts.
Utilizes: Actors; AEA Actors; Choreographers; Dancers; Five Seasonal Concerts; Grant Writers; Guest Accompanists; Guest Artists; Guest Composers; Guest Conductors; Guest Designers; Guest Lecturers; Guest Musical Directors; Guest Teachers; Instructors; Local Artists; Multimedia; Music; Original Music Scores; Performance Artists; Resident Professionals; Sign Language Translators; Soloists; Student Interns; Visual Arts
Founded: 1938
Specialized Field: Drama; Musical; Community Theater
Status: Professional; Nonprofit
Paid Staff: 25
Volunteer Staff: 300
Paid Artists: 200
Budget: 2.5 Million
Income Sources: Actors' Equity Association; Society for Stage Directors and Choreographers
Season: March - Decembers
Performs At: Mainstage; Theatre Lab; Amphitheater
Annual Attendance: 70,000+
Seating Capacity: 450
Year Built: 1938
Year Remodeled: 1992
Rental Contact: Bill Synder
Organization Type: Performing; Touring; Educational

2746
INTERACT STORY THEATRE
204 Stonegate Drive
Silver Spring, MD 20905
Phone: 301-879-9305
Toll-free: 888-501-7986
e-mail: info@interactstory.com
Management:
   Director: Lenore Blank Kelner
Mission: Our professional actors are also experienced educators helping students, parents and teachers unlock and maximize their creative potential.
Specialized Field: Youth Theater; Theater Workshops

2747
SILVER SPRING STAGE
10145 Colesville Road
Silver Spring, MD 20901
Mailing Address: PO Box 3086 Silver Spring, MD 20918-3086
Phone: 301-593-6036
Officers:
   Chairperson: Barry Hoffman
   Vice-Chairperson: Carol Leahy
   Treasurer: Christopher Carey
   Secretary: Judie Chaimson
   Vice-Chairperson: Norm Seltzer
Management:
   Chair Person: Barry Hoffman
   Vice Chairpersons: Rich Ley
   Treasurer: Seth Ghitelman
   Secretary: Pauline Griller Mitchell
   Facilities Coordinator: Bill Strein
   External/Community Affairs: Norm Seltzer
   Grants/Fund Raising: Judie Chaimson
   Membership Director: Neil Edgell

Volunteer Development: Leon Levenson
Specialized Field: Community Theater; Drama; Comedy

Massachusetts

2748
UNDERGROUND RAILWAY THEATER
41 Foster Street
Arlington, MA 02474
Phone: 781-643-6916
Fax: 781-643-7333
Web Site: www.undergroundrailwaytheatre.org
Management:
   Artistic Director: Debra Wise
   Managing Director: Catherine Carr-Kelly
   Business Manager: Tracey Clarke
Mission: Underground Railway Theater explores a changing landscape of artistic forms and social concerns, combining puppetry, music and acting to engage diverse audiences with images that challenge and delight, inform and celebrate.
Founded: 1978
Specialized Field: Musical; Puppet; Touring Company
Status: Non-Profit, Professional
Paid Staff: 5
Paid Artists: 15
Type of Stage: Proscenium
Stage Dimensions: 30' x 18'
Seating Capacity: 140
Organization Type: Performing; Touring; Educational

2749
PILGRAM THEATER RESEARCH & PERFORMANCE COLLABORATION
1948 Conway Road
Ashfield, MA 01330
Phone: 413-628-0112
Fax: 413-628-0112
e-mail: pilgrim@mit.edu
Web Site: www.pilgrimtheatre.org
Management:
   President: Kim Mancuso
   Executive Director: Kermit Dumkelberg
Founded: 1986
Specialized Field: Contemporary; Experimental
Status: Non-Profit, Professional
Paid Staff: 8
Paid Artists: 8

2750
BELMONT DRAMATIC CLUB
123 D Sycamore Street
Apartment 1
Belmont, MA 02478
Phone: 617-484-2529
e-mail: info@belmontdramaticclub.org
Web Site: www.belmontdramaticclub.org
Officers:
   President: Vern Gerig
   Vice President: Clifford Grubb
   Secretary: Roy Johnson
   Treasurer: Carter Lehmann
Management:
   President: Carolyn Binghan
Mission: Providing quality drama for the community.
Utilizes: Guest Companies
Founded: 1903
Specialized Field: Drama; New Plays
Status: Non-Profit, Non-Professional
Paid Staff: 3
Volunteer Staff: 10
Paid Artists: var

Non-paid Artists: var
Income Sources: Ticket Sales
Performs At: Payson Park Church
Organization Type: Performing

2751
NORTH SHORE MUSIC THEATRE
62 Dunham Road
Beverly, MA 01915
Phone: 978-232-7203
Fax: 978-921-0793
Toll-free: 800-926-9220
e-mail: pr@nsmt.org
Web Site: www.nsmt.org
Officers:
   President: John P Drislane
   Vice President: Donald J Short
   Treasurer: Wendell P Wood
Management:
   President: John Kimbell
   Executive Director: James K Polese
   Executive Producer: Jon Kimbell
   Marketing Director: Joesph Amaral
   Chairman: Kevin Bottomley
   Vice Chairman: Thomas S Barenboim
   Vice Chairman: David Fellows
   Secretary/Clerk: Marcia Ruderman
   Director Marketing: Joseph Amaral
Mission: To emphasize the development of new musical works and the expansion of educational programming to capture the interest of all age groups in the creative process.
Utilizes: Guest Companies
Founded: 1955
Specialized Field: Comedy; Youth Theater; Dinner Theater; Puppet; Contemporary
Status: Non-Profit, Professional
Paid Staff: 220
Volunteer Staff: 500
Paid Artists: 400
Budget: $11,000,000
Income Sources: Ticket Sales; Contributions
Season: April - December
Performs At: North Shore Music Theatre
Annual Attendance: 350,000
Type of Stage: In-the-Round
Seating Capacity: 1800
Year Built: 1955
Year Remodeled: 1990
Organization Type: Performing; Touring; Educational

2752
BOSTON CHILDREN'S THEATRE
321 Columbus Avenue
Boston, MA 02116
Phone: 617-424-6634
Fax: 617-424-7108
e-mail: info@bostonchildrenstheatre.org
Web Site: www.bostonchildrenstheatre.org
Officers:
   Board President: Valerie LaCount
   Executive Director: Patricia M. Gleeson
Mission: To promote live theatre for children, by children; Enchanted Forest. Hosted at the Franklin Park Zoo in October.
Utilizes: Guest Companies; Singers
Founded: 1951
Specialized Field: Musical; Comedy; Youth Theater; Classic; Contemporary
Status: Non-Profit, Non-Professional
Paid Staff: 20
Income Sources: New England Theatre Conference; Association of American Theatre for Youth; Massachusetts Cultural Alliance

Performs At: New England Life Hall
Organization Type: Performing

2753
HUNTINGTON THEATRE COMPANY
Boston University
264 Huntington Avenue
Boston, MA 02115
Phone: 617-266-0800
Fax: 617-421-9674
e-mail: thehuntington@huntingtontheatre.org
Web Site: www.huntingtontheatre.org
Management:
    Development Director: Howard L Breslau
    Marketing: Temple Gill
Utilizes: Actors; AEA Actors; Choreographers;
Designers; Guest Designers; Resident Professionals;
Selected Students
Founded: 1982
Status: Non-Profit, Professional
Budget: $8 milliom
Income Sources: Ticket Sales; Donations
Season: September - June
Performs At: Boston University Theatre
Annual Attendance: 175,000
Facility Category: Theatre
Type of Stage: Proscenium
Seating Capacity: 890
Rental Contact: Roger Meeker
Organization Type: Performing; Resident

2754
LYRIC STAGE COMPANY OF BOSTON
140 Clarendon Street
Boston, MA 02116
Phone: 617-437-7172
Fax: 617-536-2830
Web Site: www.lyricstage.com
Management:
    President: Ellen Carno
    Managing Director: Sara Gildden
    Producing Artistic Director: Spiro Veloudos
Mission: Offering high-quality, professional theatre to
audiences at low prices, so that they can appreciate
their theatrical heritage.
Utilizes: Actors; AEA Actors; Choreographers;
Dancers; Designers; Guest Artists; Guest Companies;
Guest Designers; Guest Musical Directors; Guild
Activities; Local Artists; Multimedia; Music; New
Productions; Organization Contracts; Resident
Professionals; Sign Language Translators; Soloists;
Student Interns
Founded: 1974
Specialized Field: Drama; Classic
Status: Professional; Nonprofit
Paid Staff: 5
Volunteer Staff: 50
Paid Artists: 55
Budget: $750,000
Income Sources: Actors' Equity Association; New
England Area Theatres
Season: September - May
Affiliations: AEA, SSOC
Type of Stage: 3/4 Thrust
Seating Capacity: 236
Organization Type: Performing

2755
PUBLICK THEATRE
165 Friend Street
Boston, MA 02134
Phone: 617-782-5425
e-mail: heydiego@aol.com
Web Site: www.publick.org

Officers:
    President: Michael McDermott
    Treasurer: Randall Filer
Management:
    Artistic Director: Spiro Veloudos
    Marketing/Development Director: Deborah
Schoenberg
    Artistic Director: Diego Arciniegas
    Artistic Associate: Susanne Nitter
    Production Manager: Maureen Heakey
Mission: To discover, develop and showcase
Boston-area theatrical talent in programs of
professional quality that are accessible to a diverse
audience.
Utilizes: Guest Companies
Founded: 1970
Specialized Field: Musical; Ensembles
Status: Professional; Nonprofit
Season: June - September
Performs At: The Publick Theatre
Organization Type: Performing; Touring; Resident;
Sponsoring

2756
WHEELOCK FAMILY THEATRE
200 The Riverway
Boston, MA 02215
Phone: 617-879-2147
Fax: 617-879-2021
e-mail: tickets@wheelock.edu
Web Site: www.wheelockfamilytheatre.org
Management:
    Producer: Susan Kosoff
    Artistic Director: Jane Staab
    Marketing Director: Charles Baldwin
Mission: To improve the lives of children and families
through the shared experience of live performance.
Founded: 1981
Specialized Field: Performance And Education For
Youth
Status: Non-Profit, Professional
Paid Staff: 7
Volunteer Staff: 100
Paid Artists: 50
Season: October - November
Affiliations: AEA; TCG; StageSource; TAMA; CBACT;
Colleges of the Fenway; Fenway Alliance
Annual Attendance: 30,000
Type of Stage: Proscenium
Seating Capacity: 650

2757
PUPPET SHOWPLACE THEATRE
32 Station Street
Brookline, MA 02445
Phone: 617-731-6400
Fax: 617-731-0526
e-mail: info@puppetshowplace.org
Web Site: www.puppetshowplace.org
Officers:
    Board Chairperson: Alice Schaefer
Management:
    Executive Director: Kris Higgins
    Artistic Director: Roxie Myhrum
    Artist-In-Residence: Brad Shurs
    Box Office Manager: Kate Ott
    Marketing Director: Ben Henry
Mission: A non-profit performing arts organization
committed to excellence in puppetry for all audiences.
Utilizes: Artists-in-Residence
Founded: 1974
Specialized Field: Puppet; Children's Theater
Status: Non-Profit, Professional
Paid Staff: 7

Income Sources: Puppeteers of America; United
International Marionette Association
Seating Capacity: 100
Organization Type: Performing; Touring; Resident;
Sponsoring

2758
AMERICAN REPERTORY THEATRE
Loeb Drama Center, Harvard University
64 Brattle Street
Cambridge, MA 02138
Phone: 617-495-2668
Fax: 617-495-1705
e-mail: info@amrep.org
Web Site: www.amrep.org
Management:
    Executive Director: Robert J Orchard
    Artistic Director: Robert Woodruff
    General Manager: Jonathan Seth Miller
    Associate Director: Francois Rochaix
Founded: 1966
Specialized Field: Ensembles; Classic; Contemporary
Status: Non-Profit, Professional
Paid Staff: 60
Paid Artists: 50
Income Sources: Major Grants, Andrew W. Mellon
Foundation; The Harold and Mimi Steir Charitable Trust;
National Endowment for the Arts; Shubert Foundation;
Massachusetts Cultural Council
Season: October - July
Type of Stage: Flexible Prosc.; Proscenium
Seating Capacity: 556; 353

2759
AMERICAN REPERTORY THEATRE
Loeb Drama Center, Harvard University
64 Brattle Street
Cambridge, MA 02138
Phone: 617-495-2668
Fax: 617-495-1705
e-mail: info@amrep.org
Management:
    Artistic Director: Robert Woodruff
    Executive Director: Robert J Orchard
    General Manager: Jonathan Seth Miller
    Associate Director: Francois Rochaix
    Associate Director: Marcus Stern
    Director Development: Jan Geidt
    Production Manager: Patricia Quinlan
    Marketing Director: Henry Lussier
    Associate Artistic Director: Gideon Lester
Mission: The American Repertory Theatre is a
separately incorporated, not-for-profit organization
chartered to provide a service to the widest possible
public in the Boston/Cambridge community and to the
theatre world in general.
Utilizes: Guest Companies
Founded: 1966
Specialized Field: Educational; Theater Workshops
Status: Professional; Nonprofit
Paid Staff: 7
Income Sources: Actors' Equity Association; League
of Resident Theatres; Subscriptions; Massachusetts
Cultural Councils
Performs At: Loeb Drama Center; A.R.T New Stages
Affiliations: Andrew W. Mellon Foundation; Harold and
Mimi Steinberg Charitable Trust; National Endowment
for the Arts; Shubert Foundation; PaineWebber Group
Organization Type: Performing; Touring; Resident;
Educational

2760
CHARLESTOWN WORKING THEATER
442 Bunker Hill Street
Charlestown, MA 02129
Phone: 617-242-3285
e-mail: info@workingtheater.org
Web Site: http://www.charlestownworkingtheater.org/
Management:
Managing Director: Kristen Johnson
Mission: To enhance the quality of life through the artistic process.
Utilizes: Guest Companies; Singers
Founded: 1972
Specialized Field: Summer Stock; Community Theater; Puppet
Status: Professional; Semi-Professional; Non-Professional; Nonprofit
Income Sources: Massachusetts Council on the Arts & Humanities
Organization Type: Performing; Touring; Resident; Educational; Sponsoring

2761
CHESTER THEATRE COMPANY
PO Box 722
Chester, MA 01011
Phone: 413-354-7770
Fax: 413-354-7825
Web Site: www.chestertheatre.org
Officers:
Chair: Cipora Feiner
Vice Chair: Harley Erdman
Treasurer: Ron Belfiglio
Management:
Artistic Director: Byam Stevens
Business Manager: Victoria Braim
Utilizes: Actors; AEA Actors; Artists-in-Residence; Collaborations; Commissioned Composers; Commissioned Music; Designers; Fine Artists; Five Seasonal Concerts; Guest Accompanists; Guest Companies; Guest Designers; Guest Lecturers; Guest Musical Directors; Guest Teachers; Instructors; Local Artists; Multimedia; Original Music Scores; Performance Artists; Playwrights; Poets; Resident Artists; Resident Professionals; Selected Students; Soloists; Student Interns; Special Technical Talent; Theatre Companies; Touring Companies; Visual Arts
Founded: 1990
Specialized Field: Summer Stock
Status: Nonprofit
Budget: $175,000
Season: July - September
Performs At: Theatre
Annual Attendance: 5,500
Facility Category: Town Hall
Type of Stage: Proscenium
Stage Dimensions: 25' x 15'
Seating Capacity: 150

2762
STRAWBERRY PRODUCTIONS
PO Box 12
Chicopee, MA 01021
Phone: 413-592-4184
Fax: 413-594-7758
e-mail: info@strawberryproductions.com
Web Site: www.strawberryproductions.com/
Officers:
President: Jack Desroches
Management:
Producer: Jack Desroches
Division Manager: Nancy J Floyd
Technical Director: Gary Bessett

Founded: 1976
Specialized Field: Drama; Classic
Status: Commercial; Non-Equity
Season: Year Round

2763
YARD
Middle Road
Chilmark, MA 02535
Mailing Address: PO Box 405
Phone: 508-645-9662
Fax: 508-645-3176
e-mail: admin@dancetheyard.org
Web Site: www.dancetheyard.org
Management:
Artistic Director: Wendy Taucher
Founder: Patricia Nanon
Artistic Director: Luis Welk
Mission: Stives to promote growth and experimentation in theatre arts with its mission to give professional artists the time and space to create and perform dance, music, theatre pieces in a concentrated and supported environment.
Founded: 1973
Specialized Field: Youth Theater; Community Theater; Contemporary
Status: Non-Profit, Professional
Paid Staff: 3
Paid Artists: 50
Season: Summer
Type of Stage: Black Box
Stage Dimensions: 34'x 28'
Seating Capacity: 100

2764
GLOUCESTER STAGE COMPANY
267 E Main Street
Gloucester, MA 01930
Phone: 508-281-4099
Fax: 508-283-5150
Management:
Artistic Director: Israel Horovitz
Publicity Director: Heidi J Dallin
Production Stage Manager: Janet Howes
Technical Director: Rob Duggan
Production Coordinator: Keri Ellis Cahill
Assistant Artistic Director: Robbie Chasitz
Mission: To support contemporary playwrights through staged readings and productions of important new plays.
Utilizes: Guest Companies; Singers
Founded: 1979
Specialized Field: Ensemble
Status: Professional; Nonprofit
Organization Type: Performing; Resident; Educational; Sponsoring; Producing

2765
ARENA CIVIC THEATRE
PO Box 744
Greenfield, MA 01302
Phone: 413-863-2281
e-mail: par@crocker.com
Web Site: www.arenacivictheatre.org
Officers:
President: Jerry Marcanio
VP (External): Phyllis Roy
VP (Internal): Steve Woodard
Secretary: Elisa Martin
Treasurer: Sondra Radosh
Management:
President: Jerry Marcanio
VP: Robert Freedman

Mission: To recognize the unique ability of theatre to provide spiritual fulfillment and personal growth for its participants.
Utilizes: Guest Companies; Singers
Founded: 1970
Specialized Field: Community Theater
Status: Non-Profit
Paid Staff: 70
Income Sources: National Association of Local Arts Agencies; Mohawk Trail Association
Performs At: Shea Theater; Turner Falls, MA
Organization Type: Performing

2766
HINGHAM HIGH SCHOOL AUDITORIUM
17 Union Street
Hingham, MA 02043
Phone: 781-741-1500
Fax: 781-741-1515
Officers:
Chair: Christine Smith
Utilizes: Guest Artists; Guest Companies; Singers
Status: Non-Profit, Non-Professional
Performs At: Hingham High School Auditorium
Organization Type: Performing; Resident; Educational

2767
CAPE COD MELODY TENT
21 W Main Street
Hyannis, MA 02601
Phone: 508-775-5630
Fax: 508-778-0899
e-mail: info@themusiccircus.org
Web Site: www.melodytent.com
Management:
President: Vince Longo
Director of Marketing: Paula Gates
Marketing Associate: Jaime Saine, jsaine@themusiccircus.org
Founded: 1950
Specialized Field: Musical; Comedy; Community Theater; Classic; Summer Stock
Status: Non-Profit, Professional
Paid Staff: 70
Paid Artists: 600
Season: June 1 - September
Seating Capacity: 2300

2768
VILLAGE PLAYERS
PO Box 81
Hyannis, MA 69350
Phone: 308-458-2701
Management:
Artistic Director: Al Davis
Mission: To present and sponsor theatre.
Utilizes: Singers
Founded: 1980
Specialized Field: Summer Stock; Musical; Dinner Theater
Status: Professional; Semi-Professional; Nonprofit; Commercial
Organization Type: Performing; Touring; Sponsoring

2769
FOOTLIGHT CLUB
Eliot Hall
7A Eliot Street
Jamaica Plain, MA 02130
Phone: 617-524-3200
Fax: 617-524-6506
e-mail: boxoffice@footlight.org
Web Site: www.footlight.org
Officers:

All listings are in alphabetical order by state, then city, then organization within the city.

President: Paul Campbell
VP: Jane Yoffe
Secretary: Derek Clark
Treasurer: Jason Sheehan
Management:
President: Carol Gallagher
VP: Laurie Fisher
Secretary: Susanna Crampton
Volunteers Director: Sarah Kary
Mission: To provide quality theatre as an integral component of a vital arts community and to offer involvement to anyone interested in theatre.
Founded: 1877
Specialized Field: Community Theater
Status: Non-Professional
Paid Staff: 200
Performs At: Eliot Hall
Organization Type: Performing; Resident

2770
SHAKESPEARE & COMPANY
70 Kemble Street
Lenox, MA 01240-2813
Phone: 413-637-3353
Fax: 413-637-4274
e-mail: general@shakespeare.org
Web Site: www.shakespeare.org
Officers:
President: Tony Simotes
Board Of Chairman: Richard Mescon
Management:
Managing Director: Nicholas J. Puma, Jr., npuma@shakespeare.org
Artistic Director: Tony Simotes, tsimotes@shakespeare.org
Founding Artisitic Director: Tina Packer, tina@shakespeare.org
General Manager: Steve Ball
Artistic Associate: Elizabeth Aspenlieder
Mission: To create a theatre of unprecedented excellence in the Elizabethan ideals of inquiry, balance and harmony. To establish a theatre company which, by its commitment to the creative impulse, is a revolutionary force in society, which connects the truths of the past to the challenges and possibilities of today, which finds its source in the performance of Shakespeare's plays and reaches the widest possible audience through trainig and education.
Founded: 1978
Specialized Field: Shakespeare; Contemporary; New Plays
Status: Non-Profit, Professional
Paid Staff: 34
Volunteer Staff: 250
Paid Artists: 180
Budget: $4.3 million
Income Sources: Earned Income; Contributions
Season: May - January
Performs At: Founders' Theatre, SpringLawn Theatre and Outdoor Space at 70 Kemble Street.
Affiliations: AEA
Annual Attendance: 52,000

2771
MERRIMACK REPERTORY THEATRE
Liberty Hall
50 E Merrimack Street
Lowell, MA 01852
Phone: 978-454-6324
Fax: 978-934-0166
e-mail: info@merrimackrep.org
Web Site: www.merrimackrep.org
Management:
Artistic Director: Charles Towers

Managing Director: Lisa B Merrill-Buttzak
General Manager: Edgar Cyrus
Marketing Manager: Paul Marsh
Mission: To present engaging, vital theatre that communicates to the audience.
Utilizes: Actors; AEA Actors; Artists-in-Residence; Choreographers; Collaborating Artists; Collaborations; Commissioned Music; Composers; Contract Actors; Dancers; Designers; Educators; Fine Artists; Guest Accompanists; Guest Artists; Guest Companies; Guest Composers; Guest Conductors; Guest Designers; Guest Directors; Guest Instructors; Guest Lecturers; Guest Musical Directors; Guest Speakers; Guest Teachers; High School Drama; Instructors; Local Artists; Local Unknown Artists; Multimedia; Music; Original Music Scores; Paid Performers; Performance Artists; Resident Professionals; Scenic Designers; Sign Language Translators; Singers; Students; Visual Arts
Founded: 1979
Specialized Field: Contemporary; Drama
Status: Non-Profit, Professional
Paid Staff: 20
Paid Artists: 50
Budget: $1.8 million
Season: September - June
Performs At: Liberty Hall
Affiliations: Society for Stage Directors and Choreographers; Actors' Equity Association; USA; Dramatists Guild
Annual Attendance: 60,000
Type of Stage: 3/4 Thrust
Stage Dimensions: 34x30
Seating Capacity: 384
Year Built: 1900
Year Remodeled: 1984
Organization Type: Performing; Resident

2772
ACTORS THEATRE OF NANTUCKET
PO Box 1297
Nantucket, MA 02554-1297
Phone: 508-228-4305
Web Site: www.nantuckettheatre.com
Management:
Associate Director: Richard Cary
Artistic Director and Founder: Richard Cary
Mission: To offer professional theatre to Nantucket Island.
Utilizes: Guest Companies; Playwrights; Singers
Founded: 1992
Specialized Field: Musical; Children's Theater
Status: Professional; Nonprofit; Non-Equity
Organization Type: Performing; Resident; Educational; Sponsoring

2773
THEATRE WORKSHOP OF NANTUCKET
PO Box 1297
Nantucket, MA 02554
Phone: 508-228-4305
Web Site: www.theatreworkshop.com
Officers:
President: Elizabeth Gilbert
Treasurer: Marie Giffin
Management:
Business Manager: Edgar A Anderson
Artistic Director: S. Warren Krebs
Mission: To bring theatrical stage entertainment to the community using local talent; to offer year-round productions.
Utilizes: Guest Companies
Founded: 1956
Specialized Field: Community Theater
Status: Non-Professional; Nonprofit

Paid Staff: 25
Performs At: Bennett Hall
Organization Type: Performing; Educational

2774
NEW REPERTORY THEATRE
54 Lincoln Street
PO Box 610418
Newton, MA 02161-0418
Phone: 617-332-7058
Fax: 617-527-5217
e-mail: info@newrep.org
Web Site: www.newrep.org
Management:
President: Laura M Crary
Managing Director: Harriet Sheets
Producing Artistic Director: Rick Lombardo
Artistic Associate: Cory Elizabeth Nelson
Mission: Producing 5 professional theatre productions each year with an emphasis on area premieres and the classics.
Founded: 1984
Specialized Field: Musical; Comedy; Classic; Contemporary
Status: Non-Profit, Professional
Paid Staff: 7
Volunteer Staff: 100
Paid Artists: 200
Season: September - June
Affiliations: TCG; NEAT; NETC; MASSK
Type of Stage: Thrust
Stage Dimensions: 20' x 30'
Seating Capacity: 160

2775
JEWISH THEATRE OF NEW ENGLAND
Leventhal-Sidman Jewish Community Center
333 Nahanton Street
Newton Center, MA 02459-3213
Phone: 617-558-6480
Fax: 617-244-8290
Management:
Performance Artistic Director: Barrie Keller
Founded: 1984
Specialized Field: Jewish; Ethnic Theater
Status: Nonprofit
Season: Fall & Spring
Type of Stage: Thrust
Stage Dimensions: 48' x 30'
Seating Capacity: 250-450

2776
NEW CENTURY THEATRE
122 Green Street
Northampton, MA 01061
Mailing Address: PO Box 186, Northampton, MA 01061
Phone: 413-587-3933
Fax: 413-585-3354
e-mail: info@newcenturytheatre.org
Web Site: www.newcenturytheatre.org
Management:
Producing Director: Sam Rush
Mission: Produces four productions from June-August and is beginning to produce productions in the fall and spring.
Founded: 1991
Specialized Field: Comedy; Youth Theater; Ethnic Theater; Contemporary
Status: Non-Profit, Professional
Paid Staff: 5
Paid Artists: 30
Budget: $200,000+
Season: June - August

Affiliations: AEA
Annual Attendance: 11,000
Type of Stage: Proscenuim
Seating Capacity: 450

2777
FIDDLEHEAD THEATRE COMPANY

109 Central Street
Norwood, MA 02062
Phone: 617-888-5365
e-mail: contactus@fiddleheadtheatre.com
Management:
President: Meg Fofonoff
Associate Producer: Stacie Moye
Business Manager: Darrell Moye
Mission: The Fiddlehead Theatre Company in Norwood, MA is a non-profit orginazation which draws its strength from the rich talents of local amateurs and volunteers as well as gifted professionals, and has already brought pleasures to thousands of Boston area residents.
Specialized Field: Community Theater; Musical
Status: Non-Profit

2778
ACADEMY OF PERFORMING ARTS

120 Main Street
PO Box 1843
Orleans, MA 02653
Phone: 508-255-3075
Fax: 508-255-3075
Web Site: www.apa1.org
Officers:
President: Edward Lewis
Vice President, Production: Dick Hatch
Treasurer: C Page McMahan
Management:
Managing Director: Peter Earle
Director: Marcia Galazzi
Executive Administrator: Ralph Bassett
Mission: To provide an educational opportunity for students and people of all ages and backgrounds to further their abilities, understanding and appreciation for jazz. To increase public awareness and appreciation for jazz as an American art form. To preserve the history and foster the development of this unique music. To bring world class performers and educators to greater Cleveland audiences.
Utilizes: Actors; Choreographers; Collaborating Artists; Collaborations; Community Talent; Composers; Educators; Guest Accompanists; Guest Artists; Guest Companies; Guest Designers; Guest Lecturers; Guest Musical Directors; Guest Musicians; Guest Speakers; Guest Teachers; Guild Activities; High School Drama; Instructors; Local Artists; Multimedia; Music; Organization Contracts; Original Music Scores; Paid Performers; Performance Artists; Playwrights; Resident Professionals; Scenic Designers; Sign Language Translators; Singers; Special Technical Talent; Visual Arts
Founded: 1975
Specialized Field: Musical; Comedy; Youth Theater; Ethnic Theater; Classic; Contemporary
Status: Non-Profit, Non-Professional
Paid Staff: 6
Income Sources: Productions; Memberships; Fundraising & Events; Private Donation
Performs At: Academy Playhouse
Affiliations: Orleans Chamber of Commerce
Annual Attendance: 21,000
Facility Category: Playhouse
Type of Stage: Arena
Seating Capacity: 162
Rental Contact: Artistic Director Peter Bartle

Organization Type: Performing; Touring; Educational; Sponsoring

2779
BARRINGTON STAGE COMPANY

30 Union Street
Pittsfield, MA 01201
Phone: 413-236-8888
Fax: 413-499-5447
e-mail: info@barringtonstageco.org
Web Site: www.barringtonstageco.org
Management:
Artistic Director: Julianne Boyd
Interim Managing Director: Tristan Wilson
Director Education: Hester Kamin
Lauraal Manager: Marketing Manager
Utilizes: Actors; Community Members; Community Talent; Dancers; Designers; Instructors; Local Artists & Directors; Original Music Scores; Resident Professionals; Sign Language Translators; Students
Founded: 1995
Specialized Field: Summer Stock
Orchestra Pit: 5
Seating Capacity: 520
Year Built: 1911

2780
PROVINCETOWN REPERTORY THEATRE

238 Bradford St
Provincetown, MA 02657
Mailing Address: PO Box 812
Phone: 508-487-0600
e-mail: operations@provincetowntheater.com
Web Site: http://www.provincetowntheater.com
Officers:
Chairman: Brian O'Malley
President: Tim McCarthy
Vice President: Joy McNulty
Management:
Director: Dave Fortuna
General Director: Ted Vitale
Administrative Director: Margie Mahrdt
Specialized Field: Summer Stock
Performs At: Pilgrim Monument

2781
ROBBINS-ZUST FAMILY MARIONETTES

20 Reservoir Road
Richmond, MA 01254
Phone: 413-698-2591
Fax: 413-698-2080
Web Site: www.berkshireweb.com/zust
Management:
President: Genie Zust
Actor/Designer: Dion Robbins-Zust
Actor/Designer: Maia Robbins-Zust
Actor/Designer: Diedre Bollinger
Actor/Director: Genie Zust
Mission: To pass on to the next generations the ancient stories and the art and craft of puppetry and to delight all ages.
Founded: 1971
Specialized Field: Puppet
Status: For-Profit, Professional
Paid Staff: 5
Paid Artists: 5
Budget: $30,000
Income Sources: Performances
Performs At: Theatres; Homes; Stores; Schools throughout New England/New York
Annual Attendance: 10,000+
Type of Stage: Marionette
Stage Dimensions: 14'x8'x10'
Organization Type: Performing; Touring

2782
SHARON COMMUNITY THEATRE

53 High Street
Sharon, MA 02067
Phone: 617-784-3721
Management:
Business Manager: Tina Koppel
Publicity: Dick Leemon
Mission: To present family-oriented, high quality, local entertainment consisting mainly of play productions to the South Shore area at reasonable prices.
Utilizes: Guest Companies; Singers
Founded: 1975
Specialized Field: Community Theater
Status: Nonprofit
Paid Staff: 60
Income Sources: New England Theatre Conference
Performs At: Sharon Recreation Department Mini-Theatre
Organization Type: Performing; Educational

2783
STUDEBAKER THEATER

9 Oliver Street
Somerville, MA 02145
Phone: 617-782-6226
e-mail: bannatyn@fas.harvard.edu
Web Site:
http://www.people.fas.harvard.edu/~bannatyn/studebaker.html
Management:
Co-Artistic Director: John Bay
Co-Artistic Director: Lesley Bannatyne
Mission: To create and tour new works in theater, and to bring innovative arts programming into the schools that helps children and adults enhance creative, perceptive and problem-solving skills.
Utilizes: Guest Companies; Singers
Founded: 1978
Specialized Field: Drama; Classic
Status: Professional
Paid Staff: 10
Income Sources: National Movement Theatre Association
Performs At: Performance Place
Organization Type: Performing; Touring; Resident; Sponsoring

2784
SUMMER THEATRE AT MT. HOLYOKE COLLEGE

Alice Withington Rooke Theatre
50 College Street
South Hadley, MA 01075
Phone: 413-538-2118
Fax: 413-538-3838
e-mail: theatre@mtholyoke.edu
Web Site: www.mtholyoke.edu/acad/theat
Officers:
President: Debra Guston
VP: Jennifer Symington
Treasurer: Roger Allard
Management:
Director: Roger Babb
Mission: To provide Western Massachusetts with the highest quality summerstock entertainment while educating and nurturing a new genetration of theatre artists.
Utilizes: Students; Special Technical Talent
Founded: 1970
Specialized Field: Summer Stock
Status: For-Profit,Non-Professional
Budget: $425,000

Income Sources: Ticket Sales; Sponsors; Donors; Businesses; Grants
Season: June - August
Annual Attendance: 15,000
Facility Category: Mainstage
Type of Stage: Thrust
Stage Dimensions: 36'x36'
Seating Capacity: 400
Year Remodeled: 2000

2785
BERKSHIRE THEATRE FESTIVAL

PO Box 797
Stockbridge, MA 01262
Phone: 413-298-5576
Fax: 413-298-3368
Toll-free: 866-811-4111
e-mail: info@berkshiretheatre.org
Web Site: www.berkshiretheatre.org
Officers:
   CO-President: Lee Perlman
   CO-President: David Lloyd
   Secretary: Randolph Hawthorne
   Treasurer: Neil Ellenoff
   Vice President: B Carger White
Management:
   Artistic Director/CEO: Kate Maguire
   Assistant Artistic Director: E Gray Simons III
   General Manager: Peter Durgin
   Director Finance/Administration: Linda Ludwig
   Director Development: Craig Smith
   Director Marketing/Public Relations: Jamie Davidson
   Box Office/Subscriptions Manager: Tara Young
Mission: To produce and promote thought-provoking theatre for its community throughout the summer through performance and educational activities.
Utilizes: Singers
Founded: 1928
Specialized Field: Drama; Classic; Contemporary; Musical
Status: Professional; Nonprofit
Paid Staff: 12
Income Sources: Actors' Equity Association; Council of Resident Summer Theatres
Season: June - September
Performs At: Playhouse, Unicorn Theatre
Type of Stage: Proscenium, Thrust
Seating Capacity: 415, 122
Organization Type: Performing; Resident; Educational; Sponsoring

2786
VINEYARD PLAYHOUSE

24 Church Street
Box 2452
Vineyard Haven, MA 02568
Phone: 508-693-6450
Fax: 508-696-9299
e-mail: info@vineyardplayhouse.org
Web Site: www.vineyardplayhouse.org
Officers:
   Chairperson: George L Cohn
   Clerk: Gerald Yukevich
   Treasurer: Ted E Desrosiers
Management:
   Artistic Director: Mj Bruder Munafo
   Artistic Associate: Jon Lipsky
Mission: Community based professional theater dedicated to developing, producing and presenting exceptional live theater for adults and children; to providing educational programs; and to encourage and supporting the work of theater artists of all ages, abilities and ethnic and social background.

Founded: 1983
Specialized Field: Summer Stock; Ensembles; Drama
Status: Nonprofit
Paid Staff: 6
Paid Artists: 100
Budget: $450,000
Season: June - October
Type of Stage: Black Box
Seating Capacity: 120

2787
SPINGOLD THEATER CENTER

Brandeis University
415 S Street
Waltham, MA 02454
Phone: 781-736-3340
Fax: 781-736-3408
e-mail: theater@brandeis.edu
Web Site: www.brandeis.edu
Officers:
   President: Jehuda Reinharz
   Chair: Susan Dibble
Management:
   Artistic Director: Eric Hill
   Director: David Colfer
   Manager: Irene Vienneau
Income Sources: New England Theatre Conference; Massachusetts Cultural Alliance
Performs At: Spingold Theater Center
Organization Type: Performing; Educational

2788
HISTORY MAKING PRODUCTIONS

100 Summer
Suite 3-6
Watertown, MA 02172
Phone: 617-924-4430
Officers:
   Chairperson: Lisa Gregory
   Secretary Clerk: Judith Einach
   Treasurer: Richard Freedberg
Management:
   Director: Linda Myer
Mission: To tour live, professional plays which dramatize historical events and people; to bring literature to life; to spark critical thinking and thoughtful discussion on gender, race, social diversity and social change.
Utilizes: Guest Companies; Singers
Founded: 1976
Specialized Field: Historical; Contemporary; Drama
Status: Professional; Nonprofit
Income Sources: Massachusetts Advocates for Arts; Sciences & Humanities; Stage Source
Organization Type: Performing; Touring; Educational

2789
WELLFLEET HARBOR ACTORS THEATER

PO Box 797
Wellfleet, MA 02667
Phone: 508-349-3011
Toll-free: 866-282-9428
e-mail: info@what.org
Officers:
   President: John Dubinsky
   Honorary Chair Person: Julie Harris
Management:
   Artistic Director: Jeff Zinn, jz@what.org
Mission: To present a most adventurous professional theater company.
Founded: 1985
Specialized Field: Drama; Comedy
Status: Nonprofit; Equity

Paid Staff: 25
Volunteer Staff: 125
Paid Artists: 50
Budget: $1.3 Million
Season: May - October
Affiliations: TCG
Type of Stage: Proscenium
Seating Capacity: 220; 90
Year Built: 2007
Cost: $5 Million
Rental Contact: Artistic Director Jeff Zinn

2790
HARWICH JUNIOR THEATRE

105 Division Street
PO Box 168
West Harwich, MA 02671
Phone: 508-432-0934
Fax: 508-432-0726
Web Site: www.hjtcapecod.org
Management:
   President: Richard Rust
   Artistic Director: Nina Schuessler
   Managing Director: Tamara Harper
Mission: To provide young people with the opportunity to explore and expand their creative talents and aspirations; to entertain, develop, and foster a love and full appreciation of theatre and the enrich lives through the theatrical experience.
Founded: 1951
Specialized Field: Musical; Comedy; Ethnic Theater; Community Theater; Classic; Contemporary
Status: Non-Profit, Non-Professional
Paid Staff: 3
Paid Artists: 50
Season: June - August
Type of Stage: Thrust
Stage Dimensions: 20' x 30'
Seating Capacity: 210

2791
NEW PHOENIX

42 Cold Spring Road
Williamstown, MA 01267
Phone: 413-458-2411
Officers:
   President: Ralph Hamman
   Vice President: Dana Swanson
Management:
   Artistic Director/Producer: Ralph Hammann
   Associate Director: Douglas Bradburd
Mission: To produce a diversity of small-cast, transportable theatre pieces; special interest in Samuel Beckett, mono dramas, psychological thrillers and black comedies.
Utilizes: Guest Companies
Founded: 1975
Specialized Field: Drama; Touring Company; Ensembles
Status: Professional; Semi-Professional; Nonprofit
Organization Type: Performing; Touring; Educational; Sponsoring

2792
WILLIAMSTOWN THEATRE FESTIVAL

PO Box 517
Williamstown, MA 01267-0517
Phone: 413-458-3200
Fax: 413-458-3147
e-mail: wtfinfo@wtfestival.org
Web Site: www.wtfestival.org
Officers:
   President: Dr. Ira Lapidus
   Vice President: Brian D Cabral

Secretary: Fred A Windover
Treasurer: Jid Sprague
Management:
Producer: Michael Ritchie
General Manager: Deborah Fehr
Business Manager: Julie Cammer
Administrative Assistant: Juliet Flynt
Development Director: Bart Reidy
Production Manager: Christopher Atkins
Workshop Director: Amanda Charlton
Company Manager: Michael Coglan
Mission: To present outstanding productions of modern classics on our main stage; to develop new acting, writing and musical talent.
Utilizes: Actors; AEA Actors; Artists-in-Residence; Choreographers; Commissioned Composers; Commissioned Music; Designers; Educators; Guest Accompanists; Guest Artists; Guest Companies; Guest Conductors; Guest Designers; Guest Ensembles; Guest Lecturers; Guest Musical Directors; High School Drama; Music; Original Music Scores; Performance Artists; Poets; Resident Artists; Resident Professionals; Singers; Soloists; Student Interns
Founded: 1954
Specialized Field: Drama; Classic; Contemporary; Musical
Status: Non-Profit, Professional
Paid Staff: 75
Volunteer Staff: 150
Paid Artists: 100
Non-paid Artists: 40
Budget: $2,500,000
Performs At: Adams Memorial Theater; Nikos Stage
Annual Attendance: 50,000
Seating Capacity: 520
Organization Type: Performing
Comments: September-May in NYC 212-395-9090

2793
KIDSTOCK CREATIVE THEATER EDUCATION CENTER
50 Cross Street
Winchester, MA 01890
Phone: 781-729-5543
Management:
Creative Director: Brian Milauskas
Mission: To empower young artists and actors to express themselves by providing them with quality resources and instruction; promoting creative problem solving, cooperative planning and public speaking skills through dramatic play.
Utilizes: Soloists
Founded: 1991
Specialized Field: Children's Theater; Educational

2794
BOOTH PRODUCTIONS
144 Granite Street
Worcester, MA 01604
Phone: 508-797-9277
Management:
Artistic Director: Richard A Booth, Senior
Technical Director: Jeff Boutiette
Chief Stage Technician: James Gagaglio
Sound Technician: Rob Steere
Music Director: Daniel Zabinski
Music Director: Robert Rucinski
Prime Theatre Director: Christine Seger
Mission: Providing the opportunity for all to learn and develop theater skills by participating in the many aspects of theater, both on stage and behind the scenes. Strengthening the value of friendship, team

effort, and a sense of community. Enabling all participants to achieve their fullest potential. Also providing the community with quality theater.
Specialized Field: Summer Stock
Performs At: Holy Name Theater

2795
FOOTHILLS THEATRE COMPANY
100 Front Street
Suite 100
Worcester, MA 01608
Phone: 508-754-3314
Fax: 508-767-0676
Web Site: www.foothillstheatre.com
Officers:
President: Guy Jones
Treasurer: James F Goulet
Clerk: Hon Mel Greenberg
Management:
Artistic Director: Brad Kenney
Business Manager: Lisa Ayotte
Mission: To provide professional regional theatre for Worcester and the Central New England Region and serve the region by providing many ancillary services including a theatre conservatory, intern/apprentice programs, youth services, services for the communicatively and physically disabled and more.
Utilizes: Guest Companies; Singers
Founded: 1974
Specialized Field: Musical; Comedy; Classic; Contemporary
Status: Non-Profit, Professional
Income Sources: Actors' Equity Association
Season: October - May
Performs At: Foothills Theatre Company
Type of Stage: Proscenium
Seating Capacity: 349
Organization Type: Performing

2796
WORCESTER CHILDREN'S THEATRE
6 Chatman Street
Worcester, MA 01609
Phone: 404-315-0235
Management:
Director Programs/Development: Mary Pantano
Managing Director: Liz Humphreys
Artistic Director: Steven Braddock
Mission: Providing performances and educational programming that educates children about theatre.
Utilizes: Guest Companies
Founded: 1968
Specialized Field: Children's Theater
Status: Professional; Semi-Professional; Nonprofit
Performs At: Worcester State College; Administration Building
Organization Type: Performing; Touring; Educational

Michigan

2797
THUNDER BAY THEATRE
400 N Second Avenue
Alpena, MI 49707
Phone: 989-354-2267
Web Site: www.deepnet.com/tbt/
Management:
President: Kathryn Kunze
VP: Maggie Lamb
Artistic Director: Hal Adams
Treasurer: Barb Bourdelais
Mission: To enhance the cultural life of Northeast Michigan.

Utilizes: Guest Companies; Singers
Founded: 1967
Specialized Field: Summer Stock; Musical; Ensembles
Status: Professional; Nonprofit; Non-Equity
Season: May - September
Performs At: Thunder Bay Theatre
Type of Stage: Proscenium
Stage Dimensions: 33' x 15'
Seating Capacity: 180
Year Built: 1930
Organization Type: Performing; Resident; Educational

2798
PERFORMANCE NETWORK OF ANN ARBOR
Performance Network Theatre
120 E Huron
Ann Arbor, MI 48104-1437
Phone: 734-663-0696
Fax: 734-663-7367
e-mail: info@performancenetwork.org
Web Site: www.performancenetwork.org
Officers:
Board President: Ron Maurer
Management:
Artistic Director: David Wolber
Executive Director: Carla Milarch
Marketing Director: Chelsea Sadler
Mission: To provide uncompromising artistic leadership in the region and produce works that engage, challenge and inspire audiences and artists.
Utilizes: Actors; AEA Actors; Choreographers; Contract Actors; Designers; Equity Actors; Local Artists; Local Artists & Directors; Original Music Scores; Performance Artists
Founded: 1981
Specialized Field: Drama, Comedy; Youth Theater; Classic; Contemporary
Status: Non-Profit, Professional
Paid Staff: 8
Volunteer Staff: 300
Paid Artists: 50
Budget: $750,000
Affiliations: AEA
Seating Capacity: 139
Year Built: 2000

2799
UNIVERSITY PRODUCTIONS: UNIVERSITY OF MICHIGAN
Department of Theatre & Drama
2550 Frieze Building
Ann Arbor, MI 48109-1265
Phone: 734-764-5350
Fax: 734-647-2297
e-mail: theatre.info@umich.edu
Web Site: www.theatre.music.umich.edu
Management:
Chairman: Erik Fredricksen
Managing Director: Jeffrey Kuras
Dean School of Music: Karen Wolff
Mission: To create 10 productions annually through the departments of Musical Theatre, Opera and Theatre and Dance.
Utilizes: Guest Choreographers; Guest Companies
Founded: 1973
Specialized Field: Drama; Educational; Theater Workshops
Status: Non-Profit, Non-Professional
Paid Staff: 22
Performs At: Power Center for the Performing Arts; Trueblood Theatre
Type of Stage: Flexible; Proscenium; Arena

Seating Capacity: 1414; 650; 200
Organization Type: Performing; Educational

2800
BARN THEATRE
13351 W Michigan 96
Augusta, MI 49012
Phone: 616-731-4545
Fax: 616-731-2306
e-mail: mibarntheatre@aol.com
Web Site: www.barntheatre.com
Management:
    Founder/Producer: Jack P Ragotzy
    Assistant Producer: Brendan Ragotzy
    Apprentice Coordinator: Penelope Aalex Ragotzy
    General Manager: Howard McBride
    Resident Manager: James B Knox
Mission: To offer high-quality professional summer theatre to Southwestern Michigan.
Utilizes: Designers
Founded: 1946
Specialized Field: Summer Stock; Musical
Status: Professional; Commercial
Paid Staff: 14
Paid Artists: 40
Income Sources: Actors' Equity Association
Organization Type: Performing; Resident

2801
BAY CITY PLAYERS
1214 Colombus Avenue
Bay City, MI 48708
Phone: 989-893-5555
e-mail: info@baycityplayers.com
Web Site: www.baycityplayers.com
Mission: To provide quality theatrical productions for our area.
Founded: 1917
Specialized Field: Musical; Community Theater
Status: Nonprofit
Income Sources: Community Theatre Association of Michigan
Facility Category: Theatre
Organization Type: Performing

2802
CALUMET THEATRE COMPANY
340 Sixth Street
PO Box 167
Calumet, MI 49913
Phone: 906-337-2166
Fax: 906-337-4073
e-mail: calumettheatre@calumettheatre.com
Web Site: www.calumettheatre.com
Officers:
    Board Director: Johnnie De Bernard
    Board Director: Andrew Gryuruch
Management:
    Executive Director: Jim Lowell
    Managing Director: Christine Fanning
    Artistic/Technical Director: Davey Holmbo
Mission: Hosting and sponsoring performing events.
Founded: 1900
Specialized Field: Musical; Comedy; Community Theater; Classic; Contemporary; Musical; Ethnic Theater
Status: Non-Profit, Non-Professional
Paid Staff: 5
Income Sources: Michigan Association of Community Arts Agencies
Organization Type: Educational; Sponsoring

2803
PURPLE ROSE THEATRE COMPANY
137 Park Street
Chelsea, MI 48118
Phone: 734-433-7673
Fax: 734-475-0802
e-mail: purplerose@purplerosetheatre.org
Web Site: www.purplerosetheatre.org
Officers:
    Executive Director: Jeff Daniels
Management:
    Artistic Director: Guy Sanville
    Managing Director: Alan Ribant
Founded: 1991
Specialized Field: Musical; Comedy; Classic; Contemporary
Status: Non-Profit, Professional
Paid Staff: 17
Paid Artists: 75
Season: September - August
Type of Stage: Thrust
Seating Capacity: 160

2804
ATTIC / NEW CENTER THEATRE
2990 W Grand Boulevard
Suite 308
Detroit, MI 48202
Phone: 313-875-8285
Officers:
    Chairman: Andy Soffel
    President: Lavinia Moyer
    Treasurer: Peter C Gray
    Secretary: Paul R. Retenbach
Management:
    Artistic Director: Lavinia Moyer
    Managing Director: Jim Moran
Mission: Attic/New Center Theatre is a resident, professional theatre company committed to the development of actors, directors, playwrights, and technicians as craftsmen in the art of theatre. It exists to create new works and to present new and challenging plays by contemporary playwrights.
Utilizes: Guest Companies; Singers
Founded: 1975
Specialized Field: Musical; Ensembles
Status: Professional; Nonprofit
Income Sources: Theatre Communications Group; Foundation for the Extension and Development of American Professional Theatre
Performs At: The New Center Theatre
Organization Type: Performing; Touring; Resident; Educational

2805
DETROIT REPERTORY THEATRE
13103 Woodrow Wilson
Detroit, MI 48238
Phone: 313-868-1347
Fax: 313-868-1705
e-mail: detrepth@aol.com
Web Site: www.detroitreptheatre.com
Officers:
    Board Chair: Shyvonne Davis
Management:
    Artistic Director: Bruce Millan
Mission: The Detroit Repertory Theatre has demonstrated that racial harmony and non-traditional casting (casting without racial distinction) can produce an artistic vitality and quality second to none and win over an audience in sufficient numbers to prove viability.

Utilizes: AEA Actors; Contract Actors; Designers; Equity Actors; High School Drama; Original Music Scores; Playwrights; Resident Companies; Resident Professionals; Touring Companies
Founded: 1956
Specialized Field: Theater; Classic; Contemporary
Status: Non-Profit, Professional
Paid Staff: 7
Volunteer Staff: 6
Paid Artists: 22
Budget: $800,000
Income Sources: Box Office; Grants; Contributors
Season: November - June
Performs At: Theatre
Affiliations: TCG, AFA, DMCVB
Annual Attendance: 30,000+
Type of Stage: Proscenium
Stage Dimensions: 28' x 26'
Seating Capacity: 194
Year Remodeled: 1990
Organization Type: Performing
Resident Groups: Hire only indigenous professional artists.

2806
HILBERRY THEATRE, WAYNE STATE UNIVERSITY
4841 Cass Avenue
Suite 3225
Detroit, MI 48202
Phone: 313-577-3510
Fax: 313-577-0935
e-mail: ac8806@wayne.edu
Officers:
    Interim Chair: James Thomas
Founded: 1963
Specialized Field: Educational; Theater Workshops
Status: Non-Professional; Nonprofit
Paid Staff: 60
Volunteer Staff: 100
Budget: $2.5 Million
Income Sources: Box Office; Fundraising; Grants; University
Performs At: Hilberry Theatre
Affiliations: Association for Theatre in Higher Education; U/RTA; National Association of Schools of Theatre
Annual Attendance: 50,000
Facility Category: Theatre
Type of Stage: Thrust
Seating Capacity: 530
Year Remodeled: 1963
Organization Type: Performing; Touring; Resident; Educational; Sponsoring
Resident Groups: Repertory Company

2807
MASONIC TEMPLE THEATRE
500 Temple Avenue
Detroit, MI 48201
Phone: 313-832-7100
Fax: 313-832-2292
Web Site: www.olympiaentertainment.com
Officers:
    President: Dana Warg
Status: Professional
Affiliations: Fisher Theatre
Facility Category: Live Stage Theatre
Type of Stage: Proscenium
Seating Capacity: 4,404
Year Remodeled: 1990

2808
PLOWSHARES THEATRE COMPANY
2870 Grand Boulevard
Suite 600
Detroit, MI 48202-3146
Phone: 313-872-0279
Fax: 313-872-0067
Web Site: www.plowshares.org
Officers:
President: Justin Klimko
VP: Mildred Morton Cross
Secretary: Johnnie Hunter
Treasurer: Bessie Burden
Management:
President: Justin Klimko
Executive Director: Gary Anderson
Production Manager: Janet Cleveland
Managing Director: Addell Anderson
Mission: To produce relevant, high quality African American theatre for a culturally and socially diverse audience through the establishment of supportive relationships within the civic, religious and business communities.
Utilizes: Actors; AEA Actors; Choreographers; Collaborations; Guest Designers; Guild Activities; High School Drama; Instructors; Local Artists; Lyricists; Music; Performance Artists; Sign Language Translators; Soloists; Theatre Companies
Founded: 1989
Specialized Field: Musical; Comedy; Ethnic Theater; Contemporary
Status: Non-Profit, Professional
Paid Staff: 4
Volunteer Staff: 140
Paid Artists: 30
Budget: $500,000
Affiliations: BTN; TCG; NCAAT; MAPT; DMVCB
Organization Type: Performing; Touring

2809
THEATER GROTTESCO
PO Box 32658
Detroit, MI 48232
Phone: 313-961-5880
Management:
Co-Artistic Director: John Flax
Co-Artistic Director: Elizabeth Wiseman
Mission: To create modern original plays; to conduct master classes and training workshops.
Founded: 1983
Specialized Field: Contemporary; New Plays; Theater Workshops
Status: Professional; Nonprofit
Income Sources: Association of Performing Arts Presenters; Theatre Communications Group; Arts Midwest; National Association for Campus Activities
Organization Type: Performing; Touring; Educational

2810
CIRCLE THEATRE
1607 Robinson Road SE
Grand Rapids, MI 49506
Phone: 616-632-1980
Fax: 616-456-8540
Web Site: www.circletheatre.org
Officers:
President: David Weinandy
Management:
Managing Director: Joe Dulin
Founded: 1953
Specialized Field: Musical; Comedy; Community Theater; Puppet; Classic; Contemporary
Status: Non-Profit, Non-Professional

2811
CIVIC THEATRE & SCHOOL OF THEATRE
30 N Division Avenue
Grand Rapids, MI 49503
Phone: 616-222-6658
Fax: 616-222-6660
Management:
Executive Director: Bruce Tinker
Associate Director: Penny Notter
Marketing Director: Eric Dawe
Utilizes: Student Interns
Founded: 1925
Specialized Field: Community Theater; Theater Workshops; Educational

2812
URBAN INSTITUTE FOR CONTEMPORARY ARTS
41 Sheldon Boulevard SE
Grand Rapids, MI 49503
Phone: 616-454-7000
Fax: 616-454-7013
Web Site: www.uica.org
Officers:
President: Tom Clinton
Vice President: Daryl Fischer
Second VP/Secretary: Heidi Holst Leeestma
Treasurer: David J. Everett
Management:
President: Jeff Meeuwsen
Executive Director: Jill Donabauer
Program Manager: Gail Philbin
Facilities Manager: Aaron Smith
Special Events Coordinator: Carole Walters
Marketing/Communications: Karen Spelling
Mission: To foster cultural dialogue and creative activity through innovative and diverse events and services.
Utilizes: Touring Companies
Founded: 1977
Specialized Field: Comedy; Youth Theater; Ethnic Theater; Community Theater; Classic; Contemporary
Status: Non-Profit, Professional
Seating Capacity: 170

2813
ACTING UP THEATRE COMPANY
PO Box 1070
Grayling, MI 49738
Phone: 989-348-3587
e-mail: chad@actingup.biz
Management:
Artistic Director: Kurt Thoma
Creative Director: Chad Patterson
Teaching Artist: Rachel Roberts
Artistic Consultant: Suzen Rosa
Teaching Artist: Dean Gibbs
Mission: Providing schools, institutions and libraries with unique brand of educational theatre. Striving to teach students about theatre by providing them with the opportunity to write, produce and act in their own plays. Involve, Inform and Entertain. 'Anything is Possible.'
Founded: 1996
Specialized Field: Children's Theater; Summer Stock; Touring Company

2814
HOPE SUMMER REPERTORY THEATRE
Hope College
141 E. 12th Street
Holland, MI 49423

Phone: 616-395-7850
Fax: 616-395-7130
Toll-free: 800-968-7850
e-mail: robins@hope.edu
Web Site: www.hope.edu
Management:
Producing Director: Mary Schafer
Artisitic Director: David Colacci
Founded: 1851
Specialized Field: Educational; Theater Workshops; Summer Stock
Status: Non-Equity; Nonprofit
Season: June - August
Type of Stage: Thrust
Seating Capacity: 500

2815
IRONWOOD THEATRE
109 E Aurora Street
Ironwood, MI 49938
Phone: 906-932-0618
Fax: 906-932-0457
Web Site: www.ironwoodtheatre.org
Officers:
President: Dale Ballone
VP: Tom Brown
Secretary: Lee Brown
Treasurer: David Sauter
Management:
Chairman: Tom Brown
Mission: To provide cultural entertainment of the highest possible quality to the greatest number of people in the Western Upper Peninsula of Michigan and Northern Wisconsin.
Utilizes: Dance Companies; Dancers; Guest Writers; Guild Activities; Multi Collaborations; Multimedia; New Productions; Original Music Scores; Sign Language Translators; Special Technical Talent; Theatre Companies
Founded: 1928
Specialized Field: Drama; Musical
Status: Non-Profit, Non-Professional
Paid Staff: 3
Budget: $125,000
Income Sources: Grants; State of Michigan; Fund Raisers
Performs At: Auditorium
Affiliations: Michigan Council for Arts-Cultural Affairs
Annual Attendance: 20,000
Facility Category: Performing Arts Center
Type of Stage: Proscenium
Stage Dimensions: 28'6"w x 23'l
Seating Capacity: 732
Year Built: 1928
Year Remodeled: 1983
Cost: $160,000
Rental Contact: Managing Director Kaye Johnson

2816
ACTORS & PLAYWRIGHTS' INITIATIVE
359 S Burdick Street
Suite 205, Epic Center
Kalamazoo, MI 49007
Phone: 616-343-8090
Fax: 616-343-8450
Management:
Artistic Director: Robert C Walker
Marketing Director: Jeremy M Morris
Founded: 1989
Specialized Field: Young Playwrights; Theater Workshops; New Plays
Paid Staff: 6
Volunteer Staff: 12
Paid Artists: 20

Non-paid Artists: 12
Performs At: Epic Center
Facility Category: Theatre
Type of Stage: Black Box
Seating Capacity: 120

2817
KALAMAZOO CIVIC PLAYERS
329 S Park Street
Kalamazoo, MI 49007
Phone: 269-343-1313
Fax: 269-343-0532
Web Site: www.kazoocivic.com
Management:
 President of the Board: Sandra Gagie
 Managing Director: Duwain Hunt
Mission: Offering the finest possible dramatic experience to the area.
Utilizes: Guest Companies
Founded: 1929
Specialized Field: Musical; Comedy; Community Theater; Classic; Contemporary
Status: Non-Profit, Non-Professional
Paid Staff: 30
Income Sources: American Association of Community Theatres; Community Theatre Association of Michigan
Performs At: Civic Auditorium; Carver Center
Organization Type: Performing

2818
BOARSHEAD THEATER
425 S Grand Avenue
Lansing, MI 48933
Phone: 517-484-7800
Fax: 517-484-2564
Web Site: www.boarshead.org
Officers:
 Chair: Larry Meyer
Management:
 Artistic Director: Kristine Thatcher
Mission: Boarshead theater exists to entertain, educate and inspire audiences of all ages throughout Michigan.
Founded: 1966
Specialized Field: Musical; Comedy; Community Theater; Puppet; Classic; Contemporary
Status: Non-Profit, Professional
Paid Staff: 10
Paid Artists: 75

2819
CHERRY COUNTY PLAYHOUSE
425 W Western
Suite 406
Muskegon, MI 49440
Phone: 231-727-8888
Fax: 231-722-0549
Toll-free: 800-686-9666
Web Site: www.cherrycountyplayhouse.org
Management:
 Producing Director: Bill Castellino
 General Manager: Gwen W Nelson
 President: Pamela Galina
Mission: To preserve the art of musical theater by presenting the most exciting classical and contemporary musicals while also creating new works that expand the range of the audience's experience.
Founded: 1955
Specialized Field: Summer Stock
Status: Professional; Commercial
Paid Staff: 3
Paid Artists: 120
Budget: $1,000,000
Income Sources: Box Office; Grants; Private Donations

Performs At: Performance Center
Annual Attendance: 35,000
Facility Category: Performing Arts Center
Type of Stage: Proscenium
Stage Dimensions: 41'6" x 29'
Seating Capacity: 1750
Year Built: 1930
Year Remodeled: 1998
Cost: 8.2 million
Rental Contact: Susan McGarry
Organization Type: Performing

2820
PORT HURON CIVIC THEATRE
701 Me Morran Boulevard
PO Box 821
Port Huron, MI 48060
Phone: 810-985-6166
Fax: 810-985-3358
Web Site: www.memorran.com
Officers:
 President: Ernest Werth
 1st Vice President: Bryan Shelby
 Second VP: Denise Selby
 Secretary: Chris Hendrickson
 Treasurer: Jennifer Dent
Management:
 Marketing Director: Sarah McCollum
 Box Office Manager: Pat David
 Marketing Director: Karen Pennewell
Mission: To offer a theatre season each year; to train and educate; to promote theatre arts.
Utilizes: Guest Companies
Founded: 1957
Specialized Field: Community Theater
Status: Semi-Professional; Nonprofit
Paid Staff: 200
Income Sources: Saint Clair County Community College
Performs At: McMorran Place Theatre
Organization Type: Performing; Educational

2821
SHELDON THEATRE
443 W 3rd Street
PO Box 34
Red Wing, MI 55066
Phone: 651-388-8701
Fax: 651-385-3663
e-mail: sdowse@sheldontheatre.org
Web Site: www.sheldontheatre.org
Officers:
 Board President: William Foot
 Executive Director: Sean Dowse
Founded: 1904
Specialized Field: Drama; Musical; Classic
Status: Non-Profit, Professional
Paid Staff: 16

2822
MEADOW BROOK THEATRE
Oakland University
Rochester, MI 48309-4401
Phone: 248-377-3300
Fax: 248-370-3344
e-mail: kgentile@mbtheatre.com
Web Site: www.mbtheatre.com
Management:
 Artistic Director: David Regal
 Managing Director: Gregg Bloomfield
 Director Marketing: Rob Gold
Mission: To present a broad variety of top-quality live theatre, ranging from classic to contemporary works; to offer seven plays each season.

Utilizes: Actors; Designers; Guest Artists; Guest Companies; Guest Conductors; Guest Designers; Guest Lecturers; Guest Writers; Local Artists; Local Unknown Artists; Multimedia; Music; Original Music Scores; Performance Artists; Poets; Resident Professionals; Selected Students; Sign Language Translators; Singers; Student Interns; Visual Arts
Founded: 1967
Specialized Field: Musical; Classic; Contemporary
Status: Non-Profit, Professional
Paid Staff: 40
Income Sources: Oakland University; Concerned Citizens for the Arts in Michigan
Season: September - May
Affiliations: LORT
Annual Attendance: 100,000+
Facility Category: Theatre
Type of Stage: Proscenium
Seating Capacity: 584
Year Built: 1963
Organization Type: Performing; Touring

2823
RED BARN PLAYHOUSE
PO Box 670
Saugatuck, MI 49453
Phone: 616-857-7707
Fax: 616-857-7803
Specialized Field: Summer Stock; Musical; Drama; Comedy
Season: June - September

2824
YOUTHEATRE
Michigan Performing Arts
15600 JL Hudson Drive
Box B
Southfield, MI 48075
Phone: 248-557-7529
Fax: 248-557-4415
Web Site: www.youtheatre.org
Management:
 President: Lou Longo
 Executive Director: Paul Berg
Mission: Youtheatre is a program of Michigan Performing arts, organization dedicated to providing the best in professional, family entertainment to its audience.
Founded: 1964
Specialized Field: Children's Theater; Youth Theater
Status: Non-Profit, Professional
Paid Staff: 5
Paid Artists: 120
Income Sources: Michigan Council of Arts & Cultural Affairs; City of Detroit Cultural Affairs Department; National Endowment for the Arts; McGregor Fund
Seating Capacity: 1,100
Cost: $900,000 (message)

2825
OLD TOWN PLAYHOUSE
148 E 8th Street
PO Box 262
Traverse City, MI 49684
Phone: 231-947-2210
Fax: 231-947-4955
e-mail: otpinfo@chartermi.net
Web Site: www.oldtownplayhouse.com
Management:
 Executive Director: Phil Murphy
 Executive Assistant: Janell Kiel Nelson
 Builing Manager: Martin Wolf

Mission: Assisting, encouraging, promoting and improving the cultural development of our community through education and entertainment.
Utilizes: Actors; Choreographers; Collaborations; Five Seasonal Concerts; Instructors; Local Artists; Music; Performance Artists; Resident Professionals; Sign Language Translators; Soloists; Student Interns
Founded: 1960
Specialized Field: Musical; Comedy; Community Theater; Classic; Contemporary
Status: Non-Profit, Non-Professional
Paid Staff: 5
Volunteer Staff: 150
Budget: $300,000
Income Sources: Ticket Sales; Season Subscribers; Donors, Fund Devlopment and Grants
Affiliations: CTAM; AACT; MACAA
Annual Attendance: 18,000
Facility Category: Community Theatre
Type of Stage: Mainstage; Black Box
Stage Dimensions: 358; 80
Seating Capacity: 358; 80
Year Built: 1903
Year Remodeled: 1997
Cost: $400,000
Organization Type: Performing; Educational
Resident Groups: Traverse City Civic Players

2826
BLUE LAKE REPERTORY THEATRE
Route #2
300 E
Twin Lake, MI 49457
Phone: 616-894-2540
Fax: 231-893-5123
Management:
President: Fritz Stansell
Treasurer: Reverend Walter Marek
Mission: To present summer-stock theatre of quality for our community.
Founded: 1966
Specialized Field: Summer Stock; Musical
Status: Semi-Professional
Income Sources: Blue Lake Fine Arts Camp
Performs At: Howmet Playhouse
Organization Type: Performing; Resident; Educational

2827
JET THEATRE
6600 W Maple Road
West Bloomfield, MI 48322-3002
Phone: 248-788-2900
Fax: 248-788-5160
e-mail: administration@jettheatre.org
Web Site: www.jettheatre.org
Management:
President: Jonathan Frank
Artistic Director: Evelyn Orbach
Managing Director: Christopher Bremer
Literary Manager: Pearl Orbach
Founded: 1989
Specialized Field: Jewish; Ethnic Theater; New Works of Social Importance
Status: Non-Profit, Professional
Paid Staff: 7
Paid Artists: 25

2828
JEWISH ENSEMBLE THEATRE
6600 W Maple Road
West Bloomfield, MI 48322-3002
Phone: 248-788-2900
Fax: 248-788-5160
Web Site: www.jettheatre.org

Management:
President: Jonathan Frank
Managing Director: Christofer Bremer
Artistic Director: Evelyn Orbach
Founded: 1989
Specialized Field: Comedy; Jewish; Classic; Contemporary
Status: Non-Profit, Professional
Paid Staff: 5
Performs At: Aaron DeRoy Theatre
Type of Stage: Thrust
Seating Capacity: 193

Minnesota

2829
THEATRE L'HOMME DIEU
PO Box 1086
Alexandria, MN 56308
Phone: 320-308-3229
Fax: 320-308-2902
e-mail: lhd@rea-alp.com
Web Site: www.alexweb.net/theatrelhommedieu
Officers:
President: Linda Roles
Secretary: Barbara Kleeper
Management:
President: Elizabeth Mohror-Hill
Artistic Director: Bruce Hyde
Marketing Director: Laveda Holtberg
Founded: 1960
Specialized Field: Musical; Comedy; Ethnic Theater; Community Theater; Contemporary
Status: Non-Profit, Professional
Paid Staff: 15
Volunteer Staff: 15
Budget: $125,000
Income Sources: Grants; Box Office; University Subsidy
Season: June-August
Affiliations: St. Claude State University
Annual Attendance: 8,000
Facility Category: Theatre
Type of Stage: Proscenium
Stage Dimensions: 40' x 18'
Seating Capacity: 265
Year Built: 1961
Year Remodeled: 2000
Cost: $50,000

2830
MATCHBOX CHILDREN'S THEATRE
407 1/2 N Main Street
PO Box 576
Austin, MN 55912
Phone: 507-437-9078
Web Site: matchboxtheatre.tripod.com
Officers:
President: Carrie Parker
VP: Barb Kasel
Treasurer: Linda Sistek
Secretary: Cindy Bellrichard
Mission: To produce creative, professional quality children's theatre on a consistent basis. Strive to produce well-rounded shows excelling in all aspects; script choice, direction, technical design and execution, costuming, make-up and the use of music. Primary focus is theatre for children, rather than by children. When appropriate roles are available children are casted.
Utilizes: Guest Companies; Singers
Founded: 1975
Specialized Field: Musical; Community Theater

Status: Non-Profit,Non-Professional
Performs At: Austin Community College Theatre
Organization Type: Performing; Resident

2831
PAUL BUNYAN PLAYHOUSE
1831 Anne Street
Suite 210
Bemidji, MN 56601
Phone: 218-444-1234
Fax: 218-444-1121
Toll-free: 800-276-8015
e-mail: info@paulbunyan.net
Web Site: www.paulbunyan.net
Officers:
President: Becky Lueben
VP: Kristine Cannon
Treasurer: Karen Moe
Secretary: Sandy Johnson
Management:
Artistic Director: Curtiss Grittner
Mission: To produce the best possible theatre utilizing local and regional talent as well as interns from Bemidji State University.
Utilizes: Guest Companies; Singers
Founded: 1951
Specialized Field: Summer Stock; Musical
Status: Professional; Nonprofit
Paid Staff: 15
Performs At: Paul Bunyan Playhouse; Old Chief Theatre
Organization Type: Performing; Educational

2832
CHANHASSEN DINNER THEATRE
501 W 78th
PO Box 100
Chanhassen, MN 55317
Phone: 952-934-1525
Fax: 612-952-1511
Toll-free: 800-362-3515
e-mail: information@chanhassentheatres.com
Web Site: www.chanassentheatres.com
Officers:
VP: Michael Brindisi
Management:
President: Thomas K Scallen
Artistic Director: Michael Brindisi
General Manager: Solveig Huseth
Director Public Relations: Kris Howland
Mission: To present fine theatre and dining.
Utilizes: Guest Companies; Singers
Founded: 1968
Specialized Field: Musical; Comedy; Dinner Theater
Status: For-Profit, Professional
Paid Staff: 250
Paid Artists: 50
Income Sources: American Dinner Theatre Institute
Performs At: Chanhassen Dinner Theatres
Annual Attendance: 250,000
Facility Category: Professional Dinner Theater
Seating Capacity: 600
Organization Type: Performing

2833
COLDER BY THE LAKE COMEDY THEATRE
PO Box 3473
Duluth, MN 55803-3473
Phone: 218-722-8867
e-mail: info@colderbythelake.com
Web Site: www.colderbythelake.com
Officers:
President: Mary Anderson

VP: Dr Scott Wolf
Secretary/Treasurer: Mary Treuer
Mission: Colder by the Lake presents all original theater, specifically: satire, comedy and the offbeat.
Utilizes: Guest Companies
Founded: 1983
Specialized Field: Comedy
Status: Nonprofit
Organization Type: Performing; Touring

2834
UNIVERSITY OF MINNESOTA DULUTH: DEPARTMENT OF THEATRE
University of Minnesota at Duluth
141 Mpac
Duluth, MN 55812
Phone: 218-726-8562
Fax: 218-726-6798
e-mail: pdennis@d.umn.edu
Web Site: www.d.umn.edu/theatre
Management:
   Chancellor: Katherine A Matine
   Department Head: Patricia Dennis
   Associate Professor: Patricia Dennis
   Directing the Dance: Ann A Bergeron
Specialized Field: Musical; Tech Theater; Educational
Status: Non-Profit, Non-Professional
Paid Staff: 17

2835
UNIVERSITY OF MINNESOTA DULUTH: DEPARTMENT OF THEATRE
University of Minnesota at Duluth
141 MPAC
Duluth, MN 55812
Phone: 218-726-8562
Fax: 218-726-6798
e-mail: pdennis@d.umn.edu
Management:
   Department Head: Patricia Dennis
   Associate Professor: Mark Harvey
   Directing The Dance: Ann A Bergeron
Specialized Field: Educational; Theater Workshops
Performs At: Marshall Performing Arts Center

2836
OLD LOG THEATER
5175 Meadville Street
PO Box 250
Excelsior, MN 55331
Phone: 952-474-5951
Fax: 952-474-1290
Web Site: www.oldlog.com
Management:
   President: Don Stolz
Mission: To offer entertainment to the public.
Utilizes: Actors; AEA Actors; Choreographers; Dancers; Designers; Grant Writers; Guest Artists; Guest Lecturers; Guest Musical Directors; Multimedia; Music; Original Music Scores; Performance Artists; Resident Artists; Resident Professionals; Selected Students; Sign Language Translators; Student Interns
Founded: 1940
Specialized Field: Dinner Theater
Status: Professional
Paid Staff: 30
Paid Artists: 12
Income Sources: Ticket sales
Performs At: Old Log Theatre
Affiliations: Actors' Equity
Type of Stage: Proscenium
Stage Dimensions: 70x80x24
Seating Capacity: 655

Year Built: 1960
Rental Contact: Don Stocz
Organization Type: Performing; Touring; Resident

2837
STAGES THEATRE COMPANY
1111 Main Street
Hopkins, MN 55343
Phone: 952-979-1123
Fax: 952-979-1124
e-mail: email@stagestheatre.org
Web Site: www.stagestheatre.org
Management:
   Chairman: G Bryan Fleming
   Artistic Director: Steve Barberio
   Managing Director: John Montilino
Mission: To provide entertainment and theatre education for families and young people.
Utilizes: Guest Companies; Singers
Founded: 1984
Specialized Field: Musical
Status: Semi-Professional; Nonprofit
Paid Staff: 30
Performs At: Eisenhower Community Center; Hopkins
Organization Type: Performing; Resident; Educational

2838
CLIMB THEATRE
6415 Carmen Avenue E
Inner Grove Heights, MN 55076
Phone: 651-453-9275
Fax: 651-453-9274
Toll-free: 800-767-9660
e-mail: mail@climb.org
Web Site: www.climb.org
Officers:
   President: Peg Wetli
Founded: 1975
Specialized Field: New Works of Social Importance
Status: Non-Profit, Professional
Paid Artists: 24
Season: July - May

2839
COMMONWEAL THEATRE COMPANY
206 Parkway Avenue N
Lanesboro, MN 55949
Mailing Address: PO Box 15
Phone: 507-467-2525
Fax: 507-467-2468
Toll-free: 800-657-7025
e-mail: info@commonwealtheatre.org
Web Site: www.commonwealtheatre.org
Officers:
   Board President: David Ruen
Management:
   Executive Director: Hal Cropp
   Marketing Director: Jill Underwood
   Media Relations/Special Events: Adrienne Sweeney
   Development Director: David Hennessey
Mission: The Commonwealth is a nonprofit professional thatre company dedicated to delighting and challenging the audiences of our region and beyond.
Utilizes: Actors; Artists-in-Residence; Commissioned Music; Designers; Educators; Fine Artists; Grant Writers; Guest Conductors; Guest Designers; High School Drama; Instructors; Multimedia; Music; Original Music Scores; Performance Artists; Resident Artists; Resident Professionals; Selected Students; Soloists
Founded: 1989
Specialized Field: Musical; Comedy; Classic; Contemporary

Status: Non-Profit, Professional
Paid Staff: 9
Paid Artists: 35
Budget: $600,000
Income Sources: 64% Contributed Income
Season: February - December
Performs At: Brand New 186-Seat Thrust Theatre Due To Be Completed In July, 2007
Annual Attendance: 18,000
Facility Category: Until July, 2007; Converted Silent Movie House
Type of Stage: Proscenium
Stage Dimensions: 23' x 30'
Seating Capacity: 126
Year Built: 1896

2840
GREEN EARTH PLAYERS
216 W Main Street
Luverne, MN 56156
Phone: 507-283-9891
Mission: To bring live theatre to the area.
Utilizes: Guest Companies
Founded: 1978
Specialized Field: Musical; Community Theater
Status: Nonprofit
Income Sources: Minnesota Arts Council; Southern Minnesota Arts & Humanities Council
Performs At: Palace Theatre
Organization Type: Performing

2841
HIGHLAND SUMMER THEATRE
Minnesota State University
201 Performing Arts Center
Mankato, MN 56001
Phone: 507-389-2118
Fax: 507-389-2922
Toll-free: 800-627-3529
e-mail: paul.hustoles@mnsu.edu
Web Site: www.msutheatre.com
Officers:
   President: Richard Davenport
Management:
   Artistic Director: Paul J Hustoles
Mission: Summer stock theatre in its 45th season
Founded: 1967
Specialized Field: Musical; Comedy; Summer Stock
Status: Non-Profit, Professional
Paid Staff: 30
Volunteer Staff: 4
Paid Artists: 15
Non-paid Artists: 20
Income Sources: Ticket Revenue; State Support
Season: May - July
Affiliations: Minnesota State University Mankato
Annual Attendance: 40,000
Facility Category: Performing Arts Center
Type of Stage: Proscenium; Black Box
Stage Dimensions: 38' x 38'; 60' x 70'
Seating Capacity: 529; 250

2842
ARTS MIDWEST
2908 Hennepin Avenue
Suite 200
Minneapolis, MN 55408-1954
Phone: 612-341-0755
Fax: 612-341-0902
e-mail: general@artsmidwest.org
Management:
   Executive Director: David Fraher
   Assistant Director: Susan T Chandler
   Program Director: Ken Carlson Carlson

Founded: 1985
Specialized Field: Educational; Community Theater
Status: Non-Profit

2843

CHILDREN'S THEATER COMPANY

2400 3rd Avenue S
Minneapolis, MN 55404-3597
Phone: 612-874-0500
Fax: 612-874-8119
e-mail: info@childrenstheatre.org
Web Site: www.childrenstheatre.org
Officers:
    Chairman: Peter Carter
    Vice Chiar: Ann Parriott
    Vice Chair: Geoff Jue
Management:
    Artistic Director: Peter C Brosius
    Managing Director: Gabriella Calicchier
Mission: To produce significant theatre experiences for young people and their families through nuturing a creative ensemble of the highest professional quality.
Utilizes: Guest Companies; Singers
Founded: 1965
Specialized Field: Youth Theater; Children's Theater
Status: Non-Profit, Professional
Paid Staff: 75
Paid Artists: 75
Budget: $9 million
Income Sources: Theatre Communications Group; International Association of Theatre for Children and Youth; Actors' Equity Association
Performs At: Children's Theatre Company
Annual Attendance: 350,000
Facility Category: Theater
Type of Stage: Proscenium
Seating Capacity: 745
Organization Type: Performing; Touring; Educational

2844

COMMEDIA THEATER COMPANY

3040 10Th Avenue S
Minneapolis, MN 55407
Phone: 612-788-2157
Management:
    General Manager: Linda Bruning
    Office/Booking Manager: Rudd Rayfield
Mission: To bring improvisational comedy with direct audience contact, into communities unfamiliar with live theater.
Founded: 1975
Specialized Field: Comedy; Improvisation
Status: Professional
Organization Type: Performing; Touring; Educational

2845

GUTHRIE THEATER

725 Vineland Place
Minneapolis, MN 55403
Phone: 612-377-2224
Fax: 612-347-1188
Toll-free: 877-447-8243
e-mail: webmaster@guthrietheater.org
Web Site: www.guthrietheater.org
Officers:
    President: Charles Zelle
    VP: Susan Engel
    Treasurer: Jay Kiedrowski
    Secretary: M. Joahn Jundt
Management:
    President: Joe Dowling
    Managing Director: Tom C Proehl
    General Manager: Thomas C Proehl

Mission: To serve as a vital artistic resource for the people of Minnesota and the region; to celebrate, through theatrical performances, the common humanity binding us all together; devoted to the traditional classical repertoire.
Utilizes: Actors; Artists-in-Residence; Choreographers; Collaborating Artists; Collaborations; Commissioned Music; Designers; Educators; Five Seasonal Concerts; Guest Accompanists; Guest Artists; Guest Choreographers; Guest Companies; Guest Conductors; Guest Designers; Guest Directors; Guest Ensembles; Guest Instructors; Guest Soloists; Guest Teachers; High School Drama; Instructors; Local Artists; Multimedia; Original Music Scores; Performance Artists; Playwrights; Resident Professionals; Selected Students; Soloists; Student Interns; Theatre Companies; Visual Arts
Founded: 1963
Specialized Field: Musical; Comedy; Classic; Contemporary
Status: Non-Profit, Professional
Season: June - February/March
Performs At: The Guthrie Theater
Affiliations: League of Resident Theatres
Type of Stage: Modified Thrust
Seating Capacity: 1300
Year Built: 1963
Year Remodeled: 1993
Cost: 3.5 Million
Organization Type: Performing; Touring; Resident

2846

HIDDEN THEATRE

4600 Oakland Avenue
Minneapolis, MN 55407-3536
Phone: 612-822-6060
Fax: 612-332-6037
Management:
    Audience Services Manager: David Pisa
Founded: 1994
Specialized Field: Drama

2847

ILLUSION THEATER

528 Hennepin Avenue
Suite 704
Minneapolis, MN 55403
Phone: 612-339-4944
Fax: 612-337-8042
e-mail: info@illusiontheater.org
Web Site: www.illusiontheater.org
Management:
    President: Michael Robins
    Managing Director: Mike Halls
    Education Director: Karen Gundlach
    Producing Director: Bonnie Morris
Utilizes: Actors; AEA Actors; Artists-in-Residence; Collaborations; Dance Companies; Dancers; Designers; Educators; Filmmakers; Five Seasonal Concerts; Grant Writers; Guest Artists; Guest Companies; Guest Conductors; Guest Lecturers; Guest Musical Directors; Guest Teachers; Local Artists; Local Unknown Artists; Multi Collaborations; Multimedia; Organization Contracts; Original Music Scores; Performance Artists; Poets; Resident Professionals; Selected Students; Sign Language Translators; Soloists; Student Interns; Visual Arts
Founded: 1974
Specialized Field: Musical; Comedy; Youth Theater; Contemporary
Status: Non-Profit, Professional
Paid Staff: 10
Paid Artists: 100
Budget: $1,500,000

Income Sources: Actors' Equity Association; Small Professional Theatre Association; Grants; Box Office
Season: September - August
Performs At: Hennepin Center for the Arts
Annual Attendance: 15,000
Facility Category: Theater
Type of Stage: Proscenium
Seating Capacity: 225
Year Remodeled: 1999
Organization Type: Performing; Touring; Resident; Educational; Sponsoring

2848

IN THE HEART OF THE BEAST PUPPET AND MASK THEATRE

1500 E Lake Street
Minneapolis, MN 55407
Phone: 612-721-2535
Fax: 612-721-7174
e-mail: info@hobt.org
Web Site: www.hobt.org
Officers:
    Chairman: Mary Lynn Puischer
    Vice Chairman: Sue Melrose
    Executive Director: Loren Niemi
Management:
    Artistic Director: Sandy Spieler
Mission: Newspaper, paint and unlimited imagination to tell stories that explore the struggles and celebrations of human existence. Drawing inspiration from the world's traditions of puppet and mask theatre and its lively roots in transformative ritual and street theatre. HOBT creates vital, poetic theater for all ages and backgrounds.
Utilizes: Actors; Artists-in-Residence; Commissioned Composers; Guest Companies; Guest Conductors; Student Interns; Special Technical Talent
Founded: 1973
Specialized Field: Puppet; Mask Theater
Status: Non-Profit, Professional
Paid Staff: 13
Volunteer Staff: 350
Non-paid Artists: 20
Income Sources: Grants from Private and Public Sectors; Ticket Revenue and Earned Fees
Performs At: Restored Movie Theater
Annual Attendance: 100,000
Facility Category: Theatre
Type of Stage: Proscenium
Seating Capacity: 300
Year Built: 1937
Year Remodeled: 1997
Rental Contact: Paul Robinson
Organization Type: Performing; Touring; Resident; Educational; Sponsoring

2849

INTERNATIONAL THEATRES CORPORATION

4701 Ids Center
Minneapolis, MN 55402
Phone: 612-340-1900
Fax: 612-340-9919
Management:
    President: Tom Scallen
    Director of Communications: Sandra Sullivan
Specialized Field: Specialty Acts; Mystery; Dinner Theater; International

2850

JACKSON MARIONETTE PRODUCTIONS

1500 E Lake Street
Minneapolis, MN 55407
Phone: 612-721-2535

Management:
Manager: Sara Jackson
Utilizes: Singers
Specialized Field: Puppet
Status: Professional
Income Sources: Puppeteers of America; United International Marionette Association; Twin City Puppeteers
Organization Type: Performing; Touring

2851
JUNGLE THEATER

2951 S Lyndale Avenue
Minneapolis, MN 55408
Phone: 612-822-7063
Fax: 612-822-9408
e-mail: info@jungletheater.com
Web Site: www.jungletheater.com
Officers:
Marketing Director: Sonja Wahlberg
Management:
Artistic Director: Bain Boehlke
Managing Director: Margo Sagisselman
Development Director: Don Sommer
Community Programs Manager: Charles Bethel
Board Chair: Eric Galatz
Vice Chair: Julie Umbarger
Mission: To produce high quality theatre in an intimate setting.
Founded: 1991
Specialized Field: Contemporary
Status: Non-Profit, Professional
Paid Staff: 15
Volunteer Staff: 80
Paid Artists: 200
Budget: $1.1 million
Income Sources: Earned; Contributions
Performs At: Theater
Affiliations: Theatre Communications Group
Annual Attendance: 26,000
Facility Category: Theater
Type of Stage: Proscenium
Seating Capacity: 135
Year Built: 1911
Year Remodeled: 1999
Rental Contact: Charlie Bethel

2852
MARGOLIS BROWN THEATRE COMPANY

3112 17th Avenue S
Minneapolis, MN 55407
Phone: 612-722-2333
e-mail: margolisbrown@aol.com
Web Site: www.margolisbrown.org
Management:
Director Of Education and Outreach: Kym Longhi
Artistic and Executive Director: Tony Brown
Artistic and Executive Director: Karl Margolis
Mission: To create original multimedia productions of movement theatre; to share our facilities with other artists.
Utilizes: Singers
Founded: 1983
Specialized Field: Multi-Media; Movement Theater
Status: Professional; Nonprofit
Income Sources: National Movement Theatre Association
Organization Type: Performing; Touring; Resident; Educational; Sponsoring; Dramatic Movement School

2853
MIXED BLOOD THEATRE COMPANY

1501 S 4th Street
Minneapolis, MN 55454

Phone: 612-338-6131
Fax: 612-338-1851
e-mail: boxoffice@mixedblood.com
Web Site: www.mixedblood.com
Management:
Artistic Director: Jack Reuler
Production Manager: Sharon Bach
Director Touring: Charlie Moore
Box Office Manager: Morgan Martin
Mission: A multiracial, professional theatre ensemble employing colorblind casting, and dedicated to fostering the spirit of Dr. Martin Luther King's dream.
Utilizes: Actors; AEA Actors; Designers; Educators; Fine Artists; Five Seasonal Concerts; Guest Companies; Instructors; Local Artists; Organization Contracts; Original Music Scores; Performance Artists; Resident Professionals; Selected Students; Soloists; Student Interns; Theatre Companies
Founded: 1976
Specialized Field: Ethnic Theater; Community Theater; Contemporary
Status: Non-Profit, Professional
Paid Staff: 8
Paid Artists: 75
Budget: $1 million
Income Sources: Society for Stage Directors and Choreographers
Season: September - May
Annual Attendance: varies
Type of Stage: Flexible
Seating Capacity: 200
Organization Type: Performing; Touring; Educational

2854
MU PERFORMING ARTS

2700 NE Winter Street
Suite 1A
Minneapolis, MN 55413
Phone: 612-824-4804
Fax: 612-824-3396
e-mail: info@muperformingarts.org
Web Site: www.muperformingarts.org
Management:
Artistic Director: Rick Shiomi
Managing Director: Kathleen Hansen
Founded: 1992
Specialized Field: Musical; Comedy; Ethnic Theater; Puppet; Contemporary
Status: Non-Profit, Professional
Paid Staff: 6
Paid Artists: 50

2855
PANGEA WORLD THEATER

711 Westlake Street
Suite 102
Minneapolis, MN 55408
Phone: 612-822-0015
Fax: 612-821-1070
e-mail: pangea@pangeaworldtheater.org
Web Site: www.pangeaworldtheater.org
Officers:
Board Chair: June LaValleur
Management:
Artistic Director: Dipankar Mukherjee
Founded: 1996
Specialized Field: Comedy; Ethnic Theater; Classic; Contemporary
Status: Non-Profit, Professional
Paid Staff: 3

2856
PILLSBURY HOUSE THEATRE

3501 Chicago Avenue S
Minneapolis, MN 55407
Phone: 612-825-0459
Fax: 612-827-5818
e-mail: info@pillsburyhousetheatre.org
Web Site: www.pillsburyhousetheatre.org
Management:
President: Tony Wagner
Managing Director: Noel Raymond
Co-Artistic Director: Faye Price
Founded: 1992
Specialized Field: Youth Theater; Ethnic Theater; Contemporary
Status: Non-Profit, Professional
Paid Staff: 8

2857
PLAYWRIGHTS' CENTER

2301 Franklin Avenue E
Minneapolis, MN 55406-1099
Phone: 612-332-7481
Fax: 612-332-6037
e-mail: info@pwcenter.org
Web Site: www.pwcenter.org
Officers:
Board President: Mary McGreevy
Board Vice President: Peter Quale
Director Development: Todd Boss
Treasurer: Joyce Bevning
Secretary: Paula Anderson
Management:
Producing Artistic Director: Jeremy Cohen, jeremyc@pwcenter.org
Mission: The Playwrights' Center champions playwrights and plays to build upon a living theater that demands new and innovative works.
Utilizes: AEA Actors; Artists-in-Residence; Collaborating Artists; Collaborations; Community Members; Community Talent; Educators; Equity Actors; Five Seasonal Concerts; Guest Accompanists; Guest Choreographers; Guest Conductors; Guest Designers; Guest Ensembles; Guest Musical Directors; Guest Soloists; High School Drama; Instructors; Local Artists & Directors; Local Talent; Multi Collaborations; Multimedia; Original Music Scores; Performance Artists; Students; Student Interns; Special Technical Talent; Volunteer Directors & Actors; Writers
Founded: 1971
Specialized Field: Musical; Comedy; Young Playwrights; Ensembles; Classic; Contemporary
Status: Non-Profit, Professional
Paid Staff: 13
Paid Artists: 100
Income Sources: Actors' Equity Association; Theatre Communications Group
Season: July - August
Year Built: 1900
Year Remodeled: 2000
Cost: $1,100,000
Organization Type: Touring; Educational; Sponsoring; Developmental Workshops; Reading

2858
RED EYE

15 W 14th Street
Minneapolis, MN 55403
Phone: 612-870-7531
e-mail: staff@theredeye.org
Web Site: www.theredeye.org
Management:
Managing Director: Miriam Must

Artistic Director: Steve Busa
Production and Facility Manager: Tim Heins
Mission: To provide experimental theatre; to develop multimedia theater productions.
Utilizes: Guest Companies; Singers
Founded: 1983
Specialized Field: Experimental; Multi-Media
Status: Professional; Nonprofit
Income Sources: National Endowment for the Arts; Dayton Hudson Foundation; Jerome Foundation; McKnight Foundation; United Artists; Metropolitan Regional Arts Council
Performs At: Red Eye's 14th Street Theatre
Organization Type: Performing; Touring; Resident; Educational

2859
THEATRE DE LA JEUNE LUNE

105 N 1st Street
Minneapolis, MN 55401
Phone: 612-332-3968
Fax: 612-332-0048
e-mail: info@junelune.org
Web Site: www.jeunelune.org
Management:
   Executive Director: Steve Richardson
   Artistic Director: Robert Rosen
   Artistic Director: Dominique Serrand
   Artistic Director: Vincent Gracieux
   Business Director: Kit Waickman
   Development Director: Jennifer Halcrow
   Marketing Director: Steve Richardson
Mission: The production of immediate, energetic, dynamic, theatre through company creations and scripted material.
Founded: 1978
Specialized Field: Musical; Comedy; Community Theater; Puppet; Contemporary
Status: Non-Profit, Professional
Paid Staff: 10
Paid Artists: 10
Income Sources: Foundation for the Extension and Development of American Professional Theatre
Season: September - June
Type of Stage: Mobile
Stage Dimensions: 60' x 100'; 47' x 30'
Seating Capacity: 500;100-150
Organization Type: Performing; Touring

2860
THEATRE IN THE ROUND

245 Cedar Avenue
Minneapolis, MN 55454-1054
Phone: 612-333-3010
e-mail: editorial@theatremania.com
Web Site: www.theatreintheround.org
Management:
   President: Diana Hellerman
   Managing Director: Steve Antenucci
Mission: To bridge the gap between professional and amateur theatre with quality drama; to entertain the community; to educate.
Utilizes: Guest Companies; Singers
Founded: 1952
Specialized Field: Drama; Educational
Status: Non-Profit, Non-Professional
Paid Staff: 3
Paid Artists: 9
Income Sources: American Association of Community Theatres; Minnesota Association of Community Theatres
Performs At: Theatre-in-the-Round
Organization Type: Performing; Resident; Educational

2861
TROUPE AMERICA

3313 Republic Avenue
Minneapolis, MN 55426
Phone: 612-333-3302
Fax: 612-333-4337
e-mail: johnt@troupeamerica.com
Web Site: www.troupeamerica.com
Officers:
   President: Curtis N Wollan
   Secretary/Treasurer: Jane Wollan
Management:
   Publicist: Linda Twiss
   Production Manager: Scott Herbst
   General Manager: John Tsadoyannis
Mission: To provide top quality theatrical experiences for our audiences, on the road and in the Twin Cities.
Utilizes: Actors; Artists-in-Residence; Choreographers; Collaborating Artists; Collaborations; Community Talent; Composers; Contract Actors; Dancers; Designers; Equity Actors; Guest Designers; Guest Lecturers; Local Unknown Artists; Multimedia; Music; Organization Contracts; Original Music Scores; Performance Artists; Resident Professionals; Selected Students; Theatre Companies
Founded: 1987
Specialized Field: Musical; Comedy; Contemporary
Status: For-Profit, Professional
Paid Staff: 23
Paid Artists: 35
Budget: $1,750,000
Income Sources: Ticket Sales; Concessions; Touring Fees
Season: September - August
Affiliations: Southeastern Theatre Conference; United Professional Theatre Association
Annual Attendance: 100,000
Facility Category: Plymouth Playhouse; and Touring Venues
Type of Stage: Semi Thrust
Stage Dimensions: 30x24
Seating Capacity: 211
Year Built: 1974
Year Remodeled: 1998
Cost: $150,000
Rental Contact: Production Manager Scott Herbst
Organization Type: Performing; Touring; Resident; Sponsoring

2862
WALKER ART CENTER

Vineland Place
Minneapolis, MN 55403
Phone: 612-375-7624
Fax: 612-375-7618
e-mail: leigha.horton@walkerart.org
Web Site: www.walkerart.org
Management:
   Director: Kathy Halbreich
   Curator Performing Arts: Philip Bither
Mission: To serve as a catalyst regionally and internationally for emerging forms of expression; to engage the audience in contemporary arts issues.
Utilizes: Artists-in-Residence; Choreographers; Collaborating Artists; Collaborations; Commissioned Composers; Commissioned Music; Composers-in-Residence; Curators; Dance Companies; Educators; Fine Artists; Guest Soloists; Instructors; Original Music Scores; Poets; Selected Students; Student Interns; Touring Companies
Founded: 1887
Specialized Field: Drama; Contemporary; Multi-Media
Status: Non-Profit, Professional

Paid Staff: 150
Income Sources: Endowment; Grants; Ticket Revenue; Donations
Performs At: Walker Art Center Auditorium
Facility Category: Multidisciplinary Arts Center
Seating Capacity: 350
Organization Type: Performing; Touring; Resident; Educational; Sponsoring; Exhibition

2863
WORLD TREE PUPPET THEATER

3305 E Calhoun Parkway
Minneapolis, MN 55408
Phone: 612-824-3112
Management:
   Director: Joan Mickelson
Mission: To use the traditions of puppetry and adaptations of folklore to entertain families and children; to employ experimental uses of puppets, dolls and masks for adult theater.
Founded: 1982
Specialized Field: Puppet
Status: Professional
Organization Type: Performing; Touring; Resident

2864
GOOSEBERRY PARK PLAYERS

PO Box 362
Moorhead, MN 56561
Phone: 218-299-3728
e-mail: jcermak@cord.edu
Web Site: www.gooseberryparkplayers.org
Officers:
   President: Ann Vandermaten
Management:
   Co-President: Gen Poehls
   Treasurer: Grace Matheson
   Managing Artistic Director: Jim Cermack
Mission: Provide a summer outdoor theatre for and by children for family entertainment providing a fun, educational experience for young people.
Utilizes: Singers
Founded: 1984
Specialized Field: Summer Stock; Children's Theater
Status: Nonprofit
Income Sources: Moorhead Parks & Recreational Department
Organization Type: Performing

2865
STRAW HAT PLAYERS

Minnesota State University Moorhead
1104 7th Avenue South
Moorhead, MN 56563
Phone: 218-477-2126
Fax: 218-477-4612
e-mail: ellngson@mnstate.edu
Web Site: www.mnstate.edu/strawhat
Management:
   Executive Director: Craig A Ellingson
Founded: 1963
Specialized Field: Classic; Musical
Status: Non-Profit, Professional
Paid Staff: 10
Paid Artists: 35
Season: May - July
Type of Stage: Thrust
Seating Capacity: 800

2866
OFF-BROADWAY MUSICAL THEATRE

3243 Flag Avenue N
New Hope, MN 55427

Phone: 612-544-3810
Fax: 612-545-3622
Mission: To offer major musicals employing local talent of all ages and degrees of proficiency.
Utilizes: Guest Artists; Guest Companies; Singers
Founded: 1979
Specialized Field: Community Theater; Musical
Status: Nonprofit
Income Sources: Minnesota State Arts Council
Performs At: New Hope Outdoor Theatre; Brooklyn Center Civic
Organization Type: Performing

2867
LITTLE THEATRE OF OWATONNA
Dunell Drive
PO Box 64
Owatonna, MN 55060
Mailing Address: PO Box 64
Phone: 507-451-0764
Web Site: http://www.littletheatreofowatonna.orr
Officers:
President: Vidette Ostermeir
Vice President: Sandee Hagan
Secretary: Lori Beadell
Management:
Executive Secretary: Sharon Stark
Mission: To bring performing arts, particularly theatre, to the community.
Utilizes: Guest Companies
Founded: 1966
Specialized Field: Drama; Community Theater
Status: Non-Professional; Nonprofit
Organization Type: Performing

2868
ROCHESTER CIVIC THEATRE
20 Civic Drive
Rochester, MN 55904
Phone: 507-282-8481
Fax: 507-282-0608
e-mail: info@rochestercivictheatre.org
Web Site: http://www.rochestercivictheatre.org/
Management:
President: Chris Gade
Executive Director: Greg Millern
Technical Director: Janet Rader
Managing Director: Mark Colbenson
Mission: Promoting interest in and appreciation of dramatic arts through programs and productions.
Utilizes: Guest Companies; Singers
Founded: 1951
Specialized Field: Musical; Comedy; Community Theater; Puppet; Classic; Contemporary
Status: Non-Profit, Non-Professional
Paid Staff: 6
Income Sources: Minnesota Association of Community Theatres
Organization Type: Performing; Touring; Educational

2869
CLIMB THEATRE - CREATIVE LEARNING IDEAS
6415 Carmen Ave E
Suite 220
Saint Paul, MN 55076
Phone: 651-453-9275
Fax: 651-453-9274
Toll-free: 800-679-60
e-mail: mail@climb.orgÿ
Web Site: http://www.climb.org/contactus.aspx
Officers:
President: Jim Gambone
Management:

Executive Director: Peg Wetli
Residency Company Manager: Peg Endres
Performance Company Sales Rep.: Susan Lund
Performance Company Director: Leigh Anne Adams
Mission: To harness and direct the creative power and artistic talents of its writers, directors, actors and educators to create and perform plays, classes and other creative works which communicate matters of social or educational significance to all citizens.
Utilizes: Singers
Founded: 1975
Specialized Field: New Works of Social Importance; Educational
Status: Professional; Nonprofit
Organization Type: Performing; Touring; Educational

2870
DUDLEY RIGGS INSTANT THEATRE COMPANY
1586 Burton Street
Saint Paul, MN 55108
Phone: 612-647-6748
Fax: 612-647-5637
Management:
Producing Director: Dudley Riggs
Founded: 1954
Specialized Field: Drama; Musical; Contemporary
Performs At: Dudley Riggs Theatre
Type of Stage: Modified Thrust
Seating Capacity: 260

2871
GREAT AMERICAN HISTORY THEATRE
30 E 10th Street
Saint Paul, MN 55101
Phone: 651-292-4323
Fax: 651-292-4322
e-mail: boxofc@historytheatre.com
Web Site: http://www.historytheatre.com/about/
Officers:
President: Jeff Perterson
VP: Connie Braziel
Treasurer: Tyler Zehring
Secretrary: Jack Flynn
Management:
Artistic Director: Ron Peluso
Managing Director: Kathleen Hansen
Production Manager: Janet Hall
Mission: To create new plays about Minnesota the Midwest and the diverse American experience.
Founded: 1978
Specialized Field: Musical; Historical
Status: Professional; Nonprofit
Paid Artists: 40
Income Sources: 70% Earned; 30% Contributed
Annual Attendance: 54,000

2872
HISTORY THEATRE
30 E 10th Street
Saint Paul, MN 55101
Phone: 651-292-4323
Fax: 651-292-4322
e-mail: pr@historytheatre.com
Web Site: www.historytheatre.com
Officers:
President: Jeff Peterson
VP: Connie Braziel
Treasurer: Tyler Zehring
Secretary: Jack Flynn
Management:
Artistic Director: Ron Peluso
Managing Director: Kathleen Hansen

Director of Development: Barbe Marshall
Marketing Director: Rachel Flynn
Mission: To create new plays about Minnesota the Midwest and the diverse American experience.
Utilizes: Guest Companies; Singers
Founded: 1978
Specialized Field: Theater; Musical; Drama; Comedy
Status: Professional; Nonprofit
Paid Staff: 20
Volunteer Staff: 200
Paid Artists: 120
Budget: $1.1 Million
Income Sources: 70% Earned; 30% Contributed
Performs At: Crawford Livingston Theatre
Annual Attendance: 30,000
Type of Stage: Thrust
Seating Capacity: 587
Rental Contact: Erik Paulson
Organization Type: Performing; Touring; Resident; Educational; Sponsoring

2873
NAUTILUS MUSIC-THEATER
308 Prince Street
#250
Saint Paul, MN 55101
Phone: 651-298-9913
Fax: 651-298-9924
e-mail: nautilus@nautilusmusictheater.org
Management:
Artistic Director: Ben Krywosz
Managing Director: Bethany Gladhill
Mission: To develop and produce new musical theater works; to nurture the creative artist.
Founded: 1986
Specialized Field: Musical; Classic; Contemporary
Status: Non-Profit, Professional
Paid Staff: 2
Paid Artists: 200
Budget: $250,000
Organization Type: Performing; Educational

2874
PARK SQUARE THEATRE COMPANY
408 Saint Peter Street
Suite 110
Saint Paul, MN 55102-1130
Phone: 651-291-7005
Fax: 651-291-9180
e-mail: parksquare@parksquaretheatre.org
Web Site: www.parksquaretheatre.org
Management:
Develoment Director: Michael Pease
Executive Director: Steven Kent Lockwood
Audience Services Director: Eric M Herr
Education Director: Mary Finnerty
Mission: Entertaining and enriching area audiences with quality productions of the classics.
Utilizes: Actors; AEA Actors; Choreographers; Commissioned Music; Designers; Guest Accompanists; Guest Artists; Guest Companies; Guest Conductors; Guest Lecturers; Local Artists; Original Music Scores; Resident Professionals; Selected Students; Student Interns
Founded: 1975
Specialized Field: Comedy; Classic; Contemporary
Status: Non-Profit, Professional
Paid Staff: 10
Paid Artists: 100
Budget: $1.2 million
Income Sources: Sales; Contributions
Season: January - August
Annual Attendance: 54,000
Facility Category: Rental

Type of Stage: Proscenium
Stage Dimensions: 34' x 30'
Seating Capacity: 340
Organization Type: Performing

2875

PENUMBRA THEATRE COMPANY
270 N Kent Street
Saint Paul, MN 55102
Phone: 651-224-3180
Fax: 612-224-7074
e-mail: lou.bellamy@penumbratheatre.org
Web Site: http://penumbratheatre.org
Management:
   Artistic Director: Lou Bellamy
   General Manager: Jayne Khalifa
Mission: To present high quality theatre from the Pan African/American viewpoint.
Utilizes: Guest Companies
Founded: 1976
Specialized Field: Musical; Ethnic Theater
Status: Professional; Nonprofit
Income Sources: Actors' Equity Association
Season: August - June
Type of Stage: Proscenium/Thrust
Stage Dimensions: 27' x 41'
Seating Capacity: 260
Organization Type: Performing; Touring; Educational

2876

RAINBO CHILDREN'S THEATRE COMPANY
688 Selby Avenue
Saint Paul, MN 55104
Phone: 651-293-9043
Management:
   Founder/Managing Artistic Director: Merline Batiste Doty
Mission: To bring children together for cultural exchange through participation in the performing arts.
Utilizes: Guest Companies; Singers
Founded: 1979
Specialized Field: Community Theater; Ethnic Theater
Status: Professional; Nonprofit
Paid Staff: 10
Organization Type: Performing; Touring; Resident; Educational; Sponsoring

2877

LAKESHORE PLAYERS
4820 Stewart Avenue
White Bear Lake, MN 55110
Phone: 651-426-3275
e-mail: info@lakeshoreplayers.com
Web Site: www.lakeshoreplayers.com
Management:
   Business Manager: Sherrie Tarble
Mission: To provide entertainment for the community.
Utilizes: Guest Companies; Singers
Founded: 1953
Specialized Field: Musical
Status: Nonprofit
Paid Staff: 25
Income Sources: Minnesota Association of Community Theatres
Performs At: Lakeshore Playhouse
Organization Type: Performing; Educational

2878

SHAKESPEARE & COMPANY
Century College, W Campus
3300 Century Avenue N
White Bear Lake, MN 55110

Phone: 651-779-5818
Fax: 651-779-5802
e-mail: info@shakespeare-company.org
Web Site: www.shakespeare-company.org
Management:
   President: Larry Litecky
   Artistic Director: George M Roesler
Mission: To provide an environment where families can come and enjoy an informal picnic atmosphere and see performances of Shakespeare and other classical plays.
Founded: 1976
Specialized Field: Educational; Shakespeare
Status: Professional
Performs At: Outdoor Theatre Complex, West Campus of Century College

Mississippi

2879

CORINTH THEATRE-ARTS
303 Fulton Drive
PO Box 127
Corinth, MS 38834
Phone: 662-287-2995
Fax: 662-287-6272
e-mail: cta@corinththeatrearts.com
Web Site: www.corinththeatrearts.com
Officers:
   Chairman: John Treadway
   Vice Chairman: Paul Schumacher
   Secretary: Laurie Prichett
   Treasurer: Jimmy Deaton
Management:
   President: Ed Lucas
   VP Of Operations: Tonya Freeman
   Artistic Director: Katie Simons
   Technical Director: Roger Bryie
Mission: To offer theatrical performances, arts education, economic stimulation and quality arts entertainment.
Founded: 1968
Specialized Field: Community Theater
Status: Non-Profit, Professional
Paid Staff: 2
Volunteer Staff: 2
Paid Artists: 10
Non-paid Artists: 500
Budget: $105,000
Income Sources: Theatre Patrons; Box Office; Grants
Performs At: Crossroads Playhouse; Coliseum Civic Center
Annual Attendance: 8500
Type of Stage: Proscenium
Stage Dimensions: 19 x 30
Seating Capacity: 204
Organization Type: Resident

2880

NEW STAGE THEATRE
1100 Carlisle Street
PO Box 4792
Jackson, MS 39202
Mailing Address: PO Box 4792 Jackson MS 39296
Phone: 601-948-3533
Fax: 601-948-3538
e-mail: mail@newstagetheatre.com
Web Site: www.newstagetheatre.com
Management:
   Artistic Director: Francine Thomas Reynolds
   General Manager: Bill McCarty
   Managing Director: Dawn Buck

Utilizes: Actors; AEA Actors; Choreographers; Collaborations; Contract Actors; Designers; Educators; Equity Actors; Five Seasonal Concerts; Grant Writers; Guest Accompanists; Guest Artists; Guest Conductors; Guest Designers; Guest Ensembles; Guest Lecturers; Guest Musical Directors; Guest Speakers; Guest Teachers; High School Drama; Instructors; Local Artists; Local Artists & Directors; Multimedia; Music; Original Music Scores; Poets; Resident Companies; Resident Professionals; Scenic Designers; Soloists; Students; Theatre Companies; Visual Designers; Volunteer Directors & Actors; Writers
Founded: 1965
Opened: 1965
Specialized Field: Musical; Comedy; Ethnic Theater; Classic; Contemporary
Status: Non-Profit, Professional
Paid Staff: 13
Paid Artists: 5
Budget: $900,000
Season: September - June
Affiliations: Actors' Equity Association
Facility Category: New Stage Theatre
Type of Stage: Proscenium
Seating Capacity: 364
Organization Type: Resident; Educational; Producing

2881

PUPPET ARTS THEATRE
1927 Springridge Drive
Jackson, MS 39211
Phone: 601-956-3414
Fax: 601-956-3414
e-mail: peter@mspuppetry.com
Web Site: www.mrzpuppets.com
Management:
   Managing Director: Peter Zapletal
   Business Manager: Jarmila Zapletal
Mission: To offer entertainment and education in the Southeast through programs featuring puppets and classical music.
Founded: 1968
Specialized Field: Puppet; Children's Theater
Status: For-Profit, Professional
Paid Staff: 10
Paid Artists: 10
Organization Type: Performing; Touring

Missouri

2882

ARROW ROCK LYCEUM THEATRE
PO Box 14
Arrow Rock, MO 65320
Phone: 660-837-3311
Fax: 660-837-3112
e-mail: lyceumtheatre@lyceumtheatre.org
Web Site: www.lyceumtheatre.org
Officers:
   President: Dave Griggs
   Vice President: Chet Breitwieser
   Treasurer: Vicki Russell
   Secretary: Michael Kateman
Management:
   Artistic Director: Quinn Gresham
   Managing Director: Steve Bertani
   Marketing Director: Erin Willis
   Box Office Manager: Alice Roselius
Mission: To touch, enrich and entertain human beings with live professional theatre.
Utilizes: Actors; AEA Actors; Artists-in-Residence; Choreographers; Designers; Guest Artists; Guest Companies; Guest Musical Directors; Instructors;

Music; Original Music Scores; Resident Artists;
Resident Professionals; Sign Language Translators;
Singers; Soloists
Founded: 1960
Specialized Field: Drama; Musical
Status: Professional; Nonprofit
Paid Staff: 25
Volunteer Staff: 80
Paid Artists: 35
Non-paid Artists: 80
Budget: $750,000
Income Sources: Actors' Equity Association
Season: June - August
Performs At: Lyceum Theatre
Annual Attendance: 35,000
Facility Category: Indoor A/C Theatre
Type of Stage: Proscenium w/thrust
Seating Capacity: 408
Year Remodeled: 1993
Rental Contact: Business Manager Elizabeth Ostrin
Organization Type: Performing; Touring; Resident

2883
SHEPHERD OF THE HILLS
W Highway 76
Branson, MO 65616-0000
Phone: 417-334-4191
Toll-free: 800-653-6288
e-mail: groups@tablerock.net
Management:
Director: Keith Thurman
General Manager: Richard Bittle
Operations Manager: Jim O'Donnell
Technical Director: Rick Swan
Mission: In 1907, a novel was published that forever
changed the way of life for Branson area residents.
That novel, The Shepherd of the Hills, sold millions of
copies and attracts many people to the Ozark hills
around which its story is centered.
Founded: 1907
Specialized Field: Summer Stock; Historical
Status: For-Profit,Professional
Season: April - October
Type of Stage: Outdoor
Seating Capacity: 1100

2884
TRILAKES COMMUNITY THEATRE
PO Box 1301
Branson, MO 65616
Phone: 417-335-4241
e-mail: board@tlctheatre.org
Web Site: http://www.tlctheatre.org
Officers:
President: John Spencer
VP Business: Gail Wehr
VP Production: Corey James
Mission: To foster the Performing Arts; to entertain the
community.
Utilizes: Singers
Founded: 1983
Specialized Field: Musical; Community Theater
Status: Nonprofit
Paid Staff: 30
Income Sources: Missouri Arts Council
Organization Type: Performing

2885
FLORISSANT CIVIC CENTER THEATER
1 James J Eagan Drive
Florissant, MO 63033

Phone: 314-921-5678
Fax: 314-921-5666
e-mail: fcct@florissantmo.com
Web Site: www.florissantmo.com
Management:
Manager: Gary Gaydos
Founded: 1972
Opened: 1972
Specialized Field: Musical; Comedy; Community
Theater; Puppet; Classic; Contemporary
Status: Non-Profit, Professional
Paid Staff: 8
Type of Stage: Proscenium; Moderate Thrust
Stage Dimensions: 40'x40'
Year Built: 1972
Year Remodeled: 2004
Cost: $1.5 Million
Rental Contact: Manager Gary Gaydos

2886
CITY THEATRE OF INDEPENDENCE
Roger T Sermon Center
201 N Dodgion Street
Independence, MO 64050
Phone: 816-325-7367
e-mail: sharonpropst@comcast.com
Officers:
President: Steve Kennedy
Treasurer: Carolyn Putsch
Secretary: Sarah Schmidt
Management:
VP Production: Trasey Propst
VP Of Marketing: Sharon Propst
Season Production Manager: RJ Parish
Founded: 1980
Specialized Field: Community Theater

2887
COTERIE THEATRE
2450 Grand Avenue
Suite 144
Kansas City, MO 64108-2520
Phone: 816-474-6552
Fax: 816-474-7112
e-mail: jeffchurch@aol.com
Web Site: www.thecoterie.com
Officers:
President: Karen Weltner
Vice President: Bob Inerman
Secretary: Mark Gilgus
Treasurer: LJ Buckner
Management:
President: Cathy Doyal
Executive Director: Jolette M Pelster
Producing Artistic Director: Jeff Church
Marketing Manager: Karen Vanasdale
Mission: To provide professional classic and
contemporary theater which challenges the audience as
well as the artist; to provide educational dramatic
outreach programs in the community.
Utilizes: Guest Companies
Founded: 1979
Specialized Field: Youth Theater
Status: Non-Profit, Professional
Paid Staff: 8
Paid Artists: 30
Income Sources: Theatre Communications Group;
International Association of Theatre for Children and
Youth
Performs At: Coterie Theatre
Type of Stage: Flexible
Seating Capacity: 240
Organization Type: Performing; Touring; Resident;
Educational

2888
FOLLY THEATER
300 W 12th Street
PO Box 26505
Kansas City, MO 64196
Phone: 816-842-5500
Fax: 816-842-8709
e-mail: gale@follytheater.org
Web Site: www.follytheater.org
Management:
Executive Director: Gale Tallis
Events Manager: Stephanie Ornburn
Box Office Manager: Linda Bowlen
Development Director: Steve Irwin
Utilizes: Lyricists; Multimedia; Original Music Scores;
Special Technical Talent; Theatre Companies
Founded: 1900
Specialized Field: Musical
Status: Non-Profit, Professional
Paid Staff: 4
Volunteer Staff: 1
Budget: $60,000-150,000
Performs At: Performing Arts
Annual Attendance: 55,000
Type of Stage: Proscenium
Stage Dimensions: 34'x31'
Seating Capacity: 1,078
Year Built: 1900
Year Remodeled: 2000
Cost: $2,500,000
Rental Contact: Events Manager Kate Egan

2889
MID-AMERICA ARTS ALLIANCE
912 Baltimore Avenue
#700
Kansas City, MO 64105
Phone: 816-421-1388
Fax: 816-421-3918
e-mail: virgina@maaa.org
Web Site: www.maaa.org
Management:
Program Manager: Jenny Tritt
Founded: 1974
Specialized Field: Drama; Musical
Status: Non-Profit, Professional

2890
MISSOURI REPERTORY THEATRE
4949 Cherry Street
Kansas City, MO 64110-2499
Phone: 816-235-2727
Fax: 816-235-5367
Toll-free: 888-502-2700
e-mail: theatre@umkc.edu
Web Site: www.kcrep.org
Management:
Executive Director: Peter Altman
Managing Director: William Preacvost
Utilizes: Guest Companies; Singers
Founded: 1964
Specialized Field: Educational; Contemporary
Status: Non-Profit, Professional
Paid Staff: 25
Volunteer Staff: 10
Paid Artists: 30
Budget: $5,000,000
Season: August - May
Performs At: Helen F. Spencer Theatre
Type of Stage: Proscenium
Seating Capacity: 700
Organization Type: Performing; Resident; Educational

2891
QUALITY HILL PLAYHOUSE
303 W Tenth Street
Kansas City, MO 64105-1615
Phone: 816-421-1700
Fax: 816-221-6556
e-mail: info@qualityhillplayhouse.com
Web Site: www.qualityhillplayhouse.com
Officers:
   President: Dale Wassergord
   VP: Jack Rosenfield
   Secretary: Debbie MacLaughlin
   Treasurer: Kent Maughan
Management:
   President of the Board of Director: Dale Wassergord
   Executive Director: J Kent Barnhart
   Managing Director: Rick Truman
   Assistant Executive Director: Nancy Nail
Utilizes: Actors; AEA Actors; Choreographers; Collaborations; Dancers; Designers; Five Seasonal Concerts; Grant Writers; Guest Artists; Guest Musical Directors; Guest Musicians; Instructors; Local Artists; Local Unknown Artists; Multimedia; Music; Organization Contracts; Original Music Scores; Resident Professionals; Selected Students; Sign Language Translators; Singers; Soloists; Student Interns; Special Technical Talent
Founded: 1995
Specialized Field: Cabaret; Musical
Status: Non-Profit, Professional
Paid Staff: 8
Volunteer Staff: 98
Paid Artists: 30
Budget: $650,000
Income Sources: Ticket Sales; Contributions
Performs At: Quality Hill Playhouse
Annual Attendance: 30,000
Facility Category: Theatre
Type of Stage: Thrust
Stage Dimensions: 12' x 28'
Seating Capacity: 153
Year Built: 1989
Rental Contact: Nancy Nail
Comments: Handicapped Accessible

2892
STARLIGHT THEATRE
4600 Starlight Road
Kansas City, MO 64132-2032
Phone: 816-363-7827
Fax: 816-361-6398
Toll-free: 800-776-1730
e-mail: starlight@kcstarlight.com
Web Site: www.kcstarlight.com
Officers:
   Chairman of the Board: John W Kennedy
   Treasurer: Howard Cohen
   Secretary: Adele Hall
Management:
   President/Executive Director: Denton Yockey
   VP Marketing/Sales & Development: Cindy Jeffries
   VP Finance: Brenda Mortensen
   Assoc Producer/Education Director: Brad Jackson
Mission: To present first quality professional entertainment and arts education to diverse audiences, while building an appreciation for the performing arts and preserving and enhancing the Starlight venue for future generations. As it carries out this mission, Starlight will remain committed to family-oriented entertainment at affordable prices, with a focus on musical theatre.
Founded: 1951
Specialized Field: Musical
Status: Non-Profit, Professional
Volunteer Staff: 193
Budget: $12 Million
Income Sources: Ticket Sales; Fundraising
Season: May-September
Performs At: Live Theatrical Performance Including Plays And Concerts
Annual Attendance: 250,000
Facility Category: Outdoor Ampitheater
Type of Stage: Proscenium
Stage Dimensions: 68'x 48'
Seating Capacity: 8,000
Year Built: 1950
Year Remodeled: 2000

2893
UNICORN THEATRE
3828 Main Street
Kansas City, MO 64111
Phone: 816-531-7529
Fax: 816-531-0421
e-mail: unicornnews@unicorntheatre.org
Web Site: www.unicorntheatre.org
Officers:
   Managing Director: Jason Kralicek
   Marketing Director: Justin M Shaw
   Development Director: Geoff Gerling
Management:
   Artistic Director: Cynthia Levin
Mission: To enhance the cultural life of Kansas City by producing professional contemporary, thought-provoking theater which inspires emotional response and stimulates discussion.
Utilizes: Guest Companies; Singers
Founded: 1974
Specialized Field: Musical; Comedy; Contemporary
Status: Non-Profit, Professional
Paid Staff: 7
Income Sources: Actors' Equity Association; Theatre Communications Group
Season: September - June
Performs At: Unicorn Theatre
Affiliations: Actors' Equity Association; National New Play Network; Arts Council of Metropolitan Kansas City; Realtors For the Arts
Annual Attendance: 20,000
Type of Stage: Thrust
Seating Capacity: 175
Organization Type: Performing
Comments: Discounts for students, seniors and working artists

2894
MEMPHIS COMMUNITY PLAYERS
125 S Main
Memphis, MO 63555
Phone: 660-465-7770
Mission: To offer summer musical theatre to our area.
Founded: 1974
Specialized Field: Musical; Community Theater
Status: Non-Professional; Nonprofit
Performs At: Memphis Cinema
Organization Type: Performing; Resident; Educational

2895
MOBERLY COMMUNITY THEATRE
212 Crest Drive
Moberly, MO 65270
Phone: 660-263-3345
e-mail: carolee@mcmsys.com
Management:
   President: Carolee Hazlet
   VP: Bob Wright
Mission: Working together as a community to promote the performing arts.
Utilizes: Guest Companies; Singers
Founded: 1979
Specialized Field: Community Theater
Status: Non-Profit, Non-Professional
Paid Staff: 50
Performs At: Moberly Municipal Auditorium; Peppermint Loft
Organization Type: Performing; Sponsoring

2896
MARK TWAIN OUTDOOR THEATRE
12665 Fox Run Place
New London, MO 63459
Phone: 573-221-5204
Management:
   Managing Director: Sharon Donegan
Founded: 1979
Specialized Field: Summer Stock
Status: Non-Equity; Commercial
Season: May - September
Type of Stage: Outdoor
Stage Dimensions: 150' x 20'
Seating Capacity: 500+

2897
OZARK ACTORS THEATRE
PO Box K
Rolla, MO 65402
Phone: 573-364-9523
Fax: 573-364-9523
e-mail: oat@ozarkactorstheatre.org
Management:
   Artistic Director: F Reed Brown
Mission: Ozark Actors Theatre is a professional, summer stock theatre. Professional actors, directors, technicians, and designers are employed by OAT on a seasonal basis.
Founded: 1988
Specialized Field: Musical; Summer Stock;
Status: Non-Profit
Season: July - August
Type of Stage: Proscenium
Stage Dimensions: 36' x 24'
Seating Capacity: 188

2898
EDISON THEATRE
Campus Box 1119
One Brookings Drive
Saint Louis, MO 63130-4899
Phone: 314-935-6518
Fax: 314-935-7362
e-mail: crobin@artsci.wustl.edu
Web Site: www.artsci.wustl.edu/edison
Management:
   Managing Director: Charles E Robin
   Operations Manager: Melinda Compton
   Marketing Manager: Aly Abrams
   Technical Director: Clinton McLanghlin
Founded: 1973
Specialized Field: Musical; Community Theater
Status: Professional; Nonprofit
Paid Staff: 12
Budget: $150,000-400,000
Performs At: Edison Theatre; Mallinckrodt Drama Studio
Facility Category: Concert Hall; Performance Theatre

Type of Stage: Proscenium
Seating Capacity: 656
Rental Contact: Melinda Compton
Organization Type: Performing; Touring; Educational; Sponsoring; Presenting

2899
HOT CITY THEATRE

3547 Olive Street
Suite #203
Saint Louis, MO 63103
Phone: 314-289-4060
Web Site: http://hotcitytheatre.org/contact.html
Officers:
President: Joseph Potter
Vice President: Charlie Lutz
Treasurer: Thomas Schroedeer
Secretary: Kendra Howard
Management:
Managing Director: John Armstrong
Artistic Director: Marty Stanberry
Mission: HotHouse's mission is to produce thought-provoking theatre dedicated to cultural enhancement.
Founded: 1997
Specialized Field: Drama; Comedy
Status: Nonprofit
Season: October - May
Type of Stage: Flexible Black Box
Seating Capacity: 90

2900
METRO THEATER COMPANY

8308 Olive Boulevard
Saint Louis, MO 63132-2814
Phone: 314-997-6777
Fax: 314-997-1811
Web Site: www.metrotheatercompany.org
Officers:
President: Janet Schoedinger
VP: Kathe Rasch
CFO/Treasurer: John Weil
Secretary: Peggy O'Brien
Management:
President: Joan T Briccetti
Artistic Director: Carol North
Booking Director: Rita Mocek
Mission: Metro Theater Company is a professional touring ensemble that develops and produces original theater pieces that respect the intelligence and emotional wisdom of young people, blend drama, movement, music, and design, and challenge both the artists who develop the work and the audience who receive it.
Utilizes: Actors; Artists-in-Residence; Collaborating Artists; Collaborations; Commissioned Composers; Composers; Contract Actors; Curators; Educators; Guest Artists; Guest Conductors; Guest Lecturers; Guest Speakers; Organization Contracts; Original Music Scores; Performance Artists; Resident Professionals; Soloists
Founded: 1973
Specialized Field: Comedy; Youth Theater; Contemporary
Status: Non-Profit, Professional
Paid Staff: 7
Paid Artists: 7
Budget: $535,000
Income Sources: Contributions; NEA; Missouri Arts Council; Regional Arts Commission of St. Louis; Arts & Education Council of Greater St. Louis
Season: August - May

Affiliations: American Alliance for Theatre & Education; International Association of Theatre for Children and Youth/USA; Theatre Communications Group, Inc.
Annual Attendance: 60,000+
Type of Stage: Proscenium
Stage Dimensions: 30x25x15
Rental Contact: Managing Director Joan T. Briccetti
Organization Type: Performing; Touring; Resident; Educational

2901
MUNICIPAL THEATER ASSOCIATION OF SAINT LOUIS

1 Theater Drive
Saint Louis, MO 63112
Phone: 314-361-1900
Fax: 314-361-0009
e-mail: munyinfo@muny.org
Web Site: www.muny.com
Management:
President: Dennis M Reagan
Executive Producer: Paul Blake
Company Manager: Sue Greenberg
Director of Marketing and Publicity: Laura P Reilly
Mission: To perform and produce musical theater shows 7 nights a week, during the summer only.
Utilizes: Selected Students; Sign Language Translators; Singers; Student Interns; Theatre Companies
Founded: 1919
Specialized Field: Summer Stock; Community Theater
Status: Non-Profit, Professional
Paid Staff: 500
Paid Artists: 200
Income Sources: NAMTP; Arts & Education Council of Greater Saint Louis
Performs At: The MUNY; Forest Park
Organization Type: Performing; Educational

2902
NEW THEATRE

634 N Grand Boulevard
Suite 10-C
Saint Louis, MO 63103
Phone: 314-531-8330
Fax: 314-533-3345
Officers:
President: DeLancey Smith
VP: Suzanne Couch
Treasurer: James F O'Donnell
Secretary: Agnes Wilcox
Management:
Artistic Director: Agnes Wilcox
Production Manager: Amy Allen
Director Public Relations: Dean Minderman
Office Manager: Joan Duggan
Mission: To provide innovative professional theatre in accessible locations for Saint Louis audiences.
Utilizes: Guest Companies; Singers
Founded: 1985
Specialized Field: New Plays; Contemporary
Status: Professional; Nonprofit
Income Sources: Theatre Communications Group: League of Saint Louis Theatres
Organization Type: Performing

2903
REPERTORY THEATRE OF SAINT LOUIS

130 Edgar Road
Box 191730
Saint Louis, MO 63119

Phone: 314-968-4925
Fax: 314-968-9638
e-mail: mail@repstl.org
Web Site: www.repstl.org
Officers:
President: Ven Houts
Public Relations: Brad Graham
Mission: Dedicated to producing live theatre of superior quality. In celebrating the joy of live performance, this theatre is committed to building and sustaining a vital connection among all its stakeholders.
Utilizes: Guest Companies; Singers
Founded: 1966
Specialized Field: Theater Workshops; Drama; Contemporary
Status: Professional
Income Sources: Actors' Equity Association; Society for Stage Directors and Choreographers; American Federation of Musicians; International Association of Theatrical Stage Employees
Season: September - April
Performs At: Loretto-Hilton Center for the Performing Arts
Type of Stage: Thrust; Flexible
Seating Capacity: 734; 125
Organization Type: Performing

2904
SAINT LOUIS BLACK REPERTORY COMPANY

634 N Grand
Suite 10F
Saint Louis, MO 63103
Phone: 314-534-3807
Fax: 314-534-8456
e-mail: stlouisblackrep@hotmail.com
Web Site: www.stlouisblackrep.org
Management:
President of Board: Debra Denham
Producing Director: Ron Himes
Bussiness Manager: Susan Hayden
Mission: To provide platforms for theatre, dance and other creative expressions from the African-American perspective that heighten the social and cultural awareness of its audiences.
Utilizes: Actors; AEA Actors; Guest Artists; Guest Designers; Guest Writers; Performance Artists; Resident Professionals; Theatre Companies
Founded: 1976
Specialized Field: Musical; African American; Community Theater; Classic; Contemporary
Status: Non-Profit, Professional
Paid Staff: 12
Volunteer Staff: 50
Performs At: Grandel Square Theatre
Affiliations: Theatre Communications Group; Actors' Equity Association
Annual Attendance: 75,000
Seating Capacity: 467
Organization Type: Performing; Touring; Educational; Sponsoring

2905
STAGES ST. LOUIS

104 N Clay
Saint Louis, MO 63122
Phone: 314-821-2412
Fax: 314-821-2191
e-mail: mailbox@stagesslouis.com
Web Site: www.stagesslouis.com
Officers:
Chairman: Betty Von Hoffmann
President: Dory Poholsky
VP: Susan Svejkosky

Secretary: Philip S. Roush
Treasurer: Carl O. Trautman
Management:
President: Betty Vonhossmann
Artistic Director: Michael Hamilton
Executive Producer: Jack Lane
Production Stage Manager: Judith Grothe Cullen
Production Manager: John Cattanach
Mission: To produce the indigenous American art form of musical theatre which artfully combines the three disciplines of music, dance and drama. Through vital and unique interpretations of classic musicals, Stages strives to keep this threatened art form alive.
Utilizes: Actors; AEA Actors; Contract Actors; Dancers; Guest Conductors; Instructors; Local Artists; Music; Original Music Scores; Resident Professionals; Selected Students; Sign Language Translators; Soloists; Student Interns
Founded: 1987
Specialized Field: Musical; Comedy; Youth Theater; Dinner Theater; Ethnic Theater; Community Theater; Puppet
Status: Non-Profit, Professional
Paid Staff: 19
Paid Artists: 100
Budget: $1,200,000
Income Sources: Ticket Revenue; Private Donors; Corporations and Foundations
Performs At: Reim Theatre
Annual Attendance: 46,000
Facility Category: Theatre
Type of Stage: Proscenium
Stage Dimensions: 24'Dx34'W
Seating Capacity: 380
Year Built: 1960
Rental Contact: Kirkwood Civic Center

2906
THEATER FACTORY SAINT LOUIS
4265 Shaw Avenue
Saint Louis, MO 63110
Phone: 314-771-0780
Management:
Artistic Director: Hope Wurdack
Managing Director: Earl D Weaver
Business Manager: Cindy Vahle
Utilizes: Guest Artists; Guest Companies; Lyricists; Singers
Founded: 1982
Specialized Field: Summer Stock
Status: Professional
Income Sources: League of St. Louis Theatres
Organization Type: Performing; Educational

2907
WEST END PLAYERS GUILD
Union Avenue Christian Church
733 Union Boulevard
Saint Louis, MO 63108
Mailing Address: 733 Union Boulevard
Phone: 314-367-0025
Web Site: http://www.westendplayers.org
Officers:
President: Renee Monesye
Vice President: John Reidy
Secretary: Sean Belt
Treasurer: Robert Ashton
Mission: Compromises two groups, the Players Guild and the West End Players, both of which originated and prospered in the city's Central West End.
Founded: 1911
Specialized Field: Drama
Status: Non-professional

2908
LIBERTY CENTER
111 W 5Th
Sedalia, MO 65301
Phone: 816-827-3228
Fax: 816-827-3103
Management:
Administrator: Patti McFatrich
Mission: Promoting the Arts and cultural activities in the community.
Utilizes: Singers
Founded: 1981
Specialized Field: Musical; Community Theater; Puppet
Status: Professional; Non-Professional; Nonprofit
Paid Staff: 100
Performs At: Liberty Center
Organization Type: Performing; Touring; Educational; Sponsoring

2909
SIKESTON LITTLE THEATRE
PO Box 126
Sikeston, MO 63801
Phone: 573-681-9400
Management:
Administrator: Lynn A Colley
Mission: To nurture theatrical arts in the Sikeston area; to provide theatre experience for students.
Founded: 1959
Specialized Field: Musical; Community Theater
Status: Non-Professional; Nonprofit
Paid Staff: 150
Income Sources: Missouri Community Theatre Association
Performs At: Chaney-Harris Cultural Center
Organization Type: Performing; Resident

2910
GOLDENROD SHOWBOAT DINNER THEATRE
1000 Riverside Drive
St. Charles, MO 63301
Phone: 636-946-2020
Fax: 636-946-0946
Specialized Field: Specialty Acts; Mystery; Dinner Theater

2911
MULE BARN THEATRE OF TARKIO COLLEGE
PO Box 114
224 Main Street
Tarkio, MO 64491
Phone: 816-736-4185
Mission: To provide cultural and educational enrichment for the area featuring the American musical and children's theatre, theatre for area residents and training for young professionals in theatre.
Utilizes: Singers
Founded: 1967
Specialized Field: Educational; Theater Workshops
Status: Professional; Nonprofit
Paid Staff: 15
Performs At: Mule Barn Theatre
Organization Type: Performing

2912
ROYAL ARTS COUNCIL
PO Box 273
107 S Monroe
Versailles, MO 65084
Phone: 573-378-6226
e-mail: royalart@advertisnet.com
Officers:
President: Richard Williott
VP: Kevin Schehr
Secretary: Michelle Gerlt
Treasurer: Cindy Davenport
Management:
Executive Director: Pam Voth
Director: Steve Bannon
Director: Mary Jo Jackson
Director: Lana James
Director: Lois Viebrock
Mission: Promote the appreciation of various art disciplines through education, presentation, organization and the provision of an appropriate facility.
Utilizes: Community Talent; Guest Companies; Guild Activities; Instructors; Local Artists; Multimedia; Paid Performers; Sign Language Translators; Singers; Theatre Companies
Founded: 1984
Specialized Field: Musical; Community Theater
Status: Non-Professional; Nonprofit
Paid Staff: 1
Budget: $60,000
Income Sources: Ticket Sales; MAC Funding; Corporate Funding; Concessions; Program Advertising; Donations
Performs At: Royal Theatre
Annual Attendance: 4,000
Facility Category: Converted movie theatre with enlarged stage
Stage Dimensions: 34'x5 1/2'x22'
Seating Capacity: 294
Year Built: 1931
Year Remodeled: 2000
Rental Contact: Executive Director Pam Voth
Organization Type: Performing; Educational; Sponsoring

Montana

2913
BIGFORK SUMMER PLAYHOUSE
PO Box 456
Bigfork, MT 59911
Phone: 406-837-4886
e-mail: dthomson@bigforksummerplayhouse.com
Web Site: www.bigforksummerplayhouse.com
Officers:
President: Don Thomson
Founded: 1960
Specialized Field: Musical; Summer Stock
Status: For-Profit, Professional
Paid Staff: 55
Paid Artists: 25
Season: May - August

2914
ALBERTA BAIR THEATER
2801 3rd Avenue
Billings, MT 59101
Mailing Address: PO Box 1556, Billings, MO. 59103
Phone: 406-256-8915
Fax: 406-256-5060
Toll-free: 877-321-2074
e-mail: bfisher@albertabairtheater.org
Web Site: www.albertabairtheater.org
Management:
President: Bruce Bhittenberg
Executive Director: Bill Fisher
Artistic Director: Corby Skinner
Technical Director: Tom Lund

Utilizes: Actors; Collaborations; Dance Companies; Dancers; Educators; Guest Accompanists; Guest Artists; Guest Choreographers; Guest Composers; Guest Directors; Guest Ensembles; Guest Instructors; Guest Musical Directors; Guest Soloists; Guest Teachers; High School Drama; Instructors; Local Artists; Lyricists; Multimedia; Original Music Scores; Playwrights; Resident Artists; Selected Students; Sign Language Translators; Singers; Special Technical Talent; Theatre Companies
Founded: 1984
Specialized Field: Drama; Musical; Contemporary
Status: Non-Profit, Professional
Paid Staff: 15
Volunteer Staff: 200
Budget: $1.2 million
Income Sources: Ticket income
Annual Attendance: 123,000

2915
MONTANA SHAKESPEARE IN THE PARKS
Montana State University
PO Box 174120
Bozeman, MT 59717-4120
Phone: 406-994-3901
Fax: 406-994-4591
e-mail: moirah_k@msn.com
Web Site: www.montana.edu/shakespeare
Management:
Artistic Director: Joel Jahnke
Development/Marketing Director: Moira Keshishian
Business Director: Daine Eagleson
Marketing Assistant: Jodee Palin
Founded: 1973
Specialized Field: Musical; Comedy; Classic
Status: Non-Profit, Professional
Paid Staff: 4
Volunteer Staff: 82
Paid Artists: 30
Budget: $400,000
Income Sources: Grants; Corporate Sponsorship; Montana State University; Indidvidual Donations; Earned Income
Season: June - September
Affiliations: Montana State University
Annual Attendance: 26,000
Facility Category: Portable Elizabethan-style wood stage

2916
VIGILANTE THEATRE COMPANY
111 S Grand
Suite 201
Bozeman, MT 59715
Phone: 406-586-3897
e-mail: vigilante@in-tch.com
Web Site: www.vigilantetheatre.com
Management:
Artistic Director: John Hosking
Marketing Director: Cathy Kohler
Office Manager: Chavon Kautzman
Mission: To stimulate, cultivate and promote interest in theatre; to tour original, professional-level theatre in the Northwest.
Utilizes: Choreographers; Collaborations; Guest Companies; Guest Conductors; Guest Designers; Guest Lecturers; Guest Teachers; Multimedia; Music; Organization Contracts; Performance Artists; Resident Professionals; Student Interns; Theatre Companies; Visual Arts; Volunteer Directors & Actors; Writers
Founded: 1981

Specialized Field: Musical; Comedy; Puppet; Contemporary
Status: Non-Profit, Professional
Paid Staff: 6
Paid Artists: 4
Income Sources: Bookings; Ticket Sales; Grants; Membership; Contributors
Season: January - December
Annual Attendance: 14,000
Organization Type: Performing; Touring; Educational

2917
ALEPH MOVEMENT THEATRE
822 E 6Th Avenue
Helena, MT 59601
Phone: 406-443-1274
Mission: To perform movement theatre; to provide an opportunity for education; to foster cultural exchange.
Utilizes: Guest Companies; Singers
Founded: 1985
Specialized Field: Movement Theater
Status: Professional; Nonprofit
Income Sources: National Mime Association
Organization Type: Performing; Touring; Educational

2918
MISSOULA CHILDREN'S THEATRE
200 N Adams Street
Missoula, MT 59802
Phone: 406-728-1911
Fax: 406-721-0637
e-mail: tour@mctinc.org
Web Site: www.mctinc.org
Officers:
President: Alane Harkin
Executive Director: Michael McGill
Chief Executive Officer: Jim Caron
Tour Marketing Director: Joanna Michelson
Mission: The development of lifeskills through participation in the performing arts
Founded: 1971
Specialized Field: Musical; Youth Theater; Children's Theater

2919
MONTANA REPERTORY THEATRE
Performing Arts Center
University of Montana
Missoula, MT 59812
Phone: 406-243-6809
Fax: 406-243-5726
e-mail: mrt@selway.umt.edu
Web Site: www.umt.edu/mrt/mrt.html
Management:
Artistic Director: Greg Johnson
Production Manager: Steve Wing
Assistant of Artistc Director: Mary Ann Riddle
Booking Agent: Rena Shagan Associates
Mission: To tell the great stories of our world to an ever expanding community.
Utilizes: Actors; AEA Actors; Choreographers; Collaborating Artists; Commissioned Composers; Contract Actors; Designers; Educators; Guest Accompanists; Guest Companies; Guest Conductors; Guest Designers; Guest Teachers; Instructors; Local Artists; Original Music Scores; Performance Artists; Resident Professionals; Soloists; Students; Student Interns
Founded: 1976
Specialized Field: Drama; Historical
Status: Professional; Nonprofit
Paid Staff: 4
Budget: $900,000
Income Sources: Box Office; Grants; State Aid

Season: November - April
Performs At: Montana Theatre; University of Montana
Affiliations: Society for Stage Directors and Choreographers; Actors' Equity Association; International Alliance of Theatrical Stage Employees
Annual Attendance: varies
Facility Category: Educational
Type of Stage: Proscenium
Seating Capacity: 499
Year Built: 1985
Organization Type: Performing; Touring; Resident; Educational

2920
WHITEFISH THEATRE COMPANY
One Central Avenue
Whitefish, MT 59937
Phone: 406-862-5371
Fax: 406-863-9200
e-mail: wtc@bigsky.net
Web Site: www.whitefishtheatreco.org
Officers:
President: Rebecca Blickenstaff
Management:
Executive Director: Carolyn Pitman
Artistic Director: Nancy Nei
Mission: To nurture the creative and artistic passions of our community by bringing the arts to life.
Founded: 1978
Specialized Field: Performing Arts; Theatre; Dance Series; Music; Film
Paid Staff: 8
Budget: $450,000
Annual Attendance: 13,000
Facility Category: 326 Multiuse-Thrust Stage
Type of Stage: Thrust
Seating Capacity: 326
Year Built: 1998

Nebraska

2921
BELLEVUE LITTLE THEATRE
PO Box 162
Bellevue, NE 68005
Phone: 402-291-1554
Fax: 402-291-3809
e-mail: cyberma609@aol.com
Web Site: www.bellevuelittletheatre.com
Officers:
President: Edward Roche
Management:
President: Edward Roche, ebroche@cox.net
Mission: To create a superior environment for the promotion of the performing arts through the presentation of comedy, drama, and musical theatre productions; and to stimulate educational and recreational programs in the technical and artistic venues of the performing arts for the citizens of the city of Bellevue, Sarpy County, and the Greater Omaha Metropolitan Area.
Utilizes: Guest Companies; Singers
Founded: 1968
Specialized Field: Musical; Comedy; Ethnic Theater; Community Theater; Contemporary
Status: Non-Profit, Non-Professional
Seating Capacity: 244
Year Built: 1942
Organization Type: Performing; Educational

2922
POST PLAYHOUSE INCORPORATED
PO Box 271
Crawford, NE 69339
Phone: 308-665-1976
Fax: 308-432-6396
e-mail: rmays@csc.edu
Web Site: www.postplayhouse.com
Management:
 Executive Director: Roger Mays
Mission: A Summer Repertory Theatre for tourists and residents.
Utilizes: Actors; Guest Artists; Guest Designers; Guest Lecturers; Resident Artists; Student Interns
Founded: 1966
Specialized Field: Summer Stock
Status: Non-Equity; Nonprofit
Paid Staff: 15
Budget: $80,000
Income Sources: Ticket Sales; Nebraska Arts Council; Chadron stage College
Season: May - August
Performs At: Proscenium Theater
Annual Attendance: 9-12,000
Type of Stage: Proscenium
Stage Dimensions: 24' x 30'
Seating Capacity: 182
Year Remodeled: 1991

2923
GOTHENBURG COMMUNITY PLAYHOUSE
10th and D Street
PO Box 15
Gothenburg, NE 69138
Mailing Address: PO Box 15
Phone: 308-537-7596
e-mail: sbooth@nebnet.net
Web Site:
http://users.connections.net/NACT/Default.htm
Management:
 President: Ryan Lovell
 VP: Jamie Ulmer
 Secretary: Candie Johnson
 Treasurer: Sue DeCamp
Mission: To offer cultural, literary and educational opportunities to residents of the community and region.
Utilizes: Guest Companies; Singers
Founded: 1967
Specialized Field: Community Theater
Status: Non-Profit, Non-Professional
Paid Staff: 3
Performs At: Sun Theatre
Organization Type: Performing; Resident; Sponsoring

2924
KEARNEY COMMUNITY THEATRE
83 Plaza Boulevard
Kearney, NE 68845
Phone: 308-234-1529
e-mail: boxoffice@kctonline.com
Web Site: www.kctonline.com
Officers:
 President: David Rozema
 VP: Mary Haeberle
 Treasurer: Mark Thomas
 Secretary: Jeff Knapp
Management:
 President: Rick Marlatt, marlattr@kctonline.com
Mission: To present five shows annually, as well as a summer children's workshop.

Utilizes: Music; Paid Performers; Sign Language Translators; Soloists; Student Interns; Visual Designers; Volunteer Artists
Founded: 1977
Specialized Field: Musical; Community Theater
Status: Non-Profit, Non-Professional
Paid Staff: 2
Volunteer Staff: 4
Income Sources: Nebraska Arts Council; Nebraska Association of Community Theatres; American Association of Community Theatres
Performs At: Kearney Community Theatre
Organization Type: Performing; Educational; Sponsoring

2925
LINCOLN COMMUNITY PLAYHOUSE
2500 S 56th Street
Lincoln, NE 68506
Phone: 402-489-7529
Fax: 402-489-1035
Web Site: www.lincolnplayhouse.com
Officers:
 President: Gary Hall
 Secretary: Olinda Boslau
 Treasurer: Shannon Meyerer
 President Elect: Randal Hawthorne
Management:
 Executive Director: Morrie Enders
 Office Manager: Bryan Johnson
 Development Director: Shelly Wachman
Mission: To offer quality theatrical experiences to the community.
Utilizes: Guest Companies
Founded: 1946
Specialized Field: Musical; Comedy; Community Theater; Puppet; Classic; Contemporary
Status: Non-Profit, Non-Professional
Paid Staff: 10
Volunteer Staff: 400
Income Sources: NE Arts Council
Performs At: Oliver T. Joy Mainstage; L.L. Coryell & Sons
Affiliations: American Association of Community Theatres; Nebraska Association of Community Theatres
Organization Type: Performing

2926
NEBRASKA REPERTORY THEATRE
215 Temple Building
12th and R Streets
Lincoln, NE 68588-0201
Phone: 402-472-2072
Fax: 402-472-9055
Toll-free: 800-432-3231
e-mail: jhagemeier1@unl.edu
Web Site: www.unl.edu/rep
Officers:
 President: Larry Frederick
 Past President: Joyce Cartmill
Management:
 President: Larry Frederick
 General Manager: Julie Hagemeier
 Production Stage Manager: Brad Buffum
Utilizes: Actors; AEA Actors; Designers; Educators; Guest Accompanists; Guest Conductors; Guest Designers; High School Drama; Instructors; Original Music Scores; Resident Professionals; Singers; Soloists; Student Interns
Founded: 1968
Specialized Field: Contemporary; Ensembles
Status: Non-Profit, Professional
Paid Staff: 6

Volunteer Staff: 30
Paid Artists: 24
Budget: $176,000
Income Sources: Ticket Sales; University; Contributions
Season: June - August
Performs At: Howell Theatre; Studio Theatre; Carson Theatre
Affiliations: TCG, ATHE, KC/ACTF, NAST, UIRTA
Annual Attendance: 6,000
Type of Stage: Proscenium; Black Box
Seating Capacity: 320; 240
Year Built: 1908
Year Remodeled: 1980
Rental Contact: Brad Buffum
Organization Type: Performing; Resident

2927
CENTER STAGE
3010 R Street
Omaha, NE 68107
Phone: 402-444-6230
Management:
 Executive Director: Linda Runice
Mission: The presentation of ethnic performances.
Utilizes: Guest Companies; Singers
Founded: 1980
Specialized Field: Community Theater
Status: Non-Professional; Nonprofit
Performs At: LaFerne Williams Center
Organization Type: Performing

2928
CIRCLE THEATRE
2015 S 60th Street
Omaha, NE 68106
Phone: 402-553-4715
Fax: 402-553-4715
e-mail: ldmarr@cox.net
Officers:
 President: Ward Peters
 VP: Robert Bradley
 Treasurer: Karen Dowell
 Secretary: Nancy Ross
Management:
 President: Nancy Bradley
 Executive Director: Laura Marr
 Artistic Director: Doug Marr
Mission: Developing and producing new plays by Nebraska playwrights, employing Nebraska artists.
Founded: 1983
Specialized Field: Comedy; Community Theater; Contemporary
Status: Non-Profit, Professional
Paid Staff: 10
Paid Artists: 10
Budget: $120,000
Income Sources: Nebraska Arts Council; Local Foundation; Private Support
Annual Attendance: 10,000
Type of Stage: Black Box
Seating Capacity: 100
Year Built: 1945
Organization Type: Performing; Touring; Resident

2929
GRANDE OLDE PLAYERS THEATRE COMPANY
2339 N 90th
Omaha, NE 68134
Phone: 402-397-5262
Fax: 402-573-7532
e-mail: lensartcpp@aol.com
Web Site: www.go.gott.org

Officers:
President: David Kistler
VP: Kieth Homan
Treasurer: Jack Kincaid
Secretary: Riza Breen
Management:
President: Ranita Lilyhorn
Executive Director: Mark Manhart
Mission: Provide live community theatre experience with and for senior citizens.
Utilizes: Actors; Choreographers; Community Talent; Dancers; Guest Artists; Guest Companies; Guest Conductors; Guest Designers; Guest Lecturers; Guest Musical Directors; Guest Speakers; Local Artists; Performance Artists; Resident Professionals; Sign Language Translators
Founded: 1984
Specialized Field: Drama; Specialty Acts
Status: Non-Profit, Non-Professional
Non-paid Artists: 125
Budget: $59,000
Income Sources: Ticket Sales
Annual Attendance: 5,000
Facility Category: Live Theatre
Type of Stage: Proscenium
Stage Dimensions: 43'x17'
Seating Capacity: 141
Year Remodeled: 1993
Rental Contact: Executive Director Warren H. Johnson
Organization Type: Performing; Touring; Educational

2930
OMAHA COMMUNITY PLAYHOUSE

6915 Cass Street
Omaha, NE 68132-2696
Phone: 402-553-4890
Fax: 402-553-6288
Toll-free: 800-964-0990
e-mail: info@omahaplayhouse.com
Web Site: www.OmahaPlayhouse.com
Officers:
President: Mike McMeekin
Executive Director: Tim Schmad
Mission: To offer the finest possible theatre to our audiences; to provide a performance outlet for amateur actors.
Utilizes: Actors; Artists-in-Residence; Choreographers; Collaborating Artists; Collaborations; Commissioned Composers; Commissioned Music; Dancers; Educators; Fine Artists; Grant Writers; Guest Accompanists; Guest Designers; Guest Ensembles; Guest Instructors; Guest Musical Directors; Guest Soloists; Guest Teachers; Guest Writers; Guild Activities; High School Drama; Instructors; Local Artists; Lyricists; Multi Collaborations; Multimedia; Music; New Productions; Organization Contracts; Original Music Scores; Poets; Resident Artists; Resident Professionals; Selected Students; Sign Language Translators; Singers; Soloists; Student Interns; Theatre Companies; Touring Companies; Visual Arts
Founded: 1924
Specialized Field: Community Theater
Status: Non-Profit, Non-Professional
Paid Staff: 40
Paid Artists: 120
Budget: $4,000,000
Income Sources: Donations; Subscribers; Single Ticket Revenue
Season: September - June
Performs At: Omaha Community Playhouse
Annual Attendance: 110,000
Facility Category: Theatre
Type of Stage: Traditional Proscenium & Black Box
Seating Capacity: 600; 235

Year Built: 1959
Year Remodeled: 1986
Organization Type: Performing; Touring

2931
OMAHA THEATRE COMPANY FOR YOUNG PEOPLE

2001 Farnam Street
Omaha, NE 68102
Phone: 402-345-4852
Fax: 402-344-7255
e-mail: boxoffice@otcmail.org
Web Site: www.otcyp.org
Officers:
President: Richard Heyman
VP Marketing: Stephen Zubrod
Past President: Tracy Stanko
Foundation Representative: Susie Buffett
Management:
Executive Director: Roberta Wilhelm
Artistic Director: James Larson
Mission: Providing quality theater for Omaha children and their families.
Utilizes: Guest Companies; Singers
Specialized Field: Youth Theater; Young Playwrights
Status: Professional; Nonprofit
Paid Staff: 32
Volunteer Staff: 15
Paid Artists: 10
Budget: $2.4 million
Income Sources: Theatre Communications Group; Nebraska Arts Council; Douglas County; National Endowment for the Arts; Corporations; Private Donations
Facility Category: Live Theatre for Children and Their Families
Type of Stage: Proscenium; Black Box
Stage Dimensions: 48'& 31' deep. Pit 11'x6'/11'X 6'
Year Built: 1927
Year Remodeled: 1994
Cost: $5.9 million
Rental Contact: Stan Kiepke
Organization Type: Performing; Touring; Resident; Educational

2932
SHAKESPEARE ON THE GREEN

Department of Fine Arts
Creighton University
Omaha, NE 68178
Phone: 402-280-2391
Fax: 402-280-2320
e-mail: neshakes@creighton.edu
Management:
Chancelor: Nancy Belck
Artistic Director: Cindy Melby Phaneuf
Managing Director: Micheal Markey
Founded: 1986
Specialized Field: Educational; Theater Workshops
Status: Non-Equity
Season: May - July
Type of Stage: Outdoor
Stage Dimensions: 100' x 300'
Seating Capacity: 5000

Nevada

2933
BREWERY ARTS CENTER

449 W King Street
Carson City, NV 89703

Phone: 775-883-1976
Fax: 775-883-1922
e-mail: phil@breweryarts.org
Web Site: www.breweryarts.org
Management:
President: Norma Conway
Executive Director: Phil Caterino
Development Director: Bill Cowee
Mission: To provide and promote the arts and culture in Carson City.
Founded: 1976
Specialized Field: Musical; Drama
Status: Non-Profit, Professional
Paid Staff: 2
Volunteer Staff: 100
Performs At: Carson City Community Center; Brewery Arts Center
Organization Type: Performing; Sponsoring

2934
ACTORS REPERTORY THEATRE

1824 Palo Alto Circle
Las Vegas, NV 89108
Phone: 702-647-7469
Fax: 702-647-3130
Officers:
President: Michael Levy
Management:
Artistic Director: Georgia Neu
Managing Director: Rob Gubbins
Mission: Dedicated to training for, and the performance of, the classics, and the best in modern and musical theatre, with special emphasis given to new works of exceptional merit.
Specialized Field: Educational; Theater Workshops
Performs At: Summerlin Performing Arts Center
Comments: Summerlin Theatre is accesible to the mobility impaired and listening assistance devices are available.

2935
LAS VEGAS LITTLE THEATRE

3920 Schiff Drive
Las Vegas, NV 89103
Phone: 702-362-7996
e-mail: info@lvlt.org
Web Site: www.lvlt.org
Management:
President: Walter Niejadli
VP: TJ Larsen
Treasurer: Frank Mengwasser
Secretary: Katie Affentranger
Mission: To educate and entertain the community; to provide hands-on training for interested artists.
Utilizes: Singers
Founded: 1978
Specialized Field: Musical; Community Theater
Status: Non-Profit
Income Sources: Nevada Community Theatre Association; Allied Arts Council of Southern Nevada; American Association of Community Theatres
Organization Type: Performing; Educational

2936
THEATER COALITION/THE LEAR THEATER

528 W 1st Street
Reno, NV 89503
Phone: 775-786-2278
Fax: 775-786-4350
Web Site: www.theatercoalition.org
Management:
Executive Director: Susan Mayes-Smith
Office Administrator: Rhonda Hernandez

Capital Campaign Coordinator: Angela
Rodriquez-Cao
Founded: 1994
Specialized Field: Drama; Comedy; Musical; Classic
Paid Staff: 5
Volunteer Staff: 50

New Hampshire

2937
MAINSTAGE CENTER FOR THE ARTS

Camden County College
PO Box 200
Blackwood, NH 08012
Phone: 856-232-1012
Fax: 856-401-1776
e-mail: stage3091@snip.net
Web Site: www.mainstage.org
Management:
President: Edward P Fiscella
Artistic Director: Susan Waldi
Managing Director: Bret Schneider
Board Director: Pat O'Neill
Founded: 1987
Specialized Field: Youth Theater; Classic; Drama
Status: Non-Profit, Professional
Paid Staff: 1
Paid Artists: 53

2938
COMMUNITY PLAYERS OF CONCORD

PO Box 681
Concord, NH 03302-0681
Phone: 603-224-4905
Officers:
President: Abby Lange
VP: Paul Bacon
Secretary: Kevin Barrett
Treasurer: Doris Ballard
Management:
President: Betty Lent
VP: Doug Schwarz
Mission: To nurture interest in all aspects of community
theater.
Founded: 1927
Specialized Field: Community Theater
Status: Nonprofit
Income Sources: New Hampshire Community Theater
Association
Performs At: Concord City Auditorium
Organization Type: Performing

2939
HAMPTON PLAYHOUSE

Winnacunnet Road
Hampton, NH 03842
Phone: 603-926-3076
Management:
Producing/Artistic Director: Alfred Christie
Producer: John Vari
Utilizes: Guest Companies; Singers
Founded: 1948
Specialized Field: Summer Stock; Musical
Status: Professional; Commercial
Income Sources: Actors' Equity Association; Society
for Stage Directors and Choreographers; Council of
Resident Summer Theatres
Season: June - September
Performs At: Hampton Playhouse Theatre Arts
Workshop
Organization Type: Performing; Resident; Educational

2940
PAPERMILL THEATRE/NORTH COUNTY CENTER FOR THE ARTS

PO Box 1060
Lincoln, NH 03251
Phone: 603-745-6032
Fax: 603-745-2564
e-mail: kbarber@papermilltheatre.org
Web Site: www.papermilltheatre.org
Management:
President: David Talbot
Business Director: Tony Ferrelli
Artistic Director: Kim Barber
Founded: 1986
Specialized Field: Summer Stock
Status: Non-Profit, Professional
Paid Staff: 50
Paid Artists: 55
Season: June - August
Type of Stage: Proscenium
Stage Dimensions: 36' x 40'
Seating Capacity: 250

2941
LAKES REGION SUMMER THEATRE

Route 25
Meredith, NH 03253
Phone: 603-279-9933
Fax: 603-279-4525
e-mail: meredith@lr.net
Specialized Field: Summer Stock
Season: June - September

2942
MOUNT WASHINGTON VALLEY THEATRE COMPANY

Box 265
North Conway, NH 03860
Phone: 603-356-5425
Fax: 603-356-8357
e-mail: pinkham@pinkhamrealestate.com
Management:
President: Linda Pinkham
Founded: 1971
Specialized Field: Summer Stock; Musical
Status: Nonprofit
Season: June - August
Type of Stage: Proscenium
Seating Capacity: 183

2943
PETERBOROUGH PLAYERS

PO Box 118
Peterborough, NH 03458
Phone: 603-924-9344
Fax: 603-924-6359
e-mail: kstevens@peterboroughplayers.org
Web Site: www.peterboroughplayers.org
Management:
President: Robert Hance
Artistic Director: Gus Kaikkonen
Managing Director: Keith Stevens
Vice President: Jim Borsari
Treasurer: Philip Grisafi
Utilizes: Guest Companies; Singers
Founded: 1933
Specialized Field: Drama; Ensembles
Status: Non-Profit, Professional
Paid Staff: 60
Paid Artists: 70
Income Sources: Actors' Equity Association; Council
of Resident Summer Theatres
Season: June - September

Organization Type: Performing; Resident; Educational

2944
PONTINE THEATRE

959 Islington Street
Portsmouth, NH 03801
Phone: 603-436-6660
Fax: 603-436-1577
e-mail: info@pontine.org
Web Site: www.pontine.org
Officers:
President: Belinda Braley
Vice President: Charlotte Colman
Management:
Co-Director: Greg Gather
Mission: Dedicated to the cultural enhancements of its
various publics, its performances and educational
programs are offered to inform the public in the art of
corporeal mime and to the preservation and
development of this exciting theatrical form.
Utilizes: Dance Companies; Dancers; Guest Directors;
Original Music Scores; Resident Artists; Student
Interns; Special Technical Talent; Theatre Companies
Founded: 1977
Specialized Field: Youth Theater; Puppet;
Contemporary
Status: For-Profit, Professional
Paid Staff: 5
Paid Artists: 2
Budget: $101,000
Performs At: McDonough Street Theater
Affiliations: New Hampshire State Council on the Arts
Annual Attendance: 1,200
Facility Category: Studio/theatre
Type of Stage: Black Box
Stage Dimensions: 20'x20'
Seating Capacity: 48
Year Built: 1900
Year Remodeled: 1987
Rental Contact: Greg Gathers
Organization Type: Performing; Touring; Resident;
Educational; Sponsoring
Resident Groups: Pontine Movement Theatre

2945
SEACOAST REPERTORY THEATRE

125 Bow Street
Portsmouth, NH 03801
Phone: 603-433-4793
Fax: 603-431-7818
Toll-free: 800-639-7650
e-mail: info@seacoastrep.org
Web Site: www.seacoastrep.org
Officers:
President: Martin Lessard
VP: John Bosen
Secretary: John Colliander, Esquire
Treasurer: Steven Scott
Management:
Producing Artistic Director: Roy Rogosin
Associate Director/Producer: Eileen Rogosin
Assistant Artistic Director: Jean Benda
Director Marketing/Publicity: Stacy Baker
Mission: To provide a safe haven for performers and
audiences.
Utilizes: Actors; AEA Actors; Artists-in-Residence;
Choreographers; Collaborating Artists; Commissioned
Music; Five Seasonal Concerts; Grant Writers; Guest
Accompanists; Guest Artists; Guest Choreographers;
Guest Companies; Guest Conductors; Guest
Designers; Guest Ensembles; Guest Musical Directors;
Instructors; Local Artists; Multimedia; Music; Original
Music Scores; Resident Professionals; Sign Language
Translators; Soloists; Student Interns; Visual Arts

Founded: 1986
Specialized Field: Drama; Musical; Comedy
Status: Non-Profit, Professional
Paid Staff: 15
Volunteer Staff: 6
Budget: $1,100,000
Income Sources: Ticket Sales; Sponsorships; Fundraising Events
Season: Summer and All - Year
Annual Attendance: 50,000
Facility Category: Live Theatre
Type of Stage: 3/4 Thrust
Seating Capacity: 235
Year Built: 1890
Year Remodeled: 1970
Rental Contact: Sandi Clark
Organization Type: Performing; Resident; Educational

2946
BARNSTORMERS

PO Box 434
Tamworth, NH 03886
Phone: 603-323-8500
Fax: 603-323-3351
e-mail: callboard@barnstormerstheatre.org
Web Site: www.barnstormerstheatre.org
Officers:
    Secretary: Cope Murphy
    Treasurer: Parker Roberts
    Vice Chair: Ann Batchelder
    Chair: Paul Chant
Management:
    Producing Artistic Director: Clayton Phillips
    Asst. Producing Artistic Director: Claire Van Cott
Mission: To provide a theatre program featuring old—and some new—plays.
Founded: 1931
Specialized Field: New Plays; Classic
Status: Professional; Nonprofit
Income Sources: Actors' Equity Association
Season: June - August
Performs At: The Barnstormers Theatre
Affiliations: AEA
Facility Category: Theatre-Proscenium
Type of Stage: Wood
Stage Dimensions: 30'x40'
Seating Capacity: 282
Year Built: 1931
Year Remodeled: 1997
Rental Contact: Clayton Phillips
Organization Type: Performing; Resident

2947
WEATHERVANE THEATRE

53 Jefferson Road
Whitefield, NH 03598
Phone: 603-837-9010
Fax: 603-837-3333
e-mail: wvtheatre@aol.com
Web Site: www.weathervanetheatre.org
Officers:
    COO: Richard Portner
Management:
    President: Pamela Remick
    Managing Director: Richard Portner
    Artistic Director: Jacques Stewart
    Producing Director: Gibbs Murray
Mission: To present 7-8 shows each season, including musicals.
Utilizes: Actors; AEA Actors; Collaborations; Guest Artists; Guest Designers; Local Artists; Multimedia; Music; Original Music Scores; Resident Artists; Soloists; Student Interns
Founded: 1965

Specialized Field: Musical; Comedy; Youth Theater; Contemporary
Status: Non-Profit, Professional
Paid Staff: 5
Paid Artists: 50
Non-paid Artists: 15
Budget: $300,000
Income Sources: Box Office; Grants; Donor Appeal
Season: July - August
Performs At: Barn Theatre
Affiliations: Actors' Equity Association
Annual Attendance: 10,000
Type of Stage: Open Thrust
Seating Capacity: 250
Year Built: 2002
Organization Type: Performing

2948
ANDY'S SUMMER PLAYHOUSE

Issac Frye Highway
PO Box 601
Wilton, NH 03086
Phone: 603-654-2613
e-mail: andyssummerplayhouse@yahoo.com
Management:
    Artistic Director: Robert Lawson
    Managing Director: Lizzie Harris
Mission: Andy's Summer Playhouse is innovative theater by children for people of all ages. We serve all of Southern New Hampshire from Nashua to Keene, and from Concord to Massachusetts.
Founded: 1970
Specialized Field: Children's Theater; Summer Stock; Educational
Season: June - August
Type of Stage: Flexible
Stage Dimensions: 40' x 50'
Seating Capacity: 152

New Jersey

2949
SURFLIGHT THEATRE

Engleside & Beach Avenue
PO Box 1155
Beach Haven, NJ 08008
Phone: 609-492-9477
Fax: 609-492-4469
e-mail: surflight@comcast.net
Web Site: www.surflight.org
Officers:
    President: Lynn E Hammond
    Vice President: Barbara K Pruittg
    Secretary: Sandy Martin
    Treasurer: Ellen Dondero Meyer
Management:
    Board President: Lynn E Hammond
    Producing Artistic Director: Roy Miller
    Associate Producer: Erin Esposito
    General Manager: Ruth Blankemeyer
    Director of Education: John Anker Bow
    Chief Financial Officer: Tim Laczynski
Utilizes: Actors; AEA Actors; Artists-in-Residence; Choreographers; Collaborations; Dancers; Designers; Five Seasonal Concerts; Guest Accompanists; Guest Artists; Guest Companies; Guest Conductors; Guest Designers; Guest Ensembles; Guest Lecturers; Guest Musical Directors; Guest Writers; High School Drama; Instructors; Local Artists; Multimedia; Music; Original Music Scores; Performance Artists; Poets; Resident Artists; Resident Professionals; Sign Language Translators; Soloists; Student Interns; Special Technical Talent

Founded: 1950
Specialized Field: Theatrical Productions, Musicals, Comedies, Dramas, Children's Theatre, Concerts, Special Events, Holiday Shows
Status: Non-Profit, Professional
Paid Staff: 25
Volunteer Staff: 25
Paid Artists: 60
Non-paid Artists: 20
Budget: $1,500,000
Income Sources: Box Office; NJSCA; Donations
Performs At: Theatre
Affiliations: New Jersey Theatre Alliance
Annual Attendance: 60,000
Facility Category: Theatre House
Type of Stage: Proscenium
Stage Dimensions: 24x35
Seating Capacity: 450
Year Built: 1987
Rental Contact: Gail Anderson Steiner
Organization Type: Performing; Resident

2950
CAPE MAY STAGE

31 Perry Street
Cape May, NJ 08204
Phone: 609-884-1341
Management:
    Artistic Director: Michael Carleton
    Managing Director: Joe Pannullo
    Associate Producer: John Alvarez
Mission: To be a professional theatre company with a spirit of community. Places emphasis on acting, directing and playwriting excellence.
Specialized Field: Drama; Comedy; Educational
Season: May - December
Performs At: Theater at Bank & Lafayette Streets

2951
CRANFORD DRAMATIC CLUB

78 Winans Avenue
PO Box 511
Cranford, NJ 07016
Phone: 908-276-7611
e-mail: info@cdctheatre.org
Web Site: http://www.cdctheatre.org/contact.html
Management:
    President: Jennifer Love
    Vice President: Joanne Gescickter
    Secretary: Madge Wittel
    Treasurer: John Duryee
Mission: To stimulate interest in theatre.
Founded: 1919
Specialized Field: Community Theater
Status: Non-Professional; Nonprofit
Performs At: Cranford Dramatic Club
Organization Type: Performing

2952
PLAYS-IN-THE-PARK

Middlesex County Department of Parks and Recreation
1 Pine Drive/Roosevelt Park
Edison, NJ 08817
Phone: 732-548-2884
Fax: 732-548-1484
e-mail: pipoffice@playsinthepark.com
Web Site: www.playsinthepark.com
Management:
    Managing Director: Gary Cohen
    Producer: Gary Cohen
Utilizes: Actors; Artists-in-Residence; Choreographers; Dance Companies; Dancers; Designers; Educators; Fine Artists; Five Seasonal Concerts; Guest Choreographers; High School Drama; Local Artists;

Multimedia; Music; Resident Artists; Resident Professionals; Selected Students; Sign Language Translators; Singers; Soloists; Student Interns; Special Technical Talent
Founded: 1963
Specialized Field: Musical; Community Theater; Contemporary
Status: Non-Profit, Non-Professional
Paid Staff: 30
Volunteer Staff: 75
Non-paid Artists: 100
Budget: $405,000
Income Sources: Middlesex County Department of Parks and Recreation; Middlesex County Taxpayers; Patrons
Season: June - August
Performs At: Indoor/Outdoor Amphitheater
Annual Attendance: 60,000
Type of Stage: Proscenium
Stage Dimensions: 40'x20'
Year Built: 1963
Year Remodeled: 1975

2953
HOLMDEL THEATRE COMPANY

36 Crawfords Corner Rd
Musical Theater; Drama;
Holmdel, NJ 07733
Mailing Address: PO Box 182
Phone: 732-946-0427
e-mail: info@holmdeltheatrecompany.org
Web Site:
http://www.holmdeltheatrecompany.org/abouthtc_peopl e.html
Officers:
President: Rebecca Flynn
Vice President: Kelly Bird
Treasurer: Michael Serluco
Management:
Creative Director: Geoff Shields
Executive Producer: Kelly Bird
Educational Director: Angela DeMatteo
General: Greg Santopadre
Mission: To provide artistic/theatrical opportunities for community residents to perform and create in a professional environment.
Founded: 1985
Specialized Field: Musical; Comedy; Drama
Status: Semi-Professional
Performs At: Duncan Smith Theatre

2954
ATTIC ENSEMBLE

83 Wayne Street
Jersey City, NJ 07302
Phone: 201-413-9200
Fax: 201-434-0568
e-mail: info@atticensemble.org
Founded: 1970
Specialized Field: Ensemble
Income Sources: Donors; New Jersey Stage Council on the Arts; Hudson County Department of Cultural & Heritage Affairs

2955
NEW JERSEY REPERTORY COMPANY

179 Broadway
Long Branch, NJ 07740
Phone: 732-229-3166
Fax: 732-229-3167
e-mail: njrep@njrep.org
Web Site: www.njrep.org
Officers:
Director Marketing: Debbie Mura

Management:
Artistic Director: Suzanne Barabas, suzanne@njrep.org
Executive Producer: Gabor Barabas, gabor@njrep.org
Managing Director: Janey Huber, janey@njrep.org
Group Sales: Doris Dunigan
Mission: The primary mission of the theater is to develop and produce new plays with diverse themes. It is also devoted to creating an atmosphere where classics can take on a fresh look and forgotten plays can find a home.
Utilizes: Actors; AEA Actors; Choreographers; Collaborations; Community Talent; Composers; Contract Actors; Designers; Equity Actors; Five Seasonal Concerts; Grant Writers; Guest Accompanists; Guest Artists; Guest Companies; Guest Conductors; Guest Designers; Guest Lecturers; Guest Musical Directors; Guest Soloists; Guest Teachers; Guest Writers; Instructors; Local Artists & Directors; Local Unknown Artists; Lyricists; Multi Collaborations; Multimedia; Music; Organization Contracts; Original Music Scores; Paid Performers; Performance Artists; Playwrights; Resident Artists; Resident Companies; Resident Professionals; Scenic Designers; Sign Language Translators; Students; Student Interns; Special Technical Talent; Visual Arts
Founded: 1997
Specialized Field: New Plays; Classic
Status: Non-Profit, Professional
Paid Staff: 6
Income Sources: Donations, Grants
Facility Category: Theater
Type of Stage: Black Box
Year Remodeled: 1998

2956
PLAYWRIGHTS THEATRE OF NEW JERSEY

33 Green Village Road
PO Box 1295
Madison, NJ 07940
Phone: 973-514-1787
Fax: 973-514-2060
e-mail: info@ptnj.org
Web Site: www.ptnj.org
Management:
President: Kermeit Smith
Executive Director: John Pietrowski
Managing Director: Elizabeth Murphy
Mission: Provides opportunities for writers to develop their work in a nurturing environment and connect with new audiences. Four step process through which playwrights, theatre artists and audiences collaborate to bring selected texts from rough draft to finished production. Education programs for students of all ages and backgrounds.
Utilizes: Actors; AEA Actors; Artists-in-Residence; Collaborations; Designers; Educators; Guest Conductors; Guest Designers; Instructors; Local Artists; Original Music Scores; Performance Artists; Playwrights; Resident Professionals; Selected Students
Founded: 1986
Specialized Field: Young Playwrights; New Plays
Status: Non-Profit, Professional
Paid Staff: 10
Volunteer Staff: 30
Paid Artists: 150
Budget: 900,000
Income Sources: Earned; Government; Corporate Foundation; Individuals
Season: September - June
Affiliations: AEA; SSDC; USA
Annual Attendance: 6,000

Type of Stage: Black Blox
Stage Dimensions: 30' x 18'
Seating Capacity: 125
Year Built: 1985

2957
SIMULATIONS

PO Box 399
Martinsville, NJ 08836
Phone: 732-356-7800
Management:
President: Margaret McGovern
Founded: 1979
Specialized Field: Educational
Status: For-Profit, Professional

2958
FORUM THEATRE

314 Main Street
Metuchen, NJ 08840
Phone: 732-548-4670
Fax: 732-548-4230
e-mail: forumtheatre@yahoo.com
Web Site: www.forumtheatrecompany.com
Officers:
Executive Director: Peter Loewy
Management:
Artistic Director: Ellen Beattie
Founded: 983
Specialized Field: Musical; Comedy; Classic; Contemporary
Status: Non-Profit, Professional
Paid Staff: 16
Paid Artists: 44
Season: October - June
Type of Stage: Proscenium/Thrust

2959
PAPER MILL PLAYHOUSE

Brookside Drive
Millburn, NJ 07041
Phone: 973-379-3636
Fax: 973-376-0825
e-mail: smiller@papermill.org
Web Site: www.papermill.org
Officers:
Chairman of the Board: Kenneth Wegner
Management:
Managing Director: Todd Schmidt
Producing Artistic Director: Mark S Hoebee
Director of Press/Public Relations: Shayne Miller
Mission: To enrich the cultural lives of a wide and diverse audience. A nationally recognized professional arts center committed to excellence and to preserving the rich heritage of plays and musicals through productions of the highest quality; to develop new works; collaborating with established and emerging artists, providing arts education for all ages; and to maintaining a leadership role in the community.
Utilizes: Guest Artists; Guest Companies; Singers
Founded: 1934
Specialized Field: Musical Theatre; Arts Education
Status: Non-Profit, Professional
Paid Staff: 45
Volunteer Staff: 30
Paid Artists: 500
Budget: $15 Million
Income Sources: Earned & Contributed
Season: September - June
Annual Attendance: 200,000
Facility Category: Theatre
Type of Stage: Proscenium
Seating Capacity: 1200
Year Built: 1938

All listings are in alphabetical order by state, then city, then organization within the city.

Year Remodeled: 1982
Organization Type: Performing; Touring; Resident; Educational; Sponsoring

2960
ARTSPOWER NATIONAL TOURING THEATRE

39 S Fullerton Avenue
Montclair, NJ 07042-3354
Phone: 973-744-0909
Fax: 973-744-3609
Toll-free: 888-278-7769
e-mail: info@artspower.org
Web Site: www.artspower.org
Officers:
    Production Manager: Ginny Bowers Coleman
Management:
    Artistic Director: Greg Gunning
    Executive Producer: Gary Blackman
    Senior Booking Associate: Stacey Sander Higgins
Utilizes: AEA Actors; Designers; Five Seasonal Concerts; Guest Designers; Music; Organization Contracts; Performance Artists; Resident Professionals; Selected Students; Soloists; Special Technical Talent; Theatre Companies
Founded: 1985
Specialized Field: Youth Theater; Touring Company
Status: Non-Profit, Professional
Paid Staff: 9
Paid Artists: 32
Budget: $1.7 million
Income Sources: Ticket Sales; Presenting Fees; Grants
Season: October - June
Performs At: Performs in 40 states across US
Affiliations: AEA
Facility Category: Touring Theatre
Organization Type: Varies

2961
YASS HAKOSHIMA MIME THEATRE

239 Midland Avenue
Montclair, NJ 07042
Phone: 973-783-9845
Fax: 973-783-0001
e-mail: yass@bellatlantic.net
Web Site: www.yasshakoshima.com
Management:
    Artistic Director: Yass Hakoshima
    Chairperson: Anne Benbow
    Assistant Director: Renate A Boue
Mission: To present the highest form of the art of mime through performances, master classes, lecture demonstrations and workshops worldwide.
Utilizes: Student Interns
Founded: 1976
Specialized Field: Mime
Status: Professional; Nonprofit
Paid Staff: 4
Organization Type: Performing; Touring; Resident; Educational

2962
GROWING STAGE THEATRE COMPANY

Route 183
7 Ledgewood Avenue
Netcong, NJ 07857
Mailing Address: PO Box 36
Phone: 973-347-4946
Fax: 973-691-7069
e-mail: exdir@growingstage.com
Web Site: http://growingstage.goes.com/
Officers:

President: Laura Baron
    Vice President: Matthew Connahan
    Secretary: Norman Penney
    Treasurer: Margaret Baumann
Mission: Bringing families together through theatre, giving children the attention they deserve and helping adults to see the importance of imagination in their lives.
Founded: 1995
Specialized Field: Children's Theater
Performs At: Historic Palace Theatre

2963
CROSSROADS THEATRE COMPANY

7 Livingston Avenue
PO Box 238
New Brunswick, NJ 08901
Phone: 732-545-8100
Fax: 732-317-2894
Web Site: www.crossroadsnb.com
Management:
    Co-Founder: Ricardo Khan
    Co-Founder: L Kenneth Richardson
Mission: To provide a professional environment to encourage public interest of all backgrounds; to present honest portrayals and uphold the highest standard of artistic excellence of professional Black Theatre.
Utilizes: Guest Artists; Guest Companies; Singers
Founded: 1978
Specialized Field: African American; Ethnic Theater
Status: Professional; Nonprofit
Income Sources: Private Foundations/Grants; Business/Corporate Donations; Box Office; Government Grants; Individual Donations
Season: September - May
Performs At: Crossroads Theatre
Affiliations: NJ Performing Arts Center, Newark; New Victory Theatre, NYC
Type of Stage: Modified Thrust
Seating Capacity: 300
Organization Type: Touring; Resident; Educational

2964
GEORGE STREET PLAYHOUSE

9 Livingston Avenue
New Brunswick, NJ 08901
Phone: 732-846-2895
Fax: 732-247-9151
e-mail: gryan@georgestplayhouse.org
Web Site: www.georgestplayhouse.org
Management:
    Artistic Director: David Saint
    Managing Director: Mitchell Kriege
    Producing Director: George Ryan
    Business Manager: Karen Price
Mission: To produce new musicals and world premieres; to revitalize contemporary classics.
Utilizes: Guest Companies; Singers
Founded: 1974
Specialized Field: Musical; Contemporary
Status: Professional; Nonprofit
Income Sources: Theatre Communications Group
Season: September - May
Performs At: George Street Playhouse
Type of Stage: Proscenium/Thrust
Seating Capacity: 367
Organization Type: Performing; Touring; Resident; Producing

2965
NEWARK PERFORMING ARTS CORPORATION/NEWARK SYMPHONY HALL

1030 Broad Street
Newark, NJ 07102
Phone: 973-643-8468
Fax: 973-643-6722
Web Site: www.newarksymphonyhall.org
Officers:
    Chairman: Miquel E Rodriguez
    Treasurer: Julian Marsh
    Secretary: J Barry Washington
Management:
    President: Marc Berson
    Executive Director: Gwen Moten
    Artistic Director: Catherine Lenix-Hooker
Mission: To enhance the cultural and community life of the citizens of the greater Newark area by presenting a program of the highest quality and artistic integrity and to complement that activity by providing first class facilities for classical, ethnic, popular and community arts groups, for arts education, and civic/social organizations.
Utilizes: Actors; Collaborating Artists; Collaborations; Dance Companies; Dancers; Designers; Five Seasonal Concerts; Grant Writers; Guest Accompanists; Guild Activities; Lyricists; Multi Collaborations; Multimedia; Original Music Scores; Resident Artists; Resident Professionals; Special Technical Talent; Theatre Companies
Founded: 1925
Specialized Field: Musical; Community Theater
Status: Non-Profit, Professional
Paid Staff: 16
Paid Artists: 96
Budget: $2,178,000
Income Sources: Box Office Receipts; State & City Government Grants; Space Rental Fees; Concessions; Foundation & Corporation Grants
Performs At: Newark Symphony Hall
Affiliations: American Society of Composers, Authors, & Publishers; Garden State Theatrical Organ Society; Broadcast Music, Inc.
Annual Attendance: 250,000+
Facility Category: Performing Arts Center
Type of Stage: Proscenium
Stage Dimensions: 63'x40'
Seating Capacity: 2,800
Year Built: 1925
Rental Contact: General Manager Oscar N. James
Organization Type: Performing; Presenting
Resident Groups: African Globe Theatre Works Company; Kabu Okai-Davies

2966
THEATRE AT RARITAN VALLEY COMMUNITY COLLEGE

Route 28 & Lamington Road
North Branch, NJ 08876
Phone: 908-725-3420
e-mail: theatre@rvccArts.org
Web Site: www.rvccArts.org
Officers:
    President: Casey Crabill
Management:
    Director: Alan Liddel
Founded: 1985
Specialized Field: Educational; Theater Workshops
Status: For-Profit, Professional
Paid Staff: 4

2967
CREATIVE THEATRE
102 Witherspoon Street
Princeton, NJ 08540
Phone: 609-924-8777
Management:
  Executive Director: Carly Tilton
  Artistic Director: Eloise Bruce
  Education Director: Jean Prall
Mission: To provide theatre and creative drama for children.
Founded: 1969
Specialized Field: Children's Theater
Status: Professional; Nonprofit
Organization Type: Performing; Touring; Resident; Educational

2968
MCCARTER THEATRE
91 University Place
Princeton, NJ 08540
Phone: 609-258-6500
Fax: 609-497-0369
Toll-free: 888-278-7932
e-mail: admin@mccarter.org
Web Site: www.mccarter.org
Management:
  Artistic Director: Emily Mann
  Managing Director: Timothy Shields
  Special Programming Director: William W Lockwood
Mission: The Theatre is one of the most active cultural centers in the nation, offering 200 performances of theatre, dance, music and special events each year.
Utilizes: Actors; AEA Actors; Artists-in-Residence; Choreographers; Dance Companies; Dancers; Designers; Educators; Fine Artists; Five Seasonal Concerts; Guest Artists; Guest Choreographers; Guest Companies; Guest Conductors; Guest Designers; Guest Directors; Guest Lecturers; Guest Musical Directors; Guest Musicians; Guild Activities; Local Unknown Artists; Multimedia; Music; Original Music Scores; Performance Artists; Poets; Resident Professionals; Sign Language Translators; Soloists; Student Interns; Theatre Companies; Visual Arts
Founded: 1930
Specialized Field: Drama; Musical
Status: Non-Profit, Professional
Paid Staff: 80
Season: September - May
Affiliations: McCarter Theatre Company
Annual Attendance: 200,000+
Facility Category: Performing Arts Center
Type of Stage: Proscenium
Stage Dimensions: 42' x 36'
Orchestra Pit: 1
Seating Capacity: 1078
Year Built: 1930
Architect: DK Este Fisher
Rental Contact: General Manager Tom Nuzan

2969
PRINCETON REP COMPANY/PRINCETON REP SHAKESPEARE FESTIVAL
1 Palmer Square
Suite 541
Princeton, NJ 08542
Phone: 609-921-3682
Fax: 609-921-3962
e-mail: prcreprap@aol.com
Web Site: www.princetonrep.org
Management:
  President: Victoria Liberatori

  Executive Director: Janice Orlandi
  Press Contact: Carol Fineman
Mission: Princeton Repertory Company was founded in 1984 and is a professional theatre company operating under a Small Professional Theatre Contract with Actors' Equity Association.
Founded: 1984
Specialized Field: Comedy; Youth Theater; Classic; Contemporary
Status: Non-Profit, Professional
Season: June - August

2970
TWO RIVER THEATER COMPANY
21 Bridge Avenue
Red Bank, NJ 07701
Phone: 732-345-1400
Fax: 732-345-1414
e-mail: info@trtc.org
Web Site: www.trtc.org
Management:
  Executive Producer: Robert Rechnitz
  Artistic Director: Aaron Posner
  Managing Director: Guy Gsell
Mission: Dedicated to presenting works, which most richly direct our gaze to the life of the human spirit. Our mission is to produce works, from the classical and contemporary canons, which are literary and intelligent. Two River's programs include not only mainstage productions, but special performances including a student matinee series (for high school classes), singles nights and sign-interpretation and audio-described performances.
Utilizes: Actors; AEA Actors; Guest Conductors; Guest Designers
Founded: 1993
Specialized Field: Classic; Contemporary; Educational
Status: Nonprofit
Season: September - May
Affiliations: AEA
Annual Attendance: 25,000
Type of Stage: Proscenium
Stage Dimensions: 35' x 35'
Seating Capacity: 300
Year Built: 2005
Rental Contact: Sales Director Sydney Mehrlander

2971
THEATRE AT RARITAN VALLEY COMMUNITY COLLEGE
Route 28 & Lamingdon Road
PO Box 3300
Somerville, NJ 08876-1265
Phone: 908-725-3420
Fax: 908-526-7890
e-mail: theatre@rvccarts.org
Officers:
  President: G Jeremiah Ryan
  Senior VP: Marie Gnage
  VP Finance/Administration: Thomas Carroll
Management:
  Director Of Theatre: Alan Liddell
  Communications Assistant: Alan Liddell
  Theatre Manager: Jacinthia Alexander
  Production Assistant: John Wiedermann
Utilizes: Artists-in-Residence; Dance Companies; Fine Artists; Special Technical Talent; Theatre Companies
Founded: 1985
Specialized Field: Educational; Theater Workshops
Status: Nonprofit
Paid Staff: 7
Volunteer Staff: 60
Paid Artists: 100
Budget: $600,000

Income Sources: Ticket Sales, Facility Rental; Contributions; Concessions
Performs At: Edward Nash Theatre; Welpe Theatre
Affiliations: APAP; IPAY; IAAM
Annual Attendance: 30,000
Stage Dimensions: 46'x40'
Seating Capacity: 984
Year Built: 1985

2972
TEANECK NEW THEATRE
PO Box 71
Teaneck, NJ 07666-0071
Phone: 201-692-0200
e-mail: tnthattie@aol.com
Web Site: www.njtheater.com
Management:
  President: Bruce Cascor
Mission: We try to introduce our audience to new playwrights while continuing to present classics along with current well known plays.
Founded: 1990
Specialized Field: Community Theater
Status: Non-Profit, Non-Professional
Volunteer Staff: 20
Non-paid Artists: var
Budget: $10,000
Income Sources: Tickets; Local Support
Performs At: Bogart Memorial Church
Annual Attendance: 900
Facility Category: Auditorium
Type of Stage: Raised Proscenium
Seating Capacity: 100

2973
PASSAGE THEATRE COMPANY
PO Box 967
Trenton, NJ 08605
Phone: 609-392-0766
Fax: 609-392-0318
e-mail: info@passagetheatre.org
Web Site: www.passagetheatre.org
Management:
  Executive Director: June Ballinger
Mission: Committed to staging dynamic works that celebrate the human experience across cultural lines.
Founded: 1985
Specialized Field: New Plays
Status: Non-Profit, Professional
Paid Staff: 3
Season: September - June
Stage Dimensions: 30' x 22'
Seating Capacity: 125

2974
PATRIOTS THEATER AT THE WAR MEMORIAL
PO Box 232
Trenton, NJ 08625
Phone: 609-984-8484
Fax: 609-777-0581
Toll-free: 800-955-5566
e-mail: thewarmemorial@sos.state.nj.us
Web Site: www.thewarmemorial.com
Management:
  Executive Director: Molly S McDonough
  Production Coordinator: Bill Nutter
  Ticketing/Sales Director: Andrew Burkett
  Ticketing/Sales Director: Rebecca Jensen
  Administrative Assistant: Stephanie Gorski
Mission: Proudly hosts a diverse and exciting array of theatrical and concert events — from comedy to ballet, from opera to gospel, from international to jazz, from classical to country to rock, pop, and folk.

Founded: 1932
Specialized Field: Drama; Historical
Status: Non-Profit, Professional
Paid Staff: 20
Volunteer Staff: 100
Income Sources: State of New Jersey
Affiliations: State of New Jersey, Department of State Division of War Memorial
Facility Category: Theater
Type of Stage: Proscenium
Stage Dimensions: 50 x 30
Seating Capacity: 1800; 12,000 sq ft
Year Built: 1932
Year Remodeled: 1998
Cost: $ 34.5 Million
Rental Contact: Executive Director Molly S. McDonough
Resident Groups: New Jersey Symphony, Greater Trenton Sympony, Boheme Opera, American Repertory Ball

2975
MONTCLAIR STATE UNIVERSITY

Montclair State University
Upper Montclair, NJ 07043-9987
Phone: 973-655-5112
Fax: 973-655-5335
Web Site: www.montclair.edu
Management:
    Stage/Production Management: Michael Allen
Mission: Evolving theatre featuring new works and American standards.
Specialized Field: Educational; Theater Workshops
Status: Nonprofit
Paid Staff: 50
Volunteer Staff: 15
Paid Artists: 40
Budget: $550,000
Income Sources: Grants; Ticket Revenue; Individuals
Season: June - August
Performs At: Alexander Kasser Theater
Affiliations: LOA; SPT
Annual Attendance: 15,000
Facility Category: Equity Theater
Type of Stage: 2 Prosceniums and Flexible
Stage Dimensions: 40' x 36'
Seating Capacity: 950 + 99
Year Remodeled: 2002
Rental Contact: John Wooten

2976
PUSHCART PLAYERS

197 Bloomfield Avenue
Verona, NJ 07044
Phone: 973-857-1115
Fax: 973-857-4366
e-mail: information@pushcartplayers.org
Web Site: www.pushcartplayers.org
Management:
    Executive Artistic Director/CoFound: Ruth Fost
    Executive Producer/Production Mgr: Goffrey Morris
    Programs/Services Director: Stephanie Carr
    Arts-In-Education Director: Harry Patrick Christian
    Associate Production Manager: Terrence P Burnett
    Development Associate: Lucile Mason
    Development Associate: Janet Mason
Mission: Pushcart Players is an award-winning professional theatre and arts-in-education company for young audiences. Pushcart programs offer the finest artists and arts educators available in the field, bringing the best of theatre arts to young viewers in schools and local theatres.

Founded: 1974
Specialized Field: Musical; Youth Theater; Touring Company; Educational
Status: Non-Profit, Professional
Paid Staff: 25
Paid Artists: 25
Season: September - June

2977
CUMBERLAND PLAYERS

Community Theatre
Sherman Avenue & SE Boulevard
PO Box 494
Vineland, NJ 08362-0494
Phone: 856-692-5626
e-mail: theatre@cumberlandplayers.com
Web Site: www.cumberlandplayers.com
Officers:
    President: Richard Curcio
    VP Finance: Mary Wijsmuller
Management:
    VP Production: Brian Garrison
Mission: Promoting opportunities for grassroots participation amoung young and old theatre lovers. Dedicated to enriching the culture life, spirit of volunteerism, community service and love for the theatre.
Utilizes: Actors; Choreographers; Community Members; Community Talent; Local Artists; Local Artists & Directors; Local Talent; Music; Performance Artists; Visual Designers
Founded: 1946
Specialized Field: Community Theater; Musical; Drama; Comedy
Status: Non-Profit
Income Sources: Grants; Donations; Ticket Sales
Seating Capacity: 143

2978
SHADOW LAWN SUMMER STAGE

Monmouth University
Woods Theatre, Cedar Ave
West Long Branch, NJ 07764
Phone: 732-571-3442
Fax: 732-263-5330
e-mail: jburke@monmouth.edu
Web Site: www.monmouth.edu; www.njtheater.com
Management:
    Chair Music/Theatre Arts: John J Burke
    Technical Director/Set Designer: Fernando Del Guercio
Utilizes: Actors; Dancers; Designers; Five Seasonal Concerts; Grant Writers; Guest Conductors; Guest Ensembles; High School Drama; Multimedia; New Productions; Original Music Scores; Resident Professionals; Soloists; Touring Companies; Visual Arts
Founded: 1979
Specialized Field: Musical; Summer Stock
Status: For-Profit, Non-Professional
Season: June - August
Performs At: Lauren K Woods Theatre
Type of Stage: Thrust
Stage Dimensions: 35' x 20'
Seating Capacity: 148

2979
MAURICE LEVIN THEATER SEASON

760 Northfield Avenue
West Orange, NJ 07052
Phone: 973-736-3200
Fax: 973-736-6871
e-mail: jrossi@jccmetrowest.org
Web Site: www.jccmetrowest.org
Management:

President: Sharon Seiden
Executive Director: Michael Hopkins
Director: Julie Rossi
Founded: 1877
Specialized Field: Drama; Specialty Acts; Summer Stock
Status: Non-Profit
Paid Staff: 100
Budget: $500,000 - $600,000
Performs At: Maurice Levin Theater

New Mexico

2980
ADOBE THEATER

9813 4th Street NW
Albuquerque, NM 87048
Mailing Address: PO Box 276, Corrales, NM. 87048
Phone: 505-898-9222
Fax: 505-892-9761
e-mail: reservations@adobetheater.com
Officers:
    President: Erin K Moots
    VP/Technical Director: Jeff Kuykendall
    Secretary: Ninetter S Mordaunt
    Treasurer: Beverly Herring
Management:
    President: Kelle Senye
    VP: Judy Buehler
Mission: To provide an educational vehicle to produce plays, musicals and other entertainments, primarily for the Westside and Greater Albuquerque Communities, including Bernalillo, Sandoval, Valencia and Cibola Counties. To furnish an opportunity for learning experiences for theater enthusiasts of all ages with any degree of experience.
Founded: 1957
Specialized Field: Community Theater; Drama; Comedy
Budget: $40 Million
Income Sources: Box Office; Individual Donations
Season: Year-round
Performs At: Adobe Theatre
Annual Attendance: 9,000
Type of Stage: Thrust
Stage Dimensions: 24 x 24
Seating Capacity: 90
Year Built: 1960

2981
ALBUQUERQUE LITTLE THEATRE

224 San Pasquale SW
Albuquerque, NM 87102
Phone: 505-242-4750
e-mail: alt@swcp.com
Officers:
    President: Jean Block
    VP: Jan Alvidrez
    Secretary: Karen Patterson
    Treasurer: Wesley Daniels, CPA
Management:
    Executive Director: Larry D Parker
    Technical Director: Andrew McHarney
    Sales/Box Office: David A Rivera
    Director Development: Marie G Hamitlon
    House Manager: Deborah Dickey
    Business Manager: Kristi Gore
Founded: 1930
Specialized Field: Community Theater; Theater Workshops
Status: Not-for-profit
Affiliations: Albuquerque Children's Theatre

2982
CITY OF ALBUQUERQUE KIMO THEATRE
423 Central NW
Albuquerque, NM 87102
Phone: 505-768-3522
Fax: 505-768-3542
e-mail: crivera@cabq.gov
Web Site: www.cabq.gov/kimo
Management:
   Managing Director: Craig Rivera
   Technical Manager: Dennis Potter
   Business Manager: Lauren Griego
Founded: 1927
Specialized Field: Drama; Classic; Contemporary
Status: For-Profit, Professional
Paid Staff: 4
Budget: $55,000
Type of Stage: Proscenium
Seating Capacity: 650
Year Built: 1927
Year Remodeled: 2000

2983
LA COMPANIA DE TEATRO DE ALBUQUERQUE
La Compania North Albuquerque
PO Box 884
Albuquerque, NM 87103-0884
Phone: 505-242-7929
Management:
   Artistic Director: Ramon A Flores
Mission: To reflect, preserve and empower the New Mexican society and culture through professional production; Southwest bilingual theatre.
Utilizes: Singers
Founded: 1977
Specialized Field: Multi-Cultural; Ethnic Theater; Spanish Language Company
Status: Semi-Professional; Nonprofit
Budget: $95,000
Performs At: KiMo Theatre; South Broadway Cutural Center
Annual Attendance: 10,000
Seating Capacity: 700; 309
Organization Type: Performing; Touring; Resident; Educational

2984
SANDSTONE PRODUCTIONS
901 Fairgrounds Road
Farmington, NM 87401
Phone: 505-327-9336
Management:
   Producer: Shawn F Lyle
Founded: 1993
Specialized Field: Summer Stock; Musical
Status: Non-Equity; Nonprofit
Season: June - August
Type of Stage: Outdoor
Stage Dimensions: 150' x 100'
Seating Capacity: 600

2985
LAS CRUCES COMMUNITY THEATRE
313 N Downtown Mall
Las Cruces, NM 88001
Phone: 505-523-1200
Web Site: www.lcctnm.org
Officers:
   President: Michael Mandel
   Secretary: Cindy Pitts
   Treasurer: Ray Carter
Management:

   President: PJ Waggaman
   Treasurer: Heather Pfeiffer
   Secretary: Faith Hutson
Mission: Las Cruces Community Theatre is an all volunteer non-profit organization with many opportunities for involvement.
Utilizes: Singers
Founded: 1963
Specialized Field: Community Theater
Status: Non-Professional; Nonprofit
Organization Type: Performing

New York

2986
BLACK EXPERIENCE ENSEMBLE
5 Homestead Avenue
Albany, NY 12203
Phone: 518-482-6683
Officers:
   President/Founder: Mars Hill
Mission: To provide cultural exposure and enrichment to the minority community through the performing arts.
Utilizes: Singers
Founded: 1968
Specialized Field: Community Theater; African American
Status: Professional; Nonprofit
Paid Staff: 5
Income Sources: Albany League of Arts
Organization Type: Performing; Touring; Sponsoring

2987
PARK PLAYHOUSE INCORPORATED
PO Box 525
Albany, NY 12201
Phone: 518-434-2035
Fax: 518-434-1048
e-mail: parkplay@aol.com
Management:
   Assistant Producer: Shirley W Aren
   Park Supervisor: Lee T Griffin
   Producer: Venustiano Borromeo
Founded: 1989
Specialized Field: Summer Stock
Status: Nonprofit
Season: July - August
Type of Stage: Proscenium
Stage Dimensions: 56' x 36'
Seating Capacity: 900

2988
AUBURN PLAYERS COMMUNITY THEATRE
PO Box 543
Auburn, NY 13021
Phone: 315-258-8275
e-mail: mgmword@twcny.rr.com
Web Site:
www.community.syracuse.com/cc/auburnplays
Officers:
   President: Deborah Scott
   Secretary: Cynthia Nagle
   Administrative Treasurer: Ellie Beck
   Production Treasurer: Dia Carabajal
Management:
   Administrative VP: Elisa Hunt
   Production VP: Andrew Rankin
Mission: To be a non-profit, educational and cultural organization; to present dramatic productions; to increase appreciation for the theatre.
Founded: 1961
Specialized Field: Community Theater

Status: Nonprofit
Paid Staff: 100
Organization Type: Performing

2989
MERRY-GO-ROUND PLAYHOUSE
PO Box 506
Auburn, NY 13021
Phone: 315-255-1305
Fax: 315-252-3815
e-mail: marketing@merry-go-round.com
Web Site: www.merry-go-round.com
Officers:
   President: Robert Nethercott
Management:
   President: Edward Sayles
   Director Of Marketing: Nancy Calocerinos
   Youth Theatre Production Manager: Mark Goodloe
Mission: The Merry-Go-Round Playhouse is a professional theatre providing a Summer Season of Broadway quality musicals.
Founded: 1975
Specialized Field: Musical
Status: Non-Profit, Professional
Paid Staff: 20
Season: June - August
Annual Attendance: 17,000
Seating Capacity: 325

2990
MOHAWK PLAYERS
PO Box 382
Babylon, NY 11702
Phone: 516-669-7605
Mission: To present live theatre to diverse groups at libraries.
Founded: 1954
Specialized Field: Community Theater; Touring Company
Status: Nonprofit
Paid Staff: 10
Income Sources: New York State Coucil on Arts
Organization Type: Performing; Touring

2991
RIVER ARTS REPERTORY
Route 212
Bearsville, NY 12409
Phone: 914-679-7693
Fax: 845-679-9239
Management:
   Managing Director: Albert Idhe
   Co-Artistic Director: Michael Cristofer
   Managing Director: Albert Idhe
Mission: To offer new interpretations of the classics; to create innovative new works.
Utilizes: Singers
Founded: 1979
Specialized Field: Summer Stock; Puppet
Status: Professional; Nonprofit
Income Sources: Actors' Equity Association; Theatre Communications Group
Performs At: Bearsville Theatre
Organization Type: Performing; Sponsoring

2992
GATEWAY PLAYHOUSE
215 S Country Road
Box 5
Bellport, NY 11713

Phone: 631-286-1133
Fax: 631-286-5806
Toll-free: 888-484-9669
e-mail: boxoffice@gatewayplayhouse.com
Management:
Producer: Paul Allan
Founded: 1950
Specialized Field: Musical; Children's Theater; Theater
Workshops
Status: Commercial
Season: May - December
Type of Stage: Proscenium
Stage Dimensions: 30' x 8'
Seating Capacity: 500

2993
AIRPORT PLAYHOUSE

218 Knickerbocker Avenue
PO Box 162
Bohemia, NY 11716-0162
Phone: 631-589-7588
Fax: 631-589-7607
e-mail: airportplayhouse@aol.com
Web Site: www.airportplayhouse.com
Management:
Executive Director: Terry Brennan
Mission: The Airport Playhouse is a year-round
professional, not-for-profit theater offering an annual
roster of 10 full scale productions and an array of
children's programs, fund-raising activities, special
events, dinner theater packages and theater classes.
Utilizes: Actors; Artists-in-Residence; Choreographers;
Collaborating Artists; Collaborations; Commissioned
Composers; Community Members; Community Talent;
Contract Actors; Contract Orchestras; Dance
Companies; Dancers; Designers; Educators; Equity
Actors; Fine Artists; Guest Accompanists; Guest Artists;
Guest Composers; Guest Designers; Guest Directors;
Guest Instructors; Guest Lecturers; Guest Musical
Directors; Guest Musicians; Guest Soloists; Instructors;
Local Artists; Local Artists & Directors; Local Unknown
Artists; Multimedia; Music; Original Music Scores; Paid
Performers; Poets; Resident Companies; Resident
Professionals; Scenic Designers; Sign Language
Translators; Singers; Soloists; Students; Student
Interns; Special Technical Talent; Touring Companies;
Visual Designers; Volunteer Artists
Founded: 1977
Specialized Field: New Plays; Musical; Contemporary
Status: Non-Profit, Professional
Season: Year-Round
Annual Attendance: 8,000
Facility Category: Theatre
Type of Stage: Proscenium
Stage Dimensions: 38' x 38'
Seating Capacity: 255

2994
BELMONT PLAYHOUSE

2385 Arthur Avenue
Bronx, NY 10458
Phone: 718-364-4700
Fax: 718-563-5053
e-mail: thebelmont@hotmail.com
Management:
Artistic Director: Dante Albertie
Founded: 1991
Specialized Field: Ethnic Theater; Classic; New Plays
Performs At: Belmont Playhouse
Type of Stage: Black Box, Platform
Seating Capacity: 75, 25-100

2995
PREGONES THEATER

571-575 Walton Avenue
Bronx, NY 10451
Phone: 718-585-1202
Fax: 718-585-1608
e-mail: info@pregones.org
Web Site: www.pregones.org
Management:
Artistic Director: Rosalba Rolon
Managing Director: Maggie Gonzales
Associate Artistic Director: Alvan Colon Lespier
Associate Director: Jorge Merced
Mission: To offer bilingual theatre mainly for Latino
audiences; to present a broad range of professional
performers.
Founded: 1979
Specialized Field: Musical; Comedy; Community
Theater; Classic; Contemporary
Status: Non-Profit, Professional
Organization Type: Performing; Touring

2996
AAI PRODUCTIONS

528 5th Street
Suite 4R
Brooklyn, NY 11215
e-mail: aaiproductions@aol.com
Management:
Artistic Director: Melanie Sutherland
Mission: To offer classical and contemporary plays
developed by theatre artists of a resident company.
Utilizes: Singers
Founded: 1976
Specialized Field: Comedy; Puppet; Classic;
Contemporary
Status: Non-Profit, Professional
Paid Staff: 1
Organization Type: Performing; Touring; Resident

2997
ADELPHIAN PLAYERS

8515 Ridge Boulevard
Brooklyn, NY 11209
Phone: 718-238-3308
Fax: 718-238-2894
Management:
Artistic Director: Russell E Bonanno
Business Manager: Philip Stone
Director Advancement: Albert C Corham
Mission: To provide quality theatre for the residents of
Brooklyn.
Founded: 1964
Specialized Field: Summer Stock
Status: Non-Professional
Paid Staff: 25
Volunteer Staff: 10
Performs At: Adelphi Academy
Organization Type: Performing; Educational

2998
BILLIE HOLIDAY THEATRE

1368 Fulton Street
PO Box 470131
Brooklyn, NY 11247-0131
Phone: 718-636-0919
Fax: 718-636-2165
e-mail: billieholidaytheatre@yahoo.com
Web Site: www.thebillieholiday.org
Management:
President: Marjorie Moon

Mission: To offer trained Black artists a professional
environment; to provide theatre that enlightens and
educates the community.
Utilizes: Singers
Founded: 1972
Specialized Field: African American
Status: Non-Profit, Professional
Paid Staff: 4
Stage Dimensions: Proscenium
Seating Capacity: 200
Organization Type: Performing; Resident

2999
CONEY ISLAND USA

1208 Surf Avenue
Brooklyn, NY 11224
Phone: 718-372-5159
Fax: 718-372-5101
e-mail: info@coneyisland.com
Web Site: www.coneyisland.com
Management:
President: Dick Zigun
Managing Director: Jennifer Upchurch
Mission: To present America's popular art forms in
innovative sideshow parades, performances and
exhibitions.
Utilizes: Singers
Founded: 1980
Specialized Field: Specialty Acts; Musical
Status: Non-Profit, Professional
Paid Staff: 12
Volunteer Staff: 4
Paid Artists: 8
Budget: 250,000
Income Sources: Alliance of Resident Theatres/New
York
Performs At: Sideshows by the Seashore, Coney
Island Museum
Annual Attendance: 75,000+
Facility Category: Sideshows by the seashore, Coney
Island Museum
Type of Stage: Arena, Cabaret
Seating Capacity: 99; 74
Organization Type: Performing; Educational;
Sponsoring

3000
RYAN REPERTORY COMPANY AT HARRY
WARREN THEATRE

2445 Bath Avenue
Brooklyn, NY 11214
Phone: 718-996-4800
Fax: 718-996-4800
e-mail: ryanrep@juno.com
Management:
Executive Director: Barbara Parisi
Technical Director: Michael Pasterneck
Artistic Director: John Sannuto
Mission: Developing new musicals and working on
new plays.
Utilizes: Actors; AEA Actors; Artists-in-Residence;
Choreographers; Collaborating Artists;
Composers-in-Residence; Designers; Educators; Five
Seasonal Concerts; Guest Designers; Music;
Organization Contracts; Performance Artists; Poets;
Resident Professionals; Sign Language Translators;
Soloists; Special Technical Talent
Founded: 1972
Specialized Field: Musical; New Plays
Status: Professional; Nonprofit
Volunteer Staff: 18
Non-paid Artists: 200
Budget: $60,000
Performs At: Harry Warren Theatre

Annual Attendance: 2000
Stage Dimensions: 12 x 12
Seating Capacity: 40
Year Built: 1990
Organization Type: Performing; Resident

3001
STAGES OF LEARNING
138 S Oxford Street
Suite 1B
Brooklyn, NY 11217
Phone: 718-398-2494
Fax: 718-398-2494
e-mail: megan@stagesoflearning.org
Web Site: www.stagesoflearning.org
Management:
   President: Floyd Rumohr
   Stages of Learning Program Manager: Terry Hofler
   Administrative Assistant: Mike Halverson
Mission: To improve the educational success, social well-being and potential for happiness of children, ages 8-13, through kinesthetic, theatre-based activities guided by the artistic principles of Michael Chekhov and to inspire and unite artists, teachers, children and families through theatre experiences.
Founded: 1994
Specialized Field: Youth Theater; Educational
Status: Non-Profit, Professional
Paid Staff: 6
Volunteer Staff: 15
Paid Artists: 10
Non-paid Artists: 3

3002
AFRICAN AMERICAN CULTURAL CENTRE
350 Masten Avenue
Buffalo, NY 14209
Phone: 716-884-2013
Fax: 716-885-2590
e-mail: aacc@wzrd.com
Officers:
   Executive Director: Agnes M. Bain
Management:
   Artistic Dir Paul Robeson Theatre: Paulette Harris
   Artistic Dir Dance/Drum Department: Linda Barr
   Artistic Dir Dance/Drum Department: Theresa Mingo
Mission: To develop and nurture an appreciation for Black Theatre in the Black community, especially among Black youth.
Utilizes: Singers
Founded: 1958
Specialized Field: African American; Ethnic Theater; Community Theater; Youth Theater; Multi-Cultural
Status: Non-Profit, Non-Professional
Paid Staff: 50
Performs At: Paul Robeson Theatre
Organization Type: Performing; Educational

3003
ALLEYWAY THEATRE
One Curtain Up Alley
Buffalo, NY 14202-1911
Phone: 716-852-2600
Fax: 716-852-2266
e-mail: email@alleyway.com
Web Site: www.alleway.com
Management:
   Executive Director: Neal Radice
   Director Public Relations: Joyce Stilson
   Director Marketing: Todd Warfield
Mission: To develop and produce new theatre.

Utilizes: Actors; AEA Actors; Artists-in-Residence; Choreographers; Collaborations; Designers; Educators; Five Seasonal Concerts; Guest Accompanists; Guest Companies; Guest Conductors; Guest Designers; Guest Soloists; Guest Teachers; High School Drama; Instructors; Local Artists; Original Music Scores; Performance Artists; Poets; Resident Professionals; Sign Language Translators; Student Interns; Visual Arts
Founded: 1980
Specialized Field: New Plays
Annual Attendance: 17,000
Type of Stage: Black Box
Seating Capacity: 100

3004
IRISH CLASSICAL THEATRE COMPANY
625 Main Street
Buffalo, NY 14203
Phone: 716-853-4282
Fax: 716-853-0592
e-mail: iclassical@aol.com
Web Site: www.irishclassicaltheatre.com
Management:
   President: Vincent O'Neill
   Business Manager: Nancy Dohry
Mission: To present the greatest works of dramatic literture, international classics, modern plays of exceptional merit, and Irish plays, both traditional and contemporary; to produce them at the highest level of artistic excellence; to offer them to the public of Buffalo, Western New York and Southern Ontario, and subsequently, for national and international audiences.
Founded: 1990
Specialized Field: Ethnic Theater; Classic
Status: Non-Profit, Professional
Paid Staff: 12
Paid Artists: 12
Annual Attendance: 25,000+
Type of Stage: In The Round
Seating Capacity: 200
Year Built: 1998

3005
KAVINOKY THEATRE
320 Porter Avenue
Buffalo, NY 14201
Phone: 716-829-7668
Fax: 716-829-7790
e-mail: kavinokytheatre@dyc.edu
Web Site: www.kavinokytheatre.com
Management:
   Artistic Director: David Lamb
   Executive and Managing Director: Steve Cooper
Founded: 1980
Specialized Field: Musical; Classic; New Plays
Status: Non-Profit, Professional
Paid Staff: 4
Volunteer Staff: 300
Paid Artists: 40
Performs At: D'Youville College campus
Type of Stage: Proscenium/Thrust
Seating Capacity: 260

3006
PANDORA'S BOX THEATRE COMPANY
One Curtain Up Alley
Buffalo, NY 14202
Phone: 716-852-2600
Fax: 716-852-2266
e-mail: jkittsley@alleyway.com
Web Site: www.alleyway.com/pandorasbox
Management:
   President of the Board: Leonard London
   Executive Director: Neal Radice

Artistic Director: Julie Kittsley
Mission: To produce plays about women and their experiences.
Utilizes: Actors; AEA Actors; Choreographers; Collaborations; Designers; Five Seasonal Concerts; Guest Conductors; Guest Designers; Instructors; Performance Artists; Playwrights; Resident Professionals; Singers; Theatre Companies; Visual Arts
Founded: 1995
Specialized Field: Women's Theater
Status: Non-Profit, Professional
Paid Staff: 2
Paid Artists: 40

3007
SHAKESPEARE IN DELAWARE PARK
PO Box 716
Buffalo, NY
Phone: 716-515-3960
e-mail: sdp_mailbox@yahoo.com
Web Site: www.shakespeareindelawarepark.com
Officers:
   Chair: Scott L Sroka
   Vice Chair: Melissa R Grainger
   Treasurer: Anne K Kyzmir
   Secretary: Marita Ronald
Management:
   Artistic Director: Saul Elkin
   Program Director: Roger Keicher
Mission: Shakespeare in Delaware Park is a not-for-profit, professional theatre company dedicated to providing free, high-quality public theatre to the widest possible audience by performing Shakespearean plays outdoors.
Utilizes: Scenic Designers; Soloists
Founded: 1976
Specialized Field: Classic; Shakespeare
Status: Professional; Nonprofit
Season: June - August

3008
STUDIO ARENA THEATRE
710 Main Street
Buffalo, NY 14202-1990
Phone: 716-856-8025
Fax: 716-856-3415
Toll-free: 800-777-8243
Officers:
   President: James Anderson
Management:
   Artistic Director: Gavin Cameron-Webb
   Executive Director: Ken Neufeld
   Director Development: Carol Halter
   Director Marketing: Bil Schroeder
Mission: To provide Western New York with a varied theatre season of the finest quality.
Utilizes: Actors; AEA Actors; Artists-in-Residence; Collaborations; Designers; Educators; Fine Artists; Five Seasonal Concerts; Guest Companies; Guest Conductors; Guest Designers; High School Drama; Instructors; Local Artists; Lyricists; Original Music Scores; Performance Artists; Resident Professionals; Scenic Designers; Singers; Soloists; Students
Founded: 1927
Specialized Field: Musical; Drama; Comedy
Status: Non-Profit
Budget: 4.5 Million
Income Sources: League of Resident Theatres; Theatre Communications Group; Actors' Equity Association
Season: September - May
Affiliations: Theatre Communications Group; League of Resident Theatres
Annual Attendance: 100,000

Type of Stage: Semi-Thrust
Seating Capacity: 637
Year Remodeled: 2001
Organization Type: Performing; Educational

3009
THEATRE OF YOUTH COMPANY
203 Allen Street
Allendale Theatre
Buffalo, NY 14201
Phone: 716-884-4400
Fax: 716-819-9653
e-mail: theatreofyouth@hotmail.com
Web Site: www.buffalo.com/toy
Officers:
President: Lynn Edelmam
VP: Kevin Brady
Secretary: Janice Dearing
Treasurer: Richard D'Arcy
Management:
Artistic Director: Meg Quinn
Director Marketing and Sales: Robert Brunschmid
Business Manager: Linda D'Agostino
Utilizes: Singers
Founded: 1972
Specialized Field: Children's Theater
Status: Non-Profit
Annual Attendance: 53,000
Facility Category: Theatre
Type of Stage: Proscenium
Year Built: 1913
Year Remodeled: 1999
Organization Type: Performing; Touring; Educational

3010
MAC-HAYDN THEATRE
Route 203
PO Box 204
Chatham, NY 12037
Mailing Address: PO Box 204
Phone: 518-392-9292
Fax: 518-392-4547
Web Site: www.machaydntheatre.org
Management:
President: Lynne Hayden
Artistic Producing Director: Linda MacNish
Founded: 1969
Specialized Field: Musical; Summer Stock
Status: Non-Profit, Professional
Season: May - September
Annual Attendance: 40,000+
Facility Category: Theatre
Type of Stage: In the Round
Seating Capacity: 350

3011
HUDSON VALLEY SHAKESPEARE FESTIVAL
155 Main Street
Cold Spring, NY 10516
Phone: 845-265-7858
Fax: 845-265-1037
e-mail: slandstreet@shakespeare.org
Web Site: www.hvshakespeare.org
Management:
Artistic Director: Terrence O'Brien
Executive Director: Susan Landstreet
Director Marketing: Abigail Adams
Mission: Dedicated to producing and performing the plays of Shakespeare with clarity, energy and invention.
Founded: 1987
Specialized Field: Shakespeare; Classic
Status: Non-Profit, Professional
Paid Staff: 25

Paid Artists: 34
Performs At: Boscabel Restoration

3012
LEATHERSTOCKING THEATRE COMPANY
Box 711
Cooperstown, NY 13775
Phone: 607-547-1363
Fax: 607-547-6144
Management:
Artistic Director: Mercedes Gotwald
Founded: 1991
Specialized Field: Summer Stock; Drama; Comedy
Status: Nonprofit
Season: July - September
Type of Stage: Proscenium
Seating Capacity: 150

3013
CORTLAND REPERTORY THEATRE
PO Box 783
Cortland, NY 13045
Phone: 607-753-6161
Fax: 607-753-0047
Toll-free: 800-427-6160
e-mail: cortlandrep@hotmail.com
Web Site: www.cortlandrep.org
Officers:
President: John Folmer
VP: Tom Knobel
Treasurer: Garry Marsted
Secretary: Dorothea Fowler
Management:
Producing Artistic Director: Kerby Thompson
Business Manager: Barclay Diamond
Mission: To offer residents of Central New York an opportunity to experience, at an accessible price, the range and scope of excellent professional theatre.
Utilizes: Actors; AEA Actors; Choreographers; Dancers; Designers; Guest Accompanists; Guest Artists; Guest Conductors; Guest Designers; Guest Lecturers; Guest Musical Directors; Guest Writers; Instructors; Local Artists; Multimedia; Music; Original Music Scores; Resident Professionals; Selected Students; Sign Language Translators; Soloists; Student Interns; Visual Arts
Founded: 1972
Specialized Field: Summer Stock Theatre; Musicals; Non Musicals
Status: Non-Profit, Professional
Paid Staff: 2
Paid Artists: 100
Budget: $480,000
Income Sources: NYSCA; Grants; Corporate Sponsors; Individual Donations
Season: June - August
Performs At: Summer Stock Theatre
Annual Attendance: 17,000
Facility Category: Converted National Historic Dance Pavilion
Type of Stage: 3/4 Thrust, Wood Floor
Seating Capacity: 250
Year Built: 1906
Year Remodeled: 1972
Organization Type: Performing

3014
ARENA PLAYERS REPERTORY THEATRE COMPANY OF LONG ISLAND
296 Route 109
East Farmingdale, NY 11735

Phone: 516-293-0674
e-mail: arena109@aol.com
Web Site: www.arenaplayers.org
Officers:
President: Frederic De Feis
Management:
Office Manager: Carolyn De Melo
Mission: To develop and encourage a love of arena theatre; to assist new playwrights as they develop original scripts.
Utilizes: Actors; Artists-in-Residence; Collaborating Artists; Commissioned Music; Organization Contracts; Original Music Scores; Performance Artists; Resident Artists
Founded: 1955
Specialized Field: Youth Theater; Ethnic Theater; Community Theater; Classic; Contemporary
Status: Non-Profit, Professional
Paid Staff: 3
Volunteer Staff: 5
Paid Artists: 10
Non-paid Artists: 5
Budget: $450,000
Income Sources: Theatre Communications Group
Season: Year-Round
Performs At: Arena Players Repertory Theater
Annual Attendance: 30,000
Facility Category: 2 stages
Type of Stage: Arena
Seating Capacity: 240; 100
Year Remodeled: 1970
Organization Type: Performing; Touring

3015
JOHN DREW THEATER AT GUILD HALL
158 Main Street
East Hampton, NY 11937
Phone: 631-324-4051
Fax: 631-324-2722
e-mail: joshgladstone@guildhall.org
Web Site: www.guildhall.org
Management:
Chairman of Board: Melville Staruss
Executive Director: Ruth Appelhof
Artistic Director: Josh Gladstone
Managing Director: Jeannine Dyner
Mission: The John Drew Theater of Guild Hall operates under an educational/arts charter; dedicated to the presentation of the finest in the performing arts.
Founded: 1931
Specialized Field: AEA LOA Prodctions; Musical; Comedy; Community Theater; Puppet; Classic; Contemporary
Status: Non-Profit, Professional
Paid Staff: 30
Volunteer Staff: 50
Paid Artists: 200
Non-paid Artists: 200
Budget: $2.3 Million
Income Sources: Actors' Equity Association
Season: May-September
Performs At: John Drew Theater
Affiliations: Film Society Lincoln Center; Hamptons International Film Festival; Playwrights Theatre of the Hampton
Annual Attendance: 20,000
Type of Stage: Proscenium
Stage Dimensions: 25'x34'
Seating Capacity: 360
Year Built: 1931
Year Remodeled: 2008
Cost: $14 Million
Rental Contact: Josh Gladstone
Organization Type: Performing; Educational

3016

SHADOWLAND ARTISTS

157 Canal Street
Ellenville, NY 12428
Phone: 845-647-5511
Fax: 845-647-3510
e-mail: mail@shadowlandstheatre.org
Web Site: www.shadowlandstheatre.org
Management:
President: William Collier
Executive Director: William Morris
Founded: 1985
Specialized Field: Drama; Musical; New Plays
Status: Non-Profit, Professional
Season: May - September
Type of Stage: Thrust
Stage Dimensions: 36' x 24'
Seating Capacity: 148

3017

QUEENS COLLEGE SUMMER THEATRE

Rathaus Hall 213
65-30 Kissena Boulevard
Flushing, NY 11367
Phone: 718-997-3185
Fax: 718-997-3095
Web Site: www.qc.cuny.edu
Management:
Production Manager: Ralph Carhart
Mission: Educational setting presenting diverse
productions and programs in the arts. Three theatre
complex with seating for 100 to 500.
Founded: 1970
Specialized Field: Drama; Summer Stock
Status: Non-Equity; Nonprofit
Season: July - August
Performs At: Two Black Boxes; One Fly Space
Affiliations: CUNY
Type of Stage: Proscenium; Thrust
Stage Dimensions: 45' x 45'; 30' x 25'
Seating Capacity: 476

3018

FORESTBURGH PLAYHOUSE

39 Forestburgh Road
Forestburgh, NY 12777
Phone: 845-794-2005
Fax: 845-794-3747
e-mail: info@fbplayhouse.com
Management:
Producer: Norman Duttweiler
Founded: 1947
Specialized Field: Summer Stock; Cabaret; Children's
Theater
Status: Equity; Commercial
Season: June - September
Type of Stage: Proscenium
Seating Capacity: 150

3019

ADIRONDACK THEATRE FESTIVAL

PO Box 3203
Glens Falls, NY 12801
Phone: 518-798-7479
Fax: 518-793-1334
e-mail: atf@atfestival.org
Web Site: www.atfestival.org
Officers:
President: Kathy Reed
VP: Rene Clements
Treasurer: David J King
Secretary: Janet Cordes
Management:

Producing Artistic Director: Mark Fleischer
General Manager: Tracy Long
Mission: A professional not-for-profit summer theatre
located in Glens Falls, NY. Strives to challenge,
entertain and nourish its audience through the
development and production of new and contemporary
musicals and plays. This relationship engages the
commnuity as audience members and participants in
workshops, discussions and educational programming.
Utilizes: Actors; AEA Actors; Choreographers;
Commissioned Composers; Designers; Local Unknown
Artists; Music; Organization Contracts; Original Music
Scores; Performance Artists; Resident Professionals;
Student Interns
Founded: 1994
Specialized Field: Theater
Status: Nonprofit
Paid Staff: 11
Volunteer Staff: 10
Paid Artists: 36
Budget: $400,000
Income Sources: Ticket Sales; Donations; Grants
Season: June - July
Performs At: Charles R Wood Theater
Affiliations: AEA
Annual Attendance: 6,100
Facility Category: Theater
Type of Stage: Proscenium
Seating Capacity: 294
Year Built: 2004

3020

YOUTHEATRE

10 Windy Hill Road
Glens Falls, NY 12801
Phone: 518-793-3521
e-mail: lgyoutheatre@aol.com
Web Site: www.lgyoutheatre.com

3021

STAGEWORKS

133 Warren Street
Hudson, NY 12534
Phone: 518-828-7843
Fax: 518-828-4026
e-mail: contact@stageworkstheater.org
Management:
Production Artistic Director: Laura Margolis
Administrative Director: Phil Gliman
Utilizes: Actors; AEA Actors; Choreographers;
Collaborations; Commissioned Composers; Designers;
Educators; Five Seasonal Concerts; Guest
Accompanists; Guest Artists; Guest Choreographers;
Guest Companies; Guest Conductors; Guest
Designers; Guest Ensembles; Guest Lecturers; Guest
Teachers; High School Drama; Instructors; Music;
Original Music Scores; Performance Artists; Resident
Professionals; Soloists; Student Interns; Visual Arts
Founded: 1993
Specialized Field: Drama; Comedy
Status: Nonprofit
Budget: $190,000
Income Sources: Earned and Unearned
Season: April - November
Affiliations: Theater Communications; Hudson Valley
East Consortium of Professional Theaters
Facility Category: North Point in Kinderhook, NY
Type of Stage: Thrust
Stage Dimensions: 40' x 20'
Seating Capacity: 100-125

3022

CORNELL UNIVERSITY THEATRE, FILM & DANCE DEPARTMENT

Cornell University
Ithaca, NY 14853-6902
Phone: 607-254-2733
Fax: 607-254-2700
e-mail: av45@cornell.edu
Web Site: http://theatrefilmdance.cornell.edu/
Specialized Field: Educational; Theater Workshops
Affiliations: Cornell Concert Series
Facility Category: Dance Hall
Resident Groups: Cornell Savoyards

3023

HANGAR THEATRE

116 N Cayuga Street
Ithaca, NY 1485
Mailing Address: PO Box 205 Ithaca NY, 14851
Phone: 607-273-8588
Fax: 607-273-4516
e-mail: rhoan@hangartheatre.org
Web Site: www.hangartheatre.org
Officers:
President: Laurel Southard
VP: Roy Decheimer
Secretary: Jeol Zumoff
Treasurer: Raymond M Schlath
Management:
President: Lisa Bushlow
Artistic Director: Kevin Moriarty
Business Director: Maryann Summer
Marketing Director: Rhoan Morgan
Mission: As a professional theatre the Hangar hires
Equity and nonequity actors, designers and directors for
each play the theatre produces during the summer.
Utilizes: Selected Students; Singers; Student Interns
Founded: 1974
Specialized Field: Musical; Comedy; Community
Theater; Puppet; Classic; Contemporary
Status: Non-Profit, Non-Professional
Paid Staff: 20
Paid Artists: 20
Budget: $900,000
Income Sources: Foundation; Individual; Grant;
Earned
Season: May - August
Performs At: Hangar Theatre; Cass Park
Affiliations: Actors Equity Association; United Scenic
Artists; Society of Stage Directors and Choreography;
Drama League
Annual Attendance: 20,000
Type of Stage: Thrust
Seating Capacity: 349
Organization Type: Performing; Educational

3024

KITCHEN THEATRE COMPANY

116 N Cayuga Street
Ithaca, NY 14850
Phone: 607-272-0403
Fax: 607-273-4816
e-mail: kitchenithaca@aol.com
Web Site: www.kitchentheatre.org
Management:
President: Percy Browning
Artistic Director: Rachel Lampert
Utilizes: Actors; AEA Actors; Collaborating Artists;
Commissioned Composers; Dancers; Designers; Five
Seasonal Concerts; Grant Writers; Guest
Accompanists; Guest Choreographers; Guest
Companies; Guest Conductors; Guest Designers;
Guest Directors; Guest Lecturers; Guild Activities;

Instructors; Local Artists; Local Unknown Artists; Multimedia; Music; Original Music Scores; Performance Artists; Playwrights; Resident Professionals; Selected Students; Soloists; Student Interns; Special Technical Talent
Founded: 1992
Specialized Field: Community Theater; New Plays
Status: Non-Profit, Professional
Paid Staff: 5
Volunteer Staff: 50
Paid Artists: 15
Season: August - May
Annual Attendance: 10,000
Type of Stage: 3/4 Thrust
Seating Capacity: 73

3025
CHINESE THEATRE WORKS
34-23 Steinway Street No 241
Jackson Heights, NY 11101
Phone: 718-392-3493
Fax: 718-392-3493
e-mail: chinesethtrwks@aol.com
Web Site: www.chinesetheaterworks.org
Management:
Executive Director: Kuang Yu Fong
Artistic Director: Stephen Katlin
Founded: 1975
Specialized Field: Musical; Ethnic Theater; Community Theater; Puppet; Multi-Cultural
Status: Non-Profit, Professional
Paid Staff: 5
Season: Year-Round

3026
YUEH LUNG SHADOW THEATRE
34-41 74Th Street
Jackson Heights, NY 11372
Phone: 718-457-1627
Fax: 718-457-1627
Management:
Executive/Artistic Director: Joe Humphrey
Assistant Director: Sarah Jonker-Burke
Mission: To preserve and perpetuate the art of shadow theatre, which began in China 2000 years ago.
Founded: 1976
Specialized Field: Ethnic Theater; Puppet; Multi-Cultural
Status: Professional; Nonprofit
Income Sources: Alliance of Resident Theatres/New York; United International Marionette Association; Queens Council on Arts; Puppeteers of America; UNIMA
Organization Type: Performing; Touring; Educational

3027
AFRIKAN POETRY THEATRE
176-03 Jamaica Avenue
Jamaica, NY 11432
Phone: 718-523-3312
Fax: 718-523-1054
e-mail: jwatusi@aol.com
Web Site: www.afrikanpoetrytheatre.org
Management:
Chairman: Ann Cheatham
Executive Director: John Watusi Branch
Administrative Assistant: Byron W Perry
Mission: To offer performances, classes, workshops, cultural reference sources and exhibits to the community.
Founded: 1976
Specialized Field: Music; Poetry; Dance; Children's Crafts
Status: Non-Profit, Professional

Paid Staff: 3
Volunteer Staff: 10
Budget: $450,000
Income Sources: Public Funds, Foundation's Sales
Performs At: Afrikan Poetry Theatre
Annual Attendance: 10,000
Type of Stage: Platform
Stage Dimensions: 18 x 20
Seating Capacity: 100
Year Built: 1930
Year Remodeled: 1979
Rental Contact: Executive Director John Watusi Branch
Organization Type: Performing; Touring; Educational; Sponsoring

3028
NEW YORK STREET THEATRE CARAVAN
8705 Chelsea Street
Jamaica Estates, NY 11432
Phone: 718-657-8070
Management:
Artistic Director of the Collective: Marketa Kimbrell
Founded: 1968
Specialized Field: Community Theater; Touring Company; Outdoor Theater
Status: Professional
Organization Type: Performing

3029
COACH HOUSE PLAYERS
12 Augusta Street
PO Box 3481
Kingston, NY 12401
Phone: 845-331-2476
e-mail: mbennett@hvc.rr.com
Web Site: http://www.coachhouseplayers.org/
Management:
Business Manager: Kay Finn
Mission: To offer the finest possible productions in every aspect of theatre.
Founded: 1950
Specialized Field: Musical; Community Theater
Status: Nonprofit
Performs At: J. Watson Bailey School
Organization Type: Performing; Educational

3030
LAKE GEORGE DINNER THEATRE
Canada Street
Lake George, NY 12845
Mailing Address: PO Box 4623, Queensbury, NY. 12804
Phone: 518-761-1092
Fax: 518-798-0735
e-mail: lgot@nycap.com
Management:
Producer: Vicky Eastwood
Founded: 1968
Specialized Field: Summer Stock; Dinner Theater
Status: Professional Equity
Paid Staff: 8
Season: June - October
Organization Type: Performing

3031
OPEN EYE THEATER
Box 959
Margaretville, NY 12455
Phone: 845-586-1660
Fax: 845-586-1660
e-mail: openeye@catskill.net
Web Site: www.theopeneye.org

Management:
President: Amie Brockway
Literary Associate: Sharone Stacy
Administrative Assistant: Vesti Snyder
Mission: To create, develop and produce plays for a diverse audience. To provide children, youth, and adults with quality hands-on theatre arts education and performance experiences.
Utilizes: Actors; Artists-in-Residence; Choreographers; Collaborating Artists; Collaborations; Commissioned Composers; Commissioned Music; Composers-in-Residence; Dancers; Designers; Educators; Five Seasonal Concerts; Grant Writers; Guest Accompanists; Guest Artists; Guest Companies; Guest Conductors; Guest Designers; Guest Ensembles; Guest Lecturers; Guest Teachers; Guild Activities; Instructors; Local Artists; Local Artists & Directors; Music; Original Music Scores; Performance Artists; Resident Professionals; Selected Students; Soloists; Student Interns
Founded: 1972
Specialized Field: Educational; Drama; Youth Theater
Status: Non-Profit, Professional
Paid Staff: 5
Volunteer Staff: 30
Paid Artists: 30
Budget: $90,000
Affiliations: TCG; ART/NY; ASS/TEJ/USA; AATE
Annual Attendance: 1,000
Facility Category: Church and Community Hall
Type of Stage: Flexible
Stage Dimensions: 12x16
Seating Capacity: 75
Year Built: 1943

3032
PERIWINKLE NATIONAL THEATRE
456 Broadway
Suite 3
Monticello, NY 12701
Phone: 845-794-1666
Fax: 845-794-0304
Toll-free: 800-888-8271
e-mail: periwinkle@hvc.rr.com
Web Site: www.periwinkle.org
Officers:
President: Robert S Kapito
VP: Patricia Sternberg
Secretary/Treasurer: Julie Hoffman
Secretary: Joel Lerber
Management:
President: Robert Kapito
Executive Director: Sunna Rasch
Director Education: Scott Laughead
Mission: To provide quality programing with a unique blend of preliminary materials, original productions and workshops designed to challenge students intellectually, imaginatively and artistically.
Utilizes: Actors; Artists-in-Residence; Collaborations; Commissioned Composers; Educators; Five Seasonal Concerts; Original Music Scores; Performance Artists; Poets; Resident Professionals; Singers; Student Interns; Theatre Companies
Founded: 1963
Specialized Field: Youth Theater; Ethnic Theater; Community Theater
Status: Non-Profit, Professional
Paid Staff: 7
Volunteer Staff: 3
Paid Artists: 25
Budget: $650,000
Income Sources: Program Fees ; Grants
Season: Feburary - May; September - December
Affiliations: AATE

Annual Attendance: 100,000
Organization Type: Performing; Touring; Educational

3033
BRISTOL VALLEY THEATER
151 S Main Street
PO Box 218
Naples, NY 14512
Phone: 585-374-9032
Fax: 585-374-8520
e-mail: bvt@bvtnaples.org
Web Site: www.bvtnaples.org
Management:
    Managing Director: Barbara Allen
Mission: Professional summer stock theater.
Founded: 1986
Specialized Field: Musical; Comedy; Contemporary;
New Plays
Status: Non-Profit, Professional
Paid Staff: 60
Paid Artists: 30
Season: June - September
Annual Attendance: 10,000
Type of Stage: Proscenium
Seating Capacity: 200

3034
THEATER BARN
PO Box 390
New Lebanon, NY 12125
Phone: 518-794-8989
Web Site: www.theaterbarn.com
Management:
    President: Teresa Brewer
    Vice President: Susan Cobb
    Treasurer: Rosie Interrante
Founded: 1984
Specialized Field: Musical; Comedy; Contemporary
Status: Non-Profit, Professional
Season: June - October
Type of Stage: Proscenium
Stage Dimensions: 30' x 16'
Seating Capacity: 134

3035
NEW PALTZ SUMMER REPERTORY
THEATRE
Department of Theatre, Ct 102
Suny At New Paltz, 75 S Manheim Boulevard
New Paltz, NY 12561-2499
Mailing Address: 1 Hawke Drive
Phone: 845-257-3865
Fax: 845-257-3882
e-mail: trezzaf@newpaltz.edu
Web Site:
http://www.newpaltz.edu/summerrep/contact.html
Management:
    Producer: Frank Trezza
Founded: 1973
Specialized Field: Educational; Theater Workshops;
Summer Stock
Status: Non-Equity; Nonprofit
Season: June - August
Type of Stage: Thrust
Stage Dimensions: 20' x 24'
Seating Capacity: 212

3036
FLEETWOOD STAGE
44 Wildcliff Drive
New Rochelle, NY 10805
Phone: 914-654-8533
Fax: 914-235-4459
e-mail: mailbox@fleetwoodstage.org
Web Site: www.fleetwoodstage.org
Management:
    Producing Director: Lewis Arlt
Founded: 1993
Specialized Field: Musical; Comedy; Youth Theater
Status: Non-Profit, Professional
Performs At: Playhouse at Wildcliff
Type of Stage: Proscenium
Seating Capacity: 100

3037
52ND STREET PROJECT
789 Tenth Avenue
New York, NY 10019
Phone: 212-333-5252
Fax: 212-333-5598
e-mail: info@52project.org
Web Site: www.52project.org
Management:
    Chairman of Board: Steven Graham
    Executive Director: Carol Ochs
    Artistic Director: Gus Rogerson
    Director of Development and Marketi: John
    Sheehy
Founded: 1981
Specialized Field: Experimental; Classic;
Contemporary; Ensembles
Status: Non-Profit, Professional
Paid Staff: 7

3038
ABINGDON THEATRE COMPANY
432 W 42Nd Street
4Th Floor
New York, NY 10036
Phone: 212-736-6604
Fax: 212-736-6608
e-mail: atcnyc@aol.com
Management:
    Artistic Director: Jan Buttram
    Managing Director: Samuel J Bellinger
Specialized Field: Staged Readings; Studio
Productions

3039
ABOUTFACE THEATRE COMPANY
835 Broadway, Suite 1516
Box 210
New York, NY 10003
Phone: 212-268-9638
Management:
    Artistic Director: Sean Burke
    Managing Director: Allison Jones
    Resident Director: Martin Fluger
    General Manager: Michael Herz
    Development: Ron O'Conner
    Development: Barry Rowell
    Development: Ralph Lewis
Mission: To create and present original plays that
explore American idealogy and mythology.
Utilizes: Singers
Founded: 1984
Specialized Field: New Works of Social Importance
Status: Professional; Nonprofit
Income Sources: Alliance of Resident Theatres/New
York; New York Foundation for the Arts
Performs At: Nat Horne Theatre and Studios
Organization Type: Resident; Sponsoring

3040
ACTING COMPANY
630 Ninth Avenue
Suite 214
New York, NY 10036
Mailing Address: PO Box 898 New York, NY
10108-0898
Phone: 212-258-3111
Fax: 212-258-3299
e-mail: mail@theactingcompany.org
Web Site: www.theactingcompany.org
Officers:
    Chairman: Edgar Lansbury
    President: Joan M Warburg
    Vice Chairman: Earl D Weiner
    VP: Robert T Goldman
    VP: John C McDonald
    VP: Elinor A Seevak
    Treasurer: Mark Levenfus
    Secretary: Wade Nichols
Management:
    Chairman of the Board: Earl Weiner
    Producing Artistic Director: Margot Harley
Mission: Dedicated to the development of classical
repertory actors and a national audience for the theatre.
Utilizes: Actors; AEA Actors; Commissioned Music;
Five Seasonal Concerts; Guest Companies; Guest
Conductors; Guest Designers; Resident Professionals;
Singers; Student Interns
Founded: 1972
Specialized Field: Comedy; Youth Theater; Classic;
Contemporary
Status: Non-Profit, Professional
Paid Staff: 17
Volunteer Staff: 2
Paid Artists: 20
Budget: $2,500,000
Income Sources: Foundations; Corporations;
Individuals
Season: September - May
Affiliations: Actor's Equity; USA; SSDC
Annual Attendance: 65,000
Organization Type: Performing; Touring; Resident;
Educational

3041
ACTING STUDIO
CHELSEA REPERTORY COMPANY
Shetler Studio & Theatre
244 W 54th Street, 12th Floor
New York, NY 10023
Phone: 212-580-6600
e-mail: info@actingstudio.com
Web Site: www.actingstudio.com
Management:
    Executive Director: James Price
    Associate Director: John Grabowski
Mission: To serve as a training institution; to develop
new scripts; to provide a resident theatre company.
Founded: 1983
Specialized Field: Meisner Technique; Theater
Workshops
Status: For-Profit, Professional
Paid Staff: 10
Organization Type: Performing; Resident; Educational

3042
ACTORS STUDIO
165 W 46th Street
Suite 509
New York, NY 10036

Phone: 212-302-1900
Fax: 212-302-1926
Toll-free: 800-884-2772
e-mail: brian@actorsstudio.com
Web Site: www.actorsstudio.com
Officers:
   Founder/CEO: Alan S Nusbaum
Management:
   Artistic Director: Estelle Parsons
   Administrator: Rebecca L Scott
Mission: To provide actors with a center where they can focus on the business of their careers in addition to learning the the necessary skills to compete as an actor.
Founded: 1986
Specialized Field: Theater Workshops; Educational
Status: Non-Profit; Professional
Organization Type: Resident

3043
ADOBE THEATRE COMPANY
453 W 16th Street
New York, NY 10011
Phone: 212-352-0441
Fax: 212-352-0441
Management:
   Literary Manager: Jordan Schildcrout
   Artistic Director: Jeremy Dobrish
   Producing Director: Christopher Roberts
Founded: 1991
Specialized Field: New Plays; Theater Workshops
Performs At: Ohio Theatre
Type of Stage: Flexible Stage
Seating Capacity: 75

3044
ALLAN ALBERT PRODUCTIONS INCORPORATED
665 Broadway
4th Floor
New York, NY 10012
Phone: 212-398-9500
Fax: 212-388-9848
Toll-free: 800-966-8881
e-mail: kcaap@aol.com
Web Site: www.allan-albert.com
Management:
   Senior Producer: Kathy Carney
Founded: 1980
Specialized Field: Musical
Status: Non-Equity; Commercial
Season: May - September
Type of Stage: Amphitheatre
Seating Capacity: 3000

3045
AMAS MUSICAL THEATRE
450 W 42nd Street
Suite 2J
New York, NY 10036
Phone: 212-563-2565
Fax: 212-239-8332
e-mail: amas@amasmusical.org
Web Site: www.amasmusical.org
Officers:
   Chairman: Erik Krebs
Management:
   Founder: Rosetta LeNoire
   Producing Director: Donna Trinkoff
Mission: To provide a starting place for new American theatrical pieces in a multi-racial environment which instills creative professionalism.
Utilizes: Singers
Founded: 1968

Specialized Field: Musical; Dinner Theater; Classic; Contemporary; Ethnic Theater
Status: Non-Profit, Non-Professional
Paid Staff: 5
Volunteer Staff: 4
Paid Artists: 40
Budget: $200,000 - 300,000
Organization Type: Performing; Touring; Resident; Educational; Sponsoring

3046
AMERICAN CENTER FOR STANISLAVSKI THEATRE ART
485 Park Avenue
New York, NY 10022
Phone: 212-308-5458
Management:
   Artistic Director: Sonia Moore
   Development Consultant: Marie Lou Catalano
Mission: Bringing Stanislavski's ultimate acting technique and solution to spontaneity, the method of Physical Actions, to American theatre.
Utilizes: Singers
Founded: 1964
Specialized Field: Theater Workshops; Stanislavski Technique; Drama
Status: Professional; Nonprofit
Paid Staff: 15
Income Sources: Alliance of Resident Theatres/New York
Performs At: Trinity Presbyterian Church
Organization Type: Performing; Touring; Educational

3047
AMERICAN ENSEMBLE COMPANY
PO Box 972
Peck Slip Station
New York, NY 10272
Phone: 212-684-7766
Fax: 212-684-7857
Management:
   Artistic Director: Robert Petito
   General Manager: Robert Dominguez
Mission: Production of plays and musicals of literary merit and development of a working ensemble of actors, directors, designers, and writers.
Utilizes: Singers
Founded: 1967
Specialized Field: Musical; Ensembles
Status: Professional; Nonprofit
Organization Type: Performing; Touring; Resident; Educational

3048
AMERICAN PLACE THEATRE
630 9th Avenue
Suite 809
New York, NY 10036
Phone: 212-594-4482
Fax: 212-594-4208
e-mail: contact@americanplacetheatre.org
Web Site: www.americanplacetheatre.org
Officers:
   Chairman: Wynn Handman
Management:
   Executive Director: David Kener
   Artistic Director: Wynn Handman
   Managing Director: Jennifer Barnette
Mission: Committed to producing high quality new work by diverse American writers and ti pursuing pluralism and diversity in all endeavors.
Utilizes: Actors; AEA Actors; Artists-in-Residence; Collaborating Artists; Designers; Educators; Guest Accompanists; Guest Conductors; Guest Designers;

Guest Teachers; Instructors; Local Artists; Original Music Scores; Performance Artists; Resident Professionals; Soloists; Student Interns
Founded: 1963
Specialized Field: Arts & Literacy
Status: Professional; Nonprofit
Paid Staff: 20
Paid Artists: 25
Budget: $1,200,000
Season: Year-Round
Performs At: Main Stage; Subplot Theatre; First Floor Theatre
Affiliations: AEA; IATSE
Annual Attendance: 10,000
Type of Stage: Proscenium; Black Box
Stage Dimensions: 55' x 35'; 40'x 30'
Seating Capacity: 199-349; 74
Year Built: 1970
Rental Contact: Genral Manager Zafra Whitcomb
Organization Type: Performing

3049
AMERICAN THEATRE OF ACTORS
314 W 54th Street
New York, NY 10019
Phone: 212-581-3044
Fax: 212-956-5761
Web Site: www.americantheatreofactors.org
Management:
   President: James Jennings
   Vice President: Jane Culley
   Secretary: James Bernet
   Treasurer: Jacqueline Pace
Mission: To help to develop new actors, playwrights and directors; to produce new plays.
Founded: 1977
Specialized Field: New Plays
Status: Non-Profit, Professional
Paid Staff: 5
Paid Artists: 120
Organization Type: Performing

3050
ATLANTIC THEATER COMPANY
336 W 20th Street
New York, NY 10011
Phone: 212-691-5919
Fax: 212-691-6280
e-mail: admissions@atlantictheater.org
Web Site: www.atlantictheater.org
Management:
   Artistic Director: Neil Pepe
   Managing Director: Andrew D Hamingson
   Literary Manager: Christian Parker
   Director Admissions: Heather Baird
Founded: 1985
Specialized Field: Comedy; Youth Theater; Contemporary
Status: Non-Profit, Professional
Performs At: Atlantic Theater Mainstage, Black Box
Type of Stage: Proscenium
Seating Capacity: 160, 70

3051
BARROW GROUP
312 W 36th Street
6th Floor
New York, NY 10018
Phone: 212-760-2615
e-mail: tbg@barrowgroup.org
Web Site: www.barrowgroup.org
Management:
   Artistic Director: Seth Barish
   Artistic Director: Lee Brock

Producing Director: Porter Pickard
School Director: Christel Ferguson
Founded: 1986
Specialized Field: Musical; Comedy; Ethnic Theater; Classic; Contemporary
Status: Non-Profit, Professional
Paid Staff: 5

3052
BAT THEATRE COMPANY

Flea Theater
41 White Street
New York, NY 10013
Phone: 212-226-0051
Fax: 212-965-1808
e-mail: theflea@thebat.com
Web Site: www.theflea.org
Management:
Artistic Director: Jim Simpson
Managing Director: Todd Rosen
Literary Manager: Gary Winter
Technical Director: Steve Kovaca
Associate Producer: Nella Vera
General Manager: Todd Rosen
Office Manager: Jen McKenna
Stage Manager: Rebecca Gura
Founded: 1996
Specialized Field: Comedy; Puppet; Contemporary
Status: Non-Profit, Professional
Paid Staff: 5

3053
BIG LEAGUE THEATRICALS, INC.

1501 Broadway
Suite 2015
New York, NY 10036
Phone: 212-575-1601
Fax: 212-575-9817
e-mail: jstarr@bigleague.org
Management:
General Manager: Carolyn Clark S
Associate General Manager: Susan Bartelt
Director Of Booking: John Starr
Booking Assistant: Doug Beeman
Director Booking: John Starr
Associate General Manager: Sue Bartelt
Specialized Field: Specialty Acts

3054
BLACK SPECTRUM

119-07 Merrick Boulevard
New York, NY 11434
Phone: 718-723-1800
Fax: 718-723-1806
Web Site: www.blackspectrum.com
Management:
Chairperson: Bob Law
1St Vice Chairman Treasurer: Timothy James
2Nd Vice Chairman: Arthur French
Secretary: Linda Adams
Mission: To present socially significant Black classical as well as contemporary works.
Utilizes: Singers
Founded: 1970
Specialized Field: Musical; Dinner Theater; African American
Status: Non-Profit,Professional
Organization Type: Performing; Touring; Educational

3055
BOND STREET THEATRE COALITION

2 Bond Street
New York, NY 10012

Phone: 212-254-4614
Fax: 212-254-4614
e-mail: info@bondst.org
Web Site: www.bondst.org
Officers:
President: Patrick Sciarratta
VP: Joanna Sherman
Management:
Executive Director: Joanna Sherman
Managing Director: Michael McGuigan
Music Director: Sean Nowell
Mission: To develop new works of theatre employing an imagistic and physical vocabulary; to explore politically relevant themes for diverse audiences.
Utilizes: Singers; Soloists; Student Interns
Founded: 1978
Specialized Field: Comedy; Youth Theater; Puppet; Contemporary; Community Theater
Status: Non-Profit, Professional
Paid Staff: 3
Volunteer Staff: 4
Paid Artists: 12
Budget: $150,000
Income Sources: Trust for Mutual Understanding; Art Link; Arts International
Affiliations: ART/NY; NPCC
Organization Type: Performing; Touring; Sponsoring; Artists' Colony

3056
BROADWAY TOMORROW

191 Claremont Avenue
Suite 53
New York, NY 10027
Phone: 212-531-2447
Fax: 212-531-2447
e-mail: solight@aorldnet.att.net
Web Site: http://home.att/~solight
Officers:
President: Elyse Curtis PhD
VP: Mitchell Robinson
Secretary/Treasurer: Norman Curtis
Management:
Artistic Director: Elyse Curtis
Music Director: Norman Curtis
Mission: To foster new musicals.
Utilizes: Singers
Founded: 1983
Specialized Field: Musical; New Plays
Status: Professional; Nonprofit
Budget: $25,000
Income Sources: Donations
Organization Type: Performing

3057
CASTILLO THEATRE

543 W 42nd Street
New York, NY 10036
Phone: 212-941-5800
Fax: 212-941-8340
e-mail: castilloth@aol.com
Web Site: www.castillo.org
Management:
Artistic Director: Fred Newman
Managing Director: Diane Stiles
Dramaturg: Dan Friedman
Founded: 1983
Specialized Field: Musical; Comedy; Community Theater; Puppet; Classic; Contemporary
Status: Non-Profit, Professional
Paid Staff: 2
Volunteer Staff: 70
Non-paid Artists: 18
Performs At: Castillo Theatre

Affiliations: TCG; ART; NY
Type of Stage: Thrust
Seating Capacity: 71
Year Built: 1989

3058
CHICAGO CITY LIMITS

318 W 53rd Street
New York, NY 10036
Phone: 212-888-5233
Fax: 212-888-0810
e-mail: info@chicagocitylimits.com
Web Site: www.chicagocitylimits.com
Officers:
Director/Executive Producer: Paul Zuckerman
Management:
Producer: Linda Gelman, info@chicagocitylimits.com
Mission: To offer satirical comedy revues that incorporate audience suggestions for an evening of improvisation, comedy and song. Chicago City Limits also teaches corporate workshops, improv classes, and performs at private events.
Utilizes: Actors; Artists-in-Residence; Composers; Dancers; Filmmakers; Multimedia; Original Music Scores; Resident Artists; Sign Language Translators; Theatre Companies; Volunteer Directors & Actors; Writers
Founded: 1977
Specialized Field: Improvisation
Status: For-Profit, Professional
Paid Staff: 3
Paid Artists: 15
Season: Year-Round
Performs At: Chicago City Limits Theater
Type of Stage: Proscenium
Seating Capacity: 75
Year Built: 1971
Rental Contact: Producer Linda Gelman
Organization Type: Performing; Touring; Resident; Educational
Resident Groups: Chicago City Limits

3059
CLASSIC STAGE COMPANY

136 E 13th Street
New York, NY 10003
Phone: 212-677-4210
Fax: 212-477-7504
e-mail: info@classicstage.org
Web Site: www.classicstage.org
Management:
Executive Director: Jessica R Jenen
Artistic Director: Brian Kulick
General Manager: Jeff Griffin
Mission: Award-winning Off-Broadway theatre committed to re-imagining the classical repertory for a contemporary American audience
Utilizes: Actors; AEA Actors; Choreographers; Collaborating Artists; Collaborations; Commissioned Composers; Commissioned Music; Dance Companies; Educators; Five Seasonal Concerts; Guest Conductors; Guest Designers; Guest Instructors; Guest Musicians; Guest Teachers; Performance Artists; Resident Professionals; Sign Language Translators; Singers; Soloists; Student Interns; Special Technical Talent
Founded: 1967
Specialized Field: Classic
Status: Non-Profit, Professional
Paid Staff: 9
Paid Artists: 100
Budget: $2,000,000
Income Sources: Various
Season: September - May

Performs At: Theater
Affiliations: Actors Equity; USA; American Guild of Musical Artists
Annual Attendance: 17,000
Facility Category: Theater
Type of Stage: 3/4 Thrust
Stage Dimensions: 25'x30'
Seating Capacity: 199
Year Built: 1800
Year Remodeled: 2000
Rental Contact: General Manager Jeff Griffin
Organization Type: Performing; Resident

3060
CREATION PRODUCTION COMPANY
127 Greene Street
New York, NY 10012
Phone: 212-674-5593
Fax: 212-974-5593
e-mail: mosakowski@creationproduction.org
Web Site: http://www.creationproduction.org/who.htm
Management:
 President: Jerald Clark
 Director: Anne Hemenway
 Co-Artistic Director: Matthew Maguire
Mission: To create experimental theatre.
Founded: 1977
Specialized Field: Contemporary; Experimental
Status: Non-Profit, Professional
Season: Year-Round
Organization Type: Performing; Touring; Educational

3061
CREATIVE ARTS TEAM
411 Lafayette Street
4th Floor
New York, NY 10003
Phone: 212-998-7380
Fax: 212-995-4151
Web Site:
http://www.cuny.edu/academics/k-to-12/cat.html
Management:
 Executive Director: Lynda Zimmerman
 Artistic Director: Chris Vine
 Managing Director: Leslie White
 Playwright-In-Residence: Jim Mirrione
Founded: 1974
Specialized Field: Musical; Comedy; Community Theater; Puppet; Classic; Contemporary
Status: Non-Profit, Professional
Paid Staff: 60
Paid Artists: 40
Income Sources: New York State Council on Arts; Theatre Communications Group; New York University
Organization Type: Performing; Touring; Resident; Educational

3062
DISNEY THEATRICAL PRODUCTIONS
1450 Broadway
#300
New York, NY 10018
Phone: 212-827-5400
Fax: 212-703-1048
e-mail: michele.gold@disney.com
 Booking Assistant/Domestic Touring: Jim Lanahan
Specialized Field: Disney Theater; Touring Company

3063
DIXON PLACE
161A Chrystie St
New York, NY 10002

Phone: 212-219-0736
Fax: 212-219-0761
e-mail: contact@dixonplace.org
Web Site: http://dixonplace.org/index2.html
Management:
 Executive Director: Ellie Covan
 Managing Director: Emily Morgan
Founded: 1986
Specialized Field: Ensembles; Contemporary
Performs At: Dixon Place
Type of Stage: Thrust
Seating Capacity: 70

3064
DO GOODER PRODUCTIONS
359 W 54th Street
Suite 4FS
New York, NY 10019
Phone: 212-581-8852
e-mail: dgp@dogooder.org
Web Site: www.dogooder.org
Management:
 Founding/Artistic Executive Directo: Mark Robert Gordon
Mission: Not for profit, off Broadway theatre company that works in partnership with designated charities.
Founded: 1994
Specialized Field: Theatre
Paid Staff: 2

3065
DON QUIJOTE CHILDREN'S THEATRE
250 W 65th Street
New York, NY 10023
Phone: 212-579-2358
Management:
 Artistic Director: Oswaldo Pradere
 Resident Director: Stefanie Scott
 Administrator: Jim Finn
 Administrative Assistant: Wendy Samuel
Mission: To inspire, entertain and educate children through theatre.
Founded: 1972
Specialized Field: Musical; Children's Theater; Puppet
Status: Professional; Nonprofit
Organization Type: Performing; Touring; Resident; Educational

3066
DOWNTOWN ART COMPANY
64 E 4Th Street
New York, NY 10003
Phone: 212-479-0085
e-mail: info@downtownart.org
Web Site: http://downtownart.org/
Management:
 Artistic Director: Ryan Gilliam
 Producing Director: Cliff Scott
 Artistic Associate: Dan Hurlin
 Artistic Associate: Dan Froot
Mission: To support the development of contemporary performance works.
Utilizes: Singers
Founded: 1987
Specialized Field: Contemporary
Status: Professional; Nonprofit
Income Sources: National Association of Artists; Alliance of Resident Theatres/New York
Organization Type: Performing; Touring; Sponsoring

3067
DRAMA DEPARTMENT
451 Greenwich Street
7th Floor
New York, NY 10013
Phone: 212-633-9108
Fax: 212-633-9578
e-mail: info@dramadept.org
Web Site: www.dramadept.org
Officers:
 Development Director: Clinton Cargill
 Ticketing Director: Cheryl French
Management:
 Artistic Director: Douglas Carter Beane
 Managing Director: Michael S Rosenberg
 Head Production: Ilene Rosen
 Director Operations: Alexis Rehrmann
 Director Development: Clinton Cargill
 Director Ticketing: Cheryl French
Mission: A collective of actors, directors, designers, writers and stage managers who collaborate to create new works and revive neglected classics.
Utilizes: AEA Actors; Choreographers; Designers; Filmmakers; Five Seasonal Concerts; Instructors; Local Unknown Artists; Multimedia; Music; Original Music Scores; Performance Artists; Poets; Resident Artists; Resident Professionals; Sign Language Translators; Visual Arts
Founded: 1995
Specialized Field: New Plays; Classic
Status: Non-Profit, Professional
Paid Staff: 2
Volunteer Staff: 2
Budget: $1,000,000
Income Sources: Ticket sales; Grants; Private contributions
Season: July - June
Annual Attendance: 10,000+
Facility Category: Great theatre in old settlement house
Type of Stage: Proscenium
Stage Dimensions: 35'x20'
Seating Capacity: 99
Year Built: 1916
Year Remodeled: 2001
Cost: $3,000,000+
Rental Contact: Alexis Rehrmann

3068
EMERGING ARTISTS THEATRE COMPANY
518 9th Avenue
Suite 2
New York, NY 10018
Phone: 212-627-5792
e-mail: info@eatheatre.org
Officers:
 President: Roland Dib
 Senior VP: Brad Punty
 VP: Leigh Giroux
 Treasurer: Dara Falco
Management:
 Artistic Director: Paul Adams
 Manager For Directors: Blake Lawrence
 Manager For Playwrights: Johnathan Reuing
 Managing Director: Brad Punty
 Sales And Marketing: Ilona Lima
 Development Director: Donna Moreau
Mission: Emerging Artists Theatre Company exists to provide a safe and secure home for new playwrights to develop their work from an idea to fully realized production and where the playwright remains the key component in the creation and birth of that work.

Founded: 1993
Specialized Field: New Plays; Young Playwrights

3069
EN GARDE ARTS
225 Rector Place
Suite 3A
New York, NY 10280
Phone: 212-941-9793
Fax: 212-274-8123
Management:
    Managing Director: Ron Aja
    Director Development: Mary McBride
Mission: To commission artists for the purpose of creating theatrical productions that are inspired by socially, historically or architecturally significant sites.
Specialized Field: Experimental; Touring Company
Status: Professional; Nonprofit
Organization Type: Performing

3070
ENSEMBLE STUDIO THEATRE
549 W 52nd Street
New York, NY 10019
Phone: 212-247-4982
Fax: 212-664-0041
e-mail: postmaster@ensemblestudiotheatre.org
Web Site: www.ensembloestudiotheatre.org
Management:
    Artistic Director: Curt Dempster
    Managing Director: John McCormick
Mission: To nurture and develop the American theatre artist.
Utilizes: Actors; AEA Actors; Choreographers; Dance Companies; Designers; Educators; Guest Designers; Guest Teachers; High School Drama; Instructors; Local Artists; Original Music Scores; Performance Artists; Resident Artists; Resident Professionals; Soloists
Founded: 1972
Specialized Field: Ensembles; New Plays
Status: Non-Profit, Professional
Paid Staff: 14
Volunteer Staff: 25
Paid Artists: 500
Budget: $ 1.3 Million
Season: October - June
Performs At: The Ensemble Studio Theatre
Type of Stage: Black Box; Proscenium
Seating Capacity: 99; 60
Organization Type: Performing

3071
ERGO THEATRE COMPANY
Times Square Station
PO Box 290
New York, NY 10108
Phone: 212-501-2710
e-mail: info@ergotheatre.org
Management:
    Artistic Director: Robert Jay Cronin
    Managing Director: Johanna Pinzler
    Business Manager: Katherine Clark Helzer
Mission: Ergo Theatre Company is making a new home for bright rising talent in the New York theatre community.
Founded: 1997
Specialized Field: Theater Workshops; Staged Readings
Status: Non-Profit

3072
FIJI COMPANY
47 Great Jones Street
New York, NY 10012

Phone: 212-254-7228
Management:
    Artistic Director: Ping Chong
    Managing Director: Joe Jeffcoat
Mission: Created out of a desire to incorporate the visual arts (dance, film, video and theater) into a multimedia show questioning the syntax of global theater.
Utilizes: Singers
Founded: 1972
Specialized Field: Multi-Cultural
Status: Professional; Nonprofit
Income Sources: Theatre Communications Group; Alliance of Resident Theatres/New York
Organization Type: Performing; Touring; Resident; Educational

3073
FREDERICK DOUGLASS CREATIVE ARTS CENTER
270 W 96th Street
New York, NY 10025
Phone: 212-864-3375
Fax: 212-864-3474
e-mail: fdcac@aol.com
Web Site: www.fdcac.org
Management:
    President: Fred Hudson
    Executive Director: Mark Johnson
    Executive Administrator: Yvonne Hudson
Mission: A writers development organization which includes a performance component.
Utilizes: Singers
Founded: 1971
Specialized Field: Community Theater; Classic; Contemporary
Status: Non-Profit, Non-Professional
Paid Staff: 25
Paid Artists: 25
Organization Type: Resident

3074
GLINES
240 W 44th Street
New York, NY 10036
Phone: 212-354-8899
e-mail: theglines@aol.com
Officers:
    President/Treasurer: John Glines
    VP: Steve Carpenter
    Secretary: Malcolm Wexchler
    Board of Director: Mark Hostetter
Management:
    Artistic Director: John Glines
Mission: To promote positive gay images and dispel negative stereotyping.
Founded: 1976
Specialized Field: Alternative
Status: Nonprofit
Organization Type: Performing

3075
HARBOR THEATRE
160 W 71st Street
PHA
New York, NY 10023
Phone: 212-787-1945
e-mail: swarmflash@harbortheatre.org
Web Site: www.harbortheatre.org
Management:
    Artistic Director: Stuart Warmflash
    Webmaster: Mark E Lang
    Artistic Associate: Marc Gellar

Mission: In 1994 a group of writers, under that artistic leadership of Stuart Warmflash, began a theatre workshop that would focus on the written word. Its purpose was to provide a safe haven for a few dedicated playwrights to express and refine their personal vision.
Founded: 1994
Specialized Field: Contemporary; Drama
Status: Non-Profit, Professional

3076
HARLEM ARTISTS DEVELOPMENT LEAGUE
207 W 133rd Street
New York, NY 10030
Phone: 212-368-9314
Fax: 212-368-9314
e-mail: harlemplayer@yahoo.com
Web Site: www.harlemplayer.org
Officers:
    Chairwoman of the Board: Delores Dixon
    CEO: Gertrude Jeanette
Management:
    Founder: Gerturde Jeanette
    Artistic Director: Janice Jenkins
    Managing Director: Eric Coleman
Mission: To offer professional theatre to residents of the Harlem community at modest prices; to train artists in speech, acting and dance.
Utilizes: Singers
Founded: 1975
Specialized Field: New Plays; African American; Theater Workshops
Status: Non-Profit, Professional
Paid Staff: 4
Volunteer Staff: 20
Non-paid Artists: 50
Income Sources: NY State Council on the Arise-NYC Cultural Affairs
Performs At: Saint Philips Church
Organization Type: Performing; Resident; Educational

3077
HENSON INTERNATIONAL FESTIVAL OF PUPPET THEATRE
584 Broadway
Suite 1007
New York, NY 10021
Phone: 212-680-1400
Fax: 212-680-1401
e-mail: info@hensonfestival.org
Web Site: www.hensonfestival.org
Management:
    President: Cheryl Henson
    VP: Jane Henson
    Development Officer: Meg Daniel
Mission: To present the finest international puppet artists to American audiences.
Founded: 1992
Specialized Field: Puppet
Status: Nonprofit
Performs At: Joseph Papp Public Theater
Organization Type: Sponsoring

3078
HERE ARTS CENTER
145 6th Avenue Front 1
New York, NY 10013
Phone: 212-647-0202
Fax: 212-647-0257
e-mail: info@here.org
Web Site: www.here.org
Management:

Executive Director: Kristen Marting
Producer: Barbara Busackijno
General Manager: Toni Marie Davis
Founder: Randy Rollison
Mission: To support emerging and mid-career artist in all disciplines.
Founded: 1993
Specialized Field: Multi-Media
Status: Nonprofit
Paid Staff: 21
Volunteer Staff: 6
Budget: $1.2 million
Income Sources: Earned; Contributions
Affiliations: Art NY Member
Annual Attendance: 75,000
Facility Category: Multi-Arts Center
Type of Stage: Flexible
Seating Capacity: 99
Year Built: 1993

3079
HISPANIC ORGANIZATION OF LATIN ACTORS

107 Suffolk Street
Suite 302
New York, NY 10002
Phone: 212-253-1015
Fax: 212-799-6718
e-mail: holagram@hellohola.org
Web Site: www.hellohola.org
Officers:
    Chairman HOLA Board: Gonzalo Armendariz
    Executive Director: Manny Alfaro
Mission: To offer workshops, advocacy-training and referrals.
Utilizes: Singers
Founded: 1975
Specialized Field: Spanish Language Company
Status: Non-Profit, Professional
Paid Staff: 4
Paid Artists: 4
Organization Type: Arts Service Organization

3080
HUDSON GUILD THEATRE

441 W 26th Street
New York, NY 10001
Phone: 212-760-9800
Fax: 212-268-9983
e-mail: info@hudsonguild.org
Web Site: www.hudsonguild.org
Officers:
    President: Arthur Aufses
    Chairman: Paul Balser
Management:
    Theatre Director: Jim Furlong
Utilizes: Actors; Commissioned Composers; Commissioned Music; Composers-in-Residence; Five Seasonal Concerts; Guest Accompanists; Guest Choreographers; Guest Conductors; Guest Designers; Local Artists; Performance Artists; Resident Professionals; Singers; Special Technical Talent
Founded: 1895
Specialized Field: Community Theater
Status: Non-Profit
Paid Staff: 1
Budget: $35,000
Facility Category: Theatre
Stage Dimensions: 28'x29'
Seating Capacity: 104
Rental Contact: Jim Furlong
Organization Type: Performing

3081
IGLOO, THE THEATRICAL GROUP

225 E 4th Street
Apartment 6
New York, NY 10009
Phone: 212-460-9055
Management:
    Artistic Director: Maria Taribassi
    Artistic Director: Chris Peditto
    Artistic Director: Paul Peditto
Mission: Dedicated to ensemble production of new and rarely seen works.
Founded: 1985
Specialized Field: Musical; New Plays
Status: Professional; Nonprofit
Paid Staff: 10
Organization Type: Performing; Resident

3082
INTAR THEATRE

500 W 52nd Street, 4th Floor
PO Box 756
New York, NY 10108
Mailing Address: PO Box 756, New York, NY, 10108
Phone: 212-695-6134
Fax: 212-268-0102
e-mail: intar@intartheatre.org
Web Site: www.intartheatre.org
Management:
    Executive Director: Editha Rosario
    Artistic Director: Eduardo Machado
    Founder: Max Ferra
Mission: INTAR brings to the public the vital and energetic voices of both promising & accomplished Latin theatre professionals.
Utilizes: Actors; AEA Actors; Curators; Designers; Fine Artists; Local Artists; Performance Artists; Resident Professionals; Singers; Visual Arts
Founded: 1966
Specialized Field: New Plays; Spanish Language Company
Status: Non-Profit, Professional
Paid Staff: 5
Income Sources: Non-profit funding
Season: October - June
Affiliations: Theatre Communications Group, Alliance of Resident Theatres (NY)
Facility Category: Off-Broadway Theater
Organization Type: Performing

3083
INTERBOROUGH REPERTORY THEATER

154 Christopher Street
Suite 3B
New York, NY 10014
Phone: 212-206-6875
Fax: 212-206-7037
e-mail: info@irttheater.org
Web Site: http://irttheater.org
Officers:
    President: Mimi Craig
    Secretary: Pamala L La Bonne
Management:
    Artistic Director: Kori Rushton
    Executive Director: Jonathan Fluck
    Development Director: Stacy Donovan
Mission: To offer adaptations of literature and history as well as issues of interest to disenfranchised audiences; to provide standard repertory for general audiences.
Utilizes: Singers
Founded: 1986
Specialized Field: Musical; Historical

Status: Semi-Professional; Nonprofit
Income Sources: Brooklyn Arts & Cultural Association; Actors' Equity Association; Encore; Saturday Theater for Children; Division of American Theater Wing
Organization Type: Performing; Touring; Educational

3084
IRISH ARTS CENTRE THEATRE

553 W 51st Street
New York, NY 10019
Phone: 212-757-3318
Fax: 212-247-0930
e-mail: info@irishartscenter.org
Web Site: http://irishartscenter.org/
Management:
    Artistic Director: Neal Jones
Mission: Preserving, celebrating and developing Irish culture in America through producing New Irish, Classic Irish, and Irish-American plays.
Founded: 1972
Specialized Field: Children's Theater; Theater Workshops
Status: Professional; Nonprofit
Paid Staff: 50
Volunteer Staff: 30
Season: Year-Round
Performs At: Irish Arts Center Theatre
Stage Dimensions: 23x15x1000
Seating Capacity: 99
Year Built: 1972
Year Remodeled: 1995
Organization Type: Performing; Resident

3085
IRONDALE ENSEMBLE PROJECT

PO Box 150604
New York, NY 11215
Phone: 718-488-9233
Fax: 718-488-9185
e-mail: irondalert@aol.com
Web Site: www.irondale.org
Officers:
    Managing Director: Maria Knapp
Founded: 1983
Specialized Field: Comedy; Youth Theater; Classic; Contemporary
Status: Non-Profit, Professional
Paid Staff: 4
Paid Artists: 8

3086
JAM AND COMPANY

331 W 38th Street
#5
New York, NY 10018
Phone: 212-714-2263
Fax: 212-594-1245
Management:
    Artistic Director: John Amudd
Founded: 1985
Specialized Field: Drama; Contemporary
Status: Semi-Professional
Organization Type: Performing

3087
JEAN COCTEAU REPERTORY

330 Bowery
New York, NY 10012
Phone: 212-677-0060
Fax: 212-777-6151
e-mail: cocteau@jeancocteaurep.org
Web Site: www.jeancocteaurep.org
Officers:
    President: David Jiranek

VP: John Horn
Secretary: Carmen Anthony
Management:
President: Mark Gamell
Artistic Director: David Fuller
Managing Director: Merediph Zolty
Director Development: Deborah Aaronson
Mission: Committed to presenting innovative productions of the world's classics; dedicated to sustaining a resident company presenting rotating repertory.
Utilizes: Actors; Artists-in-Residence; Choreographers; Collaborating Artists; Commissioned Music; Designers; Guest Artists; Guest Companies; Guest Conductors; Guest Designers; Guest Lecturers; Music; Original Music Scores; Performance Artists; Resident Artists; Resident Professionals; Soloists; Student Interns; Theatre Companies
Founded: 1971
Specialized Field: Musical; Comedy; Classic; Contemporary
Status: Non-Profit, Professional
Paid Staff: 10
Volunteer Staff: 5
Paid Artists: 20
Budget: $850,000
Income Sources: Box Office; Individuals; Corporations; Foundation
Performs At: Bouwerie Lane Theatre
Affiliations: Theatre Communications Group; Alliance of Resident Theatres/New York
Annual Attendance: 22,000
Facility Category: Theatre
Type of Stage: Proscenium
Stage Dimensions: 17'x22'x13'
Seating Capacity: 140
Year Built: 1960
Year Remodeled: 1996
Rental Contact: Ernest Johns
Organization Type: Performing; Resident; Educational
Resident Groups: Jean Cocteau Repertory

3088
JEWISH REPERTORY THEATRE

15 East 40th Street
#303
New York, NY 10016
Phone: 212-254-6564
Fax: 212-831-0082
Management:
Artistic Director: Rau Avni
Managing Director: Kathleen Germann
Assoc. Artistic Director/Literary: Richard Sabellico
Mission: To present works in English which relate to Jewish experience.
Specialized Field: Jewish; Drama; Comedy
Status: Professional; Nonprofit
Income Sources: Actors' Equity Association
Performs At: Jewish Repertory Theatre
Organization Type: Performing

3089
KOHAV THEATRE FOUNDATION

118 Riverside Drive
New York, NY 10024
Phone: 212-877-1667
Fax: 212-799-3589
Management:
President: Hava Beller
Production Assistant: Kathleen Greene
Counsel: Herbert C Kantor
Utilizes: Singers
Founded: 1979

Specialized Field: Contemporary
Status: Non-Profit, Professional
Organization Type: Performing

3090
LA MAMA EXPERIMENTAL THEATRE

74A E 4th Street
New York, NY 10003
Phone: 212-254-6468
Fax: 212-254-7597
e-mail: lamama@lamama.org
Web Site: www.lamama.org
Management:
President: Frank Carucci
Founder/Director: Ellen Stewart
Associate Director: Beverly Petty
Business Manager: Gretchen Green
Utilizes: Student Interns; Touring Companies; Visual Arts
Founded: 1961
Specialized Field: Experimental
Status: Non-Profit, Professional
Budget: $1,500,000
Income Sources: Foundations; Government; Ticket Revenue; Playwright Royalties
Performs At: Experimantal Theatre; Dance; Opera
Annual Attendance: 30,000
Facility Category: Theatre (3 venues) 1 Gallery
Seating Capacity: 100; 400
Organization Type: Performing; Producing

3091
LAMB'S THEATRE COMPANY

130 W 44th Street
New York, NY 10036
Phone: 212-575-0300
Fax: 212-302-7847
e-mail: office@lambstheatre.org
Web Site: http://www.lambstheatre.org/
Officers:
Chairman: Kendyl K Monroe
Secretary: Patricia McCorkle
Management:
Producing Director: Carolyn Rossi-Copeland
Production Manager: Clark Cameron
Mission: To develop and present the work of new American theatre artists hoping to offer positive solutions to modern ethical problems.
Founded: 1980
Specialized Field: New American Works
Status: Professional; Nonprofit
Income Sources: Theatre Communications Group; Alliance of Resident Theatres/New York
Performs At: Lamb's Theatre; Lamb's Little Theatre
Organization Type: Performing; Touring; Educational

3092
LATIN AMERICAN THEATRE EXPERIMENT & ASSOCIATES

107 Suffolk Street
New York, NY 10002
Phone: 212-529-1948
Management:
Executive Director: Margarita Toirac
Founder: Mario Pena
Mission: Our purpose is to expand the theatre movement to the Spanish and English communities.
Founded: 1970
Specialized Field: Spanish Language Company; Experimental
Status: Professional; Nonprofit
Type of Stage: Proscenium
Stage Dimensions: 25'x20'x14'
Seating Capacity: 150

Organization Type: Performing; Touring; Resident; Educational

3093
LES BALLETS GRANDIVA

101 W 67th Street
Suite 49 E
New York, NY 10023
Phone: 212-875-0951
Fax: 212-875-0952
e-mail: grandiva01@aol.com
Web Site: www.balletsgrandiva.com
Officers:
President: Suguru Aito
Management:
Artistic Director: Victor Trevino
Mission: To develop sance audiences by performing comedic parodies of a wide range of choreographic styles both classical and contemporary.
Founded: 1996
Specialized Field: Comedy; Classic; Contemporary
Status: Non-Profit, Professional
Paid Staff: 2
Paid Artists: 19
Budget: $600,000
Income Sources: Performance Fees; Donations
Annual Attendance: 80,000

3094
LIGHTNING STRIKES THEATRE COMPANY

PO Box 1545
New York, NY 10028
Phone: 212-713-5335
Management:
Artistic Director: John Mcdermott
Managing Director: Lori Funk
Literary Manager: DL Shroder
Specialized Field: Experimental; New Plays

3095
LIVING THEATRE

272 E 3rd Street
New York, NY 10009
Phone: 212-982-2335
Fax: 212-865-3234
Officers:
President: Hanon Reznikov
Management:
Executive Director: Hanon Reznikov
Artistic Director: Judith Malina
Managing Director: Joanie Fritz
Managing Associate: Isha Manna Beck
Mission: To create socially relevant theatre to be performed by an artistic ensemble of the highest calibre.
Founded: 1947
Specialized Field: New Works of Social Importance
Status: Nonprofit
Income Sources: Alliance of Resident Theatres/New York; Theatre Communications Group
Organization Type: Performing; Touring; Resident; Educational

3096
MABOU MINES

150 1st Avenue
2nd Floor
New York, NY 10009
Phone: 212-473-0559
Fax: 212-473-2410
e-mail: office@maboumines.org
Web Site: www.maboumines.org
Officers:

President: Sharon Fogarty
Management:
    President: Joe Stalkell
    Artistic Director: Ruth Maleczech
Mission: To look at theater in fresh ways by re-exploring existing theatrical works and creating new ones.
Utilizes: Singers
Founded: 1970
Specialized Field: Classic; Contemporary
Status: Non-Profit, Professional
Affiliations: Theatre Communications Group; Alliance of Resident Theatres/New York
Type of Stage: Block Box
Organization Type: Performing; Touring; Educational

3097
MANHATTAN THEATRE CLUB
311 W 43rd Street
8th Floor
New York, NY 10036
Phone: 212-399-3000
Fax: 212-399-4329
e-mail: questions@mtc-nyc.org
Web Site: www.manhattantheatreclub.com
Management:
    Artistic Director: Lynne Meadow
    Executive Producer: Barry Grove
    General Manager: Florie Seery
Mission: Encouraging, developing, and presenting important new American and international work that provides insight into culture, life and conflict.
Founded: 1970
Specialized Field: Musical; Comedy; Ethnic Theater; Contemporary
Status: Non-Profit, Professional
Paid Staff: 60
Volunteer Staff: 25
Income Sources: Theatre Communications Group; Alliance of Resident Theatres/New York; Foundation for the Extension and Development of American Professional Theatre
Organization Type: Performing

3098
MARCEL MARCEAU
253 W 73rd Street
Suite 8G
New York, NY 10023
Phone: 212-874-2030
Fax: 212-874-1175
e-mail: staff@marceau.org
Specialized Field: Mime

3099
MCC THEATER
145 W 28th Street
New York, NY 10001
Phone: 212-727-7722
Fax: 212-727-7780
e-mail: mcc@mcctheater.org
Web Site: www.mcctheater.org
Management:
    Executive Director: John Schultz
    Artistic Director: Robert Lupone
    Literary Manager: Stephen Willems
    Associate Artistic Director: William Cantler
    Office Manager: Greta Rothman
    General Manager: Jodi Schoenbrun
Founded: 1986
Specialized Field: Drama; Musical
Status: Non-Profit, Professional
Paid Staff: 9
Paid Artists: 6

3100
METROPOLITAN PLAYHOUSE
220 E 4th Street
New York, NY 10009
Phone: 212-995-8410
e-mail: connect@metropolitianplayhouse.org
Web Site: www.metropolitianplayhouse.org
Management:
    President: Alex Roe
    Comapany Manager: Ed Chemaly
    Literary Manager: Kim Wadsworth
Founded: 1992
Specialized Field: Drama; Comedy; Musical
Status: Non-Profit, Professional
Paid Artists: 4

3101
MIRROR REPERTORY COMPANY
50 E 96 Street
New York, NY 10128
Phone: 212-427-7393
Fax: 212-427-7393
Toll-free: 866-647-7371
e-mail: info@mirrorrepertoryco.com
Web Site: www.mirrorrepertoryco.com
Management:
    Board Chairman: Donna Ward
    Managing Director: Marilyn Miller
    Artistic Director: Sabra Jones
Mission: The Mirror Repertory Company, aka Mirror Theatre Ltd., was founded in 1983. It was a daring return to the European theatre style of alternating repertory theatre—a different play each night as in the ballet and the opera.
Founded: 1982
Specialized Field: Musical; Comedy; Youth Theater; Ethnic Theater; Classic; Contemporary
Status: Non-Profit, Professional
Paid Staff: 6
Income Sources: Actors' Equity Association
Performs At: Mirror Repertory Theater
Organization Type: Performing; Resident; Educational

3102
MUSIC THEATRE ASSOCIATES
1841 Broadway
Suite 914
New York, NY 10023
Phone: 212-841-9690
Fax: 212-841-9542
e-mail: jsimpson@cami.com
Web Site: www.camitheatricals.com
Management:
    President: Gary McKvay
    COO: Aldo Scrofani
    Head of Music Theatre Associates: Jann Simpson
Founded: 1981
Specialized Field: Musical; Contemporary; New Plays
Paid Staff: 100
Paid Artists: 100

3103
MUSIC THEATRE GROUP AT LENOX ARTS CENTER
30 W 26th Street #1001
New York, NY 10010
Phone: 212-366-5260
Fax: 212-366-5265
Officers:
    Co- Chairman: Katheryn Walker
    Co- Chairman: Charles Hollerith
    President: Lyn Austin

    VP: Lynda Sthrner Traum
Management:
    Producing Director: Lyn Austin
    General Director: Diane Wondisford
    Associate Producer: Charlotte Kreutz
    Development: Peter Krasny
Mission: Exclusively engaged in and dedicated to the creation of new musical theatre works with distinctive focus on developing new forms and artists through unique combinations of music, theatre, dance and visual arts.
Utilizes: Singers
Founded: 1970
Specialized Field: Musical; New Plays
Status: Professional; Nonprofit
Budget: $80,000
Income Sources: Box Office, Grants, Private Donations
Organization Type: Performing; Touring

3104
NATIONAL BLACK THEATRE
2033 5th Avenue
New York, NY 10035
Phone: 212-722-3800
Fax: 212-926-1571
e-mail: info@nationalblacktheatre.org
Web Site: http://www.nationalblacktheatre.org/
Officers:
    Founder/CEO: Barbara Ann Teer
Management:
    Executive Director: Shirley Faison
    Performing Program Director: Tunde Samuel
    Action Arts Director: Ade Faison
    Rental Program Director: Nabi Faison
Mission: To enhance human dignity by increasing the unity, appreciation and availability of Black Theatre.
Founded: 1968
Specialized Field: African American
Status: Professional; Nonprofit
Affiliations: Harlem Strategic Cultural Collaborative, Coalition of Theatres of Color and Harlem Arts Alliance

3105
NATIONAL BLACK TOURING CIRCUIT
790 Riverside Drive
Suite 3E
New York, NY 10032
Phone: 212-283-0974
Fax: 212-283-0983
Officers:
    Co-Chairman: Shaunielle Perry
Management:
    Producer/Director: Woodie King Jr
    Associate Producer: Ashia Dervisa
Mission: To tour plays to colleges, festivals, and black cultural institutions across the USA, Europe, and Africa.
Utilizes: Singers; Special Technical Talent; Theatre Companies
Founded: 1976
Specialized Field: African American; Touring Company
Status: Professional; Nonprofit
Paid Staff: 3
Paid Artists: 25
Non-paid Artists: 2
Budget: $240,000
Income Sources: Contracted Services
Organization Type: Performing; Touring; Resident; Educational

3106
NATIONAL IMPROVISATIONAL THEATRE
223 8th Avenue
New York, NY 10011

Phone: 212-243-7224
Fax: 212-366-4312
Management:
  Executive Director: Christopher Smith
  Artistic Director: Tamara Wilcox-Smith
  VP Public Relations: Robert Martin
  VP Operations: Eva Mahoney
Mission: To bring art improvisation to the highest possible level.
Founded: 1984
Specialized Field: Improvisation
Status: Professional; Nonprofit
Paid Staff: 30
Organization Type: Performing; Educational

3107
NATIONAL SHAKESPEARE COMPANY

353 W 48th Street
3Rd Floor
New York, NY 10036
Phone: 212-265-1340
Fax: 212-265-1258
e-mail: nsc62@aol.com
Management:
  Producing Director: Deborah Teller
  Tour Director: Val Sherman
  Education Director: Heather Drastal
Mission: Nurturing and developing performing arts through touring professional, live theatre to American communities.
Founded: 1963
Specialized Field: Touring Company; Shakespeare
Status: Professional
Season: September - May
Organization Type: Performing; Touring

3108
NEGRO ENSEMBLE COMPANY

154 Christopher Street
#2A-A
New York, NY 10014
Phone: 212-691-6730
Fax: 212-691-6798
e-mail: newgroup1@earthlink.net
Web Site: www.newgrouptheatre.com
Management:
  Artistic Director: Scott Elliot
  Executive Director: Geoffrey Rich
  Literary Manager: Ian Morgan
  Associate Executive Director: Josh Boggioni
Mission: To offer plays about the Black experience.
Utilizes: Singers
Founded: 1967
Specialized Field: African American; Multi-Cultural
Status: Professional; Nonprofit
Performs At: Theatre Four
Organization Type: Performing; Touring

3109
NEW DRAMATISTS

424 W 44th Street
New York, NY 10036
Phone: 212-757-6960
Fax: 212-265-4738
e-mail: newdramatists@newdramatists.org
Web Site: www.newdramatists.org
Officers:
  Chairman: Seth Gelblum
  President: Isobel Robins Koneccy
Management:
  Executive Director: Joel K Rukark
  Artistic Director: Todd London
Mission: To develop plays and playwrights.
Founded: 1949

Specialized Field: New Plays; Young Playwrights
Status: Non-Profit, Professional
Paid Staff: 7
Volunteer Staff: 50
Non-paid Artists: 55
Income Sources: National Endowment for the Arts
Performs At: New Dramatists Theater
Organization Type: Resident; Educational

3110
NEW FEDERAL THEATRE

292 Henry Street
New York, NY 10002
Phone: 212-353-1176
Fax: 212-353-1088
e-mail: newfederal@aol.com
Web Site: www.newfederaltheatre.org
Management:
  Producing Director: Woodie King Jr
  Company Director: Pat White
  Marketing Director: Shea Douglas
  Office Administrator: Andrena Hale
Mission: To present both new and unknown works; to allow unknown and known directors and actors the opportunity to work together.
Utilizes: Actors; AEA Actors; Performance Artists; Resident Professionals
Founded: 1970
Specialized Field: Musical; Comedy; Community Theater; Classic; Contemporary
Status: Non-Profit, Professional
Income Sources: Actors' Equity Association; Alliance of Resident Theatres/New York; Theatre Communications Group; Foundations; Corporate and Private Individuals
Season: September 30 - June 30
Performs At: Henry Street Settlement; New Federal Theater
Organization Type: Performing; Resident

3111
NEW GEORGES

109 W 27th Street
Suite 9A
New York, NY 10001
Phone: 646-336-8077
Fax: 646-336-8077
e-mail: info@newgeorges.org
Web Site: www.newgeorges.org
Management:
  Artistic Director: Susan Bernfield
  Associate Director: Sarah C Sunde
Founded: 1992
Specialized Field: Women's Theater
Status: Non-Profit, Professional
Paid Staff: 2
Paid Artists: 30

3112
NEW RAFT THEATER COMPANY

450 W 42nd Street
Suite 2J
New York, NY 10036
Phone: 212-268-5501
Fax: 212-967-1458
Management:
  Executive Director: Eric Krebs
  Artistic Director: Avi Ber Hoffman
  Executive Director: Eric Krebs
Mission: To find and develop original plays and musicals.
Founded: 1976
Specialized Field: Musical; New Plays
Status: Professional; Nonprofit

Performs At: Houseman Theatre Complex
Organization Type: Performing

3113
NEW VICTORY THEATER

229 W 42nd Street
10th Floor
New York, NY 10036
Phone: 646-223-3000
Fax: 646-562-0175
e-mail: info@new42.org
Web Site: www.newvictory.org
Officers:
  President: Cora Cahan
Founded: 1995
Specialized Field: Musical; Comedy; Ethnic Theater; Classic; Contemporary; Children's Theater
Status: Non-Profit, Professional
Paid Staff: 150

3114
NEW YORK STAGE & FILM

315 West 6th Street
Suite 905
New York, NY 10001
Phone: 212-736-4240
Fax: 212-736-4241
e-mail: info@newyorkstageandfilm.org
Web Site: http://www.newyorkstageandfilm.org/
Officers:
  President: Marc Segan
Management:
  Artistic Director: Johanna Pfaelzer
  Associate Producer: Kyle Frisina
Founded: 1984
Specialized Field: New Plays

3115
NEW YORK THEATRE WORKSHOP

79 E 4th Street
New York, NY 10003
Phone: 212-780-9037
Fax: 212-460-8996
e-mail: info@nytw.org
Web Site: www.nytw.org
Management:
  President: Jim Nicola
  Artistic Director: James C Nicola
  Managing Director: Lynn Moffat
Mission: To offer inventive new plays; to showcase new directors.
Founded: 1980
Specialized Field: Theater Workshops; Educational
Status: Non-Profit, Professional
Paid Staff: 25
Volunteer Staff: 25
Paid Artists: 150
Non-paid Artists: 300
Income Sources: Actors' Equity Association; Theatre Communications Group; Alliance of Resident Theatres/New York
Performs At: New York Theatre Workshop
Type of Stage: Proscenium
Seating Capacity: 189
Organization Type: Performing

3116
OHIO THEATRE

66 Wooster
New York, NY 10012
Phone: 212-966-4844
Management:
  Artistic Director: Robert Lyons
Mission: To offer experimental theatre.

Founded: 1977
Specialized Field: Experimental
Status: Professional
Income Sources: Downtown Theatre Coalition
Performs At: Ohio Theatre
Organization Type: Performing; Sponsoring

3117
ONTOLOGICAL-HYSTERIC THEATER

260 West Broadway
New York, NY 10013
Phone: 212-941-8911
Fax: 212-334-5149
e-mail: ontological@mindspring.com
Web Site: www.ontological.com
Management:
   Artistic Director: Richard Foreman
   Administrator: Mimi Johnson
Mission: Producing and presenting the works of
playwright, director and designer Richard Foreman.
Founded: 1968
Specialized Field: New Plays; Contemporary
Status: Non-Profit
Paid Staff: 1
Paid Artists: 8
Performs At: Ontological at St. Mark's Theater
Type of Stage: Black box
Seating Capacity: 85
Organization Type: Performing

3118
OPEN BOOK

525 W End Avenue
12E
New York, NY 10024-3207
Phone: 212-362-9014
e-mail: theopenbook@juno.com
Web Site: www.theopenbook.net
Officers:
   Board: Mary Higgins Clark
   Board: Mario Fratti
   Board: Rev Kathleen L Camera
   Board: Marc Lewis
   Board: Beverly Penberthy
Management:
   Artistic Director: Marvin Kaye
   Public Relations Director: Nancy Temple
   Educational Division Director: Kathleen C Szaj
Mission: Producing new and little-known literature of
quality in readers theatre format.
Founded: 1975
Specialized Field: Reading Theatre
Status: Professional; Nonprofit
Volunteer Staff: 3
Income Sources: Various
Performs At: Various
Annual Attendance: 300 - 500
Type of Stage: Modified Platform
Stage Dimensions: Varies
Seating Capacity: 70 - 100
Organization Type: Performing; Touring; Resident

3119
OPEN EYE: NEW STAGINGS

270 W 89th Street
New York, NY 10024
Fax: 212-769-4141
Officers:
   Chairman: Stephen Graham
   VP: Joan Stein
   Secretary: Elliot Brown
Management:
   Founding Director: Jean Erdman
   Artistic Director: Amie Brockway

Production Manager/Business Manager:
   Adrienne Brockway
Mission: Presents productions of new and rare plays,
plays geared for family audiences and provides
playwrights the opportunity to develop new works
through the New Stagings Lab.
Utilizes: Singers
Founded: 1972
Specialized Field: New Plays
Status: Professional; Nonprofit
Income Sources: Theatre Communications Group;
Alliance of Resident Theatres/New York; International
Association of Theatre for Children and Youth
Performs At: The Open Eye; New Stagings
Organization Type: Performing; Touting; Educational

3120
PAN ASIAN REPERTORY THEATRE

520 8th Avenue
3rd Floor, Room 314
New York, NY 10018
Mailing Address: 47 Great Jones Street, New York,
NY, 10012
Phone: 212-868-4030
Fax: 212-868-4033
e-mail: panasian@aol.com
Web Site: www.panasianrep.org
Officers:
   Chairman: Sybil Nadel
   Vice Chairman: Muzaffar Chishti
Management:
   Chairman: Sybel Nadel
   Artistic Producing Director: Tisa Chang
   Communications Director: Sylvie H Fan
   Artistic Associate: Ron Nakahara
Mission: To offer new Asian-American plays of the
highest artistic standards, as well as adaptations of
classics from around the world; to premiere Asian
masterworks in America.
Founded: 1983
Specialized Field: Asian American; Multi-Cultural
Status: Professional; Nonprofit
Paid Staff: 4
Volunteer Staff: 10
Paid Artists: 50
Income Sources: Theatre Communications Group;
Alliance of Resident Theatres/New York
Performs At: West End Theatre
Type of Stage: Proscenium
Organization Type: Performing; Touring; Resident;
Educational

3121
PAPER BAG PLAYERS

185 East Broadway
New York, NY 10002
Phone: 212-353-2332
Fax: 212-362-0431
e-mail: pbagp@verizon.net
Web Site: http://www.thepaperbagplayers.org
Officers:
   President: Alison Harmelin
   Treasurer: Judi Blitzer
   Secretary: Patricia Langer
Management:
   Managing Director: Michael Oakes
   Artistic Director: Ted Brackett
Mission: To create a contemporary theatre for children
with shows based on a child's everyday experiences
and perceptions of the world.
Founded: 1958
Specialized Field: Children's Theater
Status: Professional; Nonprofit

Organization Type: Performing; Touring; Resident;
Educational

3122
PARK AVENUE THEATRICAL GROUP

404 Park Avenue S
10th Floor
New York, NY 10016
Phone: 212-213-5270
Fax: 212-689-9140
e-mail: jkravat@parny.com
Management:
   Director Sales: Carol Bresner
Specialized Field: Drama; Contemporary

3123
PEARL THEATRE COMPANY

80 St Mark's Place
New York, NY 10003
Phone: 212-505-3401
Fax: 212-505-3404
e-mail: akaiser@pearltheatre.org
Web Site: www.pearltheatre.org
Officers:
   Chairperson: Brian Heidtke
   President: Ellen Hirsch
   Treasurer: Jean Cheever
   Secretary: Ellen Jakobson
Management:
   Executive Director: Shepard Sobel
   Director Development: Margaret Benson
   Managing Director: Amy Kaiser
   Programs Manager/Casting: Meghan Beals
   Business Manager: Amy Kaiser
   Production Manager: Dale Smallwood
Mission: To present a full-range repertory strongly
rooted in the classics with a resident acting company,
guest artists and theatre staff.
Founded: 1982
Specialized Field: Classic; Ensembles
Status: Non-Profit, Professional
Paid Staff: 8
Volunteer Staff: 50
Paid Artists: 35
Budget: $1.5 million
Income Sources: Foundations; Individual Giving;
Earned Income
Performs At: Theatre
Annual Attendance: 27,000
Facility Category: Theatre with Lobby, Box Office and
Dressing Rooms
Type of Stage: Proscenium
Stage Dimensions: 22' x 44'
Seating Capacity: 160
Rental Contact: Production Manager Dale Smallwood
Organization Type: Performing; Resident; Educational

3124
PECULIAR WORKS PROJECT

595 Broadway
2nd Floor
New York, NY 10012-3222
Phone: 212-529-3626
Fax: 212-529-3626
e-mail: info@peculiarworks.org
Web Site: www.peculiarworks.org
Management:
   President: Ralph Lewis
   Artistic Director: Catherine Porter
   Managing Director: Barry Rowell
Mission: Peculiar Works Project generates original,
multi-disciplinary performance that is accessible and fun
for diverse audiences.
Founded: 1993

Specialized Field: Multi-Media; Touring Company; New Plays
Status: Non-Profit, Professional
Paid Artists: 20

3125
PING CHONG & COMPANY
47 Great Jones Street
New York, NY 10012
Phone: 212-529-1557
Fax: 212-529-1703
e-mail: info@pingchong.org
Web Site: http://www.pingchong.org/info.html
Management:
    Artistic Director: Ping Chong
    Managing Director: Bruce Allardice
Specialized Field: Touring Company; Contemporary; Multi-Cultural

3126
PLAYWRIGHTS HORIZONS
416 W 42nd Street
New York, NY 10036
Phone: 212-564-1235
Fax: 212-594-0296
e-mail: marketing@playwrightshorizons.org
Web Site: www.playwrightshorizons.org
Officers:
    Chair: Judith Rubin
    Vice Chair: Lawrence Buttenwieser
    Secretary: Amy McIntosh
    Treasurer: Herbert Morey
Management:
    Artistic Director: Tim Sanford
    Managing Director: Leslie Marcus
    General Manager: Carol Fishman
Mission: Developing American composers, lyricists and playwrights; offering internships and training programs.
Utilizes: Singers
Founded: 1971
Specialized Field: Musical; Comedy; Contemporary
Status: Non-Profit, Professional
Paid Staff: 25
Income Sources: Actors' Equity Association; Alliance of Resident Theatres/New York; New York University
Performs At: Mainstage Theatre; Studio Theatre
Facility Category: Theater
Type of Stage: Proscenium
Seating Capacity: 141
Organization Type: Performing; Educational

3127
PRIMARY STAGES COMPANY
307 W 38th St
Ste 1510
New York, NY 10018
Phone: 212-840-9705
Fax: 212-840-9725
e-mail: info@primarystages.org
Web Site: www.primarystages.org
Management:
    Artistic Director: Andrew Leynse
    Managing Director: Elliot Fox
    Associate Artistic Director: Michelle Bossy
Mission: Discovering and producing the finest new American plays.
Utilizes: Singers
Founded: 1984
Specialized Field: Theatre
Facility Category: 199 Seats; 59 Theatres
Organization Type: Performing

3128
PROCESS STUDIO THEATRE
257 Church Street
New York, NY 10007
Phone: 212-271-0410
Management:
    Artistic Director: Bonnie Loren
    Technical Director: Anthony Sandkamp
Mission: Promoting new artists and works; offering a home to professional artists.
Utilizes: Singers
Founded: 1977
Specialized Field: Musical; New Plays
Status: Professional; Nonprofit
Organization Type: Performing; Touring; Resident; Educational; Sponsoring; Outreach

3129
PUBLIC THEATER
425 Lafayette Street
New York, NY 10003
Phone: 212-539-8500
Fax: 212-539-8705
e-mail: press@publictheater.org
Web Site: www.publictheather.org
Management:
    Artistic Director: Oskar Eustis
    Excutive Director: Mara Manus
Mission: The Public Theater produces new plays, musicals, productions of Shakespeare, as well as other classics. In addition to its theatrical programming, The Public trains the next generation of classical performers through the Shakespeare Lab, an annual summer acting intensive.
Founded: 1967
Specialized Field: Shakespeare; Classic; Summer Stock
Status: Professional; Non-Profit
Income Sources: The LuEsther T. Mertz Charitable Trust
Annual Attendance: 250,000

3130
PUBLIC THEATRE
425 Lafayette Street
Box 7
New York, NY 10003
Phone: 212-539-8500
Fax: 212-539-8705
e-mail: press@thepublictheatre.org
Web Site: www.thepublictheatre.org
Officers:
    President: Kathy Gleason
    VP: Kathy Stuchiner
    Treasurer: Thomas H Platz
    Secretary: Carol Murrell
Management:
    Artistic Director: Oskar Eustis
    Executive Director: Andrew D. Harrington
Mission: The Public Theater produces new plays, musicals, productions of Shakespeare, as well as other classics. In addition to its theatrical programming, The Public Theater trains the next generation of classical performers through The Shakespeare Lab, an annual summer acting intensive.
Founded: 1954
Opened: 1967
Specialized Field: Shakespeare; Classic; Summer Stock
Status: Non-Profit, Professional
Paid Staff: 7
Volunteer Staff: 65
Paid Artists: 8

Budget: $450,000
Income Sources: Ticket Sales; Grants; Corporate Support; Donations
Annual Attendance: 250,000
Facility Category: Theatre
Type of Stage: Proscenium
Stage Dimensions: 36' x 33'
Seating Capacity: 307

3131
PUERTO RICAN TRAVELING THEATRE COMPANY
141 W 94th Street
New York, NY 10025
Phone: 212-354-1293
Fax: 212-307-2769
e-mail: prttny@aol.com
Management:
    President: Miriam Colon Valle
    Managing Director: Michael Palma
Mission: Presenting bilingual plays; conducting workshops for underprivileged youth; providing training for playwrights.
Utilizes: Singers
Founded: 1967
Specialized Field: Musical; Touring Company; Spanish Language Company; Multi-Cultural
Status: Non-Profit, Professional
Performs At: Puerto Rican Travelling Theatre
Organization Type: Performing; Touring; Educational

3132
RAJECKAS AND INTRAUB MOVEMENT THEATRE
AKA Theatremoves
275 E 7th Street #4
New York, NY 10009
Mailing Address: PO Box 1333
Phone: 212-529-8068
Fax: 212-529-8068
e-mail: nintraub@aol.com
Web Site: www.theatremoves.com
Management:
    Co-Director: Paul Rajeckas
    Co Director: Neil Intraub
Founded: 1988
Specialized Field: Movement Theater
Status: Non-Profit, Professional
Paid Staff: 5
Paid Artists: 5

3133
RATTLESTICK THEATRE
224 Waverly Place
New York, NY 10014
Phone: 212-627-2556
Fax: 630-839-8352
Management:
    Artistic Director: Albert Harris
    Lit. Manager: Lousie Shannon
Mission: The production of new works; the presentation of neglected works by established writers.
Utilizes: Singers
Founded: 1994
Specialized Field: Musical; Ensembles; New Plays
Status: Non-Profit, Professional
Income Sources: Actors' Equity Association; Alliance of Resident Theatres/New York
Performs At: Theatre Off Park
Organization Type: Educational

3134

REPERTORIO ESPANOL
138 E 27th Street
New York, NY 10016
Phone: 212-889-2850
Fax: 212-686-3732
Management:
Artistic Director: Rene Buch
Associate Artistic Producer: Robert Federico
Producer: Gilberto Zaldivar
Specialized Field: Spanish Language Company;
Multi-Cultural

3135

RIDGE THEATER
141 Ridge Street
Suite 8
New York, NY 10002
Phone: 212-674-5485
Fax: 212-674-5485
e-mail: ridgetheater@earthlink.net
Web Site: www.ridgetheater.org
Management:
President: Laurie Olinder
Executive Director: Bob McGrath
Mission: Exploring the boundaries of theatre and
opera.
Founded: 1987
Specialized Field: Contemporary; Experimental
Status: Non-Profit, Professional
Paid Staff: 5
Paid Artists: 5
Facility Category: Theatre
Organization Type: Performing

3136

RIVER REP THEATRE COMPANY
100 E 4 Street
New York, NY 10003
Phone: 212-674-8181
Management:
Artistic Director: Warren Kelley
Managing Director: Joan Shepard
Mission: To bring 11 weeks a year of fulfilling theatre to
the shoreline of Eastern Connecticut.
Founded: 1987
Specialized Field: Drama; Musical; Comedy; Classic
Status: Non-Profit
Paid Staff: 15
Volunteer Staff: 10
Paid Artists: 18
Non-paid Artists: 5
Season: June - September
Performs At: Chester Meeting House, Chester CT
Type of Stage: Proscenium
Stage Dimensions: 18' x 30'

3137

RIVERSIDE SHAKESPEARE COMPANY
Shakespeare Center
165 W 86th Street
New York, NY 10024
Phone: 212-505-2021
Fax: 212-505-2054
Management:
Executive Director: Ann Harvey
Artistic Director: Gus Kaikkonen
Academy Director: Robert Mooney
Mission: Bringing classic works to life and making them
more accessible.
Utilizes: Singers
Founded: 1976
Specialized Field: Shakespeare

Status: Professional
Organization Type: Performing; Touring; Resident;
Educational

3138

ROGER FURMAN THEATRE
60 E 42nd Street
Suite 1336
New York, NY 10017
Phone: 212-599-1922
Fax: 212-599-2414
Management:
Executive Director: Voza Rivers
Mission: Encouraging cultural pluralism in New York
City through the presentation of high-quality,
professional Black theatre.
Utilizes: Singers
Founded: 1964
Specialized Field: African American; Multi-Cultural
Status: Professional; Nonprofit
Paid Staff: 5
Income Sources: National Endowment for the Arts;
Department of Cultural Affairs
Performs At: Roger Furman Theater; B Smiths
Rooftop Cafe
Organization Type: Performing; Touring; Resident;
Educational

3139

ROUNDABOUT THEATRE COMPANY
231 W 39th Street
Suite 1200
New York, NY 10018
Phone: 212-719-9393
Fax: 212-869-8817
e-mail: info@roundabouttheatre.org
Web Site: www.roundabouttheatre.org
Management:
President: Todd Haimes
Managing Director: Harold Wolpert
Mission: To produce the classics, both ancient and
modern.
Utilizes: Singers
Founded: 1965
Specialized Field: Musical; Comedy; Classic;
Contemporary; Renaissance
Status: Non-Profit, Professional
Affiliations: Actors' Equity Association; League of
Resident Theatres; Society for Stage Directors and
Choreographers
Facility Category: Theatre
Type of Stage: Proscenium
Seating Capacity: 700
Rental Contact: Christine Vall
Organization Type: Performing; Resident

3140

SAINT BART'S PLAYERS
109 E 50th Street
New York, NY 10022
Phone: 212-378-0248
Fax: 212-378-0281
e-mail: central@stbarts.org
Web Site: www.stbarts.org
Officers:
Co-Chair: Maryjane Baer
Co-Chair: Merrill Vaughn
Management:
Director St. Bart's Central: Veronica Shea
Utilizes: Singers
Founded: 1927
Specialized Field: Musical; Educational; Theater
Workshops
Status: Non-Profit, Non-Professional

Paid Staff: 75
Income Sources: Theatre Communications Group
Performs At: Saint Bartholomew's Community House
Organization Type: Performing; Resident; Educational

3141

SALT AND PEPPER MIME COMPANY
320 E 90th
#1B
New York, NY 10128
Phone: 212-262-4989
Fax: 212-262-4989
Management:
Artistic Manager/Producer: Scottie Davis
Director: Chuck Wise
Resident Playwright: Mark Pearce
Mission: Preserving the art forms of vaudeville and
mime through performances, exhibitions and
workshops.
Utilizes: Singers
Founded: 1978
Specialized Field: Musical; Mime; Drama; Children's
Theater
Status: Professional; Nonprofit
Income Sources: Alliance of Resident Theatres/New
York; Westside Arts Coalition
Performs At: Lincoln Square Theatre; Studio Theatre
Organization Type: Performing; Touring; Educational

3142

SARATOGA INTERNATIONAL THEATER INSTITUTE
SITI Company
520 8th Avenue
Suite 310
New York, NY 10018
Phone: 212-868-0860
Fax: 212-868-0837
e-mail: inbox@siti.org
Web Site: www.siti.org
Management:
Artistic Director: Anneeen Bogart
Managing Director: Megan Wanlass Szalla
Mission: SITI exemplifies the disciplines it practices
and the artistic values it develops in its work; to create
new works for the theater; to perform and tour these
productions nationally and internationally; to provide
ongoing training for young theater professionals in an
approach to acting that forges unique and highly
disciplined artists for the theater; to foster opportunities
for cultural exchange.
Founded: 1992
Specialized Field: New Plays; Touring Company
Status: Nonprofit
Paid Staff: 5
Volunteer Staff: 3
Paid Artists: 16

3143

SECOND STAGE THEATRE
307 W 43rd Street
New York, NY 10036
Phone: 212-787-8302
Fax: 212-397-7066
e-mail: info@secondstagetheatre.com
Web Site: www.secondstagetheatre.com
Officers:
Executive Director: Ellen Richard
Management:
Artistic Director: Carole Rothman
Mission: To produce plays of the recent past which we
feel deserve a second production; to produce world and
New York premieres by emerging authors, with
emphasis on women authors and authors of color.

Utilizes: Actors; AEA Actors; Artists-in-Residence;
Choreographers; Commissioned Composers;
Commissioned Music; Designers; Educators; Five
Seasonal Concerts; Guest Accompanists; Guest Artists;
Guest Conductors; Guest Designers; Guest Lecturers;
Instructors; Local Unknown Artists; Multimedia; Music;
New Productions; Original Music Scores; Performance
Artists; Resident Professionals; Selected Students;
Soloists; Visual Arts
Founded: 1979
Specialized Field: Musical; Comedy; Contemporary
Status: Non-Profit, Professional
Paid Staff: 20
Paid Artists: 25
Annual Attendance: 67,000
Facility Category: Theatre
Seating Capacity: 296
Year Built: 1999
Rental Contact: Producing Manager Peter Davis
Organization Type: Performing

3144
SHADOW BOX THEATRE
325 W End Avenue
New York, NY 10023
Phone: 212-724-0677
Fax: 212-724-0767
e-mail: sbt@shadowboxtheatre.org
Web Site: www.shadowboxtheatre.org
Management:
   President: Sandra Robbins
   Managing Director: Marlyn Baum
   Administrator: Elaine Brand
Mission: To serve inner city disadvantaged children
with a high quality art-in-education program.
Founded: 1967
Specialized Field: Musical; Ethnic Theater; Puppet;
Shadow Theater
Status: Non-Profit, Professional
Paid Staff: 5
Paid Artists: 10
Affiliations: NYC Board of Education Vendor
Organization Type: Performing; Touring; Resident;
Educational; Sponsoring

3145
SIGNATURE THEATRE COMPANY
630 9th Avenue
Suite 1106
New York, NY 10036
Phone: 212-967-1913
Fax: 212-967-2957
Web Site: www.signaturetheatre.org
Officers:
   Chairman: Peter Norton
   President: Michael Rauch
   VP: Christine M Millen
   VP: Marian Succoso
Management:
   Executive Director: Erika Mallin
   Artistic Director: James Houghton
   Director Development: Katherine Thomas
   Production Manager: Paul Ziemer
   General Manager: Adam Bernstein
Founded: 1991
Specialized Field: Drama; Musical; Comedy
Status: Non-Profit, Professional
Paid Staff: 13
Volunteer Staff: 1
Paid Artists: 150
Affiliations: Alliance of Resident Theatres, NY; Theatre
Communications Group
Type of Stage: Proscenium
Seating Capacity: 160

3146
SOHO REPERTORY THEATRE
86 Franklin Street
4th Floor
New York, NY 10013
Phone: 212-941-8632
Fax: 212-941-7148
e-mail: sohorep@sohorep.org
Web Site: www.sohorep.org
Management:
   Executive Director: Alexandra Conley
   Artistic Director: Daniel Aukin
   Associate Director: Sarah Benson
   Administrative Manager: Young Jean Lee
   Facility Manager: Noah Hall
Founded: 1975
Specialized Field: Comedy; Community Theater;
Contemporary; New Plays
Status: Non-Profit, Professional
Paid Staff: 3
Seating Capacity: 70

3147
SOUPSTONE PROJECT
309 E 5th Street
Suite 19
New York, NY 10003
Phone: 212-473-7584
Management:
   Director/Literary Manager: Neile Weissman
Mission: To expand the theatergoing audience through
free, trilingually-accessible presentations of new
American plays.
Founded: 1985
Specialized Field: New Plays; Multi-Cultural;
Contemporary
Status: Professional
Performs At: Henry Street Settlement; Louis Abrons
Art Center
Organization Type: Performing

3148
SPANISH THEATRE REPERTORY COMPANY
138 E 27th Street
New York, NY 10016
Phone: 212-889-2850
Fax: 212-686-3732
Web Site: http://www.repertorio.org/
Management:
   Producer: Gilbert Zaldivar
   Associate Producer: Robert Federico
   Press Agent: Ellen Jacobs
Mission: To offer Spanish-language professional
theatre; to promote Hispanic culture.
Founded: 1969
Specialized Field: Musical; Community Theater;
Spanish Language Company
Status: Professional
Income Sources: Theatre Communications Group;
American Arts Alliance; Alliance of Resident
Theatres/New York
Performs At: Gramercy Arts Theatre; Equitable Tower
Auditorium
Organization Type: Performing

3149
STAGEWRIGHTS
PO Box 4745
Rockefeller Center Station
New York, NY 10185
Phone: 212-768-8964
Mission: To develop scripts.

Founded: 1983
Specialized Field: New Plays; Young Playwrights
Status: Semi-Professional; Nonprofit
Paid Staff: 100
Organization Type: Writer's Theatre

3150
TADA!
15 W 28th Street
3rd Floor
New York, NY 10001
Phone: 212-252-1619
Fax: 212-252-8763
e-mail: info@tadatheater.com
Web Site: www.tadtheater.com
Management:
   President: Stephen T Rodd
   Executive Director: Janine Nina Trevens
Founded: 1984
Specialized Field: Youth; Musical Theatre
Paid Staff: 10
Performs At: Theater; Rehearsal; Studio
Facility Category: Theater
Type of Stage: Procenium
Stage Dimensions: 20 x 30 x 11
Seating Capacity: 99
Rental Contact: Andrew Bryant

3151
TALKING BAND
PO Box 293
Prince Street Station
New York, NY 10012
Phone: 212-295-0371
Web Site: http://talkingband.org/panic/about.html
Management:
   Artistic Director: Paul Zinet
Mission: The creation and performance of new theatre
works.
Specialized Field: New Plays
Status: Professional; Nonprofit
Organization Type: Performing; Touring

3152
TARGET MARGIN THEATER
1879 Murray Hill Station
New York, NY 10156
Phone: 212-725-4617
Fax: 212-725-4627
Management:
   Artistic Director: David Herskovits
   Managing Director: Meredith Palin
   Development Director: Tonya Canada
Specialized Field: Specialty Acts; Hellenic Drama

3153
THEATER BY THE BLIND
306 W 18th Street
New York, NY 10011
Phone: 212-243-4337
Fax: 212-243-4337
e-mail: ashiotis@panix.com
Web Site: www.tbtb.org
Management:
   Artistic Director: Ike Schambelan
Mission: To change the image of the blind from one of
dependence to independence.
Founded: 1979
Specialized Field: Alternative
Status: Non-Profit, Professional
Paid Staff: 4
Paid Artists: 17

3154
THEATER FOR THE NEW CITY
155 1st Avenue
Between 9th & 10th
New York, NY 10003
Phone: 212-245-1109
Fax: 212-979-6570
e-mail: info@theaterforthenewcity.org
Web Site: www.theaterforthenewcity.org
Management:
    Executive Director: Crystal Field
    Production Manager: Mark Marcante
    Administrator: Jerry Jaffe
    Development Director: Victoria Linchon
Mission: To embody the vision of a center for new and innovative theater arts that would be truly accessible to the community and its experimental theater artists; to discover relevant new writing and to nurture new playwrights; to be a bridge between playwright, experimental theater artist, and the ever growing audiences in the community; to create spaces where a new vision can breathe and be nourished by a working process.
Utilizes: Singers
Founded: 1970
Specialized Field: Experimental; Young Playwrights
Status: Professional; Nonprofit
Paid Staff: 5
Volunteer Staff: 20
Performs At: Four Theatre Complex
Affiliations: Alliance of Resident Theatres/New York; Theatre Communications Group; American Arts Alliance
Annual Attendance: 30,000
Facility Category: Multi-theater complex
Type of Stage: Black Box; Cabaret; Flexible Stage
Seating Capacity: 270; 99; 74; 104
Organization Type: Performing; Touring

3155
THEATRE DU GRAND-GUIGNOL DE PARIS
310 E 70th Street
New York, NY 10021
Phone: 212-861-1813
Fax: 212-861-1813
Management:
    Embassy of Montmartre: Barry Alan Richmond
Mission: Specializing in grotesquerie, shock, terror, the macabre and earthy laughter.
Utilizes: Singers
Founded: 1896
Specialized Field: Multi-Cultural; Drama; Comedy; Alternative
Status: Professional; National Theatre of Montmartre
Income Sources: State Theatre of the Republic of Montmartre
Organization Type: Performing; Touring; Resident

3156
THEATRE FOR A NEW AUDIENCE
154 Christopher Street
Suite 3D
New York, NY 10014
Phone: 212-229-2819
Fax: 212-229-2911
e-mail: info@tfana.org
Web Site: www.tfana.org
Officers:
    Founding Artistic Director: Jeffrey Horowitz
Management:
    Managing Director: Dorothy Ryan
    ':

:
Mission: Producing works of poetic imagination; building a diverse audience.
Founded: 1979
Specialized Field: New Plays
Status: Professional; Nonprofit
Income Sources: Theatre Communications Group
Performs At: Lucille Lortel Theatre
Organization Type: Performing; Educational

3157
RAJECKAS AND INTRAUB - MOVEMENT THEATRE
PO Box 1333
New York, NY 10009
Phone: 212-529-8068
Fax: 212-529-8068
e-mail: nintraub@aol.com
Management:
    Co-Artistic Director: Neil Intraub
    Co-Artistic Director: Paul Rajeckas
Mission: Increasing public exposure to the art form of movement theatre.
Specialized Field: Community Theater; Movement Theater
Status: Professional; Nonprofit
Organization Type: Performing; Touring; Educational

3158
THEATREWORKS USA
151 W 26th Street
New York, NY 10001
Phone: 212-647-1100
Fax: 212-924-5377
e-mail: info@theatreworksusa.org
Web Site: www.theatreworksusa.org
Officers:
    Chairman: Michael J. Passarella
    President: Ken Arthur
Management:
    Artistic Director: Barbara Pasternack
    Managing Director: Ken Arthur
Mission: Theatreworks/USA, a nonprofit organization and America's largest theatre creating, producing, and touring plays for young audiences, has presented more than 27,000 performances to well over 22 million young people in schools, art centers, museums and theatres, in 49 states.
Utilizes: Actors; AEA Actors; Artists-in-Residence; Choreographers; Collaborating Artists; Collaborations; Commissioned Composers; Commissioned Music; Dancers; Designers; Educators; Five Seasonal Concerts; Guest Accompanists; Guest Artists; Guest Choreographers; Guest Companies; Guest Composers; Guest Conductors; Guest Designers; Guest Ensembles; Guest Lecturers; Guest Teachers; Guild Activities; High School Drama; Local Unknown Artists; Lyricists; Music; New Productions; Original Music Scores; Performance Artists; Resident Professionals; Sign Language Translators; Singers; Soloists; Special Technical Talent; Theatre Companies; Visual Arts
Founded: 1961
Specialized Field: Musical; Comedy; Youth Theater; Community Theater; Contemporary
Status: Non-Profit, Professional
Paid Staff: 21
Budget: $10 million
Performs At: Town Hall; Promenade Theatre; Variety Arts Theatre
Affiliations: AEA, SSDC, USA, AGG, IAPAYP, APAP
Annual Attendance: 4.6 million
Organization Type: Performing; Touring; Resident; Educational; Sponsoring

3159
THERESA LANG THEATRE
Marymount Manhattan College
221 E 71 Street
New York, NY 10021
Phone: 212-774-0760
Fax: 212-774-0770
Web Site: www.mmm.edu
Management:
    President: Judson Shaver
    Executive Director: Mary Fleischer
Specialized Field: Musical; Comedy; Classic; Contemporary
Status: For-Profit, Non-Professional

3160
THUNDER BAY ENSEMBLE
Box 289
New York, NY 1029
Phone: 413-269-4201
Fax: 413-269-4201
e-mail: info@thunderbayus.org
Web Site: www.thunderbayus.org
Management:
    President: Beth Skinner
    Artistic Director: Edward Herbst
Founded: 1987
Specialized Field: Ensembles; Contemporary
Status: Non-Profit, Professional
Paid Staff: 4
Paid Artists: 8

3161
TVI ACTORS STUDIO
165 W 46th Street
Suite 509
New York, NY 10036
Phone: 212-302-1900
Fax: 212-302-1926
Toll-free: 800-884-2772
Web Site: www.tvistudios.com
Officers:
    Founder/CEO: Alan S Nusbaum
Management:
    President: Alan Nusbaum
    Executive Director: Deborah Kossler
    Managing Director: Susan Sleeper
Mission: Provide actors with a center where they can focus on the business of their careers in addition to learning the necessary skills to compete as an actor.
Founded: 1986
Specialized Field: Musical; Youth Theater
Status: For-Profit, Professional
Paid Staff: 12
Performs At: Actors Studio
Organization Type: Resident

3162
UNION SQUARE THEATRE
100 E 17th Street
New York, NY 10003
Phone: 212-505-0700
Fax: 212-505-0709
Management:
    Owner: Margaret Cotter
Specialized Field: Commuity Theater
Status: For-Profit, Professional
Paid Staff: 10
Type of Stage: Proscenium
Seating Capacity: 499
Rental Contact: Margaret Cotter

3163
VINEYARD THEATRE
108 E 15th Street
New York, NY 10003
Phone: 212-353-3366
Fax: 212-353-3803
e-mail: boxoffice@vineyardtheatre.org
Web Site: www.vineyardtheatre.org
Officers:
   Chairman: Barbara Zinn Krieger
   President: Christopher W Gould
   Treasurer: David Schwrtz
   Secretary: James J Gabbe
Management:
   Artistic Director: Douglas Aibel
   Executive Director and External Aff: Jennifer Garvey-Blackewell
   Managing Director: Bardo S Ramirez
Mission: Developing musical theatre and new plays.
Utilizes: Actors; AEA Actors; Artists-in-Residence; Choreographers; Collaborating Artists; Collaborations; Commissioned Composers; Commissioned Music; Designers; Five Seasonal Concerts; Grant Writers; Guest Accompanists; Guest Artists; Guest Companies; Guest Composers; Guest Conductors; Guest Designers; Guest Lecturers; Guest Musical Directors; Guild Activities; Instructors; Local Artists; Local Unknown Artists; Multimedia; Music; Original Music Scores; Performance Artists; Playwrights; Poets; Resident Professionals; Sign Language Translators; Soloists
Founded: 1981
Specialized Field: Musical; New Plays
Status: Non-Profit
Paid Staff: 8
Budget: $1.6 Million
Income Sources: Theatre Communications Group; Opera America
Season: Late-Fall - Spring
Affiliations: AEA, AFM, SSDC
Type of Stage: Flexible; Thrust
Seating Capacity: 129
Rental Contact: General Manager Jodi Schoenbrun
Organization Type: Performing

3164
VIVIAN BEAUMONT THEATER
150 W 65th Street
New York, NY 10023
Phone: 212-362-7600
Fax: 212-873-0761
e-mail: info@lct.org
Web Site: www.lct.org
Officers:
   Assistant Treasurer: Robert A Belkin
   Box Office Treasurer: Fred Bonis
Management:
   Artistic Director: Andre Bishop
   Director Development: Hattie K Jutagir
   Production Manager: Jeff Hamlin
   Assistant Production Manager: Paul Smithyman
   Associate General Manager: Mala Yee Mosher
   Management Assistant: Melanie Weiner
   Company Manager: Adam Siegal
   Assistant Company Manager: Anthony LaTorella
Utilizes: Singers
Founded: 1985
Specialized Field: Musical; Drama
Status: Non-Profit, Professional
Performs At: Vivian Beaumont Theater; Mitzi E Newhouse Theater
Facility Category: Theater
Organization Type: Performing

3165
WEISSBERGER THEATER GROUP
909 3rd Avenue
27th Floor
New York, NY 10022
Phone: 212-339-5529
Fax: 212-486-8996
Management:
   Producer: Jay Harris
Founded: 1992
Specialized Field: New Plays

3166
WINGS THEATRE COMPANY
154 Christopher Street
New York, NY 10014
Phone: 212-627-2960
Fax: 212-462-0024
e-mail: jcorrick@wingstheatre.com
Web Site: www.wingstheatre.com
Management:
   Literary Manager: Laura Kleeman
   President: Jeffery Corrick
   Managing Director: Robert Mooney
   Rentals Manager: Robert Mooney
Mission: To engourage artists and arts organizations other than our own-theatre and dance companies, comedy troupes, film-makers-by producing and by making our space available for productions and rentals. We receive scripts and choose 5 for each year for Equity Tier II Showcase Productions (5 week runs). We have a gay plays series as well as a new musicals series.
Founded: 1986
Specialized Field: New Plays
Status: Non-Profit, Professional
Paid Staff: 3
Volunteer Staff: 3
Paid Artists: 30
Non-paid Artists: 20
Income Sources: Box Office; Grants; Rentals
Facility Category: Fully Equipped Theatre
Type of Stage: Proscenium
Stage Dimensions: 20 x 20, 2 side stages
Seating Capacity: 74-95
Year Built: 1990
Rental Contact: Rmooney@Verizon.Net Robert Mooney

3167
WOMEN'S INTERART CENTER
549 W 52nd Street
New York, NY 10019
Phone: 212-246-1050
Management:
   Artistic Director: Margot Lewitin
   Dramaturge: Jean Rowan
   Development Director: Susan Waring Morris
Mission: To explore all avenues of theatrical expression; to emphasize the work of new playwrights.
Utilizes: Singers
Founded: 1971
Specialized Field: Women's Theater; New Plays
Status: Professional; Nonprofit
Income Sources: Actors' Equity Association
Performs At: Interart Theater
Organization Type: Performing

3168
WOMEN'S PROJECT & PRODUCTIONS
55 W End Avenue
New York, NY 10023
Phone: 212-765-1706
Fax: 212-765-2024
e-mail: info@womensproject.org
Web Site: www.womensproject.org
Management:
   Producing Artistic Director: Loretta Greco
   Associate Artistic Director: Lisa McNulty
   Managing Director: Jane Ann Crum
   Literary Manager: Karen Keagle
Mission: Promoting and developing women directors and playwrights in the theatre.
Utilizes: Singers
Founded: 1978
Specialized Field: Women's Theater; New Plays
Status: Non-Profit, Professional
Paid Staff: 10
Income Sources: Theatre Communications Group; Alliance of Resident Theatres/New York
Organization Type: Performing; Resident; Educational; Sponsoring

3169
WOOSTER GROUP
Canal Street Station
PO Box 654
New York, NY 10013
Phone: 212-966-9796
Fax: 212-226-6576
e-mail: mail@thewoostergroup.org
Web Site: www.thewoostergroup.org
Officers:
   President: Kate Valk
Management:
   Artistic Director: Elizabeth Lecompte
   Managing Director: Joel Bassin
Mission: An artists collective working together on live performances.
Founded: 1967
Specialized Field: Ensembles; New Plays
Status: Non-Profit, Professional
Paid Staff: 17
Budget: $1 Million
Income Sources: Ticket Sales; Touring; Grants & Contributions
Performs At: The Performing Garage
Annual Attendance: 15,000
Facility Category: Flexible black box
Type of Stage: Flexible floor
Seating Capacity: 100
Year Built: 1950
Organization Type: Performing; Touring; Resident; Sponsoring

3170
WORKING THEATRE COMPANY
128 East Broadway
Box 892
New York, NY 10022-0892
Phone: 212-539-5675
Fax: 212-614-9821
e-mail: email@the workingtheater.org
Officers:
   Chairman: Larry Beers
Management:
   Artistic Director: Bill Mitchelson
   Development Director: Honour Molloy
Mission: America's only professional theatre company dedicated to producing new plays of cultural diversities that reflect the issues and concerns that working people face in the modern world.
Specialized Field: Young Playwrights; Drama; Comedy
Status: Professional; Nonprofit
Organization Type: Performing; Educational

3171
WPA THEATRE
159 W 23rd Street
Suite 301
New York, NY 10001
Phone: 212-206-0523
Fax: 212-637-7154
Management:
Artistic Director: Kyle Renick
Managing Director: Donna Lieberman
Mission: Committed to fostering realistic writing, acting and design in American repertory.
Founded: 1977
Specialized Field: New Works
Status: Professional; Nonprofit
Income Sources: Alliance of Resident Theatres/New York; Theatre Communications Group
Season: September - June
Performs At: Chelsea Playhouse
Type of Stage: Proscenium
Seating Capacity: 160
Organization Type: Performing

3172
YORK THEATRE COMPANY
619 Lexington Avenue @ 54th Street
New York, NY 10022-4610
Phone: 212-935-5820
Fax: 212-832-0037
e-mail: jmorgan@yorktheatre.org
Web Site: www.yorktheatre.org
Management:
Chairman: David McCoy
Artistic Director: Jim Morgan
President: Sarah Tod Smith
Mission: A professional equity off-Broadway company dedicated to presenting great classical works as well as revivals and/or premieres of unusual, avant-garde musicals.
Utilizes: Singers
Founded: 1969
Specialized Field: Musical; Youth Theater; Contemporary
Status: Non-Profit, Professional
Paid Staff: 6
Paid Artists: 300
Affiliations: Actors' Equity Association
Organization Type: Performing

3173
YOUNG PLAYWRIGHTS
321 W 44th Street
Suite 906
New York, NY 10036
Phone: 212-307-1140
Fax: 212-307-1454
Management:
Artistic Director: Sheri Goldhirsch
Managing Director: Brett Reynolds
Project Administrator: Rebecca Sheir
Literary Associate: Ruth McKee
Specialized Field: Young Playwrights; Theater Workshops

3174
PUPPET THEATRE: DANCE AND MUSIC FROM INDONESIA
1 Sir Kenneth Court
Northport, NY 11768
Phone: 631-754-5035
Fax: 631-754-2341
e-mail: javapuppets@aol.com
Web Site: www.indonesianshadowplay.com

Management:
President: Tamara Fielding
Founded: 1975
Specialized Field: Multi-Cultural; Puppet; Ethnic Theater
Status: For-Profit, Professional
Paid Staff: 2
Paid Artists: 6

3175
TAMARA AND THE SHADOW THEATRE OF JAVA
1 Sir Kenneth Court
Northport, NY 11768
Phone: 631-754-5035
Fax: 631-754-2341
e-mail: javapuppets@aol.com
Web Site: www.indonesianshadowplay.com
Management:
Artistic Director: Tamara Fielding
Founded: 1975
Specialized Field: Multi-Cultural; Shadow Theater; Ethnic Theater; Musical
Status: For-Profit, Professional
Paid Staff: 2
Volunteer Staff: 1
Paid Artists: 20

3176
ELMWOOD PLAYHOUSE
10 Park Street
Nyack, NY 10960
Phone: 845-353-1313
Fax: 845-348-9397
e-mail: elmwoodplayhouse@aol.com
Web Site: www.elmwoodplayhouse.com
Officers:
President: Larry Beckerle
VP: Alison Costello
Management:
Operations Manager: Evelyn Russo
Founded: 1964
Specialized Field: Musical; Comedy; Community Theater
Status: Non-Profit, Non-Professional
Paid Staff: 4
Volunteer Staff: 200
Income Sources: Art Council of Rockland County
Performs At: Elmwood Playhouse
Affiliations: ACOR, AACT
Facility Category: Community Theatre
Seating Capacity: 99
Organization Type: Performing; Educational

3177
OGDENSBURG COMMAND PERFORMANCES
1100 State Street
Ogdensburg, NY 13669
Phone: 315-393-2625
Fax: 315-393-2625
e-mail: mcpalao@internetusa.net
Management:
Administrative Coordinator: Sally Palao
Mission: To offer theatrical productions, drama and music for the enjoyment and inspiration of the residents of Ogdensburg and the North Country.
Founded: 1963
Specialized Field: Drama; Classic
Status: Professional; Nonprofit
Paid Staff: 2
Performs At: George Hall Auditorium; Ogdensburg Free Academy

Organization Type: Sponsoring

3178
ORPHEUS THEATRE
31 Maple Street
PO Box 1014
Oneonta, NY 13820
Phone: 607-432-1800
Fax: 607-436-9682
e-mail: orpheus@stny.rr.com
Officers:
President: Carolyn Anderson
1st VP: Arnold Drogen
2nd VP: Duncan Smith
Secretary: Carol Detweiler
Treasurer: Rosalie Benson
CEO: Sammy Dallas Bayes
Management:
Co-Producers: Peter Macris
Founded: 1983
Specialized Field: Musical; Theater Workshops
Status: Nonprofit; Non-Equity
Season: September - August
Type of Stage: Proscenium
Stage Dimensions: 49' x 35'
Seating Capacity: 497

3179
IMAGO, THE THEATRE MASK ENSEMBLE
163 Amsterdam Avenue #121
Pawling, NY 10023
Phone: 212-799-4814
Fax: 212-874-3613
Management:
Artistic Director: Carol Trifle
Artistic Director: Jerry Mouwad
Mission: To present our unique art form.
Utilizes: Singers
Founded: 1981
Specialized Field: Summer Stock; Community Theater; Mask Theater
Status: Professional
Income Sources: Westaff Touring Program; North Carolina Touring Program; Arts Midwest; Performing Arts Touring Program of Oregon
Organization Type: Performing; Touring; Resident; Educational

3180
THEATRE THREE PRODUCTIONS
412 Main Street
PO Box 512
Port Jefferson, NY 11777
Phone: 631-928-9100
Fax: 631-928-9120
e-mail: maureen@theatrethree.org
Web Site: www.theatrethree.org
Officers:
President: Andrew Markowitz
Management:
Executive Artistic Director: Jeffrey Sanzel
Managing Director: Vivian Koutrakos
Mission: Dedicated to developing an appreciation for the art of live theatre among the residents of Long Island by involving as large a constituency as possible in a rich variety of programming which includes Mainstage, Second Stage, Cabaret and Children's Theatre productions.
Utilizes: Singers
Founded: 1969
Specialized Field: Live Theatre
Status: Non-Profit, Non-Professional
Paid Staff: 15

Volunteer Staff: 15
Paid Artists: 75
Non-paid Artists: 20
Budget: $1.1 Million
Income Sources: Port Jefferson Arts Council
Season: July - June
Type of Stage: Thrust
Seating Capacity: 247
Organization Type: Performing; Touring; Resident; Educational

3181
NEW DAY REPERTORY COMPANY
29 N Hamilton Street
PO Box 269
Poughkeepsie, NY 12602
Phone: 845-485-7399
Fax: 845-485-6544
e-mail: newdayrep@netzero.com
Officers:
   Chairman: Al Coley
   Treasurer: Dr. Tansukh Dorawala
   Secretary: Dorothy Paulin
Management:
   President: Rodney K Douglas
   Managing Director: Jerry Naple
Mission: Make quality life theatre accessible to culturally/socially diverse, economically disadvantaged, and underserved audiences of all ages
Utilizes: Student Interns
Founded: 1963
Specialized Field: Classic; Contemporary
Status: Non-Profit, Professional
Paid Staff: 2
Budget: $160,000
Performs At: Vassar Institute Theatre
Facility Category: Schools; Colleges; Community Centers; Churches
Type of Stage: Proscenium
Seating Capacity: 1,100
Year Remodeled: 1997
Organization Type: Performing; Touring; Resident; Educational

3182
POWERHOUSE THEATER AT VASSAR
Vassar College
124 Raymond Avenue
Poughkeepsie, NY 12604-0225
Phone: 845-437-5902
Fax: 845-437-7209
e-mail: powerhouse@vassar.edu
Web Site: www.powerhouse.vassar.edu
Officers:
   President: Marc Segan
Management:
   Artistic Director: Johanna Pfaelzer
   General Manager: Nathan Baynard
Status: Non-Profit, Professional
Season: June - August
Type of Stage: Black Box
Seating Capacity: 130

3183
BLACKFRIARS THEATRE
28 Lawn Street
Rochester, NY 14607
Phone: 585-454-1260
e-mail: mail@blackfriars.org
Web Site: www.blackfriars.org
Management:
   President: Katharine Fischer
   Artistic Director: John Halboupis
Mission: A professional oriented community theater.

Founded: 1950
Specialized Field: Community Theater; Musical; Comedy; Classic; Contemporary
Status: Non-Profit, Professional
Paid Staff: 4
Paid Artists: 15
Facility Category: Theatre
Type of Stage: Thrust Stage; Flexible
Stage Dimensions: 20'x40'
Seating Capacity: 99-165
Year Remodeled: 1997

3184
GEVA THEATRE
75 Woodbury Boulevard
Rochester, NY 14607-1717
Phone: 716-232-1366
Fax: 716-232-4031
e-mail: gevatalk@gevatheatre.org
Web Site: www.gevatheatre.org
Officers:
   Chairman: Peter Messner
   VP: Sergio Esteban
   Secretary: Helen Zamboni
   Treasurer: Terry Hartmann
Management:
   Artistic Director: Mark Cuddy
   Production Manager: Matt Reinert
Mission: To produce work that celebrates the human spirit.
Utilizes: Singers
Founded: 1972
Specialized Field: Drama; Musicals; New Plays; World Classics
Status: Not-For-Profit, Professional
Paid Staff: 85
Volunteer Staff: 120
Paid Artists: 125
Income Sources: Theatre Communications Group; American Arts Alliance; League of Resident Theatres
Season: September - June
Performs At: Elaine Wilson Theatre, Ronald and Donna Fielding Nextstage
Annual Attendance: 160,000
Type of Stage: Thrust, Proscenium
Stage Dimensions: 50' x 40'
Seating Capacity: 552, 180
Organization Type: Performing; Resident; Educational

3185
ROCHESTER BROADWAY THEATRE LEAGUE
885 E Main Street
Rochester, NY 14605
Phone: 585-325-7760
e-mail: info@rbtl.org
Web Site: www.rbtl.org
Officers:
   President: Donald E. Jeffries
   Executive Vice President: John C. Parkhurst
   VP, Finance: Francine Barlow
   VP, Operations: Linda Glosser
Mission: The Rochester Broadway Theatre League was founded in 1957 by a small group of volunteers to stimulate, promote and develop interest in the dramatic and musical arts for the cultural benefit of the community.
Founded: 1957
Specialized Field: Broadway Musical Revivals; Summer Stock; Touring Company
Status: Non-Profit
Seating Capacity: 2,458

3186
THEATRE ON THE RIDGE
200 Ridge Road W
Building 28
Rochester, NY 14652
Phone: 716-722-9449
Fax: 716-477-8041
Management:
   Manager: David R Dunn
Mission: To provide entertainment for Eastman Kodak Company as well as the local community.
Specialized Field: Musical; Dinner Theater; Community Theater
Status: Professional; Commercial
Organization Type: Performing; Resident; Sponsoring

3187
UNIVERSITY OF ROCHESTER THEATRE PROGRAM
107 Todd Union
Rochester, NY 14627
Phone: 716-275-4088
Fax: 716-461-4547
Management:
   Artistic Director: Mervyn Willis
   Administrator: Katherine Mcgill
   Associate Director/ Art Director: Nigel Maister
   Technical Director: John Gilfus
Mission: To offer modern, contemporary and classical plays; to provide professional training.
Utilizes: Singers
Founded: 1968
Specialized Field: Educational; Theater Workshops
Status: Semi-Professional; Nonprofit
Paid Staff: 4
Paid Artists: 10
Performs At: Black Box Theatre
Organization Type: Performing; Resident; Educational

3188
CAPITOL THEATRE SUMMERSTAGE
220 W Dominick Street
Rome, NY 13440
Phone: 315-337-6277
Fax: 315-337-6277
Web Site: www.theatreorgans.com/ny/rome
Officers:
   President: Peter Ehrnstrum
Management:
   President: Eileen Trnobis
   Executive Director: Art Pierce
Mission: Offering the community an opportuniity for participation in quality music performances.
Founded: 1928
Specialized Field: Musical; Summer Stock
Status: Non-Profit, Professional
Paid Staff: 5
Paid Artists: 50
Season: July - August
Type of Stage: Proscenium
Stage Dimensions: 40' x 25'
Seating Capacity: 1700

3189
BROADHOLLOW PLAYERS LIMITED
80 13th Avenue
Building 5, Unit 6
Ronkonkoma, NY 11779
Phone: 631-471-0064
Fax: 631-471-8276
e-mail: broadhollowweb@aol.com
Management:
   Executive Producer: Jerry Zaback

Founded: 1973
Specialized Field: Community Theater; Children's Theater; Educational
Status: Nonprofit
Season: Year-Round
Seating Capacity: 175; 288; 250;

3190
BAY STREET THEATRE

PO Box 810
Sag Harbor, NY 11963
Phone: 631-725-0818
Fax: 631-725-0906
e-mail: mail@baystreet.org
Web Site: www.baystreet.org
Management:
Executive Director: Stephen Hamilton
Artistic Director: Sybil Christopher
Literary Manager: Mia Emlen Grosjean
Artistic Director: Emma Walton
General Manager: Norman Kline
Founded: 1991
Specialized Field: Drama; Musical
Status: Non-Profit, Professional
Facility Category: Theater
Type of Stage: Thrust Stage
Seating Capacity: 299

3191
FORT SALEM THEATRE

Box 10
Salem, NY 12865
Phone: 518-854-9200
Fax: 518-854-9200
e-mail: fortsalem@aol.com
Web Site: www.salemchamberofcommerce.org
Management:
President: Kim Shernan
Artistic Director: Kathy Beaver
Mission: Bring professional theatre to the Washington county and Saratoga springs area.
Founded: 1972
Specialized Field: Musical; Comedy; Youth Theater
Status: Non-Profit, Professional
Paid Staff: 10
Volunteer Staff: 10
Paid Artists: 15
Non-paid Artists: 10
Season: June - September
Type of Stage: Proscenium
Stage Dimensions: 41' x 25'
Seating Capacity: 200

3192
METTAWEE THEATRE COMPANY

209 Dunnigan Road
Salem, NY 12865
Phone: 518-854-9357
Fax: 518-854-9321
e-mail: info@mettawee.org
Officers:
President: Stephanie Gallas
Management:
Artistic Director: Ralph Lee
Managing Director: Casey Compton
Mission: To offer original theatre works incorporating masks, live music and figures that are larger than life to illustrate the myths and legends of different cultures.
Founded: 1975
Specialized Field: New Plays; Storytelling; Ethnic Theater
Status: Professional; Nonprofit
Organization Type: Performing; Touring

3193
PENDRAGON THEATRE

15 Brandy Brook
Saranac Lake, NY 12983
Phone: 518-891-1854
Fax: 518-891-7012
e-mail: pdragon@northnet.org
Web Site: www.pendragontheatre.org
Management:
Artistic Director: Susan Neal
Managing Director: Bob Pettee
Mission: Pendragon is an ensemble of artists based in the Adirondacks dedicated to preserving the vitality and enhancing the quality of professional theatre through year round performance and education programs.
Founded: 1980
Specialized Field: Theatre
Status: Non-Profit, Professional
Paid Staff: 1
Volunteer Staff: 20
Paid Artists: 20
Budget: $280,000 - $300,000
Season: June - September
Facility Category: Black Box
Type of Stage: Proscenium
Stage Dimensions: 30' x 24'
Seating Capacity: 130

3194
SARATOGA PERFORMING ARTS CENTER

Saratoga Spa State Park
Hall of Springs
Saratoga Springs, NY 12866
Phone: 518-584-9330
Fax: 518-584-0809
e-mail: elinehan@spac.oorg
Web Site: www.spac.org
Officers:
Honorary Chairman: Cornelius Whitney
Chairman: Charles V Wait
President: Herbert A Chesbrough
Secretary: Walter M. Jeffords, Jr
Treasurer: Harold N. Langlitz
Mission: To host performing arts events.
Utilizes: Singers
Founded: 1966
Specialized Field: Drama; Musical; Comedy; Classic
Status: Professional; Nonprofit
Budget: $11 Million
Income Sources: International Association of Auditorium Managers; New York Performing Arts Association; membership ticket sales
Affiliations: Summer home of New York City Ballet, Philadelphia Orchestra and Saratoga Chamber Music Festival
Annual Attendance: 350,000
Facility Category: Ampitheatre
Type of Stage: Proscenium
Stage Dimensions: 80 W x 60 D
Seating Capacity: 5100
Year Built: 1966
Organization Type: Performing; Educational; Sponsoring

3195
PROCTOR'S THEATRE

432 State Street
Schenectady, NY 12305
Phone: 518-382-3884
Fax: 518-346-2468
e-mail: boxoffice@proctors.org
Web Site: www.proctors.org

Management:
CEO: Philip Morris
Mission: Presenting Broadway, opera, popular music, dance and classical
Founded: 1926
Specialized Field: Musical; Classic; Contemporary
Status: Non-Profit, Professional
Paid Staff: 40
Volunteer Staff: 900
Paid Artists: 35

3196
SCHENECTADY CIVIC PLAYERS

12 S Church Street
Schenectady, NY 12305
Phone: 518-382-2081
e-mail: postmaster@civicplayers.org
Web Site: www.civicplayers.org
Officers:
President: Charles Hepburn
VP: Laura Houlihan
Secretary: Gail Kitchen
Treasurer: Melissa Brown
Management:
President: Melissa Brown
Mission: Continuation of long tradition of providing non-profit community theatre.
Founded: 1928
Specialized Field: Community Theater
Status: Non-Professional; Nonprofit
Income Sources: New York State Community Theatre Association; New York State Theater Festival Association
Organization Type: Performing; Resident

3197
STERLING RENAISSANCE FESTIVAL

15385 Farden Road
Sterling, NY 13156
Phone: 315-947-5783
Fax: 315-947-6905
Toll-free: 800-879-4446
e-mail: office@sterlingfestival.com
Web Site: www.sterlingfestival.com
Officers:
President: Alisa Cook
VP: John Kissler
Secretary: Phil Holding
Treasurer: Marylee Pangman
Management:
President: Virginia Young
Executive Director: Gerald Young
Artistic Director: Gary Izzo
Sales Director: Marilyn Goldthwait
Mission: To present interactive and staged performances.
Founded: 1977
Specialized Field: Musical; Comedy; Community Theater; Renaissance; Classic
Status: Non-Profit, Professional
Paid Staff: 10
Paid Artists: 80
Season: June - August
Annual Attendance: 100,000
Facility Category: Outdoor
Type of Stage: 8 Stages
Year Built: 1977

3198
PENGUIN REPERTORY COMPANY

Crickettown Road
Box 91
Stony Point, NY 10980

Phone: 845-786-2873
Fax: 914-786-3638
e-mail: info@penguinrep.org
Web Site: www.penguinrep.org
Officers:
   President: Glen Kerslake
   VP: Bob Patrick
   Treasurer: Lorette Peto
   Secretary: Thomas Wilson
Management:
   Executive Director: Andrew Horn
   Artistic Director: Joe Brancato
Mission: To give new playwrights opportunities through mounting new plays; to stage works that are tried and true.
Founded: 1977
Specialized Field: New Plays; Classic
Status: Non-Profit, Professional
Paid Staff: 25
Paid Artists: 20
Income Sources: Actors' Equity Association; Society for Stage Directors and Choreographers
Season: May - October
Annual Attendance: 7,000-10,000
Type of Stage: Proscenium
Stage Dimensions: 23'x 25'
Seating Capacity: 108
Year Built: 1830
Year Remodeled: 1986
Organization Type: Performing

3199
THALIA SPANISH THEATRE

41-17 Greenpoint Avenue
PO Box 4368
Sunnyside, NY 11104
Phone: 718-729-3880
Fax: 718-729-3388
e-mail: info@thaliatheatre.org
Web Site: www.thaliatheatre.org
Officers:
   Chairperson/Treasurer: Walter Bracero
   President: Angel Gil Orrios
   VP: Mitchell Draizin
   Secretary: Ada Suarez
Management:
   Artistic/Executive Director: Angel Gil Orrios, agil@thaliatheatre.org
   Administrative Director: Kathryn A Giaimo
   Managing Director: Soledad Lopez, slopez@thaliatheatre.org
   Technical Director: Fabricio Saquicela
Mission: To celebrate the vibrancy and diversity of Spanish and Latin American culture and heritage with unique productions of theatre, music and dance. Every month is Hispanic Heritage Month.
Utilizes: Actors; AEA Actors; Choreographers; Collaborations; Commissioned Composers; Dance Companies; Dancers; Designers; Grant Writers; Guest Accompanists; Guest Artists; Guest Choreographers; Guest Companies; Guest Conductors; Guest Designers; Guest Directors; Guest Lecturers; Guest Musical Directors; High School Drama; Instructors; Local Artists; Multimedia; Music; Organization Contracts; Resident Professionals; Sign Language Translators; Singers; Soloists; Student Interns; Special Technical Talent; Visual Arts
Founded: 1969
Specialized Field: Musical; Community Theater; Bilingual Theatre
Status: Professional; Nonprofit
Paid Staff: 4
Volunteer Staff: 6
Paid Artists: 90

Budget: $586,000
Income Sources: National Endowment for the Arts; New York State Coucil on Arts; New York City-Department of Cultural Affairs; NY Community Trust; JP Morgan Chase Foundation; Con Edison
Annual Attendance: 7,000
Facility Category: Theatre
Type of Stage: Proscenium
Seating Capacity: 72
Year Remodeled: 1992
Organization Type: Performing; Touring; Resident

3200
OPEN HAND THEATER

518 Prospect Avenue
Syracuse, NY 13208
Phone: 315-476-0466
Fax: 315-472-2578
e-mail: info@openhandtheater.org
Web Site: www.openhandtheater.org
Officers:
   President: Samuel Gordon
Management:
   Artistic Director: Geoffrey Navias
   Producer: Leslie Archer
Founded: 1980
Specialized Field: Puppet
Status: Non-Profit, Professional
Paid Staff: 5
Volunteer Staff: 85
Paid Artists: 4
Non-paid Artists: 4

3201
REDHOUSE ARTS CENTER

201 South West Street
PO Box 11506
Syracuse, NY 13218
Phone: 315-425-0405
Fax: 315-425-0561
e-mail: info@theredhouse.org
Web Site: www.theredhouse.org
Officers:
   President: Timothy Mulver, Esq
   Executive Director: Terrance Demas
Mission: To offer contemporary drama; to encourage works-in-progress through stage readings; to provide programs in schools.
Founded: 1978
Specialized Field: Musical; Comedy; Classic; Contemporary
Status: Non-Profit, Professional
Paid Staff: 15
Paid Artists: 80
Organization Type: Performing

3202
SYRACUSE STAGE

820 E Genesee Street
Syracuse, NY 13210-1508
Phone: 315-443-4008
Fax: 315-443-9846
e-mail: syrstage@syr.edu
Web Site: www.syracusestage.org
Officers:
   President: Mark Russell
Management:
   Producing Director: James A Clark
   Assistant Production Manager: Dianna Angell
   Director Marketing/Development: Barbara Beckos
   Technical Director: Randy Steffen
   Artistic Director: Robert Moss
   Dir Communications/Special Event: Heidi Holtz

Mission: To enrich, empower and entertain our community through the creation of professional theatre and to be an essential element in affecting the lives of thoughts in our community.
Utilizes: Actors; AEA Actors; Choreographers; Collaborations; Designers; Guest Designers; Guest Writers; Lyricists; Music; Original Music Scores; Resident Professionals; Selected Students; Soloists; Touring Companies
Founded: 1974
Specialized Field: Drama; Musical; New Works of Social Importance
Status: Non-Profit, Professional
Paid Staff: 90
Paid Artists: 30
Budget: $3.3 million
Income Sources: Theatre Communications Group; League of Resident Theatres; Actors' Equity Association
Season: September - May
Performs At: The John D Archbold Theatre
Annual Attendance: 90,000
Type of Stage: Proscenium
Seating Capacity: 499
Organization Type: Performing; Touring; Educational

3203
NEW YORK STATE THEATRE INSTITUTE

37 1st Street
Troy, NY 12180
Phone: 518-274-3200
Fax: 518-274-3815
e-mail: nysti@capital.net
Web Site: www.nysti.org
Officers:
   Chairman: David Morris
Management:
   Producing Artistic Director: Patricia D Benedette Snyder
Mission: To provide production of a high quality professional theatre; extensive arts in education programs; new play development; international cultural exchange.
Utilizes: Selected Students; Soloists; Students; Theatre Companies
Founded: 1976
Specialized Field: Drama; Multi-Cultural
Status: Non-Profit, Professional
Paid Staff: 33
Volunteer Staff: 250
Annual Attendance: 50,000
Facility Category: Theatre
Type of Stage: Proscenium
Stage Dimensions: 48'x30'
Seating Capacity: 850

3204
NEW YORK RENAISSANCE FAIRE

600 Route 17A
Tuxedo, NY 10987
Phone: 845-351-5171
Fax: 845-351-5646
e-mail: chrisdetroy@rec.com
Web Site: www.renfair.com
Management:
   President: Stanley Gilbert
   Executive Director: Bob Corsett
   Artistic Director: Christopher Detroy
   Finance Manager: Douglas DeTroy
   Art Director/Web Mistress: Joni Massengale
   Office Manager: Melissa McKeever
Founded: 1977
Specialized Field: Renaissance
Status: For-Profit, Professional

Paid Staff: 200
Paid Artists: 150
Season: July - September

3205
BROADWAY THEATRE LEAGUE OF UTICA

259 Genesee Street
Utica, NY 13501
Phone: 315-724-7196
Fax: 315-724-1227
e-mail: btlutica@dreamscape.com
Web Site: www.broadwayutica.com
Management:
   President: Marolyn Wilson
   Executive Director: Robert A Lewis
Founded: 1957
Specialized Field: Touring Company; Broadway Musical Revivals; Classic
Status: Non-Profit,Professional
Paid Staff: 3

3206
WATERTOWN LYRIC THEATER PRODUCTIONS

1333 Holcomb Street
Watertown, NY 13601
Phone: 315-788-6492
Fax: 315-779-8002
e-mail: lyric_theatre@yahoo.com
Web Site: www.geocities.com/lyric_theater
Officers:
   President: James S Williams Jr
   Treasurer: Steve Hunt
Management:
   President: John Michael
   Managing Director: Joan Jones
Mission: To offer the community live theatre employing local talent; to provide young people with training in musical theatre.
Utilizes: Singers
Founded: 1959
Specialized Field: Musical; Community Theater
Status: Non-Profit, Non-Professional
Volunteer Staff: 360
Non-paid Artists: 150
Performs At: State Office Building Auditorium
Organization Type: Performing; Educational

3207
DAS PUPPENSPIEL PUPPET THEATER

1 1/2 E Main Street
Westfield, NY 14787
Phone: 716-326-2611
Fax: 716-326-2601
Toll-free: 877-326-2611
e-mail: sadpupp@puppets.org
Web Site: www.puppets.org
Management:
   Artistic Director: Myriam Mayshark
   Managing Director: Kevin Kuhlman
Founded: 1974
Specialized Field: Children's Theater; Touring Company; Puppet
Status: Non-Profit, Professional
Paid Staff: 5
Paid Artists: 4
Income Sources: United International Marionette Association; Puppeteers of America; Children's Theatre Association of America
Organization Type: Performing; Touring; Educational

3208
STREET THEATER

228 Fisher Avenue
White Plains, NY 10606
Phone: 914-761-3307
Fax: 914-422-2340
e-mail: thestreettheater@aollll.com
Management:
   Artistic Director: Gray Smith
Mission: Committed to educational programs. Mission: to insure success in school for disadvantaged students through early literacy programs. Program components: weekly performance-based instruction by professional actors, teacher training, curriculum materials, parent participation, professional touring company.
Utilizes: Singers
Founded: 1970
Specialized Field: Educational; Theater Workshops; Youth Theater
Status: Professional; Semi-Professional; Nonprofit
Income Sources: Actors' Equity Association
Organization Type: Performing; Touring; Educational

3209
COMMON STAGE THEATRE COMPANY

PO Box 1028
Woodstock, NY 12498
Phone: 845-679-9256
Mission: Developing and producing plays by women.
Utilizes: Singers
Founded: 1989
Specialized Field: Women's Theater
Status: Semi-Professional; Nonprofit
Paid Staff: 10

North Carolina

3210
BLACK SWAN THEATER

825-C Merriman Avenue
#318
Asheville, NC 28804
Phone: 828-254-6057
Fax: 828-251-6603
e-mail: swantheatre@aol.com
Web Site: blackswan.org
Management:
   Director: David B Hopes
Mission: To produce original contemporary scripts and reinterpret the classics.
Utilizes: Actors; Choreographers; Collaborating Artists; Collaborations; Commissioned Composers; Commissioned Music; Community Talent; Composers; Dance Companies; Dancers; Designers; Guest Accompanists; Guest Artists; Guest Choreographers; Guest Companies; Guest Conductors; Guest Designers; Guest Lecturers; Guest Musical Directors; Guest Musicians; Guest Writers; Instructors; Local Artists; Multi Collaborations; Organization Contracts; Original Music Scores; Paid Performers; Performance Artists; Playwrights; Resident Professionals; Sign Language Translators; Singers; Special Technical Talent; Theatre Companies; Visual Arts
Founded: 1988
Specialized Field: Contemporary; Classic; New Plays
Status: Non-Professional; Nonprofit
Paid Staff: 70
Income Sources: University of North Carolina at Asheville Creative Writing Department; Ticket Sales
Organization Type: Performing; Touring; Sponsoring

3211
DIANA WORTHAM THEATRE AT PACK PLACE

2 S Pack Square
Asheville, NC 28801
Phone: 828-257-4530
Fax: 828-251-5652
e-mail: jellis@dwtheatre.com
Web Site: www.dwtheatre.com
Management:
   Managing Director: John Ellis
Founded: 1993
Specialized Field: Youth Theater; Puppet; Classic; Contemporary
Status: Non-Profit, Professional
Paid Staff: 3
Volunteer Staff: 30
Budget: $400,000
Annual Attendance: 40,000
Facility Category: Performing Arts Center
Type of Stage: Proscenium
Stage Dimensions: 40x40
Seating Capacity: 500
Year Built: 1992

3212
SMOKY MOUNTAIN REPERTORY THEATRE

26 S Lexington Street
Asheville, NC 28801
Phone: 704-252-9661
Management:
   Managing Director: H Byron Ballard
   Business Manager: Joe Fioccola
   Technical Director: M Michael Hyatt
   Youth Director: Vivienne Conjura
Mission: Producing new works and adaptations with particular emphasis on plays of regional significance.
Utilizes: Singers
Founded: 1981
Specialized Field: Ethnic Theater; Ensembles
Status: Professional; Semi-Professional; Nonprofit
Paid Staff: 10
Performs At: First Artists Studio Theater
Organization Type: Performing; Touring; Resident; Educational

3213
LEES-MCRAE COLLEGE

Performing Arts Department
191 Main Street
Banner Elk, NC 28604
Mailing Address: PO Box 128
Phone: 828-898-8721
Fax: 828-989-3467
e-mail: joslinp@lmc.edu
Web Site: www.lmc.edu
Management:
   President: Dr. Barry M Buxton
   Summer Theatre, Artistic Director: Dr. Janet Barton Speer
   Chair, Div of Creative & Fine Arts: Dr. Kacy Crabtree
   Division Assistant: Pamela Wilder Joslin
Mission: LMST is a professional company that shows three musicals each summer.
Founded: 1900
Opened: 1984
Specialized Field: Musical Summer Stock
Status: Non-Profit, Non-Professional
Paid Staff: 13
Paid Artists: 15
Season: June - August

3214
BLOWING ROCK STAGE COMPANY
PO Box 2170
Blowing Rock, NC 28605
Phone: 828-295-9168
Fax: 828-295-9104
e-mail: theatre@blowingrock.com
Web Site: www.blowingrockstage.com
Officers:
President: Connie Baird
VP: Rebecca Wright
Treasurer: Jerry Burns
Secretary: Yvonne Myers
Management:
President: Freda Smith
Artistic Director: Kenneth Kay
General Manager: Robert Miller
Founded: 1986
Specialized Field: Musical; Comedy; Summer Stock
Status: Non-Profit, Professional
Paid Staff: 2
Paid Artists: 40
Season: June - September
Type of Stage: Proscenium
Stage Dimensions: 28'x 36'
Seating Capacity: 240

3215
ARTSCENTER
300-G E Main Street
Carrboro, NC 27510
Phone: 919-929-2787
Fax: 919-969-8574
e-mail: info@artscenterlive.org
Web Site: www.artscenterlive.org
Officers:
Chairman: Steve Benezra
Management:
Executive Director: Jon Wilner
Booking Manager: Tess O'Cana
Mission: To inspire a love of the arts through
presentation of a broad range of artists and educational
programs, and by supporting the development of young
artists; to create an environment for exploring and
appreciating artistic expression.
Utilizes: Guest Companies; Singers
Founded: 1973
Specialized Field: Young Playwrights; Youth Theater;
Community Theater; Puppet
Status: Non-Profit, Professional
Paid Staff: 6
Volunteer Staff: 30
Paid Artists: 250
Income Sources: Grants; Ticket Sales; Class Tuitions;
Donars; Foundations
Performs At: Earl Wynn Theatre
Annual Attendance: 83,750
Seating Capacity: 350
Year Built: 1972
Year Remodeled: 1986
Organization Type: Performing; Touting; Resident;
Educational; Sponsoring

3216
INSTITUTE OF OUTDOOR DRAMA
CB 3240, 1700 Airport Road
UNC
Chapel Hill, NC 27599-3240
Phone: 919-962-1328
Fax: 919-962-4212
e-mail: outdoor@unc.edu
Web Site: www.unc.edu/depts/outdoor
Management:

President: Scott J Parker
Mission: Sponsors regional auditions for performers
and technicians in outdoor dramas; hosts management
conference annually; conducts feasibility studies.
Utilizes: Singers
Founded: 1963
Specialized Field: Outdoor Theater; Drama
Status: Non-Profit, Professional
Paid Staff: 3
Organization Type: Educational; Sponsoring

3217
PLAYMAKERS REPERTORY COMPANY
Centers for Dramatic Art
CB #3235
Chapel Hill, NC 27599-3235
Phone: 919-962-7529
Fax: 919-962-5791
e-mail: prcboxoffice@unc.edu
Web Site: www.playmakersrep.org
Management:
Managing Director: Hannah Grannemann
Producing Artistic Director: Joseph Haj
General Manager: Heidi Reklis,
hreklis@email.unc.edu
Mission: To engage our community in an ongoing
exploration of and significance of theatre in
contemporary life; to investigate the theatrical events
and the methods used for its realization in performance.
Utilizes: Dancers; Guest Lecturers; Instructors; Paid
Performers; Scenic Designers; Soloists
Founded: 1976
Specialized Field: Contemporary Works; Classics;
New Works of Social Importance
Status: Professional
Paid Staff: 15
Budget: $2.4 million
Income Sources: Private Foundations; Grants;
Endowments; Business; Ccorpote Donations; Box
Office; Government Grant; Individual Donors
Performs At: Paul Green Theatre; Elizabeth Price
Kenan Theatre
Affiliations: League of Resident Theatres; Actors'
Equity Association; Society for Stage Directors and
Choreographers
Type of Stage: Thrust
Seating Capacity: 499;285
Year Built: 1976
Year Remodeled: 2010
Organization Type: Performing; Educational

3218
ACTOR'S THEATRE OF CHARLOTTE
650 E Stonewall Street
Charlotte, NC 28202
Phone: 704-342-2251
Fax: 704-342-1229
e-mail: actorstheatre@bellsouth.net
Web Site: www.actorstheatrecharlotte.org
Management:
President: Dan Shoemaker
Managing Director: Chip Decker
Mission: The mission of Actor's Theatre of Charlotte is
to produce bold and innovative new works by
contemporary playwrights.
Founded: 1989
Specialized Field: Drama; Contemporary
Status: Non-Profit, Professional
Paid Staff: 3
Volunteer Staff: 6
Paid Artists: 37
Budget: $197,000
Type of Stage: Proscenium

3219
CENTRAL PIEDMONT COMMUNITY THEATRE
1201 Elizabeth Avenue
Charlotte, NC 28204
Phone: 704-330-6534
Fax: 704-330-6290
Web Site: www.cpcc.edu
Management:
Producer and Director: Tom Vance
Director: Tom Hollis
Mission: To offer quality entertainment to the
community; to provide training for students aspiring to
careers in professional theatre.
Utilizes: Guest Companies; Singers
Founded: 1974
Specialized Field: Musical; Community Theater
Status: Non-Profit, Professional
Paid Staff: 40
Income Sources: North Carolina Theatre Conference;
Southeastern Theatre Conference
Performs At: Pease Auditorium
Organization Type: Performing; Educational

3220
CHARLOTTE REPERTORY THEATRE
2424 N Davidson Street
Suite 113
Charlotte, NC 28205
Phone: 704-333-8587
Fax: 704-333-0224
e-mail: info@charlotterep.org
Web Site: www.charlotterep.org
Officers:
President: Mike McGuire
Treasurer: Neil Glenn
Secretary: Anita Doran
Management:
Artistic Director: Terry Loughlin
Managing Director: Debbie Fitts
Founder: Matt Olin
Literary Manager: Claudia C Covington
Mission: Presenting contemporary plays, developing
and presenting new works and reviving modern drama
classics.
Utilizes: Educators; Equity Actors; Guest Companies;
Performance Artists; Singers
Founded: 1976
Specialized Field: Musical; Comedy; Classic;
Contemporary
Status: Non-Profit, Professional
Paid Staff: 20
Paid Artists: 40
Income Sources: Actors' Equity Association
Performs At: Booth Theatre at North Carolina
Blumenthal Performing Arts Center
Type of Stage: Flexible
Seating Capacity: 450
Organization Type: Performing; Resident

3221
CHILDREN'S THEATRE OF CHARLOTTE
300 East 7th Street
Charlotte, NC 28202
Phone: 704-973-2800
Fax: 703-973-2850
e-mail: info@ctcharlotte.org
Web Site: www.ctcharlotte.org
Officers:
Executive Director: Bruce LaRowe
Management:
Artistic Director: Alan Poindexter
Education Director: Valerie Rhymer

Mission: To enrich the lives of young people, ages 3-18, of all cultures, through theatre and education experiences of the highest quality.
Founded: 1948
Specialized Field: Children's Theater
Status: Non-Profit, Professional
Paid Staff: 30
Paid Artists: 80
Income Sources: Arts and Science Council; Cultural Education Collaborative; North Carolina Arts Council; National Endowment for the Arts

3222
THEATRE CHARLOTTE
501 Queens Road
Charlotte, NC 28207
Phone: 704-334-9128
Fax: 704-347-5216
e-mail: ron@theatrecharlotte.org
Web Site: www.theatrecharlotte.org
Mission: To offer community members an opportunity to participate in or attend amateur theatre productions.
Utilizes: Actors; Collaborations; Commissioned Music; Educators; Fine Artists; Grant Writers; Guest Artists; Guest Companies; Guest Conductors; Guest Lecturers; Guild Activities; Local Artists; Multi Collaborations; Organization Contracts; Singers; Touring Companies
Founded: 1927
Specialized Field: Community Theater
Status: Nonprofit
Paid Staff: 6
Income Sources: First Nighters
Facility Category: Community Theatre
Type of Stage: Proscenium
Seating Capacity: 221
Year Built: 1941
Year Remodeled: 1998
Cost: $100,000
Organization Type: Performing; Educational

3223
CAROLINA THEATRE OF DURHAM
309 W Morgan Street
Durham, NC 27701-2119
Phone: 919-560-3040
Fax: 919-560-3065
e-mail: connie@carolinatheatre.org
Web Site: www.carolinatheatre.org
Management:
   President: Ed Rose
   Executive Director: Connie Campanero
   Programming Rentals Director: Jim Carl
Mission: To manage, operate and program the creative theater for the city of Durham.
Utilizes: Dance Companies; Filmmakers; Local Artists; Original Music Scores; Theatre Companies
Founded: 1992
Specialized Field: Community Theater; Musical
Status: Non-Profit, Professional
Paid Staff: 60
Volunteer Staff: 200
Paid Artists: 30
Budget: $1,000,000
Performs At: Fletcher Hall
Annual Attendance: 150,000
Facility Category: Performance Center/Cinemas
Type of Stage: Proscenium
Stage Dimensions: 30'x 60'
Seating Capacity: 1,015
Year Built: 1926
Year Remodeled: 1994
Rental Contact: Jim Carl

3224
THEATRE PREVIEWS AT DUKE
109 Page
Durham, NC 27708-0680
Phone: 919-660-3343
Fax: 919-684-8906
e-mail: mmsauls@duke.edu
Web Site: www.theaterstudies.duke.edu
Management:
   Director of Theater: Miriam Sauls
Mission: Theatre Previews is the professional prodcing arm of the Duke University Department of Theater Studies and a laboratory for the professional development and production of new plays on Duke's campus.
Founded: 1986
Specialized Field: Musical; Comedy; Classic; Contemporary; Educational
Status: Non-Profit, Professional
Paid Staff: 1
Facility Category: Theater
Seating Capacity: 600

3225
CHILDREN'S THEATRE OF EDEN
PO Box 547
Eden, NC 27288
Phone: 336-725-4531
Fax: 336-725-4531
Mission: To provide professional plays for all children in Eden City schools at no cost.
Founded: 1971
Specialized Field: Musical; Ethnic Theater; Puppet; Children's Theater
Status: Professional; Nonprofit
Performs At: High School Auditorium
Organization Type: Sponsoring

3226
CAPE FEAR REGIONAL THEATRE
1209 Hay Street
Fayetteville, NC 28305
Phone: 919-323-4234
Fax: 919-323-0898
e-mail: bothorp@cfrt.org
Web Site: www.cfrt.org
Officers:
   Marketing Director: Claire Cheatwood Hedgecoe
Management:
   Artistic Director: Bo Thorp
Mission: To offer a diverse program of plays to the Cape Fear Region.
Utilizes: AEA Actors; Curators; Guest Artists; Guest Companies; Singers
Founded: 1962
Specialized Field: Musical; Community Theater; Puppet; Drama
Status: For-Profit,Professional
Income Sources: North Carolina Theatre Conference; Southeastern Theatre Conference; Arts Council
Seating Capacity: 327
Organization Type: Performing

3227
GILBERT THEATER
Bow Street
PO Box53704
Fayetteville, NC 28305
Phone: 910-678-7186
e-mail: gilberttheater@aol.com
Management:
   Executive Director: Gerald Ellison
   Artistic Director: Lynn Pryer

   Managing Director: Andrew Morfesis
Mission: Our purpose is to use our creativity and enthusiasm to support and inspire others as we all freely express our talents in joyfulness, harmony and love.
Founded: 1994
Specialized Field: Contemporary; Classic
Status: Non-Profit, Professional

3228
FLAT ROCK PLAYHOUSE
2661 Greenville Highway
Flat Rock, NC 28731
Phone: 828-693-0403
Fax: 828-693-6795
e-mail: frp@flatrockplayhouse.org
Web Site: www.flatrockplayhouse.org
Management:
   Producing Artistic Director: Vincent Marini
   Managing Director: Paige Posey
   Associate Artistic Director: Scott Treadway
   Production Stage Manager: Bill Munoz
Mission: To produce the highest quality professional theatre while teaching theatre arts through a multifaceted educational program.
Founded: 1937
Specialized Field: Musical; Comedy; Youth Theater; Contemporary; Theater Workshops
Status: Non-Profit, Professional
Paid Staff: 30
Volunteer Staff: 10
Paid Artists: 100
Budget: $2.6 million
Income Sources: Ticket Sales; Grants; Donations
Season: May - October
Performs At: Flat Rock Playhouse
Affiliations: Actor's Equity Association; South Eastern Theatre Conference; North Carolina Theatre Conference
Annual Attendance: 100,000
Type of Stage: Proscenium
Stage Dimensions: 30'x40'
Seating Capacity: 500
Year Built: 1956
Organization Type: Performing; Touring; Resident; Educational; Sponsoring

3229
LITTLE THEATER OF GASTONIA
238 Clay Street
PO Box 302
Gastonia, NC 28053
Phone: 704-865-0160
e-mail: ewixson@prodigy.net
Web Site: www.littletheatergastonia.org
Management:
   President: Susan Lisle
Mission: To offer entertainment as well as education in the theatre arts.
Utilizes: Singers
Founded: 1950
Specialized Field: Musical; Comedy; Community Theater; Classic; Contemporary
Status: Non-Profit, Non-Professional
Paid Staff: 50
Volunteer Staff: 6
Income Sources: Ticket Sales; Season Memberships
Performs At: The Little Theatre of Gastonia
Organization Type: Performing; Educational

3230

CITY ARTS DRAMA CENTER
200 N Davie Street
Box 2
Greensboro, NC 27401
Phone: 336-335-6426
Fax: 336-373-2659
e-mail: stephen.hyers@greensboro-nc.gov
Web Site: www.TheDramaCenter.com
Management:
   Managing Director: Stephen D. Hyers
Mission: To present six musicals annually. The programs presented are: Livestock Players, Greensboro Children's Theatre, Greensboro Playwrights' Forum, 3rd Stage Theatre Company, Greene Pictures.
Utilizes: Guest Artists; Guest Companies
Founded: 1971
Specialized Field: Musical; Drama; Ensembles; Children's Theater
Status: Non-Profit, Non-Professional
Paid Staff: 2
Paid Artists: 10
Income Sources: Southeastern Theatre Conference
Performs At: Carolina Theatre
Organization Type: Performing

3231

COMMUNITY THEATRE OF GREENSBORO
200 N Davie Street
#9
Greensboro, NC 27401
Phone: 336-333-7470
Fax: 336-333-2607
e-mail: ctgemail@aol.com
Web Site: www.ctgso.com
Officers:
   President: Scott Brewington
   VP: Randy Hanson
   Secretary: Brett Brackett
   Treasurer: Dennis Duquette
Management:
   President: Chris Lamey
   Executive Director: Mitchel Sommers
   Director Marketing/Development: Robert Ankrom
   Director Education: Pauline Cobrda
Mission: To provide an outlet in the community whereby persons may participate avocationally in a live theatrical experience of high calibre, both as talent and audience under professional guidance.
Utilizes: Actors; Choreographers; Dancers; Grant Writers; Guest Artists; Guest Composers; Guest Lecturers; Music; Resident Professionals; Student Interns
Founded: 1954
Specialized Field: Musical; Community Theater
Status: Non-Profit, Non-Professional
Paid Staff: 5
Budget: $552,000
Income Sources: United Arts Council of Greensboro; Fundraising
Performs At: Carolina Theatre; GSO Cultural Center
Annual Attendance: 35,000
Organization Type: Performing; Resident; Educational

3232

GREENSBORO CHILDREN'S THEATRE
200 N Davie Street
Greensboro, NC 27401
Phone: 336-373-2728
Fax: 336-373-2659
e-mail: barbara.britton@ci.greensboro.nc.us
Web Site:
www.ci.greensboro.nc.us/leisure/drama/gct.htm
Management:
   Director: Barbara Britton
Mission: To offer a series of drama classes and three quality plays annually by and for children and families as part of a recreation program.
Utilizes: Guest Companies
Founded: 1971
Specialized Field: Musical; Community Theater; Children's Theater
Status: Non-Professional; Nonprofit
Paid Staff: 2
Volunteer Staff: 10
Paid Artists: 50
Income Sources: City of Greensboro NC Parks and Recreation Depertment; Ticket Sales
Performs At: Weaver Education Center Theatre
Affiliations: Southeastern Theatre Conference; City Arts Drama; NC Theatre Conference
Annual Attendance: 2,500-3,000
Facility Category: Rented
Type of Stage: Proscenium Stage
Organization Type: Performing

3233

HICKORY COMMUNITY THEATRE
30 3rd Street NW
Hickory, NC 28601
Phone: 828-327-3855
Fax: 828-328-2284
e-mail: pam@hct.org
Web Site: www.hct.org
Management:
   President: Lee Pugh
   Executive Director: Pamela Livingstone
   Managing Artistic Director: Pamela Livingstone
Mission: To offer quality theatre to the community; to provide a performance outlet for talented local performers.
Utilizes: Actors; Grant Writers; Guest Artists; Guest Companies; Guest Designers; Guest Directors; Guest Lecturers; High School Drama; Local Artists; Multimedia; Music; Performance Artists; Resident Professionals; Singers; Soloists
Founded: 1949
Specialized Field: Musical; Comedy; Community Theater; Classic; Contemporary
Status: Non-Profit, Non-Professional
Paid Staff: 5
Budget: $412,000
Income Sources: Catawba County Council for the Arts; Box Office; Grants; Donatios
Performs At: Old City Hall
Affiliations: AACT; NCTC; SETA
Facility Category: Community Theatre
Type of Stage: Proscenium/Cabaret
Seating Capacity: 382; 72
Organization Type: Performing; Touring; Resident; Educational

3234

YOUTHEATRE
810 8th Street NE
Hickory, NC 28601
Phone: 828-324-5354
Management:
   Owner/Executive Director: Sylvia B Hoffmire
Mission: To provide an arena for the creative expression of young people through performance and study.

Utilizes: Guest Companies; Singers
Founded: 1976
Specialized Field: Community Theater; Youth Theater
Status: Professional; Semi-Professional; Commercial
Income Sources: Catawba County Council for the Arts
Organization Type: Performing; Touring; Educational; Sponsoring

3235

HIGH POINT COMMUNITY THEATRE
1014 Mill Avenue
Suite 190
High Point, NC 27260
Mailing Address: PO Box 1152, High Point, NC 27261
Phone: 336-882-2542
Fax: 336-882-4178
e-mail: jblevins@hpcommunitytheater.org
Web Site: www.hpcommunitytheater.org
Management:
   President: Ed Cornwell
   Executive Director: Jennifer Blevins
Mission: To promote community involvement in performing arts; to provide high quality entertainment for citizens in our area.
Utilizes: Guest Artists; Guest Companies; Singers
Founded: 1976
Specialized Field: Community Theater
Status: Non-Profit, Non-Professional
Paid Staff: 1
Paid Artists: 25
Income Sources: High Point Arts Council
Performs At: High Point Theatre
Affiliations: High Point Area Arts Council
Organization Type: Performing

3236

NORTH CAROLINA SHAKESPEARE FESTIVAL
1014 Mill Avenue
High Point, NC 27260
Phone: 336-841-2273
Fax: 336-841-8627
e-mail: pedro@ncshakes.org
Web Site: www.ncshakes.org
Officers:
   Chairman: Christine Green
Management:
   Managing Director: Pedro Silva
Mission: Seeks to serve the cultural and educational needs of North Carolina audiences through traditional and nontraditional staging of the plays of Shakespeare and other classic playwrights.
Founded: 1977
Specialized Field: Youth Theater; Classic
Status: Non-Profit, Professional
Paid Staff: 7
Paid Artists: 55
Budget: $1,400,000
Income Sources: Ticket Sales; Touring Fees; Contributors
Season: Late August - December
Performs At: High Point Theatre
Organization Type: Performing; Touring; Resident; Educational

3237

LOST COLONY
1409 National Park Drive
Manteo, NC 27954
Phone: 252-473-2127
Fax: 252-473-6000
Toll-free: 866-468-7630

Utilizes: Actors; Dancers; Grant Writers; Multimedia; Music; Selected Students; Sign Language Translators; Soloists; Student Interns
Founded: 1937
Specialized Field: Summer Stock
Status: Non-Equity; Nonprofit
Season: June - August
Type of Stage: Amphitheatre
Stage Dimensions: 80' x 40'
Seating Capacity: 1650
Year Built: 1937
Year Remodeled: 1998

3238
FOOTHILLS COMMUNITY THEATRE
24 S Main Street
PO Box 1387
Marion, NC 28752
Phone: 828-659-7529
Management:
   Artistic Director: Sandra Epperson
Mission: To offer opportunities for participation in the performing arts; to enhance cultural life and provide entertainment.
Utilizes: Guest Artists; Guest Companies; Singers
Founded: 1972
Specialized Field: Community Theater
Status: Non-Professional; Nonprofit
Income Sources: McDowell Arts & Craft Association
Performs At: McDowell East Junior High; McDowell Technical Company
Organization Type: Performing

3239
SOUTHERN APPALACHIAN REPERTORY THEATRE
Mars Hill College
PO Box 1720
Mars Hill, NC 28754
Phone: 828-689-1384
Fax: 828-689-1272
e-mail: sart@mhc.edu
Web Site: www.sartheatre.com
Management:
   President: Richard Morgan
   Artistic Director: William Gregg
   Managing Director: Rob Miller
   Production Manager: Neil St Clair
Mission: From the beginning, SART's purpose has been to produce quality theatre by a professional non-profit company in an area considered economically and culturally deprived, to present plays concerning Applachia that portray the rich culture and heritage of its people.
Utilizes: Guest Companies; Singers
Founded: 1975
Specialized Field: Comedy; Ensembles; Contemporary
Status: Non-Profit, Professional
Paid Staff: 4
Volunteer Staff: 3
Paid Artists: 60
Non-paid Artists: 4
Income Sources: Mars Hill College; Ticket Sales
Performs At: Owen Theatre
Year Built: 1887
Organization Type: Performing; Touring; Resident

3240
MATTHEWS PLAYHOUSE
PO Box 3331
Matthews, NC 28106
Phone: 704-846-8343
Management:
   President: Randy Ballard

Vice President: Roy Schumacher
Secretary: Carolanne Gooley
Treasurer: John Hurst
Artistic Director: June Bayless
Resident Director: Jamey Varnadore
Mission: To provide the good people of our community with theatrical experience, educational opportunities, and quality entertainment.
Founded: 1995
Specialized Field: Children's Theater; Educational; Musical

3241
MOORESVILLE COMMUNITY THEATRE
PO Box 194
Mooresville, NC 28115
Phone: 704-664-5254
Fax: 704-662-3344
Web Site: www.main.nc.us
Officers:
   President: Larry Gambill
   VP: Julian D'Amico
   Secretary/Treasurer: Clayton Miller
Management:
   President: Julian D'Amico
Mission: To provide live theatre for the Mooresville area.
Utilizes: Actors; Choreographers; Guest Designers; Instructors; Local Artists; Multimedia; Resident Professionals; Sign Language Translators
Founded: 1973
Specialized Field: Musical; Comedy; Community Theater; Contemporary; New Plays
Status: Non-Profit, Non-Professional
Paid Staff: 4
Volunteer Staff: 10
Paid Artists: 4
Income Sources: Box; Office Receipts
Performs At: Joe V Knox Auditorium
Organization Type: Performing

3242
UNTO THESE HILLS
PO Box 398
Pittsboro, NC 28719
Phone: 828-497-2111
Fax: 828-497-6987
Toll-free: 866-554-4557
e-mail: cheratt@dnet.net
Web Site: www.untothesehills.com/
Management:
   Artistic Director: Peter Hardy
   General Manager: Barry Hipps
Mission: America's most popular outdoor drama, Unto These Hills, is the tragic and triumphant story of the Cherokee.
Founded: 1950
Specialized Field: Drama; Multi-Cultural; Historical
Status: Non-Profit, Professional
Paid Staff: 290
Paid Artists: 70
Season: May - August

3243
ACTORS COMEDY LAB
1610 Midtown Place
Raleigh, NC 27609
Phone: 919-873-1333
Fax: 919-875-0703
e-mail: info@actorscomedylab.com
Officers:
   Board Member: Nancy Rich
Specialized Field: Comedy
Status: Nonprofit

3244
BURNING COAL THEATRE COMPANY
224 Polk Street
Raleigh, NC 27604
Phone: 919-834-4001
Fax: 919-834-4002
e-mail: burning_coal@ipass.net
Web Site: www.burningcoal.org
Officers:
   Board of Directors: Kate Day
   Board of Directors: William Lightfoot
   Board of Directors: Marvin Swirsky
   Board of Advisors: Wiliam Peeples
Management:
   Artistic Director: Jerome Davis
   Managing Director: Simmie Kastner
Mission: To produce, literate, visceral, affecting theatre that is experienced, not simply seen.
Specialized Field: Musical; Drama; Comedy
Status: Incorporated; Nonprofit
Income Sources: City of Raleigh Arts Commission; United Arts
Facility Category: Flexible Black Box

3245
NORTH CAROLINA THEATRE
One E S Street
Raleigh, NC 27601
Phone: 919-831-6941
Fax: 919-831-6951
e-mail: nct@nctheatre.com
Web Site: www.nctheatre.com
Officers:
   President: Duke Fentress
Management:
   President: Robert Monroe
   Executive Director: William Jones
   Founder: De Ann S Jones
Mission: To provide Broadway-quality professional theatre at an affordable price as well as provide available employment to theatre artists and craftsmen.
Utilizes: Actors; AEA Actors; Choreographers; Dancers; Designers; Educators; Guest Accompanists; Guest Artists; Guest Conductors; Guest Designers; Guest Directors; Guest Ensembles; High School Drama; Instructors; Local Artists; Multimedia; Music; Original Music Scores; Resident Professionals; Selected Students; Sign Language Translators; Student Interns; Theatre Companies
Founded: 1983
Specialized Field: Broadway Musical Revivals
Status: Non-Profit, Professional
Paid Staff: 10
Budget: $678,000
Income Sources: Grants; Sponsors; Donations; Ticket Sales; Kids' Programs
Facility Category: Auditorium
Seating Capacity: 2000-2500
Year Remodeled: 2002
Organization Type: Performing

3246
RALEIGH ENSEMBLE PLAYERS
201 E Davie Street
Raleigh, NC 27601
Phone: 919-832-9607
Fax: 919-821-0383
e-mail: gorep@juno.com
Web Site: www.realtheatre.org
Management:
   Managing Director: Gary Williams
   Artistic Director: Glen Mathews
Founded: 1983

Specialized Field: Ensembles; Contemporary
Status: Non-Profit, Professional
Paid Staff: 5

3247
SIDE BY SIDE
150 Fayetteville Street
PO Box 19416
Raleigh, NC 27601
Phone: 919-833-1141
Management:
Director: Paul B Conway
Mission: To provide entertainment.
Founded: 1981
Specialized Field: Musical; Dinner Theater; Community Theater; Ethnic Theater
Status: Semi-Professional; Nonprofit
Organization Type: Performing

3248
THEATRE IN THE PARK
107 Pullen Road
Raleigh, NC 27607-7367
Phone: 919-831-6936
Fax: 919-831-9475
e-mail: info@theatreinthepark.com
Web Site: www.theatreinthepark.com
Officers:
President: Bill Parmelee
VP: G Troy Page
Secretary: Camille Patterson
Treasurer: Johy Taylor
Management:
President: Van Eure
Executive Director: Ira David Wood
Financial Director: Sue R Hill
Director Of Managing: Dolly R Sickle
Mission: North Carolina's largest community theatre. Each year, theatre in the park produces humorous productions, Shakepeare and original plays.
Utilizes: Guest Companies
Founded: 1973
Specialized Field: Musical; Community Theater
Status: Non-Professional; Nonprofit
Paid Staff: 6
Volunteer Staff: 10
Non-paid Artists: 120
Income Sources: American Alliance for Theatre Arts; North Carolina Community Theatre
Performs At: Theatre In The Park
Organization Type: Performing; Touring; Resident; Educational; Sponsoring

3249
PIEDMONT PLAYERS THEATRE
213 S Main Street
PO Box 762
Salisbury, NC 28145
Phone: 704-633-5471
Fax: 704-633-4653
e-mail: bm@piedmontplayers.com
Web Site: www.piedmontplayers.com
Officers:
President: David Crook
VP: John Sofley
Treasurer: John Brincefield
Management:
President: Monica Bigsbi
Resident Director: Reid Leonard
Box Office Manager: Laura Sandridge
Volunteer Coordinator: Suzanne Burgess
Mission: To entertain and educate the community.
Utilizes: Educators; Guest Artists; Multi Collaborations; Multimedia; Organization Contracts; Singers

Founded: 1961
Specialized Field: Musical; Comedy; Youth Theater; Ethnic Theater; Community Theater; Classic; Contemporary
Status: Non-Profit, Non-Professional
Paid Staff: 2
Volunteer Staff: 100
Budget: $255,700
Income Sources: Season Memberships; Ticket Sales; Donations
Performs At: The Meroney Theatre
Affiliations: NC Center for Non-Profits
Annual Attendance: 16,000
Facility Category: Performing Arts Center
Type of Stage: Proscenium
Stage Dimensions: 24'x32'x30' deep, 12' wings
Seating Capacity: 361
Year Built: 1906
Year Remodeled: 1995
Architect: Newman & Jones
Cost: $1,800,000
Rental Contact: Faculty Manager Diana Moghrabi
Organization Type: Performing

3250
TEMPLE THEATRE COMPANY
120 Carthage Street
PO Box 1391
Sanford, NC 27330
Phone: 919-774-4512
Fax: 919-774-7531
Web Site: www.templeshows.com
Officers:
President: Cindy Boggs
VP: Mary Dossenbath
Secretary: Martha Ragsdale
Treasurer: Kathi Smith
Management:
President: Cinny Beggs
Artistic Director: Jerry Sipp
Technical Director: Brad Sizemore
Box Office Manager: Karen Brewer
Mission: To entertain, enlighten, educate, and enrich lives through the performing arts.
Utilizes: Actors; AEA Actors; Choreographers; Collaborations; Commissioned Composers; Commissioned Music; Grant Writers; Guest Artists; Guest Choreographers; Guest Companies; Guest Conductors; Guest Designers; Guest Lecturers; Guest Musical Directors; Music; Original Music Scores; Resident Professionals; Sign Language Translators; Student Interns; Theatre Companies
Founded: 1925
Specialized Field: Drama; Musical; Comedy; Classic
Status: Non-Profit, Professional
Paid Staff: 5
Volunteer Staff: 30
Paid Artists: 60
Budget: $330,000
Income Sources: State; Local Government; Corporate; Individuala Theatre Conference
Performs At: Temple Theatre
Affiliations: SETC, NCTC
Annual Attendance: 21,000
Facility Category: Theatre
Type of Stage: Proscenium
Seating Capacity: 339
Year Built: 1925
Year Remodeled: 1984
Cost: $500,000
Rental Contact: Jerry Sipp
Organization Type: Performing; Educational; Sponsoring

3251
SNOW CAMP HISTORICAL DRAMA SOCIETY
1 Drama Road
PO Box 535
Snow Camp, NC 27349
Phone: 336-376-6948
Toll-free: 800-726-5115
e-mail: snowcampot@aol.com
Web Site: www.snowcampdrama.com
Officers:
President: Carol Guthrie
Secretary/General Manager: James Wilson
Founded: 1974
Specialized Field: Outdoor Theater; Drama; Classic
Status: Non-Profit, Professional
Paid Staff: 40
Paid Artists: 20
Season: Year Round
Type of Stage: Amphitheater
Stage Dimensions: 100' x 400'
Seating Capacity: 500

3252
SANDHILLS LITTLE THEATRE
250 NW Broad Street
Southern Pines, NC 28387
Phone: 910-692-3340
Fax: 910-692-9821
e-mail: slt@pinehurst.net
Web Site: web2.sandhillsonline.com
Management:
Administrative Assistant: Karen Steerman
Mission: To please audiences.
Utilizes: Guest Companies; Singers
Founded: 1981
Specialized Field: Community Theater
Status: Non-Professional; Nonprofit
Paid Staff: 200
Income Sources: New England Theatre Conference; Southeastern Theatre Conference
Performs At: Performing Arts Center
Organization Type: Performing; Resident; Sponsoring

3253
OLD COLONY PLAYERS
PO Box 112
Valdese, NC 28690
Phone: 828-874-0176
Fax: 828-874-0176
e-mail: ocp@hci.net
Web Site: www.oldcolonyplayers.com
Officers:
President: Marvin Folger
VP: Chuck Moseley
Treasurer: Mark Rostan
Secretary: Nancy McFadden
Management:
Executive Director: Knolan Benfield
Business Manager: Knolan Benfield
Mission: To produce the historical outdoor drama from this day forward annually; to produce Dickens' A Christmas Carol annually; to produce other dramas, engage in outreach activities, and sponser workshops and cultural events.
Utilizes: Guest Artists; Guest Companies; Singers
Founded: 1936
Specialized Field: Outdoor Theater; Historical; Theater Workshops
Status: Non-Profit, Non-Professional
Paid Staff: 2
Paid Artists: 30

Income Sources: Southeastern Theatre Conference; North Carolina Theatre Conference; North Carolina Association of Professional Theatres; Burke County Chamber of Commerce; Burke Arts Council
Season: July - August
Performs At: Old Colony Players Amphitheater; Old Rock School
Organization Type: Performing; Touring; Resident; Educational

3254
MARTIN COMMUNITY PLAYERS
300 North Watts Street
Williamston, NC 27892-2099
Phone: 252-792-1521
Fax: 252-792-0826
Management:
    Artistic Director: Allan Osborne
Mission: To offer theatre to all citizens in our county, primarily through the schools, providing one selected offering annually.
Founded: 1974
Specialized Field: Musical; Community Theater
Status: Non-Professional; Nonprofit
Performs At: Martin County Auditorium
Organization Type: Performing; Resident

3255
OPERA HOUSE THEATRE COMPANY
20LI Carolina Beach Road
Wilmington, NC 28401
Phone: 910-762-4234
Fax: 910-251-9800
e-mail: ohte@wilmington.net
Management:
    Executive Director/Founder: Lou Criscuolo
Mission: To produce and promote high quality, accessible, professional theatre; to train and develop the talents of musicians, actors and technicians.
Utilizes: Actors; Choreographers; Dancers; Designers; Grant Writers; Guest Artists; Guest Companies; Guest Conductors; Guest Designers; Instructors; Local Artists; Multimedia; Music; Resident Professionals; Sign Language Translators; Singers; Student Interns
Founded: 1985
Specialized Field: Summer Stock; Musical
Status: Professional
Paid Staff: 20
Performs At: Thalian Hall Center for the Performing Arts
Organization Type: Performing; Educational

3256
CHILDREN'S THEATRE BOARD
610 Coliseum Drive
Winston-Salem, NC 27106
Phone: 336-725-4531
Fax: 336-725-2751
e-mail: ctis4me@aol.com
Web Site: www.childrenstheatre.org
Officers:
    President: Mary Harper
    President Elect: Libby Noah
    Treasurer: Leslie Madigan
    Treasurer-Elect: Ernestine Worley
    Immediate Past President: Janet Bondurant
Management:
    President: Keith Gardner
    Executive Director: Pat Land
    Director Marketing/ Development: Jennifer Lewis
Mission: To provide opportunities for students, educators and families to experience and participate in the performing arts; to offer multidisciplinary, culturally diverse programs to foster sensitivity and acceptance of others. Our programs are accessible and entertaining, our vision is to reach young people through experimental learning.
Utilizes: Singers
Founded: 1940
Specialized Field: Musical; Comedy; Youth Theater; Puppet; Classic
Status: Non-Profit, Professional
Paid Staff: 2
Performs At: The Arts Council Theatre; W-S/FC Schools
Organization Type: Performing; Educational; Sponsoring

3257
LITTLE THEATRE OF WINSTON-SALEM
610 Coliseum Drive
Winston-Salem, NC 27106
Phone: 336-748-0857
Fax: 336-727-4841
e-mail: theatre@littletheatreonline.com
Web Site: www.littletheatreonline.com
Officers:
    President: Eva Wu
Management:
    President: Christine Gorelick
    Executive Director: Mark Pirolo
    Operations Director: Cheri Vanloon
    Box Office Manager: Janice Dearth
    Education Director: Angela Chance
Mission: To provide for all within the community an avenue for education and development in all aspects of theatrical arts and to provide entertainment for the community by offering a series of well-staged performances of live theatre.
Utilizes: Guest Companies; Singers
Founded: 1935
Specialized Field: Musical; Comedy; Community Theater; Contemporary
Status: Non-Profit, Non-Professional
Paid Staff: 11
Income Sources: Winston-Salem Arts Council
Performs At: Hanes Community Center; Arts Council Theatre
Organization Type: Performing; Educational

3258
NORTH CAROLINA BLACK REPERTORY COMPANY
610 Coliseum Drive
PO Box 2793
Winston-Salem, NC 27106
Phone: 336-723-7907
Fax: 336-723-2223
e-mail: nbtf@bellsouth.net
Web Site: www.nbtf.org/history.htm
Management:
    Artistic Director: Larry Leon Hamlin
Mission: To offer professional productions of musicals and plays including original and renowned works with universal as well as ethnic (African-American) themes.
Utilizes: Guest Companies; Singers
Founded: 1979
Specialized Field: Musical; African American
Status: Professional; Nonprofit
Season: September - June
Performs At: Winston-Salem Arts Council Theatre
Type of Stage: Proscenium
Seating Capacity: 541
Organization Type: Performing; Touring; Resident; Educational; Sponsoring

3259
YADKIN PLAYERS
PO Box 667
Yadkinville, NC 27055
Phone: 336-679-2941
Fax: 336-677-3962
e-mail: yadkinarts@yadtel.net
Web Site: www.yadkinarts.org
Management:
    President: Camara Collins
    Executive Director: Michael Orsillo
Utilizes: Guest Companies
Founded: 1975
Specialized Field: Community Theater
Status: Non-Profit, Non-Professional
Paid Staff: 1
Paid Artists: 12
Organization Type: Performing; Touring; Educational

North Dakota

3260
FARGO-MOORHEAD COMMUNITY THEATRE
333 S 4th Street
Fargo, ND 58103
Phone: 701-235-1901
Fax: 701-235-2685
Toll-free: 877-687-7469
e-mail: rick@fmct.org
Web Site: www.fmct.org
Officers:
    President: Dawn Duncan
    VP: Robin Hoffer
    Treasurer: Dave Stende
    Secretary: Kim Horab
Management:
    President: Michael Lowchow
    Artistic Director: Charlene Hudgins
    Business Director: Shannyn Jacobson
    Development Director: Sherry Shadley
Mission: To provide quality avocational theatre opportunities to the cities of Fargo and Moorhead, as well as the region.
Utilizes: Actors; Choreographers; Collaborating Artists; Collaborations; Commissioned Music; Designers; Educators; Five Seasonal Concerts; Grant Writers; Guest Accompanists; Guest Artists; Guest Companies; Guest Composers; Guest Conductors; Guest Designers; Guest Ensembles; Guest Lecturers; Guest Musical Directors; Guest Soloists; Guest Writers; High School Drama; Local Artists; Multimedia; Resident Professionals; Selected Students; Singers; Soloists; Student Interns; Touring Companies
Founded: 1946
Specialized Field: Musical; Comedy; Community Theater; Classic; Contemporary
Status: Non-Profit, Professional
Paid Staff: 12
Volunteer Staff: 500
Paid Artists: 50
Income Sources: American Association of Community Theater; Lake Agassiz Arts Council; North Dakota Community Theatre Association; Minnesota Association of Community Theaters
Performs At: Emma K. Herbst Playhouse
Annual Attendance: 28,000
Facility Category: Theatre
Type of Stage: Thrust
Seating Capacity: 302-380
Year Built: 1965
Year Remodeled: 1994

Organization Type: Resident

3261
LITTLE COUNTRY THEATRE
PO Box 5691
Fargo, ND 58102-5691
Phone: 701-231-9442
Web Site: www.ndsu.edu/finearts/theatre_arts/lct.shtml
Management:
  Artistic Director: Donald Larew
  Managing Director: M Joy Erickson
Mission: To produce theatrical productions reflecting a high degree of professionalism; to develop artists in the theatre as well as responsive audiences.
Utilizes: Singers
Founded: 1914
Specialized Field: Drama; Musical
Status: Nonprofit
Paid Staff: 50
Income Sources: American College Theatre Festival; United States Institute for Theatre Technology
Performs At: Askanase Auditorium; Walsh Studio Theatre
Organization Type: Educational

3262
FORT TOTTEN LITTLE THEATRE
PO Box 97
Fort Totten, ND 58335
Phone: 701-766-4473
Web Site: www2.stellarnet.com
Officers:
  President: Carol Leevers
  VP: Jane Traynor
  Treasurer/Secretary: Dean Petska
  Artistic Director: Judy Ryan
Management:
  Community Relation: Carol Leevers
  Community Relation: Jane Traynor
  Attorney: John Traynor
  Advanced Ticket Drive: Chuck Jerome
Mission: Provide an opportunity for talented people to have theatre experience; attract tourists to a state historic site; entertainment for the citizens of rural areas.
Utilizes: Singers
Founded: 1962
Specialized Field: Musical; Community Theater
Status: Semi-Professional; Non-Professional; Nonprofit
Paid Staff: 20
Income Sources: North Dakota Council of Arts; Council of Lake Region
Season: June - August
Performs At: Cavalry Square; Historic Site
Organization Type: Performing; Resident

3263
MEDORA MUSICAL
528 Hennepin Avenue
Suite 206
Minneapolis, ND 55403
Phone: 612-333-3302
Fax: 612-333-4337
Toll-free: 800-633-0721
e-mail: cw@troopamerica.com
Web Site: www.troupeamerica.com
Management:
  President: Curtis N Wollan
  Managing Director: John Tsafoyanni
Utilizes: Actors; AEA Actors; Choreographers; Collaborations; Commissioned Composers; Commissioned Music; Dancers; Designers; Guest

Artists; Instructors; Music; Organization Contracts; Original Music Scores; Resident Professionals; Sign Language Translators; Student Interns
Founded: 1992
Specialized Field: Musical; Comedy; Contemporary
Status: For-Profit, Professional
Paid Staff: 18
Paid Artists: 15
Budget: $500,000
Income Sources: Ticket Sales; Grants; Donations
Season: June - September
Annual Attendance: 115,000
Facility Category: Ampitheatre
Type of Stage: Outdoor
Stage Dimensions: 90' x 60'
Seating Capacity: 3000
Year Built: 1992
Cost: $4 Million

Ohio

3264
CAROUSEL DINNER THEATRE
1275 E Waterloo Road
PO Box 7530
Akron, OH 44306
Phone: 330-724-9855
Fax: 330-724-2232
Toll-free: 800-362-4100
e-mail: carousel@carouseldinnertheatre.com
Web Site: www.carouseldinnertheatre.com
Officers:
  President/Owner/Executive Producer: Prescott F Griffith
Management:
  Director Sales/Marketing: Jeffrey Lynch
Mission: Elegant Dinner Theatre featuring live Broadway musical productions withprofessional New York talent.
Utilizes: Actors; AEA Actors; Choreographers; Commissioned Music; Community Talent; Contract Orchestras; Dancers; Designers; Guest Artists; Guest Conductors; Guest Designers; Guest Lecturers; Multi Collaborations; Multimedia; Music; Original Music Scores; Resident Professionals; Selected Students; Sign Language Translators; Singers; Soloists; Students; Student Interns; Visual Arts
Founded: 1973
Specialized Field: Dinner Theater
Status: For-Profit, Professional
Paid Staff: 175
Income Sources: Box Office; Ticket Sales
Affiliations: National Dinner Theatre Association; Actors' Equity Association
Annual Attendance: 200,000
Facility Category: Dinner Theatre
Type of Stage: Proscenium
Stage Dimensions: 60'x40'x18'
Seating Capacity: 1,130
Year Built: 1988
Year Remodeled: 1988
Rental Contact: Producer Marc A Resnik
Resident Groups: Sheila A Fetterman

3265
MAGICAL THEATRE COMPANY
565 W Tuscarawas Avenue
PO Box 386
Barberton, OH 44203
Phone: 330-848-3708
Fax: 330-848-5768
e-mail: magicaltheatre@aol.com
Web Site: www.magicaltheatre.org

Officers:
  President: Tim Papp
Management:
  Co-Producing Director: Holly Barkdoll
Mission: Resident and touring, educational and entertainment resource for young audiences. In partnership with schools and other organizations, we are leaders in providing a positive cultural service as a strong and energetic professional theatre serving Northeast Ohio. We enhance learning, growth and civic improvement through live theatre.
Utilizes: Actors; Choreographers; Collaborations; Community Talent; Contract Actors; Local Artists; Original Music Scores; Resident Companies; Scenic Designers; Selected Students; Soloists; Student Interns; Special Technical Talent; Theatre Companies
Founded: 1972
Specialized Field: Musical; Comedy; Ensembles; Classic; Contemporary
Status: Non-Profit, Professional
Paid Staff: 4
Volunteer Staff: 1
Paid Artists: 55
Budget: $415,000
Income Sources: Foundations; Corporate Donors; Ticket Sales
Affiliations: Akron Area Arts Alliance; Cleveland Theatre Collective Ticket Sales; Fees; Foundations; Individual & Corporate Donors
Annual Attendance: 50,000
Facility Category: Former Movie Theatre
Type of Stage: Proscenium; Thrust
Seating Capacity: 285
Year Built: 1919
Year Remodeled: 2000
Cost: $500,000
Rental Contact: Co-Producing Director Dennis O'Connell
Organization Type: Performing; Touring; Resident; Educational

3266
HUNTINGTON THEATRE
28601 Lake Road
Bay Village, OH 44140
Phone: 216-871-8333
Mission: To maintain a community theatre.
Utilizes: Guest Companies; Singers
Founded: 1958
Specialized Field: Musical; Community Theater
Status: Non-Professional; Nonprofit
Paid Staff: 100
Performs At: Huntington Playhouse
Organization Type: Performing; Educational

3267
BRECKSVILLE LITTLE THEATRE
Box 41131
Brecksville, OH 44141
Phone: 440-526-4477
e-mail: jpfuthey@earthlink.net
Web Site: www.brecksville.oh.us
Mission: To offer good theatre; to provide performance opportunities.
Utilizes: Guest Artists; Guest Companies; Singers
Founded: 1941
Specialized Field: Musical; Community Theater
Status: Non-Professional; Nonprofit
Paid Staff: 100
Performs At: Old Towne Hall; Brecksville Square
Organization Type: Performing; Resident; Educational

3268

THEATRE ON THE SQUARE

PO Box 41002
Brecksville, OH 44141
Phone: 440-526-3443
Fax: 440-526-6591
Toll-free: 800-895-4708
e-mail: theatre@btots.org
Web Site: www.btots.org
Management:
    President: Lynda Demko
    Education Director: Michele Cotner
    Business Director: Steve Demko
    Managing Director: Jean Marincic
Mission: Presenting touring and original plays.
Utilizes: Guest Companies
Founded: 1975
Specialized Field: Musical; Drama; New Plays
Status: Professional; Commercial
Performs At: Theatre on the Square
Stage Dimensions: 40x32
Seating Capacity: 750
Year Built: 1924
Organization Type: Performing; Touring

3269

PLAYERS GUILD OF CANTON

1001 Market Avenue N
Canton, OH 44702
Phone: 330-453-7619
Fax: 330-453-8368
e-mail: info@playersguildtheatre.com
Web Site: www.playersguildtheatre.com
Officers:
    President: Vivian Leggett
    President Elect: Jodi Wilson
Management:
    Artistic Manager: Tricia Ostertag
    Administrative Manager: Jean Reahm
    Technical Director: Craig M Betz
Mission: A charitable and educational institution which produces and exhibits plays and provides instruction of the theatre arts for the purpose of fostering and advancing education in and appreciation of the theatre by and among the people of the Greater Canton Area.
Utilizes: Actors; Artists-in-Residence; Choreographers; Commissioned Music; Guest Companies
Founded: 1932
Specialized Field: Musical; Comedy; Community Theater; Classic; Contemporary
Status: Non-Profit, Non-Professional
Paid Staff: 5
Volunteer Staff: 500
Paid Artists: 6
Non-paid Artists: 150
Budget: $700,000
Facility Category: Community Theatre
Type of Stage: Proscenium; Thrust
Stage Dimensions: 60'x40'; 30'x20'
Seating Capacity: 478; 139
Year Built: 1970
Rental Contact: Bil Pfuderer
Organization Type: Performing

3270

CHAGRIN VALLEY LITTLE THEATRE

40 River Street
Chagrin Falls, OH 44022
Phone: 440-247-8955
e-mail: cvlt@cvlt.org
Web Site: www.cvlt.org
Management:
    Business Manager: Rollin DeVere

Mission: To provide community theater.
Founded: 1929
Specialized Field: Community Theater
Status: Non-Professional; Nonprofit
Paid Staff: 150
Seating Capacity: 262
Organization Type: Performing

3271

TECUMSEH!

PO Box 73
Chilicothe, OH 45601
Phone: 740-775-4100
Fax: 740-775-4349
Toll-free: 866-775-0700
e-mail: tecumseh@bright.net
Web Site: www.tecumsehdrama.com
Officers:
    President: Beth Beatty
Utilizes: Actors; AEA Actors; Guest Designers; Original Music Scores; Soloists; Student Interns
Founded: 1973
Specialized Field: Outdoor Theater; Drama; Historical
Status: Non-Profit, Professional
Paid Staff: 100
Paid Artists: 60
Season: June - September
Annual Attendance: 44,000
Facility Category: Outdoors
Type of Stage: Amphitheater
Stage Dimensions: 150'x50'
Seating Capacity: 1,700
Year Built: 1971
Year Remodeled: 1998
Cost: $ 1.4 million

3272

ARTREACH: A DIVISION OF THE CHILDREN'S THEATRE OF CINCINNATI

2106 Florence Avenue
Cincinnati, OH 45206
Phone: 513-569-8080
Fax: 513-569-8084
e-mail: computertotskentco@comcast.net
Web Site: www.thechildrenstheatre.com
Management:
    Artistic Director: Kelly Germain
    Business Manager: Chris Casazza
Mission: The Children's Theatre of Cincinnati and Theatre IV merged to provide fully produced Broadway-syle productions and theatrical experiences for school aged children throughout the region.
Utilizes: Actors; Educators; Guest Companies; Local Artists; Multimedia; Original Music Scores; Resident Professionals; Singers; Theatre Companies
Founded: 1976
Specialized Field: Musical; Comedy; Youth Theater; Classic; Contemporary
Status: Non-Profit, Professional
Paid Staff: 3
Paid Artists: 14
Income Sources: Theatre Communications Group; Association of Performing Arts Presenters; American Association of Theatre Educators; Arts Midwest
Season: September - May
Performs At: Touring

3273

CINCINNATI PLAYHOUSE IN THE PARK

962 Mt Adams Circle
PO Box 6537
Cincinnati, OH 45202

Phone: 513-345-2242
Fax: 513-345-2254
Toll-free: 800-582-3208
e-mail: admin@cincyplay.com
Web Site: www.cincyplay.com
Officers:
    Board of Trustees President: Jack D Osborn
    Boarf of Trustees VP: Richard Curry
Management:
    President: Ed Stern
    Executive Director: Buzz Ward
    Public Relations Director: Christa Skiles
Mission: Produced on stage in a fiscally responsible manner, and through stimulating educational and outreach programs.
Utilizes: Guest Companies; Singers
Founded: 1960
Specialized Field: Musical; Comedy; Community Theater; Classic; Contemporary
Status: Non-Profit, Professional
Paid Staff: 74
Budget: $9 million
Performs At: Robert S Marx Theatre; Thompson Shelterhouse Theatre
Affiliations: League of Cincinnati Theatres
Annual Attendance: 250,000
Facility Category: Robert S Marx Theatre; Thomson Shelterhouse Theat
Type of Stage: Thrust
Seating Capacity: 626; 225
Rental Contact: 513-345-2242 Norma Niinemets
Organization Type: Performing; Resident

3274

ENSEMBLE THEATRE OF CINCINNATI

1127 Vine Street
Cincinnati, OH 45202
Phone: 513-421-3555
Fax: 513-562-4104
e-mail: director@cincyetc.com
Web Site: www.cincyetc.com
Management:
    Director Of Operations: Trent Kotch
    Producing Artistic Director: D Lynn Meyers
    Director Of Marketing and Public Re: Sue Cohen
Mission: Professional equity theatre dedicated to the production and development of new works and works new to the region.
Founded: 1986
Specialized Field: Ensembles; New Plays
Paid Staff: 15
Volunteer Staff: 50
Performs At: Ensemble Theatre
Type of Stage: Thrust
Seating Capacity: 202

3275

MADCAP PRODUCTIONS PUPPET THEATRE

3316 Glenmore Avenue
Cincinnati, OH 45211
Phone: 513-921-5965
Fax: 513-921-3845
Toll-free: 866-921-5965
e-mail: info@madcappuppets.com
Web Site: www.madcappuppets.com
Officers:
    President: Rosemary Schlachter
    VP: Maroene Johnson
    Secretary/Treasurer: Paul Rattermann
Management:
    President: Betsy Meyer
    Artistic Director: Jerry Handorf
    Managing Director: Vickie Francis

Booking Manager: Jim Lepscomb Jr
Mission: To present educational theatre experiences and further the art of puppet theatre.
Utilizes: Actors; Collaborations; Five Seasonal Concerts; Guest Artists; Guest Conductors; Guest Designers; Guest Musical Directors; Local Artists; Lyricists; Multimedia; Original Music Scores; Selected Students; Singers
Founded: 1981
Specialized Field: Youth Theater; Classic; Puppet
Status: Non-Profit, Professional
Paid Staff: 9
Paid Artists: 9
Performs At: Touring Company; Resident Theatre at Cincinnati Art Museum
Affiliations: Puppeteers of America; Ohio Theatre Alliance; League of Cincinnati Theatres
Annual Attendance: 450,000
Organization Type: Performing; Touring; Educational

3276
MARIEMONT PLAYERS
4101 Walton Creek Road
Cincinnati, OH 45227
Phone: 513-271-1661
Web Site: wwwk.geocities.com/mariemontplayers
Mission: To produce plays for the enrichment and enjoyment of area audiences.
Founded: 1936
Specialized Field: Community Theater
Status: Non-Professional; Nonprofit
Income Sources: American Association of Community Theatres-Cincinnati; Ohio Community Theatre Alliance
Performs At: Walton Creek Theater
Organization Type: Performing

3277
SHOWBOAT MAJESTIC
PO Box 5255
Cincinnati, OH 45205-0255
Phone: 513-241-6550
e-mail: info.crc@rcc.org
Specialized Field: Summer Stock; Musical; Comedy
Season: April - October

3278
STAGECRAFTERS
1580 Summit Road
Cincinnati, OH 45237
Phone: 513-761-7500
Fax: 513-761-0084
Mission: To provide a performance outlet and entertainment for the community.
Utilizes: Guest Companies; Singers
Founded: 1952
Specialized Field: Community Theater
Status: Non-Professional
Paid Staff: 25
Income Sources: American Association of Community Theatres; Ohio Community Theatre Alliance
Performs At: Jewish Community Center
Organization Type: Performing; Resident

3279
CLEVELAND PLAY HOUSE
8500 Euclid Avenue
Cleveland, OH 44106
Phone: 216-795-7000
Fax: 216-795-7005
Toll-free: 800-278-1274
e-mail: mbloom@clevelandplayhouse.com
Web Site: www.clevelandplayhouse.com
Officers:
   Chairman: Alan Rauss

   Secretary: Raymond M Malone
Management:
   Artistic Director: Michael Bloom
Mission: To provide the experience of a complete performing arts environment through its varied repertoire of classical and contemporary theatre, facilities and the continuance of young people's theatre training.
Utilizes: Artists-in-Residence; Collaborations; Commissioned Music; Dancers; Designers; Educators; Guest Artists; Guest Companies; Guest Composers; Guest Conductors; Guest Designers; Guest Ensembles; Guest Lecturers; Guest Writers; Guild Activities; Instructors; Local Artists; Lyricists; Music; Organization Contracts; Performance Artists; Resident Professionals; Selected Students; Sign Language Translators; Singers; Soloists; Touring Companies
Founded: 1915
Specialized Field: Musical; Comedy; Classic; Contemporary
Status: Non-Profit, Professional
Paid Staff: 150
Volunteer Staff: 300
Paid Artists: 50
Budget: $6.5 million
Income Sources: Ticket Sales; Grants; Donations
Performs At: Bolton Theatre; Drury Theatre; Brooks Theatre
Affiliations: League of Resident Theatres; Theatre Communications Group; Ohio Arts Council
Annual Attendance: 300,000
Facility Category: Regional Theatre
Type of Stage: Proscenium;
Seating Capacity: 504; 500; 120
Year Built: 1916
Year Remodeled: 1991
Rental Contact: Managing Director Dean R Gladden
Organization Type: Performing; Educational

3280
CLEVELAND PUBLIC THEATRE
6415 Detroit Avenue
Cleveland, OH 44102-3011
Phone: 216-631-2727
Fax: 216-631-2575
e-mail: info@cptonline.org
Web Site: www.cptonline.org
Officers:
   President: George H Carr
   VP: Jillian Davis
Management:
   President: James Levin
   Artistic Director: Randy Rollison
   Managing Director: Dennis Griesmer
   Director Marketing and Public Relat: Dan Kilpane
Mission: To inspire, nurture, challenge, amaze, educate and empower artists and audiences in order to make the Cleveland public a more conscious and compassionate community.
Utilizes: Guest Companies; Singers
Founded: 1983
Specialized Field: Community Theater
Status: Non-Profit, Professional
Paid Staff: 15
Volunteer Staff: 40
Paid Artists: 170
Budget: $1.2 Million
Income Sources: Foundations; Government; Individual; Corporate
Affiliations: Ohio Theatre Association; Theatre Communications Group; Ohio Arts Council; National Endowment for the Arts
Annual Attendance: 20,000
Facility Category: Multi Theatre

Type of Stage: Proscenium; Black Box
Year Built: 1920
Year Remodeled: 2000
Rental Contact: James Levin
Organization Type: Performing; Touring; Resident; Educational; Sponsoring

3281
CLEVELAND SIGNSTAGE THEATRE
8500 Euclid Avenue
Cleveland, OH 44106
Phone: 216-229-2838
Fax: 216-229-2769
e-mail: deaftheatre@signstage.org
Web Site: www.signstage.org
Management:
   President: Richard Slozar
   Executive Assistant: Erin La Fountain
   Artistic Director: William Morgan
Mission: FTD accepts the unique responsibility for providing theatrical and educational performances and workshops for deaf, hearing impaired and hearing people.
Utilizes: Actors; AEA Actors; Commissioned Music; Designers; Educators; Five Seasonal Concerts; Guest Accompanists; Guest Artists; Guest Companies; Guest Conductors; Guest Teachers; Local Artists; Lyricists; Original Music Scores; Performance Artists; Resident Artists; Resident Professionals; Selected Students; Singers; Theatre Companies
Founded: 1975
Specialized Field: Theatre for Deaf; Alternative
Status: Non-Profit, Professional
Paid Staff: 2
Volunteer Staff: 2
Paid Artists: 6
Budget: $800,000
Performs At: Cleveland Play House
Facility Category: Resident Theatre
Stage Dimensions: 25'x25'
Seating Capacity: 139
Organization Type: Performing; Touring; Resident; Educational

3282
KARAMU HOUSE
2355 E 89th Street
Cleveland, OH 44106-3403
Phone: 216-795-7070
Fax: 216-795-7073
e-mail: info@karamu.com
Web Site: www.karamu.com
Officers:
   Board Chairman: Stanley Jackson Jr
Management:
   Marketing Manager: Vivian C Wilson
   Executive Director: Gregory J Ashe
Mission: To support and encourage the preservation, celebration and evaluation of African American culture and provide a vehicle for social, economic and educational development.
Utilizes: Actors; Choreographers; Collaborations; Educators; Fine Artists; Guest Accompanists; Guest Artists; Guest Conductors; Guest Designers; Guest Lecturers; Guest Teachers; Guild Activities; High School Drama; Instructors; Local Artists; Multimedia; Music; Performance Artists; Resident Professionals; Sign Language Translators; Singers; Soloists; Student Interns; Touring Companies
Founded: 1915
Opened: 1915
Specialized Field: Multi-Cultural; Drama; Musical; African American
Status: Semi-Professional; Nonprofit

Paid Staff: 38
Volunteer Staff: 20
Paid Artists: 5
Non-paid Artists: 170
Budget: $1,795,000
Income Sources: Foundations; Corporations; Fees
Affiliations: American Alliance for Theatre Arts
Annual Attendance: 20,000
Facility Category: Multi-Cultural Arts Center
Type of Stage: Arena; Proscenium
Seating Capacity: 100/225
Year Built: 1948
Organization Type: Performing; Educational

3283
NEAR WEST THEATRE

2012 West 25th Street
Suite 908
Cleveland, OH 44113
Phone: 216-621-1919
Fax: 216-621-3202
e-mail: info@nearwesttheatre.org
Management:
   Executive Director: Stephanie Morrison-Hrbek
   Artistic Director: Bob Navis, Jr
   Technical Director: Michael Larochelle
   Development Diriector: Laura R Hammel
   Business Operations Director: Carole
   Leiblinger-Hedderson
Mission: Delivers an inclusive, self-esteem building
process that results in high-quality theatre productions
and programming that help build Cleveland's west side
and surrounding neighborhoods. Educates and raises
awareness around issues of social justice discrimation
and stigma and it provides people of all ages with the
the ability to nurture their sense of identity and
strengthen their purposes as individuals and as a
community.
Specialized Field: Community Theater; Musical

3284
PLAYHOUSE SQUARE FOUNDATION

1501 Euclid Avenue
Suite 200
Cleveland, OH 44115
Phone: 216-771-4444
Fax: 216-771-0217
Toll-free: 800-492-6048
Web Site: www.playhousesquare.com
Management:
   President: Art Falco
   Vice President And Director: Patricia Gaul
   Technical Director: Bob Rody
   Director of Marketing: Autum Tiser
Mission: The renovation and operation of five theatres
in the Playhouse Square Center.
Founded: 1970
Specialized Field: Drama; Musical; Comedy; Classic;
Touring Company
Status: Non-Profit, Non-Professional
Paid Staff: 250
Budget: $34 Million
Income Sources: Ticket Sales; Contributions
Performs At: Five historic theatres ranging in size from
750 to 3100.
Annual Attendance: 1,200,000
Facility Category: Performing Arts Center
Type of Stage: Proscenium
Rental Contact: Hallie Yavitch 216-348-5257
Organization Type: Performing; Touring; Resident;
Educational

3285
CAIN PARK THEATRE

Lee and Superior Road
Cleveland Heights, OH 44118
Mailing Address: 40 Severange Circle
Phone: 216-371-3000
Fax: 216-371-6995
Web Site: http://www.cainpark.com/contact.asp
Management:
   General Manager: Erin Cameron
Specialized Field: Outdoor Theater; Summer Stock
Season: June - August
Facility Category: Amphitheater

3286
DOBAMA THEATRE

2490 Lee Boulevard
Suite 325
Cleveland Heights, OH 44118
Phone: 216-932-6838
Fax: 216-932-3259
e-mail: dobama@dobama.org
Web Site: www.dobama.org
Management:
   Artistic/Managing Director: Joyce Casey
Mission: Produce five plays not yet available to
Cleveland Heights audiences; encourage new
American playwrights by offering staged readings and
full world premiere productions of their work; encourage
creative expression in children through annual Marilyn
Biarchi Kids Playwriting Festival.
Founded: 1959
Specialized Field: New Plays; Young Playwrights;
Drama; Contemporary
Status: Non-Profit, Professional
Paid Staff: 2
Paid Artists: 68
Income Sources: Ohio Theatre Association
Performs At: Dobama Theatre
Type of Stage: Thrust
Seating Capacity: 200
Organization Type: Performing; Resident; Educational

3287
ACTORS' THEATRE COMPANY

1000 City Park
Columbus, OH 43206
Phone: 614-444-6888
e-mail: jdoklovic@vscat.com
Web Site: www.theactorstheatre.org
Officers:
   President: Joel M Winston
   1st VP: Debbie Matan
   2nd VP: Noel C Shepard
   Treasurer: Eric A Carlson
   Secretary: Kara L Miller
Management:
   President: Geoffery Martin
   Executive Director: Frank Barnhart
   Artistic Director: John Kuhn
   Managing Director: Jeanne Earhart
Mission: To make quality theatre accessible by
providing free outdoor plays, particularly entertaining
Shakespeare productions.
Utilizes: Guest Artists; Guest Companies; Singers
Founded: 1982
Specialized Field: Shakespeare
Status: Semi-Professional; Nonprofit
Paid Staff: 100
Performs At: Schiller Park Amphitheatre
Organization Type: Performing; Touring; Resident;
Educational

3288
CATCO (CONTEMPORARY AMERICAN THEATRE COMPANY)

77 S High Street
2Nd Floor
Columbus, OH 43215
Phone: 614-469-0939
Fax: 614-461-4917
e-mail: webmaster@catco.org
Web Site: www.catco.org
Management:
   Artistic Director: Geoffrey Nelson
   Development Director: Patrick Roehrenbeck
   Executive Director: David Edelman
   Executive Assistant: Jerry Matheny
Mission: Entertaining theatre company, dramatically
different.
Founded: 1984
Specialized Field: Contemporary
Status: Nonprofit
Paid Staff: 25
Volunteer Staff: 4
Paid Artists: 7
Income Sources: Organizations; Individuals;
Foundations

3289
COLUMBUS CHILDREN'S THEATRE

512 N Park Street
Columbus, OH 43215-2224
Phone: 614-224-6672
e-mail: cctboxoffice@sbcglobal.net
Web Site: www.colschildrenstheatre.org
Officers:
   President: Olga Lucia
   VP: Linda Cochran
   Treasurer: Sue Zazon
   Secretary: Dawn Farrell
Management:
   Managing Director: Steven Bridgeland
   Executive and Artistic Director: William Goldsmith
   Education Director: Mark Mann
   Office and Touring Manager: Kathy Hyland
Mission: CCT is committed to the proposition that the
best way for young people to understand and
appreciate the theatre arts is through direct
participation. Our focus is on professionally directed,
interactive, hands-on programs that celebrate young
people's spirit, creativity and fresh perspective... to
provide creative outlets, structure and discipline for
young people to progress in the theatre arts.
Founded: 1963
Specialized Field: Children's Theater
Status: Non-Profit, Non-Professional
Paid Staff: 5
Paid Artists: 100
Annual Attendance: 100,000

3290
OHIO STATE UNIVERSITY-DEPARTMENT OF THEATRE

1089 Drake Center
1849 Cannon Drive
Columbus, OH 43210-5821
Phone: 614-292-5821
Fax: 614-292-3222
e-mail: theatre@osu.edu
Web Site: www.the.ohio-state.edu
Officers:
   Chairperson: Dan Gray
Utilizes: Actors; Artists-in-Residence; Collaborating
Artists; Collaborations; Community Talent; Curators;
Dancers; Designers; Educators; Equity Actors;

Filmmakers; Guest Designers; Guest Ensembles; Guest Instructors; Guest Soloists; High School Drama; Instructors; Local Talent; Lyricists; Multi Collaborations; New Productions; Performance Artists; Poets; Resident Professionals; Soloists; Theatre Companies; Volunteer Directors & Actors; Writers
Founded: 1870
Specialized Field: Educational; Theater Workshops
Status: Non-Profit, Professional
Paid Staff: 8
Performs At: Thuber Theatre; Bowen Theatre
Type of Stage: Proscenium; Thrust
Seating Capacity: 600; 250

3291
PHOENIX THEATRE FOR CHILDREN
39 E State Street
PO Box 06238
Columbus, OH 43206
Phone: 614-464-9400
Fax: 614-464-9402
e-mail: mail@thephoenixonline.org
Web Site: www.thephoenixonline.org
Management:
   Artistic Director: Steven C Anderson
   Education Director: Vanessa Becker
   General Manager: Lonelle Yoder
   Business Manager: Thom O'Reilly
Mission: A non-profit theatre for young audiences dedicated to providing quality arts opportunities and arts education programs for Central Ohio.
Utilizes: Actors; Community Talent; Educators; Guest Accompanists; Guest Conductors; Guest Designers; Local Artists; Original Music Scores; Resident Artists
Founded: 1993
Specialized Field: Children's Theater
Status: Professional; Nonprofit
Paid Staff: 8
Paid Artists: 10
Performs At: Vern Riffg Center for Government and the Arts
Facility Category: Government Run Facility
Type of Stage: 3/4 Thrust and Proscenium
Seating Capacity: 180 and 240
Organization Type: Performing; Educational

3292
REALITY THEATRE
Axis Nightclub
775 N High St
Columbus, OH 43215
Phone: 614-265-7337
e-mail: info@realitytheatre.com
Web Site: www.realitytheatre.com
Management:
   President: Jeffrey Smith
   VP: Randee Estep
   Executive Director: Mollie Levin
Mission: Primarily dedicated to the development of experimental plays and also the presentation of original scripts written by Ohio playwrights.
Utilizes: Guest Companies
Founded: 1985
Specialized Field: Experimental; New Plays
Status: Semi-Professional; Nonprofit
Organization Type: Performing; Resident

3293
RED HERRING THEATRE ENSEMBLE
Vern Riffe Center Theater Complex
77 South High Street, Second Floor
Columbus, OH 43215

Phone: 614-469-0939
Fax: 614-291-8654
e-mail: info@redherring.org
Management:
   President: Mo Ryan
   Managing Director: Nancy Fox
Mission: To provide unique theatre experience for audiences of central Ohio.
Specialized Field: Musical; Ensembles

3294
ROSEBRIAR SHAKESPEARE COMPANY
549 Franklin Avenue
Columbus, OH 43202
Phone: 614-470-1616
e-mail: sdvavies@ohiohistory.org
Management:
   Managing Director: Sandra Davies
   Artistic Director: John Heisel
Founded: 1990
Specialized Field: Community Theater; Shakespeare; Classic; Drama; Comedy
Income Sources: Grants from the Ohio Arts Council; Jefferson Center for Learning and the Arts
Performs At: Davis Discovery Center's Van Fleet Theatre

3295
SCARLET MASK SOCIETY
1739 N High Street
211 Ohio Union, Rm 307
Columbus, OH 43210
Phone: 614-487-8551
e-mail: colleary.1@osu.edu
Web Site: www.theatre.org.ohio-state.edu/about.html
Officers:
   Executive Artistic Director: Kelly Hartman
Management:
   Artistic Director: Eric Colleary
   Producer: Liz Botros
   Press/Publicity: Betsy Pandora
   Curator: Nena Couch
Mission: Offering Ohio State University students and community members an opportunity for participation in all areas of performing arts and affordable quality theatre productions.
Founded: 1892
Specialized Field: Musical; Community Theater
Status: Non-Professional; Nonprofit
Organization Type: Performing

3296
SHADOWBOX CABARET
164 Easton Town Center
Columbus, OH 43219
Phone: 614-416-7625
Fax: 614-416-7630
Toll-free: 888-887-4230
e-mail: info@shadowboxcabaret.com
Web Site: www.shadowboxcabaret.com
Management:
   President: Steven Guyer
   Artistic Director: Rebecca Gentile
   Managing Director: Julie Klein
   Literary Manager: Jimmy Makofsky
Mission: To change the face of live entertainment so that it meets our standards and to create a self-perpetuating organization that acts as a virus by breeding change and dynamism.
Founded: 1992
Specialized Field: Comedy; Cabaret
Status: Non-Profit, Professional
Paid Staff: 97
Volunteer Staff: 3

Paid Artists: 97
Budget: $2.5 million
Income Sources: Tickets Sales
Annual Attendance: 100,000
Facility Category: Multi-stage Theaters

3297
SRO THEATRE COMPANY
1393 E Broad Street
Suite 103
Columbus, OH 43205
Phone: 614-258-9495
Fax: 614-258-9499
e-mail: gplt@glt-theatre.org
Web Site: www.sro-theatre.org
Officers:
   President: Karen Clark-Carpenter
   Secretary: Ruth Fullen
   Treasurer: Tom Giusti
   Vice President: E Joel Wesp
Management:
   Executive/Artistic Director: Nancy S Nocks
   Administrative Assistant: Chris Kioss
   Touring Director: Ronald E Nocks
Mission: Five original shows and a home season emphatically shatters myths about aging and celebrates life experience. Create theatre that joyously takes risks, is sometimes provacative, but always truthful and unafraid.
Founded: 1985
Specialized Field: Musical; Comedy; New Plays; Contemporary
Status: Non-Profit, Semi-Professional
Paid Staff: 2
Volunteer Staff: 80
Paid Artists: 22
Non-paid Artists: 47
Budget: $94,000
Income Sources: Private Foundations; Grants; Business & Corporate Donations; Box Office; Government Grants; Individual Donations
Affiliations: Senior Theatre League Of America; Ohio Arts Presenters Network; Greater Columbs Convention and Visitors Bureau; Central Ohio Theatre Roundtable

3298
DAYTON PLAYHOUSE
1301 E Siebenthaler Avenue
Dayton, OH 45415
Phone: 937-333-7469
Fax: 930-333-2827
e-mail: dave@daytonplayhouse.com
Web Site: www.daytonplayhouse.com
Officers:
   Chair: Betty Gould
   Treasurer: Gwen Eberly
Management:
   President: Debra Strauss
   Executive Director: Dave Seyer
Utilizes: Guest Companies; Singers
Founded: 1959
Specialized Field: Musical; Community Theater
Status: Non-Professional; Nonprofit
Paid Staff: 2
Volunteer Staff: 600
Income Sources: Membership; MCACD, Culture Works
Performs At: Dayton Playhouse
Affiliations: OCTA; Culture Works
Annual Attendance: 3,000
Seating Capacity: 200
Year Built: 1987
Organization Type: Performing

3299

HUMAN RACE THEATRE COMPANY
126 N Main Street
Suite 300
Dayton, OH 45402-1710
Phone: 937-461-3823
Fax: 937-461-7223
e-mail: contact@humanracetheatre.org
Web Site: www.humanracetheatre.org
Management:
    President of the Board: Beth Schaeffer
    Executive Director: Kevin Moore
    Artistic Director: Marsha Hanna
Mission: Works to affect the conscience of our community, to see our audience as our partner in the creative experience, to provide a platform for our artists to evolve and explore and to be an educational resource for our community. As our name suggests, we present universal themes that explore the human condition and startle us all into a reward awareness of ourselves.
Founded: 1986
Specialized Field: New works of social importance; Contemporary and classic plays and musicals
Status: Non-Profit, Professional
Paid Staff: 9
Paid Artists: 200
Budget: $1.2 million
Season: September - June
Performs At: The Loft Theatre; Victoria Theatre
Affiliations: AEA
Annual Attendance: 30,000
Type of Stage: Thrust, Proscenium
Seating Capacity: 219/1139

3300

SUMMER STOCK AT THE UNIVERSITY OF FINDLAY
1000 N Main Street
Findlay, OH 45840
Phone: 419-434-4562
Fax: 419-424-4822
Toll-free: 800-472-9502
e-mail: hayes@findlay.edu
Web Site: www.findlay.edu
Management:
    Program Director: Scott Hayes
    Curtain Raiser Advisory Chair: Anne Hermiller
Mission: Provide professional theatre opportunities for pre professional thatre students, and produce quality. affordable thatre for northwest Ohio.
Utilizes: Actors; AEA Actors; Artists-in-Residence; Choreographers; Collaborations; Dancers; Grant Writers; Guest Accompanists; Guest Artists; Guest Conductors; Guest Designers; Guest Ensembles; Guest Lecturers; Guild Activities; High School Drama; Instructors; Local Artists; Multimedia; Music; Original Music Scores; Resident Professionals; Sign Language Translators; Soloists
Founded: 1977
Specialized Field: Summer Stock
Status: Non-Profit, Professional
Paid Staff: 8
Volunteer Staff: 10
Paid Artists: 8
Non-paid Artists: 15
Season: June - August
Type of Stage: Proscenium
Stage Dimensions: 28' x 30'
Seating Capacity: 222
Year Built: 1964
Year Remodeled: 2001

3301

FOSTORIA FOOTLIGHTERS
225 S Poplar Street
PO Box 542
Fostoria, OH 44830
Phone: 419-435-7501
Utilizes: Guest Companies
Founded: 1959
Specialized Field: Musical; Community Theater
Status: Non-Professional; Nonprofit
Paid Staff: 100
Income Sources: Ohio Community Theatre Alliance
Performs At: Fostoria Footlighters
Organization Type: Performing; Resident; Educational

3302

CURTAIN PLAYERS
5691 Harlem Road
Galena, OH 43021
Mailing Address: PO Box 1143 Westerville, OH 43086
Phone: 740-965-4690
e-mail: info@curtainplayers.com
Web Site: www.curtainplayers.com
Management:
    President: Jim Petsche, president@curtainplayers.com
    Production Manager: Michael Day, production@curtainplayers.com
    Business Manager: Lisa Billing, business@curtainplayers.com
Founded: 1963
Specialized Field: Community Theater
Seating Capacity: 76

3303

PORTHOUSE THEATRE COMPANY
PO Box 5190
B 149 Music & Speech Center
Kent, OH 44242
Mailing Address: Kent State
Phone: 330-672-3884
Fax: 330-672-2889
Toll-free: 800-304-2363
e-mail: porthouse@kent.edu
Web Site: www.porthousetheatre.com
Management:
    Executive Director: Cynthia Stilings
    Artistic Director: Terri Kent
    Managing Director: Rebeccath Gates
    Producing Manager: Karl Erdmann
    Managing Director: Jeff Cruszewski
Utilizes: Guest Artists; Guest Companies; Singers
Founded: 1968
Specialized Field: Summer Stock
Status: Non-Profit, Professional
Paid Staff: 100
Paid Artists: 50
Income Sources: Kent State University
Season: June - August
Performs At: Porthouse Theatre of Blossom Music Center
Affiliations: Kent State University
Type of Stage: Outdoor, Covered Pavilion Theatre
Seating Capacity: 450
Organization Type: Performing; Educational

3304

BECK CENTER FOR THE CULTURAL ARTS
17801 Detroit Avenue
Lakewood, OH 44107

Phone: 216-521-2540
Fax: 216-228-6050
Web Site: www.lkwdpl.org/beck
Officers:
    President: Rosemary Corcoran
    VP: Brian King
    Treasurer: Marjorie Wiess
Management:
    Artistic Director: Scott Spence
    Managing Director: Andrea Krist
    Executive Director: Bill Beckenbach
    Director Education: Linda Sackett
    Production/Design: Don McBride
Mission: To be a comprehensive community arts center focusing on theater, arts education, and gallery exhibitions.
Utilizes: Guest Artists; Guest Companies; Singers
Founded: 1930
Specialized Field: Multi-Cultural; Drama; Musical
Status: Non-Professional
Paid Staff: 200
Annual Attendance: 12,000
Organization Type: Performing; Touring; Resident; Educational

3305

MANSFIELD PLAYHOUSE
95 E Third Street
Mansfield, OH 44902
Phone: 419-522-2883
Fax: 419-522-8446
Web Site: www.mansfieldplayhouse.com
Officers:
    President: Steve Zigmund
    First VP: Char Hutchinson
    Second VP: Gordon Wending
    Secretary: Dauhpne Maloney
Management:
    Business Manager: Dave Rinehart
    Theatre Manager: Susie Schaus
Mission: Providing entertainment and encouraging all branches of theatre arts.
Utilizes: Guest Artists; Guest Companies; Guest Ensembles; Singers
Founded: 1929
Specialized Field: Musical; Community Theater
Status: Non-Professional
Paid Staff: 2
Volunteer Staff: 200
Income Sources: Ohio Theatre Association; Ohio Arts Council; Ohio Community Theatre Alliance
Organization Type: Performing; Touring; Resident; Educational

3306

RENAISSANCE THEATRE
138 Park Avenue W
PO Box 789
Mansfield, OH 44901-0789
Phone: 419-522-2726
Fax: 419-524-7098
e-mail: rpaa@rparts.org
Web Site: www.rparts.org
Officers:
    President/CEO: Dr. Thomas J Carto
Management:
    President: Thomas Carto
    Artistic Director: Robert Frans
    Managing Director: Darlene Taylor
    Development Director: Shelley A Mauk
    CEO: Tom Cardo
Mission: To operate a community and regional entertainment, cultural, educational and civic center; to preserve and restore the Renaissance Theatre.

Utilizes: Actors; Collaborations; Dancers; Five Seasonal Concerts; Guest Accompanists; Guest Artists; Guest Choreographers; Guest Companies; Guest Designers; Guest Directors; Guest Musical Directors; Guest Musicians; Instructors; Local Artists; Original Music Scores; Resident Professionals; Selected Students; Singers; Student Interns; Special Technical Talent; Theatre Companies
Founded: 1979
Specialized Field: Renaissance; Community Theater; Classic
Status: Non-Profit, Professional
Paid Staff: 15
Volunteer Staff: 300
Budget: $1.4 Million
Income Sources: Association of Performing Arts Presenters; ORACLE; Ohio Theatre Association
Performs At: Renaissance Theatre
Affiliations: American Symphony Orchestra league, Association of Performing Arts Presenters
Annual Attendance: 65,000
Facility Category: Performing arts theatre
Type of Stage: proscenium
Stage Dimensions: 47 x 26
Seating Capacity: 1,406
Year Built: 1928
Year Remodeled: 1982
Cost: $2.5 Million
Rental Contact: Operations Manager Darlene Taylor
Organization Type: Performing; Educational; Sponsoring

3307
SHOWBOAT BECKY THATCHER
237 Front Street
PO Box 572
Marietta, OH 45750
Phone: 740-373-6033
Fax: 740-373-6084
Toll-free: 877-746-2628
e-mail: beckythatcher@sbc.yahoo.com
Web Site: www.marietta-ohio.com/becky thatcher
Management:
   President: Craig Hartline
   Executive Director: Jena L Blair
Founded: 1975
Specialized Field: Comedy; Musical; Historical
Status: Non-Profit, Professional
Paid Staff: 6
Volunteer Staff: 25
Paid Artists: 30
Non-paid Artists: 10
Season: June - August
Type of Stage: Proscenium
Stage Dimensions: 26' x 14'
Seating Capacity: 200
Year Built: 1926

3308
PALACE THEATRE
276 W Center Street
Marion, OH 43302
Phone: 740-383-2101
Fax: 740-387-3425
Web Site: www.marionpalace.org
Officers:
   Board President: Sue Jacob
   Board VP: Mike Greeley
Management:
   Executive Director: Elaine Merchant
   Operations Director: Suzanne Walke
   Business Manager: Veronica Bodine
   Stage Manager: Steve Beltz

Mission: To stimulate, promote and develop interest in the dramatic arts by operation of a permanent theatre.
Founded: 1928
Specialized Field: Musical; Comedy; Classic; Contemporary
Status: Non-Profit, Professional
Paid Staff: 8
Income Sources: Ohio Arts Council; Private Foundations; Donations
Performs At: Palace Theatre
Affiliations: League of Historic American Theatres
Annual Attendance: 77,650
Seating Capacity: 1420
Year Built: 1928
Year Remodeled: 1976
Organization Type: Performing; Educational

3309
TRUMPET IN THE LAND
Schoenbrunn Amphitheatre
PO Box 450
New Philadelphia, OH 44663
Phone: 330-364-5111
Fax: 330-339-1132
e-mail: trumpet@tusco.net
Web Site: www.trumpetintheland.com
Officers:
   President: Linda M. Eaton
Management:
   General Manager: Margaret M. Bonamico
Founded: 1965
Specialized Field: Comedy; Contemporary
Status: Non-Profit, Professional
Paid Staff: 60
Paid Artists: 40
Season: June - August
Type of Stage: Proscenium
Stage Dimensions: 40' x 30'
Seating Capacity: 1400

3310
LICKING COUNTY PLAYERS
131 W Main Street
Newark, OH 43055
Phone: 740-345-2287
e-mail: hobbit275@alltel.net
Management:
   President: John Roberts
   Vice Pesident: Christina Barth
   Secretary: Baird Krueger
   Treasurer: Tim Gardner
Mission: To preserve, promote, and perform all types of living theater in the community.
Specialized Field: Community Theater; Musical; Drama; Comedy
Status: Non-Profit

3311
WEATHERVANE PLAYHOUSE
1301 Weathervane Lane
PO Box 607
Newark, OH 44313
Phone: 330-366-4616
Fax: 330-344-3185
e-mail: info@weathervaneplayhouse.com
Management:
   Executive Director: Elynmarie Kazle
   Supervisor: Keith Campbell
Founded: 1935
Specialized Field: Community Theater; Drama; Comedy; Musical; Children's Theater; Educational
Status: Non-Equity; Nonprofit
Season: June - August
Type of Stage: Thrust

Stage Dimensions: 30' x 30'
Seating Capacity: 333

3312
TOWNE AND COUNTRY PLAYERS
PO Box 117
Norwalk, OH 45380
Phone: 937-526-5566
e-mail: info@tcplayers.com
Web Site: www.tcplayers.com
Management:
   Executive Director: Ronn Koerper
Mission: Providing family entertainment.
Utilizes: Singers
Founded: 1973
Specialized Field: Musical; Dinner Theater; Community Theater
Status: Semi-Professional; Nonprofit
Paid Staff: 2
Performs At: Historic Shrine Theatre
Annual Attendance: 40,000
Year Remodeled: 1941
Organization Type: Performing

3313
CEDAR POINT LIVE ENTERTAINMENT
One Cedar Point Drive
Sandusky, OH 44870-5259
Phone: 419-627-2390
Fax: 419-627-2389
e-mail: liveshows@cedarpoint.com
Web Site: www.cedarpoint.com
Management:
   Vice President Live Entertainment: Marje Rody
   Manager: Herbe Donald
Utilizes: Actors; Choreographers; Dancers; Designers; Guest Artists; Guest Companies; Guest Conductors; Guest Designers; Guest Directors; Guest Ensembles; Guest Musical Directors; Guest Musicians; Guest Soloists; High School Drama; Multimedia; Music; Original Music Scores; Resident Professionals; Singers; Student Interns; Visual Arts
Founded: 1870
Specialized Field: Musical; Contemporary
Paid Staff: 100
Paid Artists: 100
Season: May - October
Annual Attendance: 3 million
Facility Category: Theme Park

3314
SANDUSKY STATE THEATRE
107 Columbus Avenue
Sandusky, OH 44870
Phone: 419-626-1950
Fax: 419-626-2994
Toll-free: 877-378-2150
e-mail: sernst@state-theatre.com
Web Site: www.state-theatre.com
Management:
   Executive Director: Terri Bergman
   Managing Director: Steve Ernst
Mission: Performing Arts Center.
Founded: 1988
Specialized Field: Musical; Comedy; Classic; Contemporary
Status: Non-Profit, Non-Professional
Paid Staff: 9
Volunteer Staff: 150
Budget: $150,000-400,000
Income Sources: Ticket Sales; Sponsorship; Grants
Type of Stage: Proscenium
Seating Capacity: 1,600

3315

RITZ THEATRE

30 S Washington Street
PO Box 289
Tiffin, OH 44883
Phone: 419-448-8544
Fax: 419-448-7410
e-mail: michael@ritztheatre.org
Web Site: www.ritztheatre.org
Officers:
    President: Dominic Fabrizio
Management:
    Executive Director: Michael Strong
    Production Manager: John Spahr
    Development Director: Jessica Dickney
Founded: 1983
Specialized Field: Musical; Community Theater; Classic; Contemporary
Status: Non-Profit, Professional
Paid Staff: 8
Volunteer Staff: 250
Budget: $1 Million
Facility Category: Restored Movie Theatre
Type of Stage: Proscenium
Stage Dimensions: 29 x 29
Seating Capacity: 1,260
Year Built: 1928
Year Remodeled: 1998
Rental Contact: Michael Strong

3316

TOLEDO REPERTOIRE THEATRE

16 10th Street
Toledo, OH 43606
Phone: 419-243-0454
Fax: 419-321-1930
e-mail: gmoulopoulos@toledorep.org
Web Site: www.toledorep.org
Officers:
    Chairman: Jori Jex
    Business Manager: Kathleen McGovern
Management:
    Artistic Director: Gloria Moulopoulos
Mission: To entertain, educate, and provide services to Toledo and the surrounding region through the disciplines of theatre.
Utilizes: Guest Artists; Guest Companies; Singers
Founded: 1933
Specialized Field: Drama; Musical
Status: Semi-Professional; Nonprofit
Income Sources: Ohio Concerned Citizens for the Arts
Organization Type: Performing; Educational

3317

MAD RIVER THEATER WORKS

PO Box 248
West Liberty, OH 43357
Phone: 937-465-6751
e-mail: madriver@bright.net
Web Site: www.madrivertheater.org
Management:
    Administrative Director: Laurie Collins
    Musical Director: Bob Lucas
    Marketing Director: Jean Hooper
    Producing Director: Jeff Hooper
Mission: Our purpose is to create and produce plays that explore the concerns of rural people and to perform these works for multi-generational, primarily rural audiences.
Utilizes: Guest Companies; Singers
Founded: 1978
Specialized Field: Musical
Status: Professional; Nonprofit

Income Sources: Theatre Communications Group
Organization Type: Performing; Touring; Resident; Educational

3318

BLUE JACKET, FIRST FRONTIER

PO Box C
Xenia, OH 45385
Phone: 937-376-4358
Fax: 937-376-5364
Toll-free: 877-465-2583
e-mail: tracy@bluejacketdrama.com
Web Site: bluejacketdrama.com
Officers:
    Board President: Tim Hancy
    Chief of Operations/Education: Tracy Leake
    CFO: Michael Stricka
Management:
    Administrative Assistant: Kerry Bush
    Business Development Manager: Joanna Stevens
Mission: Produces the Epic Outdoor Drama, Blue Jacket, along with other education works and events. First Frontier strives to preserve and promote the history of the Ohio Territory through educational programs and artistic preservations. Through our efforts, we strive to support historic preservation, provide valuable educational opportunities and provide diverse cultural enrichment.
Utilizes: Actors; AEA Actors; Commissioned Composers; Commissioned Music; Designers; Guest Conductors; Guest Designers; Multimedia; Organization Contracts; Original Music Scores; Performance Artists; Resident Artists; Resident Professionals; Selected Students; Sign Language Translators; Soloists
Founded: 1982
Specialized Field: Outdoor Theater
Status: Non-Profit, Professional
Paid Staff: 100
Paid Artists: 60
Budget: $100,000,000
Income Sources: Ticket Sales; Fundraising; Special Events
Season: June - August
Annual Attendance: 40,000
Facility Category: Outdoor Amphitheatre
Type of Stage: Amphitheater
Stage Dimensions: 3 acres
Seating Capacity: 1,400 (stadium seats)
Year Built: 1978

Oklahoma

3319

BULLSHED THEATRE PROJECT

5505 E Mountain View Road
Edmond, OK 73034
Phone: 405-341-0928
e-mail: bullshedtheatre@aol.com
Web Site: www.geocities.com/bullshedtheatre
Management:
    Artistic Director: Don Shirey
    Producing Director: Anne Lower-Shirey
Mission: Using a minimalist approach without sacrificing the artistic intent. From Shakespeare to Shepard, we produce gypsy/guerilla theatre fare. Minimal design, minimal cast equals maximum overdrive.
Founded: 1999
Specialized Field: New Plays; Contemporary; Drama
Status: For-Profit, Professional

3320

POLLARD THEATRE

120 W Harrison
PO Box 38
Guthrie, OK 73044
Phone: 405-282-2802
Fax: 405-282-0061
Management:
    President: Don Coffin
    Artistic Director: W Jerome Stevenson
    Managing Director: Donna Dickson
Founded: 1987
Specialized Field: Musical; Comedy; Classic; Contemporary
Status: Non-Profit, Professional
Paid Staff: 11
Paid Artists: 11
Season: July - June
Type of Stage: Proscenium
Stage Dimensions: 50' x 50'
Seating Capacity: 277

3321

CAMERON UNIVERSITY: THEATRE ARTS DEPARTMENT

2800 W Gore Boulevard
Lawton, OK 73505
Phone: 580-581-2211
e-mail: thescoop@cameron.edu
Officers:
    Chair: Scott Richard Klein
Specialized Field: Educational; Theater Workshops
Facility Category: Auditorium; Studio Performance; Theatre House
Type of Stage: Flexible; Proscenium
Rental Contact: Scott Hofmann

3322

SOONER THEATRE OF NORMAN

101 E Main Street
Norman, OK 73069
Phone: 405-321-9600
Fax: 405-364-0543
e-mail: tickets@soonertheatre.com
Web Site: www.soonertheatre.com
Officers:
    President: Amy Pepper
    VP: Meg Newville
Management:
    Executive Director: Jennifer Heavner Baker
    Production Manager: Brandon Adams
    Marketing Director: Jessica George
Mission: To present live entertainment and theatrical productions including music concerts, movies and other special events.
Founded: 1979
Specialized Field: Musical; Comedy; Community Theater; Classic; Contemporary
Status: Non-Profit, Non-Professional
Paid Staff: 4

3323

LYRIC THEATRE OF OKLAHOMA

1727 NW 16th Street
Civic Center Music Hall-Performance Venue
Oklahoma City, OK 73162
Phone: 405-524-9310
Fax: 405-524-9316
e-mail: amy@lyrictheatreokc.com
Web Site: www.lyrictheatreokc.com
Management:
    Executive Director: Paula Stover
    Artistic Director: Nick Demos

Pr and Marketing Director: Amy Russo
Business Manager: Deborah Minard
Mission: Oklahoma's only professional Musical Theatre for 44 years.
Utilizes: Actors; AEA Actors; Choreographers; Collaborations; Dancers; Designers; Five Seasonal Concerts; Grant Writers; Guest Accompanists; Guest Companies; Guest Composers; Guest Conductors; Guest Designers; Guest Lecturers; Guest Writers; Instructors; Local Artists; Lyricists; Music; New Productions; Organization Contracts; Original Music Scores; Poets; Resident Artists; Resident Professionals; Selected Students; Sign Language Translators; Singers; Soloists; Student Interns; Visual Arts
Founded: 1763
Specialized Field: Musical
Status: Professional; Nonprofit
Paid Staff: 10
Budget: $2 million
Income Sources: Ticket Sales; Donations from Foundations; Corporations; Individuals
Performs At: The Civic Center Music Hall
Affiliations: AEA; SSDC; IATSE
Annual Attendance: 50,000
Facility Category: Theatre
Type of Stage: Proscenium
Seating Capacity: 1,396
Year Built: 1932
Year Remodeled: 1999
Rental Contact: Bart Wells
Organization Type: Performing; Resident

3324

OKLAHOMA CHILDREN'S THEATRE

Fair Park
3000 General Pershing Boulevard
Oklahoma City, OK 73107-6202
Phone: 405-951-0000
Fax: 405-951-0003
e-mail: cacoct@swbell.net
Web Site: www.cityartscenter.org
Management:
  City Arts President: James Piskel
  Executive Director: Mary Ann Prior
Mission: To provide entertaining, educational and accessible experiences through theatrical productions, creative programming and events.
Founded: 1986
Specialized Field: Musical; Community Theater; Contemporary; Touring Company; Children's Theater
Status: Non-Profit, Professional
Paid Staff: 6
Volunteer Staff: 3
Paid Artists: 40
Performs At: City Arts Center

3325

OKLAHOMA OPERA & MUSICAL THEATER COMPANY

2501 N Blackwelder
Oklahoma City University
Oklahoma City, OK 73106
Phone: 405-521-5315
Fax: 405-521-5971
e-mail: mparker@okcu.edu
Management:
  Dean: Mark Edward Parker
Specialized Field: Educational; Musical
Budget: $10,000-20,000
Performs At: Kirkpatrick Fine Arts Auditorium; Burg Theater; Wymberly

3326

OKLAHOMA SHAKESPEARE IN THE PARK

PO Box 1437
Oklahoma City, OK 73101
Phone: 405-235-3700
Fax: 405-235-3700
e-mail: okshakespr@aol.com
Web Site: www.oklahomashakespeare.com
Officers:
  President: Larry Alley
  Artistic Director: Kathryn McGill
Management:
  Managing Director: Sue Ellen Reiman
Mission: To produce works of Shakespeare; to teach Shakespeare in school.
Founded: 1985
Specialized Field: Comedy; Classic; Shakespeare
Status: Non-Profit, Professional
Paid Staff: 10
Volunteer Staff: 20
Paid Artists: 40
Non-paid Artists: 12
Budget: $120,000
Income Sources: Ticket Sales; Donations
Season: June - September
Affiliations: Oklahoma City University
Annual Attendance: 10,000
Facility Category: Ampitheatre
Type of Stage: Amphitheatre
Stage Dimensions: 50' x 25'
Seating Capacity: 750
Year Built: 1990
Year Remodeled: 2002
Cost: $50,000

3327

STAGE CENTER

400 W California Street
Oklahoma City, OK 73102-5021
Phone: 405-270-4800
Fax: 405-270-4806
e-mail: info@stagecenter.com
Web Site: www.stagecenter.com
Management:
  Director: Ron Martin
  Operations Manager: Don Lusk
Mission: Provides a facility that bring the arts and community together.
Founded: 1970
Specialized Field: Comedy; Community Theater; Classic; Contemporary
Status: Non-Profit; Non-Professional
Budget: $60,000-150,000
Income Sources: Grants
Performs At: Mary Noble Tolbert Theatre; Arena Theatre
Annual Attendance: 79,000
Facility Category: Multi-use Facility
Type of Stage: Round; Thrust stage
Seating Capacity: 210-580
Year Built: 1970
Year Remodeled: 1987

3328

PONCA PLAYHOUSE

Ponca Playhouse Box Office 1414
Ponca City, OK 74602-1414
Mailing Address: PO Box 1414 Ponca City, OK 74602
Phone: 580-765-5360
Management:
  President: Diane Malone

Mission: To offer interested area amateurs opportunities to participate in producing live theatre for the benefit of a discriminating audience.
Utilizes: Guest Companies; Singers
Founded: 1959
Specialized Field: Musical; Comedy; Community Theater
Status: Non-Profit, Non-Professional
Paid Staff: 1
Income Sources: American Association of Community Theatres; Oklahoma Community Theatre Association; Southwest Theatre Association
Organization Type: Performing; Touring; Resident

3329

CHEROKEE NATIONAL HISTORICAL SOCIETY

PO Box 515
Tahlequah, OK 74465
Phone: 918-456-6007
Fax: 918-456-6165
Toll-free: 888-999-6007
e-mail: tourism@cherokeeheritage.org
Web Site: www.cherokeeheritage.org
Officers:
  President: Charles/Chief Boyd
  VP: Mary Ellen Meredith
Management:
  President: Richard Fields
  Drama Producer: Patrick Whelan
  Marketing Director: Marilyn Craig
Mission: Seeks to preserve the history and traditions of the Cherokee Indian tribe and to educate the public concerning the Cherokee story through the presentation of the Trail of Tears drama and other cultural presentations.
Utilizes: Actors; Dance Companies; Dancers; Designers; Filmmakers; Fine Artists; Five Seasonal Concerts; Guest Ensembles; Guest Instructors; Guest Musical Directors; Instructors; Local Artists; Sign Language Translators; Soloists; Student Interns; Special Technical Talent; Theatre Companies; Touring Companies
Founded: 1967
Specialized Field: Outdoor Theater; Historical
Status: Non-Profit, Professional
Paid Staff: 23
Volunteer Staff: 25
Income Sources: Tourism and Recreation Department, State of Oklahoma
Performs At: Cherokee Heritage Center Tsa La Gi Amphitheater
Annual Attendance: 16,000
Facility Category: Amphitheater
Stage Dimensions: 80'x40'
Seating Capacity: 1,800
Year Built: 1969
Cost: 500,000
Rental Contact: Seth Hecht
Organization Type: Resident; Educational

3330

NORTHEASTERN STATE UNIVERSITY SIZZLIN' SUMMER SHOWCASE

Northeastern State University
College of Arts & Letters
609 N Grand Avenue
Tahlequah, OK 74464
Phone: 918-456-5511
Fax: 918-458-2348
e-mail: robinska@nsuok.edu
Web Site: www.nsuok.edu
Management:

President: Larry Williams
Technical Director: Charles Seat
Founded: 1983
Specialized Field: Summer Stock
Status: Non-Profit, Non-Professional
Paid Staff: 50
Volunteer Staff: 1
Paid Artists: 35
Season: June - August
Type of Stage: Proscenium
Stage Dimensions: 35' x 40'
Seating Capacity: 200

3331
DISCOVERYLAND!

W 41St Street
Tulsa, OK 74136
Phone: 918-742-6552
Fax: 918-743-7059
Web Site: http://dland.redrockcustomhomes.com/
Management:
    Casting Director: Rosemary Beckham
Founded: 1976
Specialized Field: Summer Stock; Musical
Status: Non-Equity; Commercial
Season: June - August
Type of Stage: Arena
Seating Capacity: 2200

3332
THEATRE TULSA

207 N Main Street
Tulsa, OK 74103
Phone: 918-587-8402
Fax: 918-592-0848
e-mail: theatretul@aol.com
Web Site: www.theatretulsa.org
Officers:
    Treasurer: Jennifer Flexner
    Secretary: Barbara Kaiser
Management:
    President/Co-VP Production: Melissa Childs
    Co-VP Production: Vern Stefanic
    VP Marketing: Linda Adams
Mission: To provide enrichment, entertainment and education to all sectors of the community by facilitating participation in the theatre arts.
Utilizes: Guest Artists; Guest Companies; Singers
Founded: 1922
Specialized Field: Community Theater
Status: Non-Profit, Non-Professional
Paid Staff: 1
Income Sources: Oklahoma Community Theatre Association; State Arts Council of Oklahoma
Performs At: Tulsa Performing Arts Center
Organization Type: Performing; Touring; Resident; Educational; Sponsoring

3333
WOODWARD ARTS AND THEATRE COUNCIL

818 Main
PO Box 1523
Woodward, OK 73802-1523
Phone: 580-256-7120
Fax: 580-256-7120
e-mail: wwarts@tlvi.net
Management:
    President: Krista Gaydon
    Executive Director: Jeanie K Raymer
Mission: To foster and promote cultural arts activities in Woodward and surrounding areas; to own and operate Woodward Arts Theatre.
Utilizes: Singers

Founded: 1981
Specialized Field: Community Theater
Status: Non-Profit, Professional
Paid Staff: 1
Income Sources: State Arts Council of Oklahoma
Organization Type: Performing; Sponsoring

Oregon

3334
OREGON SHAKESPEAREAN FESTIVAL ASSOCIATION

15 S Pioneer
PO Box 158
Ashland, OR 97520
Phone: 541-482-4331
Fax: 541-482-0446
e-mail: BoxOffice@orshakes.org
Web Site: www.osfashland.org
Management:
    Executive Director: Paul Nicholson
    Artistic Director: Libby Appel
    Managing Director: Jerry Russ
    Director Marketing/Communications: Janeen Olsen
Mission: To create bold new interpretations of contemporary and classic plays in repertory, influenced by American diversity and inspired by the high standard of Shakespeare.
Utilizes: Guest Companies; Singers
Founded: 1935
Specialized Field: Shakespeare; Classic; Contemporary
Status: Non-Profit, Professional
Paid Staff: 450
Volunteer Staff: 750
Budget: 23,000,000
Income Sources: Earned; Contributed
Season: June - August
Performs At: Angus Bowmer Theatre; New Theatre; Elizabethan Theatre
Affiliations: Actors' Equity Association; ATA; University/Resident Theatre Association; Theatre Communications Group
Annual Attendance: 375,000
Type of Stage: Thrust Stage; Black Box; Outdoors
Seating Capacity: 601; 250; 1188
Organization Type: Performing; Touring; Resident; Educational

3335
QUARTZ THEATRE

392 Taylor
Ashland, OR 97520
Phone: 513-482-8119
Management:
    Artistic Director: Robert Spira
Mission: The development of playwrights.
Founded: 1976
Specialized Field: Young Playwrights; New Plays
Status: Nonprofit
Organization Type: Performing

3336
CASCADES THEATRICAL COMPANY

148 NW Greenwood
Bend, OR 97701
Phone: 541-389-0803
Fax: 541-383-2879
e-mail: ctlinfo@cascadestheatrical.org
Web Site: www.cascadestheatrical.org
Officers:
    Chair-Board of Govenors: Janie Sharpe

Treasurer: Robert Barr
Vice Chair: Jim Keaton
Secretary: Lilly Ann Foreman
Management:
    Executive/Artistic Director: E Dee Torrey
    Marketing Director: Lana Shane
Mission: To offer quality live theatre to the community and Central Oregon
Utilizes: Singers
Founded: 1978
Specialized Field: Comminity Theater
Status: Non-Profit, Non-Professional
Paid Staff: 2
Volunteer Staff: 100
Budget: $150,000
Income Sources: Oregon Theatre Association
Performs At: Theatre
Affiliations: AACT
Annual Attendance: 18,000
Facility Category: Simi Thrust
Type of Stage: Flat Floor-No
Stage Dimensions: 43' WideX20' Deep
Seating Capacity: 131
Year Built: 1920
Year Remodeled: 1978
Rental Contact: Lana Shane
Organization Type: Performing

3337
ACTORS CABARET/MAINSTAGE THEATRE COMPANY

996 Willamette Street
Eugene, OR 97401
Phone: 541-683-4368
Fax: 541-485-5503
e-mail: cabaret1@aol.com
Officers:
    Executive Director: Jim Roberts
Management:
    Artistic Director: Joe Zingo
Mission: To offer a broad range of experiences to participants and audiences in both a professional theater and community theatre atmosphere.
Founded: 1979
Specialized Field: Musical; Comedy; Cabaret; Dinner Theater; Classic; Contemporary
Status: Non-Profit, Non-Professional
Paid Staff: 10
Performs At: Downtown Cabaret; Eugene Downtown Mall
Organization Type: Performing

3338
OREGON FANTASY THEATRE

Celeste Rose
820 E 36Th Avenue
Eugene, OR 97405
Phone: 541-686-1574
Management:
    Director: Celeste Rose
Mission: Producing and performing puppet shows which combine live actors with hand puppets, marionettes, shadows and masks.
Utilizes: Singers
Founded: 1978
Specialized Field: Puppet; Musical; Community Theater
Status: Professional; Non-Professional; Commercial
Paid Staff: 3
Income Sources: Puppeteers of America
Performs At: Hult Center for the Performing Arts
Organization Type: Performing; Touring; Educational

3339

ROGUE MUSIC THEATRE

PO Box 862
980 SW 6th Street
Grants Pass, OR 97526
Phone: 541-479-2559
Fax: 541-471-0919
e-mail: info@roguemusictheatre.org
Web Site: http://www.roguemusictheatre.org
Officers:
    President: Angela Padilla
    Vice President: Molly Means
    Treasurer: Catherine Healy
    Secretary: Jim Thorpe
Management:
    Artistic Director: Richard Jessup
Mission: To provide the highest quality musical theatre to the home region and beyond.
Founded: 1982
Specialized Field: Musical; Educational
Status: Non-profit; Professional
Paid Staff: 4
Volunteer Staff: 100
Paid Artists: 110
Non-paid Artists: 10
Budget: $150,000-400,000
Annual Attendance: 11,000
Facility Category: Outdoor ampitheatre
Type of Stage: Proscenium
Stage Dimensions: 35'x70'
Seating Capacity: 1,385
Year Built: 1915
Year Remodeled: 1978

3340

LAKEWOOD THEATRE COMPANY

368 S State Street
PO Box 274
Lake Oswego, OR 97034
Phone: 503-635-3901
Fax: 503-635-2002
e-mail: center.info@lakewood-center.org
Web Site: www.lakewood-center.org
Officers:
    President: Jerry Koll
    Executive Director: Andrew Edwards
Management:
    Executive Producer: Kay Vega
Mission: Establishment and maintenance of a permanent multi-arts and theatre facility; the sponsorship and coordination of education and cultural programming in visual arts, theatre and community events.
Founded: 1952
Specialized Field: Musical; Drama; Multi-Media; Community Theater
Status: Non-Profit, Professional
Paid Staff: 14
Volunteer Staff: 150
Paid Artists: 150
Non-paid Artists: 100
Budget: $1,300,000
Income Sources: Oregon Theatre Association; Oregon Advocates for the Arts; Portland Area Theatre Alliance
Season: June - September
Annual Attendance: 30,000
Facility Category: Arts Facility
Type of Stage: Thrust
Stage Dimensions: 30'x30'
Seating Capacity: 196
Year Built: 1980
Cost: $80,000

Organization Type: Performing; Resident; Educational; Sponsoring

3341

GALLERY THEATRE OF OREGON

210 N Ford
PO Box 245
McMinnville, OR 97128
Phone: 503-472-2227
Fax: 503-434-1394
e-mail: execdirector@gallerytheatre.org
Web Site: www.gallerytheatre.org
Officers:
    President: Ken Moore
    VP: Lea New
    Secretary: Barbara Knutson
    Treasurer: Ken Myers
Management:
    President: Walt Haight
    Managing Director: Ginger Williams
Mission: To provide a performing arts center in Yamhill County.
Utilizes: Guest Companies; Singers
Founded: 1968
Specialized Field: Drama; Musical; Comedy; Contemporary
Status: Non-Profit, Non-Professional
Paid Staff: 2
Type of Stage: Black Box; Mainstage
Stage Dimensions: 20'x40'
Seating Capacity: 240-100
Year Built: 1968
Year Remodeled: 1992
Organization Type: Performing; Educational

3342

BRITT FESTIVALS

PO Box 1124
Medford, OR 97501
Phone: 541-779-0847
Fax: 541-776-3712
Toll-free: 800-882-7488
e-mail: info@brittfest.org
Web Site: www.brittfest.org
Management:
    President: Garry Sherwood
    Executive Director: Ron McUne
    Artistic Director: Peter Bay
    Development Director: Ed Foss
    Booking/Production Director: Mike Sturgill
    Education Director: David MacKenzie
Mission: To present and sponsor, in Southern Oregon, performing arts of the highest quality for the education, enrichment and enjoyment of all.
Utilizes: Guest Artists; Guest Companies
Founded: 1963
Specialized Field: Classic; Contemporary; Ethnic Theater; Comedy; Drama
Status: Non-Profit, Professional
Paid Staff: 12
Volunteer Staff: 600
Performs At: The Britt Gardens
Annual Attendance: 70,000
Facility Category: Outdoor Amphitheatre
Seating Capacity: 2200
Year Built: 1963
Year Remodeled: 1992
Organization Type: Performing; Touring; Resident; Educational; Sponsoring

3343

DOLPHIN PLAYERS

2540 Union
North Bend, OR 97459

Phone: 503-756-7088
Mission: Presenting quality theater in a comfortable intimate setting.
Founded: 1980
Specialized Field: Musical; Dinner Theater; Community Theater
Status: Non-Professional; Nonprofit
Paid Staff: 50
Organization Type: Performing; Resident; Educational; Sponsoring

3344

ARTISTS REPERTORY THEATRE

1516 SW Alder Street
Portland, OR 97205
Phone: 503-241-1278
Fax: 503-241-8268
e-mail: brad@artistsrep.org
Web Site: www.artistsrep.org
Management:
    President: Allen Nause
    Executive Director: Jill Baum
    Business Manager: Rosalie Tank
Founded: 1981
Specialized Field: Musical; Comedy; Classic; Contemporary
Status: Non-Profit, Professional
Paid Staff: 20
Paid Artists: 20
Performs At: Reiersgaard Theatre
Type of Stage: Flexible Black Box
Seating Capacity: 170

3345

BRODY THEATER

1904 NW 27th Avenue
Portland, OR 97210
Phone: 503-224-0688
e-mail: info@brodytheater.com
Web Site: www.brodytheater.com
Mission: The Brody's double focus on entertainment and experiment, marks it as a showcase for both audience-pleasing performances and cutting edge theatrical presentation.
Founded: 1996
Specialized Field: Experimental

3346

MIRACLE THEATRE GROUP

425 SE 6th Avenue
Portland, OR 97214
Phone: 503-236-7253
Fax: 503-236-4174
e-mail: miracle@milagro.org
Web Site: www.milagro.org
Officers:
    Chair Board of Directors: Ann Marcus
Management:
    President: Jose Gonzalez
    Artistic Director: Olda Sanchez
    Artistic Director and Founder: Danielle Malan
    Director Dance Education: Catherine Evleshin
Mission: Provides programming that includes public performances as well as specialized touring and education projects that currently encompass all of the Western states and the countries of Mexico and Canada. Incorporated as a nonprofit organization in 1985. The Miracle Theatre Group oversees three professional performance companies: Miracle Mainstate, Teatro Milagro, and the Milagro Bailadores.
Founded: 1985
Specialized Field: Musical; Comedy; Classic; Contemporary
Status: Non-Profit, Professional

Paid Staff: 15
Paid Artists: 10
Performs At: Miracle Theatre; 525 SE Stark
Rental Contact: Alice Snyder

3347
OREGON CHILDREN'S THEATRE
600 SW 10th
Suite 501
Portland, OR 97205-2723
Phone: 503-228-9571
Fax: 503-228-3545
e-mail: info@octc.org
Web Site: www.octc.org
Officers:
Board President: Mark Wilcox
Management:
Executive Producer: Sondra Pearlman
Director Marketing: Sharon Martell
Mission: To present professional live theatre for youth at a price affordable to schools and families; to educate young people to the wonders of live theatre.
Utilizes: Actors; High School Drama; Original Music Scores
Specialized Field: Contemporary; Children's Theater
Performs At: Keller Auditorium
Annual Attendance: 100,000

3348
PORTLAND ACTORS ENSEMBLE
PO Box 8671
Portland, OR 97207
Phone: 503-467-6573
e-mail: portlandactors@gmail.com
Web Site: www.portlandactors.com
Mission: To bring financially accessible classical theatre to Portland communities in a non-traditional environment.
Founded: 1970
Specialized Field: Shakespeare; Outdoor Theater

3349
PORTLAND CENTER STAGE
Gerding Theater at the Armory
128 NW Eleventh Avenue
Portland, OR 97209
Phone: 503-445-3700
Fax: 503-445-3720
e-mail: webmaster@pcs.org
Web Site: www.pcs.org
Management:
General Manager: Edith Love
Artistic Director: Chris Coleman
Founded: 1988
Specialized Field: Drama; Comedy; Musical; Classic
Status: Non-Profit, Professional
Season: October - April
Type of Stage: Partial Thrust
Seating Capacity: 860

3350
STARK RAVING THEATRE
Pmb 383
25 NW 23rd Place, Suite 6
Portland, OR 97210
Phone: 503-232-7072
Officers:
President: Lani Miller
Treasurer: Catherine Scheidler
Secretary: Jane Davies
Management:
Artistic Director: Matthew B Zrebski
Managing Director: Michelle Seaton
Director Of Marketing: Chris Murray

Marketing Manager: David Seitz
Business Manager: Steve Alexander
Box Office Manager: Jim Wilhite
Production Manager/Technical: Ian Smith
Founded: 1988
Specialized Field: New Plays; Staged Readings; Theater Workshops

3351
PENTACLE THEATRE
450 Court Street NE
PO Box 186
Salem, OR 97301
Phone: 503-364-7121
Fax: 503-485-4301
e-mail: tickets@pentacletheatre.org
Web Site: www.pentacletheatre.org
Officers:
Founder: Robert Putnam
Management:
President: Dave Davis
Executive Director: Angie Morris
VP: John Tawney
Production Director: Tony Zandol
Mission: Pentacle's History begin in the early 1950's when a small group of theatre enthusiasts rented a barn (that subsequently became known as The Old Barn) and mounted a four production summer season.
Founded: 1954
Specialized Field: Summer Stock
Status: Non-Profit, Non-Professional
Paid Staff: 4
Volunteer Staff: 350
Non-paid Artists: 200
Budget: $275,000
Affiliations: AACT

3352
BROADWAY ROSE THEATRE COMPANY
PO Box 231004
Tigard, OR 97281
Phone: 503-620-5262
Fax: 503-670-8512
e-mail: info@broadwayrose.com
Web Site: www.bwayrose.com
Management:
Producing Artistic Director: Sharon Maroney
General Manager: Dan Murphy
Marketing Director: Alan Anderson
Development Manager: Brisa Peters
Mission: Broadway Rose has been producing live, fun, professional summer stock theater since 1992. As the only professional theater company in Washington County, we provide accessible, quality entertainment.
Founded: 1992
Specialized Field: Summer Stock
Status: Professional; Nonprofit
Season: June - August
Performs At: Deb Fennell Auditorium

3353
ENCHANTED FOREST SUMMER THEATRE
8462 Enchanted Way SE
Turner, OR 97392
Phone: 503-371-4242
Fax: 503-363-3060
e-mail: susan@enchantedforest.com
Web Site: www.enchantedforest.com
Officers:
President: Roger Tofte
Management:
Executive Director: Susan Vasley

Mission: To make people of all ages laugh and leave our theatre with wonderful memories.
Utilizes: Actors; Choreographers; Composers; Composers-in-Residence; Contract Actors; Dancers; Designers; Local Unknown Artists; Multimedia; Organization Contracts; Original Music Scores; Performance Artists; Sign Language Translators
Founded: 1972
Specialized Field: Musical; Comedy; Contemporary; Summer Stock
Status: For-Profit, Non-Professional
Paid Staff: 10
Paid Artists: 12
Income Sources: Paid Admission
Season: May - September
Performs At: 200 Seat Outdoor, Stage Covered
Annual Attendance: 100,000
Facility Category: Theme Park
Type of Stage: Proscenium
Stage Dimensions: 22' x 25'
Seating Capacity: 200
Year Built: 1972

Pennsylvania

3354
THEATRE OUTLET
SilkWerks Bldg
930 N 4th Street
Allentown, PA 18102
Mailing Address: PO Box 715, Allentown PA 18105
Phone: 610-820-9270
Fax: 610-820-9130
e-mail: admin@theatreoutlet.org
Web Site: www.theatreoutlet.org
Officers:
President: Michael J Fegley
VP: Marilyn J Roberts
Secretary: Bill Mutimer
Management:
Producing Artistic Director: Beth Schachter
Managing Director: Kindall Goble
Marketing Director: Phil Haas
Mission: Dedicated to bringing vibrant and multicultural arts to the community while engaging patrons and cultivating artists.
Founded: 1989
Specialized Field: Contemporary; New Plays
Status: Non-Profit, Non-Professional
Paid Staff: 2
Paid Artists: 60

3355
ACT II PLAYHOUSE
56 E Butler Avenue
Ambler, PA 19002
Phone: 215-654-0200
Fax: 215-654-5001
Web Site: www.actii.org
Management:
President: Steven Blumenthal
Managing Director: Alan Blumenthal
Founded: 1999
Specialized Field: Drama; Musical; Comedy
Status: Non-Profit, Professional
Paid Staff: 6
Paid Artists: 19

3356
SOUTH PARK THEATRE
P.O. Box 133
Bethel Park, PA 15129

Phone: 412-831-8552
Fax: 412-831-1647
e-mail: sopktheat@aol.com
Officers:
  President: Robert H Craft Jr
Management:
  Executive Director: Audrey Castracane
Mission: To provide highest quality opera; to broaden public awareness and understanding of opera through education and comunity programming; to support development of young American singers; to encourage work of new composers to maintain oper as a living arts form.
Founded: 1995
Specialized Field: Musical; Drama; Comedy
Status: Non-Equity; Nonprofit
Season: May - September
Type of Stage: Proscenium
Stage Dimensions: 24' x 36'
Seating Capacity: 136

3357
TOUCHSTONE THEATRE
321 E 4th Street
Bethlehem, PA 18015
Phone: 610-867-1689
Fax: 610-867-0561
e-mail: touchstone@touchstone.org
Web Site: www.touchstone.org
Officers:
  President: Dave Rabaut
  Vice President: Denise Stangl
  Treasurer: John Fallock
  Secretary: Kelly Watkins
  Touring Mgr/Ensemble Member/Founder: Bill George
Management:
  Producing Director/Ensemble Member: Lisa Jordan
  Production Manager/Ensemble Member: James P. Jordan
  Touring Manager/Ensemble Member: Bill George
  Education Director/Ensemble Assoc.: Cathleen O'Malley
  Director Of Development: Amy Meleck
Mission: Dedicated to being an active force in the renewal of theatre as a vital art form. At our center is a resident professional acting ensemble rooted both in the local community of Bethlehem, Pennsylvania and the international community of the actor-creater.
Utilizes: Actors; Collaborating Artists; Collaborations; Community Members; Community Talent; Composers; Contract Actors; Curators; Designers; Educators; Five Seasonal Concerts; Guest Accompanists; Guest Choreographers; Guest Companies; Guest Conductors; Guest Designers; Guest Directors; Guest Ensembles; Guest Lecturers; Guest Musical Directors; Guest Speakers; Guest Teachers; High School Drama; Instructors; Local Artists; Local Artists & Directors; Local Talent; Lyricists; Multi Collaborations; Music; Organization Contracts; Original Music Scores; Paid Performers; Performance Artists; Poets; Resident Artists; Resident Companies; Soloists; Student Interns; Visual Designers
Founded: 1981
Specialized Field: Comedy; Classic; Contemporary; Ensembles
Status: Non-Profit, Professional
Paid Staff: 8
Volunteer Staff: 50
Paid Artists: 5
Income Sources: Theatre Communications Group; Theatre Association of Pennsylvania; National Mime Association

Performs At: Touchstone Theatre
Seating Capacity: 72
Year Built: 1980
Organization Type: Performing; Touring; Resident; Educational; Sponsoring

3358
BLOOMSBURG THEATRE ENSEMBLE
226 Center Street
PO Box 66
Bloomsburg, PA 17815
Phone: 570-784-8181
Fax: 570-784-4912
Toll-free: 800-282-0283
e-mail: bte@bte.org
Web Site: www.bte.org
Officers:
  President: Christina Francis PhD
  VP: Karl Meyer
  Secretary: Geeta Krishnan MD
  Treasurer: Barbara Martin
Management:
  Administrative Director: J S Atherton
  Box Office Manager: Rachel Kindt
  Director Development: Beth Larson
  Stage Manager: Michael Yerges
  Marketing: Syreeta CombsCannaday
Utilizes: Actors; Collaborations; Community Members; Community Talent; Designers; Educators; Five Seasonal Concerts; Guest Accompanists; Guest Conductors; Guest Instructors; Guest Lecturers; Guest Musical Directors; Guest Soloists; Guest Speakers; Instructors; Original Music Scores; Resident Professionals; Selected Students; Soloists; Students; Theatre Companies; Visual Arts
Founded: 1978
Specialized Field: Ensembles; Drama
Status: Nonprofit
Paid Staff: 25
Volunteer Staff: 4
Paid Artists: 7
Budget: $650,000
Performs At: Alvina Krause Theatre
Type of Stage: Proscenium
Seating Capacity: 350
Rental Contact: J S Atherton
Organization Type: Performing; Touring; Resident; Educational; Sponsoring

3359
STATE COLLEGE COMMUNITY THEATRE
Boal Barn Playhouse
PO Box 23
Boalsburg, PA 16804
Phone: 814-234-7228
e-mail: info@scctonline.org
Officers:
  President: Mark Comly
  VP: Susanna Ritti
  Treasurer: Charlie Wilson
  Secretary: Bonnie Spetzer
Management:
  President: Susanna Ritti
  VP: Barry Hutzell
Founded: 1955
Specialized Field: Educational; Theater Workshops
Status: Non-Equity; Nonprofit
Season: June - August
Annual Attendance: 2,000
Type of Stage: Arena
Seating Capacity: 201

3360
ALLENBERRY PLAYHOUSE
Resort & Playhouse
PO Box 7
Boiling Springs, PA 17007
Phone: 717-258-3211
Fax: 717-960-5280
Toll-free: 800-430-5468
e-mail: aberry@allenberry.com
Web Site: www.allenberry.com
Management:
  Producer: John J Heinze
  Artistic Director: Ed Aldridge
Mission: A repertory equity theatre with a season running from March-November.
Utilizes: Actors; AEA Actors; Artists-in-Residence; Choreographers; Commissioned Music; Dancers; Designers; Educators; Fine Artists; Grant Writers; Guest Accompanists; Guest Artists; Guest Conductors; Guest Designers; Guest Lecturers; Guest Teachers; Instructors; Local Artists; Music; Performance Artists; Poets; Resident Artists; Resident Professionals; Sign Language Translators; Soloists; Student Interns
Founded: 1949
Specialized Field: Musical; Comedy; Classic
Status: For-Profit, Professional
Paid Staff: 15
Paid Artists: 30
Income Sources: Actors' Equity Association; Society for Stage Directors and Choreographers
Season: April - November
Performs At: Allenberry Playhouse
Affiliations: AEA, SSDC, USSA
Annual Attendance: 60,000
Type of Stage: Proscenium
Stage Dimensions: 28'x60'x28'
Seating Capacity: 400
Year Built: 1949
Year Remodeled: 1988
Organization Type: Performing; Resident

3361
BRISTOL RIVERSIDE THEATRE
120 Radcliffe Street
PO Box 1250
Bristol, PA 19007
Phone: 215-785-6664
Fax: 215-785-2762
e-mail: info@brtstage.org
Web Site: www.brtstage.org
Officers:
  President: Brian McPeak
Management:
  Artistic Director: Edward Keith Baker
Founded: 1983
Specialized Field: Drama; Comedy; Musical
Status: Non-Profit, Professional
Paid Staff: 10
Budget: $35,000-60,000
Performs At: Bristol Riverside Theatre
Type of Stage: Flexible
Seating Capacity: 302

3362
PENNSYLVANIA SHAKESPEARE FESTIVAL
DeSales University
2755 Station Avenue
Center Valley, PA 18034
Phone: 610-282-9455
Fax: 610-282-2084
e-mail: sally.reith@desales.edu
Web Site: www.pashakespeare.org

Management:
  Producing/Artistic Director: Patrick Mulcahy
  General Manager: Casey William Gallagher
  Management Associate: Timothy Walling
  Office Manager: Sally Reith
Mission: A professional theatre compnay and the Official shakespeare festival of the Commonwealth of Pennsylvania. Our mission is to enrich, inspire, engage and entertain the widest possible audience through first-rate professional productions of classical and contemporary plays, with a core commitment to the works of Shalespeare and other master dramatists and through an array of educational outreach and mentorship programs.
Founded: 1991
Specialized Field: Shakespeare; Classic
Status: Non-Profit, Professional
Paid Staff: 8
Volunteer Staff: 200
Season: May - August
Type of Stage: Thrust
Stage Dimensions: 38' x 40'
Seating Capacity: 473

3363
UPPER DARBY SUMMER STAGE

601 N Lansdowne Avenue
Drexel Hill, PA 19026
Phone: 610-394-1570
Fax: 610-622-6960
e-mail: hdietzler@rcn.com
Web Site: www.udpac.org
Management:
  Executive/Artistic Director: Harry Dietzler
Mission: One of the nations most sucessfully youth theater programs, producing six children's musicals and a mainstage Broadway show. We involve more than 600 youth ages 11 through 25 and employ more than 70 professionals and staff.
Founded: 1976
Specialized Field: Musical; Summer Stock
Status: Non-Profit, Non-Professional
Paid Staff: 80
Paid Artists: 25
Budget: $300,000
Income Sources: Government; Fundraising; Ticket Sales
Season: July - August
Facility Category: Performing Arts Center
Type of Stage: Thrust
Stage Dimensions: 50' x 40'
Year Built: 1960
Year Remodeled: 1974

3364
STATE THEATRE CENTER FOR THE ARTS

453 Northampton Street
Easton, PA 18042
Phone: 610-252-3132
Fax: 610-258-2570
Toll-free: 800-999-7828
e-mail: info@statetheatre.org
Web Site: www.statetheatre.org
Officers:
  President/CEO: Shelley Brown
Management:
  Operations: Mark Rafinski
  Marketing: Jamie Balliet
Specialized Field: Children's Theater; Broadway Musical Revivals
Status: Non-Profit, Non-Professional
Paid Staff: 12
Annual Attendance: 100,000

Seating Capacity: 1,500
Year Built: 1922
Year Remodeled: 2000

3365
CRESSON LAKE PLAYHOUSE

526 W Ogle Street
PO Box 368
Ebensburg, PA 15931
Phone: 814-472-4333
Fax: 814-472-4419
e-mail: cressonlake@aol.com
Web Site: www.geocites.com
Officers:
  President: Sr Linda Karas
  Treasurer: Gary Bradley
  Vice President: Jim Pollino
Management:
  Executive Director: Elaine Mastalski
Mission: Cresson Lake Playhouse is governed by a Board of Directors. It is a not-for-profit organization. It is sponsored in part by Pennsylvania Council on the Arts. The theatre's mission since its founding in 1974 is to bring quality to live entertainment to the underserved rural areas of the Appalachian Mountains at affordable family prices.
Utilizes: Actors; Artists-in-Residence; Choreographers; Collaborations; Composers-in-Residence; Dancers; Designers; Educators; Five Seasonal Concerts; Grant Writers; Guest Artists; Guest Conductors; Guest Designers; Guest Directors; Guest Ensembles; Guest Lecturers; Guest Musical Directors; Guest Musicians; Guild Activities; High School Drama; Instructors; Local Artists; Multi Collaborations; Multimedia; Music; New Productions; Organization Contracts; Performance Artists; Resident Professionals; Sign Language Translators; Singers; Soloists; Student Interns; Touring Companies; Visual Arts
Founded: 1974
Specialized Field: Community Theater
Status: Non-Profit, Non-Professional
Paid Staff: 2
Volunteer Staff: 30
Paid Artists: 75
Non-paid Artists: 125
Season: May-December
Performs At: Historic Theatre Built In 1854, Equipped With State-Of-The-Art Sound System; Air-Conditioned And Heated; Ample Parking
Annual Attendance: 15,000-17,000
Facility Category: Indoor Theatre-Air Conditioned And Heated
Type of Stage: Alley/Black Box Theatre
Stage Dimensions: 20x17
Seating Capacity: 199
Year Built: 1850
Year Remodeled: 1974
Rental Contact: Elaine Mastalski

3366
TOTEM POLE PLAYHOUSE

9555 Golf Course Road
PO Box 603
Fayetteville, PA 17222-0603
Phone: 717-352-2164
Fax: 717-352-8870
Toll-free: 888-805-7056
e-mail: boxoffice@totempoleplayhouse.org
Web Site: www.totempoleplayhouse.org
Officers:
  President: Dana Witt
  Treasurer: Jake Kaufman
Management:
  Managing Director: Sue McMurtray

Artistic Director: Ray Ficca
  Production Manager: Michael Domme
Mission: To provide professional theatre to the Cumberland Valley.
Utilizes: Actors; AEA Actors; Artists-in-Residence; Choreographers; Designers; Grant Writers; Guest Artists; Guest Composers; Guest Conductors; Guest Designers; Guest Lecturers; Guest Musical Directors; Instructors; Resident Artists; Resident Professionals
Founded: 1950
Specialized Field: Professional Theatre
Status: Professional; Commercial
Paid Staff: 4
Volunteer Staff: 30
Paid Artists: 50
Budget: $1,100,000
Income Sources: Ticket Sales; Tax Deductible Gifts; Corporate Sponsors
Season: June - August
Performs At: Totem Pole Playhouse
Affiliations: Actors Equity Association
Annual Attendance: 29,000
Facility Category: Air-Conditioned Enclosure
Type of Stage: Proscenium
Seating Capacity: 389
Year Built: 1970
Organization Type: Performing; Resident

3367
BARROW-CIVIC THEATRE

1223 Liberty Street
PO Box 1089
Franklin, PA 16323
Phone: 814-432-5196
Fax: 814-432-6608
Toll-free: 800-537-7769
e-mail: john@barrowtheatre.com
Web Site: www.barrowtheatre.com
Management:
  President: Mary Ann Richardson
  Managing Director: John McConnell
Mission: Committed to providing leadership and education in cultural development and performing arts to the region, striving to create a legacy of quality entertainment by tapping the resources of all age group and encouraging the pursuit of artistic talents.
Founded: 1992
Specialized Field: Drama; Musical
Status: Non-Profit, Non-Professional
Paid Staff: 3
Seating Capacity: 497

3368
OPEN STAGE OF HARRISBURG

223 Walnut Street
Harrisburg, PA 17101-1711
Phone: 717-232-6736
Fax: 717-232-1505
e-mail: management@openstagehbg.com
Web Site: www.openstagehbg.com
Officers:
  President: Marianne M Fisher
Management:
  President: Susan Kadel
  Artistic Director: Donald L Alsedek
  Managing Director: Terry Sneed
  Educational Director: Anne L Alsedek
Mission: To develop and support an ensemble of theatre artists for the purpose of presenting modern, contemporary and original dramatic literature in close relationship with its audiences; to provide educational opportunites through a school and outreach program.

Utilizes: Actors; AEA Actors; Artists-in-Residence; Collaborating Artists; Guest Companies; Guest Conductors; Guest Directors; Guest Instructors; Guest Soloists; Guild Activities; High School Drama; Local Artists; Lyricists; New Productions; Original Music Scores; Student Interns; Touring Companies
Founded: 1983
Specialized Field: New Plays; Contemporary
Status: Non-Profit, Professional
Paid Staff: 5
Paid Artists: 40
Budget: $406,315
Income Sources: Theatre Communications Group; Citizens for the Arts in Pennsylvania; Theatre Association of Pennsylvania; Box Office; Student Tuition; Individual, Public and Private Fundings.
Performs At: Citizens for the Arts in PA
Affiliations: Theatre Communications Group
Annual Attendance: 9000
Facility Category: Theatre
Type of Stage: Black Box
Stage Dimensions: 18x24
Seating Capacity: 99
Year Remodeled: 1991
Rental Contact: Donald L Alscolk
Organization Type: Performing; Touring; Resident; Educational; Sponsoring

3369
THEATRE HARRISBURG
513 Hurlock Street
Harrisburg, PA 17110
Phone: 717-232-5501
Fax: 717-232-5912
e-mail: email@theatreharrisburg.com
Web Site: www.theatreharrisburg.com
Officers:
  President: Joe Rebarchak
Management:
  Executive Director: Samuel Kuba
Mission: To provide quality theatrical experiences, opportunities and education to the Capital Region.
Utilizes: Guest Companies
Founded: 1926
Specialized Field: Musical; Community Theater
Status: Non-Profit, Non-Professional
Paid Staff: 5
Income Sources: Grants
Performs At: Whitaker Center and Krevsky Production Center
Annual Attendance: 21,000
Organization Type: Performing; Educational

3370
HERSHEY THEATRE
15 E Caracas Avenue
PO Box 395
Hershey, PA 17033
Phone: 717-534-3411
Fax: 717-533-2882
e-mail: htheatre@hersheytheatre.com
Web Site: www.hersheytheatre.com
Officers:
  Executive Director: Susan R. Fowler
  Assistant Executive Director: Diane R. Paul
  Director Operations: Patrick Seeley
Management:
  Box Office Manager: Millie Morris
Mission: Premiere performing arts center presenting the finest in touring Broadway shows, classical music and dance attractions, and world-renowned entertainers.
Utilizes: Original Music Scores; Selected Students; Theatre Companies

Founded: 1933
Specialized Field: Drama; Musical; Light Theater; Classic; Children's Theater
Status: Non-Profit, Non-Professional
Paid Staff: 5
Volunteer Staff: 400
Performs At: Hershey Theatre
Annual Attendance: 75,000
Facility Category: Theatre
Type of Stage: Proscenium
Seating Capacity: 1,904
Year Built: 1933
Year Remodeled: 2002
Cost: $3,000,000
Rental Contact: Executive Director Susan Fowler
Organization Type: Touring; Sponsoring

3371
HERSHEYPARK ENTERTAINMENT
100 W Hersheypark Drive
Hershey, PA 17033
Phone: 717-534-3349
Fax: 717-534-3336
e-mail: audition@hersheypa.com
Web Site: www.hersheypa.com
Management:
  Executive Director: Cherie Vanzant
Founded: 1976
Specialized Field: Community Theater; Musical
Status: For-Profit, Professional
Season: May - September

3372
KEYSTONE REPERTORY THEATER
104 Waller Hall
Indiana, PA 15705
Mailing Address: 401 S 11th Street Indiana, PA 15705
Phone: 724-357-2547
Fax: 724-357-7899
e-mail: lively-arts@iup.edu
Web Site: www.arts.iup.edu/krt
Officers:
  Preisdent: George Fender
Management:
  Artistic Director: Barbara Blackledge
  Associate Artistic Director: Brain Jones
Mission: Professional summer theater bringing theater to rural western PA.
Founded: 1997
Specialized Field: Summer Stock
Status: Nonprofit
Paid Staff: 22
Volunteer Staff: 5
Paid Artists: 80
Budget: $45,000-60,000
Income Sources: Grants; Tickets; Subscriptions; Advertising; Donations
Season: June - July
Affiliations: AEA Special Appearence Contracts
Annual Attendance: 2000-2500
Type of Stage: Black Box
Seating Capacity: 199
Year Built: 1915
Year Remodeled: 1989
Cost: $2 Million

3373
MOUNTAIN PLAYHOUSE
PO Box 205
Jennerstown, PA 15547
Phone: 814-629-9201
Fax: 814-629-9201
e-mail: boxoffice@mountainplayhouse.com
Web Site: www.mountainplayhouse.com

Management:
  Director: Danny Gidron
  Director: Chan Harris
  Director: Guy Stroman
Utilizes: Guest Companies
Founded: 1939
Specialized Field: Dinner Theater; Comedy; Musical; Drama; Classic
Status: Non-Profit, Professional
Paid Staff: 40
Season: May - October
Performs At: Mountain Playhouse
Facility Category: Resident; Educational
Organization Type: Resident; Educational

3374
FULTON OPERA HOUSE/ACTOR'S COMPANY OF PENNSYLVANIA
12 N Prince Street
PO Box 1865
Lancaster, PA 17608-1865
Phone: 717-394-7133
Fax: 717-397-3780
e-mail: artdir@fultontheatre.org
Web Site: www.fultontheatre.org
Management:
  Artistic Director: Michael Mitchell
Founded: 1963
Specialized Field: Musical; Light Theater
Performs At: Fulton Opera House; Studio Theatre
Type of Stage: Proscenium, Black Box
Seating Capacity: 630, 100

3375
SESAME PLACE
100 Sesame Road
Langhome, PA 19047
Phone: 215-752-7070
Fax: 215-741-5307
e-mail: michael.joyce@anheuser-busch.com
Web Site: www.sesameplace.com
Officers:
  Chairman: Jan Cavanaugh
  Vice-Chairman: Ann Marie Boweyer
  Treasurer: Michael Eiser
  Secretary: Joanne Bujnoski
Management:
  EVP: Robert Caruso
  Director Entertainment: Michael Joyce
Founded: 1980
Specialized Field: Specialty Acts; Children's Theater
Status: For-Profit, Non-Professional
Season: May - October
Stage Dimensions: 30' x 32'
Seating Capacity: 1000

3376
SAINT VINCENT SUMMER THEATRE
Saint Vincent College
300 Fraser Purchase Road
Latrobe, PA 15650-2690
Phone: 724-537-8900
Fax: 724-537-4554
Web Site: www.svst.org
Officers:
  Acting Executive Director: Bonaventure Curtis
Management:
  Artistic Director: Colleen Reilly
Mission: To continue to bring quality opera to out community and to showcase it in out own opera house; to educate the general community in an appreciation of opera and send our outreach programs into the schools of both Manatee and Sarasota counties; to offer statewide touring programs.

Founded: 1969
Specialized Field: Touring Company; Drama; Musical
Status: Non-Profit, Professional
Paid Staff: 2
Paid Artists: 7
Season: May - August
Type of Stage: Half-Round
Stage Dimensions: 32' x 20'
Seating Capacity: 280

3377

PEOPLE'S LIGHT AND THEATRE COMPANY

39 Conestoga Road
Malvern, PA 19355
Phone: 610-647-1900
Fax: 610-640-9521
Web Site: http://www.peopleslight.org
Officers:
President: L Frederick Sutherland
Vice President: Kenneth Mumma
Treasurer: Brian Doerner
Secretary: Hal Real
Management:
Managing Director: Grace Grillet
General Manager: Ellen Anderson
Literary Manager: Alda Cortese
Communications Director: Mary Bashaw
Artistic Director: Abigail Adams
Marketing Director: Wendy E Worthington
Communications Assistant: Sara Montgomery
Mission: To help unify a culturally diverse society by giving the community barrier-free access to drama that celebrates our joys, terrors and dreams as we struggle to live together in difficult times.
Utilizes: Actors; AEA Actors; Artists-in-Residence; Choreographers; Collaborating Artists; Collaborations; Commissioned Composers; Commissioned Music; Designers; Grant Writers; Guest Accompanists; Guest Artists; Guest Companies; Guest Conductors; Guest Designers; Guild Activities; Instructors; Local Artists; Lyricists; Multi Collaborations; Multimedia; Music; Original Music Scores; Performance Artists; Poets; Resident Artists; Resident Professionals; Selected Students; Soloists
Founded: 1974
Specialized Field: Light Theater; Multi-Cultural
Status: Professional; Nonprofit
Income Sources: Actors' Equity Association; League of Resident Theatres
Season: Year-round
Performs At: The People's Light Theater
Organization Type: Performing; Resident; Educational

3378

HEDGEROW THEATRE

64 Rose Valley Road
Media, PA 19063
Phone: 610-565-4211
Fax: 610-565-1672
e-mail: hedgerowtheatre@comcast.net
Web Site: www.hedgerowtheatre.org
Officers:
President: Shiela Kutner
Management:
Producing Artistic Director: Penelope Reed
Managing Director: Dean Michelson
Operations Manager: Zoran Kovcic
Mission: Seeks to connect and enrich the lives of actors and audiences through the shared intimate experiences of excellence. We have a wide variety of year-round ofering between our Premier Series,

Horizon Series, and Children's Theatre, as well as classes for both children and adults through our Theatre School.
Utilizes: Guest Companies; Singers
Founded: 1923
Specialized Field: Drama; Musical; Classic
Status: Non-Profit, Professional
Paid Staff: 30
Volunteer Staff: 5
Paid Artists: 70
Performs At: Theatre
Facility Category: Theatre
Type of Stage: Proscenium
Stage Dimensions: 19'x27'
Seating Capacity: 144
Year Built: 1840
Year Remodeled: 1985
Organization Type: Performing; Touring; Resident; Educational

3379

MEDIA THEATRE FOR THE PERFORMING ARTS

104 E State Street
Media, PA 19063
Phone: 610-891-0100
e-mail: info@mediatheatre.org
Web Site: www.mediatheatre.com
Officers:
President: Jack Holefelder
Chair Person: Robert McMahon
Management:
Public Relations: Roger Ricker
Executive Director: Patrick Ward
Artistic Director: Jesse Cline
Mission: Promote and nurture the imagination, diversity and joy unique to music theatre by the production of new and classic works.
Utilizes: Actors; AEA Actors; Artists-in-Residence; Choreographers; Five Seasonal Concerts; Grant Writers; Guest Artists; Guest Conductors; Guest Designers; Guest Lecturers; Guild Activities; High School Drama; Music; Sign Language Translators; Soloists; Student Interns
Founded: 2002
Specialized Field: Musical
Status: Non-Profit, Professional
Paid Staff: 10
Paid Artists: 30
Budget: $2,000,000
Income Sources: Grants; Membership; Ticket Sales
Performs At: Proscenium
Affiliations: AEA
Annual Attendance: 80,000
Facility Category: Theatre
Type of Stage: Proscenium
Seating Capacity: 632
Year Built: 1927
Year Remodeled: 1993
Cost: $1,500,000
Rental Contact: Artistic Director Jesse Cline

3380

ROBERT MORRIS UNIVERSITY COLONIAL THEATRE

6001 University Blvd
Moon Township, PA 15108
Phone: 412-262-8445
Fax: 412-262-8606
Toll-free: 800-762-0097
e-mail: locke@rmu.edu
Web Site: www.rmu.edu/theatre
Management:

Theatre Program Communications: Robert J Locke
Events Manager/Operations: Rebecca M Diana
Events Manager/Facilities: Webley J Yeardie
Mission: Professional quality, student-focused, theatrical productions for the university and surrounding community.
Utilizes: Guest Companies; Singers
Founded: 1967
Specialized Field: Community Theater
Status: Non-Professional; Nonprofit
Paid Staff: 1
Income Sources: Fundraising
Performs At: Massey Theatre
Annual Attendance: 1,200
Organization Type: Performing; Educational

3381

VAGABOND ACTING TROUPE

PO Box 355
Morgantown, PA 19103
Phone: 610-286-5567
Fax: 610-286-5567
e-mail: vagabondactingtroupe@gmail.com
Web Site: www.vagabondactingtroupe.org
Officers:
President: Ty Furman
Secretary: April Sandor
Treasurer: Gavin McCulloch
Management:
Executive Director: Aileen McCullogh
Bookkeeper: Gavin McCullogh
Resident Music Director: Jeff Beideman
Mission: Family and adult theatre utilizing an intense physical style.
Utilizes: Students; Special Technical Talent; Theatre Companies
Founded: 1993
Specialized Field: Children's Theater; Educational; Experimental; New Plays
Status: Non-Profit, Educational
Paid Staff: 2
Paid Artists: 100
Budget: $50,000
Income Sources: Ticket Sales; Educational Tuition; Advertising; Individual Donors; Foundation; Government and Corporate Sponsorships
Affiliations: Theatre Alliance of Greater Philadelphia
Annual Attendance: 5,000
Type of Stage: Black Box
Stage Dimensions: Changeable
Seating Capacity: 200; 399
Year Built: 1970
Rental Contact: Aileen McCulloch

3382

GRETNA PRODUCTIONS

Gretna Theatre
PO Box 578
Mount Gretna, PA 17064
Phone: 717-964-3322
Fax: 717-964-2189
e-mail: willstutts@gretnatheatre.com
Web Site: www.gretnatheatre.com
Management:
Artistic Director: Will Stutts
Associate Artistic Director: Renee T Krizan
Managing Director: Larry Frenock
Musical Director: Nathan Perry
Mission: Nonprofit professional theatre dedicated to producing and presenting work that appeals to a diverse audience and community.
Utilizes: Guest Companies; Singers
Founded: 1927

Specialized Field: Musical; Classic
Status: Non-Profit, Professional
Paid Staff: 3
Paid Artists: 100
Income Sources: League of Resident Theatres; Actors' Equity Association; Theatre Association of Pennsylvania; Metro Arts of Harrisburg
Performs At: Mt. Gretna Playhouse
Organization Type: Performing; Touring

3383
TIMBERS DINNER THEATRE
Timber Road
PO Box 10
Mount Gretna, PA 17064
Phone: 717-964-3601
Management:
    President: John Briody
    Artistic Director: Andy Robert
    Production Manager: Katheleen Briody
Mission: Family entertainment, affordable price.
Founded: 1975
Specialized Field: Dinner Theater; Musical
Status: For-Profit, Professional
Paid Staff: 25
Paid Artists: 10
Season: June - September
Performs At: Timbers Summer Dinner Theatre
Facility Category: Outdoor/Under Roof
(semi-enclosed)
Type of Stage: Proscenium
Seating Capacity: 450
Year Built: 1950
Year Remodeled: 1976
Organization Type: Performing

3384
POCONO PLAYHOUSE
Playhouse Lane
Mountainhome, PA 18342
Phone: 570-595-7456
Fax: 570-595-7465
Management:
    Owner/Producer: Hubert Fryman
    General Manager: Donna McMicken
Utilizes: Guest Companies
Founded: 1947
Specialized Field: Musical; Ensembles
Status: Professional; Commercial
Season: June - October
Performs At: Pocono Playhouse
Organization Type: Performing; Educational

3385
BUCKS COUNTY PLAYHOUSE
70 S Main
PO Box 313
New Hope, PA 18938
Phone: 215-862-2046
Fax: 215-862-0220
e-mail: mail@buckscountyplayhouse.com
Web Site: www.buckscountyplayhouse.com
Officers:
    President: Ralph Miller
Management:
    Artistic Director: Stephen Casey
Utilizes: Guest Companies
Founded: 1939
Specialized Field: Musical
Status: Professional; Commercial
Performs At: Bucks County Playhouse
Organization Type: Performing; Educational;
Partial-Equity Season

3386
AMERICAN FAMILY THEATER
1429 Walnut Street
4th Floor
Philadelphia, PA 19102
Phone: 215-563-3501
Fax: 215-563-1588
Toll-free: 800-822-8487
e-mail: jkneppervp@aol.com
Web Site: www.atafy.org
Management:
    President: Bob Steck
    Artistic Director: Don Kersy
    Account Executive: Amy Wozniak
Founded: 1971
Specialized Field: Youth Theater; Classic;
Contemporary
Status: Non-Profit, Professional
Paid Staff: 35

3387
AMERICAN MUSIC THEATER
FESTIVAL/PRINCE MUSIC THEATER
100 S Broad Street
Suite 650
Philadelphia, PA 19110
Phone: 215-972-1000
Fax: 215-972-1020
e-mail: info@princemusictheater.org
Web Site: www.princemusictheater.org
Officers:
    President/Producing Director: Marjorie Samoff
Founded: 1984
Specialized Field: Musical; Classic
Status: Non-Profit, Professional
Paid Staff: 35
Performs At: Prince Music Theater
Facility Category: Theater
Type of Stage: Proscenium
Seating Capacity: 450

3388
AMERICAN THEATER ARTS FOR YOUTH
1429 Walnut Street
Philadelphia, PA 19102
Phone: 800-822-8487
Fax: 215-563-3501
e-mail: atafy@aol.com
Management:
    Artistic Director: Don Kersey
Founded: 1971
Specialized Field: Touring Company; Children's
Theater
Status: Nonprofit; Non-Equity
Season: October - May

3389
ARDEN THEATRE COMPANY
40 N 2nd Street
Philadelphia, PA 19106
Phone: 215-922-8900
Fax: 215-922-7011
e-mail: info@ardentheatre.org
Web Site: www.ardentheatre.org
Management:
    Managing Director: Amy L Murphy
    Producing Artistic Director: Terrence J Nolen
    Associate Artistic Director: Amy Dugas Brown
Mission: Dedicated to bringing to life the greatest stories by the greatest storytellers of all times.
Founded: 1988
Specialized Field: Musical; Comedy; Classic;
Contemporary

Status: Non-Profit, Professional
Paid Staff: 30
Budget: $3,000,000.00
Performs At: Hass Stage/Mainstage; Arcadia
Stage/Studio Theatre
Affiliations: LORT; AEA
Annual Attendance: 90,000
Type of Stage: Flexible Stage
Seating Capacity: 400-175
Rental Contact: General Manager Jenn Peck

3390
BIG MESS THEATRE
1112 Manning Street
Philadelphia, PA 19107
Phone: 215-829-8333
e-mail: bigmessthr@aol.com
Management:
    Artistic Director: Greg Giovanni
Mission: Big Mess Theatre dedicates itself to visionary forms of theatre and theatrical experience.
Founded: 1988
Specialized Field: New Plays; Experimental; Classic

3391
BUSHFIRE THEATRE OF PERFORMING ARTS
224 S 52nd Street
Philadelphia, PA 19139
Phone: 215-747-9230
Fax: 215-747-9236
e-mail: thebushfire@earthlink.net
Management:
    Artistic Director: Al Simpkins
Mission: Is to offer greater opportunity for black professional and non-professional actors, playwrights and other theatre personnel to develop their skills and careers.
Utilizes: Guest Companies; Singers
Founded: 1977
Specialized Field: Musical
Status: Professional; Nonprofit
Income Sources: Actors' Equity Association
Performs At: Bushfire Theatre of Performing Arts;
Writers Works
Organization Type: Performing; Educational

3392
FREEDOM REPERTORY THEATRE
1346 N Broad Street
Philadelphia, PA 19121
Phone: 215-765-2793
Fax: 215-765-4191
Web Site: www.freedomtheatre.org
Officers:
    Chair: Keith Hargreaves
Management:
    Executive Director: Sandra Haughton
Founded: 1966
Specialized Field: Drama; Musical; Educational
Performs At: John E Allen Theatre, Freedom Cabaret
Theatre
Type of Stage: Proscenium; Flexible
Seating Capacity: 299-120

3393
GERMANTOWN THEATRE GUILD
4821 Germantown Avenue
Philadelphia, PA 19144
Phone: 215-991-0419
Fax: 215-991-0419
e-mail: gtc@germantowntheatre.org
Web Site: www.germantowntheatre.org
Management:

Artistic Director: Mark Hallen
Managing Director: Darla Max
Technical Director: GA Carafelli
Mission: Germantown Theatre Center is a place for arts education in the northwest neighborhood of Philedelphia, providing classes, residencies and performances which excite and inspire a diverse economic, ethnic and racial population and enhance cultural and community revitalization.
Utilizes: Guest Companies
Founded: 1933
Specialized Field: Community Theater; Theater Workshops
Status: Professional; Nonprofit
Income Sources: Theatre Alliance of Pennsylvania; Greater Philadelphia Cultural Alliance; Citizens for the Performing Arts in Pennsylvania; Performing Arts League of Philadelphia
Organization Type: Performing; Touring; Educational; Sponsoring

3394
INDIAN RIVER THEATRE OF THE PERFORMING ARTS
32925 US Route 11
Philadelphia, PA 13673
Phone: 315-642-5521
Fax: 315-642-5658
e-mail: pdixon@mail.ircsd.org
Web Site: www.ircsd.org
Management:
Theatre Secretary: Pamela Dixon
Assistant Principal: John Davis
Technical Director: Phillip Dyke
Theater Manager: Kristi Fuller
Mission: Community Theatre arts education theatre.
Utilizes: Actors; AEA Actors; Arrangers; Artists-in-Residence; Choreographers; Collaborating Artists; Collaborations; Commissioned Composers; Commissioned Music; Community Members; Community Talent; Composers; Composers-in-Residence; Contract Actors; Contract Orchestras; Curators; Dance Companies; Dancers; Designers; Educators; Equity Actors; Fellows of Institute; Filmmakers; Fine Artists; Five Seasonal Concerts; Grant Writers; Guest Accompanists; Guest Artists; Guest Choreographers; Guest Companies; Guest Composers; Guest Conductors; Guest Designers; Guest Directors; Guest Ensembles; Guest Instructors; Guest Lecturers; Guest Musical Directors; Guest Musicians; Guest Soloists; Guest Speakers; Guest Teachers; Guest Writers; Guild Activities; High School Drama; Instructors; Local Artists; Local Artists & Directors; Local Talent; Local Unknown Artists; Lyricists; Multi Collaborations; Multimedia; Music; Musical Directors; New Productions; Organization Contracts; Original Music Scores; Paid Performers; Performance Artists; Playwrights; Poets; Resident Artists; Resident Companies; Resident Professionals; Scenic Designers; Selected Students; Sign Language Translators; Singers; Soloists; Students; Student Interns; Special Technical Talent; Theatre Companies; Touring Companies; Visual Arts; Visual Designers; Volunteer Artists; Volunteer Directors & Actors;
Founded: 1995
Specialized Field: Musical; Classic; Contemporary
Status: Non-Profit, Non-Professional
Paid Staff: 3
Facility Category: Community School Theatre
Type of Stage: Proscenium
Stage Dimensions: 60'x24'
Seating Capacity: 1400
Year Built: 1995
Rental Contact: Theatre Secretary Pamela Dixon

3395
INTERACT THEATRE COMPANY
2030 Sansom Street
Philadelphia, PA 19103
Phone: 215-568-8077
Fax: 215-568-8095
e-mail: interact@interacttheatre.org
Web Site: www.interacttheatre.org
Management:
Producing Artistic Director: Seth Rozin
General Manager: Melissa Amster
Education Director: Tom Reing
Mission: Believes in developing and producing important new plays that represent our time and place, and introducing new writers to local audiences.
Founded: 1988
Specialized Field: New Plays; New Works of Social Importance
Paid Staff: 8
Paid Artists: 75
Performs At: Adrienne
Type of Stage: Proscenium
Seating Capacity: 106

3396
MUM PUPPETTHEATRE
115 Arch Street
Philadelphia, PA 19106-2000
Phone: 215-952-8686
Fax: 215-922-5184
e-mail: info@mumpuppet.org
Management:
Chairperson: John Reddish
Operations Manager: Patrick Thrasher
Artistic Director: Robert Smythe
General Manager: Heather Rogers
Founded: 1985
Specialized Field: Puppet; Educational; Theater Workshops
Status: Nonprofit
Rental Contact: Heather Rogers

3397
PHILADELPHIA THEATRE COMPANY
230 S 15th Street
4th Floor
Philadelphia, PA 19102
Phone: 215-985-1400
Fax: 215-985-5800
e-mail: info@phillytheatreco.com
Web Site: www.phillytheatreco.com
Officers:
President: Sheldon Thompson
VP: E Gerald Riesenbach Esq
VP: Carol Saline
VP: Anita I Steen
VP: Harriet Weiss
Treasurer: Robert A Brown
Secretary: Julia Ericksen PhD
Management:
Producing Artistic Director: Sara Garonzik
General Manager: Ada Coppock
Mission: Dedicated to producing the Philadelphia and world premieres of major works by contemporary American playwrights.
Utilizes: Actors; AEA Actors; Artists-in-Residence; Collaborations; Designers; Five Seasonal Concerts; Guest Accompanists; Guest Conductors; Guest Designers; Guest Ensembles; Guest Instructors; Guest Soloists; Guest Teachers; Guild Activities; Instructors; Local Artists; Original Music Scores; Performance Artists; Poets; Resident Professionals; Selected Students; Soloists; Visual Arts

Founded: 1975
Specialized Field: Musical; Comedy; Classic; Contemporary
Status: Non-Profit, Professional
Paid Staff: 14
Volunteer Staff: 200
Budget: $1.7 million
Income Sources: Foundations; Corporations; Individuals
Performs At: Plays and Players Theater
Affiliations: AEA; LORT; TCG; PCVB; TAGP; GPCA; Philadelphia Chamber of Commerce
Annual Attendance: 40,000
Facility Category: Historic
Type of Stage: Proscenium
Stage Dimensions: 25'x25'
Seating Capacity: 324
Year Built: 1919
Organization Type: Performing; Resident

3398
PRINCE MUSIC THEATER
1412 Chestnut Street
100 S Broad Street
Philadelphia, PA 19110
Phone: 215-972-1000
Fax: 215-972-1020
e-mail: info@princemusictheater.org
Web Site: www.princemusictheater.org
Management:
Producing Artistic Director: Marjorie Samoff
Development: Amy Singer
Marketing Director: Jennifer Donnelly
Production: Jim Griffith
Mission: Dedicated to developing music theatre in its various forms.
Utilizes: Actors; AEA Actors; Choreographers; Collaborating Artists; Collaborations; Commissioned Composers; Dancers; Designers; Fine Artists; Five Seasonal Concerts; Grant Writers; Guest Accompanists; Guest Artists; Guest Companies; Guest Composers; Guest Conductors; Guest Designers; Guest Ensembles; Guest Lecturers; Guest Musical Directors; Guest Musicians; Guest Soloists; Guest Teachers; Guild Activities; Instructors; Local Artists; Local Unknown Artists; Multi Collaborations; Multimedia; Music; Organization Contracts; Original Music Scores; Performance Artists; Poets; Resident Professionals; Sign Language Translators; Singers; Soloists; Student Interns; Visual Arts
Founded: 1984
Specialized Field: Musical
Status: Nonprofit
Annual Attendance: 100,000
Seating Capacity: 450
Year Built: 1999
Rental Contact: Managing Director Joe Farina
Organization Type: Sponsoring

3399
SOCIETY HILL PLAYHOUSE
507 S Eighth Street
Philadelphia, PA 19147
Phone: 215-923-0210
Fax: 215-923-1789
e-mail: shp@erols.com
Web Site: www.societyhillplayhouse.org
Management:
Director: Deen Kogan
Mission: To present works of the finest contemporary American and European writers.
Founded: 1959
Specialized Field: New American Works; Classic; International

Status: Professional; Nonprofit
Performs At: Society Hill Playhouse
Affiliations: Theatre Communications Group; American Arts Alliance; Theatre Alliance
Annual Attendance: 100,000
Facility Category: Historic Building
Type of Stage: Proscenium; Cabaret
Seating Capacity: 250; 99
Year Built: 1900
Year Remodeled: 1979
Rental Contact: Lee Vaughn
Organization Type: Performing; Touring; Educational

3400
WALNUT STREET THEATRE

825 Walnut Street
Philadelphia, PA 19107
Phone: 215-574-3550
Fax: 215-574-3598
Web Site: www.wstonline.org
Officers:
President: Louis Fryman
Management:
Producing Artistic Director: Bernard Harvard
Managing Director: Mark Sylvester
Director Development: Rebekah A Sassi
Director Marketing and Public Relat: Cristian E David
Mission: The mission of the Walnut Street Theatre Company is to sustain the tradition of professional theatre and contribute to its future viability and vitality. It does so through: the production and presentation of professional theatre; the encouragement, training and development of artists; the development of diverse audiences; the preservation and chronicling of its theatre building, a National Historic Landmark.
Utilizes: Actors; AEA Actors; Choreographers; Collaborations; Commissioned Composers; Dancers; Designers; Educators; Filmmakers; Five Seasonal Concerts; Grant Writers; Guest Accompanists; Guest Artists; Guest Choreographers; Guest Companies; Guest Composers; Guest Conductors; Guest Designers; Guest Ensembles; Guest Lecturers; Guild Activities; High School Drama; Instructors; Local Artists; Local Unknown Artists; Multimedia; Music; Organization Contracts; Original Music Scores; Performance Artists; Poets; Resident Professionals; Sign Language Translators; Soloists; Student Interns; Special Technical Talent; Theatre Companies
Founded: 1809
Specialized Field: Drama; Comedy; Musical; Classic; Contemporary
Status: Nonprofit
Paid Staff: 100
Budget: $10 million
Income Sources: Tickets; Grants; Funders
Affiliations: Greater Philadelphia Cultural Alliance; National Alliance of Musical Theaters; Theatre Community Group; League of Historic American Theatres
Annual Attendance: 300,000
Facility Category: Mainstage; Studio
Type of Stage: Proscenium; Black Box
Seating Capacity: 1,075; 80
Year Built: 1809
Year Remodeled: 1969
Rental Contact: D Jadico

3401
WILMA THEATER

265 S Broad Street
Philadelphia, PA 19107
Phone: 215-893-9456
Fax: 215-546-7824
e-mail: info@wilmatheater.org
Management:
Artistic Director: Blanka Zizka
Artistic Director: Jiri Zizka
Managing Director: Jonathan Kline
Production Manager: Patrick Heydenburg
Technical Director: Douglas Marshall
Director Development: Brian Moore
Director Marketing: Liz Walsh
Mission: To produce innovative theatre of the highest artistic quality from international and contemporary American repertoires.
Utilizes: Actors; Choreographers; Collaborations; Commissioned Composers; Composers-in-Residence; Dance Companies; Dancers; Designers; Educators; Filmmakers; Fine Artists; Five Seasonal Concerts; Grant Writers; Guest Accompanists; Guest Artists; Guest Choreographers; Guest Companies; Guest Composers; Guest Conductors; Guest Designers; Guest Directors; Guest Ensembles; Guest Instructors; Guest Lecturers; Guest Musical Directors; Guest Musicians; Guest Soloists; Guest Speakers; Guest Teachers; Guest Writers; Guild Activities; High School Drama; Instructors; Local Artists; Local Artists & Directors; Local Unknown Artists; Lyricists; Multi Collaborations; Multimedia; Music; New Productions; Organization Contracts; Original Music Scores; Paid Performers; Performance Artists; Playwrights; Poets; Resident Artists; Resident Companies; Resident Professionals; Selected Students; Sign Language Translators; Singers; Soloists; Student Interns; Special Technical Talent; Theatre Companies; Touring Companies; Visual Arts
Founded: 1973
Specialized Field: Drama; Comedy; Theater Workshops
Status: Professional; Nonprofit
Paid Staff: 21
Budget: $1.5 Million
Income Sources: Theatre Communications Group
Facility Category: 1 Stage Studio
Type of Stage: Proscenium
Stage Dimensions: 44'x46'
Seating Capacity: 296
Year Built: 1996
Architect: Hugh Hardy
Rental Contact: Neal Racioppo
Organization Type: Performing

3402
CITY THEATRE COMPANY

1300 Bingham Street
Pittsburgh, PA 15203
Phone: 412-431-4400
Fax: 412-431-5535
e-mail: caquiline@citytheatrecompany.org
Web Site: www.citytheatrecompany.org
Management:
President: Ed Saler
Artistic Director: Tracy Brigben
Managing Director: David Jobin
Mission: To provide an artistic home for the development and production of contemporary plays of substance and ideas that engage and challenge diverse audiences.
Utilizes: Guest Companies; Singers
Founded: 1974
Specialized Field: Drama; Comedy; Contemporary
Status: Non-Profit, Professional
Paid Staff: 50
Volunteer Staff: 5
Paid Artists: 15

Income Sources: Theatre Communications Group
Performs At: City Theatre
Type of Stage: Flexible; Black Box
Seating Capacity: 272; 99
Organization Type: Performing; Resident; Educational

3403
DANCE ALLOY THEATER

5530 Penn Avenue
Pittsburgh, PA 15206
Phone: 412-363-4321
Fax: 412-363-4320
e-mail: info@dancealloy.org
Web Site: www.dancealloy.org
Officers:
President: Thomas K Whitford
VP: J Nicole Wilson
Management:
Artistic Director: Beth Corning
Managing Director: Susan Sparks
Mission: We are a performing professsional company, a studio open for dance and movement classes as well as a provider of dance education in the Pittsburgh Public Schools.
Utilizes: Choreographers; Commissioned Music; Curators; Dance Companies; Dancers; Educators; Five Seasonal Concerts; Grant Writers; Guest Artists; Guest Companies; Guest Conductors; High School Drama; Original Music Scores; Poets; Soloists
Founded: 1976
Specialized Field: Modern
Status: Professional, Nonprofit
Paid Staff: 6
Paid Artists: 5
Budget: $700,000
Income Sources: Foundations; Corporations; Government
Performs At: Kelly Strayhorn Theatre
Annual Attendance: 4,500
Organization Type: Performing; Touring; Educational

3404
PITTSBURGH INTERNATIONAL CHILDREN'S THEATER

182 Allegheny Center Mall
Pittsburgh, PA 15212
Phone: 412-321-5520
Fax: 412-321-5212
e-mail: boxoffice@pghkids.org
Web Site: www.pghkids.org
Officers:
Board Chair/President: Karen Flam
Management:
Executive Director: Pam Leberman
Founding Artistic Director: Maranne Purcell Welch
Mission: Presents a professional theater series and International Children's Festival.
Founded: 1969
Specialized Field: International; Children's Theater; Musical
Status: Non-Profit, Professional
Paid Staff: 3
Paid Artists: 40
Budget: $615,000
Income Sources: Ticket Sales; Contributions; Concession; Special Events; Program Ads
Performs At: Byham Theatre; Area Schools
Affiliations: IPAY (International Performing Arts for Youth)
Annual Attendance: 56,000

3405

PITTSBURGH IRISH & CLASSICAL THEATRE

PO Box 23607
Pittsburgh, PA 15222
Phone: 412-561-6000
Fax: 412-561-6686
e-mail: apaul@picttheatre.org
Web Site: www.picttheatre.org
Officers:
    President: Ray Werner
    VP: Andrew S Paul
    VP: Stephanie Riso
    CPA/Treasurer: Michael Regan
    Secretary: Sr. Michele O'Leary
Management:
    Artistic Director: Andrew S Paul
    General Manager: Stephanie Riso
Mission: To challenge, educate and entertain Pittsburgh audiences by providing quality, professional, text-driven theatre at a reasonable price, while respectfully utilizing and compensating local talent, and by encouraging collaborative efforts with other successful theatres and individuals, particularly focusing on theatre of an Irish, English and Classical nature.
Founded: 1996
Specialized Field: Classic
Status: Professional

3406

PITTSBURGH PUBLIC THEATER

621 Penn Avenue
Pittsburgh, PA 15222
Phone: 412-316-8200
Fax: 412-316-8216
e-mail: info@ppt.org
Web Site: www.ppt.org
Officers:
    President: Tony Bucci
    Secretary: Edward L Linder
    Treasurer: Richard L Crouch
    Counsel: Thomas M. Thompson
Management:
    President: David Madder
    Executive Director: Ted Pappas
Mission: To provide artistically diverse experiences of the highest quality, thereby holding a preeminent position among American theaters. We strive to serve, challenge, stimulate, and entertain an expanding audience while operating in a fiscally responsible manner.
Utilizes: Actors; AEA Actors; Choreographers; Collaborations; Commissioned Composers; Commissioned Music; Designers; Educators; Guest Artists; Guest Companies; Guest Composers; Guest Conductors; Guest Designers; Guest Ensembles; Guest Lecturers; Guest Soloists; Guild Activities; High School Drama; Instructors; Local Artists; Music; Organization Contracts; Original Music Scores; Performance Artists; Selected Students; Sign Language Translators; Singers; Soloists; Student Interns
Founded: 1974
Specialized Field: Musical; Comedy; Classic; Contemporary
Status: Non-Profit, Professional
Paid Staff: 44
Volunteer Staff: 400
Paid Artists: 30
Budget: $6.3 Million
Income Sources: Actors' Equity Association; League of Resident Theatres
Performs At: O'Reilly Theater

Affiliations: AEA, SSDC, USA, IATSE
Annual Attendance: 110,000
Type of Stage: Thrust
Seating Capacity: 650
Year Built: 1999
Cost: 25 Million
Rental Contact: Jason Hassell
Organization Type: Performing; Educational

3407

POINT PARK UNIVERSITY'S PITTSBURGH PLAYHOUSE

222 Craft Avenue
Pittsburgh, PA 15213
Phone: 412-392-8000
Fax: 412-621-4762
Web Site: www.pittsburghplayhouse.com
Management:
    Artistic Director: Ronald A Lindblom
    Producing Director: Earl Hughes
Mission: The performing arts cetner of the Point Park University and the Conservatory of Performing Arts. The three-theater performing arts center is home to The REP, the professional theatre company and three student companies-Conservatory Theatre Company, Conservatory Dance Company and Playhouse Jr. Maintains a rigorous performance calendar with eighteen major productions and 235 performances entertaining more than 30,000 patrons annually.
Specialized Field: Educational; Theater Workshops

3408

PRIME STAGE

PO Box 1849
Pittsburgh, PA 15230
Phone: 412-771-7373
Fax: 412-771-8585
e-mail: producerinfo@primestage.com
Web Site: www.primestage.com
Officers:
    Chairman: Thomas Wettach Esquire
    VP: Jerry Weinand Esquire
Management:
    Artistic Director: Wayne Brindag
    Assistant Producer: Lynn DeBree
Mission: We are commited to exposing and engaging young people and families in the discovery of live theatre. We accomplish this by producing new plays and other works, which celebrate the achievements of young people and adults.
Founded: 1996
Specialized Field: Youth Theater; Young Playwrights
Status: Non-Profit, Professional
Affiliations: American Alliance for Theatre and Education.
Annual Attendance: 9,000

3409

VERONICA'S VEIL PLAYERS

44 Puis Street
Pittsburgh, PA 15203-1897
Phone: 412-431-5550
Fax: 412-431-3463
e-mail: vvplayers@aol.com
Web Site: www.trfn.clpgh.org/vvp
Management:
    Managing Director: Dennis M Thompston
Mission: We are dedicated to continuing the tradition of presenting the Lenten drama Veronica's Veil as well as presenting other quality theatrical productions at affordable prices.
Utilizes: Actors; Choreographers; Collaborations; Dancers; Guest Designers; Local Artists; Multimedia; Music

Founded: 1910
Specialized Field: Classic; Historical
Status: Nonprofit
Volunteer Staff: 5
Non-paid Artists: 200
Performs At: Theater
Seating Capacity: 833
Year Built: 1900
Year Remodeled: 1925

3410

READING COMMUNITY PLAYERS

403 N 11th Street
Reading, PA 19603
Mailing Address: PO Box 1032 Reading, PA 19603-1032
Phone: 610-375-9106
e-mail: rcptheatre@gmail.com
Web Site: www.rcptheatre.org
Officers:
    President: Ruth Martelli
    VP: Tracy Bukowski
Management:
    Production Manager: Lisa Uliasz
    Publicity: Julia Parsons
Mission: To develop the community's interest in theatrical arts; provide true live community theatre; and provide artistic opportunities for local talent.
Founded: 1920
Specialized Field: Musical; Community Theater
Status: Non-Profit, Non-Professional
Paid Staff: 114
Affiliations: American Association of Community Theatre; Berks Arts Council
Organization Type: Performing; Educational

3411

NORTHEASTERN THEATRE

Box 765
Scranton, PA 18501-0765
Phone: 570-969-1770
Management:
    Producer: Alicia Grega-Pikul
Founded: 1992
Specialized Field: Drama; Comedy; Theater Workshops

3412

SHAWNEE PLAYHOUSE

PO Box 159
Shawnee Inn Golf Resort
Shawnee-on-Delaware, PA 18356
Phone: 570-421-5093
Fax: 570-421-4914
Toll-free: 800-742-9633
e-mail: request@theshawneeplayhouse.com
Web Site: www.theshawneeplayhouse.com
Management:
    Executive Director: Midge McClosky
    Sales Manager: Mary Horn
    Marketing: Becky Haskell
Mission: To provide professional quality live theatre to the residents and visitors of Shawnee.
Founded: 1978
Specialized Field: Staged Readings; Musical; Children's Theater
Status: Non-Equity; Commercial
Season: June - December
Performs At: Historic Theatre
Type of Stage: Proscenium
Seating Capacity: 200

3413
STRUTHERS LIBRARY THEATRE
302 3rd Avenue W
PO Box 6
Warren, PA 16365
Phone: 814-723-7231
Fax: 814-723-3856
e-mail: librarytheatre@westpa.net
Web Site: www.struthersibrarytheatre.com
Management:
Executive Director: Maurice J Cashman
Founded: 1883
Specialized Field: Community Theater; Classic
Status: Non-Profit, Professional
Paid Staff: 3
Season: June - August
Type of Stage: Proscenium
Stage Dimensions: 35' x 26'
Seating Capacity: 989

3414
SALTWORKS THEATRE COMPANY
2553 Brandt School Road
Wexford, PA 15090-7931
Phone: 724-934-2820
Fax: 724-934-2815
e-mail: stc@lm.com
Web Site: www.saltworks.org
Management:
Director of Marketing: Barbara Baun
Mission: To perform plays for youth and families that address social issues.
Utilizes: Actors; Choreographers; Educators; Guest Artists; Guest Lecturers; High School Drama; Local Artists; Music; Original Music Scores; Soloists; Student Interns
Founded: 1981
Specialized Field: Educational; Youth Theater; New Works of Social Importance
Status: Non-Profit, Professional
Paid Staff: 12
Paid Artists: 7
Budget: $450,000
Affiliations: ARAD; Tix for Teachers
Annual Attendance: 7,000
Seating Capacity: 150-250
Year Built: 1986
Organization Type: Performing; Touring; Educational

3415
MARY L WELCH THEATRE
700 College Place
Lycoming College, Theatre Department
Williamsport, PA 17701
Phone: 570-321-4024
Fax: 570-321-4090
e-mail: allen@lycoming.edu
Web Site: www.lycoming.edu
Management:
President: James Douthat
Artistic Director: Jerry D Allen
Production Director: Robert Graham
Founded: 1964
Specialized Field: Drama; Musical; Comedy
Status: Non-Profit, Non-Professional
Paid Staff: 3
Paid Artists: 2
Non-paid Artists: 5
Budget: $45,000
Income Sources: Ticket Sales
Season: June - July
Affiliations: Actor Equity Association; TCG
Type of Stage: Thrust

Seating Capacity: 204
Year Built: 1964

3416
MOVEMENT THEATRE INTERNATIONAL
50 Bernard Drive
Yardley, PA 19067
Phone: 215-337-9100
Fax: 215-337-9100
e-mail: MAPedretti@aol.com
Mission: Provide space for area troupes and general services to mime field.
Founded: 1979
Specialized Field: Movement Theater
Paid Staff: 1
Volunteer Staff: 3
Budget: $20,000-35,000
Income Sources: Retails, Box Office, Gifts
Type of Stage: Proscenuim
Seating Capacity: 299
Year Built: 1890
Year Remodeled: 1986
Cost: 1,000,000

Rhode Island

3417
ASTORS BEECHWOOD MANSION
580 Bellevue Avenue
Newport, RI 02840
Phone: 401-846-3772
Fax: 401-849-6998
e-mail: casting@astors-beechwood.com
Management:
Executive Director: Charlotte C Lee
Marketing: Karen Leepman
Mission: Victorian Living History
Founded: 1881
Specialized Field: Multi-Media; Drama; Historical
Paid Staff: 10
Paid Artists: 18
Season: year round
Year Built: 1851

3418
SANDRA FEINSTEIN-GAMM THEATRE
172 Exchange Street
Pawtucket, RI 02860
Phone: 401-723-4266
e-mail: info@gammtheatre.org
Web Site: www.gammtheatre.org
Officers:
President: Coline Covington
Vice President: Samuel Babbitt
Treasurer: Pia Potter
Secretary: William P. Wingate
Mission: To create intimate, professional, actor-centered theater which delights and inspires through the communal experience of the telling of great stories.
Utilizes: Guest Companies
Founded: 1984
Specialized Field: Storytelling
Status: Professional; Semi-Professional; Nonprofit
Paid Staff: 5
Volunteer Staff: 10
Paid Artists: 15
Organization Type: Performing

3419
BROWN SUMMER THEATRE
77 Waterman Street
Box 1897
Providence, RI 02912
Phone: 401-863-3284
Fax: 401-862-7529
e-mail: christopher_oneil@brown.edu
Web Site: www.brown.edu
Management:
Artistic Director: Lowry Marshal
Utilizes: Actors; Soloists
Founded: 1969
Specialized Field: Contemporary; New Plays; Summer Stock
Status: Non-Profit, Non-Professional
Season: June - August
Type of Stage: Arena
Stage Dimensions: 22' x 16'
Seating Capacity: 200

3420
BROWN UNIVERSITY THEATRE
77 Waterman Street
Box 1897
Providence, RI 02912
Phone: 401-863-2838
Fax: 401-863-7529
e-mail: boxoffice@brown.edu
Web Site: www.brown.edu/tickets
Officers:
Chairman: Spencer Golub
Management:
President: Ruth Simmon
Box Office Manager: Brian Gaston
Production Manager: Brian Gaston
Mission: To offer a balanced theatrical season during the academic year and in the summer for the university community and Providence area; to train students.
Utilizes: Guest Companies
Founded: 1901
Specialized Field: Educational; Theater Workshops
Status: Non-Profit, Non-Professional
Paid Staff: 20
Performs At: Stuart Theatre; Leeds Theatre
Organization Type: Performing; Resident; Educational; Sponsoring

3421
LOOKING GLASS THEATRE
312 Wickenden Street
Providence, RI 02093
Phone: 401-331-9080
Fax: 401-351-2051
Toll-free: 866-742-9080
e-mail: lgtinc@msn.com
Web Site: www.lookingglasstouringtheatre.org
Management:
Executive Director: Fred Sailer
Artistic Director: Diane Postoian
Managing Director: Pat McDougal
Mission: To enlighten and educate children and their families through audience participation, theater and follow-up workshops; to present new productions annually focusing on the classics and topical issues.
Founded: 1965
Specialized Field: Touring Company; Children's Theater
Status: Non-Profit, Professional
Paid Staff: 7
Paid Artists: 10
Income Sources: Theatre Communications Group
Performs At: Looking Glass Theatre

Facility Category: Touring Theatre
Organization Type: Touring; Educational; Sponsoring

3422
RITES AND REASON
Brown University
PO Box 1148
Providence, RI 02912
Phone: 401-863-3558
Fax: 401-863-3559
Management:
    Executive Director: Anthony Bogues
    Artistic Director: Elmo Terry-Morgan
    Managing Director: Karen A Baxter
    Research Director: Rhett S Jones
Mission: Developmental research theatre committed to offering new plays celebrating and exploring Africana culture and history.
Utilizes: Actors; AEA Actors; Artists-in-Residence; Choreographers; Collaborating Artists; Commissioned Composers; Commissioned Music; Curators; Designers; Educators; Filmmakers; Five Seasonal Concerts; Guest Artists; Guest Companies; Guest Conductors; Guest Designers; Guest Ensembles; Guest Instructors; Guest Lecturers; Guest Musical Directors; Guest Soloists; Guest Teachers; High School Drama; Instructors; Local Artists; Local Unknown Artists; Multimedia; Music; Original Music Scores; Performance Artists; Playwrights; Poets; Resident Professionals; Sign Language Translators; Soloists; Student Interns; Visual Arts
Founded: 1970
Specialized Field: African American; Historical
Status: Non-Profit, Non-Professional
Paid Staff: 5
Income Sources: University/Resident Theatre
Affiliations: Black Theatre Network; National Alliance for Music Theatre
Annual Attendance: 2,000
Type of Stage: Black Box
Seating Capacity: 125
Organization Type: Performing; Touring; Resident; Educational

3423
TRINITY REPERTORY COMPANY
201 Washington Street
Providence, RI 02903-3226
Phone: 401-521-1100
Fax: 401-751-5577
e-mail: info@trinityrep.com
Web Site: www.trinityrep.com
Officers:
    Chairman: Jack McConnell
Management:
    Artistic Director: Curt Columbus
    Managing Director: Michael Gennaro
Mission: Providing theatrical performances as well as educational services for Rhode Island and surrounding New England audiences.
Utilizes: Actors; AEA Actors; Artists-in-Residence; Choreographers; Collaborating Artists; Collaborations; Dance Companies; Dancers; Designers; Educators; Fine Artists; Grant Writers; Guest Accompanists; Guest Artists; Guest Choreographers; Guest Companies; Guest Designers; Guest Directors; Guest Ensembles; Guest Instructors; Guest Lecturers; Guest Musical Directors; Guest Soloists; Guest Teachers; High School Drama; Instructors; Local Artists; Multimedia; Music; New Productions; Original Music Scores; Performance Artists; Resident Artists; Resident Professionals; Selected Students; Sign Language Translators; Soloists; Student Interns; Special Technical Talent; Theatre Companies; Visual Arts

Founded: 1964
Specialized Field: Drama; Theater Workshops
Status: Non-Profit, Professional
Paid Staff: 130
Budget: 7.2 million
Income Sources: League of Resident Theatres
Performs At: Trinity Repertory Company
Affiliations: AEA, LORT, TEG, SSD&C
Annual Attendance: 145,000
Facility Category: Theater
Type of Stage: Two
Stage Dimensions: Flexible
Seating Capacity: 300;600
Year Built: 1917
Year Remodeled: 1973
Rental Contact: Bob Whitney
Organization Type: Performing; Touring; Educational

South Carolina

3424
AIKEN COMMUNITY PLAYHOUSE
126 Newberry Street
Aiken, SC 29801
Phone: 803-648-1438
e-mail: info@aikencommunityplayhouse.com
Web Site: www.aikencommunityplayhouse.com/
Management:
    Publicity: Elizabeth Mouser
Mission: To offer community members an opportunity to participate in legitimate theatre; to encourage the public's appreciation of theatre arts.
Founded: 1953
Specialized Field: Community Theater
Status: Nonprofit
Income Sources: South Carolina Theatre Association
Performs At: Aiken Community Playhouse
Organization Type: Performing

3425
SPOLETO FESTIVAL USA
14 George Street
Charleston, SC 29401-1524
Phone: 843-722-2764
Fax: 843-723-6383
e-mail: info@spoletousa.org
Web Site: www.spoletousa.org
Officers:
    Chairman: Martha Rivers Ingram
    President: Carlos E. Evans
Management:
    Artistic Director-Choral Activities: Joseph Flummerfelt
    Director, Chamber Music: Geoff Nuttall
    General Director: Nigel Redden
    Producer: Nunally Kersh
    Director Of Development: Julia Forster
    Director Marketing/Public Relations: Paula Edwards
Mission: To present opera, dance, theater, symphonic, choral and chamber music, jazz and visual arts exhibits of the higest quality; to serve as an educational environment for young artists and audiences alike.
Utilizes: Singers
Founded: 1977
Specialized Field: Jazz; Theatrical Dance
Status: Professional; Semi-Professional; Non-Profit
Paid Staff: 18
Budget: $7,000,000
Income Sources: Ticket Revenues; Contributions
Performs At: Gaillard Municipal Auditorium; Dock Street Theater
Annual Attendance: 70,000-80,000

Organization Type: Performing; Educational; Sponsoring

3426
COLUMBIA STAGE SOCIETY AT TOWN THEATRE
1012 Sumter Street
Columbia, SC 29201
Phone: 803-799-2510
Fax: 803-799-6463
e-mail: town@towntheatre.com
Web Site: www.towntheatre.com
Mission: To encourage and develop musical, vocal, and dramatic talent of those in the city and surrounding areas and to provide theatrical entertainment.
Utilizes: Guest Artists
Founded: 1919
Specialized Field: Community Theater
Status: Non-Professional; Nonprofit
Income Sources: South Carolina Theatre Association
Performs At: The Town Theatre
Annual Attendance: 20,000
Year Built: 1924
Year Remodeled: 1993
Cost: $1,200,000
Organization Type: Performing; Educational

3427
TRUSTUS
PO Box 11721
Columbia, SC 29211
Phone: 803-254-9732
Fax: 803-771-9153
e-mail: trustus@trustus.org
Web Site: www.trustus.org
Management:
    Artistic Director: Jim Thigpen
    Producing Director: Kay Thigpen
    Box Office Manager: Joe Morales
    Technical Director: Brian Riley
    Production Manager: Chad Henderson
Mission: To bring to the area a professional theatre dedicated to new works, plays of literary and artistic merit, and quality mainstream theatre in an environment that allows us to reach a broad spectrum of patrons.
Utilizes: Guest Companies; Singers
Founded: 1985
Specialized Field: Drama; Comedy
Status: Professional; Nonprofit
Paid Staff: 5
Income Sources: Theatre Communications Group; South Carolina Theatre Association
Organization Type: Performing; Resident; Educational

3428
SWAMP FOX PLAYERS
710 Front Street
PO Box 911
Georgetown, SC 29442
Phone: 843-527-2924
Fax: 843-546-6193
e-mail: swampfoxplayers@verizon.net
Officers:
    President: Robbie O'Donnell
Management:
    Theatre Manager: Foy Ford
Mission: To offer a cultural center to the area; to provide dramatic presentations for area citizens.
Founded: 1971
Specialized Field: Musical; Comedy; Classic; Contemporary
Status: Non-Profit, Non-Professional
Paid Staff: 1
Performs At: Strand Theatre

Year Built: 1937
Organization Type: Performing; Resident

3429
BOB JONES UNIVERSITY CONCERT, OPERA & DRAMA SERIES
1700 Wade Hampton Boulevard
Greenville, SC 29614
Phone: 864-242-5100
Fax: 864-770-1375
e-mail: finearts@bju.edu
Web Site: www.bju.edu
Officers:
President: Dr Stephen Jones
Management:
Dean Fine Arts/Communication: Dr Darren Lawson
Founded: 1927
Specialized Field: Educational; Drama; Theater Workshops
Status: For-Profit, Professional
Budget: $35,000-60,000
Performs At: Founder's Memorial Auditorium
Seating Capacity: 7,000

3430
CENTRE STAGE-SOUTH CAROLINA
Morgan Stanley Smith Barney Building
501 River Street
Greenville, SC 29601
Phone: 864-233-6733
Fax: 864-233-3901
Toll-free: 877-377-1339
e-mail: information@centrestage.org
Web Site: www.centrestage.org
Officers:
Board President: Tim Balden
Board Vice President: Norman Glickman
Management:
Executive & Artistic Director: Glenda ManWaring
Mission: To be a cornerstone of the performing arts by providing captivating entertainment, intellectual stimulation, and adding to the quality of life in Upstate South Carolina.
Founded: 1983
Specialized Field: Drama; Musical
Paid Staff: 5
Volunteer Staff: 200
Type of Stage: Thrust
Seating Capacity: 285

3431
WAREHOUSE THEATRE
37 Augusta Street
Greenville, SC 29601
Phone: 864-235-6948
e-mail: tix@warehousetheatre.com
Web Site: www.warehousetheatre.com
Officers:
Office Manager: Erin Stewart
Mission: To excite the imagination; to examine the signposts/symbols of our time; to test the old, explore the new; to allow our audience to test-drive parts of the human experience.
Founded: 1974
Specialized Field: Drama; Musical; Classic
Status: Nonprofit
Paid Staff: 4
Volunteer Staff: 50
Paid Artists: 20
Non-paid Artists: 50
Budget: $260,000
Season: September - June
Type of Stage: Flexible; Proscenium

Seating Capacity: 170; 349

3432
NEWBERRY COLLEGE THEATRE
Newberry College
2100 College Street
Newberry, SC 29108
Phone: 803-276-5010
Fax: 803-321-5627
Toll-free: 800-845-4955
e-mail: info@newberry.edu
Web Site: www.newberry.edu
Officers:
Director Theatre/Dept. Chair: Patrick Gagliano
Management:
Technical Fuller: Matthew Fuller
Mission: To provide a performing arts program of quality in the environment of a liberal arts college.
Utilizes: Collaborations; Fine Artists; Grant Writers; Guest Artists; Guest Companies; Guest Musical Directors; High School Drama; Instructors; Sign Language Translators; Singers; Soloists
Founded: 1856
Specialized Field: Theater Workshops; Drama; Musical
Status: College
Paid Staff: 3
Type of Stage: Proscenium; Thrust; Flexible
Seating Capacity: 100-200
Organization Type: Performing; Educational

South Dakota

3433
ABERDEEN COMMUNITY THEATRE
417 S Main
PO Box 813
Aberdeen, SD 57402-0813
Phone: 605-225-2228
Fax: 605-226-5494
e-mail: act@nvc.com
Web Site: www.pclan-sd.com/act
Management:
President: Ann Rassussman
Executive Director: Jim Walker
Mission: To educate, entertain and further performing arts through community involvement.
Utilizes: Guest Companies
Founded: 1979
Specialized Field: Musical; Comedy; Community Theater
Status: Non-Profit, Non-Professional
Paid Staff: 3
Volunteer Staff: 300
Paid Artists: 2
Income Sources: American Association of Community Theatres; South Dakota Theatre Association
Performs At: Capitol Theatre
Seating Capacity: 450
Organization Type: Performing; Educational; Sponsoring

3434
BLACK HILLS PLAYHOUSE
HC 83 Box 68
Custer, SD 57730
Phone: 605-255-4141
Fax: 605-255-4242
e-mail: bhphq@aol.com
Web Site: www.blackhillsplayhouse.com
Officers:
President: Dr. John Barlow
VP: Steven McCarthy

Secretary: Pat Stofft
Treasurer: Jo Anna Warder
Founder: Doc Lee
Management:
President: Micheal Fellner
Executive Director: Jan Swank
Mission: To offer high quality performances to audiences; to provide theatre students with intensive professional training.
Utilizes: Guest Companies; Selected Students; Singers
Founded: 1946
Specialized Field: Musical; Comedy; Theater Workshops; Summer Stock
Status: Non-Profit, Non-Professional
Paid Staff: 2
Paid Artists: 70
Budget: $400,000
Income Sources: Box Office; Grants; Donations
Season: May - August
Performs At: Black Hills Playhouse (Custer State Park)
Affiliations: University of South Dakota
Annual Attendance: 16,000
Facility Category: Theatre
Type of Stage: Modified Thrust
Seating Capacity: 360
Year Built: 1955
Organization Type: Performing; Resident; Educational

3435
BLACK HILLS COMMUNITY THEATRE
713 7th Street
Rapid City, SD 57701
Phone: 605-394-1786
Management:
Manager: Merritt Olsen
Mission: To offer quality theatre employing community talent.
Founded: 1968
Specialized Field: Community Theater
Status: Nonprofit
Paid Staff: 150
Income Sources: South Dakota Arts Council; Allied Arts Fund
Organization Type: Performing

3436
SIOUX FALLS COMMUNITY PLAYHOUSE
315 N Phillips Avenue
PO Box 600
Sioux Falls, SD 57101
Phone: 605-336-7418
Fax: 605-336-0926
e-mail: sfcp@sfcp.org
Web Site: www.sfcp.org
Management:
Executive Director: Larae Blanker
Technical Director: Dion Denevan
Artistic Assoc/Education Director: Lee Shackelford
Mission: To offer the community and the area opportunities for experiencing live theatre through participation on a variety of levels.
Founded: 1930
Specialized Field: Community Theater
Status: Nonprofit
Paid Staff: 8
Non-paid Artists: 200
Budget: $250,000
Income Sources: American Association of Community Theatres; South Dakota Arts Council
Performs At: Sioux Falls Community Playhouse
Annual Attendance: 10,000
Seating Capacity: 262
Year Remodeled: 1999

Cost: $1,200,000
Organization Type: Performing; Touring; Resident;
Educational; Sponsoring

3437
BLACK HILLS PASSION PLAY
PO Box 489
Spearfish, SD 57783
Phone: 605-642-2646
Fax: 605-642-7993
Toll-free: 800-457-0160
e-mail: bhpp@blackhills.com
Web Site: www.blackhills.com/bhpp
Management:
 President: Johanna Meier
Founded: 1932
Specialized Field: Drama; Historical; Classic
Status: For-Profit, Professional
Paid Staff: 76
Volunteer Staff: 150
Paid Artists: 24
Season: June - August
Type of Stage: Amphitheatre
Seating Capacity: 5600

3438
MATTHEWS OPERA HOUSE SOCIETY
614 Main Street
Spearfish, SD 57783
Phone: 605-642-7973
Fax: 605-642-3477
e-mail: scah@rushmore.com
Web Site: www.matthewsoperahousetheater.com
Management:
 Administrative Director: Ardis Golay
 Managing Artistic Director: R David Whitlock
Mission: To offer opportunities for talented people
interested in theatre; to continue restoration of the
Opera House.
Utilizes: Actors; Educators; Fine Artists; Instructors;
Local Artists; Music; Soloists; Touring Companies
Founded: 1906
Specialized Field: Musical; Light Theater
Status: Non-Professional; Nonprofit
Paid Staff: 2
Volunteer Staff: 12
Budget: $300,000
Income Sources: Show Fees; Festival Fees; Grants
Performs At: Senior High Theatre; Matthews Opera
House
Annual Attendance: 12,000 - 15,000
Seating Capacity: 230
Year Built: 1906
Year Remodeled: 1997
Rental Contact: Ardis Golay
Organization Type: Performing; Educational

3439
SPEARFISH CENTER FOR THE ARTS
Matthews Opera House
614 Main Street
Spearfish, SD 57783
Phone: 605-642-7973
Fax: 605-642-3477
e-mail: dmyers@matthewsoperahouse.org
Web Site: www.spearfishcenter.org
Management:
 Executive Director: Sue Gannaway
 Performing Arts Manager: Dwight Myers
Mission: To provide quality programming while
preserving the Matthews Opera House.
Utilizes: Actors; Educators; Fine Artists; Instructors;
Local Artists; Music; Soloists; Touring Companies
Founded: 1906

Specialized Field: Contemporary
Status: Non-Profit, Non-Professional
Paid Staff: 3
Volunteer Staff: 20
Paid Artists: 15
Budget: $300,000
Income Sources: Show Fees; Festival Fees; Grants;
Memberships Fees
Performs At: Senior High Theatre; Matthews Opera
House
Annual Attendance: 12,000 - 15,000
Seating Capacity: 230
Year Built: 1906
Year Remodeled: 1997
Rental Contact: Ardis Golay
Organization Type: Performing; Educational

3440
TOWN PLAYERS
5 S Broadway
Watertown, SD 57201
Phone: 605-882-2076
Fax: 605-882-2076
Management:
 President: Tom Harvey
 Manager: Nancy Johnson
Mission: To promote appreciation of dramatic arts.
Utilizes: Guest Artists; Guest Companies; Singers
Founded: 1940
Specialized Field: Community Theater; Drama
Status: Non-Profit, Non-Professional
Paid Staff: 45
Paid Artists: 1
Organization Type: Performing; Touting; Resident

3441
LEWIS & CLARK THEATRE COMPANY
328 Walnut Street
PO Box 836
Yankton, SD 57078
Phone: 605-665-4711
e-mail: lctheatr@byelectric.com
Web Site: www.lewisandclarktheatre.com
Management:
 President: Barbara Christenson
 Executive Director: Joel Vermuele
 Artistic Director: Allison Spak
Founded: 1961
Specialized Field: Musical; Comedy; Classic;
Contemporary
Status: Non-Profit, Non-Professional
Paid Staff: 5
Paid Artists: 20
Season: June - August
Type of Stage: Proscenium
Stage Dimensions: 60' x 36'
Seating Capacity: 640

Tennessee

3442
THEATRE BRISTOL
512 State Street
Bristol, TN 37620
Phone: 423-968-4977
Fax: 423-968-4978
e-mail: info@theatrebristol.org
Web Site: www.theatrebristol.org
Officers:
 President: Dorothy Havlik
 VP: Anne Koehner
 Treasurer: Holly Whitley
 Secretary: Ann Christ

Management:
 Artistic Director: Robert Dean
 General Manager: Emily Anne Thompson
 Technical Director: Jim Quensenberry
 Director Education: Amy Bussey
Mission: Theatre Bristol is a regional theatre that uses
the arts to inspire educate and entertain.
Utilizes: Actors; Artists-in-Residence; Choreographers;
Collaborations; Dancers; Designers; Educators; Guest
Accompanists; Guest Artists; Guest Companies; Guest
Conductors; Guest Designers; Guest Lecturers; Guest
Musical Directors; Guest Writers; Guild Activities; High
School Drama; Instructors; Local Artists; Lyricists;
Multimedia; Music; Performance Artists; Resident
Professionals; Sign Language Translators; Soloists;
Student Interns; Touring Companies; Visual Arts
Founded: 1965
Specialized Field: Musical; Community Theater
Status: Non-Profit, Non-Professional
Paid Staff: 3
Volunteer Staff: 20
Performs At: Paramount Center for the Arts; Theatre
Bristol Artspace
Seating Capacity: 756; 95
Organization Type: Performing; Resident; Educational;
Sponsoring

3443
ROXY THEATER
100 Franklin Street
Clarksville, TN 37040
Phone: 931-645-7699
 Artistic Director: John McDonald
Mission: To promote and produce the performing and
visual arts.
Utilizes: Guest Companies
Founded: 1983
Specialized Field: Musical; Community Theater
Status: Professional; Nonprofit
Paid Staff: 2
Organization Type: Performing; Educational

3444
CUMBERLAND COUNTY PLAYHOUSE
221 Tennessee Avenue
PO Box 484
Crossville, TN 38557
Phone: 931-484-5000
Fax: 931-484-6299
Toll-free: 877-868-8710
e-mail: info@ccplayhouse.com
Web Site: www.ccplayhouse.com
Management:
 President of the Board: Tom Weesley
 Executive Director: Jim Crabtree
 Business Manager: Janet Kluender
Mission: To provide cultural enrichment for the area
and beyond.
Utilizes: Actors; Choreographers; Collaborating Artists;
Collaborations; Dancers; Designers; Educators; Fine
Artists; Five Seasonal Concerts; Guest Accompanists;
Guest Artists; Guest Composers; Guest Conductors;
Guest Designers; Guest Ensembles; Guest Lecturers;
Guest Musical Directors; Guest Musicians; Guild
Activities; Instructors; Local Artists; Local Unknown
Artists; Multimedia; Music; Organization Contracts;
Original Music Scores; Performance Artists; Poets;
Resident Artists; Resident Professionals; Sign
Language Translators; Singers; Soloists; Student
Interns
Founded: 1965
Specialized Field: Musical; Comedy; Contemporary
Status: Non-Profit, Professional
Paid Staff: 20

Paid Artists: 35
Budget: $2.1 million
Income Sources: 80% Earned Income; Grants; Donations
Season: Year-round
Performs At: Cumberland County Playhouse
Annual Attendance: 145,000
Type of Stage: 2 indoor; 1 outdoor
Year Built: 1965
Year Remodeled: 1992
Rental Contact: Producing Director Jim Crabtree
Organization Type: Performing; Touring; Resident; Educational; Sponsoring

3445
PULL-TIGHT PLAYERS

PO Box 105
Franklin, TN 37065-0105
Phone: 615-790-6782
e-mail: thespian@pull-tight.com
Web Site: www.pull-tight.com
Officers:
President: Marianne Clark
VP: Jeanne Drone
Secretary: Heather Bottoms
Tresurer: Iain MacPhearson
Founder: Vance Ormes
Management:
President: Beth Woodruff
VP: Pat Evans
House Manager: Laurie Sackett
Mission: To provide quality community theatre for Williamson County and the surrounding area.
Utilizes: Guest Companies
Founded: 1968
Specialized Field: Community Theater
Status: Non-Professional; Nonprofit
Paid Staff: 60
Organization Type: Performing; Resident

3446
SWEET FANNY ADAMS THEATRE & MUSIC HALL

461 Parkway
Gatlinburg, TN 37738
Phone: 865-436-4039
Fax: 865-436-4038
Toll-free: 877-388-5784
e-mail: jennifer@sweetfannyadams.com
Web Site: www.sweetfannyadams.com
Management:
Manager: Jennifer MacPherson-Evans
Director: Chris MacPherson
Utilizes: Actors; Commissioned Composers; Guest Companies; Original Music Scores; Visual Arts
Founded: 1977
Specialized Field: Musical; Drama
Status: Professional
Paid Staff: 6
Paid Artists: 8
Season: May - October
Annual Attendance: 20,000
Facility Category: Theatre
Type of Stage: Thrust
Stage Dimensions: 12'x13'
Seating Capacity: 184
Year Built: 1877
Year Remodeled: 1996
Rental Contact: Don MacPherson

3447
GERMANTOWN COMMUNITY THEATRE

3037 Forest Hill-Irene Road
Germantown, TN 38138
Phone: 901-754-2680
Fax: 901-755-1185
e-mail: officemgr@germantowncommunitytheatre.org
Web Site: www.germantowncommunitytheatre.org
Officers:
Guild President: Evonne Siemer
Management:
Executive Director/Producer: Brent Davis
Education Director: Rachel King-Barr
Production Coordinator: Kerry Stahm
Founded: 1972
Specialized Field: Community Theater
Status: Non-Profit, Non-Professional
Paid Staff: 5
Volunteer Staff: 20
Income Sources: Memphis Arts Council; Germantown Arts Alliance
Seating Capacity: 112

3448
POPLAR PIKE PLAYHOUSE

7653 Old Poplar Pike
Germantown, TN 38138
Phone: 901-755-7775
Fax: 901-755-6951
e-mail: poppikeplayhouse@aol.com
Web Site: www.ppp.org
Officers:
Director: E. Frank Bluestein
Mission: To present educational theatre at Germantown High School.
Utilizes: Arrangers; Guest Accompanists; Guest Conductors; Guest Designers; Guest Ensembles; Guest Soloists; Guild Activities; High School Drama; Instructors; Local Artists; Music; Performance Artists; Poets
Founded: 1976
Specialized Field: Theater
Status: Nonprofit
Paid Staff: 10
Volunteer Staff: 5
Paid Artists: 3
Budget: $50,000
Income Sources: Shelby County Schools; Germaston Arts Alliance
Annual Attendance: 5,000
Facility Category: Theatre
Type of Stage: Proscenium
Stage Dimensions: 55'x40'
Seating Capacity: 285
Year Built: 1975
Year Remodeled: 1998
Rental Contact: Director E Frank Bluestein
Organization Type: Performing; Educational

3449
JACKSON THEATRE GUILD

314 E Main Street
PO Box 7041
Jackson, TN 38301
Phone: 731-427-3200
Fax: 731-425-8674
e-mail: info@jtgonline.com
Web Site: www.jtgonline.com
Officers:
President: Bill Worboys
VP: Brenda Poteet
Secretary: Ann Bailey
Treasurer: Sue Barnes
Mission: To promote public education appreciation and enjoyment of dramatic literature, current stage craft, and theatre by the presentation of quality productions. Also, by conducting other related activities, we reflect our diverse community.

Utilizes: Guest Companies; Singers
Founded: 1966
Specialized Field: Comedy; Youth Theater; Community Theater; Contemporary
Status: Non-Profit, Non-Professional
Paid Staff: 1
Income Sources: Tickets; Grants
Annual Attendance: 6,900
Seating Capacity: 400
Organization Type: Performing; Resident; Educational

3450
ACTORS CO-OP

P.O. Box 10192
Knoxville, TN 37939
Phone: 865-909-9300
Fax: 423-523-0900
e-mail: actorscoopinc@bellsouth.net
Management:
Artistic Director: Amy Hubbard
Board President: John Winemiller
Specialized Field: Drama; Comedy; Theater Workshops

3451
ARTS & CULTURE ALLIANCE OF GREATER KNOXVILLE

PO Box 2506
Knoxville, TN 37901
Phone: 615-523-7543
Fax: 615-523-7312
e-mail: alliance@esper.com
Web Site: www.koxarts.com
Officers:
President: Patrick Roddy
Treasurer: Kathy Hamilton
VP: Jefferson Hcapma
VP: Lila Plfleger
Management:
Executive Director: Liza Zenni
Mission: To unite, strenghen, and promote arts and culture activities in East Tennessee.
Founded: 1976
Specialized Field: Musical; Community Theater
Status: Nonprofit
Organization Type: Educational

3452
CARPETBAG THEATRE

100 S Gay Street
#106
Knoxville, TN 37902
Phone: 865-544-0447
Fax: 423-524-6631
Management:
Executive/Artistic Director: Linda Parris-Bailey
Managing/Technical Director: Jeff Cody
Mission: To give artistic voice to the underserved. We address the issues and dreams of people who have historically been silenced by racism, classism, sexism and ageism; tell stories of empowerment; celebrate our culture; and reveal hidden stories.
Utilizes: Guest Companies; Singers
Founded: 1970
Specialized Field: Ensembles; Multi-Cultural; Ethnic Theater
Status: Professional; Nonprofit
Income Sources: National Endowment for the Arts; Tennessee Arts Commision; East Tennessee Community Foundation
Organization Type: Touring

3453
CLARENCE BROWN THEATRE COMPANY
206 McClung Tower
Knoxville, TN 37996
Phone: 865-974-6011
Fax: 865-974-4867
e-mail: cbt@utk.edu
Web Site: www.clarencebrowntheatre.org
Officers:
    Chairperson: Andrew White
Management:
    Department Head: Cal MacLean
    Managing Director: Thomas A Cervone
Utilizes: Actors; AEA Actors; Artists-in-Residence; Collaborations; Educators; Guest Accompanists; Guest Companies; Guest Conductors; Guest Designers; Guild Activities; Local Artists
Founded: 1974
Specialized Field: Musical; Comedy; Ethnic Theater; Classic; Contemporary
Status: Non-Profit, Professional
Budget: $1.5 million
Income Sources: League of Resident Theatres; Theatre Communications Group; Knoxville Arts Council; University of Tennessee
Performs At: Clarence Brown Theatre, Carousel Theatre
Affiliations: Actors' Equity Association; League of Resident Theatres; SSOC
Annual Attendance: 34,000
Facility Category: Theatre
Type of Stage: Proscenium; Arena
Stage Dimensions: 60'x32'
Seating Capacity: 600; 250
Year Built: 1970
Rental Contact: Product Manager Laura Sims
Organization Type: Performing; Touring; Resident

3454
TENNESSEE STAGE COMPANY
PO Box 1186
Knoxville, TN 37901
Phone: 865-546-4280
Fax: 865-546-9677
e-mail: tennesseestage@bellsouth.net
Web Site: www.tennesseestage.com
Mission: To serve the Knoxville and East Tennessee area by producing exciting, high quality, productions of primarily American plays, both classical and current, while providing professional opportunities for regional artists.
Founded: 1989
Specialized Field: Shakespeare; Classic
Status: Non-Profit, Professional
Paid Staff: 1
Paid Artists: 30
Income Sources: Arts Council of Greater Knoxville; Community Televison of Knoxville; Comcast
Season: August
Stage Dimensions: 24' x 24'
Seating Capacity: 1,300

3455
THEATER KNOXVILLE
Bijou Theater
803 S Gay Street
PO Box 1746
Knoxville, TN 37901
Phone: 865-523-4211
Fax: 865-524-0821
Mission: To provide quality productions employing community members as actors and technicians.

Utilizes: Singers
Founded: 1976
Specialized Field: Community Theater
Status: Non-Professional; Nonprofit
Performs At: The Bijou Theater
Organization Type: Performing; Touring; Educational

3456
TENNESSEE PLAYERS
304 W Due West Avenue
Madison, TN 37115
Phone: 615-868-3738
Fax: 615-868-3738
e-mail: tennesseeplayers@webtv.net
Web Site: www.tennesseeplayers.org
Management:
    Executive Director: Thurston Moore
Mission: To create something beautiful for somebody else.
Founded: 1986
Specialized Field: Multi-Media; Classic
Status: Non-Profit, Professional
Paid Staff: 1
Volunteer Staff: 3
Annual Attendance: 15,000
Organization Type: Performing; Touring; Educational

3457
CIRCUIT PLAYHOUSE
1705 Poplar Avenue
Memphis, TN 38104
Phone: 901-726-5523
Fax: 901-272-7530
e-mail: circuit@playhouseonthesquare.org
Web Site: www.playhouseonthesquare.org
Officers:
    President: PJ Smoot
    VP: Leigh McLean
Management:
    Managing Director: Whitney Jo
    Executive Producer: Jackie Nichols
    Administrative Director: Jackie Nichols
    Managing Director: Whitney Jo
Founded: 1969
Specialized Field: New Plays; Musical; Drama; Comedy; Community Theater
Income Sources: Southeastern Theatre Conference; Theatre Communications Group; Tennessee Theatre Association; Playhouse on the Square
Performs At: Circuit Playhouse; Playhouse on the Square

3458
EWING CHILDREN'S THEATRE
2635 Avery Avenue
Memphis, TN 38112
Phone: 901-452-3968
Fax: 901-452-3805
Officers:
    President: June Scudder
    Secretary/Treasurer: Pat Barnes
Management:
    Theatre Director: Kay Lighffoot
Mission: Memphis Children's Theatre uses children, ages 5-17, and involves them in all aspects of theatre.
Utilizes: Actors; Choreographers; Collaborations; Dancers; Guest Accompanists; Guest Choreographers; Guest Companies; Guest Conductors; Guest Designers; Guest Ensembles; Guild Activities; Local Artists; Multimedia; Music; Organization Contracts; Performance Artists; Resident Professionals; Sign Language Translators; Singers; Soloists; Student Interns; Theatre Companies
Founded: 1949

Specialized Field: Community Theater
Status: Nonprofit
Paid Staff: 6
Income Sources: Memphis Park Services; American Children's Theatre Association; Tennessee Theatre Association; Southeastern Theatre Conference
Annual Attendance: 10,000
Facility Category: Theatre
Seating Capacity: 200
Year Remodeled: 1979
Organization Type: Performing; Educational

3459
PLAYHOUSE ON THE SQUARE
51 S Cooper Street
Memphis, TN 38104
Phone: 901-726-4656
Fax: 901-272-7530
e-mail: info@playhouseonthesquare.org
Web Site: www.playhouseonthesquare.org
Management:
    Founder And Executive Producer: Jackie Nichols
    Development Director: Donna Sue Shannon
    Associate Director: Davis Landis
    Managing Director: Whitney Jo
Mission: Producing live theatrical productions including new plays, Broadway and off-Broadway shows.
Utilizes: Guest Companies; Singers
Founded: 1969
Specialized Field: Drama; Broadway Musical Revivals
Status: Professional; Nonprofit
Paid Staff: 10
Income Sources: Theatre Communications Group; Circuit Playhouse
Season: Year round
Performs At: Playhouse on the Square
Organization Type: Performing; Touring; Resident; Educational

3460
MORRISTOWN THEATRE GUILD
314 S Hill Street
PO Box 1502
Morristown, TN 37816
Phone: 423-586-9260
Web Site: http://www.theatreguildinc.org/
Officers:
    Chairman: Wendy McGowen
    Vice-Chairman: Victor Thompson
    Secretary: Susan Stansberry
    Treasurer: Gregg Harrell
Management:
    Artistic Director: David Horton
Mission: To provide exposure to live theatre; to offer school-age children educational training.
Founded: 1934
Specialized Field: Musical; Dinner Theater; Community Theater
Status: Non-Professional; Nonprofit
Paid Staff: 50
Income Sources: Tennessee Theatre Association
Performs At: Theatre Guild
Organization Type: Performing; Educational

3461
CHAFFIN'S BARN DINNER THEATRE
8204 Highway 100
Nashville, TN 37221
Phone: 615-646-9977
Fax: 615-662-5439
Toll-free: 800-282-2276
Web Site: www.dinnertheatre.com
Officers:
    Co-Owner: John Chaffin

Co-Owner: Janie Chaffin
Management:
Artistic Director: Martha Wilkinson
Sales: Vanessa Wynn
Mission: To produce top quality mysteries, comedies, and musicals.
Founded: 1967
Specialized Field: Musical; Dinner Theater
Status: Non-Profit, Professional
Facility Category: Dinner Theatre
Type of Stage: In the Round
Stage Dimensions: 16'x16'
Seating Capacity: 300
Year Built: 1967
Rental Contact: Regina Brock

3462
DARKHORSE THEATER

4610 Charlotte Avenue
Nashville, TN 37209
Phone: 615-297-7113
Fax: 615-665-3336
e-mail: info@darkhorsetheater.com
Web Site: www.darkhorsetheater.com
Management:
Managing Director: Shannon Wood
Mission: To provide home to the Nashville creative performance community. Darkhouse theater presents aneclectic mix of original, classic, alternative, collorative, controversial and relevant theater and dance.
Founded: 1990
Specialized Field: Musical; Classic; Alternative; Contemporary

3463
DAVID LIPSCOMB UNIVERSITY THEATER

3901 Granny White Pike
Nashville, TN 37204-3951
Phone: 615-279-5715
Fax: 615-279-6516
e-mail: larry.brown@lipscomb.edu
Web Site: www.theatre.lipscomb.edu
Management:
President: Steven Flatt
Theater Director: Larry Brown
Founded: 1891
Specialized Field: Educational
Status: Non-Profit, Non-Professional
Paid Staff: 1
Type of Stage: Black Box
Seating Capacity: 140

3464
MOCKINGBIRD PUBLIC THEATRE

PO Box 24002
Nashville, TN 37202
Phone: 615-242-6704
Fax: 615-242-7201
e-mail: mockingbirdpublictheatre@comcast.net
Officers:
Chairman: Chris Chamberlin
Treasurer: Rueben Buck
Secratery: Pamela Crosby
Management:
Artistic Director: David Alford
Associate Artistic Director: Rene Copeland
General Manager: Kara V Kindall
Mission: To produce theatre that is relevant to the life of our community, maintain artistic integrity and pursue a standard of excellence; to promote, develop and support the culture and artists of our region.
Utilizes: Actors; AEA Actors; Collaborating Artists; Collaborations

Founded: 1994
Specialized Field: Community Theater
Status: Professional; Nonprofit
Paid Artists: 40
Budget: $250,000-$300,000
Income Sources: Foundation; Private; Government
Performs At: Tennesee Performing Arts Center
Annual Attendance: 9,000-10,000

3465
NASHVILLE CHILDREN'S THEATRE

724 2nd Avenue S
Nashville, TN 37210
Phone: 615-254-9103
Fax: 615-254-3255
e-mail: adillon@nct-dragonsite.org
Web Site: www.nashvillechildrenstheatre.org
Officers:
Chair: Paul Meyers
Vice Chair: Chris Chamberlain
Secretary: Sue Mendes
Treasurer: Joel Goldberg
Management:
Producing Director: Scot Copeland
Producing Director: Jean Johnson
Managing Director: Allison Dillon
Marketing/PR Director: Sharon Armstrong
Education Director: Martha Goodman
Office/House Manager: Lorna Turner
Mission: An ensemble of professional artists who bring unique vision and compelling voice to the creation of meaningful theatre for young audiences at NCT. We strive to make live theatre a vital part of the childhood experience for all young people in Nashville and Middle Tennessee.
Utilizes: Guest Companies; Singers
Founded: 1931
Specialized Field: Children's Theater
Status: Non-Profit, Professional
Paid Staff: 12
Paid Artists: 60
Income Sources: Box Office; Government Grants & Individual; Corporate & Foundation Support
Performs At: Hill Theatre, Cooney Playhouse
Affiliations: ASSITEJ/USA; AEA:TYA
Type of Stage: Main Stage; Black Box
Seating Capacity: 690; 300
Year Built: 1960
Organization Type: Performing; Resident; Educational

3466
NASHVILLE SHAKESPEARE FESTIVAL

161 Raine Avenue
Nashville, TN 37203
Phone: 615-255-2273
Fax: 615-248-2273
e-mail: thebard@nashvilleshakes.org
Web Site: www.nashvilleshakes.org
Officers:
Chairman: James Cartiglia
Management:
Artistic Director: Denice Hickes
Managing Director: Robert Marigza
Mission: To educate and entertain the mid-south community through professional Shakespearean experiences.
Founded: 1988
Specialized Field: Shakespeare; Outdoor Theater
Status: Professional
Paid Staff: 4
Volunteer Staff: 40
Paid Artists: 25
Non-paid Artists: 15
Budget: $330,000

Season: August
Performs At: Centennial Park Bandshell
Affiliations: Shakespeare Theatre Association of America
Annual Attendance: 18,000
Organization Type: Performing; Resident; Touring; Educational

3467
TENNESSEE REPERTORY THEATRE

161 Rains Avenue
Nashville, TN 37203
Phone: 615-244-4878
e-mail: david@tennesseerep.org
Web Site: www.tnrep.org
Management:
Executive Artistic Director: David Alford
Producing Director: Rene Copeland
Company Stage Manager: David Wilkerson
Mission: The presentation of quality, professional theatre and a complete season of plays.
Utilizes: Actors; AEA Actors; Choreographers; Collaborations; Grant Writers; Guest Artists; Guest Companies; Guest Conductors; Guest Designers; Guest Lecturers; Guest Writers; Guild Activities; Instructors; Local Artists; Music; Original Music Scores; Performance Artists; Resident Professionals; Selected Students; Soloists
Founded: 1985
Specialized Field: Drama; Musical; Classic
Status: Professional
Paid Staff: 18
Volunteer Staff: 20
Paid Artists: 40
Income Sources: Ticket Sales; Fund-raising
Performs At: James K. Polk Theater; Tennessee Performing Arts Center
Affiliations: League of Resident Theatres; Actors' Equity Association; SSD&C
Annual Attendance: 70,000
Facility Category: Performing Arts Center
Type of Stage: Proscenium
Seating Capacity: 1,000
Year Built: 1980
Organization Type: Performing; Resident

3468
OAK RIDGE PLAYHOUSE

27 E Tennessee Avenue at Jackson Square
PO Box 5705
Oak Ridge, TN 37831
Phone: 865-482-9999
Fax: 865-482-0945
e-mail: playhouse@orplayhouse.com
Web Site: www.orplayhouse.com
Officers:
President: Robert Wham
VP: Em Way
Secretary: John E Gunning
Treasurer: Eugene Spejewski
Management:
Managing Artistic Director: Reggie Law
Technical Director: Jim Prodger
Public Relations Director: Karen Brunner
Costume Shop Manager: Jennifer Taylor-Smith
Mission: To provide quality theatre for the community while maintaining volunteer status.
Utilizes: Actors; AEA Actors; Choreographers; Collaborations; Dance Companies; Dancers; Designers; Educators; Grant Writers; Guest Accompanists; Guest Artists; Guest Choreographers; Guest Companies; Guest Conductors; Guest Designers; Guest Ensembles; Guest Lecturers; Guild Activities; High School Drama; Instructors; Local Artists;

Lyricists; Multimedia; Music; Original Music Scores; Resident Professionals; Sign Language Translators; Soloists; Student Interns
Founded: 1943
Specialized Field: Drama
Status: Nonprofit
Paid Staff: 3
Volunteer Staff: 100
Paid Artists: 15
Non-paid Artists: 10
Budget: $250,000
Income Sources: Box Office; Grants; Private Donations; Corporate Donations & Sponsors; Subscription
Performs At: Oak Ridge Playhouse in Jackson Square
Affiliations: SE Theatre Conference; Knoxville Area Theatre Coalition; Arts Council of Oak Ridge; American Assoc of Community Theatres; Knoxville Arts Council
Annual Attendance: 25,000
Facility Category: Community Theatre; Children's Theatre
Type of Stage: Proscenium
Stage Dimensions: 40'x25'
Seating Capacity: 344
Year Built: 1943
Year Remodeled: 1988
Rental Contact: Reggie Law
Organization Type: Performing

3469
DIXIE STAMPEDE
3849 Parkway
PO Box 58
Pigeon Forge, TN 37868
Phone: 865-453-9473
Fax: 865-908-7061
Toll-free: 800-356-1676
Web Site: www.dixiestampede.com
Management:
    General Manager: John Shaver
Founded: 1988
Specialized Field: Dinner Theater
Status: Non-Equity; Commercial
Season: March - December
Type of Stage: Arena
Stage Dimensions: 75' x 150'
Seating Capacity: 1000

3470
LIFE OF CHRIST PASSION PLAY
329 Bethel Church Road
Townsend, TN 37882
Phone: 423-448-9080
Specialized Field: Outdoor Theater; Summer Stock

Texas

3471
WATERTOWER THEATRE
15650 Addison Road
Addison, TX 75001
Phone: 972-450-6230
Fax: 972-450-6244
e-mail: info@watertowertheatre.org
Web Site: www.watertowertheatre.org
Management:
    Producing Artistic Director: Terry Martin
Founded: 1977
Specialized Field: Musical; Comedy; Classic; Contemporary
Status: Non-Profit, Professional
Paid Staff: 7
Paid Artists: 50

Annual Attendance: 20,800

3472
FORT GRIFFIN FANDANGLE ASSOCIATION
1 Railroad Street
PO Box 155
Albany, TX 76430
Mailing Address: PO Box 2017
Phone: 915-762-3838
Fax: 915-762-3125
e-mail: fandangle@bitstreet.com
Web Site: http://www.fortgriffinfandangle.org/
Officers:
    President: John Matthews
    VP: Harold Law
    VP/Treasurer: Winifred Waller
    Executive Secretary: Debbie Hudman
Mission: To present historical narration with song and dance.
Utilizes: Singers
Founded: 1937
Specialized Field: Staged Readings; Historical
Status: Non-Professional; Nonprofit
Paid Staff: 250
Season: June
Performs At: Fort Griffin Fandangle Outdoor Theatre
Facility Category: Outdoor Ampitheater
Type of Stage: Grass
Seating Capacity: 1,800
Year Built: 1951
Organization Type: Performing

3473
CREATIVE ARTS THEATRE AND SCHOOL
1100 W Randol Mill Road
Arlington, TX 76012
Phone: 817-861-2287
Fax: 817-274-0793
e-mail: cats@creativearts.org
Web Site: www.creativearts.org
Management:
    Executive Director: Heather Simmons
    Producing Director: Merry Brewe
    Technical Director: Richard Blake
    Registrar: Gina Galante
    Box Office Manager: Gail Wooster
Mission: To develop the potential of young people from diverse backgrounds through performing arts training and performance opportunities. Devoted to professionally training, enriching and inspiring all youth by igniting within them an enduring passion for the arts. A theatre....by youth for youth.
Utilizes: High School Drama; Soloists
Founded: 1977
Specialized Field: Children's Theater; Theater Workshops
Status: Non-Profit
Income Sources: Tuition; Ticket Sales; Donations; Grants
Seating Capacity: 350

3474
THEATRE ARLINGTON
305 W Main Street
Arlington, TX 76010
Phone: 817-275-7661
Fax: 817-275-3370
e-mail: info@theatrearlington.org
Web Site: www.theatrearlington.org
Management:
    Executive Director: Todd Hart

Development Director: Kim Lawson
Marketing Director: Emmy Klein
Box Office Manager: Troy Stidham
Mission: Dedicated to the cultural enrichment, education and entertainment of the citizenry of Arlington and the North Texas Community.
Utilizes: Guest Companies; Singers
Founded: 1973
Specialized Field: Musical; Comedy; Classic; Contemporary
Status: Non-Profit, Professional
Paid Staff: 6
Volunteer Staff: 100
Paid Artists: 3
Income Sources: Texas Nonprofit Theatre
Performs At: Theatre Arlington
Organization Type: Performing; Resident; Educational

3475
AUSTIN MUSICAL THEATRE
2011 E Riverside Drive
Suite C
Austin, TX 78741
Phone: 512-428-9696
Fax: 512-428-9699
e-mail: jhammond@amtpresents.org
Web Site: www.amtpresents.com
Management:
    Producing Artistic Director: Scott Thompson
    Managing Artistic Director: Richard Byron
    Company Manager: Stuart Moultan
    Production Manager: Jeanine Lisa
    Executive Director: Jared Hammond
    Academy Coordinator: Ginger Morris
    Academy Assistant: Kevin Archambealt
    Marketing Director: Suzie Harriamn
Utilizes: Actors; Dancers; Designers; Five Seasonal Concerts; Grant Writers; Guest Ensembles; Guest Lecturers; Guest Musical Directors; High School Drama; Instructors; Local Artists; Multimedia; Music; Original Music Scores; Resident Professionals; Selected Students; Sign Language Translators; Soloists; Student Interns
Founded: 1996
Specialized Field: Musical; Theater Workshops
Paid Staff: 10
Paid Artists: 100
Budget: $3,500,000
Income Sources: Donations; Grants; Academy Revenue; Ticket Sales
Performs At: The Paramount Theatre
Affiliations: Actors' Equity Association; International Alliance of Theatrical Stage Employees
Annual Attendance: 50,000
Type of Stage: Proscenium
Seating Capacity: 1,200
Year Built: 1915
Year Remodeled: 1975

3476
AUSTIN THEATRE FOR YOUTH
5555 N Lamar
#C-125
Austin, TX 78751
Phone: 512-459-2289
Fax: 512-459-7451
Officers:
    President: Mimi Wolff Rosenthal
Management:
    Executive/Artistic Director: Rick Schiller
    Associate Artistic Director: Rod Caspers
    Director Community Outreach/PR: Regina Rosenthal
    Director Marketing/Development: Elena Coates

Mission: To create relevant, enriching and entertaining theatre experiences for Central Texas families and youth.
Specialized Field: Children's Theater

3477
FRONTERA
511 W 43rd Street
Austin, TX 78751
Phone: 512-302-4933
Fax: 512-302-5041
Management:
    Artistic Director: Vicky Boone
Founded: 1992
Specialized Field: Drama; Musical
Performs At: Hyde Park Theatre
Type of Stage: Flexible
Seating Capacity: 90

3478
RUDE MECHANICALS
2211-A Hidalgo Street
Suite 220
Austin, TX 78702
Phone: 512-476-7833
Fax: 512-477-3157
e-mail: info@rudemech.com
Web Site: www.rudemechs.com
Officers:
    President: Paul Drown
    VP: Ron Marks
    Treasurer: Alex Alford
    Secretary: Jonathan Tamez
Management:
    Venue Manager: Madge Darlington
    Development Director: Mike Henry
    Business Manager: Lana Lesley
    Marketing Director: Sarah Richardson
    Resident Producer: Shawn Sides
Specialized Field: Ensembles

3479
STATE THEATER COMPANY
719 Congress Avenue
Austin, TX 78701
Phone: 512-472-2901
Fax: 512-472-7199
e-mail: info@austintheatre.org
Web Site: www.statetheatercompany.com
Officers:
    CEO: Dan Fallon
Management:
    Producing Artistic Director: Scott Kanoff
    Associate Artistic Director: Michelle Polgar
    Technical Director: Mark Porter
    Production Manager: Jeanine Lisa
Founded: 1982
Specialized Field: Theater Workshops; Drama; Musical
Status: For-Profit,Professional
Paid Staff: 5
Paid Artists: 75
Income Sources: Corporations; Foundations; Individual Gifts
Season: March - August

3480
VORTEX REPERTORY COMPANY
2307 Manor Road
PO Box 33125
Austin, TX 78722
Phone: 512-478-5282
e-mail: ponty@jollylox.com
Web Site: www.jollylox.com/vortex/

Management:
    Managing Director: Steve Bacher
    Producing Artistic Director: Bonnie Cullum
Mission: To create new, innovative performances, including original works, new plays, revitalized classics, and to present nationally-recognized, cutting edge touring artists.
Utilizes: Guest Companies; Singers
Founded: 1988
Specialized Field: New Plays; Classic; Contemporary
Status: Professional; Nonprofit
Paid Staff: 200
Performs At: Vortex Performance Care
Organization Type: Performing; Touring; Resident; Educational; Sponsoring

3481
ZACHARY SCOTT THEATRE CENTER
1510 Toomey Road
Austin, TX 78704
Phone: 512-476-0594
Fax: 512-476-0314
e-mail: info@zachscott.com
Web Site: www.zachscott.com
Management:
    Artistic Director: Dave Steakley
    Managing Director: Ann Ciccolella
    Business Manager: Linda Wilson
Mission: To offer the finest contemporary and classical scripts and original works for young people; to maintain a multicultural company.
Utilizes: Singers
Founded: 1977
Specialized Field: Musical; Comedy; Classic; Contemporary
Status: Non-Profit, Professional
Paid Staff: 35
Paid Artists: 40
Income Sources: Theatre Communications Group; American Association of Theatre Educators; Theatre in Disability; Austin Circle of Theatres
Performs At: ZSTC Arena; ZSTC Kleberg
Organization Type: Performing; Touring; Educational

3482
BASTROP OPERA HOUSE
711 Spring Street
PO Box 691
Bastrop, TX 78602
Phone: 512-321-6283
e-mail: chester@bastropoperahouse.com
Web Site: www.bastropoperahouse.com
Management:
    Executive Director: Chester Eitze
Mission: To present dance, music and theatre in a performing arts center at the restored Old Bastrop Opera House.
Utilizes: Guest Companies; Singers
Founded: 1889
Specialized Field: Summer Stock; Musical; Dinner Theater
Status: Semi-Professional; Non-Professional; Nonprofit
Performs At: Old Bastrop Opera House
Organization Type: Performing; Sponsoring

3483
CAMILLE PLAYERS
1 Dean Porter Park
Brownsville, TX 78520
Phone: 956-542-8900
Fax: 956-986-0639
e-mail: PatCranick@aol.com
Web Site: www.freewebs.com/camilleplayhouse/
Officers:

President: John P Kinch
VP: Ben Salinas
Second VP: Fidencio Zavala
Treasurer: Dan Anderson
Management:
    Executive Director: Ben Agresti
Mission: To stimulate interest in drama through presenting plays.
Utilizes: Actors; Choreographers; Dancers; Multimedia; Music; Resident Professionals; Sign Language Translators; Soloists
Founded: 1964
Specialized Field: Musical; Classic; Contemporary
Status: Non-Profit, Non-Professional
Paid Staff: 2
Volunteer Staff: 3
Budget: $9,000
Performs At: Camille Lightner Playhouse
Annual Attendance: 5,000
Facility Category: Theatre
Type of Stage: Proscenium
Stage Dimensions: 30'x25'
Seating Capacity: 301
Year Built: 1964
Year Remodeled: 1995
Organization Type: Performing

3484
TEXAS PANHANDLE HERITAGE FOUNDATION
Palo Duro Canyon State Park
Pioneer Ampitheatre 1514 5th Avenue
Canyon, TX 79015
Phone: 806-655-2181
Fax: 806-655-4730
e-mail: info@tphf.com
Web Site: www.texas-show.com
Officers:
    Chairman of the Board: Jayne Brainard
    Vice Chairman: Martha Chow
    Secretary: Gene Morrison
Management:
    Artistic Director: David Yinak
    Executive Director: Vince Hernandez
    Office Manager: Staci Wyatt
Mission: To preserve and present Texas history and culture through education and entertainment.
Utilizes: Actors; Choreographers; Dancers; Multimedia; Original Music Scores; Sign Language Translators; Singers
Founded: 1961
Specialized Field: Musical; Historical
Status: Non-Profit, Non-Professional
Paid Staff: 11
Paid Artists: 60
Income Sources: Texas Panhandle Heritage Foundation
Performs At: Pioneer Amphitheatre
Annual Attendance: 85,000
Facility Category: Outdoor Theatre
Seating Capacity: 1723
Year Built: 1965
Rental Contact: Blaine Bertrand
Organization Type: Performing; Educational

3485
STAGECENTER
701 N Main Street
PO Box 9475
College Station, TX 77842
Phone: 979-823-4297
e-mail: stage.center@hotmail.com
Web Site: http://www.stagecenter.net
Officers:

President: Reid Self
Secretary: Kristie Hanle
Treasurer: Evelyn Callaway
Mission: To offer community members an opportunity for participation in theatre.
Utilizes: Guest Companies; Singers
Founded: 1966
Specialized Field: Community Theater
Status: Nonprofit
Paid Staff: 50
Income Sources: Arts Council of Brazos Valley
Organization Type: Performing; Educational

3486
CORSICANA COMMUNITY PLAYHOUSE
119 W 6th Avenue
Corsicana, TX 75110
Phone: 903-872-5421
Management:
President: H M Dabnpork
Executive Director: Sandra McCluremahood
Mission: To provide quality theatrical performances for Corsicana and the north and east Texas regions.
Founded: 1971
Specialized Field: Community Theater
Status: Non-Profit, Non-Professional
Paid Staff: 3
Income Sources: Texas Nonprofit Theatre
Performs At: Warehouse Living Arts Center
Organization Type: Performing; Touring

3487
CABBAGES AND KINGS
7436 Kenshine Lane
Dallas, TX 75230
Phone: 214-363-7292
Fax: 214-867-7615
Management:
Founder/Artistic Director: Linda Comess
Business Manager: Tricia Avery
Mission: To entertain and enlighten families and children; to present original plays which are based on mythology and stories and are relevant to modern life.
Utilizes: Guest Companies; Singers
Founded: 1984
Specialized Field: Children's Theater; Historical
Status: Professional; Nonprofit
Income Sources: Actors' Equity Association
Performs At: Addison Centre Theatre
Organization Type: Performing; Touring

3488
DALLAS CHILDREN'S THEATER
5938 Skillmans Street
Dallas, TX 75231
Phone: 214-978-0110
Fax: 214-978-0118
e-mail: family@dct.org
Web Site: www.dct.org
Management:
President: Kandace Winslow
Artistic Director: Robyn Flatt
Education Director: Nancy Schaeffer
Tour Director: Sally Fiorello
Mission: To enrich children's lives through theater arts.
Utilizes: Actors; AEA Actors; Artists-in-Residence; Choreographers; Collaborating Artists; Commissioned Composers; Commissioned Music; Designers; Educators; Five Seasonal Concerts; Guest Accompanists; Guest Artists; Guest Companies; Guest Conductors; Guest Designers; Guest Directors; Guest Lecturers; Instructors; Local Artists; Lyricists; Multimedia; Music; Organization Contracts; Original Music Scores; Performance Artists; Poets; Resident

Professionals; Selected Students; Sign Language Translators; Soloists; Student Interns; Special Technical Talent; Theatre Companies; Visual Arts
Founded: 1984
Specialized Field: Musical; Comedy; Youth Theater; Puppet; Educational
Status: Non-Profit, Professional
Paid Staff: 22
Volunteer Staff: 100
Paid Artists: 175
Budget: $2,500,000
Income Sources: International Association of Theatre for Children and Youth; Corporate; Foundation; Individuals; Grants; Ticket Purchases
Performs At: El Centre College Theatre; Crescent Theatre
Affiliations: TGG; AEA; AATE; TNT; ASSITEJ
Annual Attendance: 245,000
Organization Type: Performing; Touring; Educational

3489
DALLAS PUPPET THEATER
3905 Main Street
Dallas, TX 75226
Phone: 214-515-0004
Web Site: www.puppetry.org
Management:
Executive Director: Pix Smith
Artistic Director: Michael Robinson
Founding Artistic Director: James Smith
Mission: Dedicated to promoting and advancing the performing, visual, and creative art of puppetry.
Utilizes: Guest Companies; Singers
Founded: 1982
Specialized Field: Puppet
Status: Non-Profit, Professional
Paid Staff: 20
Paid Artists: 20
Organization Type: Performing; Touring; Resident; Educational; Sponsoring

3490
DALLAS THEATER CENTER
3636 Turtle Creek Boulevard
Dallas, TX 75219-5598
Phone: 214-522-8499
Fax: 214-521-7666
e-mail: comments@dallastheatercenter.org
Web Site: www.dallastheatercenter.org
Management:
General Manager: Angela Lee Gier
Managing Director: Mark Hadley
Artistic Director: Richard Hamburger
Management Assistant: Dustin McGee
Mission: To offer excellent professional theatre that produces classic, contemporary and new plays of the highest artistic quality.
Utilizes: Guest Companies; Singers
Founded: 1920
Specialized Field: Classic; Contemporary
Status: Professional; Nonprofit
Income Sources: Theatre Communications Group; League of Resident Theatres; American Arts Alliance
Performs At: Kalita Humphreys Theater; Arts District Theater
Type of Stage: Flexible; Thrust
Seating Capacity: 530; 466
Organization Type: Performing; Resident; Educational

3491
DRAMA CIRCLE THEATRE
2929 Mayhew
Dallas, TX 75228
Phone: 972-270-9255

Management:
Managing Director: Linda Boatman
Founder: Bill Green
Co-Founder: Nan Truax
Mission: To promote the theatre arts.
Founded: 1971
Specialized Field: Drama
Status: Semi-Professional; Nonprofit
Paid Staff: 30
Organization Type: Performing; Touring; Educational

3492
ECHO THEATRE
PO Box 820698
Dallas, TX 75328
Phone: 214-904-0500
e-mail: mail@echotheatre.org
Web Site: www.echotheatre.org
Officers:
Co-Founder: Linda Marie Ford
Co-Founder: Pam Myers-Morgan
Co-Founder: Suzy Blaylock
Mission: For years, theatre seasons at all levels of production have been programmed mainly wiht works by male playwrights, often resulting in an absence of the female voice.
Founded: 1997
Specialized Field: Women's Theater
Status: Non-Profit

3493
JUNIOR PLAYERS
4054 McKinney Avenue
Suite 104
Dallas, TX 75204
Phone: 214-526-4076
Fax: 214-526-0114
e-mail: info@juniorplayers.org
Web Site: www.juniorplayers.org
Management:
Executive Director: Kirsten Brandt James
Program Director: Vikas Adam
Mission: Junior Players uses the arts to provide role models, increase literacy, self-esteem and communication skills for the Dallas youth.
Specialized Field: Children's Theater; Educational; Summer Stock
Status: Nonprofit

3494
KATHY BURKS THEATRE OF PUPPETRY ARTS
5938 Skillman
Dallas, TX 75231
Phone: 214-587-7543
e-mail: kburkstx@yahoo.com
Web Site: http://www.kathyburkspuppets.com
Management:
Artistic Director: Kathy Burks
Mission: To perform using all styles of puppetry and perpetuate the art of puppetry. Material for the shows range from classic stories and fairytales to original work.
Founded: 1973
Specialized Field: Puppet
Status: Professional; Nonprofit
Income Sources: Puppeteers of America; Lone Star Puppet Guild
Performs At: The Loft Puppet Theatre at Fairview Farms
Organization Type: Performing; Resident; Educational

3495
KITCHEN DOG THEATER
3120 McKinney Avenue
Dallas, TX 75204
Phone: 214-953-1055
Fax: 214-953-1873
e-mail: admin@kitchendogtheater.org
Web Site: www.kitchendogtheater.org
Officers:
 Co-President/Board Director: Jason Ankele
 Co-President/Board Director: Susan Albritton
Management:
 President: Jayson Ankele
 Artistic Director: Dan Day
 Administrative Director: Tina Parker
Mission: It is the mission of Kitchen Dog Theater to provide a place where questions of justice, morality, and human freedom can be explored. We choose plays that challenge our moral and social consciences, and invite our audiences to be provoked, challenged, and amazed. We believe that the theater is a site of individual discovery as well as a force against conventional views of the self and experience.
Founded: 1990
Specialized Field: Comedy; Classic; Contemporary
Status: Non-Profit, Professional
Paid Staff: 4
Performs At: McKinney Avenue Contemporary
Affiliations: National New Play Network; Dallas Theatre League; Theater Communications Group
Type of Stage: Thrust; Black Box
Seating Capacity: 150; 75-100
Year Built: 1994

3496
PEGASUS THEATRE
6333 E Mockingbird Lane
Suite 147 PMB 773
Dallas, TX 75214
Phone: 214-821-6005
Fax: 214-572-7861
e-mail: comedy@pegasustheatre.com
Web Site: www.pegasustheatre.com
Management:
 Artistic Director: Kurt Kleinmann
 Producer: Barbara Weinberger,
 barb@pegasustheatre.com
Mission: A professional live stage theatre specializing in new and original comedies. They offer one main stage production each season and one black box prodution.
Utilizes: AEA Actors; Designers; Equity Actors; Guest Designers; Instructors; Local Artists; Original Music Scores; Performance Artists; Resident Professionals
Founded: 1985
Specialized Field: Musical; Classic
Status: Professional; Nonprofit
Paid Staff: 1
Budget: $150,000
Income Sources: Stage
Performs At: Eisemann Cetner
Type of Stage: Proscenium
Organization Type: Performing; Touring

3497
POCKET SANDWICH THEATRE
5400 E Mockingbird Lane
Suite 119
Dallas, TX 75206
Phone: 214-821-1860
Fax: 214-821-4742
e-mail: pst@dallas.net
Web Site: www.pocketsandwich.com

Management:
 President: Joe Dickinson
 Owner and Technical Director: Rodney Dobbs
Mission: To offer variety in live theatre performances.
Utilizes: Guest Companies; Singers
Founded: 1980
Specialized Field: Comedy; Dinner Theater
Status: For-Profit, Professional
Paid Staff: 20
Performs At: Pocket Sandwich Theatre
Organization Type: Performing

3498
TEATRO HISPANO DE DALLAS
1331 Record Crossing Road
Dallas, TX 75235
Phone: 214-689-6492
e-mail: teatro@airmail.net
Web Site: www.teatrodallas.org
Officers:
 President: Barbara Roy
 Vice President: Ruby Marrero
 Executive Director: Abigail Self
Management:
 Artistic Director/Producer: Cora Cardona
Utilizes: Actors; AEA Actors; Artists-in-Residence; Collaborating Artists; Community Members; Dance Companies; Designers; Educators; Five Seasonal Concerts; Guest Accompanists; Guest Choreographers; Guest Companies; Guest Conductors; Guest Designers; Guest Directors; Guest Ensembles; Guest Instructors; Guest Musical Directors; Guest Teachers; Lyricists; Multimedia; Original Music Scores; Performance Artists; Resident Professionals; Singers; Soloists; Student Interns; Theatre Companies
Founded: 1985
Specialized Field: Community Theater
Status: Professional; Semi-Professional; Nonprofit
Paid Staff: 2
Budget: $250,000
Performs At: Teatro Dallas
Annual Attendance: 15,000
Facility Category: Leases various venues
Organization Type: Performing

3499
TEXAS INTERNATIONAL THEATRICAL ARTS SOCIETY
3101 N Fitzhugh Avenue
Suite 301
Dallas, TX 75204
Phone: 214-528-6112
Fax: 214-528-2617
e-mail: csantos@titas.org
Web Site: www.titas.org
Management:
 Executive Director: Charles Santos
 Marketing/Public Relations: Scott Rozsa
Mission: To create opportunities otherwise unavailable in Dallas and North Texas for the community to experience an abundant mixture of the best American and international dance, performance art, and music through performances and cultural and educational outreach activities.
Founded: 1982
Specialized Field: Drama; Musical
Status: Non-Profit, Professional
Paid Staff: 8
Volunteer Staff: 70
Budget: $2,100,000
Income Sources: Private; Corporate; Foundation; Individual; Box Office
Performs At: McFarlin Auditorium; Southern Methodist University

Affiliations: Association of Performing Arts Presenters; International Society of Performing Arts
Annual Attendance: 52,000
Facility Category: Auditorium
Seating Capacity: 2,383
Rental Contact: Director Melissa Berry
Organization Type: Presenting; Educational

3500
THEATRE GEMINI
PO Box 191225
Dallas, TX 75219
Phone: 214-521-6331
Management:
 General Manager: Craig Hess
Founded: 1984
Specialized Field: Community Theater
Status: Non-Professional; Nonprofit
Paid Staff: 60
Organization Type: Performing; Educational

3501
THEATRE THREE
2800 Routh Street 168
Dallas, TX 75201
Phone: 214-871-2933
Fax: 214-871-3139
e-mail: theatre3@airmail.net
Web Site: www.theatre3dallas.com
Management:
 President: Jack Alder
 Managing Director: Tarry Dobson
Mission: To offer professional theatre as well as related activities to the Dallas-Ft. Worth area and to further the artistic careers of theatre artists who reside in North Texas.
Utilizes: Actors; AEA Actors; Choreographers; Dancers; Designers; Guest Artists; Guest Designers; Guest Musical Directors; Guest Teachers; Instructors; Local Artists; Music; Original Music Scores; Performance Artists; Poets; Resident Professionals; Sign Language Translators; Soloists; Student Interns
Founded: 1961
Specialized Field: Musical; Comedy; Classic
Status: Non-Profit, Professional
Paid Staff: 30
Budget: $1.4 million
Income Sources: Admission Earnings; Miscellaneous Earnings; Government; Corporate; Foundation; Individual Grants/Donations
Performs At: Theatre in the round
Affiliations: AEA; Southwest Theatre Association; Texas Non Profit Theatres
Facility Category: Theatre
Seating Capacity: 242; 70
Year Built: 1969
Year Remodeled: 1986
Organization Type: Performing; Touring; Resident; Educational; Sponsoring

3502
UNDERMAIN THEATRE
3100 Main Street # 16
PO Box 144466
Dallas, TX 75226
Phone: 214-747-1424
Fax: 214-747-1864
e-mail: mail@undermain.com
Web Site: www.undermain.com
Management:
 Artistic Director: Katherine Owens
 Operations Manager: Victor Ruiz

Mission: To focus on regionally and nationally premiering work that is challenging intellectually, emotionally and philosphically.
Utilizes: Guest Companies; Singers; Touring Companies
Founded: 1984
Specialized Field: Experimental; New Plays
Status: Professional; Nonprofit
Performs At: Undermain Theatre Basement
Affiliations: Actors' Equity Association; TCG; National Endowment for the Arts
Facility Category: Basement Theatre
Type of Stage: Flexible
Seating Capacity: 90
Year Built: 1900
Organization Type: Performing

3503
BREAD AND CIRCUS THEATRE
1009 Bull Run
Denton, TX 76201
Phone: 817-387-2408
Management:
Managing Director: Connie Whitt-Lambert
Mission: To offer fun theatrical experiences to children and adults through audience participation.
Utilizes: Singers
Founded: 1982
Specialized Field: Summer Stock; Community Theater; Musical
Status: Professional; Semi-Professional
Organization Type: Performing; Touring

3504
DENTON COMMUNITY CAMPUS THEATRE
214 W Hickory
PO Box 1931
Denton, TX 76201
Phone: 940-382-1915
Fax: 940-891-1691
Toll-free: 800-733-7014
e-mail: dct@campustheatre.com
Web Site: www.campustheatre.com
Officers:
President: Steve Plunkett
Management:
Executive Director: Scott Wilkinson
Mission: To offer artistic, educational experiences to participants; to provide quality theatre for audiences.
Utilizes: Actors; Choreographers; Collaborations; Dance Companies; Designers; Guest Artists; Guest Companies; Guest Conductors; Guest Lecturers; Local Artists; Original Music Scores; Resident Professionals; Singers; Special Technical Talent
Founded: 1949
Specialized Field: Community Theater
Status: Non-Professional; Nonprofit
Paid Staff: 5
Volunteer Staff: 50
Paid Artists: 300
Non-paid Artists: 300
Budget: $450,000
Income Sources: City of Denton
Performs At: Campus Theatre
Affiliations: ACT; SWTC; TNT
Annual Attendance: 30,000
Type of Stage: Proscenium
Stage Dimensions: 40'x40'
Seating Capacity: 299
Year Built: 1949
Year Remodeled: 1985
Cost: $2 million
Organization Type: Performing; Educational

3505
EL PASO ASSOCIATION FOR THE PERFORMING ARTS/VIVA EL PASO!
PO Box 31340
El Paso, TX 79931-0340
Phone: 915-565-6900
Fax: 915-565-6999
Web Site: http://www.viva-ep.org/contact.php
Management:
Managing Director: David Mills
Director of Marketing: Mario A Duron
Founded: 1978
Specialized Field: Outdoor Theater; Musical; Educational
Status: Non-Equity; Nonprofit
Season: June - August
Type of Stage: Amphitheatre
Stage Dimensions: 80' x 40'
Seating Capacity: 1500

3506
SOUTHWEST REPERTORY ORGANIZATION
1301 Texas Avenue
El Paso, TX 79901
Phone: 915-534-7653
Management:
Interim Executive/Artistic Director: Ed Hamilton
Technical Director: Glen O Brooks
Office Manager: Glenda Nevarez
Mission: To provide a main season including musicals, comedies and contemporary dramas; to offer a summer repertory featuring contemporary plays as well as classes in directing, acting and the technical aspects of theatre.
Utilizes: Guest Companies
Founded: 1978
Specialized Field: Musical; Community Theater
Status: Non-Professional; Nonprofit
Organization Type: Performing; Touring

3507
ALLIED THEATRE GROUP/STAGE WEST
1300 Gendy Street
Fort Worth, TX 76107
Phone: 817-784-9378
Fax: 817-735-4065
e-mail: stagewest@gbronline.com
Web Site: www.stagewest.org
Management:
President: J R Martinez
Executive Director: Jerry Russell
Producing Artistic Director: Jim Covault
Founded: 1979
Specialized Field: Musical; Comedy; Classic; Contemporary
Status: Non-Profit, Professional
Paid Staff: 10
Paid Artists: 35

3508
ALLIED THEATRE GROUP/STAGE WEST
3053-55 S University Drive
Fort Worth, TX 76109
Phone: 817-924-9454
Fax: 817-926-8650
e-mail: stagewest@gbronline.com
Web Site: www.stagewest.org
Officers:
President: Charles Reid
VP: Sharon Harrelson
Treasurer: Janie Frank
Past President: Maggie Knapp

Management:
Producing Artistic Director: Jim Covault
Administrative Associate: Jenae Yerger
Literary Associate: Natalie Gaupp
Mission: To produce a minimum of six major productions annually, including some musicals; to offer a broad range of works from classical to new and contemporary.
Utilizes: Guest Companies; Singers
Founded: 1979
Specialized Field: Drama; Musical
Status: Professional; Nonprofit
Paid Staff: 10
Volunteer Staff: 100
Non-paid Artists: 20
Income Sources: Actors' Equity Association; Theatre Communications Group; Texas Nonprofit Theatre; Live Theatre League of Tarrant County; Arts Council of Fort Worth & Tarrant County
Performs At: Stage West
Facility Category: Theatre-in-the-Round
Seating Capacity: 200
Year Remodeled: 1993
Organization Type: Performing

3509
CASA MANANA MUSICALS
300 W 3rd Street
Suite 1715
Fort Worth, TX 76102
Phone: 817-332-2272
Fax: 817-332-5711
Web Site: www.casamanana.org
Management:
President: Denton Yockey
Associate Producer: Scott Galbraith
Utilizes: Actors; AEA Actors; Choreographers; Dancers; Designers; Educators; Five Seasonal Concerts; Guest Artists; Guest Companies; Guest Conductors; Guest Designers; Instructors; Local Artists; Multimedia; Original Music Scores; Resident Professionals; Sign Language Translators; Singers; Soloists; Student Interns; Special Technical Talent; Theatre Companies
Founded: 1958
Specialized Field: Musical; Comedy; Youth Theater; Contemporary
Status: Non-Profit, Professional
Paid Staff: 20
Paid Artists: 100
Performs At: Casa Manana Theatre; Bass Performance Hall
Affiliations: National Alliance for Musical Theatre; Live Theatre League of Tarrant County; Texas Nonprofit Theatre Association
Organization Type: Performing; Touring; Resident; Educational

3510
CASA MANANA PLAYHOUSE
3101 W Lancaster Avenue
Fort Worth, TX 76107
Phone: 817-332-2272
Fax: 817-332-5711
Web Site: http://www.casamanana.org
Officers:
Chairman: Colby Siratt
Secretary: Elizabeth Webb
Treasurer: Connie Fagg
Management:
Executive Producer: Wally Jones
Business Manager: Leslie Bradford
Director of Development: Victor Mashburn

Mission: To present plays for children Fridays and Saturday with special weekday performances for local schools; to present Casa Kids, 15 children who provide free performances for area civic and nonprofit organizations.
Utilizes: Guest Companies
Founded: 1962
Specialized Field: Musical; Children's Theater
Status: Professional; Nonprofit
Income Sources: International Association of Theatre for Children and Youth; Actors' Equity Association; American Federation of Musicians
Performs At: Casa Manana Theatre
Organization Type: Performing; Resident; Educational

3511
CIRCLE THEATRE
230 W 4th Street
PO Box 470456
Fort Worth, TX 76147-0456
Phone: 817-921-3040
Fax: 817-877-3536
e-mail: plays@circletheatre.com
Web Site: http://www.circletheatre.com/
Officers:
    President: Joan Kline
    VP: Robert I Fenandez
    VP: Tom Gaffney
    Corresponding Secretary: Kim Kirk
    Recording Secretary: Sherry Jackson
    Treasurer: Marilyn Austin
Management:
    Executive Director: Rose Pearson
    Managing Director: Bill Newberry
    Director Public Relations/Marketing: Carlo Cuesta
Mission: Our mission is the advocacy of contemporary plays rarely seen in this community. We are commited to presenting professional, innovative theatre in an intimate setting.
Utilizes: Singers
Founded: 1981
Specialized Field: Drama; Classic
Status: Semi-Professional; Nonprofit
Organization Type: Performing; Resident

3512
FORT WORTH THEATRE
4401 Trail, Ake Drive
Fort Worth, TX 76109
Phone: 817-921-5300
Web Site: fwtheatre.homestead.com
Management:
    Artistic Director: William Garber
    Administrative Director: Brynn Bristol
Mission: To offer quality theatre to Fort Worth; to provide an outlet for talented amateurs.
Utilizes: Guest Companies
Founded: 1955
Specialized Field: Community Theater
Status: Non-Professional; Nonprofit
Performs At: William Edrington Scott Theatre
Organization Type: Performing; Resident

3513
HIP POCKET THEATRE
PO Box 136758
Fort Worth, TX 76136
Phone: 817-246-9775
Fax: 817-246-5651
e-mail: mdmole@aol.com
Web Site: www.hippocket.org
Officers:
    President: Judy Clark

President Elect: Ralph Watterson
    Secretary: Judy Golden
    Treasurer: Jessica Weaver
Management:
    President: Diana Simons
    Artistic Director: Johnny Simons
Mission: Showcasing the original work of regional composers and playwrights, as well as works rarely seen in this area.
Utilizes: Guest Companies; Singers
Founded: 1977
Specialized Field: Musical; Comedy; Puppet; Classic; Contemporary
Status: Non-Profit, Non-Professional
Paid Staff: 4
Volunteer Staff: 2
Paid Artists: 2
Non-paid Artists: 30
Budget: $165,000
Income Sources: Texas Commission on the Arts; National Endowment
Performs At: Oak Acres Amphitheatre
Affiliations: Live Theatre League Arts Council at Fort Worth
Facility Category: Outdoor Amphitheatre
Type of Stage: Multi-leveled tree house
Seating Capacity: 175
Year Built: 1978
Rental Contact: Diene Simons
Organization Type: Performing; Touring; Resident; Educational

3514
STAGE WEST
1300 Gendy Street
Fort Worth, TX 76107
Phone: 817-735-9995
Fax: 817-735-4065
e-mail: stgwest@ix.netcom.com
Web Site: www.stagewest.org
Management:
    President of the Board: J R Martinez
    Executive Director: Jerry Russel
    Artistic Director: Jim Covault
Mission: To provide Shakespeare-in-the-Park for Fort Worth residents at no cost.
Utilizes: Actors; AEA Actors; Five Seasonal Concerts; Guest Accompanists; Guest Designers; Guest Instructors; Guest Lecturers; Guest Musical Directors; Student Interns
Founded: 1979
Specialized Field: Drama; Musical
Status: Non-Profit, Professional
Paid Staff: 12
Paid Artists: 35
Income Sources: Texas Christian University; City of Fort Worth
Performs At: Indoor venue; Outdoor venue
Annual Attendance: 125,000
Facility Category: Park Site Fort Worth's Trinity Park, Stagewest
Rental Contact: Managing Director Mark Waltz
Organization Type: Performing; Touring

3515
GALVESTON OUTDOOR MUSICALS
PO Box 5253
Galveston, TX 77554
Phone: 409-737-1744
Fax: 409-737-2033
Founded: 1977
Specialized Field: Musical; Outdoor Theater
Status: Nonprofit
Season: June - August

Type of Stage: Amphitheatre
Stage Dimensions: 150' x 150'
Seating Capacity: 1766

3516
GARLAND CIVIC THEATRE
108 N 6th Street
Garland, TX 75040
Phone: 972-485-8884
Fax: 214-553-0081
Web Site: http://www.garlandcivictheatre.org/index.php
Management:
    Producing Director: James Weir
    Administrative Assistant: Linda White
    Technical Director: Dwight Swanson
Mission: To offer quality entertainment to our audiences; to provide space for community performers; to advance theatre.
Founded: 1967
Specialized Field: Musical; Community Theater
Status: Semi-Professional; Nonprofit
Income Sources: Texas Nonprofit Theatre; Theatre Communications Group
Performs At: Garland Center for the Performing Arts
Organization Type: Performing; Resident

3517
TEXAS AMPHITHEATRE
202 Bo Gibbs Boulevard
PO Box 8
Glen Rose, TX 76043
Phone: 254-897-4509
Fax: 254-897-7713
e-mail: somexto@glenrose.org
Web Site: www.glenroseexpo.org
Management:
    Facilities Manager: Mike Dooley
Founded: 1989
Specialized Field: Musical; Outdoor Theater
Status: For-Profit, Non-Professional
Paid Staff: 12
Paid Artists: 3
Season: June - October
Type of Stage: Amphitheatre
Stage Dimensions: 130' x 64'
Seating Capacity: 3200

3518
GRANBURY OPERA HOUSE THEATRE
PO Box 297
Granbury, TX 76048
Phone: 817-573-9191
Fax: 817-579-5529
Toll-free: 866-572-0881
e-mail: info@granburyoperahouse.org
Web Site: www.granburyoperahouse.org
Management:
    Managing Director And Producer: Marty Van Kleeck
    Technical Director: Adam Puglielli
    Costume Designer: Drenda Lewis
    Facilities Manager: Jake Jacobs
Founded: 1975
Specialized Field: Musical; Classic
Status: Nonprofit
Income Sources: Box Office; Texas Commission for the Arts Grant; Individual Donors
Season: Year round
Performs At: Granbury Opera House
Annual Attendance: 63,000
Organization Type: Performing; Educational

3519
A.D. PLAYERS
2710 W Alabama Street
Houston, TX 77098
Phone: 713-526-2721
Fax: 713-439-0905
e-mail: boxoffice@adplayers.org
Web Site: www.adplayers.org
Management:
   Artistic Director: Jeannette George
   Managing Director: Ric Hodgin, ric@adplayers.org
   Technical Director: Mark A Lewis,
   makr@adplayers.org
Mission: A professional theatre ministry communicating through various mediums under the creative signature of God.
Utilizes: Actors; AEA Actors; Designers; Five Seasonal Concerts; Grant Writers; Guest Accompanists; Guest Lecturers; High School Drama; Resident Artists; Resident Companies; Resident Professionals; Sign Language Translators; Soloists; Theatre Companies
Founded: 1967
Specialized Field: Musical; Comedy; Classic; Contemporary
Status: Non-Profit, Professional
Paid Staff: 45
Paid Artists: 40
Income Sources: Texas Nonprofit Theatre; Theatre Communications Group; Houston Theatre Association; Cultural Arts Council of Houston
Season: September - August
Performs At: Grave Theatre; Rotunda Theater
Type of Stage: Proscenium; Arena; Round
Seating Capacity: 220; 149
Organization Type: Performing; Touring; Resident; Educational

3520
ACTORS THEATRE OF HOUSTON
4112 Austin Street
Houston, TX 77004
Phone: 713-529-6606
e-mail: kgeorgeb@flash.net
Management:
   Producing Director: Chris Wilson
Founded: 1986
Specialized Field: Drama; Comedy; Theater Workshops

3521
ALLEY THEATRE
615 Texas Avenue
Houston, TX 77002
Phone: 713-220-5700
Fax: 713-222-6542
e-mail: webmaster@alleytheatre.org
Web Site: www.alleytheatre.org
Management:
   Artistic Director: Gregory Boyd
   Managing Director: Dean Gladden
Mission: The chief aims of the Alley, under the direction of Artistic Director Gregory Boyd and Managing Director Dean Gladden are to present a wide range of plays, embracing classic, new and neglected plays, and to produce these plays to the highest standards and to serve the widest audience.
Utilizes: Guest Companies; Singers
Founded: 1947
Specialized Field: Comedy; Contemporary
Status: Non-Profit, Professional
Paid Staff: 80
Income Sources: Sponsors; Corporations
Performs At: Alley Theatre

Affiliations: League of Resident Theatres; Actors' Equity Association; USA; Society for Stage Directors and Choreographers
Seating Capacity: 824; 310
Organization Type: Performing; Touring; Resident; Educational; Sponsoring

3522
CHANNING PLAYERS
PO Box 631363
Houston, TX 77263
Phone: 713-785-9492
Management:
   Artistic Director: Janis Halliday
   Technical Director: Donald Williams
Mission: Producing quality plays.
Utilizes: Singers
Founded: 1955
Specialized Field: Community Theater
Status: Nonprofit
Paid Staff: 50
Income Sources: Cultural Arts Council of Houston; Texas Nonprofit Theatre
Organization Type: Performing; Educational

3523
ENSEMBLE THEATRE
3535 Main Street
Houston, TX 77002
Phone: 713-520-0055
Fax: 713-520-1269
Web Site: www.ensemblehouston.org
Officers:
   Chair: Argentina James
   VP Operations: Vernon Landers
   Secretary: Alaina Benford
   Treasurer: Mary Simon
Management:
   President: Jackie Phillips
   Executive Director: Jeanette Cosley
   Artistic Director: Eileen Morris
Mission: The Ensemble Theatre is the Southwest's largest African American theatre presenting a season of classic and contemporary works featuring local and national artists.
Utilizes: Guest Companies; Singers
Founded: 1976
Specialized Field: Ethnic Theater
Status: Non-Profit, Professional
Paid Staff: 10
Paid Artists: 115
Performs At: The Ensemble Theatre
Organization Type: Performing; Touring; Resident; Educational

3524
HOUSTON SHAKESPEARE FESTIVAL
School of Theatre
University of Houston
Houston, TX 77204-5071
Phone: 713-743-3003
Fax: 713-749-1420
Web Site: www.houstonfestivalscompany.com
Officers:
   President: Annabella Sahakian
   Vice President: Bob Bourdeaux
Management:
   Producing Director: Sidney L Berger
   Secretary: Sandy Judice
   Business Administrator: Jerry Aven
Mission: To provide classical theater at no cost to citizens of Houston and surrounding areas.
Founded: 1975
Specialized Field: Shakespeare; Classic

Status: Professional; Nonprofit
Income Sources: University of Houston
Performs At: Miller Outdoor Theatre
Organization Type: Performing

3525
INFERNAL BRIDEGROOM PRODUCTIONS
2524 McKinney
Houston, TX 77003
Mailing Address: PO Box 131004 Houston, TX 77219-1004
Phone: 713-522-8443
Fax: 713-527-9538
e-mail: infernalbridegroom@hotmail.com
Web Site: www.infernalbridegroom.com
Management:
   Artistic Director: Anthony Barilla
   Managing Director: Lisa Haymes
   Associate Artistic Director: Tamarie Cooper
   Associate Artistic Director: Troy Schulze
Founded: 1993
Specialized Field: Musical; Comedy; Contemporary
Status: Non-Profit, Non-Professional
Paid Staff: 5

3526
MAIN STREET THEATER
2540 Times Boulevard
Houston, TX 77005
Phone: 713-524-3622
Fax: 713-524-3977
e-mail: info@mainstreettheatre.com
Web Site: www.mainstreettheater.com
Management:
   Artistic Director: Rebecca Greene Udden
   Production Manager: Andrew Ruthven
   Managing Director: Robbye Floyd-Archibald
   Marketing Associate: Misty Johnson
   Director Education: Angela Harris
Mission: To offer a lively year-round repertory of classic and contemporary plays for audiences of all ages; to provide a much-needed showcase for Houston theatre professionals. Main Street Theatre is a member of Theatre Communications Group, the national organization of professional not-for-profit theatres and produces under an agreement with Actors' Equity Association, the union of professional actors.
Founded: 1975
Specialized Field: Classic; Contemporary
Status: Professional; Semi-Professional; Non-Professional
Organization Type: Performing; Touring; Resident

3527
STAGES REPERTORY THEATRE
3201 Allen Parkway
Suite 101
Houston, TX 77019
Phone: 713-527-0220
Fax: 713-527-8669
e-mail: kmclaughlin@stagestheatre.com
Web Site: www.stagestheatre.com
Management:
   Producing Artistic Director: Kenn McLaughlin
   Production Manager: Kirk Markley
   Development Director: Star Massing
   Marketing/Communications Director: Lise Bohn
Mission: To present plays that are challenging to a developing company and are of social value and that set a standard of excellence.
Utilizes: Guest Companies; Singers; Students
Founded: 1978
Specialized Field: Drama; New Plays

Status: Professional; Nonprofit
Paid Staff: 27
Volunteer Staff: 2
Paid Artists: 128
Budget: $1.5 Million
Income Sources: Ticket Sales; Private Foundations; Corparations; Local and State Funding
Season: Year round
Performs At: Arena Theatre; Thrust Theatre
Affiliations: Actors' Equity Association; TCG; ASSITJ
Annual Attendance: 60,000
Facility Category: Dual Stages
Stage Dimensions: 19'x 20'; 23'x 30'
Seating Capacity: 229;171
Year Built: 1933
Year Remodeled: 1983
Rental Contact: Managing Director Thomas M. Smith
Organization Type: Performing; Touring; Resident; Educational; Sponsoring

3528
TALENTO BILINGUE DE HOUSTON

333 S Jenson
Houston, TX 77003
Phone: 713-222-1213
Fax: 713-222-1426
e-mail: info@tbhcenter.org
Web Site: www.tbhcenter.org
Management:
 President: Joeseph Cooper
 Artistic Director: Jorge Pina
 Technical Director: Rodney Becerra
 Publicity: Jim Bratton
 Special Events: Rick Camargo
 Program Manager: Fernando Perez
Mission: A non-profit cultural and educational organization.
Utilizes: Guest Companies
Founded: 1977
Specialized Field: Spanish Language Company; Multi-Cultural; Ethnic Theater
Status: Non-Profit, Professional
Paid Staff: 3
Paid Artists: 40
Organization Type: Performing; Touring; Educational; Sponsoring

3529
THEATRE SUBURBIA

4106 Way Out West Dr
Houston, TX 77018
Mailing Address: PO Box 920518
Phone: 713-682-3525
e-mail: info@theatresuburbia.org
Web Site: http://www.theatresuburbia.com
Officers:
 President: Elvin Moriarty
 Secretary: Judith Mallernee
 Treasurer: Marilyn Faulkner
Management:
 House Manager: Doris Merten
 Technical Director: Darrell Krause
 Back Stage Coordinator: Judith Mallernee
Mission: To provide the public with quality entertainment consisting of light comedy through heavy drama; to achieve recognition as a producer of the finest quality original scripts.
Utilizes: Guest Companies
Founded: 1960
Specialized Field: Light Theater; Drama
Status: Non-Professional; Nonprofit
Performs At: Theatre Suburbia
Organization Type: Performing

3530
THEATRE UNDER THE STARS

800 Bagby
Suite 200
Houston, TX 77002-2525
Phone: 713-558-2600
Fax: 713-558-2650
e-mail: boxoffice@tuts.com
Web Site: www.tuts.com
Management:
 Executive Director and Founder: Frank M Young
 Producing Director: John Holly
 Managing Director: Cissy Segall
 General Manager: Vivian Flynn
Mission: To present light opera regionally as well as on tour; to operate a school for aspiring artists; to foster the development of new musical theatre works.
Specialized Field: Musical
Status: Professional; Nonprofit
Performs At: The Music Hall
Organization Type: Performing; Touring; Educational

3531
HILL COUNTRY ARTS
FOUNDATION/POINT THEATRE

120 Point Theatre Road S
PO Box 1169
Ingram, TX 78025
Phone: 830-367-5121
Fax: 830-367-4332
Toll-free: 800-459-4223
e-mail: davidc@hcaf.com
Web Site: www.hcaf.com
Management:
 Executive Director: David Cockerell
 Business Manager: Leddy Gonzalez
Mission: To sustain a center for the visual and performing arts that promotes education and a public interest in the arts.
Utilizes: Guest Artists; Guest Companies
Founded: 1958
Specialized Field: Drama; Musical
Status: Non-Profit, Non-Professional
Paid Staff: 6
Volunteer Staff: 400
Income Sources: Texas Nonprofit Theatre; Texas Educators Theatre Association
Performs At: Smith-Ritch Point Theater
Affiliations: Hill Country Arts Foundation
Type of Stage: Outside Amphitheater; Pavilion
Seating Capacity: 722; 140
Organization Type: Performing; Touring; Educational

3532
IRVING COMMUNITY THEATER

2333 Rochelle
Irving, TX 75062
Phone: 972-594-6104
e-mail: info@irvingtheatre.org
Web Site: www.irvingtheatre.org
Mission: To promote the cultural, educational, and literary advancement of the residents of Irving and surrounding areas.
Utilizes: Guest Companies
Founded: 1971
Specialized Field: Musical; Comedy; Community Theater
Status: Non-Profit, Non-Professional
Paid Staff: 1
Income Sources: Cultural Affairs Council
Performs At: Irving Center for Cultural Arts
Organization Type: Performing; Resident

3533
TEXAS SHAKESPEARE FESTIVAL

1100 Broadway
Kilgore, TX 75662
Mailing Address: PO Box 2788, Kilgore, TX 75663
Phone: 903-983-8117
Fax: 903-983-8124
e-mail: info@texasshakespeare.com
Web Site: www.texasshakespeare.com
Officers:
 Founder: Raymond Caldwell
Management:
 Artistic Director: Raymond Caldwell
 Managing Director: John Dodd
Mission: To provide quality professional productions for East Texas of dramatic masterpieces, employing professional theatre artists from throughout the nation.
Founded: 1986
Specialized Field: Musical; Classic; Contemporary
Status: Non-Profit, Professional
Paid Staff: 2
Paid Artists: 75
Budget: $560,000
Income Sources: Kilgore College; TSF Foundation; City Of Kilgore; Grants; Donations; Ticket Sales
Season: June - July
Performs At: Indoor
Affiliations: S.T.A.A.
Annual Attendance: 8,000
Facility Category: Indoor Facility
Type of Stage: Proscenium
Stage Dimensions: 30' x 40'
Seating Capacity: 200
Year Built: 1966
Year Remodeled: 2008

3534
VIVE LES ARTS THEATRE

3401 S WS Young Drive
PO Box 10657
Killeen, TX 76547
Phone: 254-526-9090
Fax: 254-526-6906
e-mail: vh@desklink.com
Web Site: www.vlattheatre.com
Officers:
 Chairman: Mary Kliewer
Management:
 Director: Eric Shephard
 Administration: Tami Young
 WebMaster: Linda McMurray
 Children's Theatre Director: Amy Ball
Mission: To provide artistic and cultural activities in the areas of Killeen, Fort Hood, Copperas Cove and Harker Heights.
Utilizes: Guest Artists; Singers
Founded: 1976
Specialized Field: Musical; Community Theater; Children's Theater
Status: Professional; Non-Professional; Nonprofit
Paid Staff: 4
Income Sources: City of Killeen Hotel Motel Occupancy Tax; Meadows Foundation
Performs At: Vive Les Arts Center for the Arts
Type of Stage: Thrust
Seating Capacity: 400
Year Built: 1991
Rental Contact: Tam Young
Organization Type: Performing; Touring; Sponsoring

3535

MESQUITE COMMUNITY THEATRE

1527 N Galleway
Mesquite, TX 75149
Mailing Address: PO Box 870431 Mesquite, TX 75187-0431
Phone: 972-216-6444
Mission: To offer quality live theatre to the Mesquite Community.
Utilizes: Guest Companies; Singers
Founded: 1983
Specialized Field: Community Theater
Status: Professional; Semi-Professional; Nonprofit
Performs At: East Ridge Park Christian Church
Type of Stage: Black Box
Seating Capacity: 492
Year Built: 1995
Organization Type: Performing

3536

LAMP-LITE THEATER

224 Old Tyler Road
PO Box 630446
Nacogdoches, TX 75963
Mailing Address: PO Box 630446
Phone: 936-564-8300
e-mail: lamplite@netdot.com
Web Site: http://www.lamplitetheatre.org
Management:
    Director: Sarah McMullan
Mission: To provide quality live theatre for the East Texas region; to offer a dynamic creative experience for actors and related artists.
Founded: 1971
Specialized Field: Musical; Community Theater
Status: Non-Professional; Nonprofit
Volunteer Staff: 120
Income Sources: Ticket sales
Performs At: Lamp-Lite Theater
Annual Attendance: 1,500
Seating Capacity: 237
Year Built: 1979
Organization Type: Performing; Touring; Educational

3537

GLOBE OF THE GREAT SOUTHWEST THEATRE

2308 Shakespeare Road
Odessa, TX 79761
Phone: 915-332-1586
Fax: 915-332-1587
e-mail: hamlet@globesw.org
Web Site: www.globesw.org
Officers:
    President: G William Fowler
    Treasurer: La Doyce Lambert
    Secretary: Jerri Nickel
Management:
    Artistic Director: Anthony Ridley
    Office Manager: Ann Wilson
Mission: To provide Shakespearean and classical plays that are educational; to present contemporary and religious plays and musicals; to present an annual Shakespeare Festival; to advance the enjoyment, appreciation and study of great literature; to make available the Globe Building and grounds to the community for all the arts.
Utilizes: Actors; Artists-in-Residence; Commissioned Music; Guest Companies; Local Artists; Multimedia; Original Music Scores; Singers
Founded: 1958
Specialized Field: Community Theater; Shakespeare
Status: Professional; Nonprofit

Paid Staff: 4
Volunteer Staff: 100
Paid Artists: 6
Non-paid Artists: 150
Income Sources: Grants; Patron Membership Ffees; Ssponsorships
Performs At: An authentic replica of an Elizabethan Theatre
Affiliations: Shakespeare Theatre Association of America; Texas Nonprofit Theatres
Annual Attendance: 15,000
Facility Category: Elizabethan Theatre
Type of Stage: Thrust
Seating Capacity: 400
Year Built: 1968
Rental Contact: Anthony Ridley
Organization Type: Performing; Educational

3538

PERMIAN PLAYHOUSE OF ODESSA

310 W 42nd Street
PO Box 13374
Odessa, TX 79764-3374
Phone: 432-550-5456
Fax: 915-362-2678
e-mail: permianplay@yahoo.com
Web Site: www.permianplayhouse.org
Officers:
    Board President: Vicki Gomez
    First VP: Melissa Hirsch
    Second VP: Vonnie Downey
Management:
    President: Brenda Denton
    Educational Director: Laura Bond
Mission: To provide high quality, culturally diverse theatrical experiences and educational programs to enrich the lives of the people in the Permian Basin.
Utilizes: Guest Artists; Guest Companies; Singers
Founded: 1939
Specialized Field: Community Theater
Status: Non-Profit
Paid Staff: 5
Volunteer Staff: 25
Income Sources: American Association of Community Theatres; Southwest Theatre Association; Texas Nonprofit Theater; Season Membership; Ticket Sales
Performs At: Permian Playhouse of Odessa
Facility Category: Community Theatre
Seating Capacity: 400
Year Built: 1966
Organization Type: Performing; Touring; Educational

3539

PLANO REPERTORY THEATRE

1104 Capital Avenue
Suite 100
Plano, TX 75074
Mailing Address: PO Box 86185 Plano, TX 75086
Phone: 972-422-7460
Fax: 972-578-7072
e-mail: info@planorep.org
Web Site: www.planorep.org
Officers:
    Board President: Craig McKinney
    VP: Tiffany Kellerman
    Treasurer: Howard Danziger
    Secretary: Christine Henry
Management:
    Director Marketing/Development: David James
    Artistic Director: Ryan Pointer
Mission: To bring audiences and artists together through innovative productions and theatrical outreach, creating opportunities to experience our shared humanity.

Utilizes: Guest Companies
Founded: 1975
Specialized Field: Musical; Comedy; Contemporary
Status: Non-Profit, Professional
Paid Staff: 8
Volunteer Staff: 325
Paid Artists: 100
Budget: $720,000
Income Sources: Earned 75%; Contributed 25%
Performs At: Courtyard Theatre
Affiliations: Actor's Equity Association
Annual Attendance: 32,000
Facility Category: Theater
Type of Stage: Proscenium
Stage Dimensions: 51'x28'
Seating Capacity: 319
Year Built: 1935
Year Remodeled: 2002
Organization Type: Performing; Educational

3540

GUADALUPE CULTURAL ARTS CENTER

1300 Guadalupe Street
San Antonio, TX 78207
Phone: 210-271-3151
Fax: 210-271-3480
e-mail: mariat@guadalupeculturalarts.org
Web Site: www.guadalupeculturalarts.org
Officers:
    Chairman: Hector Fransto
Management:
    Managing Director: Leroy Martinez
Mission: To present and promote Mexican-American arts; to facilitate a deeper knowledge and appreciation of Native American and Latino cultures as well as their artistic expressions.
Utilizes: Actors; Artists-in-Residence; Collaborating Artists; Commissioned Music; Curators; Dancers; Filmmakers; Fine Artists; Five Seasonal Concerts; Guest Artists; Guest Companies; Guest Conductors; Guest Designers; Guest Lecturers; Guest Soloists; Guest Teachers; High School Drama; Local Artists; Multimedia; Organization Contracts; Original Music Scores; Performance Artists; Playwrights; Touring Companies
Founded: 1979
Specialized Field: Multi-Media
Status: Non-Profit, Professional
Paid Staff: 18
Paid Artists: 25
Budget: $1,500,000
Income Sources: Corporations; Foundations; City & Federal funding
Performs At: Guadalupe Theater
Annual Attendance: 190,000
Facility Category: Theater; Gallery
Seating Capacity: 372
Year Built: 1940
Year Remodeled: 1984
Organization Type: Performing; Touring; Resident; Educational; Sponsoring; Presenting
Resident Groups: Grupo Animo Youth Theatre; Folk Flamenco Dance Company

3541

JUMP-START PERFORMANCE COMPANY

108 Blue Star
San Antonio, TX 78204
Phone: 210-227-5867
Fax: 210-322-2231
e-mail: info@jump-start.org
Web Site: www.jump-start.org
Officers:
    Executive Director: Steve Bailey

Administrator: Sterling Houston
Management:
Artistic Director: S T Shimi
Managing Director: Pauline Cashion
Mission: Committed to the creation of art that is a lasting voice of many diverse cultures.
Utilizes: Guest Companies
Founded: 1985
Specialized Field: Contemporary
Status: Non-Profit, Professional
Paid Staff: 9
Paid Artists: 20
Income Sources: American Association of Community Theatres; Rural Organization of Theaters South
Performs At: Jump-Start Theater
Organization Type: Performing; Touring; Resident; Educational; Sponsoring; Commissioning

3542
MAGIK THEATRE
420 S Alamo
San Antonio, TX 78205
Phone: 210-227-2751
Fax: 210-227-2753
e-mail: info@magiktheatre.org
Web Site: www.magiktheatre.org
Officers:
Marketing Director: Asia Ciaravino
Office Manager: Tracie J Coop
Management:
President: Richard Rosen
Music Director: Mark G Johnson
Operations Manager: David Ankrom
Academy Director: Dave Cortez
Academy Director: Angela Hoeffler
Costume Manager: Greg Hinojosa
Mission: To promote literacy and learning, strengthen family life; to offer quality and affordable live theatrical presentations for the entire community and create tomorrow's live theater audience.
Utilizes: Actors; Artists-in-Residence; Collaborations; Dancers; Guest Artists; Guest Conductors; Guild Activities; Local Artists; Multi Collaborations; Multimedia; Original Music Scores; Performance Artists; Resident Artists; Resident Professionals; Sign Language Translators; Touring Companies; Visual Arts
Founded: 1984
Specialized Field: Children's Theater
Status: Non-Profit, Professional
Paid Staff: 15
Paid Artists: 11
Budget: $900,000
Income Sources: Box Office; Classes; Tours; Contributed Income
Performs At: Theatre
Affiliations: ASSITES/USA; SATCO; TNT, ATHE
Annual Attendance: 155,000
Facility Category: Theatre
Type of Stage: Thrust
Stage Dimensions: 30'x42'
Seating Capacity: 600
Year Built: 1899
Year Remodeled: 1939
Rental Contact: Operations Manager David Ankrom
Resident Groups: Magik Theatre Company

3543
SAN PEDRO PLAYHOUSE
800 W Ashby
PO Box 12356
San Antonio, TX 78212

Phone: 210-733-7258
Fax: 210-734-2651
e-mail: sanpedplay@aol.com
Web Site: www.sanpedroplayhouse.com
Officers:
President: Janet Nevenschwander
1st VP: Joe Medina
Second VP: Rickard Archer
Secretary: Susan Lelauren
Management:
President: Rick Archer
Executive Director: Diann Sneed
Artistic Director: Frank Latson
Mission: Literary and educational community theatre.
Utilizes: Actors; Choreographers; Collaborating Artists; Dancers; Designers; Educators; Five Seasonal Concerts; Grant Writers; Guest Accompanists; Guest Artists; Guest Companies; Guest Conductors; Guest Designers; Guest Directors; Guest Ensembles; Guest Instructors; Guest Lecturers; Guest Musical Directors; Guest Musicians; Guest Soloists; Guest Speakers; Guest Teachers; High School Drama; Instructors; Local Artists; Local Unknown Artists; Multimedia; Music; Original Music Scores; Performance Artists; Resident Professionals; Selected Students; Sign Language Translators; Singers; Soloists; Student Interns
Founded: 1912
Specialized Field: Musical; Comedy
Status: Non-Profit, Professional
Paid Staff: 8
Budget: $450,000
Income Sources: Private Donations; Business Donations
Annual Attendance: 35,000
Type of Stage: Proscenium; Thrust
Seating Capacity: 400; 60
Year Built: 1929
Year Remodeled: 2000
Rental Contact: Yvette Oakes
Organization Type: Performing; Educational

3544
TEMPLE CIVIC THEATRE
2413 S 13th Street
Temple, TX 76504
Phone: 254-778-4751
Fax: 254-778-4980
e-mail: tct@artstemple.com
Web Site: www.artstemple.com
Officers:
President: Richard Schneider
Management:
Executive Director: Tim Campbell
Technical Director: Jon Boles
Mission: To promote community involvement in theatre arts; to offer an outlet for talent in the community.
Utilizes: Guest Companies
Founded: 1965
Specialized Field: Community Theater
Status: Non-Profit, Non-Professional
Paid Staff: 3
Affiliations: Texas Non-Profit Theatre's; Southwest Teatre Association
Organization Type: Performing; Educational

3545
WICHITA FALLS BACKDOOR PLAYERS
501 Indiana
PO Box 896
Wichita Falls, TX 76307
Phone: 940-322-5000
Fax: 940-322-8167
e-mail: backdoor1@wf.net
Web Site: www.backdoortheatre.org

Management:
Box Office Manager: Weldon Fraker
Managing Artistic Director: Linda Bates
Mission: To offer participation in all areas of theatre to anyone interested regardless of experience.
Utilizes: Actors; Choreographers; Collaborating Artists; Designers; Grant Writers; Guest Artists; Guest Companies; Guest Designers; Guild Activities; High School Drama; Local Artists; Performance Artists; Singers
Founded: 1971
Specialized Field: Community Theater
Status: Non-Profit, Professional
Paid Staff: 3
Volunteer Staff: 200
Paid Artists: 3
Non-paid Artists: 20
Organization Type: Performing

Utah

3546
UTAH SHAKESPEAREAN FESTIVAL
351 W Center Street
Cedar City, UT 84720
Phone: 435-586-7880
Fax: 435-865-8003
Toll-free: 800-pla-ytix
e-mail: usfinfo@suu.edu
Web Site: www.bard.org
Officers:
Development Director: Jyl Shuler
Marketing Director: Donna Law
Education Director: Michael Bahr
Publications Director: Bruce Lee
Management:
Executive Producer: Fred Adams
Production Manager: Ray Inkel
Art Director: Philip Hermansen
Associate Artistic Director: JR Sullivan
Marketing Director: Donna Law
Production Manager: Ran Inkel
Director Plays-in-Progress: George Judy
Education Director: Michael Don Bahr
Publications Director: Bruce Lee
Mission: To present six classic and Shakespearean works in repertory each summer and fall.
Utilizes: Actors; Guest Conductors; Guest Designers; Guest Writers; Guild Activities; Performance Artists; Resident Professionals; Student Interns
Founded: 1961
Specialized Field: Shakespeare
Status: Professional; Nonprofit
Paid Staff: 25
Volunteer Staff: 250
Paid Artists: 200
Budget: $5 Million
Income Sources: Box Office Sales; Contributed Income; Endowment Income; Merchandise Sales
Season: June - August
Performs At: Adams Memorial Stage; Randall L. Jones Theatre; University Stage
Affiliations: USA; SSD&C; Actors' Equity Association; LORT; TCG
Annual Attendance: 155,000
Facility Category: Outdoor/Indoor
Type of Stage: Thrust; Proscenium
Stage Dimensions: 50Wx30D; 22Hx42Wx25D; 18Hx44Wx39D
Seating Capacity: 887; 769; 981
Year Remodeled: 1989
Rental Contact: Production Manager Ray Inkel
Organization Type: Performing; Resident; Educational

3547

OLD LYRIC REPERTORY COMPANY
4035 Old Main Hill
Logan, UT 84322-4035
Phone: 435-797-0085
Fax: 435-797-0086
e-mail: vicki.fowler@usu.edu
Web Site: www1.usu.edu/lyric
Management:
House Manager: LuAnn Heap
Marketing Director: Jeremy Gordon
Business Manager: Vicki Fowler
Mission: A professional theater group that produces four repertory shows through the summer months. It also serves as a training ground for advanced theatre students from Utah State University.
Utilizes: Actors; AEA Actors; Designers; Guest Accompanists; Guest Conductors; Guest Designers; Original Music Scores; Resident Professionals; Soloists; Student Interns
Founded: 1967
Specialized Field: Musical; Comedy; Classic; Contemporary; Educational
Status: Non-Profit, Professional
Paid Staff: 35
Paid Artists: 40
Season: May - August
Performs At: Legitimate Theatre
Type of Stage: Proscenium
Stage Dimensions: 22' x 18'
Seating Capacity: 380

3548

OFF BROADWAY THEATRE
272 S Main Street
Salt Lake City, UT 84101
Phone: 801-355-4628
Fax: 801-355-4641
e-mail: sandy@theobt.com
Web Site: www.theobt.com
Management:
President: Sandy Jensen
Artistic Director: Eric Jensen
Owner: Ben Poter
Owner: Sandy Jensen
Founded: 1994
Specialized Field: Musical; Comedy
Status: For-Profit, Professional
Paid Staff: 3
Volunteer Staff: 8
Paid Artists: 26

3549

PIONEER THEATRE COMPANY
University of Utah
300 S 1400 E
Salt Lake City, UT 84112-0660
Phone: 801-581-6961
Fax: 801-581-5472
e-mail: kpeterson@ptc.utah.edu
Web Site: www.pioneertheatre.org
Management:
Artistic Director: Charles Morey
Managing Director: Christopher Lino
Business Manager: Pat Wells
Development Director: Diane Parisi
Marketing Director: Kwin Peterson
Mission: Dedicated to offering high quality professional theater to Utah as well as the Northwestern United States.

Utilizes: Actors; AEA Actors; Choreographers; Composers-in-Residence; Designers; Fine Artists; Guest Companies; Guest Conductors; Guest Designers; Guest Writers; Instructors; Multimedia; Resident Artists; Resident Professionals; Singers
Founded: 1962
Specialized Field: Musical; Classic; Contemporary
Status: Non-Profit, Professional
Budget: 3.5 million
Income Sources: Ticket Sales; Donations; Grants
Performs At: Pioneer Memorial Theater
Affiliations: Theatre Communications Group
Annual Attendance: 94,000
Type of Stage: Proscenium
Seating Capacity: 932
Year Built: 1962
Year Remodeled: 2000
Organization Type: Performing; Educational

3550

PLAN - B THEATRE COMPANY
138 W 300 S
Salt Lake City, UT 84101
Phone: 801-297-4200
Fax: 801-466-3840
Web Site: www.planbtheatrecompany.org
Officers:
President: Luana Chilelli
Vice President: Tami Marquardt
Secretary: Kay Sheen
Treasurer: Patrick Commiskey
Management:
Managing Director: Cheryl Ann Cluff
Producing Director: Jerry Rapier
Stage Manager: Jennifer Freed
Specialized Field: Comedy; Radio Performances; Puppet

3551

SALT LAKE ACTING COMPANY
168 West 500 N
Salt Lake City, UT 84103
Phone: 801-363-0526
Fax: 801-532-8513
e-mail: info@saltlakeactingcompany.org
Web Site: www.saltlakeactingcompany.org
Management:
Executive Producer: Keven Myhre
Executive Producer: Cynthia Heming
Mission: Produces seasons of thoughtful, provocative, regional and world premiers; nurtures, supports and develops a community of professional artists; produces and supports emerging playwrights, and makes a significant contribution to the community and to the American theatre field by commissioning, developing and producing new plays.
Utilizes: Guest Companies
Founded: 1970
Specialized Field: Musical; Comedy; Classic; Contemporary
Status: Non-Profit, Professional
Paid Staff: 15
Income Sources: Theatre Communications Group
Performs At: The Salt Lake Acting Company Theater
Organization Type: Performing

3552

SUNDANCE INSTITUTE
PO Box 3630
Salt Lake City, UT 84110
Phone: 801-328-3456
Fax: 801-575-5175
e-mail: institute@sundance.org
Web Site: www.sundance.org

Officers:
President: Robert Redford
Chairman: Walter Weisman
Executive Director: Geoffrey Gilmore
Artistic Director: Phillip Himberg
Managing Director: Aaron Young
Press Contact: Patrick Hubley
Mission: Dedicated to the development of artists of independent vision and the exhibition of their new work.
Utilizes: Actors; Artists-in-Residence; Choreographers; Collaborating Artists; Collaborations; Composers-in-Residence; Dancers; Designers; Educators; Filmmakers; Guest Accompanists; Guest Companies; Guest Conductors; Guest Designers; Guest Directors; Guest Ensembles; Guest Instructors; Guest Lecturers; Guest Musicians; Guest Teachers; Instructors; Local Artists; Music; Organization Contracts; Original Music Scores; Performance Artists; Poets; Resident Professionals; Selected Students; Sign Language Translators; Soloists; Student Interns
Founded: 1981
Specialized Field: Musical; Comedy; Drama; Young Playwrights; New Plays; Contemporary; Experimental
Status: Non-Profit, Non-Professional
Paid Staff: 30
Budget: $10,600,000
Income Sources: 35% Earned; 65% Contributed Income
Type of Stage: Outdoor; Indoor
Organization Type: Educational

3553

SUNDANCE CHILDREN'S THEATRE
Rural Route 3
PO Box 624-D
Sundance, UT 84604
Phone: 801-328-3456
Fax: 801-225-3096
e-mail: institute@sundance.org
Web Site: www.sundance.org
Officers:
President: Robert Redford
Management:
Chairman: Walter Weisman
Executive Director: Geoffrey Gilmore
Artistic Director: Jerry Parch
Managing Director: David Kirk Chambers
Mission: To develop and produce new plays for young audiences.
Utilizes: Guest Companies
Founded: 1990
Specialized Field: Children's Theater
Status: Non-Profit, Non-Professional
Paid Staff: 65
Organization Type: Performing; Touring

3554

HALE CENTRE THEATRE AT HARMAN HALL
3333 S Decker Lake Drive
2200 W
West Valley City, UT 84119
Phone: 801-984-9000
Fax: 801-984-9009
e-mail: info@halecentretheatre.org
Web Site: www.halecentretheatre.org
Management:
President: Mark Dietlein
Executive Producer: Sally Dietlein
Executive Producer: Sally Hale
Technical Director: Andrew Barrus
Costumer Rentals: Amy Glaser
Office Manager: Tammy Morgan

Marketing Director/Building Rentals: JaceSon Barrus
Founded: 1985
Specialized Field: Musical; Comedy; Community Theater
Status: Non-Profit, Non-Professional
Paid Staff: 70
Paid Artists: 250
Performs At: Comedies; Musicals
Rental Contact: Marketing Director JaceSon Barrus

Vermont

3555
OLDCASTLE THEATRE COMPANY
Bennington Center for the Arts
Route 9 & Gypsy Lane
PO Box 1555
Bennington, VT 05201
Phone: 802-447-0564
Fax: 802-442-3704
e-mail: oldcastletheatreco@sover.org
Web Site: www.oldcastle.org
Management:
  President: Lisa Catapano-Friedman
  Producing Artistic Director: Eric Peterson
  Associate Artistic Director: Richard Howe
  Director Production: Kenneth Mooney
  Marketing Director: Daryl Kenny
  House/Box Office Manager: Jana Lillie
Mission: Resident professional theatre company.
Utilizes: Actors; AEA Actors; Choreographers; Community Talent; Contract Actors; Dancers; Designers; Guest Artists; Guest Companies; Guest Conductors; Guest Designers; Guest Lecturers; Guest Musical Directors; Guild Activities; Local Artists; Music; Original Music Scores; Performance Artists; Resident Artists; Resident Companies; Resident Professionals
Founded: 1972
Specialized Field: New Plays
Status: Non-Profit, Professional
Paid Staff: 3
Paid Artists: 35
Budget: $400,000
Income Sources: Ticket Revenue; Donations; Special Events; Corporate Underwriting; Grants
Season: March - October
Performs At: Bennington Center for the Arts
Affiliations: Actors' Equity Association; Society for Stage Directors and Choreographers
Annual Attendance: 10,000
Facility Category: Auditorium & Art Gallery
Type of Stage: Proscenium
Seating Capacity: 313
Year Built: 1994
Rental Contact: Oldcastle Theatre Company Eric Peterson
Organization Type: Performing; Touring; Resident; Educational; Sponsoring

3556
NATIONAL MARIONETTE THEATRE
350 Putney Road
Brattleboro, VT 05301
Mailing Address: PO Box 1311
Phone: 802-579-1032
Fax: 802-257-4079
Web Site: www.nationalmarionette.com
Management:
  Artistic Director: David Syrotiak
  Production Manager: Peter Syrotiak
  Managing Director: David J. Syrotiak
Utilizes: Singers

Founded: 1968
Specialized Field: Puppet
Status: Professional; Nonprofit
Income Sources: Association of Performing Arts Presenters; NECA; New England Arts Foundation
Organization Type: Performing; Touring

3557
VERMONT STAGE COMPANY
PO Box 1430
Burlington, VT 05402
Phone: 802-862-1497
Fax: 802-862-1257
e-mail: vsc@vtstage.org
Web Site: www.vtstage.org
Management:
  Artistic Director: Mark Nash
  Business Manager: Emily Rozanski
Mission: Works to make theatre that matters. By creating professional theatre that is emotionally, intellectually, and physically engaging, committing to the belief that theatre can make a positive difference in the community and in the world.
Founded: 1994
Specialized Field: Drama; Contemporary
Status: Non-Profit, Professional
Paid Staff: 2
Volunteer Staff: 50
Budget: $275,000
Income Sources: Ticket Sales; Corporate Sponsorships; Program Advertising; Private Contributions
Season: September - May
Affiliations: Flynn Center for the Performing Arts
Annual Attendance: 6,000-7,000
Type of Stage: Flexible; Black Box
Seating Capacity: 150

3558
AMERICAN THEATRE WORKS
PO Box 510
Dorset, VT 05251
Phone: 802-867-2223
Fax: 802-867-0144
e-mail: theatre@sover.net
Web Site: www.theatredirectories.com
Officers:
  President: Robert G Bushell Jr
  VP: Jean Miller
  Treasurer: Ben Weil
Management:
  Producing and Artistic Director: John Nassivera
  General Manager: Barbara Ax
Mission: To offer a season of five plays each summer, as well as a writers' colony.
Utilizes: Actors; AEA Actors; Artists-in-Residence; Designers; Guest Designers; Instructors; Music; Performance Artists; Resident Professionals; Soloists
Founded: 1976
Specialized Field: Summer Stock
Status: Non-Profit
Income Sources: Theatre Communications Group
Performs At: Dorset Playhouse
Seating Capacity: 290
Year Remodeled: 2001
Organization Type: Performing; Resident; Educational; Publishing

3559
POTOMAC THEATRE PROJECT
4 Nedde Lane
Middlebury, VT 05753
Phone: 802-388-3318
e-mail: info@olneytheatre.org

Management:
  Director: Cheryl Faraone
  Director: James Petosa
  Director: Richard Romagnoli
Mission: Producing highly theatrical new works; Providing professional theatre training.
Founded: 1977
Specialized Field: New Plays; Theater Workshops
Status: Professional; Nonprofit
Paid Staff: 15
Income Sources: Alliance of Resident Theatres/New York; Vermont Council on the Arts
Performs At: Hall of Nations
Organization Type: Performing; Resident; Educational

3560
LOST NATION THEATER
39 Main Street
Montpelier, VT 05602
Phone: 802-229-0492
Fax: 802-223-9608
e-mail: info@lostnationtheater.org
Web Site: www.lostnationtheater.org
Management:
  President: Kim Bent
  Artistic Director: Kathleen Jeenan
Founded: 1977
Specialized Field: Drama; Historical
Status: Non-Profit, Professional
Paid Staff: 7
Season: June - October
Type of Stage: Flexible Thrust
Stage Dimensions: 32' x 28'
Seating Capacity: 124

3561
GREEN MOUNTAIN GUILD
PO Box 659
Pittsfield, VT 05762
Phone: 802-746-8320
Management:
  Program Coordinator/Managing Dir: Marjorie O'Neill-Butler
  Artistic Director: Robert O'Neill-Butler
  Associate Artistic Director: Jay Berkow
Mission: Developing and promoting excellence in Northern New England's performing arts.
Utilizes: Guest Companies
Founded: 1971
Specialized Field: Summer Stock; Musical; Youth Theater
Status: Professional
Paid Staff: 3
Income Sources: New England Theatre Conference; Vermont Council on the Arts; New England Touring Foundation
Season: July - August
Performs At: Killington Playhouse
Organization Type: Performing; Touring; Resident

3562
CATAMOUNT FILM AND ARTS COMPANY
139 Eastern Avenue
PO Box 324
Saint Johnsbury, VT 05819
Phone: 802-748-2600
Fax: 802-748-0852
Toll-free: 888-757-5559
e-mail: catamountarts@charter.net
Web Site: www.catamountarts.com
Management:
  President: Robert Swortz
  Executive Director: Reg Ainsworth

Mission: To perform community-based multidisciplinary presentations.
Founded: 1975
Specialized Field: Musical; Contemporary; Mime
Status: Non-Profit, Professional
Paid Staff: 3
Volunteer Staff: 15
Paid Artists: 40
Organization Type: Performing; Educational

3563
WESTON PLAYHOUSE
703 Main Street
Weston, VT 05161
Phone: 802-824-8167
Fax: 802-824-5099
e-mail: mail@westplay.com
Web Site: www.westonplayhouse.org
Management:
    Producing Director: Malcolm Ewen
    General Manager: Stuart Duke
Founded: 1937
Specialized Field: Musical; Drama; Comedy
Status: Nonprofit
Season: June - September
Type of Stage: Proscenium
Seating Capacity: 285

3564
NORTHERN STAGE
PO Box 4287
White River Junction, VT 05001
Phone: 802-296-7000
Fax: 802-291-9156
e-mail: info@northernstage.org
Web Site: www.northernstage.org
Officers:
    Board President: Hunt Whitcare
    Treasurer: Byron Hathorn Jr
Management:
    Artistic Director: Brooke Wetzel-Ciardelli
    Production Director: Kathrein Dorothy
    Director Media/Marketing: Charlie Glazer
    Production Manager: Angelina Giudice
Mission: Dedicated to presenting new interpretations of classics, regional premires of recent and new works, and professioanl theater education.
Utilizes: Actors; AEA Actors; Artists-in-Residence; Choreographers; Collaborating Artists; Collaborations; Commissioned Composers; Designers; Educators; Filmmakers; Fine Artists; Grant Writers; Guest Accompanists; Guest Artists; Guest Companies; Guest Conductors; Guest Designers; Guest Ensembles; Guest Instructors; Guest Lecturers; Guest Musical Directors; Guild Activities; High School Drama; Instructors; Local Artists; Multimedia; Music; Original Music Scores; Performance Artists; Resident Artists; Resident Professionals; Sign Language Translators; Soloists; Student Interns; Theatre Companies; Visual Arts
Founded: 1992
Specialized Field: Musical; Comedy; Classic; Contemporary
Status: Non-Profit, Professional
Paid Staff: 25
Volunteer Staff: 60
Paid Artists: 8
Income Sources: Donations
Season: September - December
Affiliations: TCG
Annual Attendance: 12,000
Facility Category: Theater
Type of Stage: 3/4 Thrust
Stage Dimensions: 50' x 24'

Seating Capacity: 245
Year Built: 1885
Year Remodeled: 1972
Rental Contact: Charlie Glazer

Virginia

3565
BARTER THEATRE - STATE THEATRE OF VIRGINIA
Main Street
PO Box 867
Abingdon, VA 24210
Phone: 276-628-3991
Fax: 276-628-4551
e-mail: info@bartertheatre.com
Web Site: www.bartertheatre.com
Management:
    Artistic Director/Producer: Rex Partington
    Artistic Director: Richard Rose
    Business Manager: Joan Ballou
    Development Director: Lisa Alderman
    Marketing Director: Debbie Addison
    Associate Artistic Director: John Hardy
    Group Sales Reservationist: Linda Pruner
    Media Specialist/Web/Graphics: Stacy Fine
Mission: Performing the finest in contemporary and classical theatre for residents as well as visitors to our region.
Utilizes: Guest Companies
Founded: 1933
Specialized Field: Musical; Comedy; Classic; Contemporary
Status: Non-Profit, Professional
Paid Staff: 125
Income Sources: Actors' Equity Association; League of Resident Theatres; Theatre Communications Group
Performs At: Barter Playhouse; Barter Theatre House
Type of Stage: Proscenium, Flexible Stage
Seating Capacity: 508, 140
Organization Type: Performing; Touring; Resident; Educational

3566
KATHY HARTY GRAY DANCE THEATRE
PO Box 3291
Alexandria, VA 22302
Phone: 703-413-3811
Fax: 703-413-4198
e-mail: info@khgdt.org
Web Site: www.khgdt.org
Management:
    Artistic Director: Kathy Gray
Mission: Mondern dance company providing concerts, school shows, residencies and master classes.
Founded: 1978
Specialized Field: Musical; Movement Theater
Status: Professional
Paid Staff: 1
Volunteer Staff: 1
Paid Artists: 10

3567
METROSTAGE
1201 N Royal Street
Alexandria, VA 22314
Phone: 703-548-9044
Fax: 703-548-9089
e-mail: info@metrostage.org
Web Site: www.metrostage.org
Officers:
    President of Board: Mark Feldheim
Management:

    Producing Artistic Director: Carolyn Griffin
Mission: Offers comtemporary plays and musicals in an intimate theatre setting, including many new plays and musicals
Utilizes: Actors; AEA Actors; Designers; Guest Companies; Music
Founded: 1984
Specialized Field: Musical; Comedy; Contemporary
Status: Non-Profit, Professional
Paid Staff: 2
Volunteer Staff: 2
Paid Artists: 50
Budget: $500,000
Income Sources: Box Office; Contributions
Performs At: Theatre
Affiliations: League of Washington Theatres; Alexandria Convention and Visitors Association
Annual Attendance: 4,000
Facility Category: Theatre
Type of Stage: Modified Thrust
Stage Dimensions: 26'x 20'
Seating Capacity: 130
Year Remodeled: 2001
Cost: $450,000
Organization Type: Performing; Touring; Educational

3568
MOUNT VERNON COMMUNITY CHILDREN'S THEATRE
1900 Elkin Street
Suite 270
Alexandria, VA 22308
Phone: 703-360-0686
e-mail: mvcct@verizon.net
Web Site: www.mvcct.org
Management:
    Programs Coordinator: Pam Peckar
    Education Director: Beth Hauptle
Mission: Committed to providing opportunities of creative expression to children of all ages through drama education and live theatrical production.
Founded: 1980
Specialized Field: Children's Theater; Theater Workshops

3569
HORIZONS THEATRE
4350 N Fairfax Drive
Suite 127
Arlington, VA 22203
Phone: 703-243-8550
Fax: 703-243-4561
e-mail: info@horizonstheatre.org
Web Site: www.horizonstheatre.org
Management:
    Artistic Director: Leslie B Jacobson
    Managing Director: Joan Kelley
Founded: 1976
Specialized Field: Women's Theater
Status: Non-Equity; Nonprofit

3570
SIGNATURE THEATRE
4200 Campbell Ave
Arlington, VA 22206
Phone: 703-820-9771
Fax: 703-845-0236
Web Site: www.sig-online.org
Officers:
    Chair: Deborah Gandy
    Vice Chair: Paul Wojcik
    Secretary: Mary Cadagin
    Treasurer: Wes Pickard
Management:

Artistic Director: Eric D Schaeffer
Managing Director: Maggie Boland
Mission: To reinvent musical classics and premiere groundbreaking new work by today's best writers
Founded: 1990
Specialized Field: Classic; New Plays
Status: Nonprofit

3571
OFFSTAGE THEATRE

PO Box 131
Charlottesville, VA 22902
Phone: 804-295-7249
Management:
   Co-Artistic Director: Tom Coash
   Co-Artistic Director: Doug Grissom
   Resident Director: John Quinn
   Public Relations Director: Amy Lowenstein
Mission: Producing new plays of high quality in nontraditional, low-cost theatre environments.
Utilizes: Guest Companies
Founded: 1989
Specialized Field: New Plays; Contemporary
Status: Professional; Semi-Professional; Nonprofit
Organization Type: Performing; Touring; Resident; Educational

3572
SWIFT CREEK MILL PLAYHOUSE

PO Box 41
Colonial Heights, VA 23834
Phone: 804-748-5203
Fax: 804-748-4411
e-mail: roneill@swiftcreekmill.com
Web Site: www.swiftcreekmill.com
Management:
   Artistic Director: Tom Width
   Managing Director: Chip McCoull
Founded: 1965
Specialized Field: Musical; Comedy; Contemporary
Status: Non-Profit, Professional
Paid Staff: 3
Paid Artists: 25

3573
THEATER OF THE FIRST AMENDMENT

George Mason University
Mail Stop 3E6
Fairfax, VA 22030-4444
Phone: 703-993-2195
Fax: 703-993-2191
e-mail: rdavi4@gmu.edu
Web Site: www.theatreofthefirstadmendment.org
Management:
   Co-Artistic Director: Rick Davis
   Co-Artistic Director: Heather McDonald
   Managing Director: Kevin Murray
Mission: TFA's mission is to discover, develop and launch new, thought-provoking plays, and serve as an artistic home to next generation playwrights.
Utilizes: Actors; AEA Actors; Choreographers; Designers; Educators; Guest Conductors; Guest Designers; Guest Musical Directors; Instructors; Local Artists; Lyricists; Multi Collaborations; Multimedia; Music; Original Music Scores; Resident Professionals; Selected Students; Sign Language Translators; Soloists; Student Interns
Founded: 1990
Specialized Field: New Work
Status: Non-Profit, Professional
Paid Staff: 7
Paid Artists: 30
Budget: $250,000
Income Sources: George Mason University; Box Office

Season: September - April
Affiliations: AEA, SSDC, USA
Annual Attendance: 6,000
Type of Stage: Flexible
Stage Dimensions: 40' x 30'
Seating Capacity: 150
Year Built: 1975

3574
RIVERSIDE CENTER DINNER THEATER

95 Riverside Parkway
Fredericksburg, VA 22406
Phone: 540-370-4300
Fax: 540-370-4304
Toll-free: 888-999-8527
e-mail: riversided@aol.com
Web Site: www.riversidedt.com
Management:
   Music Director: Rollin Wehman
   Producer Assistant: Stephen R Hayes
   Artistic Director and General Manag: Rollin E Wehman
Mission: Presentation of Broadway musicals, children's theatre musicals, and education of youth and adults in all aspects of the performing arts, while providing an outlet for the diverse talents of area actors, musicians, and dancers.
Founded: 1998
Specialized Field: Musical; Children's Theater
Paid Staff: 12
Volunteer Staff: 8
Paid Artists: 35
Non-paid Artists: 6
Budget: $2.4 million
Income Sources: Group Sales; General Public; Bus-Tour Companies; Season Subscribers
Annual Attendance: 50,000
Type of Stage: Proscenium
Stage Dimensions: 35' x 30'
Year Built: 1998
Cost: $30 million

3575
LIME KILN ARTS

14 S Randolph Street
Lexington, VA 24450
Phone: 540-463-7088
Fax: 540-463-1082
e-mail: limekiln@cfw.com
Web Site: www.thetheatreatlimekiln.com
Officers:
   President: Paul Belo
Management:
   Executive Director: Jennifer Anderson
   Marketing Director: Alysia Graber
   Artistic Associate: Zach Hanks
   Artistic Director: John Heeley
   Touring Coordinator: Scott Fix
Mission: Promoting and preserving the traditions of the Southern Appalachian Mountains and exploring their myths as well as their potential.
Utilizes: Actors; AEA Actors; Artists-in-Residence; Choreographers; Designers; Guest Accompanists; Guest Designers; Guest Ensembles; Guest Instructors; Guest Lecturers; Guest Musical Directors; Guest Soloists; Guild Activities; Instructors; Local Artists; Multimedia; Music; Original Music Scores; Resident Artists; Resident Professionals; Sign Language Translators; Soloists; Student Interns
Founded: 1982
Specialized Field: Summer Stock; Musical; Ethnic Theater
Status: Professional; Nonprofit
Paid Staff: 6

Volunteer Staff: 100
Paid Artists: 50
Budget: $500,000
Income Sources: Private; earned; government
Season: May - September
Performs At: Lime Kiln Theater-Outdoor
Annual Attendance: 17,000
Facility Category: Theatre and Concert Venue
Type of Stage: Outdoor
Seating Capacity: 388; 700
Rental Contact: Jennifer D. Anderson
Organization Type: Performing; Touring; Resident; Educational; Sponsoring
Resident Groups: Artists-in-Residence

3576
THEATER AT LIME KILN

2 W Henry Street
Lexington, VA 24450
Phone: 540-463-7088
Fax: 540-463-1082
e-mail: limekiln@ntelos.net
Web Site: www.theateratlimekiln.com
Management:
   Artistic Director: John Healey
   Executive Director: Jennifer D Anderson
   Marketing Director: Gail Abbott
   Development Director: Cydney Davis
   Touring Coordinator: Ron Smith
Mission: To promote entertainment and education in the arts while exploring Appalachian traditions and culture.
Founded: 1983
Specialized Field: Summer Stock; Touring Company; Musical; Ethnic Theater
Status: AEA-LOA/Outdoor Drama; Professional; Nonprofit
Paid Staff: 5
Volunteer Staff: 100
Paid Artists: 50
Non-paid Artists: 4
Budget: $629,000
Income Sources: Private; Earned; Foundation; Government
Performs At: Lime Kiln Theater
Affiliations: AEA; Institute of Outdoor Drama
Annual Attendance: 17,000
Facility Category: Outdoor Theater and Concert Venue
Seating Capacity: 388; 700
Year Built: 1983
Rental Contact: Jennifer D Anderson

3577
SPENCERS: THEATER OF ILLUSION

PO Box 10396
Lynchburg, VA 24506
Phone: 434-384-4740
Fax: 434-384-8032
e-mail: booking@theatreofillusion.com
Web Site: www.theatreofillusion.com
Officers:
   President: Kevin Spencer
Management:
   Executive Director: Cindy Spencer
Founded: 1982
Specialized Field: Youth Theater; Drama; Classic
Status: For-Profit, Professional
Paid Staff: 4
Paid Artists: 2

3578
ALDEN THEATRE SERIES
1234 Ingleside Avenue
McLean, VA 22101-2817
Phone: 703-790-0123
Fax: 703-556-0547
e-mail: clare.kiley@fairfaxcounty.gov
Web Site: www.mcleancenter.org
Management:
Performing Dance Director: Clare Kiley
Utilizes: Actors; Choreographers; Dance Companies; Dancers; Designers; Grant Writers; Guest Accompanists; Guest Artists; Guest Conductors; Guest Designers; Guest Directors; Guest Ensembles; Guest Instructors; Guest Musical Directors; Guest Soloists; Instructors; Local Artists; Multimedia; Music; Original Music Scores; Resident Professionals; Sign Language Translators; Soloists; Student Interns; Special Technical Talent; Theatre Companies
Founded: 1975
Specialized Field: Musical; Comedy; Classic; Contemporary
Status: Non-Profit, Professional
Paid Staff: 20
Volunteer Staff: 30
Paid Artists: 35
Budget: $400,000
Type of Stage: Proscenium
Stage Dimensions: 28 x 35
Seating Capacity: 424
Year Built: 1975
Year Remodeled: 1988
Rental Contact: Performing Arts Director Clare Kiley

3579
WAYSIDE THEATRE
7853 Main Street
PO Box 260
Middletown, VA 22645
Phone: 540-869-1776
Fax: 540-869-1746
e-mail: info@waysidetheatre.org
Web Site: www.waysidetheatre.org
Management:
Artistic Director: Warner Rocker
Mission: Community based professional theatre which strives to enrich the lives of the people of our community through a broad spectrum of live professional theatre and performance opportunities that are entertaining, challenging, educational and accessible, and which effectively transmits that wonder to future generations.
Utilizes: Actors; AEA Actors; Choreographers; Collaborations; Grant Writers; Guest Artists; Guest Companies; Guest Designers; Guest Lecturers; Guild Activities; Local Artists; Music; Resident Professionals; Singers; Student Interns
Founded: 1961
Specialized Field: Musical; Comedy
Status: Non-Profit, Professional
Paid Staff: 5
Paid Artists: 26
Budget: $500,000
Income Sources: Ticket Sales; Corporate/Foundation Grants; Government Grants; Program Advertising, Concession Sales
Season: May - December
Affiliations: AEA
Annual Attendance: 15,000
Facility Category: Historic Proscenium
Type of Stage: Proscenium
Stage Dimensions: 24'x22'
Seating Capacity: 173

Year Built: 1942
Year Remodeled: 1962
Rental Contact: Artistic Director Warner Crocker
Organization Type: Performing; Touring; Resident

3580
2ND STORY THEATRE COMPANY
809 Brandon Avenue
Suite 210
Norfolk, VA 23517
Phone: 757-623-1776
Fax: 757-623-1777
e-mail: 2ndstory@brucehartmandesign.com
Web Site: www.brucehartmandesign.com
Management:
Co-Owner/Producer: Ethan Marten
Co-Owner/Producer: Richard Marten
Webmaster/Advertising Design: Bruce Hartman
Lighting Design: Yoni Charry
Stage Manager: Sheri Beyrau
Graphic/Web/Print Designer: Bruce Hartman
Mission: 2nd Story Theatre has functioned as a community resource encouraging the development and employment of local and regional talent, and activly fostering the performance of sister arts in Tidewater, Virginia. Committed to the concept of training and developing the talents of aspiring theatre professionals.
Specialized Field: Comedy

3581
GENERIC THEATER
912 W 21st Street
PO Box 11071
Norfolk, VA 23517
Phone: 757-441-2160
Fax: 757-441-2729
e-mail: generic@whro.net
Web Site: www.generictheater.lorg
Officers:
President: Patti Wray
Management:
Managing Director: Denise Dillard
Production Manager: Betty Xander
Mission: To produce innovative productions of contemporary works, new plays, and reinterpretations of the classics.
Utilizes: Actors; Community Talent; Designers; Guest Accompanists; Guest Conductors; Guest Designers; High School Drama; Local Artists; Original Music Scores; Performance Artists; Resident Professionals; Soloists; Student Interns
Founded: 1981
Specialized Field: Contemporary; Drama; Comedy
Paid Staff: 2
Paid Artists: 50
Non-paid Artists: 50
Budget: $100,000
Income Sources: Ticket Sales; State and Local Grant Organizations; Contributions
Performs At: Theater
Affiliations: Generic Theatre
Annual Attendance: 4,000 - 5,000
Facility Category: Black Box
Type of Stage: Proscenium
Stage Dimensions: 28'x56'
Seating Capacity: 80
Rental Contact: Artistic Director (757-441-2729) Steven Harders

3582
LITTLE THEATRE OF NORFOLK
801 Claremont Avenue
Norfolk, VA 23507

Phone: 804-627-8551
e-mail: itn@norfolk-little-theatre
Mission: To offer excellent amateur theatre and give non-professionals an opportunity to utilize their talents.
Founded: 1926
Specialized Field: Community Theater
Status: Nonprofit
Performs At: Little Theatre of Norfolk
Organization Type: Performing

3583
VIRGINIA STAGE COMPANY
254 Granby Street
PO Box 3770
Norfolk, VA 23514
Phone: 757-628-6988
Fax: 757-628-5958
e-mail: boxoffice@vastage.com
Web Site: www.vastage.com
Officers:
President: Philip Campbell
Secretary: Katherine Willis
Executive Director: Keith Stava
Management:
Marketing Director: Marilyn Johnson, mjohnson@vastage.com
Interim Managinng Director: Faye Bailey Timm
Box Office Manager: Lucy Armitstead, boxoffice@vastage.com
Assistant to Directors: Patricia Darden
Strategic Planning: Kerry Jahnou
Production Manager: Randy Foster
Production Management Aapprentice: Gretchen Schaefer
Company Manager: Kerry Jahn
Production Manager: Randy Foster
Mission: To develop and sustain a fully professional theatre serving Southeastern Virginia which enriches the region and the field through the production of theatrical art of the highest quality.
Utilizes: Artists-in-Residence; Community Talent; Guild Activities; Resident Companies; Singers; Students
Founded: 1980
Specialized Field: Musical; Comedy; Classic; Contemporary
Status: Non-Profit, Professional
Paid Staff: 22
Volunteer Staff: 50
Paid Artists: 22
Budget: $2 Million
Income Sources: Ticket Sales; Grants; Personal and Business Giving
Performs At: Wells Theatre
Affiliations: League Of Resident Theatres; Theatre Communication Group
Annual Attendance: 55,000
Facility Category: Theatre
Type of Stage: Proscenium; Hemp House
Stage Dimensions: 36'x36'
Seating Capacity: 677
Year Built: 1913
Year Remodeled: 1986
Rental Contact: Beth Spangler
Organization Type: Performing; Resident; Educational; Sponsoring

3584
ROADSIDE THEATER
PO Box 771
Norton, VA 24273
Phone: 276-679-3116
Fax: 276-679-3116
e-mail: roadsidetheater@verizon.net
Web Site: www.roadside.org

Management:
Director: Dudley Cocke
Specialized Field: Drama; Theater;

3585
LONG WAY HOME
PO Box 711
Radford, VA 24141
Phone: 540-639-0679
Fax: 540-731-8306
Management:
Technical Director: Al Shumate
Founded: 1971
Specialized Field: Historical; Outdoor Theater; Drama; Summer Stock; Storytelling
Status: Nonprofit
Season: June - August
Type of Stage: Amphitheatre, Open Stage
Seating Capacity: 500

3586
BARKSDALE THEATRE
1601 Willow Lawn Drive
Suite 301-E
Richmond, VA 23230
Phone: 804-282-2620
Fax: 804-288-6470
e-mail: development@barksdalerichmond.org
Web Site: www.barksdalerichmond.org
Management:
Managing Director: Phil Whiteway
Artistic Director: Bruce Miller
Director Development: Victoria McClure Mautinko
Box Office Manager: Pam Northrup
Mission: To produce diverse and outstanding contemporary plays to a growing regional audience.
Utilizes: Actors; AEA Actors; Choreographers; Collaborations; Dancers; Designers; Educators; Grant Writers; Guest Artists; Guest Companies; Guest Composers; Guest Conductors; Guest Designers; Guest Directors; Guest Ensembles; Guest Instructors; Guest Lecturers; Guest Musical Directors; Guest Soloists; Guest Teachers; Guild Activities; Instructors; Local Artists; Lyricists; Multimedia; Music; Organization Contracts; Original Music Scores; Performance Artists; Playwrights; Resident Professionals; Selected Students; Sign Language Translators; Singers; Soloists; Touring Companies; Visual Arts
Founded: 1953
Specialized Field: Musical
Status: Professional; Nonprofit
Paid Staff: 7
Volunteer Staff: 50
Budget: $750,000
Income Sources: Ticket Sales; Program Advertising; Charitable Contributions
Performs At: 214 Theatre-in-the-Round
Affiliations: TCG; Richmond Alliance of Professional Theatres
Annual Attendance: 30-40,000
Type of Stage: 3/4 Thrust
Seating Capacity: 190
Organization Type: Performing; Touring

3587
MYSTERY DINNER PLAYHOUSE
2025 E Main Street
Suite 206
Richmond, VA 23223
Phone: 804-649-2583
Fax: 804-649-7419
Toll-free: 888-471-4802
e-mail: info@mysterydinner.com
Web Site: www.mysterydinner.com

Management:
President: James Daab
Utilizes: Actors; Contract Actors; Local Artists; Local Artists & Directors; Organization Contracts; Original Music Scores; Performance Artists; Special Technical Talent
Founded: 1993
Specialized Field: Comedy; Dinner Theater
Status: For-Profit, Professional
Paid Staff: 7
Paid Artists: 24
Budget: $800,000
Income Sources: Ticket Sales
Performs At: Double Tree, Sheraton, Crowne Plaza, Clarrion Inn
Affiliations: RMA, WHMA, GWCTA, ACVA
Annual Attendance: 24,000
Facility Category: Hotel
Type of Stage: Promenade
Seating Capacity: 100; 150; 150
Organization Type: Commercial

3588
THEATRE IV
114 W Broad Street
Richmond, VA 23220
Phone: 804-783-1688
Fax: 804-775-2325
Toll-free: 800-235-8687
e-mail: ewilliams@theatreiv.org
Web Site: www.theatreiv.org
Management:
Managing Director: Philip Whiteway
Mission: To create exciting and innovative professional theatrical productions of high quality.
Utilizes: Guest Companies; Singers
Founded: 1975
Specialized Field: Youth Theater
Status: Non-Profit, Professional
Paid Staff: 40
Paid Artists: 100
Income Sources: Theatre Communications Group
Performs At: The Empire Theatre; The Little Theatre
Type of Stage: Proscenium; Flexible
Seating Capacity: 604; 84
Organization Type: Performing; Touring; Resident; Educational

3589
MILL MOUNTAIN THEATRE
One Market Square
Roanoke, VA 24011
Phone: 540-342-5730
Fax: 540-342-5745
Toll-free: 800-317-6455
e-mail: mmtmail@millmountain.org
Web Site: www.millmountain.org
Officers:
President: Howard Beck Jr
VP: John Jessee
Treasurer: John Light
Secretary: Ted Feinour
Management:
Producing Artistic Director: Jere Lee Hodgin
General Manager: Mary C Knapp
Director Development: John Levin
Youth Ensemble Director: David Dvorscak
General Manager: Mary Knapp
Director Finance: Jim Ayers
Director Audience Services: Dick Vipperman
Group Sales Coordinator: John Whitney
Production Manager: Doug Flinchum

Mission: Professional production of musicals, dramas and comedies with particular emphasis on the production and development of original works.
Utilizes: Actors; AEA Actors; Artists-in-Residence; Choreographers; Collaborating Artists; Collaborations; Commissioned Composers; Dancers; Designers; Grant Writers; Guest Accompanists; Guest Artists; Guest Companies; Guest Composers; Guest Conductors; Guest Designers; Guest Instructors; Guest Lecturers; Guest Soloists; Guild Activities; High School Drama; Local Artists; Multimedia; Organization Contracts; Original Music Scores; Performance Artists; Poets; Resident Professionals; Sign Language Translators; Soloists; Student Interns
Founded: 1964
Specialized Field: Musical
Status: Professional; Nonprofit
Paid Staff: 35
Volunteer Staff: 300
Budget: $2,000,000
Income Sources: Box Office Sales; Private & Public Support
Season: October - August
Performs At: Mill Mountain Theatre; Trinkle Main Stage; Waldron Stage
Affiliations: Theatre Communications Group; Southeastern Theatre Conference; Society for Stage Directors and Choreographers; Actors Equity
Annual Attendance: 60,000
Facility Category: Performing; Touring
Type of Stage: Proscenium; Black Box
Stage Dimensions: 44'x34'; 15'x20'
Seating Capacity: 400; 110
Year Built: 1983
Rental Contact: Doug Flinchum
Organization Type: Performing; Resident; Educational

3590
SHENANDOAH SHAKESPEARE
13 W Beverley Street
4th Floor
Staunton, VA 24401
Phone: 540-885-5588
Fax: 540-885-4886
Toll-free: 877-682-4236
e-mail: shsh@shenandoahshakespeare
Web Site: www.americanshakespearecenter.com
Management:
Executive Director: Ralph Alan Cohen
Artistic Director: Jim Warren
Managing Director: Sandie Nelson
Director Development: Martha P Farmer
Director Tour Operations: Bill Gordon
Director Community Relations: Susan Hawthorne
Managing Director: Sandie Nelson
Mission: Shenandoah shakespeare through its performances, its theatres, its exhibitions, and its educational programs, seeks to make Shakespeare, the joys of theatre and language, and the communal experience of the Renaissance stage accessible to all.
Utilizes: Actors
Founded: 1988
Specialized Field: Shakespeare
Status: Non-Profit,Professional
Income Sources: Sponsors; Donor

3591
BABCOCK SEASON
Box AU
Sweet Briar College
Sweet Briar, VA 24595

Phone: 804-381-6100
Fax: 804-381-6263
e-mail: Wittman@sbc.edu
Web Site: www.theatre.sbc.edu
Management:
Babcock Theatre Manager: Loretta Wittman
Utilizes: Actors; Artists-in-Residence; Choreographers; Collaborating Artists; Collaborations; Dance Companies; Dancers; Educators; Fine Artists; Grant Writers; Guest Accompanists; Guest Artists; Guest Choreographers; Guest Instructors; Guest Musical Directors; Guest Soloists; Guild Activities; High School Drama; Local Artists; Multimedia; Music; Organization Contracts; Original Music Scores; Performance Artists; Poets; Resident Professionals; Sign Language Translators; Soloists; Special Technical Talent; Theatre Companies
Specialized Field: Educational; Theater Workshops
Budget: $39,000
Income Sources: College Budget, Grants
Performs At: Babcock Auditorium
Affiliations: Association of Performing Arts Presenters; Virginia Arts Presenters
Annual Attendance: 5,000
Facility Category: General Purpose Theatre
Type of Stage: Proscenium
Seating Capacity: 652
Year Built: 1962

3592
VIRGINIA MUSICAL THEATRE

228 N Lynnhaven Road
Suite 114
Virginia Beach, VA 23452-7514
Phone: 757-340-5446
Fax: 757-340-5398
e-mail: vmtheatre@verizon.net
Web Site: www.vmtheatre.org
Management:
Managing Director: Mark Hudgins
Executive Director: Jeff Meredith
Mission: Preservation of musical theatre as a uniquely american art form
Founded: 1991
Specialized Field: Musical
Status: Non-Profit, Professional
Paid Staff: 4
Volunteer Staff: 10
Paid Artists: 300
Budget: $1 million
Income Sources: Ticket Sales; Fundraising
Season: October - July
Performs At: Performing Arts Center
Affiliations: AEA; SSD&C
Annual Attendance: 40,000
Type of Stage: Proscenium
Stage Dimensions: 50' x 35'
Seating Capacity: 1,300
Year Built: 2006
Cost: $53 Million

3593
VIRGINIA SHAKESPEARE FESTIVAL

College of William and Mary
PO Box 8795
Williamsburg, VA 23187
Phone: 757-221-2683
Fax: 757-221-2636
e-mail: clowen@wm.edu
Web Site: www.vsf.wm.edu
Management:
Producing Artistic Director: Christopher Owens

Mission: To produce professional classic theatre for Tidewater region of Virginia and provide educational opportunities for young people to learn more about the works of William Shakespeare and his contemporaries.
Utilizes: Singers
Founded: 1978
Specialized Field: Shakespeare
Status: Professional; Nonprofit
Paid Staff: 6
Volunteer Staff: 2
Paid Artists: 40
Budget: $300,000
Income Sources: 65% Earned; 35% Contributions
Season: July - August
Affiliations: AEA Guest Artist
Annual Attendance: 9,000
Type of Stage: Proscenium, Sprung, Traps
Stage Dimensions: 36' x 36'
Seating Capacity: 600
Year Built: 1957
Organization Type: Performing; Educational

Washington

3594
BAINBRIDGE PERFORMING ARTS

200 Madison Avenue N
Bainbridge Island, WA 98110
Phone: 206-842-4560
Fax: 206-842-0195
e-mail: dcantwell@bainbridgeperformingarts.org
Web Site: http://www.bainbridgeperformingarts.org
Management:
Managing Director: Domonique Cantwell
Artistic Director: Steven Fogell
Director of Operations: Kim Failla
Specialized Field: Musical; Drama; Comedy

3595
MBT STUDIO THEATRE

104 N Commercial Street
Bellingham, WA 98225
Phone: 360-733-5793
Fax: 360-671-0114
e-mail: Bauer@Mountbakertheatre.Com
Web Site: www.mountbakertheatre.com
Management:
Executive Director: Brad Burdick
Associate Artistic Director: Amy Martin
Technical Director: John Bauer
Deputy Director: Kim Laskey
Mission: Dedicated to showcasing some of the best live performing artists on both the professional and community levels for audiences in the North Puget Sound area and the Lower Mainland of British Columbia.
Founded: 1983
Specialized Field: Jazz, Cabaret, Small Theatre Acts, Chamber Ensembles
Status: Non-Profit, Professional
Paid Staff: 20
Type of Stage: Black Box
Seating Capacity: 140-200

3596
MOUNT BAKER THEATRE

104 N Commercial Street
Bellingham, WA 98225
Phone: 360-733-5793
e-mail: cindi@mountbakertheatre.Com
Web Site: www.mountbakertheatre.com
Management:
Executive Director: Brad Burdick

Technical Director: John Bauer
Exec Asst/Volunteer Coordinator: Cindi Pree
Mission: To provide arts, entertainment, and social interaction which through a wide variety of programs, results in personal enrichment, enjoyment and a sense of community for diverse audiences in the region; and to preserve the restored historic Mount Baker Theatre as a home for local performing arts organizations, film, a venue for touring performers and community events.
Founded: 1983
Specialized Field: Musical; Comedy
Status: Non-Profit, Professional
Paid Staff: 19
Volunteer Staff: 275
Facility Category: Performing Arts
Type of Stage: Proscenium
Stage Dimensions: 45'x26'
Orchestra Pit: y
Seating Capacity: 1,509
Year Built: 1927
Year Remodeled: 1995
Cost: $1.6 million

3597
WWU SUMMER STOCK

MS-9108
Bellingham, WA 98225
Phone: 360-650-3876
Fax: 360-650-3028
e-mail: theatre@cc.wwu.edu
Web Site: www.as.wwu.edu
Management:
Artistic Director: Mark Kuntz
Specialized Field: Musical; Comedy; Classic; Contemporary
Status: For-Profit, Non-Professional
Paid Staff: 20
Paid Artists: 10
Season: Jule - August

3598
ADMIRAL THEATRE FOUNDATION

515 Pacific Avenue
Bremerton, WA 98337
Phone: 360-373-6810
Fax: 360-405-0673
e-mail: admiraltheatre@msn.com
Web Site: www.admiraltheatre.org
Management:
Executive Director: Ruth Enderle
Business Manager: Brian Johnson
Technical Director: Jeff Vaughan
Music/Box Office Manager: Tim Walbel
Specialized Field: Drama; Musical
Paid Staff: 5

3599
BERMERTON COMMUNITY THEATRE

599 Lebo Boulevard
Bremerton, WA 98310
Phone: 360-373-5152
Fax: 360-373-6754
Toll-free: 800-863-1706
e-mail: sgoupil@hotmail.com
Web Site: http://www.bremertoncommunitytheatre.org/
Officers:
President: Steve Goupil
Vice President: Judy Nichols
Treasurer: Becky Lorber
Secretary: Don Bidwell
Management:
Technical: Kevin Matthew
Production Manager: Adam Matthew

Mission: Production of amateur dramas, comedies, mysteries and musicals for the local community.
Utilizes: Guest Artists; Guest Companies; Singers
Founded: 1945
Specialized Field: Musical; Community Theater
Status: Non-Professional; Nonprofit
Volunteer Staff: 12
Non-paid Artists: 100
Organization Type: Performing

3600
EVERETT THEATRE

2911 Colby
Everett, WA 98201
Mailing Address: PO Box 12 Everett, WA 98206
Phone: 425-258-6766
Fax: 425-257-0620
e-mail: boxoffice@everetttheatre.org
Web Site: www.everetttheatre.org
Officers:
President: Randy Mather
Finance: Terry Klett
Artistic Director: Victoria Walker
Founded: 1901
Specialized Field: Musical; Comedy; Classic; Contemporary
Status: Non-Profit, Professional
Paid Staff: 3

3601
VILLAGE THEATRE

2710 Wetmore Avenue
Everett, WA 98201
Phone: 425-257-6363
Fax: 425-257-6393
e-mail: feedback@villagetheatre.org
Web Site: www.villagetheatre.org
Management:
President of the Board: Gary Tomlison
Executive Producer: Robb Hunt
Artistic Director: Steve Tomkins
General Manager: Keith Daahgren
Mission: The mission of Village Theatre is to be a regionally recognized and nationally influenced center of excelent in family theatre.
Founded: 1979
Specialized Field: Musical; Educational
Status: Non-Profit, Professional
Paid Staff: 50
Paid Artists: 150
Budget: $6.1 million
Performs At: Francis J Gaudette Theatre; Everett Performing Arts Center

3602
KNUTZEN FAMILY THEATRE - CITY OF FEDERAL WAY

3200 SW Dash Point Road
Federal Way, WA 98023
Phone: 253-835-2025
Fax: 253-835-2010
e-mail: johng@fedway.org
Web Site: www.knutzenfamilytheatre.com
Management:
Coordinator of Facilities: John Gamache
Founded: 1998
Specialized Field: Youth Theater; Drama; Classic
Status: Non-Profit, Non-Professional
Paid Staff: 2

3603
SAN JUAN COMMUNITY THEATRE AND ARTS CENTER

100 Second Street
PO Box 1063
Friday Harbor, WA 98250
Phone: 360-378-3211
Fax: 360-378-2398
e-mail: sjarts@rockisland.com
Web Site: www.sanjuanarts.org
Officers:
President: David Bayley
Management:
President: Pam Nichols
Executive Director: Merritt Olsen
Mission: To maintain a center for visual and performing arts for the residents of the island.
Founded: 1989
Specialized Field: Community Theater
Status: Non-Professional; Nonprofit
Paid Staff: 6
Volunteer Staff: 350
Organization Type: Performing; Educational; Sponsoring

3604
PARADISE THEATRE

9916 Peacock Hill Avenue
PO Box 4
Gig Harbor, WA 98335
Phone: 253-851-7529
Fax: 253-851-7503
e-mail: vrichards@paradisetheatre.org
Web Site: www.paradisetheatre.org
Officers:
President: Bob Flynn
Treasurer: Lynn Bromley
Secretary: Gus Berry
Management:
Artistic Director: Jeff Richards
Mission: To promote theatre arts and cultural enrichment through performances as well as educational workshops and classes.
Utilizes: Singers
Founded: 2000
Specialized Field: Musical
Status: Semi-Professional; Nonprofit
Paid Staff: 4
Volunteer Staff: 15
Paid Artists: 16
Non-paid Artists: 15
Income Sources: Grants; Individual Donations; Ticket Sales
Performs At: Paradise Theatre
Type of Stage: Proscenium
Seating Capacity: 50 indoor; 800 outdoor
Year Built: 1900
Year Remodeled: 2000
Organization Type: Performing; Touring; Educational

3605
VILLAGE THEATRE

303 Front Street N
Issaquah, WA 98027
Phone: 425-392-2202
Fax: 425-391-3242
e-mail: boxoffice@villagetheatre.org
Web Site: www.villagetheatre.org
Mission: The mission of Village Theatre is to be a regionally recognized and nationally influenced center of excelent in family theatre.
Founded: 1979
Specialized Field: Musical

Budget: $6.1 million
Performs At: Francis J Gaudette Theatre; Everett Performing Arts Center
Facility Category: Theatre

3606
COLUMBIA THEATRE FOR THE PERFORMING ARTS

1231 Vandercook Way
Longview, WA 98632-4001
Phone: 360-423-1011
Fax: 360-423-8626
Toll-free: 888-575-8499
e-mail: info@columbiatheatre.com
Web Site: www.columbiatheatre.com
Management:
President: John Landau
Executive Director: Dan Mankin
Technical Director: Kelly Ragsdale
Mission: To provide engaging theatre experience of the highest quality that we always strive to uplift and entertain; to instill in audience and theatre members the value of our integrity as a source of inspiration and hope.
Founded: 1981
Specialized Field: Musical; Community Theater
Status: Non-Profit, Professional
Paid Staff: 10
Annual Attendance: 60,000
Facility Category: Performing Arts Center
Type of Stage: Proscenium
Seating Capacity: 1,000
Year Built: 1925
Organization Type: Performing; Sponsoring

3607
CUTTER THEATRE

PO Box 133
Metaline Falls, WA 99153-0133
Phone: 509-446-4108
Fax: 509-446-3037
e-mail: cutter@potc.net
Web Site: www.cuttertheatre.com
Officers:
President: Erin Kinney
Executive Director: Jennifer Snead
Founded: 1982
Specialized Field: Musical; Comedy; Classic; Contemporary
Status: Non-Profit, Non-Professional
Paid Staff: 2
Budget: $93,000
Seating Capacity: 156

3608
HARLEQUIN PRODUCTIONS

State Theater
202 4th Avenue E
Olympia, WA 98501
Phone: 360-786-0151
Fax: 360-534-9659
e-mail: linda@harlequinproductions.org
Web Site: www.harlequinproductions.org
Management:
Managing Artistic Director: Scot Whitney
Artistic Director: Linda Whitney
Production Manager: Jill Carter
Development Director: Trudy Soucoup
Mission: A nonprofit theater founded with the goal of producing a more challenging style of theater than what was already available in the community.
Founded: 1991
Specialized Field: Musical; Comedy; Contemporary
Status: Non-Profit, Professional

Paid Staff: 8
Season: May - December
Type of Stage: Thrust
Stage Dimensions: 48'6" x 32'
Seating Capacity: 218

3609
BEASLEY PERFORMING ARTS COLISEUM

PO Box 641710
Pullman, WA 99146-1710
Phone: 509-335-2241
Fax: 509-335-3853
e-mail: udy@wsu.edu
Web Site: www.beasley.wsu.edu
Management:
 President: Leo Udy
Founded: 1972
Specialized Field: Musical; Comedy; Classic; Contemporary
Status: Non-Profit, Professional
Paid Staff: 6

3610
PULLMAN SUMMER PALACE

Theatre Program
Washington State University
Pullman, WA 99164-2432
Phone: 509-335-5682
Fax: 509-335-7447
e-mail: caldwell@wsu.edu
Web Site: libarts.wsu.edu/musicandtheatre
Management:
 Managing Director: George Caldwell
Founded: 1977
Specialized Field: Educational; Theater Workshops
Status: Non-Equity; Nonprofit
Season: July - August
Type of Stage: Proscenium
Stage Dimensions: 45' x 45'
Seating Capacity: 460

3611
ACT THEATRE

Kreielsheimer Place
700 Union Street
Seattle, WA 98101-4037
Phone: 206-292-7660
Fax: 206-292-7670
e-mail: act@acttheatre.org
Web Site: www.acttheatre.org
Officers:
 Chairman: John Siegler
Management:
 Managing Director: Susan Trapnell
 Producing Director: Joan Toggenburger
 Artistic Director: Kurt Beattie
 Communications Director: Karen L Bystrom
Mission: To offer the best in contemporary theater.
Utilizes: Guest Companies; Singers
Founded: 1965
Specialized Field: Contemporary
Status: Professional; Nonprofit
Paid Staff: 75
Paid Artists: 170
Budget: 5,500,000
Income Sources: Actors' Equity Association; League of Resident Theatres; American Arts Alliance; Washington State Arts Alliance
Season: March - December
Performs At: A Contemporary Theatre
Annual Attendance: 125,000
Facility Category: 4 Venue Performance Facility
Type of Stage: 3/4 Thrust; Arena; Caberat

Year Built: 1925
Year Remodeled: 1996
Rental Contact: Kristina Wicke
Organization Type: Resident

3612
BATHHOUSE THEATRE

7312 W Greenlake Drive N
Seattle, WA 98103
Phone: 206-524-1300
Fax: 206-527-1942
e-mail: boxoffice@seattlepublictheater.org
Web Site: http://www.seattlepublictheater.org
Officers:
 President: Steve McCarthy
 Vice President: Chris Auty
 Treasurer: Rebecca Wakefield
 Secretary: Wendy Woolery
Management:
 Artistic Director: Shana Bestock
 Managing Director: Keith Dahlgren
Mission: To develop our full potential as a resident theatre company; to put excellent theatre within reach of the widest possible audience.
Utilizes: Guest Companies
Founded: 1970
Specialized Field: Contemporary
Status: Professional; Nonprofit
Income Sources: Theatre Communications Group; Actors' Equity Association; Small Professional Theatre Association
Performs At: Bathhouse Theatre
Organization Type: Performing; Touring; Resident

3613
EMPTY SPACE THEATRE

901 12th Avenue
PO Box 222000
Seattle, WA 98122-1090
Phone: 206-547-7500
Fax: 206-547-7635
e-mail: emptyspace@emptyspace.org
Web Site: www.emptyspace.org
Officers:
 Chair: Erik Blachford
Management:
 Managing Director: Melanie Mathews
 Artistic Director: Allison Narver
 Artisitc Associate: Shiela Daniels
 Marketing/Development Director: Christine Kolodge
Mission: Strives to make theater an event - bold, provocative, celebratory - bringing audiences and artists to a common ground through an uncommon experience.
Utilizes: Actors; AEA Actors; Artists-in-Residence; Designers; Five Seasonal Concerts; Guest Accompanists; Guest Conductors; Guest Designers; Guest Lecturers; Instructors; Local Artists; Original Music Scores; Performance Artists; Poets; Resident Professionals
Founded: 1971
Specialized Field: Musical
Status: Non-Profit
Paid Staff: 6
Volunteer Staff: 80
Paid Artists: 30
Non-paid Artists: 3
Budget: $600,000
Income Sources: Ticket Sales; Donations; Grants
Affiliations: TCG, TPS, AEA
Annual Attendance: 10,000
Facility Category: Theater
Type of Stage: Flexible Black Box

Seating Capacity: 150
Year Built: 1940
Year Remodeled: 2006
Cost: $7 million
Rental Contact: 206-296-5360 Steve Galato
Organization Type: Performing; Resident; Educational

3614
INTIMAN THEATRE COMPANY

201 Mercer Street, Seattle Center
PO Box 19760
Seattle, WA 98109
Phone: 206-269-1901
Fax: 206-269-1928
e-mail: scripts@intiman.org
Web Site: www.intiman.org
Management:
 General Manager: Rebecca Sherr
 Artistic Director: Bartlett Sher
 Managing Director: Laura Pann
 Community Programs Manager: Liza Comtois
 Managing Director: Laura Penn
 General Manager: Art Bridenstine
 Associate Managing Director: Rebecca Sherr
 Assistant/Managing Director: Precious Butiu
 Production Manager: David A Mulligan
Mission: To produce engaging dramatic work that celebrates the intimate relationship among audience and language and, through the exploration of enduring themes, illuminates the shared human experience of our diverse community.
Founded: 1972
Specialized Field: Drama; New Works of Social Importance
Season: May - December
Performs At: Intiman Playhouse
Type of Stage: Modified Thrust
Seating Capacity: 480
Year Remodeled: 1987
Cost: $1,200,000

3615
NEW CITY THEATER

1703 13th Avenue
Seattle, WA 98122
Phone: 206-328-4683
Fax: 206-328-4683
Management:
 Artistic Director: John Kazanjian
 Theater Manager: Alan Horton
Mission: Dedicated to research and development in the contemporary arts.
Utilizes: Guest Companies
Founded: 1982
Specialized Field: Contemporary
Status: Professional; Nonprofit
Income Sources: Theatre Communications Group
Performs At: The New City Theatre
Organization Type: Performing; Resident

3616
NORTHWEST PUPPET

9123 15th Avenue NE
Seattle, WA 98103
Phone: 206-523-2579
Fax: 206-783-0851
e-mail: info@nwpup.org
Web Site: www.nwpuppet.org
Management:
 Executive Co-Director: Stephen Carter
 Executive Co-Director: Chris Carter

Mission: To create professional puppet theater; to present top quality puppet theater; to teach puppet skills and cultural knowledge; to serve children and adults by providing entertainment and education.
Founded: 1985
Specialized Field: Puppet
Status: Professional; Nonprofit
Paid Staff: 2
Income Sources: Puppeteers of America; United International Marionette Association
Organization Type: Performing; Touring; Resident; Educational; Sponsoring

3617
SEATTLE CHILDREN'S THEATRE
201 Thomas Street
Seattle, WA 98109
Phone: 206-443-0807
Fax: 206-443-0442
e-mail: sctpr@sct.org
Web Site: www.sct.org
Officers:
    President: Lauie Oki
    First VP: Richard Bendix
    Second VP: Judy Bunnell
    Secretary: Marty Chilberg
Management:
    Artistic Director: Linda Hartzell
    Managing Director: Kevin Maifeld
    Public Relations: Taryn Essinger
    Public Relations: Taryn Essinger
Mission: To produce professional theater for the young with appeal to people of all ages; to provide theater education and theater arts training; to develop scripts and musical scores for new theater works.
Founded: 1975
Specialized Field: Children's Theater; Drama
Status: Non-Profit, Professional
Budget: $5,300,000
Performs At: Charlotte Martin Theatre; Eve Alvovd Theatre
Affiliations: ASSITES/USA; Actors' Equity Association/TYA; American Association of Theatre Educators; International Alliance of Theatrical Stage Employees; TCG
Annual Attendance: 250,000
Seating Capacity: 480; 285
Year Built: 1993
Rental Contact: General Manager Shelley Sanders
Organization Type: Performing; Touring; Resident; Educational

3618
SEATTLE MIME THEATRE
915 E Pine Street
Suite 419
Seattle, WA 98122
Phone: 206-324-8788
Fax: 206-322-5569
e-mail: admin@seattlemime.org
Web Site: www.seattlemime.org
Management:
    President: Richard Davidson
    Managing Director: Hal Ryder
    Artistic Director: Bruce Wylie
Mission: Dedicated to enlivening the imaginations of minds and bodies of people of all ages with its unique form of physical theater through the interlaced processes of creation, teaching and performances.
Utilizes: Actors; Artists-in-Residence; Choreographers; Collaborating Artists; Collaborations; Community Talent; Contract Actors; Dance Companies; Dancers; Educators; Guest Artists; Guest Companies; Guest

Designers; Instructors; Local Artists; Lyricists; Multi Collaborations; Performance Artists; Selected Students; Soloists; Theatre Companies
Founded: 1977
Specialized Field: Comedy; Contemporary
Status: Non-Profit, Professional
Paid Staff: 3
Paid Artists: 3
Facility Category: Offices and Theater
Type of Stage: Black Box
Stage Dimensions: 55'x40'
Seating Capacity: 49
Rental Contact: Richard Davidson
Organization Type: Performing; Touring; Educational

3619
SEATTLE REPERTORY THEATRE
155 Mercer Street
PO Box 900923
Seattle, WA 98109-9982
Phone: 206-443-2222
Fax: 206-443-2379
Toll-free: 877-900-9285
e-mail: info@seattlerep.org
Web Site: www.seattlerep.org
Management:
    Artistic Director: Sharon Ott
    Managing Director: Ben Moore
Mission: To offer professional live theatre and education for residents of the Pacific Northwest.
Utilizes: Actors; AEA Actors; Choreographers; Commissioned Composers; Commissioned Music; Designers; Five Seasonal Concerts; Guest Accompanists; Guest Artists; Guest Companies; Guest Conductors; Guest Designers; Guest Lecturers; Guest Musical Directors; Guest Soloists; Guest Teachers; High School Drama; Local Artists; Multimedia; Music; Original Music Scores; Performance Artists; Resident Professionals; Selected Students; Singers; Student Interns
Founded: 1963
Specialized Field: Musical; Comedy; Classic; Contemporary
Status: Non-Profit, Professional
Paid Staff: 150
Income Sources: Actors' Equity Association; League of Resident Theatres
Performs At: Bagley Wright Theatre
Facility Category: Theatre
Type of Stage: Proscenium
Seating Capacity: 856 and 286
Year Built: 1983
Year Remodeled: 1996
Rental Contact: Ten Eyck Swackharner
Organization Type: Performing; Resident

3620
TAPROOT THEATRE COMPANY
204 N 85th Street
PO Box 30946
Seattle, WA 98103
Phone: 206-781-9707
Fax: 206-297-6882
e-mail: info@taproottheatre.org
Web Site: www.taproottheatre.org
Officers:
    President: Scott Nolte
    Treasurer: Gary Massingill
    Chairman: Dr. George Scranton
    Vice Chairman: George Meyers
    Immediate Past Chairman: Dennis McCurley
    Secretary: Carolyn Hanson
Management:
    Artistic Director: Scott Nolte

Associate Artistic Director: Karen Lund
Mission: Taproot Theatre exists to create theatre that explores the beauty and questions of life while providing hope to our search for meaning.
Utilizes: Actors; AEA Actors; Designers; Guest Accompanists; Guest Artists; Guest Companies; Guest Conductors; High School Drama; Local Artists; Multimedia; Organization Contracts; Original Music Scores; Resident Artists; Resident Professionals; Sign Language Translators
Founded: 1976
Specialized Field: Classic
Status: Non-Profit, Professional
Paid Staff: 24
Volunteer Staff: 285
Paid Artists: 98
Affiliations: TCG; CITA; Greenwood Chamber of Commerce
Annual Attendance: 85,000
Facility Category: Renovated historic cinema
Type of Stage: Thrust
Stage Dimensions: 15'x22'
Seating Capacity: 226
Year Built: 1915
Year Remodeled: 1996
Rental Contact: Anne Hitt
Organization Type: Performing; Touring; Resident

3621
THEATER SCHMEATER
1500 Summit Avenue
Seattle, WA 98102
Phone: 206-324-5801
Web Site: http://www.schmeater.org/index.php
Officers:
    President: Mikki Kunz
    Vice President: Tiffany Pokorny
    Secretary: Andrew Bishop
Management:
    Artistic Director: J.D. Lloyd
    Managing Director: Teri Lazzara
    Production Manager: Miranda Pratt
Specialized Field: Classic; Contemporary

3622
INTERPLAYERS ENSEMBLE THEATRE
174 S Howard Street
Spokane, WA 99201
Phone: 509-455-7529
e-mail: info@interplayers.com
Web Site: www.Interplayers.com
Officers:
    Board Chairman: William Thompson
    Vice Chairman: Steve Chapman
    Business Manager: Esta Rosevear
    Secretary: Joan Parker
Mission: Serving Spokane with challenging, diverse and inspiring productions, Interplayers is a major contributor to the Inland Northwest cultural quality of life. A professional theatre listed on the National Register of Historic Places and the Washington State Historic Register, Interplayers is pivotal to the economic revitalization of downtown Spokane.
Founded: 1980
Specialized Field: Ensembles
Paid Staff: 8

3623
SPOKANE CIVIC THEATRE
1020 Howard
PO Box 5222
Spokane, WA 99205

Phone: 509-325-1413
Fax: 509-325-9287
Toll-free: 800-446-9576
e-mail: civictheatre@mindspring.com
Web Site: www.spokanecivictheatre.com
Management:
President: Denny Lordan
Artistic Director: Jack Delehanty
Managing Director: Debra McDandless
Office Administrator: Shirley Deranleau
Technical Director: Peter Hardie
Mission: To offer opportunities for participation in the art of theatre; to promote new plays.
Utilizes: Actors; Artists-in-Residence; Choreographers; Collaborations; Dancers; Designers; Fine Artists; Five Seasonal Concerts; Grant Writers; Guest Accompanists; Guest Artists; Guest Designers; Guest Ensembles; Guest Lecturers; Guest Teachers; Guild Activities; Local Artists; Multimedia; Music; Organization Contracts; Original Music Scores; Performance Artists; Selected Students; Sign Language Translators; Singers; Student Interns; Touring Companies
Founded: 1947
Specialized Field: Community Theater
Status: Non-Profit, Non-Professional
Paid Staff: 7
Budget: $625,000
Income Sources: Washington State Arts Commission; Allen Foundation; Box Office
Performs At: Spokane Civic Theatres
Affiliations: American Association of Community Theatres; WA Arts Alliance; TCG
Annual Attendance: 35,000
Facility Category: Theatre
Type of Stage: Proscenium; Black Box
Seating Capacity: 339; 100
Year Built: 1966
Year Remodeled: 1999
Rental Contact: Jack Phillips
Organization Type: Performing; Educational

3624
SPOKANE INTERPLAYERS ENSEMBLE
174 S Howard Street
Spokane, WA 99204
Phone: 509-455-7529
Fax: 509-624-9348
e-mail: info@interplayers.com
Web Site: www.interplayers.com
Management:
Executive Director: Ron Wasson
Artistic Director: Nicke Imoru
Marketing and Development: Grant Smith
Production Manager: Jason Lewis
Box Office Manager: Jennifer Laws
Mission: To maintain a resident non-profit, professional theatre company offering an annual season ranging from contemporary and classic to original works.
Utilizes: Actors; Collaborations; Designers; Fine Artists; Guest Companies; Guest Conductors; Guest Designers; High School Drama; Instructors; Local Artists; Original Music Scores; Performance Artists; Resident Professionals; Student Interns
Founded: 1980
Specialized Field: Musical; Comedy; Contemporary; Ensembles
Status: Non-Profit, Professional
Paid Staff: 14
Volunteer Staff: 150
Paid Artists: 100
Budget: $485,000
Income Sources: Ticket Sales; Grants
Performs At: Spokane Interplayers Ensemble Theatre
Affiliations: Theatre Communications Group

Annual Attendance: 25,000
Type of Stage: Thrust
Seating Capacity: 253
Year Built: 1926
Year Remodeled: 1980
Organization Type: Performing; Resident; Educational

3625
TACOMA ACTORS GUILD
901 Broadway
Suite 600
Tacoma, WA 98402
Phone: 253-272-3107
Fax: 253-272-3358
Management:
General Manager: Chris Shelton
Artistic Director: Pat Petttan
Mission: To offer quality theatre and to entertain and enrich the South Puget Sound area.
Utilizes: Actors; AEA Actors; Choreographers; Educators; Guest Companies; Guest Designers; Guest Lecturers; Guest Musical Directors; Multimedia; Music; Original Music Scores; Resident Professionals; Student Interns; Visual Arts
Founded: 1978
Specialized Field: Drama; Theater Workshops
Status: Professional; Nonprofit
Income Sources: Theatre Communications Group
Performs At: Tacoma Actors Guild
Annual Attendance: 35,000
Seating Capacity: 302
Year Built: 1998
Cost: $8,000,000
Organization Type: Performing; Resident

3626
SLOCUM HOUSE THEATRE COMPANY
605 Esther Street
Vancouver, WA 98660
Phone: 360-696-2427
e-mail: info@slocumhouse.com
Web Site: www.slocumhouse.com
Officers:
President: Tony Bump
VP: Jim Fully
Treasurer: Steve Herron
Secretary: Beth Duvall
Mission: The restoration of the Slocum House Theatre and the production of 19th-century plays.
Founded: 1966
Specialized Field: Musical; Community Theater
Status: Non-Profit
Organization Type: Resident

3627
COLUMBIA GORGE REPERTORY THEATRE
1381 Snowden Road
White Salmon, WA 98672
Phone: 503-255-7186
Fax: 509-493-1501
Toll-free: 800-405-3450
e-mail: cgrep@aol.com
Web Site: www.cgrep.com
Management:
Artistic Director: Jesse Merz
Executive Director: Jan James
Dance Director: Jennifer Seigle
Founded: 1996
Specialized Field: Summer Stock; New Plays
Status: Non-Equity; Commercial
Season: June - September
Type of Stage: Proscenium
Stage Dimensions: 30' x 40'

Seating Capacity: 150

West Virginia

3628
THEATRE WEST VIRGINIA
PO Box 1205
Beckley, WV 25802
Phone: 304-256-6800
Fax: 304-256-6807
Toll-free: 800-666-9142
e-mail: contact@theatrewestvirginia.com
Web Site: www.theatrewestvirginia.com
Officers:
President: John Rist
VP: Alice Cox
Secretary: Colleen McCalhoah
Treasurer: Brad Wartella
Marketing Director: Lola Rizer
Management:
General Manager: Gayle Bowling
Executive Director: Marina Hunley
Mission: To provide theatre of the highest quality to community and state residents as well as tourists.
Utilizes: Actors; Choreographers; Dancers; Designers; Local Artists; Music; Original Music Scores; Resident Professionals; Sign Language Translators; Soloists; Student Interns
Founded: 1961
Specialized Field: Touring Company; Marionettes; Educational
Status: Non-Profit, Professional
Paid Staff: 60
Paid Artists: 70
Season: June - August
Annual Attendance: 120,000
Facility Category: Amphitheatre; Touring
Stage Dimensions: 60'x60'
Seating Capacity: 1,259
Year Built: 1960
Year Remodeled: 1991
Organization Type: Performing; Touring; Educational; Sponsoring

3629
KANAWHA PLAYERS
5315 Maccorkle Avenue
PO Box 4575
Charleston, WV 25304
Phone: 304-925-5051
e-mail: kplayersdirector@aol.com
Web Site: www.kanawhaplayers.org
Officers:
President: Stephen E Kawash
Management:
President: Tina Vance
Artistic Director: Jeff Haught
Historian: Jimmy Stann
Utilizes: Singers
Founded: 1922
Specialized Field: Community Theater
Status: Non-Profit, Non-Professional
Paid Staff: 2
Income Sources: Arts Advocacy of West Virginia
Performs At: Charleston Civic Center-Little Theatre
Organization Type: Performing; Touring; Educational

3630
APPLE ALLEY PLAYERS
PO Box 144
Keyser, WV 26726

Phone: 304-788-1105
Fax: 304-788-5883
e-mail: lymyersaap@yahoo.com
Officers:
President: Annette Favara
VP: Bob Shadier
Secretary: Alexa Fazenbaker
Treasurer: Sandy Shadler
Management:
Manager: Vinnie Favara
Mission: To provide quality theatre for the surrounding area.
Utilizes: Singers
Founded: 1980
Specialized Field: Community Theater
Status: Nonprofit
Performs At: McKee Art Center; Potomac State College
Organization Type: Resident; Sponsoring

3631
GREENBRIER VALLEY THEATRE
113 E Washington Street
PO Box 494
Lewisburg, WV 24901
Phone: 304-645-3838
Fax: 304-645-3818
e-mail: info@gvtheatre.org
Web Site: www.gvtheatre.org
Officers:
President: Claire LaRocco
Secretary: Carolyn Rudley
Treasurer: Stephen P King
Management:
CEO: Cathey Crowell Sawyer
Equity Stage Manager: Alan Porch
Public Relations Director: Philip McLaughlin
Business Manager: Mary Buskirk
Technical Director: Devin Preston
Volunteer Director: Jane Matheny
Mission: To provide a vehicle for bringing live, professional-quality theatre experiences to our community; to explore all practical means of encouraging the performing arts and artists in our area.
Utilizes: Actors; AEA Actors; Choreographers; Collaborations; Dancers; Educators; Five Seasonal Concerts; Grant Writers; Guest Accompanists; Guest Artists; Guest Choreographers; Guest Conductors; Guest Designers; Guest Ensembles; Guest Instructors; Guest Lecturers; Guest Musical Directors; Guest Teachers; Guild Activities; Instructors; Local Unknown Artists; Multimedia; Music; Original Music Scores; Performance Artists; Playwrights; Resident Artists; Resident Professionals; Soloists; Student Interns
Founded: 1966
Specialized Field: Contemporary; Classic; Musical; Children's Theater; Educational
Status: Non-Profit, Professional
Paid Staff: 18
Budget: $400,000
Income Sources: Private Donations; Foundation
Performs At: Hollowell Theatre; Black Box Flexible Seating
Annual Attendance: 10,000
Facility Category: Black Box
Type of Stage: Flexable-Sprung Floor
Stage Dimensions: Fexible
Seating Capacity: 150; 200
Year Built: 1953
Year Remodeled: 2000
Cost: $1,700,000
Rental Contact: Cathy Sawyer
Organization Type: Performing; Touring; Educational

3632
ARACOMA STORY
311 Main Street
PO Box 2016
Logan, WV 25601
Phone: 304-752-0253
Fax: 304-752-0253
e-mail: scf05500@mail.wvnet.edu
Web Site: www.thearacomastory.com
Management:
President: Lez Spurlock
Executive Director: Jeannie Gore
Founded: 1976
Specialized Field: Musical; Puppet
Status: Non-Profit, Non-Professional
Paid Staff: 4
Volunteer Staff: 5
Paid Artists: 5
Non-paid Artists: 50
Season: June - August
Annual Attendance: 3,000
Facility Category: Amphitheatre
Type of Stage: Proscenium-Wood Walls
Stage Dimensions: 60' x 40'
Seating Capacity: 650
Year Built: 1982
Year Remodeled: 2002

3633
COLLEGE OF CREATIVE ARTS
West Virginia University
PO Box 6111
Morgantown, WV 26506-6111
Phone: 304-293-4339
Fax: 304-293-6896
e-mail: mark.oreskovich@mail.wvu.edu
Web Site: www.ccarts.wvu.edu
Management:
Director Of Recruitment: Amy Burgess
Mission: Educational facility
Utilizes: Actors; AEA Actors; Artists-in-Residence; Choreographers; Collaborating Artists; Commissioned Music; Community Talent; Composers; Curators; Dance Companies; Dancers; Designers; Educators; Guest Accompanists; Guest Artists; Guest Companies; Guest Composers; Guest Designers; Guest Directors; Guest Instructors; Guest Lecturers; Guest Speakers; High School Drama; Instructors; Multimedia; Music; Original Music Scores; Paid Performers; Performance Artists; Sign Language Translators; Singers; Students; Special Technical Talent; Theatre Companies; Visual Arts
Specialized Field: Musical
Income Sources: Stage; Private
Performs At: Lyell B. Clay Concert Theatre, Gladys G. Davis Theatre, Antoinette A. Falbo Theatre, Vivian Davis Michael Laboratory Theatre
Affiliations: NASM - National Association of Schools of Theatre; NASAD - National Association of Schools of Art and Design
Annual Attendance: 1,000
Facility Category: Educational
Type of Stage: Proscenium
Stage Dimensions: 16'x32'
Seating Capacity: 75
Year Built: 1968
Year Remodeled: 1998
Cost: $50,000

3634
WEST VIRGINIA PUBLIC THEATRE
PO Box 4270
Morgantown, WV 26504-4270

Phone: 304-598-0144
Fax: 304-594-0145
Toll-free: 877-999-WVPT
e-mail: info@wvpublictheatre.org
Web Site: www.wvpublictheatre.org
Management:
President: Ron Iannone
Managing Director: Mary Beth Sickles
Founded: 1985
Specialized Field: Drama; Musical
Status: Non-Profit, Professional
Paid Staff: 3
Paid Artists: 200
Season: June - August
Seating Capacity: 650

3635
CONTEMPORARY AMERICAN THEATER FESTIVAL
Sheperd University
PO Box 429
Shepherdstown, WV 25443
Mailing Address: PO Box 429
Phone: 304-876-3473
Fax: 304-876-5443
e-mail: eherende@shepherd.edu
Web Site: www.catf.org
Officers:
President: Jenny Ewing Allen
VP Operations: Skip Adkins
Secretary: Michael Proffitt
Treasurer: Bridget Cohee
Management:
Technical Director: Patrick Wallace
Managing Director: Catherine Irwin
Producing Director/ Founder: Ed Herendeen
Founded: 1991
Specialized Field: Contemporary
Status: Non-Profit
Performs At: Main Stage; Studio Theater
Type of Stage: Proscenium, Black Box
Seating Capacity: 350; 99

3636
BROOKE HILLS PLAYHOUSE
140 Gist Drive
PO Box 186
Wellsburg, WV 26070
Mailing Address: PO Box 186
Phone: 304-737-3344
Fax: 304-737-4247
e-mail: juliabarnhart@aol.com
Web Site: http://brookehillsplayhouse.com
Officers:
President: Rhonda Revels
Vice President: Charles Calabrese
Secretary: Julia Barnhart
Secretary: Paula Welch
Founded: 1972
Specialized Field: Musical; Contemporary
Status: Non-Profit, Non-Professional
Paid Staff: 4
Volunteer Staff: 6
Income Sources: Ticket Sales
Season: June - August
Annual Attendance: 4,000
Facility Category: Barn
Type of Stage: Proscenium
Stage Dimensions: 26' x 22'
Seating Capacity: 195

Wisconsin

3637
AL RINGLING THEATRE LIVELY ARTS SERIES
136 4th Avenue
PO Box 381
Baraboo, WI 53913
Phone: 608-356-8864
Fax: 608-356-0976
e-mail: info@alringling.com
Web Site: www.alringling.com
Management:
President: Bryant Hazard
Director: Brian Heller
Founded: 1989
Specialized Field: Musical; Comedy; Puppet
Status: Non-Profit, Non-Professional
Paid Staff: 4
Volunteer Staff: 80
Budget: $20,000-35,000
Facility Category: Vandeville/Movie Palace
Type of Stage: Proscenium
Stage Dimensions: 37' x 27'
Seating Capacity: 750
Year Built: 1915

3638
CHIPPEWA VALLEY THEATRE GUILD
102 W Grand Avenue
Eau Claire, WI 54703
Phone: 715-832-7529
Fax: 715-832-7528
e-mail: cvtgact@aol.com
Web Site: www.cvtg.org
Officers:
President: Jim Matteson
Vice President: Karen Welch
Executive Director: Ann Sessions
Mission: To bring quality theatre productions to our area, as well as allowing community members to perform in a theatrical production.
Utilizes: Singers
Founded: 1982
Specialized Field: Musical; Comedy
Status: Non-Profit, Non-Professional
Paid Staff: 2
Volunteer Staff: 300
Income Sources: Eau Claire Parks & Recreation
Performs At: The State Regional Arts Center
Annual Attendance: 10,500
Seating Capacity: 1,117
Organization Type: Performing; Educational

3639
EAU CLAIRE CHILDREN'S THEATRE
18 South Barstow Street
Eau Claire, WI 54701
Phone: 715-839-8877
e-mail: info@ecct.org
Web Site: www.ecct.org
Management:
Executive Director: Wayne Marek
Marketing/Outreach Director: Lee Heike
Costume Designer: Ann Behrens
Sound /Lighting Designer: Ron Rude
Scenic Coordinator: Mike Kolstad
Mission: Providing quality theatrical and educational experiences for western Wisconsin residents of all ages.
Specialized Field: Community Theater; Theater Workshops

3640
SUNSET PLAYHOUSE
800 Elm Grove Road
Elm Grove, WI 53122
Mailing Address: PO Box 2
Phone: 262-782-4430
Fax: 262-782-3150
e-mail: mtucker@sunsetplayhouse.com
Web Site: www.sunsetplayhouse.com
Officers:
President: James Loveridge
Vice President: Marla Eichman
Treasurer: Marta Bartolacci
Secretary: Jennifer Allen
Management:
Artistic Director: Mark Salentine
Technical Director: Michael Desper
Managing Director: Jonathan West
Mission: To introduce as many new people as possible to live entertainment.
Founded: 1954
Specialized Field: Drama; Summer Stock
Status: Non-Profit, Non-Professional
Paid Staff: 7
Performs At: Sunset Playhouse
Organization Type: Performing; Open Auditions

3641
AMERICAN FOLKLORE THEATRE
PO Box 273
Fish Creek, WI 54212
Phone: 920-854-6117
Fax: 920-854-9106
e-mail: gen@folkloretheatre.com
Web Site: www.folkloretheatre.com
Officers:
Chairman of Board: Mary Seeberg
Management:
President: M Kaye Christman
Artistic Director: Jeffrey Herbst
Technical Director: David Colby
Mission: To develop and present professional dramatic productions of a cultural and/or educational nature which will futher the knowledge and appreciation of the heritage of the United States.
Founded: 1990
Specialized Field: Musical; Ethnic Theater
Status: Non-Profit, Professional
Budget: 850,000
Income Sources: Box Office; Donations; Sponsorships; Grants
Season: May - September
Affiliations: TCG; NAMT; Theatre Wisconsin
Annual Attendance: 50,000
Facility Category: Indoor and Outdoor
Type of Stage: Proscenium
Stage Dimensions: 35' x 15'
Seating Capacity: 750
Year Built: 1962
Year Remodeled: 2003

3642
PENINSULA PLAYERS
W 4351 Peninsula Players Road
Fish Creek, WI 54212
Phone: 920-868-3287
Fax: 920-868-2295
e-mail: ticket@peninsulaplayers.com
Web Site: www.peninsulaplayers.com
Management:
President: Bill Hartman
Artistic Director: Greg Winkler
Executive Producer: Todd Schmidt
Mission: As America's oldest professional resident summer theatre, our purpose is to present the latest of Broadway fare.
Founded: 1935
Specialized Field: Musical; Comedy; Summer Stock
Status: Non-Profit, Professional
Income Sources: Council of Resident Summer Theatres; Actors' Equity Association
Season: June - October
Performs At: Theatre in a Garden; Open Air Pavilion
Organization Type: Performing; Resident; Educational

3643
NORTHERN LIGHTS PLAYHOUSE
PO Box 256
Hazelhurst, WI 54531-0256
Phone: 715-356-7173
Fax: 715-356-1851
e-mail: nlplays@newnorth.net
Management:
Managing Director: Scott Black
Founded: 1976
Specialized Field: Drama; Musical
Status: Non-Profit, Non-Professional
Season: May - October
Type of Stage: Proscenium
Seating Capacity: 299

3644
BROOM STREET THEATER
1119 Williamson Street
Madison, WI 53703
Phone: 608-244-8338
Web Site: http://www.broomstreet.org
Officers:
Chairperson: Rod Clark
Acting Chairperson/Vice Chairperson: Kurt Meyer
Treasurer: Tracy Will
Management:
Artistic Director: Callen Harty
Technical Director: Matt Kenyon
Development Director: Scott Feiner
Mission: Produces eight original plays by Madison playwrights per year. The shows are directed or supervised by the play-wrights. Our work is highly visual and physical. We are one of the oldest experimental theaters in the United States, and occasionally tour.
Founded: 1968
Specialized Field: Drama; Contemporary
Status: Professional; Nonprofit
Paid Staff: 150
Organization Type: Performing

3645
MADISON REPERTORY THEATRE
1 South Pinckney Street
Suite 340
Madison, WI 53703-2500
Phone: 608-256-0029
Fax: 608-256-7433
e-mail: postmaster@madisonrep.org
Web Site: www.madisonrep.org
Officers:
President: Tim Christen
President Elect: Robert Birkhauser
Management:
President: Lee Eisenberg
VP: Jennifer Kraemer
Artistic Director: Richard Corley
Mission: Mission is to produce, in an intimate setting, both new and classical work for a diverse audience.
Utilizes: Selected Students; Student Interns
Founded: 1969

Specialized Field: Drama; Comedy; Youth Theater
Status: Professional
Paid Staff: 20
Volunteer Staff: 350
Paid Artists: 18
Budget: $1,300,000
Income Sources: 60% Earned; 40% Conutributed
Affiliations: Actors' Equity Association; TCG
Annual Attendance: 35,000
Type of Stage: Thrust Stage
Stage Dimensions: 24'x30'
Seating Capacity: 335
Year Built: 1978
Year Remodeled: 2004
Rental Contact: Madison Civic Center
Organization Type: Performing; Resident

3646
MADISON THEATRE GUILD
2410 Monroe Street
Madison, WI 53711
Phone: 608-238-9322
e-mail: info@madisontheatreguild.org
Web Site: www.madisontheatreguild.org
Officers:
    President: Jim Chiolino
    Treasurer: Ilona Pinzke
    Vice President: Betty Diamond
    Secretary: Jordan Peterson
Management:
    Costume Shop Manager: Robby Sonzogi
Mission: To provide education and recreation through theatrical production.
Utilizes: Singers
Founded: 1946
Specialized Field: Community Theater
Status: Nonprofit
Paid Staff: 150
Income Sources: Wisconsin Theatre Association
Performs At: McDaniels Auditorium
Organization Type: Performing; Educational

3647
WISCONSIN UNION THEATER
800 Langdon Street
Madison, WI 53706
Phone: 608-262-2202
Fax: 608-265-5084
e-mail: edinur@wisc.edu
Web Site: www.union.wisc.edu/theater
Management:
    Artistic Director: Ralph Risco
    Operations Manager: Bruce Ehlinger
Mission: Cultural, entertainment and educational programming for university and community audiences.
Utilizes: Singers
Founded: 1939
Specialized Field: Classic
Status: Non-Profit, Professional
Paid Staff: 30
Volunteer Staff: 80
Budget: $900,000
Income Sources: Ticket Reserves
Performs At: Wisconsin Union Theater
Annual Attendance: 120,000
Type of Stage: Proscenium
Stage Dimensions: 36x24
Seating Capacity: 1,300
Year Built: 1934
Organization Type: Sponsoring

3648
MABEL TAINTER MEMORIAL THEATER
205 Main Street
PO Box 250
Menomonie, WI 54751
Phone: 715-235-9726
Fax: 715-235-9736
e-mail: mtainter@mabeltainter.com
Web Site: www.mabeltainter.com
Management:
    Executive Director: Laura Reisinger
    Facility Manager and Technical Dire: Jeff Torgerson
    General Manager: Maxine Terry
    Box Office Manager: Kate Donicht
Mission: Historic 1890's theater with a performing arts season.. Our mission is dedicated to promoting and enhancing the region's cultural life.
Utilizes: Actors; Artists-in-Residence; Collaborations; Dance Companies; Dancers; Designers; Educators; Fine Artists; Five Seasonal Concerts; Guest Accompanists; Guest Choreographers; Guest Directors; Guest Instructors; Guest Soloists; Instructors; Local Artists; Lyricists; Multi Collaborations; Multimedia; Original Music Scores; Playwrights; Sign Language Translators; Singers; Soloists; Student Interns; Special Technical Talent; Theatre Companies
Founded: 1890
Specialized Field: Musical; Classic
Status: Professional; Nonprofit
Paid Staff: 12
Volunteer Staff: 51
Paid Artists: 30
Budget: $330,000
Income Sources: Tickets; Tours; Rentals; Donations; City and County
Performs At: Mabel Tainter Memorial Theater
Facility Category: Theater and Gift Shop
Type of Stage: Opera House w/orchestra pit
Stage Dimensions: 26'6"x20'
Seating Capacity: 313
Year Built: 1889
Cost: $106,000
Rental Contact: Jeff Torgorson
Organization Type: Sponsoring

3649
ACACIA THEATRE
3195 S Superior St #414
Suite 227
Milwaukee, WI 53207
Phone: 414-744-5995
Fax: 414-744-5996
e-mail: acacia@acaciatheatre.com
Web Site: http://www.acaciatheatre.com/contact.php
Management:
    Artistic Director: Janet Peterson
    Business Manager: Melinda Rhodebeck
Mission: To produce plays with a Christian viewpoint.
Utilizes: Singers
Founded: 1980
Specialized Field: Contemporary
Status: Semi-Professional; Nonprofit
Paid Staff: 10
Organization Type: Touring; Resident; Educational

3650
FIRST STAGE CHILDREN'S THEATER
929 N Water Street
Milwaukee, WI 53202

Phone: 414-273-2314
Fax: 414-273-5595
e-mail: rgoodman@firststage.org
Web Site: www.firststage.org
Management:
    President: Alexander Fraser
    Artistic Director: Jeff Frank
    Producer/Managing Director: Rob Goodman
Founded: 1987
Specialized Field: Musical; Children's Theater
Status: Non-Profit, Professional
Paid Staff: 32
Paid Artists: 50
Performs At: Marcus Center for the Performing Arts's Todd Wehr Theater
Type of Stage: Thrust
Seating Capacity: 500

3651
GREAT AMERICAN CHILDREN'S THEATRE COMPANY
PO Box 92123
Milwaukee, WI 53202
Phone: 414-276-4230
Fax: 414-276-2214
Officers:
    President: Paul Medved
    VP Development: Danita Medved
    Secretary/Treasurer: Thomas Balgeman
Management:
    Managing Director: Annie Jurczyk
    Contact: Teri Solomon Mitze
Mission: To provide quality theatre for young audiences.
Utilizes: Singers
Founded: 1975
Specialized Field: Children's Theater
Status: Professional; Nonprofit
Performs At: Pabst Theatre
Organization Type: Performing; Touring; Educational; Sponsoring

3652
MILWAUKEE CHAMBER THEATRE
158 N Broadway
Milwaukee, WI 53202
Phone: 414-276-8842
Fax: 414-277-4474
e-mail: mail@chamber-theatre.com
Web Site: www.chamber-theatre.com
Management:
    Artistic Director: Davis Montgomery
    Managing Director: Charlane Hertig
    Subscription Manager: Sharon Middleton
Mission: To produce the only annual Shaw festival in the nation and is committed to employing primarily Wisconsin actors and artists. Each season Chamber Theatre offers a wide variety of plays with strong literary and philosophical merit and produces World and regional premieres.
Founded: 1975
Specialized Field: Comedy; Classic; Contemporary
Status: Non-Profit, Professional
Paid Staff: 6
Volunteer Staff: var
Paid Artists: 30
Non-paid Artists: var
Income Sources: Individual Ticket Revenue; Foundation; Corporation; Goverment Grants
Performs At: Broadway Theatre Center
Annual Attendance: 12,500
Facility Category: 2 Theatres (Cabot; Studio)
Stage Dimensions: 358; 96
Organization Type: Performing; Touring; Resident

3653
MILWAUKEE PUBLIC THEATRE
626 E Kilbourn
Suite 802
Milwaukee, WI 53202
Phone: 414-347-1685
Fax: 414-347-1690
e-mail: mpt@milwaukeepublictheatre.org
Web Site: www.milwaukeepublictheatre.org
Officers:
President: Jill Haas, CFM
Vice President: Dante Houston
Secretary: Sandra B Lind
Management:
CoFounder/Artistic/Producing Dir: Barbara Leigh
Co-Founder: Michael John Moynihan
Education Coordinator: Azeeza Islam
Outreach Coordinator: Carolyn Mello
Producer/Special Projects Director: Kathleen Stacy
Healing Arts Director: Karen Stobbe
Mission: To create and present of visual, theatrical, and performing arts productions and related activites through the developement and maintenance of a professional company.
Utilizes: Singers
Founded: 1973
Specialized Field: Musical; Puppet
Status: Non-Profit, Professional
Paid Staff: 5
Paid Artists: 30
Income Sources: Theatre Communications Group; WTA
Season: June - August
Organization Type: Performing; Touring; Resident; Educational; Sponsoring

3654
MILWAUKEE REPERTORY THEATER
108 E Wells Street
Milwaukee, WI 53202
Phone: 414-224-1761
Fax: 414-224-9097
e-mail: mailrep@milwaukeerep.com
Web Site: www.milwaukeerep.com
Officers:
President: Susan Lueger
Management:
Artistic Director: Joe Hanreddy
Managing Executive Director: Timothy Shields
Public Relations Manager: Annie Jurczyk
Mission: To play a vital role in the cultural life of our region through: creating theatrical productions of the highest standard which explore and illuminate the human condition; providing an artistic home for a diverse company of theater professionals; and providing a variety of educational programs for all ages.
Utilizes: Selected Students; Sign Language Translators; Singers; Soloists; Student Interns; Special Technical Talent; Theatre Companies; Visual Arts
Founded: 1954
Specialized Field: Drama
Status: Non-Profit, Professional
Paid Staff: 120
Volunteer Staff: 8
Paid Artists: 170
Non-paid Artists: 30
Budget: $8,800,000
Income Sources: Ticket Sales; Foundations; Corporations; Individuals; Merchandise
Performs At: Milwaukee Repertory Theater
Affiliations: Actors' Equity Association; Lort; TCG
Annual Attendance: 225,000

Type of Stage: Thrust; Black Box; Cabaret
Stage Dimensions: 3 theater complex and full support
Year Built: 1900
Year Remodeled: 1987
Rental Contact: Associate Manager Rebecca Stibbe
Organization Type: Performing; Resident; Educational

3655
MILWAUKEE THEATRE
500 W Kilbourn Avenue
Milwaukee, WI 53203
Phone: 414-908-6001
Fax: 414-908-6010
e-mail: rgeyer@wcd.org
Web Site: www.milwaukeetheatre.org
Officers:
President: Richard A Geyer
Management:
Sales Manager: Tony Dynicki
Production/Operations: Jason Borders
Box Office Manager: Donna Hrobsky
Group Sales: Molly Powell
PR/Promotions: David Snyder
Mission: The Milwaukee Theatre, the newst jewel in Milwaikee's flourishing downtown, opened in November, 2003 with seating for 4,100 and the flexibility to create a full house of as few as 2,500 patrons. The Milwaukee Theatre offers regional audiences a breathtaking and elegant seating for a wide variety of entertainment.
Opened: 1998
Specialized Field: Drama
Seating Capacity: 4,087

3656
NEXT ACT THEATRE
342 N Water Street
PO Box 394
Milwaukee, WI 53201
Phone: 414-278-7780
Fax: 414-278-5930
e-mail: info@nextact.org
Web Site: www.nextact.org
Management:
President: Dwight Ellis
Artistic Director: David Cecsarini
Executive Director: Charles Kakuk
Development Marketing Director: Susan Zellner
Mission: To produce engaging and thought-provoking up close and personal theatre, highlighting the Milwaukee area's finest talent.
Founded: 1990
Specialized Field: Musical; Comedy
Status: Non-Profit, Professional
Paid Staff: 16
Paid Artists: 25
Income Sources: Wisconsin Professional Community Theatre Association
Performs At: Off Broadway Theatre; Stiemke Theater
Affiliations: Corporate member of the United Performing Arts Fund; Wisconsin Arts Board
Organization Type: Performing

3657
REED MARIONETTES
3216 S Quincy Avenue
Milwaukee, WI 53207
Toll-free: 877-803-6575
e-mail: tim@reedmarionettes.com
Web Site: www.reedmarionettes.com
Management:
Managing Director/President: Tim Reed

Mission: A professional touring company presenting colorful, entertaining and faithful versions of children's classics, combining the best of the arts of puppetry and theatre.
Utilizes: Singers
Founded: 1950
Specialized Field: Puppet
Status: Professional
Income Sources: Puppeteers of America; Wisconsin Puppetry Guild
Organization Type: Performing; Touring

3658
RENAISSANCE THEATERWORKS
158 N Broadway
Milwaukee, WI 53202
Phone: 414-273-0800
Fax: 414-273-0801
e-mail: info@r-t-w.com
Web Site: www.r-t-w.com
Officers:
President: Angela Topetzes Strelka
Management:
Producing Director: Julie Swenson Petras
Mission: To produce classical and contemporary theater of the highest artistic quality, rooted in the humanist tradition and with particular interest in the feminine voice.
Founded: 1993
Specialized Field: Dinner Theater; Contemporary
Status: Non-Profit, Professional
Paid Staff: 2
Volunteer Staff: 35
Paid Artists: 30

3659
SKYLIGHT OPERA THEATRE
158 N Broadway
Milwaukee, WI 53202
Phone: 414-291-7811
Fax: 414-271-7815
e-mail: skylight@skylightopera.com
Web Site: www.skylightopera.com
Management:
Artistic Director: Bill Theisen
Managing Director: Christopher Libby
Mission: To bring the full spectrum of music theatre works to a wide and diverse audience in a celebration of the musical and theatrical arts and their reflection of the human condition.
Founded: 1959
Specialized Field: Musical
Status: Non-Profit, Professional
Paid Staff: 35
Budget: $2.2 million
Income Sources: Box Office; Rentals; Private Foundations/Grants/Endowments; Business/Corporate Donations; Government Grants; Individual Donations
Performs At: Cabot Theatre
Affiliations: Skylight Opera Theatre
Facility Category: Theatre House; Opera House; Room
Type of Stage: Flexible; Platform
Stage Dimensions: 12'x24' Expandable
Orchestra Pit: 1
Architect: Wenzler & Associates
Rental Contact: Artistic Administrator John VandeWalle

3660
THEATRE X
158 N Broadway
Milwaukee, WI 53202

Phone: 414-278-0555
Fax: 414-278-8233
e-mail: theatrex@sbcglobal.net
Management:
    President: David Garnham
    Executive Director: John Loscuito
    Artistic Director: John Schneider
Founded: 1969
Specialized Field: Summer Stock
Status: Non-Profit, Professional
Paid Staff: 3
Paid Artists: 65
Season: September - May
Type of Stage: Black Box
Stage Dimensions: 27' x 70'
Seating Capacity: 99

3661
PLAYTIME PRODUCTIONS

1277 County Highway Z
Mount Horeb, WI 53572
Phone: 608-437-4217
e-mail: playtime@mhtc.net
Web Site: www.playtimeproductions.org
Management:
    Founding Director: Teddy Studt
    Director: Renaye Leach
    Stage Manager/Costume Designer: Siobon Edget
    Managing/Artistic Director: Renaye Leach
    Musical Director: Bev Pizzingrilli
    Choreographer: Deb Rabin
Mission: Delighting audiences with its creative and spirited renditions of classic tales. Brings the magic of theater to thousands of people through out Dane County, Wisconsin.
Specialized Field: Children's Theater

3662
PORTAGE AREA COMMUNITY THEATRE

PO Box 263
Portage, WI 53901
Phone: 608-742-6942
Web Site: www.portageareacommunitytheatre.org
Officers:
    President: Pat Madoni
    VP: Lisa Piekarski
    Secretary/Registered Agent: Fran Malone
    Treasurer: Hans Jensen
Management:
    Director: Sheril Lannoye
Mission: To promote, encourage and increase the public's knowledge and appreciation of the arts, especially theatre, and to provide an outlet for the above.
Founded: 1971
Specialized Field: Community Theater
Status: Non-Professional; Nonprofit
Paid Staff: 300
Income Sources: Wisconsin Theatre Association; Wisconsin Council on the Arts
Organization Type: Performing

3663
SHAWANO COUNTY ARTS COUNCIL

PO Box 213
Shawano, WI 54166
Phone: 715-526-2525
e-mail: lindabl@netnet.net
Web Site: http://www.shawanoarts.com/main.html
Officers:
    President: Rusty Mitchell
    VP: Deb Lonick
    Treasurer: Jaquee Salzman
Founded: 1967

Specialized Field: Musical; Community Theater
Status: Nonprofit
Performs At: Mielke Theatre
Organization Type: Resident; Sponsoring

3664
SHEBOYGAN THEATRE COMPANY

607 S Water Street
Sheboygan, WI 53081
Phone: 920-459-3779
Fax: 920-459-4021
e-mail: mbestul@sheboygan.k12.wi.us
Web Site: www.sheboygantheatercomapny.com
Officers:
    President: Karin Gunderson
    First VP: Mike Roehl
    Second VP: Kevin Heling
    Secretary: Steve Flook
    Treasurer: Stan Seagren
Management:
    Production Manager: Dustin Uhl
    Admin Marketing Coordinator: Michelle Bestul, mbestul@sheboygan.k12.wi.us
    Business Manager: Steve Scharrer
Mission: STC exists to provide quality performances for its audiences and quality opportunities to participate and learn to all who might be interested.
Utilizes: Actors; Choreographers; Dancers; Guest Artists; Guest Lecturers; Guest Musical Directors; Music; Performance Artists; Sign Language Translators
Founded: 1934
Specialized Field: Musical; Comedy; Community Theater
Status: Non-Profit, Professional
Paid Staff: 2
Volunteer Staff: 250
Paid Artists: 5
Budget: $250,000
Income Sources: Tickets; Donations; Concessions; Program Advertisements; Rentals
Performs At: Leslie W Johnson Theatre; Horace Mann Middle School
Affiliations: Sheboygan Area School District
Annual Attendance: 18,000-20,000
Facility Category: Standard Theatre
Type of Stage: Thrust; Proscenium
Seating Capacity: 750
Year Built: 1970
Organization Type: Performing; Resident; Educational

3665
AMERICAN PLAYERS THEATRE

PO Box 819
Spring Green, WI 53588
Phone: 608-588-7401
Fax: 608-588-7085
e-mail: broth@americanplayers.org
Web Site: www.americanplayers.org
Management:
    Executive Director: Sheldon Wilner
    Artistic Director: David Frank
    Managing Director: Michael Broh
    Associate Artistic Director: Roseann Sheridan
Utilizes: Singers; Theatre Companies
Founded: 1980
Specialized Field: Classical Repertory Theatre
Status: Non-Profit, Professional
Paid Staff: 22
Volunteer Staff: 120
Budget: $4.5 Million
Income Sources: Ticket Sales; Consessions; Giftshop; Individual Giving; Corporate Giving; Grants
Season: June - October
Performs At: Classical Outdoor Repertory

Affiliations: Actors' Equity Association; Theatre Communications Group, Shakespeare Theatres Assoc. Of America; Theatre Wisconsin
Annual Attendance: 100,000
Facility Category: Outdoor Amphitheatre
Type of Stage: Thrust
Seating Capacity: 1,148
Year Built: 1980
Rental Contact: Production Manager Michael Broh
Organization Type: Performing; Touring; Resident; Educational
Resident Groups: Lort C Special

3666
WAUKESHA CIVIC THEATRE

Margaret Brate Bryant Civic Theatre
264 W Main Street
PO Box 221
Waukesha, WI 53187
Phone: 262-547-4911
Fax: 262-547-8454
e-mail: webmaster@waukeshacivictheatre.com
Web Site: www.waukeshacivictheatre.org
Management:
    Managing Artistic Director: John Cramer
    President: James Chermak
Mission: Mission is to enrich, challenge and entertain participants through the performance of live theatre.
Utilizes: Actors; Educators; Fine Artists; Five Seasonal Concerts; Grant Writers; Guest Accompanists; Guest Artists; Guest Conductors; Guest Designers; Guest Directors; Guest Ensembles; Guest Instructors; Guest Lecturers; Guest Soloists; Instructors; Local Artists; Multimedia; Music; Original Music Scores; Resident Professionals; Selected Students; Sign Language Translators; Soloists; Student Interns; Visual Arts
Founded: 1957
Specialized Field: Musical; Drama; Comedy
Organization Type: Performing; Educational

Wyoming

3667
CHEYENNE LITTLE THEATRE PLAYERS

2706 E Pershing Boulevard
PO Box 1086
Cheyenne, WY 82003
Mailing Address: PO Box 20087
Phone: 307-638-6543
Fax: 307-638-6430
e-mail: cltpinfo@cheyennelittletheatre.org
Web Site: www.cheyennelittletheatre.org
Officers:
    President: Dave Lerner
    VP of Programming: John Lyttle
    VP of Finance: Carol Pascal
Management:
    Managing and Artistic Director: Randy Bernhard
Mission: To entertain and educate through theatre; to promote creativity among volunteers.
Utilizes: Guest Companies
Founded: 1930
Specialized Field: Musical; Dinner Theater; Community Theater
Status: Non-Profit, Non-Professional
Paid Staff: 4
Volunteer Staff: 2
Non-paid Artists: 150
Budget: $350,00
Income Sources: American Association of Community Theatres
Performs At: Mary Godfrey Playhouse; Atlas Theatre
Organization Type: Performing; Educational

3668
SHERIDAN CIVIC THEATRE GUILD
419 Delphi Avenue
Sheridan, WY 82801
Mailing Address: PO Box 1
Phone: 307-672-9886
Web Site: http://www.civictheaterguild.org/
Officers:
    President: Nathan Doerr
    VP: Steve Baskin
    Secretary: Benjamin Brewer
    Treasurer: Pat Tomsovic
Management:
    Manager: Judi O'Neal
Mission: To foster community theatre in our area; to involve community members in all areas of theatre; to entertain.
Utilizes: Guest Artists; Singers
Founded: 1953
Specialized Field: Musical; Community Theater
Status: Nonprofit
Performs At: Carriage House Theatre
Organization Type: Performing; Resident

Alabama

3669
BIRMINGHAM INTERNATIONAL CENTER
1900 Third Avenue North
Suite 100
Birmingham, AL 35203
Phone: 205-252-7652
Fax: 205-252-7656
e-mail: bifstaff@bellsouth.net
Web Site: www.birminghaminternationalcenter.com
Officers:
    President: Dan Sansone
    Vice President: Frank Young, III
    Treasurer: David Salter, Jr.
Management:
    Executive Director: Iris Gross
    Development/Marketing: Kara Kennedy
Mission: Seeks to present an international festival of arts, education, and economic development programs that build bridges of understanding with nations of the world.
Utilizes: Collaborations; Curators; Dancers; Educators; Filmmakers; Five Seasonal Concerts; Guest Composers; Guest Lecturers; Guest Musical Directors; Guest Musicians; Instructors; Lyricists; Multimedia; Original Music Scores; Selected Students; Singers; Soloists; Touring Companies
Founded: 1951
Specialized Field: Series & Festivals: Cultural Diversity
Status: Non-Profit, Professional
Paid Staff: 3
Volunteer Staff: 1k+
Income Sources: Grants; Donations
Season: April 4 - 20
Performs At: Various venues throughout Alabama
Annual Attendance: 50,000
Facility Category: Public park
Seating Capacity: 1,200

3670
INDEPENDENT PRESBYTERIAN CHURCH-NOVEMBER ORGAN RECITAL SERIES
3100 Highland Aveune S
Birmingham, AL 35205
Phone: 205-933-1830
Fax: 205-933-1836
e-mail: bfillmer@bellsouth.net

3671
PRINCESS THEATRE PROFESSIONAL SERIES
112 2nd Avenue NE
Decatur, AL 35601
Phone: 256-350-1745
Fax: 256-350-1712
e-mail: lindy@princesstheatre.org
Web Site: www.princesstheatre.org
Officers:
    Executive Director: Lindy Ashwander
Management:
    Executive Director: Lindy Ashwander
    Technical Director: Penny Linville
Mission: To present and promote a variety of professional performing-arts events.
Utilizes: Collaborations; Dance Companies; Educators; Soloists; Student Interns; Special Technical Talent; Theatre Companies; Visual Arts
Founded: 1983
Specialized Field: Dance; Vocal Music; Instrumental Music; Theater
Status: Nonprofit

Paid Staff: 5
Volunteer Staff: 250
Budget: $570,000
Income Sources: Tickets; Rental; Contribution
Performs At: Princess Theatre
Annual Attendance: 50,000
Facility Category: Performing Arts Center
Type of Stage: Proscenium
Stage Dimensions: 40'x35'x18'.6"
Seating Capacity: 700
Year Built: 1919
Year Remodeled: 2000
Cost: $6 million
Rental Contact: Penny Linville
Organization Type: Performing; Educational

3672
COFFEE COUNTY ARTS ALLIANCE
PO Box 310447
Enterprise, AL 36331
Phone: 334-406-1617
e-mail: coffeecaa@aol.com
Web Site: www.coffeecountyartsalliance.com
Officers:
    President: Suzanne Sawyer
    Treasurer: Charles Canon
Mission: A nonprofit organization that brings a variety of artists, entertainment, symphonies, plays, and educational programs for the community at an affordable price.
Founded: 1974
Specialized Field: Series & Festivals: Broadbased Entertainment In Arts and Crafts Festival
Status: Non-Profit, Non-Professional

3673
WC HANDY MUSIC FESTIVAL
PO Box 1827
Florence, AL 35631
Phone: 256-766-7642
Fax: 256-776-7549
Web Site: www.wchandymusicfestival.org
Management:
    Executive Director: Nancy C Gonce
Founded: 1982
Specialized Field: Series & Festivals; Instrumental Music; Vocal Music; Theatre; Youth; Ethnic Performances
Status: Non-Profit, Professional
Paid Staff: 1

3674
CITY OF GULF SHORES ENTERTAINMENT SERIES
PO Box 299
Gulf Shores, AL 36547
Phone: 251-968-2425
e-mail: info@ci.gulf-shores.al.us
Web Site: www.ci.gulf-shores.al.us
Management:
    Mayor And Council: Mayor David L Bodenhamer
    City Administrator: Tony Rivera
    Administrative Assistant: Lisa Kennedy
    Special Events Director: Patsy Hollingsworth
Rental Contact: Kathy Van Cor

3675
OAKWOOD COLLEGE ARTS & LECTURES
Oakwood College Music Department
7000 Adventist Boulevard
Huntsville, AL 35896

Phone: 256-726-7278
Fax: 256-726-7481
e-mail: achambers@oakwood.edu
Web Site: www.oakwood.edu
Management:
    President: Dr. Leslie Pollard
    Executive Director: John Anderson
    Artistic Director: Audley Chembers
Mission: Music education & performances.
Founded: 1896
Specialized Field: Series and Festivals; Instrumental Music; Vocal Music; Music Education; Music Performance
Status: Non-Profit, Non-Professional
Paid Staff: 11
Paid Artists: 1
Budget: $8,500
Income Sources: Tuition
Performs At: Seventh-Day Adventist Church
Annual Attendance: 12,000
Facility Category: Auditorium
Seating Capacity: 400
Year Built: 1899
Year Remodeled: 1998

3676
PANOPLY ARTS FESTIVAL
Von Braun Civic Center
700 Monroe Street, Suite 2
Huntsville, AL 35801
Phone: 256-519-2787
Fax: 256-533-3811
e-mail: tac@panoply.org
Web Site: www.panoply.org
Management:
    President: Janet Watson
    Executive Director: David Todd
    Artistic Director: Joann Henderson
Founded: 1962
Specialized Field: Series and Festivals: Music
Status: Non-Profit, Professional
Paid Staff: 8
Paid Artists: 20
Performs At: Big Spring Park
Annual Attendance: 90,000
Facility Category: Three outdoor tents with stages; Concert Hall

3677
ALABAMA SHAKESPEARE FESTIVAL
One Festival Drive
Montgomery, AL 36117
Phone: 334-271-5300
Fax: 334-271-5348
Web Site: www.asf.net
Management:
    Managing Director: Alan Harrison
    Artistic Director: Kent Thompson
    Marketing Director: Catherine Gwin
Mission: Dedicated to artistic excellence in the production and performance of the classics and the best of contemporary plays, with the plays of Shakespeare forming the core of our repertoire. Through the Southern Writer's Project, ASF commissions, develops, and produces new plays that reflect the rich, diverse cultures of the South.
Utilizes: Singers
Founded: 1972
Specialized Field: Series and Festivals: Performing Arts and Theatre
Status: Non-Profit, Professional
Performs At: Alabama Shakespeare Festival
Organization Type: Performing; Touring; Resident; Educational; Sponsoring

3678
OPELIKA ARTS ASSOCIATION
1032 S Railroad Avenue
Opelika, AL 36801
Phone: 334-705-5545
Fax: 334-749-8105
e-mail: opelika.arts@mindspring.com
Web Site: www.opelikaarts.com
Management:
    President: Phillip Preston
Founded: 1965
Specialized Field: Series & Festivals; Instrumental music; Vocal music; Theater; Youth; Dance; Ethnic performances
Status: Non-Profit, Non-Professional
Paid Staff: 2

3679
SELMA COMMUNITY CONCERT ASSOCIATION
1034 Dawson Avenue
PO Box 310
Selma, AL 36701
Phone: 334-872-3527
Fax: 334-872-3504
e-mail: hollandschool@bellsouth.net
Web Site: www.selmaalabama.com
Management:
    President: Doris Holland
Mission: Dedicated to providing classical and popular performances.
Founded: 1940
Specialized Field: Concerts; Classical; Jazz
Status: Non-Profit, Professional
Paid Staff: 2

3680
TROY UNIVERSITY
Office Of Student Activities
Trojan Center, Room 233
Troy, AL 36082
Phone: 334-670-3207
Fax: 334-670-3111
e-mail: jjmiller@troy.edu
Web Site: www.troy.edu
Management:
    Office Of Student Activities: Jamie Miller
Specialized Field: Theatre
Status: Non-Profit, Non-Professional
Paid Staff: 6
Budget: Under $10,000
Performs At: Adams Center Theatre for the Performing Arts; Claudia Crosby
Annual Attendance: 700
Facility Category: Fully equipped theatres
Seating Capacity: 900
Year Remodeled: 1999

3681
ARTS COUNCIL OF TUSCALOOSA FANFARE
PO Box 1117
Tuscaloosa, AL 35403-1117
Phone: 205-758-5195
Fax: 205-345-2787
e-mail: education@tuscarts.org
Web Site: www.tuscarts.org
Management:
    Executive Director: Pamela Penick
    Education Programs Director: Sandra Wolfe
Utilizes: Artists-in-Residence; Instructors; Local Artists; Special Technical Talent; Touring Companies
Founded: 1975
Specialized Field: Series & Festivals; Instrumental Music; Vocal Music; Theatre; Youth; Dance
Status: Non-Profit, Professional
Paid Staff: 4
Budget: $20,000-35,000
Performs At: Bama Theatre
Annual Attendance: 7,500-10,000
Facility Category: Presentation House
Seating Capacity: 1000
Year Built: 1938
Year Remodeled: 1976

3682
HORIZONS PERFORMING ARTS SERIES
PO Box 6689
Tuscaloosa, AL 35486-6689
Phone: 205-348-7525
Fax: 205-348-8251
Web Site: www.up.ua.edu
Management:
    Assistant Director: Steven McCuller
Paid Staff: 4

3683
HORIZONS PERFORMING ARTS SERIES
PO Box 6689
Tuscaloosa, AL 35486-6689
Phone: 205-348-7525
Fax: 205-348-8251
Web Site: www.up.ua.edu
Management:
    Assistant Director: Steven McCuller
Mission: To provide a variety of performing art to the University of Alabama.
Paid Staff: 4
Volunteer Staff: 100

3684
UNIVERSITY OF ALABAMA SCHOOL OF MUSIC CELEBRITY SERIES
PO Box 870366
Tuscaloosa, AL 35487-0366
Phone: 205-348-7110
Fax: 205-348-1473
e-mail: ssnead@music.ua.edu
Web Site: www.music.ua.edu
Management:
    Director, School of Music: Charles G. Snead
    Events Coordinator: Joyce Coffee Grant
Founded: 1987
Budget: $60,000-150,000
Performs At: Concert Hall, Moody Music Building
Seating Capacity: 934

Alaska

3685
ANCHORAGE CONCERT ASSOCIATION
430 W 7th Avenue
Suite 200
Anchorage, AK 99501
Phone: 907-272-1471
Fax: 907-272-2519
e-mail: executive@anchorageconcerts.org
Web Site: www.anchorageconcerts.org
Management:
    Executive Director: Lissette Miles
Founded: 1950
Specialized Field: Performing Arts Presenter
Status: Non-Profit, Professional
Paid Staff: 9
Volunteer Staff: 82

3686
ANCHORAGE FESTIVAL OF MUSIC
PO Box 103251
Anchorage, AK 99510
Phone: 907-276-2465
Fax: 907-276-2540
Web Site: www.alaska.net/~anchfest
Management:
    Executive Director: Steven Alvarez
    Artistic Director: Grant Cooper
Mission: Promoting diverse musical events in Anchorage and the surrounding area.
Utilizes: Guest Artists
Founded: 1976
Specialized Field: Instrumental; Choral; Educational
Status: Professional; Nonprofit
Paid Staff: 30
Season: June
Performs At: Anchorage (Festival Site)
Affiliations: Alaska Center for the Performing Arts
Seating Capacity: 300; 800; 2,200
Organization Type: Performing

3687
FAIRBANKS CONCERT ASSOCIATION MASTER SERIES
PO Box 80547
Fairbanks, AK 99708
Phone: 907-474-8081
Fax: 907-474-0266
e-mail: info@fairbanksconcert.org
Web Site: www.fairbanksconcert.org
Officers:
    President: Scott McCrea
Management:
    Executive Director: Anne Biberman
Utilizes: Actors; Artists-in-Residence; Collaborations; Dance Companies; Dancers; Educators; Guest Accompanists; Guest Choreographers; Guest Composers; Guest Designers; Guest Ensembles; Guest Musical Directors; Guest Musicians; Guild Activities; Multimedia; Original Music Scores; Sign Language Translators; Singers; Theatre Companies
Founded: 1947
Specialized Field: Music; Dance; Speakers
Status: Non-Profit, Professional
Paid Staff: 2
Budget: $60,000-150,000
Performs At: Hering Auditorium; Charles W Davis Concert Hall
Annual Attendance: 13,000
Facility Category: Proscenium Auditorium
Type of Stage: Proscenium
Stage Dimensions: 47'10x22'x36'6"
Seating Capacity: 1305; 967

3688
FAIRBANKS SUMMER ARTS FESTIVAL
PO Box 82510
Fairbanks, AK 99708
Phone: 907-474-8869
Fax: 907-474-8617
e-mail: festival@alaska.net
Web Site: www.fsaf.org
Officers:
    Board Chair: Patty Kastelic
    Vice Chair: Don Gray
Management:
    Director: Terese Kaptur
Mission: To offer a two-week residency with approximately 100 professional guest performers/master teachers.

Utilizes: Actors; Artists-in-Residence; Choreographers; Collaborations; Dancers; Educators; Fine Artists; Grant Writers; Guest Accompanists; Guest Artists; Guest Companies; Guest Composers; Guest Designers; Guest Ensembles; Guest Lecturers; Guest Musical Directors; Guest Musicians; High School Drama; Instructors; Local Artists; Multimedia; Music; Original Music Scores; Sign Language Translators; Singers; Soloists; Touring Companies
Founded: 1980
Specialized Field: Study Performance Festivals
Status: Non-Profit
Paid Staff: 3
Volunteer Staff: 60
Paid Artists: 100
Budget: $500,000
Income Sources: Registration Fees; Corporate/Private Donations; Grants
Season: July - August
Affiliations: University of Alaska Fairbanks
Annual Attendance: 1,000
Facility Category: University of Alaska Fairbanks
Seating Capacity: 1,000
Year Built: 1917
Organization Type: Performing; Educational

3689

HAINES ARTS COUNCIL

PO Box 505
Haines, AK 99827
Phone: 907-766-2592
Officers:
   VP: Len Feldman
Management:
   Music Director: Dr. Suzanne Summerville
   Contact: Tom Morphet
   Staff Director: Theodora Mann
   Staff Conductor: Robert Luther
Mission: To provide performing arts resources for local artists; to offer concerts and festivals.
Utilizes: Guest Artists; Singers
Founded: 1983
Specialized Field: Dance; Vocal Music; Instrumental Music; Theater; Festivals; Lyric Opera
Status: Non-Professional; Nonprofit
Income Sources: Lynn Community Players
Performs At: Chilkat Center for the Arts
Organization Type: Performing; Touring; Resident; Educational; Sponsoring

3690

KENAI PENINSULA ORCHESTRA

315 W Pioneer Avenue
Homer, AK 99603
Phone: 907-235-4899
Fax: 907-235-5633
e-mail: kpoalaska@gmail.com
Web Site: www.kpoalaska.org
Officers:
   Board President: Jack Will
Management:
   Artistic Director: Tammy Vollom-Matturro
   Production Manager: Laura Norton
Mission: To provide the Kenai Peninsula community enriched, educational opportunities and cultural experiences through the study and performance of the Orchestral Arts.
Founded: 1983
Specialized Field: Symphony Orchestra
Status: Non-Profit, Non-Professional
Paid Staff: 3
Volunteer Staff: 3
Paid Artists: 8
Non-paid Artists: 80

Budget: $35,000
Seating Capacity: 200-450

3691

CROSSSOUND

1109 C Street
Juneau, AK 99801
Phone: 907-586-9601
e-mail: directors@crosssound.com
Web Site: www.crosssound.com
Management:
   President: Jocelyn Clark
   Artistic Director: Stefan Hakenberg
Mission: To commission new works for musicians from Southeast Alaska and beyond that stretch the boundaries of the planets of chamber music
Founded: 1999
Specialized Field: Sereise & Festivals; New Music; Chamber Music; Multi Media
Status: Non-Profit, Professional
Paid Staff: 2
Volunteer Staff: 10
Paid Artists: 30
Income Sources: Donations

3692

JUNEAU ARTS & HUMANITIES COUNCIL

Performing Arts & Culture Concert Series
206 N Franklin Street
Juneau, AK 99801
Phone: 907-586-2787
Fax: 907-586-2148
e-mail: info@jahc.org
Web Site: www.jahc.org
Officers:
   President: Teri Rasmussen
   Secretary: Dan Hopson
Management:
   Executive Director: Nancy DeCherney
   Program Coordinator: Mary Wood
Mission: To provide cultural opportunities for the city and surrounding communities.
Utilizes: Guest Choreographers; Guest Musical Directors; Guest Musicians; Local Artists; Original Music Scores; Touring Companies
Founded: 1973
Specialized Field: Series and Festivals; Instrumental Music; Vocal Music; Youth; Dance; Ethnic Performances; Performing Arts; Visual Arts
Status: Non-Profit, Professional
Paid Staff: 2
Volunteer Staff: 40
Paid Artists: 20
Budget: For concert series $56,000
Performs At: Juneau-Douglas H.S. Auditorium; ANB Community Hall
Facility Category: High School Auditorium
Type of Stage: Proscenium
Stage Dimensions: 40 x 50
Seating Capacity: 1,000

3693

KODIAK ARTS COUNCIL

Kodiak Baranof Productions
PO Box 1792
Kodiak, AK 99615-1792
Phone: 907-486-5291
Fax: 907-486-5591
e-mail: kodiak-arts-council@gci.net
Web Site: www.kodiakartscouncil.org
Officers:
   President: Mike Wall
   VP: Darcy Stielstra
   Secretary: Randy Busch

Treasurer: Andrew Ott
Management:
   Executive Director: Tom Quass
Founded: 1963
Status: Non-Profit, Professional
Paid Staff: 1
Volunteer Staff: 1
Paid Artists: 100
Budget: $200,000
Income Sources: Grants; Membership; Ticket Sales
Performs At: Gerald C Wilson Auditorium
Affiliations: Kenney Center
Type of Stage: Proscenium
Stage Dimensions: 40' x 35'
Seating Capacity: 750
Year Built: 1986
Cost: $10 Million

3694

SITKA SUMMER MUSIC FESTIVAL

PO Box 201988
Sitka, AK 99520
Phone: 907-747-6774
Fax: 907-277-4842
e-mail: director@sitkamusicfestival.org
Web Site: www.sitkamusicfestival.org
Management:
   Executive Director: Darleen Fernandez
   Artistic Director: Paul Rosenthal
Mission: To present chamber music festivals throughout Alaska
Utilizes: Guest Musicians
Founded: 1972
Specialized Field: Classical
Status: Professional
Volunteer Staff: 80
Paid Artists: 15
Non-paid Artists: 30
Budget: $250,000
Season: June
Performs At: Harrigan Centennial Hall
Annual Attendance: 8,000
Facility Category: Performance Hall
Seating Capacity: 500
Year Built: 1970
Year Remodeled: 1998
Organization Type: Performing; Touring

Arizona

3695

DESERT FOOTHILLS MUSICFEST

PO Box 5254
Carefree, AZ 85377
Phone: 480-488-0806
Fax: 480-488-1401
e-mail: info@azmusicfest.org
Web Site: www.azmusicfest.org
Management:
   Chairman: C J Goldthwaite
   Managing Director: Roberta Pappas
   Music Director and Conductor: Paul Perry
Mission: To assist in making the Arizona High Desert area a major winter cultural center.
Utilizes: Five Seasonal Concerts; Guest Accompanists; Guest Musical Directors; Guest Soloists; Guest Teachers; Multimedia; Music; Original Music Scores; Sign Language Translators; Singers; Soloists
Founded: 1992
Specialized Field: Series & Festivals; Instrumental Music; Vocal Music; Youth
Status: Non-Profit, Professional
Paid Staff: 3

Paid Artists: 30
Budget: $400,000
Income Sources: Individual Contributions; Corporate Sponsors; Grants; Ticket Revenue
Season: February
Performs At: Carefree; Cave Creek; North Scottsdale
Annual Attendance: 4,500
Seating Capacity: 250 - 700
Organization Type: Performing; Educational

3696
PINAL COUNTY FINE ARTS COUNCIL: ARTS IN THE DESERT

8470 N Overfield Road
Central Arizona College
Coolidge, AZ 85228
Phone: 520-426-4223
Fax: 520-426-4224
e-mail: community_services@central.az.edu
Web Site: www.centralaz.edu
Management:
 President: Terry Callaway
 Executive Director: Jim Lamb
 Cultural Events Coordinator: Cheryl R Sanborn
Utilizes: Artists-in-Residence; Dance Companies; Dancers; Fine Artists; Guest Accompanists; Instructors; Multimedia; Original Music Scores; Sign Language Translators; Singers; Soloists
Founded: 1975
Specialized Field: Series & Festivals; Instrumental Music; Vocal Music; Theatre; Youth; Dance; Ethnic Performances
Status: Non-Profit, Professional
Paid Staff: 1
Volunteer Staff: 15
Paid Artists: 135
Budget: $44,000
Income Sources: Series Subscribers
Performs At: Pence Auditorium, Central Arizona College
Annual Attendance: 6,000-7,000
Facility Category: Auditorium
Type of Stage: Proscenium
Stage Dimensions: 45'x20'
Seating Capacity: 735
Year Built: 1969
Rental Contact: Cheryl Ragsdale

3697
VERDE VALLEY CONCERT ASSOCIATION

14 S Main Street
PO Box 26
Cottonwood, AZ 86326-0026
Phone: 928-639-0636
Fax: 928-639-2185
e-mail: vvca@wildapache.net
Web Site: www.verdevalleyconcerts.com
Officers:
 President: Anna May Cory
Management:
 President: Arleen Wright
Utilizes: Artists-in-Residence; Dance Companies; Fine Artists; Grant Writers; Guest Lecturers; Original Music Scores; Singers; Theatre Companies
Founded: 1952
Specialized Field: Series & Festivals; Chamber music; Instrumental Music; Vocal Music
Status: Non-Profit, Professional
Paid Staff: 1
Performs At: Mingus Union High School Auditorium
Seating Capacity: 852

3698
FLAGSTAFF FESTIVAL OF THE ARTS

PO Box 1607
Flagstaff, AZ 86002
Phone: 520-774-7750
Fax: 520-774-2600
Web Site: www.flagstaffguide.com/festival
Management:
 Managing Director: Larry Reid
 Orchestra Conductor: Irwin Hoffman
 Theatre Artistic Director: Tal Russell
Mission: Offering professional arts programs to the Flagstaff community.
Utilizes: Guest Artists; Guest Companies; Singers
Founded: 1966
Specialized Field: Dance; Vocal Music; Instrumental Music; Theater; Festivals
Status: Professional; Semi-Professional; Nonprofit
Income Sources: Northern Arizona University
Performs At: Ardrey Auditorium; Creative Arts Theatre
Organization Type: Performing; Educational

3699
NORTHERN ARIZONA UNIVERSITY ARTIST SERIES

CAL, School of Music
Box 6040, Bldg 37, Rm 120
Flagstaff, AZ 86011
Phone: 928-523-3731
Fax: 928-523-5111
e-mail: Todd.Sullivan@nau.edu
Web Site: www.cal.nau.edu/music/
Management:
 Director: Todd Sullivan
 Associate Director: Rick Stamer
 Events Coordinator: Robbie Elliot
Mission: Presents guest and faculty artist series as well as the Jazz/Madrigal Festival.
Budget: $60,000-150,000
Performs At: Ardrey Auditorium
Seating Capacity: 1500

3700
GRAND CANYON MUSIC FESTIVAL

PO Box 1332
Grand Canyon, AZ 86023
Phone: 928-638-9215
Fax: 520-638-3373
Toll-free: 800-997-8285
e-mail: gcmf@infomagic.net
Web Site: www.grandcanyonmusicfest.org
Officers:
 President: Kenneth Bacher
 VP/Secretary: Clare Hoffman
Management:
 Director: Frances Bonfiglio
 Artistic Director: Clare Hoffman
Mission: To present a series of concerts in Grand Canyon National Park each September, maintaining high musical standards and diversity of programming; to commission new chamber music from American composers; to give a public service tour to schools in Northern Arizona.
Founded: 1984
Specialized Field: Instrumental; Jazz
Status: Nonprofit
Budget: $20,000-$35,000
Season: September
Performs At: Grand Canyon National Park (Festival Site)
Affiliations: Shrine of the Ages
Seating Capacity: 310
Organization Type: Presenting

3701
WEST VALLEY ARTS COUNCIL

PO Box 754
Litchfield Park, AZ 85340
Phone: 623-935-6384
Fax: 623-935-4327
e-mail: admin@westvalleyarts.com
Web Site: www.westvalleyarts.com
Management:
 Executive Director: Julie Richard
Mission: To develop, enhance and promote quality arts opportunities and arts education for everyone in the West Valley
Founded: 1969
Specialized Field: Series & Festivals; Visual arts; Music festivals; Dance; Theatre
Status: Non-Profit, Professional
Paid Staff: 12
Performs At: Various Community Spaces

3702
PARADISE VALLEY JAZZ PARTY

6014 N Nauni Valley Drive
Paradise Valley, AZ 85253
Phone: 480-948-7993
Fax: 480-991-5732
e-mail: dzmiller@cox.net
Web Site: www.paradisevalleyjazz.com
Management:
 President: Don Z Miller
Founded: 1978
Specialized Field: Series & Festivals: Instrumental Music & Concerts
Status: For-Profit, Professional
Paid Staff: 1
Volunteer Staff: 5

3703
ARIZONA EXPOSITION & STATE FAIR

1826 W Mcdowell Road
Phoenix, AZ 85007
Phone: 602-252-6771
Fax: 602-495-1302
e-mail: info@azstatefair.com
Web Site: www.azstatefair.com
Management:
 Event Coordinator: Stephen King

3704
PHOENIX SYMPHONY

One N. 1st Street
Phoenix, AZ 85004
Phone: 602-495-1117
Fax: 602-253-1772
e-mail: info@phoenixsymphony.org
Web Site: www.phoenixsymphony.org
Officers:
 President: Maryellen H Gleason
 Chairman: C A Howlett
 Treasurer: Michael F Casey
Management:
 Music Director: Michael Christie
 Managing Director: Jay Good
 Operations Manager: Kimberly Koniecki
 Marketing Director: Laura Schairer
 Development Director: Frank Bourget
 Assistant Conductor: Joseph Young
Mission: Evoking a passion for orchestral music within the entire community
Utilizes: Commissioned Composers; Commissioned Music; Dancers; Educators; Guest Accompanists; Guest Composers; Guest Directors; Guest Lecturers;

Guest Musical Directors; Guest Musicians; Local Artists; Original Music Scores; Sign Language Translators; Singers; Theatre Companies
Founded: 1947
Specialized Field: Symphony
Paid Artists: 75
Budget: $8,600,000
Income Sources: Private Donations; Institutional Supporters
Season: September-May
Performs At: Phoenix Symphony Hall; Orpheum Theatre; Sedona Cultural Park
Annual Attendance: 140,000
Facility Category: Symphony Hall
Stage Dimensions: 60x100
Seating Capacity: 2,587
Year Built: 1972
Organization Type: Performing; Touring; Educational

3705
SOUTHWEST ARTS & ENTERTAINMENT
PO Box 55566
Phoenix, AZ 85078-5566
Phone: 602-482-6410
Fax: 602-482-0939
e-mail: swae@southwestae.com
Web Site: www.southwestae.com
Management:
President: Charles Fischil
Utilizes: Artists-in-Residence; Collaborations; Dance Companies; Theatre Companies
Founded: 1992
Specialized Field: Presenting Organization
Status: Non-Profit, Professional
Paid Staff: 2
Budget: $555,000
Income Sources: Arts Commissions; Foundations; Corporations
Affiliations: WAA; AZ Presenters; CA Presenters
Annual Attendance: 60,000
Facility Category: Orphium Theatre
Type of Stage: Proscenium
Stage Dimensions: 30'x50'
Seating Capacity: 1,300
Year Built: 1929
Year Remodeled: 1994

3706
PRESCOTT FINE ARTS
The Corner of Marina and Willis
208 N Marina
Prescott, AZ 86301
Phone: 928-445-3286
Fax: 928-778-7888
e-mail: pfaadirector@qwest.net
Web Site: www.pfaa.net
Officers:
President: Ralph Hess
Secretary: Sandy Moss
Treasurer: John Cargill
Management:
Executive Director: Dee R Toci
Operations Manager: Suzy Campbell
Box Office: Sue Lord
Associate Director: Casey Knight
Mission: To offer cultural and artistic activities.
Utilizes: Actors; Curators; Educators; Fine Artists; High School Drama; Local Artists
Founded: 1969
Specialized Field: Theatre and Music
Status: Nonprofit
Paid Staff: 4
Non-paid Artists: 600
Budget: $225,000

Income Sources: Ticket sales, Grants, Donations
Annual Attendance: 20,000
Facility Category: Historic Church
Type of Stage: Proscenium
Seating Capacity: 194
Year Built: 1894
Resident Groups: Yavapai County, North central Arizona

3707
YAVAPAI SYMPHONY ASSOCIATION
228 N Alarcon Street
Prescott, AZ 86301
Phone: 928-776-4255
Fax: 928-778-5286
Officers:
President: Jan Spaulding
Mission: To offer an annual series featuring six to eight of the finest dance companies. Collaborates with Ballet Arizona, Arizona Opera, Arizona Theatre Company, Phoenix Bach Choir, Phoenix Boys Choir, Heard Museum and Arizona State University.
Founded: 1966
Specialized Field: Classical
Status: Nonprofit; Professional
Volunteer Staff: 400
Paid Artists: 75
Income Sources: American Symphony Orchestra League; Private Donations
Season: November-June
Performs At: Yavapai College Performance Hall
Annual Attendance: 1,100
Stage Dimensions: 60x100
Seating Capacity: 2,587
Year Built: 1972
Organization Type: Sponsoring; Performing

3708
GILA VALLEY ARTS COUNCIL
PO Box 1022
Safford, AZ 85548-1022
Phone: 520-428-1009
Fax: 520-428-2772
e-mail: pizarro@zakes.com
Web Site: www.zakes.com
Officers:
President: Joann Mortensen
Treasurer: Dorine Chancellor
Residency Chair: Cecilia Roudenbush
Recording Secretary: Mary Ann Ripplinger
Management:
Artistic Director: Jack Kukuk
Executive Director: Shelly Williams
Mission: To promote, support, and sponsor performing arts in Southeast Arizona through the School Residency Program and Public Performance.
Budget: $35,000-60,000
Performs At: Eastern Arizona College of Fine Arts Studio
Seating Capacity: 941+; 300

3709
RAGTYME-JAZZTYME SOCIETY
6835 E Kings Avenue
Scottsdale, AZ 85254-1512
Phone: 480-951-8339
Fax: 480-348-3702
Toll-free: 800-473-5396
e-mail: azragtime2001@aol.com
Web Site: www.ragtymejazztyme.com
Officers:
President: Robert Lynn
Management:
President: Robert Lynn

Newsletter Editor: Patricia Gray
Chairman: Ross Dunshee
Mission: To preserve, promote and promulgate Ragtime and Early American Jazz Music. To provide educational activities and benefits to our younger generation of musicians and music lovers.
Founded: 2001
Specialized Field: Ragime and Early American Jazz Music
Status: Non-Profit, Professional
Volunteer Staff: 12

3710
SCOTTSDALE ARTS FESTIVAL
Scottsdale Center for the Arts
7380 E 2nd Street
Scottsdale, AZ 85251
Phone: 480-874-4610
Fax: 480-874-4699
e-mail: janiceb@sccarts.org
Web Site: www.scottsdalearts.org
Management:
President: Frank Jacobson
Artistic Director: Kathy Hotchner
Managing Director: Ally Haynes
Festival Manager: Janice Bartczak
Founded: 1975
Specialized Field: Performing Arts
Status: Non-Profit, Professional

3711
CHAMBER MUSIC SEDONA
1487 W Highway 89A
Suite 9
Sedona, AZ 86336
Phone: 928-204-2415
Fax: 928-282-0893
e-mail: info@chambermusicsedona.org
Web Site: www.chambermusicsedona.org
Officers:
President: Marion Maby
Treasurer: Charles Spining
Secretary: Marilyn Thaden Dexter
Management:
Executive Director: Albert P Harclerode III
General Manager: Anna Cates
Operations Director: Ian Amberson
Mission: To preserve and foster the appreciation of chamber music in its many forms by producing world class concerts and by presenting and supporting community music education programs
Utilizes: Artists-in-Residence; Collaborating Artists; Commissioned Music; Five Seasonal Concerts; Grant Writers; Guest Companies; Guest Directors; Guest Lecturers; Guest Musical Directors; Local Artists; Multimedia
Specialized Field: Chamber; Jazz
Paid Staff: 2
Paid Artists: 52
Budget: $200,000
Performs At: St. John Vianney Church; Museum of Northern Arizona
Affiliations: CMA, ACA
Annual Attendance: 4000
Seating Capacity: 250; 200

3712
SEDONA JAZZ ON THE ROCKS
2020 Contractors Road
Suite 5
Sedona, AZ 86336

Phone: 928-282-1985
Fax: 928-282-0590
e-mail: office@sedonajazz.com
Web Site: www.sedonajazz.com
Officers:
President: Bettye Wilson
Management:
Executive Director: Carol Golden
Mission: To celebrate jazz as a living art form through education and performance programs
Utilizes: Guest Accompanists; Instructors; Original Music Scores; Sign Language Translators; Soloists
Specialized Field: Jazz
Status: Non-Profit, Non-Professional
Paid Staff: 3
Volunteer Staff: 200
Non-paid Artists: 4
Budget: $400,000
Income Sources: Box Office; Corporate Sponsors; Grants
Season: September
Performs At: Sedona Cultural Park (Festival Site)
Annual Attendance: 6,000
Facility Category: Various Venues
Seating Capacity: 200-4,500
Organization Type: Performing; Sponsoring

3713
ARIZONA STATE UNIVERSITY PUBLIC EVENTS

Arizona State University
PO Box 870205
Tempe, AZ 85287-0205
Phone: 480-965-5062
Fax: 480-965-7663
e-mail: mreed@asu.edu
Web Site: www.asugammage.com
Management:
President: Micheal Crow
Executive Director: Colleen Jennings-Roggensack
Director of Programming: Micheal Reed
Mission: To connect communities through performing arts.
Utilizes: AEA Actors; Artists-in-Residence; Choreographers; Collaborating Artists; Collaborations; Commissioned Composers; Commissioned Music; Composers-in-Residence; Curators; Dance Companies; Dancers; Educators; Grant Writers; Guest Artists; Guest Companies; Guest Conductors; Guest Directors; Guest Instructors; Guest Lecturers; Guest Soloists; Instructors; Multimedia; Organization Contracts; Original Music Scores; Playwrights; Selected Students; Singers; Soloists; Special Technical Talent; Theatre Companies; Touring Companies
Founded: 1967
Specialized Field: Performing Arts
Status: Non-Profit, Non-Professional
Paid Staff: 54
Volunteer Staff: 400
Budget: $1,000,000+
Performs At: Grady Gammage Memorial Auditorium; Sundome Center
Affiliations: Arts Presenters, ISPAA, WAA
Annual Attendance: 500,000
Facility Category: Auditorium
Type of Stage: Prosenium Sprungwood
Seating Capacity: 3011
Year Built: 1967
Rental Contact: Terri Cranmer

3714
MICHELOB COOL SUMMER JAZZ SERIES

730 N Mill Avenue
Tempe, AZ 85281
Fax: 480-829-1552
Toll-free: 800-466-6779
Web Site: www.redrivermusihall.com

3715
GREATER ORO VALLEY ARTS COUNCIL

7400 N Oracle Road
Suite 100R
Tucson, AZ 85704
Phone: 520-797-3959
Fax: 520-531-9225
Management:
Executive Director: Carmen Feriend

3716
PIMA COMMUNITY COLLEGE FOR THE ARTS

2202 W Anklam Road
Tucson, AZ 85709-0225
Phone: 520-206-6986
Fax: 520-206-6670
e-mail: cfa@pimacc.pima.edu
Web Site: www.wc.pima.edu/csa
Management:
President: Lou Albert
Dean of Performing/Visual Arts: Frank Pickard
Program Director: Leighann Langel
Technical Director: Warren Loomis
Founded: 1994
Specialized Field: Series and Festivals; Plays; Dances; Shows; Theatre
Status: Non-Profit, Professional
Budget: $20,000-35,000
Performs At: Proscenium Theatre; Black Box Theatre; Recital Hall
Seating Capacity: 425;170;120

3717
ST. PHILIP'S IN THE HILLS FRIENDS OF MUSIC

4440 N Campbell Avenue
PO Box 65840
Tucson, AZ 85728
Phone: 520-299-6421
Fax: 520-299-0712
e-mail: office@stphilipstucson.org
Web Site: www.stphilipstucson.org
Management:
Music Director: Garmon Ashby
Associate Music Director: Jeffery Campbell
Facilities Use Coordinator: Jeffri Sanders
Mission: To present concert series.
Founded: 1989
Specialized Field: Series and Festivals; Instrumental Music; Vocal Music; Youth; Ethnic Performances; Classical Ensembles
Status: Non-Profit, Professional
Paid Staff: 2
Paid Artists: 25
Budget: $10,000-20,000
Performs At: St. Philip's in the Hills Episcopal Church
Seating Capacity: 500

3718
TUCSON WINTER CHAMBER MUSIC FESTIVAL

PO Box 40845
Tucson, AZ 85717
Phone: 520-577-3769
e-mail: office@arizonachambermusic.org
Web Site: www.arizonachambermusic.org
Management:
Artistic Director: Peter Rejto
Mission: To be one of the country's most active commissioning programs
Specialized Field: Chamber
Status: Non-Profit
Budget: $60,000-$150,000
Season: February - March
Affiliations: Leo Rich Theatre; Tucson Convention Center
Seating Capacity: 550

3719
UA PRESENTS

1020 E University Boulevard
PO Box 210158
Tucson, AZ 85721-0029
Phone: 520-621-3341
Fax: 520-621-8991
e-mail: uapresents@arizona.edu
Web Site: www.uapresents.org
Officers:
Executive Director: Natalie Bohnet
Performs At: Centennial Hall

Arkansas

3720
OUACHITA BAPTIST UNIVERSITY: ARTISTS SERIES

410 Ouachita Street
Arkadelphia, AR 71998-0001
Phone: 870-246-5129
Fax: 870-245-5274
e-mail: gerberg@obu.edu
Web Site: www.obu.edu/music
Management:
Chair, Division of Music: Gary Gerber
Mission: Students are provided a wide range of performance opportunities through the artists series in the spring and other events.
Performs At: Jones Performing Arts Center; W Francis McBeth Recital Hall
Seating Capacity: 1500; 267

3721
WALTON ARTS AND IDEAS

University of the Ozarks
Clarksville, AR 72830
Phone: 479-979-1346
Fax: 501-979-1349
e-mail: gemyers@ozarks.edu
Web Site: www.ozarks.edu
Management:
President: Rick Niece
Executive Director: Ginny Myers
Specialized Field: Series and Festivals: Different Events
Status: Non-Profit, Professional
Paid Staff: 3
Performs At: Seay Thaetre
Seating Capacity: 699

3722
UNIVERSITY OF CENTRAL ARKANSAS PUBLIC APPEARANCES
201 Donaghey
Conway, AR 72035-0001
Phone: 501-450-3293
Fax: 501-450-3296
e-mail: gucch@aol.com
Web Site: www.uca.edu/cfac
Management:
President: Lu Hardin
Artistic Director: Guy Couch
Founded: 1909
Specialized Field: Higher Education
Status: Non-Profit, Professional
Paid Staff: 900
Performs At: Ida Waldran Auditorium; Conway Public Schools Auditorium
Seating Capacity: 1100-1500

3723
INSPIRATION POINT FINE ARTS COLONY
Opera in the Ozarks
16311 Highway 62 W
PO Box 127
Eureka Springs, AR 72632-3160
Phone: 479-253-8595
Treasurer: Duane Langley
Management:
Executive Director/Manager: James Swiggart
President: Carole Langley
Director: Charles Turley
Mission: To provide local students with exposure to professional opera.
Utilizes: Guest Artists; Guest Companies; Singers
Founded: 1950
Specialized Field: Instrumental Music; Lyric Opera; Grand Opera
Status: Non-Professional; Nonprofit
Paid Staff: 7
Income Sources: National Federation of Music Clubs; donations
Performs At: Inspiration Point Fine Arts Colony
Organization Type: Performing; Educational; Sponsoring

3724
SYMPHONY ORCHESTRA OF NORTHWEST ARKANSAS
605 W. Dickson Street
Fayetteville, AR 72701
Mailing Address: PO Box 1243 Fayetteville AR 72702
Phone: 479-521-4166
Web Site: www.nasymphony.org/not working try back
Officers:
Chairman: Bob Gaddy
Secretary: Joan Campbell
Treasurer: Tom Garrison
Management:
Director: Jeannine Wagar
General Manager: Aldee Marquis
Mission: To provide north Arkansas with a fully professional regional orchestra presenting quality music, education and programs to enrich the communities
Utilizes: Guest Artists; Singers
Founded: 1954
Specialized Field: Symphony
Status: Non-Profit, Professional
Paid Staff: 2
Paid Artists: 70
Performs At: Walton Arts Center
Organization Type: Educational; Sponsoring

3725
SEASON OF ENTERTAINMENT
University of Arkansas-Fort Smith
5210 Grand Avenue
PO Box 3649
Fort Smith, AR 72913
Phone: 479-788-7000
e-mail: boxoffice@uafortsmith.edu
Web Site: www.uafortsmith.edu/season/
Officers:
Vice Chancellor Campus Events: Stacey Jones
Management:
Director Bands: Charles Booker
Director Vocal Activities: Thomas Lippert
Mission: Annual concert series that combines national touring productions with UA Fort Smith productions.
Performs At: Breedlove Fine Arts Auditorium; Fort Smith Civic Center
Seating Capacity: 440; 1,300

3726
OZARK ARTS COUNCIL
PO Box 382
Harrison, AR 72602-2117
Phone: 870-391-3504
Fax: 870-391-3504
e-mail: ozarkartscouncil@alltel.net
Web Site: www.thelyricharrison.org
Officers:
Executive Director: Joe Golden
Mission: To promote arts in Northwest Arkansas.
Utilizes: Fine Artists; Grant Writers; Guest Composers; Guest Musical Directors; Multimedia; Music; Original Music Scores; Sign Language Translators; Singers
Founded: 1965
Specialized Field: Series and Festivals; Instrumental Music; Vocal Music; Theatre; Youth
Status: Non-Profit, Professional
Paid Staff: 1
Volunteer Staff: 15
Paid Artists: 40
Budget: $25,000
Income Sources: Patrons; Grants
Performs At: Harrison High Scholl Auditorium
Affiliations: Ozark Arts Council
Annual Attendance: 2,500
Seating Capacity: 600

3727
WARFIELD CONCERTS
123 Stonebrooke
Helena, AR 72342
Phone: 870-338-8327
Web Site: www.warfieldconcerts.com
Management:
Contact: Bettye W Hendrix
Mission: Musical events made available free of charge through the generosity of the late Samuel Drake Warfield.
Founded: 1968
Specialized Field: Instrumental; Multi-Media; Opera; Choral; Jazz; Dance; Theatre; Childrens'; Educational
Paid Staff: 1
Volunteer Staff: 3
Paid Artists: 160
Budget: $20,000-$35,000
Season: Late April - Early May
Performs At: Philips Colliseum Fine Arts Center (Festival Site)
Affiliations: Lily Peter Auditorium
Seating Capacity: 1,250

3728
HOT SPRINGS MUSIC FESTIVAL CHAMBER ORCHESTRA
634 Prospect Avenue
Hot Springs, AR 71901-3918
Phone: 501-623-4763
Fax: 501-624-6440
e-mail: festival@hotmusic.org
Web Site: www.hotmusic.org
Management:
Artistic Director: Richard Rosenberg
Executive Director: Laura Rosenberg
Founded: 1996
Specialized Field: Series and Festivals; Instrumental Music; Vocal Music
Status: Non-Profit, Non-Professional
Paid Staff: 3
Paid Artists: 30

3729
HOT SPRINGS MUSIC FESTIVAL CHAMBER ORCHESTRA
634 Prospect Avenue
Hot Springs, AR 71901-3918
Phone: 501-623-4763
Fax: 501-624-6440
e-mail: hsmusfest@prodig.com
Web Site: www.hotmusic.org
Management:
Artistic Director: Richard Rosenberg
Executive Director: Laura S Rosenberg

3730
HOT SPRINGS MUSIC FESTIVAL
634 Prospect Avenue
Hot Springs National Park
Hot Springs, AR 71901-3918
Phone: 501-623-4763
Fax: 501-624-6440
e-mail: festival@hotmusic.org
Web Site: www.hotmusic.org
Officers:
Chair: David Lundberg
Vice Chair: Helen Selig
President/Executive Director: Laura S Rosenberg
Secretary/Treasurer: Kenneth Wheatley III
Management:
Artistic Director: Richard Rosenberg
Mission: Dedicated to bring young international string players together in Hot Springs and to provide midwinter concerts to Hot Springs residents and holiday visitors.
Founded: 1994
Specialized Field: Classical
Status: For-Profit, Professional
Budget: $370,000
Income Sources: Corporate; Individual Contributions
Season: December-June
Performs At: Various Historic Venues
Annual Attendance: 23,000
Seating Capacity: 1,100-2,200
Organization Type: Performing; Educational

3731
FOWLER CENTER AT ARKANSAS STATE UNIVERSITY
201 Olympic Drive
PO Box 2339
Jonesboro, AR 72467
Mailing Address: PO Box 2339 State University, AR 72467
Phone: 870-910-8115

Fax: 870-910-8118
e-mail: fowlercenter@astate.edu
Web Site: www.fowlercenter.astate.edu
Management:
    Director: Jerome Biebesheimer
    Director: Lee Christensen
    Technical Director: Albert Juhrend
Mission: The mission is to present to the students, faculty and staff of Arkansas State University and the citizens of Northeast Arkansas an opportunity to exprience visual and performing arts events of national and international stature.
Utilizes: Dance Companies; Multimedia; Original Music Scores
Founded: 2001
Specialized Field: Music; Theatre; Visual Art
Status: Nonprofit
Paid Staff: 5
Budget: $400,000
Income Sources: Arkansas State University; Endowments; Ticket Sales
Performs At: Fine Arts Recital Hall; Wilson Auditorium
Facility Category: Concert Hall, Drama Theatre
Type of Stage: Proscenium
Seating Capacity: 975; 342
Year Built: 2000
Rental Contact: Manager Jerry Biebesheimer

3732
ARTSPREE
University of Arkansas At Little Rock
164 Fine Arts Building
2801 S University
Little Rock, AR 72204-1099
Phone: 501-569-3288
Fax: 501-569-8775
e-mail: fwmartin@ualr.edu
Management:
    President: Floyd Martin
    Box Office Manager: Janice Sampson
Founded: 1993
Specialized Field: Series & Festivals: Music & Dance
Status: Non-Profit, Professional
Performs At: University Theatre; Stella Boyle Smith Concert Hall
Seating Capacity: 679; 312

3733
RIVERFEST AMPHITHEATRE
Jullius Breckling Riverfront Park
Little Rock, AR
Phone: 501-375-2552
Fax: 501-375-5559
Management:
    River Market Manager: Shannon Light
    Special Events Coordinator: Mabyn Patten
Seating Capacity: 10,000

3734
HARDING UNIVERSITY CONCERT & LYCEUM SERIES
PO Box 10877
Harding University
Searcy, AR 72149
Phone: 501-279-4311
Fax: 501-279-4086
e-mail: ganus@harding.edu
Management:
    Managing Director: Clifton Ganus
Mission: Four events per season, mostly classical, for a college community.
Utilizes: Guest Accompanists; Multimedia; Theatre Companies
Founded: 1924

Specialized Field: University With Performing Series
Status: Non-Profit, Non-Professional
Budget: $11,000
Performs At: Auditorium
Annual Attendance: 1,200
Type of Stage: Proscenium
Seating Capacity: 900
Rental Contact: David Briggs

3735
JOHN BROWN UNIVERSITY LYCEUM CONCERT SERIES
2000 West University Street
Siloam Springs, AR 72761
Phone: 479-524-7358
e-mail: jbuinfo@jbu.edu
Web Site: www.jbu.edu
Officers:
    Chair Communications/Fine Arts Dept: Terri Wubbena
Management:
    Director Music Theatre: Donna Rollene
    Media Relations Coordinator: Lindsey Dikes-Larsen
Mission: Concert series highlighting the works of various artists throughout the year and usually free to the public.
Paid Staff: 1
Volunteer Staff: 3
Budget: $9,000
Income Sources: Fees (student); grants
Performs At: Jones Recital Hall; Cathedral of the Ozarks
Annual Attendance: 500-600
Facility Category: Small recital hall; large sanctuary with platform
Seating Capacity: 159; 1000
Year Built: 1991

3736
GRAND PRAIRIE FESTIVAL OF THE ARTS
PO Box 65
Stuttgart, AR 72160
Phone: 870-673-1781
Fax: 870-673-1781
Management:
    Director: Wanda Loudermilk
Mission: To provide a diverse program of performing arts for the Grand Prairie community.
Utilizes: Guest Companies
Founded: 1956
Specialized Field: Vocal Music; Instrumental Music; Theater
Status: Professional; Non-Professional
Income Sources: Grand Prairie Arts Council
Performs At: Grand Prairie War Memorial Auditorium
Organization Type: Educational; Sponsoring

California

3737
KELSONARTS PERFORMANCES
315 Crest Avenue
Alamo, CA 94507
Phone: 925-934-4566
Fax: 925-934-4536
e-mail: info@kelsonarts.com
Web Site: www.kelsonarts.com
Management:
    Managing Director: Linus Eukel
Performs At: Various Sites

Seating Capacity: 200-750

3738
ALHAMBRA PERFORMING ARTS
111 S First Street
Alhambra, CA 91801
Phone: 626-570-5044
Fax: 626-282-9419
e-mail: webmaster@cityof alhambra.org
Web Site: www.cityofalhambra.org
Management:
    Artistic Director: Cynthia Jarvis
    Managing Director: Coludine Meeker
    Director of Community Programs: Mike Macias
Mission: To administer, manage and implement leisure service programs accommodating a variety of interests, ages, cultures, and abilities
Founded: 1804
Specialized Field: Series & Festivals; Instrumental Music; Vocal Music; Youth; Dance; Ethnic Performances
Status: Non-Profit, Professional
Paid Staff: 100
Season: Summer festival; free admission and parking
Performs At: Outdoor Bandshell
Seating Capacity: 750-1000

3739
OLD PASADENA JAZZ FESTIVAL – JAZZFEST WEST
27101 Aliso Creek Road
Suite 154
Aliso Viejo, CA 92656
Phone: 949-362-3366
Fax: 949-362-5366
e-mail: info@omegaevents.com
Web Site: www.omegaevents.com
Management:
    President: Rich Sherman
Founded: 1995
Specialized Field: Producing Concerts
Status: For-Profit, Non-Professional
Income Sources: Ticket Sales; Commercial sponsorship,
Season: Two-day festival; July;
Performs At: Outdoors; Bonelli Park , San Dimas, CA;

3740
NORTH ORANGE COUNTY COMMUNITY CONCERTS ASSOCIATION
623 S Clara Street
Anaheim, CA 92804
Phone: 714-535-8925
e-mail: membership@northocconcerts.org
Web Site: www.northocconcerts.org
Officers:
    VP Memberships: John Jackson
Management:
    President: Frank Knouse
Founded: 1945
Specialized Field: Series & Festivals; Instrumental Music; Vocal Music; Ethnic Performances
Status: Non-Profit, Professional
Performs At: Fullerton First United Methodist Church
Seating Capacity: 700

3741
SHASTA COMMUNITY CONCERT ASSOCIATION
6396 Vista Del Sierra Drive
P.O. Box 493979, Redding
Anderson, CA 96049-3979

Phone: 530-247-7355
Fax: 530-365-2664
Web Site: www.shastacommunityconcerts.com
Officers:
President: Jane G Wittmann
Management:
President: Jane Wippmann
Founded: 1938
Specialized Field: Series and Festivals; Instrumental
Music; Vocal Music; Youth; Dance
Status: Non-Profit, Professional
Income Sources: Season Memberships, Patron
Donors
Performs At: Redding Convention Center

3742
PACIFIC UNION COLLEGE FINE ARTS SERIES

Music Department
102 Paulin Hall
Angwin, CA 94508
Phone: 707-965-6201
Fax: 707-965-6390
Management:
Manager: Del Case
Mission: University Department of Music Performance
Series
Performs At: Paulin Hall
Seating Capacity: 465

3743
BEAR VALLEY MUSIC FESTIVAL

PO Box 5068
Bear Valley, CA 95223
Phone: 209-753-2574
Fax: 209-753-2576
Toll-free: 800-458-1618
e-mail: music@bearvalleymusic.org
Web Site: www.bearvalleymusic.org
Officers:
Executive Director: Caroline Schirato
Offfice Manager: Pati Hendersot
Production Manager: Myke Kunkel
Controller: Kathleen Lowe
Management:
Music Director: Carter Nice
President: Randy Hanvelt
VP: Ann Hicks
Director: Robert Bess
Founded: 1968
Specialized Field: Instrumental;Symphonic concerts;
Opera; Jazz; Childrens'
Budget: $20,000-$35,000
Income Sources: Subscription and Individual Ticket
Sales;Corporate Sponsors; Individual Donors; 501C3
non-profit organization
Season: July - August
Performs At: Bear Valley (Festival Site)
Facility Category: Festival Tent
Seating Capacity: 1,200

3744
NOTRE DAME DE NAMUR RALSTON CONCERT SERIES

NDNU Music Department
1500 Ralston Avenue
Belmont, CA 94002
Phone: 650-508-3597
Fax: 650-508-3736
e-mail: mschmitz@ndnu.edu
Web Site: www.music.ndnu.edu
Officers:
President: Christopher Clausen

Management:
President: John B O'Blak
Chairman Music Department: Debra Lambert
Stage Director: ,Greg Fritsch
Mission: University Department of Music Performance
Series
Founded: 1851
Specialized Field: Series & Festivals; Instrumental
Music; Vocal Music; Theatre; Dance
Status: Non-Profit, Professional
Paid Staff: 20
Performs At: Ralston Ballroom
Seating Capacity: 200

3745
BERKELEY FESTIVAL & EXHIBITION

UC Berkeley, Cal Performances
101 Zellerbach Hall, #4800
Berkeley, CA 94720-4800
Phone: 510-642-0212
Fax: 510-643-6707
e-mail: rcole@calperfs.berkeley.edu
Web Site: www.bfx.berkeley.edu
Management:
General Director: Robert W Cole
Mission: Produced by Cal Performances in association
with University Department of Music. San Francisco
Early Music Society; Early Music America
Specialized Field: Instrumental
Budget: $150,000-$400,000
Season: June
Performs At: Berkeley; University of California
(Festival Site)
Affiliations: Various Bay Locations
Seating Capacity: 400 - 2,000

3746
CALIFORNIA SHAKESPEARE THEATER

701 Heinz Avenue
Berkeley, CA
Berkeley, CA 94710
Phone: 510-548-3422
Fax: 510-843-9921
e-mail: info@calshakes.org
Web Site: www.calshakes.org
Officers:
Director of Finance: Noralee Rockwell
Business Office manager: Joyce Fleming
Development Director: Jim Huntley
Marketing & Public Relations Dir.: Marilyn
Langbehn
Management:
Artistic Director: Jonathan Moscone
Managing Director: Susie Folk
Associate Artistic Director: Jessica Richards
Production Manager: Jean Paul Grassieux
Mission: To make boldly imagined and deeply
entertaining interpretations of Shakespeare's plays and
other works of classic theater.
Utilizes: Actors; AEA Actors; Artists-in-Residence;
Choreographers; Collaborations; Commissioned Music;
Designers; Educators; Five Seasonal Concerts; Guest
Instructors; Guest Soloists; Instructors; Local Artists;
Multimedia; Organization Contracts; Original Music
Scores; Performance Artists; Poets; Resident
Professionals
Founded: 1973
Specialized Field: Theatre: Classics
Status: Non-Profit, Professional
Paid Staff: 25
Paid Artists: 50
Budget: $3,400,000
Income Sources: Ticket Sales; Government;
Individuals; Corporations; Foundations

Season: June - October
Performs At: Bruns Memorial Amphitheater
Annual Attendance: 46,000
Facility Category: Outdoor Amphitheater
Seating Capacity: 545
Year Built: 1990
Year Remodeled: 2010
Organization Type: Performing; Touring; Educational

3747
EARLY MUSIC IN MARIN

PO Box 10151
Berkeley, CA 94709
Phone: 510-548-3422
Fax: 510-843-9921
e-mail: sfems@sfems.org
Web Site: www.sfems.org
Management:
Coordinator: Alisa Gould Sugden
Mission: To create an appreciative and supportive
environment for the study and performance of medieval,
Renaissance, and baroque music.
Founded: 1975
Specialized Field: Instrumental
Budget: $10,000
Season: June - July
Performs At: Dominican Colliseum; San Rafael
(Festival Site)
Affiliations: Angelico Hall; Meadowlands Assembly
Hall
Seating Capacity: 500; 100

3748
FOUR SEASONS CONCERTS

PO Box 507
Berkeley, CA 94701
Phone: 510-845-4444
Fax: 510-549-3504
e-mail: admin@fourseasonconcerts.com
Web Site: www.fourseasonsconcerts.com
Officers:
President: Jesse W. Anthony
Management:
President: Jesse W Anthony
Founded: 1958
Performs At: Berkeley Piano Club, Berkeley; Herbst
Theatre, San Francisco; Regents' Theatre at Valley
Center, Holy Names University, Oakla
Seating Capacity: 1497; 915; 3176

3749
SAN FRANCISCO EARLY MUSIC SOCIETY

PO Box 10151
Berkeley, CA 94709
Phone: 510-528-1725
e-mail: sfems@sfems.org
Web Site: www.sfems.org
Officers:
Board President: Meryl Sacks
Administrative Assistant: Dorothy Manly
Management:
Executive Director: Harvey Malloy,
hmalloy@sfems.org
Mission: The San Francisco Early Music Society seeks
to create an appreciative and supportive environment
for the study and performance of Medieval,
Renaissance, and Baroque music by both amateurs
and professionals of Northern California.
Founded: 1975
Specialized Field: Chamber; Ensemble
Status: Professional; Nonprofit
Paid Staff: 2
Budget: $250,000

All listings are in alphabetical order by state, then city, then organization within the city.

477

Income Sources: Private and Corporate Donations; Grants
Performs At: First Lutheran Church; St. John's Presbyterian Church; St. Mark's Lutheran Church
Seating Capacity: 400

3750
UNIVERSITY OF CALIFORNIA-BERKELEY CALIFORNIA
101 Zellerbach Hall
#4800
Berkeley, CA 94720-4800
Phone: 510-642-0212
Fax: 510-643-6707
e-mail: rcole@calperfs.berkeley.edu
Web Site: www.calperfs.berkeley.edu
Officers:
    CEO: Lori Cripps
Management:
    Executive Director: Robert Cole
    Assistant Director: Robin Tomeromce
    Associate Director: Hollis Ashby
    General Manager: Mark Heiser
    Director/Marketing/Sales: Mary Dixon
Mission: To offer professional performances in the performing arts to students.
Founded: 1904
Specialized Field: Performing Arts
Status: Non-Profit, Professional
Paid Staff: 60
Income Sources: Association of Performing Arts Presenters; International Society of Performing Arts Administrators; Western Alliance of Arts Administrators
Performs At: Zellerbach Auditorium; University of California
Organization Type: Educational; Sponsoring

3751
INTERNATIONAL CONCERTS EXCHANGE
1124 Summit Drive
Beverly Hills, CA 90210
Phone: 213-272-5539
Fax: 213-272-5539
Management:
    Producer/Managing Director: Dr. Irwin Paones
Utilizes: Singers
Founded: 1942
Specialized Field: Festivals
Status: Professional; Semi-Professional; Non-Professional; Nonprofit
Organization Type: Performing; Educational

3752
PLAYBOY JAZZ FESTIVAL
9242 Beverly Boulevard
Beverly Hills, CA 90210
Phone: 310-449-4070
Fax: 310-786-7440
Web Site: www.playboy.com/arts-entertainment/features/jazzfest2008
Officers:
    President: Richard Rosenzweig
    Public Relations: Nina Gordon
    Communications Director: Bill Farley
Management:
    Producer: Hugh Hefner
    Producer: George Wein
    Associate Producer: Darlene Chan
    Festival Manager: Jonne-Marie Switzler
Mission: Providing a community service; enabling the residents of Los Angeles to enjoy jazz.

Founded: 1979
Specialized Field: Jazz
Status: Professional
Budget: $1.5-2 Million
Season: June Weekend
Performs At: Hollywood Bowl (Festival Site)
Annual Attendance: 35,000
Seating Capacity: 18,000
Year Built: 1922
Year Remodeled: 2003
Organization Type: Sponsoring

3753
BIG SUR JAZZ FEST
PO Box 459
Big Sur, CA 93920
Phone: 831-667-1530
Fax: 831-667-1530
Web Site: www.bigsurjazz.org
Management:
    Director: Ron Birmingham

3754
MUSIC AT KOHL MANSION
2750 Adeline Drive
Burlingame, CA 94010
Phone: 650-762—113
Fax: 650-343-8464
e-mail: info@musicatkohl.org
Web Site: www.musicatkohl.org
Officers:
    Chairman: Thomas Gilman
    Vice Chairman: Ernest Littaur
    Treasurer: Thomas Rounds
Management:
    Executive Director: Carol Eggers
    Musicologist: Kai Christiansen
    Finance Officer: Donna Fetisoff
    Education Director: Anneke Gaenslen
Mission: To offer chamber music performance and music education for adults and children.
Utilizes: Guest Directors; Multimedia
Performs At: Great Hall; Kohl Mansion
Seating Capacity: 200

3755
CARMEL BACH FESTIVAL
PO Box 575
Sunset Center Theater
Carmel, CA 93921
Phone: 831-624-1521
Fax: 831-624-2788
e-mail: info@bachfestival.org
Web Site: www.bachfestival.org
Officers:
    President: Cyril Yansouni
    First Vice President: Davis Nee
    Second vice president: Mary Castagna
    CFO/Treasurer: Susan Watts DuCoeur
Management:
    Artistic Director: Bruno Weill
    Executive Director: Camille Kolles
    Finance & Administration: Elizabeth Pasquinelli
    Marketing Director: Erin Sullivan
Mission: Performing the works of Johann Sebastian Bach, as well as other classical compositions.
Founded: 1935
Specialized Field: Series & Festivals; Instrumental; Opera; Choral; Childrens'; Educational
Status: Non-Profit, Professional
Paid Staff: 4
Paid Artists: 100
Non-paid Artists: 30
Budget: $2,300,000

Income Sources: Private Donations
Season: July - August
Performs At: Carmel (Festival Site)
Affiliations: Various Sites in the vicinity of Carmel-by-the-Sea
Annual Attendance: 17,000
Facility Category: Community Auditorium
Type of Stage: Proscenium
Seating Capacity: 733; 400; 250; 200
Year Built: 1928
Organization Type: Performing; Educational

3756
CARMEL MUSIC SOCIETY
PO Box 22783
Carmel, CA 93922
Phone: 831-625-9938
Fax: 831-625-6823
e-mail: carmelmusic@sbcglobal.net
Web Site: www.carmelmusic.org
Officers:
    President: Anne Thorp
    First Vice President: Victoria Davis
    Second vice president: Rudolf Schroeter
    Third Vice President: Larry Davidson
Management:
    Director of Marketing: Ginna Gordon
    Office Administrator: Lucy Faridany
Mission: To present classical music performances and foster the appreciation of classical music across the community.
Utilizes: Fine Artists; Guest Accompanists; Guest Directors; Guest Musical Directors; Multimedia; Original Music Scores; Theatre Companies
Founded: 1927
Specialized Field: Classical Music Presentation
Status: Non-Profit, Professional
Paid Staff: 2
Volunteer Staff: 10
Paid Artists: 30
Budget: $60,000-150,000
Income Sources: Ticket Sales; Grants; Donations
Performs At: Concert Hall or Church
Seating Capacity: 300-1,200

3757
PACIFIC REPERTORY THEATRE/CARMEL SHAKESPEARE FESTIVAL
PO Box 222035
Carmel, CA 93922
Phone: 408-622-0700
Fax: 831-622-0703
Management:
    Artistic Director: Stephen Moorer
Status: Non-Equity; Nonprofit
Season: February-October
Type of Stage: Proscenium; Thrust; Arena

3758
PACREP THEATRE
Monte Verde (btwn 8th & 9th Aves)
Carmel, CA 93921
Mailing Address: PO Box 222035, Carmel CA 93922
Phone: 831-622-0700
Fax: 831-622-0703
Toll-free: 866-622-0709
e-mail: contact@pacrep.org
Web Site: www.pacrep.org
Management:
    Executive Director/Founder: Stephen Moorer, smatprt@aol.com
    Technical Director: John Rousseau, john@pacrep.org

Business Manager: Julie Hughett, julieprt@aol.com
Company Manager: Jim Webber
Mission: Produces bold and daring interpretations of the great plays from the world stage in celebration of the transforming power of the creative spirit.
Utilizes: Visual Designers
Founded: 1982
Specialized Field: Live Professional Theatre
Status: Non-Profit, Professional
Paid Staff: 11
Volunteer Staff: 100
Paid Artists: 100
Season: Year Round

3759
FUJITSU-CONCORD JAZZ FESTIVAL

PO Box 845
Concord, CA 94522
Phone: 925-682-6770
Fax: 925-682-3508
e-mail: info@concordrecords.com

3760
ORANGE COAST COLLEGE COMMUNITY EDUCATION

2701 Fairview Road
PO Box 5005
Costa Mesa, CA 92626-0120
Phone: 714-432-5154
Fax: 714-432-5902
Toll-free: 888-622-5376
e-mail: jwood@occ.cccd.edu
Web Site: occtickets.com
Management:
   Administative Dean: George Blanc
   Lead Technician: Brock Cilley
   Administrative Secretary: Helen McGinley
Mission: To offer an enriching and affordable quality performing arts season for adults and school children.
Utilizes: Dancers; Guest Accompanists; Guest Instructors; Guest Soloists; Instructors; Local Artists; Original Music Scores; Special Technical Talent; Theatre Companies
Founded: 1947
Specialized Field: Band
Status: Semi-Professional
Paid Staff: 3
Budget: $350,000 Artist Fees
Income Sources: Orange Coast College
Performs At: Robert B Moore Theatre; Fine Arts Recital Hall; Drama Lab
Affiliations: WAA
Annual Attendance: 55,000
Facility Category: Concert Hall
Stage Dimensions: 40'x 50'
Seating Capacity: 916
Year Built: 1950
Year Remodeled: 1996
Rental Contact: Brock Cilley
Organization Type: Performing; Touring; Educational

3761
DEL NORTE ASSOCIATION FOR CULTURAL AWARENESS

Performance Series
501-B H Street
Crescent City, CA 95531
Mailing Address: PO Box 1480
Phone: 707-464-1336
Fax: 707-464-4842
e-mail: dnaca@harborside.com
Web Site: www.dnaca.net

Management:
   Executive Director: Holly O Austin
Mission: The Del Norte Association for Cultural Awareness provides support and excitement for all the creative arts, to inspire community vitality and harmony.
Founded: 1981
Opened: 1983
Specialized Field: Mulit-disciplinary local arts agency
Paid Staff: 1
Volunteer Staff: 4
Performs At: Crescent Elk Auditorium; Procenium arch
Seating Capacity: 530
Year Built: 1930
Rental Contact: Del Norte County USD

3762
UC DAVIS PRESENTS

200 B Street
Suite A
Davis, CA 95616-8561
Phone: 530-757-3488
Fax: 530-757-6815
Web Site: www.ucdavispresents.ucdavis.edu
Performs At: Freeborn Hall
Seating Capacity: 1280

3763
REDWOOD COAST DIXIELAND JAZZ FESTIVAL

523 5th Street
P.O. Box 314
Eureka, CA 95502
Phone: 707-445-3378
Fax: 707-445-1240
e-mail: info@redwoodjazz.org
Web Site: www.redwoodjazz.org
Management:
   President: Russ Harris
   Executive Director: Brenda Steinberg
Founded: 1991
Specialized Field: Series & Festivals; Instrumental Music; Vocal Music
Status: Non-Profit, Professional
Paid Staff: 2
Paid Artists: 20
Income Sources: Ticket Sales, Sponsors
Performs At: Six local venues, including The Adorni Center, The Arkely Center, Municipal Auditorium, Red Lion, Francheschi Hall and Vicker

3764
FAIRFIELD CITY ARTS

Cityarts Fairfield
1000 Webster Street
Fairfield, CA 94533
Phone: 707-428-7662
Fax: 707-428-0618
e-mail: reich@ci.fairfield.ca.us
Web Site: www.ci.fairfield.ca.us/cs-artscenter.htm
Management:
   President: Robert Reich
   Executive Director: John De Lorenzo
Founded: 1990
Specialized Field: Series & Festivals; Music and Performing Arts; Recitals; Concerts
Status: Non-Profit, Non-Professional
Paid Staff: 10
Performs At: Fairfield Center for Creative Arts
Seating Capacity: 368

3765
LIVELY ARTS FOUNDATION

1379 Crown Drive, Alameda CA
Fresno, CA 94501

Toll-free: 877-608-5883
e-mail: Livelyarts2@aol.com
Web Site: www.livelyarts.org
Management:
   Artistic Director: Diane K Mosler
   Technical Director: Tom Wolfgang
   Associate Artistic Director: Yukari Thiesen
Mission: A non-profit presenting and support organization to help establish the Fresno metropolitan area as a major cultural force by providing a variety of wold-class music, dance, and drama and dance outreach.
Founded: 1989
Performs At: William Saroyan Theatre
Seating Capacity: 2300

3766
FULLERTON FRIENDS OF MUSIC

1417 Kensington Drive
Fullerton, CA 92631
Phone: 714-525-5836
Fax: 714-529-1512
e-mail: fullerton-friends-of-music@webpanache.com
Web Site: www.webpan.com/fullerton-friends-of-music
Management:
   President: Lynn Rogers
   Executive Director: Tony Dycks
   Artistic Director: Valerie Bernstein
   Membership: Laurel Stevens
Mission: Dedicated to providing live music concerts featuring professional Classical Chamber Music and Early Period ensembles and artists, free of charge to the public.
Founded: 1958
Performs At: Sunny Hills High School Performing Arts Center
Seating Capacity: 350

3767
CITRUS COLLEGE HAUGH PERFORMING ARTS CENTER

1000 W Foothill Boulevard
Glendora, CA 91741
Phone: 626-852-8046
Fax: 626-335-4715
e-mail: ghinrichsen@citruscollege.edu
Web Site: www.haughpac.com
Management:
   Performing Arts Center Director: Greg Hinrichsen
   Marketing Director: Linda Graves
Utilizes: Artists-in-Residence; Fine Artists; Guest Instructors; High School Drama; Resident Professionals; Soloists; Special Technical Talent; Theatre Companies
Founded: 1971
Specialized Field: Music, Theatre, Education, Dance
Status: Non-Profit, Professional
Paid Staff: 25
Non-paid Artists: 300
Budget: $1 Million
Income Sources: College Support & Ticket Sales; Donations; Rentals
Performs At: Proscenium Venue
Annual Attendance: 125,000
Facility Category: Proscenium Theatre
Type of Stage: Sprung Wooden
Stage Dimensions: 54' opening
Seating Capacity: 1400
Year Built: 1971
Year Remodeled: 2005
Rental Contact: Greg Hinrichsen

3768

CALIFORNIA STATE UNIVERSITY EAST BAY

CSUEB Theatre And Dance Department
25800 Carlos Bee Boulevard
Hayward, CA 94542
Phone: 510-885-3118
Fax: 510-885-4748
e-mail: thomas.hird@csueastbay.edu
Web Site: www.class.csueastbay.edu/theatre
Officers:
    President: Mohammad Qayoumi
    Program Chair: Thomas Hird
    Production Manager: Richard Olmstead
Mission: University education in the performing arts, community service (performance), occassional privately funded guest artists, and community use facility.
Founded: 1964
Specialized Field: Theatre; Dance; Music
Status: Non-Profit, Non-Professional
Paid Staff: 2
Paid Artists: 10
Budget: $100,000
Income Sources: State Institutional Funds; Activity Board; Ticket Sales
Performs At: Educational Theatre
Annual Attendance: 12,000
Facility Category: University Theatre; Studio Theatre
Type of Stage: Proscenium
Stage Dimensions: 36'x 40' x 22'
Seating Capacity: 480
Year Built: 1975
Rental Contact: Facility Reservations Cecilia Grima-Torres

3769

HEALDSBURG JAZZ FESTIVAL

PO Box 266
Healdsburg, CA 95448
Phone: 707-433-4644
Fax: 707-431-8371
e-mail: info@healdsburgjazzfestival.org
Web Site: www.healdsburgjazzfestival.com
Officers:
    Chair: Frank Carrubba
    Vice Chair: Ed Flesch
    Treasurer: Richard Carney
Management:
    Artistic Director: Jessica Felix
    President Healdsburg Arts Counsil: Janet Norton
    Community Services Director: Marla Young
    VP Of Marketing: Dan Wildermuth
Founded: 1998

3770

RAMONA BOWL AMPHITHEATRE

27400 Ramona Bowl Road
Hemet, CA 92544
Phone: 951-658-3111
Fax: 951-658-2695
Toll-free: 800-645-4465
e-mail: ramona@ramonabowl.com
Web Site: www.ramonabowl.com
Officers:
    President of the Board: Jim Pomeroy
    Board Member: Don Meak
Management:
    Artistic Director: Dennis Anderson
    General Manager: Janine Reitenbach
    Marketing & Development: Judy Zulfiqar
    Wedding Coordinator: Llinda Hoogestraat

Mission: To bring California history to life through performances highlighting the region's Indian and Spanish cultures.
Utilizes: Actors; Collaborations; Curators; Dance Companies; Dancers; Designers; Educators; Filmmakers; Guest Companies; Guest Designers; Guest Directors; Guest Musical Directors; Guild Activities; High School Drama; Instructors; Local Artists; Multimedia; Music; Original Music Scores; Poets; Resident Professionals; Selected Students; Sign Language Translators; Singers; Soloists; Student Interns; Special Technical Talent
Founded: 1923
Specialized Field: Outdoor Drama
Status: Non-Profit, Non-Professional
Paid Staff: 5
Paid Artists: 2
Non-paid Artists: 600
Income Sources: Box Office; Private Donations; Grants
Performs At: Ramona Bowl Outdoor Amphitheatre
Affiliations: NTA; INTIX; Institute of Outdoor Drama; California Arts Council
Rental Contact: Events Coordinator Linda Hoogestraat
Organization Type: Performing; Resident; Educational

3771

RAMONA HILLSIDE PLAYERS

PO Box 462
Hemet, CA 92546
Phone: 951-658-5300
e-mail: info@hillsideplayers.org
Web Site: www.ramonahillsideplayers.org
Officers:
    President: Crist Thomas
    Vice President: Jean Brown
    Treasurer: Crist Thomas
    Secretary: Peggy McQuown
Management:
    Contact Person: Peggy L McQuown
    Technical Supervisor: Kim Negrete
Mission: To offer professional education in theatre performance and a series of performances.
Utilizes: Guest Companies
Founded: 1941
Specialized Field: Vocal Music; Instrumental Music; Theater
Status: Non-Professional; Nonprofit
Performs At: Ramona Hillside Playhouse
Organization Type: Performing; Resident; Educational

3772

HOLLYWOOD BOWL SUMMER FESTIVAL

Los Angeles Philharmonic Association
2301 North Highland Avenue
Hollywood, CA 90068
Phone: 323-850-2000
Fax: 323-850-5376
Web Site: www.hollywoodbowl.org
Officers:
    Chairman: John F Hotchkis
    President/CEO: Deborah Borda
Management:
    VP/General Manager Presentations: Arvind Manocha
    Orchestra Director: John Mauceri
    Program Director World Music: Tom Schnabel
    Philharmonic Music Director: Esa-Pekka Salonen
Mission: The summer home to the Los Angeles Philharmonic, which offers pop, classical and jazz performances. Offers a variety of free or low cost summer series events for children ages 3-11, and other performances.
Founded: 1922

Specialized Field: Instrumental; Multi-Media; Opera; Choral; Jazz; Folk; Dance; Theatre; Ethnic; Educational
Status: Professional; Nonprofit
Budget: $1,000,000
Income Sources: Los Angeles Philharmonic
Season: June - September
Performs At: Hollywood (Festival Site)
Facility Category: Hollywood Bowl
Seating Capacity: 17,400
Organization Type: Performing; Touring; Resident; Educational; Sponsoring

3773

IDYLLWILD ARTS-ACADEMY & SUMMER PROGRAM

52500 Temecula Drive
PO Box 38
Idyllwild, CA 92549
Phone: 951-659-2171
Fax: 951-659-4383
e-mail: admission@idyllwildarts.org
Web Site: www.idyllwildarts.org
Management:
    Director Summer Program: Steven Fraider
    Dean of Admission: Marek Pramukar
    Dean of Admission: Tara Sechrest
    Director Marketing: Darren Schilling
Mission: To provide pre-professional training in the arts and a comprehensive college preparatory curriculum in an environment conducive to positive personal development for gifted young artists from all over the world.
Founded: 1950
Specialized Field: Arts and Academics
Status: Non-Profit, Non-Professional
Performs At: Idyllwild Arts Foundation Theatre; Holmes Amphitheater
Seating Capacity: 300
Organization Type: Performing; Educational

3774

ECLECTIC ORANGE FESTIVAL

2082 Business Center Drive
Suite 100
Irvine, CA 92612
Phone: 949-553-2422
Fax: 949-553-2421
e-mail: contactus@philharmonicsociety.org
Web Site: www.eclecticorange.org
Management:
    Executive Director: Dean Corey
    Media: Chantel Chen
    Development Director: Susan Swinburne
Mission: As a project of the Philharmonic Society of Orange County, to foster, promote and increase the knowledge and appreciation of music and the arts through the presentation of performances of national and international stature; to development and implementation of a wide variety of education outreach programs.
Founded: 1999
Specialized Field: Classical
Paid Staff: 25
Volunteer Staff: 999
Paid Artists: 45

3775

UCI CULTURAL EVENTS

320 University Tower
University Of California
Irvine, CA 92717
Phone: 714-856-5589
Fax: 714-725-2201
Management:

Manager Cultural Events: Desiree Mallory
Mission: To provide professional performances for students and residents of the surrounding area.
Founded: 1965
Specialized Field: Dance; Instrumental Music; Theater
Status: Professional; Nonprofit
Performs At: Irvine Barclay Theatre; Bren Events Center
Organization Type: Educational; Sponsoring; Presenting

3776
TAHOE JAZZ FESTIVAL

PO Box 2390
Kings Beach, CA 96143
e-mail: info@tahoejazz.org
Web Site: www.tahoejazz.org

3777
CELEBRITY PRESENTATIONS

PO Box 457
La Canada, CA 91012
Phone: 818-790-3944
Fax: 818-790-2544
Management:
President: Sunny Charla Asch
Utilizes: Dance Companies; Guest Musicians; Multimedia; Original Music Scores; Special Technical Talent
Specialized Field: Series and Festivals; Instrumental Music; Vocal Music; Theatre; Dance; Ethnic Performances
Status: Non-Profit, Non-Professional
Paid Staff: 2
Budget: $60,000-150,000
Type of Stage: Proscenium

3778
LA JOLLA MUSIC SOCIETY SUMMERFEST

7946 Ivanhoe Avenue
Suite 309
La Jolla, CA 92037
Phone: 858-459-3724
Fax: 858-459-3727
e-mail: info@LJMS.org
Web Site: www.ljms.org
Officers:
Development Director: Ferdinand Gasand
Business Manager: Chris Benavides
Promotions manager: Anne Heinlein
Board Chair: Karen Brailean
Management:
President/Artistic Director: Christopher Beach
SummerFest Music Director: Cho-Liang Lin
Artistic Administrator: Leah Z Rosenthal
Marketing Director: Kristen Sakamoto
Mission: Presents a variety of presentations year-round including jazz, classical, and contemporary music and dance.
Founded: 1941
Specialized Field: Series & Festival; Classical Music
Status: Non-Profit, Professional
Paid Staff: 16
Volunteer Staff: 50
Budget: $3.5 Million
Income Sources: Tickets, Contributions, Grants

3779
UNIVERSITY EVENTS OFFICE

9500 Gilman Drive
UCSD Campus
La Jolla, CA 92093-0078
Phone: 858-534-4090
Fax: 858-534-7665
e-mail: knlee@ucsd.edu
Web Site: ueo.ucsd.edu
Management:
Director: Martin Wollesen
Assistant Director: Brian Ross
Business Manager: Beverly Ward
Marketing Manager: Amy Thomas
Mission: University Events Office, a department of Student Affairs at UC San Diego, is dedicated to presenting entertaining performing artists and film to expose the campus and community of the various art forms and diverse cultures of the world.
Utilizes: Actors; Choreographers; Dance Companies; Dancers; Filmmakers; Fine Artists; Guest Artists; Guest Instructors; Guest Lecturers; Guest Musical Directors; Guest Soloists; Multimedia; Special Technical Talent
Founded: 1965
Paid Staff: 8
Volunteer Staff: 25
Paid Artists: 30
Budget: $120,000 presenting only
Income Sources: Student Registration Fees; Ticket Sales; Patrons
Performs At: Mandeville Center
Affiliations: California Presenters
Annual Attendance: 20,000-30,000
Facility Category: Concert
Type of Stage: Proscenium
Stage Dimensions: 100'x40'
Seating Capacity: 788
Year Built: 1968
Rental Contact: Russell King

3780
DEL VALLE FINE ARTS CONCERT SERIES

PO Box 2335
Livermore, CA 94551-2335
Phone: 925-447-3564
e-mail: info@delvallefinearts.org
Web Site: www.delvallefinearts.org
Officers:
Jr President: Ervin C Woodward
President: Jeffrey B Garberson
Mission: To present outstanding classical chamber music groups along with a bit of non-traditional music.
Founded: 1980
Performs At: First Presbyterian Church
Seating Capacity: 450

3781
CITY OF LOS ANGELES CULTURAL AFFAIRS DEPARTMENT

201 North Figueroa St
Suite 1400
Los Angeles, CA 90012
Phone: 213-202-5500
Fax: 213-202-5517
Web Site: www.culturela.org
Management:
Executive Director: Olga Garay
Assistant General Manager: Saul Romo
Marketing & Development: Will Caperton y Montoya
Mission: To promote varied performing arts performances in the Los Angeles community.
Utilizes: Guest Artists; Guest Companies; Singers
Founded: 1980
Specialized Field: Dance; Vocal Music; Instrumental Music; Theater; Festivals
Status: Nonprofit

Organization Type: Performing

3782
GRAND PERFORMANCES

350 S Grand Avenue
Suite A-4
Los Angeles, CA 90071
Phone: 213-687-2190
Fax: 213-687-2191
e-mail: Comments@grandperformances.org
Web Site: www.grandperformances.org
Officers:
Office Administrator: Zindy Landeros Valle
Production Manager: Fred Stites
Board Chair: Craig Bloomgarden
Board Treasurer: Mark Flaisher
Management:
Executive & Artistic Director: Michael Alexander
Marketing Director: Dean Porter
Associate Director: Leigh Ann Hahn
Business Manager: Lee Lawlor
Development Associate: Karlee Decima
Office Adminstrator: Michelle Diaz
Production Manager: Fred Stites
Technical Director: Mark Baker
Office Administrator: Johnny Tu
Founded: 1987
Specialized Field: Series & Festivals; Instrumental Music; Vocal Music; Theatre; Dance; Ethnic Performances; Multi Disciplinary Performing Arts Presenter
Status: Non-Profit, Professional
Paid Staff: 10
Volunteer Staff: 2
Paid Artists: 504
Budget: $1.3 million
Income Sources: Contracts; Grants
Affiliations: APAP; WAA; California Presenters; California Arts Advocates
Annual Attendance: 65,000
Facility Category: Outdoor Plaza
Type of Stage: Thrust
Seating Capacity: 2,000; 6,500
Year Built: 1992

3783
JAZZ AT DREW LEGACY MUSIC & CULTURAL MARKETPLACE

1730 E 120th Street
Charles Drew University of Medicine & Science
Los Angeles, CA 90059
Phone: 323-563-5850
Fax: 323-563-4919
e-mail: toabdul@cdrewu.edu
Web Site: www.cdrew.edu
Management:
Executive Producer/Founder: Roland H Betts
Producer Assistant: Toni Abdul-Hanson
Mission: To offer jazz performances as public relation events and fundraisers.
Founded: 1991
Specialized Field: Instrumental Music (Jazz)
Paid Staff: 2
Volunteer Staff: 125
Paid Artists: 11

3784
LMU GUITAR CONCERT & MASTERCLASS SERIES

Loyola Marymount University Music Department
One LUM Drive
Los Angeles, CA 90045-8347

Phone: 310-338-5142
Fax: 310-338-5046
e-mail: mmiranda@lmumail.lmu.edu
Web Site: www.lmu.edu/guitarseries
Management:
    President: Michael Miranda
Founded: 1999
Specialized Field: Series & Festivals: Instrumental
Music
Status: Non-Profit, Professional
Paid Staff: 1
Paid Artists: 4
Performs At: Murphy Recital Hall

3785
LOS ANGELES BACH FESTIVAL

First Congregational Church
540 S Commonwealth Avenue
Los Angeles, CA 90020-1298
Phone: 213-385-1345
Fax: 213-487-0461
e-mail: musicinfo@fccla.org
Web Site: www.fccla.org
Officers:
    Events Manager: June Flowers
Management:
    Music Director: Dr. Jonathan Talberg
Mission: To provide this city with a unique opportunity
to celebrate the musical genius of Johann Sebastian
Bach in the neo-gothic beauty of the sanctuary and
chapel of First Church.
Founded: 1934
Specialized Field: Instrumental; Choral; Folk
Budget: $20,000-$35,000
Affiliations: First Congregational Church of Los
Angeles
Seating Capacity: 150
Year Built: 1867

3786
LOS ANGELES COUNTY MUSEUM OF ART

5905 Wilshire Boulevard
Los Angeles, CA 90036
Phone: 323-857-6014
e-mail: music@lacma.org
Web Site: www.lacma.org
Officers:
    President: Michael Govan
Management:
    Director Music Programs: Mitch Glickman
    Sundays Live Programs: Bill Vestal
    Music Programs Coordinator: Ryan Zwahlen
    Music Programs Coordinator: Gregory Milliren
Mission: To produce concerts of chamber music and
jazz.
Utilizes: Guest Artists; Singers
Founded: 1939
Specialized Field: Arts Museum
Status: Non-Profit, Non-Professional
Income Sources: Los Angeles County Museum of Art
Performs At: Leo S. Bing Theatre
Organization Type: Performing

3787
LACMA MONDAY EVENING CONCERTS

5905 Wilshire Boulevard
Los Angeles, CA 90036
Phone: 323-857-6115
Fax: 323-857-6214
e-mail: dstalvey@lacma.org
Web Site: www.lacma.org
Management:
    President: Andrea Rich

    Artistic Director: Dorrance Stalvey
Founded: 1939
Specialized Field: New Music
Status: Non-Profit, Professional
Paid Staff: 3
Volunteer Staff: 5
Paid Artists: 60
Performs At: Leo S. Bing Theatre
Seating Capacity: 600

3788
MOUNT SAINT MARY'S COLLEGE - THE DA CAMERA SOCIETY

10 Chester Place
Los Angeles, CA 90007s
Phone: 213-477-2929
Fax: 213-477-2959
e-mail: mbonino@msmc.la.edu
Web Site: www.dacamera.org
Officers:
    Client Services Manager: Patrick Schirato
    Membership & Development: Wendy Gragg
    Publications & Marketing: Ed Murray
Management:
    Founder/Artistic Director: Dr. MaryAnn Bonino
    General Director: Kelly Garrison
    Associate Director of Administratio: Sherrill
Bennet Herring
    Production & Music Education Manage: Sean
Bradley
Mission: Presenting chamber music in historic sites
that include the Doheny Mansion, walking and driving
tours in Boyle Heights, San Pedro, Camarillo, and San
Fernando.
Founded: 1973
Specialized Field: Series & Festivals: Music Chamber
Concert Series
Status: Non-Profit, Professional
Performs At: Doheny Mansion; Los Angeles' Union
Station; The Queen Mary; The former Bullocks Wilshire
Seating Capacity: 50-2000

3789
MUSIC CENTER OF LOS ANGELES COUNTY

135 N Grand Avenue
Los Angeles, CA 90012
Phone: 213-972-7211
e-mail: general@musiccenter.org
Web Site: www.musiccenter.org
Officers:
    Music Director/Philharmonic: Esa-Pekka Salonen
    Music Director/Chorale: Grant Gershon
Management:
    Chairman, Board of Directors: John B Emerson
    President and CEO: Stephen D Roundtree
    Artistic Director/Theatre Group: Michael Ritchie
    Music Director/Opera: James Conlon
Founded: 1964
Specialized Field: Series and Festivals; Instrumental
Music; Dance; Ethnic Performances
Status: Non-Profit, Professional
Paid Staff: 225

3790
MUSIC GUILD

6022 Wilshire Boulevard
Suite 203
Los Angeles, CA 90036

Phone: 323-954-0404
Fax: 323-954-0303
e-mail: themusicguild@aol.com;
tickets@themusicguild.org
Web Site: www.themusicguild.org
Officers:
    President: Anne Mor
    Secretary: Eugene Golden
Management:
    Executive/Artistic Director: Eugene Golden
    Executive Administrator: Pam Pantell
Mission: To present classical music in an intimate
setting; to introduce children at an early age; to provide
free intruments ; to encourage them to study music.
Founded: 1944
Specialized Field: Series & Festivals: Chamber Music
Concerts
Status: Non-Profit, Professional
Paid Staff: 3
Volunteer Staff: 4
Budget: $250,000-$300,000
Income Sources: Ticket Sales; Private Donations
Performs At: Chamber Music Groups Presenter
Affiliations: Cal State Northridge & Long Beach;
UCLA; University Synagogue
Annual Attendance: 1,500-2,000
Seating Capacity: 1294

3791
OCCIDENTAL COLLEGE ARTIST SERIES

1600 Campus Road
Los Angeles, CA 90041
Phone: 323-259-2737
Fax: 323-341-4987
e-mail: music@oxy.edu
Web Site: www.oxy.edu/Arts
Management:
    Department Chair: Irene Girton
    Director of Instrumental Music: Allen Gross
Specialized Field: Dance; Vocal Music; Instrumental
Music; Theater; World Music
Status: Nonprofit
Performs At: Thorne Hall; Keck Theater
Organization Type: Sponsoring

3792
ROSALINDE GILBERT CONCERTS

5905 Wilshire Boulevard
Los Angeles, CA 90036
Phone: 323-857-6115
Fax: 323-857-6214
e-mail: dstalvey@lacma.org
Web Site: www.lacma.org
Management:
    Music Director: Dorrance Stalvey
Founded: 1996
Specialized Field: Chamber Music
Performs At: Leo S Bing Thaetre; LA County Museum
of Art
Seating Capacity: 600

3793
SWEET & HOT SUMMER MUSIC FESTIVAL

PO Box 642269
Los Angeles, CA 90064-2269
e-mail: sweethot@sweethot.org
Web Site: www.sweethot.org
Management:
    Executive Director: Wally Holmes
    Director: John Kennebeck
    Chief Financial Officer: Earl Hammmond
    Festival Coordinator: Laurie Whitlock

Mission: The Sweet and Hot Music Foundation is a California 501c3 non-profit corporation dedicated to American's Golden Age of Popular Music.
Founded: 1996

3794
MASS ENSEMBLE
3525 Coast View Drive
Malibu, CA 90265
Phone: 310-317-8677
Fax: 310-313-8586
e-mail: CloseSound@aol.com
Web Site: www.massensemble.com
Management:
  Production Manager: Ron Doroba
  Artistic Director: William Close
  Business Manager: Andrew Cohen
  Associate Director: Andrea Brook

3795
MAMMOTH LAKES JAZZ JUBILEE
PO Box 909
Mammoth Lakes, CA 93546-0909
Phone: 760-934-2478
Fax: 760-934-2478
e-mail: mljj@qnet.com
Web Site: www.mammothjazz.org
Management:
  Director: Ken Coulter
  Director: Flossie Coulter
Mission: To bring to a small town-big time entertainment. To keep America's true art form alive.
Founded: 1989
Specialized Field: Series & Festivals: Jazz
Status: Non-Profit, Professional
Paid Staff: 2
Volunteer Staff: 500
Paid Artists: 140
Facility Category: 10 Venues in Tents

3796
YUBA COUNTY-SUTTER COUNTY REGIONAL ARTS COUNCIL TOURING/PRESENTING PROGRAM
624 & 630 E Street
PO Box 468
Marysville, CA 95901
Phone: 530-742-2787
Fax: 530-742-1171
e-mail: email@yubasutterarts.org
Web Site: www.yubasutterarts.org
Officers:
  Board President: David Anderson
  Board Vice President: Joan Saunders
  Board Secretary: Lee Jones
Management:
  Executive Director: Robert Reich
  Business Manager: Jim Jenkins
  Arts Coordinator: Lily Noonan
Performs At: Marysville Auditorium
Seating Capacity: 1,083

3797
MENDOCINO MUSIC FESTIVAL
PO Box 1808
Mendocino, CA 95460
Phone: 707-937-2044
Fax: 707-937-1045
e-mail: music@mendocinomusic.com
Web Site: www.mendocinomusic.com
Officers:
  President: Barbara Faulkner
  VP: Roger Schwartz

Treasurer: Jim Havlena
  Secretary: Marcia Lotter
Management:
  Artistic Director: Allan Pollack
  Festival Manager: Nancy Harris
  Box Office manager: Brian Eich
Mission: To enrich, educate and entertain all ages of residents and visitors by presenting world class musicians and music on the Mendocino Coast.
Utilizes: Guest Accompanists; Guest Instructors; Multimedia; Original Music Scores; Singers
Founded: 1986
Specialized Field: Series & Festivals; Youth; Dance; Ethnic Performances; Classical Music Festival
Status: Non-Profit, Professional
Paid Staff: 5
Volunteer Staff: 250
Paid Artists: 130
Budget: $480,000
Income Sources: Ticket Revenues, Donations, Sponsorhips, Program Ads, Events
Season: July
Performs At: Mendocino Headlands State Park (Festival Site)
Annual Attendance: 10,000
Facility Category: Tent/Concert Hall
Seating Capacity: 808
Organization Type: Performing

3798
SADDLEBACK COLLEGE GUEST ARTISTS SERIES
Division of Fine Arts Media Technology
28000 Marguerite Parkway
Mission Viejo, CA 92692-3635
Phone: 949-582-4413
Fax: 949-347-8653
e-mail: nwelch@saddleback.edu
Web Site: www.saddleback.edu
Officers:
  Public Information Officer: Nina Welch
Management:
  Dean of Fine Arts: Bart McHenry
  Performing Arts Director: Kate Realista
  Fine Arts Public Information: Nina Welch
Utilizes: Actors; Artists-in-Residence; Choreographers; Collaborations; Community Members; Composers; Contract Orchestras; Dancers; Filmmakers; Fine Artists; Five Seasonal Concerts; Grant Writers; Guest Accompanists; Guest Companies; Guest Designers; Guest Musical Directors; Instructors; Local Artists & Directors; Multimedia; Music; Paid Performers; Resident Professionals; Scenic Designers; Sign Language Translators; Student Interns; Theatre Companies; Visual Arts
Founded: 1977
Specialized Field: Series & Festivals; Instrumental Music; Vocal Music; Theatre; Youth; Dance; Ethnic Performances
Status: Non-Profit, Professional
Paid Staff: 7
Performs At: McKinney Theatre
Seating Capacity: 405

3799
STARLITE PATIO THEATER SUMMER SERIES
Montclair Civic Center
Benito And Fremont
Montclair, CA 91763
Phone: 909-625-9460
Fax: 909-399-9751
Management:

Manager/Program Director: Harve Edwards
  Facility Supervisor: Shirley Wofford
Mission: Offering summer cultural entertainment (eight programs) at no charge on Tuesdays.
Founded: 1963
Specialized Field: Dance; Theater
Status: Nonprofit
Paid Staff: 3
Paid Artists: 16
Budget: $2,400
Season: July and August
Performs At: The Starlite Patio Theater, 5111 Benito Street
Facility Category: Outdoor Patio
Type of Stage: Small Outdoor; Covered
Seating Capacity: 200
Organization Type: Performing

3800
DIXIELAND MONTEREY
177 Webster Street
A-206
Monterey, CA 93940
Phone: 831-675-0298
Toll-free: 888-349-6879
e-mail: email@dixieland-monterey.com
Web Site: www.dixieland-monterey.com
Management:
  President: April DeShields
  Vice President: Steve Carlisle
  Special Events Director: Donna DaVigo
  Marketing Director: Richard Hughett
Founded: 1980

3801
MONTEREY JAZZ FESTIVAL
PO Box Jazz
Monterey, CA 93942
Mailing Address: PO Box Jazz Monterey, CA 93942
Phone: 831-373-3366
Fax: 831-373-0244
e-mail: jazzinfo@montereyjazzfestival.org
Web Site: www.montereyjazzfestival.org
Officers:
  Development Director: Paul Mondestin
  Education Director: Dr. Rob Klevan
  Marketing Director: Paul S Fingerote
  Stage Manager: Mike Wilmot
Management:
  President: Jackson Booth
  General Manager: Tim Jackson
  Production Coordinator: David Murray
Mission: To perpetuate jazz and further jazz education.
Founded: 1958
Specialized Field: Entertainment and Music Presentation
Status: Non-Profit, Professional
Paid Staff: 7
Paid Artists: 500

3802
MUSIC IN THE VINEYARDS
Napa Valley Cahmber Music Festival
PO Box 6297
Mt. Helena, CA 94581
Phone: 707-258-5559
Fax: 707-258-5566
e-mail: mitv@sonic.net
Web Site: www.musicinthevineyards.org
Officers:
  President: Greg Evans
  Secretary: Rosemary Richardson
  Treasurer: Peter McCrea
Management:

Co-Artistic Director: Daria T Adams
Co-Artistic Director: Michael Adams
Executive Director: Evie Ayers
Marketing Manager: Christy Bors
Mission: Dedicated to bringing together outstanding artists to perform in the unique vineyard settings of the Napa Valley so that both the performers and the audience can experience the intimacy of chamber music as it was intended to be performed.
Utilizes: Multimedia; Original Music Scores
Founded: 1995
Specialized Field: Chamber Music Festival
Paid Staff: 3
Volunteer Staff: 120
Paid Artists: 45
Budget: $140,000
Season: August
Performs At: Napa Valley (Festival Site)
Affiliations: Various vineyards and related venues
Seating Capacity: 150 - 250

3803
MUSIC IN THE MOUNTAINS
530 Searls Avenue, Suite A
PO Box 1451
Nevada City, CA 95959
Phone: 530-265-6173
Fax: 530-265-6810
Toll-free: 800-218-2188
e-mail: mim@musicinthemountains.org
Web Site: www.musicinthemountains.org
Officers:
President: Jeffrey Leiter
Vice President: Dan Halloran
Vice President: Lynn Kerby
Vice President: Bill Kinney
Management:
Artistic Director: Paul Perry
Executive Director: Marge Rath
Artistic Coordinator: Neil Tatman
Marketing Director: Jeanne Duerst
Mission: To present a full spectrum of classical music by including chamber music, pops, jazz, big band, and Broadway music in the repertoire.
Founded: 1982
Specialized Field: Series & Festivals; Instrumental Music; Vocal Music; Instrumental; Choral; Jazz; Educational; Childrens'
Status: Non-Profit, Professional
Paid Staff: 6
Paid Artists: 175

3804
MUSIC IN THE MOUNTAINS
530 Searls Avenue, Suite A
PO Box 1451
Nevada City, CA 95959
Phone: 530-265-6173
Fax: 530-265-6810
Toll-free: 800-218-2188
e-mail: mim@musicinthemountains.org
Web Site: www.musicinthemountains.org
Officers:
President: Hazel Shewell
Management:
Artistic Director: Paul Perry
Executive Director: Barry Bonifas
Mission: To present high-quality classical, jazz and Broadway music at affordable prices.
Utilizes: Artists-in-Residence; Collaborating Artists; Commissioned Music; Grant Writers; Guest Companies; Guest Directors; Guest Musical Directors; Guest Musicians; Instructors; Multi Collaborations;

Multimedia; Organization Contracts; Original Music Scores; Sign Language Translators; Singers; Student Interns
Founded: 1981
Specialized Field: Instrumental; Choral; Jazz; Educational; Childrens'
Status: Professional; Nonprofit
Paid Staff: 6
Volunteer Staff: 300
Paid Artists: 175
Budget: $700,000-$1,000,000
Income Sources: Donation; Grants; Ticket Sales; Benefit Events; Advertising; Sponsoring
Season: November; December; April; June; July
Performs At: Festival sites around Nevada City & Grass Valley
Affiliations: Chamber Music America; American Symphony Orchestra League; Association of California Symphony Orchestras; BMI; ASCAP
Annual Attendance: 17,000
Facility Category: Renovated Concert Hall; Outdoor Tent
Stage Dimensions: 48'x56'
Seating Capacity: 550 inside; 4,000 outside
Year Remodeled: 2001
Organization Type: Performing; Resident; Educational; Sponsoring

3805
CENTER FOR THE VISUAL AND PERFORMING ARTS
California State University, Northbridge
18111 Nordhoff Street
Northridge, CA 91330-8314
Phone: 818-677-5768
Fax: 818-677-5472
e-mail: info@ArtsNorthridge.csun.com
Web Site: www.cvpa.csun.com
Officers:
Dean: William Toultant
Associate Dean: Cynthia Raywrtch
Management:
General Director: Karen Kearns
Concert Production: Guy Fabre
Administrative Coordinator: Jill Price
Director of Public Relations: Mary Reale
Mission: To provide cultural, educational and artistic experiences that enrich lives and promote lifelong learning in and through the arts to the community we serve.
Founded: 1996
Specialized Field: Jazz Series; Dance Series; Celebrity Shows Series
Paid Staff: 10
Volunteer Staff: 75
Budget: $300,000
Income Sources: University Subsidy; Tickets Sales; Contributions
Performs At: USU, Northridge Performing Arts Center; Plaza del Sol Performance Hall
Annual Attendance: 50,000
Type of Stage: Proscenium
Seating Capacity: 500/150
Year Built: 1994
Rental Contact: Kathy Anthony

3806
MULTI-CULTURAL MUSIC AND ART FOUNDATION OF NORTHRIDGE (MCMAFN)
PO Box 280101
Northridge, CA 91328

Phone: 818-349-3431
Fax: 818-349-0716
e-mail: info@mcmafn.org
Web Site: www.mcmafn.org
Officers:
President: W M Paulin
Vice President/Historial: Paul A. Dentzel
Management:
Program Coordinator/Creative Dir: Elisabeth Waldo
Secretary: Paul Dentzel
Chief Financial Officer: William Paulin
Mission: Supporting a wide range of performing and visual arts, particularly music and dance.
Utilizes: Actors; Curators; Dancers; Educators; Filmmakers; Five Seasonal Concerts; Grant Writers; Guest Accompanists; Guest Instructors; Guest Lecturers; Guest Musical Directors; Guest Musicians; Multi Collaborations; Multimedia; Organization Contracts; Original Music Scores; Resident Professionals; Sign Language Translators; Singers; Soloists; Touring Companies; Visual Arts
Founded: 1998
Specialized Field: Dance; Vocal Music; Instrumental Music; Festivals
Status: Non-Profit,Non-Professional
Paid Staff: 2
Budget: $100,000
Income Sources: Memberships, Grants, Admissions to Theatre
Performs At: New Mission Theatre
Affiliations: All Los Angeles Museums, ASCAP, Local 47 AIF
Type of Stage: Expandable
Seating Capacity: 150, outdoors; 300 seats
Year Remodeled: 1995
Rental Contact: Booking Calendar Hengamett
Organization Type: Performing; Educational

3807
MILLS COLLEGE MUSIC DEPARTMENT
5000 Macarthur Boulevard
Oakland, CA 94613
Phone: 510-430-2171
Fax: 510-430-3228
e-mail: music@mills.edu
Web Site: www.mills.edu/music
Officers:
President: Janet L. Holmgren
Vice President Finance: Elizabeth Burwell
Management:
Concert Coordinator: Steed Cowart
Technical Director: Les Stuck
Founded: 1852

3808
REDWOOD ART COUNCIL
PO Box 449
Occidental, CA 95465
Phone: 707-874-1124
Fax: 707-544-1512
e-mail: racmusic@sonic.net
Web Site: www.redwoodarts.org
Officers:
President/Director: Kathryn Neustadter
Management:
Director: Candace Rossman
Mission: To present exceptional chamber music.
Utilizes: Guest Musical Directors; Multimedia; Original Music Scores; Sign Language Translators; Singers; Soloists
Founded: 1980
Specialized Field: Series & Festivals: Chamber Music Concerts

Status: Non-Profit, Professional
Paid Staff: 15
Volunteer Staff: 15
Paid Artists: 30
Budget: $50,000
Income Sources: Tickets, Donations, Grants
Performs At: Occidental Community Church
Annual Attendance: 1,500-2,000
Facility Category: Mostly Churches
Type of Stage: Platform
Stage Dimensions: 8' x 20'
Seating Capacity: 150
Year Built: 1876

3809
OJAI FESTIVALS
201 S Signal Street
PO Box 185
Ojai, CA 93024
Phone: 805-646-2094
Fax: 805-646-6037
e-mail: info@ojaifestival.org
Web Site: www.ojaifestival.org
Management:
   Executive Director: Jeffrey P Haydon
   Artistic Director: Thomas W Morris
Mission: Promoting contemporary music and dance
performances, from artists such as Emerson Quartet.
Utilizes: Actors; Composers-in-Residence; Educators;
Grant Writers; Guest Accompanists; Guest Artists;
Guest Companies; Guest Lecturers; Guest Musicians;
Local Artists; Lyricists; Multimedia; Original Music
Scores; Singers; Soloists
Founded: 1971
Status: Non-Profit, Professional
Paid Staff: 5
Budget: $600,000
Income Sources: American Symphony Orchestra
League; California Confederation of the Arts
Season: May - June
Performs At: Ojai Festival; Libbey Bowl
Affiliations: Libbey Bowl
Seating Capacity: 1,500
Organization Type: Educational; Sponsoring

3810
OJAI MUSIC FESTIVAL
201 S Signal Street
PO Box 185
Ojai, CA 93024
Phone: 805-646-2094
Fax: 805-646-6037
e-mail: info@ojaifestival.org
Web Site: www.ojaifestival.org
Officers:
   President: Christine T Drucker
   Vice President: Barbara Hirsch
   Vice President: Esther Wachtell
   Treasurer: Thomas A Munzig
Management:
   Executive Director: Jeffrey P Hydon
   Artistic Director: Thomas W Morris
   Festival Producer: Susan Anderson
   Director of Marketing: Gina Gutierrez
Mission: To foster a healthy spirit of eclecticism in
adventurous programs, attracting artists who are given
artistic freedom to perform exceptional pieces of
classical music.
Founded: 1947
Specialized Field: Series & Festivals: Classical Music
Status: Non-Profit, Professional
Paid Staff: 5
Paid Artists: 150
Season: June

Performs At: Libby Bowl

3811
OJAI MUSIC FESTIVAL
201 S Signal Street
PO Box 185
Ojai, CA 93024
Phone: 805-646-2094
Fax: 805-646-6037
e-mail: info@ojaifestival.org
Web Site: www.ojaifestival.org
Management:
   Executive Director: Jacqueline Saunders

3812
OJAI SHAKESPEARE FESTIVAL
160 Oak Glen Avenue
Ojai, CA 93023-3011
Phone: 805-646-9455
Fax: 805-646-9455
e-mail: info@ojaishakespeare.org
Web Site: www.ojaishakespeare.org
Officers:
   VP: Bruce Wallace
   Treasurer: Wayne Francis
   Secretary: Marilyn Wallace
   Madrigali Representative: Dave Farber
Management:
   Producer: Peter Fox
   Producer: Kathy Zotnowski
   Co-Producer: Julie Fox
   Director: Paul Amadio
   Marketing/Public Relations: Dina Pielaet
Founded: 1991
Status: Non-Profit,Non-Professional
Season: August
Type of Stage: Amphitheatre
Stage Dimensions: 38'x32'
Seating Capacity: 650

3813
OROVILLE CONCERT ASSOCIATION
29 Orchard Hill Drive
Oroville, CA 95966
Phone: 530-589-0836
e-mail: swedin@cncnet.com
Officers:
   President: Sharon Wedin
Management:
   President: Herma Barber
Mission: To offer every man, woman and child in the
community the opportunity to experience the magic of
affordable, live, quality performances.
Founded: 1952
Specialized Field: Series and Festivals: Community
Concerts
Status: Non-Profit, Professional
Income Sources: Supported by theater ticket sales,
and patron and corporate sponsorships
Performs At: State Theater, in downtown Oroville
Seating Capacity: 612

3814
CANYON INDUSTRIES
PO Box 256
Palm Springs, CA 92263
Phone: 760-778-7966
Fax: 760-778-4890
e-mail: simone@angelshq.com
Web Site: www.canyonentertainment.com
Management:
   President: Simone Sheffield

Utilizes: Actors; AEA Actors; Artists-in-Residence;
Choreographers; Collaborating Artists; Commissioned
Composers; Commissioned Music; Dance Companies;
Dancers; Designers; Filmmakers; Grant Writers; Guest
Companies; Guest Designers; Guest Musical Directors;
Guest Soloists; Local Unknown Artists; Multimedia;
Music; Original Music Scores; Performance Artists;
Poets; Selected Students; Sign Language Translators;
Soloists; Special Technical Talent; Theatre Companies
Founded: 1981
Paid Staff: 30
Volunteer Staff: 100
Paid Artists: 10
Non-paid Artists: 10
Budget: $400,000-1,000,000

3815
CATALINA ISLAND JAZZTRAX FESTIVAL
611 S Palm Canyon Drive
Suite 7-458
Palm Springs, CA 92264-7402
Phone: 760-323-1171
Fax: 760-323-5770
Toll-free: 888-330-5252
e-mail: info@jazztrax.com
Web Site: www.jazztrax.com/jazz/catalina.html
Management:
   Founder: Art Good
   Festival Director: Gregg Hudson
Mission: Jazz festival held for three weekends at the
beautiful Avalon Harbor on Catalina Island.
Founded: 1987
Season: October

3816
CALTECH PUBLIC EVENTS SERIES
Caltech Public Events
Mail Code 332-92
Pasadena, CA 91125
Phone: 626-395-3834
Fax: 626-395-1721
Toll-free: 888-225-32
e-mail: events@caltech.edu
Web Site: www.events.caltech.edu
Management:
   Public Events Administrator: Denise Nelson Nash
   Associate Director: Chris Harcourt
   Operations Coordinator: Deborah White
   Marketing and Outreach Manager: Cara Stemen
Mission: Each season Caltech presents performing
arts events ranging from theater and music to dance
and comedy. Open to the public; tickets required.

3817
CALTECH PUBLIC EVENTS SERIES
Caltech Public Events
Mail Code 332-92
Pasadena, CA 91125
Phone: 626-395-4638
Fax: 626-577-0130
e-mail: events@caltech.edu
Web Site: www.events.caltech.edu
Management:
   Director: Denise Nelson Nash
   Associate Director: Chris Harcourt
   Technical Operations Manager: Louis Lind
   Marketing/Outreach Manager: Cara Steven
   Stage Technician: Erick Ferguson
Budget: $60,000-150,000
Performs At: Beckman Auditorium; Ramo Auditorium;
Dabney Lounge
Seating Capacity: 1165; 423; 200

3818
COLEMAN CHAMBER CONCERTS
225 S Lake Avenue
Suite 300
Pasadena, CA 91101
Phone: 626-793-4191
Fax: 818-787-1294
e-mail: info@colemanchambermusic.org
Web Site: www.coleman.caltech.edu
Officers:
President: Susan Grether
Vice President: Robert Winter
Secretary: Donna Swayze
Treasurer: Jerome Hamburger M.D.
Management:
Executive Director: Kathy Freedland
Mission: To present international chamber ensembles, both established and emerging.
Utilizes: Guest Directors
Founded: 1904
Specialized Field: Chamber
Status: Nonprofit
Paid Staff: 1
Volunteer Staff: 50
Income Sources: Western Alliance of Arts Administrators; Chamber Music America; California Presenters; Ticket Sales, Membership Dues, Endowment Income and Gifts from Organizations
Season: October-April
Performs At: Caltech Beckman Auditorium
Stage Dimensions: 24x43x16
Seating Capacity: 1,150
Year Built: 1964
Organization Type: Sponsoring

3819
MONTICELLO MEDICI PERFORMING ARTS ACADEMY
200 Fern Drive
Pasadena, CA 91105-1216
Phone: 626-792-3096
Fax: 626-792-5049
e-mail: vburner@juno.com

3820
MONTICELLO MEDICI PERFORMING ARTS ACADEMY
200 Fern Drive
Pasadena, CA 91105-1216
Phone: 626-792-3096
Fax: 626-792-5049
e-mail: vburner@juno.com
Officers:
President: Dr. Victor Burner
Performs At: Monticello Medici Recital Hall
Seating Capacity: 25-75

3821
SONGFEST
Pasadena, CA 91106
Phone: 626-449-7146
Fax: 626-405-0151
e-mail: songfest@earthlink.net
Web Site: www.songfest.us
Management:
Artistic Director: Rosemary Hyler Ritter
Dean School Of Music: Elaine Chow
Mission: To advance the art of song by cultivating its musical literary traditions and promoting its contemporary development, with both artists and audiences. To provide both professional and pre-professional artists with unique opportunity of close working association with some of the world's most distinguished artists.
Founded: 1996
Specialized Field: Series & Festivals: Classical Voice and Piano
Status: Non-Profit, Non-Professional
Paid Staff: 1
Volunteer Staff: 7
Paid Artists: 10
Budget: $110,000
Income Sources: Private Donors, Tuitions, and grants for the Aaron Copland Fund for Music, The Marc and Eva Stern Foundation, and The Ann and Gordon Getty Foundation
Affiliations: Chapman University
Facility Category: Music School

3822
GOLDEN GATE INTERNATIONAL CHILDREN'S CHORAL FESTIVAL
401-A Highland Avenue
Piedmont, CA 94611
Phone: 510-547-4441
Fax: 510-547-7449
Web Site: www.piedmontchoirs.org
Officers:
President: Terry Amgott-Kwan
Vice President: Terence Howzell
Secretary: Susan R Kelley
Treasurer: Paul Swenson
Management:
Director/Founder: Robert Geary
Executive Director: Stuart Rosenthal
Program Manager: T J Togasaki
Marketing: Cynthia Doll
Mission: The GGF, the first international children's choral festival in the western U.S., promotes international understanding through music, and musical excellence in choral singing, through competition and performance.
Founded: 1991
Season: July

3823
IAI PRESENTATIONS
Peking Acrobats
PO Box 4
Pismo Beach, CA 93448-0004
Phone: 805-476-8422
Fax: 805-476-8426
Toll-free: 800-424-3454
e-mail: don@iaipresentations.com
Web Site: www.iaipresentations.com
Officers:
President: Don Hughes
Management:
Producer: Don Hughes
Artistic Director: Ken Hai

3824
PEKING ACROBATS
IAI Presentations
PO Box 4
Pismo Beach, CA 93448-0004
Phone: 805-474-8422
Fax: 805-474-8426
Toll-free: 800-424-3454
e-mail: don@iaipresentations.com
Web Site: www.iaipresentations.com
Founded: 1984

3825
CALIFORNIA INSTITUTE OF MUSIC
PO Box 9401
Rancho Santa Fe, CA 92067
Phone: 858-259-2503
Fax: 858-259-5508
e-mail: office@cimwebsite.org
Web Site: www.cimwebsite.org
Officers:
President: Michael Tseitlin
Management:
Artistic Director: Irina Tseitlin
President: Michael Tseitli
Founded: 1990
Specialized Field: Recitals: Southern California Youth Symphony and Sinfonietta
Income Sources: Tuition and individual patrons, donors, and Sponsors
Performs At: California Center for the Arts; Horizon Auditorium
Seating Capacity: 1600; 650

3826
CARMEL VALLEY LIBRARY CONCERT SERIES
PO Box 9401
Rancho Santa Fe, CA 92067
Phone: 858-259-2503
Fax: 858-259-5508
Management:
Artistic Director: Michael Tseitlin
Budget: $35,000-60,000
Performs At: Concert Hall
Seating Capacity: 300

3827
INTERNATIONAL INSTITUTE OF MUSIC FESTIVAL
Rancho Santa Fe, CA 92067
Phone: 858-259-2503
Fax: 858-259-5508
Management:
Executive Director: Michael Tseitlin
Administrative Director: Paul Lindenauer
Artistic Advisor: Giuseppe Nova
Specialized Field: Instrumental; Educational
Budget: $35,000-$60,000
Season: July
Performs At: Bayerische Musikakademie; Marktoberdorf (Festival Site)
Seating Capacity: 400 - 800

3828
RIVERCITY JAZZ FESTIVAL
4055 Oro Street
Redding, CA 96001-2937
Phone: 530-244-6033
e-mail: rhuff@c-zone.net
Web Site: www.rivercityjazz.com
Management:
President: Kathie Sanchez
Festival Director: Maurice Huff
Membership: Lorna Burke
Mission: The Redding Jazz Festival, offered in April, is one of the performance events offered by the Rivercity Jazz Society. Other performances from March through December include the Annual Youth Jazz Concert, Ken Brock & Friends, Jasscity, Delta Flyers, Jelly Roll jazz Band and Straight Ahead Big Band. These performances are held in Redding, Stockton, Sacramento, Vacaville, Emeryville, Wallace, and Fairfield
Founded: 1986

Season: April
Performs At: Mt. Shasta Mall in Redding

3829
REDLANDS BOWL SUMMER MUSIC FESTIVAL
PO Box 466
Redlands, CA 92373-0141
Phone: 909-793-7316
Fax: 909-793-5086
e-mail: bowlprogdir@aol.com
Web Site: www.redlandsbowl.org
Officers:
    Executive Director: Beverly Noerr
Management:
    President: David Breff
    Executive Director: Beverly Noerr
    Program Director: Marsha Gebara
Mission: Providing a range of performing arts to residents of Redlands at no admission charge.
Utilizes: Dance Companies; Dancers; Grant Writers; Guest Accompanists; Guest Musical Directors; Guest Musicians; Multimedia; Music; Original Music Scores; Singers; Special Technical Talent
Founded: 1923
Specialized Field: Series & Festivals; Instrumental; Opera; Choral; Traditional Jazz; Dance; Childrens'
Status: Non-Profit, Non-Professional
Paid Staff: 2
Volunteer Staff: 100
Budget: $150,000-$400,000
Income Sources: Freewill Donations; Underwriting; Grants
Season: Late June - Late August
Performs At: Redlands Open-air Amphitheatre (Festival Site)
Affiliations: Redlands Bowl
Annual Attendance: 80,000 to 100,000
Seating Capacity: 3,750
Organization Type: Performing; Sponsoring

3830
JAZZ ON THE LAKE: PEOPLE PRODUCTIONS
Mateel Commjunity Center,
PO Box 1910
Redway, CA 95560
Phone: 707-923-4599
Fax: 707-923-4509
e-mail: people@humboldt.net
Web Site: www.peopleproductions.net
Management:
    Executive Director: Carol Bruno
Founded: 1985
Specialized Field: Series & Festivals: Music Productions and Promotions
Status: For-Profit, Non-Professional
Paid Staff: 8
Paid Artists: 30
Performs At: 1976

3831
SUMMER ARTS & MUSIC FESTIVAL
Mateel Community Center
PO Box 1910
Redway, CA 95560
Phone: 707-923-3368
Fax: 707-923-3370
e-mail: office@mateel.org
Web Site: www.mateel.org
Officers:
    President: Garth Epling
    Vice President: Bruce Champie

Treasurer: Bob Stern
    Secretary: Elena Worley
Management:
    Talent and Booking: Justin Crellin
    Office Administrator: Katz Boose
    Sponsorship and Ad Sales: Cathy Miller
    Special Projects: Casandra Taliaferro
Mission: To involve segments of the community in the creative actualization of a cultural vision embracing diversity, vitality, justice, and sustainability. Our programs and events serve changing community needs, emphasizing the performing and visual arts.
Founded: 1976
Specialized Field: 100 diverse performances on 5 stages, over 150 handmade craft and food booths, fine arts showcase.
Status: Non-Profit, Professional
Paid Artists: 20
Non-paid Artists: 40
Season: Late June
Performs At: Benbow Lake State Recreation Area in Humboldt County
Facility Category: Outdoor venue
Seating Capacity: 6,000

3832
WINTER ARTS FAIRE
Maateel Community Center
PO Box 1910
Redway, CA 95560
Phone: 707-923-3368
Fax: 707-923-3370
e-mail: office@mateel.org
Web Site: www.mateel.org
Officers:
    President: Garth Epling
    Vice President: Bruce Champie
    Treasurer: Bob Stern
    Secretary: Elena Worley
Management:
    Talent and Booking: Justin Crellin
    Office Administrator: Katz Boose
    Sponsorship and Ad Sales: Cathy Miller
    Special Projects: Casandra Taliaferro
Mission: To involve segments of the community in the creative actualization of a cultural vision embracing diversity, vitality, justice, and sustainability. Our programs and events serve changing community needs, emphasizing the performing and visual arts.
Founded: 1976
Specialized Field: Series & Festivals; Instrumental Music; Vocal Music; Youth; Dance; Ethnic Performances; Instrumental; Jazz
Status: Non-Profit, Professional
Paid Artists: 1
Season: December, second weekend
Affiliations: Mateel Community Center; Redway
Annual Attendance: 1,500 per day
Facility Category: Community Center/Performance Hall

3833
INDIAN WELLS VALLEY CONCERT ASSOCIATION
PO Box 1802
Ridgcrest, CA 93556-1802
Phone: 760-375-5600
Fax: 760-375-3330
e-mail: iwvca@hotmail.com
Web Site: www.iwvca.com
Officers:
    President: Alice E Martin
    Vice President: Micki Edge-O'Bergfell
    Secretary: Yvonne M Beyer

Treasurer: Katherine Hu
Management:
    Business Manager: Carl N Helmick Jr
    Marketing Manager: Ann D Niessen
    Lighting Director: Jim Bego
    Sound Director: Clarence Dent
    Artist Selection Coordinator: Philip Mieseala
Mission: To present leading performing artists in the fields of music, dance & stage to the residents of Western Mojave Desert, since 1947
Founded: 1947
Specialized Field: Performing Artists; Primarily Music (Classical & Non-Classical); Some Dance & One Person Stage
Volunteer Staff: 11
Paid Artists: 6
Budget: $47,000
Income Sources: Season Subscriptions; Contributions
Performs At: China Lake Auditorium
Affiliations: Western Arts Alliance
Annual Attendance: 3,000
Facility Category: Parker Performing Arts Center
Type of Stage: Proscenium
Seating Capacity: 608
Year Built: 1968
Year Remodeled: 2000

3834
PERFORMING ARTS PRESENTATIONS
University of California Music Department – 0
Arts Building 121
Riverside, CA 92521-0325
Phone: 951-827-7059
Fax: 952-827-4651
e-mail: traceys@ucr.ed
Web Site: www.performingarts.ucr.edu
Management:
    Management Services Officer: Tracey J Scholtemeyer
    Department Chair: Walter Clark
    Financial Analyst: Melisa Vicario
    Publicity/Publications: Kathleen DeAtley
Mission: Providing educational and cultural resources for students and area residents.
Founded: 1973
Specialized Field: Dance; Vocal Music; Instrumental Music; Theater
Status: Professional; Nonprofit
Income Sources: Western Alliance of Arts Administrators; Association of Performing Arts Presenters; California Presenters
Performs At: University Theatre
Organization Type: Sponsoring

3835
UNIVERSITY OF CALIFORNIA AT RIVERSIDE: CULTURAL EVENTS
900 University Avenue
Riverside, CA 92521
Phone: 951-827-4629
Fax: 951-827-2221
e-mail: culturalevents@ucr.edu
Web Site: www.culturalevents.ucr.edu
Management:
    Director: Todd Wingate
Specialized Field: Performing Arts Series
Status: Non-Profit, Professional
Paid Staff: 2
Paid Artists: 40
Performs At: University Theatre
Seating Capacity: 500

3836
CALIFORNIA STATE SUMMER SCHOOL FOR THE ARTS
1010 Hurley Way
Suite 185
Sacramento, CA 95825
Phone: 916-274-5815
Fax: 916-274-5814
e-mail: rjaffe@innerspark.us
Web Site: www.innerspark.us
Officers:
  Chair: Susan Dolgen
  Vice Chair: Bret Magpiong
Management:
  Director: Robert M Jaffe
  Deputy Director: Katrina Dolenga
Mission: The California State Summer School for the Arts is a rigorous, month long training program in the visual and performing arts, creative writing, animation and film for talented artists of high school age.
Founded: 1987
Specialized Field: Arts Program for High School Kids; student performances
Status: Non-Profit, Professional

3837
CALIFORNIA STATE SUMMER SCHOOL FOR THE ARTS
4825 J Street
Suite 120
Sacramento, CA 95819-3747
Mailing Address: PO Box 1077 Sacramento, CA 98512-1077
Phone: 916-227-9320
Fax: 916-227-9455
e-mail: rjaffe@csssa.org
Web Site: www.csssa.org/
Officers:
  Chair: Susan Dolgen
  VP: Megan Chernin
  VP Finance: Bret Magpiong
  Secretary: Donna Miller Casey
Management:
  Director: Robert M Jaffe
  Deputy Director: Joseph Alameida
  Program Analyst: Katrina Dolenga
  Office Assistant: Cynthia Glenn
  Development Director: Joan Newberg
Mission: The California State Summer School for the Arts is a rigorous, month long training program in the visual and performing arts, creative writing, animation and film for talented artists of high school age.
Founded: 1987
Budget: $1.9 million
Performs At: Various Auditoriums
Facility Category: Rented College Campus

3838
FESTIVAL OF NEW AMERICAN MUSIC
Music Department, CSU
6000 J Street
Sacramento, CA 95819-6015
Phone: 916-278-5155
Fax: 916-278-7217
e-mail: fenam@csus.edu
Web Site: www.csus.edu/music
Management:
  Department Chair: Ernie Hills
  Information Secretary: Shea Grimm
  Events Manager: Glenn Disney
Mission: To showcase the works of contemporary American composers. All Festival events are free.
Founded: 1964

Specialized Field: Contemporary American Music
Status: Non-Profit, Professional
Paid Artists: 60
Budget: $60,000-$150,000
Season: Early-mid November, 12 days
Performs At: Sacremento (Festival Site)
Facility Category: Music Recital Hall
Seating Capacity: 350
Organization Type: Performing; Educational; Sponsoring

3839
FINEST ASIAN PERFORMING ARTS
PO Box 162163
Sacramento, CA 95816
Phone: 916-924-1212
Fax: 916-924-7212
Management:
  Executive Director: Anna Y Mayo
  Secretary: Lucy Nemac
  Music Director/Advisor: Yan Zhang
Mission: To expose the Western community to Eastern culture works.
Utilizes: Singers
Founded: 1988
Specialized Field: Dance; Vocal Music; Instrumental Music; Festivals
Status: Non-Profit,Professional
Paid Staff: 12
Income Sources: Finest Asian Music Festival
Organization Type: Performing; Sponsoring

3840
HUGHES STADIUM
3835 Freeport Boulevard
Sacramento, CA 95822
Phone: 916-558-2111
Fax: 916-558-2030
Management:
  President: Robert Harris
  Executive Director: Mary Leland
  Facility Manager: Vicki Byers
Founded: 1916
Specialized Field: Sub-venue of Sacramento City College
Status: Non-Profit, Professional

3841
CHAMBER MUSIC IN NAPA VALLEY
4050 Spring Mountain Road
Saint Helens, CA 94574
Phone: 707-963-1391
Fax: 707-963-4512
e-mail: jkwine@napanet.net
Web Site: www.chambermusicnapa.org
Management:
  Director: John Kongsgaard
  Director: Maggy Kongsgaard
Mission: Presenters of world-renowned artists including Emanuel Ax, Garrick Ohlsson, St Petersburg String Quartet, et cetera in an intimate concert setting.
Founded: 1979
Status: Nonprofit
Income Sources: Private and Corporate Donations, Ticket Sales, Grants
Season: October-May
Performs At: United Methodist Church, Napa Valley Opera House
Seating Capacity: 320

3842
SALINAS CONCERT ASSOCIATION
PO Box 1984
Salinas, CA 93902

Phone: 408-443-4411
e-mail: carlc93906@aol.com
Officers:
  President: Carl Christensen
Performs At: Performing Arts Centre
Seating Capacity: 550

3843
LIPINSKY FAMILY SAN DIEGO JEWISH ARTS FESTIVAL
San Diego Repertory Theatre
79 Horton Plaza
San Diego, CA 92101-6144
Phone: 619-231-3586
Fax: 619-235-0939
e-mail: artistic@sandiegorep.com
Web Site: www.sandiegorep.com
Management:
  Artistic Director: Sam Woodhouse
Founded: 1976
Status: Professional
Paid Artists: 800

3844
MAINLY MOZART FESTIVAL
2802 Juan Street
Suite 29
San Diego, CA 92110
Mailing Address: PO Box 124705 San Diego, CA 92112-4705
Phone: 619-239-0100
Fax: 619-233-4292
e-mail: admin@mainlymozart.org
Web Site: www.mainlymozart.org
Officers:
  Chair: Alexander Pearson
  President: Christopher Wier
  Secretary/Treasurer: Linda Satz
Management:
  Executive Director: Nancy Laturno Bojanic
  Artistic Director: David Atherton
  Development Director: Veronica Baker
  Director Administration: Robert Fishman
Utilizes: Educators; Guest Accompanists; Guest Musical Directors; Guest Musicians; Multimedia
Founded: 1988
Specialized Field: Series & Festivals; Instrumental Music; Classical Music; Jazz; Education
Status: Non-Profit, Professional
Paid Staff: 7
Paid Artists: 80
Budget: $700,000 - 800,000
Income Sources: Box Office Receipts; Grants; Donations; Memberships; Special Events; Retail
Season: June
Performs At: Balboa Theatre downtown
Affiliations: Spreckels Theatre; Neurosciences Institution; St Pauls Cathedral; US Grant Hotel; East County Performing Arts Center; Lambs Theatre
Annual Attendance: 26,000
Seating Capacity: 1,500

3845
POINT LOMA NAZARENE UNIVERSITY CULTURAL EVENTS SERIES
3900 Lomaland Drive
San Diego, CA 92106
Phone: 619-849-2559
Fax: 619-849-2668
e-mail: music@pointloma.edu
Web Site: www.ptloma.edu
Officers:
  President: Robert Brower

Chairman: Betsy Northam
Management:
   Cultural Events Coordinator: Betsy Northam, BetsyNortham@pointloma.edu
   Building Coordinator: Laurie Oliver, LaurieOliver@pointloma.edu
Utilizes: Fine Artists; Guest Companies; Guest Directors; Guest Instructors; Guest Soloists; Multimedia; Sign Language Translators; Singers
Founded: 1902
Specialized Field: Series & Festivals; Instrumental Music; Vocal Music
Status: Non-Profit, Professional
Paid Staff: 3
Paid Artists: 9
Performs At: Performance Hall; Chapel
Seating Capacity: 380; 1800
Year Built: 1995
Cost: $6,000,000

3846
SAN DIEGO EARLY MUSIC SOCIETY

PO Box 82008
San Diego, CA 92138
Phone: 619-291-8246
e-mail: sdems@sdems.org
Web Site: www.sdems.org
Officers:
   President: Penelope Hawkins
   Vice President: Mark Lester
   Treasurer: Peter Cramer
   Secretary: Angela Quinn
Management:
   International Series Director: Laurent Planchon
   Museum Series Director: Diemet Rose
   Conductor: Elizabeth Zuehlke
   Choral Conductor: Stephen Sturk
   Program Director: Geoffrey Brooks
   Grants Coordinator: Duane Gruber
Mission: To encourage the appreciation of medieval, renaissance, and baroque music; to present two series of six concerts each, outreach programs, and annual workshop for instrumentalists and vocalists.
Utilizes: Guest Musical Directors; Instructors; Multimedia; Original Music Scores; Sign Language Translators
Founded: 1981
Specialized Field: Early Music (Classical)
Status: Nonprofit
Paid Staff: 1
Budget: $65,000
Income Sources: Box Office; Members; Ads; Grants
Season: October-April
Performs At: St. James-by-the-Sea; Sherwood Auditorium At S.D. Museum of Contemporary Art, La Jolla; S.D. Museum of Art
Affiliations: Early Music America; San Diego Performing Arts League
Annual Attendance: 2,500
Seating Capacity: 400; 500; 100

3847
SAN DIEGO STATE UNIVERSITY-SCHOOL OF MUSIC AND DANCE

San Diego State University
5500 Campanile Drive
San Diego, CA 92182-7902
Phone: 619-594-6031
Fax: 619-594-1692
e-mail: music.dance@mail.sdsu.edu
Web Site: www.musicdance.sdsu.edu
Management:
   Director: Donna Conaty

Administrative Support Coordinator: Debbie Willis
   Student Coordinator: Sandra Konar
   Public Affairs/Communications: Rhoda Nevins
Mission: To deliver specialized educational instruction, experiences and career development for students by creating an artistic environment based on the unique strengths and knowledge ofour accomplished facility. Programs emphasize experiential development through high quality performances, professional engagement and applied practical training in music and dance.
Founded: 1897
Specialized Field: Music; Dance

3848
SAN DIEGO THANKSGIVING, DIXIELAND JAZZ FESTIVAL

PO Box 880387
San Diego, CA 92168-0387
Phone: 619-297-5277
Fax: 619-297-5281
e-mail: jazzinfo@dixielandjazzfestival.org
Web Site: www.dixielandjazzfestival.org
Officers:
   President: Hal Smith
   Vice President: Bill Adams
Management:
   Executive Director: Alan Adams
   Administrative & Media Director: Hal Smith
   Treasurer: Alice Contreras
   Secretaty: Myrna Goodwin
Mission: A non-profit organization composed of more than 1,000 members dedicated to the preservation and perpetuation of our country's only original art form – Traditional Jazz.
Founded: 1979
Season: November Jazz Festival and monthly concerts July through Jan

3849
AMERICAN INDIAN DANCE THEATRE

Gary Lindsey Artist Services
2700 15th Avenue
San Francisco, CA 94127
Phone: 415-759-6410
Fax: 415-681-9801
Toll-free: 800-949-2745
e-mail: lindseyart@aol.com
Web Site: www.lindseyartists.com/indian.htm
Management:
   American Indian Dance Theatre Artis: Hanay Geiogamah
Mission: The American Indian Dance Theatre, founded in1987, is the country's leading native American performing company.
Specialized Field: Traditional Native American Dance

3850
BALLET FOLCLORICO DO BRASIL

Gary Lindsey Artist Services
2700 15th Avenue
San Francisco, CA 94127
Phone: 415-759-6410
Fax: 415-681-9801
e-mail: lindseyart@aol.com
Management:
   Artistic Director: Amen Santo
Specialized Field: Afro-Brazilian Dance

3851
BRENDA ANGIEL AERIAL DANCE

Gary Lindsey Artist Services
2700 15th Avenue
San Francisco, CA 94127

Phone: 415-759-6410
Fax: 415-681-9801
e-mail: lindseyart@aol.com
Management:
   Artistic Director/Choreographer: Brenda Angiel
Mission: Brenda Angiel Aerial Dance Company is an important part of Argentina's avant-garde dance movement.
Founded: 1998
Specialized Field: Avant-Garde Aeriel Dance

3852
CHAMBER MUSIC MASTERS

San Francisco Conservatory of Music
50 Oak Street
San Francisco, CA 94102-6011
Phone: 415-864—732
Fax: 415-503-6299
e-mail: kayc@sfcm.edu
Web Site: www.sfcm.edu
Management:
   President: Colin Murdoch
   Assistant to the President: Laura Reynolds
   Manager, Concert Operations: Seth Ducey
   Special Events Coordinator: Trista Cunningham
Mission: Offering advanced students and faculty the opportunity to perform with outstanding guest artists and providing Bay Area audiences with concerts featuring highly imaginative programming.
Specialized Field: Chamber Master Classes and Performances
Status: Professional; Nonprofit
Organization Type: Performing; Educational

3853
CORPUS ACROBATIC THEATRE

Gary Lindsey Artist Services
2700 15th Avenue
San Francisco, CA 94127
Phone: 415-759-6410
Fax: 415-681-9801
e-mail: lindseyart@aol.com

3854
DANCE THROUGH TIME

Gary Lindsey Artist Services
2700 15th Avenue
San Francisco, CA 94127
Phone: 415-759-6410
Fax: 415-681-9801
e-mail: lindseyart@aol.com
Management:
   Executive Director: Lawrence Ewing

3855
GRACE CATHEDRAL CONCERTS

Grace Cathedral
1100 California Street
San Francisco, CA 94108
Phone: 415-749-6355
Fax: 415-749-6301
e-mail: concerts@gracecathedral.org
Web Site: www.gracecathedral.org
Management:
   President: Alan Jones
   Concerts Manager: Rebecca Nestle
Utilizes: Multimedia; Original Music Scores; Sign Language Translators; Singers
Founded: 1965
Specialized Field: Series & Festivals; Instrumental Music; Vocal Music; Youth; Dance; Ethnic Performances
Status: For-Profit, Professional
Paid Staff: 1

Paid Artists: 30
Performs At: Grace Cathedral
Facility Category: Church
Seating Capacity: 1309
Year Built: 1934

3856
IRINA DVOROVENKO

Gary Lindsey Artist Services
2700 15th Avenue
San Francisco, CA 94127
Phone: 415-759-6410
Fax: 415-681-9801
Toll-free: 800-949-2745
e-mail: LindseyArt@aol.com

3857
JOSE GRECO II FLAMENCO DANCE COMPANY

Gary Lindsey Artist Services
2700 15th Avenue
San Francisco, CA 94127
Phone: 415-759-6410
Fax: 415-681-9801
Toll-free: 800-949-2745
e-mail: LindseyArt@aol.com

3858
MASSENKOFF RUSSIAN FOLK FESTIVAL

Sandra Calvin, Artist Representative
4827 17th Street
San Francisco, CA 94117
Phone: 415-586-9654
Fax: 415-564-4602
e-mail: russianfok@aol.com
Web Site: www.nikolaimassenkoff.us
Management:
    Singer/Director: Nikolai Massenkoff
    Artist Representative: Sandra Calvin,
    sandracalvin@att.net
Mission: To provide entertainment and expand
knowledge of Russian culture and people.
Founded: 1975
Specialized Field: Russian Music; Song; Dance
Facility Category: Flexible
Type of Stage: Flexible
Seating Capacity: 500-50,000

3859
MAXIM BELOTSERKOVSKY

Gary Lindsey Artist Services
2700 15th Avenue
San Francisco, CA 94127
Phone: 415-759-6410
Fax: 415-681-9801
Toll-free: 800-949-2745
e-mail: LindseyArt@aol.com

3860
MIDSUMMER MOZART FESTIVAL

760 Market Street
#749
San Francisco, CA 94102-6011
Phone: 415-627-9141
Fax: 415-627-9142
e-mail: amadeus@midsummermozart.org
Web Site: www.midsummermozart.org
Officers:
    Chairman: Bezhad Khosrovi
    Treasurer: David Claridge
    Secretary: Tom Bria
Management:
    Executive Director: Lori Noack
    Music Director and Conductor: George Cleve

Production Coordinator: Sue Edwards
    Associate Advisory Administrator: Clark Griffith
Mission: To present the music of Wolfgang Amadeus
Mozart to expanding Bay Area audiences through
performances of unparalleled excellence.
Founded: 1975
Specialized Field: Instrumental
Status: Professional; Nonprofit
Budget: $10,000
Income Sources: American Symphony Orchestra
League; California Confederation of the Arts;
Association of California Symphony Orchestras
Season: July
Affiliations: Various venues throughout California
Seating Capacity: 928; 700; 315; 600; 300
Organization Type: Performing

3861
MORRISON ARTIST SERIES

San Francisco State University Music Departme
1600 Holloway Avenue
San Francisco, CA 94123
Phone: 415-338-1358
Fax: 415-338-6159
e-mail: sgropman@sfsu.edu
Web Site: www.musicdance.sfsu.edu/morrison
Management:
    Artistic Director: Saul Gropman
Mission: Bringing Bay Area audiences the world's
finest chamber music. The Morrison Artists Series
concert program presents six free Sunday afternoon
performances each year by acclaimed chamber music
ensembles.
Founded: 1955
Specialized Field: Series & Festivals: Chamber Music
Concerts
Status: Non-Profit, Professional
Paid Staff: 2
Performs At: McKenna Theatre
Seating Capacity: 700

3862
NATIONAL SONG AND DANCE COMPANY OF MOZAMBIQUE

Gary Lindsey Artist Services
2700 15th Avenue
San Francisco, CA 94127
Phone: 415-759-6410
Fax: 415-681-9801
Toll-free: 800-949-2745
e-mail: LindseyArt@aol.com
Management:
    Artistic Director: David Abillio

3863
NEW LANGTON ARTS

1246 Folsom Street
San Francisco, CA 94103-3817
Phone: 415-626-5416
Fax: 415-255-1453
e-mail: nla@newlangtonarts.org
Web Site: www.newlangtonarts.org
Officers:
    Chair: Timothy Collins
    President: Catherine Homsey
    Vice Chair: Kate Connally
    Vice Chair: Christopher Dean
    VP: Margaret Tedesco
Management:
    Executive Director: Sandra Percival
    Development & Communications: Sam Spiewak
    Associate Curator: Maria Del Carme Carrion
    Operations Manager: Michael Smoler
    Gallery Coordinator/Executive Asst: Sara Ayazi

Mission: To cultivate experimental and innovative
contemporary art, performance art, and time-based art,
including video installation, improvised and electronic
music, and poetry.
Utilizes: Collaborating Artists; Collaborations;
Commissioned Music; Curators; Filmmakers; Fine
Artists; Five Seasonal Concerts; Guest Instructors;
Guest Musical Directors; Guest Soloists; Instructors;
Local Artists; Lyricists; Multi Collaborations; Multimedia;
Organization Contracts; Original Music Scores;
Playwrights; Singers; Soloists; Special Technical Talent;
Touring Companies
Founded: 1975
Specialized Field: Art Gallery
Status: Non-Profit, Professional
Paid Staff: 6
Performs At: Auditorium
Seating Capacity: 80

3864
NOONTIME CONCERTS-SAN FRANCISCO'S MUSICAL LUNCH BREAK

660 California Street
San Francisco, CA 94108
Phone: 415-777-3211
Fax: 415-777-3244
e-mail: info@noontimeconcerts.org
Web Site: www.noontimeconcerts.org
Officers:
    Board Member: Robin Wirthlin
    Board Member: Michael Abrahams
    Board Member: David Rickey
    Board Member: Carol Verburg
Management:
    Executive Director: James Rittell
    Program Coordinator: Duc Joie Tran
    Production Coordinator: Kervin McGlynn
Mission: To enrich the cultural life of Sand Francisco
and the Bay Area. Performed by professional local and
international touring artists. The concerts are not
ticketed, but free-will donations are solicited.
Performances are offered at a time convenient for
downtown workers, visitors, students, shoppers, and
music lovers.
Founded: 1988
Season: Weekly on Tuesdays
Performs At: Old St. Mary's Cathedral
Seating Capacity: 900

3865
OLD FIRST CONCERTS

1751 Sacramento Street
San Francisco, CA 94109
Phone: 415-474-1608
Fax: 415-474-6533
e-mail: staff@oldfirstconcerts.org
Web Site: www.oldfirstconcerts.org
Management:
    Director: Kathy Barr
Mission: To contribute to and enhance the artistic life of
the Bay Area by offering the public a wide variety of
musical forms and expressions that ranges from
classical recital and chamber performances to blues,
folk, avant-garde, and jazz, as well as multicultural
concerts and world music.
Founded: 1970
Specialized Field: Theatre: Chamber Music
Status: Non-Profit, Professional
Paid Artists: 200
Performs At: Old First Church
Facility Category: Presbyterian Church
Type of Stage: Raised; Wooden
Seating Capacity: 450

All listings are in alphabetical order by state, then city, then organization within the city.

3866
OMNI FOUNDATION FOR THE PERFORMING ARTS
236 W Portal Avenue
#1
San Francisco, CA 94127
Phone: 415-242-4500
Toll-free: 888-400-6664
e-mail: info@omniconcerts.com
Web Site: www.omniconcerts.com
Management:
   President: Richard Patterson
Mission: To bring the world's finest acoustic guitarists to the San Francisco Bay Area. Although our series present acoustic guitarists of all genres, such as flamenco, jazz, and fingerstyle, the primary focus is on the classical guitar. Omni presents over 20 exceptional guitarists each season.
Founded: 1981
Specialized Field: Series and Festivals: Guitar Concert Series
Status: Non-Profit, Professional
Paid Staff: 2
Paid Artists: 12
Budget: $165,000
Season: September through April
Performs At: Herbst Theatre, the Green Room in the Veterans Building, the San Francisco Conservatory of Music, and The Palace of Fine Arts
Annual Attendance: 6,000
Seating Capacity: 915

3867
OTHER MINDS MUSIC FESTIVAL
333 Valencia Street
Suite 303
San Francisco, CA 94103-3552
Phone: 415-934-8134
Fax: 415-934-8136
e-mail: otherminds@otherminds.org
Web Site: www.otherminds.org
Officers:
   President: Curtis Smith
   President Emeritus, Treasurer: Jim Newman
   Vice President: Andrew Gold
   Secretary: Mitchell Yawitz
Management:
   Executive and Artistic Director: Charles Amirkhanian
   Business Manager: Betsy Teeter
   Associate Director: Adam Fong
   Development Director: Emma Moon
Mission: To support and present the works of composers of new music.
Founded: 1993
Specialized Field: Series and Festivals; Instrumental Music; Vocal Music; Ethnic Performances
Status: Non-Profit, Professional
Paid Staff: 5
Paid Artists: 25
Budget: $35,000-$60,000
Season: Late March
Annual Attendance: 2,000
Seating Capacity: 500

3868
SAN FRANCISCO BLUES FESTIVAL
PO Box 460608
San Francisco, CA 94146-0608
Phone: 415-979-5588
Fax: 415-826-6958
e-mail: SFblues@earthlink.net
Web Site: www.sfblues.com
Management:
   Director: Tom Mazzolini
   Stage Manager: Mike Dingle
   Director Of Logistics: Scott Redmond
   Director of Concessions: Lenny Ivler
Founded: 1973
Specialized Field: Blues
Annual Attendance: 18,000-20,000
Facility Category: Outdoors Lawns

3869
SAN FRANCISCO ETHNIC DANCE FESTIVAL
World Arts West, Fort Mason Center
Building D
San Francisco, CA 94123-1382
Phone: 415-474-3914
Fax: 415-474-3922
Toll-free: 888-756-0888
e-mail: info@worldartswest.org
Web Site: www.worldartswest.org
Officers:
   President: Esther Li
   Vice President: Amanda Almonte
   Vice President: Sheree Chambers
   Secreaty: Elaine Connell
Management:
   Executive Director: Julie Mushet
   Festival Arts Director: Carlos Carvajal
   Festival Arts Director: CK Ladzekpo
   Production Manager: Jack Carpenter
   Office Manager: Robert Taylor
   Marketing: Joann Driscoll
Mission: To present and to promote ethnic and cultural diversity through the performance and teaching of world dance traditions.
Founded: 1978
Specialized Field: Dance; Ethnic
Status: Professional; Non-Profit
Volunteer Staff: 15
Budget: $60,000-$150,000
Income Sources: Sponsors; Donations
Season: June
Affiliations: Palace of Fine Arts
Annual Attendance: 7,600
Seating Capacity: 1,000

3870
SAN FRANCISCO FRINGE FESTIVAL
156 Eddy Street
San Francisco, CA 94102
Phone: 415-931-1094
Fax: 415-931-2699
e-mail: mail@sffringe.org
Web Site: www.sffringe.org
Officers:
   President: Geoffrey Link
   Board Member: Chris Barnett
   Board Member: Frank Aflague
   Board Member: Carmen White
Management:
   Artistic Director: Christina Augello
   Managing Director: Richard Livingston
   Production Manager: Amanda Ortmayer
Founded: 1992
Specialized Field: Series and Festivals: Theatre
Status: Non-Profit, Professional
Paid Staff: 4
Volunteer Staff: 100
Paid Artists: 50
Season: September
Performs At: Exit Theatre
Annual Attendance: 10000

3871
SAN FRANCISCO JAZZ SPRING SEASON
SF Jazz
3 Embarcadero Center, Lobby Level
San Francisco, CA 94111
Phone: 415-398-5655
Fax: 415-398-5569
Toll-free: 800-850-7353
e-mail: mailbox@sfjazz.org
Web Site: www.wsfjazz.org
Officers:
   Chair: Srinija Srinivasan
   Vice Chair: Michael P Lazarus
   President: Randal Kline
   Treasurer: Gloria Lau
   Controller: Jennifer Schwartz
   Director Development: Donna Blakemore
   Director Marketing/PR: Jennifer Joyce
   Operations Manager: Eric Allen
   Director Production: David Coffman
Management:
   Executive Director, Artistic Direct: Randall Kline
   Artist Administrator: Laura Evans
   Director Education: Cory Combs
   Director of Operations and Finance: David Miller
Mission: Offering the finest Bay Area and national jazz performers in San Francisco venues.
Utilizes: Poets
Founded: 1983
Specialized Field: Dance; Vocal Music; Instrumental Music; Festivals; Jazz; World Class Music
Status: Professional; Nonprofit
Paid Staff: 22
Volunteer Staff: 300
Paid Artists: 40
Non-paid Artists: 25
Budget: 4.6 million
Income Sources: Private and Corporate Donations, Organizations
Season: June-March
Performs At: Various Venues
Annual Attendance: 100,000
Organization Type: Performing; Resident; Educational; Presenter

3872
SAN FRANCISCO PERFORMANCES
500 Sutter Street
Suite 710
San Francisco, CA 94102
Phone: 415-398-6449
Fax: 415-398-6439
e-mail: info@performances.org
Web Site: www.performances.org
Officers:
   Chairman: Fred M Levine
   Vice Chair: Thomas G Beischer
   Vice Chair: Patrick R McCabe
   Secretary: Roger D Miles
Management:
   President: Ruth A Felt
   Director Public Relations: Karen Hershenson
   Director Development: Michele Casau
   Director of Finance and Administrat: Christian A Jessen
   Director Education Programs: Melanie Smith
   Director Marketing: Millicent Jones
Mission: To present outstanding national, international and emerging artists; to introduce innovative programs; to build new and diversified audiences for the arts.

Utilizes: Artists-in-Residence; Collaborations; Commissioned Composers; Commissioned Music; Dance Companies; Guest Accompanists; Guest Choreographers; Lyricists; Multimedia; Original Music Scores; Sign Language Translators; Singers
Founded: 1979
Specialized Field: Series & Festivals; Instrumental Music; Vocal Music; Youth; Dance; Ethnic Performances
Status: Non-Profit, Professional
Paid Staff: 13
Budget: $2 million
Income Sources: Ticket Sales; Grants & Contributions
Season: September – May
Performs At: Herbst Theatre; St. John's Presbyterian Church, Novellus Theater, Hotel Rex
Affiliations: Association of Performing Arts Presenters; International Society of Performing Arts Administrators; Western Arts Alliance
Annual Attendance: 48,000
Organization Type: Sponsoring
Resident Groups: Alexander String Quartet; Guitarist, Manuel Barrueco; Jazz Violin, Regina Clark

3873
SAN FRANCISCO SHAKESPEARE FESTIVAL

PO Box 460937
San Francisco, CA 94159-0937
Phone: 415-558-0888
Fax: 415-865-4433
Toll-free: 800-787-29
e-mail: sfshakes@sfshakes.org
Web Site: www.sfshakes.org
Officers:
    Chair: Raymond Kutz
    Vice-Chair: Eleanor Jacobs
    CFO: Keith D Taylor
    Executive Director: Toby Leavitt
Management:
    Resident Director: Kenneth Kellenher
    Artistic Associate: Rebecca Ennals
Mission: One of the nation's premiere free Shakespeare producers and a vital regional arts organization with strong roots in the community, offering performances and arts education programs.
Founded: 1983
Specialized Field: Series & Festivals; Music; Theatre
Status: Non-Profit, Professional
Paid Staff: 6
Volunteer Staff: 5
Paid Artists: 200
Budget: $825,000
Income Sources: Camp Fees; Tour Fees; Individual; Government; Institutional Gifts
Season: July - October
Seating Capacity: 1100

3874
SFJAZZ

3 Embarcadero Center
Lower Lobby
San Francisco, CA 94111
Phone: 415-398-5655
Fax: 415-398-5569
Toll-free: 800-850-7353
e-mail: mailbox@sfjazz.org
Web Site: www.sfjazz.org
Officers:
    Chair: Srinija Srinivasan
    Vice Chair: Michael Lazarus
    President: Randal Kline
    Treasurer: Gloria Lau
Management:

Executive and Artistic Director: Randall Kline
Artistic Administrator: Laura Evans
Director of Education: Cory Combs
Director of Operations and Finance: David Miller
Founded: 1983
Specialized Field: Series & Festivals; Instrumental Music; Vocal Music; Theatre; Youth; Dance; Ethnic Performances
Status: Non-Profit, Professional
Paid Staff: 22
Season: Year Round Programs

3875
STERN GROVE FESTIVAL ASSOCIATION

44 Page Street
Suite 600
San Francisco, CA 94102
Phone: 415-252-6252
Fax: 415-252-6250
e-mail: info@sterngrove.org
Web Site: www.sterngrove.org
Officers:
    Chairman: Douglas Goldman
    Vice Chairman: Robin Michel
    Treasurer: Deborah E Gallegos
    Secretary: Gregory L Lippetz
    Governance Chair: Karla L Martin
    Development Chair: Elizabeth Goldstein
Management:
    Executive Director: Steven P Haines
    Director of Development: Pamela Sullivan
    Operations/Administration: Robb Huddleston
    Director of Programming: Judy Tsang
Mission: An independent, non-profit arts presenting organization, founded by civic activist and arts patron Rosalie M. Stern, committed to providing the people of the Bay Area with admission-free access to diverse performing arts.
Utilizes: Dance Companies; Dancers; Instructors; Lyricists; Multimedia; Original Music Scores; Sign Language Translators
Founded: 1938
Specialized Field: Intsrumental Music; Vocal Music; Dance
Status: Non-Profit
Paid Staff: 8
Volunteer Staff: 300
Paid Artists: 300
Budget: $1.1 million
Income Sources: Foundations; Individuals; Government; Corporate
Season: June - August
Performs At: Sigmund Stern Grove Amphitheater (Festival Site)
Annual Attendance: 95,000
Facility Category: Ampitheatre
Seating Capacity: 8,000 - 10,000
Year Built: 1932
Organization Type: Sponsoring

3876
SWINGDANCE AMERICA

Gary Lindsey Artist Services
2700 15th Avenue
San Francisco, CA 94127
Phone: 415-759-6410
Fax: 415-681-9801
e-mail: lindseyart@aol.com

3877
WORLD ARTS ETHNIC FESTIVAL: WEST

Fort Mason Center
Building D
San Francisco, CA 94123-1382

Phone: 415-474-3914
Fax: 415-474-3922
e-mail: info@worldartswest.org
Web Site: www.worldartswest.org
Officers:
    President: Esther Li
    Vice President: Amanda Almonte
    Vice President: Sheree Chambers
    Secreaty: Elaine Connell
Management:
    Executive Director: Julie Mushet
    Artistic Director: Carlos Carvajal
    Artistic Director: CK Ladzekipo
    Artistic Director Liaison: Tyese Wortham
Mission: The San Francisco Ethnic Dance Festival celebrates and fosters appreciation for the diverse ethnic communities in the Bay Area through an annual performance season.
Founded: 1978
Specialized Field: Series & Festivals; Dance; Ethnic Performances
Status: Non-Profit, Professional
Paid Staff: 8
Paid Artists: 300
Budget: $60,000-$150,000
Season: June
Affiliations: Palace of Fine Arts
Seating Capacity: 1,000

3878
WORLD ARTS WEST

Fort Mason Center
Building D
San Francisco, CA 94123-1382
Phone: 415-474-3914
Fax: 415-474-3922
Toll-free: 888-756-0888
e-mail: info@worldartswest.org
Web Site: www.worldartswest.org
Officers:
    President: Ester Li
    Vice President: Amanda Almonte
    Vice President: Sheree Chambers
    Secreaty: Elaine Connell
Management:
    Executive Director: Julie Mushet
    Artistic Director: Carlos Carvajal
    Artistic Director: CK Ladzekipo
    Production Manager: Jack Carpenter
Mission: To honor and celebrate culturally diverse dance forms through presentation, education, and support of artists and their traditions.
Utilizes: Dance Companies; Dancers
Founded: 1978
Specialized Field: Series & Festivals: Dance
Status: Non-Profit, Professional
Paid Staff: 8
Paid Artists: 150
Performs At: Palace of Fine Arts
Seating Capacity: 1000

3879
CAL POLY ARTS PRESENTS & GREAT PERFORMANCES

One Grand Avenue
San Luis Obispo, CA 93407
Phone: 805-756-6556
Fax: 805-756-6558
e-mail: cparts@polymail.calpoly.edu
Web Site: www.calpolyarts.org
Officers:
    President: Harry Heilenbrond
Management:
    CPA, Director: Steve Lerian

Chair, Theatre & Dance Dept: Tim Dugan
Chair, Music Department: W. Terrance Spiller
Mission: To provide a broad program of high quality, professional touring performances, exhibitions, and readings for the Central Coast community while also assisting with the educational needs of university students through various artist-in-residency and outreach activities.
Founded: 1985
Specialized Field: Series and Festivals; Instrumental Music; Vocal Music; Theater; Youth; Dance; Ethnic Performances; Presentation of Tour and Performing Arts
Status: Non-Profit, Non-Professional
Paid Staff: 5
Volunteer Staff: 175
Budget: $1 million
Income Sources: Box Office; Grants; Private Donations; Corporate Donations
Performs At: Cushman Auditorium, Harman hall, Spanos Theatre
Affiliations: California Presenters; Association of Performing Arts Presenters; Western Arts Alliance
Annual Attendance: 75,000
Facility Category: Performing Arts Center; SLO
Type of Stage: Proscenium
Stage Dimensions: 49'x23'
Seating Capacity: 1,300; 497
Year Built: 1996
Cost: $34 million
Rental Contact: Ron Regier

3880
CUESTA COLLEGE PERFORMING ARTS

PO Box 8106
San Luis Obispo, CA 93403-8106
Phone: 805-546-3132
Fax: 805-546-3968
e-mail: gstone@cuesta.edu
Web Site: www.academic.cuesta.edu/performingarts
Management:
Dean of Students, Performing Arts: Pamela Ralston
Chair: Jennifer Martin
Music Director: George Stone
Drama Director: Bree Valle
Founded: 1929
Specialized Field: Education
Status: Non-Profit, Professional
Performs At: College Auditorium; Cuesta Interact Theatre
Seating Capacity: 810; 150

3881
FESTIVAL MOZAIC

PO Box 311
3165 Broad Street, #110
San Luis Obispo, CA 93406
Phone: 805-781-3009
Fax: 805-781-3011
Toll-free: 877-818-99
e-mail: operations@festivalmozaic.com
Web Site: www.mozartfestival.com
Officers:
President: Dwyne Willis
Vice President: Charles Myers
Secretary: Peter Zaleski
Treasurer: Rodger Mastako
Management:
Music Director: Scott Yoo
Executive Director: Curtis Pendleton
Volunteer Coordinator: Nan Hamilton
Office manager: Kathy East

Mission: To present a classical music festival highlighting Mozart and other classical and contemporary composers.
Founded: 1971
Status: Non-Profit, Professional
Paid Staff: 3
Paid Artists: 100
Budget: $150,000-$400,000
Season: July - August
Performs At: Throughout San Luis Obispo County (Festival Sites)

3882
SAN LUIS OBISPO MOZART FESTIVAL

PO Box 311
San Luis Obispo, CA 93406
Phone: 805-781-3008
Fax: 805-781-3011
e-mail: info@mozartfestival.com
Web Site: www.mozartfestival.com
Management:
Music Director: Scott Yoo
Mission: To present a classical music festival highlighting Mozart and other classical and contemporary composers.
Utilizes: Commissioned Composers; Commissioned Music; Guest Composers; Guest Lecturers; Guest Musical Directors; Multimedia; Original Music Scores; Singers
Founded: 1970
Status: Professional; Nonprofit
Budget: $150,000-$400,000
Season: July - August
Performs At: Throughout San Luis Obispo County (Festival Sites)
Affiliations: San Luis Performing Arts Center; Wineries; Chapels
Seating Capacity: 1,300
Organization Type: Performing; Educational

3883
CENTERSTAGE, OSHER MARIN JCC

200 N San Pedro Road
San Rafael, CA 94903
Phone: 415-444-8000
Fax: 415-491-1235
e-mail: centerstage1@marinjcc.org
Web Site: www.marinjcc.org
Management:
Managing Director, Performing Arts: Linda Bolt
Events Manager: Pam Day
Operations Coordinator: Kathy Langrock
Production Coordinator: Josh Korbel
Utilizes: Dance Companies; Dancers; Guest Directors; Guest Instructors; Instructors; Local Unknown Artists; Multimedia; Original Music Scores; Sign Language Translators; Singers
Founded: 1990
Specialized Field: Series & Festivals; Classical; Dance; Lectures; Jazz; Broadway music; World music; One Man shows; Literary Arts and Conversation; Comedy
Status: Non-Profit, Professional
Paid Staff: 10
Performs At: Auditorium
Seating Capacity: 500

3884
COMMUNITY ARTS AND MUSIC ASSOCIATION OF SANTA BARBARA-CAMA

2060 Alameda Padre Serra
Suite 201
Santa Barbara, CA 93103
Phone: 805-966-4324
Fax: 805-962-2014
e-mail: info@camasb.org
Web Site: www.camasb.org
Officers:
President: Dolores M Hsu
First Vice-President: Andre Saltoun
Second vice president: Nancy L Wood
Treasurer: John Lundegard
Management:
Executive Director: Mark Trueblood
Concert and Publicity Manager: Justin Weaver
Director of Development: Nancy R Lynn
Office Manager/Subscriber Services: Linda Proud
Mission: To bring the world's greatest orchestras and soloists to Santa Barbara and enrich the cultural aspect of our community.
Utilizes: Guest Artists
Founded: 1919
Specialized Field: Series & Festivals; Classical Instrumental Music; Vocal Music
Status: Non-Profit, Professional
Paid Staff: 4
Budget: $1,200,000
Income Sources: Grants; Foundations; Individual Donations; Investment Income
Season: October-April
Performs At: Arlington Theatre; Lobero Theatre
Annual Attendance: 18,000
Facility Category: Historic Movie House and Concert Hall; Historic Opera House
Type of Stage: Theatre Stage; Opera Stage
Seating Capacity: 2,018
Year Built: 1923
Year Remodeled: 1976
Rental Contact: Karen Killingworth
Organization Type: Sponsoring

3885
MUSIC ACADEMY OF THE WEST FESTIVAL

1070 Fairway Road
Santa Barbara, CA 93108-2899
Phone: 805-969-4726
Fax: 805-969-0686
e-mail: festival@musicacademy.org
Web Site: www.musicacademy.org
Officers:
Chairman: James E Davidson
First Vice Chairman: Sharon Westby
Treasurer: Benjamin J Cohen
Second Vice Chairman: A Stevens Halsted
Management:
President: NancyBell Coe
VP Artistic Programs: Richard Feit
VP Marketing Communications: Susan Gwynne
VP Finance: Barbara J Robertson
Mission: To maintain a pre-professional instrumental company with vocal instruction.
Utilizes: Artists-in-Residence; Collaborating Artists; Educators; Grant Writers; Guest Artists; Guest Companies; Guest Composers; Guest Directors; Guest Instructors; Resident Professionals
Founded: 1947
Specialized Field: Instrumental; Opera; Educational
Status: Non-Profit, Non-Professional

Paid Staff: 30
Volunteer Staff: 90
Paid Artists: 40
Budget: $1,050,000 - 3,600,000
Income Sources: Individual Contributions; Foundations; Corporations
Season: June - August
Performs At: Santa Barbara (Festival Site)
Affiliations: Lobero Theatre
Annual Attendance: 17,000
Seating Capacity: 680
Year Built: 1909
Organization Type: Performing; Educational; Sponsoring
Resident Groups: The Canadian Brass

3886
SANTA BARBARA FESTIVAL BALLET

1019 B Chapala Street
Santa Barbara, CA 93101
Phone: 805-966-0711
Fax: 805-966-9521
e-mail: sbballetcenter@gmail.com
Web Site: www.santabarbaraballetcenter.com
Management:
    Artistic Director: Michele Rinaldi
    Co-Artistic Director: Denise Rinaldi
    Co-Artistic Director: Michele Anderson

3887
SUMMERDANCE SANTA BARBARA

1528 Chapala Street #308
Santa Barbara, CA 93101
Phone: 805-568-0865
Fax: 805-568-0637
e-mail: festival@summerdance.com
Officers:
    President: Megan Matthieson
    Treasurer: Daniel Vapnek
    Secretary: Randy Franks
Management:
    Executive Director: Dianne Vapnek
    Managing Director: Laurie Burnaby
Mission: A multi-week festival of contemporary dance, is to build audiences for dance, to provide a place for emerging and established choreographers to create work, and to share the inspiration of great dance through performances, educational evetns and community outreach.
Founded: 1997
Specialized Field: Contemporary Dance
Status: Non-Profit; Professional
Paid Staff: 3
Volunteer Staff: 1
Income Sources: Foundations; Ticket Sales; Grants; Donations
Performs At: Center Stage Theatre; Libaro Theatre

3888
UCSB ARTS & LECTURES

University of California
Building 402
Santa Barbara, CA 93106-5030
Phone: 805-893-3535
Fax: 805-893-8637
e-mail: aandl-info@sa.ucsb.edu
Web Site: www.artsandlectures.ucsb.edu
Management:
    Director: Celesta Billeci
    Performing Arts Manager: Cathy Oliverson
    Director Operations: Laureen Lewis
    Programming Associate: Heather Silva

Mission: To present a wide variety of professional touring artists and ensembles in dance, theater, classical music, ethnic and traditional arts, film and literature for campus and community audiences.
Utilizes: Actors; Artists-in-Residence; Collaborations; Dance Companies; Dancers; Guest Soloists; Multimedia; Special Technical Talent; Theatre Companies
Founded: 1959
Specialized Field: Dance; Vocal Music; Instrumental Music; Theater
Status: Professional; Non-Profit
Paid Staff: 14
Income Sources: Western Alliance of Arts Administrators; Arts Presenters; California Presenters
Performs At: Campbell Hall
Seating Capacity: 860
Organization Type: Performing; Educational; Presenting

3889
CABRILLO FESTIVAL OF CONTEMPORARY MUSIC

104 Walnut Avenue
Suite 206
Santa Cruz, CA 95060
Phone: 831-426-6966
Fax: 831-426-6968
e-mail: info@cabrillomusic.org
Web Site: www.cabrillomusic.org
Officers:
    President: Bruce Nicholson
    Vice President: Dina Hoffman
    Vice President: Birgit Weskamp
    CFO: Fran Fisher
Management:
    Executive Director: Ellen M Primack
    Director of Development: Tom Fredericks
    Associate Director: Jessica Frye
    Music Director/Conductor: Marin Alsop
Founded: 1963
Specialized Field: Contemporary instrumental music
Budget: $480,000
Season: July
Performs At: S. Cruz Civic Auditorium; Mission San Juan Bautista
Seating Capacity: 1,000

3890
SANTA CRUZ BAROQUE FESTIVAL

PO Box 482
Santa Cruz, CA 95061
Phone: 197-4 -
e-mail: info@scbaroque.org
Web Site: www.scbaroque.com
Management:
    Artistic Director: Linda Burman-Hall
    President: Dean Silvers
    Treasurer: Donald Wilson
    Ad Coordinator: Gertrude Fator
Mission: Offering a series of early music concerts each spring.
Founded: 1974
Specialized Field: Instrumental
Status: Professional; Nonprofit
Budget: $10,000-$20,000
Season: February - May
Facility Category: Various auditoriums
Seating Capacity: 400
Organization Type: Performing; Sponsoring

3891
UC SANTA CRUZ ARTS & LECTURES

University of California at Santa Cruz
D106 Porter
1156 High Street
Santa Cruz, CA 95064
Phone: 831-459-3861
Fax: 831-459-4521
e-mail: artslecs@ucsc.edu
Web Site: www.artslectures.ucsc.edu
Management:
    Arts and Lectures Director: Jeanette Pilak
    Production Manager: Greg Arrufat
Mission: UC Santa Cruz Arts & Lectures is the largest interdisciplinary presenting organization in the Monterey Bay region, with a mission to transform lives through excellence, innovation, and diversity in the performing arts.
Utilizes: Actors; Dance Companies; Dancers; Instructors; Multimedia; Original Music Scores; Playwrights; Selected Students; Singers; Special Technical Talent; Theatre Companies
Specialized Field: Dance; Theater; Spoken Word/Lectures; World Music; Classical; Jazz
Performs At: Performing Arts Theater
Seating Capacity: 528

3892
CONCERTS WEST

630 San Vicente Boulevard
Unit T
Santa Monica, CA 90402
Phone: 310-393-1155
Fax: 310-393-1155
e-mail: mpreston@ix.netcom.com
Management:
    Artistic Director: Howard Colf
Performs At: Unitarian Universalist Community Church of Santa Monica
Seating Capacity: 225

3893
OAKMONT CONCERT SERIES

444 Crestridge Place
Santa Rosa, CA 95409
Phone: 707-539-7066
Fax: 707-539-0894
e-mail: bartok2@sonic.net
Web Site: www.oakmontconcertseries.org
Officers:
    Secretary/Treasurer: Maurine Christ
Management:
    Artistic Director: Robert Hayden
    Associate Director: Rosemarie Waller
    Programs: Judy Burness
Founded: 1990
Specialized Field: Performing Series
Status: Non-Profit, Professional
Volunteer Staff: 4
Paid Artists: 24
Budget: $24,000
Income Sources: Entrance Fees
Season: One concert per month throughout the year , usually on the s
Performs At: Auditorium
Affiliations: Oakmont Village Association
Annual Attendance: 3,000
Facility Category: Auditorium
Type of Stage: Raised & Curtained
Seating Capacity: 400
Year Built: 1990
Year Remodeled: 2002

3894
SANTA ROSA CONCERT ASSOCIATION
PO Box 4821
Santa Rosa, CA 95402
Phone: 707-546-1152
e-mail: Jay@srconcert.org
Web Site: www.srconcert.org
Officers:
President: John Lawrence
Mission: All-volunteer organization bringing noted musicians to Santa Rosa audiences since 1948, introducing a variety of musical experiences to audiences at great prices.
Founded: 1948
Performs At: Wells Fargo Theater
Seating Capacity: 1500

3895
SANTA ROSA JUNIOR COLLEGE CHAMBER MUSIC SERIES
1501 Mendocino Avenue
Santa Rosa, CA 95401
Phone: 707-527-4249
Fax: 707-521-7988
e-mail: erussell@santarosa.edu
Web Site: www.santarosa.edu/music/chamber
Officers:
Department Chair: Dr Jon Nelson
Administrative Assistant: Elona Russell
Management:
Department Chair: Bennett Friedman
Administrative Assistant: Elona Russell
Specialized Field: Classical; Chamber
Income Sources: Private and Corporate Donations, Ticket Sales
Season: October-December
Performs At: Burbank Auditorium, Randolph Newman Auditorium
Annual Attendance: 1,200
Seating Capacity: 700, 350

3896
MOUNTAIN WINERY
14831 Pierce Road
Saratoga, CA 95070
Phone: 408-741-2822
Fax: 408-741-2818
e-mail: events@mountainwinery.com
Web Site: www.mountainwinery.com
Management:
President: Stuart Ferguson
Mission: To enhance the cultural atmosphere of the San Francisco Bay Area
Utilizes: Filmmakers; Instructors; Local Unknown Artists; Multimedia; Original Music Scores; Sign Language Translators; Theatre Companies
Founded: 1957
Specialized Field: Summer Concerts
Status: For-Profit, Non-Professional
Paid Staff: 70
Performs At: Mountain Winery
Annual Attendance: 100,000
Facility Category: Winerey
Type of Stage: Open Air
Stage Dimensions: 27'x24'
Seating Capacity: 1,700
Year Built: 1902
Rental Contact: Mark Karakas
Organization Type: Performing; Sponsoring

3897
TAHOE ARTS PROJECT
PO Box 14281
South Lake Tahoe, CA 96151
Phone: 530-542-3632
Fax: 530-542-4792
e-mail: tahoearts@aol.com
Web Site: www.tahoeartsproject.org
Officers:
President: Linda Mateas
Vice President: JoJo Conroy
Secretary: Janel Morales
Treasurer: Kerri Montgomery
Management:
Executive Director: Peggy Thompson
Executive Assistant: Jessica Perasso
Mission: To provide cultural enrichment and diversity for the community through the arts and education, with particular focus on our youth.
Utilizes: Artists-in-Residence; Dance Companies; Fine Artists; Instructors; Multimedia; Original Music Scores; Sign Language Translators; Special Technical Talent; Theatre Companies
Founded: 1987
Status: Nonprofit
Paid Staff: 2
Paid Artists: 5
Budget: $100,000
Income Sources: Grants; Donations; Fundraising Events
Facility Category: Schools
Seating Capacity: 200-1,200

3898
STANFORD JAZZ FESTIVAL & WORKSHOP
PO Box 20454
Stanford, CA 94309
Phone: 650-736-0324
Fax: 650-856-4155
e-mail: info@stanfordjazz.org
Web Site: www.stanfordjazz.org
Management:
Director: Jim Nadel
Mission: Each year the festival presents more than 30 performances by jazz masters, acclaimed contemporary standouts, and emerging stars. Renowned for presenting straight-ahead jazz, flavored with innovative modern stylings, traditional, blues, salsa, Brazilian, and other cross-cultural approaches to musical improvisation.
Specialized Field: Jazz
Season: June - August

3899
STANFORD LIVELY ARTS
537 Lomita Mall, MC 2250
Stanford University
Stanford, CA 94305-2250
Phone: 650-723-2551
Fax: 650-725-6230
e-mail: livelyarts@stanford.edu
Web Site: www.livelyarts.stanford.edu
Management:
Artistic and Executive Director: Jenny Bilfield
Special Events Coordinator: Mary Ancell
Financial Coordinator: Precy Cabanatan
Public Relations Manager: Bob Cable
Mission: To create unique experiences for diverse communities and artists to share passion, knowledge, creative inspiration, and cultural traditions through live performance and arts education.

Utilizes: Artists-in-Residence; Collaborating Artists; Collaborations; Commissioned Music; Dance Companies; Dancers; Grant Writers; Guest Choreographers; Guest Musical Directors; Guest Musicians; Lyricists; Multimedia; Singers; Special Technical Talent; Theatre Companies
Founded: 1969
Specialized Field: Series & Festivals: Chamber Music and Dance
Status: Non-Profit, Professional
Performs At: Memorial Auditorium and other campus venues
Annual Attendance: 55,000
Facility Category: Theater
Type of Stage: Proscenium
Stage Dimensions: 40'x50'
Seating Capacity: 1710

3900
UNIVERSITY OF THE PACIFIC CONSERVATORY OF MUSIC - RESIDENT ARTIST SERIES
3601 Pacific Avenue
Stockton, CA 95211
Phone: 209-946-2417
Fax: 209-946-2770
e-mail: gongaro@pacific.edu
Web Site: www.pacific.edu/conservatory
Officers:
President: Pamela Eibeck
Management:
Dean, Conservatory of Music: Giulio Ongaro
Assistant Dean: David Chase
Director of Development: Holly Stanko
Stage & Technical Director: James Gonzales
Mission: A major resource for the region with more than 120 musical performances each year featuring students, faculty, guest artists, and alumni.
Founded: 1924
Specialized Field: Conservatory
Status: Non-Profit, Professional
Performs At: Faye Spanos Concert Hall, Recital hall
Seating Capacity: FSCH-946; RH-119

3901
ARTS FOR THE SCHOOLS
PO Box 230
Tahoe Vista, CA 96148
Phone: 530-546-4602
Fax: 530-546-7832
e-mail: kyagura@sierra.net
Web Site: www.aftstahoe.org
Management:
President: Terry Yagura
Executive Director: Joanne Snarr
Mission: To provide artistic, educational and cultural opportunities for students, residents, and guests in Lake Tahoe.
Founded: 1984
Specialized Field: Series & Festivals; Instrumental Music; Vocal Music; Theater; Youth; Dance; Ethnic Performances
Status: Non-Profit, Professional
Paid Staff: 2
Paid Artists: 50
Performs At: School Auditorium; Cal-Neva
Seating Capacity: 300; 350

3902
CALIFORNIA LUTHERAN UNIVERSITY MUSIC SERIES
60 W Olsen Road No 4000
Thousand Oaks, CA 91360

Phone: 805-492-2411
e-mail: morton@clunet.edu
Web Site: www.clunet.edu
Officers:
President: John Sladek
Management:
Director: Daniel M Greeting
Music Department Chair: Wyant Morton
Professor of Music: Dorothy Elliott Schechter
Assistant Professor of Music: Mark Spraggins
Founded: 1959
Specialized Field: Performances by University
Symphony, CLU Choir, Wind Ensemble, Women's
Chorale, and Jazz Ensemble
Status: Non-Profit, Professional
Paid Staff: 23

3903
CALIFORNIA LUTHERAN UNIVERSITY MUSIC SERIES

60 W Olsen Road
Thousand Oaks, CA 91360-2787
Phone: 805-492-2411
Fax: 805-493-3479
e-mail: morton@clunet.edu
Web Site: www.clunet.edu
Management:
Orchestra Conductor: Daniel Geeting
Chair Music Department: Wyant Morton
Budget: $10,000
Performs At: Samuelson Chapel; Forum
Seating Capacity: 650; 250

3904
CONEJO RECREATION & PARK DISTRICT SUMMER CONCERT SERIES

403 W Hill Crest Drive
Thousand Oaks, CA 91360-5565
Phone: 805-495-6471
Fax: 805-497-3199
e-mail: recadmin@crpd.org
Web Site: www.crpd.org
Management:
General Manager: Jim Friedl
Recreation Services Manager: Steve Wiley
Recreation Supervisor; Cultural: Scott Buchanan
Mission: To present cultural programs including The
Young Artists Ensembles, Teen Summer Musical,
classes and workshops in visual and performing arts,
community theater, music and dance, special
performances, and gallery showings.
Founded: 1964
Status: For-Profit, Professional
Performs At: Outdoors
Annual Attendance: 12,000-15,000
Type of Stage: Stage
Seating Capacity: 4600

3905
SPRING MUSIC FESTIVAL: CALIFORNIA UNIVERSITY OF ARTS

California Institute of The Arts
24700 Mcbean Parkway
Valencia, CA 91355
Phone: 661-253-7817
Fax: 661-255-0938
e-mail: info@music.calarts.edu
Web Site: music.calarts.edu
Management:
President: Steven D Lavin
Dean School Of Music: David Rosenboom
Chair in Music: Richard Seaver
Founded: 1961

Status: Professional; Nonprofit
Organization Type: Performing; Educational

3906
VENTURA MUSIC FESTIVAL

472 E Santa Clara Street
Ventura, CA 93001
Phone: 805-648-3146
Fax: 805-648-4103
Toll-free: 888-882-8263
e-mail: contact@venturamusicfestival.org
Web Site: www.venturamusicfestival.org
Officers:
President: Ivor Davis
President-Elect: Eric Oltmann
Secretary: Virginia Norris
Treasurer: Patricia Maki
Management:
Artistic Director: Nuvi Mehta
Executive Director: Cheryl Heitmann
Operations Manager: Ann Willard-Bevans
Administrative Assistant: Sandy Carey
Mission: Annual music festival
Utilizes: Artists-in-Residence; Collaborating Artists;
Commissioned Composers; Commissioned Music;
Composers-in-Residence; Curators; Dance Companies;
Educators; Fine Artists; Grant Writers; Guest
Accompanists; Guest Companies; Guest Soloists; Local
Artists; Multimedia; Original Music Scores; Playwrights;
Singers; Student Interns
Founded: 1994
Specialized Field: Series & Festivals; Instrumental
Music; Vocal Music; Ethnic Performances
Status: Non-Profit, Professional
Paid Staff: 4
Volunteer Staff: 300
Budget: $60,000-$400,000
Season: May
Affiliations: American Symphony League; Chamber
Music America
Annual Attendance: 4,000
Facility Category: Historic buildings in downtown
Ventura
Seating Capacity: 100 - 1,100

3907
VISALIA CULTURAL PROGRAMS-ON STAGE VISALIA

303 E Acequia
Visalia, CA 93291
Phone: 559-713-4000
Fax: 559-738-3579
Toll-free: 800-225-2277
e-mail: vcc@ci.visalia.ca.us
Web Site: www.visalia.org
Management:
General Manager: Wally Roeben

3908
MOUNT SAN ANTONIO COLLEGE PERFORMING ARTS CENTER

1100 N Grand Avenue
Walnut, CA 91789
Phone: 909-594-5611
e-mail: slong@mtsac.edu
Web Site: www.performingarts.mtsac.edu
Officers:
President: Dr. Christopher O'Hearn
Management:
Chair, Music Department: Katherine Charl Calkins
Director of Instrumental Jazz: Jeffrey Ellwood
Director of Choral Activities: Bruce Rogers
Department Secretary: Jeannie DeVito

Founded: 1946
Specialized Field: Series & Festivals; Music; Dance;
Theatre; Radio; Education (Community College)
Status: Non-Profit, Professional
Paid Staff: 2

3909
COLLEGE OF THE SISKIYOUS PERFORMING ARTS SERIES

800 College Avenue
Weed, CA 96094
Phone: 530-938-5373
Fax: 530-938-5570
Toll-free: 888-397-4339
e-mail: cozzalio@siskiyous.edu
Web Site: www.siskiyous.edu
Management:
Academic Senate President: Michael Graves
Vice President of Instruction: Barry A Russell
Mission: The Performing Arts Series is carefully
planned to present the residents of Siskiyou County
with the highest quality performances, at the most
reasonable prices, within Northern California and
southern Oregon. The series provides local residents
an opportunity to see internationally renowned
performing groups at prices set especially for families.
Specialized Field: Family Programming
Status: Non-Profit, Professional
Paid Staff: 2
Performs At: Kenneth W. Ford Theatre
Seating Capacity: 584

3910
SACRAMENTO JAZZ JUBILEE

2787 Del Monte Street
West Sacramento, CA 95691
Phone: 916-372-5277
Fax: 916-372-3479
e-mail: info@sacjazz.com
Web Site: www.sacjazz.com
Officers:
President: Tom Duff
Vice President: Ron Jones
Treasurer: Lisa Negri
Secretary: Judy Hendricks
Management:
Executive Director: Greg Willett
Mission: Sacramento Traditional jazz Society, sponsors
of the Sac. Jazz Jubilee- is a non-profit organization
dedicated to the preservation and promotion of
traditional jazz, Dixieland, and classic jazz music.
Founded: 1974
Specialized Field: Music
Status: Nonprofit
Paid Staff: 5
Volunteer Staff: 4000
Budget: $1.8 million
Income Sources: Admissions, Sponsorships, Grants,
Food Concession Sales, Souvenir Sales, Private and
Corporate Donations, Memberships, Ticket Sales
Season: May
Performs At: Old Sacramento and Midtown
Affiliations: 40 Sacramento Area Venues (Indoor &
Outdoor)
Annual Attendance: 102,000
Seating Capacity: 250-2,500

3911
WHITTIER COLLEGE BACH FESTIVAL

13406 E Philadelphia Street
PO Box 634
Whittier, CA 90608

Phone: 562-907-4237
Fax: 562-464-4592
e-mail: dlozano@whittier.edu
Web Site: www.web.whittier.edu
Management:
　Music Department Chair: David J. Muller
　Associate Professor of Music: Stephen Cook
　Associate Professor of Music: Danilo Lozano
　Associate Professor of Music: Teresa LeVelle
Founded: 1936
Specialized Field: Featuring rock, classical, jazz, R&B, Latino pop, country, cowboy, Dixieland, and folk music.
Paid Artists: 20
Budget: $10,000
Season: March
Performs At: Whittier College Campus (Festival Site)
Facility Category: Whittier College Memorial Chapel & other venues
Seating Capacity: 300

3912
VALLEY CULTURAL CENTER CONCERTS IN THE PARK

21550 Oxnard Street
Suite 470
Woodland Hills, CA 91367-7110
Phone: 818-704-1358
Fax: 818-704-1604
e-mail: info@valleycultural.org
Web Site: www.valleycultural.org
Officers:
　Chairman: Jordan Rothstein
　CFO/Executive Vice Chair: Les Sumpter
　Vice Chair – Board Development: I. Allan Oberman
　Vice Chair – Community Outreach: Leslie DeBeauvais
Management:
　CEO/President: James W Kinsey III
　Director of Operations: Don Sweeney
　Executive Assistant: Wendi Gladstone Potter
　Stage Manager: Jonathan Herndon
Mission: The Valley Cultural Center serves the greater San Fernando Valley as the prominent resource in promoting the performing and visual arts, offering free concerts in the park.
Founded: 1975
Status: Non-Profit, Professional
Paid Staff: 6
Paid Artists: 300
Season: June – August
Performs At: Lou Bredlow Pavillion; Warner Park

Colorado

3913
ASPEN MUSIC FESTIVAL AND SCHOOL

2 Music School Road
Aspen, CO 81611
Phone: 970-925-3254
Fax: 970-920-1643
e-mail: festival@aspenmusic.org
Web Site: www.aspenmusicfestival.com
Officers:
　President/CEO: Don Roth
Management:
　President: Don Roth
　General Manager: James Berdahl
　Artistic Director: Asadour Santourian
　Music Director: David Zinman
Founded: 1949
Specialized Field: Vocal Music: Classical
Status: Non-Profit, Professional

Paid Staff: 100
Paid Artists: 250
Budget: $11,000,000
Performs At: Joan & Irving Harris Concert Hall; Benedict Music Tent
Seating Capacity: 500; 2,050
Year Built: 2000

3914
JAZZ ASPEN SNOWMASS

110 E Hallam Street
Suite 104
Aspen, CO 81611
Phone: 970-920-4996
Fax: 970-920-9135
e-mail: jazzaspen@jazzaspen.org
Web Site: www.jazzaspen.org
Officers:
　Executive Producer: James Honowitz
　Executive VP/Sales/Marketing: Marc Breslin
Management:
　President: Jim Horowitz
Mission: To create world-class programing of jazz, American and world music, to educate and entertain audiences of diverse tastes and backgrounds, to preserve America's musical heritage.
Founded: 1991
Specialized Field: Series & Festivals; Instrumental Music; Vocal Music; Theatre; Youth; Dance; Ethnic Performances; Music; Jazz
Status: Non-Profit, Professional
Paid Staff: 6
Paid Artists: 60
Income Sources: Ticket Sales; Grants; Donations

3915
BOULDER BACH FESTIVAL

PO Box 1896
Boulder, CO 80306
Phone: 303-652-9101
Fax: 303-652-9101
e-mail: info@boulderbachfest.org
Web Site: www.boulderbachfest.org
Management:
　President: Dalene Beaver
　Executive Director: Rebecca Gauss
　Artistic Director: Robert Spillman
Founded: 1981
Specialized Field: Music of Bach
Status: Non-Profit, Professional
Paid Staff: 1
Paid Artists: 40

3916
BOULDER INTERNATIONAL MUSIC FESTIVAL FOR YOUNG PERFORMERS

2955 Dover Drive
Boulder, CO 80305
Phone: 303-494-6975
Fax: 303-494-8225
e-mail: bimfya@uswestmail.net
Management:
　President: Elena Mathys
　Artistic Director: Denise Schaller
Founded: 1998
Specialized Field: Series & Festivals: Instrumental Music
Status: Non-Profit, Non-Professional
Season: June
Facility Category: Saint Paul United Methodist Church

3917
BOULDER PHILHARMONIC ORCHESTRA

Dairy Center for the Arts
2995 Wilderness Place Suite 100
Boulder, CO 80301-5700
Phone: 303-449-1343
Fax: 303-443-9203
e-mail: info@boulderphil.org
Web Site: www.peakarts.org
Officers:
　President: Robert McAllister
Management:
　Executive Director: Sue Levine
　Director Of Marketing And Sales: Melissa Vargas
　Director Of Operations: Glenn Ross
　Chorale Director: Timothy Kreuger
Mission: To offer music, classical dance and arts education experiences.
Status: Nonprofit

3918
COLORADO MAHLERFEST

PO Box 1314
Boulder, CO 80306-1314
Phone: 303-447-0513
e-mail: stanrutt@aol.com
Web Site: www.mahlerfest.org
Officers:
　President: Stan Ruttenberg
　VP: Barry G Knapp
Management:
　President: Stanley Ruttemberg
　Artistic Director: Robert Olson
Mission: To perform all the music of Gustav Mahler.
Utilizes: Guest Instructors; Guest Soloists; Instructors
Founded: 1988
Specialized Field: Music of Gustav Mahler
Status: Non-Profit, Professional
Budget: $45,000
Income Sources: Box Office; Grants; Donations
Season: July
Performs At: University of Colorado; Boulder (Festival Site)
Facility Category: University Auditorium
Seating Capacity: 2,000
Year Built: 1896
Year Remodeled: 1982

3919
COLORADO MUSIC FESTIVAL & ROCKY MOUNTAIN CENTER FOR MUSICAL ARTS

900 Baseline Road
Cottage 100
Boulder, CO 80302
Phone: 303-449-1397
Fax: 303-449-0071
e-mail: info@comusic.org
Web Site: www.comusic.org
Officers:
　President: T K Smith
　Executive Director: Catherine Underhill
Management:
　Music Director: Victoria Marschner
Mission: To inspire and connect community members of all ages by providing access to the best of the world's music through education and performance
Utilizes: Guest Accompanists; Guest Composers; Guest Directors; Guest Musical Directors; Guest Musicians; Instructors; Multimedia; Original Music Scores; Singers
Founded: 1977
Specialized Field: Music performance and education

Status: Non-Profit, Professional
Paid Staff: 12
Volunteer Staff: 75
Paid Artists: 100
Budget: $1.9 Million
Income Sources: Ticket Sales, Tuition, Grants and Donations
Season: June - August
Performs At: Historic landmark auditorium
Annual Attendance: 25,000
Facility Category: Chautauqua Auditorium, Boulder
Seating Capacity: 1,200
Year Built: 1898
Organization Type: Performing

3920
COLORADO SHAKESPEARE FESTIVAL

University of Colorado
1301 Grandview Avenue
277 UCB
Boulder, CO 80309-0277
Phone: 303-492-1527
Fax: 303-735-5140
e-mail: shakes@colorado.edu
Web Site: www.coloradoshakes.org
Management:
   Business Manager: Ray Kemble
   Artistic Director: Philip Charles Sneed
   General Manager: Lynn Nichols
Mission: To produce an aesthetically challenging mix of both traditional and innovative productions of Shakespeare's plays, as well as other classic and contemporary plays.
Utilizes: Actors; AEA Actors; Commissioned Music; Designers; Guest Accompanists; Guest Designers; Guest Writers; Instructors; Original Music Scores; Resident Professionals; Selected Students; Soloists
Founded: 1958
Specialized Field: Theater
Status: Professional; Nonprofit
Paid Staff: 10
Volunteer Staff: 500
Paid Artists: 150
Budget: $1 Million
Income Sources: Blue Mountain Arts
Season: June 27th - August 17th
Performs At: Mary Rippon Outdoor Theatre, University Mainstage Theatre
Annual Attendance: 41,000
Facility Category: Outdoor Theatre, Indoor Theatre
Type of Stage: Greco-Roman, Proscenium
Seating Capacity: 1,004, 406
Year Built: 1936
Organization Type: Performing

3921
CU COORS EVENTS

Conference Center
University of Colorado
Regent Drive
Boulder, CO 80309
Phone: 303-492-5316
Fax: 303-492-4801
e-mail: eggertk@spot.colorado.edu
Web Site: www.colorado.edu
Management:
   President: Steve Wells
Founded: 1979
Specialized Field: Events Setups; Event Facility
Status: Non-Profit, Non-Professional
Paid Staff: 7

3922
EARLY MUSIC COLORADO FALL FESTIVAL OF EARLY MUSIC

PO Box 19078
Boulder, CO 80308-2078
Phone: 720-304-6255
e-mail: info@earlymusiccolorado.org
Web Site: www.earlymusiccolorado.org
Officers:
   President: Leland G Hoover
   Ex-Officio: Rebecca Beshore
Management:
   President: Leland G Hoover
   VP: Mark Counts
   Artistic Director: Frank Nowell
Founded: 1992
Specialized Field: Instrumental; Choral
Status: Nonprofit; Tax-Exempt
Paid Artists: 50
Non-paid Artists: 50
Budget: $10,000
Season: February, May, July, October
Affiliations: Denver Aqmerican Recorder Society
Facility Category: Boulder Public Library
Seating Capacity: 500-700

3923
UNIVERSITY OF COLORADO CONCERTS

31 UCB
University of Colorado
Boulder, CO 80309-0301
Phone: 303-492-8008
Fax: 303-492-5619
e-mail: musictix@colorado.edu
Web Site: www.cuconcerts.org
Management:
   Executive Director: Joan McLean Braun
   Operations Manager: Laima Gaigalas
   Operations Manager: Sandra Miller
Mission: The Artsist Series offers the highest quality emerging and internationally acclaimed soloists and ensembles with related educational programs and residency activities.
Utilizes: Dance Companies; Multimedia; Singers
Founded: 1937
Specialized Field: Series & Festivals; Instrumental Music; Vocal Music; Theatre; Youth; Dance; Ethnic Performances
Status: Non-Profit, Professional
Paid Staff: 5
Performs At: Macky Auditorium

3924
BRECKENRIDGE MUSIC FESTIVAL ORCHESTRA

PO Box 1254
Breckenridge, CO 80424
Phone: 303-453-9142
Fax: 303-453-1423
e-mail: bmi@breckenridgemusicfestival.com
Web Site: www.breckenridgemusicfestival.com
Officers:
   President: Wally Ducayet
   Treasurer: Linda Hague
   Secretary: Rick Oshlo
Management:
   Music Director/Conductor: Gerhardt Zimmermann
   Executive Director: Jeff D Baum
   Concertmaster: Nathan Olson
   Production Manager: Vito Ciccone
Mission: The Breckenridge Music Festival's mission is to provide performing arts programs and arts education to the communities of Summit, Park and Lake Counties.

Utilizes: Guest Artists
Founded: 1980
Specialized Field: Jazz, Folk Music; Educational
Status: Professional, Nonprofit
Performs At: Breckenridge Event Tent
Organization Type: Performing; Educational

3925
NATIONAL REPERTORY ORCHESTRA

PO Box 6336
111 S Main Street
Breckenridge, CO 80424
Phone: 970-453-5825
Fax: 970- 45—583
e-mail: info@nromusic.com
Officers:
   Artistic & Operations Manager: Karen Munnelly
Management:
   Conductor: Carl Topilow
   Executive Director: Terese Kaptur
Mission: Education and performance.
Specialized Field: Orchestra
Paid Staff: 16
Volunteer Staff: 35
Budget: $260,000-1,050,000
Performs At: Riverwalk Center at Breckenridge
Facility Category: Amphitheater
Seating Capacity: 750

3926
COLORADO COLLEGE DANCE FESTIVAL

14 E Cache La Poudre Street
Colorado Springs, CO 80903
Phone: 719-389-6353
Toll-free: 877-894-8727
e-mail: summerdance@coloradocollege.edu
Web Site: www.ArtsFestival.ColoradoCollege.edu/dancefestival
Management:
   Festival Director: Patrizia Herminjard
Mission: To support dance education and performance by fostering a creative environment where all dancers, including students and members of the community, can come together to cultivate and discover the intrinsic value of the many facets of dance. We do this by providing a variety of training in diverse forms across the discipline of dance.
Utilizes: Guest Composers; Guest Musical Directors; Multimedia; Original Music Scores
Founded: 2001
Specialized Field: Dance
Status: Non-Profit, Professional
Paid Staff: 3
Volunteer Staff: 5
Paid Artists: 16
Budget: $50,000
Income Sources: Internal and Private Funding
Season: June 25-July 16
Performs At: Large Theater
Affiliations: Colorado Dance Alliance
Annual Attendance: 60class/1200perfor
Facility Category: Dance Studio
Type of Stage: Marley
Seating Capacity: 750
Year Built: 1975

3927
COLORADO SPRINGS FINE ARTS CENTER PERFORMING ARTS SERIES

30 West Dale
Colorado Springs, CO 80903
Phone: 719-643-5581
Fax: 719-634-0570
e-mail: rgeers@aol.com

Management:
Executive Director: Fran Holden
Executive Director: Fran Holden
Deputy Director: Nancy Sullivan
Performs At: Theatre
Seating Capacity: 450

3928
CRESTED BUTTE CHAMBER MUSIC FESTIVAL
PO Box 992
Crested Butte, CO 81224
Phone: 970-349-5864
Fax: 970-349-5864
Management:
Artistic Director: Claire Jolivet
Administrative Director: Karrie Tenley
Specialized Field: Instrumental; Choral; Folk; Ethnic

3929
CHERRY CREEK ARTS FESTIVAL
PO Box 6265
Denver, CO 80206
Phone: 303-355-2787
Fax: 303-355-2788
e-mail: management@cherryarts.org
Web Site: www.cherryarts.org
Officers:
President/CEO: Bruce Storey
Management:
Executive Director: Terry Adams
Utilizes: Dance Companies; Dancers; Fine Artists; Instructors; Multimedia; Original Music Scores; Sign Language Translators; Singers; Theatre Companies; Touring Companies
Founded: 1990
Specialized Field: Instrumental; Folk; Dance; Theatre
Status: Non-Profit
Paid Staff: 8
Volunteer Staff: 800
Non-paid Artists: 200
Budget: $60,000-$150,000
Season: July
Performs At: Cherry Creek North Business District (Festival Site)
Annual Attendance: 350,000
Facility Category: Outdoor
Stage Dimensions: 24'x 32'; 20'x16'; 20'x16'
Seating Capacity: 3,000; 1,000; 450

3930
COLORADO COUNCIL ON THE ARTS
1380 Lawrence Street
Denver, CO 80204
Phone: 303-894-2617
Fax: 303-894-2615
e-mail: coloarts@state.co.us
Web Site: www.coloarts.state.co.us
Officers:
Chairman: Donald K Bain
Management:
Program Administrator: Jeanette Albert
Executive Director: Elaine Mariner
Associate Director: Maryo Ewell
Mission: To stimulate arts development in the state, to assist and encourage artists and arts organizations, and to help make the arts more accessible statewide.
Founded: 1967
Specialized Field: Visual; Performing; Literary Arts.
Status: Professional; Nonprofit; State Agency
Paid Staff: 7
Budget: $1,900,000
Income Sources: Annual State Appropriation; Federal Grants; Foundation Grants

Affiliations: National Endowment for the Arts; Western States Arts Federation; National Association of Local Arts Agencies
Organization Type: Sponsoring; Grant Making

3931
MUSIC IN THE MOUNTAINS CLASSICAL MUSIC FESTIVAL
PO Box 3751
Durango, CO 81302
Phone: 970-385-6820
Fax: 970-382-0982
e-mail: info@musicinthemountains.com
Web Site: www.musicinthemountains.com
Management:
President: Terry Bacon
Festival Artistic Director: Greg Hustis
Music Director And Conductor: Guillermo Figueroa
Conservatory Artistic Director: Arkady Fomin
Mission: To produce an exceptional summer music festival with musicians of the highest caliber, entertain, educate and delight audiences with the richness of classical music, and complement concerts with educational programs.
Utilizes: Community Talent; Contract Orchestras; Educators; Guest Accompanists; Guest Companies; Guest Composers; Guest Musical Directors; Guest Musicians; High School Drama; Multimedia; Music; Original Music Scores; Soloists; Students
Founded: 1987
Specialized Field: Series and Festivals: Classical Music and Conservatory for Children
Status: Non-Profit, Professional
Paid Staff: 3
Volunteer Staff: 100
Paid Artists: 200
Non-paid Artists: 100
Budget: $700,000
Income Sources: Individual Donations, Foundations, Corporate Sponsors, Ticket Sales
Season: July - August
Performs At: Durango Mountain Resort (Festival Tent Site), Community Concert Hall, and more than 6 other venues throughout Durango & SW CO
Facility Category: Tent
Seating Capacity: 50-640

3932
MUSIC IN THE MOUNTAINS
465 Longs Peak Road
Estes Park, CO 80517-6422
Phone: 970-586-4031
Fax: 970-586-4031
e-mail: rrmcoffice@aol.com
Officers:
President: Mary Jane Clark
Management:
Music Director: Elizabeth Mueller Grace
Mission: To provide live classical music of the highest quality to the Four Corners of Colorado, New Mexico, Utah and Arizona.
Founded: 1986
Specialized Field: Instrumental
Status: Professional; Nonprofit
Budget: $20,000 - 35,000
Season: Late June - Late August, Sundays
Performs At: Estes Park, CO (Festival Site)
Facility Category: Rocky Ridge Music Center
Seating Capacity: 250
Organization Type: Performing; Educational

3933
ROCKY RIDGE MUSIC CENTER
465 Longs Peak Road
Estes Park, CO 80517-1790
Phone: 970-586-4031
Fax: 970-586-6685
e-mail: info@rockyridge.org
Web Site: www.rockyridge.org
Officers:
Founder: Beth Miller Harrod
President: Madison Casey
VP: Miriam Reitz Baer
Management:
President: Norman Taulu
Music Director: Carina Voly
Assistant Music Director: Connie G Cook
Mission: To offer summer programs of conservatory-level music training for young people, with emphasis on Youth Orchestra, young pianists, chamber music and composition; to offer this program simultaneously with the summer concert series, Music in the Mountains.
Utilizes: Artists-in-Residence; Guest Artists; Multimedia
Founded: 1942
Specialized Field: Series & Festivals: Instrumental Music
Status: Non-Profit, Professional
Paid Staff: 4
Annual Attendance: 300
Facility Category: Log cabins - historical
Seating Capacity: 150
Year Built: 1900
Year Remodeled: 1990
Organization Type: Performing; Educational

3934
SUMMIT JAZZ SWINGING JAZZ CONCERTS
PO Box 1150
Evergreen, CO 80437
Phone: 303-670-8471
Fax: 360-379-8811
e-mail: summitjazz1@cs.com
Web Site: www.summitjazz.org
Officers:
President: Alan P Frederickson
Secretary/Treasurer: Juanita P Greenwood
Management:
President: Alan P Frederic
Secretary and Treasurer: Juanita P Green
Mission: to foster awareness and appreciation of traditional jazz through public concert performances by internationally recognized artists who have earned their reputation as dedicated exponents of this musical genre.

3935
MESA COUNTY COMMUNITY CONCERT ASSOCIATION
1155 Lakeside Drive
#801
Grand Junction, CO 81506
Phone: 970-245-1293
e-mail: mcca@acsol.net
Officers:
Secretary: Jackie Porter
Management:
President: Jerry A M Brosier
Stage Manager: Jonathan Jones
Founded: 1944
Specialized Field: Series and Festivals: National and International Concerts
Status: Non-Profit, Professional

Paid Artists: 6
Performs At: Grand Junction High School Auditorium

3936
LOVELAND FRIENDS OF CHAMBER MUSIC
1000 King Drive
Loveland, CO 80537
Phone: 970-663-7928
e-mail: frhale@msn.com
Management:
President: Ruth J Hale
Founded: 1995
Specialized Field: Series & Festivals; Instrumental Music; Vocal Music; Youth; Chamber Music
Status: Non-Profit, Professional
Paid Artists: 25
Performs At: Private Homes

3937
MUSIC IN OURAY
PO Box 14
Ouray, CO 81427
Phone: 970-626-5506
Fax: 970-626-4341
e-mail: chimney@rmi.net
Web Site: www.musicinouray.com
Management:
Director: Soozie Arnold
Specialized Field: Instrumental
Budget: $35,000 - 60,000
Season: Early June
Facility Category: Wright Opera House, Ouray
Seating Capacity: 200

3938
SANGRE DE CRISTO ARTS AND CONFERENCE CENTER
210 North Santa Fe Avenue
Pueblo, CO 81003
Phone: 719-543-0130
Fax: 719-543-0134
Web Site: www.solc-arts.org
Management:
Director: Maggie Divelbiss
Associate Director: Jennifer Cook
Technical Director: Timothy F Gately
Founded: 1972
Specialized Field: Dance; Vocal Music; Instrumental Music; Theater; Festivals; Lyric Opera
Status: Professional; Nonprofit
Paid Staff: 40

3939
SANGRE DE CRISTO ARTS AND CONFERENCE CENTER
210 North Santa Fe Avenue
Pueblo, CO 81003
Phone: 719-543-0130
Fax: 719-543-0134
Web Site: www.solc-arts.org
Management:
Director: Maggie Divelbiss
Associate Director: Jennifer Cook
Technical Director: Timothy F Gately
Mission: Supporting diverse visual and performing arts in the Southeastern Colorado area.
Utilizes: Artists-in-Residence; Choreographers; Collaborating Artists; Collaborations; Dance Companies; Dancers; Guest Artists; Guest Ensembles; Guest Musical Directors; Guild Activities; Lyricists; Multimedia; New Productions; Resident Artists; Soloists; Special Technical Talent; Theatre Companies

Founded: 1972
Specialized Field: Dance; Vocal Music; Instrumental Music; Theater; Festivals; Lyric Opera
Status: Professional; Nonprofit
Paid Staff: 40
Volunteer Staff: 50
Income Sources: Association of Performing Arts Presenters; Western Alliance of Arts Administrators; Rocky Mountain Theatre Guild
Performs At: Sangre de Cristo Arts and Conference Center
Annual Attendance: 10,000
Facility Category: Arts Center
Type of Stage: Proscenium
Stage Dimensions: 35'x20'x22'
Seating Capacity: 496
Year Built: 1972
Rental Contact: Lorrie Marquez
Organization Type: Performing; Touring; Resident; Educational; Sponsoring

3940
TELLURIDE CHAMBER MUSIC FESTIVAL
PO Box 115
Telluride, CO 81435
Phone: 970-728-8686
Fax: 866-366-2329
Toll-free: 800-525-3455
e-mail: chambermusictelluride@yahoo.com
Web Site: www.telluride.com/chamber.html
Officers:
President: Kay Langstraff
Management:
Founder/Co-Director: Roy Malan
Co-Director: Robin Sutherland
Mission: Talented musicians visit our area each year and enrich us with their musical mastery.
Founded: 1973
Specialized Field: Instrumental
Status: Professional
Budget: $10,000
Income Sources: Individual Donations, Grants, Telluride Foundation
Season: August
Performs At: Telluride; Festival Site
Facility Category: Sheridan Opera House
Seating Capacity: 240

3941
TELLURIDE JAZZ CELEBRATION
Telluride Society for Jazz
PO Box 2132
Telluride, CO 81435
Phone: 970-728-7009
Fax: 970-728-5834
e-mail: paul@telluridejazz.com
Web Site: www.telluridejazz.com
Management:
President: John Burchmore
Executive Director: Paul Machado
Mission: Jazz music
Founded: 1977
Specialized Field: Series & Festivals: Music festival.
Status: Non-Profit, Professional
Paid Staff: 1
Volunteer Staff: 125
Paid Artists: 40
Non-paid Artists: 60
Budget: $ 300,000
Seating Capacity: 3,000

3942
TYER CHAMBER MUSIC FESTIVAL
PO Box 115
Telluride, CO 81435
Phone: 970-728-8686
Fax: 970-728-8686
Toll-free: 800-525-3455
e-mail: chambermusictelluride@yahoo.com
Web Site: www.telluridechambermusic.com
Management:
President: Ann Grady
Executive Director: Jenny Sullivan
Artistic Director: Roy Malan
Mission: We are fortunate to have very talented musicians visit our area each year and enrich us with their musical mastery.
Founded: 1973
Specialized Field: Series & Festivals: Chamber Music
Status: Non-Profit, Professional
Paid Staff: 1
Paid Artists: 500
Budget: $10,000
Income Sources: Individual Donations, Grants, Telluride Foundation
Season: August
Performs At: Telluride (Festival Site)
Facility Category: Sheridan Opera House
Seating Capacity: 240

3943
ACADEMY CONCERTS
USAFA/34TRW/SDAE
2302 Cadet Drive, Suite 12
USAF Academy, CO 80840-6099
Phone: 719-333-4497
Fax: 719-333-4597
Management:
Cultural Arts/Entertainment Directo: Candyce Thomas
Mission: To offer the Cadet Wing cultural enhancements, entertaining rock concerts, and comedians; to offer our military personnel and community cultural events.
Founded: 1959
Specialized Field: Series & Festivals: Instrumental Music
Status: Non-Profit, Professional
Paid Staff: 4
Performs At: Arnold Hall Theater
Annual Attendance: 28,000
Facility Category: Theater; Concert Hall
Type of Stage: Proscenium
Seating Capacity: 2,809
Year Built: 1957
Year Remodeled: 1999

3944
BRAVO! VAIL VALLEY MUSIC FESTIVAL
PO Box 2270
Vail, CO 81658
Phone: 970-827-5700
Fax: 970-827-5707
Toll-free: 877-827-5700
e-mail: bravo@vail.net
Web Site: www.vailmusicfestival.org
Management:
Executive Director: John W Giovando
Artistic Director: Eugenia Zukerman
Utilizes: Artists-in-Residence; Commissioned Music; Guest Companies; Guest Composers; Guest Directors; Guest Musicians; Guest Writers; Soloists
Founded: 1987
Specialized Field: Vocal Music: Classical

Status: Non-Profit, Professional
Paid Staff: 25
Budget: $2,000,000
Season: June - August
Performs At: Venues throughout Vail, Beaver Creek (Festival Site)
Annual Attendance: 48,000
Seating Capacity: 2,500; 250

3945
VAIL JAZZ FESTIVAL
PO Box 3035
Vail, CO 81658-3035
Phone: 970-479-6146
Fax: 970-477-0866
Toll-free: 800-824-5526
e-mail: vjf@vailjazz.org
Web Site: www.vailjazz.org
Officers:
    President: Howard L Stone
Management:
    Executive Director: Mia Vlaar
    Education Director: John Clayton Jr
Mission: Dedicated to the perpetuation of jazz through the presentation of jazz performances and jazz education, with special emphasis on young musicians and young audiences.
Founded: 1995
Status: Non-Profit,Professional

3946
JAZZ IN THE SANGRES
PO Box 327
Westcliffe, CO 81252
Phone: 719-783-3785
e-mail: design@creativeminds.com
Web Site: www.custerguide.com/jazz

3947
WESTMINSTER COMMUNITY ARTIST SERIES
7380 Lowell Boulevard
Westminster, CO 80030
Phone: 303-429-1999
Fax: 303-469-4599
Management:
    President: Patrick Payne
    Executive Director: Dona Waddell
Mission: To bring world class visual and performing artists to audiences in the Westminster Area.
Utilizes: Singers
Founded: 1983
Specialized Field: Performing Arts
Status: Non-Profit, Non-Professional
Organization Type: Performing

Connecticut

3948
GREAT CONNECTICUT JAZZ FEST
The Great Ct Jazz
PO Box 2426
Branford, CT 06405-1526
Phone: 203-469-8592
Fax: 203-481-2603
Toll-free: 800-468-3836
e-mail: ct.traditional.jazz@snet.net
Web Site: www.ctjazz.org
Founded: 1985
Specialized Field: Dixieland Jazz; Swing Jazz
Volunteer Staff: 375
Paid Artists: 138
Non-paid Artists: 46

Annual Attendance: 10,000
Facility Category: Tent

3949
GOODSPEED MUSICALS
6 Main Street
Box A
East Haddam, CT 06423
Phone: 860-873-8664
Fax: 860-873-2329
e-mail: info@goodspeed.org
Web Site: www.goodspeed.org
Management:
    Executive Director: Michel Price
    Technical Director: R Glen Grusmark
Mission: Preserving and advancing the American musical as an art form; developing new works to be added to the repertoire.
Founded: 1963
Specialized Field: Musical
Status: Non-Profit, Professional
Performs At: Goodspeed Opera House
Type of Stage: Proscenium
Stage Dimensions: 27'x18'
Orchestra Pit: 1
Architect: William H Goodspeed
Organization Type: Performing; Equity Theater

3950
GOODSPEED OPERA HOUSE
Route 82
PO Box A
East Haddam, CT 06423
Phone: 860-873-8664
Fax: 860-873-2329
e-mail: info@goodspeed.org
Web Site: www.goodspeed.org
Management:
    President: Michael Price
    General Manager: Hattie Guin Kittner
    Associate Producer: Sue Frost
Founded: 1963
Specialized Field: Series and Festivals: Musicals
Status: Non-Profit, Professional
Performs At: Goodspeed Opera House; Goodspeed-at-Chester
Type of Stage: Proscenium; Adaptable Proscenium
Seating Capacity: 400; 200

3951
ENFIELD CULTURAL ARTS COMMISSION
19 North Main Street
Enfield, CT 06422
Phone: 860-253-6421
Fax: 860-253-5147
Officers:
    Chairman: Priscilla D McManus
Management:
    President: Theresa Jedyniak
Specialized Field: Series and Festivals Instrumental Music; Vocal Music; Theatre; Youth; Dance; Ethnic Performances
Status: Non-Profit,Non-Professional

3952
HOT STEAMED JAZZ FESTIVAL
Valley Railroad
PO Box 293
Essex, CT 06426
Phone: 860-767-3968
Fax: 860-767-3968
Toll-free: 800-348-0003
e-mail: info@hotsteamedjazz.com
Web Site: www.hotsteamedjazz.com

Officers:
    President: Joseph Bombaci
    Tresurer: Peter Tizzie
Management:
    President: Jb Bombac
    Artistic Director: Richard Moore
    Band Contact: Dick Moore
Mission: Providing good jazz for the Whole in the Wall Camp.
Founded: 1992
Specialized Field: Series & Festivals; Instrumental Music; Vocal Music; Youth; Dance; Ethnic Performances; Traditional jazz
Status: Non-Profit, Non-Professional
Volunteer Staff: 30
Paid Artists: 50
Budget: $35,000
Income Sources: Ticket Sales; Donations
Annual Attendance: 22,000

3953
CHESTNUT HILL CONCERTS
PO Box 183; 724 Boston Post Rd
Guilford, CT 06437
Phone: 203-245-5736
Web Site: www.shorelinearts.org
Officers:
    President: John Posner
Management:
    Owner: William Donald
Mission: Brings world-class chamber music to the shoreline at the Katharine Hepburn Cultural Arts Center in Old Saybrook on the first four Fridays of August
Founded: 1969
Specialized Field: Instrumental
Paid Staff: 1
Budget: $10,000
Season: August
Performs At: Madison, CT (Festival Site)
Facility Category: First Congregational Church of Madison
Seating Capacity: 500

3954
SHORELINE ARTS ALLIANCE
725 Boston Post Road
Guilford, CT 06437
Phone: 203-453-3890
Fax: 203-453-0611
e-mail: office@shorelinearts.org
Web Site: www.shorelinearts.org
Officers:
    President: Julie McClenan
    VP: Deborah Abildsoe
    Treasurer: Armand Rossi
Management:
    Program Coordinator: Donita Aruny
    Administrative Coordinator: Jennifer Zeliff Kearney
Mission: A performance and service organization offering juried competitions for artists, photographers and writers; student scholarships within the local region; and a performance series.
Utilizes: Touring Companies
Status: Nonprofit
Budget: $100,000
Income Sources: Grants; Foundations; Memberships
Resident Groups: Connecticut Commission on the Arts

3955
FIRST NIGHT HARTFORD
750 Main Street
Suite 514
Hartford, CT 06103
Phone: 860-722-9546
Fax: 860-722-9627
e-mail: firstnighthartford@msn.com
Web Site: www.firstnighthartford.com
Management:
    President: James Gordon
    Executive Director: Pamela Amodio
Mission: Offering downtown Hartford an alcohol-free
New Year's Eve celebration.
Utilizes: Singers
Founded: 1988
Specialized Field: Series & Festivals: Produce Arts
Festival
Status: Non-Profit, Professional
Paid Staff: 1
Volunteer Staff: 200
Paid Artists: 30
Budget: $250,000
Income Sources: Corporate Sponsorships; Foundation
Grants; Admissions
Season: December - January
Performs At: Downtown Hartford (Festival Site)
Annual Attendance: 30,000
Organization Type: Performing

3956
TALCOTT MOUNTAIN MUSIC FESTIVAL, SUMMER SERIES
Hartford Symphony
228 Farmington Avenue
Hartford, CT 06105
Phone: 860-246-8742
Fax: 860-247-1720
e-mail: info@hartfordsymphony.org
Web Site: www.hartfordsymphony.org
Officers:
    President: Millard H Pryor Jr
    VP Finance: Thomas R Wildman, Esquire
    VP Marketing: Robinson A Grover
    VP Administration: John H Beers
Management:
    President: David Roth
    Executive Director: Charles Owens
    Artistic Director: Edward Cumming
Utilizes: Actors; Collaborating Artists; Collaborations;
Commissioned Composers; Commissioned Music;
Composers-in-Residence; Dancers; Five Seasonal
Concerts; Grant Writers; Guest Accompanists; Guest
Companies; Guest Composers; Guest Lecturers; Guest
Musical Directors; Guest Musicians; Instructors;
Lyricists; Multi Collaborations; Multimedia; Original
Music Scores; Sign Language Translators; Singers;
Theatre Companies
Founded: 1944
Specialized Field: Instrumental
Status: Non-Profit, Professional
Paid Staff: 178
Paid Artists: 178
Season: July
Performs At: Simsbury (Festival Site); Iron Horse
Boulevard; Simsbury
Annual Attendance: 21,300

3957
WOODLAND CONCERT SERIES
10 Woodland Street
Hartford, CT 06105

Phone: 860-527-8121
Fax: 860-293-1404
e-mail: immanvel@iccucc.org
Web Site: www.woodlandconcertseries.org
Management:
    Artistic Director: Edward Tyler
    Managing Director: Deborah Flower
Utilizes: Collaborating Artists; Commissioned Music;
Guest Accompanists; Guest Companies; Guest
Directors; Guest Instructors; Guest Musicians; Guest
Soloists; Instructors; Local Artists; Multimedia; Music;
Organization Contracts; Original Music Scores;
Playwrights; Singers; Soloists
Performs At: Immanuel Congregational Church
Seating Capacity: 700

3958
LITCHFIELD JAZZ FESTIVAL
174 W Street
PO Box 69
Litchfield, CT 06759
Phone: 860-567-4162
Fax: 860-567-3592
Management:
    Executive Director: Vita West Muir

3959
LITCHFIELD PERFORMING ARTS SERIES
40 W Street
PO Box 69
Litchfield, CT 06759
Phone: 860-567-4162
Fax: 860-567-3592
e-mail: lpai@ct1.nai.net
Management:
    Executive Director: Vita West Muir
Performs At: Church

3960
SILVERMINE GUILD ART CENTER SERIES
1037 Silvermine Road
New Canaan, CT 06840
Phone: 203-966-9700
Fax: 203-966-2763
e-mail: sgac@silvermineart.org
Web Site: www.silvermineart.org
Management:
    Executive Director: Cynthia Clair
    Program Director: Carol Nordgren
Mission: Arts, education and appreciation.
Utilizes: Collaborations; Curators; Educators; Fine
Artists; Guest Accompanists; Guest Ensembles; Guest
Instructors; Guest Musical Directors; Guest Musicians;
Guest Soloists; Guest Teachers; Guest Writers;
Instructors; Local Artists; Lyricists; Multi Collaborations;
Multimedia; Original Music Scores; Playwrights;
Singers; Soloists; Touring Companies
Founded: 1922
Specialized Field: Visual Art; Concerts
Status: Non-Profit, Professional
Paid Staff: 15
Volunteer Staff: 15
Budget: $1.6 Million
Income Sources: Tuition; Private Donations; Art Sales
Performs At: Multi-Purpose
Facility Category: Galleries; Auditorium
Seating Capacity: 125
Year Remodeled: 2000

3961
INTERNATIONAL FESTIVAL OF ARTS & IDEAS
195 Church Street
12th Floor
New Haven, CT 06510
Phone: 203-498-1212
Fax: 203-498-2220
Toll-free: 888-278-4332
e-mail: chedstrom@artidea.org
Web Site: www.artidea.org
Management:
    Program Director: Cynthia Hedstrom
Specialized Field: Instrumental; Dance; Theatre;
Childrens'; Ethnic
Season: June - July

3962
NEW HAVEN JAZZ FESTIVAL
New Haven Festivals
165 Church Street
New Haven, CT 06510
Phone: 203-946-7821
Fax: 203-946-5750
e-mail: info@newhavenjazz.com
Web Site: www.newhavenjazz.com
Management:
    Director: Barbara Lamb
Founded: 1982
Specialized Field: Music

3963
CONNECTICUT COLLEGE: ON STAGE
270 Mohegan Avenue
PO Box 5216
New London, CT 06320
Phone: 860-439-2787
Fax: 860-439-2695
e-mail: onstage@conncoll.edu
Web Site: www.onstage.conncoll.edu
Management:
    Director: Robert A Richter
Mission: To present a varied annual series of the
world's great performing artists thereby enriching and
enhancing the cultural life of our community.
Founded: 1939
Specialized Field: Series and Festivals Instrumental
Music; Theatre; Dance; Vocal Music
Status: Professional; Non-Profit
Paid Staff: 2
Budget: $139,000
Performs At: Palmer Auditorium; Evans Hall
Organization Type: Performing; Presenting

3964
CONNECTICUT EARLY MUSIC FESTIVAL
PO Box 329
New London, CT 06320
Phone: 860-444-2419
Web Site: www.ctearlymusic.org
Management:
    Artistic Director: Eric Rice
    Executive Director: Jan MacGregor
Mission: To provide performances of music from the
16th-19th centuries on period instruments.
Utilizes: Guest Artists
Founded: 1983
Specialized Field: Instrumental
Status: Professional; Nonprofit
Season: Mid June
Performs At: New London; Noank; Niantic; Waterford
Seating Capacity: 125; 500
Organization Type: Performing

All listings are in alphabetical order by state, then city, then organization within the city.

3965
SUMMER MUSIC
300 State Street
Suite 400
New London, CT 06320
Phone: 860-442-9199
Fax: 860-442-9290
e-mail: info@summer-music.org
Web Site: www.summer-music.org
Management:
    Executive Director: Paul R Bunker
    Chairman: Raymond Johnson
Founded: 1983
Specialized Field: Music festivals
Status: Non-Profit, Professional
Paid Staff: 2

3966
NEWTOWN FRIENDS OF MUSIC
PO Box 295
Newtown, CT 06470-0295
Phone: 203-426-6470
Fax: 203-426-4587
e-mail: friendsofmusic@snet.net
Web Site: www.newtownfriendsofmusic.org
Officers:
    President: Ellen Parrella
Mission: To present exquisite-superbly performed
Utilizes: Artists-in-Residence; Multimedia; Original
Music Scores
Founded: 1978
Specialized Field: Series & Festivals; Instrumental
Music; Chamber Music; Recitals; Chamber Orchestra
Status: Non-Profit, Professional
Volunteer Staff: 16
Paid Artists: 22
Performs At: Edmond Town Hall
Annual Attendance: 2,500
Seating Capacity: 450

3967
NORFOLK CHAMBER MUSIC FESTIVAL/YALE SUMMER SCHOOL OF MUSIC
Ellen Battell Stoeckel Estate
Route 44 & 272
Norfolk, CT 06058
Phone: 203-432-1966
Fax: 203-432-2136
e-mail: norfolk@yale.edu
Web Site: www.yale.edu/norfolk
Management:
    Director: Paul Hawkhaw
    General Manager: James Nelson
Founded: 1941
Specialized Field: Series and Festivals: Chamber
Music
Status: Non-Profit, Professional
Paid Staff: 12
Paid Artists: 40

3968
PROJECT TROUBADOR
374 Taconic Road
Salisbury, CT 06068
Phone: 860-435-0561
Fax: 860-435-0561
e-mail: louise@projecttroubador.org
Web Site: www.projecttroubador.org
Management:
    Executive Director: Louise Lindenmeyr
    Artistic Director: Eliot Osborn
Mission: Music, theatre and humor are powerful
universal vehicles of communication yet there is little
opportunity for cross-cultural sharing to take place on a
person-to -person level around the world. Project
Troubador is unique in its fulfillment of this need-offering
a way for both performing artists and audiences to meet
on common ground in celebration.
Founded: 1978
Specialized Field: National Development/Performance
Status: Non-Profit, Professional
Paid Staff: 2
Paid Artists: 75

3969
FALCON RIDGE FOLK FESTIVAL
POB 144
Sharon, CT 06069
Phone: 860-364-0366
Fax: 860-364-4678
e-mail: info@falconridgefolk.com
Web Site: www.falconridgefolk.com
Officers:
    Executive Director: Howard Randall
Management:
    Artistic Director: Anne Saunders
Utilizes: High School Drama; Multimedia; Original
Music Scores; Playwrights; Selected Students; Sign
Language Translators; Students
Founded: 1988
Specialized Field: Folk Music; Dance
Paid Staff: 5/6/
Paid Artists: 50
Income Sources: Ticket Sales
Performs At: Long Hill Farm
Affiliations: National Folk Alliance; International
Bluegrass; Americana Music Association
Annual Attendance: 10-15,000
Facility Category: Corporation

3970
MUSIC MOUNTAIN
PO Box 1739
Sharon, CT 06069
Phone: 860-824-7126
Fax: 860-364-2090
e-mail: ngordon@keystonebroadcasting.com
Web Site: www.musicmountain.org
Officers:
    President: Nicholas Gordon
Mission: To provide professional chamber music to
western Connecticut through a Summer Chamber
Music Festival, as well as broadcasts to over 200 radio
stations and 220 foriegn countries.
Utilizes: Guest Musical Directors; Multimedia; Original
Music Scores
Founded: 1930
Specialized Field: Series and Festivals: Chamber
Music
Status: Non-Profit, Professional
Paid Staff: 1
Volunteer Staff: 30
Paid Artists: 150
Income Sources: Ticket Sales; Donations; Bequests;
Foundations; Government Grants
Season: June - September
Performs At: Gordon Hall; Falls Village
Annual Attendance: 10,000
Facility Category: Colonial Concert Hall
Stage Dimensions: 18'x36'
Seating Capacity: 344
Year Built: 1930
Rental Contact: President Nicholas Gordon
Organization Type: Performing; Educational;
Sponsoring

3971
NORTHWEST CORNER YOUNG ARTISTS SERIES
18 Old Sharon Road
#3
Sharon, CT 06069
Phone: 860-364-0253
Management:
    Artistic Director: DeeAnne Hunstien
Performs At: Private Homes

3972
WINTERHAWK - BLUEGRASS & BEYOND
74 Modley Road
Sharon, CT 06069
Phone: 860-364-0366
Fax: 860-364-8081
Toll-free: 866-325-2744
e-mail: info@winterhawk2000.com
Web Site: www.winterhawk2000.com
Management:
    President: Howard Randall
    Executive Director: Anne Saunders
Utilizes: High School Drama; Multimedia; Original
Music Scores; Playwrights; Selected Students; Sign
Language Translators; Students
Founded: 1983
Specialized Field: Series & Festivals: Produce Music
Festivals
Status: For-Profit, Professional
Paid Staff: 2
Paid Artists: 60
Income Sources: Ticket Sales
Performs At: Long Hill Farm
Affiliations: National Folk Alliance; Interntional
Bluegrass; Americana Music Association
Annual Attendance: 2,500-7,000
Facility Category: Corporation

3973
CENTENNIAL THEATER FESTIVAL
995 Hopmeadow Street
Simsbury, CT 06070
Phone: 860-408-5300
Fax: 860-408-5301
e-mail: deanadams@msn.com
Management:
    Artistic Director: Dean Adams
Utilizes: Actors; AEA Actors; Dance Companies;
Dancers; Designers; Grant Writers; Guest
Accompanists; Guest Artists; Guest Conductors; Guest
Designers; Guest Lecturers; Multimedia; Music; Original
Music Scores; Resident Professionals; Student Interns;
Theatre Companies
Founded: 1990
Specialized Field: Festival
Status: Nonprofit
Season: June 11 - August 1
Annual Attendance: 8,000
Facility Category: Theater; Air Conditioned, Handicap
Access
Type of Stage: Proscenium
Stage Dimensions: 29' x 35'
Seating Capacity: 400
Year Built: 1989

3974
CONNECTICUT THEATER FESTIVAL
995 Hopmeadow Street
Simsbury, CT 06070

Phone: 860-651-6329
Fax: 860-408-5301
e-mail: ctfestival@hotmail.com
Web Site: www.ctfestival.com
Management:
  Producing Artistic Director: Dean Adams
Utilizes: Actors; AEA Actors; Dance Companies;
Dancers; Designers; Grant Writers; Guest
Accompanists; Guest Artists; Guest Conductors; Guest
Designers; Guest Lecturers; Multimedia; Music; Original
Music Scores; Resident Professionals; Student Interns;
Theatre Companies
Founded: 1990
Status: Nonprofit
Season: June 11 - August 1
Annual Attendance: 8,000
Facility Category: Theater; Air Conditioned, Handicap
Access
Type of Stage: Proscenium
Stage Dimensions: 29' x 35'
Seating Capacity: 400
Year Built: 1989

3975
STRATFORD FESTIVAL THEATER

1850 Elm Street
Stratford, CT 06615
Phone: 203-378-1200
Fax: 203-378-9777
Management:
  Dramaturg: J Wishnia
Founded: 1996

3976
ARMSTRONG CHAMBER CONCERTS

86 Church Hill Road
PO Box 367
Washington Depot, CT 06794
Phone: 860-868-0522
Fax: 860-868-0522
e-mail: accnct@aol.com
Web Site: www.accnct.org
Officers:
  President/Treasurer: Helen Armstrong
  VP: Ajit Hutheesing
  Secretary: Greta Pofcher
  Secretary: Ann Wade
  Secretary: Suzanne Geiss-Robbins
Management:
  President: Helen Armstrong
  Operations Manager: Kathie Plaskiewicz
  Grant Writer: Carol Mallquist
Mission: To provide concerts of professional chamber
music to diverse audiences.
Utilizes: Artists-in-Residence; Collaborations; Guest
Accompanists; Guest Musical Directors; Guest
Musicians; Multimedia; Original Music Scores; Singers
Founded: 1983
Specialized Field: Series & Festivals; Instrumental
Music; Chamber Music
Status: Non-Profit, Professional
Paid Staff: 2
Paid Artists: 15
Income Sources: Grants; Donations; Box Office
Performs At: Litchfield
Affiliations: Chamber Music America; Ulenfield Hills
Visitors Bureau; American Symphony League
Annual Attendance: 5-6,000
Organization Type: Performing; Touring; Resident;
Educational

3977
HARTT SCHOOL CONCERT SERIES

200 Bloomfield Avenue
West Hartford, CT 06117
Phone: 860-768-4454
Fax: 860-768-4441
e-mail: jessilevi@hartford.edu
Web Site: www.hartford.edu/hartt
Management:
  Dean: Malcolm Morrison
  Executive Director: Michael Yaffe
Founded: 1920
Specialized Field: Music; Dance; Theatre
Performs At: Millard Auditorium; Lincoln Theater
Rental Contact: DaVid Bell

3978
SOUTH SHORE MUSIC

PO Box 403
Westport, CT 06881
Phone: 203-227-0695
Fax: 203-454-3682
e-mail: southshoremusic@bigplanet.com
Web Site: www.southshoremusic.com
Officers:
  President/Program Chairman: Marianne
  Liberatore
Mission: To present chamber music concerts
Utilizes: Guest Musical Directors; Multimedia
Founded: 1933
Specialized Field: Classical Chamber Music
Volunteer Staff: 6
Budget: $100,000
Income Sources: Tickets; Ads; Contributions
Season: June-September
Performs At: Saugatuck Congregational Church

3979
TEMPLE ISRAEL

14 Coleytown Road
Westport, CT 06880
Phone: 203-227-1293
Fax: 203-454-2292
e-mail: finearts@tiwestport.org
Web Site: www.tiwestport.org
Management:
  Executive Director: Sandy Silstein
Status: Non-Profit, Professional
Performs At: Temple Israel

Delaware

3980
UNIVERSITY OF DELAWARE
PERFORMING ARTS SERIES

Alumni Hall
24 E Main Street
Newark, DE 19716-7101
Phone: 302-831-8741
Fax: 302-831-2045
e-mail: pas@mvs.udel.edu
Web Site: www.vdel.edu
Management:
  Assistant Director: Robert Snyder
Mission: A public service for local community.
Founded: 1979
Paid Staff: 3
Volunteer Staff: 20
Paid Artists: 20
Performs At: Mitchell Hall

3981
DELAWARE CHAMBER MUSIC FESTIVAL

PO Box 3537
Wilmington, DE 19807-3537
Phone: 302-239-8440
Fax: 302-636-9400
e-mail: dcmf@geocities.com
Web Site: www.dcmf.org
Officers:
  President: Mary P Richards
  VP: Tamara Lyn Smith
  Treasurer: Roger Cuson
  Secretary: Marcia Peoples Halio
Management:
  Music Director: Barbara Govatos
  Co-Administrator: Cher Astolfi
  Co-Administrator: Tracy Ann Smith
Paid Staff: 3
Volunteer Staff: 20
Paid Artists: 25

District of Columbia

3982
AMERICAN COLLEGE THEATER
FESTIVAL

John F Kennedy Center
for the Performing Arts
Washington, DC 20566-0001
Phone: 202-416-8864
Fax: 202-416-8802
e-mail: ghenry@kennedy-center.org
Management:
  Director: Gregg Henry

3983
AMERICAN MUSIC FESTIVAL

National Gallery of Art
2000B South Club Drive
Washington, DC 20785
Phone: 202-737-4215
Fax: 202-789-3246
e-mail: der-info@nga.gov
Web Site: www.nga.gov
Management:
  Music Director: George Manos
  Music Program Specialist: Stephen Ackert
Specialized Field: Instrumental; Choral; Jazz;
Educational
Season: May, Sundays only
Performs At: Washington, DC (Festival Site)
Seating Capacity: 500

3984
ARTS IN THE ACADEMY, NATIONAL
ACADEMY OF SCIENCES

2101 Constitution Avenue NW
Washington, DC 20418
Phone: 202-334-2439
Fax: 202-334-1687
e-mail: jtomlins@nas.edu
Web Site: www.national-acadamies.org/arts
Officers:
  Administrative Assistant: Marsha Barrett
Management:
  Director: Janis Tomlinson
Performs At: Auditorium
Seating Capacity: 670

3985
CHILDREN'S NATIONAL MEDICAL CENTER, NEW HORIZONS PROGRAM
111 Michigan Avenue NW
Washington, DC 20010-2970
Phone: 202-884-3465
Fax: 202-884-3489
e-mail: tlassite@cnmc.org
Management:
    Manager: Tina S Lassiter
    Performance Coordinator: Arabella Johnson
Mission: To provide multi-disciplined high quality arts programming to patients at bedside, in playrooms and, in the Atrium space in order to expedite the healing process.
Founded: 1978

3986
DC SPORTS & ENTERTAINMENT COMMISSION
2400 E Capitol Street
SE RFK, 4th Floor
Washington, DC 20003
Phone: 202-547-0977
Fax: 202-547-7460
e-mail: nevwa@aol.com
Web Site: www.dcsec.dcgov.org
Management:
    Executive Director: James Dalrymple
    Marketing Director: Neville Waters
    Stadium Manager: Anthony Burnett
Mission: To promote Washington, DC as a location for holding sporting events to enhanve the city's economic development and welfare, and expand the city's national and international exposure. The Commission also creates opportunities for community outreach and local recreation for all residents of the district, particularly youths.
Seating Capacity: 56; 692

3987
DISTRICT CURATORS
PO Box 14197
Washington, DC 20044
Phone: 202-783-0360
Fax: 202-783-4185
Management:
    Executive Director: Bill Warrell
    Producer: Katea Stitt
Mission: Presenting the finest new performing arts to Washington DC and mid-Atlantic audiences; advancing cultural opportunities world-wide for artists and audiences.
Specialized Field: Ethnic
Status: Nonprofit
Organization Type: Presenting

3988
DUMBARTON CONCERT
3133 Dumbarton Street NW
Washington, DC 20007
Phone: 202-965-2000
Fax: 202-965-2004
e-mail: dumbartonc@aol.com
Web Site: www.dumbartonconcerts.org
Management:
    Chairman: Charles Miller
    Executive Director: Connie Zimmer
    Managing Director: Mimi Newcastle
Mission: To provide a venue for the world's finest young musicians in the US capital.
Founded: 1978
Specialized Field: Chamber Music

Status: Non-Profit, Professional
Paid Staff: 4
Paid Artists: 25
Income Sources: Box Office; Grants; Private Donations
Performs At: Dumbarton Church
Facility Category: Historic Church
Seating Capacity: 375
Organization Type: Presenting

3989
EMBASSY SERIES
PO Box 9871
Washington, DC 20016
Phone: 202-625-2361
Fax: 301-588-6445
e-mail: concerts@embassyseries.org
Web Site: www.embassyseries.com
Management:
    Director: Jerome Barry
Mission: Presents programs at embassies with local international artists and musicians.
Founded: 1981
Specialized Field: Chamber; Vocal Music

3990
FOLGER THEATRE
201 E Capitol Street SE
Washington, DC 20003-1094
Phone: 202-544-4600
Fax: 202-544-4623
e-mail: academic@folger.edu
Web Site: www.folger.edu
Management:
    Executive Director: Kathleen Lynch
    Manager: Jane Pisano
    Production Manager: Jane Pisano
    Events Publicist: Annalisa Rosmarin
Utilizes: Actors; AEA Actors; Guest Conductors; Guest Designers; Local Artists; Original Music Scores; Resident Professionals; Selected Students; Student Interns
Performs At: The Elizabethan Theatre at the Folger
Facility Category: Theatre
Type of Stage: Elizabethan indoor
Seating Capacity: 240
Year Built: 1930

3991
GEORGE WASHINGTON'S SERIES AT MOUNT VERNON COLLEGE
2100 Foxhall Road NW
Washington, DC 20007
Phone: 202-242-6600
Fax: 202-338-1089
e-mail: mvcfw@gwu.edu
Web Site: www.gwu.edu
Management:
    Artistic Director: Carla Hubner
Performs At: Hand Chapel

3992
IMAGINATION CELEBRATION - KENNEDY CENTER PERFORMANCES FOR YOUNG PEOPLE
John F Kennedy Center for the Performing Arts
2700 F Street NW
Washington, DC 20566-0001
Phone: 202-416-8000
Fax: 202-416-8802
Web Site: www.kennedy-center.org
Officers:
    VP Education: Derek Gordon

3993
KENNEDY CENTER ANNUAL OPEN HOUSE ARTS FESTIVAL
Kennedy Center for the Performing Arts
Washington, DC 20566-0003
Phone: 202-467-4600
Fax: 202-416-8205
Toll-free: 800-444-1324
Web Site: www.kennedy-center.org
Officers:
    Chairman: James A Johnson
    President: Laurence J Wilker
    Founding Chairman: Roger L Stevens
Management:
    President: Michael Kaiser
    Music Director/Orchestra: Leonard Slatkin
Specialized Field: Series and Festivals; Instrumental Music; Vocal Music; Theatre; Youth; Dance; Ethnic Performances
Status: Non-Profit, Professional
Season: September
Performs At: Kennedy Center (Festival Site)

3994
KENNEDY CENTER/MARY LOU WILLIAMS WOMEN IN JAZZ FESTIVAL
2700 F Street NW
Washington, DC 20566
Phone: 202-416-8824
Fax: 202-416-8876
Toll-free: 800-444-1324
e-mail: kastruthers@kennedy-center.org
Web Site: www.kennedy-center.org/womeninjazz
Officers:
    President: Michael M. Kaiser
    Executive Director: Claudette Donlon
Management:
    Jazz Programming Director: Kevin A. Struthers
Founded: 1971
Specialized Field: Series and Festivals; Instrumental Music; Vocal Music; Theatre; Youth; Dance; Ethnic performances; Education; Jazz
Status: Non-Profit, Professional

3995
LIBRARY OF CONGRESS CHAMBER MUSIC CONCERT SERIES
Library of Congress Music Division
101 Independence Avenue SE
Washington, DC 20540-4710
Phone: 202-707-5503
Fax: 202-707-0621
Web Site: www.lcweb.loc.gov/concert
Management:
    Chief Music Division: Jon Newsom
    Producer: Anne McLean
Mission: To present free concerts of the highest artistic caliber, with a special emphasis on american music and musicians.
Founded: 1925
Specialized Field: Chamber Music; Jazz; America Music Theatre; Dance
Status: Non-Profit,Non-Professional
Paid Staff: 6
Volunteer Staff: 6
Paid Artists: 120

3996
NATIONAL ACADEMY OF SCIENCES CONCERTS
2100 C St NW
Washington, DC 20048

Phone: 202-334-2436
Fax: 202-334-1690
e-mail: arts@nas.edu
Web Site: www.nationalacademies.org/arts
Management:
Director: J D Talasek
Specialized Field: Series & Festivals: Instrumental Music
Status: Non-Profit, Professional
Paid Staff: 1000
Seating Capacity: 670

3997
NATIONAL GALLERY OF ART/CONCERT SERIES

2000B South Club Drive
Washington, DC 20785
Phone: 202-737-4215
Fax: 202-842-2407
e-mail: der-info@nga.gov
Web Site: www.nga.gov
Management:
Music Director: George Manos
Music Program Specialist: Stephen Ackert
Mission: To provide the public with free concerts at the National Gallery of Art.
Founded: 1941
Specialized Field: Symphony; Orchestra; Chamber; Ensemble
Status: Nonprofit
Paid Staff: 8
Performs At: Museum Garden Courts; National Gallery
Annual Attendance: 14,000
Seating Capacity: 500
Organization Type: Performing

3998
OPERA LAFAYETTE

10 Fourth Street NE
Washington, DC 20002
Phone: 202-546-9332
e-mail: operalafayette@operalafayette.org
Web Site: www.operalafayette.org
Officers:
President: Yoko Arthur
Management:
General Manager: Henry Valoris, henryvaloris@operalafayette.or
Artistic Director: Ryan Brown, ryanbrown@operalafayette.org
Mission: An American period instrument ensemble that presents 17th and 18th century opera, rediscovers masterpieces, and creates a recorded legacy of its work.
Utilizes: Actors; Dancers; Educators; Five Seasonal Concerts; Guest Accompanists; Multimedia; Original Music Scores; Singers; Soloists; Students
Specialized Field: Opera
Status: Nonprofit
Paid Staff: 1
Volunteer Staff: 2
Paid Artists: 70
Budget: $525,000
Income Sources: Ticket and CD Sales; Government and Private Grants; Corporations; Individual Donors
Season: August
Annual Attendance: 2,500
Facility Category: Concert Halls (Kennedy Center, Lincoln Center)
Type of Stage: Proscenium
Seating Capacity: 2,500

3999
PHILLIPS COLLECTION SUNDAY CONCERTS

1600 21st Street NW
Washington, DC 20009
Phone: 202-387-2151
Fax: 202-387-2436
e-mail: concerts@phillipscollection.org
Web Site: www.phillipscollection.org/music
Management:
Artistic Director: Caroline Mousset
Director of The Museum: Doroth Kosinski
Founded: 1921
Specialized Field: Modern Art Museum
Status: Non-Profit, Professional

4000
SMITHSONIAN INSTITUTION: THE SMITHSONIAN ASSOCIATES

The Smithsonian Associates
PO Box 23293
Washington, DC 20026-3293
Phone: 202-357-3030
Fax: 202-786-2034
e-mail: customerservice@residentassociates.org
Web Site: www.smithsonianassociates.org
Management:
Director: Mara Mayor
Deputy Director: Barbara Tuceling
Assoc Dir Marketing And Membership: Robert Anastasi
Educational And Cultural Programs: Carol Bogash
Associate Director: Carol Bogash
Associate Director/Marketing: Robert Anastasio
Webmaster: Dennis R Smoot
Mission: Encouraging and supporting the participation of the Washington DC community in Smithsonian Institution performing arts events.
Founded: 1964
Specialized Field: Dance; Vocal Music; Instrumental Music; Theater
Status: Professional; Nonprofit
Paid Staff: 100
Volunteer Staff: 200
Performs At: Hirshhorn Museum Auditorium; Baird Auditorium
Organization Type: Educational; Sponsoring
Resident Groups: Smithsonian Chamber Music Society

4001
SOCIETY OF THE CINCINNATI CONCERTS AT ANDERSON HOUSE

2118 Massachusetts Avenue NW
Washington, DC 20008-2810
Phone: 202-785-2040
Fax: 202-293-3350
Management:
Museum Director: Kathleen Betts
Performs At: Ballroom

4002
WASHINGTON PERFORMING ARTS SOCIETY

2000 L Street NW
Suite 510
Washington, DC 20036-4907
Phone: 202-833-9800
Fax: 202-331-7678
e-mail: wpas@wpas.org
Web Site: www.wpas.org

Officers:
Chairman: Lena Ingegerd Scott
Vice Chairman: James F Lafond
Vice Chairman: AW Smith Jr
Vice Chairman: Paul Martin Wolff
CFO/Operations Director: Teri McDonald
Management:
President: Neale Perl
Mission: To present the world's finest artists in the nation's capital; to present over 100 concerts annually on the major stages, as well as over 800 concerts each year in the schools of the metropolitan Washington area using resident artists.
Utilizes: Guest Artists; Guest Companies
Founded: 1966
Specialized Field: Performing Arts
Status: Non-Profit, Professional
Paid Staff: 50
Performs At: WPAS Is A Presenter That Presents At A Variety Of Venues In DC, VA, And MD
Organization Type: Educational; Sponsoring

Florida

4003
MIAMI INTERNATIONAL PIANO FESTIVAL

20191 E Country Club Drive
Suite 709
Aventura, FL 33180
Phone: 305-935-5115
Fax: 305-935-9087
e-mail: info@miamipianofest.com
Web Site: www.miamipianofest.com
Management:
President: Jack Brodsky
Executive Director: Barbara Muze
Managing Director: Gisela Brodsky
Founded: 1997
Specialized Field: Series & Festivals; Piano; Education; Promotion
Status: Non-Profit, Non-Professional
Paid Staff: 2
Volunteer Staff: 10
Paid Artists: 2

4004
SOUTH FLORIDA COMMUNITY COLLEGE CULTURAL SERIES

600 W College Drive
Avon Park, FL 33825
Phone: 863-453-6661
Fax: 863-784-7190
e-mail: andrewst@southflorida.edu
Web Site: www.sfcc.cc.fl.us
Officers:
Chairman Cultural Affairs: Douglas Andrews
Management:
President: Norman Steven
Artistic Director: Doug Andrews
Founded: 1965
Specialized Field: Series and Festivals; Instrumental Music; Theatre; Youth; Dance; Ethnic Performances
Status: Non-Profit, Professional
Paid Staff: 250
Paid Artists: 32
Performs At: College Auditorium

4005
CLEARWATER JAZZ HOLIDAY

PO Box 7278
Clearwater, FL 33758

Mailing Address: PO Box 7278 Clearwater, FL 33758-7287
Phone: 727-461-5200
Fax: 727-461-1292
e-mail: evelyn@clearwaterjazz.com
Web Site: www.clearwaterjazz.com
Management:
President: Larry Gerwig
VP: David Ruppel

4006
FESTIVAL MIAMI
University of Miami, Frost School of Music
PO Box 248165
Coral Gables, FL 33146-1260
Mailing Address: 5807 Ponce de Leon Boulevard, Suite 202
Phone: 305-284-4940
Fax: 305-284-3901
e-mail: festivalmiami.music@miami.edu
Web Site: www.festivalmiami.com
Management:
Marketing/Communications Director: Julia Berg
Ticket Office Coordinator: Kimberly Engelhardt
Events Director: Marianne Mijares
Asst Coordinator: Ron Wideman
Mission: To provide a high quality music education and training for its undergraduate and graduate majors as well as to expose the community to a diverse range of cultures through music. Intends to foster advancements in music performance, creativity, scholarship, and teaching among its faculty and staff.
Utilizes: Artists-in-Residence; Collaborating Artists; Collaborations; Commissioned Composers; Commissioned Music; Composers-in-Residence; Educators; Grant Writers; Guest Companies; Guest Composers; Guest Musical Directors; Guest Musicians; Local Artists; Multimedia; Organization Contracts; Original Music Scores; Resident Artists; Sign Language Translators; Special Technical Talent; Theatre Companies
Founded: 1983
Specialized Field: Series & Festivals: Concerts
Status: Non-Profit, Professional
Paid Staff: 8
Volunteer Staff: 21
Paid Artists: 20
Budget: $300,000
Income Sources: Ticket Sales; Sponsorships; Donations; Grants
Season: Mid September - Mid October
Performs At: UM Maurice Gusman Concert Hall
Affiliations: Association of Performing Arts Presenters, Arts & Business Council of Miami, Florida Festivals & Events Association
Annual Attendance: 12,000-14,000
Facility Category: Indoor/Concert Hall
Seating Capacity: 600

4007
MIAMI BACH SOCIETY/TROPICAL BAROQUE MUSIC FESTIVAL
PO Box 4034
Coral Gables, FL 33114
Phone: 305-669-1376
Fax: 305-669-1376
e-mail: jgaubatz@msn.com
Web Site: www.miamibachsociety.org
Officers:
President: Mark Hart
VP: George Berberian
Secretary: Claire Veater
Treasurer: Myriam Ribenborm
Management:

President: Michael Berke
Executive Director: Catherine Gaubatz
Artistic Director: Donald Oglesby
Mission: To perform and present the music of Johann Sebastian Bach and his baroque composer contemporaries to the people and visitors of the sociable Florida community.
Utilizes: Guest Directors; Guest Musical Directors; Guest Musicians; Multimedia; Original Music Scores
Founded: 1984
Specialized Field: Series & Festivals: Performing Music Before 1800
Status: Non-Profit, Professional
Paid Staff: 4
Paid Artists: 2
Budget: $300,000
Income Sources: Corporations; Government; Indivdual Donations; Ticket Sales
Annual Attendance: 5,000
Organization Type: Performing and Presenting Musical Organization
Resident Groups: MBS Chorus and Orchestra

4008
CENTRAL FLORIDA CULTURAL ENDEAVORS
PO Box 1310
Daytona Beach, FL 32115
Mailing Address: PO Box 1310 Daytona Beach, FL 32115-1310
Phone: 386-872-2324
Fax: 386-238-1663
e-mail: fifcfce@n-jcenter.com
Web Site: www.fif-lso.org
Officers:
President: Tippen Davidson
Treasurer: Georgia Kaney
Management:
Executive Director: Eric Lariviere
Operations Manager: Erin Bailey
Mission: To provide world class chamber music and orchestra concerts for Daytona Beach audiences.
Utilizes: Educators; Fine Artists; Guest Artists; Guest Writers; Multimedia; Original Music Scores; Sign Language Translators
Founded: 1982
Specialized Field: Series and Festivals: Instrumental Music
Status: Non-Profit, Professional
Paid Staff: 8
Budget: $240,000
Income Sources: Individuals; Corporations; City; County; State; Grants
Performs At: Peabody Auditorium
Affiliations: Association of Performing Arts Presenters; FL Arts Presenters; INTIX
Facility Category: Churches
Seating Capacity: 600-1,200
Organization Type: Sponsoring

4009
FLORIDA INTERNATIONAL FESTIVAL FEATURING THE LONDON SYMPHONY ORCHESTRA
Central Florida Cultural Endeavors
212 S Beach Street
Daytona Beach, FL 32114
Phone: 386-872-2323
Fax: 386-238-1663
e-mail: fifcfce@fif-lso.org
Web Site: www.fif-lso.org
Management:
Founder/Director: Tippen Davidson

General Manager: Eric Larivivere
Mission: To provide the citizens of Volusia County and its visitors with a high quality, broadly based performing arts series built around the biennial residency of the London Symphony Orchestra, thereby promoting Daytona Beach as a culturally diverse and informed area.
Utilizes: Artists-in-Residence; Dance Companies; Dancers; Educators; Fine Artists; Guest Accompanists; Guest Artists; Guest Companies; Guest Composers; Guest Directors; Guest Instructors; Guest Lecturers; Guest Musicians; Guest Soloists; Guest Writers; High School Drama; Instructors; Lyricists; Multimedia; Organization Contracts; Original Music Scores; Sign Language Translators; Singers; Soloists
Founded: 1974
Specialized Field: Series and Festivals; Instrumental Music; Dance; Ethnic Performances
Status: Non-Profit, Non-Professional
Paid Staff: 8
Paid Artists: 200
Budget: $2,400,700
Income Sources: Local Individuals, Corporations; City, County, State & other Grants
Performs At: Peabody Auditorium; Ocean Center; Ormond Beach, PA
Affiliations: Association of Performing Arts Presenters; FL Arts Presenters; INTIX
Seating Capacity: 200-9,000
Organization Type: Performing; Educational; Sponsoring

4010
FLORIDA INTERNATIONAL FESTIVAL FEATURING THE LONDON SYMPHONY ORCHESTRA
901 6th Street
Daytona Beach, FL 32115-1310
Mailing Address: PO Box 1310 Daytona Beach, FL 32115-1310
Phone: 386-252-1511
Fax: 386-238-1663
e-mail: fifcfce@fif-lso.org
Web Site: www.fif-lso.org
Management:
General Manager: Dewey Anderson
Utilizes: Artists-in-Residence; Dance Companies; Guest Choreographers; Guest Composers; Guest Instructors; Guest Musicians; Multimedia; Original Music Scores; Singers; Theatre Companies
Founded: 1974
Specialized Field: Music
Paid Staff: 6
Volunteer Staff: 100
Paid Artists: 200
Budget: $400,000 - 1,000,000
Income Sources: Ticket Sales; Contributions; Grants
Season: July
Performs At: Daytona Beach area [Festival Site]; Various
Annual Attendance: 2,000-40,000
Facility Category: Peabody Aud; Ocean Cntr; Ormond Beach Cntr; etc.
Seating Capacity: 250 - 8,000

4011
BEETHOVEN BY THE BEACH
Florida Philharmonic Orchestra
3401 NW 9th Avenue
Fort Lauderdale, FL 33309-5903

Phone: 954-561-2997
Fax: 954-561-1390
Toll-free: 800-930-1812
Web Site: www.floridaphilharmonic.org
Management:
    Music Director: James Judd
Specialized Field: Instrumental; Childrens'
Budget: $60,000 - 150,000
Season: July
Performs At: Fort Lauderdale [Festival Site]

4012
BROADWAY IN FORT LAUDERDALE
PO Box 4603
Fort Lauderdale, FL 33338-4603
Phone: 954-764-0700
Fax: 954-764-0708
Toll-free: 800-764-0700
e-mail:
fortlauerdalebroadwayseries@clearchannel.com
Web Site: www.broadwayacrossamerica.com
Management:
    President: Bryan Becker
    Executive Director: Fusie Krajsa
    Managing Director: John Poland
Specialized Field: Touring Broadway
Status: Non-Profit, Professional
Paid Staff: 60

4013
CORAL RIDGE PRESBYTARIAN CHURCH CONCERT SERIES
5555 N Federal Highway
Fort Lauderdale, FL 33308
Phone: 954-491-1103
Fax: 954-491-7374
Toll-free: 800-987-9818
e-mail: cboatright@crpc.org
Web Site: www.crpc.org
Management:
    Executive Director: Charlie Boatright
Utilizes: Artists-in-Residence; Grant Writers; Guest Artists; Guest Lecturers; Multimedia; Music; Organization Contracts; Original Music Scores; Sign Language Translators; Singers; Soloists
Founded: 1971
Specialized Field: Series and Festivals; Instrumental Music; Vocal Music; Theatre; Dance; Ethnic Performances
Status: Non-Profit, Professional
Paid Staff: 3
Volunteer Staff: 2
Performs At: Coral Ridge Presbytarian Church
Annual Attendance: 50,000
Facility Category: Church
Type of Stage: Chancel
Seating Capacity: 2000
Year Built: 1971

4014
FLORIDA ARTS CONCERT SERIES
146 Riverview Road
Fort Myers, FL 33905
Phone: 941-823-3758
Fax: 941-694-2787
e-mail: jimflarts@earthlink.net
Management:
    Executive Director/Chairman: James Griffith

4015
FORT MYERS COMMUNITY CONCERT ASSOCIATION SERIES
PO Box 606
PO Box 606
Fort Myers, FL 33902
Phone: 239-939-3236
Officers:
    President: George T Mann
Performs At: Barbara B Mann Performing Arts Hall

4016
FIRST ARTS SERIES
103 1st Street SE
Fort Walton Beach
Fort Walton, FL 32548
Phone: 850-863-2436
Fax: 850-243-0905
e-mail: director@firstartsconcerts.org
Web Site: ww.firstartsconcerts.org
Management:
    Director: Karen Tindall
    Concert Hospitality: Karen Tindall
    Treasurer: Joan Moody
Founded: 1989
Volunteer Staff: 12
Budget: $25,000
Income Sources: Tickets; Donations
Facility Category: Church Sanctuary

4017
NYK PRODUCTIONS
1747 Van Buren Street
Suite 700
Hollywood, FL 33028
Phone: 954-929-6010
Fax: 954-929-6399
Management:
    Chief Officer: Arie Kaduri
Performs At: Various Auditoriums

4018
SCOTT EVANS PRODUCTIONS
PO Box 814028
Hollywood, FL 33081-4028
Phone: 954-963-4449
e-mail: evansprod@aol.com
Web Site: www.theentertainmentamall.com
Officers:
    President: Evan S Resnick
Management:
    Artistic Director: Scott Evans
    Internet Marketing/Sales: Jeanne K
Utilizes: Commissioned Composers; Community Talent; Contract Orchestras; Dancers; Designers; Educators; Fine Artists; Grant Writers; Guest Artists; Guest Choreographers; Guest Composers; Guest Conductors; Guest Directors; Guest Ensembles; Guest Lecturers; Guest Musical Directors; Guest Soloists; Guest Speakers; Guest Teachers; High School Drama; Instructors; Local Talent; Lyricists; Multi Collaborations; Music; Paid Performers; Poets; Scenic Designers; Sign Language Translators; Singers; Theatre Companies; Touring Companies; Visual Designers; Volunteer Artists
Founded: 1979
Specialized Field: All Performing Arts
Paid Artists: 1000
Affiliations: Chambers of Broward County, Boynton Beach, Coral Gables, Key Biscayne, North Dade, Southeast Florida; Inten'l Assoc'n Wedding/Event Professionals

4019
DELIUS FESTIVAL
PO Box 5621
Jacksonville, FL 32247-5621
Phone: 904-384-3956
Management:
    Director: Jeff Driggers
    Director: Michael Blachly
    Education Coordinator: Elizabeth Auer
    Receptionist: Mary Monroe
    Assistant Director: Kay Holcomb
    Operations Manager: Matt Koropeckyj-Cox
    Assistant Director: Deborah C Rossi
    Accountant: Gay Hale
    Technical Director: Steve Schell
Specialized Field: Instrumental; Choral
Budget: $10,000
Season: April
Performs At: Jacksonville (Festival Site)
Facility Category: Terry Concert Hall; Friday Musicale Auditorium
Seating Capacity: 450; 250

4020
FLORIDA THEATRE PERFORMING ARTS SERIES
128 E Forsyth Street
Jacksonville, FL 32202
Phone: 904-355-5661
Fax: 904-358-1874
e-mail: stillcool@flordiatheatre.com
Web Site: www.floridatheatre.com
Management:
    Executive Director: J Erik Hart
Founded: 1985
Specialized Field: Series & Festivals; Instrumental Music; Vocal Music; Theater; Youth; Dance; Ethnic Performances
Status: Non-Profit, Non-Professional
Performs At: Flordia Theatre

4021
JACKSONVILLE UNIVERSITY MASTER-CLASS & ARTISTS SERIES
College of Fine Arts, Jacksonville University
2800 University Boulevard, North
Jacksonville, FL 32211
Phone: 904-256-7371
Fax: 904-256-7375
Toll-free: 800-225-2027
e-mail: tnetter@ju.edu
Web Site: www.ju.edu
Management:
    President: Kerry Ronberg
    Dean College Fine Arts: D Terence Netter
    Dean College of Fine Arts: Patty Aniole
Mission: Cultural enrichment of the university community and the community at large.
Founded: 1958
Specialized Field: Series & Festivals; Art; Dance; Music; Theatre
Status: Non-Profit, Non-Professional
Paid Staff: 12
Paid Artists: 20
Performs At: Terry Concert Hall

4022
KUUMBA FEST
PO Box 12001
Jacksonville, FL 92101

Phone: 904-353-2270
Fax: 904-355-0567
e-mail: kuumbafestival@kuumbafestival.org
Web Site: kuumbafestival.tripod.com

4023

WJCT JACKSONVILLE JAZZ FESTIVAL

100 Festival Park Avenue
Jacksonville, FL 32202-1397
Phone: 904-353-7770
Fax: 904-358-6344
e-mail: vic_digenti@wjct.pbs.org
Web Site: www.jaxjazzfest.com
Management:
   Executive Producer: Vic DiGenti

4024

BEACHES FINE ARTS SERIES

PO Box 51171
Jacksonville Beach, FL 32240-1171
Phone: 904-270-1771
Fax: 904-270-2074
e-mail: beachesfinearts@aol.com
Management:
   Executive Director: Kathryn Wallis
Founded: 1973
Specialized Field: Present Concerts for Community
Status: Non-Profit, Non-Professional
Paid Staff: 2
Performs At: St. Pauls By-the-Sea Episcopal Church

4025

KEY WEST COUNCIL ON THE ARTS SERIES

2932 Seidenberg Avenue
Key West, FL 33040

Management:
   Artistic Director: RJ Weiss

4026

BACH FESTIVAL OF CENTRAL FLORIDA

PO Box 2764
Lakeland, FL 33806-2764
Phone: 863-299-2555
Fax: 863-439-0759
e-mail: info@bachfestivalofcentralflorida.org
Web Site: www.bachfestivalofcentralflorida.org
Founded: 1974
Status: Non-Profit,Professional

4027

FLORIDA SOUTHERN COLLEGE

111 Lake Hollingsworth Drive
Lakeland, FL 33801
Phone: 863-680-4218
Fax: 863-680-3758
Toll-free: 800-274-4131
e-mail: fla@flsouthern.edu
Web Site: www.flsouthern.edu
Management:
   President: Nanne Kerr
   Executive Director: Robert Macdonald
Founded: 1961
Specialized Field: Series & Festivals; Classical Music;
Theatre and Art
Status: Non-Profit, Professional
Paid Staff: 6
Paid Artists: 12

4028

LAKELAND CENTER

701 W Lime Street
Lakeland, FL 33815

Phone: 863-834-8100
Fax: 863-834-8101
Web Site: www.thelakelandcenter.com
Management:
   Executive Director: Mike LaPan
   Assistant Manager: Scott Sloman
Utilizes: Collaborations; Dance Companies; Guest
Accompanists; Guest Choreographers; Multimedia;
Original Music Scores; Theatre Companies
Founded: 1974
Paid Staff: 33
Volunteer Staff: 100
Performs At: The Lakeland Center/The Youkey
Theater
Facility Category: Event, Sports & Convention
complex
Stage Dimensions: 78'x47'
Seating Capacity: 2,246 w/pit seats 2,296
Year Built: 1974
Year Remodeled: 1996
Rental Contact: Scott Sloman

4029

SUNCOAST DIXIELAND JAZZ CLASSIC

PO Box 1945
Largo, FL 33779-1945
Phone: 727-536-0064
Fax: 727-536-0064
e-mail: jazzclassic@aol.com
Web Site: www.jazzclassic.net
Management:
   Festival Director: Joan Dragon
Mission: To keep traditional jazz and the traditions of
jazz alive and provide financial assistance to youth for
musical study
Founded: 1990
Specialized Field: Series and Festivals; Dixieland
Jazz; Instrumental; Traditional
Status: Non-Profit, Professional
Paid Staff: 90
Volunteer Staff: 200
Performs At: Hotels; Indoor Venues
Affiliations: Suncoast Dixieland Jazz Society
Annual Attendance: 4,500

4030

NORTH FLORIDA COMMUNITY COLLEGE

325 NW Turner Davis Drive
Madison, FL 32340
Phone: 850-973-1613
Fax: 850-973-1685
Toll-free: 866-937-6322
e-mail: artistseries@nfcc.edu
Web Site: www.nfcc.edu
Officers:
   Artists Series Chairman: Kim Scarboro
Management:
   President: John Gross Kopf
   Performance Coordinator: Kim Scarboro
Mission: To provide cultural enrichment through live
performances for audiences of all ages residing in the
North Florida area.
Utilizes: Collaborations; Dance Companies; Dancers;
Fine Artists; Grant Writers; Guest Directors; Guest
Instructors; Guest Soloists; Guild Activities; High School
Drama; Local Artists; Multimedia; Original Music
Scores; Playwrights; Selected Students; Sign Language
Translators; Singers; Soloists; Student Interns; Special
Technical Talent; Theatre Companies
Founded: 1980
Specialized Field: Series & Festivals: Performing
Artists series - Live Performances
Status: Non-Profit, Professional
Paid Staff: 3

Volunteer Staff: 5
Paid Artists: 7
Non-paid Artists: 11
Budget: $40,000
Income Sources: Ticket Sales; Private & Corporate
Donations; Grants
Performs At: Van H. Priest Auditorium
Annual Attendance: 6,000
Facility Category: Auditorium
Type of Stage: Resilient Wood
Stage Dimensions: 29'x40'
Seating Capacity: 580
Year Built: 1992

4031

CHIPOLA COLLEGE ARTIST SERIES

3094 Indian Circle
Marianna, FL 32446-2206
Phone: 850-718-2301
Fax: 850-718-2206
e-mail: stadsklevj@chipola.edu
Web Site: www.chipola.edu
Officers:
   President: Dr. Gene Prough
   Executive Director: Joan Stadsklev
Founded: 1947
Specialized Field: Series & Festivals; Instrumental
Music; Vocal Music; Theatre; Ethnic Performances;
Fine & Performing Arts
Status: Non-Profit, Professional
Paid Staff: 8
Budget: $15,000
Performs At: Chipola Junior College Auditorium
Facility Category: Theatre
Type of Stage: Proscenium
Seating Capacity: 355

4032

KEY WEST MUSIC FESTIVAL

1057 NE 210 Terrace
Miami, FL 33179
Phone: 305-651-5525
Fax: 305-651-0885
e-mail: kwmfestival@aol.com
Web Site: www.keywestmusicfestival.com/
Budget: $10,000 - 20,000
Season: May
Performs At: Key West (Festival Site)
Facility Category: San Carlos Institute
Seating Capacity: 400

4033

MIAMI CIVIC MUSIC ASSOCIATION SERIES

5360 SW 87th Avenue
Miami, FL 33165
Phone: 305-271-8449
Fax: 305-595-9597
e-mail: miamicivic@aol.com
Management:
   Artistic Director: Rosalina Sackstein
Founded: 1932
Specialized Field: Series & Festivals; Instrumental
Music; Vocal Music; Theatre; Ethnic Performances
Status: Non-Profit, Professional
Performs At: Gusman Hall, University of Miami

4034

MIAMI DADE COMMUNITY COLLEGE

300 NE 2nd Avenue
Suite 1423
Miami, FL 33132

Phone: 305-237-3010
Fax: 305-237-7559
e-mail: caffairs@mdc.edu
Web Site: www.culture.mdc.edu
Management:
    President: Eduardo Padron
    Executive Director: Michelle H Hayes
    Artistic Director: Gregory Jackson
Utilizes: Artists-in-Residence; Choreographers; Collaborations; Commissioned Music; Dance Companies; Dancers; Guest Accompanists; Guest Choreographers; Guest Ensembles; Guest Musical Directors; Instructors; Multi Collaborations; Organization Contracts; Playwrights; Selected Students; Sign Language Translators; Soloists; Special Technical Talent; Theatre Companies
Founded: 1990
Specialized Field: Series & Festivals; Instrumental Music; Vocal Music; Theater; Youth; Dance; Ethnic Performances
Status: Non-Profit, Professional
Paid Staff: 5
Paid Artists: 75
Budget: $1,000,000
Income Sources: Miami-Dade Community College; Miami-Dade County; State of Florida
Performs At: Auditorium
Annual Attendance: 10,000
Facility Category: Various

4035
TEMPLE BETH AM SERIES

5950 North Kendall Drive
Miami, FL 33156
Phone: 305-667-6667
Fax: 305-662-8619
Officers:
    President: Michael Bittel
    Executive VP: Bea Citron
    Corresponding Secretary: Randy Fisher
    Recording Secretary: Debbie Rosenthal
    Treasurer/Financial Secretary: Irwin Katz
Management:
    Executive Director: Irene Warner
    Finance Director: Hellene Strul
    Operations: Lori Solomon
    Communications Director: Helene Layne
    Administration Secretary: Rita Diaz
    Administration Assistant: Marylin Harrison
    Donations: Barbara Hoffman
    Receptionist: Sandy Morrison
Performs At: Temple Sanctuary

4036
CONCERT ASSOCIATION OF FLORIDA

1470 Biscayne Boulevard
Miami Beach, FL 33132
Phone: 305-808-7446
Fax: 305-808-7463
e-mail: info@concertfla.org
Web Site: www.concertfla.org
Officers:
    Director Public Relations/Marketing: Craig Hall
Founded: 1967
Performs At: Dade County Auditorium

4037
PERFORMING ARTS SOCIETY OF SOUTH FLORIDA

PO Box 6304
Miami Beach, FL 33141
Phone: 305-682-4999
e-mail: passouth@earthlink.net
Web Site: www.cdg.org

Management:
    Managing Director: Darrell Calvin
Mission: To bring the best entertainment to a diverse community.
Founded: 1984
Specialized Field: Dance; Music; Theatre; Pop
Status: Nonprofit
Paid Staff: 2
Volunteer Staff: 6
Budget: $200,000
Income Sources: Box Office; Grants; Gifts; In Kind Services
Affiliations: APAP; IEG
Annual Attendance: 5,500

4038
ORLANDO-UCF SHAKESPEARE FESTIVAL

812 E Rollins Street
Suite 100
Orlando, FL 32803
Phone: 407-447-1700
Fax: 407-447-1701
e-mail: info@shakespearefest.org
Web Site: www.shakespearefest.org
Management:
    Executive Director: Mary Ann
    Artistic Director: Jim Helsinger
Mission: Will serve as a cultural resource to the community by presenting the plays of Shakespeare and other theatrical works, as well as the artistic and educational activities inspired by them. Festival presentations will reflect the highest possible artistic, educational and ethical values. We will strive fore artistic and educational excellence and innovation.

4039
SOCIETY OF THE FOUR ARTS

2 Four Arts Plaza
Palm Beach, FL 33480
Phone: 561-655-7227
Fax: 561-655-7233
e-mail: contactus@fourarts.org
Web Site: www.fourarts.org
Officers:
    President: Ervin Duggan
    Executive VP: Nancy Mato
Management:
    Marketing/Corporate Development Dir: Katie Edwards
Mission: A cultural center which features international traveling art exhibitions, a lecture series of world renowned personages, a distinguished concert series, two film series, and a young peoples series for children. Also maintains two libraries-the main Four Arts Library and a children's library, as well as a botanical garden and The Philip Hulitar Sculpture Garden.
Founded: 1936
Specialized Field: Series & Festivals: Art exhibitions.
Status: Non-Profit, Professional
Paid Staff: 30
Volunteer Staff: 6
Budget: $4.6 Million
Income Sources: Donations; Ticket Sales; Membership; Endowment Income
Annual Attendance: 111,563
Facility Category: Cultural Institution
Type of Stage: Proscenium
Stage Dimensions: 25' x 30'
Seating Capacity: 700
Year Built: 1948
Year Remodeled: 1994

4040
TREASURE COAST CONCERT ASSOCIATION

2394 SW Foxpoint Way
Palm City, FL 34990
Phone: 772-220-8400
Fax: 772-220-8401
e-mail: ehberlin@adelphia.net
Web Site: www.ovationconcerts.org
Officers:
    President: Ernest Berlin
Management:
    President: Ernest Berlin
Utilizes: Guest Directors; Guest Musical Directors; Guest Musicians; Multimedia; Original Music Scores; Singers; Theatre Companies
Founded: 1984
Specialized Field: Series & Festivals: Instrumental Music
Status: Non-Profit, Professional
Performs At: Lyric Theatre

4041
BAY ARTS ALLIANCE

PO Box 1153
Panama City, FL 32402
Phone: 850-769-1217
Fax: 850-785-5165
e-mail: jenniferjones@bayarts.org
Web Site: www.bayarts.org
Officers:
    Executive Director: Jennifer Jones
Specialized Field: Series & Festivals; Instrumental Music; Vocal Music; Theatre; Youth; Dance; Ethnic Performances
Status: Non-Profit, Non-Professional
Performs At: Marina Civic Theatre

4042
PANAMA CITY MUSIC ASSOCIATION SERIES

PO Box 133
Panama City, FL 32402
Phone: 850-769-2707
Fax: 850-913-0498
e-mail: coxjbc@bellsouth.net
Web Site: www.panamacitymusicassoc.org
Officers:
    President: Nancy Moore
    First Vice President: Bob Borich
    Talent Chairman: Joanne B Cox
Founded: 1941
Specialized Field: Series & Festivals; Classical Music; Opera; Ballet Dance; Orchestras
Status: Non-Profit, Non-Professional
Volunteer Staff: 40
Paid Artists: 5
Budget: $120,000
Income Sources: Ticket Sales(Season)
Performs At: Municipal Auditorium

4043
CLASSICFEST: PENSACOLA SUMMER MUSIC FESTIVAL

PO Box 12683
Pensacola, FL 32591
Phone: 850-432-5118
Fax: 850-434-8700
e-mail: ccpns@aol.com
Web Site: www.christ-church.net
Management:
    Rector: Rev Russell Jones Levenson
    Associate Rector: Rev D Wallace Adams Riley

Founded: 1764

4044

MUSIC HALL ARTIST SERIES

University of West Florida
11000 University Parkway
Pensacola, FL 32514
Phone: 850-474-2147
Fax: 850-474-3247
e-mail: lmay0@uwf.edu
Web Site: www.uwf.edu/cfpa
Management:
Chairman: Richard Glaze
Mission: To provide the Pensacola community with world-class performances of chamber music.
Utilizes: Actors; Choreographers; Collaborating Artists; Collaborations; Community Talent; Composers; Contract Orchestras; Curators; Dance Companies; Dancers; Designers; Educators; Fine Artists; Five Seasonal Concerts; Grant Writers; Guest Accompanists; Guest Artists; Guest Choreographers; Guest Companies; Guest Composers; Guest Conductors; Guest Designers; Guest Directors; Guest Instructors; Guest Lecturers; Guest Musical Directors; Guest Musicians; Guest Soloists; Guest Speakers; Guest Teachers; Guest Writers; Guild Activities; High School Drama; Instructors; Local Artists; Local Unknown Artists; Lyricists; Multi Collaborations; Multimedia; Music; New Productions; Original Music Scores; Paid Performers; Performance Artists; Playwrights; Resident Professionals; Scenic Designers; Selected Students; Sign Language Translators; Singers; Soloists; Students; Student Interns; Special Technical Talent; Theatre Companies; Touring Companies; Visual Arts
Founded: 1970
Specialized Field: Vocal Music: Classical
Status: Non-Profit, Professional
Paid Staff: 1
Paid Artists: 6
Budget: $10,000
Income Sources: SGA; University President; Private Funding
Performs At: Music Hall
Annual Attendance: 1,000
Facility Category: Education
Type of Stage: Proscenium; Arena; Concert Hall
Seating Capacity: 426; 120; 307
Year Built: 1992
Rental Contact: Linda May
Organization Type: Sponsoring

4045

SOUTH FLORIDA JAZZ

10460 Kestrel Street
Plantation, FL 33324
Phone: 954-424-4440
Fax: 954-424-4417
e-mail: rw@southfloridajazz.org
Web Site: www.southfloridajazz.org
Management:
President: Ronald B Weber
Founded: 1992
Specialized Field: Series and Festivals; Jazz Performance; Jazz Education
Status: Non-Profit, Professional
Paid Artists: 50

4046

FRIENDS OF MUSIC OF CHARLOTTE COUNTY CONCERT SERIES

533 Skylark Lane
Port Charlotte, FL 33952
Phone: 941-625-3177

Management:
Concert Series Director: Mauriel Van Patten
Utilizes: Artists-in-Residence; Collaborations; Fine Artists; Guest Accompanists; Guest Choreographers; Guest Musical Directors; Guest Musicians; Guild Activities; Lyricists; Multimedia; Original Music Scores; Sign Language Translators; Singers; Theatre Companies
Performs At: Port Charlotte Cultural Center Theatre
Facility Category: Concert Hall
Seating Capacity: 418

4047

BIG ARTS: GREAT PERFORMERS SERIES

900 Dunlop Road
Sanibel, FL 33957
Phone: 239-395-0900
Fax: 239-395-0330
e-mail: email@bigarts.org
Web Site: www.bigarts.org
Management:
Executive Director: Lee Ellen Harder
Utilizes: Artists-in-Residence; Dance Companies; Dancers; Fine Artists; Guest Accompanists; Guest Choreographers; Guest Directors; Guest Instructors; Guest Soloists; High School Drama; Multimedia; Singers; Soloists; Theatre Companies
Founded: 1979
Specialized Field: Series and Festivals; Instrumental Music; Vocal Music; Theatre; Dance; Ethnic Performances
Status: Non-Profit, Professional
Paid Staff: 8
Volunteer Staff: 40
Budget: $700,000
Facility Category: Cultural Center
Seating Capacity: 414
Year Built: 1979
Year Remodeled: 1997

4048

SANIBEL MUSIC FESTIVAL

PO Box 1623
Sanibel, FL 33957-1623
Phone: 239-336-7999
Fax: 941-395-1375
Web Site: www.sanibelmusicfestival.org
Management:
Artistic Director: Jim Griffith
Founded: 1980
Season: March
Performs At: Sanibel Island (Festival Site)
Facility Category: Sanibel Congregational Church
Seating Capacity: 350

4049

ASOLO THEATRE FESTIVAL

5555 N Tamiami Trail
Sarasota, FL 34243-2141
Phone: 813-351-9010
Fax: 813-351-5796
Toll-free: 800-361-8388
e-mail: asolo@asolo.org
Web Site: www.asolo.org
Officers:
Co-President: J Robert Peterson
Co-President: Lee M Peterson
Management:
Company Manager: Jacob Stan
Artistic Administrator: Corinne Gabrielson
Managing Director: Linda M Digabriele
Producing Artistic Director: Howard J Millman

Mission: To foster an appreciation for the performing arts in the community, state and country by utilizing live performances as to educate students by placing them with professional actors with whom they may learn the theatrical trade.
Utilizes: Guest Companies; Singers
Founded: 1960
Specialized Field: Theatrical Group
Status: Non-Profit
Volunteer Staff: 200
Income Sources: Theatre Communications Group; American Arts Alliance; Actors' Equity Association; League of Resident Theatres
Performs At: Harold E and Esther M Mertz Theatre; Jane B Cook Theatre
Organization Type: Performing; Educational

4050

ASOLO THEATRE FESTIVAL

5555 N Tamiami Trail
Sarasota, FL 34243
Phone: 941-351-9010
Fax: 941-351-5796
Toll-free: 800-361-8388
e-mail: asolo@asolo.org
Web Site: www.asolo.org
Officers:
President: Ron Greenbaum
Management:
Artistic Director: Howard Millman
Managing Director: Linda M Digabriele
Mission: To produce and present the highest quality professional theatre in a fiscally responsible manner for its community. The Asolo performs primarily in rotating repertory with a resident company.
Utilizes: Guest Companies; Singers
Founded: 1960
Specialized Field: Professional Theatre
Status: Non-Profit, Professional
Paid Staff: 100
Volunteer Staff: 300
Paid Artists: 15
Non-paid Artists: 60
Budget: $5 million
Income Sources: Theatre Communications Group; American Arts Alliance; Actors' Equity Association; League of Resident Theatres
Performs At: Harold E and Esther M Mertz Theatre; Jane B Cook Theatre
Affiliations: Florida State University
Annual Attendance: 92,000
Organization Type: Performing; Educational

4051

BONK FESTIVAL OF NEW MUSIC

New College of USF, Humanities Division
5700 N Tamiami Trail
Sarasota, FL 34243-2197
Phone: 813-930-8440
Fax: 941-359-4479
e-mail: info@bonkfest.org
Web Site: www.bonkfest.org
Specialized Field: Instrumental; Multi-Media; Dance; Educational
Budget: $10,000
Season: February - March
Performs At: Tampa, Sarasota, St. Petersburg (Festival Site)
Facility Category: Theatres; Auditoriums; Museums

4052

FLORIDA WEST COAST SYMPHONY SERIES

709 N Tamiami Trail
Sarasota, FL 34236
Phone: 941-953-4252
Fax: 941-953-3059
Toll-free: 800-287-9634
e-mail: symphony@fwcs.org
Web Site: www.fwcs.org
Officers:
    President: Jack Jost
    Vice President: Beatrice Friedman
    VP: Susan Weinkle
    Secretary: Ronald Jurgens
    Treasurer: Ernest Rice
Management:
    Executive Director: Joseph McKenna
    Artistic Director: Leis Vjailand
    Finance: Trevor Cramer
    Educational Director Programminfg: Rosanne McCabe
Mission: To present Florida symphonies, festivals, orchestras and youth orchestra.
Utilizes: Artists-in-Residence; Collaborating Artists; Collaborations; Commissioned Composers; Commissioned Music; Educators; Fine Artists; Five Seasonal Concerts; Grant Writers; Guest Accompanists; Guest Artists; Guest Companies; Guest Composers; Guest Directors; Guest Instructors; Guest Musical Directors; Guest Musicians; High School Drama; Instructors; Local Artists; Multimedia; New Productions; Original Music Scores; Resident Artists; Singers; Soloists
Founded: 1949
Specialized Field: Series & Festivals; Instrumental Music; Festivals
Status: Non-Profit, Professional
Paid Staff: 28
Paid Artists: 100
Budget: $3,800,000
Income Sources: Ticket Sales; Donations
Performs At: Holley Hall; Van Wezel Performing Arts Hall
Annual Attendance: 100,000
Facility Category: Concert Hall
Type of Stage: Raised Open
Stage Dimensions: 16'x32'
Seating Capacity: 500
Year Remodeled: 1985
Architect: Garry Hoyt
Cost: $800,000
Organization Type: Performing; Resident; Educational; Sponsoring

4053

LA MUSICA FESTIVAL

Sarasota, FL
Mailing Address: PO Box 5442 Sarasota, FL 34277
Phone: 941-346-2601
Fax: 941-346-2414
Web Site: www.lamusicafetival.org
Management:
    Executive Director: Sally R Faron
Mission: Bring European & American Artists together to present 5 concerts of outstanding chamber music. Daily rehearsals are open to the public.
Utilizes: Commissioned Composers; Commissioned Music; Guest Musical Directors; Multimedia
Founded: 1987
Specialized Field: Chamber Music Festival
Paid Staff: 6
Volunteer Staff: 10

Paid Artists: 15
Budget: $270,000
Income Sources: Tickets; Sponsorships; Gifts
Season: April
Performs At: University of South Florida, Sainer Center (Festival Site); Rehearsal Hall
Annual Attendance: 4,500
Facility Category: St. Thomas More Church
Seating Capacity: 770

4054

SARASOTA CONCERT

4346 Bryant'S Pond Lane
Sarasota, FL 34233
Phone: 941-925-7811
Fax: 941-925-7811
e-mail: streetleit@aol.com
Officers:
    President: Martha Leiter
Management:
    Artistic Selection Chairman: Martha Leiter
Founded: 1940
Specialized Field: Series & Festivals; Instrumental Music; Vocal Music; Dance; Ethnic Performances; Orchestra
Status: Non-Profit, Professional
Paid Staff: 26
Paid Artists: 5
Performs At: Van Wezel Performing Arts Hall

4055

SARASOTA JAZZ FESTIVAL

330 S Pineapple Avenue
Suite 111
Sarasota, FL 34236
Phone: 941-366-1552
Fax: 941-366-1553
e-mail: admin@jazzclubsarasota.com
Web Site: www.jazzclubsarasota.com
Officers:
    President: Bobby Prince
Management:
    Vice President: Wesley Bearden
Founded: 1980
Specialized Field: Series & Festivals; Instrumental Music; Vocal Music
Status: Non-Profit, Professional
Paid Staff: 1
Paid Artists: 300

4056

SARASOTA MUSIC FESTIVAL

709 N Tamiami Trail
Sarasota, FL 34236
Phone: 941-953-4252
Fax: 941-953-3059
e-mail: rmccabe@sarasotaorchestra.org
Web Site: www.sarasotaorchestra.org
Officers:
    President: Joseph McKenna
    CFO: Douglas Shanley
    CMO: Gordon Greenfield
Management:
    Artistic Director: Robert Levin
    Education Director: RoseAnne McCabe
Mission: To present chamber music, master classes and concerts by artists and students from around the world in a three week event on Florida's West Coast.
Founded: 1964
Specialized Field: Chamber; Orchestra
Status: Non-Profit, Professional, Student
Income Sources: Chamber Music America
Performs At: Holley Hall; Sarasota Opera House
Facility Category: Chamber Music; Music Education

Organization Type: Performing; Educational

4057

SEASIDE INSTITUTE SERIES

30 Smolian Circle, 2nd Floor
PO Box 4730
Seaside, FL 32459
Phone: 850-231-2421
Fax: 850-231-1884
e-mail: institute@seasidefl.org
Web Site: www.theseasideinstitute.org
Management:
    Executive Director: Phyllis Bleiweis
    Director Of Programme: Leslie W Picke
Performs At: Seaside Meeting Hall

4058

MAHAFFEY THEATER

400 First Street S
St Petersburg, FL 33701
Phone: 727-892-5708
Fax: 727-892-5858
Toll-free: 800-874-9015
e-mail: laura.kleinfeld@stpete.org
Management:
    Marketing/Booking Manager: Lauren Kleinfeld
Specialized Field: Festival
Performs At: Mahaffey Theatre for the Performing Arts

4059

MUSEUM OF FINE ARTS SERIES

255 Beach Drive NE
St Petersburg, FL 33701
Phone: 727-896-2667
Fax: 727-894-4638
e-mail: webmonkey@fine-arts.org
Web Site: www.fine-arts.org
Management:
    Director: John E Schloder
Mission: To present classical concerts.
Founded: 1896
Specialized Field: Tampa Bay
Paid Staff: 4
Volunteer Staff: 6
Paid Artists: 12

4060

ST PETERSBURG COLLEGE

6605 5th Avenue N
St Petersburg, FL 33710
Mailing Address: PO Box 13489 St Petersburg, FL 33733
Phone: 727-341-4360
Fax: 727-341-4744
e-mail: steelej@spcollege.edu
Web Site: www.spcollege.du/spg/music
Management:
    Program Director: Jonathan E Steele
    Coordinator Human Resources: Cathy Ladewig
Mission: Education
Founded: 1927
Specialized Field: Music; Choral; Instrumental; Piano; Vocal; Guitar
Paid Staff: 60

4061

TALLAHASSEE MUSEUM

3945 Museum Drive
Tallahassee, FL 32310-6325
Phone: 850-575-8684
Fax: 850-574-8243
e-mail: karen@tallahasseemuseum.org
Web Site: www.tallahasseemuseum.org
Management:

President: Russell Daws
Artistic Director: Jennifer Golden
Managing Director: Sherri Hall
Founded: 1957
Specialized Field: Education
Status: Non-Profit, Non-Professional
Paid Staff: 50
Paid Artists: 20

4062
ATLANTIC SHAKESPEARE FESTIVAL

1435 22nd Avenue
Vero Beach, FL 32960-1975
Phone: 772-559-0556
e-mail: atlanticshakes@yahoo.com
Web Site: www.geocities.com
Management:
President: Jon A Putzke
Mission: Was founded to provide classical theatrical works, with an emphasis on the works of William Shakespeare, to the residents and visitors to St. Augustine, Florida.
Founded: 1997
Specialized Field: Series & Festivals; Theatre; Youth
Status: Non-Profit, Professional
Income Sources: Program Ad Sales; Production Sponsors; Grants; Private Donations
Facility Category: Outdoor Amphitheatre
Type of Stage: Proscenium
Stage Dimensions: 60;x30'
Seating Capacity: 2200
Year Built: 1995

4063
REGIONAL ARTS MUSIC AT THE KRAVIS CENTER FOR THE PERFORMING ARTS

701 Okeechobee Boulevard
West Palm Beach, FL 33401
Phone: 561-835-4141
Fax: 561-835-0738
Toll-free: 800-572-8471
e-mail: tilley@kravis.org
Web Site: www.kravis.org
Officers:
Chief Executive Officer: Judith Mitchell
Regional Arts Programming Assoc.: Sharon McDaniel
Utilizes: Guest Musical Directors; Guest Musicians; Multimedia
Founded: 1974
Specialized Field: Vocal Music; Classical
Status: Non-Profit, Professional
Paid Staff: 2
Performs At: Kravis Center for the Arts

4064
SUNFEST OF PALM BEACH COUNTY

319 Clematis Street
West Palm Beach, FL 33401
Phone: 561-837-8065
Fax: 561-659-3567
e-mail: sunfest@sunfest.org
Web Site: www.sunfest.org
Management:
President: Gregory Fagan
Event Manager: Stewart Auville
Marketing Manager: Terri Neil
Mission: To support a variety of quality visual and performing arts festivals and entertainment events meeting the highest degree of excellence.
Utilizes: Student Interns
Founded: 1982
Specialized Field: Festivals
Status: Nonprofit

Paid Staff: 10
Paid Artists: 210
Income Sources: International Festival Association
Performs At: Along the Intracoastal Waterway; Flagler Drive
Organization Type: Resident

4065
POLK COMMUNITY COLLEGE SPECIAL PERFORMANCE SERIES

999 Avenue H NE
Winter Haven, FL 33881-4299
Phone: 863-297-1050
Fax: 863-297-1053
e-mail: sbevis@polk.edu
Web Site: www.polk.edu
Management:
President: Larry Durrence
Executive Director: William N Ryan
Founded: 1960
Specialized Field: Education
Status: Non-Profit, Non-Professional
Paid Staff: 2
Volunteer Staff: 4
Paid Artists: 6

4066
BACH FESTIVAL SOCIETY

1000 Holt Avenue-2763
Winter Park, FL 32789-4499
Phone: 407-646-2182
Fax: 407-646-2692
e-mail: info@bachfestivalflorida.org
Web Site: www.bachfestivalflorida.org
Officers:
President: John M Tiedtice
Management:
Music Director: Dr John V Sinclair
Conductor and Music Director: Dr John V Sinclair
Utilizes: Collaborating Artists; Commissioned Music; Educators; Five Seasonal Concerts; Grant Writers; Guest Accompanists; Guest Artists; Guest Choreographers; Guest Companies; Guest Conductors; Guest Instructors; Guest Musical Directors; Guest Musicians; Guest Soloists; Instructors; Local Artists; Multimedia; Music; Original Music Scores; Sign Language Translators; Singers; Soloists; Theatre Companies
Founded: 1935
Specialized Field: Performing Arts; Education
Paid Staff: 11
Volunteer Staff: 215
Paid Artists: 40
Income Sources: Box Office; Grants; Private Donations
Performs At: Annie Russell Theatre; Knowles Memorial Chapel
Affiliations: Rollins College
Annual Attendance: 26,000
Facility Category: Theatre; Chapel
Type of Stage: Proscenium
Seating Capacity: 1,500; 375

4067
BACHS FESTIVAL SOCITEY OF WINTER PARK

1000 Holt Avenue - 2763
Winter Park, FL 32789-4499
Phone: 407-646-2182
Fax: 407-646-2692
e-mail: info@bachfestivalflorida.org
Web Site: www.bachfestivalflorida.org
Officers:

President: John Tiedtke
Management:
President: John Tiedke
Artistic Director: John V Sinclair
Founded: 1937
Specialized Field: Vocal Music: Classical
Status: Non-Profit, Professional
Paid Staff: 4
Paid Artists: 20
Season: February
Performs At: Rollins Colliseum, Winter Park (Festival Site)
Facility Category: Knowles Memorial Chapel
Seating Capacity: 500

4068
FESTIVAL OF ORCHESTRAS

1353 Palmetto Avenue
Suite 100
Winter Park, FL 32789
Phone: 407-539-0245
Fax: 407-539-0525
Toll-free: 800-738-8188
e-mail: greatorchs@cfl.rr.com
Web Site: www.festivaloforchestras.com
Officers:
CEO: Joseph J Rizzo
Management:
President: Ellen Thompson
Mission: The mission of the Festival of Orchestras (FOI) is to present premier live performances to the world's great symphony orchestras to the Central Florida public, and at a reasonable price for all. Introducing young children and their teachers, from local schools to world-class orchestral concerts. We also encourage support from the local business community, by providing introductions to international business leaders.
Founded: 1984
Specialized Field: Series and Festivals: Vocal Music
Status: Non-Profit, Professional
Paid Staff: 3
Volunteer Staff: 3
Performs At: Bob Carr Performing Arts Center
Affiliations: OCCA

Georgia

4069
PORTERFIELD MEMORIAL UNITED METHODIST CHURCH - DISTINGUISHED ARTIST SERIES

2200 Dawson Road
Albany, GA 31707
Phone: 229-436-6336
Fax: 229-439-9141
e-mail: stevenjones@porterfieldchurch.org
Web Site: www.porterfieldchurch.org
Management:
Sr Pastor: Mason Gadly
Music Ministries Director: Steven Jones
Founded: 1956
Specialized Field: Series & Festivals; Instrumental Music; Vocal Music; Theatre; Youth; Dance; Ethnic Performances
Status: Non-Profit, Non-Professional
Paid Staff: 25
Seating Capacity: 850

4070
GEORGIA SOUTHWESTERN STATE UNIVERSITY CHAMBER CONCERT SERIES
800 Wheatley Street
Americus, GA 31709-4693
Phone: 229-931-2204
Fax: 229-931-2927
e-mail: jem@canes.gsw.edu
Officers:
Fine Arts Department Chairman: Julie Megginson
Specialized Field: Music
Performs At: Fine Arts Theatre
Seating Capacity: 250

4071
FORTE: THE UNIVERSITY UNION PERFORMING ARTS SERIES
Tate Center, Room 153
University of Georgia
Athens, GA 30602-3401
Phone: 706-542-6396
Fax: 706-542-5584
e-mail: joslyn@arches.uga.edu
Web Site: www.uga.edu/stuart
Management:
President: Erin Bohan
Student Coordinator: Nathan Copeland
Mission: To deliver a culturally and artistically diverse programming schedule to the University community.
Utilizes: Artists-in-Residence; Guest Soloists; Multimedia; Original Music Scores; Resident Artists; Singers; Theatre Companies
Specialized Field: Series & Festivals; Programming For Concerts; Shows
Status: For-Profit, Non-Professional
Paid Staff: 2
Volunteer Staff: 15
Paid Artists: 6
Budget: $143,850
Income Sources: Student Activity Fees; Ticket Sales

4072
ATLANTA DOWNTOWN FESTIVAL AND TOUR
Atlanta Downtown Neighborhood Association
PO Box 57021
Atlanta, GA 30343
e-mail: downtownatl@hotmail.com
Web Site: www.atlantadna.org/festival.htm
Management:
Co-Chairman: Chris Raffield
Vice President Of Special Events: Mary Elizabeth Harmon
Season: June
Performs At: Centennial Olympic Park (Festival Site)
Seating Capacity: 1,000

4073
ATLANTA JAZZ FESTIVAL
Atlantic Bureau of Cultural Affairs
675 Ponce De Leon
Atlanta, GA 30308
Phone: 404-817-6851
Fax: 404-817-6827
e-mail: bcamusic@atlantaga.gov
Web Site: www.atlantafestivals.com
Management:
President: Camille Love
Artistic Director: Alonzo Craig
Managing Director: Eddie Granderson

Mission: To offer a showcase for talented local and national performers; to provide Atlanta citizens with jazz music.
Founded: 1976
Specialized Field: Series & Festivals; Instrumental Music; Vocal Music; Theatre; Youth; Ethnic Performances
Status: Non-Profit, Professional
Paid Staff: 12
Performs At: Grant Park
Organization Type: Performing; Educational

4074
CHASTIAN PARK AMPHITHEATRE ATLANTA SYMPHONY ORCHESTRA FESTIVAL POPS
1293 Peachtree Street NE
Suite 300
Atlanta, GA 30309
Phone: 404-733-4900
Fax: 404-733-4901
e-mail: aso-info@woodruffcenter.org
Web Site: www.classicchastian.org
Officers:
Executive Director: Allison Vulgamore
Director Public Relations: Minde Herbert
Staff Accountant: April Satterfield
Management:
Music Director: Robert Spano
Conductor: Jere Flint
Conductor: Michael Krajewski
Principal Guest Conductor: Donald Runnicles
Mission: Provides young instrumentalists an opportunity to perform orchestral masterworks under the city's finest conductors.
Founded: 1945
Specialized Field: Orchestral
Status: Nonprofit
Paid Staff: 40
Volunteer Staff: 200
Budget: $6 million
Income Sources: Donations and Sponsors.
Season: June - August
Performs At: Atlanta Symphony Hall; Woodruff Arts Center
Affiliations: Atlanta Symphony Orchestra
Annual Attendance: 160,000
Facility Category: Chastian Park Amphitheatre
Type of Stage: Plywood/ Shell
Seating Capacity: 6,291
Year Built: 1933
Year Remodeled: 1989
Resident Groups: Atlanta Symphony Orchestra

4075
GEORGIA SHAKESPEARE FESTIVAL
Conant Performing Arts Center
4484 Peachtree Road NE
Atlanta, GA 30319
Phone: 404-264-0020
Fax: 404-504-3414
e-mail: boxoffice@gashakespeare.org
Web Site: www.gashakespeare.org
Management:
Managing Director: Robert Faff
Artistic Director: Richard Garner
Education Director: Kathleen McManus
Marketing Director: Stacey Colosa Lucas
Production Manager: Rob Dillard
Development Officer: Sarah Robinson
Events/Volunteer Coordinator: Carla Hyman
Company Manager: Christy Costello
Box Office Manager: Thomas Pinckney

Mission: To produce professional plays written by Shakespeare and other enduring authors.
Founded: 1985
Specialized Field: Series & Festivals; Theatre; Festivals
Status: Non-Profit, Professional
Paid Staff: 7
Income Sources: Southeastern Theatre Conference; Atlanta Theatre Coalition
Organization Type: Performing; Resident

4076
NATIONAL BLACK ARTS FESTIVAL
NABF
730 Peachtree Street NE
Suite 500
Atlanta, GA 30308
Phone: 404-730-7315
Fax: 404-730-7104
e-mail: info@nbaf.org
Web Site: www.nbaf.org
Officers:
President/CEO: Neil A. Barclay
Vice Chair: John H. Evans
Secretary: Ronald Wilson
Management:
Director, Artistic Programming: Leatrice Ellzy
Deputy Director: Muriel Hepburn
Mission: To engage, cultivate and educate diverse audiences about the arts and culture of the African Diaspora and provide opportunities for artistic and creative expression.
Utilizes: Actors; AEA Actors; Artists-in-Residence; Choreographers; Collaborating Artists; Collaborations; Commissioned Composers; Composers-in-Residence; Curators; Dance Companies; Dancers; Designers; Educators; Filmmakers; Fine Artists; Five Seasonal Concerts; Guest Accompanists; Guest Artists; Guest Choreographers; Guest Companies; Guest Composers; Guest Conductors; Guest Designers; Guest Directors; Guest Ensembles; Guest Instructors; Guest Musical Directors; Guest Musicians; Guest Soloists; Guest Teachers; High School Drama; Instructors; Local Artists; Local Unknown Artists; Lyricists; Multimedia; Music; Original Music Scores; Performance Artists; Playwrights; Poets; Resident Professionals; Sign Language Translators; Singers; Soloists; Special Technical Talent; Theatre Companies; Touring Companies; Visual Arts
Founded: 1987
Specialized Field: Multi-Disciplinary
Status: Non-Profit, Professional
Paid Staff: 10
Volunteer Staff: 200
Paid Artists: 800
Budget: $2 Million
Income Sources: Fulton County Arts Council; Ticket Sales; Corporate Sponsors; Foundations
Organization Type: Presenting

4077
OGLETHORPE UNIVERSITY-ARTS AND IDEAS AT OGLETHORPE
4484 Peachtree Road NE
Atlanta, GA 30319-4487
Phone: 404-364-8429
Fax: 404-364-8442
Toll-free: 800-428-4484
e-mail: iray@oglethorpe.edu
Web Site: www.oglethorpe.edu
Officers:
President: Lawrence Schall
Management:
President: Lawrence Schall

Music Director: W Irwin Ray
Mission: To support the programming of the university.
Founded: 1835
Specialized Field: Instrumental Music; Vocal Music; Choral; Theatre; Ethnic Performances
Status: Non-Profit; Educational; Professional
Paid Staff: 1
Volunteer Staff: 4
Performs At: Conant Center for the Performing Arts

4078
SCHWARTZ CENTER FOR PERFORMING ARTS AT EMORY

1700 N Decatur Road
Suite 251
Atlanta, GA 30322
Phone: 404-727-5050
Fax: 404-712-2296
e-mail: boxoffice@emory.edu
Web Site: www.emory.edu/arts/
Management:
Managing Director: Robert McKay
Assistant Marketing and PR Director: Sally Corbett
Assistant Director Programming: Debbie Joyal
Box Office Manager: Piper Phillips
Utilizes: Actors; AEA Actors; Choreographers; Collaborating Artists; Collaborations; Curators; Dance Companies; Dancers; Designers; Educators; Filmmakers; Fine Artists; Five Seasonal Concerts; Grant Writers; Guest Accompanists; Guest Artists; Guest Choreographers; Guest Composers; Guest Designers; Guest Directors; Guest Ensembles; Guest Instructors; Guest Lecturers; Guest Musical Directors; Guest Musicians; Guest Soloists; Guest Teachers; Guest Writers; Guild Activities; High School Drama; Instructors; Local Artists; Local Unknown Artists; Multi Collaborations; Multimedia; Music; Original Music Scores; Performance Artists; Playwrights; Poets; Resident Artists; Resident Professionals; Sign Language Translators; Singers; Soloists; Student Interns; Special Technical Talent; Theatre Companies; Touring Companies; Visual Arts
Specialized Field: Music; Dance; Theatre
Paid Staff: 9
Performs At: Glenn Memorial Auditorium; Munroe Theater; Dance Studio; Music; Dance; Theater; Schwartz Center for Performing Arts
Annual Attendance: 30,000
Facility Category: Multiple Facilities

4079
SIX FLAGS OVER GEORGIA

PO Box 43187
Atlanta, GA 30336
Phone: 770-739-3400
Fax: 770-739-3457
Web Site: www.sixflags.com
Management:
Production Coordinator: Daniel Barr
Founded: 1967
Specialized Field: Entertainment; Teen-Park
Status: Non-Profit, Non-Professional
Season: March - November
Type of Stage: Semi-Thrust
Stage Dimensions: 45' x 30'
Seating Capacity: 750

4080
SPELMAN COLLEGE FRESH IMAGES CHAMBER MUSIC SERIES

PO Box 246
350 Spelman Lane Southwest
Atlanta, GA 30314
Phone: 404-681-3643
Fax: 404-215-7771
e-mail: kjohns10@spelman.edu
Web Site: www.spelman.edu
Officers:
Chairman Music Department: Kevin Johnson
Management:
President: Dr Beverly Daniel Tatum
Associate Director: Monica Rodgers
Mission: To fully empower black women to fully use their talents to succees and to better the world.
Founded: 1881
Specialized Field: Music
Budget: $58 Million
Performs At: Sisters Chapel

4081
GREATER AUGUSTA ARTS COUNCIL

1301 Greene Street
PO Box 1776
Augusta, GA 30903
Phone: 706-826-4702
Fax: 706-826-4723
e-mail: arts@augustaarts.com
Web Site: www.augustaarts.com
Management:
Events Director: Leslie Fletcher

4082
GEORGIA PERIMETER COLLEGE GUEST ARTIST SERIES

555 N Indian Creek Drive
Clarkston, GA 30021
Phone: 404-299-4150
Fax: 404-299-4271
e-mail: ssigmon@gpc.edu
Web Site: www.gpc.edu
Management:
President: David Kauffman
Executive Director: Susan Sigmon
Managing Director: Richards Rogers
Founded: 1970
Specialized Field: Series and Festivals: Classical Music
Status: Non-Profit, Professional
Paid Staff: 13
Paid Artists: 13
Performs At: Marvin Cole Auditorium

4083
ARTS ASSOCIATION IN NEWTON COUNTY

1106 Washington Street
Covington, GA 30014
Phone: 770-786-8188
Fax: 770-784-1692
e-mail: info@newtoncountyarts.org
Web Site: www.newtoncountyarts.org
Management:
Executive Director: Buncie Lanners
Artistic Drector: Ric Chiapetta
Founded: 1989
Specialized Field: Series and Festivals; Instrumental Music; Vocal Music; Theatre; Youth; Dance; Ethnic Performances
Status: Non-Profit, Professional
Paid Staff: 4

Paid Artists: 90
Performs At: Olive Swann Porter Hall

4084
NORTH GEORGIA COLLEGE & STATE UNIVERSITY MUSIC SERIES

Student Center
101 College Circle
Dahlonega, GA 30597
Phone: 706-864-1643
Fax: 706-864-1647
e-mail: wthomas@ngcsu.edu
Web Site: www.ngc.peachnet.edu
Management:
Student Activities Director: Wesley Thomas
Professor Music/Keyboarding: Joe Chapman
Director Choral Activities: John Broman
Director Bands/Music Education: Andy David
Founded: 1970
Specialized Field: Series & Festivals; Instrumental Music; Vocal Music; Theater; Dance; Ethnic Performances; Performing Arts
Status: Non-Profit
Performs At: Student Center Auditorium

4085
GILMER ARTS & HERITAGE ASSOCIATION SERIES

200 Industrial Boulevard
Suite 103-B
Ellijay, GA 30540-3335
Phone: 706-635-5605
Fax: 706-636-5606
e-mail: gaha@ellijay.com
Web Site: www.gilmercounty.com/gaha
Management:
President: Jane Layman
Executive Director: Mary Sparks
Utilizes: Educators; Fine Artists; Guest Instructors; Guest Soloists; Guild Activities; Instructors; Local Artists; Multimedia; Original Music Scores; Playwrights; Special Technical Talent; Theatre Companies; Touring Companies
Founded: 1979
Specialized Field: Series & Festivals; Instrumental Music; Vocal Music; Theatre; Youth; Dance; Ethnic Performances
Status: Non-Profit, Professional
Paid Staff: 1
Volunteer Staff: 30
Non-paid Artists: 35
Performs At: Ellijay Elementary School Theatre
Seating Capacity: 600

4086
ARTS COUNCIL

331 Spring Street Southwest
PO Box 1632
Gainesville, GA 30503
Phone: 770-534-2787
Fax: 770-534-2973
e-mail: gladys@theartscouncil.net
Web Site: www.theartscouncil.net
Management:
Executive Director/CEO: Gladys Wyant
Mission: To enhance, educate and expand public interest in the arts.
Founded: 1970
Opened: 1972
Specialized Field: Series & Festivals; Music; Dance; Visual Arts
Status: Non-Profit, Professional
Paid Staff: 4

Volunteer Staff: 300
Paid Artists: 200
Non-paid Artists: 20
Budget: $420,000
Income Sources: Memberships; Corporate Sponsors; Foundations, Ticket Revenue; GA Council for the Arts; South Arts; Rentals; Endowment
Performs At: Pearce Auditorium; Arts Council Smithgall Arts Center; GA Mtns Center Arena & Theatre
Affiliations: Brenau University; Crawford W Lang Museum; Elachee Nature Science Center; Gainesville Ballet Company; Gainesville Chorale; Gainesville Theatre
Seating Capacity: 720
Rental Contact: Gladys Wyant

4087
MACON CONCERT ASSOCIATION

4760 Forsyth Rd
Macon, GA 31210
Phone: 478-743-6940
Officers:
VP: Edward Eikner
Management:
Executive Director: Lynn Cass
President: Stella Tsai
Founded: 1927
Specialized Field: Instrumental Music; Vocal Music; Classical Music
Status: Non-Profit,Professional
Paid Staff: 1
Performs At: Porter Auditorium

4088
MUSIC MERCER SERIES

Mercer University
1400 Coleman Avenue
Music Department
Macon, GA 31207
Phone: 478-301-2748
Fax: 478-301-5633
Toll-free: 800-342-0841
e-mail: roberts_jn@mercer.edu
Web Site: www.mercer.edu
Officers:
Music Department Chairman: Dr. John Roberts
Management:
President: Richard Fallis
Executive Director: Kirby Godsey
Artistic Director: Patty Crocker
Managing Director: John Roberts
Founded: 1833
Specialized Field: Vocal Music: Classical Music
Status: Non-Profit, Professional
Paid Staff: 27
Paid Artists: 18
Performs At: McCorkle Music Building; Recital Hall
Affiliations: NASM
Seating Capacity: 190
Year Built: 2001
Cost: 7,000,000

4089
BREWTON-PARKER COLLEGE FINE ARTS COUNCIL

US 280
Mount Vernon, GA 30445
Phone: 912-583-3133
Fax: 912-583-3136
Toll-free: 800-342-1087
e-mail: pdickens@bpc.edu
Web Site: www.bpc.edu
Officers:
Chairman: Pierce Dickens

Management:
President: David R Smith
Founded: 1903
Specialized Field: Education
Status: Non-Profit, Professional
Paid Staff: 200
Paid Artists: 7
Performs At: Gilder Recital Hall

4090
ARMSTRONG ATLANTIC STATE UNIVERSITY

11935 Abercorn Street
Savannah, GA 31419
Phone: 912-927-5325
Fax: 912-921-5492
Toll-free: 800-633-2349
e-mail: finearts@mail.armstrong.edu
Web Site: www.finearts.armstrong.edu
Management:
President: Tom Jones
Founded: 1935
Specialized Field: Series & Festivals; Instrumental Music; Vocal Music; Theater; Youth
Status: Non-Profit, Non-Professional
Performs At: AASU Fine Arts Auditorium
Seating Capacity: 960
Year Built: 1975

4091
SAVANNAH CONCERT ASSOCIATION

7209 Van Buren Ave.
Savannah, GA 31406
Phone: 912-356-8193
Officers:
President: Martin Greenburg
Management:
President: Byron Boyd
Founded: 2003
Specialized Field: Instrumental Music; Classical Music
Status: Non-Profit

4092
SAVANNAH MUSIC FESTIVAL

204 W St Julian Street
2nd Floor
Savannah, GA 31401
Mailing Address: PO Box 8105 Savannah, GA 31412-8105
Phone: 912-234-3378
Fax: 912-236-1989
Toll-free: 800-868-3378
e-mail: genepinion@gmail.com
Web Site: www.savannahmusicfestival.org
Management:
President: Rob Gibson
Managing Director: Melissa Paulsen
Mission: Music festival in historic Savannah, Georgia.
Founded: 1988
Specialized Field: Series & Festivals; Instrumental Music; Vocal Music; jazz; Youth; Dance; Ethnic Performances
Status: Non-Profit, Professional
Paid Staff: 6
Volunteer Staff: 260
Paid Artists: 75
Non-paid Artists: 78
Budget: $866,000
Income Sources: Box Office; Grants; Corporate; Foundation; Individuals; Government
Season: March
Performs At: Historic District of Savannah (Festival Site)
Annual Attendance: 20,000

Facility Category: Historic Churches; Synagogues; Recital Halls
Seating Capacity: 400 - 1,200 (indoors); 3,000 (outdoors)

4093
THOMASTON-UPSON ARTS COUNCIL PERFORMING SERIES

118 South Church Street
PO Box 211
Thomaston, GA 30286
Phone: 706-647-1605
Fax: 706-647-2187
e-mail: tuarts@alltel.net
Web Site: www.tuac.com
Management:
President: Jaye Eubanks
Executive Director: Carmen Ellerbee
Vice President: Lauri Irvin
Founded: 1986
Specialized Field: Series and Festivals; Instrumental Music; Vocal Music; Theatre; Youth; Dance; Ethnic Performances
Status: Non-Profit, Professional
Paid Staff: 2
Organization Type: Performing; Educational; Sponsoring

4094
THOMASVILLE ENTERTAINMENT FOUNDATION

600 E Washington Street
Thomasville, GA 31792
Mailing Address: PO Box 1976 Thomasville, GA 31799
Phone: 229-226-7404
Fax: 229-226-0599
e-mail: tef@rose.net
Web Site: www.tefconcerts.com
Officers:
President: Kenneth J Rebman
Management:
Executive Director: Janice Faircloth
Founded: 1937
Specialized Field: Series and Festivals; Instrumental Music; Vocal Music; Theatre; Youth; Dance; Ethnic Performances
Status: Non-Profit, Professional
Paid Staff: 1
Volunteer Staff: 12
Income Sources: Ticket Sales; Private Contributions
Performs At: Thomasville Cultural Center
Seating Capacity: 500

4095
JEKYLL ISLAND MUSICAL THEATRE FESTIVAL

Department of Communication Arts
Valdosta, GA 31698
Phone: 912-333-5820
Fax: 912-245-3799
e-mail: dguthrie@valdosta.edu
Management:
Managing Director: Duke Guthrie
Dean School of the Arts: Dr. Lanny Milbrandt
Mission: Providing Georgia's Golden Isles residents and visitors with quality musical theatre; offering college interns professional training.
Utilizes: Guest Choreographers; Guest Companies; Singers
Founded: 1990
Specialized Field: Summer Stock; Musical
Status: Professional; Nonprofit

Paid Artists: 65
Income Sources: Valdosta State University
Season: June - August
Performs At: Jekyll Island Amphitheater
Annual Attendance: 10,000
Facility Category: Professional Summer Stock Theatre
Type of Stage: Wooden, uncovered amphitheatre
Seating Capacity: 500
Year Built: 1970
Organization Type: Performing; Touring

4096
LOWNDES/VALDOSTA ARTS COMMISSION
527 N Patterson Street
Valdosta, GA 31601
Phone: 229-247-2787
Fax: 229-247-8978
e-mail: l/vac@surfsouth.com
Web Site: www.turnercentre.com
Management:
President: Paula Brown
Executive Director: Roberta George
Specialized Field: Series & Festivals: Theatre
Status: Non-Profit, Professional
Performs At: Mathis Municipal Auditorium

Hawaii

4097
HAWAII CONCERT SOCIETY
PO Box 233
Hilo, HI 96721
Phone: 808-935-5831
e-mail: jwakely@packagehomes.com
Officers:
VP: Judith Wakely
Management:
President: Tom Geballe
Founded: 1956
Specialized Field: Series & Festivals; Instrumental Music; Vocal Music; Dance; Ethnic Performances
Status: Non-Profit, Non-Professional
Performs At: University of Hawaii at Hilo Theatre
Seating Capacity: 600

4098
HONOLULU CHAMBER MUSIC SERIES
Box 2233
Honolulu, HI 96804
Phone: 808-528-8226
Fax: 808-956-9422
e-mail: tslaught@outreach.hawaii.edu
Officers:
President: Andrew Bunn
Performs At: Orvis Auditorium

4099
UNIVERSITY OF HAWAII SERIES
2530 Dole Street
Room D-406
Honolulu, HI 96822
Phone: 808-956-2036
Fax: 808-956-9422
e-mail: tslaught@outreach.hawaii.edu
Web Site: www.outreach.hawaii.edu
Management:
President: David McClain
Executive Director: Peter Tanaka
Mission: Presenting organization
Founded: 1907
Specialized Field: Series and Festivals: Ethnic Performances

Status: For-Profit, Professional
Paid Staff: 4
Performs At: Various Auditoriums

4100
MAUI COMMUNITY COLLEGE VITEC
310 Kaahumanu Avenue
Kahului, HI 96732
Phone: 808-984-3231
Fax: 808-244-9632
e-mail: brendal@hawaii.edu
Management:
Programs Coordinator: Brenda Lee

4101
MAUI COMMUNITY COLLEGE SERIES
310 Kaahumanu Avenue
Kahului, HI 96732-1617
Phone: 808-984-3500
Fax: 808-244-9632
e-mail: rwehrman@hawaii.edu
Web Site: www.maui.hawaii.edu
Management:
Assistant Music Professor: Robert Wehrman
Performs At: Maui Arts & Cultural Center

4102
HALAU HULA KA NO'EAU
Hawai'i Arts Ensemble
64-5259 Kekehau Street
PO Box 1907
Kamuela, HI 96743-1907
Mailing Address: PO Box 1907
Phone: 808-885-6525
Fax: 808-885-9018
e-mail: kanoeau@artofhula.com
Web Site: www.artofhula.com
Management:
Artistic Director: Kuma Hula
Director: Michael Pili Pang
Technical: Barbara Thompson
Mission: To promote and sustain the inherent cultural and artistic values of Hawaiian Dance.
Founded: 1986
Specialized Field: Hula; Hawaiian Chant and Music

4103
BRIGHAM YOUNG UNIVERSITY: HAWAII PERFORMANCE SERIES
PO Box 1924
Laie, HI 96762
Phone: 808-293-3550
Fax: 808-293-3374
e-mail: lucerod@byuh.edu
Web Site: www.byuh.edu
Management:
Managing Director: David Lucero
Founded: 1955
Specialized Field: Series & Festivals; Instrumental Music; Vocal Music; Dance; Ethnic Performances
Status: Non-Profit, Non-Professional
Paid Staff: 1
Performs At: David O. McKay Auditorium
Seating Capacity: 649

Idaho

4104
BOISE CHAMBER MUSIC SERIES
1910 University Drive
Boise, ID 83725-1560

Phone: 208-426-1216
Fax: 208-426-1771
e-mail: jbelfy@boisestate.edu
Management:
Artistic Director: Jeanne Belfy
Founded: 1984
Specialized Field: Chamber Music Presenting
Status: Non-Profit, Professional
Paid Staff: 1
Performs At: Morrison Center Recital Hall

4105
IDAHO SHAKESPEARE FESTIVAL
PO Box 9635
Boise, ID 83707
Phone: 208-336-9221
Fax: 208-323-0700
Web Site: www.idahoshakespeare.org
Management:
Production Manager: Philip Hendren
Artistic Director: Charles Fee
Managing Director: Mark Hofflund
Founded: 1976
Specialized Field: Theater
Status: Professional; Nonprofit
Paid Staff: 10
Season: May - September
Organization Type: Performing; Touring; Educational

4106
SHAKESPEARE FESTIVAL
520 S 9th
Boise, ID 83702
Phone: 208-345-0060
Fax: 208-429-8798
e-mail: info@idahoshakespeare.org
Web Site: www.idahoshakespeare.org
Management:
President: Nick Miller
Executive Director: Charles Fee
Managing Director: Mark Hosslund
Educational Director: Carole Whiteleather
Mission: To provide live, professional theater for the cultural enrichment and theater-arts education of children, young adults and their families at a cost which makes the programs easily accessible to all.
Utilizes: Guest Companies; Singers
Founded: 1981
Specialized Field: Theatre; Classical; Theatrical Group
Status: Non-Profit, Professional
Paid Staff: 5
Non-paid Artists: 15
Performs At: Morrison Center for the Performing Arts, Fulton St. Theatre
Annual Attendance: 25,000 - 30,000
Seating Capacity: 200; 200
Organization Type: Performing; Touring; Educational

4107
CALDWELL FINE ARTS SERIES
2112 Cleveland Boulevard
Caldwell, ID 83605
Phone: 208-454-1376
Fax: 208-459-5885
e-mail: cfa@albertson.edu
Web Site: www.caldwellfinearts.org
Officers:
President: Dr Lisa Derry
Management:
Executive Director: Sylvia Hunt
Mission: To offer professional performances in the performing arts; to provide local industry groups and schools with training and support.
Founded: 1961

Specialized Field: Series & Festivals: Classical
Status: Non-Profit, Professional
Paid Staff: 1
Income Sources: Pacific Northwest Presenters
Performs At: Jewett Auditorium
Organization Type: Educational; Sponsoring

4108
AUDITORIUM CHAMBER MUSIC SERIES
University of Idaho
PO Box 444015
Moscow, ID 83844-4015
Phone: 208-885-7557
Fax: 208-885-7254
e-mail: mdupree@uidaho.edu
Web Site: www.class.uidaho.edu/concerts
Management:
   Director: Mary DuPree
   Administrative Assistant: Matthew Pilcher
Mission: Offers a yearly concert series and we also
sponsor activities throughout the Palouse bringing
visiting artists into direct contact with school children,
university students and community members.
Status: Nonprofit
Paid Staff: 2
Paid Artists: 20
Income Sources: National Endowment for the Arts,
Idaho Commission on the Arts
Season: September-April
Performs At: University of Idaho Auditorium

4109
LIONEL HAMPTON JAZZ FESTIVAL
University of Idaho
PO Box 444257
Moscow, ID 83844-4257
Phone: 208-885-6765
Fax: 208-885-6513
Toll-free: 800-639-4160
e-mail: jazzinfo@uidaho.edu
Web Site: www.jazz.uidaho.edu
Management:
   President: Tim White
   Executive Director: Lynn J Skinner
Mission: Through four days of student competitions,
artist workshops and world class concerts, the Lionel
Hampton Jazz Festival keeps the magic, music and
spirit of jazz alive for generations to come by inspiring
students, teachers and artists of all ages and abilities to
support music education in schools and colleges
throughout the US and Canada and very directly at the
University of Idaho.
Founded: 1967
Specialized Field: Education
Status: Non-Profit, Professional
Paid Staff: 5
Volunteer Staff: 400
Paid Artists: 60
Budget: $ 1 Million
Income Sources: Ticket Sales; Sponsorships;
Registration Fees
Affiliations: University of Idaho
Annual Attendance: 25,000-30,000
Facility Category: University
Stage Dimensions: 50x100
Seating Capacity: 10,000

4110
MOUNTAIN HOME ARTS COUNCIL
935 N 12 E
Mountain Home, ID 83647
Phone: 208-587-4821
Management:
   Executive Director: Laurie Unrein

Mission: To offer diverse professional, performing arts
presentations to the Mountain Home community.
Specialized Field: Dance; Vocal Music; Instrumental
Music; Theater
Status: Non-Professional
Organization Type: Performing; Educational

4111
BRIGHAM YOUNG UNIVERSITY: IDAHO
Brigham Young University-Idaho
Rexburg, ID 83460-1660
Phone: 208-496-1152
Fax: 208-496-1884
e-mail: sparhawkd@byui.edu
Web Site: www.byui.edu
Management:
   Executive Director: Don Sparhawk
Mission: Our year round series of more than 20
performance offers a variety of music, dance and
theater that is intended to entertain, uplift and enlighten
both our students and the surrounding community.
Utilizes: Guest Musical Directors; Guest Musicians;
Multimedia; Singers
Founded: 1888
Specialized Field: Classical and Contemporary Music
Status: Non-Profit, Professional
Paid Staff: 1
Performs At: Hart Auditorium; Barrus Concert Hall;
Kirkham Auditorium

4112
SALMON ARTS COUNCIL
200 Main Street
Salmon, ID 83467
Phone: 208-756-2987
Fax: 208-756-4840
e-mail: sac1@centurytel.net
Web Site: www.salmonidaho.com
Management:
   President: Bryan Casey
   Executive Director: Janice Torrey
Founded: 1978
Specialized Field: Series & Festivals; Instrumental
Music; Vocal Music; Theatre; Youth; Dance; Ethnic
Performances
Status: Non-Profit, Professional
Paid Staff: 1
Performs At: Salmon High School Gymnasium

4113
FESTIVAL AT SANDPOINT
120 E Lake Street
Suite 207
Sandpoint, ID 83864
Mailing Address: PO Box 695
Phone: 208-265-4554
Fax: 208-263-6858
Toll-free: 888-265-4554
e-mail: festival@sandpoint.net
Web Site: www.festivalatsandpoint.com
Management:
   Executive Director: Diana Wahl
   Office Manager: Carol Winget
   Production Manager: Dave Nygren
Founded: 1983
Specialized Field: Series & Festivals: Music
Status: Non-Profit, Professional
Paid Staff: 3
Performs At: Memorial Field; Schweitzer Mountain
Resort (Festival Site)
Facility Category: Memorial Field
Seating Capacity: 2,500

4114
PEND OREILLE ARTS COUNCIL
PO Box 1694
Sandpoint, ID 83864
Phone: 208-263-6139
Fax: 208-255-1869
e-mail: poac@artsandpoint.net
Web Site: www.artsandpoint.org
Management:
   President: Carol Deaner
   Director: Kim Brown
Mission: Exists to facilitate and present the finest
quality experiences in the arts for the people of the
Sandpoint area.
Performs At: Panida Theatre

4115
SUN VALLEY SUMMER SYMPHONY
PO Box 1914
Sun Valley, ID 83353
Phone: 208-622-5607
Fax: 208-622-9149
e-mail: svss@sunvalley.net
Web Site: svsummersymphony.org
Officers:
   President: Harriet Parker-Bass
   VP: Jon Thorson
   VP: Preston Strazza
   Treasurer: Dick Porter
   Secretary: Preston Strazza
Management:
   Music Director: Alasdair Neale
   Founder: Carl Eberl
   Executive Director: Jaci Wilkins
Mission: To provide quality free, classical music
performances that have cultural, educational, and
artistic relevance.
Utilizes: Collaborations; Guest Musicians; Music;
Original Music Scores
Founded: 1985
Paid Staff: 1.5
Paid Artists: 90
Budget: $860,000
Income Sources: Individual; Business; Private
Donations
Season: Late July - Mid August
Performs At: Sun Valley (Festival Site)
Facility Category: Sun Valley Esplanade Tent
Stage Dimensions: 60'x 40'
Seating Capacity: 1,000

4116
ARTS ON TOUR SERIES
PO Box 1158
Twin Falls, ID 83303
Phone: 208-734-2787
Fax: 208-736-3015
e-mail: mvac@micron.net
Performs At: Auditorium

Illinois

4117
ARTS AT ARGONNE MUSIC SERIES
Argonne National Laboratory
9700 S Cass Avenue, Building 221
Argonne, IL 60439
Phone: 630-252-3751
Fax: 630-252-6104
e-mail: arts@anl.gov
Web Site: www.anl.gov/arts
Officers:

Chairman/President: Dr. Branko Ruscic
Mission: Supporting world class cultural presentations for employees of Argonne National laboratory and their families and for residents of neighboring communities.
Utilizes: Fine Artists; Multimedia; Original Music Scores; Singers
Founded: 1988
Specialized Field: Series & Fetivals: Instrumental Music
Status: Non-Profit, Professional
Volunteer Staff: 15
Budget: $20,000-$35,000
Income Sources: Ticket Sales; Illinois Arts Council
Performs At: Auditorium
Affiliations: Chicago Music Alliance
Facility Category: Auditorium
Seating Capacity: 400
Organization Type: Sponsoring

4118
PARAMOUNT ARTS CENTRE PERFORMING ARTS SERIES

8 E Galena Boulevard
Suite 230
Aurora, IL 60506
Phone: 630-896-7676
Fax: 630-892-1084
e-mail: info@paramountarts.com
Web Site: www.paramountarts.com
Officers:
Chairman: MW Meyer
Vice Chairman: Richard Hawks
Treasurer: Donna Williams
Secretary: Gyda Stoner
Management:
Executive Director: Diana Martinez
Theatre Services Coordinator: Jeff Wells
Box Office Manager: Don Hommowum
Box Office Manager: Jonnell Crawford
Executive Director: Janet R Bean
Mission: To present a variety of quality performances at moderate prices in a convenient location, plus educational opportunities and activities; supports other not-for-profit performing arts organizations.
Founded: 1931
Specialized Field: Series & Festivals; Theatre; Youth; Dance; Ethnic Performances
Status: Non-Profit, Professional
Budget: $3.0 million
Income Sources: Ticket Sales; Theatre Rentals; Grants; Donations; Sponsors; Program Ads; Fundraisers
Annual Attendance: 100,000
Facility Category: Performance Center
Type of Stage: Proscenium
Stage Dimensions: 48'x2" x 38'
Seating Capacity: 1888
Year Built: 1931
Year Remodeled: 1975
Rental Contact: Theatre Center Coordinator Jeff Wells (630-264-7202)

4119
FERMILAB ARTS SERIES

PO Box 500
Batavia, IL 60510-0500
Phone: 630-840-3000
Fax: 630-840-4343
e-mail: audweb@fnal.gov
Web Site: www.fnal.gov/culture
Management:
Arts Coordinator: Janet MacKay-Galbraith
Box Office Manager: Colleen Choy
Cultural Arts Supervisor: Denise M Adducci

Mission: To provide professional performing arts for the Batavia community.
Specialized Field: Dance; Instrumental Music; Theater; Comedy; Jazz
Status: Nonprofit
Paid Staff: 3
Budget: $35,000-$60,000
Income Sources: Fermi National Accel Laboratories
Performs At: Ramsey Auditorium
Organization Type: Sponsoring

4120
UNIVERSITY OF ILLINOIS: ASSEMBLY HALL

1800 S First Street
Champaign, IL 61820
Phone: 217-333-2923
Fax: 217-244-8888
e-mail: webcomment@ahmail.assembly.uiuc.edu
Web Site: www.uofiassemblyhall.com
Management:
Director: Kevin Ullestad
Specialized Field: Series & Festivals: Arena

4121
ANNUAL CHICAGO JAZZ FESTIVAL

Mayor's Office of Special Events
121 N LaSalle Street
Chicago, IL 60602
Phone: 312-744-3315
Fax: 312-744-0613
e-mail: specialevents@cityofchicago.org
Web Site: www.cityofchicago.org/specialevents
Management:
Coordinator: Jennifer J Washington
Mission: To present a festival, free to the public featuring jazz in all of its forms.
Founded: 1979
Specialized Field: Vocal Music; Instrumental Music; Jazz
Status: Professional
Season: September
Performs At: Symphony Music Shell; Petrillo Music Shell
Organization Type: Performing

4122
CHICAGO COLLEGE OF PERFORMING ARTS MUSIC CONSERVATORY SERIES

430 S Michigan Avenue
Chicago, IL 60605
Phone: 312-341-3785
Fax: 312-341-6358
e-mail: lberna@roosevelt.edu
Web Site: www.ccpa.roosevelt.edu
Management:
President: Charles Middleton
Director: Linda Berna
Founded: 1997
Specialized Field: Series & Festivals; Instrumental Music; Vocal Music; Theatre
Status: Non-Profit, Professional
Paid Staff: 80
Paid Artists: 20

4123
CHICAGO COLLEGE OF PERFORMING ARTS MUSIC CONSERVATORY SERIES

430 S Michigan Avenue
Chicago, IL 60605
Phone: 312-341-3785
Fax: 312-341-6358
e-mail: lberna@roosevelt.edu

Management:
Director/Music Conservatory/Dean: Linda Berna
Performance Activities Manager: Thomas Ballentine
Performs At: Rudolph Ganz Memorial Hall

4124
CHICAGO STUDIO OF PROFESSIONAL SINGING PERFORMANCE SERIES

Berger Cultural Mansion
6205 N Sheridan Road
Chicago, IL 60660
Phone: 773-764-5022
Fax: 773-764-5022
e-mail: info@professionalsinging.com
Web Site: www.professionalsinging.com
Management:
Director and Master Voice Teacher: Janice Pantazelos
Assistant Marketing Director: Joyce Chacko
Voice Teacher: Monique Robertson
Voice Teacher: Grace Sanchez
Mission: CSPS performance series showcase top professional singers from the Chicagoland area.
Specialized Field: Edgewater
Paid Staff: 3
Income Sources: Tickets; Advertising
Affiliations: NATS

4125
CRYSTAL BALLROOM CONCERT ASSOCIATION SERIES

410 S Michigan Avenue
#521
Chicago, IL 60605
Phone: 312-595-5434
Management:
Executive Secretary/Program Dir: Beverly DeFries-D'Albert
Mission: To provide performances of local and international artists for the Chicago community.
Founded: 1984
Specialized Field: Dance; Vocal Music; Instrumental Music; Festivals
Status: Professional; Nonprofit
Paid Staff: 50
Income Sources: Zoltan Kodaly Academy & Institute
Performs At: Crystal Ballroom
Organization Type: Performing; Educational; Sponsoring

4126
DAME MYRA HESS MEMORIAL CONCERT SERIES

30 E Adams Street
Suite 1206
Chicago, IL 60603
Phone: 312-670-6888
Fax: 312-670-9166
e-mail: info@imfchicago.org
Web Site: www.imfchicago.org
Management:
Program Coordinator: Michael Cansfield
Executive Director: Ann Murray
Founded: 1978
Specialized Field: Classical Music
Paid Staff: 3
Volunteer Staff: 4
Paid Artists: 79
Annual Attendance: 25,000

4127
DAME MYRA HESS MEMORIAL CONCERT SERIES
650 N Dearborn
Suite 350
Chicago, IL 60610
Phone: 312-670-6888
Fax: 312-670-9166
e-mail: info@imfchicago.org
Web Site: www.imfchicago.org
Management:
   Director: Ann Murray
Founded: 1978
Specialized Field: Music
Performs At: Preston Bradley Hall

4128
FRIDAY NOON CONCERT SERIES
Fourth Presbyterian Church
126 E. Chestnut Street
Chicago, IL 60611-2094
Phone: 312-787-4570
Fax: 312-787-4584
e-mail: music@fourthchurch.org
Web Site: www.fourthchurch.org
Management:
   Music Director/Organist: John W W Sherer
   Associate Organist: Thomas Gouwens

4129
GRANT PARK MUSIC FESTIVAL
205 E Randolph
Chicago, IL 60601
Phone: 312-742-7638
Fax: 312-742-7662
e-mail: info@grantparkmusicfestival.com
Web Site: www.grantparkmusicfestival.com
Management:
   Executive Director: James W Palermo
   Managing Director: Leigh Levine
Mission: To offer symphonic concerts at no cost to
Chicago residents.
Utilizes: Guest Artists
Founded: 1934
Specialized Field: Series and Festivals; Instrumental
Music; Vocal Music
Status: Non-Profit, Professional
Paid Staff: 100
Paid Artists: 100
Season: June - August
Performs At: Grant Park, Chicago
Organization Type: Performing; Resident; Educational

4130
ILLINOIS INSTITUTE OF TECHNOLOGY, UNION BOARD CONCERTS
3201 S State Street
Chicago, IL 60616
Phone: 312-567-3086
Fax: 312-567-8930
e-mail: ub@iit.edu
Web Site: www.ub.iit.edu
Management:
   Student Activities Director: Daniel DiCesare
Specialized Field: Series & Festivals: Cultural Events
Status: Non-Profit, Professional
Paid Artists: 150

4131
ILLINOIS INSTITUTE OF TECHNOLOGY, UNION BOARD CONCERTS
3241 S Federal Street
Chicago, IL 60616

Phone: 312-567-3075
Fax: 312-567-8930
e-mail: dicesare@alpha1.iit.edu
Management:
   Student Activities Director: Daniel DiCesare
Performs At: Grover M. Hermann Hall

4132
JAZZ INSTITUTE OF CHICAGO
410 S Michigan Avenue
Room 943
Chicago, IL 60605
Phone: 312-427-1676
Fax: 312-427-1684
e-mail: laurend@flash.net
Web Site: www.jazzinchicago.org
Officers:
   President: Steven Saltzman
   Executive Director: Lauren Deutsch
Founded: 1969
Specialized Field: Series & Festivals; Instrumental
Music; Vocal Music; Theatre; Youth; Dance; Ethnic
Performances; Jazz
Status: Non-Profit, Professional
Paid Staff: 3
Season: Labor Day Weekend
Performs At: Grant Park, Chicago (Festival Site)
Facility Category: Perillo Band Shell & Jazz on
Jackson Stage
Seating Capacity: 5,000 seats, 100,000 lawn seating

4133
LOYOLA UNIVERSITY OF CHICAGO SEASON SUBSCRIPTION SERIES
6525 N Sheridan Road
Chicago, IL 60626
Phone: 773-508-3833
Fax: 773-508-7126
e-mail: abrowni@luc.edu
Web Site: www.luc.edu/depts/theatre
Management:
   Chairperson: Sarah Gabel
   Technical Director: Joseph Gluecker
   Managing Director: April Browning

4134
LOYOLA UNIVERSITY OF CHICAGO SEASON SUBSCRIPTION SERIES
6525 N Sheridan Road
Chicago, IL 60626
Phone: 773-508-3833
Fax: 773-508-7126
e-mail: abrowni@luc.edu
Web Site: www.luc.edu/depts/theatre
Management:
   Managing Director: April Browning
Performs At: Kathleen Mullady Theatre

4135
NEWBERRY CONSORT
60 W Walton
Chicago, IL 60610
Phone: 312-255-3610
Fax: 312-255-3680
e-mail: consort@newberry.org
Web Site: www.newberry.org
Management:
   General Manager: Ken Perlow
Founded: 1987
Specialized Field: Series & Festivals; Instrumental
Music; Vocal Music
Status: Non-Profit, Professional
Paid Staff: 200

Paid Artists: 6

4136
NEWBERRY CONSORT
60 W Walton
Chicago, IL 60610
Phone: 312-255-3610
Fax: 312-255-3680
e-mail: consort@newberryorg
Web Site: www.newberry.org
Management:
   General Manager: Alex Bonus
Founded: 1987
Seating Capacity: 310

4137
PERFORMING ARTS ASSOCIATION
180 E Pearson Street
#5702
Chicago, IL 60611
Phone: 312-932-9566
Fax: 312-932-9566
Officers:
   President: Judys Neisser
   Executive Director: Susan Lipman
   Director: Christy Uchida
   Operations Manager: Laurell Zahrobsky
   Development Assistant: Brigid Flynn
   Treasurer: David Ellis
Management:
   President: Frederic W Schwartz
Mission: To present artists who explore the creative
tension between tradition and innovation, to nurture an
environment for and bring to performance new works
and new performers, and to remain accountable to its
community, furthering support for local artists,
engagement and education, not only for its direct
audience, but for society at large.
Utilizes: Special Technical Talent
Founded: 1954
Specialized Field: Series & Festivals: Individual
Concerts
Status: Non-Profit, Professional
Budget: $1,000,000
Performs At: The Civic Theater
Organization Type: Performing; Resident; Educational;
Sponsoring

4138
PERFORMING ARTS ASSOCIATION
180 E Pearson Street
#5702
Chicago, IL 60611
Phone: 312-932-9566
Fax: 312-932-9566
Officers:
   President: Frederic W Schwartz
Utilizes: Fine Artists
Founded: 1954

4139
ROOSEVELT UNIVERSITY PERFORMING ARTS SERIES
430 S Michigan Avenue
Chicago, IL 60605
Phone: 312-341-3785
Fax: 312-341-6358
e-mail: lberna@roosevelt.edu
Management:
   Performance Activities Manager: Thomas
   Ballentine

4140
ROOSEVELT UNIVERSITY PERFORMING ARTS SERIES
430 S Michigan Avenue
Chicago, IL 60605
Phone: 312-341-3785
Fax: 312-341-6358
e-mail: lberna@roosevelt.edu
Officers:
Director/Music Conservatory/Dean: Linda Berna
Management:
Performance Activities Manager: Thomas Ballentine
Performs At: Rudolph Ganz Memorial Hall

4141
UNIVERSITY OF CHICAGO PROFESSIONAL INSTRUMENTAL MUSIC SERIES
8627 Meadow Brook Drive
Chicago, IL 60527-1604
Phone: 630-655-9538
Fax: 630-655-8807
e-mail: philharmonia@yahoo.com
Management:
Executive Director: Mark Epstein
Artistic Director: Farobaghomi Cooper
Founded: 1985
Specialized Field: Series and Festivals: Instrumental Music
Status: Non-Profit, Professional
Paid Staff: 7
Paid Artists: 75

4142
UNIVERSITY OF CHICAGO PROFESSIONAL INSTRUMENTAL MUSIC SERIES
University Of Chicago Music Department
1010 E 59th Street
Chicago, IL 60637-1604
Phone: 773-702-8484
Fax: 773-753-0558
e-mail: jmaxwell@uchicago.edu
Web Site: www.music.uchicago.edu
Management:
Director Of Public Relations: Jennifer Maxwell
Performs At: Mandel Hall

4143
UNIVERSITY OF ILLINOIS AT CHICAGO FINE ARTS SERIES
Campus Programs Department, Room 340 S
Mailcott 118, 750 S Halsted Street
Chicago, IL 60607
Phone: 312-413-5070
Fax: 312-413-5074
Management:
Executive Director: Jill Rothamer
Artistic Director: Melissa Cfoke
Associate Director: Joey Hampton
Specialized Field: Higher Education
Status: Non-Profit, Professional
Paid Staff: 20

4144
URBAN GATEWAYS SERIES: CENTER FOR ARTS EDUCATION
200 W Jackson Boulevard
Suite 300
Chicago, IL 60606-6910
Phone: 312-922-0440
Fax: 312-922-2740
e-mail: frentdesk@urbangateways.org
Web Site: www.urbangateways.org
Management:
Executive Director: Libby Chiu
Producing Director: Tim Sauers
Mission: To provide comprehensive arts education programs, to serve locally as a resource, and nationally as a model for incorporating the arts in all levels of education for aesthetic, academic, cultural and personal development.
Founded: 1961
Specialized Field: Series & Festivals; Arts Education; Instrumental Music; Vocal Music; Theatre; Youth; Ethnic Performances
Status: Non-Profit, Professional
Paid Staff: 20
Paid Artists: 160
Budget: $2.3 million
Income Sources: Ticket Sales; Fees for Service; Grants; Corporation; Government; Contributions

4145
WILBUR COLLEGE CULTURAL EVENTS SERIES
4300 N Narragansett
Chicago, IL 60634
Phone: 773-481-8144
Fax: 773-481-8147
Seating Capacity: 200
Year Built: 1993
Rental Contact: Director Student Affairs Betty Gilbert

4146
NORTHERN ILLINOIS UNIVERSITY FINE ARTS SERIES
NIU, University Programming
Campus Life Building 150
De Kalb, IL 60115
Phone: 815-753-1421
Fax: 815-753-2905
e-mail: cabfinearts@niu.edu
Web Site: www.niu.edu/cab
Management:
Assistant Director: Mary Tosch
Utilizes: Dance Companies; Dancers; Fine Artists; Instructors; Local Artists; Multimedia; Sign Language Translators; Soloists; Special Technical Talent; Theatre Companies; Touring Companies
Founded: 1895
Specialized Field: Series & Festivals; Instrumental Music; Vocal Music; Theatre; Dance; Ethnic Performances
Status: Non-Profit, Professional
Performs At: Carl Sandburg Auditorium; Duke Ellington Ballroom

4147
PERFORMING ARTS SERIES FOR STUDENTS
125 N Water
PO Box 1607
Decatur, IL 62525
Phone: 217-423-3189
Fax: 217-423-3194
e-mail: arts4all@decaturarts.org
Web Site: www.decaturarts.org
Management:
President: Mike Gibson
Founded: 1967
Specialized Field: Facilitator for Arts
Status: Non-Profit, Non-Professional

Paid Staff: 5

4148
PERFORMING ARTS SERIES FOR STUDENTS
145 N Main
PO Box 1607
Decatur, IL 62525
Phone: 217-423-3189
Fax: 217-423-3194
e-mail: arts4all1@aol.com
Management:
Executive Director: Susan Smith
Performs At: Kirkland Fine Arts Center

4149
TRINITY COLLEGE SCHOOL OF MUSIC
2065 Half Day Road
Deerfield, IL 60015
Phone: 847-317-7035
Fax: 847-317-4786
e-mail: music@tiu.edu
Web Site: www.tiu.edu
Management:
Department Of Music Coordinator: Melody Velkuer
Department Of Music: Don Hedges
Mission: The TIU Department of Music exists to foster the understanding, teaching and performance of music as an arts & discipline, profession and a calling, and as a means to worship God and serve others.
Specialized Field: Series & Festivals; Instrumental Music; Vocal Music; Youth
Status: Non-Profit, Professional
Performs At: Arnold T. Olson Chapel

4150
MAINE TOWNSHIP COMMUNITY CONCERT ASSOCIATION
986 Jeannette Street
Des Plaines, IL 60016
Phone: 847-824-2591
Officers:
President: Anne Evans
Management:
President: Ann Evans
Founded: 1947
Specialized Field: Series & Festivals: Classical Music
Status: Non-Profit, Non-Professional
Performs At: High School Auditorium

4151
ARTISTS SHOWCASE WEST
Downers Grove Concert Association
731 59th Street
Downers Grove, IL 60516
Phone: 630-252-7160
Fax: 630-252-5986
Web Site: www.dgconcerts.org
Management:
President: Audra Hamernik
Founded: 1945
Specialized Field: Series & Festivals; Instrumental Music; Vocal Music
Status: Non-Profit, Professional

4152
DOWNERS GROVE CONCERT ASSOCIATION SERIES
PO Box 9602
Downers Grove, IL 60515

Phone: 630-963-9093
Fax: 630-252-5986
Web Site: www.dgconcerts.org
Officers:
    President: Tom Hamernik
Management:
    Artistic Director: Robert Johnson
Mission: To increase public support for performing arts in Downers Grove through the presentation of professional dancers and musicians.
Founded: 1976
Specialized Field: Dance; Instrumental Music
Status: Non-Profit
Volunteer Staff: 20
Budget: $20,000-$35,000
Income Sources: Ticket Sales; Village of Downers Grove; Illinois Art Council
Performs At: Downers Grove North High School Auditorium
Affiliations: Chicago Music Alliance
Facility Category: Auditorium
Seating Capacity: 1,000
Organization Type: Sponsoring

4153
ILLINOIS CENTRAL COLLEGE SUBSCRIPTION SERIES

Illinois Central College
Performing Arts Center
East Peoria, IL 61635
Phone: 309-694-5138
Fax: 309-694-5268
e-mail: drademaker@icc.edu
Web Site: www.icc.edu
Management:
    President: John Erwin
    Executive Director: Jeffery Hoover
    Managing Director: Dana Rademaker
Founded: 1967
Specialized Field: Series & Festivals; Traditional Jazz and Broadway Music; General Popular Entertainment
Status: Non-Profit, Professional
Paid Staff: 20
Volunteer Staff: 20
Budget: $35,000
Income Sources: Funded by the School
Performs At: Performing Arts Center
Affiliations: Illinois Presenters Network
Annual Attendance: 25,000
Type of Stage: Prosceium; Thurst
Stage Dimensions: 40'x36'
Seating Capacity: 500
Year Built: 1979
Cost: $4,000,000

4154
SOUTHERN ILLINOIS UNIVERSITY EDWARDSVILLE SERIES

Campus Box 1608
Edwardsville, IL 62026
Phone: 618-650-2626
Fax: 618-650-5050
e-mail: gandree@sive.com
Web Site: www.artsandissues.com
Management:
    Director Artist Issues: Grant Andree
Mission: Performing arts/speaker series
Founded: 1985
Status: Non-Profit, Professional
Paid Staff: 3
Paid Artists: 30
Income Sources: Association of Performing Arts Presenters

Performs At: University Center and Communications Theater
Organization Type: Educational; Sponsoring

4155
ELMHURST COLLEGE JAZZ FESTIVAL

190 Prospect Avenue
Elmhurst, IL 60126
Phone: 630-617-5534
Fax: 630-617-3738
e-mail: barbv@elmhurst.edu
Web Site: www.elmhurst.edu
Management:
    President: Bryant Cureton
    Executive Director: Doug Beach
Mission: To offer both jazz performances and the opportunity for artists to give constructive critiques, advice, demonstration of skills and guest band appearances.
Founded: 1967
Specialized Field: Series & Festivals; Instrumental Music; Vocal Music; Jazz
Status: Non-Profit;Collegiate/Professional
Paid Staff: 2
Volunteer Staff: 150
Affiliations: UCC, Community
Annual Attendance: 3,000
Facility Category: Chapel-Multi Purpose
Type of Stage: Indoor Elevated
Seating Capacity: 850
Year Remodeled: 1994

4156
PRINCIPIA COLLEGE CONCERT SERIES

Principia College
Elsah, IL 62028
Phone: 618-374-5004
Fax: 618-374-5911
e-mail: rer@prin.edu
Web Site: www.principia.edu
Management:
    Concert Coordinator: John Near
Founded: 1898
Specialized Field: Series & Festivals; Instrumental Music; Vocal Music; Theatre
Status: Non-Profit, Professional
Performs At: Cox Auditorium

4157
BACH WEEK FESTIVAL IN EVANSTON

PO Box 1832
Evanston, IL 60204-1832
Phone: 847-648-0813
Fax: 847-945-1106
e-mail: info@bachweek.org
Web Site: www.bachweek.org
Management:
    Music Director: Richard R Webster
    Festival Manager: Michael Cansfield
Founded: 1974
Season: May
Facility Category: Saint Luke's Episcopal Church, Evanston
Seating Capacity: 450

4158
NORTHWESTERN UNIVERSITY SUMMER DRAMA FESTIVAL

Theatre Department
1949 Campus Drive
Evanston, IL 60208

Phone: 847-491-3232
Fax: 847-467-7135
e-mail: n-barnett@northwestern.edu
Web Site: www.northwestern.edu
Management:
    Chairman: Rives Collins
    Managing Director: Claudia Kunin
Founded: 1954
Specialized Field: Series & Festivals: Acting and Musical Theatre
Status: Non-Profit, Non-Professional
Paid Staff: 20
Paid Artists: 28
Season: June - August
Type of Stage: Thrust
Stage Dimensions: 21' x 30'
Seating Capacity: 450

4159
KNOX-ROOTABAGA JAMM JAZZ FESTIVAL

Knox College
2 E South Street, Box 44
Galesburg, IL 61401
Phone: 309-341-7265
Fax: 309-289-2823
e-mail: nwhittak@knox.edu
Web Site: www.knox.edu/knoxjazzrootabaga
Management:
    President: Nicole Whittaker
Mission: Entertainment and education.
Founded: 1989
Specialized Field: Series & Festivals; Instrumental Music; Vocal Music; Youth
Status: Non-Profit, Professional
Paid Staff: 1
Volunteer Staff: 50
Paid Artists: 20
Non-paid Artists: 40

4160
COLLEGE OF LAKE COUNTY - PERFORMING ARTS BUILDING

19351 W Washington Street
Graylake, IL 60030-1198
Phone: 847-543-2077
Fax: 847-543-2629
e-mail: gbronner@clc.cc.il.us
Web Site: www.clc.cc.il.us
Management:
    President: Gretchen Naff
    Executive Director: Gwethalyn Bronner
    Technical Coordinator: Jeremy Eiden
    Media Coordinator: Lyla Maclean
Founded: 1997
Specialized Field: Perfoming arts
Status: Non-Profit, Professional
Paid Staff: 20
Performs At: Mainstage

4161
GREENVILLE COLLEGE GUEST ARTIST SERIES

315 E College Avenue
Greenville, IL 62246
Phone: 618-664-6582
Fax: 618-664-6580
e-mail: achaussee@greenville.edu
Management:
    Manager: Andrea Chaussee
Mission: Acts enrichment in a small community
Performs At: LaDue Auditorium

4162
RAVINIA FESTIVAL
PO Box 896
Highland Park, IL 60035
Phone: 847-266-5100
Fax: 847-266-0641
e-mail: ravinia@ravinia.org
Web Site: www.ravinia.org
Officers:
    President/CEO: Welz Kauffman
Management:
    President: Welz Kauffman
    Artistic Director: Ramsey Lewis
    Music Director: James Conlon
Mission: To present, at low cost, quality classical, jazz, folk, and pop music to the public.
Utilizes: AEA Actors; Artists-in-Residence; Choreographers; Collaborating Artists; Commissioned Composers; Commissioned Music; Dance Companies; Dancers; Designers; Five Seasonal Concerts; Guest Artists; Guest Choreographers; Guest Companies; Guest Composers; Guest Conductors; Guest Designers; Guest Directors; Guest Ensembles; Guest Instructors; Guest Lecturers; Guest Musical Directors; Guest Musicians; Guest Soloists; High School Drama; Local Artists; Multimedia; Music; Original Music Scores; Resident Professionals; Sign Language Translators; Singers; Soloists; Student Interns; Theatre Companies
Founded: 1935
Status: Professional; Nonprofit
Paid Staff: 50
Volunteer Staff: 50
Non-paid Artists: 100
Season: June - September
Performs At: Ravinia Park, Highland Park (Festival Site)
Annual Attendance: 500,000
Facility Category: Ravinia Pavilion; Martin Theatre; Bennet-Gordon Hall
Seating Capacity: 3,200; 850; 450
Year Built: 1955
Year Remodeled: 1995
Organization Type: Performing; Educational

4163
STARRY NIGHTS SUMMER CONCERT SERIES
3301 Flossmoor Road
Homewood, IL 60422
Phone: 708-957-0300
Fax: 708-957-0267
e-mail: hfinfo@hfparks.com
Web Site: www.hfparks.com/
Management:
    President: Patrick Nevins
    Director: Greg Meyer
    VP: Melissa Barrett
    Commissioner: Pete Camin
Season: June - July
Performs At: Homewood (Festival Site)
Facility Category: Marie Irwin Community Center Bandshell, Homewood
Seating Capacity: 4,000

4164
MYSTERY CAFE SERIES
231 S College Avenue
Indianapolis, IL
Phone: 317-684-0668
e-mail: info@themysterycafeindy.com
Web Site: www.mysterycafeonline.com
Founded: 1990

4165
BARAT COLLEGE PERFORMING ARTS CENTER SEASON
700 E Westleigh Road
Lake Forest, IL 60045
Phone: 847-234-3000
Fax: 847-604-6342
e-mail: drakethe@barat.edu
Web Site: www.barat.edu
Management:
    Theatre Department Chair: Steve Carmichael
    Assistant Producer: Jeannie Petkewicz
Budget: $10,000-$20,000
Performs At: Drake Theatre
Facility Category: College
Type of Stage: Proscenium
Seating Capacity: 625

4166
MCKENDREE COLLEGE FINE ARTS SERIES
Mckendree College
701 College Road
Lebanon, IL 62254
Phone: 618-537-4481
Fax: 618-537-6259
Toll-free: 800-232-7228
e-mail: nypma@mckendree.edu
Web Site: www.mckendree.edu
Officers:
    Chairperson Music Department: Dr. Nancy Ypma
Mission: For education of students and community.
Paid Staff: 2
Paid Artists: 5
Performs At: Bothwell Chapel; Pearsons Hall

4167
WESTERN ILLINOIS UNIVERSITY BCA PERFORMING ARTIST SERIES
University Union
1 University Circle
Macomb, IL 61455
Phone: 309-298-3232
Fax: 309-298-2879
e-mail: cl-steelman@wiu.edu
Web Site: www.bca.wiu.edu
Management:
    Director Performing Arts: Dan Maxwell
    Performing Arts Assistant Director: Christi Steelman
Founded: 1968
Specialized Field: Series & Festivals; Instrumental Music; Vocal Music; Theatre; Youth; Dance; Ethnic Performances
Status: Non-Profit, Professional
Paid Staff: 10
Performs At: Western Hall

4168
QUAD-CITIES JAZZ FESTIVAL
719 17th St
Moline, IL 61244
Phone: 563-324-0049
Officers:
    Chairman: Josef Fackel
Management:
    Director: Nathaniel Lawrence
Founded: 1994
Paid Staff: 1

4169
NAPERVILLE-NORTH CENTRAL COLLEGE PERFORMING ARTS SERIES
30 N Brainard Street
Naperville, IL 60566
Phone: 630-637-5100
Fax: 630-637-5121
Management:
    Director Fine Arts: Brian Lynch
Founded: 1974
Specialized Field: Dance; Vocal Music; Instrumental Music; Theater
Status: Non-Professional; Nonprofit
Income Sources: North Central College
Performs At: Pfeiffer Hall
Organization Type: Sponsoring

4170
ILLINOIS SHAKESPEARE FESTIVAL
Illinois State University
Box 5700
Normal, IL 61790-5700
Phone: 309-438-8974
Fax: 309-438-5806
e-mail: shake@ilstu.edu
Web Site: www.thefestival.org
Management:
    Managing Director: Dick Folse
    Artistic Director: Deb Alley
Utilizes: Actors; AEA Actors; Designers; Guest Conductors; Guest Designers; Guest Writers; Guild Activities; Original Music Scores; Resident Artists; Resident Professionals; Soloists; Student Interns
Founded: 1978
Specialized Field: Festivals
Status: Non-Profit
Paid Staff: 80
Paid Artists: 40
Budget: $1.2 Million
Income Sources: Box Office, Fund Raising
Season: June - August
Performs At: Ewing Manor
Affiliations: UARTA; Actors' Equity Association; SSOC
Annual Attendance: 15,000
Facility Category: Outdoor
Type of Stage: Thrust
Seating Capacity: 438
Year Built: 2000
Cost: $1.65 million
Organization Type: Performing; Educational

4171
BRADEN AUDITORIUM
100 N University Street
Campus Box 2640
Normal, IL 61790-2640
Phone: 309-438-2222
Fax: 309-438-3544
e-mail: rajohn2@ilstu.edu
Web Site: www.bsc.ilstu.edu/bsc
Management:
    Coordinator: Jennifer Booher
    Box Office Manager: Amy Johnson
Founded: 1973
Specialized Field: Education
Status: For-Profit, Professional
Paid Staff: 100
Volunteer Staff: 20
Non-paid Artists: 200
Performs At: Auditorium
Affiliations: Illinois State University
Facility Category: Auditorium
Seating Capacity: 3,457

Rental Contact: Coordinator Jennifer Booher

4172
FIRST FOLIO SHAKESPEARE FESTIVAL
146 Juliet Court
Oak Brook, IL 60514
Mailing Address: 146 Juliet Center Claredon Hill, IL 06514
Phone: 630-986-8067
Fax: 630-455-0071
e-mail: firstfolio@firstfolio.org
Web Site: www.firstfolio.org
Management:
President: Alison C Vesely
Managing Director: David Rice
Mission: Bring attention to the historic and environmental site here. Mission emphasizes a training intiative for young theatre artists, including a college intern program.
Founded: 1996
Specialized Field: Series & Festivals: Classical Theatre
Status: Non-Profit, Professional
Paid Staff: 2
Volunteer Staff: 60
Paid Artists: 30
Season: July - September
Type of Stage: Thrust
Stage Dimensions: 40' x 30'

4173
COMMUNITY CHILDREN'S THEATRE OF PEORIA PARK DISTRICT
2218 N Prospect Road
Peoria, IL 61603-2193
Phone: 309-688-3667
Fax: 309-686-3384
e-mail: lhuff@peoriaparks.org
Web Site: www.peoriaparks.org
Officers:
President: Lisa Voyles
Treasurer: Kris Griffith
Vice President: Chris Paternoga
Secretary: Sally Robertson
Management:
Fine Arts Coordinator: Linda Elegant Huff
Mission: To foster participation among the young people in the community in children's theatre activity; to present educational programs, with the purpose of raising awareness and standards of such programs.
Utilizes: Choreographers; Dancers; Educators; Grant Writers; Guest Artists; Guest Designers; Guest Lecturers; Guild Activities; High School Drama; Instructors; Local Artists; Multimedia; Music; Sign Language Translators; Soloists; Student Interns
Founded: 1957
Specialized Field: Theatre: Children's Theatre
Status: Non-Profit, Non-Professional
Paid Staff: 1
Volunteer Staff: 200
Paid Artists: 4
Non-paid Artists: 65
Budget: $20,000
Income Sources: Tickets Sales and Concessions; Donations; Grants
Performs At: Theatre; Schools
Affiliations: Illinois Theatre Association
Annual Attendance: 5,000
Facility Category: Theatre
Type of Stage: Proscenium
Seating Capacity: 360

4174
MIDWEST JAZZ HERITAGE FESTIVAL
PO Box 754
Peoria, IL 61652-0754
Phone: 309-672-2004
e-mail: bduffy@bigplanet.com
Web Site: www.midil.com/jazzpeoria.html
Management:
Prducer and Promoter: B Duffy

4175
PEORIA CIVIC CENTER
201 SW Jefferson Street
Peoria, IL 61602-1448
Phone: 309-673-8900
Fax: 309-673-3200
e-mail: dritschel@peoriaciviccenter.com
Web Site: www.peoriaciviccenter.com
Management:
Director Marketing: Marc Burnett
General Manager: Debbie Ritschal
Director Operations: Will Kenney
Founded: 1982
Specialized Field: Series and Festivals; Instrumental Music; Vocal Music; Theatre; Youth; Dance; Ethnic Performances
Status: For-Profit, Professional
Paid Staff: 500

4176
QUINCY CIVIC MUSIC ASSOCIATION
PO Box 1165
Quincy, IL 62306-1165
Phone: 217-224-5499
e-mail: cma@insightbb.com
Web Site: www.cma.home.insightbb.com
Management:
Second Vice President: Merle Crossland
First Vice President: Mary Anne Klein
President: Mowbray Allan
Founded: 1928
Specialized Field: Series & Festivals; Instrumental Music; Vocal Music; Dance; Ethnic Performances
Status: Non-Profit, Professional

4177
DOMINICAN UNIVERSITY PERFORMING ARTS CENTER
7900 W Division Street
River Forest, IL 60305
Phone: 708-524-6515
Fax: 708-524-6517
e-mail: lrodriguez@dom.edu
Web Site: www.dom.edu
Management:
Operations/Marketing Manager: Leslie Rodriguez
Technical Director: Bill Jenkins
Administrativ Associate: Julianna Mendelson
Utilizes: Actors; Artists-in-Residence; Choreographers; Collaborating Artists; Commissioned Music; Dance Companies; Dancers; Designers; Educators; Filmmakers; Fine Artists; Five Seasonal Concerts; Grant Writers; Guest Accompanists; Guest Artists; Guest Choreographers; Guest Companies; Guest Conductors; Guest Designers; Guest Ensembles; Guest Instructors; Guest Lecturers; Guest Musical Directors; Guest Musicians; Guest Soloists; Guest Teachers; High School Drama; Instructors; Local Artists; Multi Collaborations; Multimedia; Music; Original Music Scores; Performance Artists; Playwrights; Poets; Resident Professionals; Sign Language Translators; Singers; Soloists; Theatre Companies; Touring Companies; Visual Arts

Founded: 1901
Specialized Field: Theatre/Music
Paid Staff: 4
Performs At: Lund Auditorium; Martin Hall
Affiliations: Dominican University
Annual Attendance: 45,000
Facility Category: Fine Arts Building
Type of Stage: Proscenium
Seating Capacity: 1,000; 180
Year Built: 1952
Year Remodeled: 1992
Rental Contact: Bill Jenkins

4178
QUAD CITY ARTS
1715 2nd Avenue
Rock Island, IL 61201
Phone: 309-793-1213
Fax: 309-793-1265
e-mail: info@quadcityarts.com
Web Site: www.quadcityarts.com
Officers:
Executive Director: Carmen Darland
Management:
Performing Arts Director: Susan Wohlman
Mission: To offer professional concerts by area performing artists.
Utilizes: Actors; Artists-in-Residence; Collaborations; Dance Companies; Dancers; Educators; Fine Artists; Five Seasonal Concerts; Grant Writers; Guest Accompanists; Guest Choreographers; Guest Designers; Guest Ensembles; Guest Instructors; Guest Musical Directors; Guest Musicians; Guest Soloists; Guest Teachers; Guild Activities; High School Drama; Instructors; Local Artists; Local Unknown Artists; Lyricists; Multi Collaborations; Multimedia; Music; New Productions; Original Music Scores; Performance Artists; Playwrights; Sign Language Translators; Soloists; Special Technical Talent; Theatre Companies; Touring Companies
Founded: 1973
Specialized Field: Series and Festivals; Instrumental Music; Vocal Music; Theatre; Youth; Dance; Ethnic Performances; Regional arts council
Status: Non-Profit, Non-Professional
Paid Staff: 6
Budget: $130,000
Income Sources: Grants; Foundations; Fund Drive
Performs At: Deere and Company; St. Ambrose University; Augustana College
Affiliations: Association of Performing Arts Presenters; Music America; American For The Arts
Facility Category: Arts Center
Year Remodeled: 1988
Organization Type: Performing; Educational

4179
ROCK VALLEY COLLEGE LECTURE/CONCERT SERIES
3301 N Mulford Road
Rockford, IL 61114
Phone: 815-654-4290
Fax: 815-654-4402
e-mail: m.sink@rvc.cc.il.us
Management:
Program Director: Monique Aduddell

4180
ROCK VALLEY COLLEGE LECTURE/CONCERT SERIES
3301 N Mulford Road
Rockford, IL 61114

Phone: 815-654-4290
Fax: 815-654-4402
e-mail: m.sink@rvc.cc.il.us
Management:
    Program Director: Monique Aduddell
Performs At: Performing Arts Room

4181
UNIVERSITY OF ILLINOIS AT SPRINGFIELD SANGAMON PERFORMING ARTS SERIES

Sangamon Auditorium
PAC397, UIS, PO Box 19243
Springfield, IL 62794-9243
Phone: 217-206-6150
Fax: 217-206-6391
Toll-free: 800-207-6960
e-mail: sangamonauditorium@uis.edu
Web Site: www.sangamonauditorium.org
Management:
    Director: Bob Vaughn
    Event Manager: Elise Robertson
Mission: To present a varied professional performing arts program to audiences in central illinois.
Founded: 1981
Specialized Field: Series & Festivals; Instrumental Music; Vocal Music; Theatre; Dance; Ethnic Performances
Status: Non-Profit, Professional
Paid Staff: 10
Volunteer Staff: 250
Budget: $2 Million
Annual Attendance: 100,000
Facility Category: Proscenium; Black Box
Stage Dimensions: 62' x 55'
Seating Capacity: 2018
Rental Contact: Elise Robertson

4182
ST CHARLES ART & MUSIC FESTIVAL

1040 Dunham Road
The Dellora A Norris Cultural Arts Center
St Charles, IL 60174
Mailing Address: PO Box 3340
Phone: 630-584-7200
e-mail: jgranquist@norrisculturalarts.com
Web Site: www.norrisculturalarts.com
Management:
    Director Of Operations: Jo Anne Granquist
    Technical Director: John Mizanin
Performs At: St. Charles & Tri-City Area (Festival Site)
Facility Category: Norris Cultural Arts Center
Seating Capacity: 980

4183
KRANNERT CENTER MARQUEE SERIES, UNIVERSITY OF ILLINOIS

500 S Goodwin Avenue
Urbana, IL 61801
Phone: 217-333-6700
Fax: 217-244-0810
e-mail: kran-tix@uiuc.edu
Web Site: www.krannertcenter.com
Management:
    Director: Mike Ross
Founded: 1969
Specialized Field: Series and Festivals; Instrumental Music; Vocal Music; Theatre; Youth; Dance; Ethnic Performances
Status: Non-Profit, Non-Professional
Paid Staff: 80
Performs At: Foellinger Great Hall

4184
UNIVERSITY OF ILLINOIS: SUMMERFEST

4-122 Krannert Center for Performing Arts
500 S Goodwin Avenue
Urbana, IL 61801
Phone: 217-333-3538
Fax: 217-244-1861
e-mail: theater@uiuc.edu
Web Site: www.theatre.uiuc.edu
Officers:
    Head: Robert Graves
Management:
    Chairman of University: Robert Graves
    Chancellor of Unversity: Richard Herman
    Production Director: J B Harris
Utilizes: Actors; Designers; Guest Conductors; Guest Designers; Local Artists; Multimedia; Original Music Scores; Resident Professionals
Founded: 1991
Specialized Field: Theatre; Musical; Comedy; Dinner; Ethnic Theater; Theatrical Group; Classical; Contemporary; Theatre Education
Status: Non-Profit, Professional
Paid Staff: 34
Volunteer Staff: 9
Paid Artists: 8
Season: June - August
Performs At: Performing Arts Center
Facility Category: Studio Theatre
Type of Stage: Flexible
Seating Capacity: 200

4185
ARTIST SERIES AT WHEATON COLLEGE

Wheaton Conservatory of Music
501 College Avenue
Wheaton, IL 60187-5593
Phone: 630-752-5099
Fax: 630-752-5341
Toll-free: 800-325-8718
e-mail: artistseries@wheaton.edu
Web Site: www.wheaton.edu
Management:
    President: Duane Litfin
    Artistic Director: Tony Payne
    Managing Director: Rhaondas Sission
Founded: 1950
Specialized Field: Series and Festivals; Instrumental Music; Vocal Music; Theatre; Youth
Status: Non-Profit, Non-Professional
Paid Staff: 4
Volunteer Staff: 10
Paid Artists: 6
Budget: $300,000
Income Sources: Box Office; Private Donationas; Corporate Donations
Performs At: Edman Memorial Chapel
Affiliations: Wheaton College
Annual Attendance: 12,500
Facility Category: Auditorium/Hall
Type of Stage: Proscenium
Stage Dimensions: 35'x 60'
Seating Capacity: 2,350
Year Built: 1960

4186
MUSIC INSTITUTE OF CHICAGO SERIES

300 Green Bay Road
Winnetka, IL 60093
Phone: 847-446-3822
Fax: 847-446-3876
e-mail: info@musicinst.com
Web Site: www.musicinst.com

Officers:
    Chairman: William J Eichar
    President: Frank Little
    VP: Gilda Barston
Management:
    President: John Pietgras
    Executive Director: Richard Rohrer
Mission: To provide the foundation for a lifelong enjoyment of music.
Utilizes: Collaborations; Educators; Guest Instructors; Soloists
Founded: 1931
Specialized Field: Series & Festivals; Instrumental Music; Vocal Music; Theatre; Youth & Adults
Status: Non-Profit, Professional
Paid Staff: 150
Budget: 4 million
Income Sources: Tuition; Donations
Performs At: Recital Hall
Annual Attendance: 1,000+
Facility Category: Recital Hall
Seating Capacity: 150
Year Built: 1956
Rental Contact: Jim Brown

4187
WOODSTOCK FINE ARTS ASSOCIATION - MUSIC FOR A SUNDAY AFTERNOON SERIES

PO Box 225
Woodstock, IL 60098
Phone: 815-338-0175
Management:
    Contact: Mary Sircar
Founded: 1961

4188
WOODSTOCK FINE ARTS ASSOCIATION - MUSIC FOR A SUNDAY AFTERNOON SERIES

PO Box 225
Woodstock, IL 60098
Phone: 815-338-0175
Management:
    Contact: Mary Sircar
Performs At: Auditorium

4189
WOODSTOCK MOZART FESTIVAL

PO Box 734
Woodstock, IL 60098
Phone: 630-983-7072
Fax: 630-717-7782
e-mail: mozartfest@aol.com
Web Site: www.mozartfest.org
Officers:
    President: Louis La Coque
Management:
    President: Louise Le Coque
    General Director: Anita Whelan
    Artistic Advisor: Mark Peskanov
Utilizes: Guest Accompanists; Guest Composers; Guest Musicians; Multimedia; Original Music Scores
Founded: 1987
Specialized Field: Series & Festivals: Instrumental Music
Status: Non-Profit, Professional
Paid Staff: 3
Paid Artists: 40
Budget: $130,000
Income Sources: Individuals, Corporations, Foundations
Facility Category: Woodstock Opera House

Seating Capacity: 412
Year Built: 1889
Year Remodeled: 1977

Indiana

4190
FOUNTAIN/WARREN MUSICAL ARTS SERIES
PO Box 6
Attica, IN 47918
Phone: 765-762-2481
Fax: 765-762-2487
e-mail: wrghthsm@hscast.com
Officers:
    Secretary: Mike Wrighthouse
Management:
    President: Wade C Harrison
    Artistic Director: Mike Wrighthouse
Utilizes: Guild Activities; Multimedia; Sign Language Translators; Singers; Soloists
Founded: 1985
Specialized Field: Series & Festivals; Chamber Music; Solo
Status: Non-Profit, Professional
Budget: $11,000
Performs At: Harrison Hills Country Club

4191
DEARBORN HIGHLANDS ARTS COUNCIL SERIES
406 Second Street
PO Box 193
Aurora, IN 47001-0193
Phone: 812-926-1778
Fax: 812-926-4700
Toll-free: 866-818-2787
e-mail: dhac@seidata.com
Web Site: www.all4art.org
Management:
    Executive Director: Marilyn Bower
Mission: To serve, expand and enrich the lives of residents of Dearborn County and adjacent areas through education, exposure, diversity, enjoyment and participation in the performing and visual arts.
Founded: 1982
Specialized Field: Series and Festivals; Instrumental Music; Vocal Music; Theatre; Youth; Dance; Ethnic Performances; Education Programmes
Status: Non-Profit, Non-Professional
Paid Staff: 1
Volunteer Staff: 215
Budget: $100,000
Income Sources: Grants; Memberships; Ticket Sales; Corporate; Private Support
Performs At: Lawrenceburg HS Auditorium; South Dearborn HS Auditorium; Public Libraries
Annual Attendance: 4800
Facility Category: Auditorium, city park

4192
BLOOMINGTON EARLY MUSIC FESTIVAL
PO Box 734
Bloomington, IN 47402
Phone: 812-331-1263
Fax: 812-331-1263
e-mail: office@blemf.org
Web Site: www.blemf.org
Officers:
    President: Mary Tilton
    Chair, Program Commitee: Gesa Kordes
Management:
    President: Mary Tilton
    Interim Executive Director: Martha Perry
Utilizes: Choreographers; Collaborating Artists; Collaborations; Dancers; Designers; Guest Accompanists; Guest Artists; Guest Designers; Guest Directors; Guest Instructors; Guest Musical Directors; Guest Musicians; Guest Soloists; Instructors; Local Artists; Lyricists; Multi Collaborations; Multimedia; Music; Original Music Scores; Resident Professionals; Sign Language Translators; Soloists
Founded: 1992
Specialized Field: Series & Festivals: Presenting In Early Music Festival
Status: Non-Profit, Professional
Paid Staff: 2
Volunteer Staff: 25
Paid Artists: 100
Non-paid Artists: 50
Season: May
Performs At: Bloomington (Festival Site)
Facility Category: Concert Halls, Opera Theatre
Seating Capacity: 230; 450

4193
INDIANA UNIVERSITY SUMMER MUSIC FESTIVAL
Indiana University Jacobs School of Music
Bloomington, IN 47405
Phone: 812-855-9846
Fax: 812-855-9847
e-mail: musicpub@indiana.edu
Web Site: www.music.indiana.edu
Officers:
    President: Adam Herbert
Mission: To provide a program of professional performing arts events for students and community members.
Specialized Field: Ballet theatre; Music; Instrument ensemble
Status: Non-Profit, Non-Professional
Income Sources: International Association of Auditorium Managers; Association of Performing Arts Presenters
Performs At: Indiana University Auditorium
Organization Type: Educational; Sponsoring

4194
INDIANA UNIVERSITY SCHOOL OF MUSIC SUMMER FESTIVAL
Indiana University School of Music
Bloomington, IN 47405
Phone: 812-855-9846
Fax: 812-855-4936
e-mail: jkosovsk@indiana.edu
Web Site: www.music.indiana.edu
Management:
    Special Programs Coordinator: Helena Walsh
Utilizes: Choreographers; Guest Accompanists; Guest Artists; Guest Composers; Guest Designers; Guest Directors; Guest Ensembles; Guest Lecturers; Guest Musical Directors; Guest Musicians; High School Drama; Local Artists; Multimedia; Music; Original Music Scores; Resident Professionals; Sign Language Translators; Singers; Soloists
Season: Mid June - Mid August
Performs At: Bloomington (Festival Site)
Annual Attendance: 12,000
Facility Category: Musical Arts Center; Auer Concert Hall
Seating Capacity: 1,460; 480

4195
CREATIVE ARTS COUNCIL OF WELLS COUNTY
110 W Washington Street
Bluffton, IN 46714
Phone: 219-824-5222
e-mail: cac@parlorcity.com
Management:
    Executive Director: Maureen Butler
Performs At: Auditorium

4196
BROADWAY SERIES: INDIANAPOLIS
200 Medical Drive
Suite D
Carmel, IN 46032
Phone: 317-818-3970
Fax: 317-818-3961
Toll-free: 800-793-7469
Web Site: www.broadwayseries.com

4197
COLUMBUS AREA ARTS COUNCIL
302 Washington Street
Columbus, IN 47201
Phone: 812-376-2539
Fax: 812-376-2589
e-mail: caac@artsincolumbus.org
Web Site: www.artsincolumbus.org
Management:
    President: Warren Ward
Performs At: The Commons

4198
CONNERSVILLE AREA ARTISTS SERIES
3006 W 400 N
Connersville, IN 47331
Phone: 317-825-2427
Management:
    Manager: David Caldwell
Performs At: Robert Wise Auditorium

4199
CULVER MILITARY ACADEMY CONCERT SERIES
Culver Academies
CEF Suite 79
Culver, IN 46511
Phone: 219-842-8255
Fax: 219-842-7994
Management:
    Theatre Director: Richard Coven
Performs At: Eppley Auditorium

4200
FORT WAYNE PARKS & RECREATION FESTIVAL
705 E State Street
Fort Wayne, IN 46805
Phone: 219-427-6715
Fax: 219-427-6020
Management:
    Manager: Michael Thompson
Utilizes: Guest Speakers; Local Artists; Multimedia; Original Music Scores
Paid Staff: 7
Income Sources: Budget, Grants, Donations
Affiliations: Fort Wayne Parts and Recreation
Annual Attendance: 52,000
Facility Category: Outdoor Theatre
Seating Capacity: 2,500
Year Built: 1949
Year Remodeled: 1976

Rental Contact: Mike Thompson

4201
DEPAUW UNIVERSITY PERFORMING ARTS SERIES
DePauw University
709 Locust Street
Greencastle, IN 46135
Phone: 765-658-4689
Fax: 765-658-4356
e-mail: rdye@depauw.edu
Management:
    Coordinator: Ron Dye
Performs At: Auditoriums

4202
HANOVER COLLEGE COMMUNITY ARTIST SERIES
Hanover College
PO Box 108
Hanover, IN 47243-0108
Phone: 812-866-7264
Fax: 812-866-7229
e-mail: hildebrand@hanover.edu
Web Site: www.hanover.edu/arts
Management:
    Producer: Paul Hildebrand
Mission: Presents a subscription series of 4-5 public events from September through April
Utilizes: Dance Companies; Multimedia; Original Music Scores; Sign Language Translators; Special Technical Talent
Founded: 1951
Specialized Field: Series & Festivals; Music; Theatre; Performing Arts and Dance
Status: Non-Profit, Professional
Budget: $60,000
Income Sources: Ticket Sales; Donations & Sponsorships; Grants
Performs At: Recital Hall
Annual Attendance: 3,000
Type of Stage: Proscenium
Seating Capacity: 700; 350

4203
CONCESCO FIELDHOUSE
One Conseco Court
125 S Pennsylvania Street
Indianapolis, IN 46204
Phone: 317-917-2500
Fax: 317-917-2599
Web Site: www.consecofieldhouse.com
Management:
    President/CEO: Donnie Walsh
    Owner: Melvin Simon
    Owner: Herbert Simon
    VP Facilities Administration: Harry James
Specialized Field: Home of the Indiana Pacers and downtown home of the Indianpolis Ice (IHL)
Seating Capacity: 18,000
Year Built: 1999

4204
ENSEMBLE MUSIC SOCIETY OF INDIANAPOLIS SERIES
PO Box 40188
Indianapolis, IN 46240
Phone: 317-254-8915
Fax: 317-254-8915
e-mail: pamela.steele@comcast.net
Web Site: www.ensemblemusic.org
Management:
    President: Pamela Steele

Founded: 1944
Specialized Field: Sereis & Festivals: Chamber Music Concerts
Status: Non-Profit, Professional
Paid Artists: 15

4205
ENSEMBLE MUSIC SOCIETY OF INDIANAPOLIS SERIES
PO Box 40188
Indianapolis, IN 46240
Phone: 317-254-8915
Fax: 317-254-8915
e-mail: pamelasteele@earthlink.net
Officers:
    President: Pamela Steele
Founded: 1944
Specialized Field: Chamber Music Concerts
Paid Artists: 15
Non-paid Artists: 36
Performs At: Indiana Historical Society
Seating Capacity: 300
Year Built: 1999

4206
FESTIVAL MUSIC SOCIETY OF INDIANA
6471 Central Avenue
Indianapolis, IN 46220
Phone: 317-251-5190
Fax: 317-251-8027
e-mail: merfms@msn.com
Web Site: www.emimdy.org
Officers:
    President: David A Garrett
    VP: Gail Bowler
    Treasurer: Neal Rothman
Management:
    Director: Frank Cooper
    Executive Secretary: Mary Ellen Roberts
Mission: To present early music including educational programs to diverse audiences at affordable prices.
Founded: 1969
Specialized Field: Early Music; Baroque; Renaissance
Paid Staff: 2
Volunteer Staff: 27
Budget: $100,000
Income Sources: Contributions; Grants; Ticket Sales
Season: June - July
Performs At: Inside Auditorium, Indianapolis (Fesitval Site)
Annual Attendance: 1,200
Facility Category: Indiana Historical Society
Stage Dimensions: 16'x32'
Seating Capacity: 300
Year Built: 1940
Year Remodeled: 1996

4207
INDY JAZZ FESTIVAL
22 E Washington Street
Suite 103
Indianapolis, IN 46204
Phone: 317-635-6630
Fax: 317-635-2010
Toll-free: 800-983-4639
e-mail: info@indyjazzfest.org
Web Site: www.indyjazzfest.org

4208
NATIONAL WOMEN'S MUSIC FESTIVAL
PO Box 1427
Indianapolis, IN 46206

Phone: 317-713-1144
e-mail: nwmfpro@yahoo.com
Web Site: www.wiaonline.org
Management:
    Producer: Jane Weldon
    Administration: Ann Arvidson
Season: June
Performs At: Muncie (Festival Site)
Facility Category: Emens Auditorium
Seating Capacity: 2,500

4209
JASPER COMMUNITY ARTS
951 College Avenue
Jasper, IN 47546-9382
Phone: 812-482-3070
Fax: 812-634-6997
e-mail: jasperarts@psci.net
Web Site: www.jasperarts.org
Officers:
    President: Michael Jones
Management:
    Director: Kit Miracle
Mission: The mission of the Jasper Community Arts Commission is to stimulate and encourage an appreciation of and participation in the arts.
Founded: 1975
Specialized Field: Music; Theatre; Mono-Acting
Status: Non-Profit, Professional
Paid Staff: 8
Paid Artists: 12
Budget: $650,000
Performs At: Multi-Discipline Performing; Visual; Dance; Education
Affiliations: APAP; INPN; IAC
Annual Attendance: 35,000-40,000
Facility Category: Performing Arts Center; Visual; Dance
Type of Stage: Proscenium
Stage Dimensions: 30X40
Seating Capacity: 675
Year Built: 1975
Year Remodeled: 2006
Rental Contact: Doreen Lechner

4210
CANTERBURY SUMMER THEATRE/THE FESTIVAL PLAYERS GUILD
PO Box 57
807 Franklin Street
Michigan City, IN 46360
Phone: 219-874-4269
Fax: 219-879-6377
Management:
    Productions Administrator: Gerald E Peters
Founded: 1969
Specialized Field: Summer Theater
Status: Non-Equity; Nonprofit
Season: June - August
Type of Stage: Proscenium
Stage Dimensions: 26'x 26'

4211
BETHEL COLLEGE FINE ARTS SERIES
1001 W Mckinley Avenue
Mishawaka, IN 46545
Phone: 574-259-3331
Fax: 574-257-3513
Toll-free: 800-422-4101
e-mail: jacobss@bethelcollege.edu
Web Site: www.bethel-in.edu
Management:
    Director: Erin Wagler
    Assistant Director: Becky Schaut

Assistant Director: Sheila Jacobsen
Performs At: Everest-Rohrer Auditorium

4212
EMENS AUDITORIUM

Emens Auditorium
Ball State University
Muncie, IN 47306-0750
Phone: 765-285-1539
Fax: 765-285-3719
Toll-free: 877-993-6367
Web Site: www.bsu.edu/emens
Management:
    Manager: Robert Myers
    Assistant Manager: Darcy Wood
Founded: 1964
Specialized Field: Series & Festivals; Vocal Music; Theatre; Youth; Dance; Ethnic Performances
Status: Non-Profit, Professional
Paid Staff: 15
Annual Attendance: 10,000+
Facility Category: Performing Arts Center
Seating Capacity: 3309
Year Built: 1964
Rental Contact: Bob Myers

4213
SAINT MARY'S COLLEGE CULTURAL ARTS SEASON

Saint Mary's College
Moreau Center for the Arts
Notre Dame, IN 46556-5001
Phone: 574-284-4000
Fax: 219-284-4784
e-mail: webmaster@saintmarys.edu
Web Site: www.saintmarys.edu
Management:
    President: Carol Ann Mooney
Performs At: O'Laughlin Auditorium

4214
ARTS PLACE, INC.

PO Box 804
131 East Walnut Street
Portland, IN 47371
Phone: 260-726-4809
Fax: 260-726-2081
e-mail: artsland@artsland.org
Web Site: www.artsland.org
Management:
    Executive Director: Eric Rogers
Mission: To nurture the creative spirit by making arts,experiences, education, and services accessible to the regions residents, artists, and cultural organizations.
Founded: 1967
Specialized Field: Arts Council
Paid Staff: 10
Budget: $700,000
Income Sources: Private Contributions; Endowments; Grants; Tickets And Instructional Fees
Performs At: Hall Memorial Theatre
Facility Category: Arts Center
Type of Stage: Proscenium
Seating Capacity: 283
Year Built: 1985
Year Remodeled: 2000

4215
EARLHAM COLLEGE GUEST ARTIST SERIES

801 National Road W
Richmond, IN 47374

Phone: 765-983-1373
Fax: 765-983-1291
Web Site: www.earlham.edu
Management:
    President: Douglas Bennett
    VP: James McKey
    Chairman of the Board: Mark Mayers
Founded: 1847
Status: Non-Profit, Non-Professional
Performs At: Goddard Auditorium

4216
FIREFLY FESTIVAL FOR THE PERFORMING ARTS

112 W Jefferson Boulevard
Suite 511
South Bend, IN 46601
Phone: 574-288-3472
Fax: 574-288-3478
e-mail: firefly@fireflyfestival.com
Web Site: www.fireflyfestival.com
Management:
    President: Candace Butler
    Promotion Director: Wendy Little
    Office Assistant: Judy West
Mission: To promote and present to the general public artistic performanaces which have as their general theme music, dance, drama, and other arts.
Utilizes: Actors; Dance Companies; Guest Accompanists; Guest Artists; Guest Companies; Guest Musical Directors; Guild Activities; Local Artists; Multimedia; Original Music Scores; Selected Students; Singers; Special Technical Talent; Theatre Companies
Founded: 1981
Specialized Field: Series and Festivals; Music; Theatre; Dance
Status: Non-Profit, Professional
Paid Staff: 3
Volunteer Staff: 140
Budget: $330,000
Income Sources: Grants; Sponsors; Advertisers; Ticket Sales; In-kind Donations; Private Donations; Business Donations
Season: June - August
Performs At: St. Patrick's County Park, South Bend (Festival Site)
Annual Attendance: 18,000
Facility Category: Robert J Fischgrund Center for the Performing Arts
Type of Stage: Proscenium
Stage Dimensions: 30x60
Seating Capacity: 6,000
Year Built: 1986
Rental Contact: St. Patrick's County Park
Organization Type: Performing; Educational

4217
PERFORMING ARTS SERIES OF INDIANA STATE UNIVERSITY

200 North Seventh Street
Terre Haute, IN 47809
Phone: 812-237-3770
Toll-free: 877-478-8497
e-mail: david.dekolletti@indstate.edu
Web Site: www.indstate.edu
Management:
    Program Coordinator: David Dekolletti
Founded: 1865
Specialized Field: Series & Festivals; Music; Device; Theatre
Status: Non-Profit, Professional
Paid Staff: 1
Performs At: Tilson Auditorium

Seating Capacity: 1,684

4218
VALPARAISO UNIVERSITY GUEST ARTISTS SERIES

VU Center for the Arts
Valparaiso, IN 46383
Phone: 219-464-5000
Fax: 219-464-5381
e-mail: sarah.rothaar@valpo.edu
Web Site: www.valpo.edu
Management:
    President: Alan F Harre
    VP Academic Affair: Roy A Austensen
    VP Admin And Finance: Charley Gillispie
Performs At: Chapel of the Resurrection

4219
VINCENNES UNIVERSITY COMMUNITY SERIES

1002 N 1st Street
DC-38
Vincennes, IN 47591
Phone: 812-888-4354
Fax: 812-888-5942
Toll-free: 800-945-ALUM
e-mail: dclinken@vinu.edu
Management:
    President: Richard Helton
    Executive Director: Donna Clinkenbeard
Utilizes: Special Technical Talent; Theatre Companies
Founded: 1950
Specialized Field: Series & Festivals; Vocal Music; Ethnic Performances
Status: Non-Profit, Professional
Performs At: Auditorium
Facility Category: High School Auditorium
Seating Capacity: 900

4220
PURDUE UNIVERSITY CONVOCATIONS & LECTURES

1821 ENAD
Room S-103
West Lafayette, IN 47907
Phone: 765-494-9712
Fax: 765-494-0540
Web Site: www.purdue.edu/convos
Management:
    President: Todd E Wetzel
    Artistic Director: Laura Clavio
Specialized Field: Theatre: Musical
Status: Professional
Paid Staff: 13
Performs At: Edward C. Elliot Hall of Music

4221
MASTERWORKS FESTIVAL

PO Box 700
Winona Lake, IN 46590
Phone: 574-267-5973
Fax: 574-267-8315
Toll-free: 888-836-2723
e-mail: publicity@christianperformingart.org
Web Site: www.masterworksfestival.org
Management:
    Artistic Director: Dr Patrick Kavanaugh
    Music Director: Dr James Kraft
    Administrator: Rachel Center
    Office Manager: Cyd Kumi
    Publicity Coordinator: Erin Richard
Mission: To train the next generation of Christian performing artists.

Utilizes: Actors; Arrangers; Choreographers; Collaborating Artists; Community Members; Composers; Dancers; Designers; Educators; Filmmakers; Grant Writers; Guest Accompanists; Guest Composers; Guest Designers; Guest Ensembles; Guest Instructors; Guest Lecturers; Guest Musical Directors; Guest Musicians; Guest Speakers; High School Drama; Multimedia; Paid Performers; Sign Language Translators; Soloists; Students; Student Interns
Founded: 1997
Specialized Field: Classical
Status: Professional; Nonprofit; Educational; Religious
Budget: $300,000 - $500,000
Income Sources: Donations, Tuition, Foundations
Performs At: Grace College
Annual Attendance: 3,500 - 4,500
Facility Category: 4 Stages: 2 Concert, 1 Recital Hall, 1 Outdoor Ampitheater
Seating Capacity: 300, 500, 150, 300
Year Built: 1999

Iowa

4222
IOWA STATE UNIVERSITY PERFORMING ARTS COUNCIL SERIES
Iowa State Center, ISU
Ames, IA 50011
Phone: 515-294-3347
Fax: 515-294-3349
Web Site: www.center.iastate.edu
Management:
   Director: Mark North
   Performing Arts Program Manager: Patti Cotter
Founded: 1969
Specialized Field: Multi
Paid Staff: 30

4223
IOWA STATE UNIVERSITY PERFORMING ARTS COUNCIL SERIES
Iowa State Center, ISU
Ames, IA 50011
Phone: 515-294-3347
Fax: 515-294-3349
Web Site: www.center.iastate.edu
Management:
   Director: Mark North
   Performing Arts Program Manager: Patti Cotter
Utilizes: Dance Companies; Educators; Multimedia; Original Music Scores; Selected Students; Theatre Companies
Founded: 1969
Specialized Field: Multi
Paid Staff: 30
Performs At: Stephens Auditorium
Annual Attendance: 30,000
Facility Category: Auditorium
Type of Stage: Proscenium
Seating Capacity: 2720
Year Built: 1969

4224
CASS COUNTY ARTS COUNCIL
Box 255
Atlantic, IA 50022
Phone: 712-243-2527
Fax: 712-243-4182

4225
BURLINGTON CIVIC MUSIC ASSOCIATION
Box 324
Burlington, IA 52601
Fax: 319-754-6824
Toll-free: 800-397-1708
e-mail: bwilson@thehawkeye.com
Officers:
   Program Chairman: Bobby Wilson
Performs At: Memorial Auditorium

4226
UNIVERSITY OF NORTHERN IOWA ARTISTS SERIES
University of Northern Iowa
Gallagher Bluedorn Performing Arts Center
Cedar Falls, IA 50614-0801
Phone: 319-273-3660
Fax: 319-273-7470
Toll-free: 877-549-7469
e-mail: steve.carignan@uni.edu
Web Site: www.gbpac.com
Officers:
   President: Benjamin Allen
   Assistant VP Events Management: Steve Carignan
Management:
   Director Operations Performing Arts: Janelle Darst
   Director Events Complex: Heather Tousignant
Utilizes: Artists-in-Residence; Choreographers; Collaborations; Dance Companies; Dancers; Educators; Guest Accompanists; Guest Choreographers; Guest Conductors; Guest Instructors; Guest Musical Directors; Guest Musicians; Local Artists; Lyricists; Multimedia; Original Music Scores; Selected Students; Sign Language Translators; Soloists; Special Technical Talent; Theatre Companies
Founded: 2000
Specialized Field: Performing Art
Status: Non-Profit, Non-Professional
Paid Staff: 13
Volunteer Staff: 350
Budget: 1.8 Million
Income Sources: Tickets; Grants; Fundraising; State Support
Performs At: Theatre/Concert Hall
Affiliations: APAP
Annual Attendance: 120,000
Facility Category: Multi-Venue, Performing Arts Center
Type of Stage: Proscenium/Thrust
Stage Dimensions: 30'x 40'
Seating Capacity: 1,700
Year Built: 2000
Cost: $27,000
Rental Contact: Director Steve Carignan

4227
CEDAR RAPIDS COMMUNITY CONCERTS ASSOCIATION
800 35th St NE
Cedar Rapids, IA 52402
Phone: 319-540-2301
Web Site: http://www.crcommunityconcerts.org/
Management:
   President: Tony Staab
   Bruce: Ellen Pelzer 1st Vice President
   Treasurer: Ivan Chester
   Secretary: Mary Ann Wetherbee
Founded: 1930
Specialized Field: Series & Festivals; Instrumental Music; Theatre; Youth; Dance; Ethnic Performances

Status: Non-Profit, Professional
Performs At: Paramount Theatre for the Performing Arts

4228
COE COLLEGE JAZZ SUMMIT
1220 First Avenue NE
Marquis 104
Cedar Rapids, IA 52402
Phone: 319-399-8500
Fax: 319-399-8209
Toll-free: 877-CAL- COE
e-mail: btiede@coe.edu
Web Site: www.coe.edu
Management:
   Director Of Marketing: Rod Pritchard
   Associate Director Of Marketing and: Lonnie Zingula
   Director Of Production: Carole Butz
Mission: To offer student musicians the opportunity to work with renowned professional players/teachers.
Founded: 1851
Specialized Field: Jazz
Status: Nonprofit
Paid Staff: 5
Volunteer Staff: 40
Paid Artists: 6
Non-paid Artists: 20
Annual Attendance: 1,500

4229
COE COLLEGE MARQUIS SERIES
1220 1st Avenue NW
Cedar Rapids, IA 52402
Phone: 319-366-6237
e-mail: ggriffin@coe.edu
Web Site: www.coe.edu
Management:
   President: Greg Griffins
Specialized Field: Performance Arts Community
Status: Non-Profit, Professional
Paid Staff: 6

4230
COE COLLEGE MARQUIS SERIES
1220 1st Avenue NW
Cedar Rapids, IA 52402
Phone: 319-399-8682
e-mail: GCross@coe.edu
Web Site: www.coe.edu
Officers:
   Chairman: Dr. Maria Dean
   Marquis Series Committee Chair: Dr. Gavin Cross
Performs At: Sinclair Auditorium

4231
LEGION ARTS
1103 3rd Street SE
Cedar Rapids, IA 52401
Phone: 319-364-1580
Fax: 319-362-9156
e-mail: info@legionarts.org
Web Site: www.legionarts.org
Management:
   Executive Director: F John Herbert
   Producing Director: Mel Andringa, mel@legionarts.org
Mission: Promotes new and innovative expression in the visual, performing, literary and electronic arts; fosters creative interaction between artists, their communities and society; and encourages the imaginative exploration of contemporary ideas and experience.

Utilizes: Artists-in-Residence; Choreographers; Collaborating Artists; Dance Companies; Dancers; Fine Artists; Guest Accompanists; Guest Choreographers; Guest Designers; Guest Directors; Guest Ensembles; Guest Musical Directors; Guest Musicians; Multimedia; Original Music Scores; Playwrights; Resident Artists; Sign Language Translators; Student Interns; Special Technical Talent; Theatre Companies
Founded: 1981
Specialized Field: Visual Arts; Theatre; Music; Dance; Film; Spoken Word
Status: Non-Profit, Professional
Paid Staff: 4
Budget: $300,000
Income Sources: Public and Private Grants; Earned Income
Performs At: Proscenium; Black Box; Concert Halls; Cabaret
Affiliations: NPN; NAAO; APAP
Annual Attendance: 20,000
Facility Category: Contemporary Arts Center
Type of Stage: Black Box; Proscenium
Seating Capacity: 75/175
Year Built: 1893
Year Remodeled: 2010
Rental Contact: Mel Andrinca
Organization Type: Performing; Touring; Sponsoring

4232
GLENN MILLER FESTIVAL
107 E Main Street
PO Box 61
Clarinda, IA 51632
Phone: 712-542-2461
Fax: 712-542-2461
e-mail: gmbs@heartland.net
Web Site: www.glennmiller.org
Officers:
  President: Marvin Negley
Management:
  President: Marvin Negley
  Office Manager: Jodi Eberly
  Secretary of Board: Arlene Leonard
Founded: 1978
Specialized Field: Series and Festivals; Instrumental Music; Vocal Music; Youth; Dance; Life and Memory of Glenn Miller
Status: Non-Profit, Non-Professional
Paid Staff: 1
Volunteer Staff: 15

4233
BIX BIEDERBECKE MEMORIAL JAZZ FESTIVAL
311 N Ripley Street
PO Box 3688
Davenport, IA 52808
Phone: 563-324-7170
Fax: 563-326-1732
Toll-free: 888-249-5487
e-mail: info@bixsociety.org
Web Site: www.bixsociety.org
Officers:
  President: Don Estes
  Secretary: Muriel Voss
  Treasurer: Annette J Peart
Management:
  President: Raymond Voss
  Executive Director: Rich Johnson
  Festival Director: Ray Voss
Mission: To honor the memory and perpetuate the music of Leon Bix Beiderbecke, a Davenport native son, who was a world-renowned jazz cornetist, pianist and composer.

Founded: 1972
Specialized Field: Series & Festivals; Instrumental Music; Youth
Status: Non-Profit, Professional
Volunteer Staff: 450
Paid Artists: 100
Season: July
Annual Attendance: 10,000

4234
MISSISSIPPI VALLEY BLUES FESTIVAL
102 S Harrison Street
Suite 300
Davenport, IA 52801
Phone: 563-322-5837
Fax: 563-322-5832
e-mail: mvbs@revealed.net
Web Site: www.mvbs.org
Management:
  President: Robert W Covemaker
Founded: 1984
Specialized Field: Education of Blues with Residency
Status: Non-Profit, Non-Professional
Paid Staff: 1

4235
LUTHER COLLEGE CENTER STAGE SERIES
Luther College
700 College Drive
Decorah, IA 52101
Phone: 563-387-1291
Fax: 563-387-1766
Toll-free: 800-458-8437
e-mail: gertta01@luther.edu
Web Site: www.programming.luther.edu
Management:
  Director Campus Programming: Tanya M B Gertz
Founded: 1861
Specialized Field: Performing Arts
Paid Staff: 6
Volunteer Staff: 40
Performs At: Center for Faith & Life
Annual Attendance: 9,300
Facility Category: Performing Arts Facility
Type of Stage: Thrust & Perscenium
Stage Dimensions: 48'x 32'
Seating Capacity: Thrust - 1,400; Perscenium - 950
Year Built: 1977

4236
CIVIC MUSIC ASSOCIATION OF DES MOINES
1620 Pleasant Street
Suite 244
Des Moines, IA 50314
Phone: 515-280-4020
Fax: 515-286-4080
e-mail: info@civicmusic.org
Web Site: www.civicmusic.org
Management:
  Executive Director: Carrie Clogg
Founded: 1925
Specialized Field: Classical and Jazz Music
Status: Non-Profit, Professional
Paid Staff: 1
Paid Artists: 15
Seating Capacity: 770

4237
CIVIC MUSIC ASSOCIATION OF DES MOINES
221 Walnut Street
Des Moines, IA 50309
Phone: 515-288-8918
Fax: 515-243-1588
e-mail: info@civicmusic.org
Web Site: www.civicmusic.org
Management:
  Executive Director: Debra Peckumn
Founded: 1925
Specialized Field: Classical And Jazz Music
Paid Staff: 1
Seating Capacity: 2735

4238
GRAND VIEW COLLEGE-NIELSEN CONCERT SERIES
1200 Grand View Avenue
Des Moines, IA 50316
Phone: 515-263-2958
Fax: 515-263-6192
Toll-free: 800-444-6083
e-mail: kduffy@gvc.edu
Web Site: www.gvc.edu
Management:
  Chairperson of the Committee: Katherine P Duffy
Founded: 1981
Specialized Field: Series & Festivals; Instrumental Music; Vocal Music
Status: Non-Profit, Professional

4239
GRAND VIEW COLLEGE-NIELSEN CONCERT SERIES
1200 Grand View Avenue
Des Moines, IA 50316
Phone: 515-263-2958
Fax: 515-263-6192
e-mail: kduffy@gvc.edu
Management:
  Director: Dr. Katherine Pohlmann Duffy
Performs At: College Center Theatre

4240
CLARKE COLLEGE CULTURAL EVENTS SERIES
1550 Clark Drive
Dubuque, IA 52001-3198
Phone: 319-588-6330
Fax: 319-588-6789
Toll-free: 800-383-2345
Web Site: www.clarke.edu
Management:
  President: Catherine Dunn

4241
LORAS COLLEGE ARTS & LECTURE SERIES
1450 Alta Vista
PO Box 178
Dubuque, IA 52004-0178
Phone: 563-588-7100
Fax: 319-557-4086
Toll-free: 800-245-6727
e-mail: bhughes@loras.edu
Web Site: www.loras.edu
Management:
  President: Colin James
Founded: 1939

Specialized Field: Insturmental Music; Vocal Music; Dance; Multi-Cultural; Theatre; Lecture

4242
LORAS COLLEGE ARTS & LECTURE SERIES
1450 Alta Vista
Dubuque, IA 52004-0178
Phone: 319-588-7153
Fax: 319-557-4086
e-mail: bhughes@loras.edu
Web Site: www.loras.edu
Officers:
　Chairman: Brian Hughes
Management:
　Chairman: Brain Hughes
Mission: To bring high quality cultural activity to the college and community.
Founded: 1985
Specialized Field: Insturmental Music; Vocal Music; Dance; Multi-Cultural; Theatre; Lecture
Volunteer Staff: 10
Performs At: St. Joseph Auditorium

4243
WALDORF COMMUNITY ARTISTS SERIES
Waldorf College
106 S 6Th Street
Forest City, IA 50436
Phone: 641-585-8177
Fax: 641-582-8194
e-mail: thompsons@waldorf.edu
Web Site:
www.waldorf.edu/finearts/music/events/wcas.htm
Management:
　President: Richard A Hanson PhD
　Assistant To President: Cindy Carter
Mission: To offer the finest in performing arts events to the Forest City and Waldorf communities.
Founded: 1988
Specialized Field: Dance; Vocal Music; Instrumental Music; Theater; Lyric Opera; Grand Opera
Status: Nonprofit
Income Sources: Waldorf College
Organization Type: Sponsoring

4244
GRINNELL COLLEGE MUSIC DEPARTMENT CONCERT SERIES
Music Department
Grinnell, IA 50112
Phone: 641-269-4000
Fax: 641-269-4420
Web Site: www.grinnell.edu/music/
Officers:
　Music Department Chairman: Jonathan Chenette
Management:
　Chair: John Rommereim
　Music Technical Assistant: Paul Nelson
Performs At: Sebring-Lewis Hall

4245
FRIDAY NIGHT CONCERT SERIES
PO Box 3128
Iowa City, IA 52244
Phone: 319-337-7944
Fax: 319-358-9094
e-mail: info@summerofthearts.org
Web Site: www.summerofthearts.org
Officers:
　Executive Director: Katie Roche
Founded: 1991

4246
IOWA ARTS FESTIVAL
PO Box 3128
Iowa City, IA 52244
Phone: 319-337-7944
Fax: 319-358-9094
e-mail: info@summerofthearts.org
Web Site: www.summerofthearts.org
Officers:
　Executive Director: Katie Roche
Management:
　Executive Director: Lisa Barnes
Founded: 1982
Paid Artists: 20

4247
IOWA CITY JAZZ FESTIVAL
PO Box 3128
Iowa City, IA 52244
Phone: 319-337-7944
Fax: 319-358-9094
e-mail: info@summerofthearts.org
Web Site: www.summerofthearts.org
Officers:
　Executive Director: Katie Roche
Management:
　Executive Director: Lisa Barnes
Founded: 1982

4248
IOWA PICTURE SHOW
PO Box 3128
Iowa City, IA 52244
Phone: 319-337-7944
Fax: 319-358-9094
e-mail: info@summerofthearts.org
Web Site: www.summerofthearts.org
Officers:
　Executive Director: Katie Roche
Founded: 1991

4249
SAND IN THE CITY
PO Box 3128
Iowa City, IA 52244
Phone: 319-337-7944
Fax: 319-358-9094
e-mail: info@summerofthearts.org
Web Site: www.summerofthearts.org
Officers:
　Executive Director: Katie Roche
Management:
　Executive Director: Lisa Barnes
Founded: 1982
Paid Artists: 20

4250
JACKSON CONCERT SERIES
400 Iowa Avenue
Wesley United Methodist Church
Muscatine, IA 52761
Phone: 563-263-1596
Fax: 563-263-1631
e-mail: wesleymethodist@machlink.com
Web Site: www.wesleymethodist.org/jackson.htm
Management:
　Choir Director: Dr Richard Smith
　Sr Pastor Of Worship/Administration: Dr Hal Green
　Youth Director: Bob Calegan
Performs At: Wesely United Methodist Church

4251
ORANGE CITY ARTS COUNCIL
Box 202
Orange City, IA 51041
Phone: 712-707-4885
Fax: 712-707-4351
e-mail: ocarts@juno.com
Management:
　Program Director: Joyce Bloemendaal
Utilizes: Actors; Artists-in-Residence; Dance Companies; Fine Artists; Guest Accompanists; Instructors; Local Artists; Multimedia; Original Music Scores; Special Technical Talent; Theatre Companies
Founded: 1977
Specialized Field: Series and Festivals; Present Arts for Variety Music; Dance; Theatre
Status: Non-Profit, Non-Professional
Paid Staff: 1
Performs At: Christ Chapel

4252
BUENA VISTA UNIVERSITY ACADEMIC & CULTURAL EVENTS SERIES
Buena Vista University
610 W 4th Street
Storm Lake, IA 50588
Phone: 712-749-2401
Fax: 712-749-2404
Toll-free: 800-383-2821
e-mail: wagnerl@bvu.edu
Web Site: www.bvu.edu/students
Management:
　President: Fred Moore
　Managing Director: Lisa Wagner
Founded: 1988
Specialized Field: Series & Festivals; Instrumental Music; Vocal Music; Theatre; Dance; Ethnic Performances
Status: Non-Profit, Non-Professional
Paid Staff: 1
Budget: $140,000
Performs At: Anderson Auditorium
Affiliations: APAP
Annual Attendance: 3,500-4,000
Facility Category: Multi Use
Type of Stage: Proscenium
Seating Capacity: 822
Year Built: 1999
Rental Contact: Katie Schwint

4253
AMERICAFEST: ALLIANCE WORLD FESTIVAL OF SINGING
34 Fox Creek Drive
Waukee, IA 50263
Phone: 515-987-1405
Fax: 515-987-5480
e-mail: allianceforartsu@qwest.net
Web Site: www.allianceforartsandunderstanding.com
Management:
　President: Alfred Moore
　Executive Director: Donald Morse
　Artistic Director: Carol Stewart
Founded: 1993
Specialized Field: Vocal Music: Choral
Status: Non-Profit, Professional
Paid Staff: 7
Paid Artists: 5
Season: October
Performs At: St. John's University (Festival Site)
Facility Category: Abbey Cathedral
Seating Capacity: 2,000

4254
ALLIANCE WORLD FESTIVAL OF WOMEN SINGING
34 Fox Creek Drive
Waukee, IA 50263
Phone: 515-987-1405
Fax: 515-987-5480
e-mail: allianceforartsu@qwest.net
Web Site: www.allianceforartsandunderstanding.com
Management:
President: Alfred Moore
Executive Director: Donald Morse
Artistic Director: Carol Stewart
Founded: 1993
Specialized Field: Series and Festivals: Festivals of Choral Singing
Status: Non-Profit, Professional
Paid Staff: 6
Season: October
Performs At: St. John's University [Festival Site]
Facility Category: Abbey Cathedral
Seating Capacity: 2,000

4255
WARTBURG COLLEGE ARTISTS SERIES
100 Wartburg Boulevard
Waverly, IA 50677-1003
Mailing Address: PO Box 1003
Phone: 319-352-8409
Fax: 319-352-8501
Toll-free: 800-772-2085
e-mail: artistseries@wartburg.edu
Web Site: www.wartburg.edu
Officers:
President: Darrel Colson
Management:
Artistic Director: Myrna Culbertson
Mission: To provide diverse performing artists with community service and educational venues.
Founded: 1920
Specialized Field: Series & Festivals; Instrumental Music; Vocal Music; Theater; Dance; Ethnic Performances
Status: Non-Profit, Professional
Paid Staff: 1
Performs At: Neumann Auditorium
Organization Type: Sponsoring

Kansas

4256
GREAT PLAINS THEATRE FESTIVAL
PO Box 476
Abilene, KS 62410
Phone: 785-263-2903
Fax: 785-263-9960
Toll-free: 888-222-4574
e-mail: marc@greatplainstheatre.com
Web Site: www.greatplainstheatre.com
Management:
Executive Artistic Director: Richard Esvang
Associate Artistic Director: Michelle Meade
Utilizes: Actors; AEA Actors; Choreographers; Five Seasonal Concerts; Guest Designers; Guest Lecturers; Guild Activities; Instructors; Local Artists; Multi Collaborations; Multimedia; New Productions; Organization Contracts; Original Music Scores; Performance Artists; Resident Artists; Sign Language Translators; Soloists; Touring Companies
Founded: 1994
Status: Nonprofit

Performs At: Remodeled Stone Church; State of the Art Theatre.
Affiliations: Equity
Facility Category: Theatre
Type of Stage: Proscenium
Stage Dimensions: 45' x 26'
Seating Capacity: 199
Year Built: 1880
Year Remodeled: 1994

4257
COFFEYVILLE CULTURAL ARTS COUNCIL INC
912 Walnut St.
Coffeyville, KS 67337
Phone: 960-251-0088
Web Site:
http://www.coffeyville.com/Culture.htm#Center_For_the_Arts
Management:
Executive Director: Kenneth H Burchinal
President: John Isaacs
Treasurer: Robert Erickson
Secretary: Nedra Troxel
Specialized Field: Series; Youth Choir
Paid Staff: 1
Performs At: JH Benefiel Auditorium

4258
EMPORIA ARTS COUNCIL PERFORMING ARTS/CONCERT/CHILDREN'S SERIES
618 Mechanic St
Emporia, KS 66801
Phone: 620-340-6473
Management:
Executive Director: Melissa Windsor
Specialized Field: Choral, Dance, Theater, Instrumental Music, Series, Youth
Status: Non-Profit, Professional
Performs At: Albert Taylor Hall

4259
GOODLAND ARTS COUNCIL
120 W 12
PO Box 526
Goodland, KS 67735
Phone: 785-890-6442
Fax: 785-890-6335
e-mail: gidarts@st/tel.net
Web Site: www.goodlandnet.com/artcenter
Officers:
President: Jacque Schields
Executive Director: Kay Younger
Founded: 1979
Specialized Field: Visual Arts
Status: Non-Profit, Non-Professional
Paid Staff: 2
Paid Artists: 5
Performs At: Auditorium

4260
FORT HAYS STATE UNIVERSITY ENCORE SERIES
600 Park Street
Hays, KS 67601
Phone: 785-628-5801
Fax: 785-628-4007
Web Site: www.fhsu.edu
Management:
Executive Director: Carol Brock
Founded: 1981
Specialized Field: Series & Festivals: Multidisciplinary
Status: Non-Profit, Professional

Paid Staff: 2
Performs At: Felton-Start Theatre

4261
HESSTON/BETHEL PERFORMING ARTS SERIES
PO Box 3000
Hesston, KS 67062
Phone: 316-327-8158
Fax: 316-327-8300
Officers:
Chairman: Jacob Rittenhouse
Executive Secretary: David W Rhodes
Administrative Assistant: Krista Murray
Mission: To provide high quality cultural programming for the Hesston College/Bethel College student bodies and the immediate Hesston and Newton communities
Utilizes: Contract Orchestras; Educators; Guest Directors; Guest Instructors; Guest Musical Directors; Guest Musicians; Multimedia; Paid Performers; Sign Language Translators
Founded: 1982
Specialized Field: Vocal Music; Instrumental Music
Status: Nonprofit
Budget: $45,000
Income Sources: Season Tickets; Single Ticket Sales; Patrons; City Support
Performs At: Yost Center, Hesston College; Memorial Hall, Bethel College
Annual Attendance: 500
Facility Category: Gymnasium/Field House
Seating Capacity: 1,000
Year Built: 1983
Organization Type: Sponsoring

4262
MESSIAH FESTIVAL OF MUSIC
Bethany College
421 N 1st Street
Lindsborg, KS 67456
Phone: 913-227-3311
Fax: 913-721-2110
Management:
Conductor: Gregory Aune
Public Relations/Ticket Information: Jud Barclay
Music Director: Daniel Mahraun
Founded: 1882
Specialized Field: Vocal Music; Instrumental Music
Status: Nonprofit
Income Sources: Bethany College
Performs At: Presser Hall Auditorium
Organization Type: Performing; Sponsoring

4263
BOWLUS CULTURAL ATTRACTIONS SERIES
PO Box 705
205 E Madison
Lola, KS 66749
Phone: 316-365-4765
Fax: 316-365-4767
e-mail: mary.bowlus@iolaks.com
Web Site: www.bowluscenter.com
Management:
Director: Mary Martin
Seating Capacity: 752

4264
KANSAS STATE UNIVERSITY MCCAIN PERFORMANCE SERIES
McCain Auditorium
Manhattan, KS 66506-4711

Phone: 785-532-6425
Fax: 785-532-5870
e-mail: rpm@ksu.edu
Web Site: www.ksu.edu/mccain
Management:
President: Wes Sald
Artistic Director: Richard Martin
Operations Manager: Terri Lee
Founded: 1971
Specialized Field: Series & Festivals: Theatre
Status: Non-Profit, Professional
Paid Staff: 7
Seating Capacity: 1800

4265
OTTAWA MUNICIPAL AUDITORIUM ENTERTAINMENT SERIES
301 S Hickory
PO Box 462
Ottawa, KS 66067
Phone: 785-242-8810
Fax: 785-229-3760
e-mail: omalive@grapevine.net
Web Site: www.grapevine.net/~omalive
Management:
Administrative Manager: Shonda Stitt
Operations Manager: Sam Parkins
Founded: 1978
Specialized Field: Series and Festivals: Vocal Music
Status: Non-Profit, Professional
Paid Staff: 9

4266
OVERLAND PARK ARTS COMMISSION
6300 W 87th Street
Overland Park, KS 66212
Phone: 913-895-6357
Fax: 913-895-6365
e-mail: jkbilyea@opkansas.org
Web Site: www.opkansas.org
Management:
Executive Director: Julie K Bilyea
Founded: 1962
Specialized Field: Series and Festivals: Performance and Visual Arts
Status: For-Profit, Non-Professional
Paid Staff: 1

4267
PITTSBURG STATE UNIVERSITY SOLO & CHAMBER MUSIC SERIES
PSU Department of Music
1701 S Broadway
Pittsburg, KS 66762
Phone: 620-235-4476
Fax: 620-235-4468
e-mail: music@pittstate.edu
Web Site: www.pittstate.edu/music
Management:
President: Tom Bryant
Chaiman of the Music Department: Craig Fuchs
Series Director: Susan Marchant
Specialized Field: Series and Festivals; Instrumental Music; Vocal Music; Ethnic Performances
Status: Non-Profit, Professional
Paid Staff: 20
Paid Artists: 19

4268
UNIVERSITY OF NEVADA: RENO PERFORMING ARTS SERIES
UNR School Of The Arts/048
Reno, KS 89557-0048

Phone: 775-784-4278
Fax: 775-784-3566
Toll-free: 800-233-8928
e-mail: cmoney@unr.edu
Web Site: www.unr.edu/pas
Officers:
President: Fred Holman
Executive Director: C J Watler
Management:
Assistant Director Of Programs: Chris Money
Artistic Director: Dain Dragore
Founded: 1960
Specialized Field: Performing Arts
Status: Non-Profit, Professional
Paid Staff: 1
Paid Artists: 20
Budget: $62,000-80,000
Income Sources: University Administration, Students, State And Local Grants, Ticket Income, Other Sources
Performs At: Concert Hall
Affiliations: University Of Nevada, Reno
Annual Attendance: 2,200-3,000
Facility Category: Concert Hall
Type of Stage: Proscenium
Seating Capacity: 618
Year Built: 1988

4269
SALINA ARTS & HUMANITIES COMMISSION
PO Box 2181
Salina, KS 67402-2181
Phone: 785-309-5770
Fax: 785-826-7444
e-mail: sahc@salina.org
Web Site: www.riverfestival.com
Officers:
Executive Director: John Highkin

4270
STERLING COLLEGE ARTIST SERIES
Sterling College
Sterling, KS 67579
Phone: 316-278-2173
Web Site: www.sterling.edu
Management:
Chair, Music Department: Dr. Brad Nix
Specialized Field: Instrumental Music
Performs At: Culbertson Auditorium

4271
TOPEKA PERFORMING ARTS CENTER
214 SE 8th Street
Topeka, KS 66603
Phone: 785-234-2787
Fax: 785-234-2307
Web Site: www.tpactix.org
Management:
Executive Director: Barbara Wiggins
Marketing Manager: Tracie Kalkbreaner
Mission: To promote and preserve jazz.
Founded: 1991
Specialized Field: Performing Arts Center
Status: Non-Profit, Professional
Paid Staff: 6
Volunteer Staff: 60
Performs At: Theater
Seating Capacity: 2,461

4272
FRIENDS UNIVERSITY MILLER FINE ARTS SERIES
2100 University
Wichita, KS 67213
Phone: 316-295-5849
Fax: 316-295-5593
e-mail: riney@friends.edu
Web Site: www.friends.edu
Officers:
Fine Arts Division Chairman: Cecil J Riney
Management:
Chair: Ceico Raney
Assistant Chair: Toni Liphart
Specialized Field: Series & Festivals; Instrumental Music; Vocal Music; Theatre; Dance
Status: Non-Profit, Professional
Paid Staff: 15
Paid Artists: 20
Performs At: Alexander Auditorium

4273
WICHITA STATE UNIVERSITY CONNOISSEUR SERIES
College of Fine Arts, 415 Jardine Hall
1845 Fairmount
Wichita, KS 67260-0151
Phone: 316-978-3389
Fax: 316-978-3951

Kentucky

4274
ARTISTS IN CONCERT SERIES
Ashland Community and Technical College
1400 College Drive
Ashland, KY 41101-3683
Phone: 606-325-1132
Fax: 606-326-2173
e-mail: aic@artistsinconcert.com
Web Site: www.artistsinconcert.com
Management:
President: John Barker
Founded: 1983
Specialized Field: Sereis & Festivals: Classical Music
Status: Non-Profit, Non-Professional
Performs At: Ashland Community College Auditorium

4275
BEREA COLLEGE CONVOCATION SERIES
Frost Room 107 CPO 2160
Berea College
Berea, KY 40404-2160
Phone: 859-985-3359
Fax: 859-985-3642
e-mail: randall_roberts@berea.edu
Web Site: www.berea.edu/convocations/default.asp
Management:
Instructor In General Studies: Randall Roberts
Performs At: Phelps - Stokes Auditorium

4276
CAPITOL ARTS ALLIANCE
416 E Main Street
Bowling Green, KY 42101-2241
Phone: 270-782-2787
Fax: 270-782-2804
Toll-free: 877-694-2787
e-mail: mike.thomas@capitolarts.com
Web Site: www.capitolarts.com
Management:

President/Executive Director: Mike Thomas
Managing Director: Dawn Wesley
Gallery Director: Lynn Robertson
Operations Manager: Jeff Smith
Founded: 1981
Specialized Field: Series & Festivals; Instrumental Music; Vocal Music; Theatre; Youth; Dance; Ethnic Performances; Gallery
Status: Non-Profit, Professional
Paid Staff: 12
Paid Artists: 200
Seating Capacity: 840

4277
CENTRAL KENTUCKY ARTS SERIES

PO Box 383
Campbellsville, KY 42719
Phone: 207-789-5340
Fax: 270-789-5524
e-mail: aocunha@campbellsville.edu
Web Site: www.centralkentuckyarts.org
Officers:
   President: Tony Cunha
Mission: To provide professional programs in all the arts.
Founded: 1967
Specialized Field: Series & Festivals; Instrumental Music; Vocal Music; Theatre; Youth; Dance; Ethnic Performances
Status: Non-Profit, Professional
Volunteer Staff: 10
Income Sources: Individual and Corporate Donations
Facility Category: Recital Hall; Auditoriums

4278
GREAT AMERICAN BRASS BAND FESTIVAL

PO Box 429
Danville, KY 40423-0429
Phone: 859-236-4692
Fax: 859-236-9610
Management:
   Director: George Foreman

4279
FOUST ARTIST SERIES

Georgetown College
Georgetown, KY 40324-1696
Phone: 502-863-8112
e-mail: sburnett@georgetowncollege.edu
Management:
   President: William Crouch Jr
   Foust Artistic Series Director: Sonny Burnette
Founded: 1987
Specialized Field: Series & Festivals; Instrumental Music; Vocal Music; Theatre; Dance; Ethnic Performances; Music
Status: Non-Profit, Professional
Paid Staff: 1
Performs At: John L. Hill Chapel

4280
GREATER HAZARD AREA PERFORMING ARTS SERIES

C/O Hete
1 Community College Drive
Hazard, KY 41701
Phone: 606-487-3067
Fax: 606-439-3821
Toll-free: 800-246-7521
e-mail: tammy.duff@kctcs.edu
Web Site: www.hazardperformingarts.com
Officers:

Chair, Executive Council: Jan Maygard
Chair, Advisory Committee: Terry Thies
Management:
   Performing Arts Director: Tammy Duff
Mission: Assist in the development of the arts and arts education in the Southeast Kentucky region
Founded: 1974
Specialized Field: Southeast Kentucky
Status: Non-Profit, Professional
Paid Staff: 2
Budget: $100,000+
Income Sources: Ticket Sales; Corporate/Private Support; Grants
Performs At: First Federal Center
Affiliations: Hazard Community & Technical College, Hazard Independent College Foundation
Facility Category: Conference Center, Convention Hall & Theatre
Type of Stage: Proscenium/Portable
Seating Capacity: 800
Year Built: 1992

4281
PENNYROYAL ARTS COUNCIL SERIES

PO Box 1038
Hopkinsville, KY 42241
Phone: 270-887-4295
Fax: 270-887-4027
e-mail: paci@bellsouth.net
Web Site: www.pennyroyalarts.org
Management:
   Executive Director: Carol Barta
Mission: To encourage, develop and promote the appreciation of the arts through: education, support, service and presentation.
Founded: 1977
Specialized Field: Art Performances for Children and Adults
Status: Non-Profit, Non-Professional
Paid Staff: 4
Income Sources: Grants & Fund Drive
Performs At: Alhambra Theatre
Facility Category: Theatre
Type of Stage: Proscenium
Stage Dimensions: 32'x 26'
Seating Capacity: 760
Year Built: 1928
Rental Contact: Carol Barta

4282
UNIVERSITY OF KENTUCKY SINGLETARY CENTER FOR THE ARTS

126 Singletary Center
Lexington, KY 40506-0241
Phone: 859-257-1706
Fax: 859-323-9991
e-mail: michael.grice@uky.edu
Web Site: www.uky.edu/scfa
Management:
   Executive Director: Michael Grice
   Marketing Director: Summer Gossett
   Production Director: Tanya Harper
Utilizes: Collaborations; Composers; Grant Writers; Guest Accompanists; Guest Companies; Guest Composers; Guest Directors; Guest Instructors; Guest Musical Directors; Guest Musicians; Guest Soloists; Instructors; Lyricists; Multimedia; Original Music Scores; Paid Performers; Sign Language Translators; Singers; Students; Student Interns; Theatre Companies
Founded: 1979
Opened: 1979
Specialized Field: Sereis & Festivals: Music Shows
Status: Non-Profit, Non-Professional
Paid Staff: 7

Volunteer Staff: 71
Income Sources: Rentals; Ticket Revenue
Annual Attendance: 100,000
Facility Category: Concert Hall & Recital Hall
Seating Capacity: 1,467; 381
Year Built: 1979
Year Remodeled: 2003
Rental Contact: Tanya Harper

4283
UNIVERSITY OF KENTUCKY ARTISTS SERIES

University of Kentucky
Singletary Center for the Arts
Lexington, KY 40506-0241
Phone: 859-257-1706
Fax: 859-323-9991
e-mail: hbsali00@pop.uky.edu
Web Site: www.uky.edu/SCFA/
Management:
   Center for the Arts Director: Holly Salisbury
Performs At: Otis A. Singletary Center for the Arts Concert Hall

---

4284
SUE BENNETT COLLEGE, APPALACHIAN FOLK FESTIVAL

151 College Street
London, KY 40741
Phone: 606-864-2238
Fax: 606-539-4404
Management:
   Chairperson: Madge Chestnut
Mission: To offer arts, performances and events showcasing Appalachian heritage.
Founded: 1973
Specialized Field: Vocal Music; Festivals
Status: Nonprofit
Performs At: Sue Bennett College Auditorium
Organization Type: Performing; Educational

4285
KENTUCKY SHAKESPEARE FESTIVAL

1387 S 4th Street
Louisville, KY 40208
Phone: 502-583-8738
Fax: 502-583-8751
Toll-free: 877-655-2273
e-mail: info@kyshakes.org
Web Site: www.kyshakes.org
Management:
   Executive Director: Steven Renner
   Artistic Director: Curt L Toftlend
   Director Education: Doug Sumey
Mission: To provide accessible, professional, classical theatre and quality education touring programs.
Utilizes: Actors; Artists-in-Residence; Collaborating Artists; Collaborations; Designers; Educators; Five Seasonal Concerts; Guest Accompanists; Guest Conductors; Guest Ensembles; Guild Activities; High School Drama; Local Artists; Original Music Scores; Resident Artists; Resident Professionals; Selected Students; Soloists; Student Interns; Theatre Companies
Founded: 1960
Specialized Field: Free Shakespeare Performances; Educational Outreach Programming
Status: Non-Profit, Professional
Budget: $750,000
Income Sources: Corporate; Foundation; Individuals; Government; Fund; Earned
Season: May - August
Performs At: C Douglas Ramey Amphitheater
Annual Attendance: 67,500

Facility Category: Outdoor Ampitheatre
Type of Stage: Thrust
Seating Capacity: 1,000
Year Built: 1963
Year Remodeled: 1993
Cost: $1,000,000
Organization Type: Performing; Resident; Touring; Educational

4286

SOUTHERN BAPTIST THEOLOGICAL SEMINARY-INMAN JOHNSON GUEST ARTIST SERIES

2825 Lexington Road
Louisville, KY 40280
Phone: 502-897-4115
Fax: 502-897-4066
Toll-free: 800-626-5525
e-mail: chmusic@sbts.edu
Web Site: www.sbts.edu
Officers:
Manager: Linda Lancaster
Management:
President: Albert Mohler
Specialized Field: School of Church Music and Worship
Status: Non-Profit, Professional
Budget: $23,000
Income Sources: Endowment
Performs At: Recital Hall
Seating Capacity: 230

4287

MURRAY CIVIC MUSIC ASSOCIATION SERIES

Murray State University, Music Department
527 Fine Arts Center
Murray, KY 42071-3342
Phone: 270-762-6337
Fax: 270-762-3965
e-mail: robert.murray@murraystate.edu
Officers:
VP Programming: Robert Murray
Mission: To provide Murray with the finest in performing arts events.
Founded: 1959
Specialized Field: Dance; Vocal Music; Instrumental Music; Theater; Lyric Opera; Grand Opera
Status: Nonprofit
Performs At: Lovett Auditorium; Murray State University
Organization Type: Sponsoring

4288

PIKEVILLE CONCERT ASSOCIATION SERIES

147 Sycamore Street
Pikeville, KY 41501
Phone: 606-218-5250
Fax: 606-218-5269
e-mail: webmaster@pc.edu
Web Site: www.pa.pc.edu/pca/index.htm
Management:
President: Robert Eugene Schindeler
Vice President/Administration: Jeanette Anderson
Founded: 1952
Specialized Field: Series & Festivals; Instrumental Music; Vocal Music; Dance; Orchestra
Status: Non-Profit, Non-Professional
Performs At: Auditorium

4289

ALICE LLOYD COLLEGE CANEY CONVOCATION SERIES

Purpose Road
Pippa Passes, KY 41844
Phone: 606-360-6136
Fax: 606-368-6217
Performs At: Estelle Campbell Center for the Arts

4290

ASBURY COLLEGE ARTIST SERIES

Asbury College
One Macklem Drive
Wilmore, KY 40390
Phone: 859-858-3511
Fax: 859-858-3921
Toll-free: 800-888-1818
e-mail: mstratford@asbury.edu
Web Site: www.asbury.edu
Officers:
Chairman: Kevin Sparks
Management:
President: Paul Rader
Founded: 1890
Performs At: Hughes Memorial Auditorium

4291

WINCHESTER COUNCIL FOR THE ARTS SERIES

37 North Main Street
Winchester, KY 40391
Phone: 859-744-6437
Fax: 859-744-8211
Toll-free: 888-772-6985
e-mail: contact@leedscenter.org
Web Site: www.leedscenter.com
Management:
President: Fara Tyree
Executive Director: Peggy Case
Founded: 1986
Specialized Field: Series & Festivals; Instrumental Music; Vocal Music; Theatre; Youth
Status: Non-Profit, Non-Professional
Paid Staff: 1
Paid Artists: 10
Performs At: Leeds Theatre & Performing Arts Center

Louisiana

4292

L.S.U. UNION GREAT PERFORMANCES THEATER SERIES

Box 25123 LSU
Baton Rouge, LA 70894
Phone: 225-578-5118
Fax: 225-578-9311
e-mail: rdunaw1@lsu.edu
Management:
Assistant Director: Rhonda Rogers Dunaway
Founded: 1963

4293

L.S.U. UNION GREAT PERFORMANCES THEATER SERIES

Box 25123 LSU
Baton Rouge, LA 70894
Phone: 225-578-5118
Fax: 225-578-9311
e-mail: rdunaw1@lsu.edu
Management:
Program Coordinator: Rhonda Dunaway

Utilizes: Actors; Artists-in-Residence; Dance Companies; Dancers; Fine Artists; Guest Accompanists; Guest Choreographers; Guest Directors; Instructors; Local Artists; Original Music Scores; Soloists; Special Technical Talent; Theatre Companies
Founded: 1963
Annual Attendance: 5,028
Seating Capacity: 1250
Rental Contact: Cason Duke

4294

LSU UNION GREAT PERFORMANCES THEATER SERIES

PO Box 25123
Baton Rouge, LA 70894
Phone: 225-578-5128
Fax: 225-578-9311
e-mail: rdunaw1@lsu.edu
Management:
Executive Director: Rhonda R Dunaway
Program Coordinator: Joann Doolos
Founded: 1963
Specialized Field: Series and Festivals; Instrumental Music; Vocal Music; Theatre; Youth; Dance; Performances of LSU Union Theatre
Status: For-Profit, Professional

4295

FANFARE FESTIVAL

Slu 10797
500 Western Avenue
Hammond, LA 70402
Phone: 985-543-4366
Fax: 985-543-4369
e-mail: fanfare_ctpa@selu.edu
Web Site: www.selu.edu/fanfare
Management:
Associate Director For Programming: Keiron Couret
Director: Donna Gay Anderson
Business Manager: Carol Knott
Associate Director and Programming: Keiron Covrest
Founded: 1986
Paid Staff: 8
Volunteer Staff: 22
Paid Artists: 25
Non-paid Artists: 10

4296

SOUTHEASTERN LOUISIANA UNIVERSITY ARTS & LECTURES SERIES

Slu 346
Hammond, LA 70402
Phone: 504-549-3792
Fax: 504-549-5647
e-mail: jmchodgkins@selu.edu
Officers:
Chairman: Jim McHodgkins

4297

JEFF DAVIS ARTS COUNCIL

PO Box 1068
Jennings, LA 70546
Phone: 337-824-5060
Fax: 337-824-1070

4298

FESTIVAL INTERNATIONAL DE LOUISIANE

PO Box 4008
Lafayette, LA 70502

Phone: 337-232-8086
Fax: 337-233-7536
e-mail: info@festivalinternational.com
Web Site: www.festivalinternational.com
Officers:
Executive Director: Dana Canedo
Management:
Marketing Coordinator: Adrienne Stewart
Programming Coordinator: Lisa Stafford
Mission: Free family event celebrating the French cultural heritage of southern Louisiana - a combination of French, African, Caribbean and Hispanic influences.
Founded: 1986
Specialized Field: Series & Festivals; Instrumental Music; Vocal Music; Theatre; Youth; Dance; Ethnic Performances; Visual; Performing And Culinary Arts
Status: Non-Profit, Professional
Paid Staff: 3
Volunteer Staff: 1500
Paid Artists: 250
Season: April
Performs At: Kimmel Center for the Performing Arts

4299
LAFAYETTE COMMUNITY CONCERTS SERIES

PO Box 2465
Lafayette, LA 70502
Phone: 337-233-1035
Officers:
President: George E Arceneaux

4300
PERFORMING ARTS SOCIETY OF ACADIANA SERIES

PO Box 52979
Lafayette, LA 70505
Phone: 337-237-2787
Fax: 337-237-3974
e-mail: pasajll@aol.com
Web Site: www.pasa-online.org
Management:
President: Jacqueline Lyle
Managing Director: Mary Coleman
Founded: 1989
Specialized Field: Series and Festivals; Instrumental Music; Vocal Music; Theatre; Youth; Dance; Ethnic Performances
Status: Non-Profit, Professional
Paid Staff: 7

4301
PERFORMING ARTS SOCIETY OF ACADIANA SERIES

PO Box 52979
Lafayette, LA 70505
Phone: 337-237-2787
Fax: 337-237-3974
e-mail: pasajll@aol.com
Web Site: www.pasa.online.org
Performs At: Heymann Performing Arts - Convention Center

4302
UNIVERSITY OF LOUISIANA AT LAFAYETTE CONCERT SERIES

Ull Drawer 41207
Lafayette, LA 70504-1207
Phone: 337-482-5216
Fax: 337-482-5017
e-mail: pdm0677@louisiana.edu
Officers:

University Concert Committee Chair: Dr. Paul Morton

4303
UNIVERSITY OF SOUTHWESTERN LOUISIANA CONCERT SERIES

USL Drawer 41207
Lafayette, LA 70504
Phone: 337-482-5216
Fax: 337-482-5017
Management:
Assistant Professor: Paul Morton

4304
UNIVERSITY OF SOUTHWESTERN LOUISIANA CONCERT SERIES

USL Drawer 41207
Lafayette, LA 70504
Phone: 337-482-5216
Fax: 337-482-5017
Officers:
Chairman: Andrea Loewy
Management:
Assistant Professor: Paul Morton
Performs At: Angelle Hall Auditorium

4305
MAMOU CAJUN MUSIC FESTIVAL

420 E Street
Apartment 1
Mamou, LA 70554
Phone: 337-468-2258
Web Site:
http://www.mamoucajunmusicfestival.com/252.html
Mission: To offer traditional Cajun music, as well as related events.
Utilizes: Singers
Founded: 1972
Specialized Field: Vocal Music; Festivals
Status: Nonprofit
Organization Type: Performing; Resident; Educational

4306
JEFFERSON PERFORMING ARTS SOCIETY

1118 Clearview Parkway
Metairie, LA 70001
Phone: 504-885-2000
Fax: 504-885-3437
e-mail: jpasinfo@jpas.org
Web Site: www.jpas.org
Officers:
Chairman: Hannah Cunningham
President: Wayne Keating
Past President: Dr. Bud Willis
Secretary: Subhash Kulkarni
Management:
Business Manager: Donna Barber
Executive/Artistic Director: Dennis G Assaf
Chairman: Hannah J Cunningham
Mission: Supporting performance and education in the performing arts.
Utilizes: Actors; Artists-in-Residence; Choreographers; Collaborating Artists; Collaborations; Dance Companies; Dancers; Five Seasonal Concerts; Grant Writers; Guest Accompanists; Guest Artists; Guest Choreographers; Guest Companies; Guest Composers; Guest Designers; Guest Directors; Guest Lecturers; Guest Musical Directors; Guest Musicians; Instructors; Local Artists; Multi Collaborations; Multimedia; Music; Organization Contracts; Original Music Scores;

Playwrights; Sign Language Translators; Singers; Soloists; Student Interns; Special Technical Talent; Theatre Companies
Founded: 1978
Specialized Field: Series & Festivals; Instrumental Music; Vocal Music; Theatre; Youth; Dance; Ethnic Performances
Status: Non-Profit, Professional
Paid Staff: 14
Volunteer Staff: 100
Paid Artists: 100
Budget: 1.2 million
Income Sources: Box Office; Ads; Sponsorships; Grants
Affiliations: APAP; ACDA; ASOL; Conductor's Guild
Annual Attendance: 30,000
Facility Category: Theater
Type of Stage: Proscenium Arch
Stage Dimensions: 42'x 35'
Seating Capacity: 1,350
Year Built: 1952
Year Remodeled: 1999
Organization Type: Performing; Educational

4307
ULM PERFORMING ARTS SERIES

University of Louisiana in Monroe
700 University Avenue
Monroe, LA 71209
Phone: 318-342-3600
Fax: 318-342-5425
e-mail: enhaedicke@uca.edu
Management:
Chairman: Dr. Janet Haddicke
Mission: To bring to students and townspeople the best in professional cultural entertainment.
Utilizes: Actors; Collaborations; Dance Companies; New Productions; Original Music Scores; Theatre Companies
Specialized Field: Dance; Vocal Music; Instrumental Music; Theatre
Status: Nonprofit
Paid Staff: 1
Budget: $120,000
Income Sources: Season Ticket Sales
Performs At: Civic Center Theater; Brown Auditorium
Organization Type: Performing; Sponsoring

4308
UNIVERSITY OF LOUISIANA AT MONROE PERFORMING ARTS SERIES

700 University Avenue
Monroe, LA 71209
Phone: 318-342-3811
Fax: 318-342-1599
e-mail: kwhite@ulm.edu
Web Site: www.ulm.edu/vapa
Management:
Director: L Keith White
Paid Staff: 1
Paid Artists: 50

4309
UNIVERSITY OF LOUISIANA AT MONROE PERFORMING ARTS SERIES

700 University Avenue
Monroe, LA 71209
Phone: 318-342-1494
Fax: 318-342-1491
e-mail: Enhaedicke@ulm.edu
Officers:
University Concert Committee Chair: Dr. Paul Morton

Management:
Director: Dr. Janet V Haedicke
Paid Staff: 1
Volunteer Staff: 2
Paid Artists: 50

4310
NORTHWESTERN STATE UNIVERSITY CONCERT SERIES
Capa
Northwestern State University of Louisiana
Natchitoches, LA 71497
Phone: 318-357-4522
Fax: 318-357-5906
e-mail: bandcamps@nsula.edu
Web Site: www.nsula.edu
Officers:
Chairman: Bill Brent
Management:
Artistic Director: Roger Chaenler
Chairman: Bill Brant
Founded: 1886
Specialized Field: Series and Festivals: Music
Status: Non-Profit, Professional
Paid Staff: 60
Paid Artists: 3
Performs At: Fine Arts Auditorium

4311
NEW ORLEANS FRIENDS OF MUSIC SERIES
940 Turquoise Street
New Orleans, LA 70124
Phone: 504-887-1133
Fax: 504-282-4008

4312
NEW ORLEANS FRIENDS OF MUSIC SERIES
940 Turquoise Street
New Orleans, LA 70124
Phone: 504-887-1133
Fax: 504-282-4008
Officers:
President: Dr. Stuart Farber
Performs At: Dixon Hall

4313
NEW ORLEANS INTERNATIONAL PIANO COMPETITION & KEYBOARD FESTIVAL
PO Drawer 19599
New Orleans, LA 70179-0599
Phone: 504-899-4826
Fax: 504-899-4826
e-mail: director@masno.org
Web Site: masmo.org
Management:
Director: Danial Weilbaecher
Founded: 1980
Specialized Field: Classical Piano Music
Budget: $200,000

4314
NEW ORLEANS JAZZ & HERITAGE FOUNDATION
1205 N Rampart Street
New Orleans, LA 70116
Phone: 504-522-4786
Fax: 504-522-5456
Web Site: www.nojazzfest.com
Management:
Director: Quint Davis

4315
SHAKESPEARE FESTIVAL AT TULANE
Tulane University
Department of Theatre & Dance
New Orleans, LA 70118
Phone: 504-865-5105
Fax: 504-865-5205
e-mail: amichel@tulane.edu
Web Site: www.neworleansshakespeare.com
Management:
Artistic Director: Aimee K Michel
Managing Director: Clare Moncrief
Operations Director: Brad Robbert
Mission: To provide professional Shakespeare productions to the Greater New Orleans and surrounding Gulf South area along with educational programs to the schools.
Utilizes: Actors; AEA Actors; Artists-in-Residence; Choreographers; Collaborating Artists; Collaborations; Commissioned Composers; Commissioned Music; Composers; Educators; Five Seasonal Concerts; Guest Artists; Guest Companies; Guest Instructors; Guest Musical Directors; Guest Soloists; Guest Teachers; High School Drama; Local Artists; Multimedia; Organization Contracts; Original Music Scores; Performance Artists; Resident Artists; Resident Professionals; Soloists; Students; Special Technical Talent
Founded: 1993
Specialized Field: Classical Theatre; Shakespeare; New Works; Modern Classics
Status: Professional; Nonprofit
Paid Staff: 6
Paid Artists: 60
Budget: $250,000
Income Sources: Public; Private; Corporate; Foundation; Box Office; Tuition
Facility Category: Equity Small Professional Theatre
Type of Stage: Black Box; Laboratory
Seating Capacity: 150; 60

4316
LOUISIANA TECH CONCERT ASSOCIATION SERIES
Tech Station
PO Box 8608
Ruston, LA 71272
Phone: 318-257-2711
Fax: 318-257-4571
e-mail: krobbins@latech.edu
Web Site: www.performingarts.latech.edu
Management:
President: Dan Reneau
Executive Director: Kenneth Robbins
Theatre Director: Cherrie Sciro
Co-Director: Alan Goldspiel
Founded: 1944
Specialized Field: Music; Theatre; Dance
Status: Non-Profit, Non-Professional
Paid Staff: 8
Paid Artists: 1
Budget: $133,000
Income Sources: Ticket Sales
Performs At: Howard Center for the Performing Arts
Annual Attendance: 6,000
Facility Category: Conference Hall
Type of Stage: Proscenium
Seating Capacity: 1,051

4317
FRIENDS OF MUSIC SERIES
Hurley School of Music, Centenary College
2911 Centenary Boulevard
Shreveport, LA 71104
Phone: 318-869-5235
Fax: 318-869-5248
e-mail: godom@centenary.edu
Web Site: www.centenary.edu/departme/music/music.html
Management:
Manager: Dr. Gale Odom
Performs At: Hurley Recital Hall

4318
RED RIVER REVEL ARTS FESTIVAL
101 Crockett Street
Suite C
Shreveport, LA 71101
Phone: 318-424-4000
Fax: 318-226-9559
e-mail: rrr@redriverrevel.com
Web Site: www.redriverrevel.com
Officers:
President: John T Hubbard
Management:
Executive Director: Kip Holloway
Mission: Eight day celebration of the Arts.
Founded: 1976
Specialized Field: Series and Festivals; Instrumental Music; Vocal Music; Theatre; Youth; Dance; Ethnic Performances
Status: Non-Profit, Professional
Paid Staff: 4
Volunteer Staff: 6
Income Sources: Corporate Sponsors; Underwriters; State; Local Grants
Annual Attendance: 180,000-200,000
Facility Category: Outdoor Festival

4319
SLIDELL DEPARTMENT OF CULTURAL AFFAIRS
444 Erlanger Street
PO Box 828
Slidell, LA 70459
Phone: 504-646-4375
Fax: 504-646-4231
Web Site: www.slidell.la.us
Management:
Director: Kelli Gustafson
Utilizes: Dancers; Guest Musical Directors; Instructors; Special Technical Talent; Touring Companies
Performs At: Auditorium

4320
IMPRESARIO'S CHOICE-THE BROADWAY SERIES AT THE MONROE CIVIC THEATRE
267 Verhagen Road
PO Box 828
Tallulah, LA 71284-0828
Phone: 318-574-0440
Fax: 318-574-0440
Toll-free: 888-822-0440
e-mail: impresariosmail@aol.com
Web Site: www.impresarioschoice.com
Officers:
President: Raymond E Poliquit
VP: Mark Henderson
Secretary: Douglas Leporati
Trasurer: Sherry Free
Public Realtions: Ruby James

Management:
  President: Douglas Leoreti
  Executive Director: Ezekial J Moore
  Artistic Director: Raymond E Poliquit
Mission: It is our mission to bring high quality national touring Broadway musicals to Northeast Louisiana, and to expand the theatregoing audience, both in number and diversity.
Founded: 1988
Specialized Field: Series & Festivals: Theatre
Status: Non-Profit, Professional
Paid Staff: 1
Volunteer Staff: 1
Budget: $275,000
Income Sources: Corporate Sponsorship
Affiliations: Impresario's Friends
Annual Attendance: 6,200
Facility Category: Civic Center
Type of Stage: Procenium
Seating Capacity: 2,100

4321
NICHOLLS STATE UNIVERSITY ARTISTS & LECTURE SERIES

PO Box 2038
Thibodaux, LA 70310
Phone: 985-448-4273
Fax: 985-448-4271
e-mail: angela.hammerli@nicholls.edu
Web Site: www.nicholls.edu
Management:
  Director: Angela Hammerli
Specialized Field: Series & Festivals; Instrumental Music; Vocal Music; Theatre; Youth; Dance; Ethnic Performances
Status: Non-Profit
Paid Staff: 2
Performs At: Auditorium

Maine

4322
NEW MUSIK DIRECTIONS SERIES

67 Green Street
Augusta, ME 4330
Phone: 207-623-1941
Fax: 207-623-1941
Management:
  Director: Joseph Baltar
Mission: To provide a network for artists in film, video and new music.
Founded: 1981
Specialized Field: Festivals
Status: Professional; Commercial
Organization Type: Performing; Educational; Sponsoring

4323
BAR HARBOR MUSIC FESTIVAL

59 Cottage St
59 Cottage Street
Bar Harbor, ME 04609-1800
Phone: 207-288-5744
Web Site: www.barharbormusicfestival.org
Management:
  Artistic Director: Francis Fortier
Founded: 1967
Specialized Field: Vocal Music; Festivals, Opera, Instrumental Music
Paid Staff: 2

4324
CHOCOLATE CHURCH ARTS CENTER FESTIVAL

804 Washington Street
Bath, ME 04530-2617
Phone: 207-442-8455
Fax: 207-442-8637
e-mail: info@chocolatechurcharts.org
Web Site: www.chocolatechurcharts.org
Management:
  Executive Director: Claire Adams
Founded: 1975
Specialized Field: Series and Festivals; Instrumental Music; Vocal Music; Theatre; Youth; Dance; Ethnic Performances
Status: Non-Profit, Professional
Paid Staff: 2
Paid Artists: 30
Seating Capacity: 294

4325
KNEISEL HALL CHAMBER MUSIC FESTIVAL

PO Box 648
Blue Hill, ME 4614
Phone: 207-374-2811
Fax: 207-374-2811
e-mail: festival@kneisel.org
Web Site: www.kneisel.org
Management:
  President: Saul Cohen
  Executive Director: Ellen Werner
  Artistic Director: Seymour Lipkin
Mission: To foster the art of chamber music through teaching and performance.
Founded: 1902
Specialized Field: Music and Education
Status: Non-Profit, Professional
Paid Staff: 5
Paid Artists: 14
Budget: $485,000
Income Sources: Donations; Grants; Ticket Sales
Annual Attendance: 2,500
Facility Category: Historic Hall
Seating Capacity: 175
Year Built: 1922
Rental Contact: Ellen Werner

4326
BOWDOIN COLLEGE CONCERT SERIES

Music Department, Gibson Hall
9200 College Station
Brunswick, ME 04011-8492
Phone: 207-725-3747
Fax: 207-725-3748
e-mail: dsmall@bowdoin.edu
Management:
  Administrator: Delmar D Small
Specialized Field: College Music Department
Performs At: Kresge Auditorium, Pickard Theater and Chapel

4327
BOWDOIN SUMMER MUSIC FESTIVAL

6300 College Station
Bowdoin College
Brunswick, ME 4011
Phone: 207-373-1400
Fax: 207-373-1441
e-mail: info@bowdoinfestival.org
Web Site: www.bowdoinfestival.org
Officers:
  Chairman of the Board: Hugh Phelps
  Vice Chair: William A Rogers
  Treasurer: Lester Hodgdon
  Secretary: Nancy R Connery
Management:
  President: Bill Rogers
  Executive Director: Peter Simmons
  Artistic Director: Lewis Kaplan
  Admissions Director: Jen Means
Mission: To provide the most promising music students from around the world with opportunities to further their musical development, and to present chamber music performed to the highest standards by distinguished professional musicians.
Utilizes: Commissioned Music; Composers-in-Residence; Grant Writers; Guest Companies; Guest Musical Directors; Multimedia
Founded: 1964
Specialized Field: Vocal Music: Chamber Music
Status: Non-Profit, Professional
Paid Staff: 3
Paid Artists: 50
Budget: $1,100,000
Income Sources: Contributions; Ticket Sales; Tution
Performs At: Crooker Theater, Brunswick High School
Affiliations: Chamber Music America; Major Conservatories; Maine Performing Arts Network
Annual Attendance: 10,000
Seating Capacity: 600
Year Built: 1995
Organization Type: Educational; Presenting

4328
GAMPER FESTIVAL OF CONTEMPORARY MUSIC

Bowdoin Internatinal Music Festival
6300 College Station
Brunswick, ME 04011-8463
Phone: 207-373-1400
Fax: 207-373-1441
e-mail: info@bowdoinfestival.org
Web Site: www.bowdoinfestival.org
Officers:
  President: William Rogers
  Executive Director: Peter Simmons
Management:
  Artistic Director: Lewis Kaplin
  Managing Director: Chris Murray
Founded: 1964
Specialized Field: Series and Festivals: Chamber Music
Status: Non-Profit, Professional
Paid Staff: 100
Paid Artists: 50

4329
UNIVERSITY OF MAINE AT FORT KENT, INTERNATIONAL PERFORMERS SERIES

University of Maine at Fort Kent
25 Pleasant Street
Fort Kent, ME 04743
Phone: 207-834-7513
Fax: 207-834-7503
Toll-free: 888-879-8635
e-mail: rphinney@maine.edu
Web Site: www.umfkmaine.edu
Management:
  Assoc. Director Student Activities: Raymond Phinney
Paid Staff: 4
Facility Category: University
Type of Stage: Proscenium
Stage Dimensions: 30 X 24
Seating Capacity: 450

Year Built: 1965
Rental Contact: Fran Picard

4330
BATES DANCE FESTIVAL

163 Wood Street
Lewiston, ME 04240-6016
Phone: 207-786-6381
Fax: 207-786-8282
e-mail: dancefest@bates.edu
Web Site: www.bates.edu/dancefest
Officers:
    Director: Laura Faure
    Associate Director/Registrar: Nancy Salmon
Mission: The Bates Dance Festival brings an artistically and ethnically diverse group of the best contemporary dance artists to Maine during the summer season to teach, perform, and create new work; encourages and inspires established and emerging artists by providing them with a creative, supportive environment in which to work; and actively engages people from the community and region in a full range of dance activities.
Utilizes: Singers
Founded: 1982
Specialized Field: Series and Festivals; Youth; Dance; Ethnic Performances
Status: Non-Profit, Professional
Paid Staff: 8
Volunteer Staff: 14
Paid Artists: 35
Budget: $800,000
Income Sources: Public; Private; and Earned Income
Performs At: Schaeffer Theatre
Affiliations: Bates College
Annual Attendance: 4,000
Type of Stage: Proscenium
Stage Dimensions: 28'x35'
Seating Capacity: 300
Year Built: 1952
Organization Type: Resident; Educational; Sponsoring

4331
L/A ARTS

221 Lisbon Street
Lewiston, ME 4240
Phone: 207-782-7228
Fax: 207-782-8192
Toll-free: 800-639-2919
e-mail: mail@laarts.org
Web Site: www.laarts.org
Management:
    Executive Director: Richard Willing
Mission: To offer diverse performing arts to Central Maine communities.
Founded: 1973
Specialized Field: Series and Festivals; Vocal Music; Theatre; Youth; Dance; Instrumental Music; Theatre; Festivals
Status: Non-Profit, Professional
Paid Staff: 3
Income Sources: Association of Performing Arts Presenters; Maine Arts Sponsor Association
Organization Type: Performing; Educational; Sponsoring

4332
MT DESERT FESTIVAL OF CHAMBER MUSIC

PO Box 862
Northeast Harbor, ME 04662
Phone: 207-276-3988
e-mail: info@mtdesertfestival.org
Web Site: www.mtdesertfestival.org

Management:
    Founder: Matthew Raimondi
    Executive Director: Natalie Raimondi
    Music Director: Todd Crow
Founded: 1963
Specialized Field: Vocal Music: Chamber Music
Status: Non-Profit, Professional

4333
SACO RIVER FESTIVAL

PO Box 610
Parsonsfield, ME 4047
Phone: 207-625-7116
e-mail: srfa@psouth.net
Web Site: www.psouth.net/~mapleroc
Management:
    President: Judy Ingram
    Executive Director: James O'Neil
    Artistic Director: Scott Woolwever
Founded: 1974
Specialized Field: Series and Festivals: Music
Status: Non-Profit, Professional
Paid Staff: 1

4334
LARK SOCIETY FOR CHAMBER MUSIC

PO Box 11
Portland, ME 4112
Phone: 207-761-1522
Fax: 207-780-6554
e-mail: lark1@prexar.com
Web Site: www.portlandstringquartet.org
Management:
    President: Barbara Smith
    Executive Director: Gistlle Auger
Mission: Committed to supporting and presenting a Portland concert series and educational presentations by the Portland String Quartet. Presenters of the Portland Concert Series, and supporters of the PSQ's outreach activities, we promote chamber music and music education in the state of Maine.
Founded: 1980
Specialized Field: Series & Festivals; Chamber Music; Education; Performance
Status: Non-Profit, Professional
Paid Staff: 1
Income Sources: Chamber Music America
Organization Type: Performing; Touring; Resident; Educational

4335
MAINE ARTS SERIES

193 Street
Suite 3
Portland, ME 4333
Phone: 207-287-2724
Fax: 207-772-3995
e-mail: info@mainearts.org
Web Site: www.mainearts.org
Management:
    Executive Director: Mallwyn Willson
    Artistic Director: Dona McNeil
Mission: To provide artistic opportunities and to encourage the advancement of the performing and the visual arts in Maine through the presentation of a public program of services to artists.
Founded: 1977
Specialized Field: Series and Festivals: Ethnic Performances
Status: Non-Profit, Professional
Paid Staff: 9
Performs At: Downtown Portland; Thomas Point Beach
Organization Type: Sponsoring

4336
MAINE FESTIVAL

582 Congress Street
Portland, ME 4101
Phone: 207-772-9012
Fax: 207-772-3995
e-mail: nbloom@mainearts.org
Web Site: www.mainearts.org
Management:
    Director: Nicolaus Bloom

4337
PCA GREAT PERFORMANCES

477 Congress Street
Portland, ME 4101
Phone: 207-773-3150
Fax: 207-774-1018
e-mail: pcabox@pcagreatperformances.org
Web Site: www.pcagreatperformances.org
Management:
    Executive Director: Judith Adams
Founded: 1931
Specialized Field: Series & Festivals; Instrumental Music; Vocal Music; Theatre; Youth; Dance; Ethnic Performances
Status: Non-Profit, Professional
Paid Staff: 6
Volunteer Staff: 200
Annual Attendance: 35,000-50,000
Seating Capacity: 1,908
Year Remodeled: 1997

4338
PORTLAND CHAMBER MUSIC FESTIVAL

211 Marginal Way
PO Box 9715-277
Portland, ME 04101
Toll-free: 800-320-0257
e-mail: jenelo@maine.rr.com
Web Site: www.pcmf.org
Management:
    Executive/Artistic Director: Jennifer Elowitch
    Co-Artistic Director: Dena Levine
Mission: Annual summer chamber music festival presenting concerts by nationally renowned performers and composers.
Utilizes: Artists-in-Residence; Collaborations; Commissioned Music; Multimedia; Poets
Founded: 1994
Specialized Field: Performing Arts; Classical Music; Summer Festival
Paid Staff: 3
Paid Artists: 20
Budget: $71,000
Income Sources: Individual; Corporate; Grants
Performs At: Concert Hall; Ludcke Auditorium; University of New England
Annual Attendance: 1,000
Seating Capacity: 250

4339
PORTLAND STRING QUARTET CONCERT SERIES/WORKSHOP

60 Candlewyck Terrace
Portland, ME 4102
Phone: 207-774-5144
Fax: 207-780-6554
e-mail: arpeggio@worldnet.att.net
Web Site: www.portlandstringquartet.org
Management:
    LARK Society Executive Director: Giselle A Auger
Founded: 1969

4340
FORUM SERIES
84 Mechanic Street
PO Box 784
Presque Isle, ME 04769
Phone: 207-764-0491
Fax: 207-764-2525
e-mail: theforum@mfx.net
Web Site: www.presqueisleforum.com
Management:
    Director Forum: James F Kaiser
    Administrative Assistant: Sandra Bonville
Founded: 1978
Specialized Field: Auditorium and Arena
Status: For-Profit, Non-Professional
Paid Staff: 18

4341
BAY CHAMBER CONCERTS
18 Central Street
PO Box 599
Rockport, ME 04856
Phone: 207-236-2823
Fax: 207-230-0454
Toll-free: 888-707-2770
e-mail: info@baychamberconcerts.org
Web Site: www.baychamberconcerts.org
Officers:
    President: Carole Brand
    Treasurer: Laurence Novotney
    Secretary: Jacob Gerritsen
Management:
    Executive Director: Monica Kelly
Mission: To present a variety of music styles and
educational programs to reach a diverse audience
along the coast of Maine.
Utilizes: Commissioned Music; Dancers; Fine Artists;
Grant Writers; Guest Accompanists; Guest
Choreographers; Guest Directors; Guest Musical
Directors; Guest Musicians; Lyricists; Multimedia;
Original Music Scores; Resident Artists; Sign Language
Translators; Singers; Special Technical Talent
Founded: 1960
Specialized Field: Music
Status: Non-Profit, Professional
Paid Staff: 9
Budget: $500,000
Performs At: Rockport Opera House
Facility Category: Opera House; Strom Auditorium
Type of Stage: Proscenium; Auditorium
Seating Capacity: 400; 800
Organization Type: Performing

4342
COLBY MUSIC SERIES
Colby College
5670 Mayflower Hill
Waterville, ME 4901
Phone: 207-872-3236
Fax: 207-872-3141
e-mail: dlkadyk@colby.edu
Web Site: www.colby.edu/music
Management:
    President: William Adams
    Music Department Chairman: Steve Saunders
Founded: 1987
Specialized Field: Series and Festivals; Instrumental
Music; Vocal Music; Ethnic Performances
Status: Non-Profit, Professional
Paid Staff: 10
Performs At: Given Auditorium; Lorimer Chapel

Maryland

4343
ST. JOHN'S COLLEGE CONCERT SERIES
St John'S College
Music Library, Box 2800
Annapolis, MD 21404
Phone: 410-269-6904
Fax: 410-626-2886
Management:
Music Librarian: Eric Stolzfus
Performs At: Francis Scott Key Auditorium

4344
ARTSCAPE-BALTIMORE'S FESTIVAL OF THE ARTS
7 E Redwood Street
Suite 500
Baltimore, MD 21202
Phone: 410-752-8632
Fax: 410-385-0361
e-mail: kajanku@promotionandarts.com
Web Site: www.artscape.org
Management:
    Executive Assistant: Linda Blume
    Arts Education Coordinator: Kibibi Ajanku
    School 33 Art Center Director: Jody Albright
Specialized Field: Three day regional festival of the
literary; visual; and performing arts.
Status: Non-Profit

4345
BALTIMORE SYMPHONY ORCHESTRA SUMMER MUSIC FEST: OREGON RIDGE CONCERT SERIES
1212 Cathedral Street
Baltimore, MD 21201-5545
Phone: 410-783-8100
Fax: 410-783-8004
Toll-free: 877-DSO-1444
e-mail: tickets@baltimoresymphony.com
Web Site: www.baltimoresymphony.com
Officers:
    President: John Gidwitz
Management:
    President: James Glicker
    Artistic Director: Mario Venzago
    Music Director: Yuri Temirkanov
Founded: 1906
Specialized Field: Series & Festivals; Instrumental
Music; Theatre; Youth; Classical Music
Status: Non-Profit, Professional
Paid Staff: 75
Paid Artists: 100

4346
COLLEGE OF NOTRE DAME OF MARYLAND CONCERTS
Music at CND Concerts
4701 N Charles Street
Baltimore, MD 21210
Phone: 410-532-5386
Fax: 410-435-5937
e-mail: eragogini@ndm.edu
Web Site: www.ndm.edu
Officers:
    Professor of Music: Dr. Ernest Ragogini
Management:
    College President: Mary Seurkamp
    Founder/Artistic Director: Ernest Ragogini
Mission: Outreach to community by presenting free
professional concerts

Utilizes: Collaborating Artists; Collaborations;
Commissioned Composers; Composers; Grant Writers;
Guest Companies; Guest Directors; Guest Lecturers;
Guest Musical Directors; Guest Musicians; Local Artists
& Directors; Lyricists; Multimedia; Organization
Contracts; Original Music Scores; Paid Performers;
Sign Language Translators; Singers
Founded: 1969
Specialized Field: Series & Festivals; Instrumental
Music; Vocal Music; Ethnic Performances; Jazz;
Classical
Status: Non-Profit, Professional
Volunteer Staff: 1
Paid Artists: 10
Budget: $10,000-$12,000
Income Sources: Donations; College Support
Performs At: LeClerc Auditorium
Annual Attendance: 1,200
Type of Stage: Proscenium; Thrust
Stage Dimensions: 55w xc 30d
Seating Capacity: 995
Year Built: 1895
Year Remodeled: 1970
Rental Contact: Kara Yendell

4347
CONCERT ARTISTS OF BALTIMORE
1114 St Paul Street
Baltimore, MD 21202-2615
Phone: 410-625-3525
Fax: 410-625-9343
e-mail: cab@cabalto.org
Web Site: www.cabalto.org
Management:
    Artistic Director: Edward Polochick
    General Manager: Cheryl Kauffman,
    cheryl@cabalto.org
    President Of The Board: Barry Williams,
    bfw53@aol.com
Mission: To present chamber orchestra and vocal
ensemble works in the clasical music genre.
Founded: 1987
Specialized Field: Chamber; Orchestra; Vocal
Ensemble
Status: Non-Profit, Professional
Paid Staff: 4
Volunteer Staff: 10
Paid Artists: 70
Budget: $300,000
Income Sources: Grants; Ticket Sales; Corporate
Foundations; Individual Giving
Annual Attendance: 7,500-10,000
Type of Stage: Proscenium

4348
MARYLAND INTERNATIONAL CHAMBER MUSIC FESTIVAL
PO Box 28060
Baltimore, MD 21239
Phone: 410-830-2838
Fax: 410-426-6062
e-mail: intermuse@email.com
Web Site: www.internmusearts.org
Management:
    Coordinator: Barry Goldstein
    Director: Cathy Jones
Mission: To promote classical music in Maryland.
Founded: 1985
Specialized Field: Classical

4349
RES MUSICAMERICA SERIES
211 Goodwood Gardens
Baltimore, MD 21210

All listings are in alphabetical order by state, then city, then organization within the city.

Phone: 410-889-3939
Management:
President: Vivian A Rudow
Founded: 1980
Specialized Field: Series & Festivals: American Music
Status: Non-Profit, Professional

4350
RES MUSICAMERICA SERIES
211 Goodwood Gardens
Baltimore, MD 21210
Phone: 410-889-3939
Management:
Artistic Director: Vivian Adelberg Rudow
Performs At: Various Auditoriums

4351
SHRIVER HALL CONCERT SERIES
Shriver Hall 105
3400 N Charles Street
Baltimore, MD 21218-2698
Phone: 410-516-7164
Fax: 410-516-7165
e-mail: info@shriverconcerts.org
Web Site: www.shriverconcerts.org
Officers:
President: Jephta Drachman
VP: Harriet Panitz
Secretary: Sander Wise
Treasurer: Mary Ellen Robinson
Management:
Executive Director: David J Baldwin
Office Manager: Ed Heyers
Mission: Present solo and chamber music concerts.
Utilizes: Educators; Guest Musical Directors; Guest Musicians; Lyricists
Founded: 1965
Specialized Field: Series & Festivals; Chamber Music; Solo Recitals
Status: Non-Profit, Professional
Paid Staff: 3
Paid Artists: 9
Budget: $650,000
Income Sources: Ticket sales, contributions, ads, grants
Annual Attendance: 8,000+
Facility Category: Auditorium
Type of Stage: Proscenium
Stage Dimensions: 40x80
Seating Capacity: 1,100
Year Built: 1953
Rental Contact: 410-516-2224 Pat Forrester

4352
YOUNG AUDIENCES OF MARYLAND
2601 N Howard Street
Suite 320
Baltimore, MD 21218
Phone: 410-837-7577
Fax: 410-837-7579
e-mail: info@yamd.org
Web Site: www.yamd.org
Officers:
President: Lois Mark
VP: Bill Buckner
Treasurer: Michael Stein
Secretary: Thomas J Sessa
Management:
Communication Director: Stacie Sanders
Director Administration: Donna Sherman
Education Director: Pat Cruz
Director of Development: Jennifer Andiorio
Marketing/PR Manager: Michelle Clesse

Mission: Transforms the lives and education of our youth through the arts by connecting educators, professional artists, and communities. Provides artistically excellent programs, expertise and resources to ensure opportunities for all students across the state of Maryland.
Utilizes: Actors; Artists-in-Residence; Collaborating Artists; Collaborations; Dance Companies; Dancers; Educators; Fine Artists; Grant Writers; Guest Artists; Guest Companies; Guest Directors; Guest Ensembles; Guest Instructors; Guest Musical Directors; Guild Activities; Local Artists; Lyricists; Multi Collaborations; Multimedia; Original Music Scores; Playwrights; Poets; Selected Students; Sign Language Translators; Singers; Special Technical Talent; Theatre Companies; Touring Companies
Founded: 1950
Specialized Field: Series & Festivals; Vocal Music; Instrumental Music; Theatre Arts; Education
Status: Non-Profit, Professional
Paid Staff: 11
Volunteer Staff: 3
Paid Artists: 100
Budget: $1 Million
Income Sources: Programs; Special Events; Corporate; Foundations; Individual Contributions
Performs At: Maryland Schools; Libraries; Festivals
Affiliations: National Young Audiences
Annual Attendance: 200,000
Facility Category: School
Organization Type: Performing; Educational; Sponsoring

4353
MUSIC IN THE GREAT HALL SERIES
6607 Altamont Avenue
Catonsville, MD 21228
Phone: 410-747-6012
e-mail: greathall@verizon.net
Web Site: www.migh.org
Management:
President: Rosita Hill
Artistic Director: Adam Mahonske
Founded: 1973
Specialized Field: Series and Festivals: Present Chamber Music Concerts
Status: Non-Profit, Professional

4354
WASHINGTON COLLEGE CONCERT SERIES
300 Washington Avenue
Chestertown, MD 21620
Phone: 410-778-7839
Web Site:
http://news.washcoll.edu/concertandfilmseries.php
Management:
Director: Kate Bennett
Founded: 1951
Specialized Field: Instrumental Music
Performs At: Tawes Theater

4355
MARYLAND PRESENTS
University of Maryland
Clarice Smith Performing Arts Center
College Park, MD 20742-5611
Phone: 301-405-7846
Fax: 301-405-5977
Web Site: www.claricesmithcenter.umd.edu
Management:
Executive Director: Susan Farr
Associate Director Communications: Amy Harbison

Director of Cultural Participation: Ruth Waalkes
Founded: 2001
Specialized Field: Series & Festivals; Dance; Theatre; Opera; World Music; Jazz
Status: Non-Profit, Non-Professional
Paid Staff: 50
Annual Attendance: 250,000
Facility Category: Performing Arts Center with 6 stages
Year Built: 2001

4356
UNIVERSITY OF MARYLAND INTERNATIONAL WILLIAM KAPELL PIANO COMPETITION & FESTIVAL
Suite 3800
University of Maryland
College Park, MD 20742-1625
Phone: 301-405-2993
Fax: 301-405-5977
e-mail: sfarr@umd.edu
Web Site: www.claricesmithcenter.umd.edu
Management:
Executive Director: Susan Farr
Cultural Participation Director: Ruth Waalkes
Executive Administrative Assistant: Kim Thorne
Founded: 1971
Specialized Field: Series and Festivals; Instrumental Music; Vocal Music; Theatre; Youth; Dance; Ethnic Performances
Status: Non-Profit, Professional
Paid Staff: 50
Paid Artists: 100

4357
UNIVERSITY OF MARYLAND INTERNATIONAL WILLIAM KAPELL PIANO COMPETITION & FESTIVAL
Clarice Smith Performing Arts Center
University of Maryland
College Park, MD 20742
Phone: 301-405-8174
Fax: 301-405-5977
e-mail: gmoquin@deans.umd.edu
Web Site: www.claricesmithcenter.umd.edu
Management:
Director: George Moquin
Mission: Sponsoring a major international festival biennially which features recitals, lecture-recitals, master classes and symposia as well as the William Kapell Piano Competition.
Founded: 1971
Specialized Field: Instrumental Music; Festivals
Status: Nonprofit
Income Sources: University of Maryland
Performs At: Tawes Fine Arts Center
Organization Type: Educational; Sponsoring

4358
WILLIAM KAPELL INTERNATIONAL COMPETITION & FESTIVAL
Clarice Smith Performing Arts Center
Suite 3800, University of Maryland
College Park, MD 20742-1625
Phone: 301-405-2993
Fax: 301-405-5977
e-mail: rwaalkes@umd.edu
Web Site: www.claricesmithcenter.umd.edu
Management:
Contact: Brian Jose
Season: May - June

4359
BALTIMORE-WASHINGTON JAZZFEST
PO Box 1105
Columbia, MD 21044-0105
Phone: 410-730-7106
Fax: 410-715-7105
e-mail: africanartmuseum@erols.com
Web Site: www.baltowashjazzfest.org
Officers:
Chairman: Claude M Ligon
Specialized Field: Jazz

4360
COLUMBIA FESTIVAL OF THE ARTS
5575 Sterrett Place, Suite 280
Suite 300
Columbia, MD 21044
Phone: 410-715-3044
Fax: 410-715-3056
e-mail: info@columbiafestival.com
Web Site: www.columbiafestival.com
Officers:
Executive Director: Nichole J. Hickey
Mission: To present a variety of art forms and to make these accessible to the public.
Utilizes: Dancers; Singers; Touring Companies
Founded: 1987
Specialized Field: Dance; Vocal Music; Instrumental Music; Theater; Festivals
Status: Non-Profit
Volunteer Staff: 350
Paid Artists: 250
Budget: $750,000
Income Sources: Major business sponsors; individual & corporate support
Performs At: Merriweather Post Pavilion
Affiliations: The Baltimore Sun; Columbia Association; Columbia Flier
Organization Type: Presenting

4361
EASTERN SHORE CHAMBER MUSIC FESTIVAL
PO Box 461
Easton, MD 21601
Phone: 410-819-0380
Fax: 410-819-0038
e-mail: managingdirector@musicontheshore.org
Web Site: www.musicontheshore.org
Management:
President: James Campbell
Artistic Director: J Lawrie Bloom
Artistic Director: Marcy Rosen
Managing Director: Donald C Buxton
Founded: 1985
Specialized Field: Series and Festivals: Instrumental Music
Status: Non-Profit, Professional
Paid Staff: 2

4362
FREDERICK COMMUNITY COLLEGE ARTS SERIES
Arts Center
Frederick Community College
Frederick, MD 21702
Phone: 301-846-2513
Fax: 301-624-2878
e-mail: wpoindexter@frederick.edu
Web Site: www.frederick.edu
Management:
President: Patricia Stanley
Director: Wendell Poindexter

Founded: 1989
Specialized Field: Series & Festivals; Plays; Music; Lecture Series
Status: Non-Profit, Professional
Paid Staff: 12
Paid Artists: 20
Performs At: Jack B. Kussmaul Theatre
Seating Capacity: 409

4363
FROSTBURG STATE UNIVERSITY CULTURAL EVENTS SERIES
Lane Center
Frostburg State University
Frostburg, MD 21532
Phone: 301-687-4151
Fax: 301-687-7049
e-mail: wmandicott@frostburg.edu
Officers:
Chairman: Bill Mandicott
Management:
Executive Director: Bill Manvicott
Specialized Field: Series & Festivals; Instrumental Music; Vocal Music; Theatre; Youth; Dance; Ethnic Performances
Status: For-Profit, Non-Professional
Paid Staff: 11
Performs At: Physical Education Center

4364
CITY OF GAITHERSBURG CULTURAL ARTS DIVISION
506 S Frederick Road
Gaithersburg, MD 20877
Phone: 301-258-6350
Fax: 301-948-8364
e-mail: dkayser@ci.gaithersburg.md.us
Management:
Cultural Arts Director: Denise Kayser
Arts Barn Director: Marty Willey
Mission: To promote, present, and support rge arts and hummanties.
Founded: 1989
Specialized Field: All Areas
Performs At: Various Auditoriums

4365
OPEN SKY
PO Box 10356
Rockville, MD 20849

Management:
Principal: Suzan Jenkins
Principal: Willard Jenkins
Mission: Open Sky has amassed over thirty years as industry leader in various facets of the jazz, arts, the recording business and jazz media. Provides multifaceted consulting services that tap into its unrivaled acumen in the profit and nonprofit music business and recording industry arenas.
Specialized Field: Jazz

4366
CAPITAL JAZZ FESTIVAL
PO Box 2129
Upper Marlboro, MD 20773
Phone: 301-780-9300
Web Site: www.capitaljazz.com
Management:
Producer: Cliff Hunte
Specialized Field: Jazz festival (contemporary jazz and soul); jazz cruises
Status: Professional

4367
BRIGHT MOMENTS FESTIVAL
University of Massachusetts
15 Campus Center
Amherst, MA 01003
Phone: 413-545-2876
Fax: 413-545-0682
e-mail: gsiegel@stuaf.umass.edu
Web Site: www.umass.edu/fac
Management:
Director: Curry Hicks
Artistic Director: Talvin Wilks
Managing Director: Glenn Siegel

4368
MUSIC AT AMHERST SERIES
Music Department at Amherst College
Amherst, MA 01002-5000
Phone: 413-542-2195
Fax: 413-542-2678
e-mail: mhbaumgarten@amherst.edu
Web Site: www.amherst.edu/~concerts
Management:
Concert Manager: Michael Baumgarten
Specialized Field: Series & Festivals; Instrumental Music; Vocal Music; Ethnic Performances
Status: Non-Profit, Professional
Performs At: Buckley Recital Hall

4369
ANN ARBOR SUMMER FESTIVAL
522 S Fourth Avenue
Suite B
Ann Arbor, MA 48104
Phone: 734-994-5999
Fax: 734-994-5885
e-mail: rwoulfe@umich.edu
Web Site: www.mlive.com/aasf/
Management:
Executive Director: Robb Woulfe
Business/Operations Manager: Jennifer Fike
Development Director: Astrid Giese

4370
ELECTRIC SYMPHONY FESTIVAL
PO Box 1316
Arlington, MA 02474
Phone: 877-646-1304
Fax: 877-646-1304
e-mail: mail@wildflowerpublishers.com
Web Site: www.electricsymphony.com
Management:
Director: James Forte
Mission: Exploring the spirit in music since 1988

4371
JACOB'S PILLOW DANCE FESTIVAL
358 George Carter Road
Becket, MA 01223
Phone: 413-243-9919
Fax: 413-243-4744
e-mail: info@jacobspillow.org
Web Site: www.jacobspillow.org
Management:
Jazz/Musical Dance Director: Chet Walker
Marketing Director: Mariclare Hulbert
Mission: The mission of Jacob's Pillow is to support dance creation, presentation, education, and preservation and to engage and deepen public appreciation and support for dance.

Utilizes: Artists-in-Residence; Choreographers; Dance Companies; Dancers; Educators; Guest Accompanists; Guest Artists; Guest Choreographers; Guest Ensembles; Guest Instructors; Guest Soloists; Guest Speakers; Instructors; Multi Collaborations; Paid Performers; Resident Companies; Soloists; Students
Founded: 1933
Specialized Field: Dance
Status: Professional, Nonprofit
Income Sources: Corporate; Endowment; Foundations; Governments; Membership; Planned Giving
Season: June-August
Performs At: Doris Duke Theatre; Marcia & Seymour Simon Performance Space; Ted Shawn Theatre
Annual Attendance: 70,000
Type of Stage: Flexible
Seating Capacity: 620, 220

4372
BOSTON CONSERVATORY
8 The Fenway
Boston, MA 02215
Phone: 617-912-9153
Fax: 617-247-3159
e-mail: admissions@bostonconservatory.edu
Web Site: www.bostonconservatory.edu
Officers:
    President: Richard Ortner
Management:
    President: Richard Ortner
Founded: 1867
Specialized Field: Series & Festivals; Music; Dance; Theater
Status: For-Profit, Professional

4373
BOSTON UNIVERSITY EARLY MUSIC SERIES
855 Commonwealth Avenue
Boston, MA 02215
Phone: 617-353-3341
Fax: 617-353-7455
e-mail: arts@bu.edu
Web Site: www.bu.edu
Management:
    Director: Robert Dodson
Specialized Field: Series and Festivals; Musicology; Classical Performance
Status: For-Profit, Non-Professional

4374
BOSTON UNIVERSITY EARLY MUSIC SERIES
855 Commonwealth Avenue
Boston, MA 02215
Phone: 617-353-6885
e-mail: mkroll@acs.bu.edu
Management:
    Series Director: Mark Kroll
Seating Capacity: 400

4375
CHARLES RIVER CONCERT SERIES
262 Beacon Street
3rd Floor
Boston, MA 02116
Phone: 617-262-0650
Fax: 617-267-6539
Management:
    Manager: Kathleen Fay

4376
CHARLES RIVER CONCERT SERIES
262 Beacon Street
3rd Floor
Boston, MA 02116
Phone: 617-262-0650
Fax: 617-267-6539
Management:
    Manager: Kathleen Fay
Performs At: Jordan Hall, New England Conservatory of Music

4377
EMMANUEL MUSIC SERIES
15 Newbury Street
Boston, MA 02116
Phone: 617-536-3356
Fax: 617-536-3315
e-mail: music@emmanuelmusic.org
Web Site: www.emmanuelmusic.org
Management:
    Executive Director: Leonard Matczynski
    Artistic Director: Craig Smith

4378
EMMANUEL MUSIC SERIES
15 Newbury Street
Boston, MA 02116
Phone: 617-536-3356
Fax: 617-536-3315
e-mail: emmanmsc@aol.com
Web Site: www.emmanuelmusic.org
Management:
    Executive Director: Leonard Matczynski
    Artistic Director: Craig Smith
Seating Capacity: 1000

4379
FIRST NIGHT BOSTON
31 Snake James Avenue
Suite 949
Boston, MA 02116
Phone: 617-542-1399
Fax: 617-426-9531
e-mail: info@firstnight.org
Web Site: www.firstnight.org
Officers:
    Co-Chairman: Eric Schwarz
    Co-Chairman: Edwin P Tiffany
    Clerk: Royal Dunham Jr
    Treasurer: Charles A Ansbacher
Management:
    Executive Director: Geri Guardino
    Production Director: Amy Havwood
    Marketing Manager: Barbara Wojslawowicz
    Marketing Assistant: Barbara Wojslawowicz
Mission: To use a street fair venue to broaden and deepen the public's appreciation for the visual and performing arts.
Utilizes: Actors; Artists-in-Residence; Choreographers; Collaborations; Dance Companies; Dancers; Fine Artists; Guest Artists; Guest Companies; Guest Musical Directors; Guest Musicians; Instructors; Local Artists; Lyricists; Multi Collaborations; Multimedia; New Productions; Original Music Scores; Playwrights; Selected Students; Sign Language Translators; Soloists; Touring Companies; Visual Arts
Founded: 1976
Specialized Field: Series & Festivals; Instrumental Music; Vocal Music; Theatre; Dance
Status: Non-Profit, Professional
Paid Staff: 12
Volunteer Staff: 400

Paid Artists: 1000
Budget: $1,600,000
Annual Attendance: 2,000,000
Organization Type: Art Presenter

4380
FLEETBOSTON CELEBRITY SERIES
20 Park Plaza
Suite 1032
Boston, MA 02116
Phone: 617-482-2595
Fax: 617-482-3208
e-mail: info@celebrityseries.org
Web Site: www.celebrityseries.org
Officers:
    President: Martha Jones
    Chairman: Harris A Berman
    Treasurer: Norman C Nicholson, Jr
    Clerk: Joseph D Steinfield
Management:
    President and Executive Director: Martha Jones
    Senior VP Programming: Amy W Lam
    Performance Operations Manager: Karen Brown
    Program Coordinator: Carrie Cheron
    Director Marketing: David A Dalena
    Director Education: Suzanne Wilson
Mission: To bring Boston the world's greatest performing artists.
Utilizes: Actors; Artists-in-Residence; Collaborating Artists; Collaborations; Commissioned Composers; Commissioned Music; Composers-in-Residence; Dance Companies; Dancers; Designers; Educators; Five Seasonal Concerts; Guest Accompanists; Guest Choreographers; Guest Companies; Guest Conductors; Guest Directors; Guest Instructors; Guest Musical Directors; Guest Musicians; Instructors; Local Artists; Lyricists; Multi Collaborations; Multimedia; New Productions; Organization Contracts; Original Music Scores; Resident Professionals; Sign Language Translators; Singers; Special Technical Talent; Theatre Companies
Founded: 1938
Specialized Field: Dance; Vocal Music; Instrumental Music; Theater
Status: Non-Profit
Paid Staff: 22
Budget: 6.3 Million
Income Sources: Ticket Sales; Sponsorship; Fundraising
Season: October - January
Performs At: Symphony Hall; Wang Center; Jordan Hall; Shubert Theatre
Affiliations: Association of Performing Arts Presenters; International Society of Performing Arts Dance USA
Annual Attendance: 100,000+
Organization Type: Presenting

4381
HARVARD MUSICAL ASSOCIATION IN BOSTON
57A Chesnut Street
Boston, MA 02108
Phone: 617-523-2897
Fax: 617-523-2897
Management:
    President: Stephen Friedlaender
    Program Director: F Lee Eiseman
Founded: 1837
Specialized Field: Series & Festivals: Chamber Music
Status: Non-Profit, Professional
Paid Staff: 3

4382

HARVARD MUSICAL ASSOCIATION

57A Chesnut Street
Boston, MA 02108
Phone: 617-523-2897
Web Site: http://www.hmaboston.org/
Founded: 1837
Specialized Field: Concert, practice and recital spaces
Status: Private non-profit
Seating Capacity: 100

4383

KING'S CHAPEL CONCERT SERIES

58 Tremont Street
Boston, MA 02108
Phone: 617-227-2155
Fax: 617-227-4101
e-mail: frontdesk@kings-chapel.org
Web Site: www.kings-chapel.org
Management:
   Music Director: Heinrich Christensen
Mission: To offer chamber music, particularly Baroque and contemporary works.
Utilizes: Singers
Founded: 1958
Specialized Field: Series & Festivals; Instrumental Music; Vocal Music; Youth
Status: Non-Profit, Professional
Performs At: King's Chapel
Organization Type: Performing

4384

MUSEUM OF FINE ARTS CONCERTS & PERFORMANCES

465 Huntington Avenue
Boston, MA 02115
Phone: 617-267-9300
Fax: 617-267-9328
e-mail: webmaster@mfa.org
Web Site: www.mfa.org
Management:
   Concert Co-ordinator: Laurie Thomas

4385

MUSEUM OF FINE ARTS CONCERTS & PERFORMANCES

465 Huntington Avenue
Boston, MA 02115
Phone: 617-369-3291
Fax: 617-267-9328
Web Site: www.mfa.org
Management:
   Concert Co-ordinator: Laurie Thomas
Performs At: Remis Auditorium

4386

BRIDGEWATER STATE COLLEGE PROGRAM COMMITTEE

Bridgewater State College
109 Campus Center
Bridgewater, MA 02325
Phone: 508-531-1273
Fax: 508-531-1786
Toll-free: 800-531-2292
e-mail: mthorp@bridgew.edu
Web Site: www.bridgew.edu/tepte
Management:
   President: Thrish Realduto
   Executive Director: Mac Miller
Specialized Field: Series & Festivals; Instrumental Music; Vocal Music; Ethnic Performances; Comedy; Concert In Spring
Status: Non-Profit, Professional

Paid Artists: 100

4387

MASSASOIT COMMUNITY COLLEGE BUCKLEY ARTS CENTER PERFORMANCE SERIES

1 Massasoit Boulevard
Brockton, MA 02302
Phone: 508-427-1234
Fax: 508-427-1267
Management:
   Director: Michael Pevzner
Founded: 1983
Paid Staff: 3

4388

BOSTON EARLY MUSIC FESTIVAL

161 First Street
Suite 202
Cambridge, MA 02142-1207
Phone: 617-661-1812
Fax: 617-661-1816
e-mail: bemf@bemf.org
Web Site: www.bemf.org
Officers:
   Vice President: Donald E. Vaughan
   Vice President: Miles Morgan
   Vice President: Amanda Pond
Management:
   Executive Director: Kathleen Fay
   Director of Marketing: Brian Stuart, brian@bemf.org
   Artistic Director: Stephen Stubbs
   Artistic Director: Paul O'Dette
Mission: To discover and reproduce how early music originally sounded to a composer and his audience; to produce a biennial international festival in Boston; to educate youth.
Utilizes: Guest Artists; Guest Companies; Singers
Founded: 1980
Specialized Field: Series & Festivals; Instrumental Music; Vocal Music; Youth; Dance; Vocal Music; Instrumental Music
Status: Non-Profit, Professional
Paid Staff: 7
Paid Artists: 100
Seating Capacity: 557
Organization Type: Performing; Touring; Educational; Sponsoring

4389

BOSTON GLOBE JAZZ & BLUES FESTIVAL

36 Bay State Road
Cambridge, MA 02138
Phone: 617-929-7900
Web Site: www.boston.com/jazzfest
Management:
   VP: Lisa Desisto
   Director Of Product Development: Michael Manning

4390

CAMBRIDGE SOCIETY FOR EARLY MUSIC: CHAMBER MUSIC SERIES

Box 336
Cambridge, MA 02238-0336
Phone: 617-489-2062
Fax: 617-489-0686
e-mail: csem@csem.org
Web Site: www.csem.org
Management:
   Music Director: Bernard Brauchli

Mission: To entertain, enlighten, educate, and in general promote the rich musical culture of five centuries of Western music occuring up to the early nineteenth century.
Performs At: Fogg Art Museum

4391

MIT GUEST ARTISTS SERIES

77 Massachusetts Avenue
14N-207
Cambridge, MA 02139
Phone: 617-253-2906
Fax: 617-253-4523
e-mail: csnyder@mit.edu/mta
Web Site: www.mit.edu/mta
Management:
   Director: Clarise Snyder
Utilizes: Artists-in-Residence; Composers; Educators; Guest Directors; Guest Musical Directors; Instructors
Performs At: Kresge Auditorium

4392

MIT GUEST ARTISTS SERIES

77 Massachusetts Avenue
14N-207
Cambridge, MA 02139
Phone: 617-253-2906
Fax: 617-253-4523
e-mail: csnyder@mit.edu
Web Site: www.mit.edu/mta/www/
Management:
   Director: Clarise Snyder
Performs At: Kresge Auditorium

4393

REGATTABAR JAZZ FESTIVAL AT THE CHARLES HOTEL

Charles Hotel
One Bennett Street
Cambridge, MA 02138-5780
Phone: 617-864-1200
Fax: 617-864-5715
Toll-free: 800-882-1818
e-mail: generalmail@charleshotel.com
Web Site: www.charleshotel.com
Management:
   Lounge Manager: Jeffrey Keyes

4394

WORLD MUSIC FESTIVAL

720 Massachusetts Avenue
Cambridge, MA 02139
Phone: 617-876-4275
Fax: 617-876-9170
e-mail: worldmus@star.net
Web Site: www.worldmusic.org
Management:
   President: Maure Aronson
   Associate Director: Susan Weiler
Founded: 1990
Specialized Field: Series & Festivals: Concert Promoter
Status: Non-Profit, Non-Professional
Paid Staff: 7

4395

WORLD MUSIC FESTIVAL

720 Massachusetts Avenue
Cambridge, MA 02139
Phone: 617-876-4275
Fax: 617-876-9170
e-mail: worldmus@star.net
Web Site: www.worldmusic.org.html
Management:

Executive Director: Maure Aronson
Associate Director: Susan Weiler
Performs At: Auditoriums

4396
KING RICHARD'S FAIRE
PO Box 419
Carver, MA 02330
Phone: 508-866-5391
Fax: 508-866-8600
Management:
Producer: Bonnie Shapiro
General Manager: Aimee Sedley
Founded: 1982
Specialized Field: Festival
Status: Non-Equity; Commercial
Season: September - October
Performs At: Outdoor with 10 stages and a Tourney Field
Annual Attendance: 200,000

4397
FRIENDS OF THE PERFORMING ARTS
51 Walden Street
PO Box 251
Concord, MA 01742
Phone: 978-369-7911
e-mail: fopac@tiac.net
Web Site: www.tiac.net/users/fopac
Management:
Manager: Kathleen Chick
Performs At: Auditorium

4398
ASTON MAGNA FESTIVAL
323 Main Street
PO Box 28
Great Barrington, MA 01230
Phone: 732-572-5119
Fax: 732-572-5119
Toll-free: 800-875-7156
e-mail: info@astonmagna.org
Web Site: www.astonmagna.org
Management:
President: Daniel Stepner
Executive Director: Ronnie Boriskin
Founded: 1978
Specialized Field: Classical; Baroque

4399
CLOSE ENCOUNTERS WITH MUSIC SERIES
PO Box 34
Great Barrington, MA 01230
Phone: 413-392-6677
Fax: 413-392-9782
Management:
Artistic Director: Yehunda Hanani
Performs At: St. James Church, Great Barrington

4400
HUDSON COMMUNITY ARTS SERIES
155 Apsley Street
Hudson, MA 01749-1697
Phone: 978-562-1646
e-mail: arts_alliance@upwitharts.org
Web Site: www.upwitharts.org
Management:
President: Alison Doherty
Executive Director: Jan Patterson
Specialized Field: Series & Festivals; Vocal Music; Theatre; Youth; Dance; Ethnic Performances
Status: Non-Profit, Professional
Performs At: Hudson High School Auditorium

4401
CASTLE HILL SERIES
Castle Hill
290 Argilla Road
Ipswich, MA 01938
Phone: 978-356-4351
Fax: 978-356-2143
Management:
Events Manager: Jennifer Kyte
Mission: To offer a range of performing arts events at the historic R.T. Crane Estate.
Utilizes: Guest Artists; Original Music Scores; Singers
Founded: 1951
Specialized Field: Vocal Music; Instrumental Music; Limited Small Scale Performances With Local Artists
Status: Professional; Nonprofit
Performs At: Crane Memorial Reservation
Organization Type: Performing; Educational; Sponsoring

4402
TANGLEWOOD FESTIVAL
Tanglewood Music Center
297 West Street
Lenox, MA 01240
Phone: 413-637-1600
Fax: 413-637-5100
e-mail: customerservice@bso.org
Web Site: www.bso.org
Officers:
Chairman: James Levine
Management:
Managing Director: Mark Volpe
Utilizes: Guest Artists; Singers
Founded: 1940
Income Sources: Ticket sales, contributions
Season: Summer
Performs At: Tanglewood
Organization Type: Performing; Educational
Comments: Information at Tanglewood for the disabled is available at the Access Services Center at the Main Gate. The Service Center has alternate format materials, medical equipment, and trained staff available to assist patrons on an as-needed b

4403
CAPE & ISLANDS CHAMBER MUSIC FESTIVAL
216B Orleans Road
North Chatham, MA 02650
Phone: 508-945-8060
Fax: 508-945-8059
Toll-free: 800-818-0608
e-mail: contact@capecodchambermusic.org
Web Site: www.capecodchambermusic.org
Management:
President: Lawrence M Handley
Executive Director: Pamela Patrick
Artistic Director: Nicholas Kitchen
VP: George Dillon
Mission: To present the finest classical and contemporary chamber music by both world-class ensembles and exceptional young emerging artists to Cape Cod audiences; to develop new and younger audiences for chamber music.
Founded: 1980
Specialized Field: Chamber Music
Paid Staff: 2
Volunteer Staff: 30

4404
CAPE COD CHAMBER MUSIC FESTIVAL
216B Orleans Road
Nickerson Corners
North Chatham, MA 02650
Phone: 508-945-8060
Fax: 508-945-8059
Toll-free: 800-818-0608
e-mail: contact@capecodchambermusic.org
Web Site: www.capecodchambermusic.org
Officers:
President: Lawrence M Handley
Treasurer: Laura S Emmons
Secretary: George Dillion
Management:
President: Larry Handley
Executive Director: Nora Hayes
Artistic Director: Nicholas Kitchen
Managing Director: Susan Chalmers
Mission: To present the finest classical and contemporary chamber music by both world-class ensembles and exceptional young emerging artists to Cape Cod audiences; to develop new and younger audiences for chamber music; to commission new chamber works whenever possible; and to provide educational activities and programs which encourage, broaden and deepen appreciation of the chamber music art form.
Founded: 1979
Specialized Field: Series & Festivals; Instrumental Music; Vocal Music; Youth; Dance; Chamber Music
Status: Non-Profit, Professional
Paid Staff: 3
Paid Artists: 30
Facility Category: Usually churches
Seating Capacity: 250 - 300
Organization Type: Performing; Educational

4405
MASSACHUSETTS INTERNATIONAL FESTIVAL OF THE ARTS
274 Main Street
Northampton, MA 01060
Phone: 413-584-4425
Fax: 413-586-5368
Toll-free: 800-224-6432
e-mail: info@mifafestival.org
Web Site: www.mifafestival.org
Management:
Managing Director: Marta Ostapiuk
Artistic/Executive Director: Donald T Sanders
Administrative Assistant: Melissa Hays
Mission: To present the finest contemporary practice in opera, theatre, dance, music, film and the visual arts in three counties of the Pioneer Valley of Western Massachusetts.
Founded: 1993
Specialized Field: Series & Festivals; Theatre; Dance; Opera; Music; Visual arts
Status: Non-Profit, Professional
Paid Staff: 4
Volunteer Staff: 5
Paid Artists: 150

4406
SOUTH MOUNTAIN CONCERTS
PO Box 23
Pittsfield, MA 01202
Phone: 413-442-2106
Web Site: www.southmountainconcert.org
Management:
Director: Lou R Steigler
Founded: 1918

Specialized Field: Series & Festivals: Chamber Music
ConcertS
Status: Non-Profit, Professional
Paid Staff: 2
Paid Artists: 5

4407
ROCKPORT CHAMBER MUSIC FESTIVAL

PO Box 312
Rockport, MA 01966
Phone: 978-546-7391
Fax: 978-546-7391
e-mail: rcmf.info@verizon.net
Web Site: www.rcmf.org
Officers:
   President: Phillip D Cutter MD
   VP: Dianne Anderson
   VP: Barbara Sparks
   Treasurer: William Hausman
   Clerk/Secretary: Mollie Byrnes
Management:
   President: Cameron Smith
   Executive Director: Elizabeth Redmond
   Artistic Director: David Deveau
Mission: The presentation of a 16-concert series in
June, featuring chamber ensembles performing alone
and in collaboration.
Founded: 1982
Specialized Field: Series and Festivals: Chamber
Music Concerts
Status: Non-Profit, Professional
Paid Staff: 2
Paid Artists: 30
Performs At: Rockport Art Association
Organization Type: Presenting

4408
BERKSHIRE CHORAL FESTIVAL

245 N Undermountain Road
Sheffield, MA 01257
Phone: 413-229-8526
Fax: 413-229-0109
e-mail: bcf@choralfest.org
Web Site: www.choralfest.org
Officers:
   President/CEO: Debi Kennedy
Management:
   Music Director: Frank Nemhauser
Mission: A not-for-profit educational institution
dedicated to enhancing the skkills of choral singers
while extending the knowledge & appreciation of choral
singing and its tradition to singers and audiences.
Founded: 1982
Specialized Field: Classical Choral; Orchestral Works
Status: Non-Profit

4409
MOHAWK TRAIL CONCERTS/MUSIC IN DEERFIELD

75 Bridge Street
Shelburne, MA 01370
Phone: 413-625-9511
Fax: 413-625-0221
Toll-free: 888-682-6873
e-mail: info@mohawktrailconcerts.org
Web Site: www.mohawktrailconcerts.org/tickets.html
Management:
   Artistic Director-Deerfield: John Montanari
   Artistic Director-Mohawk Trail: Ruth Black
   Artistic Director-Deerfield: John Montanari
Mission: To offer professional chamber music in the fall
and summer; to provide educational music programs.

Utilizes: Collaborations; Five Seasonal Concerts;
Guest Accompanists; Guest Companies; Guest
Composers; Guest Designers; Guest Directors; Guest
Lecturers; Guest Musical Directors; Guest Musicians;
Instructors; Local Unknown Artists; Multimedia; Music;
New Productions; Organization Contracts; Original
Music Scores; Selected Students; Sign Language
Translators; Singers
Founded: 1969
Specialized Field: Vocal Music; Instrumental Music;
Festivals
Status: Professional; Nonprofit
Paid Staff: 3
Budget: $200,000
Performs At: Federated Church
Annual Attendance: 5,500
Seating Capacity: 225-500
Organization Type: Performing; Touring; Resident;
Educational; Sponsoring

4410
MUSICORDA SUMMER FESTIVAL

PO Box 557
South Hadley, MA 01075
Phone: 413-493-1465
Fax: 413-493-1944
e-mail: musicorda@comcast.net
Web Site: www.musicorda.org
Management:
   Executive Director: Janet Sadler
   Artistic Director: Rachel B Pine
Founded: 1987
Specialized Field: Series & Festivals; Violin; Viola;
Cello; Piano; Chamber Music
Status: Non-Profit, Professional
Paid Staff: 3
Paid Artists: 20

4411
AMERICAN INTERNATIONAL COLLEGE SERIES

Sprague/Griswold Cultural Arts Center
1000 State Street
Springfield, MA 01109
Phone: 413-747-6393
Fax: 413-737-2803
Management:
   Visual/Performing Arts Director: Alvin Paige
Performs At: Auditorium

4412
SPRINGFIELD PERFORMING ARTS DEVELOPMENT CORPORATION

1 Columbus Center
Springfield, MA 01103
Phone: 413-788-7646
Fax: 413-737-9991
e-mail: tdagostino@citystage.symphonyhall.com
Web Site: www.citystage.symphonyhall.com
Management:
   President: Cynthia Anzalotti
   Marketing Director: Ken Scally
   Technical Director: Chad Labombard
   Box Office Manager: Faldo Rossane
Mission: Professional presenting theatres.
Founded: 1998
Specialized Field: Series & Festivals; Theater; Youth;
Dance; Ethnic Performances
Status: Non-Profit, Professional
Paid Staff: 8
Volunteer Staff: 50

4413
BERKSHIRE THEATRE FESTIVAL

PO Box 797
Stockbridge, MA 01262
Phone: 413-298-5576
Fax: 413-298-3368
Toll-free: 866-811-4111
e-mail: info@berkshiretheatre.org
Web Site: www.berkshiretheatre.org
Officers:
   President: James W Giddens
   Vice President: B Carter White
   Secretary: Judith C Knight
   Treasurer: Robert W Trask
Management:
   Executive Director: Kate Maguire
   Artistic Director: E Gray Simons III
   Production Manager: Peter Durgin
   Director Finance/Administration: Richard
Czelusniak
   Director Development: Nina Garlington
   Director Marketing/Public Relations: Eileen
Pierce
   Box Office/Subscriptions Manager: Ronald
Nantell
Mission: To produce and promote thought-provoking
theatre for its community throughout the summer
through performance and educational activities.
Utilizes: Singers
Founded: 1928
Specialized Field: Theater; Festivals
Status: Professional; Nonprofit
Paid Staff: 12
Income Sources: Actors' Equity Association; Council
of Resident Summer Theatres
Season: June - September
Performs At: Playhouse, Unicorn Theatre
Type of Stage: Proscenium, Thrust
Seating Capacity: 415, 122
Organization Type: Performing; Resident; Educational;
Sponsoring

4414
BENTLEY COLLEGE BOWLES PREFORMANCE SERIES

STU 330, 175 Forest Street
Waltham, MA 02154
Phone: 781-891-3424
Fax: 781-891-2839
e-mail: jmorris@bentley.edu
Web Site: www.bentley.edu
Management:
   Performing Arts Coordinator: Jim Morris
Specialized Field: Series & Festivals; Instrumental
Music; Vocal Music; Theatre; Dance; Ethnic
Performances
Status: Non-Profit, Professional
Performs At: Lindsay Auditorium

4415
BRANDEIS SYMPHONY ORCHESTRA

Slosberg Musical Building MS 051
Waltham, MA 02454
Phone: 781-736-3328
Fax: 781-736-3320
e-mail: brocksym@email.msn.com
Web Site: www.brandeis.edu/departments/music
Management:
   Music Director: Neal Hampton

4416

BRANDEIS UNIVERSITY SPINGOLD THEATER CENTER SERIES

Spingold Theater Center, Brandeis University
MS072, PO Box 549110
Waltham, MA 02454-9110
Phone: 781-736-3400
Fax: 781-736-3389
e-mail: spingold@brandeis.edu
Web Site: www.brandeis.edu/theater
Management:
   Head of Department: Eric Hill
   General Manager: David Colfer
Founded: 1948
Specialized Field: Student Theatre Productions
Featureing Brandies Graduates; Undergraduate Actors;
Guest Artists
Status: Non-Profit, Professional
Seating Capacity: 744

4417

WALTHAM COMMUNITY CONCERT SERIES

124 Felton Street
Suite 2
Waltham, MA 02453-4119
Phone: 781-891-3740
Fax: 781-891-3740
e-mail: sbkilgore@mediaone.net
Management:
   Director: Stephen Kilgore
Performs At: Waltham Public Library

4418

ALL NEWTON MUSIC SCHOOL, THE ANDREW WOLF CONCERT SERIES

321 Chesnut Street
West Newton, MA 02465
Phone: 617-527-4553
Fax: 617-527-7710
e-mail: anms@allnewtonmusicschool.com
Web Site: www.allnewtonmusicschool.com
Officers:
   President: Catherine Grein
   Executive Director: Paulette Brown
   Utilizes: Collaborations; Guest Companies; Guest
Instructors; Guest Musical Directors; Guest Musicians;
Guest Writers; Multimedia
Founded: 1911
Specialized Field: Music Instruction
Status: Non-Profit, Professional
Paid Staff: 4
Paid Artists: 65
Budget: $1,500,000
Income Sources: Tuition; Grants; Donations
Performs At: Salon
Annual Attendance: 800
Facility Category: Mansion
Type of Stage: Salon in the Round
Seating Capacity: 175
Year Built: 1900

4419

WESTFIELD STATE COLLEGE MUSIC & MORE PERFORMING ARTS SERIES

Western Avenue
Westfield, MA 01086
Phone: 413-572-5438

4420

CONCERTS-AT-THE-COMMON

Harvard Unitarian Church
POBox 217; 9 Ayer Rd.
32 Coburn Road
Weston, MA 01451
Phone: 978-779-2876
Web Site:
http://www.uuharvard.org/CongregationalLife/SpecialEv
ents/Concerts.aspx
Officers:
   Concert Series Director: Bernard J Fine
Management:
   Planning Committee: Pat White
   Planning Committee: Eleanor Toth
Mission: To present community concerts.
Founded: 1979
Specialized Field: Vocal Music; Instrumental Music
Status: Nonprofit
Organization Type: Sponsoring

4421

WILLIAMS COLLEGE SERIES

Bernhard Music Center
54 Chapin Hill Drive
Williamstown, MA 01267
Phone: 413-597-2736
Fax: 413-597-3100
e-mail: eclark@williams.edu
Web Site: www.williams.edu/music
Officers:
   Music Department Chairman: David Kechley
Management:
   President: Morton Schupiro
   Executive Director: David Kechley
   Artistic Director: Ronald Feltman
   Managing Director: Ernest Clark
Founded: 1700
Specialized Field: Series & Festivals; Instrumental
Music; Vocal Music; Ethnic Performances
Status: Non-Profit, Professional
Paid Staff: 1
Paid Artists: 50

4422

WILLIAMSTOWN THEATRE FESTIVAL

PO Box 517
Williamstown, MA 01267-0517
Phone: 413-458-3200
Fax: 413-458-3147
e-mail: wtfinfo@wtfestival.org
Web Site: www.wtfestival.org
Officers:
   President: Dr. Ira Lapidus
   Vice President: Brian D Cabral
   Secretary: Fred A Windover
   Treasurer: Jid Sprague
Management:
   Producer: Michael Ritchie
   General Manager: Deborah Fehr
   Associate Producer: Jenny Gersten
   Business Manager: Julie Cammer
   Administrative Assistant: Juliet Flynt
   Development Director: Bart Reidy
   Production Manager: Christopher Atkins
   Workshop Director: Amanda Charlton
   Company Manager: Michael Coglan
Mission: To present outstanding productions of modern
classics on our main stage; to develop new acting,
writing and musical talent.
Utilizes: Actors; AEA Actors; Artists-in-Residence;
Choreographers; Commissioned Composers;
Commissioned Music; Designers; Educators; Guest

Accompanists; Guest Artists; Guest Companies; Guest
Conductors; Guest Designers; Guest Ensembles;
Guest Lecturers; Guest Musical Directors; High School
Drama; Music; Original Music Scores; Performance
Artists; Poets; Resident Artists; Resident Professionals;
Singers; Soloists; Student Interns
Founded: 1954
Specialized Field: Series & Festivals: Theatre
Status: Non-Profit, Professional
Paid Staff: 75
Volunteer Staff: 150
Paid Artists: 100
Non-paid Artists: 40
Budget: $2,500,000
Performs At: Adams Memorial Theater; Nikos Stage
Annual Attendance: 50,000
Seating Capacity: 520
Organization Type: Performing
Comments: September-May in NYC 212-395-9090

4423

WORCESTER MUSIC FESTIVAL

323 Main Street
Worcester, MA 01608
Phone: 508-754-3231
Fax: 508-754-8698
e-mail: music@musicworcester.org
Web Site: www.musicworcester.org
Management:
   Executive Director: Stasia B Hovenesian
   Marketing Coordinator: Margaret Hamilton
Founded: 1858
Specialized Field: Series & Festivals; Instrumental
Music; Vocal Music; Theatre; Youth; Dance; Ethnic
Performances; Classical Orchestras; Soloist; Chamber
Ensembles; J
Status: Non-Profit, Professional
Paid Staff: 5

4424

WORCESTER MUSIC FESTIVAL

323 Main Street
Worcester, MA 01608
Phone: 508-754-3231
Fax: 508-754-8698
e-mail: music@musicworcester.org
Web Site: www.musicworcester.org
Management:
   Executive Director: Stasia B Hovenesian
   Marketing Assistant: Avril K Waye
   Marketing Coordinator: Cynthia Wood
Mission: To present performances of the highest
quality through Worcester Music Festival, International
Artist Series, Mass Jazz Festival and Music for
Children; to educate all ages about music composers,
history, etc.
Utilizes: Collaborations; Dance Companies; Guest
Choreographers; Guest Directors; Guest Instructors;
Guest Musical Directors; Guest Musicians; Multimedia;
Original Music Scores; Sign Language Translators;
Singers; Student Interns; Theatre Companies
Founded: 1858
Specialized Field: Classical Orchestras; Soloist;
Chamber Ensembles; Jazz Groups; Dance Ensembles
Status: Nonprofit; Cultural Organization
Paid Staff: 5
Performs At: Mechanics Hall; Tuckerman Hall
Annual Attendance: 26,000
Facility Category: Concert Halls
Seating Capacity: 1,550 & 550 (2 stages)

Michigan

4425
ADRIAN COLLEGE EVENTS SERIES
Pellowe Hall
110 S Madison Street
Adrian, MI 49221
Phone: 517-264-3156
Fax: 517-264-3156
e-mail: mmoran@adrian.edu
Web Site: www.adrian.edu
Management:
   President: Stanley Paine
   Artistic Director: Thomas Hodzman
Founded: 1859
Specialized Field: Liberal Arts College
Status: Non-Profit, Non-Professional
Performs At: Dawson Auditorium

4426
ALBION PERFORMING ARTIST & LECTURE SERIES
Albion College
611 E Porter Street
Albion, MI 49224
Phone: 517-629-1000
Fax: 517-629-0566
Web Site: www.albion.edu
Management:
   President: Peter T Mitchell
Founded: 1835
Performs At: Goodrich Chapel

4427
GRAND VALLEY STATE UNIVERSITY ARTS AT NOON SERIES
Grand Valley State University
Allendale, MI 49401
Phone: 616-895-3484
Fax: 616-895-3100
e-mail: vandenwj@gvsu.edu
Management:
   Arts At Noon Coordinator: Julianne Vanden Wyngaard
Performs At: Louis Armstrong Theatre

4428
ALMA COLLEGE PERFORMING ARTS SERIES
Heritage Center
614 W Superior
Alma, MI 48801
Phone: 989-463-7111
Fax: 517-463-7277
e-mail: boxoffice@alma.edu
Web Site: www.alma.edu
Management:
   President: Dave Blanford
   Managing Director: Dave Young
Founded: 1993
Specialized Field: Musician; Lecture; Dance Groups; Theatre
Status: Non-Profit, Professional
Paid Staff: 12
Performs At: Heritage Center for the Performing Arts

4429
THUNDER BAY ARTS COUNCIL
313 1/2 N 2Nd Avenue
Alpena, MI 49707-2805
Phone: 517-356-6678
e-mail: hoarts@freeway.net
Officers:

President: Duane Beyer
Mission: The promotion of cultural arts through the coordination of events and the sponsoring of various performances.
Utilizes: Guest Artists; Guest Companies; Singers
Founded: 1971
Specialized Field: Dance; Vocal Music; Instrumental Music; Theatre; Lyric Opera
Status: Professional; Nonprofit
Organization Type: Educational; Sponsoring

4430
ANN ARBOR BLUES & JAZZ FESTIVAL
PO Box 7456
Ann Arbor, MI 48107
Phone: 734-747-9955
e-mail: info@jazzfest.org
Web Site: www.a2.blues.jazzfest.org

4431
ANN ARBOR SUMMER FESTIVAL
400 4th Street
Room 150
Ann Arbor, MI 48103
Phone: 734-647-2278
Fax: 734-936-3393
e-mail: Evyw@umich.edu
Web Site: www.annarborsummerfestival.org
Officers:
   Business Manager: Jeanne Rowlette
   Marketing Director: Colleen Murdock
   President: John C Clark
   Chairman: Anne K. Rubin
Management:
   President: Ingrid Sheldon
   Production Manager: Evy Warshawski
Mission: To offer both ticketed and free of charge performing arts events to Ann Arbor area residents.
Utilizes: Artists-in-Residence; Collaborating Artists; Dance Companies; Dancers; Guest Choreographers; Guest Directors; Guest Instructors; Guest Musicians; Lyricists; Multimedia; Original Music Scores; Sign Language Translators; Singers; Special Technical Talent; Theatre Companies
Founded: 1978
Specialized Field: Series and Festivals; Instrumental Music; Vocal Music; Theatre; Dance; Ethnic Performances; Festivals
Status: Non-Profit, Professional
Paid Staff: 5
Volunteer Staff: 100
Paid Artists: 75
Budget: $1,000,000
Income Sources: Donations from Businesses & Individuals; Grants
Performs At: Power Center; Lydia Mendelssohn; Top of the Park
Affiliations: University of Michigan; City of Ann Arbor
Annual Attendance: 50,000
Type of Stage: Thrust, Proscenium
Stage Dimensions: 40x60
Seating Capacity: 1,300
Organization Type: Performing; Sponsoring

4432
MICHIGAN ASSOCIATION OF COMMUNITY ARTS AGENCIES
107 Miller Avenue
Ann Arbor, MI 48104
Phone: 734-996-2500
Fax: 734-996-3317
Toll-free: 800-649-3777
e-mail: macaa@macaa.com
Web Site: www.macaa.com

Officers:
   President: Oliver Ragsdale, Jr
Management:
   Executive Director: Deborah E Mikula
Mission: Exists to support, strengthen, and unite community arts and organizations in Michigan.
Founded: 1977
Specialized Field: Arts Service Organization
Status: Non-Profit
Paid Staff: 7

4433
MPULSE ANN ARBOR
1100 Baits Drive
1281 Moore Building
Ann Arbor, MI 48109-2085
Phone: 734-936-2660
Fax: 734-647-0140
Toll-free: 866-936-2660
e-mail: mpulse@umich.edu
Web Site: www.music.umich.edu/special_programs/youth/mpulse
Management:
   Program Manager: Sarah Rau
   Program Coordinator: Bonnie Mills-Martin
Mission: MPulse Ann Arbor is a summer phenomenon on the University of Michigan xcampus carrying high school students to exciting new levels of excellence in usic performance, music technology, musical theatre, theatre and dance.

4434
MUSICAL SOCIETY OF THE UNIVERSITY SERIES
Burton Memorial Tower
881 N University
Ann Arbor, MI 48109-1011
Phone: 734-764-2538
Fax: 734-647-1171
Toll-free: 800-221-1239
e-mail: umstix@umich.edu
Web Site: www.ums.org
Officers:
   Chairperson: Beverley Geltner
   Vice Chair: Lester Monts
   Secretary: Pruuueu Rosentnal
   Treasurer: David Featherman
   President: Kenneth C. Fischer
Management:
   President: Ken Fisher
   Director Programming: Michael Kondziolka
   Director Administration: John Kennard
   Director Development: Christina Thoburn
   Director Education: Ben Johnson
Mission: To provide professional theatre, dance and music for Southeastern Michigan students and residents.
Utilizes: Singers; Special Technical Talent; Theatre Companies
Founded: 1879
Specialized Field: Series & Festivals: Musical Performance
Status: Non-Profit, Professional
Paid Staff: 30
Budget: $6,000,000
Income Sources: Ticket Sales; Fundraising
Performs At: Hill Auditorium; Power Center; Rackham Auditorium
Annual Attendance: 150,000
Organization Type: Performing; Educational

4435

BAY ARTS COUNCIL

915 Washington Avenue
Bay City, MI 48708
Phone: 989-893-0343
Fax: 989-893-6443
e-mail: contactus@bayartscouncil.org
Web Site: www.bayartscouncil.org
Management:
    President: Cynthia Gracey
    Managing Director: Tom Niemann
    Administrative Assistant: Laura Cunningham
Founded: 1978
Specialized Field: Series & Festivals; Vocal Music;
Theatre; Youth; Dance
Status: Non-Profit, Professional
Paid Staff: 2
Volunteer Staff: 50
Paid Artists: 25
Non-paid Artists: 10

4436

BAY VIEW MUSIC FESTIVAL

6111 Evanston Ave
Bay View, MI 46220
Mailing Address: PO Box 1596
Phone: 231-225-8877
Web Site: www.bayviewfestival.org
Management:
    Artistic Director: Chris Ludwa
Specialized Field: Vocal Music; Instrumental Music;
Opera; Chamber Music; Chamber Orchestra; Theater

4437

FERRIS STATE UNIVERSITY-ARTS & LECTURES SERIES

1201 S State
CSS 208A
Big Rapids, MI 49307
Phone: 231-591-3626
Fax: 231-591-3067
e-mail: hadley-p@ferris.edu
Web Site: www.ferris.edu
Officers:
    Chairman: Daniel Cronk
    Chairman: J Randall Groves
Management:
    President: Davis Eisler
    Executive Director: Dan Cronk
    Auditorium Manager: Michael Terry
Utilizes: Dance Companies; Dancers; Fine Artists;
Guest Musicians; Guest Soloists; Local Artists;
Multimedia; Original Music Scores; Selected Students;
Singers; Theatre Companies
Specialized Field: Series & Festivals; Instrumental
Music; Vocal Music; Theatre; Youth; Dance; Ethnic
Performances
Status: Non-Profit, Professional
Paid Staff: 2
Budget: $40,000
Income Sources: Ticket Sales; Donations; Grants
Performs At: Williams Auditorium
Affiliations: Michigan Nonprofit Presenters Network
Type of Stage: Proscenium
Seating Capacity: 1,800

4438

AMERICAN ARTISTS SERIES

435 Goodhue Road
Bloomfield Hills, MI 48304
Phone: 313-547-2230
Fax: 313-547-1525
Management:

Executive Director: Leonard Mazern
    Artistic Director: Joann Freeman
    Business Manager: Morton Malitz
Mission: Sponsoring diverse performing arts programs,
which include guest artists and native musicians.
Utilizes: Dance Companies
Founded: 1970
Specialized Field: Instrumental Music; Theatre;
Chamber Music
Status: Professional; Nonprofit
Performs At: Kingswood Auditorium
Organization Type: Performing; Touring; Sponsoring

4439

CRANBROOK MUSIC GUILD CONCERT SERIES

Lone Pine & Cranbrook Rds; PO Box 402
Bloomfield Hills, MI 48303
Phone: 248-644-6352
Web Site: www.cranbrookmusicguild.org
Officers:
    Program Chairman: Anita Demarco Goor
    President: William R Brashear
Management:
    Contact: Anita Goor
Specialized Field: Chamber Music
Performs At: Cranbrook House Library

4440

GOPHERWOOD CONCERT SERIES

119 Marble
Cadillac, MI 49601
Phone: 231-775-7084
e-mail: pbrown@michweb.net
Web Site:
www.users.michweb.net/~pbrown/gopherwood.htm
Performs At: Auditorium

4441

VILLAGE BACH FESTIVAL

PO Box 27
Cass City, MI 48726
Phone: 517-872-3465
Fax: 517-872-2301
Mission: Promoting professional musical events in
Michigan's Thumb Area.
Founded: 1979
Specialized Field: Vocal Music; Instrumental Music;
Festivals
Status: Professional; Nonprofit
Organization Type: Performing

4442

CHEBOYGAN AREA ARTS COUNCIL/OPERA HOUSE

403 N Huron Street
Cheboygan, MI 49721
Phone: 231-627-5432
Fax: 231-627-2643
e-mail: pam@theoperahouse.org
Web Site: www.theoperahouse.org
Officers:
    President: Jeff Schmidt
    Treasurer: Tom Cadwalader
Management:
    Executive Director: Pam Westover
    Manager: Dolores Kozlowski
Founded: 1877
Status: Non-Profit, Professional

4443

CASA DE UNIDAS SERIES

1920 Scotten
Detroit, MI 48209
Phone: 313-843-9598
Fax: 313-843-7307
e-mail: casadeunidad@sbcglobal.net
Web Site: www.casadeunidad.org
Officers:
    Executive Director: Veronica A. Paiz
Management:
    Program Coordinator: Marta Lagos
Mission: Providing community-based, performing arts
presentations for Detroit's Hispanic communities.
Utilizes: Guest Companies; Singers
Founded: 1981
Specialized Field: Series & Festivals; Dance; Vocal
Music; Instrumental Music; Theatre; Youth
Status: Non-Profit, Non-Professional
Paid Staff: 10
Performs At: Clark Park Theatre
Organization Type: Performing; Touring; Educational;
Sponsoring

4444

DETROIT FESTIVAL OF THE ARTS

4735 Cass Avenue
Detroit, MI 48202
Phone: 313-577-5088
Fax: 313-577-3332
e-mail: maureen.riley@wayne.edu
Web Site: www.detroitfestival.com
Officers:
    President: Susan Mosey
Management:
    President: Sue Mosey
    Executive Director: Moreen Riley
    Artistic Director: Njia Kai
Mission: To encourage use of the University Cultural
Center of Detroit, and introduce the resources of the
area to the metropoliton community.
Founded: 1976
Specialized Field: Series & Festivals: Music
Status: Non-Profit, Professional
Paid Staff: 7
Volunteer Staff: 400
Paid Artists: 60
Non-paid Artists: 150
Budget: 1,300,000
Income Sources: Corporate; Private; State
Performs At: Outdoors; 20 Blocks
Affiliations: Wayne State University and University
Cultural Center Association
Annual Attendance: 300,000
Facility Category: Various Outdoor Venues
Type of Stage: 3 Main, 1 Childrens, 2 Coffeehouses

4445

FORD DETROIT INTERNATIONAL JAZZ FESTIVAL

350 Madison Avenue
Detroit, MI 48226
Phone: 313-963-7622
Fax: 313-963-2462
Web Site: www.detroitjazzfest.com
Management:
    President: Cameron Duncan
    Artistic Director: Frank Malfitano
    Managing Director: Jeff Wilson
    Director Media Relations: Michael Vigilant
Mission: Preserving, promoting and maintaining the
understanding and appreciation of jazz music.
Founded: 1980

Specialized Field: Series & Festivals: Jazz
Status: Non-Profit, Professional
Annual Attendance: 770,000
Facility Category: Outdoor Festival
Organization Type: Performing; Sponsoring

4446
SYRACUSE JAZZ FESTIVAL
655 Brush Street
#2815
Detroit, MI 48226
Phone: 313-961-2166
Fax: 313-961-2177
e-mail: info@syracusejazzfest.com
Web Site: www.syracusejazzfest.com

4447
UNITED BLACK ARTISTS: USA SERIES
7661 Lasalle Boulevard
Detroit, MI 48206
Phone: 313-898-5574
Fax: 313-898-5574
Management:
 President: Robert Warren
 Volunteer Artistic Director: Ann Marshall
Mission: Encouraging cultural opportunities and
education among Detroit's black communities.
Founded: 1987
Specialized Field: Promotions Of Potential Black
Artists
Status: Non-Profit, Non-Professional
Paid Staff: 20
Income Sources: Harmony Park Playhouse
Organization Type: Educational; Sponsoring

4448
FLINT INSTITUTE OF MUSIC
1025 E Kearsley Street
Flint, MI 48503
Phone: 810-238-1350
Fax: 810-238-6385
Toll-free: 800-395-4849
e-mail: fim@thefim.com
Web Site: www.flintinstituteofmusic.com
Officers:
 President: Paul Torre
Management:
 President: Paul Torre
 Marketing Director: Christina Ferris
 Director Flint School Performing: Davin
Piersontorre
 Manager Flint Symphony: Tom Glasscok
 Director Ticket: Linda Tomlinson
 Director Development: Carol Hartley
Mission: Providing a lifelong continuum of music and
dance.
Utilizes: Guest Artists; Singers
Founded: 1917
Specialized Field: Music
Status: Non-Profit, Professional
Paid Artists: 75
Performs At: Whiting Auditorium
Annual Attendance: 3,500

4449
MUSIC IN THE PARKS
Flint, MI
Fax: 610-327-4786
Toll-free: 800-323-0974
e-mail: info@edprog.com
Web Site:
www.educationalprograms.com/frame_mitp.html
Management:
 President: Dr James R Wells

Program Coordinator: Kathy Bird

4450
GAYLORD AREA COUNCIL FOR THE ARTS
PO Box 249
Gaylord, MI 49734
Phone: 517-732-3242
e-mail: nordeen@avci.net
Management:
 Manager: Kate Nordeen
Performs At: Auditorium

4451
FESTIVAL OF THE ARTS
300 Waters Building
161 Ottawa NW #300
Grand Rapids, MI 49503
Phone: 616-459-2787
Fax: 616-459-7160
Management:
 Executive Director: Tammy Ramaker
Mission: To support the arts and artists of the Greater
Grand Rapids Community; to promote and support the
arts financially and through technical assistance to
organizations or individuals; to promote experiences for
participants and observers from within the general
public.
Utilizes: Instructors
Founded: 1970
Specialized Field: Dance; Vocal Music; Instrumental
Music; Theater; Festivals
Status: Professional; Nonprofit
Paid Staff: 3000
Budget: $300,000
Performs At: Calder Plaza
Annual Attendance: 300,000
Organization Type: Sponsoring
Resident Groups: Regional artists only

4452
REIF ARTS CENTER
720 Conifer Drive
Grand Rapids, MI 55744
Phone: 218-327-5780
Fax: 218-327-5798
e-mail: dmarty@reifcenter.org
Web Site: www.reifcenter.org
Officers:
 Board Chair: Kirk Adams
 President: David Marty
Mission: Stimulating arts in Northern Minnesota.
Founded: 1981
Opened: 1981
Specialized Field: Series and Festivals; Instrumental
Music; Vocal Music; Theatre; Youth; Dance; Ethnic
Performances; Multi-Disciplinary
Status: Non-Profit, Professional
Paid Staff: 8
Paid Artists: 150
Budget: $980,000
Income Sources: Sales; Grants; Tuition
Annual Attendance: 24,000
Type of Stage: Proscenium; Modified Thrust
Stage Dimensions: 50' x 38'
Seating Capacity: 642
Year Built: 1981
Year Remodeled: 2005
Rental Contact: John Miller

4453
GROSSE POINTE WAR MEMORIAL
32 Lake Shore Drive
Grosse Pointe Farms, MI 48236

Phone: 313-881-7511
Fax: 313-884-6638
e-mail: mweber@warmemorial.org
Web Site: www.warmemorial.org
Management:
 President: Mark R Weber
 Community Relations and Development: Teri L
Carroll
 Finance Director: Elizabeth A Berry
 Director Lifelong Learning: Lou Anne Wattrick
Mission: To offer outdoor performances in the summer
via Summer Music Festival and other events during the
year.
Utilizes: Guest Artists; Singers
Founded: 1949
Specialized Field: Vocal Music; Instrumental Music;
Theater; Festivals; Lyric Opera
Status: Professional; Nonprofit
Performs At: Terrace of Alger House
Organization Type: Performing; Touring; Resident

4454
PINE MOUNTAIN MUSIC FESTIVAL
PO Box 406
Hancock, MI 49930
Phone: 906-482-1542
Toll-free: 888-309-7861
e-mail: festival@pmmf.org
Web Site: www.pmmf.org
Officers:
 President: William Leder
 VP: Joy Ibsen
 Secretary: Diane Eshbach
 Treasurer: Ellen Bechthold
Management:
 Executive Director: Peter Van Pelt
 Artistic Director: Joshua Major
Mission: Serve upper Midwest with opera, symphony,
and chamber music during June and July.
Founded: 1991
Specialized Field: Series & Festivals; Instrumental
Music; Vocal Music; Youth; Classical Music; Opera
Symphony Chamber
Status: Non-Profit, Professional
Paid Staff: 4
Volunteer Staff: 200
Paid Artists: 100
Budget: $500,000
Income Sources: Grants; Box Office; Donations;
Foundations
Performs At: Rented Theaters
Affiliations: Opera America
Annual Attendance: 8,000
Facility Category: Various

4455
HOLLAND AREA ARTS COUNCIL
150 E 8th Street
Holland, MI 49423
Phone: 616-396-3278
Fax: 616-396-6298
Management:
 Executive Director: Brenda S Nienhouse

4456
HOPE COLLEGE GREAT PERFORMANCE SERIES
Hope College
PO Box 9000
Holland, MI 49422-9000
Phone: 616-395-7893
Fax: 616-395-7191
e-mail: emerson@hope.edu
Web Site: www.hope.edu/arts

Management:
President: Jim Boltman
Executive Director: Derek Emerson
Utilizes: Actors; Artists-in-Residence; Dance
Companies; Dancers; Multimedia; Playwrights; Special
Technical Talent
Founded: 1975
Specialized Field: Series & Festivals; Chamber Music;
Dance; Theatre
Status: Non-Profit, Professional
Paid Staff: 1
Paid Artists: 6
Performs At: DeWitt Center
Annual Attendance: 4000
Facility Category: 3 different venues

4457
MICHIGAN RENAISSANCE FESTIVAL
12600 Dixie Highway
Holly, MI 48442
Phone: 248-634-5552
Fax: 248-634-7590
Toll-free: 800-601-4848
e-mail: renaissancegraphics@comcast.net
Web Site: www.michrenfest.com
Management:
General Manager: Christine Daye
Site Operations/Special Events: Kathy Parker
Mission: Promoting Renaissance traditions in the area
of Southeastern Michigan.
Founded: 1980
Specialized Field: Dance; Vocal Music; Instrumental
Music; Theater; Festivals
Status: Professional; Commercial
Paid Staff: 30
Volunteer Staff: 200
Paid Artists: 100
Non-paid Artists: 100
Performs At: Hollygrove; Holly
Organization Type: Performing

4458
MTU/GREAT EVENTS SERIES
1400 Townsend Drive
Center Room 106
Houghton, MI 49931
Phone: 906-487-2844
Fax: 906-487-3552
e-mail: rozsa@mtu.edu
Web Site: www.greatevents.mtu.edu
Management:
Director Great Events: Valerie Pegg
Utilizes: Actors; Artists-in-Residence; Collaborations;
Commissioned Music; Dance Companies; Dancers;
Fine Artists; Grant Writers; Guest Accompanists; Guest
Choreographers; Guest Composers; Guest Designers;
Guest Instructors; Guest Lecturers; Guest Musical
Directors; Guest Musicians; Guest Soloists; Instructors;
Local Artists; Local Unknown Artists; Multimedia; Music;
Organization Contracts; Original Music Scores;
Playwrights; Resident Artists; Resident Professionals;
Selected Students; Sign Language Translators;
Singers; Soloists; Student Interns; Special Technical
Talent; Theatre Companies; Visual Arts
Specialized Field: Performing; Educational
Paid Staff: 7
Volunteer Staff: 60
Budget: $130,000
Income Sources: Box Office; Grants; Private
Donations
Performs At: Performing Arts Theatre; Concert Hall
Facility Category: Performing Arts Center
Seating Capacity: 1,101
Year Built: 2000

Rental Contact: Kelly Thomas

4459
INTERLOCHEN CENTER FOR ARTS
PO Box 199
Interlochen, MI 49643
Phone: 231-276-7200
Fax: 231-276-7442
e-mail: woodwr@interlochen.org
Web Site: www.interlochen.org
Management:
President: Jeffrey Kimpton
Executive Director: William Wood
Artistic Director: Tim Wade
Managing Director: Jennifer Weising
Founded: 1928
Specialized Field: All Kinds of Arts; Summercamp
Status: Non-Profit, Non-Professional
Paid Staff: 198
Paid Artists: 50

4460
INTERLOCHEN ARTS FESTIVAL
PO Box 199
Interlochen, MI 49643-0199
Phone: 231-276-4455
Fax: 231-276-4417
e-mail: paulsontm@interlochen.org
Web Site: www.interlochen.org
Officers:
Radio/Presentations VP: Thom Paulson
Mission: To offer an eight-week extension of the
National Music Camp.
Utilizes: Guest Companies; Singers
Founded: 1928
Specialized Field: Dance; Vocal Music; Instrumental
Music; Theater
Status: Semi-Professional; Nonprofit
Performs At: Kresge Auditorium; Corson Auditorium
Organization Type: Performing; Educational

4461
MICHIGAN SHAKESPEARE FESTIVAL
Box 323
Jackson, MI 49204
Phone: 517-788-5032
Fax: 517-788-5254
Toll-free: 866-705-2636
e-mail: thebard@michshakefest.org
Web Site: www.michshakefest.org
Officers:
President: Ann Green
VP: Tom Mitchell
Secretary: Rick Davies
Treasurer: Margaret Musser
Management:
Artistic Director: John Neville-Andrews
President: Rick Davies
VP: Jennifer Brunk
Mission: Quality outdoor Shakespeare.
Founded: 1995
Status: For-Profit,Professional
Paid Staff: 8
Volunteer Staff: 6
Paid Artists: 60
Season: July - August
Type of Stage: Thrust
Stage Dimensions: 40' x 30'
Seating Capacity: 350

4462
BACH FESTIVAL SOCIETY OF
KALAMAZOO
Kalamazoo College
1200 Academy Street
Kalamazoo, MI 49006
Phone: 616-337-7407
Fax: 616-337-7067
e-mail: jturner@kzoo.edu -or- bach@kzoo.edu
Management:
Artistic Director/Conductor: James Turner

4463
FONTANA FESTIVAL OF MUSIC & ART
Fontana Concert Society
821 W South Street
Kalamazoo, MI 49007
Phone: 616-382-0826
Fax: 616-382-0812
e-mail: fontana@iserv.net
Web Site: www.fontanafestival.org
Management:
Executive Director: Janet Karpus

4464
IRVING S GILMORE INTERNATIONAL
KEYBOARD FESTIVAL
359 S Kalamazoo Mall
Suite 101
Kalamazoo, MI 49007
Phone: 269-342-1166
Fax: 269-342-0968
Toll-free: 800-347-4266
e-mail: gilmore@gilmore.org
Web Site: www.gilmore.org
Officers:
President: Patti Huiskamp
Management:
Director Of Development: Alice Kemerling
Director: Dan Gustin
Operations Director: Dan Gustin
Director Public Relations and Marke: Carol
Janowicz
Box Office Manager/Secretary: Diane Gill
Mission: Identifying and supporting concert pianists;
producing a biennial festival.
Utilizes: Collaborations; Commissioned Composers;
Guest Directors; Guest Musical Directors; Guest
Musicians; Guest Soloists; Multimedia; Organization
Contracts; Original Music Scores; Singers
Founded: 1989
Specialized Field: Festivals
Status: Nonprofit
Paid Staff: 10
Income Sources: Association of Performing Arts
Presenters
Performs At: Miller Auditorium; Dalton Center Recital
Hall; others
Annual Attendance: Biennial Festival
Resident Groups: Gilmore Artist; Gilmore Young
Artists

4465
NEW YEAR'S FEST
364 W Michigan Avenue
Kalamazoo, MI 49007
Phone: 616-388-3083
Fax: 616-388-2830
Officers:
President: Chuck Wray
Entertainment Chair: David Overton
Mission: To offer an alcohol-free celebration of New
Year's Eve featuring performing arts to Kalamazoo.

Founded: 1986
Specialized Field: Dance; Vocal Music; Instrumental Music; Theatre; Festivals; Lyric Opera
Status: Nonprofit
Organization Type: Festival

4466
MATRIX: MIDLAND FESTIVAL-CELEBRATION OF THE ARTS, SCIENCES & HUMANITIES

1801 W St Andrews Drive
Midland, MI 48640
Phone: 989-631-5930
Fax: 989-631-7890
Toll-free: 800-523-7649
e-mail: sabin@mcfta.org
Web Site: www.mcfta.org
Management:
    President: Michael Tiknin
    Executive Director: Dick Jellum
    General Manager: Phyllis B Sabin
Mission: To encourage creativity of the highest level in the arts, sciences, humanties and all aspects of their interelationships.
Founded: 1978
Specialized Field: Series & Festivals; Arts; Theatre; Museum
Paid Staff: 40
Budget: $250,000
Income Sources: Corporate Sponsorships
Annual Attendance: 12,000

4467
MIDLAND COMMUNITY CONCERT SOCIETY

1801 W St Andrews Road
Midland, MI 48640
Phone: 517-631-5930
Fax: 517-631-7890
e-mail: info@mcfta.org
Web Site: www.mcfta.org/A_MPAS/index.html
Officers:
    Chairman: Dr. Alice Ralston
Management:
    Managing Director: Kimberly Dimond
    Conductor: Carlton Woods
Mission: Encouraging concert audiences; Providing students with opportunities to experience professional performances.
Utilizes: Guest Companies
Specialized Field: Vocal Music; Instrumental Music
Status: Nonprofit
Organization Type: Educational; Sponsoring

4468
MUSIC SOCIETY OF THE MIDLAND CENTER FOR THE ARTS

1801 W Saint Andrews Road
Midland, MI 48640
Phone: 989-631-8250
Fax: 989-631-7890
Toll-free: 800-523-7649
e-mail: hohmeyer@mcfta.org
Web Site: www.mcfta.org
Management:
    President: Michael Tiknis
    Artistic Director: James Hohmeyer
    Managing Director: Robb Wouose
Founded: 1971
Specialized Field: Series and Festivals; Instrumental Music; Vocal Music; Theatre; Youth; Dance; Ethnic Performances
Status: Non-Profit, Professional

Seating Capacity: 1492

4469
CROOKED TREE ARTS COUNCIL

461 E Mitchell Street
Petoskey, MI 49770
Phone: 231-347-4337
Fax: 231-347-5414
e-mail: liz@crookedtree.org
Web Site: www.crookedtree.org
Officers:
    President: Phoebea Wietzke
    VP: Stephen Palmer
    Treasurer: Richard Lent
    Secretary: Jane Miller
Management:
    President: Steve Palmer
    Executive Director: Dale Hull
    Artistic Director: Gail Lambert
    Marketing Director: Elizabeth Ahrens
Mission: To sponsor and encourage cultural and educational activities in the fine arts for Charlevoix and Emmet Counties.
Founded: 1972
Specialized Field: Visual and Performing Arts
Status: Non-Profit, Professional
Paid Staff: 10
Paid Artists: 4
Income Sources: National Guild of Community Schools of the Arts; Michigan Association of Community Arts Agencies; Michigan Council on the Arts
Performs At: Crooked Tree Arts Center
Annual Attendance: 50,000
Year Remodeled: 2002
Organization Type: Performing; Educational; Sponsoring

4470
TEMPLE THEATRE ORGAN CLUB

315 Court Street
Saginaw, MI 48602
Phone: 517-754-2575
Fax: 517-793-7225
Management:
    General Manager: Ken Wuepper
Mission: Restoring the Temple Theatre and reestablishing it as a prominent performing arts center.
Founded: 1960
Status: Nonprofit
Organization Type: Educational; Sponsoring; Historic Preservation

4471
LAKE SUPERIOR STATE UNIVERSITY CULTURAL EVENTS SERIES

Lake Superior State Univesity
Sault Sainte Marie, MI 49783
Phone: 906-635-2265
Fax: 906-635-6674
e-mail: jwilkinson@gw.lssu.edu
Officers:
    Cultural Events Chairman: John Wilkinson
Performs At: Auditoriums

4472
WEST SHORE COMMUNITY COLLEGE CULTURAL SERIES

3000 N Stiles Road
Scottville, MI 49454

Phone: 231-845-6211
Fax: 231-843-2680
Toll-free: 800-848-9722
e-mail: rjplummer@westshore.edu
Web Site: www.westshore.edu
Management:
    President: Charles Dillon
    VP: Virginia Fox
    Managing Director: Tom Davis
    Cultural Arts Director: Rick Plummer
Specialized Field: Education
Status: Non-Profit, Professional
Paid Staff: 150
Volunteer Staff: 2
Paid Artists: 19
Non-paid Artists: 35
Performs At: Media Center Auditorium
Annual Attendance: 12,000+
Type of Stage: Thrust
Seating Capacity: 279
Year Built: 1971
Year Remodeled: 1999

4473
GREAT LAKES CHAMBER MUSIC FESTIVAL

20300 Civic Center Drive
Suite 100
Southfield, MI 48076
Phone: 248-559-2097
Fax: 248-559-2098
e-mail: info@greatlakeschambermusic.com
Web Site: www.greatlakeschambermusic.com
Management:
    Executive Director: Maury Okun
    Artistic Director: James Tocco
Founded: 1994
Specialized Field: Series & Festivals; Instrumental Music; Vocal Music; Youth
Status: Non-Profit, Professional
Paid Staff: 4

4474
DOWNRIVER COUNCIL FOR THE ARTS

Downriver Council for the Arts
20904 Northline Road
Taylor, MI 48180
Phone: 734-287-6103
Fax: 734-287-6151
e-mail: info@downriverarts.org
Web Site: www.downriverarts.org
Management:
    Executive Director: Emma Jean Woodyard
    Gallery Director: Martine MacDonald
    Administrative Assistant: Linda Englund
Mission: Promoting a range of the fine and performing arts in Downriver communities.
Utilizes: Collaborations; Guest Artists; Guest Writers; New Productions; Singers; Touring Companies
Founded: 1978
Specialized Field: Dance; Vocal Music; Instrumental Music; Theater; Festivals
Status: Professional; Nonprofit
Paid Staff: 35
Income Sources: Grants, Donations, Membership
Organization Type: Educational; Sponsoring

4475
SAGINAW VALLEY STATE UNIVERSITY CONCERT: LECTURE SERIES

Campus Life
7400 Bay Road
University Center, MI 48710

Phone: 517-790-4170
Fax: 517-249-1695
e-mail: ebusch@tardis.svsu.edu
Management:
Director: Eric Buschlen
Seating Capacity: 400

4476
WATERFORD CULTURAL COUNCIL

5860 Andersonville Road
Waterford, MI 48329-1510
Phone: 248-623-9389
Fax: 248-623-7907
e-mail: waterfordcc@earthlink.net
Web Site: www.waterford.wb.mi.us/win/ncc
Management:
President: Marleen Rudolph
Program Director: Debra Berry
Mission: To strenthen, enrich and unite the community through the arts.
Founded: 1994
Specialized Field: Series & Festivals; Instrumental Music; Performing; Visual
Status: Non-Profit, Professional
Paid Staff: 4
Volunteer Staff: 120
Paid Artists: 4
Budget: $260,000
Income Sources: United Way; Waterford Township; Waterford Schools
Performs At: Waterford Mott High School Auditorium
Annual Attendance: 16,000
Facility Category: Performance Arena
Seating Capacity: 650

Minnesota

4477
ALEXANDRIA FESTIVAL OF THE LAKES

PO Box 863
Alexandria, MN 56308
Phone: 320-762-5666
Fax: 320-762-8246
e-mail: Alexfest@aol.com
Web Site: www.AlexFest.org
Management:
Artistic Director: Nina Tobias
Founded: 1993
Specialized Field: Chamber Music

4478
HOBSON UNION PROGRAMING BOARD PERFORMING ARTISTS SERIES

Bemidji State University
15th & Birchmont Drive
Bemidji, MN 56601
Phone: 218-755-3760
Fax: 218-755-3757
e-mail: hupb@hotmail.com
Web Site: www.bemidjistate.edu
Management:
President: Sara Lewanbowski
Executive Director: Lauralynn Keuchle
Specialized Field: Series & Festivals; Instrumental Music; Vocal Music
Status: Non-Profit, Non-Professional
Paid Staff: 1
Paid Artists: 1
Performs At: Various Auditoriums

4479
COLLEGE OF ST. SCHOLASTICA MITCHELL AUDITORIUM

1200 Kenwood Avenue
Duluth, MN 55811-4199
Phone: 218-723-6000
Fax: 218-723-6290
Toll-free: 800-447-5444
e-mail: ngawinsk@css.edu
Web Site: www.css.edu
Management:
President: Larry Goodwin
Office Assistant: LeAnn Jopke
Utilizes: Actors; Artists-in-Residence; Collaborations; Commissioned Composers; Commissioned Music; Dance Companies; Dancers; Educators; Fine Artists; Guest Accompanists; Guest Instructors; Guest Musical Directors; Guest Musicians; Guest Soloists; Guild Activities; Instructors; Local Artists; Multi Collaborations; Multimedia; Organization Contracts; Original Music Scores; Playwrights; Selected Students; Sign Language Translators; Singers; Soloists; Special Technical Talent; Theatre Companies; Touring Companies
Founded: 1912
Paid Staff: 12
Performs At: Mitchell Auditorium
Annual Attendance: 38,000
Facility Category: Orchestra Hall/Arts Center
Type of Stage: Sprung Wood Maple Dance Floor
Stage Dimensions: 30 deep X 60 wide
Seating Capacity: 585
Year Built: 1993
Cost: $4.6 million
Rental Contact: Director Neil A. Gawinski

4480
REIF GREENWAY SERIES

720 Conifer Drive
Grand Rapids, MN 55744
Phone: 218-327-5780
Fax: 218-327-5798
e-mail: dmarty@reifcenter.org
Web Site: www.reifcenter.org
Management:
President: David Broberg
Executive Director: David Marty
Mission: Stimulating arts in Northern Minnesota.
Founded: 1980
Specialized Field: Musical Theatre
Status: Non-Profit, Non-Professional
Paid Staff: 10
Budget: $520,000
Income Sources: Box Office; Grants; Foundations
Annual Attendance: 12,500
Facility Category: Auditorium
Type of Stage: Modified Thrust
Stage Dimensions: 45 x 46 (curtain lines)
Seating Capacity: 645
Year Built: 1980
Year Remodeled: 1999
Rental Contact: John Miller
Organization Type: Presenting

4481
BETHANY LUTHERAN COLLEGE CONCERTS & LECTURES

700 Luther Drive
Mankato, MN 56001-6163
Phone: 507-344-7365
Fax: 507-344-7380
Toll-free: 800-944-3066
e-mail: ljaeger@blc.edu
Web Site: www.blc.edu

Officers:
President: Dr. Dan Bruss
Management:
Fine Arts Director: Lois Jaeger
Founded: 1927
Specialized Field: Series & Festivals: Chamber Performances and Theatre Performances
Status: Non-Profit, Non-Professional
Paid Staff: 10
Paid Artists: 10
Performs At: Theatre

4482
INTERMEDIA ARTS

2822 Lyndale Avenue S
Minneapolis, MN 55408-2108
Phone: 612-871-4444
Fax: 612-871-6927
e-mail: info@intermediaarts.org
Web Site: www.intermediaarts.org
Officers:
Chair of the Board: Richard Ammmen
Management:
Executive Director: Daniel Gumnit
Artistic Director: Sandy Agustin
Mission: Intermedia Arts is a catalyst that builds understanding among people through art.
Founded: 1973

4483
MINNEAPOLIS PARK & RECREATION BOARD-SUMMER MUSIC IN THE PARKS

2117 W River Road
Minneapolis, MN 55411-1400
Phone: 612-230-6400
Fax: 612-230-6500
e-mail: concerts@minneapolisparks.org
Web Site: www.minneapolisparks.org
Officers:
Board President: Jon Olson
Management:
Concert Coordinator: Goeff Walsh
Concert/Events Coordinator: Jessica Berg
Founded: 1883
Specialized Field: Parks Center Recreation
Status: Non-Profit, Non-Professional
Paid Staff: 20

4484
UNIVERSITY OF MINNESOTA AT MINNEAPOLIS SERIES

84 Church Street
109 Northrop Auditorium
Minneapolis, MN 55455
Phone: 612-625-6600
Fax: 612-626-1750
e-mail: radis001@axus.umn.edu
Web Site: www.northrop.umn.edu
Management:
President: Dale Schatzlein
Operations Manager: Sally Dischinger
Specialized Field: Series & Festivals: Dance & Jazz
Status: Non-Profit, Professional
Paid Staff: 13
Performs At: Northrop Memorial Auditorium

4485
VOCALESSENCE

1900 Nicollet Avenue
Minneapolis, MN 55403

Phone: 612-547-1451
Fax: 612-547-1484
e-mail: info@vocalessence.org
Web Site: www.vocalessence.org
Management:
   Artistic Director: Philip Brunelle
   Managing Director: Mary Ann Pulk
Mission: The presentation of newly commissioned choral and orchestral works.
Founded: 1969
Specialized Field: Vocal Music: Choral Music
Status: Non-Profit, Professional
Paid Staff: 9
Paid Artists: 32
Non-paid Artists: 75
Budget: 1.2 million
Affiliations: Chorus America; IFCM
Organization Type: Performing; Educational; Sponsoring
Resident Groups: Ensamble Singers

4486
ALLIED CONCERT SERVICES
12450 Wayzata Boulevard
#200
Minnetonka, MN 55305
Phone: 952-542-8019
Fax: 952-542-8398
Officers:
   President: Paul Folin
Management:
   President: Paul Folin
Founded: 1947
Specialized Field: Series & Festivals; Instrumental Music; Vocal Music; Theatre; Youth; Dance; Ethnic Performances
Status: For-Profit, Professional
Paid Staff: 4

4487
CONCORDIA COLLEGE CULTURAL EVENTS SERIES
901 8th Street S
Moorhead, MN 56562
Phone: 218-299-4366
Fax: 218-299-3191
Web Site: www.cord.edu
Management:
   President of the University: Pamela Jolicouer
   Director of Cultural Events Series: Lowell Larson
Founded: 1985
Specialized Field: Series & Festivals; Instrumental Music; Vocal Music; Youth; Dance; Ethnic Performances; Performing Skits
Status: Non-Profit, Professional
Paid Staff: 2
Paid Artists: 8

4488
MINNESOTA STATE UNIVERSITY MOOREHEAD SERIES
250D Bridges Hall
1104 7th Avenue S
Moorhead, MN 56563
Phone: 218-477-5031
Fax: 218-287-5037
e-mail: wigtil@mnstate.edu
Web Site: www.mnstate.edu/perform
Management:
   President: Roland Barden
   Executive Director: Craig Ellingson

Mission: To provide cultural programming of the highest calibre to the community and campus audiences.
Utilizes: Collaborations; Dance Companies; Dancers; Multi Collaborations; Multimedia; Original Music Scores; Singers; Special Technical Talent; Theatre Companies
Founded: 1930
Specialized Field: Series and Festivals; Dance; Theatre; Music
Status: Non-profit, Professional
Paid Staff: 5
Budget: $80,000
Performs At: Center for the Arts
Annual Attendance: 5,000
Facility Category: Center for the Arts
Type of Stage: Proscenium
Stage Dimensions: 41'x22'x33'
Seating Capacity: 850
Year Built: 1963
Organization Type: Performing; Educational; Sponsoring

4489
UNIVERSITY OF MINNESOTA MORRIS CAC PERFORMING ARTS SERIES
Office of Student Activities, UMM
600 E 4th Street
Morris, MN 56267-2134
Phone: 320-589-6080
Fax: 320-589-6084
e-mail: haugensj@mrs.umn.edu
Performs At: Edson Auditorium

4490
CARLETON COLLEGE CONCERT SERIES
One N College Street
Northfield, MN 55057
Phone: 507-646-4347
Fax: 507-633-4347
Management:
   Concert Manager: Harry Nordstrom
Mission: Providing excellently performed music; offering an educational program.
Founded: 1945
Specialized Field: Vocal Music; Instrumental Music
Status: Professional; Nonprofit
Performs At: Carleton Concert Hall; Skinner Chapel
Organization Type: Educational; Sponsoring

4491
ST. OLAF COLLEGE ARTIST SERIES
Music Department
St Olaf College
Northfield, MN 55057
Phone: 507-646-3179
Fax: 507-646-3527
Toll-free: 800-363-5487
e-mail: music@stloaf.edu
Web Site: www.stolaf.edu
Management:
   President: Christopher Thomforde
   Music Organizations Manager: Bj Johnson
Founded: 1912
Specialized Field: Series & Festivals; Music; Band Choir
Status: Non-Profit, Non-Professional
Paid Staff: 60
Performs At: Skoglund Auditorium

4492
ROCHESTER CIVIC MUSIC
201 4th Street SE
Suite 170
Rochester, MN 55904

Phone: 507-281-6005
Fax: 507-281-6055
e-mail: sschmidt@ci.rochester.mn.us
Web Site: www.ci.rochester.mn.us/music
Management:
   General Manager: Steven J Schmidt
Utilizes: Artists-in-Residence; Collaborations; Commissioned Composers; Commissioned Music; Composers-in-Residence; Guest Accompanists; Guest Composers; Guest Directors; Guest Lecturers; Guest Musical Directors; Guest Musicians; Instructors; Local Artists; Multi Collaborations; Multimedia; Music; Organization Contracts; Original Music Scores; Selected Students; Sign Language Translators; Singers
Specialized Field: Series & Festivals; Riverside Live; Down by the Riverside; Concerts
Status: Non-Profit, Professional
Paid Staff: 5
Performs At: Mayo Civic Center

4493
ST CLOUD STATE UNIVERSITY PROGRAM BOARD PERFORMING ARTS SERIES
Edward Memorial Center 118
720 4th Avenue S
Saint Cloud, MN 56301
Phone: 320-308-2205
Fax: 320-308-1669
e-mail: upb@stcloudstate.edu
Web Site: www.stcloudstate.edu/upb
Management:
   President: Jessica Ostman
   Artistic Director: Janice Courtney
Founded: 1978
Specialized Field: Series & Festivals; Vocal Music; Theatre; Youth; Dance; Ethnic Performances
Status: Non-Profit, Professional
Paid Staff: 10
Paid Artists: 10
Performs At: Atwood Center Ballroom

4494
PACIFIC COMPOSERS FORUM
332 Minnesota Street
Suite E145
Saint Paul, MN 55101-1300
Phone: 651-228-1407
Fax: 651-291-7978
e-mail: info@composersforum.com
Web Site: www.composersforum.com
Management:
   Senior Program Director: Philip Blackbur
   Innova Assistant: Chris Campbell
   VP And Managing Directo: Glenna Dibrell
   Finance Manager: Paul Hanson
Founded: 1973

4495
SCHUBERT CLUB INTERNATIONAL ARTIST SERIES
302 Landmark Center
75 W 5th Street
Saint Paul, MN 55102
Phone: 651-292-3267
Fax: 651-292-4317
e-mail: schubert@schubert.org
Web Site: www.schubert.org
Management:
   President: Terry Hoffmann
   Executive Director: Bruce Carlson
Founded: 1882

Specialized Field: Series and Festivals; Instrumental Music; Vocal Music; Youth; Ethnic Performances
Status: Non-Profit, Professional
Paid Staff: 10

4496
SCHUBERT CLUB INTERNATIONAL ARTIST SERIES
302 Landmark Center
75 W 5th Street
Saint Paul, MN 55102
Phone: 651-292-3267
Fax: 651-292-4317
e-mail: schubert@schubert.org
Web Site: www.schubert.org
Management:
Executive Director: Bruce Carlson
Mission: To promote the art of music, particularly recital music through education, performance, and museum programs and to maintain a high standard of artistic excellence.
Founded: 1982
Specialized Field: Performing Music Series and Museum.
Paid Staff: 10
Performs At: Ordway Music Theatre

4497
GUSTAVUS ADOLPHUS COLLEGE ARTIST SERIES
Gustavus Adolphus College
800 W College Avenue
Saint Peter, MN 56082
Phone: 507-933-7363
Fax: 507-933-6253
e-mail: al@gustavus.edu
Web Site: www.gustavus.edu
Management:
President: James Peterson
Executive Director: Alan Behrends
Founded: 1862
Specialized Field: Fine Arts
Status: Non-Profit, Professional
Paid Staff: 600
Performs At: Bjorling Concert Hall

Mississippi

4498
JAZZ IN THE GROVE
PO Box 409
Bay Springs, MS 39422
Phone: 601-764-2121
Fax: 601-764-6866
Toll-free: 800-898-2782
e-mail: joeyg@tec.com
Web Site: www.bayspringstel.net
Management:
President: Joseph Fail
Director: Emily Mixon
Founded: 1996
Specialized Field: Performing Series - Jazz Festival
Status: Non-Profit, Non-Professional

4499
UNIVERSITY OF SOUTHERN MISSISSIPPI SCHOOL OF MUSIC
118 College Drive
#5081
Hattiesburg, MS 39406-0001
Phone: 601-266-5543
Fax: 601-266-6427
e-mail: music@usm.edu
Web Site: www.usm.edu/music
Management:
Director: Dr Michael Miles,
michael.a.miles@usm.edu
Associate Director: Dr Jennifer Shank,
jennifer.shank@usm.edu
Mission: Recognized for its eminence in musical artistry, education and community service. Provides a wealth of valuable opportunities for the professional and artistic growth of the students.
Utilizes: Actors; Artists-in-Residence; Choreographers; Commissioned Music; Composers-in-Residence; Dance Companies; Dancers; Educators; Grant Writers; Guest Accompanists; Guest Artists; Guest Choreographers; Guest Companies; Guest Composers; Guest Conductors; Guest Designers; Guest Directors; Guest Ensembles; Guest Instructors; Guest Lecturers; Guest Musical Directors; Guest Musicians; Instructors; Multimedia; Music; Original Music Scores; Resident Artists; Resident Professionals; Sign Language Translators; Singers; Soloists; Student Interns; Special Technical Talent; Theatre Companies; Touring Companies; Visual Arts
Founded: 1910
Specialized Field: Orchestra; Chamber; Ensemble; Choral; Band
Status: Non-Profit, Non-Professional
Budget: $35,000-60,000
Income Sources: State Funded
Seating Capacity: 1,000

4500
BELHAVEN COLLEGE PRESTON MEMORIAL SERIES
Belhaven College
1500 Peachtree Street
Jackson, MS 39202-1789
Phone: 601-968-5940
Fax: 601-968-9998
Toll-free: 800-960-5940
e-mail: admission@belhaven.edu
Web Site: www.belhaven.edu
Officers:
Music Department Chairman: Christopher Shelt
Performs At: Girault Auditorium

4501
MISSISSIPPI ARTS COMMISSION
501 North West Street
Suite 701 B Woolfolk Building
Jackson, MS 39201
Phone: 601-359-6030
Fax: 601-359-6008
e-mail: lpowell@arts.state.ms.us
Web Site: www.arts.state.ms.us
Management:
Executive Director: Malcolm White
Deputy Director: Lee Ann Powell
Founded: 1968
Specialized Field: Grant and Technical Assistance
Status: For-Profit, Professional
Paid Staff: 12

4502
WORLD PERFORMANCE SERIES: THALIA MARA FOUNDATION
1440 N State Street
Jackson, MS 39202
Phone: 601-968-0090
Fax: 601-354-2781
e-mail: mail@thaliamara.org
Web Site: www.thaliamara.org
Management:
Executive Director: Leanne Mahoney
Budget: $400,000-1,000,000

4503
MISSISSIPPI STATE UNIVERSITY LYCEUM SERIES
PO Drawer HY
Mississippi State, MS 39762
Phone: 662-325-4201
Fax: 662-325-7456
e-mail: bneubauer@cmo.msstate.edu
Web Site: www.msstate.edu/dept/lyceum
Management:
Series Coordinator: Brenda Neubauer
Founded: 1961
Specialized Field: Series and Festivals; Instrumental Music; Vocal Music; Theatre; Dance; Ethnic Performances; Orchestra
Status: Non-Profit, Professional
Paid Staff: 1
Budget: $20,000-35,000
Performs At: Humphery Coliseum

4504
NATCHEZ FESTIVAL OF MUSIC
Alcorn State University
1000 ASU Drive
Natchez, MS 39096
Phone: 601-877-6100
Fax: 601-442-9686
Toll-free: 800-647-6724
e-mail: maw@alcorn.edu
Web Site: www.alcorn.edu
Officers:
Interim President: Malvin Williams
Chairman of the Board: Robert Gage
Executive Vice President: Rudolph Walters
Management:
Executive Director: Arthur Brooks
Mission: Teach variety of research activities that focus on biotechnology, energy, meat, ecology, farming and alternative crops.
Founded: 1989
Specialized Field: Series & Festivals; Opera; Jazz; Musical Theatre; Broadways; Concerts
Status: Non-Profit, Professional
Paid Staff: 6
Paid Artists: 40
Performs At: Margaret Martin Performing Arts Center

4505
UNIVERSITY OF MISSISSIPPI ARTIST SERIES
University of Mississippi Artists Series
145 Martindale
University, MS 38677
Phone: 662-995-7226
Fax: 662-232-7830
Web Site: www.olemiss.edu/depts/music/artist.html
Officers:
Chairman: Dr. Robert Riggs
Budget: $35,000-60,000
Performs At: Fulton Chapel

Missouri

4506
FRIENDS OF HISTORIC BOONVILLE PERFORMING ARTS
614 E Morgan
PO Box 1776
Boonville, MO
Phone: 660-882-7977
Fax: 660-882-9194
Toll-free: 888-588-1477
e-mail: friends@undata.com
Officers:
President: Ron Lenz
Second VP: Barbara Holtzclaw
First VP: Gary Campbell
Secretary: Debby Koerner
Management:
President: Camt Bell
Executive Director: Marry Mcvicker
Artistic Director: Dave Para
Mission: To provide a community arts program in our historic theatre, Thespian Hall.
Utilizes: Actors; Artists-in-Residence; Collaborations; Dance Companies; Guild Activities; Instructors; Local Artists; Multimedia; Original Music Scores; Sign Language Translators; Soloists; Touring Companies
Founded: 1971
Specialized Field: Community Arts
Status: Non-Profit,Professional
Paid Staff: 1
Budget: $60,000-150,000
Income Sources: Donations; earned income
Performs At: Thespian Hall
Annual Attendance: 7,500
Facility Category: Theatre; Performing Arts Center
Type of Stage: Proscenium
Stage Dimensions: 80x100
Seating Capacity: 600
Year Built: 1857
Year Remodeled: 1980
Organization Type: Performing; Educational; Sponsoring

4507
MISSOURI RIVER FESTIVAL OF THE ARTS
PO Box 1776
614 E Morgan
Boonville, MO 65233
Phone: 660-882-7977
Fax: 660-882-9194
Toll-free: 888-588-1477
e-mail: friendsart@mid-mo.net
Web Site: www.mid-mo/friendsart
Management:
Administrator: Maryellen H McVicker
Founded: 1975
Seating Capacity: 600
Year Built: 1855
Year Remodeled: 2002

4508
SOUTHEAST MISSOURI STATE UNIVERSITY: CULTURAL SERIES
Southeast Missouri State University
Cape Girardeau, MO 63701
Phone: 573-651-2000
Fax: 573-651-2893
Management:
Dean College of Humanities: Dr. Martin Jones
Chairperson/Speech Communications: Dr. Ray G Ewing
Mission: To attract professional quality performing arts to the Southeast Missouri area; to offer professional workshops.
Founded: 1873
Specialized Field: Dance; Vocal Music; Instrumental Music; Theatre
Status: Nonprofit
Income Sources: Missouri Council on the Arts
Performs At: Academic Hall Auditorium
Organization Type: Educational; Sponsoring

4509
UNIVERSITY OF MISSOURI: COLUMBIA CONCERT SERIES
409 Jesse Hall
Columbia, MO 65211
Phone: 573-882-3875
Fax: 573-882-2636
Toll-free: 800-292-9136
e-mail: dunnm@missouri.edu
Web Site: www.concertseries.org
Officers:
Executive Director: Michael Dunn
Management:
Assistant Director: Kimberly Mouser
Utilizes: Actors; Artists-in-Residence; Collaborations; Dance Companies; Dancers; Grant Writers; Guest Composers; Guest Musicians; Multi Collaborations; Original Music Scores; Selected Students; Sign Language Translators; Theatre Companies
Specialized Field: Choral; Dance; Opera; Instrumental Music; Theatre
Status: Non-Profit, Professional
Paid Staff: 20
Volunteer Staff: 50
Paid Artists: 42
Budget: $400,000-1,000,000
Income Sources: Ticket Sales; Private Donations; Corporate Support; Grants
Performs At: Performing Arts Center
Affiliations: University Of Missouri
Annual Attendance: 65,000
Seating Capacity: 1,784

4510
CENTRAL METHODIST COLLEGE CONVOCATIONS
Central Methodist University
Fayette, MO 65248-1198
Phone: 660-248-6284
Fax: 660-248-2622
Toll-free: 877-268-1854
e-mail: mkelty@centralmethodist.edu
Web Site: www.centralmethodist.edu
Officers:
Chairman: Dr Mary Kelty
Founded: 1854
Budget: $20,000-35,000
Performs At: Little Theater; Lynn Memorial Chapel; Field House

4511
WILLIAM WOODS UNIVERSITY CONCERT & LECTURE SERIES
William Woods University
One University Avenue
Fulton, MO 65251
Phone: 573-592-4281
Fax: 573-592-1623
e-mail: jpotter@william-woods.edu
Web Site: www.williamwoods.edu
Management:
President: Jahnae Barnett
Artistic Director of Theatre: Joe Potter
Utilizes: Artists-in-Residence; Choreographers; Collaborations; Dance Companies; Dancers; Educators; Fine Artists; Grant Writers; Guest Artists; Guest Companies; Guest Conductors; Guest Designers; Guest Instructors; Guest Lecturers; Guest Soloists; Guild Activities; High School Drama; Instructors; Local Artists; Music; Original Music Scores; Playwrights; Poets; Resident Professionals; Selected Students; Sign Language Translators; Soloists; Student Interns; Special Technical Talent; Theatre Companies; Touring Companies; Visual Arts
Founded: 1870
Specialized Field: Series & Festivals; Vocal Music; Theatre; Youth; Dance; Ethnic Performances
Status: For-Profit, Non-Professional
Budget: $10,000
Performs At: Cutlip Auditorium; Dulany Auditorium

4512
HANNIBAL CONCERT ASSOCIATION
54979 Buffalo Lane
Hannibal, MO 63459
Phone: 573-267-3901
Fax: 573-221-4091
e-mail: sanorth@adams.net
Management:
President: Rita Cornelius
Founded: 1944
Specialized Field: Series and Festivals; Instrumental Music; Vocal Music; Youth; Dance; Ethnic Performances; Presenting Performances
Status: Non-Profit, Professional
Budget: $10,000-20,000

4513
CAPITAL CITY COUNCIL ON THE ARTS
PO Box 1311
Jefferson City, MO 65102
Phone: 573-635-8355
Fax: 573-634-3805
Web Site: www.capitalcityarts.org
Management:
President: Ann Littlefield
Executive Director: Joyce Neuenswander
Founded: 1957
Specialized Field: Programs for Children; Support Community Art
Status: Non-Profit, Professional
Paid Staff: 1
Paid Artists: 15
Budget: $10,000

4514
PRO MUSICA
2700 E 15th Street
Joplin, MO 64804
Phone: 417-625-1822
Fax: 417-625-1822
e-mail: athena@ipa.net
Web Site: www.promusicajoplin.org
Management:
Artistic Director: Cynthia A. Schwab
Executive Assistant: Bonnie Yetter
Founded: 1986
Specialized Field: Chamber Music
Status: Non-Profit, Professional
Paid Staff: 2
Volunteer Staff: 1
Budget: $35,000-60,000

4515
HEART OF AMERICA SHAKESPEARE FESTIVAL
3619 Broadway
Suite 2
Kansas City, MO 64111
Phone: 816-531-7728
Fax: 816-531-1911
e-mail: info@kcshakes.org
Web Site: www.kcshakes.org
Management:
   Executive Director: Lisa Cordes
   Producing Artistic Director: Sidonie Garrett
Mission: To make Shakespeare's works accesible to a diverse audience through free professional theater and educational programs. Vision is to use the power and presence of live professional performance to enhance the meaning of life and to illustrate the indomitability of the human spirit through the works of William shakespeare.
Utilizes: Actors; AEA Actors; Choreographers; Collaborations; Dancers; Designers; Educators; Guest Designers; Guest Soloists; Local Artists; Multimedia; Resident Professionals; Selected Students; Student Interns
Founded: 1991
Specialized Field: Series & Festivals: Shakespeare Theatre in the Park
Status: Professional; Non-Profit
Paid Staff: 4
Volunteer Staff: 400
Paid Artists: 55
Budget: $650,000
Income Sources: Foundations; Individuals; Corporations
Season: June - July
Performs At: Outdoor Theatre, Southmoreland Park 47th and Oak Street
Annual Attendance: 18,000-26,000
Facility Category: Outdoor Park Setting
Stage Dimensions: 45'x 30'
Seating Capacity: 2,500

4516
KANSAS CITY BLUES & JAZZ FESTIVAL
4200 Pennsylvania Avenue
Suite 230
Kansas City, MO 64111
Fax: 816-531-2583
Toll-free: 800-530-5266
e-mail: kcbluesjazz@kcbluesjazz.org
Web Site: www.kcbluesjazz.org
Management:
   Director: Greg Patterson
   Assistant Director: Connie Hemiston
Founded: 1991
Specialized Field: Music Festival
Paid Staff: 2
Volunteer Staff: 500
Paid Artists: 50

4517
KANSAS CITY RENAISSANCE FESTIVAL
207 Westport Road
Suite 206
Kansas City, MO 64111
Phone: 816-561-8005
Fax: 816-561-6493
Toll-free: 800-373-0357
e-mail: renfest@kcrenfest.com
Web Site: www.kcrenfest.com
Management:
   Executive Director: Carrie Shoptaw

Mission: To entertain and educate using a Renaissance theme.
Founded: 1977
Specialized Field: Performing Arts
Status: Professional
Paid Staff: 15
Volunteer Staff: 2
Income Sources: Ticket sales; sponsorships
Annual Attendance: 180,000
Facility Category: 12 Outdoor Stages
Type of Stage: 4 Proscenium; 1 Jousting Field
Year Built: 1977

4518
KANSAS CITY YOUNG AUDIENCES SERIES
5601 Wind Art
Kansas City, MO 64112
Phone: 816-531-4022
Fax: 816-960-1519
e-mail: dwindham@crn.org
Web Site: www.kcya.org
Management:
   President/CEO: Daniel Windham
Founded: 1962
Specialized Field: Series & Festivals: Instrumental Music
Status: Non-Profit,Professional

4519
SUMMERFEST CONCERTS
PO Box 22697
Kansas City, MO 64113-0697
Phone: 816—51-0-09
Web Site: www.summerfestconcertsinc.com
Management:
   President: John Church
   Vice President: Mary Zimmerman
   Artistic Advisor: Jane Carl
   Artistic Advisor: Shannon Finney
   Artistic Advisor: Mary Garcia Grant
   Business Manager: Shirley Quastler
Founded: 1991
Specialized Field: Chamber Music

4520
UNIVERSITY OF MISSOURI-KANSAS CITY CONSERVATORY SERIES
4949 Cherry Street
Kansas City, MO 64110-2229
Phone: 816-235-2949
Fax: 816-235-5265
e-mail: urbana@umkc.edu
Web Site: www.umkc.edu/conservatory
Management:
   Dean of Conservatory: Randall Pembrook
   Marketing Director: Al Urban
Founded: 1906
Specialized Field: Series & Festivals; Instrumental Music; Vocal Music; Dance
Status: Non-Profit, Professional
Paid Staff: 105
Paid Artists: 5
Budget: $35,000-60,000
Performs At: White Recital Hall; Center for the Performing Arts

4521
TRUMAN STATE UNIVERSITY LYCEUM SERIES
McClain 101
100 E Normal Street
Kirksville, MO 63501

Phone: 600-785-4016
Fax: 660-785-4019
e-mail: heidi@truman.edu
Web Site: www.lyceum.truman.edu
Officers:
   Lyceum Committee Co-Chairman: Winston Vanderhoof
   Lyceum Committee Co-Chair: Zach Burden
Management:
   Director of Public Relations: Heidi Templeton
Budget: $60,000-150,000
Performs At: Baldwin Hall Auditorium

4522
HARRIMAN-JEWELL COLLEGE
William Jewell College
500 College Hill, PO Box 1015
Liberty, MO 64068
Phone: 816-415-5025
Fax: 816-415-5035
Toll-free: 888-528-5521
e-mail: info@hjseries.org
Web Site: www.hjseries.org
Officers:
   President: Dave Sallee
Management:
   Executive & Artisitic Director: Clark Morris
Mission: To bring the best of the performing arts to Kansas City.
Founded: 1965
Specialized Field: Series & Festivals: Classical music
Status: Non-Profit, Professional
Paid Staff: 6

4523
NORTHWEST MISSOURI STATE UNIVERSITY PERFORMING ARTS SERIES
800 University Drive
Maryville, MO 64468
Phone: 660-562-1562
Fax: 660-562-1121
Toll-free: 800-633-1175
e-mail: desser@mail.nwmissouri.edu
Web Site: www.nwmissouri.edu
Management:
   President: Dean L Hubbard
   Managing Director: Bart Pitchford
Mission: Providing a range of lectures and performing arts for the University and area residents.
Founded: 1992
Specialized Field: Series & Festivals; Theatre; Dance; Ethnic Performances
Status: For-Profit, Non-Professional
Paid Staff: 1
Budget: $60,000-150,000
Income Sources: Missouri Arts Council
Performs At: Charles Johnson Theatre; Mary Linn Performing Arts
Organization Type: Educational; Sponsoring

4524
MOBERLY AREA COUNCIL ON THE ARTS
Moberly Area Community College
Moberly, MO 65270
Phone: 660-263-4110
Fax: 660-263-6448
Budget: $20,000-35,000

4525
COTTEY LECTURERS & ARTISTS SUPER SERIES
Cottey College
Nevada, MO 64772
Phone: 417-667-8181
Fax: 417-448-1020
e-mail: kkorb@cottey.edu
Web Site: www.cottey.edu
Officers:
President: Dr. Judy Rogers
Management:
Coord. Campus Activities: Kristi Korbrs
Founded: 1990
Specialized Field: Series & Festivals; Instrumental music; Vocal music; Theatre; Youth; Dance; Ethnic Performances
Status: Non-Profit, Professional
Paid Staff: 1
Paid Artists: 5
Budget: $20,000-35,000
Performs At: Center for the Arts
Type of Stage: Auditorium
Stage Dimensions: 40X40
Seating Capacity: 495
Year Built: 1990

4526
THERON C BENNET RAGTIME & EARLY JAZZ FESTIVAL
21554 Lawrence 1032
Pierce City, MO 65723
Phone: 417-476-5408
Web Site: www.sound.net/~gary/theron/theron.htm
Management:
Festival Organizer: Murray Bishoff

4527
PERFORMING ARTS ASSOCIATION OF SAINT JOSEPH
719 Edmond Street
Saint Joseph, MO 64501
Phone: 816-279-1225
Fax: 816-233-6704
e-mail: toihunt@paastjo.org
Web Site: www.paastjo.org
Management:
Executive Director: Teresa Fankhauser
Founded: 1962
Specialized Field: Jazz; Theater; Instrumental Music; Dance
Status: Non-Profit, Non-Professional
Paid Staff: 3
Budget: $60,000-150,000
Performs At: Missouri Theatre

4528
CITICORP SUMMERFEST
Powell Symphony Hall
718 N Grand Boulevard
Saint Louis, MO 63103
Phone: 314-533-2500
Fax: 314-286-4188
Toll-free: 800-232-1880
Web Site: www.slso.org
Management:
President: Randy Adams
Artistic Director: Kathleen Vanberger
Music Director/Conductor: David Robertson
Utilizes: Guest Artists
Founded: 1880
Specialized Field: Series & Festivals: Classical music
Status: Non-Profit, Professional
Paid Staff: 150
Paid Artists: 60
Performs At: Powell Symphony Hall At Grand Center
Affiliations: Saint Louis Symphony Orchestra
Organization Type: Performing

4529
FOX ASSOCIATES
539 N Grand Boulevard
Suite 300
Saint Louis, MO 63103
Phone: 314-534-1678
Fax: 314-534-8702
e-mail: webmaster@gabulousfox.com
Web Site: www.fabouousfox.com
Officers:
Executive Director: Richard Baker
Mission: Present live entertainment.
Founded: 1929
Specialized Field: Series & Festivals: Broadway Shows and Concerts
Status: For-Profit, Professional
Paid Staff: 100
Budget: $1,000,000+

4530
JUNETEENTH HERITAGE & JAZZ FESTIVAL
625 N Euclid
Suite 225
Saint Louis, MO 63108
Phone: 314-367-0100
Fax: 314-367-0200
Toll-free: 877-586-8684
e-mail: juntnthjaz@aol.com
Web Site: www.juneteenthjazz.org
Management:
Executive Producer: Curtis Faulkner

4531
NEW MUSIC CIRCLE SERIES
PO Box 190308
Saint Louis, MO 63119
Phone: 314-995-4963
Fax: 314-567-5384
e-mail: info@newmusiccircle.org
Web Site: www.newmusiccircle.org
Management:
Music Department: Rich O'Donnell
Utilizes: Guest Musical Directors
Founded: 1959
Paid Staff: 2
Volunteer Staff: 5
Paid Artists: 30
Budget: $34,000
Income Sources: St. Louis Regional Arts Commission, Missouri Arts Council
Annual Attendance: 1,000
Facility Category: Venues

4532
SAINT LOUIS CATHEDRAL CONCERTS
4431 Lindell Boulevard
Saint Louis, MO 63108
Phone: 314-533-7662
Fax: 314-373-8292
e-mail: concerts@cathedralstl.org
Web Site: www.stlcathedralconcerts.org
Management:
Interim Executive Dir/Operations: Scott Kennebeck
Development Director: Nicole Heerlein
Group Sales Director: Ruth Ferris

Mission: Cathedral Concerts mission is to present affordable live concerts in the Cathedral Basilica of St. Louis featuring world-class musicians and the finest repertoire of sacred and classical music for the cultural enrichment, education, and enjoyment of the entire region.
Founded: 1992
Opened: 1993
Specialized Field: Music
Status: Non-Profit, Professional
Paid Staff: 3
Volunteer Staff: 70
Paid Artists: 300
Budget: $350,000-400,000
Income Sources: Ticket Sales; Donations
Annual Attendance: 10,000
Seating Capacity: 1,500

4533
SAINT LOUIS SYMPHONY: CLASSICS IN THE LOOP FESTIVAL
Saint Louis Symphony Orchestra
718 N Grand Boulevard
Saint Louis, MO 63103
Phone: 314-533-2500
Fax: 314-286-4111
e-mail: symph@admiral.umsl.edu
Web Site: www.slso.org
Management:
President: Randy Adams
CFO: James Garrone
Artistic Director: Kathleen Van Bergen
Orchestra Manager: Susan Lim

4534
SAINT LOUIS HILLS ARTS COUNCIL
4924 Hampton Avenue
Saint Louis, MO 63109-3109
Phone: 314-352-1838
Fax: 314-352-3049
Toll-free: 866-840-1838
e-mail: johnpwalsh@aol.com
Web Site: www.blueribbonrealutor.com
Officers:
President: John Powel Walsh
Budget: $10,000-20,000
Performs At: Powell Symphony Hall

4535
UNIVERSITY OF MISSOURI: SAINT LOUIS PREMIER PERFORMANCES
8001 Natural Bridge Road
Saint Louis, MO 63121-4499
Phone: 314-516-5818
Fax: 314-516-5881
e-mail: klbmezzo@umsl.edu
Web Site: www.umsl.edu/~premier
Management:
Director: Katharine Lawton Brown
Production Associate: Gloria Kohn
Founded: 1986
Specialized Field: Series & Festivals; Instrumental Music; Vocal Music; Chamber Music
Status: Non-Profit, Professional
Paid Staff: 2
Volunteer Staff: 2
Non-paid Artists: 50
Budget: $35,000-60,000
Income Sources: Public, Private and Grants
Performs At: Sheldon Concert Hall; Ethical Society Auditorium
Seating Capacity: 700/419

4536
SCOTT JOPLIN RAGTIME FESTIVAL
113 E 4th Street
Sedalia, MO 65301
Phone: 660-826-2271
Fax: 660-826-5054
Toll-free: 866-218-6258
e-mail: ragtimer@scottjoplin.org
Web Site: www.scottjoplin.org
Management:
   President: Jody Boswell
   Managing Director: Kim Phillip
Mission: To expose a greater variety of people to the
historical and aesthetic value of Scott Joplin and
ragtime music; to enrich our understanding.
Utilizes: Singers
Founded: 1974
Specialized Field: Series & Festivals; Instrumental
Music; Vocal Music; Youth; Dance; Ethnic
Performances; Orchestra; Ensemble; Instrumental
Group; Electronic & Live
Status: Non-Profit, Professional
Paid Staff: 1
Paid Artists: 50
Organization Type: Performing; Educational

4537
EVANGEL UNIVERSITY ARTISTS & LECTURESHIP SERIES
1111 N Glenstone
Springfield, MO 65802
Phone: 417-865-2811
Fax: 417-865-9599
Toll-free: 800-382-6435
e-mail: bernetg@evangel.edu
Web Site: www.evangel.edu
Management:
   President: Robert Spence
   Executive Director: John S Shows
   Dean: Glenn Bernet
Founded: 1955
Specialized Field: Education
Status: Non-Profit, Non-Professional
Paid Staff: 100
Budget: $10,000-20,000

4538
LINDENWOOD COLLEGE MAINSTAGE SEASON
209 S Kings Highway
St. Charles, MO 63301
Phone: 636-949-4966
e-mail: ggregory@lindenwood.edu
Web Site: www.lindenwood.edu
Management:
   President: Dennis Stellmann
   Executive Director: Marsha Parker
   Manager: Ted Gregory
Founded: 1827
Specialized Field: Series & Festivals; Instrumental
Music; Vocal Music; Theatre; Youth; Dance; Ethnic
Performances
Status: Non-Profit, Non-Professional
Paid Staff: 8
Paid Artists: 5

4539
ROYAL ARTS COUNCIL
PO Box 273
Versailles, MO 65084
Phone: 573-378-6226
Fax: 573-378-6928
e-mail: royalarts@advertise.net.com

Management:
   President: Richard Leass
   Executive Director: Cindy Davenport
Founded: 1981
Specialized Field: Series & Festivals; Instrumental
Music; Vocal Music; Theatre; Youth; Dance
Status: Non-Profit, Non-Professional
Paid Staff: 1
Budget: $10,000-20,000

4540
UNIVERSITY OF CENTRAL MISSOURI
403 Humphreys
Warrensburg, MO 64093
Phone: 660-543-4263
Fax: 660-543-8333
e-mail: performing_arts_series@cmsu.edu
Web Site: www.cmsu.edu/pas
Officers:
   Associate VP: Dale Carder
Management:
   Manager: Michelle Schubert
Founded: 1988
Specialized Field: Series and Festivals; Instrumental
Music; Theatre; Youth; Dance
Status: Non-Profit, Professional
Paid Staff: 2
Budget: $60,000-150,000
Performs At: Hendricks Hall
Seating Capacity: 1300

Montana

4541
RED LODGE MUSIC FESTIVAL
2235 Saint Andrews Drive
Billings, MT 59105
Phone: 406-655-4289
e-mail: rlmf@tgrfolution.net
Web Site: www.redlodgemusicfestival.org
Officers:
   President: Kenneth Gilstrap
Management:
   President: Kennith Gilstrap
   Artistic Director: Mike Peterson
Founded: 1963
Specialized Field: Series and Festivals; Instrumental
Music; Youth
Status: Non-Profit, Non-Professional
Paid Artists: 30

4542
ASSOCIATED STUDENTS OF MONTANA STATE UNIVERSITY
Strand Union Building
Room 282-B
Bozeman, MT 59717
Phone: 406-994-5828
Fax: 406-994-6911
Utilizes: Collaborations; Dancers; Filmmakers; Guest
Instructors; Guest Soloists; Instructors; Lyricists;
Multimedia; Theatre Companies
Budget: $20,000-35,000
Performs At: Wilson Auditorium; Reynolds Recital Hall;
Northwest Lounge

4543
DILLON COMMUNITY CONCERT ASSOCIATION
PO Box 621
Dillon, MT 59725
Phone: 406-683-2285

Officers:
   Drive Chairman: Ingrid Joy Kaushagen
Specialized Field: Vocal Music; Instrumental Music
Status: Non-Profit
Budget: $10,000-20,000

4544
MONTANA TRADITIONAL JAZZ FESTIVAL
PO Box 956
Great Falls, MT 59403
Phone: 406-771-1642
Fax: 406-727-5869
e-mail: jazzfeset@montana.com
Web Site: www.montanatradjazz.com
Management:
   Director: Don West

4545
HAVRE COMMUNITY CONCERT ASSOCIATION
44 Saddle Butte Drive
Havre, MT 59501
Phone: 406-265-5254
Officers:
   President: Dan Heltne
Budget: $10,000-20,000

4546
NORTHERN SHOWCASE CONCERT ASSOCIATION
MSU-Northern
PO Box 7751
Havre, MT 59501
Phone: 406-265-3732
Fax: 406-265-3785
Toll-free: 800-662-6132
e-mail: brewer@msun.edu
Web Site: www.msun.edu
Officers:
   Chair: Denise Brewer
Management:
   Executive Director: Debbie Ritz
Mission: To provide fine arts/culture to the Havre
community and MSU Northern students.
Utilizes: Community Members; Community Talent; Five
Seasonal Concerts; Original Music Scores
Founded: 1932
Specialized Field: Havre and the Hiline community
Status: Non-Profit, Professional
Volunteer Staff: 15
Paid Artists: 6
Budget: $10,000-20,000

4547
FLATHEAD VALLEY FESTIVAL
545 Second Avenue E
Kalispell, MT 59901
Phone: 406-257-1065
Fax: 406-257-1065
e-mail: festival@cyberport.net
Web Site: www.cyberport.net/festival
Officers:
   VP: Bob Kieser
   Treasurer: Kris Fuehrer

4548
UNIVERSITY OF MONTANA PERFORMING ARTS SERIES
University Of Montana
University Center Suite 104
Missoula, MT 59812

Phone: 406-243-6661
Fax: 406-243-4905
e-mail: specialevents@umproductions.org
Web Site: www.umproductions.org
Management:
Executive Director: Dave Van
Concert Coordinator: Elizabeth Wilhelm
Advisor: Marlene Hendckson
Founded: 1918
Specialized Field: Series & Festivals; Instrumental Music; Vocal Music; Theatre; Dance; Ethnic Performances
Status: Non-Profit, Non-Professional
Paid Staff: 9
Income Sources: Student Funded
Performs At: Fieldhouse; Wilma Theatre; University Theater; UC Ballroom; Arena; Theaters
Facility Category: Theater
Type of Stage: Built In
Seating Capacity: 1,000
Year Remodeled: 1998
Rental Contact: Tom Webster

4549
YOUNG AUDIENCES OF WESTERN MONTANA SERIES
PO Box 9096
111 N Higgins #212
Missoula, MT 59807
Phone: 406-721-5924
Fax: 406-829-6432
e-mail: alaynusa@montana.com
Officers:
President: John Engen
Past President: John Bohyer
Secretary: Jack Sturgis
Treasurer: Dan Chisholm
Management:
Executive Director: Alayne Dolson
Mission: To introduce elementary school children to various performing arts.
Utilizes: Actors; Collaborations; Dance Companies; Dancers; Fine Artists; Lyricists; Multimedia; New Productions; Original Music Scores; Playwrights; Sign Language Translators
Founded: 1964
Specialized Field: Performing Arts Program for School Children
Status: Non-Profit, Professional
Paid Staff: 1
Paid Artists: 15
Budget: $43,000
Income Sources: Grants, School Fees, Individual and business donors.
Performs At: Schools
Affiliations: Young Audience, New York, NY
Organization Type: Performing; Touting; Educational

4550
OLD TIMERS CONCERT SERIES
Sheridan High School
Sheridan, MT 59749
Phone: 406-842-5226
Management:
Manager: Sue Nottingham
Mission: To encourage community talent; to raise money for scholarships and school music programs.
Utilizes: Guest Artists; Guest Companies; Singers
Founded: 1974
Specialized Field: Dance; Vocal Music; Instrumental Music; Theatre; Festivals
Status: Semi-Professional; Non-Professional
Paid Staff: 50
Performs At: Sheridan School Gym

Organization Type: Performing; Resident

4551
FLATHEAD FESTIVAL OF THE ARTS
PO Box 1780
Whitefish, MT 59937/WHIT
Phone: 406-862-1780
Management:
Executive Director: Charles Buchwalter
Artistic Director: Gordon Johnson
Administrative Director: Rebecca Grouse
Founded: 1986
Specialized Field: Vocal Music Instrumental Music; Festivals; Lyric Opera
Status: Nonprofit
Organization Type: Performing; Touring; Educational; Sponsoring

Nebraska

4552
HARLAN COUNTY ARTS COUNCIL
PO Box 166
Alma, NE 68920
Phone: 308-928-9989
Officers:
President: Cindy Kauk
Budget: $10,000-20,000

4553
BASSETT ARTS COUNCIL
Box 429
Bassett, NE 68714
Phone: 402-684-3355
Fax: 402-684-2546
Officers:
President: Linda May
VP: Kathy Jorgenser
Treasurer: Betty Hall
Secretary: Mary M. Schelkopf
Management:
Secretary/ Contact Person: Mary M Schelkopf
Utilizes: Actors; Artists-in-Residence; Choreographers; Collaborations; Commissioned Music; Curators; Dance Companies; Dancers; Educators; Fine Artists; Guest Accompanists; Guest Choreographers; Guest Instructors; Guest Soloists; Guild Activities; Instructors; Local Artists; Lyricists; Multimedia; New Productions; Original Music Scores; Playwrights; Sign Language Translators; Soloists; Special Technical Talent; Theatre Companies; Touring Companies
Paid Staff: 50
Budget: $20,000-35,000

4554
COLUMBUS FRIENDS OF MUSIC ASSOCIATION
3485 18th Avenue
Columbus, NE 68601
Phone: 402-563-1857

4555
MIDLAND LUTHERAN COLLEGE CONCERT: LECTURE SERIES
900 N Clarkson
Fremont, NE 68025
Phone: 402-721-5480
Officers:
VP Institutional Advancement: Fred Pyle

4556
ABENDMUSIK SERIES
2000 D Street
Lincoln, NE 68502-1698
Phone: 402-476-9933
Fax: 402-476-8402
e-mail: jeremy@abendmusik.org
Web Site: www.abendmusik.org
Management:
Executive Director: Jeremy Bankson
Artistic Director: Tom Trenney
Mission: Gathering to experience excellence in the performing arts
Founded: 1972
Specialized Field: Series & Festivals; Instrumental Music; Vocal Music; Concert Series
Status: Non-Profit, Professional
Paid Staff: 3
Budget: $60,000-150,000
Performs At: First-Plymouth Church
Facility Category: Church
Seating Capacity: 670-750
Rental Contact: Louise Bremers

4557
LIED CENTER FOR PERFORMING ARTS
Lied Center for Performing Arts
301 N 12th, PO Box 880151
Lincoln, NE 68588
Phone: 402-472-4747
Fax: 402-472-2725
Toll-free: 800-432-3231
e-mail: info@liedcenter.org
Web Site: www.liedcenter.org
Management:
Executive Director: Charles Henry Bethea
Artistic Director: Charles Henry Bethea
Managing Director: Charles Henry Bethea
Founded: 1989
Specialized Field: Series and Festivals; Instrumental Music; Vocal Music; Theatre; Youth; Dance; Ethnic Performances
Status: Non-Profit, Professional
Paid Staff: 30
Volunteer Staff: 300

4558
HERITAGE DAYS FESTIVAL
PO Box 337
McCook, NE 69001
Phone: 308-345-3200
Fax: 308-345-3201
e-mail: info@aboutmecook.com
Web Site: www.aboutmecook.com
Management:
Director: Moris Owen
Assistant Director: Joan Parsons
Founded: 1969
Specialized Field: Dance; Vocal Music; Instrumental Music; Arts and Crafts
Status: Non-Professional; Nonprofit
Organization Type: Sponsoring

4559
BROWNVILLE CONCERT SERIES
740 S 75th Street
Omaha, NE 68114
Phone: 402-346-1102
Fax: 402-346-1355
Officers:
Program Chairman: James Keene
Budget: $20,000-35,000

4560

CATHEDRAL ARTS PROJECT SERIES

100 N 62nd Street
Omaha, NE 68132
Phone: 402-558-3100
Fax: 402-558-3026
e-mail: dorthy@tuma.net
Web Site: www.cathedralartsproject.org
Management:
Executive Director: William Woeger
Adminstrative Assistant: Dorothy Tuma
Founded: 1985
Specialized Field: Visual/Performing
Paid Staff: 2
Volunteer Staff: 50
Budget: $10,000-20,000
Performs At: St. Cecelia Cathedral

4561

NEBRASKA SHAKESPEARE FESTIVAL

Department of Fine Arts, Creighton University
Creighton University
Omaha, NE 68178
Phone: 402-280-2391
Web Site: www.nebraskashakespeare.com
Management:
Executive Director: Mary Ann Bamber
Director of Production/Education: Thomas Lowe
Marketing Director: Nellie Sudavici MacCallum
Co-Founder and Interim Artistic Dir: Alan Klem
Specialized Field: Theater

4562

TUESDAY MUSICAL CONCERT SERIES

8543 Hickory Street
Omaha, NE 68124
Phone: 402-391-4661
Fax: 402-397-9510
e-mail: barbarataxman@aol.com
Web Site: www.tuesdaymusicomaha.org
Management:
President: Frederica Perhulste
Program Chairman: Barbara Taxman
Mission: Offering an annual professional concert
series.
Utilizes: Guest Accompanists; Multimedia
Founded: 1892
Specialized Field: Series & Festivals: Recitals Series
Status: Non-Profit, Professional
Volunteer Staff: 30
Budget: $35,000-60,000
Income Sources: Ticket sales; Donations; Grants
Performs At: Joslyn Art Museum
Annual Attendance: 600
Facility Category: Art Museum/Concert Hall
Seating Capacity: 1,000
Organization Type: Sponsoring

4563

UNIVERSITY OF NEBRASKA AT OMAHA MUSIC SERIES

Music Department
60 and Dodge Street
Omaha, NE 68182
Phone: 402-554-3427
Fax: 402-554-2252
e-mail: gperdue@mail.unomaha.edu
Web Site: www.music.unomaha.edu
Officers:
Chairman Department of Music: Melissa Berke
Management:
Event Coordinator/Performace Series: Greg
Perdue

Utilizes: Artists-in-Residence; Commissioned Music;
Guest Accompanists; Guest Companies; Guest
Directors; Guest Instructors; Guest Lecturers; Guest
Musical Directors; Guest Musicians; High School
Drama; Local Artists; Multimedia; Music; Organization
Contracts; Singers
Founded: 1918
Specialized Field: Series & Festivals: Chamber Music
Status: Non-Profit, Professional
Paid Staff: 10
Paid Artists: 20
Non-paid Artists: 50
Budget: $25,000
Income Sources: University Funds, Foundation
Support, Grants, Ticket Sales
Performs At: Strauss Performing Arts Center
Annual Attendance: 50,000+
Facility Category: Concert Hall
Type of Stage: Concert Only
Stage Dimensions: 36'8"-37'7" x 40'
Seating Capacity: 474
Year Built: 1975
Cost: $23 million
Rental Contact: Events Coordinator T. Heil

4564

CONCORDIA UNIVERSITY CONCERT SERIES

800 N Columbia Avenue
Seward, NE 68434
Phone: 402-643-7411
Fax: 402-643-4073
Budget: $10,000

4565

WAYNE STATE COLLEGE SPECIAL PROGRAMS BLACK & GOLD SERIES

Wayne State College
Wayne, NE 68787
Phone: 402-375-7359
Fax: 402-375-7204
Management:
Dean: James O'Donnell
Utilizes: Actors; Artists-in-Residence; Dance
Companies; Dancers; Fine Artists; Guest
Accompanists; Guest Directors; Guest Instructors;
Guest Musical Directors; Guest Musicians; Guest
Soloists; Multimedia; Original Music Scores;
Playwrights; Sign Language Translators; Singers;
Touring Companies
Budget: $35,000-60,000
Performs At: Ramsey Theatre; Ley Theatre

Nevada

4566

BOULDER CITY ARTS COUNCIL

PO Box 61314
Boulder City, NV 89006
Phone: 702-294-1499
Fax: 702-293-7743
Budget: $10,000

4567

NEVADA ARTS COUNCIL

716 N Carson Street
Suite A
Carson City, NV 89701

Phone: 775-687-6680
Fax: 775-687-6688
Toll-free: 800-326-6888
e-mail: rhodgkins@nevadaculture.org
Web Site: nac.nevadaculture.org
Management:
Community Development: Robin Hodgkins
Founded: 1967

4568

CHURCHILL ARTS COUNCIL

PO Box 2204
Fallon, NV 89407
Phone: 775-423-1440
Fax: 775-423-0779
e-mail: charts@phonewave.net
Web Site: www.churchillarts.org
Management:
President: Ted Balash
Executive Director: Valerie J Serpa
Founded: 1986
Specialized Field: Multidisplinary Organisation.
Status: Non-Profit, Professional
Paid Staff: 2
Volunteer Staff: 20
Paid Artists: 35

4569

REED WHIPPLE CULTURAL ARTS CENTER

821 Las Vegas Boulevard N
Las Vegas, NV 89101
Phone: 702-229-6211
Fax: 702-382-5199
Web Site: www.lasvegasnevada.gov
Management:
Manager: Nancy Deaner
Executive Director: Bob Jackson
Artistic Director: Patricia Harris
Mission: Developing the arts community via
programming, community involvement and education.
Utilizes: Singers
Founded: 1961
Specialized Field: Series and Festival; Instrumental
music; Vocal music; Theatre; Youth; Dance; Ethnic
Performances; Visual Arts
Status: Non-Profit, Professional
Paid Staff: 50
Paid Artists: 100
Income Sources: American Council for the Arts;
Nevada Recreation & Parks Society; Nevada
Presenters Network
Affiliations: Las Vegas Civic Center; Las Vegas
Woodwing Quintet
Type of Stage: Proscenium
Stage Dimensions: 18'x45'x24'
Seating Capacity: 300
Rental Contact: Patricia Harris
Organization Type: Performing; Touring; Educational;
Sponsoring
Resident Groups: Rainbow Theatre Company

4570

UNIVERSITY OF NEVADA PERFORMING ARTS CENTER

4505 Maryland Parkway
Las Vegas, NV 089154-500
Phone: 702-895-3535
Fax: 702-895-4714
Web Site: www.pac.unlv.edu
Management:
Dir Artistic Programming/Production: Larry
Henley

Technical Director: Trent Downing
Director Of Marketing: Shaun Sewell
Founded: 1976
Specialized Field: Dance; Music; Theatre
Paid Staff: 8
Non-paid Artists: 20
Performs At: Performing Arts Center Consisting Of Three Theatres
Affiliations: University Government
Annual Attendance: 132,000
Type of Stage: Concert Hall, Theatre, Blackbox
Seating Capacity: 1830; 550; 175
Rental Contact: Dir Artistic Programming/Production Larry Henley

---

4571

NEVADA SHAKESPEARE FESTIVAL

454 Glenmanor Drive
Reno, NV 89509
Phone: 775-324-4198
Fax: 775-324-2677
e-mail: information@nevada-shakespeare.org
Web Site: www.nevada-shakespeare.org
Management:
    President: Joan Walker
    Executive Director: Cameron Crain
    Artistic Director: Jeanmarie Simpson
    Communications Director: Lindsey Stedsand
Mission: Presents language-rich works that mine the core as archaeologist to soul, making a case, in these tenuous times, for the preservation of humankind and the world that we inhabit. NSC is driven to create a new action-based stagings that are theatrical rather than cinematic or realistic. Embracing principles of Universal Access, the company serves more than 100,000 children, youth and adults each year with theatre outreach.
Founded: 1989
Specialized Field: Series and Festivals; Theatre; Youth; Ethnic Performances
Status: Non-Profit, Professional
Paid Staff: 3
Paid Artists: 12

4572

UNIVERSITY OF NEVADA: RENO PERFORMING ARTS SERIES

UNR School Of The Arts/048
Reno, NV 89557-0048
Phone: 775-784-4278
Fax: 775-784-3566
e-mail: cmoney@unr.edu
Web Site: www.unr.edu/pas
Management:
    Assistant Director Of Programs: Chris Money
Utilizes: Collaborations; Multimedia
Founded: 1960
Specialized Field: Performing Arts
Paid Staff: 2
Paid Artists: 20
Budget: $62,000-80,000
Income Sources: University Administration, Students, State And Local Grants, Ticket Income, Other Sources
Annual Attendance: 3000
Facility Category: Concert Hall
Type of Stage: Proscenium
Seating Capacity: 618
Year Built: 1988

New Hampshire

4573

KEISER CONCERT SERIES

Saint Paul's School
325 Pleasant Street
Concord, NH 03301-2591
Phone: 603-229-4681
Fax: 603-229-5695
e-mail: dseaton@sps.edu
Web Site: www.sps.edu
Management:
    Music Director: David D Seaton
Mission: To bring professional solo and chamber music concerts to St. Paul's school.
Founded: 1974
Specialized Field: Series and Festivals; Instrumental Music; Vocal Music
Status: Non-Profit, Professional
Paid Staff: 5
Paid Artists: 5
Budget: $30,000
Income Sources: Funding
Performs At: Intimate Chamber Music Hall
Seating Capacity: 150
Year Built: 1979

4574

WILLIAM H GILE TRUST FUND CONCERT SERIES

17 Pleasant View Avenue
Concord, NH 03301-2555
Phone: 603-224-1217
Fax: 603-228-3901
e-mail: docdode@aol.com
Officers:
    Committee Chairman: Dr. Robert C Rainie
    Advisor: MT Mennino
Management:
    President: M T Menino
Specialized Field: Series & Festivals; Instrumental Music; Vocal Music; Theatre; Youth; Dance; Ethnic Performances
Status: Non-Profit, Professional
Paid Staff: 3
Budget: $85,000
Income Sources: Trust Fund
Performs At: Chubb Theatre; Capitol Center for the Arts
Annual Attendance: 1,400/performance
Facility Category: Capiyol Center for the Arts
Stage Dimensions: 40' wide/24 1/2' deep/4 1/2' apron
Seating Capacity: 1,425
Rental Contact: CEO M.T. Mennino

4575

NEW HAMPSHIRE SHAKESPEARE FESTIVAL

PO Box 191
Deerfield, NH 03037
Phone: 603-666-9088
e-mail: nhsf@nhsf.org
Web Site: www.nhsf.org
Management:
    Executive Director: Gail Mills
Founded: 1993
Status: Non-Equity; Nonprofit
Season: July - August

4576

UNIVERSITY OF NEW HAMPSHIRE CELEBRITY SERIES

Paul Creative Arts Center, M202
30 College Road
Durham, NH 03824-3538
Phone: 603-862-3242
Fax: 603-862-3155
e-mail: mary.deturk@unh.edu
Web Site: www.unh.edu/celebrity
Management:
    Manager: Mary Deturk
Utilizes: Dancers; Guest Directors; Multimedia; Special Technical Talent; Theatre Companies
Specialized Field: Series & Festivals; Instrumental Music; Vocal Music; Theatre; Dance
Status: Non-Profit, Non-Professional
Paid Staff: 1
Budget: $60,000-150,000
Performs At: Johnson Theatre
Type of Stage: proscenium
Stage Dimensions: 20x40
Seating Capacity: 688a
Year Built: 1963
Rental Contact: Theatre & Dance Dept. Michael Woood

4577

DARTMOUTH COLLEGE HOPKINS CENTER PERFORMING SERIES

Hopkins Center
6041 Lower Level Wilson Hall
Hanover, NH 03755-3543
Phone: 603-646-3453
Fax: 603-646-3911
e-mail: hopprogramming@dartmouth.edu
Web Site: www.hop.dartmouth.edu
Management:
    Executive Director: Lewis Crickard
    Artistic Director: Margaret Lawrence
Founded: 1962
Specialized Field: Series & Festivals; Instrumental Music; Vocal Music; Theatre; Youth; Dance; Ethnic Performances
Status: Non-Profit, Professional
Paid Staff: 43
Paid Artists: 175
Budget: $400,000-1,000,000
Performs At: The Moore Theatre; Rollins Chapel

4578

NEW ENGLAND COLLEGE CULTURAL EVENTS SERIES

24 Bridge Street
Henniker, NH 03242-0793
Phone: 603-428-2303
Budget: $10,000

4579

BELKNAP MILL SOCIETY

The Mill Plaza
25 Beacon Street E
Laconia, NH 03246
Phone: 603-524-8813
Fax: 603-528-1228
Web Site: www.belknapmill.org
Management:
    President: Dick Metz
    Executive Director: Mary Boswell
Founded: 1971
Specialized Field: Multidisciplinary Art Center
Status: Non-Profit, Professional
Paid Staff: 7

Budget: $10,000

4580
NORTH COUNTRY CHAMBER PLAYERS SUMMER FESTIVAL: MUSIC IN THE WHITE MOUNTAINS
PO Box 904
Littleton, NH 03561
Phone: 603-444-0309
Fax: 603-444-0309
e-mail: nccp@ncia.net
Web Site: www.newwww.com/org/nccp
Officers:
   President, Board of Directors: Len Reed
Management:
   Executive Director: Stephen Dignazio
   Artistic Director: Ronnie Bauch
Mission: Culturally enrich New Hamphire through chamber music performance and music education
Founded: 1978
Status: Nonprofit
Paid Staff: 1
Paid Artists: 12
Budget: $400,000-500,000
Income Sources: Earned Revenues by Government; Foundation; Corporate and Individual Donors

4581
SAINT ANSELM COLLEGE PERFORMING ARTS SERIES
Dana Humanities Center
100 Saint Anselm Drive
Manchester, NH 03102-1310
Phone: 603-641-7000
Fax: 603-641-7332
Web Site: www.anselm.edu
Management:
   President: Fr Jonathan Defelice
   VP Of Student Affairs: Joseph M Horto
Founded: 1889
Budget: $150,000-400,000
Performs At: Koonz Theatre

4582
AMERICAN STAGE FESTIVAL PEACOCK PLAYERS
14 Court Street
Nashua, NH 03060-3478
Phone: 603-886-7000
Fax: 603-889-2336
Web Site: www.peacockplayers.org
Management:
   Production Artistic Director: Robert Walsh
Founded: 2002
Specialized Field: Series & Festivals; Theatre; Youth
Status: Non-Profit, Non-Professional
Season: June - August
Type of Stage: Proscenium
Stage Dimensions: 40' x 38'
Seating Capacity: 497

4583
NASHUA COMMUNITY CONCERT ASSOCIATION
PO Box 1563
Nashua, NH 03061
Phone: 603-318-1792
Web Site: www.nashuacommunityconcerts.org
Officers:
   President: Ernest D Berube
Management:
   President: Carol P. Marshall
   Membership Secretary: Mary E. Sayre

   Vice-President: Calvin Knickerbocker
   Corresponding Secretary: Betty Williams
Founded: 1931
Specialized Field: Series & Festivals; Vocal Music; Choral; Theatre; Dance; Ethnic Performances; Orchestra
Status: Non-Profit, Professional
Budget: $35,000-60,000

4584
COLBY-SAWYER COLLEGE
Ware Campus Center
541 Maint Street
New London, NH 03257
Phone: 603-526-3759
Fax: 603-526-2135
e-mail: sazodi@colby-sawyer.edu
Web Site: www.colby-sawyer.edu
Management:
   President: Ann Ponder
   Campus Activities Director: Sharon Williamson
Founded: 1857
Specialized Field: Series & Festivals: Theatre
Status: Non-Profit, Non-Professional
Budget: $10,000-20,000

4585
SUMMER MUSIC ASSOCIATES SERIES
PO Box 603
New London, NH 03257
Phone: 603-526-8234
Web Site: www.nl-nh.com
Management:
   Program Committee Chairman: Robert Fraley
Mission: Presenter of four summer concerts.
Founded: 1974
Specialized Field: Vocal Music; Instrumental Music
Status: Nonprofit
Budget: $45,000
Income Sources: Contributions; ticket sales
Performs At: College/high schoool/church/town hall facilities
Annual Attendance: 1500
Seating Capacity: 700
Organization Type: Sponsoring

4586
MONADNOCK MUSIC
2A Concord Street
Peterborough, NH 03458
Phone: 603-924-7610
Fax: 603-924-9403
Toll-free: 800-868-9613
e-mail: mm@monadnockmusic.mv.com
Web Site: www.monadnockmusic.org
Officers:
   President: Hilary Feldstein
   Treasurer: Kevin McElhinney
   Secretary: Virginia Lee Miller
Management:
   Artistic Director: Jonathan Bagg
   Artistic Director: Laura Gilbert
   Managing Director: Christina Meinke
Mission: To make exceptional music accessible to all in intimate and informal settings through a commitment to varied and imaginative performances to keep a sense of musical daring and discovery alive.
Utilizes: Guest Directors; Guest Musicians; Multimedia; Original Music Scores; Sign Language Translators; Singers
Founded: 1966
Specialized Field: Vocal Music; Instrumental Music; Festivals; Lyric Opera
Status: Professional; Nonprofit

Paid Staff: 5
Paid Artists: 50
Budget: $350,000
Income Sources: Grants; Private Donations
Performs At: Churches; Meetinghousese
Seating Capacity: 200
Organization Type: Performing; Educational

4587
FRIENDS OF THE ARTS REGIONAL ART COUNCIL
PO Box 386
Plymouth, NH 03264-0386
Phone: 603-536-1182
Fax: 603-536-1182
e-mail: pfa@plymouth.edu
Web Site: www.friends-of-the-arts.org
Management:
   President: Margaret Turner
   Executive Director: Jane Hamor
   Artistic Director: Cynthia Robinson
Founded: 1973
Specialized Field: Series and Festivals: Ethnic Performances
Status: Non-Profit, Professional
Paid Staff: 3
Budget: $20,000-35,000
Performs At: Silver Hall

4588
PLYMOUTH STATE UNIVERSITY
Silver Center For The Arts
Plymouth State University
Plymouth, NH 03264
Mailing Address: MSC 36-17 High Street
Phone: 603-535-2801
Fax: 603-535-2917
e-mail: djeffery@plymouth.edu
Web Site: silver.plymouth.edu
Management:
   Director: Diane Jeffery
Utilizes: Artists-in-Residence; Collaborating Artists; Collaborations; Dance Companies; Dancers; Educators; Guest Accompanists; Guest Choreographers; Guest Musical Directors; Guest Musicians; Guest Soloists; Lyricists; Multi Collaborations; Multimedia; Original Music Scores; Playwrights; Selected Students; Soloists; Special Technical Talent; Theatre Companies
Specialized Field: Central NH
Paid Staff: 20
Paid Artists: 14
Budget: $35,000-60,000
Income Sources: Ticket Revenue, Sponsorships, Grants, and Donations.
Performs At: Hanaway Theatre; Smith Recital Hall; Studio Theatre
Facility Category: Performing Arts Center
Type of Stage: Proscenium
Stage Dimensions: 90' x 36'
Seating Capacity: 650
Year Built: 1992
Year Remodeled: 1992
Rental Contact: Director Diane Jeffery

4589
FRIENDS OF THE MUSIC HALL CONCERT SERIES
104 Congress Street
Suite 203
Portsmouth, NH 03801

Phone: 603-433-3100
Fax: 603-431-4103
e-mail: tlagamma@themusichall.org
Web Site: www.themusichall.org
Management:
   President: Patricia Lynch
   Artistic Director: Theresa La Gamma
Founded: 1986
Specialized Field: Series & Festivals; Music; Theatre;
Dance; Films
Status: Non-Profit, Professional
Paid Staff: 20
Budget: $150,000-400,000

4590
HARBOR ARTS JAZZ NIGHT: PORTSMOUTH JAZZ FESTIVAL

C/O 93 High Street
Suite No 1
Portsmouth, NH 03801
Phone: 603-436-8596
Fax: 603-433-2787
e-mail: richard@cuzinrichard.com
Web Site: www.jazznite.org
Officers:
   President: John Hauschildt
Management:
   Managing Director: Richard Smith
Mission: Raise funds for Harbor Arts Museum and for
school music art departments/music schools, other non
profits.
Utilizes: Collaborating Artists;
Composers-in-Residence; Guest Accompanists;
Instructors; Local Artists & Directors; Music; Original
Music Scores; Paid Performers; Playwrights; Scenic
Designers; Students; Visual Arts; Visual Designers
Founded: 1991
Specialized Field: Series & Festivals: Museum and
jazz music
Status: Non-Profit, Professional
Volunteer Staff: 25
Paid Artists: 10

4591
PRESCOTT PARK ARTS FESTIVAL

PO Box 4370
105 Marcy Street
Portsmouth, NH 03802
Phone: 603-436-2848
Web Site: www.prescottpark.org
Management:
   Executive Director: Ben Anderson
   Festival Coordinator: Ellen Foord
   Music Director: Catherine York
   Stage Manager/Production Manager: David
   D'Agostino
   President: Sandi Hennequin
   Vice President: Cathy Sununu
   Secretary: Janet Stevens
   Treasurer: Mark Rollick
Mission: To provide a professional wide-ranging arts
festival for a diverse audience combining ticketed and
free access.
Utilizes: Singers
Founded: 1974
Specialized Field: Dance; Vocal Music; Theatre;
Festivals
Status: Nonprofit
Season: July - August
Performs At: Prescott Park
Organization Type: Performing; Touring; Resident;
Educational; Sponsoring

4592
FRANKLIN PIERCE COLLEGE CRIMSON-GREY CULTURAL SERIES

Franklin Pierce College
Rindge, NH 03461
Phone: 603-899-4152
Fax: 603-899-6448
Budget: $10,000-20,000
Performs At: Fieldhouse; Ravencroft Theater

4593
WATERVILLE VALLEY FOUNDATION SUMMER FESTIVAL

1 Ski Area Road
PO Box 540
Waterville Valley, NH 03215
Phone: 603-236-8311
Fax: 603-236-4344
Toll-free: 800-468-2553
Web Site: www.waterville.com
Management:
   Town Square Manager: April Smith
Mission: To present a summer festival of the arts.
Utilizes: Singers
Founded: 1985
Specialized Field: Vocal Music; Instrumental Music;
Festivals; Concerts
Status: Nonprofit
Performs At: Town Square Concert Pavillion
Organization Type: Performing; Educational

4594
GREAT WATERS MUSIC FESTIVAL

58 N Main Street
PO Box 488
Wolfeboro, NH 03894-0488
Phone: 603-569-7710
Fax: 603-569-7715
e-mail: info@greatwaters.org
Web Site: www.greatwaters.org
Management:
   Executive Director: Ben Anderson
Mission: To present a diversified summer concert
series.
Founded: 1995
Status: Non-Profit
Facility Category: Acoustic Tent

New Jersey

4595
ASBURY PARK JAZZ FESTIVAL

1 Municipal Plaza
Asbury Park, NJ 07712
Phone: 732-502-5728
Fax: 732-502-5738

4596
GREAT GEORGE FESTIVAL

11 Elmwood Avenue
Belleville, NJ 07109
Phone: 973-759-3819
e-mail: dquinn711@aol.com
Management:
   Producer: Daniel P Quinn

4597
SCANDINAVIAN FEST

NJ Vasa Park
1 Wolfe Road
Budd Lake, NJ 07872

Phone: 610-417-1483
e-mail: info@ScanFest.org
Web Site: www.ScanFest.org
Officers:
   President: Palmer Hval
   General Chair/Entertainment Coord: Kathy Hval
   Publicity/Promotion: Carl Anderson
   Vendor Chair: Lisbet Price
Utilizes: Actors; Dance Companies; Dancers; Fine
Artists; Five Seasonal Concerts; Grant Writers; Guest
Accompanists; Guest Directors; Guest Instructors;
Guest Musical Directors; Guest Musicians; Guest
Soloists; High School Drama; Instructors; Multimedia;
Original Music Scores; Sign Language Translators;
Singers; Soloists; Student Interns; Special Technical
Talent; Theatre Companies
Founded: 1985
Volunteer Staff: 30
Paid Artists: 20
Budget: $40,000-$50,000
Income Sources: Admission Fees, Donations,
Sponsorhsip, Vendor Fees
Performs At: Outdoor park with covered/roofed
performance areas
Annual Attendance: 5,000
Facility Category: Outdoor park with covered stages, 1
Indoor stage
Type of Stage: Covered Outdoors, One Indoor
Stage Dimensions: varies to 40x80
Seating Capacity: 200-500

4598
CAPE MAY JAZZ FESTIVAL

PO Box 2065
Cape May, NJ 08204
Phone: 609-884-7277
Fax: 609-884-7248
e-mail: jodi@capemayjazz.com
Web Site: www.capemayjazz.org
Officers:
   President: Carol Stone
Management:
   President: Woody Woodland
   Executive Director: Lelah Ettenbazh
   Artistic Director: Carol Stone
Mission: To hold 2 jazz festivals per year, education
programs and promote jazz to region
Founded: 1994
Specialized Field: Series & Festivals; Instrumental
Music; Vocal Music
Status: Non-Profit, Professional
Paid Staff: 3
Volunteer Staff: 200
Annual Attendance: 15,000

4599
CAPE MAY MUSIC FESTIVAL

1048 Washington Street
PO Box 340
Cape May, NJ 08204
Phone: 609-884-5404
Fax: 609-884-0574
Toll-free: 800-275-4278
e-mail: mstewart@capemaymac.org
Web Site: www.capemaymac.org
Management:
   Chief Outreach Officer: Mary E Stewart,
   mstewart@capemaymac.org
Mission: Preservation, interpretation and cultural
enrichment
Utilizes: Commissioned Music; Community Talent;
Curators; Five Seasonal Concerts; Guest Directors
Founded: 1970
Opened: 1990

Specialized Field: Music; Instrumental
Status: Non-Profit
Paid Staff: 20
Volunteer Staff: 50
Paid Artists: 100
Budget: $250,000
Income Sources: Grants, Donationa, Admissions
Type of Stage: Altar Area
Seating Capacity: 200-400
Year Built: 1800

4600
EDISON ARTS SOCIETY
1729 Woodland Avenue
Edison, NJ 08820
Phone: 908-753-2787
Fax: 908-753-2790
e-mail: edisonarts@aol.com
Web Site: www.edisonnarts.org
Officers:
    President: Angelo A Orlando
    Vice President: Denise Persico
    Treasurer: Denise Sirna
    Secretary: Karen McNamara
Management:
    President: Angelia Orlando
    Executive Director: Hand Nina
Founded: 1998
Specialized Field: Series & Festivals: Symphonic
Orchestra
Status: Non-Profit, Professional
Paid Staff: 2
Paid Artists: 3

4601
APPEL FARM ARTS AND MUSIC CENTER
PO Box 888
Elmer, NJ 08318
Phone: 856-358-2472
Fax: 856-358-6513
Toll-free: 800-394-1211
e-mail: info@appelfarm.org
Web Site: www.appelfarm.org
Management:
    Executive Director: Mark E Packer
    Artistic Director: Sean Timmons
    Director Special Projects: Judy Henson
Utilizes: Artists-in-Residence; Multimedia; Original
Music Scores
Founded: 1960
Specialized Field: Series & Festivals; Dance; Vocal
Music; Instrumental Music; Theatre; Festivals
Status: Non-Profit, Professional
Paid Staff: 18
Volunteer Staff: 500
Paid Artists: 21
Budget: $2.3 million
Affiliations: ArtPRIDE, NJSCA, SJCA, ABP
Facility Category: Regional Performing Arts Center
Type of Stage: Indoor/Outdoor
Stage Dimensions: 40'x50'
Seating Capacity: 250/12,000
Year Built: 1965
Rental Contact: Conference Center Director Walt
Sibley
Organization Type: Performing; Resident; Educational

4602
JOHN HARMS CENTER FOR THE ARTS
30 N Van Brunt Street
Englewood, NJ 07631
Phone: 201-567-5797
Fax: 201-567-7357
Web Site: www.johnharms.org

Management:
    Executive Director: Jessica Finkelberg
    Business Manager: Steve Nemiroff
    Director Education: Cathy Roy
    Communications/Marketing: Ed Kirchdoerffer
Founded: 1976
Status: Nonprofit
Paid Staff: 14
Volunteer Staff: 150
Paid Artists: 250
Budget: $3,000,000
Income Sources: Foundations, Grants, Corporate
Support, Individuals, Earned
Annual Attendance: 300,000
Facility Category: Theater
Type of Stage: Proscenium
Stage Dimensions: 33 x 30
Seating Capacity: 1322
Year Built: 1926

4603
COLLEGE OF NEW JERSEY CENTER FOR THE ARTS
PO Box 7718
Ewing, NJ 08628-0718
Phone: 609-771-2563
Fax: 609-637-5134
e-mail: artsfac@tcnj.edu
Web Site: www.tcnj.edu/~arts/facilities
Officers:
    Dean: John C Laughton
Management:
    Director of Arts Facilities: Richard Kroth
    Coordinator of Audience Services: Susan
    O'Connor
Mission: Serves as a focal point for the Arts at the
College and will function to promote arts activities, both
on and off campus, collaborate with arts organization in
New Jersey and beyond, advocate for arts education in
schools and communities, and serve as a link to the
curricular needs of all of the schools in the College of
New Jersey.
Founded: 1855

4604
FAIR LAWN SUMMER FESTIVAL
Federated Arts Council
185 Prospect Avenue, Apartment 12M
Hackensack, NJ 07601
Phone: 201-646-1061
Fax: 201-796-5667
Management:
    Director: Isadore Freeman
Founded: 1960
Specialized Field: Series & Festivals; Instrumental
Music; Vocal Music; Theatre; Youth; Dance; Ethnic
Performances
Status: Non-Profit, Professional
Paid Staff: 2
Budget: $10,000
Annual Attendance: 1,000
Facility Category: Band Shell
Year Built: 1992

4605
SOUNDFEST CHAMBER MUSIC FESTIVAL, COLORADO QUARTET
225 Prospect Avenue
Suite B
Hackensack, NJ 07601

Phone: 508-548-2290
Fax: 201-498-0019
e-mail: cq@coloradoquartet.com
Web Site: www.coloradoquartet.com
Management:
    Director: Diane Chaplin

4606
CENTENARY STAGE COMPANY AND PERFORMING ARTS GUILD
400 Jefferson Street
Hackettstown, NJ 07840
Phone: 908-979-0900
Fax: 908-979-4297
e-mail: boxoffice@centenarystageco.org
Web Site: www.centenarystageco.org
Management:
    Artistic Director: Carl Wallnau
    Associate Artistic Director: Catherine Rust
    Development Associate: Lea Antonlini
    Office Manager: Claudia Polo
Mission: A not-for-profit professional Equity Theatre
dedicated to bringin the performing arts to the Warren,
Sussex, Morris and Hunterdon County areas. OUr
actors are a part of the Actors Equity Association, the
professional union for actors. We are an associate
member of the New Jersey Theatre Alliance.
Founded: 1987
Specialized Field: Theatre; Music; Dance
Status: Non-Profit, Professional
Paid Staff: 4
Volunteer Staff: 5

4607
COMMUNITY ARTS PARTNERSHIP SERIES WITH PEDDIE SCHOOL
The Peddie School
South Main Street PO BOX A
Highstown, NJ 08520
Phone: 609-490-7500
Fax: 609-426-9019
e-mail: sjames@peddie.org
Web Site: www.peddie.org
Management:
    Head Of School: John Green
    Director Of Athletics: Susan Cabot
    Dean Of Students: Melaine Clements
    Dean Of Faculty: Timothy Garcia
Mission: Performing and Visual Arts Presenter and
Producer
Utilizes: Actors; Collaborations; Dance Companies;
Guest Ensembles; Guest Instructors; Guest Musical
Directors; Guild Activities; Instructors; Multi
Collaborations; Original Music Scores; Sign Language
Translators; Special Technical Talent; Touring
Companies
Founded: 1864
Budget: $250,000
Performs At: William Mount-Burke Theatre; Masland
Room
Type of Stage: Proscenium
Seating Capacity: 535

4608
AM PRODUCTIONS SERIES
2 Woodland Road
Holmdel, NJ 07733
Phone: 732-264-2111
Fax: 732-264-0081
Toll-free: 800-995-8085
e-mail: amprod@aol.com
Officers:
    President: Stanley Andrucyk

All listings are in alphabetical order by state, then city, then organization within the city.

565

Management:
   President: Stanley Andrucyk
   Marketing: Terry Y McDermott
Founded: 1979
Specialized Field: Series & Festivals: Concerts
Status: For-Profit, Professional
Paid Staff: 28
Volunteer Staff: 30

4609
NEW JERSEY REPERTORY COMPANY

179 Broadway
Long Branch, NJ 07740
Phone: 732-229-3166
Fax: 732-229-3167
e-mail: info@njrep.org
Web Site: www.njrep.org
Officers:
   Director Marketing: Debbie Mura
Management:
   President: David Lumia
   Executive Director: Gabor Barabas
   Artistic Director: Suzanne Barabas
Mission: The primary mission of the theater is to develop and produce new plays with diverse themes. It is also devoted to creating an atmosphere where classics can take on a fresh look and forgotten plays can find a home.
Founded: 1997
Specialized Field: Series & Festivals: Theatre
Status: Non-Profit, Professional
Paid Staff: 12
Paid Artists: 12
Income Sources: Donation, Grants
Facility Category: Theater
Type of Stage: Black Box
Year Remodeled: 1998

4610
SHAKESPEARE THEATER OF NEW JERSEY

36 Madison Avenue (at Lancaster Road)
Madison, NJ 07940
Phone: 973-408-3278
Fax: 973-408-3361
e-mail: info@shakespearenj.org
Web Site: www.shakespearenj.org
Officers:
   Board President: Jeanne Barrett
Management:
   Artistic Director: Bonnie J Monte
   Managing Director: Stephen Klein
   Chairman of the Board: Martin Prentice
Mission: The Festival strives to illuminate the universal and lasting relevance of the classics for contemporary audiences, and its mission places an equal emphasis on education, for young artists and audiences alike.
Utilizes: Guest Companies; Singers
Founded: 1962
Specialized Field: Series and Festivals: Theatre
Status: Non-Profit, Professional
Paid Staff: 35
Paid Artists: 150
Budget: 2.6 million
Income Sources: Actors' Equity Association; Society for Stage Directors and Choreographers; New Jersey State Council on the Arts; Corporations; Foundations, Businesses; Individuals
Season: May - December
Performs At: F.M. Kirby Shakespeare Theatre
Affiliations: New Jersey Theatre Group; Theatre Communications Group; Shakespeare Association of America; ArtPride; Artsweb NJ/NY
Annual Attendance: 100,000

Stage Dimensions: 28' wide x 33' deep
Seating Capacity: 308
Year Built: 1998
Organization Type: Performing; Educational; Sponsoring; Touring

4611
ALGONQUIN ARTS

173 Main Street
Manasquan, NJ 08736
Phone: 732-528-9211
Fax: 732-528-3881
e-mail: info@algonquinarts.com
Web Site: www.algonquinarts.com
Officers:
   Board Chair: Dale Wegener
   Director Development: Patrick O'Hagan
   Director Communications: Dana Roberts
   Director Operations: Jane E. Huber
Founded: 1992
Specialized Field: Series and Festivals; Instrumental Music; Vocal Music; Theatre; Dance; Ethnic Performances
Status: Non-Profit, Professional
Paid Staff: 4
Volunteer Staff: 2
Paid Artists: 120
Non-paid Artists: 25

4612
ACADEMY OF SAINT ELIZABETH PERFORMING ARTS SERIES

Saint Elizabeth
2 Convent Road
Morristown, NJ 07960-6989
Phone: 973-290-0045
Management:
   Artist in Residence: Dr. Teresa Walters
Budget: $10,000
Performs At: Founders Hall; McGuire Lounge

4613
ARTS COUNCIL OF THE MORRIS AREA

14 Maple Avenue
Suite 301
Morristown, NJ 07960
Phone: 973-285-5115
Fax: 973-285-1199
e-mail: info@morrisarts.org
Web Site: www.morrisarts.org
Officers:
   Executive Director: Anne Aronovitch
   Board President: Alan Levitan
Mission: To significantly enhance the arts and their impact on the quality of life in the Morris Area.
Founded: 1973
Specialized Field: Series and Festivals; Instrumental Music; Vocal Music; Theatre; Dance; Ethnic Performances
Status: Non-Profit, Professional
Paid Staff: 7
Budget: $900,000-950,000

4614
RUTGERS UNIVERSITY CONCERT SERIES

33 Livingston Avenue
New Brunswick, NJ 08901
Phone: 732-932-7511
Fax: 732-932-8794
Web Site: www.masongross.rutgers.edu
Management:
   President: George Stauffer

Assistant Dean Arts Programming: Meg Frantz
Publicity Director: Ellen Saxon
Operations Manager: Kevin Coleman
Box Office Manager: Jeanne Salzman
Mission: To offer performances by contemporary musicians.
Founded: 1976
Specialized Field: Series & Festivals; Instrumental Music; Vocal Music; Theatre; Youth; Dance; Ethnic Performances; Instrumental Music; Visual Arts
Status: Non-Profit, Non-Professional
Paid Staff: 50
Paid Artists: 10
Performs At: Rutgers Arts Center
Organization Type: Presenting

4615
STATE THEATRE REGIONAL ARTS CENTER AT NEW BRUNSWICK

11 Livingston Avenue
New Brunswick, NJ 08901
Phone: 732-247-7200
Fax: 732-247-4005
Toll-free: 877-782-8311
e-mail: info@statetheatrenj.org
Web Site: www.statetheatrenj.org
Officers:
   President: Chris Butler
Management:
   President: Christopher Butler
   Education Director: Lian Farer
   General Manager: David Hartkern
Mission: To present the finest of the performing arts.
Founded: 1988
Specialized Field: Series & Festivals; Instrumental Music; Vocal Music; Theatre; Dance; Ethnic Performances; Presenting Theatre Opera; Ballet
Status: Non-Profit, Professional
Paid Staff: 35
Budget: $2,000,000
Performs At: State Theatre
Seating Capacity: 1800
Year Built: 1921
Year Remodeled: 1987
Organization Type: Performing; Educational; Sponsoring

4616
CATHEDRAL BASILICA OF THE SACRED HEART CONCERT SERIES

89 Ridge Street
Newark, NJ 07104
Phone: 973-484-2400
Fax: 973-497-9336
e-mail: jmiller@cathedralbasilica.org
Web Site: www.cathedralbasilica.org/concert/
Management:
   Director Music Ministry: John J Miller
Mission: Offering quality musical programs to Newark area residents.
Founded: 1983
Specialized Field: Symphony; Orchestra; Chamber; Ensemble

4617
NEW JERSEY SYMPHONY ORCHESTRA AMADEUS FESTIVAL

2 Central Avenue
Newark, NJ 07102

Phone: 973-624-3713
Fax: 973-624-2115
Toll-free: 800-255-3476
e-mail: kswanson@njsymphony.org
Web Site: www.njsymphony.org
Management:
    President: Simon Woods
    Music Director: Neeme Jarvi
Specialized Field: Symphony Orchestra Tickets
Status: Non-Profit, Professional

4618
NEWARK MUSEUM ASSOCIATION
49 Washington Street
PO Box 540
Newark, NJ 07102-3176
Phone: 973-596-6550
Fax: 973-596-6613
Toll-free: 800-768-7386
e-mail: pubblicrelations@newarkmusium.org
Web Site: www.newarkmuseum.org
Mission: The americas and the Pacific, Ancient Egypt, Greece and Rome, Decorative Arts, Science, Planetarium, Mini Zoo, Natural Sciences, Newark Black Film Festival, Jazz in the Garden, Family, Adult and children's programing
Founded: 1909
Specialized Field: American; Fold; Tibetan; Asian; Africa
Status: Non-Profit
Budget: $20,000-35,000
Performs At: Billy Johnson Auditorium

4619
ANNUAL OCEAN GROVE CHOIR FESTIVAL
OGCMA
PO Box 248
Ocean Grove, NJ 07756
Phone: 732-775-0035
Fax: 732-775-5689
Toll-free: 800-773-0097
e-mail: information@oceangrove.org
Web Site: www.oceangrove.org
Management:
    Music Director: Lewis A Daniels
Founded: 1954
Status: Non-Profit

4620
RARITAN RIVER MUSIC
PO Box 454
Oldwick, NJ 08858-0454
Phone: 908-213-1100
Web Site: www.raritanrivermusic.org
Management:
    Music Co-Director: Michael Newman
Mission: Offers the Raritan River Music Festival May, the Artists-in-the-Community Residency Program, and a New Music Commissioning Program
Founded: 1989
Specialized Field: Instrumental Music; Vocal Music; Chamber Music
Status: Nonprofit
Budget: $10,000

4621
RARITAN RIVER MUSIC
PO Box 454
Oldwick, NJ 08858-0454
Phone: 908-213-1100
Web Site: www.raritanrivermusic.org
Management:
    Co-Music Director: Thomas Gallant

Founded: 1989
Specialized Field: Instrumental Music; Vocal Music; Chamber Music
Status: Nonprofit

4622
JULIUS FORSTMANN LIBRARY SECOND SUNDAY SERIES
195 Gregory Avenue
Passaic, NJ 07055
Phone: 973-779-0474
Fax: 973-779-0889
Web Site: www.bccls.org/passaic
Management:
    Music Director: Laurie Sansone
Status: Non-Profit, Professional

4623
PASSAIC COUNTY COMMUNITY COLLEGE SERIES
1 College Boulevard
Paterson, NJ 07505-1179
Phone: 973-684-6555
Fax: 973-523-6085
Web Site: www.pccc.edu/culturalaffairs
Officers:
    President: Steven Rose
Management:
    Cultural Affairs Director: Maria M Gillan
Mission: To serve poets and poetry, bring performing arts to elementary schools and enjoy the arts as a community.
Utilizes: Actors; Curators; Dance Companies; Fine Artists; Original Music Scores; Playwrights; Selected Students; Special Technical Talent; Touring Companies
Founded: 1968
Specialized Field: Poetry Center; Art Gallery; Theatre & Poetry Project; Passaic County Cultural & Heritage Council
Status: Non-Profit, Non-Professional
Paid Staff: 7
Paid Artists: 45
Budget: $35,000-60,000
Income Sources: Nassaic County College; NJ State Council of the Arts; Geraldine K. Dodge Foundation
Performs At: Theater; Reading Rooms
Type of Stage: Proscenium
Seating Capacity: 300
Year Built: 1968
Year Remodeled: 1999
Rental Contact: Edna Ortiz

4624
CRESCENT CONCERTS
716 Watchung Avenue
Plainfield, NJ 07060
Phone: 908-756-2468
Fax: 908-756-3158
Web Site: www.crescentonline.org
Officers:
    President: Alan Ganun
Management:
    Executive Director: Allan Ganun
    Director: Ronald Thayer
Mission: Classical concert series, one per month from October to May, all performances at Creseent Avenue Presbyterian Chruch.
Founded: 1981
Specialized Field: Series & Fesivals: Vocal and Instrumental Music
Status: Non-Profit, Professional
Paid Staff: 1
Volunteer Staff: 12

Paid Artists: 50
Non-paid Artists: 125

4625
PRINCETON SHAKESPEARE FESTIVAL
1 Palmer Square
Suite 541
Princeton, NJ 08542
Phone: 609-921-3682
Fax: 609-921-3962
e-mail: prcreprap@aol.com
Web Site: www.princetonrep.org
Management:
    Artistic Director: Victoria Liberatori
    Executive Producer: Anne Reiss
    Press Contact: Carol Fineman
Founded: 1995
Status: Professional; Not-for-Profit

4626
PRINCETON UNIVERSITY CONCERTS
Woolworth Center
Princeton, NJ 08544
Phone: 609-258-4239
Fax: 609-258-1179
Management:
    Concert Manager: Nathan A Randall
Budget: $60,000-150,000
Performs At: Richardson Auditorium

4627
YOUNG AUDIENCES OF NEW JERSEY
12 Rpszel Road
Suite B102
Princeton, NJ 08540
Phone: 609-243-9000
Fax: 609-243-5999
e-mail: info@yanj.org
Web Site: www.yanj.org
Management:
    Executive Director: Kris Bolden Wenger
    Artistic Director: Steve Mosel
Mission: To provide arts in education programs and services to schools and other community settings.
Founded: 1973
Specialized Field: Arts Education
Status: Non-Profit, Professional
Budget: $400,000-1,000,000

4628
RINGWOOD FRIENDS OF MUSIC SERIES
PO Box 427/145 Carletondale Rd
Ringwood, NJ 07456
Phone: 973-962-9356
Budget: $10,000
Performs At: Ringwood Community Church

4629
WILLIAMS CENTER FOR THE ARTS
One Williams Plaza
Rutherford, NJ 07070
Phone: 201-939-6969
Fax: 201-939-0843
Web Site: www.williamscenter.org
Officers:
    President: Richard Theryoung
    Vice President: Carolyn Spann-Swallwood
    Secretary: Dr. Joseph DeFazi
    Treasurer: Evelyn Spath-Mercado
Management:
    Executive Director: Gw McLuckey
Mission: To provide programs of artistic excellence at affordable prices.

Utilizes: Actors; AEA Actors; Dance Companies; Local Artists; Multimedia; Original Music Scores; Student Interns; Theatre Companies
Founded: 1978
Paid Staff: 22
Budget: $650,000
Income Sources: Ticket Sales; grants; sponsorships; rentals
Performs At: Newman Theatre
Annual Attendance: 50,000
Facility Category: Performing Arts Center
Type of Stage: Black Box; Proscenium Arch
Seating Capacity: 200; 642
Year Built: 1922
Year Remodeled: 1992
Rental Contact: G.W. McLuckey

4630
WATERLOO FOUNDATION FOR THE ARTS SERIES
525 Waterloo Road
Stanhope, NJ 07874
Phone: 973-347-0900
Fax: 973-347-3573
e-mail: info@waterloovillage.org
Web Site: www.waterloovillage.org
Officers:
   Controller: Cule Jorden
Management:
   Executive Director: Gregory Gaertner
   Director Museum Operations: John Kraft
Mission: To combine history, music, art and architecture; to educate all persons in the state of New Jersey in appreciation of these arts forms.
Utilizes: Collaborations; Curators; Educators; Five Seasonal Concerts; Guest Artists; Guest Companies; Guest Directors; Guest Instructors; Guest Lecturers; Guest Musical Directors; Guest Soloists; Instructors; Multimedia; Original Music Scores; Playwrights
Founded: 1967
Specialized Field: Educational Programs for School Children
Status: Non-Profit
Paid Staff: 10
Volunteer Staff: 40
Budget: $ 2.5 Million
Income Sources: Gate Admissions; New Jersey State Council of the Arts; New Jersey Tourism Council; Business/Corporate Donations
Season: April - November
Performs At: Waterloo Music Festival Tent; Waterloo Concert Field
Affiliations: New Jersey Tourism Council
Annual Attendance: 150,000
Facility Category: Seasonal
Seating Capacity: 2,200-15,000
Year Built: 1964
Year Remodeled: 1997
Organization Type: Performing; Sponsoring

4631
CENTRAL PRESBYTERIAN CHURCH
Sanctuary Arts Series
70 Maple Street
Summit, NJ 07901
Phone: 908-273-0441
e-mail: jdaurio@centralpres.org
Web Site: www.centralpres.org
Management:
   Contact: Joyce Brandt
Mission: Friday Music (Mid-day concerts on Fridays during Advent and Lent), Special music and concerts announced through website.

Specialized Field: Series & Festivals; Instrumental Music; Vocal Music; Youth; Ethnic Performances
Status: Non-Profit,Professional

4632
OCEAN COUNTY COLLEGE FINE & PERFORMING ARTS SELECT-A-SERIES
Ocean County College
College Drive
Toms River, NJ 08754
Phone: 732-255-0500
Fax: 732-864-3853
e-mail: rkrantz@ocean.edu
Web Site: ocean.edu
Management:
   Fine Arts Center Director: Roberta F Krantz
Mission: Tol provide quality production at an amenable price for the Ocean County Community.
Utilizes: Actors; Dance Companies; Dancers; Designers; Fine Artists; Five Seasonal Concerts; Guest Accompanists; High School Drama; Instructors; Multimedia; Music; Original Music Scores; Resident Professionals; Sign Language Translators; Singers; Soloists; Special Technical Talent; Theatre Companies; Visual Arts
Paid Staff: 3
Budget: $35,000-60,000
Income Sources: Ticket Sales
Facility Category: Fine Arts Center
Type of Stage: Proscenium
Seating Capacity: 564
Year Built: 1972

4633
JETTE PERFORMANCE COMPANY
10 Raymond Terrace
Vauxhall, NJ 07008
Phone: 908-397-1714
Fax: 212-840-0344
e-mail: jettejazz@excite.com
Web Site: www.jettejazz.org
Mission: Creates a fusion of classical and commersials styles of dance and brings them to the concert stage.
Founded: 1996
Specialized Field: Dance

4634
JAZZ IT UP FESTIVAL
William Paterson University
300 Pompton Road
Wayne, NJ 07470
Phone: 973-720-2371
Web Site: www.wpunj.edu

4635
WILLIAM PATERSON COLLEGE: THE JAZZ ROOM SERIES
300 Pompton Road
Wayne, NJ 07470
Phone: 877-978-3923
e-mail: basslers@wpunj.edu
Web Site: www.ww2.wpunj.edu
Officers:
   President: Arnold Speert
   Secretary: Vincent Mazzola
   Chair: Robert Taylor
   Vice-Chair: Carla Temple
Mission: Presenting a complete range of jazz music.
Founded: 1978
Specialized Field: Series & Festivals; Instrumental Music; Vocal Music; Theatre; Youth; Ethnic Performances
Status: For-Profit, Professional

Performs At: Shea Center for the Performing Arts
Organization Type: Performing

4636
WILLOWBROOK JAZZ FESTIVAL
William Paterson College
300 Pompton Road
Wayne, NJ 07470
Phone: 201-595-2268
Fax: 201-595-2460
Management:
   Special Projects Assistant: Dr. Martin Krivin
   Director Jazz Program at William: Rufus Reid
Mission: Making jazz accessible by offering free concerts at convenient times and places.
Specialized Field: Jazz
Status: Professional; Nonprofit
Performs At: Willowbrook Mall
Organization Type: Performing

4637
YM-YWHA OF NORTH JERSEY CULTURAL ARTS SERIES
1 Pike Drive
Wayne, NJ 07470-2497
Phone: 973-595-0100
Fax: 973-595-5234
Management:
   Executive Director: Josh Samborn
   Cultural Arts Director: Sheila Hellman
Specialized Field: Series and Festivals; Instrumental Music; Theatre; Youth; Fitness
Status: Non-Profit, Professional
Paid Staff: 75
Paid Artists: 75
Budget: $60,000-150,000
Performs At: Rosen Auditorium

New Mexico

4638
CHAMBER MUSIC ALBUQUERQUE PRESENTS THE JUNE MUSIC FESTIVAL
1209 Mountain Road Place
Suite D Ne
Albuquerque, NM 87110
Phone: 505-268-1990
Fax: 505-268-6288
e-mail: cma@cma-abq.org
Web Site: www.cma-abq.org
Officers:
   President: Heidi Frost Heard
   VP: Calla Ann Pepmueller
   Secretary: Geoffrey M Kalmu
Management:
   Administrative Director: Judith O Smith
Mission: To present the world's finest chamber musicians in live performance, sharing the power of great music with the community.
Founded: 1942
Affiliations: June Music Festival; Chamber Music at the Simms

4639
NEW MEXICO JAZZ WORKSHOP
5500 Lomas Boulevard NE
Albuquerque, NM 87110
Phone: 505-255-9798
Fax: 505-232-8420
e-mail: nmjw@flash.net
Web Site: www.nmjazz.org
Officers:

Board President: Larry Schwartz
Executive Director: Charles W. Lowery II, BS, MA
Mission: To present major jazz artists January-May for performing and educational activities.
Utilizes: Educators; Fine Artists; Grant Writers; Guest Directors; Guest Instructors; Guest Musical Directors; High School Drama; Local Artists; Multimedia; Original Music Scores
Founded: 1978
Specialized Field: Series & Festivals; Instrumental Music; Youth; Ethnic Performances; Jazz
Status: Non-Profit, Professional
Paid Staff: 2
Volunteer Staff: 50
Paid Artists: 30
Performs At: Hiland Theater; Kimo Theater
Facility Category: Various local venues
Organization Type: Performing; Touring

4640
CARLSBAD COMMUNITY CONCERT ASSOCIATION
611 N 4th Street
Carlsbad, NM 88220
Phone: 505-885-8255
e-mail: jedhoward@leaco.net
Management:
President: Jared Howard
Founded: 1946
Specialized Field: Series & Festivals; Instrumental Music; Vocal Music; Dance; Ethnic Performances; Classical Music
Status: Non-Profit, Professional
Budget: $20,000-35,000

4641
DONA ANA ARTS COUNCIL
PO Box 1721
Las Cruces, NM 88004
Phone: 575-523-6403
Web Site: www.las-cruces-arts.org
Management:
President: Dorothy Rivera
Past-President: Kathleen Squires
Vice President: Annette Morales
Interim Executive Director and Prog: Ceci Vasconcellos
Rio Grande Theatre Manager: David Salcido
Finance Director: Victoria Frederick
Founded: 1974
Specialized Field: Series & Festivals; Instrumental Music; Vocal Music; Theatre; Youth; Ethnic Performances
Status: Non-Profit, Professional
Budget: $20,000-35,000

4642
PAN AMERICAN CENTER
MSC 35E
New Mexico State University, Dept 3SE
PO Box 30001
Las Cruces, NM 88003
Phone: 505-646-4413
Fax: 505-646-3605
e-mail: wlofdahl@nmsu.edu
Web Site: www.panam.nmsu.edu
Management:
President: Will Lofdahl
Mission: Special events facilities, 13,000 seat arena, 500 seat Performing Arts Center
Specialized Field: Series & Festivals: Concerts and Basketball Games
Status: Non-Profit, Professional
Paid Staff: 14

4643
LOS ALAMOS CONCERT ASSOCIATION
Box 572
Los Alamos, NM 87544
Phone: 505-662-9000
e-mail: rheller88@cybermesa.com
Web Site: www.losalamosconcert.org
Officers:
President: Ann McLaughlin
Management:
Artistic Director: Rosalie Heller
Founded: 1946
Volunteer Staff: 20
Paid Artists: 5
Budget: $35,000-60,000
Performs At: Duane Smith Auditorium

4644
PLACITAS ARTISTS SERIES
PO Box 944
Placitas, NM 87043
e-mail: information@placitasarts.org
Web Site: www.placitasarts.org
Officers:
President: Diana Shomaker
Vice President: Jean Reid
Treasurer: Jackie Ericksen
Secretary: Lois Gonzalez
Mission: Providing music of a consistently high quality, at extremely modest cost in a tranquil rural setting. The organization promotes interest in the musical and visual arts, encourages musicians and artists, and brings music, arts and theater to children in schools throughout the country.
Founded: 1986
Specialized Field: Series and Festivals: Chamber Music
Status: Non-Profit, Professional
Paid Staff: 1
Paid Artists: 90
Budget: $25,000-35,000
Seating Capacity: 185

4645
EASTERN NEW MEXICO UNIVERSITY
Station 17
Portales, NM 88130
Phone: 505-562-2153
Fax: 505-562-2822
Toll-free: 800-367-3668
e-mail: athletics@enmu.edu
Web Site: www.enmu.edu/athletics.html
Management:
President: Steven Gamble
VP Business Affiars: Scott Smart
Vp: Paul Jones
Athletic Director: Michael Mcguire
Founded: 1934
Specialized Field: Degrees and all College Eduation
Status: Non-Profit, Professional

4646
SANTA FE CHAMBER MUSIC FESTIVAL
PO Box 2227
Santa Fe, NM 87504-2227
Phone: 505-983-2075
Fax: 505-986-0251
e-mail: info@sfcmf.org
Web Site: www.santafechambermusic.org
Officers:
President: Quarrier Cook
Management:
Artistic Director: Marc Neikrug

Executive Director: Steven Ovitsky
Production Director: Linda Klosky
Volunteer Coordinator: Toni Wilkinson
Mission: To produce innovative chamber music concerts and related educational programs of exceptional artistic quality; to serve as a chamber music center attracting American musicians, composers and audiences whose combined influence, stimulation and energy will benefit American culture.
Utilizes: Sign Language Translators
Founded: 1973
Specialized Field: Chamber Music; Jazz; World Music
Status: Professional; Nonprofit
Paid Staff: 12
Budget: 1.6 k
Performs At: Saint Francis Auditorium; Museum of Fine Arts
Annual Attendance: 11,000
Organization Type: Performing; Touring; Resident; Educational

4647
SANTA FE CONCERT ASSOCIATION
210 E Marcy Street
Santa Fe, NM 87501
Mailing Address: PO Box 4626, Santa Fe, NM. 87502
Phone: 505-984-8759
Fax: 505-989-8930
e-mail: info@musicone.org
Web Site: www.musicone.org
Officers:
President: Clifford Vernick
Management:
Managing Director: William Mullen
Founded: 1937
Specialized Field: Vocal Music: Classical Music
Status: Non-Profit, Professional
Paid Staff: 1
Paid Artists: 300
Budget: $60,000-150,000
Performs At: St. Francis Auditorium; James A. Little Theatre

4648
TWENTIETH CENTURY UNLIMITED SERIES
PO Box 2631
Santa Fe, NM 87504-2631
Phone: 505-820-6401
Fax: 505-995-0941
Management:
Director: Eleanor C Eisenmenger

4649
TAOS ART ASSOCIATION
133 Paseo del Pueblo Norte
Taos, NM 87571
Phone: 505-758-2052
Fax: 505-751-3305
e-mail: jean@taoscenterforthearts.org
Web Site: www.taoscenterforthearts.org
Officers:
Treasurer: James Day
Secretary: Nancy Glasgow
President: Douglas Smith
Vice President: Loren Smith
Office Manager: Holly White
Management:
Executive Director: Jean F Marquardt
Mission: Inspires creative expression throughout this diverse community by providing facilities and programming in the visual, performing and media arts.
Founded: 1952

All listings are in alphabetical order by state, then city, then organization within the city.

569

4650
TAOS SCHOOL OF MUSIC
PO Box 2630
Taos, NM 87571
Phone: 575-776-2388
Fax: 575-776-2388
e-mail: tsofm@newmex.com
Web Site: www.taosschoolofmusic.com
Officers:
    President: R Jameson Burns
    VP: Lou Sturbois
    Secretary: Barb Wiard
    Treasurer: Judith Anderson
Management:
    Director: Kahleen Knox, tsofm@newmex.com
Mission: Study and performance of chamber music.
Utilizes: Artists-in-Residence; Composers; Educators;
Five Seasonal Concerts; Guest Directors; Guest
Musical Directors; High School Drama; Multimedia;
Poets; Singers; Soloists
Founded: 1963
Opened: 1963
Specialized Field: Series & Festivals: Instrumental
Music
Status: Non-Profit, Professional
Paid Staff: 2
Volunteer Staff: 10
Paid Artists: 15
Budget: $100,000
Income Sources: Contributions; Grants; Tuition
Performs At: Taos Community Auditorium; Hotel St.
Bernard; Taos Ski Valley
Affiliations: Chamber Music America
Annual Attendance: varies
Facility Category: Auditorium
Type of Stage: Platform
Seating Capacity: 290; 150
Organization Type: Performing; Educational
Resident Groups: Chicago String Quartet

New York

4651
ALBANY SYMPHONY ORCHESTRA AMERICAN FESITVAL
19 Clinton Avenue
Albany, NY 12207
Phone: 518-465-4755
Fax: 518-465-3711
e-mail: info@albanysymphony.com
Web Site: www.albanysymphony.com
Management:
    Chairman: Allan Goldberg
    Artistic Director: David Alan Miller
    General Manager: Sharon Walsh
Founded: 1931
Specialized Field: Series & Festivals; Instrumental
Music; Youth; Classical Music
Status: Non-Profit, Professional
Paid Staff: 7
Paid Artists: 30

4652
L'ENSEMBLE CHAMBER MUSIC
PO Box 38024
Albany, NY 12203-8024
Phone: 518-436-5321
Fax: 518-436-5322
Management:
    Executive/Artistic Director: Ida Faiella

4653
ALFRED UNIVERSITY PERFORMING ARTS
1 Saxon Drive
Alfred, NY 14802
Mailing Address: PO Box 781
Phone: 607-871-2562
Fax: 607-871-2587
e-mail: performs@alfred.edu
Web Site: www.alfred.edu
Officers:
    President: Charles Edmondson
    Performing Arts Head: S Crosby
Management:
    Admissions Director: Earl Pierce
    Tech Theater: Zachary Hamm
    Theater Designs: Marketa Fantova
Mission: To provide professional performing artists for
the area.
Founded: 1836
Specialized Field: Series and Festivals; Dance;
Instrumental Music; Theatre; Education
Status: Non-Profit, Non-Professional
Paid Staff: 3
Non-paid Artists: 4
Facility Category: Proscenium Theater, Black Box
Theater
Seating Capacity: 450; 180
Organization Type: Performing; Educational;
Sponsoring

4654
MUSIC FESTIVAL OF THE HAMPTONS
PO Box 1525
Amagansett, NY 11930
Toll-free: 800-644-4418
Web Site: http://www.musicfestivalofthehamptons.com/
Management:
    Artistic Director: Lukas Foss

4655
AMSTERDAM AREA COMMUNITY CONCERT ASSOCIATION
31 Young Avenue
Amsterdam, NY 12010
Phone: 518-843-3247
Fax: 518-842-4072
Management:
    Stage Manager: Robert Swenson
Specialized Field: Series & Festivals; Instrumental
Music; Vocal Music; Dance; Ethnic Performances;
Symphony; Classical; Choral Group
Status: Non-Profit, Non-Professional
Budget: $10,000-20,000

4656
BARD MUSIC FESTIVAL
Bard College
Annandale-on-Hudson, NY 12504
Phone: 845-758-7410
Fax: 845-758-7043
e-mail: bmf@bard.edu
Web Site: www.bard.edu/bmf
Officers:
    Executive Director: Irene Zedlacher
Management:
    Artistic Director: Leon Botstein
    Artistic Director: Christopher Gibbs
    Artistic Director: Robert Martin
Founded: 1991
Specialized Field: Series & Festivals: Classical Music
Festival
Status: Non-Profit, Professional

4657
LORRAINE PRODUCTIONS: EAST/WEST
28-04 33Th Street
Suite 8
Astoria, NY 11102
Phone: 718-721-9785
Management:
    Executive Director: Scott Douglas Morrow
Budget: $150,000-400,000

4658
GENESEE COMMUNITY COLLEGE
Genesee College for the Arts
One College Road
Batavia, NY 14020-9704
Phone: 585-343-0055
Fax: 585-345-6815
e-mail: boxoffice@genesee.edu
Web Site: www.genesee.edu
Management:
    Director of Fine/Performing Arts: Maryanne
    Arena
    Technical Director: Vincent Elliott
    Audience Services Manager: Christopher M
    Montpetit
Mission: Commits to providing educational experiences
which promote intellectual and social growth, workforce
and economic development and global citizenship.
Utilizes: Actors; Collaborations; Dance Companies;
Dancers; Educators; Fine Artists; Guest Instructors;
Guest Soloists; Guild Activities; High School Drama;
Instructors; Local Artists; Multimedia; Soloists; Student
Interns; Touring Companies
Income Sources: Ticket Sales; College Funding;
Grants
Performs At: Theatre, Rehearsal Space, Lobby Art
Exhibits
Facility Category: Theatre
Type of Stage: Proscenium
Stage Dimensions: 40' x 35'
Seating Capacity: 3400
Year Built: 1992
Rental Contact: Mary Anne Arena

4659
PROFESSIONAL PERFORMING ARTS SERIES
Queensborough Community College/Cuny
222-05 56 Avenue
Bayside, NY 11364
Phone: 718-631-6311
Fax: 718-631-6033
e-mail: agin@qcc.cuny.edu
Web Site: www.qcc.cuny.edu/boxoffice
Management:
    President: Marti Agin
    Artistic Director: Susan Agin
Utilizes: Actors; Artists-in-Residence; Dance
Companies; Dancers; Multimedia; Original Music
Scores; Theatre Companies
Founded: 1965
Specialized Field: Performing Arts
Status: Non-Profit, Professional
Paid Staff: 5
Budget: $60,000-150,000
Annual Attendance: 12,000-15,000
Facility Category: Conventional Theatre
Type of Stage: Proscenium
Stage Dimensions: 40x40
Seating Capacity: 875
Year Built: 1970
Rental Contact: Terry Doria

4660
DIA: BEACON
3 Beekman Street
Beacon, NY 12508
Phone: 845-440-0100
Fax: 845-440-0092
e-mail: info@diaart.org
Web Site: www.diacenter.org
Management:
Assistant Director/Beacon: Steven Evans
Founded: 1974
Specialized Field: Contemporary Art
Status: Non-Profit
Income Sources: Foundations; Corporations;
Affiliations: 1

4661
BINGHAMTON SUMMER MUSIC FESTIVAL
PO Box 112
Binghamton, NY 13903
Phone: 607-777-4777
Fax: 607-777-4000
e-mail: bsmf1@yahoo.com
Web Site: www.summermusic.binghamtom.edu
Officers:
President: Jim Reyer
VP: Karl Hirshman
Secretary: Jim Gacioch
Treasurer: Larry Deminster
Management:
Executive Director: Kelly Wakeman
Mission: To provide an annual summer performing arts program for audiences in New York's Southern Tier.
Founded: 1985
Specialized Field: Dance; Vocal Music; Instrumental Music; Festivals
Status: Nonprofit
Paid Staff: 1
Volunteer Staff: 24
Paid Artists: 9
Performs At: Anderson Center for Performing Arts
Organization Type: Performing; Educational

4662
STATE UNIVERSITY OF NEW YORK AT BINGHAMTON PERFORMING ARTS SERIES
Binghamton University
Anderson Center for the Arts, PO Box 6000
Binghamton, NY 13902-6000
Phone: 607-777-6802
Fax: 607-777-6771
Web Site: www.anderson.binghamton.edu
Management:
President: Llis B Befleur
Executive Director: Floyd R Herzog
Founded: 1985
Specialized Field: Series & Festivals; Instrumental Music; Vocal Music; Theatre; Youth; Dance; Ethnic Performances
Status: Non-Profit, Professional
Paid Staff: 10
Budget: $60,000-150,000
Performs At: Cmaber Hall; Watters Theater

4663
BAY SHORE-BRIGHTWATERS LIBRARY PERFORMING ARTS SERIES
1 S. Country Road
Brightwaters, NY 11718

Phone: 631-665-4350
Fax: 631-665-4958
e-mail: jcreilly@suffolk.lib.ny.us
Management:
Executive Director: Eileen Kavanagh
Secretary: Laura Carey
Founded: 1968
Specialized Field: Series and Festivals; Dance; Theatre
Status: Non-Profit, Professional
Volunteer Staff: 6
Paid Artists: 7
Budget: $35,000-60,000
Performs At: Suffolk Community College
Facility Category: Auditorium
Seating Capacity: 75-100

4664
651 ARTS
651 Fulton Street
Brooklyn, NY 11217
Phone: 718-636-4181
Fax: 718-636-4166
e-mail: info@651arts.org
Web Site: www.651arts.org
Management:
Executive Director: Georgiana Pickett
Founded: 1988
Specialized Field: Performing Arts

4665
ARTS AT ST. ANN'S
45 Main Street
Suite 315
Brooklyn, NY 11201
Phone: 718-834-8794
Fax: 718-522-2470
e-mail: info@artsatstanns.org
Web Site: www.artsatstanns.org
Management:
President: Susan Feldman
Co Producer: Kim Whitener
Founded: 1979
Specialized Field: Series and Festivals; Instrumental Music; Vocal Music; Theatre; Youth; Ethnic Performances; Performing Arts
Status: Non-Profit, Professional
Paid Staff: 11
Volunteer Staff: 10
Paid Artists: 200
Budget: $1,500,000
Income Sources: Foundation; Corporate; Government; Individual; Earned Income

4666
BROOKLYN ACADEMY OF MUSIC
30 Lafayette Avenue
Brooklyn, NY 11217
Phone: 718-636-4100
Fax: 718-857-2021
e-mail: info@bam.org
Web Site: www.bam.org
Officers:
Chairman: Neil Chrisman
Vice Chairman: Rita Hillman
Vice Chairman: Franklin Weissberg
Vice Chairman: I. Stanley Kriegel
VP: David Kleiser
Executive VP: Judith E. Daykin
Treasurer: Richard Balzano
President: Karen Brooks Hopkins
Management:
President: Karen Brooks Hopkins
Executive Director: Joseph V Melilo

Finance: Richard Balzano
Promotion/Marketing: Doug Allan
Mission: Programming policy involves a commitment to provide our audiences with quality performing arts, new and innovative theatre, and dance and music, both foreign and domestic, as well as diversified choices in all areas at affordable and accessible prices.
Utilizes: Singers
Founded: 1861
Specialized Field: Series & Festivals; Instrumental Music; Vocal Music; Theatre; Youth; Dance; Ethnic Performances
Status: Non-Profit, Professional
Paid Staff: 150
Income Sources: New York Department of Cultural Affairs
Performs At: Brooklyn Academy of Music
Organization Type: Performing; Touring; Educational; Sponsoring

4667
CELEBRATE BROOKLYN FESTIVAL
647 Fulton Street
Brooklyn, NY 11217
Phone: 718-855-7882
Fax: 718-802-9095
e-mail: celebrate@briconline.org
Web Site: www.briconline.org
Officers:
President: Nanette Rainone
Management:
Director/Producer: Jack Walsh
Mission: Supporting Brooklyn's international community through the presentation of original and professional performing arts.
Founded: 1979
Specialized Field: Series & Festivals; Instrumental Music; Vocal Music; Theatre; Dance; Ethnic Performances
Status: Non-Profit, Professional
Paid Staff: 100
Performs At: Prospect Park Bandshell and Picnic House
Annual Attendance: 200,000
Facility Category: Ampitheatre
Type of Stage: Sprung Wood
Stage Dimensions: 70x40
Seating Capacity: 10,000
Year Built: 1939
Year Remodeled: 1999
Cost: $3.4 million
Rental Contact: Director Jack Walsh
Organization Type: Performing

4668
CW POST CHAMBER MUSIC FESTIVAL
Long Island University, CW Post Campus
720 Northern Boulevard
Brookville, NY 11548
Phone: 516-299-2103
Fax: 516-299-2884
Web Site: www.liu.edu/cwpost/svpa/music/festival
Management:
Festival Director: Susan Deaver
Assistant Director: Dale Stuckenbruck
Faculty Ensemble-In-Residence: Pierrot Consort
Mission: To study and perform standard chamber music repertoire
Founded: 1981
Paid Staff: 2
Volunteer Staff: 2
Paid Artists: 15
Performs At: Tilles Center; Hillwood Recital Hall

4669
AFRICAN-AMERICAN CULTURAL CENTER
350 Masten Avenue
Buffalo, NY 14209
Phone: 716-884-2013
Fax: 716-885-2590
e-mail: aacc@pcom.net
Web Site: www.paulrobesontheatre.com
Officers:
Chairman: Darlene Badgett
Vice Chairman: Emma Bassett
Secretary: Gwendolyn Neal
Treasurer: Paulett S. Counts
Management:
Executive Director: Agnes M Bain
Artistic Director: Paulette D Harris
Mission: Developing appreciation for African traditions through cultural events and the arts.
Founded: 1958
Specialized Field: Dance; Theater
Status: Nonprofit
Paid Staff: 35
Performs At: Paul Robeson Theatre
Type of Stage: proscenium
Stage Dimensions: 40x18
Seating Capacity: 130
Organization Type: Performing; Sponsoring

4670
JUNE IN BUFFALO
222 Haird Hall
Buffalo, NY 14260-4700
Phone: 716-645-2765
Fax: 716-645-3824
e-mail: mus-info@buffalo.edu
Web Site: www.music.buffalo.edu/jib
Officers:
Secretary: Katherine Phillips
Concert Manager: Philip Rehard
Assistant to the Chair: Dusti Dean
Management:
Director of Student Programs: Karen Sausner
Business Administrator: Dusti Dean
Director Music Technology: Chris Jacob
Mission: To sponsor festival and conference dedicated to emerging composers, and the opportunity to work with outstanding professional musicians and distinguished composition faculty.
Founded: 1975
Specialized Field: Series & Festivals; Instrumental Music; Vocal Music
Status: Non-Profit, Professional
Paid Staff: 15
Paid Artists: 50

4671
VIVA VIVALDI FESTIVAL XXIII
Ars Nova Musicians Chamber Orchestra
136 Goethe Street
Buffalo, NY 14206
Phone: 716-662-3598
Fax: 716-894-2456
e-mail: arsnovamusicians@aol.com
Management:
President: Dorothy Smith
Executive/Managing Director: Marylouise Nanna
Mission: ARS Nova Musicians is dedicated to performing a varied repertoire that extends from early Baroque through contemporary music, including frequent premiers. Constantly aspire through creative

and innovative means to attract new audiences to this wonderful medium of the musical art, called Chamber Music.
Founded: 1974
Specialized Field: Series & Festivals; Instrumental Music; Vocal Music; Chamber Music
Status: Non-Profit, Professional
Paid Staff: 2

4672
CHAUTAUQUA INSTITUTION
1 Ames Avenue
Chautauqua, NY 14722
Mailing Address: Po Box 28
Phone: 716-357-6200
Fax: 716-357-9014
Toll-free: 800-836-2787
e-mail: slundine@ciweb.org
Web Site: www.ciweb.org
Officers:
President: Thomas M Becker
Chair: William F Clinger Jr.
Management:
Executive Assistant: Rindy Barmore
Mission: Combining the arts, religion, recreation and education in a Victorian community.
Utilizes: Singers
Founded: 1874
Specialized Field: Series & Festivals; Dance; Vocal Music; Instrumental Music; Theatre; Grand Opera
Status: Professional; Semi-Professional; Non-Professional; Nonprofit
Paid Staff: 300
Income Sources: Opera America; American Symphony Orchestra League; Association for Performing Arts Presenters; Music Educators National Conference; American Arts Alliance
Performs At: Amphitheater; Norton Hall
Organization Type: Performing; Resident; Educational; Sponsoring

4673
PERFORMING ARTS AT HAMILTON
Performing Arts
Hamilton College
Clinton, NY 13323
Phone: 315-859-4350
Fax: 315-859-4632
e-mail: performingarts@hamilton.edu
Web Site: www.hamilton.edu
Management:
President: Michelle Reiser-Memmer
Founded: 1985
Specialized Field: Vocal Music: Classical Music
Status: Non-Profit, Professional
Paid Staff: 2
Paid Artists: 30
Budget: $60,000-150,000
Performs At: Wellin Hall; Schambach Center

4674
HUDSON VALLEY SHAKESPEARE FESTIVAL
155 Main Street
Cold Spring, NY 10516
Phone: 845-265-7858
Fax: 845-265-1037
e-mail: slandstreet@shakespeare.org
Web Site: www.hvshakespeare.org
Management:
Executive Director: Susan Landstreet
Artistic Director: Terrence O'Brien
Director Marketing: Abigail Adams

Mission: Dedicated to producing and performing the plays of Shakespeare with energy and invention, challenging the audience to take a fresh look at what is essential in the presentations.
Utilizes: Actors; AEA Actors; Artists-in-Residence; Choreographers; Commissioned Composers; Educators; Five Seasonal Concerts; Guest Artists; Guest Companies; Guest Conductors; Guest Designers; Guest Soloists; Original Music Scores; Soloists; Student Interns; Theatre Companies
Founded: 1987
Specialized Field: Summer Theater
Status: Nonprofit
Volunteer Staff: 250
Paid Artists: 24
Non-paid Artists: 11
Budget: $735,000
Income Sources: Ticket Sales and Fundraising
Season: June, July, August
Performs At: Boscabel Restoration
Annual Attendance: 24,000
Type of Stage: Thrust
Seating Capacity: 450

4675
COOPERSTOWN CONCERT SERIES
PO Box 624
Cooperstown, NY 13326
Phone: 607-547-2918
Fax: 617-547-2918
Officers:
Co-Director: Jane Johngren
Co-Director: Donna Thomson
Treasurer: Lois Hopper
Secretary: Dottie Leslie
Management:
Co-Director: Richard Brown
Co-Director: Pamela Huntsman
Mission: To promote the cultural growth of our community by presenting live performances of high quality.
Founded: 1970
Specialized Field: Dance; Vocal Music; Instrumental Music; Theatre
Status: Nonprofit
Budget: $10,000-20,000
Performs At: Sterling Auditorium
Organization Type: Sponsoring

4676
COOPERSTOWN THEATRE & MUSIC FESTIVAL
PO Box 851
Cooperstown, NY 13326
Phone: 607-547-2335
Management:
Producer: Margarita Malinova

4677
CLARION CONCERTS IN COLUMBIA COUNTY
Box 43
Copake, NY 12516
Phone: 518-325-3815
Management:
Music Director: Sanford Allen

4678
A FESTIVAL OF ART
1 Baron Steuben Place
Suite 8, Market Street
Corning, NY 14830

Phone: 607-962-5871
Fax: 607-936-2235
e-mail: thearts@stny.lrun.com
Web Site: www.eARTS.org
Management:
Executive Director: Janet Newcomb

4679
CORNING-PAINTED POST CIVIC MUSIC ASSOCIATION
PO Box 1402
Corning, NY 14830
Phone: 607-936-9493
Fax: 607-974-7522
Web Site: www.pennynet.org/civicmus.htm
Mission: To provide professional performers at the lowest possible cost.
Founded: 1928
Specialized Field: Dance; Vocal Music; Instrumental Music; Jazz; Classical Presentation
Status: Professional
Budget: $60,000-150,000
Performs At: Corning Glass Center Auditorium
Organization Type: Performing

4680
STATE UNIVERSITY OF NEW YORK AT CORTLAND: CAMPUS ARTIST & LECTURE SERIES
Corey Union
Room 406
Cortland, NY 13045
Phone: 607-753-2321
Fax: 607-753-2808
Web Site: www2.cortland.edu/events/cals/index.dot
Management:
President: Erik Bitterbaum
Asst Director, Campus Activities: Sandra Wohlleber
Mission: To enhance the cultural awareness of the Cortland College and general community.
Founded: 1984
Specialized Field: Series & Festivals; Instrumental Music; Vocal Music; Theatre; Dance; Ethnic Performances; Dance
Status: Non-Profit, Professional
Paid Staff: 6
Budget: $45,000
Income Sources: Grant Funded
Performs At: Varied
Organization Type: Presenting

4681
GREAT PERFORMERS IN WESTCHESTER SERIES
5 Joseph Wallace Drive
Croton-on-Hudson, NY 10520
Phone: 914-271-2595
Management:
Executive Director: Beth Jennings Eggar
Budget: $10,000

4682
ROYCROFT CHAMBER MUSIC FESTIVAL
PO Box 281
East Aurora, NY 14052
Phone: 716-457-3565
Fax: 716-457-4119

4683
PIANOFEST
1701 E12th Street, 21 Tower
East Hampton, NY 44114

Mailing Address: PO Box 574, Wainscott, NY. 11975
Phone: 718-544-5891
Fax: 631-329-9115
e-mail: pschenly@aol.com
Web Site: www.pianofest.org
Management:
Director: Paul Schenly
Manager: Hyperion Knight

4684
ISLIP ARTS COUNCIL CHAMBER MUSIC SERIES
50 Irish Lane
East Islip, NY 11730
Phone: 631-224-5420
Fax: 631-224-5440
e-mail: iacouncil@aol.com
Web Site: www.islipartscouncil.org
Officers:
President: Helene Katz
VP: Nicholas Wartella
Secreatary: Jean Lipshie
Treasurer: Edward E. Wankel
Management:
President: Steve Bard
Executive Director: Lillian Barbash
Artistic Director: Dorothy Kalson
Clerk Typist: Angela Wallace
Mission: To present a variety of disciplines ranging from fine classical music to young persons' programs to avant garde performance art; to enable and emerging art organizations to gain information and assistance from the Arts Council library and staff in applying for not-for-profit status, funding, computer services, publicity, mailing lists, etc.
Utilizes: Singers
Founded: 1974
Specialized Field: Series & Festivals: Music Concerts
Status: Non-Profit, Professional
Paid Staff: 3
Budget: $250,000
Income Sources: Town of Islip; Suffolk County
Performs At: Sayville Schools; Dowling College
Type of Stage: Semi-Thurst
Organization Type: Performing

4685
COLDEN CENTER PERFORMANCES
Colden Center for the Performing Arts
Queens College
Flushing, NY 11367-1597
Phone: 718-544-2996
Fax: 718-261-7063
e-mail: v.charlop@coldcenter.org
Web Site: www.coldencenter.org
Management:
Tecnical Director: Tony Fitsch
Executive Director: Vivian Charlop
Office Manager: Gail Marcus
Operation Manager: Michael Kelleher
Founded: 1961
Budget: $150,000-400,000
Performs At: Irving & Susan Wallack Goldstein Theatre

4686
FLUSHING COUNCIL ON CULTURE & THE ARTS
Flushing Town Hall
137-35 Northern Boulevard
Flushing, NY 11354

Phone: 718-463-7700
Fax: 718-445-1920
e-mail: info@flushingtownhall.org
Web Site: www.flushingtownhall.org
Officers:
President: Howard Graf
Management:
Executive Director: Ellen Kodadek
Deputy Director: Maria Laura Leslie
Mission: Founded to be a revitalizing force for its community, a catalyst for developing and promoting the arts throughout Queens, and a bridge to promote intercultural understanding through the arts in the most culturally diverse county in the country.
Founded: 1979
Specialized Field: Music and the Arts
Status: Non-Profit, Professional
Paid Staff: 16
Volunteer Staff: 900
Seating Capacity: 340
Rental Contact: Susan Agin

4687
MERANOFEST
6911 Yellowstone Boulevard
Suite B-5
Forest Hills, NY 11375
Phone: 718-575-8998
Fax: 718-575-2132
e-mail: info@meranofest.com
Web Site: www.meranofest.com
Management:
President: Federico Steinhaus
Artistic Director: Lev Natochenny
Founded: 1988
Specialized Field: Piano Master Classes
Status: Non-Profit, Professional
Paid Staff: 1
Paid Artists: 7

4688
SPECIALIST TO THE ARTS
5 Yorktown Place
Fort Salonga, NY 11768
Phone: 631-261-1576
Fax: 631-754-4616
e-mail: reabsld@aol.com
Officers:
President: Rea Jacobs
Management:
President: Rea Jacob
Founded: 1984
Specialized Field: Series & Festivals; Instrumental Music; Vocal Music; Theatre; Youth; Dance; Ethnic Performances
Status: For-Profit, Professional
Paid Staff: 2

4689
SUFFOLK Y JCC INTERNATIONAL JEWISH ARTS FESTIVAL & THE CELEBRATION SERIES
5 Yorktown Place
Fort Salonga, NY 11768
Phone: 516-261-1576
Toll-free: 516-754-4616
e-mail: www.jewishartsfest.comsw
Management:
Specialist to the Arts: Rea Jacobs

4690
NASSAU COMMUNITY COLLEGE CULTURAL PROGRAM
Nassau Community College
1 Education Drive
Garden City, NY 11530
Phone: 516-572-7153
Fax: 516-222-2962
Management:
    Student Activities Counselor: Phyllis Kurland
Mission: On campus presentations for student body.
Founded: 1970
Budget: $10,000-20,000
Performs At: College Center-Multipurpose Room
Type of Stage: Resess
Stage Dimensions: 16 x 24
Seating Capacity: 300

4691
HUDSON HIGHLANDS MUSIC FESTIVAL
PO Box 164
Garrison, NY 10516
Phone: 845-265-4273
e-mail: HHMF@highlands.com
Web Site: www.highlands.com/MusicFestival
Management:
    Artistic Director: Heidi Stubner

4692
SUNY COLLEGE AT GENESEO LIMELIGHT ARTIST SERIES
College Union, SUNY College at Geneseo
1 College Circle
Geneseo, NY 14454
Phone: 585-245-5855
Fax: 585-245-5400
e-mail: rodgers@geneseo.edu
Management:
    Campus Activities Director: Thomas Rodgers
Budget: $60,000-150,000
Income Sources: Student Feed; Ticket Revenue
Performs At: Wadsworth Auditorium
Affiliations: Arts Presenters National Association for Campus Activities
Facility Category: Auditorium
Type of Stage: Proscenium

4693
GENEVA CONCERTS
PO Box 709
Geneva, NY 14456
Phone: 315-568-8767
Fax: 315-781-3660
e-mail: horvath_susan@hotmail.com
Web Site: www.genevaconcerts.org
Officers:
    President: Kevin Mitchell
Management:
    President: Susan Horvath
Mission: To promote the arts in Geneva and the surrounding Finger Lakes community by presenting music, dance and vocal performances.
Utilizes: Artists-in-Residence; Dance Companies; Dancers; Multimedia; Original Music Scores; Theatre Companies
Founded: 1938
Specialized Field: Series & Festivals: Music and Dance Performance
Status: Non-Profit, Non-Professional
Volunteer Staff: 22
Paid Artists: 290
Budget: $60,000-150,000
Performs At: Smith Opera House

Annual Attendance: 3,000
Facility Category: Opera House
Type of Stage: Proscenium Arts; Thrust Stage
Seating Capacity: 1,500
Year Built: 1894
Year Remodeled: 2000
Rental Contact: Kevin Mitchell
Organization Type: Educational; Sponsoring

4694
ADIRONDACK THEATRE FESTIVAL
PO Box 3203
Glens Falls, NY 12801
Phone: 518-798-7479
Fax: 518-793-1334
e-mail: atf@atfestival.org
Web Site: www.atfestival.org
Officers:
    President: Kathy Reed
    VP: Rene Clements
    Treasurer: David J King
    Secretary: Janet Cordes
Management:
    Producing Artistic Director: Mark Fleischer
    General Manager: Tracy Long
Mission: A professional not-for-profit summer theatre located in Glens Falls, NY, strives to challenge, entertain, and nourish its audience through the development and production of new and contemporary musicals and plays. This relationship engages the community as audience members and participants in workshops, discussions and educational programming.
Utilizes: Actors; AEA Actors; Choreographers; Commissioned Composers; Designers; Local Unknown Artists; Music; Organization Contracts; Original Music Scores; Performance Artists; Resident Professionals; Student Interns
Founded: 1994
Specialized Field: Theater
Status: Nonprofit
Paid Staff: 11
Volunteer Staff: 10
Paid Artists: 36
Budget: $400,000
Income Sources: Ticket Sales; Donations; Grants
Season: June - July
Performs At: Charles R Wood Theater
Affiliations: AEA
Annual Attendance: 6,100
Facility Category: Theater
Type of Stage: Proscenium
Seating Capacity: 294
Year Built: 2004

4695
LOWER ADIRONDACK REGIONAL ARTS COUNCIL
7 Lapham Place
Glens Falls, NY 12801
Phone: 518-798-1144
Fax: 518-798-9122
e-mail: gallery@larac.org
Web Site: www.laracarts.org
Management:
    President: Patricia Joyce
Mission: To lead in the improvement of the quality of life for the people of the lower Adirondack region by supporting the arts and culture.
Founded: 1972
Specialized Field: Series and Festivals
Status: Non-Profit, Non-Professional
Paid Staff: 3
Affiliations: New York State Council on the Arts

4696
GLYDE RECITALS: NEW YORK VIOLA SOCIETY
26 Green Hill Road
Golden's Bridge, NY 10526
Mailing Address: New York Viola Society, PO Box 61, New York, NY 10019
Phone: 914-232-8159
Fax: 914-232-0521
e-mail: wsalchow@computer.net
Web Site: www.viola.com/nyvs
Management:
    President: William Salchow
    Director: Chris Ims
Budget: $10,000

4697
FESTIVAL OF BAROQUE MUSIC
Foundation for Baroque Music
165 Wilton Road
Greenfield Center, NY 12833
Phone: 518-893-7527
Fax: 518-893-2351
e-mail: rconant@baroquefestival.org
Web Site: www.baroquefestival.org
Management:
    President: Robert Conant
Founded: 1959
Specialized Field: Series & Festivals; Instrumental Music; Vocal Music; Youth; Dance
Status: Non-Profit, Professional
Paid Staff: 1
Paid Artists: 18

4698
LONG ISLAND UNIVERSITY/TILLES CENTER
Route 25A
Greenvale, NY 11548-0570
Phone: 516-299-2752
Fax: 516-299-2520
e-mail: elliott.stroka@liu.edu
Web Site: www.tillescenter.org
Officers:
    Executive Director: Elliot Sroka
Management:
    General Manager: George Lindsay
Mission: Long Island's premiere concert venue and presenter of world class live performances.
Founded: 1981
Specialized Field: Series & Festivals; Instrumental Music; Vocal Music; Theatre; Youth; Dance; Ethnic Performances
Status: Non-Profit, Professional
Paid Staff: 80
Volunteer Staff: 20
Budget: $6,000,000
Income Sources: Ticket Sales; Private Donations; NYSCA
Performs At: Concert Hall; Recital Hall
Affiliations: Ticketmaster
Annual Attendance: 200,000
Facility Category: Theatre
Type of Stage: Wood
Stage Dimensions: 70 X 35
Seating Capacity: 2,242
Year Built: 1981
Rental Contact: General Manager George Lindsay

4699

COLGATE UNIVERSITY CONCERT SERIES

Colgate University, Music Department
13 Oak Drive
Hamilton, NY 13346-1398
Phone: 315-228-7642
Fax: 315-228-7557
e-mail: shealey@mail.colgate.edu
Web Site: www.colgate.edu
Officers:
Chairperson: Mariette Cheng
Director, Chenango Summer Mus. Fest: Laura Klugherz
Management:
President: Rebeca Chopp
Managing Director: Roberta Healey
Mission: To provide music concerts for Colgate students and the surrounding community.
Utilizes: Guest Companies; Guest Directors; Guest Musical Directors; Guest Musicians
Founded: 1836
Specialized Field: Series and Festivals; Instrumental Music; Vocal Music; Theatre; Ethnic Performances
Status: Non-Profit, Professional
Paid Staff: 2
Paid Artists: 40
Budget: $20,000-35,000
Income Sources: Private
Performs At: Colgate Memorial Chapel
Facility Category: chapel
Type of Stage: wooden
Seating Capacity: 750
Organization Type: Educational; Sponsoring
Resident Groups: University Orchestra, Chamber Players, Chorus, Jazz Ensemble

4700

JOSEPH G ASTMAN INTERNATIONAL CONCERT SERIES

200 Hofstra University
Student Center, Room 107
Hempstead, NY 11549
Phone: 516-463-5042
Fax: 516-463-6132
e-mail: culrts@hofstra.edu
Web Site: www.hofstra.edu
Management:
Artistic Director: Bob Spiotto
Utilizes: Actors; Collaborations; Educators; Guest Conductors; Guest Directors; Guest Instructors; Guest Lecturers; Guest Soloists; Local Artists; Lyricists; Multimedia; Organization Contracts; Original Music Scores; Performance Artists; Resident Professionals; Sign Language Translators; Soloists; Student Interns; Special Technical Talent
Specialized Field: Series & Festivals; Instrumental Music; Theatre; Ethnic Performances
Status: Non-Profit, Professional
Performs At: Monroe Lecture Center Theater

4701

BELLEAYRE MUSIC FESTIVAL

PO Box 198
Highmount, NY 12441
Mailing Address: PO Box 198
Phone: 845-254-5600
Fax: 845-254-5608
Toll-free: 800-942-6904
e-mail: festival@catskill.net
Web Site: www.belleayremusic.org
Management:
Executive/Artistic Director: Mel Litoff

Administrative Manager: Don L Myers
Mission: To bring the arts and culture to this Catskill highpeaks area
Founded: 1992
Specialized Field: All Types Of Music From Opera To Orchestra, Folk To Pop
Status: Non-Profit, Professional
Paid Staff: 4
Volunteer Staff: 30
Paid Artists: 250
Non-paid Artists: 50
Budget: $800,000
Income Sources: Ticket Sales; Contributions
Performs At: Tent & Lawn Summer Music Festival
Affiliations: Festival Is Held On The Grounds & Belleayre Ski Center
Annual Attendance: 10,000
Facility Category: Performance Tent
Type of Stage: Wood Platform
Stage Dimensions: 30'x40'
Seating Capacity: 650
Year Built: 2003

4702

HORNELL AREA ARTS COUNCIL

PO Box 298
20 Broadway
Hornell, NY 14843
Phone: 607-324-3822
Fax: 607-324-3822
Management:
Executive Director: Rene, Coombs
Budget: $10,000-20,000

4703

HOUGHTON COLLEGE ARTIST SERIES

Houghton College
Houghton, NY 14744
Phone: 716-567-9403
Fax: 716-567-9517
e-mail: BBrown@houghton.edu
Management:
Director: Dr. Bruce Brown
Mission: To offer the finest music concerts.
Utilizes: Artists-in-Residence; Dance Companies; Guest Accompanists; Guest Choreographers; Guest Composers; Guest Directors; Guest Lecturers; Multimedia; Original Music Scores; Sign Language Translators; Special Technical Talent; Theatre Companies
Founded: 1930
Specialized Field: Vocal Music; Instrumental Music; Theatre; Grand Opera
Status: Nonprofit
Budget: $20,000-35,000
Income Sources: Association of Performing Arts Presenters
Performs At: Wesley Chapel
Organization Type: Performing; Educational; Sponsoring

4704

HUNTINGTON ARTS COUNCIL

213 Main Street
Huntington, NY 11743
Phone: 631-271-8423
Fax: 631-271-8428
e-mail: info@huntingtonarts.org
Web Site: www.huntingtonarts.org
Management:
President: Harry Whittelsey
Executive Director: Diana Cherryholmes
VP: Sandi Bloomberg
Program Director: Dan Forte

Mission: The Huntington Arts Council supports and fosters the arts to enhance the lives of the citizens of Huntington Township and their visitors.
Founded: 1963
Specialized Field: Presenting; Education; Re-grants; Technical Assistance
Paid Staff: 8
Volunteer Staff: 27
Paid Artists: 57
Income Sources: Grants; Sponsorchip; Town and County Funding; Membership Dues
Annual Attendance: 90,000
Seating Capacity: 5,500
Year Built: 1979
Rental Contact: Dan Forte

4705

HUNTINGTON SUMMER ARTS FESTIVAL

Huntington Arts Council
213 Main Street
Huntington, NY 11743
Phone: 631-271-8423
Fax: 631-271-8428
e-mail: hsaf@huntingtonarts.org
Web Site: www.huntingtonarts.org
Management:
President: Victoria Carlin
Executive Director: Diana J Cherryholmes
Founded: 1962
Status: Non-Profit, Professional
Paid Staff: 7

4706

CORNELL CONCERT SERIES

Cornell University
Lincoln Hall
Ithaca, NY 14853
Phone: 607-255-4363
Fax: 607-254-2877
Web Site: www.arts.cornell.edu/ccs
Management:
Managing Director: Kiko Nobusawa
Mission: Concert events per academic year, from solo recitals to orchestras presents; musicians of international renown.
Founded: 1903
Specialized Field: Series & Festivals; Instrumental Music; Vocal Music; Dance; Ethnic Performances; Classical Music; Jazz; World Music
Status: Non-Profit, Professional
Paid Staff: 2
Volunteer Staff: 80
Paid Artists: 10

4707

ITHACA COLLEGE CONCERTS

Ithaca College School of Music
4201 Whalen Center
Ithaca, NY 14850-7240
Phone: 607-274-3717
Fax: 607-274-1727
e-mail: ekibelsbeck.ithaca.edu
Web Site: www.ithaca.edu/music
Management:
Concert Manager: Erik Kibelsheck
Founded: 1892
Specialized Field: Series & Festivals: Classical Music
Status: Non-Profit, Non-Professional
Budget: $20,000-35,000
Income Sources: Ticket Revenue
Performs At: Ford Hall
Facility Category: Concert Hall
Type of Stage: Proscenium
Seating Capacity: 737

Year Built: 1960

4708
NEW DIRECTIONS CELLO FESTIVAL
501 Linn Street
Ithaca, NY 14850
Phone: 607-277-1686
Fax: 607-277-1686
Toll-free: 877-665-5815
e-mail: info@newdirectionscello.com
Web Site: www.newdirectionscello.com
Management:
   Director: Joel Cohen
   General Director: Chris White
   Education Director: Sera Surslen
Mission: To bring together cellists and others interested in nonclassical uses of cello (jazz, blues, folk, rock, etc.). Workshops, jams, concerts.
Utilizes: Artists-in-Residence; Collaborations; Guest Accompanists; Guest Directors; Guest Musical Directors; Guest Musicians; Multimedia; Organization Contracts; Original Music Scores; Soloists
Founded: 1995
Specialized Field: Series & Festivals; Instrumental Music; Youth; Ethnic Performances; Promotion of Non Classical Usage of Cello
Status: For-Profit, Professional
Paid Staff: 3
Volunteer Staff: 10
Paid Artists: 12
Budget: Under $10,000
Income Sources: Sponsors, Participants, Donations
Season: July 11 - 13, 1999
Performs At: University of Connecticut, Storrs [Festival Site]
Annual Attendance: 100
Facility Category: Mehden Auditorium/Recital Hall
Stage Dimensions: 50x25
Seating Capacity: 500
Year Built: 1985
Cost: $150 - 3 day

4709
ARTS COUNCIL FOR CHAUTAUGUA COUNTY
116 E Third Street
Jamestown, NY 14701
Phone: 716-664-2465
Fax: 716-661-3829
e-mail: heather@artscouncil.com
Web Site: www.artscouncil.com
Management:
   Executive Director: David Schein
Founded: 1970
Status: Non-Profit, Non-Professional
Budget: $60,000-150,000
Performs At: Reg Lenna Civic Center

4710
JAMESTOWN CONCERT ASSOCIATION
315 N Main Street
Suite 200
Jamestown, NY 14701-5124
Phone: 716-487-1522
Fax: 716-483-5051
e-mail: jcamusic@excite.com
Web Site: www.jamestownconcertassociation.org
Officers:
   President: R Richard Corbin
   VP: Sally Ulrich
   Treasurer: F John Fuchs
   Secretary: Mary Weeden
Management:
   President: Richard Corbin

   Executive Director: Sally Ulrich
   Managing Director: Jack Hemink
Mission: Purpose of presenting live classical performances in the Jamestown area.
Founded: 1934
Specialized Field: Series and Festivals; Instrumental Music; Vocal Music; Youth; Ethnic Performances
Status: Non-Profit, Professional
Volunteer Staff: 16
Paid Artists: 200
Budget: $20,000-35,000
Income Sources: NYSCA; Local Foundations; PENNPAT

4711
CARAMOOR CENTER FOR MUSIC AND THE ARTS
149 Girdle Ridge Road
PO Box 816
Katonah, NY 10536
Phone: 914-232-5035
Fax: 914-232-5521
e-mail: museum@caramoor.org
Web Site: www.caramoor.org
Officers:
   Chief Executive/General Director: Michael Barrett
Management:
   Managing Director: Paul Rosenblum
Founded: 1970
Specialized Field: Vocal Music; Instrumental Music; Festivals
Status: Professional; Nonprofit

4712
CARAMOOR CENTER FOR MUSIC AND THE ARTS
Katonah, NY 10536
Phone: 914-232-1252
Fax: 914-232-5521
Web Site: www.caramoor.org
Officers:
   President/CEO: Erich Vollmer
Management:
   Executive Director: Howard Herring
   Managing Director: Paul Rosenblum
   Director Development: Susan Shine
   Director Operations: Melissa Montera
   Box Office Manager: Sal Vaccaro
Mission: To offer a performing arts venue in Bedford and New York State.
Founded: 1945
Specialized Field: Vocal Music; Instrumental Music; Festivals
Status: Professional; Nonprofit
Performs At: Museum Music Room Venetian Theatre
Organization Type: Performing; Educational; Sponsoring

4713
CARAMOOR INTERNATIONAL MUSIC FESTIVAL
PO Box 816
Katonah, NY 10536
Phone: 914-232-1252
Fax: 914-232-5521
e-mail: boxoffice@caramoor.org
Web Site: www.caramoor.com
Management:
   Chief Executive And Generaldirector: Michael Barrett
   Artistic Director: Joe Lovano
   Managing Director: Paul Rosenblum

4714
LAKE GEORGE JAZZ WEEKEND
Lake George Arts Project
1 Amherst Street
Lake George, NY 12845
Phone: 518-668-2616
Fax: 518-668-3050
Officers:
   President: Ed Ostberg
Management:
   Executive Director: John Strong
   Music Director: Paul Pines
Mission: Sponsoring a two-day jazz festival every September featuring nationally acclaimed as well as emerging jazz artists.
Founded: 1980
Specialized Field: General Arts Organisation
Status: Non-Profit, Professional
Paid Staff: 1
Paid Artists: 5
Performs At: Shepard Park Bandstand
Organization Type: Performing; Touring

4715
LUZERNE CHAMBER MUSIC FESTIVAL
PO Box 35
Lake Luzerne, NY 12846
Phone: 518-696-2771
Fax: 518-696-4903
Toll-free: 800-874-3202
e-mail: info@luzernemusic.org
Web Site: www.luzernemusic.org
Management:
   President: Bert Philips
Founded: 1980
Specialized Field: Series & Festivals; Chamber Music; Summer Music Camp
Status: Non-Profit, Professional
Paid Staff: 20
Paid Artists: 20

4716
ARTPARK
450 S 4th Street
Lewiston, NY 14092
Phone: 716-754-9000
Fax: 716-754-2741
e-mail: gosborne@artpark.net
Web Site: www.artpark.net
Officers:
   President: George D Osborn
   Director Finance: Jean Stopa
   Productions Manager: Susan Stimson
Management:
   President: George Osborne
Mission: To provide arts education and programming to nuture and develop the talents of visual and performing artists; to provide quality volunteer experiences in the arts; to produce and present a series of theatre productions and concert events that will entertain and enrich the residents of Western New York, southeastern Canada, and area tourists.
Utilizes: Actors; AEA Actors; Artists-in-Residence; Choreographers; Dance Companies; Dancers; Designers; Fine Artists; Local Artists; Multimedia; Music; Original Music Scores; Resident Professionals; Sign Language Translators; Soloists; Touring Companies; Visual Arts
Founded: 1974
Specialized Field: Series & Festivals; Dance; Vocal Music; Instrumental Music; Festivals
Status: Non-Profit, Professional
Paid Staff: 100

Volunteer Staff: 300
Paid Artists: 200
Budget: $4 Million
Income Sources: Tickets; Grants; Sponsors
Season: June - September
Affiliations: Actors' Equity Association; International Association of Theatrical Stage Employees; American Guild of Musical Artists
Annual Attendance: 300,000
Facility Category: Theater & Ampi-Theater
Type of Stage: Sprung
Seating Capacity: 2,324
Year Built: 1974
Cost: $7,200,000
Rental Contact: Productions Manager Susan Stimson
Organization Type: Performing; Resident; Sponsoring

4717
BEETHOVEN FESTIVAL

Friends of the Arts
PO Box 702
Locust Valley, NY 11560
Phone: 516-922-0061
Fax: 516-922-0770
e-mail: info@fotapresents.org
Web Site: www.fotapresents.org
Management:
Executive Director: Maryann Beaumant
Mission: Presenting Beethoven's lifetime body of work during one spectacular weekend.
Founded: 1972
Specialized Field: Series & Festivals; Concerts And Presenters; Educational Programs Jazz; Classical And Pop
Status: Non-Profit, Professional
Paid Staff: 8
Performs At: Planting Fields Arboretum
Organization Type: Performing

4718
BASKETBALL CITY

3100 47th Avenue
2nd Floor
Long Island City, NY 11103
Phone: 718-786-4242
Fax: 718-786-4252
e-mail: bruce@basketballcity.com
Web Site: www.basketballcity.com
Management:
Director: Bruce D. Radler
Founded: 1997
Specialized Field: Basketball
Status: For-Profit, Professional

4719
EMELIN THEATRE FOR THE PERFORMING ARTS

153 Library Lane
Mamaroneck, NY 10543
Phone: 914-698-3045
Fax: 914-698-1404
e-mail: emelin98@aol.com
Web Site: www.emelin.org
Management:
Managing Director: John Raymond
Founded: 1973
Status: Non-Profit,Professional
Budget: $150,000-400,000
Performs At: Emelin Theatre
Type of Stage: Proscenium
Seating Capacity: 280

4720
OYSTER BAY ARTS COUNCIL

977 Hicksville Road
Massapequa, NY 11758-1281
Phone: 516-797-7926
Fax: 516-797-7919
e-mail: jreeves@oysterbay-ny.gov
Web Site: www.tobac.org
Management:
Executive Director: Joanne Reeves
Mission: The Art Council's mission is to promote, encourage, publicize and stimulate performing & visual arts in our community.
Founded: 1973
Status: Non-Profit, Non-Professional
Volunteer Staff: 19
Budget: $10,000
Income Sources: Membership; Fundraising

4721
DOROTHY TAUBMAN SEMINAR AT LINCOLN CENTER

The Taubman Institute
245 Route 351
Medusa, NY 12120
Phone: 518-966-5558
Fax: 518-966-5998
Toll-free: 800-826-3720
e-mail: es@taubman-institute.com
Web Site: www.taubman-institute.com
Management:
Director: Enid Stettner
Mission: June 21, 22, 23, (2007)
Founded: 1977
Paid Artists: 13

4722
CHAMBER MUSIC FESTIVAL OF THE EAST

Chamber Music Conference
PO Box 6
Melville, NY 07605-0006
Phone: 201-242-1277
e-mail: chmusic@tiac.net
Management:
Chairman of Board: Stephen Reid
Music Director: Shem Guibbory
Founded: 1945
Specialized Field: Chamber Music; Study Organization
Status: Non-Profit, Professional
Paid Staff: 60

4723
MOUNT KISCO CONCERT ASSOCIATION

34 Lakeside Road
Mount Kisco, NY 10549
Phone: 914-666-9181
Fax: 914-241-0034
e-mail: djnmriii@aol.com
Officers:
Artist Selection Chairperson: Michael G Rothenberg
Management:
President: Eedee Rothenberg
Artistic Director: Micheal Rothenberg
Founded: 1967
Specialized Field: Series & Festivals: Chamber Music
Status: Non-Profit, Professional
Paid Artists: 3
Budget: $20,000-35,000

4724
PIANO SUMMER AT NEW PALTZ

SUNY at New Paltz, Music Department
75 S Manheim Boulevard, Suite 9
New Paltz, NY 12561-2443
Phone: 845-257-2700
Fax: 845-257-3121
Web Site: www.newpaltz.edu/piano
Management:
Artistic Director: Vladimir Feltsman

4725
92ND STREET Y

92nd Street Y
1395 Lexington Avenue
New York, NY 10128
Phone: 212-415-5500
Fax: 212-415-5788
e-mail: webmaster@92ndsty.org
Web Site: www.92ndsty.org
Officers:
President: Matthew Bronfman
Chairman: Philip L Milgrein
VP: Claire B Benenson
VP: Lini Lipton
Treasurer: Martin J. Rabinpwitz
Secretary: Lori A. Kasowitx
Management:
President: Michael Goldstein
Executive Director: Sol Adler
Director: Tamar C Podell
Production Manager: Zoe Markwalter
Mission: Promotes individual and family development and participation in civic life within the context of Jewish values and American pluralism; creates, provides and disseminates programs of distinction that foster physical and mental health.
Founded: 1874
Status: Nonprofit

4726
AMERICAN FESTIVAL OF MICROTONAL MUSIC

318 E 70th Street
#5FW
New York, NY 10021
Phone: 212-517-3550
Fax: 212-517-3550
e-mail: afmmjr@aol.com
Web Site: www.afmm.org
Officers:
President: Edgar E Coons
Management:
Director: Johnny Reinhard
Founded: 1981
Specialized Field: Series & Festivals; Instrumental Music; Vocal Music; Theatre; Youth; Dance; Ethnic Performances
Status: Non-Profit, Professional
Paid Artists: 30

4727
AMERICAN INDIAN COMMUNITY HOUSE SERIES

708 Broadway
8th Floor
New York, NY 10003
Phone: 212-598-0100
Fax: 212-598-4909
e-mail: akwesasne@aol.com
Web Site: www.aich.org
Management:
Executive Director: Rosemary Richmond

Performing Arts Director: Jim Cyrus
Founded: 1969
Status: Non-Profit, Professional
Paid Staff: 40
Budget: $10,000-20,000
Season: September - June

4728
AMERICAN LANDMARK FESTIVALS

26 Wall Street
New York, NY 10005
Phone: 212-866-2086
Fax: 212-866-2086
e-mail: AmLandmarKFstvls@gmail.com
Web Site: www.americanlandmarkfestivals.org
Officers:
Founding Director: Francis L Heilbut
President: Gena Rangel
Treasurer: Joe Pearce
Management:
Director: Gena Rangel
Mission: To present cultural and performing arts events in landmarks of sign, science, and to promote better understanding of landmarks and the performing arts.
Utilizes: Singers
Founded: 1973
Specialized Field: Performing Arts
Status: Professional
Paid Staff: 2
Volunteer Staff: 3
Paid Artists: 20
Non-paid Artists: 20
Organization Type: Performing

4729
ARTS INTERNATIONAL

526 W 26th Street
Suite 516
New York, NY 10001
Phone: 212-924-0771
Fax: 212-924-0773
e-mail: info@artsinternational.org
Web Site: www.artsinternational.org
Officers:
President: Noreen Tomassi
Management:
President: Noreen Tomassi
Director Of Development: Esther McGowan
Director: Renata Petroni Petroni
Founded: 1981

4730
ASIA SOCIETY

725 Park Avenue
New York, NY 10021-5025
Phone: 212-288-6400
Fax: 212-517-8315
e-mail: asiastore@asiasoc.org
Web Site: www.asiasociety.org
Management:
President: Vishakha N Desai
VP External Affairs: Carol P Herring
VP Marketing/Communications: Karen Karp
VP Finance/Administration: Shin R Miyoshi
Founded: 1956

4731
BANG ON A CAN

80 Hanson Place
New York, NY 11217
Phone: 718-852-7755
Fax: 718-852-7732
e-mail: info@bangonacan.org
Web Site: www.bangonacan.org

Management:
President: Adam Wolfensohn
Executive Director: Kenny Savelson
Artistic Director: Michael Gordon
Artistic Director: Julia Wolfe
Mission: To present contemporary musical works by emerging and young composers.
Utilizes: Choreographers; Commissioned Composers; Commissioned Music; Designers; Five Seasonal Concerts; Grant Writers; Guest Accompanists; Guest Artists; Guest Choreographers; Guest Companies; Guest Composers; Guest Conductors; Guest Designers; Guest Directors; Guest Ensembles; Guest Musical Directors; High School Drama; Instructors; Multimedia; Original Music Scores; Resident Professionals; Sign Language Translators; Singers; Student Interns; Special Technical Talent; Visual Arts
Founded: 1987
Specialized Field: Series and Festivals; Instrumental Music; Vocal Music; Presenting New Music
Status: Non-Profit, Professional
Paid Staff: 6
Income Sources: Public; Private Funding; Earned Income
Organization Type: Performing

4732
BELL ATLANTIC JAZZ FESTIVAL

74 Leonard Street
New York, NY 10013
Phone: 212-219-3006
Fax: 212-219-3401
Web Site: www.jazfest.com

4733
BLOOMINGDALE SCHOOL OF MUSIC CONCERT SERIES

323 W 108th Street
New York, NY 10025
Phone: 212-663-6021
Fax: 212-932-9429
e-mail: bvazquez@bsmny.org
Web Site: www.bsmny.org
Management:
Executive Director: Lawrence Davis
Founded: 1964
Specialized Field: Series & Festivals: Music
Status: Non-Profit, Professional
Budget: $10,000
Performs At: David Greer Recital Hall

4734
BOPI'S BLACK SHEEP/DANCE BY KRAIG PATTERSON

Jaf Station
PO Box 372
New York, NY 10116
Phone: 212-262-9499
Fax: 212-399-1349
e-mail: dancebopi@aol.com
Web Site: www.bopi.org
Management:
Artistic Director: Kraig Patterson
Booking Agent: Micocci Productions
Mission: Performance, touring and creation of works.
Specialized Field: Modern Dance
Paid Staff: 2
Paid Artists: 12

4735
BRIDGEHAMPTON CHAMBER MUSIC FESTIVAL

850 Seventh Avenue
Suite 700
New York, NY 10019
Phone: 212-741-9073
Fax: 212-741-9403
e-mail: info@bcmf.org
Web Site: www.bcmf.org
Management:
Executive Director: Derek Delaney
Artistic Director: Marya Martin
Founded: 1984
Specialized Field: Series & Festivals; Classical Music; Instumental Music
Status: Non-Profit, Professional
Paid Staff: 1
Paid Artists: 40

4736
CATHEDRAL ARTS

1047 Amsterdam Avenue
New York, NY 10025
Phone: 212-316-7563
Fax: 212-316-7445
Web Site: www.anderson.binghamton.edu
Management:
President: James A Kowski
Director: Canon Tom Miller
Founded: 1892
Specialized Field: Series & Festivals; Instrumental Music; Vocal Music; Youth; Ethnic Performances; Concerts
Status: Non-Profit, Professional
Budget: $10,000-20,000

4737
CENTRAL PARK SUMMERSTAGE

830 5th Avenue
New York, NY 10021
Phone: 212-360-2756
Fax: 212-360-2754
e-mail: info@summerstage.org
Web Site: www.summerstage.org
Management:
Director Of Marketing And Public Re: Debbie Ferraro
Executive Director: David Rivel
Director Of Operations: Josy Dussek
Production Director: John McDonald
Founded: 1986
Specialized Field: Music; Dance; Spokin Word; Opera
Status: Nonprofit
Paid Staff: 76
Volunteer Staff: 300
Paid Artists: 90
Budget: $800,000
Income Sources: Ticket Sales; State Local Grants; Memberships; Endowment Funds
Performs At: Rumsey Playfield
Annual Attendance: 350,000
Stage Dimensions: 36'x42'
Seating Capacity: 4,000-6,000
Year Built: 1986
Year Remodeled: 2000

4738
CLARION MUSIC SOCIETY

Kaye Playhouse
695 Park Avenue
New York, NY 10021

Phone: 212-463-7201
Fax: 212-463-7201
Web Site: www.kayeplayhouse.org
Management:
 Executive Director: Sandra Davis
Budget: $35,000-60,000
Performs At: Kaye Playhouse

4739
CONCERT ARTISTS GUILD NEW YORK RECITAL SERIES

850 7th Avenue
Suite 1205
New York, NY 10019
Phone: 212-333-5200
Fax: 212-977-7149
e-mail: caguild@concertartists.org
Web Site: www.concertartists.org
Officers:
 President: Richard S Weinert
 Executive VP: Amy Roberts Frawley
 Senior VP: Brian D Bumby
Management:
 President: Richard S Weinert
 Executive VP: Amy Roberts Frawley
 Senior VP Artist: Steven D Shaiman
 Comptroller: Christine Sperry
Founded: 1951
Specialized Field: Classical
Performs At: Weill Recital Hall at Carnegie Hall

4740
CONCERT SOCIALS

110 W 96th Street
Suite 9D
New York, NY 10025
Phone: 212-749-5464
Management:
 Executive Director/President: Rae Metzgar
Performs At: Weill Recital Hall at Carnegie Hall

4741
CONCERTS AT THE CLOISTERS

The Cloisters
Fort Tryon Park
New York, NY 10040
Phone: 212-650-2290
Fax: 212-795-3640
Web Site: www.metmuseum.org
Management:
 Concert Manager: Nancy Wu
Budget: $50,000-100,000
Performs At: Fuentiduena Chapel; Metropolitan Museum of Art

4742
CREATIVE TIME SERIES

307 7th Avenue
Suite 1904
New York, NY 10001
Phone: 212-206-6674
Fax: 212-255-8467
e-mail: staff@creativetime.org
Web Site: www.creativetime.org
Management:
 President: Anne Pasternak
 Producer And Curator: Alexa Coyne
 Director Of Development: Heather Duggan
 Chairman Of Executive Committee: Philip Aarons
Founded: 1973
Budget: $10,000-20,000

4743
DIA CENTER FOR THE ARTS

535 W 22nd Street 4th Floor
New York, NY 10011
Phone: 212-989-5566
Fax: 212-989-4055
e-mail: info@diacenter.org
Web Site: www.diacenter.org
Management:
 Director: Michael Govan
 Administrator Art Programs: John Bowsher
 Development Associate: Katherine Carl
 Assistant Director: Stephen Dewhurst
Founded: 1974
Specialized Field: Contemporary Art
Status: Non-Profit
Income Sources: Foundations; Corporations;
Affiliations: 1

4744
EARLY MUSIC NEW YORK (EM/NY)

10 West 68 Street
New York, NY 10023
Phone: 212-749-6600
Fax: 212-749-2848
e-mail: info@EarlyMusicNY.org
Web Site: www.EarlyMusicNY.org
Officers:
 President: Audrey Boughton
Management:
 Founder/Director: Frederick Renz,
 f.renz@EarlyMusicNY.org
 Operations Manager: Aaron Smith,
 admin@EarlyMusicNY.org
Mission: To foster historically informed performances
Founded: 1974
Specialized Field: Early Music; Dance & Music Drama;
Medieval; Renassiance; Baroque; Classical
Status: Non-Profit; Professional
Paid Staff: 4
Budget: $300,000
Income Sources: Ticket Sales; CD Sales; Private
Contributions & Grants; Government Awards
Performs At: Cathedral of Saint John the Divine
Affiliations: Early Music Foundation; New York Early
Music Central (NYEMC)

4745
ELAINE KAUFMAN CULTURAL CENTER PRESENTATIONS

129 W 67th Street
New York, NY 10023
Phone: 212-501-3386
Fax: 212-874-7865
e-mail: lhart@kaufman-center.org
Web Site: www.kaufman-center.org
Management:
 Executive Director: Lydia Kontos
 Merkin Concert Hall Director: Karen Chester
 Communications Director: Lizanne Hart
Founded: 1952
Specialized Field: Performing Arts; Presentation;
Education
Status: Non-Profit, Professional
Budget: $60,000-150,000
Performs At: Ann Goodman Recital Hall

4746
FESTIVAL OF NEW MUSIC

30 Seaman Avenue
#4M
New York, NY 10034

Phone: 646-489-0367
Fax: 212-544-0738
e-mail: info@threetwo.org
Web Site: www.threetwo.org
Management:
 Co-Director: Taimur Sullivan
Founded: 1994

4747
FOOLS COMPANY

356 W 44th Street
New York, NY 10036
Phone: 212-307-6000
Fax: 212-307-6003
e-mail: foolsco@att.net
Web Site: www.foolsco.org
Officers:
 President: James Wertheim
 VP: Marcus Bicknell
 Secretary/Treasurer: Joseph Benitez
Management:
 Executive Director: Jill Russell
 Artistic Director: Martin Russell
 Executive Administrator: Susan Cline
Mission: To produce a theatre arts festival and other
works and workshops in the performing arts.
Founded: 1970
Specialized Field: Theater; Festivals
Status: Professional; Nonprofit
Budget: $10,000
Performs At: John Houseman Theatre Studio
Organization Type: Performing; Educational

4748
FRENCH INSTITUTE ALLIANCE FRANCAISE

22 E 60th Street
New York, NY 10022
Phone: 212-355-6100
Fax: 212-935-4119
e-mail: reception@fiaf.org
Web Site: www.fiaf.org
Management:
 President: Marie Steckel-Monique
 Client Relations Manager: Kin Hernandez
 Artistic Director: Jacqueline Chambord
 Managing Director: John Franco
Founded: 1898
Specialized Field: French Classes; French Library;
French Programs; French Films
Status: Non-Profit, Professional
Paid Staff: 100
Budget: $150,000-400,000
Performs At: Theater, Dance, Music, Lecture and Film
Facility Category: Cultural Organization
Type of Stage: Proscenium
Stage Dimensions: 35'x22'
Seating Capacity: 400
Year Built: 1989
Rental Contact: Client Relations Manager Kin
Hernandez

4749
FRICK COLLECTION CONCERT SERIES

1 E 70th Street
New York, NY 10021
Phone: 212-288-0700
Fax: 212-628-4417
e-mail: bodig@frick.org
Web Site: www.frick.org
Management:
 Concerts Coordinator: Joyce Bodig
Founded: 1935

Specialized Field: Chamber; Vocal; Early; Instumental music
Status: Non-Profit, Professional
Budget: $60,000-150,000

4750
GOTHAM EARLY MUSIC FOUNDATION SERIES

PO Box 231300
Ansonia Station
New York, NY 10023
Phone: 212-595-4036
Fax: 212-875-8503
e-mail: admin@gothamemf.com
Officers:
President: Douglas K Dunn
Budget: $150,000-400,000
Performs At: Weill Recital Hall at Carnegie Hall; Ethical Culture Society

4751
GREENWICH HOUSE ARTS: NORTH RIVER MUSIC

46 Barrow Street
New York, NY 10014
Phone: 212-242-4770
Fax: 212-366-9621
e-mail: gharts@gharts.org
Web Site: www.gharts.org
Management:
Chairman: Edward Adler
Vice Chairman: Victor Futter
Founded: 1902
Specialized Field: Music; Theatre
Budget: $10,000-20,000
Performs At: Renee Weiler Concert Hall

4752
HELICON FOUNDATION

27 W 67th Street
New York, NY 10023-6258
Phone: 212-874-6438
Fax: 212-874-6438
e-mail: helicon@dti.net
Management:
Executive Director: James Roe
Artistic Director: Albert Fuller
Budget: $10,000-20,000

4753
HENSON INTERNATIONAL FESTIVAL OF PUPPET THEATRE

117 E 69th Street
New York, NY 10021
Phone: 212-794-2400
Fax: 212-439-6036
e-mail: info@hensonfestival.org
Web Site: www.hensonfestival.org
Management:
Executive Producer: Cherly Henson
General Manager: Heidi Wilenius
Development Officer: Meg Daniel
Mission: To provide some of the finest international puppetry performers for American audiences; to present the finest international puppet artists to American audiences.
Specialized Field: Theatre: Puppet Theatre
Status: For-Profit, Professional
Paid Staff: 20
Performs At: Joseph Papp Public Theater
Organization Type: Sponsoring

4754
HISTORIC BRASS SOCIETY - EARLY BRASS FESTIVAL

148 W 23rd Street
Suite 5F
New York, NY 10011
Phone: 212-627-3820
Fax: 212-627-3820
e-mail: president@historicbrass.org
Web Site: www.historicbrass.org
Management:
President: Jeff Nussbaum
Mission: To promote the study and performance of brass music.
Founded: 1988
Specialized Field: Study and History of Brass Instruments and Brass Music
Status: Non-Profit, Professional
Volunteer Staff: 20

4755
HUDSON RIVER FESTIVAL

200 Liberty Street
Lobby Level
New York, NY 10281
Phone: 212-945-2600
Fax: 212-945-3392
e-mail: info@worldfinancialcenter.com
Web Site: www.worldfinancialcenter.com
Management:
Director: Melissa Coley
Founded: 1988

4756
INTERNATIONAL OFFESTIVAL

Fools Company
423 W 46th Street
New York, NY 10036
Phone: 212-307-6000
Fax: 212-307-6003
e-mail: foolsco@att.net
Web Site: www.foolsco.org
Management:
Executive Director: Jill Russell
Artistic Director: Martin Russell

4757
JAPAN SOCIETY PERFORMING ARTS SERIES

333 E 47th Street
New York, NY 10017
Phone: 212-832-1155
Fax: 212-715-1262
e-mail: yshioya@japansociety.org
Web Site: www.japansociety.org
Management:
President: Frank Ellsworth
Artistic Director: Yoko Shioya
Founded: 1907
Specialized Field: Series & Festivals; Arts & Culture; Education; Global Affairs programming; Instrumental Music; Vocal Music; Theatre; Youth; Dance; Ethnic Performanc
Status: Non-Profit, Professional
Paid Staff: 50
Budget: $60,000-150,000
Performs At: Lila Acheson Wallace Auditorium
Annual Attendance: 6,000
Seating Capacity: 278
Year Built: 1971

4758
JAZZ AT LINCOLN CENTER: ESSENTIALLY ELLINGTON JAZZ FESTIVAL

33 W 60th Street
New York, NY 10023-7999
Phone: 212-258-9800
Fax: 212-258-9900
e-mail: ee@jalc.org
Web Site: www.jalc.org/EssentiallyEllington
Management:
President: Derek E Gordon
Artistic Director: Wynton Marsalis
Executive Director: Adrian Ellis
Specialized Field: Series & Festivals; Instrumental Music; Youth
Status: Non-Profit, Professional

4759
JAZZ IN JULY

92nd Street Y
1395 Lexington Avenue
New York, NY 10128
Phone: 212-415-5740
Fax: 212-415-5738
Web Site: www.92ndsty.org
Management:
Artistic Director: Dick Hyman

4760
JVC JAZZ FESTIVAL NEW YORK

311 W 74th Street
PO Box 1169, Ansonia Station
New York, NY 10023
Phone: 212-501-1390
Fax: 212-877-9916
e-mail: info@fpiny.com
Web Site: www.festivalproductions.net
Management:
CEO: George Wein
President: John Phillip
Founded: 1954
Specialized Field: Concert Productions
Status: For-Profit, Non-Professional

4761
LEAGUE OF COMPOSERS-ISCM NEW YORK SEASON

PO Box 250281
New York, NY 10025
Phone: 718-442-5225
e-mail: lqc5590@is9.nyu.edu
Web Site: www.unix.temple.edu/~mrimple/iscm.html
Officers:
President: Dan Wanner
Management:
Executive Director: Louis Conti
Budget: $10,000-20,000

4762
LOTUS FINE ARTS PRODUCTIONS

109 W 27th Street
8th Floor
New York, NY 10001
Phone: 212-627-1076
Fax: 212-675-7191
e-mail: info@lotusarts.com
Web Site: www.lotusarts.com
Management:
Executive Director: Edward Schoelwer
Artistic Director: Kamala Cesar
Founded: 1989

Specialized Field: Series & Festivals; Instrumental
Music; Dance; Singing
Status: Non-Profit, Professional
Paid Staff: 4
Paid Artists: 12

4763
MANNES COLLEGE OF MUSIC INTERNATIONAL KEYBOARD INSTITUTE AND FESTIVAL
150 W 85th Street
New York, NY 10024
Phone: 212-580-0210
Fax: 212-580-1738
e-mail: iki@newschool.edu
Web Site: www.mannes.edu/iki
Officers:
President: Joel Lester
Management:
Director: Jerome Rose
Specialized Field: Series & Festivals: Music
Status: Non-Profit, Non-Professional

4764
MELLON JAZZ IN PHILADELPHIA
PO Box 1169
New York, NY 10023
Phone: 212-496-9000
Fax: 212-877-9916
e-mail: dan.melnick@fpiny.com
Web Site: www.festivalproductions.net
Management:
Senior Producer: Dan Melnick

4765
METROPOLITAN MUSEUM CONCERTS AND LECTURES
1000 5th Avenue and 82nd Street
New York, NY 10028
Phone: 212-570-3717
Fax: 212-570-3973
e-mail: communications@metmuseum.org
Web Site: www.metmuseum.org
Management:
President: Dave McKinney
Executive Director: Philippe D'Montebello
General Manager: Hilde Annik Limondjian
Mission: As one of the major presenting organizations
in New York City to reflect the museum's charter in
promoting education and cultural events which reflect
the museum's holdings.
Founded: 1954
Specialized Field: Musical Concerts; Art; Music
Lectures
Status: Non-Profit, Professional
Paid Staff: 2000
Income Sources: American Association of Museums
Performs At: Grace Rainey Rogers Auditorium
Seating Capacity: 705
Organization Type: Sponsoring

4766
MIDAMERICA PRODUCTIONS
132 W 36th Street
4th Floor
New York, NY 10018
Phone: 212-239-0205
Fax: 212-563-5587
e-mail: tiboris@midamerica-music.com
Web Site: www.midamerica-music.com
Management:
General Director/Artistic Director: Petern Tiboris
Executive Director: Norman Dunfee

Budget: $1,000,000+
Performs At: Avery Fisher Hall; Lincoln Center; Lakka
Open Theatre

4767
MOSTLY MOZART FESTIVAL
70 Lincoln Center Plaza
New York, NY 10023
Phone: 212-875-5135
Fax: 212-875-5145
Web Site: www.lincolncenter.org
Management:
President: Ranold Levy
Artistic Director: Jane Moss
Managing Director: Honnako Yamaguchi
Music Director: Louis Longrey
Founded: 1966
Specialized Field: Instrumental; Dance; Opera
Status: Non-Profit, Professional
Paid Staff: 500

4768
MUSIC BEFORE 1800
Music Before 1800, Inc.
Corpus Christi Church
529 W 121st Street
New York, NY \0027
Phone: 212-666-9266
Fax: 212-666-9266
e-mail: mb1800@aol.com
Web Site: www.mb1800.org
Management:
Executive Director: Louise Basbas,
mb1800@aol.com
Mission: Offering performances of vocal and
instrumental chamber music from before 1800 on
historic instruments.
Founded: 1975
Opened: 1975
Specialized Field: Chamber; Early Music
Status: Professional
Paid Staff: 2
Volunteer Staff: 20
Paid Artists: 60
Budget: $150,000
Performs At: Corpus Christi Church
Annual Attendance: 2,600
Seating Capacity: 500
Year Built: 1935
Year Remodeled: 2007

4769
MUSIC FROM JAPAN
7 E 20th Street
Suite 6F
New York, NY 10003-1106
Phone: 212-529-1888
Fax: 212-529-7855
e-mail: mfjrc@aol.com
Web Site: www.musicfromjapan.org
Management:
Artistic Director: Naoyuki Miura
Utilizes: Guest Companies; Guest Musical Directors;
Organization Contracts
Founded: 1975
Specialized Field: Music
Status: Non-Profit, Professional
Paid Staff: 2
Volunteer Staff: 2
Budget: $270,000
Income Sources: NYSCA; Japanese Government;
Corporations; Foundations
Performs At: Merkin Concert Hall

Facility Category: Baruch Performing Arts
Center/Freer Gallery of Art

4770
MUSIC IN THE PARK: THIRD STREET MUSIC SCHOOL SETTLEMENT
235 E 11th Street
New York, NY 10003
Phone: 212-777-3240
Fax: 212-477-1808
e-mail: info@thirdstreetmusicschool.org
Web Site: www.thirdstreetmusicschool.org
Management:
Executive Director: Lee Koonce
Director of Programs: Shalisa Kline Ugaz
Dir of School/Community Partnership: Nancy
Morgan
Founded: 1894
Specialized Field: Quality Instruction in Music; Dance;
Visual Arts
Status: Non-Profit, Professional
Paid Staff: 120
Paid Artists: 100
Budget: $10,000
Performs At: Abe Lebewohl Park
Facility Category: Outdoor

4771
NOONDAY CONCERTS AT ONE
74 Trinity Place
New York, NY 10006-2088
Phone: 212-602-0768
Fax: 212-602-9630
e-mail: etucker@trinitywallstreet.org
Web Site: www.trinitywallstreet.org
Management:
President: Earl Tucker
Founded: 1697
Specialized Field: All Manner In Music
Status: Non-Profit, Professional
Paid Staff: 135
Paid Artists: 100
Budget: $35,000-60,000
Performs At: St. Paul's Chapel & Trinity Church

4772
PEOPLES' SYMPHONY CONCERTS
201 W 54th Street
Suite 1 C
New York, NY 10019
Phone: 212-586-4680
Fax: 212-581-4029
e-mail: info@pscny.org
Web Site: www.pscny.org
Officers:
Chairperson: Susan Porter
President: Richard R Howe
Treasurer: Stefan H Cushman
Secretary: Frederick Wertheim
Management:
Manager: Frank E Salomon
Production Manager: Amanda James

4773
PLURAL ARTS INTERNATIONAL
22 E 67th Street
New York, NY 10021
Phone: 212-439-9800
e-mail: info@pluralarts.org
Web Site: www.pluralarts.org
Management:
Executive Director: Todd J Fletcher

4774
PRO PIANO NEW YORK RECITAL SERIES
Pro Piano
85 Jane Street
New York, NY 10014
Phone: 212-206-8794
Fax: 212-633-1207
e-mail: ricard@propiano.com
Web Site: www.propiano.com
Management:
Founder/Executive Director: Ricard de La Rosa
Artistic Director: Chitose Okashiro
Mission: Present pianists to perform at Weill Hall NYC annually.
Budget: $60,000-150,000
Performs At: Weill Recital Hall at Carnegie Hall

4775
SCHNEIDER CONCERTS AT THE NEW SCHOOL
66 W 12th Street
New York, NY 10011
Phone: 212-243-9937
Fax: 212-243-9958
e-mail: info@schneiderconcert.org
Web Site: www.schneiderconcert.org
Management:
President: Bob Carry
Managing Director: Rohana Keninll
Administrator: Rohana Keninll
Mission: To offer young profesional classical musicians performance opportunities and exposure at a vital stage of career development and to present chamber music concerts of the highest quality at modest ticket prices.
Utilizes: Multimedia
Founded: 1957
Specialized Field: Series and Festivals: Instrumental Music
Status: Non-Profit, Professional
Paid Staff: 2
Volunteer Staff: 2
Non-paid Artists: 4
Budget: $30,000-45,000
Income Sources: Box Office; NYSCA; Private Donors; Foundations
Annual Attendance: 4,000
Facility Category: Auditorium
Type of Stage: Proscenium
Seating Capacity: 510

4776
SEVENARS CONCERTS MUSIC FESTIVAL
30 E End Avenue
Suite 3A-3D
New York, NY 10028
Phone: 212-288-4261
Fax: 212-288-4261
e-mail: sevenars@aol.com
Officers:
President/Artistic Director: Robert W Schrade
VP/Executive Director: Rolande Y Schrade
Director: David F James
Director: Robelyn Schrade-James
Director: Randolph RA Schrade
Director: Rorianne C Schrade
Executive Director: Rolande Young Schrade
Management:
Executive Director: Rolande Young Schrade
Artistic Director: Robert W Schrade
Mission: To present music of the highest quality to the widest possible audience in an atmosphere of family warmth, acoustical perfection and serene beauty.

Utilizes: Collaborating Artists; Guest Accompanists; Guest Musical Directors; Multimedia; Original Music Scores
Founded: 1968
Specialized Field: Instrumental Music
Status: Professional; Nonprofit
Budget: $70,000-$80,000
Income Sources: Individual contributions; foundations; corporations & local cultural councils
Season: May to October in Worthington, Massachusetts
Performs At: Historic Academy/Concert Hall
Affiliations: Conservatories, universities, independent schools
Annual Attendance: 250+ at 7-8 events
Facility Category: Historic Academy
Type of Stage: Raised; Acoustic
Seating Capacity: 250 - 350
Year Built: 1800
Year Remodeled: 1976
Organization Type: Performing; Educational
Resident Groups: Schrade and James family pianists
Comments: May-October: c/o Schrade, Worthington, Massachusetts, 01098, phone (413-338-5854)

4777
SHANDELEE MUSIC FESTIVAL
36 E 74th Street
New York, NY 10021
Phone: 212-288-4152
Fax: 212-879-2462
e-mail: shanfest@aol.com
Web Site: www.shandelee.org
Officers:
Founding President: Daniel Stroup
VP: Stephen Johnson
Management:
Chairperson: Daniel Stroup
Executive Assistant: Joseph Kaczmarek
Artistic Director: Lana Ivanov
Technical Operations: Christopher Kennedy
Founded: 1993
Specialized Field: Classical
Performs At: Concert Hall; Sunset Concert Pavilion
Seating Capacity: 200
Year Built: 2001

4778
ST. PATRICK'S CATHEDRAL CHAMBER MUSIC SERIES
Saint Patrick's Cathedral
460 Madison Avenue
New York, NY 10022
Phone: 212-753-2261
Fax: 212-753-3925
e-mail: rmespc@aol.com
Management:
Manager: Monica Avitsur
Executive Director: Joseph Manzella
Artistic Director: Jennifer Pascual
Manager: Robert Evers
Founded: 1879
Specialized Field: Church
Status: Non-Profit, Professional
Paid Staff: 16
Paid Artists: 3
Budget: $10,000

4779
SUMMERGARDEN
The Museum of Modern Art
11 W 53rd Street
New York, NY 10019

Phone: 212-708-9400
Fax: 212-708-9889
e-mail: info@moma.org
Web Site: www.moma.org
Management:
President: Robert Menschel
Director: Glenn Lowry
Founded: 1929
Specialized Field: Museum; Art institution
Status: Non-Profit, Professional
Paid Staff: 600

4780
SYMPHONY SPACE
2537 Broadway
New York, NY 10025-6947
Phone: 212-864-1414
Fax: 212-932-3228
e-mail: info@symphonyspace.org
Web Site: www.symphonyspace.org
Officers:
Executive VP: Joanne Cossa
Management:
President: Isaiah Sheffer
Executive Director: Cynthia Elliott
Director Marketing: Elizabeth Vilmik
Managing Director: Peggy Wreen
Producer Music/Dance Program: Maren Bethelsen
Founded: 1978
Specialized Field: Series and Festivals; Instrumental Music; Vocal Music; Theatre; Youth; Dance
Status: Non-Profit, Professional
Paid Staff: 32
Facility Category: Theater
Rental Contact: Patricia Sinnott

4781
THIRD STREET MUSIC SCHOOL SETTLEMENT FACULTY ARTISTS SERIES
235 E 11th Street
New York, NY 10003
Phone: 212-777-3240
Fax: 212-477-1808
Management:
Community Affairs/Concerts Director: Beth Flusser
Budget: $10,000
Performs At: Mark's Park

4782
TRIBECA PERFORMING ARTS CENTER
199 Chambers Street
#S110C
New York, NY 10007
Phone: 212-220-1460
Fax: 212-732-2482
e-mail: boxoffice@tribecapac.org
Web Site: www.tribecapac.org
Management:
Marketing Director: John Malatesta
Executive Director: Linda Herring
Operations Director: Carol Cleveland
Program Director: Jeff Mousseau
Utilizes: Artists-in-Residence; Dance Companies; Soloists; Special Technical Talent; Theatre Companies
Founded: 1983
Budget: $60,000-150,000

4783
USDAN CENTER FOR THE CREATIVE & PERFORMING ARTS: FESTIVAL CONCERTS
420 E 79th Street
New York, NY 10021
Phone: 212-772-6060
Web Site: www.usdan.com
Management:
President: Mrs James A Block
Executive Director: Dale Lewis
Artistic Director: Dennis Nahat
Assistant Director: Allison Bitz

4784
WASHINGTON SQUARE MUSIC FESTIVAL
Village Station
PO Box 1066
New York, NY 10014-0706
Phone: 917-855-4205
e-mail: pacrasia@aol.com
Web Site: www.washingtonsquaremusicfestival.org
Officers:
Chairman: Liama Hood
Management:
Executive Director: Peggy Friedman
Artistic Director: Lutz Rath
Music Director: Jean Lyman Geotz
Mission: To present free classical and classical jazz and salsa concerts in Washington Square Park in the summer, for the largest possible audiences. Outreach activities announce the series to as large and diverse asegment of the metropolitan population as possible.
Founded: 1953
Specialized Field: Series & Festivals; Classical Chamber; Orchestra music
Status: Non-Profit, Professional
Paid Staff: 3
Volunteer Staff: 15
Paid Artists: 50
Budget: $55,000
Income Sources: Public and Private Funds; NYSCA; NYC Cultural Affairs; Trust Fund through 802
Affiliations: Whashington Square Association
Annual Attendance: 6,000
Facility Category: Park

4785
WASHINGTON SQUARE CONTEMPORARY MUSIC SERIES
NYU Music Department Fas
268 Waverly Building
New York, NY 10003-6789
Phone: 212-998-8300
Fax: 212-995-4147
e-mail: fennellyBL@aol.com
Web Site: www.washingtonsquaremusic.org
Management:
Co-Director: Brian Fennelly
Budget: $10,000-20,000
Performs At: Merkin Hall

4786
WORLD FINANCIAL CENTER ARTS & EVENTS PROGRAM
200 Liberty Street
Lobby Level
New York, NY 10281
Phone: 212-945-2600
Fax: 212-945-3392
e-mail: info@worldfinancialcenter.com
Web Site: www.worldfinancialcenter.com
Management:
Artistic Director and VP: Melissa Coley
Founded: 1988
Budget: $150,000-400,000
Performs At: World Financial Center Winter Garden & Plaza

4787
WORLD MUSIC INSTITUTE
49 W 27th Street
#930
New York, NY 10001-6396
Phone: 212-545-7536
Fax: 212-889-2771
e-mail: wmi@heartheworld.org
Web Site: www.heartheworld.org
Management:
Executive Director: Robert Browning
Founded: 1985
Specialized Field: Series & Festivals: Ethnic Performances
Status: Non-Profit, Professional
Paid Staff: 10
Budget: $150,000-400,000
Performs At: Washington Square Church; Sylvia & Danny Kaye Playhouse

4788
YOUNG CONCERT ARTISTS SERIES
250 W 57th Street
New York, NY 10019
Phone: 212-307-6655
Fax: 212-581-8894
e-mail: yca@yca.org
Web Site: www.yca.org
Management:
Director: Susan Wadsworth
Public Relations: Karen Karush
Budget: $60,000-150,000
Performs At: Kaufmann Concert Hall; Terrace Theatre; Kennedy Center

4789
GREECE PERFORMING ARTS SOCIETY SERIES
PO Box 300
North Greece, NY 14515
Phone: 716-227-2619
Officers:
President: Rick Stein
Treasurer: William Coons
Secretary: Carol Coons
Management:
Program Coordinator: William Coons
Mission: To foster the development, in the community of Greece, of an appreciation for artistic and cultural activities, GPAS sponsors the Greece Symphony Orchestra, Greece Community Orchestra and Greece Choral Society & GPAS Summer Theatre.
Founded: 1972
Specialized Field: Vocal Music; Instrumental Music; Theatre
Status: Nonprofit
Organization Type: Sponsoring

4790
CHENANGO COUNTY COUNCIL FOR THE ARTS
27 W Main Street
Norwich, NY 13815
Phone: 607-336-2787
Fax: 607-336-1893
e-mail: info@chenangoarts.org
Web Site: www.chenangoarts.org
Management:
Executive Director: Victoria Kappel
Specialized Field: Series & Festivals; Vocal Music; Theatre; Youth; Dance; Ethnic Performances
Status: Non-Profit, Professional
Paid Staff: 7
Budget: $10,000-20,000

4791
NYACK COLLEGE PROGRAM OF CULTURAL EVENTS
Nyack College
1 S Boulevard
Nyack, NY 10960
Phone: 845-358-1710
Fax: 845-358-1718
Budget: $10,000
Performs At: Pardington Hall; Olson Auditorium

4792
OGDENSBURG COMMAND PERFORMANCES
1100 State Street
Ogdensburg, NY 13669
Phone: 315-393-2625
Fax: 315-393-2625
e-mail: manny@gisco.net
Management:
Administrative Coordinator: Sally Palao

4793
ARTS CENTER/OLD FORGE
Route 28
PO Box 1144
Old Forge, NY 13420
Phone: 315-369-6411
Fax: 315-369-2431
e-mail: info@artcenteroldforge.org
Web Site: www.artcenteroldforge.org
Management:
President: Gary Lee
Executive Director: Debra Jones
Artistic Director: Julie Tabbitas
Utilizes: Actors; Educators; Fine Artists; Guest Accompanists; Guest Instructors; Instructors; Multimedia; Selected Students; Special Technical Talent; Touring Companies
Founded: 1952
Specialized Field: Series & Festivals: Exhibition
Status: Non-Profit, Professional
Paid Staff: 6
Volunteer Staff: 6
Paid Artists: 8
Budget: $250,000-300,000
Income Sources: Private Donations; Membership; State & Local Government
Annual Attendance: 30,000
Facility Category: Community Arts Center
Stage Dimensions: varies
Seating Capacity: 150

4794

FRIENDS OF GOOD MUSIC

PO Box 222
Olean, NY 14760
Phone: 716-373-1776
Fax: 716-373-2662
Budget: $35,000-60,000

4795

FESTIVAL OF THE ARTS

248 Main Street
Upper Catskill Community Council of the Arts
Oneonta, NY 13820
Phone: 607-432-2070
Fax: 607-431-9319
Management:
    Director: Pamela Cooley
Founded: 1969
Specialized Field: Dance; Vocal Music; Instrumental
Music; Theatre; Festivals
Status: Professional; Nonprofit
Income Sources: State University of New
York-Oneonta
Performs At: Slade Auditorium; Anderson Theater
Organization Type: Educational; Sponsoring

4796

HARTWICK COLLEGE FOREMAN CREATIVE & PERFORMING ARTS SERIES

Office of Events Planning
Shineman Chapel
Oneonta, NY 13820
Phone: 607-431-4034
Fax: 607-431-4043
e-mail: markusonc@hartwick.edu
Web Site: www.hartwick.edu
Management:
    Event Planning/Stewardship Director: Cira P
    Markuson
Budget: $20,000-35,000
Performs At: Slade Theatre

4797

UPPER CATSKILL COMMUNITY COUNCIL OF THE ARTS

11 Ford Avenue
Oneonta, NY 13820
Phone: 607-432-2070
Fax: 607-431-9319
e-mail: director@uccca.com
Officers:
    President: Stan Rabbiner
Management:
    Executive Director: Kathleen Frascatore
Mission: Sponsoring community performances and
coordinating secondary and elementary school
performances.
Founded: 1970
Specialized Field: Non-Profit Arts
Status: Non-Profit, Professional
Paid Staff: 4
Paid Artists: 100
Organization Type: Educational; Sponsoring

4798

OSWEGO HARBOR FESTIVALS

41 Lake Street
Oswego, NY 13126
Phone: 315-343-6858
Fax: 315-343-7390
e-mail: info@oswegoharborfest.com
Web Site: www.oswegoharborfest.com

Management:
    Executive Director: Tom Van Schaack
    Business Manager: Barbara Manwaring
Mission: To promote and increased public awareness
of, and civic pride in, the unique history and geography
as well as the varied cultural and recreational to be
found in the City of Oswego and its waterfront, the
County of Oswego, the Oswego River and the
southeastern shore of Lake Ontario. This will include,
but not be limited to, providing a series of events or
activities that highlight the quality in this area.
Founded: 1988
Specialized Field: Series & Festivals; Instrumental
Music; Vocal Music; Theatre; Youth; Dance; Ethnic
Performances
Status: Non-Profit, Professional
Paid Staff: 4
Budget: $800,000
Income Sources: Sponsorships; Memberships; Grants
Affiliations: IFEA, New York Festival & Events
Association
Annual Attendance: 200,000
Facility Category: Outdoor Lawn

4799

PAWLING CONCERT SERIES

700 Route 22
Pawling, NY 12564
Phone: 845-855-3100
Fax: 845-855-3816
e-mail: nreade@trinitypawling.org
Web Site: www.pawlingconcertseries.org
Officers:
    President: Ned Reade
Management:
    Artistic Director: Keir Donaldson
Mission: To bring excellent live jazz, classical, folk and
ethnic music to the Eastern Dutchess, Putnam and
Westchester counties in New York.
Utilizes: Multimedia; Original Music Scores
Founded: 1973
Specialized Field: Series & Festivals; Instrumental
Music; Vocal Music
Status: Non-Profit, Professional
Paid Staff: 1
Volunteer Staff: 13
Non-paid Artists: 24
Budget: $53,000
Income Sources: Subscriptions; Private & Corporate
Grants
Performs At: Gardner Theatre, All Saints Chapel,
McGraw Pavillion
Affiliations: Trinity Pawling School
Annual Attendance: 1,200
Facility Category: Theatre
Type of Stage: Procenium
Stage Dimensions: 26X26
Seating Capacity: 200; 250; 35
Year Built: 2004
Cost: $1.3 Million
Organization Type: Sponsoring; Presenting

4800

CLASSICAL FRONTIERS

446 Pelhamdale Avenue
Pelham, NY 10803
Phone: 914-738-6537
Budget: $10,000

4801

YATES PERFORMING ARTS SERIES

PO Box 503
Penn Yan, NY 14527
Phone: 315-536-2095

Management:
    President: Sylvia Eisenhart
Mission: To provide entertainment for Yates County
residents.
Founded: 1972
Specialized Field: Series & Festivals: Vocal Music &
Instrumental Music concerts
Status: Non-Profit, Non-Professional
Performs At: Penn Yan Academy
Organization Type: Performing; Touring

4802

MUSICAL CONCERTS AT THE BURLINGHAM INN

29 Vinegar Hill Road
Pine Bush, NY 12566
Phone: 845-744-8499
Fax: 845-744-8936
e-mail: BIConcerts@aol.com
Web Site: www.burlinghaminn.com/concerts
Management:
    Director: Jonathan Bley
Budget: $10,000
Performs At: Burlingham Inn Hall

4803

MUSIC AT PORT MILFORD

288 Washington Avenue
Pleasantville, NY 10570
Phone: 914-769-9046
e-mail: director@mpmcamp.org
Web Site: www.mpmcamp.org
Management:
    Director: Meg Hill
Founded: 1987
Specialized Field: Series & Festivals; Instrumental
Music; Vocal Music; Youth
Status: Non-Profit, Professional
Paid Staff: 9
Paid Artists: 30

4804

SUMMIT MUSIC FESTIVAL

192 Edgewood Avenue
Pleasantville, NY 10570
Phone: 914-769-4111
Fax: 914-769-4111
e-mail: summitmusic2000@aol.com
Management:
    Executive Director: David Krieger
    Artistic Director: Efrem Breskin
    Administrator: Miriam Derivan
Mission: To provide an enriching musical experience
for area students and exposure to the finest in solo,
chamber, and orchestra performances.
Founded: 1991
Specialized Field: Classical Instrumental Music
Instruction and Performance for Pre - Professional High
School and College Age Students
Paid Staff: 7
Paid Artists: 20

4805

COMMUNITY PERFORMANCE SERIES

Snell Music Theatre
Bishop Hall, SUNY
Potsdam, NY 13676
Phone: 315-267-2411
Fax: 315-267-2869
e-mail: olsenka@potsdam.edu
Web Site: www.potsdam.edu/cps
Management:
    Executive Director: Kathy Olsen
    Managing Director: Amy Slack

Utilizes: Actors; Artists-in-Residence; Collaborating Artists; Collaborations; Dance Companies; Dancers; Guest Accompanists; Guest Artists; Guest Choreographers; Guest Directors; Guest Instructors; Guest Musical Directors; Guest Musicians; Lyricists; Multimedia; Original Music Scores; Singers; Theatre Companies
Founded: 1986
Specialized Field: Series & Festivals: Instrumental Music
Status: Non-Profit, Professional
Paid Staff: 4
Paid Artists: 50
Non-paid Artists: 20
Budget: $300,000
Performs At: Hosmer Concert Hall; Snell Music Theater; MaxcyHall
Annual Attendance: 7,000
Facility Category: Concert Hall
Stage Dimensions: 40 x 40
Seating Capacity: 1,200
Year Built: 1971
Year Remodeled: 2000

4806
CRANE SCHOOL OF MUSIC ANNUAL SPRING FESTIVAL OF THE ARTS

State University of NY at Potsdam
Potsdam, NY 13676
Phone: 315-267-2412
Fax: 315-267-2413
e-mail: olsenka@potsdam.edu
Web Site: www.potsdam.edu/crane
Management:
　　Executive Director: Kathleen Olsen
Founded: 1986
Specialized Field: Series & Festivals: Arts Presentation
Status: Non-Profit, Professional
Paid Staff: 4
Paid Artists: 12

4807
CLEARWATER'S GREAT HUDSON RIVER REVIVAL

112 Little Market Street
Poughkeepsie, NY 12601
Phone: 845-454-7673
e-mail: office@clearwater.org
Web Site: www.clearwater.org
Management:
　　Executive Director: Andy Mele
　　Director: Manna Jo Greene

4808
EASTMAN SCHOOL OF MUSIC

26 Gibbs Street
Rochester, NY 14604
Phone: 585-274-1110
Fax: 585-274-1073
e-mail: agreen@esm.rochester.edu
Management:
　　Director of Concert Operations: Andrew Green
Budget: $60,000-150,000
Performs At: Kilbourn Hall; Eastman Theatre

4809
NAZARETH COLLEGE ARTS CENTER SERIES

4245 E Avenue
Rochester, NY 14618-3090

Phone: 716-389-2175
Fax: 716-389-2182
e-mail: nlpeet@naz.edu
Officers:
　　Chairman: Fred E Strauss
　　President of the College: Dr. Rose Marie Beston
Management:
　　School Program Coordinator: Nancy Peet
　　Director: Dr David M Ferrell
　　Assistant Director: Terry Meyer
Mission: To present a subscription series of professional performing artists and organizations for the benefit of Nazareth students and the community of Rochester.
Founded: 1967
Specialized Field: Dance; Vocal Music; Instrumental Music; Theatre
Status: Professional; Nonprofit
Budget: $150,000-400,000
Income Sources: Association of Performing Arts Presenters
Performs At: Nazareth College Arts Center
Organization Type: Performing; Sponsoring

4810
ROBERTS WESLEYAN COLLEGE

Roberts Cultural Life Center
2301 Westside Drive
Rochester, NY 14624
Phone: 585-594-6812
Fax: 585-594-6059
e-mail: dunndr@roberts.edu
Web Site: www.rwc.edu
Management:
　　President: John Martin
　　Managing Director: Jim Cughbert
Founded: 1866
Specialized Field: Series and Festivals; Instrumental Music; Vocal Music; Theatre; Youth
Status: Non-Profit, Professional
Paid Staff: 6
Volunteer Staff: 45
Non-paid Artists: 155
Budget: $35,000-60,000
Income Sources: Ticket Sales
Performs At: Hale Auditorium
Annual Attendance: 45,000
Facility Category: Performing Arts
Type of Stage: Proscenium
Stage Dimensions: 50'x30'x25'
Seating Capacity: 1000
Year Built: 1996
Cost: $8 Million
Rental Contact: David Dunn

4811
ROCHESTER PHILHARMONIC ORCHESTRA

108 East Avenue
Rochester, NY 14604
Phone: 585-454-7311
Fax: 585-423-2256
e-mail: rpo@rpo.org
Web Site: www.rpo.org
Officers:
　　President/CEO: Rick Nowlin
Management:
　　Artistic Operations Director: Andrew Cassano
Specialized Field: Series and Festivals; Instrumental Music; Vocal Music; Youth
Status: Non-profit, Professional

4812
MUSIC FROM SALEM

HUBBARD HALL
25 East Main Street
Salem, NY 12816
Phone: 518-638-5594
e-mail: hubbardhall@juno.com
Web Site: www.musicfromsalem.org
Management:
　　Artistic Director: Lila Brown
Mission: To provide a summer home to international chamber musicians.
Founded: 1985
Specialized Field: Vocal Music; Instrumental Music
Status: Professional
Performs At: Hubbard Hall
Organization Type: Performing; Resident

4813
HILL & HOLLOW MUSIC

Weatherwatch Farm
550 #37 Road
Saranac, NY 12981
Phone: 518-293-7613
Fax: 518-293-7634
e-mail: info@hillandhollowmusic.com
Web Site: www.hillandhollowmusic.com
Management:
　　President: J Kellum Smith Jr
　　Executive Director: Angela Brown
　　Co-Director: Angela Brown
Mission: To promote and present classical chamber music in a rural area.
Utilizes: Artists-in-Residence; Grant Writers; Guest Directors; Guest Instructors; Multimedia; Singers
Founded: 1995
Specialized Field: Series & Festivals; Instrumental Music; Vocal Music; Chamber Music
Status: Non-Profit, Professional
Volunteer Staff: 2
Paid Artists: 20
Budget: $100,000
Income Sources: Box office, Grants, Private contributions
Performs At: Church in the Hollow; Highschool Auditorium
Affiliations: Chamber Music America; Country Dance & Song Society
Facility Category: Rural Venues
Seating Capacity: 220
Year Built: 1862

4814
ADIRONDACK FESTIVAL OF AMERICAN MUSIC

Gregg Smith Singers
PO Box 562
Saranac Lake, NY 12983
Phone: 518-891-1057
Fax: 518-891-1057
Management:
　　Artistic Director: Gregg Smith
　　Director Vocal Workshop: Linda Ferriera
Mission: To offer a program including American music of the present and past, and some traditional repertoire.
Specialized Field: Vocal Music; Instrumental Music; Choral
Status: Professional; Nonprofit
Performs At: Town Hall
Organization Type: Performing; Educational

4815

FREIHOFER'S JAZZ FESTIVAL AT THE SARATOGA PERFORMING ARTS CENTER

Saratoga Performing Arts Center
Saratoga Springs, NY 12866
Phone: 518-584-9330
Fax: 518-584-0809
e-mail: info@spac.org
Web Site: www.spac.org
Management:
    President: Herbert Chesbrough
Founded: 1966
Specialized Field: Series & Festivals: Classical Music
Status: Non-Profit, Non-Professional
Paid Staff: 13

4816

SKIDMORE MUSIC DEPARTMENT SERIES

Skidmore College
815 N Broadway
Saratoga Springs, NY 12866
Phone: 518-580-5320
Fax: 518-580-5340
e-mail: gthompso@skidmore.edu
Web Site: www.skidmore.edu
Officers:
    Chair: Thomas Denny
    President: Phil Glotzbach
Founded: 1922
Specialized Field: Series & Festivals; Instrumental Music; Vocal Music; Dance; Ethnic Performances
Status: Non-Profit, Professional
Paid Staff: 25
Budget: $35,000-60,000
Performs At: Filene Recital Hall

4817

SCHENECTADY MUSEUM: UNION COLLEGE CONCERT SERIES

857 Northumberland Drive
Schenectady, NY 12309
Phone: 518-372-3651
Officers:
    Chairman: Dr. Daniel Berkenblit
Budget: $35,000-60,000
Performs At: Union College Memorial Chapel

4818

SKANEATELES FESTIVAL

97 E Genesee Street
Skaneateles, NY 13152
Phone: 315-685-7418
Fax: 315-685-4802
e-mail: music@scanfest.org
Web Site: www.skanfest.org
Management:
    President: Lynn Cleary
    Executive Director: Susan Mark
    Artistic Director: Diane Walsh
    VP: Karen Veverka
Mission: Bringing world-class musicians to this lakeside community for five weeks of chamber music, chamber orchestra and children's concerts in the late summer.
Founded: 1980
Specialized Field: Festivals
Status: Professional; Nonprofit
Organization Type: Performing; Educational

4819

SPENCERTOWN ACADEMY PERFORMING SERIES

790 Route 203
Box 80
Spencertown, NY 12165
Phone: 518-392-3693
Fax: 518-392-8694
e-mail: spencertown@taconic.net
Web Site: www.spencertown.org
Officers:
    President: Roberta Reynes
    Vice President: Ben Puccio
    Secretary: Claire Verenezi
    Treasurer: Jan Steinbrenner
Management:
    President: Kate Cohen
    Executive Director: Judy Staber
    Associate Director: Susan Davis
Mission: To preserve the historic building and provide a welcoming space for all the arts.
Founded: 1972
Specialized Field: Series & Festivals; Classical; Traditional; Spoken Word; Film; Chamber Theatre Production Music series
Status: Non-Profit, Professional
Paid Staff: 3
Volunteer Staff: 10+
Paid Artists: 40
Non-paid Artists: 5
Budget: $100,000
Income Sources: Private Funds; Ticket Sales; Art Sales
Annual Attendance: 5,000
Facility Category: Performance & Visual Arts Center
Type of Stage: Proscenium
Seating Capacity: 130
Year Built: 1867
Year Remodeled: 1999

4820

STERLING RENAISSANCE FESTIVAL

15385 Farden Road
Sterling, NY 13156
Phone: 315-947-5783
Fax: 315-947-6905
Toll-free: 800-879-4446
e-mail: ad@sterlingfestival.com
Web Site: www.sterlingfestival.com
Officers:
    President: Alisa Cook
    VP: John Kissler
    Secretary: Phil Holding
    Treasurer: Marylee Pangman
Management:
    Office Manager and Sales Director: Kelli Raymond
Mission: To present interactive and staged performances.
Paid Staff: 10
Paid Artists: 80
Season: June - August
Annual Attendance: 100,000
Facility Category: Outdoor
Type of Stage: 8 Stages
Year Built: 1977

4821

STATE UNIVERSITY OF NEW YORK AT STONY BROOK CONCERT SERIES

Stony Brook
Stony Brook, NY 11794
Phone: 631-632-7235
Fax: 531-632-7354
e-mail: AInkles@stallercenter.com
Web Site: www.stallercenter.com
Management:
    Director: Alan Inkles
Budget: $150,000-400,000
Performs At: Staller Center for the Arts; Three Black Box Theatres

4822

CIVIC MORNING MUSICALS

301 Apple Street
Syracuse, NY 13204-2107
Phone: 315-422-0553
Management:
    Public Relations Coordinator: Irene Boheme
Budget: $10,000
Performs At: Hosmer Auditorium; Everson Museum of Art

4823

CULTURAL RESOURCES COUNCIL OF SYRACUSE

411 Montgomery Street
Syracuse, NY 13202
Phone: 315-435-2155
Fax: 315-435-2160
Web Site: www.cspot.org
Management:
    Executive Director: Leo Crandall
Mission: Promote cultural development in Central NY; identify, coordinate, promote, and present performing arts for a 10-county area in Cedntral New York. Education and trainging; technical assistance.
Utilizes: Singers
Founded: 1968
Specialized Field: Series & Festivals; Theatre; Youth; Ethnic Performances; Dance; Theatre; Festivals; Music; Visual Advocacy; Training; Education
Status: Non-Profit, Non-Professional
Paid Staff: 8
Paid Artists: 150
Income Sources: International Society of Performing Arts Administrators
Performs At: Civic Center of Onondaga County
Organization Type: Performing

4824

SYRACUSE SOCIETY FOR NEW MUSIC

312 Crawford Avenue
Syracuse, NY 13224
Phone: 315-446-5733
e-mail: npilgrim@aol.com
Web Site: www.societyfornewmusic.org
Management:
    President: Edward Green
    Program Advisor: Neva Pilgrim
Founded: 1971
Specialized Field: Series & Festivals: Contemproray & Classical Music
Status: Non-Profit, Professional
Paid Artists: 25
Budget: $20,000-35,000
Performs At: Everson Museum; Carrier Theatre
Annual Attendance: 13,000

4825

TICONDEROGA FESTIVAL GUILD

124 Montclaim Street
PO Box 125
Ticonderoga, NY 12883

Phone: 518-585-6716
Fax: 518-543-6654
e-mail: tfguild@capital.net
Management:
    Executive Director: Cathie Burdick
Mission: To provide cultural events for a rural area.
Founded: 1980
Specialized Field: Festivals
Status: Nonprofit
Budget: $40,000
Income Sources: Grants; Donations; Tickets
Annual Attendance: 3500
Type of Stage: Wood
Stage Dimensions: 20'x30'
Seating Capacity: 200
Organization Type: Performing

4826
HUDSON VALLEY COMMUNITY COLLEGE CULTURAL AFFAIRS PROGRAM

80 Vandenburgh Avenue
Troy, NY 12180
Phone: 518-629-8073
e-mail: boggesar@hvcc.edu
Management:
    Community Relations Director: Sarah Boggess
Budget: $10,000
Performs At: Maureen Stapleton Theatre

4827
A GOOD OLD SUMMER TIME'S GENESEE STREET FESTIVAL

520 Seneca Street
Utica, NY 13502
Phone: 315-733-6976
Fax: 315-724-3177
Web Site: www.goodoldsummertime.org
Officers:
    President: Mark Minasi

4828
MOHAWK VALLEY COMMUNITY COLLEGE CULTURAL SERIES

1101 Sherman Drive
Utica, NY 13501
Phone: 315-731-5722
Fax: 315-792-5678
e-mail: wdustin@mvcc.edu
Web Site: www.mvcc.edu/culture
Management:
    Events Administrator: Bill Dustin,
    wdustin@mvcc.edu
Founded: 2000
Specialized Field: Series & Festivals; Plays; Lectures; Music; Instrumental; Vocal; Theatre; Youth; Events; Dance; Films
Status: Non-Profit, Non-Professional
Paid Staff: 5
Paid Artists: 1
Budget: $10,000

4829
MUNSON-WILLIAMS-PROCTOR ARTS INSTITUTE

310 Genesee Street
Utica, NY 13502-4799
Phone: 315-797-0000
Fax: 315-797-5608
Toll-free: 800-754-0797
e-mail: gtrudeau@mwpi.edu
Web Site: www.mwpai.edu
Management:

President: Milton Bloch
Artistic Director: Paul Schwizer
Director Performing Arts: Robert Mortis
Mission: To provide exemplary programs and educational opportunites in the performing and cinematic arts, setting a national standard for artistic achievement.
Utilizes: Artists-in-Residence; Choreographers; Curators; Dance Companies; Dancers; Filmmakers; Fine Artists; Guest Accompanists; Guest Artists; Guest Choreographers; Guest Directors; Guest Musical Directors; Guest Musicians; Guest Soloists; High School Drama; Instructors; Multimedia; Original Music Scores; Selected Students; Sign Language Translators; Singers; Theatre Companies; Touring Companies
Founded: 1932
Specialized Field: Series & Festivals: Exhibitions of Paintings & Sculptures
Status: Non-Profit, Professional
Paid Staff: 300
Volunteer Staff: 30
Paid Artists: 270
Budget: $919,000 (performing arts)
Income Sources: Ticket sales; grants; sponsorships; program advertising; endowment
Performs At: Stanley Performing Arts Center
Affiliations: International Society of Performing Arts Administrators, INTIX, American Symphony Orchestra League, Wellinhall/Hamilton Colletge
Annual Attendance: 45,550
Facility Category: Arts center
Type of Stage: Proscenium, thrust,museum courtyad
Seating Capacity: 2,960, 271, 500
Year Built: 1960
Cost: 10 Million
Organization Type: Performing; Educational; Sponsoring

4830
WESTBURY MUSIC FAIR

960 Brush Hollow Road
Westbury, NY 11590
Phone: 516-247-5212
Fax: 516-333-7991
e-mail: westburyreplies@clearchannel.com
Web Site: www.musicfair.com
Management:
    Executive VP: Jason Stone
    Theatre Manager: John Blenn
    Marketing Director: Dan Kellachan
    Publicist: Laura Nuzzolo
    Group Sales Manager: Ed Denning
Mission: To offer the best entertainment of all kinds to metropolitan New York.
Utilizes: Singers
Founded: 1956
Specialized Field: Dance; Vocal Music; Instrumental Music; Theater
Status: Professional; Commercial
Season: year-round
Facility Category: Year-round Indoor
Type of Stage: In the round
Seating Capacity: 2,742
Year Built: 1956
Year Remodeled: 1998
Rental Contact: 516-333-2101 Ed Denning
Organization Type: Performing

4831
ARTS COUNCIL FOR THE NORTHERN ADIRONDACKS

PO Box 187
Westport, NY 12993

Phone: 518-962-8778
Fax: 518-962-8797
Toll-free: 800-661-4704
e-mail: artsco@westelcom.com
Web Site: www.artsnorth.org
Management:
    President: Caroline Rubino
Founded: 1984
Specialized Field: Art Services
Status: Non-Profit, Non-Professional
Paid Staff: 2
Budget: $10,000-20,000

4832
MAVERICK CONCERTS

Maverick Road
PO Box 102
Woodstock, NY 12498
Phone: 914-338-3074
Fax: 914-338-3074
e-mail: musicmavrk@aol.com
Web Site: www.beekman.net/maverickconcerts
Management:
    Music Director: Vincent Wagner
Mission: To provide Sunday afternoon chamber music concerts in summer.
Budget: $60,000-150,000

North Carolina

4833
ASHEVILLE CHAMBER MUSIC SERIES

25 Brook Forest Drive
Arden, NC 28704
Phone: 828-684-5976
Web Site: www.main.nc.us/ashevillechambermusic/
Officers:
    President: Dr. Harold Rotman
    VP: Philip Walker
    Secretary: Perien Gray
    Treasurer: J. H. Wynn
Management:
    Program Director: Bill van der Hoeven
Mission: To provide chamber music concerts.
Founded: 1952
Specialized Field: Instrumental Music
Status: Non-Professional; Nonprofit
Budget: $10,000-20,000
Income Sources: Chamber Music America
Organization Type: Performing

4834
UNIVERSITY OF NORTH CAROLINA AT ASHEVILLE CULTURAL & SPECIAL EVENTS

Highsmith Center
1 University Heights CPO2150
Asheville, NC 28804
Phone: 828-232-5000
Fax: 828-251-6614
e-mail: bhalton@unca.edu
Web Site: www.unca.edu/culturalarts
Management:
    Director Office Of Cultural Events: Barbara
    Halton-Subkis
Utilizes: Artists-in-Residence; Choreographers; Collaborations; Dance Companies; Dancers; Guest Accompanists; Guest Choreographers; Guest Ensembles; Guest Musical Directors; Guest Musicians; Guest Teachers; Instructors; Lyricists; Multi

Collaborations; Multimedia; Original Music Scores; Playwrights; Sign Language Translators; Singers; Soloists; Special Technical Talent; Theatre Companies
Founded: 1982
Status: Non-Profit, Professional
Paid Staff: 2
Budget: $60,000-150,000
Performs At: Lipinsky Auditorium; Thomas Wolfe Auditorium; Diana Wortham Theatre
Annual Attendance: 7,000+
Facility Category: Campus Auditorium
Type of Stage: Proscenium
Seating Capacity: 600

4835
BEAUFORT COUNTY COMMUNITY CONCERTS ASSOCIATION
1117 Whealton Point Road
Aurora, NC 27806
Phone: 252-322-5259
Officers:
President: Helen Sommerkamp
Budget: $20,000-35,000

4836
LEES-MCRAE COLLEGE FORUM
PO Box 649
Banner Elk, NC 28604
Phone: 828-898-8748
Fax: 828-898-8814
Toll-free: 800-280-4562
e-mail: ramsey@imc.edu
Web Site: www.lmc.edu
Officers:
President: Ed Hardin
Vice President: Dick Collins
Treasurer: Paul Weber
Management:
President of Forum: Ed Hardin
President of College: Earl Robinson
Special Events Coordinator: Sandy M Ramsey
Mission: To bring a stimulating series of cultural events to the area.
Utilizes: Artists-in-Residence; Dance Companies; Dancers; Instructors; Multimedia; Original Music Scores; Sign Language Translators; Singers
Founded: 1979
Specialized Field: Series & Festivals: Performing Arts
Status: Non-Profit, Professional
Paid Staff: 2
Volunteer Staff: 4
Paid Artists: 7
Budget: $40,000-45,000
Income Sources: Donations
Performs At: Hayes Auditorium
Annual Attendance: 6500
Facility Category: Concert hall/performance center
Seating Capacity: 750

4837
GARDNER-WEBB UNIVERSITY DISTINGUISHED ARTIST SERIES
Box 7298
Fine Arts Department
Boiling Springs, NC 28017
Phone: 704-406-3937
Fax: 704-406-3920
e-mail: psparti@gardner-webb.edu
Officers:
Fine Arts Department Chairman: Dr. Patricia Sparti
Budget: $10,000-20,000
Performs At: Hamrick Hall Auditorium; Dover theatre

4838
AN APPALACHIAN SUMMER FESTIVAL
Appalachian State University
Office of Arts & Cultural Programs
PO Box 32045
Boone, NC 28608-2045
Phone: 828-262-6084
Fax: 828-262-2848
Toll-free: 800-841-2787
e-mail: boxoffice@appstate.edu
Web Site: ww.appsummer.org
Management:
Director: Denise Ringler
Mission: To enrich, expand and enhance the cultural climate of Appalachian State University and the Regional Community through the ongoing presentation of intellecutally and aesthetically challenging programs which may not otherwise be available.
Founded: 1983
Specialized Field: Multi-Disciplinary;(Music; Dance; Theatre; Visual Arts)
Paid Staff: 11
Paid Artists: 30
Annual Attendance: 26,000
Facility Category: Auditorium
Seating Capacity: 1700

4839
APPALACHIAN STATE UNIVERSITY PERFORMING ARTS & FORUM SERIES
Appalachian State University
PO Box 32045
Boone, NC 28608-2045
Phone: 828-262-6084
Fax: 828-262-2848
e-mail: mixterhp@appstate.edu
Web Site: www.oca.appstate.edu/
Management:
Director: Perry Mixter
Budget: $150,000-400,000
Performs At: Farthing Auditorium; Rosen Concert Hall; Valborg Theatre

4840
HORN IN THE WEST
PO Box 295
Boone, NC 28607
Phone: 828-264-2120
Fax: 828-264-4529
e-mail: smalling@boone.net
Web Site: www.boonenc.org/saha
Management:
General Manager/Museum Director: Curtis Smalling
Assistant General Manager: Debbie Grant
Mission: To bring the past to life, with emphasis on the Revolutionary War and the struggle between settlers and Native Americans.
Founded: 1952
Specialized Field: Dance; Vocal Music; Theater; Festivals
Status: Professional; Nonprofit
Income Sources: Southern Appalachian Historical Association
Season: June - Ausust
Performs At: Horn In The West
Organization Type: Performing; Educational

4841
BREVARD MUSIC FESTIVAL
1000 Probart Street
PO Box 312
Brevard, NC 28712
Phone: 828-862-2100
Fax: 828-884-2036
e-mail: brevardmusic@citcom.net
Web Site: www.brevardmusic.org
Management:
President: John Kampler
Artistic Director: David Effron
Founded: 1936
Specialized Field: Series & Festivals; Instrumental Music; Vocal Music; Theatre; Youth; Dance; Ethnic Performances; Music
Status: Non-Profit, Non-Professional
Paid Staff: 14
Paid Artists: 25
Income Sources: Ticket Sales; Tuition; Donation
Performs At: Concert Hall
Annual Attendance: 70,000
Facility Category: Covered, Open-Sided Auditorium
Seating Capacity: 1,800
Year Built: 1965
Year Remodeled: 1998

4842
CAMPBELL UNIVERSITY COMMUNITY CONCERT SERIES
Music Department
PO Box 70, Campbell University
Buies Creek, NC 27506
Phone: 910-931-4996
Fax: 910-893-1515
Toll-free: 800-334-4111
e-mail: wilson@mailcenter.cambell.edu
Management:
Director: Charles D Wilson
Budget: $10,000-20,000
Performs At: Scott Concert Hall

4843
CAROLINA UNION PERFORMING ARTS SERIES
Carolina Union
201 Student Union Building
Chapel Hill, NC 27599-5210
Phone: 919-966-3120
Fax: 919-962-3719
e-mail: lused@email.unc.edu
Web Site: carolinaunion.unc.edu
Management:
Director: Don Luse
Production Services Ass't Director: Michael Johnson
Budget: $150,000-400,000
Performs At: Memorial Hall university of North Carolina
Annual Attendance: 10,000

4844
CAROLINAS CONCERT ASSOCIATION
PO Box 11356
Charlotte, NC 28220
Phone: 704-527-6680
Fax: 704-527-1846
e-mail: bratton@carolinasconcert.com
Web Site: www.carolinasconcert.com
Management:
President: Richard Grove
Executive Director: Ron Law
Booking Director: John Whitaker
Utilizes: Dance Companies; Fine Artists; Multimedia; Original Music Scores
Founded: 1930
Specialized Field: Series & Festivals; Instrumental Music; Orchestra
Status: Non-Profit, Professional

Paid Staff: 3
Budget: $150,000-400,000
Performs At: North Carolina Blumenthal Performing Arts Center

4845
CHARLOTTE CENTER CITY PARTNERS
128 S Tyron Street
Suite 1960
Charlotte, NC 28202
Phone: 704-332-2227
Fax: 704-342-1233
e-mail: rkrumbine@charlottecentercity.org
Web Site: www.charlottecentercity.org
Management:
    President: Tim Newnan
    VP Events: Rovbert Krumbine
Founded: 1979
Specialized Field: Downtown Development
Status: Non-Profit, Non-Professional
Paid Staff: 12

4846
QUEENS UNIVERSITY: QUEENS FRIENDS OF MUSIC CHAMBER SERIES
1900 Selwyn Avenue
Charlotte, NC 28274
Phone: 704-337-2204
Fax: 704-337-2356
e-mail: deanjm@queens.edu
Web Site: www.queens.edu/alumni/friends/music.asp
Management:
    Artistic Director: Paul Nitsch
Utilizes: Artists-in-Residence; Educators; Guest Musical Directors; Multimedia; Original Music Scores
Founded: 1983
Specialized Field: Chamber Music
Paid Staff: 1
Volunteer Staff: 28
Paid Artists: 6
Budget: $10,000-20,000
Income Sources: Donations; Ticket Sales
Performs At: Dana Auditorium
Annual Attendance: 1,200
Year Built: 1961
Year Remodeled: 1995

4847
WESTERN CAROLINA UNIVERSITY LECTURES, CONCERTS & EXHIBITIONS
Western Carolina University
University Center
Cullowhee, NC 28723
Phone: 828-227-7234
Fax: 828-227-7250
Management:
    LCE Series: Beth Johnson
Utilizes: Dance Companies; Dancers; Multimedia; Original Music Scores; Playwrights; Sign Language Translators; Special Technical Talent
Paid Staff: 1
Budget: $35,000-60,000
Performs At: Ramsey Activities Center; Hoey Auditorium

4848
AMERICAN DANCE FESTIVAL
PO Box 90772
Durham, NC 27708-0772
Phone: 919-684-6402
Fax: 919-684-5459
e-mail: adf@americandancefestival.org
Web Site: www.americandancefestival.org

Officers:
    President: Charles L Reinhart
Management:
    Director: Charles L Reinhart
    Associate Director: Jodee Nimerichter
Mission: Committed to serving the needs of dance, dancers, choreographers and professionals in dance-related fields.
Founded: 1934
Specialized Field: Series & Festivals: Modern Dance
Status: For-Profit, Professional
Budget: $2,000,000
Performs At: Page Auditorium; Reynolds Industries Theatre; others
Annual Attendance: 25,000
Stage Dimensions: 30'x 37',48'x 35'
Seating Capacity: 1232; 589
Organization Type: Educational; Sponsoring

4849
BULL DURHAM BLUES FESTIVAL
Hayti Historic Center
801 Old Fayetteville Street
Durham, NC 27702
Phone: 919-683-1709
Fax: 919-682-5869
e-mail: info@hayti.org
Web Site: www.hayti.org
Management:
    President: Dianna Pledger
Specialized Field: Series & Festivals: Cultural Arts
Status: Non-Profit, Non-Professional
Paid Staff: 8

4850
DUKE UNIVERSITY UNION BROADWAY COMMITTEE / ON STAGE COMMITTEE
Box 90834
Duke University
Durham, NC 27708-0834
Phone: 919-684-4682
Fax: 919-684-8395
e-mail: pcoyle@acpub.duke.edu
Management:
    Associate Dean: Peter Coyle
Budget: $60,000-150,000
Performs At: Page Auditorium
Seating Capacity: 1232

4851
DUKE UNIVERSITY UNION BROADWAY COMMITTEE / ON STAGE COMMITTEE
Box 90834
Duke University
Durham, NC 27708-0834
Phone: 919-684-4682
Fax: 919-684-8395
e-mail: pcoyle@acpub.duke.edu
Management:
    Associate Dean: Peter Coyle
Budget: $35,000-60,000
Performs At: Page Auditorium
Seating Capacity: 1232

4852
SUMMER FESTIVAL OF CHAMBER MUSIC AT DUKE UNIVERSITY
Box 90834
Duke University
Durham, NC 27708
Phone: 919-684-3227
Fax: 919-684-8395
Management:

Office of University Life Dean: Susan Coon

4853
TRIANGLE THEATRE FESTIVAL
100 Timber Ridge Drive
Durham, NC 27713-9330
Phone: 919-490-8603
Fax: 919-401-3565
e-mail: info@theatrefestival.org
Web Site: www.theatrefestival.org
Management:
    Director: Anthony C Caporale

4854
COA COMMUNITY CENTER AUDITORIUM
PO Box 2327
Elizabeth City, NC 27906-2327
Phone: 252-335-9050
Fax: 252-337-6622
Toll-free: 800-335-9050
e-mail: lmanning@albemarle.edu
Web Site: www.albemarle.cc.nc.us/acadaff/finearts
Management:
    Facility Supervisor: Dave Griffie
    Events Coordinator/Box Office Mgr: Leslie Manning
Paid Staff: 4
Volunteer Staff: 20
Budget: $30,000-50,000
Performs At: Proscenium House Auditorium
Seating Capacity: 1,000
Rental Contact: Dave Griffie

4855
ELIZABETH CITY STATE UNIVERSITY LYCEUM SERIES
1704 Weeksville Road
Campus Box 831
Elizabeth City, NC 27909
Phone: 252-335-3359
Fax: 252-335-3779
e-mail: gjknight@mail.ecsu.edu
Web Site: www.ecsu.edu/academics/music
Management:
    Chairperson: Gloria Knight
    Assistant Professor: Mary Hellmann
    Academic Counselor: Ellard Forrester
Specialized Field: Series & Festivals; Instrumental Music; Vocal Music; Theatre; Youth; Dance; Ethnic Performances
Status: Non-Profit, Non-Professional

4856
ELON UNIVERSITY LYCEUM COMMITTEE
2800 Campus Box
Elon, NC 27244-2010
Phone: 336-278-5607
Fax: 336-278-5609
e-mail: troxlerg@elon.edu
Web Site: www.elon.edu/e-net/cultural
Management:
    President: Leo Lambert
    Dean of Cultural and Special Progra: George Troxler
Specialized Field: Series & Festivals; Instrumental Music; Vocal Music; Dance; Theatre of Illusion
Status: For-Profit, Non-Professional
Paid Staff: 4
Budget: $35,000-60,000
Income Sources: University Funds
Performs At: McCrary Theatre; Whitley Auditorium
Seating Capacity: 572/370

4857

FARMVILLE COMMUNITY ARTS COUNCIL

PO Box 305
Farmville, NC 27828
Phone: 252-753-3832
Fax: 252-753-6910
e-mail: fcac@greenvillenc.com
Web Site: www.farmvillearts.org
Management:
Executive Director: Eraina Oakley
Founded: 1977
Specialized Field: Theatre; Community; Theatre
Status: For-Profit, Non-Professional
Paid Staff: 2
Budget: $10,000
Performs At: Stage-Theater-Arts Center

4858

ARTS COUNCIL OF FAYETTEVILLE/CUMBERLAND COUNTY

301 Hay Street
Fayetteville, NC 28301
Mailing Address: PO Box 318, Fayetteville, NC 28302
Phone: 910-323-1776
Fax: 910-323-1727
e-mail: admin@theartscouncil.com
Web Site: www.theartscouncil.com
Management:
Executive Director: Deborah M Mintz
Founded: 1973
Specialized Field: Rotating Art Exhibit; Funding agency for artists in organization
Status: Non-Profit, Professional
Paid Staff: 9
Budget: $10,000

4859

ARTS COUNCIL OF MACON COUNTY

PO Box 726
Franklin, NC 28744
Phone: 828-524-7683
Fax: 828-524-7683
Management:
Executive Director: Bobbie Contino
Budget: $10,000
Performs At: Franklin Fine Arts Center; Highlands Civic Center

4860

EASTERN MUSIC FESTIVAL & SCHOOL

PO Box 22026
Greensboro, NC 27420
Phone: 336-333-7450
Fax: 336-333-7454
e-mail: info@easternmusicfestival.org
Web Site: www.easternmusicfestival.org
Officers:
Co-Chairman Of The Board: Dr. Sam LeBauer
Co-Chairman Of The Board: Barbara Morgenstein
Executive Director: Stephanie Cordick
Management:
Music Director: Gerard Schwarz
Director Of Marketing: Carrie Miller
Mission: The EMF mission is to promote musical enrichment, excellence, professional collaboration, innovation and diversity through a nationally recognized teching program, music festival, concerts and other programs which will enchance the quality of life, health and vitality of our region.
Utilizes: Guest Artists
Founded: 1961

Specialized Field: Festival and Summer Music Academy; Orchestral; Chamber and Piano Performance Program; Special Attractions Ranging From Americana To Jazz; Blues; Etc
Status: Non-Profit, Professional
Paid Staff: 100
Paid Artists: 200
Non-paid Artists: 200
Budget: $2.5 million
Income Sources: Tickets; Tuition; Fees; Grants; Sponsorship; Private Contributions
Annual Attendance: 60,000
Organization Type: Performing; Educational

4861

GUILFORD COLLEGE ARTS

5800 W Friendly Avenue
Greensboro, NC 27410
Phone: 336-316-2301
Fax: 336-316-2949
e-mail: scrisp@guilford.edu
Web Site: www.guilford.edu
Management:
President: Kent John Chabotar
Founded: 1837
Budget: $35,000-60,000
Performs At: Dana Auditorium; Sternberger Auditorium

4862

NORTH CAROLINA A&T STATE UNIVERSITY LYCEUM SERIES

North Carolina A&T State University
Greensboro, NC 27411
Phone: 336-334-7500
Fax: 336-334-7770
e-mail: jhgarner@ncat.edu
Officers:
Chairman: Dr. Olen Cole, Jr.
Student Affairs Vice-Chancellor: Dr. Sullivan Wellbourne, Jr
Status: Nonprofit
Budget: $35,000-60,000

4863

UNITED ARTS COUNCIL OF GREENSBORO

200 N Davie Street
Greensboro, NC 27401
Mailing Address: PO Box 877 Greensboro, NC 27402
Phone: 336-373-7523
Fax: 336-373-7553
Web Site: www.uncarts.org
Management:
President: Jeanie Duncan
Marketing Director: Liz Summers
Founded: 1962
Specialized Field: Fund raising and Advocacy
Status: Non-Profit, Professional
Paid Staff: 5

4864

UNIVERSITY OF NORTH CAROLINA AT GREENSBORO CONCERT/LECTURE SERIES

Aycock Auditorium, Spring Garden at Tate Stre
PO Box 26170
Greensboro, NC 27402-6170
Phone: 336-334-5800
Fax: 336-334-3008
e-mail: ucls@uncg.edu
Web Site: www.ucls.uncg.edu
Management:
President: Bruce Michael

Associate Director: Checkle Leinwell
Utilizes: Actors; Dance Companies; Dancers; Fine Artists; Guest Composers; Guest Musical Directors; Guest Musicians; Singers; Special Technical Talent; Theatre Companies
Founded: 1891
Specialized Field: Arts and Humanities
Status: Non-Profit, Professional
Paid Staff: 16
Budget: $150,000-400,000
Income Sources: Ticket Revenue
Performs At: Aycock Auditorium
Affiliations: NCPC; APAP
Type of Stage: Black Pine
Stage Dimensions: 39'8"
Seating Capacity: 2300
Year Built: 1926
Year Remodeled: 1970
Rental Contact: 336-334-5118 Jan Hullihan

4865

EAST CAROLINA UNIVERSITY S. RUDOLPH ALEXANDER PERFORMING ART SERIES

207 Mendenhall Student Center
East Carolina University
Greenville, NC 27858
Phone: 252-328-4788
Fax: 252-328-2336
Toll-free: 800-328-2787
e-mail: clutterw@mail.ecu.edu
Web Site: www.ecuarts.com
Management:
Asst VC for Student Experiences: William B Clutter
Managing Director: Carol Woodruff
Utilizes: Dance Companies; Fine Artists; Multimedia; Original Music Scores; Selected Students; Student Interns; Theatre Companies
Founded: 1907
Specialized Field: Series and Festivals: Youth
Status: Non-Profit, Professional
Paid Staff: 2
Budget: $150,000-400,000
Performs At: Wright Auditorium
Annual Attendance: 14,000
Type of Stage: Proscenium
Seating Capacity: 1,500
Year Remodeled: 1985

4866

PITT COUNTY ARTS COUNCIL

PO Box 8191
Greenville, NC 27835
Phone: 252-757-1785
e-mail: pcac@greenville.com
Budget: $35,000-60,000

4867

NORTH CAROLINA SHAKESPEARE FESTIVAL

PO Box 6066
High Point, NC 27262
Phone: 336-841-2273
Fax: 336-841-8627
e-mail: pedro@ncshakes.org
Web Site: www.ncshakes.org
Officers:
Chairman: Christine Green
Management:
Sales Director: Casey Schmidt
Artistic Director: Pedro Silva
Production Manager: Joel Radatz

Mission: Seeks to serve the cultural and educational needs of North Carolina audiences through traditional and nontraditional staging of the plays of Shakespeare and other classic playwrights.
Founded: 1977
Specialized Field: Theater
Status: Professional; Nonprofit
Paid Staff: 10
Paid Artists: 55
Budget: $1,400,000
Income Sources: Ticket sales; Touring fees; Contributors
Season: Late August - December
Performs At: High Point Theatre
Organization Type: Performing; Touring; Resident; Educational

4868
HIGHLANDS CASHIERS CHAMBER MUSIC FESTIVAL

PO Box 1702
Highlands, NC 28741
Phone: 828-526-9060
Fax: 828-526-4893
e-mail: hccmf@frontier.com
Web Site: www.h-cmusicfestival.org
Officers:
    President: Dr. Jack Sapolsky
    Treasurer: Julian Franklin
    Executive Director: Nancy Gould-Aaron
Management:
    Artistic Director: William Ransom
Mission: To promote the performance and appreciation of chamber music.
Utilizes: Original Music Scores
Founded: 1982
Specialized Field: Series and Festivals; Instrumental Music; Vocal Music; Chamber Music
Status: Non-Profit, Professional
Paid Staff: 2
Volunteer Staff: 15
Paid Artists: 24
Budget: $250,000
Income Sources: Contributions; Ticket Sales; Fund Raising
Performs At: Highlands Performong Arts Center
Affiliations: Chamber Music America
Annual Attendance: 3500
Facility Category: Performing Arts Center
Seating Capacity: 200;100
Year Remodeled: 2001
Organization Type: Performing; Touring; Resident; Educational; Sponsoring

4869
COASTAL CAROLINA COMMUNITY COLLEGE

444 Western Boulevard
Jacksonville, NC 28546-6877
Phone: 910-455-1221
Fax: 910-455-7027
Web Site: www.coastal.cc.nc.us
Management:
    President: Ronald Lingle
    Music Instructor: Michael Daughtey
Founded: 1963
Specialized Field: Education
Status: Non-Profit, Professional
Paid Staff: 200
Budget: $10,000-20,000
Performs At: CCCC Fine Arts Auditorium
Seating Capacity: 182

4870
LINCOLN ART COUNCIL

PO Box 45
Lincolnton, NC 28093
Phone: 704-732-9044
Fax: 704-732-9057
e-mail: merrylac@bellsouth.net
Web Site: www.lincolnartcouncil.org
Officers:
    President: Madeline Elmore
    First VP: Kenneth Brown
    Second VP: Beverly McAdams
Management:
    President: Ary Lee
    Executive Director: Aryaane Howare
Mission: To develop, promote and foster all forms of creative and performing arts by arranging and offering exhibits, lectures, demonstrations, classes and performances, etc.
Founded: 1973
Specialized Field: Presentation of Art Circle
Status: Non-Profit, Professional
Paid Staff: 1
Paid Artists: 4
Income Sources: North Carolina Association of Arts Councils; North Carolina Arts Council
Performs At: Lincoln Citizens Center; Lincoln Cultural Center
Organization Type: Performing; Educational; Sponsoring

4871
LOUISBURG COLLEGE CONCERT SERIES

Louisburg College
501 N Main Street, Box 3125
Louisburg, NC 27549
Phone: 919-497-3251
Fax: 919-496-7141
Toll-free: 866-773-6354
e-mail: rpoole@louisburg.edu
Web Site: www.louisburg.edu
Officers:
    President: Dr Mark LaBranche
Management:
    Executive Director: Robert Poole
    VP Development: Kurt Carlson
    Box Office Manager: Anna Stallings
Mission: To provide cultural arts education and entertainment to the people of Franklin County and surrounding areas through music, dance, drama & visual arts.
Utilizes: Actors; Dance Companies; Dancers; Guest Instructors; Guest Musical Directors; Guest Soloists; Guild Activities; Instructors; Local Artists; Multimedia; Original Music Scores; Playwrights; Sign Language Translators; Singers; Soloists; Special Technical Talent; Theatre Companies; Touring Companies
Founded: 1957
Specialized Field: All
Status: Non-Profit, Professional
Paid Staff: 3
Volunteer Staff: 15
Paid Artists: 10
Income Sources: Ticket Sales; Patron Gifts
Performs At: Louisburg College Auditorium
Annual Attendance: 6,000
Facility Category: PAC
Type of Stage: Proscenium
Stage Dimensions: 40' x 30'
Seating Capacity: 1,180
Year Built: 1989
Rental Contact: Robert Poole

4872
ROANOKE ISLAND HISTORICAL ASSOCIATION

1409 National Park Road
Manteo, NC 27954
Phone: 252-473-2127
Fax: 252-473-6000
e-mail: info@thecolony.org
Web Site: www.thecolony.org
Officers:
    Chairman: Rick Gray
    Vice-Chairman: Norma Mills
    Secretary: Julie Daniels Nowells
    Treasurer: Stuart Bell
Management:
    Executive Production Coordinator: Rhoda Dresken
    Marketing/PR Associate: Joshua M Gilliam
    Membership/Development Associate: Bette Self
    Office Manager: Terry Fowler
Mission: To celebrate the history of the first English colonies on Roanoke Island NC; to honor the founders of The Last Colony, to promote awareness of the historical value of this event; to educate through drama and literature.
Founded: 1937
Specialized Field: Dance; Theater
Status: Non-Equity; Nonprofit
Paid Staff: 30
Paid Artists: 145
Budget: $1.5 million
Income Sources: Ticket Sales; Grants; Donations
Performs At: Waterside Theatre
Affiliations: Professional Theatre Workshop (in-house)
Annual Attendance: 60,000-70,000
Facility Category: Outdoor
Type of Stage: Amphitheatre
Stage Dimensions: 80' x 40'
Seating Capacity: 1534
Year Built: 1937
Year Remodeled: 1998
Organization Type: Performing

4873
PFEIFFER UNIVERSITY ARTIST SERIES

Pfeiffer University
Misenheimer, NC 28109
Phone: 704-463-1360
Fax: 704-463-1363
e-mail: sharrill@pfeiffer.edu
Web Site: www.pfeiffer.edu
Management:
    President: Charles Amerons
    Artistic Director: Doug Staeter
    Manager: Stephen Harrill
Founded: 1885
Specialized Field: Series & Festivals: Theatre
Status: Non-Profit, Professional
Paid Staff: 10
Paid Artists: 5
Budget: $10,000
Performs At: Henry Pfeiffer Chapel

4874
SURRY ARTS COUNCIL

PO Box 141
Mount Airy, NC 27030
Phone: 336-786-7998
Fax: 336-786-9822
e-mail: surryarts@advi.net
Management:
    Executive Director: Tanya Rees

Mission: To give direction and encouragement in the arts via performances, workshops and classroom instruction to residents of all ages in Surry County.
Utilizes: Guest Artists; Guest Companies
Founded: 1968
Specialized Field: Musical
Status: Nonprofit
Budget: $60,000-150,000
Performs At: Andy Griffith Playhouse; Mount Airy Fine Arts Center
Organization Type: Educational; Sponsoring

4875
ARTS NCSTATE

North Carolina State University
Campus Box 7306
Raleigh, NC 27695-7306
Phone: 919-513-1820
e-mail: artsncstate@ncsu.edu
Web Site: www.fis.ncsu.edu/arts
Management:
    Museum Tech/Righteous Sister: Claire Ashby

4876
ARTSPLOSURE: 2003 SPRING JAZZ & ART FESTIVAL

336 Fayetteville Street
Mall Suite 405
Raleigh, NC 27601
Phone: 919-832-8699
Fax: 919-832-0890
e-mail: info@artsplosure.org
Web Site: www.atsplosure.org
Management:
    Director: Michael Lowder
    Entry Coordinator: Christa Misenheiner
    Program Director: Terri Dollar
Founded: 1979
Specialized Field: Visual Arts; Music
Status: Nonprofit
Income Sources: Sposors; Grnats; Donations
Annual Attendance: 75,000
Facility Category: Outdoor Stages

4877
FIRST NIGHT RALEIGH

336 Fayetteville Street Mall
Suite 405
Raleigh, NC 27601
Phone: 919-832-8699
Fax: 919-832-0890
e-mail: info@artsplosure.org
Web Site: www.artsplosure.org
Management:
    Executive Director: Michael Louder
    Program Director: Terri Dollar
Mission: To offer annual arts festivals to enhance cultural life in the communities of Raleigh and Walce.
Utilizes: Actors; Artists-in-Residence; Collaborating Artists; Collaborations; Dance Companies; Dancers; Educators; Fine Artists; Five Seasonal Concerts; Guest Conductors; Guest Directors; Guild Activities; Instructors; Local Artists; Lyricists; Multi Collaborations; Multimedia; New Productions; Original Music Scores; Playwrights; Resident Artists; Selected Students; Sign Language Translators; Singers; Soloists; Student Interns; Special Technical Talent; Theatre Companies; Touring Companies
Founded: 1979
Specialized Field: Series & Festivals; Instrumental Music; Vocal Music; Theatre; Youth; Dance; Ethnic Performances
Status: Non-Profit, Professional
Paid Staff: 4

Annual Attendance: 50,000
Organization Type: Performing; Festivals

4878
GALLERY OF ART & DESIGN

North Carolina State University
Box 7306
Raleigh, NC 27695-7306
Phone: 919-515-5337
Fax: 919-515-6163
e-mail: claire_ashby@ncsu.edu
Web Site: www.gad.ncsu.edu
Management:
    Museum Tech/Righteous Sister: Claire Ashby

4879
NORTH CAROLINA ARTS COUNCIL

Mail Service Center 4632
Raleigh, NC 27699-4632
Phone: 919-733-2111
Fax: 919-733-4834
e-mail: ncarts@ncmail.net
Web Site: www.ncarts.org
Management:
    Executive Director: Mary Regan
Founded: 1967
Specialized Field: Series & Festivals; Instrumental Music; Vocal Music; Theatre; Youth; Dance; Ethnic Performances; State Arts Agency for North Carolina
Status: For-Profit, Non-Professional
Paid Staff: 25

4880
PINE CONE-PIEDMONT COUNCIL OF TRADITIONAL MUSIC

PO Box 28534
Raleigh, NC 27611
Phone: 919-664-8333
Fax: 919-664-8301
e-mail: pinecone1@mindspring.com
Web Site: www.pinecone.org
Management:
    Executive Director: Susan Newberry
    Program Associate: William Lewis
Mission: Pine Cone is dedicated to preserving, promoting, and presenting traditonal forms of music and dance and other folk performing arts in North Carolina.
Founded: 1984
Specialized Field: Series & Festivals: Concerts In Traditional Music
Status: Non-Profit, Non-Professional
Paid Staff: 2

4881
UNITED ARTS COUNCIL OF RALEIGH AND WAKE COUNTY

336 Fayetteville Street Mall
Suite 440
Raleigh, NC 27601-1743
Phone: 919-839-1498
Fax: 919-839-6002
e-mail: gzehr@unitedarts.org
Web Site: www.unitedarts.org
Officers:
    President/CEO: Eleonor Jordan
    VP Education/Community Programs: Virginia Zehr
    Campaign Director: Yvette Holmes
    Community Arts/Grants Manager: Angela Carter
    Chair: V R Ramanan
    Chair-Elect: Brad Phillips
    Vice Chair Administration: David Otteni
    Vice Chair Grants: Priscilla Tyree

Management:
    President: Eleanor H Jordan
    Community Arts and Grants Manager: Angela Carter
    Campaign Director: Yvette Holmes
    Accounting Manager: Jill Morris
Mission: Builds better communities through support and advocacy of true arts.
Utilizes: Artists-in-Residence; Guest Artists; Touring Companies
Founded: 1962
Status: Nonprofit
Volunteer Staff: 1
Budget: 1.5 million
Organization Type: Educational; Sponsoring

4882
JOHNSTON COMMUNITY COLLEGE ON STAGE CONCERT SERIES

245 College Road
PO Box 2350
Smithfield, NC 27577
Phone: 919-209-2099
Fax: 919-209-2133
e-mail: mitchellk@johnstoncc.edu
Web Site: www.johnstoncc.edu
Management:
    President: Donald L Reichard
    Executive Managing Director: Ken Mitchell
Founded: 1989
Specialized Field: Series and Festivals: National and International Events
Status: Non-Profit, Non-Professional
Paid Staff: 3
Budget: $60,000-150,000
Performs At: Paul A. Johnston Auditorium
Type of Stage: Proscenium
Seating Capacity: 1,000
Rental Contact: Ken Mitchell

4883
ARTS COUNCIL OF MOORE COUNTY

PO Box 405
Southern Pines, NC 28388
Phone: 910-692-4356
Fax: 910-693-1217
e-mail: acmc@pinehurst.net
Web Site: www.artscouncil-moore.org
Management:
    Managing Director: Kathreen McRea
    Assistant Director: Chris Dunn
Founded: 1976
Specialized Field: Series & Festivals; Arts Council; Childrens Program
Status: Non-Profit, Non-Professional
Paid Staff: 4
Budget: $20,000-35,000

4884
SWANNANOA CHAMBER MUSIC FESTIVAL

WWC 6062
701 Warren Wilson Road
Swannanoa, NC 28778
Phone: 828-771-3035
Fax: 828-254-1733
e-mail: festival1@juno.com
Management:
    Director: Frank Ell
    Administrator: Margaret Gormley-Chapman
Mission: Five weeks of chamber music featuring compositions of traditional and contempory composers.
Founded: 1969

Specialized Field: Asheville; Hendersonville;
Waynesville; North Carolina
Paid Staff: 1
Volunteer Staff: 15
Paid Artists: 9

4885
EDGECOMBE COUNTY ARTS COUNCIL
130 Bridgers Street
Tarboro, NC 27886
Phone: 252-823-4159
Fax: 252-823-6190
e-mail: edgecombearts@earthlink.net
Management:
Executive Director: Meade Horne
Mission: Promote and preserve cultural heritage of the
county.
Founded: 1985
Specialized Field: Visual Arts In School; Festival
Paid Staff: 4
Volunteer Staff: 12
Paid Artists: 1
Budget: $10,000
Income Sources: Private Donations; State and Local
Government
Facility Category: Outdoor Stage; Intimate Gallery

4886
MESSIAH 2000
PO Box 502
Troy, NC 27371
Phone: 910-576-8742
e-mail: tmusic@mc-online.net
Officers:
President: Dr. Paul Chandley

4887
TRYON CONCERT ASSOCIATION SUBSCRIPTION SERIES
PO Box 32
34 Melrose Avenue
Tryon, NC 28782
Phone: 828-859-8322
Fax: 828-859-0271
e-mail: tfac@alltel.net
Officers:
President: Philip Cooper
Budget: $20,000-35,000
Performs At: Tryon Fine Arts Center

4888
SOUTHEASTERN COMMUNITY COLLEGE PERFORMING ARTS SERIES
4564 Chadbourn Highway
PO Box 151
Whiteville, NC 28472
Phone: 910-642-7141
Fax: 910-642-5658
e-mail: rburkhardt@mail.southeast.cc.nc.us
Web Site: www.sccnc.edu
Management:
President: Brantley Briley
Founded: 1964
Specialized Field: Education
Status: Non-Profit, Non-Professional
Paid Staff: 250
Budget: $20,000-35,000
Performs At: College Auditorium; Bowers Auditorium

4889
CAPE FEAR BLUES FESTIVAL
PO Box 1487
Wilmington, NC 28402

Phone: 910-350-8822
e-mail: l.m.nichols@earthlink.net
Web Site: www.capefearblues.com
Management:
President: Lan Nichols
VP: Arthur Brown

4890
UNIVERSITY OF NORTH CAROLINA AT WILMINGTON
Kenan Auditorium
601 S College Road
Wilmington, NC 28403-3297
Phone: 910-962-3442
Fax: 910-962-3661
e-mail: bemelmansn@uncw.edu
Web Site: www.uncw.edu/arts
Management:
Director Cultural Arts: Norman Bemelmans,
bemelmansn@uncw.edu
Utilizes: Dance Companies; Dancers; Educators;
Filmmakers; Fine Artists; Guest Accompanists; Guest
Directors; Guest Instructors; Guest Musical Directors;
Guest Musicians; Guest Soloists; Guild Activities; High
School Drama; Local Artists; Multimedia; Original Music
Scores; Sign Language Translators; Singers; Soloists;
Special Technical Talent; Theatre Companies
Founded: 1970
Specialized Field: Series and Festivals; Instrumental
Music; Vocal Music; Theatre; Youth; Dance; Ethnic
Performances
Status: Non-Profit, Professional
Paid Staff: 12
Volunteer Staff: 15
Budget: $60,000-150,000
Income Sources: University Support, Ticket Sales
Performs At: Kenan Auditorium
Affiliations: Kennedy Center Arts In Education Partner
Facility Category: Auditorium/Concert Hall
Seating Capacity: 1,012
Year Built: 1970
Year Remodeled: 2005
Rental Contact: Director Cultural Arts Norman
Bemelmans

4891
BARTON COLLEGE CONCERT, LECTURE & CONVOCATION COMMITTEE SERIES
Barton College
Wilson, NC 27896
Phone: 252-399-6368
Fax: 252-399-0893
e-mail: lhutchinson@barton.edu
Web Site: www.barton.com
Management:
President: Norval Kaneten
Chaplain: Loura Hutchinson
Specialized Field: Series & Festivals; Instrumental
Music; Vocal Music; Theatre; Youth; Dance; Ethnic
Performances
Status: Non-Profit, Professional
Paid Staff: 1
Budget: $10,000
Performs At: Howard Chapel

4892
WINGATE UNIVERSITY
PO Box 159
Wingate University
Wingate, NC 28174

Phone: 704-233-8302
Fax: 704-233-8309
Toll-free: 800-755-5550
e-mail: lcoleman@wingate.edu
Web Site: www.wingate.edu
Management:
President: Jerry McGee
Mission: Educational
Founded: 1896
Performs At: Hannah Covington McGee Theatre;
Recital Hall; Helms Art Gallery; Austin Auditorium
Affiliations: NC Baptist Convention
Facility Category: Performing Arts
Type of Stage: Full Staging
Seating Capacity: 554
Year Built: 1999

4893
NORTH CAROLINA SCHOOL OF THE ARTS: SCHOOL OF MUSIC PERFORMANCE SERIES
1533 S Main Street
Winston-Salem, NC 27127-2188
Mailing Address: PO Box 12189, Winston-Salem, NC.
27117-2189
Phone: 336-770-3399
Fax: 336-770-3248
Web Site: www.ncarts.edu
Management:
Director: Sheeler Lawson
Budget: $10,000
Performs At: Crawford Hall; Stevens Center

4894
SALEM COLLEGE SCHOOL OF MUSIC
601 South Church
Winston-Salem, NC 27101
Phone: 336-721-2636
Fax: 336-721-2683
e-mail: barbara.lister-sink@salem.edu
Web Site: www.salem.edu
Management:
President, Salem College: Susan Pauly
Acting Director, School Of Music: Barbara
Lister-Sink
Founded: 1772
Specialized Field: Series & Festivals; Instrumental
Music; Vocal Music; Theatre; Dance; Ethnic
Performances
Status: Non-Profit, Professional
Budget: $10,000
Performs At: Hanes Auditorium; Shirley Recital Hall

4895
WAKE FOREST UNIVERSITY SECREST ARTISTS SERIES
Reynolda Station
PO Box 7411
Winston-Salem, NC 27109
Phone: 336-758-5757
Fax: 336-758-4935
e-mail: sheltolb@wfu.edu
Web Site: www.wfu.edu/secrestartists
Management:
Executive Director: Lillian Shelton
Founded: 1930
Specialized Field: Series & Festivals: Classical Music
Status: Non-Profit, Professional
Paid Staff: 1
Budget: $60,000-150,000
Performs At: Wait Chapel; Brendle Hall

4896

CASWELL PERFORMING ARTS SERIES

536 Main Street E
PO Box 609
Yanceyville, NC 27379-0609
Phone: 336-694-4591
Fax: 336-694-5675
e-mail: ccfta@vnet.net
Management:
President: Lee Fowlkes
Utilizes: Actors; Artists-in-Residence; Dance
Companies; Dancers; Educators; Fine Artists;
Instructors; Multimedia; Original Music Scores;
Playwrights; Sign Language Translators; Soloists;
Student Interns; Special Technical Talent; Theatre
Companies; Touring Companies
Founded: 1979
Specialized Field: Series & Festivals; Instrumental
Music; Vocal Music; Theatre; Youth; Dance; Ethnic
Performances
Status: Non-Profit, Professional
Paid Staff: 4
Volunteer Staff: 30
Budget: $150,000
Annual Attendance: 7,000
Facility Category: civic center
Type of Stage: proscenium
Stage Dimensions: 45 x 30
Seating Capacity: 912
Year Built: 1979
Rental Contact: Hilce Fowlfes

North Dakota

4897

NORTH DAKOTA STATE UNIVERSITY LIVELY ARTS SERIES

North Dakota State University
344 Menorial Union
PO Box 5476
Fargo, ND 58105-5476
Phone: 701-231-7221
Fax: 701-231-8043
e-mail: gerard.e.beaubrun@ndsu.edu
Web Site: www.ndsu.nodak.edu
Management:
Coordinator: Gerard Beaubrun
Mission: To provide a quality performing arts program
for all members of the university community including
students, faculty, staff, alumni, guests, parents and
Fargo-Moorhead community members. Performing arts
provided by the Lively Arts Series must challenge and
stimulate creativity and positive regard for a
multicultural perspective and provide students with
opportunities for experiential learning and involvement
related to performing arts.
Founded: 1910
Specialized Field: Series & Festivals; Instrumental
Music; Vocal Music; Theatre; Dance; Ethnic
Performances
Status: Non-Profit, Professional
Paid Staff: 2
Paid Artists: 50
Budget: $30,000-50,000
Income Sources: Grants; Community Support
Affiliations: Lake Agassiz Arts Council
Annual Attendance: 2,000-3,000
Facility Category: Fully Functional Concert Hall
Seating Capacity: 1,000

4898

NORTH DAKOTA MUSEUM OF ART CONCERT SERIES

Box 7305
Grand Forks, ND 58202
Phone: 701-777-4195
Fax: 701-777-4425
e-mail: ndmoa@ndmoa.com
Web Site: www.ndmoa.com
Management:
Director: Laurel Reuter
Founded: 1972
Paid Staff: 15
Volunteer Staff: 70
Budget: $20,000-30,000
Performs At: museum gallery
Facility Category: Art Museum
Seating Capacity: 300

4899

MAYVILLE STATE UNIVERSITY (ND) FINE ARTS SERIES

Mayville State University
330 Third Street NE
Mayville, ND 58257
Mailing Address: 400 Groveland Avenue Minneapolis
MN, 55403
Phone: 612-874-9238
Fax: 701-786-4748
e-mail: apthien@msn.com
Management:
Series Director: Dr. Anthony Thein
Income Sources: Student Activity Fee, Concert
Tickets, Contributions
Annual Attendance: 15-200
Facility Category: Fieldhouse
Type of Stage: Concrete
Seating Capacity: 400
Year Built: 1969

Ohio

4900

OHIO NORTHERN UNIVERSITY ARTIST SERIES

Fred Center for the Performing Arts
525 S Main Street
Ada, OH 45810
Phone: 419-772-2000
Fax: 419-772-1932
e-mail: k-baker@onu.edu
Web Site: www.onu.edu
Officers:
Chairman Music Department: Dr. Edwin Williams
Management:
President: Kendall Baker
VP: Anne Lippert
Utilizes: Actors; Artists-in-Residence; Collaborating
Artists; Collaborations; Commissioned Music; Dance
Companies; Dancers; Designers; Educators; Five
Seasonal Concerts; Grant Writers; Guest
Accompanists; Guest Artists; Guest Choreographers;
Guest Companies; Guest Composers; Guest
Conductors; Guest Designers; Guest Directors; Guest
Ensembles; Guest Instructors; Guest Lecturers; Guest
Musical Directors; Guest Musicians; Guest Soloists;
High School Drama; Local Artists; Multi Collaborations;
Multimedia; Music; Organization Contracts; Original
Music Scores; Performance Artists; Playwrights; Poets;
Resident Artists; Resident Professionals; Sign
Language Translators; Singers; Soloists; Touring
Companies

Founded: 1871
Specialized Field: Music; Dance; Theater
Paid Staff: 10
Budget: $35,000-60,000
Performs At: Freed Center for the Performing Arts
Facility Category: Concert Hall
Type of Stage: Moveable Proscenium/Black Box
Seating Capacity: 550/136
Year Built: 1990
Cost: $7,000,000
Rental Contact: Andrea Lawson

4901

CHILDREN'S CONCERT SOCIETY OF AKRON

Edwin J Thomas Performing Arts Hall
198 Hill Street
Akron, OH 44325-0501
Phone: 330-972-2504
Fax: 330-972-6571
Management:
Administrative Director: Elizabeth Butler
Budget: $60,000-150,000
Seating Capacity: 2800

4902

GREATER AKRON MUSICAL ASSOCIATION

17 N Broadway
Akron, OH 44308
Phone: 330-535-8131
Fax: 330-535-7302
e-mail: generalinformation@akronsymphony.org
Web Site: www.akronsymphony.org
Officers:
President: Wayne Knabel
Executive Vice President: Ellen Otto
Management:
President: Guy Pipitone
Executive Director: Jeff Sperry
Director of Operations and Educatio: Claire Van
Brandeghen
Music Director/Conductor: Ya-Hui Wang
Mission: To provide the Greater Akron Area with the
finest quality symphonic and choral music and related
fine arts; to educate the local public with respect to
classical and contemporary music.
Utilizes: Guest Artists
Founded: 1950
Specialized Field: Orchestra of Music
Status: Non-Profit, Professional
Paid Staff: 10
Paid Artists: 80
Performs At: E.J. Thomas Hall
Organization Type: Performing; Educational

4903

MUSIC FROM STAN HYWET

714 N Portage Path
Akron, OH 44303
Phone: 330-836-5533
Fax: 330-688-4839
Officers:
Concert Chairman: Lola Rothmann
Budget: $10,000
Seating Capacity: 160

4904

TUESDAY MUSICAL ASSOCIATION

198 Hill Street
Akron, OH 44325-0501

Phone: 330-972-2342
Fax: 330-972-2342
e-mail: tmc@uakron.edu
Officers:
    Executive Director: Barbara Feld
Budget: $60,000-150,000
Performs At: Edwin J. Thomas Performing Arts Hall

4905
UNIVERSITY OF AKRON: EJ THOMAS HALL SERIES

198 Hill Street
Akron, OH 44325-0501
Phone: 330-972-7595
Fax: 330-972-6571
Management:
    Executive Director: Dan Dahl
    Assistant Director: Cynthia Hollis
Budget: $400,000-1,000,000
Seating Capacity: 2,956

4906
OHIO UNIVERSITY PERFORMING ARTS SERIES

Office of Public Occasions
Templeton-Blackburn Alumni Memorial Auditoriu
Athens, OH 45701
Phone: 740-593-1761
Fax: 740-593-1763
e-mail: gstephensl@ohiou.edu
Management:
    President: Rodney McDavis
    Public Occassions Director: Grethen L Stephens
Specialized Field: Series & Festivals; Instrumental Music; Vocal Music; Theatre; Youth; Dance; Ethnic Performances
Status: Non-Profit, Professional
Paid Staff: 4
Budget: $60,000-150,000
Seating Capacity: 2,000

4907
LOGAN COUNTY COMMUNITY CONCERTS

PO Box 442
1200 Milligan Road
Bellefontaine, OH 43311
Phone: 937-592-5863
e-mail: barnwell@loganrec.com
Officers:
    Treasurer: Robert J Barnell
Budget: $20,000-35,000

4908
BALDWIN-WALLACE BACH FESTIVAL

Baldwin-Wallace College Conservatory of Music
96 Front Street
Berea, OH 44017
Phone: 440-826-2207
Fax: 440-826-8138
e-mail: bachfest@bw.edu
Web Site: www.bw.edu/academics/libraries/bach
Management:
    President: Mark Collier
    Executive Director: Catherine Jarjisian
    Coordinator: Mary Tuck
    Music Director: Dwight Oltman
Founded: 1930
Specialized Field: Series & Festivals; Instrumental Music; Vocal Music
Status: Non-Profit, Professional
Paid Staff: 4

4909
BALDWIN-WALLACE COLLEGE ACADEMIC & CULTURAL EVENTS SERIES

275 Eastland Road
Berea, OH 44017
Phone: 440-826-2157
Fax: 440-826-3020
e-mail: jhairsto@bw.edu
Management:
    Program Director: Jay Hairston
Specialized Field: Series & Festivals; Instrumental Music; Vocal Music; Dance; Ethnic Performances
Status: Non-Profit, Professional
Budget: $10,000
Performs At: John Patrick Theatre; Kulas Musical Arts Building

4910
BLUFFTON UNIVERSITY ARTIST SERIES

1 University Drive
Bluffton, OH 45817-2104
Phone: 419-358-3349
Fax: 419-358-3323
e-mail: schatta@bluffton.edu
Web Site: www.bluffton.edu
Officers:
    Artists Series Director: Dr. Adam J Schattschneider
Management:
    President: Lee Snyder
    Executive Director: Adam Schattschneider
    Artist Series Coordinator: Anna Stembler-Smith
Founded: 1899
Specialized Field: Series & Festivals; Instrumental Music; Vocal Music; Theatre; Youth; Dance; Ethnic Performances
Status: Non-Profit, Professional
Paid Staff: 2
Paid Artists: 6
Budget: $10,000-20,000
Performs At: Yoder Recital Hall; Founders Hall; Mosiman Hall

4911
BOWLING GREEN STATE UNIVERSITY: NEW MUSIC & ART FESTIVAL

BGSU
MidAmerican Center for Contemporary Music
Bowling Green, OH 43403
Phone: 419-372-2836
Fax: 419-372-2938
e-mail: bbeerma@bgnet.bgsu.edu
Web Site: www.bgsu.edu/colleges/music/maccm
Management:
    Director: Burton Beerman

4912
BOWLING GREEN STATE UNIVERSITY FESTIVAL SERIES

Moore Musical Arts Center
Bowling Green State University
Bowling Green, OH 43403-0290
Phone: 419-372-8654
Fax: 419-372-2938
e-mail: dfleitz@bgnet.bgsu.edu
Web Site: www.bgsu.edu/colleges/music
Management:
    President: Sidney Ribeau
    Public Events Director: Deborah L Fleitz
Founded: 1910
Specialized Field: Educational; Public University

Status: Non-Profit, Non-Professional
Budget: $60,000-150,000
Performs At: Kobacker Hall; Bryan Hall

4913
CRAWFORD COUNTY COMMUNITY CONCERT ASSOCIATION

PO Box 469
Bucyrus, OH 44820
Phone: 419-562-3719
Fax: 416-562-9098
e-mail: slater@cybrtown.com
Web Site: www.slatertours.com
Officers:
    President: Robert A Slater
Budget: $35,000-60,000
Performs At: Bucyrus Middle School Auditorium

4914
LITHOPOLIS PERFORMING ARTISTS SERIES

3825 Cedar Hill Road
Canal Winchester, OH 43110-8929
Phone: 614-837-8925
Fax: 614-837-4765
Management:
    President: Leland Smith
    Series Director: Virginia E Heffner
Founded: 1972
Specialized Field: Series & Festivals; Concert Series; School Residency
Status: Non-Profit, Professional
Paid Artists: 20
Budget: $10,000-20,000
Performs At: Wagnalss Memorial Auditorium

4915
CEDARVILLE UNIVERSITY ARTIST SERIES

251 N Main Street
Box 601
Cedarville, OH 45314
Phone: 937-766-7956
Fax: 937-766-7581
Management:
    Ass't Campus Activities Director: Jeff Beste
    Director: Scott Van Loo
Budget: $20,000-35,000
Performs At: James T. Jeremiah Chapel

4916
COLLEGE-COMMUNITY ARTS COUNCIL

7600 State Route 703E
Celina, OH 45822
Phone: 419-678-2950
Fax: 419-678-2950
e-mail: eeweber@bright.net
Officers:
    President: Eugene Weber
Budget: $10,000-20,000
Seating Capacity: 150-470

4917
CINCINNATI ARTS ASSOCIATION: ARONOFF CENTER FOR THE ARTS

650 Walnut Street
Cincinnati, OH 45202
Phone: 513-977-4123
Fax: 513-977-4150
Web Site: www.cincinnatiarts.org
Officers:
    President/Executive Director: Stephen A Loftin
    VP/General Manager: Janet L Taylor

Founded: 1992
Specialized Field: Series & Festivals; Music; Theatre; Dance; Education
Status: Non-Profit, Professional
Paid Staff: 100
Budget: $10,000,000
Performs At: Proctor & Gamble Hall; Jarson-Kaplin Theater; Fifth Third Bank Trust
Annual Attendance: 1,100,000
Seating Capacity: 2,719; 437; 150

4918
CINCINNATI FOLK LIFE SERIES
PO Box 9008
Cincinnati, OH 45209
Phone: 513-533-4822
Fax: 513-533-4828
e-mail: cfl@zoomtown.com
Web Site: www.cincinnaticalticfestival.com
Management:
  Managing Director: Joann Buck
Founded: 1981
Specialized Field: Series and Festivals: Folk Music
Status: Non-Profit, Professional
Paid Staff: 1
Budget: $20,000-35,000
Seating Capacity: 150-500

4919
CINCINNATI GARDENS
2250 Seymour Avenue
Cincinnati, OH 45212
Phone: 513-631-7793
Fax: 513-631-2666
Management:
  Director: Joseph F Jagoditz

4920
CINCINNATI MAY FESTIVAL
Music Hall
1241 Elm Street
Cincinnati, OH 45210
Phone: 513-621-1919
Fax: 513-744-3535
e-mail: information@mayfestival.com
Web Site: www.mayfestival.com
Officers:
  Chairman: Mary Margret Rochford
  Vice Chairman: Alice Sweet
  Secretary: Ruthy Korelitz
Management:
  President: Greg Ebel
  Executive Director: Steven Monder
  Music Director: James Conlon
  Chorus Director: Robert Porco
  Director Marketing/Development: Vera Menner
Mission: Cincinnati May Festival presents an exciting repertoire of choral and orchestral music featuring the May Festival Chorus, world-renowned guest soloists and conductors and the Cincinnati Symphony Orchestra.
Utilizes: Guest Artists
Founded: 1873
Specialized Field: Series & Festivals; Vocal Music; Instrumental Music; Festivals
Status: Non-Profit, Professional
Paid Staff: 200
Income Sources: Cincinnati Symphony Orchestra
Performs At: Music Hall; Cathedral Basillica of the Assumption
Organization Type: Performing; Resident; Sponsoring

4921
CINCINNATI OPERA ASSOCIATION SUMMER FESTIVAL
1241 Elm Street
Cincinnati, OH 45210
Phone: 513-621-1919
Fax: 513-744-3520
Toll-free: 888-533-7149
e-mail: info@cincinnatiopera.com
Web Site: www.cincinnatiopera.com
Management:
  President: Harry Sath
  Managing Director: Patricia Beggs
Founded: 1920
Specialized Field: Vocal Music: Opera
Status: Non-Profit, Professional
Paid Staff: 26
Paid Artists: 300

4922
CINCINNATI SHAKESPEARE FESTIVAL
719 Race Street
Cincinnati, OH 45202-4304
Phone: 513-381-2288
Fax: 513-334-2244
e-mail: info@cincyshakes.com
Web Site: www.cincyshakes.com
Officers:
  President: Doug Ignattus
Management:
  Artistic Director: Bryan I Phillips
  Managing Director: Rebecca Bromels
  Education Director: Jenna Vellaon
Founded: 1994
Specialized Field: Series & Festivals; Theatre; Youth
Status: Non-Profit, Professional
Paid Staff: 15
Volunteer Staff: 20
Paid Artists: 15
Season: August - June
Type of Stage: Proscenium
Stage Dimensions: 24' x 32'
Seating Capacity: 163

4923
CLASSICAL GUITAR SERIES
Xavier University
3800 Victoria Parkway
Cincinnati, OH 45207-2717
Phone: 513-745-3161
Fax: 513-745-3232
Toll-free: 800-344-4698
e-mail: heim@xu.edu
Web Site: www.xu.edu
Management:
  Executive Director: John P Heim S J
  Director: Jack Heim
Founded: 1976
Specialized Field: Series & Festival; Classical Piano; Classical Guitar; Swing/Jazz
Status: Non-Profit, Professional
Paid Staff: 2
Paid Artists: 20
Budget: $20,000-35,000
Performs At: University Center Theatre
Seating Capacity: 395

4924
CLASSICAL PIANO SERIES
Xavier University
3800 Victoria Parkway
Cincinnati, OH 45207-2717

Phone: 513-745-3161
Fax: 513-745-4223
e-mail: heim@admin.xu.edu
Web Site: www.xu.edu
Management:
  President: Michael Graham
  Director of Performing Arts: Catherine Springfield
  Director of Music Series: Jack Heim
Founded: 1831
Status: Non-Profit, Professional
Paid Staff: 2
Budget: $20,000-35,000
Performs At: University Center Theatre
Seating Capacity: 395

4925
FALL ARTS FESTIVAL/JEWISH FOLK FESTIVAL
2615 Clifton Avenue
Cincinnati, OH 45220
Phone: 513-221-6728
Fax: 513-221-7134
e-mail: email@hillelcincinnati.orgf
Management:
  Executive Director: Rabbi Abie Ingber
Mission: Folkmusic, Theatre and World Music especially Jewish artists.
Founded: 1977
Specialized Field: Music; Theatre; (Small Production; One Person Show)
Paid Staff: 6
Volunteer Staff: 35
Paid Artists: 3
Non-paid Artists: 3

4926
JAZZ GUITAR SERIES
Xavier University
3800 Victoria Parkway
Cincinnati, OH 45207-2717
Phone: 513-745-3161
Fax: 513-745-2083
e-mail: heim@admin.xu.edu
Web Site: www.xu.edu
Management:
  Director: Father Jack Heim

4927
JAZZ GUITAR SERIES
Xavier University
3800 Victoria Parkway
Cincinnati, OH 45207-2717
Phone: 513-745-3161
Fax: 513-745-2083
e-mail: heim@admin.xu.edu
Web Site: www.xu.edu
Management:
  Director: Father Jack Heim
Budget: $20,000-35,000
Performs At: University Center Theatre
Seating Capacity: 395

4928
JAZZ PIANO SERIES
Xavier University
3800 Victoria Parkway
Cincinnati, OH 45207
Phone: 513-745-3000
Fax: 513-745-2083
Toll-free: 800-344-4698
e-mail: heim@admin.xu.edu
Web Site: www.xu.edu
Management:
  Vice Chairperson: Robert J Kohlhepp

President: Michael J Graham

4929
JAZZ PIANO SERIES
Xavier University
3800 Victoria Parkway
Cincinnati, OH 45207-2717
Phone: 513-745-3161
Fax: 513-745-2083
e-mail: heim@admin.xu.edu
Web Site: www.xu.edu
Management:
    Director: Father Jack Heim
Budget: $20,000-35,000
Performs At: University Center Theatre
Seating Capacity: 395

4930
LINTON CHAMBER MUSIC SERIES/ENCORE
5465 N Bend Road
Suite 337
Cincinnati, OH 45247
Phone: 513-381-6868
Fax: 513-232-0949
e-mail: linton_info@lintonmusic.org
Web Site: www.lintonmusic.org
Management:
    President: Chad Wick
    Artistic Director: Richard Waller
Founded: 1977
Specialized Field: Series and Festivals: Chamber Music
Status: Non-Profit, Professional
Paid Staff: 1
Paid Artists: 20
Budget: $20,000-35,000
Performs At: First Unitarian Church; Cinicinnati City Council Chambers

4931
LINTON'S PEANUT BUTTER & JAM SESSIONS
4 W 4th Street
Cincinnati, OH 45202
Phone: 513-381-6868
Fax: 513-381-6888
e-mail: lintoninc@aol.com
Management:
    Artistic Director: Richard Waller
    Executive Director: Anne Black
Budget: $20,000-35,000
Performs At: First Unitarian Church; Cinicinnati City Council Chambers

4932
ART SONG FESTIVAL
11021 E Boulevard
Cleveland, OH 44106
Phone: 216-791-5000
Fax: 216-791-3063
e-mail: cimweb@cwru.edu
Web Site: www.cim.edu
Management:
    Executive Coordinator: Dr Joanne Uniatowski
Founded: 1985

4933
CHINA MUSIC PROJECT
334 Claymore Boulevard
Cleveland, OH 44143-1730
Phone: 216-531-2188
Management:

Director: Marjorie Ann Ciarlillo

4934
CLEVELAND MUSEUM OF ART PERFORMING ARTS SERIES
11150 East Blvd.
Cleveland, OH 44106
Phone: 216-421-7340
Fax: 216-707-6867
e-mail: perform@clevelandart.org
Web Site: www.clevelandart.org
Management:
    Director/Performing Arts,Music,Film: Massoud Saidpour
    Associate Director, Music: Thomas Welsh
Founded: 1916
Specialized Field: Art Collection
Status: Non-Profit, Professional
Paid Staff: 3
Budget: $35,000-60,000
Performs At: Gartner Auditorium
Organization Type: Educational; Sponsoring

4935
CLEVELAND MUSIC SCHOOL SETTLEMENT ARTISTS CONCERT SERIES
11125 Magnolia Drive
Cleveland, OH 44106
Phone: 216-421-5806
Fax: 216-421-5813
e-mail: cmsselee@aol.com
Web Site: www.thecmss.org
Management:
    Executive Director: Daniel Windham
Founded: 1911
Specialized Field: Series and Festivals; Instrumental Music; Vocal Music; Youth
Status: Non-Profit, Professional
Budget: $10,000
Seating Capacity: 200

4936
CLEVELAND SHAKESPEARE FESTIVAL
1300 Athens Avenue
Suite 104B
Cleveland, OH 44106
Phone: 216-732-3311
e-mail: info@cleveshakes.org
Web Site: www.cleveshakes.org
Officers:
    Chair: Rodger Govea
Management:
    Artistic Director: Tyson Douglas Rand
    Production Manager: Aaron D Elersich
Mission: To produce exceptional, accessible theater free of charge. Celebrate the talents of local artists in all aspects of production and excite contemporary audiences with the timeless themes of Shakespearean theater. Dedicated to bringing plays of professional quality to the greater Cleveland area as a way of encouraging community through theater.
Founded: 1998
Specialized Field: Free Outdoor Summer Festival

4937
DARIUS MILHAUD SOCIETY
15715 Chadbourne Road
Cleveland, OH 44120
Phone: 216-921-4548
Fax: 216-921-4548
Officers:
    President: Katherine M Warne

Budget: $10,000-20,000
Seating Capacity: 500

4938
GREAT LAKES THEATER FESTIVAL
1501 Euclid Avenue
Suite 300
Cleveland, OH 44115
Phone: 216-241-5490
Fax: 216-241-6315
e-mail: mail@greatlakestheater.org
Web Site: www.greatlakestheater.org
Officers:
    President: David Porter
    Co-Chairman: John Katzenmeyer
    Co-Chairman: Joseph Lopresti
Management:
    President: Charlie Fee
    Executive Director: Bob Taylor
    Managing Director: Greg Quinlan
    Marketing Director: Pam Mehenett
Mission: To produce theater emphasizing world classics, particularly Shakespeare and important nonclassical works of American theater.
Utilizes: Actors; Choreographers; Designers; Educators; Guest Artists; Guest Conductors; Guest Designers; Guest Lecturers; Music; Resident Professionals
Founded: 1962
Specialized Field: Series & Festivals; Theatre; Youth; Classical Theatre
Status: Non-Profit, Professional
Paid Staff: 14
Income Sources: League of Resident Theatres; American Arts Alliance
Performs At: Ohio Theatre Playhouse Square Center
Affiliations: LORT
Year Built: 1921
Organization Type: Performing; Educational

4939
TRI-C JAZZFEST
2900 Community College Avenue
Theatre 11
Cleveland, OH 44115
Phone: 216-987-4400
Fax: 216-987-4422
e-mail: jay.albert@tri-c.edu
Web Site: www.tricjazzfest.com
Management:
    Executive Director: Lawrence Simpson
    Artistic Director: Willard Jenkins
    Managing Director: Jay Albert
    Education Events Coordinator: Susan Stone
Mission: To provide an educational opportunity for students and people of all ages and backgrounds to further their abilities, understanding and appreciation for jazz. To increase public awareness and appreciation for jazz as an American art form. To preserve the history and foster the development of this unique music. To bring world class performers and educators to greater Cleveland audiences.
Utilizes: Artists-in-Residence; Collaborating Artists; Commissioned Music; Educators; Grant Writers; Guest Accompanists; Guest Companies; Guest Composers; Guest Directors; Guest Ensembles; Guest Lecturers; Guest Musical Directors; Guest Musicians; Local Artists; Multimedia; Music; Original Music Scores; Sign Language Translators; Singers; Soloists; Student Interns
Founded: 1980
Specialized Field: Series and Festivals: Jazz Music
Status: Non-Profit, Professional
Paid Staff: 4

Volunteer Staff: 20
Paid Artists: 100
Budget: 500,000
Income Sources: Foundations; Corporate;
Government; Private
Performs At: College Campus Auditorium; Severance
Hall; Metro Campus
Affiliations: Cuyahoga Community College;
International Association of Jazz Educators
Annual Attendance: 30,000-40,000
Type of Stage: Proscenium
Seating Capacity: 360-3,000
Organization Type: Performing; Educational
Resident Groups: Swing City; Tri-C Jazz Fest; High
School All-Stars

4940
SHALHAVET FESTIVAL
2140 Lee Road
Suite 218
Cleveland Heights, OH 44118
Phone: 216-932-3455
Management:
   Executive Director: Clara Amster

4941
COLUMBIANA SUMMER CONCERT ASSOCIATION
2905 Middleton Road
Columbiana, OH 44408-9550
Phone: 330-482-2978
Officers:
   Chairman: Fred A Lynn
Budget: $10,000-20,000
Performs At: Firestone Park Gazebo Entertainment
Center

4942
COLUMBUS ARTS FESTIVAL
100 E Broad Street
Suite 2250
Columbus, OH 43215
Phone: 614-224-2606
Fax: 614-224-7461
e-mail: festival@gcac.org
Web Site: www.gcac.org
Management:
   President of Arts Council: Ray Hanley
   Director of Arts Festival: Katie Lucas
Mission: To offer an annual festival of the arts.
Founded: 1961
Specialized Field: Dance; Vocal Music; Instrumental
Music; Festivals; Fine Art; Fine Craft
Status: Non-Profit, Professional
Paid Staff: 2
Volunteer Staff: 300
Income Sources: Greater Columbus Arts Council
Annual Attendance: 550,000
Facility Category: Outdoor Stage
Organization Type: Performing; Festival

4943
COLUMBUS ASSOCIATION FOR THE PERFORMING ARTS: SIGNATURE SERIES
55 E State Street
Columbus, OH 43215-4264
Phone: 614-469-1045
Fax: 614-461-0429
e-mail: meilley@capa.com
Web Site: www.capa.com
Officers:
   VP: Michael Rilley

   President: Bill Conner
Management:
   Executive Director: Douglas F Kridler
Mission: To utilize entertainment to enliven and enrich
metropolitan life through its work in all its venues,
enhance a continuing downtown renaissance and install
appreciation for diverse forms of entertainment.
Utilizes: Actors; Artists-in-Residence; Choreographers;
Collaborating Artists; Collaborations; Commissioned
Composers; Commissioned Music; Dance Companies;
Dancers; Educators; Filmmakers; Fine Artists; Grant
Writers; Guest Accompanists; Guest Artists; Guest
Choreographers; Guest Companies; Guest Composers;
Guest Designers; Guest Musical Directors; Guest
Musicians; High School Drama; Instructors; Local
Artists; Multimedia; Music; Original Music Scores;
Poets; Selected Students; Sign Language Translators;
Singers; Soloists; Special Technical Talent; Theatre
Companies
Founded: 1969
Budget: $15,000,000+
Income Sources: 90 per cent Ticket Sales; Rentals;
Grants;Contributions
Performs At: Ohio Theatre; Palace Theatre; Southern
Theatre; Riffe Center Theatre; Chicago Theatre;
Shubert Theater
Annual Attendance: 1,000,000+

4944
COLUMBUS SYMPHONY ORCHESTRA: PICNIC WITH THE POPS
Columbus Symphony Orchestra
55 E State Street
Columbus, OH 43215
Phone: 614-228-9600
Fax: 614-224-7273
Management:
   Executive Director/President: Daniel Hart
   V Chairman: Lynn Crawford
   Past Chair: Bernie Woreman
Paid Staff: 35
Volunteer Staff: 750
Paid Artists: 8

4945
COOPER STADIUM
1155 W Mound Street
Columbus, OH 43223
Phone: 614-462-5250
Fax: 614-462-3271
e-mail: info@clippersbaseball.com
Web Site: www.clippersbaseball.com
Management:
   General Manager: Ken Schnake
Seating Capacity: 15,000

4946
EARLY MUSIC IN COLUMBUS
Capital University
2199 E Main Street
Columbus, OH 43209
Phone: 614-861-4569
Fax: 614-861-4569
e-mail: mkwole@insight.rr.com
Web Site:
www.capital.edu/acad/cons/erly/earlymusic.htm
Management:
   Program Director: Katherine Wolfe
Paid Staff: 1
Volunteer Staff: 20
Paid Artists: 30
Budget: $20,000-35,000
Performs At: Mees Hall; Capital University; Huntington
Recital Hall

4947
JEFFERSON ACADEMY OF MUSIC
OSU School of Music
1866 College Road
Columbus, OH 43210
Phone: 614-292-2693
Fax: 614-292-1102
e-mail: jeffacad@osu.edu
Management:
   Executive Director: Ruth Triplett Haddock
Founded: 1979
Specialized Field: Series & Festivals; Instrumental
Music; Vocal Music; Youth; Dance
Status: Non-Profit, Professional
Paid Staff: 18
Paid Artists: 18
Budget: $10,000-20,000
Performs At: Battle Fine Arts Center; Children's
Hospital Auditorium

4948
MUSIC IN THE AIR
549 Franklin Avenue
Columbus, OH 43215
Phone: 614-645-7995
Fax: 614-645-6278
e-mail: mita@columbus.gov
Web Site: www.musicintheair.org
Management:
   Executive Director: Wayne A Roberts
   Managing Director: Karen Wiser
Mission: Presents a variety of musicians and
performers with four summer music series and Festival
Latino. All performances are free.
Founded: 1973
Specialized Field: Present Festivals and Performances
in Columbus
Status: Non-Profit, Professional
Paid Staff: 5
Paid Artists: 150
Budget: 450,000
Performs At: Outdoor Amphitheater; Mobile Stage Van
Annual Attendance: 200,000
Seating Capacity: 5,000
Rental Contact: Karen Wiser

4949
SHORT NORTH PERFORMING ARTS ASSOCIATION
PO Box 8414
Columbus, OH 43201
Phone: 614-291-5854
Fax: 614-291-5854
e-mail: strosen@excite.com
Officers:
   President: Toba Feldman
   Secretary: Cathy Huston
   Treasurer: Anita St. John
Management:
   Artistic Director: Steve Rosenberg
Mission: To present the finest chamber and folk music
and to provide after school programs in music to inner
city children.
Utilizes: Guest Directors; Instructors; Multimedia;
Original Music Scores
Founded: 1983
Specialized Field: Instrumental Music
Status: Nonprofit
Paid Staff: 2
Volunteer Staff: 1
Budget: $50,000-70,000
Income Sources: Ticket sales, grants, sponsorships,
contributions

Performs At: Short North Tavern; Little Brothers; Greek Orthodox Church

4950
TRIUNE CONCERT SERIES
St John'S Evangelical Church
59 E Mound Street
Columbus, OH 43215
Phone: 614-224-8634
Fax: 614-224-6375
Management:
Minister of Music: Mary Schwarz
Budget: $10,000
Seating Capacity: 1,000

4951
WOMEN IN MUSIC: COLUMBUS
PO Box 14722
Columbus, OH 43214
Phone: 614-470-0098
Fax: 614-430-3144
e-mail: WmcCols@cs.com
Performs At: Mees Hall; Huntington Recital Hall

4952
DAYTON'S JAZZ AT THE BEND FESTIVAL
City of Dayton
216 N Main Street
Dayton, OH 45402
Phone: 937-223-2489
Fax: 937-223-0795
e-mail: ccultural2@aol.com
Management:
President: Carol Sampson
Executive Director: Cathy Shanklin
Artistic And Festival Director: Walter Williams
Founded: 1996
Specialized Field: Series & Festivals; Cultural Events; Vocal Music; Theatre; Youth; Dance; Ethnic Performances
Status: Non-Profit, Professional
Paid Staff: 5

4953
ERVIN J NUTTER CENTER
3640 Colonel Glenn Highway
Suite 430
Dayton, OH 45435
Phone: 937-775-3498
Fax: 937-775-2060
e-mail: nutterguest@wright.edu
Web Site: www.nuttercenter.com
Founded: 1990
Specialized Field: Series & Festivals; Music Concerts; Sports (Hockey & Basketball)
Status: For-Profit, Professional
Paid Staff: 24
Performs At: Arena
Facility Category: Arena
Type of Stage: Stage Right
Seating Capacity: 11500
Year Built: 1990

4954
SOIREES MUSICALES PIANO SERIES
834 Riverview Terrace
Dayton, OH 45407-2433
Phone: 937-228-5802
Fax: 937-228-2380
e-mail: hagpia@riva.net
Web Site: www.soireesmusicales.com
Management:
Founder and Director: Donald C Hageman
Founded: 1969

Specialized Field: Series & Festivals: Piano Recitals
Status: Non-Profit, Professional
Paid Artists: 5
Budget: $10,000-20,000
Performs At: Shiloh Church

4955
UNIVERSITY OF DAYTON ARTS SERIES
University of Dayton
300 College Park
Dayton, OH 45469-1494
Phone: 937-229-2787
Fax: 937-229-3916
e-mail: arts-series@udayton.edu
Web Site: www.eventsudayton.edu/inarts-series
Management:
President: Daniel Curran
Executive Director: Barbra Lupp
Mission: To present an annual performing arts series to campus and community.
Utilizes: Collaborations; Dance Companies; Dancers; Educators; Five Seasonal Concerts; Guest Accompanists; Guest Musical Directors; Guest Musicians; Guest Soloists; Instructors; Local Artists; Multimedia; Original Music Scores; Playwrights; Sign Language Translators; Singers; Soloists; Special Technical Talent; Theatre Companies; Touring Companies
Founded: 1961
Specialized Field: Series and Festivals; Instrumental Music; Vocal Music; Theatre; Dance; Ethnic Performances
Status: Non-Profit, Professional
Paid Staff: 1
Budget: $60,000
Income Sources: Ohio Arts Council; Box Office; Montgomery County; University Subsidy
Performs At: Boll Theatre
Annual Attendance: 2,000
Facility Category: Theater
Seating Capacity: 378
Organization Type: Performing; Sponsoring

4956
VANGUARD CONCERTS
5335 Far Hills Avenue
Suite 304
Dayton, OH 45429
Phone: 937-434-6902
Fax: 937-434-6903
e-mail: vanguard@woh.rr.com
Management:
Director: Elana Bolling
Utilizes: Guest Musical Directors; Guest Musicians; Multimedia
Founded: 1961
Specialized Field: Series & Festivals: Chamber Music Series
Status: Non-Profit, Professional
Paid Staff: 3
Budget: $20,000-35,000
Performs At: Dayton Art Institute

4957
WRIGHT STATE UNIVERSITY ARTIST SERIES
Music Department
Wright State University
Dayton, OH 45435
Phone: 937-775-2787
Fax: 937-775-3786
e-mail: music@wright.edu
Web Site: www.wright.edu/academics/music
Management:

Manager: Alison Y Schray
Specialized Field: Series & Festivals: Classical Music Concerts
Status: Non-Profit, Professional
Paid Staff: 1

4958
WRIGHT STATE UNIVERSITY ARTIST SERIES
Music Department
Wright State University
Dayton, OH 45435
Phone: 937-775-2787
Fax: 937-775-3786
e-mail: alison.schray@wright.edu
Web Site: www.wright.edu/academics/music
Management:
Manager: Alison Y Schray
Budget: $20,000-35,000
Performs At: Creative Arts Center Concert Hall

4959
MIDAMERICA CHAMBER MUSIC FESTIVAL
Marblecliffchamberplayers
c/o Dept Of Music Ohio Wesleyan University
Delaware, OH 43015
Phone: 614-261-7903
Fax: 740-368-3723
e-mail: mccp@marblecliffchamberplayers.org
Web Site: www.owu.edu/~machmi
Management:
Artistic Director: Charles Wetherbee
Director: Charles Wetherber
Founded: 1995
Specialized Field: Music
Paid Staff: 2
Paid Artists: 8

4960
OHIO WESLEYAN UNIVERSITY PERFORMING ARTS SERIES
Sanborn Hall
23 Elizabeth Street
Delaware, OH 43015
Phone: 740-368-3710
Fax: 740-368-3723
e-mail: nmgamso@owu.edu
Web Site: www.music.owu.edu
Officers:
President: Mark Huddleston
Management:
Concert Chairman: Nancy Gamso
Founded: 1856
Specialized Field: Liberal Arts
Status: For-Profit, Professional
Paid Staff: 7
Budget: $20,000-35,000
Performs At: Gray Chapel

4961
LORAIN COUNTY COMMUNITY COLLEGE: STOCKER ARTS CENTER PROGRAMMING
1005 N Abbe Road
Elyria, OH 44035
Phone: 440-366-4140
Fax: 440-366-4101
e-mail: kcrooker@lorainccc.edu
Web Site: www.lorainccc.edu
Management:
President: Janet H Barlow
Founded: 1980

Specialized Field: Series & Festivals; Instrumental Music; Vocal Music; Theatre; Youth; Dance; Ethnic Performances
Status: Non-Profit, Non-Professional
Budget: $150,000-400,000
Performs At: Stocker Arts Center

4962
ARTS PARTNERSHIP OF GREATER HANCOCK COUNTY
618 South Main Street
Findlay, OH 45840
Phone: 419-422-3412
Fax: 419-424-9103
Toll-free: 800-750-0750
e-mail: director@artspartnership.com
Web Site: www.artspartnership.com
Officers:
   President: Dave Glass
   Treasurer/President Elect: Duane Donaldson
Management:
   Education Director: Peggy Grandbois
   Operations Director: Desiree Ciraldo
   Event Director: Teri Scheer
   Executive Director: Char Johannigman
Mission: To offer a variety arts and education programs for all ages.
Utilizes: Artists-in-Residence; Collaborations; Dancers; Educators; Five Seasonal Concerts; Guest Accompanists; Guest Ensembles; Guest Musical Directors; Guest Soloists; Guild Activities; High School Drama; Multimedia; Original Music Scores; Selected Students; Soloists; Special Technical Talent; Theatre Companies
Founded: 1979
Specialized Field: Performing; Educational
Paid Staff: 45
Volunteer Staff: 500
Paid Artists: 20
Budget: $500,000
Income Sources: Box office, grants, private and corporate donations
Performs At: Several Facilities but primarily Auditorium
Annual Attendance: 5,000
Facility Category: Auditorium
Type of Stage: Proscenium
Stage Dimensions: 56x23
Seating Capacity: 1418
Year Built: 1940
Year Remodeled: 1987
Cost: @$1000 per day
Rental Contact: 419-425-8257 Kelly Fletcher

4963
DENISON UNIVERSITY VAIL SERIES
Colwell House
Granville, OH 43023
Phone: 614-587-0525
Fax: 614-587-6602
e-mail: wales@denison.edu
Management:
   Director: Lorraine Wales

4964
MIAMI UNIVERSITY: HAMILTON ARTIST SERIES
1601 University Boulevard
Hamilton, OH 45011
Phone: 513-785-3264
Fax: 513-785-3145
e-mail: epsteihr@muohio.edu
Web Site: www.ham.muohio.edu/artistseries
Management:

Artistic Director: Howard Epsteis
Founded: 1968
Specialized Field: Music
Status: Non-Profit, Professional
Paid Staff: 1
Paid Artists: 9
Budget: $20,000-35,000
Performs At: Parrish Auditorium

4965
HIRAM COLLEGE CONCERT & ARTIST SERIES
Hiram College
PO Box 67
Hiram, OH 44234
Phone: 330-569-5181
Fax: 330-569-5479
e-mail: willsoneb@hiram.edu
Web Site: www.hiram.edu
Management:
   President: Tom Chema
Specialized Field: Community
Status: Non-Profit, Non-Professional
Paid Staff: 2
Budget: $10,000-20,000
Performs At: Hayden Auditorium

4966
FOOTHILLS ART FESTIVAL, SOUTHERN HILLS ARTS COUNCIL
Box 149
Jackson, OH 45640
Phone: 740-286-6355
Fax: 740-286-6355
e-mail: shac@zoomnet.net
Management:
   President: Maxine Plummer
   Executive Director: Barbara Summers
   Artistic Director: Barbara Summers
   Managing Director: Barbara Summers
Mission: Southern Hius Arts Council is Renovating a 1930 Art Deco movie house for live performances until it is ready we have 3 musical presentation per year during the festival-3rd weekend in October.
Specialized Field: Visual Performance and Musical arts
Status: Non-Profit, Non-Professional
Paid Staff: 2

4967
KENT/BLOSSOM MUSIC
Kent State University
E101 M&S, PO Box 5190
Kent, OH 44242
Phone: 330-672-2613
Fax: 330-672-7837
e-mail: kbm@kent.edu
Web Site: http://dept.kent.edu/blossom
Management:
   Director: Jerome Lacorte
Mission: Six-week summer program for young musicians embarking on professional careers for the intensive study and performance of chamber music with principles/members of The Cleveland Orchestra and other visiting artists Scholarship.
Founded: 1968
Specialized Field: Education-Chamber Music Summer (Advanced Training Institute)
Status: Non-Profit, Professional
Paid Staff: 2
Paid Artists: 30
Affiliations: The Cleveland Orchestra; Blossom Music Center

4968
KENTFEST
PO Box 248
Kent, OH 44240-0237
Phone: 330-673-1599
Officers:
   Chairman: Mary Drongowski

4969
LAKESIDE ASSOCIATION
236 Walnut Avenue
Lakeside, OH 43440
Phone: 419-798-4461
Fax: 419-798-5033
e-mail: schedule@lakesideohio.com
Web Site: www.alkesideohio.com
Management:
   Director Programs: G Keith Aody
Mission: To establish and maintain schools, conferences, institutes, lecture courses and other means of aesthetic culture.
Utilizes: Guest Artists
Founded: 1873
Specialized Field: Dance; Vocal Music; Instrumental Music; Theater
Status: Professional; Nonprofit; Commercial
Performs At: Auditorium
Type of Stage: Proscenium
Seating Capacity: 2,900
Year Built: 1929
Organization Type: Sponsoring

4970
CLEVELAND SHAKESPEARE FESTIVAL
PO Box 93494
Lakewood, OH 44101
Phone: 216-732-3311
Toll-free: 877-280-1646
e-mail: info@cleveshakes.org
Management:
   President: Park Goist
   Associate Artistic Director: Robert Hawkes
   Artistic Director: Lawrence Nehring
   Education Director: Tonya Beckman Ross
Mission: Committed to producing the plays of Shakespeare in the way that the author intened—fun, at the speed of thought, and in the midst of a vibrant community. To that end, they are committed to free admission, a festive atmosphere, and an earned attention to the work of the play.
Specialized Field: Free Outdoor Summer Festival

4971
LANCASTER FESTIVAL
127 W Wheeling Street
Lancaster, OH 43130
Phone: 740-687-4808
Fax: 740-687-1980
Toll-free: 800-LAN-FEST
e-mail: lanfest@lanfest.org
Web Site: www.lanfest.org
Officers:
   President: Steve Cox
   Executive Director: Lou Ross
Management:
   Artistic Director: Gary Sheldon
Utilizes: Actors; Artists-in-Residence; Choreographers; Collaborating Artists; Collaborations; Commissioned Composers; Commissioned Music; Curators; Dance Companies; Dancers; Fine Artists; Grant Writers; Guest Accompanists; Guest Artists; Guest Choreographers; Guest Companies; Guest Directors; Guest Instructors; Guest Musical Directors; Guest Musicians; Instructors;

Local Artists; Lyricists; Multimedia; Organization Contracts; Original Music Scores; Playwrights; Poets; Sign Language Translators; Singers; Soloists; Student Interns; Special Technical Talent; Theatre Companies; Touring Companies
Founded: 1985
Specialized Field: Orchestra; Pops; Chamber; Various
Status: Non-Profit, Professional
Paid Staff: 1
Volunteer Staff: 300
Paid Artists: 65
Budget: $800,000
Income Sources: Grants; Individual & Corporate Donations; Ticket Sales
Affiliations: Ohio Citizens For The Arts
Annual Attendance: 50,000
Facility Category: Indoor/Outdoor Festival
Stage Dimensions: 40'x60'

4972
COUNCIL FOR THE ARTS OF GREATER LIMA
130 W Elm Street
PO Box 1124
Lima, OH 45801
Phone: 419-222-1096
Fax: 419-222-3871
Web Site: www.limaartscouncil.org
Officers:
    President: Greg Phipps
    VP: Mike Hoffman
    Financial Officer: Terry Webb
    Secretary: Brenda Ellis
Management:
    Executive Director: Bart Mills
    Education Director: Sally Windle
    Operations Manager: Chris Craft
Mission: To enrich the quality of life in the Greater Lima community, the Council for the Arts will promote and encourage appreciation, respect and understanding of the arts through advocacy, education and programming.
Utilizes: Artists-in-Residence; Choreographers; Collaborations; Curators; Dance Companies; Dancers; Educators; Fine Artists; Five Seasonal Concerts; Guest Accompanists; Guest Designers; Guest Directors; Guest Ensembles; Guest Instructors; Guest Musical Directors; Guild Activities; Local Artists; Lyricists; Multi Collaborations; Multimedia; Performance Artists; Playwrights; Poets; Resident Artists; Sign Language Translators; Singers; Soloists; Special Technical Talent; Theatre Companies
Founded: 1966
Specialized Field: Dance; Vocal Music; Instrumental Music; Theater; Festivals; Lyric Opera
Status: Nonprofit
Performs At: Civic Center
Organization Type: Educational; Sponsoring

4973
LIVELY ARTS SERIES: PALACE CULTURAL ARTS ASSOCIATION
276 W Center Street
Marion, OH 43302
Phone: 740-383-2101
Fax: 740-387-3425
Web Site: www.marion.net/palace
Management:
    President: Diane Glassmeyer
    Managing Director: Elaine Merchant
Specialized Field: Performing Arts
Status: Non-Profit, Professional
Paid Staff: 8

4974
DRAKE COUNTY CENTER FOR THE ARTS
Medina County Performing Arts Foundation
222 South Broadway
Medina, OH 44256
Phone: 330-764-1999
Web Site: www.mcpaf.org
Management:
    President: Marcus L Neiman
    Vice President: Richard Graber
    Production Director: Mary F Shultz
Utilizes: Dance Companies; Fine Artists; Multimedia; Original Music Scores; Selected Students; Theatre Companies
Founded: 1978
Specialized Field: Series and Festivals: Instrumental Music
Status: Non-Profit, Professional
Paid Staff: 3
Paid Artists: 12
Budget: $60,000-150,000
Performs At: Henry St. Clair Memorial Hall
Annual Attendance: 15,000
Type of Stage: Proscenium
Stage Dimensions: 30'x24'x28'
Seating Capacity: 632
Year Built: 1912

4975
MENTOR PERFORMING ARTISTS CONCERT SERIES
6477 Center Street
Mentor, OH 44060
Phone: 440-205-3333
Fax: 440-974-5216
Web Site: www.mentorconcertseries.com
Management:
    Director: Theodore Hieronymus
Budget: $150,000-400,000
Performs At: Mentor Schools Fine Arts Center

4976
MOUNT VERNON NAZARENE COLLEGE: LECTURE ARTIST SERIES
Mount Vernon Nazarene University
800 Martinsburg Road
Mount Vernon, OH 43050
Phone: 740-397-6868
Fax: 740-392-1689
e-mail: bcochran@mvnu.edu
Web Site: www.mvnc.edu
Management:
    Dean Of School Of Arts And Humaniti: Dr David Wilke
Utilizes: Actors; Fine Artists; Guest Accompanists; Guest Directors; Guest Instructors; Guest Musical Directors; Guest Musicians; Guest Soloists; Instructors; Multimedia; Sign Language Translators; Special Technical Talent
Founded: 1970
Volunteer Staff: 10
Budget: $10,000-20,000
Income Sources: Institutional budget
Performs At: R.R. Hodges Chapel-Auditorium; Recital Hall-Theater
Annual Attendance: 3,225
Facility Category: 2 Theatres
Seating Capacity: 2,000; 300
Year Built: 1990

4977
OHIO OUTDOOR HISTORICAL DRAMA ASSOCIATION
Trumpet In The Land Outdoor Drama
PO Box 450
New Philadelphia, OH 44663
Phone: 330-364-5111
Fax: 330-339-8140
e-mail: trumpet@tusco.net
Web Site: www.trumpetintheland.com
Management:
    General Manager: Margaret M Bonamico
    Director: Joseph Bonamico
Mission: To preserve the rich history of the Tuscarawas Valley through the production of an outdoor, symphonic drama and other cultural programs. And to increase opportunities for employment in cultural programs in Mideast Ohio as well as to assist in the development of the economy through the expansion of travel and tourism in Ohio.
Utilizes: Guest Companies; Singers
Founded: 1967
Specialized Field: Musical
Status: Nonprofit
Income Sources: Actors' Equity Association
Performs At: Schoenbrunn Amphitheatre
Facility Category: Outdoor amphitheatre
Seating Capacity: 1200
Organization Type: Educational; Sponsoring

4978
CENTRAL OHIO TECHNICAL COLLEGE
1179 University Drive
Newark, OH 43055-1767
Phone: 740-364-9580
Fax: 740-364-9646
e-mail: irmscher.1@osu.edu
Management:
    Executive Director: Amy Greenland
    Assistant Director: Krista Irmscher
Specialized Field: Series and Festivals; Theatre; Ethnic Performances; Programming for Students
Status: Non-Profit, Non-Professional
Paid Staff: 1
Budget: $10,000-20,000
Performs At: Founders Hall

4979
OBERLIN BAROQUE PERFORMANCE INSTITUTE & FESTIVAL
Oberlin College Conservatory of Music
77 W College Street
Oberlin, OH 44074-1588
Phone: 440-775-8044
Fax: 440-775-6840
e-mail: ocbpi@oberlin.edu
Web Site: www.oberlin.edu/con/summer/bpi
Management:
    Artistic Director: Kenneth Slowik
Founded: 1971
Specialized Field: Series & Festivals; Instrumental Music; Vocal Music; Dance
Status: Non-Profit, Professional
Paid Staff: 25
Paid Artists: 25

4980
OBERLIN COLLEGE CONSERVATORY OF MUSIC ARTIST: RECITAL SERIES
Oberlin College
Conservatory of Music
Oberlin, OH 44074

Phone: 440-775-8293
Fax: 440-775-8942
e-mail: marci.alegant@oberlin.edu
Web Site: www.oberlin.edu
Management:
Assistant Dean: Marci Alegant
Utilizes: Guest Directors; Guest Musical Directors;
Multimedia; Singers
Budget: $60,000-150,000
Performs At: Finney Memorial Chapel

4981
MIAMI UNIVERSITY PERFORMING ARTS SERIES
102 Hall Auditorium
Oxford, OH 45056
Phone: 513-529-6333
Fax: 513-529-5482
e-mail: swoffoph@muohio.edu
Web Site: www.muohio.edu/performingartsseries
Management:
Executive Director: Patti Hannan Swofford
Budget: $150,000-400,000
Performs At: Millett Hall; Gates-Abegglen Theater; Art
Museum; Hall Auditorium
Seating Capacity: 730

4982
VALLEY ARTISTS SERIES
University Of Rio Grande
Fine & Performing Arts Center
Rio Grande, OH 45674
Phone: 740-245-7360
Fax: 740-245-7101
Toll-free: 800-282-7201
e-mail: www.gmiler@rio.edu
Management:
President: Gary Stewart
Fine and Performing Arts Coordinato: Greg Miller
Founded: 1981
Specialized Field: Series & Festivals; Instrumental
Music; Vocal Music; Theatre; Dance; Ethnic
Performances; Concerts
Status: Non-Profit, Professional
Paid Staff: 50
Paid Artists: 30
Budget: $20,000-35,000
Performs At: Fine Arts Theater

4983
LANGE TRUST
1402 Columbus Avenue
Sandusky, OH 44870
Phone: 419-625-8312
Fax: 419-625-8380
e-mail: ernst@bex.net
Officers:
Chairman: Diane Ernst
Mission: To bring events of good quality and variety to
the people of our county at no charge.
Utilizes: Collaborations; Dance Companies;
Multimedia; Original Music Scores; Theatre Companies
Founded: 1973
Paid Staff: 1
Budget: $50,000
Income Sources: Interest income from the Lange Trust
Performs At: State Theatre
Affiliations: Ohio Arts Presenter Network, Association
of Performing Arts Presenters
Facility Category: Renovated Vaudovillle House
Type of Stage: Proscenium
Stage Dimensions: 25x40
Seating Capacity: 1,570
Year Built: 1924

4984
SANDUSKY CONCERT ASSOCIATION
PO Box 1537
Sandusky, OH 44870-3521
Phone: 419-433-2399
e-mail: pedajd@aol.com
Web Site: www.sanduskyconcert.org
Management:
Talent Coordinator: Paul Dahnke
Founded: 1928
Specialized Field: Series & Festivals; Instrumental
Music; Vocal Music; Youth; Dance; Ethnic
Performances
Status: Non-Profit, Non-Professional
Budget: $30,000
Income Sources: Tickets sales, local support
Performs At: Sandusky State Theatre & Local
Churches
Affiliations: AOR Hearthland

4985
SPRINGFIELD ARTS COUNCIL BROADWAY & POPS ON TOUR & SEASON EXTRAS
8 N Limestone Street Suite-B
Springfield, OH 45502
Phone: 937-324-2712
Fax: 937-324-3170
Toll-free: 866-324-2712
e-mail: info@springfieldartscouncil.org
Web Site: www.springfieldartscouncil.org
Management:
Director Of Development: William Schwartz
Executive Director: Chris Moore
Director Of Finance: Margaret Schief
Director Of Marketing And Design: Tim Rowe
Budget: $60,000-150,000
Performs At: Kuss Auditorium; Clark State Performing
Arts Center

4986
SPRINGFIELD SUMMER ARTS FESTIVAL
PO Box 745
Springfield, OH 45501-0745
Phone: 937-324-2712
Fax: 937-324-3170
Toll-free: 866-324-2712
e-mail: sac4arts@aol.com
Web Site: www.springfieldartscouncil.org
Management:
Executive Director: J Chris Moore
Founded: 1967
Specialized Field: Series & Festivals; Instrumental
Music; Vocal Music; Theatre; Youth; Dance; Ethnic
Performances
Status: Non-Profit, Professional
Paid Staff: 7

4987
ARTS COUNCIL LAKE ERIE WEST
1700 N Reynolds Road
Toledo, OH 43615
Phone: 419-531-2046
Fax: 419-531-5049
Toll-free: 888-297-6645
e-mail: martinnagy@aol.com
Web Site: www.artscouncillew.org
Management:
President: Hugh Gaylord
Executive Director: Martin W Nagy
Mission: To support, nourish, and provide for a quality
environment for the arts to flourish in our region.
Founded: 1983

Specialized Field: Programs for Children; Paintings;
Music
Status: Non-Profit, Professional
Paid Staff: 4
Paid Artists: 4
Budget: $10,000-20,000
Income Sources: Admission; grants; donations; sales
Affiliations: Americans for the Arts
Facility Category: Auditorium
Type of Stage: Proscenium
Stage Dimensions: 16 x 44
Seating Capacity: 800
Year Built: 1920
Year Remodeled: 2001

4988
UPPER ARLINGTON CULTURAL ARTS COMMISSION
3600 Tremont Road
Upper Arlington, OH 43221
Phone: 614-583-5310
Fax: 614-442-3208
Toll-free: 888-722-5845
Web Site: www.ua.ohio.net
Management:
Arts Manager: Diane Deane
Arts Coordinator: Lynette Santoro-Au
Mission: Encouraging, promoting and providing cultural
opportunities for community enrichment.
Founded: 1972
Specialized Field: Dance; Vocal Music; Instrumental
Music; Facility; Theater; Festivals
Status: Nonprofit
Paid Staff: 2
Volunteer Staff: 78
Budget: $82,000
Income Sources: OAC; Ohio Humanities Donations; In
Kind
Performs At: Upper Arlington Municipal Center
Annual Attendance: 200-30,000
Facility Category: Schools; City Buildings
Organization Type: Sponsoring

4989
FINE ARTS COUNCIL OF TRUMBULL COUNTY
PO Box 48
Warren, OH 44482
Phone: 330-399-1212
Fax: 330-399-7710
e-mail: bbrown@trumbullarts.org
Web Site: www.trumbullarts.org
Management:
Executive Director: Bobbie Brown
Utilizes: Artists-in-Residence; Multimedia; Selected
Students
Founded: 1971
Specialized Field: Arts Council
Status: Non-Profit, Non-Professional
Paid Staff: 1
Budget: $80,000

4990
WARREN CIVIC MUSIC ASSOCIATION
PO Box 8731
Warren, OH 44484
Phone: 330-652-1118
Fax: 330-393-5348
Officers:
Talet Chairperson: Jeannine Morris
Management:
President: Kenneth Matheny
Artistic Director: Karl Morrs

Mission: Building and maintaining a permanent audience for concerts in Warren and the surrounding areas; cultivating interest in music; encouraging performance by skilled artists.
Founded: 1937
Specialized Field: Series & Festivals; Instrumental Music; Vocal Music; Theatre; Youth; Dance; Ethnic Performances
Status: Non-Profit, Professional
Budget: $60,000-150,000
Income Sources: Ohio Arts Council
Performs At: W.D. Packard Music Hall and Convention Center
Organization Type: Performing; Educational; Sponsoring

4991
OTTERBEIN COLLEGE ARTIST SERIES
Cellar House
141 W Park Street
Westerville, OH 43081
Phone: 614-823-1600
Fax: 614-823-1360
e-mail: pkessler@otterbein.edu
Web Site: www.otterbein.edu
Management:
Executive Director: Patricia Kessler
Budget: $35,000-60,000
Performs At: Cowan Hall

4992
CHAMBER MUSIC CONNECTION
242 Sinsbury Drive North
Worthington, OH 43085-3563
Phone: 614-848-3312
e-mail: artsdir@cmconnection.org
Web Site: www.cmconnection.org
Management:
Artistic Director: Deborah Barrett Price
Founded: 1992
Specialized Field: Chamber Music
Paid Staff: 3
Volunteer Staff: 5
Paid Artists: 40

4993
WORTHINGTON ARTS COUNCIL
777 High Street
2nd Floor
Worthington, OH 43085
Phone: 614-431-0329
Fax: 614-431-2491
e-mail: info@worthingtonarts.org
Web Site: www.worthingtonarts.org
Management:
Executive Director: Sean Cooper
Mission: To encourage arts appreciation, awareness and participation in Worthington.
Utilizes: Dance Companies; Dancers; Fine Artists; Guest Accompanists; Instructors; Multi Collaborations; Multimedia; Original Music Scores; Sign Language Translators; Theatre Companies; Touring Companies
Founded: 1977
Specialized Field: Community
Paid Staff: 4
Volunteer Staff: 15
Paid Artists: 4
Budget: $200,000
Income Sources: Grants; Sponserships; Ticket Sales
Performs At: Theaters
Annual Attendance: 4,000
Seating Capacity: 1,174

4994
MONDAY MUSICAL CLUB OF YOUNGSTOWN, OHIO
1000 5th Avenue
Suite 3
Youngstown, OH 44504-1603
Phone: 330-743-2717
Fax: 330-743-3745
e-mail: tickets@mondaymusical.com
Web Site: www.mondaymusical.com
Management:
President: Jane Evans
Executive Director: Kathy Doyle
Artistic Director: Gloria Mosur
Founded: 1896
Specialized Field: Series & Festivals: Concerts
Status: For-Profit, Professional
Paid Staff: 2
Volunteer Staff: 30
Paid Artists: 5
Budget: $60,000-150,000
Performs At: Stambaugh Auditorium
Seating Capacity: 2,535
Year Built: 1926

4995
YOUNGSTOWN STATE UNIVERSITY: DANA CONCERT SERIES
Youngstown University
Dana School of Music
1 University Plaza
Youngstown, OH 44555
Phone: 330-941-3640
Fax: 330-941-1490
e-mail: mdgelfand@ysu.edu
Management:
Coordinator: Michael D Gelfand

4996
YOUNGSTOWN STATE UNIVERSITY: DANA CONCERT SERIES
Dana School of Music, Youngstown University
1 University Plaza
Youngstown, OH 44555
Phone: 330-742-3640
Fax: 330-742-1490
e-mail: mgelfand@cc.ysu.edu
Management:
Coordinator: Michael D Gelfand
Budget: $20,000-35,000
Performs At: Bliss Recital Hall

4997
ZANESVILLE CONCERT ASSOCIATION
3450 S River Road
Zanesville, OH 43701
Phone: 740-452-4325
Fax: 740-453-3103
Management:
Booking Agent: Carol Boyse
Seating Capacity: 35,000-60,000

Oklahoma

4998
COMMUNITY CONCERTS OF BARTLESVILLE
PO Box 651
Bartlesville, OK 74005
Phone: 918-333-4599
e-mail: Cjswango@aol.com

4999
COMMUNITY CONCERTS OF BARTLESVILLE
PO Box 651
Bartlesville, OK 74005
Phone: 918-333-4599
e-mail: Cjswango@aol.com
Officers:
President: Carol Swango
Budget: $20,000-35,000

5000
OKLAHOMA MOZART INTERNATIONAL FESTIVAL
500 SE Dewey, Suite A
PO Box 2344
Bartlesville, OK 74005
Phone: 918-333-9900
Fax: 918-336-9525
e-mail: bwilliams@okmozart.com
Web Site: www.okmozart.com
Management:
President: Barbara Williams
Executive Director: Ginger Griffen
Artistic Director: Ransom Wilson
Development Director: Amy Livington
Utilizes: Actors; Artists-in-Residence; Collaborations; Commissioned Music; Dance Companies; Fine Artists; Grant Writers; Guest Accompanists; Guest Companies; Guest Composers; Guest Conductors; Guest Directors; Guest Instructors; Guest Musicians; Multi Collaborations; Multimedia; Original Music Scores; Sign Language Translators; Singers; Touring Companies
Founded: 1985
Specialized Field: Dance; Vocal Music; Instrumental Music; Festivals; Grand Opera
Status: Professional; Nonprofit
Paid Staff: 8
Volunteer Staff: 800
Paid Artists: 50
Budget: $890,000
Income Sources: Oklahoma State Arts Council; National Endowment for the Arts; Individuals; Businesses
Performs At: Bartlesville Community Center
Annual Attendance: 30,000
Facility Category: Concert Hall, Community Center
Seating Capacity: 1700
Year Built: 1982
Organization Type: Sponsoring
Resident Groups: New York Orchestra

5001
CHISHOLM TRAIL ARTS COUNCIL
717 W Willow
Suite 6
Duncan, OK 73533
Phone: 580-252-4160
Fax: 580-252-1631
e-mail: ctac@texhoma.net
Officers:
President: Gina Flesher
Management:
President: Gina Flesher
Executive Director: Patrick Brown
Mission: To promote the arts in all discipline in the community.
Utilizes: Actors; Artists-in-Residence; Collaborating Artists; Dance Companies; Dancers; Educators; Filmmakers; Fine Artists; Guest Instructors; Guest Soloists; Guild Activities; High School Drama; Instructors; Local Artists; Lyricists; Multimedia;

Performance Artists; Playwrights; Poets; Selected
Students; Singers; Special Technical Talent; Theatre
Companies; Touring Companies
Founded: 1976
Specialized Field: Series & Festivals; Instrumental
Music; Vocal Music; Youth; Ethnic Performances
Status: Non-Profit, Professional
Paid Staff: 1
Volunteer Staff: 50
Budget: $60,000-150,000
Income Sources: Public and private support
Performs At: Jack A. Mauer Convention Center
Seating Capacity: 750
Year Built: 1990

5002
CENTRAL OKLAHOMA CONCERT SERIES

PO Box 5272
Edmond, OK 73083
Phone: 405-340-3500
Fax: 405-844-8795
e-mail: janstan@swbell.net
Web Site: www.chopinsociety.com
Management:
 Executive Director: Jan Steele
Founded: 1986
Specialized Field: Series & Festivals: Concert
Status: Non-Profit, Professional
Budget: $20,000-35,000
Performs At: Mitchell Hall UCO Campus

5003
PHILADELPHIA FOUNDATION

PO Box 3700
Edmond, OK 73083
Phone: 405-285-1010
Fax: 405-359-6280
e-mail: info@pfconcerts.org
Web Site: www.pfconcerts.org
Management:
 Concert Series Director: Ryan Malone
Founded: 1998
Status: Nonprofit
Stage Dimensions: 21x56
Seating Capacity: 900
Year Built: 2001

5004
TRI-STATE MUSIC FESTIVAL

PO Box 5908
Enid, OK 73702
Phone: 580-237-4964
Fax: 580-237-1767
e-mail: enidtristate@aol.com
Web Site: www.tristatemusicfestival.com
Management:
 President: Jerry Allen
 Executive Director: C W Simmons Jr
Founded: 1932
Specialized Field: All Kinds of Music
Status: Non-Profit, Non-Professional
Paid Staff: 2

5005
CAMERON UNIVERSITY: LECTURE & CONCERT SERIES

2800 W Gore Boulevard
Lawton, OK 73505
Phone: 580-581-2211
Fax: 580-581-2867
e-mail: thescoop@cameron.edu
Web Site: www.cameron.edu

Management:
 President: Cindy Ross
Founded: 1908
Specialized Field: General University
Status: For-Profit, Professional
Budget: $10,000
Seating Capacity: 500

5006
LAWTON ARTS & HUMANITIES DIVISION

801 NW Ferris
Lawton, OK 73507
Phone: 580-581-3470
Fax: 580-581-3473
e-mail: scheatwood@cityos.lawton.ok.us
Web Site: www.cityos.lawton.ok.us
Management:
 Executive Director: Bobby Matchett
 Artistic Director: Sharon Cheatwood
Specialized Field: Community Theatre
Status: Non-Profit, Professional
Paid Staff: 7

5007
LAWTON ARTS & HUMANITIES DIVISION

801 NW Ferris
Lawton, OK 73507
Mailing Address: PO Box 1054, Lawton, OK. 73502
Phone: 580-581-3470
Fax: 580-581-3473
Management:
 Administrator: Margaret Chalfant
 Auditorium Coordinator: Jim McCarthy
Budget: $10,000-20,000
Performs At: McMahon Memorial Auditorium

5008
JAZZ IN JUNE

PO Box 2405
Norman, OK 73070
Phone: 405-325-3388
Fax: 405-325-7129
e-mail: dkritten@swbell.net
Web Site: www.jazzinjune.org
Management:
 Managing Director: Karen Holp
Mission: To offer Oklahoma residents a jazz festival.
Utilizes: Singers
Founded: 1985
Specialized Field: Series & Festivals; Instrumental
Music; Vocal Music; Jazz Concerts
Status: Non-Profit, Professional
Income Sources: American Federation of Musicians
Organization Type: Performing

5009
ARTS COUNCIL OF OKLAHOMA CITY

400 W California
Oklahoma City, OK 73102
Phone: 405-270-4848
Fax: 405-270-4888
e-mail: info@artscouncilokc.com
Web Site: www.artscouncilokc.com
Management:
 President: Cheryl Bought
 Executive Director: Elizabeth Eickmon
 Operations Manager: Don Busk
Utilizes: Actors; Collaborations; Dance Companies;
Educators; Fine Artists; Guest Artists; Guest
Conductors; Guest Lecturers; Instructors; Local Artists;
Multimedia; Original Music Scores; Special Technical
Talent; Theatre Companies
Founded: 1967
Status: Non-Profit, Non-Professional

Paid Staff: 17
Paid Artists: 144
Income Sources: Grants; Corporate Sponsors; Ticket
Sales
Performs At: Stage Center; 400 West Sheridan
Annual Attendance: 44,700
Facility Category: Theatre
Type of Stage: 3/4 Round; Full Round
Seating Capacity: 580; 210
Year Built: 1970
Year Remodeled: 1987
Rental Contact: Kevin Lesley

5010
CHARLIE CHRISTIAN INTERNATIONAL JAZZ FESTIVAL

PO Box 11014
Oklahoma City, OK 73136
Phone: 405-524-3800
Fax: 405-524-3800
Web Site: www.charliechristianjazz.com
Management:
 President: Fe Burroughs
 Executive Director: Anita G Arnold
Founded: 1971
Specialized Field: Series & Festivals; Instrumental
Music; Vocal Music; Theatre; Youth; Dance; Ethnic
Performances
Status: Non-Profit, Professional
Paid Staff: 1
Volunteer Staff: 3
Paid Artists: 15

5011
DUSK TILL DAWN BLUES FESTIVAL

701 DC Minner Street
Rentiesville, OK 74459
Phone: 918-473-2411
Fax: 918-473-0033
e-mail: dcminner@lakewebs.net
Web Site: www.dcminnerblues.com
Management:
 President: Selby Minner
 Executive Director: D C Minner
 Vice President: Pam Sharp
Mission: To showcase the Oklahoma blues tradition,
music strong on electric guitars and full bands.
Founded: 1988
Specialized Field: Series & Festivals; Vocal Music;
Youth; Dance; Ethnic Performances; Band Music
Status: Non-Profit, Professional
Volunteer Staff: 60
Paid Artists: 200

5012
OKLAHOMA BAPTIST UNIVERSITY ARTIST SERIES

College of Fine Arts
Box 61276
Shawnee, OK 74804
Phone: 405-878-2305
Fax: 405-878-2328
e-mail: paul.hammond@okbu.edu
Web Site: www.okbu.edu
Management:
 President: David Whitlock
 Dean: Paul Hammond
Utilizes: Guest Directors; Guest Musicians; Multimedia;
Singers
Founded: 1910
Specialized Field: Series & Festivals; Instrumental
Music; Vocal Music; Chamber Music; Solo Recitals
Status: Non-Profit, Non-Professional

Paid Staff: 2
Budget: 20,000
Performs At: Yarborough Auditorium
Facility Category: Recital Hall
Seating Capacity: 2,000/400
Year Built: 1963
Year Remodeled: 2000

5013
OKLAHOMA STATE UNIVERSITY ALLIED ARTS

Oklahoma State University
060 Student Union
Stillwater, OK 74078
Phone: 405-744-7509
Fax: 405-744-2680
e-mail: joe.ray@okstate.edu
Web Site: www.alliedarts.okstate.edu
Management:
    Special Events Coordinator: Joe Ray
    Ticketing/Marketing Manager: Amy Wavicky
Mission: Cultural and educational programming presentation.
Utilizes: Actors; Dance Companies; Dancers; Guest Directors; Guest Musical Directors; Guest Musicians; Multimedia; Original Music Scores; Sign Language Translators; Singers; Special Technical Talent; Theatre Companies
Founded: 1922
Specialized Field: Series and Festivals; Instrumental Music; Vocal Music; Dance; Ethnic Performances
Status: Non-Profit; Educational
Paid Staff: 2
Volunteer Staff: 2
Budget: $60,000-82,000
Income Sources: Student Fees; Ticket Sales; Grants
Performs At: MB Seretean Center Concert Hall
Affiliations: APAP; SWPAP
Facility Category: Concert Hall
Type of Stage: Proscenium
Stage Dimensions: 38x44
Seating Capacity: 801

5014
NORTHEASTERN OKLAHOMA STATE UNIVERSITY ALLIED ARTS SERIES

College of Liberal Arts
Tahlequah, OK 74464
Phone: 918-456-5511
Fax: 918-458-2348
Toll-free: 800-722-9614
e-mail: storerz@nsuok.edu
Web Site: www.nsuok.edu
Officers:
    Series Chairperson: Dr. Kathryn Robinson
Management:
    President: Larry Williams
    Dean: Paul Westbrooke
Specialized Field: Series and Festivals; Instrumental Music; Vocal Music; Theatre; Ethnic Performances
Status: Non-Profit, Non-Professional
Paid Staff: 100
Budget: $10,000-20,000

5015
CONCERTIME

11317 E 4th Street
Tulsa, OK 74128-2006
Phone: 918-438-2582
Fax: 918-437-1848
e-mail: organist@mciworld.com
Web Site: www.webtek.com/concertime
Management:

Manager: Alta Selvey
Budget: $20,000-35,000
Performs At: Patti Johnson Wilson Hall; Philbrook Museum

5016
LIGHT OPERA OKLAHOMA - LOOK

Harwelden
2210 S Main
Tulsa, OK 74114
Phone: 918-583-4267
Fax: 918-583-1780
e-mail: eric@lightoperaok.org
Web Site: www.lightoperaok.org
Management:
    President: Jason McIntoch
    Artistic Director: Eric Gibson
    Artistic Director Emeritus/Founder: John Everitt
Mission: To preserve and create awareness of the musical comedy/operetta art form by producing a festival of such every summer in Tulsa, OK.
Founded: 1983
Specialized Field: Series & Festival; Musical Theatre; Opera
Status: Non-Profit, Professional
Paid Staff: 3
Volunteer Staff: 10
Paid Artists: 100
Non-paid Artists: 10
Budget: $300,000-350,000
Income Sources: Foundations; Corporations
Performs At: University of Tulsa School of Theatre
Annual Attendance: 6000-7500
Seating Capacity: 375

5017
TULSA PERFORMING ARTS CENTER TRUST

110 E 2nd Street
Tulsa, OK 74103-3212
Phone: 918-596-7122
Fax: 918-596-7144
Toll-free: 800-364-7111
e-mail: shirleyelliott@ci.tulsa.ok.us
Web Site: www.tulsapac.com
Management:
    Executive Director: John E Scott
Founded: 1977
Specialized Field: Entertainment; Performing Arts
Status: Non-Profit, Professional
Paid Staff: 33

5018
TULSA PERFORMING ARTS CENTER TRUST

110 E 2nd Street
Tulsa, OK 74103-3212
Phone: 918-596-7122
Fax: 918-596-7144
Toll-free: 800-364-7111
e-mail: tgrufik@ci.tulsa.ok.us
Web Site: www.tulsapac.com
Management:
    Program Director: Terry Grufik
Budget: $150,000-400,000
Performs At: Chapman Music Hall; Williams Theatre; Doenges Theatre

5019
CHILDREN'S PERFORMING ARTS SERIES

Albany Parks & Recreation
333 Broadalbin Street SW
Albany, OR 97321-2247
Phone: 541-917-7772
Fax: 541-917-7776
Web Site: www.cityofalbany.net/parks
Management:
    Director Of Parks & Recreation: Ed Hodney
Founded: 1978
Specialized Field: Childrens Performance
Status: Non-Profit, Professional
Paid Staff: 8
Paid Artists: 6
Budget: $10,000
Performs At: Linn Benton Community College Forum

5020
CITY OF ALBANY PARKS AND RECREATION DEPARTMENT

433 SW 4th Avenue
Albany, OR 97321
Phone: 541-917-7777
Fax: 514-917-7776
Management:
    Director: Dave Clark
    Program Coordinator: Sherry Halligan
Mission: To offer an outdoor concert series in summer at no cost, as well as a concert series for children.
Utilizes: Singers
Founded: 1983
Specialized Field: Vocal Music; Instrumental Music; Festivals
Status: For-Profit,Non-Professional
Organization Type: Sponsoring

5021
RIVER RHYTHMS

Albany Parks & Recreation
333 Broadalbin Street SW
Albany, OR 97321-2247
Phone: 541-917-7772
Fax: 541-917-7776
e-mail: jan.taylor@cityofalbany.net
Web Site: www.ci.albany.or.us
Management:
    President: Ed Hodney
    Artistic Director: Jan Taylor
    Managing Director: Katie Noofhazar
Mission: To build community.
Founded: 1983
Specialized Field: Series & Festivals: Performance & Concerts
Status: Non-Profit, Professional
Paid Staff: 16
Volunteer Staff: 12
Paid Artists: 7

5022
ASHLAND FOLK MUSIC CLUB

PO Box 63
Ashland, OR 97520
Phone: 541-488-0679
Fax: 541-552-6693
e-mail: ashlandfolk@iname.com
Officers:
    President: Jay Michalson
    VP: Gordon Enns
Mission: Supporting traditional music and dance.

Founded: 1984
Specialized Field: Dance; Vocal Music; Instrumental Music
Status: Nonprofit
Volunteer Staff: 8
Performs At: Carpenter Hall
Organization Type: Performing; Sponsoring

5023
OREGON SHAKESPEAREAN FESTIVAL ASSOCIATION

15 S Pioneer Street
PO Box 158
Ashland, OR 97520
Phone: 541-482-2111
Fax: 541-482-0446
Web Site: www.osfashland.org
Management:
   President: Chuck Butler
   VP: Nancy Tait
   Artistic Director: Libby Appel
   Treasurer: Dan Thorndike
Mission: To create bold new interpretations of contemporary and classic plays in repertory, influenced by American diversity and inspired by the high standard of Shakespeare.
Utilizes: Guest Companies; Singers
Founded: 1935
Status: Professional; Nonprofit
Paid Staff: 450
Volunteer Staff: 750
Budget: $17.1 million
Season: June - August
Performs At: Angus Bowmer Theatre; Black Swan; Elizabethan Theatre
Affiliations: Actors' Equity Association; ATA; University/Resident Theatre Association; Theatre Communications Group
Annual Attendance: 375,000+
Type of Stage: Thrust Stage; Black Box; Outdoors
Seating Capacity: 601; 250; 1188
Organization Type: Performing; Touring; Resident; Educational

5024
CASCADE FESTIVAL OF MUSIC

505 NW Franklin Avenue
Bend, OR 97701
Phone: 541-382-8381
Fax: 541-388-2814
Toll-free: 888-545-7435
e-mail: musicinfo@cascademusic.org
Web Site: www.cascademusic.org
Management:
   President: Kay Lucas
   Executive Director: Sally Russenberger
   Artistic Director: Murry Sidlan
   Business Manager: Cindy Sundquist
Mission: Classical music event in Central Oregon as an eight day festival in late August
Founded: 1981
Specialized Field: Classical
Status: Non-Profit, Professional
Paid Staff: 4
Volunteer Staff: 200
Paid Artists: 90
Performs At: Tent
Annual Attendance: 7,000 - 8,000

5025
OREGON COAST MUSIC FESTIVAL

PO Box 663
Coos Bay, OR 97420

Phone: 541-267-0938
Fax: 541-267-0938
Toll-free: 877-897-9350
e-mail: info@oregoncoastmusic.com
Web Site: www.oregoncoastmusic.com
Management:
   President: Jane Hooper
   Music Director: James Paul
Mission: To present an annual Classical Music festival of the highest professional caliber and to support a wide range of year-round musical performances and educational activities.
Founded: 1979
Specialized Field: Series & Festivals; Instrumental Music; Vocal Music; Youth; Ethnic Performances; Live Music
Status: Non-Profit, Professional
Paid Artists: 100

5026
COQUILLE PERFORMING ARTS

PO Box 53
Coquille, OR 97423
Phone: 541-396-5131
e-mail: rwiese@ucinet.com
Officers:
   President: Rochelle Wiese
Budget: $10,000
Performs At: Sawdust Theatre

5027
CORVALLIS-OREGON STATE UNIVERSITY MUSIC ASSOCIATION

3328 NW Firwood Drive
Corvallis, OR 97330
Phone: 541-737-1879
Fax: 541-346-5764
e-mail: mcclintt@ucs.orst.edu
Founded: 1948
Specialized Field: Classical; Orchestra

5028
CORVALLIS-OREGON STATE UNIVERSITY MUSIC ASSOCIATION

3328 NW Firwood Drive
Corvallis, OR 97330
Phone: 541-737-1879
Fax: 541-346-5764
e-mail: mcclintt@ucs.orst.edu
Officers:
   Chairman Program Committee: Thomas C McClintock
   President: Larry Blus
   Treasurer: Len Webber
   Secretary: Midge Mueller
Utilizes: Dancers; Guest Musical Directors; Guest Musicians; Multimedia; Original Music Scores; Sign Language Translators; Singers; Theatre Companies
Founded: 1948
Specialized Field: Classical; Orchestra
Volunteer Staff: 15
Budget: $20,000-35,000
Income Sources: Ticket Sales, Member and Corporate Donations, Foundation Grants
Performs At: Austin Auditorium; LaSells Stewart Center
Annual Attendance: 20,000
Facility Category: Auditorium in Conference Center
Type of Stage: Proscenium
Seating Capacity: 1,200
Year Built: 1981

5029
OREGON BACH FESTIVAL

1257 University of Oregon
Eugene, OR 97403
Phone: 541-346-5666
Fax: 541-346-5669
Toll-free: 800-457-1486
e-mail: bachfest@uoregon.edu
Web Site: www.bachfest.uoregon.edu
Management:
   Executive Director: H Royce Saltzman
   Artistic Director: Helmuth Rilling
   Marketing Director: George Evano
Mission: To offer high quality performances that elevate the spirits of both performers and audiences.
Utilizes: Singers
Founded: 1970
Specialized Field: Choral-Orchestra
Status: Non-Profit, Professional
Paid Staff: 10
Budget: 1.3 Million
Income Sources: Box office; Grants; Private Donations
Performs At: University of Oregon School of Music; Beall Concert
Affiliations: University of Oregon School of Music
Annual Attendance: 33,000
Facility Category: Concert Hall
Type of Stage: Proscenium
Seating Capacity: 2500/550
Organization Type: Performing; Resident; Educational

5030
OREGON FESTIVAL OF AMERICAN MUSIC

The Shedd
868 High Street
PO Box 97440
Eugene, OR 97401
Mailing Address: PO Box 1497, Eugene, OR. 97440
Phone: 541-687-6526
Fax: 541-687-1589
Toll-free: 800-248-1615
e-mail: info@ofam.org
Web Site: www.ofam.org
Management:
   President: Jim Ralph
   Executive Director: James Ralph
Mission: Year-round production and presenting of American music genres.
Founded: 1991
Specialized Field: Series & Festivals; Instrumental Music; Vocal Music; Youth; Dance
Status: Non-Profit, Professional
Paid Staff: 16

5031
UNIVERSITY OF OREGON CHAMBER MUSIC SERIES

School of Music
1225 University of Oregon
Eugene, OR 97403-1225
Phone: 541-346-5666
Fax: 541-346-5669
e-mail: chambermusic@beall
Web Site: www.music.oregon.edu/emb/
Officers:
   Co-Director: John Evans
   Co-Director: Dr. Brad Foley
Mission: To present the highest quality of chamber music possible in the Eugene-Springfield area with attention to a wide range of repertoire and genres that

will enhance the educational missions of the University of Oregon School of Music and Dance and the Oregon Bach Festival.
Founded: 1974
Specialized Field: Chamber Music
Status: Non-Profit, Professional
Paid Staff: 8
Budget: $75,000
Income Sources: Ticket Revenues; Sponsorships; Private Philanthropy; University Support
Performs At: Concert Hall
Affiliations: University Of Oregon; School Of Music And Dance; Oregon Bach Festival
Annual Attendance: 3,000
Seating Capacity: 540
Year Built: 1921

5032
UNIVERSITY OF OREGON CHAMBER MUSIC SERIES
School of Music
1225 University of Oregon
Eugene, OR 97403-1225
Phone: 541-346-5679
Fax: 541-346-0723
e-mail: jjs@oregon.uoregon.edu
Web Site: www.music1.oregon.edu/cms/cmshomepage.html
Management:
    Director: Janet J Stewart
Budget: $20,000-35,000
Performs At: Beall Concert Hall

5033
MT. HOOD COMMUNITY COLLEGE
26000 SE Stark Street
Gresham, OR 97030
Phone: 503-491-7260
Fax: 503-491-6077
Web Site: www.mhcc.edu
Management:
    President: Robert Silverman
Founded: 1968
Specialized Field: Junior College
Status: Non-Profit, Non-Professional
Budget: $10,000

5034
KLAMATH COMMUNITY CONCERTS
PO Box 1214
Klamath Falls, OR 97601
Phone: 541-850-1290
Fax: 541-273-0497
e-mail: kccaklamathfalls@aol.com
Web Site: www.kcca.us
Officers:
    President: Susan Fortune
Management:
    President: Lynne D Dalla
Founded: 1936
Specialized Field: Series and Festivals; Instrumental Music; Vocal Music; Theatre; Dance
Status: Non-Profit, Professional
Budget: $20,000-35,000
Performs At: Ross Ragland Theater

5035
EASTERN OREGON STATE COLLEGE PERFORMING ARTS PROGRAM
Student Activities Office
1 University Boulevard, Hoke Center, Suite 32
La Grande, OR 97850-2899
Phone: 541-962-3704
Fax: 541-962-1849
e-mail: ese@eou.edu
Management:
    ESE Director: Shean Lattin
    Student Activities Director: Jeff Dunbar
Specialized Field: Series & Festivals; Instrumental Music; Vocal Music; Theater; Dance
Status: Non-Profit, Professional
Paid Staff: 7
Paid Artists: 9
Budget: $10,000
Performs At: Inlow Hall; Loso Hall

5036
LAKE OSWEGO FESTIVAL OF THE ARTS
368 S State Street
PO Box 385
Lake Oswego, OR 97034
Phone: 503-636-1060
Fax: 503-635-2002
Web Site: www.lakewood-center.org
Management:
    Director: Dean Denton
    Director: Andrew Edwards
Founded: 1962
Specialized Field: Art
Status: Non-Profit
Paid Staff: 1
Volunteer Staff: 22
Budget: $150,000
Income Sources: Gifts; Grants; Commisions
Annual Attendance: 22,000
Facility Category: Arts Center and Park
Type of Stage: Outdoor
Seating Capacity: 500-1,000

5037
CASCADE HEAD MUSIC FESTIVAL
PO Box 605
1226 SW 13Th
Lincoln City, OR 97367
Toll-free: 877-994-5333
Web Site: www.cascadeheadmusic.com
Management:
    Music Director: Sergiu Luca
    Manager: Mark Imscher
Founded: 1986
Paid Staff: 1

5038
MARYLHURST UNIVERSITY MUSIC DEPARTMENT
Marylhurst University
17600 Pacific Highway
Marylhurst, OR 97036
Mailing Address: PO Box 261, Marylhurst, PA. 97036
Phone: 503-636-8141
Fax: 503-636-9526
Toll-free: 800-634-9982
e-mail: music@marylhurst.edu
Web Site: www.marylhurst.edu
Officers:
    Chair: John Paul
Management:
    President: Nancy Wilgendusch
    Department Head of Music: George Paul
Utilizes: Collaborations; Guest Accompanists; Guest Companies; Guest Ensembles; Guest Musical Directors; Guest Musicians; Guest Soloists; Guest Teachers; Instructors; Local Artists; Multimedia; Original Music Scores; Playwrights; Sign Language Translators; Singers; Soloists

Specialized Field: Series and Festivals; Instrumental Music; Vocal Music; Youth; Music Therapy
Status: Non-Profit, Non-Professional
Paid Staff: 3
Performs At: St. Anne's Chapel; Wiegand Recital Hall
Annual Attendance: 1,000
Facility Category: Chapel
Seating Capacity: 325
Cost: $690/day

5039
BRITT FESTIVALS
PO Box 1124
Medford, OR 97501
Phone: 541-779-0847
Fax: 541-776-3712
Toll-free: 800-882-7488
e-mail: info@brittfest.org
Web Site: www.brittfest.org
Management:
    President: Gary Sherwood
    Executive Director: Ron McUne
    Artistic Director: Peter Bay
    Development Director: Ed Foss
    Booking/Production Director: Mike Sturgill
    Education Director: David MacKenzie
Mission: To present and sponsor, in Southern Oregon, performing arts of the highest quality for the education, enrichment and enjoyment of all.
Utilizes: Guest Artists; Guest Companies
Founded: 1963
Specialized Field: Series & Festival; Live Music; Country Music
Status: Non-Profit, Professional
Paid Staff: 12
Volunteer Staff: 600
Performs At: The Britt Gardens
Annual Attendance: 70,000
Facility Category: Outdoor Amphitheatre
Seating Capacity: 2200
Year Built: 1963
Year Remodeled: 1992
Organization Type: Performing; Touring; Resident; Educational; Sponsoring

5040
WESTERN OREGON UNIVERSITY EDGAR H SMITH FINE ARTS SERIES
Western Oregon University
345 N Monmouth Avenue
Monmouth, OR 97361
Phone: 503-838-8000
Fax: 503-838-8880
e-mail: willisk@wou.edu
Web Site: www.wou.edu/las
Management:
    President: Dr John P Minahan
    Chair-Division Of Creative Arts: Diane Tarter
Utilizes: Artists-in-Residence; Dance Companies; Dancers; Guest Choreographers; Guest Musical Directors; Multimedia; Original Music Scores; Special Technical Talent
Founded: 1976
Paid Staff: 1
Volunteer Staff: 16
Paid Artists: 4
Budget: $35,000-60,000
Performs At: Rice Auditorium
Facility Category: College Auditorium
Type of Stage: Proscenium
Stage Dimensions: 30 X 55
Seating Capacity: 617

5041
ERNEST BLOCH MUSIC FESTIVAL AT NEWPORT
PO Box 1617
Newport, OR 97365
Phone: 541-574-0614
Fax: 541-265-5008
e-mail: baymusic@newportnet.com
Web Site: www.baymusic.org
Management:
    President: Ken Combs
    Director: Mary Lee Scoville
Founded: 1994

5042
CHAMBER MUSIC NORTHWEST
522 SW 5th Avenue
Suite 725
Portland, OR 97204
Phone: 503-223-3202
Fax: 503-294-1690
e-mail: info@cmnw.org
Web Site: www.cmnw.org
Management:
    President: Peter Livingston
    Executive Director: Linda Magee
    Artistic Director: David Shifrin
    Finance Director: Katherine King
    Marketing Manager: Garen Horgend
Mission: To present an annual summer music festival (five weeks/25 concerts) with world renowned performers in residence; to present concerts and educational activities on a year-round basis.
Founded: 1971
Specialized Field: Series and Festivals: Chamber Music
Status: Non-Profit, Professional
Paid Staff: 6
Budget: One Million
Performs At: Reed College
Affiliations: Kaul Auditorium at Reed College; Cabell Theatre at Catlin Gabel Schhool
Annual Attendance: 19,000
Facility Category: Concert Hall (private college)
Seating Capacity: 550
Year Built: 1998
Organization Type: Performing

5043
MOUNT HOOD FESTIVAL OF JAZZ: THE GOVERNOR BUILDING
323 NE Roberts Avenue
Portland, OR 97030
Phone: 503-665-3827
Fax: 503-232-2336
Web Site: www.mthoodjazz.com
Management:
    Artistic Director: Kyle O Brien

5044
PORTLAND UNIVERSITY PORTLAND INTERNATIONAL: PERFORMANCE FESTIVAL
PO Box 1491
Portland, OR 97207
Phone: 503-725-5389
Fax: 503-725-4840
e-mail: griggsm@ses.pdx.edu
Web Site: www.extended.pdx.edu/pipf/index.html
Management:
    Artistic Director: Michael Griggs

5045
PORTLAND STATE UNIVERSITY PIANO RECITAL SERIES
PO Box 751
Portland, OR 97207
Phone: 503-725-5400
Fax: 503-725-8215
e-mail: zagelop@mail.pdx.edu
Web Site: www.fpa.pdx.edu/prs/
Management:
    Executive Director: Pat Zagelow
Mission: The piano recital series is dedicated to presenting the finest pianists in the world in recital settings and outreach for the purpose of enriching and educating our community.
Utilizes: Guest Directors; Multimedia; Singers
Budget: $200,000
Income Sources: Tickets; Contributions
Performs At: Lincoln Hall Auditorium
Annual Attendance: 6,000
Type of Stage: Proscenium
Seating Capacity: 476

5046
TRIANGLE PRODUCTIONS
8420 SW Canyon Lane #13
Portland, OR 97225
Phone: 503-239-5919
Fax: 503-239-5928
e-mail: trianglepro@juno.com
Web Site: www.tripro.org/general.html
Officers:
    Triangle Productions Board: Lennky Borer
    Board: Dennis Dohtery
    Board: Larry Esau
    Board: Sherman Tam
    Board: Edd Scott
    Board: Donald I Horn
    Past President: Sharon Knorr
    Honorary Member: Gus Van Sant
    Honorary Member: Dan Reed
Management:
    Managing Director and Founder: Donald I Horn
Founded: 1989
Opened: 1989
Status: Not-for-profit
Paid Staff: 1
Volunteer Staff: 50
Paid Artists: 40
Performs At: Various
Affiliations: Dramatists Guild

5047
UNIVERSITY OF PORTLAND MUSIC AT MIDWEEK
5000 N Williamette Boulevard
Portland, OR 97203
Phone: 503-943-7382
Fax: 503-943-7399
Toll-free: 800-BAP-ILOT
e-mail: doyle@up.edu
Management:
    Manager: Roger Doyle
Founded: 1901
Specialized Field: Series & Festivals; Instrumental Music; Vocal Music; Theatre; Dance; Ethnic Performances
Status: Non-Profit, Non-Professional

5048
UNIVERSITY OF PORTLAND MUSIC AT MIDWEEK
5000 N Williamette Boulevard
Portland, OR 97203
Phone: 503-943-7382
Fax: 503-943-7399
e-mail: doyle@up.edu
Management:
    Manager: Roger Doyle
Budget: $10,000
Performs At: Hunt Center Recital Hall

5049
ABBEY BACH FESTIVAL
Mount Angel Abbey
One Abbey Drive
Saint Benedict, OR 97373
Phone: 503-845-3321
Fax: 503-845-3594
e-mail: bach@mountangelabbey.org
Web Site: www.mountangelabbey.org
Officers:
    President: Abbot Gregory Duerr OSB
Management:
    Executive Director: Rev Paschal Cheline OFB
Utilizes: Multimedia; Original Music Scores; Singers
Founded: 1972
Specialized Field: Series & Festivals: Instrumental Music
Status: Non-Profit, Professional
Performs At: Damian Center
Annual Attendance: 1500
Type of Stage: Proscenium
Seating Capacity: 500
Year Built: 1936
Year Remodeled: 1983
Organization Type: Performing

5050
SUNRIVER MUSIC FESTIVAL
PO Box 4308
Sunriver, OR 97707
Phone: 541-593-1084
Fax: 541-593-6959
e-mail: tickets@sunrivermusic.org
Web Site: www.sunrivermusic.org
Officers:
    President: Jim Putney
Management:
    Executive Director: Pamela Beezley
    Office Manager: Vicki Udlock
    Ticket Office Manager: Robin Burford
Mission: To present quality performaces of classical music and support music education programs for the youth of Central Oregon.
Utilizes: Fine Artists; Guest Lecturers; Multimedia; Original Music Scores
Founded: 1971
Specialized Field: Series and Festivals: Classical Music
Status: Non-Profit, Professional
Paid Staff: 3
Volunteer Staff: 4
Budget: $250,000
Income Sources: Private; Business; Grants
Performs At: Great Hall
Annual Attendance: 3,500

5051

YACHATS MUSIC FESTIVAL

Yachats Community Presbyterian Church
360 - West 7th Street
Yachats, OR 97498
Mailing Address: Four Season Concerts, PO Box 507,
Berkeley, CA. 94701
Phone: 510-451-0775
Fax: 510-549-3504
e-mail: fourseasonsconcerts@juno.com
Web Site: www.fourseasonsconcerts.com
Officers:
    President: Jesse W Anthony
Founded: 1981

Pennsylvania

5052

ALLENTOWN COMMUNITY CONCERTS

905 S Cedar Crest Boulevard
Allentown, PA 18103
Phone: 610-432-9143
Officers:
    President: William Lazenberg
Mission: To present four annual concerts with varied
programs; membership is open to the public during the
annual campaign.
Founded: 1927
Specialized Field: Dance; Vocal Music; Instrumental
Music
Status: Nonprofit
Budget: $20,000-35,000
Income Sources: Community Concerts
Organization Type: Educational; Sponsoring

5053

MUHLENBERG COLLEGE CONCERT SERIES

2400 Chew Street
Allentown, PA 18104
Phone: 484-664-3363
Fax: 484-664-3633
Web Site: www.muhlenbergcollege.edu
Management:
    President: Randall Helms
    Executive Director: Douglas Ovens
    Theatre Director: Charles Richter
Founded: 1847
Specialized Field: Series & Festivals; Instrumental
Music; Vocal Music
Status: Non-Profit, Professional
Paid Staff: 20
Paid Artists: 20

5054

MUHLENBERG COLLEGE CONCERT SERIES

2400 Chew Street
Allentown, PA 18104
Phone: 484-664-3363
Fax: 484-664-3633
Budget: $10,000-20,000
Season: June - August

5055

BEAVER VALLEY COMMUNITY CONCERT ASSOCIATION

153 Oak Drive
Beaver Falls, PA 15010
Phone: 724-846-6814
Officers:
    President: EE Bass

Budget: $20,000-35,000

5056

ARTSQUEST

25 W 3rd Street
Bethlehem, PA 18015
Phone: 610-861-0678
Fax: 610-861-2644
e-mail: info@fest.org
Web Site: www.fest.org
Officers:
    President: Jeffrey Parks
Management:
    Director of Performing Arts: Patrick Brogan

5057

BETHLEHEM BACH FESTIVAL

423 Heckewelder Place
Bethlehem, PA 18018
Phone: 610-866-4382
Fax: 610-866-6232
Toll-free: 888-743-3100
e-mail: office@bach.org
Web Site: www.bach.org
Management:
    Artistic Director and Conductor: Greg Funfgeld
Founded: 1898

5058

MORAVIAN COLLEGE ARTS & LECTURES SERIES

1200 Main Street
Bethlehem, PA 18018
Phone: 610-861-1686
Fax: 610-861-1657
e-mail: mecat01@moravian.edu
Officers:
    Chairperson: Carol Traupman-Carr
Budget: $20,000-35,000
Seating Capacity: 400

5059

BLOOMSBURG UNIVERSITY ARTIST-CELEBRITY SERIES

Bloomsburg University
400 E 2nd Street
Bloomsburg, PA 17815
Phone: 570-389-4201
Fax: 570-389-4201
e-mail: rpress@bloomu.edu
Web Site: www.bloomu.edu
Management:
    President: Jessica Kozloff
    VP Administration/Finance: Richard Rugen
Specialized Field: Higher Education
Status: Non-Profit, Professional
Budget: $60,000-150,000
Performs At: Mitrani Hall; Haas Center for the Arts;
Gross Auditorium

5060

MONTGOMERY COUNTY COMMUNITY COLLEGE LIVELY ARTS SERIES

340 Dekalb Pike
Box 400
Blue Bell, PA 19422-0796
Phone: 215-641-6300
Fax: 215-641-6645
e-mail: livarts@mc3.edu
Web Site: www.mc3.edu
Management:
    Vice Chair: Anthony Disandro
    Chair: Paul S Bitner

Founded: 1972
Paid Staff: 2
Budget: $35,000-60,000
Performs At: Science Center Theater

5061

BRADFORD CREATIVE & PERFORMING ARTS CENTER

10 Marilyn Horne Way
PO Box 153
Bradford, PA 16701
Phone: 814-362-2522
Fax: 814-368-7040
e-mail: info@bcpac.com
Web Site: www.bcpac.com
Officers:
    President: James D Guelfi
Management:
    President: James D Guelfi
    VP: Karen Niemic Bucheit
Founded: 1984
Paid Staff: 1
Volunteer Staff: 15
Paid Artists: 5
Budget: $60,000-150,000
Income Sources: Sales; Grants; Patrons
Annual Attendance: 5,000
Seating Capacity: 1410

5062

CRS NATIONAL FESTIVAL FOR THE PERFORMING ARTS

724 Winchester Road
Broomall, PA 19008
Phone: 215-544-5920
Fax: 215-544-5921
e-mail: crsnews@erols.com
Web Site: www.erols.com/crsnews
Management:
    Artistic Advisor: Milton Babbitt
Mission: To offer performers, composers, teachers,
libraries, educational institutions, amateurs, devotees of
music and prosepective sponsors cultural enrichment
through vast musical sources.
Utilizes: Community Members; Guest Artists; Guest
Companies; Scenic Designers; Singers
Founded: 1981
Specialized Field: Dance; Vocal Music; Instrumental
Music; Festivals
Status: Professional; Semi-Professional; Nonprofit
Income Sources: Contemporary Record Society
Organization Type: Performing; Touring; Resident;
Educational

5063

BRYN MAWR COLLEGE PERFORMING ARTS SERIES

Office for the Arts
101 N Merion Avenue
Bryn Mawr, PA 19010
Phone: 610-526-5210
Fax: 610-526-5205
e-mail: lkraus@brynmawr.edu
Web Site: www.brynmawr.edu
Officers:
    President: Jane McAuliffe
Management:
    Executive Director: Linda Caruso Haviland
    Performing Arts Coordinator: Lisa Kraus
Founded: 1985
Specialized Field: Series and Festivals; Dance;
Theatre; Chamber Music
Status: Non-Profit, Professional

Paid Staff: 2
Volunteer Staff: 2
Budget: $43,350
Seating Capacity: 800

5064
PENNSYLVANIA SHAKESPEARE FESTIVAL

2755 Station Avenue
Center Valley, PA 18034
Phone: 610-282-3192
Fax: 610-282-2084
e-mail: kathryn.cousar@desales.edu
Web Site: www.pashakespeare.org
Management:
President: Paul Domalakes
VP: James P Mcfadd
Producing Artistic Director: Patrick Mulcahy
General Manager: Casey William Gallagher
Endowment Director: Gerard J Schubert, OSFS
Business Manager: Janice Hein
Founded: 1992
Status: Professional
Paid Staff: 6
Volunteer Staff: 200
Paid Artists: 100
Season: May - August
Type of Stage: Thrust
Stage Dimensions: 38' x 40'
Seating Capacity: 473

5065
WILSON COLLEGE PERFORMING ARTS SERIES

1015 Philadelphia Avenue
Chamebrsburg, PA 17201
Phone: 717-262-2003
Fax: 717-262-2038
e-mail: klehman@wilson.edu
Web Site: www.wilson.edu
Officers:
President: Lorna Edmundson
Management:
Cultural Events Director: Kathy Lehman
Mission: Provide series of artistic performances that enrich lives of students, faculty and staff, and to serve as a cultural resource to the Cumberland Valley area.
Utilizes: Artists-in-Residence; Dance Companies; Multimedia; Special Technical Talent
Founded: 1869
Specialized Field: Laird Hall
Status: Non-Profit, Professional
Paid Staff: 3
Volunteer Staff: 4
Paid Artists: 4
Budget: $12,000
Income Sources: Grants; Endowment Funds
Facility Category: Auditorium
Type of Stage: Proscenium
Stage Dimensions: 30'x30'
Seating Capacity: 300

5066
CLARION UNIVERSITY ACTIVITIES BOARD ARTS

273 Gemmell Student Center
Clarion, PA 16214
Phone: 814-393-2312
Management:
Advisor: Jamie Bero-Johnson
Budget: $10,000-20,000
Performs At: Marwick - Boyd Auditorium

5067
LEHIGH VALLEY BLUES & JAZZ FESTIVAL

PO Box G
Coplay, PA 18037
Web Site: www.lvbluesfest.org

5068
PENNSYLVANIA RENAISSANCE FAIRE

PO Box 685
Cornwall, PA 17016
Phone: 717-665-7021
Fax: 717-664-3466
e-mail: royalspk@parenaissancefaire.com
Web Site: www.parenfaire.com
Management:
Associate Producer: Thomas Roy
Utilizes: Actors; Artists-in-Residence; Choreographers; Dancers; Designers; Fine Artists; Guest Accompanists; Guest Conductors; Guest Directors; Guest Ensembles; Guest Musical Directors; Guest Musicians; High School Drama; Local Artists; Multimedia; Organization Contracts; Original Music Scores; Resident Artists; Resident Professionals; Selected Students; Sign Language Translators; Singers; Soloists; Student Interns
Founded: 1980
Status: Non-Equity; Commercial
Season: August - October
Annual Attendance: 200,000
Facility Category: Outdoor Festival
Type of Stage: Outdoor
Year Built: 1980

5069
MOUNT ALOYSIUS COLLEGE PERFORMING ARTS SERIES

7373 Admiral Peary Highway
Cresson, PA 16630
Phone: 814-886-6407
Fax: 814-886-2978
e-mail: jniebauer@mtaloy.edu
Management:
Director of Student Activities: Joyce Niebauer
Budget: $10,000-20,000

5070
DELAWARE WATER GAP CELEBRATION OF THE ARTS

PO Box 249
Delaware Water Gap, PA 18327
Phone: 717-424-2210
Web Site: www.welcome.to/cotajazz
Management:
Director: Richard C Chamberlain

5071
ALLAN KURBY SPORTS CENTER

Lafayette College
Easton, PA 18042
Phone: 610-250-5470
Fax: 610-250-7651
Web Site: www.lafayette/sports.edu
Management:
Director: Eve Atkinson

5072
LAFAYETTE COLLEGE CONCERT SERIES

Williams Center for the Arts
Easton, PA 18042

Phone: 610-250-5010
Fax: 610-250-8728
Management:
Executive Director: Dr. Ellis Finger
Budget: $60,000-150,000
Seating Capacity: 400

5073
EDINBORO UNIVERSITY OF PENNSYLVANIA PERFORMING ARTS SERIES

Music Department
Room 109
Edinboro, PA 16444
Phone: 814-732-2518
Fax: 814-732-2862
e-mail: aortega@edinboro.edu
Web Site: www.edinboro.edu
Management:
Director Performing Arts: Ann Ortega
Specialized Field: Choral; Dance; Instrumental Music
Status: Non-Profit, Professional
Budget: $35,000-60,000
Performs At: Memorial Auditorium

5074
MUSIC AT GRETNA

1 Alpha Drive
Elizabethtown, PA 17022
Phone: 717-361-1508
Fax: 717-361-1512
e-mail: music@mtgretna.com
Web Site: www.mtgretna.com/music
Officers:
Founder: Carl Ellenberger, Jr
President: Henry Kenderdine
Management:
President: David Wood
Executive Director: Michael Murray
Development Director: Suzanne Kenderdine
Founded: 1975
Specialized Field: Series & Festivals; Instrumental Music; Vocal Music; Youth; Dance; Ethnic Performances
Status: Non-Profit, Professional
Paid Staff: 3
Budget: $60,000-150,000
Income Sources: Mt. Greten Playhouse; Clyde & Perk Center
Performs At: Leffler Chapel Performance Center
Organization Type: Educational; Sponsoring; Producing

5075
ERIE CIVIC CENTER/ WARNER THEATRE

809 French Street
Erie, PA 16512
Phone: 814-453-7117
Fax: 814-455-9931
Web Site: www.erieciviccenter.com
Management:
Managing Director: John Wells

5076
ERIE CIVIC MUSIC ASSOCIATION

1833 W 33rd Street
Erie, PA 16508
Mailing Address: PO Box 143 Erie, PA 16512
Phone: 814-864-5681
Fax: 814-864-1218
e-mail: butchvick@aol.com
Web Site: www.eriecivicmusic.com
Officers:

President: Garlan Newcomb
VP: Harry Osiecki
Treasurer: Chris Mosier
Executive Secretary: Bea Hansen
Management:
Director of Advertising: Vickie Newcomb
Mission: We present the greatest international talent available at the most reasonable costs.
Founded: 1928
Specialized Field: Vocal Music; Instrumental Music; International Dancers and Nostalgia Shows
Status: Nonprofit
Volunteer Staff: 35
Budget: $50,000-90,000
Income Sources: Erie Area Fund for the Arts; Season & Single Tickets Sales
Performs At: Warner Theatre
Annual Attendance: 7,500-9,000
Organization Type: Sponsoring

5077
MESSIAH COLLEGE CULTURAL SERIES
Messiah College, One College Avenue
PO Box 3020
Grantham, PA 17027
Phone: 717-691-6027
Fax: 717-796-5371
e-mail: ehager@messiah.edu
Web Site: www.messiah.edu
Management:
President: Kim Pitts
Founded: 1909
Specialized Field: Series & Festivals; Coral; Dance; Ethnic; Opera; Educational; Instrumental Music; Jazz; Theatre; Music
Status: Non-Profit
Paid Staff: 8
Budget: $20,000-35,000
Performs At: Miller Auditorium

5078
27TH ANNUAL CENTRAL PA COMMERCE BANK JAZZ FESTIVAL
5721 Jonestown Road
Harrisburg, PA 17112
Phone: 717-540-1010
Fax: 717-540-7735
e-mail: dave@pajazz.org
Web Site: www.pajazz.org
Officers:
President: Rosemary Barrett
Management:
Executive Director: David Lazorcik
Founded: 1980
Specialized Field: Series and Festivals: Jazz Music
Status: Non-Profit, Professional
Paid Staff: 1
Paid Artists: 200

5079
HARRISBURG AREA COMMUNITY COLLEGE
1 HACC Drive
Harrisburg, PA 17110-2999
Phone: 717-780-2545
Fax: 717-780-3281
Web Site: www.hacc.edu/rose
Management:
Performing Artist Series Director: Teri Guerrisi
Utilizes: Dance Companies; Multimedia; Original Music Scores; Theatre Companies
Founded: 1975

Specialized Field: Series & Festivals; Dances; Music; Theatre; Family
Status: Non-Profit, Professional
Paid Staff: 6
Volunteer Staff: 30
Budget: $35,000-60,000
Performs At: Rose Lehrman Auditorium
Facility Category: Proscenium
Type of Stage: Hardwood, Spring Floor
Stage Dimensions: 36'x40'
Seating Capacity: 374
Year Built: 1975
Year Remodeled: 1993
Rental Contact: Teri Guerrsi

5080
MARKET SQUARE CONCERTS
225 Market Street
2nd Floor
Harrisburg, PA 17101
Mailing Address: PO Box 1292, Harrisburg, PA. 17108
Phone: 717-221-9599
Fax: 717-221-9588
e-mail: lucymiller@marketsquareconcerts.org
Web Site: www.marketsquareconcerts.org
Officers:
President: David Lehman
Management:
Executive Director: Lucy Miller
Mission: Presenting a wide range of chamber and solo music presentations by distinguished artists.
Founded: 1982
Specialized Field: Chamber Music
Status: Non-Profit, Professional
Paid Staff: 1
Budget: $60,000-150,000
Performs At: Market Square Church; Rose Lehrman Art Center; Whitaker Ctr.
Organization Type: Educational; Presenting

5081
NEXT GENERATION FESTIVAL
WITF-Inc 1982 Locust Lane
PO Box 2954
Harrisburg, PA 17105-2954
Phone: 717-236-6000
Web Site: www.nextgenerationfestival.org

5082
HERSHEYPARK ARENA/STADIUM
100 W Hersheypark Drive
Hershey, PA 17033
Phone: 717-534-8966
Fax: 717-534-3113
Web Site: www.hersheypa.com
Management:
General Manager: Matthew Ford

5083
JUNIATA PRESENTS
Juniata College
1700 Moore Street
Huntingdon, PA 16652
Phone: 814-641-3608
e-mail: herzog@juniata.edu
Web Site: www.juniatapresents.com
Officers:
President: Thomas R Kepple Jr
Executive Assistant to President: JoAnne Isenberg
Management:
Director of the Performing Arts: Chad Herzog

Mission: Providing the highest quality of liberal education and to awaken students to the empowering richness of the mind and to enable them to lead fulfilling and useful lives.
Utilizes: Actors; Artists-in-Residence; Collaborating Artists; Collaborations; Commissioned Composers; Community Members; Community Talent; Contract Actors; Contract Orchestras; Curators; Dance Companies; Dancers; Educators; Filmmakers; Fine Artists; Grant Writers; Guest Accompanists; Guest Artists; Guest Choreographers; Guest Directors; Guest Ensembles; Guest Soloists; High School Drama; Multi Collaborations; Multimedia; Original Music Scores; Paid Performers; Playwrights; Resident Companies; Scenic Designers; Soloists; Students; Student Interns; Theatre Companies; Visual Designers
Founded: 1876
Specialized Field: Educational
Status: Non-Profit, Professional
Paid Staff: 400
Budget: $35,000-60,000

5084
INDIANA UNIVERSITY OF PENNSYLVANIA ONSTAGE: ARTS AND ENTERTAINMENT
410 Sutton Hall
Indiana, PA 15705
Phone: 724-357-2315
Fax: 724-357-2593
e-mail: destefan@iup.edu
Web Site: www.onstageatiup.com
Management:
Arts/Entertainment Director: Frank Destefano
Mission: Presenting organization
Founded: 1963
Specialized Field: Series; music, theater, dance
Status: Non-Profit, Professional
Paid Staff: 3
Volunteer Staff: 60
Budget: $800,000
Income Sources: Corporate; Grants; Tickets; Donors
Performs At: Fisher Auditorium
Type of Stage: Proscenium
Seating Capacity: 1454
Year Built: 1938
Year Remodeled: 2008
Cost: $12,000,000

5085
LAUREL FESTIVAL OF THE ARTS
PO Box 206
Jim Thorpe, PA 18229
Phone: 570-325-4439
Fax: 570-325-4439
Management:
Artistic Director: Marc Mostaroy
Weeknight Concerts: Randall Perry
Publicity: Herbert Thompson
Marketing: Barbara Loeffler
Mission: To unite the finest performers in working together to present events for the public.
Founded: 1990
Specialized Field: Dance; Vocal Music; Instrumental Music; Festivals; Poetry
Status: Professional; Nonprofit
Performs At: Manch Chunk Opera House
Organization Type: Performing; Resident; Educational

5086
CAMBRIA COUNTY WAR MEMORIAL ARENA
326 Napoleon
Johnstown, PA 15901
Phone: 814-536-5156
Fax: 814-536-3670
Toll-free: 800-243-8499
e-mail: gm@warmemorialarena.com
Web Site: www.warmemorialarena.com
Management:
  President: Larry Giannone
  Executive Director: James Vautar
  Managing Director: Tom Grenell
Mission: Sports and entertainment
Founded: 1950
Specialized Field: Hockey
Status: Non-Profit, Professional
Paid Staff: 9
Paid Artists: 12
Budget: 1.5 million
Income Sources: Rental Events
Annual Attendance: 275,000
Facility Category: Arena
Type of Stage: Portable
Seating Capacity: 5,000
Year Built: 1950
Year Remodeled: 2003
Cost: $85 million
Rental Contact: Jim Vautar

5087
PASQUERILLA PERFORMING ARTS CENTER
University of Pittsburgh at Johnstown
450 Schoolhouse Road
Johnstown, PA 15904-2990
Phone: 814-269-7200
Fax: 814-269-7240
Toll-free: 800-846-2787
e-mail: upjarts@pitt.edu
Web Site: www.upj.pitt.edu/artscenter
Management:
  Executive Director: Michael Bodolosky
  Office Manager: Beverlyh Walerysiak
  Technical Director: Thomas Brubaker
Founded: 1991
Status: Non-Profit, Professional
Paid Staff: 3
Volunteer Staff: 39
Seating Capacity: 1001

5088
LONGWOOD GARDENS PERFORMING ARTS
PO Box 501
Kennett Square, PA 19348
Phone: 610-388-1000
Fax: 610-388-3833
Web Site: www.longwoodgardens.org
Management:
  Executive Director: Fred Robert
  Performing Arts Coordinator: Dara Gordon
Mission: To enhance the gardens and follow tradition of founder Pierre S duPont.
Utilizes: Actors; Choreographers; Dance Companies; Dancers; Local Artists; Multimedia; Original Music Scores; Sign Language Translators; Singers; Special Technical Talent; Theatre Companies
Founded: 1906
Specialized Field: Series & Festivals; Instrumental Music; Theatre; Dance
Status: Non-Profit, Professional
Paid Staff: 50
Budget: $60,000-150,000
Income Sources: Ticket Sales
Annual Attendance: 1 Million to Gardens
Facility Category: Outdoor Historic Theatre
Stage Dimensions: 73 x 36
Seating Capacity: 2000
Year Built: 1920
Organization Type: Performing; Educational

5089
KUTZTOWN UNIVERSITY PERFORMING ARTISTS SERIES
Office of Cultural Affairs
Kutztown University
Kutztown, PA 19530
Phone: 610-683-4510
Fax: 610-683-4010
e-mail: kupas@kutztown.edu
Web Site: www.kupas.org
Management:
  Cultural Affairs Director: Ellen Finks
Founded: 1986
Specialized Field: Series & Festivals; Instrumental Music; Vocal Music; Theatre; Youth; Dance; Ethnic Performances
Status: Non-Profit, Professional
Paid Staff: 3
Paid Artists: 30
Budget: $60,000-150,000
Performs At: Schaeffer Auditorium

5090
NEW ARTS PROGRAM
173 W Main Street
PO Box 82
Kutztown, PA 19530
Phone: 610-683-6440
Fax: 610-683-6440
e-mail: napconn@aol.com
Web Site: www.napconnection.com
Officers:
  President: James FL Carroll
  VP: Michael Kessler
  Treasurer: James FL Carroll
  Secretary: Joanne P. Carroll
Management:
  President: James Carroll
Mission: To present artists from the performing, visual and literary arts in one-to-one consultations; to offer a presentation/performance style collective consultation.
Utilizes: Artists-in-Residence; Choreographers; Dancers; Filmmakers; Fine Artists; Multimedia; Performance Artists; Playwrights; Singers
Founded: 1974
Specialized Field: Series & Festivals; Instrumental Music; Vocal Music; Dance; Ethnic Performances
Status: Non-Profit, Professional
Paid Staff: 1
Volunteer Staff: 2
Paid Artists: 8
Budget: $60,000
Income Sources: PCA, Foundations, Corporations, Individuals
Performs At: Saint Johns UCC
Annual Attendance: 3000
Facility Category: Gallery
Seating Capacity: 76 - 350
Organization Type: Performing; Resident

5091
FRANKLIN & MARSHALL COLLEGE SOUND HORIZONS CONCERT SERIES
PO Box 3003
Lancaster, PA 17604-3003
Phone: 717-291-4346
Fax: 717-358-7168
e-mail: mathew.weaver@fandm.edu
Web Site: www.fandm.edu
Officers:
  Chairman Concert Committee: Bruce Gustafson
Management:
  Concert Coordinator: Mathew Weaver
  Performance Manager: Mark Miskinis
  Chair of Concert: John Carbon
Utilizes: Artists-in-Residence; Commissioned Composers; Commissioned Music; Composers-in-Residence; Dance Companies; Dancers; Grant Writers; Guest Accompanists; Guest Companies; Guest Composers; Guest Designers; Guest Directors; Guest Ensembles; Guest Musical Directors; Guest Musicians; Guest Soloists; Local Artists; Multimedia; Music; Original Music Scores; Resident Artists; Sign Language Translators; Singers; Soloists
Founded: 1935
Specialized Field: Series & Festivals; Instrumental Music; Vocal Music; Theatre; Youth; Dance; Ethnic Performances
Status: Non-Profit, Professional
Paid Staff: 6
Volunteer Staff: 6
Budget: $35,000-50,000
Performs At: The Ann & Richard Barshinger Center; Miller Recital Hall
Facility Category: Concert Hall
Seating Capacity: 500
Year Built: 1925
Year Remodeled: 2000

5092
PHILADELPHIA SCHOOL OF MUSIC & PERFORMING ARTS
Philadelphia Biblical University
200 Manor Avenue
Langhorne, PA 19047-2990
Phone: 215-702-4329
Fax: 215-702-4342
e-mail: music@pbu.edu
Web Site: www.pbu.edu
Officers:
  President: Todd Williams
  Dean: Paul Isensee
Specialized Field: Degrees; Music Degrees; Church Music; Music Education
Status: Non-Profit, Professional
Paid Staff: 3
Paid Artists: 25
Budget: $10,000
Affiliations: NASM
Facility Category: Chapel
Seating Capacity: 750

5093
BUCKNELL UNIVERSITY: WEIS CENTER PERFORMANCE SERIES
Weis Center for the Performing Arts
Bucknell University
Lewisburg, PA 17837-2005
Phone: 570-577-3700
Fax: 570-577-3701
e-mail: boswell@bucknell.edu
Web Site: www.departments.bucknell.edu
Management:

President: Brian Mitchell
Executive Director: William Boswell
Mission: To provide the campus and region with opportunity for exposure to the essential cultural and educational values inherent in the great historical an radical traditions of the performing arts.
Founded: 1988
Specialized Field: Series & Festivals: Performing Arts
Status: Non-Profit, Professional
Paid Staff: 120
Budget: $150,000-400,000
Affiliations: APAP, CMA, PA Presenters, Others
Annual Attendance: 9000
Facility Category: Concert Hall
Type of Stage: Sprung Wood Floor
Seating Capacity: 1,200+
Year Built: 1988

5094
MIFFLIN-JUNIATA CONCERT ASSOCIATION
PO Box 870
Lewiston, PA 17044-0870
Phone: 717-248-4971
Fax: 717-248-2672
Management:
    Director Emeritus: Allen J Levin
Budget: $20,000-35,000

5095
MUSIC FOR MT.LEBANON
PO Box 817
Mac Muarry, PA 15317
Phone: 724-941-9490
Management:
    President: Elliot Davis
    Artistic Director: Carl Apone
Founded: 1945
Specialized Field: Series and Festivals: Community Musical Programs
Status: Non-Profit, Professional
Paid Staff: 2

5096
MANSFIELD UNIVERSITY FINE ARTS SERIES
Music Department
Mansfield, PA 16933
Phone: 570-662-4710
Fax: 570-662-4114
Web Site: www.music.mnsfld.edu
Management:
    President: John Halstead
    Department Chairperson: Adam Brennan
    Manager: Kenneth Sarch
Founded: 1857
Specialized Field: Series & Festivals; Instrumental Music; Vocal Music; Theatre
Status: Non-Profit, Non-Professional
Paid Staff: 24
Budget: $10,000-20,000
Performs At: Steadman Theatre

5097
MUSIC AT FISHS EDDY
875 Welsh Road
Maple Glen, PA 19002
Mailing Address: PO Box 191, Fishs Eddy, NY. 13774
Phone: 607-637-3413
Fax: 607-637-3413
e-mail: fishsmusic@aol.com
Management:
    Artistic Director: Joyce Lindorff

5098
ALLEGHENY COLLEGE PUBLIC EVENTS SERIES
Allegheny College
520 N Main Street
Box V
Meadville, PA 16335
Phone: 814-332-3101
Fax: 814-332-4320
e-mail: events@allegheny.edu
Web Site: www.allegheny.edu
Officers:
    President: Richard Cook
Management:
    Events Director: Patricia Henry
Utilizes: Dance Companies; Dancers; Guest Musical Directors; Multimedia; Original Music Scores; Special Technical Talent; Theatre Companies
Founded: 1815
Specialized Field: Series and Festivals; Instrumental Music; Vocal Music; Theatre; Youth; Dance; Ethnic Performances
Status: Non-Profit, Professional
Paid Staff: 3
Budget: $35,000-60,000
Type of Stage: Proscenium
Seating Capacity: 1,700

5099
BRODHEAD CULTURAL CENTER SUMMER SERIES
Penn State Beaver
100 University Drive
Monaca, PA 15061-2799
Phone: 724-773-3817
Fax: 724-773-3578
e-mail: amk6@psu.edu
Web Site: www.br.psu.edu/bcc
Management:
    Executive Director: Amy K Kerbs
Mission: The Brodhead Cultural Center is operated through the Penn State Beaver Offices of University Relations to provide free and low-cost programs for the public.
Founded: 1977
Specialized Field: Series & Festivals: Instrumental Music
Status: Non-Profit, Professional
Paid Staff: 1
Budget: $10,000-20,000
Affiliations: Pennsylvania State
Annual Attendance: 10,000
Facility Category: Outdoor Amphitheater
Type of Stage: Concrete
Seating Capacity: 750
Year Built: 1997

5100
ALLEGHENY VALLEY CONCERT ASSOCIATION
67 River Avenue
Natrona, PA 15065
Phone: 724-226-2155
Officers:
    President: Nora Ann Pastrick
Budget: $20,000-35,000

5101
WESTMINSTER COLLEGE CELEBRITY SERIES
Westminster College
New Wilmington, PA 16172-0001

Phone: 724-946-7371
Fax: 724-946-6243
e-mail: decatre@westminster.org
Web Site: www.westminster.edu
Management:
    President: Thomas Williamson
    Celebrity Series Director: Gene Decaprio
Founded: 1966
Specialized Field: Series & Festivals: Music and Song and Dance Performers
Status: Non-Profit, Non-Professional
Paid Staff: 2
Budget: $150,000-400,000

5102
PCCA FESTIVAL AT LITTLE BUFFALO
PO Box 354
Newport, PA 17074
Phone: 717-567-7023
Fax: 717-567-7429
e-mail: pcca@perrycountyarts.org
Web Site: www.perrycountyarts.org
Management:
    President: Joni Williamson
Founded: 1983
Specialized Field: Members Gallery and Exhibits; Joint Classes; Workshops
Status: Non-Profit
Paid Staff: 5
Volunteer Staff: 500
Paid Artists: 100
Facility Category: Multi-Cultural

5103
BUCKS COUNTY COMMUNITY COLLEGE CULTURAL PROGRAMMING
Bucks County Community College
275 Swamp Road
Newtown, PA 18940
Phone: 215-968-8132
Fax: 215-504-8530
e-mail: mengersk@storm.bucks.edu
Web Site: www.bucks.edu
Management:
    President: James Linksz
Founded: 1964
Specialized Field: Series & Festivals; Instrumental Music; Vocal Music; Theatre; Youth; Ethnic Performances
Status: Non-Profit, Professional
Paid Staff: 100
Budget: $10,000-20,000
Seating Capacity: 345

5104
AMERICAN MUSIC THEATER FESTIVAL/PRINCE MUSIC THEATER
100 S Broad Street
Suite 650
Philadelphia, PA 19110
Phone: 215-972-1000
Fax: 215-972-1020
e-mail: info@princemusictheater.org
Web Site: www.princemusictheater.org
Management:
    President: Marjorie Samoss
Founded: 1984
Specialized Field: Song Driven Musical
Status: Non-Profit, Professional
Paid Staff: 37
Performs At: Prince Music Theater
Facility Category: Theater
Type of Stage: Proscenium

Seating Capacity: 450

5105
BACH FESTIVAL OF PHILADELPHIA
8419 Germantown Avenue
Philadelphia, PA 19118
Phone: 215-247-4020
Fax: 215-247-4070
e-mail: office@bach-fest.org
Web Site: www.bach-fest.org
Officers:
   President: Toni Carey
   Treasurer: Emilio Bonelli
   VP: Samuel Swansen
   Secretary: Jeanette Cord
Management:
   President: Samuel Swansen
   Executive Director: Guido Houden
   Artistic Director: Jonathan Sternberg
Mission: The Bach Festival of Philadelphia is dedicated to enriching the community through concerts and educational programs presented by some of the best Baroque interpreters in the world.
Utilizes: Collaborations; Guest Composers; Guest Directors; Guest Musical Directors; Guest Musicians; Guest Soloists; Multimedia; Original Music Scores; Sign Language Translators; Singers
Founded: 1976
Specialized Field: Series & Festivals; Instrumental Music; Vocal Music; Youth
Status: Non-Profit, Professional
Paid Staff: 3
Volunteer Staff: 8
Paid Artists: 20
Income Sources: Government; Corporate and private foundations; Donations; Ticketsales; Advertising books
Performs At: Churches, Performance halls
Annual Attendance: 2,000-3,000
Organization Type: Educational; Presenting

5106
COMMUNITY EDUCATION CENTER
3500 Lancaster Avenue
Philadelphia, PA 19104-2434
Phone: 215-387-1911
Fax: 215-387-3701
e-mail: cec@libertynet.org
Web Site: www.cec.libertynet.org
Management:
   President: Elaine Simone
   Executive Director: Theresa Shockley
   Artistic Director: Edgar Shockley
Founded: 1973
Specialized Field: Series & Festivals; Theatre; Youth; Dance; Ethnic Performances
Status: Non-Profit, Professional
Paid Staff: 6
Paid Artists: 5

5107
COMMUNITY EDUCATION CENTER
3500 Lancaster Avenue
Philadelphia, PA 19104-2434
Phone: 215-387-1911
Fax: 215-387-3701
Budget: $10,000-20,000
Seating Capacity: 100

5108
FIRST UNION CENTER
3601 S Broad Street
Philadelphia, PA 19148
Phone: 215-336-3600
Fax: 215-389-9403
Web Site: www.comcast-spectator.com
Management:
   President: Peter Luukko
   VP Event Producer: John Page
Specialized Field: Home of the Philadelphia 76ers (NBA); Philadelphia Flyers (NFHL); and the Philadelphia Wings (NLL)
Seating Capacity: 21,000, 19,500
Year Built: 1996

5109
FOLKLIFE CENTER OF INTERNATIONAL HOUSE
3701 Chestnut Street
Philadelphia, PA 19104
Phone: 215-387-5125
Fax: 215-895-6550
e-mail: helen@ihphilly.org
Web Site: www.ihousephilly.org
Management:
   President: Osagie Imasogie
Founded: 1977
Specialized Field: Traditional Arts (ethnic)
Paid Artists: 50

5110
FOLKLIFE CENTER OF INTERNATIONAL HOUSE
3701 Chestnut Street
Philadelphia, PA 19104
Phone: 215-895-6537
Fax: 215-895-6562
e-mail: helen@ihphilly.org
Web Site: www.ihousephilly.org
Management:
   Program Director: Helen Henry
Mission: Too present the highest caliber of traditional arts.
Utilizes: Dance Companies; Dancers; Filmmakers; Local Artists; Multi Collaborations; Multimedia; Original Music Scores; Playwrights; Theatre Companies
Founded: 1977
Specialized Field: Traditional Arts (ethnic)
Paid Artists: 50
Budget: $60,000-150,000
Performs At: Hopkinson Hall
Annual Attendance: 2500
Facility Category: Multi-use
Type of Stage: Thrust
Stage Dimensions: 14 x 40
Seating Capacity: 480
Year Built: 1970
Year Remodeled: 1987
Rental Contact: Helen Henry

5111
GERMAN SOCIETY OF PENNSYLVANIA
611 Spring Garden Street
Philadelphia, PA 19123
Phone: 215-627-2332
Fax: 215-627-5297
e-mail: info@germansociety.org
Web Site: www.germansociety.org
Management:
   President: James G Mundy
Mission: Devoted to furthering the understanding of German and German-American contributions to the growth of American history and culture from the past to the present, and into the future.
Founded: 1764

Specialized Field: Series & Festivals; Instrumental Music; Dance; Ethnic Performances
Status: Non-Profit, Professional
Paid Staff: 3
Paid Artists: 10

5112
GERMAN SOCIETY OF PENNSYLVANIA
611 Spring Garden Street
Philadelphia, PA 19123
Phone: 215-627-2332
Fax: 215-627-5297
e-mail: contact@germansociety.org
Web Site: www.germansociety.org
Management:
   Executive Director: Annke Farago
Mission: Serve members and the community, espeially those who share our intrest in German and German-American culture.
Founded: 1764
Status: Nonprofit
Paid Staff: 5
Volunteer Staff: 40
Paid Artists: 10
Budget: $460,000
Facility Category: Historic Landmark Building
Seating Capacity: 370
Year Built: 1888
Year Remodeled: 1997
Organization Type: Educational; Language classes; Lectures; Concerts

5113
MARLBORO MUSIC FESTIVAL
135 S 18th Street
Philadelphia, PA 19103
Phone: 215-569-4690
Fax: 215-569-9497
e-mail: info@marlboromusic.org
Web Site: www.marlboromusic.org
Officers:
   Administrator: Anthony P Checchia
Management:
   President: Tony Checchia
   Artistic Director: Richard Goode
   Managing Director: Frank Salomon
   Manager: Philip Maneval
Mission: Artistic development of younger musicians with older, more experienced musicians.
Founded: 1951
Specialized Field: Series & Festivals; Instrumental Music; Vocal Music
Status: Non-Profit, Professional
Paid Staff: 15
Volunteer Staff: 10
Paid Artists: 80
Season: August-June
Performs At: Persons Auditorium
Organization Type: Performing; Touring; Resident; Educational; Sponsoring

5114
MIDATLANTIC ARTS FOUNDATION PENNSYLVANIA PERFORMING ARTS ON TOUR
1811 Chestnut Street, 301
Philadelphia, PA 19103
Phone: 215-496-9424
Fax: 215-496-9585
e-mail: pennpat@erols.com
Web Site: www.libertynet.org/pennpat
Management:
   Director: Katie West

5115
NORTHEAST PHILADELPHIA CULTURAL COUNCIL
Jardel Recreation Center
Penny & Cottman Avenue
Philadelphia, PA 19111
Phone: 215-686-0592
Management:
    Coordinator: James Robb

5116
NORTHEAST PHILADELPHIA CULTURAL COUNCIL
Jardel Recreation Center
Penny & Cottman Avenue
Philadelphia, PA 19111
Phone: 215-686-0592
Management:
    Coordinator: James Robb
Budget: $35,000-60,000
Performs At: Small Hall

5117
PENN PRESENTS
3680 Walnut Street
Philadelphia, PA 19104-6219
Phone: 215-898-3900
Fax: 215-573-9568
e-mail: info@pennpresents.org
Web Site: www.pennpresents.org
Management:
    Managing Director: Michael J Rose
    Facilities/Events Manager: Marie Gallagher
    Public Relations Manager: Stephanie Grant
    Box Office Manager: David Sullivan
Utilizes: Dance Companies; Five Seasonal Concerts; Guest Musicians; Multimedia; Original Music Scores; Selected Students; Singers; Student Interns; Special Technical Talent; Theatre Companies
Founded: 1971
Specialized Field: Series and Performances: Dance
Status: Non-Profit, Professional
Paid Staff: 70
Annual Attendance: 100000+
Facility Category: 5 theaters throughout Univ. of Pennsylvania
Type of Stage: Proscenium, Black Box
Seating Capacity: 120-1270
Year Built: 1971
Rental Contact: Marie Gallagher

5118
PHILADELPHIA ALL STAR-FORUM SERIES
PO Box 42276
Philadelphia, PA 19101-2276
Phone: 215-735-7506
Fax: 215-735-4129

5119
PHILADELPHIA ALL STAR-FORUM SERIES
PO Box 42276
Philadelphia, PA 19101-2276
Phone: 215-735-7506
Fax: 215-735-4129
Officers:
    Treasurer: Roy A Shubert
Budget: $400,000-1,000,000
Performs At: Academy of Music

5120
PRESIDENTIAL JAZZ WEEKEND
African-American History Museum
701 Arch Street
Philadelphia, PA 19106
Phone: 215-574-0380
Fax: 215-574-3110
Management:
    Jazz Live Director: Rhoda Blount
    Museum Director: Dr. Rowena Stewart
Mission: To celebrate the classical music of African-Americans.
Utilizes: Singers
Founded: 1989
Specialized Field: Vocal Music; Instrumental Music; Festivals; Ethnic
Status: Professional; Semi-Professional; Nonprofit
Income Sources: Greater Philadelphia Cultural Alliance; American Association of Museums; Coalition of Afro-American Organizations
Organization Type: Performing; Educational; Sponsoring

5121
SETTLEMENT MUSIC SCHOOL WEXLER CONTEMPORARY
416 Queen Street
PO Box 63966
Philadelphia, PA 19147-3094
Phone: 215-320-2600
Fax: 215-551-0483
e-mail: info@smsmusic.org
Web Site: www.smsmusic.org
Officers:
    President: Joseph Waz Jr
Management:
    Executive Director: Robert Capanna
    Branch Director: Eric t Anderson
Founded: 1908
Specialized Field: Music Education
Status: Non-Profit, Professional
Paid Staff: 250
Paid Artists: 250
Performs At: PNC Bank-Presser Recital Hall

5122
ST. STEPHEN'S
19 S 10 Street
Philadelphia, PA 19107
Phone: 215-922-3807
Fax: 215-829-4561
e-mail: ststevepa@email.msn.com
Management:
    Program Director: Mark Yurkanin
Performs At: St. Stephen's Sanctuary

5123
TONY WILLIAMS SCHOLARSHIP JAZZ FESTIVAL
PO Box 27116
Philadelphia, PA 19118
Phone: 215-848-3677
Fax: 215-842-3760
e-mail: vwedwards@worldnet.att.net
Web Site: www.maccjazz.org
Officers:
    President: Donald Clark Ph.D
    Ambassador At Large: Thelma Anderson
    Secretary: Joseph Stevenson
Management:
    President: Anthony H Williams

Mission: To increase community involvement with our youth. A commitment to helping the youth develop the proper attitude necessary in becoming a productive adult through the expressive arts with special emphasis on jazz, our only American art form.
Founded: 1977
Specialized Field: Instrumental Program
Status: Non-Profit, Professional
Paid Staff: 12
Volunteer Staff: 20
Paid Artists: 12
Non-paid Artists: 20

5124
ALLEGHENY COUNTY SUMMER CONCERT SERIES
101 County Courthouse
436 Grant Street
Pittsburgh, PA 15219-2904
Phone: 412-350-6500
Fax: 412-350-4360
e-mail: executive@county.allegheny.pa.us
Web Site: www.county.allegheny.pa.us
Management:
    County Chief Executive: Dan Onorato
Mission: Enhance quality of life for the people.
Paid Staff: 3
Volunteer Staff: 20
Paid Artists: 500

5125
CARNEGIE-MELLON CONCERTS
School of Music CFA 105
Carnegie Mellon University
Pittsburgh, PA 15213
Phone: 412-268-2372
Fax: 412-268-1431
e-mail: fletcher@andrew.cmu.edu
Web Site: www.cmu.edu/cfa/music
Management:
    Music Head: Alan Fletcher
    Assistant To The Head: Gloria Watkins
    Associate Head: Natalie Ozeas
    Concert Manager: Amy Stabenow

5126
CARNEGIE-MELLON CONCERTS
CMU School of Music
Pittsburgh, PA 15213-3890
Phone: 412-268-2383
Fax: 412-268-1431
e-mail: musicschool@andrew.cmu.edu
Web Site: www.cmu.edu/cfa/music
Management:
    Manager: Amy Stabenow
Budget: $20,000-35,000
Performs At: Carnegie Music Hall; Lecture Hall; Exhibition Hall
Seating Capacity: 450

5127
FIRST FRIDAY AT THE FRICK CONCERT SERIES
7227 Reynolds Street
Pittsburgh, PA 15208
Phone: 412-371-0600
Fax: 412-371-6030
e-mail: smartin@frickart.org
Web Site: www.frickart.org
Officers:
    Director Visitor Services: Sue Martin
Management:
    Director of Visitor Services: Sue N Martin

Executive Director: William Bodine
Utilizes: Collaborations; Instructors; Local Artists; Lyricists; Multi Collaborations; Multimedia; Original Music Scores; Playwrights; Sign Language Translators; Singers; Soloists; Student Interns
Founded: 1995
Specialized Field: Series & Festivals; Outdoor Summer Concert Series; Instrumental Music; Vocal Music; Ethnic Performance
Status: Non-Profit, Professional
Paid Staff: 50
Paid Artists: 12
Budget: $20,000
Annual Attendance: 10,000
Facility Category: Outdoor Stage
Type of Stage: Platform
Stage Dimensions: 24x40
Seating Capacity: 3,000

5128
FIRST FRIDAYS AT THE FRICK CONCERT SERIES
7227 Reynolds Street
Pittsburgh, PA 15208-2923
Phone: 412-371-0600
Fax: 412-371-6030
e-mail: smartin@frickart.org
Web Site: www.frickart.org
Management:
Visitor Services Director: Sue N Martin
Assistant Manager Visitors Services: Caito Amarose
Services Assistant: Peggy McLean
Founded: 1995
Specialized Field: Electric Mix

5129
FIRST FRIDAYS AT THE FRICK CONCERT SERIES
7227 Reynolds Street
Pittsburgh, PA 15208-2923
Phone: 412-371-0600
Fax: 412-371-6030
e-mail: smartin@frickart.org
Web Site: www.frickart.org
Management:
Visitor Services Director: Sue N Martin
Assistant Manager Visitors Services: Caito Amarose
Services Assistant: Peggy McLean
Mission: Community cultural event sposored by our museum complex.
Utilizes: Guest Musical Directors; Guest Musicians; Instructors; Multimedia; Original Music Scores; Playwrights; Sign Language Translators; Singers
Founded: 1995
Specialized Field: Electric Mix
Budget: $10,000-20,000
Performs At: Frick Art & Historical Center
Annual Attendance: 3,000 per concert
Facility Category: Outdoor
Type of Stage: Transtage
Stage Dimensions: 20x30
Organization Type: outdoor

5130
MANCHESTER CRAFTSMEN'S GUILD
1815 Metropolitan Street
Pittsburgh, PA 15233
Phone: 412-322-1773
Fax: 412-322-1075
e-mail: experiencemcg@mcg-btc.org
Web Site: www.mcjazz.org

Officers:
President/CEO: William E. Strickland, Jr
Management:
Executive Producer, MCG Jazz: Marty Ashby
Mission: To present jazz performances as well as community and educational activities.
Utilizes: Artists-in-Residence; Commissioned Composers; Commissioned Music; Educators; Guest Companies; Guest Directors; Guest Instructors; Guest Lecturers; Guest Musical Directors; Guest Soloists; Lyricists; Multimedia
Founded: 1987
Specialized Field: Series & Festivals: Jazz Concerts
Status: Non-Profit, Professional
Paid Staff: 30
Volunteer Staff: 6
Performs At: Manchester Craftmen's Guild Music Hall
Annual Attendance: 15,000
Facility Category: Concert Hall
Type of Stage: Concert stage
Stage Dimensions: 24x26
Seating Capacity: 350
Year Built: 1987
Organization Type: Educational; Presenting

5131
MUSIC FOR MT. LEBANON
2016 Worcester Drive
Pittsburgh, PA 15243-1542
Phone: 412-531-8588
Fax: 412-344-9054
Management:
Artistic Director: Carl Apone
Budget: $60,000-150,000
Seating Capacity: 1,500

5132
PITTSBURGH ARTS COUNCIL
707 Penn Avenue
2nd Floor
Pittsburgh, PA 15222-3401
Phone: 412-391-2060
Fax: 412-394-4280
e-mail: info@pittsburghartscouncil.org
Web Site: www.pittsburghartscouncil.org
Management:
CEO: Mark Swain
Director Of Arts Program: Susan Blackman

5133
POINT PARK COLLEGE GUEST ARTISTS SERIES
222 Craft Avenue
Pittsburgh, PA 15213
Phone: 412-621-4445
Fax: 412-621-4762
Web Site: www.pittsburghplayhouse.com
Management:
Artistic Producing Director: Ronald Allan-Lindblom
Specialized Field: Series & Festivals; Theatre; Dance; and Children's Theatre
Status: Non-Profit, Professional
Performs At: John Hopkins Auditorium & Library Center

5134
THREE RIVERS ARTS FESTIVAL
937 Liberty Avenue
Pittsburgh, PA 15222
Phone: 412-281-8723
Fax: 412-281-7822
e-mail: pearlman@sgi.net
Web Site: www.artsfestival.net

Management:
Executive Director: Elizabeth Reiss
Founded: 1959
Specialized Field: Series & Festivals; Instrumental Music; Vocal Music; Theatre; Youth; Dance; Ethnic Performances
Status: Non-Profit, Professional
Paid Staff: 6

5135
UNIVERSITY OF PITTSBURGH CONCERT SERIES
Music Building
Room 110
Pittsburgh, PA 15260
Phone: 412-624-4125
Fax: 412-624-4186
e-mail: musicdpt+@pitt.edu
Web Site: www.pitt.edu/""concerts.edu
Management:
Chancellor: Mark Notingburd
Founded: 1787
Specialized Field: Series & Festivals; Instrumental Music; Vocal Music; Ethnic Performances
Status: Non-Profit, Professional
Paid Staff: 1
Budget: $10,000
Performs At: Frick Fine Arts Auditorium; William Pitt Union Ballroom

5136
Y MUSIC SOCIETY OF THE JEWISH COMMUNITY CENTER
5738 Forbes Avenue
Pittsburgh, PA 15217
Phone: 412-421-6771
Fax: 412-208-9107
e-mail: mroth@jccpgh.org
Web Site: www.jccpgh.org
Management:
Director: Mayda Roth
Budget: $60,000-150,000
Performs At: Carnegie Music Hall

5137
HILL SCHOOL CENTER FOR THE ARTS LIVELY ARTS SERIES
717 E High Street
Pottstown, PA 19464-5791
Phone: 610-326-1000
e-mail: bmerriam@thehill.org
Web Site: www.thehill.org
Officers:
President: David Dougherty
Management:
Executive Director: Burton Merriam
Founded: 1854
Specialized Field: Series & Festivals; Instrumental Music; Vocal Music; Theatre; Youth; Dance; Ethnic Performances
Status: Non-Profit, Non-Professional
Budget: $20,000-35,000
Performs At: The Center Theatre

5138
CABRINI COLLEGE
610 King of Prussia Road
Radnor, PA 19087
Phone: 610-902-8380
Fax: 610-902-8285
e-mail: abethany@cabrini.edu
Web Site: www.cabrinicollege.edu
Officers:

President: Dr. Marle George
Management:
    Music Dir./Coor. Cultural Events: Dr. Adeline Bethany
Founded: 1957
Specialized Field: Vocal Music: Classical Music
Status: Non-Profit, Professional
Paid Staff: 1
Budget: $10,000
Performs At: Lecture Hall; Mansion Grand Foyer

5139
ALBRIGHT COLLEGE CONCERT SERIES

13th & Bern Streets
PO Box 15234
Reading, PA 19612-5234
Phone: 610-921-7871
Fax: 610-921-7768
e-mail: bbutler@alb.edu
Web Site: www.albright.edu/concertseries
Management:
    President: Patricia Hummel
    Executive Director: Rebecca Butler
Founded: 1995
Specialized Field: Series & Festivals; Instrumental Music; Vocal Music; Ethnic Performances
Status: Non-Profit, Professional
Budget: $10,000
Performs At: Memorial Chapel; Roop Hall

5140
FIRSTENERGY BERKS JAZZ FESTIVAL

Berks Arts Council
PO Box 854
Reading, PA 19603-0854
Phone: 610-655-6374
Fax: 610-655-6378
Toll-free: 800-523-3781
e-mail: info@berksjazfest.com
Web Site: www.berksjazzfest.com
Management:
    President: Katherine Marshall
    Executive Director: Connie Leinbach
    Managing Director: John Ernesto
Founded: 1971
Specialized Field: Arts In Berks County
Status: Non-Profit, Professional
Paid Staff: 9
Volunteer Staff: 200
Paid Artists: 100

5141
STAR SERIES ASSOCIATION

147 N 5th Street
Reading, PA 19601
Phone: 610-373-0141
Fax: 610-376-3336
e-mail: cbreaux@redrose.net
Web Site: www.berks.net
Management:
    Manager: Chip Breaux
Performs At: Rajah Theatre; Albright Coll. Theatre; Albright Coll. Chapel

5142
SCRANTON COMMUNITY CONCERTS

404 N Washington Avenue
Scranton, PA 18503
Phone: 570-342-4137
Fax: 570-342-4856
e-mail: commconcerts@aol.com
Web Site: www.scrantonconcerts.org
Management:
    President: Susan Trussler

Executive Director: Bridget Fitzpatrick
Mission: To present world-class performing arts in classical, jazz, opera and dance.
Utilizes: Collaborations; Dance Companies; Multimedia; Original Music Scores; Theatre Companies
Founded: 1928
Specialized Field: Series & Festivals: Present Concerts
Status: Non-Profit, Professional
Paid Staff: 2
Budget: $170,000
Income Sources: Grants; Donations
Performs At: Scranton Cultural Center; Mellow Theater

5143
SUSQUEHANNA UNIVERSITY ARTIST SERIES

514 University Avenue
Selinsgrove, PA 17870
Phone: 570-372-4260
Fax: 570-372-2722
Toll-free: 800-326-9672
e-mail: artistseries@susqu.edu
Web Site: www.susqu.edu/artists
Management:
    President: Jay Lemons
Founded: 1902
Budget: $35,000-60,000
Performs At: Weber Chapel Auditorium and Dogenstein Center Theatre

5144
CENTRAL COMMUNITY CONCERTS

52 E Independence Street
Shamokin, PA 17872
Phone: 570-648-3931
Officers:
    President: Irvin R Liachowitz
Budget: $20,000-35,000

5145
SLIPPERY ROCK UNIVERSITY - PERFORMING ARTS SERIES

1 Morrow Way
Slippery Rock, PA 16057
Phone: 724-738-2092
Fax: 724-738-2624
Toll-free: 800-778-9111
e-mail: cheryl.knoch@sru.edu
Web Site: www.sru.edu
Management:
    Director of Student Life: Cherly Knoch
Performs At: Miller Auditorium; Swope Music hall

5146
CENTRAL PENNSYLVANIA FESTIVAL OF THE ARTS

PO Box 1023
State College, PA 16804
Phone: 814-237-3682
Fax: 814-237-0708
e-mail: office@arts-festival.com
Web Site: www.arts-festival.com
Management:
    President: Pamela Ruest
    Executive Director: Philip L Walz
Mission: To offer an annual festival which celebrates all the arts.
Utilizes: Fine Artists; Instructors; Local Artists; Multimedia; Selected Students; Touring Companies
Founded: 1967
Specialized Field: Series & Festivals: Arts Festival
Status: Non-Profit, Professional

Paid Staff: 3
Budget: $490,000
Income Sources: Sponsorship; ticket sales; entry fees
Performs At: Indoor; Auditorium; Outdoor stages
Affiliations: PA Presenters
Annual Attendance: 100,000
Facility Category: Festival
Organization Type: Performing

5147
MUSIC AT PENN'S WOODS

Pennsylvania State University
254 Music Building
University Park, PA 16802
Phone: 814-863-1118
Fax: 814-865-6785
e-mail: pennswoods@psu.edu
Web Site: www.music.psu.edu/mpw
Management:
    Music Director: Gerardo Edelstein
    Manager: Russell Bloom
Mission: Orchestra and chamber music festival
Founded: 1985
Specialized Field: Orchestra; chamber music
Paid Staff: 3
Paid Artists: 45
Budget: $100,000
Performs At: Eisenhower Auditorium
Facility Category: Performing Arts Facility
Seating Capacity: 2500
Year Built: 1972

5148
MUSIC AT PENN'S WOODS

254 Music Building
Penn State University
University Park, PA 16802-1901
Phone: 814-863-1118
Fax: 814-865-6785
e-mail: pennswoods@psu.edu
Web Site: www.music.psu.edu/mpw
Management:
    Music Director: Gerardo Edelstein
    Manager: Russell Bloom
Founded: 1985
Specialized Field: Orchestra; Chamber Music
Paid Staff: 3
Paid Artists: 45
Budget: $100,000
Performs At: Eisenhower Auditorium
Facility Category: Performing Arts Facility
Seating Capacity: 2500
Year Built: 1972

5149
VILLANOVA UNIVERSITY CHAMBER SERIES

Office of Musical Activities
Villanova University
Villanova, PA 19085
Phone: 610-519-7214
Fax: 610-519-7596
Toll-free: 888-862-5050
e-mail: brian.meneely@villanova.com
Web Site: www.villanovamusic.com
Management:
    Executive Director: John Junphi
    Artistic Director: Peter Marino
    Managing Director: Brian Meneeli
Specialized Field: Series & Festivals; Instrumental Music; Vocal Music; Theatre; Dance
Status: Non-Profit, Non-Professional
Paid Staff: 6
Budget: $20,000-35,000

Performs At: St. Mary's Hall

5150

WILDFLOWER MUSIC FESTIVAL

PO Box 356
White Mills, PA 18473
Phone: 570-253-5500
Fax: 570-253-5196
e-mail: music01@ptd.net
Web Site: www.wildflowermusic.org
Management:
  Executive Director: Joan Gillner
  Artistic Director: Kyler Brown
Founded: 1982
Specialized Field: Series and Festivals; Instrumental
Music; Vocal Music; Ethnic Performances
Status: Non-Profit, Professional
Paid Staff: 3
Paid Artists: 8
Performs At: Outdoor Natural Amphitheater
Annual Attendance: 5,000-8,000
Type of Stage: Concrete W/Shell
Seating Capacity: 800

5151

KING'S COLLEGE EXPERIENCING THE ARTS SERIES

133 N River Street
Wilkes-Barre, PA 18711-0801
Phone: 570-208-5900
Fax: 570-208-6023
e-mail: rbmcgoni@kings.edu
Web Site: www.kings.edu
Management:
  President: Thomas O'Hara
  Artistic Director: Robert McGonigle
Utilizes: Actors; Artists-in-Residence; Guest Directors;
Guest Musical Directors; Multimedia; Original Music
Scores; Sign Language Translators
Founded: 1946
Specialized Field: Education
Status: Non-Profit, Professional
Paid Staff: 1
Paid Artists: 1
Budget: $10,000-20,000
Performs At: Campus Ministry Center; Sheeny-Farmer
Campus Center

5152

WILLIAMSPORT COMMUNITY CONCERT ASSOCIATION

1401 Washington Boulevard
Williamsport, PA 17701-5424
Phone: 570-322-7004
Officers:
  President: Terry L Ziegler
Budget: $35,000-60,000
Performs At: Scottish Rite Auditorium

5153

ARCADIA PERFORMING ARTS

1418 Graham Avenue
Windber, PA 15963
Phone: 814-467-9070
Fax: 814-467-5646
e-mail: arcadiatheater@floodcity.net
Web Site: www.arcadiatheater.net
Officers:
  Chairman of Board: Frank Consolo
  President: Frank Consolo
  Second Chair: Al Christ
Management:
  Executive Director: Frank Cunsolo

Artistic Director: Elsie Mock
Asst Artistic Director: Robert Seese
Children's/Community Theater Dir: Aspen Mock
Founded: 1998
Specialized Field: Series & Festivals; Vocal Music;
Youth; Arts
Status: Non-Profit, Professional
Paid Staff: 4
Budget: $60,000-150,000
Seating Capacity: 710
Year Built: 1921
Year Remodeled: 1998

5154

BUCKS COUNTY PERFORMING ARTRS SERIES

1140 Edgewood Road
Yardley, PA 19067
Phone: 215-493-3010
Fax: 215-968-2475
e-mail: lmpspamaryb@comcast.net
Web Site: www.lmt.org
Management:
  Executive Director: Mary Borkovitz
Founded: 1978
Specialized Field: Series & Festivals; Instrumental
Music; Vocal Music; Youth; Dance; Ethnic
Performances
Status: Non-Profit, Professional
Volunteer Staff: 10
Paid Artists: 25
Budget: $24,000
Performs At: Township Community Room
Annual Attendance: 1050
Seating Capacity: 175
Year Built: 1976

5155

STRAND-CAPITOL PERFORMING ARTS CENTER SERIES

50 N George Street
York, PA 17401
Phone: 717-846-1155
Fax: 717-843-1208
e-mail: boxoffice@strandcapitol.org
Web Site: www.strandcapitol.org
Officers:
  Chair: Michael Heine
  President/CEO: Joe Jefcoat
  Vice-Chair: Charles Wise
Management:
  Operations Director: Brian Heller
  Program Director: Carol Oppelaar
Founded: 1980
Specialized Field: Performing Arts Facility;
Instrumental Music; Vocal Music; Theatre; Youth;
Dance; Ethnic Performances
Status: Non-Profit
Paid Staff: 17
Budget: $3 million

Rhode Island

5156

CONCERTS BY THE BAY

101 Ferry Road
Route 114
Bristol, RI 02809
Phone: 401-253-2707
Fax: 401-253-0412
e-mail: info@blitheworld.org
Web Site: www.blitheworld.org

Management:
  Site Administrator: Constance Coar

5157

CULTURAL ORGANIZATION OF THE ARTS

PO Box 258
111 Pierce Street
East Greenwich, RI 02818
Phone: 401-886-4530
Management:
  COA Director: Kate Leach
Budget: $10,000

5158

KINGSTON CHAMBER MUSIC FESTIVAL AT URI

PO Box 1733
Kingston, RI 02881
Phone: 401-789-0665
Fax: 401-874-2380
e-mail: sadd@egr.uri.edu
Web Site: www.kingstonchambermusic.org
Management:
  President: Martin Sadd
  Artistic Director: David Kim
  Managing Director: Bryan Mitchell
Mission: To provide outstanding classical music
programs in New England. Offers both summer and
winter concerts, and also outreach programs at local
area schools.
Utilizes: Guest Musical Directors; Multimedia; Original
Music Scores
Founded: 1989
Specialized Field: Series & Festivals; Instrumental
Music; Youth; Classical Music
Status: Non-Profit, Professional
Paid Staff: 2
Volunteer Staff: 15
Paid Artists: 20
Budget: $60,000
Income Sources: Donations; Ticket sales
Affiliations: University of Rhode Island
Annual Attendance: 2800

5159

NEW ENGLAND PRESENTERS: UNIVERSITY OF RHODE ISLAND GREAT PERFORMANCES

105 Upper College Road
URI
Kingston, RI 02881
Phone: 401-874-2627
Fax: 401-874-2772
e-mail: rto9302u@postoffice.uri.edu
Management:
  Director: Roxana Tourigny
Budget: $35,000-60,000
Performs At: Veterans Memorial Auditorium; Edwards
Hall; Will Theatre

5160

NEWPORT MUSIC FESTIVAL

PO Box 3300
Newport, RI 02840
Phone: 401-846-1133
Fax: 401-849-1857
e-mail: staff@newportmusic.org
Web Site: www.newportmusic.org
Officers:
  President: Ms Diane S Hurley
  President Emeritus: Mrs Robert Horne Charles
  VP Emeritus: Mrs William Wood-Price

All listings are in alphabetical order by state, then city, then organization within the city.

Management:
General Manager: Mark P Malkovich IV
Mission: Presenting chamber music of the Romantic era. 65 concerts per year.
Utilizes: Collaborations; Commissioned Composers; Commissioned Music; Guest Accompanists; Guest Companies; Guest Musical Directors; Guest Musicians; Instructors; Multimedia; Original Music Scores; Sign Language Translators; Singers
Founded: 1969
Specialized Field: Series & Festivals; Vocal Music; Chamber Music
Status: Non-Profit, Professional
Paid Staff: 3
Volunteer Staff: 300
Paid Artists: 50
Budget: $1 Million
Income Sources: Box Office; Donations; Corporate & Foundation Support
Season: July
Performs At: Newport Mansions
Affiliations: Yamaha Corporation of America; Roederer Champagne; Time, Inc.; Lufthansa
Annual Attendance: 28,000
Facility Category: Various Mansions; Churches; Tents
Seating Capacity: 250 - 500
Organization Type: Performing; Sponsoring
Comments: The Newport Music Festival is listed by Cadogen Press in their Ultimate List of 1000 Best Things in America.

5161
CAPITOLARTS PROVIDENCE CULTURAL AFFAIRS
65 Weybosset Street, Mailbox 39
Suite 68
Providence, RI 02903
Phone: 401-265-5051
Fax: 401-621-1883
e-mail: info@caparts.org
Web Site: www.caparts.org
Management:
President: Randy Kass
Executive Director: Bob Rizzo
Choreographer: Nancy Compton
Web Site Development: Remo Campopiano
Mission: Dedicated to producing arts events that enliven the cityscape of Providence, Rhode Island; working together with the City of Providence, Parks Department, Office of Cultural Affairs, CapitolArts Providence produces events, both large and small, that appeal to the region's diverse community.
Founded: 1992
Specialized Field: Producing arts events
Status: Nonprofit

5162
CONVERGENCE 2000 ARTS FESTIVAL: WORKSHOP WITH TS THOMAS
Providence Parks Department
400 Westminister Street 4th Floor
Providence, RI 02903
Phone: 401-621-1992
Fax: 401-621-1883
Web Site: www.vac.igs.net
Specialized Field: Two-day workshop - poetry of Walt Whitman

5163
FIRST NIGHT PROVIDENCE
10 Dorrance Street
Suite 920
Providence, RI 02903

Phone: 401-521-1166
Fax: 401-273-5630
e-mail: firstnight@firstnightprovidence.org
Web Site: www.firstnightprovidence.org
Management:
Director: Doris Stephens
Assistant Director: Annette Robinson
Artistic Director: Kathleen Fletcher
Business Director: Carolyn Tick
Mission: Nonalcoholic family celebration of the arts on New Year's Eve.
Utilizes: Actors; Artists-in-Residence; Collaborating Artists; Collaborations; Dance Companies; Dancers; Five Seasonal Concerts; Instructors; Local Artists; Lyricists; Multi Collaborations; Multimedia; Original Music Scores; Playwrights; Sign Language Translators; Special Technical Talent; Touring Companies
Founded: 1985
Specialized Field: Dance; Vocal Music; Instrumental Music; Theater
Status: Nonprofit
Paid Staff: 4
Budget: $550,000
Income Sources: Admission Sales; Corporate Sponsors; Individual Contributions
Performs At: Theaters; Performance Halls; Churches
Annual Attendance: 50,000
Facility Category: Arts festival
Type of Stage: Multi-Purpose
Organization Type: Performing; Educational; Sponsoring

5164
NEWGATE THEATER
PO Box 41311
Providence, RI 02940
Phone: 401-454-0454
e-mail: brien@newgatetheatre.org
Management:
Artistic Director: Brien Lang
Managing Director: Joseph Mecca
Webmaster: Peter Gogol
Mission: Committed to producing new and established works which challenge both artists and audiences.
Utilizes: Guest Companies
Founded: 1982
Specialized Field: June Festival of Short Plays
Status: Semi-Professional; Nonprofit
Income Sources: New England Theatre Conference
Organization Type: Performing; Resident; Producing

5165
PROVIDENCE DIVISION OF PUBLIC PROGRAMMING DEPARTMENTS
Providence Parks Department
400 Westminster Street 4th Floor
Providence, RI 02903-3222
Phone: 401-621-1992
Fax: 401-621-1883
e-mail: info@caparts.org
Web Site: www.caparts.org
Management:
Public Programming Director: Bob Rizzo
Budget: $60,000-150,000

5166
RHODE ISLAND COLLEGE: PERFORMING ARTS SERIES
600 Mount Pleasant Avenue
301 Roberts Hall
Providence, RI 02908-1991

Phone: 401-456-8194
Fax: 401-456-8269
e-mail: mducharme@ric.edu
Web Site: www.ric.edu/pfa
Management:
Director: Michael Ducharme
Utilizes: Actors; Artists-in-Residence; Dance Companies; Dancers; Educators; Fine Artists; Grant Writers; Guest Accompanists; Guest Artists; Guest Choreographers; Guest Companies; Guest Conductors; Guest Directors; Guest Instructors; Guest Musical Directors; Guest Musicians; Guest Soloists; Instructors; Multimedia; Original Music Scores; Playwrights; Selected Students; Sign Language Translators; Singers; Soloists; Special Technical Talent; Theatre Companies
Founded: 1962
Specialized Field: Series & Festivals; Instrumental Music; Vocal Music; Theatre; Youth; Dance; Ethnic Performances
Status: Non-Profit, Professional
Paid Staff: 9
Volunteer Staff: 24
Paid Artists: 80
Budget: $60,000-$150,000
Performs At: Roberts Auditorium; Sapinsley Hall; Forman Theatre

South Carolina

5167
UNIVERSITY OF SOUTH CAROLINA: AIKEN ETHERREDGE CENTER
471 University Parkway
Aiken, SC 29801
Phone: 803-641-3328
Fax: 803-641-3691
e-mail: janes@aiken.sc.edu
Web Site: www.usca.sc.edu/ec
Management:
President: Thomas Hallmen
Executive Director: Jane Schumacher
Utilizes: Dance Companies; Dancers; Fine Artists; Instructors; Local Artists; Multimedia; Sign Language Translators; Singers; Soloists; Special Technical Talent; Theatre Companies
Founded: 1982
Specialized Field: Series & Festivals; Musical; Dance; Ballads
Status: Non-Profit, Non-Professional
Paid Staff: 3
Budget: $60,000-150,000
Affiliations: University of Saint Gerdina
Facility Category: Theater Complex
Type of Stage: Thrust Proscenium
Stage Dimensions: 38 by 24
Seating Capacity: 687
Year Built: 1986
Rental Contact: Jane Schumacher

5168
ANDERSON UNIVERSITY
316 Boulevard
Anderson, SC 29621
Phone: 864-231-2002
Fax: 864-231-2083
e-mail: dlarson@andersonuniversity.edu
Web Site: www.andersonuniversity.edu
Officers:
President: Evans Whitaker
Dean/Visual Performance Arts: David Larson
Founded: 1911

Specialized Field: Series & Festivals; Instrumental Music; Vocal Music; Theatre
Status: Non-Profit, Non-Professional
Paid Staff: 3
Volunteer Staff: 20
Paid Artists: 13
Budget: $10,000-20,000
Seating Capacity: 1100; 200; 100

5169
CIVIC CENTER OF ANDERSON
3027 Mall Road
Anderson, SC 29625
Phone: 864-260-4800
Fax: 864-260-4847
e-mail: asec@andersoncountysc.org
Web Site: www.andersonevents.com
Management:
Manager: Charles Wyatt
Specialized Field: Series & Festivals Instrumental Music; Vocal Music; Theatre; Youth; Dance; Ethnic Performances
Status: Non-Professional
Paid Staff: 15

5170
UNIVERSITY OF SOUTH CAROLINA-BEAUFORT
PO Box 482
Beaufort, SC 29902
Phone: 843-379-2787
Fax: 843-379-2789
e-mail: ellenz@hargray.com
Web Site: www.beaufortarts.com
Management:
President: John Gettys Smith
Executive Director: Ellen Zisholtz
Founded: 1991
Status: Non-Profit
Budget: $60,000-150,000
Performs At: Beaufort Waterfront Park

5171
CHARLESTON CONCERT ASSOCIATION
207 E Bay Street, Suite 213
PO Box 743
Charleston, SC 29401
Phone: 843-722-7667
Fax: 843-577-5173
e-mail: nicholscca@aol.com
Web Site: www.charlestonconcerts.org
Management:
President: John Davis
Director: Jason Nichols
Executive Assistant: Toni Franklin
Founded: 1934
Specialized Field: Series & Festivals; Instrumental Music; Vocal Music; Theatre; Youth; Dance; Ethnic Performances
Status: Non-Profit, Professional
Paid Staff: 3
Budget: $150,000-400,000
Performs At: Gaillard Municipal Auditorium

5172
CITADEL FINE ARTS SERIES
The Citadel
Charleston, SC 29409
Phone: 843-953-5065
Fax: 843-953-6797
e-mail: Grant.Staley@citadel.edu
Officers:
Chairman: Dr. Grant B Staley
Budget: $10,000-20,000

Performs At: Mark Clark Hall Auditorium

5173
PICCOLO SPOLETO FESTIVAL
Office of Cultural Affairs
133 Church Street
Charleston, SC 29401
Phone: 843-724-7305
Fax: 843-720-3967
e-mail: cultural_affairs@ci.charleston.us
Web Site: www.picoluspoleto.com
Management:
Executive Director: Ellen Dressler Moryl
Founded: 1979
Specialized Field: Series & Festivals; Instrumental Music; Vocal Music; Theatre; Youth; Dance; Ethnic Performances
Status: Non-Profit, Professional
Paid Staff: 9

5174
SPOLETO FESTIVAL USA
14 George Street
Charleston, SC 29401-1524
Phone: 843-722-2764
Fax: 843-723-6383
e-mail: info@spoletousa.org
Web Site: www.spoletousa.org
Officers:
Chairman: Martha Rivers Ingram
President: Carlos E. Evans
Management:
Artistic Director-Choral Activities: Joseph Flummerfelt
Director, Chamber Music: Geoff Nuttall
General Director: Nigel Redden
Producer: Nunally Kersh
Director Of Development: Julia Forster
Director Marketing/Public Relations: Paula Edwards
Mission: To present opera, dance, theater, symphonic, choral and chamber music, jazz and visual arts exhibits of the highest quality; to serve as an educational environment for young artists and audiences alike.
Utilizes: Singers
Founded: 1977
Specialized Field: Jazz; Theatrical Dance
Status: Professional; Semi-Professional; Non-Profit
Paid Staff: 18
Budget: $7,000,000
Income Sources: Ticket Revenues; Contributions
Performs At: Gaillard Municipal Auditorium; Dock Street Theater
Annual Attendance: 70,000-80,000
Organization Type: Performing; Educational; Sponsoring

5175
PRESBYTERIAN COLLEGE
503 S Broad Street
Clinton, SC 29325
Phone: 864-833-8523
Fax: 864-833-8600
Toll-free: 800-476-7272
e-mail: lwshealy@presby.edu
Web Site: www.presby.edu
Officers:
President: John Griffith
Management:
Cultural Events Director: Laura Shealy
Technical Director: Greg Bruce

Utilizes: Artists-in-Residence; Dance Companies; Guest Directors; Guest Instructors; Guest Musical Directors; Guest Soloists; Multimedia; Original Music Scores; Singers; Soloists
Founded: 1880
Specialized Field: Education
Status: Non-Profit, Non-Professional
Paid Staff: 3
Paid Artists: 10
Non-paid Artists: 30
Budget: $35,000-60,000
Annual Attendance: 25,000
Facility Category: Concert Hall/Recital Hall
Type of Stage: Proscenium
Stage Dimensions: 39'x24'/23'x49'
Seating Capacity: 1,100/335
Rental Contact: Not Available for Rental

5176
CAROLINA PRODUCTIONS, PERFORMING ARTS COMMISSION
Russell House University Union
Room 227
Columbia, SC 29208
Phone: 803-777-7130
Fax: 803-777-7132
Web Site: www.sa.sc.edu/cp
Officers:
President: Krista Wingard
Management:
President: Scott Fowell
Director Student Activities: Mike Duncan
Specialized Field: Series & Festivals; Instrumental Music; Vocal Music; Theatre; Youth; Dance; Ethnic Performances
Status: Non-Profit, Professional
Performs At: Koger Center for the Arts; Carolina Coliseum

5177
COLUMBIA COLLEGE POWER COMPANY SERIES
1301 Columbia College Drive
Columbia College Dance Department
Columbia, SC 29203
Phone: 803-786-3825
Fax: 803-786-3868
e-mail: mbrim@colacoll.edu
Web Site: www.columbiacollegesc.edu
Officers:
Dance Department Chair: Susan Haigler-Robles
Management:
President: Caroline Whitson
Executive Director: Laurie Hopkins
Artistic Director: Martha Brim
Utilizes: Artists-in-Residence; Choreographers; Collaborating Artists; Collaborations; Dance Companies; Dancers; Educators; Guest Artists; Guest Soloists; High School Drama; Instructors; Local Artists; Resident Artists; Soloists; Theatre Companies
Founded: 1987
Specialized Field: Series & Festivals: Contemporary Dance
Status: Non-Profit, Professional
Paid Staff: 2
Volunteer Staff: 45
Paid Artists: 5
Budget: $10,000
Performs At: Cottingham Theater, Columbia College
Affiliations: The Power Company; South Carolina Center for Dance Education
Annual Attendance: 12,000
Facility Category: Theater

Type of Stage: Proscenium
Stage Dimensions: 30 X 40
Seating Capacity: 385
Year Built: 1960
Rental Contact: Patrick Faulds

5178
KOGER CENTER FOR THE ARTS
Koger Center of the Arts
University of South Carolina
Columbia, SC 29208
Phone: 803-777-7500
Fax: 803-777-9774
Web Site: www.koger.sc.edu
Management:
  Director: Ron Pearson
  Assistant Director: Michael Gaylor
Founded: 1989
Specialized Field: Series and Festivals; Instrumental
Music; Vocal Music; Theatre; Youth; Dance; Ethnic
Performances
Status: For-Profit, Non-Professional
Paid Staff: 7
Budget: $1,000,000+

5179
ERSKINARTS (THE FINE & PERFORMING ARTS AT ERSKINE COLLEGE)
Erskine College
Due West, SC 29639
Phone: 864-379-8831
Fax: 864-379-3164
e-mail: mattman@erskine.edu
Web Site: www.erskine.edu
Officers:
  Chairman Music Department: Matthew
  Manwarren
Management:
  Director Of Choral Activities: Johnn Warre
  Chair Of The Department Of Music: Matthew
  Manwarr
Founded: 1839
Budget: $20,000-35,000
Performs At: Memorial Hall

5180
FRANCIS MARION UNIVERSITY ARTISTS SERIES
PO Box 100547
Florence, SC 29501-0547
Phone: 843-661-1385
Fax: 843-661-1529
e-mail: jfallenger@fmarion.edu
Web Site: www.fmarion.edu
Officers:
  Fine Arts Department Chairman: Lawrence P
  Anderson
Management:
  President: Luther F Carter
Founded: 1972
Specialized Field: Series & Festivals; Instrumental
Music; Vocal Music; Theatre; Dance; Classical Dance
Status: Non-Profit, Professional
Budget: $10,000-20,000
Performs At: McNair Auditorium

5181
METROPOLITAN ARTS COUNCIL
16 Augusta Street
Greenville, SC 29601
Phone: 864-467-3132
Fax: 864-467-3133
e-mail: macsc@greenvillearts.com
Web Site: www.greenvillearts.com
Management:
  Head of the Adminstrative: Kim Sholy
Mission: To stimulate and support artistic expression
and its appreciation and enjoyment in ways that enrich
all citizens, artsits, cultural organizations, and
communities of the Metropolitan area.
Utilizes: Actors; Artists-in-Residence; Choreographers;
Collaborating Artists; Collaborations; Commissioned
Composers; Commissioned Music; Curators; Dance
Companies; Dancers; Designers; Educators; Equity
Actors; Filmmakers; Fine Artists; Five Seasonal
Concerts; Guest Accompanists; Guest Choreographers;
Guest Composers; Guest Designers; Guest
Ensembles; Guest Lecturers; Guest Musical Directors;
Guest Musicians; Guest Teachers; Guild Activities; High
School Drama; Instructors; Local Artists; Local
Unknown Artists; Lyricists; Multi Collaborations;
Multimedia; Music; New Productions; Organization
Contracts; Original Music Scores; Performance Artists;
Playwrights; Poets; Resident Professionals; Sign
Language Translators; Singers; Soloists; Special
Technical Talent; Touring Companies; Visual Arts
Founded: 1973
Status: Non-Profit, Non-Professional
Paid Staff: 3
Budget: $450,000
Income Sources: City, State and Federal grants,
private donations

5182
GREENWOOD-LANDER PERFORMING ARTS
Lander University
CPO Box 6044
Greenwood, SC 29649
Phone: 864-388-8326
Fax: 864-388-8036
e-mail: glpa@lander.edu
Web Site: www.lander.edu/glpa
Management:
  Executive Director: Beverly Psomas
Founded: 1946
Specialized Field: Series & Festival; Instrumental
Music; Dance
Status: Non-Profit, Professional
Paid Staff: 1
Paid Artists: 250
Budget: $70,000-80,000
Annual Attendance: 3,500- 4,000
Facility Category: Concert Hall
Seating Capacity: 700

5183
HARTSVILLE COMMUNITY CONCERT ASSOCIATION
PO Box 2283
Hartsville, SC 29551
Phone: 843-383-8145
e-mail: gsawyer@coker.edu
Officers:
  President: David M Tavernier
Founded: 1945
Budget: $20,000-35,000

5184
ARTS CENTER OF COASTAL CAROLINA
14 Shelter Cove Lane
Hilton Head Island, SC 29928
Phone: 843-686-3945
Fax: 843-842-7877
Toll-free: 888-860-2787
e-mail: artscenter@hargray.com
Web Site: www.artscenter-hhi.org
Officers:
  President/CEO: Kathleen P Bateson
Management:
  President: Kathleen Bateson
  General Manager: Richard Feldman
Mission: Theatre and presenting.
Founded: 1996
Specialized Field: Performing; Visual Gallery; Produce
and Present Live Theatre
Status: Non-Profit, Professional
Paid Staff: 35
Paid Artists: 15
Budget: $3.2 million
Performs At: Elizabeth Wallace Theatre
Type of Stage: Proscenium
Seating Capacity: 350
Year Built: 1996
Rental Contact: Richard Feldman

5185
COASTAL CONCERT ASSOCIATION
1107 48 Avenue N
Suite 211-E
Myrtle Beach, SC 29577
Phone: 843-449-7546
Fax: 843-449-9391
e-mail: coastcon@infionline.net
Web Site: www.coastalconcert.com
Officers:
  President: John Trugdeau
  Treasurer: Kelli Shana Felt
  President: B Matt Morris
Management:
  President: Brenda Mancill
  Executive Director: Shirley Cope
  Concert Chairperson: Linda Erwin
Utilizes: Dance Companies; Multimedia; Original Music
Scores; Special Technical Talent
Founded: 1972
Specialized Field: Music
Status: Non-Profit, Professional
Paid Staff: 1
Volunteer Staff: 20
Paid Artists: 20
Budget: $35,000-60,000
Performs At: Performing Arts Center
Annual Attendance: 6,000
Seating Capacity: 1900

5186
ARTS ETC
PO Box 2692 CRS
Rock Hill, SC 29732
Phone: 803-324-8803
Fax: 803-324-8200
e-mail: karenb@infoave.net
Web Site: www.artsetc.org
Management:
  Executive Director: Karen Blankenship
Paid Staff: 5
Budget: $35,000-60,000
Performs At: Byrnes Auditorium
Type of Stage: Proscenium
Seating Capacity: 3,540
Year Built: 1938

5187
WINTHROP UNIVERSITY COLLEGE OF VISUAL & PERFORMING ARTS
College of Visual & Performing Arts
133 McLaurin Hall, Winthrop University
Rock Hill, SC 29733
Phone: 803-323-2323
Fax: 803-323-2333
e-mail: rogersd@winthrop.edu
Web Site: www.winthrop.edu
Management:
    Dean/Professor Of Dance: Libby Patenaude
    Chair Of Music/Associate Music Prof: Donald M Rogers
Budget: $35,000-60,000

5188
ARTS PARTNERSHIP OF GREATER SPARTANBURG
200 E St. John Street
Spartanburg, SC 29306-3350
Phone: 864-542-2787
Fax: 864-948-5353
e-mail: mixterhp@spartanarts.org
Web Site: www.chapmanculturalcenter.org
Management:
    President & COO: H Perry Mixter
    Director of Facilities: Jan Benjamin
    Director of Development: Jennifer Evins
Mission: The Arts Partnership inspires one true expression and educational discovery in Spartanburg County; and provides strategic and financial leadership to cultural organizations, artists and educators
Founded: 1968
Specialized Field: United Arts Council
Paid Staff: 17
Volunteer Staff: 100
Paid Artists: 12
Budget: $2,000,000
Income Sources: Annual fund; rental; grants
Affiliations: Americans for the Arts
Annual Attendance: 132,000
Facility Category: Cultural Center
Type of Stage: Proscenium
Stage Dimensions: 40 x 80
Seating Capacity: 500
Year Built: 2007
Cost: $47,000,000
Rental Contact: Kathy Campbell

5189
MUSIC FOUNDATION OF SPARTANBURG CONCERT SERIES
385 S Spring Street
Spartanburg, SC 29306
Mailing Address: Box 1274, Spartanburg, SC. 29304
Phone: 864-948-9020
Fax: 864-948-5353
e-mail: music@teleplex.net
Web Site: www.sparklenet.com/musicfoundation
Management:
    President: Robert Rainer
    Executive Director: Dana Gencarelli
Specialized Field: Series & Festivals: Instrumental Music
Status: Non-Profit, Professional
Paid Staff: 3
Budget: $60,000-150,000
Performs At: Twichell Auditorium

5190
FINE ARTS COUNCIL OF SUMTER PERFORMING ARTS SERIES
10 Mood Avenue
Sumter, SC 29150
Phone: 803-775-5580
Fax: 803-778-9664
e-mail: finearts@ftc-i.net
Web Site: www.angelfire.com/sc/finearts
Management:
    Director: Zan Fort
Mission: To enrich the cultural atmosphere of our area by presenting a Performing Arts Series; to reward students of the performing arts by sponsoring a school competition.
Utilizes: Actors; Artists-in-Residence; Dance Companies; Dancers; Fine Artists; Guest Lecturers; Guest Musical Directors; Local Artists; Multimedia; Sign Language Translators; Special Technical Talent; Theatre Companies
Founded: 1986
Paid Staff: 1
Volunteer Staff: 25
Budget: $100,000
Income Sources: Grants; ticket sales
Performs At: Patriot Hall
Facility Category: Auditorium
Type of Stage: Proscenium
Stage Dimensions: 47x21
Seating Capacity: 1,017
Year Remodeled: 1988

5191
NORTH GREENVILLE UNIVERSITY: FINE ARTS SERIES
PO Box 1892
Tigerville, SC 29688
Phone: 864-977-7001
Fax: 864-977-7021
Toll-free: 800-468-6642
e-mail: admissions@ngu.edu
Web Site: www.ngu.edu
Management:
    President: James B Epting
    Dean of Fine Arts/Head of Music: Dr. Jackie Griffin
    Head of Theater: Dr. Dale Savidge
    Head of Visual Arts: Zac Buser
Mission: Quality education in a Christian environment
Founded: 1882
Specialized Field: Music; Visual; Theatre
Status: Accredited; University
Budget: $10,000
Performs At: Fine Arts Center
Affiliations: NASM; SACS
Seating Capacity: 260/Recital; 1600/Auditorium

South Dakota

5192
ABERDEEN COMMUNITY CONCERT ASSOCIATION
1312 3rd Avenue SE
Aberdeen, SD 57401
Phone: 605-226-3143
Officers:
    Secretary: Stacy Braun
Budget: $10,000-20,000
Performs At: Johnson Fine Arts Center

5193
SOUTH DAKOTA STATE UNIVERSITY STUDENT ACTIVITIES
PO Box 2815
Brookings, SD 57007-1599
Phone: 605-688-6129
Fax: 605-688-4973
Management:
    Program Advisor: Adam Karnopp
Budget: $20,000-35,000
Performs At: David B. Doner Auditorium

5194
LAURA INGALLS WILDER PAGEANT SOCIETY
PO Box 154
De Smet, SD 57231
Phone: 605-692-2108
Management:
    Managing Director: Portia Potvin
Mission: To present an outdoor pageant depicting The Little House on the Prairie books of Laura Ingalls Wilder. The pageant takes place across from the site of the Ingalls homestead.
Founded: 1971
Specialized Field: Theatre
Status: Nonprofit
Organization Type: Performing

5195
HURON ARENA
150 5th Street SW
Huron, SD 57350
Phone: 605-353-6970
Fax: 605-353-6973
Management:
    Manager: Glen Ulvested

5196
MADISON AREA ARTS COUNCIL
PO Box 147
Madison, SD 57042
Phone: 605-256-5051
Management:
    Arts Coordinator: Eve Fisher
Mission: To promote arts appreciation; to sponsor arts activities; to offer opportunities for arts education to community members.
Utilizes: Guest Companies
Founded: 1968
Specialized Field: Dance; Vocal Music; Instrumental Music; Theater; Festivals
Status: Nonprofit
Income Sources: South Dakota Arts Council; Community Arts Council Network; South Dakota Alliance
Performs At: Dakota Prairie Playhouse
Organization Type: Educational; Sponsoring

5197
PIERRE COMMUNITY CONCERTS ASSOCIATION
PO Box 519
808 W Pleasant
Pierre, SD 57501
Phone: 605-224-5803
Budget: $10,000-20,000

5198
ATHENS AREA COUNCIL FOR THE ARTS
PO Box 95
Athens, TN 37371-0095
Phone: 423-745-8781
Fax: 423-745-8635
e-mail: aaca@bellsouth.net
Web Site: www.athensartscouncil.org
Management:
President: Lyn Thompson
Executive Director: Ellen Kimball
Founded: 1979
Specialized Field: Arts Council
Status: Non-Profit, Professional
Paid Staff: 3
Paid Artists: 30
Budget: $10,000-20,000

5199
RIVERBEND FESTIVAL
Friends of the Festival
180 Hamm Road
Chattanooga, TN 37405
Phone: 423-756-2211
Fax: 423-756-2719
e-mail: info@riverbendfestival.com
Web Site: www.riverbendfestival.com
Management:
Executive Director: Chip Baker
Artistic Director: Joe Fuller
Operations Director: Don Sharp
Mission: A huge family-oriented music festival which goes on for 9 nights, with six stages of almost every possible genre of music, fantastic fireworks and a children's village.
Founded: 1981
Specialized Field: Series & Festivals; Instrumental Music; Vocal Music; Theatre; Youth; Dance; Ethnic Performances
Status: Non-Profit, Professional
Paid Staff: 8

5200
UNIVERSITY OF TENNESSEE AT CHATTANOOGA
Fine Arts Center, Department 1351
615 Mccallie Avenue
Chattanooga, TN 37403
Phone: 423-425-4269
Fax: 423-425-5249
e-mail: Bob-Boyer@utc.edu
Web Site: www.utc.edu/finearts
Management:
Fine Arts Center Manager: Bob Boyer
Mission: Patten performances provides the Southeast Tennessee area with a professional showcase of national and international artists who perform and conduct residency activities in music, theatre and dance.
Paid Staff: 3
Paid Artists: 12
Budget: $60,000-150,000
Performs At: Roland Hayes Concert Hall
Annual Attendance: 4,000-5,000
Facility Category: Fine Arts Center
Type of Stage: Modified Proscenium
Seating Capacity: 505
Year Built: 1979
Rental Contact: Sue Carroll

5201
AUSTIN PEAY STATE UNIVERSITY
Center of Excellence for the Creative Arts
PO Box 4666
Clarksville, TN 37044
Phone: 931-221-7876
Fax: 931-221-7149
e-mail: johnsonf@apsu.edu
Web Site: www.apsu.edu
Management:
President: Cherry Hoppe
Executive Director: Jim Diehr
Managing Director: Feleesha Johnson
Founded: 1985
Specialized Field: Series & Festivals; Instrumental Music; Vocal Music; Theater; Youth; Ethnic Performances; Arts
Status: Non-Profit, Non-Professional
Paid Staff: 3
Paid Artists: 5
Budget: $700,000
Income Sources: State
Performs At: Mass Communication Building
Type of Stage: Proscenium
Seating Capacity: 600

5202
LEE UNIVERSITY PRESIDENTIAL CONCERT SERIES
Lee University
Cleveland, TN 37311
Phone: 423-614-8240
Fax: 423-614-8242
e-mail: ngoff@leeuniversity.edu
Web Site: www.leeuniversity.edu
Officers:
Dean, School Of Music: Stephen W Plate
Management:
President: Paul Conn
Vocal Chair: Luktann Holden
Instrumental Chair: Philip Thomas
Dean, School Of Music: Stephen Plate
Founded: 1991
Specialized Field: Series and Festivals; Instrumental Music; Vocal Music
Status: Non-Profit, Professional
Paid Staff: 21
Budget: $20,000-35,000
Performs At: Dixon Center
Annual Attendance: 3,000+
Facility Category: Music/Drama Performing Hall
Type of Stage: Full

5203
SOUTHERN ADVENTIST UNIVERSITY
PO Box 370
Collegedale, TN 37315
Phone: 423-236-2813
Fax: 423-236-1814
Toll-free: 800-768-8437
e-mail: wohlers@southern.edu
Web Site: www.southern.edu
Officers:
Student Services VP: William R Wohlers
Management:
President: Gordon Bietz
Executive Director: Bill Wolhers
Founded: 1892
Specialized Field: Series & Festivals; Instrumental Music; Vocal Music; Theatre; Youth; Ethnic Performances & Cultural
Status: Non-Profit, Non-Professional
Budget: $20,000-35,000

Performs At: Physical Education Center; Ackerman Auditorium

5204
BRYAN COLLEGE DEPARTMENT OF MUSIC
Bryan College
PO Box 7817
Dayton, TN 37321
Phone: 423-775-2041
Fax: 423-775-7317
Toll-free: 800-277-9522
e-mail: wilhoitm@bryan.edu
Web Site: www.bryan.edu
Officers:
Chair Music Department: Mel R Wilhoit
Founded: 1930
Specialized Field: Series and Festivals; Instrumental Music; Vocal Music; Theatre
Status: Non-Profit, Professional
Paid Staff: 80
Budget: $20,000
Performs At: Rudd Auditorium
Facility Category: Auditorium
Type of Stage: Proscenium
Seating Capacity: 750
Year Built: 1976

5205
ETOWAH ARTS COMMISSION
PO Box 193
Etowah, TN 37331
Phone: 423-263-7608
Fax: 423-263-1670
Management:
Chairman: Charles Marta
Founded: 1977
Specialized Field: Series & Festivals; Instrumental Music; Vocal Music; Theater; Youth
Status: Non-Profit, Non-Professional
Paid Staff: 1
Paid Artists: 25
Budget: $10,000
Performs At: Gem Theater

5206
GERMANTOWN PERFORMING ARTS CENTRE
1801 Exeter Road
Germantown, TN 38138
Phone: 901-751-7500
e-mail: info@gpacweb.com
Web Site: www.gpacweb.com
Management:
Executive Director: Tania Moskalenko
Founded: 1994
Specialized Field: Series & Festivals: Instumental Music
Status: Non-Profit, Professional
Paid Staff: 14
Paid Artists: 40
Budget: $400,000-1,000,000
Income Sources: Box Office; Member Support

5207
JACKSON ARTS COUNCIL
314 E Main Street
Jackson, TN 38301
Mailing Address: PO Box 7534, Jackson, TN. 38302-7534
Phone: 901-423-2787
Fax: 901-424-2040
e-mail: jac@aeneas.net

Management:
Executive Director: Judy Truex

5208
CARSON-NEWMAN COLLEGE CONCERT-LECTURE SERIES

Carson-Newman College
Box 71891
Jefferson City, TN 37760
Phone: 865-471-3435
Fax: 865-471-4849
e-mail: rscruggs@cn.edu
Web Site: www.cn.edu
Officers:
President: Randall O'Brien
Management:
Director: Richard Scruggs
Founded: 1917
Specialized Field: Series and Festivals; Instrumental Music; Vocal Music; Theatre; Dance
Status: Non-Profit, Professional
Paid Staff: 2
Budget: $20,000-35,000
Performs At: Henderson Humanities Building

5209
EAST TENNESSEE FINE AND PERFORMING ARTS SCHOLARS

Box 70589
Johnson City, TN 37614-0691
Phone: 423-439-6513
Fax: 423-439-6080
e-mail: williadj@etsu.edu
Web Site: www.estu.east-tenn-st.edu
Management:
Department Chairman: Terry Countermine
Assistant Department Chair: Martin Barrett
Executive Aide: Cathy McGinnis
Specialized Field: Series and Festivals: Instrumental Music
Status: Non-Profit, Professional
Paid Staff: 5
Performs At: Brooks Gym

5210
JOHNSON CITY AREA ARTS COUNCIL

214 E Main Street
Johnson City, TN 37604
Mailing Address: Box 1033, Johnson City, TN. 37605
Phone: 423-928-8229
Fax: 423-928-4511
e-mail: jcarts@mounet.com
Web Site: www.arts.org
Management:
President: Lee Lay
Executive Director: Sarah K Davis
Media Director: Christine Murdock
Mission: Dedicated to preserving the cultural communities in our area.
Founded: 1978
Specialized Field: Art Gallery
Status: Non-Profit, Professional
Paid Staff: 2
Volunteer Staff: 1
Budget: $10,000
Performs At: Small gallery space

5211
JUBILEE COMMUNITY ARTS

Laurel Theater
1538 Laurel Avenue
Knoxville, TN 37916

Phone: 865-522-5851
Fax: 865-522-5386
e-mail: info@jubileearts.org
Web Site: www.jubileearts.org
Management:
Executive Director: Brent Cantrell
Concert Manager: Tolby Koosman
Founded: 1969
Specialized Field: Series & Festivals; Instrumental Music; Vocal Music; Dance; Ethnic Performances
Status: Non-Profit, Non-Professional
Paid Staff: 4
Budget: $35,000-60,000

5212
UNIVERSITY OF TENNESSEE AT KNOXVILLE: CULTURAL ARTS

305 University Center
Knoxville, TN 37996-4800
Phone: 865-974-5455
Fax: 865-974-9252
e-mail: ronl@utk.edu
Web Site: www.utk.edu
Management:
President: Jon Peterson
Assistant Director: Edee Vaughan
Specialized Field: Series & Festivals: Cultural Music And Dance
Status: Non-Profit, Professional
Paid Staff: 3
Budget: $150,000-400,000
Performs At: Clarence Brown Theatre

5213
UNIVERSITY OF TENNESSEE AT MARTIN ARTS COUNCIL

102 Fine Arts Building
Martin, TN 38238
Phone: 901-587-7400
Fax: 901-587-7415
e-mail: dcook@utm.edu
Management:
Director: Douglas Cook
Budget: $20,000-35,000
Performs At: Harriet Fulton Performing Arts Theater

5214
CONCERTS INTERNATIONAL

PO Box 770522
Memphis, TN 38177-0522
Phone: 901-527-3067
Fax: 901-682-1928
e-mail: barnbeca@mindspring.com
Web Site: Http://home.midsouth.rr.com
Officers:
President: Barry White
VP: Jeff Kass
Secretary: Kacky Walton
Treasurer: Dennis Norton
Management:
Executive Director: Carol Barnett
Artistic Director: Ralph Lake
Utilizes: Guest Musical Directors; Multimedia; Original Music Scores
Specialized Field: Chamber Music
Paid Staff: 1
Budget: $35,000-60,000
Performs At: Harris Concert Hall; University of Memphis
Seating Capacity: 385
Year Remodeled: 1999

5215
MEMPHIS IN MAY INTERNATIONAL FESTIVAL

88 Union
Suite 301
Memphis, TN 38103
Phone: 901-525-4611
Fax: 901-525-4686
e-mail: mim@memphisinmay.org
Web Site: www.memphisinmay.org
Management:
President: Leigh Shockey
Executive Director: James L Holt
Director of Programming: Archana Chandoyle
Mission: To promote and celebrate Memphis culture, foster economic growth and enhance international awareness.
Founded: 1976
Specialized Field: Series & Festivals; Instrumental Music; Vocal Music; Youth; Ethnic Performances
Status: Non-Profit, Professional
Paid Staff: 14
Volunteer Staff: 999
Performs At: Tom Lee Park in downtown Memphis, Tennessee and various venues throughout town
Annual Attendance: 300,000+
Organization Type: Educational; Sponsoring

5216
RHODES COLLEGE: MCCOY VISITING ARTIST SERIES

2000 N Parkway
Memphis, TN 38112
Phone: 901-843-3875
Fax: 901-843-3553
e-mail: templeton@rhodes.edu
Web Site: www.rhodes.edu
Management:
President: William Troutt
Founded: 1848
Specialized Field: Communications
Status: Professional
Paid Staff: 15
Budget: $10,000

5217
ROBERTS W MCLEAN SCHOOL OF MUSIC SERIES

Music Department
1500 Greenland Drive
Murfreesboro, TN 37132
Phone: 615-898-2469
Fax: 615-898-5037
e-mail: jperkins@frank.mtsu.edu
Web Site: www.mtsumusic.com
Management:
President: Sidney A Necphee
Executive Director: George T Riorden
Specialized Field: Series and Festivals; Instrumental Music; Vocal Music; Music Performance
Status: Non-Profit, Professional
Paid Staff: 8
Budget: $10,000-20,000

5218
DAVID LIPSCOMB UNIVERSITY: MUSIC DEPARTMENT

David Lipscomb University
Nashville, TN 37204

Phone: 615-269-1000
Fax: 615-386-7620
Toll-free: 800-333-4358
e-mail: reedja@dlu.edu
Web Site: www.lipscomb.edu
Management:
President: Val Prill
Artistic Director: Connie Pirtle
Founded: 1891
Specialized Field: Series and Festivals; Instrumental Music; Vocal Music; Theatre; Christian Education
Status: For-Profit, Professional
Budget: $10,000-20,000
Performs At: Ward Lecture Auditorium; Alumni Auditorium

5219

FRIENDS OF MUSIC

PO Box 23593
Nashville, TN 37202-3593
Phone: 931-254-0469
Fax: 931-254-0469
Officers:
President: Joseph S Johnson, Jr
Budget: $20,000-35,000
Performs At: James K. Polk Theater; Tennessee Performing Arts Center

5220

HOWARD C GENTRY COMPLEX

Tennessee State University
3500 John Merritt Boulevard
Nashville, TN 37209
Phone: 615-963-5000
Fax: 615-963-5911
Management:
Athletic Director: Bill Thomas

5221

NASHVILLE SHAKESPEARE FESTIVAL

1604 8th Avenue S
Nashville, TN 37203
Phone: 615-255-2273
Fax: 615-248-2273
e-mail: shellie@nashvilleshakes.org
Web Site: www.nashvilleshakes.org
Officers:
Chairman: Donald Capparella
Secretary/Treasurer: Denah Shabal
Management:
President: Donald Capparrella
Artistic Director: Steve Cardamone
Managing Director: Shellie Fossick
Mission: Dedicated to community enrichment and arts in education through innovative and relevant presentations of the works of William Shakespeare and other curriculum-based programming. We focus our work to stimulate imagination and inspire conversation, which are essential elements to a healthy society.
Founded: 1988
Specialized Field: Series & Festivals: Theatre
Status: Non-Profit, Professional
Paid Staff: 3
Paid Artists: 30
Season: august
Performs At: Centennial Park Bandshell
Affiliations: Shakespeare Theatre Association of America
Annual Attendance: 14,000
Organization Type: Performing; Resident; Touring; Educational

Comments: Productions are free of charge or at a cost that makes them accesible regardless of socio-economic circumstances; Barrier free and multiculturally cast.

5222

VANDERBILT UNIVERSITY: GREAT PERFORMANCES

207 Sarratt Center
Student Center
Nashville, TN 37240
Phone: 615-322-2471
Fax: 615-343-8081
e-mail: bridgette.kohnhorst@vanderbilt.edu
Web Site: www.vanderbilt.edu/greatperformances
Management:
Executive Director: Bridgette Kohnhorst
Art&Cultural Programs Director: Bridgette Kohnhorst
Founded: 1974
Specialized Field: Series and Festivals; Instrumental Music; Vocal Music; Dance; Ethnic Performances; Theatre; Performing Art
Status: Non-Profit, Professional
Paid Staff: 8
Paid Artists: 8
Budget: $150,000-400,000

5223

OAK RIDGE CIVIC MUSIC ASSOCIATION

PO Box 4271
Oak Ridge, TN 37831
Phone: 865-483-5569
Fax: 865-483-5569
e-mail: orcma@korrnet.org
Web Site: www.korrnet.org/orcma
Management:
Managing Director: Earle Lovering
Music Director: Serge Fournier
Mission: To provide the community with quality music; to encourage community youth to enjoy good music.
Founded: 1944
Specialized Field: Series and Festivals; Symphony; Orchestra; Classical
Status: Non-Profit, Professional
Paid Staff: 2
Paid Artists: 50
Performs At: Oak Ridge High School Auditorium
Organization Type: Performing; Educational; Sponsoring

5224

SEWANEE FESTIVAL ORCHESTRAS / SEWANEE MUSIC FESTIVAL

University of the South
735 University Avenue
Sewanee, TN 37383-1000
Phone: 931-598-1225
Fax: 931-598-1706
e-mail: ssmf@sewanee.edu
Management:
Artistic Director: James Paul
Managing Director: Mark Savage
Director Admission: Katherine Lehman
Festival Coordinator: Kory Vrieze
Founded: 1957
Specialized Field: Orchestra

5225

SEWANEE SUMMER MUSIC FESTIVAL

University of the South
735 University Avenue
Sewanee, TN 37383-1000

Phone: 931-598-1225
Fax: 931-598-1706
e-mail: ssmf@sewanee.edu
Web Site: www.musicfestival.sewanee.edu
Management:
Managing Director: Katherine Lehman, klehman@sewanee.edu
Office Manager: Sally Hubbard, ssmf@sewanee.edu
Mission: Internationally acclaimed summer festival, combining a program for advanced music students and a professional concert series.
Founded: 1957
Specialized Field: Orchestra
Paid Staff: 29
Volunteer Staff: 20
Paid Artists: 5
Income Sources: Tuition, Annual Fund, Endowed Funds, Grants
Annual Attendance: 145
Facility Category: Concert Hall
Seating Capacity: 1,999

5226

UNIVERSITY OF THE SOUTH: PERFORMING ARTS SERIES

735 University Avenue
Sewanee, TN 37402
Phone: 615-598-1484
Fax: 615-598-1145
e-mail: sshrader@sewanee.edu
Management:
Chairman: Steven Shrader

5227

WATERTOWN JAZZ FESTIVAL

Watertown Bed & Breakfast
116 Depot Avenue
Watertown, TN 37184
Phone: 615-237-9999
e-mail: mccomb28@charter.net
Web Site: www.watertownjazz.com
Management:
President: Sharon McComb
Artistic Director: Glenn Martin
Founded: 1990
Specialized Field: Series & Festivals; Instrumental Music; Vocal Music; Youth; Ethnic Performances
Status: Non-Profit, Professional

Texas

5228

UNIVERSITY OF TEXAS AT ARLINGTON

Excel Campus Activities
Uta Box 19348
Arlington, TX 76019
Phone: 817-272-2963
Fax: 817-272-2962
e-mail: excel@uta.edu
Web Site: www.uta.edu
Management:
President: Kelly Earnest
Director of Student Activities: Mardie Sorensen
Artistic Director: Megan Ridley Ridley
Founded: 1992
Specialized Field: Programming
Status: Non-Profit, Non-Professional
Paid Staff: 15
Volunteer Staff: 50
Non-paid Artists: 6
Budget: $20,000-35,000

Performs At: Texas Hall; Rosebud Theatre; Blubonnet Ballroom

5229
AUSTIN CHAMBER MUSIC FESTIVAL
3814 Medical Parkway
Suite 203
Austin, TX 78756
Phone: 512-454-7562
Fax: 512-454-0029
e-mail: info@austinchambermusic.org
Web Site: www.austinchambermusic.org
Officers:
    President: Barbara Grove
    VP: Bryce Williams
    Secretary: Dee Ann Kincke
    Treasurer: Diane Post
Management:
    Executive Director: Jeri Deangelis
    Artistic Director: Felicity Coltman
    Business Manager: Ora Shay
    President: Barbara Grove
Mission: To enhance the quality of community life by nurturing and expanding knowledge, understanding, and appreciation of chamber music through education, community outreach and performance.
Founded: 1981
Specialized Field: Series & Festivals; Instrumental Music; Vocal Music; Youth; Ethnic Performances; Chamber Music
Status: Non-Profit, Professional
Paid Staff: 4
Paid Artists: 60
Budget: 265,000
Income Sources: Grants; Membership; Corporate Support; Government Funds; Individuals
Facility Category: Varies
Type of Stage: Varies

5230
AUSTIN SHAKESPEARE FESTIVAL
PO Box 683
Austin, TX 78767-0683
Phone: 512-454-2273
e-mail: info@austinshakespeare.org
Web Site: www.austinshakespeare.org
Officers:
    President: Daniel B Wilson
    VP: Susan Threadgill
    Treasurer: Jill K Sawnson
    Secretary: Sylvester L. Ruffin
Management:
    President: James E Cousar
    Administrative Director: Kelsey Kling
    Artistic Director: Guy Roberts
Mission: To produce professional quality productions of Classical theatre with an emphasis on the plays of William Shakespeare and to entertain and enrich the theatre-going public by presenting productions that are accessible, imaginative, and stimulating, while remaining true to the integrity of the plays and the author.
Founded: 1984
Status: Non-Equity; Nonprofit
Season: September - October
Type of Stage: Outdoor
Stage Dimensions: 50' x 40'
Seating Capacity: 3000

5231
CONSPIRARE, CRAIG HELLA JOHNSON & COMPANY OF VOICES
2702 McCulloum Street
Austin, TX 78703
Phone: 512-476-5775
Fax: 512-481-1676
e-mail: info@conspirare.org
Web Site: www.conspirare.org
Officers:
    Board Chairman: Fran Collmann
Management:
    Interim Executive Director: Stephanie Sheppard
Founded: 1993
Specialized Field: Series & Festivals; Concerts; Vocal Music
Status: Non-Profit, Professional
Paid Staff: 4
Paid Artists: 35
Affiliations: New Texas Music Works

5232
FRANK ERWIN CENTER/ UNIVERSITY OF TEXAS-AUSTIN
1701 Red River
PO Box 2929
Austin, TX 78768-2929
Phone: 512-471-7744
Fax: 512-471-9652
Toll-free: 800-982-2386
e-mail: erwin.center@erwin.utexas.edu
Web Site: www.uterwincenter.com
Management:
    Director: John M Graham
    Associate Director: Jimmy Earl
Founded: 1977
Specialized Field: Series & Festivals; Vocal; Instrumental Music; Theatre; Youth; Dance; Ethnic Performances
Status: Non-Profit, Non-Professional
Paid Staff: 2000
Seating Capacity: 17,800, 16,500
Year Built: 1977

5233
SALON CONCERTS
PO Box 163501
Austin, TX 78716-3501
Phone: 512-342-2785
Fax: 512-342-0515
e-mail: salonconcerts@aol.com
Web Site: www.salonconcerts.org
Management:
    Music Director: Robert Rudie
    Managing Director: Melissa Eddy
Founded: 1992
Specialized Field: Series and Festivals: Chamber Music
Status: Non-Profit, Professional
Paid Staff: 2
Budget: $10,000

5234
BAY CITY FESTIVAL ARTS ASSOCIATION
PO Box 111
Bay City, TX 77404-0111
Phone: 409-245-9062
Fax: 409-245-1622
e-mail: melvine@sat.net
Officers:
    Chairman Selection Committee: Melvin Epstein
Budget: $20,000-35,000
Performs At: Keye Ingram Auditorium

5235
FESTIVAL ARTS ASSOCIATION
PO Box 1794
Bay City, TX 77404-1794
Phone: 409-245-2727
Fax: 409-245-6966
e-mail: mseaman@alphainternet.net
Web Site: www.festarts.org
Management:
    Artistic Director: Mark Seaman

5236
BEAUMONT MUSIC COMMISSION
PO Box 7469
Beaumont, TX 77726
Phone: 409-755-3565
Fax: 409-755-3596
e-mail: bmc@exp.net
Web Site: www.beaumontmusic.org
Officers:
    President: Matthew White
    VP/Chairman: Naaman J Woodland, Jr
    Second VP: David Hitt
    Third VP: J. Robert Madden
    Fourth VP: Virginia Christopher
    Recording Secretary: Gwenn Mercer
Management:
    President: Murray Anderson
    Executive Director: Cathy Theall
Mission: To offer instrumental and vocal artists in small ensembles, recitals/concerts, opera, musicals, dance groups and small orchestras.
Utilizes: Actors; Collaborating Artists; Collaborations; Community Members; Dance Companies; Dancers; Educators; Grant Writers; Guest Artists; Guest Companies; Guest Soloists; Guest Writers; Local Artists; Local Unknown Artists; Lyricists; Multimedia; Music; New Productions; Organization Contracts; Original Music Scores; Special Technical Talent; Theatre Companies; Touring Companies
Founded: 1923
Specialized Field: Dance; Vocal Music; Instrumental Music
Status: Nonprofit
Volunteer Staff: 60
Budget: $128,000
Performs At: Julie Rogers Theatre for the Performing Arts
Annual Attendance: 8,000
Organization Type: Educational; Sponsoring

5237
YOUNG AUDIENCES OF SOUTHEAST TEXAS
595 Orleans
Suite 414
Beaumont, TX 77701
Phone: 409-835-3884
Fax: 409-835-5504
e-mail: yasetx@aol.com
Web Site: www.geocities.com
Officers:
    President: Douglas E Fierce
Management:
    President: Doug Fierce
    Executive Director: Sally Kiikpatrick
    Program Director/Business Manager: Stacie Jannice
Mission: To provide students with an opportunity to experience live performances featuring professional artists; to further arts education.
Utilizes: Actors; Artists-in-Residence; Collaborations; Curators; Dance Companies; Educators; Fine Artists; High School Drama; Local Artists; Multimedia; Original Music Scores; Playwrights; Poets; Sign Language Translators; Soloists; Special Technical Talent; Theatre Companies; Touring Companies
Founded: 1973

Specialized Field: Fine Arts Education
Status: Non-Profit, Professional
Paid Staff: 2
Paid Artists: 35
Budget: $155,598
Income Sources: Individual, Corporate, Grants/Foundations
Organization Type: Performing; Educational

5238
UNIVERSITY OF MARY HARDIN: BAYLOR
900 College Street
Box 8012, UMHB Station
Belton, TX 76513
Phone: 254-295-4678
Fax: 254-295-4158
Toll-free: 800-727-8642
e-mail: glayne@umhb.edu
Web Site: www.umhb.edu
Officers:
    Interim Chairman, Dept of Music: Ted Barnes
    President: Dr Randy O'Rear
Founded: 1845
Specialized Field: Series & Festivals; Instrumental Music; Vocal Music; Theatre
Status: Non-Profit, Non-Professional
Paid Staff: 200
Budget: $100,000
Performs At: Hughes Recital Hall

5239
BIG SPRING CULTURAL AFFAIRS COUNCIL
Box 1391
Big Spring, TX 79721
Phone: 915-263-7641
Fax: 915-264-9111
Management:
    Director: Marae Brooks
Mission: To offer balanced cultural activities to the community; to enhance natural cultural resources.
Utilizes: Guest Artists; Singers
Specialized Field: Dance; Vocal Music; Instrumental Music; Theater
Status: Nonprofit
Budget: $10,000
Organization Type: Touring

5240
ARTS COUNCIL OF WASHINGTON COUNTY
701 Milroy Drive
Brenham, TX 77833
Phone: 979-836-3120
Fax: 979-830-4030
Mission: To advance local arts in our community; to bring events to our community that are not locally available.
Utilizes: Guest Artists; Guest Companies; Singers
Founded: 1981
Specialized Field: Vocal Music; Instrumental Music; Theatre
Status: Professional; Semi-Professional; Non-Professional; Nonprofit
Income Sources: TCA
Organization Type: Touring; Resident; Educational; Sponsoring

5241
UNIVERSITY OF TEXAS AT BROWNSVILLE
80 Fort Brown
Brownsville, TX 78520
Phone: 956-544-8247
e-mail: sue.z.urbis@utb.edu
Web Site: www.utb.edu/finearts
Officers:
    President: Juliet Garcia
    Department Chairman: Sue Zanne Williamson Urbis
Management:
    Music Professor: Richard Urbis
Founded: 1992
Specialized Field: Series & Festivals; Instrumental Music; Vocal Music; Youth; Ethnic Performances
Status: Non-Profit, Professional
Paid Staff: 2
Paid Artists: 12
Budget: $10,000

5242
CITY OF BRYAN PARKS AND RECREATION
1309 Martin Luther King
PO Box 1000
Bryan, TX 77803
Phone: 979-209-5528
Fax: 979-209-5524
e-mail: cmessina@ci.bryan.tx.us
Web Site: www.bryantx.gov
Management:
    Speical Events Coordinator: Linda Giffen
    Managing Director: David Schmitz
    Special Events Coordinator: Ashley Bennett
Mission: To provide area residents with quality entertainment.
Utilizes: Singers
Founded: 1890
Specialized Field: Recreation and Part Programming for the City
Status: Non-Profit, Non-Professional
Paid Staff: 60
Performs At: Lake Byrant
Type of Stage: Amphitheatre; Outdoors
Organization Type: Performing; Touring; Resident; Educational; Sponsoring

5243
MONTGOMERY COUNTY PERFORMING ARTS SERIES
PO Box 1714
Conroe, TX 77305
Phone: 936-856-6243
Web Site: www.mcpas.org
Officers:
    President: Peggy Miller
Budget: $20,000-35,000

5244
CATHEDRAL CONCERT SERIES
505 N Upper Broadway
Corpus Christi, TX 78401
Phone: 361-888-6520
Fax: 361-883-1918
e-mail: lee.gwozdz@cccathedral.com
Web Site: www.goccn.org/ccs
Officers:
    Executive Director: Lee Gwozdz
    Administrative Assistant: Rachael Vasquez
    Administrative Assistant: Rosa M. Alfaro
Mission: Preserve, promote and provide high quality live performances to all segments, cultures and divisions of the community's population at no charge.
Utilizes: Five Seasonal Concerts; Guest Accompanists; Guest Artists; Guest Choreographers; Guest Companies; Guest Composers; Guest Musical

Directors; Guest Musicians; Guest Writers; Instructors; Multimedia; Original Music Scores; Sign Language Translators; Singers; Soloists; Student Interns; Theatre Companies
Founded: 1985
Specialized Field: Series & Festivals: Vocal music
Status: Non-Profit, Professional
Paid Staff: 2
Paid Artists: 15
Budget: $101,275.00
Income Sources: Corporate Sponsors; Grants; VIP Memberships
Performs At: Church
Annual Attendance: 6,000
Facility Category: Cathedral
Type of Stage: Portable
Seating Capacity: 1,000
Organization Type: Performing; Touring; Resident

5245
CORPUS CHRISTI COMMUNITY CONCERT
446 Troy
Corpus Christi, TX 78412
Phone: 361-992-9220
Fax: 361-992-9220
e-mail: pat@testx.net
Founded: 1935

5246
CORPUS CHRISTI COMMUNITY CONCERT
446 Troy
Corpus Christi, TX 78412
Phone: 361-992-9220
Fax: 361-992-9220
e-mail: pat@testx.net
Officers:
    President: Pat Townsend
Founded: 1935
Volunteer Staff: 20
Budget: $60,000-150,000
Income Sources: Subscriptions
Performs At: Bayfront Plaza Auditorium
Seating Capacity: 2,500

5247
DEL MAR COLLEGE STUDENT CULTURAL PROGRAMS
Del Mar College Music
Music & Drama Department, East Campus
Corpus Christi, TX 78404-3897
Phone: 361-886-1211
Budget: $10,000-20,000
Performs At: Nell Bartlett Theater

5248
TEXAS A&M UNIVERSITY: CORPUS CHRISTI, COLLEGE OF ARTS & HUMANITIES
6300 Ocean Drive
Corpus Christi, TX 78412
Phone: 361-825-2372
Fax: 361-825-6097
Web Site: www.tamucc.edu
Officers:
    Visual/Performing Arts Dept. Chair: Carey Rote
Management:
    President: Robert Fergusson
    Executive Director: Don Luna
Founded: 1947
Specialized Field: Education In Art Theatre Music
Status: Non-Profit, Professional

Paid Staff: 6
Paid Artists: 30
Budget: $10,000-20,000
Performs At: Warren Theatre

5249
TEXAS JAZZ FESTIVAL SOCIETY
PO Box 424
Corpus Christi, TX 78403
Phone: 361-808-9515
Fax: 361-853-4185
e-mail: tjfspres@email.msn.com
Web Site: www.texasjazz-fest.org/
Management:
    President: Rick Sanchez
Mission: Producing the Texas Jazz Festival to the
public annually, free of charge; promoting and
preserving American jazz.
Utilizes: Singers
Founded: 1969
Specialized Field: Vocal Music; Instrumental Music;
Festivals
Status: Professional; Nonprofit
Performs At: Bayfront Plaza Convention Center
Organization Type: Performing

5250
PINEY WOODS FINE ARTS ASSOCIATION
603 E Goliad, Suite 203
PO Box 1213
Crockett, TX 75835
Phone: 936-544-4276
Fax: 936-546-0927
e-mail: pwfaa@consolidated.net
Web Site: www.pwfaa.org
Management:
    President: J Patrick Walker
    Executive Director: J Bryan Lake
Utilizes: Actors; Collaborations; Dance Companies;
Educators; Guest Instructors; Guest Soloists; Guild
Activities; Instructors; Local Artists; Multimedia; Original
Music Scores; Poets; Resident Professionals; Sign
Language Translators; Soloists; Student Interns;
Special Technical Talent; Theatre Companies; Touring
Companies; Visual Arts
Founded: 1991
Specialized Field: Series & Festivals; Instrumental
Music; Vocal Music; Theatre; Youth; Dance; Ethnic
Performances; Performing/Visual Arts
Status: Non-Profit, Professional
Paid Staff: 2
Volunteer Staff: 80
Paid Artists: 4
Non-paid Artists: 1
Performs At: General Purpose

5251
BLACK ACADEMY OF ARTS AND LETTERS SERIES
650 S Griffin
Dallas, TX 75202
Phone: 214-743-2440
Fax: 214-743-2450
e-mail: pbaal@airmail.net
Web Site: www.pbaal.org
Management:
    Founder and President: Curtis King
    Facility Operations Manager: Gwen Hargrove
    Developmental Manager: Ken Rowe
    Membership Developer: Gail Johnson
    Publicist: Marilyn Clark
Mission: Promoting, fostering, cultivating, perpetuating
and preserving Black Americans' arts and letters.
Utilizes: Guest Artists; Guest Companies; Singers

Founded: 1977
Specialized Field: Series & Festivals; Dance; Music;
Theatre
Status: Non-Profit, Professional
Paid Staff: 100
Organization Type: Performing; Educational

5252
DALLAS FESTIVAL OF ARTS & JAZZ
Mei Festivals
2626 Cole Avenue, Suite 400
Dallas, TX 75204
Phone: 214-885-1881
Fax: 214-885-1882
e-mail: info@meifestivals.com
Web Site: www.meifestivals.com/dalfest.html
Management:
    President: Stephen Millard
Founded: 1986

5253
DALLAS SUMMER MUSICALS
Music Hall at Fair Park
909 1st Avenue Parry
Dallas, TX 75210
Phone: 214-565-1116
Fax: 214-565-0071
e-mail: jcagle@dallassummermusicals.org
Web Site: www.dallassummermusicals.org
Officers:
    VP/General Manager: Nancy J Marshall
Management:
    President: Michael A Jenkins
    Event Booking: Jayne Basse
    Facilities Services Manager: Ben Perrin
Mission: To promote the performing arts.
Utilizes: Special Technical Talent; Theatre Companies
Founded: 1940
Specialized Field: Musical Theatre
Status: Non-Profit, Professional
Paid Staff: 50
Season: June - August
Annual Attendance: 400,000+
Facility Category: Performance; Concert Hall
Type of Stage: Proscenium
Stage Dimensions: 100'x39'10'
Seating Capacity: 3,420
Year Built: 1925
Rental Contact: Jayne Basse
Organization Type: Performing

5254
DSO CLASSICAL SUMMER SAMPLER
2301 Flora Street
Suite 300
Dallas, TX 75201-2497
Phone: 214-692-0203
Fax: 214-953-1218
e-mail: customerservice@dalsym.com
Web Site: www.dallassymphony.com
Officers:
    President: Dr. Eugene Bonelli
Management:
    President: Fred Bronstein
Founded: 1900

5255
FAIR PARK
PO Box 150188
Dallas, TX 75315
Phone: 214-565-1116
Fax: 214-565-0071
e-mail: cls2nd@aol.com
Web Site: www.dallassummermusicals.org

Management:
    President: Michael Jenkins
    Assistant General Manager: JB Gassaway
    Events Manager: Les Studdard
Mission: Offers a 277 acre cultural and exhibition park
including; Cotton Bowl Stadium; eight museums; the
Old Mill Inn Restaurant; five indoor performance halls.
Specialized Field: Series and Festivals: Theatre
Status: Non-Profit, Professional
Seating Capacity: 72,500 (Cotton Bowl)
Year Built: 1936

5256
SHAKESPEARE FESTIVAL OF DALLAS
3630 Harry Hine Boulevard
3rd Floor
Dallas, TX 75219
Phone: 214-559-2778
Fax: 214-559-2782
e-mail: sotg@shakespearedallas.org
Web Site: www.shakespearedallas.org
Management:
    Artistic Director: Raphael Parry
    Managing Director: Sandra L Greenway
Utilizes: Singers
Founded: 1971
Status: Non-Profit
Paid Staff: 3
Performs At: Fair Park Band Shell
Organization Type: Performing; Educational

5257
DEL RIO COUNCIL FOR THE ARTS
120 E Garfield
Del Rio, TX 78840
Phone: 830-775-0888
Fax: 830-774-0803
e-mail: drcarts@delrio.com
Web Site: www.firehousearts.org
Management:
    Executive Director: Ann Stool
Utilizes: Actors; Artists-in-Residence; Curators; Dance
Companies; Dancers; Educators; Fine Artists; Guest
Accompanists; Guest Choreographers; Guest
Ensembles; Guest Musical Directors; Guest Musicians;
Guest Soloists; High School Drama; Instructors; Local
Artists; Multimedia; Original Music Scores; Sign
Language Translators; Singers; Soloists; Special
Technical Talent; Theatre Companies; Touring
Companies
Founded: 1977
Specialized Field: Performing Arts
Status: Non-Profit, Professional
Paid Staff: 2
Volunteer Staff: 21
Paid Artists: 105
Non-paid Artists: 15
Budget: $250,000
Income Sources: Grants; Ticket Sales; Fundraisers;
Corporate Sponsors; City; County; State; Foundation;
Performs At: Theatre, Schools, Fairgrounds,
Ampitheaters
Affiliations: Southwest Performing Arts Presenters;
Mid-America Arts Alliance, Heartland Fund
Annual Attendance: 16,000
Facility Category: Proscenium
Type of Stage: Wooden floor
Stage Dimensions: 25x27
Seating Capacity: 700
Year Built: 1930
Year Remodeled: 1980

5258
GRAYSON COUNTY COLLEGE HUMANITIES
6101 Grayson Drive
Denison, TX 75020
Phone: 903-465-6030
Web Site: www.grayson.edu
Management:
   Dean: John Dartin
   Chairman: Steve Black
   Manager: Joe Hick
Founded: 1965
Specialized Field: Series & Festivals: Theatre
Status: Non-Profit, Non-Professional
Paid Staff: 6
Paid Artists: 50
Budget: $35,000-60,000

5259
DENTON ARTS & JAZZ FESTIVAL
Denton Festival Foundation, Inc.
PO Box 2104
Denton, TX 76202
Phone: 940-565-0931
Fax: 940-566-7007
e-mail: artspatron@aol.com
Web Site: www.dentonjazzfest.com
Officers:
   Board President: Jean Stanley
Management:
   Executive Director: Carol Short
   Artistic Manager: Ray Hair
Mission: To plan, promote and produce the annual Denton Arts & Jazz Festival that is free to the public.
Founded: 1980
Specialized Field: Music; Fine Arts, Crafts and Diverse Performances
Status: Non-Profit
Paid Staff: 2
Volunteer Staff: 300
Paid Artists: 250
Budget: $400,000
Income Sources: Sponsors; Grants; Memberships; Booth Space Fees; Concessions; Souvenirs
Affiliations: City of Denton/Denton Convention & Visitors Bureau
Annual Attendance: 200,000
Facility Category: Quakertown Park
Type of Stage: 7 Stages

5260
GREATER DENTON ARTS COUNCIL
207 S Bell Avenue
Denton, TX 76201-4259
Phone: 940-382-2787
Fax: 940-566-1486
Web Site: www.dentonarts.com
Management:
   President: Randy Robinson
   Executive Director: Herbert Holl
Founded: 1975
Specialized Field: Visual Arts in Education
Status: Non-Profit, Non-Professional
Paid Staff: 7
Budget: $10,000

5261
EASTLAND FINE ARTS ASSOCIATION
PO Box 705
108 N Lamar
Eastland, TX 76448
Phone: 254-629-2102
Fax: 254-629-2247
e-mail: majestic@txol.net
Management:
   Manager: Ed Allcorn
Budget: $10,000
Performs At: Majestic Theatre

5262
EL PASO ASSOCIATION FOR THE PERFORMING ARTS
3525 Pershing Boulevard
El Paso, TX 79930
Phone: 915-565-6900
Fax: 915-565-6999
e-mail: epapa@viva-ep.org
Web Site: www.viva-ep.org
Management:
   Executive Director: Thea Chambers
   Artistic Director: Babil Gandara
Mission: An outdoor drama emphasizing dance, which celebrates the Western American, Native American, Mexican and Spanish cultures that have influenced El Paso's history. Shakespeare-on-the-Rocks presents four plays in repertory each September.
Founded: 1978
Specialized Field: Dance; Vocal Music; Theater; Ballet; Folkdance
Status: Professional; Nonprofit
Paid Staff: 15
Paid Artists: 100
Income Sources: Institute of Outdoor Drama
Season: June - August
Performs At: McKelligon Canyon Amphitheater
Organization Type: Performing; Resident

5263
EL PASO CHAMBER PRO-MUSICA FESTIVAL
PO Box 13328
El Paso, TX 79913
Phone: 915-833-9400
Fax: 915-833-9425
e-mail: info@elpasopromusica.org
Web Site: www.elpasopromusica.org
Management:
   President: Jaime Lowenbert
   Artistic Director: Zuill Bailey
Founded: 1977
Specialized Field: Series and Festivals: Chamber Music
Status: Non-Profit, Professional
Paid Staff: 3
Paid Artists: 25

5264
EL PASO PRO-MUSICA
PO Box 13328
El Paso, TX 79913
Phone: 915-833-9400
Fax: 915-833-9425
e-mail: info@elpasopromusica.org
Web Site: www.elpasopromusica.org
Management:
   Artistic/Administrative Director: Kwang-Wu Kim
Budget: $60,000-150,000

5265
IMPACT: PROGRAMS OF EXCELLENCE
444 E Robinson
El Paso, TX 79902
Phone: 915-545-5068
Fax: 915-545-5076
Management:
   Executive Director: Sally Gilbert

5266
MUSEUMS & CULTURAL AFFAIRS DEPARTMENT
2 Civic Center Plaza
6th Floor
El Paso, TX 79901
Phone: 915-541-4481
Fax: 915-541-4902
e-mail: quijanoal@elpasotexas.gov
Web Site: www.elpasoartsandculture.org
Management:
   Director: Yolanda Alameda
   Deputy City Manager: Debbie Hamlyn
   Artistic Director: Betty Jaraba
Founded: 1984
Specialized Field: Series and Festivals; Instrumental Music; Vocal Music; Theatre; Youth; Dance; Ethnic Performances
Status: Non-Profit, Professional
Paid Staff: 6
Paid Artists: 7
Budget: $150,000-400,000
Performs At: Chamizal National Memorial

5267
BROOKHAVEN COLLEGE CENTER FOR THE ARTS
3939 Valley View Lane
Farmers Branch, TX 75244
Phone: 972-860-4730
Fax: 972-860-4385
e-mail: rpbfape@dcccd.edu
Web Site: www.dcccd.edu/bmc/centerforarts
Management:
   President: Alice Villedsen
   Dean Fine Arts: Rodger Bennett
Founded: 1978
Specialized Field: Community College
Status: Non-Profit, Non-Professional
Paid Staff: 3
Budget: $35,000-60,000
Income Sources: City Grants; Tickets
Annual Attendance: 7,000
Facility Category: Performance Center
Type of Stage: Proscenium
Seating Capacity: 680
Year Built: 1978
Rental Contact: Roger Bennett

5268
FORT HOOD COMMUNITY MUSIC AND THEATER
Building 2803
Fort Hood, TX 76544
Phone: 254-287-1110
Management:
   Mucsical Director/Theater: Jean Zavoina
   Music Director: Roland Gagne
   Technical Director: Fred Baker
   Costumer: Tom Ross
Mission: To provide opportunities for military personnel, their families and other area residents to participate in talent competitions, musicals and shows.
Utilizes: Guest Artists; Guest Companies
Founded: 1950
Specialized Field: Dance; Vocal Music; Instrumental Music; Theater; Festivals
Status: Non-Professional
Organization Type: Performing; Touring

5269

CHILDREN'S UNIVERSAL MUSIC FESTIVAL

4449 Camp Bowie Boulevard
Fort Worth, TX 76107-3834
Phone: 817-732-8161
Fax: 817-732-4774
e-mail: tgc@texasgirlschoir.org
Web Site: www.texasgirlschoir.org
Management:
    Executive Director: Debi Weir
Mission: To bring together childrens choirs from all over the world to share their music in performance.
Utilizes: Arrangers; Collaborating Artists; Collaborations; Community Members; Composers; Dancers; Educators; Five Seasonal Concerts; Grant Writers; Guest Artists; Guest Companies; Guest Composers; Guest Directors; Guest Ensembles; Guest Lecturers; Guest Musical Directors; Guest Speakers; High School Drama; Local Artists; Local Artists & Directors; Multimedia; Music; Organization Contracts; Resident Companies; Sign Language Translators; Volunteer Artists
Founded: 1998
Specialized Field: Children's Choral Music
Status: Non-Profit, Non-Professional
Paid Staff: 10
Volunteer Staff: 55

5270

CLIBURN CONCERTS

Van Cliburn Foundation
2525 Ridgmar Boulevard, Suite 307
Fort Worth, TX 76116
Phone: 817-738-6536
Fax: 817-738-6534
e-mail: clistaff@cliburn.org
Web Site: www.cliburn.org
Officers:
    President: Richard Rodzinski
Management:
    President: Richard Rodzinski
    Executive Director: Maria Guralnik
    Chairman: Alann B Sampson
    Vice Chairman: Tim Carter
Mission: To produce the Cilburn Piano Series.
Founded: 1962
Specialized Field: Series & Festivals; Instrumental Music; Vocal Music
Status: Non-Profit, Professional
Paid Staff: 13
Paid Artists: 15
Budget: $150,000-400,000
Performs At: Nancy Lee & Perry R. Bass Performance Hall

5271

PERFORMING ARTS FORT WORTH

330 E 4th Street
#300
Fort Worth, TX 76102
Phone: 817-212-4200
Fax: 817-810-9294
e-mail: pbeard@basshall.com
Web Site: www.basshall.com
Management:
    Managing Director: Paul S Beard
    Director Operations: Don Fearing
    Director Communications: Carl Davis
    Sales/Sponsorship Director: Julie Curtis

Utilizes: Dance Companies; Dancers; Fine Artists; Grant Writers; Instructors; Local Artists; Original Music Scores; Resident Artists; Sign Language Translators; Special Technical Talent; Theatre Companies
Founded: 1992
Specialized Field: Series & Festivals; Instrumental Music; Vocal Music; Theatre; Youth; Dance; Ethnic Performances
Status: Non-Profit, Professional
Paid Staff: 35
Volunteer Staff: 750
Budget: $1,000,000+
Income Sources: Ticket Sales; Facility Rental; Donations
Performs At: One 2,056 seat multi-purpose theatre; Two 350 Seat Spaces For Small Productions
Annual Attendance: 500,000 - 600,000
Facility Category: Multi-purpose theater
Type of Stage: Proscenium
Stage Dimensions: see www.basshall.com
Seating Capacity: 2,056
Year Built: 1998
Cost: 67 Million
Rental Contact: Managing Director Paul Beard
Resident Groups: Five local resident companies

5272

FREDERICKSBURG MUSIC CLUB

PO Box 1214
Fredericksburg, TX 78624
Phone: 830-997-5413
Fax: 830-997-2980
Officers:
    President: Patsy Hejl
    VP: Frances Gibson
Management:
    Artistic Director: Frances Gibson
Founded: 1937
Specialized Field: Classical
Budget: $10,000-20,000
Facility Category: Church; High School Auditorium

5273

GRAND 1894 OPERA HOUSE

2020 Post Office Street
Galveston, TX 77550
Phone: 409-770-5051
Fax: 409-763-1068
Toll-free: 800-821-1894
e-mail: mpatton@thegrand.com
Web Site: www.thegrand.com
Management:
    Executive Director: Maureen M Patton
Mission: To present professional performing arts in a restored, historic structure and to maintain that structure; to serve the Galveston and the Greater Houston areas.
Utilizes: Actors; Commissioned Music; Dance Companies; Educators; Original Music Scores; Special Technical Talent; Theatre Companies
Founded: 1974
Specialized Field: Live Theatre
Status: Non-Profit, Professional
Paid Staff: 12
Volunteer Staff: 300
Budget: $3.5 million
Income Sources: Earned and Contributed Revenue
Performs At: The Grand 1894 Opera House
Affiliations: Assoc. of Performing Arts Presenters; League Of Historic American Theatres; SW Performing Arts Presenters
Annual Attendance: 100,000+
Facility Category: Historic Theatre
Type of Stage: Proscenium

Stage Dimensions: 38x36
Seating Capacity: 1,040
Year Built: 1894
Year Remodeled: 1985
Rental Contact: Maureen Patton
Organization Type: Performing; Touring; Resident; Educational; Sponsoring; Presenting
Resident Groups: Galveston Symphony Orchestra

5274

GARLAND SUMMER MUSICALS

PO Box 462049
Garland, TX 75046
Phone: 972-205-2780
Fax: 972-205-2775
Management:
    Producer: Patty Granville
    Director: Buff Shurr
Mission: To bring to the community productions of the highest quality; to continue to provide excellent family entertainment.
Utilizes: Singers
Founded: 1983
Specialized Field: Dance; Vocal Music; Instrumental Music
Status: Semi-Professional; Nonprofit
Income Sources: Actors' Equity Association
Performs At: Garland Center for the Performing Arts
Organization Type: Sponsoring

5275

SOUTHWESTERN UNIVERSITY ARTIST SERIES

Southwestern University
The Sarofim School of Fine Arts
Georgetown, TX 78626
Phone: 512-863-1379
Fax: 512-863-1422
Web Site: www.southwestern.edu
Management:
    President: Jake Schrum
    Dean: Paul Gaffney
Specialized Field: Series & Festivals; Performing Arts; Musical Concerts
Status: Non-Profit, Professional
Paid Staff: 10
Paid Artists: 10
Budget: $10,000-20,000
Performs At: Alma Thomas Theater

5276

HARLINGEN COMMUNITY CONCERT ASSOCIATION

PO Box 707
Harlingen, TX 78551
Phone: 956-748-3020
Officers:
    President: James Hough
Management:
    Publicity: Joyce Davis-Tucker
Mission: To entertain and influence community adults and students in culture and cultural events.
Founded: 1930
Specialized Field: a variety of cultural programs

5277

RIOFEST: A BLENDING OF THE ARTS AND ENTERTAINMENT

305 E Jackson, Suite 214
PO Box 531105
Harlingen, TX 78550

Phone: 956-425-2705
Fax: 956-440-0476
Toll-free: 800-746-3378
e-mail: riofest@aol.com
Web Site: www.riofest.com
Management:
    President: Gregg Henderson
    Festival Director: Kathy Preddy
Mission: To develop new audiences for the arts and provide access to the arts for all citizens.
Founded: 1982
Specialized Field: Series & Festivals; Instrumental Music; Vocal Music; Theatre; Youth; Dance; Ethnic Performances
Status: Non-Profit, Professional
Paid Staff: 1
Paid Artists: 50
Non-paid Artists: 100
Budget: $305,000
Income Sources: Gate; Sale of food & drink; Sponsors
Performs At: 40 Acre Park, One 1800 Seat Theatre & One 300 Seat Theatre
Affiliations: TFEA; TCA; City of Harlingen
Annual Attendance: 30,000
Facility Category: Multi-Venue; Indoor & Outdoor Theaters

5278
HILL COLLEGE

112 Lamar Drive
Hillsboro, TX 76645
Phone: 254-659-7882
Fax: 254-582-7591
e-mail: phillowe@hillcollege.edu
Web Site: www.hillcollege.edu
Management:
    President: Sheryl Kappus
    Executive Director: Phillip Lowe
Founded: 1963
Specialized Field: Series & Festivals; Instrumental Music; Vocal Music; Theatre; Youth; Ethnic Performances
Status: Non-Profit, Professional
Paid Staff: 2
Budget: $$8,000-$10,000
Income Sources: Donations
Annual Attendance: 1,200
Seating Capacity: 400

5279
CHILDREN'S THEATRE FESTIVAL

School of Theatre
University of Houston
Houston, TX 77204-4016
Phone: 713-743-3003
e-mail: sjudice@uh.edu
Management:
    Production Director: Sidney Berger
Founded: 1978
Specialized Field: Educational Institution Theater Department
Status: Non-Equity; Nonprofit
Season: June - August
Type of Stage: Proscenium
Stage Dimensions: 40' x 33'
Seating Capacity: 566

5280
DA CAMERA OF HOUSTON

1427 Branard
Houston, TX 77006

Phone: 713-524-7601
Fax: 713-524-4148
Toll-free: 800-233-2226
e-mail: mlaleskie@decamara.com
Web Site: www.dacamera.com
Management:
    Executive Director: Sarah Loudermilk
    Artistic Director: Sarah Rothenberg
Utilizes: Guest Companies; Multimedia; Original Music Scores; Sign Language Translators
Founded: 1987
Specialized Field: Chamber Music/Jazz
Status: Non-Profit, Professional
Paid Staff: 10
Paid Artists: 100
Budget: $1,200,000
Performs At: Cullen Theater; Wortham Center

5281
HOUSTON INTERNATIONAL JAZZ FESTIVAL

3303 S Rice
Suite 107
Houston, TX 77054
Mailing Address: PO Box 8031 Houston, TX 77288
Phone: 713-839-7000
Fax: 713-839-8266
e-mail: jazzed@jazzeducation.org
Web Site: www.jazzeducation.org
Officers:
    President/COO: Dr. James Austin
Management:
    Festival Director: Richard Dabon
Mission: To sponsor a 10-day cultural celebration in an urban setting, focusing on a different country every year.
Founded: 1974
Specialized Field: Performing Series
Status: Non-Profit
Paid Staff: 4
Paid Artists: 19
Income Sources: Cultural Arts Council of Houston; Houston Convention & Visitors Center
Organization Type: Educational; Sponsoring

5282
HOUSTON INTERNATIONAL JAZZ FESTIVAL

PO Box 8031
Houston, TX 77288-8031
Phone: 713-839-7000
Fax: 713-839-8266
e-mail: jazzed@jazzeducation.org
Web Site: www.jazzeducation.org
Management:
    Festival Director: Richard Dabon
Founded: 1990
Specialized Field: Performing Series
Paid Staff: 4
Volunteer Staff: 125
Paid Artists: 19

5283
HOUSTON SHAKESPEARE FESTIVAL

School of Theatre
University of Houston
Houston, TX 77204-4016
Phone: 713-743-3003
Fax: 713-743-2648
e-mail: sjudice@uh.edu
Web Site: www.hfac.uh.edu/theatre
Management:
    President: Sidney Berger

    Secretary: Sandy Judice
    Office Manager: Jerry Aven
    Academic Advisor: Molly Dean
    Lighting Designer: John Gow
    Scene Shop Forman: Drew Hoovler
    Costume Production Supervisor: Toni Lovaglia
    Technical Director: Mo Tuttle
Mission: To provide classical theater at no cost to citizens of Houston and surrounding areas.
Founded: 1975
Specialized Field: Series & Festivals: Theater
Status: Non-Profit, Professional
Paid Staff: 100
Paid Artists: 12
Income Sources: University of Houston
Performs At: Miller Outdoor Theatre
Organization Type: Performing

5284
HOUSTON'S ANNUAL ASIAN-AMERICAN FESTIVAL

1714 Tannehill Drive
Houston, TX 77008
Phone: 713-861-8273
Fax: 713-861-3450
Management:
    Festival Director: Glenda Joe
Mission: Promote, preserve, present Asian cultural arts.
Founded: 1980
Specialized Field: Music; Dance; Theatre; Puppetry
Paid Staff: 1
Volunteer Staff: 50
Paid Artists: 1600

5285
IMMANUEL & HELEN OLSHAN TEXAS MUSIC FESTIVAL

120 School of Music Bldg
Houston, TX 77204-4017
Phone: 713-743-3167
Fax: 713-743-3166
e-mail: tmf@uh.edu
Web Site: www.uh.edu/music/tmf
Management:
    General and Artistic Director: Alan Austin, tmf@uh.edu
    Assistant Director: Melissa Mccrimmon, mfmccrimmon@uh.edu
Mission: The Texas Music Festival is an orchestral training program for talented young musicians ages 18-30. Performs four orchestral programs under internationally recognized conductors.
Utilizes: Artists-in-Residence; Commissioned Composers; Composers; Educators; Grant Writers; Guest Accompanists; Guest Companies; Guest Composers; Guest Ensembles; Guest Musical Directors; Guest Musicians; High School Drama; Multimedia; Organization Contracts; Original Music Scores; Sign Language Translators; Singers; Soloists; Students
Founded: 1990
Specialized Field: Classical
Paid Staff: 2
Paid Artists: 60
Budget: $800,000+
Performs At: Concert Hall
Affiliations: Univ. of Houston, Moores School of Music, Houston Symphony, Houston Grand Opera Orchestra, Houston Ballet Orchestra, Shepherd School of Music
Annual Attendance: 7,000

5286
JEWISH COMMUNITY CENTER OF HOUSTON
5601 S Braeswood
Houston, TX 77096
Phone: 713-729-3200
Fax: 713-551-7223
Web Site: www.jcchouston.org
Management:
    Executive Director: Jerry Wische
Mission: To offer education, leisure activities and recreation to Southwest Houston; to promote the appreciation of theatre.
Utilizes: Guest Companies; Singers
Founded: 1935
Specialized Field: Series & Festivals; Dance; Vocal Music; Instrumental Music; Theater
Status: Non-Profit, Professional
Paid Staff: 50
Income Sources: Texas Nonprofit Theatre; National Council of Jewish Theatres
Performs At: Jewish Community Center; Kaplan Theatre; IW Marks Theatre Center; Joe Frank Theatre
Facility Category: Proscenium Theatre; Black Box Theatre
Type of Stage: Proscenium; Thrust
Seating Capacity: 330; 130
Organization Type: Performing; Educational; Sponsoring

5287
JONES HALL FOR THE PERFORMING ARTS
615 Louisiana Avenue
Houston, TX 77002
Phone: 713-227-3974
Web Site: www.ci.houston.tx.us/cef/jones.html
Management:
    Manager: Vivian Montejano
    Director: Gerald J Tollett
Opened: 1966

5288
SHEPHERD SCHOOL OF MUSIC CONCERT SERIES
Rice University
6100 Main Street
Houston, TX 77005
Phone: 713-348-4933
Fax: 713-348-5317
e-mail: littman@rice.edu
Web Site: www.rice.edu/music
Management:
    Dean: Robert Yekovich
    Concert Manager: Tom Littman
Mission: Pre-professional training for musicians in a conspiratory environment within a private university.
Founded: 1975
Specialized Field: Series & Festivals; Instrumental Music; Vocal Music; Theater; Youth
Status: Non-Profit, Non-Professional
Paid Staff: 100
Paid Artists: 75
Facility Category: Concert Hall
Seating Capacity: 780
Year Built: 1991
Rental Contact: Tom Littman

5289
SOCIETY FOR THE PERFORMING ARTS
615 Louisiana
Suite 100
Houston, TX 77002
Phone: 713-227-5134
Fax: 713-223-8301
e-mail: mattox@spahouston.org
Web Site: www.spahouston.org
Officers:
    Executive Director: Hoyt T Mattox
    Director Development: Chree Boydstun
    Director Marketing: Lynda Sanders
    Director Operations: June Christensen
    Chairman: Charles Davidson
    President: Stephen Trauber
Management:
    Executive Director: Sally Tyler
    Director Development: Priscilla Larson
    Director Marketing: Lynda Sanders
    Director Operations: June Christensen
    Director Ticketing Services: Greg Brown
Mission: To present the world's best in performing arts, whether dance, music or theatre.
Utilizes: Commissioned Composers; Commissioned Music; Dancers; Multimedia; Theatre Companies
Opened: 1966
Specialized Field: Modern; Mime; Ballet; Jazz; Ethnic; Folk
Status: Professional; Nonprofit
Budget: $2,500,000 - $4,000,000
Income Sources: Sales; Contributions
Performs At: Jones Hall; Wortham Theatre Center
Affiliations: ISPA; Arts Presenters; Dance USA
Annual Attendance: 50,000-60,0000
Type of Stage: Sprung Wood
Seating Capacity: 2912
Year Built: 1966
Year Remodeled: 1996
Cost: $9,000,000
Organization Type: Sponsoring

5290
UNIVERSITY OF ST. THOMAS GUEST RECITALS
3800 Montrose
Houston, TX 77006
Phone: 713-525-3560
Fax: 713-942-5912
e-mail: yong@stthom.edu
Web Site: www.stthom.edu
Management:
    President: Robert Ivany
    Artistic Director: Tom Crow
    Department Coordinator: Sue Young
Mission: Enrichment for students, faculty and community.
Founded: 1947
Specialized Field: School of Hire Learning
Status: Non-Profit, Non-Professional
Paid Staff: 1
Paid Artists: 2
Budget: $10,000-20,000

5291
HILL COUNTRY ARTS FOUNDATION
Highway 39
PO Box 1169
Ingram, TX 78025
Phone: 830-367-5120
Fax: 830-367-4332
Toll-free: 800-459-4223
Web Site: www.hcaf.com
Management:
    President: Nelwyn Moser
    Artistic Director: Jennifer Hayne
Mission: Promoting the performing and visual arts.
Utilizes: Guest Artists; Guest Companies; Singers
Founded: 1958
Specialized Field: Series & Festivals; Dance; Vocal Music; Instrumental Music; Theater
Status: Non-Profit, Professional
Paid Staff: 75
Income Sources: American Association of Community Theatres; Texas Nonprofit Theatre
Performs At: Outdoor Amphitheatre
Organization Type: Performing; Educational

5292
ENTERTAINMENT SERIES OF IRWING
3333 N MacArthur Boulevard
Suite 300
Irving, TX 75062
Phone: 972-252-7558
Fax: 972-570-4962
Web Site: www.ci.irving.tx.us
Officers:
    Chairman: Kim Dennis
    Vice-Chairman: Vanessa Bell
    Secretary: Laura Sanner
Management:
    President: Dotty Verept
    Technical Theater Coordinator: Ross Moroney
    Box Office Manager: Andy Pate
    Director Marketing/Publications: Jo Trizila
Founded: 1955
Specialized Field: Series and Festivals; Instrumental Music; Vocal Music; Theatre; Dance
Status: Non-Profit, Professional
Income Sources: Community Concerts
Organization Type: Sponsoring

5293
KERRVILLE FESTIVALS
Quiet Valley Ranch
PO Box 291466
Kerrville, TX 78029
Phone: 830-257-3600
Fax: 830-257-8680
e-mail: info@kerrville-music.com
Web Site: www.kerrvillefolkfestival.com
Management:
    President: Charlie Land
    Producer and Director: Dalis Allen
Mission: To offer recordings, workshops and music festivals, featuring regional national and international artists and emphasizing acoustic musicians and songwriters.
Utilizes: Singers
Founded: 1972
Specialized Field: Singer/Songwriters Music Outdoor Theatre Concerts
Status: For-Profit, Professional
Paid Staff: 4
Volunteer Staff: 600
Paid Artists: 100
Income Sources: Texas Festivals Association; Texas Music Association
Performs At: Festival Outdoor Theater
Organization Type: Performing

5294
KERRVILLE FOLK FESTIVAL
PO Box 291466
Kerrville, TX 78029
Phone: 830-257-3600
Fax: 830-257-8680
Toll-free: 800-435-8429
e-mail: staff@kerrville-music.com
Web Site: www.kerrville-music.com
Management:
    Producer: Dalis Allen
Founded: 1972

Specialized Field: Songwriters Festival
Status: For-Profit, Professional
Paid Staff: 2
Paid Artists: 10

5295
KILGORE COMMUNITY CONCERT ASSOCIATION
PO Box 47
Kilgore, TX 75663-0047
Phone: 903-983-9023
Fax: 903-984-1101
Officers:
President: WS Morris
Budget: $20,000-35,000

5296
TEXAS SHAKESPEARE FESTIVAL
1100 Broadway
Kilgore, TX 75662
Mailing Address: PO Box 2788, Kilgore, TX. 75663
Phone: 903-983-8117
Fax: 903-983-8124
e-mail: info@texasshakespeare.com
Web Site: www.texasshakespeare.com
Management:
Artistic Director: Raymond Caldwell
Managing Director: John Dodd
Mission: To serve the community by providing cultural enrichment, educational opportunities and economic benefits.
Founded: 1986
Specialized Field: Series & Festivals: Theatre
Status: Non-Profit, Professional
Paid Staff: 2
Paid Artists: 20
Season: June - July
Type of Stage: Flexible
Stage Dimensions: 30' x 30'
Seating Capacity: 240

5297
LUBBOCK ARTS ALLIANCE
2109 Broadway
Lubbock, TX 79401
Phone: 806-744-2787
Fax: 806-744-2790
e-mail: mail@lubbockarts.org
Web Site: www.lubbockarts.org
Officers:
President: Robby Vestal
Festival Chairman: Meredith McAlister
Management:
President: Meredith McAllister
Executive Director: Elizabeth Regner
Specialized Field: Promotion of the Arts
Status: Non-Profit, Professional
Paid Staff: 2
Volunteer Staff: 250
Non-paid Artists: 300
Budget: $10,000-20,000
Income Sources: Grants; Corporate Sponsors
Performs At: Lubbock Memorial Civic Center

5298
LUBBOCK CHRISTIAN UNIVERSITY
5601 W 19th Street
Lubbock, TX 79407-2099
Phone: 806-720-7726
Fax: 806-720-7255
Web Site: www.lcu.edu
Management:
President: Ken Jones
Artistic Director: Michelle Kraft

Theatre Director: Don Williams
Assistant Professor Music: Philip Camp
Professor Music: Dr. Ruth Holmes
Utilizes: Guild Activities
Founded: 1957
Specialized Field: Series & Festivals; Music; Art; Theatre
Status: Non-Profit, Non-Professional
Paid Staff: 6
Paid Artists: 2
Budget: $10,000
Type of Stage: Proscenium
Stage Dimensions: 35x20
Seating Capacity: 1,200
Year Built: 1967

5299
TEXAS TECH UNIVERSITY ARTISTS & SPEAKERS
TTU
PO Box 45014
Lubbock, TX 79409-5014
Phone: 806-742-3621
Fax: 806-742-0138
e-mail: campusactivitiesinvolvement@ttu.edu
Web Site: www.campuslife.ttu.edu
Management:
President: James Whitmore
Executive Director: Gregory Elkins
Artistic Director: Jennifer Henley
Specialized Field: Series & Festivals: Concerts and Speakers
Status: Non-Profit, Non-Professional
Paid Staff: 20

5300
MARSHALL REGIONAL ARTS COUNCIL
2501 E End Boulevard S
PO Box C
Marshall, TX 75671-3003
Phone: 903-935-4484
Fax: 903-927-2132
e-mail: arts@marshallartscouncil.org
Web Site: www.marshallartscouncil.org
Officers:
President: Nancy Simpson
Executive Director: Joyce Weekly
Mission: To support, promote, and encourage participation and involvement of all citizens of the region in quality experiences in both the arts and humanities.
Utilizes: Actors; Artists-in-Residence; Dancers; Instructors; Local Artists; Multimedia; Original Music Scores; Resident Artists; Singers; Special Technical Talent; Theatre Companies
Founded: 1979
Specialized Field: Series & Festivals; Dance; Vocal Music; Instrumental Music; Theatre; Festivals; Grand Opera
Status: Non-Profit, Professional
Paid Staff: 2
Budget: $100,000
Income Sources: Association of Performing Arts Presenters; National Association of Local Arts Agencies; Texas Arts Council; Country Music Association
Performs At: Marshall Convention Center
Facility Category: Convention Center
Type of Stage: Proscenium
Stage Dimensions: 78 x 57
Seating Capacity: 1600
Year Built: 1984
Year Remodeled: 2001
Cost: 1.5 Million
Organization Type: Educational; Sponsoring

5301
MCALLEN PERFORMING ARTS
PO Box 790
McAllen, TX 78505
Phone: 956-631-2545
Fax: 956-631-8571
Management:
Executive Director: Genevia Crow
Mission: To provide the public with professional touring theatre productions and entertainment not available through local agencies.
Specialized Field: Vocal Music; Theatre; Broadway Musicals
Status: Professional; Nonprofit
Performs At: McAllen Civic Center
Organization Type: Performing; Touring

5302
RIO GRANDE VALLEY INTERNATIONAL MUSIC FESTIVAL
PO Box 2315
McAllen, TX 78502
Phone: 956-618-6085
Officers:
Chairman: Dean R PhD Canty
Vice Chairman: Joy Judin
Secretary/Treasurer: Carol Edrington
Financial Secretary: Mildred Erhart
Mission: To present a major symphony orchestra annually, in varied concerts for students and adults, with emphasis on education of young listeners.
Utilizes: Singers
Founded: 1960
Specialized Field: Dance; Vocal Music; Instrumental Music; Festivals; Grand Opera
Status: Nonprofit
Paid Staff: 14
Performs At: McAllen International Civic Center
Organization Type: Performing; Touring; Educational; Presenting

5303
STEPHEN F AUSTIN UNIVERSITY VISUAL & PERFORMING ARTS
Box 13022 SFA
Nacogdoches, TX 75962
Phone: 936-468-2801
Fax: 936-468-1168
e-mail: jgoodall@sfasu.edu
Web Site: www.finearts.sfasu.edu
Management:
Interim Dean/Programming Officer: John Goodall
Founded: 1923
Specialized Field: Arts; Music; Theatre
Status: Non-Profit, Professional
Budget: $60,000-150,000

5304
ADVENTURES WITH THE ARTS
602 Motley Drive
Overton, TX 75684-1021
Phone: 903-834-6234
Fax: 903-834-3574
e-mail: awamwc@aol.com
Budget: $35,000-60,000

5305
PITTSBURG/CAMP COUNTY ARTS COUNCIL
Box 72
Pittsburg, TX 75686
Phone: 903-856-6653
Budget: $35,000-60,000

5306
ROUND TOP FESTIVAL INSTITUTE
James Dick Foundation for the Performing Arts
248 Jaster Road
Round Top, TX 78954
Mailing Address: PO Box 89
Phone: 979-249-3129
Fax: 979-249-5078
e-mail: info@festivalhill.org
Web Site: www.festivalhill.org
Officers:
President: James Dick
Management:
Managing Director: Richard Royal
Program Director: Alain G Declert
Director Library/Museum: Lamar Lentz
Mission: Educational project.
Utilizes: Commissioned Composers;
Composers-in-Residence; Educators; Fine Artists; Five
Seasonal Concerts; Guest Companies; Guest
Composers; Guest Ensembles; Guest Instructors;
Guest Soloists; Scenic Designers; Students
Founded: 1971
Specialized Field: Classical Music; Poetry; Theatre;
Dance
Status: Non-Profit, Professional
Paid Staff: 14
Paid Artists: 44
Budget: $2 Million
Income Sources: Individual Gifts; Foundations; Grants;
Box Office; Gift Shop
Performs At: Festival Concert Hall
Affiliations: Chamber Music of America, League of
American Orchestra, American String Teachers
Association
Type of Stage: Proscenium
Stage Dimensions: 70 x 50
Seating Capacity: 1,100
Rental Contact: Program Director Alain G Declert

5307
ANGELO STATE UNIVERSITY
2601 W Avenue N
San Angelo, TX 76909
Phone: 325-942-2062
Fax: 915-942-2354
e-mail: program@angelo.edu
Web Site: www.angelo.edu/org/ucpc/
Management:
Assistant Director Programming: Rick E Greig
Assistant Program Director: Rick E Greig
Mission: The Arts Committee of the University Center
Program Council presents performing and visual arts to
the ASU and San Angelo communities.
Budget: $20,000-35,000

5308
CACTUS JAZZ & BLUES FESTIVAL
Cactus Hotel
PO Box 2477
San Angelo, TX 76902
Phone: 325-653-6793
Fax: 325-658-6036
e-mail: sacac@wcc.net
Web Site: www.sanangeloarts.com
Management:
President: Michael Ryan
VP: Hal Noelke

5309
ALAMO CITY PERFORMING ARTS ASSOCIATION
12915 Jones Maltsberger
Suite 200
San Antonio, TX 78247
Phone: 210-495-2787
Fax: 210-495-0872
e-mail: saspa@aol.com
Web Site: www.saspa.org
Management:
President: Sherrie Aoki
Executive Director: Nancy Grossenbacher
Artistic Director: Scott Conway
Mission: To offer the best in music, both national and
international, as well as theatre, dance and music to
San Antonio year-round.
Utilizes: Actors; Choreographers; Dance Companies;
Educators; Guest Accompanists; Guest Artists; Guest
Designers; Guest Ensembles; Guest Lecturers; Guest
Writers; Local Artists; Original Music Scores; Sign
Language Translators; Singers; Soloists
Founded: 1991
Specialized Field: Series & Festivals; Dance; Vocal
Music; Instrumental Music; Theatre; Festivals
Status: Non-Profit, Professional
Paid Staff: 10
Budget: $50,000
Income Sources: TCA; National Endowment for the
Arts; City of San Antonio; Private Donations
Performs At: Theaters
Annual Attendance: 10,000
Organization Type: Sponsoring
Resident Groups: Alamo City Dance Company

5310
ARTS SAN ANTONIO
222 E Houston
Suite 400
San Antonio, TX 78205
Phone: 210-226-2891
Fax: 210-226-1981
e-mail: frank@artssanantonio.com
Web Site: www.artssanantonio.com
Officers:
Chairman: Tony Novoa
President: Frank Villani
Management:
President: Frank J Villani
Mission: To offer theatre, music, ethnic dance, opera,
ballet and family performances; to provide outreach
programs.
Utilizes: Sign Language Translators; Singers; Theatre
Companies; Visual Arts
Founded: 1992
Specialized Field: Series & Festivals; Arts Presenter;
Ballet; Opera; Concerts
Status: Non-Profit, Professional
Paid Staff: 4
Paid Artists: 50
Budget: One million
Income Sources: Ticket sales - concession sales - in
school workshops and grants
Performs At: Multiple
Affiliations: SWPAP; ISPA; Association of Performing
Arts Presenters
Annual Attendance: 40,000
Seating Capacity: 400 - 5,000

5311
CARVER CULTURAL CENTER
226 N Hackberry
San Antonio, TX 78202
Phone: 210-207-7211
Fax: 210-207-4412
e-mail: wlewis@thecarver.org
Web Site: www.thecarver.org
Officers:
Chairperson: Prenza Woods
Management:
Chairman: Robert L Jemerson
Vice Chairman: C David Kinder
President Emeritus: Betty Green
Executive Director: William Lewis
Utilizes: Actors; Artists-in-Residence; Collaborating
Artists; Collaborations; Commissioned Composers;
Commissioned Music; Dance Companies; Dancers;
Fine Artists; Five Seasonal Concerts; Guest
Accompanists; Guest Choreographers; Guest
Ensembles; Guest Musical Directors; High School
Drama; Instructors; Local Artists; Lyricists; Multimedia;
Original Music Scores; Poets; Resident Artists;
Selected Students; Special Technical Talent; Theatre
Companies; Touring Companies
Specialized Field: African American Visual and
Performing Arts
Paid Staff: 20
Volunteer Staff: 50
Paid Artists: 15
Budget: $400,000-1,000,000
Annual Attendance: 50,000
Facility Category: Theatre and Arts School
Type of Stage: Proscenium
Seating Capacity: 640
Year Built: 1929
Year Remodeled: 2000
Rental Contact: 210-207-7215 Leticia Velazquez

5312
JAZZ'SALIVE
600 Hemistair Plaza Way
Building 247
San Antonio, TX 78212
Phone: 210-212-8423
Fax: 210-212-4376
e-mail: tkeck@saparksfoundation.org
Web Site: www.saparksfoundation.org
Officers:
President: Lila Cockrell
Management:
Executive VP: Teresa Keck
Founded: 1984

5313
TUESDAY MUSICAL CLUB ARTIST SERIES
5410 Pawtucket Drive
San Antonio, TX 78230
Phone: 210-366-2464
Fax: 210-342-7748
Officers:
Booking Chairman: Mrs. Harold Cockburn
Utilizes: Fine Artists; Guest Directors; Multimedia;
Original Music Scores; Sign Language Translators;
Singers
Budget: $20,000-35,000
Income Sources: Tickets
Annual Attendance: 1,000
Facility Category: Chruch

5314
SOUTHWEST TEXAS STATE UNIVERSITY ARTS SERIES
Dance Department
San Marcos, TX 78666

Phone: 512-245-2194
Fax: 512-245-8181
e-mail: jwli@swt.edu
Officers:
   Artist Series Committee Chair: LeAnne
   Smith-Stedman
   Assistan Chair: Cary Michaels
Budget: $60,000-150,000

5315
TEXAS LUTHERAN UNIVERSITY
CULTURAL ARTS EVENTS

1000 W Court
Seguin, TX 78155
Phone: 830-372-8180
Fax: 830-372-8096
Toll-free: 800-771-8521
Web Site: www.tlu.edu
Management:
   President: John Moline
   Provost: John Masterson
   Jackson Auditorium Director: Susan Rinn
Specialized Field: Education
Status: Non-Profit, Professional
Budget: $20,000-35,000

5316
AUSTIN COLLEGE COMMUNITY SERIES

900 N Grand
Suite 61602
Sherman, TX 75090-4440
Phone: 903-813-2251
Fax: 903-813-2273
e-mail: jhicks@austinc.edu
Management:
   Manager: Joe Hicks
Utilizes: Actors; Fine Artists; Guest Directors; Guest
Instructors; Guest Musical Directors; Guest Musicians;
Multimedia; Original Music Scores; Singers; Special
Technical Talent
Founded: 1966
Paid Staff: 2
Volunteer Staff: 12
Budget: $35,000-60,000
Performs At: Wynne Chapel
Affiliations: AAAP
Annual Attendance: 7,000

5317
CROSS TIMBERS FINE ARTS COUNCIL

204 River North Boulevard
PO Box 1172
Stephenville, TX 76401
Phone: 254-965-6190
Fax: 254-965-6186
e-mail: ctfac@our-town.com
Web Site: www.crosstimbersarts.org
Officers:
   Executive Director: Debbie Reynolds
Founded: 1980
Specialized Field: Cultural Arts
Status: Non-Profit, Non-Professional
Paid Staff: 2
Budget: $60,000-150,000
Performs At: Clyde H. Wells Fine Arts Center

5318
TARLETON STATE UNIVERSITY
STUDENT PROGRAMMING

Tarleton Station
Box T-0670
Stephenville, TX 76402

Phone: 254-968-9490
Fax: 254-968-9492
e-mail: stuact@tarleton.edu
Web Site: www.tarleton.edu
Management:
   President: Merideth Lincoln
   Executive Director: Donna Strohmeyer
Specialized Field: Programming Opportunities
Status: Non-Profit, Non-Professional
Paid Staff: 3

5319
TEXARKANA REGIONAL ARTS &
HUMANITIES COUNCIL

221 Main Street
PO Box 1711
Texarkana, TX 75504
Phone: 903-792-8681
Fax: 903-793-8510
e-mail: artsinfo@trahc.org
Web Site: www.trahc.org
Management:
   Executive Director: Brian W Goesel
   Operations Director: Randal Conry
   Administrative Director: Mary Starrett
Mission: Mission is to grow people and community
through the arts.
Founded: 1978
Opened: 1924
Specialized Field: Series & Festivals; Instrumental
Music; Vocal Music; Theatre; Youth; Dance; Ethnic
Performances
Status: Non-Profit, Professional
Paid Staff: 17
Budget: $1,602,244
Performs At: Perot Theatre
Affiliations: LHAT; APAP; SWPAP
Annual Attendance: 40,000
Type of Stage: Proscenium
Stage Dimensions: 69x35
Seating Capacity: 1,606
Year Built: 1924
Year Remodeled: 1980
Cost: $2.4 Million (1980)
Rental Contact: Randal Conry

5320
TOMBALL REGIONAL ARTS COUNCIL

PO Box 1321
Tomball, TX 77377-1321
Phone: 713-351-2787
Officers:
   President: Kathi Truex
Management:
   Executive Director: Harriet Fether

5321
TYLER COMMUNITY CONCERT
ASSOCIATION

1008 W 4th St
Tyler, TX 75701
Mailing Address: PO Box 131673
Phone: 903-592-6266
Web Site: www.tcca.biz
Officers:
   President: Gini Rainey
Founded: 1933
Specialized Field: Music; Dance; Instrumental Music;
Vocal Music; Performing Arts
Budget: $35,000-60,000

5322
UNIVERSITY OF TEXAS AT TYLER

3900 University Boulevard
Department Of Music
Tyler, TX 75799
Phone: 903-566-7450
Fax: 903-566-7062
e-mail: info@mail.uttyl.edu
Web Site: www.uttyler.edu/music
Management:
   Senior Lecturer In Music: Vicki J Conway
   Music Program Coordinator: Jeffrey D Emge
   Administrative Assistant: Gail Andrews
Specialized Field: Series and Festivals; Theatre;
Dance; Ethnic Performances
Status: For-Profit, Professional
Paid Staff: 7
Budget: $35,000-60,000
Performs At: Fine & Performing Arts Center

5323
UVALDE ARTS COUNCIL

104 W North Street
Uvalde, TX 78801
Phone: 830-278-4184
Fax: 830-278-1658
e-mail: Esther@peppersnet.com
Officers:
   President: Carol Kirlcham
   VP: Michael Box
   Treasurer: Esther Trevino
Management:
   Managing Director: Esther Trevino
Utilizes: Actors; Collaborating Artists; Collaborations;
Dance Companies; Dancers; Educators; Guest
Accompanists; Guest Designers; Guest Lecturers;
Guest Musical Directors; Guest Teachers; Guild
Activities; Instructors; Local Artists; Multimedia; Music;
Resident Professionals; Sign Language Translators;
Soloists; Student Interns; Special Technical Talent;
Theatre Companies
Founded: 1981
Paid Staff: 3
Volunteer Staff: 15
Budget: $20,000 - $30,000
Income Sources: memberships, ticket sales
Performs At: Grand Opera House
Annual Attendance: 14,000
Facility Category: Performing Arts & Presenter
Seating Capacity: 370
Year Built: 1891
Year Remodeled: 1981
Cost: 650,000

5324
CULTURAL COUNCIL OF VICTORIA

PO Box 1758
Victoria, TX 77902-1758
Phone: 361-572-2787
Fax: 361-572-6739
e-mail: leee@icsi.net
Web Site: www.ccvtx.org
Management:
   President: Don Truman
   Executive Director: Leolive Rogge
Utilizes: Artists-in-Residence; Collaborations;
Educators; Original Music Scores; Soloists; Theatre
Companies; Touring Companies
Founded: 1981
Specialized Field: Series & Festivals: Council
Status: Non-Profit, Professional
Paid Staff: 2
Volunteer Staff: 200

Budget: $10,000
Facility Category: Victoria College Auditorium

5325
VICTORIA FINE ARTS ASSOCIATION
700 N. Main St
Victoria, TX 77901
Phone: 361-572-2787
Management:
Artists Selection Chairman: Joe Hewell
Artists Selection: Ruth Williams
Founded: 1946
Specialized Field: Series Festival; Youth; Jazz
Status: Non-Profit, Professional
Budget: $35,000-60,000

5326
BAYLOR UNIVERSITY DISTINGUISHED ARTIST SERIES
Baylor University
School of Music
Waco, TX 76798
Phone: 254-710-2112
Fax: 254-710-1191
Toll-free: 800-229-5678
e-mail: john_wilson@baylor.edu
Web Site: www.baylor.edu
Management:
Distinguished Artist Series Manager: Kathy Johnson
Budget: $20,000-35,000
Performs At: Jones Concert Hall; Roxy Grove Hall

5327
WHARTON COUNTY JUNIOR COLLEGE THE CENTER FOR THE ARTS SERIES
911 Boling Highway
Wharton, TX 77488
Phone: 979-532-4560
Fax: 979-532-6587
Toll-free: 800-561-9252
e-mail: marjoriek@wcjc.edu
Web Site: www.wcjc.cc.tx.us
Officers:
President: Betty McCrohan
Communications Chair: Dr Pam Speights
Founded: 1946
Specialized Field: Series & Festivals; Art; Drama; Music
Status: For-Profit, Non-Professional
Paid Staff: 5
Budget: $10,000
Performs At: Horton Foote Theatre

5328
MIDWESTERN STATE UNIVERSITY: ARTIST LECTURE SERIES
3410 Taft Boulevard
CSC Room 104
Wichita Falls, TX 76308
Phone: 940-397-4291
Fax: 940-397-4938
e-mail: jane.leishner@mwsu.edu
Management:
President: Jessy Rogers
Founded: 1922
Specialized Field: University; Musical Events
Status: Non-Profit, Professional
Paid Staff: 300
Budget: $10,000-20,000

Utah

5329
SOUTHERN UTAH UNIVERSITY SUMMER EVENING CONCERTS
Hunter Conference Center
Southern Utah University
Cedar City, UT 84720
Phone: 435-586-5483
Fax: 435-865-8087
e-mail: bingham@suu.edu
Web Site: www.suu.edu/ced/specialprojects/
Management:
Manager: Marla Bingham
Budget: $10,000-20,000
Performs At: Randall Jones Performing Arts Theatre

5330
UTAH SHAKESPEAREAN FESTIVAL
351 W Center Street
Cedar City, UT 84720
Phone: 435-586-7880
Fax: 435-865-8003
Toll-free: 800-752-9849
e-mail: ussboxoffice@suu.edu
Web Site: www.bard.org
Officers:
Development Director: Jyl Shuler
Marketing Director: Donna Law
Education Director: Michael Bahr
Publications Director: Bruce Lee
Management:
Founder: Fred Adams
Artistic Director: Jim Sullivan
Managing Director: R Scott Phillips
Associate Artistic Director: Cathleen Conlin
Marketing Director: Donna Law
Production Manager: Ran Inkel
Director Plays-in-Progress: George Judy
Education Director: Michael Don Bahr
Publications Director: Bruce Lee
Mission: To present six classic and Shakespearean works in repertory each summer.
Utilizes: Actors; Guest Conductors; Guest Designers; Guest Writers; Guild Activities; Performance Artists; Resident Professionals; Student Interns
Founded: 1961
Specialized Field: Series and Festivals; Instrumental Music; Vocal Music; Theatre; Dance
Status: Non-Profit, Professional
Paid Staff: 30
Volunteer Staff: 250
Paid Artists: 400
Budget: $5 Million
Income Sources: Box Office Sales; Contributed Income; Endowment Income; Merchandise Sales
Season: June - August
Performs At: Adams Memorial Stage; Randall L. Jones Theatre; University Stage
Affiliations: USA; SSD&C; Actors' Equity Association; LORT; TCG
Annual Attendance: 155,000
Facility Category: Outdoor/Indoor
Type of Stage: Thrust; Proscenium
Stage Dimensions: 50Wx30D; 22Hx42Wx25D; 18Hx44Wx39D
Seating Capacity: 887; 769; 981
Year Remodeled: 1989
Rental Contact: Production Manager Ray Inkel
Organization Type: Performing; Resident; Educational

5331
CACHE VALLEY CENTER FOR THE ARTS
43 S Main Street
Logan, UT 84321-4535
Phone: 435-753-6518
Fax: 435-753-1232
e-mail: wbloss@centerforthearts.us
Web Site: www.centerforthearts.us
Management:
Executive Director: Wally Bloss
Utilizes: Actors; Artists-in-Residence; Choreographers; Collaborations; Curators; Dance Companies; Dancers; Designers; Educators; Fine Artists; Five Seasonal Concerts; Grant Writers; Guest Accompanists; Guest Artists; Guest Choreographers; Guest Companies; Guest Composers; Guest Conductors; Guest Designers; Guest Directors; Guest Ensembles; Guest Instructors; Guest Lecturers; Guest Musical Directors; Guest Musicians; Guest Soloists; Guest Teachers; High School Drama; Instructors; Local Artists; Local Unknown Artists; Multimedia; Music; Original Music Scores; Performance Artists; Playwrights; Resident Artists; Resident Professionals; Selected Students; Sign Language Translators; Singers; Soloists; Student Interns; Special Technical Talent; Theatre Companies; Touring Companies; Volunteer Artists
Founded: 1989
Specialized Field: Northern Utah
Paid Staff: 10
Volunteer Staff: 50
Budget: $1,300,000
Income Sources: City and County; Foundations; Corporations and Individuals
Facility Category: Proscenium Theatre
Stage Dimensions: 36'x32'
Seating Capacity: 1,100
Year Built: 1923
Year Remodeled: 1993
Rental Contact: Mary Shope
Resident Groups: Utah Festival Opera, Alliance for the Varied Arts, Paint Utah

5332
UTAH STATE UNIVERSITY PERFORMING ARTS SERIES
Taggart Student Center, UMC-01
Logan, UT 84322-0105
Phone: 435-797-1732
Fax: 435-797-2571
Management:
Student Activities Director: Randy Jensen
Budget: $150,000-400,000
Performs At: Chase Fine Arts Center

5333
WASSERMANN PIANO FESTIVAL
Utah State University, Music Department
4015 Old Main Hill
Logan, UT 84322-4015
Phone: 435-797-3257
Fax: 435-797-1862
e-mail: musicdep@cc.usu.edu
Web Site: www.usu.edu/music
Management:
President: Bruce Saperston
Director for Festivals: R Dennis Hirst
Founded: 1965
Specialized Field: Music and Music Therapy
Status: Non-Profit, Professional
Paid Staff: 40
Paid Artists: 15

5334
MORMON MIRACLE PAGEANT
PO Box 155
Manti, UT 84642
Phone: 435-835-3000
Web Site: www.mormonmiracle.org/
Management:
Pageant Director: Laren Swensen
Mission: Portraying the religious history of the
Latter-Day Saints and relating it to national events.
Utilizes: Guest Companies
Founded: 1967
Specialized Field: Theater
Status: Non-Professional; Nonprofit
Performs At: Manti Temple Grounds Amphitheatre
Organization Type: Performing; Resident

5335
CANYONLANDS ARTS COUNCIL
59 S Main Street
#236
Moab, UT 84532
Phone: 435-259-2742
Fax: 435-259-2418
Management:
Director: Theresa King
Budget: $10,000-20,000

5336
MOAB MUSIC FESTIVAL
58 East 300 South
Moab, UT 84532
Phone: 435-259-7003
Fax: 432-259-7044
e-mail: info@moabmusicfest.org
Web Site: www.moabmusicfest.org
Officers:
President: Hank Rutter
Management:
Music Director: Michael Barrett
Artistic Director: Leslie Tomkins
Administrative Director: Theresa King
Mission: Produce music festival and provide education
outreach program to community schools.
Founded: 1991
Specialized Field: Classical Chamber Music
Status: Non-Profit, Professional
Paid Staff: 8
Volunteer Staff: 1

5337
WEBER STATE UNIVERSITY CULTURAL AFFAIRS
1909 University Circle
Ogden, UT 84408-1904
Phone: 801-626-6570
Fax: 801-626-7422
e-mail: dstern@weber.eduu
Web Site: www.weber.edu
Management:
Office Cultural Affairs Director: Diane Stern
Budget: $60,000-150,000
Seating Capacity: 1800

5338
AUTUMN CLASSIC MUSIC FESTIVAL
PO Box 354
Park City, UT 84060
Phone: 435-649-5309
e-mail: lharlow@pcmusicfestival.com
Web Site: www.cmcconcerts.org
Officers:
President: Russell Harlow

Director Development: Leslie Blackburn Harlow
Founded: 1984
Specialized Field: Series & Festivals: Chamber Music
Status: Non-Profit, Professional
Paid Staff: 1
Paid Artists: 15

5339
CONTEMPORARY MUSIC CONSORTIUM
PO Box 354
Park City, UT 84060
Phone: 435-649-5309
e-mail: lharlow@pcmusicfestival.com
Web Site: www.cmcconcerts.org
Officers:
President: Russell Harlow
Director Development: Leslie Blackburn Harlow
Founded: 1984
Specialized Field: Series & Festivals: Chamber Music
Status: Non-Profit, Professional
Paid Staff: 1
Paid Artists: 15

5340
PARK CITY & SALT LAKE MUSIC FESTIVAL
PO Box 354
Park City, UT 84060
Phone: 435-649-5309
e-mail: lharlow@pcmusicfestival.com
Web Site: www.pcmusicfestival.com
Officers:
President: Russell Harlow
Director Development: Leslie Blackburn Harlow
Founded: 1984
Specialized Field: Series & Festivals: Chamber Music
Status: Non-Profit, Professional
Paid Staff: 1
Paid Artists: 15

5341
PARK CITY FILM MUSIC FESTIVAL
PO Box 354
Park City, UT 84060
Phone: 435-649-5309
e-mail: lharlow@pcmusicfestival.com
Web Site: www.cmcconcerts.org
Officers:
President: Russell Harlow
Director Development: Leslie Blackburn Harlow
Founded: 1984
Specialized Field: Series & Festivals: Chamber Music
Status: Non-Profit, Professional
Paid Staff: 1
Paid Artists: 15

5342
PARK CITY JAZZ FESTIVAL
PO Box 680720
Park City, UT 84068-0720
Phone: 435-940-1362
Fax: 435-940-1464
Toll-free: 800-453-1360
e-mail: info@parkcityjazz.com
Web Site: www.parkcityjazz.com
Officers:
Founder: Lew Fine
Founder: Arlene Fine
Interim Chairman: Martin Marmor
Management:
Chairman: Hans Suegi
Executive Director: Tom Horrocks
Assistant To Director: Mike Andrews

Mission: Is committed to promoting jazz music through
an annual showcase of national, regional, and local jazz
musicians.
Founded: 1998
Specialized Field: Series & Festivals: Jazz Festivals
Status: Non-Profit, Professional
Paid Staff: 2
Volunteer Staff: 186
Paid Artists: 11
Annual Attendance: 15,000
Seating Capacity: 5000

5343
BRIGHAM YOUNG UNIVERSITY PERFORMING ARTS SERIES
F-315 Harris Fine Arts Center
Provo, UT 84602
Phone: 801-378-5203
Fax: 801-378-8008
Officers:
Director: Jon Hollsman
Management:
Director: Jon Hollsman
Mission: A varied production and concert season in
support of academic programs in music, dance and
theatre.
Utilizes: Guest Artists; Guest Companies; Singers
Founded: 1875
Specialized Field: Dance; Vocal Music; Instrumental
Music; Theatre; Grand Opera
Status: Professional; Semi-Professional; Nonprofit
Paid Staff: 11
Budget: $60,000-150,000
Income Sources: Association of Performing Arts
Presenters; Western Alliance of Arts Administrators
Performs At: Harris Fine Arts Center; Brigham Young
University
Facility Category: Concert hall
Type of Stage: Proscenium w/hydralic pit
Stage Dimensions: 60 x 45
Seating Capacity: 1960
Year Built: 1963
Organization Type: Performing; Touring; Educational;
Sponsoring

5344
DIXIE COLLEGE CELEBRITY CONCERT SERIES
225 S 700 E
Saint George, UT 84770
Phone: 435-652-7994
Fax: 435-656-4080
e-mail: gbunker@dixie.edu
Web Site: www.dixie.edu/conserts
Officers:
President: Bill Ostler
Management:
Director: Gail Bunker
Mission: Presents eleven to twelve professional
concerts on two consecutive nights each from October
through May 2008. Concerts are held in the 1200-seat
Cox Performing Arts Center and represent the finest
professional artists and companies available
representing various genres: opera, symphonic, dance,
choral, brass, wind and string ensembles, jazz and
string, vocal and piano soloists.
Utilizes: Artists-in-Residence; Collaborations; Dance
Companies; Dancers; Fine Artists; New Productions;
Original Music Scores; Playwrights; Sign Language
Translators; Singers; Special Technical Talent; Theatre
Companies
Founded: 1958

Specialized Field: Series & Festivals: Multi-Discipline Performance Arts
Status: Non-Profit, Non-Professional
Paid Staff: 1
Volunteer Staff: 12
Paid Artists: 12
Budget: $150,000-200,000
Income Sources: Season Memberships; Ticket Sales; Grants; Donations; Endowment Income
Performs At: Avenna Center Cox Auditorium
Annual Attendance: 14,200
Facility Category: Theatre
Type of Stage: Proscenium
Seating Capacity: 1,200
Year Built: 1980

5345
DELTA CENTER
301 W South Temple
Salt Lake City, UT 84101
Phone: 801-325-2000
Fax: 801-325-2516
Web Site: www.deltacenter.com
Management:
General Manager: Scott Williams
VP Marketing: Jay Francis
VP Event Services: Brent Allenbach
Founded: 1991
Specialized Field: Home of the Utah Jazz (NBA) and the Utah Starzz (WNBA).
Seating Capacity: 19,911
Year Built: 1991

5346
EASTERN ARTS INTERNATIONAL DANCE THEATER
PO Box 526362
Salt Lake City, UT 84152
Phone: 801-485-5824
e-mail: kstjohn@burgoyne.com
Web Site: www.easternartists.com
Officers:
Dance Director: Katherine St John
Music Director: Lloyd Miller
Management:
President: Katherine John
Mission: To promote time-honored traditions by offering concerts, lectures, and workshops of cultures from Asia and Eastern Europe.
Founded: 1960
Specialized Field: Series & Festivals: International Music and Dance
Status: Non-Profit, Professional
Paid Staff: 10
Income Sources: Western Alliance of Arts Administrators; Society for Ethno-Musicology; Middle East Studies Association; Society for Dance Ethnology
Organization Type: Performing; Educational; Sponsoring

5347
GINA BACHAUER INTERNATIONAL PIANO COMPETITION & FESTIVAL
138 W Broadway
Suite 220
Salt Lake City, UT 84101
Phone: 801-297-4250
Fax: 801-521-9202
e-mail: gina@bachauer.com
Web Site: www.bachauer.com
Management:
President of the Board: Brad Beagles
Artistic Director: Paul Pollei

Manager: Kimi Kawashima
Director: Paul C Pollei
Founded: 1977
Specialized Field: Series and Festivals; Instrumental Music; Youth
Status: Non-Profit, Professional
Paid Staff: 3
Paid Artists: 5

5348
TEMPLE SQUARE CONCERT SERIES
LDS Church Office Building, 20th Floor
50 E North Temple
Salt Lake City, UT 84150
Phone: 801-240-3323
Fax: 801-240-1994
Management:
Director: Iain B McKay
Performs At: Assembly Hall; Tabernacle at Temple Square
Seating Capacity: 1200; 5500

5349
WESTMINSTER COLLEGE
1840 S 1300 E
Salt Lake City, UT 84105
Phone: 801-832-2435
Fax: 801-484-5579
Toll-free: 800-748-4753
e-mail: wccconcerts@rider.edu
Web Site: www.wcslc.edu
Management:
President: Michael Bassis
Artistic Director: Karlyn Bard
Founded: 1874
Specialized Field: Master Programming in Community and Education
Status: Non-Profit, Professional
Paid Staff: 42
Budget: $10,000
Performs At: Jewett Center for the Performing Arts
Seating Capacity: 300

5350
WORLD ARTS/NOON CONCERTS SERIES
PO Box 526362
Salt Lake City, UT 84152
Phone: 801-485-5824
Management:
Project Coordinator: Lloyd Miller
Founded: 1990
Specialized Field: Series & Festivals; Instrumental Music; Vocal Music; Youth; Dance; Ethnic Performances
Status: Non-Profit, Professional
Paid Staff: 6
Budget: $10,000

5351
AMERICAN WEST HERITAGE FESTIVAL
4025 S Highway 89-91
Wellsville, UT 84339
Phone: 435-245-6050
Fax: 435-245-6052
Toll-free: 800-225-3378
e-mail: info@awhc.org
Web Site: www.awhc.org
Management:
Executive Director: Matt Dahl
Artistic Director: Lorraine Bowen
Mission: Educate, entertain, and enlighten guests about life from 1820-1920.
Founded: 1972

Specialized Field: Series & Festivals: Ethnic Performances
Status: Non-Profit, Professional
Paid Staff: 17
Volunteer Staff: 100
Paid Artists: 55
Non-paid Artists: 15

Vermont

5352
BRATTLEBORO MUSIC CENTER
38 Walnut Street
Brattleboro, VT 05301
Phone: 802-257-4523
e-mail: info@bmcvt.org
Web Site: www.bmcvt.org
Officers:
President: Doug Coz
Management:
Managing Director: Richard Riley
Founded: 1952
Specialized Field: Series and Festivals; Instrumental Music; Vocal Music
Status: Non-Profit, Professional
Paid Staff: 5
Paid Artists: 30

5353
BURLINGTON DISCOVER JAZZ FESTIVAL
156 College Street
Suite 202
Burlington, VT 05401
Phone: 802-863-7992
Fax: 802-864-3927
e-mail: info@discoverjazz.com
Web Site: www.discoverjazz.com
Officers:
Director, Flynn Center: Andrea Rogers
Management:
Managing Director: Brian Mital
Chief Programming Officer: Arnie Malina
Associate Director: Geeda Searfoorce
Mission: Offering the widest possible range of jazz and music educational programs; ticketed and free events.
Utilizes: Community Members; Community Talent; Composers; Educators; Guest Directors; Guest Musical Directors; Instructors; Local Artists & Directors; Lyricists; Multimedia; Music; Scenic Designers; Sign Language Translators
Founded: 1984
Specialized Field: Jazz
Status: Non-Profit, Professional
Paid Staff: 2
Volunteer Staff: 350
Budget: $600,000
Income Sources: Burlington City Arts; Flynn Center
Performs At: Multi-disciplinary
Annual Attendance: 45,000
Facility Category: City-wide (Burlington)
Organization Type: Performing; Educational; Sponsoring

5354
UNIVERSITY OF VERMONT: GEORGE BISHOP LANE SERIES
460 S Prospect Street
Burlington, VT 05401-2501

Phone: 802-656-4455
Fax: 802-656-4010
e-mail: lane.series@uvm.edu
Web Site: www.uvm.edu/laneseries
Officers:
President: Gail Haefner
Management:
Director: Jane Ambrose
Utilizes: Artists-in-Residence; Collaborations;
Commissioned Music; Composers-in-Residence;
Dancers; Educators; Fine Artists; Guest
Choreographers; Guest Musical Directors; Guest
Musicians; Lyricists; Multimedia; Original Music Scores;
Sign Language Translators; Singers; Soloists
Founded: 1954
Specialized Field: Presenter
Status: Non-Profit, Professional
Paid Staff: 3
Volunteer Staff: 20
Budget: $500,000
Income Sources: Endowment; Ticket Sales;
Fundraising
Performs At: Flynn Theatre

5355
VERMONT MOZART FESTIVAL
3 Main Street
Suite 217
Burlington, VT 05401
Phone: 802-862-7352
Fax: 802-862-2201
e-mail: info@vtmozart.com
Web Site: www.vtmozart.org
Management:
Executive Director: Timothy Riddle
Operations Assistant: Christina Brooker
PR & Development Coordinator: Rachel Mullis
Mission: Enriching people's lives through beautiful
music in special Vermont places.
Utilizes: Singers
Founded: 1973
Specialized Field: Northwestern Vermont
Status: Non-Profit, Professional
Paid Staff: 7
Volunteer Staff: 30
Paid Artists: 80
Income Sources: Ticket Sales, Sponsorship,
Membership
Organization Type: Performing

5356
CASTLETON STATE COLLEGE PERFORMING ARTS SERIES
Castleton State College
Castleton, VT 05735
Phone: 802-468-5611
Fax: 802-468-1440
e-mail: mariko.hancock@castleton.edu
Web Site: www.csc.vsc.edu
Management:
President: David Walk
Executive Director: James Fuller
Fine Arts Center Coordinator: Mariko Hancock
Founded: 1787
Specialized Field: Series & Festivals; Instrumental
Music; Vocal Music; Theatre; Youth; Dance; Ethnic
Performances
Status: Non-Profit, Professional
Budget: $10,000-20,000

5357
GREEN MOUNTAIN FESTIVAL SERIES
PO Box 561
Chester, VT 05143

Phone: 802-875-4473
Fax: 802-875-3989
e-mail: info@greenmountainfestivalseries.com
Web Site: www.greenmountainfestivalseries.com
Management:
Manager: Ann C. DiBernardo
Mission: Organized to bring quality arts to local schools
and communities.
Budget: $20,000-35,000

5358
MUSIC IN A GREAT SPACE
Saint Michael'S College
Winooski Park
Colchester, VT 05439
Phone: 802-654-2508
Fax: 802-655-3680
Management:
Music Director: Dr. William Tortolano

5359
ST. MICHAEL'S COLLEGE CONCERTS
St Michael's College
Winooski Park
Colchester, VT 05439
Phone: 802-654-2508
Fax: 802-655-3680
Management:
Music Director: Dr. William Tortolano
Budget: $10,000-20,000

5360
DORSET THEATRE FESTIVAL
PO Box 510 Dorset
Dorset, VT 05251
Phone: 802-867-2223
Fax: 802-867-0144
e-mail: theatre@sover.net
Web Site: www.theatredirectories.com
Management:
President of the Board: Robert Bushnel
Executive Director: James Faszholz
Artistic Director: William John Aupperly
Founded: 1976
Specialized Field: Series & Festivals; Instrumental
Music; Vocal Music; Theatre; Youth; Ethnic
Performances
Status: Non-Profit, Professional
Paid Staff: 5
Paid Artists: 32
Income Sources: Theatre Communications Group
Season: June-September
Performs At: Dorset Playhouse
Type of Stage: Proscenium
Seating Capacity: 218
Organization Type: Performing

5361
WAREBROOK CONTEMPORARY MUSIC FESTIVAL
276 Hillandale Road
Irasburg, VT 05845
Phone: 802-754-6335
Fax: 802-754-2562
e-mail: wcmf@sover.net
Web Site: www.warebrook.org
Management:
President: Elizabeth Doncaster
Executive Director: Sarah Doncaster
Founded: 1991
Specialized Field: Chamber and Vocal Music
Status: Non-Profit, Professional
Paid Staff: 3
Paid Artists: 22

5362
FESTIVAL OF THE ARTS
Southern Vermont Arts Center/West Coast
PO Box 672
Manchester, VT 05254
Phone: 802-362-1405
Fax: 802-362-3274
Management:
Executive Director: Christopher Madkour
Founded: 1929
Specialized Field: All Medium Arts
Status: Non-Profit, Non-Professional
Paid Staff: 9
Performs At: Southern Vermont Arts Center
Organization Type: Sponsoring

5363
MANCHESTER MUSIC FESTIVAL
42 Dillingham Avenue
PO Box 33
Manchester, VT 05254
Phone: 802-362-1956
Fax: 802-362-0711
Toll-free: 800-639-5868
e-mail: mmfvermont@adelphia.net
Web Site: www.mmfvt.org
Management:
Artistic Director: Ariel Rudiskov
Managing Director: Robyn Madison
Mission: Educating young artists for a professional
career.
Utilizes: Commissioned Composers; Composers;
Guest Artists; Guest Musical Directors; Original Music
Scores; Sign Language Translators; Students
Founded: 1974
Specialized Field: Series & Festivals: Chamber Music
Concert
Status: Non-Profit, Professional
Paid Staff: 2
Paid Artists: 15
Budget: $500,000
Income Sources: Ticket sales; contributions
Performs At: The Louise Arkell Pavilion
Annual Attendance: 4,000
Organization Type: Performing; Touring; Educational

5364
MANCHESTER MUSIC FESTIVAL
42 Dillingham Avenue
PO Box 33
Manchester Center, VT 05255
Phone: 802-362-1956
Fax: 802-362-0711
Toll-free: 800-639-5868
e-mail: info@mmfvt.org
Web Site: mmfvt.org
Management:
Artistic Director: Ariel Rudiakov
Managing Director: Robyn Madison
Education Director: Heidi Johnson
Mission: To maintain a school for gifted instrumental
musicians; to offer festival concerts.
Founded: 1974
Specialized Field: Instrumental Music; Festivals
Status: Nonprofit
Paid Staff: 2
Volunteer Staff: 10
Paid Artists: 20
Performs At: Southern Vermont Arts Center
Seating Capacity: 460
Organization Type: Performing; Educational

5365
MIDDLEBURY COLLEGE CONCERT SERIES
Middlebury College
Middlebury, VT 05753
Phone: 802-443-5307
Fax: 802-443-2084
Management:
Director: Paul Nelson
Budget: $60,000-150,000
Performs At: Wright Theatre; Dance Performance Hall

5366
ONION RIVER ARTS COUNCIL: CELEBRATION SERIES
41 Elm Street
Montpelier, VT 05602
Phone: 802-229-9408
Fax: 802-229-9408
e-mail: orac@sover.net
Web Site: www.onionriverarts.org
Management:
Executive Director: Diane Manion
Status: Non-Profit
Budget: $35,000-60,000

5367
YELLOW BARN MUSIC FESTIVAL
63 Main Street
Putney, VT 05346
Phone: 802-387-6637
Fax: 802-387-6637
Toll-free: 800-639-3819
e-mail: info@yellowbarn.org
Web Site: www.yellowbarn.org
Officers:
President: Douglas Cox
Management:
Executive Director: Daniel Lichtenfeld
Artistic Director: Seth Knopp
Administrator: Maurey McNaughton
Mission: To offer professional training and a performance festival to talented young chamber artists.
Utilizes: Guest Artists
Founded: 1969
Specialized Field: Chamber music
Status: Nonprofit
Paid Staff: 50
Volunteer Staff: 50+
Paid Artists: 22
Budget: $350,000
Income Sources: Private donations; Grants
Performs At: Concert Hall and touring events
Organization Type: Performing; Educational

5368
CHANDLER CENTER FOR THE ARTS
71-73 Main Street
Randolph, VT 05060
Phone: 802-728-9878
Fax: 802-728-4612
e-mail: chandler@innevi.com
Web Site: www.randolphvt.com
Officers:
President: Janet Watton
Management:
Program Director: Rebecca B McMeekin
Mission: Providing opportunities to the community at large for artistic expression and educational pursuit by sponsoring and producing programs in the creative and performing arts in and for Chandler Music Hall.

Utilizes: Actors; Artists-in-Residence; Collaborations; Dance Companies; Educators; Guest Directors; Guild Activities; High School Drama; Instructors; Local Artists; Multimedia; Original Music Scores; Sign Language Translators; Soloists; Touring Companies
Founded: 1978
Paid Staff: 2
Volunteer Staff: 50
Budget: $200,000
Income Sources: Individual and corporate donations; Grants; and Ticket sales
Annual Attendance: 13,000
Facility Category: Music hall and art gallery
Type of Stage: Proscenium
Stage Dimensions: 31'W x 20'H x 21'D
Seating Capacity: 589
Year Built: 1907
Rental Contact: Becky McMeekin

5369
CHAFFEE ART CENTER
16 South Main Street
Rutland, VT 05701
Phone: 802-775-0356
e-mail: director@crossroadsarts.com
Web Site: www.crossroadsarts.com
Management:
Ex-Director: Jim Boughton
Program Directory: Whitnaey Lamy
Mission: To bring performing artists to the Rutland Region.
Founded: 1971
Specialized Field: Series & Festivals; Performances; Workshop; Educational Programme
Status: Non-Profit, Professional
Paid Staff: 3
Paid Artists: 30
Budget: $225,000
Annual Attendance: 5,000+

5370
KILLINGTON MUSIC FESTIVAL
39 E Center Street
Rutland, VT 05701
Mailing Address: PO Box 386, Rutland, VT. 05702
Phone: 802-773-4003
Fax: 802-773-1168
e-mail: kmfest@sover.net
Web Site: www.killingtonmusicfestival.org
Management:
Executive Director: Maria Fish
Mission: To present a series of summer chamber music concerts; To maintain a summer school to train aspiring musicians.
Utilizes: Guest Companies
Founded: 1982
Specialized Field: Series and Festivals; Classical Chamber Music; Residency Program; Concert Series
Status: Non-Profit, Professional
Paid Staff: 2
Paid Artists: 20
Organization Type: Performing; Educational

5371
STOWE PERFORMING ARTS
1250 Waterbury Road
Stowe, VT 05672
Phone: 802-253-7792
Fax: 802-253-7140
e-mail: spa@stowearts.com
Web Site: www.stowearts.com
Management:
Executive Director: Lynn Paparella

Mission: Stowe Performing Arts is a non-profit community organization with a volunteer Board of Directors dedicated to bringing high quality performances and opportunities for cultural enrichment through the Performing Arts to the community and surrounding areas.
Utilizes: Fine Artists; Guest Musicians; Instructors; Multimedia; Original Music Scores; Sign Language Translators; Singers
Founded: 1976
Specialized Field: Series and Festivals; Present Concerts in Classical; Country; Pops; Jazz; Chamber Music
Status: Non-Profit, Professional
Paid Staff: 1
Volunteer Staff: 15
Paid Artists: 10
Budget: $100,000
Income Sources: Donations and Ticket Sales
Performs At: Outdoor venue, Church, Ice Arena
Facility Category: Open Stage
Type of Stage: Wooden Platform
Stage Dimensions: 30'x40'
Seating Capacity: 2,200

5372
PENTANGLE COUNCIL ON THE ARTS AND THE WOODSTOCK TOWN HALL THEATRE
31 The Green
PO Box 172
Woodstock, VT 05091
Phone: 802-457-3981
Fax: 802-457-4972
e-mail: pentarts@sover.net
Web Site: www.pentanglearts.org
Management:
Executive Director: Sabrina Brown
Mission: To maintain an arts program of high quality for the enrichment of our community and schools.
Utilizes: Artists-in-Residence; Collaborating Artists; Collaborations; Dance Companies; Dancers; Educators; Filmmakers; Guest Instructors; Guild Activities; Local Artists; Multi Collaborations; Multimedia; New Productions; Original Music Scores; Sign Language Translators; Soloists; Special Technical Talent
Founded: 1974
Specialized Field: Series & Festivals; Instrumental Music; Vocal Music; Theatre; Youth; Dance; Ethnic Performances
Status: Non-Profit, Professional
Paid Staff: 3
Paid Artists: 25
Budget: $275,000
Income Sources: Annual Appeal; Membership; Endowment; Ticket Sales; Grants
Performs At: Town Hall Theatre; Little Theatre
Annual Attendance: 12,000
Facility Category: Theatre
Type of Stage: Proscenium
Seating Capacity: 400
Year Built: 1901
Year Remodeled: 1979
Rental Contact: Sabrina Brown

Virginia

5373
ALEXANDRIA RECITAL SERIES
5917 Berkshire Court
Alexandria, VA 22303-1632

Phone: 703-960-0616
Fax: 703-960-6691
e-mail: RecitalSeries@aol.com
Management:
Program Director: Willis Bennett
Budget: $10,000
Performs At: The Lyceum

5374
INTERNATIONAL CHILDREN'S FESTIVAL
Arts Council of Fairfax County
4022 Hummer Road
Annandale, VA 22003
Phone: 703-642-0862
Fax: 703-642-1773
e-mail: info@artsfairfax.org
Web Site: www.artsfairfax.org
Officers:
President/CEO: Toni Winters McMahon
Management:
President: Ann Rodriguez
Performing Arts Director: Scott Fridy
Utilizes: Selected Students; Sign Language Translators; Singers; Soloists
Founded: 1964
Specialized Field: Arts and artists
Status: Non-Profit, Professional
Paid Staff: 3
Income Sources: Arts Council of Fairfax County, Inc.
Performs At: Wolf Trap Farm Park for the Performing Arts
Annual Attendance: 30,000
Facility Category: Amphitheatre in a park
Seating Capacity: 4,000
Year Built: 1971
Organization Type: Performing; Resident; Sponsoring

5375
ARLINGTON CULTURAL AFFAIRS DIVISION
3700 S Lang Street
Arlington, VA 22206-3106
Phone: 703-228-6962
Fax: 703-228-1851
e-mail: arts@arlingtonza.us
Web Site: www.arlingtonarts.org
Management:
Performing Arts Director: Jon Palmer Claridge
Specialized Field: Series & Festivals; Instrumental Music; Vocal Music; Theatre; Youth; Dance; Ethnic Performances
Paid Staff: 40
Budget: $60,000-150,000

5376
ARLINGTON'S ARTS AL FRESCO & THE INNOVATORS
3700 S 4 Mile Run Drive
Arlington, VA 22206
Phone: 703-228-1850
Fax: 703-228-1851
e-mail: arts@arlingtonva.us
Web Site: www.arlingtonarts.org
Management:
Department Director: Toni Hubbard
Artistic Director: Jon Claridge
Founded: 1985
Specialized Field: Series and Festivals; Instrumental Music; Vocal Music; Theatre; Dance; Ethnic Performances
Status: Non-Profit, Professional
Paid Staff: 25
Paid Artists: 150

Budget: $60,000-150,000
Performs At: Thomas Jefferson Theatre; Ellipse Art Center

5377
VIRGINIA TECH UNION LIVELY ARTS SEASON
Virginia Tech
325 Squires Student Center (0138)
Blacksburg, VA 24061
Phone: 540-231-5661
Fax: 540-231-7028
e-mail: vtu@vtu.org
Web Site: www.vtu.org
Management:
President: Jason Shank
Executive Director: Erik Kneubuehl
Utilizes: Dance Companies; Special Technical Talent; Theatre Companies
Founded: 1969
Specialized Field: Series & Festivals; Vocal Music; Theatre; Dance; Ethnic Performances
Status: Non-Profit, Professional
Paid Staff: 1
Volunteer Staff: 20
Budget: $150,000-400,000
Income Sources: Ticket Sales; Student Activity Fees
Annual Attendance: 14,000
Facility Category: Auditorium
Type of Stage: Proscenium
Stage Dimensions: 58x34x32
Seating Capacity: 2,950
Year Built: 1935

5378
BRIDGEWATER COLLEGE LYCEUM SERIES
E College Street
Bridgewater, VA 22812
Phone: 540-828-5303
Fax: 540-828-5637
e-mail: jhopkins@bridgewater.edu
Web Site: www.bridgewater.edu
Management:
President: Phillip Stone
Executive Director: P Hopkins
Director: Jesse E Hopkins
Specialized Field: Series & Festivals; Instrumental Music; Vocal Music; Ethnic Performances
Status: Non-Profit, Professional
Budget: $20,000-35,000
Performs At: Cole Hall

5379
ASHLAWN-HIGHLAND SUMMER FESTIVAL
1941 James Monroe Parkway
Charlottesville, VA 22902
Phone: 804-293-4500
Fax: 804-293-0736
e-mail: summerfestival@avenue.gen.va.us
Web Site: www.avenue.org/summerfestival
Management:
General Director: Judith H Walker
Founded: 1978
Status: Non-Equity; Nonprofit
Paid Staff: 4
Volunteer Staff: 100
Paid Artists: 80
Non-paid Artists: 25
Season: June - August
Stage Dimensions: 24' x 16'
Seating Capacity: 450

5380
TUESDAY EVENING CONCERT SERIES
108 5th Street SE
Suite 208
Charlottesville, VA 22902
Phone: 434-244-9505
Fax: 434-244-9510
e-mail: kpellon@virginia.edu
Web Site: www.tecs.org
Management:
Executive Director: Karen Pellon
Mission: Chamber music series with artists from around the world.
Utilizes: Guest Musicians; Multimedia
Founded: 1948
Specialized Field: Music
Status: Professional; Nonprofit
Paid Staff: 2
Paid Artists: 30
Budget: $100000+
Income Sources: Tickets; Advertising; Grants; Donations
Performs At: Concert Hall
Annual Attendance: 5,000
Facility Category: Concert Hall
Seating Capacity: 850
Year Built: 1896
Year Remodeled: 1995
Organization Type: Sponsoring

5381
ALLEGHANY HIGHLANDS ARTS COUNCIL/PERFORMING ARTS
PO Box 261
Covington, VA 24426
Phone: 540-962-6220
Fax: 540-962-4911
e-mail: artsco@aol.com
Web Site: www.alleghanyhighlands.com/arts4all
Management:
President of the Board: Gary Pillow
Executive Director: Tammy S Scruggs
Founded: 1952
Specialized Field: Series & Festivals; Instrumental Music; Vocal Music; Theater; Youth; Dance; Ethnic Performances
Status: Non-Profit, Professional
Paid Staff: 2
Budget: $35,000-60,000
Performs At: Curfman Hall

5382
AVERETT UNIVERSITY CONCERT-LECTURE SERIES
420 W Main
Danville, VA 24541
Phone: 804-791-5621
Fax: 804-791-5819
e-mail: paul.bryant@averett.edu
Management:
Dean of Students: Paul A Bryant
Utilizes: Actors; Dance Companies; Dancers; Educators; Fine Artists; Guest Accompanists; Guest Directors; Guest Instructors; Guest Soloists; Local Artists; Original Music Scores; Playwrights; Sign Language Translators; Singers
Budget: $10,000-20,000

5383

DANVILLE AREA ASSOCIATION FOR THE ARTS & HUMANITIES

435 Main Street
PO Box 3581
Danville, VA 24543
Mailing Address: PO Box 3581, Danville, VA. 24543-3581
Phone: 434-792-6965
Fax: 434-792-1307
e-mail: aandh@gamewood.net
Web Site: www.danriverartalliance.com
Officers:
   President: John W Collins
Management:
   Executive Director: Arlyne McDowell
Utilizes: Actors; Dance Companies; Dancers; Guild Activities; Multimedia; Special Technical Talent; Theatre Companies; Touring Companies
Founded: 1981
Status: Non-Profit
Paid Staff: 1
Budget: $35,000-60,000
Income Sources: Box office; Grants; Private donations
Annual Attendance: 5,500
Type of Stage: Proscenium
Stage Dimensions: 40x27
Seating Capacity: 1,119
Year Built: 1955

5384

EMORY & HENRY COLLEGE CONCERT SERIES

PO Box 947
Emory, VA 24327
Phone: 540-944-6846
Fax: 540-944-6259
e-mail: atcoulth@ehc.edu
Web Site: www.ehc.edu/inweb
Management:
   Arts Coordinator: Anita Coulthard
Mission: To provide cultural events that support the curriculum of the college.
Specialized Field: College arts organ
Paid Staff: 1
Paid Artists: 20
Non-paid Artists: 5
Budget: $20,000-35,000
Income Sources: College budget and grants
Performs At: Chapel, auditorium
Annual Attendance: 5,000
Facility Category: College campus, chapel and auditorium
Type of Stage: Proscenium
Seating Capacity: Chapel 500; auditorium - 300

5385

COLLEGE OF VISUAL AND PERFORMING ARTS

George Mason University
4400 University Drive, MSN 4C1
Fairfax, VA 22030-4444
Phone: 703-993-8877
Fax: 703-993-8883
e-mail: skruppin@gmu.edu
Web Site: www.gmu.edu/cfa
Management:
   President: Allan Mertens
   Artistic Director: Richard Davis
   Dean: William Reeder
   Assistant Dean: William Reeder
Specialized Field: Series & Festivals; Instrumental Music; Vocal Music; Theatre; Youth; Dance; Arts

Status: Non-Profit, Professional
Budget: $400,000-1,000,000
Performs At: Harris Theatre
Facility Category: Performing Arts Hall
Type of Stage: Proscenium
Seating Capacity: 1,935

5386

GEORGE MASON UNIVERSITY PATRIOT CENTER

4400 University Drive
Fairfax, VA 22030
Phone: 703-993-3000
Fax: 703-993-3079
Web Site: www.patriotcenter.com
Management:
   General Manager: Barry Geisler
Founded: 1985
Specialized Field: Basketball
Status: For-Profit, Professional
Paid Staff: 300

5387

FREDERICKSBURG MUSIC FESTIVAL

PO Box 7816
Fredericksburg, VA 22404
Phone: 540-374-5040
Fax: 540-368-1098
e-mail: fredfest@infionline.net
Web Site: www.fredfest.org
Management:
   President: Xavier Richards
   Executive Director: Susan Mullane
   Founder And Artistic Director: Heidi Lehwalder
Mission: To foster excellence and diversity in the arts in Virginia and to bring world class arts events to the residents of the greater Fredericksburg area.
Founded: 1988
Specialized Field: Chamber Music; Pops; Big Band; Ethnic; Dance
Status: Nonprofit
Paid Staff: 3
Income Sources: Corporate & Individual Donations; Grants
Annual Attendance: 2,500+

5388

HAMPDEN-SYDNEY MUSIC FESTIVAL

Hampden-Sydney College
Box 25
Hampden-Sydney, VA 23943
Phone: 804-223-6304
Fax: 804-223-6399
Management:
   Executive Director: James Kidd

5389

HAMPTON ARTS COMMISSION

4205 Victoria Boulevard
Hampton, VA 23669
Phone: 757-722-2787
Fax: 757-727-1621
e-mail: americantheatre@hampton.gov
Web Site: www.theamericantheatre.com
Management:
   Director: Michael P Curry
Mission: Presenting and promoting the finest visual and performing arts.
Utilizes: Actors; Artists-in-Residence; Dance Companies; Fine Artists; Guest Accompanists; Guest Musical Directors; Guest Musicians; Original Music Scores; Special Technical Talent; Theatre Companies
Founded: 1987

Specialized Field: Series and Festivals; Performing Arts; Visual Arts; Theatre
Status: Non-Profit, Non-Professional
Paid Staff: 9
Income Sources: Association of Performing Arts Presenters
Performs At: American Theatre
Annual Attendance: 30,000
Facility Category: Theatre
Type of Stage: Procenium
Seating Capacity: 400
Year Built: 1908
Year Remodeled: 2000
Cost: $2.8 million
Organization Type: Performing; Educational; Sponsoring

5390

HAMPTON JAZZ FESTIVAL

1000 Coliseum Drive
PO Box 7309
Hampton, VA 23666
Phone: 757-838-5650
Fax: 757-838-2595
e-mail: jtsao@hampton.gov
Web Site: www.hamptonjazzfestival.com
Management:
   Executive Director: Joe Tsao
Founded: 1968
Specialized Field: Series and Festivals; Instrumental Music; Vocal Music; Theatre; Youth; Ethnic Performances; Multipurpose
Status: For-Profit, Professional
Paid Staff: 32

5391

JAMES MADISON UNIVERSITY ENCORE SERIES

College of Visual & Performaning Arts
Forbes Center for the Arts
Harrisonburg, VA 22807
Mailing Address: 147 Warsaw Avenue, MSC 5602
Phone: 540-568-6358
Fax: 540-568-2787
Toll-free: 877-201-7543
e-mail: weaverje@jmu.edu
Web Site: www.jmu.edu/jmuartssterpiece
Management:
   Executive Assistant: Jerry Weaver
Utilizes: Actors; Artists-in-Residence; Dance Companies; Dancers; Fine Artists; Grant Writers; Guest Accompanists; Guest Directors; Guest Musical Directors; Guest Musicians; Instructors; Lyricists; Multimedia; New Productions; Organization Contracts; Original Music Scores; Resident Artists; Sign Language Translators; Soloists; Special Technical Talent; Theatre Companies; Touring Companies; Visual Arts
Specialized Field: Series & Festivals; Instrumental Music; Vocal Music; Theatre; Youth; Dance; Ethnic Performances
Status: Non-Profit, Non-Professional
Paid Staff: 6
Budget: $60,000-150,000
Affiliations: Association of Performing Arts Performers
Facility Category: Auditorium
Type of Stage: Proscenium
Stage Dimensions: 34 x 33
Seating Capacity: 1300, 500, 450

5392

SHENANDOAH VALLEY BACH FESTIVAL

Eastern Mennonite University
1200 Park Road
Harrisonburg, VA 22802

Phone: 540-432-4367
Fax: 540-432-4622
e-mail: mary.adams@emu.edu
Web Site: www.emu.edu/bach
Management:
   President: Loren Swartzentruber
   Executive Director: Mary Kay Adams,
   mary.adams@emu.edu
   Artistic Director: Kenneth Nafziger
Mission: One week festival honoring the creative spirit of Johann Sebastian Bach with first rate performances for an ever widening audience.
Utilizes: Actors; Collaborating Artists; Commissioned Composers; Community Members; Community Talent; Composers; Contract Orchestras; Educators; Five Seasonal Concerts; Grant Writers; Guest Accompanists; Guest Directors; Guest Ensembles; Guest Musical Directors; Guest Musicians; Guest Soloists; Guest Speakers; High School Drama; Instructors; Local Artists & Directors; Multimedia; Organization Contracts; Original Music Scores; Paid Performers; Scenic Designers; Sign Language Translators; Singers; Soloists; Students; Visual Designers
Founded: 1993
Specialized Field: Series & Festivals, Instrumental Music, Vocal Music, Youth, Classical Music Festival, Chamber Music, Baroque Performance Workshop
Status: Non-Profit, Professional
Paid Staff: 3
Paid Artists: 50
Budget: $185,000
Income Sources: Grants, Private Donations, Business Advertising, Tickets
Performs At: University Auditorium, Church Sanctuary
Affiliations: ASOL
Annual Attendance: 4,000
Seating Capacity: 600/400

5393
TOWN OF HERNDON

PO Box 427
Herndon, VA 20172
Phone: 703-435-6800
Fax: 703-318-8652
e-mail: holly.popple@herndon-va.gov
Web Site: www.herndon-va.gov
Management:
   Executive Director: Arthur Anselelne
Mission: Functions as a talent buyer and events director.
Founded: 1975
Specialized Field: Series & Festivals; Theatre; Youth; Dance
Status: For-Profit, Professional
Paid Artists: 80
Performs At: Industrial Strength Theatre; Worldgate Theatre

5394
WASHINGTON & LEE UNIVERSITY LENFEST SERIES

Lenfest Center, 100 Glasgow Street
Washington & Lee University
Lexington, VA 24450
Phone: 540-463-8001
Fax: 540-463-8041
e-mail: mgorman@wlu.edu
Management:
   Managing Director: Michael Gorman
Mission: Home of Theatre/Music/Dance Departments. Presenter of a few touring attractions.

Utilizes: Actors; Dance Companies; Dancers; Designers; Guest Artists; Guest Choreographers; Guest Composers; Guest Conductors; Guest Designers; Guest Directors; Guest Musical Directors; Guest Musicians; Instructors; Multimedia; Poets; Resident Professionals; Soloists; Student Interns; Theatre Companies
Founded: 1991
Specialized Field: Theatre/Dance/Music
Budget: $35,000-60,000
Income Sources: Endowment/Ticket Sales
Performs At: Keller Theatre
Facility Category: Performing Arts Center
Type of Stage: Proscenium
Seating Capacity: 415
Year Built: 1991

5395
LYNCHBURG COMMUNITY CONCERT ASSOCIATION

PO Box 1332
Lynchburg, VA 24505
Phone: 804-845-3563
Fax: 804-845-3536
Management:
   Manager: Betty Sue Moehlenkamp
Budget: $35,000-60,000
Performs At: E.C. Glass High School Auditorium

5396
TOURING CONCERT OPERA COMPANY: MARTINSVILLE-HENRY COUNTY FESTIVAL OF OPERA

730 Craig Street
Martinsville, VA 24112
Phone: 540-632-5861
Fax: 518-851-6778
e-mail: tcoc@mhonline.com
Officers:
   President: Alberto Figols
   VP: Glenn Wilder
   Secretary/Treasurer: Anne de Figols
Management:
   Managing Director: Alberto Figols
   Managing Director: Alberto Figols
   Public Relations: Ruth Johnson
   Bookkeeper: Alberto Fijolo
Mission: To bring live opera performances to audiences, internationally making it accessible to all.
Utilizes: Actors; Artists-in-Residence; Choreographers; Collaborating Artists; Collaborations; Commissioned Composers; Commissioned Music; Dance Companies; Dancers; Designers; Fine Artists; Grant Writers; Guest Accompanists; Guest Artists; Guest Companies; Guest Composers; Guest Conductors; Guest Designers; Guest Directors; Guest Ensembles; Guest Lecturers; Guest Musical Directors; Guest Musicians; Guest Soloists; Guild Activities; Instructors; Local Artists; Multimedia; New Productions; Organization Contracts; Original Music Scores; Poets; Resident Professionals; Sign Language Translators; Singers; Soloists
Founded: 1977
Specialized Field: Dance; Vocal Music; Instrumental Music; Theater; Lyric Opera; Grand Opera
Annual Attendance: 5,000 - 10,000

5397
SWIFT CREEK ACADEMY OF THE PERFORMING ARTS

2808 Fox Chase Lane
Midlothian, VA 23112
Phone: 804-744-2801
Web Site: www.swiftcreekacademy.org

Management:
   Owner/Academy Director: Cassandra Lacey
Mission: Performance school
Specialized Field: Dance, Drama, Instrumental & Music classes for all ages; student performances
Paid Staff: 15
Budget: $10,000

5398
CHRISTOPHER NEWPORT UNIVERSITY

1 University Place
Newport News, VA 23606
Phone: 757-594-7475
Fax: 757-594-7389
Web Site: www.cnu.edu
Management:
   Administrative Assistant: Margaret Donovan
Mission: The Department of Theatre & Dance offers developing theater artists a comprehensive curriculum of rigorous training with a superb faculty of professional actors, directors, play wrights and designers. Within the dedicated atmosphere of a small liberal arts university, the theater majors enjoy a unique spirit of closeness and collaboration teamed with immediate opportunities to perform and/or to work backstage.
Founded: 1960
Specialized Field: Series & Festivals; Instrumental Music; Vocal Music; Theatre; Dance
Status: Non-Profit, Non-Professional
Paid Staff: 100
Paid Artists: 100
Budget: $20,000-35,000
Performs At: John W. Gaines Theatre

5399
NORFOLK FESTEVENTS

Norfolk Festevents
120 W Main Street
Norfolk, VA 23501
Phone: 757-441-2345
Fax: 757-441-5098
e-mail: festevents@festevents.org
Web Site: www.festeventsva.org
Founded: 1982

5400
TIDEWATER PERFORMING ARTS SOCIETY

PO Box 1140
Norfolk, VA 23501-1140
Phone: 757-627-2314
Fax: 757-622-2803
e-mail: tpas@tpas.org
Web Site: www.tpas.org
Management:
   Executive Director: Karen E Levy
Budget: $35,000-60,000
Performs At: Pavilion Theatre; Wells Theatre; Harrison Opera House

5401
VIRGINIA ARTS FESTIVAL

220 Boush Street
Norfolk, VA 23510
Mailing Address: PO Box 3595, Norfolk, VA 23514
Phone: 757-282-2800
Fax: 757-282-2787
Toll-free: 877-741-2787
e-mail: lori@virginiaartsfest.com
Web Site: www.virginiaartsfest.com
Management:
   Executive Director: Robert W Cross
   Director Operations: Renae Adrian
   Marketing Manager: Lori Gubala

Mission: Brings an imaginative and eclectic line-up of world-renowned performers, complemented by the region's own cultural stars, to the Virginia waterfront. Stages events in seven cities within a 60 mile radius. More than 80 performances in dance, theatre, classical, chamber, jazz and vocalmusic each season.
Founded: 1997
Specialized Field: Series & Festivals; Instrumental Music; Vocal Music; Theatre; Youth; Dance; Ethnic Performances
Status: Non-Profit, Professional
Paid Staff: 22
Volunteer Staff: 300
Paid Artists: 700

5402
BLUEMONT CONCERT SERIES
PO Box 521
Purcellville, VA 20134
Phone: 540-338-4640
Fax: 540-338-4847
e-mail: info@bluemont.org
Web Site: www.bluemont.org
Management:
    Artistic Director: Peter Dunning
Mission: To offer a wide range of quality arts programs to the community.
Utilizes: Singers
Founded: 1975
Specialized Field: Concert Presenter
Status: Non-Profit, Professional
Paid Staff: 6
Budget: $60,000-400,000
Performs At: Outdoor venues
Organization Type: Educational; Sponsoring

5403
RADFORD UNIVERSITY PERFORMING ARTS SERIES
Box 6980
Radford University
Radford, VA 24142
Phone: 540-831-5265
Fax: 540-831-6313
e-mail: jscartel@radford.edu
Officers:
    Dean College/Visual/Performing: Dr. Joe Scartelli
Management:
    President: Douglas Covington
    Technical Director: Doug Mead
Mission: Provide high end cultural artistic experiences for the campus and surrounding communities.
Utilizes: Actors; AEA Actors; Artists-in-Residence; Choreographers; Collaborating Artists; Collaborations; Curators; Dance Companies; Dancers; Designers; Educators; Filmmakers; Fine Artists; Guest Accompanists; Guest Artists; Guest Choreographers; Guest Companies; Guest Composers; Guest Conductors; Guest Designers; Guest Directors; Guest Ensembles; Guest Instructors; Guest Musical Directors; Guest Musicians; Guest Soloists; High School Drama; Instructors; Local Artists; Multi Collaborations; Multimedia; Paid Performers; Playwrights; Poets; Resident Professionals; Sign Language Translators; Soloists; Special Technical Talent; Theatre Companies; Touring Companies; Visual Arts
Founded: 1975
Specialized Field: Series and Festivals; Instrumental Music; Vocal Music; Theatre; Youth; Dance; Ethnic Performances
Status: Non-Profit,Professional
Paid Staff: 2
Volunteer Staff: 8
Non-paid Artists: 20

Budget: $60,000-150,000
Income Sources: Student activities fees; Ticket revenues
Annual Attendance: 10,000
Facility Category: Auditorium
Type of Stage: Proscenium
Stage Dimensions: 40 x 25
Seating Capacity: 1500
Year Built: 1960

5404
CENTERSTAGE
2310 Colt Neck Road
Reston, VA 20191
Phone: 703-476-4500
Fax: 703-476-8617
e-mail: Damian.Sinclair@fairfaxcounty.gov
Web Site: www.restoncommunitycenter.com
Management:
    Executive Director: Leila Gordon
Founded: 1979
Specialized Field: General Recreation and Cultural Agency
Status: Non-Profit, Professional
Paid Staff: 284
Budget: $200,000
Income Sources: Government agency
Affiliations: Assoc. of Performing Arts Presenters
Annual Attendance: 25,000 +
Facility Category: Cultural and recreational
Type of Stage: Proscenium
Stage Dimensions: 32W x 18H x 25D
Seating Capacity: 290
Year Built: 1979
Cost: $2 MM

5405
CITYCELEBRATIONS MUSICFEST
200 S 3rd Street
Richmond, VA 23219
Phone: 804-788-6466
Fax: 804-788-6477
e-mail: info@citycelebrations.org
Web Site: www.citycelebrations.org
Management:
    Executive Director: K Alferio
    Managing Director: Pamela Wiseman
Founded: 1988
Specialized Field: Series and Festivals; Instrumental Music; Vocal Music; Youth; Dance; Ethnic Performances; Festivals; Event
Status: Non-Profit, Professional
Paid Staff: 6
Paid Artists: 100

5406
MODLIN CENTER FOR THE ARTS
University Of Richmond
28 Westhampton Way
Richmond, VA 23173
Phone: 804-287-6632
Fax: 804-287-6681
Toll-free: 800-700-1662
e-mail: modlinarts@richmond.edu
Web Site: www.oncampus.richmond.edu
Management:
    Executive Director: Kathleen Panoff
Utilizes: Actors; Artists-in-Residence; Dancers; Guest Accompanists; Guest Artists; Guest Designers; Guest Soloists; High School Drama; Instructors; Local Artists; Multimedia; Original Music Scores; Sign Language Translators; Singers; Special Technical Talent; Theatre Companies; Touring Companies
Founded: 1996

Paid Staff: 7
Paid Artists: 30
Non-paid Artists: 15
Budget: $60,000-150,000

5407
RICHMOND SHAKESPEARE FESTIVAL
PO Box 27543
Richmond, VA 23261-7543
Phone: 804-270-3310
Fax: 804-232-4400
Toll-free: 888-373-2628
e-mail: cliffick@richmondshakespeare.com
Web Site: www.richmondshakespeare.com
Management:
    President: Stephanie Meharg
    Managing Director: Cynde Liffick
Specialized Field: Shakespeare Production
Status: Non-Profit, Professional
Paid Staff: 5
Paid Artists: 20

5408
THEATREVIRGINIA
2800 Groove Avenue
Richmond, VA 23221
Phone: 804-353-6100
Fax: 804-353-8799
Web Site: www.theatreva.com
Management:
    Programming Artistic Director: Benny Ambush
    Assistant Director: Karen Brown
    Managing Director: Barbara Wells
Budget: $150,000-400,000

5409
VIRGINIA COMMONWEALTH UNIVERSITY COMMONS COLLEGE
907 Floyd Avenue
Box 842032
Richmond, VA 23284
Phone: 804-828-6500
Fax: 804-828-6182
e-mail: mhorvath@vcu.edu
Web Site: www.students.vcu.edu/commons
Management:
    Executive Director: Timothy Reed
    Artistic Director: Justin Hirsch
    Managing Director: John Leppo
    Activities Coordinator: Mary Beth Horvath
Specialized Field: Series & Festivals; Instrumental Music; Vocal Music; Theatre; Youth; Dance; Ethnic Performances
Status: For-Profit, Non-Professional
Budget: $10,000-20,000
Performs At: University Student Commons Commonwealth Ballroom

5410
HOLLINS UNIVERSITY PERFORMING ARTS SERIES
Presser Hall, 8226 Tinker Lane NE
PO Box 9643
Roanoke, VA 24020
Phone: 540-362-6511
Fax: 540-362-6648
e-mail: jcline@hollins.edu
Web Site: www.hollins.edu/academ/depts/music
Management:
    President: Nancy Gray
    Provost: Wayne Markert
    Chairman of Music Department: Judith Cline
Founded: 1842

Specialized Field: Women's Art Events and Training
Status: Non-Profit, Professional
Paid Staff: 13
Paid Artists: 8
Budget: $10,000

5411
ROANOKE COLLEGE PERFORMING ARTS SERIES
Roanoke College
221 College Lane
Salem, VA 24153
Phone: 540-375-2351
Fax: 540-375-2559
e-mail: arthur@roanoke.edu
Web Site: www.roanoke.edu
Management:
Administrator: George N Arthur
Utilizes: Actors; Artists-in-Residence; Collaborations; Commissioned Music; Dancers; Fine Artists; Multimedia; Poets; Resident Artists; Special Technical Talent
Specialized Field: Performing Arts Events
Status: Non-Profit, Professional
Paid Staff: 2
Budget: $10,000-20,000
Performs At: Olin Hall
Seating Capacity: 404

5412
CARL BROMAN CONCERTS
Mary Baldwin College
Box 1
Staunton, VA 24402
Phone: 540-887-7188
Fax: 540-885-7887
e-mail: rtallen@mbc.edu
Management:
Manager: Robert T Allen III
Founded: 1980
Specialized Field: Series & Festivals; Chambers; Recitals
Status: Non-Profit, Professional
Paid Artists: 12
Budget: $10,000-20,000
Performs At: Francis Auditorium

5413
MIDDLE PENINSULA COMMUNITY CONCERT ASSOCIATION
PO Box 198
Topping, VA 23169
Phone: 804-758-4819
Officers:
President: Carolyn Shank
Budget: $20,000-35,000

5414
WOLF TRAP FOUNDATION FOR THE PERFORMING ARTS
1645 Trap Road
Vienna, VA 22182
Phone: 703-255-1900
Fax: 703-255-1918
e-mail: wolftrap@wolftrap.org
Web Site: www.wolftrap.org
Officers:
VP, Performing Arts/Education: Ann McPherson McKee
Vp, External Affairs: Beth Brummel
Management:
President: Terrence Jones
Sr Director Comm and Marketing: Lisa Lacamera

Director Media Relations: Melissa Chotiner
Mission: To provide enrichment, education and enjoyment to diverse audiences through presentation, production and creation of a broad spectrum of performing arts activities.
Utilizes: Artists-in-Residence; Commissioned Music; Dance Companies; Five Seasonal Concerts; Guest Composers; Instructors; Multimedia; Students
Founded: 1971
Specialized Field: Series & Festivals; Instrumental Music; Vocal Music; Theatre; Youth; Dance; Ethnic Performances; Dance
Status: Non-Profit, Professional
Paid Staff: 80
Budget: $20,000,000
Performs At: Filene Center at America's National Park for the Performing Arts
Facility Category: Indoor/Outdoor Amphitheatre
Type of Stage: Proscenium
Seating Capacity: 7,023 with lawn seats
Year Built: 1971
Year Remodeled: 1984
Organization Type: Educational; Sponsoring

5415
GARTH NEWEL MUSIC CENTER
PO Box 240
Warm Springs, VA 24484
Phone: 540-839-5018
Fax: 540-839-3154
e-mail: office@garthnewel.org
Web Site: www.garthnewel.org
Management:
Artistic Director: Evelyn Grau
Managing Director: Jacod Yarrow
Artistic Director: Tobias Werner
Mission: Promoting and performing chamber music.
Utilizes: Guest Artists
Founded: 1973
Specialized Field: Series & Festivals; Youth; Ethnic Performances; Vocal Music; Festivals; Instrumental music; Concert Series; Performance and study of Classical Music
Status: Non-Profit, Professional
Paid Artists: 4
Performs At: Herter Hall
Organization Type: Performing; Touring; Resident; Educational

5416
MUSIC HOLIDAY WEEKENDS
Garth Newel Music Center
PO Box 240
Warm Springs, VA 24484
Phone: 540-839-5018
Fax: 540-839-3154
Toll-free: 877-558-1689
e-mail: office@garthnewel.org
Web Site: www.garthnewel.org
Management:
Artistic Director: Evelyn Grau
Managing Director: Jacob Yarrow
Mission: Music Holiday of offers a total experience in social civility.
Founded: 1973
Specialized Field: Educational Programs and Performances
Status: Non-Profit, Professional
Paid Staff: 7
Paid Artists: 4
Season: Fall; Winter; Spring

5417
SPECIAL MUSIC HOLIDAYS
PO Box 240
Warm Springs, VA 24484
Phone: 540-839-5018
Fax: 540-839-3154
Toll-free: 877-558-1689
e-mail: office@garthnewel.org
Web Site: www.garthnewel.org
Management:
Managing Director: Jacob Yarrow
Artistic Director: Evelyn Grau
Founded: 1973
Specialized Field: Series and Festivals; Instrumental Music; Vocal Music; Youth; Ethnic Performances; Music Classical
Status: Non-Profit, Professional
Paid Staff: 9
Paid Artists: 4
Season: November; December

5418
SPRING 2003
Garth Newel Music Center
PO Box 240
Warm Springs, VA 24484
Phone: 540-839-5018
Fax: 540-839-3154
Toll-free: 877-558-1689
e-mail: office@garthnewel.org
Web Site: www.garthnewel.org
Management:
Artistic Director: Evelyn Grau
Managing Director: Jacob Yarrow
Founded: 1973
Specialized Field: music classical
Status: Non-Profit
Season: Spring

5419
SUMMER CHAMBER MUSIC FESTIVAL
Garth Newel Music Center
PO Box 240
Warm Springs, VA 24484
Phone: 540-839-5018
Fax: 540-839-3154
Toll-free: 877-558-1689
e-mail: office@garthnewel.org
Web Site: www.garthnewel.org
Management:
Artistic Director: Evelyn Grau
Managing Director: Jacob Yarrow
Mission: A tradition since 1973, the Summer Chamber Music Festival makes Garth Newel the place to be on weekends afternoons. Each concert consist of a unique program featuring members of the Garth Newel Piano Quartet and guest artists. Performances take place in Herter Hall.
Founded: 1973
Specialized Field: Performance and Study of Chamber Music
Status: Non-Profit, Professional
Paid Staff: 7
Paid Artists: 4

5420
VIRGINIA SHAKESPEARE FESTIVAL
College of William and Mary
PO Box 8795
Williamsburg, VA 23187

Phone: 757-221-2683
Fax: 757-221-2636
e-mail: clowen@wm.edu
Web Site: www.vsf.wm.edu
Management:
   Producing Artistic Director: Christopher Owens
   Executive Director: Jerry H Bledsoe
Mission: To offer quality Shakespeare performed in the classical manner.
Utilizes: Singers
Founded: 1978
Specialized Field: Series and Festivals; Theatre; Youth; Dance; Festivals
Status: Non-Profit, Professional
Paid Staff: 20
Paid Artists: 25
Income Sources: The College of William & Mary
Season: July - August
Performs At: Phi Beta Kappa Memorial Hall; The College of Williamsburg
Organization Type: Performing; Educational

5421
WILLIAM & MARY CONCERT SERIES
The Campus Center 203
PO Box 8795
Williamsburg, VA 23187-8795
Phone: 757-221-3300
Fax: 757-221-3451
e-mail: mxcons@wm.edu
Web Site: www.wm.edu
Management:
   President: Tim Sullivan
Founded: 1950
Specialized Field: Series & Festivals; Instrumental Music; Vocal Music; Dance; Ethnic Performances
Status: For-Profit, Non-Professional
Paid Staff: 2
Budget: $60,000-150,000
Performs At: Phi Beta Kappa Memorial Hall
Seating Capacity: 763

5422
WINTERGREEN PERFORMING ARTS
Box 816
Wintergreen, VA 22958
Phone: 540-343-6221
Fax: 540-325-1464
e-mail: info@wparts.com
Web Site: www.wparts.com
Officers:
   President: Stuart C Harvey
Management:
   Artistic Director/Conductor: David Wiley
   Managing Director: Sarah McCracken

5423
WINTERGREEN SUMMER MUSIC FESTIVAL
Wintergreen Performing Arts
PO Box 816
Wintergreen, VA 22958
Phone: 434-325-8292
Fax: 804-325-1464
e-mail: info@wparts.com
Web Site: www.wintergreenmusic.org
Management:
   Artistic Director: David Wiley
Mission: Summer Orchestra Concerts.
Founded: 1996
Paid Staff: 2
Volunteer Staff: 40
Paid Artists: 70
Non-paid Artists: 10

5424
SHENANDOAH VALLEY MUSIC FESTIVAL
PO Box 528
Woodstock, VA 22664
Phone: 540-459-3396
Fax: 540-459-3730
Toll-free: 800-459-3396
e-mail: svmf@shentel.net
Web Site: www.musicfest.org
Officers:
   Executive Director: Dennis M Lynch
Management:
   President: Dennis Lynch
Mission: To foster, promote, and increase the musical knowledge of the public by organizing and presenting programs chosen primarily from the literature of symphonic music, and incidentally from folk, bog band, jazz and family programming.
Utilizes: Guest Musicians; Multimedia; Original Music Scores
Founded: 1963
Specialized Field: Series and Festivals: Symphonic Music
Status: Non-Profit, Professional
Paid Staff: 3
Budget: $7,500
Income Sources: Government & private grants
Performs At: Orkney Springs Pavilion
Annual Attendance: 10,000
Organization Type: Sponsoring

Washington

5425
AUBURN ARTS COMMISSION
Auburn City Hall
25 W Main Street
Auburn, WA 98001
Phone: 253-804-5057
Fax: 253-288-3132
Management:
   Cultural Programs Manager: Susan Sagawa
Budget: $60,000-150,000

5426
BELLINGHAM FESTIVAL OF MUSIC
1300 N State Street
Suite 101
Bellingham, WA 98225
Phone: 360-676-5997
Fax: 360-647-3521
Toll-free: 800-335-5550
Web Site: www.bellinghamfestival.org
Officers:
   Chairperson: Marty Haines
Management:
   Chairman: Milton Schayes
   Executive Director: Andrew Moquin
   Artistic Director: Micheal Palmer
Mission: To provide the area with educational opportunities to experience live music performances at the highest artistic level by nationally and internationally renowned musicians in a concentrated festival format.
Founded: 1993
Specialized Field: Series & Festivals; Summer Music Festival Featuring Classical; Chamber; Jazz; and Ethnic Music
Status: Non-Profit, Professional
Paid Staff: 3
Volunteer Staff: 6
Paid Artists: 50
Budget: $500,000

Income Sources: Grants from City; County; Private Foundations; Local Fund Drive; Ticket Sales
Performs At: Bellwether on the Bay
Annual Attendance: 9,000
Facility Category: Outdoor

5427
WESTERN WASHINGTON UNIVERSITY PERFORMING ARTS CENTER SERIES
Pac, Pa-361
516 High Street
Bellingham, WA 98225-9109
Phone: 360-650-3866
Fax: 360-650-3028
Web Site: www.pacseries.wwu.edu
Management:
   Dean: Carol Edwards
   Performing Arts Series Coordinator: Tamara McDonald
Budget: $40,000-55,000
Performs At: PAC Mainstage Theatre, PAC Concert Hall

5428
OLYMPIC COLLEGE
Student Programs
1600 Chester Avenue
Bremerton, WA 98337-1699
Phone: 360-475-7441
Fax: 360-475-7454
e-mail: jgallagher@oc.ctc.edu
Web Site: www.oc.ctc.edu
Management:
   President: David Michell
   Artistic Director: Rick White
   Managing Director: Barry Janucsh
   Associate Director: Jean Gallagher
Specialized Field: Medical Training
Status: Non-Profit, Non-Professional
Paid Staff: 250
Budget: $10,000-20,000

5429
LAKE CHELAN BACH FESTIVAL
Lake Chelan Bach Fest
PO Box 554
Chelan, WA 98816-9522
Phone: 509-667-0904
Fax: 509-682-0901
e-mail: info@bachfest.org
Web Site: www.bachfest.org
Officers:
   Co-President: Ruth Rogers
   Co-President: Karen Rich
   Secretary: Kerry Travers
Management:
   Executive Director: Beth Jensen
   Artistic Director: Dan Baldwin
Mission: To inspire, enrich and educate through live musical performances.
Founded: 1982
Specialized Field: Vocal Music; Instrumental Music; Lyric Opera
Status: Professional; Non-Professional; Nonprofit
Organization Type: Performing; Educational

5430
ORCAS THEATER & COMMUNITY CENTER
917 Mount Baker Road
PO Box 567
East Sound, WA 98245-0567

Phone: 360-376-2281
Fax: 360-376-6822
Web Site: www.rockisland.com/~orcascenter
Management:
    Director: Malissa White
Budget: $35,000-60,000

5431
EDMONDS ARTS COMMISSION
700 Main Street
Edmonds, WA 98020
Phone: 425-771-0228
Fax: 425-771-0253
e-mail: chapin@ci.edmonds.wa.us
Web Site: www.ci.edmonds.wa.us/artscommission
Management:
    Cultural Services Manager: Frances White Chapin
Founded: 1975
Specialized Field: Municipal Organizations Promotes Arts
Status: For-Profit, Non-Professional
Paid Staff: 2
Budget: $10,000-20,000

5432
JAZZ IN THE VALLEY
PO Box 214
Ellensburg, WA 98926
Phone: 509-925-2002
Toll-free: 888-925-2204
e-mail: jazzinfo@jazzinthevalley.com
Web Site: www.jazzinthevalley.com
Management:
    Director: Larry Sharpe
Status: Non-Profit

5433
ENUMCLAW ARTS COMMISSION
1339 Griffin
Enumclaw, WA 98022
Phone: 360-802-0232
Fax: 360-825-1429
Management:
    Cultural Programs Manager: DeNae McGee
Budget: $35,000-60,000
Performs At: City Hall Park (summer)

5434
SAN JUAN JAZZ
PO Box 1666
Friday Harbor, WA 98250
Phone: 360-378-5509
Fax: 360-378-7796
e-mail: jazz@sanjuanjazz.org
Web Site: www.sanjuanjazz.org
Management:
    Manager: Bud Rodewald

5435
KENT ARTS COMMISSION
220 4th Avenue S
Kent, WA 98032
Phone: 253-856-5050
Fax: 253-856-6050
e-mail: rbillerbeck@ci.kent.wa.us
Web Site: www.kentarts.com
Management:
    Cultural Programs Manager: Ronda Billerbeck
Utilizes: Collaborating Artists; Dance Companies; Fine Artists; Instructors; Local Artists; Multimedia; Original Music Scores; Special Technical Talent; Theatre Companies; Touring Companies
Founded: 1980
Specialized Field: Cultural Programs

Status: Non-Profit, Professional
Paid Staff: 7
Budget: $35,000-60,000
Annual Attendance: 50,000
Facility Category: Performing Arts Center/Outdoor Festival - various

5436
ABBEY CHURCH EVENTS
Saint Martin's Abbey
5300 Pacific Avenue SE
Lacey, WA 98503-1297
Phone: 360-438-4476
Fax: 360-438-4387
Management:
    Director: Boniface V Lazzari, OSB
Budget: $10,000-20,000

5437
ICICLE CREEK MUSIC CENTER
PO Box 2071
Leavenworth, WA 98826
Phone: 509-548-6347
Fax: 509-548-3128
Toll-free: 877-265-6026
e-mail: icicle@icicle.org
Web Site: www.icicle.org
Management:
    Executive Director: Sheila Hughes
    Artistic Director: Sally Singer
    Artistic Director: Oksana Ezhokino
    General Director: Lisa Bergman
Mission: To advance classical music, performing arts and education in a spectacular retreat setting.
Founded: 1995
Specialized Field: Music/Chamber Music
Paid Staff: 5
Volunteer Staff: 20
Paid Artists: 18
Performs At: Classical Music; Performing Arts & Education

5438
LYNNWOOD JAZZ FESTIVAL AT EDMONDS COMMUNITY COLLEGE
20000 68th Avenue W
Lynnwood, WA 98036
Phone: 425-640-1650
Fax: 425-640-1083
e-mail: kmarcy@edcc.edu
Web Site: www.music.edcc.edu
Management:
    Festival Director: Randi Irby
Founded: 1975
Specialized Field: Series & Festivals; Instrumental Music; Vocal Music; Theatre; Youth; Dance; Ethnic Performances
Status: For-Profit, Non-Professional
Paid Artists: 3

5439
MERCER ISLAND ARTS COUNCIL
2040 84th Avenue SE
Mercer Island, WA 98040
Phone: 206-236-3545
Fax: 206-236-3631
e-mail: miparks@ci.mercer-island.wa.us
Web Site: www.ci.mercer-island.wa.us
Management:
    Chairman: Barry Massoudi
    Recreation Supervisor: Jennifer Berner
Mission: To present cultural arts programs to the citizens of Mercer Island and to advocate for the arts and Mercer Island artists.

Founded: 1985
Specialized Field: Arts Council
Status: For-Profit, Non-Professional
Paid Staff: 2
Volunteer Staff: 12
Budget: $20,000-35,000

5440
EVERGREEN STATE COLLEGE EVERGREEN EXPRESSIONS
Communications Building
Room 301
Olympia, WA 98505
Phone: 360-867-6070
Fax: 360-866-6794
Toll-free: 877-787-9721
Web Site: www.evergreen.edu
Management:
    Performing/Media Arts Manager: John Robbins
    Technical Director: Jeremy Reynolds
Founded: 1967
Specialized Field: Series & Festivals; Instrumental Music; Vocal Music; Theater; Ethnic Performances
Status: For-Profit, Non-Professional
Paid Staff: 50
Paid Artists: 10
Budget: $20,000-35,000

5441
JUAN DE FUCA FESTIVAL OF THE ARTS
PO Box 796
Port Angeles, WA 98362
Phone: 360-457-5411
Fax: 360-457-5411
Management:
    Executive Director: Anna Manildi

5442
DANCE FESTIVAL: CENTRUM FESTIVAL
PO Box 1158
Port Townsend, WA 98368
Phone: 360-385-3102
Fax: 360-385-2470
Toll-free: 800-733-3608
Web Site: www.centrum.org
Management:
    President: Cindy Finnie
    Executive Director: Phacher Bailey
    Artistic Director: Greg Miller
Mission: To assist those who seek creative and intellectual growth and to present visual, literary and performing arts to the public.
Founded: 1973
Specialized Field: Arts Workshop
Status: Non-Profit, Professional
Paid Staff: 18
Volunteer Staff: 60
Paid Artists: 200

5443
JAZZ PORT TOWNSEND: CENTRUM FESTIVAL
PO Box 1158
Port Townsend, WA 98368
Phone: 360-385-3102
Fax: 360-385-2470
Toll-free: 800-733-3608
Web Site: www.centrum.org
Management:
    President: Thatcher Bailey
    Artistic Director: Gregg Miller

Mission: To assist those who seek creative and intellectual growth and to present visual, literary and performing arts to the public.
Founded: 1973
Specialized Field: Arts and Education
Status: Non-Profit, Professional
Paid Staff: 18
Volunteer Staff: 60
Paid Artists: 200

5444
PORT TOWNSEND BLUES HERITAGE FESTIVAL: CENTRUM FESTIVAL

PO Box 1158
Port Townsend, WA 98368
Phone: 360-385-3102
Fax: 360-385-2470
Toll-free: 800-733-3608
Web Site: www.centrum.org
Management:
    Executive Director: Thatcher Bailey
    Artistic Director: Gregg Miller
Mission: To assist those who seek creative and intellectual growth and to present visual, literary and performing arts to the public.
Founded: 1973
Specialized Field: Arts and Education
Status: Non-Profit, Professional
Paid Staff: 18
Volunteer Staff: 60
Paid Artists: 200

5445
WASHINGTON STATE UNIVERSITY

Washington State University
Pullman, WA 99164-1710
Phone: 509-335-2241
Fax: 509-335-3853
Web Site: www.wsu.edu/beasoey
Management:
    Executive Director: Leo Udy
Founded: 1974
Specialized Field: Series & Festivals: Performing Arts
Status: Non-Profit, Professional
Paid Staff: 200
Budget: $10,000
Performs At: Performing Arts Coliseum Theatre

5446
CORNISH COLLEGE: CORNISH SERIES

1000 Lenora Street
Seattle, WA 98121
Phone: 206-726-5030
Fax: 206-720-5183
Toll-free: 800-726-2787
Web Site: www.cornish.edu
Officers:
    Music Department Chairperson: Laura Kaminsky
Management:
    President: Sergei Tschernisch
    Department Chairman: Carol Shiffman
Founded: 1914
Specialized Field: Series and Festivals: Performing in Visual Arts
Status: Non-Profit, Non-Professional
Budget: $20,000-35,000
Performs At: Poncho Concert Hall
Seating Capacity: 200
Year Remodeled: 2000

5447
EARLY MUSIC GUILD INTERNATIONAL SERIES/RECITALS

2366 Eastlake Avenue E
Suite #335
Seattle, WA 98102
Phone: 206-325-7066
Fax: 206-860-9151
e-mail: emg@earlymusicguild.org
Web Site: www.earlymusicguild.org
Officers:
    President: Lorri Falterman
Management:
    Executive Director: August Denhard
    Office Manager/Education: Ben Albritton
Founded: 1977
Paid Staff: 2
Volunteer Staff: 11
Paid Artists: 30
Budget: $35,000-60,000

5448
EARSHOT JAZZ FESTIVAL

3429 Fremont Place
#309
Seattle, WA 98103
Phone: 206-547-6763
Fax: 206-547-6286
e-mail: jazz@earshot.org
Web Site: www.earshot.org
Management:
    Executive Director: John Gilbreath
    News Magazine Editor: Steve Cline
Founded: 1984
Status: Non-Profit

5449
GOVERNORS CHAMBER MUSIC SERIES

205 Mcgraw Street
Seattle, WA 98109
Phone: 206-281-8292
Fax: 206-285-7610
Management:
    Artistic Director: Judith Cohen
Specialized Field: Only Use Pacific Northwest Artists
Budget: $10,000-20,000
Performs At: State Theatre, Olympia, Washington and the Governor's

5450
LADIES MUSICAL CLUB

Cobb Building 1305 Fourth Avenue
Suite 500
Seattle, WA 98101
Phone: 206-622-6882
Fax: 206-622-0791
Web Site: www.lmcseattle.org
Officers:
    Concert Committee Chairperson: Barbara Sand
    President: Doris Eckert
    Recording Secretary: Susan Buttram
    Corresponding Secretary: Iris Ewing
    Treasurer: Ruth Caswell
Management:
    President: Sue Buttram
Mission: To grant scholarships to deserving music students; to sponsor a yearly International Artists Series; to foster music among its members and the community.
Utilizes: Singers
Founded: 1891
Specialized Field: Classical
Status: Non-Profit, Professional

Paid Staff: 1
Performs At: Meany Hall; University of Washington
Organization Type: Performing; Resident; Educational; Sponsoring

5451
NORTHWEST FOLKLIFE FESTIVAL

305 Harrison Street
Seattle, WA 98109
Phone: 206-684-7300
Fax: 206-684-7190
e-mail: folklife@nwfolklife.org
Web Site: www.nwfolklife.org
Officers:
    President: Scott Scher
    Vice President: Craig Beles
    VP: Ed D'Alessandro
    Secretary: Chuck Kichner
Management:
    President: Edward D Alessandro
    Executive Director: Michael Herschensohn
    Artistic Director: Deborah Fant
    Managing Director: Mea Fischelis
Mission: Preserving and presenting traditional and ethnic arts; fostering cultural understanding.
Founded: 1971
Specialized Field: Series & Festivals; Instrumental Music; Vocal Music; Theatre; Youth; Dance; Ethnic Performances; Classical
Status: Non-Profit, Professional
Paid Staff: 14
Budget: $2,200,000
Income Sources: Fees; Commissions; Donations; Grants
Performs At: Seattle Center
Annual Attendance: 200,000
Organization Type: Performing; Touring; Educational; Sponsoring

5452
OLYMPIC MUSIC FESTIVAL

PO Box 45776
Seattle, WA 98145-0776
Phone: 206-527-8839
Fax: 206-526-8621
Web Site: www.olympicmusicfest.org
Management:
    Executive Director: Alan Iglitzin
Founded: 1982
Specialized Field: Series & Festivals; Instrumental Music; Vocal Music
Status: Non-Profit, Professional
Paid Staff: 2
Paid Artists: 30

5453
ON THE BOARDS

100 W Roy Street
Seattle, WA 98119
Mailing Address: PO Box 19515 Seattle, WA 98109
Phone: 206-217-9886
Fax: 206-217-9887
e-mail: info@ontheboards.org
Web Site: www.ontheboards.org
Management:
    Artistic Director: Lane Czaplinski
    Managing Director: Sarah Wilke
Mission: Presentation oragnization featuring contemporary performance artists in dance, theater, music, multimedia and visual arts from around the globe.

Utilizes: Actors; Artists-in-Residence; Choreographers; Collaborating Artists; Composers-in-Residence; Dance Companies; Dancers; Instructors; Local Artists; Multimedia; Performance Artists; Poets; Special Technical Talent; Theatre Companies
Founded: 1978
Specialized Field: Series & Festivals: Contemporary Avanta Grade Performance
Status: Non-Profit, Professional
Paid Staff: 12
Budget: $1,200,000
Type of Stage: Black Box; Proscenium
Rental Contact: Operations Manager Brett McDowell

5454

SEATTLE CHAMBER MUSIC FESTIVAL

10 Harrison Street
Suite 306
Seattle, WA 98109
Phone: 206-283-8710
Fax: 206-283-8826
e-mail: info@seattlechambermusic.org
Web Site: www.seattlechambermusic.org
Officers:
President: Patricia Tall-Takacs
Management:
Executive Director: Connie Cooper
Artistic Director: Toby Saks
Mission: To present a four-week summer series of twelve outstanding chamber-music concerts annually.
Founded: 1982
Specialized Field: Series & Festivals; Chamber Music; String Music
Status: Non-Profit, Professional
Paid Staff: 5
Budget: $500,000
Performs At: Lakeside School; Saint Nicholas Hall; Benareya Recital Hall
Organization Type: Performing

5455

SEATTLE INTERNATIONAL CHILDREN'S FESTIVAL

305 Harrison Street
Seattle, WA 98109
Phone: 206-684-7338
Fax: 206-233-3944
e-mail: info@seattleinternational.org
Web Site: www.seattleinternational.org
Management:
Executive Director: Andrea Wagner
Artistic Director: Brian Faker
Director Education: Chris Jeffries
Mission: To offer an international festival of performing arts for children.
Founded: 1987
Specialized Field: Series & Festivals: International Performing Arts Festival
Status: Non-Profit, Professional
Paid Staff: 6
Paid Artists: 100
Income Sources: Western Alliance of Arts Administrators; International Association of Theatre for Children and Youth
Performs At: Seattle Center
Organization Type: Performing; Educational

5456

SEATTLE SHAKESPEARE FESTIVAL

1219 Westlake Avenue North
Suite 109
Seattle, WA

Phone: 206-286-0736
Fax: 206-286-0843
Web Site: www.seanet.com/~ssf/
Management:
Producing Artistic Director: Stephanie Shine
Mission: To serve the community by presenting plays essential to our common culture in stagings that are vital and accesible to all.

5457

SEATTLE YOUTH SYMPHONY ORCHESTRA'S MARROWSTONE MUSIC FESTIVAL

11065 5th NE
Seattle, WA 98125
Phone: 206-362-2300
Fax: 206-361-9254
e-mail: info@syso.org
Web Site: www.syso.org
Management:
Executive Director: Dan Pettersen
Music Director: Stephen Rogers Radcliffe
Founded: 1942
Specialized Field: Series & Festivals: Instrumental Music
Status: Non-Profit, Non-Professional
Paid Staff: 8

5458

TEATRO ZINZANNI

PO Box 9750
Seattle, WA 98109-0750
Phone: 206-281-7788
Fax: 206-281-7799
e-mail: rduff@onereel.org
Web Site: www.zinzannil.org
Management:
President/CEO/Artistic Director: Norman Langill
Associate Artistic Director: Reenie Duff
Budget: $400,000-1,000,000

5459

WATER MUSIC FESTIVAL

PO Box 524
Seaview, WA 98644-0524
Phone: 360-642-5812
Fax: 360-642-5812
Toll-free: 800-451-2542
Web Site: www.watermusicfsetival.com
Board VP: Pat Reither
Board Secretary: Sandy Jacoby
Board Treasurer: Jane Schience
Grants Coordinator: Jayne Dash
Founded: 1984
Specialized Field: Chamber Music
Volunteer Staff: 50

5460

CONNOISSEUR CONCERTS ASSOCIATION

315 W Mission Avenue
#21
Spokane, WA 99201-2325
Phone: 509-326-4942
Web Site: www.nwbachfest.com
Officers:
President: Mart K. Craft
Vice President: Verne Windham
Management:
Executive Director: Gertrude Harvey
Artistic Director: Gunther Schuller
Specialized Field: Instrumental Music; Festivals
Budget: $35,000-60,000

Income Sources: Washington State Arts Commission; donations
Performs At: Metropolitan Performing Arts Center

5461

PINESONG/SPOKANE FALLS COMMUNITY COLLEGE

3410 W Fort George Wright Drive
MS 3020
Spokane, WA 99204
Phone: 509-533-3500
Fax: 509-533-3433
e-mail: sfccinfo@spokanefalls.edu
Web Site: www.spokanefalls.edu
Management:
President: Mark Palek
Festival Director: John Thompson
Mission: To offer a multi-cultural arts festival featuring hands-on participation.
Utilizes: Singers
Founded: 1966
Specialized Field: Undergraduate Education
Status: Non-Profit, Non-Professional
Organization Type: Sponsoring

5462

BROADWAY CENTER FOR THE PERFORMING ARTS

901 Broadway
7th Floor
Tacoma, WA 98402
Phone: 253-591-5890
Fax: 253-591-2013
e-mail: administration@broadwaycenter.org
Web Site: www.broadwaycenter.org
Management:
Executive Director: David Fischer, dfischer@broadwaycenter.org
Operations Director: Scott Painter, spainter@broadwaycenter.org
Utilizes: Actors; Collaborating Artists; Collaborations; Dance Companies; Dancers; Educators; Fine Artists; Grant Writers; High School Drama; Instructors; Local Artists; Lyricists; Multimedia; Original Music Scores; Resident Artists; Selected Students; Sign Language Translators; Singers; Theatre Companies
Founded: 1983
Specialized Field: Series & Festivals; Instrumental Music; Vocal Music; Theatre; Youth; Dance; Ethnic Performances
Status: Non-Profit, Professional
Paid Staff: 25
Volunteer Staff: 100
Budget: $5 Million
Performs At: Pantages Theater; Rialto Theater; Theatre on the Square
Seating Capacity: 1169; 735; 302
Year Built: 1918
Year Remodeled: 1979
Cost: $25 Million
Rental Contact: Brenda Ramsey
Resident Groups: Tacoma Actors Guild

5463

EVERGREEN MUSIC FESTIVAL: TACOMA YOUTH SYMPHONY ASSOCIATION

901 Broadway Plaza
Suite 500
Tacoma, WA 98402-4415
Phone: 253-627-2792
Fax: 253-627-1682
Web Site: www.tacomayouthsymphony@nisn.com
Management:

Festival Music Director: Dr. Paul-Elliot Cobbs
Executive Director: Dr. Loma Mosley
Marketing Manager: Kristina Thomas
Mission: To provide an intense musical experience for younger students at the first session, and pre-professionals at the second session.
Founded: 1984
Specialized Field: Music

5464
PACIFIC LUTHERAN UNIVERSITY PROGRAM BOARD

Pacific Lutheran University
Tacoma, WA 98447
Phone: 253-535-7602
Fax: 253-535-8669
Toll-free: 877-254-7001
e-mail: music@plu.edu
Web Site: www.plu.edu
Management:
  President: Lorin Anderson
Founded: 1890
Specialized Field: Series and Festivals; Instrumental Music; Vocal Music; Theatre; Youth; Ethnic Performances
Status: Non-Profit, Non-Professional
Budget: $10,000
Performs At: Lutheran Concert Hall

5465
UNIVERSITY OF PUGET SOUND CULTURAL EVENTS

1500 N Warner
Tacoma, WA 98416
Phone: 253-879-3366
Fax: 253-879-2671
e-mail: ssolidarios@ups.edu
Web Site: www.ups.edu
Management:
  Public Events Director: Margaret Throndill
  Director of Student Programs: Serni Solidarios
Founded: 1888
Specialized Field: Education
Status: Non-Profit, Non-Professional
Budget: $20,000-35,000

West Virginia

5466
BETHANY COLLEGE

Renner Union
PO Box 37
Bethany, WV 26032
Phone: 304-829-7901
Fax: 304-829-7434
Web Site: www.bethanywv.edu
Management:
  President: Brian Fernandes
Utilizes: Commissioned Music; Dance Companies; Educators; Fine Artists; Grant Writers; Guest Directors; Guest Instructors; Guest Musical Directors; Guest Musicians; Guest Soloists; Instructors; Multimedia; Organization Contracts; Original Music Scores; Performance Artists; Playwrights; Sign Language Translators; Singers; Soloists; Touring Companies
Founded: 1860
Specialized Field: Students Activities
Status: Non-Profit, Non-Professional
Budget: $10,000-20,000
Income Sources: Private
Performs At: Sstage; Steinman Hall of Fine Arts; Hummel Field House

Annual Attendance: 750
Facility Category: College

5467
BLUEFIELD STATE COLLEGE

219 Rock Street
Bluefield, WV 24701
Phone: 304-327-4186
Fax: 304-327-4188
Management:
  Campus Life Director: JD Carpenter
Budget: $10,000

5468
CHARLESTON CIVIC CENTER

200 Civic Center Drive
Charleston, WV 25301
Phone: 304-345-1500
Fax: 304-357-7432
Management:
  General Manager: John D Robertson

5469
JEWISH CULTURAL SERIES

3828 Virginia Avenue SE
Charleston, WV 25304
Phone: 304-925-5112
Officers:
  Chairman: Dr. Steve Jubelirer
Budget: $10,000-20,000
Performs At: Temple Israel; B'nai Jacob Synagogue

5470
GLENVILLE STATE COLLEGE CULTURAL AFFAIRS COMMISSION

Glenville State College
Glenville, WV 26351-1292
Phone: 304-462-7361
Fax: 304-462-4407
Web Site: www.glenville.edu
Officers:
  Chairman Fine Arts: John S McKinney
Management:
  President: Robert Freeman
  Executive Director: Robert Hardman
  Artistic Director: Duane Chapman
Founded: 1872
Specialized Field: Education
Status: Non-Profit, Non-Professional
Paid Staff: 200
Budget: $10,000-20,000

5471
CAM HENDERSON CENTER

Marshall University
400 Hal Greer Boulevard
Huntington, WV 25755
Phone: 304-696-3170
Fax: 304-696-6448
Web Site: www.marshall.edu
Management:
  Athletic Director: Lance West

5472
HUNTINGTON CIVIC ARENA

Ogeden Entertainment
One Civic Center Plaza
Huntington, WV 25701
Phone: 304-696-5990
Fax: 305-696-4463
Web Site: www.hcarena.com
Management:
  Executive Director: Steven J Haver

5473
MARSHALL ARTISTS SERIES

Marshall University, Smith Hall 160
400 Hal Greek Boulevard
Huntington, WV 25755
Phone: 304-696-6656
Fax: 304-696-6658
e-mail: watkins@marshall.edu
Web Site: www.marshallartistsseries.org
Officers:
  President: J Wade Gilley
Management:
  Executive Director: Penny Watkins
  Administrative Assistant: Anne S Moncer
Mission: To aid, promote and contribute to the educational and cultural life of Marshall University and the surrounding area.
Founded: 1936
Specialized Field: Performing Arts
Status: Non-Profit, Professional
Paid Staff: 3
Paid Artists: 50
Budget: $150,000-400,000
Income Sources: Marshall University
Performs At: Keith-Albee Theatre
Organization Type: Educational; Sponsoring

5474
WEST VIRGINIA STATE UNIVERTISY MUSIC SERIES

Campus Box 4
PO Box 1000
Institute, WV 25112-1000
Phone: 304-766-3194
Fax: 304-766-5100
e-mail: cgiles@wvstateu.edu
Officers:
  Music Department Chairperson: Charlotte Giles
Management:
  President: Hazo Carter Jr
Founded: 1891
Specialized Field: Liberal Arts
Status: Non-Profit, Professional
Paid Staff: 4
Budget: $35,000-60,000

5475
CARNEGIE HALL

105 Church Street
Lewisburg, WV 24901
Phone: 304-645-7917
Fax: 304-645-5228
Web Site: www.carnegie-hall.com
Officers:
  President/CEO: Bruce Loving
Management:
  Artistic Director: Mary Leb
  Community Relations Director: Susan Bell
  Education Director: Christy Clemons-Rodgers
Founded: 1983
Paid Staff: 12
Volunteer Staff: 150
Budget: $35,000-60,000

5476
FAIRMONT CHAMBER MUSIC SOCIETY

359 Arbogast Lane
Morgantown, WV 26508-8801
Phone: 304-291-8277
Fax: 304-367-4248
e-mail: ashtonjohn@comcast.net
Web Site: www.fairmontchambermusic.com
Officers:

All listings are in alphabetical order by state, then city, then organization within the city.

President: John Ashton
Vice President: Alison Poland
Treasurer: Ruth Brooks
Secretary: Marcella Yarenhuk
Mission: To present the finest of classical chamber music in the North Central West Virginia area.
Founded: 1982
Specialized Field: Chamber Music; Classical
Volunteer Staff: 8
Budget: $11,000
Performs At: St. Peter's Church
Seating Capacity: 700

5477
WVU ARTS SERIES

PO Box 6017
Morgantown, WV 26506-6017
Phone: 304-293-4407
Fax: 304-293-7574
Web Site: www.events.wvu.edu
Budget: $150,000-400,000

5478
WEST VIRGINIA UNIVERSITY AT PARKERSBURG

W Virginia University at Parkersburg
300 Campus Drive
Parkersburg, WV 26104
Phone: 304-424-8248
Fax: 304-424-8354
e-mail: hg.young@mail.wvu.edu
Web Site: www.wvup.wvnet.edu
Management:
President: Marie Gnage
Executive Director: Tom Yencha
Artistic Director: H G Young III
Founded: 1961
Specialized Field: Series & Festivals; Vocal Music; Theatre
Status: Non-Profit, Non-Professional
Paid Staff: 1
Budget: $35,000-60,000

5479
CONTEMPORARY AMERICAN THEATER FESTIVAL

PO Box 429
Shepherdstown, WV 25443
Phone: 304-876-3473
Fax: 304-876-5443
Toll-free: 800-999-2283
e-mail: eherende@shepherd.edu
Web Site: www.catf.org
Management:
President: Lynn Shirley
Managing Director: Catherine Irwin
Producing Director: Ed Herendeen
Founded: 1990
Specialized Field: Theater Festival
Status: Non-Profit
Performs At: Main Stage, Studio Theater
Type of Stage: Proscenium, Black Box
Seating Capacity: 350, 99

5480
PERFORMING ARTS SERIES AT SHEPHERD

Shepherd College
101 College Center
Shepherdstown, WV 25443

Phone: 304-876-5113
Fax: 304-876-5137
e-mail: rmeads@shepherd.edu
Web Site: www.shepherd.edu/passweb
Officers:
Chairperson: Rachael Meads
Management:
President: Rachael Meads
Production Director: Patrick Wallac
Founded: 1982
Specialized Field: Series & Festivals; Instrumental Music; Vocal Music; Theatre; Dance; Ethnic Performances; Folk Art
Status: Non-Profit, Professional
Paid Staff: 2
Paid Artists: 35
Budget: $35,000-60,000

5481
CHARLESTON COMMUNITY MUSIC ASSOCIATION

PO Box 8008
South Charleston, WV 25303
Phone: 304-744-1400
Fax: 304-343-7058
Officers:
President: JB Wollenberger
Mission: Presenter.
Founded: 1933
Specialized Field: Music; Dance
Volunteer Staff: 100
Budget: $150,000
Income Sources: Ticket Sales; Contributions
Performs At: Concert Hall
Annual Attendance: 2,800-3,100
Type of Stage: Procenium
Seating Capacity: 3,450
Year Built: 1939

5482
WEST LIBERTY COLLEGE CONCERT SERIES

W Liberty College
Hall of Fine Arts
West Liberty, WV 26074-0335
Phone: 304-336-8006
Fax: 304-336-8056
Web Site: www.wlsc.edu
Officers:
Concert Committee Chairman: James C Guerriero
Management:
President: Richard Owens
VP of Academics: John McCullough
Chairman of Concert Series: James Gueraiero
Founded: 1964
Specialized Field: Series & Festivals; Instrumental Music; Vocal Music
Status: Non-Profit, Professional
Paid Staff: 1
Paid Artists: 15
Budget: $20,000-35,000

5483
OGLEBAY INSTITUTE

Oglebay Park
Wheeling, WV 26003
Phone: 304-242-4200
Fax: 304-242-4203
Toll-free: 888-696-4283
e-mail: inspire@oionline.com
Web Site: www.oionline.com
Management:
President: Mark R Williams

Director of Performing Arts: Kate Crosbie
Artistic Director: Harold O'Leary
Founded: 1930
Specialized Field: Series & Festivals; Vocal Music; Theatre; Youth; Dance; Ethnic Performances Theatre; Lyric Opera; History
Status: Non-Profit, Professional
Paid Staff: 100
Organization Type: Performing; Touring; Educational

Wisconsin

5484
PERFORMING ARTS AT LAWRENCE

115 S Drew Street
PO Box 599
Appleton, WI 54912-0599
Phone: 920-832-6589
Fax: 920-832-6783
Web Site: www.lawrence.edu
Management:
President: Jill Beck
Executive Director: Gregory Volk
Managing Director: Shana Shallue
Founded: 1847
Specialized Field: Series & Festivals: Jazz And Classical Concerts
Status: Non-Profit, Professional
Paid Staff: 2
Paid Artists: 8
Budget: $60,000-150,000
Income Sources: Ticket Revenue; Sponsorship
Annual Attendance: 10,000

5485
AL RINGLING THEATRE: LIVELY ARTS SERIES

PO Box 381
136 Fourth Avenue
Baraboo, WI 53913
Phone: 608-356-8864
Fax: 608-356-0976
Web Site: www.alringling.com
Management:
Executive Director: Larry McCoy
Founded: 1915
Status: For-Profit

5486
BELOIT COLLEGE PERFORMING ARTS SERIES

Int'l Performing Arts & Lecture Series
700 College Street
Beloit, WI 53511
Phone: 608-363-2242
Fax: 608-363-2870
Web Site: www.beloit.edu/~ipals
Officers:
President: John Burris
Management:
Director Special Events: Mary Frey
Founded: 1846
Specialized Field: Liberal Arts Education
Status: Non-Profit, Professional
Paid Staff: 1
Paid Artists: 40
Budget: $20,000-35,000
Income Sources: Beloit College
Performs At: Eaton Chapel

5487

ST. NORBERT COLLEGE PERFORMING ARTS

St. Norbert College
100 Grant Street
De Pere, WI 54115
Phone: 920-403-3950
Fax: 920-403-4081
e-mail: performingarts@snc.edu
Web Site: www.snc.edu/performingarts/
Management:
 Advisor: Garrett Grenz
Utilizes: Dance Companies; Fine Artists; Guest Instructors; Original Music Scores; Soloists
Founded: 1898
Budget: $10,000-20,000
Performs At: Abbot Pennings Hall of Fine Arts
Annual Attendance: 7,000
Facility Category: vantons

5488

HEADWATERS COUNCIL FOR THE PERFORMING ARTS

Box 1481
Eagle River, WI 54521
Phone: 715-477-6206
Fax: 715-477-1736
Officers:
 President: Bernie Hupperts
 VP: Linnea Ebann
 Secretary: Tim Niehaus
 Treasurer: David Hanselman
Management:
 Community Contact: Nancy Berg
Mission: To bring quality entertainment to our remote community.
Utilizes: Sign Language Translators; Singers; Soloists; Special Technical Talent; Theatre Companies
Founded: 1982
Specialized Field: Dance; Vocal Music; Instrumental Music; Theater
Status: Nonprofit
Volunteer Staff: 15
Budget: $24,000
Income Sources: Ticket Sales; Donations; Grants
Performs At: Northland Pines High School
Facility Category: High School Auditorium
Seating Capacity: 450
Year Built: 1980
Organization Type: Performing

5489

EAU CLAIRE REGIONAL ARTS CENTER

316 Eau Claire Street
Eau Claire, WI 54701
Phone: 715-832-2787
Fax: 715-832-0828
e-mail: info@eauclairearts.com
Web Site: www.eauclairearts.com
Management:
 Executive Director: Jen Roth
Utilizes: Choreographers; Dance Companies; Dancers; Fine Artists; Five Seasonal Concerts; Grant Writers; Guest Accompanists; Guest Choreographers; Guest Designers; Guest Directors; Guest Musicians; Guest Soloists; High School Drama; Instructors; Local Artists; Lyricists; Original Music Scores; Resident Artists; Student Interns; Special Technical Talent; Theatre Companies; Touring Companies
Founded: 1984
Opened: 1926
Status: Nonprofit
Paid Staff: 7

Budget: $300,000-400,000
Income Sources: Grants; Membership; Ticket Sales; Rentals
Annual Attendance: 80,000+
Facility Category: State Theatre
Type of Stage: Prosenium Theatre
Stage Dimensions: 50x29
Seating Capacity: 1,117
Year Built: 1926
Year Remodeled: 1986
Resident Groups: Chippewa Valley Symphony, Chippewa Valley Theatre Guild, Eau Claire Childrens Theatre

5490

UNIVERSITY OF WISCONSIN AT EAU CLAIRE ARTISTS SERIES

University of Wisconsin-Claire
Activities & Programs
Eau Claire, WI 54702-4004
Phone: 715-836-2787
Fax: 715-836-2521
Toll-free: 800-949-8932
e-mail: brockpjl@uwec.edu
Web Site: www.uwec.edu
Management:
 Arts/Events Coordinator: Jennifer Brockpahler
 Arts/Events Coordinator: Beverly Soll
Utilizes: Dancers; Guest Choreographers; Guest Directors; Guest Instructors; Guest Musicians; Guest Soloists; Multimedia; Original Music Scores; Sign Language Translators; Special Technical Talent; Theatre Companies
Founded: 1967
Specialized Field: Series & Festivals; Instrumental Music; Vocal Music; Theatre; Dance; Ethnic Performances
Status: Non-Profit, Professional
Paid Staff: 5
Budget: $60,000-150,000
Performs At: Zorn Arena; Gantner Concert Hall
Annual Attendance: varies
Facility Category: varies

5491

PENINSULA MUSIC FESTIVAL

3045 Cedar Street
PO Box 340
Ephraim, WI 54211
Phone: 920-854-4060
Fax: 920-854-1950
e-mail: musicfestival@musicfestival.com
Web Site: www.musicfestival.com
Officers:
 President: Bruce McKeefry
 Executive Director: Sharon Grutzmacher
Management:
 Music Director/Conductor: Victor Yampolsky
 Associate Conductor: Stephen Alltop
Mission: To perform quality music in a casual atmosphere and promote young, new artists.
Utilizes: Singers
Founded: 1953
Specialized Field: Series & Festivals; Instrumental Music; Festivals
Status: Non-Profit, Professional
Paid Staff: 3
Volunteer Staff: 115
Paid Artists: 75
Budget: $650,000
Income Sources: Ticket Sales; Contributions; Endowments
Season: August 6 - August 26, 2000
Performs At: Door Community Auditorium

Annual Attendance: 7,000
Facility Category: Concert Hall
Organization Type: Performing; Educational

5492

DOOR COMMUNITY AUDITORIUM SERIES

3926 Highway 42
PO Box 397
Fish Creek, WI 54212
Phone: 920-868-2728
Fax: 920-868-2590
e-mail: boxoffice@dcauditorium.org
Web Site: www.dcauditorium.org
Mission: Door Community Auditorium serves as a center to enrich, entertain and challenge through a balanced combination of performing, visual and literary arts and to provide opportunities for social educational and cultural growth.
Utilizes: Actors; Artists-in-Residence; Choreographers; Collaborating Artists; Collaborations; Dance Companies; Dancers; Educators; Filmmakers; Fine Artists; Five Seasonal Concerts; Grant Writers; Guest Accompanists; Guest Artists; Guest Choreographers; Guest Composers; Guest Designers; Guest Directors; Guest Instructors; Guest Lecturers; Guest Musical Directors; Guest Musicians; Guest Soloists; Guest Teachers; Guest Writers; Guild Activities; Instructors; Local Artists; Local Unknown Artists; Lyricists; Multi Collaborations; Multimedia; Music; New Productions; Organization Contracts; Original Music Scores; Playwrights; Resident Professionals; Sign Language Translators; Singers; Soloists; Theatre Companies; Touring Companies
Founded: 1991
Status: Non-Profit
Paid Staff: 8
Volunteer Staff: 100
Budget: $600,000
Year Built: 1991
Rental Contact: Pete Evans

5493

BROWN COUNTY CIVIC MUSIC ASSOCIATION

PO Box 5243
Green Bay, WI 54115-5243
Phone: 920-338-1801
Fax: 920-338-9702
e-mail: bccivicmusic@gmail.org
Web Site: www.bccivicmusic.org
Officers:
 President: Helen Bintz
 Executive Secretary: R Kilmer
Management:
 Artistic Director: Roger Bintz
Utilizes: Dance Companies; Dancers; Fine Artists; Guest Musical Directors; Multimedia; Original Music Scores; Sign Language Translators; Singers; Theatre Companies
Founded: 1926
Opened: 1927
Specialized Field: Classical Music Series; Instrumental Music; Vocal Music; Dance; Ethnic Performances
Status: Non-Profit, Professional
Paid Staff: 1
Volunteer Staff: 150
Budget: $50,000
Annual Attendance: 3,000
Facility Category: Auditorium
Seating Capacity: 1,522

5494

GREEN LAKE FESTIVAL OF MUSIC
PO Box 569
Green Lake, WI 54941
Phone: 920-748-9398
Fax: 920-748-6918
Toll-free: 800-662-7097
Web Site: www.greenlakefestival.org
Officers:
President: John Chapman
Executive Director: Jeannette Kreston
Administrative Director: Missy Nygaard
Mission: The Green Lake Festival of Music is a non-profit corporation founded for cultural enrichment through the creation, promotion and public performance of the musical arts.
Founded: 1979
Specialized Field: Series & Festivals: Concert Series And Music Workshop
Status: Non-Profit, Professional
Paid Staff: 3
Paid Artists: 20
Organization Type: Performing; Touring; Resident; Educational; Sponsoring

5495

JANESVILLE PERFORMING ARTS CENTER
408 South Main Street
Janesville, WI 53545
Phone: 608-758-0297
Fax: 608-758-2549
Web Site: http://www.janesvillepac.org
Officers:
President: Tobin Ryan
Vice President: Mark Gregory
Treasurer: Lynn Gardinier
Secretary: Lisa Stevens
Management:
Executive Director: Laurel Canan
Technical Director: Michael Stalsberg
Founded: 1932
Specialized Field: Events for Family Audiences
Status: Non-Profit, Professional
Paid Staff: 1
Budget: $20,000-35,000

5496

COUNCIL FOR THE PERFORMING ARTS
100 N Main Street
Suite A
Jefferson, WI 53549-1717
Phone: 920-674-2179
Fax: 920-674-5140
e-mail: info@councilfortheperformingarts.org
Web Site: www.councilfortheperformingarts.org
Management:
Executive Director: Pat Guttenberg
Mission: To provide culturally and socially valuable entertainment and educational opportunities for this area.
Utilizes: Actors; Artists-in-Residence; Choreographers; Dance Companies; Guild Activities; Instructors; Multimedia; Music; Poets; Selected Students; Sign Language Translators; Singers; Soloists; Special Technical Talent; Theatre Companies
Founded: 1977
Specialized Field: Series & Festivals; Instrumental Music; Vocal Music; Theatre; Youth; Dance; Ethnic Performances
Status: Non-Profit, Professional
Paid Staff: 3
Volunteer Staff: 100

Paid Artists: 100
Non-paid Artists: 175
Budget: $250,000
Income Sources: Ticket Sales; Grants; Donations
Affiliations: Arts Midwest
Annual Attendance: 15,000
Facility Category: Auditorium
Type of Stage: Proscenium
Stage Dimensions: 66'x44'
Seating Capacity: 996
Year Built: 1977
Organization Type: Performing; Educational

5497

CARTHAGE CHAMBER MUSIC SERIES
2001 Alford Drive
Kenosha, WI 53140-1994
Phone: 262-551-8500
Fax: 262-551-6208
Toll-free: 800-351-3058
e-mail: sjoerd1@carthage.edu
Web Site: www.carthage.edu
Officers:
Chairman Music Department: Dr. RD Sjoerdsma
Founded: 1999
Specialized Field: Series & Festivals: Music Performance & Education
Status: Non-Profit, Professional
Budget: $20,000-35,000
Performs At: Siebert Chapel

5498

CARTHAGE COLLEGE CHAMBER MUSIC & LECTURE SERIES
2001 Alford Park Drive
Kenosha, WI 53140
Phone: 262-551-8500
Web Site: www.carthage.edu
Management:
Chair, Music Department: Peter Dennee
Specialized Field: Chamber music, various lectures

5499

DISTINGUISHED GUEST SERIES
Kohler Foundation
725X Woodlake Road
Kohler, WI 53044-1334
Phone: 920-458-1972
Fax: 920-458-4280
e-mail: larry.thomas@kohler.com
Web Site: www.kohlerfdn.org
Management:
Executive Director: Terri Yorto
Admin Coordinator: Larry Thomas
Accountant: Wanda Bintzler
Paid Staff: 5
Volunteer Staff: 44
Budget: $60,000-150,000
Annual Attendance: 4,000
Facility Category: High School Theatre
Type of Stage: Wood
Stage Dimensions: 37'x30'x30'
Seating Capacity: 1,100

5500

KOHLER FOUNDATION
725X Woodlake Road
Kohler, WI 53044
Phone: 920-458-1972
Fax: 920-458-4280
e-mail: nancy.luczak@kohler.com
Web Site: www.kohlerfoundation.org
Management:
President: Ruth Kohler

Executive Director: Terri Yoho
Office Manager: Nancy Luczak
Mission: To provide cultural opportunities for the benefit of the community.
Founded: 1940
Specialized Field: Series & Festivals; Art Conservation; Dance; Vocal Music; Instrumental Music; Theatre
Status: Non-Profit, Professional
Paid Staff: 6
Income Sources: Ticket Sales
Performs At: Kohler Memorial Theater
Annual Attendance: 4,000
Type of Stage: Wood Sprung Floor
Year Built: 1968
Organization Type: Performing

5501

GREAT RIVER FESTIVAL OF ARTS
PO Box 1434
La Crosse, WI 54602-1434
Phone: 608-784-3033
e-mail: grff@juno.com
Management:
Administrator: Kathy Fitchuk
Founded: 1959
Specialized Field: Education and Cultural Events
Status: Non-Profit, Professional
Paid Staff: 1
Paid Artists: 20

5502

GREAT RIVER JAZZ FEST
1311 Badger Street #609
La Crosse, WI 54601
Phone: 608-784-7575
e-mail: jazznowt@gmail.com
Web Site: www.lacrossejazz.com
Management:
Director: Terry Rochester, jazznowt@gmail.com
Status: Non-Profit

5503

PUMP HOUSE REGIONAL ARTS
119 King Street
La Crosse, WI 54601
Phone: 608-785-1434
Fax: 608-785-1432
Web Site: www.thepumphouse.org
Officers:
President: Donald Smith
Management:
Executive Director: Toni Asher
Artistic Director: Marti Schwem
Utilizes: Educators; Fine Artists; Five Seasonal Concerts; Guest Accompanists; Guest Musical Directors; Guest Musicians; High School Drama; Instructors; Local Artists; Multimedia; New Productions; Special Technical Talent; Touring Companies
Founded: 1977
Specialized Field: Series & Festivals; Instrumental Music; Vocal Music; Theatre; Youth; Dance; Ethnic Performances
Status: Non-Profit, Professional
Paid Staff: 4
Volunteer Staff: 3
Non-paid Artists: 350
Budget: $98,000
Performs At: Dayton Gallery
Annual Attendance: 12,000
Facility Category: Arts Center
Seating Capacity: 130
Year Built: 1880
Rental Contact: Jodi Bente

5504
UNIVERSITY OF WISCONSIN AT LA CROSSE LECTURES
212 Cartwright Center
La Crosse, WI 54601
Phone: 608-785-8866
Fax: 608-785-6575
e-mail: richter.jara@uwlax.edu
Web Site:
www.uwlax.edu/StuServ/SAC/LandC/index.html
Management:
Program Adviser: Jaralee Richter
Budget: $20,000-35,000

5505
VITERBO UNIVERSITY BRIGHT STAR SEASON
900 Viterbo Drive
La Crosse, WI 54601
Phone: 608-796-3737
Fax: 608-796-3736
Web Site: www.viterbo.edu/fac
Management:
Artistic Director: Michael Ranscht
Utilizes: Artists-in-Residence; Dance Companies; Dancers; Designers; Five Seasonal Concerts; Guest Artists; Guest Conductors; Guest Instructors; Guest Soloists; Local Artists; Multimedia; Music; Resident Professionals; Singers; Soloists; Special Technical Talent; Theatre Companies
Founded: 1890
Specialized Field: Series & Festivals; Instrumental Music; Vocal Music; Theatre; Youth; Dance; Ethnic Performances; General Education
Status: Non-Profit, Professional
Paid Staff: 250
Budget: $200,000 - 250,000
Performs At: Fine Arts Center
Annual Attendance: 65,000
Facility Category: Multi-Disciplinary Arts Center
Type of Stage: Proscenium
Stage Dimensions: 40x30
Seating Capacity: 1,090
Year Built: 1971
Rental Contact: Michael Ranscht

5506
FLAMBEAU VALLEY ARTS ASSOCIATION
PO Box 343
Ladysmith, WI 54848
Phone: 715-532-5594
Web Site: www.flambeauvalley.com
Officers:
President: Charmaine Johnson
Management:
President: Karen Ek
Vice President: Margaret Foss
Treasurer: Kevin Smith
Mission: To present a season of 6-7 performing arts events to public audiences in their rural county.
Utilizes: Dance Companies; Multimedia; Original Music Scores; Sign Language Translators; Special Technical Talent; Theatre Companies
Founded: 1971
Specialized Field: Performing Arts; Dance, Instrumental Music, Vocal Music
Status: Nonprofit
Volunteer Staff: 3
Budget: $10,000-20,000
Income Sources: Admissions; Wisconsin Arts Board, Performing Arts Fund of Arts Midwest, General Mills Foundation, Land O'Lakes Foundation

Performs At: High School Auditorium
Annual Attendance: 1600-2800
Type of Stage: Multipurpose auditorium w/fly space
Stage Dimensions: 60'x40'
Seating Capacity: 450
Year Built: 1968

5507
CAPITAL CITY JAZZ FEST
PO Box 8866
Madison, WI 53708
Phone: 608-850-5400
Fax: 608-850-5401
e-mail: marsch@chorus.net
Web Site: www.madisonjazz.com
Management:
President: Linda Marty Schmitz
Founded: 1984
Specialized Field: Series and Festivals: Jazz Music
Status: Non-Profit, Non-Professional

5508
MADISON BLUES FESTIVAL
PO Box 5363
Madison, WI 53705
Phone: 608-836-0020
Fax: 608-836-8555
Web Site: www.madisonblues.com

5509
SILVER LAKE COLLEGE GUEST ARTIST SERIES
2406 S Alverno Road
Manitowoc, WI 54220
Phone: 920-684-6691
Fax: 920-684-7082
Toll-free: 800-236-4752
e-mail: wmaster@silver.sl.edu
Web Site: www.sl.edu
Officers:
Music Department Chairperson: Sr. Marella Wagner
Mission: Outreach program bringing quality music performance to the community
Founded: 1935
Specialized Field: Instrumental music; Vocal Music; Piana; Mixed Ensemble
Paid Artists: 5
Budget: $6,000
Income Sources: College Sponsorship & Ticket Sales
Performs At: Silver Lake College Chapel
Annual Attendance: 100-125
Seating Capacity: 250

5510
UNIVERSITY OF WISCONSIN LECTURES AND FINE ARTS
2000 W 5th Street
PO Box 150
Marshfield, WI 54449
Phone: 715-389-6500
Fax: 715-389-6517
Web Site: www.marshfield.uwc.edu
Management:
Dean: Andy Keogh
Music Professor: Robert I Biederwolf
Drama Director: Greg Rindfleisch
Mission: Provide performances and lectures for the University and the community.
Founded: 1962
Specialized Field: Series and Festivals; Vocal Music; Theatre; Youth; Dance; Ethnic Performances
Status: Non-Profit, Professional

Paid Staff: 50
Paid Artists: 10
Performs At: University of Wisconsin Marshfield/Wodd County Theater
Type of Stage: Black Box
Organization Type: Educational; Sponsoring

5511
UNIVERSITY OF WISCONSIN CENTER - FOX VALLEY
1478 Midway Road
Menasha, WI 54952-1297
Phone: 920-832-2671
Fax: 920-832-2674
e-mail: jkuepper@uwc.edu
Management:
Student Activities Director: Jeff Kuepper
Founded: 1972
Specialized Field: Series & Festivals; Instrumental Music; Vocal Music; Theatre; Dance; Ethnic Performances
Status: Non-Profit, Non-Professional
Budget: $10,000-20,000
Performs At: Fine Arts Theatre
Organization Type: Performing; Educational

5512
CONCORDIA UNIVERSITY WISCONSIN
12800 N Lake Shore Drive
Mequon, WI 53097
Phone: 262-243-5700
Fax: 262-243-4351
e-mail: admissions@cuw.edu
Web Site: www.cuw.edu
Officers:
Music Department Chairperson: Louis A Menchaca
President: Patrick Ferry
Utilizes: Fine Artists
Specialized Field: Series & Festivals; Instrumental Music; Vocal Music; Theatre; Youth; Dance; Ethnic Performances
Status: Non-Profit, Non-Professional
Budget: $10,000
Performs At: Chapel of Christ Triumphant

5513
MERRILL AREA CONCERT ASSOCIATION
1201 N. Sales St
Merrill, WI 54452
Phone: 715-536-3740
Management:
Manager: Chad P Premeau
Contact: Meagan Cihlar
Specialized Field: Instrumental Music; Performing Arts, Vocal Music
Budget: $20,000-35,000

5514
ALVERNO COLLEGE
3400 South 43rd Street
PO Box 343922
Milwaukee, WI 53234-3922
Phone: 414-382-6000
Fax: 414-382-6354
Toll-free: 800-933-3401
e-mail: webinfo@alverno.edu
Web Site: www.alverno.edu
Management:
President: Mary Meehan Ph D

Mission: Alverno Presents, the performing arts series of Alverno College has presented the finest artists of all disciplines since 1960. Emphasis is on contemporary dance and world music. Artists perform in one of three theatre spaces or various locations throughout Milwaukee. Mission is to engage our community in stimulating arts experiences with both established and emerging artists from a variety of perspectives and cultural backgrounds.
Utilizes: Actors; Artists-in-Residence; Collaborating Artists; Collaborations; Dance Companies; Dancers; Educators; Fine Artists; Local Artists; Lyricists; Multimedia; Original Music Scores; Playwrights; Special Technical Talent; Theatre Companies
Founded: 1887
Specialized Field: Presenter
Paid Staff: 3
Annual Attendance: 5000
Facility Category: Performing Arts Venue
Type of Stage: Proscenium
Stage Dimensions: 40'x30'
Seating Capacity: 930
Year Built: 1951
Rental Contact: Jan Kellogg

5515
ARTIST SERIES AT THE PABST

700 N Water Street
Suite 700
Milwaukee, WI 53202
Phone: 414-291-6010
Fax: 414-291-7605
Toll-free: 800-291-7605
e-mail: info@milwaukeesymphony.org
Web Site: www.milwaukeesymphony.org
Officers:
Chairman: Stephen E Richman
Immediate Past-Chairman: Stanton J Bluestone
Treasurer/Secretary: Robert A Wermuth
President/Executive Director: Steven A. Ovitsky
Management:
Chairman: Judy Jorgensen
Executive Director: Mark Hanson
Founded: 1959
Specialized Field: Symphony; Orchestra
Status: Professional; Nonprofit
Performs At: Performing Arts Center; Uihlein Hall
Organization Type: Performing; Touring; Educational; Recording

5516
BRADLEY CENTER

1001 N 4th Street
Milwaukee, WI 53203-1314
Phone: 414-227-0400
Fax: 414-227-0497
Web Site: www.bradleycenter.com
Management:
General Manager: David L Skiles
Assistant General Manager: Steve Costello
Seating Capacity: 20,000
Year Built: 1988

5517
CARDINAL STRITCH UNIVERSITY SCHOOL OF VISUAL AND PERFORMING ARTS

6801 N Yates Road
Milwaukee, WI 53217-3965
Phone: 414-410-4100
Fax: 414-410-4111
Web Site: www.stritch.edu
Officers:

Music Department Chairman: Dr. Dennis King
Chairman Art Department: Tim Abler
Chairman Theatre Arts Department: David Oswald
Utilizes: Actors; Educators; Fine Artists; Guest Composers; Guest Musical Directors; Guest Soloists; Instructors; Local Artists; Multimedia; New Productions; Organization Contracts; Playwrights; Sign Language Translators; Singers; Soloists; Special Technical Talent; Touring Companies
Specialized Field: Art; Music; Theatre; Dance; Film; Photography
Facility Category: Art Gallery
Type of Stage: Proscenium Arch
Seating Capacity: 400
Year Built: 1997
Comments: Theatre is air conditioned, handicapped accessible, infra-red hearing enhanced.

5518
EARLY MUSIC NOW

759 N Milwaukee Street
Suite 420
Milwaukee, WI 53202-1810
Phone: 414-225-3113
Fax: 414-225-3787
e-mail: info@earlymusic.org
Web Site: www.earlymusicnow.org
Officers:
President: Janet Ahrens
Management:
Executive & Artistic Director: Charles Q Sullivan
Utilizes: Guest Directors; Guest Instructors; Guest Soloists; Multimedia; Original Music Scores
Founded: 1986
Specialized Field: Series & Festivals: Vocal And Instrumental-Renaissance
Status: Non-Profit, Professional
Paid Staff: 3
Budget: $225,000
Income Sources: Ticket sales; donations; grants
Annual Attendance: 2,000-3,000
Facility Category: Various halls and churches
Seating Capacity: 300-1,000

5519
MILWAUKEE SYMPHONY ORCHESTRA

700 N Water Street
Suite 700
Milwaukee, WI 53202
Phone: 414-291-6010
Fax: 414-291-7610
Toll-free: 800-291-7605
e-mail: info@mso.org
Web Site: www.mso.org
Officers:
VP Marketing & Communications: Susan Loris
Chairman Of The Board: Chris Abele
Director Of Public Relations: Erin Kogler
Human Resources Manager: Mary Novak
Management:
Orchestra Personnel Manager: Linda Unkefer
Founded: 1959
Specialized Field: Symphony; Orchestra
Status: Professional; Nonprofit
Income Sources: Ticket Sales; Fees For Services; United Performing Arts Fund; Wisconsin Arts Board; Milwaukee County CAMPAC; Corporate And Individual Giving
Performs At: Marcus Center for The Performing Arts; Uihlein Hall
Organization Type: Performing; Touring; Educational; Recording

5520
WISCONSIN CONSERVATORY OF MUSIC

1584 N Prospect Avenue
Milwaukee, WI 53202
Phone: 414-276-5760
Fax: 414-276-6076
e-mail: info@wcmusic.org
Web Site: www.wcmusic.org
Officers:
President: Karen Deschere
Management:
President: Karen Deschere
Mission: Music education and performance opportunities.
Founded: 1899
Specialized Field: Music Education
Status: Non-Profit, Professional
Paid Staff: 16
Volunteer Staff: 50
Paid Artists: 100
Budget: $2,400,000
Performs At: Recital Hall
Affiliations: NASM; NGCSA
Annual Attendance: 5,000
Seating Capacity: 115
Year Built: 1903

5521
LAKELAND PERFORMING ARTS ASSOCIATION

PO Box 1279
Minocqua, WI 54548
Phone: 715-356-5550
Web Site: http://www.lakelandperformingarts.org/
Officers:
President: Jack Erwin
Management:
President: Ginny Andrus
Specialized Field: Vocal Music; Instrumental Music; Festivals; Lyric Opera
Budget: $10,000

5522
UNIVERSITY OF WISCONSIN AT OSHKOSH CHAMBER ARTS SERIES

Music Department N105
N105 A-C
Oshkosh, WI 54901
Phone: 920-424-4224
Fax: 920-424-1266
Web Site: www.uwosh.edu/music
Management:
President: Beverly Hassel
Mission: To offer the highest quality series of four professional classical music performances each season.
Founded: 1967
Specialized Field: Series & Festivals; Instrumental Music; Vocal Music; Music Education
Status: Non-Profit, Professional
Volunteer Staff: 10
Budget: $20,000-35,000
Income Sources: Student Allocations and Box Office
Affiliations: University of Wisconsin-Oshkosh
Annual Attendance: 2,000
Facility Category: University Recital Hall
Type of Stage: Open
Stage Dimensions: 43'x 23'
Seating Capacity: 500
Year Built: 1970

5523

UNIVERSITY OF WISCONSIN-PLATTEVILLE

Center for the Arts
Platteville, WI 53818
Phone: 608-342-1267
Fax: 608-342-1737
Web Site: www.uwplatt.edu/ARTS/cfa
Management:
Director: John Hassig
Box Office Manager: Tianna Conway
Founded: 1983
Specialized Field: Series & Festival: Instumental Music
Status: Non-Profit, Professional
Paid Staff: 30
Paid Artists: 75

5524

UNIVERSITY OF WISCONSIN-PLATTEVILLE PERFORMING ARTS

Center for the Arts
Platteville, WI 53818
Phone: 608-342-1480
Fax: 608-342-1478
Management:
Business Manager for the Arts: Kris Swanson
Budget: $35,000-60,000
Performs At: Center for the Arts-Concert Hall

5525

PRAIRIE PERFORMING ARTS CENTER

4050 Lighthouse Drive
Racine, WI 53402
Phone: 262-260-3845
Fax: 262-260-3790
Web Site: www.prairieschool.com
Management:
President: Mark Murphy
Founded: 1965
Budget: $10,000

5526

NORTHWOODS CONCERT ASSOCIATION

1960 Larsen Director
Rhinelander, WI 54501
Phone: 715-362-4912
Officers:
President: Meredith Pirazzini
Budget: $20,000-35,000

5527

RIPON COLLEGE: CAESTECKER FINE ARTS SERIES

300 Seward Street
PO Box 248
Ripon, WI 54971
Phone: 920-748-8164
Fax: 920-748-7243
Web Site: www.ripon.edu
Officers:
President: David Joyce
Mission: To present four to five performing and visual artists, representing diverse backgrounds and arts areas each season for the college and surrounding Ripon community.
Founded: 1800
Specialized Field: Series & Festivals; Dance; Vocal Music; Instrumental Music; Theatre
Status: Non-Profit, Non-Professional
Performs At: Benstead Theater; Demmer Recital Hall
Organization Type: Sponsoring

5528

UNIVERSITY OF WISCONSIN RIVER FALLS: WYMAN CONCERTS & LECTURES SERIES

River Falls 410 S 3rd Street
River Falls, WI 54022
Phone: 715-425-4911
Fax: 715-425-3296
e-mail: kaye.e.schendel@uwrf.edu
Web Site: www.uwrf.edu
Management:
Assistant Director Of Leadership: Kaye Schendel
Assistant Director of Leadership: Vicky Hajewski
Specialized Field: Series & Festivals: Variety
Status: Non-Profit
Paid Staff: 1

5529

JOHN MICHAEL KOHLER ARTS CENTER: FOOTLIGHTS

608 New York Avenue
Sheboygan, WI 53081
Phone: 920-458-6144
Fax: 920-458-4473
e-mail: jzufeltbarnes@jmkac.org
Web Site: www.jmkac.org
Management:
Executive Director: Ruth DeYoung Kohler
Specialized Field: Visual and Performing Arts
Status: Non-Profit, Professional
Paid Staff: 30
Budget: $35,000-60,000

5530

LAKELAND COLLEGE KRUEGER FINE ARTS SERIES

Lakeland College
PO Box 359
Sheboygan, WI 53082-0359
Phone: 920-565-1000
Fax: 920-565-1206
Toll-free: 800-569-2166
Web Site: www.lakeland.edu
Officers:
Fine Arts Series Co-Chair: Dr. Michael Gill
Fine Arts Series Co-Chair: Dr. JC Crawford
Management:
President: Steven Gould
Artistic Director: Bill Weidner
Kraeger Fine Arts Coordinator: Debra Fale
Founded: 1846
Specialized Field: Liberal Arts College.
Status: For-Profit, Non-Professional
Paid Staff: 100
Volunteer Staff: 4
Paid Artists: 5
Budget: $20,000-35,000
Performs At: Bradley Building
Seating Capacity: 495

5531

SHELL LAKE ARTS CENTER

802 1st Street
Shell Lake, WI 54871
Phone: 715-468-2414
Fax: 715-468-4570
e-mail: info@shelllakeartscenter.org
Web Site: www.shelllakeartscenter.org
Officers:
President of Board: William Taubman
VP: Jeanne Chamberlain
Management:

Director: Jill Johnson
Assistant Director: Tara Heckel
Mission: To provide creative arts education and enrichment experiences for diverse populations of youth and adult learners.
Founded: 1968
Specialized Field: Instrumental & Chorus Music; Visual Arts; Arts Education
Paid Staff: 4
Volunteer Staff: 104
Paid Artists: 60

5532

LUCIUS WOODS PERFORMING ARTS CENTER: MUSIC IN THE PARK

PO Box 295
Solon Springs, WI 54873
Phone: 715-378-4272
e-mail: luciuswoods@lwmusic.org
Web Site: www.lwmusic.org
Management:
Executive Director: Pat Pluntz
Founded: 1994
Specialized Field: Musical Arts Presenter
Status: Non-Profit, Professional
Paid Staff: 1
Paid Artists: 300

5533

UNIVERSITY OF WISCONSIN AT STEVENS POINT PERFORMING ARTS

Quandt Fieldhouse
Stevens Point, WI 54481
Phone: 715-346-3265
Fax: 715-346-4655
e-mail: cseefeld@uwsp.edu
Web Site: www.uwsp.edu
Management:
Manager: Chris Seefeldt
Founded: 1934
Specialized Field: Series & Festivals; Instrumental Music; Vocal Music; Theater; Youth; Dance; Ethnic Performances
Status: Non-Profit, Professional
Paid Staff: 2
Budget: $35,000-60,000
Performs At: Michelsen Concert Hall; Sentry Theatre

5534

UNIVERSITY OF WISCONSIN: SUPERIOR UNIVERSITY

1800 Grand Avenue
Superior, WI 54880-2898
Phone: 715-394-8115
Fax: 715-394-8454
Web Site: www.uwsuper.edu
Management:
Chairman: D Greg Kehl Morre
Founded: 1893
Specialized Field: Series and Festivals; Instrumental Music; Vocal Music; Theatre; Youth; Dance; Ethnic Performances
Status: Non-Profit, Non-Professional
Paid Staff: 1
Paid Artists: 26
Budget: $10,000

5535

WAUPACA FINE ARTS FESTIVAL

Box 55
Waupacu, WI 54981
Phone: 715-842-1676
Fax: 715-848-4314

Officers:
Chairman: Gerald Knoepfel
Co-Chairman: Charles Spanhauer
Treasurer: Blanche Fanik
Mission: Encouragement of active participation of musicians, artists and listeners/viewers of all the fine arts.
Founded: 1962
Specialized Field: Dance; Vocal Music; Instrumental Music; Theater
Status: Nonprofit
Paid Staff: 300
Income Sources: Wisconsin Art Council
Performs At: High School Auditorium
Organization Type: Performing

5536
PERFORMING ARTS FOUNDATION

401 4th Street
Wausau, WI 54403
Phone: 715-842-0988
Fax: 715-842-8715
Toll-free: 888-239-0421
e-mail: joconnell@grandtheater.org
Web Site: www.grandtheater.org
Management:
Executive Director: Jim O'Connell
Utilizes: Artists-in-Residence; Dance Companies; Educators; Guest Soloists; Instructors; Multimedia; Special Technical Talent; Theatre Companies
Founded: 1972
Specialized Field: Series & Festivals; Instrumental Music; Vocal Music; Theatre; Youth; Dance; Ethnic Performances; Multi-Disciplinary
Status: Non-Profit, Professional
Paid Staff: 15
Volunteer Staff: 200
Paid Artists: 30
Budget: $2,000,000
Income Sources: Ticket Sales; Theater Rental; Annual United Arts Fund Drive
Performs At: Proscenium Theater; Multi-purpose Room
Affiliations: Arts Presenters; Wisconsin Presenter's Network; Art's Wisconsin
Annual Attendance: 100,000+
Facility Category: Performing Arts Center
Type of Stage: Proscenium
Stage Dimensions: 42 x 42
Seating Capacity: 1214
Year Built: 1927
Year Remodeled: 2002
Cost: $13.1 Million
Rental Contact: Merry Little

5537
UNIVERSITY OF WISCONSIN MARATHON COUNTY

518 S 7th Avenue
Wausau, WI 54401
Phone: 715-261-6234
Fax: 715-261-6333
e-mail: jgreenwo@uwc.edu
Management:
Program Coordinator: Jean Greenwood
Utilizes: Artists-in-Residence; Guest Accompanists; Guest Instructors; Guest Soloists; Instructors; Local Artists; Multimedia; Original Music Scores; Playwrights; Sign Language Translators; Singers; Soloists; Special Technical Talent; Theatre Companies; Touring Companies
Paid Staff: 1
Budget: $15,000-25,000
Income Sources: Grants, student fees

Annual Attendance: 2500
Facility Category: Proscenium Stage
Stage Dimensions: 26 x 36
Seating Capacity: 240

5538
UNIVERSITY OF WISCONSIN AT WHITEWATER

Irvin L Young Auditorium
University of Wiscocsin at Whitewater
Whitewater, WI 53190
Phone: 262-472-4444
Fax: 262-472-4400
e-mail: youngaud@mail.uww.edu
Web Site: www.uww.edu
Management:
Program Director: Ken Kohberger
Technical Director: David Nees
Audience Services Manager: Michael Morrissey
Marketing Director: Leslie LaMuro
Mission: Performing arts series for community, on-school-time presentations for school children and academic facility for the university arts students.
Utilizes: Actors; AEA Actors; Artists-in-Residence; Dance Companies; Multimedia; Original Music Scores; Selected Students; Theatre Companies
Founded: 1896
Specialized Field: Series & Festivals; Instrumental Music; Vocal Music; Theatre; Youth; Dance; Ethnic Performances
Status: Non-Profit, Professional
Paid Staff: 6
Volunteer Staff: 200
Paid Artists: 50
Budget: $150,000-400,000
Facility Category: Multi-Purpose Auditorium
Type of Stage: Proscenium
Stage Dimensions: 48'x30'
Seating Capacity: 1,335
Year Built: 1993
Rental Contact: Malinda Hunter

5539
ARTS COUNCIL OF SOUTH WOOD COUNTY

240 Johnson Street
PO Box 818
Wisconsin Rapids, WI 54495-0818
Phone: 715-421-4552
Fax: 715-421-4245
e-mail: swcarts.wctc.net
Management:
Administrator: Mary Beth Rokus
Utilizes: Artists-in-Residence; Dance Companies; Fine Artists; Multimedia; Original Music Scores; Theatre Companies
Founded: 1976
Budget: $10,000-20,000
Performs At: Library Fine Arts Center; Performing Arts Center
Annual Attendance: 10,000
Seating Capacity: 800

Wyoming

5540
ARTCORE

PO Box 874
Casper, WY 82602
Phone: 307-265-1564
Web Site: www.artcorewy.com
Management:

Executive Director: Carolyn Deuel
President: Richard Turner
Vice President: Chuck Wilson
Secretary: Jim Brown
Treasurer: Lorrie Hogan
Specialized Field: Instrumental Music; Vocal Music; Dance; Children's Performances
Volunteer Staff: 1
Budget: $20,000-35,000

5541
WYOMING ARTS COUNCIL

2320 Capitol Avenue
Cheyenne, WY 82002
Phone: 307-777-7742
Fax: 307-777-5499
Web Site: www.wyoarts.com
Officers:
Chairman: Jim Willms
Management:
Director: John G Coe
Literature Manager: Mike Shay
Visual Arts Manager: Liliane Francuz
Visual Arts Manager: Liliane Francuz
Grants Data Manager: Donna French
Fiscal Officer: Justine Morris
Office Manager: Evangeline Bratton
Mission: Promoting performing and literary and visual arts in Wyoming.
Utilizes: Artists-in-Residence; Community Talent; Curators; Guest Accompanists; Guest Musical Directors; Guest Soloists; Guest Teachers; Instructors; Original Music Scores; Playwrights; Selected Students; Students
Founded: 1967
Specialized Field: Dance; Vocal Music; Instrumental Music; Theater; Festivals; Lyric Opera; Grand Opera
Status: Nonprofit
Paid Staff: 10
Income Sources: National Endowment for the Arts; National Association of State Arts Agencies; WESTAF; Americans for the Arts
Organization Type: Educational; Sponsoring

5542
UNIVERSITY OF WYOMING CULTURAL PROGRAMS

Box 3951 University Station
Fine Arts Buiding, Room 113
Laramie, WY 82071
Phone: 307-766-5139
Fax: 307-766-2560
Web Site:
www.uwadmnweb.uwyo.edu/culturalprograms
Management:
President: Cedric Reverand
Managing Director: Wendy Fanning
Administrative Assistant: Janelle A Fletcher-Kilmer
Utilizes: Actors; Artists-in-Residence; Dance Companies; Dancers; Fine Artists; Guest Accompanists; Guest Choreographers; Guest Composers; Guest Designers; Guest Musical Directors; Guest Musicians; Multimedia; Original Music Scores; Special Technical Talent; Theatre Companies
Founded: 1979
Specialized Field: Series & Festivals; Instrumental Music; Vocal Music; Theatre; Dance
Status: Non-Profit, Professional
Paid Staff: 3
Volunteer Staff: 6
Paid Artists: 25
Budget: $60,000-$150,000
Annual Attendance: 5,000 - 6,000

Facility Category: Concert Hall
Type of Stage: Concert Stage
Seating Capacity: 699
Year Built: 1974
Year Remodeled: 2001

5543
WESTERN ARTS MUSIC FESTIVAL
University of Wyoming Department of Music
PO Box 3037
Laramie, WY 82071
Phone: 307-766-5242
Management:
    Chairman Music Department: Fredrick Gersten
Mission: To offer quality music to audiences during the summer.
Founded: 1972
Specialized Field: Vocal Music; Instrumental Music; Festivals; Lyric Opera
Status: Professional; Nonprofit
Income Sources: Wyoming Council of the Arts
Performs At: The Fine Arts Council Hall; University of Wyoming
Organization Type: Performing; Touring; Resident; Educational

5544
NORTHWEST COLLEGE
Northwest College
231 W 6th Street
Powell, WY 82435
Phone: 307-754-6307
Fax: 307-754-6245
Toll-free: 800-560-4692
e-mail: neil.hansen@northwestcollege.edu
Web Site: www.northwestmusic.org
Management:
    Music Coordinator: Neil Hansen
Budget: $10,000-$20,000

5545
WESTERN WYOMING COLLEGE
PO Box 428
Rock Springs, WY 82902
Phone: 307-382-1729
Fax: 307-382-7665
e-mail: jyoung@wwcc.wy.edu
Web Site: www.wwcc.wy.edu
Officers:
    Chairman Cultural Affairs: Billy Smith
Management:
    President: Tex Boggs
    Executive Director: Jamie Young
Founded: 1989
Specialized Field: Theatre: Musical
Status: Non-Profit, Non-Professional
Paid Staff: 34
Paid Artists: 4
Budget: $20,000-$35,000

5546
GRAND TETON MUSIC FESTIVAL
4015 W Lake Creek Drive #1
Wilson, WY 83014
Phone: 307-733-3050
Fax: 307-739-9043
e-mail: gtmf@gtmf.org
Web Site: www.gtmf.org
Officers:
    President, GTMF Board of Directors: Pamela Rankin
Management:
    Music Director: Donald Runnicles
    Executive Director: Tracy Jacobson

Dir of Artistic Planning/Ops: Liz Kintz
    Director Marketing: Amanda Flosbach
Mission: To establish a resident ensemble of like-minded artists to perform in small ensembles in a superb symphony orchestra; to bring the musical resources of a great metropolis to the Northern Rocky Mountain region for the summer season.
Utilizes: Guest Accompanists; Guest Composers; Guest Directors; Guest Musical Directors; Guest Musicians; Original Music Scores; Singers; Theatre Companies
Founded: 1962
Specialized Field: Music: Classical
Status: Non-Profit, Professional
Paid Staff: 9
Volunteer Staff: 100
Paid Artists: 200
Budget: 1,900,00
Income Sources: Donations; Sales
Performs At: Walk Festival Hall
Affiliations: ASOL; Jackson Hole Chamber of Commerce
Annual Attendance: 50,000
Facility Category: Concert Hall
Stage Dimensions: 60'wx 40'd
Year Built: 1974
Organization Type: Performing; Sponsoring

Alabama

5547
ANNISTON MUSEUM OF NATURAL HISTORY
PO Box 1587
Anniston, AL 36202
Phone: 256-237-6766
Fax: 256-237-6776
e-mail: info@annistonmuseum.org
Web Site: www.annistonmuseum.org
Management:
   Executive Director: Cheryl H Bragg
   Marketing Manager: Margie Conner
   Development Director: Lindie K Brown
Founded: 1929
Status: Non-Profit, Professional
Paid Staff: 30
Budget: $10,000
Annual Attendance: 85,000
Seating Capacity: 175-200

5548
ALABAMA THEATRE
1817 Third Avenue N
Birmingham, AL 35203
Phone: 205-252-2262
Fax: 205-251-3155
e-mail: jhanks6349@aol.com
Web Site: www.alabamatheatre.com
Management:
   General Manager: Cecil Whitmire
Founded: 1927
Seating Capacity: 2,174
Year Built: 1927

5549
ALYS ROBINSON STEPHENS PERFORMING ARTS CENTER
1200 10th Ave S
Birmingham, AL 35294-1261
Mailing Address: ASC, 1530 3rd AVE S,
BIRMINGHAM, AL 35294-1261
Phone: 205-975-9540
Fax: 205-975-2341
Toll-free: 800-975-2787
Web Site: www.alysstephens.org
Officers:
   Chair: James R Nelson
Management:
   Executive Director: Caron Howell Thornton
   Development Director: Lili Anderson
Utilizes: Artists-in-Residence; Dance Companies;
Dancers; Guest Accompanists; Guest Choreographers;
Multimedia; Original Music Scores; Resident Artists;
Sign Language Translators; Singers; Special Technical
Talent; Theatre Companies
Founded: 1996
Status: Non-Profit, Professional
Paid Staff: 23
Seating Capacity: 1,330

5550
B & A WAREHOUSE
1531 First Avenue South
Birmingham, AL 35233
Phone: 205-326-4220
Fax: 205-326-0233
e-mail: info@bawarehouse.com
Web Site: www.bawarehouse.com
Seating Capacity: 2,235

5551
BIRMINGHAM-JEFFERSON CONVENTION COMPLEX ARENA
2100 Richard Arrington Jr Boulevard N
Birmingham, AL 35203
Phone: 205-458-8400
Fax: 205-458-8438
Toll-free: 877-843-2522
e-mail: info@bjcc.org
Web Site: www.bjcc.org
Officers:
   CEO: Jack Fields
Management:
   Sales/Marketing Director: Susette Hunter,
susette.hunter@bjcc.org
Founded: 1970
Paid Staff: 150
Performs At: Concerts; Meetings; Conventions;
Exhibits
Affiliations: ArenaNetwork; IAAM; IEBA; ACAE;
Pollstar; RCMA
Annual Attendance: 413,044
Facility Category: Arena
Type of Stage: Varies
Seating Capacity: 18,000
Year Built: 1973
Year Remodeled: 2009
Rental Contact: Contract Specialist/Administrator Tara
Roseberry

5552
BIRMINGHAM-SOUTHERN COLLEGE THEATRE
Birmingham Southern College
900 Arkadelphia Road
PO Box 549026
Birmingham, AL 35254
Phone: 205-226-4600
Fax: 205-226-3044
Toll-free: 800-523-5793
e-mail: admission@bsc.edu
Web Site: www.bsc.edu
Officers:
   Chair: Michael Flowers
Management:
   Director: Ruth S Henry
   Artistic Director: Mira Popovich

5553
COLLEGE THEATRE
Birmingham Southern College
900 Arkadelphia Road
PO Box 549026
Birmingham, AL 35254
Phone: 205-226-4600
Fax: 205-226-3044
Toll-free: 800-523-5793
e-mail: admission@bsc.edu
Web Site: www.bsc.edu
Officers:
   Chair: Michael Flowers
Management:
   Director: Ruth S Henry
   Artistic Director: Mira Popovich
Type of Stage: Split-Revolve-Lift Stage

5554
HARRISON THEATRE
Samford University
800 Lakeshore Drive
Birmingham, AL 35229

Mailing Address: 800 Lakeshore Drive, Birmingham,
Alabama 35229
Phone: 205-726-2853
e-mail: wanunnel@samford.edu
Web Site: www.samford.edu
Officers:
   Chair: Dr Don Sandley
Management:
   Theatre Director: Dr Don Sandley
   Director of media and public relati: William
Nunnelley
Opened: 1976
Specialized Field: Dance; Theatre
Type of Stage: Proscenium Thrust
Seating Capacity: 288

5555
LEGION FIELD STADIUM
400 Graymont Avenue W
Birmingham, AL 35204
Phone: 208-254-2848
Web Site:
www.informationbirmingham.com/press/legion75.jsp
Management:
   Director: Melvin Miller
   Stadium Manager: Walter Garrett
Founded: 1926
Status: Non-Profit, Professional
Paid Staff: 12
Seating Capacity: 80,673
Year Built: 1927
Year Remodeled: 1991

5556
SLOSS FURNACES NATIONAL HISTORIC THEATER
McMillan Associates
1923 3rd Avenue N
Suite 900
Birmingham, AL 35203
Phone: 205-324-6881
Fax: 205-323-7074
Web Site: www.mcmillan-associates.com
Officers:
   President: George DH McMillan
Management:
   Executive Director: Denise Lovoy Koch
Seating Capacity: 2,600

5557
THE LESLIE WRIGHT CENTER
Samford University
800 Lakeshore Drive
Birmingham, AL 35229
Phone: 205-726-2462
Fax: 205-726-2243
e-mail: dvhartle@samford.edu
Web Site: www.samford.edu
Management:
   Managing Director: David Hartley
Seating Capacity: 2,640

5558
UAB ARENA
University of Alabama
Bartow Arena
617 13th Street S BRTW 134
Birmingham, AL 35294-1160
Phone: 205-934-7296
Fax: 205-975-8015
e-mail: bartowarena@uab.edu
Web Site: www.vpad.uab.edu
Officers:
   President: Carol Garrison

Management:
Director: Steve Mitchell
Founded: 1987
Status: Non-Profit, Non-Professional
Paid Staff: 5
Paid Artists: 5
Type of Stage: Concert Stage
Seating Capacity: 9,000

5559
PRINCESS THEATRE CENTER FOR THE PERFORMING ARTS

112 2nd Avenue NE
Decatur, AL 35601
Phone: 256-350-1745
Fax: 256-350-1712
e-mail: debbie@princesstheatre.org
Web Site: www.princesstheatre.org
Management:
Executive Director: Lindy Ashwander
Office Manager: Debbie Nieberlein
Founded: 1983
Paid Staff: 5
Volunteer Staff: 250
Budget: $500,000
Affiliations: SAF
Annual Attendance: 60,000
Facility Category: Proscenium
Seating Capacity: 677
Year Built: 1919

5560
WALLACE HALL FINE ARTS CENTER

Gadsden State Community College
Wallace Hall Stage Office
PO Box 227
Gadsden, AL 35902
Phone: 256-549-8475
Fax: 256-549-9637
e-mail: jlongshore@gadsdenstate.edu
Web Site: www.gadsdenstate.edu
Mission: The mission of Wallace Hall Fine Arts Center is to serve as a meeting place for the community to engage in educational opportunities and enhance understanding and enjoyment of life through the creation and presentation of performing and visual arts.
Founded: 1968
Opened: 1968
Stage Dimensions: 40'W, 20'H, 30'D
Seating Capacity: 1,213
Year Built: 1966
Year Head Theatre Renovated: 2000
Cost: $450,000

5561
VON BRAUN CIVIC CENTER PLAYHOUSE

700 Monroe Street
Huntsville, AL 35801
Phone: 256-533-1953
Fax: 256-551-2203
e-mail: vbcinfo@vonbrauncenter.com
Web Site: www.vonbrauncenter.com
Management:
Executive Director: Steve Maples
Operations Director: Ron Grimes
Marketing/Sales: Marie Arighi
Founded: 1965
Income Sources: Private and Corporate Donations, Endowment Fund
Seating Capacity: 8,748

5562
VON BRAUN CIVIC CENTER ARENA

700 Monroe Street
Huntsville, AL 35801
Phone: 256-533-1953
Fax: 256-551-2203
e-mail: vbcinfo@vonbrauncenter.com
Web Site: www.vonbrauncenter.com
Management:
Executive Director: Steve Maples
Operations Director: Ron Grimes
Marketing/Sales: Marie Arighi
Founded: 1965
Seating Capacity: 10,000

5563
VON BRAUN CIVIC CENTER CONCERT HALL

700 Monroe Street
Huntsville, AL 35801
Phone: 256-533-1953
Fax: 256-551-2203
e-mail: vbcinfo@vonbrauncenter.com
Web Site: www.vonbrauncenter.com
Management:
Executive Director: Steve Maples
Operations Director: Ron Grimes
Marketing/Sales: Marie Arighi
Founded: 1965
Seating Capacity: 2,153

5564
VON BRAUN CIVIC CENTER EXHIBIT HALL

700 Monroe Street
Huntsville, AL 35801
Phone: 256-533-1953
Fax: 256-551-2203
e-mail: vbcinfo@vonbrauncenter.com
Web Site: www.vonbrauncenter.com
Management:
Executive Director: Steve Maples
Operations Director: Ron Grimes
Marketing/Sales: Marie Arighi
Founded: 1965

5565
PAUL SNOW MEMORIAL STADIUM

Jackson State University
700 Pelham Road N
Jacksonville, AL 36265
Phone: 256-782-5268
Fax: 256-782-5953
Toll-free: 800-231-5291
e-mail: info@jsu.edu
Web Site: www.jsu.edu
Officers:
President: William Meeham
Management:
Athletic Director: Jim Fuller
Founded: 1883
Status: Non-Profit, Professional
Paid Staff: 50
Seating Capacity: 14,000

5566
PETE MATHEWS COLISEUM

Jacksonville State University
JSU Athletic Dept
700 Pelham Road N
Jacksonville, AL 36265
Phone: 256-782-5268
Fax: 256-782-5953
Toll-free: 800-231-5291
Web Site: www.jsu.edu
Officers:
President: William Meeham
Management:
Athletic Director: Jim Fuller
Seating Capacity: 6,000

5567
ARTHUR R OUTLAW MOBILE CONVENTION CENTER

1 S Water Street
Mobile, AL 36602
Phone: 251-208-2100
Fax: 251-208-2150
e-mail: bbrazier@mobileconventions.com
Web Site: www.mobileconventions.com
Management:
General Manager: Bob Brazier
Marketing Manager: Mary Lee McCrory
Operations Manager: Jake Robinson
Facility Category: Convention Center
Seating Capacity: 6,000

5568
MITCHELL CENTER

University of South Alabama
2195 Mitchell Center
Mobile, AL 366880002
Mailing Address: 5950 Old Shell Road, Mobile, AL 36608
Phone: 251-461-1632
Fax: 251-461-1634
e-mail: vcohen@usouthal.edu
Web Site: www.mitchellcenter.com
Management:
Arena Manager: Victor Cohen
Specialized Field: Sports, Career fairs, youth concerts, adult lectures
Facility Category: Sport Arena
Seating Capacity: 10,000

5569
MOBILE CIVIC CENTER

401 Civic Center Drive
Mobile, AL 36602-0204
Phone: 251-208-7261
Fax: 334-208-7551
e-mail: mlmccrory@mobilecivicctr.com
Web Site: www.mobilecivicctr.com
Management:
General Manager: Jay Hagerman
Operations Director: Joe Delaronde
Marketing Manager: Mary Lee McCrory
Mission: Conceived from the ground up as a venue for major events
Specialized Field: professional hockey and Division I basketball tournaments to rock concerts and monster truck rallies

5570
MOBILE THEATRE GUILD

14 N Lafayette Street
Mobile, AL 36606-2206
Phone: 251-433-7513
e-mail: info@mobiletheatreguild.org
Web Site: www.mobiletheatreguild.org
Officers:
President/Treasurer: Bob Peter
VP: Cookie Baylor
Secretary: Debbie Lake

5571
USA SAENGER THEATRE
6 S Joachim Street
Mobile, AL 36602
Phone: 251-208-5600
Fax: 251-208-5607
Web Site: www.mobilesaenger.com
Management:
Theatre Manager: Chris Penton
Founded: 1927

5572
CHICHESTER BLACK BOX THEATRE
University of Montevallo
College Of Fine Arts
Station 6663
Montevallo, AL 35115
Phone: 205-665-6000
e-mail: shackelc@montevallo.edu
Web Site: www.montevallo.edu
Officers:
President: Phillip C Williams
Management:
Director of Public Relations: Cynthia K
Shackelford
Public Relations Asst: Diane Kennedy
Specialized Field: plays and musicals
Type of Stage: Black Box
Seating Capacity: 50

5573
PALMER THEATRE
University of Montevallo
College of Fine Arts
Station 6663
Montevallo, AL 35115
Phone: 205-665-6000
e-mail: shackelc@montevallo.edu
Web Site: www.montevallo.edu
Officers:
President: Phillip C Williams
Management:
Director of Public Relations: Cynthia K
Shackelford
Public Relations Asst: Diane Kennedy
Specialized Field: musicals and an occasional play
Type of Stage: Balcony Proscenium Auditorium
Orchestra Pit: Y
Seating Capacity: 1200

5574
REYNOLDS STUDIO THEATRE
University of Montevallo
College Of Fine Arts
Station 6663
Montevallo, AL 35115
Phone: 205-665-6000
e-mail: shackelc@montevallo.edu
Web Site: www.montevallo.edu
Officers:
President: Phillip C Williams
Management:
Director of Public Relations: Cynthia K
Shackelford
Public Relations Asst: Diane Kennedy
Specialized Field: main stage shows
Orchestra Pit: Y
Seating Capacity: 160
Year Stage Renovated: 2004

5575
ALABAMA SHAKESPEARE FESTIVAL - FESTIVAL STAGE
1 Festival Drive
Montgomery, AL 36117
Phone: 334-271-5353
Fax: 334-271-5348
Toll-free: 800-841-4ASF
e-mail: mlewis@asf.net
Web Site: www.asf.net
Officers:
COO: Michael Vigilant
Management:
Producing Artistic Director: Geoffrey Sherman
Company Manager: Mary Martha Ford
Marketing Director: Alicia Johnson Reed
Director of Marketing: Meg Lewis
Mission: principal performance space within the
Carolyn Blount Theatre, designed to be used in either
proscenium or thrust-staging mode.
Founded: 1985
Specialized Field: 14 world-class productions annually
Status: Non-Profit, Professional
Annual Attendance: 300,000
Seating Capacity: 750

5576
ALABAMA SHAKESPEARE FESTIVAL - OCTAGON
1 Festival Drive
Montgomery, AL 36117
Phone: 334-271-5353
Fax: 334-271-5348
Toll-free: 800-841-4273
e-mail: mlewis@asf.net
Web Site: www.asf.net
Officers:
COO: Michael Vigilant
Management:
Producing Artistic Director: Geoffrey Sherman
Company Manager: Mary Martha Ford
Marketing Director: Alicia Johnson Reed
Director of Marketing: Meg Lewis
Founded: 1985
Specialized Field: 14 world-class productions annually
Status: Non-Profit, Professional
Annual Attendance: 300,000
Seating Capacity: 225

5577
GARRET COLISEUM
1555 Federal Drive
PO Box 70026
Montgomery, AL 36107
Mailing Address: Agricultural Center Board, Garrett
Coliseum, P.O. Box 70026
Phone: 334-242-5597
Fax: 334-240-3242
e-mail: ed.wesson@garrett.alabama.gov
Web Site: www.garrett.alabama.gov
Officers:
Executive Secretary: Dianne Hall
Management:
Executive Director: William H Johnson III
Assistant Director: Ed Wesson
Mission: family entertainment that includes Rodeos,
Concerts, Social Events, Expositions, Trade Shows,
Sports Events, Horse and Cattle Shows and Sales,
Circuses and Conventions.
Founded: 1951
Status: For-Profit, Professional
Paid Staff: 10

5578
JOE L REED ACADOME
Alabama State University
Carter Hill Road
PO Box 271
Montgomery, AL 36101-0271
Mailing Address: 915 S. Jackson Street, Montgomery,
AL 36104
Phone: 334-229-4529
Fax: 334-229-4988
Web Site: www.alasu.edu
Officers:
Chair: Elton Dean
President: Dr William H Harris
Management:
Director: Gina Jobe-Ishman
Vice President Marketing: Ms. Danielle
Kennedy-Lamar
Mission: physical education instruction, entertainment
activities, conventions, cultural events and
commencement exercises
Seating Capacity: 7,400

5579
TULANE UNIVERSITY NEWCOMB DEPARTMENT OF MUSIC
102 Dixon Hall
New Orleans, AL 70118
Phone: 504-865-5267
Fax: 504-865-5270
e-mail: music@tulane.edu
Web Site: www.tulane.edu/~music
Officers:
Chair: B Michael Howard
Management:
Artisitic Director: B Michael Howard
Office Manager: Kathleen S Crago
Status: Non-Profit, Non-Professional

5580
OZARK CIVIC CENTER
320 E College Street
PO Box 789
Ozark, AL 36361
Mailing Address: 320 East College Street, PO Box
789, Ozark, AL 36361
Phone: 334-774-2618
Toll-free: 877-622-2322
Web Site: www.ozarkalabama.us
Officers:
Chairman: E M Collier
Management:
General Manager: Donald K Hallford
Director: Stanley Enfinger
Divisions Manager/Programs: Denise Ellis
Mission: concerts, circuses, wrestling and boxing
events. We are also available for conventions, expos,
pageants, trade shows, etc.
Founded: 1975
Status: Non-Profit, Non-Professional
Paid Staff: 2
Type of Stage: Concert Stage
Seating Capacity: 4,000

5581
CLAUDIA CROSBY THEATRE
Troy University
University Avenue
Troy, AL 36082
Mailing Address: 132 Malone Hall, Troy University
Phone: 334-670-3714
Fax: 334-670-3609
Web Site: www.troytheatre.org

Officers:
Department Secretary: Jane Barwood
Management:
Theatre Director: Adeena Moree
Marketing Manager: Kaylee Green
Co-Business Manager: Troy Taylor
Co-Business Manager: Jasmine Cottrell
Mission: plays, pageants, ceremonies, and commencement exercises
Type of Stage: Proscenium
Stage Dimensions: 22'H x 43'6W
Seating Capacity: 939

5582
TROJAN/ADAMS CENTER PERFORMING ARTS THEATRE
Troy University
University Avenue
Troy, AL 36082
Mailing Address: 132 Malone Hall, Troy University
Phone: 334-670-3000
Toll-free: 800-551-9716
Web Site: www.troytheatre.org
Officers:
Department Secretary: Jane Barwood
Management:
Theatre Director: Adeena Moree
Marketing Manager: Kaley Green
Co-Business Manager: Troy Taylor
Co-Business Manager: Jasmine Cottrell
Specialized Field: classical, contemporary, drama, comedy, children's theatre, and musical theatre
Type of Stage: Proscenium
Stage Dimensions: 19'H x 30'W
Seating Capacity: 296

5583
ALLEN BALES THEATRE
University of Alabama
Department of Theatre & Dance
Box 870239
Tuscaloosa, AL 35487-0239
Phone: 205-348-5283
Fax: 205-348-9048
e-mail: pmccray@bama.ua.edu
Web Site: www.as.ua.edu/theatre
Officers:
Department Chair: William Teague
Administrative Secretary: Sharon Skipper
Management:
Dance Director: Cornelius Carter
Type of Stage: Black Box
Seating Capacity: 170

5584
BAMA THEATRE PERFORMING ARTS CENTER
Bama Theatre
600 Greensboro Avenue
PO Box 1117
Tuscaloosa, AL 35401
Phone: 205-758-5195
Fax: 205-345-2787
e-mail: director@tuscarts.org
Web Site: www.tuscarts.org
Officers:
President: John Hicks
Executive VP: Rebecca Rothman
Secretary: Valery Minges
Treasurer: Mark Sullivan
Management:
Executive Director: Pamela Penick
Theatre Manager: David Allgood

Founded: 1976
Status: Non-Profit, Non-Professional
Paid Staff: 4
Seating Capacity: 1,094

5585
BRYANT DENNY STADIUM
University of Alabama
Box 870323
Tuscaloosa, AL 35487
Phone: 205-348-3600
Fax: 205-348-2196
e-mail: mmoore@ia.ua.edu
Web Site: www.roll.tide.ua.edu
Officers:
CFO: Finus Gaston
Management:
Athletic Director: Mal Moore
Founded: 1929
Seating Capacity: 92,138

5586
COLEMAN COLISEUM
University of Alabama
Box 870323
Tuscaloosa, AL 35487
Phone: 205-348-3600
Fax: 205-348-2196
e-mail: mmoore@ia.ua.edu
Web Site: www.roll.tide.ua.edu
Officers:
CFO: Finus Gaston
Management:
Athletic Director: Mal Moore
Founded: 1968
Seating Capacity: 15,043

5587
FRANK MOODY MUSIC BUILDING
University of Alabama
PO Box 870366
Tuscaloosa, AL 35487-0366
Phone: 205-348-7110
Fax: 205-348-1473
e-mail: ssnead@music.ua.edu
Web Site: www.music.ua.edu
Management:
Music Director: Charles Snead
Founded: 1987
Seating Capacity: 1,000

5588
GALLAWAY THEATRE
University of Alabama
Department of Theatre & Dance
PO Box 870239
Tuscaloosa, AL 35487-0239
Phone: 205-348-5283
Fax: 205-348-9048
Web Site: www.as.ua.edu
Officers:
Department Chair: William Teague
Administrative Secretary: Sharron Skipper
Management:
Dance Director: Cornelius Carter

5589
HUEY RECITAL HALL
University of Alabama
Frank Moody Music Building
PO Box 870366
Tuscaloosa, AL 35487-0366

Phone: 205-348-7110
Fax: 205-348-1473
e-mail: ssnead@music.ua.edu
Web Site: www.music.ua.edu
Management:
Music Director: Charles Snead
Seating Capacity: 140

5590
MARIAN GALLAWAY THEATRE
The University of Alabama
Department of Theatre & Dance
Box 870239
Tuscaloosa, AL 35487-0239
Phone: 205-348-5283
Fax: 205-348-9048
e-mail: theatre.dance@ua.edu
Web Site: www.theatre.ua.edu
Officers:
Department Chair: William Teague
Administrative Secretary: Sharon Skipper
Management:
Theatre Management Director: Christopher Montpetit
Mission: The mission of the Department of Theatre and Dance is to offer excellent teaching and resultant dynamic learning on the graduate (theatre only) and undergraduate levels of education.
Utilizes: Choreographers; Dancers; Designers; Educators; Guest Instructors; Guest Soloists; High School Drama; Resident Professionals; Soloists
Paid Staff: 25
Facility Category: University Theatre & Dance Space
Type of Stage: Proscenium
Seating Capacity: 305
Year Built: 1954

5591
MORGAN AUDITORIUM
University of Alabama
Department of Theatre & Dance
Box 870239
Tuscaloosa, AL 35487-0239
Phone: 205-348-5283
Fax: 205-348-9048
e-mail: pmccray@bama.ua.edu
Web Site: www.as.ua.edu/theatre
Officers:
Department Chair: William Teague
Management:
Dance Director: Cornelius Carter
Type of Stage: Proscenium
Seating Capacity: 600

5592
CLEVE L ABBOTT MEMORIAL ALUMNI STADIUM
Tuskegee University
321 Chappie James Center Arena
Tuskegee, AL 36088
Phone: 334-727-8150
Fax: 334-727-8202
e-mail: media@tuskegee.edu
Web Site:
www.tuskegee.edu/Global/story.asp?S=1323231
Management:
Interim Athletics Director: Emmett L Taylor
Sports Information Director: Arnold Houston
Faculty Athletic Representative: Luther Williams
Compliance Officer: George Johnson
Athletic Trainer: Rickey Hayes
Founded: 1924
Specialized Field: Sports Facility
Seating Capacity: 10,000

Alaska

5593
ALASKA CENTER FOR THE PERFORMING ARTS
621 W 6th Avenue
Anchorage, AK 99501
Phone: 907-263-2900
Fax: 907-263-2927
e-mail: fdesk@alaskapac.org
Web Site: www.myalaskacenter.com
Officers:
President/COO: Nancy Harbour
VP: Julie Millington
Management:
Development Director: Codie Costello
Founded: 1988
Status: Non-Profit, Non-Professional
Paid Staff: 30
Annual Attendance: 250,000
Type of Stage: Proscenium

5594
GEORGE M SULLIVAN SPORTS ARENA
1600 Gambell Street
Anchorage, AK 99501
Phone: 907-279-0618
Fax: 907-274-0676
Web Site: www.sullivanarena.com
Management:
Region General Manager: Joe Wooden
Operations Director: Ernest Jackson
Marketing Director: Tanya Pont
Mission: designed to be a multi-use facility
Founded: 1983
Opened: 1983
Specialized Field: Olympic-size ice rink for hockey, with an insulated floor covering for basketball, concerts, and trade shows.
Facility Category: Arena
Seating Capacity: 9,000

5595
UAA RECITAL HALL
University of Alaska Anchorage
Department of Theatre & Dance
3211 Providence Drive
Anchorage, AK 99508
Mailing Address: University of Alaska Anchorage, 3211 Providence Drive, Ancho
Phone: 907-786-1792
Fax: 907-786-1799
e-mail: theatre@uaa.alaska.edu
Web Site: http://www.uaa.alaska.edu/
Officers:
Department Chair: Tom T Skore
Management:
Director: David Edgecomb
Director: Tom T Skore
Building Manager: Cedar Cussins
Specialized Field: Music concerts
Type of Stage: Convertible Thrust

5596
WELLS FARGO SPORTS COMPLEX
University of Alaska Anchorage Athletics
3211 Providence Drive
Anchorage, AK 99508
Mailing Address: University of Alaska Anchorage, 3211 Providence Drive, Ancho
Phone: 907-786-1231

Fax: 907—78-6-11
e-mail: athletics@uaa.alaska.edu
Web Site: www.uaa.alaska.edu
Management:
Athletic Director: Steve Cobb
General Manager: Kevin Silver
Mission: exists primarily to enhance the educational athletic experience available on the Anchorage campus
Founded: 1978
Specialized Field: Gym, Swimming Pool, Ice Rink, Fitness Center, Jogging Track and Dance Studio
Status: Non-Profit, Non-Professional
Paid Staff: 40
Seating Capacity: 1,250

5597
ALASKALAND CIVIC CENTER & THEATRE
Parks & Recreation FNSB
PO Box 71267
Fairbanks, AK 99707-1267
Mailing Address: Alaskaland (or Pioneer Park), Parks & Recreation, F.N.S.B.,
Phone: 907-459-1087
Web Site: fairbanks-alaska.com
Mission: theater, art gallery and exhibition room.
Seating Capacity: 384

5598
CHARLES W DAVIS CONCERT HALL
Fairbanks Symphony Association
234 Fine Arts Complex
312 Tanna Drive
Fairbanks, AK 99775
Phone: 907-474-5733
e-mail: symphony@fairbankssymphony.org
Web Site: www.fairbankssymphony.org
Officers:
President: Chuck Lemke
VP: Ed Niewohner
Treasurer: Ted Fathauer
Secretary: Sue Evans
Management:
Executive Director: Laura Berghn
Marketing Director: George Rydlinski
Utilizes: Educators; Multimedia
Founded: 1984
Status: Nonprofit, Professional
Paid Staff: 2
Paid Artists: 23
Stage Dimensions: 30x60
Seating Capacity: 950
Year Built: 1968

5599
CHILKAT CENTER FOR THE ARTS
PO Box 1128
Haines, AK 99827
Phone: 907-766-3573
Fax: 907-766-3574
e-mail: chamber@haineschamber.org
Web Site: haineschamber.org
Management:
Business Manager: Georgia Giacobbe
General Manager: Judy Ereckson
Status: Non-Profit, Professional
Paid Staff: 2
Paid Artists: 20
Type of Stage: Flexible

5600
PIER ONE THEATRE
PO Box 894
Homer, AK 99603

Phone: 907-235-7333
e-mail: lance@xyz.net
Web Site: www.pieronetheatre.org
Officers:
President: Nancy Lander
Vice President: Phil Morin
Treasurer: Julia Clymer
Secretary: Mellisa Nill
Management:
Artistic Director: Lance Petersen

5601
CENTENNIAL HALL CONVENTION CENTER
101 Egan Drive
Juneau, AK 99801
Phone: 907-586-5283
Fax: 907-586-1135
Toll-free: 800-587-2201
e-mail: centennial_hall@ci.juneau.ak.us
Web Site: www.juneau.org/centennial
Management:
Manager: Wendi Marriott
Founded: 1985
Status: For-Profit, Professional
Seating Capacity: 3,106

5602
KODIAK ARTS COUNCIL
PO Box 1792
Kodiak, AK 99615-1792
Phone: 907-486-5291
Fax: 907-486-5591
e-mail: kodiak-arts-council@gci.net
Web Site: www.kodiak.org
Officers:
President: Mike Wall
VP: Mike Pfeffer
Secretary: Ginny Shank
Treasurer: Andrew Ott
Management:
Executive Director: Nancy Kemp
Utilizes: Artists-in-Residence; Collaborating Artists; Dance Companies; Dancers; Educators; Fine Artists; Guest Accompanists; Guest Directors; Guest Instructors; Guest Lecturers; Guest Musical Directors; Guest Musicians; Guest Soloists; High School Drama; Instructors; Local Artists; Lyricists; Multi Collaborations; Multimedia; Music; New Productions; Original Music Scores; Resident Professionals; Selected Students; Sign Language Translators; Singers; Soloists; Theatre Companies; Touring Companies
Founded: 1963
Status: Non-Profit, Professional
Paid Staff: 3
Paid Artists: 100
Budget: $190,000
Income Sources: Grants; membership; ticket sales
Facility Category: Auditorium
Type of Stage: Proscenium
Stage Dimensions: 40'x35'
Seating Capacity: 750
Year Built: 1986
Cost: 10,000,000

5603
HARRIGAN CANTENNO HALL
330 Harbor Drive
Sitka, AK 99835
Phone: 907-747-3225
Fax: 907-747-8495
Web Site: www.cityofsitka.com/dept/cent/index.html
Management:
Building Manager: Don Kouting

Founded: 1967
Status: Non-Profit, Non-Professional
Paid Staff: 5
Seating Capacity: 500

Arizona

5604
CHANDLER CENTER FOR THE ARTS
250 N Arizona Avenue
Chandler, AZ 85225
Phone: 480-782-2683
Fax: 480-782-2684
e-mail: info@chandlercenter.org
Web Site: www.chandlercenter.org
Management:
    Manager: Katrina Mueller
    Development Director: Bill Harrison
    Marketing Coordinator: Judi Johnson
Status: Non-Profit, Professional
Paid Staff: 15
Seating Capacity: 1,550

5605
PAC AUDITORIUM
Chandler-Gilbert Community College
2626 E Pecos Road
Chandler, AZ 85225-2499
Phone: 480-732-7000
Fax: 480-732-7090
e-mail: mary.day@cgcmail.maricopa.edu
Web Site: www.cgc.edu/arts
Officers:
    Administrative Secretary: Iris Ishikawa
Management:
    Director of Research Planning & Dev: Mary Day
Mission: faculty and staff offices, and performance support facilities including costuming and make-up areas, dressing rooms, a full-scale set building shop, storage and classroom space
Founded: 2000
Specialized Field: Vocal and Instrumental Music, Dance, Theater and Musical Theater.
Seating Capacity: 299

5606
RAWHIDE PAVILION & RODEO ARENA
5700 W N Loop Road
Chandler, AZ 85226
Phone: 480-502-5600
Fax: 480-502-1301
Toll-free: 800-527-1880
e-mail: info@rawhide.com
Web Site: www.rawhide.com
Management:
    President: Jerry Hirche
    General Manager: Steve Feld
    Entertainment Director: Rob Jensen
    Director Sales & Marketing: Floy Kennedy
    Operations Manager: Patty Kearney
Founded: 1971
Status: For-Profit, Professional
Paid Staff: 200
Annual Attendance: 960,000
Seating Capacity: 4,500

5607
ARDREY AUDITORIUM
Northern Arizona University
Building 37A
PO Box 6040
Flagstaff, AZ 86011

Mailing Address: College of Arts & Letters, PO Box 5064, Building 15/Room 200
Phone: 928-523-4120
Fax: 928-523-2056
e-mail: Kathleen.Battali@nau.edu
Web Site: www.cal.nau.edu/
http://www.cal.nau.edu/ardrey/
Management:
    Facility Manager: Kathy Battali
    Technical Director: Janice Gary
    Director-Community Relations: Molly Munger
Mission: performing arts auditorium
Seating Capacity: 1400

5608
ASHURST AUDITORIUM
Northern Arizona University
Building 37A
PO Box 6040
Flagstaff, AZ 86011
Mailing Address: College of Arts & Letters, PO Box 5064, Building 15/Room 200
Phone: 928-523-4120
Fax: 928-523-2056
e-mail: Kathleen.Battali@nau.edu
Web Site: www.cal.nau.edu/
http://www.cal.nau.edu/ashurst/
Management:
    Facility Manager: Kathy Battali
    Technical Director: Janice Gary
Mission: recital stage/banquet hall
Founded: 1918
Specialized Field: Musical perfomances
Seating Capacity: 300

5609
CLIFFORD E WHITE THEATRE
Northern Arizona University
Building 37 Room 120
PO Box 6040
Flagstaff, AZ 86011
Mailing Address: Department of Theatre, PO Box 6040, Building 37/Room 120, Fl
Phone: 928-523-3781
Fax: 928-523-5111
e-mail: Theatre@nau.edu
Web Site: www.nau.edu/theatre
Officers:
    Department Chair: Kathleen M McGeever
Management:
    Technical Director/Facility Manager: Ben Grohs
Mission: ""Main Stage"" shows are held.
Founded: 1998
Seating Capacity: 600
Year Remodeled: 1998

5610
COCONINO CENTER FOR THE ARTS
Po Box 296
Flagstaff, AZ 86002
Phone: 928-779-2300
Fax: 928-779-7197
e-mail: jtannous@culturalpartners.org
Web Site: www.culturalpartners.org
Officers:
    President: Ingrid Lee
    VP: Terry Hubbard
    Treasurer: Trevor Ainardi
    Secretary: Marjorie Kamine
Management:
    Executive Director: John Tannous
    Office Manager: Rpbin Cadigan
    Marketing: Colt Fulk
Seating Capacity: 200

5611
J LAWRENCE WALK-UP SKYDOME
Northern Arizona University
PO Box 15096
Flagstaff, AZ 86011
Phone: 928-523-3449
Fax: 928-523-7588
e-mail: dave.brown@nau.edu
Web Site: www.nau.edu
Management:
    Skydome Director: Dave Brown
    Athletic Director: Jim Fallis
    Marketing: Ashley Hammerstrom
Founded: 1977

5612
PROCHNOW AUDITORIUM
Northern Arizona University
Dupont Avenue
Suite 152
Flagstaff, AZ 86011
Mailing Address: University Marketing, PO Box 4101, Flagstaff, Arizona 86011
Phone: 928-523-5638
Fax: 928-523-9219
Web Site: www.nau.edu
Management:
    Operations: Rachel Cole
Mission: University movie theater
Specialized Field: comedians, concerts and weekend movies.
Facility Category: Theatre Hall
Seating Capacity: 900

5613
STUDIO THEATRE
Northern Arizona University
PO Box 6064
Flagstaff, AZ 86011
Mailing Address: Department of Theatre, PO Box 6040, Building 37/Room 120, Fl
Phone: 928-523-3781
Fax: 928-523-5111
Web Site: www.nau.edu
Officers:
    Department Chair: Kathleen M McGeever
Management:
    Technical Director/Facility Manager: Ben Grohs
Mission: ""Second Stage"" shows are held
Founded: 1998
Seating Capacity: 150
Year Built: 1998

5614
GCC PERFORMING ARTS CENTER
Glendale Community College
6000 W Olive Avenue
Glendale, AZ 85302
Mailing Address: Glendale Community College, 6000 W. Olive Ave., Glendale AZ
Phone: 623-845-3720
e-mail: college.advancement@gcmail.maricopa.edu
Web Site: www.gc.maricopa.edu/performingarts
Officers:
    Department Chair: Robert Albury PhD
    Department Secretary: Mickey Myers
Mission: dedicated to producing students capable of succeeding in today's highly competitive professional world

5615
MCC PERFORMING ARTS CENTER
Mohave Community College
1971 Jagerson Avenue
Kingman, AZ 86409
Phone: 928-757-4331
Fax: 928-757-0837
Toll-free: 866-664-2832
Web Site: www.mohave.edu
Management:
   Chancellor: Thomas C Henry Ph D
   President: Michael Ford
   Facilities Director: David Brusby
   Vice Chancellor Student Services: Billy Bates
Founded: 1971

5616
MESA CONVENTION CENTER
263 N Center Street
Mesa, AZ 85201
Phone: 480-644-2178
Fax: 480-644-2617
e-mail: rhett.evans@cityofmesa.org
Web Site: mesaconventioncenter.com
Management:
   Facilities Director: Rhett Evans
   Sales/Marketing Manager: Dyan Dwyer Seaburg
   Operations: Felix Imadiyi
Utilizes: Multimedia
Paid Staff: 23
Facility Category: Amphitheatre
Seating Capacity: 4,200
Year Built: 1978

5617
MESA CONVENTION CENTER-MESA AMPHITHEATRE
263 N Center Street
Mesa, AZ 85201
Phone: 480-644-2178
Fax: 480-644-2617
e-mail: rhett.evans@cityofmesa.org
Web Site: www.mesaconventioncenter.com
Management:
   Director: Rhett Evans
   Sales/Marketing Manager: Dyan Dwyer Seaburg
   Operations: Felix Imadiyi
Founded: 1978
Paid Staff: 80
Type of Stage: Outside Stages
Seating Capacity: 4,200
Rental Contact: Sales Specialist (480) 644-4906
Heather Murray

5618
THEATRE OUTBACK
Mesa Community College
1833 W Southern Avenue
Mesa, AZ 85202
Phone: 480-461-7000
e-mail: dutson@mc.maricopa.edu
Web Site: www.mc.maricopa.edu
Management:
   Theatre Director: Lyn Dutson
   Director: Gary Stephens
Seating Capacity: 250

5619
PEORIA SPORTS COMPLEX
16101 N 83rd Avenue
Peoria, AZ 85382
Phone: 623-773-8700
Fax: 623-412-4255
Toll-free: 800-409-1511
e-mail: sportscomplex@peoriaaz.com
Web Site: www.peoriasportscomplex.com
Management:
   Operations Manager: Chris Easom
   Marketing Supervisor: Melissa Melton
Founded: 1994
Status: Non-Profit, Professional
Paid Staff: 30
Volunteer Staff: 486
Annual Attendance: 450,000
Seating Capacity: 18,000
Year Built: 1994

5620
ARIZONA VETERANS MEMORIAL COLISEUM
1826 W McDowell Street
Phoenix, AZ 85007
Phone: 602-252-6771
Fax: 602-495-1302
e-mail: info@azstatefair.com
Web Site: www.azstatefair.com
Management:
   Executive Director: Don West
Facility Category: Arena
Seating Capacity: 14,500

5621
CELEBRITY THEATRE
440 N 32nd Street
Phoenix, AZ 85008
Phone: 602-267-1600
Fax: 602-267-4882
e-mail: Assistant@celebritytheatre.com
Web Site: www.celebritytheatre.com
Management:
   General Manager: Alycia Klein
Founded: 1963
Type of Stage: Proscenium
Seating Capacity: 2,651
Year Built: 1963
Year Remodeled: 1997
Rental Contact: Reed Glick

5622
CHASE FIELD
401 E Jefferson Street
PO Box 2095
Phoenix, AZ 85001
Mailing Address: 4300 N Miller Rd, Suite 150,
Scottsdale, AZ 85251
Phone: 602-462-6500
Fax: 602-514-8699
Toll-free: 888-777-4664
Web Site: www.dbacks.com,
http://www.azchasefield.com
Officers:
   President: Derrick Hall
   CFO: Tom Harris
Management:
   Business Operations: Tom Grlfinkel
   Senior Marketing Director: Karina Bohn
   Vice President of Stadium Operation: Tom Tygett
Mission: Baseball
Founded: 1998
Specialized Field: Sports Facility
Status: For-Profit, Professional
Paid Staff: 450
Seating Capacity: 49,500
Year Built: 1998

5623
CRICKET PAVILION
2121 North 83rd Avenue
Phoenix, AZ 85035
Phone: 602-254-7200
Fax: 602-254-6060
e-mail: tiffanygreen@livenation.com
Web Site: www.livenation.com
Officers:
   Executive Director: Brandon Sirochman
   Director of Sponsor Sales: Sterling Dortch
   Box Office Manager: Deidra Warstler
   Controller: Tonya Riley
Management:
   Premium Seats Director: Shelby Burdick
   Sponsorship Coordinator: Hollie Robbins
   Asst to the Executive Director: Tiffany Green
   Operations Manager: Billy Royal
Mission: Concert venue
Performs At: Amphitheater
Affiliations: Live Nation
Annual Attendance: 300,000
Facility Category: Amphitheater
Seating Capacity: 20,000
Rental Contact: Brandon Sirochman

5624
DODGE THEATRE
400 West Washington
Phoenix, AZ 85003
Phone: 602-379-2800
Fax: 602-379-2801
Web Site: www.dodgetheatre.com
Officers:
   General Manager: Paige Peterson
   VP Entertainment Services: Ralph Marchetta
   VP Marketing/Advertising: Cathey Moses
   Box Office Manager: Maria Kimaszewski
   Director of Theatre Operations: Maggie Harvey
Management:
   Theatre Events Manager: Bryan White
   Production Manager: Shaun Schultz
Facility Category: Theatre
Type of Stage: Wood
Stage Dimensions: 100x50
Seating Capacity: 5,000
Year Built: 2002
Rental Contact: Ralph Marchetta

5625
ETHINGTON AUDITORIUM
Grand Canyon University
3300 W Camelback Road
Phoenix, AZ 85017-1097
Phone: 602-589-2482
Fax: 602-589-2492
Toll-free: 800-800-9776
Management:
   Chairperson Music Department: Dr. Sheila Corley
   Piano Area Coordinator: Dr. Judy Lively
   Instrumental Area Coordinator: Joe Lloyd
   Choral Activities: Dr. Keith Whitlock
   Director Vocal Activities: Nathan Wight
Budget: $10,000
Seating Capacity: 300
Rental Contact: Nathan Wight

5626
JOBING.COM ARENA
9400 W Maryland
Phoenix, AZ 85303

Phone: 623-772-3200
Fax: 623-772-3201
e-mail: guest.services@jobingarena.com
Web Site: www.jobingarena.com.com
Facility Category: Arena
Seating Capacity: 20,000

5627
LEWIS AUDITORIUM

203 West Adams Street
Phoenix, AZ 85003
Phone: 602-252-9678
Fax: 602-252-1223
Web Site: http://phoenix.gov/STAGES/orpheum.html
Management:
Executive Director: Joan Weil
Director: Robert Allen
Facilities Department Director: Jay Green
Mission: The 1,364-seat Orpheum audience chamber—now known as the Lewis Auditorium, dedicated to Jewell and Delbert Lewis and family—has 1,062 seats on orchestra level, 302 in the balcony.
Founded: 1929
Paid Staff: 3

5628
PHOENIX CONVENTION CENTER - BALLROOMS

100 N 3rd Street
Phoenix, AZ 85004
Phone: 602-262-6225
Fax: 602-495-3642
Toll-free: 800-282-4842
e-mail: jaygreen@phoenix.gov
Web Site: www.phoenix.gov/phxplaza.html
Management:
Director: Jay Green
Marketing Director: Kevin Hill
Event Manager: Caron Bernard
Status: Non-Profit, Non-Professional
Volunteer Staff: 120
Seating Capacity: 8,210

5629
PHOENIX STAGES

203 West Adams Street
Phoenix, AZ 85003
Phone: 602-534-4874
Fax: 602-534-5622
e-mail: jay.green@phoenix.gov
Web Site: http://phoenix.gov/STAGES/orpheum.html
Management:
Director: Jay Green
Assistant Director: Tracey Short
Marketing Director: Kevin Hill
Sales Director: Diane McCullough
Music Director: Hermann Michael
Mission: Division of the city of Phoenix which manages the Lewis Auditorium and Symphony Hall.
Founded: 1996
Status: Non-Profit, Professional
Paid Staff: 50
Volunteer Staff: 500

5630
PVCC CENTER FOR THE PERFORMING ARTS

Paradise Valley Community College
Division Of Fine & Performing Arts
18401 North 32nd Street
Phoenix, AZ 85032
Mailing Address: Center for the Performing Arts, Paradise Valley Community Co
Phone: 602-787-6580
e-mail: Julia.devous@pvmail.maricopa.edu
Web Site: http://www.pvc.maricopa.edu/, http://www.pvc.maricopa.edu/cpa/
Officers:
Division Chair: Christopher Scinto
President: Mary Kay Kickles PhD
Division Secretary: Daral Alonzo
Management:
Director Theatre: Alan Tonget
Director of Development and Communi: Julia Devous
Mission: PAC will now provide a showplace for theater, music, dance, literature, and the visual arts.
Founded: 2005
Specialized Field: music, theater, dance productions and film presentations. In addition, the lobby space serves as an art gallery
Seating Capacity: 300
Architect: Westlake Reed Leskosky
Cost: $7.8 million

5631
SMCC PERFORMING ARTS CENTER

South Mountain Community College
7050 S. 24th Street
Phoenix, AZ 85042
Phone: 602-243-8055
Fax: 602-243-8329
e-mail: julie.holston@smcmail.maricopa.edu
Web Site: www.southmountaincc.edu
Officers:
President: Ken Atwater PhD
Management:
Theatre Faculty: Julie Holston
Mission: SMCC offers a full range of theatre classes to meet your needs, whether you plan to major in theatre at the university level or simply take theatre classes on the side while pursuing another major. Our program offers a wide variety of courses to give you both the broad background you need in theatre, as well as the focused study of your artistic and/or technical skills.
Type of Stage: Auditorium
Seating Capacity: 350

5632
SMCC STUDIO THEATRE

South Mountain Community College
7050 S. 24th Street
Phoenix, AZ 85042
Phone: 602-243-8055
Fax: 602-243-8329
e-mail: julie.holston@smcmail.maricopa.edu
Web Site: www.southmountaincc.edu
Officers:
President: Ken Atwater PhD
Management:
Theatre Faculty: Julie Holston
Mission: SMCC offers a full range of theatre classes to meet your needs, whether you plan to major in theatre at the university level or simply take theatre classes on the side while pursuing another major. Our program offers a wide variety of courses to give you both the broad background you need in theatre, as well as the focused study of your artistic and/or technical skills.
Type of Stage: Black Box
Seating Capacity: 100

5633
PHOENIX CONVENTION CENTER - SYMPHONY HALL

225 East Adams Street
Phoenix, AZ 85004
Phone: 602-534-5600
Fax: 602-495-3608
e-mail: jaygreen@phoenix.gov
Web Site: http://phoenix.gov/STAGES/symphall.html
Management:
Director: Jay Green
Assistant Director: Tracey Scott
Marketing Director: Kevin Hill
Information Officer/Symphony Hall: Sina Matthes
Sales Director: Diane McCullough
Founded: 1972
Seating Capacity: 2,387

5634
U S AIRWAYS CENTER

201 East Jefferson Street
PO Box 433
Phoenix, AZ 85004
Phone: 602-379-2000
Fax: 602-379-2002
Web Site: www.americawestarena.com
Management:
President: Jerry Cooangelo
Executive Director: Paige Peterson
Director Ticket Operations: John Walker
Sales Manager: Chris Montgomery
Founded: 1992
Status: For-Profit, Professional

5635
JOHN PAUL THEATRE

Phoenix College
1202 W. Thomas Road
Phoenix,, AZ 85013
Phone: 602-285-7500
Fax: 602-285-7309
e-mail: geoffrey.eroe@pcmail.maricopa.edu
Web Site: www.pc.maricopa.edu
Officers:
Department Chair: Liz O'Brien
President: Anna Solley EdD
Management:
Coordinator Performing Arts Center: Gary Imel
club advisor: Geof Eroe
Mission: campus club for students interested in theatre. The Phoenix College Theatre & Film Department, one of the oldest and most respected theatre programs in Arizona, offers students the opportunity to earn an undergraduate AA transferable degree with an emphasis in acting, directing, technical work and design.
Type of Stage: Modified Thrust
Seating Capacity: 300

5636
YAVAPAI COLLEGE PERFORMANCE HALL

Yavapai College
1100 East Sheldon
Prescott, AZ 86301
Phone: 520-776-2034
Fax: 520-776-2032
Web Site: www.yavapai.edu
Management:
Community Events Mamager: Debbie McCasland
Mission: To present a broad variety of music, dance and theatre.
Founded: 1976

Paid Staff: 4
Paid Artists: 300
Income Sources: Ticket Sales; Grants
Annual Attendance: 30,000
Facility Category: Theater
Type of Stage: Proscenium; Thurst
Stage Dimensions: 40'x50'
Seating Capacity: 1100
Year Built: 1992
Cost: $6.5 Million
Rental Contact: Garry Charter

5637
SCOTTSDALE CENTER FOR THE PERFORMING ARTS

7380 E 2nd Street
Scottsdale, AZ 85251
Phone: 480-994-2787
Fax: 480-874-4699
e-mail: info@sccarts.org
Web Site: www.scottsdaleperformingarts.org
Management:
VP/Director: Cory Baker
Utilizes: Artists-in-Residence; Dance Companies; Multimedia; Student Interns; Theatre Companies
Founded: 1975
Specialized Field: Performing Arts
Status: Non-Profit, Professional
Paid Staff: 60
Annual Attendance: 300,000
Facility Category: Multi-Disciplinary
Type of Stage: Proscenium/Thrust
Seating Capacity: 853
Year Built: 1975
Year Remodeled: 2009
Rental Contact: Kasey Croxton

5638
SCOTTSDALE COMMUNITY COLLEGE PERFORMING ARTS CENTER

9000 East Chaparral
Scottsdale, AZ 85256-6000
Phone: 480-423-6718
Fax: 480-423-6365
Web Site: www.sc.maricopa.edu/finearts/theatre/
Management:
Theatre Arts Director: Kimb Williamson
Associate Theatre Arts Director: Elaine Moe
Founded: 1970

5639
SEDONA CULTURAL PARK

250 Cultural Park Place
Sedona, AZ 86336
Phone: 928-282-0747
Fax: 928-220-1633
Web Site: www.sedonaculturalpark.org
Officers:
Production Director: Dallas Taylor
Operations Director: Lisa Rhodes
Seating Capacity: 5,000

5640
BUENA PERFORMING ARTS CENTER

1011 N Coronado Drive
Sierra Vista, AZ 85635
Phone: 520-417-6980
Fax: 520-417-6992
e-mail: msneary@ci.sierra-vista.az.us
Web Site: www.ci.sierra-vista.az.us
Management:
Cultural Leisure Supervisor: Megan Sneary
Status: Professional

Budget: $35,000-60,000
Type of Stage: Flexible
Seating Capacity: 1,366

5641
SIERRA VISTA THEATRE HALL

Cochise College
Cochise College
901 North Colombo Avenue
Sierra Vista, AZ 85635-2315
Phone: 520-515-5490
Toll-free: 800-966-7943
e-mail: boydcolin@cochise.edu
Web Site: www.cochise.edu
Management:
Manager: M David Meeker
Cultural/Music Events Coordinator: Carol Rivera
Director Cultural Events: Marc C Bellassai
Creative Services Dir, Marketing/Cr: Colin Boyd
Mission: as a source of personal growth and selfexpression, to fulfill general education requirements for associate's or baccalaureate degrees, to successfully transfer credit to four-year institutions.
Founded: 1961
Specialized Field: music, theater, and visual arts

5642
SUNDOME CENTER

19403 RH Johnson Blvd, Sun City West, AZ, USA
19403 RH Johnson Boulevard
Sun City West, AZ 85375
Phone: 623-584-3118
Fax: 623-584-7947
e-mail: SMOKEY.RENEHAN@asu.edu
Web Site: www.asusundome.com
Management:
Director: M Smokey Renehan
Technical Director: Rob Neyman
Event / Rental Coordinator: Melissa Schwartz
Paid Staff: 35
Volunteer Staff: 250
Paid Artists: 35
Non-paid Artists: 60
Affiliations: Arizona State University; APAP; WAA
Annual Attendance: 300,000
Facility Category: Performing Arts
Type of Stage: Proscenium
Seating Capacity: 7036
Year Built: 1978
Rental Contact: Melissa Schwartz

5643
GALVIN PLAYHOUSE

Arizona State University
Herberger College of Fine Arts
PO Box 872002
Tempe, AZ 85287-2002
Phone: 480-965-5337
Fax: 480-965-5351
e-mail: theatre@asu.edu
Web Site: www.theatre.asu.edu
Management:
Director: Linda Essig
Associate Director: Johnny Saldana
Mission: To educate imaginative, knowledgeable, skilled, and responsible artists, teachers, scholars, audience members, and advocates for the future of theatre and film arts.
Type of Stage: Proscenium
Stage Dimensions: 101' x 52'10
Orchestra Pit: Y
Seating Capacity: 500

5644
GAMMAGE AUDITORIUM

Arizona State University
Corner of Mill Avenue & Apache Boulevard
Tempe, AZ 85287
Phone: 480-965-5062
Fax: 480-965-3583
e-mail: boxoffice@asugammage.com
Web Site: www.asugammage.com/home.shtml
Management:
Executive Director Public Events: Colleen Jennings-Roggensack
Senior Director Operations: Terri Cranmer
Communications Director: Michael Porto
Events Coordinator: Larry Kovac
Public Relations Manager: Dana McGuinness
Founded: 1962
Type of Stage: Concert Stage; Flexible
Seating Capacity: 3,000

5645
LYCEUM THEATRE

Arizona State University
Herberger College of Fine Arts
PO Box 872002
Tempe, AZ 85287-2002
Phone: 480-965-5337
Fax: 480-965-5351
e-mail: theatre@asu.edu
Web Site: www.theatre.asu.edu
Management:
Director: Linda Essig
Associate Director: Johnny Saldana
Mission: To educate imaginative, knowledgeable, skilled, and responsible artists, teachers, scholars, audience members, and advocates for the future of theatre and film arts.
Type of Stage: Proscenium
Seating Capacity: 164
Year Built: 1917

5646
MARQUEE THEATRE

730 North Mill Avenue
Tempe, AZ 85281
Phone: 480-829-0607
Fax: 480-829-1552
e-mail: orion@luckymanonline.com
Web Site: www.marqueetheatre.tickets.musictoday.com, http://www.luckymanonline.com/
Officers:
Owner: Tom LaPenna
GM: Mike Lee
Talent Buyer: Will Anderson
Management:
Box Office Manager/Web: Orion Eckstrom
Specialized Field: Music concerts
Facility Category: Concert Hall
Seating Capacity: 1,001

5647
PRISM THEATRE

Arizona State University
Herberger College of Fine Arts
Cornerstone Performing/Media Arts Bldg.
Tempe, AZ 85287-2002
Phone: 480-965-5337
Fax: 480-965-5351
e-mail: theatre@asu.edu
Web Site: www.theatre.asu.edu
Management:
Director: Linda Essig

Associate Director: Johnny Saldana
Mission: To educate imaginative, knowledgeable, skilled, and responsible artists, teachers, scholars, audience members, and advocates for the future of theatre and film arts.
Type of Stage: Flexible Black Box
Seating Capacity: 74

5648
SUN DEVIL STADIUM
500 East Stadium Drive
PO Box 872405
Tempe, AZ 85287-2505
Phone: 480-965-3482
Fax: 480-965-8154
Toll-free: 888-786-3857
e-mail: athletics.director@asu.edu
Web Site: www.thesundevils.cstv.com
Management:
Vice President University Athletics: Lisa Love
Asst Athletic Director/Operations: Bill Givens
Marketing Manager: Mike Bosewell
Athletics Business Manager: Brian Milhorn
Events Coordintor: Tyrone Figaro
Founded: 1968
Specialized Field: Facility
Seating Capacity: 74,000

5649
FINE ARTS CENTER AUDITORIUM
Eastern Arizona College
615 N. Stadium Avenue
Thatcher, AZ 85552
Mailing Address: Shakespeare, comedy and musicals, as well as contemporary an
Toll-free: 800-678-3808
e-mail: todd.haynie@eac.edu
Web Site: www.eac.edu
Officers:
President: Mark Bryce
Management:
Director, Marketing and PR: Todd Haynie
Theatre Arts Faculty: Rice John
Mission: Eastern Arizona College boasts one of the most active and distinguished Fine Arts programs in Arizona. Opportunities to showcase your talents abound here, and class credits are fully transferable to universities.
Founded: 1972
Specialized Field: Music and in Theatre and Cinematic Arts
Seating Capacity: 960

5650
LEE LITTLE THEATRE
Eastern Arizona College
615 N. Stadium Avenue
Thatcher, AZ 85552
Mailing Address: Shakespeare, comedy and musicals, as well as contemporary an
Toll-free: 800-678-3808
e-mail: todd.haynie@eac.edu
Web Site: www.eac.edu
Officers:
President: Mark Bryce
Mission: Eastern Arizona College boasts one of the most active and distinguished Fine Arts programs in Arizona. Opportunities to showcase your talents abound here, and class credits are fully transferable to universities.
Seating Capacity: 305

5651
NAVAJO DINE COLLEGE PERFORMING ARTS CENTER
One Circle Drive
Route 12
Tsaile, AZ 86556
Phone: 928-724-6609
Fax: 928-724-6613
e-mail: info@dinecollege.edu
Web Site: www.dinecollege.edu/ics/
Management:
President: Serlin Clark
Vice President: Maggie Necefer
Student Programs Director: Walter Jensen
Founded: 1968
Status: Non-Profit, Professional

5652
TUBAC CENTER OF THE ARTS
9 Plaza Road
PO Box 1911
Tubac, AZ 85646
Phone: 520-398-2371
Fax: 520-398-9511
Web Site: www.tubacarts.org
Management:
President: Kim Kruger
Executive Director: Jofie Deflla
Artistic Director: Mary Watson
Volunteer/Membership Coordinator: Karin Topping
Education Coordinator: Edith Zarev
Utilizes: Actors; Collaborations; Commissioned Music; Dance Companies; Educators; Fine Artists; Five Seasonal Concerts; Guest Accompanists; Guest Ensembles; Guest Soloists; Guild Activities; High School Drama; Instructors; Local Artists; Multimedia; Original Music Scores; Playwrights; Sign Language Translators; Soloists; Special Technical Talent
Founded: 1972
Status: Non-Profit, Professional
Paid Staff: 4
Volunteer Staff: 200
Budget: $10,000
Performs At: Auditorium
Annual Attendance: 36,000
Facility Category: Regional Art Center
Type of Stage: Flexible
Seating Capacity: 175
Year Built: 1972
Year Remodeled: 1999

5653
ARIZONA STADIUM
University of Arizona
Tucson, AZ 85721
Mailing Address: The University of Arizona Athletics, McKale Center, 1 Nation
Phone: 520-621-2287
Fax: 520-621-2419
Toll-free: 800-452-2287
e-mail: schev@arizona.edu
Web Site: www.arizcats.com
Management:
President: Peter Likens
Artistic Director: Jim Livengood
Director of Marketing and Licensing: Shawn Chevreux
Assistant Dirctor of Marketing/Lice: Alixe Holcomb
Mission: Football
Founded: 1928
Specialized Field: Sports Facility

Status: For-Profit, Professional
Affiliations: NCAA, Home to University of Arizona athletics, football season games
Seating Capacity: 56,136
Year Built: 1979

5654
CENTENNIAL HALL
University of Arizona
1020 East University Boulevard
Tucson, AZ 85721-0029
Phone: 520-621-3341
Fax: 520-621-8991
e-mail: uapresents@arizona.edu
Web Site: www.uapresents.org/
Management:
Executive Director: Natalie Bohnet
Development Director: David Scott Allen
Marketing Director: Jo Alenson
Community Outreach Director: Benita Silvyn
Business Services Director: Simon White
Production Manager: Gary Lotze
Artist Relations Director: Patrice Kennedy
Seating Capacity: 2,456

5655
CROWDER HALL
University of Arizona
Music Building Room 111, Tucson
Tucson, AZ 85721
Mailing Address: College of Fine Arts, PO Box 210004
Phone: 520-621-1778
Fax: 520-621-1307
e-mail: sevigny@u.arizona.edu
Web Site: www.web.cfa.arizona.edu/students/crowder.php
Management:
Director: Peter McAllister
Vice Director: Rex Woods
Assistant Director Development: Joe Swinson
Business Manager: Elizabeth Gradillas
Mission: Faculty and student music and dance recitals
Utilizes: Collaborations; Guest Accompanists; Guest Companies; Guest Composers; Guest Directors; Guest Ensembles; Guest Instructors; Guest Musical Directors; Guest Musicians; Guest Soloists; High School Drama; Instructors; Multimedia; Sign Language Translators; Singers; Soloists
Founded: 1934
Paid Staff: 2
Performs At: Recital Hall
Seating Capacity: 544

5656
HI CORBETT FIELD
3400 East Camino Campestre
Tucson, AZ 85716
Mailing Address: Colorado Rockies, Coors Field, 2001 Blake Street, Denver, CO
Phone: 520-327-2621
Toll-free: 520-327-2371
Web Site: http://mlb.mlb.com/NASApp/mlb/col/news/spring_training_ballpark.jsp
Officers:
Chairman & Chief Executive Officer: Charles K Monfort
Vice Chairman: Richard L Monfort
Executive Vice Presidnet/Gen. Mgr.: Daniel J O'Dowd
SVP/CFO and General Counsel: Harold R Roth
Management:
Director Baseball Operations: Jeff Bridich
Business Operations: Donna Reed

Director Medical Operations: Tom Probst
Engineering/Facility Asst Director: James Wiener
AVP Commmunications/PR: Irma Thumin
Mission: Baseball
Specialized Field: Sports Facility
Seating Capacity: 8,665

5657
HOLSCLAW RECITAL HALL
University of Arizona
Theatre Arts, Drama Bldg, Room 239
1025 North Olive Road
Tucson, AZ 85721-0003
Mailing Address: P.O. Box 210004, 1017 N Olive Rd, Music Bldg, Rm 111, Tucson
Phone: 520-621-7008
Fax: 520-621-2412
e-mail: finearts@email.arizona.edu
Web Site: www.web.cfa.arizona.edu/theatre
Officers:
Dean: Maurice J. Sevigny Ph.D
Director Marketing/Development: Paula Newsome
Management:
Director Theatre: Albert Tucci
Production Manager: Laurie Kincman
Mission: The mission of the School of Theatre Arts at the University of Arizona is to provide professional training and education leading to careers in acting, musical theatre, theatre design and technology, theatre education and outreach, and theatre history and dramaturgy. The School is dedicated to educating students through a highly visible production program enriching the university and Tucson communities.
Specialized Field: Organ chamber music hall
Seating Capacity: 204

5658
MCKALE MEMORIAL CENTER
University of Arizona Athletics
1 National Championship Drive
Tucson, AZ 85721
Mailing Address: The University of Arizona Athletics, McKale Center, 1 Nation
Phone: 520-621-2200
Fax: 520-621-9690
e-mail: schev@arizona.edu
Web Site: www.arizonaathletics.com/
Management:
Athletics Director: Jim Livengood
Community Relations: Phoebe Chalk
Operations: Suzy Mason
Sales Director: Galen Hungate
Information Technology: Greg Shaffer
Specialized Field: Sports Facility
Seating Capacity: 20,000

5659
MUSIC RECITAL HALL
Pima Community College
PCC West Campus
2202 W. Anklam Road
Tucson, AZ 85709-0015
Phone: 520-206-6090
Fax: 520-206-6719
e-mail: centerforthearts@pima.edu
Web Site: www.pima.edu/performingarts/theatre
Officers:
Chancellor: Roy Flores PhD
Mission: The Theatre Arts program is house in the Center for the Arts at the West Campus. The program provides extensive experience and training in performance and all aspects of theatre production.

Specialized Field: Small-Group or Solo Performances, Readings and Lectures.
Type of Stage: Curved Amphitheater-Style
Seating Capacity: 75-120

5660
OLD TUCSON STUDIOS
201 South Kinney Road
Tucson, AZ 85735
Phone: 520-883-0100
Fax: 520-578-1269
Web Site: www.oldtucson.com
Officers:
Marketing Manager: Jeff Anderson
Facility Category: Film Studio Set
Seating Capacity: 4,000

5661
TEMPLE OF MUSIC & ART
330 South Scott Avenue
Tucson, AZ 85701
Mailing Address: PO Box 1631
Phone: 520-884-4875
Fax: 520-628-9129
e-mail: ebagnall@arizonatheatre.org
Web Site: www.arizonatheatre.org
Officers:
Facilities Manager: Eileen Bagnall
Founded: 1927
Opened: 1990
Facility Category: Theatre
Seating Capacity: 623

5662
TUCSON CONVENTION CENTER - ARENA
260 South Church Avenue
Tucson, AZ 85701
Phone: 520-791-4101
Fax: 520-791-5572
e-mail: richard.singer@tucsonaz.gov
Web Site: www.tucsonaz.gov/tcc/facilities/arena/index.html
Management:
Director: Richard Singer
General Manager: Rich Henkel
Administration: Elizabeth O'Hara Walker
Marketing/Sales Director: Kate Breck Calhoun
Event Manager: Andrew Brown
Mission: The Tucson Arena floor can also be utilized as 33,750 square feet of exhibit or banquet space.
Founded: 1981
Paid Staff: 100
Facility Category: Arena
Type of Stage: Flexible
Seating Capacity: 9,505
Year Built: 1971
Rental Contact: Marketing/Sales Director Kate Breck Calhoun

5663
TUCSON CONVENTION CENTER - EXHIBITION HALL
260 South Church Avenue
Tucson, AZ 85701
Phone: 520-791-4101
Fax: 520-791-5572
e-mail: richard.singer@tucsonaz.gov
Web Site: www.tucsonaz.gov/tcc/facilities/exhibithalls/index.html
Management:
Director: Richard Singer
General Manager: Rich Henkel

Event Manager: Andrew Brown
Marketing/Sales Director: Kate Breck Calhoun
Administration: Elizabeth O'Hara Walker
Mission: The Tucson Convention Center has a total of five (5) Exhibit Hall spaces that will provide 147,690 square feet of contiguous floor space. Each space is equipped with wireless Internet, electrical outlets, concession stands and load-in doors.
Founded: 1981
Paid Staff: 100
Facility Category: Exhibition Hall
Year Built: 1981
Rental Contact: Marketing/Sales Director Kate Breck Calhoun

5664
TUCSON CONVENTION CENTER - LEO RICH THEATRE
260 South Church Avenue
Tucson, AZ 85701
Phone: 520-791-4101
Fax: 520-791-5572
e-mail: richard.singer@tucsonaz.gov
Web Site: www.tucsonaz.gov/tcc/facilities/leorich/index.html
Management:
Director: Richard Singer
General Manager: Rich Henkel
Event Manager: Andrew Brown
Markting/Sales Director: Kate Breck Calhoun
Administration: Elizabeth O'Hara Walker
Founded: 1981
Paid Staff: 100
Type of Stage: Proscenium
Seating Capacity: 501
Rental Contact: Marketing/Sales Director Kate Breck Calhoun

5665
TUCSON CONVENTION CENTER - MUSIC HALL
260 South Church Avenue
Tucson, AZ 85701
Phone: 520-791-4101
Fax: 520-791-5572
e-mail: richard.singer@tucsonaz.gov
Web Site: www.tucsonaz.gov/tcc/facilities/musichall/index.html
Management:
Director: Richard Singer
General Manager: Rich Henkel
Events Manager: Andrew Brown
Marketing/Sales Director: Kate Breck Calhoun
Administration: Elizabeth O'Hara Walker
Mission: The auditorium has a permanent seating capacity of 2277 (1489 - orchestra level, 386 - lower balcony, 402 - upper balcony). An additional 77 seats may be added in the orchestra pit when lowered to house level bringing the total seating capacity to 2,354.
Founded: 1981
Paid Staff: 100
Facility Category: Music Hall
Type of Stage: Concert Stage
Seating Capacity: 2,354
Rental Contact: Marketing/Sales Director Kate Breck Calhoun

5666
TUCSON ELECTRIC PARK
2500 East Ajo Way
Tucson, AZ 85713

Phone: 520-434-1000
Fax: 520-434-1159
e-mail: info@kinosportscomplex.com
Web Site: www.kinosportscomplex.com
Officers:
   Director: Kate O'Rielly
   Stadium Business Manager: Tom Taylor
Facility Category: Sports Arena
Seating Capacity: 17,500

5667
UAPRESENTS CENTENNIAL HALL

1020 E University Boulevard
PO Box 210029
Tucson, AZ 85721-0029
Phone: 520-621-3341
Fax: 520-621-8991
e-mail: uapresents@arizona.edu
Management:
   Executive Director: Ken Foster
Specialized Field: Theater

5668
ARIZONA WESTERN COLLEGE AMPHITHEATRE

2020 S Avenue 8 E
PO Box 929
Yuma, AZ 85366
Phone: 928-317-6000
Fax: 928-344-7730
Toll-free: 888-293-0392
e-mail: deborah.leal@azwestern.edu
Web Site: www.azwestern.edu
Management:
   President: Donald Schoening
   Theatre Department: Forrest A Straley
   Senior Secretary: Lupe Fuentes
Founded: 1963
Status: For-Profit, Professional
Budget: $60,000-150,000
Seating Capacity: 600

5669
DESERT SUN STADIUM

1440 Desert Hills Drive
Yuma, AZ 85365
Phone: 928-373-5040
Fax: 928-344-9121
e-mail: ycc@ci.yuma.az.us
Web Site: www.yumaciviccenter.com
Officers:
   Events/Booking Supervisor: Becky Franks
   Box Office Manager: Mary Jane Chambers
   Operations Supervisor: Joe Baro
Founded: 1970
Paid Staff: 12
Volunteer Staff: 25
Income Sources: 2% Hospitality Tax; City Of Yuma
Affiliations: Owned And Operated By The City Of Yuma
Facility Category: Outdoor Stadium
Type of Stage: Portable
Stage Dimensions: varies depending on event needs
Seating Capacity: 6,000
Year Built: 1970
Rental Contact: MaryJane Chambers

5670
RAY KROC BASEBALL COMPLEX

Yuma Civic & Convention Center
1440 Desert Hills Drive
Yuma, AZ 85365

Phone: 928-344-3800
Fax: 928-344-9121
e-mail: ycc@ci.yuma.az.us
Web Site:
www.yumaconventioncenter.com/complex_facilities.htm
Management:
   Director: Anthony Guerrera
   Complex Supervisor: Joel Hubbard
   Marketing Rep: Mary Jane Chambers
   Booking Manager: Becky Franks
Seating Capacity: 6,590

5671
YUMA CIVIC AND CONVENTION CENTER - YUMA ROOM

Yuma Civic & Convention Center
1441 Desert Hills Drive
Yuma, AZ 85365
Phone: 928-373-5040
Fax: 928-344-9121
e-mail: ycc@ci.yuma.az.us
Web Site: www.yumaconventioncenter.com
Management:
   Park and Recreation Director: Steven Bills
   Managing Director: Roberta Ukura
   Marketing Director: Mary Jane Chambers
Utilizes: Instructors; Multimedia; Sign Language Translators; Theatre Companies
Founded: 1973
Status: For-Profit, Non-Professional
Paid Staff: 20
Budget: 1,200,000.00
Income Sources: Earned Revenue, Hospitality Tax
Affiliations: IAAM, MPI, SGMP
Type of Stage: Portable
Stage Dimensions: 30x40
Seating Capacity: 2,000
Year Built: 1973
Cost: 550.00

Arkansas

5672
JONES PERFORMING ARTS CENTER

Ouachita Baptist University
410 Ouachita Street
Arkadelphia, AR 71998
Mailing Address: Jones Performing Arts Center, OBU Box 3767, 410 Ouachita St.
Phone: 870-245-5000
Fax: (87-0) -245-
Toll-free: 1 8-0 D-AL O
e-mail: hosclaws@.obu.edu
Web Site: www.obu.edu/thearts
Management:
   Department Chair: Scott Holsclaw
   Production Manager Technical Direct: Joey Licklider
Mission: Ouachita's theatre arts department provides the students with practical experience which is enhanced by classroom instruction. Though rehearsals and performance, students engage in the collaborative process and continue to develop their skills under faculty direction.
Specialized Field: chapel, music events, campus social club shows, and touring productions/concerts
Type of Stage: Proscenium
Stage Dimensions: 54' X 28'
Seating Capacity: 1500

5673
OUACHITA BAPTIST UNIVERSITY HARVEY & BERNICE JONES PERFORMING ARTS CENTER

410 Ouachita Street
Arkadelphia, AR 71998
Phone: 870-245-5000
Fax: 870-245-5500
Web Site: www.obu.edu/music/facilities.asp
Management:
   President: Andy Westmoreland
   Executive Director: Charles Fuller
   Department Chair: Scott Holsclaw
   Technical Director: Joey Licklider
Founded: 1886
Status: Non-Profit, Professional
Paid Staff: 41
Paid Artists: 41
Seating Capacity: 1,500

5674
VERSER THEATER

Ouachita Baptist University
410 Ouachita Street
Arkadelphia, AR 71998
Mailing Address: Box 3771 , Arkadelphia, AR 71998
Phone: 870-245-5000
Fax: (87-0) -245-
Toll-free: 1 8-0 D-AL O
e-mail: hosclaws@.obu.edu
Web Site: www.obu.edu/thearts
Management:
   Department Chair: Scott Holsclaw
   Production Manager: Joey Licklider
Mission: Ouachita's theatre arts department provides the students with practical experience which is enhanced by classroom instruction. Though rehearsals and performance, students engage in the collaborative process and continue to develop their skills under faculty direction.
Specialized Field: Dramatic productions
Type of Stage: Proscenium Modified Thrust Stage
Stage Dimensions: 36' X 18'
Seating Capacity: 200

5675
RITZ CIVIC CENTER

306 West Main Street
Blytheville, AR 72315
Phone: 501-762-1744
Fax: 501-763-1950
Web Site: www.arkansas.com
Management:
   Director: Rae Glidewell

5676
CENTRE STAGE

University of Central Arkansas
Silas D. Snow Fine Arts Building
201 Donaghey Ave, Harrin Hall 224
Conway, AR 72035
Phone: 501-450-3162
Fax: 501-450-3296
e-mail: josepha@mail.uca.edu
Web Site: www.uca.edu/cfac/mct/theatre
Officers:
   Dean: Rollin R. Potter
   Interim Associate Dean: Gayle Seymour
Management:
   Chair: Joe Anderson

Mission: The Department of Mass Communication and Theatre offers programs that combine art and technology in four areas of emphasis: digital filmmaking, journalism, television, and theatre.
Type of Stage: Proscenium
Seating Capacity: 307

5677
DONALD W. REYNOLDS AUDITORIUM
University of Central Arkansas
Silas D. Snow Fine Arts Building
201 Donaghey Ave, Harrin Hall 224
Conway, AR 72035
Phone: 501-450-3162
Fax: 501-450-3296
e-mail: josepha@mail.uca.edu
Web Site: www.uca.edu/cfac/mct/theatre
Officers:
  Dean: Rollin R. Potter
  Interim Associate Dean: Gayle Seymour
Management:
  Chair: Joe Anderson
Mission: The Department of Mass Communication and Theatre offers programs that combine art and technology in four areas of emphasis: digital filmmaking, journalism, television, and theatre.
Opened: 2000
Type of Stage: Performance Hall
Orchestra Pit: Y
Seating Capacity: 1200
Cost: $22 million

5678
STUDIO THEATRE
University of Central Arkansas
Silas D. Snow Fine Arts Building
201 Donaghey Ave, Harrin Hall 224
Conway, AR 72035
Phone: 501-450-3162
Fax: 501-450-3296
e-mail: josepha@mail.uca.edu
Web Site: www.uca.edu/cfac/mct/theatre
Officers:
  Dean: Rollin R. Potter
  Interim Associate Dean: Gayle Seymour
Management:
  Chair: Joe Anderson
Mission: The Department of Mass Communication and Theatre offers programs that combine art and technology in four areas of emphasis: digital filmmaking, journalism, television, and theatre.
Type of Stage: Black Box
Seating Capacity: 150

5679
EL DORADO MUNICIPAL AUDITORIUM
City of El Dorado
100 West 8th Street
El Dorado, AR 71730
Phone: 870-881-4878
Fax: 870—88-1-41
e-mail: mayor@eldoradoar.org
Web Site: www.eldoradoar.org/auditorium.html
Management:
  Mayor: Bobby Beard
  Judge Union County Courthouse: Bobby Edmonds
Specialized Field: Concerts, theater, weddings

5680
SOUTH ARKANSAS ARTS CENTER
110 East 5th Street
Suite 206
El Dorado, AR 71730

Phone: 870-862-5474
Fax: 870-862-4921
Web Site: www.saac-arts.org/home.html
Officers:
  President Board of Directors: Gay Bechtelheimer
  Vice President: Dan Francis
  Secretary: Carol Wofsey
  Treasurer: John Niemann
  Chairman: Dean Inman
Management:
  Manager: Virginia Matthews

5681
CARLSON CENTER
Ogden Entertainment
2010 2nd Avenue
Fairbanks, AR 99701
Phone: 907-451-7800
Fax: 907-451-1195
e-mail: info@carlson-center.com
Web Site: www.carlson-center.com
Management:
  President: Joyce White
  Managing Director: Angie Spear
  Catering Manager: David Welborn
  Marketing/Box Office Manager: Kristin Bayer
  Operations Manager: Kyle Holder
Mission: Event Facility
Utilizes: Actors; Artists-in-Residence; Collaborating Artists; Commissioned Music; Dance Companies; Dancers; Designers; Educators; Filmmakers; Guest Companies; Guest Conductors; Guest Directors; Guest Ensembles; Guest Instructors; Guest Lecturers; Guest Musical Directors; Guest Musicians; Guest Soloists; Guest Writers; Guild Activities; Instructors; Local Artists; Multi Collaborations; Multimedia; Music; New Productions; Original Music Scores; Poets; Resident Artists; Resident Professionals; Selected Students; Sign Language Translators; Singers; Soloists; Student Interns; Special Technical Talent; Theatre Companies; Touring Companies; Visual Arts
Founded: 1990
Paid Staff: 100
Type of Stage: Concert Stage; Portable; Sico
Seating Capacity: 3,470; 6,539

5682
BUD WALTON ARENA
University of Arkansas
Fayetteville, AR 72701
Mailing Address: PO Box 7777
Phone: 479-575-2000
Fax: 501-575-3716
Web Site: www.uark.edu
Officers:
  President Razorbacks Foundation: Chuck Dicus
  Vice Presiident Razorbacks Foundtn: Norm DeBriyn
  Chief Financial Officer: Jackie Rollins
Management:
  Arena Manager: Fred Vorsanger
  Concession Manager: Mike Holbrook
  Donor Relations: Charlotte Faucette
Specialized Field: Sports Arena
Seating Capacity: 19,500

5683
STELLA BOYLE SMITH CONCERT HALL
UALR Music Department
University of Arkansas at Fayetteville
2801 South University Avenue
Fayetteville, AR 72701

Phone: 479-575-4701
Fax: 479-575-5409
e-mail: music@uark.edu
Web Site: www.ualr.edu/mudept/
Officers:
  Department Chairman: Dr. Ronda Mains
Management:
  Chancellor of University: Dave Gearhart
Status: Non-Profit, Professional
Paid Staff: 30
Paid Artists: 30
Facility Category: Concert Hall

5684
WALTON ARTS CENTER
229 N School Street
PO Box 3547
Fayetteville, AR 72701
Phone: 479-443-9216
Fax: 479-443-6461
e-mail: jburns@waltonartscenter.org
Web Site: www.waltonartscenter.org
Officers:
  President/CEO: Peter Lane
  Senior VP: Jenni Taylor Swain
  COO: Terri Trotter
Mission: Visual and performing arts center.
Utilizes: Artists-in-Residence; Collaborations; Curators; Dance Companies; Educators; Fine Artists; High School Drama; Instructors; Multimedia; Original Music Scores; Theatre Companies; Touring Companies
Founded: 1992
Status: Non-Profit, Professional
Paid Staff: 47
Volunteer Staff: 300
Non-paid Artists: 50
Budget: $4 million
Income Sources: Ticket Sales, Corporate Sponsors, Members, Grants
Performs At: 1200 Seat Hall; 200 Seat Black Box
Affiliations: APAP, Midwest Arts Alliance
Annual Attendance: 150,000+
Type of Stage: Proscenium
Stage Dimensions: 58 x 40
Seating Capacity: 1,200
Year Built: 1992
Cost: $9 Million

5685
BREEDLOVE AUDITORIUM WESTARK COMMUNITY COLLEGE
5210 Grand Avenue
PO Box 3649
Fort Smith, AR 72913
Phone: 479-788-7000
e-mail: information@uafortsmith.edu
Web Site: www.uafortsmith.edu
Management:
  President: Joe Stubblefield
  Executive Director: Stacy Jones
  Technical Director: Bob Stevenson
Founded: 1928
Status: Non-Profit, Non-Professional

5686
FORT SMITH CONVENTION CENTER
55 S 7th Street
Fort Smith, AR 72901
Phone: 479-788-8932
Fax: 479-788-8930
e-mail: khobbs@fortsmithan.gov
Web Site: www.fortsmithconventioncenter.org
Management:
  Director of Convention Center: Frankie Hamilton

Sales Director: Karen Hobbs
Sales Director: Jeremy Richey
Mission: Multipurpose facility for conventions, tradeshows, banquets, meetings, PAC performances and 40,000 square feet Exhibit Hall with riser seating.
Founded: 2001
Status: Operational
Paid Staff: 12
Income Sources: Concerts; Tradeshows; Conventions; Banquets; Rental Facilities
Annual Attendance: 500,000
Facility Category: Convention Center
Type of Stage: Hardwood on plywood substrate
Stage Dimensions: 58 x 42
Seating Capacity: 1330; 4700
Year Built: 1966
Year Remodeled: 2000
Cost: $27 Million
Rental Contact: Melanie Jordin

5687
FORT SMITH LITTLE THEATRE

401 North 6th Street
Fort Smith, AR 72913
Mailing Address: PO Box 3752
Phone: 479-783-2966
Fax: 479-783-1295
Web Site: www.fslt.20fr.com
Officers:
    President Board of Directors: Carole Rogers
    Vice President Board of Directors: Michael Richardson
    Secretary Board of Directors: Blake Young
    Treasurer Board of Directors: Paula Sharum
Founded: 1948

5688
KAY ROGERS PARK

4400 Midland Boulevard
Fort Smith, AR 72904
Mailing Address: PO Box 4145
Phone: 507-738-6176
Fax: 501-782-9944
Web Site: www.kayrogerspark.com
Management:
    Director: Jim Berry
    Accounting: Beverly Sharp
Seating Capacity: 13,000

5689
HOT SPRINGS CONVENTION SUMMIT CENTER

134 Convention Boulevard
Hot Springs, AR 71901
Phone: 501-321-2835
Fax: 501-620-5008
e-mail: hscvb@hotsprings.org
Web Site: www.hotsprings.org
Management:
    Executive Director: Steve Arrison
    Deputy Director: Gordon Manoney
    Box Office Manager: Brian Leonard
Status: Nonprofit, Professional
Paid Staff: 75
Seating Capacity: 6,500

5690
FORUM

115 East Monroe
Jonesboro, AR 72401
Phone: 870-935-2726
Fax: 870-933-9505
Web Site: www.jonesborofoa.com/fanda.html
Management:

Executive Director: Sherri Beatty
Technical Director: Gaylon Tyner
Director of Education: Heather Intres
House Manager: Kent O'Daniel
Development Coordinator: Vicki Pillow
Associate Executive Director: Amanda Drennon
Founded: 1926
Seating Capacity: 658

5691
FOUNDATION OF ARTS

115 East Monroe
PO Box 310
Jonesboro, AR 72403
Phone: 870-935-2726
Fax: 870-933-9505
Web Site: www.jonesborofoa.com
Management:
    Executive Director: Sherri Beatty
    Associate Executive Director: Amanda Drennon
    Technical Director: Gaylon Tyner
    Director of Education: Heather Intres
    House Manager: Kent O'Daniel
    Development Coordinator: Vicki Pillow
Status: Non-Profit, Non-Professional
Paid Staff: 5
Paid Artists: 5
Performs At: Auditorium
Seating Capacity: 658

5692
FOWLER CENTER AT ARKANSAS UNIVERSITY

201 Olympic Drive
PO Box 2339
Jonesboro, AR 72467
Phone: 879-972-3471
Fax: 870-972-3748
e-mail: fowlercenter@astate.edu
Web Site: www.yourfowlercenter.com
Management:
    Director: Jeff Brown
    Bradbury Gallery Director: Lee Christensen
    Technical Director: Jason Henson
Mission: To represent to the students, faculty and staff of Arkansas State University and the citizens of Northeast Arkansas an opportunity to experience visual and performing arts events of national and international stature.
Founded: 2001
Specialized Field: Music; Theatre; Visual Art
Status: Nonprofit
Paid Staff: 5
Budget: $100,000
Income Sources: Arkansas State University; Endowments; Ticket Sales
Facility Category: Concert Hall/Drama Theatre
Type of Stage: Proscenium
Seating Capacity: 975; 342
Year Built: 2000
Rental Contact: Director Jeff Brown

5693
HAISLIP ARENA THEATRE

University of Arkansas Little Rock
2801 South University Avenue
Little Rock, AR 72467
Mailing Address: PO Box 2309
Phone: 870-972-2037
Fax: 870-972-2830
e-mail: asutheatre@astate.edu
Web Site: www.ualr.edu/theatre/season2.htm
Management:
    Chancellor: Joe Anderson

Executive Director: Robert Hupp
Department Chair: Jay Raphael Ph.D
Technical Director: Carl Wick
Status: Non-Profit, Non-Professional
Paid Staff: 10

5694
RAY WINDER FIELD

War Memorial Park
PO Box 55066
Little Rock, AR 72215
Phone: 501-664-1555
Fax: 501-664-1834
e-mail: travs@travs.com
Web Site: www.travs.com
Management:
    President: Bert Parke
    Executive Director: Bill Valentine
    Assistant General Manager: Pete Laven
    Superintendant: Greg Johnson
    Director Stadium Operations: Mike Green
    Assistant Park Supervisor: Reggi Temple
    Director Media Relations: Phil Elson
    Director of Tickets: David Kay
    Director of Group Sales: Paul Allen
Founded: 1932
Status: Non-Profit, Professional
Paid Staff: 8
Seating Capacity: 6,083

5695
ROBINSON CENTER MUSIC HALL

Markham and Broadway
PO Box 3232
Little Rock, AR 72203
Phone: 501-376-4781
Fax: 501-374-2255
Toll-free: 800-844-4781
e-mail: lrcvb@littlerock.com
Web Site: www.littlerock.com
Management:
    Chief Operating Officer: Jim Rice
    Chief Executive Officer: Barry Travis
Affiliations: Arkansas Symphony Orchestra Celebrity Attractions
Year Built: 1939
Year Remodeled: 1989
Rental Contact: Lisa Simmons

5696
WAR MEMORIAL STADIUM

Markham and Van Buren Street
1 Stadium Drive
Little Rock, AR 72225
Mailing Address: PO Box 250222
Phone: 501-663-6385
Fax: 501-663-6387
e-mail: jerry.cohen@arkansas.goc
Web Site: www.state.ar.us/wms.facilities.html, http://www.wmstadium.com/
Management:
    Stadium Manager: Charlie Staggs
    Assistant Manager: Wayne Dyer
Mission: Football
Founded: 1948
Specialized Field: Sports facility, concerts
Status: Non-Profit, Non-Professional
Paid Staff: 5
Seating Capacity: 53,727

5697
WILDWOOD PARK FOR THE PERFORMING ARTS
20919 Denny Road
Little Rock, AR 72223
Phone: 501-821-7275
Fax: 501-821-7280
Toll-free: 888-821-7225
Web Site: www.wildwoodpark.org
Officers:
Chairman Emeritus: Lucy C Cabe
Chairman: Bill Morton
President: Ellen M Gary
VP: Melissa Thoma
Secretary: Dolores Bruce
Founder/Artistic Director: Ann Chotard
Director of Finance: Benny Cagle
Conductor: Pioir Sulkowski
Utilizes: AEA Actors; Artists-in-Residence; Collaborations; Commissioned Composers; Commissioned Music; Dancers; Designers; Educators; Fine Artists; Five Seasonal Concerts; Grant Writers; Guest Accompanists; Guest Artists; Guest Choreographers; Guest Composers; Guest Conductors; Guest Designers; Guest Instructors; Guest Lecturers; Guest Musical Directors; Guest Musicians; Guest Soloists; Guest Writers; Guild Activities; Instructors; Local Artists; Lyricists; Multimedia; Music; New Productions; Organization Contracts; Original Music Scores; Poets; Resident Artists; Resident Professionals; Sign Language Translators; Singers; Soloists; Student Interns; Special Technical Talent; Touring Companies; Visual Arts
Founded: 1991
Status: Non-Profit, Professional
Paid Staff: 6
Paid Artists: 10
Budget: $1.2 Million
Income Sources: Friends of Wildwood, Grants, City and State Fundings
Affiliations: Opera America
Annual Attendance: 3,750
Facility Category: Opera House
Type of Stage: Thrust
Seating Capacity: 625
Year Built: 1996
Cost: $6 Million

5698
WILKINS STADIUM
Southern Arkansas University
100 East University
Magnolia, AR 71753-5000
Phone: 870-235-4000
Fax: 870-235-5005
e-mail: muleriders@saumag.edu
Web Site: www.saumag.edu
Management:
Executive Assistant to President: Ronnie Birdsong
Director Development: Sharon Eichenberger
University Editor: Mark Trout
Athletic Director: Jay Adcox
Assistant Athletic Director: Houston Taylor
Sports Information Director: Houston Taylor
Director Wellness Center: Leonard Biddle
Seating Capacity: 6,000

5699
ARTS AND SCIENCE CENTER FOR SOUTHEAST ARKANSAS
701 S Main Street
Pine Bluff, AR 71601

Phone: 870-536-3375
Fax: 870-536-3380
e-mail: info@artssciencecenter.org
Web Site: www.artsssciencecenter.org
Management:
Executive Director: Janelle Powell
Utilizes: Actors; Choreographers; Curators; Dance Companies; Dancers; Designers; Educators; Grant Writers; Guest Artists; Guest Conductors; Guest Designers; Guest Ensembles; Guest Musical Directors; Guest Musicians; Guild Activities; High School Drama; Instructors; Local Artists; Multimedia; Music; Resident Professionals; Sign Language Translators; Soloists; Student Interns; Theatre Companies; Touring Companies
Founded: 1966
Status: Non-Profit, Non-Professional
Paid Staff: 10
Volunteer Staff: 300
Paid Artists: 3
Non-paid Artists: 80
Budget: $110,000
Income Sources: Ticket Sales; Sponsorship; Grants
Annual Attendance: 5,500
Facility Category: Multi-use
Seating Capacity: 232
Year Built: 1994

5700
GOLDEN LION STADIUM
University of Arkansas Pine Bluff
1200 North University Drive
Pine Bluff, AR 71601
Phone: 870-575-8000
Fax: 870-575-4607
Web Site: www.uapb.edu/athletics/index.html
Management:
President: Lawrence Davis Jr/Ph.D
Athletic Director: Craig Cury
Sports Information Director: Carl Whimper
Faculty Athletic Representative: George Herts
Senior Women's Administrator: Betty Hayes
Founded: 2000
Status: Non-Profit, Non-Professional

5701
HESTAND STADIUM
420 North Blake
Pine Bluff, AR 71601
Phone: 870-535-2900
Fax: 870-534-2864
Web Site: www.pinebluffonline.com/hestand.htm
Management:
President: Dale Dixon
Executive Director: Pier Ponder
Managing Director: Brent Lacy
Convention Center Event Booking Mgr: Marian Anderson
Convention Meeting Information Mgr: Sheri Storie
Festival/Special Events Information: Greg Gustek
City/Tourist/Information: Susie Madsen
Status: Non-Profit, Professional
Paid Staff: 6
Paid Artists: 6
Seating Capacity: 7,000

5702
PINE BLUFF CONVENTION CENTER AUDITORIUM
500 E 8th Street
701 Main Street
Pine Bluff, AR 71601

Phone: 870-536-7600
Fax: 870-535-4867
Toll-free: 800-536-7660
e-mail: pbinfo@pinebluff.com
Web Site: www.pinebluffonline.com/conv/auditorium.html
Management:
President: Bob Purvis
Festival/Special Events Information: Greg Gustek
Tourist Information: Susie Madsen
Event Booking Information: Marian Anderson
Convention Meeting Information: Sheri Storie
Founded: 1976
Status: Non-Profit, Non-Professional
Paid Staff: 28

5703
PINE BLUFF CONVENTION CENTER ARENA
1 Convention Center Plaza
701, Main Street
Pine Bluff, AR 71601
Phone: 870-536-3375
Fax: 870-536-3380
Toll-free: 800-536-7660
e-mail: pbinfo@pinebluff.com
Web Site: www.pinebluffonline.com/conv/arena.html
Management:
Tourist/Travel Information: Susie Madsen
Festival/Special Events Manager: Greg Gustek
Convention/Meeting Manager: Sheri Storie
Events Manager: Marion Anderson
Paid Staff: 26
Seating Capacity: 9,000

5704
ARKANSAS RIVER VALLEY ARTS CENTER
PO Box 2112
Russellville, AR 72811
Phone: 479-968-2452
Fax: 479-968-5015
e-mail: artscenter@centurytel.net
Web Site: www.artcenter.org
Officers:
President: Emory Molitorx
Management:
Executive Director: Betty Lagrone
Artistic Director: Winston Taylor
Founded: 1981
Opened: 1981
Status: Non-Profit, Professional
Paid Staff: 4
Paid Artists: 2
Annual Attendance: 5,000
Seating Capacity: 400

5705
JOHN E TUCKER COLISEUM
Arkansas Tech Athletic Department
Tucker Coliseum, 1604 Coliseum Drive
Russellville, AR 72801
Phone: 479-968-0345
Fax: 479-964-0829
Web Site: http://athletics.atu.edu/tucker.htm
Management:
President: Robert Brown
Athletic Director: Steve Mullins
Faculty Athletic Representative: Thomas DeBlack Ph.D
Director Corporate Relations: Kelly Davis
Founded: 1976
Seating Capacity: 3,500

5706

WITHERSPOON ARTS ARENA

Arkansas Tech University
1505 North Boulder Avenue
Russellville, AR 72801
Phone: 479-968-0368
Fax: 501-964-0812
Web Site: http://lfa.atu.edu/music.htm
Management:
   Music Department Head: Andy Anders
   Director of Bands: Hal Cooper
   Director of Choirs: Gary Morris

5707

ARTS CENTER OF THE OZARKS

214 South Main Street
PO Box 725
Springdale, AR 72765-0725
Phone: 479-751-5441
Fax: 479-927-0308
e-mail: info@artscenteroftheozarks.org
Web Site: www.artscenteroftheozarks.org
Management:
   President: James Blount
   Executive Director: Cathy Blundell
   Theatre Director: Harry Blundell
   Music Director: Bill Burrows
Mission: To provide opportunities to be or see the arts in Northwest Arkansas, Southwest Missouri, Northeast Oklahoma and Southeast Kansas.
Founded: 1967
Specialized Field: Multi Disciplinary; Performing; Visual Arts
Status: Non-Profit, Non-Professional
Paid Staff: 9
Paid Artists: 3
Budget: $500,000

5708

CONVOCATION CENTER

Arkansas State University
217 Olympic Drive
State University, AR 72467
Mailing Address: PO Box 880
Phone: 870-972-3870
Fax: 870-972-3825
Web Site: www.convo.astate.edu
Management:
   Booking Manager: Lesa Carmack
   Senior Administrative Secretary: Edna Holt
   Computer Support Specialist: Michelle Lynne Minton
   Director: Tim L Dean
Founded: 1987
Budget: $1 million
Annual Attendance: 350,000
Facility Category: Arena
Type of Stage: Sico
Stage Dimensions: 60'x40'
Seating Capacity: 10,500
Year Built: 1987
Year Remodeled: 2001
Cost: $18.6 million
Rental Contact: Tim Dean

California

5709

ANAHEIM CONVENTION CENTER - ARENA

800 West Katella Avenue
Anaheim, CA 92802
Phone: 714-765-8950
Fax: 714-765-8965
e-mail: slowry@anaheim.net
Web Site: www.anaheimconventioncenter.com/
Management:
   City Manager: David M Morgan
   Assistant City Manager: Thomas J Wood
   Deputy City Manager: Joel Fick
Mission: The Anaheim Convention Center houses 815,000 square feet of exhibit space; Meeting and Ballroom space totals 130,000, Arena Capacities are 28,140 total square feet and the seating capacity is 9,100.
Opened: 1967

5710

EDISON INTERNATIONAL FIELD OF ANAHEIM

2000 Gene Autry Way
Anaheim, CA 92806
Phone: 714-634-2000
Fax: 714-940-2001
Toll-free: 888-796-4256
Web Site: www.angelsbaseball.com
Officers:
   Owner: Arturo Moreno
   President: Dennis Kuhl
   Chief Financial Officer: Bill Beverage
   SVP/Sales & Marketing: John Carpino
   VP/General Manager: Bill Stoneman
   VP/Communications: Tim Mead
   VP/Finance: Molly Taylor
Management:
   Manager Baseball Operation: Abe Flores
   Director Player Development: Tony Reagins
   Assistant General Manager: Ken Forsch
   Communications Director: Nancy Mazmanian
   Marketing Director: Robert Alvarado
Founded: 1966
Specialized Field: Home to the Anaheim Angels (MLB) and many other events and consumer shows.
Seating Capacity: 45,050
Year Built: 1966
Year Remodeled: 1998

5711

CABRILLO CROCKER THEATER

Cabrillo College
6500 Soquel Drive
Aptos, CA 95003
Phone: 831-479-6146
Fax: 831-464-8382
e-mail: mahopkins@cabrillo.edu
Web Site: www.cabrillovapa.com
Management:
   Theatre Manager: Mark Hopkins
   Marketing & Communications: Jana Marcus
   Assistant Theatre Manager: Anya Finke
   Theatre Manager: Sean C McCullough
Founded: 1959
Opened: 2009
Specialized Field: Music/Theater/Dance
Seating Capacity: 527
Year Built: 2009

5712

CENTERARTS

Humboldt State University
1 Harpst Street
Arcata, CA 95521-8299
Phone: 707-826-4411
Fax: 707-826-5980
e-mail: rmf7001@humboldt.edu
Web Site: www.humboldt.edu/~carts/

Management:
   President: Rollin Richmond
   Director: Roy Furshpan
   Event Coordinator: Michael Moore Jr
   Sound Manager: Russ Cole
   Administrative Coordinator: Tiffany O'Connell
   Ticket Officer Manager: Jason Henry
   Technical Director: Greta Welsh
Mission: Facilities include the Van Duzer Theatre with a seating capacity of 862; Fulkerson Recital Hall With a seating capacity of 201; and the Kate Buchanan Room with a seating capacity of 600.

5713

EAST GYMNASIUM

Humboldt State University
1 Harpst Street
Arcata, CA 95521
Phone: 707-826-4411
Fax: 707-826-5980
e-mail: rmf7001@humboldt.edu
Web Site: www.humboldt.edu
Management:
   Director: Roy Furshpan
   Event Coordinator: Michael Moore Jr
   Sound Manager: Russ Cole
   Administrative Coordinator: Tiffany O'Connell
   Ticket Office Manager: Jason Henry
   Technical Director: Greta Welsh
Seating Capacity: 1,400

5714

FULKERSON RECITAL HALL

Humboldt State University
1 Harpst Street
Arcata, CA 95521
Phone: 707-826-4411
Fax: 707-826-5980
e-mail: rmf7001@humboldt.edu
Web Site: www.humboldt.edu
Management:
   Director: Roy Furshpan
   Event Coordinator: Michael Moore Jr
   Sound Manager: Russ Cole
   Administrative Coordinator: Tiffany O'Connell
   Technical Director: Greta Welsh
Seating Capacity: 201

5715

JOHN VAN DUZER THEATRE

Humboldt State University
1 Harpst Street
Arcata, CA 95521
Phone: 707-826-4411
Fax: 707-826-5980
e-mail: rmf7001@humboldt.edu
Web Site: www.humboldt.edu
Management:
   Director: Roy Furshpan
   Event Coordinator: Michael Moore Jr
   Sound Manager: Russ Cole
   Administrative Coordinator: Tiffany O'Connell
   Ticket Office Manager: Jason Henry
   Technical Director: Greta Welsh
Seating Capacity: 862

5716

KATE BUCHANAN ROOM

Humboldt State University
1 Harpst Street
Arcata, CA 95521

Phone: 707-826-4411
Fax: 707-826-5980
e-mail: rmf7001@humboldt.edu
Web Site: www.humboldt.edu
Management:
    Director: Roy Furshpan
    Event Coordinator: Michael Moore Jr
    Sound Manager: Russ Cole
    Administrative Coordinator: Tiffany O'Connell
    Ticket Office Manager: Jason Henry
    Technical Director: Greta Welsh
Seating Capacity: 600

5717
APU THEATER
Azusa Pacific University
West Campus
701 East Foothill Boulevard
Azusa, CA 91702
Mailing Address: APU Theater, Azusa Pacific
University, PO Box 7000, Azusa, C
Phone: 626-815-5035
Web Site: www.apu.edu/theater
Management:
    Director Theater Arts: Bart McHenry
    General Manager Theater Arts: Brian Mercer
Mission: APU Theater offers, on average, six quality
productions a semesters, featuring a combination of
family-friendly comedy, drama, and musical
performances.
Seating Capacity: 450

5718
BAKERSFIELD CIVIC AUDITORIUM
Bakersfield Convention Center
1001 Truxton Avenue
Bakersfield, CA 93301
Phone: 661-852-7300
Fax: 661-861-9904
Toll-free: 888-255-2200
Web Site: http://production.centennialgarden.com/
Management:
    Executive Director: Jim Foss
    Event Manager: Adam Miller
    Marketing Director: Scott Norton
    Operations Director: Claudia Goodsell
    Director of Security: Sam Cornejo
    Finance Director: Steve Womack
Mission: Convention Hall has a seating capacity of
3,000, Convention Arena has a seating capacity of
2,200.
Seating Capacity: 3,000

5719
DORE THEATRE/MADIGAN GALLERY
California State University
Theatre Department, Music Bldg 102
9001 Stockdale Hwy
Bakersfield, CA 93311-1022
Mailing Address: DEPARTMENT, California State
University, Bakersfield, 9001 S
Phone: 661-654-3093
Fax: 661-665-6901
Web Site: http://www.csub.edu
Management:
    Dor: Ray Finnell
    Robinson: Theatre Techni Frank
    Plunkett: Stage Technicia Kathryn
Founded: 1977
Specialized Field: Theatre
Seating Capacity: 500

5720
BENJIMAN IDE WHEELER AUDITORIUM
University of California, Berkeley
101 Zellerbach Hall
Suite 4800
Berkeley, CA 94720-4800
Phone: 510-642-0212
Fax: 510-643-6707
e-mail: lbaqir@calperfs@calperfs.berkeley.edu
Web Site: www.berkeley.edu
Officers:
    Director Development: Katie Neubauer
Management:
    Director: Robert W Cole
    Facility Manager: Xavier Raya De Zarate
    Production Director: Tom Hansen
Mission: The mission of Cal Performances is to inspire,
nurture and sustain a lifelong appreciation for the
performing arts.
Specialized Field: Concerts, Dance, Music, Theatre,
and other performing arts disciplines
Status: Nonprofit, Professional
Paid Staff: 50
Type of Stage: Proscenium
Stage Dimensions: 15' X 30'
Seating Capacity: 760

5721
BERKELEY COMMUNITY THEATRE
Berkley High School
1930 Allston Way
Berkeley, CA 94710
Phone: 415-346-7222
Fax: 415-771-9719
e-mail: rcagan@berkeley.k12.ca.us
Web Site: www.premiertickets.com/berkeley
Management:
    President: Bryan Rotton
    Lead Teacher: Ray Cagan
Founded: 2003
Specialized Field: Concerts, theater
Status: Non-Profit, Professional
Paid Staff: 87

5722
JULIA MORGAN CENTER FOR THE ARTS
2640 College Avenue
Berkeley, CA 94704
Phone: 510-845-8542
Fax: 510-845-3133
Web Site: www.juliamorgan.org
Management:
    President: Timothy Choate
    Executive Director: Sabrina Klein
    Production Coordinator: Bridget Frederick
    Technical Director: Chris Paulina
Mission: The Julia Morgan Center for the Arts is a
home for artists, educators, learners and the
community.
Founded: 1980
Status: Non-Profit, Professional
Paid Staff: 8
Budget: $700,000
Type of Stage: Proscenrum
Stage Dimensions: 39'4" x 31'6"
Seating Capacity: 400
Year Built: 1908
Year Remodeled: 1990
Cost: $650-$1250
Rental Contact: Bridget Frederick

5723
LA PENA CULTURAL CENTER
3105 Shattuck Avenue
Berkeley, CA 94705
Phone: 510-849-2568
Fax: 510-849-9397
e-mail: info@lapena.org
Web Site: www.lapena.org
Management:
    Contact: Paul B Chin
Mission: To present cultural educational programs that
increase understanding of different cultures and support
efforts to build a more just society based on respect for
human, social and economic rights for all people; to
operate a multi-use cultural center/community gathering
place where people of all races and cultures can share
the rich and diverse heritages of the Americas and learn
about conditions in the US, Latin American and the
world.
Utilizes: Artists-in-Residence; Dancers; Filmmakers;
Guest Directors; Guest Musical Directors; Instructors;
Lyricists; Original Music Scores; Playwrights
Founded: 1973
Specialized Field: Latin American Music
Status: Non-Profit,Professional
Paid Staff: 7
Volunteer Staff: 20
Paid Artists: 4
Annual Attendance: 25,000
Facility Category: Black Box
Type of Stage: Raised Platform
Stage Dimensions: 24'x14'
Seating Capacity: 170
Year Built: 1932
Year Remodeled: 1990
Cost: $100,000
Rental Contact: Paul Chin

5724
WILLIAM RANDOLPH HEARST GREEK THEATRE
University of California, Berkeley
101 Zellerbach Hall
Suite 4800
Berkeley, CA 94720-4800
Phone: 510-642-0212
Fax: 510-643-6707
e-mail: lbaqir@calperfs@calperfs.berkeley.edu
Web Site: www.berkeley.edu
Officers:
    Director Development: Katie Neubauer
Management:
    Director: Robert W Cole
    Facility Manager: Xavier Raya De Zarate
    Production Director: Tom Hansen
Mission: The mission of Cal Performances is to inspire,
nurture and sustain a lifelong appreciation for the
performing arts.
Specialized Field: Concerts, Dance, Music, Theatre,
and other performing arts disciplines
Status: Nonprofit, Professional
Paid Staff: 50
Type of Stage: Amphitheater
Stage Dimensions: 127' X 28'
Seating Capacity: 8500

5725
ZELLERBACH AUDITORIUM
University of California, Berkeley
101 Zellerbach Hall
Suite 4800
Berkeley, CA 94720-4800

Phone: 510-642-0212
Fax: 510-643-6707
e-mail: lbaqir@calperfs@calperfs.berkeley.edu
Web Site: www.berkeley.edu
Officers:
Director Development: Katie Neubauer
Management:
Director: Robert W Cole
Facility Manager: Xavier Raya De Zarate
Production Director: Tom Hansen
Mission: The mission of Cal Performances is to inspire, nurture and sustain a lifelong appreciation for the performing arts.
Specialized Field: Concerts, Dance, Music, Theatre, and other performing arts disciplines
Status: Nonprofit, Professional
Paid Staff: 50
Type of Stage: Proscenium
Stage Dimensions: 63'x30'
Orchestra Pit: y
Seating Capacity: 2,089

5726
ZELLERBACH PLAYHOUSE
University of California, Berkeley
101 Zellerbach Hall
Suite 4800
Berkeley, CA 94720-4800
Phone: 510-642-0212
Fax: 510-643-6707
e-mail: lbaqir@calperfs@calperfs.berkeley.edu
Web Site: www.berkeley.edu
Officers:
Director Development: Katie Neubauer
Management:
Director: Robert W Cole
Facility Manager: Xavier Raya De Zarate
Production Director: Tom Hansen
Mission: The mission of Cal Performances is to inspire, nurture and sustain a lifelong appreciation for the performing arts.
Specialized Field: Concerts, Dance, Music, Theatre, and other performing arts disciplines
Status: Nonprofit, Professional
Paid Staff: 50
Type of Stage: Proscenium or Thrust
Seating Capacity: 547

5727
BEVERLY HILLS PLAYHOUSE
254 South Robertson Boulevard
Beverly Hills, CA 90211
Phone: 310-855-1556
Fax: 310-652-4889
Web Site: www.beverlyhillsplayhouse.com/
Officers:
Founder/President: Milton Katselas
Management:
Executive Director: Allen Barton
Artistic Director: Gary Grossman
Paid Staff: 10
Paid Artists: 10
Season: Year Round
Type of Stage: Proscenium

5728
BIG BEAR LAKE PERFORMING ARTS CENTER
39707 Big Bear Boulevard
PO Box 10000
Big Bear Lake, CA 92315
Phone: 909-866-5381
Fax: 909-878-6766
Web Site: www.citybigbearlake.com/bblpac/index.htm

Management:
Theatre Director: Don Gavitte
City Manager: Jeff Mathieu
Assistant City Manager: Kathy Jefferies
Utilizes: Dance Companies; Guild Activities; Local Artists; Original Music Scores; Playwrights; Resident Artists; Special Technical Talent; Theatre Companies
Founded: 1987
Status: Non-Profit, Professional
Paid Staff: 3
Volunteer Staff: 10
Annual Attendance: 18,000
Facility Category: Performing Arts Center
Type of Stage: Wood
Stage Dimensions: 40'x55'
Seating Capacity: 398
Year Built: 1988
Cost: $3 million
Rental Contact: Manager Don Gavitte

5729
CURTIS THEATRE
1 Civic Center Circle
Brea, CA 92821
Phone: 714-990-7722
Fax: 714-990-7635
e-mail: curtistheatre@ci.brea.ca.us
Web Site: www.ci.brea.ca.us
Management:
HR Manager: Emily Keller
Technical Director: Kevin Clowes
Box Office Manager: Vertira Johns
Utilizes: Actors; AEA Actors; Dance Companies; Dancers; Guest Accompanists; Guest Artists; Guest Choreographers; Guest Designers; Guild Activities; Original Music Scores; Selected Students; Soloists; Theatre Companies
Founded: 1980
Status: Non-Profit, Professional
Paid Staff: 10
Paid Artists: 10
Affiliations: Western Arts Alliance; California Presenters; Association of Performing Arts
Facility Category: Theatre
Type of Stage: Procenium
Stage Dimensions: 42W X 36D
Seating Capacity: 199
Year Built: 1981
Rental Contact: Manager Christian Wolf

5730
AIA ACTOR'S STUDIO
1918 Magnola Boulevard
Suite 204
Burbank, CA 91506
Phone: 818-563-4142
Fax: 818-563-4318
Web Site: www.aiastudios.com
Officers:
VP/Director: Emily Yost
Management:
President: Katy Wallin
Executive Director: Anita Jhonson
Managing Director: Autrey Legassik
Mission: Mission is help actors achieve professional excellence. Has sucessfully integrated the business of acting with formal training. Instructors from the worlds of casting, producing, directing, writing and acting teach a diverse array of classes.
Utilizes: Actors; Educators; Filmmakers; Guest Instructors; Guest Soloists; Guest Teachers; Guild Activities; High School Drama
Founded: 1990
Status: For-Profit, Professional

Paid Staff: 10
Facility Category: Actor's Studio
Rental Contact: VP/Director Emily Yost

5731
SUNSET CULTURAL CENTER
PO Box 1950
Carmel, CA 93921
Phone: 831-620-2040
Fax: 831-624-0147
Web Site: www.sunsetcenter.org
Management:
Executive Director: Jack Globenfelt
Theater Manager: Michelle Edmunson
Mission: To provide performing arts experiences to the greater Monteray County area.
Founded: 2004
Specialized Field: Concerts; Recitals; Dance; Theater; Lectures
Paid Staff: 12
Paid Artists: 50
Budget: $1,850,000
Income Sources: Ticket Sales; Rent; Office Leases; Sponsorships; Governmental Supports

5732
CERRITOS CENTER FOR THE PERFORMING ARTS
12700 Center Court Drive
Cerritos, CA 90703
Phone: 562-916-8510
Fax: 562-916-8514
Toll-free: 800-300-4345
Web Site: www.cerritoscenter.com
Management:
Theatre Administrator: Dianne Cheney
Marketing Manager: Lauriey Kajiwana
Operations: Tom Hamilton
Performance Manager: Michael Wolfe
Utilizes: Special Technical Talent; Theatre Companies
Founded: 1993
Specialized Field: Present Pop; Jazz; Classical; Opera; Dance; Broadway; Holiday; Special Attractions
Status: For-Profit, Professional
Paid Staff: 100
Volunteer Staff: 500
Paid Artists: 100
Budget: $11,000,000
Income Sources: Ticket Sales; Rental Revenue
Affiliations: California Presenters; Western Arts Alliance; APAP; ISPA; IAAM; IATT
Annual Attendance: 200,000
Facility Category: Multi-configuration auditorium
Seating Capacity: 950-1800
Year Built: 1992
Cost: $105,000,000
Rental Contact: Cynthia Doss

5733
HARLEN ADAMS THEATRE
California State University, Chico
400 West First Street
Chico, CA 95929
Mailing Address: Department Name, if known, California State University, Chic
Phone: 530-898-4636
Fax: 530-898-6824
e-mail: darangoodsell@csuchico.edu
Web Site: http://www.csuchico.edu/thea
Officers:
President: Paul Zingg
Management:
Technical Director: Michael Johnson
Performing Arts Technician: Sandra L. Barton

Mission: Harlen Adams Theatre is used for cultural offerings in drama, opera, recitals, and choral programs.
Specialized Field: Dance, Music, Theatre
Type of Stage: Traditional Proscenium
Stage Dimensions: 40 foot
Orchestra Pit: y
Seating Capacity: 507

5734
LARRY WISMER THEATRE
California State University, Chico
400 West First Street
Chico, CA 95929
Mailing Address: Department Name, if known, California State University, Chic
Phone: 530-898-4636
Fax: 530-898-6824
e-mail: darangoodsell@csuchico.edu
Web Site: http://www.csuchico.edu/thea
Officers:
   President: Paul Zingg
Management:
   Technical Director: Michael Johnson
   Performing Arts Technician: Sandra L. Barton
Mission: Harlen Adams Theatre is used for cultural offerings in drama, opera, recitals, and choral programs.
Specialized Field: Dance, Music, Theatre
Type of Stage: Black Box
Seating Capacity: 200

5735
LAXSON AUDITORIUM
California State University, Chico
400 West First Street
Chico, CA 95929
Mailing Address: Department Name, if known, California State University, Chic
Phone: 530-898-4636
Fax: 530-898-6824
e-mail: darangoodsell@csuchico.edu
Web Site: http://www.csuchico.edu/thea
Officers:
   President: Paul Zingg
Management:
   Technical Director: Michael Johnson
   Performing Arts Technician: Sandra L. Barton
Mission: The Theatre Arts Department produces its spring musical in Laxson Auditorium. Many theatre students gain valuable experience as stage hands for the many events which are produced in Laxson.
Founded: 1931
Specialized Field: Dance, Music, Theatre
Type of Stage: Proscenium
Orchestra Pit: y
Seating Capacity: 1200

5736
ROLAND TAYLOR THEATRE
California State University-Chico
400 West 1st Street
Chico, CA 95929
Phone: 530-898-4636
Fax: 530-898-4797
e-mail: mus@csuchico.edu
Web Site: www.csuchico.edu/mus/
Officers:
   President: Paul Zingg
   Chairman: David J Colson
Management:
   Director: Dan De Wayne
   Managing Director Music: James Venkhead

Utilizes: Actors; Artists-in-Residence; Choreographers; Collaborating Artists; Collaborations; Commissioned Composers; Commissioned Music; Dance Companies; Dancers; Guest Accompanists; Guest Artists; Guest Instructors; Guild Activities; Instructors; Lyricists; Multi Collaborations; Multimedia; Original Music Scores; Sign Language Translators; Singers; Soloists; Special Technical Talent
Founded: 1887
Status: Nonprofit, Non-Professional
Budget: $400,000-$1,000,000
Performs At: Laxson Auditorium; Adams Theatre
Facility Category: Pit Stage; Proscenium
Seating Capacity: 1300; 500

5737
ROWLAND-TAYLOR RECITAL HALL
California State University, Chico
400 West First Street
Chico, CA 95929
Mailing Address: Department Name, if known, California State University, Chic
Phone: 530-898-4636
Fax: 530-898-6824
e-mail: darangoodsell@csuchico.edu
Web Site: http://www.csuchico.edu/thea
Officers:
   President: Paul Zingg
Management:
   Technical Director: Michael Johnson
   Performing Arts Technician: Sandra L. Barton
Mission: Ruth Rowland-Taylor Recital Hall is presently used for operas, recitals, concerts, choral workshops, performance art shows, and other university gatherings.
Specialized Field: Dance, Music, Theatre
Seating Capacity: 218

5738
GARRISON THEATRE
Scripps College
1030 Columbia Avenue
Claremont, CA 91711-3948
Mailing Address: PO Box 1229
Phone: 909-621-8187
Fax: 909-607-0001
e-mail: James_Taylor@pomona.edu
Web Site: www.scrippscol.edu/dept/conferences/PAC/garrison.html
Officers:
   President: Nancy Y Bekavac
   Public Relations/Communications: Mary Bartlett
   Planning & Research Director: Janel Hastings
   Vice President Business Affairs: James Manifold
   Chair Theatre/Dance Department: James P Taylor
Management:
   Chair Theatre/Dance Department: James P Taylor
Comments: Scripps College purchased Garrison Theater in 1999.

5739
MABEL SHAW BRIDGES AUDITORIUM
Claremont College
450 North College Way
Claremont, CA 91711
Phone: 909-621-8031
Fax: 909-621-8398
Web Site: www.cuc.claremont.edu/bridges/contact/index.html
Management:
   Director: Tim Morrison
   Events Manager: Sharon Kuhn
   Production Manager: Kurt Beardsley

Mission: 60,000 square feet of inside floor space; 14,000 square feet of porches and walks; seating of 2,494.

5740
SLEEP TRAIN PAVILLION AT CONCORD
2000 Kirker Pass Road
Concord, CA 94521
Phone: 925-676-8742
Fax: 925-676-8742
Web Site: www.chroniclepavilion.com/
Management:
   General Manager: Trevor Ralph
   Director Premium Seat Sales: Javier Olazaba
   Director Promotions: Aaron Siuda
   Director of Sponsorship Sales: Molly Manin
   Box Office Manager: Jozee Perrelli
   Office Manager: Loretta Hill
Opened: 1975

5741
WILLOWS THEATRE
1425 Gasoline Alley
Concord, CA 94520
Phone: 925-798-1300
Fax: 925-676-5726
e-mail: info@willowstheatre.org
Web Site: www.willowstheatre.org
Management:
   Artistic Director: Richard Elliot
   Managing Director: Andrew Holtz
   Development Director: Barbara Grant
   Production Manager: Chris Butler
   Education/Casting Director: Cassidy Brown
   Patron Services Director: Dan Uroff
   Associate Director Education: Becky Potter
   Box Office Manager: Jonathan Spencer
   Technical Director: Adam Puglieli
Founded: 1975
Status: Non-Profit, Professional
Paid Staff: 9
Paid Artists: 50
Season: January - December
Annual Attendance: 48,000
Type of Stage: Proscenium; Amphitheater
Stage Dimensions: 40' x 26'
Seating Capacity: 210; 1200

5742
ORANGE COUNTY PERFORMING ARTS CENTER
600 Town Center Drive
Costa Mesa, CA 92626
Phone: 714-556-2122
Fax: 714-556-8984
e-mail: info@ocpac.org
Web Site: www.ocpac.org
Officers:
   Chairman: Michael S Gordon, PhD
   Interim President: Judith O'Shea
   Treasurer: John R Evans
Management:
   Artistic Director: Paul Solino
   VP Programming: Judy Morr
Founded: 1986
Status: Non-Profit, Professional
Paid Staff: 75

5743
SOUTH COAST REPERTORY SEGERSTROM AUDITORIUM
655 Town Center Drive
Costa Mesa, CA 92628-2197

Mailing Address: PO Box 2197
Phone: 714-708-5500
Fax: 714-545-0391
e-mail: theatre@scr.org
Web Site: www.scr.org
Officers:
Chairman: Michael S Gordon
Interim President: Judith O'Dea Morr
Treasurer: John R Evans
Management:
Artistic Director: Martin Benson
Managing Director: Paula Tomei
Producing Artistic Director: David Emmes
Development Director: 0elaine Bennett
Marketing/Communications Director: Bill
Schroeder
Production Manager: Jeff Gifford
Operations Manager: Alan Almeida
Casting Director: Joanne DeNaut
Literary Manager: Megan Monaghan
Founded: 1954
Status: Non-Profit, Professional
Paid Staff: 75
Seating Capacity: 507

5744
VETERAN'S MEMORIAL COMPLEX

4117 Overland Avenue
Culver City, CA 90230
Phone: 310-253-6625
Fax: 310-253-6629
Web Site:
www.culvercity.org/citygov/humanservices/fac_reserv.ht
ml
Management:
City Parks & Recreation Director: Don Rogers
Veteran's Memorial Complex Manager: Pam
Robinson
City Recreation Manager: Marty Nicholson
City Parks Supervisor: Taks Matsurra
City Senior Management Analyst: Patti Mooney
Mission: The Veterans' Memorial Complex is a
Community and Recreation facility that includes a 1500
seat auditorium, 13 meeting and banquet rooms, a
basketball court, a Teen Center and a Senior Citizens
Center.
Founded: 1917
Status: For-Profit, Non-Professional

5745
FLINT CENTER FOR THE PERFORMING
ARTS

De Anza College
21250 Stevens Creek Boulevard, 4th Floor
Cupertino, CA 95015
Mailing Address: PO Box 1897
Phone: 408-864-8820
Fax: 408-864-8918
Web Site: www.flintcenter.com
Officers:
Dean Creative Arts Department: Nancy J Canter,
Ph.D
Management:
General Manager: Paula J Davis
Founded: 1971
Annual Attendance: 265,000
Type of Stage: Proscenium
Seating Capacity: 2,300

5746
BARBARA K & W TURRENTINE
JACKSON HALL

Mondavi Center
One Shields Avenue
Davis, CA 95616-8543
Mailing Address: University of California/Davis
Phone: 530-752-6071
Fax: 530-752-3055
Web Site:
http://hector.ucdavis.edu/ucdso/04Always/AboutJackso
nMondavi.htm
Management:
Executive Director: Don Roth Ph.D
Programming Director: Jeremy Genter
Campus Engagement Director: David Webbs
Marketing Manager: Rebecca Summers
Arts Education Community Director: Joyce
Donaldson
Director of Development: Silvia M H Lester
Director of Technology Services: Shaun Owens
Director Audience Services: Kelly Denny
Facility Director: John Dorsey
Founded: 1977
Status: Non-Profit, Non-Professional
Paid Staff: 240
Seating Capacity: 1,801

5747
ROBERT & MARGRIT MONDAVI CENTER
FOR THE PERFORMING ARTS

Mondavi Center Admin Bldg
One Shields Avenue
Davis, CA 95616-8543
Mailing Address: University of California/Davis
Phone: 530-754-2787
Fax: 530-756-3041
e-mail: droth@ucdavis.edu
Web Site: www.mondaviarts.org/
Management:
Executive Director: Don Roth
Programming Director: Jeremy Ganter
Director Campus Engagement: David Webb
Marketing Manager: Rebecca Summers
Director of Development: Silvia M H Lester
Ticketing Manager: Rickey Booker
Facility Director: John Dorsey
Director Business Services: Debbie Armstrong
Director Technology Services: Shaun Owens
Founded: 1961
Status: Non-Profit, Professional
Paid Staff: 5
Annual Attendance: 50,000
Seating Capacity: 200

5748
STUDIO THEATRE

University of California, Davis
Administration Building
One Shields Avenue
Davis, CA 95616-8543
Phone: 530-754-9055
Fax: 530-754-5519
e-mail: mcrentals@ucdavis.edu
Web Site: http://www.mondaviarts.org/
Officers:
President: Garry P. Maisel
Executive Director: Don Roth, PhD
Director Programming: Jeremy Ganter
Director of Facilities: John Dorsey
Management:
Production Stage Manager: Steve Lorick
Assistant Production Manager: Rick Berger

Mission: Presents a full range of campus-based and
international musical, theatrical and dance
performances and is a learning laboratory for students
of the performing arts.
Utilizes: Resident Artists
Specialized Field: Dance, Music, Theatre
Type of Stage: Adaptable Stage
Seating Capacity: 250
Year Built: 2002

5749
VETERANS' MEMORIAL THEATRE

203 East 14th Street
Davis, CA 95616
Phone: 530-757-5664
Fax: 530-758-9218
Web Site:
www.davisvisitor.com/brochures/Facility%20Guide%20a
nd%20Map
Management:
Executive Director: Robert Stephenson
Seating Capacity: 325

5750
W. TURRENTINE AND BARBARA K.
JACKSON HALL

University of California, Davis
Administration Building
One Shields Avenue
Davis, CA 95616-8543
Phone: 530-754-9055
Fax: 530-754-5519
e-mail: mcrentals@ucdavis.edu
Web Site: http://www.mondaviarts.org/
Officers:
President: Garry P. Maisel
Executive Director: Don Roth, PhD
Director Programming: Jeremy Ganter
Director of Facilities: John Dorsey
Management:
Production Stage Manager: Steve Lorick
Assistant Production Manager: Rick Berger
Mission: Presents a full range of campus-based and
international musical, theatrical and dance
performances and is a learning laboratory for students
of the performing arts.
Utilizes: Resident Artists
Specialized Field: Classical
Type of Stage: Adaptable Stage
Seating Capacity: 1800
Year Built: 2002

5751
EAST COUNTY PERFORMING ARTS
CENTER - THEATRE

210 E Main Street
El Cajon, CA 92020
Phone: 619-440-2277
Fax: 619-440-6429
Web Site: www.ecpac.com
Officers:
President/CEO: Dick Zellner
Management:
Executive Director: Paul Russell
Managing Director: Cathie Stanner
Operations Director: Melissa Hill
Technical Director: Kristina Claar
Marketing Director: Roxanne Fulkerson
Mission: Performing arts presenter and rental house.
We book nationally and internationally recognized
performers, from the Dixie Chicks to Bob Newhart, from
Alvin Ailey to Dave Kue.

Utilizes: Artists-in-Residence; Dance Companies; Fine Artists; Instructors; Local Artists; Multimedia; Original Music Scores; Special Technical Talent; Theatre Companies
Founded: 1977
Specialized Field: Concert Presenter; Arts Education; Visual Arts; Touring Theatres
Status: Non-Profit, Professional
Paid Staff: 8
Budget: $1,900,000
Income Sources: Ticket revenues; Corporate sponsors; Individual donors; Foundations
Performs At: East County Performing Arts Center
Affiliations: Western Alliance of Arts Admistrators, International Association ofAuditorium Managers
Annual Attendance: 100,000
Facility Category: Concert Hall
Type of Stage: Proscenium
Stage Dimensions: 40 x 70
Seating Capacity: 1,142
Year Built: 1977
Year Remodeled: 1998
Rental Contact: Director of Operations Melissa Hill

5752
SOUTHWEST PERFORMING ARTS THEATRE
2001 Ocotillo Drive
El Centro, CA 92243
Phone: 760-336-4228
Fax: 760-336-4244
e-mail: theatres@cuhsd.net
Web Site: www.southwesttheatre.com
Management:
President: Orland Foote
Theatre Manager: Ron Newhouse
Founded: 1996
Status: Non-Profit, Non-Professional
Paid Staff: 2
Seating Capacity: 1,150

5753
CALIFORNIA CENTER FOR THE ARTS-ESCONDIDO
340 N Escondido Boulevard
Escondido, CA 92025
Phone: 760-839-4138
Fax: 760-739-0205
Toll-free: 800-988-4253
Web Site: www.artcenter.org
Officers:
VP/General Manager: Vicky Basehore
Performing Arts Director: Joanne Ewan-Kroeger
Utilizes: Actors; Dance Companies; Multimedia; Singers; Student Interns; Special Technical Talent; Theatre Companies; Touring Companies
Founded: 1994
Status: Non-Profit, Professional
Paid Staff: 100

5754
FONTANA PERFORMING ARTS CENTER
9460 Sierra Avenue
Fontana, CA 92335
Phone: 909-428-8360
Fax: 909-428-2546
e-mail: kherron @ fontana.org
Web Site: www.fontana.org/main/parks_rec/rec_home.htm
Management:
Director: Ken Herron
Manager: Ray Gonzales
Status: Non-Profit, Professional

Paid Staff: 15

5755
GARY SOREN SMITH CENTER FOR THE FINE AND PERFORMING ARTS
43600 Mission Boulevard
Fremont, CA 94539
Phone: 510-659-6031
Fax: 510-659-6188
Web Site: www.smithcenter.com
Management:
Dean Fine Arts: Walt Birkedahl
Director Theatre Operations: Christopher Booras
Technical Coordinator: Jasper Gong
Mission: The Gary Soren Smith Center for the Fine and Performing Arts houses the G. Craig Jackson main stage theater with a seating capacity of 405, the NUMMI studio theater, the Louie Art Gallery, an outdoor amphitheater, a dance studio, television studios, and a radio station.
Founded: 1995
Opened: 1995
Specialized Field: Performing Arts

5756
BULLDOGS STADIUM
5305 North Campus Drive NG27
Fresno, CA 93740
Phone: 559-278-2643
Fax: 559-278-6611
Web Site: http://gobulldogs.cstv.com/
Management:
Director Athletics Department: Thomas Boeh
Facilities Operations Director: John Kriebs
Athletic Development Director: Gregory Walaitis
Operations Manager: Richard Enns
Athletic Compliance Director: John Lucier
Marketing Director: Sarah Teachey
Director Media Relations: Steve Weakland
Director External Affairs: Paul Ladwig
Founded: 1980
Seating Capacity: 41,031

5757
FRESNO CONVENTION & ENTERTAINMENT CENTER
848 M Street
2nd Floor
Fresno, CA 93721
Phone: 559-445-8100
Fax: 559-445-8110
e-mail: bill.overfelt@fresno.gov
Web Site: www.fresnoconventioncenter.com/index2.asp
Management:
Director Finance: Lyn Higginson
General Manager: Bill Overfelt
Director Sales Marketing: Claudia Arquelles
Director Events Services: Wilhelmina Santana
Director Operations: Theresa Kraus
Box Office Manager: Matt Heinks
Sales Manager Sports Council: Kelly Carr
Mission: Robert A. Schoettler Conference Center, with a 13,129 square foot ballroom which can accommodate 1,200 theatre style seats or 900 for a banquet; William Saroyan Theatre With 2,353 luxuriously upholstered seats; Convention Center features 67,000 square feet of uninterrupted exhibit space with an additional 16,000 square feet of available exhibit space in the first and second floor lobbies; and the Selland Arena with a seating capacity of 11,300.
Founded: 1966
Paid Staff: 60

Volunteer Staff: 150
Budget: $2 Million
Income Sources: Rentals
Performs At: Performing Arts Theater
Year Built: 1966
Year Remodeled: 1992
Cost: $ 3 Million
Rental Contact: Mercy Tritian

5758
RATCLIFFE STADIUM
1101 East University Avenue
Fresno, CA 93741
Phone: 559-442-4600
Fax: 559-237-4232
Toll-free: 866-245-3276
e-mail: susan.yates@fresnocitycollege.edu
Web Site: www.fresnocitycollege.edu/athletics/html
Management:
Athletic Director: Susan Yates
Sports Publicist: Woody Wilk
Communications/Marketing Director: Cris Monahan Bremer
Public Information Officer: Kathleen Bonilla
Business Manager: Michael Guerra
Founded: 1926
Seating Capacity: 13,500

5759
WARNOR'S THEATER
1400 Fulton Street
Fresno, CA 93721
Phone: 559-264-6863
Fax: 559-264-5643
e-mail: paul@warnors.com
Web Site: www.warnors.com/
Management:
General Manager: Paul Fountaine
Mission: Warnors Theatre, located in downtown Fresno, has a rich heritage reaching back to its inaugural year of 1928, having a seating capacity of 2,100.
Founded: 1928

5760
WHALBERG RECITAL HALL
California State University Fresno
2380 East Keats
Fresno, CA 93740
Mailing Address: Department of Theatre Arts, 5201 N. Maple Ave., M/S SA46, Fr
Phone: 559-278-4240
Fax: 559-.27-8.72
e-mail: pamd@csufresno.edu
Web Site: www.csufresno.edu, http://www.csufresno.edu/theatreart
Management:
President: John Welty
Executive Director: Deborah Adishian-Astone
Director Human Resources: Jeannine Raymond
AVP Government/Public Relations: Mark Aydelotte
Public Information Specialist: Tom Uribes
Director Publications/New Media: Bruce Whitworth
Director Campaign Communications: Shannon Puphal
Mission: Theatre Arts students work side-by-side with faculty to create exciting productions
Founded: 1911
Specialized Field: Dance, Music, Theatre
Status: For-Profit, Professional
Seating Capacity: 100

5761
HALLBERG THEATRE
California State University, Fullerton
800 N. State College Blvd
Fullerton, CA 92831-3599
Mailing Address: CSU Fullerton, Visual Arts
Department, P.O. Box 6850, Fuller
Phone: 714-278-2011
Fax: 714-278-2649
e-mail: gaildawson@fullerton.edu
Web Site: www.fullerton.edu/arts
Officers:
   President: Milton A. Gordon
   Dean Performing Arts: Jerry D. Samuelson
Management:
   Chair: Marc R. Dickey
   Department Administrative Coordinat: Gail
   Dawson
   Department Chair: Larry Johnson
Mission: The new performing arts center will expand
the theatre, dance and music programs' physical
capabilities, but allow imaginations to soar and explore
new artistic possibilities.
Specialized Field: Experimental Productions and will
showcase new plays, ballet
Type of Stage: Black Box
Seating Capacity: 150
Architect: Pfeiffer Partners

5762
MENG CONCERT HALL
California State University, Fullerton
800 N. State College Blvd
Fullerton, CA 92831-3599
Mailing Address: CSU Fullerton, Department of Music,
P.O. Box 6850, Fullerton
Phone: 714-278-2011
Fax: 714-278-2649
e-mail: gaildawson@fullerton.edu
Web Site: www.fullerton.edu/arts
Officers:
   President: Milton A. Gordon
   Dean Performing Arts: Jerry D. Samuelson
Management:
   Chair: Marc R. Dickey
   Department Administrative Coordinat: Gail
   Dawson
   Department Chair: Larry Johnson
Mission: The new performing arts center will expand
the theatre, dance and music programs' physical
capabilities, but allow imaginations to soar and explore
new artistic possibilities.
Specialized Field: Choral and Instrumental Ensembles
Seating Capacity: 800
Architect: Pfeiffer Partners

5763
MUCKENTHALER CULTURAL CENTER
1201 W Malvern Avenue
Fullerton, CA 92833
Phone: 714-738-6595
Fax: 714-738-6366
Toll-free: 866-411-1212
e-mail: info@themuck.org
Web Site: www.themuck.org
Officers:
   President: Fred A Weelen
Management:
   Executive Director: Zoot Velasco
   Director Of Exhibitions: Matthew Leslie
   Marketing Director: Kevin Stanlec
   Lead Artist: Willie Tabath

Mission: To provide our community experiences that
stimulate creativity and imagination, and to conserve
the heritage and architecture of the Muckenthaler
estate.
Founded: 1965
Specialized Field: Multi-Cultural/Multi Discipline
Status: For-Profit, Professional
Paid Staff: 11
Volunteer Staff: 600
Paid Artists: 9
Budget: $724,968
Income Sources: City, Corporation and Foundation
Grants; Generated Revenue
Performs At: Outdoor Amphitheatre
Annual Attendance: 25,000
Facility Category: Historic Mansion

5764
PLUMMER AUDITORIUM
201 East Chapman Avenue
Fullerton, CA 92838
Mailing Address: PO Box 5786
Phone: 714-870-2813
Fax: 714-870-3768
e-mail: marilyn@fclo.com
Web Site: www.fclo.com
Officers:
   President: John Bedell
   Vice President: Norma Jones
   Secretary: Doris Winters
   Treasurer: Gordon Haag, MD
Management:
   Producer: Griff Duncan
   Artistic Director: Jan Duncan
   Resident Stage Manager: Donna Parsons
   Costume Rental Manager: Faye Robinson
   Scenic Operations Manager: Larry Knigge
   Public Relations/Marketing/Sales: Marilyn
   Gianetti
Mission: Plummer Auditorium is home to the Fullerton
Civic Light Opera, the mission of which is to present live
stage musicals for the enjoyment and cultural
enrichment of the general public at affordable prices. A
key focus of their mission is to educate youth in this
distinctly American art form, and create a lasting
interest and appreciation for it in addition to providing
access for under priviledged youth and adults.
Founded: 1930
Specialized Field: Theater, Musicals
Status: non- profit
Annual Attendance: r
Seating Capacity: 1,300

5765
YOUNG THEATRE
California State University, Fullerton
800 N. State College Blvd
Fullerton, CA 92831-3599
Mailing Address: CSU Fullerton, Department of
Theater and Dance, P.O. Box 685
Phone: 714-278-2011
Fax: 714-278-2649
e-mail: ddombrow@fullerton.edu
Web Site: www.fullerton.edu/arts
Officers:
   President: Milton A. Gordon
   Dean Performing Arts: Jerry D. Samuelson
Management:
   Chair: Marc R. Dickey
   Department Administrative Coordinat: Debbie
   Dombrow
   Department Chair: Bruce Goodrich
   Graduate Coordinator: David Nevell

Mission: The new performing arts center will expand
the theatre, dance and music programs' physical
capabilities, but allow imaginations to soar and explore
new artistic possibilities.
Specialized Field: Dramatic Productions from the
Classics to Contemporary
Type of Stage: Thrust Stage Theatre
Seating Capacity: 250
Architect: Pfeiffer Partners

5766
ALEX THEATRE
216 North Brand Boulevard
Glendale, CA 91203
Phone: 818-243-7700
Fax: 818-243-3622
Toll-free: 818-243-ALEX
e-mail: admin@alextheatre.org
Web Site: www.alextheatre.org
Officers:
   Chairman: Ted Osborn
   Vice Chairman: David Simon
   VP Finance/Treasurer: John Simpson
   Secretary: Helene Dervishian
   VP Membership: Marcia Hanford
Management:
   Executive Director: Barry McComb
   Director Theatre Operations: Jack Allaway
   Marketing/Resource Development: Elissa
   Glickman
   Assistant Technical Director: Stepanie Losleben
   Box Office Manager: Judith Baker
   Controller: Sandy Leitao
   Maintenance Supervisor: Hector Martinez
   Master Electrician: David Robkin
   Event Services Manager: Karen Smith
Founded: 1925
Seating Capacity: 1,460

5767
HAUGH PERFORMING ARTS CENTER
Citrus College
1000 West Foothill Boulevard
Glendora, CA 91741
Phone: 626-963-9411
Fax: 626-335-4715
e-mail: hpac@citruscollege.edu
Web Site: www.haughpac.com
Officers:
   President: Dr Geraldine Perri
Management:
   Performing Arts Director: Greg Hinrichsen
   Marketing/Ticketing Supervisor: Linda Graves
Founded: 1971
Status: Nonprofit, Non-Professional
Paid Staff: 6
Paid Artists: 10
Annual Attendance: 100,000
Type of Stage: Flexible; Proscenium
Seating Capacity: 1,400

5768
CALIFORNIA STATE
UNIVERSITY-HAYWARD - MAIN THEATRE
Theatre & Dance Department
220 Robinson Hall CSUEB
Hayward, CA 94542
Mailing Address: 25800 Carlos Bee Boulevard
Phone: 510-885-3118
Fax: 510-885-4748
e-mail: applycsh@csuhayward.edu
Web Site: http://class.csueastbay.edu/theatre
Officers:
   President: Norma Reese

Department Chairman: Thomas Hird
College/Department Dean: Alden Reimonenq, Ph.D
Management:
Director New Music Theatre: Darryl V Jones
Artistic Director: Timothy Smith
Mission: Built in 1971, the theatre building houses two theatres - the 480-seat main University Theatre and the flexible Studio Theatre, which can seat between 150 to 250.
Status: Non-Profit, Non-Professional
Paid Staff: 35
Paid Artists: 18

5769
CHABOT COLLEGE PERFORMING ARTS CENTER
Chabot College
25555 Hesperian Boulevard
Hayward, CA 94545
Phone: 510-723-6976
Fax: 510-723-7157
e-mail: kmcallister@chabotcollege.edu
Web Site: www.chabotcollege.edu/PAC/
Officers:
Dean: Gary Carter
Management:
Theatre Manager: Kari McAllister
Stage Technician: Gene Hale
Community Education Specialist: Judy Vetters
Director Community Education/Mrktng: Susan May
Mission: First opened in 1967, the Performing Arts Center is a 1,432-seat auditorium, which functions as a full featured theater. The Little Theater, located in Building 1200, is a 200 seat capacity intimate viewing space that is ideal for meetings, movies and other smaller scaled productions.
Founded: 1967
Status: Non-Profit, Professional
Paid Staff: 15
Income Sources: Rentals
Annual Attendance: 100,000
Type of Stage: Proscenium
Stage Dimensions: 36'x45'
Seating Capacity: 1,432
Year Built: 1967
Cost: $1.8 million

5770
STUDIO THEATRE
California State University, East Bay
Theatre And Dance Department
220 Robinson Hall, 25800 Carlos Bee Blvd
Hayward, CA 94542
Phone: 510-885-3118
e-mail: thomas.hird@csueastbay.edu
Web Site: http://class.csueastbay.edu/theatre/
Officers:
President: Mo Qayoumi
Management:
Department Chair: Tom Hird
Mission: Performance at Cal State is an important aspect of the department's undergraduate curriculum. The program leading to the Bachelor or Arts in Theatre degree provides comprehensive instruction in the theatre arts.
Specialized Field: Dance, Music, Theatre
Type of Stage: Flexible
Seating Capacity: 250

5771
UNIVERSITY THEATRE
California State University, East Bay
Theatre And Dance Department
220 Robinson Hall, 25800 Carlos Bee Blvd
Hayward, CA 94542
Phone: 510-885-3118
e-mail: thomas.hird@csueastbay.edu
Web Site: http://class.csueastbay.edu/theatre/
Officers:
President: Mo Qayoumi
Management:
Department Chair: Tom Hird
Mission: Performance at Cal State is an important aspect of the department's undergraduate curriculum. The program leading to the Bachelor or Arts in Theatre degree provides comprehensive instruction in the theatre arts.
Specialized Field: Dance, Music, Theatre
Seating Capacity: 480

5772
RAMONA BOWL AMPHITHEATRE
27400 Ramona Bowl Road
Hemet, CA 92544
Phone: 909-658-3111
Fax: 909-658-2695
Toll-free: 800-645-4465
e-mail: ramona@ramonabowl.com
Web Site: www.ramonabowl.com
Officers:
President: James A Pomeroy Jr
Vice President: Louis Amestoy
Secretary: Rose Salgado
Treasurer: Ron Hoffman
Management:
General Manager: D Janine Mundwiler
Artistic Director: Dennis Anderson
Business Manager: Kathy Long
Mission: To promote and produce The Ramona Pageant, America's longest running outdoor drama; to promote the Ramona Bowl Amphitheatre for events.
Founded: 1927
Status: Non-Profit, Non-Professional
Seating Capacity: 6,500

5773
HOLLYWOOD BOWL
2301 N Highland Avenue
Hollywood, CA 90078
Phone: 323-850-2000
Fax: 323-850-2155
e-mail: dborda@laphil.org
Web Site: www.hollywoodbowl.com
Management:
President: Debra Borda
Artistic Director: Esa Pekka Salonen
Director Development: Emily Laskin
Founded: 1922
Status: For-Profit, Professional
Seating Capacity: 18,000

5774
HOLLYWOOD COMPLEX THEATRE
6476 Santa Monica Boulevard
Hollywood, CA 90038
Phone: 323-465-0383
Fax: 323-469-5408
Web Site: www.complexhollywood.com
Management:
President/Director: Matt Chait

Mission: The Hollywood Complex Theatres consists of: the Ruby Theatre with a seating capacity of 55; Dorie Theatre - seating capacity of 55; Flight Theatre - seating capacity of 49; Theatre 6470 - seating capacity of 42; and the East Theatre with a seating capacity of 49.
Founded: 1989
Status: For-Profit, Non-Professional
Paid Staff: 1
Paid Artists: 1

5775
HOLLYWOOD PALLADIUM
6215 W Sunset Boulevard
Hollywood, CA 90028
Phone: 323-962-7600
Fax: 323-962-7502
Web Site: www.hollywoodpalladium.com
Management:
President: Allan Shuman
Mission: We are an all purpose revue that has music acts as well as conventions and dinner events.
Founded: 1940
Status: For-Profit, Non-Professional

5776
JOHN ANSON FORD THEATRES
2580 Cahauga Boulevard E
Hollywood, CA 90068
Phone: 323-856-5793
Fax: 323-464-1158
e-mail: dpiern@bos.co.la.ca.us
Web Site: www.fordamphitheatre.org
Management:
Managing Director: David Pier
Director Development: Mark Stambler
Founded: 1920
Status: Volunteer
Facility Category: Amphitheatre/ Black Box
Seating Capacity: 1245/87
Rental Contact: David Pier

5777
KODAK THEATRE
6801 North Hollywood Boulevard
Suite 180
Hollywood, CA 90028
Mailing Address: 6801 Hollywood Boulevard, Hollywood, CA 90028, Level One of
Phone: 323-308-6300
Fax: 323-308-6381
e-mail: info@kodaktheatre.com
Web Site: www.kodaktheatre.com
Management:
Managing Director: Jay Thomas
Marketing/Event Services Manager: Natalie Vo
Box Office Manager: Ly Pham
Technical Director: Alys Holden
Mission: Kodak Theatre is the crown jewel of the Hollywood & Highland Center retail, dining and entertainment complex located in the heart of historic Hollywood.
Founded: 2001
Specialized Field: Concerts, Comedians, American Ballet Theatre and various touring Broadway productions, award events
Seating Capacity: 3.400

5778
RICARDO MONTALBAN THEATER
Will and Company
1615 North Vine Street
Hollywood, CA 92262

Mailing Address: 1615 North Vine Street
Phone: 323-465-4167
e-mail: margacannon@yahoo.com
Web Site: http://www.themontalban.com/
Officers:
President: Jerry G Velasco
1st Vice President: Felipe Alejandro
2nd Vice President: Jesse Arranda
Secretary: Lina Madero
Treasurer: Louis Hernandez
Management:
Nosotros Talent Directory Manager: Alex Castillo
Casting/Membership Director: Elizabeth Miera
American Latino Film Festival Mgr: Felipe Alejandro
Showcase/E-Group Manager: Jesse Aranda
Artistic Director: Margarita Cannan
Managing Producer: Gilbert A. Smith
Mission: The program, designed to inspire children's imaginations through reading and live performance
Founded: 1926
Specialized Field: Movies, theater, concerts, sports, award ceremonies.
Seating Capacity: 1,200

5779
THEATRE EAST
6760 Lexington Avenue
Hollywood, CA 90038
Phone: 323-957-5720
Web Site:
www.theatreeast.com/interface/index.php?action=home
Officers:
President: Chris White
Director: Leif Gantvoort
Director: Peter Haskell
Director: Alan Naggar
Director: Walter Novak
Director: Tabatha Sheltra
Director: Pag Shirley
Mission: Theatre East was founded in 1960 to provide a forum and workshop for professional artists in the theatrical and allied arts to develop their talents and skills through live performance and evaluation. The Lex, where Theate East is housed, is a versatile, 49-seat black-box theatre space that can be variously configured to suit your staging requirements.
Founded: 1960

5780
GOLDEN WEST COLLEGE MAINSTAGE THEATRE
15744 Golden West Street
Huntington Beach, CA 92647-2748
Phone: 714-892-7711
Fax: 714-895-8784
e-mail: tamen@.gwc.cccd.edu
Web Site: www.gwctheater.com/
Management:
Director: Tom Amen
Director: Martie Ramm
Stage Crew/Set Construction: Sigrid Wolf
Costuming/Makeup: Susan Babb
Production Secretary: Pat Stingle
Usher: Ann Yarchin
Status: Non-Profit, Professional
Paid Staff: 800
Seating Capacity: 367

5781
GREAT WESTERN FORUM
3900 West Manchester Boulevard
Inglewood, CA 90301

Mailing Address: 3900 West Manchester Blvd.,
Inglewood, Ca 90305
Phone: 310-330-7300
Fax: 310-679-2375
e-mail: info@thelaforum.com
Web Site: www.thelaforum.com/index.php
Management:
General Manager: Gene Felling
Director Event Services: Denise Williams
Director Finance: Richard Nissenbaum
Director Operations: Bill Rydum
Human Resources: Molly Pascucci
Mission: The venue now serves as the home of Faithful Central Bible Church's congregation as well as a gathering place for concerts and community events
Founded: 1968
Opened: 1968
Specialized Field: Home of the Los Angeles Sparks (WNBA)
Seating Capacity: 18,000

5782
BREN EVENTS CENTER
University of California, Irvine
100 Bren Events Center
Irvine, CA 92697
Phone: 949-824-5050
Fax: 949-824-5097
e-mail: bmstrobe@uci.edu
Web Site: www.bren.uci.edu
Management:
Director: Bernadette Strobel-Lopez
Business Manager: Kristina Engel
Office Manager: Sheryl Suarez
Technical Manager: David Da Costa
Maintenance Supervisor: Jack Brooks
Production/Events Manager: Carla Gonzalez
Booking Manager: Jeff Grady
Events/Operations Manager: Daniel Spitzer
Manager: Marko Popovich
Mission: The Bren Center has a maximum capacity of 5,700 for concert and entertainment events with 4,984 for court sports such as basketball and volleyball. There are 2,610 fixed seats, 2,374 in retracting or telescopic bleachers.
Founded: 1987
Status: For-Profit, Non-Professional
Paid Staff: 80
Annual Attendance: 175,000
Type of Stage: Portable

5783
CLAIRE TREVOR SCHOOL OF THE ARTS
University of California, Irvine
4000 Mesa Road
Irvine, CA 92697
Web Site: www.arts.uci.edu
Officers:
Director Marketing: Wendy Day-Brown
Director Development: Ryan Marsh
Production Manager: Toby F. Weiner
Facilities Manager: Anthony E. Marquez
Mission: Dedicated to the study of the visual and performing arts.
Specialized Field: Arts; Live Music; Performance; Stage; Theater
Type of Stage: Proscenium
Seating Capacity: 285

5784
IRVINE BARCLAY THEATRE
4199 Campus Drive
Suite 680
Irvine, CA 92612

e-mail: info@thebarclay.org
Web Site: www.thebarclay.org
Officers:
President: Douglas C. Rankin
Vice President: Domenick Ietto
General Manager: Chris Burrill
Dir Communications/Program Dvlpment: Karen Drews Hanlon
Production Manager: Jim Laird
Mission: The mission of the Irvine Barclay Theatre is to be a presenter featuring the work of diverse and exceptional artists and providing a state-of-the-art venue for community cultural organizations and University programs, thus broadening the scope, availability and appreciation of the performing arts in Orange County.
Specialized Field: Dance; Music; Theatre
Status: Private, Not-for-Profit
Type of Stage: Proscenium
Stage Dimensions: 87'3W x 40'6D
Orchestra Pit: Y
Seating Capacity: 750

5785
WINIFRED SMITH HALL
University of California
4000 Mesa Road
Irvine, CA 92697
Web Site: www.arts.uci.edu
Officers:
Director Marketing: Wendy Day-Brown
Director Development: Ryan Marsh
Production Manager: Toby F. Weiner
Facilities Manager: Anthony E. Marquez
Mission: Dedicated to the study of the visual and performing arts.
Specialized Field: Arts; Live Music; Performance; Stage; Theater
Type of Stage: Modified Thrust Platform Stage
Seating Capacity: 230

5786
ATHENAEUM MUSIC & ARTS LIBRARY
1008 Wall Street
La Jolla, CA 92037
Phone: 858-454-5872
Fax: 858-454-5835
e-mail: athlib@pacbell.net
Management:
Managing Director: Erika Torri
Program Director: Geoffrey Brooks
Utilizes: Artists-in-Residence; Commissioned Composers; Commissioned Music; Curators; Fine Artists; Grant Writers; Guest Companies; Guest Directors; Guest Ensembles; Guest Instructors; Guest Musical Directors; Guest Musicians; Guest Soloists; High School Drama; Instructors; Local Artists; Multi Collaborations; Multimedia; Organization Contracts; Original Music Scores; Playwrights; Sign Language Translators; Singers; Touring Companies
Founded: 1898
Status: Non-Profit, Professional
Paid Staff: 20
Volunteer Staff: 150
Paid Artists: 80
Non-paid Artists: 20
Budget: $ 1.2 Million
Income Sources: Memberships; Donations
Performs At: Athenaem; Neurosciences Institute
Facility Category: Library
Seating Capacity: 140; 350
Rental Contact: Susan Dilts

5787
DANCE STUDIO 3
University of California, San Diego
Molli and Arthur Wagner Dance Building
9500 Gilman Drive MC0344
La Jolla, CA 92093
Phone: 858-534-3791
Fax: 858-534-1080
e-mail: promotions@ucsd.edu
Web Site: http://www-theatre.ucsd.edu/facilities/
Officers:
   Chancellor: Marye Anne Fox
Management:
   Assistant Production Manager: Michael D. Francis
Mission: UCSD's theatre and dance facilities are among the best. We share our home, The Mandell Weiss Center for the Performing Arts, with the La Jolla Playhouse.
Specialized Field: Dance, Theatre
Type of Stage: Black Box
Seating Capacity: 120

5788
GALBRAITH HALL STUDIO THEATRE 157
University of California, San Diego
Galbraith Hall, First Floor
9500 Gilman Drive MC0344
La Jolla, CA 92093
Phone: 858-534-3791
Fax: 858-534-1080
e-mail: promotions@ucsd.edu
Web Site: http://www-theatre.ucsd.edu/facilities/
Officers:
   Chancellor: Marye Anne Fox
Management:
   Assistant Production Manager: Michael D. Francis
Mission: UCSD's theatre and dance facilities are among the best. We share our home, The Mandell Weiss Center for the Performing Arts, with the La Jolla Playhouse.
Specialized Field: Dance, Theatre
Type of Stage: Thrust
Seating Capacity: 99

5789
MANDELL WEISS FORUM STUDIO
University of California, San Diego
Department of Theatre and Dance
9500 Gilman Drive MC0344
La Jolla, CA 92093
Phone: 858-534-3791
Fax: 858-534-1080
e-mail: promotions@ucsd.edu
Web Site: http://www-theatre.ucsd.edu/facilities/
Officers:
   Chancellor: Marye Anne Fox
Management:
   Assistant Production Manager: Michael D. Francis
Mission: UCSD's theatre and dance facilities are among the best. We share our home, The Mandell Weiss Center for the Performing Arts, with the La Jolla Playhouse.
Specialized Field: Dance, Theatre
Type of Stage: Black Box
Seating Capacity: 100

5790
MANDELL WEISS FORUM
University of California, San Diego
Department of Theatre and Dance
9500 Gilman Drive MC0344
La Jolla, CA 92093
Phone: 858-534-3791
Fax: 858-534-1080
e-mail: promotions@ucsd.edu
Web Site: http://www-theatre.ucsd.edu/facilities/
Officers:
   Chancellor: Marye Anne Fox
Management:
   Assistant Production Manager: Michael D. Francis
Mission: UCSD's theatre and dance facilities are among the best. We share our home, The Mandell Weiss Center for the Performing Arts, with the La Jolla Playhouse.
Specialized Field: Dance, Theatre
Type of Stage: Thrust
Seating Capacity: 400
Architect: Antoine Predock

5791
MANDELL WEISS THEATRE
University of California, San Diego
Department of Theatre and Dance
9500 Gilman Drive MC0344
La Jolla, CA 92093
Phone: 858-534-3791
Fax: 858-534-1080
e-mail: promotions@ucsd.edu
Web Site: http://www-theatre.ucsd.edu/facilities/
Officers:
   Chancellor: Marye Anne Fox
Management:
   Assistant Production Manager: Michael D. Francis
Mission: UCSD's theatre and dance facilities are among the best. We share our home, The Mandell Weiss Center for the Performing Arts, with the La Jolla Playhouse.
Specialized Field: Dance, Theatre
Type of Stage: Proscenium
Stage Dimensions: 40'x 23'
Orchestra Pit: y
Seating Capacity: 500

5792
MANDEVILLE THEATRE
University of California San Diego
Department of Theatre and Dance
La Jolla, CA 92093
Phone: 858-534-3791
Fax: 858-534-1080
e-mail: theatrefrontdesk@ucsd.edu
Web Site:
http://hds.ucsd.edu/conference/mandeville.html
Management:
   President: Walt Jones
   Executive Director: Mark Maltby
   Production Manager: Tom Aberger
Mission: The Mandeville Center has two theatres; the Auditorium, which seats 785 and the Recital Hall, which seats 150.
Founded: 1963
Status: Non-Profit, Non-Professional
Paid Staff: 35
Paid Artists: 50

5793
SHEILA & HUGHES POTIKER THEATRE
University of California, San Diego
Department of Theatre and Dance
9500 Gilman Drive MC0344
La Jolla, CA 92093
Phone: 858-534-3791
Fax: 858-534-1080
e-mail: promotions@ucsd.edu
Web Site: http://www-theatre.ucsd.edu/facilities/
Officers:
   Chancellor: Marye Anne Fox
Management:
   Assistant Production Manager: Michael D. Francis
Mission: UCSD's theatre and dance facilities are among the best. We share our home, The Mandell Weiss Center for the Performing Arts, with the La Jolla Playhouse.
Specialized Field: Dance, Theatre
Type of Stage: Thrust, Round, Proscenium, Traverse
Stage Dimensions: 70' x 80'
Seating Capacity: 417

5794
SHERWOOD AUDITORIUM
Museum of Contemporary Art - San Diego
700 Prospect Street
La Jolla, CA 92037
Phone: 858-454-3541
Fax: 858-729-0912
e-mail: events@mcasd.org
Web Site: www.mcasd.org/aboutg/host-you-event
Management:
   Hospitality & Events Manager: Edie Nehls
   Hospitality & Events Coordinator: Eric Reichman
Founded: 1940
Status: Non-Profit, Professional
Paid Staff: 50
Performs At: Auditorium
Type of Stage: Proscenium
Stage Dimensions: 45' X 25'
Seating Capacity: 492

5795
CHASE GYMNASIUM
Biola University
13800 Biola Avenue
La Mirada, CA 90639
Phone: 562-903-6000
Fax: 562-903-4746
e-mail: georgeboesflug@truth.biola.edu
Web Site: www.biola.edu
Officers:
   President: Clide Cook
Management:
   Music Department Chairman: George Boespflug
Founded: 1908
Income Sources: Ticket sales
Performs At: Lansing Auditorium
Seating Capacity: 450

5796
LA MIRADA THEATRE FOR THE PERFORMING ARTS
14900 La Mirada Boulevard
La Mirada, CA 90638
Phone: 714-994-6310
Fax: 714-994-5796
e-mail: jbrown@lamiradatheatre.com
Web Site: www.lamiradatheatre.com
Management:
   Executive Director: Jeff Brown

Ticketing Services Manager: Debbie J Walker
Technical Director: David Cruise
Founded: 1947
Status: City Owned Professional Theatre
Paid Staff: 50
Volunteer Staff: 100
Annual Attendance: 200,000
Facility Category: Performing Arts
Type of Stage: Proscenium
Stage Dimensions: 46'x26'x40'
Seating Capacity: 1,251
Year Built: 1977
Year Remodeled: 1999
Rental Contact: Laura Moore

5797
LAGUNA PLAYHOUSE

606 Laguna Canyon Road
Laguna Beach, CA 92652
Mailing Address: PO Box 1747
Phone: 949-494-8021
Fax: 949-376-8185
Toll-free: 800-946-5556
Web Site: www.lagunaplayhouse.com
Management:
   Executive Director: Richard Stein
   Business Manager: Kat Hicklin
   Artistic Director: Andrew Barnicle
   Technical Director: Jerry Stratton
   Director Development/Marketing: Greg Patterson
   Director Youth Theatre: Donna Inglima
   Production Manager: Jim Ryan
Founded: 1920
Annual Attendance: 100,000
Type of Stage: Open Proscenium
Seating Capacity: 420

5798
LANDCASTER PERFORMING ARTS CENTER

750 West Lancaster Boulevard
Lancaster, CA 93534
Fax: 661-723-5945
Web Site: www.ipac.org
Management:
   Manager: Mary Tanner
   Marketing Manager: Danise Baker
   Technical Director: Rodney Stickrod
   Business Operation Manager: Judy Kepa
   Education/Rental Coordinator: Tanya Stows
Seating Capacity: 792

5799
LONG BEACH CONVENTION AND ENTERTAINMENT CENTER

300 East Ocean Boulevard
Long Beach, CA 90802
Phone: 562-436-3636
Fax: 562-436-9491
e-mail: dspellens@longbeachcc.com
Web Site: www.longbeachcc.com/mainmenu.asp
Management:
   Director Operations: Rob Collins,
      rcollins@longbeachcc.com
   General Manager: David G Gordon,
      dgordon@longbeachcc.com
   Box Office Manager: Vicky Hanssen,
      vhanssen@longbeachcc.com
   Director Of Event Services: Taylor Marcellaus
   Catering Sales Manager: Alyssa Rosen
   Sales Director: Ellen Swartz
   Director-Theatres & Entertainment: Dan Spellins
   Assistant General Manager: Dan Lee

Mission: The Convention & Entertainment Center's
Arena has seating capacity of 13,500, and 46,000
square feet of exhibit space and the Arena Concourse
has 29,000 square feet of exhibit space. There are also
3 exhibit halls providing 224,0000 square feet of space
for all types of conventions, tradeshows, consumer
shows and special events; the Terrace Theatre, a full
production proscenium theatre that seats 3,051 and a
thrust stage seating 825.
Utilizes: Actors; Choreographers; Dance Companies;
Dancers; Grant Writers; Guest Composers; Guest
Designers; Guest Instructors; Guest Lecturers; Guest
Musical Directors; Guest Musicians; Multimedia; Music;
Original Music Scores; Resident Artists; Selected
Students; Sign Language Translators; Singers; Special
Technical Talent; Theatre Companies
Facility Category: Performing Arts Center
Type of Stage: Permanent; Proscenium
Stage Dimensions: 66 x 35
Year Built: 1928
Year Remodeled: 1999
Rental Contact: Director-Theatres & Entertainment
Dan Spellens

5800
LONG BEACH PLAYHOUSE

5021 East Anaheim Street
Long Beach, CA 90804
Phone: 562-494-1014
Fax: 562-961-8616
e-mail: boxoffice@lbplayhouse.org
Web Site: www.lbplayhouse.org
Officers:
   President: David Haberbush
   Vice President: Braden Phillips
   Secretary: Betty Karnette
   Treasurer: Margo Carter
   Chairman: Bill Friedrichs
Management:
   Managing Director: Lauren Morris
   Artistic Director: Andrew Vonderschmitt
   Designer/Costume Shop Manager: Donna
   Fritsche
   Head Ticket Services: Christa Svorinich
   Public Relations Manager: Cort Huckabone
   Community Outreach: Michael Ross
Mission: To nuture and cultivate new and traditional
audiences, as well as emerging and established artists;
encourage the participation of all interested individuals;
maintain a strong theater which includes traditional
plays and classics, new works and thought-provoking,
socially significant productions, and is accessible to our
socially and economically diverse community.
Founded: 1929
Status: Non-Profit, Professional
Paid Staff: 12
Volunteer Staff: 200
Budget: $700,000
Income Sources: Ticket Sales; Grants; Individual
Contributions
Performs At: Main Stage
Annual Attendance: 34,000
Type of Stage: Proscenium
Seating Capacity: 200

5801
RICHARD & KAREN CARPENTER PERFORMING ARTS CENTER

6200 Atherton Street
Long Beach, CA 90815-4500
Phone: 562-985-2488
Fax: 562-985-7024
Web Site: www.carpenterarts.org
Management:

Executive Director: Peter Lesnik
Managing Director: Michele Roberge
Mission: Presenting organization. Also, home to four
resident companies.
Utilizes: Actors; AEA Actors; Artists-in-Residence;
Choreographers; Collaborating Artists; Collaborations;
Commissioned Composers; Commissioned Music;
Dance Companies; Dancers; Designers; Educators;
Filmmakers; Five Seasonal Concerts; Guest
Accompanists; Guest Artists; Guest Choreographers;
Guest Conductors; Guest Designers; Guest Musical
Directors; Guest Soloists; Instructors; Local Artists;
Lyricists; Multi Collaborations; Multimedia; Music;
Original Music Scores; Poets; Resident Artists;
Selected Students; Sign Language Translators;
Soloists; Special Technical Talent; Theatre Companies;
Visual Arts
Founded: 1994
Status: Non-Profit, Professional
Paid Staff: 15
Paid Artists: 40
Budget: $1,800,000
Income Sources: Individual Donor; Corporations;
Rental Clients; Ticket Buyers
Performs At: Performing Arts Center with continental
seating.
Affiliations: CSALB
Annual Attendance: 150,000
Type of Stage: Proscenium
Stage Dimensions: 70'x70'
Seating Capacity: 1,065
Year Built: 1994
Rental Contact: 562-985-7047 Glennis Watceman

5802
RICHARD AND KAREN CARPENTER PERFORMING ARTS CENTER

California State University, Long Beach
6200 Atherton Blvd
Long Beach, CA 90815
Phone: 562-985-4274
Fax: 562-985-7203
e-mail: cpac@carpenterarts.org
Web Site: http://www.csulb.edu/depts/theatre/
Officers:
   Executive Director: Peter Lesnick
   Events Manager: Aimee Bramble
   Director Development: Michelle Sprokkereef
Management:
   Chair: Joanne Garden
   Production Manager: Kathryn Harvey
Mission: The mission of the Richard and Karen
Carpenter Performing Arts Center is to guarantee the
citizens of Long Beach, CSULB students, faculty, and
staff, and surrounding communities access to the entire
spectrum of performing arts experiences through
resident companies, arts outreach, and unique
programming.
Specialized Field: Cabaret, Comedy, Dance, Music
Seating Capacity: 1074

5803
ROBERT C SMITHWICK THEATRE

12345 El Monte Road
Los Altos Hills, CA 94022-4599
Phone: 650-949-7252
Fax: ² - -
Toll-free: 888-892-4599
e-mail: thomaslori@foothill.edu
Web Site: www.foothill.edu/fa/theater/smithwick.html
Management:
   Publications/Publicity Coordinator: Lori Thomas
   Director Marketing/Communications: Kurt Hueg
Seating Capacity: 950

5804

BING THEATRE

University of Southern California
School of Theatre
1029 Childs Way
Los Angeles, CA 90089-0791
Phone: 213-821-2744
Fax: 213-740-8888
e-mail: thtrinfo@usc.edu
Web Site: www.usc.edu
Officers:
   Dean: Madeline Puzo
Management:
   Dean School of Theater: Robert Scales
Mission: The School of Theatre offers professional and scholarly training in the theatre, stressing the interdependence of production experience with academic knowledge .
Founded: 1945
Specialized Field: Concerts, Theatre
Type of Stage: Proscenium
Stage Dimensions: 20' x 47'6
Orchestra Pit: y
Seating Capacity: 551

5805

CELEBRATION THEATRE

7985 Santa Monica Boulevard
#109-1
Los Angeles, CA 90046
Phone: 323-957-1884
Fax: 323-957-1826
Web Site: www.celebrationtheatre.com/
Officers:
   President: Rusty Hamrick
   Vice President: Scott Monson
   Treasurer: Nicholas Caprio
   Secretary: Larry Dean Harris
Management:
   Artistic Director: Michael Matthews
   Managing Director: David Tarlow
   Marketing Director: Rob Mello
   Development Director: Michael O'Hara
   Literary Manager: Allain Rochel
   Facilities Manager: Timothy Swiss
   Grants Coordinator: Luke Sandler
Founded: 1982

5806

DODGER STADIUM

1000 Elysian Park Avenue
Los Angeles, CA 90012
Phone: 323-224-1500
Fax: 323-224-1833
Web Site: www.dodgers.com
Officers:
   Chairman: Frank McCourt
   Vice Chairman/President: Jamie McCourt
   Special Advisor to the Chairman: Tommy Lasorda
   Chief Operating Officer: Martin Greenspun
   General Manager: Ned Colletti
   SVP/Chief Financial Officer: Cristine Hurley
   SVP/Public Affairs: Howard Sunkin
   SVP/Communications: Camille Johnston
   Vice President/Sales & Marketing: Serfio Del Prado
Management:
   Director Public Relations: Josh Rawitch
   Director Community Relations: Don Newcombe
   Vice President/Stadium Operations: Lon Rosenberg
   Director Ticket Operations: Bill Hunter
   Director Sponsorship Sales: Karen Marumoto

   Director Premium Sales: David Siegel
   Publications Director: Jorge Martin
   Publications Editor/Team Historian: Mark Langill
   Director Accounting: Mike Litvack
Mission: Baseball and concerts
Founded: 1962
Specialized Field: Home of the Los Angeles Dodgers (MLB). Available For Rental And Concerts.
Seating Capacity: 56,000
Year Built: 1962

5807

FORD AMPHITHEATRE

2580 Cahuenga Boulevard East
Los Angeles, CA 90068
Mailing Address: John Anson Ford Theatres, 2580 Cahuenga Blvd. East, Hollywoo
Phone: 323—85-6-57
Fax: 323-871-5904
e-mail: lchiavaroli@arts.lacounty.gov
Web Site: www.fordamphitheatre.com
Management:
   Managing Director: Dave Pier
   Box Office Manager: Susanna Erdos
   Production Manager: Arthur Trowbridge
   Ford Theatre Foundation: Mary Jo Buchanan
   Director of Communications: Linda Chiavaroli
   Interim Productions Marketing Manag: Kim Glann
Mission: Its programs nurture artists, arts organizations and community, and provide a gateway for the people of greater Los Angeles to discover and appreciate cultures of their region and the world.
Founded: 1964
Specialized Field: music, dance and film events
Seating Capacity: 1,241

5808

GETTY CENTER

1200 Getty Center Drive
Los Angeles, CA 90049-1679
Phone: 310-440-7300
Fax: 310-440-7751
Web Site: www.getty.edu
Officers:
   Interim President/CEO: Deborah Marrow
   VP/Chief Investment Offcr/Treasurer: James M Williams
   Secretary/VP/General Counsel: Peter Erichsen
   VP/Communications: Ron Hartwig
   Interim VP/Finance: Robert Abeles
Management:
   Director: Michael Brand
   Asst Director Museum Advancement: Mikka Gee Conway
   Asst Director Educational Programs: Peggy Fogelman
   Asst Director Public Programs: Quincy Houghton
   Associate Director Administration: Thomas Rhoads
Founded: 1953

5809

GREEK THEATRE

2700 North Vermont Avenue
Los Angeles, CA 90027
Phone: 323-665-5857
e-mail: yourcontact@greektheatrela.com
Web Site: www.greektheatrela.com/
Management:
   Owner/President/Chairman: James M Nederland
   Marketing/Sales/Public Relations: James L Nederland
Founded: 1929
Seating Capacity: 6,162

5810

HARRIET & CHARLES LUCKMAN FINE ARTS COMPLEX

California State University, Los Angeles
5151 State Unviersity Drive
Los Angeles, CA 90032
Phone: 323-343-6611
Fax: 323-343-6423
e-mail: info@luckmanarts.org
Web Site: www.luckmanarts.org
Management:
   Executive Director: Wendy A Baker
   Marketing Director: Nicholas A Viski Mestas
Mission: The Luckman Theatre, home of the Luckman Jazz Orchestra, seats up to 1,152, and, the Intimate Theatre has a seating capacity of 250.
Utilizes: Choreographers; Community Talent; Contract Orchestras; Curators; Dance Companies; Designers; Fine Artists; Five Seasonal Concerts; Grant Writers; Guest Artists; Guest Choreographers; Guest Composers; Guest Directors; Guest Lecturers; Guest Musical Directors; Guest Soloists; Guest Speakers; Guest Writers; Instructors; Multi Collaborations; Multimedia; Paid Performers; Sign Language Translators; Special Technical Talent; Theatre Companies; Touring Companies
Founded: 1994
Seating Capacity: 1,152 in Theatre/250 in Luckman Intimate

5811

HARRIET AND CHARLES LUCKMAN FINE ARTS COMPLEX

California State University, Los Angeles
Harriet & Charles Luckman Fine Arts Complex
5151 State University Drive
Los Angeles, CA 90032
Phone: 323-343-6611
Fax: 323-343-6670
Web Site: http://www.luckmanfineartscomplex.org
Officers:
   Executive Director: Wendy A. Baker
Management:
   Director: Julie Joyce
Mission: Cal State L.A. is more than academics it offers students music, dance and theatre performances.
Specialized Field: Dance, Film, Music, Theatre, Video, Visual Arts
Type of Stage: Proscenium
Stage Dimensions: 60 foot wide
Orchestra Pit: y
Seating Capacity: 1,152
Year Built: 1994
Architect: Luckman Partnership

5812

INTIMATE THEATRE

California State University, Los Angeles
Harriet & Charles Luckman Fine Arts Complex
5151 State University Drive
Los Angeles, CA 90032
Phone: 323-343-6611
Fax: 323-343-6670
Web Site: http://www.luckmanfineartscomplex.org
Officers:
   Executive Director: Wendy A. Baker
Management:
   Director: Julie Joyce
Mission: Cal State L.A. is more than academics it offers students music, dance and theatre performances.
Specialized Field: Dance, Jaz
Type of Stage: Flexible Stage
Seating Capacity: 250

Year Built: 1994
Architect: Luckman Partnership

5813
JAPANESE AMERICAN CULTURAL & COMMUNITY CENTER
244 South San Pedro Street
Suite 505
Los Angeles, CA 90012
Phone: 213-628-2725
Fax: 213-617-8576
e-mail: info@jaccc.org
Web Site: www.jaccc.org
Officers:
Chairman: Thomas Iino
Vice Chairman/Treasurer: Gary Kawaguchi
Secretary: Frances K Hashimoto
Management:
Artistic Director: Hirokagu Kosaka
Managing Director: Victor Wong
Producing Director: Johnny Mori
Marketing/Communications Director: Gail Matsui
Business Manager: Kathy Tokudomi
Chief Engineer: Arthur Granados
Board/Donor Relations: Robert Hori
Founded: 1971
Status: Non-Profit, Professional
Paid Staff: 30
Performs At: Japan America Theatre; Plaza
Seating Capacity: 878; 2000

5814
KECK THEATRE
Occidental College
Theater Department
1600 Campus Road
Los Angeles, CA 90041
Phone: 323-259-2771
Fax: 323-341-4987
e-mail: beatrice@oxy.edu
Web Site: http://www.oxy.edu/
Officers:
Dean: Kenyon S. Chan
Management:
Production Manager: Brian Fitzmorris
Mission: Students explore the art of theater through theory, performance, and production. Our students develop a rich understanding of the enactment of the written word and of various forms of theatrical expression, with each student combining theoretical studies with intensive performance and production experiences.
Specialized Field: Theatre
Type of Stage: Adjustable Lambda Platforms
Seating Capacity: 412
Year Built: 1987

5815
L'ERMITAGE FOUNDATION STAGE
12287 San Vicente Boulevard
Los Angeles, CA 90049
Phone: 310-472-3330
Fax: 310-476-8003
Management:
Director/Chairperson: Renee Cherniak
Utilizes: Dancers; Guest Accompanists; Guest Companies; Guest Instructors; Guest Lecturers; Guest Musical Directors; Guest Musicians; Guest Soloists; Instructors; Multimedia; Sign Language Translators; Singers
Income Sources: Member Donations
Performs At: Salon Setting
Annual Attendance: 100
Facility Category: Hotel Salon

Seating Capacity: 200-250

5816
LOS ANGELES MEMORIAL COLISEUM & SPORTS ARENA
3911 South Figueroa Street
Los Angeles, CA 90037
Phone: 213-747-7111
Fax: 213-746-9346
e-mail: info@lacoliseum.com
Web Site: www.lacoliseum.com
Management:
General Manager: Patrick J Lynch
Assistant General Manager: Ron Lederkramer
Marketing/Sales Director: Jonathan Lee
Event Coordinator: 7rene Asalde
Event Director: Todd Destefano
Mission: Sports/Entertainment
Founded: 1959
Status: Non-Profit, Non-Professional
Paid Staff: 32
Type of Stage: Proscenium
Seating Capacity: 16,500
Year Built: 1923
Year Remodeled: 1994
Comments: Main office is located at 3911 South Figueroa Street.

5817
LOS ANGELES PERFORMING ARTS THEATRES
433 S Spring Street
10th Floor
Los Angeles, CA 90013
Mailing Address: Department of Cultural Affairs, City of Los Angeles, 201 Nor
Phone: 213-473-7700
Fax: 213-473-8352
Web Site: www.culturela.org
Management:
President: Charles Ster
VP: Dennis R Martinez
General Manager: Margie J Reese
Performing Arts Director: Ernest Dillihay
Founded: 1925
Specialized Field: Theatre; Dance; Music; Variety
Volunteer Staff: 12
Budget: 13.2 million
Income Sources: Rentals, Ticket Sales, Municipal Fund
Performs At: Theatre, 1; 2; 3; 4; Madrid Theatre; Warner Grand Theatre
Affiliations: Theatre LA; CALAA
Annual Attendance: 80,000
Facility Category: Theatre Complex
Type of Stage: Trust; Proscenium
Seating Capacity: 500; 296; 323; 90; 471; 1500

5818
LOS ANGELES TENNIS CENTER
555 Westwood Plaza
Los Angeles, CA 90095
Phone: 310-825-4403
Fax: 310-825-5775
e-mail: jhenson@ucla.edu
Web Site: http://uclabruins.cstv.com/genrel/062200aag.html
Management:
Executive Director: David Sefton
Director Rental Events: John Henson
Information Technology Manager: Pranay Bhatacharyya

Marketing/Communications Director: Shana Mathur
Public Information Officer: Nicole Cavazos
Patron Services Manager: David McGrath
Box Office Manager: Matthew Poe
Technical Director: David Muller
House Audio Engineer: Keith Endo
Seating Capacity: 6,800

5819
MARK TAPER FORUM
Center Theatre Group
601 W Temple Street
Los Angeles, CA 90012
Phone: 213-628-2772
Fax: 213-628-2796
e-mail: tickets@ctgla.com
Web Site: www.taperahmanson.com
Officers:
Chairman: Martin Massmann
President Board of Directors: William H Ahmanson
VP: Ava Fries
Secretary: Martin C Washton
Treasurer: Dr Steven Nagelberg
Management:
Artistic Director: Michael Ritchie
Managing Director: Charles Dillingham
Mission: To serve the diverse audiences of Los Angeles by producing and presenting theatre of the highest caliber, by nurturing new artists, by attracting new audiences, and by developing youth outreach and arts education programs. This mission is based on a belief that the art of theatre is a cultural force with the capacity to transform the lives of individuals and society at large.
Utilizes: Actors; AEA Actors; Arrangers; Artists-in-Residence; Choreographers; Collaborating Artists; Collaborations; Community Members; Contract Actors; Dancers; Designers; Educators; Equity Actors; Five Seasonal Concerts; Guest Accompanists; Guest Artists; Guest Companies; Guest Composers; Guest Conductors; Guest Designers; Guest Lecturers; Guest Musical Directors; Guest Teachers; Instructors; Local Artists; Local Artists & Directors; Local Unknown Artists; Lyricists; Multi Collaborations; Multimedia; Music; Organization Contracts; Original Music Scores; Paid Performers; Performance Artists; Poets; Resident Artists; Resident Companies; Resident Professionals; Scenic Designers; Selected Students; Sign Language Translators; Singers; Soloists; Students; Student Interns; Special Technical Talent; Theatre Companies; Touring Companies; Visual Arts; Visual Designers; Volunteer Directors & Actors; Writers
Founded: 1967
Opened: 1967
Specialized Field: Musical; Comedy; Drama
Status: Non-Profit, Professional
Paid Artists: 100
Affiliations: Ahmanson Theatre, Kirk Douglas Theatre
Annual Attendance: 750,000
Facility Category: Music Center of Los Angeles
Type of Stage: Thrust
Stage Dimensions: 190Wx47Dx67H; 40Wx28H
Seating Capacity: 739
Year Built: 1967
Year Remodeled: 2008

5820
MARTIN MASSMAN THEATRE
University of Southern California
School of Theatre
1029 Childs Way
Los Angeles, CA 90089-0791

Phone: 213-821-2744
Fax: 213-740-8888
e-mail: thtrinfo@usc.edu
Web Site: www.usc.edu
Officers:
   Dean: Madeline Puzo
Management:
   Dean School of Theater: Robert Scales
Mission: The School of Theatre offers professional and scholarly training in the theatre, stressing the interdependence of production experience with academic knowledge .
Founded: 1945
Specialized Field: Theatre
Type of Stage: Black Box
Seating Capacity: 65

5821
MUNICIPAL ART GALLERY THEATER
Barnsdall Art Park
4800 Hollywood Boulevard
Los Angeles, CA 90027
Phone: 213-473-8432
Fax: 213-473-8527
Web Site: www.culturela.org
Management:
   Media Relations: Mark Greenfield
   Media Relations: Scott Canty

5822
MUSIC CENTER/ PERFORMING ARTS CENTER OF LOS ANGELES COUNTY
135 North Grand Avenue
Los Angeles, CA 90012
Phone: 213-972-7211
Fax: 213-481-1176
e-mail: general@musiccenter.org
Web Site: www.musiccenter.org
Management:
   President/COO: Joanne Corday Kozberg
   VP Education Division: Mark Slaukin
   Director Marketing/Communications: Leticia Rhi Buckley
   Public Relations L A Philharmonic: Adam Crane
   L A Opera: Gary W Murphy
   Press Director Center Theatre Group: Nancy Hereford
   Sr Press Associate Mark Taper Forum: Phyllis Moberly
   Publicist L A Chorale: Libby Huebner
Mission: The Music Center of Los Angeles, which encompasses the Dorothy Chandler Pavilion (capacity of 3,189), the Ahmanson Theatre (capacity of 2,115) and the Mark Taper Forum (capacity of 747), and the Walt Disney Concert Hall (capacity 2,265), lies at the heart of downtown Los Angeles.
Founded: 1964
Specialized Field: Los Angeles Philharmonic; Los Angeles Opera; Los Angeles Master Chorale; Center Theatre Group (Mark Taper & Ahmanson Theatre)

5823
PAULEY PAVILION
University California - Los Angeles/UCLA
164 Pauley Pavilion
Los Angeles, CA 90095
Mailing Address: PAULEY PAVILION, 555 Westwood Plaza, Los Angeles, CA 90095
Phone: 310-825-4546
Fax: 310-825-5775
Web Site:
http://uclabruins.cstv.com/genrel/062200aai.html
Management:
   Acting Chancellor: Norman Abrams Ph.D

Athletics Director: Daniel G Guerrero
Facilities Director: Kevin Borg
Management Information Systems: Bob Park
Asst. Director Events Operations: Paul Brown
Sports Information Director: Marc Dellins
Marketing/New Revenues: Scott Mitchell
External Relations: Ross Bjork
Compliance Director: Rich Herczog
Mission: Pauley Pavilion contains 10,337 permanent upholstered seats and retractable bleachers for 2,482 spectators.
Founded: 1965
Specialized Field: Recreation, concerts, basketball, volleyball, award shows

5824
PLAZA GRAND PERFORMANCES
350 South Grand Avenue
Suite A-4
Los Angeles, CA 90071
Phone: 213-687-2159
Fax: 213-687-2191
e-mail: comments@grandperformances.org
Web Site: www.grandperformances.org
Officers:
   Chairman: Craig Bloomgarden
   Vice Chair: John McAniff
   Secretary: Dorothy Herbst
   Treasurer: Mark Flaisher
Management:
   Executive Director: Michael Alexander
   Technical Manager: Mark Baker
   Programming Director: Leigh Ann Hahn
   Business Manager: Paula Jones
   Development Director: Alice Platt
   Marketing Director: Dean Porter
   Production Manager: Fred Stites
Founded: 1986
Specialized Field: Southern California
Paid Staff: 10
Volunteer Staff: 3
Paid Artists: 40
Annual Attendance: 70,000
Type of Stage: Amphitheater; Thrust-Style
Seating Capacity: 6,500

5825
SCENE DOCK THEATRE
University of Southern California
1030 West 37th Street
Los Angeles, CA 90089
Phone: 213-821-2744
Fax: 213-740-8888
e-mail: thtrinfo@usc.edu
Web Site: www.usc.edu
Officers:
   Dean: Madeline Puzo
Management:
   Dean School of Theater: Robert Scales
Mission: The School of Theatre offers professional and scholarly training in the theatre, stressing the interdependence of production experience with academic knowledge .
Founded: 1945
Specialized Field: Theatre
Type of Stage: Proscenium, Round, Thrust
Seating Capacity: 100

5826
SHRINE AUDITORIUM AND EXPOSITION CENTER
665 West Jefferson Boulevard
Los Angeles, CA 90007

Phone: 213-748-5116
Fax: 213-742-9922
Web Site: www.shrineauditorium.com/expo.html
Management:
   Operations Manager: Andy Stamatin
   Administration: Kimberly Walker
   Ticket Coordinator: Andrew Johnston
Mission: The Shrine Auditorium seats atotal of 6,300 with 3,044 on the main floor and 3,256 in the balcony. The Expo Center features over 54,000 square feet, with 34,000 square feet on the main floor and another 20,000 on the mezzanine. The center will accommodate up to 4,000 people, approximately 250 booths; has a 21,160 square foot dance floor; accommodates banquet dining for 1,800 and has a ceiling height of 49 feet.
Utilizes: Actors; AEA Actors; Choreographers; Collaborations; Dance Companies; Dancers; Designers; Educators; Filmmakers; Fine Artists; Guest Accompanists; Guest Artists; Guest Companies; Guest Composers; Guest Conductors; Guest Designers; Guest Directors; Guest Instructors; Guest Lecturers; Guest Musical Directors; Guest Musicians; Guest Soloists; Guest Writers; Guild Activities; High School Drama; Instructors; Local Artists; Lyricists; Multi Collaborations; Multimedia; Music; New Productions; Organization Contracts; Original Music Scores; Performance Artists; Playwrights; Resident Professionals; Selected Students; Sign Language Translators; Singers; Soloists; Student Interns; Special Technical Talent; Theatre Companies; Touring Companies; Visual Arts
Founded: 1920
Specialized Field: Los Angeles
Facility Category: Auditorium with adjoining Expo Center
Type of Stage: Concerts; Masonite; Wood
Stage Dimensions: 193'x73'
Year Built: 1926
Cost: $2,500,000
Rental Contact: Douglas Worthington

5827
STAPLES CENTER
1111 South Fugueroa Street
Los Angeles, CA 90015
Phone: 213-742-7300
Fax: 213-624-3054
e-mail: media@staplescenter.com
Web Site: www.staplescenter.com
Management:
   President: Tim Leiweke
   SVP/General Manager: Bobby Goldwater
   Community Development: Jackie Baca Geary
Seating Capacity: 16,096

5828
THORNE HALL
Occidental College
1600 Campus Road
Los Angeles, CA 90041
Phone: 323-259-2500
Fax: 323-259-2958
e-mail: abart@oxy.edu
Web Site: www.oxy.edu/x888.xml
Management:
   President: Ted Mitchell
   Artistic Director: Allen Freeman
Founded: 1938
Status: Non-Profit, Non-Professional
Seating Capacity: 835

5829
TOM BRADLEY INTERNATIONAL HALL
330 De Neve Drive
Suite L-16
Los Angeles, CA 90095-1492
Phone: 213-627-6500
Fax: 213-847-3169
e-mail: catering@ha.ucla.edu
Web Site:
http://map.ais.ucla.edu/portal/site/UCLA/menuitem
Officers:
   Acting Chancellor: Norman Abrams
   Executive Vice Chancellor/Provost: Daniel
   Neuman
Management:
   Business/Administrative Services: Sam Morabito
   Capital Programs: Peter Blackman
   External Affairs: Rhea Turteltaub
   Academic Personnel: Thomas H Rice
Mission: The 5,270 square foot International Room is
divisible into six smaller salons. The East and West
Galleries are excellent locations for meeting
registration, poster sessions, or refreshment breaks.
Several multi-purpose rooms are versatile spaces for
smaller events.
Type of Stage: Black Box; Flexible

5830
UCLA PERFORMING ARTS
Royce Hall, B100
PO Box 951529
Los Angeles, CA 90095
Phone: 310-794-4046
Fax: 310-206-3843
Web Site: www.uclalive.org
Management:
   Executive Director: David Sefton
Founded: 1929
Status: Non-Profit, Professional
Paid Staff: 60
Annual Attendance: 200,000
Seating Capacity: 1,818

5831
UNIVERSITY OF SOUTHERN CALIFORNIA
School of Theatre
1029 Childs Way
Los Angeles, CA 90089-0791
Phone: 213-821-2744
Fax: 213-740-8888
e-mail: thtrinfo@usc.edu
Web Site:
http://theatre.usc.edu/aboutus/contact-info.html
Management:
   Technical Theatre Manager: Sue Brandt
   Theatre Reservations: Alexandra Bristrow
Mission: The School's active production program
utilizes the Bing Theatre, a traditional proscenium
575-seat house; the Massman Theatre, a flexible space
that seats 50-75; and the Scene Dock Theatre, which is
also a flexible space, with seating for 99 people.
Founded: 1880
Specialized Field: Dance; Theatre; Drama
Status: For-Profit, Non-Professional

5832
VETERANS WADSWORTH THEATRE
Veterans Park Conservancy
11611 San Vincente Boulevard, Suite 204
Los Angeles, CA 90049

Phone: 310-820-5366
Fax: 310-820-1486
e-mail: info@veteransparkconservancy.org
Web Site:
www.veteransparkconservancy.org/wadsworth.htm
Mission: The Wadsworth Theatre is owned by the West
Los Angeles Department of Veteran's Affairs and is
located on the Veteran's Administration campus. Built in
1939, in Spanish Colonial/Mission Revival architectural
style, with its stucco finish and red clay tile roofing,
makes the Wadsworth not only aesthetically pleasing,
but also a historic landmark.
Founded: 1919
Seating Capacity: 1,356

5833
PEPPERDINE UNIVERSITY SMOTHERS THEATRE
24255 Pacific Coast Highway
Malibu, CA 90263
Phone: 310-506-4138
Fax: 310-506-4998
e-mail: pr@pepperdine.edu
Web Site: www.pepperdine.edu
Management:
   Director: Jerry Derloshon
   Assistant Director: Wileen Wong
   Public Relations Specialist: Jaclyn Tully
   University Photographer: Ron Hall
Utilizes: Actors; Dance Companies; Dancers; Fine
Artists; Guest Accompanists; Guest Choreographers;
Guest Designers; Guest Directors; Guest Musical
Directors; Guest Musicians; Guest Writers; Instructors;
Multimedia; Original Music Scores; Sign Language
Translators; Singers; Soloists; Special Technical Talent;
Theatre Companies; Touring Companies
Founded: 1937
Seating Capacity: 450
Year Built: 1980
Rental Contact: Managing Director Marnie Mitze

5834
HELEN SCHOENI THEATER
Mendocino Art Center
45200 Little Lake Street
Mendocino, CA 95460
Mailing Address: PO Box 765
Phone: 707-937-5818
Fax: 707-937-1764
Toll-free: 800-653-3328
e-mail: mendoart@mcn.org
Web Site: www.mendocinoartcenter.org
Officers:
   Acting President: Norman DeVall
   Vice President: Leona Walden
   Acting Treasurer: Lucia Zacha
   Secretary: Dale Moyer
Management:
   Executive/Education Director: Peggy Templer
   Marketing Director: Mike McDonald
   Music Events Coordinator: Gayle Caldwell
   Registrar: Linn Bottorf
Founded: 1959
Status: Non-Profit, Professional
Paid Staff: 15

5835
MODESTO JUNIOR COLLEGE PERFORMING ARTS CENTER
435 College Avenue
Division Office
Modesto, CA 95350

Mailing Address: Art Building Room 105
Phone: 209-575-6081
Fax: 209-575-6086
e-mail: mjcinfo@mail.yosemite.cc.ca.us
Web Site: http://mjc.yosemite.cc.ca.us/
Management:
   President: Bill Scroggins
   Interim Dean: Michael Sundquist
Mission: Recital Hall 300 seats.
Founded: 1967
Status: For-Profit, Non-Professional
Paid Staff: 80

5836
STARLITE PATIO THEATRE
Montclair Civic Center
5111 Benito Street
Montclair, CA 91763
Mailing Address: 5111 Benito Street. Montclair, CA
91763
Phone: 909-625-9457
Fax: 909-399-9751
e-mail: lphillips@cityofmontclair.org
Web Site:
www.ci.montclair.ca.us/depts/human_services/hours.as
p
Management:
   Community Development Director: Robert W
   Clark
   Administrative Services Director: Edward C Starr
   Redevelopment Director: Marilyn J Staats
   Facility Supervisor: Shirley Wofford
   Manager: Harve Edwards
   Benefits Coordinator: Leslie Phillips
Specialized Field: Concerts

5837
MOUNTAIN VIEW CENTER FOR THE PERFORMING ARTS
PO Box 7540
500 Castro Street
Mountain View, CA 94039
Phone: 650-903-6565
Fax: 650-962-9900
e-mail: performingarts@mvcpa.com
Web Site: www.mvcpa.com
Officers:
   Executive Director: W. Scott Winslow
Management:
   Marketing/Public Relations Manager: Michele
   Roberts
   Business Manager: Cindy Miksa
   Interim Operations Manager: Bernadette Fife
   Interim Technical Services Manager: Candice
   Moenich
   Ticket Services Director: Barbara Schrug
   Community Services Director: David Muela
Mission: Seeks to enrich Silicon Valley audiences
through enjoyment, celebration and interaction with the
arts.
Founded: 1991
Paid Staff: 50
Volunteer Staff: 300
Budget: 1.3 Million
Performs At: Theaters
Affiliations: United States Institute for Theater
Technolgies Inc., International Assocation of Auditorium
Managers
Annual Attendance: 170,000
Type of Stage: Black Box; Mainstage-proscenium
Seating Capacity: Mainstage 600, Black Box 200, Park
300
Year Built: 1991
Rental Contact: Booking Coordinator Jenn Poret

Resident Groups: Theatre Works, Peninsula Youth Theatre

5838
NAPA VALLEY OPERA HOUSE
Administrative Office
1040 Main Street, Suite 110
Napa, CA 94559
Mailing Address: Theatre Address: 1030 Main Street
Phone: 707-226-7372
Fax: 707-226-5392
e-mail: evy@nvoh.org
Web Site: www.nvoh.org
Management:
  Artistic Director: Evy Warshawski, evy@nvoh.org
  President, Board of Trustees: Gary Grace, gg@zbbs.com
Mission: The Napa Valley Opera House enriches the cultural experience of a diverse community - offering distinctive performing arts and preserving a unique historic theater.
Utilizes: Collaborating Artists; Collaborations; Community Members; Community Talent; Dance Companies; Guest Accompanists; Guest Designers; Guest Instructors; Guest Musicians; Guest Soloists; Guild Activities; Instructors; Local Artists & Directors; Lyricists; Multi Collaborations; Scenic Designers; Soloists; Students; Student Interns; Special Technical Talent
Founded: 1879
Opened: 2003
Specialized Field: Multi-Disciplinary
Budget: $2.1 Million
Income Sources: Revenue; Donations; Grants
Annual Attendance: 65,000
Type of Stage: Proscenium, Thrust
Stage Dimensions: 80' x 12'
Seating Capacity: 467; 150
Year Built: 1879
Year Remodeled: 2003
Cost: $16+ Million
Rental Contact: Artistic Director Evy Warshawski

5839
BALBOA PERFORMING ARTS THEATER
PO Box 752
Newport Beach, CA 92661
Phone: 949-673-0895
Fax: 949-673-0838
e-mail: ctrela@thebalboatheater.org
Web Site: www.balboaperformingartstheaterfoundation.org/
Officers:
  Chairman: Nancy Gardner
  Vice Chairman: Stan Kafka
  Secretary: Jo King
  Treasurer: Bill Wren
Management:
  Executive Director: Mary Lynch
  Marketing/Development Director: Christopher Trela
  Operations Director: Shana Bannert
Seating Capacity: 350

5840
EL PORTAL THEATRE
5269 Lankershim Boulevard
North Hollywood, CA 91601
Mailing Address: El Portal Theatre, 11206 Weddington St., North Hollywood, CA 91601
Phone: 818-508-4234
Fax: 818-508-5113
e-mail: THE ELPORTAL@AOL.COM
Web Site: http://www.elportaltheatre.com/

Officers:
  President: Thomas H Cole
  Vice President: Carol Rowen
  Secretary: Sunny Caine
Management:
  Artistic Director: Jeremiah Morris
  Managing Director: Robert Caine
Utilizes: Guest Companies; Singers
Founded: 1971
Specialized Field: Theater
Status: Professional; Nonprofit
Paid Staff: 65
Income Sources: Los Angeles Theatre Alliance; California Theater Council
Performs At: Alley Theater (Pavilion, Circle Forum)
Type of Stage: Proscenium, Thrust, Flexible
Seating Capacity: 350, 99, 42
Organization Type: Performing; Resident

5841
PLAZA DEL SOL PERFORMANCE HALL
California State University, Northridge
Nordhoff Hall
18111 Nordhoff Street
Northridge, CA 91330
Phone: 818-677-1200
e-mail: theatre@csun.edu
Web Site: http://www.csun.edu/theatre/
Officers:
  President: Jolene Koester
Management:
  Theatre Manager: William Taylor
Mission: Bachelor of Arts in theatre at California State University, Northridge offers an integrative, balanced program of studies that prepares students to enter the field of theatre, to undertake specialized graduate study, or to draw upon their theatre education in other fields and pursuits.
Specialized Field: Theatre
Seating Capacity: 500

5842
HENRY J KAISER CONVENTION CENTER
10 10th Street
Oakland, CA 94607
Phone: 510-238-7765
Fax: 510-238-7767
Web Site: www.hjkevents.com
Management:
  Facility Manager: Michael Lange
  Booking Manager: Gwendolyn Singleton
  Finance Director: Neil Mitchell
  Operations Manager: Albert M Plaza
  Event Manager: Rose Goodrich
  House Technician: Elijah Morgan
  Security Chief: Michael A Campbell
Mission: The Henery J Kaiser Convention Center is a sophisticated, diverse avenue which can accomodate all types of events from pefforming arts, to entertainment, sports and private receptions. Arena: 25,000 square feet floor space; Ballroom seating capacity: reception/350, banquet/150, dance/200, theatre/325, classroom/120.
Founded: 1984
Specialized Field: multi - use facility with theatre and arena space

5843
MCAFEE COLISEUM
7000 Coliseum Way
Oakland, CA 94621
Mailing Address: McAfee Coliseum, 7000 Coliseum Way, Oakland, California 9462
Phone: 510-569-2121

Fax: 510-569-4246
Web Site: http://oakland.athletics.mlb.com/NASApp/mlb/oak/ballpark/index.jsp
Officers:
  President: Michael Crowley
Management:
  Stadium Operations Director: David Avila
  Stadium Operations Events Manager: Kristy Ledbetter
  Public Relations Director: Jim Young
  Finance Director: Kasey Miraglia
  Information Systems Manager: Debbie Dean
  Vice President Marketing/Sales: Jim Leahy
  Vice President/General Manager: Billy Beane
  General Counsel: Steve Johnston
Founded: 1966
Specialized Field: Sports Events Stadium (Oakland Athletics/Oakland Raiders)
Status: For-Profit, Professional
Seating Capacity: 63,146

5844
MILLS COLLEGE CONCERT HALL
5000 Macarthur Boulevard
Oakland, CA 94613
Phone: 510-430-2296
Fax: 510-430-3314
e-mail: music@mills.edu
Web Site: www.mills.edu/academics/undergraduate/mus/center_contemporary_music.php
Management:
  Department Head: David Bernstein
  Technical Director: Les Stuck
  Faculty Administrator: Vi Smith
  Concert Coordinator: Steed Cowart
Founded: 1852
Status: Non-Profit

5845
PARAMOUNT THEATRE
2025 Broadway
Oakland, CA 94612
Phone: 510-893-2300
Fax: 510-893-5098
e-mail: lstewart@paramounttheatre.com
Web Site: www.paramounttheatre.com
Management:
  General Manager: Leslee Stewart
Founded: 1931
Status: Non-Profit, Professional
Paid Staff: 7

5846
OROVILLE STATE THEATER
1489 Myers Street
Oroville, CA 95965
Phone: 530-538-2470
Fax: 530-534-1609
e-mail: orovillestatetheatre@ncen.org
Web Site: www.orovillestatetheatre.org
Management:
  Manager: Jim Christensen, jschristensen@ncen.org
Founded: 1928
Seating Capacity: 608

5847
OXNARD CIVIC AUDITORIUM
800 Hobson Way
Oxnard, CA 93030

Phone: 805-486-2424
Fax: 805-483-7303
Web Site: www.oxnardpacc.com
Officers:
Vice President: Dale Belcher
Treasurer: Gary Blum
Management:
Executive Director: Bob Holden
Stage Manager: Brad McElmurry
Chief Engineer: Victor Rasmussen
Business Services Manager: Cindy Crowell
Box Office Manager: Dan Crouse
Event Coordinator: Bevera Skelton
House Senior Manager: Jessie Lucio
Founded: 1968
Specialized Field: Concert-Plays-Meetings
Status: Non-Profit, Professional
Paid Staff: 55
Seating Capacity: 1,604

5848
MCCALLUM THEATRE FOR THE PERFORMING ARTS
73000 Fred Waring Drive
Palm Desert, CA 92260
Phone: 760-346-6505
Fax: 760-341-9508
Toll-free: 866-889-2787
e-mail: information@mccallum-theatre.org
Web Site: www.mccallum-theatre.com/
Officers:
President/CEO: Ted Giatas
Management:
Development Director: Barbara Hemingway
Production Director: Keith Smith
Presentations/Theatre Director: Mitchell Gershenfield
Marketing/Sales Manager: Rick Darius
Business Operations/Facilities: H Cameron Smith
Assistant Development Director: Marcia Stone
Education Director: Kajsa Thuresson Frary
Manager of Special Events: Judi Pofsky
Box Office Manager: Barbara Dawson
Utilizes: Actors; Collaborating Artists; Collaborations; Dance Companies; Educators; Local Artists; Original Music Scores; Soloists; Student Interns; Special Technical Talent; Theatre Companies
Founded: 1988
Paid Staff: 64
Volunteer Staff: 425
Income Sources: Earned; Contributed revenues
Performs At: Presenting Theatre
Annual Attendance: 250,000
Type of Stage: Proscenium
Stage Dimensions: 41'D x 84'W
Seating Capacity: 1,127

5849
ANNENBERG THEATER
Palm Springs Art Museum
101 Museum Drive
Palm Springs, CA 92262
Mailing Address: PO Box 2310
Phone: 760-325-7186
Fax: 760-327-5069
Web Site:
www.psmuseum.org/performances_venue.shtml
Management:
Executive Director: Janice Lyle
Chief Curator/Liaison: Katherine Hough
Development Director: Scott Schroeder
Communications Director: Kimberly Nichols
Education Director: Robert Brasier
Director Theater Operations: John Finkler

Business Services Director: Fred Clewell
Publications Manager: Roy Komassa
Founded: 1976
Status: Non-Profit, Professional
Affiliations: APAP
Stage Dimensions: 50x30
Seating Capacity: 433
Year Built: 1976
Year Remodeled: 1999
Rental Contact: Bill Witte

5850
PALM SPRINGS CONVENTION CENTER
277 North Avenida Caballeros
Palm Springs, CA 92262
Phone: 760-325-6611
Fax: 760-778-4102
Toll-free: 800-333-7535
Web Site: www.palmspringscc.com
Management:
Vice President/General Manager: James Dunn
Director of Sales: Rick Leson
Marketing Director: Mary Perry
Director of Catering: Lynne Toles
Chief of Engineering: John Miller
Seating Capacity: 6.500

5851
SPANGENBURG THEATRE
Gunn High School
780 Arastradero Road @ Foothill Expressway
Palo Alto, CA 94306
Phone: 650-354-8263
Fax: 650-354-8277
Web Site: www.spangenbergtheatre.com
Management:
Theatre Manager: Jorgen Wedseltoft
Founded: 1965
Specialized Field: Movie House
Status: Non-Profit, Non-Professional
Paid Staff: 1
Facility Category: Performance Center; Art House; Cinema
Type of Stage: Proscenium
Seating Capacity: 953
Year Remodeled: 2002

5852
CALIFORNIA INSTITUTE OF TECHNOLOGY PERFORMING ARTS CENTER
1200 East California Boulevard
Pasadena, CA 91125
Phone: 626-395-6811
Fax: 626-577-0130
Toll-free: 888-222-5832
e-mail: events@caltech.edu
Web Site:
http://events.caltech.edu/preview/venues/adp
Management:
President: David Baltimore
Asst Vice President Public Events: Denise N Nash
Operations Coordinator: Deborah White
Technical Operations Manager: Louis Lind
Network Administrator: Dwayne Miles
Senior House Manager: Chuck Barnes
Marketing/Outreach Manager: Cara Stemen
Associate Director: Chris Harcourt
Mission: Provides a broad spectrum of high quality multi-disciplinary cultural, educational and information programs. These programs are designed to compliment

the Caltech experience of Institutes, students, faculty and staff, as well as serving as cultural enhancement to the greater Pasadena community.
Founded: 1891
Status: Non-Profit, Professional
Paid Staff: 60
Paid Artists: 100

5853
PASADENA CIVIC AUDITORIUM
300 East Green Street
Pasadena, CA 91101
Phone: 626-449-7360
Fax: 626-395-7132
e-mail: boxoffice@thepasadenacivic.com
Web Site: www.thepasadenacivic.com/.htm
Management:
CEO Pasadena Center Operations: Michael Ross
Founded: 1931
Opened: 1932
Seating Capacity: 3,029

5854
PASADENA PLAYHOUSE - MAINSTAGE THEATRE
39 S El Molino Avenue
Pasadena, CA 91101
Phone: 626-356-7529
Fax: 626-792-7343
Web Site: www.pasadenaplayhouse.org
Management:
Artistic Director: Sheldon Epps
Managing Director: Brian Colburn
Producing Director: Thomas Ware
Founded: 1917
Seating Capacity: 682
Year Built: 1925
Rental Contact: Thomas Ware

5855
ROSE BOWL STADIUM
1001 Rose Bowl Drive
Pasadena, CA 91103
Phone: 626-577-3100
Fax: 626-405-0992
Web Site: www.rosebowlstadium.com
Officers:
President: William E Thomson Jr
Vice President: Fred Claire
Treasurer: Robert Monk
Secretary: Ann Marie Hickambottom
Chief Financial Officer: Larry Madden
Chief Operations Officer: Jess Waiters
Management:
General Manager: Darryl Dunn
Asst General Manager/Operations: Jess Waiters
Corporate Communications: Charles Thompson Jr
Event Manager: Julie Benavidez
Maintenance Superintendent: Will Schnell
Founded: 1921
Status: Non-Profit, Professional
Seating Capacity: 92,542

5856
CALIFORNIA POLYTECHNIC UNIVERSITY THEATRE
3801 West Temple Avenue
University Theatre, Technical Services
Pomona, CA 91768

Mailing Address: Building 25
Phone: 909-869-3900
Fax: 909-869-3184
e-mail: dlogan@csupomona.edu
Web Site: www.class.csupomona.edu/th/cpframes.htm
Officers:
Department Chairman: Bill Morse
Management:
Director Technical Facilities: Dennis Logan
Director Scenic Operations: Joyce Ehrenberg
Publicity: Kellee Flanders
Mission: University theatre with continental seating - university theatre arts education, concerts, dance, on-campus activities and outside lease.
Founded: 1972
Seating Capacity: 516

5857
POWAY CENTER FOR THE PERFORMING ARTS

15498 Espola Road
Poway, CA 92064
Phone: 858-748-0505
Fax: 858-748-0826
e-mail: foundation@powayarts.org
Web Site: www.powayarts.org/
Officers:
Chairperson: Eileen Haag
President: Liza Pille
Management:
Executive Director: Henry Korn
Associate Director: Michael Rennie
Controller: Arlene Lund
Administration: Lynn Wolsey
Sales: Tom Johnson
Founded: 1990
Status: For-Profit, Non-Professional
Performs At: Poway Center for the Performing Arts
Seating Capacity: 815

5858
REDDING CIVIC AUDITORIUM

777 Auditorium Drive
Redding, CA 96001
Phone: 530-225-4100
Fax: 530-225-4354
Toll-free: 800-874-7562
e-mail: kstarman@ci.redding.ca.us
Web Site: www.ci.redding.ca.us/cm/major_pr/civic_center.html
Management:
Executive Director/City Manager: Kurt Starman
Senior Redevelopment Project Drctor: Larry Morgon
Services Supervisor: Teresa Rudolph
Assistant City Manager: Randy Bachman

5859
SHASTA COLLEGE FINE ARTS THEATRE

Center for Fine Arts & Communication
11555 Old Oregon Trail
Redding, CA 96049-6006
Mailing Address: PO Box 496006
Phone: 530-225-4761
Fax: 530-225-4763
e-mail: info@shastacollege.edu
Web Site: www.shastacollege.edu
Management:
Dean: Ronald G Johnson
President: Mary Retterer
Managing Director: Robert Soffian
Founded: 1948
Status: Non-Profit, Non-Professional
Paid Staff: 230

5860
GLENN WALLICHS THEATRE

University of Redlands
1200 East Colton Avenue
P.O. Box 3080
Redlands, CA 92373-0999
Mailing Address: University of Redlands, Glenn Wallichs Theatre, P.O. Box 308
Phone: 909-748-8028
Fax: 909-335-4092
Web Site: www.redlands.edu/theatrearts.xml
Management:
Professor Theatre: Nephelie Andonyadis
Professor Theatre: Chris Beach
Mission: Seeks to provide opportunities for all students who enjoy the theater to be more involved on campus.
Founded: 1907
Specialized Field: Departmental and Guest Artist Productions
Status: Private
Seating Capacity: 326

5861
REDLANDS COMMUNITY MUSIC ASSOCIATION

25 Grant Street
PO Box 466
Redlands, CA 92373
Phone: 909-793-7316
Fax: 909-793-5086
e-mail: redlandsbowl@verizon.net
Web Site: www.redlandsbowl.org
Officers:
President: Janet M. Weder
Management:
Executive Director: Beverly Noerr
Founded: 1923
Status: Non-Profit, Professional
Paid Staff: 2
Seating Capacity: 6,000

5862
REDONDO BEACH PERFORMING ARTS CENTER

1935 Manhattan Beach Boulevard
Redondo Beach, CA 90278
Phone: 310-318-0644
Fax: 310-643-0096
e-mail: john.larockr@redondo.org
Web Site: www.rbpac.com
Management:
Theatre Manager: John La Rock
Technical Director: Jack Meyer
Utilizes: Actors; AEA Actors; Choreographers; Collaborating Artists; Commissioned Composers; Commissioned Music; Dance Companies; Dancers; Designers; Educators; Filmmakers; Fine Artists; Grant Writers; Guest Accompanists; Guest Artists; Guest Choreographers; Guest Companies; Guest Composers; Guest Conductors; Guest Designers; Guest Directors; Guest Lecturers; Guest Musical Directors; Guest Musicians; Guest Soloists; High School Drama; Instructors; Local Artists; Local Unknown Artists; Multimedia; Music; Original Music Scores; Playwrights; Poets; Resident Professionals; Sign Language Translators; Singers; Soloists; Student Interns; Theatre Companies
Founded: 2003
Specialized Field: Performing Arts Center
Status: For-Profit, Professional
Paid Staff: 10
Type of Stage: Proscenium
Seating Capacity: 1,457

5863
MATEEL COMMUNITY CENTER

PO Box 1910
Redway, CA 95560
Phone: 707-923-3368
Fax: 707-923-3370
e-mail: office@mateel.org
Web Site: www.mateel.org/home.php
Officers:
President: Bruce Champie
Vice President: Garth Epling
Treasurer: Bob Stern
Secretary: Elena Worley
Management:
Executive Director: Taunya Stapp
Hall Manager: Glenn Gradin
Marketing: Justin Crellin
Administration: Katz Boose
Founded: 1978
Status: Non-Profit
Annual Attendance: 45,000
Seating Capacity: 300

5864
RICHMOND MEMORIAL CONVENTION CENTER

403 Civic Center Plaza
Side Rooms, 2533 Nevin Avenue
Richmond, CA 94804
Mailing Address: Richmond Memorial Auditorium and Convention Center, 403 Civi
Phone: 510-620-6904
Fax: 510-620-6583
Web Site: www.ci.richmond.ca.us/index.asp?NID=425
Management:
Reservations/Rental Coordinator: Jerry Anderson
Mission: to be a focal point for the Community of Richmond. This magnificent facility has played host to a number of different activities including concerts, car shows, boxing exhibitions, basketball games, mixed martial arts events, and a host of others.
Founded: 1949
Specialized Field: dance, reunion, reception, concert, pageant, party, sporting event, or banquet

5865
ARTS PERFORMANCE LAB

University Of California, Riverside
Arts Administrative Center
Building 121
Riverside, CA 92521-0324
Mailing Address: Program Promotions Manager, 900 University Ave.,ARTS 119 , R
Phone: 951-827-7193
Fax: 951-827-4651
e-mail: kathleen.deatley@ucr.edu
Web Site: http://www.theatre.ucr.edu/
Officers:
Chair: D. Eric Barr
Facilities Manager: Paul Richardson
Management:
Production Manager: Marc Longlois
Program Promotions Manager: Kathleen DeAtley
Mission: Theatre students have the opportunity and are encouraged to perform, direct, and design for departmental productions and student playwrights have their work staged in the annual Playworks Festival.
Specialized Field: Dance, Theatre
Type of Stage: Adaptable
Seating Capacity: 140

5866

BARN THEATRE

University Of California, Riverside
Arts Administrative Center
Building 121
Riverside, CA 92521-0324
Mailing Address: Program Promotions Manager, 900
University Ave.,ARTS 119 , R
Phone: 951-827-7193
Fax: 951-827-4651
e-mail: kathleen.deatley@ucr.edu
Web Site: http://www.theatre.ucr.edu/
Officers:
   Chair: D. Eric Barr
   Facilities Manager: Paul Richardson
Management:
   Production Manager: Marc Longlois
   Program Promotions Manager: Kathleen DeAtley
Mission: Theatre students have the opportunity and
are encouraged to perform, direct, and design for
departmental productions and student playwrights have
their work staged in the annual Playworks Festival.
Specialized Field: Movement Classes in Tap and
Dances of Mexico
Seating Capacity: 50

5867

DANCE STUDIO THEATRE

University Of California, Riverside
Arts Administrative Center
Building 121
Riverside, CA 92521-0324
Mailing Address: Program Promotions Manager, 900
University Ave.,ARTS 119 , R
Phone: 951-827-7193
Fax: 951-827-4651
e-mail: kathleen.deatley@ucr.edu
Web Site: http://www.theatre.ucr.edu/
Officers:
   Chair: D. Eric Barr
   Facilities Manager: Paul Richardson
Management:
   Production Manager: Marc Longlois
   Program Promotions Manager: Kathleen DeAtley
Mission: Theatre students have the opportunity and
are encouraged to perform, direct, and design for
departmental productions and student playwrights have
their work staged in the annual Playworks Festival.
Specialized Field: Movement Classes
Type of Stage: Adaptable
Seating Capacity: 130

5868

RIVERSIDE CONVENTION CENTER

3443 Orange Street
Riverside, CA 92501
Phone: 909-787-7950
Fax: 909-222-4706
e-mail: riversidecb@linkline.com
Web Site: www.riversidecb.com
Management:
   President: Scott Megna
   Executive Director: Debbie Megna,
   dmegna@riversidecvb.com
   Sales Manager: Anne Seymour
   Visitor Center Manager: Pam Seinturier
Status: For-Profit, Non-Professional
Paid Staff: 200
Facility Category: Convention Center
Seating Capacity: 2,000
Rental Contact: Pamela Sturrock

5869

RIVERSIDE MUNICIPAL AUDITORIUM

3485 Mission Inn Avenue
Riverside, CA 92501
Phone: 909-787-7678
Fax: 909-682-8464
Web Site: www.riversidemunicipalauditorium.com
Officers:
   President: Robert Stein
   Executive Director: Carlos Vonfrankemberg
Founded: 1987
Status: For-Profit, Professional
Paid Staff: 8
Annual Attendance: 50,000
Type of Stage: Proscenium
Seating Capacity: 1,776

5870

UNIVERSITY THEATRE

University Of California, Riverside
Arts Administrative Center
Building 121
Riverside, CA 92521-0324
Mailing Address: Program Promotions Manager, 900
University Ave.,ARTS 119 , R
Phone: 951-827-7193
Fax: 951-827-4651
e-mail: kathleen.deatley@ucr.edu
Web Site: http://www.theatre.ucr.edu/
Officers:
   Chair: D. Eric Barr
   Facilities Manager: Paul Richardson
Management:
   Production Manager: Marc Longlois
   Program Promotions Manager: Kathleen DeAtley
Mission: Theatre students have the opportunity and
are encouraged to perform, direct, and design for
departmental productions and student playwrights have
their work staged in the annual Playworks Festival.
Specialized Field: Art History, Dance, Music, Studio
Art, and Theatre
Type of Stage: Proscenim
Seating Capacity: 484
Year Built: 2001
Architect: Israel, Callas, Shortridge Design Associates
of Los Angeles
Cost: $35 Million

5871

NORRIS CENTER FOR THE PERFORMING ARTS

27570 Crossfield Drive
Rolling Hills Estates, CA 90274
Phone: 310-544-0403
Fax: 310-377-2997
e-mail: emarketing@norristheatre.org
Web Site: www.norriscenter.com
Management:
   Artistic Director: James W Gruessing
   Sales Director: Nancy Nassimbene
   Marketing Director: Diane Slome
Mission: The Norris Theatre is a 450-seat, state of the
art facility that has become the cornerstone of the
performing arts on the Palos Verdes Peninsula, bringing
leading entertainers and performing artists to the region
and reinforcing these efforts with high-quality
educational outreach programs for children and adults.
Utilizes: Actors; Dance Companies; Educators; Fine
Artists; Guest Choreographers; Guest Composers;
Guest Designers; Guest Ensembles; Guest Instructors;
Guest Lecturers; Guest Soloists; High School Drama;
Instructors; Multimedia; Music; Original Music Scores;
Soloists; Student Interns; Special Technical Talent;
Theatre Companies; Touring Companies
Founded: 1978
Specialized Field: All Performing Arts - Presenting
House
Status: Non-Profit, Professional
Paid Staff: 7
Volunteer Staff: 80
Income Sources: Private donations and ticket sales
Annual Attendance: 14,000
Facility Category: Presenting; Producing; Rental
Type of Stage: Proscenium
Year Built: 1983
Rental Contact: Box Office Manager David Barr

5872

ARCO ARENA

One Sports Parkway
Sacramento, CA 95834
Phone: 916-928-3650
Fax: 916-928-6936
e-mail: tickets@arcoarena.com
Web Site: www.arcoarena.com
Officers:
   President: John Thomas
Management:
   SVP/Business Operations: John Rinehart
   SVP Arena Services: Mark Stone
   SVP Sales/Service: Jeff Morander
   VP Marketing/Business Operations: Danette
   Leighton
   VP Service Development: Tom Peterson
   VP Strategic Alliances: Tom Hunt
   VP Human Resources: Donna Ruiz
Founded: 1988
Specialized Field: Sports Facility Also hosts Numerous
Concerts; Ice Shows; Festivals; and Other Family
Events.
Affiliations: Home of the Sacramento Kings,
Sacramento Monarchs and Sacramento Knights.
Seating Capacity: 17,317
Year Built: 1985

5873

ARDEN PLAYHOUSE

2120 Royale Road
Sacramento, CA 95815
Mailing Address: 5640 Roseville Road Suite D - -
Sacramento, CA 95842
Phone: 916-927-0942
Fax: 916-782-1072
e-mail: admin@ardenplayhouse.com or
arden@ardenplayhouse.com
Web Site: http://www.ardenplayhouse.co
Management:
   Owner/Producer: Michael Messmer
   Marketing Director: Barbara Messmer
Mission: We will continue our tradition of presenting the
best in comedy, including some original plays, for your
entertainment.
Founded: 1998
Specialized Field: comedies and farces

5874

CROCKER ART MUSEUM BALLROOM

216 O Street
Sacramento, CA 95814
Phone: 916-264-5423
Fax: 916-264-7372
Toll-free: 800-735-2929
e-mail: cam@cityofsacramento.org
Web Site: www.crockerartmuseum.org
Officers:

President: Tom Weborg
Vice President: Marc Sussman
Treasurer: Bobbi Nathanson
Secretary: Linda Merksamer
Management:
    Executive Director: Lial Jones
    Director of Administration: Cheri Johnson
    Finance Director: David Separovich
    Development Director: Lynn Upchurch
    Marketing/Communications Director: LeAnne Ruzzamenti
    Human Resoureces Manager: Laurie Rodriguez
Mission: Providing performances in an intimate museum setting.
Founded: 1885
Specialized Field: Dance; Vocal Music; Instrumental Music; Theater
Status: Non-Profit, Non-Professional
Performs At: Crocker Museum Ballroom
Annual Attendance: 140,000
Organization Type: Sponsoring

5875

SACRAMENTO COMMUNITY CENTER THEATRE

City Of Sacramento
1301 L Street
Sacramento, CA 95814
Mailing Address: 1030 15th Street, Sacramento CA 95814
Phone: 916-808-5481
Fax: 916-808-7687
e-mail: bchatterton@cityofsacramento.org
Web Site: www.sacramentoconventioncenter.org
Management:
    Theater Manager: Bryan Chatterton
    Director Convention/Culture/Leisure: Barbara E Bonebrake
    General Manager: Judy Goldbar
    Deputy General Manager: Matthew Voreyer
Founded: 1974
Opened: 1974
Performs At: Variety
Annual Attendance: 350,000
Type of Stage: Proscenium Arch
Seating Capacity: 2,350
Year Built: 1974
Rental Contact: Theater Manager Bryan Chatterton

5876

SACRAMENTO CONVENTION CENTER

1030 15th Street
Suite 100
Sacramento, CA 95814
Phone: 916-449-5291
Fax: 916-264-7687
e-mail: mvoreyer@cityofsacramento.org
Web Site: www.sacramentoconventioncenter.com
Management:
    Deputy General Manager: Matthew W. Voreyer
Mission: The Sacramento Convention Center includes 134,000 square feet of contiguous exhibit space, 31 meeting rooms, an outdoor garden terrace adjacent to an elegant 24,000 square-foot ballroom, and two separate 10,000 square-foot regisration/prefunction areas. The complex also includes the 4,000 seat Memorial Auditorium and the 2,452 seat Community Center Theatre. All venues are located conveniently near City parking facilities.
Founded: 1926
Type of Stage: Proscenium Arch

5877

CALIFORNIA THEATRE OF PERFORMING ARTS

562 West 4th Street
San Bernardino, CA 92402-0270
Mailing Address: PO Box 270
Phone: 909-885-5152
Fax: 909-885-8672
Toll-free: 800-511-6449
Web Site: www.theatricalarts.com
Management:
    President: Joseph Hansen
    Executive Director: Alan Edenson
Founded: 1998
Status: Non-Profit, Professional

5878

BALBOA PARK RECITAL HALL

2005 Pan American Road Plaza
San Diego, CA 92101
Phone: 619-544-7827
Fax: 619-544-7832
e-mail: boxoffice@starlighttheatre.org
Web Site: www.sandiego.gov/park-and-recreation/parks/balboa/recitalhall.shtml
Management:
    Executive Director: Cecilia Soriano
    Box Office Manager: Stephan Lewicki
    Finance Manager: Karen Dalton
    Artistic/Production Director: Brian Wells
    Marketing/Community Relations: Annette Grieshaber
Mission: The Recital Hall is located in the Palisades Building, a historic building which was built for the second exposition. There is one large, open hall with a stage and high truss beamed ceiling. It is approximately 5,400 sq ft. Maximum Capacity: 200 banquet-style, 300 meeting.

5879

BALBOA PARK STARLIGHT THEATER

PO Box 3519
San Diego, CA 92163
Phone: 619-544-7800
e-mail: artistic@starlighttheatre.org
Web Site: www.starlighttheatre.org
Management:
    Executive Director: Cecilia Soriano
    Producing Artistic Director: Brian Wells
    Finance Manager: Karen Dalton
    Marketing/Community Relations: Annette Grieshaber
Founded: 1945

5880

CAFE DEL REY MORO

House of Hospitality
1549 El Prado
San Diego, CA 92101
Phone: 619-557-9441
Web Site: www.sandiegohistory.org/bpbuildings/hospitality.htm
Management:
    Director Of Operations: Shanon Brant

5881

COX ARENA AT AZTEC BOWL

5500 Canyon Crest Drive
San Diego, CA 92182
Phone: 619-594-0234
Fax: 619-594-6423
Web Site: www.cox-arena.com/welcome.html

Management:
    Director: John Kolek
    Assistant Director: Tim Ripke
    Operations Manager: Tom Granucci
    Event Services Manager: Aaron Woods
    Facility Operations: Adrian Munoz
    Facility Services: Julio Pina
    Financial Administrator: Stacy Desmond
    Ticket Office Manager: June Barreras
Mission: Facility - 12,000 seat multi-purpose area.
Founded: 1997
Status: Professional
Seating Capacity: 12,000

5882

DON POWELL THEATRE

San Diego State University
5500 Campanile Drive
San Diego, CA 92182-7601
Mailing Address: San Diego State University, 5500 Campanile Drive, DA 201, Sa
Phone: 619-594-5200
Fax: 594—74-31
e-mail: aparkhur@mail.sdsu.edu
Web Site: http://theatre.sdsu.edu/
Officers:
    Director: Nick Reid
    Facilities Manager: Peter Nordyke
Management:
    TTF Coordinator: Angie Parkhurst
Mission: The Theatre Program provides its students with an understanding of the great legacy of dramatic literature, technical skills as they relate to public performance, training in critical thinking and the means to express themselves with clarity and grace.
Specialized Field: Theatre
Type of Stage: Proscenium
Seating Capacity: 500

5883

EXPERIMENTAL THEATRE

San Diego State University
5500 Campanile Drive
San Diego, CA 92182-7601
Mailing Address: San Diego State University, 5500 Campanile Drive, DA 201, Sa
Phone: 619-594-5200
Fax: 594—74-31
e-mail: aparkhur@mail.sdsu.edu
Web Site: http://theatre.sdsu.edu/
Officers:
    Director: Nick Reid
    Facilities Manager: Peter Nordyke
Management:
    TTF Coordinator: Angie Parkhurst
Mission: The Theatre Program provides its students with an understanding of the great legacy of dramatic literature, technical skills as they relate to public performance, training in critical thinking and the means to express themselves with clarity and grace.
Specialized Field: Theatre
Type of Stage: Flexible
Seating Capacity: 175

5884

HORTON GRAND THEATRE

444 Fourth Avenue
San Diego, CA 92101
Phone: 619-234-3588
Fax: 619-234-3587
Web Site: www.tripleespresso.com
Management:
    President/Executive Producer: Dennis Babcock
    Associate Producer: Rosalie Miller

Operations Manager: Hector Roberts
Group Sales Manager: Emilia Zellmer
Marketing Manager: Megan Paulek
Controller: Greg Triplett
Audience Services Manager: Ben Netzley
Artistic Director: William Partlan
Utilizes: Actors; Designers; Educators; Fine Artists; Guest Accompanists; Guest Musical Directors; Guest Soloists; High School Drama; Instructors; Local Unknown Artists; Multimedia; Original Music Scores; Performance Artists; Resident Artists; Resident Professionals; Sign Language Translators; Special Technical Talent; Theatre Companies; Visual Arts
Founded: 1985
Paid Staff: 20
Paid Artists: 20
Income Sources: Ticket Sales
Affiliations: San Diego Performing Arts League; San Diego Chamber of Commerce; San Diego Convention & Visitors Bureau
Annual Attendance: 50,000
Facility Category: Rental house
Type of Stage: Proscenium
Stage Dimensions: 29'9" x 18'x22'6"
Seating Capacity: 250
Year Built: 1983
Rental Contact: General Manager Matt Boden

5885
LYCEUM THEATRES COMPLEX

San Diego Repertory Theatre
79 Horton Plaza
San Diego, CA 92101-6144
Phone: 619-231-3586
Fax: 619-235-0939
e-mail: artistic@sandiegorep.com
Web Site: www.sandiegorep.com
Management:
    Artistic Director: Sam Woodhouse
    Managing Director: Karen Wood
    Associate Artistic Director: Todd Salovey
Founded: 1976
Annual Attendance: 50,000
Seating Capacity: 545

5886
PRADO AT BALBOA PARK

House of Hospitality
1549 El Prado
San Diego, CA 92101
Mailing Address: 1549 El Prado, San Diego CA 92101
Phone: 619-557-9441
Web Site:
www.sandiegohistory.org/bpbuildings/hospitality.htm
Management:
    Property General Manager: Rita Gallant
Mission: The Prado, an award-winning, full-service restaurant located in the House of Hospitality, offers charming indoor and outdoor dining
Specialized Field: Theater, Ballet, Symphonies, Weddings, Dance,
Status: Non profit

5887
QUALCOMM STADIUM

9449 Friars Road
San Diego, CA 92108
Phone: 619-641-3100
Fax: 619-283-0460
e-mail: stadium@sandiego.gov
Web Site: www.sandiego.gov/qualcomm/index.shtml
Management:
    General Manager: Mike McSweeney
    Centerplate: Scott Marshall

Director Sales: Lynn Abramson
Founded: 1967
Specialized Field: Stadium; Performances
Status: Non-Profit, Professional
Paid Staff: 38
Performs At: Football Stadium
Facility Category: Stadium
Seating Capacity: 70,500
Year Remodeled: 1997
Rental Contact: General Manager Michael McSweeney

5888
SAN DIEGO CIVIC THEATRE

1100 Third Avenue
San Diego, CA 92101
Phone: 619-570-1100
Fax: 619-615-4001
e-mail: dontefford@sandiegotheatre.org
Web Site: www.sandiegotheatres.org
Officers:
    Chair: M Faye Wilson
    Vice Chair: Kevin Tilden
    Director: Cheryl Fisher
    Director: Bob Nelson
    Director: Matthew Strauss
Management:
    President/CEO: Donald Telford
    Event Manager: Cindy Bowers
    Ticket Sales Manager: Debbie McDonald
    Production Services Manager: Carolyn Satter
Founded: 1965
Seating Capacity: 2,976

5889
SAN DIEGO MUSEUM OF ART AUDITORIUM

1450 El Prado
Balboa Park
San Diego, CA 92101
Mailing Address: PO Box 122107, San Diego, CA. 92112-2107
Phone: 619-232-7931
Fax: 619-232-9367
e-mail: information@sdmart.org
Web Site: www.sdmart.org
Management:
    Executive Director: Derrick Curtwright
    Interim Director Communications: Chris Zook
Utilizes: Dance Companies; Dancers; Filmmakers; Guest Choreographers; Guest Instructors; Guest Soloists; Multi Collaborations; Multimedia; Original Music Scores; Playwrights; Special Technical Talent; Touring Companies
Founded: 1925
Specialized Field: Visual
Status: Non-Profit, Professional
Paid Staff: 85
Budget: 9.0 Million
Performs At: James Copley Auditorium
Annual Attendance: 400,000
Facility Category: Auditorium
Type of Stage: Proscenium
Seating Capacity: 425
Year Remodeled: 1999

5890
SAN DIEGO SPORTS ARENA

3500 Sports Arena Boulevard
San Diego, CA 92110-4919
Phone: 619-224-4171
Fax: 619-224-3010
e-mail: pvallin@sandiegoarena.com
Web Site: www.sandiegoarena.com

Management:
    President: Ron Hahn
    General Manager: Ernie Hahn
    VP: Bob Brown
    Director Public Relations: Stephanie Coolich
    VP/Operations: John Sanders
    Event Manager: Jason Lebdetter
    Marketing & Sponsorship Director: Kathy Padilla
    Marketing Coordinator: Dana Cappello
Founded: 1967
Status: Non-Profit, Professional
Paid Staff: 60
Affiliations: Clear Channel Entertainment
Facility Category: Arena
Stage Dimensions: 60' x 40'
Seating Capacity: 14,000
Year Built: 1966
Cost: 6.4 million
Rental Contact: Sean Saadeh

5891
SAN DIEGO SYMPHONY

1245 7th Avenue
750 B Street
San Diego, CA 92101
Phone: 619-235-0800
Fax: 619-231-0935
e-mail: marketing@sandiegosymphony.org
Web Site: www.sandiegosymphony.com
Management:
    Chairman of the Board: Mitchell R Woodbury
    Executive Director: Ward Gill
    Music Director: Jahja Ling
    Artistic Administrator: Tommy Phillips
Founded: 1929
Specialized Field: Symphonic; Pops; Concert Music
Status: Non-Profit, Professional
Paid Staff: 33
Paid Artists: 79
Budget: $15 million
Performs At: Copley Symphony Hall (Concert Hall)
Type of Stage: Proscenium
Seating Capacity: 2,255
Year Built: 1929
Year Remodeled: 1988
Rental Contact: Dennis Legg

5892
SAN DIEGO THEATRES/BALBOA & CIVIC THEATRES

1100 Third Avenue
San Diego, CA 92101
Phone: 619-615-4000
Fax: 619-615-4001
e-mail: info@sandiegotheatres.org
Web Site: www.sandiegotheatres.org
Officers:
    President/COO: Don Telford
Paid Staff: 43

5893
AFRICAN AMERICAN ART AND CULTURE COMPLEX

762 Fulton Street
Suite 300
San Francisco, CA 94102
Phone: 415-922-2049
Fax: 415-922-5130
e-mail: info@aaacc.org
Web Site: www.aaacc.org
Management:
    Executive Director: London Breed
    Program Manager: Tamika Chenier

Office Manager: Melorra Green
Executive Director: Amber Hughes
Youth Coordinator: Nicola Higgins
Office Manager: Tamiko Johnson
Mission: Mission is to empower our community through Afro-centric artistic and cultural expression, mediums, education and programming. Dedicated to inspiring children and youth to serve as agents of change, cultivating their leadership skills and fostering a commitment to community service and activism.
Founded: 1989
Status: Non-Profit, Professional
Paid Staff: 10

5894
ALCAZAR THEATRE
650 Geary Street
San Francisco, CA 94102
Phone: 415-441-4042
Fax: 415-441-9567
e-mail: AlcazarTheatre@aol.com
Management:
    Artistic Director: Steve Dobbins
    Administrative Director: Alan Ramos
    Casting Director: Kim Parolari
    House Manager: Bernadette Lopes
Utilizes: Actors; AEA Actors; Choreographers; Designers; Grant Writers; Guest Accompanists; Guest Artists; Guest Companies; Guest Designers; Guest Teachers; Instructors; Local Artists; Lyricists; Multimedia; Organization Contracts; Original Music Scores; Resident Professionals; Sign Language Translators; Soloists; Special Technical Talent
Founded: 1978
Status: Commercial
Volunteer Staff: 3
Budget: Varies
Season: Year Round
Performs At: Commercial, For-Profit Theatre
Annual Attendance: 200,000
Type of Stage: Proscenium
Stage Dimensions: 45'x31'
Seating Capacity: 520
Year Built: 1917
Year Remodeled: 1991
Cost: $2.5 million
Rental Contact: Artistic Director Steve Dobbins

5895
AT&T PARK
24 Willie Mays Plaza
San Francisco, CA 94107
Mailing Address: AT&T Park, 24 Willie Mays Plaza, San Francisco, California 9
Phone: 415-972-2000
Toll-free: 800-544-2687
Web Site: http://sanfrancisco.giants.mlb.com/NASApp/mlb/sf/ballpark/index.jsp
Officers:
    President: Peter A Magowan
    EVP/Chief Operating Officer: Laurence M Baer
    VP/Chief Information Officer: Bill Schlough
    SVP/Chief Financial Officer: John F Yee
    SVP/General Counsel: Jack F Bair
Management:
    SVP/General Manager: Brian R Sabean
    SVP/Ballpark Operations: Jorge Costa
    VP Communications: Staci A Slaughter
    Public Affairs/Community Relations: Shana Daum
    SVP Consumer Marketing: Tom McDonald
    Vice President Finance: Lisa Pantages
Mission: Open aired baseball park

Founded: 2000
Specialized Field: Concerts
Status: For-Profit, Professional
Paid Artists: 25
Seating Capacity: 41,503

5896
BAYVIEW OPERA HOUSE
4705 3rd Street
San Francisco, CA 94124
Phone: 415-824-0386
Fax: 415-824-7124
Toll-free: 877-227-5544
e-mail: sbbpr@pacbell.net
Web Site: www.bayviewoperahouse.org
Officers:
    President: Edward Donaldson
Management:
    Executive Director: Shelley Bradford-Bell
    Program Director: Eugene Steptoe
Utilizes: Actors; Artists-in-Residence; Collaborating Artists; Collaborations; Dance Companies; Dancers; Designers; Educators; Filmmakers; Fine Artists; Five Seasonal Concerts; Guest Directors; Guest Lecturers; High School Drama; Local Artists; Lyricists; Multi Collaborations; Multimedia; Music; Original Music Scores; Performance Artists; Playwrights; Sign Language Translators; Soloists; Student Interns; Special Technical Talent; Touring Companies; Visual Arts
Founded: 1968
Specialized Field: Series & Festivals; Dance; Instrumental Music; Musical Theatre; Theatrical Group; Vocal Music
Status: Non-Profit, Non-Professional
Seating Capacity: 300

5897
BILL GRAHAM CIVIC AUDITORIUM
99 Grove Street
San Francisco, CA 94102
Phone: 415-974-4000
Fax: 415-974-4073
e-mail: miendaro@moscone.com
Web Site: www.billgrahamcivic.com
Management:
    General Manager: Richard Shaff
    Sales Director: Melody Lendaro
    Communications Manager: Naina Ayya
Seating Capacity: 7,000

5898
COMMUNITY MUSIC CENTER
544 Capp Street
San Francisco, CA 94110
Phone: 415-647-6015
Fax: 415-647-3890
e-mail: info@sfcmc.org
Web Site: www.sfcmc.org
Officers:
    Chairperson: Kay Kleinerman
    President: Albert W Wald
    Vice President: Robert H Hersey
    Secretary/Treasurer: Catharine L Kalin
Management:
    Executive Director: Stephen Shapiro
    Business Officer: Holly Herr
    Development Director: Fran Hilderand
    Marketing Director: Ann Smith
    Grant Writer: Linda Hitchcock
    Registrar: Kathy Cole
Founded: 1921
Status: Non-Profit, Professional
Paid Staff: 137

Paid Artists: 125
Type of Stage: Proscenium
Seating Capacity: 90

5899
COW PALACE
2600 Geneva Street
PO Box 34206
San Francisco, CA 94134-0206
Phone: 415-404-4111
Fax: 415-469-6111
e-mail: info@cowpalace.com
Web Site: www.cowpalace.com
Officers:
    Chief Executive Officer: Walter Haub
Management:
    President: Michael Wegher
    Managing Director: William Mendes
Founded: 1941
Specialized Field: Home of the Grand National Rodeo; Horse and Stock Show. Hosts ice events; basketball; motorcycle races
Status: Non-Profit, Non-Professional
Paid Staff: 25
Type of Stage: Proscenium
Seating Capacity: 8,849
Year Built: 1941

5900
COWELL THEATER
Fort Mason Center
Building A
San Francisco, CA 94123
Phone: 415-345-7500
Fax: 415-441-3405
e-mail: cowell@fortmason.org
Web Site: www.fortmason.org
Officers:
    Chair, Board Of Trustees: Sally P McNulty
    Vice Chair: David Becker
Management:
    Executive Director: Ann Lazarus
    Sales Manager: Julie Enright
    Marketing Director: Pat S Kilduff
Mission: Support-reflect the evolving cultural fabric of the San Francisco Bay Area.
Founded: 1976
Specialized Field: Dance; Theater; Music; Film
Status: Non-Profit, Professional
Paid Staff: 30
Annual Attendance: 1.7 Million
Facility Category: Cultural Center
Stage Dimensions: 40' x 30' 20'
Seating Capacity: 437
Year Built: 1989
Rental Contact: Amanda Matthews

5901
CURRAN THEATRE
445 Geary Street
PO Box 7110
San Francisco, CA 94102
Mailing Address: 445 Geary St., , San Francisco, CA, 94102
Phone: 415-512-7770
Fax: 415-431-5052
Web Site: www.bestofbroadway-sf.com, http://www.shnsf.com/theatres/index.asp?key=44
Officers:
    CEO: Greg Holland
Management:
    Public Relations/Communications: Anne Abrams
    Ticket Manager: David Cushing
    Operations: Regina Guggenheim

Marketing/Sales: Scott Kane
Mission: The officail site of broadaway in San Francisco
Founded: 1922
Specialized Field: Theater
Seating Capacity: 1,667

5902
FLORENCE GOULD THEATRE
Lincoln Park
100 34th Avenue
San Francisco, CA 94121
Phone: 415-863-3330
e-mail: smurphy@famsf.org
Web Site:
www.thinker.org/legion/about/subpage.asp?subpagekey=64
Management:
Facility Rental Manager: Shannon Murphy
Mission: Originally called the Little Theater, the Florence Gould Theater opened at the California Palace of the Legion of Honor in 1924. The Gould Theater hosts numerous concerts, plays, operas, lectures, and symposiums, and has seen performances by such diverse artists as Andr,s Segovia, Marcel Marceau, Joan Baez, the Philharmonia Baroque Orchestra, and Duke Ellington.
Opened: 1924
Seating Capacity: 316

5903
GOLDEN GATE THEATRE
1 Taylor Street
San Francisco, CA 94102
Mailing Address: One Taylor St., , San Francisco, CA, 94102
Phone: 415-512-7770
Fax: 415-431-5052
Web Site: www.bestofbroadway-sf.com, http://www.shnsf.com/theatres/index.asp?key=48
Management:
CEO: Greg Holland
Founded: 1922
Specialized Field: Theater
Seating Capacity: 2,297

5904
HERBEST THEATRE
401 Van Ness Avenue
Suite 110
San Francisco, CA 94102
Phone: 415-621-6600
Fax: 415-621-5091
e-mail: info@sfwmpac.org
Web Site: www.sfwmpac.org
Management:
Stage Manager: John Bott
Managing Director: Beth Murray
Assistant Director: Greg Ridenour
Booking Director: Jennifer Norris
Founded: 1932
Status: For-Profit, Professional
Paid Staff: 100
Affiliations: Owned and operated by the War Memorial, a department of the city of San Francisco
Annual Attendance: 127,000
Facility Category: theatre
Type of Stage: proscenium
Stage Dimensions: 33 x 40
Seating Capacity: 916
Year Built: 1937
Year Remodeled: 1979
Rental Contact: Jennifer Norris

5905
NOB HILL MASONIC CENTER
1111 California Street
San Francisco, CA 94108
Phone: 415-776-4702
Fax: 415-776-3945
Web Site: www.sfmasoniccenter.com
Management:
Executive Director: Michael Grive
Founded: 1958
Status: Non-Profit, Professional
Paid Staff: 10
Facility Category: Event Center

5906
ODC THEATRE
3153 17th Street @ Shotwell Street
San Francisco, CA 94110
Phone: 415-626-6745
Fax: 415-863-9833
e-mail: info@odctheater.org
Web Site: www.odctheater.org/v5/home.html
Management:
Director: Rob Bailis
Artistic Director: Brenda Way
Marketing Director: Liz Charlson
Production Manager: Lynda Reiman
General Manager: Lori Laqua
Theater Manager: Brittany Brown Ceres
Theater Publicist: Lori Perkovich
Seating Capacity: 187

5907
ORPHEUM THEATRE
1192 Market Street
San Francisco, CA 94102
Mailing Address: 1192 Market Street., San Francisco, CA 94102
Phone: 415-512-7770
Fax: 415-431-5052
Web Site: www.shnsf.com/theatres/index.asp?key=52
Officers:
CEO: Greg Holland
Management:
President: Carole Shorenstein Hays
Chief Executive Officer: Greg Holland
VP Public Relations/Communications: Anne Abrams
VP Ticketing: David Cushing
VP Production/Theatre Operations: Regina Guggenheim
VP Marketing & Sales: Scott Kane
Founded: 1926
Specialized Field: Theater
Seating Capacity: 2,203

5908
PALACE OF FINE ARTS THEATRE
3301 Lyon Street
San Francisco, CA 94123
Phone: 415-563-6504
Fax: 415-567-4062
e-mail: info@palaceoffinearts.org
Web Site: www.palaceoffinearts.org
Officers:
President: Jerry Firedman
Management:
Executive Director: Kevin J O'Brien
Technical Director: Kevin Taylor
House Manager: David Young
Founded: 1970
Specialized Field: Multidiscipliary; Multi-Use
Paid Staff: 15

Income Sources: Rental and concession fees
Performs At: Rental Theatre
Annual Attendance: 120,000
Facility Category: Theatre
Type of Stage: Proscenium
Stage Dimensions: 73'x54'
Seating Capacity: 1,000
Year Built: 1970
Rental Contact: Kevin O'Brien

5909
SAN FRANCISCO COUNTY FAIR ARENA
Lincoln Way & 9th Avenue
Golden Gate Park
San Francisco, CA 94122
Mailing Address: San Francisco Recreation and Park Commission, 501 Stanyan St
Phone: 415-666-7079
Fax: 415—22-1-80
Web Site: www.sfgov.org
Officers:
Director Sales: Melody Lendaro
General Manager: Richard Shaff
Building Manager: Thaddeus Watkins
Mission: Special events.
Utilizes: Student Interns; Theatre Companies
Founded: 1961
Affiliations: City of San Francisco
Annual Attendance: 300,000
Facility Category: Multi-Use Arena
Type of Stage: Flexible
Seating Capacity: 7,000
Year Built: 1918
Year Remodeled: 1986
Rental Contact: Melody Lendaro

5910
YERBA BUENA CENTER FOR THE ARTS
701 Mission Street @ 3rd
San Francisco, CA 94103-3138
Phone: 415-978-2700
Fax: 415-978-9635
Web Site: www.yerbabuenaarts.org/
Management:
Executive Director: Kenneth J Foster
Marketing/Communications Director: Mary Beth Smith
Finance Administration Director: Roberta Beier
Community Engagement Director: Joel Tan
Development Director: Charles Ward
Events Manager: Lisa Elliot
Assistant Facility Manager: Adil Fartas
Production Manager: Jose Maria Francos
Visual Arts Director: Rene De Guzman
Mission: Theater has a seating capacity of 757 and The Forum and East Garden have 6,700 square feet of space.
Utilizes: Artists-in-Residence; Collaborating Artists; Collaborations; Commissioned Music; Curators; Dance Companies; Fine Artists; Instructors; Local Artists; Multi Collaborations; Selected Students; Student Interns; Special Technical Talent; Theatre Companies; Touring Companies
Founded: 1993
Status: Non-Profit, Non-Professional
Paid Staff: 55
Volunteer Staff: 100
Budget: $7,300,000
Income Sources: Contributions; Rental Revenue; Ticket Revenue
Affiliations: LATSE
Annual Attendance: 205,000
Facility Category: Theater ; Multi-Use Forum
Type of Stage: Proscenium and Flexible

Stage Dimensions: 43'x93'
Year Built: 1993

5911
HP PAVILION AT SAN JOSE
525 W Santa Clara Street
San Jose, CA 95113
Mailing Address: 525 W. Santa Clara Street, San Jose, CA 95113
Phone: 408-287-7070
Fax: 408-999-5797
Toll-free: 800-755-5050
Web Site: www.hppavilion.com
Management:
   President: Greg Jamison
   Managing Director: Jim Goddard
   Director Booking/Events: Steve Kirsner
Founded: 1993
Specialized Field: concerts and sporting events
Status: For-Profit, Professional
Paid Staff: 35
Performs At: Sports/Entertainment Arena
Affiliations: IAAM; Arena Network; MPI
Facility Category: Arena
Type of Stage: Portable
Seating Capacity: 4,500-18,000
Year Built: 1995
Rental Contact: Steve Kirsner

5912
MONTGOMERY THEATRE
271 South Market Street
San Jose, CA 95113
Mailing Address: 271 S. Market St., San Jose, CA 95113
Phone: 408-277-5277
Fax: 408-277-3535
Toll-free: 888-726-5673
Web Site:
http://sanjose.org/meetings/facilities/montgomery.php
Management:
   Acting General Manager: Julie Mark
   Facilities/Rental Manager: Bill Fisher
Mission: home of the San Jose Children's Musical Theater, the Montgomery Theater hosts a variety of cultural and performing arts events
Founded: 1936
Specialized Field: cultural and performing arts events
Seating Capacity: 536

5913
SAN JOSE CENTER FOR THE PERFORMING ARTS
255 Almaden Boulevard
San Jose, CA 95110-2715
Mailing Address: 255 Almaden Blvd., , San Jose, CA, 95113
Phone: 408-277-5277
Fax: 408-277-3535
Toll-free: 800-533-2345
Web Site:
http://sanjose.org/meetings/facilities/montgomery.php
Officers:
   Chairman: Patrick J D'Angelo
   President: Stewart Slater
   Immediate Past-Chairman: Frank S Greene, Jr
   Artistic Director: Dianna Shuster
   Associate Artistic Director: Marc Jacobs
   Technical Director: Nick Nichols
   Marketing Associate: Kari Henrichsen
   Director: Dan Fenton
Status: Nonprofit, Non-Professional
Paid Staff: 150
Seating Capacity: 2,665

5914
SAN JOSE MUNICIPAL STADIUM
San Jose Giants Baseball
588 East Alma Avenue & Senter Road
San Jose, CA 95112
Phone: 408-297-1435
Fax: 408-297-1453
e-mail: info@sjgiants.com
Web Site: www.sjgiants.com
Management:
   President/CEO: Jim Weyermann
   General Manager/COO: Mark Wilson
   CMO: Juliana Paoli
   Player Relations Director: Linda Pereira
   Stadium Operations: Lance Motch
   Ticket Services Manager: Kellen Minteer
Founded: 1988
Status: For-Profit, Professional
Annual Attendance: 154,324
Type of Stage: Baseball Stadium
Seating Capacity: 4,500

5915
SAN JOSE STATE UNIVERSITY THEATRE
One Washington Square
San Jose, CA 95192-0098
Phone: 408-924-4530
Fax: 408-924-4574
e-mail: info@tvradiofilmtheatre.com
Web Site: www.tvradiofilmtheatre.com
Management:
   President/Chairman: Mike Adams
   Executive Director: Barnaby Dallas
   Artistic Director: Laura Long
   Technology Director: Jim Lefever
Founded: 1904
Status: Non-Profit, Non-Professional
Paid Staff: 30

5916
CAL POLY STATE UNIVERSITY PERFORMING ARTS CENTER
Cal Poly State University
Bldg 6 Room 208
San Luis Obispo, CA 93407
Mailing Address: 1 Grand Avenue, San Luis Obispo, CA 93407-0441
Phone: 805—75-6-72
Fax: 805-756-6088
Toll-free: 800-289-8425
e-mail: mrklemin@calpoly.edu
Web Site: www.pacslo.org
Management:
   Managing Director: Ron Regler
   Ticketing Services Manager: Terri Hopson
   Technical Services Manager: Jim Chernoff
   Theatre Operations Manager: Nancy Cochran
   Assistant Director: Chris McBride
Mission: The Artistic Mission of the Performing Arts Center is to:,To actively encourage full, broad-based facility use, featuring a schedule of varied, high quality arts events designed to serve diverse audience interests. ,To actively support local arts groups, providing a range of quality services, which encourage and enable them to reach their maximum potential. ,To promote use of the Center and its services to potential clients from outside the commu
Founded: 1996
Seating Capacity: 1277

5917
SAN MATEO PERFORMING ARTS CENTER
600 North Delaware Avenue
San Mateo, CA 94401
Phone: 650-762-0258
Fax: 650-762-0218
e-mail: info@peninsulasymphony.org
Web Site: www.peninsulasym.org/locations.html
Management:
   Executive Director: Margrit Rinderknecht
   Marketing Associate: Trudy Taliaferro
   Development Associate: Emily Carr
Founded: 1968
Status: Non-Profit, Professional
Paid Staff: 12
Paid Artists: 2
Seating Capacity: 1,600

5918
ANGELS GATE CULTURAL CENTER
3601 S Gaffey Street
San Pedro, CA 90731
Phone: 310-519-0936
Fax: 310-519-8698
e-mail: info@angelsgateart.org
Web Site: www.angelsgateart.org
Management:
   President of the Board: Rae Wyman
   Executive Director: Nathan Birnbaum
   Development & Programming Associate: Clare Davis
Mission: Angels Gate Cultural Center, a nonprofit corporation, serves to develop an active environment mutually nourishing to the growth of artists, cultural arts and the community.
Founded: 1982
Status: Non-Profit, Non-Professional
Paid Staff: 4
Volunteer Staff: 6
Paid Artists: 15

5919
WARNER GRAND THEATRE
478 West 6th Street
San Pedro, CA 90731
Phone: 310-548-7672
Fax: 310-548-2498
Web Site: www.warnergrand.org
Mission: Built in 1931, the Warner Grand is the only one of the three Warner Brothers art deco theaters in Los Angeles that is still intact and fully functioning with a calendar of events appealing to a wide range of interests, including classic and foreign films, youth programs, and contemporary and classical music.
Status: Non-Profit, Non-Professional
Seating Capacity: 1,500

5920
DOMINICAN COLLEGE AUDITORIUM
50 Acacia Avenue
San Rafael, CA 94901
Phone: 415-457-4440
Fax: 415-485-3205
Toll-free: 888-323-6763
e-mail: anderson@dominican.edu
Web Site: www.dominican.edu
Management:
   Operations Manager: Crystal Anderson
   Executive Assistant: Laverne Dicker
Founded: 1890

5921
MARIN CENTER SHOWCASE THEATRE
10 Avenue of the Flags
San Rafael, CA 94903
Phone: 415-499-6400
Fax: 415-499-3700
e-mail: webmaster@co.marin.ca.us
Web Site: www.marincenter.org
Management:
    Director: Jim Farley
    Deputy Director: Marion Boyd
    Senior Events Coordinator: Christian Gutt
    Technical Coordinator: Tony Taubert
Founded: 1971
Status: For-Profit, Professional
Paid Staff: 214
Performs At: Theatre
Seating Capacity: 348

5922
ARLINGTON CENTER FOR THE PERFORMING ARTS
1317 State Street
Santa Barbara, CA 93101
Phone: 805-963-4408
Fax: 805-966-4688
Founded: 1931
Facility Category: Theatre
Seating Capacity: 2,018
Year Built: 1931
Year Remodeled: 1977
Rental Contact: Karen Killingsworth

5923
ELLEN PORTER HALL
Westmont College
955 La Paz Road
Santa Barbara, CA 93108
Phone: 805-565-6040
e-mail: theater@westmont.edu
Web Site: http://www.westmont.edu
Management:
    Professor of Theatre Arts: John Blondell
    Associate Professor Theatre Arts: Erlyne Whiteman
    Adjunct Instructor Theatre Arts: Victoria Finlayson
Mission: The program is distinct for many reasons. We couple traditional theatrical methods with innovative practices, engaging in a dynamic and lively approach to the study and practice of the art of the theatre.
Specialized Field: Theatre
Type of Stage: Auditorium
Seating Capacity: 180

5924
HARDER STADIUM
University of California, Santa Barbara
Santa Barbara, CA 93106
Phone: 805-893-4156
Fax: 805-893-8640
e-mail: customer.service@pf.ucsb.edu
Web Site: www.facilities.ucsb.edu
Management:
    Acting Director: Jon Cook
    Associate Director/Operations: Jim Dewey
    Athletics Director: Gary Cunningham
    Associate Athletic Director: Bobby Castagna
    Development Director: Gil Picciotto
    Assistant Athletic Director & Media: Bill Mahoney
    Assist. Athletic Director & Finance: Sally Orsua
    Facilities/Operations Manager: Joe Ballesteros
    Assistant Director & Marketing: Jeff Kim

Opened: 1966
Seating Capacity: 17,000

5925
HATLEN THEATRE
University of California, Santa Barbara
Dramatic Art & Division Of Dance
552 University Road
Santa Barbara, CA 93106-7060
Mailing Address: University of California, Theater & Dance, Mail Code 7060, 5
Phone: 805-893-5515
Fax: 803-893-7029
e-mail: smcmillan@theaterdance.ucsb.edu
Web Site: http://www.dramadance.ucsb.edu
Officers:
    Chair: Simon Williams
Mission: Dedicated to the study and practice of theatre in all its phases, the Department of Dramatic Art offers a wide range of classes appropriate for non-majors pursuing a liberal arts education and for majors preparing for a professional or educational career.
Specialized Field: Dance, Theatre
Type of Stage: Proscenium
Orchestra Pit: y
Seating Capacity: 340

5926
LOBERO THEATRE FOUNDATION
33 East Canon Perdido Street
Santa Barbara, CA 93101
Phone: 805-966-4946
Fax: 805-963-8752
Toll-free: 888-456-2376
Web Site: www.lobero.com
Officers:
    Board President: George Burtness
Management:
    Executive Director: David Asbell
Utilizes: Collaborating Artists; Collaborations; Commissioned Music; Dance Companies; Educators; Lyricists; Multimedia; Original Music Scores; Resident Artists; Theatre Companies
Founded: 1873
Specialized Field: California Central Coast
Status: Non-Profit, Professional
Paid Staff: 15
Volunteer Staff: 100
Paid Artists: 2
Affiliations: APAP WAA Ca. Presenters
Annual Attendance: 100,000
Seating Capacity: 680
Year Built: 1924
Year Remodeled: 1996
Cost: 3 Million

5927
MUSIC THEATER OF SANTA BARBARA
1216 State Street
#200
Santa Barbara, CA 93101
Mailing Address: P.O. Box 1028, Santa Barbara CA
Phone: 805-962-1922
Fax: 805-963-3510
Web Site: www.santabarbara.com/community/art/sb_theater/
Management:
    Executive Producer: Anthony Rhine
Mission: To enrich the community through musical theater.
Founded: 1989
Paid Staff: 15
Volunteer Staff: 20
Paid Artists: 100

Budget: $5 million
Income Sources: Tickets and Donations
Performs At: Granada Theater
Affiliations: National Association of Musical Theatre
Annual Attendance: 120,000
Facility Category: Theater
Type of Stage: Proscenium
Stage Dimensions: 60x40
Seating Capacity: 953
Year Built: 1908
Resident Groups: Santa Barbara Civic Light Opera

5928
PERFORMING ARTS THEATRE
University of California, Santa Barbara
Dramatic Art & Division Of Dance
552 University Road
Santa Barbara, CA 93106-7060
Mailing Address: University of California, Theater & Dance, Mail Code 7060, 5
Phone: 805-893-5515
Fax: 803-893-7029
e-mail: mrklemin@calpoly.edu
Web Site: http://www.dramadance.ucsb.edu
Officers:
    Chair: Simon Williams
Mission: Dedicated to the study and practice of theatre in all its phases, the Department of Dramatic Art offers a wide range of classes appropriate for non-majors pursuing a liberal arts education and for majors preparing for a professional or educational career.
Opened: 1996
Specialized Field: Acting and Directing Classes
Type of Stage: Black Box
Seating Capacity: 150

5929
SANTA BARBARA CONTEMPORARY ARTS FORUM
653 Paseo Nuevo
Santa Barbara, CA 93101
Phone: 805-966-5373
Fax: 805-962-1421
e-mail: sbcaf@sbcaf.org
Web Site: www.sbcaf.org
Officers:
    President: Ian Smith
    1st Vice President: Candice Assassi
    2nd Vice President: Glenn Miller
    Secretary: Carolyn Glasoe
    Treasurer: Kendra Epley
Management:
    Executive Director: Miki Garcia
    Gallery Manager: Dena Beard
    Development Manager: Holly Mackay
    Assistant Curator: Elizabeth Lovero
    Head Preparator: Saul Gray Hildenbrand
Mission: To provide an arena for the presentation, documentation and support of a broad variety of visual, media and performing arts representing a wide range of attitudes.
Founded: 1976
Specialized Field: Visual and Performing Arts Organization
Status: Non-Profit, Professional
Paid Staff: 6
Volunteer Staff: 30
Budget: $300,000
Income Sources: Membership; Business Sponsorship
Performs At: Center Stage Theater
Facility Category: Black Box
Year Built: 1990

5930
STUDIO THEATRE
University of California, Santa Barbara
Dramatic Art & Division Of Dance
552 University Road
Santa Barbara, CA 93106-7060
Mailing Address: University of California, Theater &
Dance, Mail Code 7060, 5
Phone: 805-893-5515
Fax: 803-893-7029
e-mail: mrklemin@calpoly.edu
Web Site: http://www.dramadance.ucsb.edu
Officers:
   Chair: Simon Williams
Mission: Dedicated to the study and practice of theatre
in all its phases, the Department of Dramatic Art offers a
wide range of classes appropriate for non-majors
pursuing a liberal arts education and for majors
preparing for a professional or educational career.
Specialized Field: Acting and Directing Classes

5931
FESS PARKER STUDIO THEATRE
Santa Clara University
Center of Performing Arts
500 El Camino Real
Santa Clara, CA 95053-0341
Mailing Address: Center of Performing Arts, Santa
Clara University, 500 El Ca
Phone: 408-554-4565
Fax: 408-554-2171
e-mail: RJigour@scu.edu
Web Site: http://www.scu.edu/cpa
Management:
   Chair Dept of Theatre: Aldo Billingslea
   Interim Director Arts/Sciences: Amy Shacter
   Managing Director: Lisa Rademacher
Mission: Santa Clara University's Center of Performing
Arts presents a diverse season of dance, music, and
theatre events featuring the talent and artistry of our
students and faculty.
Specialized Field: Theatre
Type of Stage: Black Box
Seating Capacity: 130

5932
LOUIS B. MAYER THEATRE
Santa Clara University
Center of Performing Arts
500 El Camino Real
Santa Clara, CA 95053-0341
Mailing Address: Center of Performing Arts, Santa
Clara University, 500 El Ca
Phone: 408-554-4565
Fax: 408-554-2171
e-mail: RJigour@scu.edu
Web Site: http://www.scu.edu/cpa
Management:
   Chair Dept of Theatre: Aldo Billingslea
   Interim Director Arts/Sciences: Amy Shacter
   Managing Director: Lisa Rademacher
Mission: Santa Clara University's Center of Performing
Arts presents a diverse season of dance, music, and
theatre events featuring the talent and artistry of our
students and faculty.
Specialized Field: Theatre
Type of Stage: Proscenium
Orchestra Pit: y
Seating Capacity: 500

5933
EXPERIMENTAL THEATER
University of California, Santa Cruz
Theater Arts Department
J-106 Theater Arts Center
Santa Cruz, CA 95064
Phone: 831-459-2974
Fax: 831-459-5359
e-mail: theater@ucsc.edu
Web Site: http://theater.ucsc.edu/contact/
Officers:
   Event Manager: Trink Praxell
Mission: The Theater Arts Department combines
drama, dance, critical studies, and theater design,
technology offering students an intensive, unified
undergraduate program.
Specialized Field: Theatre
Type of Stage: Black Box
Seating Capacity: 200

5934
KUUMBWA JAZZ CENTER
320-2 Cedar Street
Santa Cruz, CA 95060
Phone: 831-427-2227
Fax: 831-427-3342
e-mail: kuumbwa@kuumbwajazz.org
Web Site: www.kuumbwajazz.org
Management:
   Artistic Director: Tim Jackson
   Managing Director: Bobbi Todaro
   Marketing Director: Sandy Sloan
Mission: To present jazz and educational opportunities
to Santa Cruz County and surrounding areas.
Utilizes: Commissioned Music; Educators; Grant
Writers; Guest Ensembles; Guest Musical Directors;
Guest Musicians; Instructors; Local Artists; Multimedia;
Music; Sign Language Translators; Singers; Soloists;
Touring Companies
Founded: 1975
Specialized Field: Jazz Music
Status: Non-Profit
Paid Staff: 7
Volunteer Staff: 50
Budget: $950,000
Income Sources: Membership; Grants
Performs At: Music
Stage Dimensions: 20'x14'6"
Seating Capacity: 200
Rental Contact: Sandy Sloan

5935
MAINSTAGE THEATER
University of California, Santa Cruz
Theater Arts Department
J-106 Theater Arts Center
Santa Cruz, CA 95064
Phone: 831-459-2974
Fax: 831-459-5359
e-mail: theater@ucsc.edu
Web Site: http://theater.ucsc.edu/contact/
Officers:
   Event Manager: Trink Praxell
Mission: The Theater Arts Department combines
drama, dance, critical studies, and theater design,
technology offering students an intensive, unified
undergraduate program.
Specialized Field: Theatre
Type of Stage: Proscenium, Thrust
Seating Capacity: 528

5936
MUSIC CENTER RECITAL HALL
University of California, Santa Cruz
Theater Arts Department
J-106 Theater Arts Center
Santa Cruz, CA 95064
Phone: 831-459-2974
Fax: 831-459-5359
e-mail: theater@ucsc.edu
Web Site: http://theater.ucsc.edu/contact/
Officers:
   Event Manager: Trink Praxell
Mission: The Theater Arts Department combines
drama, dance, critical studies, and theater design,
technology offering students an intensive, unified
undergraduate program.
Opened: 1997
Specialized Field: Dance
Type of Stage: Variable
Seating Capacity: 396

5937
SANTA CRUZ CIVIC AUDITORIUM
307 Church Street
Santa Cruz, CA 95060
Phone: 831-420-5240
Fax: 831-420-5261
Web Site: www.santacruzcivic@cityofsantacruz.com
Management:
   Auditorium Supervisor: Andrea Botsford
Founded: 1940
Affiliations: Owned and operated by the City of Santa
Cruz
Annual Attendance: 87,000
Type of Stage: Proscenium
Seating Capacity: 1,957

5938
SECOND STAGE
University of California, Santa Cruz
Theater Arts Department
J-106 Theater Arts Center
Santa Cruz, CA 95064
Phone: 831-459-2974
Fax: 831-459-5359
e-mail: theater@ucsc.edu
Web Site: http://theater.ucsc.edu/contact/
Officers:
   Event Manager: Trink Praxell
Mission: The Theater Arts Department combines
drama, dance, critical studies, and theater design,
technology offering students an intensive, unified
undergraduate program.
Specialized Field: Student Dance and Theater
Productions
Seating Capacity: 231

5939
STANLEY-SINSHEIMER FESTIVAL GLEN
University of California, Santa Cruz
Shakespeare Santa Cruz
Theater Arts/UCSC, 1156 High Street
Santa Cruz, CA 95064
Phone: 831-459-5810
e-mail: theater@ucsc.edu
Web Site: http://shakespearesantacruz.org/
Officers:
   Director Development: Matt Henry
Management:
   Artistic Director: Paul Whitworth

Mission: The Theater Arts Department combines drama, dance, critical studies, and theater design, technology offering students an intensive, unified undergraduate program.
Specialized Field: Theatre
Type of Stage: Amphitheater
Seating Capacity: 625

5940
UNIVERSITY OF CALIFORNIA SANTA CRUZ PERFORMING ARTS CENTER
1156 High Street
Santa Cruz, CA 95064
Phone: 831-459-0111
Fax: 831-459-3502
Web Site: www.ucsc.edu
Management:
    Director of Media Services: Henry J Burnett Ed.D
Founded: 1965
Seating Capacity: 527

5941
PACIFIC CONSERVATORY OF THE PERFORMING ARTS
800 S College Drive
PO Box 1700
Santa Maria, CA 93454
Phone: 805-928-7731
Fax: 805-928-7506
Toll-free: 800-727-2123
e-mail: pcpa@pcpa.org
Web Site: www.pcpa.org
Management:
    Artistic Director: Mark Booher
    Managing Director: Mike Black
    Marketing Director: Maria Centrella
Founded: 1964
Specialized Field: Professional Live Theatre; Conservatory Training Program

5942
MORGAN-WIXSON THEATRE
2627 Pico Boulevard
Santa Monica, CA 90405
Phone: 310-828-7519
Fax: 310-828-6209
e-mail: info@morgan-wixson.org
Web Site: www.morgan-wixson.org/contact-us.cfm
Officers:
    Chairman: Patricia Ibsen
    President: Harold Breslow
    Executive Vice President: Saul Saladow
    First VP Publicity: Deb Verla
    Second VP Production: Larry Gesling
    Treasurer: Anne Gesling
    Secretary: Al Barlaan
Management:
    Marketing/Development Director: Joshua Schulz
    Volunteer/Membership Coordinator: Thomas A Brown

5943
SANTA MONICA CIVIC AUDITORIUM
1855 Main Street
Santa Monica, CA 90401-3209
Phone: 310-458-8551
Fax: 310-394-3411
e-mail: carole.curtin@smgov.net
Web Site: www.santamonicacivicauditorium.org/
Management:
    Manager: Carole Curtin
    Business Administrator: Glennis Waterman

5944
WELLS FARGO CENTER FOR THE ARTS
50 Mark West Springs Road
Santa Rosa, CA 95403
Phone: 707-527-7006
Fax: 707-545-0518
e-mail: shekeynab@wellsfargocenterarts.com
Web Site: www.wellsfargocenterarts.com
Management:
    Executive Director: Richard Nowhn
    Director of Programming: Anita Wiglesworth
    Human Resources Manager: Julie Bova
    Rentals Manager: Shekeyna Black
Mission: Enrich, Educate, Entertain
Founded: 1981
Performs At: Performing Arts, Small Concert Venue
Seating Capacity: R.F. Finley-1600; Metro-399; Cabaret-220

5945
FALLON HOUSE THEATRE
Columbia State Historic Park
PO Box 3030
Sonora, CA 95370
Phone: 209-532-3120
Fax: 209-532-7270
e-mail: admin@sierrarep.org
Web Site: www.sierrarep.org/
Officers:
    President: Bill Green
    Vice President: Mike Jones
    Treasurer: Eric Carlson
Management:
    Producing Director: Dennis Jones
    Artistic Director: Scott Viets
    Managing Director: Sara Jones
    Development Director: Amy Nilson
    Marketing/Educational Director: Sonia Hurt
    Resident Stage Manager: Doug Brennan
    Production Manager: Benjamin Loverin
    Technical Director: Patrick Conley
    Box Office Manager: Bert Simonis
Mission: To produce a year-round season of professional theatre including musicals, drama and comedy.
Founded: 1980
Specialized Field: Theatre
Status: Non-Profit, Professional
Paid Staff: 25
Paid Artists: 200
Annual Attendance: 50,000
Type of Stage: Proscenium
Seating Capacity: 270

5946
ANNENBERG AUDITORIUM
Stanford University
Nathan Cummings Art Building
Stanford, CA 94305-2018
Mailing Address: 435 Lasuen Mall
Phone: 650-723-3404
Fax: 650-725-0140
e-mail: eimboden@stanford.edu
Web Site: www.stanford.edu
Officers:
    Chairman: Joel Leivick
Management:
    Department Administrator: Elis Imboden
    Facilities Administrator: Rory Brown
    Studio Manager: Moira Murdock
    Academic Technology Specialist: Michael Gonzalez
    Publicist: Lisa Vestal

Seating Capacity: 351

5947
CAMPBELL RECITAL HALL
Stanford University
Braun Music Center
Stanford, CA 94305-3076
Mailing Address: 541 Lasuen Mall
Phone: 650-723-3811
Fax: 650-725-2686
e-mail: marioch@stanford.edu
Web Site: http://music.stanford.edu/DeptInfo/index.html
Officers:
    Chairman: Stephen M Sano
    Financial Officer: Jaime Marconette
Management:
    Administrative Director: Mario Champagne
    Facilities/Production Manager: Mark Dalrymple
    Publicist: Beth Youngdoff
    Academic Administrator: Debbie Barney
Seating Capacity: 221

5948
DINKELSPIEL AUDITORIUM
Stanford University
Braun Music Center
Stanford, CA 94305-3076
Mailing Address: 541 Lasuen Mall
Phone: 650-723-3811
Fax: 650-725-2686
e-mail: sano@stanford.edu
Web Site: http://music.stanford.edu/DeptInfo/index.html
Officers:
    Chairman: Stephen M Sano
Management:
    Administrative Director: Mario Champagne
    Technical Services Director: Scott Kepley
    Academic Administration: Debbie Barney
    Financial Officer: Velda Williams
Performs At: Multi-Use Auditorium
Seating Capacity: 716
Year Built: 1957

5949
MEMORIAL AUDITORIUM
Stanford University
Memorial Hall
Stanford, CA 94305-5010
Mailing Address: 551 Serra Mall
Phone: 650-725-2576
Fax: 650-723-0843
Web Site: www.stanford.edu/dept/drama/maps.html#memaud
Management:
    Department Administrator: Ron Davies
    Technical Director/Operations: Ross Williams
    Financial Administrator: Mitzi Woods
    Academic Technology Specialist: Michael Gonzalez
Seating Capacity: 2000

5950
STANFORD UNIVERSITY DEPARTMENT OF MUSIC
Stanford University Braun Music Center
541 Lasuen Mall
Stanford, CA 94305-3076
Phone: 650-723-3811
Fax: 650-725-2686
e-mail: sano@stanford.edu
Web Site: www.music.stanford.edu
Officers:
    Professor & Chair, Dept Of Music: Stephen M Sano

Management:
Administrative Director: Mario Champagne
Technical Services Director: Scott Kepley
Academic Administration: Debbie Barney
Utilizes: Arrangers; Artists-in-Residence; Collaborating Artists; Collaborations; Commissioned Composers; Community Members; Community Talent; Composers; Contract Orchestras; Educators; Fellows of Institute; Guest Accompanists; Guest Companies; Guest Composers; Guest Directors; Guest Ensembles; Guest Instructors; Guest Musical Directors; Guest Musicians; Guest Soloists; Guest Speakers; Guest Writers; Instructors; Local Artists & Directors; Multi Collaborations; Multimedia; Music; Organization Contracts; Original Music Scores; Resident Companies; Scenic Designers; Sign Language Translators; Singers; Students; Student Interns
Founded: 1947
Specialized Field: Music
Performs At: Auditorium; Recital Halls; Church; Concert Hall

5951
FAYE SPANOS CONCERT AND RECITAL HALLS

University of the Pacific Music Conservatory
3601 Pacific Avenue
Stockton, CA 95211
Phone: 209-946-2415
e-mail: sperdicaris@pacific.edu
Web Site: www.pacific.edu/conservatory/facilities.asp
Officers:
Dean: Stephen C Anderson
Assistant Dean: David Chase
Management:
Operations Manager: Stephens Perdicaris
Technical Director: James Gonzales
Director of Development: Renna Beinoris
Administration: Patricia Eckert
Mission: Located within the Conservatory of Music, the Faye Spanos Concert Hall has a seating capacity of 950 and the Recital Hall seats 120.
Utilizes: Actors; Artists-in-Residence; Collaborating Artists; Commissioned Music; Educators; Grant Writers; Guest Accompanists; Guest Artists; Guest Designers; Guest Lecturers; Guild Activities; High School Drama; Music; Organization Contracts; Resident Professionals; Sign Language Translators; Soloists
Founded: 1927
Non-paid Artists: 19
Income Sources: Tickets, University
Annual Attendance: 1,800
Facility Category: Black Box
Type of Stage: Flexible

5952
LONG THEATRE

University of the Pacific
3601 Pacific Avenue
Stockton, CA 95211
Phone: 209-946-2054
Fax: 209-946-2118
Web Site: www.uop.edu
Management:
Theatre Manager: Jack Platt
Utilizes: Actors; Choreographers; Dance Companies; Dancers; Designers; Educators; Grant Writers; Guest Accompanists; Guest Artists; Guest Designers; Guild Activities; High School Drama; Instructors; Multimedia; Performance Artists; Resident Professionals; Sign Language Translators; Singers; Soloists; Student Interns
Founded: 1976
Paid Staff: 1

Non-paid Artists: 19
Performs At: Proscenium
Annual Attendance: 8-10,000
Facility Category: Proscenium
Type of Stage: Proscenium
Stage Dimensions: 40 x 80
Seating Capacity: 400
Year Built: 1950
Year Remodeled: 1998

5953
WARREN ATHERTON AUDITORIUM

5151 Pacific Avenue
San Joaquin County Delta Community College
Stockton, CA 95207
Phone: 209-954-5151
Fax: 209-954-5600
Web Site: www.deltacollege.edu
Management:
Managing Director: Don Bennett
Mission: Atherton Auditorium is one of the finest theater facilities in California. It maintains an independent staff of technical personnel who coordinate the productions presented on stage.
Specialized Field: Performing arts facility
Status: Non-Profit, Non-Professional
Type of Stage: Proscenium
Stage Dimensions: 60 W x 26 L x 40 D
Seating Capacity: 1,456
Year Built: 1977
Rental Contact: Philenia Francis

5954
PREUS-BRANDT FORUM

California Lutheran University
60 West Olsen Road
Thousand Oaks, CA 91360
Phone: 805-493-3195
Fax: 805-493-3513
e-mail: www@clunet.edu
Web Site: www.callutheran.edu/event_services/venues/
Management:
Facility Operations/Planning: Ryan Van Ommeren
Facility Operations Assistant: Diane Noble
Seating Capacity: 200

5955
THOUSAND OAKS CIVIC ARTS PLAZA

2100 Thousand Oaks Boulevard
Thousand Oaks, CA 91362
Phone: 805-449-2787
Fax: 805-449-2750
e-mail: tmitze@toaks.org
Web Site: www.civicartsplaza.com
Management:
Technical Director: Gary Mintz
Box Office Supervisor: Sharon Lauritzen
Theatre House Supervisor: Nancy Loncto
Marketing Manager: Vanessa Pellegrino
Utilizes: Community Talent; Dance Companies; Dancers; Equity Actors; Fine Artists; Grant Writers; Guest Accompanists; Guest Choreographers; Guest Instructors; Guest Musical Directors; Instructors; Local Artists & Directors; Multi Collaborations; Multimedia; Original Music Scores; Resident Artists; Selected Students; Sign Language Translators; Student Interns; Special Technical Talent; Theatre Companies; Touring Companies
Founded: 1994
Performs At: Performing Arts Center
Affiliations: City of Thosand Oaks
Annual Attendance: 300,000+
Facility Category: Performing Arts Center
Type of Stage: Proscenium

Seating Capacity: 1800; 400
Year Built: 1994
Rental Contact: Tom Mitze
Resident Groups: Cabrillo Music Theatre and New West Symphony

5956
EL CAMINO COLLEGE CENTER FOR THE ARTS

16007 South Crenshaw Boulevard
Torrance, CA 90506
Phone: 310-329-5345
Fax: 310-660-3734
e-mail: artstickets@elcamino.edu
Web Site: www.elcamino.edu/commadv/centerforarts/Index.htm
Officers:
President: Tom Fallow
Theatre Manager: Barbara Riser
Ticket Office Assistant: Terri Dixon
Management:
Executive Director: Bruce Spain
Production Manager: Nancy Adler
Stage Manager: Jerry Root
Theatre Manager: Barbara Riser
Event Specialist: Georgi Levine
Mission: The El Camino College Center for the Arts consists of Marsee Auditorium, a 2,000 seat, multi-purpose performance facility, the 350 seat Campus Theatre and the 180 seat Robert Haag Recital Hall.
Founded: 1967
Organization Type: Performing; Educational

5957
JAMES R ARMSTRONG THEATRE

Torrance Cultural Arts Center
3330 Civic Center Drive
Torrance, CA 90503-9998
Mailing Address: PO Box 10416
Phone: 310-781-7150
Fax: 310-618-2399
e-mail: Info@TorranceArts.com
Web Site: www.ci.torrance.ca.us/9028.htm
Officers:
President: Jean Adelsman
Management:
Executive Director: Ray Solley
Facility Booking Manager: Lisa Morales
Cultural Services Manager: Robert Myers
Utilizes: Collaborations; Curators; Educators; Guest Writers; High School Drama; Local Artists; Organization Contracts; Soloists; Touring Companies
Founded: 1991
Status: Non-Profit, Professional
Paid Staff: 50
Volunteer Staff: 200
Income Sources: Facility rentals
Performs At: Theatre, Visual & Performing Arts Studios(dance,crafts,etc)
Affiliations: City of Torrance, Torrance Cultural Arts Center Foundation
Facility Category: Multi-purpose complex (theater, art studios, rental)
Type of Stage: Proscenium
Stage Dimensions: 47 Feet Wide
Seating Capacity: 502
Year Built: 1991
Cost: $12 Million

5958
CALIFORNIA STATE UNIVERSITY STANISLAUS PERFORMING ARTS CENTER
801 W Monte Vista Avenue
Turlock, CA 95382
Phone: 562-951-4060
Fax: 209-667-3782
e-mail: summerarts@calstate.edu
Web Site: www.calstate.edu/summerarts
Management:
Chancellor: Charles B Reed
Founded: 1986
Seating Capacity: 50-800

5959
VISALIA CONVENTION CENTER ROTARY THEATRE
303 East Acequia Avenue
Visalia, CA 93291
Phone: 559-713-4000
Fax: 559-713-4804
Toll-free: 800-225-2277
e-mail: vcc@ci.visalia.ca.us
Web Site: www.visalia.org
Management:
Convention Center Manager: Wally Roeben
Sales Manager: Leticia Garcia
Convention Center Bureau Sales Rep: Danika Heatherly
Sr. Convention Center Technician: Anthony Morfin
Box Office Manager: Teresa Villarreal
Mission: The Visalia Convention Center offes over 114,000 square feet of flexible meeting and convention space and is adjacent to The marriott Hotel.
Seating Capacity: 2,000 to 4,000 telescopic seating

5960
MOONLIGHT AMPHITHEATRE
600 Eucalyptus
Vista, CA 92084
Phone: 760-724-2110
Fax: 760-643-2897
e-mail: moonlight@ci.vista.ca.us
Web Site: www.moonlightstage.com
Management:
Artistic Director: Kathy Brombacher
Managing Director: Daniel Kays
Technical Director: Justin Hall
Marketing Director: Jennifer Burgstaler
Ticket Supervisor: Terry Breen
Rental Coordinator: Alex Scollon
Founded: 1976
Paid Staff: 4
Paid Artists: 20
Seating Capacity: 899

5961
COLLEGE OF THE SISKIYOUS THEATRE
800 College Avenue
Weed, CA 96094
Phone: 530-938-5366
Fax: 530-938-5227
Toll-free: 888-397-4339
Web Site: www.siskiyous.edu/theatre/
Management:
President: David Telhan
Head of Department: Anna Budd
Technical Director/Theater Manager: Keith Ronge
Costume Designer: Sharon Swingle

Mission: Facilities include the Kenneth W. Ford Theater with 584 permanent seats and the Studio Theater, a small black box studio theater that can accomodate up to 100 people.
Founded: 1969
Status: Non-Profit, Non-Professional
Paid Staff: 4

5962
MERTON WRAY THEATRE
Rio Hondo College
3600 Workman Mill Road
Whittier, CA 90601
Phone: 562-692-0921
Fax: 562-908-3446
e-mail: slohr@riohondo.edu
Web Site: www.riohondo.edu/facilities/rentals.htm
Management:
Facilities Services Director: Steven Lohr Ph.D
Facilities Services Asst. Director: Gus Gonzalez
Facilities Rentals/Scheduler: Eva Cabral
Transportation Coordinator: Liz Haney
Manager Mechanical Services: Stephen J Gabriel
Manager Grounds/Parking/Security: George Lopez
Status: Non-Profit, Non-Professional

5963
PICO RIVERA SPORTS ARENA
11003 Rooks Road
Whittier, CA 90605
Mailing Address: 11003 Rooks Road, Whittier, California 90605
Phone: 562-695-0509
Fax: 562-699-0005
Web Site: www.lasports.org/lafacilities/list.php?s=Arena
Management:
President/Manager: Ralph Hauser Jr
Assistant Manager/Director: Elaine Hauser
Marketing Director: Malu Elizondo
Concessions Manager: Anothony Hauser
Sound Engineer: Daniel Esparza
Opened: 1979
Status: For-Profit, Professional
Paid Staff: 4
Paid Artists: 1
Seating Capacity: 5,000

5964
ROBINSON THEATRE
Whittier College
Ruth B. Shannon Center
13406 Philadelphia
Whittier, CA 90608-0634
Phone: 562-907-4202
Fax: 562-698-4067
e-mail: lwagner@whittier.edu
Web Site: http://web.whittier.edu/academic/Theatre
Officers:
Dean: Susan D. Gotsch
Management:
Assistant Professor Theatre Arts: Jennifer Holmes
Associate Professor Theatre Arts: Brian Allan Reed
Mission: The Department of Theatre and Communication Arts offers a wide array of courses in the areas of performance, directing, theatre history and dramatic literature, and stage design and technology.
Specialized Field: Theatre
Type of Stage: Proscenium
Seating Capacity: 400

5965
STUDIO THEATRE
Whittier College
Ruth B. Shannon Center
13406 Philadelphia
Whittier, CA 90608-0634
Phone: 562-907-4202
Fax: 562-698-4067
e-mail: lwagner@whittier.edu
Web Site: http://web.whittier.edu/academic/Theatre
Officers:
Dean: Susan D. Gotsch
Management:
Assistant Professor Theatre Arts: Jennifer Holmes
Associate Professor Theatre Arts: Brian Allan Reed
Mission: The Department of Theatre and Communication Arts offers a wide array of courses in the areas of performance, directing, theatre history and dramatic literature, and stage design and technology.
Specialized Field: Theatre
Type of Stage: Black Box
Seating Capacity: 100

5966
WOODLAND OPERA HOUSE
340 2nd Street
PO Box 1425
Woodland, CA 95776
Phone: 530-666-9617
Fax: 530-666-4783
e-mail: operahouse@afes.com
Web Site: www.wohtheatre.org/
Officers:
President: Chris Taloff
Vice President: Nancy Lohse
Secretary: Gus Bush
Treasurer: Becky Kleinhans
Management:
Executive Director: Jeff Kean
Education Director: Angela Shellhammer
Manager: Cathy Oliver
Costume Manager: Laurie Everly Klassen
Box Office Coordinator: Rosemary O'Brien
House Manager: Pam McCullaugh
Founded: 1885

5967
YREKA COMMUNITY THEATRE CENTER
810 North Oregon Street
Yreka, CA 96097
Phone: 916-842-2355
Fax: 916-842-4836
Web Site: www.yrekachamber.com/city.html
Management:
Community Theatre Center Manager: Jeff Shinn
Director City of Yreka: David Phillipe
Seating Capacity: 300

Colorado

5968
ARVADA CENTER FOR THE ARTS AND HUMANITIES
6901 Wadsworth Boulevard
Arvada, CO 80003
Phone: 720-898-7285
Fax: 720-898-7217
Web Site: www.arvadacenter.org
Management:
Executive Director: Deborah Eloerman

Artistic Director: Rod Lansderry
Performing Arts Director: Kathy Kuehn
Founded: 1976
Status: Non-Profit, Professional
Paid Staff: 30
Paid Artists: 50
Seating Capacity: 500

5969
BENEDICT MUSIC TENT AT ASPEN MUSIC SCHOOL

2 Music School Road
Aspen, CO 81611
Phone: 970-925-3254
Fax: 970-925-3802
Web Site: www.aspenmusicfestival.com
Management:
President/CEO: Alan Fletcher
Artistic Director: David Zinman
General Director: James N Berdahl
Director of Operations: Megan Manning
Director of Ticket Services: Karen Smart
Director of Finance/Administration: Jennifer Brown Elliot
Manager of Information Services: Fritz Grueter
Director of Development: Mimi Teschner
Communications/Corporate Support: Laura Smith
Founded: 1949
Status: Non-Profit, Professional
Paid Staff: 30
Seating Capacity: 2,050

5970
WHEELER OPERA HOUSE

320 E Hyman Avenue
Aspen, CO 81611
Phone: 970-920-5790
Fax: 970-920-5780
e-mail: grams@ci.aspen.co.us
Web Site: www.wheeleroperahouse.com
Management:
Executive Director: Gram Slaton
Operations Manager: Gail Mason
Founded: 1889
Specialized Field: Raoring Folk Valley
Status: Non-Profit, Professional
Paid Staff: 12
Performs At: Proc Theatre
Facility Category: Theatre
Type of Stage: Proscenium
Stage Dimensions: 28'x28'
Seating Capacity: 503
Year Built: 1889
Year Remodeled: 2006
Rental Contact: Operations Manager Gail Mason

5971
AURORA FOX ARTS CENTER

9900 East Colfax Avenue
PO Box 9
Aurora, CO 80010
Phone: 303-739-1970
Fax: 303-361-2909
e-mail: foxbox@auroragov.org
Web Site:
www.auroragov.org/AuroraGov/Departments/index.htm
Management:
Executive Director: Robert Salisbury
Producer: Charles Packard
Box Office/House Manager: Bobbie Rubin
Children's Theater Coordinator: Lisa Mumpton
Technical Director: Mike Haas

Mission: The Aurora Fox Arts Center, a historic landmark, is a 245-seat performing arts facility, with attached rehearsal and scenery shop facilities. A former movie theatre that was built in 1946, the Aurora Fox was completely renovated and reopened in March of 1985 and currently serves as the home for the Aurora Fox Theatre Company, and the Aurora Fox Children's Theatre Company.

5972
BICENTENNIAL ART CENTER

13655 East Alameda
Aurora, CO 80012
Mailing Address: Library and Cultural Services, 14949 E. Alameda Parkway - Au
Phone: 303-344-1776
Fax: 303-341-7985
e-mail: culturalservices@auroragov.org
Web Site:
www.auroragov.org/AuroraGov/Departments/in
Mission: The Bicentennial Art Center was originally a satellite building operated as part of the Lowery Air Force Base. Now this facility is a fully functioning pottery studio. The staff at Bicentennial not only coordinates pottery programs but also coordinate music and fine arts programs, held at City of Aurora libraries and recreation centers.

5973
BOULDER MUSEUM OF CONTEMPORARY ART GALLERIES AND THEATER

1750 13th Street
Boulder, CO 80302
Phone: 303-443-2122
Fax: 303-447-1633
e-mail: info@bmoca.org
Web Site: www.bmoca.org
Management:
Director of Operations: Travis Allison
Co-Exec. Director/Sr. Administrator: Penny Barnow
Co-Exec. Director/Sr. Curator: Joan Markowitz
Visitor Services Liaison: Laura Feuillebois
Publicity & Outreach Coordinator: Elizabeth Marglin
Associate Curator: Kirsten Gerdes
Finance/Membership Coordinator: Kent Nowlin
Director of the Collection: Keleigh Asbury
Performance Coordinator: Judson Webb
Mission: The Boulder Museum of Contemporary Art was originally called the Boulder Arts Center. It was founded in 1972 by a group of local artists as a venue to showcase and promote the visual arts in Boulder. The West Gallery has a capacity of 125; East Gallery capacity of 75; Union Works Gallery capacity of 50, and Theatre 13 has a seating capacity of 100.
Founded: 1972
Status: Non-Profit, Professional

5974
FOLSOM FIELD/COORS EVENTS CONFERENCE CENTER/STADIUM CLUB

University of Colorado, Boulder
Colorado & Folsom
Boulder, CO 80309
Phone: 303-492-5318
e-mail: Gail.Pederson@Colorado.edu
Web Site: www.CUBuffs.com
Management:
Scheduling: Karl Eggert
Office of Athletic Director: Gail Pederson

5975
MACKY AUDITORIUM CONCERT HALL

University of Colorado
UCB 285
Boulder, CO 80309-0285
Phone: 303-492-8423
Fax: 303-492-1651
Web Site: www.colorado.edu/macky
Management:
Director: Kristin Anderson
Assistant Director: Sara Krumwiede
Mission: Offers a broad range of performances including University ensembles of band, choir, and orchestra, the Artist Series, the Boulder Philharmonic, internationally known jazz, dance, classical, pop artists, and lectures.
Facility Category: Concert Hall
Type of Stage: Proscenium
Stage Dimensions: 37x28
Seating Capacity: 2,047
Year Built: 1914
Year Remodeled: 1986

5976
NAROPA UNIVERSITY PERFORMING ARTS CENTER

2130 Araphoe Avenue
Boulder, CO 80302
Phone: 303-444-0202
Fax: 303-444-0410
e-mail: infodesk@naropa.edu
Web Site: www.naropa.edu
Officers:
President: Thomas Coburn
Management:
Performing Arts Center Director: David Ortolano
PAC Production Manager: Donald Stikeleather
Founded: 1974
Status: Nonprofit, Professional
Performs At: Performing Arts Center

5977
BACKSTAGE THEATRE

The Breckenridge Theatre
121 South Ridge Street
Breckenridge, CO 80424
Mailing Address: PO Box 297
Phone: 970-453-0199
Fax: 970-453-4382
e-mail: info@backstagetheatre.org
Web Site: www.backstagetheatre.org
Officers:
President: Cindy Nelson
Vice President: Phil Kopp
Treasurer: Ann Gagen
Secretary: Patti Casey
Management:
Artistic Director: Christopher Willard
Business Manager: Jean Krak
Reservation Manager: Sandra Willis
Founded: 1974

5978
COORS EVENTS CONFERENCE CENTER

Regent Drive & 28th Street
Colorado, CO 80309
Phone: 303-492-5316
Fax: 303-492-4801
e-mail: steven.wells@colorado.edu
Web Site: www.totalboulder.com/resources/8.html
Management:
Director: Steve Wells
Asst Director Facilities Scheduling: Karl Eggert

Technical Coordinator: Brett McQueen
Mission: The facility features 37,000 square feet of meeting space.

5979
ARNOLD HALL THEATER UNITED STATES AIR FORCE

2302 Cadet Drive
Colorado Springs, CO 80840
Mailing Address: 2302 Cadet Drive, United States Air Force Academy, CO 80840
Phone: 719-472-4497
Fax: 719-472-4597
Web Site:
www.usafa.af.mil/10abw/10msg/svk/cadets/concerts.cfm?catname=10abw
Management:
   Director of Staff: Colonel Douglas Kreulen
   Director of Communications: Johnny Whitaker
Specialized Field: Theater, concerts
Seating Capacity: 3,000

5980
COLORADO SPRINGS CITY AUDITORIUM

221 East Kiowa Street
Colorado Springs, CO 80903
Phone: 719-385-5969
Fax: 719-385-6584
e-mail: jcarricato@springsgov.com
Web Site: www.springsgov.com/Page.asp?NavID=5569
Management:
   Manager: Bob Lillie
Founded: 1923
Paid Staff: 4
Volunteer Staff: 6
Annual Attendance: 125,000
Type of Stage: Raised Stage
Seating Capacity: 2,500

5981
COLORADO SPRINGS FINE ARTS CENTER SAGAJI THEATRE

30 West Dale Street
Colorado Springs, CO 80903
Phone: 719-634-5581
Fax: 719-634-0570
e-mail: info@csfineartscenter.org
Web Site: www.csfineartscenter.org
Management:
   President: Michael De Marsche Ph.D
   Chief Operations Officer: Ken Weiland
   Artistic Director Performing Arts: Alan Osburn
   Technical Director: Chris Sheley
   Theatre Administrator: Nathan Willers
   Facilities Director: Charlie Hagen
   Grant Manager: Laura Hines
   Marketing Director: Pam Gentile
Founded: 1936
Status: Non-Profit, Professional
Paid Staff: 65
Seating Capacity: 400

5982
PIKES PEAK CENTER EL POMAR GREAT HALL

190 South Cascade Avenue
Colorado Springs, CO 80903
Phone: 719-477-2100
Fax: 719-477-2199
e-mail: anyquist@worldarena.com
Web Site: www.pikespeakcenter.org
Management:
   General Manager: Dorothea Lischick
   Assistant General Manager: Tuesda Heslop
   Director Sales/Marketing/Promotions: Andrea Nyquist
   Group Sales Manager: Kimberly Barberi
Mission: The El Pomar Great Hall is the main auditorium of the Pikes Peak Center. Continental seating on all three levels will accommodate 2,000 patrons for performances. Annual performances at the Center cover the entire entertainment spectrum: symphony, opera, musical theatre, drama, rock, country, variety, and ballet.
Utilizes: Theatre Companies
Founded: 1982
Status: Non-Profit, Non-Professional
Paid Staff: 10
Annual Attendance: 200,000
Facility Category: Theat7e
Type of Stage: Proscenium
Seating Capacity: 2,000
Year Built: 1982
Cost: 13.2 Million
Rental Contact: Booking Manager Cindy Ballard

5983
SKY SOX STADIUM

4385 Tutt Boulevard
Colorado Springs, CO 80922
Phone: 719-597-1449
Fax: 719-597-2491
e-mail: info@skysox.com
Web Site: www.skysox.com
Officers:
   EVP: Rai Henniger
Management:
   Stadium Operations Director: Kevin Bannan
Founded: 1988
Status: For-Profit, Professional
Paid Staff: 14
Annual Attendance: 265,000
Facility Category: Baseball Stadium
Seating Capacity: 8,500
Year Remodeled: 2005
Cost: $7 million

5984
CREEDE REPERTORY THEATRE

124 North Main Street
PO Box 269
Creede, CO 81130
Phone: 719-658-2540
Fax: 719-658-2343
Toll-free: 866-658-2540
Web Site: www.creederep.com
Officers:
   President: Robert W Slater
   Vice President: Arvin VanRy
   VP/Secretary: Charlene Ameel
   VP/Treasurer: Tom Brummett
   VP/Community Relations: Stan Letz
   VP/Development: Phil Lack
Management:
   Executive/Artistic Director: Maurice LaMee
   Managing Director: Tristan Wilson
   Development Director: Lynna Jackson
   Education Director: Cody Cosmic
Founded: 1966
Type of Stage: Black Box; Proscenium
Seating Capacity: 313

5985
CRESTED BUTTE MOUNTAIN THEATRE

403 2nd Street
PO Box 611
Crested Butte, CO 81224
Phone: 970-349-0366
e-mail: mttheatre@crestedbutte.net
Web Site: www.cbmountaintheatre.org
Management:
   Managing Director: Elizabeth Bond
Mission: To entertain, educate and enrich the Crested Butte community and greater Gunnison Valley providing a well-balanced theatrical season of high quality every year.
Utilizes: Choreographers; Collaborating Artists; Collaborations; Community Members; Community Talent; Dancers; Designers; Five Seasonal Concerts; Grant Writers; Guest Designers; Guest Musical Directors; Guest Speakers; Guest Teachers; Guild Activities; Instructors; Local Artists; Local Artists & Directors; Local Talent; Lyricists; Multimedia; Music; Performance Artists; Playwrights; Resident Professionals; Scenic Designers; Sign Language Translators; Singers; Students; Student Interns; Visual Designers; Volunteer Artists
Founded: 1972
Specialized Field: Community Theatre
Status: Non-Profit
Paid Staff: 1
Budget: $100,000
Income Sources: Ticket Sales; Grants; Donations; Member/Friends
Affiliations: AACT; SWCCT; RMTA
Annual Attendance: 4,000
Facility Category: Modified Black Box
Stage Dimensions: 22' x 12'
Seating Capacity: 100
Year Built: 1883
Year Remodeled: 2008

5986
BUTTE OPERA HOUSE

139 East Bennett Avenue
Cripple Creek, CO 80813
Mailing Address: PO Box 743
Phone: 719-689-6402
Fax: 719-689-1008
e-mail: bjmac@peakinet.net
Web Site: www.butteoperahouse.com/
Management:
   Board Member: Judith McPherosn
   Board Member: Brandi Larsen
   Board Member: Michelle Fouts
   Board Member: Rick Wood
   Board Member: Bob Jeffries
   Board Member: Butch Ward
Seating Capacity: 174

5987
AUGUSTANA ARTS CENTER

5000 E Alameda Avenue
Denver, CO 80246
Phone: 303-388-4678
Fax: 303-388-1338
Web Site: www.augustanaarts.org
Officers:
   President: Cindy Linden Martin
   VP: Margaret Aarestad
   Treasurer: Donald Fink
   Secretary: Joel Haas
   Executive Director: Donald Tallman
   Artistic Director: Michael Shasberger
   Education Director: Alfred Born
Mission: To enhance the cultural life of the Denver Community: by supporting the efforts of local performing artists; by presenting performers of international renown; and performing arts outreach and educational programming.

Utilizes: Actors; Collaborating Artists; Collaborations; Fine Artists; Grant Writers; Guest Accompanists; Guest Composers; Guest Designers; Guest Lecturers; Guest Musical Directors; Guest Musicians; High School Drama; Local Artists; Multimedia; Music; Organization Contracts; Poets; Sign Language Translators; Singers; Soloists
Founded: 1997
Specialized Field: Series & Festivals; Music Instrumental; Vocal; Opera
Status: Non-Profit, Professional
Paid Staff: 6
Paid Artists: 6
Budget: $250,000
Income Sources: Ticket Sales; Grants; Donations
Performs At: Primary - Church
Annual Attendance: 8,000
Seating Capacity: 700

5988
BOETTCHER CONCERT HALL
Denver Center for the Performing Arts
1101 13th St
Denver, CO 80204
Phone: 303-893-4000
Fax: 303-640-2397
Toll-free: 800-641-1222
e-mail: dwitherspoon@dcpa.org
Web Site: www.artcomplex.com
Officers:
Chairman: Donald R. Seawell
President: Randy Weeks
Director Events/Facilities: Susan Hennessy
Management:
Artistic Director: Kent Thompson
Mission: Dedicated to excellence in the arts, The Denver Center for the Performing Arts (DCPA) is a showcase for live theatre, a nurturing ground for new plays, a preferred stop on the Broadway touring circuit, an award-winning multi-media production facility, a national training school for actors, and the site of a voice clinic and research facility.
Founded: 1972
Specialized Field: Theatre
Status: Not-For-Profit
Facility Category: Concert Hall
Type of Stage: 360-Degree-Surround
Orchestra Pit: y
Seating Capacity: 2,700
Year Built: 1978
Rental Contact: Susan Hennessy

5989
COORS FIELD
2001 Blake Street
Denver, CO 80205
Phone: 800-388-ROCK
Fax: 303-312-2116
e-mail: tickets@rockies.mlb.com
Web Site: www.colorado.rockies.mlb.com
Officers:
Chairman & Chief Executive Officer: Charles K Monfort
Vice Chairman: Richard L Monfort
President: Keli S McGregor
EVP/General Manager: Daniel J O'Dowd
SVP/Business Operations: Gregory D Feasel
SVP/Chief Financial Officer: Harold R Roth
VP/Communications/Public Relations: Jay Alves
Management:
Director Stadium Operations: Paul Egins
Director Administration/Development: Dave Moore
Director Senior Scouting: Bill Schmidt

Information Systems Director: Bill Stephani
Promotions/Broadcasting Sr Director: Alan Bossart
Operations/Service Senior Director: Kevin G Fenton
Facilities Director: Scott Amerman
Founded: 1960
Annual Attendance: 7,701,861
Seating Capacity: 50,445
Year Built: 1995

5990
DENVER BOTANIC GARDENS AMPHITHEATRE
1005 York Street
Denver, CO 80206
Mailing Address: Denver Botanic Gardens, 909 York Street, Denver, Colorado 80
Phone: 720-865-3500
Fax: 720-865-3725
e-mail: pr@botanicgardens.org
Web Site: www.botanicgardens.org
Management:
Interim CEO: Linda Greene
Facility Rentals: Daphne Webb
Marketing/Public Relatons: Rhetta Shead
Mission: Denver Botanic Gardens offers a broad range of programs for all ages. Choose from hands-on workshops, certificate courses, public lectures, professional development seminars or learning for personal enrichment
Founded: 1951
Seating Capacity: 2,200

5991
DENVER BRASS
2253 Downing Street
Denver, CO 80205
Phone: 303-832-4676
Fax: 303-829-4676
e-mail: info@denverbrass.org
Web Site: www.denverbrass.org
Management:
Executive Directory: Kathleen Aylsworth Brantigan
Founded: 1908
Affiliations: Colorado Ballet, Colorado Symphony, Center Attractions
Annual Attendance: 1,500,000
Seating Capacity: 2,100
Year Built: 1908
Rental Contact: Bobbi McFarland

5992
DENVER BRONCOS STADIUM: INVESCO FIELD AT MILE HIGH
1701 Bryant Street
Denver, CO 80204
Mailing Address: Denver Broncos Marketing Department, INVESCO Field at Mile H
Phone: 720-258-3333
Fax: 720-258-3335
Web Site: www.denverbroncos.com/
Officers:
Chairman: Pat Bowlen
Management:
EVP/Business Operations: Joe Ellis
General Manager: Ted Sundquist
VP Stadium Operations: Mac Freeman
VP Public Relations: Jim Saccomano
VP Marketing: Greg Carney
VP Finance: Jim Barlow
VP Community Development: Cindy Galloway Kellogg

VP Operations: Chip Conway
VP Information Technology: Rick Schoenhals
Founded: 1999
Status: Non-Profit, Non-Professional
Paid Staff: 1
Seating Capacity: 76,125

5993
DENVER CENTER FOR THE PERFORMING ARTS
1101 13th Street
Denver, CO 80204-2104
Phone: 303-893-4000
e-mail: denvercenter@dcpa.org
Web Site: www.denvercenter.org
Officers:
Chairman/CEO: Daniel L. Ritchie
President: Randy Weeks
Executive Vice President: Dorothy Denny
Chief Financial Officer: Vicky Miles
Management:
Artistic Director: Kent Thompson
Founded: 1972
Status: Nonprofit; Professional
Seating Capacity: 1,577

5994
DENVER VICTORIAN PLAYHOUSE
4201 Hooker Street
Denver, CO 80211
Phone: 303-433-4343
e-mail: tawx@msn.com
Web Site: www.denvervic.com/about.htm
Management:
Owner/Producer: Wade P Wood
Office Manager: Terry Ann Watts
Mission: Presenting a season of plays with five productions, including a variety of comedy and drama.
Utilizes: Guest Companies
Founded: 1911
Specialized Field: Community; Theatrical Group
Status: Semi-Professional; Nonprofit; Commercial
Paid Staff: 30
Season: Year Round
Seating Capacity: 73
Organization Type: Performing; Sponsoring

5995
EL CENTRO SU TEATRO
4725 High Street
Denver, CO 80216
Phone: 303-296-0219
Fax: 303-296-4614
e-mail: elcentro@suteatro.org
Web Site: www.suteatro.org
Management:
Executive Artistic Director: Anthony Garcia
Development Director: Tanya Marina Mote
Technical Director: Rafael Martinez
Founded: 1971

5996
ELIZABETH ERIKSEN BYRON THEATRE
University of Denver
Robert And Judi Newman Center
2199 S. University Blvd
Denver, CO 80208
Mailing Address: Department of Theatre, 2199 S. University Blvd. Denver, CO 8
Phone: 303-871-2518
Fax: 303-871-2505
e-mail: thea01@denver.du.edu
Web Site: http://www.du.edu/thea/reedhall.htm
Officers:

Associate Professor/Chair: William Temple Davis
Mission: At the University of Denver, you will explore a broad spectrum of theatre crafts and theories within the context of a liberal arts education.
Specialized Field: Theatre
Type of Stage: Alley. Thrust
Seating Capacity: Bench/modular seating
Architect: Mark Rodgers

5997
ELLIE CAULKINS OPERA HOUSE

1245 Champa Street
First Floor
Denver, CO 80204
Phone: 720-865-4220
Fax: 720-865-4246
Toll-free: 800-641-1222
e-mail: jeannette.murrietta@ci.denver.co.us
Web Site: www.artscomplex.com
Management:
 Director Theatres/Arenas: Jack Finlaw
 Marketing Director: Erik Dyce
 Director Event Services: Tad Bowman
 Booking Manager: Jeannette Murrietta
Mission: Dedicated to excellence in the arts, The Denver Center for the Performing Arts (DCPA) is a showcase for live theatre, a nurturing ground for new plays, a preferred stop on the Broadway touring circuit, an award-winning multi-media production facility, a national training school for actors, and the site of a voice clinic and research facility.
Founded: 1972
Specialized Field: Opera
Status: Not-For-Profit
Facility Category: Opera House
Type of Stage: Proscenium
Stage Dimensions: 20' x 40'
Orchestra Pit: y
Seating Capacity: 2,245
Year Restored: 1979
Rental Contact: Susan Hennessy

5998
HISTORIC PARAMOUNT THEATRE

1631 Glenarm Place
Suite 200
Denver, CO 80202
Phone: 303-623-0106
Fax: 303-623-8062
Web Site: www.historicparamounttheatre.netfrims.com
Management:
 Executive Director: Jim Sprinkle
Founded: 1930
Seating Capacity: 2,000

5999
HOUSTON FINE ARTS CENTER

Lamont School of Music
7111 Montview Boulevard
Denver, CO 80220
Phone: 303-871-6404
Fax: 303-871-3118
e-mail: nryan@du.edu
Web Site: www.du.edu/maps/houston.html
Management:
 Marketing director: Natalie Kate Ryan
 Event & Community Outreach Mgr: Deirdre A. Lopez
 Executive Director: Stephen Seifert
Specialized Field: play, an opera or a musical
Rental Contact: Jennifer L. Olcott
Resident Groups: The Climb ((jazz), Davinici Quartet string ensemble)

6000
JONES THEATRE

Denver Center for the Performing Arts
Helen Bonfils Theatre Complex
1101 13th St
Denver, CO 80204
Phone: 303-572-4466
Fax: 303-640-2397
Toll-free: 800-641-1222
e-mail: dwitherspoon@dcpa.org
Web Site: www.artscomplex.com
Officers:
 Chairman: Donald R. Seawell
 President: Randy Weeks
 Director Events/Facilities: Susan Hennessy
Management:
 Artistic Director: Kent Thompson
Mission: Dedicated to excellence in the arts, The Denver Center for the Performing Arts (DCPA) is a showcase for live theatre, a nurturing ground for new plays, a preferred stop on the Broadway touring circuit, an award-winning multi-media production facility, a national training school for actors, and the site of a voice clinic and research facility.
Founded: 1972
Opened: 1979
Specialized Field: Theatre
Status: Not-For-Profit
Facility Category: Concert Hall
Type of Stage: Thrust
Seating Capacity: 200
Year Built: 1978
Rental Contact: Susan Hennessy

6001
MAY BONFILS STANTON CENTER FOR THE PERFORMING ARTS

3001 S Federal Boulevard
Denver, CO 80110
Phone: 303-935-9110

6002
MILE HIGH STADIUM

1701 Bryant Street Suite 100
Denver, CO 80204
Phone: 720-258-3333
Fax: 720-258-3335
e-mail: tickets@broncos.nfl.com
Web Site: www.denverbroncos.com
Management:
 President: Pat Bowlen
 Director Operations: Gary Jones
Founded: 1970
Seating Capacity: 76,098

6003
MIZEL CENTER FOR ARTS AND CULTURE

350 S Dahlia Street
Denver, CO 80246-8102
Phone: 303-316-6360
Fax: 303-320-0042
e-mail: info@jccdenver.org
Web Site: www.mizelarts.org
Management:
 Executive Director: Steve Wilson
 Technical Director: C J Hosier
 Education Director: Roberta Bloom
 Arts Center Director: Joanne Kauvar
Utilizes: Actors; Choreographers; Commissioned Composers; Curators; Designers; Educators; Fine Artists; Grant Writers; Guest Artists; Guest Companies; Guest Composers; Guest Conductors; Guest

Designers; Guest Directors; Guest Ensembles; Guest Instructors; Guest Lecturers; Guest Soloists; Guild Activities; High School Drama; Instructors; Local Artists; Multimedia; Original Music Scores; Resident Professionals; Selected Students; Sign Language Translators; Soloists; Student Interns; Touring Companies
Status: Non-Profit
Paid Staff: 6
Budget: $300,000
Income Sources: Ticket Sales; Grants; City; State
Annual Attendance: 20,000
Type of Stage: Proscenium; Thrust
Seating Capacity: 300; 95
Year Built: 1970
Year Remodeled: 1995

6004
NEWMAN CENTER FOR THE PERFORMING ARTS

University Of Denver
2344 East Iliff Avenue
Denver, CO 80208
Phone: 303-871-6200
Fax: 303-871-6507
e-mail: newman_center@du.edu
Web Site: www.du.edu/newmancenter
Management:
 Executive Director: Stephen W Seifert
 Operations Director: Tracy Wagner
Mission: To assist music and theater schools in performances; to rent theaters to community organizations; to select and present performing artists from around the world.
Founded: 2002
Specialized Field: Multi-Disciplinary
Paid Staff: 12
Volunteer Staff: 160
Budget: $1.4 Million
Performs At: Multi-Purpise; Multi-Venue Performing Arts Center
Facility Category: Theatre
Type of Stage: Proscenium
Stage Dimensions: 49'widex50'd; 90' to the grid
Seating Capacity: 977
Year Built: 2002
Cost: $65 Million
Rental Contact: Tracy Wagner

6005
PEPSI CENTER

1000 Chopper Place
Denver, CO 80204
Phone: 303-405-1111
Fax: 303-893-6685
e-mail: webmaster@pepsicenter.com
Web Site: www.pepsicenter.com
Officers:
 President: Don Elliman
Management:
 Owner: E Stanley Kroenke
 Executive VP: David Ehrlich
 Senior VP: Doug Ackerman
 VP Business Affairs: Mike Benson
Founded: 1999
Type of Stage: Concert Stage
Seating Capacity: 20,000

6006
RED ROCKS AMPHITHEATRE

1245 Champa Street
First Floor
Denver, CO 80204

Phone: 720-865-4220
Fax: 720-865-4246
e-mail: jeannette.murrietta@ci.denver.co.us
Web Site: www.redrocksonline.com
Management:
Director Theatres/Arenas: Jack Finlaw
Marketing Director: Erik Dyce
Director Event Services: Tad Bowman
Booking Manager: Jeannette Murrietta
Founded: 1941
Status: Non-Profit, Professional
Paid Staff: 26

6007
RICKETSON THEATRE
Denver Center for the Performing Arts
Helen Bonfils Theatre Complex
1101 13th St
Denver, CO 80204
Phone: 303-572-4466
Fax: 303-640-2397
Toll-free: 800-641-1222
e-mail: dwitherspoon@dcpa.org
Web Site: www.artscomplex.com
Officers:
Chairman: Donald R. Seawell
President: Randy Weeks
Director Events/Facilities: Susan Hennessy
Management:
Artistic Director: Kent Thompson
Mission: Dedicated to excellence in the arts, The Denver Center for the Performing Arts (DCPA) is a showcase for live theatre, a nurturing ground for new plays, a preferred stop on the Broadway touring circuit, an award-winning multi-media production facility, a national training school for actors, and the site of a voice clinic and research facility.
Founded: 1972
Opened: 1979
Specialized Field: Theatre
Status: Not-For-Profit
Facility Category: Concert Hall
Type of Stage: Proscenium
Seating Capacity: 250
Year Built: 1978
Rental Contact: Susan Hennessy

6008
SPACE THEATRE
Denver Center for the Performing Arts
Helen Bonfils Theatre Complex
1101 13th St
Denver, CO 80204
Phone: 303-572-4466
Fax: 303-640-2397
Toll-free: 800-641-1222
e-mail: dwitherspoon@dcpa.org
Web Site: www.artscomplex.com
Officers:
Chairman: Donald R. Seawell
President: Randy Weeks
Director Events/Facilities: Susan Hennessy
Management:
Artistic Director: Kent Thompson
Mission: Dedicated to excellence in the arts, The Denver Center for the Performing Arts (DCPA) is a showcase for live theatre, a nurturing ground for new plays, a preferred stop on the Broadway touring circuit, an award-winning multi-media production facility, a national training school for actors, and the site of a voice clinic and research facility.
Founded: 1972
Opened: 1979
Specialized Field: Theatre

Status: Not-For-Profit
Facility Category: Concert Hall
Seating Capacity: 450
Year Built: 1978
Rental Contact: Susan Hennessy

6009
STAGE THEATRE
Denver Center for the Performing Arts
Helen Bonfils Theatre Complex
1101 13th St
Denver, CO 80204
Phone: 303-572-4466
Fax: 303-640-2397
Toll-free: 800-641-1222
e-mail: dwitherspoon@dcpa.org
Web Site: www.artscomplex.com
Officers:
Chairman: Donald R. Seawell
President: Randy Weeks
Director Events/Facilities: Susan Hennessy
Management:
Artistic Director: Kent Thompson
Mission: Dedicated to excellence in the arts, The Denver Center for the Performing Arts (DCPA) is a showcase for live theatre, a nurturing ground for new plays, a preferred stop on the Broadway touring circuit, an award-winning multi-media production facility, a national training school for actors, and the site of a voice clinic and research facility.
Founded: 1972
Opened: 1979
Specialized Field: Theatre
Status: Not-For-Profit
Facility Category: Concert Hall
Type of Stage: Thrust
Seating Capacity: 778
Year Built: 1978
Rental Contact: Susan Hennessy

6010
TEMPLE HOYNE BUELL THEATRE
Denver Center for the Performing Arts
Quigg Newton Denver Municipal Auditorium
1101 13th St
Denver, CO 80204
Phone: 720-865-4220
Fax: 303-640-2397
Toll-free: 800-641-1222
e-mail: dwitherspoon@dcpa.org
Web Site: www.artscomplex.com
Officers:
Chairman: Donald R. Seawell
President: Randy Weeks
Director Events/Facilities: Susan Hennessy
Management:
Artistic Director: Kent Thompson
Mission: Dedicated to excellence in the arts, The Denver Center for the Performing Arts (DCPA) is a showcase for live theatre, a nurturing ground for new plays, a preferred stop on the Broadway touring circuit, an award-winning multi-media production facility, a national training school for actors, and the site of a voice clinic and research facility.
Founded: 1972
Specialized Field: Theatre
Status: Not-For-Profit
Facility Category: Theatre
Type of Stage: Proscenium
Stage Dimensions: 20' x 67'
Orchestra Pit: y
Seating Capacity: 2,884
Year Built: 1978
Rental Contact: Susan Hennessy

6011
FORT LEWIS COLLEGE COMMUNITY CONCERT HALL
1000 Rim Drive
College Heights
Durango, CO 81301
Phone: 970-247-7162
Fax: 970-247-7058
e-mail: leslie_c@fortlewis.edu
Web Site: www.durangoconcerts.com
Management:
Director: Charles Leslie
Mission: To provide Durango, CO and the Four Corners with an eclectic presenting program and to provide a high-quality, low-cost production venue for our community
Founded: 1997
Specialized Field: Southwest Colorado; Four Corners
Status: Non-Profit, Professional
Paid Staff: 3
Volunteer Staff: 200
Annual Attendance: 35,000-40,000
Facility Category: Presenting & Rental
Type of Stage: Proscenium
Stage Dimensions: 46W x 28D
Seating Capacity: 560
Year Built: 1997

6012
COORS AMPHITHEATRE COMFORT DENTAL AMPHITHEATRE
6350 Greenwood Plaza Blvd
Englewood, CO 80111
Mailing Address: 6350 Greenwood Plaza Blvd, Englewood, CO 80111
Phone: (30-3) -220-
Fax: 303-220-7407
Web Site: www.hob.com
Management:
General Manager: Kyle Svanda
Operations Manager: Jack Ahrens
Assistant Operations Manager: Trevor Herasingh
Administration: Christian Lewis
Founded: 1988
Specialized Field: Concerts
Seating Capacity: 16,283

6013
COLORADO STATE UNIVERSITY THEATRE
Campus Delivery 1778
Fort Collins, CO 80523
Mailing Address: School of the Arts, University Center for the Arts, 1778 Cam
Phone: 970-491-5562
Fax: 970-493-4363
e-mail: jennifer.clary@colostate.edu
Web Site: www.colostate.edu, http://www.theatre.colos
Management:
President: Larry Penley
Director of marketing: Jennifer Clary
Production manager: Jimmie Robinson
Mission: The Theatre Program at Colorado State University offers a curriculum that allows students numerous opportunities to study, train, and explore theatre in all performance and design/technical fields
Specialized Field: Theater
Status: Non-Profit, Non-Professional
Paid Staff: 8
Type of Stage: Black Box

6014
HUGHES STADIUM
Colorado State University
McGraw Athetic Building
Fort Collins, CO 80523
Mailing Address: 1800 South Overland Trail, Fort Collins, CO 80526
Phone: 970-491-6211
Fax: 970-491-1348
e-mail: ben.chulick@colostate.edu
Web Site: www.csurams.com
Management:
    Assistant Athletic: Doug Max
    Director of marketing and sales: Ben Chulick
    Assistant director of marketing and: Michelle Farger Clark
Founded: 1968
Specialized Field: Concerts

6015
LINCOLN CENTER
417 W Magnolia
Fort Collins, CO 80521
Mailing Address: Lincoln Center, 417 W. Magnolia, Fort Collins, CO 80521
Phone: 970-221-6735
Fax: 970-484-0424
Web Site: www.lctix.com
Management:
    Director: Gill Stilwell
Mission: The mission of the Lincoln Center is to be a leader in cultural experience and make it an essential value to the community
Founded: 1979
Specialized Field: professional theatre, dance, music, visual arts and children's programs
Status: Non-Profit, Professional

6016
UNIVERSITY CENTER FOR THE ARTS
Colorado State University
1400 Remington Street
Fort Collins, CO 80524
Phone: 970-491-5529
Fax: 970-491-7541
e-mail: mtdinfo@colostate.edu
Web Site: www.csuSchooloftheArts.com
Management:
    Chair, Music, Theatre And Dance: Todd Queen
    Marketing Director: Jennifer Clary
    Event Director: Eileen Kirby
Utilizes: Actors; Artists-in-Residence; Choreographers; Collaborating Artists; Commissioned Composers; Commissioned Music; Composers; Composers-in-Residence; Curators; Dance Companies; Dancers; Designers; Educators; Fine Artists; Grant Writers; Guest Accompanists; Guest Artists; Guest Companies; Guest Composers; Guest Designers; Guest Directors; Guest Ensembles; Guest Instructors; Guest Lecturers; Guest Musical Directors; Guest Musicians; Guest Soloists; High School Drama; Local Unknown Artists; Lyricists; Multimedia; Original Music Scores; Performance Artists; Poets; Resident Professionals; Scenic Designers; Sign Language Translators; Singers; Soloists; Students; Student Interns; Theatre Companies; Touring Companies; Visual Arts; Volunteer Directors & Actors; Writers
Founded: 1870
Opened: 2008
Specialized Field: University Center for the Arts
Performs At: Concert Hall, Theatre,Dance Theatre, Museums
Annual Attendance: 35,000

Type of Stage: 5 Performance Spaces
Year Remodeled: 2008
Cost: $45,000,000

6017
LINCOLN PARK STOCKER STADIUM
250 N 5th Street
Grand Junction, CO 81501
Phone: 970-244-1542
Fax: 970-242-1637
e-mail: cross@mesastate.edu
Web Site: www.mesastate.edu
Management:
    Director: Erik Joe Stevens
Seating Capacity: 6,600

6018
MESA EXPERIMENTAL THEATRE
Mesa State College
Moss Performing Arts Center
1100 North Avenue
Grand Junction, CO 81501
Phone: 970-248-1604
Toll-free: 800-982-6372
Web Site: http://www.mesastate.edu/index.htm
Officers:
    President: Tim Foster
Management:
    Associate Professor Theatre Arts: Richard R. Cowden
    Professor Theatre Arts: David M. Cox
Mission: Our mission is to prepare students for careers in theatre and from your first day on campus there are abundant opportunities for you to gain the experience you need to take your place in the American Theatre scene.
Specialized Field: Drama
Type of Stage: Black Box

6019
MESA RECITAL HALL
Mesa State College
Moss Performing Arts Center
1100 North Avenue
Grand Junction, CO 81501
Phone: 970-248-1604
Toll-free: 800-982-6372
Web Site: http://www.mesastate.edu/index.htm
Officers:
    President: Tim Foster
Management:
    Associate Professor Theatre Arts: Richard R. Cowden
    Professor Theatre Arts: David M. Cox
Mission: Our mission is to prepare students for careers in theatre and from your first day on campus there are abundant opportunities for you to gain the experience you need to take your place in the American Theatre scene.
Specialized Field: Chamber Music, Piano, Vocalists
Seating Capacity: 300

6020
WALTER WALKER AUDITORIUM
Mesa College
1100 N Avenue
Grand Junction, CO 81501
Phone: 970-248-1233
Fax: 970-248-1159
e-mail: chofer@mesastate.edu
Web Site: www.mesastate.edu
Management:
    Head of Department: Calvin Hofer
Founded: 1974

Status: For-Profit, Professional
Paid Staff: 36
Paid Artists: 36

6021
WILLIAM S. ROBINSON THEATRE
Mesa State College
Moss Performing Arts Center
1100 North Avenue
Grand Junction, CO 81501
Phone: 970-248-1604
Toll-free: 800-982-6372
Web Site: http://www.mesastate.edu/index.htm
Officers:
    President: Tim Foster
Management:
    Associate Professor Theatre Arts: Richard R. Cowden
    Professor Theatre Arts: David M. Cox
Mission: Our mission is to prepare students for careers in theatre and from your first day on campus there are abundant opportunities for you to gain the experience you need to take your place in the American Theatre scene.
Specialized Field: Dance, Music, Theatre
Seating Capacity: 600
Cost: $5.1 Million

6022
FRAZIER HALL
University of Northern Colorado
501 20th Street
Greeley, CO 80639
Phone: 970-351-1890
Fax: 303-351-1923
Web Site: www.unco.edu
Founded: 1954

6023
UNION COLONY CIVIC CENTER
701 10th Avenue
Greeley, CO 80631
Phone: 970-350-9454
Fax: 970-350-9475
Toll-free: 800-315-2787
Web Site: www.ucstars.com
Management:
    Cultural Affairs Director: Jill Rosentrater
    Cultural Affairs Director: Lonnie EJ Cooper
    Event Coordinator: Jill Droetemueller
    Event Coordinator: Julianne Givan
Utilizes: Actors; Artists-in-Residence; Collaborations; Fine Artists; Grant Writers; Guest Soloists; Guest Writers; Guild Activities; Local Artists; Lyricists; Multimedia; Organization Contracts; Original Music Scores; Sign Language Translators; Soloists; Student Interns; Special Technical Talent; Theatre Companies; Touring Companies
Founded: 1988
Status: Non-Profit, Non-Professional
Paid Staff: 14
Volunteer Staff: 250
Budget: $1.5 Million
Income Sources: Ticket Sales; Rentals; Sponsorships; City Subsidy
Annual Attendance: 110,000
Facility Category: Concert Hall; Auditorium; Performance
Stage Dimensions: 50 x 60
Seating Capacity: 1660
Year Built: 1988
Cost: $9.2 Million
Rental Contact: Julie Givan

6024
UNIVERSITY OF NORTHERN COLORADO
College of Performing and Visual ARTS
501 20th Street, Campus Box 30
Greeley, CO 80639
Phone: 970-351-2515
Fax: 970-351-1923
e-mail: susan.nelson@unco.edu
Web Site: www.arts.unco.edu
Management:
Community Arts Director: Susan Nelson
Founded: 1954

6025
OTERO JUNIOR COLLEGE HUMANITIES CENTER THEATRE
1802 Colorado
La Junta, CO 81050
Phone: 719-384-6831
Fax: 719-384-6933
e-mail: tim.walsh@ojc.edu
Web Site: www.ojc.edu
Management:
President: Jim Rizzugo
VP: Brad Franz
Theatre Arts Director: Ben Sisler
Managing Director: Tom Armstrong
Founded: 1941
Status: Non-Profit, Professional
Paid Staff: 100
Paid Artists: 5

6026
PICKETWIRE PLAYERS COMMUNITY THEATRE
802 San Juan Avenue
La Junta, CO 81050
Mailing Address: Picketwire Players, 802 San Juan/
P.O. Box 912, La Junta, CO
Phone: 719-384-8320
Web Site: http://picketwireplayers.org/default.aspx
Mission: ""WHEREAS, there being a group of individuals desiring to produce, direct, act and otherwise participate in a theater group, we do hereby organize and establish ourselves as the Picketwire Players.""
Founded: 1968
Status: Non- profit
Seating Capacity: 350-394

6027
TOWN HALL ARTS CENTER
2450 W Main Street
Littleton, CO 80120
Phone: 303-794-2787
Fax: 303-794-6580
e-mail: bilroded@aol.com
Web Site: www.townhallartscenter.com
Management:
Executive Director: Bill Rodgers
Mission: Offering live broadway musicals in an intimate setting for families.
Specialized Field: Live Theater; Art Gallery

6028
DICKENS OPERA HOUSE
302 Main Street
Longmont, CO 80501
Mailing Address: 300 Main St. Longmont, CO 80501
Phone: 303-651-7773
Fax: 303-651-7774

e-mail: charlie.operahouse@gmail.com
Web Site:
http://www.myspace.com/dickensoperahouseco
Founded: 1879
Specialized Field: live music

6029
BUDWEISER EVENTS CENTER
5290 Arena Circle
Loveland, CO 80538
Phone: 970-619-4100
Fax: 970-619-4123
e-mail: scadwell@budweisereventscenter.com
Web Site: www.budweisereventscenter.com
Management:
General Manager: Rick Hontz
Assistant General Manager: Shane Cadwell
Director of Marketing: Ryan Young
Director of Operations: Thom Jones
Founded: 2003
Paid Staff: 20
Facility Category: Multi-Purpose
Type of Stage: Stage Right Rolling Stage
Seating Capacity: 6,500
Year Built: 2003
Rental Contact: Shane Cadwell

6030
SANGRE DE CRISTO ARTS AND CONFERENCE CENTER
210 N Santa Fe Avenue
Pueblo, CO 81003
Phone: 719-295-7200
Fax: 719-543-0134
e-mail: mail@sdc-arts.org
Web Site: www.sdc-arts.org
Management:
Executive Director: Maggie Divelbiss
Associate Director: Desi Vial
Founded: 1972

6031
NORTHEASTERN JUNIOR COLLEGE THEATRE
Northeastern Junior College
100 College Avenue
Sterling, CO 80751
Phone: 970-521-6600
Fax: 970-521-6703
e-mail: melissa.bornhoft@njc.edu
Web Site: www.njc.edu
Type of Stage: Proscenium
Seating Capacity: 566

Connecticut

6032
ARENA AT HARBOR YARD
600 Main Street
Bridgeport, CT 06604
Phone: 203-345-2300
Fax: 203-333-8811
e-mail: booking@arenaatharboryard.com
Web Site: www.arenaatharboryard.com
Management:
General Manager: Lynn Carlotto
Booking Manager: Stephanie Panico
Director Of Operations: Tom Saunders
Founded: 2001
Facility Category: Arena
Seating Capacity: 10,000
Rental Contact: Booking Manager Stephanie Panico

6033
BERNHARD CENTER
University of Bridgeport
84 Iranistan Avenue
Bridgeport, CT 06601
Phone: 203-576-4000
Fax: 203-576-4051
e-mail: nas@bridgeport.edu
Web Site: www.bridgeport.edu
Founded: 1971

6034
DOWNTOWN CABARET THEATRE
263 Golden Hill Street
Bridgeport, CT 06604
Phone: 203-576-1636
Fax: 203-576-1444
e-mail: mail@dtcab.com
Web Site: www.DowntownCabaret.org
Management:
Executive Producer: Hugh Hallinan
Utilizes: Actors; AEA Actors; Choreographers; Dancers; Designers; Guest Artists; Guest Lecturers; Guild Activities; Local Artists; Music; Original Music Scores; Resident Professionals; Student Interns
Founded: 1975
Status: Non-Profit, Professional
Paid Staff: 12
Season: Year Round
Annual Attendance: 80,000
Type of Stage: Proscenium
Seating Capacity: 276
Year Remodeled: 1995

6035
KLEIN MEMORIAL AUDITORIUM
910 Fairfield Avenue
Bridgeport, CT 6605
Mailing Address: The Klein Memorial Auditorium, c/o The Fairfield Theatre Com
Phone: 203-576-8115
Fax: (20-3) -259-
e-mail: kleinmemorial@fairfieldtheatre.org
Web Site: http://www.theklein.org
Founded: 1940
Specialized Field: symphonies, operas, and theatre, to local dance recitals, graduations, and union meetings

6036
CHARLES IVES CENTER PAVILION
PO Box 2957
Danbury, CT 06813
Phone: 203-837-9226
Fax: 203-837-9230
e-mail: ivescenter@aol.com
Web Site: www.ivesconcertpark.com
Management:
Board of Director: Robert Parker
Executive Director: Liz Durkinsalvador
Founded: 1974
Status: Non-Profit, Professional
Paid Staff: 2
Type of Stage: Concert Stage
Seating Capacity: 5,500

6037
O'NEILL CENTER
Western Connecticut State University
Lake Avenue & University Boulevard
Danbury, CT 06811

Phone: 203-837-8343
Fax: 203-837-8345
e-mail: murphyj@wcsu.edu
Web Site: www.wcsu.edu
Management:
President: James Schmotter
Managing Director: Jan Murphy
Founded: 1995
Status: Non-Profit, Professional
Paid Staff: 5
Seating Capacity: 3,500

6038
GOODSPEED OPERA HOUSE

Route 82
PO Box A
East Haddam, CT 06423
Phone: 860-873-8664
Fax: 860-873-2329
e-mail: info@goodspeed.org
Web Site: www.goodspeed.org
Management:
President: Michael P Price
General Manager: Hattie Unguin-Kittner
Associate Producer: Sue Frost
Founded: 1963
Specialized Field: Opera House
Status: Non-Profit, Professional
Performs At: Goodspeed Opera House,
Goodspeed-at-Chester
Type of Stage: Proscenium, Adaptable Proscenium
Seating Capacity: 400, 200

6039
EDGERTON CENTER FOR THE PERFORMING ARTS

Sacred Heart University
5151 Park Avenue
Fairfield, CT 06825-1000
Mailing Address: 5151 Park Avenue I Fairfield,
Connecticut 06825-1000
Phone: 203-371-7908
Fax: 203-.36-5.48
Web Site: www.sacredheart.edu
Officers:
Executive Director: Jerry Goehring
Director Marketing: Brendan Lynch
Mission: Dedicated to creating and presenting high
quality programming for families, students and the
community that will entertain, educate and challenge.
Opened: 1986
Specialized Field: Jazz, Musical, Theatre
Status: professional
Type of Stage: Proscenium
Seating Capacity: 776

6040
KELLEY THEATRE

Fairfield University
Regina A Quick Center for the Arts
1073 N Benson Road
Fairfield, CT 06824
Phone: 203-254-4242
Fax: 203-254-4113
Toll-free: 877-278-1396
e-mail: info@quickcenter.com
Web Site: www.quickcenter.com
Officers:
President: Rev Jeffrey P von Arx SJ
Management:
Events Coordinator: Christian Kaplan,
rentals@quickcenter.com
VP Marketing/Communications: Rama Sudhakar
Media Relations Director: Mark Gregorio

Mission: Department of Visual and Performing Arts,
theatre program classes examine the history, theory,
and literature of theatre while considering artistic
methods and techniques. We put that knowledge to
work in our theatre laboratory, Theatre Fairfield.
Specialized Field: Dance; Music; Theatre
Seating Capacity: 741
Year Built: 1990
Rental Contact: Events Manager Christian Kaplan

6041
PEPSICO THEATRE

Fairfield University
1073 N Benson Road
Fairfield, CT 06824
Phone: 203-254-4000
Fax: 205-254-4167
Web Site: www.fairfield.edu
Officers:
President: Rev Jeffrey P von Arx SJ
Management:
Professor Theatre: Lynne Porter
Department Coordinator: Caitlin Doyle
Media Relations Director: Mark Gregorio
Mission: Department of Visual and Performing Arts,
theatre program classes examine the history, theory,
and literature of theatre while considering artistic
methods and techniques. We put that knowledge to
work in our theatre laboratory, Theatre Fairfield.
Specialized Field: Theatre
Seating Capacity: 70

6042
QUICK CENTER FOR THE ARTS

Fairfield University
1073 N Benson Road
Fairfield, CT 06824-6195
Phone: 203-254-4242
Fax: 203-254-4113
Toll-free: 877-278-7396
e-mail: info@quickcenter.com
Web Site: www.quickcenter.com
Officers:
President: Rev Jeffrey P von Arx SJ
Management:
Events Manager: Christian Kaplan
VP Marketing/Communications: Rama Sudhakar
Media Relations Director: Mark Gregorio
Mission: A year round Regional Arts Center that
provides professional performances in all disciplines,
outreach and educational programs and a 6'exhibit
visual arts gallery.
Utilizes: AEA Actors; Artists-in-Residence;
Choreographers; Collaborating Artists; Collaborations;
Commissioned Composers; Commissioned Music;
Dance Companies; Dancers; Designers; Educators;
Fine Artists; Grant Writers; Guest Accompanists; Guest
Artists; Guest Companies; Guest Composers; Guest
Conductors; Guest Designers; Guest Directors; Guest
Ensembles; Guest Instructors; Guest Musical Directors;
Guest Musicians; Guest Soloists; Guest Teachers; High
School Drama; Instructors; Local Artists; Lyricists; Multi
Collaborations; Multimedia; New Productions; Original
Music Scores; Performance Artists; Playwrights; Poets;
Resident Professionals; Selected Students; Sign
Language Translators; Singers; Soloists; Student
Interns; Special Technical Talent; Theatre Companies;
Visual Arts
Founded: 1990
Specialized Field: University Owned; Performing; and
Visual Educational
Status: Non-Profit, Professional
Paid Staff: 10
Volunteer Staff: 100

Budget: $2 Million
Income Sources: Ticket Revenue; Rentals;
Sponsorships; Donations; Grants
Performs At: Kelley Theatre, Wien Experimental
Theatre, Walsh Art Gallery
Affiliations: New England Presenters, National
Association of Gallerys, Museums, Connecticut Dance
Alliance, Association of Preforming Arts Presenters
Annual Attendance: 90,000
Facility Category: Two theatres
Type of Stage: Proscenium & Black Box
Seating Capacity: 741
Year Built: 1990
Rental Contact: Events Manager Christian Kaplan

6043
WIEN EXPERIMENTAL THEATRE

Fairfield University
Regina A Quick Center for the Arts
1073 N Benson Road
Fairfield, CT 06824
Phone: 203-254-4242
Fax: 203-254-4113
Toll-free: 877-278-1396
e-mail: info@quickcenter.com
Web Site: www.quickcenter.com
Officers:
Chair: Jesus Escobar
President: Rev. Jeffrey P Von Arx, S.J.
Director Media Relations: Nancy Habetz
Management:
Events Manager: Christian Kaplan,
rentals@quickcenter.com
VP Marketing/Communications: Rama Sudhakar
Media Relations Director: Mark Gregorio
Mission: Department of Visual and Performing Arts,
theatre program classes examine the history, theory,
and literature of theatre while considering artistic
methods and techniques. We put that knowledge to
work in our theatre laboratory, Theatre Fairfield.
Founded: 1990
Specialized Field: Dance; Music; Theatre
Type of Stage: Black Box
Seating Capacity: 150
Year Built: 1990
Rental Contact: Events Manager Christian Kaplan

6044
ALBANO BALLET AND PERFORMING ARTS CENTER

15 Girard Avenue
Hartford, CT 6105
Mailing Address: Albano Ballet, 15 Girard Avenue,
Hartford, Connecticut 06105
Phone: 860-232-8898
e-mail: albanoballet@netzero.net
Web Site: http://www.albanoballet.org/contact.html
Founded: 1971
Specialized Field: ballet

6045
AUSTIN ARTS CENTER

Trinity College
300 Summit Street
Hartford, CT 06106-3100
Phone: 860-297-2199
Fax: 860-297-5380
Web Site: www.austinarts.org
Management:
Austin Arts Center Director: Jeffrey Walker
Mission: The Austin Arts Center (AAC) is Trinity
College's premier venue for the performing and visual
arts. Centrally-located on campus, it houses two
performance spaces (Goodwin Theater and Garmany

Hall) and the Widener Gallery. Annually presenting over 40 public events featuring guest artists, facility and students, programming can range from the creation of Tibetan mandalas to modern opera to political theater.
Paid Staff: 4
Facility Category: Performing; Visual Arts
Type of Stage: Proscenium; Black Box

6046
BUSHNELL CENTER FOR THE PERFORMING ARTS
166 Capitol Avenue
Hartford, CT 06106
Phone: 860-987-6000
Fax: 860-987-6070
e-mail: info@bushnell.org
Web Site: www.bushnell.org
Management:
   Executive Director: David Fay
   Associate Executive Director: Donna Reynolds
   Programs Director: Dorothy Bertoni
   Programs Coordinator: Megan Fitzgerald
   Service Director/Facility Sales: Paige Rubino
   Marketing Director: Carolynn Hebert
   Box Office Manager: Margaret Rush
Founded: 1930
Status: Non-Profit, Professional
Paid Staff: 100
Volunteer Staff: 700
Annual Attendance: 350,000
Facility Category: Performing Arts Center
Type of Stage: Proscenium
Seating Capacity: 2,800
Year Built: 1929
Year Remodeled: 2001
Rental Contact: Jodi Arnmark

6047
CHARTER OAK CULTURAL CENTER
21 Charter Oak Avenue
Hartford, CT 06106
Phone: 860-249-1207
Fax: 860-524-8014
Web Site: www.charteroakcentre.org
Officers:
   President: Raymond Baker
Management:
   Executive Director: Rabbi Donna Berman PhD
Utilizes: Artists-in-Residence; Collaborations; Dance Companies; Five Seasonal Concerts; Playwrights; Touring Companies
Specialized Field: Dance; Visual Arts; Music; Theatre; Exhibits; Film
Status: Non-Profit, Non-Professional
Paid Staff: 2
Volunteer Staff: 1
Budget: $200,000
Income Sources: Private Foundations; Grants; Business and Individual Donations; Box Office; Government; Endowments
Affiliations: Greater Hartford Arts Council; Dance Connecticut
Annual Attendance: 2,500
Facility Category: Former Synagogue
Type of Stage: Stage and Dance Floor
Stage Dimensions: 40'x60'
Seating Capacity: 200
Year Built: 1876

6048
HARTFORD CIVIC CENTER
One Civic Center Plaza
Hartford, CT 06103

Phone: 860-249-6333
Fax: 860-241-4210
e-mail: hccinfo@thegarden.com
Web Site: www.hartfordciviccenter.com
Officers:
   SVP/General Manager: Marty Brooks
Management:
   Director Facility Booking: Corey Humpage
Founded: 1977
Status: For-Profit, Professional
Paid Staff: 400
Seating Capacity: 16,500
Year Built: 1978
Year Remodeled: 1998

6049
HORACE BUSHNELL MEMORIAL HALL
166 Capitol Avenue
Hartford, CT 06106
Phone: 860-987-5900
Fax: 860-987-6080
Toll-free: 888-824-2874
e-mail: info@bushnell.org
Web Site: www.bushnell.org
Management:
   CEO: David Fay
Founded: 1929
Status: For-Profit, Non-Professional
Annual Attendance: 350,000
Type of Stage: Flexible; Proscenium

6050
MASHANTUCKET PEQUOT MUSEUM & RESEARCH CENTER
110 Pequot Trail
PO Box 3180
Mashantucket, CT 06338-3180
Phone: 860-396-6835
Fax: 860-396-6570
Toll-free: 800-411-9671
e-mail: dholahan@mptn.org
Web Site: www.pequotmuseum.org
Management:
   Executive Director: Kimberly Hatcher-White
   Head Curator: Steven Cook
   Marketing/Development Director: Steve Dennin
Founded: 1998
Status: Non-Profit, Professional
Paid Staff: 80
Paid Artists: 75
Annual Attendance: 300,000
Seating Capacity: 320

6051
CENTER FOR THE ARTS
Wesleyan University
283 Washington Terrace
Middletown, CT 06459-0442
Phone: 860-685-3355
Fax: 860-685-2061
e-mail: boxoffice@wesleyan.edu
Web Site: www.wesleyan.edu/cfa
Management:
   President: Douglas Bennet
   Events Manager: Barbara Ally
Utilizes: Artists-in-Residence; Collaborating Artists; Collaborations; Dance Companies; Dancers; Guest Companies; Lyricists; Multi Collaborations; Multimedia; Singers; Special Technical Talent; Theatre Companies; Touring Companies
Founded: 1973
Specialized Field: Music; dance; theatre; visual arts
Status: Non-Profit, Professional
Paid Staff: 20

Performs At: Crowell Concert Hall/Theater
Annual Attendance: 41,000
Facility Category: Concert Hall, Theatre
Type of Stage: Flexible
Seating Capacity: 1,799
Year Built: 1973

6052
CFA THEATER
Wesleyan University
Center for the Arts
Wesleyan Station
Middletown, CT 06459
Phone: 860-685-2000
e-mail: boxoffice@wesleyan.edu
Web Site: http://www.wesleyan.edu/theater
Officers:
   President: Douglas J. Bennett
   Director Facilities: Mark Gawlak
Management:
   Professor of Theater: John F. Carr
   Director: Pamela Tatge
Mission: Wesleyan sponsors an active program in the dramatic arts within the Theater Department, which produces theater in a liberal arts setting.
Specialized Field: Art, Dance, Music, Theater
Type of Stage: Proscenium, Thrust
Seating Capacity: 400-550
Year Built: 1973
Architect: John Dinkeloo Architects

6053
CROWELL CONCERT
Wesleyan University
Center for the Arts
Wesleyan Station
Middletown, CT 06459
Phone: 860-685-2000
e-mail: boxoffice@wesleyan.edu
Web Site: http://www.wesleyan.edu/theater
Officers:
   President: Douglas J. Bennett
   Director Facilities: Mark Gawlak
Management:
   Professor of Theater: John F. Carr
   Director: Pamela Tatge
Mission: Wesleyan sponsors an active program in the dramatic arts within the Theater Department, which produces theater in a liberal arts setting.
Specialized Field: Lectures and Music Performances
Seating Capacity: 414

6054
WORLD MUSIC HALL
Wesleyan University
Center for the Arts
Wesleyan Station
Middletown, CT 06459
Phone: 860-685-2000
e-mail: boxoffice@wesleyan.edu
Web Site: http://www.wesleyan.edu/theater
Officers:
   President: Douglas J. Bennett
   Director Facilities: Mark Gawlak
Management:
   Professor of Theater: John F. Carr
   Director: Pamela Tatge
Mission: Wesleyan sponsors an active program in the dramatic arts within the Theater Department, which produces theater in a liberal arts setting.
Specialized Field: Music Performances
Seating Capacity: 175-250

6055
BLACK BOX THEATRE
Central Connecticut State University
Department of Theatre
1615 Stanley Street
New Britain, CT 06050
Phone: 860-832-3150
e-mail: thompsonchr@ccsu.edu
Web Site: http://www.theatre.ccsu.edu
Officers:
  Chair: Lani Johnson
Mission: Dedicated to forging the highest quality
graduates in all aspects of theatre.
Specialized Field: Classical Works, Dance/Musicals,
Modern, Realism, and Originals
Type of Stage: Thrust
Seating Capacity: 100

6056
THADDEUS TORP THEATRE
Central Connecticut State University
Department of Theatre
1615 Stanley Street
New Britain, CT 06050
Phone: 860-832-3150
e-mail: thompsonchr@ccsu.edu
Web Site: http://www.theatre.ccsu.edu
Officers:
  Chair: Lani Johnson
Mission: Dedicated to forging the highest quality
graduates in all aspects of theatre.
Specialized Field: Classical Works, Dance/Musicals,
Modern, Realism, and Originals
Type of Stage: Proscenium

6057
INGALLS RINK
Yale University
PO Box 208216
New Haven, CT 06520
Phone: 203-432-0876
Fax: 203-432-7772
Web Site: www.yale.edu/athletic
Management:
  President: Howard Levin
  Managing Director: Joseph Snecinski
Founded: 1958
Status: Non-Profit, Non-Professional
Seating Capacity: 3,486

6058
KENDALL DRAMA LAB
Southern Connecticut State University
John Lyman Center for the Performing Arts
501 Crescent Street
New Haven, CT 6515
Mailing Address: Theatre Department, Southern CT
State Univ., 501 Crescent St
Phone: 203-392-6161
Fax: 203-392-6158
e-mail: fordr2@southernct.edu
Web Site: www.southernct.edu,
http://www.southernct.edu/theat
Officers:
  President: Cheryl J. Norton
Management:
  Administrative Support: Rebecca Ford
Mission: The John Lyman Center for the Performing
Arts is a multi-use performing arts facility. It consists of
two performing spaces and a lobby art gallery. It is also
home to the Department of Theatre with its costume
and scenery shops.
Specialized Field: Drama

Type of Stage: Black Box
Seating Capacity: 125

6059
LONG WHARF THEATRE STAGE II
222 Sargent Drive
Exit 46 Off I-95
New Haven, CT 06511
Phone: 203-787-4282
Fax: 203-776-2287
Toll-free: 800-782-8497
e-mail: info@longwharf.org
Web Site: www.longwharf.org
Management:
  Artistic Director: Gordon Edelstein
  Managing Director: Michael Stotts
Founded: 1960
Annual Attendance: 100,000
Type of Stage: Thrust; Proscenium
Seating Capacity: 487; 201

6060
LYMAN CENTER
Southern Connecticut State University
501 Crescent Street
New Haven, CT 06515
Phone: 203-392-6161
Fax: 203-392-6158
e-mail: tomascak@southernct.edu
Web Site: www.lymansouthernct.com
Management:
  Director: Cynthia Disano
Status: Non-Profit, Professional
Paid Staff: 4
Type of Stage: Thrust
Seating Capacity: 1,568

6061
MAIN STAGE
Southern Connecticut State University
John Lyman Center for the Performing Arts
501 Crescent Street
New Haven, CT 6515
Mailing Address: Theatre Department, Southern CT
State Univ., 501 Crescent St
Phone: 203-392-6161
Fax: 203-392-6158
e-mail: fordr2@southernct.edu
Web Site: www.southernct.edu,
http://www.southernct.edu/theat
Officers:
  President: Cheryl J. Norton
Management:
  Administrative Support: Rebecca Ford
Mission: The John Lyman Center for the Performing
Arts is a multi-use performing arts facility. It consists of
two performing spaces and a lobby art gallery. It is also
home to the Department of Theatre with its costume
and scenery shops.
Specialized Field: Broadway, Dance, Drama, Music
Type of Stage: Thrust
Seating Capacity: 1,568

6062
NEW HAVEN VETERANS MEMORIAL COLISEUM
275 South Orange Street
New Haven, CT 6510
Mailing Address: DEMOLISHED IN 2007
Phone: 203-772-4200
Fax: 203-495-7745
Web Site: www.nhcoliseum.com
Management:
  Executive Director: James E Perillo

Marketing: Jan Barese
Assistant Director: Stephanie Panico
Facility Coordinator: Jason Smith
Founded: 1972
Seating Capacity: 11,000

6063
PALACE THEATRE
248 College Street
New Haven, CT 6510
Mailing Address: Palace Theater, 100 East Main
Street, Waterbury, CT 06702
Phone: 203-789-2120
Fax: 203-773-0478
Web Site: http://www.palacetheaterct.org/
Management:
  Marketing & Public Relations Office: Sheree
  Marcucci
Mission: The Palace Theater's vision is to stimulate a
cultural and economic renaissance in the region
through the celebration of arts, education and
community. Our mission is to build a strong sense of
community and an appreciation for the arts by
operating, maintaining and sustaining the Palace
Theater as a financially viable not-for-profit performing
arts center that provides positive artistic, cultural,
educational, social and financial impact to the
Founded: 1922
Specialized Field: Broadway, comedy, lecture,
celebrity, education and family programming
Status: Non-Profit

6064
SHUBERT THEATER
247 College Street
New Haven, CT 06510-2419
Phone: 203-562-5666
Fax: 203-789-2286
Toll-free: 800-228-6622
Web Site: www.shubert.com
Officers:
  President/CEO: William Conner
  VP: John F Fisher
Status: Non-Profit, Professional
Facility Category: Theater
Type of Stage: Proscenium
Seating Capacity: 1,655
Year Built: 1914
Year Remodeled: 1997
Rental Contact: Debbi Rosenthal

6065
YALE BASEBALL STADIUM
Yale University
PO Box 208216
New Haven, CT 06520
Phone: 203-432-1420
Fax: 203-432-7772
Web Site: www.yale.edu/athletic
Management:
  President: Richard Levin
  Athletic Director: Kenneth Place
Founded: 1928
Status: Non-Profit, Professional
Seating Capacity: 6,200

6066
YALE BOWL
Yale Athletic Department
PO Box 208216
New Haven, CT 06520-8216

Phone: 203-432-4747
Fax: 203-432-7772
e-mail: thomas.beckett@yale.edu
Web Site: www.yale.edu/athletic/
Management:
Athletic Director: Tom Beckett
Assistant Athletic Director: Kenneth Place
Founded: 1914
Seating Capacity: 64,269

6067
YALE REPERTORY THEATRE
1120 Chapel Street
PO Box 1257
New Haven, CT 06505
Phone: 203-432-1234
Fax: 203-432-6423
Toll-free: 800-824-9710
e-mail: yalerep@yale.edu
Web Site: www.yalerep.org
Management:
Artistic Director: James Bundy
Managing Director: Victoria Nolan
Founded: 1966
Seating Capacity: 487

6068
GARDE ARTS CENTER
325 State Street
New London, CT 06320
Phone: 860-444-6766
Fax: 860-447-0503
Toll-free: 888-061-2033
Web Site: www.gardearts.org
Management:
Executive Director: Steve Sigel
Director Operations: George Dowker
Technical Director: Mark Comito
Box Office Manager: Lynn Hill
Founded: 1976
Status: Non-Profit, Non-Professional
Paid Staff: 15
Volunteer Staff: 200
Budget: $2,200,000
Income Sources: Ticket Sales; Sponsorships
Affiliations: Easter Connecticut Symphony Orchestra; Summer Music
Annual Attendance: 72,000
Type of Stage: Proscenium
Stage Dimensions: 41'x 36'
Seating Capacity: 1,471
Year Built: 1926
Year Remodeled: 1999
Cost: $13,000,000
Organization Type: Proscenium Theatre

6069
PALMER AUDITORIUM
Connecticut College
270 Mohegan Avenue
New London, CT 06320
Mailing Address: PO Box 5512
Phone: 860-439-2605
Fax: 860-439-2595
Toll-free: 888-553-8760
e-mail: dthol@conncoll.edu
Web Site: www.conncoll.edu
Management:
President: Norman Sainscein
Executive Director: Linda Herr
Founded: 1911
Specialized Field: Theatre
Status: Non-Profit, Non-Professional
Paid Staff: 4

6070
RIDGEFIELD PLAYHOUSE FOR MOVIES & THE PERFORMING ARTS
80 E Ridge Avenue
Ridgefield, CT 06877
Phone: 203-438-5739
Fax: 203-438-5739
e-mail: info@ridgefieldplayhouse.org
Web Site: www.ridgefieldplayhouse.org
Management:
Programming Director: Andrea Jabara
Founded: 1938
Seating Capacity: 509

6071
SHERMAN PLAYHOUSE
PO Box 471
Sherman, CT 06784
Phone: 860-354-3622
Web Site: www.geocities.com
Founded: 1926
Annual Attendance: 3,200
Type of Stage: Proscenium
Seating Capacity: 120

6072
THEATRE PROJECT CONSULTANTS
25 Elizabeth Street
South Norwalk, CT 06854
Phone: 203-299-0830
Fax: 203-299-0835
Officers:
President: Victor Gotesman
Management:
President: Richard Pilbrow
Mission: We are stage managers, theatre technicians, designers, producers, arts administrators and architects.
Founded: 1947
Specialized Field: Theater
Status: For-Profit, Non-Professional
Paid Staff: 20

6073
SOUTHINGTON COMMUNITY THEATRE
1237 Marion Avenue
PO Box 411
Southington, CT 06444
Phone: 860-276-1961
Web Site: www.southingtoncommunitytheatre.org
Management:
President: Chad E Valk
VP: Adrianne Giammatteo
Technical Director: Tom Harwood
Founded: 1957

6074
RICH FORUM
307 Atlantic Street
Stamford, CT 6901
Mailing Address: SCA Administrative Offices, 61 Atlantic Street, Stamford, CT
Phone: 203-358-2305
Fax: 203-358-2313
e-mail: jpowers@scalive.org
Web Site: http://www.stamfordcenterforthearts.org/home.cfm
Management:
President: Michael J Cacace
Chairman: Frank D Rich Jr
Director: Carlos A Barbi
Founded: 1992

Specialized Field: Broadway, comedy, lecture, celebrity, education and family programming
Status: Non-Profit
Type of Stage: Proscenium
Seating Capacity: 757

6075
STAMFORD CENTER FOR THE ARTS
307 Atlantic Street
Stamford, CT 6901
Mailing Address: SCA Administrative Offices, 61 Atlantic Street, Stamford, CT
Phone: 203-358-2305
Fax: 203-358-2313
e-mail: jpowers@scalive.org
Web Site: http://www.stamfordcenterforthearts.org/home.cfm
Management:
Executive Director: Doug Evans
Artistic Director: George Moredock
Artisic Administration: Gail Mason
Public Relation Manager: Richard Pheneger
Director Operations: Mike Moran
Production Manager: Gene Ricciardi
Mission: Dedicated to serving as the region's center for performing arts. Operates two facilities, the Palace Theatre and the Rich Forum.
Founded: 1927
Specialized Field: Broadway, comedy, lecture, celebrity, education and family programming
Status: Non-Profit
Seating Capacity: 1,580

6076
HARRIET S. JORGENSEN THEATRE
University of Connecticut
Jorgensen Center For The Performing Arts
2132 Hillside Road
Storrs, CT 06269-3104
Phone: 860-486-4226
Fax: 860-486-3110
Web Site: www.uconn.edu
Officers:
President: Philip E. Austin
Facilities Manager: Gary Yakstis
Management:
Artistic Director: Gary English
Mission: Jorgensen Center for the Performing Arts has presented the communities of eastern New England with the best the world of the performing arts has to offer, from world-renowned masters to rising stars.
Specialized Field: Ballet, Comedy, Dance, Music, Symphony, Theatre
Status: Nonprofit, Professional
Paid Staff: 10
Type of Stage: Proscenium
Seating Capacity: 500

6077
JORGENSEN CENTER FOR THE PERFORMING ARTS
University of Connecticut
2132 Hillside Road Unit 3104
Storrs, CT 06269-3104
Phone: 860-486-1983
Fax: 860-486-6781
e-mail: rodney.rock@uconn.edu
Web Site: www.jorgensen.ct-arts.com
Management:
President: Phillip Austin
Executive Director: Rodney Rock
Operations Director: Gary Yakstis
Box Office Director: Lucy Clarke

Mission: Through the presentation fo the performing arts, enlightens, entertains and inspires the intellectual curiosity in the university's students, faculty and staff, as well as the community at large.
Founded: 1955
Specialized Field: Multi-Disciplinary
Status: Non-Profit, Professional
Paid Staff: 13
Volunteer Staff: 8
Paid Artists: 50
Budget: $2 million
Income Sources: Sales; University Fees; Grants
Performs At: Jorgensen Center For The Performing Arts; Von Der Mehden Recital Hall
Affiliations: NEP, APAP
Annual Attendance: 70,000
Facility Category: Auditorium
Type of Stage: Proscenium
Seating Capacity: 2,630/500

6078
UNIVERSITY OF CONNECTICUT SPORTS COMPLEX - HARRY A GAMPEL PAVILION

2095 Hillside Road,U-78
Storrs, CT 06269
Phone: 860-486-3530
Fax: 860-486-1204
e-mail: mike.enright@uconn.edu
Web Site:
www.uconnhuskies.com/MainLinks/Facilities/facilities.html
Management:
  Director of Athletics: Neal Eskin
  Communications/Assoc Drtr Athletics: Mike Enright
  Ticket Operations: Kyle Kravchuk
  Internal Operations: Dino Mattessich
Mission: The Harry A. Gampel Pavilion, opened in January of 1990, totals more than 171,000 square feet in the domed area of the entire UConn Sports Center Complex with a seating capacity of 10,127. The entire UConn Sports Center Complex measures 320 feet in diameter in the circular domed arena area. The brilliant aluminum dome of the Gampel Pavilion towers more than 130 feet in the air from ground level.
Founded: 1881
Status: Non-Profit

6079
VON DER MEHDEN RECITAL HALL

University of Connecticut
875 Coventry Road
Storrs, CT 06269-1128
Phone: 860-486-4228
Fax: 860-486-1979
Web Site: http://www.sfa.uconn.edu/vdm
Officers:
  President: Philip E. Austin
  Facilities Manager: Gary Yakstis
Management:
  Director: Rod Rock
  Artistic Director: Gary English
  Contact: Patricia Thurber
Mission: Jorgensen Center for the Performing Arts has presented the communities of eastern New England with the best world of the performing arts has to offer, from world-renowned masters to rising stars.
Specialized Field: Concerts
Status: Nonprofit, Professional
Paid Staff: 10
Type of Stage: Proscenium
Seating Capacity: 488

6080
COE PARK CIVIC CENTER

101 Litchfield Street
Torrington, CT 6790
Mailing Address: Torrington Armory, 153 South Main Street, Torrington, CT 067
Phone: 860-489-2274
Fax: 489—25-88
e-mail: BRETT_SIMMONS@Torringtonct.org
Web Site: http://www.coeparkgardens.com/ and http://ww
Management:
  Superintendent of Parks & Recreatio: J. Brett Simmons
  Recreation director: Donna Winn
Founded: 1973
Specialized Field: Summer Concerts-on-the-Green

6081
WARNER THEATRE

68 Main Street
PO Box 1012
Torrington, CT 06790
Phone: 860-489-7180
Fax: 860-482-4076
e-mail: info@warnertheatre.org
Web Site: www.warnertheatre.org
Management:
  Executive Director: James Patrick
Founded: 1931
Status: Non-Profit, Professional
Paid Staff: 16
Annual Attendance: 10,000
Seating Capacity: 80

6082
OAKDALE THEATRE

95 South Turnpike Road
Wallingford, CT 06492
Phone: 203-269-8721
Fax: 203-294-6988
Web Site: www.oakdale.com
Management:
  Booking: Anna Cappala
  Marketing: Jim Bozzi
Seating Capacity: 4,800

6083
PAUL MELLON ARTS CENTER

Choate Rosemary Hall
333 Christian Street
Wallingford, CT 06492
Phone: 203-697-2000
Fax: 203-697-2396
e-mail: rbrandt@choate.edu
Web Site: www.choate.edu
Management:
  Director: Ray Diffley
Founded: 1890
Annual Attendance: 45,000
Type of Stage: Proscenium
Seating Capacity: 750

6084
HOFFMAN AUDITORIUM

Saint Joseph College
Carol Autorino Center
1678 Asylum Avenue
West Hartford, CT 06117
Phone: 860-231-5555
Fax: 860-231-6719
e-mail: rsmith@sjc.edu
Web Site: https://ticketing.sjc.edu

Officers:
  Director: Dr. Robert Smith
  Events Assistant: Andrea Hotes
Mission: The Center serves both the academic needs of the College and the cultural needs of the greater community. In keeping with the College's rich tradition in the liberal arts, students attend and participate in a wide variety of artistic and cultural events.
Opened: 2001
Specialized Field: Ballet, Classical Guitar, Concert Opera, Dance, Gospel, Theatre
Season: Year Round
Seating Capacity: 365

6085
LINCOLN THEATRE

University of Hartford
200 Bloomfield Avenue
West Hartford, CT 06117
Phone: 860-768-4073
Fax: 860-768-4229
e-mail: dbell@mail.hartford.edu
Web Site: www.hartford.edu
Officers:
  Managing Director: David Bell
  Director Audience Services: Robert Thompson
Facility Category: Concert Hall
Seating Capacity: 1,100

6086
UNIVERSITY OF HARTFORD SPORTS CENTER

200 Bloomfield Avenue
West Hartford, CT 6117
Mailing Address: University of Hartford Sports Center, 200 Bloomfield Ave., W
Phone: 860-768-4536
Fax: 860-768-4229
e-mail: tstavropo@hartford.edu
Web Site:
http://uhaweb.hartford.edu/sportsctr/home%20page.h
Management:
  Director: Daivd Bell
Seating Capacity: 3,545

6087
LEVITT PAVILION FOR THE PERFORMING ARTS

260 South Compo Road
Westport, CT 06880
Phone: 203-226-7600
Fax: 203-226-2330
Web Site: www.levittpavilion.com
Management:
  Executive Director: Freda Walsh
Mission: The Pavilion provides over 50 nights of diverse, top-quality entertainment every summer, at no charge, plus 1-5 special ticketed events, to the residents of Connecticut and beyond.
Utilizes: Actors; Dance Companies; Dancers; Grant Writers; Guest Accompanists; Guest Choreographers; Guest Composers; Guest Lecturers; Guest Musical Directors; Guest Musicians; Multimedia; Original Music Scores; Playwrights; Sign Language Translators; Singers; Special Technical Talent
Founded: 1973
Specialized Field: Performing Arts
Status: Nonprofit
Paid Staff: 6
Volunteer Staff: 20
Budget: $490,000
Income Sources: Fundraising Events; Foundation Grants; Corporate Donations; Individual Donations

Affiliations: Friends of the Levitt Pavilion and the Town of Westport
Annual Attendance: 50,000
Facility Category: Outdoor
Type of Stage: Proscenium
Stage Dimensions: 26'x45'
Seating Capacity: 2,500
Year Built: 1973
Year Remodeled: 1990

6088
WESTPORT COMMUNITY THEATRE

110 Myrtle Avenue
Westport, CT 6880
Mailing Address: Westport Community Theatre, Town Hall Westport 110 Myrtle Av
Phone: 203-226-1983
Web Site: http://www.westportcommunitytheatre.com/
Management:
    President: Janet Adams
Founded: 1978
Specialized Field: theater

6089
WESTPORT COUNTRY PLAYHOUSE

25 Powers Court
PO Box 629
Westport, CT 06880
Phone: 203-227-5137
Fax: 203-221-7482
e-mail: info@westportplayhouse.org
Web Site: www.westportplayhouse.org
Founded: 1931
Seating Capacity: 707

Delaware

6090
SCHWARTZ CENTER FOR THE ARTS

Wesley College
Friends of the Capitol Theater
PO Box 1449
Dover, DE 19903
Phone: 302-678-3583
Fax: 302-678-1267
Toll-free: 800-778-5078
e-mail: thearts@schwartzcenter.com
Web Site: www.schwartzcenter.com
Officers:
    Chair: Scott D. Miller
    Vice Chair: D. Wayne Holden
    Treasurer: William Winters
Mission: In 2004, a strategic alliance was formed to partner the resources of Wesley College, Delaware State University, The Grand Opera House and The Friends of the Capital Theater, to maximize usage and position the historic treasure as the premiere performing arts center south of Wilmington.
Founded: 2001
Specialized Field: Comedy, Dance, Music, Theater
Status: Non-Profit, Professional
Paid Staff: 2
Volunteer Staff: 50
Seating Capacity: 600
Year Built: 1904
Year Restored: 2001
Cost: $8.3 Million

6091
BOB CARPENTER CENTER

University of Delaware
631 S College Avenue
Newark, DE 19716
Phone: 302-831-4016
Fax: 302-831-4019
e-mail: dbs@udel.edu
Web Site: www.udel.edu/bcc
Officers:
    President: Patrick Harker
Management:
    Managing Director: Domenick Sicilia
    Box Office Manager: Denita Patrick
Mission: To provide a venue for University of Deleware home basketball games, convocations, entertainment and special events.
Founded: 1992
Specialized Field: Rock; Pop; Country; Contemprary and Christian Concerts; Rock
Status: Non-Profit, Professional
Paid Staff: 25
Volunteer Staff: 5
Paid Artists: 3
Facility Category: Arena
Rental Contact: Domenick B Sicilia

6092
CFA STUDIO

University of Delaware
Center for the Arts
413 Academy Street
Newark, DE 19716
Mailing Address: 413 Academy Street, Second Floor, University of Delaware, Ne
Phone: 302-831-2201
e-mail: ud-pttp@udel.edu
Web Site: http://www.udel.edu/theatre
Officers:
    President: Patrick Harker
Management:
    Media contact: Nadine Howett
Mission: The University of Delaware Professional Training Program/Resident Ensemble Players is a powerful and unique marriage of a resident professional acting company and a conservatory training program.
Specialized Field: Theatre
Type of Stage: Black Box

6093
CFA THOMPSON THEATRE

University of Delaware
Center for the Arts
413 Academy Street
Newark, DE 19716
Phone: 302-831-2201
Web Site: http://www.udel.edu/theatre
Officers:
    President: Patrick Harker
Mission: The University of Delaware Professional Training Program/Resident Ensemble Players is a powerful and unique marriage of a resident professional acting company and a conservatory training program.
Specialized Field: Theatre
Type of Stage: Proscenium
Seating Capacity: 450

6094
HARTSHORN THEATER

University of Delaware
Center for the Arts
413 Academy Street
Newark, DE 19716
Phone: 302-831-2201
Web Site: http://www.udel.edu/theatre
Officers:
    President: Patrick Harker

Mission: The University of Delaware Professional Training Program/Resident Ensemble Players is a powerful and unique marriage of a resident professional acting company and a conservatory training program.
Specialized Field: Theatre
Type of Stage: Black Box

6095
DUPONT THEATRE

Tenth & Market Street
Wilmington, DE 19801
Phone: 302-656-4401
Fax: 302-594-1437
Toll-free: 800-338-0881
e-mail: Carolyn.F.Grubb@usa.dupont.com
Web Site: www.duponttheatre.com
Management:
    General Manager: John Gardner
    Marketing Manager: Carolyn Grubb
    Box Office Manager: Barbara Slavin
    Technical Director: Terry Gray
Founded: 1913
Status: For-Profit, Professional
Paid Staff: 17
Seating Capacity: 1,251

6096
FRAWLEY STADIUM

818 North Market Street
Wilmington, DE 19805
Phone: 302-658-7897
Fax: 302-652-5346
e-mail: grandopera@grandopera.org
Web Site: www.grandopera.org
Management:
    Executive Director: Ken Wesler
    Associatge Director/Booking: Stephen Baile
    Marketing Director: Mary K Davis
    Box Office Manager: Terru Cruz
Seating Capacity: 7,000

6097
GRAND OPERA HOUSE

818 N Market Street
Wilmington, DE 19801-3080
Phone: 302-658-7897
Fax: 302-652-5346
e-mail: grandopera@grandopera.org
Web Site: www.grandopera.org
Management:
    Executive Director: Kenneth Wesl
    Associate Director: Stephen Bailey
    Controller: Barbara Kell
    Assistant Controller: Ismay Dacosta
Founded: 1871
Type of Stage: Proscenium
Seating Capacity: 1,190

District of Columbia

6098
AMERICAN UNIVERSITY - MCDONALD RECITAL HALL

4400 Massachusetts Avenue NW
Washington, DC 20016
Phone: 202-885-3420
Fax: 202-885-1092
Web Site: www.american.edu

6099
BAIRD AUDITORIUM
Smithsonian Institution
10th and Constitution Avenue NW
Washington, DC 20560
Phone: 202-633-1000
e-mail: info@si.edu
Web Site: www.mnh.si.edu

6100
BENDER ARENA
American University
4400 Massachusetts Avenue NW
Washington, DC 20016
Phone: 202-885-3075
Fax: 202-885-3033
Web Site: www.aueagles.com
Management:
    Athletic Director: Benjamin Ladner
    Assistant Athletic Director: Ed McLaughlin
Founded: 1988
Seating Capacity: 5,000 to 6,000

6101
CARMICHAEL AUDITORIUM
Smithsonian Institution
14th and Constitution Avenue NW
Washington, DC 20560
Phone: 202-357-1300
Web Site: www.mnh.si.edu

6102
CHARLES E SMITH CENTER
George Washington University
600 22nd Street NW
Washington, DC 20052
Phone: 202-994-6650
Fax: 202-994-6818
e-mail: gwsports@gwu.edu
Web Site: www.gwu.edu
Management:
    Athletic Director: Jack Kvancz
Status: Non-Profit, Professional
Paid Staff: 100

6103
CONSTITUTION HALL
1776 D Street NW
Washington, DC 20006
Mailing Address: National Society Daughters of the
American Revolution, 1776
Phone: 202-628-4780
Fax: 202-628-2570
Web Site: www.dar.org/conthall
Management:
    President: Presley Wagner
Founded: 1929
Specialized Field: theater, concerts
Status: Non-Profit, Professional

6104
CRAMTON AUDITORIUM
Howard University
Lulu Vere Childers Hall
2455 6th Street NW
Washington, DC 20059
Phone: 202-806-7050
Fax: 202-806-9183
e-mail: ddsaunders@howard.edu
Web Site: www.howard.edu
Officers:
    Interim Executive Director: Steven G. Johnson
    Technical Director: Michael C. Stepowany

    Production Manager: Charles Coward
    House Operations Coordinator: Kim E. Banks
Management:
    Manager: Denise Saunders Thompson
Mission: Cramton Auditorium has provided the
Institution and the community with the means to enrich
the lives of both students and visitors academically,
culturally, and socially.
Opened: 1961
Specialized Field: Theatre
Performs At: Performing Arts; Educational Event;
Keynote Speakers
Affiliations: Association of Performing Arts Presenters
Type of Stage: Proscenium
Seating Capacity: 1,508

6105
DC ARMORY
2400 E Capitol Street, SE
Washington, DC 20003
Phone: 202-547-9077
Fax: 202-547-7460
Web Site: www.dcsportscommission.com
Management:
    Executive Director: James Dalrymple
Seating Capacity: 10,000

6106
ENVIRONMENTAL THEATRE SPACE
Howard University
Lulu Vere Childers Hall
2455 6th Street NW
Washington, DC 20059
Phone: 202-806-7050
Fax: 202-806-9183
e-mail: ddsaunders@howard.edu
Web Site: www.howard.edu
Officers:
    Interim Executive Director: Steven G. Johnson
    Technical Director: Michael C. Stepowany
    Production Manager: Charles Coward
    House Operations Coordinator: Kim E. Banks
Management:
    Manager: Denise Saunders Thompson
Mission: The Department continues to present a rich
mix of high quality theatre productions to the greater
Washington community.
Opened: 1961
Specialized Field: Theatre
Performs At: Performing Arts; Educational Event;
Keynote Speakers
Affiliations: Association of Performing Arts Presenters
Type of Stage: Proscenium

6107
FOLGER CONSORT
201 E Capitol Street, SE
Washington, DC 20003
Phone: 202-544-4600
Fax: 202-544-4623
e-mail: webmaster@folger.edu
Web Site: www.folger.edu
Management:
    Manager: Susanne Oldham
Founded: 1970

6108
GASTON HALL
37th and O Streets NW
Washington, DC 20057
Phone: 202-687-4081
Fax: 202-687-2191
e-mail: lignellr@georgetown.edu
Web Site: www.georgetown.edu

Founded: 1789
Annual Attendance: 15,000
Type of Stage: Black Box
Seating Capacity: 728

6109
GEORGETOWN UNIVERSITY
PERFORMING ARTS CENTER
Davis Arts Center
Room 108, Box 571063
Washington, DC 20057-1063
Phone: 202-687-3838
Fax: 202-687-5757
e-mail: lignellr@georgetown.edu
Web Site: www.performingarts.georgetown.edu
Management:
    President: Jack Degioia
    Executive Director: Maya Rag
    Administrative Director: Ron Lignelli
Utilizes: Artists-in-Residence; Choreographers;
Collaborating Artists; Collaborations; Dance
Companies; Dancers; Guest Artists; Guest Directors;
Guest Musical Directors; Guest Musicians; High School
Drama; Instructors; Multimedia; Music; Original Music
Scores; Performance Artists; Sign Language
Translators; Soloists; Student Interns
Founded: 1989
Specialized Field: All
Status: Non-Profit, Professional
Paid Staff: 40
Performs At: 2 Music Halls, 4 Theatres, 1 Multipurpose
Annual Attendance: 20,000
Facility Category: Black Box, Recital, Concert Hall,
Multipurpose

6110
IRA ALDRIDGE THEATER
Howard University
Lulu Vere Childers Hall
2455 6th Street NW
Washington, DC 20059
Phone: 202-806-7050
Fax: 202-806-9183
e-mail: ddsaunders@howard.edu
Web Site: www.howard.edu
Officers:
    Interim Executive Director: Steven G. Johnson
    Technical Director: Michael C. Stepowany
    Production Manager: Charles Coward
    House Operations Coordinator: Kim E. Banks
Management:
    Manager: Denise Saunders Thompson
Mission: The Department continues to present a rich
mix of high quality theatre productions to the greater
Washington community.
Opened: 1961
Specialized Field: Theatre
Performs At: Performing Arts; Educational Event;
Keynote Speakers
Affiliations: Association of Performing Arts Presenters
Type of Stage: Proscenium
Seating Capacity: 300

6111
JOHN F KENNEDY CENTER FOR THE
PERFORMING ARTS
2700 F Street NW
Washington, DC 20566
Phone: 202-416-8000
Fax: 202-416-8018
Toll-free: 800-444-1324
Web Site: www.kennedy-center.org
Management:

President: Michael M Kiser
Chairman: Stephen A Schwarzman
Program Director/ SR/Youth/Family: Kim Peter Kovac
Program Manager/Performance Plus: Marlene Cooper
Mission: The Kennedy Center is America's living memorial to President Kennedy-presenting the greatest performers and performances from across America and around the world, nurturing new works and young artists, and serving as a leader in arts education.
Founded: 1971
Specialized Field: Theatre Dance Musics; Commercial Arts
Status: Non-Profit, Professional

6112
LINCOLN THEATRE
1215 U Street North West
Washington, DC 20009
Phone: 202-397-7328
Fax: 202-328-9245
Web Site: www.thelincolntheatre.org
Management:
  General Manager: Deneene Brockington
  Facility Booking: Darlene Brown
Founded: 1922
Seating Capacity: 1,250

6113
LISNER AUDITORIUM
George Washington University
730 21st Street NW
Washington, DC 20052
Phone: 202-994-6800
Fax: 202-994-6906
Web Site: www.lisner.org
Management:
  President: Rosanna Ruscetti
  Managing Director: Carl Graci
Status: Non-Profit, Professional
Paid Staff: 10
Paid Artists: 75
Affiliations: George Washington University
Annual Attendance: 200,000
Facility Category: Auditorium
Seating Capacity: 1490
Year Built: 1942
Year Remodeled: 1990
Rental Contact: Rosanna Ruscetti

6114
MCDONALD RECITAL HALL
American University
4400 Massachusetts Avenue NW
Washington, DC 20016
Phone: 202-885-3420
Fax: 202-885-1092
Web Site: www.american.edu

6115
VERIZON CENTER
601 F Street NW
Washington, DC 20004
Mailing Address: Verizon Center, 601 F Street, NW, Washington, DC 20004
Phone: 202-628-3200
Fax: 301-808-3002
Web Site: http://www.verizoncenter.com/
Officers:
  President: John Stranix
Management:
  VP/Executive Director: Nancy Lacy
  Booking Director: Patt Darr

Assistant General Manager: Fritz Smith
Director Executive Seating: Bernie Deluca
Mission: sports and entertainment arena
Founded: 1997
Specialized Field: Sports and concerts
Seating Capacity: 19,000

6116
NEW LECTURE HALL
American University
4400 Massachusetts Avenue NW
Washington, DC 20016
Phone: 202-885-3420
Fax: 202-885-1092
Web Site: www.american.edu
Founded: 1968

6117
SHAKESPEARE THEATRE
516 8th Street SE
Washington, DC 20003-2207
Phone: 202-547-1122
Fax: 202-638-3869
Toll-free: 877-487-8849
e-mail: web_admin@shakespearetheatre.org
Web Site: www.shakespearetheatre.org
Management:
  Artistic Director: Michael Kahn
  Managing Director: Nicholas T Goldsborough
  Director Information Technology: Valeria J Donegan
  Public Relations & Martketing: Barry M Colfelt
Mission: The Theatre's core mission is to present classic theatre in an accessible, skillful, imaginative, American style that honors playwrights' language and intentions while viewing their plays through a 21st-century lens.
Founded: 1986
Status: Non-Profit, Professional
Paid Staff: 90
Paid Artists: 75
Seating Capacity: 451

6118
THEATER J
Jewish Community Center
1529 16th Street NW
Washington, DC 20036
Phone: 202-518-9400
Fax: 202-518-9420
e-mail: theaterj@dtheaterj.org
Web Site: www.theaterj.org
Management:
  Group Sales Director: Becky Peters
  Artistic Director: Ari Roth
  Managing Director: Patricia Jenson
  Director Marketing/Communications: Grace Overbeke
Mission: Theater J produces thought-provoking, publicly engaged, personal, passionate and entertaining plays and musicals that celebrate the distinctive urban voice and social vision that are part of the Jewish cultural leagacy. Acclaimed as one of the nation's premiere playwrights' theaters, Theater J presents cutting edge contemporary work alongside spirited revivals and is a nurturing home for the development and production of new work.
Utilizes: Actors; AEA Actors; Collaborating Artists; Filmmakers; Guest Conductors; Local Artists; Original Music Scores; Performance Artists
Founded: 1990
Specialized Field: Theater
Status: 501c3
Season: October - May

Annual Attendance: 25,000
Facility Category: Theatre
Type of Stage: Thrust/Proscenium
Stage Dimensions: 20' x 20'
Seating Capacity: 258
Year Built: 1925
Year Remodeled: 1996
Rental Contact: Wanda ChiChester

6119
GEORGETOWN UNIVERSITY DEPARTMENT OF PERFORMING ARTS
Davis Arts Center
Room 108, Box 571063
Washington, DC 20057-1063
Phone: 202-687-3838
Fax: 202-687-5757
e-mail: lignellr@georgetown.edu
Web Site: www.performingarts.georgetown.edu
Management:
  Managing Director: Ron Lignelli
Type of Stage: Black Box; Masonite
Seating Capacity: 200

6120
WARNER THEATRE
1299 Pennsylvania Avenue
NW Suite 111
Washington, DC 20004
Phone: 202-783-4000
Fax: 202-783-0204
Toll-free: 202-783-4000
Web Site: www.warnertheatre.com
Mission: Rental facility for local and touring presenters.
Utilizes: Theatre Companies
Founded: 1924
Performs At: Rental
Facility Category: Theater
Type of Stage: Proscenium
Seating Capacity: 1,847
Year Built: 1924
Year Remodeled: 1992
Rental Contact: 202-626-8250 B Newman

6121
WASHINGTON CONVENTION CENTER
801 Mount Vernon Place NW
Washington, DC 20001
Phone: 202-249-3000
Fax: 202-249-3112
Web Site: www.dcconvention.com
Management:
  General Manager/CEO: Allen Lew
  Deputy General Manager: Claud Bailey
  Senior Sales Manager: Stacey Fleming
  Director Exhibition: Steve Schwartz

Florida

6122
ISLAND PLAYERS THEATRE
10009 Gulf Drive, Anna Maria, Florida
PO Box 2059
Anna Maria, FL 34216
Mailing Address: Carol Heckman, President, c/o P.O. Box 2059, Anna Maria, FL
Phone: 941-778-5755
e-mail: hjscan@aol.com
Web Site: http://home.earthlink.net/~islandplayers/
Management:
  Chairman for Publicity: Hugn Scanlon
Specialized Field: plays and musicals
Status: Non profit

6123
DOLLY HANDS CULTURAL ARTS CENTER
M091920010ge Drive
Belle Glade, FL 33430
Phone: 561-992-6160
Fax: 407-992-6179
Web Site: www.pbcc.cc.fl.us
Management:
Manager: Leigh Woodham

6124
PALM BEACH COMMUNITY COLLEGE PERFORMING ARTS CENTER
1977 College Drive
Belle Glade, FL 33430
Phone: 561-993-1160
Fax: 561-993-1162
Web Site: www.pbcc.edu
Management:
President: Dennis P Gallon
Executive Director: Leigh Woodham
Founded: 1982
Specialized Field: Performing
Status: Non-Profit, Professional
Paid Staff: 2

6125
WT NEAL CIVIC CENTER
1773 NE Pear Street
Blountstown, FL 32424
Phone: 850-674-4500
Fax: 850-674-1714
Management:
President: Howell Montgomery
Founded: 1983
Status: Non-Profit, Professional
Paid Staff: 4

6126
CENTURY VILLAGE THEATERS
19296 Lyons Road
Boca Raton, FL 33434
Phone: 561-451-1227
Fax: 561-883-2624
e-mail: akoffler@cencec.com
Web Site: www.centuryvillagetheater.com
Officers:
VP: Abby Koffler
Management:
Entertainment Director: Abby C Koffler
Status: For-Profit, Professional

6127
MIZNER PARK AMPHITHEATRE
590 Plaza Real
Boca Raton, FL 33432
Phone: 561-962-4109
Fax: 561-832-2043
e-mail: fantasma@fantasma.com
Web Site: www.miznerparkamp.com
Management:
Sponsorship: Randy LaVenia
Marketing: Rachel Schrift
Box Office/Operations: Jason Morey
Production: Brian Custer
Seating Capacity: 5,000

6128
UNIVERSITY CENTER AUDITORIUM
500 NW 20th Street
Boca Raton, FL 33432

Phone: 561-297-3730
Fax: 561-297-3733
Web Site: www.fau.edu
Founded: 1987

6129
HARBORVIEW CENTER
300 Cleveland Street
Clearwater, FL 33755
Phone: 727-462-6778
Fax: 462-679-8
Web Site: www.harborv.com
Management:
General Manager: David Nadeau
Director Operations: John Gerard
Food/Beverage Sales: Fran Iosa
Seating Capacity: 1,600

6130
RUTH ECKERD HALL
1111 McMullen Booth Road
Clearwater, FL 33759
Phone: 727-791-7060
Fax: 727-724-5976
Web Site: www.rutheckerdhall.com
Officers:
President/CEO: Robert Freedman
Executive Director: Kathy Rabon
Director Entertainment: Bobby Rossi
Director Marketing/Communication: Lex Poppens
Mission: To present major national and international artists and attractions year-round in a fine acoustic hall; to present educational programming, visual arts exhibits and senior citizen programs.
Utilizes: Actors; Artists-in-Residence; Choreographers; Collaborating Artists; Collaborations; Commissioned Music; Dance Companies; Dancers; Fine Artists; Guild Activities; High School Drama; Local Artists; Multi Collaborations; Multimedia; New Productions; Organization Contracts; Original Music Scores; Resident Artists; Selected Students
Founded: 1978
Specialized Field: Series & Festivals; Dance; Vocal Music; Instrumental Music; Theatre
Status: Non-Profit, Professional
Paid Staff: 50
Paid Artists: 120
Budget: $9 million
Income Sources: Association of Performing Arts Presenters; International Society of Performing Arts Administrators; Florida Professional Presenters Association
Annual Attendance: 200,000
Facility Category: Performing Arts Center
Seating Capacity: 2,173
Year Built: 1982
Year Remodeled: 2002
Rental Contact: Gregory Wright
Organization Type: Performing; Educational; Sponsoring

6131
COCOA EXPO SPORTS CENTER
500 Friday Road
Cocoa, FL 32926
Phone: 321-639-3976
Fax: 321-639-0598
e-mail: gilesmalone@cocoaexpo.com
Web Site: www.cocoaexpo.com
Management:
President/General Manager: Giles Malone
Utilizes: Local Artists; Multimedia; Original Music Scores
Founded: 1985

Specialized Field: Brevard County/Space Coast
Performs At: 25,000 Square Foot Arena
Annual Attendance: 225,000
Facility Category: Multi-Purpose
Type of Stage: Concert Stage
Seating Capacity: 5000; 1500

6132
COCOA VILLAGE PLAYHOUSE
300 Brevard Avenue
Cocoa, FL 32922
Phone: 321-636-5050
Fax: 321-636-5050
Web Site: www.playhouse.cocoavillage.com
Management:
Executive Director: Staci Hawkins
Founded: 1924
Status: Non-Profit, Non-Professional
Paid Staff: 20
Volunteer Staff: 250
Paid Artists: 35

6133
OMNI AUDITORIUM
Broward Community College
1000 Coconut Boulevard
Coconut Creek, FL 33066
Mailing Address: 1000 Coconut Creek Boulevard, Coconut Creek, FL 33066
Phone: 954-973-2233
Fax: (95-4) -201-
Web Site: www.broward.cc.fl.us
Mission: true multi-purpose facility, capable of hosting events ranging from opera to basketball tournaments.
Specialized Field: theater, opera
Type of Stage: Flexible
Seating Capacity: 1900+

6134
WYNMOOR RECITAL HALL
1300 Avenue of the Stars
Coconut Creek, FL 33066
Phone: 954-978-2632
Fax: 954-978-2626
Officers:
Chairman Fine Arts Committee: Murray Ross
Management:
Chairman: Murray Ross
Utilizes: Dance Companies; Fine Artists; Guest Accompanists; Guest Musical Directors; Guest Musicians; Multimedia; Sign Language Translators; Singers; Theatre Companies
Founded: 1974
Budget: $100,000
Income Sources: Ticket sales
Performs At: Recital Hall
Annual Attendance: 12,000
Facility Category: Concert Hall
Type of Stage: Double thrust
Stage Dimensions: 38' 10' x 21' 9'
Seating Capacity: 950
Year Built: 1979

6135
BLACK BOX THEATRE
University of Miami
Department Of Theatre Arts
P.O. Box 248273
Coral Gables, FL 33124-4820
Phone: 305-284-4474
Fax: 305-284-5702
e-mail: theatredepartment@miami.edu
Web Site: http://www.as.miami.edu/theatrearts/ring
Management:

Chair/Artistic Director: Vincent J. Cardinal
Mission: University of Miami Theatre is strictly an undergraduate training program. Our students study directly with Professors, not graduate assistants. Our Professors remain active in the profession working in the country's leading regional theaters, in New York, and in film and television. Our students do not take a back seat to graduate students in casting, design assignments, directing opportunities, or in research opportunities.
Specialized Field: Musicals, Plays
Type of Stage: Black Box
Seating Capacity: 60

6136
JERRY HERMAN RING THEATRE
University of Miami
Department Of Theatre Arts
P.O. Box 248273
Coral Gables, FL 33124-4820
Phone: 305-284-4474
Fax: 305-284-5702
e-mail: theatredepartment@miami.edu
Web Site: http://www.as.miami.edu/theatrearts/ring
Management:
Chair/Artistic Director: Vincent J. Cardinal
Mission: University of Miami Theatre is strictly an undergraduate training program. Our students study directly with Professors, not graduate assistants. Our Professors remain active in the profession working in the country's leading regional theaters, in New York, and in film and television. Our students do not take a back seat to graduate students in casting, design assignments, directing opportunities, or in research opportunities.
Specialized Field: Musicals, Plays
Type of Stage: Proscenium/Thrust/Arena
Seating Capacity: 311

6137
UNIVERSITY OF MIAMI CONVOCATION CENTER
1245 Walsh Avenue
Coral Gables, FL 33146
Phone: 305-284-8686
Fax: 305-284-6547
e-mail: convocationcenter@miami.edu
Web Site: www.umconvocationcenter.com
Officers:
General Manager: Patrick McGrew
Marketing Director: Christi Soltz
Opened: 2003
Seating Capacity: 7,900

6138
CORAL SPRINGS CENTER FOR THE ARTS
2855 Coral Springs Drive
Coral Springs, FL 33065
Phone: 954-344-5999
Fax: 954-344-5980
e-mail: info@coralspringscenterforthearts.com
Web Site: www.coralspringscenterforthearts.com
Management:
General Manager: Kevin Barrett
Founded: 1989
Specialized Field: Theatre Venue; Museum
Status: For-Profit, Professional
Paid Artists: 1
Annual Attendance: 200,000
Type of Stage: Proscenium
Seating Capacity: 1,456

6139
DAYTONA BEACH COMMUNITY COLLEGE THEATRE CENTER
1200 Volusia Avenue
Daytona Beach, FL 32115
Mailing Address: NO LONGER AROUND.
Phone: 904-254-3000
Fax: 904-254-3044

6140
DAYTONA PLAYHOUSE
100 Jessamine Boulevard
Daytona Beach, FL 32118
Phone: 386-255-2431
Fax: 386-255-2432
Web Site: www.daytonaplayhouse.com
Founded: 1946
Status: Non-Profit, Non-Professional

6141
JACKIE ROBINSON BALL PARK
108 E Orange Avenue
Daytona Beach, FL 32114
Mailing Address: Jackie Robinson Ballpark, 105 E. Orange Ave., Daytona Beach,
Phone: 386-322-5133
Fax: 904-239-6550
e-mail: jrlaub@daytonacubs.com
Web Site: http://web.minorleaguebaseball.com/team1/page.jsp?
Management:
Manager: Hillary Rowley
Founded: 1914

6142
MARY MCLEOD BETHUNE PERFORMING ARTS CENTER
Bethune-Cookman College
640 Drive Mary McLeod Bethune Boulevard
Daytona Beach, FL 32114
Phone: 386-481-2710
Fax: 386-481-2877
Web Site: www.mmbcenter.com
Officers:
Performing Arts Director: Robert Rothman
Operations Manager: Arndrea Anderson
Seating Capacity: 2,500

6143
OCEAN CENTER
101 N Atlantic Avenue
Daytona Beach, FL 32118
Phone: 386-254-4500
Fax: 386-254-4512
Toll-free: 800-858-6444
e-mail: tbuckley@oceancenter.com
Web Site: www.oceancenter.com
Management:
Sales Manager: Tim Buckley
Director: Donald Poor
Founded: 1985
Annual Attendance: 525,000
Facility Category: Multi-Purpose
Type of Stage: Sico
Seating Capacity: 9,500
Year Built: 1985
Rental Contact: Sales Manager Tim Buckley

6144
PEABODY AUDITORIUM
600 Auditorium Blvd
PO Box 551
Daytona Beach, FL 32118

Phone: 904-255-1318
Fax: 904-258-3169
e-mail: rigerh@codb.us
Web Site: http://www.peabodyauditorium.org
Management:
Marketing: Helen Riger
Founded: 1919
Specialized Field: Broadway, concerts, opera, drama, and comedy shows
Seating Capacity: 2,560

6145
DELRAY BEACH PLAYHOUSE
950 NW 9th Street
PO Box 1056
Delray Beach, FL 33444
Phone: 561-272-1281
Fax: 561-272-5884
Web Site: www.delraybeachplayhouse.com
Founded: 1948
Status: Non-Profit
Seating Capacity: 238

6146
MESA PARK ARENA
100 Mesa Park Boulevard
Fellsmere, FL 32948
Phone: 954-777-4091
Fax: 954-777-4197
e-mail: barbara.kelleher@dot.state.fl.us
Web Site: www.dot.state.fl.us/emo/scenichwy/designated/indianriver/activities.htm
Management:
Public Information Officer FDOT: Barbara Kelleher
Director Transportation Operations: Hesham Ali
Director Transportation Development: Gery O'Reilly
Mission: This 50-acre park features an amphitheater, festival area, Mesa Village and the motorsport arena. Mesa Park also provides a venue of events such as a Bluegrass/Fiddler's convention, a Valentine's Day Tea Dance, Cinco de Mayo Festival, Fourth of July Extravaganza, a Blues Festival and a Special Christmas Showcase.

6147
BAILEY CONCERT HALL
3501 SW Davie Road
Fort Lauderdale, FL 33314
Phone: 954-475-6884
Fax: 954-424-3154
Toll-free: 888-475-6884
e-mail: tjones@broward.edu
Web Site: www.broward.cc.fl.us

6148
BROWARD CENTER FOR THE PERFORMING ARTS
201 SW Fifth Avenue
Fort Lauderdale, FL 33312
Phone: 954-462-0222
Fax: 954-468-3282
Toll-free: 800-564-9539
e-mail: mnerenhausen@curtainup.org
Web Site: www.browardcenter.org
Management:
President: Mark Nerenhausen
General Manager: Kelley Shanley
Founded: 1991
Specialized Field: Series & Festivals; Dance; Instrumental Music; Musical Theater; Theatrical Group; Vocal Music

Status: Non-Profit, Professional
Type of Stage: Concert Stage
Seating Capacity: 2,700

6149
FORT LAUDERDALE STADIUM
Lockhart Stadium
1401 NW 55th Street
Fort Lauderdale, FL 33309
Phone: 954-828-4980
Fax: 305-938-4979
Web Site: www.ci.ftlaud.fl.us
Management:
 Stadium Manager: Vincent Gizzi
Founded: 1962

6150
PARKER PLAYHOUSE
707 NE Eighth Street
PO Box 4603
Fort Lauderdale, FL 33304
Mailing Address: 707 NE 8th Street, Fort Lauderdale, FL 33304
Phone: 954-763-2444
Fax: 954-764-0708
Web Site: http://www.parkerplayhouse.com/
Founded: 1967
Status: Non-Profit, Professional
Paid Staff: 2
Seating Capacity: 1,200

6151
WAR MEMORIAL AUDITORIUM
800 NE 8th Street
Fort Lauderdale, FL 33301
Mailing Address: War Memorial Auditorium 800 NE 8th Street Fort Lauderdale, F
Phone: 954-761-5380
Fax: 954-761-5361
Web Site: www.ci.ftlaud.fl.us/warmemorial.com
Management:
 Manager: Robert Stried
Founded: 1949
Seating Capacity: 2,110

6152
SQUITIERI STUDIO THEATRE
Florida Gulf Coast University
FGCU Arts Complex South
10501 FGCU Blvd
Fort Meyers, FL 33965-6565
Mailing Address: Phillips Center, 315 Hull Road, PO Box 112750, Gainesville,
Phone: 239-590-7268
e-mail: adouglas@performingarts.ufl.edu
Web Site: http://www.fgcu.edu/CAS/blackbox/
Officers:
 President: Bill Merwin
Management:
 Marketing Director: Amy Douglas
Mission: Theatre at Florida Gulf Coast University provides students with opportunities to experience performance and production as artists completing a major in theatre to prepare themselves for graduate study or professional work.
Founded: 1992
Specialized Field: Theater and dance
Type of Stage: Black Box
Seating Capacity: 120

6153
BARBARA B MANN PERFORMING ARTS HALL
13350 Edison Parkway
Fort Myers, FL 33919
Phone: 239-481-4849
Fax: 239-489-0326
Toll-free: 800-440-7469
Web Site: www.bbmannpah.com
Management:
 General Manager: Mary Bensel
 Director Marketing: Peg Welty
 Operations Manager: Eva Calhoun
 Technical Director: Robb McCoy
Mission: The Barbara B. Mann Performing Arts Hall countinues to improve the quality and accessiblity of touring broadway and star performing artists to the communities of Southwest Florida.
Founded: 1985
Specialized Field: Broadway; variety theatre
Paid Staff: 9
Volunteer Staff: 150
Paid Artists: 500
Affiliations: League of American Theatres & Producers; Florida Facility Managers; Southern Arts, APAP
Facility Category: Performing Arts Hall
Type of Stage: Non-Sprung
Stage Dimensions: 160'x47'
Seating Capacity: 1,753
Year Built: 1985
Year Remodeled: 1998

6154
FORT MYERS HARBORSIDE
1375 Monroe Street
Fort Myers, FL 33901
Phone: 239-332-6888
Fax: 239-322-2242
Web Site: www.fmharborside.com

6155
WILLIAM H HAMMOND STADIUM
Lee County Parks & Recreation
3410 Palm Beach Boulevard
Fort Myers, FL 33916
Phone: 941-338-3300
Fax: 941-339-3333
Web Site: www.lee-county.com
Management:
 Director: John Yardbrough
 Manager: Ed McLntyre
Seating Capacity: 7,600

6156
WILLIAM R FRIZZELL CULTURAL CENTRE CLAIBORNE & NED FOULDS THEATRE
10091 McGregor Boulevard
Fort Myers, FL 33919
Phone: 239-939-2787
Fax: 239-939-0794
e-mail: administration@artinlee.org
Management:
 Executive Director: Lydia Black
Founded: 1975
Opened: 1985
Status: Non-Profit
Paid Staff: 5
Volunteer Staff: 2
Budget: $700,000
Performs At: Amphitheatre; Indoor theater; Studio space

Rental Contact: Jamie Golob

6157
SAINT LUCIE COUNTY CIVIC CENTER
2300 Virginia Avenue
Fort Pierce, FL 34982
Phone: 772-462-1538
Fax: 772-462-1526
Web Site: www.stlucieco.gov/leisure/civiccenter.htm
Seating Capacity: 4,000

6158
ROSE AND ALFRED MINIACI PERFORMING ARTS CENTER ON THE NOVA SOUTHEASTERN UNIVERSITY
Nova Southeastern University
3301 Ray Ferrero Jr Boulevard
Ft. Lauderdale, FL 33314
Phone: 954-262-5480
Fax: 954-262-3809
e-mail: miniaci@nova.edu
Web Site: www.miniacipac.com
Mission: Our mission is to provide more cultural programming opportunities for Broward County residents and university students and faculty members.
Seating Capacity: 500

6159
CURTIS M PHILLIPS CENTER FOR PERFORMING ARTS
315 Hull Road
PO Box 112750
Gainesville, FL 32611
Phone: 352-392-1900
Fax: 352-392-3775
Toll-free: 800-904-2787
Web Site: www.performingarts.ufl.edu
Management:
 Director: Michael Blachly
Status: Non-Profit, Professional
Annual Attendance: 6,800
Type of Stage: Black Box; Proscenium
Seating Capacity: 1,754

6160
CURTIS M. PHILLIPS CENTER
University of Florida
Performing Arts
315 Hull Road, PO Box 112750
Gainesville, FL 32611-2750
Mailing Address: Curtis M. Phillips Center, 315 Hull Road, PO Box 112750, Gai
Phone: 352-392-1900
Fax: 352-392-3775
e-mail: adouglas@performingarts.ufl.edu
Web Site: http://www.performingarts.ufl.edu
Officers:
 Director: Michael Blachly
 Assistant Director: Elizabeth Auer
 Director Marketing: Deborah C. Rossi
 Director Operations: Matt Koropeckyj-Cox
 Technical Director: Chuck Turner
Management:
 Marketing Director: Amy Douglas
Mission: To provide an unparalleled experience where the very best performing artists create and share knowledge to serve the students, residents and visitors to North Central Florida.
Founded: 1992
Opened: 1992
Specialized Field: Theatre
Type of Stage: Proscenium
Seating Capacity: 1,754

All listings are in alphabetical order by state, then city, then organization within the city.

Architect: Flad & Associates

6161
HIPPODROME STATE THEATRE
25 SE Second Place
Gainesville, FL 32601
Phone: 352-375-4477
Fax: 352-371-9130
Web Site: www.hipp.gator.net
Management:
 Producing Director: Mary Hausch
 Artistic Director: Lauren Caldwell
 General Manager: Mark Sexton
Mission: To explore the truth of human experience and the human spirit through the examination and presentation of dramatic work. Our purpose is to accomplish this through our commitment to create an artistic home.
Utilizes: Actors; AEA Actors; Artists-in-Residence; Choreographers; Collaborating Artists; Commissioned Composers; Commissioned Music; Dancers; Designers; Educators; Five Seasonal Concerts; Grant Writers; Guest Accompanists; Guest Artists; Guest Companies; Guest Conductors; Guest Designers; Guest Ensembles; Guest Lecturers; Guest Musical Directors; High School Drama; Instructors; Local Artists; Multi Collaborations; Music; Original Music Scores; Poets; Resident Professionals; Selected Students; Sign Language Translators; Soloists; Touring Companies; Visual Arts
Founded: 1973
Specialized Field: Theatre
Status: Professional; Nonprofit
Paid Staff: 38
Volunteer Staff: 63
Budget: $243,074,800
Income Sources: Ticket sales; Concession sales; Corporate support, Federal, State and local grants
Season: Year round
Performs At: Hippodrome
Annual Attendance: 167,000
Facility Category: Live stage and movie theatre
Type of Stage: Thrust
Seating Capacity: 266
Year Built: 1911
Year Remodeled: 1980
Architect: $1.5 Million
Rental Contact: General Manager Mark Sexton
Organization Type: Performing; Touring; Resident; Educational; Sponsoring

6162
SAMUEL P HARN MUSEUM OF ART
University of Florida, SW 34th Street & Hull
PO Box 112700
Gainesville, FL 32611-2700
Phone: 352-392-9826
Fax: 352-392-3892
e-mail: chale@harn.ufl.edu
Web Site: www.harn.ufl.edu
Management:
 Director: Rebecca M Nagy Ph.D
 Marketing/Public Relations Director: Christine Hale
 Development Director: Phyllis Delaney
 Museum Store Manager: Tim Smith
Mission: The Samuel P. Harn Museum of Art promotes the power of the arts to inspire and educate people and enrich their lives. To this purpose the museum builds and maintains exemplary art collections and produces a wide variety of challenging, innovative exhibitions and stimulating educational programs. In addition, the Mary

Ann Harn Cofrin Pavilion has 11,620 square feet of exhibition gallery and 7,800 square feet of cafe and curatorial spaces.
Founded: 1987
Specialized Field: Art Museum
Status: Non-Profit, Non-Professional
Paid Staff: 45

6163
STEPHEN C O'CONNELL CENTER
University of Florida, Gale Lemerand Drive
Suite 1232
Gainesville, FL 32611-5850
Mailing Address: PO Box 115850 Gainesville, FL 32611
Phone: 352-392-5500
Fax: 352-392-7106
Web Site: www.oconnellcenter.ufl.edu
Management:
 Director: Lionel J Dubey
 Associate Director: Darius Dunn
 Business Manager: Renee Musson
Founded: 1980
Specialized Field: Entertainment - Concets-Indoor Sports-Shows
Status: Non-Profit, Non-Professional
Paid Staff: 12
Budget: $2.3 million
Performs At: Multi-Purpose Arena
Facility Category: Multi-Purpose/Arena
Type of Stage: Portable
Seating Capacity: 12,000
Year Built: 1980
Year Remodeled: 1998
Cost: $16.5 million
Rental Contact: Associate Director Darius Dunn

6164
YOUNG CIRCLE PARK AND BANDSHELL
Art and Cultural center of hollywood
US Highway 1 and Hollywood Boulevard
Hollywood, FL 33020
Mailing Address: Art and Culture Center of Hollywood, 1650 Harrison St., Holl
Phone: 954-921-3404
Fax: 305-921-3233
e-mail: alesh@artandculturecenter.org
Web Site: http://www.hollywoodfl.org/parks_rec/Cultlo
Management:
 Marketing: Alesh Houdek
Specialized Field: Theater and musicals

6165
HOMESTEAD SPORTS COMPLEX
1601 SE 28th Avenue
Homestead, FL 33030
Mailing Address: CURRENTLY VACANT
Phone: 305-247-1801
Fax: 305-246-3200
Management:
 Director Parks/Recreation: Alan Ricke
Founded: 1991

6166
EVERBANK FIELD
One Alltel Stadium Place
Jacksonville, FL 32202
Phone: 904-633-6100
Fax: 904-633-6113
Web Site: www.jaguars.com/alltelstadium
Management:
 President: Bob Downey
 Managing Director: Tracy Evans
 General Manager: Robert Downing

Founded: 1995
Status: Non-Profit, Professional
Seating Capacity: 80,000
Year Built: 1995
Resident Groups: Home to the Jacksonville Jaguars

6167
FLORIDA NATIONAL PAVILION
Metropolitan Park
1410 E Adams Street
Jacksonville, FL 32202
Mailing Address: Metropolitan Park, 1410 Gator Bowl Blvd., Jacksonville, Flor
Phone: 904-630-0837
Fax: 904-630-0538
e-mail: cgoodell@coj.net
Web Site: http://www.coj.net/Departments/Recreation+and+Community+

6168
FLORIDA THEATRE
128 E 40th Street
Suite 300
Jacksonville, FL 32202
Phone: 904-355-2787
Fax: 904-358-1874
e-mail: info@floridatheatre.com
Web Site: www.floridatheatre.com
Management:
 President: J Erik Hart
Founded: 1927
Status: Non-Profit, Professional
Paid Staff: 13
Annual Attendance: 250,000
Type of Stage: Flexible

6169
GATOR BOWL
1 Alltel Stadium Place
Jacksonville, FL 32202
Mailing Address: One Gator Bowl Blvd., Jacksonville, FL 32202
Phone: 904-690-0335
Fax: 904-633-6113
e-mail: erik@gatorbowl.com
Web Site: http://www.gatorbowl.com
Management:
 Director Sports Complex: Doug Hall
 Vice President of Marketing: Erik Dellenback
 Marketing Event: Kaitlin White
Mission: The Gator Bowl Association's mission is to provide Northeast Florida with the very best in college athletics and related activities in order to maximize positive impact on the area's economy, national image and community pride.
Founded: 1945

6170
UNF ARENA
University of North Florida
4567 Saint Johns Bluff Road
Jacksonville, FL 32224
Mailing Address: South Building 34
Phone: 904-620-2998
Fax: 904-620-1705
Web Site: www.unf.edu/groups/osprod/
Officers:
 Arena Manager: Becky Purser
 Programming Coordinator: Lindsay Bryant
Facility Category: Sports Arena
Seating Capacity: 6,000

6171
VETERANS MEMORIAL ARENA
300 A Phillip Randall Boulevard
Jacksonville, FL 32202
Phone: 904-630-3900
Fax: 904-630-3913
e-mail: rtimothy@coj.net
Web Site: www.jaxevents.com
Management:
    Director: Robin Timothy
    Event/Operations Coordinator: Jamie Nice
    Production Manager: Lyle Klemmt
Status: For-Profit, Professional
Seating Capacity: 10,276

6172
TENNIS CENTER AT CRANDON PARK
7300 Crandon Boulevard
Key Biscayne, FL 33149
Phone: 305-365-2300
Fax: 305-365-2327
e-mail: parks@miamidade.gov
Web Site: www.co.miami-dade.fl.us
Seating Capacity: 14,000

6173
SOUTH FLORIDA CENTER FOR THE ARTS
29 Jolly Rodger Drive
PO Box 2540
Key Largo, FL 33037
Phone: 350-453-4224
Fax: 305-853-7122

6174
RED BARN THEATRE
319 Duval Street
Rear Key West
Key West, FL 33040
Phone: 305-296-9911
Fax: 305-293-3035
Toll-free: 866-870-9911
Web Site: www.redbarntheatre.com
Status: Non-Profit
Seating Capacity: 88

6175
TENNESSEE WILLIAMS THEATRE
Florida Keys Community College
5901 Junior College Road
Key West, FL 33040
Phone: 305-296-1520
Fax: 305-292-3725
e-mail: info@twpac.com
Web Site: www.tennesseewilliamstheatre.com
Management:
    President: Rebecca Tomlinson
    Technical Director: Isaac Castille
    Resident Lighting Designer: Matthew Rawls
    Production Director: Mike Boyer
Founded: 1977
Specialized Field: Performing Arts
Status: Non-Profit, Professional
Paid Staff: 6
Affiliations: Performing Arts Centers for Key West
Rental Contact: Rebecca Tomlinson

6176
OSCEOLA CENTER FOR THE ARTS
2411 E Bronson Highway
PO Box 451088
Kissimmee, FL 34745-1088

Phone: 407-846-6257
Fax: 407-846-7902
Web Site: www.ocfta.com
Management:
    President: Carolyn Scott
    Executive Director: Cathy Machado
    Artistic Director: Phyllis Ross
Mission: To promote, cultivate and foster interest and participation in the arts by providing affordable and accessible programs and facilities that encourage artistc expression in the diverse community we serve.
Founded: 1963
Specialized Field: Visual Arts; Music; Craft; Local Art Council
Status: Non-Profit, Non-Professional
Paid Staff: 6
Volunteer Staff: 150
Paid Artists: 240
Non-paid Artists: 125
Budget: $580,000
Performs At: Theatre; Tours
Affiliations: Artexhibits
Facility Category: Art Center
Seating Capacity: 250
Year Built: 1913
Year Remodeled: 2002

6177
OSCELOA COUNTY STADIUM & SPORTS COMPLEX
1000 Bill Beck Boulevard
Kissimmee, FL 34744
Phone: 407-933-5400
Fax: 407-847-6237
Management:
    Director: Don Miers
Mission: Florida home of the Houston Astros.
Seating Capacity: 5,200

6178
WALT DISNEY WIDE WORLD OF SPORTS STADIUM
700 Victory Way
Lake Buena Vista, FL 34747-1000
Phone: 407-939-7810
Fax: 407-363-7000
e-mail: wdw.disney.sports.travel@disney.com
Web Site: www.disneyworldsports.com
Management:
    President: Al Weiss
    Vice President Walt Disney Sports: Reggie Williams
    Director/Event Programming: Mike Millay
    Manager Sports Programming: John Bisignano
    CEO: Michael Eisner
Founded: 1998
Status: For-Profit, Professional

6179
DUNCAN THEATRE
Palm Beach Community College
4200 S Congress Avenue MS #62
Lake Worth, FL 33461
Phone: 561-868-3309
Fax: 561-868-3317
Web Site: www.pbcc.edu/duncan
Management:
    Theatre Manager: Mark Alexander
    Administrative Assistant: Jamie Ziegele
Founded: 1986
Status: Non-Profit/Professional/Collegiate
Paid Staff: 6
Type of Stage: Proscenium

Seating Capacity: 720

6180
BRANSCOMB MEMORIAL AUDITORIUM
Florida Southern College
111 Lake Hollingsworth Drive
Lakeland, FL 33801
Phone: 863-680-4296
Fax: 813-680-3758
Toll-free: 800-274-4131
Web Site: www.flsouthern.edu
Management:
    President: Anne Kerr
    Executive Director: Anthony Harris
    Artistic Director: Robert MacDonald
Founded: 1959
Status: Non-Profit
Paid Staff: 4
Annual Attendance: 2,000
Type of Stage: Proscenium
Seating Capacity: 1,700

6181
BUCKNER THEATRE
Florida Southern College
111 Lake Hollings Worth Drive
Lakeland, FL 33801
Phone: 863-680-4296
Fax: 863-680-4120
Web Site: www.flsouthern.edu
Management:
    Office Manager: Kity Oelker
    Department Chair: James Beck
    Costumer/Faculty: Mary Albright
Status: Student Theater
Paid Staff: 3
Budget: $30,000
Income Sources: College/Academic Budget
Affiliations: Florida Southern College
Facility Category: Line Theatre Production
Year Built: 1971
Year Remodeled: 2000

6182
LAKELAND CENTER
Lakeland Center
701 W Lime Street
Lakeland, FL 33815-4534
Phone: 863-834-8100
Fax: 863-834-8101
e-mail: allen.johnson@lakelandgov.net
Web Site: www.thelakelandcenter.com
Management:
    Executive Director: Allen Johnson
    Operations Manager: Tony Postiglion
Founded: 1880
Seating Capacity: 10,000

6183
KING CENTER FOR THE PERFORMING ARTS
Brevard Community College
3865 N Wickham Road
Melbourne, FL 32935
Phone: 321-433-5719
Fax: 321-433-5817
e-mail: sjanicki@kingcenter.com
Web Site: www.kingcenter.com
Management:
    Executive Director: Steven G Janicki
Founded: 1988
Paid Staff: 10
Volunteer Staff: 400
Type of Stage: Proscenium

Seating Capacity: 2,001

6184
MELBOURNE AUDITORIUM
625 Hibiscus Boulevard
Melbourne, FL 32901
Phone: 321-674-5700
Fax: 321-953-6287
e-mail: auditorium@melbourneflorida.org
Web Site: www.melbourneflorida.org
Management:
    Manager: Ron Hayes
Founded: 1964
Specialized Field: Civic Events; Dance; Instrumental
Music; Musical Theatre; Theatrical Group; Vocal Music
Status: Non-Profit
Paid Staff: 12

6185
AMERICAN AIRLINES ARENA
601 Biscayne Boulevard
Miami, FL 33132
Phone: 786-777-1000
Fax: 786-777-4080
e-mail: guestservices@heat.com
Web Site: www.aaarena.com
Management:
    President: Pat Riley
    President Bus Operations: Eric S Woolworth
    General Manager: Alex M Diaz
Founded: 1999
Status: For-Profit, Professional
Paid Staff: 250
Paid Artists: 20
Seating Capacity: 20,000

6186
DADE COUNTY AUDITORIUM
2901 West Flagler Street
Miami, FL 33135
Phone: 305-547-5414
Fax: 305-541-7782
Web Site: www.orlando@miamidade.gov
Management:
    General Manager: Orlando Castellano
    Asst. General Manager: Patricia Arbeluez
Founded: 1951
Paid Staff: 11
Budget: $1,000,000
Performs At: Performing Arts Theatre
Affiliations: IAAM; FPPC
Annual Attendance: 125,000
Facility Category: Fixed Seat Theatre
Type of Stage: Proscenium
Stage Dimensions: 60'X40'
Seating Capacity: 2,372
Year Built: 1951
Year Remodeled: 2009

6187
GOLDEN PANTHER SPORTSPLEX
Florida International University
Room 255 University Park
Miami, FL 33199
Mailing Address: Florida International University,
Golden Panther SportsPlex
Phone: 305-348-2756
Fax: 305-348-2963
Web Site: http://www.fiu.edu/
Management:
    Athletic Director: Jose Sotolongo

6188
GUSMAN CENTER FOR THE PERFORMING ARTS
174 E Flagler Street
Miami, FL 33131
Phone: 305-374-2444
Fax: 305-374-0303
e-mail: mwharton@gusmancenter.org
Web Site: www.gusmancenter.org
Management:
    Executive Director: Mike Warren
    Artistic Director: Jerry Kinsey
Founded: 1970
Specialized Field: Series and Festivals; Dance;
Instrumental Music; Musical Theatre; Theatrical Group;
Vocal Music
Status: For-Profit, Professional
Paid Staff: 5
Seating Capacity: 1,700

6189
JAMES L KNIGHT CENTER
400 SE Second Avenue
Miami, FL 33131
Phone: 305-372-4633
Fax: 305-350-7910
e-mail: info@jlknightcenter.com
Web Site: jlknightcenter.com
Founded: 1982
Specialized Field: Music; Theatre; Dance

6190
MIAMI ARENA
701 Arena Boulevard
Suite 415
Miami, FL 33136
Mailing Address: DEMOLISHED IN 2008
Phone: 305-530-4400
Fax: 305-530-4429
Web Site: www.miamiarena.com
Management:
    President: Jim Jenkins
    Assistant Director Entertainment: Brenda Carter
Founded: 1989
Specialized Field: Concerts; Family Shows;
Exhibitions
Status: Non-Profit, Professional
Paid Staff: 30
Facility Category: Arena
Seating Capacity: 15,500
Year Built: 1986
Rental Contact: Mike Carr

6191
ORANGE BOWL STADIUM
1501 NW 3rd Street
Suite 415
Miami, FL 33125
Phone: 305-643-7100
Fax: 305-643-7115
Web Site: www.orangebowlstadium.com
Management:
    President: Ileana Gomez
Founded: 1937
Specialized Field: Bowling; Sports
Status: Professional
Seating Capacity: 82,000

6192
PERFORMING ARTS CENTER OF GREATER MIAMI FOUNDATION
1300 Biscayne Boulevard
Miami, FL 33132

Phone: 786-468-2000
Fax: 786-468-2001
e-mail: info@carnivalcenter.org
Web Site: www.pacfmiami.org
Officers:
    Executive Director/CEO: Tom Tomlinson
Management:
    President/CEO: Michael C Hardy
    Chief Of Staff: Valerie Riles-Robinson
Status: Non-Profit, Non-Professional
Paid Staff: 8

6193
JACKIE GLEASON THEATER
1700 Washington Avenue
Miami Beach, FL 33139
Phone: 305-673-7300
Fax: 305-588-6810
Web Site: www.gleasontheater.com
Management:
    Managing Director: Mitchell Morales
Founded: 1950
Status: For-Profit, Professional
Paid Staff: 20
Annual Attendance: 185,000
Type of Stage: Proscenium
Seating Capacity: 2,705

6194
MOBILE CIVIC CENTER - EXPOSITION HALL
401 Civic Center Drive
Mobile, FL 33602
Mailing Address: 401 Civic Center Drive, Mobile, AL
36602-0204
Phone: 251-208-7261
Fax: 334-208-7551
e-mail: mlmccrory@mobilecivicctr.com
Web Site: www.mobilecivicctr.com
Management:
    Marketing Manager: Mary Lee McCrory
Mission: Expo Hall is the Mobile Civic Center's
multi-use facility. The portable stage and public address
system, along with retractable seating, allow for
maximum flexibility in event planning. Expo Hall is the
perfect venue for exhibits, conventions, dances and
sporting events.
Specialized Field: exhibits, conventions, dances and
sporting events
Type of Stage: Concert Stage; Portable
Seating Capacity: 3,000

6195
MOBILE CIVIC CENTER - THEATRE
401 Civic Center Drive
Mobile, FL 33602
Mailing Address: 401 Civic Center Drive, Mobile, AL
36602-0204
Phone: 251-208-7261
Fax: 334-208-7551
e-mail: mlmccrory@mobilecivicctr.com
Web Site: www.mobilecivicctr.com
Management:
    Marketing Manager: Mary Lee McCrory
Mission: Mobile Civic Center Theater is a comfortably
elegant location for performances ranging from solo
artists to symphony orchestras.
Specialized Field: Concerts
Seating Capacity: 1,940

6196
MONTICELLO OPERA HOUSE
Courthouse Square
PO Box 518
Monticello, FL 32345
Phone: 904-997-4242
Fax: 904-997-7142
e-mail: moperahouse@juno.com

6197
PHILHARMONIC CENTER FOR THE ARTS
5833 Pelican Bay Boulevard
Naples, FL 34108
Phone: 239-597-1900
Fax: 239-597-7856
Toll-free: 800-597-1900
e-mail: info@thephil.org
Web Site: www.thephil.org
Officers:
President/CEO: Myra Janco Daniels
Mission: To enlighten, educate and entertain people of alla ges and backgrounds in Southwest Florida by presenting the very best of the visual and performing arts.
Founded: 1989
Opened: 1989
Seating Capacity: 1,421

6198
CENTER FOR THE ARTS AT RIVER RIDGE
11646 Town Center Road
New Port Richey, FL 34654
Phone: 727-774-7382
Fax: 727-774-7389
Performs At: Auditorium

6199
ATLANTIC CENTER FOR THE ARTS
1414 Art Center Avenue
New Smyrna Beach, FL 32168
Phone: 386-427-6975
Toll-free: 800-393-6975
e-mail: program@atlanticcenterforthearts.org
Web Site: www.atlanticcenterforthearts.org
Management:
Executive Director: Ann Brady
Program Manager: Nicholas Conroy
Program/Marketing Manager: Jim Frost
Utilizes: Artists-in-Residence; Choreographers; Collaborations; Filmmakers; Fine Artists; Guest Artists; Guest Companies; Multi Collaborations; Playwrights; Touring Companies
Founded: 1977
Specialized Field: Florida; National; All disciplines
Status: Non-Profit, Professional
Paid Staff: 14
Volunteer Staff: 15
Budget: $1 million
Income Sources: Grants; Donations; Fundraisers
Annual Attendance: 250
Facility Category: 5 studios
Type of Stage: Black Box
Year Built: 1996
Rental Contact: Frankie Robert

6200
ARTS CENTER
Okaloosa Walton College
100 College Boulevard
Niceville, FL 32578
Phone: 850-678-5111
Fax: 850-729-5286
Toll-free: 888-838-2787
Web Site: www.owc.edu/arts
Management:
Executive Director: Clifford Herron

6201
LEE CIVIC CENTER ARENA
11831 Bayshore Road
North Fort Myers, FL 33917
Phone: 239-543-8368
Fax: 239-543-4110
Web Site: www.leeciviccenter.com
Management:
General Manager: Alta Mosley
Operations Manager: Simon Train
Seating Capacity: 7,800

6202
LEE CIVIC CENTER - SMALL THEATER
11831 Bayshore Road
North Fort Myers, FL 33917
Phone: 239-543-8368
Fax: 239-543-4110
Web Site: www.leeciviccenter.com
Seating Capacity: 7,800

6203
VICTORY PARK AUDITORIUM
17011 NE 19th Avenue
North Miami Beach, FL 33162
Phone: 305-948-2957
Fax: 305-787-6037

6204
BLACK BOX
University of Central Florida
UCF Conservatory Theatre, UCF Campus
4000 Central Florida Blvd.
Orlando, FL 32826
Phone: 407-823-2862
Web Site: http://www.cas.ucf.edu/theatre
Officers:
Interim Chair: Diane Chase
Interim Associate Chair: Joseph Rosnock
Management:
Interim Artistic Director: Kate Ingram
Mission: The UCF Conservatory Theatre seeks to develop theatre artists of the highest quality. We provide our students with the training, education, and experiences necessary for the successful pursuit of professional theatre careers
Specialized Field: Theatre
Type of Stage: Black Box
Seating Capacity: 200

6205
BLACK BOX THEATER
Valencia Community College
East Campus, 701 North Econlockhatchee Trail
Orlando, FL 32825
Mailing Address: P.O. BOX 3028, Orlando, Florida 32802-3028
Phone: 407-299-5000
Fax: 407-277-0621
Web Site: www.valenciacc.edu

6206
BOB CARR PERFORMING ARTS CENTER
600 West Amelia Street
Orlando, FL 32801-1113
Phone: 407-849-2577
Fax: 407-849-2329
e-mail: sharon.clayton@cityoforlando.net
Web Site: www.orlandocentroplex.com
Management:
Director: Allan Johnson
Deputy Director: Jon Dorman
Box Office Manager: Sharon Clayton
Advertising/Promotions Manager: Tanya Bowley
Mission: This fully functional theatre/concert hall features continental style seating for 2518. It's acoustics and sound capabilities make it ideal for concerts, Broadway presentations, the Symphony, Ballet and Opera as well as a business conference or general session.
Founded: 1926
Status: For-Profit, Non-Professional
Paid Staff: 6
Type of Stage: Proscenium

6207
MAIN STAGE
University of Central Florida
UCF Conservatory Theatre, UCF Campus
4000 Central Florida Blvd.
Orlando, FL 32826
Phone: 407-823-2862
Web Site: http://www.cas.ucf.edu/theatre
Officers:
Interim Chair: Diane Chase
Interim Associate Chair: Joseph Rosnock
Management:
Interim Artistic Director: Kate Ingram
Mission: The UCF Conservatory Theatre seeks to develop theatre artists of the highest quality. We provide our students with the training, education, and experiences necessary for the successful pursuit of professional theatre careers
Specialized Field: Theatre
Type of Stage: Proscenium
Orchestra Pit: y

6208
ORANGE COUNTY CONVENTION CENTER
PO Box 691509
Orlando, FL 32869-1509
Phone: 407-685-9800
Toll-free: 800-345-9845
e-mail: info@occc.net
Web Site: www.occc.net
Management:
Executive Director: Thomas Ackert
General Manager: Jessie Allen
Utilizes: New Productions
Founded: 1996
Status: For-Profit, Professional
Income Sources: Conventions, Tradeshows, Seminars/Workshops, Tourist Development Tax
Affiliations: Orange County Government
Facility Category: Performance Auditorium
Type of Stage: Performance Stage with Dock Access
Stage Dimensions: 26'x145'5"x49'6"
Seating Capacity: 2,643
Year Built: 1983
Year Remodeled: 1996
Rental Contact: Sales Assistant Willie Nelson

6209
ORLANDO CENTROPLEX
600 W Amelia Street
Orlando, FL 32801

Phone: 407-849-2000
Fax: 407-849-2329
Web Site: www.orlandocentroplex.com
Management:
    Director: Allan Johnson
    Deputy Director: Bill Becker
    Events Manager: Michael Thompson
    Convention Sales/Booking: Robin R Handlan
Status: For-Profit, Non-Professional
Seating Capacity: 17,500
Year Built: 1989

6210
AMWAY ARENA
Orlando Centroplex
600 W Amelia Street
Orlando, FL 32801
Mailing Address: CLOSED SEPTEMBER 30, 2010
Phone: 407-849-2000
Fax: 407-849-2329
Web Site: www.orlandocentroplex.com
Management:
    Director: Allen Johnson
    Concessions Manager: Jim Breig
    Deputy Director: Jon Dorman
    Business Manager: Cindy Mitchum
Founded: 1989
Status: For-Profit, Professional
Paid Staff: 60
Seating Capacity: 17,320

6211
UCF ARENA
Building 50 North Gemini Boulevard
PO Box 161500
Orlando, FL 32816
Mailing Address: PO Box 161500
Phone: 407-823-3070
Fax: 407-823-0248
Web Site: www.ucfarena.com
Management:
    General Manager: Lexie Boone
    Director Of Marketing: Melissa Schaaf
Founded: 1991
Status: For-Profit, Non-Professional
Seating Capacity: 10,000
Year Built: 2007

6212
UNIVERSITY THEATRE
University of Central Florida
UCF Conservatory Theatre, UCF Campus
4000 Central Florida Blvd.
Orlando, FL 32826
Phone: 407-823-2862
Web Site: http://www.cas.ucf.edu/theatre
Officers:
    Interim Chair: Diane Chase
    Interim Associate Chair: Joseph Rosnock
Management:
    Interim Artistic Director: Kate Ingram
    Manager: Meredith Beaupre
Mission: The UCF Conservatory Theatre seeks to
develop theatre artists of the highest quality. We provide
our students with the training, education, and
experiences necessary for the successful pursuit of
professional theatre careers
Specialized Field: Musical Concerts
Type of Stage: Concert
Seating Capacity: 867
Year Built: 1920

6213
VALENCIA COMMUNITY COLLEGE PERFORMING ARTS CENTER
PO Box 3028
Orlando, FL 32802
Mailing Address: P.O. BOX 3028, Orlando, Florida
32802-3028
Phone: 407-299-5000
Fax: 407-277-0621
e-mail: alapietra@valenciacc.edu
Web Site: www.valenciacc.edu
Management:
    Chair of Performing Arts: Ann Stichler
Founded: 1967

6214
FLAGLER AUDITORIUM
5500 E Highway 100
Palm Coast, FL 32164
Phone: 386-437-7547
Fax: 386-437-7551
Toll-free: 866-352-4537
e-mail: flaglerpromotion@aol.com
Web Site: www.flaglerauditorium.org
Officers:
    President: Jack Marcussen
    President Elect: Charles Ebel
    Vice President: Joel Schwalb
    Secretary: Sandra Madden
    Treasurer: Beverly Alleman
Management:
    Executive Director: Lisa McDevitt
Mission: Provide a favorable, healthy climate for the
simulation, promotion and growth of culture and the
arts.
Founded: 1989
Status: Non-Profit, Professional
Paid Staff: 6
Type of Stage: Concert Stage
Seating Capacity: 1,000

6215
MARINA CIVIC CENTER
8 Harrison Avenue
Panama City, FL 32401
Phone: 850-763-4696
Fax: 850-785-5165
Web Site: www.marinaciviccenter.com
Management:
    General Manager/Booking: Chris Cockrill
    Executive Director: Jennifer Jones
    House Manager: Carol Cheshire
    Technical Director: Shawn Perry
    Executive Assistant: Joy Adama
Seating Capacity: 2,500

6216
PENSACOLA CIVIC CENTER
201 East Gregory Street
Pensacola, FL 32502
Phone: 850-432-0800
Fax: 850-432-1707
e-mail: webmaster@pensacolaciviccenter.com
Web Site: www.pensacolaciviccenter.com
Management:
    Event Services Director: Cyndee Pennington
Founded: 1985
Paid Staff: 219
Facility Category: Arena
Seating Capacity: 10,000

6217
PENSACOLA JUNIOR COLLEGE PERFORMING ARTS CENTER
Music and Drama Department
1000 College Boulevard
Pensacola, FL 32504
Phone: 850-484-1800
Fax: 850-484-1835
Toll-free: 888-897-3605
e-mail: dsnowden@pjc.edu
Web Site: www.pjc.edu
Management:
    President: Tom Delaino
    Executive Director: Stan Dean
Founded: 1958
Status: Non-Profit, Non-Professional
Paid Staff: 35
Performs At: Ashmore Fine Arts Auditorium
Annual Attendance: 7,000
Type of Stage: Proscenium
Seating Capacity: 314
Year Built: 1990

6218
SAENGER THEATRE
118 S Palafox Place
Pensacola, FL 32501
Phone: 850-444-7699
Fax: 850-444-7684
Web Site: www.pensacolasaenger.com
Management:
    Executive Director: Doug Lee
Utilizes: Dance Companies; Multimedia; Original Music
Scores; Theatre Companies
Founded: 1925
Annual Attendance: 150,000
Facility Category: performing arts theatre
Type of Stage: Proscenium
Seating Capacity: 1,802
Year Built: 1925
Year Remodeled: 1981
Rental Contact: Douglas Lee

6219
UNIVERSITY OF WEST FLORIDA CENTER FOR FINE & PERFORMING ARTS
Art, Music, and Theatre Departments
11000 University Parkway, Building 82
Pensacola, FL 32514
Phone: 850-474-2147
Fax: 850-474-3247
e-mail: kmarrero@uwf.edu
Web Site: www.uwf.edu/cfpa
Officers:
    Vice President: Dr. Kyle Marrero
Management:
    Asst. Dir for Fine/Performing Arts: Jerre Brisky
Mission: To support and educate the students and the
community.
Utilizes: Actors; Designers; Educators; Fine Artists;
Guest Conductors; Guest Ensembles; Guest Soloists;
High School Drama; Multi Collaborations; Multimedia;
Music; Resident Professionals; Sign Language
Translators; Singers; Soloists; Student Interns; Special
Technical Talent; Touring Companies
Founded: 1970
Status: Non-Profit, Professional
Paid Staff: 3
Volunteer Staff: 10
Paid Artists: 5
Budget: $40,000

Income Sources: SGA Funds; State and Private Donations; Black Box Theatre
Performs At: Music Hall; Concert Hall
Annual Attendance: 33,000
Facility Category: Performance
Type of Stage: Proscenium; Black Box
Seating Capacity: 309
Year Built: 1992
Rental Contact: Asst. Director Fine/Performing Arts Jerre Brisky
Organization Type: Education

6220
CHARLOTTE HARBOR EVENT AND CONFERENCE CENTER
75 Taylor Street
Punta Gorda, FL 33950
Phone: 941-833-5444
Fax: 941-833-5451
Toll-free: 800-329-9988
e-mail: amy.issersohn@charlottefl.com
Web Site: www.charlotteharborecc.com
Seating Capacity: 2,000
Year Built: 2009
Rental Contact: Sales Manager Amy Issersohn
Organization Type: a Multipurpose 19,000 Sq Ft Ballroom with full rigging, lighting and multiple staging configurations. 18,000 Sq Ft Great Lawn with full performance capabilities along the waters edge.

6221
SEMINOLE COUNTY SPORTS TRAINING CENTER
1101 E First Street
Sanford, FL 32771
Phone: 407-869-5966
Fax: 407-324-4317
Web Site: www.co.seminole.fl.us
Management:
    Sports/Events Manager: John Giantonio

6222
ED SMITH STADIUM/ SPORTS COMPLEX
City of Sarasota
1565 1St Street
Sarasota, FL 34236
Phone: 941-954-4102
Fax: 941-365-1587
Web Site: www.sarasotagov.com
Management:
    Sports Facility Manager: Patrick M Calhoon
Founded: 1839

6223
FLORIDA STUDIO THEATRE
1241 N Palm Avenue
Sarasota, FL 34236
Phone: 941-366-9017
Fax: 941-955-4137
Web Site: www.fst2000.org
Management:
    Casting and Literary Coordinator: James Ashford
Founded: 1973
Paid Staff: 40
Volunteer Staff: 100
Paid Artists: 70

6224
PLAYERS THEATRE
838 North Tamiami Trail
Sarasota, FL 34236

Phone: 941-365-2494
Fax: 941-954-0282
e-mail: info@theplayers.org
Web Site: www.theplayers.org
Officers:
    President: Ken Shelin
    Vice President: Barbara Johnson
    Treasurer: Michael G Brown
Management:
    Managing Director: Michelle Bianchi Pingel
Founded: 1930
Status: Non-Profit, Non-Professional
Paid Staff: 7
Volunteer Staff: 700
Budget: $1.2 Million
Income Sources: Earned Income; Donations
Performs At: Community Theatre
Annual Attendance: 65,000
Type of Stage: Proscenium
Seating Capacity: 497
Year Built: 1970

6225
VAN WEZEL PERFORMING ARTS HALL
777 N Tamiami Trail
Sarasota, FL 34236
Phone: 941-955-7676
Fax: 941-951-1449
Toll-free: 800-826-9303
Web Site: www.vanwezel.org
Management:
    Executive Director: Mary Bensel
    Marketing Director: Julia Mays
    Events Coordinator: Charmaine McVicker
    Technical Director: Stephen Brown
    Education Director: Robert Warren
    General Manager/Box Office Manager: Loreda Williams
    Business Manager: Anthony Becich
Mission: Present a broad spectrum of the world's finest artists, educational outreach programs for the community and provide a quality home for the other local groups.
Utilizes: AEA Actors; Dance Companies; Dancers; Guest Accompanists; Guest Choreographers; Guest Ensembles; Guest Musicians; Multimedia; Original Music Scores; Singers; Special Technical Talent; Theatre Companies
Founded: 1970
Specialized Field: Theatre; Dance; Music; Education; Comedy
Status: Non-Profit, Professional
Paid Staff: 100
Volunteer Staff: 300
Paid Artists: 500
Budget: $9,000,000
Income Sources: Ticket Sales; Grants; Donations, Sponsorships; Food & Beverage rentals
Performs At: Performing Arts Hall
Affiliations: Broadway League, Florida Facilities Managers, City of Sarasota, Fla Presents
Annual Attendance: 200,000
Facility Category: Performing Arts Hall
Type of Stage: Proscenium
Stage Dimensions: 60' wide x 30' high x 49' deep
Seating Capacity: 1709
Year Built: 1969
Year Remodeled: 2000
Rental Contact: Charmaine McVicker

6226
SPRINGSTEAD THEATRE
3300 Mariner Boulevard
Spring Hill, FL 34609

Phone: 352-797-7010
Fax: 352-797-7110
Web Site: www.springsteadtheatre.com
Management:
    President: Mark Pennington
Founded: 1976
Status: Non-Profit, Non-Professional
Paid Staff: 2

6227
TIMES/MAHAFFEY THEATRE FOR THE PERFORMING ARTS
400 1st Street S
St Petersburg, FL 33701
Phone: 727-893-7111
Fax: 727-892-5858
e-mail: lauren.kleinfeld@stpete.org
Web Site: www.stpete.org/venues.htm
Management:
    Director Facilities: Michael R Barber
    Booking/Marketing Manager: Lauren Kleinfeld
Facility Category: Theatre/Arena

6228
TROPICANA FIELD
One Tropicana Drive
St Petersburg, FL 33705
Phone: 888-326-7297
Fax: 727-825-3167
e-mail: dugout1@verizon.net
Web Site: www.devilrays.com
Management:
    VP Operations/Facilities: Rick Nafe
    Event Manager: Rick Nafe
    VP Sales/Marketing: John Brown
Seating Capacity: 45,200

6229
MAINSTAGE THEATRE
Flagler College
Theatre Department
P.O.Box 1027
St. Augustine, FL 32085-1027
Phone: 904-819-6217
Fax: 904-826-0094
e-mail: theatredept@flagler.edu
Web Site: http://www.flagler.edu
Management:
    Chair/Associate Professor: Phyllis Gibbs
    Assistant Professor: Andrea McCook
    Technical Director: Britton Corry
Mission: Flagler College's Theatre Arts Department educates students as theatre generalists in the areas of performance, technology, design, literature, history, management and directing.
Specialized Field: Theatre

6230
RAHNER-GIBBS SECOND STAGE THEATRE
Flagler College
Flagler College Auditorium
14 Granada Street
St. Augustine, FL 32085-1027
Phone: 904-819-6217
Fax: 904-826-0094
e-mail: theatredept@flagler.edu
Web Site: http://www.flagler.edu
Management:
    Chair/Associate Professor: Phyllis Gibbs
    Assistant Professor: Andrea McCook
    Technical Director: Britton Corry

Mission: Flagler College's Theatre Arts Department educates students as theatre generalists in the areas of performance, technology, design, literature, history, management and directing.
Specialized Field: Theatre

6231
STUDIO THEATER
Eckerd College
4200 54th Avenue South
St. Petersburg, FL 33711
Mailing Address: Eckerd College, 4200 54th Avenue South, St. Petersburg, Flor
Phone: 727-867-1166
Toll-free: 800-456-9009
Web Site: http://www.eckerd.edu/academics/theatre/
Officers:
    President: Donald R. Eastman, III
Management:
    Professor Theater: Cynthia Totten
    Theater Coordinator: Eric Haak
Mission: Theatre at Eckerd is designed to prepare students for the 'real world' of professional theatre, and the varied demands of the global workplace.
Specialized Field: Theatre
Type of Stage: Flexible Black Box
Seating Capacity: 50-80

6232
BININGER THEATRE
Eckerd College
4200 54th Avenue South
St. Petersburg, FL 33711
Mailing Address: Eckerd College, 4200 54th Avenue South, St. Petersburg, Flor
Phone: 727-867-1166
Toll-free: 800-456-9009
Web Site: http://www.eckerd.edu/academics/theatre/
Officers:
    President: Donald R. Eastman, III
Management:
    Professor Theater: Cynthia Totten
    Theater Coordinator: Eric Haak
Mission: Theatre at Eckerd is designed to prepare students for the 'real world' of professional theatre, and the varied demands of the global workplace.
Specialized Field: Theatre
Type of Stage: Proscenium/Thrust
Seating Capacity: 350

6233
KINGS POINT THEATRE AT THE CLUBHOUSE
1900 Clubhouse Drive
Sun City Center, FL 33573
Phone: 813-634-9229
Fax: 813-633-3759
Management:
    Entertainment Director: Marvin Donner
Specialized Field: Theater

6234
CENTER THEATER COMPANY OF TAMPA BAY
1010 N W.C. MacInnes Place
Tampa, FL 33602
Phone: 813-222-1000
Fax: 813-222-1057
e-mail: rick.criswell@tbpac.org
Management:
    Production Stage Manager: Rick Criswell

Utilizes: Actors; AEA Actors; Artists-in-Residence; Choreographers; Collaborations; Commissioned Composers; Dancers; Designers; Educators; Five Seasonal Concerts; Guest Accompanists; Guest Artists; Guest Companies; Guest Composers; Guest Conductors; Guest Designers; Guest Ensembles; Guest Lecturers; Guest Musical Directors; Guest Musicians; Guest Soloists; Guest Teachers; Instructors; Local Artists; Multi Collaborations; Multimedia; New Productions; Organization Contracts; Original Music Scores; Poets; Resident Companies; Selected Students; Sign Language Translators; Soloists; Student Interns; Special Technical Talent; Touring Companies; Visual Arts
Founded: 1995
Specialized Field: Performing Arts Complex
Status: Nonprofit
Type of Stage: Thrust
Stage Dimensions: 40' x 24'
Seating Capacity: 300
Rental Contact: Bobbi Warnick

6235
TAMPA BAY PERFORMING ARTS CENTER
1010 North Macinnes Place
PO Box 518
Tampa, FL 33602
Phone: 813-229-7827
Fax: 813-222-1057
Toll-free: 800-955-1045
Web Site: www.tbpac.org
Management:
    President: Judith Lisi
    Executive Vice President: Lorrin Shepard
    Programming Director: Judy Joseph
    Vice President Marketing: Michael Kilgore
    Director Ticketing: Tonyh Walters
Seating Capacity: 2,550

6236
TAMPA THEATRE
711 Franklin Street
PO Box 172188
Tampa, FL 33602
Phone: 813-274-8286
Fax: 813-274-8978
e-mail: john@tampatheatre.org
Web Site: www.tampatheatre.org
Management:
    Director: John C Bell
    House Manager: Mitchell Martin
    Box Office Manager: Cathy Prance
    Stage Manager: Gary Ratliff
Founded: 1976
Seating Capacity: 1,446

6237
USF SPECIAL EVENTS CENTER
University of South Florida
4202 East Fowler Avenue
Tampa, FL 33620
Phone: 813-574-5538
Fax: 813-574-5466
e-mail: kriegler@admin.usf.edu
Web Site: www.ctr.usf.edu/cab
Officers:
    Program Coordinator: Keri Kriegler
    Reservations: Greg Jackson
Seating Capacity: 1,950

6238
USF SUN DOME
University Of South Florida
4202 East Fowler Avenue
Tampa, FL 33620
Phone: 813-974-3111
Fax: 813-974-3813
e-mail: receptionist@sundome.org
Web Site: www.sundome.org
Officers:
    Director: Scott Glaser
Management:
    Director, Event Services: Seth Benalt
    Facilities Director: Chris Paras
Founded: 1980
Opened: 1981
Paid Staff: 30
Facility Category: Arena
Seating Capacity: 11,324
Year Built: 1980
Rental Contact: Director Event Services Seth Benalt

6239
RIVERSIDE THEATRE
3250 Riverside Park Drive
Vero Beach, FL 32963
Phone: 772-231-5860
Fax: 772-234-5298
Toll-free: 800-445-6745
e-mail: info@riversidetheatre.com
Web Site: www.riversidetheatre.com
Officers:
    President: Thomas Slaughter
    Vice President: Gay Bain
    Vice President: David Baldwin
    Secretary: Richard Stark
    Treasurer: Fred Wonham
Management:
    Producing Artistic Director: Allen D Cornell
    Managing Director: Jon R Moses
    Education Director: Linda Downey
Mission: Riverside Theatre is committed to providing a total theatre arts experience that entertains, challenges, and educates both adults and children.
Utilizes: AEA Actors; Arrangers; Choreographers; Collaborating Artists; Composers; Contract Actors; Designers; Equity Actors; Guest Accompanists; Guest Artists; Guest Companies; Guest Conductors; Guest Designers; Guest Instructors; Guest Lecturers; Guest Musical Directors; Guest Musicians; Guest Soloists; Guest Speakers; High School Drama; Local Artists; Local Artists & Directors; Multi Collaborations; Multimedia; Music; New Productions; Original Music Scores; Resident Professionals; Sign Language Translators; Soloists; Students; Student Interns; Visual Arts
Founded: 1973
Status: Non-Profit, Professional
Paid Staff: 75
Volunteer Staff: 600
Paid Artists: 135
Budget: $6,000,000
Income Sources: Corproate and Private Donations; Rentals; Grants; Fund-Raising Events; Ticket Sales
Season: October - May
Affiliations: Florida Professional Theatres Association; Florida Division of Cultural Affairs
Annual Attendance: 100,000
Type of Stage: Proscenium
Seating Capacity: 672 & 250 (2 stages)
Year Built: 1973
Year Remodeled: 2007
Cost: $20 Million

Rental Contact: Jon R Moses
Organization Type: Professional; Regional producing
Theatre that occasionally serving as a presenter
Resident Groups: The Acting Company

6240
VERO BEACH CONCERT ASSOCIATION
PO Box 4024
Vero Beach, FL 32964
Phone: 561-231-6990
Fax: 561-231-2186
e-mail: CWITTEN@SUNET.com
Officers:
   President: Cora Witten

6241
KRAVIS CENTER FOR THE PERFORMING ARTS
701 Okeechobee Boulevard
West Palm Beach, FL 33401-6323
Phone: 561-833-8300
Fax: 561-833-3901
Toll-free: 800-572-8471
e-mail: kravis@kravis.org
Web Site: www.kravis.org
Officers:
   CEO: Judith Mitchell
   CFO: Kyle Roberts
Founded: 1994
Paid Staff: 75
Volunteer Staff: 800
Annual Attendance: 500,000
Facility Category: Performing Arts Center
Type of Stage: Proscenium
Seating Capacity: 2,200
Year Built: 1992
Cost: $68 million
Rental Contact: Shirnette Ball

6242
POMPANO BEACH AMPHITHEATRE
1801 North East 6th Street
West Palm Beach, FL 33060
Phone: 561-832-6397
Fax: 561-832-2043
e-mail: fantasma@fantasma.com
Web Site: www.fantasma.com
Management:
   Sponsorship: Randy Lvenla
   Marketing/Advisor: Rachel Schrift
   Box Office/Operations: Jason Morey
   Production: Brian Cutler
Seating Capacity: 3,000

6243
STEPHEN FOSTER STATE FOLK CULTURE CENTER
US 41 N
PO Drawer G
White Springs, FL 32096
Mailing Address: Stephen Foster State Folk Culture Center, Post Office Drawer
Phone: 904-397-2733
Fax: 904-397-4262
Web Site:
http://www.abfla.com/parks/StephenFoster/stephenfoster.html

6244
ANNIE RUSSELL THEATRE
Rollins College
Department Theatre and Dance
1000 Holt Avenue - 2735
Winter Park, FL 32789-4499
Phone: 407-646-2501
Fax: 407-646-2257
e-mail: jnassif@rollins.edu
Web Site: http://www.rollins.edu/theatre/
Management:
   Chair: Thomas Ouellette
Mission: The Rollins College Department of Theatre and Dance provides for the development of imaginative, purposeful, and skilled expression in the theatre, and for students' artistic, intellectual, and personal growth.
Utilizes: Actors; AEA Actors; Artists-in-Residence; Choreographers; Collaborating Artists; Commissioned Music; Dance Companies; Dancers; Designers; Educators; Guest Accompanists; Guest Artists; Guest Lecturers; Guest Soloists; High School Drama; Multimedia; Performance Artists; Poets; Resident Professionals; Sign Language Translators; Singers; Soloists; Visual Arts
Founded: 1932
Opened: 1932
Specialized Field: Comedy, Drama, Musicals
Income Sources: Ticket Sales; Donations
Season: August-April
Performs At: Theatre Stages/Dance Studios
Annual Attendance: 15,000
Type of Stage: Proscenium/Thrust
Seating Capacity: 377
Year Built: 1932
Year Remodeled: 1978
Cost: $1,000,000

6245
FRED STONE THEATRE
Rollins College
Department Theatre and Dance
Chase Ave. & Fairbanks Ave
Winter Park, FL 32789-4499
Phone: 407-646-2501
Fax: 407-646-2257
e-mail: jnassif@rollins.edu
Web Site: http://www.rollins.edu/theatre/
Management:
   Chair: Thomas Ouellette
Mission: The Rollins College Department of Theatre and Dance provides for the development of imaginative, purposeful, and skilled expression in the theatre, and for students' artistic, intellectual, and personal growth.
Utilizes: Actors; AEA Actors; Artists-in-Residence; Choreographers; Collaborating Artists; Commissioned Music; Dance Companies; Dancers; Designers; Educators; Guest Accompanists; Guest Artists; Guest Lecturers; Guest Soloists; High School Drama; Multimedia; Performance Artists; Poets; Resident Professionals; Sign Language Translators; Singers; Soloists; Visual Arts
Founded: 1932
Opened: 1932
Specialized Field: Comedy, Drama, Musicals
Income Sources: Ticket Sales; Donations
Season: August-April
Performs At: Theatre Stages/Dance Studios
Annual Attendance: 15,000
Type of Stage: Proscenium/Thrust
Seating Capacity: 377
Year Built: 1932
Year Remodeled: 1978
Cost: $1,000,000

6246
ALBANY JAMES H GRAY SR CIVIC CENTER
100 W Oglethorpe Boulevard
Albany, GA 31701
Phone: 912-430-5200
Fax: 912-430-5163
Web Site: www.albanyciviccenter.com
Management:
   Director: Matty B Goddar

6247
DEPARTMENT OF FINE ARTS ALBANY STATE UNIVERSITY PERFORMING ARTS CENTER
Albany State University
504 College Drive
Albany, GA 31705
Mailing Address: University at Albany, State University of New York, 1400 Was
Phone: 229-430-4849
Fax: 229-430-0425
e-mail: pferlo@albany.edu
Web Site: http://www.albany.edu/pac/
Officers:
   Chairman: Dr. Marcia Mitchell Hood
Management:
   Director: Patrick Ferlo
   Assistant Director: Kim Engel
Mission: To provide high quality academic and artistic education for the members of the ASU community. The department's mission is central to the University, because the arts are at the heart of intellectual, social and personal development and human interaction.
Founded: 1903
Specialized Field: theater, concerts
Status: Non-Profit, Professional
Paid Staff: 21
Paid Artists: 32
Performs At: Albany Municipal Auditorium

6248
HUGH MILLS MEMORIAL STADIUM
PO Box 1470
Albany, GA 31703
Phone: 912-431-3308
Fax: 912-431-3309
Management:
   Athletic Director: Frank Orgel
Founded: 1936

6249
THEATRE ALBANY
514 Pine Avenue
Albany, GA 31701
Mailing Address: PO Box 552 Albany, GA 31702
Phone: 229-439-7193
Web Site: www.theatrealbany.com
Management:
   Artistic Director: Mark Costello
   Technical Director: Steve Felmet
Mission: To expose young people to the art of live performance.
Founded: 1932
Seating Capacity: 314

6250
HUGH HODGSON CONCERT HALL
University of Georgia
230 River Road
Athens, GA 30602-7280

Mailing Address: 212 Performing Arts Center, UGA, Athens GA 30605
Phone: 706-542-1668
Toll-free: 888-289-8497
e-mail: ugaarts@uga.edu
Web Site: www.uga.edu/pac
Management:
    Interim Director: David Levenson
    Marketing Director: Bobby Tyler Jr.
Mission: The Performing Arts Center serves as a showcase for world-class performers and ensembles. It also provides a home for UGA's faculty and student performers.
Type of Stage: Concert Hall
Seating Capacity: 1,100

6251
RAMSEY CONCERT HALL

University of Georgia
230 River Road
Athens, GA 30602-7280
Mailing Address: 212 Performing Arts Center, UGA, Athens GA 30605
Phone: 706-542-1668
Toll-free: 888-289-8497
e-mail: ugaarts@uga.edu
Web Site: www.uga.edu/pac
Management:
    Interim Director: David Levenson
    Marketing Director: Bobby Tyler Jr.
Mission: The Performing Arts Center serves as a showcase for world-class performers and ensembles. It also provides a home for UGA's faculty and student performers.
Specialized Field: Solo Recitals, Chamber Music
Type of Stage: Concert Hall
Seating Capacity: 360

6252
SANFORD STADIUM

University of Georgia
110 Field Street
Athens, GA 30602
Mailing Address: 110 Field Street, Athens, GA 30602
Phone: 706-542-1231
Fax: 706-542-9388
Toll-free: 877-542-1231
Web Site: www.georgiadogs.com
Mission: To continue to be the world-famous home of the University of Georgia Bulldogs football team and to continue to rank in the top five in the country among on-campus stadium venues.
Founded: 1929
Seating Capacity: 86,117

6253
UNIVERSITY OF GEORGIA PERFORMING ARTS CENTER

230 River Road
Athens, GA 30602-7280
Phone: 706-542-1668
Fax: 706-542-8497
e-mail: ugaarts@uga.edu
Web Site: www.uga.edu/pac
Management:
    Interim Director: David Levenson
    Marketing Director: Bobby Tyler Jr.
Mission: The UGA Performing Arts Center serves as a showcase for world class performers and ensembles. It also provides a home for UGA's faculty and student performers.
Status: Non-Profit, Professional
Paid Staff: 10
Paid Artists: 30

Performs At: Hugh Hodgson Concert Hall; Ramsey Concert Hall; Fine Arts Theatre; UGA Chapel; Franklin College Chamber Music Series
Seating Capacity: 1100

6254
14TH STREET PLAYHOUSE

173 14th Street
Atlanta, GA 30309
Phone: 404-733-4754
e-mail: 14thplay@woodruffcenter.org
Web Site: www.14thstplayhouse.org
Management:
    Administrative Assistant: April Walace-Gibbs
Mission: A thriving three-theatre complex is open to performing artists work and corporate events alike.
Specialized Field: Performing Arts; Corporate Venues

6255
BOBBY DODD STADIUM AT GRANT FIELD

Georgia Institute Of Technology
142 North Avenue NW
Atlanta, GA 30313
Phone: 404-894-5447
e-mail: whogan@athletics.gatech.edu
Web Site: ramblinwreck.cstv.com
Management:
    Director Of Athletics: Dan Radakovich
    Public Relations: Wayne Hogan
Mission: Georgia Tech's storied football facility has been a cornerstone of college football for nearly a century. Cozily nestled among Atlanta's skyscrapers, Bobby Dodd Stadium at Historic Grant Field is easily one of the nation's most unique settings for college football.
Founded: 1913
Specialized Field: Concerts

6256
DELTA CLASSIC CHASTAIN PARK AMPHITHEATRE

4469 Stella Drive North West
Atlanta, GA 30342
Phone: 404-733-4900
Fax: 404-733-4999
e-mail: chastain-info@woodruffcenter.org
Web Site: www.classicchastain.com
Officers:
    Chairman: Ben F Johnson
    Vice Chairman: Clayton F Jackson
Mission: The venue's cozy confines create the perfect rendezvous for spreading out with friends and family, hanging out with a group of co-workers or members of a special group; entertaining clients; or getting away for a romantic idyll amid music and moonlight.
Founded: 1973
Seating Capacity: 6,900

6257
FERST CENTER FOR THE ARTS

Georgia Tech University
349 Ferst Drive NW
Atlanta, GA 30332-0468
Phone: 404-894-9600
Fax: 404-864-9864
e-mail: info@ferstcenter.org
Web Site: www.ferstcenter.gatech.edu
Management:
    Director: George Thompson
    Marketing Director: Stephanie Lee
    Event Manager: Chris Dreger

Mission: As a presenter, the Ferst Center for the Arts is dedicated to bringing to the Georgia Tech Campus world class performances and artist residency programs that will enhance the total learning experience of the Georgia Tech student body, serve as a bridge to the surrounding Atlanta community and engage artists in a way that is uniquely Georgia Tech.
Utilizes: Actors; Artists-in-Residence; Choreographers; Collaborating Artists; Dance Companies; Dancers; Designers; Educators; Guest Directors; Guest Instructors; Guest Soloists; Instructors; Multimedia; Original Music Scores; Resident Professionals; Soloists; Special Technical Talent
Founded: 1992
Performs At: 1,155 seat theatre
Annual Attendance: 60,000
Facility Category: Theatre & 2 galleries
Type of Stage: Proscenium
Stage Dimensions: 37x52
Seating Capacity: 1,155
Rental Contact: Tori Wallingford

6258
FOX THEATRE

660 Peachtree Street NE
Atlanta, GA 30308
Phone: 404-881-2100
Fax: 404-872-2972
e-mail: information@foxtheatre.org
Web Site: www.foxtheatre.org
Management:
    Publicity Manager: Deborah Garner
Mission: Known throughout the Southeast as the premier venue for musicals, plays, concerts and ballets.
Founded: 1928
Status: Non-Profit, Professional
Paid Staff: 100
Seating Capacity: 4,000

6259
GEORGIA DOME

One Georgia Dome Drive
Atlanta, GA 30313-1591
Phone: 404-223-4636
Fax: 404-223-4011
e-mail: info@gadome.com
Web Site: www.gadome.com
Management:
    Executive Director: Dan Graveline
    General Manager: Carl Adkins
    COO: Khalil Johnson
Mission: To constantly earn our reputation as one of the worlds finest convention, sports and entertainment venues.
Founded: 1992
Status: For-Profit, Professional
Paid Staff: 120
Seating Capacity: 71,500
Year Built: 1992

6260
OGLETHORPE UNIVERSITY THEATRE

Oglethorpe University
4484 Peachtree Road NE
Atlanta, GA 30319
Mailing Address: 4484 Peachtree Road NE, Atlanta, GA 30319
Phone: 404-261-1441
Toll-free: 800-428-4484
e-mail: vweiss@oglethorpe.edu
Web Site: www.oglethorpe.edu/arts/theatre
Officers:
    President: Lawrence Schall
Management:

Theatre Department Director: Deborah Merola
Director of Musical Activities: Dr W Irwin Ray Jr
Mission: Oglethorpe is committed to supporting the success of all students in a diverse community characterized by civility, caring, inquiry and tolerance.
Utilizes: Resident Artists
Opened: 1997
Specialized Field: Theatre
Type of Stage: Modified-Thrust
Seating Capacity: 511

6261
PHILIPS ARENA

1 Philips Drive
Atlanta, GA 30303
Phone: 404-878-3000
Toll-free: 800-326-4000
e-mail: philipsarena-questions@atlantaspirit.com
Web Site: www.philipsarena.com
Officers:
 President: Bob Williams
 Senior VP: Trey Feazell
Management:
 Production Coordinator: Catie Scott
Mission: To leave a lasting impression upon the public before, during and after the events hosted at the Arena.
Founded: 1999
Specialized Field: Arena
Seating Capacity: 20,000

6262
RIALTO CENTER FOR THE ARTS

Georgia State University
80 Forsyth Street NW
Atlanta, GA 30303
Mailing Address: PO Box 2627 Atlanta GA 30301-2627
Phone: 404-651-1234
Fax: 404-651-1332
e-mail: info@rialtocenter.org
Web Site: www.rialtocenter.org
Management:
 Marketing Manager: Kara Keene Cooper
 Assistant Director: Jennifer Moore
 Director: Leslie Gordon
Mission: To inspire, educate and entertain diverse audiences by presenting innovative and exceptional arts programming and cultivating community partnerships.
Founded: 1916
Status: Non-Profit, Professional

6263
SEVEN STAGES THEATRE

1105 Euclid Avenue
Atlanta, GA 30307
Mailing Address: 7 Stages Theatre, 1105 Euclid Avenue, Atlanta, GA, 30307
Phone: 404-523-7647
Web Site: www.7stages.org
Management:
 Artistic Director: Del Hamilton
 Producing Director: Faye Allen
Mission: devoted to engaging artists and audiences by focusing on the social, political, and spiritual values of contemporary culture. 7 Stages gives primary emphasis to international work and the support and development of new plays, new playwrights, and new methods of collaboration.
Specialized Field: Theater
Status: Non profit
Volunteer Staff: 2
Paid Artists: 65
Budget: $850,000

Income Sources: Theatre Communications Group; National Endowment for the Arts; Georgia Council of the Arts; City of Atlanta Bureau of Cultural Affairs; Trust for Mutual Understanding; AT&T
Affiliations: Theatre Communications Group; Atlanta Coalition for the Performing Arts
Annual Attendance: 15,000
Facility Category: 2 Performing Arts Theatres
Type of Stage: Black Boxes
Seating Capacity: 99; 202
Year Built: 1928
Year Remodeled: 1994
Architect: $1.6 million
Rental Contact: Del Hamilton

6264
THE BOISEFEUILLET JONES ATLANTA CIVIC CENTER

395 Piedmont Avenue
Atlanta, GA 30308
Phone: 404-523-6275
Fax: 404-525-4634
e-mail: information@atlantaciviccenter.com
Web Site: www.atlantaciviccenter.com
Management:
 Director: Ann Marie Moraitakis
 Event Coordinator: Joyce Whisenant
 Public Relations Manager: Keisha McCotry
Mission: The Atlanta Civic Center has played host to some of the worlds most highly anticipated productions. In 2001, the Atlanta Civic Center was renamed as a lasting tribute to on of Atlanta's most beloved philanthropists, Boisfeuillet Jones.
Facility Category: procenium theatre
Type of Stage: Proscenium
Seating Capacity: 86,520
Year Built: 1968
Year Remodeled: 2001
Cost: 2 million
Rental Contact: Joyce Whisenant

6265
THEATER AT EMORY

Emory University
Donna and Marvin Schwartz Center
1700 North Decatur Road
Atlanta, GA 30322
Mailing Address: Theater Studies, Theater at Emory, or Theater Emory, Rich Me
Phone: 404-727-6751
e-mail: hhanger@emory.edu
Web Site: www.theater.emory.edu
Management:
 Program Admin Assistant: Hunter Hanger
 Director Of Technical Theater: Scott Little
Mission: a professional theater company in residence at the University, undergraduates collaborate on significant and challenging artistic projects and plays with professional artists: directors, actors, designers, playwrights, dramaturgs, technicians, and stage managers, including the Department-s core faculty
Founded: 1982
Specialized Field: theater
Status: Professional
Seating Capacity: 135
Architect: Michael Dennis and Associates
Cost: $35 Million
Acoustical Consultant: Kirkegaard and Associates

6266
TURNER FIELD

755 Hank Aaron Drive
Atlanta, GA 30315

Phone: 404-522-7630
Web Site: mlb.mlb.com/atl/ballpark
Officers:
 President: John Schuerholz
Founded: 1997
Specialized Field: Baseball Stadium
Seating Capacity: 52,007

6267
WOODRUFF ARTS CENTER

1280 Peachtree Street NE
Atlanta, GA 30309-3552
Mailing Address: Woodruff Arts Center, 1280 Peachtree St. NE, Atlanta, GA 303
Phone: 404-733-4200
Web Site: www.woodruffcenter.org
Officers:
 President/CEO: Joseph Bankoff
 Executive VP: Beauchamp Carr
Management:
 Artistic Director: Susan Booth
Specialized Field: Theater, symphony, art
Status: Non-Profit, Professional
Paid Staff: 200
Paid Artists: 125

6268
AUGUSTA ENTERTAINMENT COMPLEX

James Brown Arena
601 7th Street
Augusta, GA 30901
Mailing Address: James Brown Arena, 601 Seventh Street, Augusta GA 30901
Phone: 706-722-3521
Fax: 706-724-7545
e-mail: kwells@arccc.com
Web Site: www.augustaentertainmentcomplex.com
Management:
 Director of Marketing: Kayla Ott
 Director of Event Services: Josh Small
 General Manager: Monty Jones
 Director of Marketing: Kate Wells
Specialized Field: Concerts
Type of Stage: Proscenium
Seating Capacity: 8500 Arena, 2690 Auditorium
Year Built: 1979
Rental Contact: Mike McGhee (713)623-4583

6269
GROVER C. MAXWELL PERFORMING ARTS THEATRE

Augusta State University
2500 Walton Way
Augusta, GA 30904-2200
Mailing Address: Augusta State University, 2500 Walton Way, Augusta, GA 30904
Phone: 706-737-1405
e-mail: kthoma12@aug.edu
Web Site: www.aug.edu
Management:
 Director: Kelly Thomas
 Theatre Production Coordinator: Steve Proctor
 Theatre Production Coordinator: A. Todd Sullivan
Mission: The Grover C. Maxwell Performing Arts Theatre is the cultural heart of the ASU campus, and students take center stage
Specialized Field: Theater
Type of Stage: Proscenium/Thrust
Orchestra Pit: y
Seating Capacity: 750

6270

IMPERIAL THEATRE

749 Broad Street
Augusta, GA 30901
Mailing Address: The Imperial Theatre, 749 Broad St,
Augusta GA
Phone: 706-722-8341
Web Site: www.imperialtheatre.com
Management:
Director: Lara Plocha
Founded: 1918

6271

ACADEMY THEATRE

119 Center Street
Avondale Estates, GA 30002
Phone: 404-525-4111
Fax: 404-296-9511
Web Site: www.academytheatre.org
Management:
Managing Director: Lorenne Fey
Artistic Director: John Stephens
Producer: Tim Stoltenberg
Mission: To enrich the metropolitan community by
providing a space for the exploration of the arts,
producing educational youth focused outreach and
nurturing appreciation for the performing and visual arts
through presentation of quality professional artistic
work.
Founded: 1956
Status: Non-Profit, Professional
Paid Staff: 6
Paid Artists: 4

6272

TOWNSEND CENTER FOR THE PERFORMING ARTS

University of West Georgia
1601 Maple Street
Carrollton, GA 30118-1400
Phone: 678-839-4722
Fax: 678-839-4805
e-mail: tcpa@westga.edu
Web Site: www.townsendcenter.org
Management:
Artistic Director: Robert B. Jennings
Business Manager: Renet Jones
Founded: 1989
Specialized Field: Performing Arts
Facility Category: Performing Arts Center
Type of Stage: Procenium & Black Box
Seating Capacity: 250
Year Built: 1989
Rental Contact: Business Manager Renet Jones

6273

CEDARTOWN PERFORMING ARTS CENTER

205 East Avenue
Cedartown, GA 30125
Phone: 770-748-4168
e-mail: gm@ccauditorium.com
Web Site: www.ccauditorium.com
Management:
Director: Patrick Moore
Utilizes: Actors; AEA Actors; Collaborating Artists;
Collaborations; Community Members; Community
Talent; Contract Actors; Contract Orchestras; Dance
Companies; Designers; Educators; Equity Actors; Fine
Artists; Grant Writers; Guest Accompanists; Guest
Choreographers; Guest Directors; Guest Ensembles;
Guest Musical Directors; Guest Soloists; Guild
Activities; High School Drama; Instructors; Local Artists

& Directors; Local Talent; Multi Collaborations;
Multimedia; New Productions; Original Music Scores;
Paid Performers; Resident Professionals; Selected
Students; Soloists; Students; Student Interns; Special
Technical Talent; Theatre Companies; Touring
Companies; Visual Arts; Visual Designers; Volunteer
Artists
Paid Staff: 3
Volunteer Staff: 30
Income Sources: City of Cedartown; Ticket Sales;
Donations; Grants
Performs At: Auditorium; Performing Arts Theatre;
Professional Touring Shows
Affiliations: City of Cedartown; Georgia Council for the
Arts; Southeast Arts Federation
Type of Stage: Proscenium
Seating Capacity: 940
Year Built: 1976
Year Remodeled: 1992
Rental Contact: Director Patrick Moore

6274

MARVIN COLE AUDITORIUM

Georgia Perimeter College
555 North Indian Creek Drive
Clarkston, GA 30021-2361
Mailing Address: 555 N. Indian Creek Dr., Bldg.
CF-2230, Clarkston, GA 30021
Phone: 678-891-3200
e-mail: jjenkins@gpc.edu
Web Site: www.gpc.edu/~clafa/
Management:
Chair Of Fine Arts: David Koffman
Facilities Manager: Jennifer Jenkins
Mission: transform the lives of students to thrive in a
global society by providing them with outstanding
instruction, excellent facilities and technology, and
opportunities within a diverse liberal arts environment
Utilizes: Resident Artists
Type of Stage: Proscenium
Orchestra Pit: y
Seating Capacity: 500

6275

COLUMBUS CIVIC CENTER

400 4th Street
Columbus, GA 31901
Mailing Address: Columbus Civic Center, 400 4th
Street, (also known as Victor
Phone: 706-653-4482
Fax: 706-653-4481
e-mail: rwalker@columbusga.org
Web Site: www.columbusciviccenter.org
Management:
Director: Dale Hester
Operations Manager: Brian Giffin
Marketing Manager: Robin Walker
Founded: 1996
Seating Capacity: 10,000

6276

RIVERCENTER FOR THE PERFORMING ARTS

935 First Avenue
Columbus, GA 31901
Mailing Address: PO Box 2425 Columbus GA
31902-2425
Phone: 706-256-3620
Fax: 706-653-8664
e-mail: information@rivercenter.org
Web Site: www.rivercenter.org
Management:
Executive Director: William Bullock
Director of Programming: Jim Rutland

Technical Director: John Camp
Founded: 2002
Specialized Field: Multi-Disciplinary
Seating Capacity: 1,988

6277

THREE ARTS THEATRE

1020 Talbotton Road
Columbus, GA 31901
Phone: 706-653-4183

6278

AGNES SCOTT COLLEGE

141 E College Avenue
Decatur, GA 30030
Phone: 404-471-6000
Fax: 404-868-8602
Toll-free: 800-868-8602
e-mail: info@agnesscott.edu
Web Site: www.agnesscott.edu
Management:
Chairperson: Harriet King
Special Events/Conferences Director: Demetrice
Parks
Founded: 1889

6279

DANA FINE ARTS BUILDING

Agnes Scott College
141 East College Avenue
Decatur, GA 30030
Phone: 404-471-6285
Fax: 404-471-6298
Toll-free: 800-868-8602
e-mail: info@AgnesScott.edu
Web Site: www.AgnesScott.edu
Management:
Cultural Programs Coordinator: James Boynton
Special Events/Conferences Director: Demetrice
Parks
Founded: 1889
Performs At: Gaines Chapel

6280

GWINNETT CENTER

6400 Sugarloaf Parkway
Duluth, GA 30097
Phone: 770-813-7500
Fax: 770-813-7501
Toll-free: 800-224-6422
e-mail: info@gwinnettcenter.com
Web Site: www.gwinnettcenter.com
Officers:
Executive Director: Joseph Dennis, Jr.
Management:
Director Of Marketing: Laura Zacharias
Managing Director: Preston Williams
Founded: 1992
Status: For-Profit, Professional
Income Sources: Ticket Sales
Annual Attendance: 75,000
Type of Stage: Proscenium
Seating Capacity: 702
Rental Contact: Sales Manager Chris Muller

6281

WILD BILL'S ATLANTA

2975 Market Street
Duluth, GA 30096
Phone: 678-473-1000
Fax: 678-417-0477
e-mail: info@wildbillsatlanta.com
Web Site: www.wildbillsatlanta.com
Management:

Marketing Manager: Tom Siliven
Event Planner: Amanda Edwards
Event Planner: Tammie Nielson
Seating Capacity: 5,127

6282
ED CABELL THEATRE
Gainesville State College
Gainesville Theatre Alliance
3820 Mundy Mill Road
Gainesville, GA 30566
Mailing Address: PO Box 1358 Gainesville GA 30503
Phone: 678-717-3624
Fax: 678-717-3675
Web Site: www.gainesvilletheatrealliance.org
Management:
    Artistic Director: James Hammond
    Director of Theatre: Ann Demling
Mission: Gainesville Theatre Alliance will provide its artists and audiences quality theatrical experiences that educate, inspire, enrich and unite
Specialized Field: Theater
Budget: $400,000
Annual Attendance: 20,000
Type of Stage: Thrust
Seating Capacity: 225

6283
GEORGIA MOUNTAINS CENTER
301 Main Street SW
PO Box 2496
Gainesville, GA 30501
Phone: 770-534-8420
Fax: 770-534-8425
e-mail: cmoore@gainesville.org
Web Site: www.georgiamountainscenter.com
Management:
    Director: Carol Moore
Seating Capacity: 2.500

6284
HOSCH THEATRE
Brenau University\ Gainesville State College
John S. Burd Center for the Performing Arts
500 Washington Street SE
Gainesville, GA 30501
Mailing Address: PO Box 1358 Gainesville GA 30503
Toll-free: 800-252-5119
Web Site: www.gainesvilletheatrealliance.org
Management:
    Director of Theatre: Dr. Michelle Roueche
    Professor of Theatre: Ann Demling
    Professor of Theatre: Jim Hammond
Mission: Gainesville Theatre Alliance will provide its artists and audiences quality theatrical experiences that educate, inspire, enrich and unite
Specialized Field: Theater
Type of Stage: Proscenium
Seating Capacity: 350

6285
PEARCE AUDITORIUM
Brenau University\ Gainesville State College
500 Washington Street SE
Gainesville, GA 30501
Mailing Address: PO Box 1358 Gainesville GA 30503
Toll-free: 800-252-5119
Web Site: www.gainesvilletheatrealliance.org
Management:
    Chair: Dr. Michelle Roueche
    Professor of Theatre: Ann Demling
    Professor of Theatre: Jim Hammond

Mission: Gainesville Theatre Alliance will provide its artists and audiences quality theatrical experiences that educate, inspire, enrich and unite
Specialized Field: theater
Seating Capacity: 750
Year Head Theatre Renovated: 1981
Year Restored: 1984

6286
CENTER FOR THE CREATIVE & PERFORMING ARTS
Wesleyan College
4760 Forsyth Road
Macon, GA
Phone: 478-757-5259
Toll-free: 800-447-6610
e-mail: communications@wesleyancollege.edu
Web Site: www.wesleyancollege.edu
Officers:
    President: Ruth A Knox
    Vice President: Vivia Fowler
    Vice President: Deborah Smith
Management:
    Director of Communications: Susan Welsh
Utilizes: Actors; Artists-in-Residence; Collaborating Artists; Curators; Designers; Educators; Fine Artists; Five Seasonal Concerts; Grant Writers; Guest Composers; Guest Directors; Guest Ensembles; Guest Lecturers; Guest Musical Directors; Guest Musicians; Guest Soloists; Guest Speakers; Guest Teachers; High School Drama; Instructors; Local Artists; Local Artists & Directors; Multimedia; Music; Playwrights; Poets; Sign Language Translators; Soloists; Students; Student Interns; Touring Companies; Volunteer Directors & Actors; Writers
Founded: 1836
Opened: 2008
Specialized Field: Music; Theatre; Studio Arts
Paid Staff: 12
Paid Artists: 10
Income Sources: Tuitions; Grants; Donations
Performs At: Multi-use Fine Arts Center
Type of Stage: Auditorium; Black Box
Seating Capacity: 1,200

6287
THE GRAND OPERA HOUSE
Mercer University
651 Mulberry Street
Macon, GA 31201
Mailing Address: The Grand Opera House, 651 Mulberry Street, Macon, GA U.S.A.
Phone: 478-301-5470
Web Site: www.thegrandmacon.com
Management:
    Chairman of the Board: Mark Stevens
Mission: The Grand has hosted vaudeville performances, Broadway touring companies, community theatre, concerts, movies, and numerous other events
Founded: 1884
Specialized Field: Theater

6288
MADISON MORGAN CULTURAL CENTER
434 S Main Street
Madison, GA 30650
Phone: 706-342-4743
Fax: 706-342-1154
Web Site: www.mmcc-arts.org
Management:
    Executive Director: Judith Barber
    Marketing Director: Patricia DuBose

6289
THEATRE IN THE SQUARE
11 Whitlock Avenue
Marietta, GA 30064
Mailing Address: Theatre in the Square- 11 Whitlock Ave. - Marietta, GA 30064
Phone: 770-422-8369
Fax: 770-424-2637
Web Site: www.theatreinthesquare.com
Management:
    Producing Director: Palmer Wells
    Managing Director: Raye Varney
    Assistant Artistic Director: Jessica Phelps West
    Marketing: Andrea Gardenhire
Utilizes: Actors; AEA Actors; Artists-in-Residence; Choreographers; Collaborating Artists; Collaborations; Dancers; Designers; Educators; Grant Writers; Guest Artists; Guest Companies; Guest Conductors; Guest Designers; Guest Lecturers; Guest Musical Directors; Guest Writers; Guild Activities; High School Drama; Instructors; Lyricists; Multimedia; Music; Original Music Scores; Performance Artists; Resident Professionals; Sign Language Translators; Soloists; Student Interns
Founded: 1982
Specialized Field: Theater

6290
SPIVEY HALL
Clayton State University
2000 Clayton State Boulevard
Morrow, GA 30260
Phone: 678-466-4200
Fax: 628-466-4494
e-mail: JohnShiffert@clayton.edu
Web Site: www.spiveyhall.org
Management:
    Executive/Artistic Director: Sam Dixon
    Production Manager: Lorenzo Callahan
    Marketing Director: Susan Volkert
Mission: Spivey Hall is home to the award-winning Spivey Hall Children's Choir and Spivey Hall Young Artists
Founded: 1991
Specialized Field: Concerts
Performs At: Music Only, No Theatre, Dance Or Attractions
Seating Capacity: 392

6291
COLQUITT COUNTY ARTS CENTER
491 7th Avenue SW
Moultrie, GA 31768
Phone: 229-985-1922
Fax: 229-890-6746
Web Site: www.colquittcountyarts.com
Management:
    Executive Director: Jeffery Ophime
    Assistant Director: Lin Sheffield
    Visual Arts Director: Jane Simpson
    Curator: Candace Underwood
Mission: A creative and cultural resource that makes quality visual and performing art available to a diverse population. Provides engaging arts education for children and adults, acts as a steward of permanent collections, and maintains a landmark facility that enriches the whole community.
Paid Staff: 3

6292
FREDERICK BROWN JR AMPHITHEATER
201 McIntosh Trail
Peachtree City, GA 30269

Mailing Address: Frederick Brown Jr. Amphitheater ,
201 McIntosh Trail , Peac
Phone: 770-631-0630
Fax: 770-631-0430
Web Site: amphitheater.org
Management:
    Manager: Nancy Price
    Facilities Manager: Billy Burke
    Box Office Manager: Sarah Davenport
Mission: The Fred has established itself as one of the leading outdoor entertainment venues in the metro Atlanta area and has hosted hometown favorites, national and touring acts for more than thirty years
Seating Capacity: 2,213

6293
ROME CITY AUDITORIUM

601 Broad Street
Rome, GA 30161
Phone: 706-236-4416
Web Site: www.romega.us
Management:
    City Manager: John Bennett
Facility Category: Auditorium
Type of Stage: Wood
Seating Capacity: 1,112

6294
ARMSTRONG STATE COLLEGE FINE ARTS AUDITORIUM

11935 Abercorn Street
Savannah, GA 31419
Phone: 912-334-2503
Toll-free: 800-633-2349
e-mail: finearts@armstrong.edu
Web Site: www.finearts.armstrong.edu
Management:
    Associate Professor Of Drama: Dr. Peter Mellen
Status: Non-Profit, Non-Professional
Paid Staff: 40
Paid Artists: 40
Seating Capacity: 1,000

6295
JENKINS THEATRE

Armstrong Atlantic State University
11935 Abercorn Street
Savannah, GA 31419
Phone: 912-344-2503
Toll-free: 800-633-2349
e-mail: finearts@mail.armstrong.edu
Web Site: www.finearts.armstrong.edu
Management:
    Associate Professor of Drama: Dr Peter Mellen
    Associate Professor of Theatre: Dr Roger Miller
    Assistant Professor of Theatre: Pamela Sears
Type of Stage: Black Box
Seating Capacity: 200

6296
LUCAS THEATRE FOR THE ARTS

Savannah College of Art and Design
32 Abercorn Street
Savannah, GA 31401
Mailing Address: 32 Abercorn St., Savannah, GA 31401 USA
Phone: 912-525-5040
Fax: 915-525-5030
e-mail: carter@lucastheatre.com
Web Site: www.lucastheatre.com
Officers:
    Production Manager: David Harris
    Executive Director: Kenneth F. Carter, Jr.
Management:

Technical Director: Jim Prodger
Managing Director: Meaghan Walsh
Founded: 1921
Season: Year Round
Annual Attendance: 12,000
Type of Stage: Proscenium
Stage Dimensions: 48.3 x 26.11
Orchestra Pit: y
Seating Capacity: 1,237
Year Built: 1921
Architect: C.K. Howell
Cost: $14 Million

6297
SAVANNAH CIVIC CENTER

301 W Ogelthorpe Avenue
Savannah, GA 31401
Mailing Address: 301 West Oglethorpe Avenue, Savannah, Georgia 31401
Phone: 912-651-6550
Fax: 912-651-6552
Web Site: www.savannahcivic.com
Management:
    Executive Director: Marty Johnston
Mission: The facility has two venues: The Martin Luther King Arena and the Johnny Mercer Theater
Founded: 1974
Seating Capacity: 3,500-9,600

6298
TRUSTEES THEATER

Savannah College of Art and Design
216 E Broughton Street
Savannah, GA 31401
Phone: 912-525-5051
Fax: 912-525-5052
e-mail: trusteestheater@scad.edu
Web Site: www.trusteestheater.com
Management:
    Executive Director: Dannya Filson
    Managing Director: Christina Downs Routhier
Season: Year Round
Type of Stage: Proscenium
Stage Dimensions: 26' H x 35' W
Seating Capacity: 1,105

6299
GEORGIA SOUTHERN UNIVERSITY PERFORMING ARTS CENTER

PO Box 8159
Statesboro, GA 30460-8159
Mailing Address: Performing Arts Center, Georgia Southern University, PO Box
Phone: 912-478-0830
Fax: 912-478-1480
e-mail: apertalion@georgiasouthern.edu
Web Site: ceps.georgiasouthern.edu
Management:
    Director: Albert Pertalion
    Assistant Director: Carol Thompson
    House Manager: LeAnn Ransbotham
Specialized Field: Dance, Music, Theater
Paid Staff: 8

6300
THOMASVILLE CULTURAL CENTER

600 E Washington Street
Thomasville, GA 31799
Mailing Address: Thomasville Cultural Center, 600 East Washington Street, P.O
Phone: 229-226-0588
Fax: 229-226-0599
Web Site: www.thomasvilleculturalcenter.com
Officers:

President: Dan Autry
VP: Margo Bindhardt
Management:
    Executive Director: Charles Glassick
    Director of Development: Susan O'Neal
Mission: The Thomasville Cultural Center is dedicated to enriching creative life through the visual, performing, literary, and applied arts
Paid Staff: 12
Performs At: Thomasville Cultural Center
Seating Capacity: 500

6301
SAWYER THEATRE

Valdosta State University
1500 N Patterson Street
Valdosta, GA 31698
Phone: 229-333-5307
Fax: 229-249-2602
e-mail: dguthrie@valdosta.edu
Web Site: www.valdosta.edu
Management:
    Managing Director: H Duke Guthrie
    Artistic Director: Jacque Wheeler
Seating Capacity: 225

6302
WHITEHEAD AUDITORIUM

Valdosta State University
1500 N Patterson Street
Valdosta, GA 31698
Phone: 229-333-5800
Toll-free: 800-618-1878
Web Site: www.valdosta.edu
Management:
    Artistic Director: Jacque Wheeler
    Managing Director: H Duke Guthrie
Founded: 1970
Specialized Field: Theater, Symphony
Type of Stage: Proscenium
Seating Capacity: 773

6303
DOBBS THEATRE

Young Harris College
1 College Street
Young Harris, GA 30582
Mailing Address: 1 College Street,Po Box 68, Young Harris, GA 30582
Phone: 706-379-3111
Toll-free: 800-241-3754
Web Site: www.yhc.edu
Management:
    Professor of Theatre: Roberta Rankin
    Professor of Theatre: Tom Jeffrey
Mission: Utilized by Theatre Young Harris, the 175-seat Dobbs Theatre is a state-of-the-art flexible space that can be easily adjusted for arena or thrust staging
Specialized Field: Theater
Type of Stage: Thrust
Seating Capacity: 175

6304
HILDA D GLENN AUDITORIUM

Young Harris College
1 College Street
Young Harris, GA 30582
Mailing Address: 1 College Street,Po Box 68, Young Harris, GA 30582
Phone: 706-379-3111
Toll-free: 800-241-3754
Web Site: www.yhc.edu
Management:
    Professor of Theatre: Roberta Rankin

Professor of Theatre: Tom Jeffrey
Mission: The Clegg Building contains the Hilda D. Glenn Auditorium with a seating capacity of 1,060 and a large stage and orchestra pit for theatre and music presentations. In addition, the Clegg Fine Arts Building houses fully-equipped scenery and costume shops.
Specialized Field: Theater
Type of Stage: Proscenium
Seating Capacity: 1,200

Hawaii

6305
UHH THEATRE
University of Hawaii at Hilo
UH Hilo Performing Arts Center
200 W Kawili Street
Hilo, HI 96720-4091
Phone: 808-974-7310
Fax: 808-974-7350
e-mail: artsctr@hawaii.edu
Web Site: artscenter.uhh.hawaii.edu
Management:
    Technical Director: Robert H Abe
    General Manager: Lee Dombroski
    Performing Arts Department Chair: Jaquelyn Johnson
Season: Year Round
Type of Stage: Proscenium
Stage Dimensions: 40 ft x 20 ft
Orchestra Pit: y
Seating Capacity: 600

6306
ALOHA STADIUM
99-500 Salt Lake Boulevard
Honolulu, HI 96818
Mailing Address: PO Box 30666 Honolulu HI 96820-0666
Phone: 808-483-2500
Fax: 808-483-2823
Web Site: alohastadium.hawaii.gov
Management:
    Stadium Manager: Scott Chan
    Deputy Manager: Lois Manin
    Chairperson: Kevin Chong Kee
Mission: Honolulu's largest outdoor arena in the State of Hawaii
Founded: 1975
Specialized Field: large concerts and events
Affiliations: NCAA; NFL Pro Bowl; Hawaii Bowl Concerts
Seating Capacity: 50,419
Year Built: 1975
Rental Contact: Edwin K. Hayashi

6307
ANDREWS OUTDOOR THEATRE
University of Hawaii at Manoa
2600 Campus Road
Honolulu, HI 96822-2385
Phone: 808-956-8975
Web Site: manoa.hawaii.edu
Officers:
    President: David McClain
Management:
    Director of Education: Richard Hogeboom
    Marketing/Communications Director: Xina Ma
Seating Capacity: 3,800

6308
HAWAII THEATRE
1130 Bethel Street
Honolulu, HI 96813-2201
Phone: 808-528-0506
e-mail: burtonwhite@hawaiitheatre.com
Web Site: www.hawaiitheatre.com
Officers:
    President: Sarah M Richrds
Management:
    Artistic Director/General Manager: Burton White
    Director of Development: Elaine Evans
Seating Capacity: 1,400

6309
HONOLULU ACADEMY OF ARTS
900 S Beretania Street
Honolulu, HI 96814-1495
Mailing Address: 900 South Beretania St., Honolulu, HI 96814
Phone: 808-532-8700
Fax: 808-532-8787
e-mail: ksumner@honoluluacademy.org
Web Site: www.honoluluacademy.org
Management:
    Executive Director: Stephen Little
    Managing Director: Robert White
Mission: The Academy is accredited by the American Association of Museums and registered as a National and State Historical site. In 1990, the Academy Art Center was opened to provide a program of studio art classes and workshops. In 2001, the Henry R. Luce Pavilion Complex opened with the Pavilion Caf,, Academy Shop, and Henry R. Luce Wing with 8,000 square feet (740 m2) of gallery space. In 2005, the Asian Painting Conservation Center was opened to prov
Founded: 1922
Paid Staff: 80
Annual Attendance: 250,000

6310
KENNEDY THEATRE
University of Hawaii at Manoa
Department of Theatre and Dance
1770 East-West Road
Honolulu, HI 96822
Phone: 808-956-7677
Fax: 808-956-4234
e-mail: theatre@hawaii.edu
Web Site: www.hawaii.edu/theatre
Officers:
    Chairman: Gregg Lizenbery
Management:
    Director: Dennis Carroll
    Technical Director: Gerald R. Kawaoka
    General Manager: Marty Myers
Mission: Provide performance component for theatre and dance students
Specialized Field: Theatre; Dance
Annual Attendance: 15,000
Facility Category: Educational/College
Type of Stage: Proscenium
Seating Capacity: 600
Year Built: 1963
Architect: I.M. Pei

6311
NEAL S BLAISDELL CENTER
777 Ward Avenue
Honolulu, HI 96814

Mailing Address: Department of Enterprise Services, City & County of Honolulu
Phone: 808-527-5400
Fax: 808-527-5433
Web Site: www.blaisdellcenter.com
Management:
    Director Enterprise Services: Sidney A Quintal
    Deputy Director Enterprise Services: Gail Y Haraguchi
    Director of Production: Mary E Lewis
Mission: The multi-purpose complex is composed of an internationally renowned arena, concert hall, conference rooms, galleria and exhibition hall. It was remodeled and expanded in 1994. It is also the home of the Hawaii Basketball League Honolulu Bandits.
Founded: 1964
Specialized Field: multi functional space
Paid Staff: 150

6312
SAINT LOUIS CENTER FOR THE PERFORMING ARTS
3142 Waialae Avenue
Honolulu, HI 96816-1579
Phone: 808-739-4886
Fax: 808-739-4821
e-mail: mamiya@saintlouishawaii.org
Web Site: www.saintlouishawaii.org
Officers:
    CFO: Nancy Lacambra
Management:
    Principal: Gayle Burgher
    Dean: Sione Thompson
    Theatre Manager: Kyle Kakuno

6313
MAUI ARTS & CULTURAL CENTER
1 Cameron Way
Kahului, HI 96732
Phone: 808-242-2787
Fax: 808-242-4665
Web Site: www.mauiarts.org
Officers:
    President: Karen A Fischer
    Executive VP: Art Vento
Management:
    Marketing Director: Barbara Trecker
    Development Director: Lisa Varde
Utilizes: Actors; Collaborations; Curators; Dance Companies; Dancers; Educators; Fine Artists; Five Seasonal Concerts; Guest Choreographers; Guest Directors; Guest Musical Directors; Guild Activities; Instructors; Local Artists; Multimedia; Original Music Scores; Sign Language Translators; Student Interns; Special Technical Talent; Theatre Companies; Touring Companies
Annual Attendance: 250,000
Facility Category: Visual and performing arts
Type of Stage: Proscenium and open air
Seating Capacity: 5,000 + 1,200 + 300
Year Built: 1994
Cost: $32 million
Rental Contact: Candace Croteau

6314
KAHILU THEATRE FOUNDATION
67 1186 Lindsey Road
Kamuela, HI 96743
Mailing Address: PO Box 549 Kamuela HI 96743
Phone: 808-885-6017
Fax: 808-885-0546
e-mail: janet@kahilutheatre.org
Web Site: www.kahilutheatre.org
Officers:

President: Evarts Fox
VP Governace: Rhoady Lee
Secretary: Vicki McManus
Management:
Managing Director: Janet Coburn
Operations Director: Alva Kamalani
Development Director: Alethea Lai
Mission: the theatre serves as a center for residents and visitors alike to come to experience other cultures and explore the incredibly rich, diverse, imaginative and exciting realm of artistic expression.
Utilizes: Actors; Artists-in-Residence; Dance Companies; Dancers; Educators; Fine Artists; Guest Accompanists; Instructors; Lyricists; Multimedia; Organization Contracts; Original Music Scores; Poets; Resident Artists; Resident Professionals; Selected Students; Sign Language Translators; Singers; Soloists; Special Technical Talent; Theatre Companies; Visual Arts
Founded: 1981
Specialized Field: Theater
Paid Staff: 15
Volunteer Staff: 10
Budget: $1.2 million
Performs At: Proscenium Theatre
Affiliations: WA; APAP
Annual Attendance: 12,000
Facility Category: Theater
Type of Stage: Proscenium
Stage Dimensions: 35 x 65
Seating Capacity: 490
Year Built: 1981
Rental Contact: Operations Director Alva Kamalani
Organization Type: Performing; Sponsoring

6315
PAUL AND VI LOO THEATRE
Hawaii Pacific University
45-045 Kamehameha Highway
Kaneohe, HI 96745
Mailing Address: Hawai'i Pacific University, 1164 Bishop Street, Suite #200,
Phone: 808-544-0200
Toll-free: 866-225-5478
e-mail: KArchibald@hpu.edu
Web Site: www.hpu.edu
Officers:
President: Chatt G Wright
Management:
Theater Manager: Karen Archabald
Theater Director: Joyce Maltby
Specialized Field: Theater

6316
LAHAINA CIVIC CENTER
1840 Hanopilani Highway
Lahaina, HI 96761
Mailing Address: 1840 Honoapiilani Hwy, Lahaina, HI 96761
Fax: 808-661-9316
Web Site: www.co.maui.hi.us
Management:
Supervisor: Jeff Anderson
Booking: Robbie Wares
Mission: The Lahaina Civic Center is a sports, convention and entertainment complex
Seating Capacity: 2,500

6317
DAVID O MCKAY AUDITORIUM
Brigham Young University Hawaii
55-220 Kulanui Street
Laie, HI 96762

Mailing Address: Brigham Young University-Hawaii, 55-220 Kulanui Street, Laie
Phone: 808-675-3211
Web Site: www.byuh.edu
Officers:
President: Steven C B Wheelwright
VP of Academics: Max L Checketts
VP of Administrative Services: Michael B Bliss
VP of Student Development & Affairs: Debbie Hippolite Wright
Specialized Field: Concerts
Type of Stage: Auditorium
Orchestra Pit: y
Seating Capacity: 800
Architect: Paul Louie & Associates
Cost: $6 Million

6318
LCC THEATRE
Leewood Community College
96-045 Ala Ike
Pearl City, HI 96782
Phone: 808-455-0380
Fax: 808-455-0384
e-mail: lcctheatre@lcc.hawaii.edu
Web Site: www.lcctheatre.hawaii.edu
Officers:
Chancellor: Manuel Cabral
VC: Michael Pecsok
Paid Staff: 5
Seating Capacity: 50-65
Year Built: 1974

Idaho

6319
DANNY PETERSON THEATRE
Boise State University
Morrison Center for the Performing Arts
2201 Cesar Chavez Lane
Boise, ID 83725
Mailing Address: 1910 University Drive, Boise ID 83725-1050
Phone: 208-426-1609
Fax: 208-426-3021
e-mail: scottbodmer@boisestate.edu
Web Site: mc.boisestate.edu
Officers:
Department Chair/Director: Richard Klautsch
Management:
Executive Director: Jan Allan Zarr
Marketing Director: Scott Bodmer
Mission: the Morrison Center for the Performing Arts is to encourage cultural and intellectual activities for the benefit and enjoyment of all Idaho citizens
Utilizes: Resident Artists
Founded: 1984
Type of Stage: Flexible Black Box
Seating Capacity: 200

6320
MORRISON CENTER FOR THE PERFORMING ARTS
Boise State University
2201 Cesar Chavez Lane
Boise, ID 83725
Mailing Address: 1910 University Drive, Boise ID 83725-1050
Phone: 208-426-1609
Fax: 208-426-3021
e-mail: scottbodmer@boisestate.edu
Web Site: mc.boisestate.edu
Officers:

Department Chair/Director: Richard Klautsch
Management:
Executive Director: Jan Allan Zarr
Marketing Director: Scott Bodmer
Mission: the Morrison Center for the Performing Arts is to encourage cultural and intellectual activities for the benefit and enjoyment of all Idaho citizens
Founded: 1984
Specialized Field: Concerts, ballet, theater
Paid Staff: 50
Type of Stage: Proscenium
Seating Capacity: 2,000

6321
QWEST ARENA
233 S Capitol Boulevard
Boise, ID 83702
Mailing Address: 455 N. 10th Street, Omaha, NE 68102
Phone: 208-424-2200
Fax: 208-424-2222
e-mail: mzaborski@qwestarenaidaho.com
Web Site: www.qwestarenaidaho.com
Officers:
President: John Cunningham
VP: Michael DiPalma
Management:
General Manager: Travis Turner
Marketing/Promotions Director: Nick St John
Mission: Qwest Arena (formerly Bank of America Centre) is multi-purpose arena in Boise, Idaho. It holds 5,300 fans for ice hockey and basketball, 5,732 for end-stage concerts, 6,400 for boxing and up to 6,800 for center-stage concerts
Founded: 1997
Specialized Field: Concerts
Seating Capacity: 5,100
Year Built: 1997

6322
STUDENT UNION SPECIAL EVENTS CENTER
Boise State University
Morrison Center for the Performing Arts
2201 Cesar Chavez Lane
Boise, ID 83725
Mailing Address: 1910 University Drive, Boise ID 83725-1050
Phone: 208-426-1609
Fax: 208-426-3021
e-mail: scottbodmer@boisestate.edu
Web Site: mc.boisestate.edu
Officers:
Department Chair/Director: Richard Klautsch
Management:
Executive Director: Jan Allan Zarr
Marketing Director: Scott Bodmer
Mission: the Morrison Center for the Performing Arts is to encourage cultural and intellectual activities for the benefit and enjoyment of all Idaho citizens
Utilizes: Resident Artists
Type of Stage: Proscenium
Seating Capacity: 400

6323
TACO BELL ARENA
Boise State University
1910 University Drive
Boise, ID 83725
Mailing Address: Taco Bell Arena at Boise State University, 1910 University D
Phone: 208-426-1900

Fax: 208-426-1998
e-mail: mcolsen@boisestate.edu
Web Site: www.tacobellarena.com
Management:
    Executive Director: Lisa Cochran
    Marketing Director: McQ Olsen
Founded: 1980
Seating Capacity: 13,000

6324
THE MORRISON CENTER FOR THE PERFORMING ARTS
Boise State University
2201 Cesar Chavez
Boise, ID 83725-1050
Mailing Address: 1910 University Drive, Boise ID 83725-1050
Phone: 208-426-1609
Fax: 208-426-3021
e-mail: morrisoncenter@boisestate.edu
Web Site: www.mc.boisestate.edu
Management:
    Interim Executive Director: Rosemary Reinhardt, rosemaryreinhardt@boisestate.e
Utilizes: Resident Artists
Founded: 1984
Type of Stage: Proscenium
Orchestra Pit: y
Seating Capacity: 2000
Rental Contact: Virginia Treat

6325
THEATRE LAB
Boise State University
Morrison Center for the Performing Arts
2201 Cesar Chavez Lane
Boise, ID 83725
Mailing Address: 1910 University Drive, Boise ID 83725-1050
Phone: 208-426-1609
Fax: 208-426-3021
e-mail: scottbodmer@boisestate.edu
Web Site: mc.boisestate.edu
Officers:
    Department Chair/Director: Richard Klautsch
Management:
    Executive Director: Jan Allan Zarr
    Marketing Director: Scott Bodmer
Utilizes: Resident Artists

6326
AMPHITHEATRE
The College of Idaho
2112 Cleveland Boulevard
Caldwell, ID 83605
Mailing Address: Theatre, Box #111, 2112 Cleveland Blvd., Caldwell, ID 83
Phone: 208-459-5011
Fax: 208-459-5175
Toll-free: 800-244-3246
e-mail: mhartwell@collegeofidaho.edu
Web Site: www.collegeo
Officers:
    President: Robert Hoover
    Chair: Joe Golden
Management:
    Technical Theatre/Design: Michael Hartwell
Mission: This beautiful space is used by students for quiet study and is utilized by the Program Council for staging outdoor band concerts. While the theatre department has yet to produce a play here, the opportunity exists for staging classical Greek works in this setting! Wait and see!

6327
EROS THEATRE
The College of Idaho
McCain Student Center
2112 Cleveland Boulevard
Caldwell, ID 83605
Mailing Address: Theatre, Box #111, 2112 Cleveland Blvd., Caldwell, ID 83
Phone: 208-459-5011
Fax: 208-459-5175
Toll-free: 800-244-3246
e-mail: mhartwell@collegeofidaho.edu
Web Site: www.collegeo
Officers:
    President: Robert Hoover
    Chair: Joe Golden
Management:
    Technical Design/Theatre: Michael Hartwell
Mission: The Eros is a versatile space where seats can be arranged or removed depending upon the director's and designer's vision
Founded: 1998

6328
JEWETT AUDITORIUM
The College of Idaho
McCain Student Center
2112 Cleveland Boulevard
Caldwell, ID 83605
Mailing Address: Theatre, Box #111, 2112 Cleveland Blvd., Caldwell, ID 83
Phone: 208-459-5011
Fax: 208-459-5175
e-mail: mhartwell@collegeofidaho.edu
Web Site: www.collegeofidaho.edu
Officers:
    President: Robert Hoover
    Chair: Joe Golden
Management:
    Technical Design/Theatre: Michael Hartwell
Mission: The college hold various ceremonies in the hall as well as music concerts, guest speakers and other functions. The Caldwell Fine Arts organization frequently brings in touring companies who perform on stage.
Type of Stage: Proscenium
Seating Capacity: 850

6329
RECITAL HALL
The College of Idaho
McCain Student Center
2112 Cleveland Boulevard
Caldwell, ID 83605
Mailing Address: Theatre, Box #111, 2112 Cleveland Blvd., Caldwell, ID 83
Phone: 208-459-5011
Fax: 208-459-5175
e-mail: mhartwell@collegeofidaho.edu
Web Site: www.collegeofidaho.edu
Officers:
    President: Robert Hoover
    Chair: Joe Golden
Management:
    Technical Design/Theatre: Michael Hartwell
Mission: The Recital Hall is a 200-seat, proscenium performance space designed for optimum sound quality. The CofI Theatre and Music departments have joined forces to stage musicals and operas in this lovely theatre
Type of Stage: Proscenium
Seating Capacity: 200

6330
STUDIO THEATRE
The College of Idaho
McCain Student Center
2112 Cleveland Boulevard
Caldwell, ID 83605
Mailing Address: Theatre, Box #111, 2112 Cleveland Blvd., Caldwell, ID 83
Phone: 208-459-5011
Fax: 208-459-5175
e-mail: mhartwell@collegeofidaho.edu
Web Site: www.collegeofidaho.edu
Officers:
    President: Robert Hoover
    Chair: Joe Golden
Management:
    Technical Theatre/Design Director: Michael Hartwell
Mission: This Black Box Theatre located in the Langroise Center for the Performing and Fine Arts converts to thrust, stadium and arena configurations with movable seating sections. The Studio Theatre serves as the primary playing space for Mainstage Theatre productions and classroom work for acting and directing classes at CofI
Type of Stage: Thrust, Stadium, Arena
Stage Dimensions: 50' X 52'
Seating Capacity: 90 - 145

6331
CIVIC AUDITORIUM
501 S Holmes
Idaho Falls, ID 83405
Mailing Address: 501 S. Holmes, P.O. Box 50220, Idaho Falls, Idaho 83405
Phone: 208-612-8396
Web Site: http://www.idahofallsidaho.gov/city/the-civic-auditorium.html
Management:
    Manager: Ed Morgan
Paid Staff: 2
Seating Capacity: 1,892

6332
COLONIAL THEATRE
450 A Street
Idaho Falls, ID 83402
Phone: 208-522-0471
Web Site: www.idahofallsarts.org
Officers:
    Chair: Steve Carr
    Vice Chair: Laurel Hall
    Secretary: Carol Ormond
    Treasurer: Steve Parry
Management:
    Executive Director: Carrie Getty Schied
    Operations Manager: Jill Barnes
Seating Capacity: 970

6333
SUN VALLEY CENTER FOR THE ARTS
191 5th Street E
Ketcham, ID 83340
Mailing Address: PO Box 656, Sun Valley ID 83353
Phone: 208-726-9491
Fax: 208-726-2344
Web Site: www.sunvalleycenter.org
Officers:
    President: Trina Peters
    VP: Larry Helzel
    Treasurer: Sara Nelson
    Secretary: Marybeth Flower

Management:
Artistic Director: Kristin Poole
Development Director: Sally Boettger
Marketing Director: Kristine Bretall
Mission: Our mission is 'to provoke and stimulate the imagination while opening hearts and minds through excellence in diverse arts programming.' We do this by offering exhibitions, lectures, classes and performing arts events that touch on issues relevant to our times and by bringing some of the world's most interesting artists, writers and thinkers to our small community in central Idaho.
Founded: 1971
Paid Staff: 12
Budget: $60,000-$150,000
Performs At: Sun Valley Center for the Arts and Humanities
Organization Type: Presenting

6334
HARTUNG THEATRE
University of Idaho
Department of Theatre & Film
6th And Rayburn Streets
Moscow, ID 83844-2008
Mailing Address: PO Box 443074, Moscow ID 83844-2008
Phone: 208-885-6465
Fax: 208-885-2558
e-mail: theatre@uidaho.edu
Web Site: www.uidaho.edu
Officers:
Chair: Dean Panttaja
Management:
Design Director: Stephanie Miller
Technical Director: Justin Walsh
Marketing Director: Micki Panttaja
Utilizes: Resident Artists
Type of Stage: Semi-Thrust Proscenium
Seating Capacity: 417
Year Built: 1973

6335
KIBBIE-ASUI ACTIVITY CENTER
University of Idaho
PO Box 442302
Moscow, ID 83844-2302
Mailing Address: Christopher Cooney, P.O. Box 443221, Moscow, ID 83844-3221
Phone: 208-885-6466
e-mail: drew@uidaho.edu, ccooney@uidaho.edu
Web Site: govandals.comu
Management:
Athletic Director: Rob Spear
General Manager: Tom Morris
Senior Director of Marketing: Christopher Coonet
Mission: multi-purpose indoor athletic stadium in Moscow, Idaho, on the campus of the University of Idaho
Founded: 1975
Paid Staff: 75
Seating Capacity: 8,500

6336
KIVA THEATRE
University of Idaho
Department of Theatre & Film
6th And Rayburn Streets
Moscow, ID 83844-3074
Mailing Address: PO Box 443074, Moscow ID 83844-3074
Phone: 208-885-6465

Fax: 208-885-2558
e-mail: theatre@uidaho.edu
Web Site: www.uidaho.edu
Officers:
Chair: Dean Panttaja
Management:
Design Director: Stephanie Miller
Technical Director: Justin Walsh
Marketing Director: Micki Panttaja
Utilizes: Resident Artists
Type of Stage: Theatre-In-The-Round
Seating Capacity: 125
Year Built: 1973

6337
UNIVERSITY OF IDAHO THEATRE ARTS
University of Idaho
6th and Rayburn Streets
Moscow, ID 83844-2008
Mailing Address: PO Box 443074 Moscow ID 83844-2008
Phone: 208-885-6465
Fax: 208-885-2558
e-mail: theatre@uidaho.edu
Web Site: www.uitheatre.com
Officers:
Chair: Dean Panttaja
Management:
Design Director: Stephanie Miller
Technical Director: Robert Valliere
Marketing Director: Micki Panttaja
Utilizes: Actors; Artists-in-Residence; Choreographers; Collaborations; Community Members; Contract Actors; Dancers; Designers; Educators; Fine Artists; Guest Artists; Guest Choreographers; Guest Lecturers; Guest Soloists; Guest Teachers; Guest Writers; High School Drama; Instructors; Local Artists; Local Unknown Artists; Multimedia; Paid Performers; Performance Artists; Resident Artists; Resident Professionals; Sign Language Translators; Soloists; Students; Student Interns; Special Technical Talent; Visual Arts; Volunteer Directors & Actors; Writers
Specialized Field: Theatre
Type of Stage: Black Box
Seating Capacity: 50
Year Built: 1973

6338
MOUNTAIN HOME ARTS COUNCIL
PO Box 974
Mountain Home, ID 83647
Phone: 208-587-3706
e-mail: mh-arts@qwestoffice.net
Web Site: www.mharts.org
Officers:
President: Barb Checkets
First VP: Joe Lasuen
Second VP: Denise Barresi
Treasurer: Erika Pedrosa
Management:
Executive Director: Sally Cruser
Marketing Committee: Scotta Groggett
Marketing Committee: Christy Groggett
Paid Staff: 1

6339
GRAND LOBBY
Northwest Nazarene University
Brandt Center
623 Holly Street
Nampa, ID 83686-5897

Mailing Address: Northwest Nazarene University, 623 S University Boulevard, N
Phone: 208-467-8790
e-mail: hmlindner@nnu.edu
Web Site: www.nnu.edu
Officers:
President: Dr David Alexander
VP: Dr Samuel Dunn
Dean: Ron Ponsford
Management:
Marketing Director: Hollie Lindner
Mission: The 9,000 square-foot Grand Lobby is a beautiful setting for your banquet or annual meeting. With seating for up to 250, fresh and unique menues from Sodexho, and our signature customer service, your banquet will be an event to remember
Type of Stage: Auditorium
Seating Capacity: 1,500

6340
IDAHO CENTER
16200 Idaho Center Boulevard
Nampa, ID 83687
Mailing Address: 16114 Idaho Center Boulevard Suite 2, Nampa ID 83687
Phone: 208-468-1000
Web Site: www.idahocenter.com
Management:
Executive Director: Ron Oroson
Mission: The Idaho Center, at the Crossroads of the Northwest, is one of the most versatile and accessible facilities of its kind in the West. Whether you're attending a Convention, a Sporting Event, a Concert, a Trade Show, a Conference, an Equestrian Event, or a Theatrical Production
Seating Capacity: 13,500

6341
NAMPA CIVIC CENTER
311 3rd Street S
Nampa, ID 83651
Phone: 208-468-5500
Fax: 208-465-2255
e-mail: info@nampaciviccenter.com
Web Site: www.nampaciviccenter.com
Management:
Director/General Manager: William K Stephan
Paid Staff: 23
Seating Capacity: 640

6342
SWAYNE AUDITORIUM
Northwest Nazarene University
Brandt Center
623 Holly Street
Nampa, ID 83686-5897
Mailing Address: Northwest Nazarene University, 623 S University Boulevard, N
Phone: 208-467-8790
e-mail: hmlindner@nnu.edu
Web Site: www.nnu.edu
Officers:
President: Dr David Alexander
VP: Dr Samuel Dunn
Dean: Ron Ponsford
Management:
Marketing Director: Hollie Lindner
Mission: With over 1,500 plush theatre seats, complete backstage support spaces, state of the art technology, and a production staff dedicated to providing our clients with a quality experience, Swayne Auditoroium is the ideal venue for your concert, graduation ceremony, organization-wide training session, or theatrical performance.

Type of Stage: Auditorium
Seating Capacity: 1,500

6343
BILYEU THEATRE
Idaho State University
921 S 8th Avenue
Pocatello, ID 83209
Mailing Address: Theatre/Dance ISU, 921 S 8th Ave, Stop 8006 | Pocatello, ID
Phone: 208-282-3595
Web Site: http://www.isu.edu/theatreisu/index.shtml
Officers:
   Chair: Sherri R Dienstfrey
Management:
   Technical Director: Chad Gross
   Dance Director: Lauralee Zimmerly
Mission: The Bilyeu Theatre, previously called Frazier Auditorium, is a 790-seat proscenium theatre housed in Frazier Hall. Since its completion in 1924, Frazier has been the site for numerous theatre productions.
Utilizes: Poets
Founded: 1924
Specialized Field: Theater
Type of Stage: Proscenium
Seating Capacity: 790
Cost: $34 Million

6344
BISTLINE FAMILY THEATRE
Idaho State University
921 S 8th Avenue
Pocatello, ID 83209
Mailing Address: Theatre/Dance ISU, 921 S 8th Ave, Stop 8006 | Pocatello, ID
Phone: 208-282-3595
Web Site: www.isu.edu
Officers:
   Chair: Sherri R Dienstfrey
Management:
   Technical Director: Chad Gross
   Dance Director: Lauralee Zimmerly
Utilizes: Poets
Type of Stage: Thrust
Seating Capacity: 450
Cost: $34 Million

6345
BISTLINE THRUST THEATRE
Idaho State University
Stephens Performing Arts Center
1002 Sam Nixon Avenue, Building 88
Pocatello, ID 83209
Mailing Address: Theatre/Dance ISU, 921 S 8th Ave, Stop 8006 | Pocatello, ID
Phone: 208-282-3595
Web Site: www.isu.edu
Management:
   Events Director: George Casper
   Event Technical Manager: William Stanton
   Technical Director: Chad Gross
   Dance Director: Lauralee Zimmerly
Paid Staff: 8
Performs At: Student Union Ballroom
Affiliations: Alpha Psa Omega
Type of Stage: Proscenium Thrust

6346
GORANSON HALL
Idaho State University, Department of Music
921 S 8th Avenue
Box 8099
Pocatello, ID 83209

Phone: 208-282-3636
Fax: 208-282-4884
e-mail: music@isu.edu
Web Site: www.isu.edu
Officers:
   President: Arthur C Vailas
   Chair: Dr Randy Earles
Type of Stage: Proscenium
Seating Capacity: 446

6347
HOLT ARENA
Idaho State University
558 Memorial Drive
Building 60
Pocatello, ID 83209
Mailing Address: Theatre/Dance ISU, 921 S 8th Ave, Stop 8006 | Pocatello, ID
Phone: 208-236-2831
Web Site: www.isu.edu
Management:
   Athletic Director: Paul Bubb
   Assistant Director of Athletics: Jeff Tingey
   Marketing Director: KaLee Kopp
   Athletic Facilities Director: Mike Pritchett

6348
IDAHO STATE UNIVERSITY
921 S 8th Avenue
PO Box 8281
Pocatello, ID 83209
Phone: 208-282-0211
Fax: 208-282-4741
e-mail: kovarudo@isu.edu
Web Site: www.isu.edu
Officers:
   President: Dr. Arthur Vailas
Founded: 1900
Status: Non-Profit, Professional
Paid Staff: 650

6349
POWELL LITTLE THEATRE
Idaho State University
921 S 8th Avenue
Pocatello, ID 83209-8026
Mailing Address: Theatre/Dance ISU, 921 S 8th Ave, Stop 8006 | Pocatello, ID
Phone: 208-282-3595
Web Site: www.isu.edu
Officers:
   Chair: Sherri R Dienstfrey
Management:
   Technical Director: Chad Gross
   Dance Director: Lauralee Zimmerly

6350
ROGERS BLACK BOX THEATRE
Idaho State University
Stephens Performing Arts Center
921 S 8th Avenue
Pocatello, ID 83209
Mailing Address: Theatre/Dance ISU, 921 S 8th Ave, Stop 8006 | Pocatello, ID
Phone: 208-282-3595
Web Site: www.isu.edu
Officers:
   Chair: Sherri R Dienstfrey
Management:
   Technical Director: Chad Gross
   Dance Director: Lauralee Zimmerly
Paid Staff: 8
Performs At: Student Union Ballroom
Affiliations: Alpha Psa Omega

Type of Stage: Proscenium Thurst

6351
STEPHENS PERFORMING ARTS CENTER
Idaho State University
921 S 8th Avenue
Pocatello, ID 83209
Mailing Address: Theatre/Dance ISU, 921 S 8th Ave, Stop 8006 | Pocatello, ID
Phone: 208-282-3595
Web Site: www.isu.edu
Officers:
   Chair: Sherri R Dienstfrey
Management:
   Technical Director: Chad Gross
   Dance Director: Lauralee Zimmerly

6352
ELIZA R SNOW PERFORMING ARTS CENTER
Bringham Young University-Idaho
246 Snow Building
Rexburg, ID 83460-1210
Mailing Address: Snow Building 126, Rexburg, ID 83460-1215
Phone: 208-496-1259
Fax: 208-496-1249
e-mail: cliffordr@byui.edu
Web Site: www.byui.edu
Officers:
   Chair: Kevin Brower
Management:
   Stage/Recording Managament: Tyler McNiven
   Department Chair: Richard J Clifford
Mission: The building is home to the Music and Performing Arts departments of BYU-Idaho, as well as the famed Barrus Concert Hall.
Utilizes: Dancers; Guest Lecturers; Guest Musical Directors; Multimedia; Sign Language Translators; Theatre Companies
Specialized Field: Theater, Music, dance
Paid Staff: 21
Income Sources: Church Of Jesus Christ Of Latter-Day Saints; Donations
Facility Category: Concert Hall
Type of Stage: Raised
Stage Dimensions: 53'x 48'
Seating Capacity: 700
Year Built: 1981
Rental Contact: Denise Green

Illinois

6353
METROPOLIS PERFORMING ARTS CENTRE
111 W Campbell Street
Arlington Heights, IL 60005
Mailing Address: 111 W. Campbell St., Second Floor, Arlington Heights, IL 600
Phone: 847-577-5982
Web Site: www.metropolisarts.com
Officers:
   President: Phil Collins
   VP: Kathy Monnich
   Secretary: Lauree Harp
   Treasurer: Kevin Seifert
Management:
   Executive Director: Jim Jarvis
   Director of Production: Joe Mohamed
   Company Manager: Robin Hughes

Mission: Each year, Metropolis produces 4 shows for our Subscription Series. We also present a wide variety of shows including music performances (such as cabaret nights), comedy shows (including shows from The Second City), and family and holiday programming.
Founded: 2000
Specialized Field: Theater
Paid Staff: 25

6354
PARAMOUNT THEATRE
23 East Galena Boulevard
Aurora, IL 60508
Mailing Address: Paramount Theatre, 23 East Galena Boulevard, Aurora, IL 6050
Phone: 630-896-6666
Fax: 630-892-6751
e-mail: melissam@paramountarts.com
Web Site: www.paramountaurora.com
Officers:
    Chair: Richard Hawks
    Treasurer: Donna Williams
    Secretary: Chris Goerlich-Weber
Management:
    Executive Director: Diana Martinez
    Marketing Director: Melissa Mercado
    Production Director: Val Devine
Mission: The theatre continues to be an anchor in the city bringing in approximately $3.3 million in ancillary revenue as well as hosting many free community events including the Midwest Literary Festival, the Air Force Band Concert, the Aurora Idol Competition and staging the annual Fox Valley Park District children's production.
Founded: 1931
Specialized Field: Theater, General Entertainment.
Seating Capacity: 1,794

6355
MCPHERSON THEATRE
Illinois Wesleyan University
1312 Park Street
Bloomington, IL 61701
Phone: 309-556-1000
e-mail: webmaster@iwu.edu
Web Site: www.iwu.edu
Officers:
    President: Richard F Wilson
Paid Staff: 38
Seating Capacity: 300
Year Built: 1963

6356
WESTBROOK AUDITORIUM
Illinois Wesleyan University
Presser Hall
1312 Park Street
Bloomington, IL 61701
Phone: 309-556-1000
e-mail: webmaster@iwu.edu
Web Site: www.iwu.edu
Officers:
    President: Richard F Wilson
Paid Staff: 38
Seating Capacity: 600

6357
SHRYOCK AUDITORIUM AND ARENA PROMOTIONS
Southern Illinois University
1050 S Normal Avenue
Mail Code 4326
Carbondale, IL 62901

Phone: 618-453-3379
Fax: 618-453-8164
e-mail: shryock@siu.edu
Web Site: www.siuc.edu
Officers:
    President: Glenn Poshard
Management:
    Director: Bryan L Rives
    Production Manager: Seth Kohlhaas
Founded: 1917
Status: Non-Profit, Non-Professional
Seating Capacity: 1,249

6358
SIU ARENA
Southern Illinois University
1050 S Normal Avenue
Carbondale, IL 62901
Phone: 618-453-3379
Fax: 618-453-8164
e-mail: shryock@siu.edu
Web Site: www.siuc.edu
Management:
    Director: Bryan L Rives
    Production Manager: Seth Kohlhaas
Status: Non-Profit, Professional
Seating Capacity: 10,014

6359
ASSEMBLY HALL
University of Illinois
1800 S First Street
Champaign, IL 61820
Mailing Address: University of Illinois Assembly Hall, 1800 South First Stree
Phone: 217-333-2923
Fax: 217-244-8888
e-mail: slyman@illinois.edu
Web Site: www.uofiassemblyhall.com
Officers:
    President: B Joseph White
Management:
    Director: Kevin Ullestad
    Marketing Director: Jennifer Larson
    Marketing Director: Sue Lyman
    Marketing: Jennifer Larson
Founded: 1963
Specialized Field: General Entertainmnet
Paid Staff: 42
Seating Capacity: 16,000 to 17,200

6360
LANTZ ARENA
Eastern Illinois University
600 Lincoln Avenue
Charleston, IL 61920
Mailing Address: Eastern Illinois Athletic Department, 600 Lincoln Avenue, Ch
Phone: 217-581-6014
e-mail: rlmoser@eiu.edu
Web Site: www.eiupanthers.edu
Officers:
    President: William L Perry
Management:
    Athletic Director: Barbara Burke
    Marketing Director: Ryan Gilmore
    Associate Athletic Director/Media &: Rich Moser
Founded: 1967
Seating Capacity: 5,200

6361
O'BRIEN FIELD
Eastern Illinois University
600 Lincoln Avenue
Charleston, IL 61920
Mailing Address: Eastern Illinois Athletic Department, 600 Lincoln Avenue, Ch
Phone: 217-581-6014
e-mail: rlmoser@eiu.edu
Web Site: www.eiupanthers.com
Officers:
    President: William L Perry
Management:
    Athletic Director: Barbara Burke
    Marketing Director: Ryan Gilmore
    Associate Athletic Director/Media &: Rich Moser
Founded: 1970
Seating Capacity: 10,000

6362
APOLLO THEATER CENTER
2540 N Lincoln Avenue
Chicago, IL 60614
Phone: 773-935-9336
Fax: 773-935-6214
e-mail: info@apollochicago.com
Web Site: www.apollochicago.com
Officers:
    President: Rob Kolson
Utilizes: Actors; Collaborations; Designers; Instructors; Local Artists; Multimedia; Music; New Productions; Original Music Scores; Resident Professionals; Selected Students; Sign Language Translators; Student Interns; Special Technical Talent; Theatre Companies
Income Sources: League of Chicago Theatres
Facility Category: Theater
Type of Stage: thrust
Seating Capacity: 450
Rental Contact: Rob Kolson
Organization Type: Sponsoring; Presenting

6363
ARIE CROWN THEATRE
Lakeside Center/McCormick Place
2301 S Lake Shore Drive
Chicago, IL 60616
Phone: 312-567-8136
e-mail: dgilmore@mpea.com
Web Site: www.ariecrown.com
Management:
    Executive Director: Dulcie C Gilmore
Founded: 1967
Status: Non-Profit, Non-Professional
Paid Staff: 3
Type of Stage: Proscenium

6364
ATHENAEUM THEATRE
2936 N Southport Avenue
Chicago, IL 60657
Phone: 773-935-6860
Fax: 773-935-6878
Toll-free: 800-433-7285
Web Site: www.athenaeumtheatre.com
Management:
    Director: Dan Solari
    Marketing Director: Clyde Foster
Founded: 1972
Status: Non-Profit, Professional
Paid Staff: 21
Paid Artists: 100
Annual Attendance: 20,000+
Type of Stage: Proscenium

Seating Capacity: 1,325

6365
AUDITORIUM THEATRE
Roosevelt University
50 E Congress Parkway
Chicago, IL 60605
Phone: 312-922-2110
Fax: 312-431-2360
e-mail: info@auditoriumtheatre.org
Web Site: www.auditoriumtheatre.org
Officers:
  Chairman: Mel Katten
  CEO: Margaret Walsh
Management:
  Executive Director: Brett Batterson
  General Manager: Jennifer Turner
  Marketing Manager: Megan Flanagan
Utilizes: Resident Artists
Founded: 1945
Type of Stage: Flexible Configuration
Seating Capacity: 1,400
Year Built: 1889
Architect: Louis Sullivan and Dankmar Adler

6366
BANK OF AMERICA THEATRE
Broadway In Chicago
18 W Monroe Street
Chicago, IL 60602
Phone: 312-986-6821
e-mail: customerservice@broadwayinchicago.com
Web Site: www.broadwayinchicago.com
Officers:
  President: Lou Raizin
Founded: 1906

6367
BEVERLY ARTS CENTER
2407 W 111th Street
Chicago, IL 60655
Phone: 773-445-3838
Fax: 773-445-0386
Web Site: www.beverlyartscenter.org
Officers:
  President: William Figel
  Treasurer: Deborah Cernauskas PhD
  Secretary: Tony Kelly
Management:
  Executive Director: Michael Nix
  Development Director: Kate Coughlin
Founded: 1968
Seating Capacity: 422

6368
CHICAGO SYMPHONY ORCHESTRA SYMPHONY CENTER
220 S Michigan Avenue
Chicago, IL 60604
Mailing Address: 220 S. Michigan Avenue, Chicago, IL, 60604
Phone: 312-294-3000
Fax: 312-294-3035
Toll-free: 800-223-7114
Web Site: www.cso.org
Officers:
  President: Deborah F Rutter
  Chairman: William A Osborn
Management:
  Music Director: Riccardo Muti
  Choral Director: Duain Wolfe
Founded: 1891
Specialized Field: Orchestra

6369
COURT THEATRE
University of Chicago
5535 S Ellis Avenue
Chicago, IL 60637
Phone: 773-702-7005
e-mail: info@courttheatre.org
Web Site: www.courttheater.org
Officers:
  Chairman: Lawrence E Strickling
  Secretary: Mary Anton
  Treasurer: Russell Campbell
Management:
  Artistic Director: Charles Newell
  Executive Director: Dawn Helsing
Utilizes: Guest Companies; Singers
Paid Staff: 18
Budget: $2.7 Million
Income Sources: Actors' Equity Association; League of Chicago Theatres; Theatre Communications Group; Producers Association of Chicago Area Theatres
Performs At: Court Theatre
Annual Attendance: 35,000
Seating Capacity: 250
Organization Type: Performing; Educational

6370
CURTISS HALL
Fine Arts Building Gallery
410 S Michigan Avenue
Suite 904
Chicago, IL 60605
Phone: 312-939-3380
Web Site: www.fineartsbuilding.tv
Management:
  General Manager: Kyle Walsh
  Director: Blake Biggerstaff
Founded: 1912
Specialized Field: Music
Paid Staff: 1

6371
DANCE CENTER
Columbia College Chicago
1306 S Michigan Avenue
Chicago, IL 60605
Mailing Address: Columbia College Chicago, 600 S. Michigan Avenue, Chicago, I
Phone: 312-639-8350
e-mail: skauffman@colum.edu
Web Site: www.colum.edu
Officers:
  Chair: Bonnie Brooks
Management:
  Executive Director: Phil Reynolds
  Marketing Director: Liqia Himebaugh
Mission: The mission of The Dance Center of Columbia College Chicago is to provide our students with a superior contemporary dance education in the context of higher learning. We fulfill this mission through the work of a qualified, professional faculty, a comprehensive curriculum that offers both Bachelor of Arts and Bachelor of Fine Arts tracks, world-class guest artists, and a nationally recognized dance performance season
Seating Capacity: 275
Year Built: 1930

6372
ENSEMBLE ESPANOL
Northeastern Illinois University
5500 N St Louis
Chicago, IL 60625-4699

Phone: 773-442-5930
Fax: 773-442-5908
e-mail: ensemble-espanol@neiu.edu
Web Site: www.ensembleespanol.org
Management:
  Executive Director: Jorge Perez
Mission: The preservation, presentation and promotion of the classical, folkloric, Flamenco and contemporary traditions of Spain which includes the exploration of the countty's hisotry and identifies its influence on Latin American arts heritage as living sources of cultural pride and education.
Founded: 1976
Specialized Field: Dance
Status: Non-Profit
Paid Staff: 7
Volunteer Staff: 25
Paid Artists: 40

6373
KATHLEEN MULLADY MEMORIAL THEATRE
Loyola University
Lake Shore Campus Department of Theatre
1125 W Loyola Avenue
Chicago, IL 60626
Phone: 773-508-3847
e-mail: boxoffice@luc.edu
Web Site: www.luc.edu
Officers:
  President: Michael J Garanzini SJ
Management:
  Director: Mark Lococo
Type of Stage: Proscenium
Seating Capacity: 297

6374
LYRIC OPERA OF CHICAGO
The Civic Opera House
20 N Wacker Drive
Chicago, IL 60606
Mailing Address: 20 N. Wacker Drive,Chicago, IL 60606
Phone: 312-332-2244
Fax: 312-419-8345
Web Site: www.lyricopera.org
Management:
  General Director: William Mason
  Development Director: Mary Ladish Selander
  Marketing Director: J Philip Koester
Founded: 1952
Specialized Field: Opera

6375
MERLE RESKIN THEATRE
DePaul University
60 E Balbo Drive
Chicago, IL 60605
Mailing Address: Anna Ables, Director of Marketing/Public Relations, The The
Phone: 773-325-7917
e-mail: aables@depaul.edu
Web Site: theatreschool.depaul.edu
Officers:
  President: Rev Dennis H Holtschneider CM
Management:
  Theatre Manager: Leslie Shook
  Marketing Director: Anna Ables
  Development Director: Tessa Craib-Cox
Founded: 1910
Specialized Field: Theater

All listings are in alphabetical order by state, then city, then organization within the city.

6376

NEW STUDIO THEATRE
Columbia College Chicago
600 S Miochigan Avenue
Chicago, IL 60605
Mailing Address: Theater Office:, 3rd Floor Room 300, 72 East 11th Street, Ch
Phone: 312-369-6240
Fax: 312-369-8078
Web Site: www.colum.edu
Officers:
President: Warrick L Carter
Chairman: Richard Dunscomb
Management:
Executive Director: HE Baccus
Opened: 2000
Specialized Field: Instrumentals, Recitals
Seating Capacity: 40-70

6377

O'ROURKE CENTER FOR THE PERFORMING ARTS
Truman College
1145 W Wilson Avenue
Chicago, IL 60640
Mailing Address: O'Rourke Center, Truman College, 1145 West Wilson Avenue, Ch
Phone: 773-907-4000
Web Site: www.trumancollege.edu
Officers:
President: Lynn M Walker
Founded: 1984

6378

PATRICK L O'MALLEY THEATRE
Roosevelt University
430 S Michigan Avenue
Chicago, IL 60605
Phone: 312-341-3789
e-mail: theatre@roosevelt.edu
Web Site: www.roosevelt.edu
Officers:
President: Chuck Middleton
Dean: Rudy Marcozzi
Management:
General Manager: Kelley Kendall
Production Manager: Emily Humphreys
Founded: 1945
Status: Non-Profit, Non-Professional
Paid Artists: 50

6379

PETRILLO MUSIC SHELL
City of Chicago
235 S Columbus Drive
Chicago, IL 60604
Mailing Address: 235 S. Columbus Dr., Chicago
Phone: 312-742-4763
Officers:
Mayor: Richard M Daley
Management:
General Manager: Tracy Jones
Director: Miguel Del Valle
Mission: It serves as host to many large annual music festivals in the city such as Chicago Blues Festival, Chicago Jazz Festival, Taste of Chicago and Lollapalooza
Founded: 1933
Specialized Field: Music Festivals

6380

RECITAL HALL
Northeastern Illinois University
Fine Arts Department
Chicago, IL 60625-4699
Mailing Address: Northeastern Illinois University, 5500 N. St. Louis, Chicago
Phone: 773-442-5900
Fax: 773-442-5910
e-mail: B-Harms1@neiu.edu
Web Site: www.neiu.edu
Officers:
President: Sharon K Hahs
Secretary: Gladys Yvette Lopez
Dean: Michael T Kelly
Chair: Dr R Shayne Cofer
Management:
Director: Jorge Perez
Specialized Field: Theater

6381

SOLDIER FIELD
1410 S Museum
Campus Drive Gate 14
Chicago, IL 60605
Phone: 312-235-7000
Fax: 312-235-7030
e-mail: kmcgregor@soldierfield.net
Web Site: www.soldierfield.net
Officers:
Mayor, City of Chicago: Richard M Daley
Management:
General Manager: Tim LeFevour
Operations Director: Michael Ortman
Marketing Director: Kate McGregor
Founded: 2003
Seating Capacity: 66,950

6382

STAGE CENTER THEATRE
Northeastern Illinois University
5500 N Street Louis Avenue
Chicago, IL 60625-4699
Phone: 773-442-4274
Fax: 773-442-5960
e-mail: a-antaramian@neiu.edu
Web Site: www.neiu.edu
Officers:
President: Sharon K Hahs
Secretary: Gladys Yvette Lopez
Chair: Katrina E Bell-Jordan
Management:
Artistic/Managing Director: Anna Antaramian
Type of Stage: Thrust
Orchestra Pit: y
Seating Capacity: 100

6383

STUDIO THEATRE
Loyola University
1125 West Loyola Avenue, Chicago, IL 60626
1125 W Loyola Avenue
Chicago, IL 60626
Mailing Address: 1032 W. Sheridan Road, Chicago, IL 60660
Phone: 773-508-3000
e-mail: sgabel1@luc.edu
Web Site: www.luc.edu
Officers:
President: Michael J Garanzini SJ
Board President/General Manager: Joseph J Ahern
Chair: Sarah Gabel PhD

Management:
Director: Mark Lococo
Utilizes: Resident Artists
Type of Stage: Black Box
Seating Capacity: 50

6384

SYMPHONY CENTER
220 S Michigan Avenue
Chicago, IL 60604
Phone: 312-294-3333
Fax: 312-294-3329
e-mail: patronservices@cso.org
Web Site: www.cso.org
Officers:
President: Deborah Rutter
Management:
Director of Programming: James M Fahey
Rental Events Manager: Michael Lavin
VP Marketing: Kevin Giglinto
Box Office Manager: Joe Garnett
Seating Capacity: 2,521

6385

THE CHICAGO THEATRE
175 N State Street
Chicago, IL 60601
Mailing Address: 175 N. State Street, Chicago, IL 60601
Phone: 312-462-6300
Toll-free: 888-235-2990
Web Site: www.thechicagotheatre.com
Management:
General Manager: Mike Godina
Founded: 1921
Specialized Field: General Entertainmnet
Seating Capacity: 3,604

6386

THE MUSIC CENTER
Columbia College Chicago
1014 S Michigan Avenue
Chicago, IL 60605
Phone: 312-369-6240
Fax: 312-369-8078
e-mail: music@colum.edu
Web Site: www.colum.edu
Officers:
President: Warrick L. Carter
Chairman: Allen M Turner
Treasurer: Tom Kallen
Secretary: Averill Leviton
Type of Stage: Concert Hall
Seating Capacity: 125
Year Built: 1912

6387

STAGE 773
1225 W Belmont Avenue
Chicago, IL 60657
Phone: 773-929-5252
e-mail: info@stage773.com
Web Site: http://www.stage773.com/Default.aspx
Officers:
Secretary: Arthur Don
Treasurer: Arla Ebeling
Management:
Executive Director: Joan Mazzonelli
Artistic Director: John Sparks
Marketing Director: Jeff DeLong
Utilizes: Actors; AEA Actors; Choreographers; Collaborations; Commissioned Composers; Five Seasonal Concerts; Guest Soloists; High School Drama; Instructors; Local Artists; Local Unknown

Artists; Lyricists; Multimedia; Music; Organization Contracts; Original Music Scores; Performance Artists; Resident Artists; Resident Professionals; Sign Language Translators; Soloists; Student Interns; Special Technical Talent; Theatre Companies
Founded: 1969
Specialized Field: Theater
Paid Staff: 10
Volunteer Staff: 800
Paid Artists: 200
Non-paid Artists: 107
Budget: $1,000,000
Annual Attendance: 35,000
Facility Category: multiplex
Type of Stage: 3 black box
Seating Capacity: 444
Year Built: 1962
Year Remodeled: 2002
Cost: 100,000
Rental Contact: Lorraine Townsend

6388
UIC PAVILION

University of Illinois at Chicago
525 S Racine Avenue
Chicago, IL 60607
Phone: 312-413-5740
Web Site: www.uicpavilion.com
Officers:
    President: B Joseph White
Management:
    Director: Kevin O'Finn
    Manager: Matt Liskh
Mission: The Pavilion provides an adaptable setting for a variety of educational, recreational, cultural, entertainment and civic events. These may include university events, e.g., commencements and athletic events, or non-university events
Seating Capacity: 10,000

6389
UIC THEATRE

University of Illinois at Chicago
Department of Performing Arts EPASW Building
1040 West Harrison Street MC-255
Chicago, IL 60607
Mailing Address: UIC Department of Performing Arts , College of Architecture
Phone: 312-996-2977
Fax: 312-996-0954
e-mail: dpa@uic.edu
Web Site: www.uic.edu
Officers:
    President: B Joseph White
    Secretary: Michele M Thompson
    Chair: Michael J Anderson
Management:
    Events Director: Neal McCollam
Mission: The Theatre curriculum emphasizes a balance between practice and theory from originating impulse or idea to realization in performance. The areas of Acting, Voice, Movement, Physical Theatre Techniques, Directing, Playwriting, and Design within the context of their artistic, social, political, and historical environments form the nucleus of the curriculum.
Specialized Field: Theater
Type of Stage: Black Box
Seating Capacity: 250

6390
UNITED CENTER

1901 W Madison Street
Chicago, IL 60612

Phone: 312-455-4500
e-mail: sschanwald@bulls.com
Web Site: www.unitedcenter.com
Management:
    General Manager: Jim Koehler
    Marketing Director: Steve Schanwald
    Operations Director: Terry Savarise
    Operations Manager: Erica Schisler
Seating Capacity: 20,500

6391
US CELLULAR FIELD

Chicago White Sox
333 W 35th Street
Chicago, IL 60616
Phone: 312-674-1000
Web Site: www.whitesox.com
Officers:
    Chairman: Jerry Reinsdorf
    Secretary: Gerald Penner
Management:
    Chief Marketing Officer: Brooks Boyer
Seating Capacity: 44,321
Year Built: 1991

6392
VICTORY GARDENS THEATER

2257 N Lincoln Avenue
Chicago, IL 60614
Phone: 773-549-5788
e-mail: information@victorygardens.org
Web Site: www.victorygardens.org
Officers:
    President: Jeffrey C Rappin
    Secretary: Sylvia Margolies
    Treasurer: A Kirk Twiss
Management:
    Artistic Director: Dennis Zacek
    Managing Director: Marcelle McVay
    Managing Director: Barbara Harris
    Marketing Director: Jay Kelly
Founded: 1974
Paid Staff: 24
Annual Attendance: 60,000
Type of Stage: Black Box; Thrust
Seating Capacity: 195

6393
WRIGLEY FIELD

1060 W Addison Street
Chicago, IL 60613
Phone: 773-404-2827
Web Site: chicago.cubs.mlb.com
Officers:
    Chairman: Crane Kenney
Management:
    Director: Scott Nelson
    Marketing Director: Matthew Wszolek
    Manager: Chuck Wasserstrom
    Facility Director: Carl Rice
Founded: 1914
Seating Capacity: 38,710

6394
CONVOCATION CENTER

North Illinois University
1525 W Lincold Highway
DeKalb, IL 60115
Phone: 815-752-6800
Fax: 815-752-6830
e-mail: hpriest2@niu.edu
Web Site: www.niuconvo.com
Officers:
    President: John G Peters

    Chair: Robert T Boey
Management:
    Director: John A Gordon
    Marketing Director: Heather Priest
Mission: As the center for social, academic, and athletic events on campus, the Convocation Center is the single venue that can bring the university community together at one place and one time to share an experience: the very definition of community.
Seating Capacity: 10,000

6395
EGYPTIAN THEATRE

135 N Second Street
DeKalb, IL 60115
Mailing Address: PO Box 385, DeKalb IL 60115
Phone: 815-758-1215
e-mail: info@egyptiantheatre.org
Web Site: www.egyptiantheatre.org
Officers:
    President: Mary Brown
    Secretary: Linda Groat
    Treasurer: Keith Deal
Management:
    Operations Director: Alex Nerad
Seating Capacity: 1,475

6396
O'CONNELL THEATRE

Northern Illinois University
1425 W Lincoln Highway
DeKalb, IL 60115
Phone: 815-753-1334
Fax: 815-753-8415
Web Site: www.niu.edu
Officers:
    President: John G Peters
Management:
    Director: Alexander Gelman
    Marketing Director: David W Booth
Specialized Field: Theatre
Seating Capacity: 450

6397
PLAYERS THEATRE

Northern Illinois University
1425 W Lincoln Highway
DeKalb, IL 60115
Phone: 815-753-1334
Fax: 815-753-8415
Web Site: www.niu.edu
Officers:
    President: John G Peters
Management:
    Director: Alexander Gelman
    Marketing Director: David W Booth
Type of Stage: Black Box
Seating Capacity: 180

6398
SCHOOL OF THEATRE AND DANCE

Northern Illinois University
Stevens Building, Gable Hall
DeKalb, IL 60115
Phone: 815-753-1334
Fax: 815-753-8415
e-mail: theatreinfo@niu.edu
Web Site: www.niu.edu/theatre/
Officers:
    President: Dr. John G. Peters
    Director: Alexander Gelman
    Assistant Director: Terrence McClellan
Management:
    Technical Director: Tracy Nunnally

Director Of Marketing: David W. Booth
Mission: Provides intensive artistic & academic training for students preparing for careers in theatre & theatre-related areas. The course of study is rigorous and realistic, designed to develop, challenge & broaden the skills and attitudes off all theatre students, but especially the highly motivated student who takes responsibility for his/her own growth. Each year we present a full season of stage productions on three stages.
Specialized Field: Performance Theatre; Classical; Modern Dance
Status: Educational; Performance
Performs At: Education; Performing
Affiliations: University/Resident Theatre Assoc.; National Assoc. of Schools of Theatre; Illinois Arts Council; American Assoc. of Community Theatre
Type of Stage: Proscenium, Black Box, 1/4 Round
Seating Capacity: Theatre - 443; Corner Theatre - 145
Rental Contact: Technical Director Tracy Nunnally

6399
ALBERT TAYLOR THEATRE

Millikin University
Kirkland Fine Arts Center
1184 W Main Street
Decatur, IL 62522-2084
Mailing Address: Kirkland Fine Arts Center, 1184 West Main St, Decatur, IL 62
Toll-free: 800-373-7733
Web Site: www.millikin.edu
Officers:
    President: Douglas E Zemke
    Chair: Laura Ledford
Management:
    Marketing Director: William Warren
    General Manager: Mary Spencer
Mission: The Albert Taylor Theatre has served as the main stage for many Millikin University activities from the opening of the University in 1903 on through to today.
Utilizes: Artists-in-Residence; Dance Companies; Fine Artists; Local Artists; Lyricists; Multimedia; Music; Original Music Scores; Resident Artists; Selected Students; Soloists; Special Technical Talent; Theatre Companies; Touring Companies
Founded: 1903
Specialized Field: Theater
Paid Staff: 6
Volunteer Staff: 12
Paid Artists: 20
Annual Attendance: 60,000
Facility Category: Fine Arts Center
Seating Capacity: 750
Architect: Patton and Miller
Year Restored: 2006

6400
KIRKLAND FINE ARTS CENTER

Millikin University
1184 W Main Street
Decatur, IL 62522
Mailing Address: Kirkland Fine Arts Center, 1184 West Main St, Decatur, IL 62
Toll-free: 800-373-7733
Web Site: www.millikin.edu
Officers:
    President: Douglas E Zemke
    Chair: Laura Ledford
Management:
    Marketing Director: William Warren
    General Manager: Mary Spencer

Mission: houses several music and choral facilities, lecture halls, art galleries, and other multipurpose rooms.
Utilizes: Actors; Artists-in-Residence; Dance Companies; Dancers; Fine Artists; Guest Writers; Instructors; Local Artists; Lyricists; Multimedia; Music; Original Music Scores; Resident Artists; Selected Students; Soloists; Special Technical Talent; Theatre Companies; Touring Companies
Founded: 1969
Specialized Field: Theater, Dance, Musical
Paid Staff: 6
Volunteer Staff: 12
Paid Artists: 20
Annual Attendance: 60,000
Facility Category: Fine Arts Center
Type of Stage: Proscenium
Stage Dimensions: 53' x 23'
Orchestra Pit: y
Seating Capacity: 1,902
Rental Contact: Scheduling & Events Coordinator Lynne Kickle

6401
PIPE DREAMS STUDIO THEATRE

Millikin University
Kirkland Fine Arts Center
1184 W Main Street
Decatur, IL 62522
Mailing Address: Pipe Dreams Studio Theatre 1099 West Wood Street
Toll-free: 800-373-7733
Web Site: www.millikin.edu
Officers:
    President: Douglas E Zemke
    Chair: Laura Ledford
Management:
    Marketing Director: William Warren
    General Manager: Mary Spencer
Mission: student operated business with help and guidance by Department of Theatre & Dance faculty
Utilizes: Artists-in-Residence; Dance Companies; Fine Artists; Local Artists; Lyricists; Multimedia; Music; Original Music Scores; Resident Artists; Selected Students; Soloists; Special Technical Talent; Theatre Companies; Touring Companies
Specialized Field: Theater, Dance
Paid Staff: 6
Volunteer Staff: 12
Paid Artists: 20
Annual Attendance: 60,000
Facility Category: Fine Arts Center

6402
ROSEMONT THEATRE

5400 N River Road
Des Plaines, IL 60018
Phone: 847-671-5100
Fax: 847-671-6405
Toll-free: 800-852-7771
e-mail: info@rosemonttheatre.com
Web Site: www.rosemonttheatre.com
Management:
    Executive Director: Harry Pappas
    General Manager: Ron Stern
    Operations Director: Ken Lennstrom
Seating Capacity: 4,300

6403
DUNHAM HALL THEATER

Southern Illinois University at Edwardsville
6 S State Route 157
Edwardsville, IL 62026

Mailing Address: College of Arts and Sciences, Campus Box 1608, Southern Illi
Phone: 618-650-2000
Toll-free: 888-328-5168
e-mail: Kbozark@siue.edu
Web Site: www.siue.edu
Officers:
    Chair: Peter Cocuzza
    Secretary: Debbie Brown-Thompson
Management:
    Director: Kathryn Bentley
    Marketing Director: Mr. Kim Bozark
    General Manager: Valerie Goldston
Mission: Katherine Dunham Hall houses the departments of Theater and Dance, Music, and Mass Communications. Plays, musicals, recitals, band concerts and choral clinics are held here. Students make make use of the building's TV studio, multimedia computer lab, video editing lab and photojournalism dark room.
Specialized Field: Dance
Type of Stage: Proscenium
Orchestra Pit: y
Seating Capacity: 400

6404
JAMES F METCALF STUDENT EXPERIMENTAL THEATER

Southern Illinois University at Edwardsville
6 S State Route 157
Edwardsville, IL 62026
Mailing Address: College of Arts and Sciences, Campus Box 1608, Southern Illi
Phone: 618-650-2000
Toll-free: 888-328-5168
e-mail: Kbozark@siue.edu
Web Site: www.siue.edu
Officers:
    Chair: Peter Cocuzza
    Secretary: Debbie Brown-Thompson
Management:
    Director: Kathryn Bentley
    Marketing Director: Mr. Kim Bozark
    General Manager: Valerie Goldston
Founded: 1984
Seating Capacity: 200

6405
ELGIN COMMUNITY COLLEGE VISUAL & PERFORMING ARTS CENTER

Elgin Community College
1700 Spartan Drive
Elgin, IL 60123-7193
Mailing Address: 1700 Spartan Drive, Elgin, IL 60123-7193
Phone: 847-622-0300
e-mail: marketing@elgin.edu
Web Site: www.elgin.edu
Officers:
    President: David Sam PhD JD
Management:
    Director: Steven A Duchrow
    Marketing Director: Paula Amenta MS
    Operations/Theater Director: Cynthia Gaspardo
Mission: The Visual and Performing Arts Center provides residents of Chicago's Fox Valley a refreshingly different arts experience than can be found in the city or other regional arts center. Our CenterStage lineup avoids tired reruns in favor of fresh, artistically relevant acts. Only the ECC Arts Center pairs club amenities-including gourmet dinners and a wine bar-with performances of the highest caliber. We aim to inspire, engage and spark your cr

Paid Staff: 20
Volunteer Staff: 80
Paid Artists: 15
Annual Attendance: 40,000
Type of Stage: Proscenium
Seating Capacity: 662

6406
HEMMENS CULTURAL CENTER

45 Symphony Way
Elgin, IL 60120
Phone: 847-931-5900
Web Site: www.hemmens.org
Officers:
   Chair: Kathleen A Weber
   Secretary: Cathy Malm
   Treasurer: Jeff Grosser
Founded: 1969
Paid Staff: 33
Volunteer Staff: 35
Type of Stage: Proscenium Arch
Seating Capacity: 1,200

6407
BECKER AUDITORIUM

Eureka College
Donald B Cerf Center
300 E College Avenue
Eureka, IL 61530
Mailing Address: Eureka College, 300 East College Avenue, Eureka, Illinois 61
Phone: 309-467-6407
Toll-free: 888-438-7352
Web Site: www.eureka.edu
Officers:
   President: David J Arnold
   Chair: Rhea Edge
Management:
   Director: Dr Joseph Henry
Mission: nested at the heart of the Cerf Center, this largest of Eureka's performance spaces seats over 400.
Seating Capacity: 400

6408
PRITCHARD THEATER

Eureka College
Pritchard Hall
300 E College Avenue
Eureka, IL 61530
Mailing Address: Eureka College, 300 East College Avenue, Eureka, Illinois 61
Phone: 309-467-6407
Toll-free: 888-438-7352
Web Site: www.eureka.edu
Officers:
   President: David J Arnold
   Chair: Rhea Edge
Management:
   Director: Dr Jospeh Henry
Mission: is a flexible, 300 seat, black box theater. This is the space used for most productions and is located within Pritchard Hall, near the center of Eureka's academic halls
Type of Stage: Black Box
Seating Capacity: 300
Year Restored: 1995

6409
RAYMOND F MCCALLISTER HALL

Eureka College
300 E College Avenue
Eureka, IL 61530

Mailing Address: Eureka College, 300 East College Avenue, Eureka, Illinois 61
Phone: 309-467-6407
Toll-free: 888-438-7352
Web Site: www.eureka.edu
Officers:
   President: David J Arnold
   Chair: Rhea Edge
Management:
   Director: Dr Joseph Henry
Mission: is a 300 seat performance space that has been used for such productions as The Little Red Devils improv troupe. It is ideal for cabaret settings and one person shows.
Seating Capacity: 300

6410
RINKER OUTDOOR AMPHITHEATRE

Eureka College
300 E College Avenue
Eureka, IL 61530
Mailing Address: Eureka College, 300 East College Avenue, Eureka, Illinois 61
Phone: 309-467-6407
Toll-free: 888-438-7352
Web Site: www.eureka.edu
Officers:
   President: David J Arnold
   Chair: Rhea Edge
Management:
   Director: Dr Joseph Henry
Mission: seats well-over 900, features ideal natural acoustics and a topiary, backdrop, and wings. Used most commonly now for convocations and graduation ceremonies, Rinker was an interegral part of Woodford County's traditional pageantry.
Type of Stage: Amphitheatre
Seating Capacity: 900

6411
CAHN AUDITORIUM

Northwestern University
633 Clark Street
Evanston, IL 60208
Phone: 847-491-3471
Web Site: www.northwestern.edu
Officers:
   President: Henry S Bienen
Management:
   Director: Joseph Appelt
   Managing Director: Barbara Butts
Mission: The largest performance space on campus, the Cahn Auditorium seats more than a thousand people and contains an orchestra pit and a balcony. The annual Waa-Mu Show, Northwestern's large-scale student musical revue that has spawned international talent throughout the years, is staged here, as are many other productions each year
Opened: 1980
Orchestra Pit: y
Seating Capacity: 1,000

6412
ETHEL M BARBER THEATRE

Northwestern University
30 Arts Circle Drive
Evanston, IL 60208
Phone: 847-491-3170
Fax: 847-467-2019
Web Site: www.northwestern.edu
Officers:
   President: Henry S Bienen
Management:
   Director: Joseph Appelt

Managing Director: Barbara Butts
Type of Stage: Thrust
Seating Capacity: 439

6413
JOSEPHINE LOUIS THEATER

Northwestern University
20 Arts Circle Drive
Evanston, IL 60208
Mailing Address: 20 Arts Circle Drive Evanston 60208
Phone: 847-491-3170
Fax: 847-467-2019
Web Site: www.northwestern.edu
Officers:
   President: Henry S Bienen
Management:
   Director: Joseph Appelt
   Managing Director: Barbara Butts
Type of Stage: Proscenium
Seating Capacity: 369

6414
MARJORIE WARD MARSHALL DANCE CENTER

Northwestern University
10 Arts Circle Drive
Evanston, IL 60208
Phone: 847-491-3170
Fax: 847-467-2019
Web Site: www.northwestern.edu
Officers:
   President: Henry S Bienen
Management:
   Director: Joseph Appelt
   Managing Director: Barbara Butts
Mission: The Marjorie Ward Marshall Dance Center is a state-of-the-art teaching and performance facility that contains two dance studios used for productions and classes. It forms part of the Theatre and Interpretation Center. In addition to presenting regular student concerts, the Marjorie Ward Marshall Dance Center hosts exciting master classes and performance residencies by alumni and visiting international artists.
Opened: 1980

6415
PICK-STAIGER CONCERT HALL

Northwestern University
50 Arts Circle Drive
Evanston, IL 60208
Mailing Address: Pick-Staiger Concert Office, 50 Arts Circle Drive, Evanston,
Phone: 847-491-5441
Fax: 847-491-1831
e-mail: lnielsen@northwestern.edu
Web Site: www.pickstaiger.com
Officers:
   President: Henry S Bienen
Management:
   Director: Richard Van Kleeck
   Marketing Director: Laura Paisley
   Operations Director: Erin Hemingway
   Marketing Manager: Laura Nielson
Mission: Since its inception the hall has functioned as both a classroom and performance facility for Bienen School of Music performing ensembles, Music/Theater productions, faculty recitals, festivals and professional guest artists. A typical season of programming includes Orchestral, Choral, Opera, Chamber, Jazz, Contemporary, Brass, and Percussion concerts as well as solo recitals, lectures, master classes, and other related events.
Founded: 1975
Paid Staff: 50

6416

RYAN FIELD

Northwestern University
1501 Central Street
Evanston, IL 60201
Phone: 847-491-7887
Web Site: www.nusports.com
Officers:
   President: Henry S Bienen
   Secretary: Debbie Robert
Management:
   Athletic Director: Jim Phillips
Founded: 1942

6417

FORD CENTER FOR THE FINE ARTS

Knox College
2 E South Street
Galesburg, IL 61401-4999
Mailing Address: Knox College, 2 East South Street,
Galesburg, IL 61401-4999
Phone: 309-341-7000
e-mail: kheartle@knox.edu
Web Site: www.knox.edu
Officers:
   President: Roger Taylor
   Executive Secretary: Denise Bailey
   Chair: Janet M Koran
   Secretary: Deborah S DeGraff
Management:
   director of marketing: Kathleen Heartlein
Mission: Knox College's Ford Center for the Fine Arts
is a superbly endowed facility for art, theatre, dance,
and music

6418

HARBACH THEATER

Knox College
Ford Center for the Fine Arts
2 E South Street
Galesburg, IL 61401-4999
Mailing Address: Knox College, 2 East South Street,
Galesburg, IL 61401-4999
Phone: 309-341-7000
e-mail: kheartle@knox.edu
Web Site: www.knox.edu
Officers:
   President: Roger Taylor
   Executive Secretary: Denise Bailey
   Chair: Janet M Koran
   Secretary: Deborah S DeGraff
Management:
   director of marketing: Kathleen Heartlein
Mission: Knox's ""main stage"" theatre. It is a
dual-configuration space: the stage and a section of the
audience are situated on a 72 ft diameter turntable,
capable of rotating 180 degrees to provide a
proscenium configuration that seats 600 and a thrust
configuration that seats 450. Designers over the years
have developed many unique and non-traditional ways
of working with the space. Harbach is home to each
term's main-stage production as well as the S
Specialized Field: Theater
Type of Stage: Revolving Proscenium and Thrust
Seating Capacity: 400-600

6419

KRESGE RECITAL HALL

Knox College
Ford Center for the Fine Arts
2 E South Street
Galesburg, IL 61401-4999

Mailing Address: Knox College, 2 East South Street,
Galesburg, IL 61401-4999
Phone: 309-341-7000
e-mail: kheartle@knox.edu
Web Site: www.knox.edu
Officers:
   President: Roger Taylor
   Executive Secretary: Denise Bailey
   Chair: Janet M Koran
   Secretary: Deborah S DeGraff
Management:
   director of marketing: Kathleen Heartlein
Mission: Kresge is home to music ensemble concerts
including the Knox College Choir, Jazz Band, Concert
Band, and Jazz Ensemble and to student recitals as
well as numerous visiting performance groups and
events
Specialized Field: Music
Seating Capacity: 325

6420

STUDIO THEATRE

Knox College
Ford Center for the Fine Arts
2 E South Street
Galesburg, IL 61401-4999
Mailing Address: Knox College, 2 East South Street,
Galesburg, IL 61401-4999
Phone: 309-341-7000
e-mail: kheartle@knox.edu
Web Site: www.knox.edu
Officers:
   President: Roger Taylor
   Executive Secretary: Denise Bailey
   Chair: Janet M Koran
   Secretary: Deborah S DeGraff
Management:
   director of marketing: Kathleen Heartlein
Mission: black box"" theatre-a room within which the
arrangement possibilities are nearly endless, seating
about 100 people on average. Studio Theatre is student
run, directed, and designed. This space also
occasionally plays home to visiting companies and
productions for the edification and enjoyment of the
campus at large. Studio productions range from simple
bare-stage shows to full-length productions complete
with specific scenery and lighting.
Specialized Field: Theater
Type of Stage: Flexible Black Box
Stage Dimensions: 40ft x 60ft
Seating Capacity: 100

6421

MCANINCH ARTS CENTER THEATER 2

College of DuPage
425 Fawell Boulevard
Glen Ellyn, IL 60137-6599
Mailing Address: McAninch Arts Center at College of
DuPage, Fawell and Park B
Phone: 630-942-4000
Fax: 630-790-9806
e-mail: raffel@cod.edu
Web Site: www.cod.edu
Officers:
   President: Robert L Breuder
Management:
   Director: Stephen Cummins
   Marketing Director: Roland Raffel
   Artistic Director: Kirk Muspratt
Mission: This unique facility has presented theater,
music, dance and visual arts to more than 1.5 million
people
Founded: 1986
Specialized Field: Theater

6422

MCANINCH ARTS CENTER MAINSTAGE

College of DuPage
425 Fawell Boulevard
Glen Ellyn, IL 60137-6599
Mailing Address: McAninch Arts Center at College of
DuPage, Fawell and Park B
Phone: 630-942-4000
Fax: 630-790-9806
e-mail: raffel@cod.edu
Web Site: www.cod.edu
Officers:
   President: Robert L Breuder
Management:
   Director: Stephen Cummins
   Marketing Director: Roland Raffel
   Artistic Director: Kirk Muspratt
Utilizes: Actors; AEA Actors; Dance Companies;
Educators; Multimedia; Sign Language Translators;
Soloists; Special Technical Talent; Theatre Companies
Founded: 1986
Specialized Field: Theater
Seating Capacity: 793

6423

**MCANINCH ARTS CENTER STUDIO
THEATRE**

College of DuPage
425 Fawell Boulevard
Glen Ellyn, IL 60137-6599
Mailing Address: McAninch Arts Center at College of
DuPage, Fawell and Park B
Phone: 630-942-4000
Fax: 630-790-9806
e-mail: raffel@cod.edu
Web Site: www.cod.edu
Officers:
   President: Robert L Breuder
Management:
   Director: Stephen Cummins
   Marketing Director: Roland Raffel
   Artistic Director: Kirk Muspratt
Utilizes: Actors; Educators; Soloists
Founded: 1986
Specialized Field: Theater
Type of Stage: Black Box
Seating Capacity: 75
Resident Groups: Buffalo Theatre Ensemble

6424

**SOUTHEASTERN ILLINOIS COLLEGE
VISUAL & PERFORMING ARTS CENTER**

3575 College Road
Harrisburg, IL 62946
Mailing Address: Southeastern Illinois College, 3575
College Rd, Harrisburg,
Phone: 618-252-5400
Toll-free: 866-338-2742
e-mail: donna.patton@sic.edu
Web Site: www.sic.cc.il.us
Officers:
   President: Raymond V Cummiskey PhD
   Chair: Krystal Tison
   Secretary: JoAnna Lane
Management:
   Director: Allan Kimball
   Marketing Director: Donna Patton
Mission: The George T. Dennis Visual and Performing
Arts Center serves as the artistic home of the
Department of Theatre at SIC featuring a wide variety of
productions ranging from traditional drama, to children's
theatre, to Broadway musicals

6425
SIBERT THEATRE
Illinois College
1101 W College Avenue
Jacksonville, IL 62650
Phone: 214-245-3010
Web Site: www.ic.edu
Officers:
    President: Dr Axel D Steuer
Management:
    Artistic Director: Dr Nancy Taylor Porter PhD
Type of Stage: Modified Thrust
Seating Capacity: 250

6426
RIALTO SQUARE THEATRE
102 N Chicago Street
Joliet, IL 60432
Phone: 815-726-7171
e-mail: information@rialtosquare.com
Web Site: www.rialtosquare.com
Management:
    General Manager: Randall Green
    Marketing Director: Annette Parker
    Development Director: Tina Postel
Utilizes: Actors; AEA Actors; Collaborations; Dancers; Educators; Five Seasonal Concerts; Guest Musical Directors; Guild Activities; Lyricists; Multi Collaborations; Original Music Scores; Selected Students; Special Technical Talent; Theatre Companies
Paid Staff: 11
Volunteer Staff: 300
Paid Artists: 40
Budget: $2,000,000
Income Sources: Corporate; Individual; Foundations
Facility Category: Performing Arts
Type of Stage: Proscenium
Stage Dimensions: 52' 0" wide x 23' 6" high
Seating Capacity: 1,000
Year Built: 1926
Year Remodeled: 1981
Cost: $7,000,000
Rental Contact: Mary Beth DeGrush

6427
ALLAN CARR THEATRE
Lake Forest College
Hixon Hall
555 N Sheridan Rd
Lake Forest, IL 60045
Phone: 847-735-5141
Web Site: www.lakeforest.edu
Officers:
    President: Stephen D Schutt
    Chair: Peter G Schiff
Management:
    Marketing Director: Elizabeth Libby
    Director: D Ohlandt
Year Built: 1912

6428
DAVID ADLER MUSIC AND ARTS CENTER
1700 N Milwaukee Avenue
Libertyville, IL 60048
Mailing Address: The David Adler Music and Arts Center, 1700 North Milwaukee
Phone: 847-367-0707
Fax: 847-367-0804
Web Site: www.adlercenter.org
Officers:
    Chairman: Patrick Davidson
    Secretary: Judy Moriarty

    Treasurer: Greg Pinter
Management:
    Executive Director: Dianna Monie
Mission: dedicated to promoting music and the arts as an integral part of everyday life. Its year-round activities are designed to foster critical thinking and interpretation, participation, entertainment, and achievement in music and the arts for the people
Organization Type: Performing; Edcuational

6429
HORRABIN HALL THEATRE
Western Illinois University
Horrabin Hall
1 University Circle
Macomb, IL 61455
Phone: 309-298-1543
Fax: 309-298-2695
e-mail: theatre@wiu.edu
Web Site: www.wiu.edu
Officers:
    President: Alvin Goldfarb
    Chairman: David E Patrick
    Secretary: Wendi Mattson
Type of Stage: Thrust
Seating Capacity: 161
Year Restored: 1995

6430
SIMPKINS THEATRE
Western Illinois University
Simpkins Hall
1 University Circle
Macomb, IL 61455
Phone: 309-298-1543
Fax: 309-298-2695
e-mail: theatre@wiu.edu
Web Site: www.wiu.edu
Officers:
    President: Alvin Goldfarb
    Chairman: David E Patrick
    Secretary: Wendi Mattson
Type of Stage: Proscenium/Thrust

6431
WESTERN ILLINOIS UNIVERSITY THEATRE AND DANCE DEPARTMENT
Western Illinois University
Browne Hall
1 University Circle
Macomb, IL 61455
Phone: 309-298-1543
Fax: 309-298-2695
e-mail: theatre@wiu.edu
Web Site: www.wiu.edu
Officers:
    President: Alvin Goldfarb
    Chairman: David E Patrick
    Secretary: Wendi Mattson
Type of Stage: Proscenium
Seating Capacity: 387

6432
MARION CULTURAL AND CIVIC CENTER
800 Tower Square
Marion, IL 62959
Mailing Address: P O Box 51, Marion, IL 62959
Phone: 618-997-4030
Web Site: www.marionccc.org
Management:
    Executive Director: Joshua S Benson
    Director: Mike Bennett
Utilizes: Dance Companies; Guild Activities; New Productions; Special Technical Talent

Founded: 2004
Paid Staff: 4
Budget: $200,000
Income Sources: Donations
Annual Attendance: 52,000
Type of Stage: Proscenium
Stage Dimensions: 45'x36'
Seating Capacity: 1,100
Year Built: 2004
Cost: $8 Million

6433
I WIRELESS CENTER
1201 River Drive
Moline, IL 61265
Mailing Address: i wireless Center, 1201 River Drive, Moline, IL. 61265
Phone: 309-764-2001
Fax: 309-764-2192
Web Site: www.iwirelesscenter.com
Management:
    Executive Director: Scott Mullen
    Marketing Director: Gary Baron
Specialized Field: General Entertainment
Paid Staff: 450
Annual Attendance: 700,000
Seating Capacity: 12,000

6434
WELLS THEATER
Monmouth College
700 E Broadway
Monmouth, IL 61462
Phone: 309-457-2340
Fax: 309-457-2310
e-mail: info@monm.edu
Web Site: www.monm.edu
Officers:
    President: Dr Mauri Ditzler
Management:
    Director: Douglas B Rankin
Founded: 1790
Paid Staff: 2
Budget: $15,000
Income Sources: Budget Allocation From Institution
Type of Stage: Proscenium
Stage Dimensions: 32' X 25'
Seating Capacity: 175
Year Built: 1990
Year Remodeled: 2010
Cost: 1.6 Million
Rental Contact: Douglas Raneiu

6435
BARBARA PFEIFFER MEMORIAL HALL
North Central College
310 E Benton Avenue
Naperville, IL 60540
Mailing Address: North Central College, 30 N. Brainard Street, Naperville, IL
Phone: 630-637-5100
Toll-free: 800-411-1861
e-mail: omc@noctrl.edu
Web Site: www.northcentralcollege.edu
Officers:
    President: Dr Harold R Wilde
    Chair: Deborah L Palmes
Management:
    Director: Brian T Lynch
Mission: The DuPage Symphony Orchestra and Naperville-North Central College Performing Arts Association have called it home for decades, as have numerous community arts groups, schools, churches, organizations and the College's musical and theatrical

programs. Recitals, choral and instrumental performances, and theatrical productions are hosted throughout the year
Founded: 1926
Type of Stage: Proscenium
Seating Capacity: 1,055
Year Built: 1926

6436
HEININGER AUDITORIUM

North Central College
Larrance Academic Center
309 E School Street
Naperville, IL 60540
Mailing Address: North Central College, 30 N. Brainard Street, Naperville, IL
Phone: 630-637-5100
Toll-free: 800-411-1861
e-mail: omc@noctrl.edu
Web Site: www.northcentralcollege.edu
Officers:
President: Dr Harold R Wilde
Chair: Deborah L Palmes
Management:
Director: Brian T Lynch
Mission: Great for small group presentations, dance instruction and performance rehearsals
Specialized Field: Dance
Seating Capacity: 100

6437
BRADEN AUDITORIUM

Illinois State University
100 N University Street
Normal, IL 61761-4441
Mailing Address: Bone Student Center, Campus Box 2640, 100 N University St, N
Phone: 309-438-4636
Fax: 309-438-3147
Web Site: www.bsc.ilstu.edu
Officers:
President: Dr Al Bowman
Director: Jay D Bergman
Mission: Braden hosts Broadway shows, touring companies, concerts, ballets, conferences and much more
Performs At: Auditorium
Affiliations: Illinois State University
Seating Capacity: 3,457
Rental Contact: Coordinator Jennifer Booher

6438
HANCOCK STADIUM

Illinois State University
College Avenue and Main Street
Normal, IL 61761
Phone: 309-438-8000
Fax: 309-438-3513
Web Site: goredbirds.cstv.com
Officers:
President: Dr Al Bowman
Management:
Athletic Director: Dr Sheahon Zenger
Marketing Director: Brad Ledford
Operations Director: Peyton Deterding
Development Director: Doug Banks
Founded: 1963
Seating Capacity: 15,000

6439
MABEL CLAIRE ALLEN THEATRE

Illinois State University College of Fine Arts
School of Theatre
100 N University Street
Normal, IL 61790-5700
Mailing Address: Campus Box 5700 Normal IL 61790-5700, Office of the Dean, C
Phone: 309-438-8783
Fax: 309-438-5806
Web Site: www.ilstu.edu
Officers:
President: Dr Al Bowman
Management:
Director: John Poole
Marketing Director: Christopher Peak
Mission: The Allen Theatre offers black box opportunities for performance. The space serves as a rehearsal hall and classroom building for dance classes
Type of Stage: Black Box

6440
MFA DIRECTING STUDIO

Illinois State University College of Fine Arts
School of Theatre
100 N University Street
Normal, IL 61790-5700
Mailing Address: Campus Box 5700 Normal IL 61790-5700, Office of the Dean, C
Phone: 309-438-8783
Fax: 309-438-5806
Web Site: www.ilstu.edu
Officers:
President: Dr Al Bowman
Management:
Director: John Poole
Marketing Director: Christopher Peak
Type of Stage: Proscenium
Seating Capacity: 50

6441
REDBIRD ARENA

Illinois State University
College Avenue and Main Street
Normal, IL 61790-2660
Mailing Address: Campus Box 2660 Normal IL 61790-2660
Phone: 309-438-8000
Web Site: goredbirds.cstv.com
Officers:
President: Dr Al Bowman
Management:
Athletic Director: Dr Sheahon Zenger
Marketing Director: Brad Ledford
Operations Director: Peyton Deterding
Development Director: Doug Banks
Seating Capacity: 10,500

6442
THEATRE AT EWING

Illinois State University College of Fine Arts
School of Theatre
100 N University Street
Normal, IL 61790-5700
Mailing Address: Campus Box 5700 Normal IL 61790-5700, Office of the Dean, C
Phone: 309-438-8783
Fax: 309-438-5806
Web Site: www.ilstu.edu
Officers:
President: Dr Al Bowman
Management:
Director: John Poole

Marketing Director: Christopher Peak
Type of Stage: Proscenium
Seating Capacity: 450

6443
WESTHOFF EXPERIMENTAL THEATRE

Illinois State University College of Fine Arts
School of Theatre
100 N University Street
Normal, IL 61790-5700
Mailing Address: Campus Box 5700 Normal IL 61790-5700, Office of the Dean, C
Phone: 309-438-8783
Fax: 309-438-5806
Web Site: www.ilstu.edu
Officers:
President: Dr Al Bowman
Management:
Director: John Poole
Marketing Director: Christopher Peak
Type of Stage: Proscenium
Orchestra Pit: y
Seating Capacity: 525

6444
SHEELY CENTER FOR THE PERFORMING ARTS

Glenbrook North High School
2300 Shermer Road
Northbrook, IL 60062
Phone: 847-509-2446
Web Site: gbn.glenbrook.k12.il.us
Officers:
President: Paul Pryma

6445
MORAINE VALLEY COMMUNITY COLLEGE FINE & PERFORMING ARTS CENTER

9000 W College Parkway
Palos Hills, IL 60465-0937
Mailing Address: Moraine Valley Community College, 9000 W. College Pkwy., Pal
Phone: 708-974-5755
Web Site: www.morainevalley.edu
Officers:
President: Dr Vernon O Crawley
Chairman: Nicholas Thomas
Management:
Managing Director: Tommy Hensel
Mission: The mission of the Fine and Performing Arts center, through its public presentations of dance, music, theater and the visual arts, is to enrich the members of the college community by providing opportunities for people of all ages to experience and grow through the arts.
Founded: 1994
Specialized Field: Theater, Dance, Music
Seating Capacity: 780

6446
FREEDOM HALL: NATHAN MANILOW THEATRE

410 Lakewood Boulevard
Park Forest, IL 60466
Phone: 708-747-0580
Web Site: www.freedomhall.org
Management:
General Manager: Naomi Ferr
Mission: Freedom Hall is proud to bring you childrens theatre, musical theatre, senior theatre and performances for all ages
Founded: 1976

Specialized Field: Theater
Paid Staff: 4
Paid Artists: 50

6447
ILLINOIS THEATRE CENTER
371 Artist's Walk
Park Forest, IL 60466
Mailing Address: PO Box 397 Park Forest IL 60466
Phone: 708-481-3510
e-mail: ilthctr@sbcglobal.net
Web Site: www.ilthctr.org
Officers:
Founder: Steve Billig
Management:
Director: Etel Billig
Founded: 1976
Paid Staff: 15
Paid Artists: 42

6448
LAB THEATRE
Bradley University
Hartmann Center for the Performing Arts
1501 W Bradley Avenue
Peoria, IL 61625
Phone: 309-677-2660
Fax: 309-677-3505
Toll-free: 800-447-6460
e-mail: theatre@bradley.edu
Web Site: theatre.bradley.edu
Officers:
President: Joanne K Glasser
Chairman: Gerald L Shaheen
Secretary: Debbie Perry
Management:
Director: George H Brown
Type of Stage: Black Box
Seating Capacity: 70

6449
MEYER JACOBS THEATRE
Bradley University
Hartmann Center for the Performing Arts
1501 W Bradley Avenue
Peoria, IL 61625
Phone: 309-677-2660
Fax: 309-677-3505
Toll-free: 800-447-6460
e-mail: theatre@bradley.edu
Web Site: theatre.bradley.edu
Officers:
President: Joanne K Glasser
Chairman: Gerald L Shaheen
Secretary: Debbie Perry
Management:
Director: George H Brown
Seating Capacity: 250-275

6450
PEORIA CIVIC CENTER
201 SW Jefferson Street
Peoria, IL 61602-1448
Mailing Address: Peoria Civic Center, 201 SW
Jefferson Ave., Peoria, IL 61602
Phone: 309-673-8900
e-mail: mburnett@peoriaciviccenter.com
Web Site: www.peoriaciviccenter.com
Management:
General Manager: Debbie Ritschel
Marketing Director: Mark Burnettl
Operations Director: Will Kenney
Founded: 1982
Specialized Field: General Entertainment

Paid Staff: 450
Annual Attendance: 20,000
Facility Category: Theater
Seating Capacity: 2127

6451
BERGMAN THEATRE
Concordia University Chicago
7400 Augusta Street
River Forest, IL 60305-1499
Mailing Address: 7400 Augusta St, River Forest, IL
60305-1402
Phone: 708-771-8300
e-mail: pr@CUChicago.edu
Web Site: www.cuchicago.edu
Officers:
President: John F Johnson
Chair: Eunice R Eifert
Management:
General Manager: Julie E Hinz
Marketing Director: Krisse L Paulson
Mission: provides a more intimate setting for smaller
scale productions, student one-acts, as well as space
for classroom lab opportunities. As a truly flexible
performance space, past productions have enjoyed
arena, alley and proscenium stagings
Type of Stage: Alley, Arena, Proscenium

6452
ELOISE MARTIN RECITAL HALL
Dominican University
Fine and Performing Arts
7900 Division Street
River Forest, IL 60305
Mailing Address: Performing Arts Center, 7900 West
Division St., River Forest
Phone: 708-524-6814
Fax: 708-488-5056
Web Site: www.dom.edu
Officers:
President: Donna M Carroll
Secretary: Cordelia Pottinger-Walters
Management:
Artistic Director: Krista Hansen
Managing Director: Leslie Rodriguez
Seating Capacity: 200

6453
LUND AUDITORIUM
Dominican University
Fine and Performing Arts
7900 Division Street
River Forest, IL 60305
Mailing Address: Performing Arts Center, 7900 West
Division St., River Forest
Phone: 708-524-6814
Fax: 708-488-5056
Web Site: www.dom.edu
Officers:
President: Donna M Carroll
Secretary: Cordelia Pottinger-Walters
Management:
Artistic Director: Krista Hansen
Managing Director: Leslie Rodriguez
Seating Capacity: 1,200

6454
WERNER AUDITORIUM
Concordia University Chicago
7400 Augusta Street
River Forest, IL 60305-1499

Mailing Address: 7400 Augusta St, River Forest, IL
60305-1402
Phone: 708-771-8300
e-mail: pr@CUChicago.edu
Web Site: www.cuchicago.edu
Officers:
President: John F Johnson
Chair: Eunice R Eifert
Management:
General Manager: Julie E Hinz
Marketing Director: Krisse L Paulson
Mission: is a proscenium space dedicated to bringing
large scale productions to life. Many off campus groups
utilize this space in conjunction with our campus chapel
Type of Stage: Proscenium

6455
ROBERT M COLLINS CENTER
Triton College
2000 5th Avenue
River Grove, IL 60171
Phone: 708-456-0300
e-mail: triton@triton.edu
Web Site: www.triton.edu
Officers:
President: Dr Patricia Granados
Chairman: Mark R Stephens
Secretary: Diane Viverito

6456
TRITON COLLEGE PERFORMING ARTS CENTER
Triton College
2000 5th Avenue
River Grove, IL 60171
Phone: 708-456-0300
e-mail: triton@triton.edu
Web Site: www.triton.edu
Officers:
President: Dr Patricia Granados
Chairman: Mark R Stephens
Secretary: Diane Viverito
Management:
Department Chair: Angelee Johns,
ajohns39@triton.edu
Mission: Education and entertainment of students and
public
Utilizes: Actors; Dance Companies; Dancers; Guest
Choreographers; Guest Musical Directors; High School
Drama; Instructors; Local Artists; Multimedia; Original
Music Scores; Sign Language Translators; Singers;
Soloists; Special Technical Talent; Theatre Companies
Specialized Field: Music; Theatre
Paid Staff: 10
Volunteer Staff: 10
Paid Artists: 25
Non-paid Artists: 20
Income Sources: College Budget; Ticket Sales
Performs At: Mid-Size Auditorium; Black Box Theatre
Facility Category: Performing Arts Center
Type of Stage: Proscenium; Thrust
Seating Capacity: 412; 75
Rental Contact: Manager Maria Correa

6457
AUGUSTANA THEATRE
Augustana College
Department of Theatre Arts
639 38th Street
Rock Island, IL 61201

Mailing Address: 639 38th Street, Rock Island, IL 61201
Phone: 307-794-7611
Toll-free: 800-798-8100
Web Site: www.augustana.edu
Officers:
    President: Steven C Bahls
    Chair: Jeffrey L Coussens
    Secretary: Anna Hurty
Specialized Field: Theatre
Type of Stage: Modified Thrust
Seating Capacity: 150
Year Restored: 1998

6458
CENTENNIAL HALL

Augustana College
639 38th Street
Rock Island, IL 61201
Mailing Address: 639 38th Street, Rock Island, IL 61201
Phone: 309-794-7000
Toll-free: 800-798-8100
Web Site: www.augustana.edu
Officers:
    President: Steven C Bahls
Founded: 1860

6459
STUDIO THEATRE

Augustana College
Department of Theatre Arts
639 38th Street
Rock Island, IL 61201
Mailing Address: 639 38th Street, Rock Island, IL 61201
Phone: 307-794-7611
Toll-free: 800-798-8100
Web Site: www.augustana.edu
Officers:
    President: Steven C Bahls
    Chair: Jeffrey L Coussens
    Secretary: Anna Hurty
Specialized Field: Theatre
Year Restored: 1998

6460
CHEEK THEATRE

Rockford College
Clark Arts Center
5050 E State Street
Rockford, IL 61108
Mailing Address: Rockford College, Performing Arts, J263Clark Arts Center, 50
Phone: 815-226-4000
Web Site: www.rockford.edu
Officers:
    President: Dr Robert Head
    Chair: Noel Rennerfeldt
Management:
    Manager: Elizabeth Drog
Mission: Cheek Theatre is a 40' by 50' flexible seating black box theater. The department produces faculty directed and student directed shows, our Three-Penny Theatre, in Cheek Theatre annually.
Specialized Field: Theater
Type of Stage: Flexible Black Box
Stage Dimensions: 40' by 50'

6461
CORONADO PERFORMING ARTS CENTER

314 N Main Street
Rockford, IL 61101-0476

Mailing Address: PO Box 1976 Rockford IL 61110-0476
Phone: 815-968-2722
Fax: 815-968-1318
e-mail: tixmanager@coronadopac.org
Web Site: www.coronadopac.org
Management:
    Executive Director: Michael Goldberg
    Operations Director: Mike Walsh
Founded: 2006
Paid Staff: 5314
Volunteer Staff: 100
Budget: $1.1 Million
Type of Stage: Proscenium
Stage Dimensions: 53' x 45'
Seating Capacity: 2,309
Year Built: 1927
Year Remodeled: 2001
Rental Contact: Janice Bartik

6462
MADDOX THEATRE

Rockford College
Clark Arts Center
5050 E State Street
Rockford, IL 61108
Mailing Address: Rockford College, Performing Arts, J263Clark Arts Center, 50
Phone: 815-226-4000
Web Site: www.rockford.edu
Officers:
    President: Dr Robert Head
    Chair: Noel Rennerfeldt
Management:
    Manager: Elizabeth Drog
Mission: Maddox Theatre is a fully equipped 572 seat proscenium theater which is home to a variety of performing arts events. Each year the department produces faculty directed shows, choral concerts and recitals in Maddox Theatre. It also hosts the College forum series and many community cultural events
Specialized Field: Theater
Type of Stage: Proscenium
Seating Capacity: 572

6463
ROCKFORD METROCENTRE

300 Elm Street
Rockford, IL 61101
Phone: 815-968-5600
Fax: 815-968-5451
e-mail: info@metrocentre.com
Web Site: metrocentre.com
Officers:
    Chairman: Rita Pirrello Epperson
    Treasurer: Brian Peterson
    Secretary: Erin Jenkins
Management:
    General Manager: Corey Pearson
    Marketing Director: Matt Mohr
    Operations Director: Susan Campbell
Seating Capacity: 9,952

6464
PHILIP LYNCH THEATRE

Lewis University
1 University Parkway
Romeoville, IL 60446-2200
Mailing Address: One University Parkway, Romeoville, IL 60446
Phone: 815-838-0500
Toll-free: 800-897-9000
Web Site: www.lewisu.edu
Officers:

    President: Br James Gaffney FSC
Management:
    Director: Keith White
Paid Staff: 1
Budget: $6,000
Performs At: Philip Lynch Theatre
Facility Category: Educational Theatre
Type of Stage: 3/4 Thrust
Seating Capacity: 240
Year Built: 1976

6465
ALLSTATE ARENA

6920 N Mannheim Road
Rosemont, IL 60018
Mailing Address: 6920 N. Mannheim Road , Rosemont, IL 60018
Phone: 847-635-6601
Web Site: www.allstatearena.com
Officers:
    President: Edward M Liddy
Management:
    Marketing Director: Phil Chihoski
Founded: 1980
Paid Staff: 400
Annual Attendance: 1,500,000
Seating Capacity: 18,500

6466
PRAIRIE CENTER FOR THE ARTS

201 Schaumburg Court
Schaumburg, IL 60193
Mailing Address: Prairie Center for the Arts, 201 Schaumburg Ct., Schaumburg,
Phone: 847-895-3600
Fax: 847-895-1837
e-mail: rpileckis@ci.schaumburg.il.us
Web Site: www.prairiecenter.org
Management:
    Director: Betsy Armstead
    Development Director: Lucinda Floodin
    PR: Rob Pileckis
Mission: is an ideal venue to see a concert, play or musical. A full season of entertainment including music, dance and theatre and a free, outdoor summer concert series
Founded: 1986
Specialized Field: Concert, play, musicals
Paid Staff: 20
Volunteer Staff: 50
Paid Artists: 100
Budget: $1 million
Income Sources: Tickets; Rentals; Foundation Support
Annual Attendance: 75,000
Type of Stage: Proscenium
Year Built: 1986
Rental Contact: Pat DeBartolo

6467
NORTHSHORE CENTER FOR THE PERFORMING ARTS

9501 Skokie Boulevard
Skokie, IL 60077
Phone: 847-679-9501
e-mail: info@nscpas.org
Web Site: www.northshorecenter.org
Management:
    General Manager: Michael Pauken
    Operations Manager: Tony Scheurich
    Marketing Director: Joseph Alaimo
Utilizes: Dancers; Educators; Original Music Scores; Special Technical Talent; Theatre Companies
Paid Staff: 4
Volunteer Staff: 8

Seating Capacity: 848
Year Built: 1996

6468
MUSIC HALL
Springfield College
1500 N Fifth Street
Springfield, IL 62702
Phone: 217-525-1420
Toll-free: 800-635-7289
Web Site: www.sci.edu
Officers:
President: William J Carroll
Paid Staff: 70

6469
STUDIO THEATRE
University of Illinois at Springfield
Sangamon Auditorium
One University Plaza MS PAC 292
Springfield, IL 62703-5407
Phone: 217-206-6160
Fax: 217-206-6391
Toll-free: 800-207-6960
Web Site: www.uis.edu
Officers:
President: B Joseph White
Management:
Director: Robert Vaughn
Type of Stage: Flexible
Seating Capacity: 100-318

6470
NORRIS CULTURAL ARTS CENTER
1040 Dunham Road
St Charles, IL 60174
Mailing Address: PO Box 3340 St Charles IL 60174
Phone: 630-584-7200
Fax: 630-584-7262
e-mail: director@norrisculturalarts.com
Web Site: www.norrisculturalarts.com
Officers:
Chairman: James L Collins
Secretary: Joanne deSimone
Treasurer: Mark D Smith
Management:
Operations Director: JoAnne Granquist
Founded: 1978
Paid Staff: 4
Volunteer Staff: 10
Budget: $300,000
Income Sources: Tickets Sales; Rentals; Donors; Grants
Performs At: Live Theatre
Annual Attendance: 20,000
Facility Category: Performing Arts & Gallery
Type of Stage: Persimon
Stage Dimensions: 40x50
Seating Capacity: 1,052
Year Built: 1978
Year Remodeled: 2001
Rental Contact: JoAnne Granquist

6471
STERLING CENTENNIAL AUDITORIUM
Sterling High School
1608 4th Avenue
Sterling, IL 61081
Phone: 815-625-6800
Web Site: www.centennialauditorium.org
Management:
Director: Chuck Price
Development Director: Tim Schlegel

6472
MAINSTAGE
Governors State University
The Center for Performing Arts
1 University Parkway
University Park, IL 60466-0975
Phone: 708-235-2222
Fax: 708-235-2121
e-mail: tickets@govst.edu
Web Site: www.centertickets.net
Officers:
President: Elaine P Maimon PhD
Executive Director: Burton Dikolsky
Management:
Theatre Manager: Jon Cobb
Founded: 1994
Specialized Field: Dance; Music; Drama; Broadway
Annual Attendance: $45,000
Facility Category: Professional Venue
Type of Stage: Proscenium
Seating Capacity: 1,176
Year Built: 1994
Cost: $8.5 Million
Rental Contact: Theatre Manager Jon Cobb

6473
THE CENTER FOR THE PERFORMING ARTS
Governors State University
1 University Parkway
University Park, IL 60466-0975
Phone: 708-235-2222
Fax: 708-235-2121
e-mail: tickets@govst.edu
Web Site: www.centertickets.net
Officers:
President: Elaine P Maimon PhD
Management:
Executive Director: Burton Dikelsky
Development Director: Jaquelyn Small
General Manager: Loretta Jones
Utilizes: Actors; Dance Companies; Five Seasonal Concerts; Guest Accompanists; Guest Choreographers; Guest Directors; Guest Musical Directors; Guest Musicians; Guild Activities; Instructors; Local Artists; Multimedia; New Productions; Original Music Scores; Student Interns; Special Technical Talent; Theatre Companies
Founded: 1995
Paid Staff: 7
Volunteer Staff: 50
Paid Artists: 40
Budget: $975,000
Income Sources: Tickets; Rentals; Donations; Sales
Annual Attendance: 60,000
Facility Category: Theater
Type of Stage: Proscenium
Stage Dimensions: 45'x35'
Seating Capacity: 1,171
Year Built: 1995
Cost: $8,000,000
Rental Contact: Les Alberts
Organization Type: Performing

6474
KRANNERT CENTER FOR THE PERFORMING ARTS - THEATRE 3
500 S Goodwin Avenue
Urbana, IL 61801-3788
Phone: 217-333-6700
Fax: 217-244-0810
e-mail: kran-tix@illinois.edu
Web Site: www.krannertcenter.com

Officers:
President: B Joseph White
Management:
Director: Mike Ross
Founded: 1969
Type of Stage: Proscenium
Seating Capacity: 4,000

6475
KRANNERT CENTER FOR THE PERFORMING ARTS - STUDIO
500 S Goodwin Avenue
Urbana, IL 61801
Phone: 217-333-6700
Fax: 217-244-0810
e-mail: kran-tix@illinois.edu
Web Site: www.krannertcenter.com
Officers:
President: B Joseph White
Management:
Director: Mike Ross

6476
KRANNERT CENTER FOR THE PERFORMING ARTS - THEATRE 2
500 S Goodwin Avenue
Urbana, IL 61801
Phone: 217-333-6700
Fax: 217-244-0810
e-mail: kran-tix@illinois.edu
Web Site: www.krannertcenter.com
Officers:
President: B Joseph White
Management:
Director: Mike Ross
Type of Stage: Proscenium
Seating Capacity: 4,000; (200 to 2,094)

6477
ODEUM SPORTS & EXPO CENTER
1033 N Villa Avenue
Villa Park, IL 60181
Phone: 630-941-9292
Fax: 630-831-9183
e-mail: phil@odeumexpo.com
Web Site: www.odeumexpo.com
Officers:
President: Phil Greco
Management:
General Manager: Brad Walsh
Seating Capacity: 5,500

6478
JACK BENNY CENTER FOR THE ARTS
39 Jack Benny Drive
Waukegan, IL 60087
Phone: 847-360-4740
Fax: 847-662-0592
Web Site: www.waukeganparks.org
Officers:
President: Wayne B Motley
Treasurer: Terry Duffy
Management:
Executive Director: Greg Petry
Mission: provides fine arts instruction for music, dance, theatre, art, and traditional craft and lecture programming through the Bowen Heritage Circle.
Founded: 1986
Seating Capacity: 100

6479
ARENA THEATER
Wheaton College
501 College Avenue
Wheaton, IL 60187-5593
Phone: 630-752-5000
Web Site: www.wheaton.edu
Officers:
President: Dr Duane Liftin
Chairman: C William Pollard
Secretary: Hon Daniel R Coats
Management:
Executive Director: Ken Chase PhD
Founded: 1973

6480
EDMAN CHAPEL
Wheaton College
501 College Avenue
Wheaton, IL 60187-5593
Phone: 630-752-5000
Web Site: www.wheaton.edu
Officers:
President: Dr Duane Liftin
Chairman: C William Pollard
Secretary: Hon Daniel R Coats
Founded: 1860

6481
DILLER STREET THEATER
North Shore Country Day School
310 Green Bay Road
Winnetka, IL 60093
Phone: 847-446-0674
Fax: 847-446-0675
Web Site: www.nscds.pvt.k12.il.us
Officers:
President: Tom Doar III
Management:
Development Director: Molly Ingram McDowell
Marketing Director: Tura Cottingham
Operations Director: Cindy Hooper
Founded: 1919
Seating Capacity: 480

6482
CHRISTIAN ARTS AUDITORIUM
2500 Dowie Memorial Drive
Zion, IL 60099
Phone: 847-746-1411
Fax: 847-746-1452
e-mail: frontoffice@ccczion.org
Web Site: www.ccczion.org
Officers:
Senior Pastor: Ken Langley
Secretary: Katy Lee
Management:
Artistic Director: Barbara Johnson
Seating Capacity: 522

Indiana

6483
REARDON AUDITORIUM
1015 E Fifth Street
Anderson, IN 46012
Phone: 765-641-4144
Fax: 765-641-3647
Toll-free: 866-316-8949
Web Site: www.anderson.edu
Officers:
President: Dr James L Edwards

Treasurer: Sena Landey
Management:
Director: Cheryl Shank
General Manager: Jill Goodwin
Founded: 1983
Paid Staff: 4
Paid Artists: 4
Income Sources: University Administration; Facility Rental
Facility Category: Auditorium
Stage Dimensions: 52' x 75'
Seating Capacity: 23,000
Year Built: 1983
Cost: $5.1 million

6484
ASSEMBLY HALL
1001 E 17th Street
Bloomington, IN 47405-7000
Phone: 812-855-4848
Web Site: www.iuhoosiers.edu
Officers:
President: Michael A McRobbie
Management:
Athletic Director: Rick Greenspan
Marketing Director: Jeff Cieply
Development Director: M Grace Calhoun
Performs At: Athletics Arena
Facility Category: Intercollegiate Athletics
Type of Stage: Basketball Court
Seating Capacity: 17,466
Year Built: 1971
Cost: $14.6 Million
Rental Contact: Assistant Director Facilities Chuck Crabb

6485
B C PLAYHOUSE
Indiana University
Department of Theatre & Drama
275 North Jordan
Bloomington, IN 47405-1101
Phone: 812-855-4535
Web Site: www.theatre.indiana.edu
Officers:
President: Michael A McRobbie
Chairman: Jonathan R Michaelsen
Secretary: Charlene McGlashan
Management:
General Manager: Trish Hausmann
Paid Staff: 20
Paid Artists: 30
Type of Stage: Black Box
Orchestra Pit: y

6486
MUSICAL ARTS CENTER
Indiana University
Jacobs School of Music
1201 E Thrid Street
Bloomington, IN 47405
Phone: 812-855-1583
e-mail: musicpub@indiana.edu
Web Site: music.indiana.edu
Officers:
President: Michael A McRobbie
Management:
Marketing Director: Alain Barker
Development Director: Melissa Korzec
General Manager: Tridib Pal
Founded: 1972
Paid Staff: 60
Annual Attendance: 88,390
Type of Stage: Proscenium Arch

Seating Capacity: 3,200

6487
RUTH N HALLS THEATRE
Indiana University
Department of Theatre & Drama
275 North Jordan
Bloomington, IN 47405-1101
Phone: 812-855-4535
Web Site: www.theatre.indiana.edu
Officers:
President: Michael A McRobbie
Chairman: Jonathan R Michaelsen
Secretary: Charlene McGlashan
Management:
General Manager: Trish Hausmann
Paid Staff: 20
Paid Artists: 30
Type of Stage: Proscenium
Orchestra Pit: y
Seating Capacity: 443

6488
WELLS-METZ THEATRE
Indiana University
Department of Theatre & Drama
275 North Jordan
Bloomington, IN 47405-1101
Phone: 812-855-4535
Web Site: www.theatre.indiana.edu
Officers:
President: Michael A McRobbie
Chairman: Jonathan R Michaelsen
Secretary: Charlene McGlashan
Management:
General Manager: Trish Hausmann
Paid Staff: 20
Paid Artists: 30
Type of Stage: Flexible
Orchestra Pit: y
Seating Capacity: 236

6489
WORKSHOP THEATRE
Indiana University
Department of Theatre & Drama
275 N Jordan
Bloomington, IN 47405-1101
Phone: 812-855-4535
e-mail: theatre@indiana.edu
Web Site: www.theatre.indiana.edu
Officers:
President: Michael A McRobbie
Chairman: Jonathan R Michaelsen
Secretary: Charlene McGlashan
Management:
General Manager: Trish Hausmann
Utilizes: Actors; AEA Actors; Designers; Educators; Fine Artists; Guest Accompanists; Guest Ensembles; Guest Instructors; Guest Soloists; Guild Activities; High School Drama; Original Music Scores; Performance Artists; Resident Professionals; Soloists
Specialized Field: Theatre and drama

6490
BALL THEATER
Wabash College
PO Box 352
Crawfordsville, IN 47933
Phone: 765-361-6100
Web Site: www.wabash.edu
Officers:
President: Patrick White
Treasurer: Larry Griffith

Management:
Artistic Director: Michael S Abbott
Type of Stage: Proscenium
Seating Capacity: 370

6491
EXPERIEMNTAL THEATER
Wabash College
PO Box 352
Crawfordsville, IN 47933
Phone: 765-361-6100
Web Site: www.wabash.edu
Officers:
President: Patrick White
Treasurer: Larry Griffith
Management:
Artistic Director: Michael S Abbott
Type of Stage: Black Box
Seating Capacity: 125

6492
SALTER CONCERT HALL
Wabash College
PO Box 352
Crawfordsville, IN 47933
Phone: 765-361-6100
Web Site: www.wabash.edu
Officers:
President: Patrick White
Treasurer: Larry Griffith
Management:
Artistic Director: Michael S Abbott
Seating Capacity: 275

6493
EVANSVILLE AUDITORIUM AND CONVENTION CENTRE
715 Locust Street
Evansville, IN 47708
Phone: 812-435-5770
Web Site: www.smgevansville.com
Management:
General Manager: Todd Denk
Operations Director: Harry Cochran
Marketing Director: Kathy Embry
Paid Staff: 40

6494
HELEN MALLETTE STUDIO THEATRE
University of Southern Indiana
Liberal Arts Center
8600 University Boulevard
Evansville, IN 47712-3596
Phone: 812-464-8600
Web Site: www.usi.edu
Officers:
President: H Ray Hoops
Chair: Elliot H Wasserman
Type of Stage: Black Box
Seating Capacity: 100

6495
ROBERTS MUNICIPAL STADIUM
2600 Division Street
Evansville, IN 47714
Phone: 812-476-1383
Web Site: www.smgevansville.com
Management:
General Manager: Todd Denk
Operations Director: Kevin McAlister
Marketing Director: Kathy Embry
Seating Capacity: 12,500

6496
SOLDIERS & SAILORS MEMORIAL COLISEUM
300 Court Street
Evansville, IN 47708
Phone: 812-424-5879
Fax: 812-424-2798
Web Site: www.ssmcoliseum.org
Management:
Director: Mark Acker
General Manager: Jay Ball
Seating Capacity: 4,055

6497
VICTORY THEATRE
600 Main Street
Evansville, IN 47708
Phone: 812-435-5770
e-mail: edmason@smgevansville.com
Web Site: www.smgevansville.com
Management:
General Manager: Todd Denk
Operations Director: Ed Mason
Marketing Director: Kathy Embry
Seating Capacity: 1,950

6498
EMBASSY CENTRE
125 West Jefferson Boulevard
Fort Wayne, IN 46802
Phone: 260-424-6287
Fax: 260-424-4806
e-mail: etflori@embassycentre.org
Web Site: www.embassycentre.org
Management:
Executive Director: Lori Lobsinger
Business Manager/Booking: Mahlon Houihan
Marketing/Advisor: Eileen Ahlersmeyer
Box Office Manager: Colette Conrad
Founded: 1928
Seating Capacity: 2,477

6499
FOELLINGER THEATER IN FRANKE PARK
3411 Sherman Boulevard
Fort Wayne, IN 46805
Phone: 219-427-6715
Web Site: www.fortwayneparks.org
Founded: 1949
Annual Attendance: 52,000

6500
PERFORMING ARTS CENTER
303 E Main Street
Fort Wayne, IN 46802
Phone: 219-422-8641
Fax: 219-422-6699
Web Site: www.fwcvb.org
Seating Capacity: 150

6501
SCOTTISH RITE CENTER
431 W Berry Street
Fort Wayne, IN 46802
Phone: 260-423-2593
Fax: 260-426-4126
Toll-free: 877-480-8020
Web Site: www.srcenter.org
Management:
President: Hans Sheridan
Artistic Director: Samantha Teter
Managing Director: Colleen O'Linger

Utilizes: Dance Companies; Multimedia; Original Music Scores; Special Technical Talent; Theatre Companies
Founded: 1925
Status: Non-Profit, Professional
Paid Staff: 8
Volunteer Staff: 20
Facility Category: Theater, Ballroom, Banquet Rooms
Type of Stage: Proscenium
Stage Dimensions: 90 w x 30 d
Seating Capacity: 50 to 2,086
Year Built: 1928
Year Remodeled: 2001
Rental Contact: Director of Marketing & Events Samantha Teter

6502
WILLIAMS THEATRE
Indiana University-Purdue
Department of Theatre
2101 E. Coliseum Blvd
Fort Wayne, IN 46805-1499
Phone: 260-481-4739
Toll-free: 800-324-4739
Web Site: http://www.ipfw.edu/vpa/theatre/
Officers:
Chancellor: Michael A. Wartell
Management:
Chair/Artistic Director: Larry L. Life
Technical Director: Sean Stewart
Box Office Manager: Reuben Aubaugh
Mission: Degree programs offered by the Department of Theatre provide comprehensive training for the theatre profession and explore theatre's 2,000-year history and literature.
Specialized Field: Broadway, Shakespeare Musicals
Type of Stage: Thrust
Seating Capacity: 299

6503
THEATRE MARGOT
Franklin College
Johnson Center for Fine Arts
101 Branigin Boulevard
Franklin, IN 46131-2623
Phone: 317-738-8000
Toll-free: 800-852-0232
Web Site: www.franklincollege.edu
Management:
Director: Robin Roberts
Mission: Students not only play most of the roles in campus production, but they also get a taste of set and prop construction, lighting and sound design, costume management, state management, front-of-house management and publicity.
Founded: 1834
Specialized Field: Comedies, Drama, Historic Classics, Modern Plays, Musicals
Paid Staff: 65
Type of Stage: Black Box
Seating Capacity: 200
Year Built: 2001

6504
ALLEN COUNTY WAR MEMORIAL COLISEUM
4000 Parnell Avenue
Ft. Wayne, IN 46805
Phone: 260-482-9502
Fax: 260-484-1637
e-mail: rbrown@memorialcoliseum.com
Web Site: www.memorialcoliseum.com
Management:
VP Sales & Marketing/COO: Garnett Miller
Executive VP/General Manager: Randy L Brown

All listings are in alphabetical order by state, then city, then organization within the city.

Founded: 1952
Specialized Field: Concerts; Family Shows; Trade/Consumer Shows; Private Meetings and Banquets
Status: Professional
Paid Staff: 300
Annual Attendance: 1.1 Million
Facility Category: Complex
Type of Stage: Stageright
Stage Dimensions: variable
Seating Capacity: 13,000
Year Built: 1952
Year Remodeled: 202
Cost: $34.5 Million
Rental Contact: Garnett Miller

6505
IUDONS

3400 Broadway
PO Box 64622
Gary, IN 46408
Phone: 219-980-7120
Fax: 219-981-4208
Toll-free: 888-968-7486
e-mail: vesmith@iun.edu
Web Site: www.iun.edu
Officers:
 President: Dr. Vernon G Smith
Founded: 1963
Budget: $5,000 -$10,000
Annual Attendance: 2,000
Facility Category: University Auditorium
Type of Stage: Professional
Seating Capacity: 2,000; 300
Year Built: 1980

6506
JOHN S. UMBLE CENTER

Goshen College
1700 South Main Street
Goshen, IN 46526
Phone: 574-535-7000
Fax: 574-535-7609
Toll-free: 800-348-7422
Web Site: http://www.goshen.edu/theater
Officers:
 President: James E. Brenneman
Management:
 Department Chair: Doug Caskey
 Production Manager: Brian Mast
Mission: The theater program at Goshen College has a strong liberal arts emphasis grounded in communication and performance theory.
Founded: 1894
Specialized Field: Operas, Plays, Theatre
Status: Private, Co-Educational
Facility Category: Theatre
Type of Stage: Proscenium/Thrust
Stage Dimensions: 70'x40'
Orchestra Pit: y
Seating Capacity: 419
Year Built: 1978

6507
KRESGE AUDITORIUM

DePauw University
Performing Arts Center
701 S. College Ave.
Greencastle, IN 46135-0037
Phone: 765-658-4827
e-mail: pacboxoffice@depauw.edu
Web Site: http://www.depauw.edu/pac/generalinfo
Officers:
 President: Robert G. Bottoms

 Coordinator Publicity/Marketing: Gigi Fenlon
Management:
 Department Chair: Steven Timm
 Director: M. Susan Anthony, PhD
 Technical Director: G. Duane Skoog
 Event Coordinator: Janice Bagwell
Mission: The DePauw University Performing Arts Center strives to create a place of learning, appreciation and love for the arts by providing artistically diverse, stimulating and accessible programs to the university, local and regional communities.
Specialized Field: Concerts, Theatre
Seating Capacity: 1,500

6508
MOORE THEATER

DePauw University
Performing Arts Center
701 S. College Ave.
Greencastle, IN 46135-0037
Phone: 765-658-4827
e-mail: pacboxoffice@depauw.edu
Web Site: http://www.depauw.edu/pac/generalinfo
Officers:
 President: Robert G. Bottoms
 Coordinator Publicity/Marketing: Gigi Fenlon
Management:
 Department Chair: Steven Timm
 Director: M. Susan Anthony, PhD
 Technical Director: G. Duane Skoog
 Event Coordinator: Janice Bagwell
Mission: The DePauw University Performing Arts Center strives to create a place of learning, appreciation and love for the arts by providing artistically diverse, stimulating and accessible programs to the university, local and regional communities.
Utilizes: Resident Artists
Specialized Field: Theatre
Type of Stage: Wrap-Around Stage
Seating Capacity: 400

6509
THOMPSON RECITAL HALL

DePauw University
Performing Arts Center
701 S. College Ave.
Greencastle, IN 46135-0037
Phone: 765-658-4827
e-mail: pacboxoffice@depauw.edu
Web Site: http://www.depauw.edu/pac/generalinfo
Officers:
 President: Robert G. Bottoms
 Coordinator Publicity/Marketing: Gigi Fenlon
Management:
 Department Chair: Steven Timm
 Director: M. Susan Anthony, PhD
 Technical Director: G. Duane Skoog
 Event Coordinator: Janice Bagwell
Mission: The DePauw University Performing Arts Center strives to create a place of learning, appreciation and love for the arts by providing artistically diverse, stimulating and accessible programs to the university, local and regional communities.
Specialized Field: Recitals
Type of Stage: 40 Foot Semi-Circular
Seating Capacity: 220

6510
EASTERN HOWARD PERFORMING ARTS SOCIETY

120 South Green Street
Greentown, IN 46936

Phone: 765-628-4025
Fax: 765-628-5017
Toll-free: 888-649-2787
Web Site: www.ehpas.com
Management:
 Executive Director: Kelli Austin
Mission: Be catalysts for the cultural enrichment of the community by presenting performing arts programs to entertain and enrich all audiences: futhermore, the society hopes to foster intrest and development of the arts in the schools.
Founded: 1999
Status: Non-Profit
Paid Staff: 2
Volunteer Staff: 27
Type of Stage: Proscenium
Year Built: 1999

6511
FITZGIBBON RECITAL HALL

Hanover College
Lynn Center For Fine Arts
PO Box 108
Hanover, IN 47243
Phone: 812-866-7260
Web Site: http://www.hanover.edu/theatre/facilities
Officers:
 President: Russell Nichols
Management:
 Department Chair: Jim Stark
 Director: Paul Hildebrand
 Production Supervisor: Rob Doenges
Mission: The Hanover College Theatre approach to theatre training is production-intensive. Our curriculum includes courses in acting, directing, playwriting, design, technical theatre, history, and literature.
Specialized Field: Concerts, Recitals, Soloists
Seating Capacity: 300

6512
PARKER AUDITORIUM

Hanover College
PO Box 108
Hanover, IN 47243
Phone: 812-866-7260
Web Site: http://www.hanover.edu/theatre/facilities
Officers:
 President: Russell Nichols
Management:
 Department Chair: Jim Stark
 Director: Paul Hildebrand
 Production Supervisor: Rob Doenges
Mission: The Hanover College Theatre approach to theatre training is production-intensive. Our curriculum includes courses in acting, directing, playwriting, design, technical theatre, history, and literature.
Specialized Field: Theatre
Type of Stage: Arena, Thrust, Stadium Stages
Seating Capacity: 750

6513
UNIVERSITY THEATRE

Valparaiso University
Center for the Arts
Hayward, IN
Phone: 219-464-5213
Web Site: http://www.valpo.edu/theatre
Officers:
 President: Alan F. Harre
Founded: 1859
Specialized Field: Musicals, Operas, Plays
Status: Private
Orchestra Pit: y
Seating Capacity: 280

6514
ZURCHER AUDITORIUM

Huntington College
Merillat Centre for the Arts
2303 College Avenue
Huntington, IN 46750
Phone: 260-356-6000
Web Site: http://www.huntington.edu/mca/theatre
Management:
Merillat Centre Director: Steve Pozezanac
Technical Director: Justin Spitler
Mission: Our Department of Theatre Arts offers degree programs in general Theatre, Performance, Design/Technology and Theatre Education. As a theatre student at Huntington University, you will combine classroom study, studio work and production experience to gain a balanced education.
Specialized Field: Theatre
Type of Stage: Proscenium
Seating Capacity: 697

6515
PEPSI COLISEUM

Indiana State Fairgrounds
1202 East 38th Street
Indianapolis, IN 46205
Phone: 317-927-7536
Fax: 317-927-7695
e-mail: dhummel@indianastatefair.com
Web Site: www.indianastatefair.com
Management:
Executive Director: William Stinson
Operations Director: Dave Hummel
Marketing Director: Cindy Hoye
Box Office Manager: Marty Gaddis
Seating Capacity: 7,000

6516
BUTLER UNIVERSITY

Jordan College of Fine Arts
4600 Sunset Avenue
Indianapolis, IN 46208
Phone: 317-940-9231
Fax: 317-940-9658
e-mail: info@butler.edu
Web Site: www.butler.edu
Officers:
President: Bobby Fong
Management:
Dean, Jordan College of Fine Arts: Peter Alexander
Founded: 1928
Status: Non-Profit, Non-Professional
Paid Staff: 50

6517
CLOWES MEMORIAL HALL

Butler University
4602 Sunset Avenue
Indianapolis, IN 46208-3485
Phone: 317-940-9697
Fax: 317-940-9820
e-mail: info@cloweshall.org
Web Site: www.cloweshall.org
Officers:
President: Dr Bobby Fong
Management:
Executive Director: Elise J Kushigian
Operations Director: Karen Steele
Marketing Director: John Lingenfelter
Mission: Clowes Memorial Hall of Butler University, a professional performing arts facility, is dedicated to lifelong learning in and through the arts. Our mission is

to educate, enrich and entertain the citizens of Indiana and the Butler University community by presenting, promoting and hosting culturally, artistically and internationally diverse programs, events and collaborations.
Utilizes: Resident Artists
Founded: 1963
Specialized Field: Ballet, Concerts, Musical, Theatre
Paid Staff: 22
Volunteer Staff: 165
Budget: $3,417,714
Income Sources: Admissions plus Developed Income
Performs At: Auditorium
Annual Attendance: 162,431
Facility Category: Auditorium
Type of Stage: Proscenium
Orchestra Pit: y
Seating Capacity: 2,172
Year Built: 1963
Cost: $3 Million
Rental Contact: Karen Steele

6518
EIDSON-DUCKWALL RECITAL HALL

Butler University
Performing Arts Complex
4600 Sunset Avenue
Indianapolis, IN 46208-3485
Phone: 317-940-9659
Fax: 317-940-9930
e-mail: info@butler.edu
Web Site: http://www.butler.edu/theatre/
Officers:
President: Dr. Bobby Fong
Management:
Department Chair: John C. Green, PhD
Technical Director: Glen Thoreson
Mission: The program of study in theatre combines stage experience with core studies in: acting, directing, voice, movement, playwriting; scenic, lighting and costume design; stagecraft and make-up; theatre history, play analysis and critical theory.
Founded: 1885
Specialized Field: Recitals
Seating Capacity: 140
Year Built: 2004
Architect: Browning Day Mullins Dierdorf
Cost: #3 Million

6519
EITELJORG MUSEUM

500 W Washington Street
Indianapolis, IN 46204
Phone: 317-636-9378
Fax: 317-264-1724
Web Site: www.eiteljorg.org
Management:
President: John Vanausdall
VP/Chief Curator: James Nottage
Director Education: Cathy Burton
Mission: To inspire an appreciation and understanding of the arts, history and cultures of the American West and the indigenous people of North America. The Eiteljorg Museum collects and preserves Western art and Native American art cultural objects of the highest quality, and serves the public through ongoing exhibitions, educational programs, cultural exchanges, and entertaining special events.
Founded: 1989
Specialized Field: American Indian and Western Art
Status: Non-Profit, Professional

6520
HINKLE FIELDHOUSE

Butler University
4602 Sunset Avenue
Indianapolis, IN 46208
Phone: 317-940-9375
Fax: 317-940-9734
Management:
Director: Elise Kushigian
Founded: 1928

6521
INDIANAPOLIS ARTS GARDEN

Arts Council of Indianapolis
47 S Pennsylvania Street Suite 303
Indianapolis, IN 46204
Phone: 317-631-3301
Fax: 317-624-2559
e-mail: indyarts@indyarts.org
Web Site: www.indyarts.org
Mission: To enable a large and diverse audience to see, understand and enjoy the best of the worlds visual arts; to this end, the Museum collects, preserves, exhibits and interprets original works of art.
Founded: 1995

6522
LILLY HALL STUDIO THEATRE

Butler University
Performing Arts Complex
4603 Clarendon Rd.
Indianapolis, IN 46208-3485
Phone: 317-940-9659
Fax: 317-940-9930
e-mail: info@butler.edu
Web Site: http://www.butler.edu/theatre/
Officers:
President: Dr. Bobby Fong
Management:
Department Chair: John C. Green, PhD
Technical Director: Glen Thoreson
Mission: The program of study in theatre combines stage experience with core studies in: acting, directing, voice, movement, playwriting; scenic, lighting and costume design; stagecraft and make-up; theatre history, play analysis and critical theory.
Founded: 1885
Specialized Field: Student Directed Productions
Type of Stage: Black Box
Seating Capacity: 350
Year Built: 2003
Architect: Browning Day Mullins Dierdorf

6523
MARKEY SQUARE ARENA

Pacers Basketball Corporation
300 E Market Street
Indianapolis, IN 46204
Phone: 317-639-6411
Fax: 317-261-6299
Web Site: www.marketsquaresarena.com
Management:
VP/General Manager: Rick Fuson
Communications Manager: Jeff Johnson
VP/Scheduling/Production Manager: Jeff Bowen
Concessions Manager: Rich Kapp
Seating Capacity: 16,900

6524
OLD NATIONAL CENTRE

502 North New Jersey Street
Indianapolis, IN 46204

Phone: 317-231-0000
Fax: 317-231-9410
Web Site: www.livenation.com/oldnationalcentre
Management:
Executive Director/Booking: Terry Hennessey
Events Director: Debbie Hennessey
Box Office Manager: Chris O'Connor
Production Manager: Chris Dicke
Mission: The Old National Centre, formerly the Murat Centre, is a multi-purpose facility offering great versatility for events of all sizes.
Seating Capacity: 2,600

6525
PIKE PERFORMING ARTS CENTER

6701 Zionsville Road
Indianapolis, IN 46268
Phone: 317-216-5450
Fax: 317-216-5460
e-mail: ppac@pike.k12.in.us
Web Site: www.pikePAC.org
Management:
Executive Director: Don Steffy
Technical Director: Kyle Bredehoeft
Box Office Manager: Lorna Startzman
Bookkeeper: Sue Thatcher
Mission: To offer quality performances and educational activities for the enjoyment and enlightenment of its public.
Utilizes: Actors; Collaborations; Dance Companies; Guest Musical Directors; Guild Activities; Local Artists; Multimedia; Special Technical Talent; Theatre Companies
Founded: 1996
Paid Staff: 5
Budget: $200,000+
Income Sources: Box Office, Grants, Sponsors
Affiliations: Association of Performing Arts Presenters; Indiana Presenters Network; League of Indianapolis Theatres
Annual Attendance: 7,800
Facility Category: Performance Center
Type of Stage: Proscenium
Stage Dimensions: 52'w x 24'h x 36'8"d
Seating Capacity: 1,449
Year Built: 1997

6526
RANSBURG AUDITORIUM

University of Indianapolis
Esch Hall Theatre
1400 East Hanna Avenue
Indianapolis, IN 46227
Phone: 317-788-2183
Toll-free: 800-232-8634
e-mail: arts@uindy.edu
Web Site: www.arts.uindy.edu
Officers:
President: Beverly Pitts
Management:
Dir Christel DeHann Fine Arts Ctr: Christie Beckmann
Department Chair: Jim Ream
Director Theatre: Brad Bright
Technical Director: Jeffrey Barnes
Administrative Asst Theatre Dept: Deb Denning
Faculty Box Office Manager: Jennifer Alexander
Mission: The goal of the Department of Theatre at the University of Indianapolis is to develop the skills, crafts, and imaginations of our students within the liberal arts context.
Founded: 1902
Specialized Field: Bands, Choir Concerts, Conferences, Dance Productions, Lectures, Theatrical

Type of Stage: Traditional Proscenium
Seating Capacity: 780
Year Restored: 1997

6527
RCA DOME

100 S Capitol Avenue
Indianapolis, IN 46225
Phone: 317-262-3403
Fax: 317-262-3455
Web Site: www.iccrd.com
Management:
Executive Director: Barney Levengood
Marketing Director: Linda Addaman
Stadium Director: Micheal A Fox
Suites/Special Services Manager: Heidi Mallin
General Manager/Volume Service: Dennis Cullinane
Ticket Manager: Mary Dyer
Founded: 1972
Status: Non-Profit, Non-Professional
Paid Staff: 140
Seating Capacity: 60,500

6528
RUTH LILLY PERFORMANCE HALL

University of Indianapolis
Christel DeHaan Fine Arts Center
1400 East Hanna Avenue
Indianapolis, IN 46227
Phone: 317-788-2183
Toll-free: 800-232-8634
e-mail: arts@uindy.edu
Web Site: www.arts.uindy.edu
Officers:
President: Beverly Pitts
Management:
Dir Christel DeHann Fine Arts Ctr: Christie Beckmann
Department Chair: Jim Ream
Director Theatre: Brad Bright
Technical Director: Jeffrey Barnes
Administrative Asst Theatre Dept: Deb Denning
Faculty Box Office Manager: Jennifer Alexander
Mission: The goal of the Department of Theatre at the University of Indianapolis is to develop the skills, crafts, and imaginations of our students within the liberal arts context.
Founded: 1902
Opened: 1994
Specialized Field: Chamber, Classical, Jazz Music
Type of Stage: Proscenium
Seating Capacity: 600

6529
STUDIO THEATRE

University of Indianapolis
Esch Hall Theatre
1400 East Hanna Avenue
Indianapolis, IN 46227
Phone: 317-788-2183
Toll-free: 800-232-8634
e-mail: arts@uindy.edu
Web Site: www.arts.uindy.edu
Officers:
President: Beverly Pitts
Management:
Dir Christel DeHann Fine Arts Ctr: Christie Beckmann
Department Chair: Jim Ream
Director Theatre: Brad Bright
Technical Director: Jeffrey Barnes
Administrative Asst Theatre Dept: Deb Denning
Faculty Box Office Manager: Jennifer Alexander

Mission: The goal of the Department of Theatre at the University of Indianapolis is to develop the skills, crafts, and imaginations of our students within the liberal arts context.
Founded: 1902
Specialized Field: Faculty, Student Productions
Type of Stage: 3/4 Thrust Black Box
Seating Capacity: 80

6530
VICTORY FIELD: INDIANAPOLIS BASEBALL CLUB

501 W Maryland Street
Indianapolis, IN 46225
Phone: 317-269-3542
Fax: 317-269-3541
Web Site: www.indyindians.com
Management:
Chairman/President: Max B Schumacher
General Manager: D Cal Burleson
Business Manager: Brad Morris
Assistant General Manager: Randy Lewandowski
Office Manager: Scott Rubin
Media Relations Director: Tim Harms
Director Advertising: Daryle Keith
Director Special Projects: Bruce Schumacher
Director Ticket Operations: Mike Schneider
Founded: 1887
Status: For-Profit, Professional
Paid Staff: 15
Seating Capacity: 15,500

6531
WARREN PERFORMING ARTS CENTER

9500 East 16th Street
Indianapolis, IN 46229
Phone: 317-532-6280
Fax: 317-532-6440
e-mail: pmitchel@warren.k12.in.us
Web Site: www.warrenpac.com
Management:
Manager: Penny Miritell
Mission: Providing education and cultural programs for the students and community of Warren Township and Greater Indianapolis.
Performs At: Grand Stage Auditorium, Studio Theatre
Type of Stage: Flexible
Seating Capacity: 1000; 150

6532
JASPER ARTS CENTER

951 College Avenue
Jasper, IN 47546
Phone: 812-482-3070
Fax: 812-634-6997
e-mail: jasperarts@psci.net
Web Site: www.jasperarts.org
Founded: 1975
Type of Stage: Proscenium

6533
HAVENS AUDITORIUM

Indiana University Kokomo
Main Building
2300 S. Washington Street
Kokomo, IN 46904-9003
Phone: 765-453-2000
Web Site: http://www.iuk.edu/~koautrm/
Officers:
Chancellor: Ruth Person
Management:
Technical Director: Jeffrey Gegner

Mission: Havens Auditorium is a community cultural center, used for dramatic presentations, concerts, lectures.
Founded: 1945
Opened: 1965
Specialized Field: Concerts, Lectures, Theatre
Type of Stage: Proscenium
Stage Dimensions: 50' x 24'
Orchestra Pit: y
Seating Capacity: 868

6534
LONG CENTER FOR THE PERFORMING ARTS

111 N 6th Street
Lafayette, IN 47902
Phone: 765-742-5664
Fax: 765-742-1724
Toll-free: 877-490-7761
e-mail: info@longcentertheater.com
Web Site: www.longcentertheater.com
Officers:
    President: Dave Lahr
Management:
    Executive Director: Doug Kern
    Secretary/Ticket Sales: Brenda Shuttz
    Accountant: Shelly McConnaughey
    Operations: Shannon Sabel
Mission: Performing Arts Center that enhances the community's cultural life.
Founded: 1921
Specialized Field: Series & Festivals; Dance; Instrumental Music; Musical Theatre; Theatrical Group; Vocal Music
Status: Non-Profit, Professional
Paid Staff: 15
Volunteer Staff: 40
Budget: $250,000
Income Sources: Rentals; Donations
Performs At: Theater, Performing Arts
Annual Attendance: 40,000
Facility Category: Theater, Performing Arts
Type of Stage: Wood
Stage Dimensions: 35' x 30'
Seating Capacity: 1190
Year Built: 1921
Year Remodeled: 2000
Rental Contact: Doug Kern

6535
HERMAN BAKER RECITAL HALL

Indiana Wesleyan University
Phillippe Performing Arts Center
4229 South Nebraska Street
Marion, IN 46953
Phone: 765-667-2610
Web Site: www.indwes.edu
Officers:
    President: Dr. Henry L. Smith
    University Relations Director: Alan Miller
Mission: Our goal continues to be to provide a diversity of music and theater programming for the enjoyment of students, friends and neighbors of all ages.
Opened: 1996
Specialized Field: Chamber Music, Senior Recitals, Student Performances
Orchestra Pit: y
Seating Capacity: 176

6536
PHILLIPPE AUDITORIUM

Indiana Wesleyan University
Phillippe Performing Arts Center
4229 South Nebraska Street
Marion, IN 46953
Phone: 765-667-2610
Web Site: www.indwes.edu
Officers:
    President: Dr. Henry L. Smith
    University Relations Director: Alan Miller
Mission: Our goal continues to be to provide a diversity of music and theater programming for the enjoyment of students, friends and neighbors of all ages.
Opened: 1996
Specialized Field: Recitals, Theatre
Type of Stage: Versatile
Orchestra Pit: y
Seating Capacity: 1,155

6537
RCA BLACK BOX THEATRE

Indiana Wesleyan University
Phillippe Performing Arts Center
4229 South Nebraska Street
Marion, IN 46953
Phone: 765-667-2610
Web Site: www.indwes.edu
Officers:
    President: Dr. Henry L. Smith
    University Relations Director: Alan Miller
Mission: Our goal continues to be to provide a diversity of music and theater programming for the enjoyment of students, friends and neighbors of all ages.
Opened: 1996
Specialized Field: Theatre
Type of Stage: Black Box
Orchestra Pit: y
Seating Capacity: 125

6538
EVEREST-ROHRER AUDITORIUM

Bethel College
Fine Arts Center
1001 West McKinley Avenue
Mishawaka, IN 46545
Phone: 574-259-8511
Web Site: http://www.bethelcollege.edu/academics/undergrad/theatr
Management:
    Director: Barbara Stith
    Technical Director: Derek Null
    Production Manager: Lisa Staples
Mission: An evangelical Christian college affiliated with the Missionary Church, Bethel is uniquely qualified to provide educational opportunities for all students, traditional and adult, who are interested in a liberal arts program of studies with career and personal growth orientations.
Specialized Field: Comedy, Drama, Musical, Theatre
Type of Stage: Proscenium
Stage Dimensions: 48' x 32'
Orchestra Pit: y
Seating Capacity: 860
Year Built: 1996
Cost: $5 Million

6539
OCTORIUM

Bethel College
Fine Arts Center
1001 West McKinley Avenue
Mishawaka, IN 46545
Phone: 574-259-8511
Web Site:
http://www.bethelcollege.edu/academics/undergrad/theatr
Management:
    Director: Barbara Stith
    Technical Director: Derek Null
    Production Manager: Lisa Staples
Mission: An evangelical Christian college affiliated with the Missionary Church, Bethel is uniquely qualified to provide educational opportunities for all students, traditional and adult, who are interested in a liberal arts program of studies with career and personal growth orientations.
Specialized Field: Plays
Type of Stage: Black Box
Seating Capacity: 160

6540
CAVE THEATRE

Ball State University
Department of Theatre and Dance, AC 306
2000 West University Avenue
Muncie, IN 47306
Phone: 765-285-8740
Fax: 765-285-4030
e-mail: theatrestu@bsu.edu
Web Site: http://www.bsu.edu/theatre
Officers:
    President: Jo Ann M. Gora
Management:
    Chair: Bill Jenkins
    Technical Director: Curtis Mortimore
Mission: Ball State University's Department of Theatre and Dance is a program of choice for the serious undergraduate theatre and dance student. Our theatre major features options in acting, musical theatre, design and technology, production (directing and stage management), theatrical studies, and theatre education.
Specialized Field: Classes, Student Productions
Paid Staff: 15

6541
EDWARD S. STROTHER THEATRE

Ball State University
Department of Theatre and Dance, AC 306
2000 West University Avenue
Muncie, IN 47306
Phone: 765-285-8740
Fax: 765-285-4030
e-mail: theatrestu@bsu.edu
Web Site: http://www.bsu.edu/theatre
Officers:
    President: Jo Ann M. Gora
Management:
    Chair: Bill Jenkins
    Technical Director: Curtis Mortimore
Mission: Ball State University's Department of Theatre and Dance is a program of choice for the serious undergraduate theatre and dance student. Our theatre major features options in acting, musical theatre, design and technology, production (directing and stage management), theatrical studies, and theatre education.
Specialized Field: Theatre
Paid Staff: 15
Type of Stage: Black Box
Seating Capacity: 100

6542
EMENS AUDITORIUM
Ball State University
Worthen Arena 140
Muncie, IN 47306
Phone: 765-285-1539
Fax: 765-285-3719
Web Site: www.bsu.edu
Officers:
President: Bob Myers
Management:
General Manager: Dan P Bymes
Assistant Manager: Julie Strider
Stage Manager: Keven Byral
Mission: To provide cultural, fine arts and entearinment opportunities for East Central Indiana.
Founded: 1964
Status: Nonprofit, Professional
Paid Staff: 10
Performs At: Emens Auditorium
Type of Stage: Black Box
Seating Capacity: 3,581

6543
UNIVERSITY THEATRE
Ball State University
Department of Theatre and Dance, AC 306
2000 West University Avenue
Muncie, IN 47306
Phone: 765-285-8740
Fax: 765-285-4030
e-mail: theatrestu@bsu.edu
Web Site: http://www.bsu.edu/theatre
Officers:
President: Jo Ann M. Gora
Management:
Chair: Bill Jenkins
Technical Director: Curtis Mortimore
Mission: Ball State University's Department of Theatre and Dance is a program of choice for the serious undergraduate theatre and dance student. Our theatre major features options in acting, musical theatre, design and technology, production (directing and stage management), theatrical studies, and theatre education.
Specialized Field: Dance, Theatre
Paid Staff: 15
Seating Capacity: 410

6544
CENTER FOR VISUAL AND PERFORMING ARTS
1040 Ridge Road
Theatre At The Center
Munster, IN 46321
Phone: 219-836-3258
Fax: 219-836-9073
e-mail: cgessert@comhs.org
Web Site: www.cvpa.org
Management:
Production Manager: Chuck Gessert
Artistic Director: William Pullinsi
Mission: To touch, enrich and entertain human beings with live professional theatre.
Founded: 1989
Type of Stage: Thrust
Seating Capacity: 450

6545
BROWN COUNTY PLAYHOUSE
Indiana University at Bloomington
Theatre & Drama
70 Van Buren St South
Nashville, IN 47448
Phone: 812-988-2123
Fax: 812-856-0698
Web Site: www.indiana.edu/~thtr
Officers:
Interim Provost: Michael A. McRobbie
Events Manager: Maria Talbert
Management:
Department Chair: Jonathan R. Michaelson
Assistant Technical Director: I. Christopher Berg
Mission: The Brown County Playhouse, a professional theatre operated in conjunction with the Indiana University Department of Theatre and Drama, is located in the center of scenic Nashville.
Founded: 1949
Specialized Field: Comedy, Contemporary, Theatre
Status: Non-Profit, Professional
Paid Staff: 20
Paid Artists: 30
Seating Capacity: 400

6546
AMPHITHEATRE
Indiana University Southeast
Knobview Hall
4201 Grant Line Road
New Albany, IN 47150
Phone: 812-941-2333
Fax: 812-941-2660
e-mail: setheatr@ius.edu
Web Site: http://www.ius.edu/Theater/
Management:
Assistant Professor Scenic Design: Rebekkah Meixner
Adjunct Lecturer Theatre: Dru Pilmer
Adjunct Lecturer Theatre: Gregory Maupin
Mission: The Theatre program at Indiana University Southeast is committed to providing a wide variety of opportunities for students to explore and develop expertise in performance and design.
Specialized Field: Graduation
Seating Capacity: 6,000
Cost: $12 Million

6547
PAUL G. ROBINSON THEATER
Indiana University Southeast
Paul W. Ogle Cultural and Community Center
4201 Grant Line Road
New Albany, IN 47150
Phone: 812-941-2333
Fax: 812-941-2660
e-mail: setheatr@ius.edu
Web Site: http://www.ius.edu/Theater/
Management:
Assistant Professor Scenic Design: Rebekkah Meixner
Adjunct Lecturer Theatre: Dru Pilmer
Adjunct Lecturer Theatre: Gregory Maupin
Mission: The Theatre program at Indiana University Southeast is committed to providing a wide variety of opportunities for students to explore and develop expertise in performance and design.
Specialized Field: Dance, Theatre
Type of Stage: Thrust
Seating Capacity: 340
Cost: $12 Million

6548
PAUL W OGLE CULTURAL & COMMUNITY CENTER
Indiana University Southeast
4201 Grant Line Road
New Albany, IN 47150-6405
Phone: 812-941-2544
e-mail: oglemail@ius.edu
Web Site: www.ius.indiana.edu
Management:
Executive Director: Kyle Ridout
Founded: 1996
Status: Non-Profit, Non-Professional
Paid Staff: 11
Volunteer Staff: 15
Performs At: Concert Hall

6549
RECITAL HALL
Indiana University Southeast
Paul W. Ogle Cultural and Community Center
4201 Grant Line Road
New Albany, IN 47150
Phone: 812-941-2333
Fax: 812-941-2660
e-mail: setheatr@ius.edu
Web Site: http://www.ius.edu/Theater/
Management:
Assistant Professor Scenic Design: Rebekkah Meixner
Adjunct Lecturer Theatre: Dru Pilmer
Adjunct Lecturer Theatre: Gregory Maupin
Mission: The Theatre program at Indiana University Southeast is committed to providing a wide variety of opportunities for students to explore and develop expertise in performance and design.
Specialized Field: Community Meetings, Conferences, Faculty and Student Recitals
Seating Capacity: 96
Cost: $12 Million

6550
RICHARD K. STEM CONCERT HALL
Indiana University Southeast
Paul W. Ogle Cultural and Community Center
4201 Grant Line Road
New Albany, IN 47150
Phone: 812-941-2333
Fax: 812-941-2660
e-mail: setheatr@ius.edu
Web Site: http://www.ius.edu/Theater/
Management:
Assistant Professor Scenic Design: Rebekkah Meixner
Adjunct Lecturer Theatre: Dru Pilmer
Adjunct Lecturer Theatre: Gregory Maupin
Mission: The Theatre program at Indiana University Southeast is committed to providing a wide variety of opportunities for students to explore and develop expertise in performance and design.
Specialized Field: Concerts, Drummer Series, Music Department
Type of Stage: Proscenium
Orchestra Pit: y
Seating Capacity: 500
Cost: $12 Million

6551
CORDIER AUDITORIUM
Manchester College
604 East College Avenue
North Manchester, IN 46962
Phone: 260-982-5000
Fax: 219-982-6868
Web Site: www.manchester.edu
Officers:
President: Jo Young Switzer
Event Specialist: Alexis Leininger
Facilities Coordinator: Paula Finton
Management:

Chair: Scott K. Strode
Dir Performing Art Technologies: Matt Unger
Mission: As a primarily undergraduate, residential, liberal arts community rooted in the tradition of the Church of the Brethren, Manchester College values: Learning, Faith, Service, Integrity, Diversity, Community.
Founded: 1889
Specialized Field: Presentations, Theatre Productions
Seating Capacity: 1,300
Year Built: 1978

6552
CHRIS AND ANNE REYES ORGAN AND CHORAL HALL

University of Notre Dame
Marie P. Debartolo Performing Arts Center
100 Performing Arts Center
Notre Dame, IN
Phone: 574-631-2800
Web Site: http:/performingarts.nd.edu
Officers:
  President: Rev. John I. Jenkins, CSC
Management:
  Interim Director Debartolo Center: Howard Hanson
  Director Technical Services: Sarah Schreiber Prince
  Production Manager: Jenny Goetz
Mission: The DeBartolo Center for the Peforming Arts was carefully designed for both public performance and for teaching and learning. Our mission is rooted in the conviction that the arts are an indispensable element of a liberal education and an enlightened society.
Opened: 2004
Specialized Field: Sacred Music
Seating Capacity: 80

6553
EDMUND P. JOYCE ATHLETIC & CONVOCATION CENTER

University of Notre Dame
C113 Joyce Center
Notre Dame, IN 46556
Phone: 574-631-6107
Fax: 574-631-8596
e-mail: develop@nd.edu
Web Site: www.nd.edu
Management:
  Assistant Business Manager: Heidi Uebelhor
Founded: 1842
Status: Non-Profit, Professional
Paid Staff: 13
Seating Capacity: 9,800

6554
JUDD AND MARY LOU LEIGHTON CONCERT HALL

University of Notre Dame
Marie P. Debartolo Performing Arts Center
100 Performing Arts Center
Notre Dame, IN
Phone: 574-631-2800
Web Site: http:/performingarts.nd.edu
Officers:
  President: Rev. John I. Jenkins, CSC
Management:
  Interim Director Debartolo Center: Howard Hanson
  Director Technical Services: Sarah Schreiber Prince
  Production Manager: Jenny Goetz

Mission: The DeBartolo Center for the Peforming Arts was carefully designed for both public performance and for teaching and learning. Our mission is rooted in the conviction that the arts are an indispensable element of a liberal education and an enlightened society.
Opened: 2004
Specialized Field: Choir, Jazz Band, Shakespeare, Symphony Orchestra
Type of Stage: Concert Hall Stage
Stage Dimensions: 58' x 40'
Orchestra Pit: y
Seating Capacity: 952

6555
MARIE P. DEBARTOLO CENTER FOR THE PERFORMING ARTS

University of Notre Dame
100 Performing Arts Center
Notre Dame, IN 46556
Phone: 574-631-2995
Fax: 574-631-9411
e-mail: performingarts.nd.edu
Web Site: www.performingarts.nd.edu
Officers:
  Executive Director: Anna M. Thompson
  Business Program Manager: Tom Barkes
  Senior Associate Director: Ted Barron
Mission: The Marie P. DeBartolo center for the Performing Arts facilitates learning reflective of the University of Notre Dame's distinctive liberal arts tradition through the informed exploration of universal truth and beauty. We serve to encourage and celebrate the human spirit through the performing and cinematic arts, which connect, stimulate and enrich our communities.
Utilizes: Dance Companies; Touring Companies
Founded: 2004
Specialized Field: Professional Music/Dance Theatre; Academic Music Dance Theatre; Art House Cinema
Paid Staff: 24
Volunteer Staff: 55
Paid Artists: 25
Budget: $2-3 Million
Income Sources: Ticket Sales; Endowment; Grants; Donations; University Support
Performs At: Regis Philbin Studio Theatre, Judd and Mary Lou Leighton Concert Hall, Patricia George Decio Mainstage Theatre
Affiliations: ISPA; APAP; CMA; Dance USA; INMX; Cavco; Cavort
Annual Attendance: 50,000
Facility Category: Concert Hall; Proscenium; Black Box; Cinema; Organ Hall
Type of Stage: Proscenium; Black Box
Seating Capacity: 100, 900, 350
Year Built: 2004
Cost: $64 Million

6556
MICHAEL BROWNING FAMILY CINEMA

University of Notre Dame
Marie P. Debartolo Performing Arts Center
100 Performing Arts Center
Notre Dame, IN
Phone: 574-631-2800
Web Site: http:/performingarts.nd.edu
Officers:
  President: Rev. John I. Jenkins, CSC
Management:
  Interim Director Debartolo Center: Howard Hanson
  Browning Cinema Manager: Jon Vickers
  Director Technical Services: Sarah Schreiber Prince

Production Manager: Jenny Goetz
Mission: The DeBartolo Center for the Peforming Arts was carefully designed for both public performance and for teaching and learning. Our mission is rooted in the conviction that the arts are an indispensable element of a liberal education and an enlightened society.
Opened: 2004
Specialized Field: Art House Theatre, Current and Historic Films
Type of Stage: Cinema
Seating Capacity: 202

6557
NOTRE DAME STADIUM

University of Notre Dame
Notre Dame, IN 46556
Phone: 574-631-5000
Fax: 574-631-6772
e-mail: develop.1@nd.edu
Web Site: www.und.com
Management:
  Director Athletic Facilities: Michael J Danch
Seating Capacity: 80,530

6558
PATRICIA GEORGE DECIO THEATRE

University of Notre Dame
Marie P. Debartolo Performing Arts Center
100 Performing Arts Center
Notre Dame, IN
Phone: 574-631-2800
Web Site: http:/performingarts.nd.edu
Officers:
  President: Rev. John I. Jenkins, CSC
Management:
  Interim Director Debartolo Center: Howard Hanson
  Director Technical Services: Sarah Schreiber Prince
  Production Manager: Jenny Goetz
Mission: The DeBartolo Center for the Peforming Arts was carefully designed for both public performance and for teaching and learning. Our mission is rooted in the conviction that the arts are an indispensable element of a liberal education and an enlightened society.
Opened: 2004
Specialized Field: Professional and Amateur Productions
Type of Stage: Proscenium
Stage Dimensions: 32' and 42' x 24'
Orchestra Pit: y
Seating Capacity: 360

6559
REGIS PHILBIN STUDIO THEATRE

University of Notre Dame
Marie P. Debartolo Performing Arts Center
100 Performing Arts Center
Notre Dame, IN
Phone: 574-631-2800
Web Site: http:/performingarts.nd.edu
Officers:
  President: Rev. John I. Jenkins, CSC
Management:
  Interim Director Debartolo Center: Howard Hanson
  Director Technical Services: Sarah Schreiber Prince
  Production Manager: Jenny Goetz
Mission: The DeBartolo Center for the Peforming Arts was carefully designed for both public performance and for teaching and learning. Our mission is rooted in the conviction that the arts are an indispensable element of a liberal education and an enlightened society.

Opened: 2004
Specialized Field: Classes, Workshops, Rehearsals, and Impromptu Performances
Type of Stage: Black Box
Stage Dimensions: 53'3 x 43'8
Seating Capacity: 100

6560
WASHINGTON HALL AUDITORIUM

University of Notre Dame
Marie P. Debartolo Performing Arts Center
100 Performing Arts Center
Notre Dame, IN
Phone: 574-631-2800
Web Site: http://performingarts.nd.edu
Officers:
　President: Rev. John I. Jenkins, CSC
Management:
　Interim Director Debartolo Center: Howard Hanson
　Director Technical Services: Sarah Schreiber Prince
　Production Manager: Jenny Goetz
Mission: The DeBartolo Center for the Peforming Arts was carefully designed for both public performance and for teaching and learning. Our mission is rooted in the conviction that the arts are an indispensable element of a liberal education and an enlightened society.
Opened: 2004
Specialized Field: Musicals, Theatre
Type of Stage: Semi Thrust Stage
Stage Dimensions: 26'8 x 25'
Seating Capacity: 571

6561
CIVIC HALL PERFORMING ARTS CENTER

380 Hub Etchison Parkway
Richmond, IN 47374
Phone: 765-973-3350
Fax: 765-973-3346
Toll-free: 888-248-4242
Web Site: www.civichall.com
Management:
　Facilities Director: Jeffrey Thorne
　Technical Director: Mike Rogan
Founded: 1993
Specialized Field: Multi-discipline; School System; Entertainment
Status: Non-Profit, Professional
Paid Staff: 5
Volunteer Staff: 150
Seating Capacity: 924

6562
RICHMOND CIVIC THEATRE

1003 E Main Street
Richmond, IN 47374
Phone: 765-962-1816
Fax: 765-939-2572
e-mail: office@richmondcivictheatre.org
Web Site: www.richmondcivictheatre.org
Management:
　President: Steve Holthouse, Pres@richmondcivictheatre.org
Mission: To produce high quality theatrical productions that will engage, entertain, educate, and inspire the people of Richmond and the surrounding community, participants and audience alike.
Founded: 1941
Specialized Field: A Community Theatre
Status: Non-Profit, Non-Professional
Paid Staff: 3
Type of Stage: Concert Stage

6563
CENTURY CENTER RECITAL HALL

120 S St. Joseph Street
South Bend, IN 46601
Phone: 219-235-9711
Fax: 219-235-9185
Web Site: www.centurycenter.com

6564
CENTURY CENTER CONVENTION HALL

120 S St. Joseph Street
South Bend, IN 46601
Phone: 574-235-9711
Fax: 574-235-9185
Web Site: www.centurycenter.com
Founded: 1977
Type of Stage: Thrust
Seating Capacity: 694

6565
MORRIS PERFORMING ARTS CENTER

211 N Michigan Street
South Bend, IN 46601
Phone: 574-235-9198
Fax: 574-235-5604
Toll-free: 800-537-6415
e-mail: info@morriscenter.org
Web Site: www.morriscenter.org
Officers:
　Executive Director: Dennis J. Audres
　Asst. Director/Admin & Marketing: Mary Ellen Smith
Management:
　Asst. Director/Booking & Event Ops.: Denise Zigler
　:
Mission: It is the mission of the Morris Performing Arts Center to be the premier performing arts center in the region; to provide a cornucopia of diverse events throughout the year fulfilling the needs and wishes of all who might use the facilities; and to be recognized as one of the best theatre rental venues in the nation.
Founded: 1921
Specialized Field: Live Entertainment; National Broadway Touring Shows; Concerts; Symphony; Comedians; Family Shows
Status: Professional
Paid Staff: 11
Volunteer Staff: 150
Performs At: Theater
Affiliations: Register Of Historic Places; Ranked By Pollstar Magazine Top 100; Facilities Magazine; IAAM; League Of American Historic Theatres
Facility Category: Restored 1921 Vaudeville Theatre With Ballroom
Type of Stage: Proscenium, Orchestra
Stage Dimensions: 54'X25"
Seating Capacity: 2,564
Year Built: 1921
Year Remodeled: 2000
Rental Contact: Denise Zigler

6566
COMMUNITY THEATRE OF TERRE HAUTE

1431 S 25th Street
Terre Haute, IN 47803
Phone: 360-373-5152
Fax: 360-373-6754
Web Site: www.mama.indstate.edy
Officers:
　President: Sonni Crawford
　VP: Tim Porter

　Secretary: Marti Cornelius
　Treasurer: Wayne Huston

6567
DREISER THEATRE

Indiana State University
Department of Theatre
540 North 7th Street
Terre Haute, IN 47809
Phone: 812-237-3331
Web Site: http://web.indstate.edu/theatre/
Officers:
　President: Lloyd W. Benjamin, III
Management:
　Department Chair: Arthur Feinsod
　Director: Christopher Berchild
　Technical Director: David G. Del Colletti
Mission: At ISU Theater, our goal is to offer our students a challenging artistic and academic environment which allows them to grow as both theater artists and people. Our course offerings are diverse, exposing our students to a number of exciting concentrations and fields of study.
Specialized Field: Theatre
Type of Stage: Thrust/Arena
Seating Capacity: 200

6568
HULMAN CENTER

Indiana State University
200 N 8th Street
Terre Haute, IN 47809
Phone: 812-237-3770
Fax: 812-237-3741
Web Site: www.indstate.edu/hctaf
Management:
　Director: Cliff Lambert
　Facility Marketing/Ticket Sales: Jennifer Cook
　Operations/Event Services Manager: Judy Price
　Technical Services Supervisor: Don Knott
Founded: 1973
Specialized Field: Multi Purpose Venue
Seating Capacity: 11,000
Year Built: 1973

6569
NEW THEATER

Indiana State University
Department of Theatre
540 North 7th Street
Terre Haute, IN 47809
Phone: 812-237-3331
Web Site: http://web.indstate.edu/theatre/
Officers:
　President: Lloyd W. Benjamin, III
Management:
　Department Chair: Arthur Feinsod
　Director: Christopher Berchild
　Technical Director: David G. Del Colletti
Mission: At ISU Theater, our goal is to offer our students a challenging artistic and academic environment which allows them to grow as both theater artists and people. Our course offerings are diverse, exposing our students to a number of exciting concentrations and fields of study.
Specialized Field: Theatre
Type of Stage: Proscenium
Seating Capacity: 240

6570
STUDIO THEATRE

Valparaiso University
1700 Chapel Drive
Valparaiso, IN 46383-5244

Phone: 219-464-5213
Fax: 219-464-5244
Web Site: www.valpo.edu
Officers:
   President: Mark A Heckler
   Chair: Lee F Orchard
Management:
   Development Director: Markus Jennings
Type of Stage: Black Box
Stage Dimensions: 40' x 40'
Seating Capacity: 65

6571
HONEYWELL CENTER
275 W Market Streeet
Wabash, IN 46992
Phone: 260-563-1102
Fax: 260-563-0873
Toll-free: 800-626-6345
Web Site: www.honeywellcenter.org
Officers:
   President: Bruce Ingraham
   VP: Steve Downs
   Treasurer: Tom Hodson
Mission: Serve the local and surrounding communities through cultural and educational programs.
Utilizes: Actors; Choreographers; Dance Companies; Dancers; Fine Artists; Grant Writers; Guest Accompanists; Guest Artists; Guest Choreographers; Guest Companies; Guest Composers; Guest Directors; Guest Instructors; Guest Lecturers; Guest Musical Directors; Guest Musicians; Guest Soloists; Instructors; Local Artists; Multimedia; Original Music Scores; Playwrights; Sign Language Translators; Singers; Soloists; Special Technical Talent; Theatre Companies
Founded: 1940
Status: Nonprofit
Paid Staff: 24
Volunteer Staff: 150
Budget: $3,100,000
Income Sources: Earned
Annual Attendance: 30,000
Facility Category: cultural arts/ conference
Type of Stage: Proscenium
Stage Dimensions: 50' x 30' x45'
Seating Capacity: 1500
Year Built: 1994
Year Remodeled: 1994
Cost: $17,000,000
Rental Contact: Shannon Shrider

6572
CAROLE AND GORDON MALLETT THEATRE
Purdue University Main Campus
Yue-Kong Pao Hall of Visual & Performing Arts
552 W. Wood Street
West Lafayette, IN 47907-2002
Phone: 765-494-3074
Fax: 765-494-1766
Web Site: http://www.cla.purdue.edu/theatre
Officers:
   President: Martin C. Jischke
Management:
   Dean Liberal Arts: John J. Contreni
   Theatre Division Mktging Relations: Peggy Felix
Mission: There are three readily identifiable components of the Theatre Division: the undergraduate program, the graduate program and the production program. The latter also serves as a laboratory for the whole division. Each program has distinct goals, although the objectives of all the programs are inter-related.
Opened: 2006

Specialized Field: Theatre
Type of Stage: Arena, Thrust, End Stage
Seating Capacity: 100-150

6573
ELLIOTT HALL OF MUSIC
Purdue University
West Lafayette, IN 47907
Phone: 765-494-3920
Fax: 317-494-6621
e-mail: sdhall@purdue.edu
Web Site: www.purdue.edu
Management:
   Assistant Director, Administrative: Jennifer Molden
   Director: Steve Hall
   Assistant Director: Jim Chapman
   Box Office Manager: Carolanne Robinson
   Fiscal Administrator: Michael Smolen
   Account Clerk: Kay Gohn
   House Manager: Joyce Banta
Mission: To serve our customers in West Lafayette, IN by providing an environment which enhances their Purdue university experience while supporting the University's overall objectives of Education, Research, and Service.
Founded: 1940
Type of Stage: Proscenium
Seating Capacity: 6,025

6574
MACKEY ARENA
Purdue University
1790 Mackey Arena
West Lafayette, IN 47907
Phone: 765-494-4600
Fax: 765-784-4497
Web Site: www.purdue.edu
Management:
   Athletic Director: Morgan Burke
Seating Capacity: 14,121

6575
NANCY T. HANSEN THEATRE
Purdue University Main Campus
Yue-Kong Pao Hall of Visual & Performing Arts
552 W. Wood Street
West Lafayette, IN 47907-2002
Phone: 765-494-3074
Fax: 765-494-1766
Web Site: http://www.cla.purdue.edu/theatre
Officers:
   President: Martin C. Jischke
Management:
   Dean Liberal Arts: John J. Contreni
   Theatre Division Mktging Relations: Peggy Felix
Mission: There are three readily identifiable components of the Theatre Division: the undergraduate program, the graduate program and the production program. The latter also serves as a laboratory for the whole division. Each program has distinct goals, although the objectives of all the programs are inter-related.
Opened: 2006
Specialized Field: Theatre
Type of Stage: Proscenium
Stage Dimensions: 36' x 28'
Orchestra Pit: y
Seating Capacity: 300

6576
ROSS-ADE STADIUM
Purdue University
West Lafayette, IN 47907

Phone: 765-494-3189
Fax: 765-496-1280
Web Site: www.purduesports.com
Management:
   Athletic Director: Morgan Burke
   Senior Associate Athletic Director: Glenn Tompkins
   Senior Associate Athletic Director: Nancy Cross
   Associate Athletic Director: Roger Blalock
Founded: 1869
Seating Capacity: 67,332

Iowa

6577
AMES CITY AUDITORIUM
Ames Parks & Recreation
515 Clark Avenue
Ames, IA 50010
Mailing Address: 515 Clark Avenue
Phone: 515-239-5365
Fax: 515-239-5325
e-mail: MKing@city.ames.ia.us
Web Site: www.amesparkrec.org/Auditorium.htm
Management:
   Auditorium/Bandshell Manager: Mike King
Mission: To enrich lives by providing exceptional parks, facilities and programs for current and future generations.
Utilizes: Instructors; Local Talent; Resident Professionals; Student Interns; Special Technical Talent
Founded: 1990
Opened: 1992
Specialized Field: Theater Music
Status: Non-Profit, Non-Professional
Paid Staff: 17
Budget: $85,000
Income Sources: Rental; City Subsidy; Ticket Sales
Affiliations: IAAM
Facility Category: Proscenium Theater
Type of Stage: Concert Stage
Stage Dimensions: 37' x 24'
Seating Capacity: 881
Year Built: 1938
Year Remodeled: 1992
Rental Contact: Mike King

6578
BENTON AUDITORIUM
Iowa State University
Iowa State Center
Scheman Building, Suite 4
Ames, IA 50011-1113
Phone: 515-294-8478
Fax: 515-294-3349
Toll-free: 877-843-2368
Web Site: http://www.theatre.iastate.edu
Officers:
   President: Gregory L. Geoffroy
Management:
   Executive Director Iowa State Ctr: Mark North
   Director Marketing: Angela Ossian
   Technical Director: Steve Harder
   Audio Technical Director: Jake Ewalt
Mission: To provide a comprehensive undergraduate education in Theatre and the Performing Arts. This program prepares the student for graduate school, professional theatre training programs, and the teaching of Theatre at the secondary education level.
Specialized Field: Social Events
Seating Capacity: 450
Year Built: 1969

6579
FISHER THEATRE
Iowa State University
Iowa State Center
Scheman Building, Suite 4
Ames, IA 50011-1113
Phone: 515-294-8478
Fax: 515-294-3349
Toll-free: 877-843-2368
Web Site: http://www.theatre.iastate.edu
Officers:
  President: Gregory L. Geoffroy
Management:
  Executive Director Iowa State Ctr: Mark North
  Director Marketing: Angela Ossian
  Technical Director: Emily Brainerd
  Production Manager: Jim Trenberth
Mission: To provide a comprehensive undergraduate education in Theatre and the Performing Arts. This program prepares the student for graduate school, professional theatre training programs, and the teaching of Theatre at the secondary education level.
Specialized Field: Dance, Drama, ISU Theatre Productions
Type of Stage: Proscenium
Orchestra Pit: y
Seating Capacity: 451

6580
HILTON COLISEUM
Iowa State University
Iowa State Center
Scheman Building, Suite 4
Ames, IA 50011-1113
Phone: 515-294-8478
Fax: 515-294-3349
Toll-free: 877-843-2368
Web Site: http://www.theatre.iastate.edu
Officers:
  President: Gregory L. Geoffroy
Management:
  Executive Director Iowa State Ctr: Mark North
  Director Marketing: Angela Ossian
  Technical Director: Mike Broich
  Assistant Technical Director: Mike Cronin
Mission: To provide a comprehensive undergraduate education in Theatre and the Performing Arts. This program prepares the student for graduate school, professional theatre training programs, and the teaching of Theatre at the secondary education level.
Specialized Field: Concerts
Type of Stage: Arena Circle, Portable
Seating Capacity: 14,500

6581
IOWA STATE CENTER
Iowa State University
Scheman Building, Suite 4
Ames, IA 50011
Phone: 515-294-3347
Fax: 515-294-3349
Toll-free: 877-843-2368
Web Site: www.center.iastate.edu
Management:
  Executive Director: Mark North
  Director Business/Finance: Patrick Kennedy
  Director Marketing: Curt Miller
  Director Operations: Randy Baumeister
  Director Programing: Mark E Ewalt
  Technical Director: James B Ewalt Ewalt

Mission: To develop and support the programming facilities and services necessary to establish the Iowa State Center as the premier university public assembly complex in the United States.
Type of Stage: Concert Stage; Flexible
Seating Capacity: 3,650
Year Built: 1971

6582
STEPHENS AUDITORIUM
Iowa State University
Iowa State Center
Scheman Building, Suite 4
Ames, IA 50011-1113
Phone: 515-294-8478
Fax: 515-294-3349
Toll-free: 877-843-2368
Web Site: http://www.theatre.iastate.edu
Officers:
  President: Gregory L. Geoffroy
Management:
  Executive Director Iowa State Ctr: Mark North
  Director Marketing: Angela Ossian
  Technical Director: Steve Harder
  Audio Technical Director: Jake Ewalt
Mission: To provide a comprehensive undergraduate education in Theatre and the Performing Arts. This program prepares the student for graduate school, professional theatre training programs, and the teaching of Theatre at the secondary education level.
Specialized Field: Broadway Musicals, Concerts, Dance, Music, Orchestras, Theatre
Type of Stage: Proscenium
Stage Dimensions: 70' x 30'
Orchestra Pit: y
Seating Capacity: 2,747
Year Built: 1969

6583
STEPHENS AUDITORIUM
Iowa State University
Scheman Building, Suite 4
Ames, IA 50011
Phone: 515-294-8123
Fax: 515-294-8997
Toll-free: 877-843-2368
Web Site: www.center.iastate.edu
Seating Capacity: 2,750

6584
BURLINGTON MEMORIAL AUDITORIUM
200 Front Street
Burlington, IA 52601
Fax: 319-753-8166
e-mail: morlanb@burlingtonauditorium.com
Web Site: www.burlingtonauditorium.com
Management:
  Stage Manager/Marketing Director: Mike Courtney
  Building Manager: Milt Yeiter
  Booking/Marketing Assistant: Betty Moritan
Seating Capacity: 2,311

6585
BERTHA MARTIN THEATRE
University of Northern Iowa
Department of Theatre
1227 West 27th Street
Cedar Falls, IA 50614
Phone: 319-273-6381
Web Site: http://www.uni.edu/theatre/
Officers:
  President: Benjamin J. Allen
Management:

Theatre Department Head: Eric Lange
Technical Director: Mark A. Parrott
Director Mktg/Production Manager: Jascenna Haislet
Mission: The mission of the Department of Theatre is to provide university students with an experiential, liberal arts education in theatre through coursework and productions which are diverse, creative and participatory.
Founded: 1876
Specialized Field: Theatre
Type of Stage: Modular Black Box
Seating Capacity: 126

6586
GALLAGHER BLUEDORN PERFORMING ARTS CENTER
University of Northern Iowa
Cedar Falls, IA 50614
Phone: 319-273-3660
Fax: 319-273-7470
Toll-free: 877-549-7469
e-mail: gbpac@uni.edu
Web Site: www.uni.edu/gbpac
Officers:
  Finance Director: Jocelyn Moeller
Management:
  Executive Director: Steve Carignan
  Event Management Director: Chris Kremer
  Technical Director: Sandy Nordahl
  Assistant Technical Director: Chris Tuzicka
  Education Director: Amy Hunzelman
  Assistant House Manager: Vee Shaffer
  Audio Engineer: Travis Duncan
  Programming Assistant: Molly Hackenmiller
  Marketing Director: Janelle Darst
Founded: 2000
Specialized Field: Present Arts
Paid Staff: 10
Volunteer Staff: 350
Type of Stage: Tongue-in-groove oak
Stage Dimensions: 55'W X 40'H
Seating Capacity: 1,680
Year Built: 2000
Rental Contact: Chris Kremer

6587
STRAYER-WOOD THEATRE
University of Northern Iowa
Department of Theatre
1227 West 27th Street
Cedar Falls, IA 50614
Phone: 319-273-6381
Web Site: http://www.uni.edu/theatre/
Officers:
  President: Benjamin J. Allen
Management:
  Theatre Department Head: Eric Lange
  Technical Director: Mark A. Parrott
  Director Mktg/Production Manager: Jascenna Haislet
Mission: The mission of the Department of Theatre is to provide university students with an experiential, liberal arts education in theatre through coursework and productions which are diverse, creative and participatory.
Founded: 1876
Specialized Field: Theatre
Type of Stage: Proscenium, Thrust
Seating Capacity: 525

6588
STRAYER-WOOD THEATRE

University of Northern Iowa
Department of Theatre, 125 SWT
Cedar Falls, IA 50614-0371
Phone: 319-273-6386
Fax: 319-273-6390
e-mail: eric.lange@uni.edu
Web Site: www.uni.edu
Management:
    Department Head: Eric Lange
Mission: To create theatre which excites, and which illuminates the human condition in ways that are relevant to students, audiences, community members, teachers and guest artists. Offers coursework and productions that are diverse, creative and particpatory, serving students who want to prepare for a life in the theatre and also students who want to prepare a place for theatre in their lives. We create theatre and, in this process, educate.
Utilizes: Actors; Collaborations; Designers; Educators; Five Seasonal Concerts; Guest Accompanists; Guest Artists; Guest Conductors; Guest Ensembles; Guest Lecturers; Performance Artists; Resident Companies; Resident Professionals
Founded: 1976
Specialized Field: Theatre
Paid Staff: 3
Paid Artists: 11
Facility Category: Theater house
Type of Stage: Proscenium
Stage Dimensions: 22 x 84 x 39
Seating Capacity: 500
Year Built: 1978
Rental Contact: Eric Lange

6589
UNI-DOME

University of Northern Iowa
Business Office NE
Cedar Falls, IA 50613
Phone: 319-273-6307
Fax: 319-273-2913
e-mail: gerald.peterson@uni.edu
Web Site: www.uni.edu
Management:
    Facility Coodinator: Dave Kohrs
    Special Events Coordinator: Shandon Hoffmeier
    Assistant Operations Coordinator: Ryan McKernan
Founded: 1976
Seating Capacity: 25,000
Rental Contact: Ryan McKernan

6590
DOW THEATRE

Coe College
Dows Fine Arts Center
1220 1st Avenue NE
Cedar Rapids, IA 52402
Phone: 319-399-8500
e-mail: coeboxoffice@coe.edu
Web Site: www.coe.edu/academics/TheatreArts
Officers:
    President: James R. Phifer
Management:
    Professor of Theatre: Susan Wolverton
    Associate Professor of Theatre: Steven Marc Weiss
    Assistant Professor of Theatre: Dennis Barnett

Mission: Coe offers a Theatre Arts degree with emphasis in Acting, Directing or with Technical & Design Production emphasis. Additionally, students may opt to focus on the Playwriting or Dramaturgy areas of study.
Founded: 1851
Opened: 1974
Specialized Field: Plays, Musicals
Status: Private
Paid Staff: 80
Seating Capacity: 300
Year Built: 1974
Year Remodeled: 1994

6591
US SAILORS CENTER

370 1st Avenue NE
Cedar Rapids, IA 52401
Phone: 319-398-5211
Fax: 319-362-2102
e-mail: s.cummins@ussailorscenter.com
Web Site: www.ussailorscenter.com
Management:
    President: Steve Peters
    Executive Director: Sharon Cummins
    Director Marketing: Tammky Koolbeck
Founded: 1979
Status: For-Profit, Professional
Paid Staff: 200
Paid Artists: 150
Type of Stage: Wood
Seating Capacity: 1,901
Year Built: 1979

6592
MILLS EXPERIMENTAL THEATRE

Coe College
Dows Fine Arts Center
1220 1st Avenue NE
Cedar Rapids, IA 52402
Phone: 319-399-8500
e-mail: coeboxoffice@coe.edu
Web Site: http://www.coe.edu/academics/TheatreArts
Officers:
    President: James R. Phifer
Management:
    Professor of Theatre: Susan Wolverton
    Associate Professor of Theatre: Steven Marc Weiss
    Assistant Professor of Theatre: Dennis Barnett
Mission: Coe offers a Theatre Arts degree with emphasis in Acting, Directing or with Technical & Design Production emphasis. Additionally, students may opt to focus on the Playwriting or Dramaturgy areas of study.
Founded: 1851
Opened: 1974
Specialized Field: Dance
Status: Private
Paid Staff: 80
Seating Capacity: 50

6593
PARAMOUNT THEATRE

123 3rd Avenue SE
Cedar Rapids, IA 52401
Mailing Address: 370 1st Avenue NE Cedar Rapids IA, 52401
Phone: 319-398-5211
Fax: 319-362-2102
Web Site: www.uscellularcenter.com
Management:
    Executive Director: Sharon Cummins
    Assistant Executive Director: Thomas Fesenmey

General Manager: Tim Westemeier
Affiliations: Home of Cedar Rapids Symphony Orchestra, Cedar Rapids Area Theatre Organ Society, Community Concerts, Broadway Series, School Programming Series

6594
SINCLAIR AUDITORIUM

Coe College
1220 1st Avenue NE
Cedar Rapids, IA 52402
Phone: 319-399-8500
e-mail: coeboxoffice@coe.edu
Web Site: http://www.coe.edu/academics/TheatreArts
Officers:
    President: James R. Phifer
Management:
    Professor of Theatre: Susan Wolverton
    Associate Professor of Theatre: Steven Marc Weiss
    Assistant Professor of Theatre: Dennis Barnett
Mission: Coe offers a Theatre Arts degree with emphasis in Acting, Directing or with Technical & Design Production emphasis. Additionally, students may opt to focus on the Playwriting or Dramaturgy areas of study.
Founded: 1851
Status: Private
Paid Staff: 80
Seating Capacity: 1,100

6595
US CELLULAR CENTER

370 1st Avenue NE
Cedar Rapids, IA 52401
Phone: 319-398-5211
Fax: 319-362-2102
Web Site: www.uscellularcenter.com
Management:
    President: Steve Peter
    Executive Director: Sharon Cummins
    Manager: Christy Frost
    Director Programming: Tammy Nowerkoolbeck
Founded: 1979
Status: Non-Profit
Paid Staff: 100
Facility Category: Arena
Type of Stage: Stageright
Seating Capacity: 914
Year Built: 1978
Rental Contact: R Nowers

6596
RIVERVIEW STADIUM

PO Box 1295
Clinton, IA 52733
Phone: 563-242-0727
Fax: 563-242-1433
e-mail: lumberkings@lumberkings.com
Web Site: www.lumberkings.com
Management:
    President: Doug Smith
    Managing Director: Ted Tornow
Founded: 1937
Status: For-Profit, Professional
Paid Staff: 50
Seating Capacity: 3,600

6597
ALLAERT AUDITORIUM

St. Ambrose University
518 West Locust Street
Davenport, IA 52803

Phone: 563-333-6000
e-mail: webmaster@sau.edu
Web Site: www.sau.edu
Officers:
President: Edward Rogalski PhD
Assistant VP Communications/Mktging: Linda Hirsch
Mission: We are committed to the richness of the liberal arts tradition through quality instruction that fosters development of a broad awareness of humanity in all its dimensions. Ambrosians use their knowledge, talents, and career skills in service to others.
Founded: 1882
Specialized Field: Musicals, Performing Arts Series, Theatre
Status: Private
Paid Staff: 292
Budget: $70,000,000
Seating Capacity: 1,200
Year Remodeled: 1971

6598
GALVIN FINE ARTS CENTER
Saint Ambrose College
518 West Locust Street
Davenport, IA 52803
Phone: 563-333-6427
Web Site: www.web.sau.edu/theatre
Officers:　　　'
Chairperson: Dr. Corinne Johnson
Management:
Director: Lance Sadlek
Founded: 1971

6599
LYCEUM HALL
Palmer College of Chiropractic
1000 Brady Street
Davenport, IA 52803
Phone: 563-884-5656
Fax: 563-884-5414
Toll-free: 800-722-3648
e-mail: pcadmit@palmer.edu
Web Site: www.palmer.edu
Officers:
President: Donald Kern DC PhC
Dean: Daniel Weinert MS DC
Seating Capacity: 4,000

6600
QUAD CITY RIVER BANDITS BASEBALL STADIUM
PO Box 3496
209 S Gaines Street
Davenport, IA 52808
Phone: 563-324-3000
Fax: 319-324-3109
e-mail: bandit@riverbandits.com
Web Site: www.riverbandits.com
Management:
General Manager: Dave Ziedells
Sales Director: Pete Cunico
Marketing Director: Matt Beatty
Seating Capacity: 6,200

6601
RIVER CENTER/ADLER THEATRE
136 E 3rd Street
Davenport, IA 52801
Phone: 319-326-8500
Fax: 319-326-8505
Management:
Executive Director: Mike Hartman
Specialized Field: Theater

6602
STUDIO THEATRE
St. Ambrose University
Galvin Fine Arts Center
518 West Locust Street
Davenport, IA 52803
Phone: 563-333-6255
Web Site: http://web.sau.edu/theatre/
Officers:
President: Edward Rogalski PhD
Management:
Associate Professor/Chair: Kristofer Eitrheim
Professor of Theatre: Corinne Johnson
Mission: We are committed to the richness of the liberal arts tradition through quality instruction that fosters development of a broad awareness of humanity in all its dimensions. Ambrosians use their knowledge, talents, and career skills in service to others.
Founded: 1882
Specialized Field: Theatre
Status: Private
Paid Staff: 292
Budget: $70,000,000
Type of Stage: Black Box
Seating Capacity: 50

6603
JEWEL THEATRE
Luther College
Center for the Arts
700 College Drive
Decorah, IA
Phone: 563-387-2000
Fax: 563-387-2158
Toll-free: 800-258-8437
e-mail: thdance@luther.edu
Web Site: http://theatre.luther.edu/contactus
Officers:
President: Richard L. Torgerson
Management:
Dept Head Theatre/Dance: Jeff Dintaman
Department Coordinator: Alice Palmer
Professor of Theatre: Bob Larsonan
Associate Professor of Theatre: Jane Hawley
Associate Professor of Theatre: Jeff Dintaman
Assistant Professor of Theatre: Lisa Lantz
Assistant Technical Director: Tom Berger
Mission: Drawing from the two distinctive art forms of theatre and dance, the Luther College Theatre/Dance Department focuses on empowering and enlivening the creative imagination in self and community. In so doing, the department is a partner within a liberal arts environment that seeks to develop whole persons who emerge as informed artists and capable, passionate, accountable citizens.
Founded: 1861
Specialized Field: Theatre
Paid Staff: 191
Type of Stage: Flexible
Seating Capacity: 225

6604
LUTHER COLLEGE
Luther College Center For The Arts
700 College Drive
Decorah, IA
Phone: 563-387-2000
Fax: 563-387-2158
Toll-free: 800-258-8437
e-mail: thdance@luther.edu
Web Site: http://theatre.luther.edu/contactus
Officers:
President: Richard L. Torgerson
Management:
Dept Head Theatre/Dance: Jeff Dintaman
Department Coordinator: Alice Palmer
Professor of Theatre: Bob Larsonan
Associate Professor of Theatre: Jane Hawley
Associate Professor of Theatre: Jeff Dintaman
Assistant Professor of Theatre: Lisa Lantz
Assistant Technical Director: Tom Berger
Mission: Drawing from the two distinctive art forms of theatre and dance, the Luther College Theatre/Dance Department focuses on empowering and enlivening the creative imagination in self and community. In so doing, the department is a partner within a liberal arts environment that seeks to develop whole persons who emerge as informed artists and capable, passionate, accountable citizens.
Founded: 1861
Specialized Field: Theatre
Paid Staff: 191
Performs At: Flexible Theatre
Seating Capacity: 1,600
Year Built: 1978

6605
RECITAL HALL
Luther College
Center for Faith and Life
700 College Drive
Decorah, IA
Phone: 563-387-2000
Fax: 563-387-2158
Toll-free: 800-258-8437
e-mail: thdance@luther.edu
Web Site: http://theatre.luther.edu/contactus
Officers:
President: Richard L. Torgerson
Management:
Dept Head Theatre/Dance: Jeff Dintaman
Department Coordinator: Alice Palmer
Professor of Theatre: Bob Larsonan
Associate Professor of Theatre: Jane Hawley
Associate Professor of Theatre: Jeff Dintaman
Assistant Professor of Theatre: Lisa Lantz
Assistant Technical Director: Tom Berger
Mission: Drawing from the two distinctive art forms of theatre and dance, the Luther College Theatre/Dance Department focuses on empowering and enlivening the creative imagination in self and community. In so doing, the department is a partner within a liberal arts environment that seeks to develop whole persons who emerge as informed artists and capable, passionate, accountable citizens.
Founded: 1861
Specialized Field: Theatre
Paid Staff: 191
Seating Capacity: 200
Year Built: 1978

6606
WESTON H. NOBLE RECITAL HALL
Luther College
Jenson-Noble Hall of Music
700 College Drive
Decorah, IA
Phone: 563-387-2000
Fax: 563-387-2158
Toll-free: 800-258-8437
e-mail: thdance@luther.edu
Web Site: http://theatre.luther.edu/contactus
Officers:
President: Richard L. Torgerson
Management:
Dept Head Theatre/Dance: Jeff Dintaman
Department Coordinator: Alice Palmer

Professor of Theatre: Bob Larsonan
Associate Professor of Theatre: Jane Hawley
Associate Professor of Theatre: Jeff Dintaman
Assistant Professor of Theatre: Lisa Lantz
Assistant Technical Director: Tom Berger
Mission: Drawing from the two distinctive art forms of theatre and dance, the Luther College Theatre/Dance Department focuses on empowering and enlivening the creative imagination in self and community. In so doing, the department is a partner within a liberal arts environment that seeks to develop whole persons who emerge as informed artists and capable, passionate, accountable citizens.
Founded: 1861
Specialized Field: Music
Paid Staff: 191
Type of Stage: Black Box
Seating Capacity: 300

6607
CIVIC CENTER OF GREATER DES MOINES
221 Walnut Street
Des Moines, IA 50309
Phone: 515-246-2300
Fax: 515-246-2305
e-mail: info@civiccenter.org
Web Site: www.civiccenter.org
Officers:
    President: Jeff Chelesvig
Management:
    General Manager: Bill McElrath
Mission: Engage the Midwest in world-class entertainment, education and cultural activities.
Founded: 1979
Opened: 1979
Status: Non-Profit, Professional
Paid Staff: 30
Volunteer Staff: 40
Budget: $14 Million
Income Sources: Ticket Sales; Rentals; Concessions; Sponsorship; Public & Private Support
Performs At: Theater
Annual Attendance: 300,000
Facility Category: Theater
Type of Stage: Proscenium
Seating Capacity: 2,744
Year Built: 1979
Year Remodeled: 2007
Cost: $12.5 Million
Rental Contact: General Manager Bill McElrath

6608
DES MOINES WOMEN'S CLUB
Hoyt Sherman Place
1501 Woodland
Des Moines, IA 50309
Phone: 515-244-0507
Fax: 515-237-3582
Web Site: www.hoytsherman.org
Management:
    Executive Director: Leisha Barcus
Founded: 1875
Specialized Field: Theatre
Status: Non-Profit, Professional
Paid Staff: 10
Annual Attendance: 200,000
Type of Stage: Proscenium
Seating Capacity: 1,400

6609
DRAKE STADIUM
Drake University
2507 University Avenue
Des Moines, IA 50311
Phone: 515-271-2889
Fax: 515-271-3015
Web Site: www.drakebulldogs.org
Management:
    Athletic Director: Dave Blank
Founded: 1925
Seating Capacity: 18,000

6610
HARMON FINE ARTS CENTER
Drake University
2507 University Avenue
Des Moines, IA 50311-4505
Phone: 515-271-2018
Fax: 515-271-3977
e-mail: Marilyn.dean@drake.edu
Web Site: www.drake.edu
Officers:
    President: Dr. David Maxwell
    Director Marketing/Communications: Brooke Benschoter
    Director Public Relations: Lisa Lacher
    Facilities Manager: Marilyn Dean
Management:
    Department Chair: John Pomeroy
    Assistant Professor of Theatre: Deena Conley
    Associate Professor of Theatre: John W. Holman
    Assistant Professor of Theatre: Tony Humrichouser
Mission: The mission of the College of Arts & Sciences is to provide an exceptional learning environment for students to develop the talents and skills necessary for personal and professional success.
Founded: 1881
Specialized Field: Musicals, Theatre
Paid Staff: 246
Seating Capacity: 460

6611
JORDAN STAGE
Drake University
Sheslow Auditorium
2507 University Avenue
Des Moines, IA 50311-4505
Phone: 515-271-2018
Fax: 515-271-3977
e-mail: Marilyn.dean@drake.edu
Web Site: www.drake.edu
Officers:
    President: Dr. David Maxwell
    Director Marketing/Communications: Brooke Benschoter
    Director Public Relations: Lisa Lacher
    Facilities Manager: Marilyn Dean
Management:
    Department Chair: John Pomeroy
    Assistant Professor of Theatre: Deena Conley
    Associate Professor of Theatre: John W. Holman
    Assistant Professor of Theatre: Tony Humrichouser
Mission: The mission of the College of Arts & Sciences is to provide an exceptional learning environment for students to develop the talents and skills necessary for personal and professional success.
Founded: 1881
Specialized Field: Concerts, Recitals
Paid Staff: 246
Seating Capacity: 773

6612
SHESLOW AUDITORIUM IN OLD MAIN
Drake University
2507 University Avenue
Des Moines, IA 50311
Phone: 515-271-3939
Fax: 515-271-3977
e-mail: lisa.lacher@drake.edu
Web Site: www.drake.edu
Management:
    President: David Maxwell
Mission: Drake's mission is to provide an exceptional learning environment that prepares students for meaningful personal lives, professional accomplishments, and responsible global citizenship. The Drake experience is distinguished by collaborative learning among students, faculty, and staff and by the integration of the liberal arts and sciences with professional preparation.
Founded: 1881
Status: Non-Profit, Professional
Paid Staff: 25
Seating Capacity: 100-200

6613
VETERANS MEMORIAL AUDITORIUM
Regional Facilities, Polk County
833 5th Avenue
Des Moines, IA 50309
Phone: 515-323-5400
Fax: 515-323-5401
Web Site: www.co.polk.ia.us
Management:
    General Manager: Andy Long
    Director: F Michael Grimaldi
    Managing Director: Joy Giudicessi
Founded: 1954
Status: Non-Profit, Professional
Paid Staff: 40
Facility Category: Arena
Type of Stage: Concert
Seating Capacity: 7,200
Year Built: 1954
Year Remodeled: 1997

6614
FIVE FLAGS CENTER ARENA
405 Main Street
Dubuque, IA 52001
Phone: 563-589-4254
Fax: 563-589-4351
Toll-free: 888-412-9758
e-mail: info@fiveflagscenter.com
Web Site: www.fiveflagscenter.com
Management:
    General Manager: Joyce While
    Marketing Coord/Admin Support: Ali Levasseur
Mission: To provide the best entertainment to Dubuque Area; including all national touring, regional and local talent
Founded: 1971
Status: Non-Profit, Professional
Paid Staff: 80
Affiliations: A SMG Managed Facility
Facility Category: Historical Theater & Sporting Arena
Seating Capacity: 5,200

6615
FIVE FLAGS CENTER - THEATRE
4th and Main Streets
PO Box 628
Dubuque, IA 52001

Phone: 563-589-4258
Fax: 563-589-4351
Web Site: www.cityofdubuque.org

6616
MAHARISHI UNIVERSITY PERFORMING ARTS CENTER
1000 North Fourth Street
Maharishi University of Management, SU 361
Fairfield, IA 52557
Phone: 641-472-1104
Fax: 641-472-7000
e-mail: student_activities@mum.edu
Web Site: www.mum.edu
Management:
    Administrator: David Stried
Founded: 1971
Status: Non-Profit, Non-Professional

6617
HAROLD AND CHARLOTTE SMTIH THEATRE
Waldorf College
Thorson Hall
106 South 6th Street
Forest City, IA 50436
Phone: 641-585-8585
Toll-free: 800-292-1903
Web Site: http://www.waldorf.edu/finearts/theatre
Officers:
    President: Richard A. Hanson, PhD
Management:
    Director: Robert AuFrance
    Technical Director: Damian Ernest
Mission: As a liberal arts college Waldorf offers a core curriculum to help students develop a broad base of knowledge in a variety of disciplines, an interest in intellectual pursuits, the ability to reason and communicate, and a growing awareness of the global community.
Founded: 1903
Opened: U
Specialized Field: Fheatre
Status: KF
Paid Staff: 0925
Seating Capacity: 180

6618
RECITAL HALL
Waldorf College
Odvin Hagen Music Center
106 South 6th Street
Forest City, IA 50436
Phone: 641-585-8585
Toll-free: 800-292-1903
Web Site: http://www.waldorf.edu/finearts/theatre
Officers:
    President: Richard A. Hanson, PhD
Management:
    Director: Robert AuFrance
    Technical Director: Damian Ernest
Mission: As a liberal arts college Waldorf offers a core curriculum to help students develop a broad base of knowledge in a variety of disciplines, an interest in intellectual pursuits, the ability to reason and communicate, and a growing awareness of the global community.
Founded: 1903
Specialized Field: Music
Seating Capacity: 129

6619
OLD CREAMERY THEATRE
39 38th Avenue
Suite 200
Garrison, IA 52203
Phone: 319-622-6194
Toll-free: 800-352-6262
Web Site: www.oldcreamery.com
Officers:
    President-Amana: Bruce Eickhacker
    VP-Cedar Rapids: Richard Welch
    Secretary - Vinton: Ron Baldwin
    Treasurer-Amana: Vic Rathje
Management:
    Producing and Artistic Director: Thomas P Johnson
    Associate Artistic Director: Meg Merckens
    Associate Artistic Director: Sean McCall
    General Manager: Pat Wagner
Founded: 1971
Status: Non-Profit
Seating Capacity: 275

6620
HALLIE B. FLANAGAN STUDIO THEATRE
Grinnell College
Bucksbaum Center for the Arts
Grinnell, IA 50112-1690
Phone: 641-269-4000
Fax: 641-269-4420
Web Site: http://web.grinnell.edu/theatre/facilities
Officers:
    President: Russell K. Osgood
Management:
    Department Chair: Lesley Delmenico
    Technical Director: Erik Sanning
Mission: The study of theatre and movement at Grinnell embraces all aspects of the dramatic art as part of a liberal arts education.
Founded: 1846
Specialized Field: Theatre
Status: Private
Seating Capacity: 126

6621
ROBERTS THEATRE
Grinnell College
Bucksbaum Center for the Arts
Grinnell, IA 50112-1690
Phone: 641-269-4000
Fax: 641-269-4420
Web Site: http://web.grinnell.edu/theatre/facilities
Officers:
    President: Russell K. Osgood
Management:
    Department Chair: Lesley Delmenico
    Technical Director: Erik Sanning
Mission: The study of theatre and movement at Grinnell embraces all aspects of the dramatic art as part of a liberal arts education.
Founded: 1846
Specialized Field: Theatre
Status: Private
Type of Stage: Semi-Thrust
Seating Capacity: 450
Year Remodeled: 2000
Architect: Cesar Pelli and Associates

6622
WALL PERFORMANCE LAB
Grinnell College
Bucksbaum Center for the Arts
Grinnell, IA 50112-1690

Phone: 641-269-4000
Fax: 641-269-4420
Web Site: http://web.grinnell.edu/theatre/facilities
Officers:
    President: Russell K. Osgood
Management:
    Department Chair: Lesley Delmenico
    Technical Director: Erik Sanning
Mission: The study of theatre and movement at Grinnell embraces all aspects of the dramatic art as part of a liberal arts education.
Founded: 1846
Specialized Field: Student Productions
Status: Private
Type of Stage: Black Box
Seating Capacity: 72

6623
BARNUM STUDIO THEATRE
Simpson College
Blank Performing Arts Center
701 North C Street
Indianola, IA 50125
Phone: 515-961-1653
Fax: 515-961-1758
Toll-free: 800-362-2454
Web Site: http://www.simpson.edu/theatre
Officers:
    President: John W. Byrd
    Executive Dir College Relations: John Fuller
Management:
    Department Chair: Thomas Woldt
    Professor of Theatre: Jennifer Ross Nostrala
    Associate Professor: Steven J. McLean
    Technical Director: Nicholas Johnson
    Department Secretary: Kathy Teigland
Mission: Theatre Simpson is a dynamic community that views theatre as an avenue for personal discovery, self-discipline, creative expression and artistic excellence. Departmental courses and projects provide students with dynamic cultural and artistic experiences and help develop their abilities to observe, reflect, think critically and express themselves.
Founded: 1860
Specialized Field: Theatre
Type of Stage: Flexible Black Box
Seating Capacity: 125

6624
POTE THEATRE
Simpson College
Blank Performing Arts Center
701 North C Street
Indianola, IA 50125
Phone: 515-961-1653
Fax: 515-961-1758
Toll-free: 800-362-2454
Web Site: http://www.simpson.edu/theatre
Officers:
    President: John W. Byrd
    Executive Dir College Relations: John Fuller
Management:
    Department Chair: Thomas Woldt
    Professor of Theatre: Jennifer Ross Nostrala
    Associate Professor: Steven J. McLean
    Technical Director: Nicholas Johnson
    Department Secretary: Kathy Teigland
Mission: Theatre Simpson is a dynamic community that views theatre as an avenue for personal discovery, self-discipline, creative expression and artistic excellence. Departmental courses and projects provide students with dynamic cultural and artistic experiences and help develop their abilities to observe, reflect, think critically and express themselves.

Founded: 1860
Specialized Field: Opera, Theatre Arts
Type of Stage: Proscenium/Thrust
Seating Capacity: 500

6625
SVEN AND MILDRED LEKBERG RECITAL HALL

Simpson College
Amy Robertson Music Center
701 North C Street
Indianola, IA 50125
Phone: 515-961-1653
Fax: 515-961-1758
Toll-free: 800-362-2454
Web Site: http://www.simpson.edu/theatre
Officers:
President: John W. Byrd
Executive Dir College Relations: John Fuller
Management:
Department Chair: Thomas Woldt
Professor of Theatre: Jennifer Ross Nostrala
Associate Professor: Steven J. McLean
Technical Director: Nicholas Johnson
Department Secretary: Kathy Teigland
Mission: Theatre Simpson is a dynamic community that views theatre as an avenue for personal discovery, self-discipline, creative expression and artistic excellence. Departmental courses and projects provide students with dynamic cultural and artistic experiences and help develop their abilities to observe, reflect, think critically and express themselves.
Founded: 1860
Opened: 1983
Specialized Field: Jazz Ensembles, Music Convocations, Student Recitals
Seating Capacity: 200

6626
DAVID THAYER THEATRE

University of Iowa
Department of Theatre Arts
100 Theatre Building
Iowa City, IA 52242-1795
Phone: 319-335-2700
Fax: 319-335-3568
Toll-free: 800-553-4692
e-mail: theatre@uiowa.edu
Web Site: http://www.uiowa.edu/~theatre/about
Officers:
Interim President: Gary C. Fethke
Management:
Department Chair: Alan Macvey
Director Theatre: Eric Forsythe
Technical Director: Ojin Kwon
Stage Manager: David McGraw
Mission: The purpose of the Division of Performing Arts is to support the mission, objective, and visibility of the Department of Dance, the School of Music, and the Department of Theatre Arts through coordinated artistic activities, academic activities, public communications and outreach, student recruitment, and fundraising.
Opened: 1985
Specialized Field: Artistry, Dance, Drama, Music
Type of Stage: Semiflexible
Seating Capacity: 150-225
Year Built: 1935
Year Remodeled: 1985
Cost: $6.7 Million
Rental Contact: Stage Manager Daivd McGraw

6627
HANCHER AUDITORIUM

University of Iowa
PO Box 4550
Iowa City, IA 52244
Phone: 319-335-3305
Toll-free: 800-648-6973
Web Site: www.uifoundation.org/hancher
Management:
Executive Director: Charles Swanson
Artistic Director: Judith Hurtig
Associate Development Director: Pat Hanick
Founded: 1972
Status: Nonprofit, Professional
Annual Attendance: 20,000+

6628
KINNICK STADIUM

University of Iowa
157 Carver-Hawkeye Arena
Iowa City, IA 52242
Phone: 319-335-9411
Fax: 319-335-9333
e-mail: gohawks@hawkeyesports.com
Web Site: www.hawkeyesports.com
Management:
President: David Skorton
Facility Manager: Damian Simcox
Founded: 1847
Specialized Field: Home of University of Iowa Athletics
Status: Non-Profit, Non-Professional
Seating Capacity: 70,111

6629
MABIE THEATRE

University of Iowa
Department of Theatre Arts
100 Theatre Building
Iowa City, IA 52242-1795
Phone: 319-335-2700
Fax: 319-335-3568
Toll-free: 800-553-4692
e-mail: theatre@uiowa.edu
Web Site: http://www.uiowa.edu/~theatre/about
Officers:
Interim President: Gary C. Fethke
Management:
Department Chair: Alan Macvey
Director Theatre: Eric Forsythe
Technical Director: Ojin Kwon
Stage Manager: David McGraw
Mission: The purpose of the Division of Performing Arts is to support the mission, objective, and visibility of the Department of Dance, the School of Music, and the Department of Theatre Arts through coordinated artistic activities, academic activities, public communications and outreach, student recruitment, and fundraising.
Opened: 1936
Specialized Field: Artistry, Dance, Drama, Music
Type of Stage: Proscenium
Seating Capacity: 477
Year Built: 1935
Year Remodeled: 1985
Cost: $6.7 Million
Rental Contact: Stage Manager Daivd McGraw

6630
STUDIO THEATRE

University of Iowa
Department of Theatre Arts
100 Theatre Building
Iowa City, IA 52242-1795

Phone: 319-335-2700
Fax: 319-335-3568
Toll-free: 800-553-4692
e-mail: theatre@uiowa.edu
Web Site: http://www.uiowa.edu/~theatre/about
Officers:
Interim President: Gary C. Fethke
Management:
Department Chair: Alan Macvey
Director Theatre: Eric Forsythe
Technical Director: Ojin Kwon
Stage Manager: David McGraw
Mission: The purpose of the Division of Performing Arts is to support the mission, objective, and visibility of the Department of Dance, the School of Music, and the Department of Theatre Arts through coordinated artistic activities, academic activities, public communications and outreach, student recruitment, and fundraising.
Specialized Field: Theatre
Type of Stage: Flexible
Seating Capacity: 50
Year Built: 1935
Year Remodeled: 1985
Cost: $6.7 Million
Rental Contact: Stage Manager Daivd McGraw

6631
THEATRE B

University of Iowa
Department of Theatre Arts
100 Theatre Building
Iowa City, IA 52242-1795
Phone: 319-335-2700
Fax: 319-335-3568
Toll-free: 800-553-4692
e-mail: theatre@uiowa.edu
Web Site: http://www.uiowa.edu/~theatre/about
Officers:
Interim President: Gary C. Fethke
Management:
Department Chair: Alan Macvey
Director Theatre: Eric Forsythe
Technical Director: Ojin Kwon
Stage Manager: David McGraw
Mission: The purpose of the Division of Performing Arts is to support the mission, objective, and visibility of the Department of Dance, the School of Music, and the Department of Theatre Arts through coordinated artistic activities, academic activities, public communications and outreach, student recruitment, and fundraising.
Opened: 1985
Specialized Field: Workshop Productions
Type of Stage: Black Box
Seating Capacity: 144
Year Built: 1935
Year Remodeled: 1985
Cost: $6.7 Million
Rental Contact: Stage Manager Daivd McGraw

6632
SHAW CENTER AUDITORIUM

Graceland University
Shaw Center for the Performing Arts
1 University Place
Lamoni, IA 50140
Phone: 641-784-5000
Fax: 641-784-5487
e-mail: finearts@graceland.edu
Web Site: http://www.graceland.edu/finearts/theatre
Officers:
President: Steven L. Anders, PhD
Mission: The Department of Theatre in the Division of Fine Arts at Graceland University offers a Bachelor of Arts in Theatre as well as a Theatre minor. Theatre

students develop creative skills, practice critical thinking and problem solving, and develop personal discipline through coursework and production.
Founded: 1895
Specialized Field: Theatre
Seating Capacity: 800

6633
STUDIO THEATRE
Graceland University
Shaw Center for the Performing Arts
1 University Place
Lamoni, IA 50140
Phone: 641-784-5000
Fax: 641-784-5487
e-mail: finearts@graceland.edu
Web Site: http://www.graceland.edu/finearts/theatre
Officers:
President: Steven L. Anders, PhD
Management:
Coordinator: Rebecca M. Foster
Director: Robert A. Hamel
Mission: The Department of Theatre in the Division of Fine Arts at Graceland University offers a Bachelor of Arts in Theatre as well as a Theatre minor. Theatre students develop creative skills, practice critical thinking and problem solving, and develop personal discipline through coursework and production.
Founded: 1895
Specialized Field: Theatre
Seating Capacity: 150

6634
CHARLES H MACNIDER ART MUSEUM
303 2nd Street SE
Mason City, IA 50401
Phone: 641-421-3666
Fax: 641-422-9612
Web Site: www.macniderart.org
Management:
Director: Sheila Perry
Education Coordinator: Linda Willeke
Financial Secretary: Audrey Gabel
Founded: 1966
Status: Non-Profit, Non-Professional
Paid Staff: 9

6635
NORTH IOWA COMMUNITY AUDITORIUM
500 College Drive
Mason City, IA 50401-7299
Phone: 641-423-1264
Fax: 641-423-1711
Toll-free: 888-466-4222
e-mail: request@niacc.edu
Web Site: www.niacc.edu
Management:
President: Michael Morrison
Artistic Director: Elizabeth Gales
Founded: 1918
Status: Non-Profit, Professional

6636
KIMMEL THEATRE
Cornell College
Armstrong Hall of Fine Arts
600 First Street West
Mount Vernon, IA 52314
Phone: 319-895-4232
e-mail: theatre@cornellcollege.edu
Web Site: http://cornellcollege.edu/theatre/
Officers:
President: Leslie H. Garner, Jr.
Director Media Relations: Dawn Goodlove

Management:
Department Chair: Mark Hunter
Technical Director: Ben Alexander
Production Manager: Scott Olinger
Mission: Cornell College endorses liberal education as an end in itself and as a means of empowering students for leadership through productive careers and humane service in the global community.
Founded: 1853
Specialized Field: Jazz, Theatre
Paid Staff: 76
Seating Capacity: 266
Cost: $8.9 Million
Year Restored: 2003

6637
PLUM FLEMING STUDIO THEATRE
Cornell College
Armstrong Hall of Fine Arts
600 First Street West
Mount Vernon, IA 52314
Phone: 319-895-4232
e-mail: theatre@cornellcollege.edu
Web Site: http://cornellcollege.edu/theatre/
Officers:
President: Leslie H. Garner, Jr.
Director Media Relations: Dawn Goodlove
Management:
Department Chair: Mark Hunter
Technical Director: Ben Alexander
Production Manager: Scott Olinger
Mission: Cornell College endorses liberal education as an end in itself and as a means of empowering students for leadership through productive careers and humane service in the global community.
Founded: 1853
Specialized Field: Theatre
Paid Staff: 76
Type of Stage: Black Box
Cost: $8.9 Million
Year Restored: 2003

6638
DEWITT THEATRE ARTS CENTER
Northwestern College
101 7th Street Southwest
Orange City, IA 51041
Phone: 712-707-7000
Web Site: www.nwciowa.edu
Officers:
President: Bruce Murphy
Vice President: Eric Elder
Management:
Artistic Director: Tim McGarvey
Mission: To provide a distinctively Christian liberal arts education of recognized quality in a primarily undergraduate, co-educational, multicultural, residential environment.
Founded: 1882
Status: Nonprofit, Professional
Paid Staff: 250
Paid Artists: 24

6639
MAIN STAGE THEATRE
Central College
Kruidenier Center for Theatre
812 University
Pella, IA
Phone: 641-628-9000
Toll-free: 877-462-3687
Web Site: http://departments.central.edu/theatre/
Management:
Department Chair: Mary Jo Sodd

Professor of Theatre/Production Mgr: Treva Reimer
Technical Director: Tom E. Thatcher
Theatre Arts Associate: Ann Wilkinson
Mission: Theatre Central offers a broad range of course work across the theatre discipline. We believe that the undergraduate student should learn the whole of theatre within the larger context of the world. That is why we are very proud of the liberal arts emphasis which encourages broader thinking and creativity for the theatre artist.
Founded: 1853
Specialized Field: Theatre
Type of Stage: Black Box
Seating Capacity: 200

6640
STUDIO THEATRE
Central College
Kruidenier Center for Theatre
812 University
Pella, IA
Phone: 641-628-9000
Toll-free: 877-462-3687
Web Site: http://departments.central.edu/theatre/
Management:
Department Chair: Mary Jo Sodd
Professor of Theatre/Production Mgr: Treva Reimer
Technical Director: Tom E. Thatcher
Theatre Arts Associate: Ann Wilkinson
Mission: Theatre Central offers a broad range of course work across the theatre discipline. We believe that the undergraduate student should learn the whole of theatre within the larger context of the world. That is why we are very proud of the liberal arts emphasis which encourages broader thinking and creativity for the theatre artist.
Founded: 1853
Specialized Field: Theatre
Type of Stage: Black Box
Seating Capacity: 75

6641
B.J. HAAN AUDITORIUM
Dordt College
498 4th Avenue NE
Sioux Center, IA 51250-1606
Phone: 712-722-6002
Fax: 712-722-1198
Toll-free: 800-343-6738
e-mail: lmoerman@dordt.edu
Web Site: http://www.dordt.edu/arts/theatre
Officers:
President: Carl E. Zylstra, PhD
Management:
Department Chair: Jeri Schelhaas
Assistant Professor of Theatre: Dr. Teresa Ter Haar
Auditorium Manager/Technical Dir: Jim Van Ry
Theatre Arts Secretary: Karen Vreugdenhil
Mission: Dordt's Theatre Arts Department is small but very active theatre program serves our community with two fully mounted mainstage shows each year, as well as numerous smaller student-directed or classroom-based projects.
Founded: 1937
Specialized Field: Concerts, Organ Recitals
Seating Capacity: 1,500
Year Built: 1979

6642

KLINGER-NEAL THEATRE

Morningside College
3700 Peters Avenue
Sioux Center, IA 51106
Phone: 712-274-5199
e-mail: skewis@morningside.edu
Web Site: http://webs.morningside.edu/theatre
Officers:
President: John C. Reynders
Management:
Department Chair: Bette Skewis-Arnett
Assistant Professor of Theatre: Arthur H. Moss
Mission: The theatre curriculum includes courses emphasizing the inter-dependence of all aspects of production: acting, directing, and technical theatre.
Specialized Field: Ballets, Musicals, Plays, Recitals
Type of Stage: Proscenium, Thrust, Arena
Seating Capacity: 360
Year Built: 1964

6643

NEW WORLD THEATRE

Dordt College
498 4th Avenue NE
Sioux Center, IA 51250-1606
Phone: 712-722-6002
Fax: 712-722-1198
Toll-free: 800-343-6738
e-mail: lmoerman@dordt.edu
Web Site: http://www.dordt.edu/arts/theatre
Officers:
President: Carl E. Zylstra, PhD
Management:
Department Chair: Jeri Schelhaas
Assistant Professor of Theatre: Dr. Teresa Ter Haar
Auditorium Manager/Technical Dir: Jim Van Ry
Theatre Arts Secretary: Karen Vreugdenhil
Mission: Dordt's Theatre Arts Department is small but very active theatre program serves our community with two fully mounted mainstage shows each year, as well as numerous smaller student-directed or classroom-based projects.
Founded: 1937
Specialized Field: Theatre
Type of Stage: Black Box

6644

TE PASKE THEATRE

Dordt College
498 4th Avenue NE
Sioux Center, IA 51250-1606
Phone: 712-722-6002
Fax: 712-722-1198
Toll-free: 800-343-6738
e-mail: lmoerman@dordt.edu
Web Site: http://www.dordt.edu/arts/theatre
Officers:
President: Carl E. Zylstra, PhD
Management:
Department Chair: Jeri Schelhaas
Assistant Professor of Theatre: Dr. Teresa Ter Haar
Auditorium Manager/Technical Dir: Jim Van Ry
Theatre Arts Secretary: Karen Vreugdenhil
Mission: Dordt's Theatre Arts Department is small but very active theatre program serves our community with two fully mounted mainstage shows each year, as well as numerous smaller student-directed or classroom-based projects.
Founded: 1937
Specialized Field: Theatre

Type of Stage: Modified Thrust
Seating Capacity: 414

6645

BRIAR CLIFF THEATRE

Briar Cliff University
Department of Theatre
3303 Rebecca Street
Sioux City, IA 51104
Phone: 712-279-5542
Web Site: http://www.briarcliff.edu/departments/theatre
Officers:
President: Beverly A. Wharton
Management:
Program Director: Richard L. Poole
Mission: The goal of the Theatre Department is to provide students with theatre training to prepare them for a life in professional, community or educational theatre.
Founded: 1930
Specialized Field: Theatre

6646

ROBERTS STADIUM

2600 Division Street
PO Box 3183
Sioux City, IA 47711
Phone: 712-279-6651
Fax: 712-279-6651
Web Site: www.robertstadium.com
Management:
Manager Public Schools: Ray Rowe
Seating Capacity: 7,000

6647

BLACK HAWK CHILDREN'S THEATRE

PO Box 433
Waterloo, IA 50704
Phone: 319-235-0367
Fax: 319-235-7489
Web Site: www.cedarnet.org/wcpbhct
Officers:
President: Bryan Molinaro-Blonigan
VP Fund Developement: Stephen Saladrigas
VP Marketing: Beverly McCusker
Secretary: Linda Neese
Treasurer: Chad Abbas
Management:
Artistic/Managing Director: Charles Stilwill
Production Manager: Katrina Sanddik
Marketing/Development Director: Kristin Teig-Torres
Founded: 1916
Status: Non-Profit, Non-Professional
Paid Staff: 15

6648

WATERLOO RIVERFRONT STADIUM

850 Park Road
Waterloo, IA 50704
Phone: 319-232-5633
Fax: 319-232-6140
Management:
Manager: Eric Snider
Seating Capacity: 4,000

6649

MCCASKEY LYCEUM

Wartburg College
100 Wartburg Boulevard
Waverly, IA 50677
Phone: 319-352-8691
e-mail: webmaster@wartburg.edu
Web Site: www.wartburg.edu/vtour/vr/neumann.html

Officers:
Art Department Chairman: Thomas Payne
Management:
Music Department Chair: Karen Black, PhD
Art Department Chair: Thomas Payne
Seating Capacity: 1,400

6650

NEUMANN AUDITORIUM

Wartburg College
100 Wartburg Boulevard
Waverly, IA 50677
Phone: 319-352-8691
e-mail: webmaster@wartburg.edu
Web Site: www.wartburg.edu/vtour/vr/neumann.html
Officers:
Art Department Chairman: Thomas Payne
Management:
Music Department Chair: Karen Black, PhD
Art Department Chair: Thomas Payne
Seating Capacity: 1,400

6651

CHARLES KOCH ARENA

1845 Fairmount
Wichita, IA 67260
Fax: 316-978-3443
Web Site: www.goshockers.com
Management:
Facilities Manager: Jesse Torres
Assistant Facilities Director: Roland Banks
Media Relations Director: Larry Rankin
Athletics Director: Rege Klitze
Seating Capacity: 10,400

Kansas

6652

MEMORIAL AUDITORIUM

101 S Lincoln
PO Box 907
Chanute, KS 66720
Phone: 316-431-5229
Fax: 316-431-5239
Toll-free: 800-735-5229
e-mail: city@chanute.org
Web Site: www.chanute.org
Management:
Auditorium Manager: Ruth Ports
Founded: 1925
Paid Staff: 2
Seating Capacity: 1,243

6653

FLORAL HALL

PO Box 1629
Coffeyville, KS 67337
Phone: 316-251-9794
Stage Dimensions: 8x15 (meters)

6654

DODGE CITY FESTIVALS

PO Box 818
311 W Spruce
Dodge City, KS 67801
Phone: 620-227-9501
Fax: 620-338-8734
Toll-free: 800-381-3690
e-mail: jknight@dodgedev.org
Web Site: www.dodgedev.org
Founded: 1999

6655
ALBERT TAYLOR HALL
Emporia State University
Plumb Hall
1200 Commercial Street
Emporia, KS 66801
Phone: 620-341-5228
e-mail: idambro@emporia.edu
Web Site: www.emporia.edu/theatre
Officers:
President: Dr Michael R Lane
Management:
Director Theatre: Jim Bartruff
Public Service Executive: Indy Dambro
Mission: Campus venue for convocations, theatre performances and road shows.
Founded: 1863
Opened: 1916
Specialized Field: Concerts, Dance, Productions
Type of Stage: Proscenium
Stage Dimensions: 40' x 18'
Orchestra Pit: y
Seating Capacity: 1,281

6656
BRIGHTON THEATRE
Emporia State University
Brighton Lecture Hall
1200 Commercial Street
Emporia, KS 66801
Phone: 620-342-5374
e-mail: jbartruf@emporia.edu
Web Site: http://www.emporia.edu/theatre/
Officers:
President: Dr. Michael R. Lane
Management:
Director Theatre: Jim Bartruff
Professor of Theatre: James D. Ryan
Associate Professor of Theatre: Theresa Mitchell
Associate Professor of Theatre: Nancy Pontius
Associate Professor of Theatre: Susan J. Mai
Assistant Professor of Theatre: Ron Fowlkes
Mission: At ESU, students can earn a BFA or BA in theatre, or gain certification to become a secondary teacher in our BSE program in speech and theatre. We are proud to be a part of an outstanding department, Communication and Theatre.
Opened: 2001
Specialized Field: Musicals, Theatre
Seating Capacity: 189

6657
KARL C. BRUDER THEATRE
Emporia State University
King Hall
1200 Commercial Street
Emporia, KS 66801
Phone: 620-342-5374
e-mail: esutheatre@emporia.edu
Web Site: www.emporia.edu/theatre
Officers:
President: Dr Michael R Lane
Management:
Director Theatre: Jim Bartruff
Technical Director: Craig Moxon
Mission: At ESU, students can earn a BFA or BA in theatre, or gain certification to become a secondary teacher in our BSE program in speech and theatre. We are proud to be a part of an outstanding department, Communication and Theatre.
Specialized Field: Theatre
Type of Stage: Proscenium
Stage Dimensions: 39'6 x 18'

Orchestra Pit: y
Seating Capacity: 402
Year Built: 1967

6658
RONALD Q. FREDERICKSON THEATRE
Emporia State University
Roosevelt Hall
1200 Commercial Street
Emporia, KS 66801
Phone: 620-342-5374
e-mail: esutheatre@emporia.edu
Web Site: www.emporia.edu/theatre
Officers:
President: Dr Michael R Lane
Management:
Director Theatre: Jim Bartruff, jbartruf@emporia.edu
Technical Director: Craig Moxon, cmoxon@emporia.edu
Mission: At ESU, students can earn a BFA or BA in theatre, or gain certification to become a secondary teacher in our BSE program in speech and theatre. We are proud to be a part of an outstanding department, Communication and Theatre.
Founded: 2001
Opened: 2001
Specialized Field: Theatre
Type of Stage: Black Box
Seating Capacity: 100-125

6659
BEACH-SCHMIDT PERFORMING ARTS CENTER
Fort Hays State University
Sheridan Hall
600 Park Street
Hays, KS 67601-4099
Phone: 785-628-5365
Fax: 785-628-4227
Web Site: http://www.fhsu.edu/communication/theatreinfo
Officers:
President: Edward H. Hammond
Management:
Chair Communications Studies: Carrol Haggard, PhD
Assistant Professor: Bruce Bardwell
Mission: Theatre provides you with an opportunity to excel on stage. You can develop your talents in acting, directing, costuming, stage design and theatre management. You may take part in up to five major productions each year and a variety of one-act plays. In addition to performance, a broad range of courses are offered in acting, directing, stagecraft, and dramatic literature.
Specialized Field: Concerts, Recitals
Seating Capacity: 1,100
Year Remodeled: 1998

6660
FELTEN-START THEATRE
Fort Hays State University
Malloy Hall
600 Park Street
Hays, KS 67601-4099
Phone: 785-628-5365
Fax: 785-628-4227
Web Site: http://www.fhsu.edu/communication/theatreinfo
Officers:
President: Edward H. Hammond
Management:

Chair Communications Studies: Carrol Haggard, PhD
Assistant Professor: Bruce Bardwell
Mission: Theatre provides you with an opportunity to excel on stage. You can develop your talents in acting, directing, costuming, stage design and theatre management. You may take part in up to five major productions each year and a variety of one-act plays. In addition to performance, a broad range of courses are offered in acting, directing, stagecraft, and dramatic literature.
Specialized Field: Music, Theatre
Seating Capacity: 350

6661
FELTON CENTER
Fort Hays State University
600 Park Street
Hays, KS 67601
Phone: 785-628-5801
Fax: 785-628-4007
Web Site: www.fhsu.edu
Management:
Special Events Coordinator: Carol Brock

6662
HAL PALMER RECITAL HALL
Fort Hays State University
Malloy Hall
600 Park Street
Hays, KS 67601-4099
Phone: 785-628-5365
Fax: 785-628-4227
Web Site: http://www.fhsu.edu/communication/theatreinfo
Officers:
President: Edward H. Hammond
Management:
Chair Communications Studies: Carrol Haggard, PhD
Assistant Professor: Bruce Bardwell
Mission: Theatre provides you with an opportunity to excel on stage. You can develop your talents in acting, directing, costuming, stage design and theatre management. You may take part in up to five major productions each year and a variety of one-act plays. In addition to performance, a broad range of courses are offered in acting, directing, stagecraft, and dramatic literature.
Specialized Field: Student Recitals
Seating Capacity: 115

6663
FOX THEATRE
18 East First Avenue
Hutchinson, KS 67501
Phone: 620-663-5861
Fax: 620-663-5371
Toll-free: 877-369-7469
e-mail: thefox@hutchinsonfox.com
Web Site: www.hutchinsonsonfox.com
Management:
Executive Director: Mary Hemmings
Box Office: Carrie Rodgers
Technical Director: John Davies
Seating Capacity: 1,221

6664
KANSAS STATE FAIR - GRANDSTAND
2000 N Poplar Street
Hutchinson, KS 67502-5598
Phone: 620-669-3600
Fax: 620-669-3640
Web Site: www.kansasstatefair.com

Management:
General Manager: Denny Stoecklein
Mission: The annual Kansas State Fair is held annually beginning the Friday following Labor Day and lasts for 10 days at the Kansas State Fairgrounds in Hutchinson, Kansas. The largest single event in the State, the Fair annually attracts approximately 350,000 people from all 105 Kansas counties and several other states.
Founded: 1913
Status: Non-Profit, Professional
Paid Staff: 25
Paid Artists: 20

6665
BOWLUS FINE ARTS CENTER
205 E Madison
Iola, KS 66749
Phone: 316-365-4765
Web Site: www.bowluscenter.com
Management:
Marketing/Finance Director: Tammu Porter
Executive Director: Mary Martin
Mission: Attracts nationally-acclaimed performers to the area. Also houses a fine arts education center. The Bowlus provides display areas for local and visiting artists, while maintaining a permanent collection of distinctive paintings.

6666
ALLEN FIELDHOUSE
University of Kansas
1651 Naismith Drive, Lawrence
Lawrence, KS 66045
Phone: 785-864-3143
Fax: 785-864-5517
e-mail: KUAthletics@KU.edu
Web Site:
www.kuathletics.cstv.com/facilities/kan-allen-fieldhouse.html
Management:
Chancellor: Robert Hemenway
Athletics Director: Lew Perkins
Founded: 1955
Seating Capacity: 16,300

6667
CRAFTON-PREYER THEATRE
University of Kansas
1530 Naismith Drive, Murphy Hall
Lawrence, KS 66045
Phone: 785-864-3381
Fax: 785-864-6007
e-mail: cjenkins@ku.edu
Web Site: www.kutheatre.com
Management:
Public Relations Director: Charla Jenkins
Tech Director: Jim Peterson
Utilizes: Collaborations; Guest Accompanists; Guest Conductors; Guest Designers; Guest Writers; Multi Collaborations; Soloists
Founded: 1923
Specialized Field: Theatre
Paid Staff: 13
Income Sources: State of Kansas and Box Office
Annual Attendance: 65,000
Facility Category: University Theatre
Type of Stage: Proscenium
Seating Capacity: 1,188
Year Built: 1957
Rental Contact: Tech Director Jim Peterson

6668
LIED CENTER OF KANSAS
University of Kansas
1600 Stewart Drive, Lawrence
Lawrence, KS 66045
Phone: 785-864-3469
Fax: 785-864-5031
e-mail: lied@ku.edu
Web Site: www.lied.ku.edu
Management:
Executive Director: Tim Van Leer
Associate Director: Karen Lane Christilles
Founded: 1993
Specialized Field: Presenting
Status: Non-Profit, Professional
Paid Staff: 100
Type of Stage: Proscenium
Seating Capacity: 2,018

6669
XAVIER HALL THEATRE
University of Saint Mary
4100 S 4th Street
Leavenworth, KS 66048
Phone: 913-682-5151
Fax: 913-758-6140
Toll-free: 913-752-7043
e-mail: enroll@stmary.edu
Web Site: www.stmary.edu
Officers:
President: Sister Diane Steel
Management:
Program Director: Van Ibsen
Instructor/Fine Arts-Theatre: Danielle Trebus
Mission: Seeks to prepare students for value-centered lives and careers that contribute to the well being of the global society.
Founded: 1859
Specialized Field: Greater Kansas City Metropolitan Area
Status: Non-Profit, Non-Professional
Paid Staff: 2
Paid Artists: 6
Budget: $10,000
Income Sources: Annual budget provided by the University plus Gifts; Donations; Season Tickets and Single Ticket Revenue
Performs At: Theatre
Annual Attendance: 4,000
Facility Category: Theatre
Type of Stage: Proscenium/Thrust
Stage Dimensions: 40' x 20'
Seating Capacity: 349
Year Built: 1918
Year Remodeled: 2007

6670
BURNETT THEATRE
Bethany College
Burnett Center for Religion & Performing Arts
421 North First Street
Lindsborg, KS 67456-1897
Phone: 785-227-3311
Fax: 785-227-2004
Toll-free: 800-826-2281
e-mail: legaultg@bethanylb.edu
Web Site: www.bethanylb.edu
Officers:
President: Paul Formo
Director Operations: Jeff Barkman
Management:
Assistant Professor of Theatre: Greg Legault

Mission: Bethany College offers a small but highly flexible hands-on Theater Program.
Founded: 1881
Specialized Field: Theatrical
Status: Non-Profit, Professional
Seating Capacity: 250
Year Built: 1974

6671
FRED BRAMLAGE COLISEUM
Kansas State University
1800 College Avenue Suite 137
Manhattan, KS 66502
Phone: 785-532-7600
Fax: 785-532-7655
e-mail: bramlage@ksu.edu
Web Site: www.k-state.edu/bramlage
Management:
Executive Director: Charles E Thomas
Artistic Director: James Muller
Founded: 1988
Status: Non-Profit, Professional
Paid Staff: 200
Type of Stage: Concert Stage
Seating Capacity: 14,000

6672
MANHATTAN ARTS CENTER
1520 Poyntz Avenue
Manhattan, KS 66502
Phone: 785-537-4420
Fax: 785-539-3356
e-mail: director@manhattanarts.org
Web Site: www.manhattanarts.org
Officers:
Executive Director: Penny Senftem
Mission: To make arts activities available to all.
Utilizes: Actors; Collaborations; Community Members; Community Talent; Designers; Educators; Fine Artists; Five Seasonal Concerts; Grant Writers; Guest Accompanists; Guest Musical Directors; Guild Activities; High School Drama; Local Artists; Local Artists & Directors; Local Talent; Multimedia; Music; Original Music Scores; Paid Performers; Resident Professionals; Sign Language Translators; Soloists; Special Technical Talent; Theatre Companies; Touring Companies; Visual Designers; Volunteer Directors & Actors; Writers
Founded: 1996
Specialized Field: Galleries; Live Theatre; Concerts; Classes
Status: Non-Profit, Non-Professional
Paid Staff: 3
Volunteer Staff: 75
Budget: $290,000
Income Sources: Kansas Arts Commission; City of Manhattan; Foundations; Private Donations; Admissions; Tuition
Performs At: Multi-use Arts Center
Annual Attendance: 11,000
Type of Stage: Black Box
Seating Capacity: 145-160
Year Remodeled: 1996
Organization Type: Educational; Sponsoring

6673
MCCAIN AUDITORIUM
Kansas State University
207 McCain Auditorium
Manhattan, KS 66506
Phone: 785-532-6425
Fax: 785-532-5870
e-mail: mcctxt@ksu.edu
Web Site: www.ksu.edu

Officers:
President: Barbara Gatewood
President-Elect: Peggy Anderson
Management:
Director: Richard P. Martin
Assistant Director: Terri L. Lee
Mission: The mission of the theatre program is to develop human potential, expand knowledge, and enrich cultural understanding and expression through high quality undergraduate and graduate education.
Founded: 1858
Specialized Field: Dance, Theatre
Orchestra Pit: y
Seating Capacity: 900-1,800
Year Built: 1970

6674
NICHOLS THEATRE
Kansas State University
Manhattan, KS 66506
Phone: 785-532-6769
Web Site: http://www.k-state.edu/sctd/theatre/
Officers:
President: Jon Wefald
Management:
Director Theatre: Kate Anderson
Associate Professor of Theatre: Marci Maullar
Associate Professor of Theatre: John S. Uthoff
Mission: The mission of the theatre program is to develop human potential, expand knowledge, and enrich cultural understanding and expression through high quality undergraduate and graduate education.
Founded: 1858
Specialized Field: Theatre
Type of Stage: Arena-Thrust
Seating Capacity: 240-280
Year Built: 1985

6675
PURPLE MASQUE
Kansas State University
Manhattan, KS 66506
Phone: 785-532-6769
Web Site: http://www.k-state.edu/sctd/theatre/
Officers:
President: Jon Wefald
Management:
Director Theatre: Kate Anderson
Associate Professor of Theatre: Marci Maullar
Associate Professor of Theatre: John S. Uthoff
Mission: The mission of the theatre program is to develop human potential, expand knowledge, and enrich cultural understanding and expression through high quality undergraduate and graduate education.
Founded: 1858
Specialized Field: Student Productions
Type of Stage: Thrust
Orchestra Pit: y
Seating Capacity: 100

6676
BROWN AUDITORIUM
McPherson College
1600 East Euclid
McPherson, KS 67460
Mailing Address: PO Box 1402
Phone: 316-241-0731
Fax: 316-241-8443
Toll-free: 800-365-7402
e-mail: admiss@mcpherson.edu
Web Site: www.mcpherson.edu
Management:
Computer Services Director: David D Gitchell
Business Manager: Shirley Reissig

Library/Media Services Director: Rowena Olsen
Founded: 1887

6677
NEODESHA ARTS ASSOCIATION
PO Box 65
5th Street & Indiana
Neodesha, KS 66757
Phone: 316-325-3422
Fax: 316-325-3122
e-mail: neodeshaart@yahoo.com
Management:
Executive: Teresa Railsback
Mission: The mission is to improve the quality of life in Neodesha and surrounding area through presentation of cultutral activities in which the arts flourish.
Founded: 1973
Paid Staff: 1
Volunteer Staff: 13
Paid Artists: 1
Non-paid Artists: 3

6678
OTTAWA MUNICIPAL AUDITORIUM
301 S Hickory Street
PO Box 462
Ottawa, KS 66067
Phone: 785-242-8810
Fax: 785-229-3760
e-mail: onalide@gratevine.net
Web Site: www.gratevine.net/~omalide
Management:
Administration Manager: Shonda Stitt
Founded: 1890
Status: Non-Profit, Professional
Paid Staff: 9
Paid Artists: 100
Seating Capacity: 840

6679
PERFORMING ARTS SERIES
Johnson County Community College
12345 College Boulevard
CC 109
Overland Park, KS 66210
Phone: 913-469-4450
Fax: 913-469-2252
e-mail: tickets@jccc.edu
Web Site: www.jccc.edu/TheSeries
Officers:
Chairperson: Dan Weiss
Vice Chair: Jon Stewart
President: Terry A. Calaway
Management:
General Manger: Emily Behrmann, ebehrman@jccc.edu
Founded: 1990
Opened: 1990
Specialized Field: Multi-discipline, performing arts presenter
Paid Staff: 15
Volunteer Staff: 150
Budget: $22,000,000
Income Sources: Ticket revenue, private donations, institutional support
Performs At: Yardley Hall, Polsky Theatre
Affiliations: APAP, INTIX, KS Arts Alliance/Kennedy Center
Annual Attendance: 100,000
Type of Stage: Proscenium & Thrust
Orchestra Pit: y
Seating Capacity: Polsky-400; Yardley-1300
Year Built: 1990
Cost: $22,000,000

Rental Contact: Anthony Perry

6680
CARNIE SMITH STADIUM
Pittsburg State University
1701 S Broadway
Pittsburg, KS 66762
Phone: 620-231-7000
Fax: 316-235-4661
e-mail: acad@pittstate.edu
Web Site: www.pittstate.edu
Management:
Athletic Director: Chuck Broyles
Annual Attendance: 238,911
Seating Capacity: 8,343

6681
MEMORIAL AUDITORIUM AND CONVENTION CENTER
503 N Pine
Pittsburg, KS 66762
Phone: 316-231-7827
Fax: 316-231-5967
Web Site: www.pittks.org
Management:
Manager: Judy Collins
Office Manager: Janice Arthur
Technical Director: David Stubbs
Founded: 1925
Paid Staff: 5
Annual Attendance: 10,000
Facility Category: Concert Hall, Children's theater
Type of Stage: Proscenium
Stage Dimensions: 90 x 37
Seating Capacity: 1588
Year Built: 1923
Year Remodeled: 1984
Architect: Seidler, Owsley and Associates
Cost: $3.4 million
Rental Contact: Manager Judy Collins

6682
WEEDE ARENA
Pittsburgh State University
1701 South Broadway
Pittsburg, KS 66762
Phone: 316-235-4646
Fax: 316-235-4661
Web Site: www.oitstate.edu
Management:
Athletic Director: Chuck Broyles
Sports Information Director: Dan Wilkes
Head Basketball Coach (M): Swede Trenkle
Head Basketball Coach (W): Steve High
Assistant Director Athletics: Steve Bever
Marketing/Promotions Director: Tommy Riggs
Seating Capacity: 6,000

6683
SALINA BICENTENNIAL CENTER
800 The Midway
PO Box 1727
Salina, KS 67402
Phone: 785-826-7200
Fax: 785-826-7207
Toll-free: 888-826-7469
Web Site: www.bicentennial.org
Management:
President: Keith Rawlings
Founded: 1979
Status: For-Profit, Non-Professional
Paid Staff: 20
Seating Capacity: 2,000

6684

STIEFEL THEATRE FOR THE PERFORMING ARTS

151 South Santa Fe
Salina, KS 67401
Fax: 785-827-3478
Web Site: www.stiefeltheatre.com
Management:
  Executive Director: Michele Douglas
Seating Capacity: 1,286

6685

KANSAS EXPOCENTRE

One Expocentre Drive
Topeka, KS 66612
Phone: 785-235-1986
Fax: 785-235-2967
e-mail: roym@ksexpo.com
Web Site: www.ksexpo.com
Management:
  Managing Manager: HR Cook
  Director Operations: Roy Mitchell
  Director Marketing: Shannon Reilly
Founded: 1986
Specialized Field: Multi-Purpose Facility
Status: For-Profit, Professional
Paid Staff: 200
Seating Capacity: 10,000
Year Built: 1987

6686

LEE ARENA

Washburn University
1700 College Avenue
Topeka, KS 66621
Phone: 785-670-1134
Fax: 785-670-1091
Web Site: www.washburn.edu
Management:
  Athletic Director: Loren Ferre
  Facilities Manager: Gilbert Herrera
Seating Capacity: 3,804

6687

TOPEKA PERFORMING ARTS CENTER

214 Se 8th Avenue
Topeka, KS 66603
Phone: 785-234-2787
Fax: 785-234-2307
Web Site: www.tpactix.org
Management:
  Executive Director: Robert Seitz
  Development Director: John Esau
  Marketing Manager: Melaine Kitchner
Founded: 1990
Seating Capacity: 4,200

6688

KANSAS COLISEUM

1229 E 85th Street N
Valley Center, KS 67147
Phone: 316-755-1243
Fax: 316-755-2869
e-mail: info@kansascoliseum.com
Web Site: www.kansascoliseum.com
Management:
  Managing Director: John W Nath
  Assistant Director: David Rush
Founded: 1975
Specialized Field: Multi-Purpose Arena; Home of the
Wichita Thunder (CHL); and Wichita Stealth
Status: For-Profit, Professional
Paid Staff: 50

Annual Attendance: 700,000
Seating Capacity: 9,600; 12,400
Year Built: 1978

6689

COLUMBIAN THEATRE: MUSEUM & ART CENTER

521 Lincoln Avenue
PO Box 72
Wamego, KS 66547
Phone: 785-456-2029
Fax: 785-456-9498
Toll-free: 800-899-1893
e-mail: boxoffice@columbiantheatre.com
Web Site: www.columbiantheatre.com
Officers:
  President: Lance White
Management:
  Executive Director: Vivian Orndorff
  Artistic Director: Ariane Chapman
  Marketing/Events Director: Kayla Oney
Founded: 1989
Status: Non-Profit, Non-Professional
Paid Staff: 4
Annual Attendance: 12,000
Rental Contact: Marketing/Events Director Kayla Oney

6690

WELLINGTON MEMORIAL AUDITORIUM

PO Box 564
Wellington, KS 67152
Phone: 316-326-3303
Fax: 316-326-8506
Management:
  Manager: Ellen McCue

6691

CENTURY II CIVIC CENTER EXHIBITION HALL

225 W Douglas Avenue
Wichita, KS 67202
Phone: 316-264-9121
Fax: 316-268-9268
Web Site: www.century2.org
Type of Stage: 62,500 Sq Ft
Seating Capacity: 2,000

6692

CENTURY II CIVIC CENTER MARY JANE TEALL THEATRE

225 W Douglas Avenue
Wichita, KS 67202
Phone: 316-264-9121
Fax: 316-268-9268
Web Site: www.century2.org
Type of Stage: Proscenium
Seating Capacity: 646

6693

CENTURY II PERFORMING ARTS & CONVENTION CENTER

225 W Douglas Avenue
Wichita, KS 67202-3100
Phone: 316-264-9121
Fax: 316-268-9268
e-mail: DLWILLIAMS@wichita.gov
Web Site: www.century2.org
Management:
  General Manager: Debbie Williams
Founded: 1960
Status: Non-Profit, Non-Professional
Paid Staff: 35
Seating Capacity: 5,244; 2,178

Rental Contact: Kathy Pearson

6694

HENRY LEVITT ARENA

Wichita State University
1845 Fairmount Street
Wichita, KS 67260
Mailing Address: Campus Box 12
Phone: 316-978-STET
Fax: 316-978-3336
Web Site: www.twsu.edu
Management:
  Director Athletics: Jim Schalf

6695

MILLER CONCERT HALL

Wichita State University
Duerksen Fine Arts Center
1845 Fairmount Street
Wichita, KS 67260
Phone: 316-978-3233
e-mail: webmaster@wichita.edu
Web Site: www.wichita.edu
Officers:
  President: Donald L. Beggs
Founded: 1895
Seating Capacity: 10,432

6696

WIEDEMANN RECITAL HALL

Wichita State University
1845 Fairmount Street
Wichita, KS 67260
Phone: 316-978-3233
e-mail: webmaster@wichita.edu
Web Site: www.wichita.edu
Officers:
  President: Donald L. Beggs
Founded: 1895
Seating Capacity: 10,432

6697

WILNER AUDITORIUM

Wichita State University
1845 Fairmount Street
Wichita, KS 67260
Phone: 316-978-3233
e-mail: webmaster@wichita.edu
Web Site: www.wichita.edu
Officers:
  President: Donald L. Beggs
Founded: 1895
Seating Capacity: 10,432

Kentucky

6698

PARAMOUNT ARTS CENTER

1300 Winchester Avenue
PO Box 1546
Ashland, KY 41105
Phone: 606-324-3175
Fax: 606-324-1233
e-mail: jenny@paramountartscenter.com
Web Site: www.paramountartscenter.com
Management:
  Executive Director: Kathleen Timmons
  Marketing Director: Jenny Holmes,
  Jenny@paramountartscenter.com
  Managing Director/Rental Contact: Cindy Collins
Mission: Originally designed and built to show talking
pictures, has provided an intimate venue for a variety of
performaning arts since it re-opened in 1972.

Utilizes: Collaborations; Dance Companies; Dancers; Guest Accompanists; Guest Musical Directors; Guest Soloists; Guest Writers; Guild Activities; Instructors; Local Artists; Lyricists; Multimedia; New Productions; Original Music Scores; Playwrights; Sign Language Translators; Soloists; Special Technical Talent; Theatre Companies; Touring Companies
Founded: 1931
Specialized Field: Multi Disciplinary Presenter
Status: Nonprofit, Professional
Paid Staff: 10
Volunteer Staff: 100
Annual Attendance: 115,000
Facility Category: Performing Arts
Type of Stage: Proscenium
Stage Dimensions: 46x52
Seating Capacity: 1400
Year Built: 1931
Year Remodeled: 2001
Cost: $ 9 Million
Rental Contact: Cindy Collins

6699
STEPHEN FOSTER PRODUCTIONS

My Old Kentucky Home State Park
Bardstown, KY 40004
Phone: 502-348-5971
Fax: 502-349-0574
e-mail: info@stephenfoster.com
Web Site: www.stephenfoster.com
Management:
    General Manager: Betty Kelley
Founded: 1959
Status: Non-Profit, Professional
Paid Staff: 100
Paid Artists: 60
Season: June - August
Seating Capacity: 1450
Year Built: 1959
Year Remodeled: 1997
Cost: $1.6 million

6700
PHELPS-STOKES AUDITORIUM AT BEREA COLLEGE

Berea College Campus
CPO 2220
Berea, KY 40404
Phone: 606-985-3000
Fax: 606-985-3512
Toll-free: 800-326-5948
e-mail: linda_avery@berea.edu
Web Site: www.berea.edu

6701
CAPITOL ARTS CENTER

416 E Main Street
Bowling Green, KY 42101
Phone: 270-782-2787
Fax: 270-782-2804
Toll-free: 877-694-2787
Web Site: www.capitolarts.com
Management:
    President: Steve Jones
Founded: 1981
Status: Non-Profit, Professional
Paid Staff: 9

6702
DIDDLE ARENA

Western Kentucky University
1 Big Red Way Academic Athletic Building
Bowling Green, KY 42101
Phone: 502-745-3542
Fax: 502-745-6187
e-mail: western@wku.edu
Web Site: www.wku.edu/athletics
Management:
    Director: Wood Selid
Founded: 1963

6703
LT SMITH STADIUM

Western Kentucky University
1 Big Red Way
Bowling Green, KY 42101
Phone: 502-745-3542
Fax: 502-745-6187
Web Site: www.wku.edu/athletics.html
Management:
    Director: Wood Selid
    Associate Athletic Director: Pam Herriford
    Associate Athletic Director: Matt Pope
    Coordinator Marketing/Promotions: Wayne Orscheln
Founded: 1968
Seating Capacity: 17,000

6704
MADISON THEATER

730 Madison Avenue
Covington, KY 41011
Phone: 859-655-4807
Fax: 859-655-4808
Web Site: www.madisontheateronline.com
Management:
    Owner: Ester Johnson
    Operations: Howard Hodge
Founded: 1912
Seating Capacity: 1,200
Year Remodeled: 2001

6705
NORTON CENTER FOR THE ARTS

Centre College
600 W Walnut Street
Danville, KY 40422
Phone: 859-236-4692
Fax: 859-238-5448
Toll-free: 877-448-7469
e-mail: chafin@centre.edu
Web Site: www.centre.edu/nc
Management:
    President: John Rosh
    Managing Director: George Foreman
Founded: 1973
Status: Non-Profit, Professional
Seating Capacity: Newlin Hall-1500; Weisiger Theatre-360
Year Built: 1973
Year Remodeled: 1994

6706
HENDERSON FINE ARTS CENTER

2660 S Green Street Center
Henderson, KY 42420
Phone: 270-827-1867
Fax: 270-831-9802
Toll-free: 800-696-9958
Web Site: www.hencc.kctcs.edu
Management:
    Director: Rachael Baar
Founded: 1993
Status: Non-Profit, Professional
Paid Staff: 3

6707
COMMONWEALTH STADIUM

University of Kentucky
University Drive, Room 23
Lexington, KY 40506
Phone: 859-257-3838
Fax: 859-323-4310
Web Site: www.ukathletics.com
Management:
    President: Lee Todd
    Executive Director: Mitch Barnhart
    Managing Director: Rodney Stiles
Mission: Home of Kentucky Wildcats
Founded: 1973
Status: For-Profit, Non-Professional
Paid Staff: 250
Seating Capacity: 67,530
Year Built: 1973

6708
LEXINGTON CENTER

430 W Vine Street
Lexington, KY 40507
Phone: 859-233-4567
Fax: 859-253-2718
e-mail: webmaster@rupparena.com
Web Site: www.lexingtoncenter.com
Officers:
    President/CEO: William B Owen
Management:
    Director Arena Management: Carl Hall
    Program Dir/Lexington Opera House: Luanne A. Franklin
Seating Capacity: 23,500

6709
LEXINGTON OPERA HOUSE

430 W Vine Street
Lexington, KY 40507
Phone: 859-233-4567
Fax: 859-253-2718
Web Site: www.lexingtonoperahouse.com
Management:
    President: William B Owen
Founded: 1886
Status: For-Profit, Professional
Paid Staff: 3
Seating Capacity: 1,000
Year Built: 1886
Year Remodeled: 1972

6710
LUCILLE C LITTLE THEATER

Transylvania University
300 North Broadway
Lexington, KY 40508
Phone: 859-233-8300
Fax: 859-233-8797
e-mail: admissions@transy.edu
Web Site: www.transy.edu
Founded: 1780

6711
MITCHELL FINE ARTS CENTER

Transylvania University
300 N Braodway
Lexington, KY 40508
Phone: 859-233-8300
Fax: 859-233-8797
Toll-free: 800-872-6798
e-mail: admissions@transy.edu
Web Site: www.transy.edu
Management:

President: Charles Shearer
Artistic Director: Tim Soulis
Managing Director: Devin Query
Founded: 1780
Status: Non-Profit, Non-Professional
Paid Staff: 250

6712
SINGLETARY CENTER FOR THE ARTS
University of Kentucky
Rose Street & Euclid Avenue
Lexington, KY 40503-0241
Phone: 859-257-1706
Fax: 859-323-9991
Web Site: www.uky.edu/SCFA/
Management:
  Director: Holly Salisbury
Mission: Host over 350 programs a year.
Founded: 1979
Paid Staff: 71
Volunteer Staff: 70
Annual Attendance: 112,000
Seating Capacity: Concert Hall-1500; Recital Hall-400

6713
UNIVERSITY OF KENTUCKY MEMORIAL COLISEUM
Lexington Avenue
Room 111
Lexington, KY 40506
Phone: 859-257-8000
Fax: 859-257-6303
Toll-free: 800-928-2287
e-mail: mbarn@uky.edu
Web Site: www.ukathletics.com
Management:
  President: Lee T Todd Jr
  Athletic Director: Mitch Barnhart
  Associate Director Athletics: Kathleen DeBoer
  Associate Director: Bob Bradley
Founded: 1950
Seating Capacity: 8,500

6714
CARDINAL STADIUM
Kentucky Fair & Exposition Center
937 Phillips Lane
Louisville, KY 40209-1398
Mailing Address: PO Box 37130
Phone: 502-367-5000
Fax: 502-367-5139
Web Site: www.kyfairexpo.org
Management:
  President/CEO: Harold Workman
  Operations Director: Larry Faue
  VP Sales/Marketing: Linda Edwards
Founded: 1900
Specialized Field: Sports Stadium for baseball and NCAA
Status: For-Profit, Non-Professional
Seating Capacity: 47,925
Year Built: 1956
Year Remodeled: 1981

6715
FREEDOM HALL ARENA
Kentucky Fair & Exposition Center
937 Phillips Lane
Louisville, KY 40209-1398
Mailing Address: PO Box 37130 Louisville, KY 40233
Phone: 502-367-5000
Fax: 502-367-5139
Web Site: www.kyfairexpo.org
Management:

President/CEO: Harold Workman
Operations Director: Larry Faue
VP Sales/Marketing: Linda Edwards
Founded: 1956
Specialized Field: Home of University of Louisville Athletics (NCAA)
Status: For-Profit, Professional
Paid Staff: 300
Seating Capacity: 19,169
Year Built: 1956
Year Remodeled: 1984

6716
KENTUCKY CENTER FOR THE ARTS ROBERT S WHITNEY HALL
501 West Main Street
Louisville, KY 40202
Phone: 502-562-0100
Fax: 502-562-0150
Toll-free: 800-775-7777
e-mail: info@kentuckycenter.org
Web Site: www.kentuckycenter.org/rent/theater.asp
Management:
  President: Arthur Jacobus
  Managing Director: Kim Baker
  Sales: Chris Long
  Rental Information: Vickie Dorsey
Mission: A 2,406-seat, multipurpose concert facility, Whitney Hall can accommodate everything from the most elaborate touring Broadway extravaganzas to the more modest requirements of a chamber music ensemble. Named for the eminent former conductor of the Louisville Orchestra, this theater has exemplary acoustics, comfortable seats and uninterrupted sight lines to ensure that every patron enjoys their theatrical experience to the fullest.
Founded: 1984
Status: Non-Profit, Professional
Rental Contact: Vickie Dorsey

6717
KENTUCKY CENTER FOR THE ARTS BOMHARD THEATRE
501 W Main Street
Louisville, KY 40202
Phone: 502-562-0100
Fax: 502-562-0150
Web Site: www.kentuckycenter.org
Seating Capacity: 619

6718
LOUISVILLE MEMORIAL AUDITORIUM
970 S 4th Street
Louisville, KY 40203
Phone: 502-584-4911
Fax: 502-574-4318
Management:
  Director: Dale Royer
Founded: 1929
Specialized Field: Gospel Shows; Stage Plays; Small Concerts; Children's Shows; Dance and Talent Competitions
Status: Non-Profit, Professional
Paid Staff: 3
Annual Attendance: 100,000
Facility Category: Auditorium
Stage Dimensions: 50' x 85'
Year Built: 1929
Rental Contact: Dale Royer

6719
LOUISVILLE PALACE THEATRE
625 Fourth Avenue
Louisville, KY 40202
Phone: 502-361-3100
Fax: 502-583-9955
Web Site: www.louisvillepalace.com
Management:
  General Manager/Booking: David Bartlett
  Sales/Marketing Director: Jennifer Crutcher
  Box Office Manager: Cindy Brown
  Production Manager: Casey Clark
  Operations Manager: Christie Lunsford
  Accounting: Jennifer Hunt
Seating Capacity: 2,715

6720
W L LYONS BROWN THEATRE
315 West Broadwy
Louisville, KY 40202
Phone: 502-562-0100
Fax: 502-581-9213
e-mail: wrichards@kentuckycenter.org
Web Site: www.kentuckycenter.org
Management:
  Manager/Booking: Will Richards
  Box Office Manager: Michell Karlin
Seating Capacity: 1381

6721
GLEMA MAHR CENTER FOR THE ARTS
Madisonville Community College
2000 College Drive
Madisonville, KY 42431
Phone: 270-824-8651
Fax: 270-824-1868
e-mail: bradley.downall@kctcs.edu
Web Site: www.glemacenter.org
Management:
  Director: Brad Downall
Mission: To enhance the quality of life in Madisonville and surrounding communities by developing and presenting a wide range of arts programming and arts education opportunities for all ages and interests.
Founded: 1990
Status: Non-Profit, Professional
Paid Staff: 7
Facility Category: Performing & Visual Arts Center
Type of Stage: Proscenium
Seating Capacity: 1017

6722
JAYNE STADIUM
150 Playforth Place
Morehead, KY 40351
Phone: 606-783-2221
Fax: 606-783-5035
Toll-free: 800-585-6781
e-mail: t.stevens@moreheadstate.edu
Web Site: www.morehead-st.edu
Officers:
  President: Dr Wayne Andrews

6723
MURRAY STATE UNIVERSITY LOVETT AUDITORIUM
1401 State Route 121 North
PO Box 9
Murray, KY 42071-3362
Phone: 270-762-5577
Fax: 270-762-5511
e-mail: rsec@murraystate.edu
Web Site: www.murraystate.edu

Management:
Facility Manager: Jason Pittman
Founded: 1926
Facility Category: Auditorium

6724
RACER ARENA
Murray State University
Athletic Department
Murray, KY 42071
Phone: 502-762-6800
Fax: 270-762-5498
e-mail: webmaster@murraystate.edu
Web Site: www.murraystate.edu
Management:
President: F King Alexander
Athletic Director: E W Dennison
Founded: 1997
Seating Capacity: 5,500

6725
REGIONAL SPECIAL EVENTS CENTER
Murray State University
1401 State Route 121 North
Murray, KY 42071
Phone: 270-762-5577
Fax: 270-762-5511
e-mail: rsec@murraystate.edu
Web Site: www.murraystate.edu
Management:
President: King Alexander
Director Sales/Marketing: Shelly Todd
Founded: 1998
Status: Non-Profit, Professional
Paid Staff: 30
Seating Capacity: 8,600

6726
ROY STEWART STADIUM
Murray State University
Murray, KY 42071
Mailing Address: Box 2002 University Station
Phone: 270-762-6951
Fax: 270-762-6952
e-mail: jeanie.morgan@murraystate.edu
Web Site: www.murraystate.edu
Officers:
Student Activities Coordinator: Jeanie Morgan
Opened: 1973
Facility Category: Sports Arena
Seating Capacity: 16,800

6727
OWENSBORO SPORTS
101 East 4th Street
PO Box 10003
Owensboro, KY 42302
Phone: 270-687-8600
Fax: 270-687-8787
Web Site: www.owensboro.com
Management:
Facility Manager: Hal L Mischel
Seating Capacity: 5,000

6728
RIVERPARK CENTER
101 Daviess Street
Owensboro, KY 42303
Phone: 270-687-2770
Fax: 270-687-2775
e-mail: info@riverparkcenter.org
Web Site: www.riverparkcenter.org
Officers:
President: Zev Buffman

Management:
General Manager: Roxi Witt,
rwitt@riverparkcenter.org
Technical Director: Phillip Poe,
pope@riverparkcenter.org
Box Office Manager: Dana Wheeler,
dwheeler@riverparkcenter.org
Mission: Riverpark Center is a non-profit organization seeking to improve the quality of life by hosting and presenting diverse arts and civic events, focusing on arts and education.
Founded: 1992
Status: Non-Profit
Paid Staff: 16
Volunteer Staff: 200
Performs At: State-Of-The-Art Broadway Style Theater In Addition To A Cabaret Theater And Reception Areas.
Facility Category: Performing Arts
Seating Capacity: 1,497/300 in cabaret theater
Year Built: 1992

6729
FOUR RIVERS CENTER FOR THE PERFORMING ARTS
417 S 4th Street, Suite 1
PO Box 2194
Paducah, KY 42003-2194
Phone: 270-443-9932
Fax: 270-443-9947
Web Site: www.fourriverscenter.org
Officers:
Chairman: Ted Borodofsky
Vice Chairman: Mike Livingston
Treasurer: Linda Miller
Secretary: Anne Gwinn
Management:
Operations Director: Jeff Foreman
Events Coordinator: Suzanne Clinton
Events Coordinator: Tara Camacho
Founded: 1996
Specialized Field: Performing Arts
Status: Non-Profit, Non-Professional
Paid Staff: 19
Seating Capacity: 1,800

6730
PADUCAH COMMUNITY COLLEGE FINE ARTS CENTER
4810 Alben Barkley Drive
PO Box 7380
Paducah, KY 42002-7380
Phone: 270-554-9290
Fax: 270-552-6310
e-mail: PCC.PR@kctcs.edu
Web Site: www.pccky.com
Management:
Chairman/Director: Gail Robinson
Founded: 1983
Performs At: Auditorium
Type of Stage: Proscenium
Seating Capacity: 500

6731
EATSERN KENTUCKY UNIVERSITY ALUMNI COLISEUM
521 Lancaster Avenue
Richmond, KY 40475
Phone: 859-622-2122
Fax: 859-622-5108
Web Site: www.ekusports.com
Management:
Athletic Director: John J Shafer

Busines Manager: David Parke
Founded: 1963
Paid Staff: 2
Volunteer Staff: 4

Louisiana

6732
RAPIDES COLISEUM
5600 Coliseum Boulevard
Alexandria, LA 71303
Phone: 318-443-1110
Fax: 318-443-0611
Web Site: www.louisianarangers.com
Management:
Executive Director: Don Guillory
Seating Capacity: 6,000

6733
ALEX BOX STADIUM
Louisiana State University
S Stadium Drive
Baton Rouge, LA 70803
Phone: 225-578-8226
Fax: 225-578-2430
e-mail: jkersh2@lsu.edu
Web Site: www.lsu.sports.net
Management:
President: William Jenkins
Athletic Facilities Manager: Jeff Kershaw
Founded: 1938
Status: Non-Profit, Professional
Seating Capacity: 7,760

6734
LSU UNION THEATER
Louisiana State University
Raphael Semmes Road
Baton Rouge, LA 70803-2504
Phone: 225-578-5128
Fax: 225-578-0612
e-mail: mderr@lsu.edu
Web Site: www.lsu.edu
Management:
General Manager: Michael Derr
Mission: The generation, preservation, dissemination, and application of knowledge and cultivation of the arts for the benefit of the people of the state, the nation, and the global community.
Founded: 1861
Seating Capacity: 1,250

6735
PETE MARAVICH ASSEMBLY CENTER
Louisiana State University
N Stadium Drive
Baton Rouge, LA 70803
Phone: 225-578-8205
Fax: 225-578-8437
e-mail: jkersh2@lsu.edu
Web Site: www.lsu.sports.net
Management:
Executive Director: Dwight Johnson
Assistant Director: Jeff Campbell
Operations Manager: Eddie Crawford
Assistant Operations Manager: Nathan Hanson
Athletic Facilities Manager: Jeff Kershaw
Founded: 1972
Status: For-Profit, Non-Professional
Paid Staff: 15
Seating Capacity: 4,500 - 14,164

6736
RIVER CENTER ARENA
275 S River Road
Baton Rouge, LA 70802
Phone: 225-389-3030
Fax: 225-389-4954
Web Site: www.brcentroplex.com
Seating Capacity: 8,500 - 12,000

6737
RIVER CENTER EXHIBITION HALL
275 S River Road
Baton Rouge, LA 70810
Phone: 225-389-3030
Fax: 225-389-4954
Web Site: www.brcentroplex.com
Type of Stage: 70,000 Sq Ft

6738
RIVER CENTER GRAND BALLROOM
275 S River Road
Baton Rouge, LA 70810
Phone: 225-389-3030
Fax: 225-389-4954
Web Site: www.brcentroplex.com
Seating Capacity: 2,100

6739
RIVER CENTER THEATRE FOR PERFORMING ARTS
275 S River Road
Baton Rouge, LA 70802
Phone: 225-389-3030
Fax: 225-389-4954
Web Site: www.brcentroplex.com
Founded: 1977
Seating Capacity: 1,900

6740
TIGER STADIUM
Louisiana State University
Athletic Department
Baton Rouge, LA 70894-5095
Mailing Address: PO Box 25095
Phone: 225-334-4578
Fax: 225-388-2430
e-mail: jkersh2@lsu.edu
Web Site: www.lsu.sports.net
Management:
   Athletic Facilities Manager: Jeff Kershaw
   Athletic Director: Stanley Bertman
Founded: 1924
Seating Capacity: 91,600

6741
EUNICE PLAYERS THEATRE
PO Box 306
Eunice, LA 70535
Phone: 337-546-0163
Fax: 337-457-3081
Management:
   President: David Manuel
Founded: 1970
Status: Non-Profit, Non-Professional

6742
GRAMBLING UNIVERSITY MEMORIAL GYMNASIUM
403 Main Street
PO Box 1193
Grambling, LA 71245
Phone: 318-274-2294
Fax: 318-274-6053
e-mail: daniew@gram.edu
Web Site: www.gram.edu
Management:
   University President: Horece Judson
   Human Resources Director: Karen Emmanuel
   Facility Director: Mark Blake
   Associate Director: Betty Jones
Founded: 1901
Status: Non-Profit, Professional
Paid Staff: 15
Seating Capacity: 2,200

6743
SOUTHEASTERN LOUISIANA UNIVERSITY STRAWBERRY STADIUM
910 Galloway Drive
Hammond, LA 70402
Mailing Address: PO Box 309
Phone: 504-549-2253
Fax: 504-549-2253
Management:
   Director: Tom Douple
Founded: 1936
Seating Capacity: 7,400

6744
SOUTHEASTERN LOUISIANA UNIVERSITY CENTER
800 W University Avenue
SLU 10309
Hammond, LA 70402
Phone: 985-549-2142
Fax: 985-549-3774
Web Site: www.lionsports.net/content/facilities
Officers:
   President: Randy Moffett
Management:
   Head Basketball Coach (M): Bill Kennedy
   Director: Larry M Hymel
   Athletic Director: Frank Pergolizzi
   Head Basketball Coach (W): Lori Davis Jones
   Event Operations Coordinator: Tiffany Rauschkolb
Founded: 1982
Status: Nonprofit, Non-Professional
Paid Staff: 60
Seating Capacity: 7,500

6745
HOUMA TERREBONNE CIVIC CENTER
346 Civic Center Boulevard
Houma, LA 70360
Phone: 985-850-4657
Fax: 985-850-4663
Toll-free: 888-771-4822
e-mail: info@houmaciviccenter.com
Web Site: www.houmaciviccenter.com
Management:
   Director: David M. Ohlmeyer
   Buisness Manager: Christopher Moore
   Event Coordinator: Betsy Breerwood
   Marketing Manager: Tammy Usie
Utilizes: Original Music Scores; Theatre Companies
Paid Staff: 15
Annual Attendance: 200,000+
Facility Category: Civic Center
Type of Stage: Portable
Stage Dimensions: 40x80x150
Seating Capacity: 5,000
Year Built: 1999
Cost: $20 million

Rental Contact: Linda McCarthy

6746
BLACKHAM COLISEUM
2330 Johnston Street
Lafayette, LA 70506
Phone: 337-482-2001
Fax: 337-482-5830
Management:
   General Manager: Joseph Evans
Founded: 1894
Status: Non-Profit, Non-Professional
Seating Capacity: 9,800

6747
CAJUN STADIUM
University of Southwestern Louisiana
Lafayette, LA 70506

Management:
   General Manager: Mike Broussard
Mission: UL football
Founded: 1971
Seating Capacity: 31,000

6748
CAJUNDOME AND CONVENTION CENTER
444 Cajundome Boulevard
Lafayette, LA 70506
Phone: 337-265-2100
Fax: 337-265-2311
e-mail: pdeville@cajundome.com
Web Site: www.cajundome.com
Management:
   Finance Director: Giselle Cormier
   Assistant Director: Pam DeVille
   Marketing Manager: Heidi Romero
Founded: 1984
Seating Capacity: 13,232

6749
HEYMANN PERFORMING ARTS CONVENTION CENTER
1373 South College Road
Lafayette, LA 70503
Phone: 337-291-5540
Fax: 337-291-5580
e-mail: eplumbar@lafayettegov.net
Web Site: www.heymann-center.com/
Management:
   Manager: Frank Bradshaw
   Box Office Manager: Elnora Plumbar
   Event Coordinator: Phillip Lukinovich
   Stage Manager: Dennis Skerrett
Mission: Located within the center of Lafayette, the Heymann Performing Arts Center is a theatre with a seating capacity of 2,230. Located adjacent to Lafayette's Oil Center, the auditorium provides bi-monthly performances by the Acadiana Symphony, a Broadway series and dozens of other community functions throughout the year.
Status: Non-Profit, Non-Professional
Paid Staff: 10

6750
LAFAYETTE COMMUNITY THEATRE
529 Jefferson Street
Lafayette, LA 70501
Phone: 318-235-1532

6751
ARTISTS CIVIC THEATRE AND STUDIO
One Reid Street
PO Box 278, Lake Charles
Lake Charles, LA 70602
Phone: 337-433-2287
e-mail: information@actstheatre.com
Web Site: www.actstheatre.com
Officers:
    Board Member: Rebecca Pack
Specialized Field: Community Theatre
Organization Type: Performing; Educational

6752
BURTON COLISEUM
McNeese State University
7001 Gulf Highway
Lake Charles, LA 70607
Phone: 337-562-4040
Fax: 337-562-4070
Toll-free: 800-622-3352
e-mail: webmaster@mcneese.edu
Web Site:
www.mcneesesports.cstv.com/facilities/mcne-mbb.html
Management:
    Executive Director: Mark Ethridge
Founded: 1976
Status: Non-Profit, Non-Professional
Paid Staff: 10
Seating Capacity: 8,000

6753
COWBOY STADIUM
McNeese State University
PO Box 91989
Lake Charles, LA 70609
Phone: 337-475-5200
Fax: 337-475-5202
Web Site: www.mcneese.edu
Management:
    Director: John Suydam

6754
LAKE CHARLES CIVIC CENTER - JAMES E SUDDUTH COLISEUM
900 Lakeshore Drive
PO Box 900, Lake Charles
Lake Charles, LA 70602
Phone: 337-491-1256
Fax: 337-491-1534
Web Site: www.lakecharlesciviccenter.bigstep.com
Seating Capacity: 7,450

6755
LAKE CHARLES CIVIC CENTER - EXHIBITION HALL
900 Lakeshore Drive
PO Box 900, Lake Charles
Lake Charles, LA 70602
Phone: 337-491-1256
Fax: 337-491-1534
Web Site: www.lakecharlesciviccenter.bigstep.com
Management:
    Director: Joe Toups
    Operations: Don Zimmerman
    Building Supervisor: Roger Sensat
    Marketing Manager: James Mayo
Mission: The Civic Center structure is a 3-level, 3-part complex housing the Rosa Hart Theatre, which has a fixed seating capacity of 2000, the Contraband and Jean Lafitte Rooms have a capacity of up to 500 each,

the Buccaneer has a capacity of up to 1000, the Exhibition Hall has a capacity of up to 1400, and the James E. Sudduth Coliseum has a capacity of 8000.

6756
LAKE CHARLES CIVIC CENTER - ROSA HART THEATRE
900 Lakeshore Drive
PO Box 900, Lake Charles
Lake Charles, LA 70602
Phone: 337-491-1256
Fax: 337-491-1534
Web Site: www.lakecharlesciviccenter.bigstep.com
Seating Capacity: 2,050

6757
FANT-EWING COLISEUM
University of Louisiana at Monroe
700 University Avenue
Monroe, LA 71209
Phone: 318-342-1000
Web Site: www.ulmathletics.com
Officers:
    President: James E Cofer Sr
Management:
    Athletic Director: Bobby Staub
    Marketing Director: Patti Thrumon
    Executive Director: Toni Bacon
Paid Staff: 50
Type of Stage: Wood
Seating Capacity: 8,000

6758
MALONE STADIUM
University of Louisiana at Monroe
308 Stadium Drive
Monroe, LA 71209
Phone: 318-342-5360
Fax: 318-342-5367
Web Site: www.nlu.edu
Management:
    Facilities Director: Richard Arnold
    Media Relations Director: Judy Wilson
    Tickets/Events Manager: Sharon Traxler
    Business Manager: Frank Galardo
Mission: Named in memory of James L Malone, the University of Louisiana/Monroe's winningest football coach, the first game was played on September 16, 1978. The seating capacity of the stadium is 30,427.
Founded: 1978
Status: Non-Profit, Professional
Paid Staff: 50
Paid Artists: 10

6759
MONROE CIVIC CENTER
401 Lea Joyner Memorial Expressway
Monroe, LA 71201
Phone: 318-329-2225
Fax: 318-329-2548
Web Site: www.ci.monroe.la.us/civiccenter.php
Management:
    Technical Services Director: Chris Kidd
    Marketing Manager: Melissa Thaxton
    Director: John Benedict
Mission: The Arena provides 44,000 square feet of exhibit space and seats 5,600 (Standard Concert Configuration). Larger Capacities available for events in the round. The Arena may be used for a multitude of events including Concerts, Large Banquets, Basketball, Circuses, Ice Events, Trade Shows, and Rodeos.

6760
PRATHER COLISEUM
NSU Athletic Department
Natchitoches, LA 71497
Phone: 318-357-5251
Fax: 318-357-4221
Web Site: www.nsudemons.com
Management:
    Director of Athletic Facilities: Charles Bourg
    Director of Sports Information: Doug Ireland
    Vice President External Affairs: Jerry Pierce
Mission: Prather Coliseum, an athletic facility for sporting events in basketball, volleyball and soccer, is the home of the Louisiana Sports Hall of Fame and the Graduate N Club Hall of Fame.
Founded: 1894
Status: For-Profit, Professional
Paid Staff: 80
Seating Capacity: 3,500

6761
TURPIN STADIUM
Northweatern Stare University
Nsu Athletic Field House
Natchitoches, LA 71497
Phone: 318-357-5251
Fax: 318-357-4221
Web Site: www.nsudemons.com
Management:
    VP: Jerry Pierce
    Director Athletics: Greg Burke
    Associate Director: Donnie Cox
    Business Manager: Roxanne Freeman
Seating Capacity: 16,000

6762
CONTEMPORARY ARTS CENTER
900 Camp Street
New Orleans, LA 70130
Phone: 504-528-3805
Fax: 504-528-3828
e-mail: info@cacno.org
Web Site: www.cacno.org
Management:
    President: Allen Eskew
    Executive Director: Jay Weigel
    Associate Director: Aimee Smallwood
    Director Development: Luisa Adelfio
Founded: 1976
Status: Non-Profit, Professional
Paid Staff: 30
Type of Stage: Concert Stage; Flexible
Seating Capacity: 200-3,500

6763
KIEFER UNO LAKEFRONT ARENA
University of New Orleans
6801 Franklin Avenue
New Orleans, LA 70122
Phone: 504-280-7171
Fax: 540-280-7178
e-mail: arena@uno.edu
Web Site: www.arena.uno.edu
Officers:
    GM: Marco Perez
    Facilities Manager: David Lendermon
Seating Capacity: 10,000

6764
LE PETIT THEATRE DU VIEUX CARRE
616 St Peter
New Orleans, LA 70116

Phone: 504-522-9958
Fax: 504-524-9027
Web Site: www.lepetittheatre.com
Management:
   President: Erol Lbarde
   Managing Director: Jim Word
   Executive Artistic Director: Sonny Borey
   Technical Director: Bill Walker
   Box Office Manager: Jenny Richardson
   House Manager: Linda Wegmann
Founded: 1917
Specialized Field: Community/Regional Theatre
Status: Non-Profit, Non-Professional
Paid Staff: 11
Seating Capacity: 325

6765
LOUIS J. ROUSSEL PERFORMANCE CENTER

Loyola University
6363 Saint Charles Avenue
New Orleans, LA 70118
Phone: 504-865-3037
e-mail: music@loyno.edu
Web Site: www.loyno.edu
Seating Capacity: 600

6766
LOUISIANA SUPERDOME

Sugar Bowl Drive
New Orleans, LA 70112
Phone: 504-587-3663
Fax: 504-587-3848
Toll-free: 800-756-7074
Web Site: www.superdome.com
Management:
   General Manager: Glenn Menard
   Assistant General Manager: Danny Vincens
   Media Relations Coordinator: Bill Curl
Founded: 1975
Type of Stage: Concert Stage
Seating Capacity: 87,500
Year Built: 1975
Year Remodeled: 1997

6767
LOYOLA UNIVERSITY THEATRE

Loyola University
6363 St Charles Avenue
New Orleans, LA 70118
Phone: 504-865-3840
Fax: 504-865-2284
Toll-free: 800-456-9652
e-mail: drama@loyno.edu
Web Site: www.loyno.edu
Management:
   President: Kevin S J Wildes
   Artistic Director: Georgia Gersham
   Dean, College of Music & Fine Arts: Dr. Donald Boomgaarden
   Associate Dean: Dr. Tony Decuir
Mission: The mission of the Department of Theatre Arts and Dance at Loyola University New Orleans is to educate and develop the whole person, focusing on undergraduate education that prepares students for meaningful lives, professional accomplishments, and responsible world citizenship. The Department distinguishes itself as a noteworthy center of learning by creating and structuring a collaborative learning environment.
Specialized Field: Theatre Arts; Dance
Status: Non-Profit, Non-Professional
Paid Staff: 14
Affiliations: ATHE; USITT

Type of Stage: Proscenium; Flexible Theatre
Seating Capacity: 150

6768
MAHALIA JACKSON THEATRE OF PERFORMING ARTS

New Orleans Cultural Center
1201 Saint Peter Street
New Orleans, LA 70116
Fax: 504-565-7477
Web Site: kturner@neworleansculturalcenter.com
Management:
   General Manager: Kathleen Turner
   Director Operations: Fred Hill
   Office Manager: Margo Baum
Seating Capacity: 2,300

6769
MORRIS FX JEFF SR MUNICIPAL AUDITORIUM

New Orleans Cultural Center
1201 Saint Peter Street
New Orleans, LA 70116
Phone: 504-218-0150
Fax: 504-218-0160
Management:
   Executive Director: Gene Blaun
Founded: 1930
Status: Non-profit, Professional
Paid Staff: 20
Seating Capacity: 6,500

6770
NEW ORLEANS ARENA

1501 Girod Street
New Orleans, LA 70113
Mailing Address: PO Box 52439 New Orleans, LA 70152
Phone: 504-587-3663
Fax: 504-587-3848
Web Site: www.neworleansarena.com
Management:
   Assistant General Manager: Mike Schilling
   General Manager: Glenn Menard
Founded: 1999
Seating Capacity: 17,232

6771
SAENGER THEATRE

143 N Rampart Street
New Orleans, LA 70112
Phone: 504-525-1052
Fax: 504-569-1533
Web Site: www.saengertheatre.com
Management:
   Booking Manager: Patricia Baham
Founded: 1927
Status: For-Profit, Professional
Paid Staff: 14
Seating Capacity: 2,794
Year Built: 1927
Year Remodeled: 1980

6772
STATE PALACE THEATRE

1108 Canal Street
PO Box 55278
New Orleans, LA 70112
Fax: 504-522-5880
e-mail: brunet-co@att.net
Web Site: www.statepalace.com
Management:
   Director/Booking: Robert Brunet

Theatre Manager: Douglas Castro
Seating Capacity: 3,000

6773
TULANE UNIVERSITY ALBERT LUPIN EXPERIMENTAL THEATRE

Department of Theatre and Dance
215 Mcwilliams Hall
New Orleans, LA 70118
Phone: 504-314-7760
Fax: 504-865-6737
Toll-free: 800-873-9283
e-mail: amichel@tulane.edu
Web Site: www.tulane.edu
Management:
   Artistic Director: Aimee Michel
   Artistic Director Dance Faculty: Alice Escher
Founded: 1937
Performs At: Albert Lupin Experimental Theatre, Dixon Hall
Type of Stage: Proscenium; Black Box
Seating Capacity: 1,000

6774
TULANE UNIVERSITY DEPARTMENT OF THEATRE AND DANCE

Tulane University
15 McWilliams Hall
New Orleans, LA 70118
Phone: 504-314-7760
Fax: 504-865-6737
Toll-free: 800-873-9283
e-mail: music@tulane.edu
Web Site: www.tulane.edu/~music
Management:
   Department Chair: Barbara Hayley
Founded: 1834
Seating Capacity: 3,600

6775
UNIVERSITY OF NEW ORLEANS PERFORMING ARTS CENTER

Lakefront
2000 Lakeshore Drive
New Orleans, LA 70148
Phone: 504-280-6317
Fax: 504-280-6318
Toll-free: 888-514-4275
e-mail: pkarnell@uno.edu
Web Site: www.uno.edu
Management:
   Chair: Phillip E. Karnell
Founded: 1956

6776
AILLET STADIUM

1450 W Alabama
Ruston, LA 71272
Phone: 318-257-3144
Fax: 318-257-3456
Management:
   Director Athletic Facilities: Tommy Sisemore
Founded: 1968
Seating Capacity: 30,200

6777
HOWARD CENTER FOR PERFORMING ARTS

Louisiana Tech
Corner of Arizona & Adams
Ruston, LA 71272

Mailing Address: PO Box 8608
Phone: 318-257-2711
Fax: 318-257-4571
e-mail: krobbins@latech.edu
Web Site: www.performingarts.latech.edu
Management:
  Director SPA: Kenneth Robbins
Founded: 1898
Paid Staff: 6
Annual Attendance: 2,000
Type of Stage: Proscenium
Seating Capacity: 150
Year Built: 1938
Year Remodeled: 2001

6778
THOMAS ASSEMBLY CENTER
Louisiana Tech University
PO Box 3042
Ruston, LA 71272
Phone: 318-257-4111
Fax: 318-257-4437
Management:
  Manager: Tommy Sisemore
Seating Capacity: 8,698

6779
CENTENARY COLLEGE RECITAL HALL
Hurley School of Music
PO Box 41188
Shreveport, LA 71134
Phone: 318-869-5011
Fax: 318-869-5248
e-mail: music@centenary.edu
Web Site: www.centenary.edu
Management:
  Dean: Gale Odom
Founded: 1852
Status: Non-Profit, Professional
Paid Staff: 35
Paid Artists: 12

6780
HIRSCH MEMORIAL COLISEUM
State Fair of Louisiana
3701 Hudson Avenue
Shreveport, LA 71109
Phone: 318-635-1361
Fax: 318-631-4909
e-mail: info@statefairoflouisiana.com
Web Site: www.statefairoflouisiana.com
Officers:
  General Manager: Sam Giordano
  Assistant Manger: Chris Giordano
  Administrative Assistant: Mary M Gasper
  Secretary/Treasurer: James Elrod
Management:
  Chairman: George McInnis
  Vice Chairman: William T Cawthorne
Mission: To serve as the State Fair of Louisiana's
prime facility; to host-year round events such as major
concerts, circuses, rodeos, ice shows, sporting events
and motor thrill shows.
Founded: 1954
Status: Non-Profit
Paid Staff: 10
Budget: $80,000
Income Sources: Concerts; Rodeos; Circuses
Annual Attendance: 300,000
Facility Category: Multi-Purpose
Type of Stage: Portable
Seating Capacity: 10,300
Year Built: 1954
Year Remodeled: 1994

Cost: $300,000
Rental Contact: Mary M Gasper

6781
SHREVEPORT CIVIC THEATRE
600 Clyde Fant Parkway
Shreveport, LA 71101
Phone: 318-673-5100
Fax: 318-673-5105
e-mail: spar@ci.shreveport.la.us
Web Site: www.ci.shreveport.la.us
Management:
  President: Ronnie Hammond
Specialized Field: Municipal Performance Theater
Status: Non-Profit, Professional
Paid Staff: 50
Type of Stage: Proscenium
Stage Dimensions: 49 x 41
Seating Capacity: 1,725
Year Built: 1965
Year Remodeled: 1997

6782
SHREVEPORT MUNICIPAL AUDITORIUM
705 Elvis Presley Avenue
Shreveport, LA 71101
Phone: 318-673-5100
Fax: 318-673-5105
e-mail: spar@ci.shreveport.la.us
Web Site: www.cishreveport.la.us
Founded: 1900
Status: Non-Profit, Professional
Type of Stage: Proscenium
Stage Dimensions: 58'x 29'x 37'
Seating Capacity: 3,007
Year Built: 1929

6783
STRAND THEATRE
619 Louisiana Avenue
PO Box 1547
Shreveport, LA 71165
Phone: 318-226-1481
Fax: 318-424-5434
Toll-free: 800-313-6373
e-mail: strand@thestrandtheatre.com
Web Site: www.thestrandtheatre.com
Officers:
  President: Ron Weems
  Executive Director: Danny Fogger
  Administrative Assistant: Teresa Carmack
Management:
  Technical Director: Bill Gaston
  Assistant Director: Lily Herd
Founded: 1925

6784
NICHOLLS STATE UNIVERSITY GYM
PO Box 2032
Thibodaux, LA 70310
Phone: 504-448-4794
Fax: 504-448-4814
Toll-free: 877-642-6557
e-mail: nichweb@nicholls.edu
Web Site: www.nicholls.edu
Management:
  Athletic Director: Robert J Bernardi
  Senior Administrator: Louise Bonin
  Sports Information Director: Bobby Galinsky
Founded: 1948
Seating Capacity: 15,500

6785
AUGUSTA CIVIC CENTER NORTH STAGE
76 Community Drive
Augusta, ME 04330
Phone: 207-626-2405
Fax: 207-626-5968
e-mail: info@augustaciviccenter.org
Web Site: www.augustaciviccenter.org
Management:
  Director: Dana Colwill
  Office Manager: Betty L Brann
  Reservation Coordinator: Nancy M Dumont
Mission: To promote and facilitate various events and
group functions in order to enhance area trade and
commerce.
Seating Capacity: 6,433

6786
AUGUSTA CIVIC CENTER ARENA CENTER STAGE
76 Community Drive
Augusta, ME 4330
Phone: 207-626-2405
Fax: 207-626-5968
Web Site: www.augustaciviccenter.org
Management:
  Director: Dana Colwill
Seating Capacity: 7,264

6787
AUGUSTA CIVIC CENTER HALF HOUSE CONCERT STAGE
76 Community Drive
Augusta, ME 4330
Phone: 207-626-2405
Fax: 207-626-5968
Web Site: www.augustaciviccenter.org
Management:
  Director: Dana Colwill
Seating Capacity: 3,653

6788
BANGOR CIVIC CENTER & AUDITORIUM
Bass Park Complex
100 Dutton Street
Bangor, ME 04401
Phone: 207-947-5555
Fax: 207-947-5105
Web Site: www.bangorciviccenter.com
Mission: To serve as Maine's premier multi-purpose
convention, tradeshow, meeting and entertainment
show place.
Founded: 1954
Type of Stage: Portable
Seating Capacity: 6,000

6789
MORRELL GYM
Bowdoin College
6200 College Station
Brunswick, ME 04011
Phone: 207-725-3000
Fax: 207-725-3477
Web Site: www.bowdoin.edu
Officers:
  Director: Burgwell Howard
  Associate Director: Susan Leonard
Seating Capacity: 2,000

6790
PICKARD THEATRE
Bowdoin College
22 Elm Street
Brunswick, ME 04011
Phone: 207-725-8769
Fax: 207-725-1199
e-mail: info@msmt.org
Web Site:
www.msmt.org/default.asp?contentID=617&rc=589&zm
=617
Management:
   Executive Director: Steven C Peterson
   Artistic Director: Charles Abbott
   General Manager: Stephanie Dupal
   Company Manager: Kathi Kacinski
Mission: Historic Pickard Theater, located on the
beautiful Bowdoin College campus within walking
distance of downtown Brunswick, was originally
constructed to honor the memory of the Bowdoin
students who served on both sides during the Civil War.
Maine State Music Theatre had its genesis at The
Pickard in 1959. The theatre is air-conditioned and
offers comfortable seating with an excellent view of the
stage.
Founded: 1794
Status: Non-Profit, Non-Professional
Paid Staff: 10
Type of Stage: Proscenium
Seating Capacity: 600

6791
CAMDEN OPERA HOUSE
29 Elm Street
PO Box 1207
Camden, ME 04843
Phone: 207-236-7963
Fax: 207-236-7956
Web Site: www.camdenoperahouse.com
Officers:
   President: Jean Friedman White
Management:
   Manager: Kerry Hadley
Mission: Elegant, historic yet practical facility for rental;
providing affordable space for local nonprofit groups to
perform and meet; conference and meeting facility,
wedding parties.
Founded: 1894
Specialized Field: Theatre; Concerts; and Conference
Rentals
Status: Non-Profit, Professional
Paid Staff: 2
Volunteer Staff: 12
Budget: $100,000
Income Sources: Rentals; Show Production
Performs At: Proscenium Stage w/Thrust
Annual Attendance: 12,000
Facility Category: Performing Arts
Type of Stage: Thrust
Stage Dimensions: 37'x34'
Seating Capacity: 500
Year Built: 1894
Year Remodeled: 1994
Cost: $250-$800+
Rental Contact: Kenny Hedley
Resident Groups: Maine Grand Opera

6792
OLIN ARTS CENTER
Bates College
75 Russell Street
Lewiston, ME 04240
Phone: 207-786-6135
Fax: 207-786-8335
Web Site: www.bates.edu/tour-olin-arts-center.xml
Mission: addition to the Bates College Museum of Art
and a 300-seat concert hall, Olin houses a slide library,
classrooms, faculty offices, individual and group
practice rooms for musicians, art studios (including a
drawing studio with a panoramic view of Lake
Andrews), and two photographic darkrooms.
Year Built: 1986

6793
UNIVERSITY OF MAINE PERFORMING
ARTS CENTER
Arts Downeast
9 O'Brien Avenue
Machias, ME 04654
Phone: 207-255-1200
Fax: 207-255-4864
e-mail: stewartb@maine.edu
Web Site: www.umm.maine.edu
Mission: Host to many campus and community
meetings, seminars, festivals and performing arts. Also
the home of the UMM Theater and Music Programs, as
well as the Down River Theater production company
and the Maine Youth Summer Theater Institute.
Presents a variety of dramas, comedies and musicals.
Founded: 1909
Facility Category: Amphitheater
Seating Capacity: 358
Organization Type: Amphitheater Auditorium

6794
JOHN LANE'S OGUNQUIT PLAYHOUSE
PO Box 915
Ogunquit, ME 03907
Phone: 207-646-2402
Fax: 207-646-4732
e-mail: bkenney@ogunquitplayhouse.org
Web Site: www.ogunquitplayhouse.org
Officers:
   President: Karen M Maxwell
   1st VP: Donna L Lewis
   2nd VP: Elizabeth M Hirshom
   Secretary: Cathy J Brown
   Treasurer: Jeffrey Troiano
   Assistant Treasurer: Henry J Weller
   Clerk: Ronald J Schneider, Jr, Esq
   Guild President: Patti Levenson
Management:
   Executive Artistic Director: Bradford T Kenney
   Associate Artistic Director: Kimberly Starling
   Marketing/Publicity: Tammy J Heon
   Playbill Advertising Sales: Jaclynn Hones
   Assistant to the Directors: Jean Benda
   Business Manager: Gary Ng
Founded: 1933
Year Built: 1933

6795
MAINE CENTER FOR THE ARTS AT THE
UNIVERSITY OF MAINE
5746 Maine Center for the Arts
Orono, ME 04469
Phone: 207-581-1755
Fax: 207-581-1837
Toll-free: 877-486-2364
e-mail: john.patches@umit.maine.edu
Web Site: www.ume.maine.edu/mca
Management:
   Executive Director: John I Patches
   Associate Director, MCA: Adele Adkins
   Ticket Services Director: Mary Addison
   Manager of Theater Operations: Joe Cota
   Accounting Supervisor: Peggy Ford
   Box Office Assistant: Susan Melvin
   Technical Director: Jeffrey Richards
   Assistant Technical Director: Scott Stitham
   Outreach/Education Coordinator: Stephen Wicks
Mission: Hosts a wide variety of events, presenting
classical and contemporary music, dance, theatre,
comedy and lectures.
Founded: 1986
Specialized Field: Performing Arts
Paid Staff: 10
Volunteer Staff: 60
Seating Capacity: 1,629

6796
UNIVERSITY OF MAINE ALUMNI
STADIUM
Memorial Gymnasium
Orono, ME 04469
Phone: 207-581-1110
Fax: 207-581-3070
e-mail: john.gregory@umit.maine.edu
Web Site: www.umaine.edu
Management:
   Athletic Director: Suzanne Tyler

6797
CUMBERLAND COUNTY CIVIC CENTER
1 Civic Center Square
Portland, ME 4101
Phone: 207-775-3481
Fax: 207-828-8344
Web Site: www.theciviccenter.com
Officers:
   Chair: Dale Olmstead, Jr
   Vice Chair: Neal Pratt
   Treasurer: Richard Ranaghan, Jr
Management:
   General Manager: Steve Crane
   Controller: Mark Eddy
   Box Office Manager: Mark Warner
   Operations Manager: James Leo
   Marketing Manager: Roberta Wright
Mission: A multi-purpose entertainment and sports
facility that hosts a wide variety of family shows,
concerts, sporting events, and trade shows.
Founded: 1977
Paid Staff: 212

6798
HADLOCK FIELD
271 Park Avenue
Portland, ME 4102
Phone: 207-874-8200
Fax: 207-874-8130
e-mail: arl@portlandmaine.gov
Web Site: www.portlandevents.com
Management:
   Director Event Services: Dennis E Sargen
   Technical Director: Patty Grass
   Director Operations: Robert Leeman
   Acting Division Director: Authur H Stephenson
Founded: 1994
Facility Category: Arena
Type of Stage: Sports Arena
Stage Dimensions: 60x40
Seating Capacity: 7,000
Year Built: 1915
Year Remodeled: 1990

6799
MERRILL AUDITORIUM
20 Myrtle Street
Portland, ME 4101
Phone: 207-874-8200
Fax: 207-874-8130
Web Site: www.portlandevents.com
Management:
Executive Director: Arthur Stevenson
Founded: 1997
Status: Non-Profit, Professional
Facility Category: Upscale Arts Facility
Type of Stage: Proscenium
Seating Capacity: 1900
Year Built: 1912
Year Remodeled: 1996

6800
PORTLAND EXPOSITION BUILDING
239 Park Avenue
Portland, ME 04102
Phone: 207-874-8200
Fax: 207-874-8130
Web Site: www.portlandevents.com
Officers:
Division Director: Arthur Stephenson
Management:
Booking Coordinator: Andrea Smith
Founded: 1915
Specialized Field: Series & Festivals; Dance; Instrumental Music; Musical Theatre; Theatrical Group; Vocal Music
Status: Non-Profit, Professional
Facility Category: Arena
Type of Stage: Portable
Stage Dimensions: 60' wide x 40' deep
Seating Capacity: 3,000
Year Built: 1914

6801
STATE THEATRE
609 Congress Street
PO Box 4152
Portland, ME 04101
Phone: 207-780-8265
Web Site: www.liveatthestate.com
Management:
Owner: Grant Wilson
House Manager: John Octera
Seating Capacity: 1,750

6802
ROCKPORT OPERA HOUSE
Central St
Rockport, ME 04856
Phone: 207-236-2514
Web Site: http://town.rockport.me.us/operahouse
Management:
Executive Director: Thomas Wolf
Administrative Director: Ann Tani
Director Marketing: Kathy Maloney
Mission: Music, dance, poetry and plays are performed in the air-conditioned auditorium.
Founded: 1961
Type of Stage: Flexible
Seating Capacity: Auditorium 400; Meeting Room 100
Year Built: 1891
Year Remodeled: 1993
Cost: $1 million

6803
CELEBRATION BARN THEATER
190 Stock Farm Road
South Paris, ME 04281
Phone: 207-743-8452
e-mail: info@celebrationbarn.com
Web Site: www.celebrationbarn.com
Officers:
President: Davis Robinson
VP: Barbara Taylor
Secretary: Fritz Grobe
Treasurer: Connie Allen
Executive Director: Amanda Huotari
Management:
Executive Director: Amanda Huotari
Mission: Celebration Barn is a center for creating or performing original theatre. Performances, workshops and residencies are offered May-October.
Utilizes: Actors; Artists-in-Residence; Collaborating Artists; Collaborations; Community Members; Contract Actors; Dance Companies; Dancers; Five Seasonal Concerts; Guest Choreographers; Guest Designers; Guest Directors; Guest Ensembles; Guest Speakers; High School Drama; Instructors; Local Artists; Local Artists & Directors; Local Talent; Lyricists; Multi Collaborations; Original Music Scores; Paid Performers; Poets; Resident Artists; Resident Companies
Founded: 1972
Seating Capacity: 125
Year Built: 1902

6804
STRIDER THEATER
Colby College
4520 Mayflower Hill
Waterville, ME 04901-8845
Phone: 207-859-4520
Fax: 207-859-4533
Web Site: www.colby.edu/theater
Management:
Adjunct Professor/Chair: Christine Wentzel
Technical Director/Associate Chair: John D Ervin
Assistant Professor: Laura Chakravarty Box
Adjunct Associate Professor: James C Thurston
Administrative Secretary: Debi Ward
Professor: Joylynn Wing
Mission: To promote the historical, theoretical, and experiential study of these performing arts as vital and important areas of inquiry for liberal arts students.
Founded: 1817
Status: Non-Profit, Non-Professional
Paid Staff: 9
Facility Category: Proscenium
Type of Stage: Proscenium
Seating Capacity: 262
Year Built: 1976

6805
WATERVILLE OPERA HOUSE
93 Main Street
Waterville, ME 04901
Phone: 207-873-5381
Fax: 207-861-7096
Web Site: www.operahouse.com
Officers:
Chairman: Earle Bessey III
President: Tom Misner
Treasurer: Kathleen Livollen
Management:
Executive Director: Diane Bryan
Office Manager: Bridgett Campbell
Development Director: Barbara Allen
Production Coordinator: Joan Phillips-Sandy
Mission: The purpose of which is to maintain, restore and enhance the Opera House as a public facility for the Arts and cultural enrichment of the community.
Founded: 1902
Status: Nonprofit, Professional
Annual Attendance: 80,000
Type of Stage: Proscenium
Seating Capacity: 924

Maryland

6806
FRANCIS SCOTT KEY AUDITORIUM
60 College Avenue
St. John's College
Annapolis, MD 21401
Phone: 410-626-2547
Fax: 410-626-2885
Web Site: www.sjca.edu/college
Management:
Facilities Director: Diane Ensor
Founded: 1657
Status: Non-Profit, Non-Professional
Paid Staff: 200
Seating Capacity: 600
Year Built: 1958

6807
MARYLAND HALL FOR THE CREATIVE ARTS
801 Chase Street
Annapolis, MD 21401
Phone: 410-263-5544
Fax: 410-263-5114
Toll-free: 866-438-3808
e-mail: info@mdhallarts.org
Web Site: www.marylandhall.org
Officers:
Preisdent: Robert Leib
VP: Bill Hughes
Treasurer: Bud Billups
Secretary: Cathy Belcher
Mission: Provides a broad range of arts-related programming for people of all ages, backgrounds and socio-economic levels.
Founded: 1972
Specialized Field: Theatre; School
Status: Non-Profit, Professional
Paid Staff: 20
Year Built: 1979

6808
US NAVAL ACADEMY ALUMNI HALL
US Naval Academy
675 Decatour Road
Annapolis, MD 21402
Phone: 410-293-2234
Fax: 410-293-3218
Web Site: www.usna.edu
Management:
Manager: Gregory B Zingler
Founded: 1845
Status: Non-Profit, Non-Professional

6809
ARENA PLAYERS PLAYHOUSE
801 McCulloh Street
Baltimore, MD 21201
Phone: 410-728-6500
Fax: 410-383-2692
Web Site: www.thearenaplayers.org

6810

CENTER STAGE

700 North Calvert Street
Baltimore, MD 21202
Phone: 410-986-4000
Fax: 410-539-3912
e-mail: info@centerstage.org
Web Site: www.centerstage.org
Management:
    Artistic Director: Irene Lewis
    Managing Director: Michael Ross
    Associate Managing Director: Del W Risberg
    Operations Director: Harry DeLair
Mission: An artistically driven institution, producing and developing an eclectic repertory in collaboration with leading theater artists for a diverse audience, interested in challenging, bold, thought-provoking work.
Utilizes: Actors; AEA Actors; Artists-in-Residence; Guest Accompanists; Guest Companies; Guest Conductors; Guest Designers; Guest Instructors; Guest Lecturers; Guest Musical Directors; Guest Soloists; Instructors; Original Music Scores; Performance Artists; Selected Students; Student Interns
Founded: 1963
Budget: $6.2 million
Affiliations: BACVA, Baltimore Tourism Association, Baltimore Theatre Alliance, TCG, AEA
Type of Stage: Semi-Thrust and Flexible
Stage Dimensions: 40'x36' and 67'x118'
Seating Capacity: 541 and 850
Year Remodeled: 2000
Rental Contact: Harry Delair

6811

DUNBAR PERFORMING ARTS CENTER

1400 Orleans Street
Baltimore, MD 21231
Phone: 410-534-6614

6812

FIRST MARINER ARENA

201 W Baltimore Street
Baltimore, MD 21201
Phone: 410-347-2020
Fax: 410-347-2042
Web Site: www.firstmarinerarena.com
Management:
    General Manager: Donna P Julian
    Contracts Coordinator: Trish Howerton
Founded: 1999
Status: For-Profit, Professional
Performs At: Entertainment; Sports
Seating Capacity: 14,000
Year Built: 1962
Year Remodeled: 1984

6813

JOHNS HOPKINS

Wolman House
3213 N Charles Street
Baltimore, MD 21218
Phone: 410-516-7159
e-mail: thehop@jhu.edu
Management:
    Director: Suzanne Pratt

6814

JOHNS HOPKINS UNIVERSITY HOMEWOOD FIELD

3400 N Charles Street
Baltimore, MD 21218

Phone: 410-516-7490
Fax: 410-516-7482
e-mail: andrew.harrington@jhu.edu
Web Site: www.hopkinssports.com
Officers:
    President: Ronald S Daniels
Management:
    Managing Director: Andrew Harrington
    Athletic Director: Tom Calder
Founded: 1876
Specialized Field: Education
Status: Non-Profit, Non-Professional

6815

KRAUSHAAR AUDITORIUM

Goucher College
1021 Delaney Valley Road
Baltimore, MD 21204
Phone: 410-769-5054
Fax: 410-337-6123
Web Site: www.goucher.edu/conferenceservices
Officers:
    Director: Margaret Ermer
    Assistant Director: Ann Grabenstein
Seating Capacity: 980

6816

LYRIC OPERA HOUSE

140 W Mount Royal Avenue
Baltimore, MD 21201
Phone: 410-685-5086
Fax: 410-332-8234
Web Site: www.lyricoperahouse.com
Management:
    President: Sandy Ichmond
    Executive Director: Tim Kormberger
Founded: 1896
Status: Non-Profit, Professional

6817

MCMANUS THEATER

Loyola College
4501 N Charles Street
Baltimore, MD 21210
Phone: 410-617-5077
Fax: 410-617-2211
Web Site: www.loyola.edu
Officers:
    President: Fr Brian Linnane, SJ
Management:
    Event Services Director: Jospeh Bradley
Founded: 1852
Specialized Field: Series & Festivals:
Status: Non-Profit, Non-Professional

6818

MEYERHOFF SYMPHONY HALL

1212 Cathedral Street
Baltimore, MD 21201
Fax: 410-783-8004
e-mail: darmor@baltimoresymphony.org
Web Site: www.baltimoresymphony.org
Management:
    House Manager: Allen McCallum
    Facility Booking: Dori Armor
    Box Office Manager: Kathy Marciano
Seating Capacity: 2,443

6819

REITZ ARENA

Loyola College Maryland
4501 North Charles Street
Baltimore, MD 21210

Phone: 410-617-5077
Fax: 410-617-2211
e-mail: jflllynn@loyola.com
Web Site: www.loyola.edu
Management:
    Director Event Services: Joan Flynn
Specialized Field: Series & Festivals
Seating Capacity: 3,500

6820

BOWIE STATE UNIVERSITY MARTIN LUTHER KING JR. CENTER

14000 Jericho Park Road
Bowie, MD 20715-9465
Phone: 301-464-3441
Toll-free: 877-772-6943

6821

PRINCE GEORGE'S STADIUM

Bowie Baysox
4101 Crain Highway
Bowie, MD 20716
Phone: 301-805-6000
Fax: 301-464-4911
e-mail: info@baysox.com
Web Site: www.baysox.com
Management:
    General Manager: Brian Shallcross
    Assistant General Manager: Phil Wrye
    Box Office Manager: Charlene Fewer
Founded: 1993
Opened: 1993
Facility Category: Minor League Baseball Facility
Seating Capacity: 10,000
Rental Contact: Brian Shallcross

6822

CLARICE SMITH PERFORMING ARTS CENTER

University of Maryland
Clarice Smtih Performing Arts Center
Suite 3800
College Park, MD 20742-1625
Phone: 301-405-7794
e-mail: contact.claricesmith@umd.edu
Web Site: claricesmithcenter.umd.edu
Management:
    Executive Director: Susie Farr
    Director Marketing/Communications: Erica Bondarev
    Director, Artistic Initiatives: Paul Brohan
Mission: The Clarice Smith Performing Arts Center transforms lives through sustained engagement with the arts.
Utilizes: Artists-in-Residence; Choreographers; Collaborations; Commissioned Composers; Educators; Five Seasonal Concerts; Instructors; Paid Performers; Soloists; Students; Student Interns
Founded: 2001
Paid Staff: 50
Budget: $6.1 Million
Performs At: 6 Venues
Year Built: 2001
Rental Contact: Nicholas Roberts
Organization Type: The Clarice Smith Performing Arts Center has six performance venues. In addition to offering a presenting series, the Center serves as home to the UM School of Music, Departments of Dance and Theatre, and the Michelle Smith Perf

6823
TOBY'S DINNER THEATRE
5900 Symphony Woods Road
PO Box 1003
Columbia, MD 21044
Phone: 410-730-8311
Fax: 410-730-8311
Toll-free: 800-888-6297
e-mail: info@tobysdinnertheatre.com
Web Site: www.tobysdinnertheatre.com
Founded: 1980

6824
JOHN ADDISON CONCERT HALL
10701 Livingston Road
Fort Washington, MD 20744
Phone: 301-203-6070
Fax: 301-203-6071
Web Site: www.pgparks.com
Management:
Managing Director: Lawrence J Knowles
Founded: 1989
Status: Non-Profit, Non-Professional

6825
MARYLAND THEATRE
21-27 South Potomac Street
Hagerstown, MD 21740
Phone: 301-790-3500
Fax: 301-791-6114
e-mail: tix@mdtheatre.org
Web Site: www.mdtheatre.org
Management:
Executive Director: Brian Sullivan
Mission: Performances include country artists, comedians, orchestra concerts, children's shows, musicians, recitals, stage shows, and others.
Founded: 1915
Seating Capacity: 1,300

6826
COLLEGE OF SOUTHERN MARYLAND FINE ARTS CENTER
8730 Mitchell Road
La Plata, MD 02646
Phone: 301-934-7828
Fax: 301-934-7682
Toll-free: 800-933-9177
e-mail: bxoffice@csmd.edu
Web Site: www.csmd.edu
Officers:
Chair Communication Arts/Humanities: Ronald Brown
Management:
Technical Director: Keith Hight
Founded: 1959
Status: Non-Profit, Professional
Paid Staff: 100
Paid Artists: 100
Type of Stage: Proscenium
Seating Capacity: 404
Year Built: 1983

6827
STRATHMORE
5301 Tuckerman Lane
North Bethesda, MD 20852
Phone: 301-581-5200
e-mail: concerts@strathmore.org
Web Site: www.strathmore.org
Officers:
President/CEO: Eliot Pfanstiehl
Management:

VP Artistic Director: Shelley Brown
Director Fine Arts: Millie S Shott
Mission: Presents a lively and diverse program of art exhibitions, concerts and performing arts programs, and literary lectures and events.
Founded: 1983
Status: Non-Profit, Professional
Paid Staff: 30

6828
ROLAND E POWELL CONVENTION CENTER
4001 Coastal Highway
40th Street
Ocean City, MD 21842
Phone: 410-289-8311
Fax: 410-289-0058
Toll-free: 800-626-2326
Web Site: www.ococean.com
Management:
Director: Mike Noah
Status: For-Profit, Professional
Paid Staff: 75

6829
GORDON CENTER FOR PERFORMING ARTS
3506 Gwynbrook Avenue
Owings Mills, MD 21117
Phone: 410-356-7469
Fax: 410-356-7605
e-mail: gordoncenter@hotmail.com
Web Site: www.gordoncenter.com
Management:
Executive Director: Nancy Goldberg
Technical Director: Dave Eske
Mission: To offer professional, high-quality performances in all genres to all ages.
Utilizes: Dance Companies; Dancers; Filmmakers; Guest Accompanists; Guest Companies; Guest Soloists; Multi Collaborations; Multimedia; Original Music Scores; Singers; Special Technical Talent; Theatre Companies; Touring Companies
Founded: 1995
Specialized Field: Varied
Status: Nonprofit
Income Sources: Grants; Endowments
Annual Attendance: 35,000
Facility Category: Performing Arts Center
Type of Stage: Proscenium
Stage Dimensions: 70'x 40'
Seating Capacity: 550
Year Built: 1995
Rental Contact: Nancy Goldberg

6830
GILDENHORN/SPEISMAN CENTER FOR THE ARTS
Jewish Community Center of Greater Washington
6125 Montrose Road
Rockville, MD 20852
Phone: 301-881-0100
Fax: 301-881-5512
Web Site: www.jccgw.org
Management:
President: Marcy Cohen
CEO: Arnie Sohniki
Director Adult Services: Selma Sweetbaum
Founded: 1923
Status: Non-Profit, Professional
Paid Staff: 60
Performs At: Gliddenhorn/Speisman Center for the Arts

6831
MONTGOMERY COLLEGE ROBERT E PARILLA PERFORMING ARTS CENTER
51 Mannakee Street
Rockville, MD 20850-1195
Phone: 301-251-5301
Fax: 301-251-7542
e-mail: boffice@montgomerycollege.edu
Web Site: www.montgomerycollege.edu/PAC/
Management:
President: Charlene Munley
Executive Director: William Campbell
Artistic Director: Deborah Fyodorov
Mission: The theater facility of Montgomery College hosts visiting artists as well as collegiate productions. Fully handicapped accessible.
Founded: 1984
Status: Non-Profit, Non-Professional
Paid Staff: 7
Paid Artists: 10

6832
WICOMICO CIVIC CENTER
500 Glen Avenue
Salisbury, MD 21804
Phone: 410-548-4900
Fax: 410-546-0490
Web Site: www.wicomicociviccenter.org
Management:
Manager: Charles R Rousseau
Director Marketing/Public Relations: Amanda Beck
Operations Engineer: Bryan Furches
Founded: 1950
Status: Non-Profit, Professional
Paid Staff: 25

6833
STEPHENS AUDITORIUM
Towson State University
8000 York Road
Towson, MD 21252
Phone: 410-830-3289
Fax: 410-830-3914
Web Site: www.towson.edu/theatre
Founded: 1915
Year Remodeled: 1991

6834
TOWSON CENTER ARENA
Towson University
8000 York Road
Towson, MD 21252
Phone: 410-704-2763
Fax: 410-704-5069
Web Site: www.towson.edu
Officers:
Director: Bill Murphy
Ticket Office Manager: Joanne Repasi
Opened: 1976
Seating Capacity: 5,000

Massachusetts

6835
AMHERST COLLEGE LEFRAK GYM
Amherst College
220 S Pleasant Street
PO Box 5000
Amherst, MA 01002

Phone: 413-542-5773
Fax: 413-542-5845
e-mail: info@amherst.edu
Web Site: www.amherst.edu
Officers:
President: Anthony W Marx
Chairman: Jide J Zeitlin
Management:
Director: Suzanne Coffey
Seating Capacity: 2,400

6836
UNIVERSITY OF MASSACHUSETTS FINE ARTS CENTER

151 Presidents Drive
Amherst, MA 01003-9336
Phone: 413-545-2511
Fax: 413-545-2018
Web Site: www.fineartscenter.com
Management:
Director: Dr Willie L Hill Jr
Development Director: Lucia Miller
General Manager: Sonia Kudia
Utilizes: Artists-in-Residence; Collaborations; Dance Companies; Lyricists; Multi Collaborations; Multimedia; Theatre Companies; Touring Companies
Founded: 1975
Status: Non-Profit
Paid Staff: 50
Facility Category: Concert Hall; Bowker Auditorium
Type of Stage: Proscenium
Seating Capacity: 1980; 700

6837
WILLIAM D MULLINS MEMORIAL CENTER

University of Massachusetts
200 Commonwealth Avenue
Amherst, MA 01003
Phone: 413-545-3001
Fax: 413-545-3005
Web Site: www.mullinscenter.com
Management:
General Manager: Bob Weiss
Operations: J R Westveer
Marketing: Scott Sasenbury
Founded: 1994
Status: For-Profit, Professional
Seating Capacity: 10,500

6838
BERKLEE PERFORMANCE CENTER

Berklee College of Music
136 Massachusetts Avenue
Boston, MA 02115
Phone: 617-747-2261
Fax: 617-375-9228
e-mail: bpc@berklee.edu
Web Site: www.berkleebpc.com
Officers:
President: Roger H Brown
Chair: Jeff Shames
Management:
Manager: Ed Liberatore
Seating Capacity: 1,220

6839
BOSTON CENTER FOR THE ARTS PLAZA THEATRE

539 Tremont Street
Boston, MA 02116

Phone: 617-426-5000
Fax: 617-426-5336
e-mail: info@bcaonline.org
Web Site: www.bcaonline.org
Officers:
Chair: Philip Lovejoy
Management:
Director Development/Marketing: James K Marko
Mission: A nonprofit performing and visual arts complex that supports working artists to create, perform and exhibit new work; builds new audiences; and connects arts to community
Founded: 1968
Status: Non-Profit, Professional

6840
CITI PERFORMING ART CENTER WANG THEATRE

270 Tremont Street
Boston, MA 02116
Phone: 617-482-9393
Fax: 617-451-1436
e-mail: info@citicenter.org
Web Site: www.citicenter.org
Officers:
President/CEO: Josiah A Spaulding Jr
Management:
General Manager: Michael Szczepkowski
Marketing: Jill Kremins
Development Director: Nancy Skinner
Utilizes: Community Members; Community Talent; Educators; High School Drama; Scenic Designers; Theatre Companies
Founded: 1988
Status: Non-Profit, Professional
Paid Staff: 50
Facility Category: Theatre
Type of Stage: Proscenium
Stage Dimensions: 80 x 60
Seating Capacity: 3561
Year Built: 1910
Year Remodeled: 1996

6841
CUTLER MAJESTIC THEATRE AT EMERSON COLLEGE

219 Tremont Street
Boston, MA 02116-4117
Phone: 617-824-8000
Fax: 617-824-3209
Toll-free: 800-233-3123
e-mail: majestic@emerson.edu
Web Site: www.maj.org
Management:
General Manager: Lance Olson
Marketing: Erica Laird
Director: Warren West
Founded: 1984
Status: Non-Profit, Non-Professional
Paid Staff: 40
Volunteer Staff: 40
Annual Attendance: 150,000
Facility Category: Opera/Dance Theatre
Type of Stage: Proscenium
Stage Dimensions: 40'x 40'
Seating Capacity: 1,000
Year Built: 1903
Year Remodeled: 2003
Rental Contact: Manager Lance Olson
Resident Groups: Dance Umbrella, World Music, BAM Opera, Celebrity Series, Jose Mateo's Ballet Theatre, The Revels...

6842
HUNTINGTON THEATRE COMPANY

Boston University
264 Huntington Avenue
Boston, MA 02115
Phone: 617-266-0800
Fax: 617-421-9674
e-mail: thehuntington@huntingtontheatre.org
Web Site: www.huntingtontheatre.org
Management:
Development Director: Howard L Breslau
Marketing: Temple Gill
Utilizes: Guest Accompanists; Guest Companies; Guest Composers; Guest Musical Directors; Guest Soloists; Instructors; Sign Language Translators; Soloists
Founded: 1982
Status: Non-Profit; Professional

6843
ISABELLA STEWART GARDNER MUSEUM

280 The Fenway
Boston, MA 02115
Phone: 617-566-1401
Fax: 617-566-7653
e-mail: information@isgm.org
Web Site: www.gardnermuseum.org
Management:
Marketing: Anna Lowi
Utilizes: Artists-in-Residence; Composers-in-Residence; Fine Artists; Grant Writers; Guest Directors; Guest Instructors; Guest Soloists; Multimedia; Original Music Scores; Sign Language Translators; Touring Companies
Founded: 1903
Status: Nonprofit
Budget: $130,000
Performs At: Museum Gallery
Annual Attendance: 200,000
Facility Category: Museum
Seating Capacity: 250
Organization Type: Sponsoring

6844
JORDAN HALL AT NEW ENGLAND CONSERVATORY

290 Huntington Avenue
Boston, MA 02115
Phone: 617-585-1260
Fax: 617-585-1270
Web Site: www.newenglandconservatory.edu
Management:
Director: Brian Yankee
Founded: 1903
Annual Attendance: 125,000
Facility Category: Performance Hall
Seating Capacity: 1,013
Year Remodeled: 1995
Architect: Ann Beha Associates
Cost: $8.2 million

6845
SYMPHONY HALL

301 Massachusetts Avenue
Boston, MA 02115
Phone: 617-266-1492
Fax: 617-637-9367
Toll-free: 800-266-1492
e-mail: customerservice@bso.org
Web Site: www.bso.org
Officers:
Chairman: Ed Linde

Management:
Managing Director: Mark Volpe
Artistic Director: Dennis Alves
Marketing: Sarah L Manoog
Operations: Victoria Dominguez
Founded: 1881
Status: Non-Profit, Professional

6846
TD BANKNORTH GARDEN
100 Legends Way
Boston, MA 02114
Phone: 617-624-1050
Fax: 617-624-1818
e-mail: customerservice@tdbanknorthgarden.com
Web Site: www.tdbanknorthgarden.com
Officers:
Chairman/CEO: Jeremy Jacobs
President: Charles Moran Jr
Founded: 1995
Status: For-Profit, Professional
Paid Staff: 1000
Seating Capacity: 18,600
Year Built: 1995
Year Restored: 2006

6847
AGASSIZ THEATRE
10-12 Holyoke Street
Cambridge, MA 02138
Phone: 617-495-8726
Fax: 617-495-8728
e-mail: theatre@fas.harvard.edu
Web Site: www.fas.harvard.edu
Management:
Director: Thomas Morgan
Founded: 1904

6848
LOEB DRAMA CENTER
64 Brattle Street
Cambridge, MA 02138
Phone: 617-495-2668
Fax: 617-495-1705
e-mail: information@amrep.org
Web Site: www.amrep.org
Management:
Executive Director: Robert J Orchard
Artistic Director: Diane Paulus
General Manager: Jonathan Seth Miller
Founded: 1960
Status: Non-Profit, Professional
Paid Staff: 60
Paid Artists: 30
Type of Stage: Proscenium
Stage Dimensions: 26 x 60
Seating Capacity: 556
Year Built: 1960

6849
BOSTON COLLEGE ALUMNI FIELD STADIUM
140 Commonwealth Avenue
Chestnut Hill, MA 02467
Phone: 617-552-3004
Fax: 617-552-4903
e-mail: mahonebe@bc.edu
Web Site: www.bceagles.com
Management:
General Manager: Barry McNulty
Athletic Director: Gene Defillippo
Founded: 1957
Seating Capacity: 8,606

6850
MARGARET L JACKSON ARTS CENTER
Bristol Community College
777 Elsbree Street
Fall River, MA 02720
Phone: 508-678-2811
Fax: 508-730-3284
e-mail: president@bristol.mass.edu
Web Site: bristolcc.edu
Officers:
President: John J Sbrega
Status: Non-Profit, Professional

6851
HIGHFIELD THEATRE
Cape Cod Conservatory of Music
60 Highfield Drive
PO Box 233
Falmouth, MA 02541
Phone: 508-540-0611
Fax: 508-495-0025
Web Site: www.capecodconservatory.org
Officers:
President: Kevin Howard
Management:
Director: Richard Casper

6852
ORPHEUM THEATRE
Bay Colony Productions
1 School Street
PO Box 266
Foxboro, MA 02035
Phone: 508-543-4434
e-mail: boxoffice@baycolonyproductions.com
Web Site: www.orpheum.org
Management:
Executive Director: Bill Cunningham
Founded: 1993
Status: Nonprofit

6853
THE MAHAIWE PERFORMING ARTS CENTER THEATRE
14 Castle Street
Great Barrington, MA 01230
Phone: 413-528-6415
Fax: 413-528-8352
Web Site: www.mahaiwe.org
Management:
Executive Director: Beryl Jolly
General Manager: Karin Watkins
Founded: 1904
Opened: 1905
Status: Non-Profit; Professional

6854
LAWRENCE ACADEMY THEATRE
Powderhouse Road
PO Box 992
Groton, MA 01450
Phone: 978-448-1530
Fax: 508-448-6535
e-mail: thawgood@lacademy.edu
Web Site: www.lacademy.edu
Officers:
Chair: Steve Peisch
Management:
Director: Tony Hawgood

6855
HINGHAM HIGH SCHOOL AUDITORIUM
17 Union Street
Hingham, MA 02043
Phone: 781-741-1500
Fax: 781-741-1515
Web Site: www.hinghamschools.com
Officers:
Chair: Christine Smith
Status: Non-Profit, Non-Professional

6856
TANGLEWOOD MUSIC CENTER
297 West Street
Lenox, MA 01240
Phone: 413-637-1600
Fax: 413-637-5100
e-mail: customerservice@bso.org
Web Site: www.bso.org
Officers:
Chairman: James Levine
Management:
Managing Director: Mark Volpe
Founded: 1940
Seating Capacity: 18,000

6857
LOWELL MEMORIAL AUDITORIUM
50 E Merrimack Street
Lowell, MA 01852
Phone: 978-937-8688
Fax: 978-452-7342
e-mail: boxoffice@lowellauditorium.com
Web Site: www.lowellauditorium.com
Management:
Director: Peter Lally
Manager: Thomas McKay
Status: For-Profit, Professional
Paid Staff: 20
Seating Capacity: 3,000

6858
UNIVERSITY OF MASSACHUSETTS CENTER FOR THE ARTS
35 Wilder Street
Suite 1
Lowell, MA 01854-3081
Phone: 978-934-4444
Fax: 978-934-2017
Web Site: www.uml.edu
Management:
Director: Christine Heaton Brown
Marketing: Joan Sherman

6859
LYNN CITY HALL MEMORIAL AUDITORIUM
3 City Hall Square
Lynn, MA 01901
Phone: 781-598-4000
Fax: 781-599-8875
e-mail: jmarsh@ci.lynn.ma.us
Web Site: www.lynnauditorium.com
Management:
Development Director: James Marsh
Opened: 1948

6860
TWEETER CENTER FOR THE PERFORMING ARTS
885 S Main Street
Mansfield, MA 02048

Phone: 508-339-2331
Fax: 508-339-0550
Web Site: www.livenation.com
Facility Category: Open Air Amphitheater
Seating Capacity: 19,900

6861
ZEITERION THEATRE

684 Purchase Street
New Bedford, MA 02741
Phone: 508-997-5664
Fax: 508-999-5956
e-mail: info@zeiterion.org
Web Site: www.zeiterion.org
Management:
 Development Director: Robin Cabral
 Marketing: Anne Burnett
Founded: 1923
Status: Non-Profit, Professional

6862
FIREHOUSE CENTER FOR THE ARTS

Market Square
Newburyport, MA 01950
Phone: 978-462-7336
Fax: 978-462-9911
e-mail: info@firehouse.org
Web Site: www.firehouse.org
Management:
 Director of Productions: Kimm Wilkinson
 Director of Development: Beth Falconer
Founded: 1991
Seating Capacity: 195
Year Remodeled: 1991

6863
MASSACHUSETTS MUSEUM OF CONTEMPORARY ART

87 Marshall Street
North Adams, MA 01247
Phone: 413-662-2111
Fax: 413-663-8548
e-mail: info@massmoca.org
Web Site: www.massmoca.org
Officers:
 Chairman: Duncan Brown
Management:
 Director: Joseph C Thompson
Founded: 1999
Status: Non-Profit, Professional

6864
CALVIN THEATRE AND PERFORMANCE ARTS CENTER

19 King Street
Northampton, MA 01060
Phone: 413-584-1444
Fax: 413-586-1162
Web Site: www.iheg.com
Management:
 Creative Director: Jordi Herold

6865
JOHN M GREENE HALL

Smith College
30 Balmont Avenue
Northampton, MA 01063
Phone: 413-585-2163
Fax: 413-585-6990
e-mail: events@email.smith.edu
Web Site: www.smith.edu
Officers:
 President: Carol T Christ

Management:
 Director: Peg Pitzer
Seating Capacity: 2,046

6866
ACADEMY PLAYHOUSE

120 Main Street
Orleans, MA 02653
Phone: 508-255-3075
Fax: 508-255-8704
Web Site: www.apacape.org
Management:
 Artistic Director: Peter Earle
 Marketing: Gayle Kenerson
Founded: 1975
Status: Non-Profit, Non-Professional
Paid Staff: 10
Volunteer Staff: 150
Facility Category: Arena Theatre
Type of Stage: Arena
Seating Capacity: 164

6867
KOUSSEVITZKY PERFORMING ARTS CENTER

Berkshire Community College
1350 W Street
Pittsfield, MA 01201
Phone: 413-499-4660
Fax: 413-496-9511
Toll-free: 800-816-1233
Web Site: www.berkshirecc.edu
Officers:
 President: Paul Raverta
Management:
 Director: Christopher Gregory
Founded: 1960
Status: Non-Profit, Professional
Type of Stage: Proscenium
Stage Dimensions: 56'x46'x66'
Comments: Best contact method for info on Theatre is by telephone.

6868
GRISWOLD THEATRE

American International College
Sprague Cultural Arts Center
1000 State Street
Springfield, MA 01109
Phone: 413-747-6393
Fax: 413-737-2803
Toll-free: 800-242-3142
Web Site: www.aic.edu
Officers:
 President: Vincent Maniaci

6869
MASSMUTUAL CENTER

1277 Main Street
Springfield, MA 01103
Phone: 413-787-6610
Fax: 413-787-6645
e-mail: mmeinfo@massconvention.com
Web Site: www.massmutualcenter.com
Management:
 General Manager: Matt Hollander
 Operations: Scott Griffith
 Marketing: Marissa Tomalonis
Founded: 1972
Status: For-Profit, Professional
Affiliations: Global Spectrum
Facility Category: Arena & Convention Center
Type of Stage: Various
Seating Capacity: 8,000

Year Remodeled: 2005

6870
SPRINGFIELD SYMPHONY HALL

1 Columbus Center
Springfield, MA 01103
Phone: 413-788-7646
Fax: 413-737-9991
e-mail: tickets@citystage.symphonyhall.com
Web Site: www.symphonyhall.com
Officers:
 President: Cindy Anazalotti
Management:
 Director: Chad LaBumbard
 Manager: Sue Burris
 Marketing: Tina D'Agostino
Founded: 1912
Type of Stage: Proscenium
Orchestra Pit: Y
Seating Capacity: 2,611
Year Built: 1912
Year Remodeled: 2004

6871
GOSMAN SPORTS & CONVOCATION CENTER

Brandeis University
415 S Street
Waltham, MA 02254
Phone: 781-736-4300
Fax: 781-736-4305
Web Site: www.brandeis.edu
Officers:
 President: Jehuda Reinharz

6872
SPINGOLD THEATER CENTER

Brandeis University
415 S Street
Waltham, MA 02454
Phone: 781-736-3340
Fax: 781-736-3408
e-mail: theater@brandeis.edu
Web Site: www.brandeis.edu
Officers:
 President: Jehuda Reinharz
 Chair: Susan Dibble
Management:
 Artistic Director: Eric Hill
 Director: David Colfer
 Manager: Irene Vienneau

6873
CAPE COD CONSERVATORY OF MUSIC & ARTS

2235 Ivanough Road
West Barnstable, MA 02668
Phone: 508-362-2772
Fax: 508-362-4071
e-mail: capecodconservatory@comcast.net
Web Site: www.capecodconservatory.org
Officers:
 Founder/President: Paul Giuliana PhD
 Treasurer: Bill Janovitz
Founded: 1956
Status: Non-Profit, Professional

6874
REGIS COLLEGE FINE ARTS CENTER

235 Wellesley Street
Weston, MA 02493

Phone: 781-768-7034
Fax: 781-768-7030
e-mail: fac@regiscollege.edu
Web Site: www.regiscollege.edu
Officers:
   President: Mary Jane England MD
Management:
   Director: Steven Hall
Opened: 1993
Status: Non-Profit, Professional

6875
PRISCILLA BEACH THEATRE
796 Rocky Hill Road
White Horse Beach, MA 02381
Phone: 508-224-4888
e-mail: pbt@thinktheatre.org
Web Site: www.thinktheatre.org
Officers:
   Founder: Franklin Trask PhD
Founded: 1937

6876
CHAPIN HALL
William College
Bernhard Music Center
54 Chapin Hall Drive
Williamstown, MA 01267-2687
Phone: 413-597-2415
Fax: 413-597-3100
Web Site: www.music.williams.edu
Officers:
   Chair: David S Kechley
Founded: 1910
Status: Non-Profit, Professional

6877
STERLING & FRANCINE CLARK ART INSTITUTE
225 S Street
Williamstown, MA 01267
Phone: 413-458-2303
Fax: 413-458-2318
e-mail: info@clarkart.edu
Web Site: www.clarkart.edu
Officers:
   President: Morton Owen Schapiro PhD
Management:
   Executive Director: Michael Conforti
Founded: 1955
Status: Non-Profit, Professional
Performs At: Auditorium
Annual Attendance: 200,000
Seating Capacity: 320
Year Built: 1973

6878
MECHANICS HALL
321 Main Street
Worcester, MA 01608
Phone: 508-752-5608
Fax: 508-754-8442
e-mail: info@mechanicshall.org
Web Site: www.mechanicshall.org
Management:
   Executive Director: Robert M Kennedy
Mission: To preserve Mechanics Hall as a world-class performance center and community meeting space.
Status: Non-Profit, Non-Professional
Paid Staff: 8
Volunteer Staff: 20
Budget: $1 Million
Income Sources: Rental Income; Membership; Foundations; Businesses

Annual Attendance: 200,000
Type of Stage: Thrust
Seating Capacity: 1,6484
Year Built: 1857
Year Remodeled: 2000
Cost: $8 Million

6879
PERFORMING ARTS SCHOOL OF WORCESTER
29 High Street
Worcester, MA 01608
Phone: 508-755-8246
Fax: 508-795-0640
Web Site: www.pasow.org
Officers:
   Chair: Christine Cuccaro
   Treasurer: Nigel Belgrave
Management:
   Executive Director: Fred Dowling
   Manager: Pieter Struyk
Utilizes: Actors; Choreographers; Collaborations; Commissioned Composers; Commissioned Music; Dancers; Educators; Five Seasonal Concerts; Grant Writers; Guest Companies; Guest Composers; Guest Ensembles; Guest Instructors; Guest Soloists; Guest Writers; High School Drama; Instructors; Lyricists; Music; New Productions; Organization Contracts; Sign Language Translators; Student Interns
Status: Non-Profit, Non-Professional

Michigan

6880
DAWSON AUDITORIUM
Adrian College
110 S Madison Street
Adrian, MI 49221
Phone: 517-264-3156
Fax: 517-264-3331
Toll-free: 800-877-2246
e-mail: jdocking@adrian.edu
Web Site: www.adrian.edu
Officers:
   President: Jeffrey R Docking PhD
Seating Capacity: 1,000
Year Built: 1962
Year Remodeled: 2004

6881
COMMUNITY THEATRE ASSOCIATION OF MICHIGAN
4619 W Van Buren Road
Alma, MI 48801-9556
Phone: 989-463-1252
e-mail: info@communitytheatre.org
Web Site: www.communitytheatre.org
Officers:
   President: Art Nemitz
   Treasurer: Christy Frick
Founded: 1951
Status: Non profit
Affiliations: Arts Council For Chautauqa County
Annual Attendance: 5000
Organization Type: Service Organization

6882
ARTHUR MILLER THEATRE
Univeristy of Michigan
911 N University
Ann Arbor, MI 48109-1265

Phone: 734-764-0583
Fax: 734-763-5097
e-mail: sberritt@umich.edu
Web Site: www.music.umich.edu
Officers:
   President: Mary Sue Coleman
Management:
   Manager: Shannon Rice
Affiliations: UM School of music
Type of Stage: Black Box

6883
CRISLER ARENA
University of Michigan
333 E Stadium Bolevrd
Ann Arbor, MI 48104
Phone: 734-764-0247
Fax: 734-936-8942
e-mail: mtickets@umich.edu
Web Site: www.mgoblue.com
Officers:
   President: Mary Sue Coleman
Management:
   Director: William C Martin
Founded: 1967
Seating Capacity: 13,750

6884
HILL AUDITORIUM
University of Michigan
825 N University Avenue
Ann Arbor, MI 48109
Phone: 734-763-3333
Fax: 734-763-5097
Web Site: www.music.umich.edu
Officers:
   President: Mary Sue Coleman
Management:
   Manager: Shannon Rice
Opened: 1913
Seating Capacity: 4,163

6885
KERRYTOWN CONCERT HOUSE
415 N Fourth Avenue
Ann Arbor, MI 48104
Phone: 734-769-2999
Fax: 734-769-7791
e-mail: kch@kerrytown.com
Web Site: www.kerrytownconcerthouse.com
Management:
   Executive Director: Deanna Relyea
Founded: 1984
Status: Non-Profit, Professional

6886
LYDIA MENDELSSOHN THEATRE
University of Michigan
911 N University
Ann Arbor, MI 48109-2085
Phone: 734-764-0583
Fax: 734-763-5097
Web Site: www.music.umich.edu
Officers:
   President: Mary Sue Coleman
Management:
   Manager: Shannon Rice
Founded: 1929
Performs At: Intimate, shoe-box theatre with a cyclorama.
Type of Stage: Proscenium
Stage Dimensions: 29'11" x 16'10"
Seating Capacity: 640
Year Built: 1929

Year Remodeled: 1995

6887
MICHIGAN THEATER
603 E Liberty Street
Ann Arbor, MI 48104
Phone: 734-668-8397
Fax: 734-668-7136
Web Site: www.michtheater.com
Management:
Executive Director: Russell Collins
Marketing: Jenny Jackson
Development: Laura Barnes-Gabriel
Founded: 1928
Status: Non-Profit
Paid Staff: 12
Volunteer Staff: 300
Paid Artists: 3
Non-paid Artists: 4
Budget: $ 2 Million
Income Sources: 20% Memberiship; Contributions; Grants
Affiliations: National Association of Theater Owners
Annual Attendance: 2,100,000
Facility Category: Historic Movie Palace
Type of Stage: Proscenium
Stage Dimensions: 55x30
Seating Capacity: 1710
Year Built: 1928
Year Remodeled: 2000
Cost: $ 8.4 Million

6888
POWER CENTER FOR THE PERFORMING ARTS
University of Michigan
1100 Baits Drive
Ann Arbor, MI 48109-2085
Phone: 734-764-0583
Fax: 734-763-5097
Web Site: www.music.umich.edu
Management:
Facilities Coordinator/Manager: Perry Titus
Facilities/Booking Manager: Shannon Rice
Mission: Most technically sophisticated performance space. It is a fully functioning theatre able to handle the most complex sales meetings, product roll-outs, and corporate presentations.
Founded: 1971
Status: For-Profit, Non-Professional

6889
YOST ICE ARENA
University of Michigan
1000 S State Street
Ann Arbor, MI 48109
Phone: 734-764-4600
Fax: 734-764-4597
e-mail: yostice@umich.edu
Web Site: www.umich.edu
Management:
Manager: Craig Wotta
Founded: 1923
Status: For-Profit, Professional
Seating Capacity: 6,637

6890
PALACE AT AUBURN HILLS
Palace Sports & Entertainment
5 Championship Drive
Auburn Hills, MI 48326
Phone: 248-377-0100
e-mail: feedback@palacenet.com
Web Site: www.palacenet.com

Officers:
President/CEO: Tom Wilson
Management:
Director: Laura Passariello
Marketing: Dave Neitzer
Status: For-Profit, Professional
Seating Capacity: 21,454

6891
BATTLE CREEK CIVIC THEATRE
PO Box 519
Battle Creek, MI 49106
Phone: 269-441-2708
e-mail: info@bccivic.org
Web Site: www.bccivic.org
Officers:
President: Andy Helmboldt
Treasurer: Steve Parks

6892
CO BROWN STADIUM
189 Bridge Street
Battle Creek, MI 49017
Phone: 269-962-0735
Fax: 269-962-0741
e-mail: info@battlecreekbombers.com
Web Site: www.battlecreekbombers.com
Management:
General Manager: Brian Colopy
Founded: 1990
Status: For-Profit, Professional

6893
KELLOGG ARENA
1 McCamly Square
Battle Creek, MI 49017
Phone: 269-963-4800
Fax: 269-968-8840
e-mail: kschreibler@kelloggarena.com
Web Site: www.kelloggarena.com
Management:
General Manager: Kevin Scheibler
Operations: Fred Ogle
Marketing: Lindsay Taylor
Status: Non-Profit, Professional
Paid Staff: 50
Seating Capacity: 6,000

6894
MENDEL CENTER
Lake Michigan College
2755 E Napier Avenue
Benton Harbor, MI 49022
Phone: 269-927-1221
Fax: 269-927-6710
e-mail: boxoffice@lakemichigancollege.edu
Web Site: www.lakemichigancollege.edu
Management:
Manager: Deedy Fowler
Seating Capacity: 1,505

6895
WINK ARENA
Ferris State University
210 Sports Drive
Big Rapids, MI 49307
Phone: 231-591-2888
Fax: 231-591-2869
Web Site: www.ferris.edu
Officers:
President: David L Eisler
Chair: James K Haverman Jr
Management:
Director: Tom Kirinovic

Development: Tarrance Price
Facility Category: Sports Arena
Seating Capacity: 2,434

6896
CHEBOYGAN OPERA HOUSE
403 N Huron Street
Cheboygan, MI 49721
Phone: 231-627-5432
Fax: 231-627-2643
e-mail: pam@theoperahouse.org
Web Site: www.theoperahouse.org
Officers:
President: Jane Roe
Treasurer: Alice Barron
Management:
Executive Director: Pam Westover
Box Office: Dolores Kozlowski
Founded: 1877
Status: Non-Profit, Professional
Paid Staff: 6
Budget: $250,000
Income Sources: Ticket Sales; Contributions; Annual Campaigns; Grants
Affiliations: Association of Performing Arts Presenters
Type of Stage: Proscenium
Stage Dimensions: 34 x 23
Seating Capacity: 582
Year Built: 1877
Year Remodeled: 1984
Rental Contact: Executive Director Pamela Westover

6897
MACOMB CENTER FOR THE PERFORMING ARTS
44575 Garfield Road
Clinton Township, MI 48038-1139
Phone: 586-286-2141
Fax: 586-286-2272
e-mail: macombarts@macomb.edu
Web Site: www.macombcenter.com
Management:
Director: Christine Guarino
Operations: Elaine Adams
Marketing: Sandy Hazelton
Opened: 1982
Status: Professional
Type of Stage: Proscenium
Stage Dimensions: 48'-6" X 29'
Orchestra Pit: Y
Seating Capacity: 1,273

6898
COBO ARENA
301 Civic Center Drive
Detroit, MI 48226
Phone: 313-471-6606
Fax: 313-396-7998
Web Site: www.olympiaentertainment.com
Officers:
President: Dana Warg
Seating Capacity: 12,200
Year Built: 1959

6899
DETROIT SYMPHONY ORCHESTRA HALL
3711 Woodward Avenue
Detroit, MI 48201
Phone: 313-576-5111
Fax: 313-576-5109
Web Site: www.detroitsymphony.com
Officers:

Chairman: James B Nicholson
Management:
Executive Director: Anne Parsons
Artistic Director: Charles Burke
Marketing: Ross Binnie
Founded: 1914
Status: Non-Profit, Professional
Paid Staff: 60
Paid Artists: 100

6900
FISHER THEATRE
3011 W Grand Boulevard
Detroit, MI 48202
Phone: 313-872-1111
Fax: 313-872-0632
e-mail: groupsales@nederlanderdetroit.com
Web Site: www.nederlanderdetroit.com
Management:
Operations: Ray Harris
Utilizes: Theatre Companies
Status: For-Profit, Professional
Paid Staff: 12
Income Sources: Box Office
Facility Category: Live Stage Theater
Type of Stage: Proscenium House
Stage Dimensions: 50' 0" x 32' 6"
Seating Capacity: 2,089
Year Remodeled: 2001
Architect: Rapp & Rapp of Chicago

6901
FORD FIELD
2000 Brush Street
Suite 200
Detroit, MI 48226
Phone: 313-262-2225
Fax: 313-262-2239
e-mail: guestservices@detroitlions.com
Web Site: www.fordfield.com
Management:
Manager: Connie Kladja
Seating Capacity: 65,000

6902
FOX THEATRE
2211 Woodward Avenue
Detroit, MI 48201
Phone: 313-471-6490
Fax: 313-471-3220
Web Site: www.olympiaentertainment.com
Officers:
President: Dana Warg
Status: For-Profit, Professional

6903
JOE LOUIS ARENA
600 Civic Center Drive
Detroit, MI 48226
Phone: 313-396-7000
Fax: 313-396-7998
Web Site: www.olympiaentertainment.com
Officers:
President: Dana Warg
Status: For-Profit, Professional
Seating Capacity: 19,965
Year Built: 1979

6904
MASONIC TEMPLE THEATRE
500 Temple Avenue
Detroit, MI 48201

Phone: 313-832-7100
Fax: 313-832-2292
Web Site: www.olympiaentertainment.com
Management:
President: Dana Wang
Status: Professional

6905
MUSIC HALL CENTER FOR THE PERFORMING ARTS
350 Madison
Detroit, MI 48226
Phone: 313-887-8503
Fax: 313-887-8502
e-mail: info@musichall.org
Web Site: www.musichall.org
Officers:
President: Vincent Paul
Management:
Events Director: Karen McBride
Founded: 1928
Seating Capacity: 1701
Year Built: 1928
Year Remodeled: 1995
Organization Type: Performing

6906
UNIVERSITY OF DETROIT MERCY CALIHAN HALL
4001 W McNichols
Detroit, MI 48219
Phone: 313-993-1700
Fax: 313-993-2449
Web Site: www.udmercy.edu
Officers:
President: Gregory L Stockhausen PhD
Management:
Operations: Tamara Batcheller
Marketing: Elizabeth Patterson
Development: Gregory Cascione
Founded: 1877
Status: Non-Profit, Professional

6907
WAYNE STATE UNIVERSITY THEATRE
4841 Cass Avenue
Suite 3225
Detroit, MI 48202
Phone: 313-577-3508
Fax: 313-577-0935
e-mail: theatre@wayne.edu
Web Site: theatre.wayne.edu
Officers:
President: Jay Noren
Management:
Director: Blair Anderson
Utilizes: Actors; AEA Actors; Choreographers; Collaborating Artists; Collaborations; Commissioned Composers; Commissioned Music; Composers-in-Residence; Curators; Dance Companies; Dancers; Designers; Educators; Filmmakers; Fine Artists; Five Seasonal Concerts; Grant Writers; Guest Accompanists; Guest Artists; Guest Choreographers; Guest Companies; Guest Composers; Guest Conductors; Guest Designers; Guest Directors; Guest Ensembles; Guest Instructors; Guest Lecturers; Guest Musical Directors; Guest Musicians; Guest Soloists; Guest Teachers; High School Drama; Instructors; Local Artists; Local Unknown Artists; Lyricists; Multi Collaborations; Multimedia; Music; Organization Contracts; Original Music Scores; Performance Artists; Playwrights; Poets; Resident Artists; Resident Professionals; Selected Students; Sign Language

Translators; Singers; Soloists; Student Interns; Special Technical Talent; Theatre Companies; Touring Companies; Visual Arts

6908
JACK BRESLIN STUDENT EVENTS CENTER
One Birch Road
East Lansing, MI 48824
Phone: 517-432-1989
Fax: 517-432-1510
e-mail: bement@msu.edu
Web Site: www.breslincenter.com
Management:
Sales Manager: Nanci Yeadon
Stage Manager: Joel Wilkiins
Acting Breslin Center Manager: Ken Horvath
Founded: 1989
Status: Non-Profit
Performs At: Sports & Entertainment
Seating Capacity: 15,085

6909
SPARTAN STADIUM
Michigan State University
200 Spartan Way
East Lansing, MI 48824
Phone: 517-355-1610
Fax: 800-464-7336
Toll-free: 800-467-8273
Web Site: www.msuspartans.com
Management:
Director: Mark Hollis
Operations: Peggy Brown
Development: Chuck Sleeper
Seating Capacity: 72,027

6910
WHARTON CENTER FOR PERFORMING ARTS
Michigan State University
Shaw Lane at Bogue Street
East Lansing, MI 48824-1318
Mailing Address: 320 Wharton Center, MSU, East Lansing, MI 48824
Phone: 517-353-1982
Fax: 517-353-5329
Toll-free: 800-942-7866
e-mail: wharton@msu.edu
Web Site: www.whartoncenter.com
Management:
Executive Director: Mike Brand, brandmi@msu.edu
Programming Manager: D Bryan Jao, jao@msu.edu
Director of Development: Doug Miller, mille756@msu.edu
Director of Communications: Kent Love
Director of Education: Bert Goldstein
Senior Production Manager: Sandy Thomley
Senior House Manager: Nina Silbergleit
General Manager: Diana Baribeau
Utilizes: Artists-in-Residence; Choreographers; Collaborating Artists; Collaborations; Commissioned Composers; Composers; Contract Actors; Contract Orchestras; Dance Companies; Educators; Equity Actors; Five Seasonal Concerts; Guest Accompanists; Guest Artists; Guest Choreographers; Guest Conductors; Guest Designers; Guest Directors; Guest Instructors; Guest Musical Directors; Guest Musicians; Guest Soloists; Guest Speakers; Lyricists; Multimedia; Original Music Scores; Paid Performers; Performance

Artists; Resident Artists; Selected Students; Singers; Soloists; Students; Special Technical Talent; Theatre Companies
Founded: 1982
Opened: 1982
Status: Non-Profit
Paid Staff: 30
Volunteer Staff: 300
Budget: $12,000,000 - $17,000,000
Income Sources: Ticket Sales, Funding, Rentals
Performs At: Great Hall
Affiliations: Michigan State University; APAP; ISPA; IAAM
Annual Attendance: 250,000
Facility Category: Performing Arts Center
Type of Stage: Proscenium; Thrust; Auditorium
Seating Capacity: 2,420, 600, 3739
Year Built: 1982
Year Remodeled: 2009
Rental Contact: Baribeau@msu.edu Diana S Baribeau

6911
1515 BROADWAY PERFORMANCE VENUE
29205 Greening Boulevard
Farmington Hills, MI 48334
Phone: 248-932-0090
Fax: 248-932-8763
Toll-free: 877-683-4452
Web Site: www.the-feds.com
Management:
    President: Chris Jazczak
    Managing Director: Joseph S Ajlouny Jr
    Marketing Director: Angela Booterbaugh
Mission: Urban performance venue.
Founded: 1990
Specialized Field: Music; Theatre
Status: Non-Profit, Non-Professional
Paid Staff: 3
Volunteer Staff: 10
Budget: $160,000
Income Sources: Tickets; Sponsorship
Annual Attendance: 4,000
Facility Category: Independent Theater
Type of Stage: Proscenium; In-the-Round; Black Box
Stage Dimensions: 18' x 16' with Thrust
Seating Capacity: 120
Year Built: 1979
Year Remodeled: 1989

6912
FLINT INSTITUTE OF MUSIC
1025 E Kearsley Street
Flint, MI 48503
Phone: 810-238-1350
Fax: 810-238-6385
Toll-free: 800-395-4849
e-mail: fim@fim.com
Web Site: www.flintinstituteofmusic.com
Management:
    Markeying Director: Christina Mooney
    Audience Services Manager: Cathy Prevett
    Symphony Manager: Tom Glassock
    Manager Flint Symphony: Tom Glasscok
Founded: 1917
Status: Non-Profit, Non-Professional
Performs At: Whiting Auditorium
Annual Attendance: 3,500

6913
PERANI SPORTS ARENA
3501 Lapeer Road
Flint, MI 48503

Phone: 810-744-0580
Fax: 810-744-2906
Web Site: www.peraniarena.com
Officers:
    President: Khaled Shukairy
Founded: 1969

6914
CITY OF GRAND HAVEN COMMUNITY CENTER
421 Columbus Street
Grand Haven, MI 49417
Phone: 616-842-2550
Fax: 616-844-5287
Web Site: www.grandhaven.org
Management:
    Manager: Sandy Katt
Status: Non-Profit, Non-Professional
Paid Staff: 8
Seating Capacity: 450
Year Remodeled: 2006

6915
CALVIN COLLEGE FINE ARTS CENTER
1795 Knollcrest Circle SE
Grand Rapids, MI 49546-4404
Phone: 616-526-6253
Fax: 616-526-6266
e-mail: music@calvin.edu
Web Site: www.calvin.edu
Officers:
    Chair: Bert Polman
Management:
    Marketing: Melissa Reiffer
Founded: 1966
Status: Non-Profit, Professional
Paid Staff: 45
Seating Capacity: 1,065

6916
DELTAPLEX ENTERTAINMENT & EXPO CENTER
2500 Turner NW
Grand Rapids, MI 49544
Phone: 616-364-9000
Fax: 616-559-8001
e-mail: rich@deltaplex.com
Web Site: www.deltaplex.com
Management:
    Executive Director: Rich Baylie
    Operations Manager: Andy Boggs
Status: For-Profit, Professional
Stage Dimensions: 60'x56'
Seating Capacity: 6,500

6917
DEVOS PERFORMANCE HALL
303 Monroe Avenue NW
Grand Rapids, MI 49503
Phone: 616-742-6500
Fax: 616-742-6590
e-mail: webmaster@smggr.com
Web Site: www.devosperformancehall.com
Management:
    General Manager: Richard MacKeigan
    Marketing Director: Lynne Ike, like@smggr.com
    Operations Manager: Ryan Schultz
    Facilities Director: Rod Weeber
    Director of Finance: Chris Machuta
Founded: 1980
Opened: 1980
Paid Staff: 34

Income Sources: Performing Arts Groups; Touring Productions
Affiliations: Grand Rapids Symphony, Opera Grand Rapids, Broadway Grand Rapids & Grand Rapids Ballet
Facility Category: Performing Arts Theater
Type of Stage: Proscenium
Stage Dimensions: 58'9" x 33' x 42'5"
Seating Capacity: 2,404
Year Built: 1980
Year Remodeled: 2002
Cost: $5 Million
Rental Contact: Director of Finance Chris Machuta

6918
FOUNTAIN STREET CHURCH
24 Fountain Street NE
Grand Rapids, MI 49503
Phone: 616-459-8386
Fax: 616-459-4809
e-mail: office@fountainstreet.org
Web Site: www.fountainstreet.org
Management:
    Executive Director: Pamela Clark
Founded: 1879
Status: Non-Profit, Non-Professional

6919
URBAN INSTITUTE FOR CONTEMPORARY ARTS
41 Sheldon Boulevard SE
Grand Rapids, MI 49503
Phone: 616-454-7000
Fax: 616-459-9395
e-mail: info@uica.org
Web Site: www.uica.org
Officers:
    President: Scott Vander Leek
    Secretary: Luanne Datema
Management:
    Executive Director: Jeffrey Meeuwsen
    Development Director: Jill May
    Marketing Director: Michael Lyman
Founded: 1977
Status: Non-Profit, Professional
Paid Staff: 6

6920
VAN ANDEL ARENA
130 W Fulton Street
Grand Rapids, MI 49503
Phone: 616-742-6600
Fax: 616-742-6197
e-mail: rmackeigan@smggr.com
Web Site: www.vanandelarena.com
Management:
    Operations Manager: Keven Abbott
    General Manager: Richard MacKeigan
    Facilities Director: Rod Weeber
Founded: 1996
Status: For-Profit, Professional
Paid Staff: 29
Performs At: Sports & Entertainment Arena
Affiliations: AHL & AFL
Annual Attendance: 1 million
Facility Category: Arena
Type of Stage: Varies
Stage Dimensions: varies
Seating Capacity: 12,048
Year Built: 1996
Rental Contact: Rich MacKeigan

6921

HOPE COLLEGE THEATRE

141 E 12 Street
Holland, MI 49423
Phone: 616-395-7600
Fax: 616-395-7180
e-mail: robins@hope.edu
Web Site: www.hope.edu
Officers:
    Chair: Daina Robins
Management:
    Director: Michelle Bombe
Founded: 1866
Status: Non-Profit, Professional
Type of Stage: Proscenium; Thrust

6922

INTERLOCHEN CENTER FOR THE ARTS
KRESGE AUDITORIUM

4000 Highway M-137
PO Box 199
Interlochen, MI 49643-0199
Phone: 231-276-7200
e-mail: boxoffice@interlochen.org
Web Site: www.interlochen.org
Officers:
    Chair: Steve Hayden
Facility Category: Open Sided Ampitheatre
Type of Stage: Proscenium
Stage Dimensions: 64'x 20'
Seating Capacity: 3,943
Year Built: 1940

6923

INTERLOCHEN CENTER FOR THE ARTS
DENDRINOS CENTER

4000 Highway M-137
PO Box 199
Interlochen, MI 49643-0199
Phone: 231-276-7200
Fax: 231-276-6321
e-mail: www.interlochen.org
Web Site: boxoffice@interlochen.org
Officers:
    Chair: Steve Hayden
Founded: 1981
Seating Capacity: 200
Year Built: 1981

6924

IRONWOOD THEATRE

109 E Aurora Street
Ironwood, MI 49938
Phone: 906-932-0618
Fax: 906-932-0457
Web Site: www.ironwoodtheatre.net
Officers:
    President: Joan Borcherdt
    Secretary: Kathy Skolasinski
    Treasurer: Helen Martin
Management:
    Managing Director: Deb Kallunki Gotham
Founded: 1928
Status: Non-Profit, Non-Professional
Paid Staff: 2
Budget: $125,000
Income Sources: Grants; State of Michigan; Fund Raisers
Performs At: Auditorium
Affiliations: Michigan Council for Arts-Cultural Affairs
Annual Attendance: 20,000
Facility Category: Performing Arts Center
Type of Stage: Proscenium

Stage Dimensions: 28'6wx23'l
Seating Capacity: 732
Year Built: 1928
Year Remodeled: 1983
Cost: $160,000

6925

POTTER CENTER

Jackson Community College
2111 Emmons Road
Jackson, MI 49201-8399
Phone: 517-796-8612
Web Site: www.jccmi.edu
Management:
    Director: Cindy Allen
Seating Capacity: 1,543

6926

JAMES W MILLER AUDITORIUM

Western Michigan University
1903 W Michigan Avenue
Kalamazoo, MI 49008-5344
Phone: 269-387-2311
Fax: 269-387-2317
Toll-free: 800-228-9858
e-mail: miller-comments@wmich.edu
Web Site: www.millerauditorium.com
Management:
    Executive Director: Elaine M Williams
    Marketing Director/Development: Tracey Lawie
    Technical Director: Guy Barks
Mission: To enlighten, entertain and educate
Founded: 1968
Specialized Field: Southwest Michigan
Status: Non-Profit, Non-Professional
Paid Staff: 20
Facility Category: Auditorium
Seating Capacity: 3423

6927

KALAMAZOO CIVIC AUDITORIUM

329 S Park Street
Kalamazoo, MI 49007
Phone: 616-343-1313
Fax: 616-343-0532
Web Site: www.kazoocivic.com
Management:
    Managing Director: Kristen Chefak

6928

NELDA K BALCH PLAYHOUSE

Kalamazoo College Theatre Department
1200 Academy Street
Kalamazoo, MI 49006
Phone: 269-337-7000
Fax: 269-337-7305
Toll-free: 800-253-3602
Web Site: www.kzoo.edu
Management:
    Director: Ed Menta
Founded: 1833
Status: Non-Profit, Non-Professional
Paid Staff: 400

6929

WINGS STADIUM

3600 Vanrick Drive
Kalamazoo, MI 49001
Phone: 269-345-1125
Fax: 269-383-8029
e-mail: ppickard@wingsstadium.com
Web Site: www.wingsstadium.com
Officers:
    President: Paul Pickard

Management:
    Facility Manager: Kathy Rosner
    Public Relations Director: Mike Modugno
Founded: 1974
Seating Capacity: 5,113
Year Built: 1974

6930

BERRY EVENTS CENTER

Northern Michigan University
1401 Presque Isle Avenue
Marquette, MI 49855
Phone: 906-227-2850
e-mail: cbammert@nmu.edu
Web Site: www.nmu.edu
Officers:
    University President: Les Wong
Management:
    Athletic Director: Ken Godfrey
    Facilities Director: Carl Bammert
    Operations Director: Steve Reed
Founded: 1999
Seating Capacity: 3,800
Year Built: 1999

6931

LAKEVIEW ARENA

Marquette Parks and Recreation
401 E Fair Avenue
Marquette, MI 49855
Phone: 906-228-0460
Fax: 906-228-0493
e-mail: parks@mqtcty.org
Web Site: www.mqtcty.org
Management:
    Director: Karl Zueger
    Manager: Doug Smith
Paid Staff: 5
Seating Capacity: 600

6932

MIDLAND CENTER FOR THE ARTS

1801 W St Andrews Road
Midland, MI 48640-2695
Phone: 989-631-5930
Toll-free: 800-523-7649
e-mail: info@mcfta.org
Web Site: www.mcfta.org
Officers:
    President/CEO: Bill Henninger
Management:
    Marketing Director: Linda Basque
    Facilities Mangager: Larry Salva
Founded: 1966
Status: Non-Profit
Paid Staff: 100

6933

RIVER RAISIN CENTRE FOR THE ARTS

114 S Monroe Street
Monroe, MI 48161
Phone: 734-242-7722
Fax: 734-242-9238
e-mail: rrca@riverraisincentre.org
Web Site: www.riverraisincentre.org
Officers:
    Board: Rebecca Mehregan
    Board: Linda McCormick
    Board: Kris Zuckerman
    Board: Joe Bellino
Founded: 1988
Status: Non-Profit

6934

KELLY SHORTS STADIUM

Central Michigan University Athletics
100 Rose Center
Mount Pleasant, MI 48859
Phone: 989-774-3041
e-mail: heeke1dw@cmich.edu
Web Site: www.cmuchippewas.com
Officers:
President: Michael Rao
Management:
Athletics Director: Dave Heeke
Marketing Director: Mike Dabbs
Founded: 1892
Status: Non-Profit, Professional
Paid Staff: 10
Paid Artists: 100
Seating Capacity: 30,000

6935

PLACHTA AUDITORIUM

Central Michigan University
Warriner Hall
Mount Pleasant, MI 48859
Phone: 517-774-3355
Fax: 517-774-7957
e-mail: Robert.J.Ebner@cmich.edu
Web Site: www.cmich.edu
Officers:
President: Michael Rao
Management:
University Events Director: Robert Ebner

6936

ROSE ARENA

Central Michigan University
100 Rose Center
Mount Pleasant, MI 48859
Phone: 989-774-3041
e-mail: heeke1dw@cmich.edu
Web Site: www.cmuchippewas.com
Officers:
University President: Michael Rao
Management:
Athletics Director: Dave Heeke
Marketing Director: Mike Dabbs
Status: Non-Profit, Non-Professional
Paid Staff: 6
Seating Capacity: 5,200

6937

FRAUENTHAL CENTER FOR THE PERFORMING ARTS

425 W Western Avenue
Muskegon, MI 49440
Phone: 231-722-2890
e-mail: info@frauenthal.org
Web Site: www.frauenthal.org
Management:
Building Manager: Scott Bartoszek
Operations Manager: Bill Bodell
Marketing Manager: Linda Medema
Utilizes: Lyricists; Special Technical Talent; Theatre Companies
Founded: 1974
Status: Non-Profit, Professional
Paid Staff: 7
Volunteer Staff: 385
Budget: $890,000
Income Sources: Ticket Sales; Endowments
Affiliations: League of Historic American Theatres; American Association of Arts Presenters
Annual Attendance: 185,000

Facility Category: Historic Theater
Type of Stage: Proscenium
Stage Dimensions: 41'6'x30H
Seating Capacity: 1,748
Year Built: 1930
Year Remodeled: 1998
Cost: $8,500,000
Rental Contact: Linda Medema
Organization Type: Performing; Resident; Educational; Sponsoring; Presenter
Resident Groups: Muskegon Community Concert Association, Muskegon Civic Theatre, Cherry County Playhouse, West Shore

6938

OVERBROOK THEATER

Muskegon Community College
221 S Quarterline Road
Muskegon, MI 49442
Phone: 231-773-9131
Fax: 231-777-0324
e-mail: webmaster@muskegoncc.edu
Web Site: www.muskegoncc.edu
Officers:
President: David Rule
Management:
Artistic Director: Sheila Kulp Wahamaki
Founded: 1926
Specialized Field: Fine Arts
Status: Non-Profit, Professional
Paid Staff: 12
Paid Artists: 5
Seating Capacity: 344

6939

WALKER ARENA

955 Fourth Street
Muskegon, MI 49440
Phone: 231-726-2939
Fax: 231-726-4620
Web Site: www.lcwalkerarena.com
Management:
Director: Neil Hawryliw
Seating Capacity: 6,400

6940

MCMORRAN PLACE THEATRE

701 McMorran Boulevard
Port Huron, MI 48060
Phone: 810-985-6166
Fax: 810-985-3358
Toll-free: 800-858-6166
Web Site: www.mcmorran.com
Management:
General Manager: Larry Krabach
Operations Director: Jerry Hamilton
Founded: 1957
Specialized Field: Theatre; Community; Theatrical Group
Status: Non-Profit, Professional
Paid Staff: 10
Income Sources: College
Facility Category: Performing Arts
Type of Stage: Procenium
Stage Dimensions: 50x30
Seating Capacity: 1159
Year Built: 1959

6941

KIRTLAND CENTER FOR THE PERFORMING ARTS

Kirtland Community College
10775 N Saint Helen Road
Roscommon, MI 48653

Phone: 989-275-6777
e-mail: kcpa@kirtland.edu
Web Site: www.kirtland.edu
Officers:
President: Thomas Quinn
Management:
Director: Don Wray
Utilizes: Actors; Artists-in-Residence; Collaborations; Dance Companies; Educators; Grant Writers; Guest Accompanists; Guest Artists; Guest Companies; Guest Conductors; Guest Ensembles; Guild Activities; Instructors; Original Music Scores; Selected Students; Sign Language Translators; Soloists; Student Interns; Special Technical Talent; Theatre Companies
Founded: 1966
Status: Non-Profit
Paid Staff: 4
Volunteer Staff: 30
Budget: 300,000
Income Sources: Ticket Sales; Donations; College Funding
Affiliations: Arts Midwest; APAP; USITT; MACAA
Annual Attendance: 30,000
Facility Category: Theatre
Type of Stage: Modified Thrust
Seating Capacity: 846
Year Built: 1966
Rental Contact: Director Gary Carlton

6942

HERITAGE THEATER

Dow Event Center
303 Johnson Street
Saginaw, MI 48607
Phone: 989-759-1320
Fax: 989-759-1322
e-mail: info@DowEventCenter.com
Web Site: www.doweventcenter.com
Officers:
Director of Finance: Matthew Rick
Management:
General Manager: Matt Blasy
Utilizes: Dancers; Local Artists; Multimedia; Original Music Scores; Theatre Companies
Founded: 1970
Status: Non-Profit, Professional
Paid Staff: 200
Facility Category: Theater, Arena
Seating Capacity: 2,276
Year Built: 1970
Year Remodeled: 2002
Rental Contact: Matt Blasy

6943

FREEDOM HILL AMPHITHEATRE

14900 Metropolitan Parkway
Sterling Heights, MI 48312
Phone: 586-268-7820
Fax: 586-268-0729
e-mail: ezerba@freedomhill.net
Web Site: www.freedomhill.net
Officers:
President: Joe Bolanca
Status: Professional
Seating Capacity: 7,000

6944

TECUMSEH CENTER FOR THE ARTS

400 N Maumee Street
Tecumseh, MI 49286
Phone: 517-423-6617
Fax: 517-423-3610
e-mail: boxoffice@theTCA.org
Web Site: www.thetca.org

Management:
Executive Director: Johanna B Walker
Marketing Director: Rebecca Peach
Status: Profit
Seating Capacity: 572

6945
DENNOS MUSEUM CENTER MILLIKEN AUDITORIUM
Northwest Michigan College
1701 E Front Street
Traverse City, MI 49686
Phone: 231-995-1055
Fax: 231-995-1597
e-mail: boxoffice@nmc.edu
Web Site: www.dennosmuseum.org
Officers:
President: Timothy Nelson
Management:
Museum Director: Eugene Jenneman
Utilizes: Actors; Collaborations; Curators; Dance Companies; Dancers; Educators; Fine Artists; Grant Writers; Guest Accompanists; Guest Artists; Guest Choreographers; Guest Directors; Guest Ensembles; Guest Instructors; Guest Musical Directors; Guest Musicians; Guest Soloists; High School Drama; Instructors; Local Artists; Lyricists; Multimedia; Sign Language Translators; Singers; Soloists; Special Technical Talent; Theatre Companies; Touring Companies; Visual Arts
Founded: 1991
Specialized Field: Visual & Performing Arts
Status: Non-Profit
Paid Staff: 9
Volunteer Staff: 160
Paid Artists: 12
Budget: $900,000
Affiliations: Northwestern Michigan College
Annual Attendance: 600,000
Facility Category: Museum & Concert Hall
Stage Dimensions: 30' X 50'
Seating Capacity: 367
Year Built: 1991
Rental Contact: Assistant to the Director Judith Albers

6946
PARK PLACE HOTEL
300 E State Street
Traverse City, MI 49684
Phone: 231-946-5000
Fax: 231-941-9812
e-mail: hotel@park-place-hotel.com
Web Site: www.park-place-hotel.com
Management:
General Manager: Amy Parker
Marketing Director: Margaret Morse
Founded: 1930
Status: For-Profit, Professional

6947
JAMES E O'NEIL JR ARENA
Saginaw Valley State University
7400 Bay Road
University Center, MI 48710
Phone: 989-964-7300
e-mail: sid@svsu.edu
Web Site: www.svsu.edu
Officers:
President: Eric Gilbertson
Management:
Athletic Director: Mike Watson
Operations: Matt Oberlin
Status: Non-Professional

6948
JEWISH COMMUNITY CENTER OF METROPOLITAN DETROIT
D Dan & Betty Kahn Building
6600 W Maple Road
West Bloomfield, MI 48322-3002
Phone: 248-661-1000
e-mail: mlit@jccdet.org
Web Site: www.jccdet.org
Officers:
President: Todd Sachse
Management:
Executive Director: Mark A Lit
Development: Wendy Strip
Marketing Director: Suzanne Lichtman
Founded: 1926
Status: Non-Profit
Paid Staff: 491
Volunteer Staff: 999

6949
YACK ARENA
3131 Third Street
Wyandotte, MI 48192
Phone: 734-324-7290
e-mail: recreation@wyan.org
Web Site: www.wyandotte.net
Officers:
Chairman: Molly Exner
Management:
Operations: Fred Pischke
Founded: 1800
Status: Non-Profit, Non-Professional
Paid Staff: 150
Seating Capacity: 3,800

6950
EASTERN MICHIGAN UNIVERSITY CONVOCATION CENTER
799 N Hewitt Road
Ypsilanti, MI 48197
Phone: 734-487-5386
Fax: 734-487-6898
e-mail: mmonahan@emich.edu
Web Site: www.emich.edu
Officers:
President: Susan Martin
Management:
Director: Mark Monahan
Marketing Director: Marcy Szabo
Founded: 1998
Seating Capacity: 9,500

Minnesota

6951
ALBERT LEA CITY ARENA
701 Lake Chapeau Drive
Albert, MN 56007
Phone: 507-377-4370
e-mail: jhutchison@city.albertlea.org
Web Site: www.city.albertlea.org
Management:
Facility Manager: Robert Furland
Director: Jay Hutchison
Founded: 1976
Specialized Field: 377-4370 work
Status: Non-Profit, Non-Professional
Paid Staff: 12
Paid Artists: 6

6952
ALBERT LEA COMMUNITY THEATRE
Marion Ross Performing Arts Center
147 N Broadway
Albert Lea, MN 56007
Phone: 507-377-4372
e-mail: mrpac@charterinternet.com
Web Site: www.city.albertlea.org
Management:
Theatre Manager: Patrick Rasmussen
Director: Jay Hutchison
Utilizes: Actors; Guest Artists; Guest Designers; Guest Instructors; Guest Soloists; Guild Activities; Instructors; Local Artists; Playwrights; Resident Artists; Special Technical Talent; Theatre Companies
Status: Profit
Paid Staff: 1
Facility Category: Theatre
Type of Stage: Proscenium
Stage Dimensions: 29' 6" x 23' x 28'
Seating Capacity: 255
Year Remodeled: 1989

6953
RIVERSIDE ARENA
501 2nd Avenue NE
Austin, MN 55912
Phone: 507-433-1881
Fax: 507-433-9078
Management:
Director: Kim A Underwood
Status: Non-Professional
Facility Category: Arena
Type of Stage: Portable
Seating Capacity: 4,200

6954
BEMIDJI STATE UNIVERSITY THOMPSON RECITAL HALL
Bangsberg Fine Arts Complex
1500 Birchmont Drive NE
Bemidji, MN 56601-2699
Phone: 218-755-2915
Fax: 218-755-4369
e-mail: plogan@bemidjistate.edu
Web Site: www.bemidjistate.edu
Officers:
Chair: P Bradley Logan
President: Jon Quistgaard
Specialized Field: Fine Arts
Status: Non-Professional
Type of Stage: Main Stage; Black Box

6955
NATIONAL SPORTS CENTER
1700 105th Avenue NE
Blaine, MN 55449
Phone: 763-785-5600
Fax: 763-785-5699
e-mail: webmaster@nscsports.org
Web Site: www.nscsports.com
Management:
Executive Director: Paul Erickson
Marketing Director: Jean Maybrey
Operations Manager: Brandon Radeke
Founded: 1990
Status: Non-Profit, Non-Professional
Paid Staff: 150
Seating Capacity: 12,000

6956
ARTS IN THE PARKS PORTABLE STAGE
2215 W Old Shakopee Road
Bloomington, MN 55431
Phone: 952-948-3925
Fax: 612-887-9695

6957
BROOKLYN CENTER COMMUNITY CENTER
6301 Shingle Creek Parkway
Brooklyn Center, MN 55430
Phone: 763-569-3400
Fax: 763-569-3494
e-mail: info@ci.brooklyn-center.mn.us
Web Site: www.cityofbrooklyncenter.org
Management:
    Director: Jim Glasoe
Status: Non-Profit

6958
NORTH HENNEPIN COMMUNITY COLLEGE THEATER
7411 85th Avenue N
Brooklyn Park, MN 55445
Phone: 763-424-0775
Fax: 763-493-0542
e-mail: info@nhcc.edu
Web Site: www.nhcc.edu
Officers:
    Dean: Jane Wilson
Status: Non-Professional

6959
DULUTH ENTERTAINMENT CONVENTION CENTER
350 Harbor Drive
Duluth, MN 55802
Phone: 218-722-5573
Fax: 218-722-4247
Toll-free: 800-628-8385
Web Site: www.decc.org
Management:
    Executive Director: Dan Russel
    Operations Director: Bob Hom
Founded: 1990
Status: For-Profit, Professional

6960
ST LOUIS COUNTY HERITAGE AND ARTS CENTER
Duluth Depot
506 W Michigan Street
Duluth, MN 55802
Phone: 218-727-8025
Web Site: www.duluthdepot.org
Management:
    Executive Director: Ken Buehler
Founded: 1892

6961
FAIRMONT OPERA HOUSE
45 Downtown Plaza
PO Box 226
Fairmont, MN 56031
Phone: 507-238-4900
e-mail: director@fairmontoperahouse.com
Web Site: www.fairmontoperahouse.com
Management:
    Managing Director: Tom Dodge
Founded: 1901
Status: Non-Profit, Professional

Paid Staff: 2
Paid Artists: 10

6962
GRAND CASINO HINCKLEY AMPHITHEATER
777 Lady Luck Drive
Hinckley, MN 55037
Toll-free: 800-472-6321
Web Site: www.grandcasinomn.com
Seating Capacity: 5,644

6963
PRAIRIE ARTS CENTER
PO Box 94
310 1st Avenue North
Long Prairie, MN 56347
Phone: 320-732-6080
Officers:
    President: Linda Kielty

6964
ELIAS J HALLING RECITAL HALL
Minnesota State University
202 Performing Arts Center
Mankato, MN 56001
Phone: 507-389-2118
Fax: 507-389-2922
e-mail: music@mnsu.edu
Web Site: www.intech.mnsu.edu
Management:
    Events Coordinator/Music: Dale Haefner
Utilizes: Artists-in-Residence; Educators; Fine Artists; Guest Musical Directors; Guest Musicians; Instructors; Multimedia; Original Music Scores
Founded: 1867
Paid Staff: 13
Paid Artists: 11
Budget: $55,000
Income Sources: Gate Receipts; Grants; Advertising; Corporate Contributions
Annual Attendance: 14,000
Facility Category: Performing Arts Center
Type of Stage: Proscenium
Stage Dimensions: 80'x40'
Seating Capacity: 350
Year Built: 1968
Rental Contact: 507-398-5549 Dale Haefner

6965
MIDWEST WIRELESS CIVIC CENTER
One Civic Center Plaza
Mankato, MN 56001
Phone: 507-389-3000
Fax: 507-345-1627
Web Site: www.midwestwirelessciviccenter.com
Management:
    Executive Director: Burt Lyman
    Marketing Manager: Mona Will
    Operations Manager: Dave Randalls
    Food/Beverage Director: Scott Schonike
Seating Capacity: 7,310

6966
GUTHRIE THEATER
818 South 2nd Street
Minneapolis, MN 55415
Phone: 612-225-6000
Fax: 612-225-6004
Toll-free: 877-447-8243
Web Site: www.guthrietheater.org
Officers:
    President: Douglas M Steenland
    VP: Randall Hogan

Treasurer: Jay Kiedrowski
    Secretary: Robert A Rosenbaum
Management:
    Director: Joe Dowling
    Associate Artistic Director: John Miller-Stephany
    Production Director: Frank Butler
Mission: An American center for theater performance, production, education and professional training. By presenting both classical literature and new work from diverse cultures, the Guthrie illuminates the common humanity connecting Minnesota to the peoples of the world.
Founded: 1963
Status: Non-Profit, Professional
Paid Staff: 326
Seating Capacity: 1,293
Year Built: 1963

6967
HENNEPIN CENTER FOR THE ARTS
528 Hennepin Avenue
Minneapolis, MN 55403
Phone: 612-332-4478
Fax: 612-332-8131
Web Site: www.artspaceusa.org
Founded: 1979
Status: Non-Profit, Professional
Paid Staff: 6

6968
HISTORIC ORPHEUM THEATRE
910 Hennepin Avenue
Minneapolis, MN 55402-1800
Phone: 612-373-5600
Fax: 612-339-5917
Web Site: www.hennepintheatredistrict.org
Management:
    Operations Manager: Dave Marietta
    COO: Tom Hoch
Founded: 1921
Seating Capacity: 2,579

6969
HISTORIC STATE THEATRE
805 Hennepin Avenue
Minneapolis, MN 55402
Phone: 612-373-5600
Fax: 612-252-0601
Web Site: www.hennepintheatredistrict.com
Management:
    Operations Manager: Mark Kroening
    COO: Tom Hoch
Status: For-Profit, Non-Professional
Paid Staff: 100

6970
HUBERT H HUMPHREY METRODOME
900 South Fifth Street
Minneapolis, MN 55415
Phone: 612-332-0386
Fax: 612-332-8334
e-mail: lesterb@msfc.com
Web Site: www.msfc.com
Management:
    Executive Director: William J Lester
    Director Operations: Dennis Alfton
Founded: 1982
Status: For-Profit, Non-Professional
Seating Capacity: 65,000 (football), 55,500 (basketball)
Year Built: 1982

6971

MACPHAIL CENTER FOR THE ARTS

1128 LaSalle Avenue
Minneapolis, MN 55403
Phone: 612-321-0100
Management:
 Assistant Director: Joanna Cortright
Mission: Lessons and classes in music to both adults and children.
Founded: 1907
Specialized Field: Vocal Music; Instrumental Music
Status: Semi-Professional; Nonprofit
Income Sources: University of Minnesota; National Guild of Community Schools of Music
Organization Type: Educational

6972

NORTHROP AUDITORIUM

University of Minnesota
84 Church Street Southeast
Minneapolis, MN 55455
Phone: 612-625-9878
Fax: 612-626-1750
Web Site: www.northrop.umn.edu
Officers:
 GM: Dale Schatzlein
 Publicity Office: Linda Brandt
Founded: 1928
Seating Capacity: 4,767

6973

ORCHESTRA HALL

1111 Nicollet Mall
Minneapolis, MN 55403
Phone: 612-371-5600
Toll-free: 800-292-4141
e-mail: info@mnorch.com
Web Site: www.minnesotaorchestra.org
Officers:
 President: David H Hyslop
 VP: E Benton Gill
 General Manager: Robert Meu
Mission: To enrich lives with great music.
Founded: 1903
Status: Non-Profit, Professional
Paid Staff: 150
Paid Artists: 100
Budget: $28,000,000
Annual Attendance: 400,000
Facility Category: Concert Hall
Type of Stage: Proscenium
Seating Capacity: 2,450
Year Built: 1974

6974

TARGET CENTER

600 1st Avenue
Minneapolis, MN 55403-1416
Phone: 612-673-1300
Fax: 612-673-1370
e-mail: info@targetcenter.com
Web Site: www.targetcenter.com
Management:
 Executive Director: Steve Mattson
 VP: Kevin McHale
 Marketing Director: Sandy Sweetser
 Concessions Manager: Ajay Sekhran
Mission: There are 18,467 theatre-style permanent seats in Target Center and in addition there are over 114 wheelchair and accessible seating located on all concourse levels of Target Center. The Minnesota

Timberwolves played their first game in their new home, Target Center, on October 16, 1990 vs. the Philadelphia 76ers.
Founded: 1990
Status: For-Profit, Non-Professional
Paid Staff: 500

6975

TED MANN CONCERT HALL

University of Minnesota
2106 Fourth Street South
Minneapolis, MN 55455
Phone: 612-626-1892
Fax: 612-626-7375
e-mail: tedmann@tc.umn.edu
Web Site: www.tedmann.umn.edu
Officers:
 Facilities Manager: Craig Carnahan
Seating Capacity: 1,100

6976

THEATRE IN THE ROUND PLAYERS

245 Cedar Avenue
Minneapolis, MN 55454-1054
Phone: 612-333-2919
Web Site: www.theatreintheround.org
Management:
 President: Diana Hellerman
 Executive Director: Steven Antenucci
Mission: To produce excellent theatre in, with, and for the community.
Founded: 1952
Status: Non-Profit, Non-Professional
Paid Staff: 3
Paid Artists: 9
Seating Capacity: 249

6977

UNIVERSITY OF MINNESOTA SPORTS PAVILLION

1923 University Avenue SE
Minneapolis, MN 55455
Phone: 612-625-5804
Fax: 612-624-5887
Management:
 Director/Athletic Facilities: Scott P Ellison
 Assistant Program Director: Leon Freese
Seating Capacity: 5,700

6978

WALKER ART CENTER

1750 Hennepin Ave
Minneapolis, MN 55403
Phone: 612-375-7656
Fax: 612-375-7618
e-mail: info@walkerart.org
Web Site: www.walkerart.org
Mission: A catalyst for the creative expression of artists and the active engagement of audiences, examines the questions that shape and inspire us as individuals, cultures, and communities.
Founded: 1927

6979

NEW HOPE OUTDOOR THEATRE

4401 Xylon Avenue N
New Hope, MN 55428
Phone: 763-531-5151
Fax: 763-531-5136
Web Site: www.ci.new-hope.mn.us
Management:
 Director Arts Creation: Shery French
Founded: 1970
Status: Non-Profit

6980

MARTIN LUTHER COLLEGE LYCEUM

1995 Luther Court
New Ulm, MN 56073
Fax: 507-354-8225

6981

MAYO CIVIC CENTER ARENA

30 Civic Center Drive SE
Rochester, MN 55904
Phone: 507-281-6184
Fax: 507-281-6277
Toll-free: 800-422-2199
e-mail: info@mayociviccenter.com
Web Site: www.mayociviccenter.com
Management:
 Executive Director: Donna Drews
 Operations Manager: David Silker
 Managing Director: Andy Krogstad

6982

MAYO CIVIC CENTER AUDITORIUM THEATRE

30 Civic Center Drive SE
Rochester, MN 55904
Phone: 507-281-6184
Fax: 507-281-6277
Toll-free: 800-422-2199
e-mail: info@mayociviccenter.com
Web Site: www.mayociviccenter.com
Management:
 Executive Director: Donna Drews
 Managing Director: Andy Krogstad
 Operations Manager: David Silker

6983

PARAMOUNT THEATRE

913 W Saint Germain Street
Saint Cloud, MN 56301
Phone: 320-240-0836
e-mail: boxoffice@paramountarts.org
Web Site: www.paramountarts.org
Officers:
 CFO: Lea Leneau
Management:
 Executive Director: Tony Goddard
 Performing Arts Director: Laurie Johnson
Founded: 1998
Performs At: Historic Theatre
Seating Capacity: 700

6984

BENEDICTA ARTS CENTER

College of Saint Benedict
37 South College Avenue
Saint Joseph, MN 56374
Phone: 320-363-5777
Fax: 320-363-6097
Web Site: www.csbsju.edu/finearts
Management:
 Executive Director: Anna Thompson
 Director of Fund Raising/Marketing: Nicole Gram
 Director of Operations: Mary Darnall
 Production Manager: Jack Dempsey
 Technical Director: Brian White
 Box Office Systems Manager: Deb Wolford
Utilizes: Actors; Artists-in-Residence; Choreographers; Collaborating Artists; Collaborations; Commissioned Music; Dance Companies; Dancers; Designers; Educators; Filmmakers; Fine Artists; Five Seasonal Concerts; Grant Writers; Guest Accompanists; Guest Artists; Guest Choreographers; Guest Companies; Guest Composers; Guest Conductors; Guest

Designers; Guest Directors; Guest Ensembles; Guest Instructors; Guest Lecturers; Guest Musical Directors; Guest Musicians; Guest Soloists; Guest Teachers; High School Drama; Instructors; Local Artists; Lyricists; Multimedia; Music; Organization Contracts; Original Music Scores; Performance Artists; Playwrights; Resident Artists; Selected Students; Sign Language Translators; Singers; Soloists; Student Interns; Special Technical Talent; Theatre Companies; Touring Companies; Visual Arts
Paid Staff: 13
Volunteer Staff: 20
Paid Artists: 9
Non-paid Artists: 400
Income Sources: NEA, MSAB, Heartland Arts Fund, Target Stores, local corporations, fees and tickets
Annual Attendance: 15,000
Facility Category: Performing Arts Center
Type of Stage: Proscenium
Stage Dimensions: 59' X 38
Seating Capacity: 1,084
Year Built: 1963
Cost: 2.5 million
Rental Contact: Mary Darnall

6985
FITZGERALD THEATER
10 E Exchange Street
Saint Paul, MN 55101
Phone: 651-290-1200
Fax: 651-290-1195
e-mail: fitzgerald@mpr.org
Web Site: www.fitzgeraldtheater.org
Management:
  President: Brian Sanderson
  Production Manager: Thomas Campbell
  Box Office Manager: Shane Wethers
Mission: The theater has, over the years, played host to Broadway musicals, vaudeville shows, film festivals, and concerts of all sorts.
Utilizes: AEA Actors; Choreographers; Collaborations; Dance Companies; Dancers; Designers; Guest Choreographers; Multimedia; Music; Resident Professionals; Sign Language Translators; Special Technical Talent; Theatre Companies
Founded: 1980
Specialized Field: Concerts; Theater; Broadcasting; Dance
Status: Non-Profit, Professional
Paid Staff: 15
Volunteer Staff: 15
Budget: 350,000
Income Sources: Box Office; Rent; Concession; Grant from Parent Company
Facility Category: Rental-Performing Arts
Type of Stage: Sprung Floor
Stage Dimensions: 36'x30'
Year Built: 1910
Year Remodeled: 1986
Rental Contact: Manager, General Services Shane Wethers

6986
LEGENDARY ROY WILKINS AUDITORIUM AT SAINT PAUL RIVERCENTRE
175 W Kellogg Boulevard
Suite 501
Saint Paul, MN 55102
Phone: 651-265-4800
Fax: 651-265-4899
e-mail: info@rivercentre.org
Web Site: www.theroy.org
Management:
  Vice President/General Manager: Jim Ibister

Director Booking: Susan Hubbard
Founded: 1930
Facility Category: Auditorium with flat floor and balcony seating
Type of Stage: portable
Stage Dimensions: 6' x 8'x 8' sections
Seating Capacity: 5,500
Year Built: 1931
Year Remodeled: 1984

6987
MIDWAY STADIUM
1771 Energy Park Drive
Saint Paul, MN 55108
Phone: 651-644-3517
Fax: 651-644-1627
e-mail: funsgood@saintsbaseball.com
Web Site: www.saintsbaseball.com
Management:
  GM: Bill Fanning
Seating Capacity: 14,000

6988
O'SHAUGHNESSY THEATRE
St. Catherine University
2004 Randolph Avenue F-24
Saint Paul, MN 55105
Phone: 651-690-6700
Fax: 651-690-6769
e-mail: oshuaghnessy@stkate.edu
Web Site: www.stkate.edu/oshaughnessy
Officers:
  Managing Director: Brandie Greig
  Production Manager: Greg Morrissey
Founded: 1970
Status: Nonprofit. Professional
Paid Staff: 11
Paid Artists: 20
Seating Capacity: 1,817

6989
ORDWAY CENTER FOR THE PERFORMING ARTS
345 Washington Street
Saint Paul, MN 55102
Phone: 651-282-3000
Fax: 651-224-5319
Web Site: www.ordway.org
Management:
  President: David Galligan
  Director Marketing/Sales: Ron Smith
Founded: 1985
Paid Staff: 80
Volunteer Staff: 100
Performs At: Ordway Music McKnight Theatre

6990
RIVERCENTER
175 W Kellogg Boulevard
Saint Paul, MN 55102
Phone: 651-265-4800
Fax: 651-265-4899
e-mail: info@rivercentre.org
Web Site: www.rivercentre.org
Management:
  Managing Director: Jim Ivester
  Interim Director: Erich Mische
Founded: 1996
Status: For-Profit, Professional
Paid Staff: 200
Seating Capacity: 16,000

6991
XCEL ENERGY CENTER
Xcel Energy Center
7th Street
Saint Paul, MN 55102
Phone: 651-222-9453
Fax: 651-265-4899
Web Site: www.wild.com
Management:
  President: Doug Raisebrough
  Executive Director: Jack Larson
  Director Marketing: Peter Johns
  Arena Project Director: Ray Chandler
Founded: 1997
Status: Professional
Seating Capacity: 18,600

6992
SCHAEFFER FINE ARTS CENTER
Gustavus Adolphus College
800 W College Avenue
Saint Peter, MN 56082
Phone: 507-933-7363
Fax: 507-933-6253
e-mail: al@gac.edu
Web Site: www.gustavus.edu
Management:
  President: James Peterson
  Fine Arts Director: Alan Behrends
Founded: 1862
Status: Non-Profit, Professional
Paid Staff: 700
Paid Artists: 32

6993
I-90 EXPO CENTER
1010 70th Avenue
Sherburn, MN 56171
Phone: 507-736-2761
Fax: 507-764-4990
Web Site: www.i90expocenter.com
Officers:
  Co-Owner: Mike Johnson
  Co-Owner: Greg Johnson
Seating Capacity: 7,000

6994
LAKESHORE PLAYHOUSE
4820 Stewart Avenue
White Bear Lake, MN 55110
Phone: 651-426-3275
Fax: 651-429-5674
e-mail: office@lakeshoreplayers.com
Web Site: www.lakeshoreplayers.com
Officers:
  President: Frank Mabley
Founded: 1952
Status: Non-Profit, Non-Professional
Paid Staff: 4

Mississippi

6995
DEPOT THEATRE
110 Magnolia Street
Belzoni, MS 39038
Phone: 662-247-1976
Season: June - September

6996
BEAU RIVAGE THEATRE
875 Beach Boulevard
Biloxi, MS 39530
Mailing Address: PO Box 7777
Phone: 228-386-7712
Fax: 228-386-7619
Web Site: www.beaurivage.com
Officers:
Executive Director Of Entertainment: Anthony
Gibson
Founded: 1999
Seating Capacity: 1,500
Year Built: 2006

6997
HARLEY OUTDOOR AMPHITHEATRE
942 Cedar Lake Road
Biloxi, MS 39532
Phone: 228-547-4239
Fax: 985-646-1662
Management:
GM: Shannon Elias
Seating Capacity: 20,000

6998
SAENGER THEATRE OF THE PERFORMING ARTS
170 Reynoir Street
PO Box 775
Biloxi, MS 39530
Phone: 228-432-1601
e-mail: rchester@biloxi.ms.us
Web Site: www.biloxi.ms.us/saenger/
Management:
Manager: Ron Chester
Technical Director: Bob Montgomery
Founded: 1929

6999
BOLOGNA PERFORMING ARTS CENTER
Delta State University
PO Box 3213
Cleveland, MS 38733
Phone: 662-846-4625
Fax: 662-846-4627
e-mail: ddallas@deltastate.edu
Web Site: www.bolognapac.com
Management:
Executive Director: David Dallas
Production Coordinator: Paula H Lindsey
Arts Education Coordinator: Tennie Lester
Asst Dir/Audience Dev Coordinator: Jolana R
Gibbs
Senior Secretary: Kimberly Potts
Mission: The center attracts quality programming,
superb artists and powerful performances to enrich,
entertain and strengthen our Delta community. In
addition, the Bologna Center has demonstrated its
commitment to arts education and developed the
Janice Wyatt Mississippi Summer Arts Institute, which
provides a comprehensive training program in all arts
disciplines.
Founded: 1994
Specialized Field: Education; Dance; Speakers;
Musical Shows; Broadway Shows; Performances
Status: Non-Profit, Professional
Paid Staff: 10
Paid Artists: 12

7000
WHISTLE STOP PLAYHOUSE
Cleveland Community Theatre
PO Box 44
Cleveland, MS 38732
Phone: 601-843-3096

7001
COLUMBIA EXPOSITION CENTER
150 Industrial Park Drive
Columbia, MS 39429
Phone: 601-736-6204
Fax: 601-736-6259
e-mail: expocenter@cblink.com
Management:
Manager: Linda Martin
Manager: Paul Pounds
Seating Capacity: 3,200

7002
PRINCESS THEATRE
5th Street S
Columbus, MS 39701
Phone: 662-328-7860

7003
COLISEUM CIVIC CENTER
404 Taylor Street
PO Box 723
Corinth, MS 38834
Phone: 662-287-6079
Fax: 662-286-0903

7004
LEFLORE COUNTY CIVIC CENTER
Highway 7 N
PO Box 1659
Greenwood, MS 38930
Phone: 662-453-4065
Fax: 662-453-4067
Management:
Executive Director: Andrew McQueen
Booking: Flo Long
Founded: 1979
Status: Non-Profit, Professional
Paid Staff: 5
Budget: $350,000
Income Sources: Leflore County
Facility Category: Arena/Meeting Rooms
Type of Stage: Proscenium
Seating Capacity: 3000
Year Built: 1980

7005
SAENGER THEATRE
201 Forrest Street
Hattiesburg, MS 39401
Phone: 601-584-4888
Fax: 601-296-7740
e-mail: saenger@hattiesburg.org
Web Site: www.hattiesburgmsaenger.com
Mission: To accommodate both live performancesamd
film and to evoke images of romantic for away places
Utilizes: Actors; Collaborating Artists; Collaborations;
Dance Companies; Dancers; Grant Writers; Guest
Accompanists; Guest Artists; Guest Composers; Guest
Designers; Guest Instructors; Guest Lecturers; Guest
Musical Directors; Guest Musicians; Guest Soloists;
Guild Activities; Instructors; Local Artists; Multimedia;
Music; New Productions; Original Music Scores; Sign
Language Translators; Singers; Soloists; Special
Technical Talent; Theatre Companies
Paid Staff: 13

Volunteer Staff: 10
Paid Artists: 10
Budget: $100,000
Income Sources: Revenue Taxes
Annual Attendance: 100,000+
Facility Category: Theatre
Seating Capacity: 1000
Year Built: 1929
Year Remodeled: 2000
Cost: $3.75 Million
Rental Contact: H. Allen Sanders

7006
UNIVERSITY OF SOUTHERN MISSISSIPPI SCHOOL OF MUSIC
118 College Drive
#5081
Hattiesburg, MS 39406-0001
Phone: 601-266-5543
Fax: 601-266-6427
e-mail: music@usm.edu
Web Site: www.usm.edu\music
Management:
Director: Dr Michael Miles,
michael.a.miles@usm.edu
Associate Director: Dr Jennifer Shank,
jennifer.shank@usm.edu
Mission: Recognized for its eminence in musical
artistry, education and community service. Provides a
wealth of valuable opportunities for the professional and
artistic growth of the students.
Founded: 1920
Specialized Field: Orchestra; Chamber; Ensemble;
Choral; Band
Status: Non-Profit, Non-Professional
Paid Staff: 150
Seating Capacity: 1,000

7007
INDIANOLA LITTLE THEATRE
Main and Sunflower Avenue
Indianola, MS 38751
Phone: 662-887-9920
Management:
President: Andy Dineals
Executive Director: Wildon Aultman
Managing Director: Kathreen Parcel
Founded: 1978
Status: Non-Profit, Non-Professional
Paid Staff: 30

7008
JACKSON MUNICIPAL AUDITORIUM THALIA MARA HALL
255 E Pacagoula Street
Jackson, MS 39201
Mailing Address: PO Box 288
Phone: 601-960-1537
Fax: 601-960-1583
Management:
Booking Coordinator: Vicki Carter
Manager: Maxine Dilday
Mission: Theatre style venue for operas, ballets,
symphony, plays, small seminars, concerts and
broadway musicals.
Founded: 1968
Status: For-Profit, Non-Professional
Paid Staff: 4
Affiliations: City of Jackson
Annual Attendance: 160,000
Facility Category: Theatre
Seating Capacity: 2,350
Year Built: 1968

Rental Contact: Vicki Carter

7009

MISSISSIPPI VETERANS MEMORIAL STADIUM
2531 N State Street
Jackson, MS 39296
Phone: 601-354-6021
Fax: 601-354-6019
Web Site: www.mveteransstadium.com
Management:
    Director: Matt Watley
Seating Capacity: 60,492

7010

WOOD COLLEGE THEATRE
Wood College Road
PO Box 289
Mathiston, MS 39752
Phone: 662-263-5352
Fax: 662-263-4964

7011

MERIDIAN COMMUNITY COLLEGE THEATRE
910 Harvey 19 N
Meridian, MS 39307
Phone: 601-483-8241
Fax: 601-482-3936
Management:
    Chair/Fine Arts: Ronnie Miller
Founded: 1937
Specialized Field: Visual Arts; Music; Theatre
Paid Staff: 5

7012

HUMPHREY COLISEUM
Mississippi State University
College View Street
Mississippi State, MS 39762
Mailing Address: PO Box HY
Phone: 662-325-4201
Fax: 662-325-7456
Web Site: www.humphreycoliseum.msstate.edu
Officers:
    Director: Todd Hunt
    Assistant Director: Raymond Brooks
Opened: 1974
Seating Capacity: 11,000

7013

FULTON CHAPEL
University of Mississippi
Oxford, MS 38677
Phone: 662-232-7411
Fax: 662-232-5082
Web Site: www.olemiss.edu
Founded: 1927
Seating Capacity: 915
Year Built: 1927

7014

MEEK AUDITORIUM
University of Mississippi
Oxford, MS 38677
Phone: 662-232-7268
Fax: 662-915-7443
e-mail: music@olemiss.edu

7015

UNIVERSITY OF MISSISSIPPI STUDIO THEATRE
PO Box 1848
Oxford, MS 38677
Phone: 662-232-7411
Fax: 662-232-5082
Web Site: www.olemiss.edu

7016

PANOLA PLAYHOUSE
212 S Main Street
PO Box 43
Sardis, MS 38666
Phone: 662-487-3975
Fax: 662-487-1421
e-mail: lee@panola.com
Web Site: www.panolaplayhouse.com
Mission: To provide an outlet for entertainment and performance for the mostly rural area of Panola County and the surrounding area of North Mississippi.
Founded: 1963
Specialized Field: Community Theatre
Status: Active
Paid Staff: 2
Volunteer Staff: 3
Budget: $20,000
Income Sources: Membership; Donations; Box Office; Fundraising
Affiliations: Mississippi Arts Commission
Annual Attendance: 1,200
Seating Capacity: 163
Year Built: 1946
Year Remodeled: 1970
Rental Contact: Lee Dixon

7017

BANCORP SOUTH ARENA
375 East Main Street
Tupelo, MS 38804
Mailing Address: PO Box 7288
Phone: 601-841-6573
Fax: 601-841-6413
e-mail: dskinner@bcsarena.com
Web Site: www.bcsarena.com/
Management:
    Director: David Skinner
    Director of Operations: Craig Russell
    Director of Marketing: Kevan Kirkpatrick
    Box Office Manager: Jeanie Friday
Mission: The spacious 32,000 square foot arena seats nearly 10,000 for concerts and 8,000 for sporting events. The arena floor can accommodate wood, ice or dirt for events ranging from basketball to skating to rodeos.

7018

TRIANGLE CULTURAL CENTER
322 North Main Street
Yazoo City, MS 39194
Phone: 662-746-2273
Fax: 662-746-2838
Toll-free: 800-381-0662
e-mail: kkyazoo@gmail.com
Web Site: www.trianglecultercenter.com
Management:
    Director: K K Hill
Mission: To provide the community with a venue for performing arts.
Founded: 1978
Paid Staff: 3
Paid Artists: 1
Non-paid Artists: 3

Seating Capacity: 200

Missouri

7019

LYCEUM THEATRE
PO Box 14
Arrow Rock, MO 65320
Phone: 660-837-3311
Fax: 660-837-3112
Web Site: www.lyceumtheatre.org
Officers:
    President: Dave Griggs
    VP: Chet Breitwieser
    Treasurer: Vicki Russell
    Secretary: Michael Kateman
Management:
    Artistic Director: Quin Gresham
    Managing Director: Steve Bertani
    Marketing Director: Erin Willis
    Box Office Manager: Alice Roselius
Mission: To provide the loyal audience with the best theatrical experience possible.
Status: Professional
Seating Capacity: 408

7020

CULVER-STOCKTON COLLEGE PERFORMING ARTS HALL
One College Hill
Canton, MO 63435
Phone: 573-288-6352
Fax: 573-288-6614
Toll-free: 800-537-1883
Web Site: www.culver.edu
Officers:
    Fine Arts Department Chair: Joseph Deiker
Management:
    President: William Fox
Mission: Private liberal Arts college with a strong progam in Art, Theatre and Music.
Utilizes: Actors; AEA Actors; Dancers; Designers; Educators; Fine Artists; Five Seasonal Concerts; Grant Writers; Guest Accompanists; Guest Artists; Guest Choreographers; Guest Companies; Guest Composers; Guest Conductors; Guest Directors; Guest Ensembles; Guest Instructors; Guest Lecturers; Guest Musicians; Guest Soloists; Guild Activities; High School Drama; Instructors; Local Artists; Local Unknown Artists; Multi Collaborations; Multimedia; Music; New Productions; Playwrights; Resident Professionals; Sign Language Translators; Singers; Soloists; Student Interns; Special Technical Talent; Theatre Companies; Touring Companies; Visual Arts
Founded: 1853
Specialized Field: Art; Music; Theatre
Status: Non-Profit, Non-Professional
Paid Staff: 12
Paid Artists: 8
Budget: $10,000-20,000
Performs At: Alexander Campbell Auditorium; Meriallat Recital Hall
Annual Attendance: 5,000
Facility Category: College Campus
Type of Stage: Recital Hall; Proscenium; Black Box
Stage Dimensions: 60'x40'
Seating Capacity: 200; 969; 150
Year Built: 1966
Year Remodeled: 1990
Rental Contact: 217-231-6346 Judy Garkie

7021

SHOW ME CENTER

1333 N Sprigg Street
Cape Girardeau, MO 63701
Phone: 573-651-2297
Fax: 573-651-5054
e-mail: dross@semo.edu
Web Site: www.showmecenter.biz
Officers:
Business Manager/Executive Director: Greg
Talbut
Management:
Director: David Ross, dross@semo.edu
Operations Supervisor: Jim Barbatti,
jbarbatti@semo.edu
Marketing Director: Shannon Buford,
sbuford@semo.edu
Founded: 1987
Opened: 1987
Paid Staff: 13
Facility Category: Multi-Purpose Arena
Type of Stage: Portable SICO Stage
Stage Dimensions: 60'x40'
Seating Capacity: 7,000
Year Built: 1987
Cost: $16.5 Million
Rental Contact: David Ross

7022

FAUROT FIELDHOUSE

University of Missouri
600 Stadium Boulevard, Room 260
Columbia, MO 65211
Phone: 573-882-2056
Fax: 573-882-4298
e-mail: hickmantl@missouri.edu
Web Site: www.mutigers.com
Management:
Director: Timothy L Hickman
Facility Category: Stadium
Stage Dimensions: 67,000 sq ft

7023

HEARNES CENTER

University of Missouri
600 Stadium Boulevard
Columbia, MO 65211
Phone: 573-882-2056
Fax: 573-882-4298
Web Site: www.hearnescenter.com
Management:
Director: Timothy L Hickman
Operations Manager: Jeff Roberts
Seating Capacity: 13,500
Year Built: 1972

7024

JESSE AUDITORIUM

University of Missouri
311 Jesse Hall
Columbia, MO 65211
Phone: 573-884-9044
Fax: 573-884-5446
e-mail: murrayjs@missouri.edu
Web Site: www.missouri.edu/~jesseaud
Management:
Booking Contact: John Murray
Events Assistant: Marlys Johnson
Seating Capacity: 1,798

7025

MISSOURI THEATRE

203 S Ninth St
Columbia, MO 65201
Phone: 573-875-0600
Fax: 573-449-4214
e-mail: info@motheatre.org
Web Site: www.motheatre.org
Officers:
President: Doug Moore
President-Elect: Cortney Wright
Secretary: Jeff Keevil
Treasurer: Jim Weaver
Past President: Nancy Bedan
Management:
Executive Director: David A White, III
Mission: Providing an artistic home for the visual and
performing arts - produced by local, regional and
nationally-recognized arts organizations; Providing arts
education for the community's youth and adults;
Preserving the community's cultural heritage within the
timeless structure of the historic Missouri Theatre;
Enhancing downtown Columbia's economic base.

7026

OKOBOJI SUMMER THEATRE

Stephens College
1200 E Broadway
Columbia, MO 65215
Mailing Address: Box 341, Spirit Lake, IA. 51360
Phone: 573-442-2211
Toll-free: 800-876-7207
e-mail: bleonard@stephens.edu
Web Site:
www.stephens.edu/news/stephensevents/okoboji.php
Management:
Box Office/Tickes Manager: Beth Leonard
Mission: Stephens College began operating the
Okoboji Summer Theatre in 1958 for the purpose of
providing commercial summer stock experience for
advanced theatre students.
Founded: 1833

7027

ELIZABETH T CHAMP AUDITORIUM

Westminster College
501 Westminster Avenue
Fulton, MO 65251
Phone: 573-592-5319
Fax: 573-592-5138
e-mail: webmaster@westminster-mo.edu
Web Site:
www.westminster-mo.edu/explore/about/buildings.html
Management:
President: Dr. Fletcher M Lamkin
Mission: The Elizabeth T. Champ Auditorium, built in
1966, seats 1,400 persons for concerts, lectures,
dramatic productions, movies and other college events
such as Commencement. The lower level houses the
bookstore, an audio-visual classroom and the Office of
Enrollment Services.
Founded: 1851

7028

WILLIAM WOODS COLLEGE CAMPUS CENTER DULANY AUDITORIUM

200 W 12th Street
Fulton, MO 65251
Phone: 573-642-2251
Fax: 612-690-3279
Toll-free: 800-995-3159
Web Site: www.williamwoods.edu
Management:

President: Jahnae Barnett
VP: Robert Fredler
Artistic Director: Joe Potter
Founded: 1825
Status: Non-Profit, Professional
Paid Staff: 200
Paid Artists: 10

7029

WINSTON CHURCHILL MEMORIAL HALL

Westminster College
7th and Westminster
Fulton, MO 65251
Phone: 314-642-3361

7030

AMERICAN ROYAL CENTER KEMPER ARENA

Global Spectrum
1800 Genessee
Kansas City, MO 64102
Phone: 816-513-4000
Fax: 816-513-4001
e-mail: jlewis@kemperarenakc.com
Web Site: www.kemperarenakc.com
Officers:
Media/Public Relations Manager: Ken Gies
Executive Director: William Lamette
Management:
General Manager: Larry Hovick
Assistant General Manager: Todd Mitchell
Director of Operations: Thom Jones
Box Office Manager: Brian Wholf
Event Manager: Danny Burns
Marketing Manager: Ryan McCarthy
Founded: 1973
Specialized Field: Sports and Entertainment Arena.
Home of the Kansas City Comets (MisI)
Status: For-Profit, Professional
Paid Staff: 60
Seating Capacity: 19,500
Year Built: 1974
Year Remodeled: 1997

7031

FOLLY THEATER

300 W 12th Street
Kansas City, MO 64105
Mailing Address: PO Box 26505 Kansas City, MO
64196
Phone: 816-842-5500
Fax: 816-842-8709
Web Site: www.follytheater.com
Management:
Events Director: Lisa Lillig
Mission: The Folly is the premier Kansas City
showplace for business meetings, events, and
performances.
Founded: 1981
Status: Non-Profit, Professional
Paid Staff: 5
Seating Capacity: 1,078

7032

GOPPERT THEATRE

Avila College
11901 Wornall Road
Kansas City, MO 64145
Phone: 816-501-2411
Fax: 816-501-2442
Toll-free: 800-462-8452
e-mail: Robert.Foulk@Avila.edu
Web Site: www.avila.edu/theatre/goppert.htm
Officers:

Dean of the College Performing Arts: Dr. Charlene Gould
Management:
Theatre Director: Robert Foulk
Director Design & Technical Theatre: Jason Harris
Mission: Avila University offers state of the art performance facilities including the newly remodeled Goppert Theatre providing an exceptional performance venue.
Founded: 1973
Specialized Field: Goppert Theatre
Budget: $10,000
Performs At: Goppert Theater

7033
KANSAS CITY MUNICIPAL AUDITORIUM MUSIC HALL

301 W 13th Street
Suite 100
Kansas City, MO 64105
Phone: 816-513-5000
Fax: 816-513-5001
Toll-free: 800-821-7060
Web Site: www.kcconvention.com
Management:
Sales Associate: Sue Hides
Sales Associate: Felecia Fremont
Marketing Manager: Liz Bouman
Executive Director: William H LaMette
Deputy Director: Bill Langley
Director Sales/Marketing: Kathleen Lee
Assistant Director Sales/Marketing: Alan Schmelzle
Utilizes: Dance Companies; Dancers; Fine Artists; Grant Writers; Guest Accompanists; Guest Composers; Guest Instructors; Guest Soloists; Instructors; Local Artists; Multimedia; Original Music Scores; Singers; Special Technical Talent; Theatre Companies
Founded: 1936
Paid Staff: 120
Income Sources: Rental and User Fees
Performs At: Performance Hall
Facility Category: Fine Arts Performing Arts
Type of Stage: Proscenium
Stage Dimensions: 85'6"wx35'lx46'h
Seating Capacity: 2,400
Year Built: 1936
Year Remodeled: 1981
Architect: $1,200,000
Rental Contact: Sales Associate Sue Hodes

7034
KANSAS CITY MUNICIPAL AUDITORIUM

Convention Center
301 W 13th Street Suite 100
Kansas City, MO 64105
Phone: 816-513-5000
Fax: 816-513-5001
Toll-free: 800-821-7060
Web Site: www.kcconvention.com
Management:
Sales Manager: Larry Joneshill
Box Office Manager: Angie Blaisdell
Contract Administrator: Felicia Fremont-Alexiou
Marketing Manager: Liz Bowman
Seating Capacity: 10,700

7035
KAUFFMAN STADIUM

One Royal Way
Kansas City, MO 64129

Mailing Address: PO Box 419969 Kansas City, MO 64141-6969
Phone: 816-921-8000
Fax: 816-921-1366
Toll-free: 800-676-9257
Web Site: www.kcroyals.com
Founded: 1969
Specialized Field: Home of the Kansas City Royals (MLB)
Status: For-Profit, Professional
Paid Staff: 88
Seating Capacity: 40,625
Year Built: 1973

7036
STARLIGHT THEATRE

4600 Starlight Road
Kansas City, MO 64132
Phone: 816-363-7827
Fax: 816-361-4324
Web Site: www.umbbankpavilion.com
Management:
Executive Producer: Robert M Rohlf
VP Events/Entertainment: Bill Hartnett
Seating Capacity: 8,108

7037
UNICORN THEATRE

3828 Main Street
Kansas City, MO 64111
Phone: 816-531-7529
Fax: 816-531-0421
e-mail: unicornnews@unicorntheatre.org
Web Site: www.unicorntheatre.org
Management:
Producing Artistic Director: Cynthia Levin
General Manager: Jeffrey Blaha
Marketing Director: Justin M Shaw
Development Director: Julie E Milner
Technical Supervisor: Jeffrey Cady
Box Office Manager: Paula Simkins
Mission: Exists to enhance the cultural life of Kansas City by producing professional contemporary, thought-provoking theater, which inspires emotional response and stimulates discussion.

7038
LIBERTY PERFORMING ARTS THEATRE

1600 S Withers Road
Liberty, MO 64068-4604
Phone: 816-792-6130
Fax: 816-792-6148
e-mail: info@lpat.org
Web Site: www.lpat.org
Management:
Mayor: Steven Hawkins
Recreation Director: Chris Deal
Managing Director: Paul Miler
Technical Director: Hunter Burgess
Mission: A rental venue hosting a wide range of dance, music, drama, ceremonial, and other special events; striving to provide the best in personnel, services, and equipment. The theatre also serves as a co-presenter of high quality, family-oriented art events.
Utilizes: Collaborations; Guest Directors; Guild Activities; Instructors; Local Artists; Multimedia; Original Music Scores; Soloists; Student Interns; Theatre Companies
Founded: 1992
Specialized Field: All performing Arts Disciplines
Status: Non-Profit, Professional
Paid Staff: 10
Budget: $110,000

Income Sources: Rental Sales; Ticket Revenue; Private Donations
Performs At: Liberty Performing Arts Theatre
Affiliations: Kansas City Jazz Ambassadors, Plain Presenters Consortium, local Chamber of Commerce
Annual Attendance: 80,000
Facility Category: Multi-discipline Theatrical Space
Type of Stage: Proscenium
Stage Dimensions: 85x41
Seating Capacity: 725 (700 permanent)
Year Built: 1992
Cost: $1.5 milion
Rental Contact: Theatre Coordinator Paul Miller

7039
UMB BANK PAVILION

14141 Riverport Drive
Maryland Heights, MO 63043
Phone: 314-962-4000
Fax: 314-291-4719
Web Site: www.umbbankpavilion.com
Management:
Executive Director: Eric Blockie
Box Office Manager: Larry Pearson
Seating Capacity: 21,202

7040
MARY LINN PERFORMING ARTS CENTER

Northwest Missouri State University
800 University Drive
Maryville, MO 64468
Phone: 660-562-1317
Fax: 660-562-1346
e-mail: music@mail.nwmissouri.edu
Web Site: www.nwmissouri.edu
Officers:
President: Dean Hubbart
Management:
Department Chair/Music: Dr. Ernest Woodruff
Mission: Educational
Founded: 1905
Specialized Field: Instrumental Music; Vocal Music
Affiliations: National Association of Schools of Music

7041
PRICE CUTTER PARK

4400 North 19th Street
Ozark, MO 65721
Mailing Address: PO Box 1472
Phone: 417-581-2868
Fax: 417-581-8342
e-mail: tclegg@centurytel.net
Web Site: www.ducksprobaseball.com
Management:
GM: Tim Clegg
Seating Capacity: 6,000

7042
GRAHAM TYLER MEMORIAL CHAPEL

Park College
8700 River Park Drive
Parkville, MO 64152
Phone: 816-741-2000
Web Site: www.park.edu
Management:
President: Beverly Byer Pevitts
Founded: 1875
Status: Non-Profit, Non-Professional

7043
PARK COLLEGE ALUMNI HALL THEATRE
8700 River Park Drive
Parkville, MO 64152
Phone: 816-741-2000
Fax: 816-587-5585
Web Site: www.park.edu
Management:
   President: Beverley Byers-Pevitts
   Executive Director: Michael Droge
   Artistic Director: Marsha Morgan
Founded: 1875
Specialized Field: Series & Festivals; Intrumental Music; Vocal Music; Theaterical Group
Status: Non-Profit, Non-Professional
Paid Staff: 10

7044
JONES AUDITORIUM
College of the Ozarks
PO Box 17
Point Lookout, MO 65726
Phone: 417-334-6411
Fax: 417-335-2618
Web Site: www.coso.edu
Management:
   President: Jerry Davis
Founded: 1906
Status: For-Profit, Non-Professional

7045
LEACH THEATRE
University of Missouri-Rolla
121 Fulton
Rolla, MO 65409-1130
Phone: 573-341-4141
Fax: 573-341-6127
Web Site: web.umr.edu/~upas/
Officers:
   Chair Campus Performing Arts: Paula M Lutz
Management:
   Administrative Assistant: Barbara Palmer
   House Manager: Barbara Griffin
Utilizes: Dance Companies; Multimedia; Special Technical Talent; Theatre Companies
Budget: $60,000-150,000
Income Sources: Box Office; Subscriptions; Grants
Affiliations: Plains Presenters
Annual Attendance: 3,900
Facility Category: Theater/Concert Hall
Type of Stage: Proscenium
Stage Dimensions: 45'x21'
Seating Capacity: 656
Year Built: 1991
Rental Contact: House Manager Barbara Griffen

7046
UNIVERSITY OF MISSOURI PERFORMING ARTS SERIES
University of Missouri
College of Arts & Sciences
121 Fulton
Rolla, MO 65409-1130
Phone: 573-341-4141
Fax: 573-341-6127
Web Site: www.campus.umr.edu/cpas
Management:
   Dean: Paula Lutz
   Production Manager: Shelley Dotson
Founded: 1873
Status: Non-Profit, Non-Professional

7047
MISSOURI THEATER
717 Edmond Street
Saint Joseph, MO 64501
Phone: 816-271-4717
Fax: 816-232-9213
Toll-free: 800-821-5052
Web Site: www.ci.st-joseph.mo.us
Management:
   Manager: Kathy Brock
   Maintenance/Operations: Steve O'Neal
   Assistant: Carolyn Hitchings
Founded: 1980
Specialized Field: Performing Art Association
Paid Staff: 5
Income Sources: City Owned Facility
Facility Category: Performing Arts Facility
Type of Stage: Permanent
Seating Capacity: 1,200
Year Built: 1927
Year Remodeled: 1995
Resident Groups: Robidouk Resident Theatre

7048
MISSOURI WESTERN STATE COLLEGE FINE ARTS THEATRE
Music Department
4525 Downs Drive
Saint Joseph, MO 64507
Phone: 816-271-4420
Fax: 816-271-5974
e-mail: gilmour@missouriwestern.edu
Web Site: www.missouriwestern.edu/Music/
Management:
   President: James Scaoom
   Music Department Chair: Matt Gilmour
Mission: The Thompson E. Potter Fine Arts Building houses the Departments of Art, Music, and Theatre. The music wing, recently receiving an acoustic renovation, houses the Fine Arts Theatre and the Kemper Recital Hall.
Founded: 1969
Status: Non-Profit, Professional
Paid Staff: 30
Paid Artists: 5
Budget: $10,000

7049
SAINT JOSEPH CIVIC ARENA
100 N 4th Street
Saint Joseph, MO 64501
Phone: 816-271-4717
Fax: 816-232-9213
Toll-free: 800-821-5052
Web Site: www.ci.st-joseph.mo.us
Management:
   Manager: Kathy Brock
   Assistant: Carolyn Hitchings
   Operations Supervisor: Chad Dumphrey
Founded: 1980
Specialized Field: Music; Trade Shows
Status: For-Profit, Non-Professional
Paid Staff: 4
Income Sources: City Owned Facility/Arena
Facility Category: multi-use facility/arena
Type of Stage: Portable
Stage Dimensions: 36'x48'
Seating Capacity: 5000
Year Built: 1980
Year Remodeled: 1997

7050
AMERICAN THEATRE
1401 S Brentwood Boulevard
Suite 700
Saint Louis, MO 63144
Phone: 314-962-4000
Fax: 314-436-0483

7051
BUSCH STADIUM
Saint Louis Cardinals
250 Stadium Plaza
Saint Louis, MO 63102
Phone: 314-421-3060
Fax: 314-425-0640
Web Site: www.stlcardinals.com
Management:
   President: Mark Lamping
   General Manager: Walt Jockety
   Director: Marian Rhodes
   VP Stadium Operations: Joe Abernathky
Specialized Field: Operated by St. Louis Cardinals
Status: Non-Profit, Professional
Paid Staff: 500
Paid Artists: 100
Seating Capacity: 49,625
Year Built: 1966
Year Remodeled: 1997

7052
BUSCH STUDENT CENTER
Saint Louis University
20 North Grand Suite 335
Saint Louis, MO 63103
Phone: 314-977-7176
Fax: 314-977-7177
e-mail: grabaucr@slu.edu
Web Site: www.slu.edu
Officers:
   Activities Coordinator: Chris Grabau
Opened: 2003
Seating Capacity: 2,900

7053
CATHEDRAL OF SAINT LOUIS
4431 Lindell Boulevard
Saint Louis, MO 63108-2496
Phone: 314-373-8200
Fax: 314-533-2844
e-mail: concerts@cathedralstl.org
Web Site: www.cathedralstl.org

7054
CENTER OF CREATIVE ARTS
524 Trinity Avenue
Saint Louis, MO 63130
Phone: 314-724-1834
Fax: 314-725-6222
e-mail: info@cocastl.org
Web Site: www.cocastl.org
Management:
   Executive Director: Stephanie Riven
   Director of Performing Arts: Rebecca Carson
Mission: Provides meaningful arts experiences to St. Louisans and their family for nearly two decades. COCA has become the largest multidisciplinary arts institution and one of the most valuable community assets in the St. Louis metropolitan area
Founded: 1986
Status: Non-Profit, Professional
Paid Staff: 20
Paid Artists: 5

7055
EDISON THEATRE
Washington University
One Brookings Dr
Saint Louis, MO 63130-4899
Mailing Address: Campus Box 1119
Phone: 314-935-6543
Fax: 314-935-7362
e-mail: edison@artsci.wustl.edu
Web Site: http://edisontheatre.wustl.edu
Management:
Executive Director: Charlie Robin
Operations Manager: Bill Larson
Marketing Manager: Jennifer Killion
Technical Director/Facility Manager: Michael Hensley
Mission: To provide the highest caliber national and international artists in music, dance and theater, performing new works as well as innovative interpretations of classical material not otherwise seen in St. Louis. Focusing on presentations that are interdisciplinary, multicultural and/or experimental, Edison Theatre presents work intended to challenge, educate and inspire.
Founded: 1971
Status: Non-Profit, Professional
Paid Staff: 30
Seating Capacity: 656

7056
FABULOUS FOX THEATRE
Grand Center
527 N Grand Boulevard
Saint Louis, MO 63103
Phone: 314-534-1111
Fax: 314-534-8702

7057
GRAND CENTER GRANDEL THEATRE
3610 Grandel Square
Saint Louis, MO 63103
Phone: 314-533-8825
Fax: 314-533-3345
e-mail: info@grandcenter.org
Web Site: www.grandcenter.org
Officers:
President/CEO: Vincent Schoemehl, Jr
Management:
Manager: Merrell Wiegraffe
Budget: $60,000-150,000
Seating Capacity: 450

7058
HILTON CENTER FOR THE ARTS
Webster University
130 Edgar Road
Saint Louis, MO 63119
Phone: 314-968-6933
Fax: 314-963-6102
e-mail: luekinar@webster.edu
Management:
Director: Arthur L. Lueking
Founded: 1963
Specialized Field: Theater and Opera
Status: Non-Profit, Professional
Paid Staff: 110
Paid Artists: 300

7059
JEWISH COMMUNITY CENTER OF SAINT LOUIS
Cultural Arts Department
2 Millstone Campus Drive
Saint Louis, MO 63146
Phone: 314-432-5700
Fax: 314-432-5825
Management:
Theatre Coordinator: Kathleen Sitzer

7060
MISSOURI BOTANICAL GARDEN AMPHITHEATRE
4344 Shaw Boulevard
Saint Louis, MO 63110
Phone: 314-577-9400
Toll-free: 800-642-8842
e-mail: firstname.lastname@mobot.org
Web Site: www.mobot.org
Management:
Director: Peter H Raven
Senior Development Manager: Sharon Cognac Mertzlufft
Administrative Assistant: Laura De Young
Develpoments Event Manager: Brenda Zonola
Mission: To discover and share knowledge about plants and their environment, in order to preserve and enrich life.
Founded: 1859
Paid Staff: 385
Volunteer Staff: 99+
Income Sources: Admission Charges; Membership Fees; Grants; Private Donations
Annual Attendance: 750,000
Facility Category: Auditorium; Outdoor Ampitheatre
Type of Stage: Proscenium
Seating Capacity: 300

7061
MUNY AMPHITHEATRE
Forest Park
Saint Louis, MO 63112
Phone: 314-361-1900
Fax: 314-361-0009
Web Site: www.muny.com
President/CEO: Dennis M Reagan
Executive Producer: Paul Blake
Marketing Director: Laura Peters Reilly
Mission: Broadway-style musical theatre productions
Founded: 1919
Specialized Field: Theatre
Status: Non-Profit, Professional
Paid Staff: 550
Paid Artists: 200
Non-paid Artists: 200
Season: June - August
Annual Attendance: 400,000
Facility Category: Outdoor Amphitheatre
Type of Stage: Traditional
Seating Capacity: 11,000
Year Built: 1919
Year Remodeled: 2000

7062
POWELL SYMPHONY HALL
Grand Center
718 N Grand Boulevard
Saint Louis, MO 63103
Phone: 314-533-2500
Fax: 314-286-4142
Toll-free: 800-232-1880
Web Site: www.slso.org

Officers:
President: Randy Adams
CFO: James Garrone
VP Maketing: Kristi Kovalak
VP Development: Faith D Maddy
VP/Orchestra Manager: Robert McGrath
Director of Communications: Jeff Trammel
VP Education/Community Partnerships: Marc C Thayer
Management:
Executive Director: Randy Adams
Founded: 1880
Specialized Field: Symphony Music; Classical Music
Status: Non-Profit, Professional
Paid Staff: 150
Paid Artists: 92
Seating Capacity: 2,689

7063
SAVIS CENTER
1401 Clarke Avenue
Saint Louis, MO 63103
Phone: 314-622-5400
Fax: 314-589-5981
e-mail: webmaster@gw.kiel.com
Web Site: www.saviscenter.net
Management:
Sr VP/General Manager Savis Center: Dennis Petrullo
Sr VP Marketing: Jim Woodcockne
Food/Beverage Director: Skip Aurell
VP/Operations: Fred Corsi
Box Office Director: Carol Chilton
Boc Offive Manager: Debra Freking
Publicity/Special Events Manager: Cindy Underwood
Director Manager: Gayle Leonard
Marketing Manager: Michele Peck
Seating Capacity: 20,000
Year Built: 1994

7064
SHELDON CONCERT HALL AND BALLROOM
3648 Washington Avenue
Saint Louis, MO 63108
Phone: 314-533-9900
Fax: 314-533-2958
Web Site: www.sheldonconcerthall.org
Management:
Executive Director: Paul Reuter
Director Events (Rentals): Laurie Hasty
Mission: To present concerts of jazz, folk and classical music, art exhibits in the Sheldon Galleries and community events in 500 and 250 seat rental spaces.
Founded: 1912
Specialized Field: Series & Festivals: Instrumental and Vocal Concerts
Status: Non-Profit
Paid Staff: 14
Budget: $2.4 million
Income Sources: Subscriptions; Rentals; Contributions
Annual Attendance: 100,000
Facility Category: Concert Hall
Type of Stage: Flexible; Platform
Stage Dimensions: 17 x 24
Seating Capacity: 702
Year Built: 1912
Year Remodeled: 1998
Rental Contact: Director Events Laurie Hasty

7065
TRANSWORLD DOME AT AMERICAS' CENTER
701 Convention Plaza
Saint Louis, MO 63101
Phone: 314-342-5036
Fax: 314-342-5040
Management:
Director: Bruce Sommer
Director Sports Entertainment: Jack Croghan
General Manager/Sports Service: Tom Schlaker
Executive Suites Director/Catering: Gregory Lee
Seating Capacity: 65,600

7066
UNION AVENUE OPERA THEATRE
733 North Union Boulevard
Saint Louis, MO 63108
Phone: 314-361-8844
Fax: 314-361-3036
Web Site: http://union-avenue.org/uaot.html
Officers:
President: Clela Anderson
First Vice President: Catherine Davis
Second Vice President: Roger Duncan
Secretary: George Sublette
Finance: Eric Koch
Mission: The mission of the Union Avenue Opera Theatre is to provide a professional level opera experience for talented singers, directors, orchestra musicians, and technicians pursuing careers in the theater, and to provide quality, affordable opera for the metropolitan St. Louis community. The company operated under the auspices of the Arts Group of Union Avenue Christian Church until gaining not-for-profit status in 2003.

7067
HAMMONS STUDENT CENTER
661 S John Q Hammons Parkway
Springfield, MO 65807
Phone: 417-836-5240
Fax: 417-836-6344
Web Site: www.missouristate.edu/hsc
Management:
Executive Director: Randy Blackwood
Director: Keith Boaz
Assistant Director: Laree Moore
Administrative Secretary: Brenda O'Connell
Mission: The mission of HSC is continually supporting the recreational needs of enrolled Missouri State University students, faculty and staff members, and supporting the intramural and intercollegiate athletic programs.
Founded: 1976
Status: Non-Profit, Professional
Paid Staff: 10
Seating Capacity: 8,846

7068
JUANITA K HAMMONS HALL
Missouri State University
901 South National
Springfield, MO 65897
Phone: 417-836-6776
Fax: 417-836-6891
e-mail: jackwheeler@missouristate.edu
Web Site: www.hammonshall.com
Management:
Events Coordinator: Jack Wheeler
Founded: 1992
Paid Staff: 15
Volunteer Staff: 250

Budget: $400,000-1,000,000
Annual Attendance: 125,000
Type of Stage: Proscenium
Seating Capacity: 2,215
Year Built: 1992
Cost: $17.3 million
Rental Contact: Jack Wheeler

7069
SPRINGFIELD LITTLE THEATRE AT THE LANDERS
311 E Walnut Avenue
Springfield, MO 65806
Phone: 417-869-3869
Fax: 417-869-4047
Web Site: www.landerstheatre.org
Officers:
President: Sharon Matney Brown
First VP: Mike Bridges
Second VP: Dawn Cosby
Third VP: Cary Cummings
Secretary: Cindy Lear
Treasurer: Steve Bullard
Immediate Past President: Jason Brown
Management:
Artistic Director: Beth Domann
Education Director: Lorianne Dunn
Designer/Technical Director: John R Rogers
Technical Director: Jamie Bower
Community Relations Director: Annie Carlyn
Marketing Director: Rachel Peacock-Young
Box Office Manager: Leah Macioce
Admin Asst/Volunteer Coordinator: Heather Shannon
Mission: A volunteer driven organization, energized by the highest artistic ideals, that strives to entertain, educate and involve the community in live productions and in the preservation of the historic Landers Theatre.
Utilizes: Actors; AEA Actors; Choreographers; Commissioned Composers; Dance Companies; Dancers; Designers; Grant Writers; Guest Artists; Guest Companies; Guest Conductors; Guest Designers; Guest Lecturers; Local Artists; Music; Original Music Scores; Resident Professionals
Founded: 1934
Specialized Field: Southwest Missouri
Status: Non-Profit, Non-Professional
Paid Staff: 9
Budget: $750,000
Income Sources: Tickets; Underwriting; Grants
Annual Attendance: 35,000
Facility Category: Theatre
Type of Stage: Proscenium

7070
FAMILY ARENA
2002 Arena Parkway
St. Charles, MO 63303
Phone: 636-896-4200
Fax: 636-896-4205
Web Site: www.familyarena.com
Management:
Director: Steven R. Rosenblatt
Founded: 1999
Specialized Field: Arena/Facility
Status: Non-Profit, Professional
Paid Staff: 100
Income Sources: Tickets; Concessions; Suites; Advertising
Affiliations: St. Charles County Government
Annual Attendance: 750,000
Facility Category: Arena
Type of Stage: Stageright
Seating Capacity: 11,000

Year Built: 1999
Cost: $32 million

7071
BLANCHE M. TOUHILL PERFORMING ARTS CENTER
University of Missouri-St.Louis
8001 Natural Bridge Road
St. Louis, MO
Phone: 314-516-4949
Fax: 314-516-4110
Toll-free: 866-516-4949
Web Site: www.touhill.org
Officers:
Vice Chancellor Univer. Relations: Dixie Kohn
Director Operations: John Cattanach
Director Development: Bill George
Director Stage Services: Jason Stahr
Assistant Director Marketing: Rachel Queen
Events Services Manager: Patrick McKeon
Mission: The Touhill Performing Arts Center at the University of Missouri-St. Louis creates opportunities for the people of our region to experience, appreciate and embrace the transformational power of the performing arts. It is a welcoming place, a leading cultural partner in our community and a symbol of this University's commitment to integrate education, innovation and excellence.
Specialized Field: Classical; Soloists; Ensemble
Status: Non Profit
Performs At: Anheuser-Busch Performance Hall, E. Desmond and Mary Ann Lee Theater
Type of Stage: Proscenium
Seating Capacity: 1625, 360
Architect: Wischmeyer Architects/Pei Cobb Freed & Partners
Acoustical Consultant: Kirkegaard & Associates

7072
MULE BARN THEATRE
224 Main
Tarkio, MO 64491
Phone: 660-736-4430

7073
COGER THEATRE
Southwest Missouri State University
128 Garfield
West Plains, MO 65775
Phone: 417-836-5000
Fax: 417-257-7682
e-mail: marktempleton@missouristate.edu OR jimgrider@missouristate.edu
Web Site: www.theatreanddance.missouristate.edu
Management:
Theater/Events Coordinator: Jim Grider
Theatre & Dance Marketing Director: Mark Templeton
Mission: A performing arts center theatre located within Craig Hall on the campus of Southwest Missouri State University.
Budget: $20,000-35,000

Montana

7074
BIGFORK CENTER FOR THE PERFORMING ARTS
PO Box 1230
Bigfork, MT 59911
Phone: 406-837-4885

7075
ALBERTA BAIR THEATRE FOR THE PERFORMING ARTS
PO Box 1556
Billings, MT 59103
Phone: 406-256-8915
Fax: 406-256-5060
Toll-free: 877-321-2074
e-mail: hbergeson@albertabairtheater.org
Web Site: www.albertabairtheatre.org
Management:
    Executive Director: Bill Fisher
    Artistic Director: Corby Skinner
    Technical Director: Tom Lund
Mission: In its brief history, the Alberta Bair Theater has brought to audiences the finest performers in every discipline of the performing arts, including classical and popular music, country music and jazz, opera, ballet, modern and ethnic dance, comedy, drama and musical theater.
Utilizes: Actors; Collaborations; Dance Companies; Dancers; Educators; Guest Accompanists; Guest Artists; Guest Choreographers; Guest Composers; Guest Directors; Guest Ensembles; Guest Instructors; Guest Musical Directors; Guest Soloists; Guest Teachers; High School Drama; Instructors; Local Artists; Lyricists; Multimedia; Original Music Scores; Playwrights; Resident Artists; Selected Students; Sign Language Translators; Singers; Special Technical Talent; Theatre Companies
Founded: 1983
Status: Non-Profit, Professional
Paid Staff: 15
Volunteer Staff: 200
Budget: $1.2 million
Income Sources: Ticket Sales
Annual Attendance: 123,000
Facility Category: Performing Arts
Type of Stage: Proscenium
Stage Dimensions: 54 x 30
Seating Capacity: 1416
Year Remodeled: 1987
Cost: $ 5-6 million
Rental Contact: Bill Fisher

7076
METRAPARK
308 6th Avenue N
PO Box 2514
Billings, MT 59103
Phone: 406-256-2400
Fax: 406-254-2479
e-mail: shawke@metrapark.com
Web Site: www.metrapark.com
Management:
    Asst GM/Director of Operations: Bill Dutcher
    Admin Assistant to GM: Nancy Charbonneau
    Marketing Director: Sandra Hawke
    Box Office Manager: Sue Devries
Seating Capacity: 12,000

7077
BREENDEN FIELD HOUSE/WORTHINGTON ARENA
Montna State University, Sports Facilities
PO Box 3380
Bozeman, MT 59717-3380
Phone: 406-994-7117
Fax: 406-994-4400
Web Site: www.montana.edu/wwwsfac
Management:
    Sports Facilities Director: Melanie Stocks
    Events/Operations Manager: Brad Murphy

    Event Coordinator: Brooks Phillips
Founded: 1956
Status: Professional

7078
RENO H SALES STADIUM
Montana State University Sports Facilities
1 Bobcat Circle
Bozeman, MT 59717
Phone: 406-994-4221
Fax: 406-994-2278
Web Site: www.montana.edu
Management:
    President: Jeffery Gamble
    Director Sports Facilities: Melanie Stocks
    Operations Manager: Brad Murphy
    Sports Information Director: Tom Schulz
Status: Non-Profit, Non-Professional
Paid Staff: 60
Seating Capacity: 12,500

7079
BUTTE CIVIC CENTER
1340 Harrison Avenue
Butte, MT 59701
Phone: 406-497-6400
Fax: 406-497-6404
e-mail: bmelvin@bsb.mt.gov
Web Site: www.buttciviccener.com
Management:
    Manager: Bill Melvin
Performs At: Multi-Purpose
Seating Capacity: 7,200

7080
FOUR SEASONS ARENA
400 3rd St NW
Great Falls, MT 59404
Mailing Address: PO Box 1888 Great Fall, MT 59403
Phone: 406-727-8900
Fax: 406-452-8955
Web Site: www.goexpopark.com
Management:
    General Manager: Bill Ogg
    Asst General Manager: Stan Steen
    Operations Manager: John Scott
    Box Office Manager: Debby Wigger
    Marketing/Development: Lori Cox
    Event Coordinator: Amy Robbins
Mission: Events include concerts, trade shows, rodeos, circuses, wrestling and boxing, basketball tournaments and ice shows.
Status: For-Profit, Non-Professional
Paid Staff: 18
Seating Capacity: 6,134

7081
GREAT FALLS CIVIC CENTER THEATER
PO Box 5021
Great Falls, MT 59403
Phone: 406-454-3915
Fax: 406-454-3468

7082
CARROLL COLLEGE THEATRE
North Benton Avenue
Helena, MT 59625
Phone: 406-442-3450
Fax: 406-447-4533
Toll-free: 800-942-3648

7083
HELENA CIVIC CENTER
340 Neill Avenue
Helena, MT 59601
Phone: 406-447-8481
Fax: 406-447-8480
Web Site: www.ci.helena.mt.us
Management:
    Manager: Diane Stavnes
    Director Communications/Technical: Gery Carpenter
    Administrative Assistant: Barb Olsen
Founded: 1936
Status: Non-Profit, Non-Professional
Paid Staff: 7
Income Sources: City of Helena; Ticket Sales; Rental Income.
Performs At: Auditorium
Facility Category: Rental
Stage Dimensions: 45'x38'x17'6"
Seating Capacity: 2,000
Year Built: 1921
Year Remodeled: 1995
Rental Contact: Manager Diane Stavnes

7084
HELENA CIVIC CENTER AUDITORIUM
340 Neill Avenue
Helena, MT 59601
Phone: 406-447-8481
Fax: 406-447-8480
Web Site: www.ci.helena.mt.us
Management:
    Manager: Diane Stavnes
    Director Comm Facility/Tech Direct: Gery Carpenter
    Administrative Assistant: Barb Olsen
Founded: 1936
Paid Staff: 7
Performs At: Auditorium
Facility Category: Rental
Stage Dimensions: 25'x15'x12'
Seating Capacity: 2,000
Year Built: 1920
Year Remodeled: 1995
Rental Contact: Manager Diane Stavnes

7085
MYRNA LOY CENTER
15 North Ewing
Helena, MT 59601
Phone: 406-443-0287
Fax: 406-443-6620
e-mail: myrnaloy@mt.net
Web Site: www.myrnaloycenter.com
Officers:
    President: Brett Jakovac
    Immediate Past President: Ali Bovingdon
    VP Business: Shalon Hastings
    VP Program: Robin Shropshire
    Secretary: Annie Hull
    Treasurer: Bob Shepard
Management:
    Executive Director: Ed Noonan
    Development Associate: Marilyn Alexander
Mission: To present the arts, including media, performing, literary and visual, in an educational context, challenging and culturally enriching programs that would not otherwise appear in the Helena area or in Montana.
Utilizes: Actors; Artists-in-Residence; Collaborating Artists; Commissioned Music; Dance Companies; Dancers; Educators; Filmmakers; Fine Artists; Guest

Teachers; Instructors; Local Artists; Lyricists; Multi
Collaborations; Multimedia; Original Music Scores;
Performance Artists; Playwrights; Poets; Sign
Language Translators; Soloists; Student Interns;
Special Technical Talent; Theatre Companies
Founded: 1976
Specialized Field: Series & Festivals; Dance; Vocal
Music; Instrumental Music; Theater; Festivals; Lyric
Opera; Film House
Status: Non-Profit, Professional
Paid Staff: 12
Budget: $400,000
Income Sources: Ticket Sales; Grants; Fundraising
Affiliations: NPN
Annual Attendance: 8000
Facility Category: Media and Performance Center
Type of Stage: Proscenium
Seating Capacity: 250
Year Built: 1875
Year Remodeled: 1990
Cost: $ 1.6 Million
Rental Contact: Rental Coordinator Christy Stile
Organization Type: Performing; Touring; Resident;
Educational; Sponsoring

7086
MAJESTIC VALLEY ARENA
3630 Highway 93 North
Kalispell, MT 59901
Phone: 406-755-5366
Fax: 406-755-5399
e-mail: bparker@majesticvalleyarena.com
Web Site: www.majesticvalleyarena.com
Management:
    GM: Bob Parker
    Booking: Jim Volke
Opened: 2002
Seating Capacity: 4,000

7087
ADAMS EVENT CENTER
University of Montana-Missoula
Adams Center 103
Missoula, MT 59812
Phone: 406-243-5355
Fax: 406-243-4265
Toll-free: 888-666-8262
e-mail: bettyjo.miller@mso.umt.edu
Web Site: www.adamseventcenter.com
Management:
    Executive Director: Mary Muse
    Asst Director Operations: Jackie Hedtke
    Executive Assistant: Betty Jo Miller
Mission: The premier multi-use facility in Western
Montana, providing first-class customer service in
support of a broad range of quality events for the public,
the University of Montana and the public.
Founded: 1955
Specialized Field: Sports; Concerts; Flatshows;
Special Events
Status: Non-Profit, Professional
Paid Staff: 12
Budget: $1.5 Million
Income Sources: Rent; Services
Facility Category: Arena
Seating Capacity: 7,500
Year Built: 1955
Year Remodeled: 1999
Cost: $15,000,000
Rental Contact: Director Mary Muse

7088
UNIVERSITY OF MONTANA THEATRE
University of Montana
Department of Drama and Dance
Missoula, MT 59812-8736
Phone: 406-243-4481
Fax: 406-243-5726
Web Site: www.umt.edu/drama
Utilizes: Actors; AEA Actors; Dance Companies;
Designers; Educators; Guest Conductors; Guest
Designers; Guest Ensembles; High School Drama;
Instructors; Local Artists; Original Music Scores;
Resident Artists; Resident Professionals; Soloists;
Student Interns

7089
WILMA THEATRE
131 South Higgins
Room 200
Missoula, MT 59802
Phone: 406-728-2521
Fax: 406-728-7903
Web Site: www.thewilma.com
Management:
    General Manager: Bill Emerson
Seating Capacity: 1,100

Nebraska

7090
COMMUNITY PLAYERS THEATER
412 Ella Street
Beatrice, NE 68310
Phone: 402-228-1801
Fax: 402-228-9121
Web Site: www.beatricene.com/communityplayers/
Management:
    Artistic Director: Jamie Ulmer
Founded: 1975
Status: Non-Profit, Non-Professional
Paid Staff: 2
Paid Artists: 1

7091
BELLEVUE LITTLE THEATRE
PO Box 162
Bellevue, NE 68005
Phone: 402-291-1554
Fax: 402-291-3809
e-mail: cyberma609@aol.com
Web Site: www.bellevuelittletheatre.com
Management:
    President: Edward Roche, ebroche@cox.net
Mission: To create a superior environment for the
promotion of the performing arts through the
presentation of comedy, drama and musical theatre
productions; and to stimulate educational and
recreational programs in the technical and artistic
venues of the performing arts for the citizens of the city
of Bellevue, Sarpy County, and the Greater Omaha
Metropolitan Area.
Founded: 1968
Specialized Field: Musical; Comedy; Ethnic Theatre;
Community Theatre; Contemporary
Status: Non-Profit, Non-Professional
Seating Capacity: 244
Year Built: 1942

7092
BLADEN OPERA HOUSE
Main Street
Bladen, NE 68928

7093
CHADRON STATE COLLEGE MEMORIAL HALL
10th and Main
Chadron, NE 69337
Toll-free: 800-242-3766

7094
KEARNEY COMMUNITY THEATRE
83 Plaza Boulevard
Kearney, NE 68847
Phone: 308-234-1529
Web Site: www.

7095
UNIVERSITY OF NEBRASKA THEATRE
2506 12th Avenue
Kearney, NE 68849
Phone: 308-865-8618
Fax: 308-865-8806
Web Site: www.unk.edu
Management:
    President: Doug Kristensen
Founded: 1905
Status: Non-Profit, Professional
Paid Staff: 800

7096
UNK SPORTS CENTER
University of Nebraska
2506 12th Avenue
Kearney, NE 68849
Phone: 308-865-8514
Fax: 308-865-8806
e-mail: jamesonj@unk.edu
Web Site: www.unk.edu
Management:
    Chancellor: Doug Kristensen
    Vice Chancellor: Finnie Murray
    Vice Chancellor Finances: Randy Haack
    Music Professor: Nathan Buckner
Founded: 1905
Status: Non-Profit, Professional
Paid Staff: 24
Seating Capacity: 5,842

7097
BOB DEVANEY SPORTS CENTER
University of Nebraska-Lincoln
103 South Stadium
Lincoln, NE 68588-0119
Phone: 402-472-4224
Fax: 402-472-9675
Web Site: www.huskerwebcast.com
Management:
    Director Athletic Facilities: John M Ingram

7098
LIED CENTER FOR PERFORMING ARTS
12th And R Streets
PO Box 880151
Lincoln, NE 68588-0151
Phone: 402-472-4700
Fax: 402-472-4730
Toll-free: 800-432-3231
Web Site: www.liedcenter.org
Management:
    Executive Director: Charles Bethea
Founded: 1988
Status: Non-Profit, Non-Professional
Paid Staff: 80

7099

LINCOLN MEMORIAL STADIUM
University of Nebraska-Lincoln
118 South Stadium
Lincoln, NE 68588-0119
Phone: 402-472-1960
Fax: 402-472-4662
Web Site: www.huskerwebcast.com
Management:
   Director Athletic Facilities: John M Ingram
   Director Athletics Events: Butch Hug
Seating Capacity: 73,650

7100

PERSHING CENTER
226 Centennial Mall S
Lincoln, NE 68508
Phone: 402-441-7500
Fax: 402-441-7913
e-mail: info@pershingauditorium.com
Web Site: www.pershingauditorium.com
Management:
   Manager: Tom Lorenz
   Marketing Director: Derek Andersen
   Event Director: Phil Potter
   Operations Director: Fred McCoy
   Assistant General Manager: Howard Feldman
Founded: 1956
Paid Staff: 12
Performs At: Multi-purpose arena and exhibit hall
Stage Dimensions: 42'x105'
Seating Capacity: 6,818
Year Built: 1956
Rental Contact: Manager Tom Lorenz

7101

UNIVERSITY OF NEBRASKA-LINCOLN: KIMBALL RECITAL HALL
University of Nebraska-Lincoln
108 Westbrook
PO Box No 880100
Lincoln, NE 68588-0100
Phone: 402-475-5775
Fax: 402-472-2997
e-mail: rbowlin1@unl.edu
Web Site: www.unl.edu/music
Management:
   Professor/Director School of Music: John W. Richmond, PhD
   Events Coordinator, School of Music: Ron Bowlin
Founded: 1894
Status: Non-Profit, Non-Professional
Paid Staff: 50
Paid Artists: 50

7102

AL CANIGLIA STADIUM
University of Nebraska-Omaha
6001 Dodge
Omaha, NE 68182
Phone: 402-554-2305
Fax: 402-554-3694
Web Site: www.cidunomaha.edu/cyberman/
Management:
   Sports Information Director: Gary Anderson
   Athletic Director: Bob Danenhauer
   Head Football Coach: Pat Behrns
   Head Basketball Coach (M): Kevin McKenna
Seating Capacity: 3,800

7103

JEWISH COMMUNITY CENTER OF OMAHA
333 S 132nd Street
Omaha, NE 68154
Phone: 402-334-6426
Fax: 402-334-6466
e-mail: info@jewishomaha.org
Web Site: www.jewishomaha.org
Officers:
   President: Michael W Miller
Management:
   Executive Director: Jeffrey Aizenburg
   Associate Executive Director: Lisa Shkolnick
Mission: To create a positive Jewish environment in which to build, strengthen and preserve Jewish identity and traditions. The Center reaches out to the Jewish community and provides its members with the unique opportunity to associate through a variety of social, cultural, recreational, educational and physical fitness programs, activities and services.
Budget: $10,000

7104

OMAHA CIVIC AUDITORIUM
1804 Capitol Avenue
Omaha, NE 68102
Phone: 402-599-6500
Fax: 402-444-4739
e-mail: info@omahacivic.com
Web Site: www.omahacivic.com
Management:
   Manager: Lawrence Lahaie
   Manager: Jeff Treney
Seating Capacity: 10,950

7105

ORPHEUM THEATRE
409 S 16th Street
Omaha, NE 68102
Phone: 402-444-4750
Fax: 402-444-4739

7106

QWEST CENTER
455 North 10th Street
Omaha, NE 68102
Phone: 402-341-1500
Fax: 402-991-1501
e-mail: info@qwestcenter.com
Web Site: www.qwestcenteromaha.com
Officers:
   President/CEO: Roger Dixon
Management:
   VP Corporate Sales: Tom O'Gorman
Seating Capacity: 17,000

7107

WEST NEBRASKA ARTS CENTER
106 East 18th Street
Scottsbluff, NE 69363-0062
Mailing Address: PO Box 62
Phone: 308-632-2226
Fax: 308-632-2226
e-mail: wneartsed@earthlink.net OR wneartsmb@earthlink.net
Web Site: www.nebraskarts.com/wnac/aboutus.php
Officers:
   President: Pamela Kabalin
   Vice President: Steve Frederick
   Secretary: Christie Shaver
   Treasurer: Clark Wisniewski
Management:

   Executive Director: Peggy Millay
   Assistant Director: Mason Burbach
   Office Manager: Jo Haslow
Mission: The West Nebraska Arts Center (WNAC) is a regional cultural center, committed to the awareness and the fostering of excellence in the arts.
Budget: $10,000-20,000

7108

PAVILION & EVENTS CENTER INC.
1580 County Road K
Wahoo, NE 68502
Phone: 402-560-9230
Fax: 402-474-5055
Web Site: www.thepavilioninc.com
Officers:
   President/CEO: Paul Ramirez
Management:
   Events Director: Bob Glantz
Seating Capacity: 35,000

7109

WAYNE STATE COLLEGE ARENA
1111 Main Street
Wayne, NE 68787
Phone: 402-375-7520
Fax: 402-375-7120
Toll-free: 800-228-9972
Web Site: www.wsc.edu
Management:
   President: Richard Collings
   Athletic Director: Eric Schoh
   Assistant Athletic Director: Mike Barry
   Head Football Coach: Scott Hoffman
   Head Basketball Coach (M): Greg McDermott
Founded: 1910
Status: Non-Profit, Non-Professional
Paid Staff: 30
Seating Capacity: 6,000

Nevada

7110

BREWERY ARTS CENTER
449 West King Street
Carson City, NV 89703
Phone: 775-883-1976
Fax: 775-883-1922
Web Site: www.breweryarts.org
Management:
   Executive Director: John Procaccini
   Senior Administrator: Laura Guberman
   Program Manager/Rentals: Christopher Wilson
   Technical Services: Eric Klug
Mission: Facilities include the 1864 Grand Ballroom that accomdates meetings, receptions, intimate performances up to 100 people; and the Performance Hall that accomodates 300 people.
Founded: 1976
Budget: $10,000
Performs At: Carson City Community Center

7111

CAESARS PALACE
3570 Las Vegas Boulevard S
Las Vegas, NV 89109
Phone: 702-731-7320
Fax: 702-731-7328
Web Site: www.caesarspalace.com
Management:
   Director: Charry Kennedy

7112
CHARLESTON HEIGHTS ARTS CENTER
800 S Brush
Las Vegas, NV 89107
Phone: 702-229-6383
Fax: 702-258-8286
Management:
    Center Coordinator: Joanne Lentino
Budget: $35,000-60,000
Facility Category: Ballroom; Theater
Seating Capacity: 365
Year Built: 1979
Year Remodeled: 1989
Rental Contact: 702-229-5256 Roy Ramirez

7113
HUNTRIDGE THEATRE
1208 East Charleston Boulevard
Las Vegas, NV 89104
Phone: 702-678-6800
Fax: 702-678-6808
Web Site: www.thehuntridge.com
Management:
    Talent Buyer: Eli Mizrachi
    Marketing Manager: Kim Garcia
Seating Capacity: 1,090

7114
LAS VEGAS CONVENTION AND VISITORS AUTHORITY
850 Las Vegas Boulevard N
Las Vegas, NV 89101
Phone: 702-386-7100
Fax: 702-386-7126
Toll-free: 800-332-5333
Web Site: www.vegasfreedom.com
Management:
    President: Rossi Ralenkotter
    Managing Director: Phil Simmons
Founded: 1959
Status: Non-Profit, Non-Professional
Paid Staff: 112

7115
MANDALAY BAY EVENTS CENTER
Mandalay Bay Resort & Casino
3950 Las Vegas Boulevard South
Las Vegas, NV 89119
Phone: 702-632-7551
Fax: 702-632-7508
Web Site: www.mandalaybay.com
Management:
    Executive Director: H. C. Rowe
    VP Entertainment: Glenn Medas
Seating Capacity: 12,000

7116
MGM GRAND GARDEN ARENA
3799 Las Vegas Boulevard S
Las Vegas, NV 89109
Phone: 702-891-7824
Fax: 702-891-7831
e-mail: prowsm@aol.com
Web Site: www.mgmmirage.com
Officers:
    President: Terry Lanni
    Vice President: Mark W. Prows
    Executive Director: Karen Prescia
    Assistant Vice President: Rich Baccellieri
    Senior Event Manager: Dick Hill
Founded: 1993
Status: For-Profit, Professional
Seating Capacity: 15,200

7117
REED WHIPPLE CULTURAL ARTS CENTER
821 Las Vegas Boulevard N
Las Vegas, NV 89101
Phone: 702-229-6211
Fax: 702-382-5199
Web Site: www.lasvegasnevada.gov
Management:
    Director of Dept: Barbara Jackson
    Supervisor: Dale Barbeau
    Manager Cultural Division: Nancy Deaner
Founded: 1975
Status: Non-Profit, Professional
Paid Staff: 30
Paid Artists: 100

7118
SAM BOYD STADIUM
4505 Maryland Parkway
Las Vegas, NV 89145-0003
Phone: 702-895-3716
Fax: 702-895-1099
Web Site: www.thomasandmackcenter.com
Management:
    Director: Patrick J Christenson
    Assistant Director: Robert P Anderson
    Assistant Director/Booking: Daren Libonati
    Assistant Director/Sports Marketing: Steve Stallworth
    Assistant Director Operations: Rick Picone
    Promotions/Public Relations Manager: Cliff Clinger
Seating Capacity: 42,500

7119
THOMAS & MACK CENTER
4505 Maryland Parkway
Las Vegas, NV 89154-0003
Phone: 702-895-3725
Fax: 702-895-1099
Web Site: www.thomasandmack.com
Management:
    Managing Director: Daren Libonati
    Artistic Director: Nevada Colwell
    Associate Director Operations: Rick Picone
    Public Relations: Angela Gomes
    Event Services Director: Todd Clawson
    Event Services Manager: Mike Newcomb
    Event Coordinator: Jim Sanders
    External Coordinator: Kenny Sasaki
Founded: 1983
Status: For-Profit, Professional
Paid Staff: 100
Seating Capacity: 18,500

7120
UNIVERSITY OF NEVADA-LAS VEGAS PERFORMING ARTS CENTER ARTEMUS HAM CONCERT HALL
4505 Maryland Parkway
Box 455005
Las Vegas, NV 89154-5005
Phone: 702-895-3535
Fax: 702-895-4714
e-mail: henley@ccmail.nevada.edu
Web Site: www.pac.nevada.edu
Management:
    Director Artistic Programming: Larry Henley
    Technical Director: Trent Downing
Founded: 1976
Specialized Field: Present World's Greatest Talent
Status: Non-Profit, Professional

7121
CHURCH OF FINE ARTS
University of Nevada-Reno
Reno, NV 89557
Phone: 775-784-6847

7122
LAWLOR EVENTS CENTER
University of Nevada Athletic Department
Legacy Hall/232
Reno, NV 89557
Phone: 775-784-4659
Fax: 775-784-4428
Web Site: www.unr.edu
Management:
    Athletic Director: Chris Ault
Seating Capacity: 12,400

7123
MACKEY STADIUM
University of Nevada
Legacy Hall 232
Reno, NV 98557
Phone: 775-784-6900
Fax: 775-784-4497
Web Site: www.nevadawolfpack.com
Management:
    Athletic Director: Chris Ault
Seating Capacity: 30,000

7124
PIONEER CENTER FOR THE PERFORMING ARTS
100 S Virginia Street
Reno, NV 89501
Phone: 702-686-6010
Fax: 702-686-6630

7125
RENO LITTLE THEATER
690 N Sierra
PO Box 2088
Reno, NV 89505
Phone: 775-329-0661

7126
RENO SPARKS CONVENTION CENTENNIAL COLISEUM
4590 South Virginia Street
Reno, NV 89502
Phone: 775-825-2627
Fax: 775-825-3726
Web Site: www.visitrenotahoe.com/facilities/reno_sparks_cc/tours/
Officers:
    President/CEO: Ellen Oppenheim
Management:
    EVP Facilities & General Manager: Lynn Thompson
    Executive Director Convention Sales: Philip D'Amico
    Vice President Finance: Tim Smith
    Vice President Marketing & Sales: Knud Svendsen
Mission: Facility overview of the Reno Convention Center includes 500,000 square feet of fully adaptable exhibition and meeting space; 53 meeting rooms with 110,000 square feet of space; and 381,000 square feet of contiguous exhibit space.
Status: For-Profit, Professional
Paid Staff: 400

7127

PIPER'S OPERA HOUSE

12 N B Street
PO Box J
Virginia City, NV 89440
Phone: 775-847-0433
Fax: 775-847-9668
Web Site: www.pipers.opera.org
Management:
    President: Ron Waicul
    Executive Director: Sam Folio
    Artistic Director: William Beeson
Founded: 1878
Status: Non-Profit, Non-Professional
Paid Staff: 2
Paid Artists: 2

New Hampshire

7128

CLAREMONT OPERA HOUSE

City Hall on Tremont Square
PO Box 664
Claremont, NH 03743
Phone: 603-542-0064
Fax: 603-542-7014
Web Site: www.claremontoperahouse.com
Management:
    President: John Bennett
Mission: Multi-use performing arts center.
Utilizes: Guest Accompanists; Guest Musical Directors;
Local Artists; Multimedia; Original Music Scores;
Soloists; Special Technical Talent; Theatre Companies
Opened: 1977
Status: Non-Profit, Professional
Paid Staff: 1
Budget: $150,000
Income Sources: Tickets; Membership; Sponsors
Affiliations: APAP; APNNE
Annual Attendance: 15,000
Facility Category: Theatre
Type of Stage: Proscenium
Seating Capacity: 780
Year Built: 1897
Year Remodeled: 1975

7129

CAPITOL CENTER FOR THE ARTS

44 S Main Street
Concord, NH 03301
Phone: 603-225-1111
Fax: 603-224-3408
e-mail: mtmennino@ccanh.com
Web Site: www.ccanh.com
Management:
    Executive Director: Mary-Therese Mennino
Mission: To inspire, educate and entertain audiences
by providing both the finest venue for the performing
arts and a wide range of professioanlly excellent and
artistically significant presentations.
Founded: 1995
Status: Non-Profit, Professional
Paid Staff: 15
Budget: $1.8 Million
Annual Attendance: 100,000
Seating Capacity: 1300
Year Built: 1927
Year Remodeled: 1995

7130

CONCORD CITY AUDITORIUM

The Friends of the Concord City Auditorium
2 Prince Street
Concord, NH 03301
Mailing Address: PO Box 652 Concord, NH
03302-0652
Phone: 603-225-2164
e-mail: infO@concordcityauditorium.org
Web Site: www.theaudi.org
Officers:
    Treasurer: Merwyn Bagan
Management:
    Friends Information Chair: David Murdo,
    nhdm40@comcast.net
    Friends Marketing Chair: Carol Bagan,
    carolbagam@comcast.net
Mission: To restore and renovate our historic theatre
and to foster its use for the benefit of all the people in
our community. The Friends of the Audi will assist all
presenters who wish to book the City Auditorium.
Utilizes: Actors; Arrangers; Choreographers;
Collaborating Artists; Collaborations; Community
Members; Community Talent; Composers; Contract
Actors; Contract Orchestras; Dance Companies;
Dancers; Designers; Educators; Filmmakers; Five
Seasonal Concerts; Grant Writers; Guest
Accompanists; Guest Choreographers; Guest
Companies; Guest Conductors; Guest Designers;
Guest Directors; Guest Ensembles; Guest Instructors;
Guest Lecturers; Guest Musical Directors; Guest
Musicians; Guest Soloists; Guest Speakers; Guild
Activities; Instructors; Local Artists; Local Artists &
Directors; Local Talent; Local Unknown Artists; Multi
Collaborations; Multimedia; Music; New Productions;
Organization Contracts; Original Music Scores; Paid
Performers; Performance Artists; Playwrights; Poets;
Resident Artists; Resident Professionals; Scenic
Designers; Selected Students; Sign Language
Translators; Singers; Soloists; Students; Student
Interns; Special Technical Talent; Theatre Companies;
Touring Companies; Visual Arts; Visual Designers;
Volunteer Artists; Volunteer Directors & Actors;
Founded: 1904
Specialized Field: Theatre; Music; Dance; Series;
Community Based A and E
Status: Non-Profit, Professional
Performs At: Auditorium; Adjoining Reception Lobby
Annual Attendance: 75,000
Facility Category: Municipal Theatre
Type of Stage: Proscenium
Stage Dimensions: 25'x 25'
Seating Capacity: 850
Year Built: 1904
Year Remodeled: 1991
Rental Contact: 230-3851 Nina Piroso

7131

BRATTON RECITAL HALL

University of New Hampshire-Durham
4 Ballard Street
Durham, NH 03824
Phone: 603-862-3038
Fax: 603-862-3038

7132

HENNESSY CENTER

University of New Hampshire-Durham
4 Ballard Street
Durham, NH 03824
Phone: 603-862-3038
Fax: 603-862-3038
Web Site: www.unh.edu/theatre-dance

Seating Capacity: 150

7133

PAUL CREATIVE ARTS CENTER

University of New Hampshire-Durham
30 College Road
Durham, NH 03824-2617
Phone: 603-862-3712
Fax: 603-862-2191
e-mail: museum.of.art@unh.edu
Web Site: www.unh.edu/moa
Management:
    Interim Director: Weston LaFountain
    Assistant Director: Astrida Schaeffer
    Education & Publicity Coordinator: Catherine A
    Mazur
    Administrative Assistant III: Cindy Farrell
Mission: A professional managed museum providing
exhibitions and programs in the visual arts, the Museum
of Art is a vitally important component of the University
of New Hampshire. Role encompasses two major
areas: academic and community outreach. As a
teaching unit, the Museum provides the opportunity for
universitystudents to gain knowledge and experience in
dealing with works of art on a first hand basis.
Founded: 1960
Paid Staff: 4
Volunteer Staff: 6
Affiliations: AAM; AAMG
Annual Attendance: 6,846
Year Built: 1960
Year Remodeled: 1973
Cost: $2.5 Million

7134

WHITTEMORE CENTER

University of New Hampshire
Main Street
Durham, NH 03824
Phone: 603-862-1850
Fax: 603-862-4069
Web Site: www.unh.edu/athletics
Management:
    Athletic Director: Judith Ray
    Marketing Director: Dan Raposa
    Media Relations Director: Scott Stapin
Seating Capacity: 6,000

7135

HAMPTON PLAYHOUSE THEATRE ARTS WORKSHOP

357 Winnacunnet Road
Hampton, NH 03842
Phone: 603-926-3073

7136

HAMPTON BEACH CASINO BALLROOM

169 Ocean Boulevard
Hampton Beach, NH 03843
Phone: 603-929-4100
Fax: 603-926-9505
e-mail: fschaake@casinoballroom.com
Web Site: www.casinoballroom.com
Management:
    GM: Fred Schaake Jr
    Marketing Director: Heather Shea
Seating Capacity: 2,200

7137

MEMORIAL STADIUM

Dartmouth College
7 Lebanon Street, Suite 201
Hanover, NH 03755

Phone: 603-646-3661
Fax: 603-646-2850
e-mail: office.of.public.affairs@dartmouth.edu
Web Site: www.dartmouth.edu
Management:
President: James Wright
Director Athletics: Joann Harper
Director Sports Information: Kathy Slattery
Dean: James Larimore
Founded: 1969
Seating Capacity: 20,416

7138
COLONIAL THEATRE
95 Main Street
Keene, NH 03431
Phone: 603-357-1233
Fax: 603-357-7817
e-mail: info@thecolonial.org
Web Site: www.thecolonial.org
Officers:
Executive Director: Alec Doyle
Director Of Marketing: Jessica Reeves
Management:
Production & Facility Director: Greg Moore
Founded: 1924
Status: Non-Profit
Paid Staff: 12
Volunteer Staff: 150
Season: year round
Annual Attendance: 60,000
Type of Stage: Proscenium
Stage Dimensions: 24X60
Seating Capacity: 900
Year Built: 1924
Year Remodeled: 1998
Rental Contact: Executive Director Alec Doyle

7139
REDFERN ARTS CENTER ON BRICKYARD POND
Keene State College
229 Main Street
Keene, NH 03435-2401
Phone: 603-358-2167
Fax: 603-358-2145
e-mail: bmenezes@keene.edu
Web Site: www.keene.edu/racbp
Management:
President: Stanley Yarosewick
Director: William Menezes
Mission: Educational
Founded: 1979
Specialized Field: Theatre; Dance; Music
Status: Non-Profit, Non-Professional
Paid Staff: 4
Budget: $250,000
Income Sources: Tickets Sales, College Subscriptions, Corparate Sponsors, Private Donations
Affiliations: Green Mountain Consortium; New England Presenters; Associated Performing Arts Presenters
Annual Attendance: 15,000
Facility Category: Multipurpose
Type of Stage: Proscenium
Stage Dimensions: 36'x 30'x 56'
Seating Capacity: 572
Year Built: 1979
Rental Contact: B Denehy

7140
LEBANON OPERA HOUSE
51 N Park Street
PO Box 384
Lebanon, NH 03766
Phone: 603-448-0400
Fax: 603-448-0444
e-mail: lebanon.opera.house@valley.net
Web Site: www.lebanonoperahouse.org
Management:
President: Bonnie Robinson
Executive Director: Partridge Boswell
Founded: 1991
Specialized Field: Series and Festivals; Music; Theatre; Dance
Status: Non-Profit, Professional
Paid Staff: 5

7141
LOON MOUNTAIN
RR 1 Box 41
Lincoln, NH 03251
Phone: 603-745-8111
Fax: 603-745-8214
e-mail: info@loonmtn.com
Web Site: www.loonmtn.com
Management:
Events Coordinator: Stacey Lopes
Seating Capacity: 6,000

7142
NCCA PAPERMILL THEATRE
PO Box 1060
Lincoln, NH 03251
Phone: 603-745-6032
Fax: 603-745-2564
e-mail: info@papermilltheatre.org
Web Site: www.papermilltheatre.org
Officers:
President: Bill Hollager
VP: John Hettinger
Management:
President: David Talvot
Artistic Director: Kim Barber
Business Director: Tony Ferrelli
Mission: To provide theatre, cultural programming and theatre education for children and adults.
Utilizes: Guest Companies
Founded: 1986
Specialized Field: Theater; Festivals; Touring Children's Theatre; Art Gallery
Status: Non-Profit, Professional
Paid Staff: 3
Volunteer Staff: 50
Paid Artists: 50
Non-paid Artists: 20
Organization Type: Performing; Touring; Educational

7143
VERIZON WIRELESS ARENA
555 Elm Street
Manchester, NH 03101
Phone: 603-644-5000
Fax: 603-644-1575
Web Site: www.verizonwirelessarena.com
Management:
General Manager: Timothy Bechert
Director Sales/Marketing: Jason Perry
Founded: 2001
Paid Staff: 300
Performs At: Sports & Entertainment
Affiliations: Manchester Monarch; Manchester Wolves
Annual Attendance: 550,000

Facility Category: Arena
Type of Stage: Standard
Stage Dimensions: various
Seating Capacity: 11,000
Year Built: 2001
Cost: $70 million

7144
NEW LONDON BARN PLAYHOUSE
209 Main Street
PO Box 285
New London, NH 03257
Phone: 603-526-6710
Fax: 603-526-2849
Web Site: www.nlbarn.com/
Management:
Artistic Managing Director: Nancy Barry
Music Director: Neil Ginsberg
Costume Designer: Steven Epstein
Scenic Designer: Thom Bumblauskas
Mission: The New London Barn Playhouse in New London, New Hampshire has operated continuously since 1933 and functions as a true summer stock theatre.
Season: June - August

7145
EASTERN SLOPE INN PLAYHOUSE
Main Street
PO Box 265
North Conway, NH 03860
Phone: 603-356-5776
Fax: 603-356-8357
Mission: To keep the tradition of line performance, especially musical.

7146
MUSIC HALL
28 Chestnut Street
Portsmouth, NH 03801-4078
Phone: 603-433-3100
Fax: 603-431-4103
Web Site: www.themusichall.org
Management:
Artistic Director: Patricia Lynch
Founded: 1876
Specialized Field: Seacoast, NH
Status: Non-Profit, Professional
Paid Staff: 12
Volunteer Staff: 274

New Jersey

7147
BAYONNE VETERANS MEMORIAL STADIUM
W 26th Street
Bayonne, NJ 07002
Phone: 201-858-6164
Fax: 201-858-6092
Management:
Director: Steve Gallo

7148
ARMSTRONG HIPKINS CENTER FOR THE ARTS
Blair Academy
2 Park Street
Blairstown, NJ 07825

Mailing Address: PO Box 600
Phone: 908-362-6121
Fax: 908-362-2029
e-mail: habers@blair.edu
Web Site: www.blair.edu/performing_arts
Management:
President: Chandler Chardwick
Executive Director: Sam Backon
Artistic Director: Craige Evens
Managing Director: Jim Frick
Mission: Educational insititution.
Founded: 1997
Status: Non-Profit, Professional
Paid Staff: 150
Type of Stage: Black Box
Seating Capacity: 500

7149
CALDWELL COLLEGE STUDENT UNION BUILDING
9 Ryerson Avenue
Caldwell, NJ 07006
Phone: 973-618-3000
Fax: 201-228-3851

7150
RUTGERS-CAMDEN CENTER FOR THE ARTS GORDON THEATER
Rutgers University Fine Arts Building
3rd and Pearl Streets
Camden, NJ 08102-1403
Phone: 856-225-6676
Fax: 856-225-6597
e-mail: arts@camden.rutgers.edu
Web Site: www.rcca.camden.rutgers.edu
Management:
Director: Virginia Steel
Founded: 1996
Status: Non-Profit, Professional
Paid Staff: 8
Paid Artists: 50

7151
WALT WHITMAN CULTURAL ARTS CENTER
2nd and Cooper Streets
Camden, NJ 08102
Phone: 856-964-8300
Fax: 856-964-2953
Web Site: www.waltwhitmancenter.org/
Management:
Executive Director: Pamela Bridgeforth
Artistic Director: Ozzie Jones
Finance & Administration Director: Tony Lewis
Public Relations/External Affairs: Maureen L Mullin
Mission: The Walt Whitman Arts Center, a non-profit, multi-cultural literary, performing and visual arts center in Camden, New Jersey, is dedicated to continuing its namesake's legacy of artistic excellence. The organization also is committed to ensuring that its programming is accessible to Camden and its surrounding communities.
Founded: 1975
Status: Non-Profit, Professional
Paid Staff: 7
Budget: $60,000-150,000

7152
MID-ATLANTIC CENTER FOR THE ARTS & HUMANITIES
1048 Washington Street
PO Box 340
Cape May, NJ 08204
Mailing Address: PO Box 340, Cape May NJ 08204
Phone: 609-884-5404
Fax: 609-884-0574
Toll-free: 800-275-4278
e-mail: mstewart@capemaymac.org
Web Site: www.capemaymac.org
Management:
Chief Outreach Officer: Mary Stewart, mstewart@capemaymac.org
Mission: Dedicated to promoting preservation, awareness and interpretation of the Victorian era and its customs, heritage and architecture, as well as striving to promote the performing arts.
Utilizes: Community Members; Curators; Educators; Five Seasonal Concerts; Guest Directors; Original Music Scores
Founded: 1970
Opened: 1990
Specialized Field: Series & Festivals; Instrumental Music; Special Events
Status: Non-Profit, Professional
Paid Staff: 25
Volunteer Staff: 50
Paid Artists: 100
Performs At: Cape May Convention Hall
Organization Type: Sponsoring

7153
MIDDLE TOWNSHIP PERFORMING ARTS CENTER
1 Penkethman Way
Cape May, NJ 08210
Phone: 609-463-1924
Fax: 609-463-1928
Management:
Executive Director: Richard Ludwig
Founded: 1992
Status: Non-Profit, Professional
Paid Staff: 4
Budget: $60,000-150,000

7154
CRANFORD DRAMATIC CLUB THEATRE
78 Winans Avenue
PO Box 511
Cranford, NJ 07016
Phone: 908-276-7611

7155
DOVER LITTLE THEATRE
Elliott Street
PO Box 82
Dover, NJ 07801
Phone: 973-328-9202

7156
CONTINENTAL AIRLINES ARENA
Meadowlands
50 Route 120
East Rutherford, NJ 07073
Phone: 201-460-4374
Fax: 201-507-8122
e-mail: mbell@njsea.com
Web Site: www.meadowlands.com
Management:
President/CEO: George Zoffinger
Senior VP/General Manager: Timothy D Hassett

VP Event Booking: Ron Vandeveen
Founded: 1976
Status: For-Profit, Non-Professional
Paid Staff: 300
Budget: $3 million
Facility Category: Arena
Seating Capacity: 20,029
Year Built: 1981
Rental Contact: Ron VanDeVeen

7157
GIANTS STADIUM
Meadowlands
50 Route 120
East Rutherford, NJ 07073
Phone: 201-460-4355
Fax: 201-460-4294
e-mail: webmaster@meadowlands.com
Web Site: www.meadowlands.com
Management:
President/CEO: George Zoffinger
Senior VP/CFO: Joseph Consolazio
Senior VP Sales/Marketing: Kathleen Francis
Senior VP/Stadium Arena GM: Timothy D Hassett
Mission: Home of the New York Giants and the New York Jets, The Metro Stars, college football and concerts.
Founded: 1971
Status: For-Profit, Professional
Paid Staff: 100
Seating Capacity: 80,242
Year Built: 1976

7158
MEADOWLANDS THEATER
Meadowlands
50 Route 120
East Rutherford, NJ 07073-0700
Phone: 201-240-4038
Fax: 201-507-8130
Web Site: www.meadowlands.com
Management:
President/CEO: George Zoffinger
General Manager: Timothy D Hassett
Mission: For smaller, more intimate venues.
Founded: 2004

7159
APPEL FARM ARTS AND MUSIC CENTER
PO Box 888
Elmer, NJ 08318
Phone: 609-358-2472
Fax: 609-358-6513

7160
JOHN HARMS CENTER FOR THE ARTS
30 N Van Brunt Street
Englewood, NJ 07631
Phone: 201-567-5797
Fax: 201-567-7357
Web Site: www.johnharms.org
Management:
Executive Director: Jessica Finkelberg
Business Manager: Steve Nemiroff
Director Education: Cathy Roy
Communications/Marketing: Ed Kirchdoerffer
Founded: 1976
Status: Nonprofit
Paid Staff: 14
Volunteer Staff: 150
Paid Artists: 250
Budget: $3,000,000
Income Sources: Foundations, Grants, Corporate Support, Individuals, Earned

Annual Attendance: 300,000
Facility Category: Theater
Type of Stage: Proscenium
Stage Dimensions: 33 x 30
Seating Capacity: 1322
Year Built: 1926

7161
GLASSBORO CENTER FOR THE ARTS
Rowan University
Wilson Hall, Room 211
Glassboro, NJ 08028
Phone: 856-256-4548
Fax: 856-256-4919
e-mail: fields@rowan.edu
Web Site: www.users.rowan.edu/~benson/centerart
Management:
    Office Manager: Ginny Allen
    Director: Mark Fields
Mission: To provide several different professional
cultural events for the Southern New Jersey area.
Utilizes: Collaborations; Dance Companies; Guest
Choreographers; Guest Directors; Guest Musical
Directors; Guest Musicians; Multimedia; Original Music
Scores; Singers; Special Technical Talent; Theatre
Companies
Founded: 1989
Specialized Field: Dance; Vocal Music; Instrumental
Music; Theater; Lyric Opera; Grand Opera; Jazz
Status: Professional
Budget: $950,000
Income Sources: New Jersey State Council on the
Arts; Bergen Foundation; PSEG;
Performs At: Wilson Concert Hall
Annual Attendance: 35,000
Facility Category: Auditorium
Type of Stage: Proscenium
Stage Dimensions: 50' X 35'
Seating Capacity: 895
Year Built: 1971
Rental Contact: Stu McKee
Organization Type: Performing; Touring; Resident;
Educational; Sponsoring

7162
ORRIE DE NOOYER AUDITORIUM
Bergen County Academic
200 Hackensack Avenue
Hackensack, NJ 07601
Phone: 201-343-6000
Fax: 201-343-8884
Web Site: www.bergen.org
Management:
    Principal: Patricia Cosgroze
Founded: 1990
Status: For-Profit, Non-Professional

7163
RICHARD L SWIG ARTS CENTER
Peddie School
S Main Street Box A
Highstown, NJ 08520
Phone: 609-490-7550
Fax: 609-944-7910
Web Site: www.peddie.org
Management:
    Director: Robert Rund
Founded: 2000
Status: Non-Profit, Professional
Paid Staff: 3

7164
NORTHERN STAR ARENA
Six Flags Great Adventure
Route 537
Jackson, NJ 08527
Phone: 732-928-2000
Fax: 732-928-0937
Web Site: www.sixflags.com
Management:
    Entertainment Director: Bob O'Neill
Seating Capacity: 10,000

7165
LIBERTY SCIENCE CENTER
251 Phillip Street
Liberty State Park
Jersey City, NJ 07305-4699
Phone: 201-200-1000
Fax: 201-451-6383
e-mail: events@lsc.org OR guestcomments@lsc.org
Web Site: www.lsc.org
Management:
    President: Emlyn Koster
    Events/Rentals Director: Alison Marcon
Mission: The Central Railroad of New Jersey (CRRNJ)
Concourse Hall is suitable for a wide variety events,
from dinners and festivals to trade shows and
fund-raisers and more and can hold up to 1,000 people.
Founded: 1993
Status: Non-Profit, Non-Professional
Paid Staff: 200

7166
STRAND THEATRE
400 Clifton Avenue
Lakewood, NJ 08701
Phone: 732-367-7789
Fax: 732-367-7819
Web Site: www.strandlakewood.com
Management:
    Executive Director: Theresa Beaugard
    Event Manager: Patti Curtis
    Technical Director: Chris Staton
    Office Manager: Judy Jensen
    House Manager: Jose Pastrana
Utilizes: Collaborations; Five Seasonal Concerts;
Guest Writers; Guild Activities; Instructors; Local Artists;
Multi Collaborations; Multimedia; Special Technical
Talent; Theatre Companies
Founded: 1922
Status: Non-Profit, Professional
Paid Staff: 25
Volunteer Staff: 30
Non-paid Artists: 80
Income Sources: Rentals; Grants; Ticket Sales
Facility Category: Theatre
Seating Capacity: 1,042
Year Built: 1922
Year Remodeled: 2001
Cost: $5,000,000
Rental Contact: Linda Hassa

7167
YVONNE THEATER
Rider University
2083 Lawrenceville Road
Lawrenceville, NJ 08648
Phone: 609-896-5168
Fax: 609-896-5232
e-mail: millsm@rider.edu
Web Site: www.theatre.rider.edu
Management:
    Theater Director: Tharyle Prather

Professor: Miriam Mills
Mission: To produce outstanding Theater, Dance and
Music events for the university and the surrounding
communities. This venue provides the university with
the opportunity to learn the theater process from
concept to performance. In addition, the theater also
offers outside cultural and intellectual events, as time
permits.
Specialized Field: Theater; Dance; Music
Type of Stage: Proscenium
Seating Capacity: 440
Rental Contact: Tharyle Prather

7168
BOWNE THEATRE
Drew University
36 Madison Avenue
Madison, NJ 07940
Phone: 908-272-0100
Fax: 908-272-3949
e-mail: info@dgdco.com

7169
BERRIE CENTER FOR PERFORMING AND VISUAL ARTS
Ramapo College of New Jersey
505 Ramapo Valley Road
Mahwah, NJ 07430
Phone: 201-684-7844
Fax: 201-684-7979
e-mail: eeloi@ramapo.edu
Web Site: www.ramapo.edu/berriecenter/index.html
Management:
    Manager of Berrie Center Operations: Edonard A
    Eloiffer
    Theater Technical Director: Jason Hughes
    Assistant Technical Director: Jonathan Ginnow
    Gallery Director: Sidney O Jenkins
Mission: Constructed in 1999, the Performing Arts
Center houses the Sharp Theater, a 350-seat
proscenium theater engineered without obstructions to
visibility or sound; the Myron and Elaine Adler Theater,
a blackbox theater which can seat up to 100; The
Kresge and Pascal Art Galleries, mounting exhibitions
of museum, international, student, faculty, and
community artwork; and The Curtain Call Cafe serving
beverages and light fare.
Status: For-Profit, Professional
Paid Staff: 30
Paid Artists: 50

7170
CULTURE HALL OF MEDFORD NEW JERSEY
2 Friends Avenue
Medford, NJ 08055
Phone: 609-654-7587
Web Site: www.medfordstation.com
Specialized Field: Performing Arts Center; Banquet
Facility

7171
PAPER MILL PLAYHOUSE
Brookside Drive
Millburn, NJ 07041
Phone: 973-379-3636
Fax: 973-376-2359
Web Site: www.papermill.org
Management:
    President: Michael Gennaro
    Casting Director: Alison Franck
    Associate Artistic Director: Mark S Hoebee
    Director Development: Nina S Jacobs

7172

BICKFORD THEATRE AT THE MORRIS MUSEUM

6 Normandy Heights Road
Morristown, NJ 07960
Phone: 978-921-5706
Fax: 973-538-0154
e-mail: info@bockfordtheatre.org
Web Site: www.bickfordtheatre.org
Management:
    Artistic Director: Eric Hafen
    Public Relations Manager: Stephen Kantrowitz
Mission: A 312-seat professional theatre located within the Morris Museum. The theatre produces 4 main stage productions each year that include classic and contemporary comedies, mysteries and musicals. The company is affiliated with the Actors Equity Association and the Society of Stage Directors and Choreographers. In addition, Bickford Theatre presents year-round Children's theatre, music concerts and the acclaimed Wyeth Jazz Concert Series.
Utilizes: Actors; AEA Actors; Choreographers; Curators; Dance Companies; Dancers; Educators; Guest Conductors; Guest Designers; Guest Instructors; Guest Lecturers; Guest Soloists; Instructors; Original Music Scores; Touring Companies
Founded: 1983
Specialized Field: Theatre; Performing Arts
Status: For-Profit, Professional
Paid Staff: 20
Type of Stage: Proscenium
Stage Dimensions: 40x80
Seating Capacity: 300
Year Built: 1975
Year Remodeled: 1987
Rental Contact: Rental Coordinator Kristin Granade
Resident Groups: The Bickford Theatre

7173

COMMUNITY THEATRE

100 South Street
Morristown, NJ 07960
Phone: 973-539-0345
Fax: 973-455-1607
Web Site: www.communitytheatrenj.org
Officers:
    Board President: Bud Mayo
Management:
    Executive Director: Alison Larena
Founded: 1994
Status: Non-Profit, Professional
Paid Staff: 12

7174

WILLIAM G MENNEN SPORTS ARENA

161 E Hanover Avenue
Morristown, NJ 07962
Phone: 973-326-7651
Fax: 973-829-8698
Web Site: www.morrisparks.net
Management:
    Executive Director: Dave Helmer
    Skating School Director: Jackie Kulik
Founded: 1975
Status: For-Profit, Professional
Paid Staff: 70
Seating Capacity: 3,500

7175

HISTORIC PALACE THEATRE

Route 183
7 Ledgewood Avenue
Netcong, NJ 07857

Mailing Address: PO Box 36
Phone: 973-347-4946
Fax: 973-691-7069
Web Site: www.growingstage.com
Utilizes: Special Technical Talent; Theatre Companies
Founded: 1995

7176

RUTGERS ARTS CENTER

George Street and Route 18
New Brunswick, NJ 08903
Phone: 732-932-4636

7177

STATE THEATRE

15 Livingston Avenue
New Brunswick, NJ 08901-1903
Mailing Address: 11 Livingston Avenue
Phone: 732-246-7469
Fax: 732-745-5653
e-mail: info@statetheatrenj.org
Web Site: www.statetheatrenj.org
Officers:
    Chairman, Board of Trustees: Warren Zimmerman
Management:
    Director of Operations: Dave Hartken
    COO: Marlon Combs
    VP of Marketing: Daniel Grossman
    VP of Education: Lian Farrer
    Director of Production: Larry Dember
    Ticket Office Manager: Don McKim
Mission: Exists to enrich the lives of people from diverse backgrounds in New Jersey and to contribute to a vital urban environment by: presenting the finest national and international performing artists; providing arts education programs to inform and build future audiences; and to providing a major performing arts venue in central New Jersey that encourages and enables members of the community to have a life-long association with the performing arts.
Utilizes: Artists-in-Residence; Guest Musicians; Guest Soloists; Multimedia; Original Music Scores; Special Technical Talent; Theatre Companies
Founded: 1921
Specialized Field: Music; Dance; Live Performing Arts
Status: Non-Profit, Professional
Paid Staff: 45
Volunteer Staff: 20
Paid Artists: 100
Budget: $5 million
Income Sources: Individuals, Government, Corporations
Affiliations: League of Historic Theatres New Brunswick Cultural Center, others
Annual Attendance: 275,000
Facility Category: Performing Arts Center
Type of Stage: Procenium
Stage Dimensions: 45'x28'
Seating Capacity: 1,800
Year Built: 1921
Year Remodeled: 1988
Rental Contact: David Hartkern

7178

NEW JERSEY PERFORMING ARTS CENTER

1 Center Street
Newark, NJ 07102
Phone: 973-642-8989
Fax: 973-648-6724
Toll-free: 888-466-5722
e-mail: ldenmark@njpac.org
Web Site: www.njpac.org
Officers:

President/CEO: Lawrence P Goldman
COO: M John Richard
Treasurer: Leonard Lieberman
Assistant Treasurer: Marc E. Berson
Secretary: Clive S. Cummis
Co-Chairman: Raymond G. Chambers
Co-Chairman: Arthur E. Ryan
VP Programming: Leon Denmark
VP Development: Diane Nixa
VP Finance: Bobbie Arbesfeld
VP Operations: Audrey Winkler
Vice President Public Affairs: Jeffrey Norman
Mission: To be a world class cultural complex and center stage for New Jersey's best performing artists; to aid in providing economic revitalization in Newark.
Utilizes: Actors; AEA Actors; Artists-in-Residence; Collaborating Artists; Collaborations; Commissioned Composers; Commissioned Music; Community Talent; Composers; Contract Actors; Contract Orchestras; Curators; Dance Companies; Dancers; Designers; Educators; Guest Accompanists; Guest Choreographers; Guest Composers; Guest Designers; Guest Instructors; Guest Musical Directors; Guest Musicians; Guest Soloists; Guest Teachers; High School Drama; Instructors; Local Artists; Lyricists; Multimedia; Music; Original Music Scores; Performance Artists; Scenic Designers; Sign Language Translators; Singers; Students; Special Technical Talent; Theatre Companies
Founded: 1988
Specialized Field: Series & Festivals; Classical; Jazz; Pop; Broadway Dramatic Theatre; Modern and Classical Dance
Status: Non-Profit, Professional
Paid Staff: 130
Budget: $22 million
Income Sources: Earned Revenue: Ticket Sales, Fees, Parking, Restaurant Commission and Philanthropy
Performs At: New Jersey Performing Arts Center
Annual Attendance: 550,000
Type of Stage: Proscenium
Stage Dimensions: 37'x 39'4'x 3'2'/116' x 49'x 3'6'
Seating Capacity: 514/2,750
Year Built: 1997
Year Remodeled: N/A
Cost: $187 million
Organization Type: Performing, Resident, Educational, Sponsoring, Touring

7179

NEWARK SYMPHONY HALL

1030 Broad Street
Newark, NJ 07102
Phone: 973-643-8009

7180

THEATRE AT RARITAN VALLEY COMMUNITY COLLEGE

Raritan Valley Community College
Route 28 and Lamington Road
North Branch, NJ 08876-1265
Phone: 908-725-3420
e-mail: theatre@rvccarts.org
Web Site: www.rvccArts.org
Management:
    Director Theatre: Alan Liddell
Founded: 1985
Status: Non-Profit, Professional
Paid Staff: 4
Seating Capacity: 1,000

7181
GREAT AUDITORIUM
Pilgrim Pathway
Ocean Grove, NJ 07756
Phone: 732-775-0035
Fax: 732-775-5689
Web Site: www.oceangrove.org
Management:
GM: David Shotwell
Entertainment Director: Shelley Bellusar
Seating Capacity: 5,500

7182
LOUIS BROWN ATHLETIC CENTER
Rutgers University
83 Rockafeller Road
Piscataway, NJ 08854
Phone: 732-445-4220
Fax: 732-445-4623
Web Site: www.scarletknights.com
Management:
President: Richard McCormick
Athletic Director: Bob Mulcahy
Founded: 1776
Status: Non-Profit, Professional
Seating Capacity: 8,400

7183
RUTGERS ATHLETIC CENTER
Rutgers University
83 Rockefeller Road
Piscataway, NJ 08854
Phone: 732-932-9360
Fax: 732-445-2990
Web Site: www.recreation.rutgers.edu
Management:
Dean: Diane Bunano
Founded: 1766
Status: Non-Profit, Professional
Paid Staff: 75
Seating Capacity: 9,000

7184
RUTGERS STADIUM
Rutgers University
PO Box 1149
Piscataway, NJ 08855-1149
Phone: 732-445-4223
Fax: 732-445-2990
Management:
Assistant Athletic Director: Douglas S Kokoskie
Seating Capacity: 42,000

7185
SILVER CENTER FOR THE ARTS
Plymouth State University
Plymouth, NJ 03264
Fax: 603-535-2917
e-mail: djeffrey@mail.plymouth.edu
Web Site: www.silver.plymouth.edu
Management:
President: Sara Jayne Steen
Director of the Silver Center: Diane Jeffrey
Founded: 1992
Status: Non-Profit, Non-Professional
Paid Staff: 7

7186
STOCKTON PERFORMING ARTS CENTER
Jim Leeds Road
PO Box 195
Pomona, NJ 08240-0195
Phone: 609-652-4607
Fax: 609-626-5523
Web Site: www.stockton.edu
Officers:
President: Herman Saatkamp
Management:
Executive Director: Michael Cool
Artistic Director: Harley Halpern
Director Ticketing Services: David T. Buzza
Founded: 1963
Status: Non-Profit, Professional
Paid Staff: 8
Budget: $150,000-400,000

7187
JADWIN GYMNASIUM
Princeton University
Princeton, NJ 08544
Phone: 609-258-3000
Fax: 609-258-4477
Web Site: www.nj.com/princeton/basketball/stadium
Management:
President: Shirley Tilghman
Athletic Director: Gary D Walters
Founded: 1969
Status: Non-Profit, Non-Professional
Paid Staff: 80

7188
MCCARTER THEATRE
91 University Place
Princeton, NJ 08540
Phone: 609-258-6500
Fax: 609-497-0369
Toll-free: 888-ART-SWEB
e-mail: admin@mccarter.org
Web Site: www.mccarter.org
Management:
Artistic Director: Emily Mann
Founded: 1929
Status: For-Profit, Professional
Paid Staff: 80
Paid Artists: 10

7189
RICHARDSON AUDITORIUM
Princeton University
Alexander Hall
Princeton, NJ 08544
Phone: 609-258-4239
Fax: 609-258-6793

7190
UNION COUNTY ARTS CENTER
1601 Irving Street
Rahway, NJ 07065
Phone: 732-499-0441
Fax: 732-499-8227
Web Site: www.ucac.org
Management:
Executive Director: Sandy Erwin
Mission: Dedicated to providing world class entertainment that is exciting, educational, affordable and responsive to the diverse interests of the communities we serve.
Specialized Field: Performing Arts Presenter
Status: Non-Profit, Professional
Paid Staff: 8
Volunteer Staff: 50
Budget: 1.5 million
Performs At: 1,350 Seat Historic Theatre
Seating Capacity: 1,350
Year Built: 1928
Year Remodeled: 1996

7191
COUNT BASIE THEATRE
99 Monmouth Street
Red Bank, NJ 07701
Phone: 732-842-9000
Fax: 732-842-9323
e-mail: info@countbasietheatre.org
Web Site: www.countbasietheatre.org
Management:
CEO: Numa Saisselin
Marketing Director: Regina Paleau
Education Director: Yvonne Lamb Scudiery
General Manager: Vantony Jenkins
Utilizes: Collaborations; Dance Companies; Fine Artists; Soloists; Special Technical Talent
Founded: 1991
Specialized Field: Dance; Theatre; Vocal Music; Instrumental Music
Status: Non-Profit, Non-Professional
Paid Staff: 109
Seating Capacity: 1,400
Year Built: 1926
Rental Contact: Annette Bartolomeo

7192
WILLIAMS CENTER FOR THE ARTS NEWMAN THEATRE
One Williams Plaza
Rutherford, NJ 07070
Phone: 201-939-6969
Fax: 201-939-0843
Web Site: www.williamscenter.org
Officers:
President: Joseph Desazio
Treasurer: Evelyn Spath-Mercado
Management:
Executive Director: G W McLuckey
Mission: To provide programs of artistic excellence at affordable prices.
Utilizes: Actors; AEA Actors; Dance Companies; Local Artists; Multimedia; Original Music Scores; Student Interns; Theatre Companies
Founded: 1978
Paid Staff: 22
Budget: $650,000
Income Sources: Ticket Sales; Grants; Sponsorships; Rentals
Annual Attendance: 50,000
Facility Category: Performing Arts Center
Type of Stage: Black Box; Proscenium Arch
Seating Capacity: 200; 642
Year Built: 1922
Year Remodeled: 1992

7193
TD BANK ARTS CENTRE
519 Hurffville-Crosskeys Road
Sewell, NJ 08080
Phone: 856-256-8660
Fax: 856-256-8659
e-mail: jweiner@wtps.org
Web Site: www.tdbankarts.com
Management:
Theatre Manager: James Weiner
Technical Direector: Mike Simpson, mike@simpsonsound.net
Founded: 1998
Specialized Field: Philadelphia; Southern New Jersey
Paid Staff: 5
Volunteer Staff: 40
Facility Category: Indoor Performing Arts Center
Seating Capacity: 2,450

7194
KAPLAN JCC ON THE PALISADES
JCC School of Performing Arts
411 E Clinton Avenue
Tenafly, NJ 07670
Phone: 201-408-1492
Fax: 201-569-7448
e-mail: droberts@jccotp.org
Web Site: www.jcconthepalisades.org
Management:
    Artistic Director: Deborah Roberts,
    droberts@jccotp.org
    Program Director: Carol Leslie, cleslie@jccotp.org
Mission: The JCC School of Performing Arts offers
classes, workshops and performance opportunities for
the pre-professional as well as the recreational student
from early childhood to adult. The School is ethnically
diverse and welcomes serious students of all
backgrounds and walks of life. Instructors are at the top
of their profession, in collaboration with Strasberg and
New York City's working professionals.Agents &
Managers attend programs each year
Founded: 1981
Opened: 1982
Specialized Field: Theatre; Musical Theatre; Private
Singing; Dance
Status: Non-Profit, Professional
Paid Staff: 3
Volunteer Staff: 3
Paid Artists: 20
Non-paid Artists: 4
Performs At: Fixed-seat 188 Seat Theatre; Auditorium
That Seats 700
Affiliations: Kaplan JCC on the Palisades
Type of Stage: Proscenium
Stage Dimensions: 23'x18'; 28'x40'
Seating Capacity: 700; 188
Year Built: 1994
Year Remodeled: 2003
Rental Contact: Artistic Director Deb Roberts

7195
NEW JERSEY STATE MUSEUM AUDITORIUM
205 W State Street
PO Box 530
Trenton, NJ 08625-0530
Phone: 609-292-6464
Fax: 609-599-4098
e-mail: feedback@sos.state.nj.us
Web Site: www.state.nj.us/state/museum/
Officers:
    President: Kenneth Newcomb
    Vice President: Doug Setzer
    Treasurer: Charles Moseley
    Secretary: Louise Barrett
Management:
    Acting Director: Lorraine E Williams
Mission: To produce the historical outdoor drama From
This Day Forward annually; to produce Dickens' A
Christmas Carol annually; to produce other dramas,
engage in outreach activities, and sponsor workshops
and cultural events.
Founded: 1895

7196
PATRIOTS THEATER AT THE WAR MEMORIAL
PO Box 232
Trenton, NJ 08625

Phone: 609-984-8484
Fax: 609-777-0581
Toll-free: 800-955-5566
e-mail: thewarmemorial@sos.state.nj.us
Web Site: www.thewarmemorial.com
Management:
    Executive Director: Molly S McDonough
    Production Coordinator: Bill Nutter
    Ticketing/Sales Director: Andrew Burkett
    Ticketing/Sales Director: Rebecca Jensen
    Administrative Assistant: Stephanie Gorski
Mission: Proudly hosts a diverse and exciting array of
theatrical and concert events — from comedy to ballet,
from opera to gospel, from international to jazz, from
classical to country to rock, pop, and folk.
Founded: 1932
Status: Non-Profit, Professional
Paid Staff: 20
Volunteer Staff: 100
Income Sources: State of New Jersey
Affiliations: State of New Jersey, Department of State
Division of War Memorial
Facility Category: Theater
Type of Stage: Proscenium
Stage Dimensions: 50 x 30
Seating Capacity: 1800; 12,000 sq ft
Year Built: 1932
Year Remodeled: 1998
Cost: $ 34.5 Million
Rental Contact: Executive Director Molly S.
McDonough
Resident Groups: New Jersey Symphony, Greater
Trenton Sympony, Boheme Opera, American Repertory
Ball

7197
SOVEREIGN BANK ARENA
81 Hamilton Avenue
Trenton, NJ 08611
Phone: 609-656-3200
Fax: 609-656-3201
Web Site: www.sovereignbankarena.com
Management:
    Managing Director: Mike Scanlon
    Assistant General Manager: Rick Hontz
    Operations Manager: Jason Robertson
    Event Coordinator: Chad Jeffrey
Mission: Theatre events, concerts, sports, family
shows and community events.
Founded: 1999
Seating Capacity: 8,600
Year Built: 1999

7198
WILKENS THEATRE
Kean College of New Jersey
1000 Morris Avenue
Union, NJ 07083
Phone: 908-527-2000
Fax: 908-527-8345
Web Site: www.kean.edu
Mission: To offer theatre to all citizens in our county,
primarily through the schools, providing one selected
offering annually.

7199
PARK THEATRE PERFORMING ARTS CENTRE
560 32nd Street
Union City, NJ 07087
Phone: 201-865-6980
Fax: 201-865-5339
Web Site: www.passionplayusa.org
Management:

Artistic Director: Meriam Lobel
Theatre Director: Sixto Perez
Executive Director: Kevin Ashe
Founded: 1983
Status: Non-Profit, Professional
Paid Staff: 3
Budget: $400,000
Income Sources: Earned Income; State Grants;
Private Funds
Stage Dimensions: 70x40
Seating Capacity: 1400
Year Built: 1933

7200
MONTCLAIR STATE COLLEGE MEMORIAL AUDITORIUM
1 Normal Avenue
Upper Montclair, NJ 07043
Phone: 973-655-4000
Fax: 973-655-7371
Toll-free: 800-624-7780
e-mail: webmaster@montclair.edu
Web Site: www.montclair.edu
Management:
    President: Susan Cole
Mission: Producing and promoting high quality,
accesible, professional theater; training and developing
the talents of musicians, actors and technicians.
Status: For-Profit, Professional

7201
HUNZIKER BLACK BOX THEATER
William Patterson University
300 Pompton Road
Wayne, NJ 07470
Phone: 973-720-2000
Web Site: ww2.wpunj.edu
Officers:
    President: Mary Harper
    Treasurer: Leslie Madigan
    Immediate Past President: Janet Bondurant
Mission: Children's Theatre Board provides
opportunities for students, educators and families to
experience and participate in the perforoming arts.
CTB offers multidisciplinary, culturally diverse programs
to foster sensitivity and acceptance.

7202
POLLAK THEATRE
Monmouth University
400 Cedar Avenue
West Long Branch, NJ 07764
Phone: 732-571-3554
Fax: 732-263-5262
e-mail: vpeck@monmouth.edu
Web Site: www.monmouth.edu/performingarts
Management:
    Director: Vaune Peck
    Assistant Director: Alice Arnts
Seating Capacity: 700

7203
MAURICE LEVIN THEATER
Jewish Community Center Metrowest
760 Northfield Avenue
West Orange, NJ 07052
Phone: 973-736-3200
Fax: 973-736-6871
Web Site: www.jccmetrowest.org
Officers:
    President: Michael Hopkins
Management:
    Program Supervisor: Jo Golstein
    Program Assistant: Marsha Fleisch

Mission: To provide for all within the community an avenue for education and development in all aspects of theatrical arts and to provide entertainment for the community by offering a series of well-staged performances of live theatre.
Founded: 1877
Specialized Field: Vocal Music; Instrumental Music; Theater; Festivals; Film Series
Status: Non-Profit, Non-Professional
Paid Staff: 6
Paid Artists: 8

7204
BARRON ARTS CENTER
582 Rahway Avenue
Woodbridge, NJ 07095
Phone: 732-634-0413
Fax: 732-634-8633
e-mail: barronarts@twp.woodbridge.nj.us
Officers:
    President: Sigmund Molis
Management:
    Executive Director: Cynthia Knight
Mission: To offer professional music and spoken word performances free of charge to the central New Jersey community.
Founded: 1976
Status: Non-Profit, Professional
Paid Staff: 3
Volunteer Staff: 30
Income Sources: Municipal & Not-For-Profit Organization
Performs At: Small Multipurpose Building Used As An Center For The Arts Featuring Concerts, Poetry Readinga & Art Exhibits.
Annual Attendance: 10,000
Facility Category: Small Victorian Building
Type of Stage: Temporary 6" Riser Stage
Seating Capacity: 95
Year Built: 1877

New Mexico

7205
FLICKINGER CENTER FOR PERFORMING ARTS
1110 New York Avenue
Alamogordo, NM 88310
Phone: 505-437-2202
Fax: 505-434-0067
e-mail: flickinger@zianet.com
Web Site: www.flickingercenter.org
Officers:
    President, Board of Directors: Lonnie Jarrett
Management:
    Executive Director: Vicki Rogers
Utilizes: Dance Companies; Guest Writers; Guild Activities; Lyricists; New Productions; Original Music Scores; Special Technical Talent; Theatre Companies; Touring Companies
Founded: 1988
Status: Non-Profit, Professional
Paid Staff: 5
Volunteer Staff: 60
Non-paid Artists: 200
Facility Category: Performing Arts Center
Type of Stage: Proscenium
Stage Dimensions: 30 x 40
Seating Capacity: 675
Year Built: 1954
Year Remodeled: 1991
Rental Contact: Vicki Rogers

7206
ALBUQUERQUE CONVENTION CENTER
401 Second Street NW
Albuquerque, NM 87103
Phone: 505-768-4575
Fax: 505-768-3239
e-mail: cchavez@cabq.gov@cabq.gov
Paid Staff: 56
Facility Category: Convention Center; Ballroom; Auditorium
Type of Stage: Flexible, Platform/Proscenium
Seating Capacity: 3000
Year Built: 1972
Year Remodeled: 1990
Rental Contact: Scheduling Manager Carol Chavez

7207
JOURNAL PAVILION
5601 University Boulevard Southeast
Albuquerque, NM 87105
Phone: 505-452-5100
Fax: 505-452-0900
Web Site: www.journalpavilion.com
Management:
    Executive Director: Laura Loghry
    Marketing Director: Christine Lorello
Seating Capacity: 12,000

7208
NATIONAL HISPANIC CULTURAL CENTER OF NEW MEXICO
Quickel Building
600 Central SW, Suite 201
Albuquerque, NM 87102-3194
Phone: 505-246-2261
Fax: 505-246-2613
e-mail: rlove@state.nm.us
Web Site: www.nmhcc.org
Management:
    President: Tom Kevis
    Artistic Director: Reve Love
    Managing Director: Gene Hemley
Founded: 1987
Status: Non-Profit, Professional
Paid Staff: 52
Paid Artists: 12

7209
POPEJOY HALL
University of New Mexico
Center for the Arts
Albuquerque, NM 87131-3176
Phone: 505-277-3824
Fax: 505-277-7353
Web Site: www.popejoyhall.com
Officers:
    President: Carol Leevers
    VP: Jane Traynor
    Treasurer/Secretary: Dean Petska
Management:
    Director: Tom Tkach
    Public Relations Manager: Terry Davis
    Technical Director: Billy Tubb
    Artistic Director: Judy Ryan
Mission: To present Touring Broadway, plus national as well as international music and dance.
Paid Staff: 12
Volunteer Staff: 200
Budget: $2,000,000
Income Sources: State Legislature; Event Revenue
Affiliations: University of New Mexico-Center for the Arts
Annual Attendance: 100,000

Seating Capacity: 2044
Year Built: 1966
Year Remodeled: 1996
Rental Contact: Thomas Tkach
Resident Groups: Musical Theatre Southwest & New Mexico Symphony Orchestra

7210
SANTA FE OPERA HOUSE
Routes 285 and 84
Albuquerque, NM 87506
Phone: 505-986-5955
Fax: 505-986-5999
e-mail: tmorris@santafeopera.org
Web Site: www.santafeopera.org
Management:
    Administrative Director: Tom Morris
Founded: 1957
Seating Capacity: 2,234

7211
SOUTH BROADWAY CULTURAL CENTER
1025 Broadway SE
Albuquerque, NM 87102
Phone: 505-848-1320
Fax: 505-848-1329
e-mail: lulibarri@cabq.gov
Web Site: www.cabq.gov/sbec
Management:
    Director: Linda Ulibarri
    Technical Director: Antonio Aragon
    Gallery Curator: John Peterson
Mission: To produce theatrical productions reflecting a high degree of professionalism; to develop artists in the theatre as well as responsive audiences.
Founded: 1970
Status: Non-Profit, Non-Professional
Paid Staff: 8

7212
TINGLEY COLISEUM
New Mexico State Fairgrounds
300 San Pedro NE
Albuquerque, NM 87108
Mailing Address: PO Box 8546
Phone: 505-265-1791
Fax: 505-268-6753
Web Site: www.expelnm.com
Management:
    General Manager: Fred Teralte
    Media Director: Veronica Valencia
Founded: 1942
Status: For-Profit, Professional

7213
UNIVERSITY OF NEW MEXICO STADIUM
1414 University Boulevard SE
Albuquerque, NM 87131
Phone: 505-925-5500
Fax: 505-925-5559
Web Site: www.enm.edu/lobo
Management:
    Sports Information: Greg Remington
    Head Football Coach: Rocky Long
    Head Basketball Coach: Fran Fraschilla
    Head Basketball Coach (M): Don Flanahan
Seating Capacity: 18,018

7214
SPENCER THEATER FOR THE PERFORMING ARTS
PO Box 140
Alto, NM 88312

Phone: 505-336-4800
Fax: 505-336-4001
Toll-free: 888-818-7872
e-mail: ccentilli@spencertheater.com
Web Site: www.spencertheater.com
Management:
    Executive Director: Charles Centilli
Utilizes: Actors; Artists-in-Residence; Dance
Companies; Dancers; Educators; Five Seasonal
Concerts; Guest Soloists; Guest Writers; Guild
Activities; Original Music Scores; Resident
Professionals; Sign Language Translators; Singers;
Soloists; Student Interns; Special Technical Talent;
Theatre Companies; Visual Arts
Founded: 1997
Status: Non-Profit, Professional
Paid Staff: 13
Volunteer Staff: 30
Income Sources: Private Contributions
Annual Attendance: 5,000
Facility Category: Theater
Stage Dimensions: 50 x 80
Seating Capacity: 514
Year Built: 1979
Cost: $22 Million
Rental Contact: Charles Centilli

7215
FARMINGTON CIVIC CENTER

200 W Arrington
Farmington, NM 87401
Phone: 505-599-1150
Fax: 505-599-1146
Toll-free: 877-599-3331
e-mail: lparks@fmtn.org
Web Site: www.farmington.nm.us
Officers:
    Foundation President: Melissa Sharpe
Management:
    Supervisor: Loretta J Parks
Mission: To further promote the cultural enrichment of
the citizens of the City of Farmington and surrounding
area.
Utilizes: Actors; Dance Companies; Dancers;
Educators; Fine Artists; Guest Instructors; Guest
Soloists; Guild Activities; High School Drama; Local
Artists; Multimedia; Original Music Scores; Playwrights;
Sign Language Translators; Singers; Soloists; Theatre
Companies; Touring Companies
Founded: 1976
Specialized Field: Performing and Visual
Status: Non-Profit, Professional
Paid Staff: 16
Budget: $571,000
Income Sources: Division of City of Farmington Tax
Revenue
Performs At: Broadway Musicals, SJ Community
Concert & Symphony League
Affiliations: WAA and IAAM
Annual Attendance: 150,000
Facility Category: Performing Arts Theatre &
Convention Center
Type of Stage: Proscenium
Stage Dimensions: 52 w x 72 deep
Seating Capacity: 1200
Year Built: 1976

7216
AMERICAN SOUTHWEST CENTER

New Mexico State University
PO Box 3072
Las Cruces, NM 88003

Phone: 505-646-4517
Fax: 505-646-5767
Toll-free: 800-525-2782
Web Site: www.nmsu.edu
Management:
    President: Michael Martin
    Artistic Director: Michael Wise
    Managing Director: Ruth Cantrell
Status: Non-Profit, Professional
Paid Staff: 10
Paid Artists: 10

7217
PAN AMERICAN CENTER

New Mexico State University
PO Box 30001
Las Cruces, NM 88003
Phone: 505-646-4413
Fax: 505-646-3605
Web Site: www.nmnathletics.com
Management:
    President: Will Lofdahl
    Artistic Director: Gary Rachele
    Box Office Manager: Patrick Kennedy
Founded: 1968
Status: For-Profit, Professional
Paid Staff: 600
Seating Capacity: 13,007

7218
DUANE SMITH AUDITORIUM

1300 Diamond Drive
Los Alamos, NM 87544
Phone: 505-662-9000
Web Site: www.losalamos.org/laca
Management:
    Artistic Director: Rosalie Heller
Utilizes: Dance Companies; Fine Artists; Multimedia;
Sign Language Translators
Founded: 1946
Volunteer Staff: 30
Paid Artists: 5

7219
PEARSON AUDITORIUM

New Mexico Military Institute
101 W College Boulevard
Roswell, NM 88201
Phone: 505-622-6250
Fax: 505-624-8459
Web Site: www.nmmi.cc.nm.us
Officers:
    President: Ken Haarstad
    VP: Shirley Olson
    Secretary: Lori Garnes
    Treasurer: Jerry Jorgenson
Mission: Community theatre to promote adult
education and provide theatre arts to surroundings
communities children's educational performing arts.
Income Sources: State Education Funds
Annual Attendance: 20,000
Facility Category: Auditorium
Seating Capacity: 1,100

7220
GREER GARSON THEATRE CENTER

College of Santa Fe
1600 Saint Michael's Drive
Santa Fe, NM 87505
Phone: 505-473-6439
Fax: 505-473-6016
Toll-free: 800-456-2673
Web Site: www.csf.edu
Management:

    Assistant Director: Jennifer Kilbourn
    Chair: John Weckesser
Mission: Provide undergraduate degrees, BA and BFA
in Theatre, Acting, Music Theatre, Design Tech and
Theatre Management.
Founded: 1936
Specialized Field: Acting; Musical Theatre; Technical
Theatre; Theatre Management; Stage Management
Paid Staff: 25

7221
GUADALUPE HISTORIC FOUNDATION (SANTUARIO DE GUADALUPE) DINNER THEATER

100 S Guadalupe Street
Santa Fe, NM 87501
Phone: 505-988-2027
Management:
    Owner/President: Prescott F Griffith
Mission: Elegant dinner theatre featuring live
Broadway musical productions.

7222
SANTA FE CONVENTION AND VISITORS BUREAU SWEENEY CENTER

201 W Marcy
PO Box 909
Santa Fe, NM 87501
Phone: 505-955-6200
Fax: 505-955-6222
Toll-free: 800-777-2489
e-mail: santafe@santafenm.gov
Web Site: www.santafe.org
Management:
    Executive Director: Darlene Greigo
Status: Non-Profit, Non-Professional
Paid Staff: 12

7223
SANTA FE STAGES

422 W San Francisco Street
Santa Fe, NM 87501
Phone: 505-982-6680
Fax: 505-982-6682
e-mail: info@santafestages.org
Web Site: www.santafestages.org
Management:
    Technical Director: Mike Curtis
    Development Manager: Susan Apker
    Marketing Director: Aimee Gwynne Franklyn
    Producing Director: Craig Strong
Founded: 1994

New York

7224
ALBANY PERFORMING ARTS CENTER

SUNY
1400 Washington Avenue
Albany, NY 12222
Phone: 518-442-3995
Fax: 518-442-4206
Facility Category: Recital Hall; Theater

7225
CAPITAL REPERTORY THEATRE

111 N Pearl Street
Albany, NY 12207
Phone: 518-462-4531
Fax: 518-465-0213
e-mail: info@capitalrep.org
Web Site: www.capitalrep.org

Management:
Production Manager: Brandon Curry
Artistic Director: Margaret Mancinelli-Cahill
Managing Director: Elizabeth Doran
Utilizes: Actors; Choreographers; Designers; Guest Accompanists; Guest Lecturers; Music; Original Music Scores; Resident Professionals; Theatre Companies
Founded: 1981
Status: Non-Profit, Professional
Paid Staff: 25
Budget: 2,100,000
Income Sources: Corporate Sponsors; Individual Donors; Subscriptions; Ticket Sales
Season: July - May
Affiliations: LORT
Annual Attendance: 63,000+
Facility Category: Theatre
Type of Stage: Thrust
Seating Capacity: 285

7226
EGG-EMPIRE STATE PERFORMING ARTS CENTER
Empire State Plaza
PO Box 2065
Albany, NY 12220
Phone: 518-473-1061
Fax: 518-473-1848
e-mail: info@theegg.org
Web Site: www.theegg.org
Management:
Executive Director: Peter Lesser
Founded: 1978
Status: Professional
Paid Staff: 20

7227
PALACE PERFORMING ARTS CENTER
19 Clinton Avenue
Albany, NY 12207
Phone: 518-465-3335
Fax: 518-427-0151
Web Site: www.palacealbany.com
Management:
House Manager: Bill O'Donnell
Director Of Development: George P Kansas
Founded: 1931

7228
PEPSI ARENA
51 S Pearl Street
Albany, NY 12207
Phone: 518-487-2000
Fax: 518-487-2020
e-mail: info@pepsiarena.com
Web Site: www.pepsiarena.com
Management:
General Manager: Robert Belber
Seating Capacity: 17,000

7229
UNIVERSITY AT ALBANY PERFORMING ARTS CENTER (PAC)
SUNY
Ten Broeck 107, Dutch Quad
Albany, NY 12222
Phone: 518-442-3995
Fax: 518-442-5099
e-mail: pferlo@albany.edu
Web Site: www.albany.edu/pac/
Management:
Executive Director: Patrick Ferlo
Assistant Director: Kim Engel

Technical Operations Director: Bryan Robinson
Event Supervisor: Frank Barone
Mission: The mission at the University at Albany Performing Arts Center is to maintain a state-of-the-art facility that enhances the quality of learning for University of Albany students as well as one that offers cultural opportunities to all in the Capital Region. The Main Theatre auditorium seats 500 people; the Recital Hall seats 242 people; the Arena Theatre auditorium seats 196; the Studio Theatre seats 153 people; and the Lab Theatre seats 200.
Founded: 1983
Status: Non-Profit, Professional
Paid Staff: 4
Budget: $10,000

7230
MERRILL FIELD
Alfred University, Saxon Drive
Office of Conferences Carnegie Hall
Alfred, NY 14802-1205
Phone: 607-871-2183
Fax: 607-871-2293
Web Site: www.alfred.edu
Officers:
President: Charles Edmondson
Management:
Director: William T Emrick
Founded: 1836
Seating Capacity: 3,000

7231
MUSICAL FARE THEATRE
Daemen College
4380 Main Street, Suite 810
Amherst, NY 14226
Phone: 716-839-8540
Fax: 716-839-8539
e-mail: musicalfare@daemen.edu
Web Site: www.musicalfare.com
Management:
Executive Director: Randall Kramer
Marketing Coordinator: Doug Weyand
Administrative Director: Debbie Pappas
Mission: To bringing quality musical theatre to Western NY, and to becoming a significant regional theatre with national prominence by developing and presenting new musicals, new versions of traditional musicals and area premieres.
Founded: 1990
Specialized Field: Musical Theatre
Status: Non-Profit, Professional
Paid Staff: 5
Paid Artists: 50
Affiliations: AEA; SSDC; Buffalo Theatre Alliance
Annual Attendance: 20,000
Facility Category: Theatre
Type of Stage: Proscenium
Seating Capacity: 13
Year Built: 2000

7232
RICHARD B FISHER CENTER FOR THE PERFORMING ARTS AT BARD COLLEGE
60 Manor Avenue
Annadale-on-Hudson, NY 12504
Phone: 845-758-7950
Fax: 845-758-7920
e-mail: fishercenter@bard.edu
Web Site: www.fishercenter.bard.edu
Officers:
Director: Tambra Dillon
Managing Director: Nancy Cook
Director Communications: Mark Primoff

Production Manager: Robert Airhart
Mission: This facility will be devoted primarily to teaching and college events during the academic year and used as a public performing arts facility and venue for the college's graduate programs in the arts during the summer months.
Opened: 2003
Specialized Field: Dance; Music; Theater
Status: Non-Profit
Season: Summer
Performs At: Sosnoff Theater, Theater Two
Facility Category: Academics Facilities
Type of Stage: Proscenium
Orchestra Pit: Y
Seating Capacity: 900, 200
Year Built: 2003
Architect: Frank O Gehry & Associates
Cost: $62 Million

7233
US MILITARY ACADEMY
Wells College
Student Activities
Aurora, NY 13026
Phone: 315-364-3330
Fax: 315-364-3325

7234
JUNE COMPANY
28 Coolidge Way
Averil Park, NY 12018
Phone: 518-447-5414
Fax: 518-447-5446

7235
QUEENSBOROUGH COMMUNITY COLLEGE THEATER
222-05 56th Avenue
Bayside, NY 11364-1497
Phone: 718-631-6311
Fax: 718-631-6033
e-mail: agin@qcc.cuny.edu
Web Site: www.qcc.cuny.edu
Management:
Executive Director: Sophie Foglia
Founded: 1965
Status: For-Profit, Professional
Paid Staff: 5
Annual Attendance: 15,000+
Facility Category: Conventional Theatre
Type of Stage: Proscenium
Stage Dimensions: 40x40
Seating Capacity: 875
Year Built: 1970

7236
BROOME COUNTY VETERANS MEMORIAL ARENA
1 Stuart Street
Binghamton, NY 13901
Phone: 607-778-1528
Fax: 607-778-6041
e-mail: bhoffman@co.broome.ny.us
Web Site: www.gobroomecounty.com
Management:
Arena Manager: Brian Hoffman
Founded: 1972
Status: Non-Profit, Professional
Paid Staff: 55
Budget: 800,000
Income Sources: Sports; Concerts, Government; State; County; Concessions; Trade Shows
Performs At: Multipurpose

Affiliations: AHL Binghamton Senators
Facility Category: Arena

7237
STATE UNIVERSITY OF NEW YORK-BINGHAMPTON: ANDERSON CENTER FOR THE ARTS

Binghamton University
PO Box 6000
Binghamton, NY 13902-6000
Phone: 607-777-6802
Fax: 607-777-6771
e-mail: mmack@binghamton.edu
Web Site: www.binghamton.edu
Management:
    Director: Floyd Herzog
    Assistant Director: Mary Mack
    Adiminstrative Assistant: Patricia J Benjamin
    Development Director: Marcia Steinbrecher
Mission: Designed to meet the needs of every performing group such as soloists, chamber ensembles, symphonies, dance or large theatrical productions complemented by a full scale orchestra.
Founded: 1986
Status: Non-Profit, Non-Professional
Paid Staff: 10

7238
ADIRONDACK LAKES CENTER FOR THE ARTS

Route 28
PO Box 205
Blue Mountain Lake, NY 12812
Phone: 518-352-7715
Fax: 518-352-7333
Web Site: www.adk-arts.org
Officers:
    President: Roland B Stearns
    Vice President: Cathleen Collins
    Treasurer: Polly Fagan
    Secretary: Jamie Nile
Management:
    Executive Director: Ellen C Butz
    Program Director: Alicia Giuliani
Mission: To promote visual and performing arts through programs and services in our region, to serve established professional and aspiring artists.
Utilizes: Dancers; Educators; Fine Artists; High School Drama; Local Artists; Multimedia; Original Music Scores; Selected Students; Sign Language Translators; Soloists; Student Interns; Special Technical Talent; Theatre Companies; Touring Companies
Founded: 1967
Status: Non-Profit, Professional
Paid Staff: 5
Income Sources: Membership; grants; admission fees
Annual Attendance: 3,500
Facility Category: Concert Hall; Performance Center; Theatre
Type of Stage: Platform
Stage Dimensions: varible
Seating Capacity: 170
Year Remodeled: 1991

7239
SPECIAL OLYMPICS STADIUM

SUNY
350 New Campus Drive
Brockport, NY 14420-2989
Phone: 716-395-2218
Fax: 716-395-2160
e-mail: mandriat@brockport.edu
Web Site: www.brockport.edu

Management:
    Sports Information Director: Kelly Vergin
Seating Capacity: 10,000

7240
TOWER FINE ARTS CENTER AND HARTWELL HALL

Suny Brockport
350 New Campus Drive
Brockport, NY 14420-2983
Phone: 716-395-2797
Fax: 716-395-5872
e-mail: ssoloway@brockport.edu
Web Site: www.brockport.edu/finearts
Type of Stage: procenium/dance stage/black box
Stage Dimensions: 45'x30'
Seating Capacity: 400; 270; 100
Year Built: 1968
Year Remodeled: 1999

7241
LEHMAN CENTER FOR THE PERFORMING ARTS

250 Bedford Park Boulevard W
Bronx, NY 10468
Phone: 718-960-8232
Fax: 718-960-8233
e-mail: eva.bornstein@lehman.cuny.edu
Web Site: www.lehmancenter.org
Management:
    Executive Director: Eva Bornstein
Utilizes: Actors; Dance Companies; Dancers; Educators; Grant Writers; Guest Accompanists; Guest Artists; Guest Choreographers; Guest Companies; Guest Directors; Guest Instructors; Guest Musical Directors; Guest Musicians; Guest Soloists; Instructors; Local Artists; Multimedia; Original Music Scores; Singers; Special Technical Talent; Theatre Companies
Founded: 1980
Status: Non-Profit, Professional
Paid Staff: 10
Budget: $400,000-$1 Million
Facility Category: Concert Hall
Type of Stage: Proscenium
Seating Capacity: 2,310
Year Built: 1979
Rental Contact: Operations Manager Janet Sanchez

7242
YANKEE STADIUM

One East 161st Street
Bronx, NY 10451
Phone: 718-293-4300
Fax: 718-293-7431
Web Site: www.yankees.com
Management:
    SVP/General Manager: Brian Cashman
    SVP Marketing: Deborah Tymon
    SVP Community Relations: Brian Smith
    SVP Marketing: Deborah Tymon
    Senior Director Stadium Operations: Michael Bonner
    Senior Director Ticket Operations: Irfan Kirimica
    Director, Non-Baseball Events: Emily Hamel
Mission: Home stadium of the New York Yankees major league baseball team.
Facility Category: Baseball Stadium
Seating Capacity: 50,086
Year Built: 2009
Architect: Populous
Cost: $1.5 billion

7243
BROOKLYN ACADEMY OF MUSIC: CAREY PLAYHOUSE

30 Lafayette Avenue
Brooklyn, NY 11217
Phone: 718-636-4100
Fax: 718-857-2021
e-mail: info@bam.org
Web Site: www.bam.org
Management:
    President: Carron Hopkins
Founded: 1851
Status: Non-Profit, Professional
Paid Staff: 150

7244
BROOKLYN ACADEMY OF MUSIC: CAREY PLAYHOUSE

30 Lafayette Avenue
Brooklyn, NY 11217
Phone: 718-636-4100
Fax: 718-857-2021

7245
BROOKLYN ACADEMY OF MUSIC: OPERA HOUSE

30 Lafayette Avenue
Brooklyn, NY 11217
Phone: 718-636-4100
Fax: 718-857-2021

7246
BROOKLYN CENTER FOR THE PERFORMING ARTS

Broolyn College
Campus Road & Hillel Place
Brooklyn, NY 11210
Mailing Address: PO Box 100163
Phone: 718-951-4600
Fax: 718-951-4437
e-mail: richardg@brooklyn.cuny.edu
Web Site: www.brooklyncenter.com
Management:
    Director/General Manager: Richard Grossberg
    Producing Director: Julie Pareles
Budget: $400,000-1,000,000
Performs At: Walt Whitman Hall
Seating Capacity: 2,400
Rental Contact: Director/General Manager Richard Grossberg

7247
BROOKLYN CONSERVATORY OF MUSIC

58 7th Avenue
Brooklyn, NY 11217
Phone: 718-622-3300
Fax: 718-622-3957
Web Site: www.brooklynconservatory.com
Officers:
    President: David Rivel
Founded: 1897

7248
PRATT INSTITUTE: AUDITORIUM

200 Willoughby Avenue
Brooklyn, NY 11205
Phone: 718-636-3422
Fax: 718-399-4578
e-mail: help@pratt.edu
Web Site: www.pratt.edu
Management:
    President: Thomas Shutte

Founded: 1887
Status: Non-Profit, Professional

7249
SAINT JOSEPH'S COLLEGE CENTER FOR ARTS
Brooklyn Campus
245 Clinton Avenue
Brooklyn, NY 11205
Phone: 718-636-6868
e-mail: suffolkas@sjcny.edu
Web Site: www.sjcny.edu
Officers:
President: Elizabeth A Hill
Vice President of Academic Affairs: Loretta McGrann
Chair: Sheila Baird
Vice Chairman: Frank Lourenso
Secretary: Stephan Hochberg
Mission: Providing a strong academic and value-oriented education at the undergraduate and graduate levels, a liberal arts tradition that supports provision for career preparation and enhancement.
Founded: 1916

7250
HICKOX FIELD
CW Post Campus
Brookville, NY 11548
Phone: 516-299-2289
Fax: 516-299-3155
Management:
Athletic Director: Vincent Salamone

7251
AFRICAN-AMERICAN CULTURAL CENTER: PAUL ROBESON HALL
350 Masten Avenue
Buffalo, NY 14209
Phone: 716-884-2013
Fax: 716-885-2590

7252
BUFFALO STATE COLLEGE PERFORMING ARTS CENTER
1300 Elmwood Avenue
Rockwell Hall 210
Buffalo, NY 14222
Phone: 716-878-3032
Fax: 716-878-4234
e-mail: rhpac@bscmail.buffalostate.edu
Web Site: www.buffalostate.edu
Management:
Director Operations: Jeff Marsha
Technical Director: Thomas Kostusiak
Mission: To provide a first class professional performing arts facility that enhances the quality of life for the campus and the citizens of Western New York.
Founded: 1987
Specialized Field: Series & Festivals; Music; Dance; Theatre
Status: Non-Profit, Non-Professional
Paid Staff: 5

7253
GREATER BUFFALO YOUTH BALLET THEATER
328 Kenmore Avenue
Buffalo, NY 14223
Phone: 716-835-3585
e-mail: GBYBallet@hotmail.com
Web Site: www.gbyballet.org
Management:

Artistic Director: Elizabeth DiStasio-Waddell
Mission: A pre-professional ballet company which provides western New York dancers with a quality education in the performing art of dance. Offering children of diverse ethnic and socioeconomic backgrounds the opportunity to achieve artistic excellence through dance.
Founded: 1997

7254
HSBC ARENA
1 Seymore H Knox III Plaza
Buffalo, NY 14203-3007
Phone: 716-855-4100
Fax: 716-855-4120
Toll-free: 888-223-6000
e-mail: info@hsbcarena.com
Web Site: www.hsbcarena.com
Management:
Director Building Operations: Stan Makowski
Director Arena Booking: Jennifer Van Rysdam
Status: For-Profit, Professional

7255
KLEINHANS MUSIC HALL
Symphony Circle
Buffalo, NY 14201
Phone: 716-883-3560
Fax: 716-883-7430
Management:
Manager of the Hall: Kristen Carlson
Founded: 1941
Status: Non-Profit, Professional
Paid Staff: 40
Paid Artists: 3
Facility Category: Music Hall/Theater
Seating Capacity: 2,839
Rental Contact: Kristen R Carlsen

7256
LIPPES CONCER HALL IN SLEE HALL
University at Buffalo
105 Slee Hall Music Department
Buffalo, NY 14260-4800
Phone: 716-645-2921
Fax: 716-645-3175
e-mail: rehard@buffalo.edu
Web Site: www.slee.buffalo.edu
Management:
Assistant Concert Manager: Alana Janus
Concert Manager: Phil Rehard
Mission: Dedicated to performing both new and traditional chamber music in an intimate setting.
Founded: 1955
Specialized Field: Classical
Status: Non-Profit, Professional
Paid Staff: 11
Volunteer Staff: 15
Paid Artists: 13
Income Sources: Endowment; State
Affiliations: Chamber Music America; ECMEA
Annual Attendance: 10,000
Facility Category: 670 Seat Concert Hall; 215 Seat Recital Hall
Rental Contact: Concert Manager Phil Rehard

7257
MARINE MIDLAND ARENA
1 Seymour H Knox III Plaza
Buffalo, NY 14203-3007
Phone: 716-855-4100
Fax: 716-855-4120
e-mail: info@hsbcarena.com
Web Site: www.hsbcarena.com

Management:
Director Building Operations: Stan Makowski
Director Arena Booking: Jennifer Stich
Founded: 1969
Status: For-Profit, Professional
Paid Staff: 100

7258
SHEA'S PERFORMING ARTS CENTER
646 Main Street
Buffalo, NY 14202
Phone: 716-847-1410
Fax: 716-847-1644
Web Site: www.sheas.org
Officers:
CEO: Anthony Conte
Management:
Development Manager: Linda Sroka
Production Manager: Bill Hendrick
Marketing Manager: Lisa Grisanti
Founded: 1926
Status: Non-Profit

7259
SUNY CENTER FOR THE ARTS
Department of Theatre and Dance
285 Alumni Arena
Buffalo, NY 14260
Phone: 716-645-6898
Fax: 716-645-6992
e-mail: clwhelan@buffalo.edu
Web Site: www.cas.buffalo.edu/depts/theatredance
Management:
Department Chairman: Robert Knopf
Director Music Theater: Lynne Kurdziel-Formato
Utilizes: Dance Companies; Dancers; Designers; Educators; Guest Artists; Guest Designers; Guest Directors; Guest Ensembles; Guest Instructors; Guest Musical Directors; Guest Soloists; High School Drama; Local Artists; Multimedia; Resident Artists; Soloists
Status: Non-Profit, Non-Professional
Paid Staff: 5
Paid Artists: 28
Affiliations: Irish Classical Theatre Company; Shakespeare in Delaware Park; Kavinoky; Musical Fare; Art Park
Type of Stage: Proscenium; Black Box
Seating Capacity: 120; 388
Year Built: 1995
Cost: $500,000,000
Rental Contact: S. Fazekas

7260
UNIVERSITY AT BUFFALO CENTER FOR THE ARTS
103 Center for the Arts
Buffalo, NY 14260-6000
Phone: 716-645-6259
Fax: 716-645-6973
e-mail: info@ubcta.org
Web Site: www.ubcta.org
Management:
Executive Director: Thomas Burrows
Assistant Director: Rob Falgiano
Mission: Mission is to create an environment for the visual and performing arts to flourish through education, exploration, collaboration, and presentation, while enriching cultural opportunities for the surrounding community.
Utilizes: Actors; Artists-in-Residence; Dance Companies; Original Music Scores; Singers; Special Technical Talent; Theatre Companies
Founded: 1994
Status: Non-Profit, Professional

Paid Staff: 30
Volunteer Staff: 300
Budget: $2 million
Income Sources: Rental, ticket sales, 60% salaries.
Affiliations: State University of New York at Buffalo
Annual Attendance: 130,000
Facility Category: Performing and Visual Arts
Type of Stage: Proscenium
Stage Dimensions: 42' X 102'
Seating Capacity: 1,748
Year Built: 1994
Cost: $2,500 commercial & labor
Rental Contact: Katherine Trapanovski
Organization Type: Mainstage 1748; Drama Theatre 388; Screening Room 210; Black Box 185.

7261
AUGSBURY CENTER

Saint Lawrence University
Park Street
Canton, NY 13617
Phone: 315-229-5423
Fax: 315-229-5589
Web Site: www.stlawu.edu
Management:
Associate Director Athletics: Randolph W LaBrake
Athletic Director: Margie Strait
Sports Information Director: Walter Johnson
Head Football Coach: Chris Phelps
Head Basketball Coach (M): Chris Downs
Head Basketball Coach (W): GP Bromacki
Seating Capacity: 3,500

7262
NORTON HALL

Chautauqua Institution
Chautauqua, NY 14722
Phone: 716-357-6000
Fax: 716-357-4175

7263
HAMILTON COLLEGE: MINOR THEATRE

198 College Hill Road
Clinton, NY 13323
Phone: 315-859-4421
Fax: 315-859-4457
Toll-free: 800-843-2655
e-mail: admission@hamilton.edu
Web Site: www.hamilton.edu
Officers:
President: Joan Hinde Stewart
Chairman: Stuart Scott
Vice Chairman: Chester Siuda
Executive Assistant to the Presiden: Meredith Harper Bonham
Management:
Events Coordinator: Sue Campanie
Mission: A liberal arts college with an emphasis on individualized instruction and independent research and a national leader in teaching effective writing and persuasive speaking.
Status: Non-Profit, Non-Professional

7264
KIRKLAND ART CENTER

E Park Row
PO Box 213
Clinton, NY 13323-0213
Phone: 315-853-8871
e-mail: kacinc@centralny.twcbc.com
Officers:
President Executive Director: Annette Clarke
Founded: 1961

Specialized Field: Series & Festivals; Dance; Instrumental Music; Musical Theatre; Theatrical Group; Vocal Music
Status: Non-Profit, Professional
Paid Staff: 5

7265
171 CEDAR ARTS CENTER

171 Cedar Street
Corning, NY 14830
Phone: 607-936-4647
Fax: 607-936-2081
Web Site: www.171cedararts.com
Management:
Executive Director: Susan O'Leary
Founded: 1968
Status: Non-Profit, Professional
Paid Staff: 10
Paid Artists: 50
Budget: $60,000-150,000

7266
DARIEN LAKE PERFORMING ARTS CENTER

9993 Allegheny Road
Darien Center, NY 14040
Phone: 585-599-4641
Fax: 585-599-3444
Web Site: www.darienlakeconcerts.com
Management:
GM: Peter O'Donnell
Operations: Joan Passaro
Seating Capacity: 21,000

7267
MERCY COLLEGE: LECTURE HALL

555 Broadway
Dobbs Ferry, NY 10566
Phone: 914-693-9455

7268
EARLVILLE OPERA HOUSE

6-22 East Main Street
Earlville, NY 13332
Phone: 315-691-3550
Fax: 315-691-4111
e-mail: info@earlvilleoperahouse.com
Web Site: www.earlvilleopenhouse.com
Officers:
President: Putter Cox
Management:
Executive Director: Patricia Lockwood Blais
Mission: To promote the arts in a rural region of Central New York State by offering programs of cultural, educational and historical significance.
Founded: 1970
Status: Non-Profit, Professional
Paid Staff: 1
Volunteer Staff: 2
Paid Artists: 79
Non-paid Artists: 600
Performs At: Multi-Arts Center w/Galleries, Workshops, Arts Cafe, Gift Shop
Affiliations: NYMACC, NYS Arts, NYSCa
Facility Category: Multi Arts Center
Type of Stage: Proscenium
Stage Dimensions: 20' x 20'
Seating Capacity: 300
Year Built: 1892

7269
CLEMENS CENTER

207 Clemens Center Parkway And Gray Street
PO Box 1046
Elmira, NY 14902
Phone: 607-733-5639
Fax: 607-737-1162
Toll-free: 800-724-0159
e-mail: info@clemenscenter.com
Web Site: www.clemenscenter.com
Management:
President: Jerald M Stemerman
Executive Director: Thomas Weidemann
Associate Executive Director: Julie Kriston
Director Facility: Julie Kriston
Marketing Director: Jensen Monroe
Mission: To enhance the performing arts and the entertainment experiences for the people of our region by providing superior facilities and programs.
Founded: 1977
Specialized Field: Year-Round Presenter 10; 5 Canty Region; Resident Companies And Rentals
Paid Staff: 17
Volunteer Staff: 200

7270
GIBSON THEATRE

Elmira College
1 Park Place
Elmira, NY 14901
Phone: 607-735-1814
Fax: 607-735-1757
e-mail: jseeley@elmira.edu
Web Site: www.elmira.edu
Management:
Performing Arts Director: Ms. Misheaila Neil
Mission: Performing Arts program established as a graduation requirement for freshmen and sohomores. We want to keep the arts alive through making them a necessary part of their college education. Community patrons may purchase tickets also.
Founded: 1855
Status: Educational Institution
Paid Staff: 4
Volunteer Staff: 25
Income Sources: Course Fees; Ticket Sales
Type of Stage: Proscenium
Stage Dimensions: 28'x30'x15'
Seating Capacity: 448
Year Remodeled: 1995

7271
WESTCHESTER BROADWAY THEATRE

One Broadway Plaza
Elmsford, NY 10523
Phone: 914-592-2268
Fax: 914-592-6917
Toll-free: 800-729-7469
e-mail: hgiarlo@cloud9.net
Web Site: www.broadwaytheatre.com
Management:
Owner/Executive Producer: Bob Funking
Owner/Executive Producer: Bill Stutler
Director: Carol Waaser
Founded: 1974
Status: For-Profit,Professional

7272
ARTHUR ASHE STADIUM

USTA National Tennis Center
Flushing Meadows, Corona Park
Flushing, NY 11368

Phone: 718-760-6200
Fax: 718-592-9488
Web Site: www.usta.com
Management:
    Executive Director: Lee Hamilton
    Facility Managing Director: Dan Zausner Dan
    Zausner

7273
BROOKLYN-QUEENS CONSERVATORY OF MUSIC

42-76 Main Street
Flushing, NY 11355
Phone: 718-461-8910
Fax: 718-886-2450
Web Site: www.brooklynconservatory.com
Officers:
    President: David Rivel
Management:
    Executive Director: Jennifer Newell
Founded: 1955
Specialized Field: Music
Status: Non-Profit, Professional

7274
CITI FIELD

126th Street & Roosevelt Avenue
Flushing, NY 11368
Phone: 718-507-6387
Fax: 718-507-6395
Toll-free: 800-221-1155
Web Site: www.mets.com
Management:
    President: Saul Katz
    Chairman: Fred Wilpon
    EVP: Dave Howard
    SVP/Treasurer: Harry O'Shaughnessy
    VP/Ticket Sales/Service: Bill Ianniciello
    Director Media Relations: Jay Horowitz
    VP Venue Services: Mike Landeen
    VP Facilities: Karl Smolarz
    VP Guest Services: Pat McGovern
Mission: Home stadium for New York Mets major
league baseball team.
Opened: 2009
Status: For-Profit, Professional
Seating Capacity: 41,800
Year Built: 2009
Architect: Populous
Cost: $900 million

7275
COLDEN CENTER FOR THE PERFORMING ARTS

65-30 Kissena Boulevard
Kissena Boulevard
Flushing, NY 11367-1597
Phone: 718-544-2996
Fax: 718-261-7063
Web Site: www.coldencenter.org
Management:
    Executive Director: Vivian Charlop
    Operations Manager: Michael Kelleher
    Technical Director: Tony Fitsch
    Box Office Manager: Stephanie McWoods
Utilizes: Collaborations; Dance Companies; Dancers;
Fine Artists; Multimedia; Original Music Scores; Sign
Language Translators; Singers; Special Technical
Talent; Theatre Companies
Founded: 1961
Status: Non-Profit
Paid Staff: 9
Performs At: Auditorium w/permanent acoustical shell

Facility Category: Performing Arts
Seating Capacity: 2143
Year Built: 1961
Rental Contact: Stephen Mallalieu

7276
MICHAEL C ROCKEFELLER ARTS CENTER

SUNY Fredonia
Fredonia, NY 14063
Phone: 716-673-3217
Fax: 716-673-3617
e-mail: arts.center@fredonia.edu
Web Site: www.fredonia.edu/rac
Management:
    Artistic Director: Jefferson Westwood
Founded: 1969
Specialized Field: Pop Series; Family Caladoscope
Series; Travelog Series Dance; Theatrical Group; Vocal
Music; Musial Theartre
Status: Non-Profit, Professional
Paid Staff: 6
Volunteer Staff: 100
Budget: $400,000
Income Sources: State Of New York; Ticket Sales;
Gifts
Performs At: Multi Arts Venue
Annual Attendance: 58,000
Seating Capacity: 1,145; 400; 200

7277
WADSWORTH AUDITORIUM

SUNY-Geneseo
1 College Circle
Geneseo, NY 14454
Phone: 716-245-5855
Fax: 716-245-4500
Web Site: www.geneseo.edu~sopa

7278
SMITH OPERA HOUSE

82 Seneca Street
Geneva, NY 14456
Phone: 315-789-5483
Fax: 315-789-6360
Toll-free: 866-355-LIVE
Web Site: www.thesmith.org
Management:
    Executive Director: Kevin Schoonover
    Technical Director: Bruce Purdy
Mission: A 107-year-old, fully restored, acoustically
perfect performing arts venue and movie theatre
catering to college students, senior citizens, families,
and children.
Founded: 1894
Specialized Field: Series & Festivals; Music; Theatre;
Dance; Film; Childrens Programing
Status: Non-Profit, Non-Professional
Paid Staff: 4
Paid Artists: 80

7279
GLENS FALLS CIVIC CENTER

1 Civic Center Plaza
Glens Falls, NY 12801
Phone: 518-798-0366
Fax: 518-793-7750
Web Site: www.glensfallscc.com
Management:
    Executive Director: Suzanna M Burn
Founded: 1979
Status: Non-Profit, Non-Professional
Paid Staff: 30

7280
TILLES CENTER FOR THE PERFORMING ARTS

Long Island University
720 Northern Boulevard
Greenvale, NY 11548
Phone: 516-299-2752
Fax: 516-299-2520
e-mail: george.lindsay@liu.edu
Web Site: www.tillescenter.org
Management:
    Executive Director: Elliott Sroka
    GM: George Lindsay
Seating Capacity: 2,200

7281
ANDY KERR STADIUM

Colgate University
Hamilton, NY 13346
Phone: 315-228-7611
Fax: 315-228-7008
Web Site: www.athletics.colgate.edu
Management:
    Athletic Director: Mark Murphy

7282
DANA ARTS CENTER UNIVERSITY THEATRE

Colgate University
13 Oak Drive
Hamilton, NY 13346
Phone: 315-228-1000
Fax: 315-228-7932
e-mail: admission@mail.colgate.edu
Web Site: www.colgate.edu
Management:
    President: Rebecca Chopp
Founded: 1819
Status: Non-Profit,Professional
Paid Staff: 267

7283
HOFSTRA UNIVERSITY STADIUM & ARENA

200 Hofstra University
Room 112
Hempstead, NY 11549
Phone: 516-463-6625
Fax: 516-463-6520
Web Site: www.hofstra.edu
Management:
    Associated Director: Ann Baller

7284
FAIR & EXPO CENTER

2695 E Henrietta Road
Henrietta, NY 14467
Phone: 585-334-4000
Fax: 585-334-3005
e-mail: mcfair@rochester.rr.com
Web Site: www.fairandexpocenter.org
Officers:
    President: Bruce Radley
    VP: Sharlene Reeves
    Secretary: Carolyn Gauvin
    Treasurer: Christine Miller
Management:
    Executive Director: Frances Tepper
    Events Director: Michael Wettach
    Marketing/Development Director: Tom Gamble

Mission: To build community through the affirmation, advancement and support of youth, agriculture and technology culminating in the annual celebration of the Monroe County Fair
Utilizes: Dancers; Guest Directors; Guest Musical Directors; Guest Musicians; Guest Soloists; Local Artists; Multimedia; Original Music Scores; Sign Language Translators; Singers; Soloists; Theatre Companies
Founded: 1823
Status: Non-Profit, Professional
Paid Staff: 11
Volunteer Staff: 256
Budget: $1,172,000
Income Sources: Trade Shows
Performs At: Arena
Affiliations: IAFE; OABA
Annual Attendance: 300,000
Facility Category: Arena
Type of Stage: Portable
Stage Dimensions: varied
Seating Capacity: 3200
Year Built: 1973
Year Remodeled: 2006
Rental Contact: Executive Director Fran Tepper

7285
WESLEY CHAPEL
Houghton College
Houghton, NY 14744
Phone: 585-567-9400
Fax: 716-567-9517
Toll-free: 800-777-2556
e-mail: music@houghton.edu
Web Site: www.houghton.edu
Officers:
President: Shirley A. Mullen
Management:
Executive Director: Ben King
Founded: 1960
Status: Non-Profit, Professional
Paid Staff: 300

7286
INTER-MEDIA ART CENTER
370 New York Avenue
Huntington, NY 11743
Phone: 631-549-9666
Fax: 631-549-9423
Web Site: www.imactheater.org
Management:
President: Michael Rothbard
Founded: 1973
Status: Non-Profit, Professional
Paid Staff: 25

7287
ALICE STATLER HALL
Statler School of Hotel Administration
Cornell University
Ithaca, NY 14853-6902
Phone: 607-254-2604
Fax: 607-257-6432

7288
BEN LIGHT GYM
Ithaca College
319 Egbert Hall
Ithaca, NY 14850
Phone: 607-274-3222
Fax: 607-274-1725
e-mail: boc@ithaca.edu
Web Site: www.ithaca.edu/boc
Management:

Advisor: Karen Coleman
Seating Capacity: 3,000

7289
HANGAR THEATRE
Cass Park
PO Box 205
Ithaca, NY 14851
Phone: 607-273-8588
Fax: 607-273-4516
e-mail: info@hangartheatre.org
Web Site: www.hangartheatre.org
Management:
Executive Director: Lisa Bushlow
Artistic Director: Kevin Moriarty
Director Marketing: Rhoan Morgan
Production Manager: Adam Zonder
Founded: 1975

7290
DILLINGHAM CENTER FOR THE PERFORMING ARTS
Ithaca College
201 Dillingham Center
Ithaca, NY 14850
Phone: 607-274-3345
Fax: 607-274-3672
e-mail: theatrearts@ithaca.edu
Web Site: www.ithaca.edu/theatre
Management:
Chairman/Director Theatre: Lee Byron
Founded: 1962
Specialized Field: Theatre Education
Status: Non-Profit, Professional
Paid Staff: 25
Paid Artists: 3

7291
JIM BUTTERFIELD STADIUM
201 Ceracchie Athletic Center
Ithaca College
Ithaca, NY 14850-7198
Phone: 607-274-3209
Fax: 607-274-1667
Web Site: www.ithaca.edu
Management:
President: Peggy Williams
Director of Athletics: Ken Kutler
Founded: 1892
Specialized Field: Education for College
Status: Non-Profit, Non-Professional

7292
ALUMNI HALL GYMNASIUM
Saint John's University
8000 Utopia Parkway
Jamaica, NY 11439
Phone: 718-990-6217
Management:
Director: Edward J Manetta
Sr Associate Director: Kathleen Meehan
Associate Director: Charlie Elwood
Sports Information Director: Dominic Scianna
Seating Capacity: 6,008

7293
JAMAICA CENTER FOR THE PERFORMING & VISUAL ARTS
161-04 Jamaica Avenue
Jamaica, NY 11432
Phone: 718-658-7400
Fax: 718-658-7922
Web Site: www.jcal.org

Management:
President of Board: Wingson Wong
Presenting Program Manager: McKaie Szuri
Founded: 1972
Status: Non-Profit, Professional
Paid Staff: 24

7294
ST. JOHN'S UNIVERSITY
8000 Utopia Parkway
Jamaica, NY 11439
Phone: 718-990-6250
Fax: 718-990-2075
Web Site: www.sjur.com
Management:
President: Fab Ozzi
Associate Director: Charlie Elwood
Sports Information Director: Dominic Scianna
Status: Non-Profit, Non-Professional
Paid Staff: 30
Paid Artists: 25

7295
LUCILLE BALL LITTLE THEATRE
18-24 E Second Street
Jamestown, NY 14701
Phone: 716-483-1095
Fax: 716-483-1099
e-mail: lblittletheatre@juno.com
Officers:
President: Carla Kayes
Management:
Office Manager: Autumn Eccles
Director: Helen Merrill
Mission: Produce five plays and musicals from September through May.
Utilizes: Actors
Founded: 1936
Status: Non-Profit, Non-Professional
Paid Staff: 4
Budget: $150,000
Income Sources: Ticket sales, grants
Annual Attendance: 12,000
Facility Category: Auditorium theatre house
Type of Stage: Proscenium
Stage Dimensions: 80 x 40 x 24
Seating Capacity: 400
Year Built: 1925
Year Remodeled: 1968
Cost: $230,000

7296
CARAMOOR CENTER FOR MUSIC AND THE ARTS VENETIAN THEATRE
149 Girdle Ridge Road
Katonah, NY 10536
Phone: 914-232-5035
Fax: 914-232-5521
Web Site: www.caramoor.org
Officers:
President/CEO: Erich Vollmer
Management:
Executive Director: Howard Herring
Managing Director: Paul Rosenblum
Director Development: Susan Shine
Director Operations: Melissa Montera
Box Office Manager: Sal Vaccaro
Mission: To offer a performing arts venue in Bedford and New York State.
Founded: 1945
Specialized Field: Vocal Music; Instrumental Music; Festivals
Status: Professional; Nonprofit
Performs At: Museum Music Room Venetian Theatre

Organization Type: Performing; Educational; Sponsoring

7297
ULSTER PERFORMING ARTS CENTER
601 Broadway
Kingston, NY 12401
Phone: 845-339-6088
Fax: 845-339-3814
Web Site: www.upac.org
Management:
    Facilities Director: Will Pittmant
    Technical Director: Todd Renedette
    Assistant to the Executive Director: Jodi Longto
    Executive Artisitic Director: Ron Marquette
Year Remodeled: 2001
Rental Contact: Jodi Longto

7298
LAKE GEORGE DINNER THEATRE
2223 Route 9
PO Box 266
Lake George, NY 12845
Phone: 518-668-5781
Fax: 518-668-9213
Web Site: www.lakegeorgedinnertheatre.com
Management:
    Producer: Victoria Eastwood
Founded: 1968

7299
LAKE PLACID CENTER FOR THE ARTS THEATER
17 Algonquin Drive
Lake Placid, NY 12946
Phone: 518-523-2512
Fax: 518-523-2521
e-mail: info@lakeplacidarts.org
Web Site: www.lakeplacidarts.org
Management:
    Director: Nadine Duhaime
Mission: Dedicated to presenting and fostering quality arts which inspire, enrich, educate and entertain people of all ages.
Founded: 1972
Specialized Field: Multi-Purpose Arts Center
Status: Non-Profit, Professional
Paid Staff: 8
Volunteer Staff: 50
Budget: $750,000
Income Sources: Grants; Rentals
Annual Attendance: 35,000
Facility Category: Theatre/Gallery/Studio
Type of Stage: Proscenium
Seating Capacity: 355
Year Built: 1971
Rental Contact: Nadine Danaime

7300
OLYMPIC CENTER
Olympic Regional Development Authority
2634 Main Street
Lake Placid, NY 12946
Phone: 518-523-1655
Fax: 518-523-9275
Toll-free: 800-462-6236
Web Site: www.orda.org
Management:
    President: Ted Blazer
    General Manager: Dennis R Allen
Status: Non-Profit, Professional
Paid Staff: 150
Paid Artists: 150
Seating Capacity: 11,100

7301
LANCASTER NEW YORK OPERA HOUSE
21 Central Avenue
Lancaster, NY 14086
Phone: 716-683-1776
Fax: 716-683-8220
Web Site: www.lancopera.org
Management:
    Executive Director: Thomas Kazmierczak
Founded: 1981
Status: Non-Profit, Non-Professional
Paid Staff: 10

7302
STUDIO THEATRE
141 S Wellwood Avenue
Lindenhurst, NY 11757
Phone: 631-226-1833

7303
MOHAWK VALLEY CENTER FOR THE ARTS
401 S Ann Street
Little Falls, NY 13365
Phone: 315-823-0808
e-mail: director@mohawkvalleyarts.org
Web Site: www.mohawkvalleyarts.org
Management:
    President: Michael Guidice
    Executive Director: Marjorie Balder
Founded: 1983
Status: Non-Profit, Non-Professional
Paid Staff: 1
Paid Artists: 220

7304
KENAN CENTER
433 Locust Street
Lockport, NY 14094
Phone: 716-433-2617
Fax: 716-433-6645
e-mail: info@kenancenter.org
Web Site: www.kenancenter.org
Officers:
    President: Selena Truax
Management:
    Executive Director: Susan Przybyl
Founded: 1969
Status: Non-Profit, Professional
Paid Staff: 20

7305
LAGUARDIA PERFORMING ARTS CENTER
31-10 Thomson Avenue
Room E-241
Long Island City, NY 11101
Phone: 718-482-5151
Fax: 718-482-5155
e-mail: lpac@lagcc.cuny.edu
Web Site: www.lagcc.cuny.edu/lpac
Management:
    President: Gale Mellow
    General Director: Barbara Carson
Status: Non-Profit, Professional
Paid Staff: 15
Paid Artists: 75
Budget: $60,-150,000
Performs At: Little Theatre

7306
EMELIN THEATRE FOR THE PERFORMING ARTS
Library Lane
Mamaroneck, NY 10543
Phone: 914-698-3045
Fax: 914-698-1404

7307
HARLEM STAGE
Harlem Stage At The Gatehouse
150 Convent Avenue At West 135th Street
New York, NY 10031
Phone: 212-650-6900
Fax: 212-862-4600
Web Site: www.aarondavishall.org
Management:
    General Manager: Gregory Shanck
    Front of House Manager: Edwin Matos
    Director Of Development: Robin Semple
Specialized Field: Series & Festivals; Dance; Instrumental Music; Musical Theatre; Theatrical Group; Vocal Music
Status: Non-Profit, Professional
Performs At: Marian Anderson Theater

7308
AMBASSADOR THEATRE
215 W 49th Street
New York, NY 10019
Phone: 212-944-3700

7309
AMERICAN PLACE THEATRE
266 W 37th Street
22nd Floor
New York, NY 10018
Phone: 212-594-4482
Fax: 212-594-4208
e-mail: edu@americanplacetheatre.org
Web Site: www.americanplacetheatre.org
Management:
    Executive Director: David Kener
    Artistic Director: Wynn Handman
    Managing Director: Jennifer Barnette
Status: Non-Profit, Professional
Paid Staff: 3
Annual Attendance: 90,000
Facility Category: Three Theatres; Cabaret; Black Box
Seating Capacity: 74/74/350
Year Built: 1971

7310
ANPSACHER STAGE
Public Theater
425 Lafayette Street
New York, NY 10003
Phone: 212-539-8500
Fax: 212-539-8705
e-mail: press@publictheater.org
Web Site: www.publictheater.org
Management:
    Artistic Director: Oskar Eustis
    Executive Director: Andrew D Hamingson
    General Manager: Andrea Nellis
Mission: The Public Theater is dedicated to achieving artistic excellence while developing an American thester that is accessible and relevant to all people through productions of challenging new plays, musicials and innovative stagings of the classics.
Founded: 1967
Specialized Field: Plays, Musicals, Shakespeare

Performs At: LuEsther Hall, Martinson Hall, Shiva Theater, Newman Theater
Type of Stage: Thrust
Stage Dimensions: 23' X 32'
Seating Capacity: 275

7311
APOLLO THEATRE
253 W 125th Street
New York, NY 10027
Phone: 212-531-5300
Fax: 212-749-2743

7312
ASCAP
One Lincoln Plaza
New York, NY 10023
Phone: 212-621-6000
Fax: 212-724-9064
Toll-free: 800-652-7227
e-mail: ascapfoundation@ascap.com
Web Site: www.ascap.com
Management:
President: Marilyn Bergman
Chairman and CEO: Irwin Robins

7313
BAKER FIELD
Columbia University
533 W 218th Street
New York, NY 10027
Phone: 212-942-0431
Fax: 212-854-2988
Web Site: www.columbia.edu

7314
BERNARD B JACOBS THEATRE
242 W 45th Street
New York, NY 10036
Phone: 212-239-6200
Seating Capacity: 1,068
Year Built: 1927

7315
BMI (BROADCAST MUSIC, INC.)
7 World Trade Center
250 Greenwich Street
New York, NY 10007
Phone: 212-220-3000
e-mail: classical@bmi.com
Web Site: www.bmi.com
Officers:
President/CEO: Frances W Preston
Senior VP Performing Rights: Del R Bryant
VP Corporate Relations: Robbin Ahrold
President BMI Foundation: Ralph N Jackson
Management:
Artisitic Director: Howard Levitt
Asst. VP, Classical Music: Barbara A. Petersen
VP Writer Publisher Relations: Charles Feldman
Mission: BMI is a performing rights licensing organization representing composers, songwriters and publishers with a repertory of more than 4.5 million musical works.
Founded: 1940
Specialized Field: Music
Status: Non-Profit, Professional
Paid Staff: 150

7316
BOOTH THEATRE
222 W 45th Street
New York, NY 10036
Phone: 212-239-6200

7317
BROADHURST THEATRE
235 W 44th Street
New York, NY 10035
Phone: 212-239-6200

7318
BROADWAY THEATRE
1681 Broadway
New York, NY 10019
Phone: 212-239-6200

7319
BROOKS ATKINSON THEATRE
256 W 47th Street
New York, NY 10036
Phone: 212-719-4099

7320
CARNEGIE HALL CORPORATION
881 7th Avenue
New York, NY 10019
Phone: 212-903-9600
Fax: 212-581-6539
Web Site: www.carnegiehall.org
Management:
Artistic Director: Ara Guzelimian
Mission: To continue to be one of the world's leading institutions in presenting great music and in promoting music education, music creation and music enjoyment in landmark concert hall.
Founded: 1891
Specialized Field: Arts
Status: Non-Profit, Professional
Paid Staff: 250
Volunteer Staff: 150

7321
CENTER FOR TRADITIONAL MUSIC & DANCE
32 Broadway
Suite 1314
New York, NY 10004
Phone: 212-571-1555
Fax: 212-571-9052
e-mail: traditions@ctmd.org
Web Site: www.ctmd.org
Management:
Executive Director: Peter Rushefsky
Artistic Director: Ehtel Raim
Mission: Works to preserve and present the performing arts traditions of New Yor's immigrant communities through research-based educational programming, public performance and community partnerships.
Founded: 1976
Specialized Field: World Music; Dance
Status: Non-Profit, Professional
Paid Staff: 8
Volunteer Staff: 2

7322
CIRCLE IN THE SQUARE
Broadway & 50th Street
New York, NY 10019
Phone: 212-307-0388
Fax: 212-307-0257
e-mail: admissions@circleinthesquare.org
Web Site: www.circlesquare.org
Officers:
President: Paul Libin
Management:
Executive Director: E Colin O'Leary
Artistic Director: Theodore Mann

Mission: School of training.
Founded: 1961
Status: Non-Profit, Non-Professional
Paid Staff: 25
Facility Category: Broadway Theatre

7323
CITY CENTER OF MUSIC AND DRAMA
70 Lincoln Central Plaza
4Th Floor
New York, NY 10023
Phone: 212-870-4266
Fax: 212-870-4286
Management:
Director Finance: Michael Edwards
Mission: To provide ballet, theatre and opera for the community at low cost or no charge.
Founded: 1943
Specialized Field: Dance; Vocal Music; Instrumental Music; Theatre
Status: Professional; Nonprofit
Performs At: New York State Theater
Organization Type: Performing; Touring; Educational

7324
CORT THEATRE
138 W 48th Street
New York, NY 10036
Phone: 212-239-6200
Fax: 212-239-5134

7325
DANCE THEATER WORKSHOP
219 W 19th Street
New York, NY 10011
Phone: 212-691-6500
Fax: 212-633-1974
Web Site: www.dtw.org
Management:
Executive Director: Marion Dienstag
Artistic Director: Cathy Edwards
Senior Associate Producer: David Sheingild
Founded: 1965
Specialized Field: Dance; Theater
Status: Non-Profit, Professional
Paid Staff: 30

7326
DELACORTE THEATER IN CENTRAL PARK
81st Street at Central Park W
New York, NY 10003
Phone: 212-539-8750
Fax: 212-839-8505
Web Site: www.publictheater.org
Officers:
Producer: George C Wolfe
Managing Director: Mark Litvin
Management:
Executive Director: Mara Manus
General Manager: Michael Hurst
Founded: 1954
Season: June - September
Facility Category: Amphitheatre (open air)
Type of Stage: Thrust
Seating Capacity: 1900
Year Built: 1962
Year Remodeled: 1999
Rental Contact: General Manager Michael Hurst
Comments: The Delacorte Theater is operated by the Joseph Papp Public Theater/New York Shakespeare Festival Shakespeare productions. Free tickets are distributed starting at 1 PM on days of performances.

7327

EDEN'S EXPRESSWAY

537 Broadway
New York, NY 10012
Phone: 212-226-8988

7328

ENSEMBLE STUDIO THEATRE

549 W 52nd Street
New York, NY 10019
Phone: 212-247-4982
Web Site: www.ensemblestudiotheatre.org
Management:
    Founder/Artistic Director: Curt Dempster
Founded: 1972
Specialized Field: Theatre; Marathon; one act plays;
Open Theatre; focousing on developing news plays;
Festivals
Status: Non-Profit, Professional

7329

ETHEL BARRYMORE THEATRE

243 W 47th Street
New York, NY 10036
Phone: 212-239-6200

7330

FREDERICK P ROSE HALL

33 W 60th Street
Floor 11
New York, NY 10023
Phone: 212-258-9800
Fax: 212-258-9900
e-mail: marketing@jalc.org
Web Site: www.jalc.org
Officers:
    Chairman: Lisa Schiff
    Vice Chair: Diane M Coffey
    Vice-Chair: Shahara Ahmad-Llewellyn
    Treasurer: Alan D Cohn
    Secretary: Michael D Fricklas
Management:
    Artistic Director: Wynton Marsalis
    Executive Director: Adrian Ellis
Mission: Features three distinct concert or
performance venues: Rose Theater, Allen Room seats
300-600 and Dizzy's Club Coca Cola seats 140.
Utilizes: Artists-in-Residence; Poets; Resident Artists
Founded: 2004
Status: Professional
Income Sources: Private and Corporate Donations,
Endowment Fund
Type of Stage: Proscenium
Stage Dimensions: 100x43
Seating Capacity: 1,100-1,231
Organization Type: Resident, Performing

7331

GERALD SCHOENFELD THEATRE

236 W 45th Street
New York, NY 10036
Phone: 212-239-6200
Seating Capacity: 1080
Year Built: 1917
Comments: Formerly Plymouth Theater

7332

GERSHWIN THEATRE

222 W 51st Street
New York, NY 10019
Phone: 212-586-6510
Web Site: www.gershwintheatre.com

7333

GOETHE-INSTITUT NEW YORK/GERMAN CULTURAL CENTER

72 Spring Street
11th Floor
New York, NY 10012
Phone: 212-439-8700
Fax: 212-439-8705
Toll-free: 877-463-8431
e-mail: info@newyork.goethe.org
Web Site: www.goethe.de/newyork
Officers:
    President: Klaus-Dieter Lehmann
Management:
    Director: Gabriele Becker
Founded: 1951
Status: Non-Profit, Professional
Paid Staff: 25
Budget: $10,000

7334

HAMMERSTEIN BALLROOM

Manhattan Center Studios
311 W 34th Street
New York, NY 10001
Phone: 212-279-7740
Fax: 212-564-1072
e-mail: info@mcstudios.com
Web Site: www.mcstudios.com
Management:
    Director of Sales & Marketing: Sarah-Jane
    Bennison
    Sales & Marketing Executive: Tara Cohn
Founded: 1906
Stage Dimensions: 54' x 24'
Seating Capacity: 2,200

7335

HB PLAYWRIGHTS FOUNDATION THEATRE HOUSE

124 S Bank Street
New York, NY 10014
Phone: 212-989-6540
Fax: 212-627-4288

7336

IMPERIAL THEATRE

249 W 45th Street
New York, NY 10036
Phone: 212-944-3700

7337

JEWISH MUSEUM

1109 5th Avenue at 92nd street
New York, NY 10128
Phone: 212-423-3200
Fax: 212-423-3232
Web Site: www.thejewishmuseum.org
Management:
    Media and Public Programs Director: Aviva
    Weintraub

7338

JOE'S PUB AT THE PUBLIC THEATER

425 Lafayette Street
New York, NY 10003
Phone: 212-539-8778
Fax: 212-539-8507
e-mail: info@joespub.com
Web Site: www.joespub.com
Management:
    Director: Shanta Thake
    Managing Director: Kevin Abbott

Mission: One of New York City's most celebrated and
in-demand showcase venues for live music and
performance. With its genre-blind booking and vast
diversity of interests, the stage at Joe's Pub gives voice
to a world of varied and stellar artists.
Founded: 1998
Performs At: Newman Theater, Anspacher Theater,
Martinson Hall, LuEsther Hall, Shiva Theater
Type of Stage: Thrust
Stage Dimensions: 23' X 32'
Seating Capacity: 275

7339

JOHN GOLDEN THEATRE

252 W 45th Street
New York, NY 10036
Phone: 212-944-4136

7340

JOYCE THEATER

175 Eighth Avenue
New York, NY 10011
Phone: 212-691-9740
e-mail: staff@joyce.org
Web Site: www.joyce.org
Management:
    Executive Director: Linda Shelton
    Director of Marketing: Martha Cooper
Mission: To serve and support the art of dance and
choreography, promote the richness and variety of the
art form in its fullest expression, and enhance the public
interest in, and appreciation of, dance and the allied
arts of music, design, and theater
Founded: 1982
Specialized Field: Dance
Annual Attendance: 136,000
Facility Category: Theater
Type of Stage: Proscenium
Stage Dimensions: 64x35
Seating Capacity: 472
Year Built: 1930
Year Remodeled: 1982

7341

KATHRYN BACHE MILLER THEATRE

Columbia University, 2960 Broadway
Mail Code 1801
New York, NY 10027
Phone: 212-854-1633
Fax: 212-854-7740
Management:
    Executive Director: George Steel
    Director Of Development: Bill Kramer
    Production Manager: Barbara J Wohl
Mission: To provide high quality presentations of
contemporary, classical and early music to the greater
New York City audience.
Founded: 1998
Specialized Field: Theater
Facility Category: Concert Hall
Seating Capacity: 688
Rental Contact: Gary Caruana

7342

KAYE PLAYHOUSE AT HUNTER COLLEGE

695 Park Avenue
New York, NY 10021
Phone: 212-772-5207
Fax: 212-650-3919
Web Site: www.kayplayhouse.hunter.cuny.edu
Management:
    General Manager: Nancy B Dodds
Status: Non-Profit, Non-Professional

7343

KAZUKO HIRABAYASHI DANCE THEATRE

330 Broome Street
New York, NY 10002
Phone: 212-966-6414

7344

KITCHEN

512 W 19th Street
New York, NY 10011
Phone: 212-255-5793
Fax: 212-645-4258
e-mail: info@thekitchen.org
Web Site: www.thekitchen.org
Officers:
   Chairman: Philip Glass
   President: Chris Ahearn
   VP: Melissa Schiff Soros
   Vice-Chairman: Molly Davis
   Treasurer: Greg S Feldman
   Secretary: Douglas A Hand
Management:
   Executive Director/Chief Curator: Debra Singer
   Associate Director: Kerry Scheidt
   Marketing Director: Justin Neal
Mission: A non-profit, interdisciplinary organization that provides innovative artists working in the media, literary, and performing arts with exhibition and performance opportunities to creat and present new work. Identifies, supports, and presents emerging and under-recognized artists who are making significant contributions to their perspectives fields as well as serves as a safe space for mre established artists to take unusual creative risks.
Founded: 1971
Specialized Field: Dance; Music; Performance; Literature; Film and Video; New Media Arts
Status: Non-Profit, Professional
Paid Staff: 20
Volunteer Staff: 10
Paid Artists: 40

7345

LAMB'S THEATRE

130 W 44th Street
New York, NY 10036
Phone: 212-997-1780
Fax: 212-997-1082

7346

LEHMAN CENTER FOR THE PERFORMING ARTS

250 Bedford Park Boulevard W
New York, NY 10468
Phone: 718-960-8232
Fax: 718-960-8233
e-mail: eva.bornstein@lehman.cuny.edu
Web Site: www.lehmancenter.org
Founded: 1980
Status: Non-Profit; Professional
Paid Staff: 10
Type of Stage: Proscenium
Seating Capacity: 2,310
Year Built: 1979
Rental Contact: Operations Manager Janet Sanchez

7347

LINCOLN CENTER THEATER

150 W 65th Street
New York, NY 10023

Phone: 212-362-7600
Fax: 212-873-0761
e-mail: info@lct.org
Web Site: www.lct.org
Officers:
   Chairman: J Tomlinson Hill
   President: Eric M Mindich
   Vice Chairman: Daryl Roth
   Treasurer: John W Rowe
   Secretary: Brooke Garber Neidich
Management:
   Artistic Director: Andre Bishop
   Executive Producer: Bernard Gersten
   General Manager: Adam Siegel
   Production Manager: Jeff Hamlin
   Marketing Director: Linda Mason Ross
Founded: 1985
Specialized Field: Theater
Performs At: Vivian Beaumont, Mitzi E. Newhouse
Type of Stage: Thrust
Seating Capacity: 1000, 300

7348

LONGACRE THEATRE

220 W 48th Street
New York, NY 10036
Phone: 212-239-6200

7349

LUCILLE LORTEL THEATRE

121 Christopher Street
New York, NY 10014
Phone: 212-924-2817
Fax: 212-939-0036

7350

LUESTHER HALL

Public Theater
425 Lafayette Street
New York, NY 10003
Phone: 212-539-8500
Fax: 212-539-8705
e-mail: marketing@publictheater.org
Web Site: www.publictheater.org
Management:
   Artistic Director: Oskar Eustis
   Executive Director: Andrew D Hamington
   General Manager: Andrea Nellis
Mission: The Public Theater is dedicated to achieving artistic excellence while developing an American theater that is accessible and relevant to all people through productions of challenging new plays, musicals and innovative stagings of the classics.
Founded: 1967
Specialized Field: Plays, Musicals, Shakespeare
Performs At: Newman Theater, Anspacher Theater, Martinson Hall, LuEsther Hall, Shiva Theater
Type of Stage: Loft Space
Stage Dimensions: 67' X 27'
Seating Capacity: 160

7351

LUNT-FONTANNE THEATRE

205 W 46th Street
New York, NY 10036
Phone: 212-575-9200
Mission: To promote and increase awareness and interest in the theatre and performing arts locally, nationally and globally.
Founded: 1955
Status: For-Profit, Professional

7352

LYCEUM THEATRE

149 W 45th Street
New York, NY 10036
Phone: 212-239-6200

7353

MADISON SQUARE GARDEN

4 Pennsylvania Plaza
New York, NY 10001
Phone: 212-465-6741
Fax: 212-465-6029
e-mail: feedback.msg@thegarden.com
Web Site: www.thegarden.com
Officers:
   Executive Chairman: James L Dolan
   President/CEO: Hank J Ratner
   Executive VP/CFO: Robert M Pollichino
Mission: Madison Square Garden is part of Madison Square Garden, L.P. Cablevision Systems Corporation owns a majority interest in MSG.

7354

MAJESTIC THEATRE

245 W 44th Street
New York, NY 10036
Phone: 212-239-6200

7355

MANHATTAN THEATRE CLUB

261 W 47th Street
8th Floor
New York, NY 10036
Phone: 212-399-3000
Fax: 212-399-4329
e-mail: questions@mtc-nyc.org
Web Site: www.mtc-nyc.org
Management:
   General Manager: Florie Seery
   Artistic Director: Lynne Meadow
   Executive Producer: Barry Grove
   Production Manager: Kurt Gardner
   Theatre Manager: Jim Joseph
Mission: To produce a season of innovative work with a series of productions as broad and diverse as New York itself; to encourage significant new work by creating an environment in which writers and theatre artists are supported by the finest professionals producing theatre today; to nurture new talent in playwriting, musical composition, directing, acting and design; and to reach out to young audiences with innovative programsin education
Founded: 1970

7356

MARQUIS

211 W 45th Street
New York, NY 10036
Phone: 212-382-0100

7357

MARTIN BECK THEATER

302 W 45th Street
New York, NY 10036
Phone: 212-239-6200

7358

MARTINSON THEATRE

Public Theater
425 Lafayette Street
New York, NY 10003

Phone: 212-539-8500
Fax: 212-539-8705
e-mail: press@publictheater.org
Web Site: www.publictheater.org
Management:
Artistic Director: Oskar Eustis
Executive Director: Andrew D Hamingson
General Manager: Andrew Nellis
Mission: The Public Theater is dedicated to achieving artistic excellence while developing an American theater that is accessible and relevant to all people through productions of challenging new plays, musicals and innovative stagings of the classics.
Founded: 1967
Specialized Field: Plays, Musicals, Shakespeare
Performs At: Newman Theater, Anspacher Theater, Martinson Hall, LuEsther Hall, Shiva Theater
Type of Stage: Set Black Box
Stage Dimensions: 68' X 28'
Seating Capacity: 199

7359
MARYMOUNT MANHATTAN COLLEGE
221 E 71st Street
New York, NY 10021
Phone: 212-517-0475
Fax: 212-517-0541
Toll-free: 800-627-9686
Web Site: www.marymountmmm.edu
Management:
President: Judson Shaver PhD
Founded: 1961
Status: Non-Profit, Non-Professional

7360
MERKIN CONCERT HALL AT KAUFMAN CENTER
Goodman House
129 W 67Th Street
New York, NY 10023
Phone: 212-501-3340
Fax: 212-501-3317
e-mail: info@kaufman-center.org
Web Site: www.ekcc.org
Officers:
Honorary Chair: Leonard Goodman
Honorary Chair: Elaine Kaufman
Chairman: Bethany Millard
Management:
Executive Director: Lydia Kontos
Booking Manager: Andrea Murray
Mission: To awaken and enhance appreciation of and participation in music and other arts; seeks to further this mission as an independent concert hall. Merkin Hall's programming reflects a diverse society and encompasses a breath of musical styles, periods, and traditions, with emphasis on new work, new artists, events and programs which draw on our rich Jewish cultural heritage.
Utilizes: Actors; AEA Actors; Artists-in-Residence; Collaborating Artists; Collaborations; Commissioned Composers; Commissioned Music; Composers; Dance Companies; Educators; Fine Artists; Five Seasonal Concerts; Grant Writers; Guest Accompanists; Guest Choreographers; Guest Companies; Guest Composers; Guest Designers; Guest Directors; Guest Ensembles; Guest Instructors; Guest Lecturers; Guest Musical Directors; Guest Musicians; Guest Soloists; Guild Activities; High School Drama; Instructors; Local Unknown Artists; Multimedia; Music; Organization Contracts; Original Music Scores; Resident Artists; Resident Professionals; Singers; Soloists
Founded: 1952
Specialized Field: Concert Hall

Status: Professional; Nonprofit
Paid Staff: 19
Paid Artists: 500
Budget: $720,000
Income Sources: Earned and Contributed; Foundation; Individual; Government Support
Performs At: Merkin Concert Hall
Affiliations: Chamber Music America
Annual Attendance: 60,000
Facility Category: Professional Concert Hall
Type of Stage: Fixed Proscenium
Stage Dimensions: 35'x57'x20'
Seating Capacity: 443
Year Built: 1978
Rental Contact: Booking Manager Andrea Murray
Resident Groups: Poppyseed Players

7361
MICHAEL SCHIMMEL CENTER FOR THE ARTS
3 Spruce Street, Pace University
1 Pace Plaza
New York, NY 10038
Phone: 212-346-1398
Fax: 212-346-1645
e-mail: galleries@pace.edu
Web Site: www.pace.edu/culture
Management:
Director for Cultural Affairs: David G Watson
Theater Manager: Joy Besozzi
Mission: Presents a wide range of cultural progrtams and public events for the campus and surrounding community. In addition to student productions and special events, the Center also hosts professional theatre, music and dance, as well as international companies such as the Beijing People's Art Theatre.
Founded: 1969
Specialized Field: Series & Festivals; Dance; Jazz; Theatrical Student Productions; Location for Film and TV
Status: Non-Profit, Professional
Paid Staff: 5
Seating Capacity: 743

7362
MINETTA LANE THEATRE
18 Minetta Lane
New York, NY 10012
Phone: 212-420-8000
Fax: 212-254-4963
Management:
President: Margaret Carter
Status: For-Profit, Professional
Paid Staff: 10

7363
MINSKOFF THEATRE
200 W 45th Street
New York, NY 10036
Phone: 212-869-0550
Fax: 212-944-8644
Status: Professional
Seating Capacity: 1685

7364
MUSIC BOX
239 W 45th Street
New York, NY 10036
Phone: 212-239-6200

7365
NEDERLANDER THEATRE
208 W 41st Street
New York, NY 10036

Phone: 212-921-8000
Web Site: www.siteforrent.com

7366
NEIL SIMON THEATRE
250 W 52nd Street
New York, NY 10019
Phone: 212-757-8646
Fax: 212-262-2400
Seating Capacity: 1334

7367
NEW DRAMATISTS
424 W 44th Street
New York, NY 10036
Phone: 212-757-6960
Fax: 212-265-4738
Web Site: www.newdramatists.org
Management:
Executive Director: Joe Ruark
Artistic Director: Todd London
Founded: 1949
Status: Non-Profit, Professional
Paid Staff: 8

7368
NEW YORK CITY CENTER
130 W 56th Street
New York, NY 10019
Phone: 212-581-1212
Fax: 212-541-7979
e-mail: elowery@nycitycenter.org
Web Site: www.nycitycenter.org
Officers:
Chairman: Raymond A Lamontagne
President/CEO: Arlene Shuler
Management:
Senior VP/Managing Director: Mark Litvin
Artistic Director: Jack Viertel
Music Director: Rob Berman
Director of Production: Mark Mongold
Mission: To make the finest in the performing arts accessible to the broadest possible audience, while insuring that its landmark facility remains an active and welcoming venue to both audiences and artists throughout the year.
Founded: 1943
Status: Non-Profit, Professional
Paid Staff: 32
Budget: $1,000,000+
Income Sources: Ticket Sales; Donations
Annual Attendance: 200,000
Facility Category: Theater
Type of Stage: Proscenium
Stage Dimensions: 43'x45'
Seating Capacity: 2,684
Year Built: 1923
Rental Contact: Eugene Lowery

7369
NEWMAN STAGE
Public Theater
425 Lafayette Street
New York, NY 10003
Phone: 212-539-8500
Fax: 212-539-8705
e-mail: marketing@publictheater.org
Web Site: www.publictheater.org
Management:
Artistic Director: Oskar Eustis
Executive Director: Andrew D Hamingson
General Manager: Andrea Nellis

Mission: The Public Theater is dedicated to achieving artistic excellence while developing an American theater that is accessible and relevant to all people through productions of challenging new plays, musicals and innovative stagings of the classics.
Founded: 1967
Specialized Field: Plays, Musicals, Shakespeare
Performs At: Newman Theater, Anspacher Theater, Martinson Hall, LuEsther Hall, Shiva Theater
Type of Stage: Proscenium
Stage Dimensions: 40' X 36'
Seating Capacity: 299

7370
OPEN EYE: NEW STAGINGS
270 W 89th Street
New York, NY 10024
Phone: 212-226-8435
Fax: 212-343-1065

7371
ORPHEUM THEATRE
126 2nd Avenue
New York, NY 10003
Phone: 212-477-2477
Fax: 212-871-9094
Management:
    President: Margaret Carter
Founded: 1980
Status: For-Profit, Professional

7372
PALACE THEATRE
1564 Broadway
New York, NY 10036
Phone: 212-730-8200
Fax: 212-730-7932

7373
PAN AMERICAN MUSICAL ART RESEARCH
330 E 49th Street
Suite 11-J
New York, NY 10017
Phone: 212-688-6862
Fax: 212-688-6862
e-mail: info@pamar.org
Web Site: www.pamar.org
Officers:
    Honorary President: Placido Domingo
    Chairman: Diego Recalde
    Vice Chairman: Daniel Doura
    Secretary: Aurora Belliard
    Treasurer: Roberto Krell
Management:
    Founder/Artistic Director: Polly Ferman
Mission: A non-profit organization seeking to promote a better knowledge, understanding and coexistence, between the various cultures and countries of the americas, primarily through an ongoing and vital exchange of their artistic fields including music, dance, theater, film, visual arts and literature, and through educational programs.
Founded: 1984
Status: Non-Profit

7374
PERFORMANCE SPACE 122
150 First Avenue
New York, NY 10009
Phone: 212-477-5829
Fax: 212-353-1315
e-mail: ps122@ps122.org
Web Site: www.ps122.org

Officers:
    President: Ivan Martinez
    Treasurer: Jason C Tsou
Management:
    Artistic Director: Vallejo Ganter
    Director of Production: Derek Lloyd
    Marketing/Communications Director: Carliegh Welsh
Mission: Dedicated to supporting and presenting artists whose work challenges the traditional boundaries of dance, theatre, music and performance. Committed to exploring innovative form as well as material, PS 122 is steadfast in its search for pioneering artists from a diversity of cultures and points of view.
Founded: 1979
Status: Non-Profit, Professional
Paid Staff: 16

7375
PROMENADE THEATRE
2162 Broadway
New York, NY 10023
Phone: 212-707-8270
Fax: 212-707-8775

7376
QUEBEC GOVERNMENT HOUSE
1 Rockefeller Plaza
26th Floor
New York, NY 10020
Phone: 212-843-0985
Fax: 212-376-8984
Web Site: www.quebecusa.org
Management:
    General Delegate: Michel Robicaille
Founded: 1940
Status: Non-Profit, Non-Professional
Paid Staff: 35

7377
RADIO CITY MUSIC HALL
1260 6th Avenue
New York, NY 10020
Phone: 212-307-7171
Web Site: www.radiocity.com
Mission: Since 1932, Radio City Hall has been synonymous with the very in entertainment.
Founded: 1933
Resident Groups: Radio City Rockettes

7378
RICHARD ROGERS THEATRE
226 W 46th Street
New York, NY 10036
Phone: 212-221-1211
Web Site: www.movinoutonbroadway.com
Management:
    President: James Nederlander
Founded: 1965
Status: For-Profit, Professional

7379
SAINT CLEMENT'S CHURCH
423 W 46th Street
New York, NY 10036
Phone: 212-246-7277
Fax: 212-307-1442
Web Site: www.saintclement'snyc.org
Management:
    Incharge of Theater Operations: Rob Alberson
    President: Pamela J Nelson
Founded: 1860
Status: Non-Profit, Professional
Paid Staff: 10

Paid Artists: 200

7380
SAINT JAMES THEATER
246 W 44th Street
New York, NY 10036
Phone: 212-239-6200

7381
SHIVA THEATRE
Public Theater
425 Lafayette Street
New York, NY 10003
Phone: 212-539-8500
Fax: 212-539-8705
e-mail: marketing@publictheater.org
Web Site: www.publictheater.org
Management:
    Artistic Director: Oskar Eustis
    Executive Director: Andrew D Hamingson
    General Manager: Andrea Nellis
Mission: The Public Theater is dedicated to achieving artistic excellence while developing an American theater that is accessible and relevant to all people through productions of challenging new plays, musicals and innovative stagings of the classics.
Founded: 1967
Specialized Field: Plays, Musicals, Shakespeare
Performs At: Newman Theater, Anspacher Theater, Martinson Hall, LuEsther Hall, Shiva Theater
Type of Stage: Black Box
Stage Dimensions: 58' X 40'
Seating Capacity: 99

7382
SHUBERT THEATRE
225 W 45th Street
New York, NY 10036
Phone: 212-239-6200
Seating Capacity: 1,513

7383
SOHO REP
401 Broadway
Suite 300
New York, NY 10013
Phone: 212-941-8632
Fax: 212-941-7148
e-mail: sohorep@sohorep.org
Web Site: www.sohorep.org
Officers:
    Chair: Jon Dembrow
Management:
    Artistic Director: Sarah Benson
    Executive Director: Tania Camargo
    Producer: Rob Marcato
    Production/Facilities Manager: Robbie Saenz de Viteri
Mission: Committed to nuturing innovative and umcompromising new york from first impulse through fully mounted production.
Founded: 1975
Status: Non-Profit, Professional
Season: March - August
Stage Dimensions: 25' x 35'
Seating Capacity: 99

7384
SULLIVAN STREET PLAYHOUSE
181 Sullivan Street
New York, NY 10012
Phone: 212-674-3838
Fax: 212-674-4706
Seating Capacity: 153

7385
SUPPER CLUB THEATER
240 W 47th Street
New York, NY 10036
Phone: 212-921-1940
Web Site: www.thesupperclub.com
Management:
   Operations Manager: Kevin Sharpe
   Executive Chef: Peter Garst
   Technical Director: Jeremy Schaffer
Status: For-Profit, Professional

7386
SURDNA FOUNDATION
330 Madison Avenue
30Th Floor
New York, NY 10017
Phone: 212-557-0010

7387
TISCH CENTER FOR THE ARTS
92nd Street Y
1395 Lexington Avenue
New York, NY 10128
Phone: 212-415-5739
Fax: 212-415-5738
Web Site: www.92ndsty.org
Management:
   Director: Hanna Arie-Gaifman
Budget: $400,000-1,000,000
Performs At: Theresa L. Kaufmann Concert Hall

7388
TOWN HALL CONCERT HALL
123 W 43rd Street
New York, NY 10036
Phone: 212-997-1003
Fax: 212-997-1929
e-mail: info@the-townhall-nyc.org
Web Site: www.the-townhall-nyc.org
Management:
   Executive Director: Lawrence C Zucker
   Marketing Director: E A Kafkalas
Mission: To offer affordable entertainment to all ages.
Utilizes: Dance Companies; Dancers; Educators;
Filmmakers; Guest Instructors; Guest Musical Directors;
Guest Soloists; Guild Activities; Multimedia;
Playwrights; Soloists; Theatre Companies
Founded: 1921
Status: Non-Profit, Non-Professional
Paid Staff: 20
Annual Attendance: 500,000
Facility Category: Concert Hall
Type of Stage: Proscenium
Seating Capacity: 1,500
Year Built: 1921

7389
TRIBECA PERFORMING ARTS CENTER
199 Chambers Street
Suite S110c
New York, NY 10007
Phone: 212-220-1459
e-mail: info@tribecapac.org
Web Site: www.tribecapac.org
Officers:
   President of the Board: Richard Kennedy
   VP of the Board: Grace L Anderson-Spivey
   Secretary: Dr Sadie Bragg
   Treasurer: G Scott Anderson
Management:
   Executive Director: Linda Herring
   Operations Director: Carol Cleveland

Marketing Director: Eli Abdallah
Mission: Strives to present a broad global perspective
through the presentation of high quality artistic work in
music, theatre, dance, film and visual arts. Supports
emerging and established artists who create works that
inspire creativity and imagination, celebrate diversity
and change as well as instill emotional, social and
political awareness.
Utilizes: Artists-in-Residence; Dance Companies;
Soloists; Special Technical Talent; Theatre Companies
Founded: 1983
Specialized Field: Performing Arts
Paid Staff: 14
Paid Artists: 5
Budget: $600,000
Income Sources: Earned Income; Rental Income;
Charitable Contributions
Affiliations: TCG; ART New York
Annual Attendance: 40,000
Facility Category: Multi-theatre Performing Arts
Type of Stage: Proscenium; Thrust
Seating Capacity: 913/262
Year Built: 1983
Rental Contact: Carol Cleveland

7390
UNION SQUARE THEATRE
126 2nd Avenue
New York, NY 10003
Phone: 212-505-0700
Fax: 212-477-7732

7391
UNIVERSITY SETTLEMENT
184 Eldridge Street
New York, NY 10002
Phone: 212-674-9120
Fax: 212-475-3278
e-mail: info@universitysettlement.org
Web Site: www.universitysettlement.org
Officers:
   Chairman: Alan P Winters
   Treasurer: Paul W Brandow
   Secretary: Nancy Drosd
Management:
   Executive Director: Michael H Zisser PhD
   Director of Development: Nicole P Sharpe
Mission: Serves people of all ages, from infants to
senior citizens throughout the multi-racial and
multi-ethnic community.
Founded: 1886
Status: Non-Profit, Professional

7392
VIRGINIA THEATER
245 W 52nd Street
New York, NY 10019
Phone: 212-840-8181

7393
WALTER KERR THEATRE
219 W 48th Street
New York, NY 10036

7394
WEB CONCERT HALL
2565 Broadway
Suite 316
New York, NY 10025
Phone: 212-280-8187
Fax: 212-280-8187
e-mail: webconcerthall@usa.com
Web Site: www.webconcerthall.com

Management:
   Producer/Director: Dr Yoon-Il Auh
   Music Director: Dr Mi-Jung Im
Budget: $10,000

7395
WESTBETH STUDIO THEATRE
111 W 17th Street
3rd Floor
New York, NY 10011
Phone: 212-691-2272
Fax: 212-924-7185
Web Site: www.westbeththeatre.com
Season: Year-Round
Type of Stage: Thrust and Arena
Seating Capacity: 60-300

7396
WESTBETH THEATRE CENTER
151 Bank Street
New York, NY 10014
Phone: 212-691-2272
Fax: 212-924-7185
Web Site: www.westbeththeatre.com

7397
WESTSIDE THEATRE
407 W 43rd Street
New York, NY 10036
Phone: 212-315-2302
Fax: 212-315-2307
Type of Stage: proscenium/ thrust
Stage Dimensions: 40'x 26' 6"/ 40'x 18'3"
Seating Capacity: 299/ 250
Organization Type: Theatre Complex; Performance
Center; Commercial Rental Theatre

7398
WHITNEY MUSEUM OF ART THEATER
120 Park Avenue at 42 Street
New York, NY 10017
Phone: 212-878-2475
Fax: 212-907-5770

7399
WIEN STADIUM
Columbia University, Dodge Fitness Center
3030 Broadway, Mail Code 1902
New York, NY 10027
Phone: 212-854-2538
Fax: 212-854-2988
Management:
   Athletic Director: John Reeves
Seating Capacity: 3,405

7400
WINTER GARDEN THEATRE
1634 Broadway
New York, NY 10019
Phone: 212-944-3700

7401
HERSHELL CARROUSEL FACTORY
MUSEUM
180 Thompson Street
PO Box 672
North Tonawanda, NY 14120
Phone: 716-693-1885
Fax: 716-743-9018
e-mail: info@carrouselmuseum.org
Web Site: www.carrouselmuseum.org
Founded: 1915
Status: For-Profit

7402

HELEN HAYES PERFORMING ARTS CENTER

PO Box 229
Nyack, NY 10960
Phone: 914-358-2847
Management:
Artistic Director: Rod Kaats
Managing Director: Joel Warren
Founded: 1996
Status: Nonprofit
Season: October - July
Type of Stage: Proscenium
Stage Dimensions: 60' x 28'
Seating Capacity: 600

7403

RALPH WILSON STADIUM

One Bills Drive
Orchard Park, NY 14127
Phone: 716-648-1800
Fax: 716-649-6446
Web Site: www.buffalobills.com
Management:
President: Tom Donahoe
VP Operations: William G Munson
VP Marketing: Russ Brandon
Director Stadium Operations: Joe Frandina
Founded: 1960
Status: For-Profit, Professional
Seating Capacity: 79,902

7404

PARAMOUNT CENTER FOR THE ARTS

1008 Brown Street
Peekskill, NY 10566
Phone: 914-739-2333
Fax: 914-736-9674
e-mail: info@paramountcenter.org
Web Site: www.paramountcenter.org
Management:
President: Paul Rubin
Executive Director: Jon Yanofsky
Mission: To provide quality programming in live perfromance and the visual arts. Serving the interest of the Hudson Valley and raising the level of cultural enrichment of all who enter this unique theater.
Founded: 1930
Status: Non-Profit
Seating Capacity: 1024
Year Built: 1930

7405

THEATRE THREE PRODUCTIONS SECOND STAGE

412 Main Street
PO Box 512
Port Jefferson, NY 11777
Phone: 631-928-9202
Fax: 631-928-9120
Facility Category: Theatre House
Rental Contact: Vivian Koutrakas

7406

BARDAVON 1869 OPERA HOUSE

35 Market Street
Poughkeepsie, NY 12601-9990
Phone: 845-473-5288
Fax: 845-473-4259
e-mail: slamarca@bardavon.org
Web Site: www.bardavon.org
Management:
President: Patrick Moore

Executive Director: Chris Silva
Managing Director: Ameri Foust
Managing Director Production: Stephen Lamarca
Utilizes: Actors; AEA Actors; Artists-in-Residence; Choreographers; Dance Companies; Dancers; Designers; Educators; Filmmakers; Five Seasonal Concerts; Grant Writers; Guest Accompanists; Guest Artists; Guest Choreographers; Guest Companies; Guest Composers; Guest Conductors; Guest Designers; Guest Directors; Guest Ensembles; Guest Instructors; Guest Lecturers; Guest Musical Directors; Guest Musicians; Guest Soloists; Guest Teachers; Guild Activities; Instructors; Local Artists; Lyricists; Multi Collaborations; Multimedia; New Productions; Organization Contracts; Original Music Scores; Performance Artists; Playwrights; Resident Professionals; Sign Language Translators; Singers; Soloists; Student Interns; Special Technical Talent; Theatre Companies
Founded: 1979
Status: Non-Profit, Professional
Paid Staff: 17
Volunteer Staff: 80
Paid Artists: 270
Seating Capacity: 944
Year Built: 1869

7407

MID-HUDSON CIVIC CENTER

14 Civic Center Plaza
Poughkeepsie, NY 12601
Phone: 845-454-9800
Fax: 845-454-5877
Web Site: www.midhudsonciviccenter.com
Management:
President: John S Morgan
Executive Director: Amy Sloan
Controller: Chris Sasser
Status: Non-Profit, Professional
Paid Staff: 100

7408

PURCHASE COLLEGE PERFORMING ARTS CENTER

735 Anderson Hill Road
Purchase, NY 10577-0140
Mailing Address: MPO Box 140
Phone: 914-251-6222
Fax: 914-251-6171
e-mail: brian.mccurdy@purchase.edu
Web Site: www.artscenter.org
Officers:
Executive Director: Wiley Hausam
Management:
General Manager: Harry McFadden
Director Of Operations: Dan Sedgwick

7409

BLUE CROSS ARENA

1 War Memorial Square
Rochester, NY 14614
Phone: 585-758-5330
Fax: 716-758-5327
Web Site: www.bluecrossarena.com
Management:
General Manager: Jeffrey E Calkins

7410

EASTMAN THEATRE

University of Rochester
26 Gibbs Street
Rochester, NY 14604

Phone: 585-274-1110
Fax: 585-274-1073
e-mail: concerts@esm.rochester.edu
Web Site: www.rochester.edu/eastman
Management:
Director Concert Operations: Andrew Green
Assistant Director: Julia Ng
Founded: 1921
Seating Capacity: 3,094

7411

FRONTIER FIELD

333 N Plymounth Avenue
Rochester, NY 14608
Phone: 716-262-2009
Fax: 716-232-3453
Management:
Director: Jim Lebeau
Seating Capacity: 10,500

7412

NAZARETH ARTS CENTER

Nazareth College
4245 East Avenue
Rochester, NY 14618
Phone: 716-586-2483

7413

PYRAMID ARTS CENTER

Cultural Quarter
Palmyra Square South
Rochester, NY 14603
Phone: 192-544-2345
Fax: 912-544-2888
e-mail: pyramid@warrington.gov.uk
Web Site: www.pyramidparrhall.com
Management:
Administration Manager: Richard Fleming
Event Coordinator: Vicky Turner
Drama Development Officer: Owen Hutchings
Music Development Officer: Stuart Smith

7414

STRONG THEATRE

University of Rochester-River Campus
Rochester, NY 14627
Phone: 716-275-2330
Fax: 716-273-5306

7415

CAPITOL THEATRE

220 W Dominick Street
Rome, NY 13440
Phone: 315-337-6277
Fax: 315-337-6277
Management:
President: Eileen Prnoeis
Executive Director: Art Pierce
Founded: 1928
Status: Non-Profit, Professional
Paid Staff: 4
Paid Artists: 150

7416

RYE ARTS CENTER

51 Milton Road
Rye, NY 10580
Phone: 914-967-0700
Fax: 914-967-4495
e-mail: ryearts@bestweb.net
Web Site: www.ryeartscenter.org
Management:
President: Marilyn Gasparini
Executive Director: Peggy Hill

Founded: 1960
Status: Non-Profit, Non-Professional
Paid Staff: 6

7417
SARATOGA PERFORMING ARTS CENTER
Saratoga Spa State Park
Hall of Springs
Saratoga Springs, NY 12866
Phone: 518-584-9330
Fax: 518-584-0809
Web Site: www.spac.org
Officers:
    Vice Chairman: Wallace A Graham
    Chairman: Charles E Matter
    President: Herbert A Chesbrough
    Secretary/Treasurer: Edward P. Swyer
Mission: To host performing arts events.
Utilizes: Singers
Founded: 1966
Specialized Field: Series & Festivals; Dance; Vocal Music; Instrumental Music; Theatre; Opera
Status: Non-Profit, Professional
Paid Staff: 13
Budget: $11 Million
Income Sources: International Association of Auditorium Managers; New York Performing Arts Association; Membership ticket sales
Affiliations: Summer home of New York City Ballet, Philadelphia Orchestra and Saratoga Chamber Music Festival
Annual Attendance: 350,000
Facility Category: Ampitheatre
Type of Stage: Proscenium
Stage Dimensions: 80 W x 60 D
Seating Capacity: 5100
Year Built: 1966
Organization Type: Performing; Educational; Sponsoring

7418
PROCTOR'S THEATRE
432 State Street
Schenectady, NY 12305
Phone: 518-382-3884
Fax: 518-346-2468
Web Site: www.proctors.org
Management:
    CEO: Philip Morris
    Director Annual Programs: Dan Hanifin
    Finance Director: Kathleen Cetnar
    Production Manager: Dan Sheehan
Founded: 1926

7419
SCHENECTADY CIVIC PLAYERS THEATER
12 S Church Street
Schenectady, NY 12305
Phone: 518-382-2081

7420
SHEA THEATRE
Suffolk County Community College
533 College Road
Selden, NY 11784
Phone: 631-451-4163
Fax: 631-451-4601
Web Site: www.sunysuffolk.edu
Management:
    Theatre Director: Charles Wittreich
Status: Non-Profit, Non-Professional

7421
LONG ISLAND UNIVERSITY: FINE ARTS THEATRE
Southampton Campus
Montauk Highway
Southampton, NY 11968
Phone: 516-283-4000

7422
REILLY CENTER ARENA
St Bonaventure University
PO Box BZ
St. Bonaventure, NY 14778
Phone: 716-375-2514
Fax: 716-375-3583
Web Site: www.fbu.edu
Management:
    President: Margaret Carney
    Director: Steve Pleasec
Founded: 1960
Status: Non-Profit, Professional
Seating Capacity: 6,500

7423
CENTER FOR THE ARTS RECITAL HALL
College of Staten Island
2800 Victory Boulevard
Staten Island, NY 10314
Mailing Address: Building 1P-116
Phone: 718-982-2787
Fax: 718-982-2251
Web Site: www.csi.cuny.edu/arts
Officers:
    President: Marlene Springer
Management:
    Managing/Artistic Director: Lisa Reilly
    Theatre Operations Manager: John Jankowski
    Marketing Manager: Michele Maglio
    Box Office Manager: Hallie Smith DiLiberto
Mission: An intimate room seating 150, The Recital Hall is the Center's space for chamber music, solo recitals, and lectures.
Founded: 1996
Paid Staff: 10
Budget: $850,000
Income Sources: Ticket sales; other earned revenue; grants and contributions
Affiliations: Association of Performing Arts Presenters, onsortium of Eastern Regional Theatres
Annual Attendance: 100,000
Facility Category: Performing Arts Center
Type of Stage: Theatre
Seating Capacity: 150
Year Built: 1996
Cost: $35 million
Resident Groups: Staten Island Symphony; Staten Island Ballet, NeverLand Theatre Company; Enrichment Through the Arts

7424
CENTER FOR THE ARTS LECTURE HALL
College of Staten Island
2800 Victory Boulevard
Staten Island, NY 10314
Mailing Address: Building 1P-116
Phone: 718-982-2787
Fax: 718-982-2251
Web Site: www.csi.cuny.edu/arts
Management:
    Manager/Artistic Director: Lisa Reilly
    Theatre Operations Manager: John Jankowski
    Contracts/Reservations: Rita Balsamo
    Marketing Manager: Michele Maglio
Mission: An intimate room seating 150 and equipped with the latest audio- visual equipment, The Lecture Hall is the Center's venue for academic programs, and is also a frequent site of public hearings .
Founded: 1996
Paid Staff: 10
Budget: $850,000
Income Sources: Ticket sales; other earned revenue; grants and contributions
Affiliations: Association of Performing Arts Presenters, onsortium of Eastern Regional Theatres
Annual Attendance: 100,000
Facility Category: Performing Arts Center
Type of Stage: Lecture Hall
Seating Capacity: 150
Year Built: 1996
Cost: $35 million
Resident Groups: Staten Island Symphony; Staten Island Ballet, NeverLand Theatre Company; Enrichment Through the Arts

7425
SNUG HARBOR CULTURAL CENTER
1000 Richmond Terrace
Staten Island, NY 10301-1116
Phone: 718-448-2500
Fax: 718-442-8534
Management:
    Presentations Director: Ellen Kodadek
    Presentations Associate: Elizabeth LaCause
Budget: $60,000-150,000
Performs At: Veterans Memorial Hall; Performance Meadow; Cabaret

7426
VETERANS MEMORIAL HALL
1000 Richmond Terrace
Staten Island, NY 10301
Phone: 718-448-2500
Fax: 718-442-8534

7427
SPORTS COMPLEX
Stony Brook University
Stony Brook, NY 11794-3500
Phone: 516-632-7174
Fax: 516-632-7122
Management:
    Managing Director: Kay Don
Seating Capacity: 5,000

7428
ALLIANCE BANK STADIUM
One Tex Simone Drive
Syracuse, NY 13208
Phone: 315-474-7833
Fax: 315-474-2658
e-mail: baseball@syracusechiefs.com
Web Site: www.syracusechiefs.com
Officers:
    President: Tex Simone
Management:
    Director Group Sales: Victor Gallucci
    General Manager: John Simone
Founded: 1961
Specialized Field: Professional Baseball Club
Status: For-Profit, Professional
Paid Staff: 12
Seating Capacity: 11,071

7429
CARRIER DOME
Syracuse University
900 Irving Avenue
Syracuse, NY 13244
Phone: 315-443-4634
Fax: 315-443-5203
Web Site: carrierdome.syr.edu
Management:
Managing Director: Patrick M Campbell
Seating Capacity: 50,000 Football, 32,000 Basketball
Year Built: 1980

7430
CIVIC CENTER OF ONONDAGA COUNTY CROUSE-HIND HALL
411 Montgomery Street
Syracuse, NY 13202
Phone: 315-435-2121
Fax: 315-435-8099

7431
CIVIC CENTER OF ONONDAGA COUNTY CARRIER THEATRE
411 Montgomery Street
Syracuse, NY 13202
Phone: 315-435-2121
Fax: 315-435-8099

7432
GOLDSTEIN AUDITORIUM
Syracuse University
303 University Place
Syracuse, NY 13244
Phone: 315-443-2044
Fax: 315-443-5458
Web Site: www.syracuse.edu/ets/goldstein/html
Management:
Talent Buyer: Alison Weinflash
Seating Capacity: 1,500

7433
MULROY CIVIC CENTER
800 S State Street
Syracuse, NY 13202
Phone: 315-435-8000
Fax: 315-435-8099
e-mail: C_Tucciarone@oncenter.org
Web Site: www.oncentercomplex.com
Officers:
President/CEO: Jerry Gallagher
Management:
Director Of Sales/Marketing: Christine Tucciarone
Account Executive: Mike Spaulding
Founded: 1976
Specialized Field: Onondage County / Central New York
Status: Non-Profit, Professional
Paid Staff: 100
Volunteer Staff: 300
Paid Artists: 200
Non-paid Artists: 250

7434
SYRACUSE AREA LANDMARK THEATRE
362 S Salina Street
Syracuse, NY 13202
Phone: 315-475-7979
Fax: 315-473-7993
e-mail: denise@landmarktheatre.org
Web Site: www.landmarktheatre.org
Management:
President: Denise Fresina

Status: Non-Profit, Professional
Paid Staff: 12

7435
KNICKERBACKER RECREATIONAL FACILITY AND ICE ARENA
191 103rd Street
Troy, NY 12180
Phone: 518-235-7761
Fax: 518-235-0219
Web Site: www.troynet.net
Officers:
President: Bruce Arnold
VP: Steven Angle
Management:
Facility Manager: Irma A Magee
Mission: To provide the public with recreation and special events in a healthy atmosphere.
Founded: 1990
Specialized Field: Figure Skating; Speed Skaters; Hockey
Status: Non-Profit, Professional
Paid Staff: 10
Income Sources: City of Troy
Season: Year Round
Affiliations: City of Troy
Facility Category: Ice arena, baseball field, softball fields
Rental Contact: Facility Manager Irma Magee
Organization Type: Ice arena, baseball and softball fields, tennis courts, pool, basketball courts, 400 meter oval, out-door rink, street hockey suface, sand volleyball courts, children's playground
Resident Groups: Predominantly Figure Skaters

7436
RENSSELAER POLYTECHNIC INSTITUTE: HOUSTON FIELD HOUSE
1900 Peoples Avenue
Troy, NY 12180
Phone: 518-276-6262
Fax: 518-276-2833
Management:
President: Sherly Jackson
Manager: Norris A Pearson
Box Office Manager: Dorothy Conroy
Department Specialist: Kim M Forette
Status: Non-Profit, Professional
Seating Capacity: 6,900

7437
RENSSELAER NEWMAN FOUNDATION CHAPEL AND CULTURAL CENTER
2125 Burden Avenue
Troy, NY 12180
Phone: 518-274-7793
Fax: 518-274-5945
Management:
President: Eric Smith
Founded: 1968
Status: Non-Profit, Professional
Paid Staff: 5

7438
TROY SAVINGS BANK MUSIC HALL
7 State Street
Troy, NY 12180-3920
Phone: 518-273-0038
Fax: 518-273-1564
e-mail: info@troymusichall.org
Web Site: www.troymusichall.org
Management:
Executive Director: Laura Kratt

Founded: 1875
Status: Non-Profit, Professional
Paid Staff: 6

7439
NASSAU VETERANS MEMORIAL COLISEUM
1255 Hempstead Turnpike
Uniondale, NY 11553
Phone: 516-794-9303
Fax: 516-794-9389
Web Site: www.nassaucoliseum.com
Management:
General Manager: Scott Mullen
Founded: 1972
Seating Capacity: 16,285

7440
STANLEY PERFORMING ARTS CENTER
259 Genesee Street
Utica, NY 13501
Phone: 315-724-5919
Fax: 315-724-3854
Web Site: www.cnyarts.com
Management:
Owner: Ronald Puerte
Manager: John Fausaut
Founded: 1928
Status: Non-Profit, Non-Professional

7441
UTICA MEMORIAL AUDITORIUM
400 Oriskany Street W
Utica, NY 13502
Phone: 315-738-0164
Fax: 315-738-9597
e-mail: uticaaud@aol.com
Management:
Executive Director: Will Berkeiser
Director Operations: Frank Labella
Arena Administrator: Betsy Woish
Utilizes: Dance Companies; Multimedia; Original Music Scores; Sign Language Translators; Soloists
Founded: 1996
Status: Non-Profit,Non-Professional
Paid Staff: 90
Facility Category: Arena
Type of Stage: Wenger
Stage Dimensions: 56x44
Year Built: 1959
Rental Contact: Will Berkheiser/Gen.Mgr.

7442
EUGENE O'NEILL THEATER CENTER
305 Great Neck Road
Waterford, NY 6385
Phone: 860-443-5378
Fax: 860-443-9653
e-mail: info@theoneill.org
Web Site: www.theoneill.org
Management:
Executive Director: Amy Sullivan
Artistic Director: Richard Kuranda
Founded: 1964
Status: Non-Profit,Professional

7443
JEFFERSON COMMUNITY COLLEGE MCVEAN STUDENT CENTER
Jefferson Community College
Watertown, NY 13601

Phone: 315-786-2289
Fax: 315-788-0716
Web Site: www.sunyjefferson.edu
Management:
    President: Joseph Olson
    Asst Director Student Development: Mary Kinne
Status: Non-Profit, Non-Professional
Paid Staff: 1

7444
LUMIERE BALLET

64 East Nancy Street
West Babylon, NY 11704
Phone: 631-643-6549
Web Site: www.lumiereballet.net
Management:
    Founder/Artistic Director: Svetlana Caton-Noble
    Co-Founder/Artistic Director: Ventzislav Petrov
Mission: To foster excellence in present and future generations of talented young people and promote the appreciation for classical music and dance. The organization has initiated a fully graded training program and a performing youth ballet company which has become important and respected in the dance community.

7445
US MILITARY ACADEMY MICHIE STADIUM

Odia Building 639
West Point, NY 10996
Phone: 914-938-3002
Fax: 914-938-2210
Web Site: www.usma.com
Management:
    Director: Ben Russell
Seating Capacity: 41,000

7446
KLEINERT/JAMES ARTS CENTER

34 Tinker Street
Woodstock, NY 12498
Phone: 845-679-2079
Fax: 845-679-4529
e-mail: info@woodstockguild.org
Web Site: www.woodstockguild.org
Management:
    President: Henry T Ford
    Executive Director: Matthew Leaycraft
Mission: The Woodstock Byrdcliffe Guild (WBG) provides the opportunity for people to discover and develop their creative and artistic spirit. We are dedicated to the preservation of the Byrdcliffe Arts Colony as an arts haven, natural enviorment, and historic site. Our goal is to present and foster the creative arts for the enjoyment and education of the people of Woodstock, the region, and beyond.
Founded: 1939
Status: Non-Profit, Professional
Paid Staff: 4
Budget: $25,000
Income Sources: Concerts; Rentals
Annual Attendance: 1,500
Facility Category: Indoor
Seating Capacity: 135
Year Built: 1957
Year Remodeled: 1994
Rental Contact: Carla Smith

7447
MAVERICK CONCERT HALL

PO Box 102
Woodstock, NY 12498
Phone: 845-679-8217

7448
HUDSON RIVER MUSEUM

511 Warburton Avenue
Yonkers, NY 10701-1899
Phone: 914-963-4550
Fax: 914-963-8558
Web Site: www.hrm.org
Management:
    Managing Director: Dan Gillespe
    President: Michael Botwinick
Founded: 1919
Status: Non-Profit, Professional
Paid Staff: 40
Volunteer Staff: 100
Paid Artists: 200
Season: Seasonal

North Carolina

7449
STANLY COUNTY AGRI-CIVIC CENTER

26032-B Newt Road
Albemarle, NC 28001
Phone: 704-986-3666
Fax: 704-986-3817
Web Site: www.stanlyciviccenter.com
Management:
    Director: Edmund Roush
    Secretary: Lee Thompson
Utilizes: Actors; Dance Companies; Dancers; Educators; Grant Writers; Guest Soloists; Guest Writers; Guild Activities; Instructors; Local Artists; Multimedia; Sign Language Translators; Soloists; Special Technical Talent; Theatre Companies
Founded: 1988
Specialized Field: Music; Theater; Dance; Meetings
Status: Non-Profit, Non-Professional
Paid Staff: 3
Performs At: Performing Arts Theatre
Facility Category: Performing Arts Theatre
Type of Stage: Pine
Stage Dimensions: 53 x 38
Seating Capacity: 1200
Year Built: 1988
Rental Contact: Tim Harris

7450
ASHEVILLE CIVIC CENTER

87 Haywood Street
Asheville, NC 28801
Phone: 828-259-5544
Fax: 828-259-5777
Web Site: www.ashvilleciviccenter.com
Management:
    Director: David Pisha
Status: For-Profit, Professional

7451
HAYES AUDITORIUM

Lees McRae College
Main Street
Banner Elk, NC 28604
Phone: 828-898-5241
Fax: 704-898-8814
e-mail: joslinp@lmc.edu
Web Site: www.lmc.edu
Officers:
    President: Dr Barry M Buxton
    VP Advancement: Caroline Hart
Management:
    Artistic Director: Dr Janet Barton Speer
    Assistant to Summer Theatre: Pam Wilder Joslin

    Executive Director, Summer Theatre: Dr Kacy Crabtree
Founded: 1884
Status: Non-Profit, Non-Professional
Paid Staff: 13
Paid Artists: 15
Seating Capacity: 700

7452
FARTHING AUDITORIUM

Appalachian State University
Rivers Street
Boone, NC 28608
Phone: 704-262-6372
Fax: 704-262-2848

7453
KIDD BREWER STADIUM

Appalachian State University
Department of Athletics
Boone, NC 28608
Phone: 828-262-4010
Fax: 828-651-2556
Management:
    Director: Rachel Laney
Seating Capacity: 18,000

7454
THE HOLMES CENTER

Appalachian State University
111 Rivers Street
Boone, NC 28608
Mailing Address: ASU Box 32141
Phone: 828-262-7890
Fax: 828-262-7894
e-mail: parkerjc@appstate.edu
Web Site: www.theholmescenter.com
Management:
    Director: Eddie Crawford
    Assistant Director: Jason Parker
Founded: 1968
Seating Capacity: 8,325

7455
PORTER CENTER FOR PERFORMING ARTS

Brevard College
1 Brevard College Drive
Brevard, NC 28712
Phone: 828-884-8330
Fax: 828-883-4185
Web Site: www.brevard.edu/portercenter
Management:
    Managing Director: Steve MacQueen
Budget: $20,000-35,000
Performs At: The Concert Hall; Porter Center for Performing Arts

7456
STRAUS AUDITORIUM

Brevard Music Center
Probart Street
Brevard, NC 28712
Mailing Address: PO Box 592
Phone: 704-884-2011
Fax: 704-884-2036

7457
WHITTINGTON-PFOHL AUDITORIUM

Brevard Music Center
1000 Probart Street
Brevard, NC 28712

Mailing Address: PO Box 312
Phone: 828-862-2100
Fax: 828-884-2036
Toll-free: 888-384-8682
e-mail: bmc@brevardmusic.org
Web Site: www.brevardmusic.org
Management:
President: John Candler
Artistic Director: David Effron
Founded: 1936
Status: Non-Profit
Paid Staff: 100

7458
J. CLYDE TURNER AUDITORIUM
Campbell University
414 Judge Taylor Road
Buies Creek, NC 27506
Mailing Address: PO Box 95
Phone: 910-893-1554
Fax: 910-893-1534
Web Site: www.campbell.edu
Management:
Director Student Activities: Tracie Renfrow
Seating Capacity: 1,066

7459
CAMP THEATER
Building 19
Camp Lejeune, NC 28542
Phone: 919-451-1759
Fax: 919-451-1879

7460
TOWN OF CARY CULTURAL ARTS DIVISION
PO Box 8005
Cary, NC 27512-8005
Phone: 919-469-4061
Fax: 919-469-4344
Web Site: www.townofcary.org
Management:
Artistic Director: Deb Royals
Cultural Arts Supervisor: Lyman Collins
Mission: Present high quality cultural arts events musical and theatrical in the Town of Cary.
Founded: 1994
Specialized Field: Music; Classical; Jazz; Pop
Status: For-Profit, Non-Professional
Paid Staff: 6

7461
DEANE E SMITH CENTER
University of North Carolina-Chapel Hill
Chapel Hill, NC 27515
Phone: 919-962-7777
Fax: 919-966-3173
Web Site: www.smithcenter.unc.edu
Management:
Managing Director: Angelyn S Bitting

7462
KENAN STADIUM
University of North Carolina-Chapel Hill
Chapel Hill, NC 27515-2126
Mailing Address: PO Box 2126
Phone: 919-966-2575
Fax: 919-962-0393
Web Site: www.tarheelblue.com
Management:
Athletic Director Game Operations: William Scroggs
Associate Athletic Director: Bob Savod
Ticket Manager: Darren Lucas

Specialized Field: Home of University of North Carolina football (NCAA)
Seating Capacity: 60,000
Year Built: 1927
Year Remodeled: 1997

7463
AFRO-AMERICAN CULTURAL CENTER
401 N Myers Street
Charlotte, NC 28202-2910
Phone: 704-374-1565
Fax: 704-374-9273
Web Site: www.aacc-charlotte.org
Officers:
President: Michael Vaughn
VP: Angeline Clinton
Second VP: Dee Merrill
Treasurer: Chris Carter
Management:
Executive Director: Beverley Cureton
Director Operations: Lisa Rowland
Direct External Affairs: Sherry Walter
Director Development: Alecia Bracy
Mission: To preserve, promote and present African-American art, history and culture.
Founded: 1976
Specialized Field: Multi-disciplinary
Status: Non-Profit, Professional
Paid Staff: 7
Paid Artists: 200
Budget: $35,000-60,000

7464
BANK OF AMERICA STADIUM
800 S Mint Street
Charlotte, NC 28202
Phone: 704-358-7407
Fax: 704-358-7619
e-mail: pauls@panthers.nfl.com
Web Site: www.panthers.com
Management:
President: Mark Richardson
Executive Director: Jackie Jeffries
Director Tickets: Phil Youtsey
Founded: 1995
Specialized Field: Home of the Carolina Panthers (NFL)
Status: For-Profit, Professional
Paid Staff: 200
Seating Capacity: 73,250
Year Built: 1996

7465
BELK THEATER
PO Box 37322
Charlotte, NC 28237
Phone: 704-333-4686
Fax: 704-376-2289
Web Site: www.blumenthalcenter.org
Management:
President: Tom Jabbart
Status: Non-Profit, Professional

7466
CHARLOTTE COLISEUM
100 Paul Buck Boulevard
Charlotte, NC 28217
Phone: 704-357-4701
Fax: 704-357-4757
Web Site: www.charlottecoliseum.com
Management:
Managing Director: Michael E Crum
Director Marketing: Ereka Crawford

Mission: Home of the Charlotte Hornets and the Charlotte Sting. Also hosts family shows, motorsports and concert events.
Founded: 1959
Status: Professional
Seating Capacity: 23,698

7467
CRICKET ARENA
2700 E Independent Boulevard
Charlotte, NC 28205
Phone: 704-372-3600
Fax: 704-335-3118
Web Site: www.cricketarenacharlotte.com
Management:
Managing Director: Michael E Crum
Director Marketing: Eric Scott
Director Marketing: Ereka Cranford
Founded: 1955
Status: For-Profit, Non-Professional
Paid Staff: 25

7468
GRADY COLE CENTER
310 North Kings Drive
Charlotte, NC 28204
Phone: 704-336-8979
Fax: 704-336-3876
Web Site: www.parkandrec.com
Management:
Facility Manager: Greg Clemmer
Customer Service: Shirley Floyd
Seating Capacity: 3,000

7469
HALTON ARENA
UNC Charlotte
9201 University City Boulevard
Charlotte, NC 28223
Phone: 704-687-4805
Fax: 704-687-4803
e-mail: ndsimmon@uncc.edu
Web Site: www.haltonarena.com
Management:
Event Director: Nina Simmons
Seating Capacity: 10,000

7470
NORTH CAROLINA BLUMENTHAL PERFORMING ARTS CENTER
PO Box 37322
Charlotte, NC 28237
Phone: 704-379-1279
Fax: 704-444-2111
Web Site: www.performingartsctr.org
Officers:
President: Judith Allen
Management:
President: Tom Gabbard

7471
OVENS AUDITORIUM
2700 E Independence Boulevard
Charlotte, NC 28205
Phone: 704-372-3600
Fax: 704-372-3620

7472
SPIRIT SQUARE CENTER FOR THE ARTS
345 N College Street
Charlotte, NC 28202
Phone: 704-333-4686
Fax: 704-377-9808

7473
SUMMER THEATRE
Central Piedmont Community College
Box 55009
Charlotte, NC 28235-5009
Phone: 704-330-2722
Web Site: www.cpcc.edu
Management:
    President: Tony Ziess
Status: For-Profit, Professional

7474
VERIZON WIRELESS AMPHITHEATRE
707 Pavilion Boulevard
Charlotte, NC 28262
Phone: 704-549-1292
Fax: 704-549-1043
Web Site: www.blockconcerts.com
Management:
    Executive Director: Della Rowser
    Director Sponsorships: Shiela Fletcher
Seating Capacity: 18,500

7475
RAMSEY REGIONAL ACTIVITY CENTER
Western Carolina University
Cullowhee, NC 28723
Phone: 828-227-7677
Fax: 828-227-7680
Toll-free: 866-928-3378
Web Site: www.ramsey.wcu.edu
Management:
    Director: Bill Clarke
    Operations Manager: Jim Irvin
    Ticket Office Manager: Laura Sellers
Founded: 1986
Status: Non-Profit, Professional
Paid Staff: 10
Budget: $35,000-60,000
Annual Attendance: 100,000
Facility Category: Multipurpose
Seating Capacity: 8000
Year Built: 1986

7476
ST. JOSEPH'S HISTORIC FOUNDATION/HAYTI HERITAGE CENTER
804 Old Fayetteville Street
Durham, NC 27701
Mailing Address: PO Box 543, Durham, NC. 27702
Phone: 919-683-1709
Fax: 919-682-5869
e-mail: hayti@hayti.org
Web Site: www.hayti.org
Officers:
    President/CEO: Dianne Pledger
    Programs Director: Darrell Stover
Utilizes: Actors; Artists-in-Residence; Choreographers; Collaborating Artists; Collaborations; Dance Companies; Dancers; Educators; Filmmakers; Fine Artists; Guest Instructors; Guest Musical Directors; Guest Musicians; Guest Teachers; Instructors; Local Artists; Lyricists; Multi Collaborations; Multimedia; Original Music Scores; Performance Artists; Playwrights; Sign Language Translators; Soloists; Special Technical Talent; Theatre Companies; Touring Companies
Founded: 1975
Status: Non-Profit, Professional
Paid Staff: 10
Budget: 1.2 Million
Seating Capacity: 450

7477
COA COMMUNITY AUDITORIUM
College of the Albemarle
1208 North Road Street
Elizabeth City, NC 27909
Phone: 252-335-9050
Fax: 252-337-6622
Web Site: www.albemarle.edu
Management:
    GM: Sam Johnson
    Superintendent: Sandra Boyce
Seating Capacity: 1,000

7478
CUMBERLAND COUNTY COLISEUM COMPLEX
1960 Coliseum Drive
PO Drawer 64549
Fayetteville, NC 28306
Phone: 910-323-5088
Fax: 919-323-0489
Web Site: www.crowncoliseum.com
Management:
    President: Rick Reno
    Executive Director: Max Peers
Founded: 1997
Status: For-Profit, Non-Professional
Paid Staff: 20
Seating Capacity: 13,500
Year Built: 1997

7479
AYCOCK AUDITORIUM
University of North Carolina at Greensboro
Greensboro, NC 27412
Phone: 919-334-5800
Fax: 919-334-3008

7480
CAROLINA THEATRE
310 S Greene Street
Greensboro, NC 27401
Phone: 336-333-2600
Fax: 336-333-2604
e-mail: comments@carolinatheatre.com
Web Site: www.carolinatheatre.com
Officers:
    President/CEO: Keith Holliday
Management:
    Executive Director: Brian Gray
    Marketing Director: Meagan Kopp
Founded: 1927
Annual Attendance: 83,000+
Seating Capacity: 1075
Year Built: 1927

7481
GREENSBORO COLISEUM: WAR MEMORIAL AUDITORIUM
1921 W Lee Street
PO Box 5447
Greensboro, NC 27403
Phone: 336-373-7400
Fax: 336-373-2170
Web Site: www.greensborocoliseum.com
Management:
    Deputy Director: Scott Johnson
    Booking Assistant: Robin Crews
    Production Manager: Scott Polkinhorn
Founded: 1959
Income Sources: City
Performs At: Multi-Purpose
Seating Capacity: 23,500

Year Built: 1959
Year Remodeled: 1994

7482
HENDRIX THEATRE
Mendenhall Student Center
Greenville, NC 27858
Phone: 919-757-4702
Fax: 919-757-4778

7483
WRIGHT AUDITORIUM
E Carolina University
Campus Circle
Greenville, NC 27858
Phone: 919-757-6269
Fax: 919-757-4778

7484
LENOIR - RHYNE COLLEGE FACILITIES
7th Avenue and 8th NE
Hickory, NC 28601
Phone: 828-328-7254
Fax: 828-328-7329
Web Site: www.lrc.edu
Management:
    Director: Caroline Cauthen
    Athletic Facilities Coordinator: Joe Fisher
Seating Capacity: 3,000

7485
HIGH POINT THEATRE AND EXHIBITION CENTER
220 E Commerce Street
High Point, NC 27260
Phone: 336-883-3401
Fax: 336-883-3533
Web Site: www.ci.high-point.nc.us
Management:
    Executive Director: Louisa Hart
Utilizes: Actors; Collaborations; Dance Companies; Guest Instructors; Instructors; Local Artists; Original Music Scores; Special Technical Talent; Theatre Companies
Annual Attendance: 60,000+
Facility Category: Theatre and Exhibition Center
Seating Capacity: 967
Year Built: 1975
Rental Contact: Louisa Hart

7486
HIGHLANDS PLAYHOUSE
PO Box 896
Highlands, NC 28741
Phone: 828-526-9443
Web Site: www.highlandsplayhouse.org
Management:
    President: Dwight E Bryant
Founded: 1939
Status: Non-Profit, Professional
Paid Staff: 10
Paid Artists: 30
Season: June - August

7487
GRAINER STADIUM
400 E Grainer Avenue
Kinston, NC 28501
Phone: 252-527-9111
Fax: 919-527-2328
Web Site: www.kinstinindians.com
Management:
    Director/Manager: North Johnson

7488
JE BROYHILL CIVIC CENTER
Caldwell Community College
1913 Hickory Boulevard Southeast
Lenoir, NC 28645
Mailing Address: PO Box 600
Phone: 828-726-2401
Fax: 828-726-2405
e-mail: dbriggs@caldwell.cc.nc.us
Web Site: www.broyhillcenter.com
Management:
    Director: David Briggs
    Program Assistant: Cheryl Bolt
    Technical Director: Jeff Bentley
Utilizes: Collaborations; Dance Companies; Dancers;
Educators; Guild Activities; Instructors; Lyricists;
Multimedia; New Productions; Original Music Scores;
Selected Students; Singers; Theatre Companies
Founded: 1993
Paid Staff: 7
Budget: $350,000
Income Sources: Tickets, local and state support,
sponsors and advertising.
Annual Attendance: 80,000
Facility Category: Performing Arts/ Meeting Center
Type of Stage: Procenium
Stage Dimensions: 42W X 45D X 22H
Seating Capacity: 999
Year Built: 1993
Cost: 6.1 million
Rental Contact: Jean Rondeau

7489
LINCOLN CULTURAL CENTER
403 E Main Street
Lincolnton, NC 28092
Phone: 704-732-9055
Fax: 704-732-9057
Management:
    Executive Director: Valarie King
    Artistic Director: Andrea Tripvoi
Status: Non-Profit, Non-Professional
Paid Staff: 4

7490
MOORE AUDITORIUM
Mars Hill College
Marshall Highway
Mars Hill, NC 28754
Phone: 704-689-1260
Fax: 704-689-1474

7491
CITY OF MORGANTON MUNICIPAL AUDITORIUM
401 S College Street
PO Box 3448
Morganton, NC 28680
Phone: 828-438-5294
Fax: 828-438-5246
Toll-free: 800-939-7469
Web Site: www.ci.morganton.nc.us
Management:
    Director: John W Wilson III
Founded: 1986
Status: For-Profit, Professional
Paid Staff: 5

7492
MOUNT AIRY FINE ARTS CENTER
ANDY GRIFFITH PLAYHOUSE
218 Rockford Street
Mount Airy, NC 27030

Phone: 336-786-7998
Fax: 919-986-9822

7493
MCDOWELL COLUMNS AUDITORIUM
Chowan College
Jones Drive
Murfreesboro, NC 27855
Phone: 919-398-4101
Fax: 919-398-1190

7494
GIVENS PERFORMING ARTS CENTER
University of North Carolina-Pembroke
1 University Drive
Pembroke, NC 28372
Mailing Address: PO Box 1510
Phone: 910-521-6287
Fax: 910-521-6552
e-mail: gpac@uncp.edu
Web Site: www.uncp.edu/gpac
Management:
    Director: Patricia Fields
    Booking Manager: David Thaggard
Seating Capacity: 1,636

7495
A.J. FLETCHER OPERA THEATER
Progress Energy Ctr for the Performing Arts
2 East South Street
Raleigh, NC 27601
Phone: 919-831-6011
Fax: 919-831-6661
e-mail: holly.jacques@raleighconvention.com
Web Site: www.progressenergycenter.com
Management:
    Booking Coordinator: Holly Jacques

7496
CARTER FINLEY STADIUM
North Carolina State University-Raleigh
103 Dunn Avenue
Raleigh, NC 27695
Phone: 919-515-3050
Fax: 919-515-1161
Web Site: www.athletics.ncsu.edu

7497
JS DORTIN ARENA
1025 Blue Ridge Boulevard
Raleigh, NC 27607
Phone: 919-733-2626
Fax: 919-733-5079
Web Site: www.arg.state.nc.us/fair
Management:
    Manager: Wesley Rowley

7498
KENNEDY THEATRE
Progress Energy Ctr for the Performing Arts
2 East South Street
Raleigh, NC 27601
Phone: 919-831-6011
Fax: 919-831-6661
e-mail: holly.jacques@raleighconvention.com
Web Site: www.progressenergycenter.com
Management:
    Booking Coordinator: Holly Jacques

7499
MEMORIAL AUDITORIUM
Progress Energy Ctr for the Performing Arts
2 East South Street
Raleigh, NC 27601

Phone: 919-831-6011
Fax: 919-831-6661
e-mail: holly.jacques@raleighconvention.com
Web Site: www.progressenergycenter.com
Management:
    Booking Coordinator: Holly Jacques

7500
MEYMANDI CONCERT HALL
Progress Energy Ctr for the Performing Arts
2 East South Street
Raleigh, NC 27601
Phone: 919-831-6011
Fax: 919-831-6661
e-mail: holly.jacques@raleighconvention.com
Web Site: www.progressenergycenter.com
Management:
    Booking Coordinator: Holly Jacques

7501
NORTH CAROLINA STATE UNIVERSITY CENTER STAGE
Campus Box 7306
Raleigh, NC 27695-7306
Mailing Address: 4630 Mail Service Center, Raleigh,
NC. 27699-4630
Phone: 919-513-3030
Fax: 919-515-1390
e-mail: centerstage@ncsu.edu
Web Site: www.ncsu.edu/arts
Management:
    Interim Director: Dennis Kekas
Utilizes: Actors; Artists-in-Residence; Choreographers;
Collaborations; Commissioned Composers;
Composers-in-Residence; Curators; Dance Companies;
Dancers; Designers; Educators; Filmmakers; Fine
Artists; Five Seasonal Concerts; Grant Writers; Guest
Accompanists; Guest Artists; Guest Choreographers;
Guest Companies; Guest Composers; Guest
Conductors; Guest Designers; Guest Directors; Guest
Ensembles; Guest Instructors; Guest Musical Directors;
Guest Musicians; Guest Soloists; High School Drama;
Instructors; Local Artists; Lyricists; Multi Collaborations;
Multimedia; Original Music Scores; Playwrights; Poets;
Selected Students; Sign Language Translators;
Singers; Soloists; Student Interns; Theatre Companies;
Touring Companies
Specialized Field: Multi-Disciplinary
Volunteer Staff: 50
Budget: $275,000
Income Sources: Ticket; Sponsorships
Performs At: Outdoor Theatre
Affiliations: NC Museum of Art
Annual Attendance: 40,000+
Facility Category: Outdoor Theatre/cinema
Type of Stage: Open Air/Concert
Seating Capacity: 3,000
Year Built: 1997
Cost: 3,000,000

7502
RALEIGH CIVIC CENTER COMPLEX
500 Fayetteville Street Mall
Raleigh, NC 27601
Phone: 919-831-6011
Fax: 919-831-6013
Web Site: www.raleighconvention.com
Management:
    Executive Director: Roger Krupa
    Marketing/Promotions Director: James G Lavery
Founded: 1977
Status: Non-Profit, Non-Professional
Paid Staff: 35
Seating Capacity: 3,800

7503
RALEIGH LITTLE THEATRE
301 Pogue Street
PO Box 5637
Raleigh, NC 27607
Phone: 919-821-4579
Fax: 919-821-7961
e-mail: info@raleighlittletheatre.org
Web Site: www.raleighlittletheatre.com
Officers:
President, Board Of Directors: Scott Sutton
Management:
Managing Director: Ellen Landau
Artistic Director: Haskell Fitz-Simons
Mission: The purpose is to enrich, educate and entertain our community by providing a superior theatrical experience. The professionally directed, non-profit community theatre produces a variety of productions each season with 11 fully-staged shows, ranging from Broadway and Off-Broadway style musicals and non-musicals to family programs.
Founded: 1936
Specialized Field: Performing Arts - Theatre
Paid Staff: 15
Volunteer Staff: 600
Paid Artists: 40
Non-paid Artists: 160
Budget: $850,000
Income Sources: Ticket Sales; Corporate & Individual Contributions
Performs At: Two Indoor Theatres; Outdoor Amphitheatre
Annual Attendance: 36,000
Facility Category: Live Theatre
Type of Stage: Proscenium; Blackbox; Amphitheatre
Year Built: 1940
Year Remodeled: 1989
Rental Contact: Office Manager Wayne Olsen

7504
RBC CENTER
1400 Edwards Mill Road
Raleigh, NC 27607
Phone: 919-467-7825
Fax: 919-462-7030
Toll-free: 888-645-8494
Web Site: www.caneshockey.com
Management:
President: Peter Karmanos
General Manager: Jim Rutherford
Founded: 1999
Status: For-Profit, Professional
Paid Staff: 100
Seating Capacity: 19,000

7505
REYNOLDS COLISEUM
North Carolina State University-Raleigh
103 Dunn Avenue
Raleigh, NC 27695
Phone: 919-515-3050
Fax: 919-515-1161
Web Site: www.ecsu.edu
Management:
Athletic Director: Les Robinson
Seating Capacity: 11,400

7506
THEATRE IN THE PARK
107 Pullen Road
Raleigh, NC 27607
Phone: 919-831-6936
Fax: 919-831-9475
Web Site: www.theatreinthepark.com
Founded: 1947
Status: Non-Profit, Professional
Paid Staff: 4

7507
DUNN CENTER FOR THE PERFORMING ARTS
Wesleyan College
3400 North Wesleyan Boulevard
Rocky Mount, NC 27804
Phone: 252-985-5248
Fax: 252-985-5249
e-mail: dunnevents@ncwc.edu
Web Site: www.dunncenter.com
Management:
Executive Director: Don Briscar
Seating Capacity: 1,180

7508
CATAWBA COLLEGE COMMUNITY CENTER THEATRE
2300 W Inves Street
Salisbury, NC 28144
Phone: 704-637-4200
Fax: 704-637-4211
Toll-free: 800-228-2922
Web Site: www.catawba.edu
Management:
President: Robert Knott
Artistic Director: Woody Hood
Managing Director: Christopher Zinc
Utilizes: Actors; Dance Companies; Educators; Fine Artists; Grant Writers; Guest Instructors; Guest Soloists; Guild Activities; High School Drama; Multimedia; New Productions; Original Music Scores; Resident Professionals; Selected Students; Soloists; Special Technical Talent
Founded: 1851
Status: Non-Profit, Non-Professional
Paid Staff: 5
Annual Attendance: 20,000+
Facility Category: Theatre
Type of Stage: Proscenium
Stage Dimensions: 48'x35'
Seating Capacity: 1,451
Year Built: 1963
Year Remodeled: 1998
Rental Contact: Clark Current

7509
TEMPLE THEATRE COMPANY
120 Carthage Street
PO Box 1391
Sanford, NC 27331-1391
Phone: 919-774-4512
Fax: 919-774-7531
Toll-free: 800-752-2765
Web Site: www.transoftinc.com/temple
Management:
President: Jerry Sitt
Managing Director: Sheila Bruer
Founded: 1982
Status: Non-Profit, Professional
Paid Staff: 6
Paid Artists: 50

7510
ISOTHERMAL COMMUNITY COLLEGE PERFORMING ARTS CENTER
286 ICC Loop Road
PO Box 804
Spindale, NC 28160
Phone: 828-286-3636
Fax: 828-287-8090
e-mail: pacc@isothermal.edu
Web Site: www.isothermal.edu
Management:
President: Willard Lewis
Director: Russell J Wicker
Founded: 1999
Status: Non-Profit, Non-Professional
Paid Staff: 5

7511
TRYON FINE ARTS CENTER
208 Melrose Avenue
Tryon, NC 28782
Phone: 828-859-8322

7512
JOHN A WALKER COMMUNITY CENTER
PO Box 120
Wilkesboro, NC 28697-0120
Phone: 336-838-6133
Fax: 336-838-6277
Web Site: www.walkercenteronline.org
Officers:
President: Arnold Lakey
Mission: To provide an entertainment facility, and banquet & meeting facility.
Founded: 1985
Specialized Field: Dance; Vocal Music; Instrumental Music; Theater; Festivals
Status: Non-Profit, Non-Professional
Budget: $150,000-400,000
Income Sources: Association of Performing Arts Presenters; North Carolina Arts Council
Organization Type: Performing; Touring; Resident; Educational; Sponsoring

7513
LEGION STADIUM
PO Box 1810
Wilmington, NC 28402
Phone: 910-341-7855
Fax: 910-341-7854
Web Site: www.ci.wilmington.nc.us
Management:
Manager Director: Gary Shell
Status: Non-Profit, Professional
Seating Capacity: 6,500

7514
THALIAN HALL CENTER FOR THE PERFORMING ARTS
310 Chestnut Street
Wilmington, NC 28401
Phone: 910-632-2241
Fax: 910-343-3662
Toll-free: 800-523-2820
e-mail: trivenbark@thalianhall.org
Web Site: www.thalianhall.org
Officers:
President: Ronna Zimmer
Management:
Executive Director: Tony Rivenbark
Founded: 1858
Status: Non-Profit, Non-Professional
Paid Staff: 17

Annual Attendance: 75,000
Facility Category: Historic Theatre
Type of Stage: Proscenium
Stage Dimensions: 32' x 32'
Seating Capacity: 546
Year Built: 1858
Year Remodeled: 2010

7515
BOWMAN GRAY STADIUM

Winston-Salem Entertainment-Sports Complex
2825 University Parkway
Winston-Salem, NC 27105
Phone: 336-725-5635
Fax: 336-727-2922
e-mail: info@wscvb.com
Web Site: www.ljvm.com
Management:
    Coliseum Director: Benjamin Dame
    Assistant Dir Booking/Marketing: Gerry Duncan
Seating Capacity: 15,290

7516
CE GAINES COMPLEX

Winston Salem State University
601 Martin Luther King Drive
Winston-Salem, NC 27110
Mailing Address: Campus Box 19529
Phone: 336-750-2000
Fax: 336-750-2144
Web Site: www.wssu.edu
Management:
    Chancellor: Harolt Martin
Status: Non-Profit, Non-Professional

7517
DIXIE CLASSIC FAIRGROUNDS

Winston-Salem Entertainment-Sports Complex
2825 University Parkway
Winston-Salem, NC 27105
Phone: 336-725-5635
Fax: 336-727-2922
e-mail: info@wscvb.com
Web Site: www.ljvm.com
Management:
    Coliseum Director: Benjamin Dame
    Assistant Dir Booking/Marketing: Gerry Duncan
Seating Capacity: 15,290

7518
ERNIE SHORE FIELD

Winston-Salem Entertainment-Sports Complex
2825 University Parkway
Winston-Salem, NC 27105
Phone: 336-725-5635
Fax: 336-727-2922
e-mail: info@wscvb.com
Web Site: www.ljvm.com
Management:
    Coliseum Director: Benjamin Dame
    Assistant Dir Booking/Marketing: Gerry Duncan
Seating Capacity: 15,290

7519
GROVES STADIUM

Wake Forest University
499 Deacon Boulevard
Winston-Salem, NC 27105
Phone: 336-759-5000
Fax: 336-759-6090
Management:
    Athletic Director: Ron Wellman

7520
K.R. WILLIAMS AUDITORIUM

Winston-Salem State University
601 Martin Luther King Jr Drive
Winston-Salem, NC 27110
Mailing Address: PO Box 19402
Phone: 336-750-3350
Fax: 336-750-3355
Management:
    Thompson Center Director: Willie A Cumbo
Budget: $20,000-35,000

7521
LAWRENCE JOEL VETERANS MEMORIAL COLISEUM

Winston-Salem Entertainment-Sports Complex
2825 University Parkway
Winston-Salem, NC 27105
Phone: 336-725-5635
Fax: 336-727-2922
e-mail: info@wscvb.com
Web Site: www.ljvm.com
Management:
    Coliseum Director: Benjamin Dame
    Assistant Dir Booking/Marketing: Gerry Duncan
Seating Capacity: 15,290

7522
NORTH CAROLINA SCHOOL OF THE ARTS - ROGER

1533 South Main Street
Winston-Salem, NC 27127-2188
Phone: 336-770-3399
Fax: 336-722-7240
Web Site: www.ncarts.edu/stevens_center
Annual Attendance: 175,000
Facility Category: Theatre
Seating Capacity: 1,380
Year Built: 1979
Year Remodeled: 1983
Rental Contact: Scott Spencer

7523
REYNOLDS MEMORIAL AUDITORIUM

301 N Hawthorne Road
Winston-Salem, NC 27104
Phone: 336-727-2061
Fax: 336-727-2053

7524
CASWELL COUNTY CIVIC CENTER

Intersection of Highway 158 & Highway 62
PO Box 609
Yanceyville, NC 27379
Phone: 910-694-4591
Fax: 910-694-5675

North Dakota

7525
BISMARK CIVIC CENTER

601 E Sweet Avenue
PO Box 1075
Bismarck, ND 58504-5660
Phone: 701-222-6487
Fax: 701-222-6599
e-mail: bccdp@btinet.net
Web Site: www.bismarckciviccenter.com
Management:
    President: Richard L Petersen
    Sales/Marketing Director: Ross Horner
    General Manager: Dick Petersen

Events Coordinator: Darla Pelton
Operations Manager: Ron Staiger
Founded: 1969
Status: Non-Profit, Professional
Paid Staff: 20

7526
FARGODOME

1800 N University Drive
Fargo, ND 58102
Phone: 701-241-9100
Fax: 701-237-0987
Web Site: www.fargodome.com
Management:
    President: Keith Bjerke
    VP: Marilyn Guy
Founded: 1992
Status: Non-Profit

7527
FESTIVAL CONCERT HALL

University of North Dakota
1241 North University Drive
Fargo, ND 58105
Phone: 701-231-8011
Fax: 701-237-8043

7528
ALERUS CENTER

1200 42nd Street South
Grand Forks, ND 58201
Phone: 701-792-1200
Fax: 701-746-6511
Web Site: www.aleruscenter.com
Management:
    Executive Director: Charles Jeske
    Marketing Director: Kellie Snaith
Seating Capacity: 22,000

7529
CHESTER FRITZ AUDITORIUM

University of North Dakota
Grand Forks, ND 58202-9028
Mailing Address: 3475 University Avenue Stop 9028
Phone: 701-777-3076
Fax: 701-777-4710
Web Site: www.cfa.und.edu
Management:
    Director: Betty Allan
    Box Office Manager/Asst Director: Tom Swanglier
Founded: 1972
Status: Non-Profit, Professional
Paid Staff: 6

7530
HYSLOP SPORTS CENTER

University Sports Center
Grand Forks, ND 58202
Mailing Address: PO Box 9013
Phone: 701-777-2234
Fax: 701-777-4352
Web Site: www.fightingsioux.com
Management:
    Director: Roger Thomas

7531
JAMESTOWN CIVIC CENTER

212 3rd Avenue NE
PO Box 389
Jamestown, ND 58402
Phone: 701-252-8088
Fax: 701-252-8089
e-mail: jmstnd@jamestownnd.com
Web Site: www.jamestownnd.com

Management:
President: Lori Anderson
Marketing/Sales Manager: Fred Walker
Founded: 1973
Status: Non-Profit, Professional
Paid Staff: 5
Seating Capacity: 5,500
Year Built: 1973

7532
BURNING HILLS AMPHITHEATRE
3422 Chateau Road
Medora, ND 58645
Phone: 701-223-4800
Fax: 701-623-4494
e-mail: medora@medora.com
Web Site: www.medora.com
Management:
PR/Marketing Director: Wade Weston
Seating Capacity: 2,854

7533
ALL SEASONS ARENA
2005 Burdick Expressway
Minot, ND 58701
Phone: 701-857-7620
Fax: 701-857-7622
e-mail: ndsf@minot.com
Web Site: www.ndstatefair.com
Management:
Manager: Renae Korslien
Marketing Director: Shannon Pearson
Seating Capacity: 6,200

Ohio

7534
AKRON CIVIC THEATRE
182 S Main Street
Akron, OH 44308
Phone: 330-535-3179
Fax: 330-535-9828
e-mail: hparr@akroncivic.com
Web Site: www.akroncivic.com
Officers:
President: Ralph Palmisano
VP: Mark Watkins
Management:
Executive Director: Howard Parr
Assistant Director/Finance Admin: Brian Cummings
Status: Non-Profit

7535
EJ THOMAS PERFORMING ARTS HALL
University of Akron
198 Hill Street
Akron, OH 44325-0501
Phone: 330-972-7570
Fax: 330-972-2700
Web Site: www.ejthomashall.com
Management:
Executive Director: Dan Dahl
Managing Director: Cynthia Hollis
Marketing Manager: Nancy Logan Barton
Founded: 1973
Opened: 1973
Status: Non-Profit, Non-Professional
Paid Staff: 15

7536
DAIRY BARN CULTURAL ARTS CENTER
8000 Dairy Lane
Athens, OH 45701
Phone: 740-592-4981
Fax: 740-592-5090
e-mail: artsinfo@dairybarn.org
Web Site: www.dairybarn.org
Officers:
President: David Reiser
Management:
Executive Director: Andrea Lewis
Utilizes: Artists-in-Residence; Curators; Educators; Fine Artists; Guest Accompanists; Guest Conductors; Guest Soloists; Instructors; Local Artists; Multimedia; Original Music Scores; Playwrights; Soloists; Touring Companies
Founded: 1977
Specialized Field: Arts; Crafts; Cultural
Status: Non-Profit
Paid Staff: 6
Paid Artists: 24
Budget: $320,000
Income Sources: Grants, membership, private donations
Annual Attendance: 15,000
Facility Category: Cultural Arts Center
Type of Stage: wood/rented
Seating Capacity: 200
Year Built: 1914
Year Remodeled: 2000
Rental Contact: Mark Rice

7537
OHIO UNIVERSITY: SCHOOL OF MUSIC CENTER
440 Robert Glidden Hall
Athens, OH 45701
Phone: 740-593-4244
Fax: 740-593-1429
e-mail: reilly@ohio.edu
Web Site: www.ohiou.edu
Officers:
Graduate Chair: Richard Wetzel
Management:
Director: W Michael Parkinson
Founded: 1917
Status: Non-Profit, Non-Professional
Paid Staff: 42

7538
CALICO THEATRE
UC Clermont College
4200 Clermont College Drive
Batavia, OH 45103
Phone: 513-732-5200
Web Site: www.ucclermont.com
Officers:
President: Michael Carroll
VP: William Mulvill
Secretary/Treasurer: William Henrich
Utilizes: Collaborations; Dance Companies; Educators; Fine Artists; Guest Writers; Guild Activities; Instructors; Lyricists; Soloists; Special Technical Talent; Touring Companies
Opened: 1972
Specialized Field: Musical; Theatre; Dance
Status: Non-Profit
Paid Staff: 1
Income Sources: Grants; Ticket Sales
Facility Category: Auditorium
Type of Stage: procenium
Stage Dimensions: 20x30

Seating Capacity: 400
Rental Contact: Katie Turning

7539
HUNTINGTON PLAYHOUSE
28601 Lake Road
Bay Village, OH 44140
Phone: 440-871-8333
Fax: 216-221-9495
e-mail: huntingtonplayhouse@huntingtonplayhouse.com
Web Site: www.huntingtonplayhouse.com
Management:
Managing Director: Tom Meyrose
Founded: 1971
Status: Non-Profit

7540
MANDEL JEWISH COMMUNITY CENTER OF CLEVELAND
Mayfield JCC
26001 S Woodland Road
Beachwood, OH 44122
Phone: 216-831-0700
Fax: 216-831-7796
e-mail: info@clevejcc.org
Web Site: www.clevejcc.org
Management:
Executive Director: Michael Hyman
Mission: To provide opportunities through the arts for persons of all ages to explore and strengthen Jewish identity, arts expertise, and human-relation skills.
Utilizes: Actors; AEA Actors; Choreographers; Collaborations; Dancers; Designers; Educators; Fine Artists; Grant Writers; Guest Artists; Guest Companies; Guest Conductors; Guest Designers; Guest Directors; Guest Instructors; Guest Lecturers; Guest Musical Directors; Guest Soloists; Instructors; Local Artists; Lyricists; Music; Original Music Scores; Performance Artists; Playwrights; Resident Professionals; Selected Students; Sign Language Translators; Soloists; Student Interns; Touring Companies; Visual Arts
Founded: 1889
Status: Professional, Non Professional, Nonprofit
Income Sources: Jewish Community Center; Ohio Arts Council
Annual Attendance: 10,000
Facility Category: Theatre; Community Theatre
Type of Stage: Proscenium
Stage Dimensions: 29x35
Seating Capacity: 270
Year Built: 1960
Organization Type: Performing; Resident; Educational

7541
KULAS MUSICAL ARTS
Baldwin Wallace College
96 Front Street
Berea, OH 44017
Phone: 440-826-2369
e-mail: thecon@bw.edu
Web Site: www.bw.edu/con
Management:
Director: Peter Landgren
Mission: To educate and train undergraduate musicians.
Utilizes: Commissioned Composers; Commissioned Music; Composers-in-Residence; Educators; Grant Writers; Guest Accompanists; Guest Companies; Guest Composers; Guest Designers; Guest Directors; Guest Ensembles; Guest Instructors; Guest Musicians; High School Drama; Instructors; Local Artists; Multimedia; Original Music Scores; Sign Language Translators; Singers

Founded: 1845
Specialized Field: Music
Paid Staff: 4
Performs At: Recital Hall
Affiliations: United Methodist Church
Facility Category: Conservatory of Music
Type of Stage: Concert
Stage Dimensions: 35x41
Seating Capacity: 650
Year Built: 1913
Year Remodeled: 1988
Rental Contact: Ellen Hansen-Ellis

7542
ANDERSON ARENA
Bowling Green State University
14 College Park
Bowling Green, OH 43403
Phone: 419-372-6792
e-mail: online@bgsu.edu
Web Site: www.bgsu.edu
Officers:
    VP/CFO: Sherideen S Stoll
Management:
    Athletic Director: Gregory Christopher
Opened: 1910

7543
DOYT L PERRY FIELD
Sebo Atheletic Center
1610 Stadium Drive
Bowling Green, OH 43403
Phone: 419-372-2401
Fax: 419-372-6015
Web Site: www.bgsufalcons.com
Officers:
    Interim Unviversity President: Carol Cartwright
Management:
    Student Affairs/Asst Vice President: Gregory Christopher

7544
CANTON MEMORIAL CIVIC CENTER
1101 Market Avenue N
Canton, OH 44702
Phone: 330-489-3090
Fax: 330-471-8840
Web Site: www.cantonciviccenter.com
Management:
    Manager: Geoff M Thompkins
Status: For-Profit, Professional
Seating Capacity: 4500

7545
CINCINNATI MUSIC HALL
1241 Elm Street
Cincinnati, OH 45202
Phone: 513-744-3344
Fax: 513-744-3345
e-mail: ssantangelo@cincinnatiarts.org
Web Site: www.cincinnatiarts.org
Officers:
    President: Steve Lofton
    VP: Tina Carroll
Management:
    Development Director: Joan Wasserman
    Development Manager: Sabrina Sutton
Founded: 1992
Status: Non-Profit, Professional
Performs At: Concert Hall
Annual Attendance: 270,000
Stage Dimensions: 48x112
Seating Capacity: 3,500
Year Built: 1875

Rental Contact: 513-744-3242 Terri Kidney
Organization Type: Performing; Touring; Resident; Educational

7546
CINTAS CENTER
Xavier University
1624 Herald Avenue
Cincinnati, OH 45207
Phone: 513-745-3394
e-mail: jonesp@xu.edu
Web Site: cintascenter.com
Management:
    Director: Dr Phillip Jones
Facility Category: Arena
Seating Capacity: 10,250
Year Built: 2000
Cost: $50 MM
Rental Contact: Phillip Jones

7547
CORBETT AUDITORIUM
University of Cincinnati
Corbett Center for the Performing Arts
Cincinnati, OH 45221-0003
Phone: 513-556-6638
Web Site: www.ccm.uc.edu
Founded: 1867

7548
PAUL BROWN STADIUM
Two Paul Brown Way
Cincinnati, OH 45202
Phone: 513-455-4800
Fax: 513-455-4801
Web Site: www.paulbrownstadium.com
Management:
    Managing Director: Eric J Brown
Founded: 2000
Status: For-Profit, Professional
Seating Capacity: 65,600

7549
RIVERBEND MUSIC CENTER
6295 Kellogg Avenue
Cincinnati, OH 45230
Phone: 513-232-5882
Fax: 513-232-7577

7550
ROBERT J WERNER RECITAL HALL
University of Cincinnati
PO Box 210003
Cincinnati, OH 45221-0003
Phone: 513-556-6638
Web Site: www.ccm.uc.edu

7551
US BANK ARENA
100 Broadway
Cincinnati, OH 45202
Phone: 513-421-4111
Fax: 513-333-3040
e-mail: info@usbankarena.com
Web Site: www.usbankarena.com
Officers:
    Prseident: Kristen Ropp
Management:
    General Manager: Kristen Ropp
Founded: 1975
Status: Non-Profit, Professional
Performs At: Arena
Seating Capacity: 17,566
Year Built: 1975

Year Remodeled: 1997

7552
CLEVELAND BROWNS STADIUM
76 Lou Groza Boulevard
Cleveland, OH 44114
Phone: 440-891-5000
Fax: 440-891-5009
Web Site: www.clevelandbrowns.com
Officers:
    Pres: Michael Keeman
    Vp: Lew Merletti
Management:
    Staff Writer: Zac Jackson
Founded: 1999
Specialized Field: Home of the Cleveland Browns
Status: For-Profit, Professional
Paid Staff: 135
Seating Capacity: 62m799
Year Built: 1999

7553
CLEVELAND MUSEUM OF ART: GARTNER AUDITORIUM
11150 E Boulevard
Cleveland, OH 44106
Phone: 216-421-7340
Fax: 216-707-6867
Toll-free: 888-CMA-0033
e-mail: info@clevelandart.org
Web Site: www.clevelandart.org
Officers:
    President: Alfred M Rankin
    VP: Sarah S Cutler
    Secretery: Stephen J Knerly Jr
    Treasurer: Janet Ashe
Management:
    Director: Timothy Rub
Founded: 1916
Status: Non-Profit, Professional
Paid Staff: 500

7554
CLEVELAND PLAY HOUSE
8500 Euclid Avenue
Cleveland, OH 44106
Phone: 216-795-7000
Fax: 216-795-7005
e-mail: mbloom@clevelandplayhouse.com
Web Site: www.clevelandplayhouse.com
Officers:
    Chair: Peter Kuhn
    Vp: Robert Blattner
    Treasurer: Robert Blattner
    Secretery: Raymond Malone
Management:
    Director: Jsssie O'Neill Arose
    Director: Laura Baxter- Heuer
    National Director: Alan Alda
Founded: 1915
Specialized Field: theatrical
Status: Non-Profit,Professional
Paid Staff: 175

7555
CLEVELAND PLAY HOUSE BOLTON THEATRE
8500 Euclid Avenue
Cleveland, OH 44106
Phone: 216-795-7000
Fax: 216-795-7005
e-mail: mbloom@clevelandplayhouse.com
Web Site: www.clevelandplayhouse.com

Officers:
  Chair: Peter Kuhn
  VP/Treasure: Robert Blatten
  Secretary: Raymond Malone
Management:
  Artistic Director: Michael Bloom
  Company Manager: Betty Brooks
Founded: 1915

7556
CLEVELAND PLAY HOUSE BROOKS THEATRE

8500 Euclid Avenue
Cleveland, OH 44106
Phone: 216-795-7000
Fax: 216-795-7005
e-mail: mbloom@clevelandplayhouse.com
Web Site: www.clevelandplayhouse.com
Officers:
  Chair: Peter A Kuhn
  VP/Treasure: Robert A Blattner
  Secretary: Raymond Malone
Management:
  Artistic Director: Michael Bloom
Founded: 1915

7557
CLEVELAND PLAY HOUSE DRURY THEATRE

8500 Euclid Avenue
Cleveland, OH 44106
Phone: 216-795-7000
Fax: 216-795-7005
e-mail: MBLOOM@CLEVELANDPLAYHOUSE.COM
Web Site: WWW.CLEVELANDPLAYHOUSE.COM
Officers:
  Chair: Peter A Kuhn
  VP/Treasure: Robert A Blattner
  Secretary: Raymond Malone
Management:
  Artistic Director: Michael Bloom
  Company Manager: Betty Brooks
Founded: 1915

7558
CLEVELAND PUBLIC THEATRE

6415 Detroit Avenue
Cleveland, OH 44102
Phone: 216-631-2727
Fax: 216-631-2575
Web Site: www.cptonline.org
Officers:
  President: Carrie Carpenter
  VP: Collette Appolito
  Treasure: Davida S Howard
  Secretary: Patricia Leebove
Management:
  Executive Artistic Director: Raymond Bobgan
Founded: 1981
Status: Non-Profit, Professional

7559
CLEVELAND STATE UNIVERSITY: CONVOCATION CENTER

2121 Euclid Avenue
Cleveland, OH 44115-2214
Phone: 216-687-2000
Web Site: www.csuohio.edu
Officers:
  President: Michael Schwartz
Founded: 1991
Status: Non-Profit, Non-Professional

7560
ELDRED HALL

Case Western Reserve University
Department of Theater
10900 Euclid Avenue
Cleveland, OH 44106-7077
Phone: 216-368-4868
Fax: 216-368-5184
Toll-free: 800-421-3681
e-mail: ksg@po.cwru.edu
Web Site: www.case.edu/artsci/thtr
Officers:
  Chair, Dept of Theater/Dance: Ron Wilson
Utilizes: Choreographers; Dancers; Designers;
Educators; Grant Writers; Guest Accompanists; Guest
Artists; Guest Conductors; Guest Designers; Guest
Ensembles; Guest Musical Directors; Guest Soloists;
Guest Speakers; High School Drama; Instructors;
Resident Professionals; Soloists; Student Interns;
Visual Arts
Opened: 1826
Status: Nonprofit
Performs At: College Theater
Type of Stage: Proscenium
Seating Capacity: 152
Year Built: 1898
Year Remodeled: 1997

7561
GUND ARENA

1 Center Court
Cleveland, OH 44115-4001
Phone: 216-420-2000
Fax: 216-420-2260
Web Site: www.gundarena.com
Management:
  Executive VP/General Manager: Roy Jones
  Senior VP Sales/Marketing: Jim Kahler
Mission: Home of the Cleveland Cavaliers and the
Cleveland Lumberjacks.
Seating Capacity: 20,600
Year Built: 1994

7562
JACOBS FIELD

Cleveland Indians
2401 Ontario Street
Cleveland, OH 44115-4003
Phone: 216-420-4200
Fax: 216-420-4430
Web Site: www.indian.com
Management:
  President: Larry Dolan
  Director Ballpark Operations: Jim Folk
  Senior Director Corporate Marketing: Jon Starrett
  Concession General Manager: Charlie
  Henningsen
Mission: Home of the Cleveland Indians. Offers
ballpark signage and branded products opportunities.
Founded: 1901
Seating Capacity: 43,368
Year Built: 1994

7563
KARAMU HOUSE PERFORMING ARTS THEATRE: PROSCE HALL

2355 E 89th Street
Cleveland, OH 44106
Phone: 216-795-7070
Fax: 216-795-7073
Web Site: www.karamu.com
Officers:
  Chair: Vickie Eaton Johnson

Treasurer: Michael Beedless
Secretary: Anelia Smith
Founded: 1915

7564
KARAMU HOUSE PERFORMING ARTS THEATRE: AMPHITHEATRE

2355 E 89th Street
Cleveland, OH 44106
Phone: 216-795-7070
Fax: 216-795-7073
Web Site: www.karamu.com
Officers:
  Chair: Vickie Eaton-Johnson
  Treasurer: Michael Beedles
  Secretary: Anelia Smith
Founded: 1915

7565
KARAMU HOUSE PERFORMING ARTS THEATRE: ARENA

2355 E 89th Street
Cleveland, OH 44106
Phone: 216-795-7070
Fax: 216-795-7073
Web Site: www.karamu.com
Officers:
  Chair: Vickie Eaton-Johnson
  Treasurer: Michael Beedles
  Secretary: Anelia Smith
Founded: 1915

7566
PLAYHOUSE SQUARE CENTER: OHIO THEATRE

1501 Euclid Avenue
Suite 200
Cleveland, OH 44115
Phone: 216-771-4444
Fax: 216-771-0217
Web Site: www.playhousesquare.com
Officers:
  President: Art Falco
  Secretary/Treasurer: Thomas Stevens
Founded: 1921
Status: Non-Profit, Non-Professional

7567
PLAYHOUSE SQUARE CENTER: PALACE THEATRE

1501 Euclid Avenue
Suite 200
Cleveland, OH 44115
Phone: 216-771-4444
Fax: 216-771-0217
e-mail: reeds@playhousesquare.com
Web Site: www.playhousesquare.com
Officers:
  President: Art Falco
  Secretary/Treasurer: Thomas Stevens
Founded: 1921

7568
PLAYHOUSE SQUARE CENTER: STATE THEATRE

1501 Euclid Avenue
Suite 200
Cleveland, OH 44115
Phone: 216-771-4444
Fax: 216-771-0217
e-mail: reeds@playhousesquare.com
Web Site: www.playhousesquare.com
Officers:

President: Art Falco
Secretary/Treasurer: Thomas Stevens
Founded: 1921

7569
SEVERANCE HALL
Cleveland Orchestra
11001 Euclid
Cleveland, OH 44106-1796
Phone: 216-231-1111
Fax: 216-231-4038
Toll-free: 800-686-1141
e-mail: webpatrons@clevelandorchestra.com
Web Site: www.clevelandorch.com
Management:
Executive Director: Gary Hanson
Operations: Charles Laszlo
Development: Christina Walker

7570
CAIN PARK THEATRE
Cleveland Heights City Hall
40 Severance Circle
Cleveland Heights, OH 44118
Phone: 216-291-5796
Fax: 216-291-3705
e-mail: cainpark@clvhts.com
Web Site: www.cainpark.com
Utilizes: Actors; AEA Actors; Choreographers;
Curators; Dance Companies; Dancers; Designers;
Educators; Fine Artists; Grant Writers; Guest Artists;
Guest Companies; Guest Lecturers; Local Artists;
Multimedia; Music; Original Music Scores; Resident
Professionals; Selected Students; Sign Language
Translators; Touring Companies
Founded: 1938
Status: For-Profit, Professional
Budget: $630,000
Income Sources: Ticket sales; Grants; City of
Cleveland Heights
Performs At: Evans Amphitheater; Alma Theater
Affiliations: Ohio Arts Council; Arts Midwest;
Association of Performing Arts Presenters; Ohio Arts
Presenters Network
Annual Attendance: 125,000+
Facility Category: Summer outdoor, covered open-air
theatres
Type of Stage: Proscenium, Thrust
Seating Capacity: 1,222 + lawn; 262
Year Built: 1938
Year Remodeled: 1989
Organization Type: Sponsoring

7571
DOBAMA THEATRE
2490 Lee Boulevard
Suite 325
Cleveland Heights, OH 44118
Phone: 216-932-6838
Fax: 216-932-3259
e-mail: dobama@dobama.org
Web Site: www.dobama.org
Management:
Artistic Director: Joyce Casey
Founded: 1959
Status: Non-Profit, Professional
Paid Staff: 1

7572
CREW STADIUM
One Black & Gold Boulevard
Columbus, OH 43211
Phone: 614-447-2739
Fax: 614-447-4109
Web Site: www.thecrew.com
Officers:
President: John Wagner
VP: Tom Patton
Management:
General Manager: Mark McCullers
Founded: 1999
Status: For-Profit, Professional

7573
FRANKLIN COUNTY VETERANS MEMORIAL
300 W Broad Street
Columbus, OH 43215
Phone: 614-221-4341
Fax: 614-221-8422
Web Site: www.fcvm.com
Officers:
President: Marilyn Brown
Budget: $1.6 million
Income Sources: Self Generator Revenue
Facility Category: Auditorium and Exhibition Facility
Type of Stage: Proscenium
Stage Dimensions: 32'x26'
Seating Capacity: 3916
Year Built: 1955
Year Remodeled: 2000
Cost: $11.5 million
Rental Contact: Richard Nolan

7574
JEROME SCHOTTENSTEIN CENTER
Ohio State University
555 Borror Drive
Columbus, OH 43210
Phone: 614-688-3939
Fax: 614-292-5067
e-mail: osuarena@osu.edu
Web Site: www.schottensteincenter.com
Management:
Director: Michael Gatto
Founded: 1996
Annual Attendance: 1,000,000
Facility Category: Arena
Type of Stage: Portable
Stage Dimensions: 60x80
Seating Capacity: 20,000
Year Built: 1998
Rental Contact: Sharon Rone

7575
NATIONWIDE ARENA
200 W Nationwide Boulevard
Columbus, OH 43215
Phone: 614-246-2000
Fax: 614-246-4300
Web Site: www.nationwidearena.com
Management:
General Manager: Eric Granger
Marketing Manager: Jim Riley
Mission: Multi-purpose sports and entertainment
venue.
Founded: 2000
Performs At: Arena
Annual Attendance: 1+ Million
Facility Category: Arena
Seating Capacity: 18,500
Year Built: 2000
Cost: $150 Million

7576
OHIO STADIUM
Ohio State University
411 Woody Hayes Drive
Columbus, OH 43210
Phone: 614-292-7572
Fax: 614-292-0506
e-mail: penner.2@osu.edu
Web Site: www.ohiostatebuckeyes.com
Management:
Sr Assoc Athletic Director: Ben Jay,
jay.21@osu.edu
Associate Athletics Director: Mike Penner,
penner.2@osu.edu
Asst Direcotor Event Management: Brittan Roth,
roth.199@osu.edu
Seating Capacity: 98,000

7577
OHIO THEATRE
55 E State Street
Columbus, OH 43215-4264
Phone: 614-469-1045
Fax: 614-461-0429
Web Site: www.capa.com
Officers:
VP: John Fisher
Management:
General Manager: Sheri Kaplan
Marketing Director: Elisabeth Rivers
Opened: 1928
Seating Capacity: 2,779

7578
WEXNER CENTER FOR THE ARTS
Ohio State University
1871 N High Street
Columbus, OH 43210-1393
Phone: 614-292-0330
Fax: 614-292-3369
Web Site: www.wexarts.org
Officers:
Chairman: Leslie H Wexner
Management:
Director: Sherri Geldin
Opened: 1989
Budget: $150,000-400,000
Performs At: Mershon Auditorium; Weigel Hall
Auditorium
Type of Stage: Black Box
Rental Contact: Claudia Bonham

7579
POMERENE CENTER FOR THE ARTS
The Corner Of 3rd & Mulberry Streets
Coshocton, OH 43812
Phone: 740-622-0326
Fax: 740-622-0326
e-mail: acornell@pomerenearts.org
Web Site: www.pomerenearts.org
Officers:
President: Mike Mc Cullough
VP: Ed Keifer
Treasurer: Roger Eastman
Management:
Director: Anne Cornell
Office Manager: Katheleen Goode
Founded: 1984
Status: Non-Profit, Professional
Paid Staff: 3
Paid Artists: 2
Budget: $10,000
Seating Capacity: 75-900

7580
DAYTON HARA ARENA
1001 Shiloh Springs Road
Dayton, OH 45415
Phone: 937-278-4776
Fax: 937-278-4633
e-mail: harapr@haracomplex.com
Web Site: www.haracomplex.com
Founded: 1964
Facility Category: Arena; Exhibtion Centers
Seating Capacity: 7,000
Year Built: 1964
Year Remodeled: 1997
Rental Contact: Corey Rose

7581
DAYTON PLAYHOUSE
1301 E Siebenthaler Avenue
Dayton, OH 45414
Phone: 937-424-8477
Fax: 937-424-0062
Web Site: www.daytonplayhouse.com
Officers:
   Chair: John Beck
   President: Becky Lamb
Management:
   Executive Director: Amy Brown
Founded: 1959

7582
ERVIN J NUTTER CENTER
3640 Colonel Glenn Highway
Suite 430
Dayton, OH 45435
Phone: 937-775-3498
Fax: 937-775-2060
Web Site: www.nuttercenter.com
Management:
   Executive Director: John Siehl
Seating Capacity: 12,000
Year Built: 1990

7583
VICTORIA THEATRE ASSOCIATION
138 N Main Street
Dayton, OH 45402
Phone: 937-228-7591
Fax: 937-449-5068
Web Site: www.victoriatheatre.com
Officers:
   President/CEO: Dianne Kennedy
   VP: Michael Roediger
   CFO: David Schrodi
Management:
   Human Resource Director: Rhonda Hess
Status: Non-Profit
Budget: $1,000,000+
Performs At: Victoria Theatre; Schuster Performing
Arts Center
Annual Attendance: 375,000
Facility Category: Theatre
Type of Stage: Proscenium
Seating Capacity: 1,154/2,319
Year Built: 1868
Year Remodeled: 1990
Rental Contact: Mechele Pritchard

7584
DELAWARE COUNTY CULTURAL ARTS CENTER
190 W Winter Street
Delaware, OH 43015
Phone: 740-369-2787
Fax: 740-363-2733
Web Site: www.artscastle.org
Management:
   Executive Director: Kevin L Greenwood
Founded: 1989
Status: Non-Profit, Non-Professional
Budget: $10,000
Seating Capacity: 2,000

7585
MEMORIAL ATHLETIC & CONVOCATION CENTER
Kent State University
Kent, OH 44242
Phone: 330-672-3000
Web Site: www.kent.edu
Officers:
   President: Lester Lefton
   VP: Gregg Floyd
   Secretary: Charlene Reed
Founded: 1910
Seating Capacity: 6,327

7586
FRAZE PAVILION FOR THE PERFORMING ARTS
Lincoln Park Center
695 Lincoln Park Boulevard
Kettering, OH 45429
Phone: 937-296-3300
Fax: 937-296-3302
e-mail: fraze@ketteringoh.org
Web Site: www.fraze.com
Management:
   General Manager: Karen Durham
Utilizes: Guest Accompanists; Guest Lecturers;
Instructors; Local Artists; Multimedia; Original Music
Scores
Founded: 1991
Status: For-Profit, Professional
Paid Staff: 300
Budget: $400,000-1,000,000
Income Sources: Ticket sales
Annual Attendance: 200,000
Facility Category: Amphitheatre
Seating Capacity: 4,300
Year Built: 1991

7587
KENNETH C BECK CENTER FOR THE PERFORMING ARTS
17801 Detroit Avenue
Lakewood, OH 44107
Phone: 216-521-2540
e-mail: grumio85@aol.com
Web Site: www.beckcenter.org
Officers:
   President/CEO: Lucinda B Einhouse
Management:
   Artistic Director: Scott Spence
Founded: 1930
Status: Non-Profit, Non-Professional

7588
VETERANS MEMORIAL CIVIC AND CONVENTION CENTER
7 Town Square
Lima, OH 45801
Phone: 419-224-5222
Fax: 419-224-6964
e-mail: jrohr@limaciviccenter.com
Web Site: www.limaciviccenter.com
Officers:
   President: Donald Reeseann
   VP: James Bourk
   Treasurer: William Massa
   Executive Director: Cynthia Wood
Management:
   Marketing Services Manager: Jenni Rohr
Specialized Field: Performing Arts
Status: Non-Profit, Professional
Income Sources: 50% earned; 50% subsidy
Affiliations: I.A.A.M.
Annual Attendance: 250,000
Facility Category: Multi-Purpose
Type of Stage: Proscenium
Stage Dimensions: 60'x40'
Seating Capacity: 1700
Year Built: 1984
Cost: $9 Million
Rental Contact: Joe Shaffnerr
Resident Groups: Lima Symphony Orchestra

7589
PALACE CIVIC CENTER
617 Broadway Ave
Lorain, OH 44052
Phone: 440-245-2323
Fax: 440-246-6076
e-mail: suzanne@lorainpalace.com
Web Site: www.lorainpalace.org
Founded: 1928

7590
MARION PALACE THEATRE
276 W Center Street
Marion, OH 43302
Phone: 740-383-2101
Fax: 740-387-3425
Web Site: www.marionpalace.org
Officers:
   President: Brenda Johnston
   VP: Don Smith
   Secretary: Jill Frey
Management:
   Executive Director: Elaine Merchant
   Business Manager: Veronica Bodine
Founded: 1928
Status: Non-Profit, Professional

7591
TRUMBULL NEW THEATRE
5883 Youngstown-Warren Road
Niles, OH 44446
Phone: 330-652-1103
Web Site: www.trumbullnewtheatre.com
Officers:
   President: John Timmins
   Treasurer: Susan Gillespie
   Secretary: Lisa Bennett
Founded: 1948
Status: Non Profit

7592
FAIRMOUNT CENTER FOR THE CREATIVE AND PERFORMING ARTS
8400 Fairmount Road
Novelty, OH 44072
Phone: 440-338-3171
Fax: 440-338-4218
Web Site: www.fairmountcenter.org
Management:
   Artistic Director: Tom Fulton
   Director: Fred Sternfeld
Founded: 1970
Status: Non-Profit, Professional

7593
MILLETT HALL
501 E High Street
Oxford, OH 45056
Phone: 513-529-1809
Officers:
President: David Hodge
Secretary: S Kay Geiger
Treasurer: David Herche
Founded: 1809
Status: Non-Profit, Non-Professional
Seating Capacity: 10,000

7594
CUYAHOGA COMMUNITY COLLEGE: WESTERN CAMPUS THEATRE
11000 Pleasant Valley Road
Western Campus
Parma, OH 44115
Toll-free: 800-954-8742
Web Site: www.tri-c.edu
Officers:
President: Jerry Sue Thornton
Management:
Artistic Director: Robert Ellis
Founded: 1966
Status: Non-Profit, Professional

7595
SOUTHERN OHIO MUSEUM & CULTURAL CENTER
825 Gallia Street
PO Box 990
Portsmouth, OH 45662
Phone: 740-354-5629
Fax: 740-354-4090
Management:
Director: Sarah Johnson
Founded: 1979
Status: Non-Profit, Professional

7596
VERN RIFFE CENTER FOR THE ARTS
940 2nd Street
Portsmouth, OH 45662
Phone: 740-351-3622
Fax: 740-351-3414
e-mail: info@vrcfa.org
Web Site: www.vrcfa.org
Officers:
President: Bob Mascari
Management:
Executive Director: Carl Daehler
Box Office Manager: Casey Glenn
Technical Director: Leo Schlosser
Founded: 1995
Paid Staff: 4
Volunteer Staff: 110
Paid Artists: 50
Budget: $720,000
Performs At: Proscenium Theater Concert Hall
Affiliations: AAPA, OAPN
Annual Attendance: 75,000
Type of Stage: Proscenium and Concert Hall
Stage Dimensions: 58'x 30'
Seating Capacity: 1,139
Year Built: 1995
Cost: $16,000,000
Rental Contact: Regina Bradley

7597
CLARK STATE PERFORMING ARTS CENTER
PO Box 570
Springfield, OH 45501-0570
Phone: 937-328-3857
Fax: 937-328-3879
Web Site: www.clarkstate.edu
Officers:
President: Andy Bell
Chair: James Doyle
Management:
Director: Corey Holliday
Founded: 1962
Status: Non-Profit, Professional
Budget: $660,000
Income Sources: Box Office, Rentals, Grants, Sponsorships, Donations
Performs At: Kuss Auditorium; Turner Studio Theatre
Affiliations: Association of Performing Arts Presenters; Ohio Arts Performers Network
Annual Attendance: 90,000
Facility Category: Auditorium Studio Theatre
Type of Stage: Proscenium/ Studio Theatre
Stage Dimensions: 55'x 40'
Seating Capacity: 1,500/200
Year Built: 1993
Cost: $15.1 million
Rental Contact: Operations Manager Karen Clark
Organization Type: Arts Center

7598
FRANCISCAN CENTER
6832 Convent Boulevard
Sylvania, OH 43560
Phone: 419-824-3975
Fax: 419-882-2981
Web Site: www.franciscancenter.org
Officers:
President: Robert Helmer
Chairman: Larry Ulrich
Secretary: Ann Anderson Stranahan
Treasurer: William Carroll
Management:
Advising Director: Mary Douglas
Founded: 1958
Status: Non-Profit, Professional

7599
COLLINGWOOD ARTS CENTER
2413 Collingwood Boulevard
Toledo, OH 43620
Phone: 419-244-2787
Fax: 419-244-2820
Web Site: www.collingwoodartscenter.org
Officers:
President: Micahael Szuberla
Treasurer: Dr Robert Brundage
Secretary: Laura Gerdenich
Status: Non-Profit

7600
GLASS BOWL STADIUM
2801 W Bancroft
Toledo, OH 43606-3390
Phone: 419-530-4226
Fax: 419-530-4428
Web Site: www.utoledo.edu
Officers:
President: Dr Lloyd A Jacobs
Chairman: Rick Stansley
Founded: 1872

7601
JOHN F SAVAGE HALL
2801 W Bancroft
Toledo, OH 43606-3390
Phone: 419-530-4226
Fax: 419-530-4428
Web Site: www.utoledo.edu
Officers:
President: Dr Lloyd A Jacobs
Chairman: Rick Stansley
Founded: 1872
Seating Capacity: 9,600

7602
SEAGATE CENTRE
401 Jefferson Avenue
Toledo, OH 43604
Phone: 419-255-3300
Fax: 419-255-7731
Web Site: www.toledo~seagate.com
Officers:
Chairman: Scott Shook
CFO: Terry Dachenhaus
Management:
General Manager: Steve Miller
Founded: 1987
Status: Non-Profit, Professional
Seating Capacity: 7,500

7603
STRANAHAN THEATER GREAT HALL
4645 Heather Downs Boulevard
Toledo, OH 43614
Phone: 419-381-8851
Fax: 419-381-9525
Toll-free: 866-381-7465
Web Site: stranahantheater.org
Management:
Executive Director: Ward Whiting
Marketing Director: Elizabeth Sudheimer
Box Office Manager: Cherie Byrne
Founded: 1965
Specialized Field: Music; Dance; Theatre
Facility Category: Performing Arts
Type of Stage: Proscenium
Stage Dimensions: 60 x 46
Seating Capacity: 2424
Year Built: 1969
Year Remodeled: 2000
Cost: $1,900
Rental Contact: General Manager Ward Whiting

7604
TOLEDO CULTURAL ARTS CENTER VALENTINE THEATRE
410 Adams Street
Toledo, OH 43604-1402
Phone: 419-242-3490
Fax: 419-242-2791
Web Site: www.valentinetheatre.com
Specialized Field: Theater
Paid Staff: 20
Volunteer Staff: 185
Paid Artists: 20

7605
TOLEDO MUSEUM OF ART
PO Box 1013
Toledo, OH 43697

Phone: 419-255-8000
Fax: 419-254-5089
Toll-free: 800-644-6862
e-mail: information@toledomuseum.org
Web Site: www.toledomuseum.org
Officers:
 Chair of the Board: Elizabeth Brady
 Vice Chair of the Board: Steven R Coffin
 Vice Chair of the Board: Cynthia B Thompson
 Secretary: John S Szuch
 Treasurer: George L Chapman
Management:
 President/Director/CEO: Brian P Kennedy
 COO: Carol Bintz
 Collections Director: Carolyn Putney
 Development Director: Susan Palmer
 Communications Director: Kelly Garrow
Mission: Through our collection and programs, we strive to integrate art into the lives of people.
Founded: 1901
Specialized Field: Painting; Sculpture; Glass; Works on Paper; Decorative Arts
Status: Nonprofit
Paid Staff: 232
Volunteer Staff: 531

7606
HOBART ARENA
255 Adams Street
Troy, OH 45373
Phone: 937-339-2911
Fax: 937-335-0046
Web Site: www.hobartarena.com
Management:
 Director: Charles R Sharrett
Status: For-Profit, Non-Professional

7607
TROY HAYNER CULTURAL CENTER
301 W Main Street
Troy, OH 45373
Phone: 937-339-0457
Fax: 937-335-6373
e-mail: troyhaynercenter@troyhayner.org
Web Site: www.troyhayner.org
Management:
 Executive Director: Linda Lee Jolly
 Artistic Director: Theresa Boehringer
Founded: 1976
Status: Non-Profit, Professional
Paid Staff: 8
Paid Artists: 25

7608
BEEGHLY GYM
1 University Plaza
Youngstown, OH 44555
Phone: 330-941-3000
Toll-free: 877-468-6978
Web Site: www.ysu.edu
Officers:
 Prresident: David C Sweet
Management:
 Executive Director: Ron Strollo

7609
DEYOR PERFORMING ARTS CENTER
Youngstown Symphony Society
260 W Federal Street
Youngstown, OH 44503-1256
Phone: 330-744-4269
Fax: 330-744-1441
e-mail: symphony@youngstownsymphony.com
Web Site: www.youngstownsymphony.com

Management:
 Director: Randall Craig Fleischer
Status: Non-Profit, Professional

7610
FORD THEATRE
Youngstown State University
One University Plaza
Youngstown, OH 44555
Phone: 330-941-3000
e-mail: theatre@cc.ysu.edu
Web Site: www.fpa.ysu.edu
Officers:
 Department Chair: Frank Castronovo
Management:
 Director: Michele Lepore-Hagan

7611
SPOTLIGHT ARENA
Youngstown State University
One University Plaza
Youngstown, OH 44555
Phone: 330-941-3000
e-mail: theatre@cc.ysu.edu
Web Site: www.fpa.ysu.edu
Officers:
 Department Chair: Frank Castronovo
Management:
 Director: Michele Lepore-Hagan

7612
STAMBAUGH AUDITORIUM
1000 5th Avenue
Youngstown, OH 44504-1603
Phone: 330-747-5175
Fax: 330-747-1981
e-mail: info@stambaughauditorium.com
Web Site: www.stambaughonline.com
Officers:
 President: Douglas Wittenauer
 VP: William Conti
 Secretary: Jeanne Simeone
 Treasurer: David Konik
Management:
 Executive Director: Phil Cannaits
Mission: To present events for the enjoyment, entertainment and education of the people of Youngstown and the surrounding communities.
Founded: 1926
Paid Staff: 6
Volunteer Staff: 30

7613
SECREST AUDITORIUM
334 Shinnick Street
Zanesville, OH 43701
Phone: 740-454-6851
Fax: 740-454-6852
e-mail: auditorium@coz.org
Web Site: www.secrestonline.com
Management:
 Manager: John Kunkel
 Marketing Director: Ann Combs
Status: Non-Profit, Non-Professional
Paid Staff: 2

7614
ZANESVILLE ART CENTER
620 Military Road
Zanesville, OH 43701
Phone: 740-452-0741
Web Site: www.zanesvilleartcenter.org
Officers:
 Secretary: Vanessa Brosie

Management:
 Director: Susan Talbot-Stanaway
Utilizes: Collaborations; Commissioned Composers; Curators; Dancers; Educators; Filmmakers; Fine Artists; Guest Accompanists; Guest Composers; Guest Designers; Guest Ensembles; Guest Instructors; Guest Musical Directors; Guest Musicians; Guest Writers; High School Drama; Instructors; Lyricists; Multi Collaborations; Multimedia; New Productions; Organization Contracts; Poets; Sign Language Translators; Singers; Soloists; Special Technical Talent; Touring Companies
Paid Staff: 7
Volunteer Staff: 50
Paid Artists: 5
Budget: $300,000
Income Sources: Multiple Sources
Annual Attendance: 15,000
Facility Category: Auditorium
Stage Dimensions: 30'x
Seating Capacity: 80
Year Built: 1984
Rental Contact: Debbie Lowe

Oklahoma

7615
DOROTHY I SUMMERS AUDITORIUM
East Central University
1100 E 14th Street
Ada, OK 74820
Phone: 580-332-8000
Fax: 580-436-3329
Utilizes: Educators; Soloists
Founded: 1911
Status: Non-Profit, Non-Professional
Paid Staff: 3
Annual Attendance: 1200 - 1500
Seating Capacity: 430

7616
ALVA PUBLIC LIBRARY AUDITORIUM
504 7th Street
Alva, OK 73717
Phone: 580-327-1833
Fax: 580-327-5329
e-mail: lthorne@alva.lib.ok.us
Web Site: www.alvaok.org
Management:
 Director: Larry Thorne

7617
BARTLESVILLE COMMUNITY CENTER
300 SE Adams Boulevard
Bartlesville, OK 74003
Toll-free: 800-618-2787
Web Site: www.bartlesvilleok.com
Officers:
 Chairman: Bob Fraser
 Vice Chairman: Dan Stope
 Secretary: Bud Sexson
 Treasurer: Sherry Musselman-Cox
Management:
 Managing Director: Bud Sexson
 Facility Manager: Pat Patterson
 Marketing Director: Jo Yates Baughman
Utilizes: Actors; Artists-in-Residence; Choreographers; Collaborations; Dance Companies; Dancers; Educators; Fine Artists; Five Seasonal Concerts; Grant Writers; Guest Accompanists; Guest Artists; Guest Choreographers; Guest Companies; Guest Composers; Guest Designers; Guest Ensembles; Guest Instructors; Guest Lecturers; Guest Musical Directors; Guest

Musicians; Guest Soloists; Guest Teachers; Guest Writers; Guild Activities; Instructors; Local Artists; Lyricists; Multi Collaborations; Multimedia; Music; New Productions; Organization Contracts; Original Music Scores; Performance Artists; Playwrights; Poets; Resident Professionals; Selected Students; Sign Language Translators; Singers; Soloists; Student Interns; Special Technical Talent; Theatre Companies; Touring Companies; Visual Arts
Founded: 1982
Specialized Field: Performing Arts Hall and Rental Facility
Status: Non-Profit, Non-Professional
Paid Staff: 15
Volunteer Staff: 400
Budget: $860,000
Income Sources: Interest Income; Endowment; Rental Income; Hotel/Motel Tax Revenue; Donations; Admissions; Rentals
Affiliations: City of Bartlesville
Annual Attendance: 130,000
Facility Category: Performing Arts Hall; Rental Facility
Type of Stage: Proscenium
Stage Dimensions: 40-60wx30d
Seating Capacity: 1,702
Year Built: 1982
Cost: $13,000,000
Rental Contact: Events Coordinator Shallan John

7618
CARL WOOTEN STADIUM
PO Box 430
Goodwell, OK 73939
Phone: 580-349-2611
Fax: 580-349-2302
Toll-free: 800-664-6778
e-mail: webmaster@opsu.edu
Web Site: www.opsu.edu
Officers:
President: David Bryant
VP: Wayne Manning
Founded: 1909
Status: Non-Profit, Non-Professional

7619
GREAT PLAINS COLISEUM
920 Sheridan Road
Lawton, OK 73502
Phone: 580-357-1483
Fax: 580-357-1192
Web Site: www.gpcoliseum.com
Officers:
Chairman: David Dorrell
Treasurer: Jerry Krasser
Management:
Executive Director: Richard Pool
Status: For-Profit, Professional
Paid Staff: 10

7620
MCMAHON MEMORIAL AUDITORIUM
801 NW Ferris
Lawton, OK 73507
Phone: 580-581-3472
Web Site: www.lawtonok.com
Officers:
Co-Founder: Louise McMahon
Founded: 1954
Affiliations: Lawton Philharmonic Society
Type of Stage: Proscenium
Stage Dimensions: 92'Wx40'D
Orchestra Pit: 1
Architect: Paul Harris
Rental Contact: Jim McCarthy

7621
ROSE STATE COLLEGE PERFORMING ARTS THEATRE
6420 SE 15th Street
Midwest City, OK 73110-2799
Phone: 405-733-7673
Web Site: www.rose.edu
Officers:
President: Terry Britton
Chair: James Howell
Secretary: Aarone Corwin
Treasurer: Robert Croak
Management:
Director: John Cain
Marketing: Donna Syth
Seating Capacity: 1,400

7622
MUSKOGEE CIVIC CENTER
425 Boston
PO Box 2361
Muskogee, OK 74401
Phone: 918-684-6363
Fax: 918-684-6364
Toll-free: 888-687-6137
e-mail: cassandra.gaines@muskogeeciviccenter.com
Web Site: www.cityofmuskogee.com
Management:
Manager: Cassandra Gaines
Seating Capacity: 3,710

7623
MUSKOGEE LITTLE THEATRE
PO Box 964
Muskogee, OK 74402
Phone: 918-683-5332
Management:
Executive Director: Coni Wetz

7624
LLYOD NOBLE CENTER
660 Parrington Oval
Norman, OK 73019-0390
Phone: 405-325-0311
Fax: 405-325-7605
Web Site: www.ou.edu
Officers:
President: David L Boren
VP: Nicholas Hathaway
CFO: Chris Kwitsky
Founded: 1975
Seating Capacity: 12,000

7625
OKLAHOMA ARTS INSTITUTE
2600 Van Buren
Suite 2606
Norman, OK 73072
Phone: 405-321-9000
Fax: 405-321-9001
Web Site: www.okartinst.org
Officers:
President: Julie Cohen
VP: Emily Clinton
Management:
Director Development: Shana Rutz
Program Director: Emily Clinton
Founded: 1976

7626
UNIVERSITY THEATRE
University of Oklahoma
563 Elm Street
Norman, OK 73019-0310
Phone: 405-325-4021
Fax: 405-325-0400
Web Site: www.ou.edu
Management:
Director: James Garner
Marketing: Sandra Bent
Budget: $8,000; $1,500
Seating Capacity: 600; 144

7627
BLACK LIBERATED ARTS CENTER
PO Box 11014
Oklahoma City, OK 73136
Phone: 405-524-3800
Web Site: www.blacinc.org
Officers:
President: F E Berroughs
Management:
Executive Director: Anita G Arnold
Founded: 1970
Status: Non-Profit, Professional
Paid Staff: 1
Budget: $35,000-60,000
Performs At: Civic Center Music Hall

7628
BURG THEATRE
Oklahoma City University
2501 N Blackwelder
Oklahoma City, OK 73106-1493
Phone: 405-208-5000
e-mail: visitocu@okcu.edu
Web Site: www.okcu.edu
Officers:
President: Dr Tom J McDaniel
Chair: William F Shdeed
Secretary: Josephine Freede
Treasurer: Roy W Chandler
Management:
Theatre Department Director: Donald Childs

7629
CIVIC CENTER MUSIC HALL
201 N Walker Avenue
Oklahoma City, OK 73102
Phone: 405-297-2584
Fax: 405-297-3890
Management:
General Manager: Jim Brown
Operations: Marlon Davis
Marketing: Jennifer Lindsey-McCintock

7630
COX CONVENTION CENTER
One Myriad Gardens
Oklahoma City, OK 73102-9219
Phone: 405-602-8500
Fax: 405-602-8505
e-mail: info@coxconventioncenter.com
Web Site: www.coxconventioncenter.com
Management:
General Manager: Gary Desjardins
Operations Director: Teddy Faulkinberry
Marketing Director: Tim Linville
Founded: 1972
Seating Capacity: 14,380

7631

KIRKPATRICK AUDITORIUM

Oklahoma City University
2501 N Blackwelder
Oklahoma City, OK 73106-1493
Phone: 405-208-5000
e-mail: visitocu@okcu.edu
Web Site: www.okcu.edu
Officers:
    President: Dr Tom J McDaniel
    Chair: William F Shdeed
    Secretary: Josephine Freede
    Treasurer: Roy W Chandler
Management:
    Theatre Department Director: Donald Childs

7632

OKLAHOMA CITY ZOO AMPHITHEATRE

2101 NE 50th Street
Oklahoma City, OK 73111
Phone: 405-364-3700
Officers:
    President: Howard Pollack
    VP: Cesar Morales
    CFO: Tom Schadegg
Management:
    Promotions Director: David Beerley

7633

PONCA PLAYHOUSE

301 S First
PO Box 1414
Ponca City, OK 74602
Phone: 580-765-5360
Web Site: www.poncaplayhouse.com
Officers:
    President: Karen Brown
    VP: Ron Davis
    Treasurer: Sheila Foxworthy
    Secretary: John Dalton
Opened: 1959

7634

STILLWATER COMMUNITY CENTER

315 W 8th Street
Stillwater, OK 74074
Phone: 405-533-8433
Fax: 405-533-8022
e-mail: swalker@stillwater.org
Web Site: www.stillwater.org
Management:
    Manager: Stephanie Walker
Status: Non-Profit, Professional
Budget: $10,000
Performs At: Continental Auditorium

7635

MABEE CENTER ARENA

Oral Roberts University
7777 S Lewis Avenue
Tulsa, OK 74171
Phone: 918-495-6400
e-mail: twinters@oru.edu
Web Site: www.mabeecenter.com
Management:
    Operations Director: Crispin Ngenda
    Managing Director: Tony Winters
Founded: 1972
Status: Non-Profit, Professional
Seating Capacity: 11,763

7636

MOHAWK PARK

175 E 2nd Street
Suite 690
Tulsa, OK 74103
Phone: 918-596-2100
Web Site: www.tulsaparks.org
Management:
    Director: Monica Hamilton
    Manager: Kim MacLeod
Seating Capacity: 30,000

7637

RIVER PARKS AMPHITHEATRE

717 S Houston
Suite 510
Tulsa, OK 74127
Phone: 918-596-2001
Fax: 918-596-2004
e-mail: staff@riverparks.org
Web Site: www.riverparks.org
Officers:
    Chairman: Chet Cadieux
    Vice Chairman: Ken Levit
    Treasurer: Bobby G Lorton III
Management:
    Executive Director: Matt Meyer,
    staff@riverparks.org
    Administrative Manager: Janet Kendall
Founded: 1974
Seating Capacity: 3,000

7638

SKELLY STADIUM

600 S College Avenue
Tulsa, OK 74104-3189
Phone: 918-631-2381
Web Site: www.tulsahurricane.com
Officers:
    President: Kevin Chunley
    VP: Bob Leekly
    Treasurer: Chris Kaiser
    Secretary: Karen Ham
Management:
    Athletic Director: Bubba Cunningham
Seating Capacity: 40,235

7639

TULSA PERFORMING ARTS CENTER

110 E 2nd Street
Tulsa, OK 74103
Phone: 918-596-7122
Fax: 918-596-7144
Toll-free: 800-364-7122
e-mail: tulsapac@cityoftulsa.org
Web Site: www.tulsapac.com
Management:
    Director: John E Scott
    Assistant Director: Steven J Fendt
Opened: 1977

7640

TULSA PERFORMING ARTS CENTER: JOHN H WILLIAM HALL

110 E 2nd Street
Tulsa, OK 74103
Phone: 918-596-7122
Fax: 918-596-7144
e-mail: tulsapac@cityoftulsa.org
Web Site: www.tulsapac.com
Management:
    Director: John E Scott
    Assistant Director: Steven J Fendt

Opened: 1977

7641

TULSA PERFORMING ARTS CENTER: DOENGES THEATER

110 E 2nd Street
Tulsa, OK 74103
Phone: 918-596-7122
Fax: 918-596-7144
e-mail: tulsapac@cityoftulsa.org
Web Site: www.tulsapac.com
Management:
    Director: John E Scott
    Assistant Director: Steven J Fendt
Opened: 1977

7642

TULSA PERFORMING ARTS CENTER: STUDIO II

110 E 2nd Street
Tulsa, OK 74103
Phone: 918-596-7122
Fax: 918-596-7144
e-mail: tulsapac@cityoftulsa.org
Web Site: www.tulsapac.com
Management:
    Director: John E Scott
    Assistant Director: Steven J Fendt
Opened: 1977

7643

TYRRELL HALL

University of Tulsa
600 S College Avenue
Tulsa, OK 74104
Phone: 918-631-2262
Fax: 918-631-3589
e-mail: schoolofmusic@utulsa
Web Site: www.utulsa.edu
Officers:
    President: Dr Steadman Upham

7644

WALTER ARTS CENTER

Holland Hall
5666 E 81 Street
Tulsa, OK 74137-2099
Phone: 918-481-1111
Fax: 918-481-1193
Web Site: hollandhall.org
Officers:
    President: Tammie L Maloney
    VP: Roger B Collins
    Treasurer: Phil Frottlich
Utilizes: Artists-in-Residence; Guild Activities; High
School Drama; Instructors; Soloists; Touring Companies
Founded: 1922
Budget: $10,000
Performs At: Branch Theatre
Facility Category: Arts Education
Type of Stage: Proscenium
Seating Capacity: 1,119
Year Built: 1992
Rental Contact: Jackie Hewitt

7645

TULSA COMMUNITY COLLEGE PERFORMING ARTS CENTER FOR EDUCATION

10300 E 81st Street
Tulsa, OK 74133

Phone: 918-595-7000
e-mail: webteam@tcc
Web Site: www.tulsacc.edu
Officers:
    President: Tom McKeon

7646
MILAN STADIUM

Southwestern Oklahoma State University
100 Campus Drive
Weatherford, OK 73096
Phone: 580-774-3766
Fax: 580-774-7101
Web Site: www.swosu.edu
Officers:
    President: John M Hayes
Founded: 1903
Seating Capacity: 9,000

Oregon

7647
ONE WORLD PERFORMING ARTS

Southern Oregon University
1250 Siskiyou Boulevardity
Ashland, OR 97520
Phone: 541-552-7672
Fax: 541-552-6440
Web Site: www.sou.edu
Officers:
    President: Mary Cullinan

7648
OREGON SHAKESPEARE FESTIVAL

15 S Pioneer
PO Box 158
Ashland, OR 97520
Phone: 541-482-2111
Fax: 541-482-0446
Toll-free: 800-219-8161
e-mail: media@osfashland.org
Web Site: www.osfashland.org
Officers:
    President: Jerry Taylor
Management:
    Artistic Director: Bill Rauch
    Executive Director: Paul Nicholson
    Manager Media/Communications: Amy Richards,
    media@osfashland.org
    Director Marketing/Communications: Mallory
    Pierce
    Director Administration/Finance: Jerry Roos
Founded: 1935
Specialized Field: Shakespeare; Classic;
Contemporary
Status: Non-Profit; Professional
Paid Staff: 550
Volunteer Staff: 600
Budget: $23,000,000
Income Sources: Earned; Contributions
Performs At: Angus Bowmer Theatre; New Theatre;
Elizabethan Theatre
Affiliations: Actors' Equity Association; ATA;
University/Resic Theatre Association; Theatre
Communications Group
Annual Attendance: 400,000
Type of Stage: Thrust Stage; Black Box; Outdoors
Seating Capacity: 601; 275; 1188

7649
OREGON SHAKESPEARE FESTIVAL: BLACK SWAN THEATER

15 S Pioneer
Ashland, OR 97520
Phone: 541-482-2111
Fax: 541-482-0446
e-mail: brochures@osfashland.org
Web Site: www.orshakes.org
Officers:
    President: Jerry Taylor
Management:
    Artistic Director: Bill Rauch
Founded: 1935

7650
SOUTHERN OREGON UNIVERSITY

1250 Siskiyou Boulevard
Ashland, OR 97520
Phone: 541-552-7672
Fax: 541-552-6440
Toll-free: 800-482-7672
Web Site: www.sou.edu
Officers:
    President: Mary Cullinan

7651
CLATSOP COMMUNITY COLLEGE PERFORMING ARTS CENTER

1653 Jerome Avenue
Astoria, OR 97103
Phone: 503-325-0910
Toll-free: 866-252-8767
e-mail: admissions@clatsopcc.edu
Web Site: www.clatsopcc.edu
Officers:
    President: Dr Gregory Hamann
Facility Category: Theatre
Type of Stage: Plywood
Seating Capacity: 255
Year Built: 1920

7652
COASTER THEATRE

108 N Hemlock
PO Box 643
Cannon Beach, OR 97110
Phone: 503-436-1242
Fax: 503-436-9653
e-mail: boxoffice@coastertheatre.com
Web Site: www.coastertheatre.com
Management:
    Artistic Director: Craig Shepherd
Founded: 1972
Status: Non-Profit; Professional

7653
GILL COLISEUM

Oregon State University
123 Gill Coliseumersity
Corvallis, OR 97331
Phone: 541-737-2370
Fax: 541-737-2929
e-mail: rfrank@oregonstate.edu
Web Site: www.osubeavers.com
Officers:
    President: Anjeanette Brown
    VP: Ray Brooks
    Treasurer: Jim Renton

7654
LASELLS STEWART CENTER

Oregon State University
600 Kerr Administration Building
Corvallis, OR 97331-2128
Phone: 541-737-4133
Fax: 541-737-3033
e-mail: life@osu
Web Site: www.oregonstate.edu
Officers:
    President: Dr Edward Ray
Management:
    Executive Director: Elizabeth Grubb
Income Sources: Rental And Fees
Performs At: Concert Hall
Facility Category: Auditorium
Type of Stage: Hardwood Concert
Stage Dimensions: 53x42
Seating Capacity: 1200
Year Built: 1981
Rental Contact: Vi Anderson

7655
RESER STADIUM

Oregon State University
123 Gill Coliseum
Corvallis, OR 97331
Phone: 541-737-2370
Fax: 541-737-2929
e-mail: rfrank@oregonstate.edu
Web Site: www.osubeavers.com
Officers:
    President: Anjeanette Brown
    VP: Ray Brooks
    Treasurer: Jim Renton
Seating Capacity: 35,000

7656
AUTZEN STADIUM

University of Oregon
2727 Leo Harris Parkway
Eugene, OR 97401
Phone: 541-346-5433
Fax: 541-346-5466
Web Site: www.goducks.com
Officers:
    President: Dave Frohamayer
Management:
    Athletics Director: Pat Kilkenny
    Assistant Director: Julie Larson

7657
BEALL CONCERT HALL

University of Oregon
E 18th Avenue
Eugene, OR 97403-1225
Phone: 541-346-3761
Fax: 541-346-0723
e-mail: mushelp@uoregon.edu
Web Site: www.music.uoregon.edu
Officers:
    Director: Brad Foley
Mission: Educational/professional
Founded: 1921
Opened: 1921
Specialized Field: Miscellaneous
Paid Staff: 4
Volunteer Staff: 1
Paid Artists: 200
Non-paid Artists: 200
Income Sources: Ticket Revenues; Grants; Donors
Performs At: Concert Hall
Affiliations: University Of Oregon

Type of Stage: Proscenium
Stage Dimensions: 38 X 42
Seating Capacity: 520
Year Built: 1921
Year Remodeled: 1978

7658
COMMUNITY CENTER FOR THE PERFORMING ARTS

WOW Hall
291 W 8th Avenue
Eugene, OR 97401
Phone: 541-687-2746
Fax: 541-687-1664
e-mail: info@wowhall.org
Web Site: www.wowhall.org
Officers:
   Chair: Liora Sponko
   Secretary: Laura Poueymirou
   Treasurer: Mike Tugwell
Management:
   Manager: Lily Lamadore
Founded: 1975
Status: Non-Profit, Professional

7659
HULT CENTER FOR THE PERFORMING ARTS

One Eugene Center
Eugene, OR 97401
Phone: 541-682-5087
Fax: 541-682-5426
e-mail: hultcenter@ci.eugene.or.us
Web Site: www.hultcenter.org
Management:
   Manager: Karm Hagedorn
   Facilities Services Manager: Mark D Loigman
   Marketing & PR Manager: Libby Tower
Founded: 1982
Status: City Owned Venue
Income Sources: City of Eugene; Lodging Tax
Seating Capacity: 2,500; 500

7660
JAQUA CONCERT HALL

John C Shedd Institute for the Arts
868 High Street
PO Box 1497
Eugene, OR 97401-1497
Phone: 541-687-6526
Fax: 541-687-1589
e-mail: info@ofam.net
Web Site: www.ofam.org
Management:
   Executive Director: Ken Peplowski
Status: Non-Profit, Professional
Facility Category: Concert Hall; Recital Hall; Gymnasium
Seating Capacity: 750; 175; 300
Year Built: 1926
Year Remodeled: 02/3
Rental Contact: Erik Martin

7661
FLORENCE EVENTS CENTER

715 Quince Street
Florence, OR 97439
Phone: 541-997-1994
Fax: 541-902-0991
Toll-free: 888-968-4086
e-mail: kevin@eventcenter.org
Web Site: www.eventcenter.org
Management:

Director: Kevin Rhodes, kevin@eventcenter.org
Marketing: Paula Becker, paula@eventcenter.org
Manager: Tara Haley, tara@eventcenter.org
Founded: 1996
Status: Non-Profit, Non-Professional
Paid Staff: 4
Volunteer Staff: 50
Stage Dimensions: 33' x 44', 20' x 40' proscenium
Seating Capacity: 457
Year Built: 1996
Rental Contact: Kevin Rhodes

7662
TAYLOR-MEADE PERFORMING ARTS CENTER

Pacific University
2034 College Way
Forest Grove, OR 97116
Phone: 503-352-2216
Fax: 503-352-2056
e-mail: tuomis1@pacificu.edu
Web Site: www.pacificu.edu
Officers:
   Chair: Scott Tuomi PhD
Management:
   Director: Bryce Seliger PhD

7663
THEATRE IN THE GROVE

2028 Pacific Avenue
PO Box 263
Forest Grove, OR 97116
Phone: 503-359-5349
e-mail: info@theatreinthegrove.org
Web Site: www.theatreinthegrove.org
Officers:
   Chairman: Jeff Zimmerman
   Treasurer: Susan Munger
   Secretary: Anita Boudreau-Zijdemans
Management:
   Manager: Jeanna Van Dyke

7664
TOM MILES THEATRE

Pacific University
2043 College Way
Forest Grove, OR 97116
Phone: 503-352-2216
Fax: 503-352-2056
e-mail: theatredance@pacificu.edu
Web Site: www.pacificu.edu
Officers:
   Chair: Ellen Margolis
Management:
   Director: Jennifer L Camp

7665
ROSS RAGLAND THEATER & CULTURAL CENTER

218 N 7th Street
Klamath Falls, OR 97601
Phone: 541-884-0651
Fax: 541-884-8574
e-mail: media@rrtheater.org
Web Site: www.rrtheater.org
Management:
   Marketing: Lauren Gailis
Founded: 1989
Status: Non-Profit, Professional
Budget: $600,000
Facility Category: Performing Arts Center
Type of Stage: Proscenium
Stage Dimensions: 51x45

Seating Capacity: 700
Year Remodeled: 1989
Rental Contact: Kelly Buckles

7666
LAKE OSWEGO PARKS & REC

PO Box 369
Lake Oswego, OR 97304
Phone: 503-636-9673
Fax: 503-697-6579
e-mail: cic@ci.oswego.or.us
Web Site: www.ci.oswego.or.us
   Managing Director: Kim Gilmer
Status: For-Profit, Professional
Paid Staff: 75
Paid Artists: 1

7667
LAKEWOOD CENTER FOR THE ARTS

368 S State Street
Lake Oswego, OR 97034
Phone: 503-635-3901
Fax: 503-635-2002
e-mail: center.info@lakewood-center.org
Web Site: www.lakewood-center.org
Officers:
   President: Mark Birge
   Treasurer: Jerry Koll
Management:
   Executive Director: Andrew Edwards
Founded: 1952

7668
YAMHILL COUNTY FAIRGROUNDS

2070 Lafayette Avenue
McMinnville, OR 97128
Phone: 503-434-7524
Fax: 503-435-1860
e-mail: ycec@onlinemac.com
Web Site: www.yamhillcountyfair.com
Officers:
   Board Member: Bruce Distler
   Fair Board Chairman: Larry Collver
   Secretary: Gary Wetz
   Fair Board Vice Chairman: Russ Christensen
Management:
   Fairgrounds Manager: Darcie Vanderyacht
   Maintenance Foreman: Kevin Rose
Mission: Yamhill County Fair and rodeo, horse shows, weddings, wedding receptions, horse boarding, concerts, canine training, master gardeners test garden, saturday market, talent contests during Yamhill County Fair, flea maret and rodeo.
Founded: 1854
Paid Staff: 2
Volunteer Staff: 6
Income Sources: Horseshows; Horseboarding; Fairs & Rodeos; USDA or Lottery; Receptions; Weddings; Banquets
Performs At: Fairgrounds
Seating Capacity: 4,000
Rental Contact: Darcie Vanderyacht

7669
BRITT PAVILION

Britt Festivals
216 W Main Street
Medford, OR 97501
Phone: 541-773-6077
Fax: 541-776-3712
Toll-free: 800-882-7488
Web Site: www.brittfest.org
Management:
   Executive Director: Jim Fredericks

Development Director: Donna Briggs
Seating Capacity: 2,200

7670
CRATERIAN GINGER ROGERS THEATER
23 S Central Avenue
Medford, OR 97501
Phone: 541-779-3000
Fax: 541-779-8175
e-mail: stephen@craterian.org
Web Site: www.craterian.org
Officers:
   President: Ron Silverman
   Secretary: Lisa James
   Treasurer: John Dailey
Management:
   Executive Director: Stephen McCandless
   Development: Maureen Esser
Status: Non-Profit, Non-Professional

7671
MCARTHUR SPORTS FIELD
Western Oregon University
345 N Monmouth Avenue
Monmouth, OR 97361
Phone: 503-838-8327
Fax: 503-838-8370
Toll-free: 877-877-1593
e-mail: pubsports@wou.edu
Web Site: www.wou.edu
Officers:
   President: John P Minahan
Management:
   Director: Jon Carey
   Marketing: Denise Visuano
Seating Capacity: 2,500

7672
RICE AUDITORIUM
Western Oregon University
345 N Monmouth Avenue
Monmouth, OR 97361
Phone: 503-838-8275
Fax: 503-838-8880
e-mail: wolfgram@wou.edu
Web Site: www.wou.edu
Officers:
   President: John P Minahan PhD
   Chair: Diane Baxter PhD
Management:
   Marketing: Denise Visuano

7673
NEWPORT PERFORMING ARTS CENTER
777 W Olive Street
PO Box 1315
Newport, OR 97365
Phone: 541-265-9231
Fax: 541-265-9464
Toll-free: 888-701-7123
e-mail: occa@coastarts.org
Web Site: coastarts.org
Officers:
   President: Bernice Barnett
Management:
   Executive Director: Catherine Rickbone
   Manager: Polly Ivers
   Operations: Ron Miller
Utilizes: Actors; Artists-in-Residence; Choreographers; Collaborating Artists; Collaborations; Commissioned Composers; Commissioned Music; Curators; Dance Companies; Dancers; Designers; Educators; Filmmakers; Fine Artists; Five Seasonal Concerts; Grant Writers; Guest Accompanists; Guest Artists; Guest Choreographers; Guest Companies; Guest Composers; Guest Conductors; Guest Designers; Guest Directors; Guest Ensembles; Guest Instructors; Guest Lecturers; Guest Musical Directors; Guest Musicians; Guest Soloists; Guest Teachers; Guest Writers; Guild Activities; High School Drama; Instructors; Local Artists; Local Unknown Artists; Lyricists; Multi Collaborations; Multimedia; Music; New Productions; Organization Contracts; Original Music Scores; Performance Artists; Playwrights; Resident Artists; Resident Professionals; Sign Language Translators; Singers; Soloists; Student Interns; Special Technical Talent; Theatre Companies; Touring Companies; Visual Arts
Facility Category: Live performance venue
Type of Stage: Proscenium
Stage Dimensions: 23 x 42
Seating Capacity: 393
Year Built: 1988
Year Remodeled: 2000
Rental Contact: Jan Eastman
Resident Groups: 8 major resident presenting organizations

7674
PENDLETON CONVENTION CENTER
1601 Westgate
Pendleton, OR 97801
Phone: 541-276-6569
Fax: 541-278-1317
Toll-free: 800-863-9358
e-mail: tracy.bosen@ci.pendleton.or.us
Web Site: www.pendleton.or.us
Management:
   Development Director: Tracy Bosen
   Manager: Larry Lehman
Status: Non-Profit, Professional
Paid Artists: 3
Seating Capacity: 128,193

7675
ARLENE SCHNITZER CONCERT HALL
Portland Center for the Performing Arts
1111 SW Broadway
Portland, OR 97205
Phone: 503-248-4335
Fax: 503-274-7490
e-mail: info@pcpa.com
Web Site: www.pcpa.com
Officers:
   Chairman: Ronald K. Ragan
Management:
   Executive Director: Robyn Williams
   Public Relations Coordinator: Alicia Loos
Opened: 1984
Budget: $8 Million
Income Sources: Hotel/Motel Tax; City; County & Regional Government
Affiliations: Oregon Symphony
Annual Attendance: 300,000
Facility Category: Concert Hall
Type of Stage: Proscenium
Stage Dimensions: 54'x40'
Seating Capacity: 2,992
Year Built: 1928
Year Remodeled: 1984
Cost: $10,000,000
Rental Contact: Lori Kramer
Resident Groups: Oregon Symphony Orchestra

7676
COLUMBIA MEADOWS
63701 Southwest Columbia River Highway
Portland, OR 97054

Phone: 503-221-0288
Fax: 503-227-4418
e-mail: lowell@doubletree.com
Web Site: www.doubletree.com
Management:
   President: David Leiken
   GM: Lowell MacGregor
Seating Capacity: 25,000

7677
COMMUNITY MUSIC CENTER
3350 SE Francis Street
Portland, OR 97202
Mailing Address: 503
Phone: 530-823-3177
Fax: 503-228-7034
e-mail: symphony@orsymphony.org
Web Site: www.orsymphony.org
Management:
   General Manager: Mary Crist
   Operations: Susan Nielsen
   Marketing: Michael Granados

7678
DOLORES WINNINGSTAD THEATRE
Portland Center for the Performing Arts
1111 SW Broadway
Portland, OR 97205
Phone: 503-248-4335
Fax: 503-274-7490
e-mail: info@pcpa.com
Web Site: www.pcpa.com
Officers:
   Chairman: Ronald K Ragen
Management:
   Executive Director: Robyn Williams
   Public Relations Coordinator: Alicia Loos
Budget: $8 Million
Income Sources: City; County; Regional Government; Hotel-Motel Tax
Annual Attendance: 200,000
Facility Category: Black box
Type of Stage: Black Box
Seating Capacity: 292
Year Built: 1987

7679
EARLE A CHILES CENTER
University of Portland
5000 N Willamette Boulevard
Portland, OR 97203-5798
Phone: 503-943-7525
Fax: 503-943-7451
Toll-free: 800-227-4568
e-mail: williams@up.edu
Web Site: www.portlandpilots.com
Officers:
   President: E William Beauchamp
Management:
   Director: Larry Williams
   Marketing: Tricia Miller
Status: Non-Profit, Non-Professional

7680
EVANS AUDITORIUM
Lewis and Clark College
0615 Palatine Hill Road
Portland, OR 97219
Phone: 503-768-7460
Fax: 503-768-7475
e-mail: music@lclark.edu
Web Site: www.lclark.edu
Officers:
   Chair: David Becker

President: Thomas Hochstettler
Management:
    Artistic Director: Amy Drill
    Marketing: Joe Becker

7681
MEMORIAL COLISEUM
1 Center Court
Portland, OR 97227
Phone: 503-235-8771
Fax: 507-736-2182
e-mail: rq.boxoffice@rosequarter.com
Web Site: www.rosequarter.com
Officers:
    President: Paul G Allen
    CEO: Tod Leiweke
Management:
    General Manager: Mike Scanlon
Seating Capacity: 12,500

7682
NEWMARK THEATRE
Portland Center for the Performing Arts
1111 SW Broadway
Portland, OR 97205
Phone: 503-248-4335
Fax: 503-274-7490
e-mail: info@pcpa.com
Web Site: www.pcpa.com
Officers:
    Chairman: Ronald K Ragen
Management:
    Executive Director: Robyn Williams
    Public Relations Coordinator: Alicia Loos
Budget: $8 Million
Income Sources: City; County; Regional Government; Hotel-Motel Tax
Performs At: Theatre, dance, choral, chamber music
Affiliations: Oregon Symphony Orchestra
Annual Attendance: 200,000
Facility Category: Concert Hall
Type of Stage: Proscenium
Stage Dimensions: 48'6" x 56'
Orchestra Pit: 1
Seating Capacity: 880
Year Built: 1987
Architect: Rapp & Rapp
Cost: $18,000,000

7683
PGE PARK
1844 SW Morrison Street
Portland, OR 97205
Phone: 503-553-5400
Fax: 503-553-5405
e-mail: info@pgepark.com
Web Site: www.pgepark.com
Officers:
    President: Merritt Paulson
Management:
    Operations: Ken Puckett
    Development: Ryan Brach
    Marketing: Cory Dolich
Seating Capacity: 30,500

7684
PIONEER COURTHOUSE SQUARE
715 SW Morrison Street
Suite 702
Portland, OR 97205
Phone: 503-223-1613
Fax: 503-222-7425
e-mail: webmaster@pioneercourthousesquare.org
Web Site: www.pioneercourthousesquare.org

Management:
    Executive Director: Jennifer Polver
    Production Director: Ben Wall
    Marketing Director: Theresa Vetsch-Sandoval
Budget: $400,000-1,000,000
Annual Attendance: 7.6 million
Facility Category: Outdoor
Seating Capacity: 3,000

7685
PORTLAND CENTER FOR THE PERFORMING ARTS
Portland Center for the Performing Arts
1111 SW Broadway
Portland, OR 97205
Phone: 503-248-4335
Fax: 503-274-7490
e-mail: info@pcpa.com
Web Site: www.pcpa.com
Officers:
    Chairman: Ronald K Ragen
Management:
    Executive Director: Robyn Williams
    Public Relations Coordinator: Alicia Loos
Annual Attendance: 400,000
Facility Category: Theatre
Type of Stage: Proscenium
Seating Capacity: 2,992
Year Built: 1952
Year Remodeled: 1968
Rental Contact: Booking Manager Lori Kramer

7686
PORTLAND CIVIC STADIUM
1844 SW Morrison
Portland, OR 97205
Phone: 503-244-8434
Fax: 503-221-3983
Web Site: www.civicstadium.org
Management:
    Operations Manager: Eric Eriksen
    Interim Stadium Manager: Barry J Strafacci
Founded: 1923
Seating Capacity: 13,000

7687
PORTLAND INSTITUTE FOR CONTEMPORARY ART
224 NW 13th Avenue
Suite 305
Portland, OR 97209
Phone: 503-242-1419
Fax: 503-243-1167
e-mail: pica@pica.org
Web Site: www.pica.org
Officers:
    Chair: Michael Tingley
    Treasurer: Nancy Barrows
    Secretary: Sally Lawrence
Management:
    Executive Director: Victoria Frey
Founded: 1995
Status: Non-Profit, Professional

7688
REED THEATRE
Reed College
3203 SE Woodstock Boulevard
Portland, OR 97202
Phone: 503-777-7356
Fax: 503-777-7769
e-mail: worleyk@reed.edu
Web Site: www.reed.edu

Officers:
    Chairman: Daniel B Greenberg
    President: Colin Diver
    Treasurer: Edwin McFarlane
    Secretary: E Randolph Labbe
Management:
    General Manager: Kathleen Worley

7689
ROSE QUARTER
1 Center Court
Portland, OR 97227
Phone: 503-235-8771
Fax: 503-736-2182
e-mail: rq.boxoffice@rosequarter.com
Web Site: www.rosequarter.com
Officers:
    President: Paul G Allen
    CEO: Tod Leiweke
Management:
    General Manager: Mike Scanlon
Status: For-Profit, Professional
Seating Capacity: 12,000

7690
WILSON CENTER FOR THE PERFORMING ARTS
1111 SW 10th
Portland, OR 97205
Phone: 503-746-9293

7691
SEASIDE CIVIC AND CONVENTION CENTER
415 1st Avenue
Seaside, OR 97138
Phone: 503-738-8585
Fax: 503-738-0198
Toll-free: 800-394-3303
e-mail: sales@seasideconvention.com
Web Site: www.seasideconvention.com
Management:
    Manager: Karen Murray
Status: Non-Profit, Non-Professional

7692
BROADWAY ROSE THEATRE
12850 SW Grant Avenue
Tigard, OR 97281
Phone: 503-620-5262
Fax: 503-670-8512
e-mail: brisa@broadwayrose.com
Web Site: www.broadwayrose.com
Officers:
    President: Lisa Francolini
Management:
    Executive Director: Brisa Trinchero
    Artistic Director: Sharon Maroney
    Marketing: Alan Anderson
Founded: 1992

Pennsylvania

7693
ALLENTOWN SYMPHONY HALL
23 N 6th Street
Allentown, PA 18101
Phone: 610-432-6715
Fax: 610-432-6735
Web Site: www.allentownsymphony.org
Officers:
    President: Kristine Burfeind

Secretary: Frank Heston
Treasurer: Joan B Cole
Management:
Development Director: Maureen S Joly
Marketing: Lucy Bloise
Manager: Tracy Damiani
Opened: 1953
Status: Non-Profit, Professional

7694
J BIRNEY CRUM STADIUM
31 S Penn Street
Allentown, PA 18105
Phone: 484-765-4000
Fax: 610-871-6052
Web Site: www.allentownsd.org
Management:
Operations: George R Crawford
Development: John R Clark

7695
MISHLER THEATRE
1212 12th Avenue
Altoona, PA 16601
Phone: 814-949-2787
Fax: 814-949-3909
e-mail: blrartsorg@aol.com
Web Site: www.mishlertheatre.org
Officers:
President: Diane Osgood
Treasurer: Gerald Hymes
Secretary: Jane Hite
Management:
Executive Director: Katherine Shaffer
Development Director: Karen Volpe
Founded: 1906
Status: Non-Profit, Professional

7696
ARTS GUILD AT NEUMANN COLLEGE
Neumann College
1 Neumann Drive
Aston, PA 19014-1298
Phone: 610-558-5626
Fax: 610-459-1370
e-mail: dimarinn@neumann.edu
Web Site: www.neumann.edu
Officers:
President: Rosalie Mirenda
Management:
Marketing: Stephen T Bell

7697
FRED P MEAGHER THEATRE
Neumann College
One Neumann Drive
Aston, PA 19014-1298
Phone: 610-558-5625
Fax: 610-459-1370
Web Site: www.neumann.edu
Officers:
President: Rosalie Mirenda PhD
Management:
Director: Sara Melisi
Marketing: Stephen T Bell

7698
MORAVIAN COLLEGE: MUSIC INSTITUTE
1200 Main Street
Bethlehem, PA 18018
Phone: 610-861-1650
Fax: 610-861-1657
e-mail: music@moravian.edu
Web Site: www.moravian.edu

Officers:
Chair: Larry Lipkis
Management:
Operations: Blair Flintom
Founded: 1742

7699
STABLER ARENA
Leghigh University
124 Goodman Drive
Bethlehem, PA 18015
Phone: 610-758-3770
Fax: 610-866-8070
e-mail: info@stablerarena.com
Web Site: www.stablerarena.com
Officers:
President: Alice P Gast
Management:
Director: Karen Adams
Founded: 1979
Seating Capacity: 6,700

7700
TOUCHSTONE THEATRE
321 E 4th Street
Bethlehem, PA 18015
Phone: 610-867-1689
e-mail: touchstone@touchstone.org
Web Site: www.touchstone.org
Officers:
President: Dave Rabaut
Vice President: Denise Stangl
Treasurer: John Fallock
Secretary: Kelly Watkins
Management:
Producing Director/Ensemble Member: Lisa Jordan
Production Manager/Ensemble Member: James P Jordan
Touring Manager/Ensemble Member: Bill George
Education Dir/Ensemble Associate: Cathleen O'Malley
Director Of Development: Amy Meleck
Founded: 1981
Opened: 1981
Status: Non-Profit, Professional

7701
ZOELLNER ARTS CENTER
Lehigh University
420 E Packer Avenue
Bethlehem, PA 18015
Phone: 610-758-5323
Fax: 610-758-6537
e-mail: els7@lehigh.edu
Web Site: www.zoellnerartscenter.org
Officers:
Executive Director: Elizabeth Scofield
Management:
Development Director: Maureen Connelley
Program Director: Deborah Sacaratis
Utilizes: Artists-in-Residence; Collaborations; Composers-in-Residence; Dance Companies; Dancers; Fine Artists; Five Seasonal Concerts; Guest Choreographers; Guest Musical Directors; Guest Musicians; Instructors; Local Artists; Multi Collaborations; Original Music Scores; Sign Language Translators; Singers; Soloists; Special Technical Talent; Theatre Companies
Founded: 1997
Status: Non-Profit, Professional
Paid Staff: 20
Volunteer Staff: 180
Paid Artists: 20

Budget: $2.2MM
Income Sources: Ticket Sales; Rentals; Development; Playbill
Performs At: Baker Hall; Diamond Theater; Black Box Theatre; Presenting Series
Affiliations: Lehigh University
Annual Attendance: 30,000
Type of Stage: Proscenium & Thrust
Stage Dimensions: 37x25
Seating Capacity: 1,000
Year Built: 1997
Architect: 33,000,000
Rental Contact: Annette Stolte

7702
BRADFORD CREATIVE & PERFORMING ARTS CENTER
10 Marilyn Home Way
PO Box 153
Bradford, PA 16701
Phone: 814-362-2522
Fax: 814-362-2556
e-mail: arts@bcpac.com
Web Site: www.bcpac.com
Officers:
President: Shane Oschman
Treasurer: Marcia Morrison
Secretary: Pat Ryan
Management:
Executive Director: James D Guelfi
Marketing: Tim Ziaukas
Assistant Manager: Christin Davis
Founded: 1984
Status: Non-Profit
Paid Staff: 17
Budget: $275,000
Income Sources: Grants; Corporate & Individual Donations Ticket Sales
Annual Attendance: 6,000

7703
ALUMNI AUDITORIUM
Widener University
14th and Chestnut Street
Chester, PA 19013
Phone: 610-499-4000
Fax: 610-499-4196
e-mail: cmmccormick@widener.edu
Web Site: www.widener.edu
Officers:
President: James T Harris III
Management:
Executive Director: Cecilia M McCormick
Operations: Carl G Pierce
Founded: 1961

7704
MARWICK BOYD AUDITORIUM
Clarion University
840 Wood Street
Clarion, PA 16214-1232
Phone: 814-393-2000
Fax: 814-393-2039
Toll-free: 800-672-7171
e-mail: info@clarion.edu
Web Site: www.clarion.edu
Officers:
President: Joe Grunenwald
Chair: R Lee James
Secretary: Richard Hilinski
Management:
Director: James Stockman

7705
UPPER DARBY PERFORMING ARTS CENTER

601 N Lansdowne Avenue
Drexel Hill, PA 19026
Phone: 610-622-1189
Fax: 610-622-6960
e-mail: udpac@mac.com
Web Site: www.udpac.org
Management:
Executive Director: Harry Dietzler

7706
STATE THEATRE CENTER FOR THE ARTS

453 Northampton Street
Easton, PA 18042-3562
Phone: 610-252-3132
Fax: 610-258-2570
Toll-free: 800-999-7828
e-mail: info@statetheatre.org
Web Site: www.statetheatre.org
Officers:
President/CEO: Shelley Brown
Management:
Operations: Mark Rafinski
Marketing: Jamie Balliet
Annual Attendance: 10,000
Facility Category: Performing Arts Theatre
Seating Capacity: 1,400
Year Built: 1922
Year Remodeled: 2000

7707
ERIE CIVIC CENTER: LJ TULLIO ARENA

809 French Street
Erie, PA 16501
Phone: 814-452-4857
Fax: 814-455-9931
e-mail: casey@erieevents.com
Web Site: www.erieevents.com
Officers:
Chair: Thomas Doolin
Treasurer: Bruce Q Whitehair
Secretary: Gwen White
Management:
Executive Director: John A Casey Wells
Operations: Barry Copple
Founded: 1983
Status: Professional
Budget: $600,000
Annual Attendance: 140,000
Facility Category: Historic Performing Arts Center
Type of Stage: Proscenium
Stage Dimensions: 60x32
Seating Capacity: 2506
Year Built: 1931
Cost: $ 1.5 Milion

7708
MARY D'ANGELO PERFORMING ARTS CENTER

Mercyhurst College
501 E 38th Street
Erie, PA 16546
Phone: 814-824-3000
Fax: 814-824-3098
e-mail: mfuhrman@mercyhurst.edu
Web Site: www.mercyhurst.edu
Management:
Director: Michael Fuhrman
Marketing: Michelle Ellia
Manager: Annette Gardner

Status: Non-Profit, Professional

7709
TOTEM POLE PLAYHOUSE

9555 Golf Course Road
PO Box 603
Fayetteville, PA 17222-0603
Phone: 717-352-2164
Fax: 717-352-8870
Toll-free: 888-805-7056
e-mail: boxoffice@totempoleplayhouse.org
Web Site: www.totempoleplayhouse.org
Officers:
President: Dana Witt
Treasurer: Judy Kaufman
Management:
Managing Director: Sue McMurtray
Artistic Director: Ray Ficca
Production Manager: Michael Domme
Founded: 1950
Specialized Field: Professional Theatre
Status: Non-Profit, Professional
Paid Staff: 4
Volunteer Staff: 30
Paid Artists: 50
Budget: $1,100,000
Income Sources: Ticket Sales; Tax Deductible Gifts; Corporate Sponsors
Affiliations: Actors Equity Association
Annual Attendance: 29,000
Facility Category: Air-Conditioned Enclosure
Type of Stage: Proscenium
Year Built: 1969

7710
MUSSELMAN STADIUM

Gettysburg College
300 N Washington Street
Gettysburg, PA 17325
Phone: 717-337-6000
Fax: 717-337-6528
e-mail: dwright@gettysburg.edu
Web Site: www.gettysburg.edu
Officers:
President: Janet Morgan Riggs
Management:
Director: David Wright
Founded: 1965
Status: Non-Profit
Seating Capacity: 6,000

7711
PALACE THEATRE

21 W Otterman Street
Greensburg, PA 15601
Phone: 724-836-8000
Fax: 724-836-5833
e-mail: palace@earthlink.net
Web Site: www.thepalacetheatre.org
Officers:
President: Michael J Langer
Chairman: T Terrance Reese
Treasurer: Sean Cassidy
Secretary: Jamie McHugh
Management:
Manager: Linda Kubas
Marketing/Programming Director: Teresa Baughman
Founded: 1926
Specialized Field: Pittsburgh Metro
Status: Non-Profit, Non-Professional
Paid Staff: 10
Volunteer Staff: 80
Performs At: Multi-disciplinary; In-House & Rentals

Annual Attendance: 60,000
Facility Category: Performing Arts Center
Type of Stage: Proscenuim
Stage Dimensions: 40' x 37'
Seating Capacity: 1369
Year Built: 1926
Year Remodeled: 2010
Rental Contact: Teresa Baughman

7712
FARM SHOW COMPLEX AND EXPO CENTER

2300 N Cameron Street
Harrisburg, PA 17110-9443
Phone: 717-787-5373
Fax: 717-783-8710
e-mail: farmshow@state.pa.us
Web Site: www.pafarmshowcomplex.com
Management:
Executive Director: Patrick Kerwin
Mission: To host a full lineup of exciting events including arena events, business meetings, conferences and expositions.
Status: For-Profit, Professional
Facility Category: Expo and Conference Center
Seating Capacity: 7,400
Year Built: 1938
Rental Contact: Heidi Cragera

7713
STATE MUSEUM OF PENNSYLVANIA

300 N Street
Harrisburg, PA 17120-0024
Phone: 717-787-4980
Fax: 717-783-4558
e-mail: hpollman@state.pa.us
Web Site: www.statemuseumpa.org
Management:
Marketing: Howard Pollman
Facility Category: Auditorium

7714
WHITAKER CENTER FOR SCIENCE AND THE ARTS

222 Market Street
Harrisburg, PA 17101
Phone: 717-214-2787
Fax: 717-214-2791
e-mail: info@whitakercenter.org
Web Site: www.whitakercenter.org
Officers:
President/CEO: Michael L Hanes PhD
Management:
Operations: Lisa Kreider
Development: Susan L Stuart
Marketing: Kathleen Keller
Utilizes: Original Music Scores; Resident Artists; Theatre Companies; Touring Companies
Opened: 1999
Status: Non-Profit, Non-Professional
Facility Category: Theater
Type of Stage: Proscenium
Stage Dimensions: 45 x 80
Seating Capacity: 636
Year Built: 1997

7715
HERSHEY THEATRE

15 E Caracas Avenue
PO Box 395
Hershey, PA 17033

Phone: 717-534-3405
Fax: 717-533-2882
e-mail: pseeley@hersheypa.com
Web Site: www.hersheytheatre.com
Management:
Operations: Patrick Seeley
Marketing: Brian Bucciarelli
Founded: 1933
Status: Non-Profit, Professional

7716
MOUNTAIN PLAYHOUSE

7690 Somerset Pike
PO Box 205
Jennerstown, PA 15547
Phone: 814-629-9201
Fax: 814-629-9201
e-mail: info@mountainplayhouse.com
Web Site: www.mountainplayhouse.org
Officers:
Chairman: Joseph Beer
Treasurer: Kevin McQuillan
Secretary: Jane Laks Gleason
Management:
Development: Erica Roslonski
Manager: Lori Kishlock
Status: Non-Profit, Professional

7717
PASQUERILLA PERFORMING ARTS CENTER

University of Pittsburgh at Johnsontown
450 Schoolhouse Road
Johnstown, PA 15904-2990
Phone: 814-269-7200
Fax: 814-269-7240
Toll-free: 800-846-2787
e-mail: upjarts@pitt.edu
Web Site: www.upj.pitt.edu/artscenter
Management:
Executive Director: Michael Bodolosky
Office Manager: Beverly Walerysiak
Technical Director: Thomas Brubaker
Founded: 1991
Status: Non-Profit, Professional
Paid Staff: 3
Volunteer Staff: 39
Seating Capacity: 1001

7718
POINT STADIUM

City Hall Recreation Department
401 Main Street
Johnstown, PA 15901
Phone: 814-533-2104
Fax: 814-533-2111
Management:
Director: Clifford Kitner
Founded: 1926
Status: Non-Profit, Non-Professional
Paid Staff: 151
Seating Capacity: 10,500

7719
LONGWOOD GARDENS

PO Box 501
Kennett Square, PA 19348
Phone: 610-388-1000
Fax: 610-388-3833
e-mail: emoody@longwoodgardens.org
Web Site: www.longwoodgardens.org
Status: Non-Profit, Professional
Paid Staff: 200

7720
LONG'S PARK AMPHITHEATRE

Harrisburg Pike & Route 30
Lancaster, PA 17608
Mailing Address: PO Box 1553
Phone: 717-295-7054
Fax: 717-290-7123
Web Site: www.longspark.org
Management:
Music Director: Stella Reno
Operations Manager: Carol Barton
Income Sources: Donations; Sponsorships
Seating Capacity: 30,000

7721
WEIS CENTER FOR THE PERFORMING ARTS

Bucknell University
Lewisburg, PA 17837-2005
Phone: 570-577-3700
Fax: 570-577-3701
e-mail: boswell@bucknell.edu
Web Site: http://www.departments.bucknell.edu
Management:
Director Cultural Events: William Boswell
Mission: To provide the campus and region with opportunity for exposure to the essential cultural and educational values inherent in the great historical and radical traditions of the performing arts.
Founded: 1846
Budget: $150,000-400,000
Affiliations: APAP, CMA, PA Presenters, Others
Annual Attendance: 9000
Facility Category: Concert Hall
Type of Stage: Sprung Wood Floor
Seating Capacity: 1,200+
Year Built: 1988

7722
SHAFER AUDITORIUM

Allegheny College
Box H
Meadville, PA 16335
Phone: 814-332-2754
Web Site: www.allegheny.edu
Management:
Director Student Activities: Ellen Kauffman
Seating Capacity: 1,750

7723
MILLBROOK PLAYHOUSE

Country Club Lane
PO Box 161
Mill Hall, PA 17751
Phone: 570-748-8083
Web Site: www.millbrookplayhouse.org
Management:
President: Paul Walison
Founded: 1952
Status: Non-Profit
Season: May - August

7724
LACKAWANNA COUNTY STADIUM

235 Montage Mountain Road
Moosic, PA 18507
Phone: 570-969-2255
Fax: 570-963-6564
Web Site: www.redbarons.com
Management:
General Manager: Tom Vanschaak
Founded: 1989
Status: Non-Profit, Professional

Paid Staff: 200
Seating Capacity: 10,800

7725
POCONO PLAYHOUSE

Playhouse Lane
Mountainhome, PA 18342
Phone: 570-595-7456
Fax: 570-595-7465

7726
BUCKS COUNTY PLAYHOUSE

70 S Main
PO Box 313
New Hope, PA 18938
Phone: 215-862-2041
Fax: 215-862-0220
e-mail: mail@buckscountyplayhouse.com
Web Site: www.buckscountyplayhouse.com
Management:
President: Ralph Miller
Founded: 1938
Status: Professional

7727
BEEGHLY THEATER

Westminster College
New Wilmington, PA 16172
Phone: 724-946-8761

7728
WILL W ORR AUDITORIUM

Westminster College
Market Street
New Wilmington, PA 16172
Phone: 724-946-7270
Fax: 724-946-6270
Web Site: www.westminster.edu/music
Management:
President: Thomas Williamson
Artistic Director: Nancy Desalvo
Status: Non-Profit, Professional
Paid Staff: 200
Paid Artists: 50

7729
ACADEMY OF MUSIC: MAIN AUDITORIUM

Broad and Locust Streets
Philadelphia, PA 19102
Phone: 215-893-1935
Fax: 215-545-4588

7730
ANNENBERG CENTER

University of Pennsylvania
3680 Walnut Street
Philadelphia, PA 19104
Phone: 212-898-6702
Fax: 215-573-9568
e-mail: mjrose@pobox.upenn.edu
Web Site: www.annenbergcenter.org
Management:
Managing Director: Dr. Michael J Rose
Facilities/Events Manager: Marie Gallagher
Founded: 1971
Seating Capacity: 2,500

7731
CURTIS INSTITUTE OF MUSIC

1726 Locust Street
Philadelphia, PA 19103

Phone: 215-893-5252
Fax: 215-893-9065
Web Site: www.curtis.edu
Founded: 1924
Specialized Field: classical music conservatory
Status: Non-Profit,Professional

7732
ESTHER BOYER PERFORMING ARTS CENTER
Temple University
Philadelphia, PA 19122
Phone: 215-204-8301
Fax: 215-204-4957
Officers:
Associate Dean: Steven Kreinberg

7733
FORREST THEATRE
1114 Walnut Street
Philadelphia, PA 19107
Phone: 215-923-1515
Web Site: www.forrest-theatre.com
Management:
President: Philip Smith
Managing Director: Mark Schweppe
Founded: 1928
Specialized Field: Broadways Production
Status: For-Profit, Professional

7734
FRANKLIN FIELD
University of Pennsylvania
235 South 33rd Street
Philadelphia, PA 19104
Phone: 215-898-9231
Fax: 215-573-2161
e-mail: kowalski@pobox.upenn.edu
Web Site: www.pennathletics.com
Management:
Director: Dave Bryan
Associate Director: Peggy Kowalski
Specialized Field: Home of University of Pennsylvania athletics (NCAA); Site of the Penn Relays; one of the largest track and field events in the country.
Seating Capacity: 52,593
Year Built: 1996

7735
IRVINE AUDITORIUM
University of Pennsylvania
3401 Spruce Street
Philadelphia, PA 19104
Phone: 215-573-4638
Fax: 215-898-2143
Web Site: www.upenn.edu
Management:
Event Coordinator: Laura Carney
Seating Capacity: 1,246

7736
KIMMEL CENTER FOR THE PERFORMING ARTS
260 S Broad Street
Suite 901
Philadelphia, PA 19102
Phone: 215-790-5800
Fax: 215-790-5801
Web Site: www.kimmelcenter.org
Management:
VP Programming/Education: Mervon Mehta
VP Theatrical Presentations: Jordan Fiksenbaum

Mission: The Regional Performing Arts Center manages The Kimmel Center for the Performing Arts Academy of Music in Philadelphia, and presents a wide variety of programming including jazz, dance, theatre, classical and world music.
Founded: 2001
Specialized Field: Facility/Presenter
Status: Non-Profit, Professional
Paid Staff: 350

7737
MANN CENTER FOR THE PERFORMING ARTS
5201 Parkside Avenue
Suite 1930
Philadelphia, PA 19131
Phone: 215-546-7900
Fax: 215-546-9524
e-mail: info@manncenter.org
Web Site: www.manncenter.org
Management:
President: Peter B Lane
General Manager: Jerry W Gralbey
Director Marketing: Rosie Vergilio
Director Development: Nancy Newman
Founded: 1925
Specialized Field: Presenter; venue address; 52nd and Parkside
Status: Nonprofit
Paid Staff: 7
Budget: $4.2 Million
Income Sources: Ticket sales, grants, sponsorships
Annual Attendance: 275,000
Facility Category: Amphitheatre
Type of Stage: Proscenium
Stage Dimensions: 263 x 200 x 107
Year Remodeled: 1975
Rental Contact: Director Marketing & Dprogramming Rosie Vergilio

7738
MCCARTHY STADIUM
Lasalle University
1900 W Oleny Avenue
Philadelphia, PA 19141-1199
Phone: 215-951-1694
Fax: 215-951-1694
e-mail: athletics@lasalle.edu
Web Site: www.lasalle.edu
Management:
Director Athletics: Tom Brennan
Seating Capacity: 7,500

7739
MERRIAM THEATER
250 S Broad Street
Philadelphia, PA 19102
Phone: 215-732-5446
Fax: 215-732-1396
Toll-free: 888-451-5761
Web Site: www.broadwayseries.com
Management:
General Manager: DeVida Jenkins
Marketing Director: Collie Andrew
Utilizes: Dance Companies; Multimedia; Special Technical Talent; Theatre Companies
Founded: 1987
Paid Staff: 35
Income Sources: Ticket Sales
Performs At: Procenium Theater
Annual Attendance: 301,847
Facility Category: Road House
Type of Stage: Proscenium
Stage Dimensions: 45'x25',44'x85'

Seating Capacity: 1870
Year Built: 1910
Year Remodeled: 1986
Rental Contact: General Manager DeVida Jenkins

7740
PAINTED BRIDE ART CENTER
230 Vine Street
Philadelphia, PA 19106
Phone: 215-925-9914
Fax: 215-925-7402
Web Site: www.paintedbride.org
Management:
Executive Director: Laurel Raczka
Managing Director: Lisa Nelson
Director Programs: Ellen Rosenholtz
Mission: The Painted Bride Art Center works with artists to create and present programs that affirm the intrinsic values of all cultures, the inspirational and healing powers of the arts, and their ability to effect social change.
Founded: 1969
Specialized Field: Multi-Disciplinary
Status: Non-Profit, Professional
Paid Staff: 15
Paid Artists: 20

7741
SOCIETY HILL PLAYHOUSE
507 S 8th Street
Philadelphia, PA 19147
Phone: 215-923-0210
Fax: 215-923-1789
e-mail: shp@erols.com
Web Site: www.societyhillplayhouse.com
Management:
Director: Deen Kogan
Mission: To present works of the finest contemporary American and European writers.
Founded: 1959
Opened: 1959
Specialized Field: New American Works; Classic; International
Status: Professional; Non-Profit
Performs At: Society Hill Playhouse
Affiliations: Theatre Communications Group; American Arts Alliance; Theatre Alliance
Annual Attendance: 100,000
Type of Stage: Proscenium; Black Box
Seating Capacity: 250; 99
Year Built: 1900
Year Remodeled: 1979
Rental Contact: Lee Vaughn

7742
THE PALESTRA
University of Pennsylvania
233 South 33rd Street
Philadelphia, PA 19104
Phone: 215-898-6121
Fax: 215-898-6117
Web Site: www.upenn.edu/athletics
Management:
Athletic Director: Steve Bilsky
Seating Capacity: 8,700

7743
VETERANS STADIUM
3501 S Broad Street
Philadelphia, PA 19148
Phone: 215-463-2500
Fax: 215-393-5464
Management:
Director Sales: Rory McNeil

Ogden Entertainment Services: Brian Hastings
VP/Sales: Vic Gregovitz
Director Penthouse Operations: Christy Noyalas
Seating Capacity: 62,382

7744
WACHOVIA SPECTRUM
3601 S Broad Street
Philadelphia, PA 19148
Phone: 215-336-3600
Fax: 215-389-9506
Web Site: www.spectacor.com
Management:
    President: Peter Luukko
    VP Marketingducer: Bob Schwartz
Founded: 1967
Status: For-Profit, Professional
Paid Staff: 750
Paid Artists: 65
Seating Capacity: 18,000
Year Built: 1965

7745
WALNUT STREET THEATRE
825 Walnut
Philadelphia, PA 19107
Phone: 215-574-3550
Fax: 215-574-3598
Web Site: www.wstonline.org

7746
WALNUT STREET THEATRE: MAINSTAGE
825 Walnut
Philadelphia, PA 19107
Phone: 215-574-3550
Fax: 215-574-3598
Web Site: www.wstonline.org

7747
WALNUT STREET THEATRE: STUDIO 3
825 Walnut
Philadelphia, PA 19107
Phone: 215-574-3550
Fax: 215-574-3598
Web Site: www.wstonline.org

7748
WALNUT STREET THEATRE: STUDIO 5
825 Walnut
Philadelphia, PA 19107
Phone: 215-574-3550
Fax: 215-574-3598
Web Site: www.wstonline.org

7749
A.J. PALUMBO CENTER
Duquesne University
1304 Forbes Avenue
Pittsburgh, PA 15282
Phone: 412-396-5140
Fax: 412-396-5855
Web Site: www.duq.edu
Management:
    Executive Director: David DiPetro
    Associate Director: Scott Richards
Seating Capacity: 6,200

7750
BENEDUM CENTER
803 Liberty Avenue
Pittsburgh, PA 15222

Phone: 412-471-6070
Fax: 412-471-6917
e-mail: ciavarra@pgharts.org
Web Site: www.pgharts.org
Management:
    President: Kevin McMahon
    Executive Director: Jude Rau
    Programming Director: Fran Egler
Utilizes: Guild Activities; Selected Students; Touring Companies
Founded: 1981
Specialized Field: Performing Arts
Status: Non-Profit, Professional
Paid Staff: 18
Volunteer Staff: 550
Facility Category: Proscenium theater
Type of Stage: FIR
Stage Dimensions: 75x142
Seating Capacity: 2,889
Year Built: 1927
Year Remodeled: 1987
Cost: $42 million
Rental Contact: Gene Ciavarra

7751
CARNEGIE: LECTURE HALL
4400 Forbes Avenue
Pittsburgh, PA 15213
Phone: 412-622-6274
Fax: 412-622-1923
Web Site: www.carnegielibrary.org
Management:
    President: Susan Brladhust
    Executive Director: Herd Lish
Founded: 1895
Status: Non-Profit, Non-Professional

7752
CARNEGIE: MUSEUM OF ART THEATRE
4400 Forbes Avenue
Pittsburgh, PA 15213
Phone: 412-622-3360
Fax: 412-688-8664
Web Site: www.carnegiemuseum.org
Founded: 1895
Status: Non-Profit, Non-Professional

7753
CARNEGIE: MUSIC HALL
4400 Forbes Avenue
Pittsburgh, PA 15213
Phone: 412-622-3360
Fax: 412-688-8664

7754
FITZGERALD FIELDHOUSE
University of Pittsburgh
Pittsburgh, PA 15213
Phone: 412-648-8200
Fax: 412-648-8306
Management:
    Athletic Director: Steve Pederson

7755
HEINZ HALL FOR THE PERFORMING ARTS
600 Penn Avenue
Pittsburgh, PA 15222
Phone: 412-392-4900
Fax: 412-392-4909
Web Site: www.pittsburghsymphony.org
Management:
    President: Lawrence Tamburri
Founded: 1927

Status: Non-Profit, Professional

7756
MANCHESTER CRAFTSMEN'S GUILD
1815 Metropolitan Street
Pittsburgh, PA 15233
Phone: 412-322-1773
Fax: 412-322-1075
e-mail: experiencemcg@mcg-btc.org
Web Site: www.mcgjazz.org
Management:
    President: William E Strickland Jr
    EVP: Jesse Fefe
    Artistic Director: Marty Ashby
    Associate Producer: Renee Govanucci
Founded: 1986
Status: Non-Profit, Professional
Paid Staff: 100

7757
MELLON ARENA
300 Auditorium Place
Pittsburgh, PA 15219
Phone: 412-642-2062
Fax: 412-562-9913
Web Site: www.civiccenter.com
Management:
    Directir: Rich Engler
Seating Capacity: 18,000

7758
PITT STADIUM
University of Pittsburgh
PO Box 7436
Pittsburgh, PA 15213-0436
Phone: 412-648-8200
Fax: 412-648-8306
Management:
    Athletic Director: Steve Pederson
    Excutive Athletic Director: Marc Boehm
    Senior Associate Athletic Director: Carol Sprague
    Associate Athletics for Business: Jim Earle
Seating Capacity: 56,500

7759
PITTSBURGH CIVIC ARENA
Gate Number 9
66 Mario Lemieux Place
Pittsburgh, PA 15219
Phone: 412-642-1800
Fax: 412-642-1925
Web Site: www.civicarena.com
Management:
    General Manager: Hank Abate
    Director Operations: Jay Roberts
    Comcessions Manager: Rob Sunday
Seating Capacity: 17,500

7760
PNC PARK
115 Federal Street
Pittsburgh, PA 15212
Phone: 412-323-5000
Fax: 412-323-5009
Toll-free: 800-289-2827
Web Site: www.pirateball.com
Management:
    President: Kevin McClatchy
Founded: 1887
Paid Staff: 75
Seating Capacity: 38,127

7761

RAJAH THEATRE

136 North Sixth Street
Reading, PA 19601
Phone: 610-371-8820
Fax: 610-371-8691

7762

SOVEREIGN CENTER

700 Penn Street
Reading, PA 19602
Phone: 610-898-7210
Fax: 610-898-1141
Web Site: www.sovereigncenter.com
Management:
   GM: Robert Cavalieri
   Marketing Director: Dolly Vogt
Seating Capacity: 9,146

7763

SCRANTON CULTURAL CENTER AT THE MASONIC TEMPLE

420 North Washington Avenue
Scranton, PA 18503
Phone: 570-346-7369
Fax: 570-346-7365
e-mail: info@scrantonculturalcenter.org
Web Site: www.scrantonculturalcenter.org
Management:
   Executive Director: Jo Ann Fremiotti
   Facilities/Technical Director: John Cardoni
Utilizes: AEA Actors; Artists-in-Residence;
Collaborating Artists; Dancers; Designers; Filmmakers;
Five Seasonal Concerts; Guest Accompanists; Guest
Choreographers; Guest Directors; Guest Ensembles;
Guest Musical Directors; Guest Soloists; High School
Drama; Instructors; Local Artists; Multimedia; New
Productions; Original Music Scores; Performance
Artists; Resident Professionals; Selected Students; Sign
Language Translators; Soloists; Student Interns;
Special Technical Talent; Theatre Companies
Founded: 1996
Specialized Field: Mid Atlantic
Status: Non-Profit, Professional
Paid Staff: 12
Volunteer Staff: 100
Paid Artists: 50
Annual Attendance: 140,000+
Facility Category: Theatre
Type of Stage: Proscenium
Stage Dimensions: 48x32x64
Seating Capacity: 1,866
Year Built: 1927

7764

LAUREL ARTS/THE PHILIP DRESSLER CENTER

214 S Harrison Avenue
PO Box 414
Somerset, PA 15501-0414
Phone: 814-443-2433
Fax: 814-443-3870
e-mail: arts@laurelarts.org
Web Site: www.laurelarts.org
Officers:
   Board of Directors: Hank Parke
Management:
   President: Hank Parke
Founded: 1976
Status: Non-Profit, Non-Professional
Paid Staff: 14

7765

BEAVER STADIUM

Penn State University
100 University Drive
University Park, PA 15061-2799
Phone: 724-773-3500
Fax: 814-863-8569
Toll-free: 877-564-6778
Web Site: www.psu.edu
Management:
   President: Michelle Kramer-Fitzgerald
Specialized Field: Home Of Penn State University
Athletics.

7766

BRYCE JORDAN CENTER

127 Bryce Jordan Center
University Park, PA 16802
Phone: 814-865-5555
Fax: 814-863-1820
Toll-free: 800-863-3336
e-mail: jordancenter@psu.edu
Web Site: www.bjc.psu.edu
Management:
   President: Graham Stanier
   Executive Director: Bob Howard
Founded: 1996
Specialized Field: Music

7767

EISENHOWER AUDITORIUM

Pennsylvania State University
University Park, PA 16802
Phone: 814-863-0388
Fax: 814-865-4365
Web Site: www.cpa.psu.edu
Officers:
   Director: George Trudeau
Management:
   Calendar Coordinator: Lisa Faust
   Marketing Director: Laura Sullivan
   Assistant Director: Lea Asbell-Swanger
Founded: 1974
Status: Non-Profit, Professional
Paid Staff: 135
Volunteer Staff: 150
Facility Category: Auditorium (Continental Seating)
Seating Capacity: 2,500
Year Built: 1974

7768

PENNSYLVANIA CENTRE STAGE

106 Arts Building
University Park, PA 16802
Phone: 814-863-0381
Fax: 814-863-7327
Season: June - August

7769

FARREL STADIUM

West Chester University
West Chester, PA 19383
Phone: 610-436-3463
Fax: 610-436-2171
e-mail: jberkowitz@wcupa.edu
Web Site: www.wcupa.edu
Management:
   President: Madeleine Edler
Status: Non-Profit, Professional
Paid Staff: 1

7770

DOROTHY DICKSON DARTE CENTER

Wilkes University
South Street
Wilkes-Barre, PA 18766
Phone: 717-824-4651
Fax: 717-408-7842

7771

FM KIRBY CENTER FOR THE PERFORMING ARTS

71 Public Square
Wilkes-Barre, PA 18701
Mailing Address: PO Box 486, Wilkes-Barre, PA.
18703
Phone: 570-823-4599
Fax: 570-823-4890
Web Site: www.kirbycenter.org
Officers:
   Board Chairman: Robert Cioruttoli
   Vice Chairman: Denise Ceasare
   Treasurer: Dr. Wallace Steitler
Management:
   Executive Director: Marilyn Santarelli
   Program Manager: Mark Thomas
   Technical Director: Fran McMullen
   Director Operations: Brew Taylor
Mission: To promote and present the performing arts in
our region.
Founded: 1986
Status: Non-Profit, Professional
Paid Staff: 15
Budget: $400,000-$1,000,000
Performs At: Film, concerts, broadway
Type of Stage: Proscenium
Stage Dimensions: 47'3" x 30' x 30' deep30'
Seating Capacity: 1800
Year Built: 1936
Year Remodeled: 1986
Rental Contact: Director of Operations John Domzalski

7772

STRAND-CAPITOL PERFORMING ARTS CENTER

50 N George Street
York, PA 17401
Phone: 717-846-1155
Fax: 717-843-1208
e-mail: boxoffice@strandcapitol.org
Web Site: www.strandcapitol.org
Management:
   President: Maureen Shallcross
Status: Non-Profit, Professional
Paid Staff: 20

Rhode Island

7773

RYAN CENTER

1 Lincoln Almond Plaza
Kingston, RI 02881
Phone: 401-788-3220
Fax: 401-788-3210
e-mail: info@theryancenter.com
Web Site: www.theryancenter.com
Management:
   GM: Terry Butler
   Facilities Director: James Hathaway
Seating Capacity: 7,700

7774

UNIVERSITY OF RHODE ISLAND FINE ARTS CENTER

105 Upper College Road
Fine Arts Center
Kingston, RI 02881
Phone: 401-874-5921
Fax: 401-874-5618
Management:
Chairman: Paula McGlasson
Administrative Assistant: Bonnie Bosworth
Founded: 1950
Paid Staff: 4
Volunteer Staff: 20
Paid Artists: 10
Non-paid Artists: 10
Type of Stage: Proscenium; Black Box
Rental Contact: Bonnie Besworth

7775

NEWPORT YACHTING CENTER

America's Cup Avenue
Newport, RI 02840
Mailing Address: PO Box 550
Phone: 401-846-1600
Fax: 401-847-7754
e-mail: gm@newportyachtingcenter.com
Web Site: www.newportfestivals.com
Management:
GM: Chris Perrotti
Director Sales/Marketing: Gail Alofsin
Seating Capacity: 2,000

7776

AS220

115 Empire Street
Providence, RI 02903
Phone: 401-831-9327
Fax: 401-454-7445
e-mail: info@as220.org
Web Site: www.as220.org
Management:
Artistic Director: Umberto Crenca
Managing Director: Shawn Wallace
Founded: 1984
Status: Non-Profit
Paid Staff: 25

7777

BROWN STADIUM

235 Hope Street
Providence, RI 02912
Phone: 401-863-2295
Fax: 401-863-1436
Management:
Athletic Director: David Roach

7778

PERISHABLE THEATRE

95 Empire Street
PO Box 23132
Providence, RI 02903
Phone: 401-331-2695
Fax: 401-331-7811
e-mail: info@perishable.org
Web Site: www.perishable.org
Management:
Artistic Director: Mark Lerman
Managing Director: Carol Drowne
PR Director: Marya Jones
PR Director: Marilyn Dubois

Mission: Perishable Theatre brings together artists from all media and provides them with the opportunity to perform and develop their craft. The theatre offers a mainstage season of new plays, a theatre arts school, and touring children's theatre.
Utilizes: Actors; AEA Actors; Artists-in-Residence; Choreographers; Collaborating Artists; Collaborations; Commissioned Composers; Dancers; Designers; Educators; Five Seasonal Concerts; Guest Artists; Guest Choreographers; Guest Companies; Guest Conductors; Guest Designers; Guest Directors; Guest Ensembles; High School Drama; Instructors; Local Artists; Lyricists; Multi Collaborations; Music; Original Music Scores; Performance Artists; Poets; Resident Professionals; Selected Students; Sign Language Translators; Soloists; Student Interns; Special Technical Talent; Theatre Companies; Visual Arts
Founded: 1982
Status: Non-Profit, Professional
Paid Staff: 5
Volunteer Staff: 4
Paid Artists: 20
Budget: $500,000
Performs At: Theatre Arts Center
Affiliations: TCG
Annual Attendance: 3,000
Facility Category: Performing Arts Center
Type of Stage: Black Box
Seating Capacity: 75

7779

PROVIDENCE DUNKIN DONUTS CENTER

1 Lasalle Square
Providence, RI 02903
Phone: 401-331-0700
Fax: 401-751-6792
e-mail: dtolselli@dunkindonutscenter.com
Web Site: www.dunkindonutscenter.com
Management:
Executive Director: Larry Lapore
Ceo: Ed Anderson
Status: Non-profit, Professional
Seating Capacity: 14,500

7780

PROVIDENCE PERFORMING ARTS CENTER

220 Weybosset Street
Providence, RI 02903
Phone: 401-421-2997
Fax: 401-421-5767
e-mail: info@ppacri.org
Web Site: www.ppacri.org
Officers:
President: JL Singleton
Technical Director: William Darckett
General Manager: Alan Chille
Specialized Field: Touring Broadway; Concerts; Film
Status: Non-Profit, Professional
Paid Staff: 50

7781

TRINITY ARTS CENTER

55 Locust Street
Providence, RI 02906
Phone: 401-272-1595

7782

VETERANS MEMORIAL AUDITORIUM

Brownell Street and Park Streets
Providence, RI 02903
Phone: 401-831-3123
Fax: 401-277-1466
Web Site: www.tickets.com

Management:
President: Terriann Greenwood
Founded: 1950
Status: Non-Profit, Non-Professional
Paid Staff: 6

7783

STADIUM THEATRE PERFORMING ARTS CENTER

28 Monument Square
PO Box 665
Woonsocket, RI 02895
Phone: 401-762-4545
Fax: 401-765-4949
e-mail: info@stadiumtheatre.com
Web Site: www.stadiumtheatre.com
Officers:
Marketing Director: Jeffrey Polucha
President: Robert P Picards
Events Chairman/First VP: Jean Rondeau
Second VP: Joan Gahan
Secretary: Donna Palreiro
Management:
President: Bob Picard
Executive Director: Adell Marchbank
Managing Director: Anne Choquette
Utilizes: Actors; Community Talent; Contract Orchestras; Educators; Filmmakers; Guest Accompanists; Guest Companies; Guest Musical Directors; Guest Musicians; Guest Soloists; Instructors; Multimedia; Original Music Scores; Performance Artists; Resident Artists; Sign Language Translators; Singers; Special Technical Talent; Theatre Companies
Founded: 1996
Specialized Field: Performing Arts
Status: Non-Profit, Professional
Paid Staff: 2
Volunteer Staff: 200
Income Sources: Rentals; Donations; Grants; Box Office
Performs At: Live theatre, classic films, local & national entertainment
Affiliations: Encore Repertory Company
Annual Attendance: 60,000-100,000
Facility Category: Performing arts center
Seating Capacity: 1100
Year Built: 1926
Year Remodeled: 2000
Cost: $2.5 Million
Rental Contact: Jean Rondeau
Resident Groups: Encore Reportory Company

South Carolina

7784

ABBEVILLE OPERA HOUSE

Court Square
PO Box 247
Abbeville, SC 29620
Phone: 864-366-2157
Fax: 803-459-9266
e-mail: operahouse@wctel.net
Management:
President: Shirley Emven
Managing Director: Kathy Genevie
Founded: 1908
Status: Non-Profit, Non-Professional
Paid Staff: 3

7785

ANDERSON SPORTS CENTER

3027 Mall Road
Anderson, SC 29625

Phone: 864-260-4800
Fax: 864-260-4847
e-mail: asec@andersoncountysc.org
Web Site: www.andersonevents.com
Management:
    Director: Charles Wyatt
    Assistant Manager: Dan Brawley
Seating Capacity: 15,000

7786
FINE ARTS CENTER OF KERSHAW COUNTY
PO Box 1498
Camden, SC 29020
Phone: 803-425-7676
Fax: 803-425-7679
Web Site: www.fineartscenter.org
Management:
    President: Edwin Kohn
    Executive Director: Susan Duplessis
    Artistic Director: Steve Levan
    Managing Director: Diane Edward
Founded: 1974
Status: Non-Profit, Non-Professional
Paid Staff: 5
Paid Artists: 40

7787
DOCK STREET THEATRE
135 Church Street
Charleston, SC 29401
Phone: 843-720-3968
Fax: 843-720-3967

7788
FOOTLIGHT PLAYERS THEATRE
20 Queen Street
PO Box 62
Charleston, SC 29401
Phone: 843-722-7521
Fax: 843-722-3777
e-mail: footlightplayers@aol.com
Web Site: www.footlightplayers.net
Officers:
    President: Christy Loftin
    Vice President: Tracey Todd
    Business Manager: Gail Pike
Founded: 1931
Specialized Field: Theatre
Status: Non-Profit, Non-Professional
Paid Staff: 2

7789
GAILLARD MUNICIPAL AUDITORIUM
77 Calhoun Street
Charleston, SC 29403
Phone: 843-577-7400
Fax: 843-724-7389
Web Site: www.ci.charleston.sc.us
Management:
    Executive Director: Cam Patterson
Founded: 1969
Status: For-Profit, Non-Professional
Paid Staff: 17

7790
JOHNSON HAGOOD STADIUM
The Citadel Athletic Department
171 Moultrie Street
Charleston, SC 29409
Phone: 843-953-5030
Fax: 843-953-6727
Web Site: www.citadel.edu
Management:

President: John Granold
Executive Director: Ray Whiteman
Artistic Director: Robbie Bennet
Athletic Director: Les Robinson
Founded: 1842
Status: Non-Profit, Non-Professional
Seating Capacity: 22,500

7791
MCALISTER FIELDHOUSE
The Citadel Athletic Department
171 Moultrie Street
Charleston, SC 29409
Phone: 843-536-5030
Fax: 843-953-6727
Web Site: www.thecitadel.edu
Management:
    Associate Athletic Director: Robert Bennett
Seating Capacity: 6,000

7792
BROOKS CENTER FOR THE PERFORMING ARTS
Clemson University
Box 340526
Clemson, SC 29634-0526
Phone: 864-656-3043
Fax: 864-656-1013
e-mail: harderl@clemson.edu
Web Site: www.clemson.edu/Brooks
Management:
    Director: Lillian U Harder

7793
CLEMSON MEMORIAL STADIUM
Clemson University
602 University Union
Clemson, SC 29634
Mailing Address: PO Box 344056
Phone: 864-656-5827
Fax: 864-656-1858
e-mail: mkern@clemson.edu
Web Site: www.clemson.edu
Management:
    Director: Marty Kern
Mission: Successfully produce area shows with capacity of 20,000-70,000

7794
LITTLEJOHN COLISEUM
Clemson University
Jarvey Athletic Center
Clemson, SC 29633
Mailing Address: PO Box 31
Phone: 864-646-1935
Fax: 864-646-0299
Management:
    Director Programs/Services: Michael Arnold
Seating Capacity: 10,820

7795
TILLMAN AUDITORIUM
Clemson University
210 Hendrix Student Center
Clemson, SC 29364-4056
Phone: 864-656-6676
Fax: 864-656-1414
e-mail: mkern@clemson.edu
Web Site: www.clemsonmajorevents.com
Management:
    Director Major Events: Marty S Kern
    Marketing Director: Tina LeMay
Seating Capacity: 800

7796
CAPITOL CITY STADIUM
301 South Assemble Street
Columbia, SC 29201
Phone: 803-256-4110
Fax: 803-256-4338
Web Site: www.bomberball.com
Management:
    GM: Tim Swain
    Ticketing Director: Luis Gonzalez
Seating Capacity: 10,000

7797
CAROLINA COLISEUM
University of South Carolina
701 Assembly Street
Columbia, SC 29201
Phone: 803-777-5113
Fax: 803-777-5114
Web Site: www.coliseum.sc.edu
Management:
    Director: John Bolin
    Business Manager: Dick Marks
Specialized Field: Home to USC basketball.
Seating Capacity: 12,500
Year Built: 1969

7798
DRAYTON HALL
University of South Carolina
Green and Sumter Streets
Columbia, SC 29208
Phone: 803-777-4288
Fax: 803-777-6669
Web Site: www.cla.sc.edu/thea
Management:
    President: Andrew Sorensen
    Chairman: Jim Hunter
Status: Non-Profit, Non-Professional

7799
KOGER CENTER FOR THE ARTS
University of South Carolina
Columbia, SC 29208
Phone: 803-777-7500
Fax: 803-777-5774

7800
LONGSTREET THEATRE
University of South Carolina
Green and Sumter Streets
Columbia, SC 29208
Phone: 803-777-4288

7801
WILLIAMS-BRICE STADIUM
University of South Carolina
701 Assembly Street
Columbia, SC 29201
Phone: 704-223-8193
Fax: 704-233-8170
Web Site: www.wingate.edu
Management:
    Head Basketball Coach (W): Johnny Jacumin
    Managing Director/CEO: John C Bondi
    Director Marketing: Connie O Scrivens
    Athletic Director: Beth Lawrence
    Sports Information Director: David Sherwood
    Head Football Coach: Doug Malone
    Head Basketball Coach (M): Jeff Reynolds
Seating Capacity: 72,000

7802
FLORENCE CIVIC CENTER
3300 W Radio Drive
Florence, SC 29501-7802
Phone: 843-679-9417
Fax: 843-679-9429
e-mail: info@florenceciviccenter.com
Web Site: www.florenceciviccenter.com
Management:
   General Manager: Kendell Wall,
   kwall@florenceciviccenter.com
   Director Of Operations: Russell Infinger
   Director Sales/Marketing: Tina Dean,
   tdean@florenceciviccenter.com
   Director Sales/Marketing: Karen Johnson
Mission: The Florence Civic Center is the hub for entertainment, exhibitions & civic events for the Florence area. With over 50,000 square feet of multi-purpose space, the center can accomodate events of all shapes, types and sizes. The facility is also close to dozens of national chain hotels, and is located across the street from Florence's premier shopping plaza.
Opened: 1993
Specialized Field: Theatre Ballroom
Affiliations: Ticketmaster
Annual Attendance: 245,000
Facility Category: Adaptable to nearly any events needs
Seating Capacity: 1,400 - 10,000
Year Built: 1993
Year Remodeled: 2008
Rental Contact: Director Of Sales & Marketing Tina Dean

7803
CHARLOTTE KNIGHTS BASEBALL STADIUM
2280 Deerfield Drive
Ft. Hill, SC 29715
Phone: 803-548-8050
Fax: 803-548-8055
Web Site: www.charlotteknights.com
Management:
   President: Don Beaver
   Assistant General Manager/Facility: Jon Percival
Status: For-Profit, Professional
Paid Staff: 20
Seating Capacity: 10,000
Year Built: 1990

7804
BI-LO CENTER
650 N Academy Street
Greenville, SC 29601
Phone: 864-241-3800
Fax: 864-250-4939
Web Site: www.bilocenter.com
Management:
   Executive Director: Ed Rubenstein
   Director Operations: Steve Chastain
   Marketing Director: Jill Weninger
Founded: 1998
Specialized Field: Sports and entertainment arena in upstate South Carolina.
Status: For-Profit, Professional
Paid Staff: 100
Seating Capacity: 16,000
Year Built: 1998

7805
GREENVILLE MUNICIPAL STADIUM
One Braves Avenue
Greenville, SC 29607
Phone: 864-299-3456
Fax: 864-277-7369
Web Site: www.gbraves.com
Management:
   General Manager: Steve Desalvo

7806
MCALISTER AUDITORIUM
Furman University
3300 Poinsett Highway
Greenville, SC 29613
Phone: 864-294-2000
Fax: 864-294-3035
Web Site: www.furman.edu
Management:
   President: David E Shi
   VP: Tom Kazee
   Artistic Director: Bill Thomas
Founded: 1826
Specialized Field: vocal music
Status: Non-Profit, Professional
Paid Staff: 700
Paid Artists: 50

7807
PEACE CENTER FOR THE PERFORMING ARTS
101 W Broad Street
Greenville, SC 29601
Phone: 864-467-3030
Fax: 864-467-3040
Toll-free: 800-888-7768
e-mail: administration@peacecenter.org
Web Site: www.peacecenter.org
Officers:
   President: Megan Riegel
Mission: Providing a world-class home for Resident Companies
Founded: 1985
Specialized Field: Performing
Paid Staff: 130
Volunteer Staff: 57
Budget: $400,000
Income Sources: Board, Edowment, Patrons
Annual Attendance: 97,000
Facility Category: Performing Arts7
Type of Stage: Proscenium
Stage Dimensions: 34' x 58'
Seating Capacity: 2089
Year Built: 1985
Year Remodeled: 2002
Cost: 4 million
Rental Contact: Tom Bugg

7808
TIMMONS ARENA
Furman University
3300 Poinsett Highway
Greenville, SC 29613
Phone: 864-294-3267
Fax: 864-294-3269
e-mail: todd.duke@furman.edu
Web Site: www.timmonsarena.com
Management:
   GM: Mike Arnold
   Booking/Business Manager: Todd Duke
Seating Capacity: 5,000

7809
GREENWOOD CIVIC CENTER
PO Box 740
Greenwood, SC 29648
Phone: 864-942-8606
Fax: 864-942-8595
Management:
   Executive Director: Ron Plemmons
   Managing Director: Tracy Upton
Founded: 1978
Status: For-Profit, Non-Professional
Paid Staff: 7

7810
CENTER THEATER
212 N 5th Street
Hartsville, SC 29550
Phone: 843-332-5721
Management:
   Executive Director: Den Latham
Founded: 1936
Status: Non-Profit, Non-Professional
Paid Staff: 1

7811
THE PALACE THEATRE
1420 Celebrity Circle
Myrtle Beach, SC 29577
Phone: 843-448-9224
Fax: 843-626-9659
e-mail: admin@palacetheatremyrtlebeach.com
Web Site: www.palacetheatremyrtlebeach.com
Management:
   GM: Cynthia Sweeney
Founded: 1995
Seating Capacity: 2,638
Rental Contact: Cheryl Holowacz

7812
NEWBERRY OPERA HOUSE
1201 McKibben Street
Newberry, SC 29108
Phone: 803-276-5179
Fax: 803-276-9993
e-mail: debra@newberryoperahouse.com
Web Site: newberryoperahouse.com
Management:
   Executive Director: Debra Smith
   Technical Director: Jason Osborne
   Lighting Director: Denise Simpson- Osborne
Utilizes: Artists-in-Residence; Commissioned Composers; Dance Companies; Dancers; Five Seasonal Concerts; Grant Writers; Guest Accompanists; Guest Choreographers; Guest Composers; Guest Designers; Guest Musical Directors; Guest Musicians; Guest Writers; Instructors; Local Artists; Multimedia; Original Music Scores; Resident Professionals; Sign Language Translators; Singers; Soloists; Student Interns; Special Technical Talent; Theatre Companies
Founded: 1881
Status: Non-Profit
Budget: $400,000-1,000,000
Stage Dimensions: 29'x25'
Seating Capacity: 426
Year Built: 1881
Year Remodeled: 1996

7813
NORTH CHARLESTON PERFORMING ARTS CENTER
5001 Coliseum Drive
North Charleston, SC 29418

Phone: 843-529-5050
Fax: 843-529-5010
Web Site: www.coliseumpac.com
Officers:
   General Manager: Dave Holscher
Founded: 1993
Status: For-Profit, Non-Professional
Type of Stage: Proscenium
Seating Capacity: 2254
Year Built: 1999
Rental Contact: Dave Holscher

7814
OLIVER C DAWSON STADIUM
South Carolina State University
300 College Avenue
Orangeburg, SC 29115
Phone: 803-536-8998
Fax: 803-533-3661
Web Site: www.scsu.edu
Management:
   Athletics Director: Timothy Autry
Seating Capacity: 2,500

7815
JAMES F BYRNES AUDITORIUM
Winthrop College
129 Conservatory
Rock Hill, SC 29733
Phone: 803-323-2255
Fax: 803-323-2343
e-mail: rogersd@winthrop.edu
Web Site: www.winthrop.edu/music
Management:
   Chairman of the Department: Donald Rogers
Status: Non-Profit, Non-Professional
Paid Staff: 30
Paid Artists: 2

7816
SPARTANBURG MEMORIAL AUDITORIUM: THEATRE
385 N Church Street
Po Box 1410
Spartanburg, SC 29304
Phone: 803-582-8107
Fax: 803-583-9850

7817
SPARTANBURG MEMORIAL AUDITORIUM: ARENA
385 North Church Road
PO Box 1410
Spartanburg, SC 29304
Phone: 803-582-8107
Fax: 803-583-9850

7818
SUMTER COUNTY CULTURAL CENTER
135 Haynsworth
Sumter, SC 29150
Phone: 803-436-2260
Fax: 803-436-2258
e-mail: patriot_hall@sumtercountysc.org
Web Site: www.sumtercounty.org
Management:
   President: Anthony Coyne
   Managing Director: Martha Greenway
Founded: 1974
Status: For-Profit, Non-Professional
Paid Staff: 3
Paid Artists: 3
Income Sources: Sumter County Government

Facility Category: Auditorium
Type of Stage: Proscenium
Stage Dimensions: 47wx21hx26-38l
Seating Capacity: 1,013
Year Built: 1935
Year Remodeled: 1986
Cost: $4 million
Rental Contact: Martha Greenway

7819
MCCELVEY CENTER OF YORK
212 E Jefferson Street
York, SC 29745
Phone: 803-684-3948
Fax: 803-684-0230
e-mail: lifundbrburk@chmuseums.org
Web Site: www.chmuseums.org
Management:
   Executive Director: Mary Norton
   Managing Director: Liz Funderburk
Founded: 1988
Status: Non-Profit, Professional
Paid Staff: 2
Paid Artists: 12

South Dakota

7820
COUGHLIN ALUMNI STADIUM
16th Avenue and 11th Street
Brookings, SD 57007
Phone: 605-688-5625
Fax: 605-688-5999
Web Site: www.gojacks.com
Management:
   President: Peggy Miller
   Athletic Director: Fred Oien
Founded: 1881
Specialized Field: Engineering
Status: Non-Profit, Non-Professional

7821
SOUTH DAKOTA ART MUSEUM
PO Box 2250
Brookings, SD 57007
Phone: 605-688-5423
Fax: 605-688-4445

7822
SWIFTEL CENTER
824 32nd Avenue
Brookings, SD 57006
Phone: 605-692-7539
Fax: 605-697-6393
Web Site: www.swiftelcenter.com
Management:
   Executive Director: Tom Richter
   Sales/Marketing Manager: Jenny Hammrich
Seating Capacity: 7,000

7823
CORN PALACE
612 N Main Street
Mitchell, SD 57301
Phone: 605-995-8427
Fax: 605-995-8443
e-mail: mschilling@cornpalace.com
Web Site: www.cornpalace.com
Management:
   Director: Mark A Schilling
Founded: 1892
Opened: 1892
Status: Non-Profit, Professional

Paid Staff: 25
Volunteer Staff: 75
Paid Artists: 4
Budget: $1,809,000
Income Sources: Rentals; Commissions; Donations
Annual Attendance: 500,000
Stage Dimensions: 32x70
Seating Capacity: 3,148
Year Built: 1921
Year Remodeled: 1965
Rental Contact: Mark Schilling

7824
RUSHMORE PLAZA CIVIC CENTER
444 Mount Rushmore Road N
Rapid City, SD 57701
Phone: 605-394-4115
Fax: 605-394-4119
Toll-free: 800-468-6463
Web Site: www.gotmine.com
Management:
   Director Events: Jayne Kraemer
   General Manager: Brian Maliske
Founded: 1977
Status: For-Profit, Professional
Paid Staff: 300
Seating Capacity: 11,000

7825
SIOUX FALLS ARENA
Odgen Entertainment
1201 W Avenue N
Sioux Falls, SD 57104
Phone: 605-367-7288
Fax: 605-338-1463
Toll-free: 800-338-3177
e-mail: info@sfarena.com
Web Site: www.sfarena.com
Management:
   Executive Director: Russ Decurtins
   Assistant Director: Debra D Esche
Specialized Field: Concerts; sporting events; trade shows
Status: For-Profit, Professional
Paid Staff: 300
Seating Capacity: 8,000

7826
SIOUX FALLS COMMUNITY PLAYHOUSE
315 N Phillips
PO Box 600
Sioux Falls, SD 57101
Phone: 605-336-7418
Fax: 605-336-2243

7827
WASHINGTON PAVILION OF ARTS & SCIENCE
301 S Main Avenue
Sioux Falls, SD 57104
Mailing Address: PO Box 984, Sioux Falls, SD. 57101-0984
Phone: 605-367-7397
Fax: 605-367-7399
Toll-free: 877-927-4728
e-mail: info@washingtonpavilion.org
Web Site: www.washingtonpavilion.org
Officers:
   President: Larry Toll
Management:
   Director Marketing/Public Relations: Michelle Wellman
   Manager, Performing Arts Center: Regina Ruhberg

Mission: To educate, entertain and inspire community by making arts and science part of our lives.
Founded: 1999
Specialized Field: South Dakota; Northwest Iowa; Southwest Minnesota; Northeast Nebraska
Paid Staff: 85
Volunteer Staff: 200
Budget: $5 Million
Income Sources: Donors; Grants; Ticket Sales
Affiliations: APAP; AAM; ASTC; IAAM
Annual Attendance: 100,000
Facility Category: Theater, Science Center, Visual Arts Center
Type of Stage: Proscenium
Seating Capacity: 1,904
Year Built: 1999
Year Remodeled: 1999
Cost: $32 Million
Rental Contact: Regina Ruhberg

7828
DAKOTA DOME
University of South Dakota
414 East Clark
Vermillion, SD 57069
Phone: 605-677-5309
Fax: 605-677-5618
e-mail: urelate@usd.edu
Web Site: www.usd.edu
Officers:
VP: Royce Engstrom
Management:
Athletic Director: Kelly Higgins
Founded: 1862

7829
NATIONAL MUSIC MUSEUM
414 E Clark Street
Vermillion, SD 57069
Phone: 605-677-5306
Fax: 605-677-6995
e-mail: nmm@usd.edu
Web Site: www.nmmusd.org
Management:
Assistant to the Director: Barbara Stark
Director: Andre Larson
Mission: The NMM serves the people of South Dakota and the world as an international center for collecting and conserving musical instruments of all cultures and bringing people together to study, enjoy, and understand our diverse musical heritage.
Founded: 1973
Specialized Field: Musical instruments
Status: Non-Profit, Professional
Paid Staff: 12
Performs At: Concert Hall
Seating Capacity: 125

7830
SLAGLE AUDITORIUM
University of South Dakota
414 East Clark
Vermillion, SD 57069
Phone: 605-677-5481
Fax: 605-677-5988

7831
WARREN M LEE CENTER
University of South Dakota
414 East Clark
Vermillion, SD 57069
Phone: 605-677-5481
Fax: 605-677-5988

7832
VIKING HALL CIVIC CENTER
1100 Edgemont Avenue
Bristol, TN 37620
Phone: 423-764-4171
Fax: 423-765-3299
Web Site: www.vikinghall.com
Management:
Director: Terrie Smith
Box Office Manager: Sarah Buckles
Founded: 1981
Status: Non-Profit, Professional
Paid Staff: 100
Seating Capacity: 6,200

7833
ROLAND HAYES CONCERT HALL
University of Tennessee
615 McCallie Avenue/FAC #324
Chattanooga, TN 37403
Phone: 423-755-4269
Fax: 615-755-5249

7834
TIVOLI THEATRE
709 Broad Street
Chattanooga, TN 37402
Phone: 423-757-5457
Fax: 615-757-5326
Web Site: www.chattanooga/showplaces.gov
Management:
Manager: Wolly Robinson
Founded: 1921
Status: For-Profit, Non-Professional
Paid Staff: 15

7835
UTC MCKENZIE ARENA
University of Tennessee-Chattanooga
615 McCallie Avenue, Department 3403
Chattanooga, TN 37403
Phone: 423-425-4706
Fax: 423-425-4783
e-mail: ken-kapelinski@utc.edu
Web Site: www.utc.edu/utcarena
Management:
Director Arena: Ken Kapelinski
Assistant Director: Obie Webster
Founded: 1982
Paid Staff: 11
Volunteer Staff: 30
Budget: $.8 Million
Income Sources: Rental, Concessions, Services
Affiliations: University of Tennessee, Chatanooga
Annual Attendance: 240,000
Facility Category: Arena
Type of Stage: Flexible
Stage Dimensions: 64 x 48
Seating Capacity: 12,000
Year Built: 1982
Rental Contact: Ken Kapelinski

7836
APSU CONCERT HALL
Austin Peay State University
Center of Excellence for the Creative Arts
PO Box 4666
Clarksville, TN 37044

Phone: 931-221-7643
Fax: 931-221-7149
e-mail: burawac@apsu.edu
Web Site: www.apsu.edu/creativearts
Management:
Director: Christopher Burawa, burawac@apsu.edu
Mission: To inspire an appreciation of the creative arts with APSu students and the Clarksville community.
Utilizes: Artists-in-Residence; Choreographers; Collaborations; Commissioned Composers; Community Members; Composers; Curators; Dancers; Educators; Five Seasonal Concerts; Guest Accompanists; Guest Companies; Guest Directors; Guest Musicians; Guest Soloists; Guest Teachers; Instructors; Multimedia; Music; Organization Contracts; Paid Performers; Playwrights; Poets; Resident Companies; Sign Language Translators; Singers; Soloists; Students; Volunteer Directors & Actors; Writers
Founded: 1985
Facility Category: Concert Hall; Dance and Theatre Venue

7837
HOOPER EBLEN CENTER
Tennessee Tech University
Cookeville, TN 38505
Mailing Address: PO Box 5057
Phone: 931-372-3940
Fax: 931-372-3114
Management:
Athletic Director: David Larimore

7838
TULANE UNIVERSITY
Tennessee Tech University
PO Box 5057
Cookeville, TN 38505
Phone: 931-372-3940
Fax: 931-372-3114
Management:
Director: David Lorimore

7839
GATLINBURG CONVENTION CENTER
Historic Nature Trail
Gatlinburg, TN 37738
Phone: 865-436-2392
Fax: 865-436-3704
e-mail: debbieo@ci.gatlinburg.tn.us
Web Site: www.gatlinburg-tennessee.com
Management:
Director: Vickie Blake
Event Manager: Pattie Baker
Seating Capacity: 28,767

7840
TEX TURNER ARENA
Lincoln Memorial University
Highway 25 East
Harrogate, TN 37752
Phone: 423-869-6355
Fax: 423-869-6356
e-mail: lcarter@lmunet.edu
Web Site: www.lmutickets.com
Management:
Director Special Events: Larry Carter
Operations Director: Travis Moody
Seating Capacity: 5,500

7841
JACKSON CIVIC CENTER
400 South Highland Avenue
Jackson, TN 38301

Phone: 901-425-8580
Fax: 901-425-8385

7842

LAMBUTH THEATRE

Lambuth College
705 Lamburth Boulevard
Jackson, TN 38301
Phone: 901-425-2500
Fax: 901-423-3493

7843

AMAN ARENA

City of Jackson
179 Lane Avenue
Jackson, TN 38301
Phone: 901-425-8390
Fax: 701-425-8390
Web Site: www.cj.jacksoin.tn.us
Management:
    Manager: Martha A Pope
Seating Capacity: 5,612

7844

DERTHICK THEATRE

Milligan College
Johnson City, TN 37682
Mailing Address: PO Box 210
Phone: 423-461-8782
Fax: 423-461-8755

7845

FREEDOM HALL CIVIC CENTER

1320 Pactolas Road
Johnson City, TN 37604
Phone: 423-461-4855
Fax: 423-461-4867
e-mail: director@freedomhall-tn.com
Web Site: www.freedomhall-tn.com
Management:
    Director: Lisa Chamness
    Box Office Manager: Bobbie Shirley
Mission: To provide venue space for public assembly, cultural arts, sports and entertainment opportunities.
Founded: 1974
Status: For-Profit, Professional
Paid Staff: 6
Performs At: Arena
Affiliations: City Of Johnson City, TN
Annual Attendance: 150,000
Facility Category: Arena
Type of Stage: Wenger Portable
Seating Capacity: 7,500

7846

MINI DOME

E Tennessee State University
Johnson City, TN 37614
Phone: 423-439-4343
Fax: 423-439-5294
Management:
    Director: Bill Toohey
Seating Capacity: 16,000

7847

SEEGER CHAPEL CONCERT HALL

Milligan College
Johnson City, TN 37682
Mailing Address: PO Box 210
Phone: 423-461-8782
Fax: 423-461-8755

7848

BIJOU THEATRE

PO Box 1746
803 S Gay Street
Knoxville, TN 37901-1746
Phone: 865-522-0832
Fax: 865-522-0238
Toll-free: 800-738-0832
e-mail: info@knoxbijou.com
Web Site: www.knoxbijou.com
Management:
    Director: Beverly Snukals
Utilizes: Theatre Companies
Founded: 1984
Specialized Field: Theater
Paid Staff: 7
Volunteer Staff: 60
Paid Artists: 40
Budget: $35,000-60,000
Facility Category: Performing Arts
Type of Stage: Proscenium
Stage Dimensions: 35'x 51'
Seating Capacity: 750
Year Built: 1909
Year Remodeled: 1998

7849

BIJOU THEATRE CENTER

803 S Gay Street
Knoxville, TN 37901
Phone: 865-522-0832
Fax: 615-524-0821
Management:
    Producer: Laura Williams

7850

KNOXVILLE CIVIC AUDITORIUM AND COLISEUM-AUDITORIUM

500 East Howard Baker Jr Avenue
PO Box 37901
Knoxville, TN 37901
Phone: 865-215-8900
Fax: 865-215-8989
Web Site: www.knoxvillecoliseum.com
Management:
    Executive Director: Bob Polk
    Event Services Coordinator: Robbie Sandoval
    General Manager: Dale J Dunn
    Stage Manager: Chuck Ward
Utilizes: Actors; AEA Actors; Artists-in-Residence; Choreographers; Collaborating Artists; Commissioned Composers; Commissioned Music; Composers-in-Residence; Curators; Dance Companies; Dancers; Designers; Educators; Filmmakers; Fine Artists; Five Seasonal Concerts; Grant Writers; Guest Accompanists; Guest Artists; Guest Choreographers; Guest Companies; Guest Composers; Guest Conductors; Guest Designers; Guest Directors; Guest Ensembles; Guest Instructors; Guest Lecturers; Guest Musical Directors; Guest Musicians; Guest Soloists; Guest Teachers; Guest Writers; Guild Activities; High School Drama; Instructors; Local Artists; Local Unknown Artists; Lyricists; Multi Collaborations; Multimedia; Music; New Productions; Organization Contracts; Original Music Scores; Performance Artists; Playwrights; Resident Artists; Resident Professionals; Selected Students; Sign Language Translators; Singers; Soloists; Student Interns; Special Technical Talent; Theatre Companies; Touring Companies; Visual Arts
Founded: 1962
Status: Non-Profit, Professional
Paid Staff: 20

Facility Category: Auditorium and Arena
Stage Dimensions: Auditorium 57x57x27, Arena 60x40
Seating Capacity: Auditorium- 2,500 Arena- 6,000
Year Built: 1961
Year Remodeled: 1987
Rental Contact: Robbie Sandoval

7851

NEYLAND STADIUM

University of Tennessee
1600 Stadium Drive
Knoxville, TN 37996
Phone: 723-974-0953
Fax: 423-974-2800
Management:
    Manager: Tim Reese
    Associtae Director Athletics: Robert J Dobell
Seating Capacity: 103,000

7852

TENNESSEE THEATER

604 S Gay Street
Knoxville, TN 37902
Phone: 865-522-1174
Fax: 615-523-3954

7853

THOMPSON-BOLING ARENA

University of Tennessee
1600 Stadium Drive, Suite 202
Knoxville, TN 37996
Phone: 423-974-0953
Fax: 423-974-2800
Web Site: www.knoxvilletickets.com
Management:
    Manager: Timothy L Reese
Seating Capacity: 24,451

7854

UNIVERSITY OF TENNESSEE MUSIC HALL

1741 Volunteer Boulevard
Knoxville, TN 37996
Phone: 865-974-5110

7855

CUMBERLAND UNIVERSITY AUDITORIUM

1 Cumberland Square
Lebanon, TN 37087
Phone: 615-444-2562
Fax: 615-444-2569
Toll-free: 800-467-0562
Web Site: www.cumberland.edu
Management:
    President: Harvill Eaton
    Artistic Director: Steve Farnsley
Founded: 1842
Status: Non-Profit, Professional
Paid Staff: 30
Paid Artists: 10

7856

SKYHAWK ARENA

University of Tennessee-Martin
1020 Elam Center
Martin, TN 38238
Phone: 901-587-7745
Fax: 901-587-7725
Web Site: www.utm.edu
Management:

Interim Director Campus Recreation: Gina Warren
Seating Capacity: 6,600

7857
MARYVILLE COLLEGE
502 E Lamar
Alexander Parkway
Maryville, TN 37804
Phone: 865-981-8000
Fax: 865-981-8010
Toll-free: 800-597-2687
Web Site: www.maryvillecollege.edu
Management:
    President: Gerald Gibson
Founded: 1819
Status: Non-Profit, Professional

7858
WILSON CHAPEL COMPLEX
Maryville College
Maryville, TN 37801
Phone: 865-981-8000
Fax: 865-981-8001
Toll-free: 800-597-2687

7859
EWING CHILDREN'S THEATRE
2599 Avery Avenue
Memphis, TN 38112
Phone: 901-452-3968
Fax: 901-452-3805
Utilizes: Actors; Choreographers; Collaborations; Dancers; Guest Accompanists; Guest Choreographers; Guest Conductors; Guest Designers; Guest Ensembles; Guild Activities; Local Artists; Multimedia; Music; Organization Contracts; Performance Artists; Resident Professionals; Sign Language Translators; Soloists; Student Interns; Theatre Companies
Founded: 1949
Income Sources: Memphis Park Services
Annual Attendance: 10,000
Facility Category: Theatre
Type of Stage: Proscenium
Seating Capacity: 193
Year Built: 1982
Rental Contact: Kay Lightfoot

7860
LIBERTY BOWL MEMORIAL STADIUM
335 S Hollywood
Memphis, TN 38104
Phone: 901-729-4344
Fax: 901-276-2756
Web Site: www.libertybowl.org
Management:
    Administrator: Terry Norman
    Ground Manager: Johnny Sowell
Founded: 1965
Paid Staff: 5
Seating Capacity: 64,000
Year Built: 1963
Year Remodeled: 1965

7861
MEMPHIS COOK CONVENTION CENTER COMPLEX
Cannon Center for the Performing Arts
255 North Main Street
Memphis, TN 38103
Phone: 901-576-1200
Fax: 901-576-1212
Toll-free: 800-726-0915
Web Site: www.memphisconvention.com

Management:
    General Manager: Pierre Landaich
Mission: They are a full service convention center with a performing arts center.
Founded: 1974
Status: For-Profit, Non-Professional
Paid Staff: 40
Seating Capacity: 2,100
Year Built: 2002

7862
MID-SOUTH COLISEUM
996 Early Maxwell Boulevard
Memphis, TN 38104
Phone: 901-274-3982
Fax: 901-276-8653
Web Site: www.midsouthcoliseum.com
Management:
    Managing Director: Steve Fox
    Food/Beverage Manager: Jim Orcholski
Founded: 1964
Status: For-Profit, Professional
Seating Capacity: 12,000

7863
MUD ISLAND RIVER AMPHITHEATRE
125 North Front Street
Memphis, TN 38103
Phone: 901-576-7232
Fax: 901-576-7235
e-mail: trey@mudisland.com
Web Site: www.mudisland.com
Management:
    GM: Trey Giuntini
    Operations Manager: Alisa Bradley
Seating Capacity: 5,061

7864
ORPHEUM THEATRE
203 S Main Street
PO Box 3370
Memphis, TN 38173
Phone: 901-525-7800
Fax: 901-526-0829
Web Site: www.orpheum-memphis.com
Officers:
    Chief Administrative Officer: Donna Darwin
Management:
    President: Pat Halloran
    Director Education/Programs: Alica Donohoe
    Technical Director: Richard Reinach
Founded: 1978
Status: Non-Profit, Non-Professional
Paid Staff: 25

7865
PYRAMID ARENA
One Auction Avenue
Memphis, TN 38105
Phone: 901-521-9675
Fax: 901-528-0153
Web Site: www.pyramidarena.com
Management:
    General Director: Alan Freeman
    Assistant General Manager: Chuck Jabbour
    Office Manager/Booking Coordinator: Terri Knight
    Director Sales/Marketing: Greg Lowry
    Director Finance: Mary Burd
    Director Operations: Denise Brown
    Director Event Services: Eric Granger
    Box Office Manager: Anita Biles
Founded: 1991
Status: For-Profit, Professional
Paid Staff: 20

Seating Capacity: 22,000

7866
THEATRE MEMPHIS
630 Perkin Extended
Memphis, TN 38117
Phone: 901-682-8601
Fax: 901-763-4096
Web Site: www.theatrememphis.org
Management:
    Executive Producer: Debbie Litch
    Artistic Director: Kell Christie
    Operations Manager: Lisa Hayes
Utilizes: Actors; Artists-in-Residence; Choreographers; Dancers; Designers; Grant Writers; Guest Accompanists; Guest Artists; Guest Conductors; Guest Designers; Guest Ensembles; Guest Lecturers; Guest Musical Directors; Guest Writers; Guild Activities; High School Drama; Local Artists; Music; Organization Contracts; Original Music Scores; Performance Artists; Resident Artists; Resident Professionals; Student Interns
Founded: 1920
Specialized Field: Theatre
Status: Non-Profit, Non-Professional
Paid Staff: 13
Paid Artists: 4
Budget: $1,100,000
Income Sources: Ticket sales, Contributions, Foundation
Season: Year-Round
Performs At: Live Theatre
Annual Attendance: 40,000
Type of Stage: Proscenium; Flexible
Seating Capacity: 400
Year Built: 1975
Year Remodeled: 2004
Rental Contact: Mimi Morgrey

7867
THEATRE GUILD
314 S Hill Street
Morristown, TN 37814
Phone: 423-586-9260

7868
CHARLES M MURPHY ATHLETIC CENTER
Tennessee State University
Tennesse Boulevard
Murfreesboro, TN 37132
Mailing Address: PO Box 203
Phone: 615-898-2873
Fax: 615-898-2873
Management:
    Director Activities: Harold Smith

7869
JOHNNY 'RED' FLOYD STADIUM
MTSU Box 11
Murfreesboro, TN 37132
Phone: 615-898-2551
Fax: 615-898-2873
e-mail: cdoman@mtsu.edu
Web Site: www.mtsu.edu
Management:
    Box Office Manager: John Brooks
Seating Capacity: 31,000

7870

Murfreesboro, TN

7871
ADELPHIA STADIUM
1 Titans Way
Nashville, TN 37213
Phone: 615-565-4000
Fax: 615-565-4444
Web Site: www.titansonline.com
Management:
 Managing Director: Dempsey Henderson
Founded: 1999
Status: For-Profit, Professional
Paid Staff: 300

7872
ALLEN ARENA
Lipscomb University
3901 Granny White Pike
Nashville, TN 37204
Phone: 615-279-6670
Fax: 615-279-7071
Web Site: www.lipscomb.edu
Management:
 GM: Trish Stapp
 Box Office Manager: Janet Grimes
Seating Capacity: 5,534

7873
CHAFFIN'S BARN DINNER THEATRE
8204 Highway 100
Nashville, TN 37221
Phone: 615-646-9977
Fax: 615-662-5439
Toll-free: 800-282-2276
Web Site: www.dinnertheatre.com
Officers:
 Co-Owner: John Chaffin
 Co-Owner: Janie Chaffin
Management:
 Artistic Director: Martha Wilkinson
 Sales: Dietz Osborne
Mission: Offers a package price for professional non-equity theatre and buffet dining. The dinner theatre was Nashville's first professional theatre and continues to produce high quality productions.
Utilizes: Guest Companies
Founded: 1967
Specialized Field: Musical; Dinner Theatre
Status: Non-Profit, Professional
Performs At: Chaffin's Barn
Organization Type: Performing

7874
CURB EVENT CENTER
Belmont University
2002 Belmont Boulevard
Nashville, TN 37212
Phone: 615-460-5545
Fax: 615-460-8008
e-mail: curbeventcenter@mail.belmont.edu
Web Site: www.belmont.edu/curbeventcenter/
Management:
 Director: Jeff Hunter
 Booking Coordinator: Liz Parris
Seating Capacity: 5,900

7875
GAYLORD ENTERTAINMENT CENTER
501 Broadway
Nashville, TN 37203
Phone: 615-770-2000
Fax: 615-770-2010
Web Site: www.gaylordentertainmentcenter.com
Management:

General Manager/COO: Hugh Lombardi
 Senior Director Booking: Brock James
Specialized Field: Home of the Nashville Predators (NHL) and the Nashville Kats (AFL)
Seating Capacity: 17,298, 20,000
Year Built: 1996

7876
GORDON JEWISH COMMUNITY CENTER
801 Percy Warner Boulevard
Nashville, TN 37205
Phone: 615-356-7170
Fax: 615-353-2659
e-mail: info@nashvillejcc.org
Web Site: www.nashvillejcc.org
Officers:
 President: Didi Biesman
 President-Elect: Howard Kirshner
 Executive Director: Eric Goldstein
Founded: 1902
Status: Non-Profit, Non-Professional

7877
GRAND OLE OPRY HOUSE
2804 Opryland Drive
Nashville, TN 37214
Phone: 615-871-6612
Fax: 615-871-5719
Web Site: www.opry.com
Management:
 General Manager: Pete Fisher
 Event Manager: Sally Williams
Founded: 1974
Status: For-Profit, Professional
Facility Category: Threatre
Type of Stage: Procenium
Stage Dimensions: 80w x 60d
Seating Capacity: 4400
Year Built: 1974
Cost: 4,500 vs 12% gbr

7878
GREER STADIUM
534 Chestnut Street
Nashville, TN 37203
Phone: 615-242-4371
Fax: 615-256-5684
Web Site: www.nashvillesounds.com
Management:
 President: Glen Yearger
 Manager: Chris Snyder
Founded: 1978
Paid Staff: 20

7879
LANGFORD AUDITORIUM
Garland Avenue
Nashville, TN 37232
Phone: 615-322-2170
Founded: 1978
Status: Non-Profit, Non-Professional

7880
NASHVILLE CONVENTION CENTER
601 Commerce Street
Nashville, TN 37203
Phone: 615-742-2000
Fax: 615-742-2014
e-mail: conventioncenter@nashville.gov
Web Site: www.nashvilleconventioncenter.com
Management:
 Executive Director: Theresa Horgon
Founded: 1987
Status: For-Profit, Non-Professional

Paid Staff: 45

7881
NASHVILLE MUNICIPAL AUDITORIUM
417 4th Avenue N
Nashville, TN 37201
Phone: 615-862-6392
Fax: 615-862-6394
e-mail: sharon.hill@nashville.gov
Web Site: www.nashvilleauditorium.com
Officers:
 Chairman: John Lander
 Vice Chair: Adrrenne Newman
Management:
 Director of Ticketing: Bill Williams
 Auditorium Manager: Robert C Skoney
 Operations Manager: Jim Raver
 Director of Sales/Marketing: Sharon Hill
Mission: To provide the highest degree of patron services in a cost effective manner in order to promote the macimum use of the venue.
Founded: 1962
Specialized Field: Concerts
Status: For-Profit, Non-Professional
Paid Staff: 8
Volunteer Staff: 1
Budget: $1.5 Million
Income Sources: Ticket Sales
Affiliations: Nashville Convention & Visitors Bureau
Annual Attendance: 232,000
Facility Category: Arena
Type of Stage: Portable
Stage Dimensions: 60' x 40'
Seating Capacity: 9,600
Year Built: 1962
Year Remodeled: 2005
Cost: $5 million
Rental Contact: Sharon Hill

7882
RYMAN AUDITORIUM
116 5th Avenue N
Nashville, TN 37219
Phone: 615-458-8700
Fax: 615-458-8701
e-mail: rymaninfo@oprylandusa.com
Web Site: www.ryman.com
Management:
 President: Colin Reed
Utilizes: Actors; Artists-in-Residence; Choreographers; Collaborating Artists; Commissioned Music; Dance Companies; Educators; Fine Artists; Grant Writers; Guest Accompanists; Guest Artists; Guest Choreographers; Guest Companies; Guest Composers; Guest Conductors; Guest Designers; Guest Directors; Guest Instructors; Guest Lecturers; Guest Musical Directors; Guest Musicians; Guest Soloists; Local Artists; Lyricists; Multi Collaborations; Multimedia; Music; New Productions; Organization Contracts; Original Music Scores; Performance Artists; Sign Language Translators; Singers; Soloists; Special Technical Talent; Theatre Companies
Founded: 1892
Specialized Field: Museum; Concert Hall
Status: For-Profit, Professional
Paid Staff: 100
Year Built: 1892
Year Remodeled: 1994
Rental Contact: Brian Gavron

7883

TENNESSEE PERFORMING ARTS CENTER

505 Deaderick Street
PO Box 190660
Nashville, TN 37219
Phone: 615-782-4000
Fax: 615-782-4001
e-mail: sgreil@tpac.org
Web Site: www.tpac.org
Officers:
    President/CEO: Steven J Greil
    Executive VP/Manager: Ted DeDee
    Director: Brent Hing

7884

TENNESSEE PERFORMING ARTS CENTER: ANDREW JACKSON HALL

505 Deaderick Street
Nashville, TN 37219
Phone: 615-741-7975
Fax: 615-741-1266

7885

VANDERBILT STADIUM

25th & Kensington Place
Nashville, TN 37212
Phone: 615-322-4727
Fax: 615-343-1805
Web Site: www.zucomodores.com
Management:
    Chancellor: Gordon Gee
    Vice Chancellor: David Williams
Status: Non-Profit, Non-Professional
Seating Capacity: 41,203

7886

VANDERBILT UNIVERSITY: MEMORIAL GYM

2601 Jess Neely Drive
Nashville, TN 37212
Phone: 615-322-4727
Fax: 615-343-8738
Web Site: www.vanderbilt.edu
Management:
    Chancellor: Gordon Gee
    Executive Director: David Williams
    Athletic Director: Todd Turner
Founded: 1873
Status: Non-Profit, Non-Professional
Paid Staff: 200
Paid Artists: 300
Seating Capacity: 15,626

7887

W.J. HALE STADIUM

Tennessee State University
3500 John Merrit Boulevard
Nashville, TN 37209
Phone: 615-320-3598
Management:
    Athletic Director: Bill Thomas
Seating Capacity: 16,500

7888

LOUISE MANDRELL THEATER

2046 Parkway
Pigeon Forge, TN 37863
Phone: 865-453-3534
Fax: 865-453-9641
Web Site: www.louisemandrell.com
Management:
    GM: Sande Weiss

Facility Contact: Debbie Glandon
Seating Capacity: 1,400

7889

SIOUX FALLS STADIUM

1001 North West Avenue
Sioux Falls, TN 57104
Phone: 605-333-0179
Web Site: www.canariesbaseball.com
Management:
    President: Jeff Loeble
    GM: John Hindle
Seating Capacity: 20,000

7890

SOUTH JACKSON CIVIC CENTER

Corner of S Jackson and Decherd Streets
Tullahoma, TN 37388
Phone: 931-455-7239
Fax: 931-455-9340
Web Site: www.southjackson.org
Management:
    President: Shirley Moore
    Managing Director: Patty Wimsatt
Founded: 1977
Status: Non-Profit, Professional
Paid Staff: 1

Texas

7891

ABILENE CIVIC CENTER: THEATER

1100 N 6th Street
PO Box 60
Abilene, TX 79604
Phone: 915-676-6211
Fax: 915-676-6343

7892

ABILENE CIVIC CENTER: EXHIBIT HALL

1100 North 6th Street
PO Box 60
Abilene, TX 79604
Phone: 915-676-6211
Fax: 915-676-6343

7893

AZTEC

Albany Chamber of Commerce
PO Box 185
Albany, TX 76430
Phone: 915-762-3838
Fax: 915-762-3125

7894

FORT GRIFFIN FANDANGLE OUTDOOR THEATRE

PO Box 155
#1 Railroad Street
Albany, TX 76430
Phone: 915-762-3838
Fax: 915-762-3125

7895

OLD JAIL ART CENTER

201 S 2nd Street
Albany, TX 76430
Phone: 915-762-2269
Fax: 915-762-2260
Web Site: www.albanytexas.com
Management:
    Education Assistant: Kathryn Mitchell

Mission: To serve as an educational and cultural center focused on the visual arts through collections, interpretation, programs and regional history resources to enhance the education of the audience.
Founded: 1980
Specialized Field: Art Meseum
Paid Staff: 8
Volunteer Staff: 89
Paid Artists: 28
Non-paid Artists: 20

7896

AMARILLO CIVIC CENTER: MUSIC HALL

401 S Buchanan
Amarillo, TX 79101
Phone: 806-378-4297
Fax: 806-378-4234
Web Site: www.panhandletickets.com
Management:
    Managing Director: Chris Miller
Paid Staff: 25
Affiliations: Western Professional Hockey League
Seating Capacity: 4900 Sporting Events, 7000 Concerts
Year Built: 1968

7897

AMARILLO CIVIC CENTER: ARENA

401 South Buchanan
Amarillo, TX 79101
Phone: 806-378-4297
Fax: 806-378-4234

7898

BALLPARK IN ARLINGTON

1000 Ballpark Way
Suite 400
Arlington, TX 76011
Phone: 817-273-5222
Fax: 817-273-5174
Web Site: www.texasrangers.com
Management:
    VP Event Services: Tim Murphy
    Director Facility Event Operations: Kevin Jimison
Specialized Field: Sports Facility; home of the Texas Rangers; Also includes a baseball museum; youth baseball park; amphitheatre; and an office building.
Seating Capacity: 49,166
Year Built: 1994

7899

MAVERICK STADIUM

University of Texas at Arlington
1409 W Mitchell Street
Arlington, TX 76013
Phone: 817-272-2261
Fax: 817-272-5037
Web Site: www.uta.edu/athletics
Management:
    Athletic Director: Pete Carlon
    Director: Kathryn Beeler
Mission: Pre-professional training program for theatre.
Utilizes: Actors; Artists-in-Residence; Choreographers; Collaborating Artists; Designers; Educators; Grant Writers; Guest Accompanists; Guest Artists; Guest Companies; Guest Designers; Guest Instructors; Guest Lecturers; Guest Soloists; Performance Artists; Resident Professionals; Soloists; Student Interns
Affiliations: University of Texas system
Facility Category: Mainstage Theater; Black Box Theater
Type of Stage: Proscenium; Black Box
Seating Capacity: 12,800

All listings are in alphabetical order by state, then city, then organization within the city.

7900
MUSIC MILL AMPHITHEATRE
2201 Road To Six Flags
Arlington, TX 76011
Mailing Address: PO Box 191
Phone: 817-640-8900
Fax: 817-607-6144
Web Site: www.sixflags.com
Seating Capacity: 10,200

7901
THEATRE ARLINGTON
305 W Main Street
Arlington, TX 76010
Phone: 817-275-7661
Fax: 817-275-3370
e-mail: info@theatrearlington.org
Web Site: www.theatrearlington.org
Management:
Executive Producer: Todd Hart
Development Director: Kim Lawson
Marketing Director: Emmy Klein
Box Office Manager: Troy Stidham
Mission: Dedicated to the cultural enrichment, education and entertainment of the citizenry of Arlington and the North Texas community.
Founded: 1973
Status: Non-Profit, Professional
Paid Staff: 6
Volunteer Staff: 100
Paid Artists: 3

7902
DARRELL K ROYAL-TEXAS MEMORIAL STADIUM
University of Texas at Austin
Austin, TX 78713-7399
Mailing Address: PO Box 7399
Phone: 512-471-9405
Fax: 512-471-+130
Web Site: www.texassports.com
Management:
Facility Director: Doug Wilson
Assistant Director: Larry Falk
Assistant Director: Mike Korth
Specialized Field: Home of University of Texas athletics (NCAA).
Seating Capacity: 79,450
Year Built: 1924
Year Remodeled: 1998

7903
FRANK C ERWIN JR SPECIAL EVENTS CENTER
1701 Red River
PO Box 2929
Austin, TX 78701
Phone: 512-471-7744
Fax: 512-471-9652
Web Site: www.uterwincentre.com
Management:
President: Jimmy Earl
Athletic Director: John Graham
Artistic Director: Holley Barnes
Managing Director: Liz Land
Founded: 1977
Status: Non-Profit, Professional
Paid Artists: 2

7904
ONE WORLD THEATRE
7701 Bee Caves Road
Austin, TX 78746
Phone: 512-330-9500
Fax: 512-330-9600
e-mail: info@oneworldtheatre.org
Web Site: www.oneworldtheatre.org
Management:
Executive Director: Hartt Stearns
Founded: 1999
Status: Non-Profit, Non-Professional
Paid Staff: 6

7905
PARAMOUNT THEATER FOR THE PERFORMING ARTS
713 Congress Avenue
Austin, TX 78701
Phone: 512-472-2901
Fax: 512-472-5824
Web Site: www.austintheatrealliance.org
Management:
Artistic Director: Ken Tein
Director Programming: Paul Bewtel
Mission: Presenting performing arts and film.
Founded: 1975
Status: Non-Profit, Professional
Paid Staff: 25
Volunteer Staff: 200
Paid Artists: 40
Performs At: Proscenium Theatre
Affiliations: APAP; LHAT
Type of Stage: Proscenium
Seating Capacity: 1,300
Year Built: 1915
Year Remodeled: 1980
Rental Contact: Paul Bentel

7906
UNIVERSITY OF TEXAS AT AUSTIN PERFORMING ARTS CENTER
PO Box 7818
Austin, TX 78713-7818
Phone: 512-471-1194
Fax: 512-471-3636
e-mail: nbarclay@mail.utexas.edu
Web Site: www.utpac.org
Officers:
President: Larry Faulkner
Executive Director: Pebbles Wadsworth
Assistant /Associate Director: JB Tuttle
Assistant Director: Suzanne Cooper
Production Manager: Charles Leslie
Associate Director: Neil Barclay
Events Manager: Peter Melnick
Mission: The University of Texas at Austin Performing Arts Center is a fully professional presenter of the performing arts. The PAC also seeks to educate, enlighten and entertain residents of the state with diverse and innovative programs that reflect the traditional and evolving culture of the United States and of the world.
Founded: 1981
Status: Non-Profit, Professional
Paid Staff: 70
Budget: $1,000,000+
Performs At: Bass Concert Hall; Bates Recital Hall; McCullough Theatre
Facility Category: Performance Center; Opera House
Type of Stage: Proscenium
Stage Dimensions: 30'Wx36'D; 30'Wx18'H
Rental Contact: Pebbles Wadsworth

7907
UNIVERSITY OF TEXAS AT AUSTIN: THEATRE ROOM
Winship Drama Building
Austin, TX 78712
Phone: 512-471-5793
Fax: 512-471-0824

7908
OLD BASTROP OPERA HOUSE
711 Spring
PO Box 691
Bastrop, TX 78602
Phone: 512-321-6283

7909
BEAUMONT CIVIC CENTER COMPLEX: JULIE ROGERS THEATRE
765 Pearl Street
Beaumont, TX 77701
Phone: 409-838-3435
Fax: 409-838-3715
Toll-free: 800-782-3081
Web Site: www.beaumont-tx-complex.com

7910
CARDINAL STADIUM
Lamar University
4400 MLK Parkway
Beaumont, TX 77710
Phone: 409-880-2329
Fax: 409-880-1814
Web Site: www.athletics.lamar.edu
Management:
Athletic Director: Dean Billick

7911
CIVIC CENTER COMPLEX
701 Main Street
Beaumont, TX 77701
Mailing Address: PO Box 3827, Beaumont TX 77704
Phone: 409-838-3435
Fax: 409-838-3715
Toll-free: 800-782-3081
e-mail: bmtciviccenter@ci.beaumont.tx.us
Web Site: www.beaumont-tx-complex.com
Management:
Division Manager: Mark Arrington,
marrington@ci.beaumont.tx.us
Operations Coordinator: Tommie Minkins,
tminkins@ci.beaumont.tx.us
Director: Claudie D Hawkins,
chawking@ci.beaumont.tx.us

7912
LAMAR UNIVERSITY STUDIO THEATRE
PO Box 10044
Beaumont, TX 77710
Phone: 409-880-8037
Fax: 409-880-8091
Management:
Theatre Director: Dr Adonia D Placette
Mission: Educational
Specialized Field: Theatre
Paid Staff: 5

7913
MONTAGNE CENTER
Lamar University
4400 Mlk Parkway
Beaumont, TX 77710
Phone: 409-880-2329
Fax: 409-880-8990

Management:
Athletic Director: Dean Billick
Seating Capacity: 10,080

7914
GERTRUDE RUSSELL JONES AUDITORIUM
Coastal Bend College
3800 Charco Road
Beeville, TX 78102
Phone: 361-358-2838
Fax: 361-358-3971
Web Site: www.cbc.cc.tx.us
Officers:
Performing Arts Division Chair: James L Lee

7915
BELL COUNTY EXPO CENTER
301 West Loop 121
Belton, TX 76513
Phone: 254-933-5353
Fax: 254-933-5354
e-mail: tims@bellcountyexpo.com
Web Site: www.bellcountyexpo.com
Management:
General Manager: Tim Stephens
Assistant Director: John Dungan
Founded: 1987
Specialized Field: Concerts
Paid Staff: 16
Budget: $1.4 Million
Income Sources: County
Performs At: Arena
Affiliations: IAVM; IEBA; IAFE
Annual Attendance: 400,000+
Facility Category: Arena
Stage Dimensions: 60' x 40'
Seating Capacity: 8,000
Year Built: 1987
Cost: $12 million
Rental Contact: Tim Stephens

7916
CAMILLE PLAYHOUSE
1 Dean Porter Park
Brownsville, TX 78520
Phone: 956-542-8900
Fax: 956-542-0567
e-mail: camilleplayhouse@aol.com
Web Site: www.camilleplayhouseonline.com
Officers:
President: Stephen Shull
Management:
Executive Director: Ben Agresti
Business Manager: Penny Bridger
Mission: To stimulate an interest in the performing arts through the presentation of live theatre, utilizing the talents of the entire Valley community.
Founded: 1963
Specialized Field: Live theatre
Status: Non-Profit, Non-Professional
Paid Staff: 2
Volunteer Staff: 3
Facility Category: Theatre house
Type of Stage: Thrust, proscenium
Stage Dimensions: 20 x 48 x 28
Seating Capacity: 301
Year Built: 1964
Rental Contact: Executive Director Joel Humphries

7917
BROWNWOOD COLISEUM
500 E Baker
Brownwood, TX 76801

Phone: 915-646-3586
Fax: 915-646-0938
Management:
General Manager: David Withers
Facility Manager: Kevin Dearling
Facility Category: Arena; Multy- Purpose
Type of Stage: flexible
Stage Dimensions: 60 4'x 8' stage segments
Seating Capacity: 3,000
Year Built: 1963
Rental Contact: David Withers

7918
KIMBROUGH MEMORIAL STADIUM
West Texas A&M University
PO Box 60049
Canyon, TX 79016
Phone: 806-651-2069
Fax: 806-651-2688
Management:
Athletic Director: Ed Harris
Seating Capacity: 20,000

7919
PIONEER AMPHITHEATRE
Palo Duro Canyon State Park
PO Box 268
Canyon, TX 79015
Phone: 806-488-2421
Fax: 806-655-7425

7920
WTAMU THEATRE
West Texas A&M University
WT 60747
Canyon, TX 79016
Phone: 806-651-2799
Fax: 806-651-2818
e-mail: rbrantley@wtamu.edu
Web Site: www.wtamu.edu/bit
Management:
Theatre Director: Royal Brantley
Technical Director: John Landon
Mission: Education of theatre educators and professionals of the Texas Panhandle
Founded: 1910
Specialized Field: Theatre; Performace; Technical Theatre; Music Theatre; Theatre Education
Status: Non-Profit, Non-Professional
Paid Staff: 6
Budget: $70,000
Income Sources: Student Fees; Box Office
Performs At: University Theatre
Affiliations: TETA; USITT; APO
Annual Attendance: 6,000
Facility Category: Performing Arts
Type of Stage: Pro Arch & Black Box
Stage Dimensions: 38x70; 51x51
Seating Capacity: 304/100
Year Built: 2006
Cost: $33 Million
Rental Contact: Perry Crafton

7921
G ROLLIE WHITE COLISEUM
Texas A&M University
Athletic Department
College Station, TX 77843-1128
Phone: 409-845-2313
Fax: 409-845-6825
Web Site: sports.tamu.edu
Management:
Athletic Director: Wally Groff

7922
KYLE FIELD
Texas A&M Athletic Department
161 Wellborn Road
College Station, TX 77843
Phone: 979-845-5725
Fax: 979-845-0564
e-mail: dsouth@athletics.tamu.edu
Web Site: www.sports.tamu.edu
Management:
Associate Athletic Director: Dave South
Sr Associate Athletic Director: Billy Pickard
Specialized Field: Home of Texas A&M University athletics NCAA
Seating Capacity: 58,000
Year Built: 1927
Year Remodeled: 1998

7923
UNIVERSITY CENTER THEATRE COMPLEX AND CONFERENCE CENTER
Texas A&M University
College Station, TX 77843
Phone: 979-845-8903
Fax: 979-845-7312
Web Site: www.tamus.edu
President: Robert Gates
Managing Director: Bill Bielamowicz
Founded: 1975
Status: Non-Profit, Non-Professional
Paid Staff: 30

7924
BAYFRONT PLAZA CONVENTION CENTER: AUDITORIUM
1901 N Shoreline Drive
Corpus Christi, TX 78401
Phone: 361-883-8543
Fax: 361-883-0788
Web Site: www.americanbankcenter.com
Management:
General Manager: Mark Solis
Status: For-Profit, Professional
Paid Staff: 30

7925
RICHARDSON AUDITORIUM
101 Baldwin Avenue
Corpus Christi, TX 78404
Phone: 512-855-0264
Fax: 512-886-1276

7926
WAREHOUSE LIVING ARTS CENTER
119 W 6th
Corsicana, TX 75110
Phone: 903-872-5421
Fax: 903-874-2923
Web Site: www.corsicanaarts.com
Founded: 1971
Status: Non-Profit, Non-Professional
Paid Staff: 3

7927
DISCOVER HOUSTON COUNTY VISITORS CENTER: MUSEUM
303 S 5st
Crockett, TX 75835
Phone: 936-544-9520

7928

BATH HOUSE CULTURAL CENTER

521 E Lawther Drive
Dallas, TX 75218
Phone: 214-670-8749
Fax: 214-670-8751
Web Site: www.bathhousecultural.com
Management:
   Visual Arts Coordinator: Enrique Fernand
   Manager: David Fisher
Utilizes: Actors; Artists-in-Residence; Collaborating
Artists; Collaborations; Curators; Dance Companies;
Fine Artists; Guest Conductors; Local Artists;
Performance Artists; Playwrights; Student Interns;
Special Technical Talent; Touring Companies; Visual
Arts
Founded: 1930
Paid Staff: 3
Facility Category: Art/Cultural Center
Type of Stage: Thrust
Stage Dimensions: 13' x 20'
Seating Capacity: 120
Year Built: 1930
Year Remodeled: 1997
Rental Contact: Manager David Fisher

7929

BIBLICAL ARTS CENTER

7500 Park Lane
Dallas, TX 75225
Phone: 214-691-4661
Fax: 214-691-4752
Web Site: www.biblicalarts.org
Management:
   Executive Director: Scott Peck
   Director: R J Machacek
Status: Non-Profit, Professional

7930

BOB HOPE THEATRE

Southern Methodist University
Owen Fine Arts Center
Dallas, TX 75275
Phone: 214-692-3383
Fax: 214-692-4138

7931

BRONCO ARENA

2600 Fort Worth Avenue
Dallas, TX 75211
Phone: 214-943-1777
Fax: 214-943-2014
Web Site: www.broncobull.com
Management:
   Director: Susan Palmer

7932

CARUTH AUDITORIUM

Southern Methodist University
Owen Fine Arts Center
Dallas, TX 75275
Phone: 214-692-2713
Fax: 214-692-4138

7933

COTTON BOWL/FAIR PARK

3809 Tower Building
PO Box 159090
Dallas, TX 75315
Phone: 214-670-8400
Fax: 214-670-8907
Web Site: www.tgimaps.com
Management:

General Manager: Eddie Hueston
Sales/Event Manager: Leslie Studard
Seating Capacity: 22,528 Soccer, 67,000 Football
Year Built: 1935

7934

DALLAS CONVENTION CENTER: THEATER

650 S Griffin
Dallas, TX 75202
Phone: 214-939-2700
Fax: 214-939-2795
Web Site: www.dallasconventioncenter.com
Founded: 1970

7935

DALLAS CONVENTION CENTER: ARENA

650 South Griffin
Dallas, TX 75202
Phone: 214-939-2700
Fax: 214-939-2795

7936

DALLAS THEATER CENTER: KALITA HUMPHREYS THEATRE

3636 Turtle Creek Boulevard
Dallas, TX 75219
Phone: 214-526-8210
Fax: 214-521-7666

7937

MAJESTIC THEATRE

1925 Elm Street
Dallas, TX 75201
Phone: 214-880-0137
Fax: 214-880-0097
e-mail: jwilborn@dallassummermusicals.org
Web Site: www.dallassummermusicals.org

7938

MCFARLIN MEMORIAL

Southern Methodist University
6400 Hillcrest Avenue
Dallas, TX 75275
Mailing Address: PO Box 152
Phone: 214-692-3129
Fax: 214-692-4138

7939

MOODY COLISEUM

Southern Methodist University
6405 Boaz Lane, Suite 101
Dallas, TX 75275
Phone: 214-768-2864
Fax: 214-768-2044
Web Site: www.smu.edu
Management:
   Assistant Manager: Kevin Diggs
Status: Non-Profit,Non-Professional
Seating Capacity: 9,500

7940

MORTON H MEYERSON SYMPHONY CENTER

2301 Flora Street
PO Box 26207
Dallas, TX 75201
Phone: 214-871-4000
Fax: 214-670-4334
e-mail: customerservice@dalsym.com
Web Site: www.dallassymphony.com
Management:
   President: Fred Bronstein

Founded: 1900
Status: Non-Profit, Professional
Paid Staff: 100

7941

MUSIC HALL AT FAIR PARK

909 Frist Avenue Parry
Dallas, TX 75315
Phone: 214-565-1116
Fax: 214-428-4526
Web Site: www.dallassummermusicals.org
Paid Staff: 10

7942

REUNION ARENA

777 Sports Street
Dallas, TX 75207
Phone: 214-939-2770
Fax: 214-800-3040
Management:
   General Manager: David R Brown
   Director Events/Booking: Ken Kurl
   Director Operations: Bob Jordan
   Concessions Manager: David Jenkins
   Director Marketing: Vicki Huxel
   Box Office Manager: Mike Chilers
   EVP/CFO: Graig Courson
   Group Sales Assistant: Melissa Mezger
Seating Capacity: 18,042

7943

SOUTH DALLAS CULTURAL CENTER

3400 S Fitzhugh
Dallas, TX 75210
Phone: 214-939-2787
Fax: 214-670-8118
Web Site: www.dallasblack.com
Management:
   Manager: Vicki Meek
Founded: 1986
Status: Non-Profit, Non-Professional
Paid Staff: 4

7944

THANKSGIVING SQUARE: COURTYARD AT THANKSGIVING

PO Box 131770
Dallas, TX 75313-1770
Phone: 214-969-1977
Fax: 214-754-0152
Web Site: www.thanksgiving.org
Management:
   President/CEO: Tatiana Anderson
Founded: 1977
Status: Non-Profit, Non-Professional
Paid Staff: 7

7945

DECATUR CIVIC CENTER THEATRE

2010 W US 380
PO Box 894
Decatur, TX 76234
Phone: 940-627-2369
Fax: 940-267-2600
e-mail: info@decaturciviccenter.com
Web Site: www.decaturciviccenter.com
Management:
   Director: Duffy Terry
   Sales Director: Krista Lewis
Founded: 1854

7946

DECATUR CIVIC CENTER - VENUE

2010 W US 380
PO Box 894
Decatur, TX 76234
Phone: 940-627-2369
Fax: 940-267-6400
e-mail: info@decaturciviccenter.com
Web Site: www.decaturciviccenter.com
Management:
    Administrative Assistant: Krista Lewis

7947

REDBUD THEATRE

Texas Woman's University
TWU Station
Denton, TX 76204
Mailing Address: PO Box 23865
Phone: 817-898-2500
Fax: 817-898-3198

7948

UNIVERSITY OF NORTH TEXAS PERFORMING ARTS CENTER

PO Box 310710
Denton, TX 76203-0710
Phone: 940-565-3815
Fax: 940-565-3773
e-mail: Keffer@unt.edu
Web Site: www-lan.unt.edu/usl/home/www
Officers:
    Chairman: Lindsay Keffer
Founded: 1924
Specialized Field: Performing; Visual; Literary
Paid Staff: 1
Volunteer Staff: 9
Budget: $60,000-150,000
Income Sources: Grants; Ticket Sales; Underwriting; Student Service Fees
Affiliations: A.A; APA
Type of Stage: Thrust; Proscenium
Seating Capacity: 200/8,000

7949

UNIVERSITY OF TEXAS-PAN AMERICAN: THEATER

1201 West University Drive
Edinburg, TX 78539
Phone: 512-381-3581
Fax: 956-381-3472

7950

CHAMIZAL NATIONAL MEMORIAL: THEATER

800 S San Marcial
PO Box 722
El Paso, TX 79905
Phone: 915-532-7273
Fax: 915-532-7240
Web Site: www.nps.gov/cham
Management:
    Artistic Director: Virginia Nef
Founded: 1967
Status: Non-Profit, Non-Professional
Paid Staff: 26

7951

COHEN STADIUM

9700 Gateway North Boulevard
El Paso, TX 79924
Phone: 915-755-2000
Fax: 915-757-0671
Web Site: www.diablos.com

Management:
    General Manager: Jimmy Hicks
Founded: 1989
Status: For-Profit, Non-Professional
Paid Staff: 32

7952

DON HASKINS CENTER

Baltimore & Mesa STS
500 W University Avenue
El Paso, TX 79968-0557
Phone: 915-747-5265
Fax: 915-747-5228
e-mail: dhc@utep.edu
Web Site: www.utep.edu/venues
Management:
    President: Diana Natalicio
    Executive Director: Mike Spence
Utilizes: Dance Companies; Designers; Educators; Guest Accompanists; Soloists; Student Interns; Theatre Companies
Status: Non-Profit, Professional
Paid Staff: 9
Affiliations: University of Texas at El Paso
Facility Category: SICO
Seating Capacity: 12,000
Year Remodeled: 2001
Rental Contact: (915)747-5481 Carol Roberts-Spence

7953

DUDLEY FIELD

PO Box 4797
El Paso, TX 79914
Phone: 915-544-1950
Management:
    Owner: Jim Paul

7954

EL PASO CIVIC CENTER: EXHIBITION HALL

1 Civic Center Plaza
El Paso, TX 79901
Phone: 915-534-0600
Fax: 915-534-0686
Web Site: www.elpaso.com

7955

EL PASO CIVIC CENTER: THEATRE

1 Civic Center Plaza
El Paso, TX 79901
Phone: 915-541-4920
Fax: 915-534-0686

7956

EL PASO CONVENTION & PERFORMING ARTS CENTER

1 Civic Center Plaza
El Paso, TX 79901
Phone: 915-534-0609
Fax: 915-534-0671
Toll-free: 800-351-6024
Web Site: www.elpasocvb.com
Management:
    General Manager: William Blaziek
    Facility Sales Manager: Esther Portillo
Founded: 1972
Status: Non-Profit, Professional

7957

EL PASO COUNTY COLISEUM

4100 Paisano
El Paso, TX 79905

Phone: 915-534-4229
Fax: 915-532-4048
Web Site: www.elpasosports.org
Management:
    President: Bryan Kennedy
Founded: 2003
Status: Non-Profit, Professional
Paid Staff: 15

7958

MAGOFFIN AUDITORIUM

University of Texas
302 Union East
El Paso, TX 79968
Phone: 915-747-5481
Fax: 915-747-7469
Web Site: www.utep.edu/events/venues
Management:
    Special Events Director: Carol Roberts-Spence
Seating Capacity: 1,200

7959

SUN BOWL

500 W University Avenue
El Paso, TX 79968-0557
Phone: 915-747-5265
Fax: 915-747-5228
e-mail: events@utep.edu
Web Site: www.utep.edu.
Management:
    Director: Mike Spence
    Interim Director: Jorge Vazquez
Founded: 1913
Status: Non-Profit, Professional
Paid Staff: 3000
Seating Capacity: 52,000

7960

UNIVERSITY OF TEXAS AT EL PASO: MAIN PLAYHOUSE

500 W University
El Paso, TX 79968
Phone: 915-747-5146
Fax: 915-747-5134
Web Site: www.utep.edu
Management:
    Department Chairman: Mimi Gladstein
Status: Non-Profit, Non-Professional

7961

AMOIN G CARTER STADIUM

Texas Christian University
3500 Bellaire Drive North
Fort Worth, TX 76129
Phone: 817-257-7965
Fax: 817-257-7656
Web Site: www.gofrogs.com
Management:
    Athletic Director: Eric Hyman

7962

CARAVAN OF DREAMS

312 Houston Street
Fort Worth, TX 76102
Phone: 817-877-3000
Fax: 817-877-3752

7963

CASA MANANA THEATRE

3101 W Lancaster
Fort Worth, TX 76107
Phone: 817-332-9319
Fax: 817-332-5711
Season: june - august

7964
DANIEL-MEYER COLISEUM
Texas Christian University
2800 S University Drive
Fort Worth, TX 76129
Phone: 817-257-7000
Fax: 817-257-7656
Web Site: www.tcu.edu
Management:
    Chancellor: Victor Boschini

7965
ED LANDRETH AUDITORIUM
Texas Christian University
School of Fine Arts
Fort Worth, TX 76129
Mailing Address: PO Box 32928
Phone: 817-921-7625
Fax: 817-921-7333

7966
FORT WORTH COMMUNITY ARTS CENTER
WE Scott Theater
1300 Gendy Drive
Fort Worth, TX 76107
Phone: 817-738-1938
Fax: 817-738-3766
e-mail: marla@fwcac.org
Web Site: www.fwcac.com
Management:
    Business Development Manager: Marla
    Fleischmann Owen
Mission: To provide accessible and affordable
exhibition, performance, workshop, classroom space to
artists and arts organizations in the region and to serve
the community in a user friendly environment.
Founded: 1964
Specialized Field: Theater
Status: Non-Profit, Professional
Paid Staff: 8
Paid Artists: 50
Facility Category: Rental Facility

7967
HIP POCKET THEATRE
1950 Silver Creek Road
At Loop 820 N
Fort Worth, TX 76108
Phone: 817-246-9775
Fax: 817-246-5651
e-mail: hippockettheatre@aol.com
Web Site: www.hippocket.org
Management:
    Executive Director: Diane Simons,
    mdmolemo@aol.com
    Artistic Director: Johnny Simons,
    hippockettheatre@aol.com
Mission: Produce live theatre events
Utilizes: Actors; AEA Actors; Artists-in-Residence;
Choreographers; Collaborating Artists; Collaborations;
Commissioned Composers; Community Members;
Community Talent; Composers; Dancers; Designers;
Educators; Equity Actors; Filmmakers; Five Seasonal
Concerts; Guest Accompanists; Guest Conductors;
Guest Designers; Guest Musical Directors; Local
Artists; Local Artists & Directors; Lyricists; Multi
Collaborations; Music; Organization Contracts; Original
Music Scores; Paid Performers; Performance Artists;
Poets; Resident Artists; Sign Language Translators;
Soloists; Visual Designers
Founded: 1977
Status: Non-Profit, Professional

Paid Staff: 10
Income Sources: Grants, Box Office

7968
SOUTHWESTERN BAPTIST THEOLOGICAL SEMINARY
PO Box 22390
Fort Worth, TX 76122-0390
Phone: 817-923-1921
Fax: 817-921-8762
Toll-free: 800-792-8701
e-mail: scmusic@swbts.edu
Web Site: www.swbts.edu
Officers:
    Dean, School of Church Music: Stephen P
    Johnson
    Assoc Dean, Academic Division: William Colson
    Assoc Dean, Performance Division: William
    MacDavis
    President: Paige Patterson
    Exec VP/Provost: Craig Blaising
    Assoc Dean, Undergraduate Music: Tom Song
Founded: 1908
Specialized Field: Sacred Music
Status: Non-Profit, Professional
Paid Staff: 60
Paid Artists: 20
Performs At: Graduate School Recital Hall
Facility Category: Concert Halls, Auditorium, Studio
Seating Capacity: 500
Year Built: 1933
Year Remodeled: 1960
Rental Contact: Ext 3130 William MacDavis

7969
TEXAS WESLEYAN COLLEGE: FINE ARTS
Rosedale and Wesleyan
PO Box 50010
Fort Worth, TX 76105
Phone: 817-531-4443
Fax: 817-531-6583

7970
GRAND 1894 OPERA HOUSE
2020 Postoffice Street
Galveston, TX 77550
Phone: 409-765-1894
Fax: 409-763-1068
Toll-free: 800-821-1894
e-mail: thegrand@thegrand.com
Web Site: www.thegrand.com

7971
MOODY CIVIC CENTER: EXHIBITION HALL
2100 Seawall Boulevard
Galveston, TX 77550
Phone: 409-762-8626
Fax: 406-762-8911

7972
GARLAND CENTER FOR THE PERFORMING ARTS: THEATRE
PO Box 469002
Garland, TX 75046
Phone: 972-205-2780
Fax: 972-205-2775

7973
GRANBURY OPERA HOUSE
116 E Pearl Street
PO Box 297
Granbury, TX 76048
Phone: 817-579-5529
Fax: 817-573-9717
Toll-free: 866-572-0881
Web Site: www.granburyoperahouse.org
Management:
    President: Max Jones
    Executive Producer: Marty Van Kleeck
Founded: 1975
Status: Non-Profit, Professional
Paid Staff: 8

7974
CAPITAL BASEBALL STADIUM
Harlingen Municipal Auditorium Complex
1204 Fair Park Boulevard
Harlingen, TX 78550
Phone: 956-430-6690
Fax: 956-364-2975
e-mail: harlingenarts@xanadu2.net
Web Site: www.harlingenarts.org
Management:
    Director: Susan Thomae-Morphew
    Executive Director: Joel Humphries
Founded: 1992
Status: Non-Profit, Professional
Paid Staff: 3

7975
HARLINGEN CULTURAL ARTS CENTER: AUDITORIUM
576'76 Drive
PO Box 609
Harlingen, TX 78551
Phone: 210-423-9736

7976
ALLEY THEATRE: HUGO V NEUHAUS ARENA STAGE
615 Texas Avenue
Houston, TX 77002
Phone: 713-228-9341
Fax: 713-222-6542
Web Site: www.alleytheatre.org or www.teatroalley.org
Year Remodeled: 2001

7977
ALLEY THEATRE
615 Texas Avenue
Houston, TX 77002
Phone: 713-228-9341
Fax: 713-222-6542
Management:
    Artistic Director: Gregory Boyd
    Managing Director: Paul Tetreault
    Direction Production: Sean Skeeman

7978
ALLEY THEATRE: LARGE STAGE
615 Texas Avenue
Houston, TX 77002
Phone: 713-228-9341
Fax: 713-222-6542
Web Site: www.alleytheatre.org or teatroalley.org

7979
ASTRODOME
PO Box 288
Houston, TX 77001

Phone: 713-259-8000
Fax: 713-799-9722
Web Site: www.astros.com
Management:
    President/CEO: Mike Puryear
    VP Marketing/Sales: George Coenig
Seating Capacity: 53,000 (Stadium, 6,000 [Arena])
Year Built: 1963
Year Remodeled: 1988

7980
COMMUNITY MUSIC CENTER

3100 Cleburne
Houston, TX 77004
Phone: 713-523-9710
Fax: 713-523-0507
Web Site: www.cmch.com
Management:
    President of the Board: Kathy Wilson
    Executive Director: Gary Wilkins
    Music Director: Anne Lundy
Founded: 1979
Status: Non-Profit, Professional
Paid Staff: 2
Paid Artists: 100

7981
COMPAQ CENTER

10 Greenway Plaza
Houston, TX 77046
Phone: 713-843-3900
Fax: 713-843-3989
Web Site: www.compaqcenter.com
Management:
    Presiden: Wes Westley
    VP Human Resources: Maureen Ginty
Seating Capacity: 17,000
Year Built: 1975
Year Remodeled: 1994

7982
CULLEN PERFORMANCE HALL

University Of Houston
4800 Calhoon Road
Houston, TX 77204-2003
Phone: 713-743-5186
Fax: 713-743-5194
e-mail: cphinfo@uh.edu
Web Site: www.uh.edu/cph
Management:
    Acting Manager/Technical Director: Charlie Matthew
Founded: 1949
Paid Staff: 10
Budget: $400,000
Income Sources: Facility Rental
Performs At: Rental Facility
Affiliations: University Of Houston
Annual Attendance: 125,000
Facility Category: Rental
Type of Stage: Proscenium Theatre
Seating Capacity: 1,536
Year Built: 1949
Year Remodeled: 1987
Rental Contact: Acting Manager Charlie Matthew

7983
DELMAR STADIUM COMPLEX

2020 Magnum
Houston, TX 77092
Phone: 713-957-7700
Fax: 713-957-7704
Management:
    Director: Mike Truelove

7984
DIVERSEWORKS

1117 E Freeway
Houston, TX 77002
Phone: 713-223-8346
Fax: 713-223-4608
Web Site: www.diverseworks.org
Management:
    President: Susan Linberg
    Executive Director: Sara Kellner
    Artistic Director: Diane Barber
    Performing Arts Director: Sixto Wagan
Mission: Dedicated to presenting new visual, performing, and literary art. A place where the process of creating art is valued and where artists can test new ideas in the public arena. By encouraging the investigation of current artistic, cultural and social issues, they build, educate, and sustain audiences for contemporary art.
Founded: 1982
Specialized Field: Multidisciplinary Performance and Visual
Status: Non-Profit, Professional
Paid Staff: 7
Paid Artists: 2

7985
ENRON FIELD

PO Box 288
Houston, TX 77001-0288
Phone: 713-799-9500
Fax: 713-799-9881
Web Site: www.astros.com
Management:
    Facility Manager: Don Collins
    Senior VP Marketing Advertising: Pam Gardner
Founded: 1962
Specialized Field: Home of the Houston Astros (MLB).
Seating Capacity: 42,000
Year Built: 2000

7986
HAMMAN HALL

Rice University
PO Box 1892
Houston, TX 77251-1892
Phone: 713-348-7529
Fax: 713-348-4609
e-mail: hamman@rice.edu
Web Site: www.rice.edu/players
Management:
    Theatre Director: Trish Rigdon
Founded: 1914
Status: Non-Profit, Non-Professional
Paid Staff: 3

7987
HOFHEINZ PAVILION

3100 Cullen Boulevard
Houston, TX 77204-6742
Phone: 713-743-9370
Fax: 713-743-9375
Web Site: www.uhcougars.com
Management:
    President: Jay Gague
    Athletic Director: Dave Maggard
Status: Non-Profit, Non-Professional
Paid Staff: 100

7988
HOUSTON CIVIC CENTER: GUS WORTHAM THEATER

510 Preston 4th Floor
Houston, TX 77002
Phone: 713-237-1439
Fax: 713-237-9313
Web Site: www.worthamcenter.org
Management:
    Building Director: Down Ullrich
Founded: 1987
Status: Non-Profit, Professional
Paid Staff: 13

7989
HOUSTON CIVIC CENTER: JESSE H JONES HALL FOR THE PERFORMING ARTS

615 Louisiana
PO Box 61469
Houston, TX 77208
Phone: 713-227-3974
Fax: 713-228-9629

7990
HOUSTON CIVIC CENTER: GEORGE R BROWN CONVENTION CENTER

1001 Convention Center Boulevard
Houston, TX 77010
Phone: 713-853-8000
Fax: 713-583-8011

7991
MILLER OUTDOOR THEATRE

Hermann Park
PO Box 1562
Houston, TX 77251
Phone: 713-284-8358

7992
RICE STADIUM

Rice University
6100 S Main Street
Houston, TX 77005
Phone: 713-527-4077
Fax: 713-527-6019
Web Site: www.riceowls.com
Management:
    Athletic Director: Bobby May
Seating Capacity: 70,000

7993
ROBERTSON STADIUM

University of Huston
3100 Cullen Boulevard
Houston, TX 77204-6742
Phone: 713-743-9370
Fax: 713-743-9375
Web Site: www.uhcougars.com
Management:
    Athletic Director: Chet Gladchuk
    Sports Information Director: Chris Burkholter
    Head Football Coach: Kim Helton
    Head Basketball Coach (M): Claude Drexler
    Head Basketball Coach (W): Joe Curl
Seating Capacity: 22,000

7994
STAGES REPERTORY THEATRE

3201 Allen Parkway
Suite 101
Houston, TX 77019

Phone: 713-527-0123
Fax: 713-527-8669
e-mail: kmclaughlin@stagestheatre.com
Web Site: www.stagestheatre.com
Management:
    Producing Artistic Director: Kenn McLaughlin
    Production Manager: Kirk Markley
    Development Director: Star Massing
    Marketing/Communications Director: Lise Bohn
Mission: To present new works, interpret established works in new ways, and encourage and cultivate culture for the community.

7995
THEATRE SUBURBIA
1410 W 43rd
Houston, TX 77018
Phone: 713-682-3525

7996
BERNARD G JOHNSON COLISEUM
Sam Houston State University
Avenue H & Bowers Boulevard
Huntsville, TX 77341
Phone: 936-294-1740
Fax: 936-294-4833
e-mail: rca_elc@shsu.edu
Web Site: www.shsu.edu
Management:
    Managing Director: Ed Chatal
Founded: 1976
Status: For-Profit, Professional
Paid Staff: 18

7997
SAM HOUSTON STATE UNIVERSITY THEATRE
Theatre & Dance Department
Box 2297
Huntsville, TX 77341
Phone: 936-294-1329
Fax: 936-294-3898
e-mail: drm_pah@shsu.edu
Web Site: www.shsu.edu/~ndrm
Officers:
    President: James Gartner
Utilizes: Grant Writers; Guest Artists; Guest Conductors; Guest Designers; Guest Instructors; Guest Lecturers; Guest Soloists
Founded: 1871
Status: Non-Profit, Non-Professional
Paid Staff: 20
Type of Stage: Proscenium and Thrust
Seating Capacity: 396, 96
Year Built: 1976
Year Remodeled: 2001

7998
IRVING ARTS CENTER
3333 N Macarthur Boulevard
Suite 300
Irving, TX 75062
Phone: 972-252-7558
Fax: 972-570-4962
Web Site: www.ci.irving.tx.us/arts
Management:
    Executive Director: Richard E Huff
    Director Marketing/Publication: Jo Trizila
    Facilities Director: Kass Price
Mission: To serve the citizens of Irving through the support and development of artistic opportunities.
Founded: 1986
Status: Non-Profit, Professional
Paid Staff: 25

Volunteer Staff: 800
Affiliations: City of Irving
Annual Attendance: 100,000
Type of Stage: Proscenium; Black Box
Seating Capacity: 700; 450; 500
Year Built: 1990

7999
TEXAS STADIUM
2401 E Airport Freeway
Irving, TX 75062
Phone: 972-438-7676
Fax: 975-785-4709
Management:
    VP/General Manager: Bruce Hardy
    Concessions Manager: Amy Bersen
Seating Capacity: 63,855

8000
KERRVILLE OUTDOOR THEATRE
Quiet Valley Ranch
PO Box 291466
Kerrville, TX 78029-1466
Phone: 830-257-3600
Fax: 830-257-8680
Toll-free: 800-435-8429
Web Site: www.festival/music.com
Management:
    President: Charlie Land
    Managing Director: Dalis Allen
Founded: 1970
Status: For-Profit, Professional
Paid Staff: 5

8001
ALLEN THEATRE
Texas Tech University
15th and Boston Avenue
Lubbock, TX 79409
Mailing Address: PO Box 42031
Phone: 806-742-3636
Fax: 806-742-0655
e-mail: felix.moore@ttu.edu
Web Site: www.uc.ttu.edu
Utilizes: Actors; AEA Actors; Choreographers; Collaborating Artists; Dance Companies; Dancers; Designers; Educators; Filmmakers; Grant Writers; Guest Accompanists; Guest Artists; Guest Choreographers; Guest Companies; Guest Composers; Guest Conductors; Guest Designers; Guest Directors; Guest Ensembles; Guest Instructors; Guest Lecturers; Guest Musical Directors; Guest Musicians; Guest Soloists; Guest Teachers; High School Drama; Instructors; Local Artists; Local Talent; Local Unknown Artists; Multimedia; Music; Original Music Scores; Performance Artists; Playwrights; Resident Professionals; Sign Language Translators; Singers; Soloists; Student Interns; Special Technical Talent; Theatre Companies; Visual Arts
Paid Staff: 10
Facility Category: rental
Type of Stage: proeswien
Stage Dimensions: 60 x 20
Seating Capacity: 928
Year Built: 1976

8002
JONES AT&T STADIUM
Texas Tech Athletics Department
6 & Boston Avenue
Lubbock, TX 79409

Phone: 806-742-3355
Fax: 806-742-1970
e-mail: chris.cook@ttu.edu
Web Site: www.texastech.edu
Management:
    Athletic Director: Gerald Myers
    Senior Associate Athletic Director: Steve Uryasz
    Associate Athletics: Judi Henry
    Senior Associate Athletic Director: Bobby Gleason
    Assistant Athletic Director: Richard Kilwien
    Assistant Athletic Director: Byron Waters
    Associate Athletic Director: Ron Famrom
    Assistant Athletic Director: Russell Warren
    Associate Athletic Director: Steve Uryasz
Seating Capacity: 52,882
Year Built: 1947
Year Remodeled: 2003

8003
LUBBOCK MEMORIAL CIVIC CENTER THEATER
1501 MacDavis Lane
Lubbock, TX 79401
Phone: 806-775-2242
Fax: 806-775-3240
e-mail: DebraJustice@mylubbock.us
Web Site: www.lubbockciviccenter.com
Management:
    Director: Freddy Chavez
    Assistant Director: Debra Justice
    Senior Events Coordinator: Leslie Timmons
    Technical Coordinator: John James
Founded: 1976
Specialized Field: Performance
Status: Non-Profit, Professional
Paid Staff: 31
Performs At: Theatre; Auditorium
Affiliations: IAAM
Annual Attendance: 500,000+
Facility Category: Convention Center
Type of Stage: Proscenium
Stage Dimensions: 40x80; 96x45
Seating Capacity: 1397; 2803
Rental Contact: Leslie Timmons

8004
LUBBOCK MEMORIAL CIVIC CENTER BANQUET HALL
1501 6th Street
Lubbock, TX 79401
Phone: 806-770-2000

8005
LUBBOCK MEMORIAL CIVIC CENTER COLISEUM
4th and Boston
Lubbock, TX 79457
Phone: 806-770-2000
Fax: 806-765-5803

8006
LUBBOCK MEMORIAL CIVIC CENTER EXHIBIT HALL
1501 6th Street
Lubbock, TX 79457
Phone: 806-770-2000
Fax: 806-765-5803

8007
LUBBOCK MEMORIAL CIVIC CENTER MUNICIPAL AUDITORIUM
4th and Boston
Lubbock, TX 79457
Phone: 806-770-2000
Fax: 806-765-5803

8008
TEXAS TECH UNIVERSITY PERFORMING ARTS CENTER
18th and Boston
Box 42033
Lubbock, TX 79409-2033
Phone: 806-742-2270
Fax: 806-742-2294
Web Site: www.ttu.edu/~music

8009
UNITED SPIRIT ARENA
Texas Tech University
1701 Indiana Avenue
Lubbock, TX 79409
Phone: 806-742-7362
Fax: 806-742-7557
e-mail: unitedspiritarena@ttu.edu
Web Site: www.unitedspiritarena.com
Management:
Director: Kent Meredith
Assistant Director: Cindy Harper
Seating Capacity: 15,000

8010
MARSHALL CIVIC CENTER
2501 E End Boulevard S
Marshall, TX 75670
Phone: 903-935-4472
Fax: 903-935-0538
e-mail: jcarpenter@marshalltexas.net
Web Site: www.marshallphysics.com
Management:
Managing Director: Jennifer Carpenter
Event Facilites Director: Ardis Wright
Founded: 1976
Status: Non-Profit, Non-Professional
Paid Staff: 5
Paid Artists: 5

8011
RESISTOL ARENA/RODEO CENTER EXHIBIT HALL
SW Sports Group
1818 Rodeo Drive
Mesquite, TX 75149
Phone: 972-285-8777
Fax: 972-289-2999
Web Site: www.mesquiterodeo.com
Officers:
President: Jack B Beckman
Management:
President: Mark Miller
Status: For-Profit, Professional
Paid Staff: 20
Seating Capacity: 5,300

8012
CHAPARRAL CENTER
Midland College
3600 North Garfield
Midland, TX 79705
Phone: 915-685-4584
Fax: 915-685-4740
e-mail: mstevens@midland.edu
Management:
Director: Michael J Stevens
Founded: 1978
Affiliations: Midland College
Facility Category: Small arena with curtain system
Type of Stage: Stageright Portable
Stage Dimensions: 60' x 40'
Seating Capacity: 1800; 2400; 5000
Year Built: 1978

8013
MIDLAND CENTER
105 North Main
Midland, TX 79701
Phone: 915-682-6234
Fax: 915-686-9830
e-mail: irece@visitmidlandtx.com
Web Site: www.visitmidlandtx.com
Management:
Manager: Irece Jordan
Seating Capacity: 1,400

8014
HOMER BRYCE STADIUM
Stephen F. Austin State University
PO Box 13010, SFA Station
Nacogdoches, TX 75962
Phone: 409-468-3501
Web Site: www.athletics.sfasu.edu
Management:
Athletic Director: Steve McCarty

8015
WILLIAM R JOHNSON COLISEUM
Stephen F Austin State University
PO Box 13010-SFA Station
Nacogdoches, TX 75962
Phone: 936-468-3501
Fax: 936-468-4070
Web Site: sfajacks.com
Management:
Athletic Operations Director: Jeremy Stolfa
Founded: 1973
Type of Stage: Portable
Seating Capacity: 7,200

8016
LUTCHER THEATER
707 W Main Street
Orange, TX 77630
Phone: 409-886-5535
Fax: 409-886-5537
Toll-free: 800-828-5535
e-mail: lutcher@exp.net
Web Site: www.lutcher.org

8017
PALESTINE CIVIC CENTER COMPLEX
Highway 287-19N
Palestine, TX 75801
Phone: 903-723-3014
Fax: 903-729-6067
Toll-free: 800-659-3484
Web Site: www.visitpalestine.com
Management:
Events Coordinator: Heather Hrebec
Founded: 1986
Status: For-Profit, Non-Professional
Paid Staff: 3

8018
MK BROWN MEMORIAL AUDITORIUM & CIVIC CENTER
1100 W Coronado Drive
Pampa, TX 79066-2499
Mailing Address: PO Box 2499
Phone: 806-669-5790
Fax: 806-669-5842
e-mail: ecabrales@cityofpampa.org
Web Site: www.cityofpampa.org
Management:
Auditorium Manager: Enrique Cabrales
Founded: 1972
Status: Non-Profit, Non-Professional
Paid Staff: 10
Stage Dimensions: 3,150 square feet
Seating Capacity: 1,500

8019
PARIS JUNIOR COLLEGE
2400 Clarksville
Paris, TX 75460
Phone: 903-785-7661
Fax: 903-784-9370

8020
SLOCOMB AUDITORIUM
San Jacinto College Central
8060 Spencer Highway
Pasadena, TX 77501-2007
Mailing Address: PO Box 2007
Phone: 281-476-1829
Fax: 281-476-1892
Web Site: www.sjtd.edu
Management:
President: Jerry Ivin
Executive Director: Jerry Dyess
Artistic Director: Bob Robert
Managing Director: Louie Sal
Founded: 1969
Status: For-Profit, Professional
Paid Staff: 236
Paid Artists: 240

8021
CHARLES W. EISEMANN CENTER FOR PERFORMING ARTS & CORPORATE PRESENTATIONS
2351 Performance Drive
Richardson, TX 75082
Phone: 972-744-4600
Fax: 972-744-5823
e-mail: bruce_macpherson@cor.gov
Web Site: www.eisemanncenter.com
Management:
Managing Director: Bruce MacPherson

8022
ROUND TOP FESTIVAL INSTITUTE
James Dick Foundation for the Performing Arts
248 Jaster Road
Round Top, TX 78954
Mailing Address: PO Box 89
Phone: 979-249-3129
Fax: 979-249-5078
e-mail: info@festivalhill.org
Web Site: www.festivalhill.org
Officers:
President: James Dick
Management:
Managing Director: Richard Royal
Program Director: Alain G Declert
Director Library/Museum: Lamar Lentz

Mission: Educational project.
Utilizes: Commissioned Composers; Composers-in-Residence; Educators; Fine Artists; Five Seasonal Concerts; Guest Companies; Guest Composers; Guest Ensembles; Guest Instructors; Guest Soloists; Scenic Designers; Students
Founded: 1971
Specialized Field: Classical Music; Poetry; Theatre; Dance
Status: Non-Profit, Professional
Paid Staff: 14
Paid Artists: 44
Budget: $2 Million
Income Sources: Individual Gifts; Foundations; Grants; Box Office; Gift Shop
Performs At: Orchestral and Chamber Music Concerts, Theatre, Dance
Affiliations: Chamber Music of America, League of American Orchestra, American String Teachers Association
Annual Attendance: 20,000
Type of Stage: Proscenium
Stage Dimensions: 70 x 50
Seating Capacity: 1100
Rental Contact: Program Director Alain G. Declert

8023
ANGELO STATE UNIVERSITY AUDITORIUM

2601 W Avenue N
San Angelo, TX 76909
Phone: 915-942-2021
Fax: 915-942-2229
e-mail: it@angelo.edu
Web Site: www.angelo.edu
Management:
  Library Director: Maurice Fortin

8024
HOUSTON HARTE UNIVERSITY CENTER

Angelo State University
1910 Rosemont Drive
San Angelo, TX 76909
Phone: 325-942-2021
Fax: 325-942-2229
e-mail: david.rosipal@angelo.edu
Web Site: www.angelo.edu
Officers:
  Executive Director, Business Svcs.: Greg Pecina
  Associate Director, Special Events: David Rosipal
Management:
  Assistant Director, Special Events: Jessica Manning
  Events Manager: Ashley Wallace
  Events Manager: Don Cheek
Mission: To support the mission of Angelo State University
Status: Student Union
Paid Staff: 9
Income Sources: Student Fees; Rentals
Performs At: Conference Center
Type of Stage: Portable
Stage Dimensions: 20'x8' sections
Seating Capacity: 900
Year Remodeled: 2000
Year Restored: 2000
Rental Contact: Shayna Lopez

8025
SAN ANGELO CITY AUDITORIUM

500 Rio Concho Drive
72 West College
San Angelo, TX 76903

Phone: 915-653-9577
Fax: 915-659-0900
Web Site: www.sanangelotexas.org

8026
ALAMODOME

100 Montana
San Antonio, TX 78203
Phone: 210-207-3663
Fax: 210-207-3646
Toll-free: 800-884-3663
e-mail: dmarketing@alamodome.com
Web Site: www.alamodome.com
Management:
  Director: Goerge Abington
  Operations Manager: Jim Mery
  Booking Manager: Carol Pollock
Founded: 1993
Status: For-Profit, Professional
Paid Staff: 50
Type of Stage: Stadium
Seating Capacity: 65,000

8027
ARNESON RIVER THEATRE

418 Villita Street
San Antonio, TX 78205
Phone: 210-212-6771
Fax: 210-299-8444

8028
BEETHOVEN HALL: SAN JOSE CONVENTION CENTER

200 E Market
San Antonio, TX 78205
Phone: 210-299-8500
Fax: 210-223-1495

8029
CARVER COMMUNITY CULTURAL CENTER

226 N Hackberry
San Antonio, TX 78202
Phone: 210-207-7211
Fax: 210-207-4412
Web Site: www.thecarver.org
Management:
  Executive Director: William Lewis
Mission: To celebrate the diverse cultures of our world, nation and community, with emphasis on its African American heritage by providing challenging artistic presentations, community outreach activities and educational programs.
Founded: 1976
Specialized Field: Multi-ethnic and multi-cultural performing and visual arts center
Status: Non-Profit, Professional
Paid Staff: 18
Paid Artists: 10

8030
CARVER COMPLEX

226 N Hackberry
San Antonio, TX 78202
Phone: 210-207-7211
Fax: 210-207-4412
Web Site: www.thecarver.org
Management:
  Executive Director: William Lewis III
  Marketing Director: Chris Novosad
  Director Development: Annalisa Peace

8031
FREEMAN COLISEUM

3201 E Houston
PO Box 200283
San Antonio, TX 78219
Phone: 210-226-1177
Fax: 210-226-5081
e-mail: info@freemancoliseum.com
Web Site: www.freemancoliseum.com
Management:
  Executive Director: Derrick Howard
  General Manager: JC Hrubetz
  General Operations Manager: Mackie McCullen
Mission: Multi-purpose concert and performance facility
Founded: 1949
Specialized Field: Dance; Music; Facility

8032
LAURIE AUDITORIUM

Trinity University
San Antonio, TX 78212
Phone: 210-736-8119
Fax: 210-736-8100

8033
MUNICIPAL AUDITORIUM

100 Auditorium Circle
San Antonio, TX 78205
Phone: 210-207-8500
Fax: 210-223-1495
Toll-free: 877-504-8895
Web Site: www.sanantonio.gov/convfac
Management:
  Executive Director: Michael J Sawaya
  Operations Director: Wanda Williamsons
Founded: 1926
Status: Non-Profit

8034
NELSON W WOLFF MUNICIPAL STADIUM

5757 New Highway 90 W
San Antonio, TX 78227
Phone: 210-207-3750
Fax: 210-670-8251
e-mail: tmcafee@alamodome.com
Web Site: www.alamodome.com
Management:
  Director: Mike Abingeon
  Stadium Manager: James G Mery
Founded: 1994
Status: Non-Profit, Professional
Paid Staff: 5
Seating Capacity: 6,100

8035
SAN ANTONIO CONVENTION CENTER LILA COCKRELL HALL

200 E Market Street
San Antonio, TX 78205
Phone: 210-731-6611
Fax: 210-223-1495

8036
SUNKEN GARDEN AMPHITHEATRE

3875 North Saint Mary's
San Antonio, TX 78212
Phone: 210-735-4824
Fax: 210-735-4850
Management:
  Supervisor: Peter Georgiev
Seating Capacity: 4,800

8037

STRAHAN COLISEUM

Southwest Texas State University
174 Jowers Center
San Marcos, TX 78666
Phone: 512-245-2023
Fax: 512-245-2967
Management:
Director Facility/Game Operations: Timothy Atkinson
Director Facility: Adam Alonzo
Seating Capacity: 7,739

8038

JACKSON AUDITORIUM

1000 W Court
Seguin, TX 78155
Phone: 210-372-8180
Fax: 210-372-8096

8039

CULTURAL ACTIVITIES CENTER

3011 N 3rd Street
Temple, TX 76501
Phone: 254-773-9926
Fax: 254-773-9929
Web Site: www.cacarts.org
Management:
President: Rolinda Brindley
Executive Director: Terri Matthew
Artistic Director: Marilyn Ritchie
Mission: Provide area residents, especially children, with opportunities to expirence visual and performing arts.
Utilizes: Actors; Artists-in-Residence; Collaborations; Dance Companies; Dancers; Educators; Fine Artists; Guest Accompanists; Guest Directors; Guest Instructors; Instructors; Local Artists; Multi Collaborations; Multimedia; Original Music Scores; Resident Artists; Sign Language Translators; Soloists; Special Technical Talent; Touring Companies; Visual Arts
Founded: 1958
Specialized Field: Visual Arts; Performing Arts
Status: Non-Profit, Professional
Paid Staff: 10
Budget: $500,000
Income Sources: Heartland Fund; Texas Commission on the Arts; Foundations; Grants; Memberships
Affiliations: Southwest Performing Arts Presenters; Texas Association of Museums; Texas Alliance for Education & The Arts
Annual Attendance: 80,000
Facility Category: Auditorium
Type of Stage: Proscenium
Stage Dimensions: 38Wx30D
Seating Capacity: 487
Year Built: 1978
Rental Contact: Aileen Snyder
Organization Type: Performing; Touring; Resident; Educational; Sponsoring

8040

TEMPLE CIVIC THEATRE

2413 S 13th Street
Temple, TX 76504
Phone: 254-778-4751
Fax: 254-778-4980
Web Site: www.artstemple.com
Management:
Artistic Director: Tim Campbell
Founded: 1977
Status: Non-Profit, Non-Professional

Paid Staff: 4

8041

PEROT THEATRE

221 Main Street
PO Box 1171
Texarkana, TX 75501
Phone: 903-792-4992
Fax: 903-793-8510
e-mail: mstarrett@trahc.org
Web Site: www.trahc.org
Management:
Operations Director: Randal Conry
Executive Director: Brian Goesl, artsinfo@trahc.org
Administrative Director: Mary Starrett, mstarrett@trahc.org
Mission: To enrich the human experience in the region by increasing public awareness of, exposure to and participation in the arts and humanities in their many diverse forms.
Utilizes: Artists-in-Residence; Community Talent; Five Seasonal Concerts; Guest Writers; Guild Activities; Local Artists; Original Music Scores; Student Interns; Touring Companies
Founded: 1981
Status: Non-Profit, Professional
Paid Staff: 14
Volunteer Staff: 114
Paid Artists: 3
Year Built: 1924
Year Remodeled: 1980
Cost: $2.4 Million
Rental Contact: Operations Director Randall Conroy

8042

CYNTHIA WOODS MITCHELL PAVILION

2005 Lake Robbins Drive
The Woodlands, TX 77380
Phone: 281-363-3300
Fax: 281-364-3011
e-mail: info@woodlandscenter.org
Web Site: www.woodlandcenter.org
Officers:
President/CEO: Jerry MacDonald
Founded: 1990
Status: Non-Profit, Professional
Paid Staff: 19
Paid Artists: 70
Performs At: Amphitheatre
Annual Attendance: 500,000
Facility Category: Amphitheatre/Fine Arts Theatre
Type of Stage: Proscenium
Stage Dimensions: 60x40
Seating Capacity: 16,500
Year Built: 1990
Year Remodeled: 2008

8043

REGIONAL ARTS CENTER

PO Box 1321
500 Malone, Suite B
Tomball, TX 77377-1321
Phone: 281-351-2787
Fax: 281-351-2702
Web Site: www.regional-arts.org
Management:
President: Elaine Chrisnan
Founded: 1987
Specialized Field: Theatre: Community Performances
Status: Non-Profit, Professional
Paid Staff: 1

8044

COWAN FINE & PERFORMING ARTS CENTER

University of Texas at Tyler
3900 University Boulevard
Tyler, TX 75701
Phone: 903-566-7191
Fax: 903-566-7264
Web Site: www.uttyler.edu/cowan; www.cowancenter.org
Management:
Managing Director: Susan Thomas-Morphew
Box Office Manager: Terri Holland
Founded: 1997
Paid Staff: 6
Performs At: Theatre
Seating Capacity: 2,036
Year Built: 1997

8045

ROSE STADIUM

PO Box 2035
Tyler, TX 75710
Phone: 903-531-3602
Fax: 765-496-1280
Management:
Athletic Director: Billy Hall
Seating Capacity: 12,018

8046

FERREL CENTER

Baylor University
150 Bear Run
Waco, TX 76711
Phone: 254-710-1011
Fax: 254-710-1968
Toll-free: 800-BAY-LORU
Web Site: www.baylor.edu
Management:
President: Robert B Sloan Jr
Associate Athletic Director: Jim Trego
Founded: 1845
Status: For-Profit, Non-Professional

8047

WACO CONVENTION CENTER CHISHOLM HALL

100 Washington Avenue
PO Box 2570
Waco, TX 76703
Phone: 254-299-0630
Fax: 817-750-5801

8048

WACO HIPPODROME

724 Austin Avenue
Waco, TX 76701
Phone: 254-752-7745
Fax: 254-752-9806
Toll-free: 800-701-2787
Web Site: www.wacohippodrome.com
Management:
Executive Director: Teresa Ford
Artistic Director: Richard Aslanian
Technical Director: Len Howard
Mission: To preserve the historic Waco Hippodrome, originally a vaudeville show house; to provide quality Broadway entertainment and nationally known children's shows based on children's literature at an affordable price.
Founded: 1913
Status: Non-Profit, Professional
Paid Staff: 5

Volunteer Staff: 60
Budget: $150,000-400,000
Annual Attendance: 21,000-35,000
Facility Category: Performing Arts Center
Seating Capacity: 943
Rental Contact: Facilities Manager Len Howard

8049
MEMORIAL AUDITORIUM
1300 7th Street
Wichita Falls, TX 76307
Phone: 940-716-5500
Fax: 940-716-5509
Management:
Manager: George Casper

Utah

8050
CENTRUM ARENA
Southern Utah University
351 West Center Street
Cedar City, UT 84720
Phone: 435-586-7763
Fax: 435-865-8542
e-mail: benson_m@suu.edu
Web Site: www.suu.edu
Management:
Director Student Activities: Mindy Benson
Box Office: Shron Spevak
Seating Capacity: 5,022

8051
ECCLES COLISEUM
Southern Utah University
351 West Center Street
Cedar City, UT 84720
Phone: 435-586-1937
Fax: 435-586-5444
Management:
Athletic Director: Tom Douple

8052
LAGOON ENTERTAINMENT DIVISION
375 N Lagoon Drive
Farmington, UT 84025
Phone: 801-451-8059
Fax: 801-451-8015
Toll-free: 800-748-5246
Web Site: www.lagoonpark.com
Status: For-Profit, Professional
Paid Staff: 15
Paid Artists: 30

8053
CAINE LYRIC THEATRE
Utah State University Caine College of the Arts
CCA Production Services
4030 Old Main Hill
Logan, UT 84322-4030
Phone: 435-797-3041
Fax: 435-797-0107
e-mail: jarrod.larsen@usu.edu
Web Site: arts.usu.edu
Management:
Director: Jarrod Larsen, jarrod.larsen@usu.edu
Technical Director: Timothy North,
timothy.north@usu.edu
Scheduling Director: Kris Bushman,
kris.bushman@usu.edu
Scheduling Coordinator: Gwen Scott
Marketing Director/Box Office Mgr: Denise
Albiston

Mission: Connect the artist work of students with audiences
Utilizes: Actors; Artists-in-Residence; Collaborations;
Community Members; Composers; Contract
Orchestras; Dancers; Educators; Five Seasonal
Concerts; Guest Artists; Guest Composers; Guest
Directors; Guest Lecturers; Guest Soloists; Guest
Teachers; Guest Writers; Instructors; Local Talent;
Lyricists; Multi Collaborations; Paid Performers; Scenic
Designers; Soloists; Theatre Companies; Touring
Companies; Volunteer Directors & Actors; Writers
Founded: 1913
Opened: 1913
Specialized Field: Theatre; Music; Lectures; Dance
Status: Non-Profit; Non-Professional
Paid Staff: 5
Volunteer Staff: 100
Paid Artists: 40
Budget: $600,000
Income Sources: Ticket Sales; Rental Revenue;
Grants; Donations; State-Appropriated Funds
Annual Attendance: 10,000
Type of Stage: Proscenium
Stage Dimensions: 21'x21'x14'
Seating Capacity: 380
Year Built: 1913
Year Remodeled: 1996
Cost: $5 million
Rental Contact: Gwen Scott

8054
CHASE FINE ARTS CENTER
Utah State University
Logan, UT 84322
Phone: 435-797-1094

8055
D GLEN SMITH SPECTRUM
Utah State University
7400 Old Main Hill
Logan, UT 84322-7400
Phone: 435-797-1850
Fax: 435-797-2615
Web Site: www.utahstateuniversity.edu
Management:
Director: Rance Pugmire
Marketing Director: Michelle Wilson
Seating Capacity: 10,270

8056
KENT CONCERT HALL
Utah State University Caine College of the Arts
CCA Production Services
4030 Old Main Hill
Logan, UT 84322-4030
Phone: 435-797-3041
Fax: 435-797-0107
e-mail: jarrod.larsen@usu.edu
Web Site: arts.usu.edu
Management:
Director: Jarrod Larsen, jarrod.larsen@usu.edu
Technical Director: Timothy North,
timothy.north@usu.edu
Scheduling Director: Kris Bushman,
kris.bushman@usu.edu
Scheduling Coordinator: Gwen Scott
Marketing Director/Box Office Mgr: Denise
Albiston
Utilizes: Actors; Artists-in-Residence; Collaborations;
Community Members; Composers; Contract
Orchestras; Dancers; Educators; Five Seasonal
Concerts; Guest Artists; Guest Composers; Guest
Directors; Guest Lecturers; Guest Soloists; Guest
Teachers; Guest Writers; Instructors; Local Talent;

Lyricists; Multi Collaborations; Paid Performers; Scenic
Designers; Soloists; Theatre Companies; Touring
Companies; Volunteer Directors & Actors; Writers
Founded: 1967
Opened: 1967
Specialized Field: Theatre; Music; Lectures; Dance
Status: Non-Profit; Professional
Paid Staff: 5
Volunteer Staff: 100
Paid Artists: 40
Income Sources: Ticket Sales; Rental Revenue;
Grants; Donations; State-Appropriated Funds
Type of Stage: Proscenium
Stage Dimensions: 72'x46'x21'
Cost: $4 million
Rental Contact: Gwen Scott

8057
MANON CAINE RUSSELL KATHRYN CAINE WANLASS PERFORMANCE HALL
Utah State University Caine College of the Arts
CCA Production Services
4030 Old Main Hill
Logan, UT 84322-4030
Phone: 435-797-3041
Fax: 435-797-0107
e-mail: jarrod.larsen@usu.edu
Web Site: arts.usu.edu
Management:
Director: Jarrod Larsen, jarrod.larsen@usu.edu
Technical Director: Timothy North,
timothy.north@usu.edu
Scheduling Director: Kris Bushman,
kris.bushman@usu.edu
Scheduling Coordinator: Gwen Scott
Marketing Director/Box Office Mgr: Denise
Albiston
Mission: Connect the artist work of students with
audiences
Utilizes: Actors; Artists-in-Residence; Collaborations;
Community Members; Composers; Contract
Orchestras; Dancers; Educators; Five Seasonal
Concerts; Guest Artists; Guest Composers; Guest
Directors; Guest Lecturers; Guest Soloists; Guest
Teachers; Guest Writers; Instructors; Local Talent;
Lyricists; Multi Collaborations; Paid Performers; Scenic
Designers; Soloists; Theatre Companies; Touring
Companies; Volunteer Directors & Actors; Writers
Founded: 2006
Opened: 2006
Specialized Field: Theatre; Music; Lectures; Dance
Status: Non-Profit; Non-Professional
Paid Staff: 5
Volunteer Staff: 100
Paid Artists: 40
Budget: $600,000
Income Sources: Ticket Sales; Rental Revenue;
Grants; Donations; State-Appropriated Funds
Annual Attendance: 45,000
Type of Stage: Proscenium
Stage Dimensions: 30'x30'
Seating Capacity: 421
Year Built: 2006
Cost: $13 million
Rental Contact: Gwen Scott

8058
MORGAN THEATRE
Utah State University Caine College of the Arts
CCA Production Series
4030 Old Main Hill
Logan, UT 84322-4030

Phone: 435-797-3041
Fax: 435-797-0107
e-mail: jarrod.larsen@usu.edu
Web Site: arts.usu.edu
Management:
Director: Jarrod Larsen, jarrod.larsen@usu.edu
Technical Director: Timothy North,
timothy.north@usu.edu
Scheduling Director: Kris Bushman,
kris.bushman@usu.edu
Marketing Director/Box Office Mgr: Denise
Albiston
Utilizes: Actors; Artists-in-Residence; Collaborations;
Community Members; Composers; Contract
Orchestras; Dancers; Educators; Five Seasonal
Concerts; Guest Artists; Guest Composers; Guest
Directors; Guest Lecturers; Guest Soloists; Guest
Teachers; Guest Writers; Instructors; Local Talent;
Lyricists; Multi Collaborations; Paid Performers; Scenic
Designers; Soloists; Theatre Companies; Touring
Companies; Volunteer Directors & Actors; Writers
Founded: 1967
Opened: 1967
Specialized Field: Theatre; Music; Lectures; Dance
Status: Non-Profit, Non-Professional
Paid Staff: 5
Volunteer Staff: 100
Paid Artists: 40
Budget: $600,000
Income Sources: Ticket Sales; Rental Revenue;
Grants; Donations; State-Appropriated Funds
Annual Attendance: 30,000
Type of Stage: 3/4 Round Modified Thrust
Stage Dimensions: Full 72'x72'; Thrust 42'x50'
Seating Capacity: 669
Year Built: 1967
Year Remodeled: 2001
Cost: $4.5 Million
Rental Contact: Gwen Scott

8059
MANTI TEMPLE GROUNDS AMPHITHEATRE

Manti, UT 84642
Phone: 435-835-3000

8060
DEE EVENTS CENTER

Weber State University
4400 Harrison Boulevard, Box 3401
Ogden, UT 84408-3401
Phone: 801-626-6665
Fax: 801-626-7190
e-mail: jlake@weber.edu
Web Site: www.weber.edu
Management:
Manager: Jody G Lake
Founded: 1977
Status: Non-Profit, Non-Professional
Paid Staff: 30

8061
ECCLES COMMUNITY ART CENTER

2580 Jefferson Avenue
Ogden, UT 84401
Phone: 801-392-6935
e-mail: eccles@ogden4arts.org
Web Site: www.ogden4arts.org
Management:
Executive Director: Sandy Havas
Founded: 1959
Specialized Field: Visual Arts
Status: Non-Profit, Non-Professional
Paid Staff: 3

8062
PEERY'S EGYPTIAN THEATRE

2415 Washington Boulevard
Ogden, UT 84401
Phone: 801-395-3227
Fax: 801-395-3201
e-mail: boxoffice@peerysegyptiantheater.com
Web Site: www.peerysegyptiantheater.com
Management:
Technical Director: H C Sorensen
Mission: Performing arts and movie theater.
Utilizes: AEA Actors
Founded: 1920
Paid Staff: 8
Budget: $60,000-150,000
Season: June - August
Facility Category: Historic Theater
Type of Stage: Proscenium
Stage Dimensions: 36' x 40'
Seating Capacity: 850
Year Built: 1924
Year Remodeled: 1997
Rental Contact: Director Kathryn Maguet

8063
VAL A BROWNING CENTER FOR THE PERFORMING ARTS

Weber State University
Ogden, UT 84408-1901
Phone: 801-626-7000
Fax: 801-626-8901
Web Site: www.browningcenter.weber.edu
Management:
Executive Director: Scott Jemson
Status: Non-Profit

8064
MCKAY EVENTS CENTER

Utah Valley State College
800 West University Parkway
Orem, UT 84058
Phone: 801-863-8767
Fax: 801-863-8769
Web Site: www.uvsc.edu/mec
Management:
Director: Mark Hilderbrand
Seating Capacity: 7,500

8065
DEER VALLEY RESORT AMPHITHEATRE

2250 Deer Valley Drive South
Park City, UT 84060
Mailing Address: PO Box 1525
Phone: 435-645-6939
Fax: 435-645-6939
e-mail: marketing@deervalley.com
Web Site: www.deervalley.com
Management:
Events Manager: Carrie Budding
Seating Capacity: 5,000

8066
MARRIOTT CENTER/COUGAR STADIUM

Brigham Young University
PO Box 20530
Provo, UT 84602-0530
Phone: 801-422-6022
Fax: 801-378-2042
Toll-free: 800-322-2981
Web Site: www.byu.edu
Management:
Executive Director: Larry R Duffin
Assistant Manager: Mary Jean Draper

Founded: 1964
Status: Non-Profit, Non-Professional
Paid Staff: 13
Seating Capacity: 65,524

8067
DIXIE COLLEGE FINE ARTS CENTER

225 S 700th E
Saint George, UT 84770
Phone: 435-652-7790
Fax: 435-656-4021
Web Site: www.dixie.edu
Management:
President: Robert Huddleston
Artistic Director: Eric Young
Status: Non-Profit, Non-Professional

8068
DIXIE COLLEGE ARENA THEATRE

225 S 700th E
Saint George, UT 84770
Phone: 435-652-7790
Fax: 435-656-4021

8069
DIXIE COLLEGE PROSCENIUM THEATRE

225 S 700th E
Saint George, UT 84770
Phone: 435-652-7790
Fax: 435-656-4021

8070
TUACAHN CENTER FOR THE ARTS

1100 Tuacahn Drive
Saint George, UT 84738
Phone: 435-652-3300
Fax: 435-652-3227
Toll-free: 800-746-9882
e-mail: tuacahn@infowest.com
Web Site: www.tuacahn.org
Officers:
CEO: Kevin Smith
COO: Kevin Warnick
Management:
Chairman and CEO: Fred Lampropoulos
Sales and Marketing Coordinator: Donna
Casebolt
Mission: Was established to awaken the mobility of the
hman soul and transmit light and hope to people
everywhere through the arts and education. The theatre
wishes to preserve and project the legacy of the
American Musical into the 21st century.
Founded: 1992
Specialized Field: Theater
Status: Nonprofit
Season: June - September
Facility Category: Ampitheatre; Highschool
Type of Stage: Proscenium
Stage Dimensions: 75' x 60'
Seating Capacity: 1920

8071
ABRAVANEL HALL

123 West South Temple
Salt Lake City, UT 84101
Phone: 801-323-6871
Fax: 801-538-2272
Web Site: www.arttix.org
Management:
Event Coordinator: Terri McGhee
Event Coordinator: Mindy Nielson
Seating Capacity: 2,800

8072
ABRAVANEL SYMPHONY HALL
123 W South Temple
Salt Lake City, UT 84101
Phone: 801-323-6800
Fax: 801-538-2272
Toll-free: 888-451-2787
Web Site: www.arttix.org
Management:
Executive Director: Chris Crowley
Status: Non-Profit, Professional
Paid Staff: 200

8073
CAPITOL THEATRE
48 W Second S
Salt Lake City, UT 84101
Phone: 888-451-2787
Fax: 801-538-2272

8074
ENERGY SOLUTIONS ARENA
301 W South Temple
Salt Lake City, UT 84101
Phone: 801-325-2000
Fax: 801-325-2516
Web Site: www.energysolutionsarena.com
Officers:
President: Randy Rigby
CFO/Facilities Executive VP: Bob Hyde
Management:
Senior VP Marketing: Jim Olson
VP Event Services: Mark Powell
Founded: 1990
Facility Category: Sports & Entertainment
Seating Capacity: 20,400

8075
JON M HUNTSMAN CENTER
University of Utah
1825 East South Campus Drive, Front
Salt Lake City, UT 84112
Phone: 801-581-5155
Fax: 801-581-6670
Management:
Director: Richard L James
Box Office Supervisor: Jon Jabobsen
Founded: 1969
Specialized Field: Athletics and Concerts
Status: For-Profit, Non-Professional
Seating Capacity: 15,000

8076
KINGSBURY HALL
University of Utah
1395 East Presidents Circle, Room 190
Salt Lake City, UT 84112-0040
Phone: 801-581-6261
Fax: 801-585-5464
Web Site: www.kingsburyhall.org
Management:
Director: Greg Gailmann
Manager Events/Operations: Lynda Christensen
Development Director: Kathleen Harmon Gardner
Technical Director: Randy Rasmussen
Utilizes: Dance Companies; Guest Instructors; Guest
Soloists; Special Technical Talent; Theatre Companies
Founded: 1930
Specialized Field: Performing Arts Center
Paid Staff: 20
Income Sources: Rentals
Affiliations: University of Utah Music Department
Annual Attendance: 200,000

Facility Category: Auditorium
Type of Stage: Proscenium
Stage Dimensions: 120 x 48 x 72
Seating Capacity: 1,913
Year Built: 1930
Year Remodeled: 1996
Rental Contact: Manager of Events & Operations
Lynda Christensen
Resident Groups: University of Utah Associated
Students (Ballet, Organization theaters, operat, etc.)

8077
RICE-ECCLES STADIUM
University of Utah
451 South 1400 East, Suite 600
Salt Lake City, UT 84112
Phone: 801-581-5445
Fax: 801-585-1417
e-mail: mburk@stadium.utah.edu
Web Site: www.rice-ecclesstadium.com
Management:
Director: Mark Burk
Event Services: Kristy Holt
Seating Capacity: 45,734

Vermont

8078
BARRE OPERA HOUSE
6 N Main Street
PO Box 583
Barre, VT 05641
Phone: 802-476-8188
Fax: 802-476-5648
e-mail: staff@barreoperahouse.org
Web Site: www.barreoperahouse.org
Management:
Executive Director: Carol Dawes
Utilizes: Dance Companies; Instructors; Local Artists;
Poets; Student Interns; Special Technical Talent;
Theatre Companies
Paid Staff: 2
Annual Attendance: 22,000
Facility Category: Performance Hall
Type of Stage: Proscenium
Stage Dimensions: 32x30
Seating Capacity: 645
Year Built: 1899
Year Remodeled: 1993
Rental Contact: Carol Dawes

8079
BURLINGTON MEMORIAL AUDITORIUM
250 Main Street
Burlington, VT 05401
Phone: 802-864-6044
Fax: 802-863-4322
e-mail: memorial@ci.burlington.vt.us
Management:
President: Peter Clazelle
Executive Director: Alan Campbell
Founded: 1928
Status: Non-Profit, Professional
Paid Staff: 3

8080
FLYNN CENTER FOR THE PERFORMING ARTS
153 Main Street
Burlington, VT 05401

Phone: 802-652-4500
Fax: 802-863-8788
e-mail: amalina@flynncenter.org
Web Site: www.flynncenter.org
Management:
Executive Director: Andrea Rogers
Artistic Director: Arnie Malina
Utilizes: Actors; Artists-in-Residence; Choreographers;
Collaborating Artists; Collaborations; Commissioned
Composers; Commissioned Music; Dance Companies;
Dancers; Educators; Guest Writers; Guild Activities;
High School Drama; Instructors; Local Artists;
Multimedia; Original Music Scores; Resident Artists;
Sign Language Translators; Soloists; Special Technical
Talent; Theatre Companies
Founded: 1981
Status: Non-Profit, Non-Professional
Paid Staff: 35
Volunteer Staff: 300
Annual Attendance: 100,000+
Facility Category: 150 Seat Modular Black Box
Type of Stage: Proscenium
Seating Capacity: 1,450; 150
Year Built: 1930
Year Remodeled: 2000
Rental Contact: Aimee Petrin

8081
UNIVERSITY OF VERMONT: RECITAL HALL
Music Building
Redstone Campus - S Prospect Street
Burlington, VT 05405
Phone: 802-656-3040

8082
DEPARTMENT OF THEATRE AND DANCE
Middlebury College
Middlebury, VT 05753
Phone: 802-443-5601
Fax: 802-443-2137
Web Site: www.middlebury.edu
Management:
Chair: Mark Evancho
Status: For-Profit, Non-Professional
Performs At: Seeler Studio Theatre, Wright Memorial
Theatre

8083
YELLOW BARN
63 Main Street
Putney, VT 05346
Phone: 802-387-6637
Fax: 802-387-6637
e-mail: info@yellowbarn.org
Web Site: www.yellowbarn.org
Management:
Artistic Director: Seth Knopp
Founded: 1969
Status: Non-Profit, Professional

8084
CHANDLER MUSIC HALL AND CULTURAL CENTER
71-73 Main Street
Randolph, VT 05060
Phone: 802-728-9878

8085
THE GREEN AT SHELBURNE MUSEUM
Shelburn Museum
Route 7
Shelburne, VT 05482

Phone: 802-654-7079
Fax: 802-655-6137
e-mail: alex@highergroundmusic.com
Web Site: www.highergroundmusic.com/shelburne
Seating Capacity: 3,000

Virginia

8086
BARTER PLAYHOUSE/THEATRE HOUSE
Main Street
PO Box 867
Abingdon, VA 24210
Phone: 540-628-3991
Fax: 540-676-6064

8087
RACHEL M. SCHLESINGER CONCERT HALL AND ARTS CENTER
North Virginia Community College
3001 North Beauregard Street
Alexandria, VA 22311
Phone: 703-845-6156
Fax: 703-845-6154
e-mail: lvitello@nvcc.edu
Web Site: www.schlesingercenter.com
Management:
  Marketing/PR Manager: Linda M Vitello
  Production Manager: Stephen Shetler
  Managing Director: Dr Leslie White
Founded: 2001
Opened: 2001
Specialized Field: Washington, DC Metropolitan Area; Northern Virginia
Performs At: Rental Venue Providing Concert Hall Space For Vocal, Instrumental, Dance And Drama Performances.
Facility Category: Concert Hall And Arts Center
Type of Stage: Proscenium
Seating Capacity: 1,000 concert hall/80 reception areas

8088
BURRUSS AUDITORIUM
Virginia Tech University
225 Squires Center
Blacksburg, VA 24061
Phone: 703-231-5431
Fax: 703-231-5430

8089
CASELL COLISEUM
Virginia Tech University
Washington Street
Blacksburg, VA 24061
Phone: 540-231-9963
Fax: 540-231-3060
e-mail: caraw@vt.edu
Web Site: www.hokiesports.com
Management:
  President: Charles Steger
  Executive Director: Jim Weaver
Founded: 1872
Status: For-Profit, Non-Professional

8090
LANE STADIUM
Virginia Tech University
Jamerson Center
Blacksburg, VA 24061-0502
Phone: 540-231-6796
Fax: 540-231-3060
Web Site: www.hokiesports.com

Management:
  Director Athletics: Jim Weaver
  Senior Associate Director Athletics: Sharon McCloskey
  Associate Director Athletics: Tom Gabhard
  Associate Director Athletics: Jon Jaudon
  Director Fiance Affairs: Randy Butt
  Assistant Director Athletics: Tim East
Specialized Field: Athletics
Status: Non-Profit, Professional
Paid Staff: 500
Volunteer Staff: 250
Seating Capacity: 50,000

8091
NISSAN PAVILION AT STONE RIDGE
7800 Cellar Door Drive
Bristow, VA 20136
Phone: 703-754-6400
Fax: 703-754-6429
e-mail: boxoffice@nissanpavilion.com
Web Site: www.nissanpavilion.com
Management:
  GM: Bruce Edwards
Seating Capacity: 25,000

8092
SAINT ANNE'S-BELFIELD SCHOOL SUMMER MUSIC ACADEMY
1503 Wilton Farm Road
Charlottesville, VA 22911
Phone: 804-295-5499
Fax: 804-963-9964
Management:
  Executive Director: Susan Black

8093
SCOTT STADIUM
University of Virginia
PO Box 3785
Charlottesville, VA 22903
Phone: 804-982-5100
Fax: 804-982-5213
Management:
  Athletic Director: M Terry Holland
Seating Capacity: 40,000

8094
UNIVERSITY OF VIRGINIA HALL
University of Virginia
PO Box 400846
Charlottesville, VA 22904-4846
Phone: 804-924-3791
Fax: 804-982-5212
Web Site: www.virginiasports.com
Management:
  Associate Athletic Director: Mark Fletcher
  Athletic Director: Craig Littlepage
  Sports Information Director: Rich Murray
  Head Football Coach: George Welsh
  Head Men's Basketball Coach: Pete Gillen
  Head Women's Basketball Coach: Debbie Ryan
  Associate Athletic Director: Mike Thomas
  Ticket Manager: Dick Mathias
Seating Capacity: 8,450

8095
GEORGE MASON UNIVERSITY DEPARTMENT OF THEATER
College of Visual and Performing Arts
4400 University Drive, MSN 3E6
Fairfax, VA 22030

Phone: 703-993-1120
e-mail: theater@gmu.edu
Web Site: theater.gmu.edu
Officers:
  Department Chair: Ken Elston
  Associate Dean, AASA: Linda Miller
Mission: Provides a rigorous, creative and nuturing environment where we encourage conceptual and cultural diversity. Students establish a professional work ethic, collaborate with others, and take responsibility for individuals as well as group efforts as they prepare for a life and career beyond graduation.
Founded: 1990
Opened: 1990
Status: Non-Profit, Professional
Performs At: TheaterSpace, Black Box Theater, Harris Theater
Seating Capacity: 150, 460

8096
PATRIOT CENTER
George Mason University
4400 University Drive
Fairfax, VA 22030-4444
Phone: 703-993-3009
Fax: 703-993-3079
e-mail: bgeisler@gmu.edu
Web Site: www.patroitcenter.com
Management:
  President: Paolin Abe
  General Manager: Barry H Geisler
  Director Operations: John Gabbert
Founded: 1985
Seating Capacity: 10,200

8097
FORT EUSTIS MUSIC AND VIDEO CENTER - JACOBS THEATRE
ATZF-PRC-MT BUILDING 224
Fort Eustis, VA 23604
Phone: 757-878-3436

8098
RIVERSIDE CENTER DINNER THEATER AND CONFERENCE FACILITY
95 Riverside Parkway
Fredericksburg, VA 22406
Phone: 540-370-4300
Fax: 540-370-4304
Toll-free: 888-999-8527
e-mail: riverside@aol.com
Web Site: www.riversidedt.com
Founded: 1998
Specialized Field: Musical Theatre
Status: For-Profit, Professional

8099
INNSBROOK PAVILION
4600 Cox Road
Suite 109
Glen Allen, VA 23060
Phone: 804-217-8800
Fax: 804-217-8802
e-mail: dak@alcnet.com
Web Site: www.innsbrook.com
Management:
  Executive Director: Denise Kranich
Seating Capacity: 6,000

8100

HAMPTON COLISEUM

1000 Coliseum Drive
PO Box 7309
Hampton, VA 23666
Phone: 757-838-5650
Fax: 757-838-2595
e-mail: jtsao@hampton.gov
Web Site: www.hamptoncoliseum.org
Management:
   Director: Joe Tsao
Founded: 1969
Status: Non-Profit, Professional
Paid Staff: 200

8101

HAMPTON UNIVERSITY

121 Holland Hall
Hampton, VA 23668
Phone: 757-727-5641
Fax: 757-728-6995
Web Site: www.hamptonu.edu
Officers:
   Admin Secretary for Athletics: Yakina Parker
Management:
   Director of Athletics: Lonza Hardy Jr
   Business Manager: Petra Klimplova
   Asst AD/SWA: Tianna Scott
Founded: 1868
Status: For-Profit, Non-Professional
Paid Staff: 200
Paid Artists: 50

8102

BRIDGEFORTH STADIUM

Godwin Hall, MSC 2301
Harrisonburg, VA 22807
Phone: 540-568-6164
Fax: 540-568-3489
Web Site: www.jmusports.com
Officers:
   President: Linwood Rose
Management:
   Athletic Director: Jeffrey Boume
   Athletic Facilities Director: Ty Phillips
Founded: 1908
Status: Non-Profit, Professional

8103

EXPERIMENTAL THEATRE

James Madison University
Theatre II Building
Theatre II, MSC 5601
Harrisonburg, VA 22807
Phone: 540-568-6342
Fax: 540-568-6598
e-mail: buckwj@jmu.edu
Web Site: www.jmu.edu/theatre
Management:
   Director: William Buck
   Technical Director: Charlie Lawlor
Mission: The James Madison University Theatre program has a liberal arts orientation directed specifically toward undergraduate students. We have three basic emphases: instruction in the theory and history of drama; instruction in the practice of theatre arts; and a full production program.
Status: Professional
Type of Stage: Black Box
Seating Capacity: 150

8104

LATIMER-SHAEFFER THEATRE

James Madison University
Duke Hall
Theatre II, MSC 5601
Harrisonburg, VA 22807
Phone: 540-568-6342
Fax: 540-568-6598
e-mail: buckwj@jmu.edu
Web Site: www.jmu.edu/theatre
Management:
   Director: William Buck
   Technical Director: Charlie Lawlor
Mission: The James Madison University Theatre program has a liberal arts orientation directed specifically toward undergraduate students. We have three basic emphases: instruction in the theory and history of drama; instruction in the practice of theatre arts; and a full production program.
Status: Professional
Type of Stage: Proscenium
Seating Capacity: 324
Year Built: 1967
Year Restored: 1988

8105

ALUMNI MEMORIAL FIELD

Virginia Military Institute
North Main Street
Lexington, VA 24450
Phone: 540-464-7230
Fax: 540-464-7622
e-mail: brannerwh@vmi.edu
Web Site: www.vmi.edu
Officers:
   President: J H Binford Peay, III
Management:
   Director Communications/Marketing: COL Grover O Craven, Jr
   Sports Information Director: Wade Branner
Founded: 1839
Opened: 1962
Status: Non-Profit, Non-Professional
Paid Staff: 103
Seating Capacity: 10,000
Cost: $250,000
Year Restored: 1985

8106

CAMERON HALL

Virginia Military Institute
North Main Street
Lexington, VA 24450
Phone: 540-464-7529
Fax: 540-646-7622
Toll-free: 866-539-3387
Web Site: www.vmi.edu
Management:
   President: J Binford Peay
   Executive Director: Dennis Toney
   Director: Donny White
Founded: 1839
Status: Non-Profit, Professional
Paid Staff: 50

8107

LYNCHBURG FINE ARTS CENTER

1815 Thomson Drive
Lynchburg, VA 24501
Phone: 434-846-8451
Fax: 434-846-3806
Web Site: www.lynchburgbiz.com/fac
Officers:

Chairman: Michael Gillette
   Interim Executive Director: Judy Wynne
Management:
   Executive Director: Mary Brumbaugh
Utilizes: Actors; Choreographers; Collaborations; Curators; Dance Companies; Dancers; Fine Artists; Grant Writers; Guest Artists; Guest Designers; Guest Lecturers; Guest Musical Directors; Instructors; Local Artists; Music; Selected Students; Soloists; Touring Companies
Founded: 1962
Paid Staff: 12
Paid Artists: 100
Budget: $640,000
Income Sources: contributions, rentals, classes, performances
Annual Attendance: 50,000
Facility Category: arts center
Type of Stage: proscenium
Stage Dimensions: 20x40x30
Seating Capacity: 501
Year Built: 1962
Rental Contact: Fred Saheib

8108

VINES CENTER

Liberty University
1971 University Boulevard
Lynchburg, VA 24502
Phone: 434-582-2000
Fax: 434-582-2076
Toll-free: 800-543-5317
Web Site: www.liberty.edu
Management:
   EVP: Dave Young
   Director: Woody Galbreath
Founded: 1971
Status: Non-Profit, Non-Professional
Seating Capacity: 9,000

8109

WILLIAM STADIUM

Liberty University
1971 University Boulevard
Lynchburg, VA 24502
Phone: 804-582-2100
Fax: 804-582-2076
Management:
   Director: Woody Galbreath
Seating Capacity: 12,000

8110

PRINCE WILLIAM COUNTY STADIUM

14420 Bristow Road
Manassas, VA 22191
Phone: 703-792-7060
Fax: 703-792-4219
Management:
   Director: Rich Artenian
   Sports Marketing Coordinator: Marvin Vann
Seating Capacity: 6,000

8111

TULTEX CORPORATION

101 Commonwealth Boulevard
Martinsville, VA 24112
Phone: 540-632-2961
Fax: 510-632-9123

8112

ALDEN THEATRE AT MCLEAN COMMUNITY CENTER

1234 Ingleside Avenue
McLean, VA 22101

Phone: 703-790-0123
Fax: 703-556-0547
e-mail: clare.kiley@fairfaxcounty.gov
Web Site: www.mcleancenter.org
Management:
    Executive Director: Bill Bersie
    Artistic Director: Clare Kiley
Founded: 1975
Status: Non-Profit, Non-Professional
Paid Staff: 30

8113
ATTUCKS THEATRE

City of Norfolk
1010 Church Street
Norfolk, VA 23510
Phone: 757-664-6464
Fax: 757-664-6990
e-mail: john.rhamstine@norfolk.gov
Web Site: www.sevenvenues.com
Management:
    Director: John Rhamstine
    Events Manager: Scott Warren
    Marketing Manager: Melissa Skinner
Mission: To present the best in sports, family and cultural entertainment.
Founded: 2004
Opened: 2004
Status: Non-Profit, Professional
Paid Staff: 56
Budget: $400,000
Income Sources: City Budget
Facility Category: Theater
Type of Stage: Proscenium
Seating Capacity: 624
Year Built: 1919
Year Remodeled: 2002
Cost: $8 Million
Rental Contact: John Rhamstine

8114
CHRYSLER HALL

City of Norfolk
215 St Pauls Boulevard
Norfolk, VA 23510
Phone: 757-664-6464
Fax: 757-664-6990
e-mail: john.rhamstine@norfolk.gov
Web Site: www.norfolkscope.com
Management:
    Director: John Rhamstine
    Events Manager: Scott Warren
    Marketing Manager: Melissa Skinner
Mission: To present the best in sports, family and cultural entertainment.
Founded: 1971
Specialized Field: Concerts, Theatre
Status: Non-Profit, Professional
Paid Staff: 56
Budget: $6 million
Income Sources: City Budget
Annual Attendance: 200,000
Facility Category: Performing Arts Theater
Type of Stage: Proscenium
Orchestra Pit: y
Seating Capacity: 2,500
Year Built: 1969
Cost: $33 Million
Rental Contact: John Rhamstine

8115
CONSTANT CONVOCATION CENTER

Old Dominion College
4320 Hampton Boulevard
Norfolk, VA 23529
Phone: 757-683-6541
Fax: 757-683-6544
Web Site: www.constantcenter.com
Management:
    Regional VP/GM: Doug Higgons
Seating Capacity: 8,500
Year Built: 2002

8116
GENERIC THEATER

912 W 21st Street
PO Box 11071
Norfolk, VA 23517
Phone: 757-441-2729
Fax: 757-441-2729
Web Site: www.generictheater.org
Management:
    President: Jeff Russell
    Artistic Director: Staci Robbins
    Technical Director: Patricia S Ellison
Founded: 1981
Status: Non-Profit, Professional
Paid Staff: 5

8117
HARBOR PARK STADIUM

City Of Norfolk
150 Park Avenue
Norfolk, VA 23510
Mailing Address: 201 East Brambleton Avenue
Phone: 757-664-6464
Fax: 757-664-6990
e-mail: john.rhamstine@norfolk.gov
Web Site: www.sevenvenues.com
Management:
    Director: John Rhamstine
    Events Manager: Scott Warren
    Marketing Manager: Melissa Skinner
    Marketing Manager: Melissa Skinner
Mission: To present the best in sports, family and cultural entertainment.
Founded: 1993
Opened: 1993
Specialized Field: Professional AAA Baseball Facility
Status: Non-Profit, Professional
Paid Staff: 56
Budget: $6 Million
Performs At: Stadium
Annual Attendance: 400,000
Seating Capacity: 12,067
Year Built: 1993
Cost: $16 Million
Rental Contact: Director John Rhamstine

8118
HARRISON OPERA HOUSE

City of Norfolk
160 Virginia Beach Boulevard
Norfolk, VA 23510
Mailing Address: 201 E Brambleton Ave Norfolk VA 23510
Phone: 757-664-6464
Fax: 757-664-6990
e-mail: john.rhamstine@norfolk.gov
Web Site: www.sevenvenues.com
Management:
    Director: John Rhamstine
    Events Manager: Scott Warren

Marketing Manager: Melissa Skinner
Mission: To present the best in sports, family and cultural entertainment.
Founded: 1994
Opened: 1994
Specialized Field: Opera
Status: Non-Profit, Professional
Paid Staff: 56
Budget: $6 Million
Income Sources: City Budget
Annual Attendance: 100,000
Facility Category: Opera House
Type of Stage: Proscenium
Seating Capacity: 1,632
Year Built: 1945
Year Remodeled: 1994
Cost: $10 Million
Rental Contact: John Rhamstine

8119
LITTLE THEATRE OF NORFOLK

801 Claremont Avenue
Norfolk, VA 23508
Phone: 757-627-8551

8120
NORFOLK SCOPE ARENA

City of Norfolk
201 E Brambleton Avenue
Norfolk, VA 23510
Phone: 757-664-6464
Fax: 757-664-6990
e-mail: john.rhamstine@norfolk.gov
Web Site: www.sevenvenues.com
Management:
    Director: John Rhamstine
    Events Manager: Scott Warren
    Marketing Manager: Melissa Skinner
Mission: To present the best in sports, family and cultural entertainment.
Founded: 1971
Opened: 1971
Specialized Field: Series & Festivals; Instrumental Music; Vocal Music; Theatre; Performing Series; Sports; Concerts
Status: Non-Profit, Professional
Paid Staff: 56
Budget: $6 Million
Income Sources: City Budget
Annual Attendance: 500,000
Facility Category: Arena
Type of Stage: Wegner
Stage Dimensions: adjustable
Seating Capacity: 13,600; 11,500
Year Built: 1969
Cost: $33 Million
Rental Contact: John Rhamstine

8121
WELLS THEATRE

254 Granby Street
Norfolk, VA 23510
Phone: 757-664-6464
Fax: 757-664-6990
e-mail: john.rhamstine@norfolk.gov
Web Site: www.sevenvenues.com
Management:
    Director: John Rhamstine
    Events Manager: Scott Warren
    Marketing Manager: Melissa Skinner
Mission: To present the best in sports, family and cultural entertainment.
Founded: 1971
Status: Non-Profit, Professional

Paid Staff: 56
Seating Capacity: 600

8122
ROGERS STADIUM
Virginia State University
PO Box 9058
Petersburg, VA 23806
Phone: 804-524-5030
Fax: 804-524-5763
Web Site: www.vsu.edu
Management:
President: Eddie N Moore Jr
Interim Athletic Director: Peggy Davis
Founded: 1882
Status: Non-Profit, Non-Professional
Seating Capacity: 13,500

8123
RADFORD UNIVERSITY THEATRE
E Main Street
PO Box 6969
Radford, VA 24142
Phone: 540-831-5012
Fax: 540-831-6313
Web Site: www.radford.edu
Management:
President: Douglas Covington
Status: Non-Profit, Non-Professional
Paid Staff: 7

8124
CENTER STAGE
2310 Colts Neck Road
Reston, VA 22091
Phone: 703-476-4500
Fax: 703-476-8617
Web Site: www.westerncommunitycenter.com
Management:
Executive Director: Dennis Kern
Artistic Director: Leila Gordon
Founded: 1979
Status: For-Profit, Professional

8125
CARPENTER CENTER FOR THE PERFORMING ARTS
600 E Grace Street
Richmond, VA 23219
Phone: 804-225-9000
Fax: 804-649-7402
Web Site: www.carpentercenter.com
Management:
President: Martin Rust
Executive Director: Joel Katz
Business Manager: Maria Donaldson
Director Marketing: Torra Holnan
Facility Manager: Joe Yarborough
Founded: 1983
Status: Non-Profit, Non-Professional
Paid Staff: 10
Annual Attendance: 180,000
Type of Stage: proscenium
Stage Dimensions: width 76'6", depth 26'6"
Seating Capacity: 2,041
Year Built: 1928
Year Remodeled: 1983
Rental Contact: Joel Katz

8126
EMPIRE THEATRE COMPLEX
Theatre IV
114 W Broad Street
Richmond, VA 23220

Phone: 804-344-8040
Fax: 804-643-2671
e-mail: j.daugherty@theatreivrichmond.org
Web Site: www.theatreivrichmond.org
Officers:
President: Anne Murphy Douglas
Management:
Artistic Director: Bruce Miller
Managing Director: Thomas H. Tullidge, Jr
Business Development Manager: Thomas Hogg
Mission: We provide outstanding educational entertainment designed to tour and innovative instructional programs that enrich our nation's schools.
Founded: 1975
Opened: 1911
Specialized Field: Broadway
Status: Non-Profit, Professional
Paid Staff: 50
Paid Artists: 30
Annual Attendance: 80,000

8127
EMPIRE THEATRE COMPLEX: EMPIRE STAGE
118 W Broad Street
Richmond, VA 23220
Phone: 804-344-8040
Fax: 804-643-2671

8128
EMPIRE THEATRE COMPLEX: LITTLE THEATRE
114 W Broad Street
Richmond, VA 23220
Phone: 804-783-1688
Fax: 804-775-2325

8129
GREATER RICHMOND CONVOCATION CENTER
403 North 3rd Street
Richmond, VA 23219
Phone: 804-783-7311
Fax: 804-225-0508
e-mail: nsimmonds@greaterrichmondcc.com
Web Site: www.richmondcenter.com
Management:
GM: Michael A Meyers
Assistant GM: Carmen Barefoot
Seating Capacity: 10,000

8130
JAMES L CAMP MEMORIAL
University of Richmond
Modlin Center for the Arts
Richmond, VA 23173
Phone: 804-289-8263
Fax: 804-287-1841
e-mail: dmullin@richmond.edu
Web Site: theatre.richmond.edu
Management:
Technical Director: Reed West
Status: Non-Profit, Non-Professional
Paid Staff: 10
Paid Artists: 2

8131
RICHMOND COLISEUM
City of Richmond
601 E Leigh Street
Richmond, VA 23219

Phone: 804-780-4970
Fax: 804-780-4606
Web Site: www.richmondcoliseum.net
Management:
Operations Director: David Black
General Manager: Larry Wilson
Founded: 1979
Status: For-Profit, Professional
Paid Staff: 25
Seating Capacity: 15,523

8132
RICHMOND STADIUM
University of Richmond
3200 Maple Avenue
Richmond, VA 23221
Phone: 804-289-8371
Fax: 804-289-8820
e-mail: athletic@richmond.edu
Web Site: www.richmond.edu/~athletic
Management:
President: William Cooper
Athletic Director: Jim Miller
Founded: 1830
Status: Non-Profit, Non-Professional
Seating Capacity: 22,319

8133
ROBINS CENTER
University of Richmond
28 Westhampton Way
Richmond, VA 23173
Phone: 804-289-8371
Fax: 804-289-8820
Web Site: www.richmond.edu
Management:
Athletic Director: Charles S Boone
Head Basketball Coach (M): John Beilein
Head Football Coach: Jim Reid
Head Basketball Coach (W): Bob Foley
Seating Capacity: 9,171

8134
STUART C. SIEGEL CENTER
Virginia Commonwealth University
1200 West Broad Street
Richmond, VA 23284
Mailing Address: PO Box 843013
Phone: 804-827-1000
Fax: 804-827-1001
e-mail: events@vcu.edu
Web Site: www.siegelcenter.com
Management:
GM: Tim Lampe
Assistant GM: Nate Doughty
Seating Capacity: 8,000

8135
THEATREVIRGINIA
Virginia Museum of Fine Arts
2800 Grove Avenue
Richmond, VA 23221-2466
Phone: 804-353-6161
Fax: 804-353-8799
Toll-free: 877-353-6161
Management:
Producing Artistic Director: Benny Sato Ambush
Utilizes: Guest Companies; Singers
Founded: 1955
Specialized Field: Ballet
Status: Professional; Nonprofit
Income Sources: League of Resident Theatres; Actors' Equity Association; Society for Stage Directors and Choreographers

Organization Type: Performing; Resident

8136
JEFFERSON THEATRE CENTER

541 Luck Avenue
Suite 221
Roanoke, VA 24016
Phone: 540-343-2624
Fax: 540-343-3744
e-mail: info@jeffcenter.org
Web Site: www.jeffcenter.org
Management:
   Managing Director: Geoffrey Woodward
Mission: Strives to be the destination of choice in the Blue Ridge for cultural and artistic opportunities within a dynamic environment that nurtures creativity, facilitates community events and presents diverse programming.
Founded: 1924
Specialized Field: Theater
Status: Non-Profit

8137
ROANOKE CIVIC CENTER

710 Williamson Road Northeast
PO Box 13005
Roanoke, VA 24016
Phone: 540-853-2241
Fax: 540-853-2748
Web Site: www.roanokeciviccenter.com
Management:
   Executive Director: Willhomina Boyd
   Head of Department: Menna Boyd
   Booking Manager: Susan Owens
   Business Manager: Mae Huff
   Event Services Manager: Lisa Moorman
   Catering Manager: Jed McCracken
   Box Office Manager: Judy Jennings
   Operations Superintendent: Gary Hannabass
Utilizes: Dancers; Soloists; Special Technical Talent; Theatre Companies
Founded: 1971
Status: Non-Profit, Non-Professional
Paid Staff: 35
Annual Attendance: 500,000
Facility Category: Public Assembly - Coliseum, Auditorium, Ex. Hall
Seating Capacity: 11,000
Year Built: 1971
Cost: $14 million
Rental Contact: Booking Manager Tricia Downie

8138
SALEM CIVIC CENTER

James E. Taliaferro Sports/Entertainment Complex
1001 Boulevard
PO Box 886
Salem, VA 24153
Phone: 540-375-3004
Fax: 540-375-4011
e-mail: sales@salemciviccenter.com
Web Site: www.salemciviccenter.com
Management:
   Director Civic Facilities: Carey Harveycutter
   Assistant Director Civic Facilities: John Saunders
   Operations Supervisor: Brian Horsely
Mission: Multi-purpose entertainment facility with arena, ballroom and parlors.
Founded: 1967
Status: Non-Profit, Non-Professional
Paid Staff: 25

8139
BABCOCK AUDITORIUM

Sweet Briar College
Box AU
Sweet Briar, VA 24595
Phone: 804-381-6123
Fax: 804-381-6173
e-mail: Whittman@sbc.edu
Management:
   Manager: Loretta Whittman

8140
WOLF TRAP FARM PARK FOR THE PERFORMING ARTS

1645 Trap Road
Vienna, VA 22182
Phone: 703-255-1900
Fax: 703-255-1918
Web Site: www.wolftrap.org
Management:
   President: Terrence Jones
   CEO: Charles Walters
   Service President Performing Arts: Ann McKee
Status: Non-Profit, Professional
Paid Staff: 480

8141
VIRGINIA BEACH PAVILION CONVENTION CENTER

1000 19th Street
Virginia Beach, VA 23458
Phone: 804-428-8000
Fax: 804-422-8860

8142
CARY FIELD

Willian and Mary College
Williamsburg, VA 23187
Mailing Address: PO Box 399
Phone: 804-221-3400
Fax: 413-545-3412
Web Site: www.wm.edu
Management:
   President: Timothy J Sullivan
   Director: Bettie S Adams

8143
WILLIAM & MARY HALL

College of Williams & Mary
PO Box HC
Williamsburg, VA 23187
Phone: 804-221-3355
Fax: 413-545-3005
Management:
   Director: Bettie S Adams
Seating Capacity: 11,300

Washington

8144
BISHOP CENTER FOR PERFORMING ARTS

Grays Harbor College
1620 Edward P Smith Drive
Aberdeen, WA 98520
Phone: 360-538-4026
Fax: 360-538-4293
Toll-free: 800-562-4830
e-mail: mhood@ghc.edu
Web Site: www.ghc.ctc.edu/bishop
Officers:
   President: Edward Brewster

Management:
   Director Public Relations: Jane Goldberg
Founded: 1974
Specialized Field: Grays Harbor Symphony Orchestra, Ballet, Opera, Jazz, Theater, Classical and Popular Music
Status: Non-Profit, Non-Professional
Paid Staff: 5
Seating Capacity: 440

8145
INTERURBAN CENTER FOR THE ARTS

12401 SE 320th Street
Auburn, WA 98092-3699
Phone: 253-833-9111
Fax: 253-288-3481
e-mail: pthomas@greenriver.edu
Web Site: www.interurbancenterforthearts.org
Management:
   President: Rich Rukowski
   Executive Director: Patricia Thomas
Founded: 1978
Status: Non-Profit, Professional
Paid Staff: 1
Budget: $10,000

8146
WHITE RIVER AMPHITHEATRE

40601 Auburn Enumclaw Road
Auburn, WA 98092
Phone: 360-825-6200
Fax: 360-825-6203
Web Site: www.whiteriverconcerts.com
Management:
   Executive Director: Lance Miller
   VP Booking: Alex Kochan
Seating Capacity: 20,000

8147
THEATRE AT MEYDENBAUER

11100 NE 6th Street
Bellevue, WA 98004
Phone: 425-450-3810
Fax: 425-637-0166
e-mail: theatre@meydenbauer.com
Web Site: www.meydenbauer.com/theatre
Management:
   Chairman: Clare Nordquist
   Vice-Chairman: Roger Anderson
   Treasurer: George Northcro
Founded: 1989
Specialized Field: Theater

8148
CITY OF BELLINGHAM FACILITIES

2221 Pacific Street
Bellingham, WA 98226
Phone: 360-676-6854
Fax: 360-647-6367
Web Site: www.cob.org
Management:
   Director: Jack Gamer

8149
MOUNT BAKER THEATRE

104 N Commercial
Bellingham, WA 98225
Phone: 360-733-5793
Web Site: www.mountbakertheatre.com
Management:
   President: Kim Marvocca
   Executive Director: Brad Burdick
   Deputy Director: Kim Laskey

Mission: To provide arts, entertainment and social interaction through a wide variety of programs, results in personal enrichment, enjoyment and a sense of community, for diverse audiences in the region, and to preserve the restored historic Mount Baker Theatre as a home for local performing arts organizations, film, a venue for touring performers, and community events.
Founded: 1927
Status: Non-Profit, Professional
Paid Staff: 20
Volunteer Staff: 175

8150
OLD MAIN THEATER
Western Washington University
CFPA Performing Arts Center
516 High Street
Bellingham, WA 98225
Phone: 360-650-2829
Fax: 360-650-3028
Toll-free: 800-998-2372
e-mail: courtney.hiatt@wwu.edu
Web Site: www.wwu.edu/~cfpa
Officers:
 Dean: Carol D. Edwards, PhD
 Assistant to Dean: Jane M. Friesen
Management:
 CFPA Media/PAC Series Manager: Courtney M. Hiatt
 Facilities Operations Manager: Fred Ramage
Mission: Our College is committed to a central mission of quality arts education for Western students through the mentoring and creative talents of our dedicated faculty.
Founded: 1975
Opened: 1950
Type of Stage: Proscenium
Stage Dimensions: 30'x11'
Seating Capacity: 200

8151
PAC CONCERT HALL
Western Washington University
CFPA Performing Arts Center
516 High Street
Bellingham, WA 98225
Phone: 360-650-2829
Fax: 360-650-3028
Toll-free: 800-998-2372
e-mail: courtney.hiatt@wwu.edu
Web Site: www.wwu.edu/~cfpa
Officers:
 Dean: Carol D. Edwards, PhD
 Assistant to Dean: Jane M. Friesen
Management:
 CFPA Media/PAC Series Manager: Courtney M. Hiatt
 Facilities Operations Manager: Fred Ramage
Mission: Our College is committed to a central mission of quality arts education for Western students through the mentoring and creative talents of our dedicated faculty.
Founded: 1975
Opened: 1950
Type of Stage: Amphitheater Style
Seating Capacity: 700

8152
PAC MAINSTAGE THEATER
Western Washington University
CFPA Performing Arts Center
516 High Street
Bellingham, WA 98225

Phone: 360-650-2829
Fax: 360-650-3028
Toll-free: 800-998-2372
e-mail: courtney.hiatt@wwu.edu
Web Site: www.wwu.edu/~cfpa
Officers:
 Dean: Carol D. Edwards, PhD
 Assistant to Dean: Jane M. Friesen
Management:
 CFPA Media/PAC Series Manager: Courtney M. Hiatt
 Facilities Operations Manager: Fred Ramage
Mission: Our College is committed to a central mission of quality arts education for Western students through the mentoring and creative talents of our dedicated faculty.
Founded: 1975
Opened: 1950
Type of Stage: Proscenium
Stage Dimensions: 40' x 21'
Seating Capacity: 1,100

8153
UNDERGROUND THEATRE
Western Washington University
CFPA Performing Arts Center
516 High Street
Bellingham, WA 98225
Phone: 360-650-2829
Fax: 360-650-3028
Toll-free: 800-998-2372
e-mail: courtney.hiatt@wwu.edu
Web Site: www.wwu.edu/~cfpa
Officers:
 Dean: Carol D. Edwards, PhD
 Assistant to Dean: Jane M. Friesen
Management:
 CFPA Media/PAC Series Manager: Courtney M. Hiatt
 Facilities Operations Manager: Fred Ramage
Mission: Our College is committed to a central mission of quality arts education for Western students through the mentoring and creative talents of our dedicated faculty.
Founded: 1975
Opened: 1950
Type of Stage: Thrust
Seating Capacity: 104

8154
WESTERN WASHINGTON UNIVERSITY MAIN STAGE
Performing Arts Center
Bellingham, WA 98225
Phone: 360-650-3000
Fax: 206-676-3028

8155
WESTERN WASHINGTON UNIVERSITY OLD MAIN THEATRE
High Street
Bellingham, WA 98225
Phone: 360-650-3000

8156
COMMUNITY THEATRE
599 Lebo Boulevard
Bremerton, WA 98310
Phone: 360-373-5152
Fax: 360-373-6754
Toll-free: 800-865-1706
Web Site: www.silverlink.net/bet

8157
CORBET THEATRE
Centralia College
600 Centralia College Boulevard
Centralia, WA 98531
Phone: 360-736-9391
Fax: 360-330-7501
e-mail: clayman@centralia.edu
Web Site: www.centralia.edu
Officers:
 President: James Walton
Management:
 Artistic Director: Tony Petzold
 Events Coordinator: Candy Lunke
Mission: To creat a richer, fuller educational experience with professional performers and community groups.
Founded: 1925
Status: Non-Profit, Non-Professional
Paid Staff: 225

8158
EWU PAVILION
Eastern Washington University
215 Pub
Cheney, WA 99004
Phone: 509-359-7919
Fax: 509-359-4673
e-mail: sennis@mail.ewu.edu
Web Site: www.ewu.edu
Management:
 Director Facilities: Karry Pease
 Booking Contact: Stephanie Ennis
Seating Capacity: 5,000

8159
EDMONDS CENTER FOR THE ARTS
410 4th Ave. N
Edmonds, WA 98020
Phone: 425-275-4483
Fax: 425-771-0252
e-mail: joe@edmondscenterforthearts.org
Web Site: www.edmondscenterforthearts.org
Officers:
 President: Terry Vehrs
 Treasurer: John McGibbon
Management:
 Executive Director: Joe Mclalwain
 Technical Director: Jeff Vaughan
Mission: A cultural resource for the entire region, Edmonds Center for the Arts inspires creativity, learning and growth through performing arts presentations, community partnerships and education outreach programs.
Opened: 2006
Status: Non-Profit
Annual Attendance: 80,000
Seating Capacity: 700

8160
EVERETT CIVIC AUDITORIUM
2415 Colby Avenue
Everett, WA 98201
Phone: 425-388-4746
Fax: 425-339-4675

8161
EVERETT PARKS AND RECREATION DEPARTMENT
2930 Wetmore Avenue
Everett, WA 98201
Phone: 425-257-8720
Fax: 425-257-8607
Web Site: www.everettwa.org/parks

Management:
Director: Susan Francisco
Mission: The Everett Cultural Commission was established by city ordinance in 1974 to provide focus, visibility and direction for arts and cultural related activities of the City of Everett.

8162
7TH STREET THEATRE
313 7th Street
Hoquiam, WA 98550
Phone: 360-532-0302

8163
TRI-CITIES COLISEUM
7000 West Grandridge Boulevard
Kennewick, WA 99336
Phone: 509-783-9999
Fax: 509-735-4699
Web Site: www.tricitiescoliseum.com
Management:
GM: Jim Barbatti
Booking/Sales Manager: Megan Talbot
Seating Capacity: 7,587

8164
KENT CIVIC AND PERFORMING ARTS CENTER
PO Box 1617
Kent, WA 98035
Phone: 253-520-2525
Fax: 253-520-2424
e-mail: cmiller@ci.kent.wa.us
Web Site: www.kcpac.org
Management:
Executive Director: Christopher Miller

8165
KIRKLAND PERFORMANCE CENTER
350 Kirkland Avenue
Kirkland, WA 98033-6504
Phone: 425-828-0422
Fax: 425-889-9827
e-mail: slerian@kpcenter.org
Web Site: www.kpcenter.org
Officers:
Executive Director: Daniel Mayer
Mission: KPC provides cultural enrichment by offering a home for the presentation, support and promotion of the performing arts.
Founded: 1998
Specialized Field: Series & Festivals; Theatre; Dance; Music
Status: Non-Profit, Professional
Paid Staff: 12
Paid Artists: 120
Seating Capacity: 402

8166
MCCLELLAND ARTS CENTER
951 Delaware
Longview, WA 98632
Phone: 360-577-3345
Fax: 360-577-4002

8167
LINCOLN THEATRE CENTER
712 S 1st Street
PO Box 2312
Mt. Vernon, WA 98273
Phone: 360-336-2858
Fax: 360-336-2408
e-mail: info@lincolntheatre.org
Web Site: www.lincolntheatre.org

Management:
Executive Director: Carol Hays
Artistic Director: Vicky Young
Founded: 1987
Status: Non-Profit, Professional
Paid Staff: 5

8168
WHIDBEY PLAYHOUSE
1094 Midway Boulevard
Oak Harbor, WA 98277
Phone: 360-679-2237
e-mail: playhouse@whidbey.net

8169
BLACK BOX
South Puget Sound Community College
Kenneth J. Minnaert Center for the Arts
2011 Mottman Rd. SW
Olympia, WA 98512
Phone: 360-596-5508
Fax: 360-596-5501
Web Site: www.spscc.ctc.edu
Management:
Director: Cassie Welliver
Mission: The Minnaert Center provides an important point of contact for the college and the community. It serves as a community resource and asset, and offers an additional choice for spectators and patrons of the arts.
Founded: 1962
Type of Stage: Flexible
Stage Dimensions: 38'x38'
Seating Capacity: 100

8170
MAIN STAGE
South Puget Sound Community College
Kenneth J. Minnaert Center for the Arts
2011 Mottman Rd. SW
Olympia, WA 98512
Phone: 360-596-5508
Fax: 360-596-5501
Web Site: www.spscc..ctc.edu
Management:
Director: Cassie Welliver
Mission: The Minnaert Center provides an important point of contact for the college and the community. It serves as a community resource and asset, and offers an additional choice for spectators and patrons of the arts.
Founded: 1962
Type of Stage: Proscenium
Orchestra Pit: y
Seating Capacity: 500

8171
WASHINGTON CENTER FOR THE PERFORMING ARTS
512 Washington Street SE
Olympia, WA 98501
Phone: 360-753-8585
Fax: 360-754-1177
e-mail: info@washingtoncenter.org
Web Site: www.washingtoncenter.org
Officers:
Executive Director: Thomas Iovanne
Founded: 1985
Status: Non-Profit, Professional
Paid Staff: 25
Type of Stage: Proscenium
Seating Capacity: 1,000
Year Remodeled: 1985
Rental Contact: Janet Freeman

8172
BEASLEY PERFORMING ARTS COLISEUM
Washington State University
1 North Fairway Road
Pullman, WA 99164
Mailing Address: PO Box 641710
Phone: 509-335-3525
Fax: 509-335-3853
e-mail: udy@wsu.edu
Web Site: www.beasley.wsu.edu
Management:
Director: Leo Udy
Seating Capacity: 12,000

8173
GORGE AMPHITHEATRE
754 Silica Road Northwest
Quincy, WA 98848
Phone: 425-990-0222
Fax: 425-990-0221
Web Site: www.hob.com
Management:
GM: Bill Parsons
Marketing Director: Tim McGrath
Seating Capacity: 20,000

8174
RAYMOND THEATER
323 Third Street
Raymond, WA 98577
Phone: 360-942-5536
Fax: 360-942-5616
Specialized Field: Theater; Community Center

8175
MARYMOOR AMPHITHEATRE
6046 West Lake Sammamish Parkway
Redmond, WA 98073
Phone: 425-990-0222
Fax: 425-990-0221
e-mail: jeff.trisler@hobconcerts.com
Web Site: www.concertsatmarymoor.com
Management:
House of Blues Concerts: Dave Litrell
House of Blues Concerts: Jeff Trisler
Seating Capacity: 5,000

8176
A CONTEMPORARY THEATRE
700 Union Street
Seattle, WA 98101
Phone: 206-292-7660
Fax: 206-292-7676
Web Site: www.tickets.com/venue_info

8177
BATHHOUSE THEATRE
7312 W Greenlake Drive N
Seattle, WA 98103
Phone: 206-524-3608
Fax: 206-527-1942

8178
HEC EDMUNDSON PAVILION
University of Washington
208 Graves Building
Seattle, WA 98195
Mailing Address: Box 354070
Phone: 206-543-7373
Fax: 206-616-1523
Web Site: www.gohuskies.com
Management:

Assistant Athletic Director: Chip Lydum
Year Built: 1927
Year Remodeled: 1999

8179
HUSKY STADIUM
University of Washington
208 Graves Building, Room 207
Seattle, WA 98195-4070
Mailing Address: Box 35407
Phone: 206-543-2246
Fax: 206-616-1523
Web Site: www.gohuskies.com
Management:
    Assistant Athletics: Chip Lydum
    Event Manager: Steve Harper
Mission: Home of the University of Washington
athletics (NCAA).
Seating Capacity: 72,484
Year Built: 1920

8180
KEYARENA AT SEATTLE CENTER
305 Harrison Street
Seattle, WA 98109
Phone: 206-684-7200
Fax: 206-684-7366
e-mail: sccomm@seattle.gov
Web Site: www.seattlecenter.com
Management:
    Director: Virginia Anderson
    Director Event Producer: John Rhamstine
    Associate Director: Margaret Wetter
Mission: Home to Seattle Supersonics (NBA) and
Seattle Thunderbirds (WHL).
Seating Capacity: 15,000, 6000
Year Built: 1995

8181
MERCER ARENA AT SEATTLE CENTER
305 Harrison Street
Seattle, WA 98109
Phone: 206-684-7200
Fax: 206-684-7342
e-mail: eventsales.seattlecenter@ci.seattle.wa.us
Web Site: www.seattlecenter.com
Management:
    Director: Virginia Anderson
    Associate Director: Margaret Wetter

8182
NESHOLM FAMILY LEATURE HALL
Marion Oliver McCaw Hall at Seattle Center
305 Harrison Street
Seattle, WA 98109
Phone: 206-684-7202
Fax: 206-684-7366
e-mail: alison.mcguire@seattle.gov
Web Site: www.seattlecenter.com
Management:
    Sr Event Sales Representative: Alison McGuire
Utilizes: Actors; Choreographers; Commissioned
Composers; Contract Orchestras; Curators; Dance
Companies; Dancers; Designers; Educators; High
School Drama; Multi Collaborations; Multimedia;
Original Music Scores; Performance Artists; Resident
Artists; Sign Language Translators; Singers; Soloists;
Special Technical Talent; Theatre Companies
Founded: 1962
Opened: 2003
Specialized Field: Multi-Media
Status: For-Profit, Professional
Seating Capacity: 400

8183
SAFECO FIELD
PO Box 4100
Seattle, WA 98194-4100
Phone: 206-346-4000
Fax: 206-346-4400
Management:
    President: Chuck Armstrong
    Chairman: Howard Lincoln
    General Manager: Bill Batasi
    Manager Events Services: Toni Pereira
    VP/Ballpark Planning: John Palmer
    VP/Ballpark Operations: Neil Campbell
Founded: 1977
Status: For-Profit, Professional
Paid Staff: 170
Seating Capacity: 47,000

8184
SEATTLE CENTER OPERA HOUSE
321 Mercer Street
Seattle, WA 98109
Phone: 206-684-7200
Fax: 206-615-0306
Seating Capacity: 17,000

8185
SEATTLE REPERTORY THEATRE
155 Mercer Street
PO Box 900923
Seattle, WA 98109-9982
Phone: 206-443-2222
Fax: 206-443-2379
Toll-free: 877-900-9285
e-mail: info@seattlerep.org
Web Site: www.seattlerep.org
Management:
    Artistic Director: Sharon Ott
    Managing Director: Ben Moore
Founded: 1963

8186
SUSAN BROTMAN AUDITORIUM
Marion Oliver McCaw Hall at Seattle Center
305 Harrison Street
Seattle, WA 98109
Phone: 206-684-7202
Fax: 206-684-7366
e-mail: alison.mcguire@seattle.gov
Web Site: www.seattlecenter.com
Management:
    Sr Event Sales Representative: Alison McGuire
Mission: Marion Oliver McCaw Hall is a renovation of
the Opera House at Seattle Center.
Utilizes: Actors; Choreographers; Commissioned
Composers; Contract Orchestras; Curators; Dance
Companies; Dancers; Designers; Educators; High
School Drama; Multi Collaborations; Multimedia;
Original Music Scores; Performance Artists; Resident
Artists; Sign Language Translators; Singers; Soloists;
Special Technical Talent; Theatre Companies
Founded: 1962
Opened: 2003
Specialized Field: Concerts
Status: For-Profit, Professional
Paid Staff: 200
Type of Stage: Proscenium
Stage Dimensions: 60'x35'
Orchestra Pit: y
Seating Capacity: 2,900
Organization Type: Grand Lobby available for special
events

8187
UW WORLD SERIES
University of Washington
Box 351150
Seattle, WA 98195-1150
Phone: 206-543-3044
Fax: 206-685-2759
e-mail: krashan@u.washington.edu
Web Site: www.uwworldseries.org
Management:
    Director: Matthew Krashan
Founded: 1974
Paid Staff: 26

8188
AVISTA STADIUM
602 N Havana
Spokane, WA 99202
Phone: 509-535-2922
Fax: 509-534-5368
e-mail: mail@spokaneindiansbaseball.com
Web Site: www.spokaneindiansbaseball.com
Management:
    President: Andy Billig
    Managing Director: Paul Barbeau
Founded: 1985
Status: For-Profit, Professional
Paid Staff: 10

8189
INB PERFORMING ARTS CENTER
Spokane Public Facilities District
334 W Spokane Falls Boulevard
Spokane, WA 99201
Phone: 509-324-7000
Fax: 509-324-7050
e-mail: kbooth@spokanepfd.org
Web Site: http://www.spokanecenter.com
Management:
    General Manager: Johnna Boxley
    Marketing Manager: Kelsey Booth
    Tech Specialist: Mike Tucker
Mission: To operate as a community facility - providing
first class performing and meeting surroundings with
excellent service at affordable use rates to local
performing arts groups, event presenters, meeting
planners and school districts, thereby enhancing the
quality of life for all citizens and serving the economic
well-being of the community and enhancing the quality
of life.
Opened: 1995
Specialized Field: Symphony Concerts, Ballet, Grand
Opera, Country and Rock Music, Musical Stage
Productions
Status: For-Profit, Professional
Paid Staff: 30
Seating Capacity: 2,700

8190
METROPOLITAN PERFORMING ARTS CENTER
901 W Sprague
Spokane, WA 99204
Phone: 509-835-2638

8191
RUSSELL THEATRE
Gonzaga University
Jundt Art Center and Museum
502 East Boone Avenue
Spokane, WA 99258

Phone: 509-323-6553
Fax: 509-323-5718
Web Site: www.gonzaga.edu
Officers:
    President: Fr. Robert J. Spritzer, S.J.
Management:
    Professor Theatre Arts: Dr. Kevin Bradshaw
    Associate Professor Theatre Arts: John Hofland
Founded: 1887
Specialized Field: Theatre
Status: Non-Profit, Non-Professional
Paid Staff: 6
Paid Artists: 6
Type of Stage: Black Box
Seating Capacity: 200

8192
SPOKANE CONVENTION CENTER
334 W Spokane Falls Boulevard
Spokane, WA 99201
Phone: 509-353-6500
Fax: 509-353-6511
Web Site: www.spokanecenter.com
Management:
    Executive Director: Kevin Twohig
    Events Manager: Maxey D Adams
Founded: 1974
Status: Non-Profit, Professional

8193
SPOKANE OPERA HOUSE
334 W Spokane Falls Boulevard
Spokane, WA 99201
Phone: 509-353-6500
Fax: 509-353-6511
Web Site: spokanecenter.com
Management:
    Director: Johnna Boxley
    Events Manager: Maxey Adams
Performs At: Performing Arts
Annual Attendance: 315,000
Facility Category: Performing Arts
Type of Stage: Wood
Stage Dimensions: 149.5'x59'
Seating Capacity: 2,700
Year Built: 1974
Rental Contact: Events Manager Maxey Adams

8194
SPOKANE VETERANS MEMORIAL ARENA
West 720 Mallon Avenue
Spokane, WA 99201
Phone: 509-324-7000
Fax: 509-324-7050
e-mail: kbooth@spokanepfd.org
Web Site: www.spokanearena.com
Management:
    Executive Director: Kevin J Twohig
    Manager Events/Booking: Matt Gibson
    Marketing Manager: Kelsey Booth
    Operations Director: Dave Gebhardt
Opened: 1995
Specialized Field: Multi-Purpose Arena
Status: For-Profit, Professional
Paid Staff: 30
Seating Capacity: 12,500

8195
STAR THEATRE
Spokane Veterans Memorial Arena
West 720 Mallon Avenue
Spokane, WA 99201

Phone: 509-324-7000
Fax: 509-324-7050
e-mail: kbooth@spokanepfd.org
Web Site: www.spokanearena.com
Management:
    Executive Director: Kevin J Twohig
    Manager Events/Booking: Matt Gibson
    Marketing Manager: Kelsey Booth
    Operations Director: Dave Gebhardt
Opened: 1995
Specialized Field: Theatre, Concerts, Broadway, Family Shows
Status: For-Profit, Professional
Paid Staff: 30
Seating Capacity: 5,900

8196
CHENEY STADIUM
Tacoma Rainiers Baseball Club
2502 South Tyler Street
Tacoma, WA 98405
Phone: 253-752-7707
Fax: 253-752-7135
Toll-free: 800-281-3834
Web Site: www.tacomarainiers.com
Management:
    General Manager: Dave Lewis
    Chief Financial Officer: Laurie Yarbroug
    Director Marketing: Rachel Marecle
Mission: The rental of the stadium, parking area and/or meeting rooms for as many outside events as possible. Includes concerts, car shows, travelling performers, etc.
Founded: 1960
Facility Category: Baseball Stadium
Rental Contact: Philip Cowan

8197
TACOMA DOME
2727 East D Street
Tacoma, WA 98421
Phone: 253-272-3663
Fax: 253-593-7620
Web Site: www.tacomadome.org
Management:
    Executive Director: Mike Combs
    Assistant Director: Jody Hodgson
    Marketing Manager: Beth Sylves
Founded: 1983
Status: Non-Profit, Professional
Paid Staff: 45
Seating Capacity: 20,200

8198
UPS FIELDHOUSE
University of Puget Sound
1500 North Warner
Tacoma, WA 98416
Phone: 253-879-3366
Fax: 253-879-2671
e-mail: ssolidarios@ups.edu
Web Site: www.ups.edu
Management:
    Director Student Programs: Serni Solidarios
    Box Office Manager: Kristi Maplethorpe
Seating Capacity: 3,400

8199
CORDINER HALL
Whitman College
345 Boyer
Walla Walla, WA 99362
Phone: 509-527-5279
Fax: 509-522-4406
Web Site: www.whitmancollege.org

Management:
    President: Timothy Cromin
    Artistic Director: Nancy Simon
    Managing Director: Tom Hines
Founded: 1823
Status: Non-Profit, Non-Professional
Paid Staff: 8

8200
CAPITAL THEATRE
19 South 3rd Street
PO Box 102
Yakima, WA 98907
Phone: 509-575-6267
Fax: 509-575-6251

8201
CAPITOL THEATRE
19 S 3rd Street
PO Box 102
Yakima, WA 98901
Phone: 509-853-8000
Fax: 509-575-6251
e-mail: arts@capitoltheatre.org
Web Site: www.capitoltheatre.org
Management:
    CEO: Steven J Caffery
    President: Keith Riffe
    VP: Darell Blue
    VP: Brian Roberts
Specialized Field: Theater
Budget: $400,000-1,000,000

8202
YAKIMA VALLEY SUNDOME
1301 S Fair Avenue
Yakima, WA 98901
Phone: 509-248-7160
Fax: 509-248-8093
Web Site: www.fairfund.com
Management:
    General Manager: Greg Stewart
    Assistant General Manager: Greg Lybeck
    Events Manager: Ray Mata
Seating Capacity: 8,000

West Virginia

8203
ATKINSON AUDITORIUM
West Virginia Wesleyan College
59 College Avenue
Buckhannon, WV 26201
Phone: 304-473-8000
Fax: 304-472-2571

8204
OLD OPERA HOUSE THEATRE COMPANY
204 N George Street
Charles Town, WV 25414
Phone: 304-725-4420
Fax: 304-725-4420
Toll-free: 888-900-7469
e-mail: ooh@oldoperahouse.org
Web Site: www.oldoperahouse.org
Management:
    Manager/Artistic Director: Steven Brewer
Founded: 1973
Status: Non-Profit, Non-Professional
Paid Staff: 1

8205
CAPITOL CENTER
West Virginia State College
123 Summers Street
Charleston, WV 25301
Phone: 304-342-6522
Fax: 304-766-5718
Web Site: www.wvstateu.edu
Management:
President: Hazo Carter
Program Coordinator: Laura McCullough
Founded: 1840
Status: Non-Profit, Non-Professional
Paid Staff: 2

8206
CHARLESTON CIVIC CENTER
200 Civic Center Drive
Charleston, WV 25301
Phone: 304-345-1500
Fax: 304-345-3492
Web Site: www.charlestonwvciviccenter.com
Management:
Executive Director: John D Robertson
Founded: 1959
Status: Non-Profit, Professional
Paid Staff: 25

8207
CLAY CENTER FOR THE ARTS & SCIENCES
1 Clay Square
Charleston, WV 25301
Phone: 304-561-3500
Fax: 304-561-3599
e-mail: lcook@theclaycenter.org
Web Site: www.theclaycenter.org
Officers:
President: Sue Sergi
Programming Director: Lakin Cook
Opened: 2003
Seating Capacity: 1,883

8208
GEARY AUDITORIUM
2300 MacCorkle Avenue SE
Charleston, WV 25304
Phone: 304-357-4807
Fax: 304-357-4915

8209
LAIDLEY FIELD ATHLETIC RECREATIONAL CENTER
200 Elizabeth Street
Charleston, WV 25311
Phone: 304-348-1134
Fax: 304-348-6559
Management:
Facility Director: Lou Ann Lanham
Seating Capacity: 22,000

8210
WATT POWELL STADIUM
35th Street & Mac Corkle Avenue
Charleston, WV 25304
Phone: 304-925-8222
Fax: 304-344-0083
Web Site: www.charlestonallycats.com
Management:
General Manager: Tim Bordein
Seating Capacity: 7,500

8211
BIG SANDY SUPER STORE ARENA
1 Civic Center Plaza
Huntington, WV 25701
Phone: 304-696-5990
Fax: 304-696-4463
Web Site: www.bigsandyarena.com
Management:
President: Elliot Murnick
Director Marketing: Pete Wenzel
Director of Operations: Steve Kessick
Ticket Director: Martha Lunsford
Utilizes: Dance Companies; Guest Soloists; Instructors; Multimedia; Original Music Scores; Sign Language Translators; Singers; Special Technical Talent; Theatre Companies
Founded: 1976
Status: Non-Profit, Professional
Paid Staff: 120
Facility Category: civic arena\ conference center
Year Built: 1977
Year Remodeled: 1999
Rental Contact: Pete Wenzel

8212
HUNTINGTON MUSEUM OF ART AUDITORIUM
2033 McCoy Road
Huntington, WV 25701
Phone: 304-529-2701
Fax: 304-529-7447
e-mail: jgillisp@hmoa.org
Web Site: www.hmoa.org
Management:
Executive Director: Margaret Mary Layne
Mission: To provide services and education in the fine and performing arts.
Founded: 1952
Status: Non-Profit, Professional
Paid Staff: 27
Volunteer Staff: 400
Budget: $1.9 million
Income Sources: Endowment; Gifts; Grants
Affiliations: AAM Accredited
Annual Attendance: 60,000
Facility Category: Museum with 300-seat auditorium
Type of Stage: Proscenium
Seating Capacity: 300
Year Built: 1970
Cost: $1 million
Rental Contact: Jennifer Wheeler

8213
JOAN C EDWARDS PLAYHOUSE
Marshall University
400 Halgreer Boulevard
Huntington, WV 25755
Phone: 304-696-2787

8214
JOAN C. EDWARDS PERFORMING ARTS CENTER
Marshall University
Department of Theatre
One John Marshall Drive
Huntington, WV 25755
Phone: 304-696-2546
Fax: 304-696-6582
e-mail: reynoldsh@marshall.edu
Web Site: www.marshall.edu
Management:
Chair: Howard Lang Reynolds
Director Theatre Facilities: James Morris-Smith
Technical Director: Edward Leo Murphy
Mission: The Marshall University Theatre Department offers students opportunities to earn a Bachelor of Fine Arts Degree in Fine Arts with a major in Theatre in two areas of emphasis: Performance and Production.
Opened: 1992
Status: Non-Profit, Professional
Paid Staff: 30
Type of Stage: Auditorium
Seating Capacity: 530

8215
KEITH-ALBEE THEATRE
925 4th Avenue
Huntington, WV 25720
Phone: 304-525-4440

8216
JOAN C EDWARDS STADIUM
Marshall Athletics
2001 3rd Avenue
Huntington, WV 25703
Phone: 304-696-6448
Fax: 304-676-6448
Web Site: www.herdzone.com
Management:
Athletic Director: Lance A West
Seating Capacity: 30,000

8217
SMITH RECITAL HALL
Marshall University
Department of Theatre
One John Marshall Drive
Huntington, WV 25755
Phone: 304-696-2546
Fax: 304-696-6582
e-mail: reynoldsh@marshall.edu
Web Site: www.marshall.edu
Management:
Chair: Howard Lang Reynolds
Director Theatre Facilities: James Morris-Smith
Technical Director: Edward Leo Murphy
Mission: The Marshall University Theatre Department offers students opportunities to earn a Bachelor of Fine Arts Degree in Fine Arts with a major in Theatre in two areas of emphasis: Performance and Production.
Opened: 1967
Status: Non-Profit, Professional
Paid Staff: 30
Seating Capacity: 490

8218
VETERANS MEMORIAL FIELD HOUSE
PO Box 5455
Huntington, WV 25703
Phone: 304-528-5173
Fax: 304-528-5185
Management:
Manager: Donald S Ewanus
Seating Capacity: 6,800

8219
WEST VIRGINIA STATE COLLEGE THEATRE
Fine Arts Building
Institute, WV 25112
Phone: 304-766-3186
Fax: 304-766-5100
Web Site: www.wvstateu.edu
Management:
President: Hazo W Carter Jr
Founded: 1890
Status: Non-Profit, Non-Professional

8220
CARNEGIE HALL
105 Church Street
Lewisburg, WV 24901
Phone: 304-645-7917
Fax: 304-645-5228

8221
ANTOINETTE E. FALBO THEATRE
West Virigina University
College of Creative Arts
PO Box 6111, One Evansdale Drive
Morgantown, WV 26506-6111
Phone: 304-293-4841
Fax: 304-293-6896
e-mail: mark.oreskovich@mail.wvu.edu
Web Site: www.ccarts.wvu.edu
Management:
   Dean/Director: J Bernard Schultz
   Associate Dean: William Winsor
   Assistant Director: Mark S. Oreskovich
Mission: Educational facility.
Utilizes: Actors; AEA Actors; Artists-in-Residence; Choreographers; Commissioned Composers; Community Members; Composers; Composers-in-Residence; Contract Actors; Curators; Dance Companies; Dancers; Designers; Educators; Equity Actors; Fine Artists; Grant Writers; Guest Accompanists; Guest Artists; Guest Companies; Guest Composers; Guest Conductors; Guest Designers; Guest Directors; Guest Ensembles; Guest Instructors; Guest Lecturers; Guest Musical Directors; Guest Musicians; Guest Soloists; Guest Speakers; High School Drama; Instructors; Multi Collaborations; Multimedia; Music; Organization Contracts; Paid Performers; Performance Artists; Poets; Resident Professionals; Selected Students; Sign Language Translators; Singers; Soloists; Students; Student Interns; Theatre Companies; Touring Companies; Visual Arts
Founded: 1969
Opened: 1969
Specialized Field: Visual Art & Design; Music; Theatre & Dance
Performs At: Black Box
Affiliations: NASAD, NAST, NASM
Annual Attendance: 3,000
Facility Category: Educational
Type of Stage: Black Box
Stage Dimensions: 5000 sq. ft.
Seating Capacity: 104
Year Built: 1972

8222
BLOCH LEARNING AND PERFORMANCE HALL
College of Creative Arts
PO Box 6111
Morgantown, WV 26506-6111
Phone: 304-293-4841
Fax: 304-293-6896
e-mail: mark.oreskovich@mail.wvu.edu
Web Site: www.ccarts.wvu.edu
Management:
   Assistant Director: Mark Oreskovich,
   mark.oreskovich@mail.wvu.edu
   Chairman, Division of Music: Keith Jackson
   Associate Director, Finance: Vicki Grim
Mission: Educational facility.
Utilizes: Actors; AEA Actors; Artists-in-Residence; Choreographers; Commissioned Composers; Community Members; Composers; Composers-in-Residence; Contract Actors; Curators;

Dance Companies; Dancers; Designers; Educators; Equity Actors; Fine Artists; Grant Writers; Guest Accompanists; Guest Artists; Guest Companies; Guest Composers; Guest Conductors; Guest Designers; Guest Directors; Guest Ensembles; Guest Instructors; Guest Lecturers; Guest Musical Directors; Guest Musicians; Guest Soloists; Guest Speakers; High School Drama; Instructors; Multi Collaborations; Multimedia; Music; Organization Contracts; Paid Performers; Performance Artists; Poets; Resident Professionals; Selected Students; Sign Language Translators; Singers; Soloists; Students; Student Interns; Theatre Companies; Touring Companies; Visual Arts
Founded: 1969
Opened: 1969
Specialized Field: Visual Art; Design; Music; Theatre; Dance
Income Sources: Stage and private
Performs At: Concert Theatre
Affiliations: National Association of Schools of Theatre; National Association of Schools of Art and Design, NASM
Annual Attendance: 200,000
Facility Category: Educational
Type of Stage: Proscenium
Stage Dimensions: 58 x 42
Seating Capacity: 1441
Year Built: 1968

8223
CHORAL RECITAL HALL
College of Creative Arts
1 Evandale Drive
Morgantown, WV 26506-6111
Mailing Address: PO Box 6111
Phone: 304-296-4841
Fax: 304-293-6896
e-mail: mark.oreskovich@mail.wvu.edu
Web Site: www.wvu.edu/nccarts/
Management:
   Facilities Manager: Mark Oreskovich
   Interim Chairman Division Music: David Bess
   Associate Director/Finance: Linda Queen
Mission: Educational facility
Utilizes: Actors; AEA Actors; Artists-in-Residence; Choreographers; Collaborating Artists; Commissioned Music; Community Talent; Composers; Curators; Dance Companies; Dancers; Designers; Educators; Guest Accompanists; Guest Artists; Guest Companies; Guest Composers; Guest Designers; Guest Directors; Guest Instructors; Guest Lecturers; Guest Speakers; High School Drama; Instructors; Multimedia; Music; Original Music Scores; Paid Performers; Performance Artists; Sign Language Translators; Singers; Students; Special Technical Talent; Theatre Companies; Visual Arts
Specialized Field: Visual art; music theatre; dance
Income Sources: Stage and private
Performs At: Choral Recital Hall
Affiliations: NASM - National Association of Schools of Theatre - NASAD
Annual Attendance: 22,500
Facility Category: Educational
Type of Stage: Indoor amphitheatre
Stage Dimensions: 18 x 56
Seating Capacity: 180
Year Built: 1968
Year Remodeled: 2000
Cost: $500,000

8224
GLADYS G. DAVIS THEATRE
West Virigina University
College of Creative Arts
PO Box 6111, One Evansdale Drive
Morgantown, WV 26506-6111
Phone: 304-293-4841
Fax: 304-293-6896
e-mail: mark.oreskovich@mail.wvu.edu
Web Site: www.ccarts.wvu.edu
Management:
   Dean/Director: J Bernard Schultz
   Associate Dean: William Winsor
   Assistant Director: Mark S. Oreskovich
Mission: Educational facility.
Utilizes: Actors; AEA Actors; Artists-in-Residence; Choreographers; Commissioned Composers; Community Members; Composers; Composers-in-Residence; Contract Actors; Curators; Dance Companies; Dancers; Designers; Educators; Equity Actors; Fine Artists; Grant Writers; Guest Accompanists; Guest Artists; Guest Companies; Guest Composers; Guest Conductors; Guest Designers; Guest Directors; Guest Ensembles; Guest Instructors; Guest Lecturers; Guest Musical Directors; Guest Musicians; Guest Soloists; Guest Speakers; High School Drama; Instructors; Multi Collaborations; Multimedia; Music; Organization Contracts; Paid Performers; Performance Artists; Poets; Resident Professionals; Selected Students; Sign Language Translators; Singers; Soloists; Students; Student Interns; Special Technical Talent; Theatre Companies; Touring Companies; Visual Arts
Founded: 1969
Opened: 1969
Specialized Field: Visual Art & Design; Music; Theatre & Dance
Income Sources: Stage and private
Performs At: Concert Theatre
Affiliations: National Association of Schools of Theatre; National Association of Schools of Art and Design, NASM
Annual Attendance: 200,000
Facility Category: Educational
Type of Stage: Proscenium
Stage Dimensions: 58 x 42
Seating Capacity: 1441
Year Built: 1968

8225
LYELL B CLAY CONCERT THEATRE
West Virigina University
College of Creative Arts
PO Box 6111, One Evansdale Drive
Morgantown, WV 26506-6111
Phone: 304-293-4841
Fax: 304-293-6896
e-mail: mark.oreskovich@mail.wvu.edu
Web Site: www.ccarts.wvu.edu
Management:
   Dean/Director: J Bernard Schultz
   Associate Dean: William Winsor
   Assistant Director: Mark S. Oreskovich
Mission: Educational facility.
Utilizes: Actors; AEA Actors; Artists-in-Residence; Choreographers; Commissioned Composers; Community Members; Composers; Composers-in-Residence; Contract Actors; Curators; Dance Companies; Dancers; Designers; Educators; Equity Actors; Fine Artists; Grant Writers; Guest Accompanists; Guest Artists; Guest Choreographers; Guest Companies; Guest Composers; Guest Conductors; Guest Designers; Guest Directors; Guest

Ensembles; Guest Instructors; Guest Lecturers; Guest Musical Directors; Guest Musicians; Guest Soloists; Guest Speakers; High School Drama; Instructors; Multi Collaborations; Multimedia; Music; Organization Contracts; Paid Performers; Performance Artists; Resident Professionals; Selected Students; Sign Language Translators; Singers; Soloists; Students; Student Interns; Special Technical Talent; Theatre Companies; Touring Companies; Visual Arts
Founded: 1969
Opened: 1969
Specialized Field: Visual Art& Design; Music; Theatre & Dance
Performs At: Concert Theatre
Affiliations: NASAD, NAST, NASM
Annual Attendance: 200,000
Facility Category: Educational
Type of Stage: Proscenium
Stage Dimensions: 58 x 42
Seating Capacity: 1441
Year Built: 1968
Year Remodeled: 2003
Cost: $1.4M

8226
MONTAINEER FIELD
West Virginia University
Room 107
Morgantown, WV 26507-0877
Phone: 307-293-5621
Fax: 717-337-6528
Web Site: www.msnsportsnet.com
Management:
Athletic Director: Ed Pastilong
Seating Capacity: 63,500

8227
VIVIAN DAVIS MICHAEL LABORATORY THEATRE
West Virigina University
College of Creative Arts
PO Box 6111, One Evansdale Drive
Morgantown, WV 26506-6111
Phone: 304-293-4841
Fax: 304-293-6896
e-mail: mark.oreskovich@mail.wvu.edu
Web Site: www.ccarts.wvu.edu
Management:
Dean/Director: J Bernard Schultz
Associate Dean: William Winsor
Assistant Director: Mark S. Oreskovich
Mission: Educational facility.
Utilizes: Actors; AEA Actors; Artists-in-Residence; Choreographers; Community Members; Community Talent; Composers; Composers-in-Residence; Contract Actors; Curators; Dance Companies; Dancers; Designers; Educators; Equity Actors; Fine Artists; Grant Writers; Guest Accompanists; Guest Artists; Guest Companies; Guest Composers; Guest Conductors; Guest Designers; Guest Directors; Guest Ensembles; Guest Instructors; Guest Lecturers; Guest Musical Directors; Guest Musicians; Guest Soloists; Guest Speakers; Guild Activities; High School Drama; Instructors; Local Unknown Artists; Multi Collaborations; Multimedia; Music; Organization Contracts; Original Music Scores; Paid Performers; Performance Artists; Poets; Resident Professionals; Selected Students; Sign Language Translators; Singers; Soloists; Students; Student Interns; Special Technical Talent; Theatre Companies; Touring Companies; Visual Arts
Founded: 1969
Opened: 1969
Specialized Field: Visual Art & Design; Music; Theatre & Dance

Performs At: Classroom Lab
Affiliations: NASAD, NAST, NASM
Annual Attendance: 500
Facility Category: Educational
Type of Stage: Proscenium
Stage Dimensions: 24 x 18
Seating Capacity: 50
Year Built: 1968

8228
WEST VIRGINIA UNIVERSITY COLISEUM
West Virginia University
PO Box 6017
Morgantown, WV 26506-6017
Phone: 304-293-4407
Fax: 304-293-7574
Web Site: www.events.wvu.edu
Management:
Program Manager: Eric Andrews
Seating Capacity: 15,000

8229
WEST VIRGINIA UNIVERSITY CREATIVE ARTS CENTER
One Evansdale Drive
PO Box 6111
Morgantown, WV 26506-6111
Phone: 304-293-4841
Fax: 304-293-6896
e-mail: mark.oreskovich@mail.wvu.edu
Web Site: www.wvu.edu
Management:
Dean: Bernard Schultz
Assistant Director: Mark Oreskovich
Mission: Educational facility
Utilizes: Actors; AEA Actors; Artists-in-Residence; Choreographers; Collaborating Artists; Commissioned Composers; Community Members; Community Talent; Composers; Composers-in-Residence; Contract Actors; Contract Orchestras; Curators; Dance Companies; Dancers; Designers; Educators; Equity Actors; Fine Artists; Five Seasonal Concerts; Grant Writers; Guest Accompanists; Guest Artists; Guest Choreographers; Guest Companies; Guest Composers; Guest Conductors; Guest Designers; Guest Directors; Guest Ensembles; Guest Instructors; Guest Lecturers; Guest Musical Directors; Guest Musicians; Guest Soloists; Guest Speakers; High School Drama; Instructors; Local Artists & Directors; Lyricists; Multi Collaborations; Multimedia; Music; New Productions; Organization Contracts; Paid Performers; Performance Artists; Poets; Resident Professionals; Selected Students; Sign Language Translators; Singers; Soloists; Students; Student Interns; Theatre Companies; Touring Companies; Visual Arts; Volunteer Directors & Actors; Writers
Founded: 1969
Opened: 1969
Specialized Field: Visual Art & Design; Music; Theatre & Dance
Status: Professional
Annual Attendance: 300,000
Facility Category: Performing and Educational Arts Center
Year Built: 1968
Year Remodeled: 2003
Cost: $9,000,000

8230
SUNSHINE DAYDREAMS CAMPGROUND
Terra Alta, WV 26764
Mailing Address: Route 2 Box 6E
Phone: 304-789-2292
Web Site: www.sunshinedreams.com

Management:
Owner: Kevin "Trip" McClenny
Seating Capacity: 7,000

8231
CAPITOL MUSIC HALL & JAMBOREE USA
1015 Main Street
Wheeling, WV 26003
Phone: 304-232-1170
Fax: 304-234-0067
Toll-free: 800-624-5456
Web Site: www.jamboreeusa.com
Officers:
VP/General Manager: Larry Anderson
Management:
Tour Director: Kathy Tucker-Cupp
Sales/Account Manager: Kelly Tucker-Jones
Mission: Entertainment from country music artists, Broadway productions, comedy acts, Las Vegas-style acts and pop groups.
Utilizes: Dancers; Multimedia; Theatre Companies
Founded: 1933
Specialized Field: Comedy, Country Music, Broadway
Budget: $400,000-1,000,000
Seating Capacity: 2,500
Year Built: 1928

8232
WHEELING CIVIC CENTER
Two 14th Street
Wheeling, WV 26003
Phone: 304-223-7000
Fax: 304-233-7001
Web Site: www.wheelingciviccenter.com
Management:
Executive Director: Dennis R Magruder
Assistant Director: Philip D Campbell
Operations Director: Mark A George
Seating Capacity: 8,000

8233
WHEELING ISLAND STADIUM
S Front Street
Wheeling, WV 26003
Phone: 304-243-0431
Fax: 304-243-0328
e-mail: rconaway@access.k12.wv.us
Web Site: www.wphs.ohio.k12.wv.us
Management:
Executive Director: George Krelis
Manager: Robert Conaway
Founded: 1987
Status: Non-Profit, Non-Professional
Seating Capacity: 10,000

Wisconsin

8234
LAWRENCE UNIVERSITY MUSIC-DRAMA CENTER
420 E College Avenue
PO Box 599
Appleton, WI 54912-0599
Phone: 920-832-7000
Fax: 920-832-6633
Web Site: www.lawrence.edu
Status: Non-Profit,Professional

8235

CEDARBURG PERFORMING ARTS CENTER

W 68 N 611 Evergreen Boulevard
Cedarburg, WI 53012
Phone: 262-376-6162
Fax: 262-376-6163
e-mail: kkoster@cedarburg.k12.wi.us
Web Site: www.cedarburgpac.com
Management:
    Technical Director: Paul Thur
Founded: 1999
Status: Non-Profit, Professional
Paid Staff: 2
Volunteer Staff: 40
Paid Artists: 8
Income Sources: Ticket Revenue; District Funding
Performs At: School District Functions; Tear 1 &2 Arts; Local Talent
Annual Attendance: 50,000
Facility Category: Performing Arts Center
Stage Dimensions: 50x22x34
Seating Capacity: 580
Year Built: 1998
Cost: 1.5 million
Rental Contact: Kathleen Pier

8236

NORTHLAND PINES HIGH SCHOOL

1800 Pleasure Island Road
PO Box 1269
Eagle River, WI 54521
Phone: 715-479-4473
Fax: 715-479-5808
Web Site: www.npsd.k12,wi.us
Management:
    Advisor for Drama Club: David Strong
Status: Non-Profit, Non-Professional
Paid Staff: 1

8237

ALPINE VALLEY MUSIC THEATRE

2699 Highway D
East Troy, WI 53120
Mailing Address: PO Box 921
Phone: 262-642-4400
Fax: 414-223-4531
Web Site: www.alpinevalleymusic.com
Management:
    VP: Karl Adams
    Executive Director: David Shaw
Seating Capacity: 35,144

8238

WL ZORN ARENA

University of Wisconsin: Eau Claire
105 Garfield Avenue
Eau Claire, WI 54702
Phone: 715-836-2637
Fax: 715-836-4268
Web Site: www.uwec.edu
Management:
    Conference Manager: Karen Stuber
Seating Capacity: 3,200

8239

BIRCH CREEK MUSIC PERFORMANCE CENTER

PO Box 230
Egg Harbor, WI 54209

Phone: 920-868-3763
Fax: 920-868-1643
e-mail: mainoffice@birchcreek.org
Web Site: www.birchcreek.org
Officers:
    President: Gregory Mox
Management:
    Executive Director: Kaye Wagner
Mission: To provide intensive, performance-based instruction to promising young musicians by immersing them in a professional, mentoring environment.
Utilizes: Artists-in-Residence; Collaborating Artists; Community Members; Composers; Educators; Five Seasonal Concerts; Guest Musical Directors; High School Drama; Instructors; Local Talent; Multimedia; Music; Paid Performers; Poets; Resident Companies; Scenic Designers; Singers; Soloists; Students; Student Interns
Founded: 1976
Opened: 1976
Specialized Field: Music Education & Performance
Status: Non-Profit, Professional
Paid Staff: 6
Volunteer Staff: 150
Paid Artists: 95
Budget: $808,565
Income Sources: Ticket Sales; Student Tuition
Affiliations: League of American Orchestras
Annual Attendance: 6,000
Facility Category: Live Music: Symphony, Percussion/Steel Band, Jazz
Type of Stage: Thrust
Seating Capacity: 300; 500
Year Built: 1897
Year Remodeled: 1976
Rental Contact: Executive Director Kaye Wagner

8240

BROWN COUNTY ARENA

University of Wisconsin
2420 Nicolet Drive
Green Bay, WI 54311-7001
Phone: 920-494-6868
Fax: 920-465-2178
Management:
    Director: Les Raduenz

8241

COFRIN FAMILY HALL

Weidner Center for the Performing Arts
2420 Nicolet Drive
Green Bay, WI 54311-7001
Phone: 920-465-2726
Fax: 920-465-2619
Toll-free: 800-922-9272
e-mail: nevermab@uwgb.edu
Web Site: www.weidnercenter.com
Management:
    General Manager: Brock Neverman
    Event Manager: Kasha Huntowski
    Technical Director: Josh Koleske
Mission: To present cultural entertaining and educational programs to Northeast Wisconsin and serve as home for university and local performing arts organizations.
Opened: 1993
Facility Category: Road House
Type of Stage: Proscenium
Stage Dimensions: 54'4" x 48'
Seating Capacity: 2,021
Year Built: 1993
Rental Contact: Kasha Huntowski
Organization Type: Performing

8242

FORT HOWARD HALL

University of Wisconsin-Green Bay
Weidner Center for the Performing Arts
2420 Nicolet Drive
Green Bay, WI 54311-7001
Phone: 920-465-2726
Fax: 920-465-2619
Toll-free: 800-922-9272
e-mail: nevermab@uwgb.edu
Web Site: www.uwgb.edu/weidner/
Management:
    General Manager: Brock Neverman
    Director Of Events: Kasha Huntowski
    Technical Director: Josh Koleski
Mission: To present cultural entertaining and educational programs to Northeast Wisconsin and serve as home for university and local performing arts organizations.
Opened: 1993
Specialized Field: Recitals; Lectures
Stage Dimensions: 45 x 54
Seating Capacity: 200
Organization Type: Performing

8243

LAMBEAU FIELD

Green Bay Packers
1265 Lombardi Avenue
Green Bay, WI 54304
Phone: 920-496-5700
Fax: 920-496-5712
Web Site: www.packers.com
Management:
    President: Robert Harland
    Public Relations Executive Director: Lee Remmel
    Stadium Manager: Ted Eisenreich
    Marketing Director: Jeff Cieply
Specialized Field: Home of the Green Bay Packers
Seating Capacity: 60,790
Year Built: 1957
Year Remodeled: 1990

8244

P BROWN COUNTY ARENA

University of Wisconsin
2420 Nicolet Drive
Green Bay, WI 54311-7001
Phone: 920-494-6868
Fax: 920-465-2178
Management:
    Director: Les Raduenz

8245

STUDIO ONE

University of Wisconsin-Green Bay
Weidner Center for the Performing Arts
2420 Nicolet Drive
Green Bay, WI 54311
Phone: 920-465-2726
Fax: 920-465-2619
Toll-free: 800-922-9272
e-mail: nevermab@uwgb.edu
Web Site: www.uwgb.edu/weidner
Management:
    General Manager: Brock Neverman
    Event Manager: Kasha Huntowski
    Stage Manager: Josh Koleske
Mission: To present cultural entertaining and educational programs to Northeast Wisconsin and serve as home for university and local performing arts organizations.
Founded: 1993

Opened: 1993
Stage Dimensions: 34 x 34
Seating Capacity: 100
Organization Type: Performing

8246
PHIPPS CENTER FOR THE ARTS
109 Locust Street
Hudson, WI 54016
Phone: 715-386-2305
Fax: 715-381-2177
e-mail: info@thephipps.org
Web Site: www.thephipps.org
Officers:
   President: Sarah J Andersen
   VP: Mark J Gherty
   Secretary: Roberta Pominville
   Treasurer: James Steel
Management:
   Executive Director: John H Potter
   Artistic Director: Anastasia Shartin
Mission: To celebrate the creative spirit.
Founded: 1981
Specialized Field: Multi-Disciplinary
Status: Non-Profit, Non-Professional
Paid Staff: 7
Volunteer Staff: 500
Paid Artists: 100
Non-paid Artists: 200
Budget: $900,000
Income Sources: Earned and Contributed
Affiliations: Wisconsin Presenters Network
Annual Attendance: 22,500
Facility Category: Arts Center
Type of Stage: Proscenium
Stage Dimensions: 36' x 34'/247
Year Built: 1983
Year Remodeled: 1992
Cost: $7 million
Rental Contact: Executive Director John H Potter

8247
COMMUNICATION ARTS THEATRE
University of Wisconsin at Parkside
900 Wood Road
Kenosha, WI 53141-2000
Mailing Address: Box 2000
Phone: 262-595-3339
Fax: 262-595-2202
Web Site: www.uwp.edu
Management:
   Activities Assistant Director: Stephanie Sirovatka
Founded: 1968
Status: Non-Profit, Professional
Paid Staff: 2
Budget: $35,000-60,000
Performs At: Communication Arts Theatre

8248
MITCHELL HALL GYMNASIUM
University of Wisconsin-Lacrosse
1725 State Street
La Crosse, WI 54601
Phone: 608-785-8000
Fax: 608-785-8674
e-mail: webmaster@uwlax.edu
Web Site: www.uwlax.edu
Management:
   President: Katharine C Lyall
Seating Capacity: 3,400

8249
CAMP RANDALL STADIUM
1440 Monroe Street
Madison, WI 53711
Phone: 608-262-1866
Fax: 608-265-3036
Web Site: www.uwbadgers.com
Management:
   Interim Athletic Director: Andrea Nilsen
   Facility Director: Barry Fox
Specialized Field: Home of University of Wisconsin athletics.
Seating Capacity: 77,745
Year Built: 1917
Year Remodeled: 1968

8250
FREDRIC MARCH PLAY CIRCLE
University of Wisconsin-Madison
Memorial Union
800 Langdon St
Madison, WI 53706
Phone: 608-262-2201
Fax: 608-265-5084
e-mail: rfrusso@wisc.edu
Web Site: http://www.uniontheater.wisc.edu/
Management:
   Cultural Arts Directory: Ralph Russo
   Technical Directory: Jeff Macheel
   Operations Manager: Bruce Ehlinger
   Marketing/Communications Manager: Esty Dinur
   Box Office Manager: Ted Harks
Mission: The Department of Theatre and Drama/University Theatre is a collaborative community of artists and scholars — faculty, staff and students — aiming to achieve the highest level of excellence in their teaching and learning, research and creative endeavors, and outreach to the community and the state.
Opened: 1939
Specialized Field: Films, Plays
Seating Capacity: 168

8251
GILBERT V. HEMSLEY THEATRE
University of Wisconsin-Madison
Department of Theatre and Drama
821 University Avenue
Madison, WI 53706-1497
Phone: 608-263-2329
Fax: 608-263-2463
e-mail: gradsec@theatre.wisc.edu
Web Site: www.theatre.wisc.edu
Management:
   Director: Tony Simotes
   General Manager: Michele Traband
   Production Manager: David Stewart
   Technical Director: Dan Lisowski
Mission: The Department of Theatre and Drama/University Theatre is a collaborative community of artists and scholars — faculty, staff and students — aiming to achieve the highest level of excellence in their teaching and learning, research and creative endeavors, and outreach to the community and the state.
Specialized Field: Drama, Theatre
Type of Stage: Black Box
Seating Capacity: 125

8252
KOHL CENTER
601 W Dayton Street
Madison, WI 53715-1233

Phone: 608-263-5645
Fax: 608-265-4700
Toll-free: 800-223-4377
Web Site: www.uwbadgers.com
Management:
   Managing Director: Douglas Beard
   Associate Athletic Director: Jamie Pollard
   Facility Director: Barry Fox
Founded: 1848
Status: Non-Profit, Non-Professional
Seating Capacity: 17,142
Year Built: 1998

8253
NORMAN MITBY THEATER
Madison Area Technical College
Truax Campus
3550 Anderson Road
Madison, WI 53704-2599
Phone: 608-246-6529
Fax: 608-243-4011
e-mail: dhelser@matcmadison.edu
Web Site: http://matcmadison.edu/mitbytheater/HTM
Officers:
   President: Bettsey L. Barhorst, PhD
Management:
   Managing Director: D Corey Helser
   Technical Coordinator: Matt Breaux
   Box Office: Dee Traxler
Founded: 1932
Specialized Field: Concerts, Theater
Status: Non-Profit, Professional
Paid Staff: 11
Type of Stage: Contemporary Proscenium
Orchestra Pit: y
Seating Capacity: 976

8254
OVERTURE CENTER FOR THE ARTS
201 State Street
Madison, WI 53703-2214
Phone: 608-258-4141
Fax: 608-258-4971
Web Site: www.overturecenter.com
Officers:
   President/CEO: Bob D'Angelo
   VP Finance: Reynold Peterson
   Director Marketing/Public Relations: Anna Hahm
   Director Education/Outreach: Susan Crofton
   Director Building Facilities/Ops: Glenn Weihert
   Building Systems Manager: Rick Bidlingmaier
   Director Theatre Ops/Facilities: Rudy Lienau
   Technical Director: Steve Schroeder
   Rental Contact: Brenda Malisch
Mission: Presenting internationally acclaimed jazz, classical, opera, musicals, dance, world music, family entertainment and more. The Overture Center is currently home to seven resident performing arts organizations adn two visual arts organizations. The Playhouse seats 350, Capitol Theater seats 400-600.
Seating Capacity: 2,251
Organization Type: Resident, Presenters

8255
RONALD E. MITCHELL THEATRE
University of Wisconsin-Madison
Department of Theatre and Drama
821 University Avenue
Madison, WI 53706-1497
Phone: 608-263-2329
Fax: 608-263-2463
e-mail: gradsec@theatre.wisc.edu
Web Site: www.theatre.wisc.edu
Management:

Director: David Furumoto
Technical Director: Dan Lisowski
Mission: The Department of Theatre and Drama/University Theatre is a collaborative community of artists and scholars — faculty, staff and students — aiming to achieve the highest level of excellence in their teaching and learning, research and creative endeavors, and outreach to the community and the state.
Specialized Field: Drama, Theatre
Type of Stage: Thrust
Seating Capacity: 321

8256
UNION THEATER
University of Wisconsin
800 Langdon Street
Madison, WI 53706
Phone: 608-262-2202
Fax: 608-265-5084
e-mail: bruce@wut.org
Web Site: www.union.wisc.edu/theater
Management:
Director: Ralph Russo
Facility Booking Contact: Bruce Ehlinger
Seating Capacity: 1,300

8257
UNIVERSITY OF WISCONSIN FIELDHOUSE
University of Wisconsin
1440 Monroe Street
Madison, WI 53711
Phone: 608-262-1866
Fax: 608-265-3036
Web Site: www.wisc.ed/ath/
Management:
Sports Information Director: Tam Flarup
Athletic Director: Pat Richter
Head Football Coach: Barry Alvarez
Head Basketball Coach (M): Dick Bennett
Head Basketball Coach (W): Jane Albright/Dieterl
Seating Capacity: 11,500

8258
WISCONSIN UNION THEATRE
University of Wisconsin-Madison
Memorial Union
800 Langdon St
Madison, WI 53706
Phone: 608-262-2202
Fax: 608-265-5084
e-mail: edinur@wisc.edu
Web Site: www.union.wisc.edu/theater
Management:
Cultural Arts Directory: Ralph Russo
Technical Directory: Jeff Macheel
Operations Manager: Bruce Ehlinger
Marketing/Communications Manager: Esty Dinur
Box Office Manager: Ted Harks
Mission: The Department of Theatre and Drama/University Theatre is a collaborative community of artists and scholars — faculty, staff and students — aiming to achieve the highest level of excellence in their teaching and learning, research and creative endeavors, and outreach to the community and the state.
Founded: 1939
Specialized Field: Classical, World, Jazz and other music, drama, dance
Status: Non-Profit; Professional
Type of Stage: Proscenium
Stage Dimensions: 36'x23'7
Orchestra Pit: y

Seating Capacity: 1,300

8259
CAPITOL CIVIC CENTRE
913 S 8th Street
PO Box 399
Manitowoc, WI 54221-0399
Phone: 920-683-1937
Fax: 920-683-0272
e-mail: ccc@cccshows.org
Web Site: www.cccshows.org
Management:
Executive Director: Jian Paul Morelli
Assistant Director: Peggy Krey
Utilizes: Actors; Artists-in-Residence; Commissioned Composers; Dance Companies; Dancers; Instructors; Local Artists; Multimedia; Original Music Scores; Sign Language Translators; Soloists; Special Technical Talent; Theatre Companies
Founded: 1987
Status: Non-Profit, Professional
Paid Staff: 9
Budget: $60,000-150,000
Seating Capacity: 1,150
Year Built: 1921
Year Remodeled: 1987

8260
SILVER LAKE COLLEGE
2406 S Alverno Road
Manitowoc, WI 54220
Phone: 920-684-6691
Fax: 920-684-7082
Web Site: www.sl.edu
Management:
President: Sr. Marella Wagner
Mission: Outreach program bringing quality music performance to the community
Founded: 1935
Specialized Field: Instrumental Music; Vocal Music; Piano; Mixed Ensemble
Status: Non-Profit, Professional
Paid Staff: 5
Paid Artists: 10
Budget: $6,000.00
Income Sources: College Sponsorship & Ticket Sales
Performs At: Chapel
Annual Attendance: 100-125

8261
MUSIC LIBRARY ASSOCIATION
8551 Research Way
Suite 180
Middletown, WI 53562
Phone: 608-836-5825
Fax: 608-831-8200
e-mail: mla@areditions.com
Web Site: www.musiclibraryassoc.org
Officers:
President: James P Cassaro
Treasurer/Executive Secretary: Laura Gayle Green
Recording Secretary: Lynn Gullickson
Founded: 1931
Status: Non-Profit, Professional

8262
BRADLEY CENTER
1001 North Fourth Street
Milwaukee, WI 53203
Phone: 414-227-0400
Fax: 414-227-0497
Web Site: www.bradleycenter.com
Management:

CEO: David Skiles
GM: Stephen Costello
Founded: 1986
Opened: 1988
Seating Capacity: 20,000

8263
COOLEY AUDITORIUM
Milwaukee Area Technical College
700 West State Street
Milwaukee, WI 53233
Phone: 414-297-6600
Fax: 414-271-2195

8264
MARCUS CENTER FOR THE PERFORMING ARTS
929 N Water Street
Milwaukee, WI 53202-3122
Phone: 414-273-7121
Fax: 414-273-5480
Toll-free: 888-612-3500
e-mail: hlofy@marcuscenter.org
Web Site: www.marcuscenter.org
Officers:
President: Paul Mathews
Operations VP: Richard Hecht
Finance/Human Resource VP: Carol Hayden
Sales & Marketing VP: Heidi Lofy
Management:
Director Of Programming: John Hassig
Director Of Facility Relations: Jerold Fox
Mission: To serve the community, offer facilities and services of the highest quality, also makes a wide range of performing arts available.
Utilizes: Actors; Artists-in-Residence; Choreographers; Collaborating Artists; Collaborations; Commissioned Composers; Dance Companies; Dancers; Designers; Educators; Fine Artists; Five Seasonal Concerts; Grant Writers; Guest Accompanists; Guest Artists; Guest Choreographers; Guest Companies; Guest Composers; Guest Conductors; Guest Designers; Guest Directors; Guest Ensembles; Guest Instructors; Guest Lecturers; Guest Musical Directors; Guest Musicians; Guest Soloists; Guest Teachers; Guest Writers; High School Drama; Instructors; Local Artists; Lyricists; Multimedia; Music; New Productions; Original Music Scores; Performance Artists; Poets; Resident Artists; Resident Professionals; Selected Students; Sign Language Translators; Singers; Soloists; Special Technical Talent; Theatre Companies; Touring Companies; Visual Arts
Income Sources: Technical income; County grants; Facility Rental
Affiliations: Milwaukee Ballet Company; Florentine Opera Company; First Stage Children's Theatre; Milwaukee Youth Symphony Orchestra
Resident Groups: Milwaukee Ballet Co.; Florentine Opera Co.; Milwaukee Symphony Orch.; First Stage Children's Theater

8265
MILLER PARK
1135 S 70th Street
Suite 500
Milwaukee, WI 53214
Phone: 414-607-4040
Fax: 414-607-4044
Web Site: www.millerpark.org
Management:
COB: Robert Trunzo
Executive Direector: Michael Duckett

8266
MILWAUKEE COUNTY STADIUM
201 W 46th Street
Milwaukee, WI 53214
Phone: 414-933-4114
Fax: 414-933-2604
Web Site: www.milwaukeebrewery.com
Management:
   Director Operations: Steve Ethier
   Marketing Director: Dean Rennick
   Suites Director: Geoff Campion
   Concessions Manager: Tom Olsen
Seating Capacity: 55,000

8267
MILWAUKEE RIVERSIDE THEATER
Milwaukee Center Complex
116 West Wisconsin Avenue
Milwaukee, WI 53202
Phone: 414-286-3663
e-mail: gwitt@pabsttheater.org
Web Site: www.pabsttheater.org
Officers:
   President: Michael Cudahy
Management:
   Executive Director: Gary Witt
Founded: 1895
Specialized Field: Broadway, Pop, Country Artists
Paid Staff: 12
Orchestra Pit: y
Seating Capacity: 2,460

8268
MILWAUKEE THEATRE
Wisconsin Center District
400 West Wisconsin Avenue
Milwaukee, WI 53203
Phone: 414-908-6000
Fax: 414-908-6010
e-mail: slange@wcd.org
Web Site: www.milwaukeetheatre.com
Officers:
   President: Richard A Geyer
Management:
   Director Marketing/Sales: Sandra A Lange
   Director Event Services: David Anderson
   Box Office Manager: Donna Piotrowski
   Director Business Development: Richard Freiberg
Facility Category: Theatre
Type of Stage: Proscenium
Seating Capacity: 4,200
Year Built: 1905
Year Remodeled: 2002
Cost: $34 million
Rental Contact: Director Marketing/Sales Sandra Lange

8269
PABST THEATRE
Milwaukee Center Complex
144 E Wells Street
Milwaukee, WI 53202
Phone: 414-286-3663
Fax: 414-286-2154
Toll-free: 800-511-1552
e-mail: gwitt@pabsttheater.org
Web Site: www.pabsttheater.org
Officers:
   President: Michael Cudahy
Management:
   Executive Director: Gary Witt
Founded: 1895

Specialized Field: Chamber Music
Status: Non-Profit, Professional
Paid Staff: 12
Type of Stage: Proscenium
Orchestra Pit: y
Seating Capacity: 1,279

8270
PITMAN THEATRE
Pitman Theatre
3401 S 39th Street
Milwaukee, WI 53234
Mailing Address: PO Box 343922
Phone: 414-382-6044
Fax: 414-382-6354
e-mail: boxoffice@alverno.edu
Web Site: www.alverno.edu
   Director: Amanda Lang
   Assistant Director: Jan Kellogg
Utilizes: Actors; Artists-in-Residence; Collaborating Artists; Collaborations; Dance Companies; Dancers; Educators; Fine Artists; Local Artists; Lyricists; Multimedia; Original Music Scores; Playwrights; Special Technical Talent; Theatre Companies
Paid Staff: 3
Annual Attendance: 5000
Facility Category: Performing Arts Venue
Type of Stage: Proscenium
Stage Dimensions: 40' x 30'
Seating Capacity: 930
Year Built: 1951
Rental Contact: Jan Kellogg

8271
U.S. CELLULAR ARENA
400 W Kilbourn Avenue
Milwaukee, WI 53203
Phone: 414-908-6001
Fax: 414-908-6010
e-mail: rgeyer@wcd.org
Web Site: www.uscellulararena.com
Officers:
   President: Richard A Geyer
Management:
   Sales Manager: Tony Dynicki
   Production/Operations: Jason Borders
   Box Office Manager: Donna Hrobsky
   Group Sales: Molly Powell
   PR/Promotions: David Snyder
Mission: The US Cellular Arena, home to decades of sports legends and rock and roll history, has undergone over $13 million in technilogical, accessibility and aesthetic improvements since 1998, maintaining its place as a vibrant center for Milwaukee entertainment, sports and culture
Opened: 1998
Seating Capacity: 4,087

8272
US CELLULAR ARENA
Wisconsin Center District
400 W Winconsin Avenue
Milwaukee, WI 53203
Phone: 414-908-6000
Fax: 414-908-6010
Web Site: www.wed.org
Officers:
   President: Richards A Geyer
Management:
   Box Office Manager: Donna Piotrowski
   Director Marketing/Sales: Sandra A Lange
   Director Event Services: David Anderson
   Director Business Development: Richard Freiberg

Seating Capacity: 12,600

8273
MONROE ARTS CENTER
PO Box 472
Monroe, WI 53566
Phone: 608-325-5700
Fax: 608-325-5701
e-mail: info@monroeartscenter.com
Web Site: www.monroeartscenter.com
Management:
   President: Barbara Woodriff
   Executive Director: Richard Daniels
   Assistant Director: Lori Grinnell
Founded: 1976
Status: Non-Profit, Professional
Paid Staff: 5
Paid Artists: 18

8274
GRAND OPERA HOUSE
100 High Avenue
PO Box 1004
Oshkosh, WI 54903
Phone: 920-424-2350
Fax: 920-424-2357
Toll-free: 866-964-7263
e-mail: grandinfo@grandoperahouse.org
Web Site: www.grandoperahouse.org
Officers:
   President: Kelly Laux
   President-Elect: Ron Johnson
   Secretary: James Macy
   Treasurer: Randy Hedge
Management:
   Executive Director: Joseph A Ferlo
   Development Manager: Jeff Potts
   Event Manager: David Lange
Founded: 1883
Specialized Field: All
Status: Non-Profit, Professional
Paid Staff: 7
Volunteer Staff: 100
Non-paid Artists: 20
Budget: $500,000
Income Sources: Public; Private
Affiliations: City of Oshkosh
Stage Dimensions: 30'x30'
Seating Capacity: 668
Year Built: 1883
Year Remodeled: 1986
Rental Contact: Merry Little

8275
PIONEER FIELD
University of Wisconsin
1 University Plaza
Platteville, WI 53818-3099
Phone: 608-342-1125
Fax: 608-342-1122
Toll-free: 800-362-5515
e-mail: admit@uwplatt.edu
Web Site: www.uwplatt.edu
Management:
   Athletic Director: Mark Wolesworth
Seating Capacity: 10,000

8276
RICHARD & HELEN BRODBECK CONCERT HALL
University of Wisconsin-Platteville
Center for the Arts
One University Plaza
Platteville, WI 53818-3099

Phone: 608-342-1298
Fax: 608-342-1478
Toll-free: 800-362-5515
Web Site: http://www.uwplatt.edu/arts/cfa/
Management:
    Director Performing/Visual Arts: John Hassig
    Public Relations: Krystle Kurdi
Mission: The Center for the Arts (CFA) provides a professional performing arts environment for the campus and community to experience the arts through classroom learning and quality cultural and performing arts performances.
Founded: 1866
Specialized Field: Dance, Drama, Children's Theater, Orchestra Concerts, Choral, Jazz, Recitals, Performing Arts Series, and the Heartland Festival
Paid Staff: 1
Income Sources: Box office, grants, student support
Facility Category: Concert Hall, Theatre House
Type of Stage: Proscenium
Orchestra Pit: y
Seating Capacity: 565

8277
THEATER
University of Wisconsin-Platteville
Center for the Arts
One University Plaza
Platteville, WI 53818-3099
Phone: 608-342-1298
Fax: 608-342-1478
Toll-free: 800-362-5515
Web Site: http://www.uwplatt.edu/arts/cfa/
Management:
    Director Performing/Visual Arts: John Hassig
    Public Relations: Krystle Kurdi
Mission: The Center for the Arts (CFA) provides a professional performing arts environment for the campus and community to experience the arts through classroom learning and quality cultural and performing arts performances.
Founded: 1866
Specialized Field: Dance, Drama, Children's Theater, Orchestra Concerts, Choral, Jazz, Recitals, Performing Arts Series, and the Heartland Festival
Paid Staff: 1
Income Sources: Box office, grants, student support
Facility Category: Concert Hall, Theatre House
Type of Stage: Flexible
Orchestra Pit: y
Seating Capacity: 200

8278
DEMMER RECITAL HALL
Ripon College
Rodman Arts Center, 300 Seward Street
Ripon, WI 54971
Mailing Address: Box 248
Phone: 414-748-8120
Fax: 414-748-9262

8279
FINE ARTS THEATRE
One University Drive
Sheboygan, WI 53081
Phone: 414-459-6600
Fax: 920-459-6602

8280
JOHN MICHAEL KOHLER ARTS CENTER
608 New York Avenue
Sheboygan, WI 53081

Phone: 920-458-6144
Fax: 920-458-4473
Web Site: www.jmkac.org
Management:
    President: Marty Crneckiy
    Director: Ruth Deyoung
Founded: 1967
Status: Non-Profit, Professional
Paid Staff: 35

8281
LUCILLE TACK CENTER FOR THE ARTS
300 School Street
PO Box 337
Spencer, WI 54479
Phone: 715-659-4499
Fax: 715-659-5470
Web Site: www.spencer.kiz.wi.us/ltca
Management:
    Executive Director: Deborah Janz
Mission: To provide an environment that encourage a variety of opportunities to enlighten, enrich and develop activity growth for community members of all ages.
Founded: 1995
Status: Non-Profit, Professional
Paid Staff: 1
Volunteer Staff: 50
Seating Capacity: 500

8282
ST. CROIX FESTIVAL THEATRE
PO Box 801
St. Croix Falls, WI 54024
Phone: 715-294-2991
Web Site: www.festivaltheatre.org
Founded: 1990
Specialized Field: Theater
Status: Non-Equity; Nonprofit
Season: July - December
Type of Stage: Thrust
Seating Capacity: 260

8283
QUANDT FIELDHOUSE
University of Wisconsin-Stevens Point
2050 Fourth Avenue
Stevens Point, WI 54481
Phone: 715-346-4343
Fax: 715-346-4365
e-mail: gdiekroe@uwsp.edu
Web Site: www.uwsp.edu
Management:
    Assistant Director: Greg Diekroeger
Seating Capacity: 3,500

8284
MANION THEATRE
University of Wisconsin-Superior
Superior, WI 54880
Mailing Address: PO Box 2000
Phone: 715-394-8369
Fax: 715-394-8065
Web Site: www.uwsuperior.edu
Management:
    Theatre Director: Cathy Fank
Status: Non-Profit, Non-Professional

8285
WAUKESHA CIVIC THEATRE
Margaret Brate Bryant Civic Theatre
264 W Main Street
Waukesha, WI 53186

Phone: 262-547-4911
Fax: 262-547-8454
e-mail: planious@waukeshacivictheatre.com
Web Site: ww.waukeshacivictheatre.com
Founded: 1957

8286
IRVIN L. YOUNG AUDITORIUM
University of Wisconsin-Whitewater
930 West Main Street
Whitewater, WI 53190
Phone: 262-472-2222
Fax: 262-472-4400
e-mail: youngaud@uww.edu
Web Site: www.uww.edu/youngauditorium
Management:
    Director: Ken Kohberger
    Marketing: Leslie LaMuro
Opened: 1991
Seating Capacity: 1,289

8287
WARHAWK STADIUM
University of Wisconsin
800 W Main Street
Whitewater, WI 53190
Phone: 414-472-1234
Fax: 414-472-2791
e-mail: myersw.wwwvax.uww.edu
Web Site: www.uww.edu
Management:
    Athletic Director: Willie Myers
    Athletic Director/Women's: Dianne Jones
Seating Capacity: 11,500

Wyoming

8288
CASPER EVENTS CENTER
1 Events Drive
PO Box 128
Casper, WY 82602
Phone: 307-577-3030
Fax: 307-235-8445
Toll-free: 800-442-2256
e-mail: tcanepa@cityofcasperwy.com
Web Site: www.caspereventscenter.com
Management:
    Director: Max Torbert
    Marketing Director: Tiffine Canepa
    Box Office Manager: Carmen Mills
    Operations Manager: Bud Dovala
Seating Capacity: 10,452
Year Built: 1982

8289
DURHAM HALL
Casper College
125 College Drive
Casper, WY 82601
Phone: 307-268-2110
Fax: 307-268-3023
Toll-free: 800-442-2963
Web Site: www.caspercollege.edu
Management:
    Executive Director: Eric Unruh
Founded: 1940
Status: Non-Profit, Professional
Paid Staff: 23

8290
CHEYENNE CIVIC CENTER
2101 O'Neil Avenue
Cheyenne, WY 82001
Phone: 307-637-6364
Fax: 307-637-6365
e-mail: drohla@cheyennecity.org
Web Site: www.cheyenneciviccenter.org
Management:
    Executive Director: Dru A Rohla
Founded: 1981
Status: Non-Profit, Professional
Paid Staff: 105

8291
FRONTIER PARK
4610 Carey Avenue
Cheyenne, WY 82001
Mailing Address: PO Box 2477
Phone: 307-778-7200
Fax: 307-778-7213
e-mail: dave@cfdrodeo.com
Web Site: www.cfdrodeo.com
Management:
    Director: Dave Johansen
    Marketing Manager: Nicole Gamst
Seating Capacity: 24,000

8292
THE IKON CENTER
1530 West Lincolnway
Cheyenne, WY 82001
Phone: 307-433-0024
Fax: 307-433-0027
Web Site: www.ikoncenter.com
Management:
    GM: Ron Byrne
Opened: 2000
Seating Capacity: 2,500

8293
CAM-PLEX HERITAGE CENTER
1635 Reata Drive
Gillette, WY 82718
Phone: 307-682-0552
Fax: 307-682-8418
Toll-free: 800-358-1897
e-mail: camplex@vcn.com
Web Site: www.cam-plex.com
Management:
    Theatre Manager: Phyllis Colpitts

8294
ARENA AUDITORIUM
University of Wyoming
University Station
Laramie, WY 82071
Phone: 307-766-2292
Fax: 307-766-5414
e-mail: wyosid@uwyo.edu
Web Site: www.uwyo.edu/om/ath/inercol/index.htm
Management:
    Head Football Coach: Vick Koenning
    Head Basketball Coach (M): Steve McClain
    Head Basketball Coach (W): Cindy Fisher
    Athletic Director: Lee Moon
    Associate Athletic Director: Keener Fry
    Sports Information Director: Kevin McKinney
    Senior Women's Adminstrator: Barbara Burke
    Executive Director: Randy Woliniak
Seating Capacity: 15,028

8295
UNIVERSITY OF WYOMING: ARTS AND SCIENCES AUDITORIUM
PO Box 3254
Laramie, WY 82071
Phone: 307-766-5242
Fax: 307-766-5326

8296
UNIVERSITY OF WYOMING: FINE ARTS CONCERT HALL
PO Box 3037
Laramie, WY 82071
Phone: 307-766-5242

8297
WAR MEMORIAL STADIUM (WY)
University of Wyoming
Dept 3414, 1000 E University Avenue
Laramie, WY 82071
Phone: 307-766-2292
Fax: 307-766-5414
e-mail: wyosid@uwyo.edu
Web Site: www.wyomingathletics.com
Management:
    President: Philip Dubois
    Athletic Director: Gary A Barta
    Sports Informations Director: Kevin McKinney
Founded: 1869
Status: For-Profit, Non-Professional
Paid Staff: 100
Seating Capacity: 33,500

8298
COMMUNITY FINE ARTS CENTER
400 C Street
Rock Springs, WY 82901
Phone: 307-362-6212
Fax: 307-382-4101
Web Site: www.cfac4art.com
Management:
    Executive Director: Debra Soule
Founded: 1970
Specialized Field: American Art Work
Status: Non-Profit, Professional
Paid Staff: 3

8299
WYO THEATER
42 North Main Street
PO Box 528
Sheridan, WY 82801
Phone: 307-672-9083
Fax: 307-672-8074
e-mail: execdir@wyotheater.com
Web Site: www.wyotheater.com
Officers:
    Chairman: Jerry Pilch
    Vicechairman: Liana Huey
    Secretary: Rock Sathre
    Treasurer: Cheri Wilson
Management:
    Executive Director: Nick Johnson
    Technical Director: Pam Thompson
    Box Office Manager: Curt Sare
    Business Office: Carlyn King
Mission: Since reopening in 1989 the WYO has brought countless hours of live entertainment, cultural enrichment, and educational opportunities to the greater Sheridan community.
Founded: 1923
Status: Non-Profit, Professional
Paid Staff: 1

Associations

9001
Academy of Country Music
5500 Balboa Blvd
Suite 200
Encino, CA 91316-1505
818-788-8000
FAX 818-788-0999
E-Mail: info@acmcountry.com
Home Page: www.acmcountry.com

Gayle Holcomb, Chairman
David Young, Director Operations
Tiffany Moon, Secretary
Brandi Brammer, Project Manager
Tree Paine, Director Marketing

Involved in numerous events and activities promoting country music. Presents annual awards.
4M Members
Founded in 1964

9002
Academy of Motion Picture Arts and Sciences
8949 Wilshire Blvd
Beverly Hills, CA 90211-1972
310-247-3000
FAX 310-271-3395
Home Page: www.oscars.org

The Academy was founded to advance the arts and sciences of motion pictures; foster cooperation among creative leaders for cultural, educational and technological progress; recognize outstanding achievments; cooperate on technical research and improvement of methods and equipment; provide a common forum and meeting ground for various branches and crafts; represent the viewpoint of actual creators of the motion picture. Hosts annual Academy Awards.
6000 Members
Founded in 1927

9003
Academy of Science Fiction Fantasy and Horror Films
334 W 54th St
Los Angeles, CA 90037-3806
323-752-5811
FAX 323-752-5811
E-Mail: scifiacademy@ca.rr.com
Home Page: www.saturnawards.org

Robert Holguin, President
Roger Fenton, VP
Michael Laster, Director

Culminated from the Count Dracula Society, the Academy hosts the annual Science Fiction Film Awards, called the Saturn Awards.
Founded in 1972

9004
Accordian Federation of North America
14126 E Rosencrans Boulevard
Santa Fe Springs, CA 90670
562-921-5058
E-Mail: afna@musician.org
Home Page: www.afnafestival.org

Madeleine D'Ablaing, President
Debbie Gray, VP
Oakley Yale, Secretary
Prisscilla Martinez, Treasurer
Larry Demian, Parliamentarian

Members are primarily teachers and music school owners with the primary purpose to encourage young people to pursue their music study. Holds festivals and competitions
75 Members
Founded in 1972

9005
Accordion Teachers Guild
2312 West 71 Terrace
Prairie Village, KS 66208-3322
913-722-5625
Home Page: www.accordions.com/atg

Joan C Sommers, President
Dee Langley, First VP
Stas Venglevski, Second VP
Joanna Arnold Darrow, Executive Secretary
Stanley Darrow, Historian

ATG members are accordian teachers and professionals committed to furthering the progress of the accordion by improving teaching standards, music and all phases of music education.
Founded in 1940

9006
Actors Equity Association
165 W 46th St
New York, NY 10036-2500
212-764-7647
FAX 212-719-9815
Home Page: www.actorsequity.org

Alan Eisenberg, CEO
Mark Zimmerman, President
David Lotz, National Director of Communications
Mary Lou Westerfield, Natioanl Director Policy
Flora Stamatiades, National Director Organizing

A labor union that represents Actors and Stage Managers in the United States. Seeks to advance, promote and foster the art of live theatre as an essential component of our society. Negotiates wages and working conditions and provides a wide range of benefits, including health and pension plans.
45000 Members
Founded in 1913

9007
American Alliance for Theatre and Education
7475 Wisconsin Ave
Suite 300A
Bethesda, MD 20814-3474
301-654-0008
FAX 301-968-0144
E-Mail: info@aate.com
Home Page: www.aate.com

Steve Barberio, President

The national voice for theatre and education, representing artists and educators serving young people in theatre and education. Its members play a vital role in advocating for the interests of children who benefit from theatre in their communities and classrooms. AATE embraces diversity and encourages inclusion of all races, social classes, ages, genders, religions, sexual orientations, national organizations and abilities.
700 Members
Founded in 1986

9008
American Association of Community Theatre
8402 BriarWood Circle
Lago Vista, TX 78645
512-267-0711
866-687-2228
FAX 512-267-0712

E-Mail: info@aact.org
Home Page: www.aact.org

Julie Angelo, Executive Director
Mary Britt, President
William P Muchow, Executive VP
Frank Peot, Secretary
Gary Walker, Treasurer

The national voice of community theatre, representing the interests of its members and over 7,000 theatres across the US and with the armed services overseas. Its mission is to foster the encouragement and development of, and commitment to, the highest standards by community theatres, including standards of excellence for production, management, governance, community relations and service.
1800 Members
Founded in 1986

9009
American Choral Directors Association
PO Box 2720
Oklahoma City, OK 73101-2720
405-232-8161
FAX 405-232-8162
E-Mail: acda@acdaonline.org
Home Page: www.acdaonline.org

Gene Brooks, Executive Director
Michele Holt, President
Mitzi Groom, VP
Julie Morgan, Treasurer
Olga Funderburk, Secretary

Nonprofit music-education organization whose central purpose is to promote excellence in choral music through performance, composition, publication, research and teaching. In addition, ACDA strives to elevate choral music's position in American society through arts advocacy. Holds annual convention.
Cost: $90.00
19500 Members
Founded in 1959

9010
American Cinema Editors
100 Universal City Plaza
Verna Fields Building 2282 Room 190
Universal City, CA 91608
818-777-2900
FAX 818-733-5023
E-Mail: americancinema@earthlink.net
Home Page: www.ace-filmeditors.org

Alan Heim, President
Michael Tronick, VP
Christopher Cooke, Secretary
Ed Abroms, Treasurer

A non-profit corporation committed to the encouragement of mutually-beneficial dialogue with other members of the motion picture industry and to educating the general public. Holds the annual ACE Eddie Awards honoring the nominees for the Film Editing Award given by the Academy of Motion Pictures Arts and Sciences.
Founded in 1951

9011
American College of Musicians
PO Box 1807
Austin, TX 78767
512-478-5775
FAX 512-478-5843
E-Mail: ngpt@pianoguild.com
Home Page: www.pianoguild.com

Richard Allison, President
Julia Kruger, VP

Provides student awards and teachers benefits.

Founded in 1929

9012
American Dance Therapy Association
10632 Little Patuxent Pkwy
Suite 108
Columbia, MD 21044-3263
410-997-4040
FAX 410-997-4048
E-Mail: info@adta.org
Home Page: www.adta.org

Gloria Farrow, Manager
Sharon Goodhill, VP
Gloria J Farrow, Operations Director

Professional organization of dance movement therapists, with members both nationally and internationally; offers training, research findings, and a newsletter. Holds annual conference.
1.1M Members
Founded in 1966

9013
American Disc Jockey Association
20118 N 67th Avenue
Suite 300-605
Glendale, AZ 85308
888-723-5776
E-Mail: office@adja.org
Home Page: www.adja.org

Rob Snyder, Director

An association of professional mobile entertainers. Encourages success for its members through continuous education, camaraderie, and networking. The primary goal is to educate Disc Jockeys so that each member acts ethically and responsibly.

9014
American Federation of Musicians of the United States and Canada
1501 Broadway
Suite 600
New York, NY 10036-5501
212-869-1330
FAX 212-764-6134
E-Mail: info@afm.org
Home Page: www.afm.org

Thomas Lee, President
Linda Patterson, Executive Secreaty to President

AFM is an association of professional musicians united through their locals so that they can live and work in dignity; produce work that will be fulfilling and compensated fairly; have a meaningful voice in decisions that affect them; have the opportunity to develop their talents and skills; whose collective voice and power will be realized in a democratic and progressive union; and who oppose the forces of exploitation through their union solidarity.
10K Members
Founded in 1896

9015
American Federation of Violin and Bow Make rs
1201 South Main Street
Mount Airy, MD 21771
301-607-9020
FAX 301-607-9020
E-Mail: info@germainviolins.com
Home Page: www.afvbm.com

Christopher Germain, President
David Van Zandt, Secretary

William Scott, Treasurer
Christopher Reuning, VP

Members are those with recognized professional abilities and experience in either making or repairing violins and bows. They are elected to the Federation and are entitled to all privileges and duties of membership. The Federation has designed programs to held develop the technical skills and knowledge of the membership through seminars and regular meeting events. The Federation sponsors exhibitions as a forum for makers, musicians and the general public.
Cost: $300.00
Founded in 1980

9016
American Guild of Music
PO Box 599
Warren, MI 48090
248-686-1975
E-Mail: agm@americanguild.org
Home Page: www.americanguild.org

Barry Carr, President
Joanne Darby, Treasurer
Lorelei Eccleston Dart, First VP
Steve Petrunak, Second VP

The worls's oldest international music organization. Its membership is oipen to independent music teachers, music store owners and their teaching staffs, music publishers and instrument manufacturers and music students.
6000 Members

9017
American Guild of Musical Artists
1430 Broadway
14th Floor
New York, NY 10018-3308
212-265-3687
FAX 212-262-9088
E-Mail: agma@musicalartists.org
Home Page: www.musicalartists.org

James Odom, President
Ray Menard, Treasurer
Louis Perry, Recording Secretary

AGMA is a labor union. It negotiates collective bargaining agreements for its members that provide them with these vital benefits: guaranteed salaries; rehearsal and overtime pay; regulated work hours; vacation and sick pay; access to low-cost health benefits; good-faith resolution of disputes; and protection of their legal and contractual rights.
5700 Members
Founded in 1936

9018
American Guild of Organists
475 Riverside Drive
Suite 1260
New York, NY 10115-0055
212-870-2310
FAX 212-870-2163
E-Mail: info@agohq.org
Home Page: www.agohq.org

James Thomashower, Executive Director
Marcia Van Oyen, Director

Membership in the American Guild of Organists is primarily through local chapters, which hold regular meetings featuring performances, lectures, seminars, and discussions on a wide variety of topics. Many chapters also offer monthly newsletters, scholarship programs, musician placement services, and substitute referrals to employing institutions. Membership can also be without chapter affiliation.

20000 Members
Founded in 1896

9019
American Harp Society
PO Box 38334
Los Angeles, CA 90038-0334
323-469-3050
E-Mail: kmoon@uclalumni.net
Home Page: www.harpsociety.org

Kathleen Moon, Executive Secretary

Promotes and fosters the appreciation of the harp as a musical instrument, to encourage the composition of music for the harp and to improve the quality of performance of harpists.
Cost: $50.00
3000 Members
Founded in 1962

9020
American Indian Registry for the Performing Arts
1717 N Highland
Suite 614
Los Angeles, CA 90028
213-962-6574

Organization of American Indian performers and technical personnel in the entertainment field.

9021
American Institute of Organbuilders
PO Box 130982
Houston, TX 77219
713-529-2212
FAX 713-529-2212
E-Mail: pipes@pipeorgan.org
Home Page: www.pipeorgan.org

Sponsors training seminars, quarterly journal and annual convention for pipe organ builders and service technicians.
385 Members
Founded in 1974
Mailing list available for rent: 350 names at $250 per M

9022
American Music Therapy Association
8455 Colesville Rd
Suite 1000
Silver Spring, MD 20910-3392
301-589-3300
FAX 301-589-5175
E-Mail: info@musictherapy.org
Home Page: www.musictherapy.org

Andrea Farbman, Executive Director
Brian Abrams, Mid Atlantic Region President

The mission of the American Music Therapy Association is to advance public awareness of the benefits of music therapy and increase access to quality music therapy services in a rapidly changing world.
3800 Members
Founded in 1998

9023
American Musical Instrument Society
389 Main Street
Suite 202
Malden, MA 2148
781-397-8870
FAX 781-397-8887
E-Mail: amis@guildassoc.com
Home Page: www.amis.org

Stewart Carter, President
Joanne Kopp, Treasurer

Promotes better understanding of all aspects of history, design, construction, restoration, and usage of musical instruments in all cultures and from all periods. The membership of AMIS includes collectors, historians, curators, performers, instrument makers, restorers, dealers, conservators, teachers, students, and many institutional members.
Founded in 1971

9024
American Musicological Society
6010 College Station
Brunswick, ME 04011-8451
207-798-4243
877-679-7648
FAX 877-679-7648
E-Mail: ams@ams-net.org
Home Page: www.ams-net.org

Robert Judd, Executive Director

Advances research in the various fields of music as a branch of learning and scholarship.
3600 Members
Founded in 1934

9025
American Orff-Schulwerk Association
PO Box 391089
Cleveland, OH 44139-8089
440-543-5366
FAX 440-543-2687
E-Mail: info@aosa.org
Home Page: www.aosa2.org

Cindi Wobig, Executive Director
Sue Mueller, President
JeElla Hug, VP
Suzette Swallow, Treasurer

Professional organization of music and movement educators dedicated to the creative teaching approach developed by Carl Orff and Gunild Keetman.
Cost: $70.00

9026
American School Band Directors Association
227 N 1st Street
PO Box 696
Guttenberg, IA 52052-0696
563-252-2500
FAX 563-252-2500
E-Mail: asbda@alpinecom.net
Home Page: www.asbda.com

Jeffrey T Phillips, President
Kevin Beaken, Secretary
Blair Callaway, Treasurer

Nationwide organization dedicated to the support of professional and college band conductors. Membership by invitation only.
1200 Members
Founded in 1952

9027
American Society of Cinematographers
1782 N Orange Drive
PO Box 2230
Hollywood, CA 90028
323-969-4333
800-448-0145
FAX 323-882-6391
E-Mail: office@theasc.com
Home Page: www.theasc.com

Daryn Okadaan, President
Michael Negrin, Secretary
Victor J Kemper, Treasurer

The ASC is not a labor union or guild, but is an educational, cultural and professional organization. Membership is possible by invitation and is extended only to directors of photography with distinguished credits in the industry. Publishes 'American Cinematographer' magazine.
Founded in 1919

9028
American Society of Composers, Authors and Publishers
1 Lincoln Plaza
New York, NY 10023-7097
212-621-6027
FAX 212-724-9064
E-Mail: info@ascap.com
Home Page: www.ascap.com

Marilyn Bergman, President/Chairman
Arnold Broidon, Treasurer
Kathyr Spanberger, Secretary
John Lofrumento, CEO

Performing rights organization created and controlled by composers, songwriters and music publishers. Protects the rights of its members by licensing and distributing royalties for the non-dramatic public performances of their copyrighted works. An online newsletter is also available filled with the most up-to-date information about professional opportunities, legislative issues, member benefits and more.
26000 Members
Founded in 1914

9029
American Society of Music Arrangers and Composers
5903 Noble Ave
Van Nuys, CA 91411-3026
818-994-4661
FAX 818-994-6181
E-Mail: asmac@theproperimageevents.com
Home Page: www.asmac.org

Scherr Lillico, Executive Director
Duane L Tatro, Vice President
Ray Charles, Vice President

Professional society for arrangers, composers, orchestrators, and musicians. Monthly meetings with great speakers from the music industry.
500 Members
Founded in 1938

9030
American String Teachers Association
4153 Chain Bridge Rd
Fairfax, VA 22030-4102
703-279-2113
FAX 703-279-2114
E-Mail: asta@astaweb.com
Home Page: www.astaweb.com

Donna Hale, Executive Director
Beth Danner-Knight, Deputy Director
Jody McNamara, Deputy Director

A membership organization for string and orchestra teachers and players, helping them to develop and refine their careers. Members range from budding student teachers to artist-status performers, businesses who supply goods and services to the string and orchestra world plus colleges, universities, music programs and conservatories.
11300 Members
Founded in 1946

9031
American Symphony Orchestra League
33 W 60th Street
5th Floor
New York, NY 10023-7905
212-262-0638
FAX 212-262-5198
E-Mail: league@symphony.org
Home Page: www.symphony.org

Henry Fogel, CEO
Shirley McCrary, Secretary
Bruce E Clinton, Treasurer
Peter D Cummings, Vice Chair
Robert J Wagner, Vice Chair

Provides leadership and service to American orchestras while communicating to the public the value and importance of orchestras and the music they perform. The League links a national network of thousands of musicians, conductors, managers, board members, volunteers, staff members and business partners, providing a wealth of services, information, and educational opportunities to its members.
1000 Members
Founded in 1942
Mailing list available for rent

9032
American Viola Society
14070 Proton Rd
Suite 100
Dallas, TX 75244-3601
972-233-9107
FAX 972-490-4219
E-Mail: info@avsnationaloffice.org
Home Page: www.americanviolasociety.org

Helen Callus, President
Madeline Crouch, General Manager

An association for the promotion of viola performance and research. AVS membership is accompanied by two print issues of the Journal of the American Viola Society (JAVS) each year.
1000 Members

9033
Art Directors Guild
11969 Ventura Blvd
Suite 200
Studio City, CA 91604-2619
818-762-9995
FAX 818-762-9997
E-Mail: lydia@artdirectors.org
Home Page: www.artdirectors.org

Scott Roth, Executive Director
Lisa Frazza, Secretary
Michael Baugh, Treasurer
Alexandra Schaaf, Manager Membership Department

The creative talents that concieve and manage the background and settings for most films and television projects are members of the Art Directors Guild, Local 800. They and most other crafts of the entertainment industry are members of the International Alliance of Theatrical Stage Employees, Moving Picture Technicians, Artists and Allied Crafts of the United States, its Territories and Canada.
935 Members
Founded in 1937

9034
Assistant Directors Training Program
14724 Ventura Boulevard
Suite 775
Sherman Oaks, CA 91403

818-386-2545
FAX 818-386-2876
E-Mail: mail@trainingplan.org
Home Page: www.trainingplan.org

Tom Joyner, Chair

Provides motion picture and television industry training as directed by the Alliance of Motion Picture and Television Producers and the Directors Guild of America.
Founded in 1965

9035
Associated Pipe Organ Builders of America
PO Box 155
Chicago Ridge, IL 60415
800-473-5270
Home Page: www.apoba.com

A professional association of North American firms engaged in building traditional pipe organs. Members are a select group of organbuilders who have passed stringent memembership requirements which include commitment to principles regarding the use of electronic technology in organ building.
27 Members

9036
Association for Theatre in Higher Education
PO Box 1290
Boulder, CO 80306-1290
303-530-2167
888-284-3737
FAX 303-530-2168
E-Mail: info@athe.org
Home Page: www.athe.org

Karen Berman, President

ATHE serves the interests of its diverse individual and organization members. Its vision is to advocate for the field of theatre and performance in higher education. It serves as an intellectual and artistic center for producing new knowledge about theatre and performance-related disciplines. cultivating vital alliances with other scholarly and creative disciplines, linking with professional and community-based theatres, and promoting access and equity.
1700 Members
Founded in 1986

9037
Association of Arts Administration Educato rs
Bolz Center for Arts Administration
975 University Avenue
Madison, WI 53706
608-263-4161
FAX 608-265-2735
E-Mail: ataylor@bus.wisc.edu
Home Page: www.artsadministration.org

Andrew Taylor, President/Director
John McCann, VP
Phyllis Johnson, Treasurer
Stephen Boyle, Secretary

The Association of Administration Educators (AAAE) is an international organization incorporated as a nonprofit institution within the United States. Its mission is to represent college and university graduate and undergraduate programs in the arts administration, encompassing training in the management of visual, performing, literary, media, cultural and arts service organizations.
Founded in 1975

9038
Association of Cinema and Video Laboratori es
Bev Wood C/O Deluxe Laboratories
1377 North Serrano Avenue
Hollywood, CA 90027
323-462-6171
FAX 323-461-0608
E-Mail: beverly.wood@bydeluxe.com
Home Page: www.acvl.org

Bev Wood, President
Chip Wilkenson, First VP
John Carlson, Second VP
Kevin Dillon, Treasurer
Bob Olson, Secretary

Provides opportunities for discussion and exchange of ideas in connection with administrative, technical and managerial problems in the motion picture and video industry. The Association is concerned with improvements in technical practices and procedures, public and industry relations, product specifications to vendors, the impact of current and impending governmental regulations, and any and all other areas of interest to the laboratory industry.
80 Members
Founded in 1953

9039
Association of Concert Bands
6613 Cheryl Ann Drive
Independence, OH 44131-3718
800-726-8720
FAX 216-524-1897
Home Page: www.acbands.org

Allen Beck, President
Nada Vencl, Secretary
Mike Montgomery, CIO
Howard Habenicht, Treasurer

The purpose of ACB is to encourage and foster adult concert community, municipal, and civic bands and to promote the performance of the highest quality traditional and contemporary literature for band.
750 Members
Founded in 1977

9040
Association of Hispanic Arts
P.O.Box 7
Bronx, NY 10464-0007
212-876-1242
888-876-1240
FAX 212-876-1285
E-Mail: informacion@latinoarts.org
Home Page: www.latinoarts.org

Nicholas L Arture, Executive Director
Julia L Gutierrez-Rivera, Program Officer/Arts Service Coord.
Crystal Chaparro, Office Assistant
Gregory Castro, Comptroller
Brenda L Jiminez, Board Chair

A nonprofit arts service organization serving the Latino arts and cultural community. AHA was established out of the need to create funding and presenting opportunities for individual Latino artists and cultural organizations whose contributions were unrecognized and whose efforts were underserved by mainstream public and private institutions.
Founded in 1975

9041
Association of Performing Arts Presenters
1211 Connecticut Ave NW
Suite 200
Washington, DC 20036-2716
202-833-2787
888-820-2787
FAX 202-833-1543
E-Mail: info@artspresenters.org
Home Page: www.artspresenters.org

Sandra Gibson, President
Sean Handerhan, Marketing

A national membership and advocacy organization dedicated to bringing performing artists and audiences together.
1900 Members
Founded in 1957

9042
Association of Talent Agents
9255 W Sunset Blvd
Suite 930
Los Angeles, CA 90069-3317
310-274-0628
FAX 310-274-5063
E-Mail: shellie@agentassociation.com
Home Page: www.agentassociation.com

Sandy Bresler, President
Sheldon Sroloff, VP
Jim Gosnell, Secretary/Treasurer
Karen Stuart, Executive Director
Shellie Jetton, Administrative Director

A non-profit trade association representing talent agencies in the industry. ATA is the voice of unified talent and literary agencies. ATA agencies represent the vast majority of working artists, including actors, directors, writers, and other artists in film, stage, television, radio, commercial, literary work, and other entertainment enterprises.
Founded in 1937

9043
Blues Foundation
49 Union Ave
Memphis, TN 38103-2492
901-527-2583
FAX 901-529-4030
E-Mail: jay@blues.org
Home Page: www.blues.org

Jay Sieleman, Executive Director
Paul Benjamin, President
Chip Eagle, VP
Chadd Webb, Treasurer

A nonprofit corporation which serves as the hub for the worldwide passion for Blues Music.
Founded in 1980

9044
Broadcast Music Incorporated
320 W 57th St
New York, NY 10019-3705
212-586-2000
FAX 212-246-2163
E-Mail: webmaster@bmi.com
Home Page: www.bmi.com

Del Bryant, CEO
John E Cody, COO/Executive VP

American performing rights organization that represents approximately 300,000 songwriters, composers and music publishers in all genres of music. The nonprofit company collects license fees on behalf of those Ameri-

can creators it represents, as well as thousands of creators from around the world who chose BMI for representation in the US. These fees are then distributed as royalties to the writers, composers and copyright holders it represents.
300m Members
Founded in 1939

9045
Casting Society of America
606 N Larchmont Blvd
Los Angeles, CA 90004-1309
323-463-1925
FAX 323-463-4753
E-Mail: info@castingsociety.com
Home Page: www.castingsociety.com

Larry Raab, Manager

CSA is the largest professional association of Casting Directors in the world. They work in all areas of entertainment in film, television and theatre. CSA continually seeks to expand their standing in the industry by providing information and opportunities that support is members.
500+ Members
Founded in 1982

9046
Chamber Music America
305 7th Avenue
5th Floor
New York, NY 10001
212-242-2022
FAX 212-242-7955
Home Page: www.chamber-music.org

Susan Dadian, Program Director
Margaret M Lioi, CEO
Louise Smith, Chair

Promotes artistic excellence and economic stability within the profession and to ensure that chamber music is a vital part of American life. Their vision is that chamber music serves as a model of cooperation and collaboration, that audiences become more committed to supporting chamber music and the professionals who devote their lives to this art form, and that opportunities for the performance of chamber music increase in traditional concert venues and beyond.
Founded in 1977

9047
Chinese Music Society of North America
PO Box 5275
Woodridge, IL 60517-0275
630-910-1551
FAX 630-910-1561
Home Page: www.chinesemusic.net

Sin-Yan Shen, President
Kok-Koon Ng, VP
Yuan-Yuan Lee, Executive Director
Billie Jefferson, Artistic Administrator
Der-Tung Yuan, Membership

A national nonprofit organization founded to increase and diffuse the knowledge of Chinese music and performing arts. Today it has grown to become the national association of Chinese musicians and scholars and National and International organization specializing in Research and Educational Material in English concerning Music/Theater/Dance and Musical Instruments from China and Non-Western Cultures.
Founded in 1969

9048
Chorus America
1156 15th St NW
Suite 310
Washington, DC 20005-1747
202-331-7577
FAX 202-331-7599
E-Mail: service@chorusamerica.org
Home Page: www.chorusamerica.org

Ann Meier Baker, President & Chief Executive Officer

Chorus America's mission is to strengthen choruses and increase appreciation of choral music so that more people are enriched by its beauty and power.
1600 Members
Founded in 1977

9049
Cincinnati Arts Association
650 Walnut St
Cincinnati, OH 45202-2517
513-621-2787
FAX 513-977-4150
E-Mail: info@cincinnatiarts.org
Home Page: www.cincinnatiarts.org

Steve Loftin, Executive Director
Van Ackerman, Director Marketing/Public Relations

Oversees the programming and management of two of the Tri-state's finest performing arts venues - the Arnoff Center for the Arts and Music Hall - and is dedicated to supporting performing and visual arts.
Founded in 1992

9050
Classical Action
165 W 46th St
Suite 1310
New York, NY 10036-2514
212-997-7717
FAX 212-997-7897
E-Mail: classicalaction@bcefa.org
Home Page: www.classicalaction.org

Charles Hamlen, Founding Director
Chris Kenney, Associate Director

Since 1993, Classical Action has provided a unified voice for all those within the performing arts community to help combat HIV/AIDS and the devastating effects of this epidemic.
Founded in 1993

9051
College Music Society
312 E Pine St
Missoula, MT 59802-4624
406-721-9616
FAX 406-721-9419
E-Mail: cms@music.org
Home Page: www.music.org

Robby D Gunstream, Executive Director
Cynthia Taggart, President

A consortium of college, conservatory, university and independent musicians and scholars interested in all disciplines of music. Its mission is to promote music teaching and learning, musical creativity and expression, research and dialogue, and diversity and interdisciplinary interaction.
9500 Attendees
Founded in 1958

9052
Conductors Guild
5300 Glenside Drive
Suite 2207
Richmond, VA 23228-3983
804-553-1378
FAX 804-553-1876
E-Mail: guild@conductorsguild.org
Home Page: www.conductorsguild.org

Amanda Burton Winger, Executive Director
Scott Winger, Assistant Director

The Conductors Guild is the only music service organization devoted exclusively to the advancement of the art of conducting and to serving the artistic and professional needs of conductors.
1850+ Members
Founded in 1975

9053
Congress on Research in Dance
SUNY College of Brockport
Department of Dance
350 New Campus Drive
Brockport, NY 14420-2939
585-395-2590
FAX 585-395-5134
E-Mail: gcarlson@brockport.edu
Home Page: www.cordance.org

Ray Miller, President
Julie Malnig, Chair, Editorial Board

A not-for-profit, interdisciplinary organization with an open, international membership. Its purposes are: to encourage research in all aspects of dance, including related fields; to foster the exchange of ideas, resources, and methodology, through publication, international and regional conferences and workshops; to promote the accessibility of research materials.
Cost: $35.00
750 Members
Founded in 1965
Mailing list available for rent

9054
Contemporary Record Society
724 Winchester Road
Broomall, PA 19008
610-544-5920
FAX 915-808-4232
E-Mail: crsnews@verizon.net
Home Page:
mysite.verizon.net/vzeeewvp/contemporaryrecordsociety/

Caroline Hunt, Contact

Promotes both a fellowship in the musical arts between artists, composers and presenters and commercial recordingsa of participants in this endeavor. The intent of the Society is to advance the cause of music in the United States and throughout the world, promoting an association among its constituents. The scope of the Society's repertoire includes the musical masterworks of both well-known and relatively unknown composers of all periods.
Cost: $45.00
Founded in 1981

9055
Country Dance & Song Society
132 Main Street
PO Box 338
Haydenville, MA 01039-0338
413-268-7426
FAX 413-268-7471

E-Mail: office@cdss.org
Home Page: www.cdss.org

Brad Foster, Executive/Artistic Director
Carol Compton, Financial Manager
Robin Hayden, Memberhsip Services Coordinator

A national organization dedicated to the preservation and promotion of English and Anglo-American traditional and historical folk dance, music and song. Composed of individual members and affiliate groups, it functions both as an international service bureau and as a facilitator in building and maintaining local and regional dance, music and song communities. It exists to meed needs for community-based activity, for active participation, and for sharing and keeping historical and folk
3400 Members
Founded in 1915

9056
Country Music Association
One Music Circle S
Nashville, TN 37203
615-244-2840
FAX 615-726-0314
Home Page: www.cmaworld.com

Mike Dungan, Chairman
Clarence Spalding, President

CMA is dedicated to bringing the poetry and emotion of Country Music to the World. They will continue a tradition of leadership and professionalism, promotoing the music and recognizing excellence in all its forms. They foster a spirit of community and sharing, and respect and encourage creativity and the unique contributions of everyone. It is a place to have fun and celebrate success.
5000+ Members
Founded in 1958

9057
Country Radio Broadcasters
819 18th Ave S
Nashville, TN 37203-3218
615-327-4487
FAX 615-329-4492
E-Mail: news@crb.org
Home Page: www.crb.org

Ed Salamon, Executive Director
Chasity Crouch, Business Manager
Bill Mayne, VP
Carole Bowen, Secretary
Jeff Walker, Treasurer

A nonprofit eductional organization. It is the principal entity that brings Country radio together with the Country music industry for learning opportunities that promote growth.
Founded in 1969

9058
Creative Musicians Coalition
PO Box 6205
Peoria, IL 61601-6205
309-685-4843
800-882-4262
FAX 309-685-4879
E-Mail: aimcmc@aol.com
Home Page: www.creativemusicianscoalition.com

Ronald Wallace, Founder/President

An international organization dedicated to the advancement of new music and the success of independent musicians.
1000 Members
Founded in 1984

9059
Dance Critics Association
Old Chelsea Station
PO Box 1882
New York, NY 10011
732-643-4008
E-Mail: contactus@dancecritics.org
Home Page: www.dancecritics.org

Kena Herod, Co-Chair
Linda Traiger, Co-Chair

Encourages excellence in dance criticism through education, research and the exchange of ideas. Produces quarterly newsletter.
Cost: $50.00
300 Members
Founded in 1974

9060
Dance Educators of America
340 5th Avenue
Pelham, NY 10803
914-636-3200
800-329-3868
FAX 914-636-5895
E-Mail: dea@deadance.com
Home Page: www.deadance.com

Vickie Sheer, Executive Director
Vic D'Amore, President
Charles Kelley, Treasurer

Dedicated to improving the quality and teaching abilities of its member teachers and enhancing their education of students, as well as furthering the professional and ethical standards in the performing arts and of dance in all its form. Membership is limited to qualified teachers.
Cost: $150.00
1800 Members
Founded in 1932

9061
Dance Films Association
48 W 21st St
Suite 907
New York, NY 10010-6989
212-727-0764
FAX 212-727-0764
E-Mail: info@dancefilms.org
Home Page: www.dancefilms.org

Deidra Towers, Executive Director
Latika Young, Education Director
Anna Brady Nuse, Festival Coordinator
Julian Barnett, Research/Development

Supports all those professionals in both the dance and the film community. Publishes bi-monthly magazine.
Cost: $50.00
Founded in 1956

9062
Dance Masters of America
PO Box 610533
Bayside, NY 11361
718-254-4013
FAX 718-225-4293
E-Mail: dmamann@aol.com
Home Page: www.dma-national.org

Mimi Costa-White, National President
Robert Mann, National Executive Secretary
Charleen Locascio, National Treasurer

An international organization of dance educators who have been certified by test to teach whose main focus is advancing the art of dance and improving the practice of its teaching.

2.5M Members
Founded in 1884

9063
Dance USA
1111 16th St NW
Suite 300
Washington, DC 20036-4830
202-833-1717
FAX 202-833-2686
E-Mail: danceusa@danceusa.org
Home Page: www.danceusa.org

Andrea Snyder, Executive Director
Tom Thielen, Director Finance/Operations
Katherine Fabian, Membership Manager

Provides a forum for the discussion of issues of concern to members and a support network for exchange of information.
400 Members
Founded in 1982

9064
Directors Guild of America
7920 W Sunset Blvd
Los Angeles, CA 90046-3347
310-289-2000
800-421-4173
FAX 310-289-2029
E-Mail: LDavis@dga.org
Home Page: www.dga.org

Jay Roth, President
Steven Soderbergh, National VP
Gilbert Cates, Secretary/Treasurer

The DGA represents Film and Television Directors, Unit Production Managers, First Assistant Directors, Second Assistant Directors, Technical Coordinators and Tape Associate Directors, Stage Managers and Production Assistants.

9065
Dramatists Guild of America
1501 Broadway
Suite 701
New York, NY 10036-5505
212-398-9366
FAX 212-944-0420
E-Mail: igor@dramaguild.com
Home Page: www.dramatistsguild.com

Ralph Sevush, Executive Director Business Affairs
Gary Garrison, Executive Director Creative Affairs
Abby Marcus, Managing Director
Roland Tec, Director of Membership

The Dramatists Guild of America was established over eighty years ago, and is the only professional association that advances the interests of playwrights, composers, lyricists and librettists writing for the living stage.
6000+ Members
Founded in 1964

9066
East-2-West Marketing & Promotion
559 Wanamaker Road
Jenkintown, PA 19046-2219
215-884-3308
FAX 215-884-1083

Jackie Paul, President/CEO

Marketing and promotion.
Mailing list available for rent

9067
Educational Theatre Association
2343 Auburn Ave
Cincinnati, OH 45219-2819
513-421-3900
FAX 513-421-7077
Home Page: www.edta.org

Michael Peitz, Executive Director

EdTA's mission is to make theatre a lifelong part of learning. The Association's major areas of effort - educational development, teacher training, and advocacy - serve to accomplish this mission by helping to improve the learning environment in the theatre arts.
4600+ Members
Founded in 1929

9068
Esperanza Performing Arts Association
Po Box 502591
San Diego, CA 92150
858-391-1311
E-Mail: info@esperanzaarts.org
Home Page: esperanzaarts.org

Alan Cox, Executive Director
Adam Stout, Assistant Director

9069
Film Society of Lincoln Center
70 Lincoln Center Plz
New York, NY 10023-6583
212-875-5781
FAX 212-875-5636
E-Mail: marketing@filmlinc.com
Home Page: www.filmlinc.com

Serge Joseph, Manager
Daniel H Stern, President
Wendy Keys, Secreaty
James Bouras, Treasurer
Claudia Bonn, Executive Director

Celebrates American and international cinema, recognizes and supports new filmmakers, and enhances awareness, accessibility and understanding of the art among a broad and diverse film going audience. The Film Society is best known for two international festivals - the New York Film Festival and the New Directors/New Films festival.
Founded in 1969

9070
Folk Alliance
510 S Main St
First Floor
Memphis, TN 38103-6417
901-522-1170
FAX 901-522-1172
E-Mail: fa@folk.org
Home Page: www.folkalliance.org

Lewis Meyers, Executive Director
Van Denn, VP
Alan Korolenko, Secretary
Mark Moss, Treasurer

The service association for the field, working on behalf of the folk music and dance industry year round. They offer a business directory of contacts for members, and a non-profit group exemption program for US-based organizations.
Cost: $70.00
Founded in 1989

9071
Fritz and Lavinia Jensen Foundation
Foundation for the Carolinas

217 S Tryon Street
Charlotte, NC 28202
704-973-4500
FAX 704-973-4599
E-Mail: info@jensenfoundation.org
Home Page: www.jensenfoundation.org

Ann Todd, Competition Coordinator

Sponsors voice competitions supporting opera and other classical singers.

9072
Gina Bachauer International Piano Foundation
138 W Broadway
Suite 220
Salt Lake City, UT 84101-1913
801-297-4250
FAX 801-521-9202
E-Mail: gina@bachauer.com
Home Page: www.bachauer.com

Paul Polleli, Manager
Kimi Kawashima, Manager
Linda Harrison, Secretary
James Woolley, Treasurer

The mission of the Foundation is to further the pianistic art, foster excellence in performance and teaching, develop opportunities for pianists beyond the scope of the organization and offer leadership in developing a musically-educated community.
Founded in 1976

9073
Gospel Music Association
1205 Division St
Nashville, TN 37203-4011
615-242-0303
FAX 615-254-9755
Home Page: www.gospelmusic.org

John Styll, President

Our mission is to expose, promote and celebrate the gospel through music. GMA serves as a voice for the Christian music community. It provides an atmosphere in which artists, industry leaders, retail stores, radio stations, concert promoters and local churches can coordinate their efforts for the purpose of benefitting the industry as a whole, while remaining true to the purpose of communicating the gospel message.
Cost: $85.00
5000 Members
Founded in 1964

9074
Greek Americans in the Arts and Entertainment
1551 Midvale Avenue
Los Angeles, CA 90024-5501
310-477-7188
Home Page: www.yasas.com

Follows the legacy of Greek-Americans in the arts and entertainment field.

9075
Guild of American Luthiers
8222 S Park Ave
Tacoma, WA 98408-5298
253-472-7853
FAX 253-472-7853
E-Mail: orders@luth.org
Home Page: www.luth.org

Debra G Olsen, Executive Director
Tim Olsen, Editor
Kurt Kendall, Membership

Manufacturers and repairs stringed instruments; offers quarterly journal and triennial meeting.
Cost: $45.00
3000 Members
Founded in 1972

9076
Guitar Accessory and Marketing Association (GAMA)
Po Box 757
New York, NY 10033
212-795-3630
FAX 212-795-3630
E-Mail: assnhdqs@earthlink.net
Home Page: www.discoverguitar.com

Membership is comprised of guitar and guitar accessory manufacturers and various consumer magazines.

9077
Guitar Foundation of America
P.O.Box 2270
Huntington Beach, CA 92647-0270
877-570-1651
FAX 877-570-3409
E-Mail: info@guitarfoundation.org
Home Page: www.guitarfoundation.org

Brian Head, President
Jill Winchell, Operations Manager
Martha Masters, Executive VP
Jeff Cogan, VP
Robert Lane, Vice President/Secretary

Provides its members the combined advantages of a guitar society, a library, a publisher, a continuing education resource, and an artis council. The GFA is a non-profit educational and literacy organization devoted to furthering the knowledge of and interest in the guitar and its music.
Cost: $40.00
Founded in 1973

9078
Historians Film Committee
Rural Route 3
Box 80
Cleveland, OK 74020-9515
918-243-7637
FAX 918-243-5995
E-Mail: rollinspc@aol.com
Home Page: www.filmandhistory.org

Peter C Rollins, Editor-in-Chief

The Committee exists to further the use of film sources in teaching and research, to disseminate information about film and film use to historians and other social scientists, to work for an effective system of film preservation so that scholars may have ready access to film archives, and to organize periodic conferences dealing with film.
Founded in 1970

9079
Hollywood Arts Council
PO Box 931056
Hollywood, CA 90093
323-462-2355
FAX 323-465-9240
E-Mail: admin@hollywoodartscouncil.org
Home Page: www.hollywoodartscouncil.org

Nyla Arslanian, President
Nancy J Brown, VP
Gary Borton, Treasurer
Andre Miripolsky, Secretary

Promotes, nurtures and supports the arts in Hollywood. Has served the community through advocacy, coalition

building, free public arts events and after school programs.
450 Members
Founded in 1978

9080
Independent Film & Television Alliance
10850 Wilshire Blvd
9th Floor
Los Angeles, CA 90024-4628
310-446-1000
FAX 310-446-1600
E-Mail: info@ ifta-online.org
Home Page: www.ifta-online.org

Jean Prewitt, CEO
Jonathan Wolfe, Executive VP/Managing Director
Michael Ryan, Chairman
Lew Horwitz, Vice Chairman Finance

A non-profit association whose mission is to provide the independent film and television industry with high-quality marketplace-oriented services and worldwide representation. The Alliance actively lobbies the United States and Eurpoean governments and the international organizations on measures that impact production and distribution.
Founded in 1980

9081
International Animated Film Society
2114 W Burbank Blvd
Burbank, CA 91506-1232
818-842-8330
FAX 818-842-5645
E-Mail: info@asifa-hollywood.org
Home Page: www.animationarchive.org

Amtran Manoogian, President

A California nonprofit organization established to promote and encourage the art and craft of animation. They support and encourage animation education, supports the preservation and critical evaluation of animation history, recognize achievement of excellence in the art and field of animation, strive to increase the public awareness of animation, act as a liaison to encourage the free exchange of ideas within the animation community, as well as a variety of other goals.
350 Members
Founded in 1974

9082
International Association of Electronic Keyboard Manufacturers
305 Maple Avenue
Wyncote, PA 19095-3228
617-747-2816
Home Page: www.iaekm.org

An association that comprises the global manufacturers of electronic keyboards and affiliated software and publications.

9083
International Association of Jazz Education
PO Box 724
Manhattan, KS 66505
785-776-8744
FAX 785-776-6190
E-Mail: bill@iage.org
Home Page: www.iaje.org

Bill McFarlin, Executive Director
Chuck Owen, President
Ronald Carter, VP
Laura Johnson, Treasurer
Brian Coyle, Secretary

To ensure the continued development and growth of jazz through education and outreach.
Cost: $70.00
8000 Members

9084
International Association of Round Dance Teachers
176 S Cole Road
Boise, ID 83709-0932
208-377-1232
800-346-7522
FAX 208-377-1236
E-Mail: roundalab@roundalab.org
Home Page: www.roundalab.org

Gil & Judy Martin, General Chairman
Brent & Judy Moore, Vice Chairman
Chuck & Becky Jaworski, Marketing Membership

Supports all those involved in the field of square dancing. Publishes quarterly magazine.

9085
International Bluegrass Music Association
2 Music Cir S
Suite 100
Nashville, TN 37203-4381
615-256-3222
888-438-4262
FAX 615-256-0450
E-Mail: info@ibma.org
Home Page: www.ibma.org

Dan Hayes, Executive Director
Stan Zdonik, Vice Chair/Associations
Peter D'Addario, Treasurer
Lee Michael Demsey, Secretary

IBMA works together for high standards of professionalism, a greater appreciation for our music, and the success of the worldwide bluegrass community.

9086
International Cinematographers Guild
7755 W Sunset Boulevard
Hollywood, CA 90046
323-876-0160
FAX 323-876-6383
E-Mail: admin@camerguild.com
Home Page: www.cameraguild.com

Steven Poster, President
Tom Weston, National VP
Paul V Ferrazzi, Secretary/Treasurer
Bruce C Doering, Executive Director

The International Cinematographers Guild welcomes camera professionals from across the United States and around the world.

9087
International Clarinet Association
PO Box 1310
Lyons, CO 80540-2650
801-867-4336
FAX 212-457-6124
E-Mail: membership@clarinet.org
Home Page: www.clarinet.org

Lee Livengood, President
Diane Barger, Treasurer
Kristina Belisle, Secretary
So Rhee, Executive Director

A community of clarinetists and clarinet enthusiasts that supports projects that will benefit clarinet performance; provides opportunities for the exchange of ideas, materials and information among its members; fosters the

composition, publication, recording, and distribution of music for the clarinet; encourages the research and manufacture of a more definitive clarinet; and encourages and promotes the perfomance and teaching of a wide variety of repertoire for the clarinet.
4000 Members
Founded in 1990

9088
International Computer Music Association
1819 Polk Street
Suite 390
San Francisco, CA 94109
FAX 734-878-3031
E-Mail: icma@umich.edu
Home Page: www.computermusic.org

An international affiliation of individuals and institutions involved in the technical, creative and performance aspects of computer music. It serves composers, engineers, researchers and musicians who are interested in the integration of music and technology.
Cost: $63.52
700 Members

9089
International Documentary Association
Ste M270
1201 W 5th St
Los Angeles, CA 90017-1476
213-534-3600
FAX 213-534-3610
E-Mail: sandra@documentary.org
Home Page: www.documentary.org

Sandra J Ruch, Executive Director
Maria Arzola, Membership Coordinator

A nonprofit membership organization dedicated to supporting th eefforts of nonfiction film and video makers throughout the United States and the world; promoting the documentary form; and expanding opportunities for the production, distribution, and exhibition of documentary.
2800+ Members
Founded in 1982

9090
International Festivals and Events Association
2603 W Eastover Ter
Boise, ID 83706-2800
208-433-0950
FAX 208-433-9812
E-Mail: nia@ifea.com
Home Page: www.ifea.com

Steven Schmader, President
Nia Forster, VP/Marketing

A voluntary association of events, event producers, event suppliers, and related professionals and organizations whose common purpose is the production and presentation of festivals, events, and civic and private celebrations.
2000 Members
Founded in 1956

9091
International Horn Society
E-Mail: exec-secretary@hornsociety.org
Home Page: www.hornsociety.org

Jeffrey Snedeker, President
Bruno Schneider, VP
Nancy Jordan Fako, Secretary/Treasurer
Heidi Vogal, Membership
Cost: $35.00

3500 Members

9092

International Music Products Association NAMM

5790 Armada Dr
Carlsbad, CA 92008-4608
760-438-9267
800-767-6266
FAX 760-438-7327
E-Mail: info@namm.org
Home Page: www.namm.org

An association whose mission is to unify, lead and strengthen the international music products industry and increase active participation in music making.
9000 Members
Founded in 1901

9093

International Piano Guild

808 Rio Grande Street
PO Box 1807
Austin, TX 78767
512-478-5775
E-Mail: ngpt@pianoguild.com
Home Page: www.pianoguild.com

Richard Allison, President

A division of the American College of Musicians Professional society of piano teachers and music faculty members. Its primary function is to establish definite goals and awards for students of all levels, from the earliest beginner to the gifted prodigy. Its purpose is to encourage growth and enjoyment through the study of piano.
118m Members
Founded in 1929

9094

International Planned Music Association

5900 S Salina Street
Syracuse, NY 13205
315-469-7711
FAX 315-469-8842
Home Page: www.ipmanet.com

Roy Salgado, President
Steve Seiden, VP
Larry Zaiser, Secretary
Jon Baker, Treasurer

IPMA is a trade organization made up of providers of planned and programmed music services and key vendors. The Associatin exists to provide members with a common ground on which to share informatio about running exciting, profitable franchises and to provide associate members with opportunities to expand their sales in markets all over the world.
200 Members

9095

International Polka Association

4608 S Archer Ave
Chicago, IL 60632-2932
773-254-7771
800-867-6552
E-Mail: ipa@internationalpolka.com
Home Page: www.internationalpolka.com

Dave Ulczycki, President
Rick Rzeszutko, First VP
Fred Kenzierski, Second VP
Marlene Gill, Secretary
Linda Niewierowski, Treasurer

An educational and charitable organization for the preservation, promulgation and advancement of polka music and to promote, maintain and advance public interest in polka entertainment; to advance mutual interests and encourage greater cooperation among its members who are engaged in polka entertainment; and to encourage and pursue the study of polka music, dancing and traditional folklore. Responsible for the continued operation and growth of the Polka Music Hall of Fame and Museum.
Cost: $15.00
8M Members
Founded in 1968

9096

International Society for the Performing Arts

17 Purdy Avenue Suite 200
PO Box 909
Rye, NY 10580
914-921-1550
FAX 914-921-1593
E-Mail: info@ispa.org
Home Page: www.ispa.org

Martha H Jones, Chair
Willem Brans, Treasurer
Horacio Lecona, Secretary
Johann Zietsman, CEO
Lynne Caruso, Membership Manager

A nonprofit organization of executives and directors of concert and performance halls, festivals, performing companies, and artists competitions; government cultural officials; artists' managers; and other interested parties with a professional involvement in the performing arts around the world, and in every arts disciplie. The purpose of ISPA is to develop, nurture, energize and educate an international network of arts leaders and professionals who are dedicated to advancing its field.
600 Members
Founded in 1949

9097

International Society of Folk Harpers and Craftsmen

1614 Pittman Drive
Missoula, Mt 59803
406-542-1976
E-Mail: harps@thorharp.com
Home Page: www.folkharpsociety.org

Dave Woodworth, President
Chuck Wilson, First VP
Verlene Schermer, Second VP
Alice Williams, Secretary
Bette Virdrine, Treasurer

The mission of the ISFHC is: to promote the playing and enjoyment of the folk harp by all; to promote education, creation and development in the building of the folk harp; to increase awareness of professional folk harpers; and to increase public awareness of the music and joys of the folk harp.
Cost: $30.00
Founded in 1985

9098

International Stunt Association

11331 Ventura Boulevard
Suite 100
Studio City, CA 91604
818-760-2072
FAX 818-760-2217
E-Mail: info@isastunts.com
Home Page: www.isastunts.com

Leading the industry in exciting action while holding safety above all else, ISA is a fraternal organization whose membership is by invitation only. It is comprised of the top stuntment, stunt coordinators and second unit directors that Hollywood has to offer and a safety record that is second to none.

9099

International Theatre Equipment Association

770 Broadway
5th Floor
New York, NY 10003-9595
646-654-7680
FAX 646-654-7694
E-Mail: info@itea.com
Home Page: www.itea.com

Robert Sunshine, Executive Director
Barry Ferrell, President
Jack Panzeca, VP
Joe DeMeo, Treasurer
Sarah Fuller, Secretary

Fosters and maintains professional, business and social relationships among its members within all segments of the motion picture industry. Bestows annual Teddy Award to manufacturer of the year and the annual Rodney Award to dealer of the year.
Cost: $375.00
180 Members
Founded in 1971

9100

International Ticketing Association

330 W 38th St
Suite 605
New York, NY 10018-8592
212-629-4036
FAX 212-628-8532
E-Mail: info@intix.org
Home Page: www.intix.org

Maureen Andersen, President
Kathleen O'Donnell, Director

Non-profit association committed to the improvement, progress and advancement of ticket management. Provides educational programs, trade shows, conducts surveys, conference proceedings, and its valuable membership directory.
1200 Members
Founded in 1979

9101

Jazz Education

3303 South Rice, Suite 107
PO Box 8031
Houston, TX 77288
713-397-7800
FAX 715-839-8266
E-Mail: jazzed@jazzedcation.org
Home Page: www.jazzeducation.org

Tracy Scott, Executive Director

Nonprofit music organization providing worthwhile educational activities for school-aged youth in the field of music. Includes many subjects not covered by school systems. Promotes appreciation and understanding of Jazz.
Founded in 1970

9102

Keyboard Teachers Association Internationa l

361 Pin Oak Lane
Westbury, NY 11590-1941
516-333-3236
FAX 516-997-9531

Dr. Albert DeVito, President

9103
League of American Theatres and Producers
226 W 47th St
6th Floor
New York, NY 10036-1413
212-764-1122
FAX 212-944-2136
E-Mail: league@broadway.org
Home Page: www.livebroadway.com

Charolette St Martin, Executive Director
Colin Gibson, Director Finance
Jane Svendsen, Director Marketing
Ed Sandler, Director Membership Services

National trade association for the commercial theatre industry whose principal activity is negotiation of labor contracts and government relations.
400 Members
Founded in 1930

9104
League of Historic American Theatres
334 N Charles St
2nd Floor
Baltimore, MD 21201-4372
410-659-9533
877-627-0833
FAX 410-837-9664
E-Mail: info@lhat.org
Home Page: www.lhat.org

Frances Holden, Executive Director
Thomas Johnson, VP
Lance Olson, Treasurer

The League of Historic American Theatres, a nonprofit membership association, promotes the rescue, rehabilitation and sustainable operation of historic theatres throughout North America. Founded in 1976, the League serves its members through educational programs, publications, specialized services and an annual conference and theatre tour.
500+ Members
Founded in 1976

9105
Literary Managers and Dramaturgs of the Americas
PO Box 728
New York, NY 10014
212-561-0315
E-Mail: lmdanyc@hotmail.com
Home Page: www.lmda.org

Liz Engelman, Chair
Brian Quirt, President
Louise McKay, Administrative Director
Daniella Topol, Treasurer

The mission of the LMDA is to affirm the role of dramaturg, to expand the possibilities of the field to other media and institutions and to cultivate, develop and promote the function of dramaturgy and literary management.
500 Members

9106
Metropolitan Opera Guild
70 Lincoln Center Plz
New York, NY 10023-6577
212-769-7000
FAX 212-769-7007
E-Mail: info@metguild.org
Home Page: www.metoperafamily.org/guild/

David Dik, Manager

Seeks to encourage the appreciation of opera and to support the Metropolitan Opera. The guild provides programs and services in many areas designed to further these goals. Publishes monthly magazine and organizes special events throughout the year to raise funds.
100M Members
Founded in 1935

9107
Mid Atlantic Arts Foundation
201 N Charles Street
Suite 401
Baltimore, MD 21201-4102
410-539-6656
FAX 410-837-5517
E-Mail: info@midatlanticarts.org
Home Page: www.midatlanticarts.org

Alan Cooper, Executive Director
Anthony Gittens, Secretary

MAAF celebrates, promotes and supports the richness and diversity of the region's art resources and works to increase access to the arts and other cultures of the region and the world.
40000 Members
Founded in 1979
Mailing list available for rent: 30,000 names

9108
Motion Picture Association of America
15503 Ventura Boulevard
Eucine, CA 91436
818-995-6600
FAX 818-382-1795
Home Page: www.mpaa.org

Dan Glickman, President/CEO

Serves as the voice and advocate of the American motion picture, home video and television industries. The association advocates for strong protection of the creative works produced and distributed by the industry, fights copyright theft around the world, and provides leadership in meeting new and emerging industry challenges.
7 Members
Founded in 1922

9109
Motion Picture Editors Guild
7715 Sunset Boulevard
Suite 200
Hollywood, CA 90046
323-876-4770
800-705-8700
FAX 323-876-0861
E-Mail: webmester@editorsguild.com
Home Page: www.editorsguild.com

Lisa Zeno Churgin, President
Carol Littleton, VP
Martin Levenstein, Second Vice Presdient
Diane Adler, Secretary
Rachel B Igel, Treasurer

A national labor organization representing freelance and staff post-production professionals. MPED negotiates new collective bargaining agreements and enfoces existing agreements with employers involved in post-production. They provide assistance for securing better conditions, including but not limted to financial, medical, safety and artistic concerns.
6000 Members
Founded in 1937

9110
Motion Picture Pilots Association
7435 Valjean Avenue
Van Nuys, CA 91406
818-947-5454
E-Mail: moviepilots@cox.com
Home Page: www.moviepilots.com

Cliff Fleming, Board Director
Dirk Vahle, Board Director
Steve Hinton, Board Director
Neil Looy, Board Director
Kevin LaRosa, Board Director

The MPPA promotes aviation safety and the interest of aviators working in the motion picture, television and entertainment industries; establishes, conducts and maintains such activities which promote higher aviation standards and better business methods as may assist in the advancement of aviation in the Entertainment Aviation Profession; cooperates with those government agencies, industry organizations, entities or association whose objective is the betterment or advancement of the industry.
Founded in 1997

9111
Music Distributors Association
1026 Northwood Drive
Effingham, IL 62401
217-347-6699
FAX 217-347-6699
E-Mail: geobev@consolidated.net
Home Page: www.musicdistributors.org

An international nonprofit trade association representing and serving manufacturers, wholesalers, importers and exporters of musical instruments and accessories, sound reinforcement products and published music.
Cost: $675.00
Founded in 1939

9112
Music Library Association
8551 Research Way
Suite 180
Middleton, WI 53562
608-836-5825
FAX 608-831-8200
E-Mail: mla@areditions.com
Home Page: www.musiclibraryassoc.org

Philip Vandermeer, President

Provides a forum for issues surrounding music, music in libraries, and music librarianship.
Cost: $90.00
Founded in 1931

9113
Music Performance Fund
1040 Avenue of the Americas
New York, NY 10018-3703
212-391-3950
FAX 212-221-2604
E-Mail: info@Musicpf.org
Home Page: www.musicpf.org

A nonprofit public service organization headquartered in New York City. MPF is the world's largest sponsor of live, admission-free musical programs.
Founded in 1948

9114
Music Publishers Association
245 5th Ave
Suite 236
New York, NY 10016-8728

212-675-7354
FAX 212-675-7381
E-Mail: mpa-admin@mpa.org
Home Page: www.mpa.org

Lauren Kaiser, President
Lynn Sengstack, Treasurer
Kathleen Marsh, Secretary

The MPA fosters communication among publishers, dealers, music educators, and all ultimate users of music. It is a nonprofit association which addresses itself to issues pertaining to every area of music publishing with an emphasis on the issues relevant to the publishers of print music for concert and educational purposes.
75 Members
Founded in 1895

9115
Music Teachers National Association
441 Vine St
Suite 3100
Cincinnati, OH 45202-2813
513-421-1420
888-512-5278
FAX 513-421-2503
E-Mail: mtnanet@mtna.org
Home Page: www.mtna.org

Gary L Ingle, Executive Director
Gail Berenson, President
Janice Wenger, VP

The mission of the MTNA is to advance the value of music study and music making to society and to support the professionalism of music teachers.
24000 Members
Founded in 1876
Mailing list available for rent: 23,000 names at $85 per M

9116
Music for All Foundation
16 Mount Bethel Road
Suite 202
Warren, NJ 07059-5604
908-542-9396
FAX 908-542-9476
E-Mail: info@music-for-all.org
Home Page: www.music-for-all.org

Committed to expanding the role of music and the arts in education, to heightening the public's appreciation of the value of music and arts education, and to creating a positive environment for the arts through societal changes.

9117
Musical Box Society International
MBSI Member Registration
PO Box 10196
Springfield, MO 65808-0196
FAX 417-886-8839
Home Page: www.mbsi.org

A nonprofit organization dedicated to the enjoyment, sstudy and preservation of all automatic musical instruments. Members receive the bimonthly scholarly journal, Mechanical Music, covering educational articles, relevant events, activities, news, information, and advertisements and the biennial, Directory of Members, Museums and Dealers. Hosts annual convention.
Cost: $55.00
2.8M Members
Founded in 1949

9118
Musicians Foundation
875 Avenue of the Americas
Room 2303
New York, NY 10001-3507
212-239-9137
FAX 212-239-9138
E-Mail: info@musiciansfoundation.org
Home Page: www.musiciansfoundation.org

BC Vermeersch, Executive Director

Representing interests on the condition and social welfare of professional musicians and their families. Provides emergency financial assistance to meet current living, medical and allied expenses.
Founded in 1914

9119
National Association for Drama Therapy
21991 Sunstone Ct
Broadlands, VA 20148-4587
585-381-5618
FAX 585-383-1474
E-Mail: answers@nadt.org
Home Page: www.nadt.org

Barbara McKechnie, President
Kate Hurd, VP
Juliette Zaiser, Secretary
Red Rubenstein, Treasurer
Nancy Sondag, Membership

A nonprofit association which establishes and upholds high standards of professional competence and ethics among drama therapists; to develop criteria for training and registration; to sponsor publications and conferences; and to promote the profession of drama therapy through information and advocacy.
Founded in 1979

9120
National Association for Music Education
1806 Robert Fulton Drive
Reston, VA 20191
703-860-4000
800-336-3768
FAX 703-860-1531
Home Page: www.menc.org

Lynn M Brinckmeyer, President

The mission of MENC is to advance music education by encouraging the study and making of music by all. MENC offers more than 100 books, videos and compact discs, as well as two general-interest magazines on music education and four more closely targeted journals.
Founded in 1907
Mailing list available for rent: 60,000 names

9121
National Association of Band Instrument Manufacturers
281 W 21st Street
5th Floor
New York, NY 10010-6906
212-924-9175
FAX 212-675-3577

Jerome Hershman, Contact

A trade association of band instrument manufacturers, importers and distributors including accessories selling to the trade only.
34 Members
Founded in 1920

9122
National Association of College Wind and Percussion Instructors
Division of Fine Arts
Truman State University
Kirksville, MO 63501
660-785-4442
FAX 660-785-7463
E-Mail: cmoore@fsu.edu
Home Page: www.nacwpi.org

Chris Moore, President
Michael Dean, VP
Richard K Weerts, Executive Secretary/Treasurer

A forum for communication within the profession of applied music on the college campus. The Association is composed of university, college, and conservatory teachers.
Cost: $35.00
600 Members
Founded in 1951

9123
National Association of Negro Musicians
11551 South Laflin Street
PO Box 43053
Chicago, IL 60643-5029
773-568-3818
FAX 773-785-5388
E-Mail: nanm@nanm.org
Home Page: www.nanm.org

Roland M Carter, President
David Morrow, First VP
Serita Lattimore, Second VP
Ona B Campbell, Executive Secretary
Dan Long, Treasurer

Dedicated to the preservation, encouragement and advocacy of all genres of the music of African Americans. Holds a national convention in a different city eac year, offering a chance to participate in workshops, seminars, lectures and performances. NANM invites the professional artists, the educator, the student, the amateur, the lover of music to become a part of this organization's 'Pride in a Cultural Heritage.'
2.5M Members
Founded in 1919

9124
National Association of Pastoral Musicians
962 Wayne Ave
Suite 210
Silver Spring, MD 20910-4461
240-247-3000
FAX 240-247-3001
E-Mail: npmsing@npm.org
Home Page: www.npm.org

J Michael Mc Mahon, President
Kathleen Haley, Director Membership Services
Lowell Hickman, Office Manager/Executive Assistant
Joseph Lively, Comptroller

Fosters the art of musical liturgy. The members of NPM serve the Catholic Church in the United States as musicians, clergy, liturgists, and other leaders of prayer.
9000 Members
Founded in 1976

9125
National Association of Professional Band Instrument Repair Technicians
2026 Eagle Road
PO Box 51
Normal, IL 61761

309-452-4257
FAX 309-452-4825
E-Mail: napbirt@napbirt.org
Home Page: www.napbirt.org

Bill Mathews, President

A nonprofit international educational association dedicated to the advancement of the craft of band instrument repair. Their mission is to promote the highest possible standards of band instrument repair, restoration and maintenance by providing members with multi-level professional development by offering technical training, continuing education and the publication of their bi-monthky trade journal.
Cost: $95.00
1300 Members
Founded in 1976

9126
National Association of Recording Merchandisers

9 Eves Drive
Suite 120
Marlton, NJ 08053-3130
856-596-2221
FAX 859-596-3268
E-Mail: donio@narm.com
Home Page: www.narm.com

Sue Peterson, Chair
Scott Wilson, Vice Chairman
Bob Schneider, Treasurer
Rachelle Friedman, Secretary
Jim Donio, President

A not-for-profit trade association that serves the music retailing community in the areas of networking, advocacy, information, education and promotion. Membership includes music and other entertainment retailers, wholesalers, distributorsm record labels, multimedia suppliers, and suppliers of related products and services, as well as individual professionals and educators in the music business field.
Founded in 1958

9127
National Association of Schools of Music

11250 Roger Bacon Drive
Suite 21
Reston, VA 20190-5248
703-437-0700
FAX 703-437-6312
E-Mail: info@arts-accredit.org
Home Page: www.arts-accredit.org

Don Gibson, President
Mark Wait, VP
Mellasenah Y Morris, Treasurer

An organization of schools, conservatories, colleges and universities. NASM provides information to potential students and parents, consultations, stastistical information, professional development and policy analysis. It is the national accrediting agency for music and music-related disciplines.
635 Members
Founded in 1924

9128
National Association of Teachers of Singing

9957 Moorings Drive
Suite 401
Jacksonville, FL 32257-2416
904-262-2065
888-262-2065
FAX 904-262-2587
Home Page: www.nats.org

Allen Henderson, Executive Director
Deborah Guess, Director of Operations

To encourage the highest standards of the vocal art and of ethical principles in the teaching of singing; and to promote vocal education and research at all levels, both for the enrichment of the general public and for the professional advancement of the talented.
6500 Members
Founded in 1944

9129
National Association of Theatre Owners

750 1st St NE
Suite 1130
Washington, DC 20002-4241
202-962-0054
FAX 202-962-0370
E-Mail: nato@natodc.com
Home Page: www.natoonline.org

John Fithian, President
G Kendrick Macdowell, VP
Kathy Conroy, Executive Director

Professional trade association serving the business interests of theatre owners domestically and around the world. Assists theatre owners, works with picture distribution and issues such as new technologies, legislation, marketing and First Ammendment issues.
600 Members
Founded in 1948

9130
National Ballroom and Entertainment Association

2799 Locust Road
Decorah, IA 52101-7600
563-382-3871
E-Mail: nbea@oneota.net
Home Page: www.nbea.com

John Matter, Executive Director

National nonprofit association which advocates that social dancing is a life-long activity that contributes to the physical, mantal, and social well-being of an individual. They believe that social dancing should be preserved for current and future generations and introduced to today's youth as an alternate form of social interaction.
450 Members
Founded in 1947

9131
National Band Association

Membership Office
PO Box 25136
Baton Rouge, LA 70894
601-297-8168
FAX 601-266-6185
E-Mail: info@nationalbandassociation.org
Home Page: www.nationalbandassociation.org

Bobby Adams, President
Finley Hamilton, First VP
Mark Heidel, Second VP
Linda Moorehouse, Secretary/Treasurer
David Gregory, Advisor to the President

The purpose of the NBA to promote the musical and educational significance of bands and is dedicated to the attainment of a high level of excellence for bands and band music. It is open to anyone and everyone interested in bands, regardless of the length if his/her experience, type of position held, or the specific area at which he/she works. The membership roster includes men and women from every facet of the band world.
3M Members
Founded in 1960

9132
National Costumers Association

121 N Bosart Avenue
Indianapolis, IN 46201-3729
317-351-1940
800-622-1321
FAX 317-351-1941
E-Mail: office@costumers.org
Home Page: www.costumers.org

Debbie Lyn Owens, President
Nancy Cox, First Vive President
Adrienne Anderson, Second VP
Jennifer Skarstedt, Secretary/Treasurer

The objectives on the NCA are to establish and maintain professional and ethical standards of business in the costume industry. They encourage and promote a greater and more diversified use of costumes in all fields of human activity. They provide trade information, cooperation and friendship among its members together with a sound public relations policy.
400 Members
Founded in 1923

9133
National Dance Association

1900 Association Dr
Reston, VA 20191-1502
703-476-3436
800-213-7193
FAX 703-476-9527
E-Mail: nda@aahperd.org
Home Page: www.aahperd.org/nda

Colleen Dean, Manager
Marcey E Siegel, VP Dance Education
Mary Ann Laverty, VP Dance Performance

A nonprofit service organization dedicated to increasing knowledge, improving skills and encouraging sound professional practices in dance education while promoting and supporting creative and healthy lifestyles through high quality dance programs.
2000 Members
Founded in 1932

9134
National Dance Education Organization

8609 2nd Avenue
Suite 203 B
Silver Spring, MD 20910
301-585-2880
FAX 301-585-2888
E-Mail: info@ndeo.org
Home Page: www.ndeo.org

Susan McGreevy-Nichols, Executive Director
Patricia Cohen, Treasurer

A nonprofit organization dedicated to promoting standards of excellence in dance education.
2000 Members
Founded in 1998

9135
National Endowment for the Arts

1100 Pennsylvania Ave NW
Washington, DC 20004-2501
202-682-5400
FAX 202-682-5611
E-Mail: webmgr@arts.endow.gov
Home Page: www.arts.endow.gov

Dana Gioia, CEO
Guilomar Barbi, Scheduler
Sarah Cook, Executive Assistant
Jon P Peede, Counselor to the Chairman
Sydney Smith, Administrative Specialist

The National Endowment for the Arts, an investment in America's living heritage, serves the public good by nurturing the expression of human creativity, supporting the cultivation of community spirit, and fostering the recognition and appreciation of the excellence and diversity of our nation's artistic accomplishments.

9136
National Federation of Music Clubs
1646 W Smith Valley Rd
Greenwood, IN 46142-1550
317-638-4402
FAX 317-638-0503
E-Mail: info@nfmc-music.org
Home Page: www.nfmc-music.org

Elizabeth Paris, President
Lana Bailey, First VP
Kay Hawthorne, Secretary
Barbara Hildebrand, Treasurer
Jennifer Keller, Administrative Manager

NFMC provides opportunities for musical study, performance and appreciation to more than 200,000 senior, student and junior members in 6,500 music-related clubs and organizations nationwide. Members are professional and amateur musicians, vocalists, composers, dancers, performing artists, arts and music educators, music students, generous music patrons and benefactors, and music lovers of all ages.
170M Members
Founded in 1898

9137
National Music Publishers Association
101 Constitution Avenue NW
Suite 705 East
Washington, DC 20001
202-742-4375
FAX 202-742-4377
E-Mail: pr@nmpa.org
Home Page: www.nmpa.org

David M Israelite, President/CEO
John Eastman, Director

The NMPA is committed to promoting and advancing the interests of music publishers and their songwriting partners. Their goal is to foster a business climate that allows its members to thrive creatively and financially.
800 Members
Founded in 1917

9138
National Opera Association
PO Box 60869
Canyon, TX 79016-0869
806-651-2857
FAX 806-651-2958
Home Page: www.noa.org

Robert Hansen, Executive Director
JoElyn Wakefield-Wright, President
Carole Notestine, Secretary
Robert Thieme, Editor Opera Journal
Philip Hagemann, Treasurer

The NOA seeks to promote a greater appreciation of opera and music theatre, to enhance pedagogy and performing activities, and to increase performance opportunities by supporting projects that improve the scope and quality of opera. Members in the United States, Canada, Europe, Asia and Australia participate in a wide array of activities in support of this mission.
775 Members
Founded in 1955

9139
National Piano Travelers Association
401 Sawkill Road
PO Box 2264
Kingston, NY 12401-2264
845-338-1464
FAX 845-338-5751

Bob Smith, President

Buys and sells pianos.
110 Members

9140
New England Theatre Conference
215 Knob Hill Drive
Hamden, CT 6518
617-851-8535
FAX 203-288-5938
E-Mail: mail@netconline.org
Home Page: www.netconline.org

James Quinn, President
Jeffrey Watts, Executive VP
Charles Emmons, VP Administration/Finance

Non-profit corporation, composed of individuals and organizations in the six-State region of New England, who are active and interested in the performing arts. The NETC promotes excellence in theatre for their region, and supports quality theatre and performance in all of its diversity.
500 Members
Founded in 1952

9141
North American Performing Arts Managers and Agents
459 Columbus Ave
Suite 114
New York, NY 10024-5129
212-362-8304
E-Mail: info@napama.org
Home Page: www.napama.org

Richard Barth, Owner
Laura Colby, VP
Eleanor Oldham, VP
Barrie Steinberg, Secretary
Jennifer Morris, Treasurer

National nonprofit trade association dedicated to promoting the professionalism of its members and the vitality of the performing arts. NAPAMA promotes the mutual advancement and the best interests of performing arts managers and agents; promotes open discourse among members and within the larger field; gives active consideration and expression of opinion on questions affecting the industry and develops and encourages ethical and sound business practices.
Cost: $150.00
Founded in 1979

9142
Opera America
330 7th Ave
16th Floor
New York, NY 10001-5248
212-796-8620
FAX 212-796-8631
E-Mail: frontdesk@operaamerica.org
Home Page: www.operaamerica.org

Marc Scorca, President
Charles MacKay, Chairman
David McIntosh, Treasurer
Susan Danis, Secretary
Rebecca Ackerman, Membership Manager

Opera America serves and strengthens the field of opera by providing a variety of informational, technical, and administrative resources to the greater opera community. Its fundamental mission is to promote opera as exciting and accessible to individuals from all walks of life.

9143
Oratorio Society of New York
1440 Broadway
23rd Floor
New York, NY 10018-9759
212-400-7255
E-Mail: webmaster@oratoriosocietyofny.org
Home Page: www.oratoriosocietyofny.org

Richard Pace, President
Marie Gangemi, Treasurer
Jay Jacobson, Secretary
Kent Tritle, Music Director

New York City's second oldest cultural organization. On December 25, 1874 the society began what has become an unbroken tradition of annual performances of Handel's Messiah"" (at Carnegie Hall since its opening in 1891).""
Founded in 1873

9144
Organization of American Kodaly Educators
through the improvment of music education in scho
1612 29th Ave S
, Mo MN
565-0 5-42
218-227-6253
FAX 218-227-6254
E-Mail: www.oake.org

Social Media: o,

, Dahlin
Manager Penny, Whalen
VP Paul, Baumann
Secretary Greg, Williams
Treasurer Joan, Dahlin

The purpose of this organization is to promote Zoltan Kodaly's concept of Music for Everyone
1973 Members
Founded in 0

9145
Pedal Steel Guitar Association
PO Box 20248
Floral Park, NY 11002-0248
516-616-9214
FAX 516-616-9214
E-Mail: bobpsga@optonline.net
Home Page: www.psga.org

Bob Maickel, President
John DeMaille, VP
Jeff De Maio, Treasurer
Darlene DeMaille, Secretary
Doug Mack, Newsletter Editor

A nonprofit organization whose primary purpose is to share information on playing the steel guitar and in particular the pedal steel guitar. Publishes the Pedal Steel Newsletter ten times per year
1540 Members
Founded in 1973

9146
Percussive Arts Society
701 NW Ferris Avenue
Lawton, OK 73507-5442

580-353-1455
FAX 580-353-1456
E-Mail: percarts@pas.org
Home Page: www.pas.org

Richard Holly, President
Steve Houghton, VP
Lisa Rogers, Secretary
Michael Balter, Treasurer
Michael Kenyon, Executive Director

A music service organization promoting percussion education, research, performance and appreciation throughout the world. Offers two print publications, the Percussive Arts Society International Headquarters/Museum and the annual Percussive Arts Society International Convention.
Cost: $85.00
7000 Members
Founded in 1961

9147
Performing Arts Association
719 Edmond St
St Joseph, MO 64501-2268
816-279-1225
E-Mail: info@paastjo.org
Home Page: www.paastjo.org

Mary Ingersoll, Manager
William Wright, VP

Mission is to provide a diverse selection of performing arts in the St. Joseph area by presenting programs that foster, increase and promote public knowledge and appreciation of music, theatre and dance and lectures on subjects of cultural interests.

9148
Performing Arts Medicine Association
Po Box 61228
Denver, CO 80206
303-632-9255
E-Mail: artsmed@comcast.net
Home Page: www.artsmed.org

Mary Fletcher, Executive Director

Organization for physicians and other professionsl persons who are involved in treatment and/or research in the field of Performing Arts Medicine.
Founded in 1989

9149
Piano Manufacturers Association
5960 W Parker Road
Suite 278 #233
Plano, TX 75093-7792
972-625-0110
FAX 972-625-0110
Home Page: www.pianonet.com

Donald W Dillon, Executive Director

Piano industry trade association.
Founded in 1991

9150
Piano Technicians Guild
4444 Forest Avenue
Kansas City, KS 66106
913-432-9975
FAX 913-432-9986
E-Mail: ptg@ptg.org
Home Page: www.ptg.org

Barbara Cassaday, Executive Director
Allan Gilbreath RPT, President
Jim Coleman Jr RPT, VP

A nonprofit organization serving piano tuners, technicians, and craftsman throughout the world, organized to promote the highest possible service and technical standards among piano tuners and technicians.
4100 Members
Founded in 1957

9151
Producers Guild of America
8530 Wilshire Blvd
Suite 450
Beverly Hills, CA 90211-3115
310-358-9020
FAX 310-358-9520
E-Mail: info@producersguild.org
Home Page: www.producersguild.com

Marshall Herskovitz, President
Vance Van Paten, Executive Director
Grant Stoner, Director Membership
Courtney Cowan, Treasurer
Gale Ann Hurd, Secretary

The PGA represents, protects and promotes the interests of all members of the producing team by providing employment opportunities and health and welfare benefits for all members of the producing team; combating deceptive or uneraned credits within the producing team; and representing the interests of the entire producing team. The producing team consists of all those whose interdependency and support of each other are necessary for the creation of motion pictures and television programs.
500 Members
Founded in 1950

9152
Production Music Library Association
8551 Research Way
Suite 180
Middleton, WI 53562
608-836-5825
FAX 608-831-8200
E-Mail: mla@areditions.com
Home Page: www.musiclibraryassoc.org

Philip Vandermeer, President

Provides a forum for issues surrounding music, music in libraries, and music librarianship. Members include music librarians, librarians who work with music as part of their responsibilities, composers and music scholars, and others interested in the program of the association.
20 Members
Founded in 1931

9153
Professional Women Singers Association
PO Box 884
New York, NY 10024
212-969-0590
FAX 928-395-2560
E-Mail: info@womensingers.org
Home Page: www.womensingers.org

Elissa Weiss, President
Allison Atteberry, First VP
Sarah Downs, Second VP
Ruth Ann Cunningham, Secretary
Mary Lou Zobel, Treasurer

Non-profit networking organization for professional women singers. The group sponsors concerts, master classes and seminars for both singers and the community at large.
40 Members
Founded in 1982

9154
Retail Print Music Dealers Association
14070 Proton Rd
Suite 100
Dallas, TX 75244-3601
972-233-9107
FAX 972-490-4219
E-Mail: office@printmusic.org
Home Page: www.printmusic.org

Madeleine Crouch, Owner
Lori Supinie, VP/Secretary
Gayle Beackock, VP/Treasurer

A professional trade organization founded to address the special needs and interests of the print music industry. RPMDA provides a common meeting ground for the congenial interchange of ideas among print music dealers; promotes ethical standards and policies in dealing with music publishers; promotes better dealer/publisher relations; serves the public and encourages music education; provides association-sponsored activities and publications that help its members prepare for future trends.
275 Members
Founded in 1976

9155
Rhythm and Blues Foundation
100 S Broad St
Suite 620
Philadelphia, PA 19110-1017
215-568-1080
FAX 215-561-1026
E-Mail: paden@rhythmblues.org
Home Page: www.rhythm-n-blues.org

Patricia Wilson Aden, Executive Director
Jim Fifield, Vice Chairman
Shawn Gee, Treasurer
David Nathan, Secretary

Nonprofit service organization dedicated to the historical and cultural preservation of Rhythm and Blues music. The Foundation provides financial support, medical assistance and educational outreach through various grants and programs to support R&B amd Motown artists of the 40s, 50s, 60s and 70s.
Founded in 1988

9156
Screen Actors Guild
5757 Wilshire Blvd
Suite 7
Los Angeles, CA 90036-3681
323-954-1600
FAX 323-549-6656
Home Page: www.sag.org

Allen Rosenburg, President
Kent McCord, First VP
Paul Christie, Second VP
Steve Fried, Third Vice President
Connie Stevens, Secretary/Treasurer

Labor union affiliated with AFL-CIO which represents actors in film, television and commercials. The Guild exists to enhance actors' working conditions, compensation and benefits and to be a powerful, unifed voice on behalf of artists' rights.
120M Members
Founded in 1933

9157
Society for Cinema Studies
640 Parrington Oval
Old Science Hall Room 302
Norman, OK 73019

405-325-8075
FAX 405-325-7135
Home Page: www.cmstudies.org

Stephen Prince, President
Eric Schaefer, Secretary
Amy Villarejo, Treasurer
Jane Dye, Administrative Coordinator

A professional organization of college and university educators, filmmakers, historians, critics, scholars, and others devoted to the study of the moving image. The gaols of SCMS are to promote all areas of media studies within universities and two- and four-year colleges; to encourage and reward excellence in scholarship and writing; to facilitate and improve the teaching of media studies as disciplines and to advance multi-cultural awareness and interaction.
1M Members
Founded in 1959

9158
Society of American Magicians
PO Box 510260
Saint Louis, MO 63151-0260
314-846-5659
FAX 314-846-5659
E-Mail: rmblowers@aol.com
Home Page: www.magicsam.com

Andy Dallas, President
Bruce Kalver, First VP
Mike Miller, Second VP
Chuck Lehr, Secretary
Mary Ann Blowers, Treasurer

Founded to promote and maintain harmonious fellowship among those interested in magic as an art, to improve ethics of the magical profession, and to foster, promote and improve the advancement of magical arts in the field of amusement and entertainment. Membership includes professional and amateur magicians, manufacturers of magical apparatus and collectors.
5.5M Members
Founded in 1902

9159
Society of Camera Operators
PO Box 2006
Toluca Lake, CA 91610
818-382-7070
FAX 323-856-9155
E-Mail: info@soc.org
Home Page: www.soc.org

Dan Dodd, Director

Non-profit organization which advances the art and creative contribution of the operating cameraman in the Motion Picture and Television Industries.
Founded in 1978

9160
Society of Motion Picture & Television Eng ineers
3 Barker Ave
White Plains, NY 10601-1509
914-761-1100
FAX 914-761-3115
E-Mail: smpte@smpte.org
Home Page: www.smpte.org

The SMPTE is the leading technical society for the motion imaging industry. It was founded to advance theory and development in the motion imaging field. Today, it publishes ANSI-approved Standards, Recommended Practices, and Engineering Guidelines. SMPTE holds conferences and local Section meetings to bring people and ides together, allowing for useful interaction and information exchange.

100 Members
Founded in 1916

9161
Society of Professional Audio Recording Services
9 Music Square S
Suite 222
Nashville, TN 37203
800-771-7727
FAX 615-296-0386
E-Mail: spars@spars.com
Home Page: www.spars.com

Karen Brinton, President
Eric W Johnson, Secretary
Andrew Kautz, Treasurer

SPARS is dedicated to excellence through innovation, education and communication.
200 Members
Founded in 1979

9162
Society of Stage Directors and Choreographers
1501 Broadway
Suite 1701
New York, NY 10036-5653
212-391-1070
800-541-5204
FAX 212-302-6195
E-Mail: info@ssdc.org
Home Page: www.ssdc.org

Laura Penn, Executive Director
Sue Lawless, Secretary
Doug Hughes, Treasurer
Barbara Hauptman, Executive Director
Gretchen M Michelfeld, Membership Coordinator

An independent labor union representing directors and choreographers in American theatre.
1700 Members
Founded in 1959

9163
Songwriters Guild of America
promote and benefit the profession."""
209 10th Ave S
Suite 534, Na TN
372-3 0-43
615-329-1782
FAX 615-742-9945
E-Mail: www.songwritersguild.com

Social Media: *n,*

, Whitt

Provides agreements between songwriters, composers and publishers. The SGA will take such lawful actions as will advance
1931 Members
4000 Attendees
Founded in 0

9164
Southern Arts Federation
1800 Peachtree St NW
Suite 808
Atlanta, GA 30309-2512
404-874-7244
FAX 404-873-2148
Home Page: www.southarts.org

Gerri Combs, Executive Director
Scott Shanklin-Peterson, Secretary

Richard Ranta, Treasurer
David Batley, Marketing/Communications Director

In partnership with nine state arts agencies: promotes and supports arts regionally, nationally and internationally; enhances the artistic excellence and professionalism of Southern Arts Organizations and artists; serves the diverse population of the south.
Founded in 1975

9165
Stuntmen's Association of Motion Pictures
10660 Riverside Dr
2nd Floor, Suite E
North Hollywood, CA 91602-2352
818-766-4334
FAX 818-766-5943
E-Mail: info@stuntmen.com
Home Page: www.stuntmen.com

Chris Doyle, Manager
Kurt Lott, First VP
Alex Daniels, Second VP
Toby Holguin, Secretary
Harry Wowchuk, Treasurer

Seeks to improve working conditions for stuntmen. Encourages members to uphold high professional standards.
135 Members
Founded in 1961

9166
Stuntwomen's Association of Motion Pictures
12457 Ventura Boulevard
Suite 208
Studio City, CA 91604-2411
818-762-0907
888-817-9267
FAX 818-762-9534
E-Mail: stuntwomen@stuntwomen.com
Home Page: www.stuntwomen.com

Jane Austin, President

A professional association for stuntwomen and stunt coordinators which seeks to uphold professional standards and improve working conditions.
Founded in 1967

9167
Sundance Institute
1835 Three Kings Drive
PO Box 684429
Park City, UT 84068
435-658-3456
FAX 435-658-3457
E-Mail: Institute@sundance.org
Home Page: www.sundance.org

Robert Redford, President
Kenneth Brecher, Executive Director
Geoffrey Gilmore, Director Sundance Film Festival
Brooke McAffee, Director Finance
Ellen Oh, Associate Director Marketing

Non-profit organization dedicated to the discovery and development of independent artists and audiences. The Institute seeks to discover, support, and inspire independent film and theatre artists from the United States and around the world, and to introduce audiences to their new work. The Institutes programs include the annual Sundance Film Festival, held in Park City, Utah each January.
Founded in 1981

9168
Sweet Adelines International
PO Box 470168
Tulsa, OK 74147-0168
918-622-1444
800-992-7464
FAX 918-665-0894
E-Mail: admin@sweetadelineintl.org
Home Page: www.sweetadelineintl.org

Donna Kerley, Dicector Finance/Administration
Kelly Kirchoff, Director Communications
Jane Hanson, Marketing/Membership Coordinator

A worldwide organization of women singers committed to advancing the musical art form of barbershop harmony through education and performances. Their motto is to 'Harmonize the World.'
27000 Members
Founded in 1945

9169
Theatre Authority
6464 W Sunset Blvd
Suite 590
Los Angeles, CA 90028-8001
323-462-5761

Presides over theatrical agencies and performing arts organizations.

9170
Theatre Bay Area
1663 Mission Street
Suite 525
San Francisco, CA 94103
415-430-1140
FAX 415-430-1145
E-Mail: tba@theatrebayarea.org
Home Page: www.theatrebayarea.org

Karen Mc Kevitt, Executive Director
Dale Albright, Director, Member Services
Clayton Lord, Director, Audience Development

Theatre Bay Area's mission is to unite, strengthen and promote the theatre community in the San Francisco Bay Area, working on behalf of their conviction that the performing arts are an essential public good, critical to a healthy and truly democratic society, and invaluable as a source of personal enrichment and growth.
3,000 Members
Founded in 1976

9171
Theatre Communications Group
520 8th Ave
24th Floor
New York, NY 10018-8666
212-609-5900
FAX 212-609-5901
E-Mail: tcg@tcg.org
Home Page: www.tcg.org

Theresa Eyring, Executive Director
Elizbeth Morrow Selfridge, Director Finance/Administration
Jennifer Cleary, Director of Membership

The mission of the TCG is to strengthen, nurture and promote the professional not-for-profit American theatre. TCG believes that their diversity as a field is their greatest strength. They celebrate differences in aesthetic, culture, organizational structure, and geography. They believe that every theatre makes a contribution to the greater field as a whole, that every performance expands the artistic vocabulary for us all, and that we all benefit from one another's presence.
Cost: $39.95

17000 Members
Frequency: Monthly
Founded in 1961

9172
Theatre Development Fund
1501 Broadway
21st Floor
New York, NY 10036-5652
212-210-0013
E-Mail: info@tdf.org
Home Page: www.tdf.org

Not-for-profit service organization for the performing arts. TDF administers a wide range of audience development and financial assistance programs that encourage production of new plays and musicals and enable more New Yorkers and visitors to enjoy the riches and variety of the city's theatre, dance and music.
Cost: $25.00
Founded in 1968

9173
Theatre Library Association
Shubert Archive 149 West 45th Street
New York, NY 10036
Home Page: tla.library.unt.edu

Martha S LoManaco, President
Kenneth Schlesinger, VP
Nancy E Friedland, Secretary
Paul Newman, Treasurer

The Association supports librarians and archivists affiliated with theatre, dance, performance studies, popular entertainment, motion picture and broadcasting collections. TLA promotes professional best practices in acquistionm, organization, access and preservation of performing arts resources in libraries, archives, museums, private collections, and the digital environment.
500 Members
Founded in 1937

9174
US Institute for Theatre Technology
315 S Crouse Ave
Suite 200
Syracuse, NY 13210-1835
315-463-6463
800-938-7488
FAX 315-463-6525
E-Mail: info@office.usitt.org
Home Page: www.usitt.org

Carol Carrigan, Manager
Patricia Dennis, Secretary
Travis DeCastro, Treasurer

Association of design, production and technology professionals in the performing arts and entertainment industry whose mission is to promote the knowledge and skills of its members. International in scope, USITT draws its board of directors from across the US and Canada. Sponsors projects, programs, research, symposia, exhibits and annual conference. Disseminates information on aesthetic and technical developments.
3700 Members
Founded in 1960

9175
USA Dance
PO Box 152988
Cape Coral, FL 33915-2988
800-447-9047
FAX 239-573-0946
Home Page: usadance.org

Lydia Scardina, National President
Stan Andrews, National Secretary

Nonprofit organization working to promote ballroom dancing, both as a recreational activity and as a competitive sport, and to educate the public about the mental, physical and social benefits of dance.
23000 Members
Founded in 1965

9176
University Film and Video Association
UFVA Membership Office C/O Cheryl Jestis
University of Illinois Press
1325 South Oak Street
Champaign, IL 61820-6903
217-244-0626
866-244-0626
FAX 217-244-9910
Home Page: www.ufva.org

Karla Berry, President
Thomas Tomasulo, Executive VP
Beverly Seckinger, Secretary
Peter Bukalski, Treasurer
Cheryl Jestis, Membership Coordinator

Supports those interested in the fields of film and video production, history, criticism, and aesthetics. Provides training, education, and a quarterly magazine.
Cost: $75.00

9177
Women in Film
6100 Wilshire Blvd
Suite 201
Los Angeles, CA 90048-5107
323-935-2211
FAX 310-657-5154
E-Mail: info@wif.org
Home Page: www.wif.org

Tichi Wilkerson-Kassel, Founder
CiCi Holloway, President
Glen Alpert, VP Membership
Nicole Katz, CFO
Gayle Nachlis, Executive Director

WIFs purpose is to empower, promote, nurture, and mentor women in the industry through a network of valuable contacts, events, and programs.
10000 Members
Founded in 1974

9178
Women in the Arts Foundation
C/O E Butler
32-35 30th Street
D24
Long Island City, NY 11106
212-941-0130
E-Mail: reginas@anny.org
Home Page: www.anny.org/2/orgs/womeninarts/

Regina Stewart, Executive Director
Eric Butler, Executive Coordinator
Linda Butti, Executive Coordinator
Sari Menna, Financial Coordinator

WIA works to overcome discrimination against women artists. They provide information to help women function effectively as professional artists. WIA is open to all women interested in the arts.
150 Members
Founded in 1971

9179
World Piano Competition/AMSA
441 Vine St
Suite 1030
Cincinnati, OH 45202-2832

513-421-5342
FAX 513-421-2672
E-Mail: info@amsa-wpc.orgm
Home Page: www.amsa-wpc.org

Gloria Ackerman, Founder, CEO
William Selnick, Treasurer
Stanley Aronoff, Event Chair
Leon Fleisher, President

Provides an continuum of services and role models to assist youth in need. Their task is to provide a venue of excitement and compassion to teach them to do their best to prepare for the enormous challenges they will face as they approach adulthood.
2.5M Members
Founded in 1956

Newsletters

9180
American Dance
P.O.Box 357
New York, NY 10024-0357
212-932-2789
E-Mail: info@americandanceguild.org
Home Page: www.americandanceguild.org

Deborah Mauldin, President

Contains articles on member news, dance, and education.
Frequency: 4 per year
Founded in 1956

9181
American Guild Associate News Newsletter
American Guild of Music
PO Box 599
Warren, MI 48090-4905
248-686-1975
FAX 630-968-0197
E-Mail: agm@americanguild.org
Home Page: www.americanguild.org

Richard Chizmadia, Editor-in-Chief

Offers information and news for professionals in the music profession.
Cost: $25.00
Frequency: Quarterly
Founded in 1901

9182
American Music Center Opportunity Update
American Music Center
322 8th Ave
Suite 1001
New York, NY 10001-6774
212-366-5263
FAX 212-366-5265
E-Mail: center@amc.net
Home Page: www.amc.net

Joanne Cossa, Executive Director

A listing of composition competitions, calls for scores, workshops, and other opportunities delivered every month via e-mail to members of the American Music Center.
Frequency: Monthly
Founded in 1939

9183
American Musical Instrument Society Newsletter
389 Main Street
Suite 202
Malden, MA 2148
781-397-8870
FAX 781-397-8887
E-Mail: amis@guildassoc.com
Home Page: www.amis.org

Stewart Carter, Presdient
Joanne Kopp, Treasurer

Official notices and news of the Society's activites; short articles and communications; recent acquisition lists from member institutions; news of members; and classified ads.
Frequency: 2x/Year

9184
American Musicological Society Newsletter
University of Iowa
Arts Center Relations
300 Plaza Center One
Iowa City, IA 52242
FAX 319-384-0024
E-Mail: peter-alexander@uiowa.edu
Home Page: www.ams-net.org

Peter Alexander, Editor

The AMS Newsletter is published simiannually in February and August. The February Newsletter is mailed with the new Directory and Ballot each year. The August Newsletter is mailed with the Annual Meeting information and registration form each year.
Frequency: Semi-Annually
Founded in 1934

9185
American School Band Directors Association Newsletter
American School Band Directors Association
227 N 1st Street
PO Box 696
Guttenberg, IA 52052-0696
563-252-2500
FAX 563-252-2500
E-Mail: asbda@alpinecom.net
Home Page: www.asbda.com

Jeffrey T Phillips, President
Kevin Beaken, Secretary
Blair Callaway, Treasurer

Reports and information for members of the ASBDA
Frequency: Quarterly
Founded in 1953
Printed in 2 colors on matte stock

9186
American Viola Society Newsletter
American Viola Society
14070 Proton Rd
Suite 100
Dallas, TX 75244-3601
972-233-9107
FAX 972-490-4219
E-Mail: stemple@comcast.net
Home Page: www.madcrouch.com

Madeleine Crouch, President

A monthly e-newsletter. It contains announcements from the AVS, upcoming local chapter events, and other important items.
Frequency: Monthly

9187
Artsearch
Theatre Communications Group
520 8th Ave
Suite 305
New York, NY 10018-8666
212-609-5900
FAX 212-609-5901
E-Mail: tcg@tcg.org
Home Page: www.tcg.org

Theresa Eyring, Executive Director

Artsearch is divided into five main categories: Administration, Artistic, Production/Design, Career Development, and Education.
Cost: $75.00
Frequency: Bi-Monthly
ISSN: 0730-9023
Founded in 1961
Printed in on newsprint stock

9188
Banjo Newsletter
PO Box 3418
Annapolis, MD 21403-0418
800-759-7425
E-Mail: Bnl@annap,infi.net
Home Page: www.banjonews.com

Newletter focusing on Bluegrass banjo music.

9189
Bluegrass Music Profiles
Bluegrass Publications
PO Box 850
Nicholasville, KY 40340-0850
859-333-6456
E-Mail: info@bluegrassmusicprofiles.com
Home Page: www.bluegrassmusicprofiles.com

Information on Bluegrass music.

9190
Bluegrass Now
PO Box 2020
Rolla, MO 65402
573-341-7335
E-Mail: Bgn@fidnet.com
Home Page: www.bluegrassnow.com

Information on Bluegrass music.

9191
Bluegrass Unlimited
PO Box 771
Warrenton, VA 20188-0771
540-349-8181
800-256-7427
E-Mail: info@bluegrassmusic.com
Home Page: www.bluegrassmusic.com

Information on Bluegrass music.

9192
Broadside
Theatre Library Association
C/O New York Public Library for Performing Arts
40 Lincoln Center Plaza
New York, NY 10023
Home Page: tla.library.unt.edu

Nancy Friedland, Executive Secretary

Available only to members of the Theatre Library Association. Fosters creative and ethical use of performing arts materials to enhance research, live performance, and scholarly communication.
Frequency: Monthly
Founded in 1937

9193
Brooklyn Institute for Studies in American Music
Brooklyn College
2900 Bedford Ave
Brooklyn, NY 11210-2889
718-951-5000
Home Page:
www.brooklyn.cuny.edu/bb/fac/american.htm

Karen L Gould, President

Music news and Academy activities.
Frequency: Semi-Annual
Founded in 1861

9194
Country Dance and Song Society News
Country Dance and Song Society
132 Main Street
PO Box 338
Haydenville, MA 01039-0338
413-268-7426
FAX 413-268-7471
E-Mail: news@cdss.org
Home Page: www.cdss.org

Caroline Batson, Editor
Bradley Foster, Executive Director

A selection of articles, letters and poems. CDSS News is available as a benefit of membership in the Country Dance and Song Society.
ISSN: 1070-8251
Founded in 1915

9195
DNBulletin
151 W 30th Street
Suite 202
New York, NY 10001
212-564-0985
FAX 212-216-9027
E-Mail: dnbinfo@dancenotation.org
Home Page: www.dancenotation.org

Senta Driver, Editor

Dance news for consumers and professionals.
Founded in 1940
Printed in 2 colors on matte stock

9196
Dancedrill
3101 Poplarwood Court
Suite 310
Raleigh, NC 27604-1010
919-872-7888
FAX 919-872-6888

Susan Wershing, Publisher
Kay Crawford, Editor

Publication informs members of dance drill teams and their directors.
Frequency: 4 per year

9197
Dirty Linen
PO Box 6660
Baltimore, MD 21239-6600
410-583-7973
E-Mail: office@dirtylinen.com
Home Page: www.dirtylinen.com

Information on Bluegrass music.

9198
Dramatists Guild Newsletter
Dramatists Guild of America

1501 Broadway
Suite 701
New York, NY 10036-5505
212-398-9366
FAX 212-944-0420
Home Page: www.dramaguild.com

Ralph Sevush, Executive Director

Supplement to 'The Dramatist,' available only to Guild members, includes bi-monthly reports from New York and Los Angeles, advice from the Business Affairs Department, the latest information on submission and career development opportunities, and reminders of approaching deadlines.

9199
Early Keyboard Studies Newsletter
Westfield Center for Early Keyboard Studies
Westminster College
Box 154
New Wilmington, PA 16172
E-Mail: harrisea@westminster.edu
Home Page: www.westfield.org

Elizabeth Harrison, Editor

E-newsletter providing information to professional keyboard musicians.
12 Pages
Frequency: Monthly
Founded in 1979

9200
Early Music Newsletter
New York Recorder Guild
145 W 93 Street
New York, NY 10025-7559
212-662-2946
E-Mail: mzumoff@nyc.rr.com
Home Page: www.priceclan.com/nyrecorderguild/

Michael Zumoff, Executive Director

A publication of the New York Recorder Guild
10 Pages
Frequency: Monthly

9201
Film Advisory Board Monthly
Film Advisory Board
263 W Olive Avenue
#377
Burbank, CA 91502
323-461-6541
FAX 323-469-8541
Home Page: www.filmadvisoryboard.org

Janet Stokes, President

Information and news on the entertainment industry.
Frequency: Monthly
Founded in 1975
Printed in one color on glossy stock

9202
Flatpicking Guitar
High View Publications
PO Box 51960
Pulaski, VA 24301
540-980-0338
E-Mail: Highview@flatpick.com
Home Page: www.flatpick.com

Information on Bluegrass music and the Flatpick guitar.

9203
GMA Update
Gospel Music Association
1205 Division St
Nashville, TN 37203-4011

615-242-0303
FAX 615-254-9755
Home Page: www.gospelmusic.org

John Styll, President

GMA's industry e-newsletter available to any non-GMA member who wishes to receive it. Sent out once a month, GMA Update contains the latest news about the Christian music industry and valuable information about the GMA.
Frequency: Monthly

9204
GMAil
Gospel Music Association
1205 Division St
Nashville, TN 37203-4011
615-242-0303
FAX 615-254-9755
Home Page: www.gospelmusic.org

John Styll, President

E-newsletter sent weekly to GMA members. Includes weekly music sales, charts, news, links to valuable resources, and information about upcoming GMA and industry events.
Frequency: Weekly
Founded in 1964

9205
Girl Groups Gazette
PO Box 69A04
Department HSND
West Hollywood, CA 90069-0066

Louis Wendruck, Editor/Publisher

For fans of girl groups and female singers of the 1960's and 70's including photos, discographies, records, t-shirts, postcards, and videos.
Cost: $20.00
Frequency: Quarterly
Founded in 1988

9206
Hollywood Arts Council
PO Box 931056
Hollywood, CA 90093
323-462-2355
FAX 323-465-9240
E-Mail: bianca@hollywoodartcouncil.org
Home Page: www.hollywoodartscouncil.org

Promotes, nurtures and supports the arts field in Hollywood. Newsletter is included with membership.
Founded in 1978
Printed in 4 colors on glossy stock

9207
INTIX Bulletin
International Ticketing Association
330 W 38th St
Suite 605
New York, NY 10018-8592
212-629-4036
FAX 212-628-8532
E-Mail: info@intix.org
Home Page: www.intix.org

Maureen Andersen, President
Kathleen O'Donnell, Director

E-bulletin provides news from the International Ticketing Association including information about upcoming events, conferences and exhibitions, industry news.
1200 Members
Frequency: Monthly
ISSN: 1071-6254

Founded in 1979
Printed in 4 colors on glossy stock

9208

In Focus
National Association of Theatre Owners

9209

In Theater
Parker Publishing & Communications
214 Sullivan St
Suite 2C
New York, NY 10012-1354
212-228-1225
FAX 212-719-4477
E-Mail: intheater@aol.com
Home Page: www.parkerhodges.com

Emily Parker, President

Offers the reader a behind-the-scenes perspective of how a show is technically conceived, rehearsed and staged. Regular departments center on drama and musical reviews, listings of shows in major cities and columnist options.
Cost: $78.00
Frequency: Weekly
Circulation: 71,068

9210

In the Groove
Michigan Antique Phonograph Society
60 Central St
Battle Creek, MI 49017-3704
269-968-1299
E-Mail: ITG@michiganantiquephonographsociety.org
Home Page:
www.michiganantiquephonographsociety.org

Phil Stewart, Editor
Eileen Stewart, Editor

The Newsletter of the Michigan Antique Phonograph Society. Includes show, sales and auction announcements, MAPS chapter news, President's message, monthly feature articles, letters to the editor, and swap shop.
Cost: $25.00
24 Pages
Frequency: Monthly
Founded in 1976

9211

InLEAGUE
League of Historic American Theatres
334 N Charles St
Suite 2
Baltimore, MD 21201-4372
410-659-9533
877-627-0833
FAX 410-837-9664
E-Mail: info@lhat.org
Home Page: www.lhat.org

Frances Holden, Executive Director
Thomas Johnson, VP, Treasurer

Quarterly newsletter which reports news from historic theatre progects around the country and features articles on all facets of historic theatre restoration and operation. The newsletter solicits articles and information from the membership.
Frequency: Quarterly
Founded in 1976

9212

International Bluegrass
IBMA

2 Music Cir S
Suite 100
Nashville, TN 37203-4381
615-256-3222
888-438-4262
E-Mail: nancyc@ibma.org
Home Page: www.ibma.org

Dan Hays, Executive Director

Information on Bluegrass music from the IBMA

9213

Job Contact Bulletin
Southeastern Theatre Conference
1217 W Bessemer Avenue
PO Box 9868
Greensboro, NC 27429-0868
336-272-3645
FAX 336-272-8810
E-Mail: arpil@setc.org
Home Page: www.setc.org

April J'C Marshall, Contact
April Marshall, Editor

On-line employment listing of Classified Ads for theatrical positions, auditions, and more.
Founded in 1949

9214

Marketing Through Music
Rolling Stone Magazine
1290 Ave of the Americas
2nd Floor
New York, NY 10104-0295
212-484-1616
800-283-1549
FAX 212-484-1771
E-Mail: rollingstone@real.com
Home Page: www.rssoundingboard.com

Jann Wenner, President

A monthly newsletter geared for marketing, advertising and music exexecutives. It includes information on such matters as rock tours and musician endorsements, ad campaigns and rock contests.
Cost: $50.00
Frequency: Monthly
Founded in 1967

9215

Music for the Love of It
67 Parkside Drive
Berkeley, CA 94705-2409
510-654-9134
FAX 510-654-4656
E-Mail: tedrust@musicfortheloveofit.com
Home Page: www.musicfortheloveofit.com

Edgar Rust, Publisher/Editor
Janet Telford, Co-Editor

A newsletter for people everywhere who love making music. Every issues brings new enthusiasm, new ideas and new opportunities for making music.
Frequency: Bi-Monthly
ISSN: 0898-8757
Founded in 1988
Printed in on matte stock

9216

National Music Museum Newsletter
National Music Museum
414 E Clark St
Vermillion, SD 57069-2307
605-677-5306
FAX 605-677-6995

E-Mail: smm@usd.edu
Home Page: www.usd.edu/smm/

Andre Larson, Director

Quarterly Newletter which includes feature articles written by the curatorial staff and lists recent acquisitions. Published in February, May, August and November. It is available with basic museum membership.
Cost: $35.00
Printed in 4 colors

9217

No Depression
908 Halcyon Avenue
Nashville, TN 37204
615-292-7084
Home Page: www.nodepression.net

Information on Bluegrass music

9218

Notes a Tempo
West Virginia University
Division of Music
PO Box 6111
Morgantown, WV 26506-6111
304-293-4841

David Bess, Co-Editor
Becky Terry, Co-Editor

The official publication of the West Virginia Music Educators. Published Fall, Winter and Spring
20-32 Pages
Frequency: 3 per year
Circulation: 1115

9219

Old Time Herald
P.O.Box 61679
Durham, NC 27715-1679
919-402-8495
E-Mail: agerrard@mindspring.com
Home Page: www.oldtimeherald.org

Information on Bluegrass music

9220

Pedal Steel Newsletter
Pedal Steel Guitar Association
PO Box 20248
Floral Park, NY 11002-0248
516-616-9214
FAX 516-616-9214
E-Mail: bobpsga@optonline.net
Home Page: www.psga.org

Doug Mack, Editor
Bob Maickel, President

Dedicated to the art of playing pedal steel guitar. Every issue contains tablature arrangements of songs for the steel guitar as well as coming events, record reviews, product reports and news concerning the instrument.
Frequency: 10 x Per Year
ISSN: 1088-7954
Founded in 1973

9221

Percussion News
Percussive Arts Society
701 NW Ferris Avenue
Lawton, OK 73507-5442
580-353-1455
FAX 580-353-1456
E-Mail: percarts@pas.org
Home Page: www.pas.org

Rick Mattingly, Editor
Hillary Henry, Art Director
Rich Holly, President

Newsletter devoted to membership activities. This colorful newsletter also features a Classified Advertising section. Percussion News is published in January, March, May, July, September and November.
Frequency: 6 Editions Per Year
Founded in 1961
Mailing list available for rent

9222
Performing Arts Insider
PAI C/O Total Theater
PO Box 62
Hewlett, NY 11557-0062
516-295-1511
800-536-0099
E-Mail: totalpost@totaltheater.com
Home Page: www.totaltheater.com

A leading source of information about the performing arts in New York City and around the country. Each issue includes day-by-day calendar listings of shows on broadway, off and off-off broadway, plus dance, opera, cabaret and special events. Also includes comprehensive theatre guides, listing the author, director, cast, designers, synopsis, theater and box office details, as well as contact information for producers, press agents, general managers and casting directors.
Cost: $275.00
Frequency: Monthly+9 Mid-Month Updat
Founded in 1944
Printed in on matte stock

9223
Preview Family Movie & TV Review
Movie Morality Ministries
PO Box 407
Pomona, KS 66076-2561
785-255-4314
800-807-8071
FAX 785-255-4316
E-Mail: preview@fni.com
Home Page: www.reviewonline.org

Dave Haverty, President
Greg Shull, Editor
Susan Haverty, Desktop Publisher/Office Manager

Reviews current films and TV series from a Christian and family values perspective.
Cost: $34.00
Frequency: Monthly
ISSN: 0892-6468
Printed in 2 colors on matte stock

9224
Roots and Rhythm Newsletter
Roots and Rhythm
PO Box 837
El Cerrito, CA 94530
510-526-8373
888-766-8766
FAX 510-526-9001
E-Mail: roots@toast.net
Home Page: www.rootsandrhythm.com

Frank Scott, Owner
Nancy Scott-Noennig, Co-Owner

Lists, reviews and makes available for sale, recordings of blues, rhythm and blues, rockabilly, country, folk, ethnic, nostalgia and jazz music. Each newsletter reviews about 400 items and lists another 500 without reviews.
Frequency: Bi-Monthly
Circulation: 10000

Founded in 1974
Printed in 2 colors on newsprint stock

9225
SETC News
Southeastern Theatre Conference
1217 W Bessemer Avenue
PO Box 9868
Greensboro, NC 27429
336-272-3645
FAX 336-272-8810
E-Mail: deanna@setc.org.net
Home Page: www.setc.org

Deanna Thompson, Editor

Provides news and important information to members of the Southeaster Theatre Conference on upcoming SETC events, advocacy efforts, awards and competitions as well as items of special interest to the various divisions and interest areas. In addition, SETC News publishes news about people and organizations based in the Southeast.
Circulation: 4000
Founded in 1949

9226
Sing Out!
PO Box 5253
Bethlehem, PA 18015-5253
610-865-5366
E-Mail: info@singout.org
Home Page: www.singout.org

Information on Bluegrass music

9227
Spotlight
American Association of Community Theatre
8402 Briar Wood Circle
Lago Vista, TX 78645-4118
512-267-0711
866-687-2228
FAX 512-267-0712
E-Mail: info@aact.org
Home Page: www.aact.org

Julie Angelo, Executive Director
John Sullivan, President

News and updates on issues pertinent to community theatre.
Cost: $2.00
24 Pages
Circulation: 2000
Founded in 1958
Mailing list available for rent: 9,500 names at $180 per M
Printed in on matte stock

9228
Technical Brief
Yale School of Drama
222 York Street
PO Box 208244
New Haven, CT 6520
203-432-9664
FAX 203-432-8332
E-Mail: bronislaw.sammler@yale.edu
Home Page: www.technicalbrief.org

Ben Sammler, Editor
Dan Harvey, Editor

Produced for technical managers in theater. Written by professionals for professionals, its purpose is simple: communication. Technical Brief provides a dailogue between technical practitioners from the several performing arts who all share similar problems.
Cost: $15.00

Frequency: 3 X Year
Founded in 1924

9229
Tempo
Academy of Country Music
5500 Balboa Blvd
Suite 200
Encino, CA 91316-1505
818-788-8000
FAX 818-788-0999
E-Mail: info@acmcountry.com
Home Page: www.acmcountry.com

Devoted exclusively to the country music industry.
12 Pages
Frequency: Quarterly
Circulation: 4500
Founded in 1964

9230
Women in Bluegrass Newsletter
PO Box 2498
Winchester, VA 22604
E-Mail: Nmhentry@visuallink.com
Home Page:
www.murphymethod/com/womeninbluegrass.cfm

Information on women in bluegass music

9231
Women in the Arts Bulletin
Women in the Arts Foundation
32-35 30th Street
D24
Long Island City, NY 11106
212-941-0130
E-Mail: reginas@anny.org
Home Page: www.anny.org

Erin Butler, Editor
Regina Stewart, Executir Director
Sandra Cockerham, President

Gallery information and reviews. Women in the Arts Foundation works to overcome discrimination against women artists.
Frequency: Monthly
Founded in 1971

Magazines & Journals

9232
AfterTouch: New Music Discoveries
Music Discovery Network
PO Box 6205
Peoria, IL 61601-6205
309-685-4843
800-882-4262
FAX 309-685-4878
E-Mail: aimcmc@aol.com
Home Page: www.musicdiscoveries.com

Ronald Wallace, Editor

A magazine for music lovers who would like to experience new sights and sounds and would like to keep their fingers on the pulse of the music industry.
Frequency: Annual
Circulation: 10,000
Founded in 1984
Printed in on glossy stock

9233
American Cinematographer
American Society of Cinematographers

1782 North Orange Drive
PO Box 2230
Hollywood, CA 90078-2230
323-969-4333
800-448-0145
FAX 323-876-4973
E-Mail: office@theasc.com
Home Page: www.theasc.com

Covers feature films, television, commercials, music videos, digital video, new equipment, DVD and book releases and much more. An exploration and a reflection of today's cinematography. A publication of the American Society of Cinematographers.
Cost: $29.95
Frequency: Monthly
Circulation: 42000
Founded in 1919

9234

American Dancer
PO Box 152988
Cape Coral, FL 33915-2988
800-447-9047
FAX 239-573-0946
Home Page: usadance.org

Lydia Scardina, National President
Stan Andrews, National Secretary
23000 Members
Frequency: Bi-Monthly
Circulation: 23000
Founded in 1965

9235

American Music
University of Illinois Press
Chicago Distribution Center
11030 South Langley Avenue
Chicago, IL 60628
800-621-2736
FAX 800-621-8476
E-Mail: journals@uillinois.edu
Home Page: www.press.uillinois.edu

Michael Hicks, Editor
Daniel Felsenfeld, Book Review Editor
Caroline Benser, Recording Review Editor
Jennifer DeLapp Brikett, Multimedia Review Editor
Jeff McArdle, Journals Marketing/Advertising Mgr

Publishes articles on American composers, performers, publishers, institutions, events, and the music industry as well as book and recording reviews, bibliographies, and discographies.
Cost: $45.00
Frequency: Quarterly
Circulation: 1650
ISSN: 0734-4392
Founded in 1981
Mailing list available for rent: 1,650 names at $100 per M
Printed in 2 colors on glossy stock

9236

American Music Teacher
Music Teachers National Association
441 Vine St
Suite 505
Cincinnati, OH 45202-2813
513-421-1420
888-512-5278
FAX 513-421-2503
E-Mail: mtnanet@mtna.org
Home Page: www.mtna.org

Gary L Ingle, Executive Director
Gail Berenson, President
Janice Wenger, VP

Provides articles, reviews and regular columns that inform, educate and challenge music teachers and foster excellence in the music teaching profession.
Cost: $30.00
Circulation: 35000
Founded in 1876
Mailing list available for rent: 24000 names at $85 per M
Printed in 4 colors on glossy stock

9237

American Organist
American Guild of Organists
475 Riverside Dr
Suite 1260
New York, NY 10115-0055
212-870-2310
800-246-5115
FAX 212-870-2163
E-Mail: info@agohq.org
Home Page: www.agohq.org

James Thomashower, Executive Director

Most widely read journal devoted to organ and choral music in the world. Official journal of the American Guild of Organists, the Royal Canadian College of Organists, and the Associated Pipe Organ Builders of America.
Cost: $ 52.00
Frequency: Monthly
Circulation: 24000
ISSN: 0164-3150
Founded in 1967

9238

American String Teachers Journal
American String Teachers Association
4153 Chain Bridge Rd
Fairfax, VA 22030-4102
703-279-2113
FAX 703-279-2114
E-Mail: asta@astaweb.com
Home Page: www.astaweb.com

Donna Hale, Executive Director
Beth Danner-Knight, Deputy Director

Available to members. Provides an overview of current articles featured in the journal. Also answers questions about content, advertising, and contact information.
Cost: $90.00
Frequency: Quarterly
Circulation: 11,300
Mailing list available for rent: 10M+ names

9239

American Theatre Magazine
Theatre Communications Group
520 8th Ave
Suite 305
New York, NY 10018-8666
212-609-5900
FAX 212-609-5901
E-Mail: custserve@tcg.org
Home Page: www.tcg.org

Theresa Eyring, Executive Director
Sarah Hart, Managing Editor
Randy Gener, Senior Editor
Nicole Estvanik, Associate Editor
Cassandra Johnson, Play Editor

A vital repository of information for anyone and everyone concerned with contemporary theatre. Speaks to actors and directors, producers and artistic directors, teachers and students, designers and technicians, writers and dramaturges, theatre administrators, theatre lovers and more. Provides sophisticated insight and in-depth reporting that informs and inspires. A forum

where artists talk about their work and reflect on the creative process itself and what it means to be an artist.
Cost: $39.95
64 Pages
Circulation: 17,000
Printed in 4 colors

9240

American Viola Society Journal
American Viola Society
14070 Proton Rd
Suite 100LB
Dallas, TX 75244-3601
972-233-9107
FAX 972-490-4219
E-Mail: info@avsnationaloffice.org
Home Page: www.madcrouch.com

Madeleine Crouch, President
Kathryn Steely, Webmaster

Peer reviewed journal which promotes interest in the viola.
Cost: $42.00
Frequency: Annually
Circulation: 1500
Founded in 1984

9241

Animation Magazine
Animation Magazine
30941 Agoura Rd
Suite 102
Westlake Villag, CA 91361-4637
818-991-2884
FAX 818-991-3773
E-Mail: info@animationmagazine.net
Home Page: www.animationmagazine.net

Jean Thoren, President

Promotes the art and business of animation and gives recognition to those animators and technicians who make the world of animation what it is today.
Cost: $50.00
Frequency: Monthly
Circulation: 30000
ISSN: 1041-617X
Founded in 1986
Printed in 4 colors on glossy stock

9242

Applause Magazine
Denver Center for Performing Arts
1101 13th St
Denver, CO 80204-5319
303-893-3272
800-641-1222
FAX 303-893-3206
Home Page: www.denvercenter.org

Randy Weeks, President

A publication of the Denver Center Theatre Company and Dever Center Attractions
Frequency: 8-10 per year
Founded in 1988
Printed in 4 colors on glossy stock

9243

Asian Pacific American Journal
Asian American Writers Workshop
16 W 32nd St
Suite 10A
New York, NY 10001-1093
212-494-0061
FAX 212-494-0062
E-Mail: desk@aaww.org
Home Page: www.aaww.org

Ken Chen, Executive Director
Jeannie L Wong, Adminstrative Director
Anjali Goyal, Programs Assistant
Jeffrey Lin, Designer
Hanya Yanagihara, Journal Editor

Features include short fiction, poems, essays, stage scripts, translations and artwork.
Frequency: Semi-Annual
ISSN: 1067-778X
Founded in 1992

9244
BMI Musicworld
Broadcast Music
320 W 57th St
Suite 3
New York, NY 10019-3705
212-586-2000
FAX 212-246-2163
Home Page: www.bmi.com

Del Bryant, CEO
John E Cody, COO/EVP

Performing rights organization. Articles of interest to the songwriting community.
Founded in 1985

9245
Back Stage
Neilsen Business Media
770 Broadway
Suite 200
New York, NY 10003-9557
646-654-5700
FAX 646-654-5744
E-Mail: advertising@backstage.com
Home Page: www.backstage.com

Charles Weiss, Manager
Jamie Painter Young, Editor-in-Chief
Jenelle Riley, Film/TV Editor
Leonard Jacobs, Theatre Editor
Sherry Eaker, Editor-at-Large

Four print, four interactive and two face-to-face publications. Provides casting, news, articles and other resources for working actors, cingers, dancers and behind-the-scenes staff and crew.
Cost: $84.00
Circulation: 30,000
Founded in 1960

9246
Billboard Magazine
Billboard Subscription
PO Box 15158
North Hollywood, CA 91615-5158
818-487-4582
800-562-2706
E-Mail: info@billboard.com
Home Page: www.billboard.com

Scott McKenzie, Group Editorial Director
Tamara Conniff, Exec Editor & Associate Publisher

Packed with in-depth music and entertainment features including the latest in new media and digital music, global coverage, music and money, touring, new artists, radio news and retail reports.
Cost: $299.00
Frequency: Weekly

9247
Bomb Magazine
New Art Publications
80 Hanson Pl
Suite 703
Brooklyn, NY 11217-1506

718-636-9100
866-354-0334
FAX 718-636-9200
E-Mail: info@bombsite.com
Home Page: www.bombsite.com

Betsy Sussler, Publisher/Editor
Mary-Ann Monforton, Associate Publisher
Nell McClister, Senior Editor
Lucy Raven, Managing Editor
Paul W Morris, Director Marketing/Special Projects

Focuses on contemporary art, literature, theater, film, music.
Cost: $495.00
Frequency: Quarterly
Circulation: 60,000
Founded in 1981
Printed in 4 colors on matte stock

9248
Box Office
National Association of Theatre Owners
750 1st St Ne
Suite 1130
Washington, DC 20002-4241
202-962-0054
FAX 202-962-0370
E-Mail: nato@natodc.com
Home Page: www.natoonline.org

John Fithian, President
G Kendrick Macdowell, VP
Kathy Conroy, Executive Director

Keeps readers apprised of current events within the cinema industry, with a range of departments and recurring features designed to interest those who make exhibition their business.
Cost: $59.00
29000 Members
Frequency: Monthly
Printed in on glossy stock

9249
Boxoffice
PO Box 1634
Des Plaines, IL 60019
212-627-7000
FAX 626-396-0248
E-Mail: editorial@boxoffice.com
Home Page: www.boxoffice.com

Peter Cane, Publisher
Anlee Ellingson, Editor
Francesca Dinglasan, Senior Editor
Bob Vale, VP Advertising/Sales

Authoritative voice on The Business of Movies since before talkies.
Cost: $59.95
Frequency: Monthly
ISSN: 0006-8527
Founded in 1920
Printed in on glossy stock

9250
CCM Magazine
Salem Publishing
750 Old Hickory Blvd
Suite 150-1
Brentwood, TN 37027-4514
615-386-3011
FAX 615-386-3380
E-Mail: info@ccmcom.com
Home Page: www.ccmmagazine.com

Jim Cumbee, President

The voice of Contemporary Christian Music. Each monthly issue features music news, exclusive inter-

views, and an in-depth look at the spiritual lives of today's leading Christian music artists.
Cost: $19.95
Frequency: Monthly
Founded in 1978
Printed in 4 colors on glossy stock

9251
Callaloo
Johns Hopkins University Press
2715 N Charles St
Baltimore, MD 21218-4319
410-516-6900
800-537-5487
FAX 410-516-6998
Home Page: www.press.jhu.edu/journals/callaloo

William Brody, President
Kyle G Dargan, Managing Editor

Journal of African and African-American issues. Content includes original works by, and critical studies of, black writers worldwide. Offers a rich mixture of fiction, poetry, plays, critical essays, cultural studies, interviews, and visual art, as well as special thematic issues.
Frequency: Quarterly
Circulation: 2,500
ISSN: 0161-2492
Founded in 1976

9252
Callboard
Theatre Bay Area
1663 Mission St
Suite 525
San Francisco, CA 94103-2487
415-430-1140
FAX 415-430-1145
E-Mail: tba@theatrebayarea.org
Home Page: www.theatrebayarea.org

Karen Mc Kevitt, Manager

Provides trade information for professionals in the Bay Area. The magazine contains the following departments: Letterbox, Inside the Industry, Community News, How Did They Do That, Keep An Eye On, Editors' Picks and Encore.
Cost: $65.00
Frequency: Monthly
ISSN: 1064-0703
Founded in 1976
Printed in 2 colors on matte stock

9253
Canadian Theatre Review
University of Toronto Press
5201 Dufferin Street
Toronto, ON M3H-5T8
416-667-7777
FAX 416-667-7881
E-Mail: journals@utpress.utoronto.ca
Home Page: www.utpjournals.com

Anne Marie Corrigan, VP
Audrey Greenwood, Advertising/Marketing Coordinator

Provides critical analysis and innovative coverage of current developments in Canadian theatre. Advocates new issues and artists. Publishes at least one significant new playscript per issue. Each issue includes at least one complete playscript related to the issue theme, insightful articles, and informative reviews.
Cost: $40.00
Frequency: Quarterly
ISSN: 0315-0836
Founded in 1974
Mailing list available for rentat $250 per M

9254

Celebrity Service

8833 W Sunset Boulevard
Suite 401
Los Angeles, CA 90069-2171
213-883-3671
FAX 310-652-9244

Robert Dean, Manager/Director

A listing of celebrities names and addresses. Publisher of the Celebrity Bulletin informing the entertainment and news industry of which celebrities are traveling to Hollywood and New York
Frequency: Bi-Monthly

9255

Chamber Music Magazine

Chamber Music America
305 7th Avenue
5th Floor
New York, NY 10001
212-242-2022
FAX 212-242-7955
Home Page: www.chamber-music.org

Susan Dadian, Program Director
Margaret M Lioi, CEO
Louise Smith, Chair
Cost: $5.95
Frequency: Bi-Monthly
Circulation: 6000
Founded in 1977

9256

Choral Journal

American Choral Directors Association
PO Box 2720
Oklahoma City, OK 73101-2720
405-232-8161
FAX 405-232-8162
E-Mail: chojo@acdaonline.org
Home Page: www.acdaonline.org

Gene Brooks, Executive Director
Nina Gilbert, Associate Editor
Ron Granger, Managing Editor

The official publication of the American Choral Directors Association. Articles that embrace both scholarly and practical approaches to understanding issues affecting choral directors and their craft. Prints reviews of octavos, compact discs, and books related to choral music. Members of the association teach choral music in public and private schools as well as in colleges and universities.
Circulation: 21,000
ISSN: 0009-5028
Founded in 1959
Mailing list available for rent: 18500 names
Printed in 4 colors on glossy stock

9257

Cineaste

Cineaste Magazine
246 5th Ave
Suite 706
New York, NY 10001-7603
212-366-5720
FAX 212-366-5724
E-Mail: cineaste@cineaste.com
Home Page: www.cineaste.com

Gary Crowdus, Editor-in-Chief
Cynthia Lucia, Editor
Richard Porton, Editor
Dan Georgakas, Consulting Editor
Vicki Robinson, Production Assistant

An internationally recognized independent film magazine. Features contributions from many of America's most articulate and outspoken writers, critics and scholars. Focussing on both the art and politics of the cinema.
Cost: $ 20.00
Frequency: Quarterly
Circulation: 11000
ISSN: 0009-7004
Founded in 1967

9258

Cinefantastique

CFQ Media
PO Box 34425
Los Angeles, CA 90034-0425
310-204-0825
FAX 310-204-5882
E-Mail: info@cfq.com
Home Page: www.cfq.com

Frederick Clarke, Editor

Provides coverage of genre entertainment. Each issue features in-depth coverage of sci-fi, fantasy and horror films, TV, DVDs, games, toys, books, comics and more.
Cost: $34.95
Frequency: Monthly
Circulation: 40,000

9259

Cinefex

79 Daily Drive
#309
Camarillo, CA 93010
805-383-0800
FAX 805-383-0803
E-Mail: advertising@cinefex.com
Home Page: www.cinefex.com

A quarterly magazine devoted to motion picture special effects.
Cost: $32.00
180 Pages
Frequency: Quarterly
Circulation: 30000
ISSN: 0198-1056
Founded in 1980
Printed in 4 colors

9260

Cinema Journal

University of Texas Press
2100 Comal
PO Box 7819
Austin, TX 78713-7819
512-471-7233
800-252-3206
FAX 512-232-7178
E-Mail: utpress@uts.cc.utexas.edu
Home Page: www.utexas.edu/utpress

Sponsored by the Society for Cinema and Media Studies. The journal presents recent scholarship by SCMS members. It publishes essays on a wide variety of subjects from diverse methodological perspectives. A 'Professional Notes' section informs Society of Cinema and Media Studies readers about upcoming events, research opportunities, and the latest published research. Cinema Journal is a member of the CELJ, the Conference of Editors of Learned Journals.
Cost: $42.00
144 Pages
Frequency: Quarterly
Circulation: 2800
ISSN: 0009-7101
Founded in 1950
Printed in on matte stock

9261

Cinematograph

San Francisco Cinematheque
PO Box 880338
San Francisco, CA 94188-0338
415-552-1990
FAX 415-552-2067
E-Mail: sfc@sfcinematheque.org
Home Page: www.sfcinematheque.org

Stephen Anker, Executive Director

Supports risk-taking art, cutting edge artists and the boundless potential of creative expression.
Cost: $15.00
Frequency: Monthly
Founded in 1961

9262

Clarinet Journal

International Clarinet Society
PO Box 5039
Wheaton, IL 60189-5039
630-665-3602
FAX 630-665-3848
E-Mail: info@clarinet.org
Home Page: www.clarinet.org

James Gillespie, Editor
So Rhee, Executive Director

Contains articles in wide variety of areas written by performers and scholars.
Cost: $25.00
Frequency: Quarterly
Circulation: 3000

9263

Clavier

Instrumentalist Publishing Company
200 Northfield Road
Northfield, IL 60093-3390
847-446-5000
888-446-6888
FAX 847-446-6263
Home Page: www.instrumentalistmagazine.com

James Rohner, Publisher
Judy Nelson, Editor

Provides new ideas and advice for piano teachers from leading educators. The focus of each issue is to offer practical advice for teachers. Articles include interviews with prominent performers, teachers and composers, the latest teaching methods, tributes to great artists of the past, and reviews of newly publshed music, educational software and videos.
Cost: $17.00
Frequency: 10X Per Year
Circulation: 16000
Founded in 1965

9264

Close Up Magazine

Country Music Association
One Music Circle S
Nashville, TN 37203
615-244-2840
FAX 615-726-0314
E-Mail: international@cmaworld.com
Home Page: www.cmaworld.com

Profiles of country music artists, various songwriters and industry news. Members of the Association receive the magazine as a benefit of their membership.
Circulation: 8000
Founded in 1958

9265

Confrontation

CW Post Campus English Department
720 Northern Blvd
Greenvale, NY 11548-1300
516-626-0099
FAX 516-299-3566
E-Mail: confrontation@liu.edu
Home Page: www.liunet.bkstore.com

Jayne Mo, Manager

Brings new talent to light in the shadows cast by well-known authors. Each issue contains orignal work by famous and by lesser known writers.
Cost: $10.00
Frequency: Twice Yearly
Founded in 1968

9266

Contact Quarterly Journal of Dance and Improvisation

Contact Collaborations
PO Box 603
Northampton, MA 1061
413-586-1181
FAX 413-586-9055
E-Mail: info@contactquarterly.com
Home Page: www.contactquarterly.com

Lisa Nelson, Co-Editor
Nancy Stark Smith, Co-Editor
Melinda Buckwalter, Associate Editor
Kristin Horrigan, Operations Manager/Advertising
Bill McCully, Development/Marketing

A journal of dance, improvisation, performance and contemporary movement arts. Presents materials that spring from the experience of doing. Encourages articulation and dialogue and stimulates activity and exploration within the field of movement and its performance.
Cost: $22.00
Frequency: BiAnnual
Founded in 1975

9267

Country Weekly Magazine

American Media Inc
1000 American Media Way
T-Rex Technology Center
Boca Raton, FL 33464-1000
561-997-7733
FAX 561-989-1298
Home Page: www.nationalenquirer.com

David J Pecker, CEO

Devoted to country music and entertainment. Packed with feature articles and photos of country music personalities, music and video reviews, tour dates and late breaking news from the world of country music.
Cost: $34.95
Frequency: Bi-Weekly

9268

Cue Magazine

PO Box 2027
Burlingame, CA 94011-2027
415-348-8004
FAX 650-348-7781

Devoted to the Northern California, Seattle and Portland commercial film, video and multimedia industries and locations that support production.
Frequency: Monthly

9269

DJ Times

Testa Communications

25 Willowdale Avenue
Port Washington, NY 11050-3779
516-767-2500
800-937-7678
FAX 516-767-9335
E-Mail: testa@testa.com
Home Page: www.djtimes.com

Colorful tabloid magazine dedicated to professional mobile and club DJs. Specialized music sections, new product departments for sound and lighting, record reviews, business columns, informative entertainer profiles and more.
Cost: $19.40
Frequency: Monthly
Circulation: 30000
Founded in 1988

9270

Daily Variety - Gotham Edition

Reed Business Information
5700 Wilshire Boulevard
Suite 120
Los Angeles, CA 90036-3659
323-857-6600
FAX 323-857-0494
E-Mail: vtccustserv@cdsfulfillment.com
Home Page: www.variety.com

Peter Bart, Editor-in-Chief
Timothy M Gray, Editor
Ted Johnson, Managing Editor
Kathy Lyford, Managing Editor
Phil Gallo, Associate Editor

Focus is on Broadway theater, network television headquarters, regional music business, and local film production. Explores the role of New York City in relation to the national and global entertainment industries.
Cost: $259.00
Frequency: Daily
Founded in 1905

9271

Dance Chronicle

Taylor & Francis Group
270 Madison Ave
Floor 4
New York, NY 10016-0601
212-679-3853
FAX 212-564-7854
Home Page: www.summitcom.com

George Dorris, Co-Editor
Jack Anderson, Co-Editor
Edwin Bayrn, Associate Editor

Covers a wide variety of topics, including dance and music, theater, film, literature, painting and aesthetics.
Cost: $465.00
Frequency: TriAnnual
ISSN: 0147-2526

9272

Dance Magazine

Macfadden Performing Arts Media
110 William St
Suite 23
New York, NY 10038-3900
646-459-4800
FAX 646-459-4900
E-Mail: dancemag@dancemagazine.com
Home Page: www.dancemagazine.com

Karla Johnson, President
Wendy Perron, Editor-in-Chief
DeDe Pochos, Associate Publisher/Sales
Jessie Petrov, Publishing Manager

Provides entertaining, beautiful, up-to-date, in-the-know information for serious and aspiring dancers, dance teachers and professionals.
Cost: $34.95
Frequency: Monthly
Circulation: 300,000
ISSN: 0011-6009
Founded in 1927
Printed in 4 colors on glossy stock

9273

Dance Research Journal

University of North Carolina at Greensboro
Deparment of Dance
323 HHP Building, PO Box 26170
Greensboro, NC 24702-6170
336-334-3266
E-Mail: drj@uncg.edu
Home Page: www.cordance.org

Ann Dils, Co-Editor
Jill Green, Co-Editor

Published twice a year by the Congress on Research in Dance, this journal carries scholarly articles, book reviews, lists of books and journals received, and reports of scholarly conferences, archives and other projects of interest to the field.
Cost: $65.00
Frequency: Bi-annually
ISSN: 0149-7677
Founded in 1965
Mailing list available for rent: 750+ names at $75 per M

9274

Dance Spirit

McFadden Performing Arts Media
110 William St
23rd Floor
New York, NY 10038-3900
646-459-4800
FAX 646-459-4900
Home Page: www.dancespirit.com

Karla Johnson, President
Mary Evelyn Holder, Associate Publisher

Provides training tips, advice from experts, exercises designed for dancers, combinations and competition news and results.
Cost: $16.95
Frequency: 10 Per Year
Founded in 1980

9275

Dance Teacher Magazine

Macfadden Performing Arts Media
110 William St
23rd Floor
New York, NY 10038-3900
646-459-4800
FAX 646-459-4900
Home Page: www.dance-teacher.com

Karla Johnson, President
Jessie Petrov, Publishing Manager
Dede Pochos, Associate Publisher/Sales

A magazine for professional dance educators, senior students, and other professionals on practical information for the teacher and/or business owner, economic and historical issues related to the profession. Profiles of schools, methods and people who are leaving their marks on dance.
Cost: $24.95
Frequency: Monthly
Circulation: 60000
Founded in 1979
Printed in 4 colors

9276
Dance on Camera Journal
Dance Films Association
48 W 21st St
Suite 907
New York, NY 10010-6989
212-727-0764
FAX 212-727-0764
E-Mail: info@dancefilms.org
Home Page: www.dancefilms.org

Deidra Towers, Executive Director

Subjects range from reviews and essays, news items regarding dance films, festivals, opportunites, and issues facing artists
Frequency: Bi-Monthly
Founded in 1956

9277
Dance/USA Journal
Dance/USA
1111 16th St Nw
Suite 300
Washington, DC 20036-4830
202-833-1717
FAX 202-833-2686
E-Mail: danceusa@danceusa.org
Home Page: www.danceusa.org

Andrea Snyder, Executive Director
Tom Thielen, Director Finance/Operations
Katherine Fabian, Membership Manager

The journal features articles on issues of importance to the dance community; news stories relating to arts and dance; essays from leaders in the dance field; notes on changes, transitions and opportunities in the field; calendar of up coming events; and highlights of Dance/USA sponsored events. Subscription is free to members of Dance/USA.
Cost: $40.00
28-36 Pages
Frequency: Quarterly
Founded in 1982
Printed in 2 colors on glossy stock

9278
Descant
50 Baldwin Street
PO Box 314 Station P
Toronto, ON M5S-2S8
416-593-2557
FAX 416-593-9362
E-Mail: info@descant.on.ca
Home Page: www.descant.on.ca

Karen Mulhallen, Editor-in-Chief
Mark Laliberte, Managing Editor
Mary Newberry, Project Manager
Stacey May Fowles, Circulation Manager
Pasha Malla, Director of Outreach

A quarterly journal publishing new and established contemporary writers and visual artists from Canada and around the world. Devoted to the discovery and development of new writers, and places their work in the company of celebrated writers.
Cost: $28.00
Frequency: Quarterly
Circulation: 1200
ISSN: 0382-909X
Founded in 1970

9279
Diapason
Scranton Gillette Communications

3030 W Salt Creek Ln
Suite 201
Arlington Hts, IL 60005-5025
847-298-6622
FAX 847-390-0408
E-Mail: jbutera@sgcmail.comom
Home Page: www.thediapason.com

Edward Gillette, CEO
Joyce Robinson, Associate Editor
Vicki Pierce, Subscriptions

An international journal dealing with organ, harpsichord, carillon and church music.
Cost: $35.00
Frequency: Monthly
ISSN: 0012-2378
Founded in 1909

9280
Discoveries
700 East State Street
Ioal, WI 54990-0001
715-445-2214
800-258-0929
FAX 715-445-4087
E-Mail: wayne.youngblood@fwpubs.com
Home Page: www.discoveriesmag.com

Mark Willliams, Publisher
Wayne Youngblood, Editorial Director
Cathy Bernardy, Associate Editor
Todd Whitesel, Associate Editor
Trevor Lauber, Advertising Sales Manager

Keeps close watch on market trends for collectible records, CDs and memorabilia. The Market Watch pages serve to interpret the mass of information available online and break it down to the most useful data collectors need. Each monthly issue is full of personality and opinion, with many reviews to help you determine where to spend your money. Coverage includes rock 'n' roll, rhythm &Æblues, pop, doo-wop, classic jazz and country western recordings.
Cost: $28.00
Frequency: Monthly
Circulation: 10,859
Founded in 1988

9281
Downbeat
102 N Haven Road
PO Box 906
Elmhurst, IL 60126
630-941-2030
800-554-7470
FAX 630-941-3210
E-Mail: service@downbeat.com
Home Page: www.downbeat.com

Kevin Maher, CEO

Monthly magazine includes such features as Readers Poll results, festival reviews, CD reviews, feature articles and more.
Cost: $29.95
Frequency: Monthly

9282
Drama Review
MIT Press
238 Main St
Suite 500
Cambridge, MA 02142-1410
617-253-2864
800-207-8354
FAX 617-258-5028
E-Mail: journals-info@mit.edu
Home Page: www.mitpress.mit.edu

Rebbecca Mc Leod, Owner

TDR focuses on performances in their social, economic, and political conctexts. It emphasizes experimental, avant-garde, intercultural and interdisciplinary performance. TDR covers dance, theatre, performance art, visual art, popular entertainment, media, sports, rituals, and performance in politics and everyday life.
Frequency: Quarterly
Founded in 1955

9283
Dramatics
Educational Theatre Association
2343 Auburn Ave
Cincinnati, OH 45219-2819
513-421-3900
FAX 513-421-7077
Home Page: www.edta.org

Michael Peitz, Executive Director

The Educational Theatre Association's magazine for theatre students and teacher. Published monthly nine times a year (September through May), the magazine contains practical articles on acting, directing, design, and other facets of theatre; profiles of working professionals that offer insights into theatre careers; new plays; book reviews; news about new productions in New York and other major theatre centers; and a monthly calendar of EdTA events.
Cost: $24.00
Frequency: 9 Times per Year
Circulation: 36500
ISSN: 0012-5989
Founded in 1929
Printed in 4 colors

9284
Electronic Musician
PRIMEDIA
6400 Hollis Street
Suite 12
Emeryville, CA 94608-1086
510-653-3307
E-Mail: emeditorial@prismb2b.com
Home Page: www.emusician.com

Steve Oppenheimer, Editor-in-Chief
Joe Perry, Associate Publisher
Marie Briganti, List Manager

Magazine for musicians recording and producing music in a home or personal studio environment. They are a source of user-friendly technical information for musicans. Features include: Tech Page, ProFile, Working Musician, Sound Design Workshop, Making Tracks, Square One, Reviews, What's New, Master Class, Final Mix, and Editors Choice Awards.
Cost: $23.97
Frequency: Monthly
Circulation: 61102
Founded in 1986

9285
Encore Performance Publishing
PO Box 95567
South Jordan, UT 84095-0567
801-282-8159
E-Mail: encoreplay@aol.com
Home Page: www.encoreplay.com

Michael C Perry, President

Publishes a variety of publications for those professionals in the performing arts industry.

9286
Film & History
Historians Film Committee

Rural Route 3
Box 80
Cleveland, OK 74020-9515
918-243-7637
FAX 918-243-5995
E-Mail: rollinspc@aol.com
Home Page: www.h-net.org/~filmhis

Peter C Rollins, Director
Deborah Carmichael, Editor-in-Chief
Cynthia Miller, Associate Editor-in-Chief

An Interdisciplinary Journal of Film and Television Studies concerned with the impact of motion pictures on our society. Film and History focuses on how feature films and documentary films both represent and interpret history. Types of articles include: Analysis of individual films and/or television programs from a historical perspective, survey of documents related to the production of films, or analysis of history as explored through film.
Cost: $50.00
Frequency: Bi-annually
Circulation: 1000
ISSN: 0360-3695
Founded in 1970

9287_____
Film & Video Magazine
110 William Street
11th Floor
New York, NY 10038
212-621-4900
FAX 212-621-4635
Home Page: www.studiodaily.com/filmandvideo

Bryant Frazer, Editor-in-Chief
Pete Putman, Senior Editor
Alison Johns, Editor-in-Chief
Scott Gentry, Group Publisher
Jarrett Cory, Classified Sales

Covers new ideas in creating entertainment by focusing on technique in the production and finishing of features, TV programming, music videos and commercials. No longer publishes print copies, magazine is 100% digital
Frequency: Monthly
Founded in 1983
Printed in 4 colors

9288_____
Film Journal International
VNU Business Media
30 E 23rd St
Suite 5
New York, NY 10010-4442
212-673-1100
FAX 212-673-7074
E-Mail: filmjournal@espcomp.com
Home Page: www.filmjournal.com

Penny Vane, President
Sid Holt, Editorial Director
Robert Sunshine, Publisher/Editor
Robin Klamfoth, Advertising Director
Kevin Lally, Executive Editor

A trade publication covering the motion picture industry, including theatrical exhibition, production, distribution, and allied activities. Articles report on US and international news, with features on current production, industry trends, theatre design, equipment, concessions, sound, digital cinema, screen advertising, and other industry-related news. Each issue also includes the Buying and Booking Guide, with comprehensive feature film reviews.
Cost: $65.00
Frequency: Monthly

9289_____
Film Threat
Film Threat International Headquarters
5042 Wilshire Boulevard
PMB 1500
Los Angeles, CA 90036
FAX 310-274-7985
E-Mail: advertise@filmthreat.com
Home Page: www.filmthreat.com

Mark Bell, Editor-in-Chief
Eric Campos, Senior Contributing Editor
Chris Gore, Founder/Publishjer

The print edition of Film Threat retired in 1997, but the legend has lived on as an internet journalism mainstay. FilmThreat.com delivers film reviews, film festival coverage, exclusive filmmaker interviews and original video content.
Cost: $10.50
Frequency: Bi-Monthly
Circulation: 100,000
Founded in 1985

9290_____
Flute Talk
Instrumentalist Company
200 Northfield Road
Northfield, IL 60093-3390
847-446-5000
888-446-6888
FAX 847-446-6263
E-Mail: fteditor@instrumentalistmagazine.com
Home Page: www.instrumentalistmagazine.com

Flute Talk is written for professional flute players, teachers, and advanced students. Frequent topics include performance analyses of flute repertoire, current teaching techniques, piccolo articles, interviews with prominent performers and teachers, and reviews of new music, recordings, and books for flutists.
Cost: $13.00
Frequency: 10 x Per Year
Circulation: 12000
Founded in 1981

9291_____
Goldmine
a listing of upcoming record-and-CD-collector con
album reviews
hobby and music news
a collecting column, a and ""Col
700 E State Street
FAX lol- -
FAX WI
E-Mail: 715-445-2214
Home Page: 54990

Social Media: 8, 7,

The world's largest marketplace for collectible records, CDs, and music memorabilia covering Rock N' Roll, Blues, Country, Folk, and Jazz. Large volumes of For Sale"" and ""Wanted"" ads are placed by collectors and dealers. Includes articles on recording stars of the past and present with discographies listing all known releases
Frequency: goldmine@krause.com
Circulation: www.gold
ISSN: 1702-

9292_____
Gospel Today
Gospel Today
286 Highway 314
Suite C
Fayetteville, GA 30214-7831
770-716-2660
800-472-6731
FAX 770-716-2660
E-Mail: gospeltodaymag@aol.com
Home Page: www.gospeltoday.com

Teresa Hairston, Publisher

The Voice of the Urban Christian Community. The publication focuses on the holistic Christian lifestyle including health, fashion, fitness, spirituality, music, entertainment and more.
Cost: $24.00
Frequency: 8 Per Year
Circulation: 250000
Founded in 1989
Printed in 4 colors on glossy stock

9293_____
Guitar One
Cherry Lane Magazines
6 E 32nd St
Suite 11
New York, NY 10016-5422
212-561-3000
800-825-4942
FAX 212-447-6885
E-Mail: guitarshop@worldnet.att.net
Home Page: www.guitarmag.com

Peter W Primont, CEO
Jonathan Simpson-Bint, President
Holly Klingel, VP Circulation
Steve Aaron, Publishing Director
Greg Di Benedetto, Publisher

Information on everything from the guitar equipment evaluations to news on the latest trends and technological developments to special insider pieces covering the sound secrets of today's top players.
Cost: $24.95
Frequency: Monthly
Circulation: 105,000
Founded in 1985

9294_____
Guitar Review
Albert Augustine Limited
151 W 26th St
Suite 4
New York, NY 10001-6810
917-661-0220
FAX 917-661-0223
E-Mail: mail@guitarreview.com
Home Page: www.albertaugustine.com

Steven Griesgraber, President
Eliot Fisk, Associate Editor
David Starobin, Associate Editor
Ian Gallagher, Music Editor
Matthew Hough, Circulation

Scholarly articles related to the classical guitar.
Cost: $28.00
48 Pages
Frequency: Quarterly
Circulation: 4000
Founded in 1946

9295_____
Hispanic Arts News
Association of Hispanic Arts
P.O.Box 7
Bronx, NY 10464-0007
212-876-1242
888-876-1240
FAX 212-876-1285
E-Mail: informacion@latinoarts.org
Home Page: www.latinoarts.org

Features in depth articles on the local and national arts community, including artist profiles and a calendar of events.
Frequency: 9 Per Year
Mailing list available for rent: 5000 names at $80 per M

9296
Hollywood Life
Movieline Magazine
10537 Santa Monica Blvd
Suite 250
Los Angeles, CA 90025-4952
310-234-9501
FAX 310-234-0332
E-Mail: hollywoodlife@pcspublink.com
Home Page: www.hollywoodlive.net

Anne Volokh, President

Formerly called Movieline, an entertainment lifestyle featuring interviews with stars, directors and producers; as well as information on celebrity shopping, up and coming talent, soundtracks, electronics and fashion associated with hollywood style and trends.
Cost: $13.75
Frequency: Monthly
Founded in 1989
Printed in 4 colors on glossy stock

9297
Hollywood Reporter
5055 Wilshire Blvd
Suite 600
Los Angeles, CA 90036-4396
323-525-2000
888-900-3782
FAX 323-525-2377
E-Mail: mailbox@hollywoodreporter.com
Home Page: www.hollywoodreporter.com

Michael Laur, VP
Tommaso Campione, Executive Director
Vicki Robles, Marketing

Gives fresh ideas for film and TV. Covers the full spectrum of craft and commerce in the entertainment industry.
Cost: $299.00
Frequency: Daily
Circulation: 34770

9298
Instrumentalist
Instrumentalist Company
200 Northfield Road
Northfield, IL 60093-3390
847-446-5000
888-446-6888
FAX 847-446-6263
E-Mail: insteditor@instrumentalistmagazine.com
Home Page: www.instrumentalistmagazine.com

A magazine school band and orchestra directors can depend on for practical information to use for then ensembles. The articles written by veteran directors and performers cover a wide range of topics, including rehearsal techniques, conducting tips, programming ideas, instrument clinics, repertoire analyses, and much more. Monthly new music reviews guide directors to selecting the best music for their students.
Cost: $21.00
Frequency: Monthly
Circulation: 16,000
Founded in 1945
Printed in 4 colors

9299
International Cinematographers Guild Magazine
7755 W Sunset Blvd
Suite 300
Los Angeles, CA 90046-3911
323-876-0160
FAX 323-876-6383
E-Mail: info@icgmagazine.com
Home Page: www.cameraguild.com

Steven Poster, President
John McCarthy, Marketing

Serves as the journal of 'how to' for film and digital techniques. It incorporates a wide range of editorial for specific job categories in relation to cinematography for Film/Hi-Def/Digital production and defines the tools and technology necessary for advancement in this field. The magazine is written for members of the International Cinematographers Guild, including cinematographers, camera operators, camera assistants, still photographers, publicists, film loaders, and others in the field.
Cost: $48.00
Frequency: Monthly
Founded in 1929

9300
International Documentary Magazine
International Documentary Association
Ste M270
1201 W 5th St
Los Angeles, CA 90017-1476
213-534-3600
FAX 213-534-3610
E-Mail: tom@documentary.org
Home Page: www.documentary.org

Thomas White, Editor
Tamara Krinsky, Associate Editor
Jodi Pais Montgomery, Manager Advertising Sales

Devoted exclusively to nonfiction media.
Frequency: Monthly
Founded in 1982
Printed in 4 colors on glossy stock

9301
International Musician
American Federation of Musicians
1501 Broadway
Suite 600
New York, NY 10036-5501
212-869-1330
FAX 212-764-6134
E-Mail: info@afm.org
Home Page: www.afm.org

Thomas Lee, President

Delivers the latest happenings in music. Focuses on the overall well-being of all musicians. Provides news pertaining to symphonic, rock, freelance, recording and touring musicians. IM features aricles on pressing issues sich as piracy, legislation, on-the-job struggles, and the effects of technology.
Cost: $25.00
Frequency: Monthly
Circulation: 110000
Founded in 1896
Printed in on n stock

9302
JAMIA
American Musical Instrument Society
389 Main Street
Suite 202
Malden, MA 2148

781-397-8870
FAX 781-397-8887
E-Mail: amis@guildassoc.com
Home Page: www.amis.org

Stewart Carter, President
Joanne Kopp, Treasurer

Presents peer-reviewed articles that assist in both professionals and students to develop and apply biomedical and health informatics to patient care, teaching, research, and health care administration.
Frequency: Bi-Monthly

9303
Jazz Education Journal
International Association for Jazz Education
2803 Claflin Road
Manhattan, KS 66502
785-776-8744
FAX 785-776-6190
E-Mail: karen@iage.org
Home Page: www.iaje.org

Leslie M Sabina, Editor
Karen Mayse, Advertising

Provides news and information in the field of jazz education. Contains information of today's top jazz artists, reviews, transcriptions, industry news, and articles on improvisation, teaching techniques, history, performance, composition, arranging and music business.
Cost: $23.95
100 Pages
Circulation: 10,000
Founded in 1968
Printed in on glossy stock

9304
JazzTimes
JazzTimes
PO Box 8457
Silver Spring, MD 20907-8457
301-588-4114
800-866-7664
FAX 301-588-5531
Home Page: www.jazztimes.com

Glen Sabin, CEO
Eric Wynne, Consumer Advertising Director

JazzTimes contains extensive news coverage, award winning jazz journalism, hundreds of CD, Book and Video reviews, World class photography and award winning graphics, informative features and columns, special theme issues, special directories, readers poll and critic pics, and sound$weeps giveaways and prizes.
Cost: $23.95
Frequency: 10 Issues per y
Circulation: 86000
Founded in 1980

9305
Journal of American Organbuilding
American Institute of Organ Builders
627 McKinley Ave NW
Canton, OH 44703-3498
713-529-2212
FAX 713-529-2212
E-Mail: editor@pipeorgan.org
Home Page: www.pipeorgan.org

Jeffrey L Weiler, Editor

Features technical articles, product and book reviews, and a forum for the exchange of building and service information and techniqes. Subscriptions are provided free to AIO members, and are available to non-members for $24.00 per year.
Cost: $24.00

Frequency: Quarterly
Founded in 1974
Mailing list available for rent: 350 names at $250 per M
Printed in on glossy stock

9306
Journal of Arts Management, Law, Society

Heldref Publishers
1319 18th St Nw
Washington, DC 20036-1802
202-296-6267
800-365-9753
FAX 202-296-5149
E-Mail: subscribe@heldref.org
Home Page: www.heldref.org

James Denton, Executive Director

A resource for arts policymakters and analysts, sociologists, arts and cultural administrators, educators, trusteed, artists, lawyers, and citizens concerned with the performing, visual, and media arts as well as cultural affairs. Articles, commentaries, and reviews of publications address marketing, intellectual property, arts policy, arts law, governance, and cultural production and dissemination, from a variety of philosophical, disciplinary, and national and international perspectives.
Cost: $79.00
Frequency: Monthly
ISSN: 1063-2921
Founded in 1956

9307
Journal of Dance Education

National Dance Education Organization
8609 2nd Avenue
Suite 203 B
Silver Spring, MD 20910
301-585-2880
FAX 301-585-2888
E-Mail: info@ndeo.org
Home Page: www.ndeo.org

Susan McGreevy-Nichols, Executive Director
Jane Bonbright EdD, Executive Director
Patricia Cohen, Treasurer
Cost: $90.00
Frequency: Quarterly
Circulation: 2000
ISSN: 1529-0824

9308
Journal of Film and Video

University Film and Video Association
University of Illinois Press
1325 S Oak Street
Champaign, IL 61820
217-244-0626
866-244-0626
FAX 217-244-9910
E-Mail: journals@uiuc.edu
Home Page: www.ufva.org

Stephen Tropiano, Editor
Cheryl Jestis, Membership

Focuses on scholarship in the fields of film and video production, history, criticism, and aesthetics. Topics include film and related media, education in these fields, and the function of film and video in society.
Cost: $40.00
Frequency: Quarterly
Circulation: 1200

9309
Journal of Music Theory

Yale University

Department of Music
PO Box 208310
New Haven, CT 06520-8310
203-432-2985
FAX 203-432-2983
E-Mail: jmt.editor@yale.edu
Home Page: www.yale.edu/jmt/

Ian Quinn, Editor
David Clampitt, Associate Editor
Richard Cohn, Associate Editor
Daniel Harrison, Associate Editor
Patrick McCreless, Associate Editor

Publishes peer-reviewed reseach in Music Theory.
Cost: $30.00
Frequency: Annual
Founded in 1957

9310
Journal of Music Therapy

American Music Therapy Association
8455 Colesville Rd
Suite 1000
Silver Spring, MD 20910-3392
301-589-3300
FAX 301-589-5175
E-Mail: info@musictherapy.org
Home Page: www.musictherapy.org

Andrea Farbman, Executive Director

Research in the area of music therapy and rehabilitation, a forum for authoratative articles of current music therapy research and theory, use of music in the behavioral sciences, book reviews, and guest editorials.
Cost: $120.00
Frequency: Quarterly
Circulation: 6000
ISSN: 0022-2917
Founded in 1998

9311
Journal of Popular Film and Television

Heldref Publications
1319 18th St Nw
Suite 2
Washington, DC 20036-1802
202-296-6267
800-365-9753
FAX 202-296-5149
E-Mail: subscribe@heldref.org
Home Page: www.heldref.org

James Denton, Executive Director
Gary Edgerton, Co-Executive Editor

Articles discuss networks, genres, series and audiences, as well as celebrity stars, directors and studios. Regular features include essays on the social and cultural background of films and television programs, filmographies, bibliographies, and commisioned book and video reviews.
Cost: $51.00
Frequency: Quarterly
ISSN: 0195-6051
Founded in 1956

9312
Journal of Research in Music Education

MENC Subscription Office
PO Box 1584
Birmingham, AL 35201
800-633-4931
E-Mail: menc@ebsco.com
Home Page: www.menc.org

Keeps members informed of the latest music education research. Offers a collection of reports that includes

thorough analyses of theories and projects by respected music researchers. Issued four times yearly.
Frequency: Quarterly
Founded in 1907
Printed in on matte stock

9313
Journal of Singing

National Association of Teachers of Singing
9957 Moorings Dr
Suite 401
Jacksonville, FL 32257-2416
904-262-2065
888-262-2065
FAX 904-262-2587
Home Page: www.nats.org

Allen Henderson, Executive Director
Deborah L Guess, Director of Operations

Provides current information regarding the teaching of singing as well as results of recent research in the field. The Journal serves as a historical record and a venue for teachers of singing and other scholars to share the resilts of their work in areas such as history, diction, voice science, medicine, and voice pedagogy.
Cost: $45.00
6500 Members
Frequency: 5x times/year
Founded in 1944

9314
Journal of the American Musicological Soci ety

University of California Press, Journals Division
2000 Center Street Way
Suite 203
Berkeley, CA 94704-1223
510-643-7154
FAX 510-642-9917
E-Mail: journals@ucpress.edu
Home Page: www.ucpressjournals.com

Bruce Alan Brown, Editor
Louise Goldberg, Assistant Editor
Julie Cumming, Book Review Editor

The JAMS publishes scholarship from all fields of musical inquiry: from historical musicology, critical theory, music analysis, iconography and organology, to performance practice, aesthetics and hermeneutics, ethnomusicology, gender and sexuality, popular music and cultural studies. Each issue includes articles, book reviews, and communications.
Cost: $42.00
Frequency: Tri-Annual
Circulation: 5000
ISSN: 0003-0139
Founded in 1893

9315
Jukebox Collector Magazine

2545 SE 60th Court
Pleasant Hill, IA 50327-5099
515-265-8324
FAX 515-265-1980
E-Mail: JukeboxCollector@att.net
Home Page: www.jukeboxmagazine.com

Rick Botts, Editor

Focuses on collectors of jukeboxes from the 40's, 50's, and 60's. There are approximately 150 jukeboxes for sale each month, along with show events information. Accepts advertising.
Cost: $33.00
36 Pages
Frequency: Monthly

Circulation: 1800
Founded in 1977

9316
Keyframe Magazine
DMG Publishing
2756 N Green Valley Pkwy
Suite 261
Henderson, NV 89014-2120
702-990-8656
FAX 702-992-0471
E-Mail: info@dmgpublishing.com
Home Page: www.dmgpublishing.com

Dariush Derakhshani, Editor-in-Chief
Cheri Madison, Managing Editor
Charles Edgin, Editorial Director
Alice Edgin, Executive Editor

In response to reader requests, Keyframe is adding to its LightWave and Photoshop tutorials and content additional bonus pages covering other tools used by digital artists. As Keyframe evolves into this larger, better magazine, its new title with be HDRI 3D.
Cost: $54.00
Circulation: 9000
Founded in 1997

9317
Lighting Dimensions
Primedia Business
249 W 17th St
New York, NY 10011-5382
212-206-1894
800-827-3322
FAX 212-514-3719
Home Page: lightingdimensions.com

Doug MacDonald, Group Publisher
David Johnson, Associate Publisher/Editorial
Marian Sandberg-Dierson, Editor
Mark Newman, Managing Editor

Trade publication for lighting professionals in film, theatre, television, concerts, clubs, themed environments, architectural, commercial, and industrial lighting. Sponsors of the LDI Trade Show and the Broadway Lighting Master Classes.
Cost: $34.97
Frequency: 12/year
Circulation: 14,177
Founded in 1989

9318
Live Sound International
169 Beulah Street
San Francisco, CA 94117
415-387-4009
FAX 415-752-8144
E-Mail: amclean@livesoundint.com
Home Page: www.livesoundint.com

Mark Herman, Publisher
Jeff MacKay, Editor
Mitch Gallagher, Associate Editor
Sara Elliott, Advertising

The editorial focus is performance audio and event sound. Contains audio production techniques, new products, equipment applications and associated commercial concerns.
Cost: $60.00
Frequency: Monthly
Circulation: 20,000
Printed in on glossy stock

9319
Mid-Atlantic Events Magazine
1800 Byberry Road
Suite 901
Huntingdon Valley, PA 19006
215-947-8600
800-521-8588
FAX 215-947-8650
E-Mail: editor@eventsmagazine.com
Home Page: www.eventsmagazine.com

Jim Cohn, Publisher
Rich Kupka, Editor
Fred Cohn, VP Sales
Katie O'Connell, Director Sales/Marketing
Dana Kurtbek, Production

Focused on Hospitality in the Mid-Atlantic area. It assists the Associations, Corporations, Government, Group and Independent Meeting, Event and Travel Planners who are responsible for arranging Conventions, Trade Shows, Hotel Accommodations, Corporate/Group Travel, Meetings, Seminars, Conferences, Symposiums, Site Selections, Special Events, Banquets, Entertainment, Corporate Golf Outings and Golf Tournaments, Company Picnics, Team Building, Retreats, Board Meetings, Training & Development.
Circulation: 26000
ISSN: 0896-3967
Founded in 1987
Printed in 8 colors on glossy stock

9320
Millimeter Magazine
PO Box 2100
Skokie, IL 60076-7800
847-763-9504
866-505-7173
FAX 847-763-9682
E-Mail: millimeter@pbinews.com
Home Page: www.millimeter.com

Cynthia Wisehart, Editor

In a fast-changing and challenging industry, Millimeter anticipates the future. Its early coverage of important technology-driven trends such as 24p production, desktop post, and digital cinema has helped readers remain competitive and plan their business investments. Millimeter is an authoritative resource for professionals in production, postproduction, animation, streaming, and visual effects for motion pictures, television and commercials.
Cost: $70.00
Frequency: Monthly

9321
Mix
Prism Business Media
6400 Hollis St
Suite 9
Emeryville, CA 94608-1052
510-658-3793
866-860-7087
FAX 510-653-5142
E-Mail: mixeditorial@prismb2b.com
Home Page: www.mixonline.com

Melinda Paras, Owner
Erika Lopez, Associate Publisher
Tom Kenny, Editor
Dave Reik, Publisher
Christen Pocock, Marketing Director

Mix covers a wide range of topics including: recording, live sound and production, broadcast production, audio for film and video, and music technology. In addition, Mix includes coverage of facility design and construction, location recording, tape/disc manufacturing, edu-

cation, and other topics of importance to audio professionals. Distributed in 94 countries.
Cost: $35.97
Frequency: Monthly
Circulation: 45244
Founded in 1977

9322
Modern Drummer
Modern Drummer Publications
12 Old Bridge Rd
Cedar Grove, NJ 07009-1288
973-239-4140
FAX 973-239-7139
E-Mail: mdinfo@moderndrummer.com
Home Page: www.moderndrummer.com

Isabel Spagnardi, Owner
Tracy A Kearns, Associate Publisher
Bill Miller, Editor-in-Chief
Rick Van Horn, Senior Editor
Adam Budofsky, Managing Editor

Every issue of Modern Drummer includes interviews with the world's leading drummers, a full roster of columns on all facets of drumming, complete drum charts, solos and patterns performed by your favorite players, insightful reviews on the hottest new geat, the best in CDs, books, and DVDs for drummers, and giveaways worth thousands of dollars.
Cost: $29.97
Frequency: Monthly
Circulation: 6000
ISSN: 1078-1757
Founded in 1993
Printed in 4 colors on glossy stock

9323
Movie Collectors World
Arena Publishing
PO BOX 309
Fraser, MI 48026
586-774-4311
FAX 703-940-4566
E-Mail: mail@mcwonline.com
Home Page: www.mcwonline.com

Brian Bukantis, Editor

Leading collector's publication for collectors of movie memorabilia, with an emphasis on collectible movie posters. Each issue is filled with ads from dealers and collectors all over the world. In any monthly issue, you will find movie posters common and rare - everything from the 'Golden Age' to today's blockbusters.
Cost: $36.00
36-44 Pages
Frequency: Monthly
Circulation: 6000

9324
MovieMaker
MovieMaker Magazine
121 Fulton Street
Fifth Floor
New York, NY 10038
212-766-4100
FAX 212-766-4102
Home Page: www.moviemaker.com

Timothy Rhys, Publisher/Editor-in-Chief
Jennifer M Wood, Editor
Phillip Williams, Editor at Large
Ian Bage, New Marketing Services

MovieMaker is the world's most widely - read independent movie magazine that focuses on the art and business of making movies. Its editorial mix is a progressive mix of in depth interviews and criticism combined by

practical techniques and advice on financing, distribution and production strategies.
Cost: $18.00
Frequency: Quarterly
Circulation: 54000
Founded in 1993

9325
Music
102 N Haven Road
PO Box 906
Elmhurst, IL 60126-2932
630-941-2030
FAX 630-941-3210
E-Mail: subscriptions@musicincmag.com
Home Page: www.musicincmag.com

Zach Phillip, Editor
Kevin Maher, CEO
John Cahill, Eastern Advertising
Tom Burns, Western Advertising
Chris Maher, Classified Ads

Offered free to those involved in music products retailing. Delivers news you can use for the musical products industry. Geared toward store owners and managers in musical product retail and repair shops in the United States and Canada.
Frequency: 11 Per Year
Circulation: 8,949
Founded in 1934

9326
Music & Sound Retailer
Testa Communications
25 Willowdale Avenue
Port Washington, NY 11050
516-767-2500
800-937-7678
FAX 516-767-9335
E-Mail: testa@testa.com
Home Page: www.testa.com

Brian Berk, Editor

News magazine serving owners, managers and sales personnel in retail musical-instument and sound-product dealershops. The magazine's emphasis is on full-line and combo dealerships offering guitars, drums, electronic keyboards and digital pianos, recording and sound-reinforcement products, lighting, DJ equipment, software, print and accessories. Recurring features include 'MI Spy,' 'Top Ten,' 'Veddatorial,' 'Selling Points,' and editor's letter
Cost: $18.00
Frequency: Monthly
Circulation: 11000
Founded in 1985

9327
Music Row
1231 17th Avenue S
PO Box 158542
Nashville, TN 37215-8542
615-321-3617
FAX 615-329-0852
E-Mail: sales@musicrow.com
Home Page: www.musicrow.com

David M Ross, CEO/President

Written for people who work in the music business. Contents include record reviews, current news items, timely interviews or discovering hot talent first. Music Row subscriptions include six print issues per year, daily Afternoon News updates via e-mail and @Musicrow reports every Tuesday, Thursday and Friday via e-mail.
Cost: $159.00

Frequency: Six Per Year
Circulation: 14000
Founded in 1981
Printed in 4 colors on glossy stock

9328
Music Trades Magazine
Music Trades
PO Box 432
Englewood, NJ 07631-0432
201-871-1965
800-423-6530
FAX 201-871-0455
E-Mail: music@musictrades.com
Home Page: www.musictrades.com

Brian Majeski, Publisher
Richard T Watson, Managing Editor
Juanita Hampton, Circulation Manager

A blend of industry news, hard sales and marketing data, trend analysis and management tips in every issue. Target audience is retailers, distributors, and manufacturers of musical instruments, professional audio equipment and related products, worldwide.
Cost: $16.00
Frequency: Monthly
Circulation: 7500
Founded in 1890

9329
Music and Sound Journal
912 Carlton Road
Tarpon Spring, FL 34689
727-938-0571
E-Mail: sound@masj.com
Home Page: www.masj.com

Don Kulak, Founder/Owner

Brings readers the future of sound today, with new music, experimental sound, cutting edge audio and acoustics and alternative media. MSJ is written for people who are discriminating about music, audio, and sound - people who want to improve their sonic environments on all levels, without having to study pages of data - people who want to more fully understand the profound impact sound has on every aspect of their daily lives.
ISSN: 1541-8545
Founded in 1988

9330
Musical Merchandise Review
21 Highland Circle
Suite One
Needham, MA 2494
781-453-9310
800-964-5150
FAX 781-453-9389
E-Mail: mprescott@symphonypublishing.com
Home Page: www.mmrmagazine.com

Lee Zapis, President
Sidney L Davis, Group Publisher
Richard E Kessel, Publisher/Advertising Sales
Maureen Johan, Classified Sales

Serves retailers of musical instruments, accessories, and related services as well as wholesalers, importers/exporters and manufacturers of related products. Its purpose is to communicate facts and ideas that will benefit musical merchandisers and their daily business operations as well as help them enhance their growth. Its editorial approach includes features on industry trends and innovations, new product promotion, in-store display techniques, financing, planning and dealer surveys.
Cost: $32.00

Frequency: Monthly
Founded in 1879
Printed in 4 colors

9331
National Squares
National Square Dance Convention
C/O Gene and Connie Triplett
2760 Polo Club Boulevard
Matthews, NC 28105
704-847-1265
E-Mail: Richp27890@aol.com
Home Page: www.nationalsquaredanceconvention.com

Dick/Linda Peterson, Editors
Gene/Connie Triplett, Circulation Managers
Dick/Linda Peterson, Public Relations

A national square dance magazine published by the National Executive Committee of the National Square Dance Convention.
Cost: $7.00
Frequency: Quarterly

9332
New England Theatre Journal
New England Theatre Conference
215 Knob Hill Drive
Hamden, CT 6518
617-851-8535
FAX 203-288-5938
E-Mail: mail@netconline.org
Home Page: www.netconline.org

James Quinn, President
Jeffrey Watts, Executive VP
Charles Emmons, VP Administration/Finance

Scholarly publication produced once per year. Includes book and theatre reviews, historical analyses, and other well-written articles by noted authors. Free to NETC members. Specifically designed to provide members, and others interested in live theatre arts, with the information and resources they need to enhance their careers, promote their groups, and sharpen their theatre skills.
Cost: $10.00
Frequency: Annual
Founded in 1952

9333
New on the Charts
Music Business Reference
70 Laurel Place
New Rochelle, NY 10801-7105
914-632-3349
FAX 914-633-7690
E-Mail: lenny@notc.com
Home Page: www.notc.com

Leonard Kalikow, Publisher/Editor

Circulation limited to professionals only, provides major signings, contracts and directories.
Cost: $365.00
Frequency: Monthly
Circulation: 5,000
ISSN: 0276-7031
Founded in 1976

9334
Nouveau Magazine
Barbara Tompkins
5933 Stoney Hill Rd
New Hope, PA 18938-9602
215-794-5996
FAX 215-794-8305
E-Mail: info@nouveaumagazine.com
Home Page: www.nouveaumagazine.com

Barbara Tompkins, Publisher

Features theater reviews.
Frequency: Monthly
Founded in 1981
Printed in 4 colors on glossy stock

9335
OffBeat
OffBeat
421 Frenchmen St
Suite 200
New Orleans, LA 70116-2039
504-944-4300
877-944-4300
FAX 504-944-4306
E-Mail: offbeat@offbeat.com
Home Page: www.offbeat.com

Jan Ramsy, Publisher
Joseph L Irrera, Managing Editor
Bunny Matthews, Senior Editor
Michael Jastroch, Magazine Design/Production
Doug Jackson, Distribution Manager

Consumer-oriented music magazine focusing on New Orleans and Louisiana music. Regular columns on Cajun music, zydeco, traditional and contemporary jazz, brass band (Mardi Gras second-line music), New Orleans R & B, Louisiana and delta blues, Gospel, modern and roots rock and our internationally-appreciated culture and cusine. Information on music fairs and festivals in the region is given.
Cost: $29.00
Frequency: Monthly
Circulation: 50000
ISBN: 1-090081-0 -
Founded in 1985
Printed in 4 colors on newsprint stock

9336
Opera America Newsline
Opera America
330 7th Ave
Suite 1600
New York, NY 10001-5248
212-796-8620
FAX 212-796-8631
E-Mail: frontdesk@operaamerica.org
Home Page: www.operaamerica.org

Marc Scorca, President

Provides company news from around the world, articles on issues affecting the field, professional opportunities, and updates on OPERA America programs and activities. Complimentary subscription with all membership levels, excluding stand-alone professional subscriptions.
Frequency: 10X Per Year
Founded in 1970

9337
Opera News
Metropolitan Opera Guild
70 Lincoln Center Plz
New York, NY 10023-6577
212-769-7000
FAX 212-769-7007
E-Mail: info@metguild.org
Home Page: www.metoperafamily.org

David Dik, Manager

Monthly magazine that reports on opera around the world. Issues include reviews of commercial recordings and live performances, profiles of artists and articles by eminent writers on the music scene.
Cost: $29.95

Frequency: Monthly
Circulation: 60000
Founded in 1883

9338
Percussive Notes
Percussive Arts Society
701 NW Ferris Avenue
Lawton, OK 73507-5442
580-353-1455
FAX 580-353-1456
E-Mail: percarts@pas.org
Home Page: www.pas.org

Rick Mattingly, Editor
Hillary Henry, Managing Editor

The official journal of the Percussive Arts Society. Published in February, April, June, August, October and December, this magazine features a variety of articles and advertising aimed at professional and student percussionists. Regular sections are devoted to drumset, marching percussion, world percussion, symphonic percussion, technology, keyboard, health and wellness, research and reviews.
Cost: $85.00
Frequency: 6 Times Per Year
Circulation: 8000
Founded in 1961
Mailing list available for rent

9339
Performing Arts Insider Magazine
PAI C/O Total Theater
PO Box 62
Hewlett, NY 11557-0062
516-295-1511
E-Mail: totalpost@totaltheater.com
Home Page: hometown.aol.com/paipress/

David Lefkowitz, Publisher/Editor
Richmond Shepard, Publisher
Steven Fisch, Advertising Sales

Includes day-by-day calendar listings of shows on Broadway, Off and Off-Off Broadway, plus dance, opera, cabaret and special events. Also included are comprehensive theater guides, listing the author, director, cast, designers, synopsis, theater and box office details, as well as contact information for producers, press agents, general managers and casting directors.
Cost: $275.00
Frequency: Monthly+9 Updates
Circulation: 2000
Founded in 1944

9340
Piano Guild Notes
Piano Guild Publications
PO Box 1807
Austin, TX 78767-1807
512-478-5775
FAX 512-478-5843
E-Mail: ngpt@pianoguild.com
Home Page: www.pianoguild.com

Richard Allison, President

Music industry publication focusing on Piano Guild members and activities.
Cost: $16.00
Frequency: Quarterly
Circulation: 11000
Founded in 1929
Printed in 2 colors

9341
Piano Technicians Journal
Piano Technicians Guild

4444 Forest Avenue
Kansas City, KS 66106
913-432-9975
FAX 913-432-9986
E-Mail: ptg@ptg.org
Home Page: www.ptg.org

Barbara Cassaday, Executive Director
Allan Gilbreath RPT, President
Jim Coleman Jr RPT, VP

Monthly technical magazine covering all phases of working on pianos. Articles explore new tools, industry news and organizational issues. Feature articles range from setting up a repair shop to rebuilding techniques.
Cost: $ 150.00
Frequency: Monthly
Circulation: 4300
ISSN: 0031-9562

9342
Pitch Pipe
Sweet Adelines International
9110 S Toledo
PO Box 470168
Tulsa, OK 74137-0168
918-622-1444
800-992-7464
FAX 918-665-0894
E-Mail: Joey@sweetadelineintl.org
Home Page: www.sweetadelineintl.org

Pat LeVezu, President
Joey Mechell Stenner, Editor
Kelly Kirchhoff, Director Communications

Official publication of Sweet Adelines International, the world's largest singing performance and music education organization for women. The Pitch Pipe informs, educates and recognizes the members who have made the organization a success. The subscription price for members is included in the annual per capita fee.
Cost: $12.00
Frequency: Quarterly
Circulation: 30,000
Founded in 1947
Mailing list available for rent: 30M names
Printed in 4 colors on glossy stock

9343
Playback
American Society of Composers, Authors & Publisher
1 Lincoln Plz
New York, NY 10023-7097
212-621-6027
800-952-7227
FAX 212-362-7328
E-Mail: Playback@ascap.com
Home Page: www.ascap.com

Marilyn Bergman, President
Phil Crossland, Executive Editor
Jin Moon, Deputy Editor
Mike Barsky, Advertising
David Pollard, Design

The Society's magazine is loaded with full-color photos, features the latest news on ASCAP events, new member listings, legislative updates, feature articles on members, distribution info, upcoming workshops and showcases and much more.
Cost: $12.00
Frequency: Annual
Circulation: 100,000
ISSN: 1080-1391

9344

Playbill
52 Vanderbilt Avenue
11th Floor
New York, NY 10017-3808
212-557-5757
FAX 212-682-2932
E-Mail: agans@playbill.com
Home Page: www.playbill.com

Andrew Gans, Editor

The exclusive magazine for Broadway and Off-Broadway theatregoers, providing the information necessary for the understanding and enjoyment of each show, including features articles and columns by and about theatre personalities, entertainment, travel, fashion, dining and other editorial pieces geared to the lifestyle of the upscale, active theatre attendee. Playbill also serves New York's three most prominent performing arts venues - the Metropolitan Opera House, Lincoln Center and Carnegie Hall
Cost: $24.00
Frequency: Monthly
Founded in 1884

9345

Plays: Drama Magazine for Young People
Plays Magazine
PO Box 600160
Newton, MA 2460
617-630-9100
800-630-5755
FAX 617-630-9101
E-Mail: lpreston@playsmag.com
Home Page: www.playsmag.com

Elizabeth Preston, Editor

Includes eight to ten royalty-free one-act plays, arranged by age level. Modern and traditional plays for the celebration of all important holidays and occasions. Adaptable to all cast sizes with easy to follow instructions for settings and costumes. A complete source of original plays and programs for school-age actors and audiences.
Cost: $39.00
Frequency: 7 X Per Year
Circulation: 6000
Founded in 1940
Printed in on matte stock

9346

Pollstar: Concert Hotwire
Pollstar
4697 W Jacquelyn Ave
Fresno, CA 93722-6443
559-271-7900
FAX 559-271-7979
E-Mail: info@pollstar.com
Home Page: www.pollstar.com

Gary Smith, CEO
Shari Rice, VP
Chris Shugart, Marketing
Pat Lewis, Director

Trade publication for the concert industry offering global coverage and information including concert tour schedules, ticket sales information and more.
Cost: $449.00
Frequency: Weekly
Circulation: 20000
Printed in 4 colors

9347

Post
Advanstar Communications

641 Lexington Ave
Suite 8
New York, NY 10022-4503
212-951-6600
FAX 212-951-6793
E-Mail: info@advanstar.com
Home Page: www.advanstar.com

Joseph Loggia, CEO

News and features emphasize innovation in equipment technology and creative technique for editing, graphics, and special effects. Covers all budget levels from desktop post to feature films.
130 Pages
Frequency: Monthly
Circulation: 31464
Founded in 1986

9348

Pro Audio Review
IMAS Publishing
5827 Columbia Pike
Third Floor
Falls Church, VA 22041
703-998-7600
FAX 703-998-2966
E-Mail: letters@proaudioreview.com
Home Page: www.proaudioreview.com

John Gatski, Publisher/Executive Editor
Brett Moss, Managing Editor
Claudia Van Veen, Advertising

Reviews of the latest new equipment written by audio professionals in the field, from bench tests checking the specs, to new product announcements.
Cost: $24.95
Frequency: Monthly
Circulation: 26000
ISSN: 1083-6241
Founded in 1995
Printed in 4 colors on glossy stock

9349

Pro Sound News
United Business Media
810 Seventh Avenue
27th Fl
New York, NY 10019
212-378-0400
FAX 212-378-2160
E-Mail: sedorusa@optonline.net
Home Page: www.governmentvideo.com

Gary Rhodes, International Sales Manager

Provides timely and accurate news, industy analysis, features and technology updates to the expanded professional audio community.
Cost: $30.00
Frequency: Monthly
Circulation: 250003
Printed in 4 colors

9350

Produced By
The Producers Guild of America
8530 Wilshire Blvd
Suite 450
Beverly Hills, CA 90211-3115
310-358-9020
FAX 310-358-9520
E-Mail: info@producersguild.org
Home Page: www.producersguild.com

Vance Van Petter, Executive Director
Audra Whaley, Director Operations
Kyle Katz, Director Member Benefits

Chris Greenr, Director Communications
Dan Dodd, Advertising

Provided as a benefit with membership to the Producers Guild of America.
Frequency: Quarterly
Circulation: 325
Founded in 1962

9351

Producer
Testa Communications
25 Willowdale Avenue
Port Washington, NY 11050-3779
516-767-2500
FAX 516-767-9335
Home Page: avvproducersguide.com

Randi Altman, Editor
Sande Seidman, Advertising Manager

Magazine aimed at producers, directors and creative people in the image and sound realms, with production stories on feature films, television, commercials, documentary, and corporate video projects. Accent is on the creative application of technology, following producers into the field and onto the studio set.
Cost: $15.00
Frequency: Bi-Monthly
Circulation: 18,300

9352

RePlay Magazine
PO Box 7004
Tarzana, CA 91357-7004
818-776-2880
FAX 818-776-2888
E-Mail: editor@replaymag.com
Home Page: www.replaymag.com

Edward Adlum, President
Barry Zweben, Marketing

A trade publication for those within the coin-operated amusement machine industry, primarily distributors, manufacturers and operators of jukeboxes and games.
Cost: $65.00
Frequency: Monthly
Circulation: 36000
ISSN: 1534-2328
Founded in 1975
Printed in 4 colors on glossy stock

9353

Rolling Stone Magazine
1290 Ave of the Americas
Floor 2
New York, NY 10104-0295
212-484-1616
FAX 212-484-1771
Home Page: www.rssoundingboard.com

Jann Wenner, President

Covers pop culture, politics etc in a massive amount of music articles, interviews, news, reviews, photos, and sound clips.

9354

SMPTE Journal
Society of Motion Picture & Television Engineers
3 Barker Ave
Suite 5
White Plains, NY 10601-1509
914-761-1100
FAX 914-761-3115
E-Mail: smpte@smpte.org
Home Page: www.smpte.org

Kimberly Maki, Executive Director
Charlie Barone, Administrative Assistant

Featuring industry-leading papers and standards, each month the Journal keeps its members on the cutting edge of the industry. Each issue provides the latest research and papers, ranging in style from technical, scientific, and tutorial, to applications/practices. Readers are kept up-to-date on events and meetings, the latest publications and brochures, and new products and developments.
Cost: $140.00
Frequency: Monthly
Circulation: 10000
Founded in 1916
Printed in on glossy stock

9355
Script
Forum
5638 Sweet Air Road
Baldwin, MD   21013-9009
410-592-3466
888-245-2228
FAX 410-592-8062
E-Mail: scriptmg@erols.com
Home Page: www.scriptmag.com

Mark Madnick, Publisher
David Geatty, Founding Publisher
Shelly Mellot, Editor-in-Chief
Andrew Schneider, Managing Editor
Maureen Green, Editor

A leading source of information on the crage and business of writing for film and television. Each issues delivers informative articles on writing, developing and marketing screenplays and television scripts. Most articles are written by working writers. Additionally, development executives, agents, managers and entertainment attorneys contribute regularly.
Cost: $24.95
Frequency: Bi-Monthly
Circulation: 12000

9356
Shakespeare Bulletin
University of North Carolina
Department of English
9201 University City Boulevard
Charlotte, NC   28223
E-Mail: sbeditor@email.uncc.edu
Home Page: www.shakespeare-bulletin.org

Seymour Isenberg, Founding Editor
Andrew James Hartley, Editor
Jeremy Lopez, Theatre Review Editor
Genevieve Love, Book Review Editor
Kirk Melnikoff, Shakespeare on Film Editor

A peer-reviewed journal of performance and criticism and scholarship which provides commentary on Shakespeare and Renaissance drama through feature articles, thatre and film reviews, and book reviews. The journal is a member of the Conference of Editors of Learned Journals.
Cost: $35.00
Frequency: Quarterly
ISSN: 0748-2558
Founded in 1982
Printed in on matte stock

9357
Sheet Music Magazine
PO Box 58629
Boulder, CO   80323
914-244-8500
800-759-3036

FAX 914-244-8560
Home Page: www.sheetmusicmagazine.com

Ed Shanaphy, Publisher

Features actual reproduction of popular songs, both words and music, articles on various aspects of musical performance and interest for many types of musicians, and self improvement features for keyboard and fretter instrument players. A single year's subscription brings you at least 66 great songs best-loved standards and today's most lyrical hits.
Cost: $22.97
Frequency: Bi-Monthly
Circulation: 50,000

9358
Show Music
Po Box A
East Haddam, CT   06423-0466
860-873-8664
FAX 860-873-2329
E-Mail: rklink@goodspeed.org
Home Page: www.showmusic.org

Ryan Klink, Managing Editor
Maz O Preeo, Editor-In-Chief

Internationally acclaimed by professionals and fans as the premier magazine covering musical theatre around the world. Show music combines insightful interviews and reviews of productions, recordings, videos and books.
Cost: $ 25.00
80 Pages
Frequency: Quarterly
Circulation: 5,000

9359
Society News
Contemporary Record Society
724 Winchester Road
Broomall, PA   19008
610-544-5920
FAX 915-808-4232
E-Mail: crsnews@verizon.net
Home Page:
mysite.verizon.net/vzeeewvp/contemporaryrecordsociety/id3.

Jack M Shusterman, Advertising

Offers opportunities to CRS consitituents, progress notes on its associates, various awards and performance possibilities. The Society News offers feature articles of renowned composers/performers and reviews of music, recordings and music books.
Founded in 1983
Mailing list available for rentat $50 per M

9360
Sondheim Review
PO Box 11213
Chicago, IL   60611-0213
773-275-4254
800-584-1020
FAX 773-275-4254
E-Mail: info@sondheimreview.com
Home Page: www.sondheimreview.com

Dedicated to the work of the musical theater and Broadway's foremost composer and lyricist, Stephen Sondheim. Each issue contains news, interviews, upcoming productions in the area, puzzles and more.
Cost: $19.95
Frequency: Quarterly
Circulation: 40000
ISSN: 1076-450X
Founded in 1994
Printed in on glossy stock

9361
Southern Theatre
Southeastern Theatre Conference
1217 W Bessemer Avenue
PO Box 9868
Greensboro, NC   27429-868
336-272-3645
FAX 336-272-8810
E-Mail: setc@setc.org
Home Page: www.setc.org

Elizabeth Baun, Executive Director
April J'Callahan Marshall, Professional Theatre Services Mgr
Hardy Koenig, Educational Services Manager

Spotlights people, places and organizations within the region that are paving new paths in theatre. Includes low-cost strategies for design success, tips on hot markets for playwrights, new books of special interest, innovative ideas for marketing theatre, inside track on new trends and some of the region's up-and-coming theatre stars. Subscription is free with SETC membership.
Cost: $18.75
Frequency: Quarterly
Circulation: 4000+
Founded in 1949

9362
Southwestern Musician
Texas Music Educators Association
7900 Centre Park
PO Box 140465
Austin, TX   78714-0465
512-452-0710
888-318-8632
FAX 512-451-9213
E-Mail: rfloyd@tmea.org
Home Page: www.tmea.org

Robert Floyd, Executive Director
Karen Kneten, Communications Manager
Tesa Harding, Advertising/Exhibit Manager
Laura Kocian, Financial Manager
Maura Langan, Membership Assistant

The official magazine of the TMEA. Publsihed monthly August through May. Included with membership. A President's newsletter is published each June when necessary to provide an update on TMEA activities. The purposed of this publication is to serve the music educators of Texas as a means of communication or professional philosophy and action and to promote the field of music education within the state.
Circulation: 14000
Founded in 1938
Mailing list available for rent: 10,000 names
Printed in 4 colors on glossy stock

9363
Spectrum
110 S Jefferson Street
Dayton, OH   45402-3412
937-220-1600
800-247-1614
FAX 937-220-1642
E-Mail: mservices@thinktv.org
Home Page: www.thinktv.org

ThinkTV's monthly member magazine. Contains program listings for both ThinkTV 16 and ThinkTV14 as well as interesting feature stories, station news and more.
Frequency: Weekly
Circulation: 18000
Founded in 1959

9364

Stage Directions
Macfadden Performing Arts Media
110 William St
Suite 23
New York, NY 10038-3900
646-459-4800
FAX 646-459-4900
E-Mail: sd@lifestylemedia.com
Home Page: www.stagedirections.com

Karla Johnson, President
Jessica Hodges, Advertising

Serves the strategic, practical and technical information needs of small theaters across the country.
Cost: $26.00
Frequency: Monthly
Circulation: 7000
Founded in 1988

9365

Stage of the Art
American Alliance for Theatre and Education
7475 Wisconsin Ave
Suite 300
Bethesda, MD 20814-3474
301-654-0008
FAX 301-968-0144
E-Mail: info@aate.com.edu
Home Page: www.aate.com

David Young, Editor
JoBeth Gonzalez, Director Publications/Research

Published by the American Alliance for Theatre and Education.
Cost: $28.00
Frequency: Quarterly
Circulation: 1000
ISSN: 0892-9092
Mailing list available for rent: 700 names at $150 per M

9366

Stagebill
Stagebill
144 E 44th Street
7th Floor
New York, NY 10017-4031
212-476-0640
FAX 212-983-5976
E-Mail: bmattison@stagebill.com
Home Page: www.avant-rus.com/stagebill

Gerry Byrne, CEO
Frederick W Becker III, Associate Publisher
John Istel, Editor-in-Chief
Robert Sandla, Executive Editor
Tricia Maher, Senior Managing Editor

Publisher of the program magazines for the leading, theaters, symphonies, dance companies and performing arts centers in the United States. A national performing arts magazine.
Frequency: Monthly
Founded in 1924

9367

Stages
Curtains
301 W 45th Street
Apartment 5A
New York, NY 10036-3825
FAX 201-836-4107

Frank Scheck, Editor
Cost: $20.00
Frequency: Monthly
Circulation: 35,000

9368

Starlog
1372 Broadway
2nd Floor
New York, NY 10018
212-689-2830
800-934-6788
E-Mail: rita@starloggroup.com
Home Page: www.starlog.com

David McDonnel, Editor
Norman Jacobs, Founder

Information on science fiction happenings in the movies and television industries.
Cost: $56.97
Frequency: Monthly
Circulation: 350000

9369

Symphony Magazine
American Symphony Orchestra League
33 W 60th St
Suite 5
New York, NY 10023-7905
212-262-0638
FAX 212-262-5198
E-Mail: editor@symphony.org
Home Page: www.symphony.org

Henry Fogel, CEO
Stephen Alter, Advertising Manager
Michael Rush, Production Manager

Bimonthly magazine of the American Symphony Orchestra League. Discusses issues critical to the orchestra community and communicates the value and importance of orchestras and the music they perform. Publishes articles on compelling issues and trends relevant to the entire orchestra field. Its readers include professional staff, musicians, and board members in the orchestra industry and related fields; orchestra patrons and volunteers; and music critics and arts and media professionals.
Cost: $22.00
Frequency: Bi-Monthly
Circulation: 18000
Founded in 1942
Printed in 4 colors

9370

Symposium
312 E Pine Street
Missoula, MT 59802
406-721-9616
800-729-0235
FAX 406-721-9419
E-Mail: cms@music.org
Home Page: www.music.org

Robby D Gunstream, Executive Director
Cynthia Taggart, President
Glenn Stanley, Editor

Serves as a vehicle for the dissemination of information and ideas on music in higher education. The content of the publication highlights concerns of general interest and reflects the work of the Society in the areas of music represented on its Board of Directors.
Frequency: One Per Year
Circulation: 8000
Founded in 1968
Printed in one color on matte stock

9371

TD & T: Theatre Design & Technology
US Institute for Theatre Technology
3001 Springcrest Drive
Louisville, KY 40241-2755
502-426-1211
FAX 502-423-7467
E-Mail: info@oficce.usitt.org
Home Page: www.usitt.org

David Roger, Editor
Arnold Wengrow, Book Review Editor
Michelle Smith, Membership/Advertising Manager
N Deborah Hazlett, Art Director

Published by United States Institute for Theatre Technology. Focuses on USITT's ten interest areas: architecture, costume design and technology, education, engineering, health and safety, lighting, management, scene design, sound design, and technical production.
Frequency: Quarterly

9372

Teaching Theatre
Educational Theatre Association
2343 Auburn Ave
Cincinnati, OH 45219-2819
513-421-3900
FAX 513-421-7077
Home Page: www.edta.org

Michael Peitz, Executive Director

Educational Theatre Association's journal for theatre teachers. Includes articles on acting, directing, playwriting, technical theatre; profiles of outstanding educational theatre programs; pieces on curriculum design, assessment or teaching methodology; and reports on current trends or issues in the field, such as funding, standards, or certification. Subscription are available only as a benefit of membership in the Educational Theatre Association. Libraries and other institutions may subscribe.
Cost: $34.00
Frequency: Quarterly

9373

Technical Brief
Yale School of Drama
222 York Street
PO Box 208244
New Haven, CT 6520
203-432-9664
FAX 203-432-8332
E-Mail: bronislaw.sammler@yale.edu
Home Page: www.technicalbrief.org

Ben Sammler, Co-Editor
Don Harvey, Co-Editor

Written by professionals for professionals, providing a dialogue between technical practitioners from the several performing arts. The succinct articles, complete with mechanical drawings, represent the best solutions to recurring technical problems. Published October, January and April.
Cost: $15.00
Frequency: 3X Per Year
Founded in 1924

9374

Theater Magazine
Yale School of Drama
222 York Street
PO Box 208244
New Haven, CT 6520
203-432-1568
FAX 203-432-8336
E-Mail: theater.magazine@yale.edu
Home Page: www.yale.edu/drama

Tom Sellar, Editor
Laraine Sammler, Business Manager
Alex Grennan, Director of Business/Comm

Periodicals, essays and articles of the Yale School of Drama.
Cost: $22.00
Frequency: Annual+
Circulation: 2500
Founded in 1924
Mailing list available for rent: 1.5M names
Printed in one color on matte stock

9375
Theatre Bay Area Magazine
1663 Mission Street
Suite 525
San Francisco, CA 94103
415-430-1140
FAX 415-430-1145
E-Mail: tba@theatrebayarea.org
Home Page: www.theatrebayarea.org

Karen Mc Kevitt, Executive Director
Dale Albright, Director, Member Services
Clayton Lord, Director, Audience Development
Cost: $5.95
Frequency: Monthly
Circulation: 4500

9376
Theatre Bill
Jerome Press
332 Congress St
Suite 2
Boston, MA 02210-1217
617-423-3400
FAX 617-423-7108
Home Page: www.showofthemonthtravel.com

Jerome Rosenfeld, Owner

9377
Theatre Journal
Johns Hopkins University Press
2715 N Charles St
Baltimore, MD 21218-4319
410-516-6900
800-548-1784
FAX 410-516-6998
E-Mail: wmb@press.jhu.edu
Home Page: www.press.jhu.edu

William Brody, President
David Z Saltz, Co-Editor
Sonja Arsham Kuftinec, Performance Review Editor
James Peck, Book Review Editor
Bob Kowkabany, Managing Editor

One of the most authoritative and useful publications of theatre studies available today. Theatre Journal features social and historical studies, production reviews, and theoretical inquiries that analize dramatic texts and production. Official journal of the Association for Theatre in Higher Education.
Cost: $40.00
Frequency: Quarterly
Circulation: 2492
ISSN: 0192-2882
Founded in 1878

9378
Theatre Symposium
Auburn University
Department of Theatre
211 Telfair Peet Theatre
Auburn, AL 36849
336-272-3645
FAX 336-272-8810
E-Mail: phillm2@auburbn.edu
Home Page: www.setc.org

M Scott Phillips, Editor

An annual publication of works of scholarship resulting from a single topic meeting held on a southeastern university campus each year. Available to adult members only. A copublication of the Southeaster Theatre Conference and the University of Alabama Press.

9379
Theatre Topics
Johns Hopkins University Press
2715 N Charles St
Baltimore, MD 21218-4319
410-516-6900
800-548-1784
FAX 410-516-6998
E-Mail: jonathc@bgsu.edu
Home Page: www.press.jhu.edu

William Brody, President
Sandra G Shannon, Co-Editor
DeAnna Toten Beard, Book Review Editor
Elanore Lampners, Managing Editor
Beverley Pevitts, Founding Editor

Focuses on performance studies, dramaturgy, and theatre pedagogy. Concise and timely articles on a broad array of practical, performance-oriented subjects, with special attention to topics of current interest to the profession. Keeps readers informed of the latest developments on the stage and in the classroom. The official journal of the Association for Theatre in Higher Education. Published in March and September.
Cost: $32.00
Frequency: Semi-Annually
Circulation: 1528
ISSN: 1054-8378
Founded in 1878

9380
Variety
Reed Business Information
5700 Wilshire Boulevard
Suite 120
Los Angeles, CA 90036-3659
323-857-6600
866-698-2743
FAX 323-857-0494
E-Mail: VTCCustserv@cdsfulfillment.com
Home Page: www.variety.com

Charles C Koones, Publisher
Peter Bart, Editor-in-Chief
Timothy Gray, Editor
Kathy Lyford, Managing Editor
Christopher Wessel, Circulation Director

Variety covers all aspects of film, television and cable, homevideo, music, new media and technolgy, theater and finance. Topics run from people, companies, products and performances, to development, financing, distribution, regulation and marketing.
Cost: $259.00
Frequency: Weekly
Circulation: 35168
Founded in 1905

9381
Vibe
E-Mail: vbecustserv@cdsfulfillment.com
Home Page: www.vibe.com

Mimi Valdez, Editor-In-Chief

Covers the trends, the events, and culture of the urban scene. Film, fashion and art to politics and music-pop, jazz, R&B, dance, hip hop, rap, house and more.
Cost: $11.95
Frequency: Monthly

9382
Youth Theatre Journal
American Alliance for Theatre and Education
7475 Wisconsin Ave
Suite 300
Bethesda, MD 20814-3474
301-654-0008
FAX 301-968-0144
E-Mail: info@aate.com
Home Page: www.aate.com

Manon van de Water, Editor

Scholarly Journal of the American Alliance for Theatre and Education. A juried publication dedicated to advancing the study and practice of theatre and drama, with, for, and by people of all ages. It is concerned with all forms of scholarship of the highest quality that inform the fields of theatre for young audiences and drama/theatre education.
Cost: $25.00
Frequency: Annual
Circulation: 1000
ISSN: 0892-9092
Mailing list available for rent: 700 names at $150 per M

Trade Shows

9383
ASTA National Conference
American String Teachers Association
4153 Chain Bridge Road
Fairfax, VA 22030
703-279-2113
FAX 703-279-2114
E-Mail: asta@astaweb.com
Home Page: www.astaweb.com

Donna Sizemore Hale, Executive Director
Beth Danner-Knight, Deputy Director
Jody McNamara, Deputy Director

Recognizing the wealth of our rich traditions as well as offer members new horizons in teaching and performing strings. Cost of attendance begins at $255. 150 exhibitors.
2000 Attendees
Frequency: Annual/March

9384
American Choral Directors Association National Convention
American Choral Directors Association
545 Couch Drive
PO Box 2720
Oklahoma City, OK 73101-2720
405-232-8161
FAX 405-232-8162
E-Mail: acda@acdaonline.org
Home Page: www.acdaonline.org

Gene Brooks, Executive Director
Hilary Apfelstadt, Planning Committee
Galen Darrough, Planning Committee
Rebecca Reames, Planning Committee
Leane Defrancis, Membership

Features distinguished auditioned choirs and experienced clinicians, three tracks for the attendess, an exhibit hall, the ACDA Wall of Honor, and concessions which will be open in the exhibit hall throughout the convention.
20000 Attendees
Frequency: Biennial
Founded in 1959

9385
American Film Institute Festival: AFI Fest
American Film Institute
2021 N Western Avenue
Los Angeles, CA 90027-1657
323-856-7896
866-234-3378
FAX 323-856-9118
E-Mail: festpublicity@AFI.com
Home Page: afifest.com

Jennifer Morgerman, Publicity Director
Stacey Leinson, Publicity Manager
Lagan Sebert, Publicity Coordinator
John Wildman, Filmmaker Press Liaison
Alison Deknatel, Director Communications

A 10-day event held each November, the festival features a rich slate of films from emerging filmmakers, nightly red-carpet gala premieres and global showcases of the latest work from the great film masters. AFI runs concurrently with the American Film Market. Together, AFT Fest and AFM provide the film industry with the only concurrent festival/market event in North America.
60000 Attendees
Frequency: November
Founded in 1986

9386
American Guild of Organists, National Conference
475 Riverside Drive
Suite 1260
New York, NY 10115
212-870-2310
FAX 212-870-2163
E-Mail: info@agohq.org
Home Page: www.agohq.org

James Thomashower, Executive Director
Jennifer Madden, Manager Membership
Harold Calhoun, Mgr Competitions

Over 20 exhibits and a workshop for professional, amatuer and student organists.
Frequency: Biennial

9387
American Harp Society National Conference
PO Box 38334
Los Angeles, CA 90038-0334
323-469-3050
FAX 323-469-3050
E-Mail: kmoon@uclalumni.net
Home Page: www.harpsociety.org

Christa Grix, National Conference Chair
Lynne Aspnes, Conference Program Advisory Chair

Conference will explore the mind-body-music connection, the creative process, and the connection between creativity and learning. The conference will include multiple disciplines including educators, composers, performers, therapists and practioners.
300 Attendees
Frequency: Annual
Founded in 1962

9388
American Institute of Organbuilders Annual Convention
American Institute of Organ Builders
PO Box 130982
Houston, TX 77219
713-529-2212
FAX 713-529-2212

E-Mail: pipes@pipeorgan.org
Home Page: convention.pipeorgan.org

Rene Marceau, Convention Committee Chairman

Annual convention includes supplier exhibits, technical lectures, sight-seeing tours, professional examinations, lectures and organ demonstrations.
Frequency: October
Founded in 1974
Mailing list available for rent: 350 names at $250 per M

9389
American Music Therapy Conference
National Music Therapy Association
8445 Colesville Road
Suite 1000
Silver Spring, MD 20910
301-589-3300
FAX 301-589-5175
Home Page: www.musictherapy.org

Seminar and exhibits of publications, musical instruments, books, learning aids and recordings.
Frequency: November

9390
American Musical Instrument Society
Guild Associates
389 Main Street
Suite 202
Malden, MA 2148
781-397-8870
FAX 781-397-8887
E-Mail: amis@guildassoc.com
Home Page: www.amis.org

Susan Thompson, Program Co-Chair
Kathryn Libin, Program Co-Chair

A broad range of topics include the history, design, use, care and acoustics of musical instruments in all cultures and from all periods.
Frequency: Annual

9391
American Musicological Society Annual Meeting
American Musicological Society
6010 College Station
Brunswick, ME 04011-8451
207-798-4243
877-679-7648
FAX 877-679-7648
E-Mail: ams@ams-net.org
Home Page: www.ams-net.org

Robert Judd, Executive Director

A society of professional musicologists and university educators. The annual meetings are held in the fall each year; 2007- Quebec; 2008- Nashville; 2009- Philadelphia.
Cost: $45.00
2000 Attendees
Frequency: Annual
Founded in 1948
Mailing list available for rent: 3515 names at $100 per M

9392
American Orff-Schulwerk Association National Conference
American Orff-Schulwerk Association
PO Box 391089
Cleveland, OH 44139-8089
440-543-5366
FAX 440-543-2687

E-Mail: info@aosa.org
Home Page: www.aosa2.org

Karen Medley, Conference Chair

One hundred exhibits of music, music books, software, insturments, and gifts in addition to National Conference of 2000+ music educators.
2400 Attendees
Frequency: November
Founded in 1969

9393
American Symphony Orchestra League Natina l Conference
33 W 60th Street
5th Floor
New York, NY 10023
212-262-5161
FAX 212-262-5198
E-Mail: league@symphony.org
Home Page: www.symphony.org

Stephen Alter, Advertising and Meetings Manager
Meghan Whitbeck, Advertising/Meetings Coordinator
Henry Fogel, President/CEO

Ninety booths incorporating all facets of classical music industries including industry suppliers, music publishers and computer technology.
1200 Attendees
Frequency: June

9394
Chamber Music America National Conference
Chamber Music America
305 7th Avenue
5th Floor
New York, NY 10001
212-242-2022
FAX 212-242-7955
Home Page: www.chamber-music.org

Susan Dadian, Program Director
Margaret M Lioi, CEO
Louise Smith, Chair
Cost: $235.00
700 Attendees
Frequency: Annual

9395
Chorus America Annual Conference
910 17th Street NW
Washington, DC 20006
202-776-0215
FAX 202-776-0224
E-Mail: service@chorusamerica.org
Home Page: www.chorusamerica.org

Ann Meier Baker, President/CEO
Melanie Garrett, Membership Services Manager

This four day conference offers seminars, workshops, concerts, expert consultations and peer-group meetings in a friendly, dynamic environment.
500 Attendees
Frequency: June
Printed in 2 colors on matte stock

9396
College Music Society/Association for Tech nology in Music
College Music Society
312 E Pine Street
Missoula, MT 59802
406-721-9616
FAX 406-721-9419

E-Mail: cms@music.org
Home Page: www.music.org

Robby D Gunstream, Executive Director
Peter Park, Professional Activities
Tod Trimble, Professional Development

Covers a broad array of topics such as advocacy, composition, cultural diversity, ethnomusicology, gender issues, music education, musicology, pedagogy, performance, music theory, teacher training, the latest technologies, and world music. Attendees includes adminstrators, publishers and music business personnel.
350 Attendees
Frequency: Annual
Founded in 1958

9397
Country Radio Seminar
Country Radio Broadcasters
819 18th Avenue S
Nashville, TN 37203
615-327-4487
FAX 615-329-4492
E-Mail: info@crb.org
Home Page: www.crb.org

Ed Salamon, Executive Director
Chasity Crouch, Business Manager

Conference attendess include major radio groups and record labels as well as independents, Features include exhibits, seminars and shows.
2300 Attendees
Frequency: Annual
Founded in 1969

9398
EXPO
Theatre Bay Area
870 Market Street
Suite 375
San Francisco, CA 94102-3002
415-430-1140
FAX 415-430-1145
E-Mail: dale@theatrebayarea.org
Home Page: www.theatrebayarea.org

Dale Albright, Director of Individual Services

Theatre Bay Area's EXPO is where attendees can meet those kinds of businesses that might offer services to the theatre community: theatre companies, actors, etc. There are also break-out sessions discussing issues of interest to the theatre community.
500+ Attendees
Frequency: May

9399
Folk Alliance Annual Meeting
Folk Alliance
510 South Main
1st Floor
Memphis, TN 38103
901-522-1170
FAX 901-522-1172
E-Mail: fa@folk.org
Home Page: www.folkalliance.org

200+ artists, 4 nights of show cases, four days of feature concerts, exhibit hall parties, panels, workshops, clinics and much more all under one roof.
Cost: $650.00
3000 Attendees

9400
Gospel Music Week
Gospel Music Association

1205 Division Street
Nashville, TN 37203-4011
615-242-0303
FAX 615-242-9374
Home Page: www.gospelmusic.org

Listen to new music as you experience over 100 eclectic performances throughout the week from today's top artists and tomorrow's hit-makers, invent new waysof enhancing your ministry through educational opportunities found in over 100 seminars and panels and through the sharing of your ideas with colleagues. Connect with your industry peers and friends at various networking opportunities including receptions, roundtables and more.
3,000 Attendees
Frequency: April
Founded in 1964

9401
Gospel Music Workshop America
speakers
preachers and over 100 courses offered during
preaching and various recordings b
Men's Division, Y
PO -ox -4635
Det-oit-
FAX MI - -
FAX 48208
Home Page: 313-898-6900

Social Media: *3, www.gmwanational.org*
, Rev Albert L
Jamison, Sr Chair, Board of Direct, Sheila
Smith Director Operations, Mark
Smith Convention Manager

Conferences open with a highly spirited service including Sacraments, music from choirs within the GMWA, Psalmists and the preachedr 'Word. This is followed by lectures
Circulation: manager@
ISSN: Augu-t

9402
Horns Over the Sea
Central Washington University Music Department
400 E University Way
Ellensburg, WA 98926-7458
509-963-1226
FAX 509-963-1239
E-Mail: gross@music.ucsb.edu
Home Page: www.hornsociety.org

Jeffrey Snedeker, President
Steven Gross, Conference Coordinator
Heidi Vogel, Membership Coordinator

Features renowned hornists, guest ensembles, recitals and master classes
450 Attendees
Frequency: August

9403
International Association of Jazz Educators Conference
International Association of Jazz Education
PO Box 724
Manhattan, KS 66505
785-776-8744
FAX 785-776-6190
E-Mail: info@iage.org
Home Page: www.iaje.org

Bill McFarlin, Executive Director

This four-day conference fatures a 75,000 square-food music industry exposition, commission premieres, technology presentations, research papers, award ceremo-

nies, and performances by over 500 of the world's most respected professional jazz groups and musicians.
Cost: $375.00
8000 Attendees
Frequency: Annual

9404
International Cinema Equipment (ICECO) Showest
Magna-Tech Electronic Company
5600 NW 32nd Avenue
Miami, FL 33142
305-573-7339
FAX 305-573-8101
E-Mail: www.iceco@iceco.com
Home Page: www.showest.com

Steven H Krams, President
Dara Reusch, VP
Julio Urbay, VP International Sales/Marketing
Fancisco Blanco, VP Technical Services
Arturo Quintero, Architectural Design/Development

Annual convention for the Motion Picture industry. It is an international gathering devoted exclusively to the movie business. It is also the single largest international gathering of motion picture professionals and theatre owners in the world, with delegates from more than 50 countries in attendance each year.
Frequency: March
Founded in 1975

9405
International Cinema Equipment Company ICECO Show East
Magna-Tech Electronic Company
5600 NW 32nd Avenue
Miami, FL 33142
305-573-7339
FAX 305-573-8101
E-Mail: iceco@aol.com
Home Page: www.iceco.com

Steven H Krams, President
Dara Reusch, VP
Julio Urbay, VP International Sales/Marketing
Francisco Blanco, VP/Technical Services
Arturo Quintero, Architectural Design & Development

This annual convention brings together over 1300 colleagues from the motion picture industry in the United States, Latin America and the Caribbean. The convention provides information on industry trends, screen films and product reels, state-of-the-art theatre equipment along with services and technologies vital to the industry.
1300 Attendees
Founded in 1975

9406
International Horn Competition of America
BGSU Continuing and Extended Education
14 College Park
Bowling Green, OH 43403-0200
509-963-1226
FAX 509-963-1239
Home Page: www.ihcamerica.org

Jeffrey Snedeker, President
Andrew Pelletier, Host

International competition specifically for the horn as a solo instrument.
450 Attendees
Frequency: July

9407

International Steel Guitar Convention

College Music Society
9535 Midland Boulevard
Saint Louis, MO 63114-3314
314-427-7794
FAX 314-427-0516
E-Mail: scotty@scottymusic.com
Home Page: www.music.org

Dewitt Scott Sr, President
Mary Scott, Secretary

Sixty-five booths that provide entertainment from steel guitarists and various instruments including the bass guitar.
3M Attendees
Frequency: August

9408

Mid-South Horn Conference

Central Washington University Music Department
400 E University Way
Ellensburg, WA 98926-7458
509-963-1226
FAX 509-963-1239
E-Mail: campbellel@umkc.edu
Home Page: www.hornsociety.org

Jeffrey Snedeker, President
Ellen Campbell, Event Host
Heidi Vogel, Membership Coordinator

Features renowned hornists, guest ensembles, recitals and master classes
450 Attendees
Frequency: March

9409

Midwest International Band & Orchestra Clinic

Midwest International Band & Orchestra Clinic
828 Davis Street
Suite 100
Evanston, IL 60201
847-424-4163
FAX 847-424-5185
E-Mail: info@midwestclinic.org
Home Page: www.midwestclinic.org

The purpose to the clinic is to raise the standards of music education, to develop new teaching techniqes, to examine, analyze, analyze and appraise literature dealing with music, demonstrations for the betterment of music education. 350 exhibitors, 565 booths, 30 concerts, and 50 instructional clinics.
Cost: $90.00
12000 Attendees
Frequency: December

9410

Moondance Film Festival

970 9th Street
Boulder, CO 80302
303-545-0202
E-Mail: director@moondancefilmfestival.com
Home Page: www.moondancefilmfestival.com

Elizabeth English, Festival Founder/Executive Director
Kyle/Erica Saylors, Festival Director/Event Coordinator
Karina Pyudik, Registration Coordinator
Douglis C Garvin, Special Events Coordinator
Roy Bodner, Publicist/Media Relations

The Festival's primary goal is to present films and scripts which have the power to raise awareness about vital social issues, educating writers and filmmakers, as well as festival audiences, and inspiring them to take positive action. The Festival's objective is to promote

and encourage independent filmmakers, screenwriters and playwrights, and the best works in films, screenplays, stageplays, TV scripts, radioplays, film scores, lyrics, librettos, music videos, and short stories.
Frequency: Annual

9411

Music Teachers National Association Convention

441 Vine Street
Suite 3100
Cincinnati, OH 45202
513-421-1420
888-512-5278
FAX 513-421-2503
E-Mail: mtnanet@mtna.org
Home Page: www.mtna.org

Gary L Ingle, Executive Director
Gail Berenson, President
Janice Wenger, VP

Atendees include independent music teachers, college faculty, students and parents from all over North America.
2500 Attendees
Frequency: Annual
Founded in 1876
Mailing list available for rent: 23000 names at $85 per M

9412

NAMM: International Music Products Association

5790 Armada Drive
Carlsbad, CA 92008-4608
760-438-8001
800-767-6266
FAX 760-438-7327
E-Mail: tradeshow@namm.com
Home Page: www.thenammshow.com

Joe Lamond, President

NAMM's trade shows are all about the experience. The experience of checking out the latest gear, of networking with other music product professionals, of attending free business-boosting classes. From the cook exhibits to the sizzling hot nightlife, music and music making always take center stage.
80000 Attendees
Frequency: January

9413

NDEO National Conference

National Dance Education Organization
8609 2nd Avenue
Suite 203 B
Silver Spring, MD 20910
301-585-2880
FAX 301-585-2888
E-Mail: info@ndeo.org
Home Page: www.ndeo.org

Susan McGreevy-Nichols, Executive Director
Jane Bonbright EdD, Executive Director
Patricia Cohen, Treasurer

Provides 200+ professional development sessions for artists, educators and administrators teaching or supporting dance education programs in PreK-12, colleges/universities, private studio/schools of dance, community centers and performing arts organizations.
800 Attendees
Frequency: Annual

9414

National Association for Music Education Conference

1806 Robert Fulton Drive
Reston, VA 20191-4348
703-860-4000
800-336-3768
FAX 703-860-1531
Home Page: www.menc.org

John J Mahlmann, Executive Director
Margaret Jamborsky, Director Meetings/Conventions
Elizabeth Lasko, Director Public Relations/Marketing
Amanda Kidwell, Membership Director

To advance music education by encouraging the study and making of music by all.
5M Attendees
Frequency: April

9415

National Association of Pastoral Musicians Convention

National Association of Pastoral Musicians
962 Wayne Avenue
Suite 210
Silver Spring, MD 20910-4461
240-247-3000
FAX 240-247-3001
Home Page: www.npm.org

J Michael McMahon, President
Kathleen Haley, Membership Services Director
Paul H Colloton, Continuing Education Director
Lowell Hickman, Executive Assistant/Office Manager

200 workshop sessions, 5 major addresses, music education classes, clinics, new music showcases and exhibits, musical performances, prayer and songs, adult and children's choirs, handbells, youth gatherings, Liturgical Space Tour.
4000 Attendees
Frequency: July

9416

National Association of Recording Merchandising Trade Show

9 Eves Drive
Suite 120
Marlton, NJ 08053-3130
856-596-2221
FAX 859-596-3268
E-Mail: still@narm.com
Home Page: www.narm.com

Jim Donio, President
Pat Daly, Meeting Planner
Evelyn Dichter, Membership Coordinatorsusan, VP Communications/Marketing

One-on-One meeting opportunities, welcome reception, keynote speakers, marketplace exhibits, live performances, forums, receptions and awards dinner
3M Attendees
Frequency: April/May

9417

National Association of Schools of Music Annual Meeting

National Association of Schools of Music
11250 Roger Bacon Drive
Suite 21
Reston, VA 20190-5248
703-437-0700
FAX 703-437-6312
E-Mail: info@arts-accredit.org
Home Page: www.arts-accredit.org

Don Gibson, President
Mark Wait, VP
Mellasenah Y Morris, Treasurer
Frequency: November

9418

National Black Theatre Festival

610 Coliseum Drive
Suite 1
Winston-Salem, NC 27106
336-723-2266
E-Mail: nbtf@bellsouth.net
Home Page: www.nbtf.org

Patrice Toney, President
Frequency: Annual, Winston-Salem

9419

National Opera Association Conference

National Opera Association
PO Box 60869
Canyon, TX 79016
806-651-2857
FAX 806-651-2958
E-Mail: rhansen@mail.wtamu.edu
Home Page: www.noa.org

Robert Hansen, Executive Director
Robert Thieme, Editor

Annual conference and exhibits of opera related equipment, supplies and services.
775 Attendees
Frequency: Annual
Founded in 1954

9420

National Square Dance Convention

PO Box 5790
Topeka, KS 66605-5790
317-635-4455
Home Page: www.57nsdc.com

250 booths and 250 exhibitors.
20M+ Attendees
Frequency: June

9421

New England Theatre Conference

215 Knob Hill Drive
Hamden, CT 6518
617-851-8535
FAX 203-288-5938
E-Mail: mail@netconline.org
Home Page: www.netconline.org

James Quinn, President
Jeffrey Watts, Executive VP
Charles Emmons, VP Administration/Finance

Promoting excellence in theatre, a conference of New England's oldest, largest regional theatre association.
800+ Attendees
Frequency: November
Founded in 1952

9422

Northeast Horn Workshop

Central Washington University Music Department
400 E University Way
Ellensburg, WA 98926-7458
509-963-1226
FAX 509-963-1239
E-Mail: rdodsonw@mansfield.edu
Home Page: www.hornsociety.org

Jeffrey Snedeker, President
Rebecca Dodson, Workshop Host
Heidi Vogel, Membership Coordinator

Features renowned hornists, guest ensembles, recitals and master classes
450 Attendees
Frequency: February

9423

Opera America Conference

Opera America
330 7th Avenue
16th Floor
New York, NY 10001-5248
212-796-8620
FAX 212-796-8631
Home Page: www.operaamerica.org

Session topics include identifying ways to harness the power of the best new technologies, how to reach current and prospective audiences, how to gain support from donors, and how to enrich the lives of children and adults who are now downloading podcasts, reading blogs, and designing their own multimedia communications.
275 Attendees
Frequency: April

9424

Performing Arts Facility Administrators Se minar

International Association of Assembly Managers
635 Fritz Drive
Suite 100
Coppell, TX 75019
972-906-7441
800-935-4226
FAX 972-906-7418
E-Mail: mike.meyers@iaam.org
Home Page: www.iaam.org

Steven Peters, President
Robyn Williams, First Vice President
Frequency: Annual

9425

Piano Technicians Guild Annual Convention

Piano Technicians Guild
4444 Forest Avenue
Kansas City, KS 66106
913-432-9975
FAX 913-432-9986
E-Mail: ptg@ptg.org
Home Page: www.ptg.org

Barbara J Cassaday, Executive Director
Allan Gilbreath RPT, President
Jim Coleman Jr RPT, VP

Come for the learning: find a hands-on class for your skill level; pick from sessions covering every type of piano service; squeeze in a mini-tech; prepare for the RPT exams; see the latest and greatest piano products.
650 Attendees
Frequency: June

9426

Prescott Park Arts Festival

Po Box 4370
Portsmouth, NH 03802-4370
603-436-2848
FAX 603-436-1034
E-Mail: info@prescottpark.org
Home Page: www.artfest.org

Deborah Lielasus Tombleson, Executive Director
Russell Bolian, Festival Production Manager

Provide a financially accessible, quality multi-arts festival to a diverse audience.

9427

Southeastern Theatre Conference

1217 W Bessemer Avenue
PO Box 9868
Greensboro, NC 27429-0868
336-272-3645
FAX 336-272-8810
E-Mail: setc@setc.org
Home Page: www.setc.org

David Thompson, President
Betsey Baun, Executive Director

Join over 4,000 Theatre Artists for education, exchanges, ideas, products, networking and great theatre. Convention activities include keynote speakers, auditions, guest speakers, festivals, design competition, commercial and educational expo exhibits, scholarship awards, social events and workshops.
4000+ Attendees
Frequency: March

9428

Sundance Film Festival

Sundance Institute
1825 Three Kings Drive
PO Box 684426
Park City, UT 84068
801-328-3456
FAX 801-575-5175
E-Mail: Institute@sundance.org
Home Page: www.sundance.org

Robert Redford, Founder

Annual festival held in Park City, Utah as a US showcase for American and International independent film. The Institute is dedicated to the development of artists of independent vision and the exhibition of their new work. Since its inception, the Institute has grown into an internationally recognized resource for thousands of independent artists.
Frequency: January
Founded in 1981

9429

Sweet Adelines International Convention

Sweet Adelines International
PO Box 470168
Tulsa, OK 74147-0168
918-622-1444
800-992-7464
FAX 918-665-0894

Kathy Hayes, Director Meetings/Corporate Service
Ruth Cameron, Meetings/Exhibits Coordinator
Jane Hanson, Marketing Coordinator
Connie Heyer, Membership Registrar
Kellye Kirchhoff, Director Communications

Heart-pounding chorus competitions, the rush and excitement of the quartet competition, education classes, shopping in the Harmony Bazaars and good times with old friends and new are all included in the International Convention.
8M Attendees
Frequency: October

9430

US Institute for Theatre Technology Annual Conference & Stage Expo

USITT
315 S Crouse Avenue
Suite 200
Syracuse, NY 13210
315-463-6463
800-938-7488
FAX 315-463-6525

E-Mail: info@office.usitt.org
Home Page: www.usitt.org

Carl Lefko, President
Patricia Dennis, Secretary
Travis DeCastro, Treasurer

The Conference offers over 175 sessions featuring design, technology, costume, sound, architecture, management, engineering, and production. The Stage Expo showcases businesses, products, services, and eductional opportunities in the performing arts and entertainment industry. With over 150 exhibitors, Stage Expo provides conference attendees with the opportunity to see the newest and best products and services on the market today.
Cost: $314.00
3800 Attendees
Frequency: March

9431
Winter Music Conference
3450 NE
12th Terrace
Fort Lauderdale, FL 33334
954-563-4444
FAX 954-563-1599
E-Mail: info@wintermusicconference.com
Home Page: www.wintermusicconference.com

Regarded as the singular networking event in the dance music industry, attracting professionals from over 60 different countries.

9432
World of Bluegrass
International Bluegrass Music Association
2 Music Circle South
Suite 100
Nashville, TN 37203
615-256-3222
888-438-4262
FAX 615-256-0450
E-Mail: info@ibma.org
Home Page: www.ibma.org

Dan Hays, Executive Director
Nancy Cardwell, Special Projects Coordinator
Jill Snider, Member/Convention Services

Build relationships with event producers, record label reps, agents and managers, broadcasters, association leaders, educators, the media, instrument builders, artists and composers. Educational and networking events like seminars, facilitated discussions and workshops are the primary focus of the conference. Browse through 100+ booths in the Exhibit Hall. You will hear bluegrass music around the clock for seven days. The Highpoint of the Conference is the International Bluegrass Music Awards.
1,800 Attendees
Frequency: October

Directories & Databases

9433
Academy Players Directory
2210 W Olive Avenue
Suite 320
Burbank, CA 91506
310-247-3058
FAX 310-550-5034
E-Mail: info@playersdirectory.com
Home Page: www.playersdirectory.com

The Players Directory appeared in 1937 as the first reliable casting directory that listed both featured stars and extras. Today, more than 16,000 actors are included.
Cost: $75.00
Founded in 1937

9434
American Association of Community Theatre Membership Directory
8402 Briar Wood Circle
Lago Vista, TX 78645-4118
512-267-0711
866-687-2228
FAX 512-267-0712
E-Mail: info@aact.org
Home Page: www.aact.org

Julie Angelo, Executive Director
Mary Britt, President
Carole Ries, VP Public Relations
Frank Peot, Secretary
Gary Walker, Treasurer

The database includes addresses for over 7,000 community theatre organizations in the USA. Only available to members.
Mailing list available for rent: 10000 names at $180 per M

9435
American Music Center Directory
American Music Center
322 8th Ave
Suite 1001
New York, NY 10001-6774
212-366-5263
FAX 212-366-5265
E-Mail: center@amc.net
Home Page: www.amc.net

Joanne Cossa, Executive Director
Lyn Liston, Director New Music Information Svce
Peter Shavitz, Director Development
Lisa Taliano, Director Information Technology
Carlos Camposeco, Director Finance and Administration

Mailing lists include all United States members; all International and United States members; Composer Members in the United States; Members in the New York City Metropolitan area; and Members in the United States and Canada.

9436
American Society of Composers, Authors and Publishers
American Soc. of Composers, Authors & Publishers
1 Lincoln Plz
New York, NY 10023-7097
212-621-6027
FAX 212-724-9064
E-Mail: ACE@ascap.com
Home Page: www.ascap.com

Marilyn Bergman, President
Johnny Mandel, Writer Vice Chairman
Jay Morgenstern, Publisher Vice Chairman
Arnold Broido, Treasurer
Kathy Spanberger, Secretary

ASCAP created the dial-up ACE system as a useful tool for music professionals. An enhanced World Wide Web version of this database is now available. The database contains information on all compositions in the ASCAP repertory which have appeared in any of ASCAP's domestic surveys, including foreign compositions licensed by the ASCAP in the United States.
Frequency: Annual
Founded in 1993

9437
Americans for the Arts Field Directory
Americans for the Arts
1 E 53rd St
6th Floor
New York, NY 10022-4242
212-223-2787
FAX 212-980-4857
Home Page: www.artsactionfund.org

Suzanne Niemeyer, Editor
Robert L Lynch, President/CEO
Liz Bartolomeo, Public Relations/Marketing Coord
Chad Bauman, Director Print/Multimedia Commun
Graham Dunstan, Assoc Director Publication Sales

A must-have resource for anyone working in the arts and community development. The directory provides contact information for local, state, regional, and national arts service organizations-more than 4,000 entries broken down by state and region. Also includes contact information for professional consultants working in the nonprofit arts field. A great networking tool.
Cost: $35.00
262 Pages

9438
Annual Index to Motion Picture Credits
Academy of Motion Picture Arts and Sciences
8949 Wilshire Blvd
Beverly Hills, CA 90211-1972
310-247-3000
FAX 310-271-3395
Home Page: www.oscars.org

The Index is closely tied to the annual Academy Awards presentation. As part of the Academy Awards process, the Academy of Motion Picture Arts and Sciences gathers credits for each film hoping to qualify for awards. These credits, compiled and verified by the film's producer or distributor, are the core of the Annual Index and IMPC database. In addition to personal credits, IMPC also records index production and releasing dates, MPAA ratings, running times, color, language, and more.
Frequency: Annual
ISBN: 0-942102-37-1
ISSN: 0163-5123
Founded in 1934

9439
Association of Performing Arts Presenters Membership Directory
APAP
1211 Connecticut Ave NW
Suite 200
Washington, DC 20036-2716
202-833-2787
888-820-2787
FAX 202-833-1543
E-Mail: info@artspresenters.org
Home Page: www.artspresenters.org

Sandra Gibson, President
Sean Handerhan, Marketing

An invaluable resource for keeping in touch with colleagues. Puts more than 1,450 presenters, service organizations, artists, management companies, consultants, and vendors at your fingertips. An excellent networking tool for everyone on your staff.
1900 Members
Frequency: Annual
Founded in 1957

9440
AudArena International Guide
Billboard Directories

PO Box 15158
North Hollywood, CA 91615
818-487-4582
800-562-2706
E-Mail: info@billboard.com
Home Page: www.billboard.com/directories

Arkady Fridman, Inside Sales Manager

Complete data on over 4,400 venues worldwide, including Amphitheaters, Arenas, Stadiums, Sports Facilities, Concert Halls and New Constructions. Also includes complete listings of companies offering services to the touring industry in the Facilty Buyer's Guide. The guide features contact names, phone and fax numbers, e-mail and web site addresses, market population, facility capacities and staging configurations, and rental fees and ticketing rights.
Cost: $99.00
325 Pages
Frequency: Annual

9441_____

Billboard Subscriber File
Edith Roman Associates
PO Box 1556
Pearl River, NY 10965
845-620-9000
800-223-2194
FAX 845-620-9035
E-Mail: john.logiudice@edithroman.com
Home Page: www.edithroman.com

Steve Roberts, President
Wayne Nagrowski, E-Mail List Info Contact

Directory listees include booking agencies and agents, clubs, music publishers, promoters, radio stations, record labels, sound and lighting services, retailers, video, venues, wholesalers, equipment and manufacturing and general services.
Frequency: Annual

9442_____

Blu-Book Production Directory
Hollywood Creative Directory
5055 Wilshire Blvd
Los Angeles, CA 90036-6103
323-525-2369
800-815-0503
FAX 323-525-2398
E-Mail: hcdcustomerservice@hcdonline.com
Home Page: www.hcdonline.com

Valencia McKinley, Manager

A comprehensive directory for professionals in the production and post-production industries. Provides current contact information needed to produce a film, TV program, commercial, or music video. The directory contains a special tabbed section on premier below-the-line craft professionals, along with selective credits, and has been expanded to include New York production facilities and services, making it one of the only bi-coastal resources of its kind.
Cost: $39.95
450 Pages
Frequency: Annual
ISBN: 1-928936-44-X

9443_____

Bluegrass Resource Directory
International Bluegrass Music Association
2 Music Cir S
Suite 100
Nashville, TN 37203-4381
615-256-3222
888-438-4262
FAX 615-256-0450

E-Mail: info@ibma.org
Home Page: www.ibma.org

Member Directory can only be accessed by IBMA members.
Cost: $25.00
88 Pages
Frequency: Annual

9444_____

Boxoffice: Buyers Directory Issue
Boxoffice
PO Box 1634
Des Plains, IL 60019
212-627-7000
Home Page: www.boxoffice.com

Peter Cane, Publisher
Joe Policy, CEO
Annlee Ellingson, Editor
Francesca Dinglasan, Senior Editor
Bob Vale, VP Advertising and Sales

Guide to equipment, supplies and services. Available to subscribers of Boxoffice Magazine.
Cost: $59.95
Frequency: Annual
Founded in 1990

9445_____

Boxoffice: Circuit Giants
Boxoffice
PO Box 1634
Des Plains, IL 60019
212-627-7000
Home Page: www.boxoffice.com

Peter Cane, Publisher
Joe Policy, CEO
Annlee Ellingson, Editor
Francesca Dinglasan, Senior Editor
Bob Vale, VP Advertising and Sales

Directory of the largest exhibition chains. Available to subscribers of Boxoffice magazine
Cost: $59.95
Frequency: Annual
Founded in 1990

9446_____

Boxoffice: Distributor Directory
Boxoffice
PO Box 1634
Des Plains, IL 60019
212-627-7000
Home Page: www.boxoffice.com

Peter Cane, Publisher
Joe Policy, CEO
Annlee Ellingson, Editor
Francesca Dinglasan, Senior Editor
Bob Vale, VP Advertising and Sales

Listings of studio and independent film suppliers. Available to subscribers of Boxoffice magazine
Cost: $59.95
Frequency: Annual
Founded in 1990

9447_____

Complete Catalogue of Plays
Dramatists Play Service
440 Park Ave S
New York, NY 10016-8012
212-683-8960
FAX 212-213-1539
E-Mail: publications@dramatists.com
Home Page: www.dramatists.com

Stephen Fultan, President
Rafael J Rivera, VP Finance/Administration
Michael Q Fellmeth, VP Publications/IT
Tamra Feifer, Director Operations

The Complete Catalogue is published in odd years and the Supplement of New Plays in even years. Both books are distributed, without charge, to current customers in the Fall of each year.
412 Pages

9448_____

Costume Designers Guild Directory
Costumer Designers Guild
4730 Woodman Avenue
Suite 430
Sherman Oaks, CA 91423-2400
818-905-1557
FAX 818-905-1560
E-Mail: cdgia@earthlink.net
Home Page: www.costumedesignersguild.com

Cheryl Downey, Executive Director
Deborah N Landis, President

Directory includes members' names, classification, and other statistical information.
Frequency: Annual

9449_____

Dance Annual Directory
Dance Magazine
333 7th Ave
11th Floor
New York, NY 10001-5109
212-979-4803
FAX 212-979-4817
E-Mail: emacel@dancemagazine.com
Home Page: www.dancemagazine.com

Karla Johnson, Publisher
Emily Macel, Editor
Karen Hildebrand, Editorial Director
Wendy Perron, Editor-in-Chief
Hanna Rubin, Managing Editor

Reach 300,000+ dancers, dance teachers, and dance professionals in the dance world.
Cost: $100.00
Frequency: Annual

9450_____

Dance Magazine College Guide
Dance Magazine
110 William St
23rd Floor
New York, NY 10038-3900
646-459-4800
FAX 212-979-4817
E-Mail: subscriptions@dancemagazine.com
Home Page: www.dancemagazine.com

Karla Johnson, President
Karen Hildebrand, Editorial Director
Wendy Perron, Editor-in-Chief
Hanna Rubin, Managing Editor
Kate Lydon, Education Editor

With over 500+ listings, Dance Magazine College Guide is a comprehensive source for dance degree programs in higher education. Find application deadlines and audition dates. Get student perspectives and career advice. Online database offers the ability to identify programs that match an individual's personal criteria for degree, type of dance, location, department size, tuition and more.
Cost: $29.95
Frequency: Annual

9451

Dance Magazine: Summer Dance Calendar Issue

Dance Magazine
33 W 60th Street
Floor 10
New York, NY 10023-7905
212-245-9050
800-331-1750
Home Page: www.dancemagazine.com

A list of dance workshops and special programs for students are listed.
Cost: $3.95
Frequency: Annual
Circulation: 100,000

9452

Dance/USA Annual Directory and List-Serv

Dance/USA
1111 16th St NW
Suite 300
Washington, DC 20036-4830
202-833-1717
FAX 202-833-2686
E-Mail: danceusa@danceusa.org
Home Page: www.danceusa.org

Andrea Snyder, Executive Director
Tom Thielen, Director Finance/Operations
Katherine Fabian, Membership Manager

On-going list-servs keep many peer councils in touch throughout the year, by providing a quick and easy connection to peer counseling when members have an immediate question or problem. Information about dance companies, schools, presenters, service organizations and commercial suppliers is included in the annual copy of Dance Annual Directory.
Frequency: Annual
Circulation: 400+

9453

Directors Guild of America Directory of Members

Directors Guild of America
7920 W Sunset Blvd
Los Angeles, CA 90046-3347
310-289-2000
800-421-4173
FAX 310-289-2029
Home Page: www.dga.org

Jay Roth, President
Morgan Rumpf, Director Communications/Media Relat
Paul Zepp, Membership Administrator
Darrell L Hop, Editor DGA Monthly/Website

The DGA represents Film and Television Directors, Unit Production Managers, First Assistant Directors, Second Assistant Directors, Technical Coordinators and Tape Associate Directors, Stage Managers and Production Associates. The Directory is available in print and on-line
Cost: $25.00
Frequency: Annual

9454

Directory of Theatre Training Programs

Theatre Directories
P.O.Box 2409
Manchester Center, VT 05255-2409
802-867-9333
FAX 802-867-2297
E-Mail: info@theatredirectories.com
Home Page: www.theatredirectories.com

Peg Lyons, Editor
PJ Tumielewicz, Editor

Profiles admissions, tuition, faculty, curriculum, facilities, productions and philosophy of training at 475 programs in the US, Canada and abroad: Colleges, Universities, Conservatories, Undergraduate and Graduate degrees. Includes Combined Auditions information. Indexed by degrees offered in each program.
Cost: $39.50
ISBN: 0-933919-61-1

9455

Dramatics College Theatre Directory

Educational Theatre Association
2343 Auburn Ave
Cincinnati, OH 45219-2819
513-421-3900
FAX 513-421-7077
Home Page: www.edta.org

Michael Peitz, Executive Director

Lists more than 250 college, university, and conservatory theatre programs, offering a sketch of each based on information provided by the schools. The listings can be used to measure each school against one's own criteria for location, setting, courses of study, admission requirements, and cost. Find out which programs offer merit scholarships and grants and how these funds are awarded. Use the contact information to get in touch with the programs that seem to offer the best fit for your needs
Cost: $9.00
Frequency: Annual

9456

Dramatics Magazine: Summer Theatre Directory

Educational Theatre Association
2343 Auburn Ave
Cincinnati, OH 45219-2819
513-421-3900
FAX 513-421-7077
Home Page: www.edta.org

Michael Peitz, Executive Director

Lists nearly 200 summer theatre programs and stock companies, offering a sketch of each based on factual information provided by the schools, camps, and theatre companies. The listings can be used to measure each program against one's own criteria for location, setting, housing, courses of study, admission requirements and fees.
Cost: $9.00
Frequency: Annual

9457

Dramatist's Sourcebook

Theatre Communications Group
520 8th Ave
24th Floor
New York, NY 10018-8666
212-609-5900
FAX 212-609-5901
E-Mail: tcg@tcg.org
Home Page: www.tcg.org

Theresa Eyring, Executive Director
Kelly Haydon, Database Manager
Jennifer Cleary, Director Membership
Terence Nemeth, Publisher
Kathy Sova, Editorial Director

Completely revised, with more than 900 opportunities for playwrights, translators, composers, lyricists, and librettists, as well as opportunities for screen, radio, and television writers. Thoroughly indexed, with a calendar of deadlines. The Sourcebook contains scrip-submis-

sion procedures for more than 350 theatres seeking new plays; guidelines for more than 150 prizes; and sections on agents, fellowships and residencies.
Cost: $22.95
Frequency: Annual
ISBN: 1-559362-94-4
Founded in 1980

9458

Dramatists Guild Annual Resource Directory

Dramatists Guild of America
1501 Broadway
Suite 701
New York, NY 10036-5505
212-398-9366
FAX 212-944-0420
Home Page: www.dramaguild.com

Ralph Sevush, Executive Director

The Resource Directory is an annual sourcebook available only to Guild members, sent automatically as one of the privileges of Guild members. It includes lists of conferences and festivals, contests, producers, publishers, agents and attorneys, fellowships and grants, and workshops throughout the US and the world.
Frequency: Annual

9459

Editors Guild Directory

Motion Picture Editors Guild
7715 Sunset Boulevard
Suite 200
Hollywood, CA 90046
323-876-4770
800-705-8700
FAX 323-876-0861
E-Mail: mail@editorsguild.com
Home Page: www.editorsguild.com

Ron Kutak, Executive Director
Tomm Carroll, Publications Director
Serena Kungr, Director Membership Services
Adriana Iglesias-Dietl, Membership Administrator
Tris Carpenter, Manager

An invaluable resource for producers, directors and post production professionals alike. It lists contact, credit, award and classification information for all of the Guild's active members at the time of publication, as well as a list of Oscar and Emmy winners for every year since the awards began. It also includes a retirees section.
Cost: $25.00
Frequency: Bi-Annual
Founded in 1994

9460

Encyclopedia of Exhibition

National Association of Theatre Owners
750 1st St Ne
Suite 1130
Washington, DC 20002-4241
202-962-0054
FAX 202-962-0370
E-Mail: nato@natodc.com
Home Page: www.natoonline.org

John Fithian, President
G Kendrick Macdowell, VP
Kathy Conroy, Executive Director

Publication contains listings of North American cinema operators including contact and staff information, an index of companies that service the cinema industry, exhibition statistics, box office data and more.
Cost: $500.00

29000 Members
474 Pages
Frequency: Annual
Founded in 1948
Printed in on glossy stock

9461
Fame Index
Hollywood Madison Group
11684 Ventura Boulevard
#258
Studio City, CA 91604-2499
818-762-8008
FAX 818-762-8089
Home Page: holllywood-madison.com

Jonathan Holiff, Founder/President/CEO

Search over 10,000 celebrities from actors to athletes to find every performer who meets your needs. The Index has more than 250 searchable criteria including: age, sex, children, birthplace, genre, fees, ethnicity/heritage, biography, statistics, interests, hobbies, sports, personality attributes, charity affiliations, medical conditions, and endorsement histories. Contact information includes agent, manager, publicist, business manager, attorney, and personal assistant.
Founded in 1996

9462
Feedback Theatrebooks and Prospero Press
Feedback Theatrebooks & Prospero Press
PO Box 174
Brooklin, ME 4616
207-359-2781
FAX 207-359-5532

Publishes theatre histories, cookbooks, directories, anthologies of plays, plays published before WWII, and format guidelines for playwrights.

9463
Film Journal: Distribution Guide Issue
Film Journal International
770 Broadway
5th Floor
New York, NY 10003-9595
646-654-7680
FAX 646-654-7694
Home Page: www.filmjournal.com

Robert Sunshine, Publisher/Editor
Kevin Lally, Executive Editor
Rex Roberts, Associate Editor
Andrew Sunshine, Advertising Director
Katey Rich, Editorial Assistant

The International Distribution and subdistribution Guide supplements the regular monthly Buying and Booking Guide. It is designed to furnish ready reference information on the who, what, where and how of theatrical sales. It lists the names, addresses, personnel, telephone numbers and product of domestic and international distributors, both major and independent, along with similar information on regional exchanges together with national companies they handle.
Frequency: Annual

9464
Film Journal: Equipment Guide
Film Journal International
770 Broadway
5th Floor
New York, NY 10003-9595
646-654-7680
FAX 646-654-7694
Home Page: www.filmjournal.com

Robert Sunshine, Publisher/Editor
Kevin Lally, Executive Editor
Robin Klamfoth, Advertising Director
Rex Roberts, Associate Editor
Katey Rich, Editorial Assistant

The Equipment, Concessions and Services Guide is designed to provide ready reference information on the theatrical equipment and concessions industry. It lists in detail the company names, addresses, telephone numbers, personnel, affiliations and products of equipment and concession manufacturers and service companies, along with similar information on US and foreign service dealers and suppliers, arranged in alphabetical order according to state or country.
Frequency: Annual

9465
Film Journal: Exhibition Guide
Film Journal International
770 Broadway
5th Floor
New York, NY 10003-9595
646-654-7680
FAX 646-654-7694
Home Page: www.filmjournal.com

Robert Sunshine, Publisher/Editor
Kevin Lally, Executive Editor
Robin Klamfoth, Advertising Director
Rex Roberts, Associate Editor
Katey Rich, Editorial Assistant

The exhibition Guide is an alphabetical listing designed to provide ready reference information on the leading theatrical motion picture circuits. It lists in comprehensive detail such data as company names, addresses and phone numbers, total screens and new screens projected, division office locations, top personnel, recent circuit acquisitions, and a state-by-state breakdown of screens.
Frequency: Annual

9466
Film Superlist: Motion Pictures in the Public Domain
Hollywood Film Archive
8391 Beverly Blvd
PMB 321
Los Angeles, CA 90048-2633
323-655-4968

Richard Baer, Executive Director

Created by Walter E. Hurst and updated by Richard Baer. 1992-1994. Three volumes to date, covering 50,000 films from the years 1894-1939, 1940-1949 and 1950-1959.

9467
Gospel Music Industry Directory
Gospel Music Association
1205 Division St
Nashville, TN 37203-4011
615-242-0303
FAX 615-254-9755
E-Mail: GMAToday@aol.com
Home Page: www.gospelmusic.org

John Styll, President

Formerly called the Networking Guide, the GMA Music Industry Directory is a comprehensive listing of Christian and Gospel music artists, managers, booking agents, record companies, publishing companies and more. Active GMA Professional members get a copy of the directory free. Associate and Student GMA members can purchase one for a discounted rate.

9468
Grey House Performing Arts Directory
Grey House Publishing
4919 Route 22
PO Box 56
Amenia, NY 12501
518-789-8700
800-562-2139
FAX 845-373-6390
E-Mail: books@greyhouse.com
Home Page: www.greyhouse.com

Leslie Mackenzie, Publisher
Richard Gottlieb, Editor

The Grey House Performing Arts Directory is the most comprehensive resource covering the Performing Arts. This important directory provides current information on over 8,500 Dance Companies, Instrumental Music Programs, Opera Companies, Choral Groups, Theater Companies, Performing Arts Series, Performing Arts Facilities and Artist Management Groups.
Cost: $185.00
1200 Pages
Frequency: Annual
ISBN: 1-592373-76-3
Founded in 1981

9469
Hollywood Creative Directory
VNU Business Media
5055 Wilshire Blvd
Los Angeles, CA 90036-6100
323-525-1752
800-815-0503
FAX 323-525-2398
E-Mail: hcdcustomerservice@hcdonline.com
Home Page: www.hcdonline.com

Contact information for studios and networks, film and TV executives, production companies, independent producers, TV shows and staff, projects in development, production tracking and selected credits. Includes 11,000 producers and studio and network executives, more than 2,000 production companies, mobile content producers. Updated mid-January, end of May and end of September.
Cost: $64.95
480 Pages
Frequency: 3 per year
ISBN: 1-928936-50-4

9470
Hollywood Distribution Directory
Hollywood Creative Directory
5055 Wilshire Blvd
Los Angeles, CA 90036-6103
323-525-2369
800-815-0503
FAX 323-525-2398
E-Mail: hcdcustomerservice@hcdonline.com
Home Page: www.hcdonline.com

Valencia McKinley, Manager

Expanded listings include more entertainment finance companies and over 300 new domestic and international distributors, plus newly added information for mobile and internet distributors. The directory includes more than 2,000 companies, more than 10,000 names and job title information, domestic and international distributors, mobile/internet distributors, entertainment financing companies, TV syndicatoprs, network and cable channels, film festivals/markets and more. Published every summer.
Cost: $59.95

404 Pages
Frequency: Annual
ISBN: 1-928936-52-0

9471
Hollywood Music Industry Directory
Hollywood Creative Directory
5055 Wilshire Blvd
Los Angeles, CA 90036-6103
323-525-2369
800-815-0503
FAX 323-525-2398
E-Mail: hcdcustomerservice@hcdonline.com
Home Page: www.hcdonline.com

Valencia McKinley, Manager

For aspiring musicians and professionals, this directory will assist in finding record executives, A&R staff, soundtrack personnel, music publishers, music supervisors and recording studios. Accurate and complete contact information including company name, job title, address, phone, fax, email, assistants' names, and web site. Every individual's name is indexed.
Cost: $39.95
350 Pages
Frequency: Annual
ISBN: 1-928936-45-8

9472
Hollywood Representation Directory
Hollywood Creative Directory
5055 Wilshire Blvd
Los Angeles, CA 90036-6103
323-525-2369
800-815-0503
FAX 323-525-2398
E-Mail: hcdcustomerservice@hcdonline.com
Home Page: www.hcdonline.com

Valencia McKinley, Manager

A complete, reliable and comprehensive reference book on Hollywood talent and literary agents and managers. In addition to talent agents and managers, the directory has been expanded to include separate tab sections an Entertainment Attorneys, Publicity Companies and Casting Directors. Released every Arpil and October. Includes over 2,000 companies, over 7,000 individuals, as well as addresses, staff and titles, e-mail addresses and web sites, phone and fax numbers.
Cost: $64.95
440 Pages
Frequency: Bi-Annual
ISBN: 1-928936-47-4

9473
International Buyers Guide
Billboard Directories
PO Box 15158
North Hollywood, CA 91615
818-487-4582
800-562-2706
E-Mail: info@billboard.com
Home Page: www.billboard.com/directories

Arkady Fridman, Inside Sales Manager

A must-have resource for doing business in the music industry, covers every aspect of the recording business worldwide. The latest edition includes contact information on: record labels, video and digital music companies, distributors and importers/exporters; music publishers and rights organizations - blank media manufacturers, pressing plants and services; manufacturers of jewel boxes and other packaging and equipment services; and suppliers of store fixtures, security and accessories.
Cost: $179.00

340 Pages
Frequency: Annual

9474
International Motion Picture Alamanc
Quigley Publishing Company
64 Wintergreen Lane
Groton, MA 1450
860-228-0247
800-231-8239
FAX 860-228-0157
E-Mail: quigleypub@aol.com
Home Page: www.quigleypublishing.com

William J Quigley, President/Publisher
Eileen Quigley, Editor

Contains over 400 pages of biographies and 500 pages of reference material. From 1928 to the present day, the complete set contains the biography of everyone who has ever been of importance to the Industry. Each edition includes thousands of company listings, credits for current films and films released in the prior ten years, statistics and awards and complete coverage of all aspects of the indiustry, including production, distribution and exhibition.
Cost: $175.00
Frequency: Annual

9475
International Talent and Touring Guide
Billboard Directories
PO Box 15158
North Hollywood, CA 91615
818-487-4582
800-562-2706
E-Mail: info@billboard.com
Home Page: www.billboard.com/directories

Arkady Fridman, Inside Sales Manager

A reference guide for anyone who books, promotes or manages talent. Features over 30,000 listings, including 12,900 artists, managers and agents worldwide, including the USA and Canada. The guide includes contact names, phone and fax numbers, e-mail and website addresses, artists and their record labels, managers and agents, tour services and merchandise, sound and lighting vendors, equipment and instrument rentals, limo rentals, security services, plus national promoters and their key personnel
Cost: $139.00
242 Pages
Frequency: Annual

9476
International Television and Video Almanac
Quigley Publishing Company
64 Wintergreen Lane
Groton, MA 1450
860-228-0247
800-231-8239
FAX 860-228-0157
E-Mail: quigleypub@aol.com
Home Page: www.quigleypublishing.com

William J Quigley, President/Publisher
Eileen Quigley, Editor

Each edition contains over 400 pages of biographies and an additional 500 pages of reference material on television programs, broadcast, cable and satellie, production services, the video industry, statistics and awards. Included are detailed listings for thousands of companies, as well as coverage outside the United States.
Cost: $175.00

Frequency: Annual
Founded in 1955

9477
Keyboard Teachers Association International
Dr. Albert DeVito
361 Pin Oak Lane
Westbury, NY 11590-1941
516-333-3236
FAX 516-997-9531

Albert DeVito, President

Music teachers and those related to keeping members updated as to activity going on in music world.
Frequency: Quarterly
Founded in 1963

9478
MLA Membership Handbook
Music Library Association
8551 Research Way
Suite 180
Middleton, WI 53562
608-836-5825
FAX 608-831-8200
E-Mail: mla.areditions.com
Home Page: www.musiclibraryassoc.org

Philip Vandermeer, President

A mailing list that is available for rental in a variety of formats.
Cost: $25.00

9479
Mini Reviews
Cineman Syndicate
31 Purchase St
Suite 203
Rye, NY 10580-3013
914-967-5353
Home Page: www.minireviews.com

John P McCarthy, Editor

An easy to read, easy to use guide for movie watchers updated weekly.
Frequency: Weekly
Founded in 2000

9480
Money for Film and Video Artists
Americans for the Arts
1 E 53rd St
6th Floor
New York, NY 10022-4242
212-223-2787
FAX 212-980-4857
Home Page: www.artsactionfund.org

Suzanne Niemeyer, Editor
Robert L Lynch, President/CEO
Liz Bartolomeo, Public Relations/Marketing Coord
Chad Bauman, Director Print/Multimedia Commun
Graham Dunstan, Assoc Director Publication Sales

A comprehensive resource guide to fellowships, grants, awards, low-cost facilities, emergency assistance programs, technical assistance, and support services. Entries include contact information; type of award and/or scope of service; eligibilty requirements; application procedures; deadlines and more.
Cost: $14.95
317 Pages
ISBN: 1-879903-09-1

9481

Money for International Exchange in the Arts
Americans for the Arts
1 E 53rd St
6th Floor
New York, NY 10022-4242
212-223-2787
FAX 212-980-4857
Home Page: www.artsactionfund.org

Suzanne Niemeyer, Editor
Robert L Lynch, President/CEO
Liz Bartolomeo, Public Relations/Marketing Coord
Chad Bauman, Director Print/Multimedia Commun
Graham Dunstan, Assoc Director Publication Sales

This resource includes grants, fellowships and awards for travel and work abroad; support and technical assistance for international touring and exchange; international artists' residencies; programs that support artists' professional development, and more. Indexed by region, discipline and type of support.
Cost: $14.95
122 Pages
ISBN: 1-879903-01-6

9482

Money for Performing Artists
Americans for the Arts
1 E 53rd St
6th Floor
New York, NY 10022-4242
212-223-2787
FAX 212-980-4857
Home Page: www.artsactionfund.org

Suzanne Niemeyer, Editor
Robert L Lynch, President/CEO
Liz Bartolomeo, Public Relations/Marketing Coord
Chad Bauman, Director Print/Multimedia Commun
Graham Dunstan, Assoc Director Publication Sales

Lists awards, grants, fellowships, competitions, auditions, workshops, and artists' colonies, as well as emergency and technical assistance programs.
Cost: $12.00
240 Pages
ISBN: 0-915400-96-0
Founded in 1991

9483

Money for Visual Arts
Americans for the Arts
1 E 53rd St
6th Floor
New York, NY 10022-4242
212-223-2787
FAX 212-980-4857
Home Page: www.artsactionfund.org

Suzanne Niemeyer, Editor
Robert L Lynch, President/CEO
Liz Bartolomeo, Public Relations/Marketing Coord
Chad Bauman, Director Print/Multimedia Commun
Graham Dunstan, Assoc Director Publication Sales

A guide to grants, fellowships, awards, artist colonies, emergency and technical assistance, and support services. Entries include contact information; type of award and/or scope of service; eligibility requirements; application procedures; deadlines; and more.
Cost: $14.95
340 Pages

9484

Motion Picture TV and Theatre Directory
Motion Picture Enterprises

PO Box 276
Tarrytown, NY 10591-0276
212-245-0969
FAX 212-245-0974
E-Mail: info@mpe.net
Home Page: www.mpe.net

Neal R Pilzer, Publisher

The Guide is mailed to members of 59 trade associations, unions and professional societies; decision-makers at advertising agencies, production companies, TV stations, and government agencies; faculty and students of nearly 200 film schools; and other prime purchasers of film and TV equipment and services nationwide. Companies are listed both by category and company name. Listings include company name, address and telephone number as well as fax numbers, e-mail addresses, and web site URLs.
Cost: $18.80
335 Pages
Frequency: Annual
Circulation: 82500
Founded in 1963

9485

Movie World Almanac
Hollywood Film Archive
8391 Beverly Blvd
PMB 321
Los Angeles, CA 90048-2633
323-655-4968

Richard Baer, Executive Director

Lists over 200 major American and foreign film distributors who handle old and contemporary films.

9486

Music Library Association Membership Directory
Music Library Association
8551 Research Way
Suite 180
Middleton, WI 53562
608-836-9000
FAX 608-831-8200
E-Mail: mla@areditions.com
Home Page: www.musiclibraryassoc.org

Bonna Boettcher, President

The MLA mailing list is available for rental in a variety of formats. Members include music librarians, librarians who work with music as part of their responsibilities, composers and music scholars, and others interested in the program of the association.

9487

Musical America Directory
Musical America
400 Windsor Corporate Center
Suite 200
East Windsor, NJ 8520
609-371-7877
800-221-5488
FAX 609-371-7879
E-Mail: info@musicalamerica.com
Home Page: www.musicalamerica.com

Lynn Wall, Subscription Information
Bob Hudoba, Contact

Provides thousands of names, phone numbers, addresses, and Email and Web site addresses for manangers, orchestras, opera companies, festivals, presenters, venues and more around the world.
Cost: $125.00

9488

Musical America International Directory of the Performing Arts
Commonwealth Business Media
50 Millstone Rd
Suite 200
East Windsor, NJ 08520-1418
609-371-7700
800-221-5488
FAX 609-371-7879
E-Mail: info@musicalamerica.com
Home Page: www.cbizmedia.com

Alan Glass, CEO
Bob Hudoba, Listings

Features over 14,000 detailed listings of worldwide arts organizations, including key contact information such as name, address, phone, fax, Web site and E-mail addresses, budget category, type of event and seating capacity. In addition, through advertising, over 10,000 artists are indexed in the alphabetical and categorical indexes. Categories include artist managers, orchestras, opera companies, concert series, festivals, competitions, music schools and departments, record companies, and more.
Founded in 1898

9489

Musician's Guide
Billboard Directories
PO Box 15158
North Hollywood, CA 91615
818-487-4582
800-562-2706
E-Mail: info@billboard.com
Home Page: www.billboard.com/directories

Arkady Fridman, Inside Sales Manager

Everything the working musician needs to book gigs, contact record labels, find a manager, and locate tour services. The latest edition includes A & R Directory, Music Business Services, and City by City listings.
Cost: $15.95
170 Pages
Frequency: Annual

9490

NYC/On Stage
Theatre Development Fund
1501 Broadway
21st Floor
New York, NY 10036-5652
212-221-0885
E-Mail: info@tdf.org
Home Page: www.tdf.org

Theater, dance, and music companies and performing arts centers in New York City.

9491

National Directory of Arts Internships
National Network for Artist Placement
935 W Avenue 37
Los Angeles, CA 90065
323-222-4035
800-354-5348
E-Mail: info@artistplacement.com
Home Page: www.artistplacement.com

Warren Christensen, Consultant

Internship opportunities in dance, music, theatre, art and film.
Cost: $85.00
375 Pages
Frequency: Bi-Annual
ISBN: 0-945941-13-7

9492

National Opera Association Membership Directory
PO Box 60869
Canyon, TX 79016
806-651-2857
FAX 806-651-2958
E-Mail: rhansen@mail.wtamu.edu
Home Page: www.noa.org

Robert Hansen, Executive Director
JoElyn Wakefield Wright, President
Edith Kirkpatrick Vrenios, VP Resources
Philip Hageman, Treasurer
Carol Notestine, Recording Secretary

Members of the National Opera Association are entitled to receive the NOA Freelance Artists and Production Resources databases, the NOA membership directory, and access to the NOA e-mail listserve.
Frequency: Annual

9493

Opera America Membership Directory
Opera America
330 7th Ave
16th Floor
New York, NY 10001-5248
212-796-8620
FAX 212-796-8631
E-Mail: frontdesk@operaamerica.org
Home Page: www.operaamerica.org

Marc Scorca, President

Directory of Opera America's Company, Business, Library, and Affilliate Members, indexed alphabetically and geographically. Includes the Annual Report to Members, a description of Opera America's programs and services, and a list of individual members.
Cost: $25.00
Frequency: Annual

9494

Orion Blue Book: Guitars and Musical Instruments
Orion Research Corporation
14555 N Scottsdale Rd
Suite 330
Scottsdale, AZ 85254-3487
480-951-1114
FAX 480-951-1117
E-Mail: orion@orionbluebook.com
Home Page: www.orionbluebook.com

Roger Rohrs, Owner

77,834 products listed; products listed from 1970s to present; over 450 manufacturers listed; 2 volumes - hardbound or on CD-ROM. Lists musical instruments from Accordians to Xylophones
Cost: $195.00
Frequency: Annual
Founded in 1981

9495

Orion Blue Book: Professional Sound
Orion Research Corporation
14555 N Scottsdale Rd
Suite 330
Scottsdale, AZ 85254-3487
480-951-1114
800-844-0759
FAX 480-951-1117
E-Mail: orion@orionbluebook.com
Home Page: www.orionbluebook.com

Roger Rohrs, Owner

Features over 48,964 products from the 1950's to present. Over 350 manufacturers listed. Comes in hardbound or on CD-ROM. Lists products from Cartridge Players to Wireless Microphone Systems.
Cost: $150.00
970 Pages
Frequency: Annual
Founded in 1973

9496

Orion Blue Book: Vintage Guitar
Orion Research Corporation
14555 N Scottsdale Rd
Suite 330
Scottsdale, AZ 85254-3487
480-951-1114
800-844-0759
FAX 480-951-1117
E-Mail: orion@orionbluebook.com
Home Page: www.orionbluebook.com

Roger Rohrs, Owner

Features more than 11,413 products from the 1800's to present. Over 30 manufacturers listed. Comes in hardbound or CD-ROM, Lists products from Banjos to Ukuleles.
Cost: $50.00
Frequency: Quarterly
Founded in 1990

9497

Performing Arts Resources
Theatre Library Association
The New York Public Library for Performing Arts
40 Lincoln Center Plaza
New York, NY 10023
212-870-1630
E-Mail: nef4@columbia.edu
Home Page: tla.library.unt.edu/

Nancy Friedland, Executive Secretary
Martha S LoManaco, President
Maryann Chach, Editor Membership Directory
Louis A Rachow, Historian
Paul Newman, Treasurer

Annual publication featuring articles on resource materials in the field of theatre, popular entertainment, film, television and radio, information on public and private collections, and essays on conservation and collection management of theatre arts materials. Also includes rare historical documents and out-of-print works that might otherwise be lost to theatre scholarship.
Frequency: Annual

9498

Plays and Playwrights
International Society of Dramatists
1638 Euclid Avenue
Miami Beach, FL 33139-7744
305-882-1864

Offers valuable information on over 1,000 dramatists producing works in English.
Cost: $29.95
200 Pages
Frequency: Annual
Circulation: 10,000

9499

Record Retailing Directory
Billboard Directories
PO Box 15158
North Hollywood, CA 91615
818-487-4582
800-562-2706

E-Mail: info@billboard.com
Home Page: www.billboard.com/directories

Arkady Fridman, Inside Sales Manager

Over 5,500 listings covering the entire retailing community. Provides access to major chain headquarters and local outlets; complete coverage of independent retailers; hard-to-find audiobook retailers; and the booming world of online record retailing, plus store genre or specialization; executives, owners, buyers and planners; address, phone, fax, email and web.
Cost: $215.00
Frequency: Annual

9500

Reel Directory
Lynetta Freeman
PO Box 1910
Boyes Hot Springs, CA 95416
415-531-9760
FAX 707-581-1725
E-Mail: ivisual@aol.com
Home Page: www.reeldirectory.com

Lynetta Freeman, Manager

Source for Film, Video and Multimedia in Northern California.
Cost: $25.00
700 Pages
Frequency: Annual
Circulation: 5,000
Founded in 1979

9501

Regional Theatre Directory
Theatre Directories
P.O.Box 2409
Manchester Center, VT 05255-2409
802-867-9333
FAX 802-867-2297
E-Mail: info@theatredirectories.com
Home Page: www.theatredirectories.com

Peg Lyons, Editor
PJ Tumielewicz, Editor

Profiles over 400 theatres including dinner theatres, equity and non-equity. Find out when/where auditions are held, when resumes shoul be sent, housing and transportation policy, and general description of company. If you want to find a job or an internship as an actor, designer, technician or staff in a professional regional or dinner theatre anywhere in the country, this directory can help you.
Cost: $29.50
Frequency: Annual
ISBN: 0-933919-63-8
Founded in 1984

9502

ShowBiz Bookkeeper
Theatre Directories
P.O.Box 2409
Manchester Center, VT 05255-2409
802-867-9333
FAX 802-867-2297
E-Mail: info@theatredirectories.com
Home Page: www.theatredirectories.com

The tax record-keeping system for professionals working in the arts.
Cost: $22.95

9503

Source Directory of Books, Records and Tapes
Sutton's Super Marketplace

153 Sutton Lane
Fordsville, KY   42343
270-276-9880
E-Mail: mtsutton32@earthlink.net
Home Page: www.pubdisco.com

Jerry Sutton, Owner/Founder

Publishers, recording studios, wholesalers, distributors, manifacturers and importers. Approximatley 450 records. Changes daily as updated.
Cost: $55.20

9504

Source Directory of Musical Instruments
Sutton's Super Marketplace
153 Sutton Lane
Fordsville, KY   42343
270-276-9880
E-Mail: mtsutton32@earthlink.net
Home Page: www.pubdisco.com

Jerry Sutton, Owner/Founder

Listings in directory include names, addresses, phone and fax numbers, and product descriptions from wholesale distributors, Importers, Manufacturers, Close-out houses and Liquidators. Updated daily.
Cost: $55.20

9505

Stars in Your Eyes...Feet on the Ground
Theatre Directories
P.O.Box 2409
Manchester Center, VT   05255-2409
802-867-9333
FAX 802-867-2297
E-Mail: info@theatredirectories.com
Home Page: www.theatredirectories.com

PJ Tumielewicz, Editor
Peg Lyons, Editor

For teens who want to act...Practical advice for young actors: learning how show business works; agents and managers; local cable shows and television commercials; auditioning for stage, student films and TV; choosing a school; dealing with rejection; parental support and more. Written by a 19-year old professional actress.
Cost: $16.95
ISBN: 0-933919-42-5

9506

Student's Guide to Playwriting Opportuniti es
Theatre Directories
P.O.Box 2409
Manchester Center, VT   05255-2409
802-867-9333
FAX 802-867-2297
E-Mail: info@theatredirectories.com
Home Page: www.theatredirectories.com

Michael Write, Directory Editor
Christi Pyland, Directory Editor
PJ Tumielewicz, Theatre Directories, Inc Editor
Peg Lyons, Theatre Directories, Inc Editor

An essential tool for every high shool or college student with an interest in playwriting. Comprehensive listings of 79 academic programs and another 80 professional development programs geared for the young writer. New essays on the art, process and business of playwriting.
Cost: $23.95
128 Pages
ISBN: 0-933919-53-0

9507

Studio Report: Film Development
Hollywood Creative Directory
5055 Wilshire Blvd
Los Angeles, CA   90036-6103
323-525-2369
800-815-0503
FAX 323-525-2398
E-Mail: hcdcustomerservice@hcdonline.com
Home Page: www.hcdonline.com

Valencia McKinley, Manager

The only directory of its kind, in print for the first time. A complete breakdown of film development project tracking. A-Z listings by title, spec screenplays sold, hot studio projects, cross-referenced by studio, production company and genre. The directory's main body consists of an alphabetical listing of all in-development projects that have achieved a forward-moving milestone some time in the last five months. Subsequent sections sort and cross-reference the information to highlight aspects
Cost: $19.95
190 Pages
ISBN: 1-928936-49-0

9508

Summer Theatre Directory
Theatre Directories
P.O.Box 2409
Manchester Center, VT   05255-2409
802-867-9333
FAX 802-867-2297
E-Mail: info@theatredirectories.com
Home Page: www.theatredirectories.com

Opportunities at over 350 summer theatres, theme parks, and summer training programs.
Cost: $29.50

9509

Theatre Profiles
Theatre Communications Group
520 8th Ave
24th Floor
New York, NY   10018-8666
212-609-5900
FAX 212-609-5901
E-Mail: tcg@tcg.org
Home Page: www.tcg.org

Theresa Eyring, Executive Director
Warren Nichols, Director Information Systems
Janelle Bernard, Customer Service/Circulation Mgr
Rebecca Marzalek-Kelly, Membership Coordinator
Phillip Matthews, Director Communications

A benefit available to TCG Member Theatres, listing in included in annual TCG Theatre Directory.
Frequency: Annual

9510

Theatre Profiles Database
Theatre Communications Group
520 8th Ave
24th Floor
New York, NY   10018-8666
212-609-5900
FAX 212-609-5901
E-Mail: tcg@tcg.org
Home Page: www.tcg.org

Theresa Eyring, Executive Director
Kelly Haydon, Database Manager
Jennifer Cleary, Director Membership
Terence Nemeth, Publisher
Kathy Sova, Editorial Director

Online database of more than 400 theatre members in 47 states, 17,000 individual members, 100 Trustee Leadership Network members and a growing number of University, Funder and Business Affiliates.
Frequency: Annual

9511

Whole Arts Directory
Midmarch Arts Press
300 Riverside Dr
Apartment 8A
New York, NY   10025-5279
212-666-6990
FAX 212-865-5510
E-Mail: info@midmarchpress.org
Home Page: www.midmarchartspress.org

Cynthia Navaregga, Manager

Directory to arts resources, organiztions, museums, galleries, colonies, retreats, art therapy, information services, and much more. Highly useful material for all artists, students, organizations and institutions.
Cost: $12.95
175 Pages
ISBN: 0-960247-67-x
Founded in 1987
Printed in on matte stock

Industry Web Sites

9512

www.aact.org
American Association of Community Theatre

Non-profit corporation fostering excellence in community theatre productions and governance through community theatre festivals, educational opportunity publications, network, resources, and website.

9513

www.aahperd.org/nda
National Dance Association

A nonprofit service organization dedicated to increasing knowledge, improving skills and encouraging sound professional practices in dance education while promoting and supporting creative and healthy lifestyles through high quality dance programs.

9514

www.aate.com
American Alliance for Theatre and Education

Members are artists, teachers and professionals who serve youth theatres and theatre educational programs.

9515

www.absolutewrite.com
Absolute Write

Advice for writers, including playwrights.

9516

www.acdaonline.org
American Choral Directors Association

Nonprofit music-education organization whose central purpose is to promote excellence in choral music through performance, composition, publication, research and teaching.

9517

www.acmcountry.com
Academy of Country Music

Involved in numerous events and activities promoting country music. Presents annual awards.

9518

www.actioncutprint.com

Action-Cut-Print

Website for filmmakers. filmmaking resources, free ezine for directors, film and TV bookstore. The Director's Chair magazine by director Peter D. Marshall.

9519

www.actorsequity.org

Actors Equity Association

Labor union affiliated with AFL-CIO which represents actors in film, television and commercials.

9520

www.actorsite.com

Actor Site

Audition and other information.

9521

www.actorsource.com

Actorsource

Extensive information and resources for actors.

9522

www.actorstheatre.org

Actors Theatre of Louisville

Supports new playwrights. For information on entering a play, click Humana Festival.

9523

www.adta.org

American Dance Therapy Association

Founded in 1966; professional organization of dance movement therapists, with members both nationally and internationally; offers training, research findings, and a newsletter.

9524

www.afm.org

American Federation of Musicians of the United **States and Canada**

Union representing over 100,000 professional musicians, performing in all genres of music.

9525

www.afvbm.com

American Federation of Violin and Bow Makers

Strives to elevate professional standards of craftmanship and ethical conduct among members. Helps members develop technical skills and knowledge.Research and study organization.

9526

www.agohq.org

American Guild of Organists

Promotes the organ in its historic and evolving roles and provides a forum for mutual support, inspiration, education and certification.

9527

www.aislesay.com

Aislesay

Internet magazine of stage reviews and opinions.

9528

www.americandanceguild.org

American Dance Guild

Non-profit membership organization; sponsors professional seminars, workshops, a student scholarship and other projects and institutes programs of national significance in the field of dance.

9529

www.americantheaterweb.com

American Theater Web

Find theaters, Broadway shows and musicals.

9530

www.answers4dancers.com

Answers for Dancers

Dance Magazine sponsors this site.

9531

www.artdirectors.org

Art Directors Guild

Conceive and manage the background and settings for most films and television projects.

9532

www.artsmed.org

Performing Arts Medicine Association

Organization for physicians and professionals interested in the research of Performing Arts Medicine.

9533

www.artspresenters.org

Association of Performing Arts Presenters

Celebrates rich and diverse performing arts to the public.

9534

www.artstabilization.org

National Arts Strategies

Offers training and technical assistance to arts organizations.

9535

www.asatalent.com

ASA/Affordable Services

Entertainment services are brought to you as you need them and when you need them at the best price available. Security services, studio teachers, and medical services.

9536

www.ascap.com

American Society of Composers Authors & Publishers

Membership association of more than 260,000 US composers, song writers, lyricists and music publishers.

9537

www.asmac.org

American Society of Music Arrangers and Composers

Professional society for arrangers, composers, orchestrators, and musicians. Monthly meetings with great speakers from the music industry.

9538

www.bachauer.com

Gina Bachauer International Piano Foundation

Produce a yearly piano international competition

9539

www.backstage.com

Backstage.com

Information for actors, casting calls, film reviews, auditions and acting jobs.

9540

www.backstagejobs.com

Theatre Design and Technical Jobs Page

Employment opportunities.

9541

www.backstageworld.com

Backstage World

Post your resume and search for design and technical job opportunities worldwide.

9542

www.billboard.com

The ultimate music industry research tool and information source. The Member Service database is state-of-the-art electronic information service, enabling users to efficiently access information from a variety of music industry databases via the World Wide Web.

9543

www.bmi.com

BMI

Secures the rights of songwriters/composers. Collects license fees for the public performance of music and pays royalties to its copyright owners.

9544

www.castingsociety.com

Casting Society of America

An organization representing casting directors.

9545

www.catf.org

Contemporary American Theater Festival

Dedicated to providing and developing new American Theater.

9546

www.chorusamerica.org

Chorus America

National service for orchestral choruses, independent choruses and professional choruses.

9547

www.cincinnatiarts.org

Cincinnati Arts Association

Dedicated to supporting performing and visual arts.

9548

www.clarinet.org

International Clarinet Association

Seeks to focus attention on the importance of the clarinet and to foster communication of the fellowship between clarinetists.

9549

www.classicalaction.org

Classical Action

Provides a unified voice for all those within the performing arts community to help combat HIV/AIDS.

9550

www.cmaworld.com

Country Music Association

Promotes and publicizes country music.

9551

www.conductorsguild.org

Conductors Guild

Dedicated to encouraging the highest standards in the art and profession of conducting. Founded in 1975.

9552

www.contactimprov.net

Contact Improv

Improvisation for dancers.

9553

www.costume-con.org

Costume Connections

Costume conferences.

9554

www.costume.org

International Costumers' Guild

An affiliation of amateur hobbyist and professional costumers.

9555

www.costumegallery.com

Costume Gallery

A central location on the web for fashion and costume since 1996.

9556

www.costumers.org

National Costumers Association

Seeks to establish and maintain professional and ethical standards of business in the costume industry.

9557

www.costumes.org

Costumer's Manifesto

Online book, information and links.

9558

www.costumesocietyamerica.com

Costume Society of America

Education, research, presentation and design.

9559

www.creativedir.com

Creative Directory Services

Diectory of suppliers for costumes, sets, special effects and stunts.

9560

www.creativemusicalcoalition.com

Creative Musician Coalition

A national organization that brings the world of new music to its readers. Includes in depth music reviews, informative artist interviews, interesting articles and feature columns, and valuable resource material.

9561

www.criticaldance.com

Dance Critics Association

Critical dance forum and ballet dance magazine

9562

www.csulb.edu/~jvancamp/copyrigh.html

Csulb.edu

Copyrighting choreographic works.

9563

www.csusa.org/face/index.htm

Friends of Active Copyright Education

Playwrights should click on Words, then Copyright Basics.

9564

www.cyberdance.org

Cyber Dance

Collection of links to modern dance and classical ballet resources.

9565

www.danceart.com/edancing

Danceart.com

Ballet and dance art, features, chat and more.

9566

www.dancenotation.org

Dance Notation Bureau

Notation basics, Notated Theatrical Dances Catalogue and links.

9567

www.dancepages.com

Dance Pages.com

Offers resources to dance teachers.

9568

www.dancer.com/dance-links

Dance Links

Links to many dance sites.

9569

www.danceusa.org

Dance/USA

Provides a forum for the discussion of issues of concern to membersand a support network for exchange of information; also bestows awards.

9570

www.deadance.com

Dance Educators of America

Promotes the education of teachers in the performing arts.

9571

www.discoverhollywood.com

Hollywood Arts Council

Promotes, nurtures and supports the arts field in Hollywood. Discover Hollywood on line.

9572

www.dma-national.org

Dance Masters of America

An organization of dance teachers.

9573

www.documentary.org

International Documentary Association

A nonprofit association founded to promote non-fiction film and video, to support the efforts of documentary film and video makers around the world, and to increase public appreciation and demand for the documentary.

9574

www.dramaguild.com

Dramatists Guild

Comprehensive organization that deals solely with Broadway and off-Broadway producers, off-off-Broadway groups, agents, theatres and sources of grants.

9575

www.dramaleague.org

Drama League

Seeks to strengthen American theatre through the nurturing of stage directors.

9576

www.dtw.org

Dance Theater Workshop

Identifies, presents and supports independent contemporary artists and dance companies to advance dance and live performances in New York and worldwide.

9577

www.edta.org

Educational Theater Association

Theater educators working to increase support for theater programs in the educational system.

9578

www.esperanzaarts.org

Esperanza Performing Arts Association

9579

www.etecnyc.net

Entertainment Technology Online

For employment in design and technical theatre, click on Classifieds. Also offers resources and buyers guides for theatrical lighting.

9580

www.flmusiced.org

Florida Music Educators Association

Florida Music Educators Association and Florida School Music Association.

9581

www.folkharpsociety.org

International Society of Folk Harpers and **Craftsmen**

Conducts technical and artistic programs and promotes craft exchange.

9582

www.gmn.com

Global Music Network

Go backstage, watch rehearsals, listen to performances of classical and jazz artists.

9583

www.goldmime.com

Goldston Mime Foundation: School for Mime

Holds summer seminars and workshops.

9584

www.gospelmusic.org

Gospel Music Association

Dedicated to providing leadership, direction and unity for all facets of the gospel music industry. Through education, communication, information, promotion and recognition, the GMA is striving to help those involved in gospel music.

9585

www.greyhouse.com

Grey House Publishing

Authoritative reference directories for direct marketing, demographics, business, research, health care, international trade, food industry and education. Users can search the online databases with varied search criteria allowing for custom searches by product category, geographic area, sales volume, keyword, subject and more. Full Grey House catalog and online ordering also available.

9586

www.guitarfoundation.org

Guitar Foundation of America

Supports the serious studies of the guitar.

9587

www.harada-sound.com/sound/handbook

Kai's Sound Handbook

Information for sound designers.

9588

www.harpsociety.org

American Harp Society

Improves the quality of the instrument and performance.

9589

www.hawaii.edu

Association for Theatre in Higher Education

Promotes quality in theatre education.

9590

www.heniford.net/1234

Small Cast One-Act Guide Online

List of short plays.

9591

www.horndoggie.com/horn

International Horn Society

A national organization that focuses on music industry news and information.

9592

www.iaekm.org

International Association of Electronic Keyboard **Manufacturers**

Global manufacturers of electronic kayboards and affiliated software and publications.

9593

www.ibma.org

World of Bluegrass

IBMA: working together for high standards of professionalism, a greater appreciation for our music, and the success of the world-wide bluegrass   community.

9594

www.ifea.com

International Festivals and Events Association

Network for planning events and exchange programs; publishes quarterly magazine.

9595

www.imeamusic.org

Indiana Music Educators Association

Supports and advances music education in Indiana.

9596

www.internationalpolka.com

International Polka Association

Educational organization concerned with the preservation and advancement of polka music. Operates the Polka Music Hall of Fame and Museum, and presents the International Polka Fesitval every year during the complete first weekend of August.

9597

www.intix.org

International Ticketing Association

Not-for-profit association representing 22 countries worldwide and more than 1,200 members. Committed to the improvement, progress and advancement of ticket management, and to reach this goal provides educational programs, trade shows, conducts surveys and conference proceedings and produces a membership directory.

9598

www.iqfilm.org

International Quorum of Film and Video Producers

Fosters the exchange of information and ideas. Seeks to raise professional standards. Disseminates information on new concepts and technology.

9599

www.ispa.org

International Society for the Performing Arts **Foundation**

Supports international cooperation, facilitates networking and enhances professional dialogue.

9600

www.jensenfoundation.org

Fritz and Lavinia Jensen Foundation

Sponsors competitions.

9601

www.latinoarts.org

Association of Hispanic Arts

A multidisciplary organization which supports Hispanic arts organizations and individual artists with technical assistance. The organization facilitates projects and programs designed to foster the appreciation, growth, and well being of the Latino cultural community. It's quarter publication, AHA; Hispanic Arts News, features in depth articles on the local and national arts community, including artist profiles and a calendar of events.

9602

www.lib.colum.edu/costwais.html

Costume Image Database

Access costume images.

9603

www.light-link.com

Lightsearch.com

Lists of lighting equipment suppliers.

9604

www.livebroadway.com

League of American Theatres and Producers

National trade association for the commercial theatre industry whose principal activity is negotiation of labor contracts and government relations.

9605

www.lmda.org

Literary Managers and Dramaturgs of the Americas

Voluntary membership organization.

9606

www.luth.org

Guild of American Luthiers

Manufacturers and repairs stringed instruments; offers quarterly journal and triennial meeting.

9607

www.lycos.com

Lycos

Click Arts and Entertainment, then Dance, Theatre or Performing Arts.

9608

www.magicsam.com

Society of American Magicians

Founded to promote and maintain harmonious fellowship among those interested in magic as an art, to improve ethics of the magical profession, and to foster, promote and improve the advancement of magical arts in the field of amusement and entertainment. Membership includes professional and amateur magicians, manufacturers of magical apparatus and collectors.

9609

www.makeupmag.com

Make-Up Artist Magazine

Make-up artist magazine online.

9610

www.members.aol.com/thegoop/gaff.html

Gaff Tape Webring

Tech theatre.

9611

www.metguild.org

Metropolitan Opera Guild

Seeks to promote greater understanding and interest in opera.

9612

www.midatlanticarts.org

Mid Atlantic Arts Foundation

Provides leadership and support for artists and arts organizations in the Mid-Atlantic region and beyond.

9613

www.milieux.com/costume

Costume Source

Provides online sources for materials, costumes, accessories and books.

9614

www.millimeter.com

Millimeter Magazine

Authoritative resource for more than 33,000 qualified professionals in production, postproduction, animation, streaming and visual effects for motion pictures, television and commercials.

9615

www.mpa.org

Music Publishers Association of the United States

Encourages understanding of the copyright laws and works to protect musical works against infringements and piracy.

9616

www.mpaa.org

Motion Picture Association of America

Promotes high moral and artistic standards in motion picture production. Maintains Motion Picture Association Political Action Committee.

9617

www.mtishows.com

Music Theatre International

Scripts, cast recordings, study guides, production slides and other resources.

9618

www.mtna.org

Music Teachers National Association

This is a nonprofit organization of independent and collegiate music teachers committed to furthering the art of music through teaching, performance, composition and scholarly research.

9619

www.music.org

College Music Society

The Society is a national service organization for college conservatory and university music teachers.

9620

www.musicalamerica.com
Musicalamerica.com

Late-breaking industry news, full search capabilities, immediate interaction between Presenter and Artist Manager/Artist.

9621

www.musicalartists.org
American Guild of Musical Artists

Exclusive bargaining agent for all concert musical artists.

9622

www.musicdistributors.org
Music Distributor Association

A trade association of 160 manufactures, importers, wholesalers of musical instruments and accessories, domestic and international selling to the trade only

9623

www.musicianshealth.com
Chiropractic Performing Arts Association

To educate amateur and professional entertainers, musicians and dancers about reaching optimum health potential through natural, drug-free, conservative chiropractic care.

9624

www.musiclibraryassoc.org
Music Library Association

Promotes growth and establishment in the use of music libraries, musical instruments and musical literature.

9625

www.nacwpi.org
National Association of College Wind and **Percussion Instructors**

Teachers of wind and percussion instruments in American colleges and universities.

9626

www.nadt.org
National Association for Drama Therapy

Promotes the profession of Drama Therapy.

9627

www.namm.org
NAMM-International Music Products Association

Offers professional development seminars; sells musical instruments and allied products.

9628

www.napama.org
North American Performing Arts Managers and Agents

A cooperative voice in a competitive business.

9629

www.napbirt.org
National Association of Professional Band **Instrument Repair Technicians**

Promotes technical integrity in the craft. Surveys tools and procedures to improve work quality. Makes available emergency repair of band instruments. Provides placement services.

9630

www.narm.com
National Association of Recording Merchandisers

Not-for-profit trade association that represents the retailers, wholesalers, and distributors of prerecorded music in the United States.

9631

www.nbea.com
National Ballroom and Entertainment Association

Provides exchange for owners and operators of ballrooms.

9632

www.nbtf.org
National Black Theatre Festival

9633

www.netconline.org
New England Theatre Conference

Non-profit educational corporation founded to develop, expand and assist theatre activity in community, educational and professional levels in New England. Holds annual auditions.

9634

www.netsword.com/stagecombat.html
Netsword

Lessons on stage combat.

9635

www.newplaysforchildren.com
New Plays Online

Plays for children and young adults.

9636

www.nmpa.org
National Music Publishers' Association

Publishes a quarterly newsletter and holds an annual meeting.

9637

www.noa.org
National Opera Association

To advance the appreciation, composition and production of opera.

9638

www.notam@2.no/icma
International Computer Music Association

Supports the performance aspects of computer music; publishes newsletter and holds annual conferance.

9639

www.npm.org
National Association of Pastoral Musicians

Membership organization primarily composed of musicians, musician-liturgist, clergy, and other leaders of prayer devoted to serving the life and mission of the Church through fosterering the art of musical liturgy in Roman Catholic worshiping communities in the United States.

9640

www.ntcp.org
Non-Traditional Casting Project

Promotes inclusive practices in television, theatre and film.

9641

www.nyfa.com
New York Film Academy

Educational institution devoted to providing focused filmmaking and acting instructions. Geared to offer an intensive, hands-on experience which gives students

the opportunity to develop their creative skills to the fullest extent possible.

9642

www.nyfa.org
New York Foundation for the Arts

Employment openings in the arts.

9643

www.nypl.org/reseach/lpa/lpa.html
New York Public Library for the Performing Arts

Primary research collection.

9644

www.nyssma.org
New York State School Music Association

Advocates and improves the education in music of all people in New York State.

9645

www.nytimes.com
New York Times on the Web

Arts and Theatre contains play reviews.

9646

www.oobr.com
Off-Off-Broadway Review

Lists information on off-off broadway shows such as: title of show, author, director, producing company, theatre, address, box-office phone number, dates and times, admission price and contact info.

9647

www.opencasting.com
Open Casting

Bulletin board containing auditions, crew calls, casting notices and links.

9648

www.oscars.org
Academy of Motion Picture Arts and Sciences

Current information on motion pictures, the arts and sciences, events and screenings.

9649

www.paastjo.org
Performing Arts Association

Provides a diverse selection of performing arts.

9650

www.pas.org
Percussive Arts Society

Promotes drums and percussion through a viable network of performers, teachers, students, enthusiasts and sustaining members. Offers publications, a worldwide network of the World Percussion Network, the Percussive Arts Society International Headquarters/Museum and the annual Percussive Arts Society International Convention.

9651

www.pen.org
PEN: American Center

Site of the international literary community organization.

9652

www.performingarts.net
Performing Arts Online

Dedicated to the perpetuation of quality performing arts.

9653

www.pianoguild.com
International Piano Guild

A division of the American College of Musicians Professional society of piano teachers and music faculty members. Sponsers national examinations.

9654

www.pianonet.com
Piano Manufacturers Association International

Manufacturers and suppliers of pianos and parts; holds annual trade show.

9655

www.pipeorgan.org
American Institute of Organ Builders

Sponsers training seminars, quarterly journal and annual convention for pipe organ builders and service technicians.

9656

www.plasa.org
Professional Lighting and Sound Association

Web site for PLASA, a leading trade body for Lighting and Sound Professionals.

9657

www.playbill.com
Playbill Online

Listings for Broadway and off Broadway theatre productions. Also guides for sites, including summer stock, national touring shows and regional theatres worldwide.

9658

www.playwrights.org
Playwrights Center of San Francisco

Playwrites directory.

9659

www.playwrightshorizons.org
Playwrights Horizon

At home page click arrow. On next page click working with PH. You will see Writing Submissions.

9660

www.playwrightsproject.com
Playwrights Project

Promotes literacy, creativity and communication skills in young people through drama-based activities.

9661

www.press.jhu.edu/press/journals/paj
Johns Hopkins University Press

A journal of performance and art.

9662

www.press.jhu.edu/press/journals/tj
Johns Hopkins University Press

Theatre Journal

9663

www.press.jhu.edu/press/journals/tt
Johns Hopkins University Press

Theatre Topics

9664

www.printmusic.org
Retail Print Music Dealers Association

The voice of the print music industry.

9665

www.producersguild.com
Producers Guild of America

Members are producers of motion pictures and television shows mainly in the Los Angeles area.

9666

www.proppeople.com
Proppeople.com

Online home for props professionals.

9667

www.ptg.org
Piano Technicians Guild

Conducts technical institutes at conventions and seminars. Promotes public education in piano care. Bestows awards. Publishes monthly technical journal by subscriptions.

9668

www.renfaire.com/Language/index.html
Renfaire.com

Lessons on proper Elizabethan accents.

9669

www.resumegenie.com

Motion Pictures job listings, salary information and job search tips.

9670

www.rigging.net
Rigger's Page

Technical information on stage rigging equipment.

9671

www.roundalab.org
Roundalab

A professional international society of individuals who teach round dancing at any phase.

9672

www.safd.org
Society of American Fight Directors

Promotes safety in directing staged combat and theatrical violence.

9673

www.sag.org
Screen Actors Guild

Labor union affiliated with AFL-CIO which represents actors in film, television and commercials.

9674

www.sapphireswan.com/dance
Dance Directory

Dance resources.

9675

www.setc.org
Southeastern Theatre Conference

Annual conventions include auditions.

9676

www.sfballet.org
San Francisco Ballet Association

Provides a repertoire of classical and contemporary ballet; to provide educational opportunities for professional dancers and choreographers; to excel in ballet, artistic direction and administration.

9677

www.smpte.org
Society of Motion Picture & Television Engineers

Advances the practice and theory of engineering in television and film industry.

9678

www.southarts.org
Southern Arts Federation

Serves as the leadership voice to increase the regional, national and international awareness and prominence of Southern arts. Creates mechanisms and partnerships to expand local, regional, national and international markets for Southern arts.

9679

www.spars.com
Society of Professional Audio Recording Services

Members are individuals, companies and studios connected with the professional recording industry.

9680

www.spolin.com
Spolin Center

Information on improvisational theatre.

9681

www.ssdc.org
Society of Stage Directors and Choreographers

An independent labor union representing directors and choreographers in American theatre.

9682

www.stage-directions.com
Stage Directions Magazine

The practical and technical side of theatrical operations.

9683

www.stageplays.com/markets.htm
Playwrights Noticeboard

Information on contests, publishing and production opportunities.

9684

www.stetson.edu/csata/thr_guid.html
McCoy's Guide to Theatre and Performance Studies

A brief guide to internet resources in theatre and performance studies put out by Stetson University.

9685

www.stuntnet.com
International Stunt Association

Represents those involved in stunt work for the entertainment industry.

9686

www.stuntwomen.com
Stuntwomen's Association of Motion Pictures

A professional association for stuntwomen and stunt coordinators which seeks to uphold professional standards and improve working conditions.

9687

www.summertheater.com
Directory of Summer Theater in the United States

Search for summer theater opportunities by alphabetized listings or geographic region.

9688

www.sundance.org
Sundance Institute

Nonprofit corporation dedicated to the support and development of emerging screenwriters and directors of vision. Hosts the Sundance Film Festival.

9689
www.symphony.org
American Symphony Orchestra League

The national nonprofit service and educational organization dedicated to strengthening symphony and chamber orchestras. It provides artistic, organizational and financial leadership and service to orchestral conductors, managers, volunteers and staff.

9690
www.talkinbroadway.com
Talkin' Broadway

Theatrical events and information on and off Broadway and other selected geographical locations.

9691
www.tcg.org
Theatre Communications Group

Supports alliances among playwrights, theatres and communities. Promotes not-for-profit theatre and offers resources to jobseekers. Offers financial support to designers and directors through its Career Development Program.

9692
www.tdf.org
Theatre Development Fund

Not-for-profit service organization. Provides support for every area of the dance, music and professional theatre field. Founded 1968.

9693
www.teleport.com/~bjscript/index.htm
Essays on the Craft of Dramatic Writing

Essays on writing a screenplay, play or novel.

9694
www.theatre-resource.com
Theatre Resource

Career and employment information.

9695
www.theatrebayarea.org
Theatre Bay Area

Serving more than 400 member theatre companies and 3,000 individual members in the San Francisco Bay Area and Northern California, Theatre Bay Area provides monthly classes, workshops, events, information and publications.

9696
www.theatrecrafts.com
Theatrecrafts.com

Practical information about technical theatre techniques for theatre folk at any level.

9697
www.theatrejobs.com
Theatrejobs.com

Online job placement. Festival listings, summer stock, assistantships, apprenticeships, fellowships and internships.

9698
www.theatrelibrary.org/links
Performing Arts Links

General resources including applied and interactive theatre, performing arts data service and art sites. Digital librarian includes glossary of technical theatre terms.

9699
www.theatrelibrary.org/links/index.html
Theatrelibrary.org

Master categories are Theatre, Dance, Cinema and Reviews.

9700
www.thecastingnetwork.com/webring.html
Casting Network.com

By and for actors.

9701
www.theplays.org
Electronic Literature Foundation

William Shakespeare's plays online.

9702
www.tmea.org
Texas Music Educators Association

Promoting excellence in music education.

9703
www.top20performingarts.com
Top 20 Performing Arts

Online directory for Perfoming Arts education.

9704
www.towson.edu/worldmusiccongresses
World Music Congresses

1997-2010 World Cello Congress' II-V, 2004 The First World Guitar Congress and 2008 World Guitar Congress II. Celebrations of music with international gatherings of the world's greatest musicians, composers, conductors, instrument manufacturers students, and music lovers from around the globe.

9705
www.unc.edu/depts/outdoor
Institute of Outdoor Drama

Summer jobs for all theatrical personnel.

9706
www.ups.edu/professionalorgs/dramaturgy
Dramaturgy Northwest

Relevant information for all dramaturgs.

9707
www.urta.com
University/Resident Theatre Association

Coalition of theatre training programs. Sponsors unified auditions.

9708
www.usabda.org
USA Dance

Non-profit organization working to promote ballroom dancing, both as a recreational activity and as a competetive sport.

9709
www.usitt.org
United States Institute for Theatre Technology

The association of design, production and technology professionals in the performing arts and entertainment industry whose mission is to promote the knowledge and skills of its members. International in scope, USITT draws its board of directors from across the US and Canada. Sponsors projects, programs, research, symposia, exhibits, and annual conference. Disseminates information on aesthetic and technical developments.

9710
www.variety.org
Variety

e-version of the show business newspaper.

9711
www.vcu.edu/artweb/playwriting
Playwriting Seminars

An opinionated web companion on the art and craft of playwriting for theatre and dance.

9712
www.vl-theatre.com
WWW Virtual Library

Links to theatre and drama resources. Updated daily.

9713
www.wif.org
Women in Film

For global entertainment,communication and media industries. Focuses on contemporary issues facing women and provides an extensive network of valuable contacts, educational programs, scholars, film finishing funds, grants, community outreach, advocacy and practical services that promote, nurture and mentor women to achieve their highest potential.

9714
www.writersguild.com
Writers Guild of America

List of Agents and information on Mentor program.

9715
www.wwar.com
World Wide Arts Resources

Links to Theatre and Dance.

9716
www2.sundance.org
Sundance Institute

Information on the Sundance Theatre Laboratory summer workshop for directors, playwrights, choreographers, solo performers and composers. For information on submitting a play, click Theatre Program on home page.

Entry Index

Entry Index

Home, William, 662
Hommowum, Don, 4118
Homsey, Catherine, 3863
Honbach, Melissa, 2506
Honegger PhD, Dr. Greta, 2406
Hones, Jaclynn, 6794
Honka, Rita, 430
Honorof, Debbie, 1257
Honowitz, James, 3914
Hontz, Rick, 6029, 7197
Hood, Frank, 2068
Hood, Liama, 4784
Hood, Woody, 7508
Hoogestraat, Llinda, 3770
Hook, Don, 253
Hooker, Mary Anne, 526
Hooks, Gayle, 35
Hoomes, John, 2056
Hooper, Cindy, 6481
Hooper, Jane, 5025
Hooper, Jean, 3317
Hooper, Jeff, 3317
Hoops, H Ray, 6494
Hoose, David, 1858
Hoover, Darla, 437
Hoover, Jeffery, 4153
Hoover, Leland G, 3922
Hoover, Robert, 6326, 6327, 6328, 6329, 6330
Hoover, Wanda, 2133
Hoovler, Drew, 5283
Hope, Jr, Walter, 2050
Hopes, David B, 3210
Hopkins, Carron, 7243
Hopkins, Jesse E, 5378
Hopkins, Karen Brooks, 4666
Hopkins, Laurie, 5177
Hopkins, Liz, 1789
Hopkins, Mark, 5711
Hopkins, Michael, 2979, 7203
Hopkins, P, 5378
Hopkins, Richard, 851, 2478
Hoppe, Cherry, 5201
Hoppenstedt, Robert, 2366
Hopper, Alan T, 995
Hopper, Lois, 4675
Hopson, Dan, 3692
Hopson, Pamela, 660
Hopson, Terri, 5916
Horab, Kim, 3260
Horgan, Bernadette, 1039
Horgend, Garen, 1448, 5042
Horgon, Theresa, 7880
Hori, Robert, 5813
Horiuchi, Gen, 247
Horn, Andrew, 3198
Horn, Donald I, 5046
Horn, John, 3087
Horn, Mary, 3412
Horn, Olivia, 2497
Hornbaker, Eleanor, 1425
Horne, Meade, 4885
Horne Charles, Mrs Robert, 5160
Horner, Ross, 7525
Hornstein, Dr. Daniel, 1361
Horntvedt, Lester, 1903
Horovitz, Dr. Len, 1279
Horovitz, Israel, 2764
Horowitz, Gigi, 2160
Horowitz, Jay, 7274
Horowitz, Jeffrey, 3156
Horowitz, Jim, 3914
Horrocks, Tom, 5342
Horsely, Brian, 8138
Horsley, Alison, 2170
Horsley, Leigh, 2586
Horsman, Robert B, 1701
Horto, Joseph M, 4581
Horton, Alan, 3615
Horton, David, 3460
Horton, Sean, 2303
Horvath, Ken, 6908
Horvath, Mary Beth, 5409
Horvath, Susan, 4693
Hosale, Cindy, 2100
Hosier, C J, 6003
Hosking, John, 2916
Hoskinson, Tim, 824
Hosmer, Craig, 1763
Hosseinioun, Mishana, 43

Hosslund, Mark, 4106
Hostetter, Mark, 3074
Hotchkin, Brian, 1719
Hotchkis, John F, 3772
Hotchner, Kathy, 3710
Hotes, Andrea, 6084
Hottendorf, Diane, 123
Hottenstein, Bunny, 1471
Houdek, Alesh, 6164
Houden, Dr Guido, 1483
Houden, Guido, 5105
Hough, James, 5276
Hough, Katherine, 5849
Houghton, Brian, 2214
Houghton, Bruce, 8367
Houghton, James, 3145
Houghton, Jim, 2389
Houghton, Quincy, 5808
Houihan, Mahlon, 6498
Houlihan, Laura, 3196
Houlihan, Mahlon, 2641
Houlton, Lise, 240
Houston, Arnold, 5592
Houston, CiCi, 246
Houston, Dante, 3653
Houston, Ron, 2080
Houston, Sterling, 3541
Houts, Ven, 2903
Hovenesian, Stasia B, 4423, 4424
Hovermale, Marion, 1513
Hovick, Larry, 7030
Howard, B Michael, 206, 5579
Howard, Bob, 7766
Howard, Burgwell, 6789
Howard, Dave, 7274
Howard, Davida S, 7558
Howard, Derrick, 8031
Howard, Jared, 4640
Howard, Kendra, 2899
Howard, Kevin, 6851
Howard, Kevin T, 1853
Howard, Len, 8048
Howard, Lois, 8332
Howard, Mark, 174
Howard, Michael, 1419
Howard, Robert Charles, 885
Howard, Valarie, 2382
Howare, Aryaane, 4870
Howatt, Nadine, 2398
Howe, Lisa, 246
Howe, Marion B, 4791
Howe, Richard, 3555
Howe, Richard R, 1294, 4772
Howe, Wendy, 611
Howell, James, 7621
Howell Thornton, Caron, 5549
Howerton, Trish, 6812
Howes, Janet, 2764
Howett, Nadine, 6092
Howland, Kris, 2832
Howlett, C A, 579, 3704
Howzell, Terence, 3822
Hoye, Cindy, 6515
Hoyt, Charles E, 1755
Hoyt, Sally, 2099
Hoyt Chapman, Megan, 159
Hrebec, Heather, 8017
Hrobsky, Donna, 3655, 8271
Hrubetz, JC, 8031
Hsu, Dolores M, 3884
Hsu, Johson, 930
Hu, Katherine, 3833
Huang, June, 1301
Huang, Wen, 1046
Hubbard, Amy, 3450
Hubbard, Cindi, 705
Hubbard, Dean L, 4523
Hubbard, Joel, 5670
Hubbard, John T, 4318
Hubbard, Martin G, 1717
Hubbard, Sally, 5225
Hubbard, Susan, 6986
Hubbard, Terry, 5610
Hubbard, Toni, 5376
Hubbart, Dean, 7040
Huber, Jane E., 4611
Huber, Janey, 2955
Huber, Mark, 730
Hubley, Patrick, 3552

Hubner, Carla, 3991
Huckabone, Cort, 5800
Hucko, Stephen, 1961
Hudak, Holly H., 893
Huddleston, Mark, 4960
Huddleston, Robb, 3875
Huddleston, Robert, 8067
Huddleston, Will, 2315
Hudgins, Charlene, 3260
Hudgins, Mark, 3592
Hudman, Debbie, 3472
Hudson, Fred, 3073
Hudson, Gregg, 3815
Hudson, John, 823
Hudson, Richard, 1135
Hudson, Yvonne, 3073
Huebner, Libby, 5822
Hueg, Kurt, 5803
Hueston, Eddie, 7933
Huey, Liana, 8299
Huff, Joseph H., 863
Huff, Mae, 8137
Huff, Maurice, 3828
Huff, Richard E, 7998
Huffman, Elissa, 1364
Hug, Butch, 7099
Huggett, Monica, 1454
Huggins, Cynthia, 2721
Hugh, Jennifer, 800
Hughes, Amber, 5893
Hughes, Bill, 6807
Hughes, Brain, 4242
Hughes, Brian, 4242
Hughes, Christopher, 1878
Hughes, David, 1785
Hughes, Devin, 762
Hughes, Don, 3823
Hughes, Earl, 2458, 3407
Hughes, Jason, 7169
Hughes, Ralph, 1695
Hughes, Robin, 6353
Hughes, Sandra, 2508
Hughes, Sheila, 5437
Hughes, Thomas, 1999
Hughett, Julie, 3758
Hughett, Richard, 3800
Hugo, John, 1601
Hugo Martinez, Gay, 696
Huiskamp, Patti, 4464
Hukill, David, 437
Hula, Kuma, 4102
Hulbert, Mariclare, 4371
Hull, Annie, 7085
Hull, Dale, 4469
Hull, Richard, 1777
Hull, Rochelle, 1344
Hullette, Suzette, 2712
Hultman, Irene, 374
Hume, Leslie P., 1710
Hume, Pattie, 77
Humiston, Marilyn K, 1150
Humleker, William, 1345
Hummel, Alice, 787
Hummel, Dave, 6515
Hummel, Patricia, 5139
Humpage, Corey, 6048
Humphrey, Joe, 3026
Humphreys, Emily, 6378
Humphreys, Liz, 2796
Humphries, Joel, 7974
Humphries Breeskin, Gail, 2404
Humrichouser, Tony, 6610, 6611
Hungate, Galen, 5658
Hunkins, Marcia, 1876
Hunley, Marina, 3628
Hunnicutt, James, 2733
Hunsberger, Donald, 1314
Hunstien, DeeAnne, 3971
Hunt, Bill, 1114, 1452
Hunt, Calvin, 296
Hunt, Duwain, 2817
Hunt, Elisa, 2988
Hunt, Jeffrey, 926
Hunt, Jennifer, 6719
Hunt, Lawrence J., 1181
Hunt, Robb, 3601
Hunt, Sheila, 404
Hunt, Steve, 3206
Hunt, Sylvia, 4107

Hunt, Todd, 7012
Hunt, Tom, 5872
Hunte, Cliff, 4366
Hunter, Bill, 5806
Hunter, Christine F, 1973
Hunter, Greg, 124
Hunter, Jeff, 7874
Hunter, Jim, 7798
Hunter, Johnnie, 2808
Hunter, Mark, 6636, 6637
Hunter, Mrs. Cristine F, 1766
Hunter, Susette, 5551
Hunter Ritchie, Gwen, 447
Hunter, Esquire, David, 1402
Hunterfields, Emilye, 2568
Huntington, Dorri, 2266
Huntley, Jim, 3099
Huntley, Lance, 85
Huntley, Walter R, 2511
Huntowski, Kasha, 8241, 8242, 8245
Huntsman, Pamela, 4675
Hunzelman, Amy, 6586
Huotari, Amanda, 6803
Hupe, Don, 1345
Hupp, Robert, 2133, 2134, 5693
Hupperts, Bernie, 5488
Hurlburt, Norma, 1270
Hurley, Cristine, 5806
Hurley, Fran, 1565
Hurley, Kathleen, 196
Hurley, Linda, 1069
Hurley, Ms Diane S, 5160
Hurley, Thomas, 1069
Hurlin, Dan, 3066
Hurst, Carroll, 526
Hurst, John, 3240
Hurst, Michael, 7326
Hurt, Martha R, 2034
Hurt, Sonia, 5945
Hurtig, Judith, 6627
Hurty, Anna, 6457, 6459
Hurty, Jon, 920, 1820
Huscroft, Sue, 1697
Huseman, Sue, 2721
Huseth, Solveig, 2832
Hussie-Taylor, Judy, 321
Hussong, Jennifer, 2541
Hustis, Greg, 3931
Hustoles, Paul J, 2841
Huston, Cathy, 4949
Huston, Wayne, 6566
Hutchings, Owen, 7413
Hutchinson, Char, 3305
Hutchinson, Leland E, 1808
Hutchinson, Loura, 4891
Hutchison, Jay, 6951, 6952
Hutheesing, Ajit, 3976
Hutson, Faith, 2985
Hutten, Marshall, 2529
Hutzell, Barry, 3359
Huxel, Vicki, 7942
Huyck, Catherine, 2059
Hval, Kathy, 4597
Hval, Palmer, 4597
Hwang, Nai, 699
Hwang-Williams, Yumi, 760
Hyatt, M Michael, 3212
Hyatt Mazon, Gina, 156
Hyatt-Mazon, Gina, 156
Hyde, Bob, 8074
Hyde, Bruce, 2829
Hydon, Jeffrey P, 3810
Hyer, Warren W, 1400
Hyers, Stephen D., 3230
Hyland, Jim, 2099
Hyland, Kathy, 3289
Hyland, Louise, 1924
Hyler Ritter, Rosemary, 3821
Hyman, Carla, 4075
Hyman, Dick, 4759
Hyman, Eric, 7961
Hyman, Michael, 7540
Hymel, Larry M, 6744
Hymes, Gerald, 7695
Hynson, Richard, 2099
Hyslop, David H, 6973

Kalaf, Jerry, 35
Kalam, Tonu, 1563
Kalbfleisch, Jon, 1426
Kaler, Ilia, 1314
Kaletta, Mary, 793
Kalfus, Donald, 258
Kalin, Catharine L, 707, 5898
Kalkbreaner, Tracie, 4271
Kalkor, Dr. Alan, 1348
Kallen, Tom, 6386
Kallunki Gotham, Deb, 6924
Kalmu, Geoffrey M, 4638
Kalogeras, Alexandros, 1036
Kalson, Dorothy, 1242, 4684
Kaltenbach, Janet, 1931
Kamalani, Alva, 6314
Kambalov, Pavel, 119
Kamin, Hester, 2779
Kamine, Marjorie, 2120, 5610
Kaminsky, Laura, 5446
Kampler, John, 4841
Kampmeier, Jenny, 1264
Kanaga, Sarah R, 1874
Kanazawa, Chris, 2536
Kancianic, Phil, 1021
Kane, Angela, 231
Kane, Joe, 1841
Kane, John, 1513
Kane, Scott, 5901, 5907
Kaneten, Norval, 4891
Kaney, Georgia, 4008
Kang, Grace, 824
Kanoff, Scott, 3479
Kansas, George P, 7227
Kantar, Ned, 8363
Kantor, Herbert C, 3089
Kantrowitz, Mark, 1929
Kantrowitz, Stephen, 7172
Kao, Henry, 1197
Kapask, Dick, 2228
Kapelinski, Ken, 7835
Kapito, Robert, 3032
Kapito, Robert S, 3032
Kaplan, Christian, 6040, 6042, 6043
Kaplan, Deborah, 43
Kaplan, Lewis, 1005, 1263, 4327
Kaplan, Melvin, 8489
Kaplan, Michelle, 8457
Kaplan, Sheri, 7577
Kaplan, Thomas S, 1302
Kapley, Emma, 559
Kaplin, Lewis, 4328
Kaplin, Van, 2047
Kapp, Barbara, 1303
Kapp, Rich, 6523
Kapp, Richard, 1303
Kappas, Mike, 8325
Kappel, Mark, 8428
Kappel, Victoria, 4790
Kappus, Sheryl, 5278
Kaptur, Terese, 765, 3688, 3925
Karacson, Annamaria, 754
Karalus, Carol, 532
Karas, Sr Linda, 3365
Karidoyanes, Steven, 1069
Karinski, Edna, 640
Karlin, Eve, 358
Karlin, Jan, 681
Karlin, Michell, 6720
Karmanos, Peter, 7504
Karnell, Phillip E., 6775
Karnes, Kevin, 862
Karnette, Betty, 5800
Karnopp, Adam, 5193
Karnosh, Patricia, 1410
Karoub, Carl, 1106
Karoui, Faycal, 357
Karp, Benjamin, 985
Karp, Karen, 4730
Karp, Nancy, 71
Karp, Steve, 2382
Karpus, Janet, 4463
Karter, Jerome, 1080
Karush, Karen, 4788
Karuskopf, Fred, 2639
Karutz, Peter, 246
Kary, Sarah, 2769
Kasch, Marya, 1674
Kasel, Barb, 2830

Kashkin, MD, Kenneth B., 1928
Kasowitx, Lori A., 4725
Kasper, Lewis, 1422
Kass, Jeff, 5214
Kass, Linda, 1393
Kass, Randy, 5161
Kastelic, Patty, 3688
Kastla, Margaret, 2037
Kastle, Margaret, 2037
Kastner, G Ronald, 2089
Kastner, Simmie, 3244
Kateman, Michael, 2882, 7019
Kathryn, Stage Technica, 5719
Katlin, Stephen, 3025
Katona, Cathy, 2419
Katseanes, Alan, 879
Katselas, Milton, 5727
Katt, Sandy, 6914
Katten, Mel, 6365
Katz, Bill, 310
Katz, Danny, 2669
Katz, Gerry, 1867
Katz, Helene, 1242, 4684
Katz, Irwin, 4035
Katz, Joel, 8125
Katz, Norberto, 836
Katz, Roberta, 710
Katz, Saul, 7274
Katz, Sherman, 2419
Katzenmeyer, John, 4938
Kauffman, Cheryl, 1016, 4347
Kauffman, David, 4082
Kauffman, Ellen, 7722
Kauffman, Rhona S, 674
Kauffman, Welz, 4162
Kaufman, Elaine, 7360
Kaufman, Jake, 3366
Kaufman, Judy, 7709
Kaufman, Richard, 723
Kauk, Cindy, 4552
Kaushagen, Ingrid Joy, 4543
Kautzman, Chavon, 2916
Kauvar, Joanne, 6003
Kavafian, Ida, 1218
Kavanagh, Eileen, 4663
Kavanaugh, Dr Patrick, 4221
Kawabata, Maiko, 1292, 1297
Kawaguchi, Gary, 34, 5813
Kawaguchi Dunn, Cynthia, 688
Kawakami, Ed, 851
Kawano, Hirofumi, 28
Kawaoka, Gerald R., 6310
Kawash, Stephen E, 3629
Kawashima, Kimi, 1580, 5347
Kay, Alan, 1293
Kay, David, 5694
Kay, Kenneth, 3214
Kay, Wanda L, 597
Kaye, Marvin, 3118
Kaye, Michael, 1852
Kayes, Carla, 7295
Kayler, Kyle, 1237
Kaylor, Hugh, 8423
Kays, Daniel, 5960
Kayser, Denise, 4364
Kazanjian, John, 3615
Kazee, Tom, 7806
Kazez, Daniel, 1416
Kazis, Eearle W, 1984
Kazle, Elynmarie, 3311
Kazmierczak, Thomas, 7301
Keagle, Karen, 3168
Kean, Jeff, 5966
Kearney, Patty, 5606
Kearns, Gene, 2685
Kearns, Karen, 3805
Kearns, Patrick Alan, 2349
Kearns, Robert F, 1259
Keary, David, 245
Keating, L, 1608
Keating, Thomas P., 1780
Keating, Wayne, 1838, 4306
Keaton, Charles, 2695
Keaton, Jim, 3336
Kechley, David, 4421
Kechley, David S, 6876
Keck, Teresa, 5312
Keden, H Michael, 776
Keebler, Paul, 762

Keedy, Paige, 1814
Keefe, Matthew, 268
Keefer, Krissy, 64
Keelan, Hugh, 1468
Keeler, Janet E, 1407
Keeley, Dawn, 2537
Keeman, Michael, 7552
Keenan, Cecilie, 2606
Keenan, John, 7111
Keene, James, 4559
Keene Cooper, Kara, 6262
Keeney, Sally J, 1329
Keevil, Jeff, 7025
Keffer, Lindsay, 7948
Kehler, David, 1543
Keicher, Roger, 3007
Keilbach, Kurt, 2351
Keilitz, Douglas, 1937
Keimach, Brad, 641
Keiser, Anne, 1755
Keith, Daryle, 6530
Kekas, Dennis, 7501
Kell, Barbara, 6097
Kellachan, Dan, 4830
Kelleher, Barbara, 6146
Kelleher, Leslie, 724
Kelleher, Michael, 4685, 7275
Kellenher, Kenneth, 3873
Keller, Barrie, 2775
Keller, Emily, 5729
Keller, Joel E, 1517
Keller, Kathleen, 7714
Keller, Linda, 1424
Keller, Werner, 1726
Kellerman, Tiffany, 3539
Kellett, Brett, 2131
Kelley, Betty, 2681, 6699
Kelley, Brian, 2437
Kelley, Dorothea, 1542
Kelley, Heidi, 823
Kelley, Joan, 3569
Kelley, John, 1633
Kelley, John A., 1706
Kelley, Karla, 208
Kelley, Robert, 97, 2213, 2226
Kelley, Steve, 1835
Kelley, Susan R, 3822
Kelley, Tim, 641
Kelley, Wade, 2073
Kelley, Warren, 3136
Kellner, Sara, 7984
Kellogg, Jan, 8270
Kelly, Ann, 470, 517
Kelly, Barbara, 1751
Kelly, Brenda, 2595
Kelly, Cynthia K, 1227
Kelly, Fred, 470
Kelly, Jackie, 2667
Kelly, Jay, 6392
Kelly, Kathleen, 1868
Kelly, Laura, 576
Kelly, M Wade, 992
Kelly, Michael T, 6380
Kelly, Monica, 210, 1011, 1845, 4341
Kelly, Rebecca, 364
Kelly, Ryan M, 1891
Kelly, Sue, 641
Kelly, Tina, 807
Kelly, Tony, 2278, 6367
Kelner, Russell, 1183
Keltner, Karen, 1701
Kelty, Dr Mary, 4510
Kemble, Ray, 3920
Kemerling, Alice, 4464
Kemp, Heather, 1913
Kemp, Judy, 2598
Kemp, Kimberly, 488
Kemp, Nancy, 5602
Kemson, J, 1053
Kenaston, Kimberly, 1462
Kendall, Christopher, 1021, 1084
Kendall, Janet, 7637
Kendall, Kelley, 6378
Kendall, Paulette, 2159
Kenderdine, Henry, 5074
Kenderdine, Suzanne, 5074
Kendrick, Donald, 1674
Kener, David, 3048, 7309

Kenerson, Gayle, 6866
Keninll, Rohana, 4775
Kennard, John, 1883, 4434
Kennebeck, John, 3793
Kennebeck, Scott, 4532
Kennedy, Bill, 6744
Kennedy, Brian P, 7605
Kennedy, Bryan, 7957
Kennedy, Charry, 7111
Kennedy, Christopher, 4777
Kennedy, Courtney, 157
Kennedy, David, 715
Kennedy, Debi, 4408
Kennedy, Diane, 5572, 5573, 5574
Kennedy, Dianne, 7583
Kennedy, Elizabeth, 1682
Kennedy, Floy, 5606
Kennedy, Jim, 1656
Kennedy, John W, 2892
Kennedy, Kara, 3669
Kennedy, Karen, 876, 1794
Kennedy, Lisa, 3674
Kennedy, Patrice, 5654
Kennedy, Patrick, 6581, 7217
Kennedy, Richard, 7389
Kennedy, Robert M, 6878
Kennedy, Steve, 2886
Kennedy Smith, Jean, 809, 811
Kennedy-Lamar, Ms. Danielle, 5578
Kenner, Doug, 1150
Kenney, Brad, 2795
Kenney, Bradford T, 6794
Kenney, Crane, 6393
Kenney, Micheal, 131
Kenney, Wes, 764, 765
Kenney, Will, 2617, 4175, 6450
Kenny, Daryl, 3555
Kenny, Fionnuala, 2291
Kenny, Sheila, 2691
Kenny, Wes, 1736
Kent, George, 2051
Kent, George A, 567
Kent, Jill, 812
Kent, Sidney E, 1002
Kent, Terri, 3303
Kenworthy, Jane E, 740
Kenyan, Thomas, 3976
Kenyon, Matt, 3644
Keogh, Andy, 5510
Kepa, Judy, 5798
Kepl, Daniel, 725
Kepley, Scott, 737, 5948, 5950
Kepple Jr, Thomas R, 5083
Kerbs, Amy K, 5099
Kerby, Lynn, 3803
Kerby, Rick, 2427
Kerkhof, Lynn, 3
Kerley, Jean, 1935
Kerlin, Bill, 2458
Kern, Dennis, 8124
Kern, Doug, 6534
Kern, Gary, 589
Kern, Kathy, 7666
Kern, Marty, 7793
Kern, Marty S, 7795
Kern DC PhC, Donald, 6599
Kern Paste, Gail, 2409
Kernaghan, Maryellen, 8399
Kernodle, Jr, John R, 1344
Kerr, Allan, 483
Kerr, Anne, 6180
Kerr, Donna, 1419
Kerr, Jonathan, 1755
Kerr, Nanne, 4027
Kersey, Don, 3388
Kersey, Wade, 2538
Kersh, Nunally, 463, 1515, 3425, 5174
Kershaw, Jeff, 6733, 6735, 6740
Kershaw, Stewart, 3531
Kerslake, Glen, 3198
Kersy, Don, 3386
Kerwin, Patrick, 7712
Keshishian, Moira, 2915
Kessick, Steve, 8211
Kessler, Allan, 2277
Kessler, Laura, 180
Kessler, Lawrence, 2432
Kessler, Martin, 1369
Kessler, Melvin P, 816

Lamphere, Carla, 1087
Lamping, Mark, 7051
Lampitelli, Jude, 2537
Lampropoulos, Fred, 8070
LaMuro, Leslie, 5538, 8286
Lamy, Whitnaey, 5369
Lan Tong, Shu, 260
Lanahan, Jim, 3062
Lancaster, Bob, 2679
Lancaster, Christopher, 310
Lancaster, Dona, 2679
Lancaster, Linda, 4286
Lancaster, Mike, 1554
Lancaster, Sharon, 408
Lance, Cindy, 182
Lance, Jean, 639
Land, Charlie, 5293, 8000
Land, Liz, 7903
Land, Pat, 3256
Land, Ronald, 1746
Landaich, Pierre, 7861
Landau, Ellen, 7503
Landau, John, 3606
Lande, Aaron, 768
Landeen, Mike, 7274
Lander, John, 7881
Lander, Nancy, 5600
Landeros Valle, Zindy, 3782
Landers, Vernon, 3523
Landeverk, Wayne, 1457
Landey, Sena, 6483
Landgren, Peter, 1370, 7541
Landis, Davis, 3459
Landon, John, 7920
Landon, Mark, 910
Landow, Brett, 1835, 2676
Landrella, James N, 2192
Landry, Drew, 1178
Landry, Joan, 876
Landsman, Dennis, 198
Landsman, Kathy, 198
Landstreet, Susan, 3011, 4674
Lane, Dr Michael R, 6655, 6657, 6658
Lane, Dr. Michael R., 6656
Lane, Jack, 2905
Lane, JoAnna, 6424
Lane, Marcia, 2516
Lane, Peter, 5684
Lane, Peter B, 7737
Lane Christilles, Karen, 6668
Laney, Rachel, 7453
Lang, Amanda, 8270
Lang, Brien, 5164
Lang, Kathy, 940
Lang, Mark E, 3075
Lang, Michael, 418
Langan, Lorie, 923
Langbehn, Marilyn, 3746
Langdon, Robert B, 2516
Lange, Abby, 2938
Lange, David, 8274
Lange, Eric, 6585, 6587, 6588
Lange, Michael, 5842
Lange, Michelle, 619
Lange, Sandra A, 8268, 8272
Langel, Leighann, 3716
Langer, Michael J, 7711
Langer, Patricia, 3121
Langford, Rebecca, 2478
Langill, Mark, 5806
Langill, Norman, 5458
Langley, Bill, 7033
Langley, Carole, 3723
Langley, Duane, 3723
Langley, Jeff, 2234
Langley, Ken, 6482
Langlitz, Harold N., 3194
Langrock, Kathy, 3883
Langstraff, Kay, 3940
Lanham, Lou Ann, 8209
Lanier, Greg, 2471
Lanier, Kym, 507
Lann, Nonie, 2144
Lannamann, Richard S, 1293
Lanners, Buncie, 4083
Lanni, Terry, 7116
Lannoye, Sheril, 3662
Lansbury, Edgar, 3040
Lansderry, Rod, 5968

Lansky, David, 301
Lantz, Dr. Gordon D, 1433
Lantz, Jere, 1903
Lantz, Lisa, 6603, 6604, 6605, 6606
Lanza, Ruth, 262
Lanzilotti, Louise, 2538
LaPan, Mike, 4028
Lapedes, Richard, 409
LaPenna, Tom, 5646
Lapidas, Jerry, 2437
Lapidus, Dr. Ira, 2792, 4422
Lapine, Edward, 2334
Lapinski, Doris, 1476
Lapore, Larry, 7779
Lappin, Robert, 854
Laqua, Lori, 5906
Laredo, Jaime, 1588
Larena, Alison, 7173
Larew, Donald, 3261
Largess, Bill, 2422
Larimore, David, 7837
Larimore, James, 7137
Larison, Tamara, 432
Lariviere, Eric, 821, 4008
Larivivere, Eric, 4009
Larmore, Stephen, 1150
LaRocco, Claire, 3631
Larochelle, Michael, 3283
LaRowe, Bruce, 3221
Larsen, Brandi, 5986
Larsen, Georganne, 1019
Larsen, Honey, 2476
Larsen, Jarrod, 8053, 8056, 8057, 8058
Larsen, Rick, 730
Larsen, Robert L, 1833
Larsen, Steven, 887, 922, 923
Larsen, TJ, 2935
Larson, Andre, 7829
Larson, Beth, 3358
Larson, Bill, 7055
Larson, David, 5168
Larson, Heather, 1728
Larson, Jack, 6991
Larson, James, 2931
Larson, Jennifer, 6359
Larson, Julie, 7656
Larson, Kenneth A, 1743
Larson, Leslie Ann, 39
Larson, Lowell, 4487
Larson, Nicki, 1917
Larson, Priscilla, 5289
Larsonan, Bob, 6603, 6604, 6605, 6606
LaRue, Jaclyn, 429
Lasansky, Enrique, 594
Lash, Shari, 2013
Lasher, Robert W, 711
Laska, Marianne, 776
Laskey, Kim, 3595, 8149
Laskin, Emily, 5773
Lasorda, Tommy, 5806
Lassiter, Tina S, 3985
Laster, Liz, 11
Lasuen, Joe, 6338
Laszlo, Charles, 7569
Lata, Matthew, 1778
Latham, Den, 7810
LaTorella, Anthony, 3164
Latshaw, Charles, 933
Latson, Frank, 3543
Lattarulo, Craig, 397
Lattin, Shean, 5035
Laturno Bojanic, Nancy, 695
Lau, Clara, 1546
Lau, Diana, 530
Lau, Gloria, 3871, 3874
Lau, Tina, 874
Lauderdale, Joe, 2173
Lauffer, Bruce, 1480
Laughead, Scott, 3032
Laughton, John C, 4603
Laun, Michael, 2244
Lauridsen, Diane, 98
Lauritzen, Sharon, 5955
Lautenberger, Fran, 2116
Lauterbach, Gregg, 1223
Laux, Kelly, 8274
LaValleur, June, 2855
Lave, Roy, 2178
Lavelle, Jim, 2476

Laven, Pete, 5694
Lavender, Fred, 1364
LaVenia, Randy, 6127
Lavery, James G, 7502
Lavery, Sharon, 632
Lavey, Martha, 2588
LaVigne-Roan, Desiree, 425
Lavin, Michael, 6384
Lavin, Steven D, 3905
Lavine, Steven D, 744
Lavoie, Patricia, 256
Law, Bill, 1127
Law, Bob, 3054
Law, Donna, 3546, 5330
Law, Harold, 3472
Law, Reggie, 3468
Law, Ron, 4844
Lawie, Tracey, 6926
Lawlor, Charlie, 8103, 8104
Lawlor, Deborah, 2190
Lawlor, Lee, 3782
Lawrence, Beth, 7801
Lawrence, Blake, 3068
Lawrence, Daniel L, 2156
Lawrence, John, 3894
Lawrence, Margaret, 4577
Lawrence, Naomi, 12
Lawrence, Nathaniel, 4168
Lawrence, Sally, 7687
Lawrence Rivera, Jon, 2203
Lawrencfe, Richard, 734
Lawrey, Cathy, 1140
Laws, Jennifer, 3624
Lawson, Dr Darren, 3429
Lawson, Eric, 1360
Lawson, H Ray, 2733
Lawson, Joanne W, 1976
Lawson, John, 1976
Lawson, Kim, 3474, 7901
Lawson, Martha, 532
Lawson, Michael, 1191
Lawson, Robert, 2948
Lawson, Sheeler, 4893
Lawton, Dana, 65
Lawton, Jacqueline, 2403
Lawton, Maryi, 2442
Lawton Brown, Katharine, 4535
Laxalt, Mrs. Paul, 2410
Lay, Lee, 5210
Layendecker, Col Dennis M, 804, 1753
Layman, Jane, 4085
Layne, Helene, 4035
Layne, Margaret Mary, 8212
Layton, Richard, 955
Lazar, Elie, 6
Lazar, Joel, 1032
Lazarus, Ann, 5900
Lazarus, Michael, 710, 3874
Lazarus, Michael P, 3871
Lazenberg, William, 5052
Lazin, Steve, 443
Lazo, Christina, 2267
Lazorcik, Dave, 1471
Lazorcik, David, 5078
Lazzara, Teri, 3621
Lazzari, OSB, Boniface V, 5436
Lbarde, Erol, 6764
Le Coque, Louise, 4189
Leach, Alan, 1135
Leach, Howard H., 1710
Leach, Kate, 5157
Leach, Renaye, 3661
Leahy, Carol, 2741, 2747
Leahy, Jim, 5843
Leahy, Mary, 555
Leahy, Sharon, 410
Leake, Tracy, 3318
Leaming, Jim, 2553
Lear, Cindy, 7069
Leass, Richard, 4539
Leavitt, Toby, 3873
Leaycraft, Matthew, 7446
Leb, Mary, 5475
LeBauer, Dr. Sam, 4860
Lebdetter, Jason, 5890
Lebeau, Jim, 7411
Leberman, Pam, 3404
Lecompte, Elizabeth, 3169
Ledbetter, Kristy, 5843

Leder, William, 4454
Lederkramer, Ron, 5816
Ledford, Brad, 6438, 6441
Ledford, Laura, 6399, 6400, 6401
Ledingham, Allan, 2424
Ledingham, Joyce, 2424
Ledri-Aguilar, Lisa, 2149
Lee, Ary, 4870
Lee, Brenda, 4100
Lee, Bruce, 3546, 5330
Lee, Charlene, 1273
Lee, Charlotte C, 3417
Lee, Cindy, 353
Lee, Dan, 5799
Lee, Doc, 3434
Lee, Doug, 6218
Lee, Dr. Yuan-Yuan, 929
Lee, Gary, 4793
Lee, Genevieve, 625
Lee, Gregory, 7065
Lee, Ingrid, 5610
Lee, Irene S, 152
Lee, James L, 7914
Lee, Joe, 563
Lee, Jonathan, 5816
Lee, Joseph, 564
Lee, Josephine, 1800
Lee, Kathleen, 7033
Lee, Katy, 6482
Lee, Larry E, 1433
Lee, Leeheng, 1301
Lee, Mike, 5646
Lee, Patricia Taylor, 707
Lee, Ralph, 3192
Lee, Rhoady, 6314
Lee, Robert M, 2102
Lee, Ronald, 1507
Lee, Ruth, 181
Lee, Ryan, 651
Lee, Song, 376
Lee, Stephanie, 6257
Lee, Suzanne, 876
Lee, Terri, 4264
Lee, Terri L., 6673
Lee, William, 779
Lee, Young Jean, 3146
Lee Gier, Angela, 3490
Lee, Jr, George, 1542
Leebove, Patricia, 7558
Leeestma, Heidi Holst, 2812
Leehey, David, 916
Leekly, Bob, 7638
Leeman, Robert, 6798
Leemon, Dick, 2782
Leeping, Richard, 1637
Leepman, Karen, 3417
Leerstang, Carmen, 1840
Leevers, Carol, 3262, 7209
Lefebvre, Pat, 1055
Lefever, Jim, 5915
LeFevour, Tim, 6381
Leff, Judy, 2249
Lefton, Lester, 7585
Lefton Esq, Ira S, 442
Legassik, Autrey, 5730
Legault, Greg, 6670
Leggett, Vivian, 3269
Lehan Siegel, Pamela, 428
Lehan-Siegel, Pamela, 428
Lehman, David, 5080
Lehman, Katherine, 5224, 5225
Lehman, Kathy, 5065
Lehman, Larry, 7674
Lehmann, Carter, 2750
Lehmann, Klaus-Dieter, 7333
Lehr, Lester E, 621
Lehr, Linda, 1950
Lehwalder, Heidi, 5387
Leib, Robert, 6807
Leiblinger-Hedderson, Carole, 3283
Leidig, Irma, 1916
Leifer, Mel, 316
Leigh, Barbara, 3653
Leighton, Danette, 5872
Leighton Smith, Lawrence, 758
Leiken, David, 7676
Leinbach, Connie, 5140
Leiniger, John, 770
Leininger, Alexis, 6551

Martell, Sharon, 3347
Martelli, Ruth, 3410
Marten, Ethan, 3580
Marten, Richard, 3580
Martin, Alice E, 3833
Martin, Amy, 3595
Martin, Barbara, 3358
Martin, BJ, 187
Martin, Bruce W., 1103
Martin, Carol, 2353
Martin, Craig, 2261
Martin, Danita, 2131
Martin, Dennis, 1758
Martin, Dr Alice, 2587
Martin, Eff W., 1712
Martin, Elisa, 2765
Martin, Emily, 161
Martin, Floyd, 3732
Martin, Geoffery, 3287
Martin, Glenn, 5227
Martin, Harolt, 7516
Martin, Helen, 6924
Martin, Jason Keith, 187
Martin, Jennifer, 3880
Martin, Jill, 2314
Martin, Jill Cary, 2159
Martin, Joan, 458
Martin, John, 4810
Martin, John W, 2443
Martin, Jonathan, 1335
Martin, Jorge, 5806
Martin, Karla L, 3875
Martin, Keith J, 187
Martin, Kent, 2667
Martin, Linda, 7001
Martin, Martha, 1685
Martin, Mary, 4263, 6665
Martin, Marya, 4735
Martin, Michael, 7216
Martin, Michelle, 485
Martin, Mitchell, 6236
Martin, Morgan, 2853
Martin, Richard, 4264
Martin, Richard P., 6673
Martin, Rick, 2278
Martin, Robert, 3106, 4656
Martin, Ron, 3327
Martin, Russ, 1624
Martin, Sandy, 2949
Martin, Sharon, 1001
Martin, Steve, 2124
Martin, Sue, 5127
Martin, Sue N, 5127, 5128, 5129
Martin, Susan, 6950
Martin, Terry, 3471
Martin, Wesley, 1671
Martin, William C, 6883
Martin, William C., 2362
Martin Blackwell, Angela, 524
Martin-Palmo, Kathy, 529
Martin-Wilkins, Danita, 2131
Martindale, Diane, 1966
Martinez, Dennis R, 5817
Martinez, Diana, 2622, 4118, 6354
Martinez, Francisco, 100
Martinez, Hector, 5766
Martinez, Ivan, 7374
Martinez, J R, 3507, 3514
Martinez, Leroy, 3540
Martinez, Rafael, 5995
Martinez Rivera, Isabel, 342
Marting, Kristen, 3078
Martini, Philip, 168
Martins, Peter, 357
Martinson, Leslie, 2213, 2226
Martorano, Joseph F, 1326
Marturano, Janice, 1898
Martus, Ketty, 2546
Marty, David, 4452, 4480
Martynuk, Nusha, 414
Marumoto, Karen, 5806
Marvel Loskot, Chris, 508
Marvocca, Kim, 8149
Marx, Anthony W, 6835
Mascari, Bob, 7596
Maschino, Janine, 229
Mash, Fraizer, 2694
Mashburn, Victor, 3510
Masini, Jim, 2583

Maslich, Meredith, 805
Mason, Ann F, 1499
Mason, Ed, 6497
Mason, Gail, 5970, 6075
Mason, Janet, 2976
Mason, Lucile, 2976
Mason, Martha, 227
Mason, Mary Ellen, 2606
Mason, Suzy, 5658
Mason, William, 6374
Mason, William A, 1807
Mason Gregg, Lynette, 495
Masone, David, 1692
Massa, William, 7588
Massaro, John, 1658
Massengale, Joni, 3204
Massenkoff, Nikolai, 3858
Massey, Barbara, 333
Massey, Janet, 1543
Massing, Star, 3527, 7994
Massingill, Gary, 3620
Massman, Martin, 2152, 2182, 2198
Massmann, Martin, 5819
Massod, Al, 1465
Massoudi, Barry, 5439
Mast, Brian, 6506
Mastako, Rodger, 718, 3881
Mastalski, Elaine, 3365
Masten, John, 1287
Mastenbrook, Ellen, 225
Masterson, John, 5315
Masterson, Marc, 2694
Masterson, Veronica, 2263
Mata, Ray, 8202
Matan, Debbie, 3287
Matchett, Bobby, 5006
Matczynski, Leonard, 4377, 4378
Mateas, Linda, 3897
Mateo, Jose, 226
Matheny, Jane, 3631
Matheny, Jerry, 3288
Matheny, Kenneth, 4990
Mather, Randy, 3600
Mather, Toni, 823
Matheson, Grace, 2864
Mathews, Blair, 558
Mathews, Glen, 3246
Mathews, Louise, 1583
Mathews, Melanie, 3613
Mathews, Paul, 8264
Mathews, Sharon, 203
Mathias, Dick, 8094
Mathieu, Jeff, 5728
Mathis, Paige, 1785
Mathur, Shana, 5818
Mathwich, Lowell A, 408
Mathys, Elena, 3916
Matichak, Joe, 2265
Matin, Beatrice, 1449
Matine, Katherine A, 2834
Matison, Katie, 1612
Matney Brown, Sharon, 7069
Mato, Nancy, 4039
Matos, Edwin, 7307
Matpaliano, Christopher, 2030
Matson, L, 1053
Matsui, Gail, 5813
Matsui, Nancy, 34
Matsumoto, David, 874
Matsurra, Taks, 5744
Matter, Charles E, 7417
Matteson, Jim, 3638
Matteson, Steve, 2076
Mattessich, Dino, 6078
Matthes, Sina, 5633
Matthew, Adam, 3599
Matthew, Charlie, 7982
Matthew, Kevin, 3599
Matthew, Terri, 8039
Matthews, Benjamin, 1982
Matthews, Ingrid, 1616
Matthews, John, 3472
Matthews, Michael, 2322, 5805
Matthews, Virginia, 601, 5680
Matthies, David, 630
Matthieson, Megan, 3887
Mattison, Donald C, 908
Mattison, Mike, 2667
Matton, Annie, 1620

Mattoon, Bill, 2353
Mattox, Hoyt T, 5289
Mattson, Steve, 6974
Mattson, Wendi, 6429, 6430, 6431
Matuskey, Alison, 1853
Matuszeski, John, 726
Mauceri, Jhon, 2048
Mauceri, John, 3772
Maughan, Kent, 2891
Mauk, Shelley A, 3306
Maull, George Marriner, 1208
Maullar, Marci, 6674, 6675
Maupin, Gregory, 6546, 6547, 6549, 6550
Maur, Elsie von, 962
Maurer, Ron, 2798
Mauro, Roberto, 1887
Mauroff, David, 2258
Max, Darla, 3393
Max, Doug, 6014
Maxbauer, William, 1083
Maxey, B. William, 1103
Maxon, Barbara, 169
Maxwell, Amy, 1444
Maxwell, Carla, 336
Maxwell, Dan, 4167
Maxwell, David, 6612
Maxwell, Dr. David, 6610, 6611
Maxwell, Jennifer, 4142
Maxwell, Karen M, 6794
Maxwell, Martha Ellen, 1528
Maxwell, Mihael D, 2109
Maxwell, Mitchell, 2335
May, Bobby, 7992
May, Eileen, 241
May, Eldonna, 1087
May, Jill, 6919
May, Jonathan P, 1302
May, Linda, 4553
May, Robin, 610
May, Susan, 5769
May, Thomas D, 1037
Maybrey, Jean, 6955
Mayer, Daniel, 8165
Mayer, Debbie, 211
Mayer, Diane, 2702
Mayer, Janice, 8421
Mayer, Lisa, 418
Mayers, Mark, 4215
Mayes, Doug, 1528
Mayes, Joseph, 1489
Mayes, Tony, 302
Mayes-Smith, Susan, 2936
Mayfield, Maryhelen, 392
Maygard, Jan, 4280
Mayleas, William, 1699
Maynard, Marci, 4967
Mayne, Joseph, 1635
Mayo, Anna Y, 3839
Mayo, Bud, 7173
Mayo, James, 6755
Mayor, Mara, 4000
Mays, Julia, 6225
Mays, Roger, 2922
Mayshark, Myriam, 3207
Mayta, Dave, 1140
Mazern, Leonard, 4438
Mazmanian, Nancy, 5710
Mazonson, Eric, 1870
Mazur, Catherine A, 7133
Mazur, Penny, 984
Mazur, Richard, 285
Mazyck, Arthur, 567
Mazza, Lynne S, 1218
Mazzola, Michael, 309, 434
Mazzola, Vincent, 4635
Mazzolini, Tom, 3868
Mazzonelli, Joan, 2590, 6387
Mc Cullough, Mike, 7579
McAdams, Beverly, 4870
McAdams, Charles, 1155
McAfee, Charlie, 2366
McAlister, Joseph, 1794
McAlister, Kevin, 6495
McAlister, Meredith, 5297
McAllister, Kari, 5769
McAllister, Meredith, 5297
McAllister, Peter, 5655
McAllister, Robert, 3917
McAniff, John, 5824

McAnuff, Des, 2170
McArdle Malock, Suzanne, 1559
McArver, R Dennis, 1593
McAuliffe, Jane, 5063
McAuliffe, Nancy, 457
McAuliffe, Warren, 457
McBeth, Christopher, 2081, 2082
McBride, Chris, 5916
McBride, Don, 3304
McBride, Howard, 2800
McBride, Karen, 6905
McBride, Mary, 3069
McBride, Patricia, 390
McCabe, Patrick R, 3872
McCabe, Rosanne, 4052
McCabe, Rose Ann, 842
McCabe, RoseAnne, 4056
McCabe, Terry, 2564
McCaffrey MD, Brian, 663
McCalhoah, Colleen, 3628
McCall, Sean, 2661, 6619
McCallum, Allen, 6818
McCandless, Stephen, 7670
McCann, Margo, 493
McCarthy, Anne, 174
McCarthy, Jim, 5007
McCarthy, Ryan, 7030
McCarthy, Steve, 3612
McCarthy, Steven, 3434
McCarthy, Tim, 2780
McCarty, Bill, 2880
McCarty, Steve, 8014
McCaskey, Raymond, 2562
McCasland, Debbie, 5636
McCellan, Roberta, 690
McClain, David, 4099, 6307
McClain, Emily, 850
McClain, Steve, 8294
McClanahan, Susan, 1883
McClatchy, Kevin, 7760
McClaugherty, John L, 1628
McClellan, Casey L, 1288
McClellan, Cathie, 2311
McClellan, James, 419
McClellan, Terrence, 6398
McClements, Nancy, 548
McClenan, Julie, 3954
McClenny, Kevin "Trip", 8230
McClintock, Thomas C, 5028
McCloskey, Sharon, 8090
McClosky, Midge, 3412
McClure, Shannon, 2018
McClure Mautinko, Victoria, 3586
McCluremahood, Sandra, 3486
McClusky, Lynette, 936
McCollam, Neal, 6389
McCollum, Michael, 937
McCollum, Sarah, 2820
McCollum, Timothy, 1639
McComb, Barry, 5766
McComb, Sharon, 5227
McConnaughey, Shelly, 6534
McConnell, Jack, 3423
McConnell, John, 3367
McConnell, Mark, 1783
McConnell, Robert, 969
McCook, Andrea, 6229, 6230
McCorkle, Michael W, 2408
McCorkle, Monica S, 2408
McCorkle, Patricia, 3091
McCorkle, Sharon, 1716
McCormick, Cecilia M, 7703
McCormick, James, 1674
McCormick, John, 3070
McCormick, Linda, 6933
McCormick, Marilyn, 2156
McCormick, Richard, 7182
McCotry, Keisha, 6264
McCoull, Chip, 3572
McCourt, Frank, 5806
McCourt, Jamie, 5806
McCoy, David, 3172
McCoy, Donita, 958
McCoy, Fred, 7100
McCoy, Jerry, 2066
McCoy, Larry, 5485
McCoy, Robb, 6153
McCoy, Susan, 525
McCracken, Jed, 8137

Mistri, Jeffrey, 646
Mital, Brian, 1586, 5353
Mitchell, Brian, 5093
Mitchell, Bryan, 5158
Mitchell, Cheri, 404
Mitchell, CJ, 898
Mitchell, Clyde, 1466
Mitchell, Deborah, 258
Mitchell, Henry, 1349, 2743
Mitchell, Jack, 2244
Mitchell, Judith, 4063, 6241
Mitchell, Katheleen, 1851
Mitchell, Kathleen, 1851
Mitchell, Kathryn, 7895
Mitchell, Ken, 4882
Mitchell, Kevin, 4693
Mitchell, Lisa, 762
Mitchell, Michael, 3374
Mitchell, Neil, 5842
Mitchell, Pauline Griller, 2747
Mitchell, Peter T, 4426
Mitchell, Rachel, 58
Mitchell, Roy, 6685
Mitchell, Rusty, 3663
Mitchell, Ruth, 157
Mitchell, Scott, 5823
Mitchell, Steve, 5558
Mitchell, Ted, 5828
Mitchell, Theresa, 6656
Mitchell, Todd, 7030
Mitchell, Tom, 4461
Mitchell Hood, Dr. Marcia, 6247
Mitchelson, Bill, 3170
Mitchko, Eric, 1783
Mitchko, Janet, 2720
Mitchum, Cindy, 6210
Mittelman, Arnold, 2458
Mitze, Teri Solomon, 3651
Miura, Naoyuki, 4769
Mixon, Emily, 4498
Mixsell, Maggie, 2293
Mixter, H Perry, 5188
Mixter, Perry, 4839
Miyamura, Henry, 874
Miyoshi, Shin R, 4730
Mizanin, John, 4182
Mizerany, Michael, 59
Mizrachi, Eli, 7113
Moats, Ellen, 2733
Moberly, Phyllis, 5822
Mocek, Rita, 2900
Mock, Aspen, 5153
Mock, Elsie, 5153
Modugno, Mike, 6929
Moe, Elaine, 5638
Moe, Joan, 689
Moe, Karen, 2831
Moehlenkamp, Betty Sue, 5395
Moehring, Albert E, 1334, 1998
Moehring, Patricia, 1334
Moeller, Jocelyn, 6586
Moeller, Katherine, 766
Moenich, Candice, 5837
Moffat, Lynn, 3115
Moffatt, Michael, 2645
Moffett, Randy, 6744
Moffitt, James, 872
Mohamed, Joe, 6353
Mohebbizadeh, Henriette, 1578
Mohler, Albert, 4286
Mohoney, Ruth, 1244
Mohr, Ann, 1364
Mohr, Matt, 6463
Mohrmann, Peter, 2242
Mohror-Hill, Elizabeth, 2829
Mohylsky, Katherine, 1375
Moiola, Leigh, 274
Molden, Jennifer, 6573
Molina, Carlos, 831
Molinaro-Blonigan, Bryan, 6647
Moline, John, 5315
Molis, Sigmund, 7204
Molitorx, Emory, 5704
Mollard, Kerri, 1395
Molloy, Honour, 3170
Molnar, Jane, 2557
Monaghan, Kate, 2402
Monaghan, Megan, 5743
Monahan, Arleene, 213

Monahan, Mark, 6950
Monahan Bremer, Cris, 5758
Monas, Anna, 1873
Moncer, Anne S, 5473
Moncrief, Clare, 2710, 4315
Moncrieff, Susan, 221
Mond, Laurie, 1903
Monder, Steven, 4920
Mondestin, Paul, 3801
Monestere, Noralee, 721, 722
Monesye, Renee, 2907
Money, Chris, 4268, 4572
Monfort, Charles K, 5656, 5989
Monfort, Richard L, 5656, 5989
Mongold, Mark, 7368
Monie, Dianna, 6428
Monk, Robert, 5855
Monnich, Kathy, 6353
Monnier, Liz, 189
Monroe, Barbara, 690
Monroe, James, 1879
Monroe, Jensen, 7269
Monroe, Kendyl K, 3091
Monroe, Mary, 4019
Monroe, Parker E, 703
Monroe, Robert, 1839, 3245
Monsky, Marie, 844, 846, 847, 848
Monson, Judy, 1171
Monson, Scott, 5805
Montana, Robert, 1833
Montanari, John, 4409
Monte, Bonnie J, 4610
Monte, Elisa, 325
Montejano, Vivian, 5287
Montera, Melissa, 4712, 7296
Monteux, Claude, 1006
Monteux-Barendse, Nancie, 1006
Montgomery, Bob, 6998
Montgomery, Chris, 5634
Montgomery, Davis, 3652
Montgomery, Howell, 6125
Montgomery, J Sherwood, 1699
Montgomery, Kerri, 3897
Montgomery, Mathew, 455
Montgomery, Nicole, 500
Montgomery, Sara, 3377
Montilino, John, 2837
Montpetit, Christopher, 5590
Montpetit, Christopher M, 4658
Monts, Lester, 4434
Montville, William, 1568
Moody, Dwain, 2106
Moody, Gloria N, 559
Moody, Joan, 4016
Moody, Robert, 1010, 1358, 2008
Moody, Sherie M., 2474
Moody, Travis, 7840
Moon, Emma, 3867
Moon, Lee, 8294
Moon, Marjorie, 2998
Moon, Nulson, 2680
Mooney, Carol Ann, 4213
Mooney, Christina, 6912
Mooney, Kenneth, 3555
Mooney, Kevin, 2475
Mooney, Patti, 5744
Mooney, Robert, 3137, 3166
Moore, Alfred, 4253, 4254
Moore, Ben, 3619, 8185
Moore, Brian, 3401
Moore, Carol, 6283
Moore, Charles, 280, 1225
Moore, Charles R, 1544
Moore, Charlie, 2853
Moore, Chris, 4985
Moore, Christopher, 6745
Moore, Dave, 5989
Moore, Dick, 3952
Moore, Don, 2205
Moore, Doug, 7025
Moore, Douglas B, 1078
Moore, Dr Brain, 1166
Moore, Ezekial J, 4320
Moore, Fred, 4252
Moore, Greg, 7138
Moore, Helen, 220
Moore, J Chris, 4986
Moore, Jeff, 2682
Moore, Jennifer, 6262

Moore, Kathleen, 268, 539
Moore, Ken, 3341
Moore, Kevin, 3299
Moore, Kimberly, 650
Moore, Laree, 7067
Moore, Linda G, 1073
Moore, Mal, 5585, 5586
Moore, Mary, 607
Moore, Nancy, 4042
Moore, Pamela, 220
Moore, Patrick, 6273, 7406
Moore, Paul, 534
Moore, Rachael, 301
Moore, Rhonda, 423
Moore, Richard, 3952
Moore, Rita, 1063
Moore, Shirley, 7890
Moore, Sonia, 3046
Moore, Thurston, 3456
Moore, Walter, 1617
Moore, Wiley, 2570
Moore Jr, Eddie N, 8122
Moore Jr, Michael, 5712, 5713, 5714, 5715, 5716
Moore Morton, Amy, 482
Moorer, Stephen, 3757, 3758
Moorman, Lisa, 8137
Moors, Cat, 189
Moots, Erin K, 2980
Moquin, Andrew, 5426
Moquin, George, 4357
Mor, Anne, 3790
Morabito, Sam, 5829
Morado, Ana-Lupe, 16
Moraitakis, Ann Marie, 6264
Morales, Annette, 4641
Morales, Cesar, 7632
Morales, Janel, 3897
Morales, Joe, 3427
Morales, Lisa, 5957
Morales, Mitchell, 6193
Morales, Phoebe, 1427
Morales Matos, Jamie, 1400
Moran, Eve, 2563
Moran, Jim, 2804
Moran, Marty, 429
Moran, Mike, 6075
Moran Jr, Charles, 6846
Morander, Jeff, 5173
Moravec, Dorothea, 1655
Mordaunt, Ninetter S, 2980
Mordine, Shirley, 168
More Glagov, Jennifer, 1808
Moreau, Donna, 3068
Moredock, George, 6075
Moree, Adeena, 5581, 5582
Morel, Penelope, 2043
Morelli, Jian Paul, 8259
Moreno, Arturo, 5710
Moreno, Rolando, 2434
Morenoff, Jerry, 2737
Morer, Paul, 2191
Morey, Charles, 3549
Morey, Herbert, 3126
Morey, Jason, 6127, 6242
Morey, Melissa, 1894
Morfesis, Andrew, 3227
Morfin, Anthony, 5959
Morgan, Bennett, 8384
Morgan, Chris, 1905
Morgan, David L, 2646
Morgan, David M, 5709
Morgan, Ed, 6331
Morgan, Elijah, 5842
Morgan, Emily, 3063
Morgan, Emily R, 1603
Morgan, Ian, 3108
Morgan, James, 1005
Morgan, Jeanie, 6726
Morgan, Jim, 3172
Morgan, John S, 7407
Morgan, Julie, 1965
Morgan, Marsha, 7043
Morgan, Michael, 669, 670, 691, 1724, 1725
Morgan, Miles, 4388
Morgan, Nancy, 4770
Morgan, Rhoan, 3023, 7289
Morgan, Richard, 3239
Morgan, Sharron, 1543
Morgan, Steve, 2172

Morgan, Tammy, 3554
Morgan, Thomas, 6847
Morgan, Victoria, 397
Morgan, William, 3281
Morgan Riggs, Janet, 7710
Morgenstein, Barbara, 4860
Morgenstern, Polly, 763
Morgenstern, Shirley, 1367
Morgon, Larry, 5858
Mori, Johnny, 5813
Moriarty, Elvin, 3529
Moriarty, John, 571, 1731
Moriarty, Judy, 6428
Moriarty, Kevin, 3023, 7289
Morin, Joseph, 1018
Morin, Lindsey, 2211
Morin, Mark, 460
Morin, Phil, 5600
Morineau, Gastin, 2247
Morisi, Michael, 524
Moritan, Betty, 6584
Morley, Dave, 675
Moroney, Ross, 5292
Morphet, Tom, 3689
Morr, Judy, 5742
Morre, D Greg Kehl, 5534
Morrelli, Marietta, 2382
Morrill, Dr. Michael J, 986
Morris, Angie, 3351
Morris, B Matt, 5185
Morris, Bonnie, 2847
Morris, Brad, 6530
Morris, Chip, 221
Morris, Clark, 4522
Morris, Curtis, 720
Morris, David, 3203
Morris, Eileen, 3523
Morris, Eric, 2692
Morris, Gary, 5706
Morris, Ginger, 3475
Morris, Goffrey, 2976
Morris, Jeannine, 4990
Morris, Jeremiah, 5840
Morris, Jeremy M, 2816
Morris, Jill, 4881
Morris, Jim, 4414
Morris, Justine, 5541
Morris, Lauren, 5800
Morris, Mark, 283
Morris, Marley, 2315
Morris, Millie, 3370
Morris, Philip, 3195, 7418
Morris, Samantha, 756
Morris, Steven, 359
Morris, Susan Waring, 3167
Morris, Thomas W, 3809, 3810
Morris, Tom, 6335, 7210
Morris, William, 2670, 3016
Morris, William C, 1973
Morris, WS, 5295
Morris-Smith, James, 8214, 8217
Morrisey, Linda, 1259
Morrison, Chris, 1175
Morrison, Gene, 3484
Morrison, Gillian, 1860
Morrison, Lawan, 530
Morrison, Malcolm, 3977
Morrison, Marcia, 7702
Morrison, Michael, 6635
Morrison, Sandy, 4035
Morrison, Sarah, 402
Morrison, Tim, 5739
Morrison-Hrbek, Stephanie, 3283
Morrissey, Charles, 2049
Morrissey, Greg, 6988
Morrissey, Michael, 5538
Morrow, Christopher, 951
Morrow, Jew, 2457
Morrs, Karl, 4990
Morse, Bill, 5856
Morse, Donald, 4253, 4254
Morse, Harvey, 820
Morse, Margaret, 6946
Morse, William, 766
Morss, Anthony, 1925, 1926
Morten, Ivonne, 2447
Mortensen, Brenda, 2892
Mortensen, Joann, 3708
Mortensen, Robert E, 2041

Executive Name Index

Poole, Natalie, 681
Poole, Richard L., 6645
Poole, Robert, 4871
Pooler, Mark, 2024
Poor, Donald, 6143
Pope, Martha A, 7843
Pope, Matt, 6703
Popejoy, James, 1360
Popov, Mikhail, 404
Popovich, Marko, 5782
Popovich, Mira, 5552, 5553
Poppe, Melinda, 9
Poppens, Lex, 6130
Poppers, Ari, 2258
Porat, Ami, 627, 645
Porch, Alan, 3631
Porco, Reobert, 1384
Porco, Robert, 1384, 4920
Porter, Allen, 201
Porter, Amylou, 1528
Porter, Catherine, 3124
Porter, David, 4938
Porter, Dean, 3782, 5824
Porter, Dick, 4115
Porter, Jackie, 3935
Porter, Josh, 1211
Porter, Lynne, 6041
Porter, Mark, 3479
Porter, Susan, 404, 1294, 4772
Porter, Tammu, 6665
Porter, Tim, 6566
Portillo, Esther, 7956
Portner, Richard, 2947
Porto, Michael, 5644
Ports, Ruth, 6652
Posey, Elsa, 378
Posey, Paige, 3228
Posey, Phil, 1136
Poshard, Glenn, 6357
Posner, Aaron, 2970
Posner, John, 3953
Posnock, Jason, 1480
Post, Arthur, 763
Post, Diane, 5229
Post, Vincent, 2458
Postel, Tina, 6426
Postema, Beth, 2009
Poster, June, 372
Poster, Robert L, 1289
Postiglion, Tony, 6182
Postoian, Diane, 3421
Posvar, Mildred, 2045
Potapov, Michael, 201
Poteet, Brenda, 3449
Poter, Ben, 3548
Potter, Becky, 5741
Potter, Dennis, 2982
Potter, Joe, 4511, 7028
Potter, John H, 8246
Potter, Joseph, 2899
Potter, Lynn, 2492
Potter, Phil, 7100
Potter, Pia, 3418
Potter, Rollin R., 5676, 5677, 5678
Potter, Wendi Gladstone, 3912
Pottinger-Walters, Cordelia, 6452, 6453
Potts, Jeff, 8274
Potts, Kimberly, 6999
Potts, Patricia, 521
Potvin, Portia, 5194
Poueymirou, Laura, 7658
Poullada, Leila, 244
Poulshock, Norm, 5459
Pounds, Paul, 7001
Pourfarrokh, Ali, 294
Pov, Dr. David, 2713
Pov, Jan, 2713
Powell, Celia, 1600
Powell, Gregg Emerson, 1083
Powell, Janelle, 5699
Powell, Lee Ann, 4501
Powell, Mark, 8074
Powell, Molly, 3655, 8271
Powell, Troy, 296
Power, Katharine, 2364
Powers, Daniel, 955
Powers, Earl E, 816
Powers, James, 2086
Powers, Marc, 2490

Powers, Paul C, 950
Pozezanac, Steve, 6514
Pradere, Oswaldo, 3065
Prall, Jean, 2967
Pramukar, Marek, 3773
Prance, Cathy, 6236
Prange, Stephen E, 436
Prather, Tharyle, 7167
Prather, Will, 2442
Pratt, Miranda, 3621
Pratt, Neal, 6797
Pratt, Suzanne, 6813
Praxell, Trink, 5933, 5935, 5936, 5938
Pray, Robert, 1110
Preacvost, William, 2890
Preddy, Kathy, 5277
Pree, Cindi, 3596
Preheim, Doyle, 1941
Premeau, Chad P, 5513
Prenatt, Susan L, 942
Prentice, Martin, 4610
Prescia, Karen, 7116
Presley, Joseph K, 1529
Press, Beth, 1751
Pressentin Wright, Carol von, 787
Prestamo, Dr Manuel, 1424
Preston, Christine, 821
Preston, Devin, 3631
Preston, Frances W, 7315
Preston, J Brad, 1407
Preston, Marvin, 268
Preston, Phillip, 3678
Preucil, William, 1384
Prevett, Cathy, 6912
Prevette, Thom, 524
Price, Beth, 507
Price, Bonnie, 749
Price, Brent, 756
Price, Calvin S, 1741
Price, Chuck, 6471
Price, Dennis, 216
Price, Faye, 2856
Price, James, 3041
Price, Jill, 3805
Price, Judy, 6568
Price, Karen, 2964
Price, Kass, 7998
Price, Lisbet, 4597
Price, Michael, 3950
Price, Michael P, 6038
Price, Michel, 3949
Price, Nancy, 6292
Price, Tarrance, 6895
Price, Tim, 2608
Prichett, Laurie, 2879
Pride, Paul, 1369
Priest, Heather, 6394
Prieto, Carlos Miguel, 563
Prill, Val, 5218
Primack, Ellen M, 3889
Primoff, Mark, 7232
Prince, Bobby, 4055
Prince, Charles, 1199
Prince, Liz, 310
Prior, Mary Ann, 3324
Prior, Richard, 862
Pritchard, David M, 2349
Pritchard, Rod, 4228
Pritchett, Mike, 6347
Prnoeis, Eileen, 7415
Probst, Tom, 5656
Procaccini, John, 7110
Proctor, Steve, 6269
Prodger, Jim, 3468, 6296
Productions, Micocci, 4734
Proehl, Thomas C, 2845
Proehl, Tom C, 2845
Proffitt, Michael, 3635
Propst, Sharon, 2886
Propst, Trasey, 2886
Prostein, Zac, 2160
Protopap, Kostis, 1665
Proud, Linda, 3884
Prough, Dr. Gene, 4031
Prouty, Erin, 731
Provancher, Scott, 922
Prows, Mark W., 7116
Pruitt, Alison, 2455
Pruittg, Barbara K, 2949

Pruner, Linda, 3565
Pruzek, Kate, 1945
Pryer, Lynn, 3227
Pryma, Paul, 6444
Pryor Jr, Millard H, 3956
Przybyl, Susan, 7304
Psomas, Beverly, 5182
Puc, Iowna, 167, 896, 1805
Pucci, B.J., 2429
Puccio, Ben, 4819
Puccio, Cindy, 1262
Puckett, Carine, 145
Puckett, Ken, 7683
Pudil, Brian, 2586
Puerte, Ronald, 7440
Pugh, Gloria, 1398
Pugh, Lee, 3233
Puglieli, Adam, 5741
Puglielli, Adam, 3518
Pugliese, AC, 2037
Pugmire, Rance, 8055
Puischer, Mary Lynn, 2848
Pulice, David, 1889
Pulk, Mary Ann, 1898, 4485
Pullen, Emma, 37
Pulliam, Kristi, 12
Pullinsi, William, 6544
Pulvermacher, Neta, 355
Puma, Jr., Nicholas J., 2770
Punty, Brad, 3068
Punzi, Debra, 384
Puphal, Shannon, 5760
Purcell, Joesph F, 1259
Purcell, Keith, 2608
Purcell, Nancy, 442
Purcell Welch, Maranne, 3404
Purdie, Doris, 906
Purdin, Rebecca, 2283
Purdy, Bruce, 7278
Purnell, Deborah, 2173
Purser, Becky, 6170
Purvis, Bob, 5702
Puryear, Mike, 7979
Puryear, Molly, 59
Pusateri, Joe, 989
Putnam, Robert, 3351
Putney, Carolyn, 7605
Putney, Jim, 1463, 5050
Putsch, Carolyn, 2886
Putzke, Jon A, 4062
Puzo, Madeline, 2207, 5804, 5820, 5825
Pyke, Pat, 878
Pyle, Fred, 4555
Pyles, Kristin, 1413
Pyrzynski, Vicky, 1885

Q

Qayoumi, Mo, 5770, 5771
Qayoumi, Mohammad, 3768
Qi, Jiang, 314
Quackenbush, Bets, 382
Quaid, Andrea, 2720
Quaife, Evelyn, 1926
Quail, Chloe, 1860
Quale, Peter, 2857
Quarles, Patricia G, 1517
Quartuccio, Anthony, 639
Quass, Tom, 3693
Quastler, Shirley, 4519
Queen, Kelin, 1736
Queen, Linda, 8223
Queen, Rachel, 7071
Queen, Todd, 1736, 6016
Queler, Eve, 1984
Quensenberry, Jim, 3442
Query, Devin, 6711
Quibell, Jeff, 1140
Quick, Wendy, 2130
Quigley, Dawn, 411
Quigley, Jill, 1633
Quilleon, David, 854
Quilleux, Irene, 825
Quinlan, Greg, 4938
Quinlan, Patricia, 2759
Quinley, John, 2674
Quinn, Angela, 697, 3846
Quinn, Daniel P, 4596
Quinn, Jeffrey, 2727

Quinn, John, 3571
Quinn, Kerrie, 160
Quinn, Marta, 691
Quinn, Meg, 3009
Quinn, Siobhan, 1854
Quinn, Thomas, 6941
Quintal, Sidney A, 6311
Quintom, Dan, 2308
Quisenberry, Dr. Karl S, 1329
Quistgaard, Jon, 6954

R

Rabaut, Dave, 3357, 7700
Rabbiner, Stan, 4797
Raben, Norman, 1984
Rabin, Deb, 800
Rabin, Sol, 2202
Rabinpwitz, Martin J., 4725
Rabito, Gia, 1
Rabon, Kathy, 6130
Racanelli, Karen, 2141
Rachele, Gary, 7217
Rachelle, Tamar, 439
Racheu in, Daniel, 1440
Rachleff, Larry, 905
Raczka, Laurel, 7740
Radakovich, Dan, 6255
Radatz, Joel, 4867
Radcliffe, Mary J, 780
Radeke, Brandon, 6955
Rademacher, Lisa, 5931, 5932
Rademaker, Dana, 4153
Rader, Janet, 2868
Rader, Paul, 4290
Radice, Neal, 3003, 3006
Raditz, Edward, 1190
Radke, Jay, 54
Radke, Kirk, 374
Radke, Scott, 402
Radler, Bruce D., 4718
Radley, Bruce, 7284
Radley, Katherine, 1063
Radosh, Sondra, 2765
Radr, Steve, 2049
Raduenz, Les, 8240, 8244
Raffaelli, Gino, 1391
Raffel, Roland, 907, 6421, 6422, 6423
Raffield, Chris, 4072
Rafinski, Mark, 3364, 7706
Rag, Maya, 6109
Ragalia, Ed, 626
Ragan, Joe, 1029, 1431
Ragan, Ronald K., 7675
Ragen, Ronald K, 7678, 7682, 7685
Ragir, John, 2576
Ragni, Angela, 652
Ragogini, Dr. Ernest, 4346
Ragogini, Ernest, 4346
Ragotzy, Brendan, 2800
Ragotzy, Jack P, 2800
Ragsdale, Kelly, 3606
Ragsdale, Martha, 3250
Ragsdale, Jr, Oliver, 4432
Rahman, Zeyba, 376
Rahmatian, Sasan, 636
Rahn, Don, 1637
Rahn, Frank, 652
Rai, Susan S, 1289
Railsback, Teresa, 6677
Raim, Ehtel, 7321
Raimondi, Matthew, 4332
Raimondi, Natalie, 4332
Rainer, Robert, 5189
Rainey, Gini, 5321
Rainie, Dr. Robert C, 4574
Rainone, Nanette, 4667
Raisebrough, Doug, 6991
Raish, Don, 1941
Raizin, Lou, 6366
Rajagopalan, Hema, 171
Rajagopalan, Krithika, 171
Rajeckas, Paul, 3132, 3157
Rakestraw, Jennifer, 2602
Ralenkotter, Rossi, 7114
Ralls Forcher, Jacquelyn, 502
Ralon, Marketing, 390
Ralph, David, 1976
Ralph, James, 5030

Rubenstein, Eric, 2601
Rubienstien, Kim, 2371
Rubin, Anne K., 4431
Rubin, Bobbie, 5971
Rubin, Holli, 2486
Rubin, Judith, 3126
Rubin, Paul, 7404
Rubin, Peter, 2015
Rubin, Peter L, 2013
Rubin, Scott, 6530
Rubino, Caroline, 4831
Rubino, Paige, 6046
Rubio, Domingo, 181
Rubsam, Henning, 370
Rucinski, Robert, 2794
Ruck, Maryann, 765
Rudd, Wiss, 1553
Rude, Ron, 3639
Ruderman, Marcia, 2751
Rudiakov, Ariel, 5364
Rudie, Evelyn, 2300
Rudie, Robert, 5233
Rudiskov, Ariel, 5363
Rudley, Carolyn, 3631
Rudolph, Ellen, 7386
Rudolph, Marleen, 4476
Rudolph, Teresa, 5858
Rudow, Vivian A, 4349
Rudsill, Guy, 2006
Rueff, Rusty, 2256
Ruen, David, 2839
Ruest, Pamela, 5146
Ruffin, Sylvester L., 5230
Rugen, Richard, 5059
Ruggiero, Marianne, 225
Ruggirello, Kelly, 1718
Rugolo, Edye, 613
Ruhberg, Regina, 7827
Ruhle, Jeannette, 1507
Ruigomez, Christopher W, 1037
Ruiz, Donna, 5872
Ruiz, Suzanne, 876
Ruiz, Victor, 3502
Rukark, Joel K, 3109
Rukowski, Rich, 8145
Rule, David, 6938
Rulison, Mark, 1802
Rumbough, Leah, 795
Rumohr, Floyd, 3001
Rumsey, David, 1144
Rund, Robert, 7163
Runice, Linda, 2927
Runnicle, Donald, 1710
Runnicles, Donald, 861, 1713, 4074, 5546
Rupp, Mark, 2641
Ruppel, David, 4005
Ruppenthal, Stephen, 686
Ruscetti, Rosanna, 6113
Ruscic, Dr. Branko, 4117
Rush, David, 6688
Rush, Margaret, 6046
Rush, Patty, 1411
Rush, Sam, 2776
Rushefsky, Peter, 7321
Rushton, Kori, 3083
Rusnak, G Alan, 1839
Rusnak, Jeff, 754
Rusnock, Joseph, 2469
Russ, Jerry, 3334
Russ, Steve, 2451
Russel, Dan, 6959
Russel, Jerry, 3514
Russell, Anne, 1529
Russell, Barry A, 3909
Russell, Ben, 7445
Russell, Bill, 2682
Russell, Craig, 7017
Russell, Dr. Timothy, 1396
Russell, Elona, 3895
Russell, Jeff, 8116
Russell, Jerry, 3507
Russell, Jill, 4747, 4756
Russell, John T, 1259
Russell, Mark, 3202
Russell, Martin, 4747, 4756
Russell, Paul, 2154, 5751
Russell, Peter, 1733
Russell, Sheryl, 2154
Russell, Steve, 1649

Russell, Tal, 3698
Russell, Timothy, 586, 587
Russell, Vicki, 2882, 7019
Russenberger, Sally, 5024
Russo, Amy, 3323
Russo, Evelyn, 3176
Russo, Karen, 408
Russo, Ralph, 8250, 8256, 8258
Rust, Catherine, 4606
Rust, Martin, 8125
Rust, Richard, 2790
Rutenberg, Peter, 1680
Ruthenbeck, Lorin, 1121
Rutherford, Jim, 7504
Rutherford, Mary J, 1429
Ruthven, Andrew, 3526
Rutishauser, Martin, 1995
Rutkowski, Rebecca, 685
Rutland, Jim, 6276
Rutland, John, 1155
Ruttemberg, Stanley, 3918
Ruttenberg, Stan, 3918
Rutter, Deborah, 6384
Rutter, Deborah F, 6368
Rutter, Kevin, 5336
Rutter, Martha, 517
Rutz, Shana, 7625
Ruzzamenti, LeAnne, 5874
Ryan, Arthur E., 7178
Ryan, Benita, 1478
Ryan, Debbie, 8094
Ryan, Denise, 934
Ryan, Dorothy, 3156
Ryan, Elizabeth, 1212
Ryan, G Jeremiah, 2971
Ryan, George, 2964
Ryan, Grace, 1431
Ryan, James D., 6656
Ryan, Jim, 2173, 5797
Ryan, Judy, 3262, 7209
Ryan, Leigh, 648
Ryan, Michael, 5308
Ryan, Mo, 3293
Ryan, Natalie Kate, 5999
Ryan, Pat, 7702
Ryan, Tobin, 5495
Ryan, William N, 4065
Ryberg, William A, 1094, 1781
Ryder, Hal, 3618
Ryder, Judith, 2013
Ryder, Linda, 1908
Ryder, Tim, 525
Rydlinski, George, 572, 5598
Rydum, Bill, 5781
Rylyk, Andrew, 517
Ryno, W Douglas, 8393
Rystrom, Nancye, 1123
Ryvkin, Valery, 2002

S

Saar, David, 2124
Saatkamp, Herman, 7186
Sabah, C J, 1162
Sabean, Brian R, 5895
Sabel, Shannon, 6534
Sabellico, Richard, 3088
Sabin, Phyllis B, 4466
Sacaratis, Deborah, 7701
Saccomano, Jim, 5992
Sachs, Dana, 2354
Sachs, Stephen, 2190
Sachse, Todd, 6948
Sackett, Laurie, 3445
Sackett, Linda, 3304
Sacks, Meryl, 609, 3749
Sackstein, Rosalina, 4033
Sadd, Martin, 5158
Sadeg, Eitan, 641
Sadewhite, James, 1203
Sadlek, Lance, 6598
Sadler, Chelsea, 2798
Sadler, Janet, 1867, 4410
Saenz de Viteri, Robbie, 7383
Saetta, Mary Lou, 1222
Safonovs, Jurijs, 524
Sagawa, Susan, 5425
Saggar, Sandeep, 2745
Sagisselman, Margo, 2851

Sagman, A.J., 8366
Sagon, Patrica B, 1755
Sahakian, Annabella, 3524
Saibel, Natalie, 2272
Saidpour, Massoud, 4934
Sailer, Fred, 3421
Saine, Jaime, 2767
Sainscein, Norman, 6069
Saint, David, 2964
Saintpeter, Richard, 2690
Saisselin, Numa, 7191
Sakai Hazzard, Claire, 876
Sakamoto, Kristen, 3778
Sakamoto, Sandra, 34
Saks, Toby, 5454
Sal, Louie, 8020
Saladow, Saul, 5942
Saladrigas, Stephen, 6647
Salamone, Vincent, 7250
Salamun, Betty, 553
Salanski, Charles, 1146
Salazar, Daniel, 782
Salchow, William, 4696
Salcido, David, 4641
Sald, Wes, 4264
Saldana, John, 2123
Saldana, Johnny, 5643, 5645, 5647
Salentine, Mark, 3640
Saler, Ed, 3402
Salerno, Lee, 1079
Salesky, Brian, 2054
Salgado, Rose, 5772
Salganek, Maya, 2118
Salimpour, Suhaila, 15
Salinas, Ben, 3483
Saline, Carol, 3397
Salisbury, Diane, 649
Salisbury, Holly, 4283, 6712
Salisbury, Robert, 5971
Sallee, Dave, 4522
Salmon, Nancy, 209, 1027, 4330
Salmonsen, Robert, 790
Salomon, Christie C, 1965
Salomon, Frank, 1294, 5113, 8412
Salomon, Frank E, 4772
Salonen, Esa Pekka, 5773
Salonen, Esa-Pekka, 658, 3772, 3789
Salovey, Todd, 5885
Salter, Jr., David, 3669
Saltoun, Andre, 3884
Saltzman, H Royce, 5029
Saltzman, Steven, 4132
Salva, Larry, 6932
Salzman, Jaquee, 3663
Salzman, Jeanne, 4614
Sam PhD JD, David, 6405
Samay, Lawrence R, 1476
Samborn, Josh, 4637
Sammis, Erin, 1776
Sammis, III, Jesse F, 1588
Samoff, Marjorie, 3387, 3398
Samoss, Marjorie, 5104
Sampson, Alann B, 5270
Sampson, Carol, 4952
Sampson, Janice, 3732
Samson, Bruce, 1457
Samson, Suzanne, 1181
Samuel, Tunde, 3104
Samuel, Wendy, 3065
Samuels, Janie, 1002
Samuelson, Jerry D., 5761, 5762, 5765
Sanborn, Cheryl R, 3696
Sanchez, Grace, 4124
Sanchez, Kathie, 3828
Sanchez, Mario Ernesto, 2434
Sanchez, Olda, 3346
Sanchez, Rick, 1539, 5249
Sand, Barbara, 5450
Sandack, Susan, 513
Sandberg, Dr. Hershel, 1097
Sanddik, Katrina, 6647
Sander Higgins, Stacey, 2960
Sanderling, Stefan, 850, 1418
Sanders, Donald T, 4405
Sanders, Dudley, 2524
Sanders, Dudley W, 2524
Sanders, Jeffri, 3717
Sanders, Jim, 7119
Sanders, John, 5890

Sanders, Lynda, 5289
Sanders, Stacie, 4352
Sanders, Terry, 489
Sanders, Wayne, 1982
Sanderson, , 106
Sanderson, Brian, 6985
Sandkamp, Anthony, 3128
Sandler, Deborah, 1835
Sandler, Luke, 5805
Sandley, Dr Don, 5554
Sandor, April, 3381
Sandoval, Gema, 48
Sandoval, Robbie, 7850
Sandretto Hull, Jennifer, 2280, 2283
Sandridge, Laura, 3249
Sands, Jr, Resita M, 897
Sandvik, Katrina, 2669
Sanferrare, Bob, 1075
Sanfilippo, Phyllis, 551
Sanford, Julia, 477
Sanford, Sara, 5
Sanford, Tim, 3126
Sankey, Jean, 1470
Sanner, Laura, 5292
Sanning, Erik, 6620, 6621, 6622
Sannuto, John, 3000
Sano, Stephen M, 737, 5947, 5948, 5950
Sansone, Dan, 3669
Sansone, Laurie, 4622
Sant, Victoria P, 810
Santana, Wilhelmina, 5757
Santarelli, Marilyn, 7771
Santillo, Elizabeth, 2043
Santo, Amen, 3850
Santomo, Melissa, 397
Santopadre, Greg, 2953
Santora, Mischa, 1376
Santora, Phil, 2226
Santora, Philip, 2621
Santoro, Angelo, 1366
Santoro-Au, Lynette, 4988
Santos, Charles, 3499
Santourian, Asadour, 3913
Sanville, Guy, 2803
Sanzel, Jeffrey, 3180
Saperston, Bruce, 5333
Sapinski, Paula, 180
Sapolsky, Dr. Jack, 4868
Saquicela, Fabricio, 3199
Sara, Elizabeth C, 1761
Sarasvati, Bala, 148
Sarch, Kenneth, 5096
Sare, Curt, 8299
Sargen, Dennis E, 6798
Sarrgeri, Jacqueline, 727
Sasaki, Kenny, 7119
Sasenbury, Scott, 6837
Saslav, Ann, 5304
Sasser, Chris, 7407
Sasser, John, 1803
Sassi, Rebekah A, 3400
Sath, Harry, 4921
Sathre, Rock, 8299
Sato Ambush, Benny, 2260, 8135
Satrang Hoel, Roger, 1900
Satter, Carolyn, 5888
Satterburg, Joanne, 685
Satterfield, April, 861, 4074
Satya, Girish, 43
Satz, Linda, 695, 3844
Satzger, Bruce, 684
Sauber, Rachael, 400
Sauer, Sharon, 1930
Sauers, Tim, 4144
Saul, Randal L, 1154
Saul, Tom, 2529
Sauls, Miriam, 3224
Saunders, Anne, 3969, 3972
Saunders, Jacqueline, 3811
Saunders, Joan, 3796
Saunders, John, 8138
Saunders, Robert, 663
Saunders, Ryan, 2051
Saunders, Steve, 4342
Saunders, Tom, 6032
Saunders Thompson, Denise, 6104, 6106, 6110
Sausner, Karen, 4670
Sauter, David, 2815
Savage, Donna, 2395

Savage, Laura Q, 955
Savage, Mark, 5224
Savage, William U, 86
Savarise, Terry, 6390
Savathphoun, Friday, 2261
Savelson, Kenny, 4731
Saver, Susan, 1531
Savidge, Dr. Dale, 5191
Savod, Bob, 7462
Sawallisch, Wolfgang, 1490
Sawaya, Michael J, 8033
Sawka, Ilyana, 1744
Sawnson, Jill K, 5230
Sawyer, A, 1109
Sawyer, Suzanne, 3672
Saxon, Ellen, 4614
Saxton, Susan, 582
Sayegh, Abdo, 240
Sayles, Edward, 2989
Saylor, Brian, 2113
Sayre, Mary E., 4583
Sayyad, Banafsheh, 95
Sbrega, John J, 6850
Scaglione, Case, 613
Scaglione, Louis, 1491
Scaife, Georgia, 489
Scala, Pat, 1229
Scales, Robert, 5804, 5820, 5825
Scallen, Thomas K, 2832
Scallen, Tom, 2849
Scally, Ken, 4412
Scanlon, Hugn, 6122
Scanlon, Mike, 7197, 7681, 7689
Scanlon, Thomas J, 1367
Scannell, Cheryl, 517
Scaoom, James, 7048
Scarboro, Kim, 4030
Scarborough, Margaret, 1436
Scarlata, Estela, 2184
Scarlato, Amy, 926
Scarrow, Susan, 2071
Scartelli, Dr. Joe, 5403
Scatterday, Mark David, 1310
Scavuzzo, Jennifer, 1467
Scerbo, Richard, 1021
Schaaf, Melissa, 6211
Schaake Jr, Fred, 7136
Schachter, Beth, 3354
Schadegg, Tom, 7632
Schaefer, Al, 1209
Schaefer, Alice, 2757
Schaefer, Carol D, 1278
Schaefer, Gary, 2702
Schaefer, Gretchen, 3583
Schaeffer, Astrida, 7133
Schaeffer, Beth, 3299
Schaeffer, Eric D, 3570
Schaeffer, Nancy, 3488
Schaetzle, Tricia, 2200
Schafer, Dr. Ronald E, 1473
Schafer, Mary, 2814
Schaffer, Jeremy, 7385
Schaffer, Karl, 92
Schaffhausen, Dick, 2655
Schairer, Laura, 579, 3704
Schalf, Jim, 6694
Schall, Lawrence, 4077, 6260
Schaller, Denise, 3916
Schallern, Sarah N, 1032
Schambelan, Ike, 3153
Schantz, Ellen, 942
Schantz, Jack, 1382
Schanwald, Steve, 6390
Schaper, Julie, 923
Schapiro PhD, Morton Owen, 6877
Schario, Christopher, 2720
Scharrer, Steve, 3664
Scharres, John, 1824
Scharres, John H, 2628
Schattschneider, Adam, 4910
Schattschneider, Dr. Adam J, 4910
Schatzlein, Dale, 4484, 6972
Schaus, Susie, 3305
Schaut, Becky, 4211
Schayes, Milton, 5426
Schechter, Dorothy Elliott, 3902
Scheele, Marian, 2094
Scheer, Teri, 4962
Scheer, Tracey, 787

Schehr, Kevin, 2912
Scheib, Charles W, 1842
Scheible, William, 1198
Scheibler, Kevin, 6893
Scheidler, Catherine, 3350
Scheidt, Kerry, 7344
Scheil, Chuck, 3233
Schein, David, 4709
Scheirle, Alexander, 759
Schelhaas, Jeri, 6641, 6643, 6644
Schelhammer, Robert, 2476
Schelkopf, Mary M, 4553
Schelkopf, Mary M., 4553
Schell, Steve, 4019
Schempf, Kevin, 1371
Schendel, Kaye, 5528
Schenkman, Bryon, 1616
Schenly, Paul, 4683
Scher, Scott, 5451
Schermerhorn, Kenneth, 1529, 2057
Schesiuk, Volodymyr, 1106
Scheurich, Tony, 6467
Schewe Jr, Joseph, 2044
Schief, Margaret, 4985
Schields, Jacque, 4259
Schieman, Sue, 1391
Schience, Jane, 5459
Schieve, Cecelia, 1773
Schiff, Lisa, 7330
Schiff, Peter G, 6427
Schiff Soros, Melissa, 7344
Schifferdecker, Kristen, 355
Schiffmacher, Jennifer, 1943, 1944
Schilb, Brian, 2639
Schildcrout, Jordan, 3043
Schilke, Melissa Z, 2366
Schiller, Heidi, 2470
Schiller, Rick, 3476
Schillhammer, David, 837
Schilling, Darren, 3773
Schilling, Mark A, 7823
Schilling, Mike, 6770
Schimpf, Chris, 1265
Schindeler, Robert Eugene, 4288
Schirato, Caroline, 3743
Schirato, Patrick, 3788
Schirle, Joan, 2143
Schirm, Ted, 1938, 2444
Schisgall Currier, Lesley, 2290
Schisler, Erica, 6390
Schlachter, Rosemary, 1376, 3275
Schlack, Lawrence, 1103
Schladweiler, John, 893
Schlaker, Tom, 7065
Schlangen, Charlie, 736
Schlath, Raymond M, 3023
Schlegel, Jane, 2646
Schlegel, Tim, 6471
Schleicher, Donald, 962, 963
Schleicher, Marissa, 752
Schlenker, John, 2223
Schleuning, Maria, 1545
Schloder, John E, 4059
Schloegel, Peggy, 1133
Schlosberg, Dr Theodore K, 1211
Schlosberg, Dr. Ted, 1211
Schlosser, Leo, 7596
Schlough, Bill, 5895
Schmad, Tim, 253, 2930
Schmeling, Pete, 1633
Schmeltz, Allen, 2231
Schmelzle, Alan, 7033
Schmid-Salm, Brigit, 8374
Schmidt, Bernard, 356, 375
Schmidt, Bill, 5989
Schmidt, Casey, 4867
Schmidt, Gordon Peirce, 232
Schmidt, Jeff, 4442
Schmidt, Judy, 1685
Schmidt, Marlene, 2353
Schmidt, Sarah, 2886
Schmidt, Stephen, 28
Schmidt, Steven J, 4492
Schmidt, Susan, 1865
Schmidt, Todd, 2959, 3642
Schmitz, David, 5242
Schmitz, Linda Marty, 5507
Schmotter, James, 6037
Schmuck, Tobin, 1961

Schnabel, Tom, 3772
Schnake, Ken, 4945
Schneider, Bekki Jo, 2636
Schneider, Bret, 2937
Schneider, Cindi, 1193
Schneider, Jack, 1716
Schneider, John, 3660
Schneider, Mike, 6530
Schneider, Peggy, 887
Schneider, Richard, 3544
Schneider, Victoria, 1116
Schneider, Jr, Esq, Ronald J, 6794
Schnell, Will, 5855
Schnepp, Mary, 694
Schnobrick, Eric, 1953
Schnur, Joel, 2608
Schoeder, Collen, 1174
Schoedinger, Janet, 2900
Schoeffler, a Diane, 1465
Schoeffler-Warren, Diane, 408
Schoelwer, Edward, 4762
Schoemaker, Tiffany, 724
Schoemehl, Jr, Vincent, 7057
Schoenberg, Deborah, 2755
Schoenbrun, Jodi, 3099
Schoenhals, Rick, 5992
Schoening, Donald, 5668
Schoephoerster, Kristin, 1123
Schofield, Scott, 2115
Schoh, Eric, 7109
Scholl, Elizabeth, 2439
Scholtemeyer, Tracey J, 3834
Scholwalter, Courtenay, 1286
Scholze, Elizabeth, 2380
Schonike, Scott, 6965
Schoonover, Kevin, 7278
Schott, Randy, 2111
Schotten, Yizhak, 773
Schotz, Laurie, 2652
Schrade, Randolph RA, 4776
Schrade, Robert W, 4776
Schrade, Rolande Y, 4776
Schrade, Rorianne C, 4776
Schrade-James, Robelyn, 4776
Schraff, Paul, 2537
Schram, Andrew, 1744
Schray, Alison Y, 4957, 4958
Schreck, Matthew, 1742
Schreiber Prince, Sarah, 6552, 6554, 6556, 6558, 6559, 6560
Schrickel, William, 1124
Schrift, Rachel, 6127, 6242
Schrodi, David, 7583
Schroedeer, Thomas, 2899
Schroeder, Bil, 2150, 3008
Schroeder, Bill, 5743
Schroeder, Charlotte, 8405
Schroeder, Scott, 5849
Schroeder, Steve, 8254
Schroeder, Sue, 154
Schroer, Dee, 593
Schroeter, Rudolf, 3756
Schroeter, Steve, 1698
Schrug, Barbara, 5837
Schrum, Jake, 5275
Schubert, Barbara, 900, 906
Schubert, Michelle, 4540
Schubert, OSFS, Gerard J, 5064
Schuerholz, John, 6266
Schuessler, Nina, 2790
Schuette, Lynn, 61
Schuldmann, Sanda, 591
Schuler, Roche, 2573
Schuler Hint, Kristin, 1699
Schuller, Gunther, 5460
Schultz, Bernard, 8229
Schultz, Caron, 1157
Schultz, J Bernard, 8221, 8224, 8225, 8227
Schultz, Jeanne, 244
Schultz, John, 3099
Schultz, Kimberly, 1729
Schultz, Ryan, 6917
Schultz, Shaun, 5624
Schultz, Todd, 1701
Schulz, Eva, 1948
Schulz, Joshua, 5942
Schulz, Tom, 7078
Schulze, Dr. Otto, 939
Schulze, Dr. Richard, 939

Schulze, Elizabeth, 576, 1028
Schulze, Theodora, 939
Schulze, Troy, 3525
Schumach, August, 1764
Schumacher, Bruce, 6530
Schumacher, Jane, 5167
Schumacher, Max B, 6530
Schumacher, Paul, 2879
Schumacher, Roy, 3240
Schuman Silver, Jo, 2275
Schumann, Laura E, 1409
Schumann, Michelle, 1533
Schupiro, Morton, 4421
Schurulst, Carolyn, 1663
Schutt, Stephen D, 6427
Schuyler, Lynden, 910
Schwab, Cynthia A., 4514
Schwalb, Joel, 6214
Schwartz, Bob, 7744
Schwartz, Ethan, 8403
Schwartz, Frederic W, 4137, 4138
Schwartz, Jennifer, 3871
Schwartz, Larry, 4639
Schwartz, Melissa, 5642
Schwartz, Michael, 399, 7559
Schwartz, Roger, 3797
Schwartz, Steve, 6121
Schwartz, Susan M, 1381
Schwartz, William, 4985
Schwarz, Doug, 2938
Schwarz, Eric, 4379
Schwarz, Gerard, 4860
Schwarz, Horace W, 1488
Schwarz, Mary, 4950
Schwarzman, Stephen A, 809, 811, 6111
Schweizer II, Al, 2086
Schwem, Marti, 5503
Schwendiman, Scott, 513
Schwenk-Berman, Laura, 232
Schweppe, Bebe, 274
Schweppe, Mark, 7733
Schwerin, Michael, 767
Schwizer, Paul, 4829
Schwrtz, David, 3163
Scianna, Dominic, 7292, 7294
Sciarratta, Patrick, 3055
Scinto, Christopher, 5630
Scippione, Don, 2015
Sciro, Cherrie, 4316
Scofield, Elizabeth, 7701
Scoggins, Gene, 1578
Scolamiero, Michael, 444
Scollon, Alex, 5960
Scotland, Jeffrey, 1663
Scott, Bert, 2469
Scott, Carolyn, 6176
Scott, Catie, 6261
Scott, Cliff, 3066
Scott, Debbie, 520
Scott, Deborah, 2988
Scott, Douglas, 151
Scott, Edd, 5046
Scott, Eric, 7467
Scott, Eugene L, 1287
Scott, Gwen, 8053, 8056, 8057
Scott, Jamie, 1470
Scott, John, 7080
Scott, John E, 5017, 7639, 7640, 7641, 7642
Scott, John T., 2707
Scott, L Brett, 1951
Scott, Lois, 1186
Scott, Rebecca L, 3042
Scott, Richard, 1166
Scott, Sean Vaughn, 2142
Scott, Stefanie, 3065
Scott, Steve, 2573
Scott, Steven, 2945
Scott, Stuart, 7263
Scott, Tianna, 8101
Scott, Tracey, 5633
Scotto, Lisa, 302
Scoville, Mary Lee, 5041
Scranton, Dr. George, 3620
Scribner, Louise, 1228
Scribner, Norman, 1755
Scribner, William, 1228
Scrivens, Connie O, 7801
Scrofani, Aldo, 3102
Scrofani, Robert, 1746

Shull, Stephen, 7916
Shulman, Ivan, 657
Shultz, Mary F, 4974
Shuman, Allan, 5775
Shumate, Al, 3585
Shumway, Beth, 426
Shurr, Buff, 5274
Shurs, Brad, 2757
Shuster, Dianna, 1704, 5913
Shutte, Thomas, 7248
Shuttz, Brenda, 6534
Shwab, Robert M, 403
Shwartz, Benjamin, 712
Sibley, Thomas E, 2003
Sichak, Jr., Stephen, 1197
Sicilia, Domenick, 6091
Sicilian, Peter, 1946
Siciliani, Alessandro, 1393
Sickle, Dolly R, 3248
Sickles, Mary Beth, 3634
Sides, Shawn, 3478
Sidlan, Murry, 5024
Sidle, Daryl, 1849
Siebeking, Brad, 1289
Sieberling, David, 1331
Siebert, Cynthia, 1141
Siebrecht, Kyle, 1615
Siegal, Adam, 3164
Siegel, Adam, 7347
Siegel, David, 5806
Siegel, Glenn, 4367
Siegel, Marc, 428
Siegler, John, 3611
Siegroth, Debbie, 1366
Siehl, John, 7582
Siek, Matt, 1716
Siemer, Evonne, 3447
Siena, Jane, 1029
Sierichs, Lt Col Alan C, 804
Siff, Ira, 1972
Sigel, Steve, 6068
Sigma, Tau Beta, 1571
Sigmon, Susan, 4082
Sikina, Tom, 221
Silber, Jerry, 1358, 2008
Silber, Merry, 1770
Silbergleit, Nina, 6910
Silberman, Chris, 762
Siliven, Tom, 6281
Silker, David, 6981, 6982
Sill, Andrews, 1564
Silon, Alan, 1396
Silow, Alan, 736
Silstein, Sandy, 3979
Silva, Albert, 2264
Silva, Chris, 1307, 7406
Silva, Gail, 2273
Silva, Heather, 3888
Silva, Pedro, 3236, 4867
Silva Stegall, Marie-Louise, 306
Silver, Kevin, 5596
Silverman, Robert, 5033
Silverman, Ron, 7670
Silverman, Stephen, 61
Silvers, Dean, 3890
Silvia, David, 458
Silvyn, Benita, 5654
Sim, Claudia, 760
Simcox, Damian, 6628
Simeone, George M, 1257
Simeone, Jeanne, 7612
Simeral, Bill, 1477
Simkins, Paula, 7037
Simmet, Karla, 1213
Simmon, Ruth, 3420
Simmons, Beverly, 1272
Simmons, Bill, 2645
Simmons, Carter, 1642
Simmons, Dianne, 1872
Simmons, Heather, 3473
Simmons, J. Brett, 6080
Simmons, Jeffrey T, 1580
Simmons, Kenneth, 2570
Simmons, Michael, 1489
Simmons, Nina, 7469
Simmons, Peter, 1005, 4327, 4328
Simmons, Phil, 7114
Simmons, Scott, 1124
Simmons, William, 926

Simmons Jr, C W, 5004
Simolij, Mariusz, 1478
Simon, Barbara, 8403
Simon, Benjamin, 610
Simon, Beverly, 1276
Simon, Brad, 8403
Simon, David, 2202, 5766
Simon, Dennis, 1211
Simon, Eli, 2167
Simon, Ellen B, 260
Simon, Herbert, 4203
Simon, Howard, 726
Simon, Mary, 2605, 3523
Simon, Melvin, 4203
Simon, Nancy, 8199
Simone, Denise, 2547
Simone, Elaine, 5106
Simone, Gianni, 1926
Simone, Giovanni, 1926
Simone, John, 7428
Simone, Tex, 7428
Simonis, Bert, 5945
Simons, Annette, 732
Simons, Dennis, 1002
Simons, Diana, 3513
Simons, Diane, 7967
Simons, Johnny, 3513, 7967
Simons, Karma, 616
Simons, Katie, 2879
Simons III, E Gray, 2785, 4413
Simonson, Lynn, 317
Simotes, Tony, 2770, 8251
Simpkins, Al, 3391
Simpkins, James, 1612
Simpkins, John, 2379
Simpson, Bruce, 202
Simpson, Jane, 6291
Simpson, Jann, 3102
Simpson, Jeanmarie, 4571
Simpson, Jim, 3052
Simpson, John, 2276, 5766
Simpson, Lawrence, 4939
Simpson, Mike, 7193
Simpson, Nancy, 5300
Simpson, Robert, 2068
Simpson Kraft, Barbara, 7
Sims, David, 2379
Sims, Larry, 865
Sinclair, Dr John V, 4066
Sinclair, James, 788, 799
Sinclair, John V, 4067
Singer, Amy, 3398
Singer, Debra, 7344
Singer, Isabelle G, 790
Singer, Joan, 1083
Singer, Ken, 1588
Singer, Matt, 2282
Singer, Paulette, 1958, 1960
Singer, Richard, 5662, 5663, 5664, 5665
Singer, Sally, 5437
Singer, Valerie, 2282
Singleton, Doug, 390
Singleton, Gwendolyn, 5842
Singleton, Jacki, 2587
Singleton, Jim, 1537
Singleton, JL, 7780
Singleton, Sean, 852
Sink, Christopher, 2551
Sink, Mark, 2086
Sinn, Rose, 1143
Sinniger, Elisabeth, 1257
Siples, David, 2639
Sipp, Jerry, 3250
Siragusaal, Sheila, 2368
Siratt, Colby, 3510
Sircar, Mary, 4187, 4188
Sirna, Denise, 4600
Sirochman, Brandon, 5623
Sirovatka, Stephanie, 8247
Sisemore, Tommy, 6776, 6778
Sisler, Ben, 6025
Sission, Rhaondas, 4185
Sisson, Ray, 1146
Sistek, Linda, 2830
Sitkovetsky, Dmitry, 1342
Sitt, Jerry, 7509
Situ, Gang, 68
Sitzer, Kathleen, 7059
Siu, Sissie, 1061

Siuda, Aaron, 5740
Siuda, Chester, 7263
Sizemore, Amy, 185
Sizemore, Brad, 3250
Sjoerdsma, Dr. RD, 1634, 5497
Skala, Gary, 2555
Skeeman, Sean, 7977
Skelton, Bevera, 5847
Skerrett, Dennis, 6749
Skewis-Arnett, Bette, 6642
Skey, Carol M, 818
Skiles, Christa, 3273
Skiles, David, 8262
Skiles, David L, 5516
Skiles, Tracy, 185
Skinner, Anita Sims, 1405
Skinner, Beth, 6840
Skinner, Corby, 2914, 7075
Skinner, David, 7017
Skinner, Eric, 431
Skinner, Halcyon E, 826
Skinner, Judy, 130
Skinner, Lynn J, 4109
Skinner, Melissa, 8113, 8114, 8117, 8118, 8120, 8121
Skinner, Nancy, 6840
Skinner, Terra, 185
Skipper, Sharon, 5583, 5590
Skipper, Sharron, 5588
Skirvin, Don, 2091
Sklute, Adam, 511
Skolasinski, Kathy, 6924
Skoney, Robert C, 7881
Skoog, G. Duane, 6507, 6508, 6509
Skorton, David, 6628
Skov, Kent, 2305
Skrabalak, Duane, 1946
Slack, Amy, 4805
Sladek, John, 3902
Slagle, Richard J, 780
Slanigan, Cheri, 2217
Slater, Deana, 945
Slater, Robert, 2331
Slater, Robert A, 4913
Slater, Robert W, 5984
Slater, Stewart, 5913
Slatkin, Leonard, 1090, 1152, 3993
Slaton, Gram, 1728, 5970
Slaton, Pam, 865
Slattery, Kathy, 7137
Slaughter, Staci A, 5895
Slaughter, Thomas, 2668, 6239
Slaughter, Tim, 877
Slaughter, Timothy, 4098
Slaukin, Mark, 5822
Slavin, Barbara, 6095
Slechta, Lisa, 1664
Sleeper, Chuck, 6909
Sleeper, John, 1701
Sleeper, Susan, 3161
Slipkovich, Dan, 484
Slipp, Eric, 1033
Sloan, Amy, 7407
Sloan, Chris, 852
Sloan, Sandy, 5934
Sloan Jr, Robert B, 8046
Slobodin, Karen, 1207
Slocomb, Teresa N, 437
Slocum, William B, 1386
Sloman, Scott, 4028
Slome, Diane, 5871
Sloss, David, 634
Slowik, Kenneth, 1251, 4979
Slozar, Richard, 3281
Smaczny, Carrie A, 38
Small, Delmar D, 4326
Small, Jaquelyn, 6473
Small, Josh, 6268
Small, Norman, 2495
Smalling, Curtis, 4840
Smallwood, Aimee, 6762
Smallwood, Dale, 3123
Smarelli, David, 1366
Smart, Karen, 5969
Smart, Roger, 2586
Smart, Scott, 4645
Smentek, Susan, 1806
Smerud, Jennifer, 649

Smith, Aaron, 1274, 1967, 2812, 4744
Smith, Aaron Nigel, 1676
Smith, Alan, 1212
Smith, Alayne D, 1912
Smith, Amanda, 517
Smith, Andrea, 6800
Smith, Andrew, 2256
Smith, Anelia, 7563, 7564, 7565
Smith, Angela, 876
Smith, Ann, 5898
Smith, Annette, 2119
Smith, April, 4593
Smith, Arks, 1065
Smith, Ashley, 1385
Smith, Barbara, 4334
Smith, Billy, 5545
Smith, Brian, 7242
Smith, Cameron, 4407
Smith, Chad, 644, 658
Smith, Cherlyn, 331
Smith, Chris, 2265
Smith, Christian, 2163
Smith, Christine, 1237, 2766, 6855
Smith, Christopher, 3106
Smith, Craig, 2785, 4377, 4378
Smith, Curtis, 3867
Smith, Dalouge, 699
Smith, David R, 4089
Smith, Deborah, 6286
Smith, Debra, 7812
Smith, DeLancey, 2902
Smith, Diana, 2204
Smith, Don, 7590
Smith, Donald, 5503
Smith, Dorothy, 4671
Smith, Doug, 6596, 6931
Smith, Douglas, 4649
Smith, Dr Richard, 4250
Smith, Dr. Henry L., 6535, 6536, 6537
Smith, Dr. J Arlen, 1334
Smith, Dr. Robert, 6084
Smith, Dr. Vernon G, 6505
Smith, Duncan, 3178
Smith, Edward, 2730
Smith, Elaine, 2173
Smith, Eric, 7437
Smith, Freda, 3214
Smith, Frederick J., 2002
Smith, Fritz, 6115
Smith, Gilbert A., 5778
Smith, Grant, 3624
Smith, Gray, 3208
Smith, Gregg, 189, 4814
Smith, H Cameron, 5848
Smith, Hal, 3848
Smith, Harold, 7868
Smith, Henry, 371
Smith, Ian, 3350, 5929
Smith, James, 3489
Smith, James R, 1638
Smith, Jason, 6062
Smith, Jeanie, 503, 879
Smith, Jeff, 4276
Smith, Jeffrey, 3292
Smith, John Gettys, 5170
Smith, Joseph A, 360
Smith, Judith, 43
Smith, Judith O, 4638
Smith, Justin, 1862
Smith, Karen, 5766
Smith, Kathi, 3250
Smith, Kathryn, 2094
Smith, Keith, 5848
Smith, Kenyard, 1918
Smith, Kermeit, 2956
Smith, Kevin, 1895, 5506, 8070
Smith, Kevin W, 2024
Smith, Larry, 2725
Smith, Laura, 5969
Smith, Leland, 4914
Smith, Linda, 198
Smith, Linda C, 513
Smith, Loren, 6649
Smith, Marc, 2734
Smith, Mark D, 6470
Smith, Mark Russell, 1600
Smith, Mary, 2285
Smith, Mary Beth, 5910
Smith, Mary Ellen, 6565

Welborn, David, 5681
Welch, David M, 1041
Welch, Doris Fritz, 1041
Welch, Karen, 3638
Welch, Nina, 3798
Welch, Paula, 3636
Welch, Richard, 2661, 6619
Welch, Roger, 2546
Welch, Stanton, 498
Weldon, Jane, 4208
Welk, Luis, 2763
Wellbaum, Ray F, 1038
Wellbourne, Jr. Dr. Sullivan, 4862
Weller, Henry J, 6794
Weller, Jerrold, 695
Weller PhD, David, 247
Wellin, Thomas, 1359
Wellington, Judy, 2096
Welliver, Cassie, 8169, 8170
Wellman, Alan, 1811
Wellman, Michelle, 7827
Wellman, Ron, 7519
Wells, Barbara, 5408
Wells, Barbara C, 2464
Wells, Bob, 2332
Wells, Brian, 5878, 5879
Wells, Christine, 1069
Wells, Debbie, 2178
Wells, Dr James R, 4449
Wells, Jeff, 4118
Wells, John, 5075
Wells, John a Casey, 7707
Wells, Kate, 6268
Wells, Ken, 1446
Wells, Kermit, 1817
Wells, Larry, 1452
Wells, Palmer, 2528, 6289
Wells, Pat, 3549
Wells, Steve, 3921, 5978
Welsh, Carliegh, 7374
Welsh, George, 8094
Welsh, Greta, 5712, 5713, 5714, 5715, 5716
Welsh, John, 1604
Welsh, Josie, 12
Welsh, Melody, 990
Welsh, Susan, 6286
Welsh, Thomas, 4934
Welter, Bonnie, 1631
Welter, Charles J, 1905
Weltner, Karen, 2887
Welty, John, 5760
Welty, Peg, 6153
Wending, Gordon, 3305
Wendt Lasota, Kay, 163
Weninger, Jill, 7804
Wenta, Stefan, 30
Wente, Philip R, 650
Wentworth, Kenneth, 8387
Wentzel, Christine, 6804
Wenzel, Pete, 8211
Werch, Shifra, 1803
Werlinich, Lucille, 1303
Wermuth, Robert A, 5515
Wernecke, Susan, 1642
Werner, Ellen, 4325
Werner, Joseph, 1314
Werner, Ray, 3405
Werner, Tobias, 5415
Werner, Warren, 2461
Wernimont, Kathleen, 959
Wers, Theresa, 2250
Werth, Ernest, 2820
Wertheim, Frederick, 1294, 4772
Wertheim, James, 4747
Wertheimer Esq, Spencer, 445
Wertzer, Carla, 2689
Werz, Andreas, 638
Weskamp, Birgit, 3889
Wesl, Kenneth, 6097
Wesler, Ken, 1485, 6096
Wesler, Kenneth A, 1751
Wesley, Barbara, 1685
Wesley, Dawn, 4276
Wesp, E Joel, 3297
Wesson, Dr Matthew, 1138
Wesson, Ed, 5577
West, Don, 4544, 5620
West, George, 1177
West, Jonathan, 3640

West, Judy, 79, 4216
West, Katie, 5114
West, Lance, 5471
West, Lance A, 8216
West, Linda, 39
West, Martha, 1353
West, Morgayne, 361
West, Philip, 483
West, Reed, 8130
West, Sally, 595
West, Warren, 6841
West Muir, Vita, 3958, 3959
Westbrooke, Paul, 5014
Westby, Sharon, 3885
Westemeier, Tim, 6593
Westerman, Kit, 354
Westerwick, Bob, 1734
Westley, Wes, 7981
Westmoreland, Andy, 5673
Weston, Wade, 7532
Westover, Pam, 4442, 6896
Westover, Pamela, 1885
Westveer, J R, 6837
Westwood, Donald, 1983
Westwood, Jefferson, 7276
Wetherall, T K, 2484
Wetherbee, Charles, 4959
Wetherbee, Mary Ann, 4227
Wetherber, Charles, 4959
Wethers, Shane, 6985
Wetli, Peg, 2838, 2869
Wettach, Michael, 7284
Wettach Esquire, Thomas, 3408
Wetter, Margaret, 8180, 8181
Wetz, Coni, 7623
Wetz, Gary, 7668
Wetzel, Richard, 7537
Wetzel, Todd E, 4220
Wetzel-Ciardelli, Brooke, 3564
Wexchler, Malcolm, 3074
Wexler, Larry, 2506
Wexner, Leslie H, 7578
Weyand, Doug, 7231
Weyermann, Jim, 5914
Weyrauch, Maria, 380
Whalen, Anita, 931
Whalen, Tim M., 2256
Whaley, Ron, 773
Whalley, Brenda, 1524
Wham, Robert, 3468
Wharton, Beverly A., 6645
Wheatley III, Kenneth, 3730
Wheeland, Charles, 959
Wheeler, Curt, 828
Wheeler, Dana, 6728
Wheeler, Dick, 2366
Wheeler, Jack, 7068
Wheeler, Jacque, 2532, 6301, 6302
Wheeler, Roger, 883
Wheeler, Ronald, 1434
Wheeler, Sandra, 614
Wheeler, Scott, 1040
Wheelwright, Martin, 1932
Wheelwright, Steven C B, 6317
Whelan, Anita, 4189
Whelan, Mike, 740
Whelan, Patrick, 3329
Wheldom, Sue, 1997
Whidden, Caroline, 1589
Whidden, Shannon, 1658
Whiddon, Jerry, 2738
While, Joyce, 6614
Whimper, Carl, 5700
Whipple, Robert, 961
Whisenant, Joyce, 6264
Whisted, Don, 2740
Whitaker, Don, 950
Whitaker, Evans, 5168
Whitaker, Jennifer, 1611
Whitaker, John, 4844
Whitaker, Johnny, 5979
Whitcare, Hunt, 3564
Whitco, Dana, 309
Whitcombe, Holly, 13
White, Andrew, 2577, 3453
White, Arthur, 8342
White, B Carger, 2785
White, B Carter, 4413

White, B Joseph, 6359, 6388, 6389, 6469, 6474, 6475, 6476
White, Barry, 5214
White, Brian, 6984
White, Bryan, 5624
White, Burton, 2537, 6308
White, C. Julian, 2230
White, Carmen, 3870
White, Chris, 1254, 4708, 5779
White, Coral, 1521
White, D Patton, 153, 154
White, David, 1782
White, Deborah, 3816, 5852
White, Donny, 8106
White, Dr Leslie, 8087
White, Elizabeth, 418
White, Gwen, 7707
White, Holly, 4649
White, Jeffrey G, 1112
White, John, 440, 2129
White, Joyce, 5681
White, Kaitlin, 6169
White, Keith, 6464
White, L Keith, 4308
White, Lance, 2677, 6689
White, Leslie, 3061
White, Linda, 3516
White, LuAnn, 1832
White, Lyla L, 2227
White, Malcolm, 4501
White, Malissa, 5430
White, Marcia J., 1315
White, Mary Ann, 1031
White, Mary T, 1421
White, Matthew, 5236
White, Michael, 2549
White, Miles B., 166
White, Pat, 3110, 4420
White, Patrick, 6490, 6491, 6492
White, Rick, 5428
White, Robert, 6309
White, Roger, 557
White, Simon, 5654
White, Steven, 1648
White, Teresa A, 2570
White, Tim, 4109
White, Wrenn, 2043
White Chapin, Frances, 5431
White Thomson, Ian, 660
White, III, David A, 7025
White-Spunner, Merv, 1649
Whitehair, Bruce Q, 7707
Whitehall, James, 516
Whitehill, Joanne, 516
Whiteleather, Carole, 4106
Whiteman, Erlyne, 5923
Whiteman, Ray, 7790
Whitener, Kim, 4665
Whitener, William, 249
Whitesell, Jim, 699
Whiteway, Phil, 2701, 3586
Whiteway, Philip, 3588
Whiteway, Preston, 2388, 2389
Whitfield, Suan, 197
Whitford, Thomas K, 446, 3403
Whiting, Ward, 7603
Whitley, Benjamin, 768
Whitley, Holly, 3442
Whitley, Ran, 4842
Whitlock, Bobbi, 953
Whitlock, David, 5012
Whitlock, Dr. Keith, 5625
Whitlock, Laurie, 3793
Whitlock, Mary, 1644
Whitlock, R David, 3438
Whitman, Ann, 796
Whitman, Robert F, 8360
Whitmer, Lou, 1361
Whitmire, Cecil, 5548
Whitmore, James, 5299
Whitmore, Tyler, 2741
Whitney, Cornelius, 3194
Whitney, John, 3589
Whitney, Linda, 3608
Whitney, Scot, 3608
Whitson, Caroline, 5177
Whitson, Gwen, 50
Whitt-Lambert, Connie, 3503
Whittaker, Nicole, 4159

Whittelsey, Harry, 4704
Whittemore, Mary, 1726
Whittle-Utter, Jesse, 2268
Whittman, Loretta, 8139
Whittry, Diane M, 1464
Whitver, Josh, 968
Whitworth, Bruce, 5760
Whitworth, Paul, 5939
Wholf, Brian, 7030
Wiard, Barb, 4650
Wiatt, James A., 8304, 8444, 8482
Wick, Carl, 5693
Wick, Chad, 4930
Wicke Davis, Kelli, 454
Wicker, Russell J, 7510
Wicks, Stephen, 6795
Widdelow, Jim, 1351
Widdifield, Terra, 1128
Wideman, Ron, 4006
Width, Tom, 3572
Wiedermann, John, 2971
Wiegraffe, Merrell, 7057
Wiemken, Robert, 1492
Wiener, James, 5656
Wiener, Matthew, 2122
Wier, Christopher, 3844
Wier, Richard, 2558
Wierzel, Robert, 310
Wiese, Rochelle, 5026
Wiesen, Ruth, 142
Wiess, Marjorie, 3304
Wietzke, Phoebea, 4469
Wigger, Debby, 7080
Wiggins, Barbara, 4271
Wiggins, Judy H, 1647
Wight, Nathan, 5625
Wiglesworth, Anita, 5944
Wijsmuller, Mary, 2977
Wilberg, Mark, 2078
Wilbrecht, Dick, 1901
Wilcosky, James E., 1368
Wilcox, Agnes, 2902
Wilcox, Ericka, 8357
Wilcox, Mark, 3347
Wilcox-Smith, Tamara, 3106
Wild, William, 2650
Wilde, Dr Harold R, 6435, 6436
Wildenthal, Dr. Kern, 2062
Wilder, Bruce, 1496
Wilder, Glenn, 5396
Wilder, Jim, 2376
Wilder, Kit, 2281
Wilder Joslin, Pam, 7451
Wilder Joslin, Pamela, 3213
Wildermuth, Dan, 4940
Wildes, Kevin S J, 6767
Wildman, Esquire, Thomas R, 3956
Wilenius, Heidi, 4753
Wiley, Bert, 1347
Wiley, David, 1259, 1601, 5422, 5423
Wiley, Ella, 2142
Wiley, Hannah C, 533
Wiley, Mike, 1934
Wiley, Scott Jackson, 1950
Wiley, Steve, 3904
Wiley Pickett, Kyle, 575
Wilford, Ronald A, 8406
Wilgendusch, Nancy, 5038
Wilhelm, Elizabeth, 4548
Wilhelm, Roberta, 2931
Wilhelmus, Tom, 2637
Wilhite, Jim, 3350
Wilhoit, Mel R, 5204
Wilk, Woody, 5758
Wilke, Dr David, 4976
Wilke, Sarah, 5453
Wilker, Laurence J, 3993
Wilkerson, David, 3467
Wilkes, Dan, 6682
Wilkes, Sue, 580
Wilkiins, Joel, 6908
Wilkins, Christopher, 1569
Wilkins, Corey, 1673
Wilkins, Gary, 7980
Wilkins, Helen, 531
Wilkins, Jaci, 4115
Wilkins, John, 531
Wilkins, Thomas, 1169, 1170
Wilkinson, Ann, 6639, 6640

Facilities Index

Facilities Index

Facilities Index

Theater

Vocal Music

Folk Music
Biotzetik Basque Choir, 1795
Colorado Children's Chorale, 1732
Dallas Symphony Chorus, 2063
Hawaii Ecumenical Chorale, 1791
Klezmer Conservatory Band, 1863
Matapat, 1988
Saint Sava Free Serbian Orthodox Church, 2016
Wheeler Opera House, 1728

Gilbert and Sullivan
New York Gilbert and Sullivan Players, 1978
Opera a La Carte, 1683
Washington Savoyards, 1851

Grand Opera
Adrian Symphony Orchestra, 1880
Amato Opera Theatre, 1957
Anchorage Opera Company, 1653
Arizona Opera, 1662
Aspen Opera Theater Center, 1727
Atlanta Symphony Orchestra Chorus, 1784
Augusta Opera Association, 1789
Austin Lyric Opera, 2058
Baltimore Opera Company, 1847
Beaumont Civic Opera, 2060
Berkshire-Hudson Valley Festival of Opera, 1947
Chattanooga Symphony and Opera Association, 2053
Chautauqua Opera, 1987
Chicago Children's Choir, 1800
Cimarron Circuit Opera Company, 2024
Cincinnati Opera, 2012
Commonwealth Opera, 1867
Connecticut Opera, 1741
Dallas Opera, 2062
Dayton Opera Association, 2018
Eugene Opera, 2029
Florida State Opera at Florida State University, 1778
Glimmerglass Opera, 1954
Greensboro Opera Company, 2002
Gulf Coast Opera Theatre, 1906
Hawaii Ecumenical Chorale, 1791
Honolulu Children's Opera Chorus, 1793
Houston Grand Opera, 2069
Indianapolis Opera, 1825
Kentucky Opera, 1835
Knoxville Opera Company, 2054
Long Beach Opera, 1679
Lyric Opera of Kansas City, 1910
Macallister, 1827
Master Singers, 1870
Merola Opera Program, 1703
Metro Lyric Opera, 1923
Michigan Opera Theatre, 1887
Millikin University Opera Theatre, 1812
Mississippi Opera, 1907
Mobile Opera, 1650
Nashville Opera Association, 2056
Nevada Opera, 1920
New Rochelle Opera, 1956
Oklahoma Opera and Music Theater Company, 2026
Opera Birmingham, 1648
Opera Ebony, 1982
Opera Lite, 1889
Opera Omaha, 1919
Opera Pacific, 1717
Opera San Jose, 1716
Opera Southwest, 1940
Opera Theater of Pittsburgh, 2045
Opera Theatre of No Virginia, 2085
Opera Theatre of Saint Louis, 1913
Orlando Opera, 1774
Pala Opera Association, 1986
Philomusica Choir, 1924
Piedmont Opera Theatre, 2006
Pocket Opera, 1704
Portland Opera, 2030
San Francisco Opera Center, 1710
Sarasota Opera Association, 1777
Smith College Glee Club & Choirs, 1873
Sro - a Lyric Theatre Company, 1916
Syracuse Opera, 1994
Texas A&M University Opera & Performing Arts, 2061
Townsend Opera Players, 1685
Tulsa Opera, 2028

University of Southern California Thornton Opera, 1684
Utah Festival Opera Company, 2077
Utah Opera Company, 2082
Verismo Opera/New Jersey Association of Verismo Opera, 1926
Virginia Opera, 2087
Westminster Choir College, 1933
Wolf Trap Opera Company, 2090

International
International Music Camp, 2010

Jazz
International Music Camp, 2010

Light Opera
Amato Opera Theatre, 1957
Anchorage Opera Company, 1653
Arch-Opera House of Sandwich, 1821
Arizona Opera, 1662
Aspen Opera Theater Center, 1727
Augusta Opera Association, 1789
Austin Lyric Opera, 2058
Baltimore Opera Company, 1847
Beaumont Civic Opera, 2060
Berkshire Lyric Theatre, 1875
Chattanooga Symphony and Opera Association, 2053
Chautauqua Opera, 1987
Chicago Children's Choir, 1800
Children's Opera Theater, 1852
Cimarron Circuit Opera Company, 2024
College Light Opera Company, 1866
Columbus Symphony Chorus, 2017
Comic Opera Guild, 1882
Community Opera, 1936
Connecticut Opera, 1741
Dallas Opera, 2062
Dallas Symphony Chorus, 2063
Dayton Opera Association, 2018
Diablo Light Opera Company, 1723
Dupage Opera Theater, 1815
Eugene Opera, 2029
Gulf Coast Opera Theatre, 1906
Honolulu Children's Opera Chorus, 1793
Houston Grand Opera, 2069
Indianapolis Opera, 1825
International Music Camp, 2010
Kentucky Opera, 1835
Knoxville Opera Company, 2054
Light Opera Oklahoma - Look, 2027
Long Beach Civic Light Opera, 1678
Lyric Opera of Kansas City, 1910
Macallister, 1827
Millikin University Opera Theatre, 1812
Mississippi Opera, 1907
Moline Boys Choir, 1817
Nashville Opera Association, 2056
Nevada Opera, 1920
New England Lyric Operetta, 1738
New Rochelle Opera, 1956
North Star Opera, 1904
Ohio Light Opera, 2023
Oklahoma Opera and Music Theater Company, 2026
Opera Ebony, 1982
Opera Lite, 1889
Opera New England, 1861
Opera Omaha, 1919
Opera Pacific, 1717
Opera Southwest, 1940
Opera Theatre of No Virginia, 2085
Opera Theatre of Saint Louis, 1913
Orlando Opera, 1774
Philomusica Choir, 1924
Piedmont Opera Theatre, 2006
Pittsburgh Civic Light Opera, 2047
Pocket Opera, 1704
San Francisco Opera Center, 1710
Sarasota Opera Association, 1777
Schenectady Light Opera Company, 1990
Smith College Glee Club & Choirs, 1873
Spanish Lyric Theater, 1780
Sro - a Lyric Theatre Company, 1916
Starlight Musical Theatre, 1702
Syracuse Opera, 1994
Texas A&M University Opera & Performing Arts, 2061
Townsend Opera Players, 1685
University of Southern California Thornton Opera, 1684
Utah Festival Opera Company, 2077

Utah Opera Company, 2082
Verismo Opera/New Jersey Association of Verismo Opera, 1926
Virginia Opera, 2087
Washington Savoyards, 1851
Westminster Choir College, 1933

Lyric Opera
Academy of Vocal Arts Opera Theatre, 2034
Adrian Symphony Orchestra, 1880
American Opera Music Theater, 1959
American-International Lyric Theatre, 1960
Anchorage Opera Company, 1653
Arch-Opera House of Sandwich, 1821
Arizona Opera, 1662
Aspen Opera Theater Center, 1727
Augusta Opera Association, 1789
Austin Lyric Opera, 2058
Baltimore Opera Company, 1847
Berkshire-Hudson Valley Festival of Opera, 1947
Boston Camerata, 1857
Chamber Singers of the Colorado Springs Chorale, 1729
Chattanooga Symphony and Opera Association, 2053
Chautauqua Opera, 1987
Chicago Children's Choir, 1800
Cimarron Circuit Opera Company, 2024
Cincinnati Opera, 2012
Columbus Symphony Chorus, 2017
Commonwealth Opera, 1867
Community Opera, 1936
Dallas Opera, 2062
Dallas Symphony Chorus, 2063
Dayton Opera Association, 2018
Dupage Opera Theater, 1815
Eugene Opera, 2029
Florida State Opera at Florida State University, 1778
Glimmerglass Opera, 1954
Gulf Coast Opera Theatre, 1906
Houston Grand Opera, 2069
Indianapolis Opera, 1825
Kentucky Opera, 1835
Knoxville Opera Company, 2054
Long Beach Opera, 1679
Lyric Opera of Kansas City, 1910
Macallister, 1827
Merola Opera Program, 1703
Millikin University Opera Theatre, 1812
Mississippi Opera, 1907
Nashville Opera Association, 2056
Nevada Opera, 1920
New Rochelle Opera, 1956
North Star Opera, 1904
Ohio Light Opera, 2023
Oklahoma Opera and Music Theater Company, 2026
Opera Birmingham, 1648
Opera Ebony, 1982
Opera Lite, 1889
Opera New England, 1861
Opera Omaha, 1919
Opera Pacific, 1717
Opera Southwest, 1940
Opera Theatre of Saint Louis, 1913
Philomusica Choir, 1924
Piedmont Opera Theatre, 2006
Pocket Opera, 1704
San Francisco Opera Center, 1710
Sarasota Opera Association, 1777
Smith College Glee Club & Choirs, 1873
Spanish Lyric Theater, 1780
Sro - a Lyric Theatre Company, 1916
Syracuse Opera, 1994
University of Southern California Thornton Opera, 1684
Verismo Opera/New Jersey Association of Verismo Opera, 1926
Virginia Opera, 2087
Westminster Choir College, 1933

Medieval
Early Music New York (Em/Ny), 1967

Men's Chorus
Orpheus Male Chorus of Phoenix, 1659
Philadelphia Gay Men's Chorus, 2040

Multi-Disciplinary
Dorian Music Festivals, 1831

Music
Revels, 1878

Musical Performance
University Musical Society Choral Union, 1883

Musical Theatre
American Opera Music Theater, 1959
American-International Lyric Theatre, 1960
Arch-Opera House of Sandwich, 1821
Aspen Opera Theater Center, 1727
Augusta Opera Association, 1789
Austin Lyric Opera, 2058
Baltimore Opera Company, 1847
Boston Camerata, 1857
Chamber Singers of the Colorado Springs Chorale, 1729
Chautauqua Opera, 1987
Chicago Children's Choir, 1800
College Light Opera Company, 1866
Colorado Children's Chorale, 1732
Columbus Symphony Chorus, 2017
Comic Opera Guild, 1882
Community Opera, 1936
Dallas Opera, 2062
Dayton Opera Association, 2018
Diablo Light Opera Company, 1723
Dorian Music Festivals, 1831
Florida State Opera at Florida State University, 1778
Fulton Opera House, 2032
Gloriae Dei Artes Foundation, 1874
Grand Opera House Season at the Grand, 1790
Greensboro Opera Company, 2002
Gulf Coast Opera Theatre, 1906
Indianapolis Opera, 1825
Jpas Children's Chorus/Youth Chorale, 1838
Kentucky Opera, 1835
Knoxville Opera Company, 2054
Light Opera Oklahoma - Look, 2027
Lyric Opera of Cleveland, 2015
Lyric Opera of Kansas City, 1910
Lyric Opera Theatre Street, 2037
Michigan Opera Theatre, 1887
Millikin University Opera Theatre, 1812
Mississippi Opera, 1907
Moline Boys Choir, 1817
New England Lyric Operetta, 1738
New Rochelle Opera, 1956
New York Gilbert and Sullivan Players, 1978
Ohio Light Opera, 2023
Opera a La Carte, 1683
Opera Ebony, 1982
Opera Illinois, 1818
Opera Lite, 1889
Opera Music Theater International, 1760
Opera Omaha, 1919
Opera Pacific, 1717
Opera San Jose, 1716
Opera Theater of Pittsburgh, 2045
Opera Theatre of Saint Louis, 1913
Pala Opera Association, 1986
Pella Opera House, 1828
Philomusica Choir, 1924
Pittsburgh Civic Light Opera, 2047
Regina Opera Company, 1950
Sarasota Opera Association, 1777
Smith College Glee Club & Choirs, 1873
Spanish Lyric Theater, 1780
Starlight Musical Theatre, 1702
Summer Opera Theatre Company, 1761
Texas A&M University Opera & Performing Arts, 2061
Utah Festival Opera Company, 2077
Verismo Opera/New Jersey Association of Verismo Opera, 1926
Vocalessence, 1898
West Bay Opera, 1693
Western Opera Theater, 1714
Westminster Choir College, 1933
Windy City Performing Arts, 1811
Woodstock Opera House, 1824

Opera
Claremont Opera House, 1921
Cleveland Orchestra Chorus, 2014
Fulton Opera House, 2032
Grand Opera House Season at the Grand, 1790
Grand Youth Chorus, 1751
Jpas Children's Chorus/Youth Chorale, 1838
Lyric Opera of Cleveland, 2015
New Jersey Association of Verismo Opera, 1925

Oakland Youth Chorus, 1691
Opera a La Carte, 1683
Opera Camerata of Washington, 1759
Opera Illinois, 1818
Opera in The Ozarks at Inspiration Point, 1665
Opera Music Theater International, 1760
Opera Northeast/Children's Opera Theatre, 1983
Paul Madore Chorale, 1876
Pella Opera House, 1828
Regina Opera Company, 1950
San Diego Comic Opera/Lyric Opera San Diego, 1699
Summer Opera Theatre Company, 1761
West Bay Opera, 1693
Western Opera Theater, 1714
Wheeler Opera House, 1728
Wolf Trap Opera Company, 2090
Woodstock Opera House, 1824

Operetta
Adrian Symphony Orchestra, 1880
Atlanta Symphony Orchestra Chorus, 1784
Beaumont Civic Opera, 2060
Chattanooga Symphony and Opera Association, 2053
Cincinnati Opera, 2012
College Light Opera Company, 1866
Dallas Symphony Chorus, 2063
Diablo Light Opera Company, 1723
Eugene Opera, 2029
Florida State Opera at Florida State University, 1778
Houston Grand Opera, 2069
Indianapolis Opera, 1825
Long Beach Civic Light Opera, 1678
Los Angeles Concert Opera Association, 1668
Lyric Opera of Kansas City, 1910
Macallister, 1827
Metro Lyric Opera, 1923
Michigan Opera Theatre, 1887
Millikin University Opera Theatre, 1812
Mississippi Opera, 1907
Mobile Opera, 1650
New York Gilbert and Sullivan Players, 1978
North Star Opera, 1904
Oklahoma Opera and Music Theater Company, 2026
Opera Camerata of Washington, 1759
Opera Southwest, 1940
Piedmont Opera Theatre, 2006
Pocket Opera, 1704
San Francisco Opera Center, 1710
Sro - a Lyric Theatre Company, 1916
Syracuse Opera, 1994
University of Southern California Thornton Opera, 1684
Utah Festival Opera Company, 2077
Washington Savoyards, 1851

Orchestra
Rochester Symphony Orchestra & Chorale, 1903

Period Instruments
Bach Vespers at Holy Trinity, 1961

Religious
Arch-Opera House of Sandwich, 1821
Baltimore Opera Company, 1847
Bel Canto Chorus, 2099
Bella Voce, 1798
Canterbury Choral Society, 1963
Carolina Voices, 1997
Cathedral Choral Society, 1754
Chamber Singers of the Colorado Springs Chorale, 1729
Chicago Children's Choir, 1800
Choral Society of Greensboro, 2001
Cimarron Circuit Opera Company, 2024
Cincinnati Boychoir, 2011
Connecticut Choral Artists, 1742
Fairbanks Choral Society, 1654
Fairfield County Chorale, 1739
Gloriae Dei Artes Foundation, 1874
Gulf Coast Opera Theatre, 1906
Holland Chorale, 1891
International Music Camp, 2010
Kentucky Opera, 1835
Lindenwood Concerts, 2055
Maine Music Society, 1842
Master Singers, 1870
Minnetonka Chamber Choir, 1899

Moline Boys Choir, 1817
Mormon Tabernacle Choir, 2078
National Lutheran Choir, 1896
New Rochelle Opera, 1956
Opera Ebony, 1982
Opera Lite, 1889
Philomusica Choir, 1924
Radcliffe Choral Society, 1864
Saint Louis Symphony Children's Choirs, 1914
Saint Sava Free Serbian Orthodox Church, 2016
Santa Fe Desert Chorale, 1942
Smith College Glee Club & Choirs, 1873
St Olaf Choir, 1902
Symphony Chorus of New Orleans, 1840
Texas Girls' Choir, 2067
the New York Virtuoso Singers, 1992
Valparaiso University Chorale, 1829
Verismo Opera/New Jersey Association of Verismo Opera, 1926
Vocalessence, 1898
Westminster Choir College, 1933

Renassiance
Early Music New York (Em/Ny), 1967

Sea Chanteys
Sea Chanters, 1768

Series & Festivals
University Musical Society Choral Union, 1883

Theatre
Revels, 1878

Theatrical Dance
American International Lyric Theatre, 1958
Broadway Center Stage, 1935

Traditional Choral Music
Canticum Novum Singers, 1991
Chicago a Cappella, 1799
Sea Chanters, 1768
Texas Bach Choir, 2076
Westchester Oratorio Society, 1993

Vocal Music
Los Angeles Concert Opera Association, 1668

World Music
American International Lyric Theatre, 1958

Youth Chorus
All American Boys Youth Chorus, 1671
American Boychoir, 1931
American Opera Music Theater, 1959
Austin Lyric Opera, 2058
Baltimore Opera Company, 1847
Berkshire-Hudson Valley Festival of Opera, 1947
Boychoir of Ann Arbor, 1881
Boys Choir of Harlem, 1962
Chicago Children's Choir, 1800
Children's Aid Society Chorus, 1964
Cimarron Circuit Opera Company, 2024
Cincinnati Boychoir, 2011
Colorado Children's Chorale, 1732
Columbus Symphony Chorus, 2017
Dallas Opera, 2062
Glen Ellyn Children's Chorus, 1816
Greensboro Opera Company, 2002
Gulf Coast Opera Theatre, 1906
Handel Choir of Baltimore, 1849
International Music Camp, 2010
Jpas Children's Chorus/Youth Chorale, 1838
Kentucky Opera, 1835
Lindenwood Concerts, 2055
Lira Chamber Chorus, 1804
Minnetonka Chamber Choir, 1899
Moline Boys Choir, 1817
New Rochelle Opera, 1956
Oakland Youth Chorus, 1691
Opera Birmingham, 1648
Opera in The Ozarks at Inspiration Point, 1665
Opera Lite, 1889
Opera Northeast/Children's Opera Theatre, 1983
Opera Omaha, 1919
Opera Pacific, 1717
Opera Theater of Pittsburgh, 2045
Opera Theatre of Saint Louis, 1913
Orlando Opera, 1774
Radcliffe Choral Society, 1864
Saint Louis Children's Choirs, 1915
Saint Louis Symphony Children's Choirs, 1914
San Diego Children's Choir, 1698
San Francisco Girls Chorus, 1708
Santa Fe Desert Chorale, 1942

Sarasota Opera Association, 1777
Smith College Glee Club & Choirs, 1873
Tar River Choral & Orchestral Society, 2004
Texas A&M University Opera & Performing Arts, 2061
Texas Girls' Choir, 2067
Townsend Opera Players, 1685
Tulsa Opera, 2028
Verismo Opera/New Jersey Association of Verismo Opera, 1926
Westminster Choir College, 1933

Colorado

Indiana

Iowa

Maine

Maryland

Massachusetts

Michigan

Jewish Community Center of Saint Louis, 7059
Jones Auditorium, 7044
Juanita K Hammons Hall, 7068
Juneteenth Heritage & Jazz Festival, 4530
Kansas City Ballet, 249
Kansas City Blues & Jazz Festival, 4516
Kansas City Chamber Orchestra, 1142
Kansas City Municipal Auditorium, 7034
Kansas City Municipal Auditorium Music Hall, 7033
Kansas City Renaissance Festival, 4517
Kansas City Symphony, 1143
Kansas City Symphony Chorus, 1911
Kansas City Young Audiences Series, 4518
Kansas City Youth Symphony Association of Kansas, 1153
Kauffman Stadium, 7035
Kirkwood Symphony Orchestra, 1147
Leach Theatre, 7045
Liberty Center, 2908
Liberty Performing Arts Theatre, 7038
Liberty Symphony Orchestra, 1145
Lindenwood College Mainstage Season, 4538
Lyceum Theatre, 7019
Lyric Opera of Kansas City, 1910
Mark Twain Outdoor Theatre, 2896
Mary Linn Performing Arts Center, 7040
Memphis Community Players, 2894
Metro Theater Company, 2900
Mid-America Arts Alliance, 2889
Missouri Botanical Garden Amphitheatre, 7060
Missouri Repertory Theatre, 2890
Missouri River Festival of the Arts, 4507
Missouri Symphony Society, 1139
Missouri Theater, 7047
Missouri Theatre, 7025
Missouri Western State College Fine Arts Theatre, 7048
Moberly Area Council on The Arts, 4524
Moberly Community Theatre, 2895
Mule Barn Theatre, 7072
Mule Barn Theatre of Tarkio College, 2911
Municipal Theater Association of Saint Louis, 2901
Muny Amphitheatre, 7061
New Music Circle, 1148
New Music Circle Series, 4531
New Theatre, 2902
Northland Symphony Orchestra, 1144
Northwest Missouri State University Performing Arts Series, 4523
Okoboji Summer Theatre, 7026
Opera Theatre of Saint Louis, 1913
Ozark Actors Theatre, 2897
Park College Alumni Hall Theatre, 7043
Performing Arts Association of Saint Joseph, 4527
Powell Symphony Hall, 7062
Price Cutter Park, 7041
Pro Musica, 4514
Quality Hill Playhouse, 2891
Repertory Theatre of Saint Louis, 2903
Royal Arts Council, 2912, 4539
Saint Joseph Civic Arena, 7049
Saint Joseph Symphony Society, 1146
Saint Louis Ballet, 247
Saint Louis Black Repertory Company, 2904
Saint Louis Cathedral Concerts, 4532
Saint Louis Chamber Chorus, 1908
Saint Louis Children's Choirs, 1915
Saint Louis Classical Guitar Society, 1149
Saint Louis Hills Arts Council, 4534
Saint Louis Philharmonic Orchestra, 1150
Saint Louis Symphony Children's Choirs, 1914
Saint Louis Symphony Orchestra, 1151
Saint Louis Symphony Youth Orchestra, 1152
Saint Louis Symphony: Classics in The Loop Festival, 4533
Savis Center, 7063
Scott Joplin Ragtime Festival, 4536
Sheldon Concert Hall and Ballroom, 7064
Shepherd of the Hills, 2883
Show Me Center, 7021
Sikeston Little Theatre, 2909
Southeast Missouri State University: Cultural Series, 4508
Springfield Ballet, 251
Springfield Little Theatre at the Landers, 7069

Springfield Symphony Association, 1154
Sro - a Lyric Theatre Company, 1916
Stages St. Louis, 2905
Starlight Theatre, 2892, 7036
Summerfest Concerts, 4519
Theater Factory Saint Louis, 2906
Theron C Bennet Ragtime & Early Jazz Festival, 4526
Transworld Dome at Americas' Center, 7065
Trilakes Community Theatre, 2884
Truman State University Lyceum Series, 4521
Umb Bank Pavilion, 7039
Unicorn Theatre, 2893, 7037
Union Avenue Opera Theatre, 7066
University of Central Missouri, 4540
University of Missouri Performing Arts Series, 7046
University of Missouri-Kansas City Conservatory Series, 4520
University of Missouri: Columbia Concert Series, 4509
University of Missouri: Saint Louis Premier Performances, 4535
West End Players Guild, 2907
William Woods College Campus Center Dulany Auditorium, 7028
William Woods University Concert & Lecture Series, 4511
Winston Churchill Memorial Hall, 7029

Montana

Adams Event Center, 7087
Alberta Bair Theater, 2914
Alberta Bair Theatre for the Performing Arts, 7075
Aleph Movement Theatre, 2917
Associated Students of Montana State University, 4542
Bigfork Center for the Performing Arts, 7074
Bigfork Summer Playhouse, 2913
Billings Symphony Orchestra & Chorale, 1917
Billings Symphony Society, 1156
Breenden Field House/Worthington Arena, 7077
Butte Civic Center, 7079
Carroll College Theatre, 7082
Dillon Community Concert Association, 4543
Flathead Festival of the Arts, 4551
Flathead Valley Festival, 4547
Four Seasons Arena, 7080
Great Falls Civic Center Theater, 7081
Great Falls Symphony Association, 1158
Havre Community Concert Association, 4545
Helena Civic Center, 7083
Helena Civic Center Auditorium, 7084
Helena Symphony Society, 1159
Majestic Valley Arena, 7086
Metrapark, 7076
Missoula Children's Theatre, 2918
Missoula Symphony Association, 1160
Montana Ballet Company, 252
Montana Chorale, 1918
Montana Repertory Theatre, 2919
Montana Shakespeare in The Parks, 2915
Montana Traditional Jazz Festival, 4544
Myrna Loy Center, 7085
Northern Showcase Concert Association, 4546
Old Timers Concert Series, 4550
Red Lodge Music Festival, 4541
Reno H Sales Stadium, 7078
University of Montana Performing Arts Series, 4548
University of Montana Theatre, 7088
Vigilante Theatre Company, 2916
Whitefish Theatre Company, 2920
Wilma Theatre, 7089
Yellowstone Chamber Players, 1157
Young Audiences of Western Montana Series, 4549

Nebraska

Abendmusik Series, 4556
Al Caniglia Stadium, 7102
Bassett Arts Council, 4553
Bellevue Little Theatre, 2921, 7091
Bladen Opera House, 7092
Bob Devaney Sports Center, 7097

Brownville Concert Series, 4559
Cathedral Arts Project Series, 4560
Center Stage, 2927
Chadron State College Memorial Hall, 7093
Circle Theatre, 2928
Columbus Friends of Music Association, 4554
Community Players Theater, 7090
Concordia University Concert Series, 4564
Gothenburg Community Playhouse, 2923
Grande Olde Players Theatre Company, 2929
Harlan County Arts Council, 4552
Hastings Symphony Orchestra, 1161
Heritage Days Festival, 4558
Jewish Community Center of Omaha, 7103
Kearney Area Symphony Orchestra, 1162
Kearney Community Theatre, 2924, 7094
Lied Center for Performing Arts, 4557, 7098
Lincoln Civic Orchestra, 1163
Lincoln Community Playhouse, 2925
Lincoln Friends of Chamber Music, 1164
Lincoln Memorial Stadium, 7099
Lincoln Symphony Orchestra, 1165
Lincoln Youth Symphony, 1166
Midland Lutheran College Concert: Lecture Series, 4555
Nebraska Jazz Orchestra, 1167
Nebraska Repertory Theatre, 2926
Nebraska Shakespeare Festival, 4561
Nebraska Theatre Caravan, 253
Omaha Area Youth Orchestras, 1168
Omaha Civic Auditorium, 7104
Omaha Community Playhouse, 2930
Omaha Symphony, 1169
Omaha Symphony Chamber Orchestra, 1170
Omaha Theatre Company for Young People, 2931
Opera Omaha, 1919
Orpheum Theatre, 7105
Pavilion & Events Center Inc., 7108
Pershing Center, 7100
Post Playhouse Incorporated, 2922
Qwest Center, 7106
Shakespeare on The Green, 2932
Tuesday Musical Concert Series, 4562
University of Nebraska at Omaha Music Series, 4563
University of Nebraska Theatre, 7095
University of Nebraska-Lincoln: Kimball Recital Hall, 7101
Unk Sports Center, 7096
Wayne State College Arena, 7109
Wayne State College Special Programs Black & Gold Series, 4565
West Nebraska Arts Center, 7107

Nevada

Actors Repertory Theatre, 2934
Boulder City Arts Council, 4566
Brewery Arts Center, 2933, 7110
Caesars Palace, 7111
Carson City Symphony, 1171
Charleston Heights Arts Center, 7112
Church of Fine Arts, 7121
Churchill Arts Council, 4568
Huntridge Theatre, 7113
Las Vegas Civic Symphony, 1172
Las Vegas Convention and Visitors Authority, 7114
Las Vegas Little Theatre, 2935
Las Vegas Philharmonic, 1173
Lawlor Events Center, 7122
Mackey Stadium, 7123
Mandalay Bay Events Center, 7115
Mgm Grand Garden Arena, 7116
Nevada Arts Council, 4567
Nevada Ballet Theatre, 254
Nevada Opera, 1920
Nevada Shakespeare Festival, 4571
Nevada Symphony Orchestra, 1174
Pioneer Center for the Performing Arts, 7124
Piper's Opera House, 7127
Reed Whipple Cultural Arts Center, 4569, 7117
Reno Chamber Orchestra, 1175
Reno Little Theater, 7125
Reno Philharmonic, 1176
Reno Sparks Convention Centennial Coliseum, 7126

Sam Boyd Stadium, 7118
Theater Coalition/The Lear Theater, 2936
Thomas & Mack Center, 7119
University of Nevada Performing Arts Center, 4570
University of Nevada-Las Vegas Performing Arts Center Artemus Ham Concert Hall, 7120
University of Nevada: Reno Performing Arts Series, 4572

New Hampshire

American Stage Festival Peacock Players, 4582
Andy's Summer Playhouse, 2948
Apple Hill Center for Chamber Music, 1178
Ballet New England, 257
Barnstormers, 2946
Belknap Mill Society, 4579
Bratton Recital Hall, 7131
Capitol Center for the Arts, 7129
Claremont Opera House, 1921, 7128
Colby-Sawyer College, 4584
Colonial Theatre, 7138
Community Players of Concord, 2938
Concord City Auditorium, 7130
Dartmouth College Hopkins Center Performing Series, 4577
Eastern Slope Inn Playhouse, 7145
Franklin Pierce College Crimson-Grey Cultural Series, 4592
Friends of the Arts Regional Art Council, 4587
Friends of the Music Hall Concert Series, 4589
Great Waters Music Festival, 4594
Hampton Beach Casino Ballroom, 7136
Hampton Playhouse, 2939
Hampton Playhouse Theatre Arts Workshop, 7135
Harbor Arts Jazz Night: Portsmouth Jazz Festival, 4590
Hennessy Center, 7132
Keiser Concert Series, 4573
Lakes Region Summer Theatre, 2941
Lebanon Opera House, 7140
Loon Mountain, 7141
Mainstage Center for the Arts, 2937
Memorial Stadium, 7137
Monadnock Music, 4586
Mount Washington Valley Theatre Company, 2942
Music Hall, 7146
Nashua Community Concert Association, 4583
Ncca Papermill Theatre, 7142
Nevers' 2nd Regiment Band, 1177
New England College Cultural Events Series, 4578
New Hampshire Philharmonic Orchestra, 1179
New Hampshire Shakespeare Festival, 4575
New Hampshire Symphony Orchestra, 1180
New London Barn Playhouse, 7144
North Country Chamber Players Summer Festival: Music in The White Mountains, 4580
Northern Ballet Theatre, 256
Opera North, 1922
Papermill Theatre/North County Center for the Arts, 2940
Paul Creative Arts Center, 7133
Peterborough Players, 2943
Plymouth State University, 4588
Pontine Theatre, 2944
Prescott Park Arts Festival, 4591
Redfern Arts Center on Brickyard Pond, 7139
Saint Anselm College Performing Arts Series, 4581
Seacoast Repertory Theatre, 2945
St. Paul's School Ballet Company, 255
Summer Music Associates Series, 4585
University of New Hampshire Celebrity Series, 4576
Verizon Wireless Arena, 7143
Waterville Valley Foundation Summer Festival, 4593
Weathervane Theatre, 2947
Whittemore Center, 7134
William H Gile Trust Fund Concert Series, 4574

Wilma Theater, 3401
Wilson College Performing Arts Series, 5065
Y Music Society of the Jewish Community
 Center, 5136
Zoellner Arts Center, 7701

Rhode Island

As220, 7776
Astors Beechwood Mansion, 3417
Brown Stadium, 7777
Brown Summer Theatre, 3419
Brown University Orchestra, 1508
Brown University Theatre, 3420
Capitolarts Providence Cultural Affairs, 5161
Chorus of Westerly, 2051
Concerts by The Bay, 5156
Convergence 2000 Arts Festival: Workshop With
 Ts Thomas, 5162
Cultural Organization of the Arts, 5157
Everett Dance Theatre, 459
Festival Ballet Providence, 460
First Night Providence, 5163
Fusionworks Dance Company, 455
Island Moving Company, 458
Kelli Wicke Davis/Shoda Moving Theatre, 454
Kingston Chamber Music Festival at Uri, 1506,
 5158
Looking Glass Theatre, 3421
New England Presenters: University of Rhode
 Island Great Performances, 5159
Newgate Theater, 5164
Newport Music Festival, 5160
Newport Yachting Center, 7775
Perishable Theatre, 7778
Providence Division of Public Programming
 Departments, 5165
Providence Dunkin Donuts Center, 7779
Providence Performing Arts Center, 7780
Rhode Island Chamber Music Concerts, 1509
Rhode Island Civic Chorale & Orchestra, 1510
Rhode Island Civic Chorale and Orchestra, 2050
Rhode Island College Symphony Orchestra,
 1511
Rhode Island College: Performing Arts Series,
 5166
Rhode Island Philharmonic Orchestra and Music
 School, 1512
Rhode Island's Ballet Theatre, 457
Rites and Reason, 3422
Ryan Center, 7773
Sandra Feinstein-Gamm Theatre, 3418
Stadium Theatre Performing Arts Center, 7783
State Ballet of Rhode Island, 456
Trinity Arts Center, 7781
Trinity Repertory Company, 3423
University of Rhode Island Fine Arts Center,
 7774
University of Rhode Island Symphony Orchestra,
 1507
Veterans Memorial Auditorium, 7782

South Carolina

Abbeville Opera House, 7784
Aiken Community Playhouse, 3424
Anderson Sports Center, 7785
Anderson Symphony Orchestra, 1513
Anderson University, 5168
Arts Center of Coastal Carolina, 5184
Arts Etc, 5186
Arts Partnership of Greater Spartanburg, 5188
Bi-Lo Center, 7804
Bob Jones University Concert, Opera & Drama
 Series, 3429
Brooks Center for the Performing Arts, 7792
Capitol City Stadium, 7796
Carolina Ballet, 476
Carolina Ballet Theatre, 473
Carolina Coliseum, 7797
Carolina Productions, Performing Arts
 Commission, 5176
Carolina Youth Symphony, 1516
Center Theater, 7810
Centre Stage-South Carolina, 3430
Charleston Concert Association, 5171
Charleston Symphony Orchestra, 1514
Charlotte Knights Baseball Stadium, 7803

Citadel Fine Arts Series, 5172
Civic Center of Anderson, 5169
Clemson Memorial Stadium, 7793
Coastal Concert Association, 5185
Columbia City Ballet, 464
Columbia City Jazz Dance Company & School,
 465
Columbia College Power Company Series, 5177
Columbia Community Arts Centre, 466
Columbia Stage Society at Town Theatre, 3426
Columbia's Ballroom Company, 467
Converse Symphony Orchestra, 1518
Dance Station, 461
Dock Street Theatre, 7787
Drayton Hall, 7798
Erskinarts (The Fine & Performing Arts at
 Erskine College), 5179
Fine Arts Center of Kershaw County, 7786
Fine Arts Council of Sumter Performing Arts
 Series, 5190
Florence Civic Center, 7802
Footlight Players Theatre, 7788
Francis Marion University Artists Series, 5180
Gaillard Municipal Auditorium, 7789
Gilbert Studio of Dance Arts, 472
Greenville Ballet School and Company, 474
Greenville Municipal Stadium, 7805
Greenville Symphony Orchestra, 1517
Greenwood Civic Center, 7809
Greenwood-Lander Performing Arts, 5182
Hartsville Community Concert Association, 5183
James F Byrnes Auditorium, 7815
Johnson Hagood Stadium, 7790
Koger Center for the Arts, 5178, 7799
Littlejohn Coliseum, 7794
Longstreet Theatre, 7800
Mcalister Auditorium, 7806
Mcalister Fieldhouse, 7791
Mccelvey Center of York, 7819
Metropolitan Arts Council, 5181
Music Foundation of Spartanburg Concert
 Series, 5189
Newberry College Theatre, 3432
Newberry Opera House, 7812
North Charleston Performing Arts Center, 7813
North Greenville University: Fine Arts Series,
 5191
Oliver C Dawson Stadium, 7814
Peace Center for the Performing Arts, 7807
Piccolo Spoleto Festival, 5173
Presbyterian College, 5175
Robert Ivey Ballet, 462
Sc Christian Dance Theater, 468
Southeastern School of Ballet, 469
Spartanburg Memorial Auditorium: Arena, 7817
Spartanburg Memorial Auditorium: Theatre, 7816
Spoleto Festival Usa, 463, 1515, 3425, 5174
Stepping Out Dance Studio, 470
Sumter County Cultural Center, 7818
Swamp Fox Players, 3428
The Palace Theatre, 7811
The Southern Strutt Studio, 475
Tillman Auditorium, 7795
Timmons Arena, 7808
Trustus, 3427
University of South Carolina-Beaufort, 5170
University of South Carolina: Aiken Etherredge
 Center, 5167
Vista Ballroom, 471
Warehouse Theatre, 3431
Williams-Brice Stadium, 7801
Winthrop University College of Visual &
 Performing Arts, 5187

South Dakota

Aberdeen Community Concert Association, 5192
Aberdeen Community Theatre, 3433
Black Hills Community Theatre, 3435
Black Hills Passion Play, 3437
Black Hills Playhouse, 3434
Black Hills Symphony Orchestra, 1521
Brookings Chamber Music Society, 1519
Corn Palace, 7823
Coughlin Alumni Stadium, 7820
Dakota Dome, 7828
Huron Arena, 5195
Laura Ingalls Wilder Pageant Society, 5194

Lewis & Clark Theatre Company, 3441
Madison Area Arts Council, 5196
Matthews Opera House Society, 3438
National Music Museum, 7829
Pierre Community Concerts Association, 5197
Rushmore Plaza Civic Center, 7824
Sioux Falls Arena, 7825
Sioux Falls Community Playhouse, 3436, 7826
Slagle Auditorium, 7830
South Dakota Art Museum, 7821
South Dakota State University Civic Symphony,
 1520
South Dakota State University Student Activities,
 5193
South Dakota Symphony, 1522
Spearfish Center for the Arts, 3439
Swiftel Center, 7822
Town Players, 3440
Warren M Lee Center, 7831
Washington Pavilion of Arts & Science, 7827

Tennessee

, 7870
Actors Co-Op, 3450
Adelphia Stadium, 7871
Allen Arena, 7872
Aman Arena, 7843
Appalachian Ballet Company, 482
Apsu Concert Hall, 7836
Arts & Culture Alliance of Greater Knoxville, 5198
Athens Area Council for the Arts, 5198
Austin Peay State University, 5201
Ballet Memphis, 483
Ballet Tennessee, 477
Bijou Theatre, 7848
Bijou Theatre Center, 7849
Bryan College Department of Music, 5204
Carpetbag Theatre, 3452
Carson-Newman College Concert-Lecture
 Series, 5208
Chaffin's Barn Dinner Theatre, 3461, 7873
Charles M Murphy Athletic Center, 7868
Chattanooga Ballet, 478
Chattanooga Boys Choir, 2052
Chattanooga Symphony and Opera, 1523
Chattanooga Symphony and Opera Association,
 2053
Circuit Playhouse, 3457
City Ballet, 480
Clarence Brown Theatre Company, 3453
Concerts International, 5214
Cumberland County Playhouse, 3444
Cumberland University Auditorium, 7855
Curb Event Center, 7874
David Lipscomb University Theater, 3463
David Lipscomb University: Music Department,
 5218
Derthick Theatre, 7844
Dixie Stampede, 3469
East Tennessee Fine and Performing Arts
 Scholars, 5209
Etowah Arts Commission, 5205
Ewing Children's Theatre, 3458, 7859
Freedom Hall Civic Center, 7845
Friends of Music, 5219
Gatlinburg Convention Center, 7839
Gaylord Entertainment Center, 7875
Germantown Community Theatre, 3447
Germantown Performing Arts Centre, 5206
Gordon Jewish Community Center, 7876
Grand Ole Opry House, 7877
Greer Stadium, 7878
Hooper Eblen Center, 7837
Howard C Gentry Complex, 5220
Jackson Arts Council, 5207
Jackson Civic Center, 7841
Jackson Symphony Association, 1524
Jackson Theatre Guild, 3449
Johnny 'red' Floyd Stadium, 7869
Johnson City Area Arts Council, 5210
Johnson City Symphony Orchestra, 1525
Jubilee Community Arts, 5211
Kingsport Symphony Orchestra, 1526
Knoxville Civic Auditorium and
 Coliseum-Auditorium, 7850
Knoxville Opera Company, 2054

Knoxville Symphony Orchestra, 1527
Lambuth Theatre, 7842
Langford Auditorium, 7879
Lee University Presidential Concert Series, 5202
Liberty Bowl Memorial Stadium, 7860
Life of Christ Passion Play, 3470
Lindenwood Concerts, 2055
Louise Mandrell Theater, 7888
Maryville College, 5857
Memphis Cook Convention Center Complex,
 7861
Memphis in May International Festival, 5215
Memphis Symphony Orchestra and Youth
 Symphony Orchestra, 1528
Mid-South Coliseum, 7862
Mini Dome, 7846
Mockingbird Public Theatre, 3464
Morristown Theatre Guild, 3460
Mud Island River Amphitheatre, 7863
Nashville Ballet, 484
Nashville Children's Theatre, 3465
Nashville Convention Center, 7880
Nashville Municipal Auditorium, 7881
Nashville Opera Association, 2056
Nashville Shakespeare Festival, 3466, 5221
Nashville Symphony, 1529
Nashville Symphony Chorus, 2057
Neyland Stadium, 7851
Oak Ridge Civic Music Association, 1530, 5223
Oak Ridge Playhouse, 3468
Orpheum Theatre, 7864
Playhouse on The Square, 3459
Poplar Pike Playhouse, 3448
Pull-Tight Players, 3445
Pyramid Arena, 7865
Rhodes College: Mccoy Visiting Artist Series,
 5216
Riverbend Festival, 5199
Roberts W Mclean School of Music Series, 5217
Roland Hayes Concert Hall, 7833
Roxy Theater, 3443
Ryman Auditorium, 7882
Seeger Chapel Concert Hall, 7847
Sewanee Festival Orchestras / Sewanee Music
 Festival, 5224
Sewanee Summer Music Festival, 5225
Sioux Falls Stadium, 7889
Skyhawk Arena, 7856
South Jackson Civic Center, 7890
Southern Adventist University, 5203
Sweet Fanny Adams Theatre & Music Hall, 3446
Tennessee Association of Dance, 479
Tennessee Children's Dance Ensemble, 481
Tennessee Performing Arts Center, 7883
Tennessee Performing Arts Center: Andrew
 Jackson Hall, 7884
Tennessee Players, 3456
Tennessee Repertory Theatre, 3467
Tennessee Stage Company, 3454
Tennessee Theater, 7852
Tex Turner Arena, 7840
Theater Knoxville, 3455
Theatre Bristol, 3442
Theatre Guild, 7867
Theatre Memphis, 7866
Thompson-Boling Arena, 7853
Tivoli Theatre, 7834
Tulane University, 7838
University of Tennessee at Chattanooga, 5200
University of Tennessee at Knoxville: Cultural
 Arts, 5212
University of Tennessee at Martin Arts Council,
 5213
University of Tennessee Music Hall, 7854
University of the South: Performing Arts Series,
 5226
Utc Mckenzie Arena, 7835
Vanderbilt Stadium, 7885
Vanderbilt University: Great Performances, 5222
Vanderbilt University: Memorial Gym, 7886
Viking Hall Civic Center, 7832
W.J. Hale Stadium, 7887
Watertown Jazz Festival, 5227
Wilson Chapel Complex, 7858

Texas

A.D. Players, 3519

1095

Sherman Symphony Orchestra, 1572
Slocomb Auditorium, 8020
Society for the Performing Arts, 5289
South Dallas Cultural Center, 7943
South Texas Symphony Association, 1547
Southwest Repertory Organization, 3506
Southwest Texas State University Arts Series, 5314
Southwestern Baptist Theological Seminary, 7968
Southwestern University Artist Series, 5275
Stage West, 3514
Stagecenter, 3485
Stages Repertory Theatre, 3527, 7994
State Theater Company, 3479
Stephen F Austin University Visual & Performing Arts, 5303
Strahan Coliseum, 8037
Sun Bowl, 7959
Sunken Garden Amphitheatre, 8036
Symphony North of Houston, 1560
Symphony of Southeast Texas, 1536
Talento Bilingue De Houston, 3528
Tapestry Dance Company, 487
Tarleton State University Student Programming, 5318
Teatro Hispano De Dallas, 3498
Temple Civic Theatre, 3544, 8040
Texarkana Regional Arts & Humanities Council, 5319
Texas A&M University Opera & Performing Arts, 2061
Texas A&M University: Corpus Christi, College of Arts & Humanities, 5248
Texas Amphitheatre, 3517
Texas Bach Choir, 2076
Texas Ballet Theater, 493
Texas Girls' Choir, 2067
Texas International Theatrical Arts Society, 3499
Texas Jazz Festival Society, 1539, 5249
Texas Lutheran University Cultural Arts Events, 5315
Texas Panhandle Heritage Foundation, 3484
Texas Shakespeare Festival, 3533, 5296
Texas Stadium, 7999
Texas Tech University Artists & Speakers, 5299
Texas Tech University Performing Arts Center, 8008
Texas Wesleyan College: Fine Arts, 7969
Thanksgiving Square: Courtyard at Thanksgiving, 7944
Theatre Arlington, 3474, 7901
Theatre Gemini, 3500
Theatre Suburbia, 3529, 7995
Theatre Three, 3501
Theatre Under the Stars, 3530
Tomball Regional Arts Council, 5320
Tuesday Musical Club Artist Series, 5313
Turtle Creek Chorale, 2064
Twin Mountain Tonesmen, 2075
Tyler Civic Ballet, 507
Tyler Community Concert Association, 5321
Undermain Theatre, 3502
United Spirit Arena, 8009
University Center Theatre Complex and Conference Center, 7923
University of Mary Hardin: Baylor, 5238
University of North Texas Performing Arts Center, 7948
University of St. Thomas Guest Recitals, 5290
University of Texas at Arlington, 5228
University of Texas at Austin Performing Arts Center, 7906
University of Texas at Austin: Theatre Room, 7907
University of Texas at Brownsville, 5241
University of Texas at El Paso: Main Playhouse, 7960
University of Texas at Tyler, 5322
University of Texas-Pan American: Theater, 7949
Uvalde Arts Council, 5323
Victoria Fine Arts Association, 5325
Vive Les Arts Theatre, 3534
Voices of Change, 1545
Vortex Repertory Company, 3480
Waco Convention Center Chisholm Hall, 8047
Waco Hippodrome, 8048
Waco Symphony Orchestra, 1575

Walden Piano Quartet/Walden Chamber Music Society, 1546
Warehouse Living Arts Center, 7926
Watertower Theatre, 3471
Wharton County Junior College the Center for the Arts Series, 5327
Wichita Falls Backdoor Players, 3545
Wichita Falls Ballet Theatre, 508
Wichita Falls Symphony Orchestra, 1576
William R Johnson Coliseum, 8015
Wtamu Theatre, 7920
Young Audiences of Southeast Texas, 5237
Youth Orchestra of Greater Fort Worth, 1552
Youth Orchestras of San Antonio, 1570
Zachary Scott Theatre Center, 3481

Utah

Abravanel Hall, 8071
Abravanel Symphony Hall, 8072
American West Heritage Festival, 5351
Autumn Classic Music Festival, 5338
Ballet West, 511
Brigham Young University Performing Arts Series, 5343
Cache Valley Center for the Arts, 5331
Caine Lyric Theatre, 8053
Canyonlands Arts Council, 5335
Capitol Theatre, 8073
Centrum Arena, 8050
Chamber Music Society of Salt Lake City, 1578
Chase Fine Arts Center, 8054
Clog America, 515
Contemporary Music Consortium, 5339
D Glen Smith Spectrum, 8055
Dee Events Center, 8060
Deer Valley Resort Amphitheatre, 8065
Delta Center, 5345
Dixie College Arena Theatre, 8068
Dixie College Celebrity Concert Series, 5344
Dixie College Fine Arts Center, 8067
Dixie College Proscenium Theatre, 8069
Eastern Arts International Dance Theater, 1579, 5346
Eccles Coliseum, 8051
Eccles Community Art Center, 8061
Energy Solutions Arena, 8074
Gina Bachauer International Piano Competition & Festival, 5347
Gina Bachauer International Piano Foundation, 1580
Granite Youth Symphony, 1581
Hale Centre Theatre at Harman Hall, 3554
International Dance Theater, 512
Jon M Huntsman Center, 8075
Kent Concert Hall, 8056
Kingsbury Hall, 8076
Lagoon Entertainment Division, 8052
Manon Caine Russell Kathryn Caine Wanlass Performance Hall, 8057
Manti Temple Grounds Amphitheatre, 8059
Marriott Center/Cougar Stadium, 8066
Mckay Events Center, 8064
Moab Music Festival, 5336
Morgan Theatre, 8058
Mormon Miracle Pageant, 5334
Mormon Tabernacle Choir, 2078
Odyssey Dance Theatre, 509
Off Broadway Theatre, 3548
Old Lyric Repertory Company, 3547
Oratorio Society of Utah, 2079
Orchestra at Temple Square, 1582
Park City & Salt Lake Music Festival, 5340
Park City Film Music Festival, 5341
Park City Jazz Festival, 5342
Peery's Egyptian Theatre, 8062
Pioneer Theatre Company, 3549
Plan - B Theatre Company, 3550
Repertory Dance Theatre, 513
Rice-Eccles Stadium, 8077
Ririe Woodbury Dance Company, 514
Salt Lake Acting Company, 3551
Salt Lake Symphonic Choir, 2080
Salt Lake Symphony, 1583
Southern Utah University Summer Evening Concerts, 5329
Sundance Children's Theatre, 3553
Sundance Institute, 3552

Temple Square Concert Series, 5348
Tuacahn Center for the Arts, 8070
University of Utah: School of Music, 1584
Utah Classical Guitar Society, 1577
Utah Festival Opera Company, 2077
Utah Opera, 2081
Utah Opera Company, 2082
Utah Regional Ballet, 510
Utah Shakespearean Festival, 3546, 5330
Utah State University Performing Arts Series, 5332
Utah Symphony, 1585
Val A Browning Center for the Performing Arts, 8063
Wassermann Piano Festival, 5333
Weber State University Cultural Affairs, 5337
Westminster College, 5349
World Arts/Noon Concerts Series, 5350

Vermont

American Theatre Works, 3558
Banjo Dan and The Mid-Nite Plowboys, 1590
Barre Opera House, 8078
Brattleboro Music Center, 2083, 5352
Burklyn Ballet Theatre, 516
Burlington Discover Jazz Festival, 1586, 5353
Burlington Memorial Auditorium, 8079
Castleton State College Performing Arts Series, 5356
Catamount Film and Arts Company, 3562
Chaffee Art Center, 5369
Chandler Center for the Arts, 5368
Chandler Music Hall and Cultural Center, 8084
Department of Theatre and Dance, 8082
Dorset Theatre Festival, 3560
Festival of the Arts, 5362
Flynn Center for the Performing Arts, 8080
Green Mountain Festival Series, 5357
Green Mountain Guild, 3561
Killington Music Festival, 5370
Lost Nation Theater, 3560
Manchester Music Festival, 5363, 5364
Middlebury College Concert Series, 5365
Music in A Great Space, 5358
National Marionette Theatre, 3556
North Country Chorus, 2084
Northern Stage, 3564
Oldcastle Theatre Company, 3555
Onion River Arts Council: Celebration Series, 5366
Pentangle Council on The Arts and The Woodstock Town Hall Theatre, 5372
Potomac Theatre Project, 3559
Sky Blue Boys, 1591
St. Michael's College Concerts, 5359
Stowe Performing Arts, 5371
The Green at Shelburne Museum, 8085
University of Vermont: George Bishop Lane Series, 5354
University of Vermont: Recital Hall, 8081
Vermont Mozart Festival, 1587, 5355
Vermont Stage Company, 3557
Vermont Symphony Orchestra, 1588
Vermont Youth Orchestra Association, 1589
Warebrook Contemporary Music Festival, 5361
Weston Playhouse, 3563
Yellow Barn, 8083
Yellow Barn Music Festival, 5367

Virginia

Alden Theatre at Mclean Community Center, 8112
Alden Theatre Series, 3578
Alexandria Recital Series, 5373
Alexandria Symphony Orchestra, 1592
Alleghany Highlands Arts Council/Performing Arts, 5381
Alumni Memorial Field, 8105
American Balalaika Symphony, 1594
Arlington Cultural Affairs Division, 5375
Arlington Dance Theatre, 517
Arlington's Arts Al Fresco & the Innovators, 5376
Ashlawn-Highland Summer Festival, 5379
Attucks Theatre, 8113
Averett University Concert-Lecture Series, 5382
Babcock Auditorium, 8139

Babcock Season, 3591
Barksdale Theatre, 3586
Barter Playhouse/Theatre House, 8086
Barter Theatre - State Theatre of Virginia, 3565
Bluemont Concert Series, 5402
Bridgeforth Stadium, 8102
Bridgewater College Lyceum Series, 5378
Burruss Auditorium, 8088
Cameron Hall, 8106
Carl Broman Concerts, 5412
Carpenter Center for the Performing Arts, 8125
Cary Field, 8142
Casell Coliseum, 8089
Center Stage, 8124
Centerstage, 5404
Charlottesville Classical Guitar Society, 1596
Christopher Newport University, 5398
Chrysler Hall, 8114
Citycelebrations Musicfest, 5405
College of Visual and Performing Arts, 5385
Concert Ballet of Virginia, 525
Constant Convocation Center, 8115
Dancevert, 519
Danville Area Association for the Arts & Humanities, 5383
Emory & Henry College Concert Series, 5384
Empire Theatre Complex, 8126
Empire Theatre Complex: Empire Stage, 8127
Empire Theatre Complex: Little Theatre, 8128
Experimental Theatre, 8103
Fairfax Symphony Orchestra, 1593
Fort Eustis Music and Video Center - Jacobs Theatre, 8097
Fredericksburg Music Festival, 5387
Garth Newel Music Center, 5415
Generic Theater, 3581, 8116
George Mason University Department of Theater, 8095
George Mason University Patriot Center, 5386
Greater Richmond Convocation Center, 8129
Hampden-Sydney Music Festival, 5388
Hampton Arts Commission, 5389
Hampton Coliseum, 8100
Hampton Jazz Festival, 5390
Hampton Roads Civic Ballet, 520
Hampton University, 8101
Harbor Park Stadium, 8117
Harrison Opera House, 8118
Hesperus, 1595
Hollins University Performing Arts Series, 5410
Horizons Theatre, 3569
Innsbrook Pavilion, 8099
International Children's Festival, 5374
James L Camp Memorial, 8130
James Madison University Encore Series, 5391
Jane Franklin Dance, 518
Jefferson Theatre Center, 8136
Kathy Harty Gray Dance Theatre, 3566
Lane Stadium, 8090
Latimer-Shaeffer Theatre, 8104
Lime Kiln Arts, 3575
Little Theatre of Norfolk, 3582, 8119
Long Way Home, 3583
Loudoun Ballet Company, 521
Lynchburg Community Concert Association, 5395
Lynchburg Fine Arts Center, 8107
Malini's Dances of India Troupe, 522
Metrostage, 3567
Middle Peninsula Community Concert Association, 5413
Mill Mountain Theatre, 3589
Modlin Center for the Arts, 5406
Mount Vernon Community Children's Theatre, 3568
Music Holiday Weekends, 5416
Music in Motion®Academy of Dance, 528
Mystery Dinner Playhouse, 3587
Nissan Pavilion at Stone Ridge, 8091
Norfolk Festevents, 5399
Norfolk Scope Arena, 8120
Offstage Theatre, 3571
Opera Roanoke, 2089
Opera Theatre of No Virginia, 2085
Patriot Center, 8096
Prince William County Stadium, 8110
Rachel M. Schlesinger Concert Hall and Arts Center, 8087

Washington

West Virginia

Wisconsin

Information Resources Index

Information Resources Index

Y

Grey House Publishing
2010 Title List

Visit **www.greyhouse.com** for Product Information, Table of Contents and Sample Pages

General Reference

American Environmental Leaders: From Colonial Times to the Present
An African Biographical Dictionary
Encyclopedia of African-American Writing
Encyclopedia of American Industries
Encyclopedia of Emerging Industries
Encyclopedia of Global Industries
Encyclopedia of Gun Control & Gun Rights
Encyclopedia of Invasions & Conquests
Encyclopedia of Prisoners of War & Internment
Encyclopedia of Religion & Law in America
Encyclopedia of Rural America
Encyclopedia of the United States Cabinet, 1789-2010
Encyclopedia of Warrior Peoples & Fighting Groups
Environmental Resource Handbook
From Suffrage to the Senate: America's Political Women
Global Terror & Political Risk Assessment
Historical Dictionary of War Journalism
Human Rights in the United States
Nations of the World
Political Corruption in America
Speakers of the House of Representatives, 1789-2009
The Environmental Debate: A Documentary History
The Evolution Wars: A Guide to the Debates
The Religious Right: A Reference Handbook
The Value of a Dollar: 1860-2009
The Value of a Dollar: Colonial Era
University & College Museums, Galleries & Related Facilities
Weather America
World Cultural Leaders of the 20th & 21st Centuries
Working Americans 1880-1999 Vol. I: The Working Class
Working Americans 1880-1999 Vol. II: The Middle Class
Working Americans 1880-1999 Vol. III: The Upper Class
Working Americans 1880-1999 Vol. IV: Their Children
Working Americans 1880-2003 Vol. V: At War
Working Americans 1880-2005 Vol. VI: Women at Work
Working Americans 1880-2006 Vol. VII: Social Movements
Working Americans 1880-2007 Vol. VIII: Immigrants
Working Americans 1770-1869 Vol. IX: Revol. War to the Civil War
Working Americans 1880-2009 Vol. X: Sports & Recreation
Working Americans 1880-2010 Vol. XI: Entrepreneurs & Inventors

Bowker's Books In Print®Titles

Books In Print®
Books In Print® Supplement
American Book Publishing Record® Annual
American Book Publishing Record® Monthly
Books Out Loud™
Bowker's Complete Video Directory™
Children's Books In Print®
El-Hi Textbooks & Serials In Print®
Forthcoming Books®
Large Print Books & Serials™
Law Books & Serials In Print™
Medical & Health Care Books In Print™
Publishers, Distributors & Wholesalers of the US™
Subject Guide to Books In Print®
Subject Guide to Children's Books In Print®

Business Information

Directory of Business Information Resources
Directory of Mail Order Catalogs
Directory of Venture Capital & Private Equity Firms
Food & Beverage Market Place
Grey House Homeland Security Directory
Grey House Performing Arts Directory
Hudson's Washington News Media Contacts Directory
New York State Directory
Sports Market Place Directory
The Rauch Guides – Industry Market Research Reports

Statistics & Demographics

America's Top-Rated Cities
America's Top-Rated Small Towns & Cities
America's Top-Rated Smaller Cities
Comparative Guide to American Suburbs
Comparative Guide to Health in America
Profiles of... Series – State Handbooks

Health Information

Comparative Guide to American Hospitals
Comparative Guide to Health in America
Complete Directory for Pediatric Disorders
Complete Directory for People with Chronic Illness
Complete Directory for People with Disabilities
Complete Mental Health Directory
Directory of Health Care Group Purchasing Organizations
Directory of Hospital Personnel
HMO/PPO Directory
Medical Device Register
Older Americans Information Directory

Education Information

Charter School Movement
Comparative Guide to American Elementary & Secondary Schools
Complete Learning Disabilities Directory
Educators Resource Directory
Special Education

TheStreet.com Ratings Guides

TheStreet.com Ratings Consumer Box Set
TheStreet.com Ratings Guide to Bank Fees & Service Charges
TheStreet.com Ratings Guide to Banks & Thrifts
TheStreet.com Ratings Guide to Bond & Money Market Mutual Funds
TheStreet.com Ratings Guide to Common Stocks
TheStreet.com Ratings Guide to Credit Unions
TheStreet.com Ratings Guide to Exchange-Traded Funds
TheStreet.com Ratings Guide to Health Insurers
TheStreet.com Ratings Guide to Life & Annuity Insurers
TheStreet.com Ratings Guide to Property & Casualty Insurers
TheStreet.com Ratings Guide to Stock Mutual Funds
TheStreet.com Ratings Ultimate Guided Tour of Stock Investing

Canadian General Reference

Associations Canada
Canadian Almanac & Directory
Canadian Environmental Resource Guide
Canadian Parliamentary Guide
Financial Services Canada
History of Canada
Libraries Canada

Grey House Publishing
4919 Route 22, PO Box 56, Amenia NY 12501-0056 | (800) 562-2139 | www.greyhouse.com | books@greyhouse.com